PRINCIPLES OF MEDICAL LAW

PRINCIPLES OF MEDICAL LAW

FOURTH EDITION

Edited by

JUDITH M. LAING

Reader in Law and Co-Director of the Centre for Health, Law, and Society, University of Bristol

JEAN V. MCHALE

Professor of Health Care Law and Director of the Centre for Health Law Science and Policy, Universityof Birmingham

Consultant Editors

PROFESSOR SIR IAN KENNEDY QC (HON), FBA, LLD

DR ANDREW GRUBB FMEDSCI,

Judge of the Upper Tribunal, Deputy High Court Judge and Recorder

OXFORD
UNIVERSITY PRESS

OXFORD
UNIVERSITY PRESS

Great Clarendon Street, Oxford, ox2 6dp,
United Kingdom

Oxford University Press is a department of the University of Oxford. It furthers the University's objective of excellence in research, scholarship, and education by publishing worldwide. Oxford is a registered trade mark of Oxford University Press in the UK and in certain other countries

Third Edition published in 2010
Fourth Edition published in 2017
Impression: 1

Published in the United States of America by Oxford University Press
198 Madison Avenue, New York, NY 10016, United States of America

British Library Cataloguing in Publication Data
Data available

Library of Congress Control Number: 2017933983

ISBN 978–0–19–873251–8

Printed and bound by CPI Group (UK) Ltd, Croydon, CR0 4YY

LIST OF CONTRIBUTORS

Editors

Judith M. Laing
Reader in Law and Co-Director of the Centre for Health, Law, and Society, University of Bristol

Jean V. McHale
Professor of Health Care Law and Director of the Centre for Health Law Science and Policy, Birmingham University

Consultant Editors

Professor Sir Ian Kennedy QC (hon), FBA, LLD

Dr Andrew Grubb FMEDSCI,
Judge of the Upper Tribunal, Deputy High Court Judge and Recorder

Contributors

Neil Allen
Barrister, 39 Essex Chambers Senior Lecturer in Law, University of Manchester

Paula Case
Senior Lecturer in Law, University of Liverpool

Murray Earle
School of Law, University of Edinburgh

Jessica Elliott
Barrister, One Crown Office Row, London

Michael Freeman
Professor of English Law, University College London

Nicola Glover-Thomas
Professor of Medical Law, University of Manchester

Richard Goldberg
Professor of Law, University of Durham

Philip Havers QC
Barrister, One Crown Office Row, London

Jonathan Herring
Professor of Law, University of Oxford

Christopher Hodges
Professor of Justice Systems, University of Oxford

Emily Jackson
Professor of Law, London School of Economics

Rachael Mulheron
Professor of Law, Queen Mary, University of London

Keith Syrett
Professor of Public Health Law, University of Cardiff

Mark Taylor
Senior Lecturer, University of Sheffield

Stephen Todd
Professor of Law, University of Canterbury, New Zealand

Amanda Warren-Jones
Senior Lecturer, University of Sheffield

FOREWORD

As proud parents do, we delight at the flourishing of our off-spring that we brought into the world all those years ago. It now enters its 4th Edition and runs to over 1300 pages. And, to think that, compared to many subjects in the legal lexicon, it is still a relative new-comer. One of us (IK) can remember writing, tongue in cheek, that, as a subject, Medical Law barely existed, such that you were free to make it up as you went along!

No such freedom exists now. It is a subject rich in case-law and statute, surrounded by regulation and routinely picked over in the media. It needs careful navigation. Both of us are now at some remove from the day-to-day hurly burly of developments in Medical Law which once so engrossed us both. We are delighted that the present editors, Judith and Jean, along with the contributors, are such perceptive and able navigators.

Medical law remains the fascinating product of individual court decisions, legislation and policy and regulation of a variety of forms. It remains, as it always has been, a mosaic of legal sources that is, for many, its attraction as an area of study but which can present the busy practitioner with a logistical problem or even nightmare to obtain a sound grip on the principles, let alone the detail. This work always had in its genesis an ambition to serve academics, practitioners and judges alike. The depth of scholarship and coverage in this edition more than maintains a claim to have fulfilled that ambition with style.

The structural, architectural changes which periodically befall the National Health Service, while continuing to perplex lawyers (and feed them), continue the habit we long ago lamented of losing sight of the interests of the people for whom the NHS exists – patients and those who look after them. In this regard, we welcome the continued emphasis on human rights as a unifying strand and strength in Medical Law. In this context, the Supreme Court's decision in *Montgomery v Lanarkshire Health Board* is particularly to be welcomed, reflecting the stand taken by us in the 1st edition.

Public inquiries continue to proliferate in this, as other areas, of concern that affect our lives. Many have made important and real contributions to changes in law, policy and perceptions in the health care context: e.g. Bristol Royal infirmary; Alder Hey; Shipman etc. Distance now lends a perspective on developments arising from the Mid Staffs Inquiry. While it is axiomatic that a culture should be created which puts patients and their needs and interests at the centre of everything, it is less clear that creating new legal duties or new crimes will facilitate such a cultural change. One of the hardest tasks of the lawyer is to wrestle with the limits of what the law can or should try to do.

This edition maintains its strength in analysing and seeking to structure the law and uncover the applicable principles. Some are clear and even certain (unless and until changed by the Supreme Court of course); much is not. Quite rightly, the editors comment on the uncertainties which still dog mental health law. It was ever thus, but it was ever wrong that it is and remains so.

Of course, if you are looking for uncertainties, Brexit takes the biscuit. Its future effects on Medical Law will need to be mulled over with care and documented. That will be a task for the 5th Edition.

Meanwhile, we repeat our thanks to the Editors and to all the contributors for nurturing this work. Its subject-matter remains, as the modern vernacular would have it, 'relevant'.

Ian Kennedy
Andrew Grubb

PREFACE

The publication of a new edition of this volume brings with it many new legal changes and challenges. In the 7 years since the previous edition reached the bookshelves, the landscape of the NHS has continued to shift beyond recognition. We have witnessed the introduction of the Care Act 2014 and considerable upheaval with the provision of care and structures of the healthcare system. Chapter 1 charts all these recent changes and their implications for the organization and governance of health care in the Twenty First century. The frameworks for professional regulation have also faced a number of notable challenges since 2010, particularly in the wake of the Francis Inquiry into Mid Staffordshire NHS Trust, which are considered by Paula Case in Chapter 2. The impact of the Inquiry in relation to such matters as the new statutory duty of candour may change, at least to some extent, the clinician-patient dynamic in the future. Research regulation too continues apace as the role of the Health Research Authority, now embedded in statute, continues to evolve, as considered by Jean McHale in Chapter 13.

We charted the shift towards a fundamental rights-based approach in the courtroom in the previous edition. This shift has continued to evolve with the Supreme Court decision in *Montgomery v Lanarkshire* on the doctor's duty to provide information to patients, as well as Jackson J's autonomy focused articulation of best interests in *Wye Valley NHS Trust v B*. These cases and the implications of this shift more generally are considered in a number of contributions to this new edition. Indeed, the impact of the European Convention on Human Rights continues to be felt in several areas of clinical practice. For example, in Chapter 21, Jonathan Herring considers the decisions in *Purdy* and *Nicklinson* and the human rights challenges posed by healthcare decision-making at the end of life, and its impact in relation to decisions concerning adults lacking mental capacity is explored by Neil Allen in Chapters 9 and 10. While the book charts the impact of EU law in various areas e.g. from patient mobility as discussed by Keith Syrett (in Chapter 1); to medicines regulations examined by Christopher Hodges (in Chapter 17); and through the new data protection regulation explored by Mark Taylor (in Chapter 12), the implications of Brexit for health law in general may prove a significant challenge for policy makers, lawyers and regulators in the years to come.

The Mental Capacity Act 2005 and Mental Health Act 1983 (as amended in 2007) continue to evolve and have resulted in considerable jurisprudence, which is discussed in Chapters 10 and 11. The Deprivation of Liberty safeguards have proved to be extremely complex and controversial, and prompted considerable judicial and academic debate, as Neil Allen explores in Chapter 10. The lack of clarity surrounding the concept of 'deprivation' and the resulting professional confusion has prompted the Law Commission to make recommendations for change in a recent consultation paper. At the time of writing, the proposals are still under consideration and we will no doubt be able to write about the outcome more fully in the next edition.

It has indeed been a period of great flux as there have been several changes to the writing team since the last edition. We are pleased to welcome new contributors: Neil Allen, Paula Case, Murray Earle, Mark Taylor and Amanda Warren-Jones; and we are sorry to say goodbye to others, some of whom have been long-standing contributors to the text since the very first edition in 1998: Derek Beyleveld, Jonathan Holl-Allen, Graeme Laurie, David Lock, J.K. (Ken) Mason, Sir James Munby, Christopher Newdick, Shaun Pattinson, Mary O'Rourke and Harvey Teff. We would also like to gratefully acknowledge the contributions made by authors who were involved in previous editions of this volume, and whose work in some instances is still contained within certain chapters. And, of course, our thanks must also go to the many contributors who have continued their involvement with this new edition of the book. It is with great sadness that we record the death of Ken Mason, who died in January 2017 at the age of 97 as this book was going to press. He was a wonderful scholar of both law and medicine and a kind and generous colleague who will be greatly missed.

We are delighted that Andrew Grubb continues to be involved with the text and has now joined Ian Kennedy as a Consultant Editor for this edition. We are grateful that they have both contributed the *Foreword* to this book.

This edition has taken some time to come to fruition and we are extremely grateful to the production team at Oxford University Press for their proficiency and patience. Our particular thanks go to Rachel Holt, Katherine Hooper, Faye Mousley, and Andy Redman for their invaluable advice and assistance throughout the entire production process.

The law is stated as at 1st October 2016, with some minor changes incorporated since then at proof stage.

Judith Laing & Jean McHale
Editors
January 2017

CONTENTS—SUMMARY

CONTENTS

PART IV

TABLE OF CASES

TABLE OF LEGISLATION

TABLE OF STATUTORY INSTRUMENTS

TABLE OF TREATIES AND CONVENTIONS

TABLE OF EUROPEAN LAW

Regulations (in chronological order)

Directives (in chronological order)

TABLE OF LEGISLATION FROM OTHER JURISDICTIONS

Singapore

South Africa

United States

PART I

1

THE ORGANIZATION OF HEALTH CARE

Keith Syrett

Chapter 1 considers the organization of the National Health Service (NHS) by examining (A) the structure of the NHS, and (B) NHS governance. Judicial review of priority-setting by NHS institutions, previously considered in this chapter, is covered in Chapter 7.[1]

A. Structure of the NHS

This section describes the major institutions of the NHS and their relationship with one another.[2] It considers: (1) the general duties of the Secretary of State; (2) the commissioning (or purchasing) of NHS services; (3) the provision of NHS services by general practitioners, NHS Trusts and Foundation Trusts, private providers and overseas institutions; and (4) the NHS Constitution. **1.01**

1. General duties of Secretary of State

A number of general statutory duties are imposed on the Secretary of State by the National Health Service Act 2006. These have now been significantly amended by the Health and Social Care Act 2012. The most fundamental of those duties are set out in ss 1(1) and (2), which provide that the Secretary of State must continue the promotion in England of a comprehensive health service designed to secure improvement (a) in the physical and mental health of the people in England, and (b) in the prevention, diagnosis, and treatment of physical and mental illness, and for that purpose to exercise the functions conferred by the Act so as to secure that services are provided in accordance with it. **1.02**

Section 1(3) emphasizes that the Secretary of State retains ministerial responsibility for the provision of the health service in England. This provision was inserted in response to **1.03**

[1] See Chapter 7, paras 7.64–7.116.

[2] This chapter considers the structure of the NHS in England. While the Service elsewhere in the United Kingdom is based upon similar fundamental precepts, health is a devolved matter and the structure of the NHS in Scotland, Wales, and Northern Ireland is increasingly diverging from that in England. For discussion, see N Timmins, *The Four UK Health Systems: Learning from Each Other* (King's Fund 2013).

concerns that the removal of an explicit duty imposed upon the Secretary of State to 'provide' services (as further set out in s 3 of the 2006 Act), which duty—as discussed below—now falls upon the NHS Commissioning Board and Clinical Commissioning Groups (CCGs), effectively denuded the minister of any accountability for the NHS in Parliament.[3] Section 1(4) maintains the NHS's founding principle of free provision, except where provision is made for the making and recovery of charges.[4]

1.04 Further duties are imposed upon the Secretary of State by ss 1A to G of the 2006 Act, as inserted by ss 2 to 8 of the 2012 Act. These comprise obligations to secure continuous improvement in the quality of services, to have regard to the NHS Constitution, to have regard to the need to reduce inequalities with respect to the benefits which can be obtained from the health service, to have regard to the desirability of securing 'autonomy' in the exercise of functions or provision of services in relation to the NHS, to promote research on matters relevant to the NHS and the use of evidence derived from such research, to secure an effective system for the planning and delivery of education and training to employees, or potential employees, of the NHS, and to report to Parliament, and keep under review, the treatment of providers of NHS health care as respects any matter (including taxation) which might affect their ability to provide NHS services or their reward for doing so.

1.05 In addition to conferral of a general power upon the Secretary of State (and the NHS Commissioning Board and CCGs) to 'do anything else which is calculated to facilitate, or is conducive or incidental to the discharge of any function' exercised under the Act,[5] the Act imposes a duty to protect or improve public health. This new obligation has two dimensions. First, the Secretary of State must take such steps as are considered appropriate for the purpose of protecting the public in England from 'disease or other dangers to health'.[6] It will be noted that this amounts to an 'all hazards' approach which does not exhaustively list the dangers to health in respect of which action may be taken;[7] thus, 'other dangers' may comprise matters as diverse as radiation, poisons, or the health impacts of climate change. The steps which may be taken are listed as including the conduct of research, provision of microbiological or other technical services, provision of vaccination, immunization or screening services, provision of other services or facilities for the prevention, diagnosis and treatment of illness, provision of training, provision of information and advice, and making available the services of any person or any facilities.

1.06 While this is a rather narrow vision of the function of law in respect of public health,[8] a more expansive approach is taken by s 2B,[9] which obliges both the Secretary of State and local authorities to take such steps as they consider appropriate for improvement of health, nationally, or within a relevant local area. Several of the steps listed are similar to those stated in subsection (1), thus including provision of information and advice, provision of services and facilities for the prevention, diagnosis, and treatment of illness, provision of (or participation in the provision of) training, and making available the services of any

[3] See House of Lords Constitution Committee, Eighteenth Report, (2010–12), *Health and Social Care Bill* (HL 197).

[4] The principle that the service should be available without charge is subject to exceptions in respect of prescription, dental and ophthalmic charges.

[5] National Health Service Act 2006, s 2.

[6] ibid, s 2A, inserted by Health and Social Care Act 2012, s 11.

[7] Contrast Public Health (Control of Disease) Act 1984, prior to amendment by Health and Social Care Act 2008, Part 3.

[8] For a broader perspective, see J Coggon, K Syrett, and AM Viens, *Public Health Law: Ethics, Governance, and Regulation* (Routledge 2016).

[9] Inserted by Health and Social Care Act 2012, s 12.

person or any facilities. Additional options which reflect the health-promoting orientation of public health comprise provision of services or facilities designed to promote healthy living and provision of financial incentives to encourage individuals to adopt healthy lifestyles, while steps may also be taken to provide assistance (including of a financial nature) to help individuals minimize any risk to health arising from their accommodation or environment.

(i) To whom is the duty owed?

The duty to promote a comprehensive health service is owed to the people of England who are 'ordinarily resident' in Great Britain, their spouses, and children.[10] The meaning of the phrase was considered in the case of a failed asylum seeker who, it was said, had not come to the country because of a fear of persecution, but to receive NHS care. He had lived here for four years and could not be returned to his home in the Palestinian occupied territories because the Israeli authorities would not assist his return. For this reason, he was likely to remain in the UK indefinitely. Nevertheless, in *YA*, Ward LJ stated: **1.07**

> The words are to be given their ordinary meaning. Asylum seekers are clearly resident here but is the manner in which they have acquired and enjoy that residence ordinary or extraordinary? Normal or abnormal? Were they detained, then no-one would suggest they were ordinarily resident in the place of their detention. While they are here under sufferance pending investigation of their claim they are not, in my judgment, ordinarily resident here. Residence by grace and favour is not ordinary. The words must take some flavour from the purpose of the statute under consideration and, as I have set out above, the purpose of the National Health Act is to provide a service for the people *of* England and that does not include those who ought not to be here. Failed asylum seekers ought not to be here. They should never have come here in the first place and after their claims have finally been dismissed they are only here until arrangements can be made to secure their return, even if, in some cases, like the unfortunate YA, that return may be a long way off.[11]

As to charging overseas visitors for NHS services, Regulations provide that: 'a relevant NHS body must make and recover charges for any relevant service it provides to an overseas visitor from the person liable'.[12] The person liable is defined as the person to whom the services are provided, unless working on a ship, or as an air crew member (in which case, the employer is liable), or a child (in which case liability falls upon the person with parental responsibility).[13] It will be noted that the responsibility to recover the costs of the care provided is expressed in the form of a duty, rather than a discretion.[14] However, there is an extensive range of exemptions. First, a number of specified services are exempted from charge, for example: accident and emergency care; family planning services; treatment for specified communicable diseases;[15] treatment for sexually transmitted diseases; and treatment of conditions caused by torture, female genital mutilation, domestic violence, or sexual violence (provided, in this last case, that the person has not travelled to the UK to seek **1.08**

[10] See National Health Service Act 2006, s 175. Lord Scarman described the phrase in *R v Barnett LBC, ex p Shah* [1983] 2 AC 308, 343 as follows: 'a man's abode in a particular place or country which he has adopted voluntarily and for settled purposes as part of the regular order of his life for the time being, whether of short or of long duration'.

[11] *R (on the application of YA) v Secretary of State for Health* [2009] EWCA Civ 225, [61].

[12] National Health Service (Charges to Overseas Visitors) Regulations 2015, SI 2015/238, reg 3(1). See also Department of Health, *Guidance on Implementing the Overseas Visitors Hospital Charging Regulations 2015* (2015).

[13] ibid, reg 4.

[14] Discussed in *R v Hammersmith Hospitals NHS Trust, ex p Reffell* (2000) 55 BMLR 130, 135. Guidance now specifies that 'there is no option, nor is there the authority, to waive the charge on the part of the NHS body': Department of Health, n 12, [2.17].

[15] National Health Service (Charges to Overseas Visitors) Regulations 2015, Schedule 1.

such treatment).[16] Also, various categories of overseas visitors are exempted, for example those granted or applying for asylum or temporary or humanitarian protection in the UK (eg refugees or asylum seekers),[17] those detained in prison or by the immigration authorities,[18] and those whose services are provided under reciprocal arrangements between the UK and an overseas country.[19] However, non-European Economic Area individuals who apply to reside in the UK for longer than six months—including those who were previously exempt, such as those with at least twelve months' lawful residence in the UK but without indefinite leave to remain, those working in the UK for a UK-based employer, and students on a full-time course of at least six months' duration or which is substantially-funded by the UK government—are now subject to an 'immigration health charge'.[20] Payment of this charge, which is mandatory when making an immigration application (subject to exemptions for certain categories of person and the discretion of the Home Secretary to waive, reduce, or refund all or part of a payment), entitles the payer to NHS-funded health care on the same basis as someone who is ordinarily resident.

1.09 Patients treated as overseas visitors are not private patients. The responsible doctor may not charge a fee for his or her treatment unless the patient wishes to be treated under a private contract (eg a contract of insurance). Those treated as overseas visitors may be asked to sign an undertaking to pay and should be treated with the same urgency and priority as NHS patients. NHS bodies must ensure that treatment which is classified by the treating clinician as 'immediately necessary' is provided, regardless of whether the overseas visitor has been informed of, or agreed to pay, charges; such treatment must be provided even where the patient has indicated that s/he cannot afford to pay and it should not be withheld or delayed in order to establish chargeable status or seek payment—to act otherwise might amount to a violation of the Human Rights Act 1998.[21] Wherever possible, patients undergoing immediately necessary treatment should be stabilized, allowing them to be safely discharged and returned home for any further treatment. By contrast, where treatment is classified as 'urgent', every effort should be made to secure payment prior to treatment, although treatment should not be delayed or withheld if this is not possible.[22] As for routine, elective treatment, NHS bodies are under no obligation to provide this if the patient does not pay in advance, and should not do so until the full estimated cost of treatment has been paid;[23] but if the patient's return date or medical condition changes, a reassessment of this position may be needed.[24]

1.10 Clearly, these rules may give rise to distressing circumstances for overseas visitors, for example, those who have been diagnosed with a potentially fatal condition for which treatment will not be available in their own country. The matter was considered by the European Court of Human Rights in *D v United Kingdom*,[25] in which the applicant had obtained a visitors' visa but was detained on arrival in the UK and was convicted to a term of imprisonment. During that time, he was discovered to be suffering from AIDS and was treated, in accordance with the Regulations, as an NHS patient. On completion of his sentence, the Secretary of State ordered his deportation from the UK, but the applicant resisted under the provisions of

[16] ibid, reg 9.
[17] ibid, reg 15.
[18] ibid, reg 19.
[19] ibid, reg 14. The relevant countries are listed in Schedule 2 of the Regulations.
[20] See Immigration Act 2014, s 38; Immigration (Health Charge) Order 2015, SI 2015/792.
[21] See Department of Health, n 12, paras 8.2–8.5.
[22] ibid, para 8.8.
[23] ibid, para 8.9.
[24] ibid, para 8.18.
[25] (1997) 24 EHRR 423.

Article 3 of the European Convention on Human Rights. His country of residence was St Kitts in the West Indies, which could not continue to provide him with the care that he needed. In finding for the applicant, the Court confirmed that, as a general rule, nation states had no obligation to provide care for 'aliens' who had no right to receive it under domestic law. Nevertheless, in the extreme circumstances of this case, in which care had commenced within the UK, it would have been inhuman and degrading to return a man in the terminal stages of an illness to a country which had no facilities to provide adequate medical and palliative care.

However, in *N v Secretary of State for the Home Department*,[26] the House of Lords expressed a number of concerns about this decision. The case concerned a patient suffering from HIV who had been treated by the NHS and whose symptoms were, as a result, well controlled. In these circumstances, it was decided the applicant's health was such that he could be returned home to a country in which further treatment would not be available. Lord Hope said that to extend the right to remain in the UK would have the effect of affording all those in the appellant's condition a right of asylum until the standard of medical facilities available in their home countries had reached that which is available in Europe: **1.11**

> It would risk drawing into the United Kingdom large numbers of people already suffering from HIV in the hope that they too could remain here indefinitely so that they could take the benefit of the medical resources that are available in this country. This would result in a very great and no doubt unquantifiable commitment of resources which it is, to say the least, highly questionable the states parties to the Convention would ever have agreed to.[27]

The European Court of Human Rights has endorsed the decision in *N* and distinguished *D*. Conscious of the balance between the rights of individual patients and those of the community as a whole, and recognizing that the standards of medical care available in Contracting States could vary considerably, it said that 'Article 3 does not place an obligation on the Contracting State to alleviate such disparities through the provision of free and unlimited health care to all aliens without a right to stay within its jurisdiction. A finding to the contrary would place too great a burden on the Contracting States'.[28] Therefore, the Convention does not generate an entitlement for 'aliens' to receive medical, social or other assistance in other Contracting States: **1.12**

> The fact that the applicant's circumstances, including his life expectancy, would be significantly reduced if he were to be removed from the Contracting State is not sufficient in itself to give rise to breach of Article 3. The decision to remove an alien who is suffering from a serious mental or physical illness to a country where the facilities for the treatment of that illness are inferior to those available in the Contracting State may raise an issue under Article 3, but only in a very exceptional case, where the humanitarian grounds against the removal are compelling. In the *D* case the very exceptional circumstances were that the applicant was critically ill and appeared to be close to death, could not be guaranteed any nursing or medical care in his country of origin and had no family there willing or able to care for him or provide him with even a basic level of food, shelter or social support. The

[26] [2005] UKHL 31.

[27] ibid, [53]. See also *Bensaid v United Kingdom* (2001) 33 EHRR 205, concerning the deportation of a long-term schizophrenic patient to Algeria: 'The Court accepts the seriousness of the applicant's medical condition. Having regard however to the high threshold set by Article 3, particularly where the case does not concern the direct responsibility of the contracting state for the infliction of harm, the Court does not find that there is a sufficiently real risk that the applicant's removal in these circumstances would be contrary to the standards of Article 3. It does not disclose the exceptional circumstances of the *D* case . . . where the applicant was in the final stage of a terminal illness, AIDS, and had no prospect of medical care or family support on expulsion to St Kitts': at [40].

[28] *N v United Kingdom* [2008] ECHR 453, [44].

> Court . . . considers that it should maintain the high threshold set in *D v United Kingdom* and applied in its subsequent case-law, which it regards as correct in principle, given that in such cases the alleged future harm would emanate not from the intentional acts or omissions of public authorities or non-State bodies, but instead from a naturally occurring illness and the lack of sufficient resources to deal with it in the receiving country.[29]

(ii) NHS patients wishing to supplement NHS treatment with additional private care

1.13 A particular difficulty has arisen with respect to the duty owed to those who wish to supplement their NHS treatment by paying for part of their care privately. This can arise, for example, in a situation where a clinician recommends treatment for a particular condition which is not routinely funded (perhaps, because appraisal by the National Institute for Health and Care Excellence (NICE) has not yet taken place), or where the outcome of the NICE appraisal is negative,[30] and an individual funding request has been rejected.[31] The patient may choose to pay for the drug him/herself but may wish also to remain in an NHS hospital for medical, nursing, and other care (including monitoring and supervision of the 'additional' drug). That is, the costs of care are 'shared' between the NHS and the patient. What, if any, is the duty of the Secretary of State to patients in these circumstances?

1.14 Previous guidance on this matter stated that 'a patient cannot be both a private and a NHS patient for the treatment of one condition during a single visit to a NHS organization'.[32] Although the implications of this were not explicitly spelled out, a number of NHS bodies had interpreted the guidance, read together with the founding principle of free care at the point of delivery in what is now s 1(4) of the 2006 Act, as necessitating withdrawal of all free NHS care, and continuation as a private patient.

1.15 In light of adverse publicity relating to this situation,[33] the Secretary of State ordered a review,[34] the outcome of which was publication of new guidance, which reaffirms the founding principles that 'the NHS should never subsidise private care with public money' and that 'patients should never be charged for their NHS care, or be allowed to pay towards an NHS service (except where specific legislation is in place to allow this)'.[35] Reversing the previous policy, it continues:

> Patients may pay for additional private health care while continuing to receive care from the NHS. However, in order to ensure that there is no risk of the NHS subsidising private care:
>
> (1) It should always be clear whether an individual procedure or treatment is privately funded or NHS funded.
> (2) Private and NHS care should be kept as clearly separate as possible.
> (3) Private care should be carried out at a different time to the NHS care that a patient is receiving.
> (4) Private care should be carried out in a different place to NHS care, as separate from other NHS patients as possible. A different place would include the facilities of a

---

29 ibid, [42]–[43].

30 See further paras 1.92–1.94.

31 See further Chapter 7, para 7.91.

32 Department of Health, 'A Code of Conduct for Private Practice: Recommended Standards of Practice for NHS Consultants' (2004), para 2.31.

33 For discussion, see K Syrett, 'Mixing Private and Public Treatment in the UK's National Health Service: a challenge to core constitutional principles?' (2010) 17 European Journal of Health Law 235.

34 Department of Health, 'Improving Access to Medicines for NHS Patients' (2008).

35 Department of Health, 'Guidance on NHS Patients Who Wish to Pay for Additional Private Care' (2009), para 2.3. See also, now, NHS Commissioning Board, 'Commissioning Policy: Defining the Boundaries between NHS and Private Healthcare' (2013).

private health care provider, or part of an NHS organization which has been permanently or temporarily designated for private care, such as a private wing, amenity beds or a private room.[36]

While the guidance represents a pragmatic response to a particular, albeit limited,[37] policy problem, application of it raises certain awkward practical questions. To take just one example, noted by the Health Select Committee, while it may be a relatively simple matter to separate provision of a hip replacement on the NHS from privately purchased physiotherapy, it is much less easy to separate the administration of drugs, especially on an intravenous basis.[38] A further problem relates to the additional costs which may be incurred by the NHS as a consequence of allowing patients to 'top up' with private care; for example in staff training or allocation of time for administration of privately funded drugs and subsequent monitoring of the condition of patients.[39] Difficulties may also arise regarding the attribution of legal liability between the private sector and the NHS when mistakes are made in the treatment of a patient who has combined NHS care with privately purchased drugs. **1.16**

2. The commissioning of NHS services

An important change in form, though not of substance, made by the 2012 Act is that the duty to provide specific health services, set out in section 3(1) of the 2006 Act, no longer falls upon the Secretary of State. In practice, this duty was not exercised directly by government but rather was delegated to a variety of organizations over the lifetime of the NHS, the most recent incarnations of which (in England), were Primary Care Trusts and Strategic Health Authorities, both now abolished. The duty has been reformulated as one 'to arrange for the provision . . . to such extent as it considers necessary to meet the reasonable requirements of the persons for whom it has responsibility', thus emphasizing that the primary obligation is to commission services for a local population, rather than to deliver them. The services in question remain unaltered, namely: **1.17**

(a) hospital accommodation;
(b) other accommodation for the purpose of any service specified under this Act;
(c) medical, dental, ophthalmic, nursing, and ambulance services;
(d) such other services or facilities for the care of pregnant women, women who are breastfeeding and young children as . . . are appropriate as part of the health service;
(e) such other facilities for the prevention of illness, the care of persons suffering from illness and the after-care of persons who have suffered from illness as are . . . appropriate as part of the health service; [and]
(f) such other services as are required for the diagnosis and treatment of illness.

(i) Clinical Commissioning Groups

The duty under s 3(1) is expressed to fall upon Clinical Commissioning Groups (CCGs), the replacement for Primary Care Trusts.[40] CCGs, of which there are 211 in England, control the majority of the NHS budget,[41] and are composed of GP practices within a locality **1.18**

[36] Department of Health, ibid, para 4.2. Examples of cases in which these principles apply are suggested in the guidance document.
[37] The problem was described as 'very rare indeed': see Syrett, n 33, 238.
[38] House of Commons Health Committee, Fourth Report (2008–09), *Top-Up Fees* (HC 194-I) para 58.
[39] ibid, paras 68–72.
[40] CCGs are established by Part 2, Chapter A2 of the National Health Service Act 2006, inserted by Health and Social Care Act 2012, s 25(1).
[41] Approximately two-thirds: see C Naylor § *Clinical Commissioning Groups: supporting improvement in general practice?* (King's Fund 2013), ix.

which contract (with the NHS Commissioning Board—see further paras 1.21–1.27) to provide primary care services to NHS patients. Membership of a CCG is mandatory for every such practice and a health care professional must be appointed to act on its behalf in its dealings with the CCG.[42] A CCG is a corporate body and the arrangements for discharge of its functions, its key processes for decision-making (including arrangements for securing transparency) and the arrangements for discharging its duties with regard to registers of interest and management of conflicts of interest, must be set out in a constitution.[43] Its governing body must have at least six members, and these must include at least one each of: a person with 'a professional qualification in accountancy and the expertise or experience to lead the financial management of the CCG'; a registered nurse; a secondary care specialist; one layperson with qualifications, expertise, or experience such as to enable the person to express informed views about financial management and audit matters; and another with knowledge about the area specified in the CCG's constitution such as to enable the person to express informed views about the discharge of the CCG's functions.[44]

1.19 In addition to performance of the obligations under s 3(1), a number of further duties are imposed upon CCGs by ss 14P to 14Z1 of the 2006 Act.[45] These comprise acting with a view to securing that health services are provided in a way which promotes the NHS Constitution, and promoting awareness of the Constitution among patients, staff, and public; exercising their functions effectively, efficiently, and economically; securing continuous improvement in the quality of services provided; assisting the NHS Commissioning Board in discharging its duties in respect of securing continuous improvement in the quality of primary medical services; having regard to the need to reduce inequalities between patients with respect to access to health services and to the outcomes achieved; promoting the involvement of patients, their carers, and their representatives in decisions relating to the prevention or diagnosis of illness and care or treatment; acting with a view to promoting patient choice; obtaining appropriate advice from persons with expertise in the prevention, diagnosis, or treatment of illness, or the protection or improvement of public health to enable the CCG effectively to discharge its functions; promotion of innovation in the provision of health services; promotion of research on matters relevant to the NHS and the use in the NHS of evidence obtained from research; promotion of education and training so as to assist the Secretary of State in respect of his duty in that regard; and promotion of integration, either within health services or between health and social services. Further, a CCG must make arrangements to secure public involvement,[46] and may arrange with another CCG to exercise functions on its behalf or jointly; joint exercise of functions with Local Health Boards operating in Wales is also permissible.

1.20 Each CCG is required to prepare and publish a commissioning plan, setting out how it proposes to exercise its functions, before the beginning of each financial year.[47] This plan must set out in particular how the CCG proposes to exercise its duties in respect of improvement

[42] National Health Service Act 2006, s 89(1A), inserted by Health and Social Care Act 2012, s 28; National Health Service (General Medical Services Contract) Regulations 2004. SI 2004/291, reg 20A, inserted by National Health Service (Primary Medical Services) (Miscellaneous Amendments and Transitional Provisions) Regulations 2013, SI 2013/363, reg 15.

[43] See National Health Service Act 2006, Schedule 1A, inserted by Health and Social Care 2012, Sch 2.

[44] See National Health Service Act 2006, s 14L, inserted by Health and Social Care Act 2012, s 25(1); National Health Service (Clinical Commissioning Groups) Regulations 2012, SI 2012/1631, regs 11 and 12.

[45] As inserted by Health and Social Care Act 2012, s 26.

[46] See further paras 1.111–1.115.

[47] National Health Service Act 2006, s 14Z11, inserted by Health and Social Care Act 2012, s 26.

of the quality of services, reduction in inequalities and public involvement and consultation. A copy must be provided to the NHS Commissioning Board and to those Health and Wellbeing Boards established by local authorities whose areas coincide with, or include the whole or any part of the CCG's area.[48] The plans may be revised; if the revision is considered by the CCG to be 'significant', the revised plan must be published and submitted to the NHS Commissioning Board and Health and Wellbeing Boards; if not significant, a document summarizing the changes may be published and submitted.[49] There are obligations to consult the local population and relevant Health and Wellbeing Boards when plans are being prepared and/or revised.[50] The CCG must also prepare and publish an annual report on how it has discharged its functions in the previous financial year; this must be submitted to the NHS Commissioning Board and to relevant Health and Wellbeing Boards, and a public meeting held for the purpose of presenting it to the public.[51]

(ii) NHS Commissioning Board

Section 1H of the 2006 Act, inserted by s 9(1) of the 2012 Act, establishes the National Health Service Commissioning Board (known for operational purposes as 'NHS England'). The Board is an executive non-departmental public body, a status which is intended to confer upon it a degree of independence from central government intervention and thus to meet the government's stated vision of 'a lean and expert organization, free from day-to-day political interference'.[52] **1.21**

However, s 13A of the 2006 Act, inserted by s 23(1) of the 2012 Act, requires the Secretary of State, following consultation with the Board, the Healthwatch England committee of the Care Quality Commission, and such other persons as considered appropriate, to publish and lay before Parliament a 'mandate', which forms the 'main basis of ministerial instruction to the NHS'.[53] This document specifies the objectives that the Secretary of State considers the Board should seek to achieve in the exercise of its functions during the following financial year (and subsequent financial years as considered appropriate),[54] any requirements considered necessary to impose on the Board for the purpose of ensuring that it achieves those objectives, its revenue and capital budgets, and matters by which the Secretary of State proposes to assess the Board's performance. The Board is obliged to seek to achieve the objectives specified in the mandate and to comply with any specified requirements, but the latter only have effect if so provided by Regulations.[55] **1.22**

The Board is subject to the duty under s 1(1) of the 2006 Act to promote a comprehensive health service concurrently with the Secretary of State, except in relation to matters relating to public health.[56] It discharges this duty in large part by commissioning services, the most **1.23**

---

48 For discussion of Health and Wellbeing Boards, see further paras 1.118–1.120.

49 National Health Service Act 2006, s 14Z12, inserted by Health and Social Care Act 2012, s 26.

50 ibid, s 14Z13.

51 ibid, s 14Z15.

52 Department of Health, *Equity and Excellence: Liberating the NHS* (Cm 7881, 2010), para 4.10.

53 Department of Health, *The Mandate* (2012), para 6.

54 The first such mandate: ibid, covered the period April 2013 to March 2015, and set (quite broad) objectives relating to preventing people from dying prematurely; enhancing quality of life for those with long-term conditions; helping people to recover from periods of ill health or following injury; ensuring a positive experience of care; treating people in a safe environment and protecting them from avoidable harm; freeing the NHS to innovate; and the broader role of the NHS in society.

55 See, eg, National Health Service (Mandate Requirements) 2014, SI 2014/3487.

56 National Health Service Act 2006, s 1H(2), inserted by Health and Social Care Act 2012, s 9(1). For analysis of the meaning of the public health exception in this subsection, see *R (on the application of National Aids Trust) v NHS Commissioning Board* [2016] EWCA Civ 1100.

important of which are primary care services delivered by practitioners such as GPs, dentists, optometrists, and pharmacists, as provided in Parts 4–7 of the 2006 Act. These will be discussed further in paras 1.36–1.48. The Board also commissions 144 specialized services for 'rare and very rare conditions',[57] such as services for adult secure mental health; adult specialist renal treatment; complex spinal surgery; cystic fibrosis; foetal medicine; gender identity disorder; heart, lung, and liver transplantation; radiotherapy and spinal cord injury; 'services or facilities for persons who are detained in prison or in other accommodation of a prescribed description';[58] services for members of the armed forces and their families;[59] community and secondary dental services;[60] and high security psychiatric hospital accommodation and services.[61]

1.24 Although s 1H(2) of the 2006 Act specifies that the Board does not exercise public health functions concurrently with the Secretary of State, s 7A, inserted by s 22 of the 2012 Act, enables the minister to delegate the exercise of such functions to local authorities, CCGs, and the Board. Although the major role in relation to public health is played by local authorities, the Board undertakes commissioning of certain services, notably many vaccination and screening programmes.[62]

1.25 In addition to its commissioning functions, the Board also has functions in relation to CCGs. Section 1H(3)(b) states that, in order to discharge its duty of promoting a comprehensive health service, the Board must exercise its functions relating to CCGs in a manner which secures that services are provided; this might include its obligation to publish guidance on commissioning to CCGs.[63]

1.26 Other duties of the Board under this head are specified in ss 14A to 14I of the 2006 Act.[64] These include determination of applications for the establishment of CCGs; powers to grant or refuse variations of a CCG's constitution, or to vary it without application by the CCG;[65] determination of applications for merger and dissolution of CCGs; and transfer of property,

---

[57] See National Health Service Commissioning Board and Clinical Commissioning Groups (Responsibilities and Standing Rules) Regulations 2012, SI 2012/2996, reg 11. The phrase is that used in Schedule 4 of the Regulations, which lists the services. The decision on whether it is appropriate for the Board (rather than CCGs) to commission a service rests with the Secretary of State and is based upon the number of individuals requiring the service, the cost of providing it, the number of persons providing it and the financial implications for CCGs if they were required to commission it: see National Health Service Act 2006, s 3B(3). These services cost approximately £14 billion per year, which represents approximately 14 per cent of the total NHS budget in England: see NHS England, *Consultation Guide: Investing in Specialised Services* (2015).

[58] National Health Service Act 2006, s 3B(1)(c); National Health Service Commissioning Board and Clinical Commissioning Groups (Responsibilities and Standing Rules) Regulations 2012, reg 10. In addition to prisons, the settings include immigration removal centres, secure homes and training centres for children and young people, and (from April 2016) police custody.

[59] National Health Service Act 2006, s 3B(1)(b); National Health Service Commissioning Board and Clinical Commissioning Groups (Responsibilities and Standing Rules) Regulations 2012, reg 7.

[60] National Health Service Act 2006, s 3B(1)(a); National Health Service Commissioning Board and Clinical Commissioning Groups (Responsibilities and Standing Rules) Regulations 2012, reg 6 and Schedule 4.

[61] National Health Service Act 2006, s 4, as amended. See also High Security Psychiatric Services (NHS Commissioning Board) Directions 2013.

[62] See Department of Health/NHS England, *NHS Public Health Functions Agreement 2016–17* (2015). See also *R (on the application of National Aids Trust) v NHS Commissioning Board*, n 56.

[63] National Health Service Act, s 14Z8, inserted by Health and Social Care Act 2012, s 26.

[64] Inserted by Health and Social Care Act 2012, s 25.

[65] For example, to change the geographical area covered by a CCG. Note that s 14A(2) requires the Board to ensure that the areas specified in CCG constitutions, taken together, cover the whole of England and do not coincide or overlap. This removes any ambiguity which might arise, for example, when an individual is not registered with a GP practice or requires emergency care.

staff, or associated rights and liabilities from the CCG to the Board or another CCG. As noted previously, the Board has oversight of CCG commissioning plans and annual reports.

A range of general duties similar to those imposed on CCGs[66] are set out in ss 13C to 13P of the 2006 Act.[67] The Board is obliged to make arrangements for public involvement and consultation in respect of its planning of commissioning arrangements; the development and consideration of proposals for service change where they would have an impact upon the range or manner of the services provided; and decisions affecting the operation of commissioning arrangements.[68] It must publish a business plan setting out how it is to exercise its functions over three years with a view to fulfilling its statutory duties and the Mandate; and an annual report, to which response must be made by the Secretary of State.[69] Section 13Z of the 2006 Act enables the Board to exercise any of its functions through or jointly with a Special Health Authority, CCG or other body, while s 13Z2 (which is not intended to be used regularly) enables the Secretary of State to intervene in case of significant failure of the Board to discharge its functions properly (including failure to do so consistently with what the Secretary of State considers to be in the interests of the NHS),[70] or at all. **1.27**

(iii) Budgeting and financial arrangements

The budget for the NHS in England, allocated to the Department of Health by the Treasury, is largely administered by the Board;[71] for 2016/17 this amounted to over £106 million.[72] Approximately one-third of this sum is retained by the Board for the services which it commissions directly, including primary care, and for its own running costs. The remainder is allocated to CCGs to enable them to commission services for their populations. The Board has a duty to ensure that total health expenditure (that is, expenditure on services which it commissions, and by CCGs) does not exceed the aggregate of the amount allotted to it by government and any other income it derives.[73] In effect, this functions as a 'cash limit' on NHS commissioning. **1.28**

Financial arrangements for CCGs are set out in ss 223G to 223K of the 2006 Act.[74] As was the case with Primary Care Trusts, funds are allocated to CCGs according to a 'weighted capitation' formula,[75] which seeks to measure relative need between different geographical areas. The formula is calculated on the basis of (i) the size of the CCG's population; (ii) an adjustment for need for health care services related to age; (iii) an adjustment for other need (thus, areas with poorer health have higher need per head): (iv) an adjustment for unmet need and health inequalities; (v) an adjustment for unavoidable differences in cost based upon location alone (eg higher staff, land, and building costs, such as in London) and the cost of providing emergency ambulance services in sparsely populated areas.[76] In determining the allocation, the Board may take into account the expenditure of the CCG **1.29**

---

[66] See para 1.19.
[67] Inserted by Health and Social Care Act 2012, s 23.
[68] National Health Service Act 2006, s 13Q. See further para 1.112.
[69] ibid, ss 13T and 13U.
[70] ibid, s 13Z2(5).
[71] Some money is retained by the Department of Health for public health funding, covering departmental and arm's length body running costs and for centrally-managed projects and services.
[72] Department of Health, *The Government's Mandate to NHS England for 2016-17* (2016) para 3.1.
[73] National Health Service Act 2006, s 223C, inserted by Health and Social Care Act 2012, s 24. Other income might arise, for example, from the Board's power to generate its own income: see National Health Service Act 2006, s 13W.
[74] Inserted by Health and Social Care Act 2012, s 27.
[75] Allocation takes place under s 223G of the 2006 Act.
[76] See NHS England, *Technical Guide to Allocation Formulae and Pace of Change for 2016–17 to 2020–21 revenue allocations to Clinical Commissioning Groups and commissioning areas* (2016).

in the previous financial year, enabling it to reduce or increase the amount to reflect any overspends or underspends respectively.[77] The Board may make an in-year adjustment in the allocation;[78] in such circumstances, it may direct that the adjusted amount be spent in a particular way, for example to make a specific treatment or service more widely available to its population.[79]

1.30 Section 223H obliges CCGs to break even on their commissioning budget. Additionally, s 223I requires them to ensure that their use of resources (that is, capital and revenue) does not exceed an amount specified by the Board. These obligations have not always been fulfilled; eighteen CCGs were forecast to be in cumulative deficit at the end of the financial year 2014–15.[80] However, the Board also possesses incentivizing powers under s 223K, which enable it to pay a 'quality premium' to a CCG after the end of a financial year, assessed on the basis of at least one of the quality of services provided; improvements in quality; outcomes achieved; or improvements in outcomes.[81]

(iv) Patient-based commissioning—personal health budgets

1.31 A significantly different way of commissioning health care is through patients themselves. A 'personal health budget' is intended to allow the NHS to 'tailor services and support for people to enable them to have choice, control, and flexibility over their care'.[82] Pilot studies carried out across England between 2009 and 2012 found that there were significant improvements in quality of life and psychological wellbeing for patients operating such budgets, while costs of inpatient care were lower.[83] On this basis, government has initiated a phased introduction of personal health budgets, beginning with those with greatest levels of need. From October 2014, everyone in receipt of NHS continuing health care or children and young people's continuing care has a 'right to have' a personal health budget, if they wish.[84] The *NHS Mandate* envisages a further roll-out of the programme such that 'everyone with long-term conditions, including people with mental health problems, will be offered a personalized care plan that reflects their preferences and agreed decisions'.[85]

1.32 A personal health budget is defined as:

> an amount of money to support a person's identified health and wellbeing needs, the application of which is planned and agreed between the individual, their representative, or, in the case of children, their families or carers and the local NHS team. It is not new money, but is money

---

[77] National Health Service Act 2006, s 223G(2).

[78] ibid, s 223G(4).

[79] ibid, s 223G(6).

[80] House of Commons Health Committee, *Oral Evidence: Public Expenditure on Health and Social Care (2014–15)* (HC 679) (28 October 2014, Q8 (P Baumann)).

[81] For example, the quality premium paid in 2015/16, reflecting the quality of services commissioned in 2014/15, was based upon measures including reduction of potential years of life lost through causes considered amenable to healthcare and addressing local priorities for reducing premature mortality; improvement of access to psychological therapies; reduction in avoidable emergency admissions; and improvement in the reporting of medication-related safety incidents: NHS England, *Quality Premium: 2014/15 Guidance for CCGs* (2014), para 11.

[82] NHS England, *Guidance on the 'right to have' a Personal Health Budget in Adult NHS Continuing Healthcare and Children and Young People's Continuing Care* (2014), 9.

[83] J Forder et al, *Evaluation of the personal health budget pilot programme* (2012), Executive Summary paras 12, 16.

[84] National Health Service Commissioning Board and Clinical Commissioning Groups (Responsibilities and Standing Rules) Regulations 2012, regs 32A and B, inserted by National Health Service Commissioning Board and Clinical Commissioning Groups (Responsibilities and Standing Rules) (Amendment) Regulations 2013, SI 2013/2891.

[85] Department of Health, n 53, para 2.6.

that would normally have been spent by the NHS on a person's care being spent more flexibly to meet their identified needs.[86]

The budget may be arranged in one of three ways:[87] via direct payment,[88] in which money is transferred direct to the patient or a representative/nominee who contracts for the necessary services; through a notional budget, in which the commissioner (such as a CCG) retains the funds but uses it to purchase services based on the outcome of discussions with the patient; and through a third party independent of the individual and the NHS (such as a voluntary organization). Although discussion and agreement should take place with the patient as to the most appropriate way to manage the budget, the use of direct payments should always be considered when personal health budgets are being provided.[89] **1.33**

Where a person has the 'right to have' a personal health budget, there is an expectation that such provision will be made. Only in limited circumstances will this expectation be displaced, for instance, where specialized clinical care is required.[90] If a request for a personal health budget is refused, the CCG must set out the reasons in for doing so in writing; the patient and/or representative may request that the decision be reconsidered, providing additional information if relevant.[91] If, following reconsideration, the patient/representative remains dissatisfied, they may pursue the matter via the NHS complaints process. The CCG may agree to some elements of care being covered by the budget, but not others; where it does so, it must also give reasons for its decision and reconsider if requested to do so.[92] **1.34**

Certain services are excluded from coverage within a personal health budget: these include vaccination or immunization; screening; unplanned inpatient admissions to hospital; or treatment in accident and emergency departments. It may also not be used to purchase alcohol or tobacco; for gambling; to repay a debt; or to purchase anything illegal or unlawful.[93] Otherwise, in principle, the budget can be 'spent on a broad range of things that will enable the person to meet their health and wellbeing needs'.[94] As far as possible, the patient, supported where necessary by carers and professionals, should make choices about how needs are met. **1.35**

3. The provision of NHS services

(i) Primary care services

Section 83 of the 2006 Act, as amended by the 2012 Act, imposes a duty upon the NHS Commissioning Board to 'secure the provision of primary medical services throughout England'. The effect of this provision is that the Board will enter into contractual arrangements with GP practices which agree to provide primary medical services in their local areas. However, from 1 April 2015, CCGs have been empowered to commission primary medical services themselves via delegation from the Board. This will enable them to undertake contracting functions, including design of PMS and APMS contracts (see paras 1.45–1.48); **1.36**

[86] NHS England, n 82, 8.
[87] ibid, 10.
[88] See National Health Service Act 2006, s 12A.
[89] NHS England, *Guidance on Direct Payments for Healthcare: Understanding the Regulations* (2014) para 2.2.
[90] NHS England, n 82, 15.
[91] National Health Service Commissioning Board and Clinical Commissioning Groups (Responsibilities and Standing Rules) Regulations 2012, regs 32B(7) and (8).
[92] NHS England, n 82, 16.
[93] National Health Service (Direct Payments) Regulations 2013, SI 2013/1617, reg 8(5). Note that the Regulations only address the direct payment method of funding a personal health budget, but Guidance indicates that the exclusions should apply to all forms of budget: NHS England, n 82, 12.
[94] NHS England, n 89, para 3.3.

monitoring of contracts; taking contractual action; and removing contracts, but not to manage the performance of individual GPs.[95] Since the Board retains legal responsibility for securing provision under s 83, it must approve all proposals for assumption of such delegated powers, with CCGs being required to enter into a legally binding agreement with the Board to confirm the details of delegation,[96] and subject to an ongoing assurance framework.[97]

1.37 The 'contractual arrangements with any person' which may be made under s 83(2) take various forms. These will now be described.

1.38 (a) **General Medical Services (GMS)** Under s 84 of the Act, the Board may enter into contracts for provision of GMS. Such a 'GMS contract' may be made with a doctor; a medical partnership; or a limited company, provided at least one of the shares is owned by a doctor.[98] The contractor 'shall carry out its obligations under the contract with reasonable care and skill'[99] but the nature and extent of the GMS services provided depends upon the agreement entered into. The GMS Regulations provide for three levels of service: essential, additional, and enhanced. 'Essential' services are the minimum level of services that may be provided by a GMS contractor. They are:

> services required for the management of its registered patients and temporary residents who are (a) ill, or believe themselves to be ill, with conditions from which recovery is generally expected, (b) terminally ill, or (c) suffering from chronic disease, delivered in the manner determined by the practice in discussion with the patient.[100]

1.39 It will be noted that the obligation of the contractor is the 'management' of patients and temporary residents. 'Management' is defined as including:

> (a) offering consultation and, where appropriate, physical examination for the purpose of identifying the need, if any, for treatment or further investigation; and (b) the making available of such treatment or further investigation as is necessary and appropriate, including the referral of the patient for other services under the Act and liaison with other health care professionals involved in the patient's treatment and care.[101]

1.40 Essential services must be provided in 'core hours' (ie 8.00am to 6.30pm on any day from Monday to Friday except Good Friday, Christmas Day, or bank holidays)[102] to such extent as is appropriate to meet the reasonable needs of its patients, in addition to having arrangements in place for access throughout the core hours in case of emergency.[103]

1.41 The contractor may also undertake more extensive additional services by agreeing to provide one or more of the following: cervical screening; contraceptive services; vaccines and immunizations; childhood vaccines and immunizations; child health surveillance services; maternity medical services; and minor surgery.[104] In addition, the contractor may provide

---

[95] NHS England, *Next Steps towards Primary Care Co-Commissioning* (2014), para 4.4.
[96] ibid, para 7.4.
[97] ibid, para 9.1.
[98] National Health Service Act, 2006, s 86.
[99] National Health Service (General Medical Services Contracts) Regulations 2004, SI 2004/291, Sch 6, para 67.
[100] ibid, reg 15(3).
[101] ibid, reg 15(4).
[102] ibid, reg 2.
[103] ibid, reg 20. Out of hours services are commissioned by CCGs, not by the Board, except where GP practices have opted in to provision of such services. There have been calls by government for seven day, 8am to 8pm access to GPs: see 'GPs offered a "new deal" if they agree seven-day opening', *BBC News* (19 June 2015).
[104] ibid, reg 2, as amended by National Health Service (Primary Medical Services) (Miscellaneous Amendments) Regulations 2012, SI 2012/970, Part 2, reg 2(b), Sch 2. The right to opt out of 'additional services' may be refused if those services are not locally available elsewhere, see Sch 2, para 3(1).

enhanced services beyond those covered by the essential or additional categories: there is no limit to these services, provided that they can be considered to fall within the health service.

While there is a right under the NHS Constitution to choose a GP practice,[105] patients have the right only to 'express a preference' as to the particular practitioner by whom they wish to be treated.[106] The contractor shall endeavour to comply with any reasonable preference expressed: 'but need not do so if the performer (a) has reasonable grounds for refusing to provide services to the patient; or (b) does not routinely perform the service in question within the practice'.[107] Further, doctors have the right to refuse patients admission to, or remove them from, their lists on 'reasonable grounds'.[108] However, given the Secretary of State's duty to promote a comprehensive service, contractors cannot be entirely free to refuse patients access to care, and the GMS contract reserves to the Board the right to 'assign' patients to contractors without their agreement.[109] Of course, this is not a desirable solution to a problem, since the forcing of one party on another is hardly conducive to a productive relationship. Nevertheless, especially in areas in which there are few contractors, a small number of practices may find that patients with whom they have a poor relationship are regularly assigned to their lists.[110] **1.42**

With respect to violent patients, speedier procedures are available to remove those who have committed an 'act of violence' against, or behaved in such a way that there is a fear for safety on the part of, doctors, practice staff, or patients. In such cases the Board is to be notified of the request for removal, and the patient informed of the request unless it is not reasonably practicable to do so or the contractor has reasonable grounds for believing that doing so would be harmful to the physical or mental health of the patient or that it will put doctors, practice staff or patients at risk of safety. The Board is required to give written notice to the patient of removal from the list. [111] **1.43**

(b) Primary medical services (PMS) PMS offers greater flexibility as to the agreements that may be entered into with primary care providers.[112] The rights and duties **1.44**

---

[105] Department of Health, *NHS Constitution for England* (2015), s 3(a). See also National Health Service (General Medical Services Contracts) Regulations 2004, Sch 6, para 15.

[106] Department of Health, *NHS Constitution for England* (2015).

[107] National Health Service (General Medical Services Contracts) Regulations 2004, Sch 6, para 18(2).

[108] ibid, Sch 6, paras 17(1) and 20(1). The reasons must not relate to 'the applicant's race, gender, social class, age, religion, sexual orientation, appearance, disability, or medical condition'. The patient is entitled to a warning before removal and an explanation in writing within fourteen days if they are refused admission to the list, see Sch 6, paras 20(3) and 17(3).

[109] ibid, Sch 6, Part 2, para 32, as amended by National Health Service (Primary Medical Services (Miscellaneous Amendments and Transitional Provisions) Regulations 2013, SI 2013/363, Part 2, reg 27(26)(a).

[110] Before making such an assignment the Board must have regard to: '(a) the wishes and circumstances of the patient ... (b) the distance between the patient's place of residence and the contractor's practice premises; (c) any request made by any contractor to remove the patient from its list of patients within the preceding period of 6 months starting on the date on which the application for assignment is received by the Board; (d) whether, during the preceding period of 6 months, the patient's name has been removed ... under para 20 [removal from the list at the request of the contractor] or para 21 [violent patients]... ; (e) [where the patient's name has been removed under para 21] whether the contractor has appropriate facilities to deal with such patients; and (f) such other matters as the Board considers relevant': ibid, Sch 6, para 34, as substituted by National Health Service (Primary Medical Services (Miscellaneous Amendments and Transitional Provisions) Regulations 2013, Part 2, reg 27(28).

[111] ibid, Sch 6, para 21, as amended by National Health Service (Primary Medical Services (Miscellaneous Amendments and Transitional Provisions) Regulations 2013, Part 2, reg 27(14)(a).

[112] The power to enter into such agreements is conferred upon the Board by s 92 of the 2006 Act, as amended by Sch 4, para 36 of the 2012 Act.

of PMS contractors are set down by Regulations[113] broadly comparable to the GMS Regulations.[114] PMS providers may elect to provide practice-based, 'essential' services on the model described in the GMS Regulations, or provide different services to particular patient groups: eg disease-specific, a client group such as homeless people or drug addicts, or a wider service in a drop-in centre. PMS are essentially local contracts designed to respond to local needs, although they may also compare closely to GMS contracts. Clearly, if a PMS provider agreed to supply a less than comprehensive range of services, a commissioner would be required to arrange for the remaining services to be provided by other providers. Accordingly, it is crucial for the contract to describe accurately the services to be provided, to whom and how performance is to be assessed and remunerated (and it may do so by means of an 'NHS contract', or a private contract enforceable in the courts). So far as patients are concerned, the difference in the range and quality of the services provided should be insignificant.

1.45 (c) **Alternative provider medical services (APMS)** Section 83(2) of the 2006 Act gives the NHS Commissioning Board power to 'make such arrangements for the provision of primary medical services as it considers appropriate; and it may, in particular, make contractual arrangements with any person'.[115] APMS extends the opportunity to provide primary care to a range of other organizations such as private companies and not-for-profit organizations, voluntary and community sector organizations, and NHS and Foundation Trusts.[116] The logic of APMS is to encourage innovation in areas of historical underprovision where, for example, there has been difficulty recruiting and retaining GP practices. As in the case of PMS agreements, the nature and extent of the agreement will depend on local needs and interests, but again, some mandatory terms must be included in every APMS contract, for example: whether or not it is an NHS contract; the services to be provided; where and to whom; and how performance will be assessed and remunerated. Many of the mandatory terms included in the PMS regulations are also to be included in APMS contracts. In particular, the duty to prescribe is the same as in PMS (ie to prescribe the drugs and appliances which are needed), as are rights of entry and inspection of premises, the duty to cooperate with investigations, and provisions as to termination.

1.46 Given that APMS may be provided by commercial parties, special provision is made to exclude financial interests from the contract. In particular, the Board shall ensure that APMS contracts prohibit the demanding of fees or other payments for treatment or prescriptions (other than as permitted by the PMS regulations) and that decisions to refer patients for other services are made without regard to the party's own financial interests. Presumably, the Board and other regulators will wish to be reassured that these terms are properly observed (and there is a mandatory duty to participate in an appropriate appraisal system).[117]

1.47 The award of APMS contracts by the NHS Commissioning Board has proved controversial. Initially, the Board's policy appears to have been that all new GP contracts (thus excluding those which reverted to GMS from PMS, or where PMS were varied) would take the form

[113] Such Regulations are made under s 94 of the 2006 Act, as amended by s 28(2) and Sch 4, para 38 of the 2012 Act.

[114] The National Health Service (Personal Medical Services Agreements) Regulations 2004, SI 2004/627. These have been amended on a number of occasions, with substantial amendments consonant upon the Health and Social Care Act 2012 being effected by National Health Service (Primary Medical Services (Miscellaneous Amendments and Transitional Provisions) Regulations 2013. Contractual terms are set out in Part 5 and Schedule 5 of the 2004 Regulations, as amended.

[115] As amended by Sch 4, para 30 of the Health and Social Care Act 2012.

[116] See the Alternative Provider Medical Services Directions 2013.

[117] ibid, directions, 9, 10, and 8 respectively.

of APMS contracts, allowing for open competition in compliance with NHS procurement law[118] and the overarching EU principle of non-discrimination. The legality of this 'blanket approach' was questioned by the General Practitioners Committee of the British Medical Association,[119] noting that the Procurement Regulations required account to be taken of 'securing the needs of the people who use the services' and 'best value for money',[120] neither of which were served by the award of an APMS contract (which typically lasts for only five years) after an expensive tendering process. In response, the Board indicated that it had not made a decision to end the use of GMS or PMS contracts, but would 'continue to review on a case-by-case basis, depending on local circumstances'.[121]

Contractors may enter into agreements with the Board as 'health service bodies' and therefore outside the ambit of the private law of contract, or as private contractors.[122] With respect to 'health service bodies', the GMS and PMS regulations permit deductions from monies payable under the agreement for non-performance of terms in excess of the damage caused.[123] In *R v Secretary of State for Health, ex p Hickey*,[124] a doctor was subject to a £2,000 deduction for failing to be on duty as required by his terms of service, although he had caused no serious financial damage to the health authority. The court reasoned this was consistent with the regulatory nature of the (previous) GMS contract. However, with respect to those that contract under the private law of contract, awards of damages are limited to the loss actually inflicted by the breach on the innocent party. And penalty clauses in excess of reasonable compensation, intended simply to penalize the contract-breaker, will not be enforced.[125] This would limit the deductions that could be made from 'non-NHS contract' contractors for non-performance and, to this extent, makes them more attractive to private contractors. **1.48**

(ii) NHS Trusts and Foundation Trusts

Section 179 of the Health and Social Care Act 2012 repeals the legal framework establishing NHS Trusts in England.[126] All NHS Trusts are expected to become Foundation Trusts as soon as clinically feasible. In order to assist them in making this transition, a NHS Trust Development Authority (now part of the NHS Improvement organization) was set up as a **1.49**

[118] See National Health Service (Procurement, Patient Choice and Competition) (No. 2) Regulations 2013, SI 2013/500, reg 3(2)(b).

[119] See Monitor, *Substantive Guidance on the Procurement, Patient Choice and Competition Regulations* (2013) para 3.2: 'There is no default process that commissioners should use to secure services. In particular, the Procurement, Patient Choice and Competition Regulations do not establish a competitive tender process as the default mechanism that commissioners should use to buy services.'

[120] National Health Service (Procurement, Patient Choice and Competition)(No.2) Regulations, regs 2 and 3(3).

[121] See 'NHS managers backtrack on vow that all new GP contracts will be APMS' *Pulse* (17 September 2014).

[122] See National Health Service (General Medical Services Contracts) Regulations 2004, reg 10 (as amended by National Health Service (Primary Medical Services (Miscellaneous Amendments and Transitional Provisions) Regulations 2013, reg 10; National Health Service (Personal Medical Services Agreements) Regulations 2004 (as amended by National Health Service (Primary Medical Services (Miscellaneous Amendments and Transitional Provisions) Regulations 2013, reg 37).

[123] See NHS England, *Contract breaches, sanctions and termination for primary medical services* (2013). The relevant provisions are National Health Service (General Medical Services Contracts) Regulations 2004, Sch 6, para 117 and National Health Service (Personal Medical Services Agreements) Regulations 2004, Sch 5, para 109, as amended by National Health Service (Primary Medical Services (Miscellaneous Amendments and Transitional Provisions)) Regulations 2013.

[124] (1993) 10 BMLR 12.

[125] See *Dunlop Pneumatic Tyre Co Ltd v New Garage and Motor Co Ltd* [1915] AC 79.

[126] The section is to be commenced by an order made by the Secretary of State; until this is issued, National Health Service Act 2006, s 25 remains in force.

Special Health Authority under s 28 of the 2006 Act with additional functions of monitoring the performance of Trusts, of assurance of clinical quality, governance and risk, and of appointment of chairs, non-executive directors and special trustees.[127]

1.50 There is one situation in which an organization can remain a NHS Trust even after the transition has been made by all others. Section 179(3) of the 2012 Act provides that Trusts which have entered into 'franchise arrangements' (that, is with the private sector) are exempt from having to achieve Foundation Trust status for the duration of the arrangement, and for three years after it has ended. The franchising route has not proved popular, no doubt because of the financial pressures confronting the NHS; only one hospital had previously been franchised and it has now been returned to NHS control.[128]

1.51 The first NHS Foundation Trust hospitals were created in 2004 and now take their authority from the National Health Service Act 2006, as amended by the 2012 Act.[129] They provide over half of all NHS hospital, mental health, and ambulance services,[130] and give (in the government's words):

> proper accountability to the local community so that both public and staff have a direct say in how their local services are provided. They will offer a new form of social ownership by the public not by the state—not for private profit but in the public interest.[131]

They are therefore intended to have freedom from governmental control in reaching decisions upon strategy and the way in which services are run. They can retain their surpluses,[132] and are not legally required to break even every year.[133]

1.52 How do Foundation Trust hospitals permit local control over NHS hospitals? Like any other corporate body, Foundation Trusts require a constitution which provides for two things: (1) who owns it and what are its objectives; and (2) how is it governed and to whom is it accountable. To this extent, the challenge of Foundation Trusts is similar to any corporate body. In the private sphere, corporate objectives are identified by the board of directors which is accountable to shareholders, and any director may be removed for poor performance. There are no shareholders of Foundation Trusts, so who governs them?

1.53 (a) **Ownership and objectives** A Foundation Trust is a 'public benefit corporation' constituted in accordance with the 2006 Act.[134] Ownership is vested in 'members', namely, people who live in an area specified in the constitution (the 'public constituency'); who are employed (or engaged) by the corporation (the 'staff constituency'); or have attended the corporation's hospital as either a patient or as a carer of a patient (the 'patient constituency').[135] The statute does not define the precise nature and extent of the members' rights in respect of NHS foundation hospitals because 'each Foundation Trust will have considerable

---

[127] National Health Service Trust Development Authority (Establishment and Constitution) Order 2012, SI 2012/901.

[128] See 'Hinchinbrooke Hospital: Britain's only privately-run NHS hospital appeals for £10m taxpayer-funded bailout' *The Independent* (10 February 2015).

[129] See ch 5 of the 2006 Act and s 180 of the 2012 Act, which repeal provisions for authorization of Foundation Trusts, on the basis that these will no longer be necessary once all Trusts attain such status.

[130] 'What are foundation trusts?' at <https://www.gov.uk/government/publications/nhs-foundation-trust-directory/nhs-foundation-trust-directory>.

[131] Department of Health, *A Guide to Foundation Trusts* (2002), para 1.10.

[132] ibid, para 5.14.

[133] In contrast to CCGs and NHS Trusts. For CCGs, see above, para 1.30. For NHS Trusts, see National Health Service Act 2006, Sch 5, para 2(1).

[134] See s 30 and Sch 7.

[135] National Health Service Act 2006, Sch 7, para 3(1).

freedom as to how it implements arrangements for social ownership'.[136] However, each Trust must prepare an annual report for the independent regulator explaining what steps have been taken to secure that the membership of the public constituency and of the patient constituency is representative of those eligible.[137]

The corporate objectives of NHS Foundation Trusts are specified by each Trust's constitution and enforced by the independent regulator, Monitor (now part of the NHS Improvement organization).[138] However, their salient duty is to promote the objectives of the NHS. Section 43(1) of the 2006 Act[139] provides that the 'principal purpose of an NHS Foundation Trust is the provision of goods and services for the purposes of the health service in England', further defined by subsection (2) as being the prevention, diagnosis, and treatment of illness and the promotion and protection of public health. However, it is empowered to carry on other activities for the purpose of raising additional income to enable it better to carry on this principal purpose,[140] provided that it raises the majority of its income from undertaking the principal purpose.[141] Additionally, it may do anything which appears to it to be necessary or expedient in connection with its functions. 'In particular, it may (a) acquire and dispose of property, (b) enter into contracts, (c) accept gifts of property . . . [and] (d) employ staff'[142] and borrow and invest money.[143] **1.54**

(b) Governance and accountability Although the 'members' of NHS Foundation Trusts have statutory ownership, they have little direct control and less influence than do shareholders over private companies. Operational power in NHS Foundation Trusts is exercised by a Board of Directors; indeed: 'all the powers of the corporation [are] exercisable by the Board of Directors'.[144] The Board, and the Directors individually, have a general duty to 'act with a view to promoting the success of the corporation so as to maximize the benefits for the members of the corporation as a whole and for the public'.[145] Members elect a Council of Governors according to the rights vested in their respective constituencies.[146] In turn, the Council holds the non-executive Directors individually and collectively to account for the performance of the Board and represents the interests of the members and of the public.[147] It also appoints, or removes, the chairman and the non-executive members of the Board of Directors; the executive directors are appointed, or removed, by the chairman, chief executive, and other non-executive members.[148] **1.55**

Considerable discretion has been left to the local bodies to develop their own systems of governance.[149] However, Monitor operates a Code of Practice, which seeks to 'bring best **1.56**

[136] House of Commons Health Committee, Second Report, (2002-03), *Foundation Trusts*, (HC 395-I) para 32.
[137] National Health Service Act 2006, Sch 7, para 26(2).
[138] For further discussion of Monitor, see paras 1.131–1.140.
[139] As amended by Health and Social Care Act 2012, s 164.
[140] National Health Service Act 2006, s 43(3).
[141] ibid, s 43(2A), inserted by Health and Social Care Act 2012, s 164(1).
[142] ibid, s 47.
[143] ibid, s 46.
[144] ibid, Sch 7, para 15(2).
[145] ibid, Sch 7, para 18A, inserted by Health and Social Care Act 2012, s 151(1). There are particular duties imposed upon Directors to avoid conflicts of interest and not to accept a benefit by reason of being a Director: Sch 7, para 18B(1).
[146] ibid, Sch 7, para 7, as amended by Health and Social Care Act 2012, s 151(1).
[147] ibid, Sch 7, para 10A, inserted by Health and Social Care Act 2012, s 151(4).
[148] ibid, Sch 7, para 17.
[149] See Department of Health, n. 131, para 2.16: 'It will be up to applicants to develop proposals on the size and composition of its Board of Governors to suit its local circumstances'.

practice from the private sector to the NHS Foundation Trust sector, with the ultimate goal of ensuring a strong governance structure is in place to ensure high-quality patient care'.[150] The Code does not take a mandatory form, but Trusts are expected to explain their reasons for non-compliance.

1.57 NHS Foundation Trusts enter legal contracts with CCGs (and the NHS Commissioning Board) which are regulated by law, rather than 'NHS contracts' which are unenforceable in law. The need to agree contractual terms is necessary because NHS Foundation Trusts are not subject to Secretary of State's directions. As a result, outputs need to be agreed and formalized under legally binding contracts. The contract should specify the range of services that are to be provided by the Trust, the volumes and cost of services to be provided and include penalty and incentive clauses to encourage prompt and efficient performance.[151] Disputes relating to failures to agree a contract for a new financial year may, by agreement between the parties, be referred into the dispute resolution process described below; in-year disputes are managed through the process set out in the contract, and are ultimately enforceable by the courts.[152]

(iii) NHS 'contracts'

1.58 The National Health Service and Community Care Act 1990 first introduced the 'NHS contract' as a means of setting out the relationship between commissioners and providers of care within the Service. This is now defined by s 9(1) of the 2006 Act as 'an agreement under which one health service body ("the commissioner") arranges for the provision to it by another health service body ("the provider") of goods and services which it reasonably requires for the purposes of its functions'. Subsection (4) provides a list of bodies which are considered as health service bodies for the purposes of this provision; this includes the NHS Commissioning Board, CCGs, NHS Trusts, Special Health Authorities, the Care Quality Commission, NICE, the Secretary of State, and Scottish and Welsh ministers.

1.59 The key feature of such contracts is that they do not give rise to legally enforceable rights in the civil courts. This is made clear by s 9(5) of the 2006 Act, which provides that 'whether or not an arrangement which constitutes an NHS contract would apart from this subsection be a contract in law, it must not be regarded for any purpose as giving rise to contractual rights or liabilities'. Rather, 'if any dispute arises with respect to any such arrangement, either party may refer the matter to the Secretary of State for determination';[153] the Secretary of State, in turn, may determine the matter himself or appoint a person to do so.[154] The process of resolution varies somewhat according to whether the dispute arises in-year, or in the process of contract negotiation. In the former case, a written offer to negotiate ('escalated negotiation') will be followed by mediation and, if necessary, expert determination;[155] in the latter, advice and/or mediation precedes arbitration.[156] In both instances, the determination at the last stage is final and not subject to appeal.[157]

---

[150] Monitor, *The NHS Foundation Trust Code of Governance* (2014) para 1.3.

[151] Department of Health, n. 131, para 4.9.

[152] NHS England/NHS Trust Development Authority/Monitor, *Dispute Resolution Process for the 2015/16 Contracting Process* (2015), para 2.2.

[153] National Health Service Act 2006, s 9(6). Section 9(7) provides that similar determination may be made if issues arise in the process of negotiation due to inequality of bargaining position.

[154] ibid, s 9(8).

[155] NHS England, *NHS Standard Contract 2016/17: General Conditions* (2015), GC 14.

[156] NHS England/NHS Trust Development Authority/Monitor, n 152, ss 4 and 5.

[157] Except in the case of the Standard Contract, where there is 'fraud, collusion, bias, manifest error or material breach of instructions on the part of the Expert', in which case a party may apply to court for an

A standard NHS contract was introduced for the first time in 2007. 'The standard contract was the government's attempt to make health care contracts more detailed or 'complete' in the expectation that, by specifying in detail performance, productivity and quality indicators, greater transparency, accountability and risk allocation would be achieved'.[158] The NHS Commissioning Board now has responsibility for its preparation and publication, and the contract (which is republished each year) is mandated for use by commissioners for all health care services regardless of duration or value, except for primary care services.[159] The contract is divided into three parts: general conditions; particulars; and service conditions. The particulars (which include matters such as the details of the parties and schedules relating to payment, quality and information) are agreed locally; the service conditions vary according to the service which is the subject of the contract (thus, some clauses will only be relevant to particular services or types of provider; those which are not relevant can be deleted); while the general conditions must all be included and cannot be locally varied. **1.60**

(iv) Private providers

The NHS has long made extensive use of private providers. Most of primary care is contracted from independent GP practices, most nursing home care is provided in private nursing homes, and medicines are purchased from the pharmaceutical industry. Section 12ZA of the 2006 Act provides that commissioning arrangements made by the NHS Commissioning Board or by CCGs may be made 'with any person or body';[160] comparable provisions were contained in previous versions of the National Health Service Act.[161] Facilities and the services of other NHS bodies may be made available for this purpose on such terms as may be agreed, including the making of payments by, or to, the Board and CCGs.[162] As the use of private facilities has become more common, the traditional split between public and private providers has become more difficult to recognize. NHS patients may receive treatment in private hospitals, and staff engaged by private health companies may provide NHS care. This has created problems, as noted above.[163] **1.61**

There has, therefore, been a mixed economy of providers operating within the NHS for some time. However, recent years have witnessed a considerable increase in the role of competition in the commissioning and provision of services. For example, in 2007, the Department of Health published the first edition of non-binding guidance on the expected behaviour and rules governing cooperation and competition in the provision of NHS services. This was structured around a series of general principles, such as 'Commissioners must commission services from the providers who are best placed to deliver the needs of their patients and populations' and 'payment regimes and financial intervention in the system must be transparent and fair'.[164] An advisory board, the Cooperation and Competition Panel, was also established to help support delivery to patients and taxpayers of the benefits of competition, **1.62**

order that the Expert reconsider all or part of his decision, or that the decision be set aside in total or in part: NHS England, n 155, GC 14.17.

[158] C Petsoulas, O Allen, D Hughes, P Vincent-Jones, and J Roberts, 'The Use of Standard Contracts in the English National Health Service: A Case Study Analysis' (2011) 73 Social Science and Medicine 185, 186.

[159] National Health Service Commissioning Board and Clinical Commissioning Groups (Responsibilities and Standing Rules) Regulations 2012, reg 17(3).

[160] As inserted by Health and Social Care Act 2012, Sch 4, para 9. Emphasis added.

[161] See National Health Service Act 1977, s 23.

[162] National Health Service Act 2006, ss 12ZA(3), (8).

[163] See paras 1.13–1.16.

[164] Department of Health, *Principles and Rules for Cooperation and Competition* (2010), 7, 10.

making recommendations to the Department of Health on mergers, anti-competitive conduct, failures to co-operate, and other breaches of the Principles and Rules.[165]

1.63 The Coalition Government's reforms to the NHS were controversial in large part because of a perception that the role of the private sector in the provision of healthcare was being significantly enhanced. The White Paper which presaged the reforms stated that 'our aim is to free up provision of healthcare, so that in most sectors of care, any willing provider can provide services, giving patients greater choice and ensuring effective competition stimulates innovation and improvements, and increases productivity within a social market'.[166]

1.64 Chapter 1 of Part 3 of the 2012 Act establishes Monitor as the economic regulator with responsibility for promotion of provision of health services which are economic, efficient, and effective.[167] A clause in the Bill which would have imposed an additional duty upon it to promote competition where possible was dropped in light of political opposition; nonetheless, Monitor was given concurrent power with the Office of Fair Trading[168] to conduct investigations into anti-competitive practices or abuses of dominant position in relation to the provision of healthcare services in England, whether under the Competition Act 1998 or EU law.[169]

1.65 Section 75 of the 2012 Act empowers the Secretary of State to make Regulations which impose requirements on the NHS Commissioning Board and CCGs, when commissioning services, to adhere to good practice in relation to procurement; to protect and promote the right of patients to make choices with respect to treatment or other health care services; and not to engage in anti-competitive behaviour which is against the interests of the people who use those services. The Regulations made under this section set out an objective of procurement, in providing that the Board and CCGs must act with a view to securing the needs of people who use the services, improving the quality of the services and improving efficiency in the use of the services, including through provision of services in an integrated manner.[170] In pursuing this objective, CCGs and the Board must act transparently and proportionately, and treat providers equally and in a non-discriminatory way; must procure the services from one or more providers that are most capable of delivering the objective and provide best value for money in doing so; must consider ways of improving services; and must maintain records of how contracts awarded comply with duties in relation to effectiveness, efficiency, etc, improvement in quality of services, and promotion of integration.[171] Further specific requirements are imposed including, significantly, a prohibition upon engagement in anti-competitive behaviour when commissioning services, 'unless to do so is in the interests of people who use health care services for the purposes of the NHS'; 'interests' of this type may include provision of services in an integrated way or of cooperation between providers in order to improve quality of services.[172]

---

165 The Panel was disbanded by Monitor in 2014.

166 Department of Health, n 52, para 4.26.

167 Monitor is discussed further in paras 1.131–1.140.

168 The Office of Fair Trading's functions in this regard were assumed by the Competition and Markets Authority in April 2014.

169 Health and Social Care Act 2012, s 72.

170 National Health Service (Procurement, Patient Choice and Competition) (No. 2) Regulations 2013, reg 2.

171 ibid, reg 3. These duties are imposed upon the Board and CCGs respectively by ss 13D, E and N and 14Q, R and Z1 of the 2012 Act. See further discussion in para 1.27.

172 ibid, reg 10. The Explanatory Memorandum to the Regulations states that these savings 'reflect the Government's firm view that competition is a means to improving services and not an end in itself'.

Monitor has published guidance for commissioners on how to comply with the Regulations and on how it will utilize its enforcement powers.[173] This states that 'it is for commissioners to decide what services to procure and how best to secure them in the interests of patients within the framework of the Regulations'.[174] However, there is evidence that such local discretion is giving rise to uncertainty as to the extent of the obligation to comply with procurement rules and when and how to do so. The consequence appears to be that some CCGs have made use of procurement whereas others tend to work with existing providers.[175] **1.66**

More broadly, the impact of the 2012 Act's provisions relating to competition upon the provision of services within the NHS remains unclear. Research suggests that the proportion of services provided outside the NHS remains relatively small; one study showed that a third of contracts awarded between April 2013 and August 2014 went to private sector providers—however, most of these were small in scale and the value of those for which financial information was provided was merely 5 per cent of the total.[176] The Chief Executive of the NHS Commissioning Board has expressed the view that private sector involvement in provision 'is at the margins' and has issued a 'firm prediction that the vast majority of care will continue to be provided by NHS providers'.[177] **1.67**

(v) Provision of treatment overseas

While the UK remains in the European Union, there are two primary routes by which NHS patients may be provided with non-emergency treatment outside of the country.[178] The S2 (formerly E112) route is a direct arrangement between the NHS and state healthcare providers in European Economic Area (EEA) countries and Switzerland, which operates under Regulation 883/2004/EC on the co-ordination of social security schemes. Prior approval from the NHS Commissioning Board is required. An application must be supported by a written recommendation from an NHS consultant with an indication that a full clinical assessment has been undertaken which demonstrates that the treatment abroad meets the specific needs of the patient. An NHS England Cross Border Health Care team determines the application on the basis of whether the costs of sending the individual abroad for treatment are justified; only those eligible for treatment on the NHS are covered, and only in respect of treatment available in the other country's state healthcare system. Treatment is provided under the same conditions of care and payment as for residents of the country in question, with the consequence that the patient may be liable for payment of any co-payment charge. However, the patient may be reimbursed for any such payment upon return to the UK upon application to the Board. **1.68**

The second route is now governed by Directive 2011/24/EU on the application of patients' rights in cross-border health care.[179] Under the Directive, treatment can be provided either in the state or private sector, and prior authorization is required only in certain circumstances. The patient normally pays the cost of treatment and then seeks reimbursement from the NHS Commissioning Board (which, as under the S2 route, determines the application); **1.69**

---

173 Such guidance is published under s 78 of the 2012 Act.

174 Monitor, n 119, 6.

175 R Addicott, *Commissioning and Contracting for Integrated Care* (King's Fund 2014), 45.

176 G Iacobbuci, 'A Third of NHS Contracts Have Gone to Private Sector since Health Act Came into Force' (2014) 349 BMJ g7473.

177 G Iacobucci, 'Simon Stevens: The Man Charged with Saving the NHS' (2014) 349 BMJ g6895.

178 Emergency medical care is provided through the European Health Insurance Card scheme for EEA countries, and via reciprocal healthcare agreements between the UK and several countries outside the EEA.

179 The Directive is implemented by way of the National Health Service (Cross-Border) Regulations 2013, SI 2013/2269.

the Board then reclaims the cost from the relevant CCG.[180] Reimbursement is only available up to the cost of the equivalent NHS service or the actual cost of treatment, where this is lower than the NHS cost. Unlike the S2 route, reimbursement is only available in respect of treatments or services to which the patient would be entitled on the NHS.

1.70 Article 8 of the Directive specifies the circumstances in which prior authorization (which must be necessary and proportionate to the objective to be achieved and must not constitute a means of arbitrary discrimination or an unjustified obstacle to the free movement of persons) is permissible as a condition of reimbursement. Prior authorization is limited to health care which:

(a) is made subject to planning requirements relating to the object of ensuring sufficient and permanent access to a balanced range of high-quality treatment in the Member State concerned or to the wish to control costs and avoid, as far as possible, any waste of financial, technical and human resources and:
  (i) involves overnight hospital accommodation of the patient in question for at least one night; or
  (ii) requires use of highly specialized and cost-intensive medical infrastructure or medical equipment;

(b) involves treatments presenting a particular risk for the patient or the population; or

(c) is provided by a health care provider that, on a case-by-case basis, could give rise to serious and specific concerns relating to the quality or safety of the care, with the exception of health care which is subject to Union legislation ensuring a minimum level of safety and quality throughout the Union.

1.71 Based upon these criteria, the NHS Commissioning Board has drawn up a list of services which are subject to prior authorization.[181] Authorization may only be refused (a) where the patient will be exposed with reasonable certainty to a patient safety risk that cannot be regarded as acceptable; (b) where the general public will be exposed with reasonable certainty to a substantial safety hazard as a result of the cross-border health care; (c) where the health care is to be provided by a provider that raises serious and specific concerns relating to respect of standards and guidelines on quality of care and patient safety; or (d) where the health care can be provided within the 'home' health system within a time-limit which is medically justifiable taking into account the current state of health and the probable course of illness of the patient.[182]

1.72 The effect of condition (d) is that authorization must be given under the Directive if there would be 'undue delay' in providing treatment on the NHS. The same is true of treatment being sought via the S2 route. This is a consequence of a line of European jurisprudence culminating in the case of *R (on the application of Watts) v Bedford Primary Care Trust*,[183] in which it was held that a refusal to grant authorization cannot be based merely upon the need to plan and manage the supply of health services through waiting lists which give effect to general clinical priorities. Rather, refusal of authorization is only permissible if the waiting period for treatment on the NHS is 'medically justifiable'. This is to be established by reference to the patient; specifically by way of 'an objective assessment of the patient's medical condition, the history and probable course of the patient's illness, the degree of the

[180] See National Health Service and Public Health (Functions and Miscellaneous Provisions) Regulations 2013, SI 2013/261, reg 7(4).

[181] See Department of Health, *Cross Border Healthcare and Patient Mobility in Europe* (2013), Annex A.

[182] Article 8(6).

[183] [2006] QB 667 (ECJ). See further Chapter 7, paras 7.112–7.114.

patient's pain and/or the nature of the patient's disability at the time the request for authorization was made.[184]

In addition to these relatively common routes for treatment abroad, there is one specialized avenue. Proton beam therapy for cancer is currently only provided for patients with eye tumours within the UK, although NHS facilities are being developed in London and Manchester.[185] For patients with other forms of cancer, suitable cases are funded for treatment abroad[186] by a service commissioned nationally by the NHS Commissioning Board.[187] A Proton Clinical Reference Panel considers whether there is clinical justification for treatment abroad upon referral by a consultant clinical oncologist who has seen and assessed the patient;[188] if so, costs of travel and accommodation for the patient and one or two carers (for adults and children respectively) will be funded, plus the cost of travel insurance for those receiving treatment at centres in the USA. **1.73**

4. The NHS Constitution

One of the recommendations of the 'Next Stage Review' of the NHS in 2008, which sought to 'develop a vision of a service fit for the 21st century',[189] was the introduction of a Constitution. The stated rationales for this development were to set out the purpose, principles and values of the Service so as to preserve these for the future; to clarify the rights and responsibilities of patients and staff (thus 'empowering' them) by codification; and to strengthen accountability by specifying expectations and lines of responsibility.[190] **1.74**

The Constitution, which applies only to the NHS in England, was first published in 2009, with revised versions published in 2010, 2012, 2013, and 2015.[191] There is a statutory obligation for the Secretary of State to review the Constitution every ten years, following consultation with patients, staff, carers, local authorities, members of the public, NHS bodies, and such other persons as are considered appropriate. The first such review must be completed no later than 5 July 2018 (the seventieth anniversary of the establishment of the NHS).[192] **1.75**

So that it can remain a relatively high-level and stable instrument, the Constitution is accompanied by further documents which provide additional detail on its provisions. A 'Handbook to the NHS Constitution' provides further information on the rights, pledges, and responsibilities contained in the Constitution and explains where they originate; there is an obligation to review this document every three years.[193] A 'Statement of NHS Accountability', commitment to the availability of which is made in the Constitution, seeks to make transparent the system of responsibility and accountability for taking decisions in the NHS.[194] There is also a supplement produced to assist those working for local authorities **1.76**

[184] Article 8(5). See further National Health Service Act 2006, s 6BB(6), inserted by National Health Service (Cross-Border) Regulations 2013, reg 7.

[185] Private facilities are likely to open sooner than those being developed by the NHS: see 'Investors back £100m plan for UK proton-beam cancer centres' *Financial Times* (3 April 2015).

[186] Three facilities are presently used for this purpose: in Oklahoma, Florida, and Switzerland; the majority of patients have been sent to the USA.

[187] See NHS England, *Clinical Commissioning Policy: Funding policy for travel and accommodation proton overseas programme* (2013).

[188] For the controversial case of Aysha King, in which no such referral was made, see 'Time Running Out for Missing Boy with Brain Tumour, Say Police' *The Guardian* (29 August 2014).

[189] Department of Health, *High Quality Care for All* (CM 7432, 2008), 3.

[190] ibid, and see Chapter 7.

[191] Department of Health, *The Handbook to the NHS Constitution* (2015) 9.

[192] Health Act 2009 s. 3. Other revisions may take place within the ten-year period: s 4.

[193] ibid, s 5.

[194] See Department of Health, *Guide to the Healthcare System in England* (2013).

and Public Health England in understanding the Constitution, to which they must have regard when discharging their public health functions.[195]

1.77 The Constitution is primarily a 'declaratory' document; that is, it simply codifies existing rights and responsibilities drawn from various common law and statutory sources (which are detailed in the Handbook). The exception is the establishment of a new right to 'make choices about the services commissioned by NHS bodies and to information to support these choices',[196] which gives effect to a commitment to shared decision-making (captured by the slogan 'no decision about me, without me'), which has been central to recent reforms to the Service.[197]

1.78 The Constitution contains various forms of statements. The most general (and abstract) are NHS 'values', developed by staff, patients, and the public, which are those 'that inspire passion in the NHS and that should underpin everything it does':[198] these include 'respect and dignity'; 'compassion'; and 'improving lives'. Somewhat more specific are the 'principles' of the NHS, which are described as 'the enduring high-level "rules" that govern the way that the NHS operates, and define how it seeks to achieve its purpose'.[199] These are seven in number: (1) that the NHS provides a comprehensive service available to all; (2) that access to NHS services is based upon clinical need, not an individual's ability to pay; (3) that the NHS aspires to the highest standards of excellence and professionalism; (4) that the NHS aspires to put patients at the heart of everything it does; (5) that the NHS works across organizational boundaries and in partnership with other organizations in the interests of patients, local communities, and the wider population; (6) that the NHS is committed to providing best value for taxpayers' money and the most effective, fair and sustainable use of finite resources; and (7) that the NHS is accountable to the public, communities, and patients that it serves. Section 4(4) of the Health Act 2009 provides that any amendment to these principles can only be made by way of Regulations; this was done in 2013, when the explanatory text accompanying Principles 1, 3, 4, and 5 was amended.[200]

1.79 At a more specific level, the Constitution codifies a range of 'rights', or 'legal entitlement[s] protected by law', either conferred explicitly via statute or 'derived from legal obligations imposed on NHS bodies and other health care providers'.[201] There are several of these, described in s 3a of the Constitution: they include the right to access NHS services; the right to be treated with a professional standard of care; the right to expect local decisions on funding of drugs and treatments to be made rationally following proper consideration of the evidence; the right of access to health records; and the right to compensation when harmed by negligent treatment. Additionally, ss 3a and 4a contain 'pledges' to patients and the public, and staff respectively: these are matters which the NHS is committed to achieve, supported by its management and regulatory systems. They are not legally binding 'and cannot be guaranteed for everyone all of the time, because they express an ambition to improve, going above and beyond legal rights'.[202] These include making decisions in a clear

[195] Department of Health/Local Government Association/Public Health England, *Public Health Supplement to the NHS Constitution* (2013).

[196] National Health Service Commissioning Board and Clinical Commissioning Groups (Responsibilities and Standing Rules) Regulations 2012, Part 8.

[197] See Department of Health, n 52, ch 2; Department of Health, *Liberating the NHS: No decision about me, without me* (2012).

[198] Department of Health, n 191, 3.

[199] ibid.

[200] National Health Service (Revision of NHS Constitution—Principles) Regulations 2013, SI 2013/317.

[201] Department of Health, n 191, 4.

[202] ibid.

and transparent way; sharing correspondence sent between clinicians relating to a patient's care; ensuring that organizations learn lessons from complaints and use them to improve services; providing a positive working environment; engaging staff in decisions that affect them and the services they provide; and operating a process to enable staff to raise an internal grievance. Finally, there is a series of 'responsibilities', or 'expectations of how patients, the public and staff can help the NHS work effectively and ensure that finite resources are used fairly'.[203] These include taking responsibility for one's own health and wellbeing; treating NHS staff and patients with respect; keeping appointments; aiming to be open with patients, families, carers, or representatives; and to inform patients about use of their confidential information and to record objections, consent, or dissent.

The legal underpinning of the Constitution is to be found in the Health Act 2009, now amended and supplemented by the Health and Social Care Act 2012. Under section 2(1) of the statute,[204] particular NHS bodies, which are specified in subsection (2), 'must, in performing . . . health service functions,[205] have regard to the NHS Constitution'. Those bodies are now listed as the NHS Commissioning Board; CCGs; local authorities (in respect of their public health functions); Special Health Authorities; the National Institute for Health and Care Excellence; the Health and Social Care Information Centre; NHS Foundation Trusts; Monitor; the Care Quality Commission; and Health Education England;[206] s 3 of the Health and Social Care Act 2012 adds the Secretary of State.[207] The duty also extends to providers from whom care has been commissioned by the Board, CCGs or the Secretary of State (including voluntary organizations); those providing primary care services; those providing public health services under arrangements made by a local authority; and to those working under subcontracting arrangements.[208] A further duty—to promote the Constitution—is imposed upon the NHS Commissioning Board and CCGs by the 2012 Act.[209] This entails acting with a view to securing that services are provided in a way which promotes the Constitution, and promoting awareness of it amongst patients, staff and members of the public. **1.80**

The nature of the duty to have regard to the Constitution has been explored in case law. In *R (on the application of Booker) v NHS Oldham and Direct Line Insurance plc*,[210] the court was required to consider the lawfulness of a decision to withdraw provision of NHS continuing healthcare to a tetraplegic, prior to the commencement of periodic payments under an out-of-court settlement which would enable her to fund her health and social care needs privately. One of the rationales for this decision was that the claimant no longer had 'reasonable requirements' giving rise to a duty to provide services under s 3(1)(e) of the National Health Service Act 2006 in light of the terms of the settlement and having regard to available resources and the Primary Care Trust's duty to break even financially. This argument was rejected on the basis that the NHS is not a means-tested Service; the decision taken by the Trust could not rationally have been reached had it had due regard both to s 1(3) (now s1(4)) of the 2006 Act, which provides that health services are to be provided free of charge, **1.81**

[203] ibid.

[204] As amended by Health and Social Care Act 2012, s 55(2) and Schedule 5.

[205] These are defined as 'any function under an enactment which is a function concerned with, or connected to, the provision, commissioning or regulation of health services': s 2(3), as amended by Health and Social Care Act 2012, s 55(2) and Schedule 5.

[206] For the latter body, see Care Act 2014, Part 3, ch 1.

[207] Inserting s 1B into National Health Service Act 2006.

[208] Health Act 2009, ss 2(4) and (5), as amended by Health and Social Care Act 2012, s 55(2).

[209] National Health Service Act 2006, ss 13C and 14P, as inserted by Health and Social Care Act 2012, ss 23(1) and 26. Health Education England is also required to promote the Constitution.

[210] [2010] EWHC 2593 (Admin).

and to the Constitution's principles of comprehensiveness and access based upon clinical need rather than ability to pay and its right to access health services free of charge.

1.82 By contrast, in *R (on the application of Tracey) v Cambridge University Hospitals NHS Trust*,[211] the Court of Appeal held that there had been no breach by the Secretary of State of his duty to have regard to the Constitution. Here, it was alleged that failure to publish national guidance to ensure that: the process of making 'Do Not Attempt Cardio-Pulmonary Resuscitation' decisions was sufficiently clear, accessible, and foreseeable; that patients were involved in discussions and choices about such decisions; and that they were given information to enable them to be so involved, amounted to a failure to have regard to the right, contained in the Constitution, 'to be involved in discussions and decisions about your health and care, including your end of life care, and to be given information to enable you to do this'.[212] The Court rejected this argument, noting that the 'duty to have regard' did not imply prescription of the means by which patient involvement was to be achieved.[213] The Secretary of State had commended a joint statement on the matter from the British Medical Association and the Royal College of Nursing as an appropriate basis for a policy,[214] and this was sufficient to discharge his statutory duty.

1.83 As required by s 6(1) of the Health Act 2009, the government reported on the effect of the Constitution upon patients, staff, carers, and members of the public in July 2012.[215] The Report concluded that 'overwhelmingly, patients and staff think a Constitution for the NHS is a great idea',[216] and argued that 'three years on from the launch of the Constitution, the NHS remains true to its fundamental principles and values as expressed in the Constitution ... the Constitution remains a focal point to what the health service is all about and continues to remind us of what the NHS is striving to achieve every day'.[217] Yet it also noted that awareness of the Constitution was low (although staff awareness was higher),[218] and that patients did not, in general, utilize the Constitution as a benchmark against which to complain.[219]

1.84 Particularly in light of these last findings, it is tempting to conclude (as, strikingly, has the government), that 'the NHS Constitution is not yet having the effect originally intended. Put simply, people are not using the Constitution as a way of upholding their expectations of the NHS'.[220] However this negative evaluation requires some qualification. First, as the 2012 Report noted, in many respects 'the effect of the Constitution was meant to be longer term';[221] to 'reinforce and safeguard the NHS for the future',[222] rather than to have a direct causal effect upon NHS performance. It may therefore still be premature to assess the worth of the Constitution in this regard, although some critics might argue that the reforms encapsulated in the 2012 Act, which the Report claimed would underpin

211 [2014] EWCA Civ 822.
212 Section 3a of the Constitution.
213 n 211, [83] (Dyson MR).
214 British Medical Association/Royal College of Nursing, *Decisions Relating to Cardiopulmonary Resuscitation: a joint statement* (1999).
215 Department of Health, *Report on the effect of the NHS Constitution* (2012). Such reports, which must be laid before Parliament: Health Act 2009, s 6(3), must be published every three years.
216 ibid, para 143.
217 ibid, para 132.
218 ibid, ch 2. See also Patients Association, *Patient and Public Awareness of the NHS Constitution* (2014).
219 ibid, para 140.
220 ibid.
221 ibid, para 125.
222 ibid, para 128.

the constitutional values and principles, in fact served to undermine them.[223] Second, as also noted in the Report, assessment of the impact of the Constitution is hampered by the difficulty of mapping NHS performance data onto the rights and pledges contained in the document; further evidential work may therefore be required, which government has asked the NHS Commissioning Board to undertake.[224] But finally—and most positively—there is some indication that the Constitution occupies an increasingly important position in debates on accountability, and its enhancement, in the NHS. Most notably, one may point to the recommendations contained in the Report of the Inquiry on the Mid-Staffordshire NHS Foundation Trust that 'the NHS Constitution should be the first reference point for all NHS patients and staff and should set out the system's common values, as well as the respective rights, legitimate expectations and obligations of patients' and that 'the core values expressed in the NHS Constitution should be given priority of place and the overriding value should be that patients are put first, and everything done by the NHS and everyone associated with it should be informed by this ethos'.[225] Accordingly, it seems likely that the Constitution will remain a distinctive feature of the organizational landscape of the NHS for the foreseeable future.

B. NHS 'Governance'

The past two decades have seen a substantial increase in the number of institutions and mechanisms tasked with regulation of the NHS, in large part (though not exclusively) in response to significant failures such as those involving children's heart surgery at Bristol Royal Infirmary, the conviction for murder of the GP Harold Shipman, and high mortality rates at Stafford Hospital. Prior to these events, government was largely content to delegate discretion to local health authorities. In practice, particularly before the introduction of the 'internal market' for health care in 1992, this meant that managerial power in the NHS was dominated by the medical profession. Supervision of clinical standards was available to the General Medical Council,[226] and clinical audits were undertaken locally in hospitals, but the system tended to be reactive, in that it was motivated by concerns as to the performance of individuals after the event. There was no supervision of standards in the system as a whole, and no means by which performance in one place could be reliably compared with that of another. *Learning from Bristol* says: 'We cannot say that the external system for assuring and monitoring the quality of care was inadequate. There was, in truth, no such system.'[227] The report remarks that: **1.85**

> In the decades after the establishment of the NHS (in fact right up until the late 1980s) central government, through the Department of Health . . . interpreted its responsibility for the NHS largely in terms of planning and allocating resources. It did not see itself as being responsible for, and thus accountable for, the quality of clinical care, either in terms of setting standards or of monitoring clinical performance. Quality was regarded by government

223 See, eg J Davis and R Tallis (eds.), *NHS SOS* (Oneworld Publications 2013).

224 Department of Health, n 215, paras 152–153.

225 *Report of the Mid-Staffordshire NHS Foundation Trust Public Inquiry* (HC 898-III, 2013) 1436.

226 J Allsop and L Mulcahy, *Regulating Medical Work, Formal and Informal Controls* (Open University Press 1996).

227 *Learning from Bristol: The Report of the Public Inquiry into Children's Heart Surgery at Bristol Royal Infirmary, 1984–95* (Cm 5207, 2001), 192. The report also comments on the Department of Health: 'it [had] a role in which the factors which were set out and monitored were focused on finance and the volume of patients treated. The quality and performance of clinical services were regarded as matter for the local hospital or health service, not the DoH': 186.

as a matter for individual health care professionals. For their part, health care professionals, particularly hospital doctors, had deeply embedded in their culture the notion of professional autonomy, often expressed in the form of 'clinical freedom'.[228]

1.86 NHS governance is concerned to focus attention on systems to monitor, assess and improve quality in the NHS. There is a considerable range of opinion as to the theory on which such a system of regulation should be based. Should it pursue a 'light-touch' based on mutual trust and confidence between regulator and regulated, or a more aggressive 'arm's length' approach in which nothing is left to trust, or a combination of such approaches? How should the costs and burden of regulation be assessed so that the service is not deflected from its core duty? Should the regulator be independent of government and, if so, to whom should it be accountable? What range of sanctions should exist to encourage improvement and how should success and failure be measured, and by whom?[229]

1.87 This section considers governance of the NHS under three broad headings: (1) priority setting, (2) public and patient involvement, and (3) oversight of performance and standards.

1. NHS priority setting

1.88 Successive governments have consistently refused to confront squarely the dilemma of the hard choices that routinely have to be made throughout the NHS. This reluctance was the subject of sharp criticism in *Learning from Bristol*:

> Governments of the day have made claims for the NHS which were not capable of being met on the resources available. The public has been led to believe that the NHS could meet their legitimate needs, whereas it is patently clear that it could not. Healthcare professionals, doctors, nurses, managers, and others, have been caught between the growing disillusion of the public on the one hand and the tendency of governments to point to them as scapegoats for a failing service on the other . . . The NHS was represented as a comprehensive service which met all the needs of the public. Patently it did not do so.[230]

1.89 This passage encapsulates one of the central tensions in health care. If redistributive ethics are at the heart of politics, so politics is endemic to disputes about access to health care and, to this extent, government is inevitably, albeit unwillingly, drawn into the debate. Unsurprisingly, politicians are concerned with public perceptions and tend to favour short-term solutions. Health authorities, on the other hand, have long-term duties to entire communities. When the media, with its desire for a 'human interest' story rooted in the (sometimes desperate) individual need for access to treatment, is factored into the equation, it becomes apparent that these are genuinely multifaceted choices which are certain to generate significant public controversy.

1.90 The profoundly contentious character of priority setting (or 'rationing'), coupled with the high stakes for individuals for whom such decisions may literally be matters of life and death, has inevitably led to litigation. This is especially the case given that such choices have become more visible in recent years, as a shift from 'implicit' to 'explicit' modes of priority-setting has taken place in the NHS. The primary vehicle through which legal challenges to such decisions are articulated is via the process of judicial review of administrative action.

---

228 ibid, 303.

229 See generally K Walshe, *Regulating Healthcare—A Prescription for Improvement* (Open University Press 2003); J Healy, *Improving Health Care Safety and Quality: Reluctant Regulators* (Ashgate 2011). The literature on regulation is vast: for useful general introductions to the field, see R Baldwin, C Scott, and C Hood (eds.), *A Reader on Regulation* (Oxford University Press 1998); B Morgan and K Yeung, *An Introduction to Law and Regulation: Texts and Materials* (Cambridge University Press 2007).

230 n 227, 57. The report urges we should 'make explicit that which has been implicit': 261.

Since such cases engage the liability (in public law) of the institutions which provide health care in the NHS, they are analysed in detail in Chapter 7, which addresses that topic.

However, notwithstanding the traditionally limited role played by government in directing how and where NHS resources should be spent, key reforms undertaken by the Labour Governments of 1997–2010 have had a significant impact upon the setting of priorities in the NHS. These sought to address two problems related to resources. First, advances in medical technology—both in respect of equipment (such as magnetic resonance imaging systems), and forms of treatment (such as therapies for cancer which 'target' small subgroups of the patient population)—had begun to place growing pressure on the available budget for health care, pointing to the need for some mechanism to regulate access and availability on the NHS. Secondly, one of the causes of concern for the system that developed within the 'internal market' from 1990 onward was the tendency for there to be unequal access to care across geographical boundaries—the so-called 'postcode lottery'—which called into question the Service's founding principles of universality and comprehensiveness (although it should be noted, as discussed earlier, that delegation of the Secretary of State's duty to provide a comprehensive health service to bodies at local level has necessarily always resulted in some inequity of access and provision). 1.91

(i) National Institute for Health and Care Excellence (NICE)

Part 8 of the Health and Social Care Act 2012 places NICE, which was created in 1999 out of concern for the postcode differentials in access to care that may exist throughout the NHS, on a statutory footing as a non-departmental public body. The Institute's Charter describes it as being 'responsible for developing national guidance, standards and information on providing high-quality health and social care, and preventing ill health'.[231] To this end, it disseminates quality standards,[232] issues evidence-based guidelines on a wide range of topics in health and social care, and makes recommendations on the use of new medicines and medical technologies (technology appraisal guidance).[233] The Institute has a responsibility to 'ensure careful and targeted use of finite resources',[234] which is statutorily expressed as a duty to have regard to 'the broad balance between the benefits and costs of the provision of health services',[235] and it notes that 'following our recommendations can help ... organizations [with responsibility for commissioning or providing healthcare] to reduce variations in practice across the country'.[236] 1.92

NICE's various outputs possess differing legal status. Technology appraisal guidance carries a mandatory funding obligation,[237] such that a commissioning body must provide funding to ensure that the technology is made available for the purposes of treating patients within three months of the date of publication of the recommendation,[238] unless the Institute specifies a longer period (eg to enable training, infrastructure, or resources to be put in place, or if the technology is not yet available).[239] By contrast, other forms of advice and guidance are 1.93

231 NICE, *NICE Charter* (2013), [1].
232 See Health and Social Care Act 2012, s 234.
233 ibid, s 237.
234 NICE, above n 231, para 3.
235 Health and Social Care Act 2012, s 233(1)(a).
236 NICE, above n 231, para 8.
237 National Institute for Health and Care Excellence (Constitution and Functions) Regulations and the Health and Social Care Information Centre (Functions) Regulations 2013, SI 2013/259, regs 7(6) and 8(6).
238 ibid, regs 7(3) and 8(3).
239 ibid, regs 7(5) and 8(5).

not, in principle, binding.[240] Nonetheless, they may inform the standard of care required of clinical professionals, and commissioning bodies may be expected to comply absent provision of robust reasons justifying any departure. These matters will be considered further in Chapter 7.[241]

1.94 NICE places particular emphasis upon the importance of procedural justice in securing legitimacy for its decisions, to which end it seeks to make its decision-making process transparent and commits itself to an extensive process of consultation before issuing its guidance.[242] However, this may involve the submission to NICE of information in confidence and, as a general rule, such information will not be disclosed during the consultation process. The balance between transparency and confidentiality has given rise to dispute in respect of the economic evaluation models on which the cost-effectiveness of treatments are assessed. Pharmaceutical companies have argued that they cannot test the accuracy of NICE's estimates of the cost-effectiveness of their products unless the models by which they have been assessed are made available to them. Accordingly, NICE should not normally give undertakings as to confidentiality; however, where the importance of the material to the robustness and quality of the appraisal is sufficiently great, it may exceptionally do so when circumstances so require.[243] Nonetheless, even here NICE must still take all reasonable steps to seek the permission of those to whom it owes duties of confidentiality to make the information available.[244]

(ii) National Service Frameworks

1.95 Alongside NICE, government sought to address variations in the standard of care and to achieve greater consistency in the availability and quality of health services through the publication of National Service Frameworks. These are intended to define standards of care, based upon evidence of effectiveness, for certain services or groups: thus, for example, there are Frameworks covering coronary heart disease, mental health, older people, long-term conditions, etc. Additionally, the Frameworks establish programmes to support implementation and act as a form of performance measurement. In respect of the latter function, it should be noted that the Frameworks occupy the status of influential guidance and, in principle, there is discretion to depart from them.[245] There is evidence to suggest that, while the rationale for the introduction of such Frameworks was welcomed, their impact may have been limited, at least in certain areas of medical practice.[246]

240 ibid, reg 5.

241 See Chapter 7, paras 7.61–7.63 and 7.109–7.110.

242 See NICE, n 231, paras 13–14 and NICE, *Social Value Judgements* (2008), paras 2.3, 3.2. For critical analysis, see K Syrett, 'A Technocratic Fix to the "Legitimacy Problem"? The Blair Government and Health Care Rationing in the United Kingdom' (2003) 28 Journal of Health Politics, Policy and Law 715; and K Syrett, 'Deconstructing Deliberation in the Appraisal of Medical Technologies: NICEly does it?' (2006) 69 MLR 869.

243 *R (on the application of Servier Laboratories Ltd) v National Institute for Health and Clinical Excellence* [2009] EWHC 281 (Admin), [115].

244 ibid, [123]. See also *R (on the application of Eisai Ltd) v National Institute for Health and Clinical Excellence* [2007] EWCA Civ 438, but contrast *R (on the application of Bristol-Myers Squibb Pharmaceuticals Limited) v National Institute for Health and Clinical Excellence* [2009] EWHC 2722 (Admin), in which the company was deemed to have had full opportunity to make meaningful representations during the consultation process. For analysis of these cases, see K Syrett, 'Health Technology Appraisal and the Courts: Accountability for Reasonableness and the Judicial Model of Procedural Justice' (2011) 6 Health Economics, Policy and Law 469.

245 See further the discussion in Chapter 7, paras 7.101–7.112.

246 See K Checkland, 'National Service Frameworks and UK General Practitioners: Street Level Bureaucrats at Work?' (2004) 26 Sociology of Health and Illness 951.

(iii) GPs' Prescribing rights and duties

The various arrangements through which provision is made for primary care services were considered above. Here, the focus is on the position of general practitioners (and other non-medical prescribers) in respect of (a) their prescribing rights and duties and (b) the 'black' and 'grey' lists which restrict the medicines available to be prescribed. **1.96**

(a) The duty to prescribe CCGs are responsible for setting prescribing budgets for each GP practice within their organization. Practices are subject to indicative amounts, or 'target budgets', and should seek to ensure that these are not exceeded in any financial year. 'Excessive' prescribing, where the cost or quantity of the drug or appliance is 'in excess of that which was reasonably necessary for the proper treatment of the patient', is precluded.[247] The NHS Commissioning Board may withhold, or make deductions from, payments owed to the contractor for breach of this term;[248] such breaches, and the attached financial sanctions, are subject to dispute resolution in the Family Health Service Appeals Unit (which acts on behalf of the NHS Litigation Authority), or the courts. What is 'excessive' and how should prescribers react to patients with expensive needs? Instances have been said to include prescriptions where the treatment is switched with the effect that reimbursement is based on a product which provides a larger purchase margin for the prescriber and the product costs the NHS more, unless there is good clinical evidence for the switch; and consistent prescription of high-cost products or inappropriate, high quantities of medicines which are significantly at variance with comparable clinical scenarios and where the prescriber is unable to provide a reasonable explanation.[249] **1.97**

On the other hand, the terms of service also require that: 'a prescriber shall order any drugs, medicines or appliances which are needed for the treatment of any patient who is receiving treatment under the contract by issuing to that patient a prescription form or a repeatable prescription'.[250] Do these words permit the prescriber to prescribe treatment, irrespective of cost, that s/he reasonably believes the patient needs? Or could it be argued that the duty should be read in a more 'population-based' sense, thus permitting the doctor to ration treatment in the interests of the local community of patients as a whole? Two analogous cases which have considered the issue of needs and resources point to different conclusions. **1.98**

In *R v Gloucestershire CC, ex p Barry*[251] the applicant had been assessed by the local authority as requiring specific services under the Chronically Sick and Disabled Persons Act 1970. Section 2(1) provides that: 'Where . . . it is necessary in order to meet the needs of [a] person for [an] authority to make arrangements [for that person] . . . it shall be the duty of that authority to make those arrangements'. Owing to reductions in its block grant from central government, the authority proposed to reduce the services it provided, despite the fact that the applicant's needs remained unchanged. Notably, the needs in question did not relate to health care, but to the adaptation of the person's home, meals on wheels, and, inter alia, access to radio, television, and library facilities, various leisure activities, and occasional holidays. Should these 'needs' be interpreted by reference to the individual needs of the person **1.99**

---

247 National Health Service (General Medical Services Contracts) Regulations 2004, Sch 6, para 46.

248 ibid, Sch 6, para 117(2), as amended by National Health Service (Primary Medical Services) (Miscellaneous Amendments and Transitional Provisions) Regulations 2013, reg. 27.

249 British Medical Association/NHS Employers, *Revisions to the GMS Contract 2006/07: Annex 8: Excessive or Inappropriate Prescribing: Guidance for Health Professionals on Prescribing NHS Medicines* (2007).

250 National Health Service (General Medical Services Contracts) Regulations 2004, Sch 6, para 39(1). 'The prescriber' means (a) a doctor, (b) an independent nurse prescriber, and (c) a supplementary prescriber, see reg 2.

251 [1997] AC 584.

concerned (the 'patient'-led approach), or subject to the resources available to the authority (the 'resources'-led approach)? The House of Lords considered that the word 'needs' in the 1970 Act should be given a flexible, resource-based interpretation. Lord Clyde stated:

> The words 'necessary' and 'needs' are both relative expressions, admitting in each case a considerable range of meaning. They are not defined in the 1970 Act . . . In deciding whether there is a necessity to meet the needs of the individual some criteria have to be provided . . . In the framing of the criteria to be applied . . . the severity of the condition may have to be matched against the availability of resources.[252]

1.100 Thus, the authority was entitled to adjust the services it provided to take account of its resources because the applicant's statutory 'needs' could diminish, even though his actual needs were the same.

1.101 However, a more demanding approach was taken in *R v East Sussex CC, ex p Tandy*.[253] The case concerned analogous statutory duties imposed by the Education Act 1993 on a local education authority to provide sick children with 'suitable education' at home. The applicant was a teenage girl suffering with ME. She had previously received five hours' tuition a week at home. Owing to resource constraints, the authority proposed to reduce her home tuition to three hours. Was the Education Authority entitled to take its limited resources into account in determining what was a suitable education for the girl? In the context of this statute, the House of Lords rejected the argument that this particular duty was resource-based. Lord Browne-Wilkinson said:

> there is nothing in the Act of 1993 to suggest that resource considerations are relevant to the question of what is suitable education . . . The duty is to make arrangements for what constitutes a suitable education for each child. That duty will not be fulfilled unless the arrangements do in fact provide suitable education for each child.[254]

1.102 Significantly, his Lordship warned against using the judiciary to re-organize the order of social priorities which had been identified by Parliament. He said:

> Parliament has chosen to impose a statutory duty, as opposed to a power, requiring the local authority to do certain things. In my judgment, the courts should be slow to downgrade such duties into what are, in effect, discretions over which the courts would have very little control. If Parliament wishes to reduce public expenditure on meeting the needs of sick children, then it is up to Parliament so to provide. It is not for the courts to adjust the order of priorities as between statutory duties and statutory discretion.[255]

1.103 Accordingly, the local authority was obliged to divert resources away from those activities over which it had discretion, in order to comply with the duties imposed upon it. Which of these cases has most persuasive weight in the interpretation of prescribers' duties in the NHS? Certainly, the government appears to consider that the GP's duty to prescribe is not constrained by resources. In relation to the creation of PCTs, it was said that:

> The new system will continue to allow individual GPs to decide what is best for the patient, whether for example, to prescribe drugs or refer patients to hospital on the basis of their clinical judgment. The freedom to refer and prescribe remains unchanged. Patients will continue to be guaranteed the drugs, investigations and treatments they need. There will be no question of anyone being denied the drugs they need because the GP or Primary Care Group have run out of cash.[256]

---

252 ibid, 610. Note, however, that the Court of Appeal had taken the opposite view.
253 [1998] AC 714.
254 ibid, 746–47.
255 ibid, 749.
256 Department of Health, *Developing Primary Care Groups* (1998), HSC 1998/139, paras 52–53.

It should also be noted, as discussed further in Chapter 7, that guidance issued by NICE which does not recommend a treatment or service, or recommends its use only in limited circumstances—which may be on grounds that it is not cost-effective—does not override clinical judgment: hence:

> if, having considered the guidance, a health professional considers that the treatment or procedure would be the appropriate option in a given case, there is no legal bar on the professional recommending the treatment or on the NHS funding it.[257]

The only NHS case to have considered the question was in relation to the previous GMS regulations. The matter arose when a new medicine for erectile dysfunction (sildenafil, sold as 'Viagra') received a licence. The Secretary of State, concerned at the possibility that there might be excessive demand for the medicine, issued guidance urging that GPs: **1.104**

> should not prescribe sildenafil. Health Authorities are also advised not to support the provision of sildenafil at NHS expense to patients requiring treatment for erectile dysfunction, other than in exceptional circumstances which they should require to be cleared in advance with them.[258]

The manufacturer challenged the guidance as unlawful in that it contradicted the GP's duties contained in the terms of service, which were amenable to change only through Parliament. Collins J considered two provisions of the previous terms of service; that (under the old para 43) 'a doctor shall order any drugs or appliances which are needed for the treatment of any patient to whom he is providing treatment under these terms of service by issuing to that patient a prescription form', and that (under the old para 12): 'a doctor shall render to his patients all necessary and appropriate personal medical services of the type usually provided by general practitioners'.[259] The judge held that the Secretary of State's letter was unlawful and declared it void for contradicting Parliament's will as expressed in the regulations governing the duties of GPs in the NHS. Curiously, he considered that duty was contained in para 12, rather than para 43. He said: **1.105**

> paragraph 43 in my judgment does not impose a duty to prescribe a drug . . . The doctor's duty is contained in paragraph 12(1) . . . The doctor must give such treatment as he, exercising the professional judgment to be expected from an average GP considers necessary and appropriate . . . If a GP decides that a particular treatment is necessary, it must inevitably be appropriate.[260]

Exactly why the duty did not arise from the clear words of para 43 is not explained. Nevertheless, whether contained in para 12 or para 43, its impact is the same. The duty to respond to patient need will not always be straightforward, especially if there is a difference of opinion between doctor and patient. Nevertheless, the doctor's duty is to consider all the clinical circumstances of the case, including the patient's preferences, but to make a decision within his/her own reasonable discretion. Nor should doctors exceed their expertise by attempting treatment which should be undertaken by a specialist by means of a referral to hospital. With these caveats, however, the Secretary of State's guidance was declared unlawful for trespassing upon the proper statutory responsibilities imposed on GPs by the GMS regulations. It would have been permissible for the Secretary of State to advise doctors to be cautious in using the drug, but such advice must make clear that 'the GP's clinical judgment is supreme'.[261] The duties contained in the 2004 Regulations would seem likely to provoke a similar judicial response. **1.106**

[257] NICE, *The Legal Implications of NICE Guidance* (2009). See further para 7.63.
[258] Department of Health, *Treatment for Impotence* (1998), HSC 1998/158.
[259] Both were contained in the National Health Service (General Medical Services) Regulations 1992, SI 1992/635, Sch 2.
[260] *R v Secretary of State for Health, ex p Pfizer Ltd.* (1999) 51 BMLR 189, 198–99.
[261] ibid, 199.

1.107 Prescribing costs in primary care have been regulated by other means. Formerly, incentive payments were made available to GPs whose prescribing costs did not exceed indicative budgets,[262] encouraging 'switching' and/or prescription of generic treatments. While such schemes are no longer obligatory,[263] CCGs may choose to continue to utilize them; a challenge to their lawfulness under European law having failed in *R (on the application of ABPI) v MHRA*.[264] In addition, the NHS Commissioning Board pays a 'quality premium' to CCGs to be deployed in ways which improve patient care or health outcomes and/or reduce inequalities. This represents a means by which CCGs could, in turn, influence, support, and incentivize cost-effective activities within GP practices in their area, especially given that it is a precondition of payment of such premiums that CCGs remain within the resources allocated to them.[265]

1.108 **(b) The 'black' and 'grey' lists** The general duty to prescribe in primary care is subject to qualification by two lists, one of which contains treatments which may never be prescribed within the NHS (the 'black' list), the other of which contains treatments which may be prescribed in specific circumstances only (the 'grey' list).[266] The right to prescribe does not operate in relation to a specific 'basket' of treatments available within the NHS—there is no 'white list'. Instead, the matter is for GPs acting within their reasonable clinical discretion. The black list contains thousands of items, some of which suggest that GPs must have taken a very flexible view of their patients' needs in the past. Excluded from the NHS, therefore, are cosmetic products; soaps; shampoos; sun-screens; mild analgesics; mild cough remedies; toothpastes; baby foods; cranberry juice; vitamin supplements; decaffeinated coffee; herbal tea; powdered milk; Ribena; Lucozade; 'wines'; and Flora margarine! By contrast, the 'grey' list contains a very small number of restrictions. Most of these are concerned with clinical safety, but some—treatments for erectile dysfunction and for influenza—provide therapeutic value to patients. Their inclusion on the list might thus be regarded as a form of rationing.

1.109 The lists therefore enable Parliament to restrict the treatments available to GPs under the terms of service. However, with limited exceptions (as noted above), they have not functioned as a significant tool of rationing in the NHS. This supports the argument that the duty to prescribe is intended to enable doctors to respond to the needs of their individual patients. If Parliament wishes to restrict that freedom for reasons of cost, it is at liberty to do so within the Regulations. However, in the absence of Parliamentary intervention, doctors should not presume that an obligation to limit expenditure by controlling prescription costs falls upon them. This is significant because the NHS Commissioning Board has power to remove doctors from the medical list if 'continued inclusion in that performers list would be prejudicial to the efficiency of the services which those included in that performers list perform'.[267] In the light of this discussion, such a right of removal presumably exists in respect of GPs who prescribe irresponsibly in the sense that they prescribe treatments of no therapeutic value, perhaps because they simply offer what patients demand, or prescribe

---

[262] National Health Service (Functions of Health Authorities) (Prescribing Incentive Schemes) Amendment Regulations 2000, SI 2000/1645.

[263] See General Medical Services and Personal Medical Services Transitional and Consequential Provisions Order 2004, SI 2004/865, Sch 2.

[264] Case C-62/09, [2010] ECR I-3603.

[265] National Health Service (Clinical Commissioning Groups—Payments in Respect of Quality) Regulations 2013, SI 2013/474.

[266] See National Health Service (General Medical Services Contracts) Regulations 2004, Sch 6, paras 42 and 43. The 'black' and 'grey' lists are contained in the National Health Service (General Medical Services Contracts) (Prescription Drugs) Regulations 2004, SI 2004/629.

[267] Health and Social Care Act 2001, s 25.

irresponsible doses to patients, duplicate treatment, or routinely treat for very rare adverse reactions to medicines. Such cases deserve censure because they waste limited resources and are probably negligent in their approach to treatment.[268] On the other hand, expensive but responsible prescribers ought not to be censured under these Regulations.

2. Public and patient involvement in the NHS

Significant emphasis has been placed upon engagement between patients and public and the NHS in recent times. The NHS Commissioning Board has boldly stated that 'participation is not only about legal requirements. It underpins everything that the NHS in England does',[269] an aspiration which is reflected in the right, contained in the NHS Constitution, 'to be involved, directly or through representatives, in the planning of healthcare services commissioned by NHS bodies, the development and consideration of proposals for changes in the way those services are provided, and in decisions to be made affecting the operation of those services'.[270] Yet the NHS has often been perceived to have fallen short in this regard, in large part because its founding commitment to universal access based upon need rendered both centralization and expertise—which stand in tension with localized participatory arrangements—fundamental to its operation. Thus, 'while the NHS was set up to democratize access to health care, it is also a monument to the values of enlightened paternalism'.[271] It remains to be seen whether the arrangements described in this section will effect a lasting alteration to this picture, or whether they will go the way of previous participatory mechanisms, such as Community Health Councils.[272] **1.110**

(i) Public involvement and consultation

Section 242(2) of the National Health Service Act 2006 imposes a duty on relevant bodies (NHS Trusts and NHS Foundation Trusts) to: **1.111**

> make arrangements, as respects health services for which it is responsible, which secure that users of those services, whether directly or through representatives, are involved (whether by being consulted or provided with information, or in other ways) in—
>
> (1) the planning of the provision of those services,
> (2) the development and consideration of proposals for changes in the way those services are provided, and
> (3) decisions to be made by that body affecting the operation of those services.

Although the policy of this section is to strengthen local engagement with the NHS, new sub-ss (1B)–(1H) were introduced in 2007 limiting the duties in sub-ss (1)–(3) above to consult only with respect to '(a) the manner in which the services are delivered to users of those services, or (b) the range of health services available to those users'.[273] This limits the duty to consult to issues concerning the *delivery* and *range* of the services provided, but not to more general concerns about the nature of the *provider* of the services themselves. As Collins J observed in *Smith v North Eastern Derbyshire PCT*, not every change will engage

[268] See 'GPs should face disciplinary action for prescribing antibiotics to "pushy patients", says NICE Director' *The Independent* (18 August 2015).

[269] NHS England, *Transforming Participation in Health and Care* (2013), 7.

[270] Department of Health, n 105, 9.

[271] R Klein, 'The Politics of Participation' in T Marmor and R Klein, *Politics, Health and Health Care: Selected Essays* (Yale University Press 2002), 406.

[272] Community Health Councils were established in 1974. Increasingly seen as an irrelevance, especially in view of evolution of policies which gave patients a more direct, active voice in their care, they were abolished in England by National Health Service Reform and Health Care Professions Act 2002, s 22.

[273] Local Government and Public Involvement in Health Act 2007, s 233(2).

the duty:[274] trivially, retirement of or introduction of a new GP into a practice will not do so.[275] More controversially, the 2007 amendments would seem to preclude the necessity to consult with respect to the *nature* of the provider—for example, where a private, rather than NHS, provider of medical services is engaged, as was the case in *Smith*.

1.112 As regards CCGs, a duty of public engagement is set out in s 14Z2 of the National Health Service Act 2006.[276] This provides that:

> The clinical commissioning group must make arrangements to secure that individuals to whom the services are being or may be provided are involved (whether by being consulted or provided with information or in other ways)—
>
> (a) in the planning of the commissioning arrangements by the group,
> (b) in the development and consideration of proposals by the group for changes in the commissioning arrangements where the implementation of the proposals would have an impact on the manner in which the services are delivered to the individuals or the range of health services available to them, and
> (c) in decisions of the group affecting the operation of the commissioning arrangements where the implementation of the decisions would (if made) have such an impact.

It should be noted that this section does not permit involvement to take place by way of representatives; those to whom the services are being, or may be, provided, must be *directly* involved.

1.113 A description of the arrangements made to give effect to this duty must be contained in the constitution of the CCG,[277] and regard must be had to any guidance issued by the NHS Commissioning Board on the matter.[278] There is also an obligation to report annually on discharge of the duty.[279]

1.114 As to the nature and extent of consultation, whether or not consultation of interested parties and the public is a statutory requirement, if it is embarked upon it must be carried out properly:

> To be proper, consultation [1] must be undertaken at a time when proposals are still at a formative stage; [2] must include sufficient reasons for particular proposals to allow those consulted to give intelligent consideration and an intelligent response; [3] adequate time must be given for this purpose; [4] the product of consultation must be conscientiously taken into account when the ultimate decision is taken.[280]

1.115 The public authority may be quite advanced in its preference for one solution rather than another, but there must be possibility of a change of view.[281] Difficulty may arise with respect to the proper remedy available following a failure of consultation. Once a decision has been taken within the range of options reasonably available to the health authority, courts are

---

[274] Here, under the equivalent provisions of Health and Social Care Act 2001, s 11.
[275] [2006] EWHC 1338 (Admin), [15].
[276] As inserted by Health and Social Care Act 2012, s 26. Comparable obligations are imposed on the NHS Commissioning Board: see National Health Service Act 2006, s 13Q.
[277] National Health Service Act 2006, s 14Z2(3).
[278] ibid, s 14Z2(5). For such guidance, see NHS England, n 269.
[279] ibid, s 14Z15.
[280] See *R v North and East Devon Health Authority, ex parte Coughlan* [1999] EWCA Civ 1871, [108]; *R v Brent LBC, ex p Gunning* [1986] 84 LGR 168, 189; and *R (on the application of Moseley) v London Borough of Haringey* [2014] UKSC 56, [25]; and further Chapter 7, paras 7.97–7.100.
[281] See *Sardar v Watford Borough Council* [2006] EWHC 1590 (Admin), [29] and *R (on the application of F) v Healthy Futures Joint Committee of Primary Care Trusts* [2007] EWHC 1611.

reluctant to reverse the decision in order for proper consultation to be take place.[282] Exactly how the health service body should respond to the product of the consultation is a matter for local discretion. A decision to close an old and well-liked hospital is likely to generate hostility, yet the need to do so may be irrefutable, for example, because standards of safety can no longer be maintained given the small numbers and cross-section of patients admitted for care. Nevertheless, the decision must remain open for reconsideration or modification. Ultimately, however, it is the health body, and not a democratic expression of opinion, which must make the difficult decisions that confront the health service.

(ii) Local Healthwatch

Section 182 of the Health and Social Care Act 2012 amends s 221 of the Local Government and Public Involvement in Health Act 2007, replacing health services and social services Local Involvement Networks (LINKS) with independent local Healthwatch organizations, whose 'aim . . . is to give citizens and communities a stronger voice to influence and challenge how health and social care services are provided within their locality'.[283] These organizations are assisted and advised by a committee of the Care Quality Commission, Healthwatch England.[284] **1.116**

Local Healthwatch bodies are responsible for promoting and supporting the involvement of people in the commissioning, provision, and scrutiny of local care services; enabling people to monitor the standard of provision of local services, whether and how they could be, and ought to be, improved and to review, for those purposes, the commissioning and provision of local care services; obtaining the views of people about their needs for, and their experiences of, local care services; and making such views known and reporting to those responsible for commissioning, providing, managing, or scrutinizing local services and to Healthwatch England on how they should be improved.[285] Additionally, they provide advice and information about access to local care services and choices which can be made in respect of those services; make recommendations to Healthwatch England (or, exceptionally, directly to the Care Quality Commission) about special reviews and investigations; make recommendations to Healthwatch England to publish a report on a particular health or social care matter; and provide such assistance to Healthwatch England as it may require to perform its functions effectively, efficiently, and economically.[286] **1.117**

(iii) Local government involvement

Section 194(1) of the Health and Social Care Act 2012 requires each upper-tier local authority to establish a Health and Wellbeing Board, as a committee of the authority.[287] The government has stated that 'the ambition behind the introduction of Health and Wellbeing Boards is to build strong and effective partnerships, which improve the commissioning and delivery of services across NHS and local government, leading in turn to improved health and wellbeing for local people'.[288] Membership consists of at least one councillor; **1.118**

[282] In *R (on the application of Fudge) v South West Strategic Health Authority* [2007] EWCA Civ 803, a failure in the duty to consult was identified but the court declined any relief and said, at [67]: 'Our conclusion as to the law has been reached at the cost of a disproportionate amount of time and energy . . . the costs might have been better deployed in securing and maintaining health services within the region concerned'.

[283] Local Government Association, *Delivering Effective Local Healthwatch* (2013), 5.

[284] Health and Social Care Act 2012, s 181.

[285] Local Government and Public Involvement in Health Act 2007, s 221, as amended by Health and Social Care Act 2012, s 182.

[286] Health and Social Care Act 2012, s 182(4).

[287] ibid, s 194(11).

[288] Department of Health, *The General Duties and Powers relating to Health and Wellbeing Boards* (2013), 1.

the director of adult social services; the director of children's services; the director of public health; a representative of the local Healthwatch organization; and a representative from each CCG whose area falls within or coincides with the local authority area.[289] This core statutory membership can be expanded upon either by the Board itself or by the local authority where it is thought appropriate to do so;[290] for example, to include local representatives of the voluntary sector or those working in criminal justice agencies.

1.119 The functions of the Board are set out in ss 195 and 196 of the Act. The former imposes a duty to encourage persons who arrange for the provision of health or social care services to work 'in an integrated manner' for the purpose of advancing the health and wellbeing of the people in its area. Such 'integration' extends to the broader social determinants of health: sub ss 3 and 4 enable Boards to encourage persons who arrange for the provision of 'health-related services' (defined as 'services that may have an effect on the health of individuals but are not health services or social care services'),[291] to work closely with the Board and with health and social care providers. More specifically, s 196(1) requires the Board to perform the functions specified in ss 116 and 116A of the Local Government and Public Involvement in Health Act 2007,[292] that is, preparation respectively of the Joint Strategic Needs Assessment and Joint Health and Wellbeing Strategy for the local authority area,[293] for which purposes a representative of the NHS Commissioning Board must also be appointed.[294] A local authority is also empowered to delegate any of its functions to the Board;[295] in such cases, a Board may also be able to exercise functions in relation to the wider determinants of health (eg housing).

1.120 There is no statutory obligation for a Board to become directly involved in the commissioning process. Nonetheless, 'there is a clear expectation that [the Joint Strategic Needs Assessment and Joint Health and Wellbeing Strategy] be reflected in plans for commissioning in relation to the area'.[296] CCGs must provide a copy of their commissioning plan, and any revised plan, to the Board.[297] More onerously, they must involve the Board in the planning or revision process, providing it with a draft of the plan or revised plan and consulting it on whether the plan or revision takes account of the Joint Health and Wellbeing Strategy.[298] The Board must provide its opinion on this matter,[299] and this statement of opinion must be published in the commissioning plan;[300] the Board may also refer its opinion on whether

---

[289] Health and Social Care Act 2012, s 194(2). Note that the same person may represent more than one CCG, with the approval of the Board: s 194(7). CCGs are required to co-operate with the Board in the exercise of its functions: s 194(10).

[290] ibid, ss 194(8) and (2)(g) respectively, In the latter instance, the Board must be consulted prior to the appointment: s 194(9).

[291] ibid, s 195(6).

[292] The latter section is inserted by Health and Social Care Act 2012, s 193.

[293] A Joint Strategic Needs Assessment is described as 'a process that identifies current and future health and wellbeing needs in light of existing services, and informs future service planning taking into account evidence of effectiveness', it 'identifies the "big picture" in terms of the health and wellbeing needs and inequalities of the local population': Department of Health, *Guidance on Joint Strategic Needs Assessment* (2007), 7. The Joint Health and Wellbeing Strategy establishes the priorities for action based upon this assessment, informing commissioning decisions and influencing the commissioning of services beyond health in order to impact upon wider social determinants: see Department of Health, *Joint Strategic Needs Assessments and Joint Health and Wellbeing Strategies Explained* (2011), 19.

[294] Health and Social Care Act 2012, ss 197(1), (2).

[295] ibid, s 196(2).

[296] Department of Health, n 288, 2.

[297] National Health Service Act 2006, ss 14Z11 and 14Z12.

[298] ibid, ss 14Z13(3) and (4).

[299] ibid, s 14Z13(5).

[300] ibid, s 14Z13(8)(c).

the commissioning plan takes proper account of the Strategy to the NHS Commissioning Board.[301] The CCG must review the extent to which it has complied with the Strategy in its annual report, consulting the Board in doing so.[302] Finally, the annual performance assessment of each CCG by the NHS Commissioning Board will include an evaluation of how well the Group has discharged its duties to have regard to the Assessment and Strategy, the Health and Wellbeing Board being consulted in preparing this evaluation.[303]

Local authority Overview and Scrutiny Committees, whose functions are broadly akin to those of parliamentary select committees, are no longer a statutory requirement, but the government regards health scrutiny, whose primary aim it defines as 'to act as a lever to improve the health of local people, ensuring their needs are considered as an integral part of the commissioning, delivery and development of health services' as 'even more important in the new system' established by the Health and Social Care Act 2012.[304] To this end, s 190 of that Act amends s 244 of the National Health Service Act 2006 to enable local authorities to discharge health scrutiny functions in various ways, thus increasing flexibility. In particular, local authorities which have moved from executive governance arrangements (comprising a mayor/leader and cabinet) to a committee system of governance,[305] are not obliged to operate overview and scrutiny committees, although they may choose to do so. Most councils have, to date, retained executive governance arrangements and continue to discharge health scrutiny functions through an Overview and Scrutiny Committee.[306] **1.121**

Regulations create a duty on 'responsible persons' (which include CCGs; the NHS Commissioning Board; local authorities providing health services; NHS Trusts and NHS Foundation Trusts; GP practices; other providers of primary care; and private and voluntary sector bodies commissioned to provide NHS or public health services) to provide such information about the planning, provision, and operation of health services in its area as a local authority may reasonably require.[307] Members and employees of the bodies previously named may be required to attend to answer 'such questions as appear to the authority to be necessary for the discharge of its [scrutiny] functions'.[308] Reports and recommendations may be made to any of the bodies covered by the legislation;[309] where a response is requested, it must be provided in writing within 28 days.[310] **1.122**

Proposals for substantial development, or variation in the provision, of health services necessitate consultation with the local authority,[311] unless 'a decision has to be taken without allowing time for consultation because of a risk to safety or welfare of patients or staff'.[312] It should be noted that this is a distinct legal duty from that of public engagement set out in paras 1.111–1.115 above.[313] No definitions are provided of 'substantial development' or 'substantial variation': the matter will be one for discussion between the responsible person **1.123**

[301] ibid, s 14Z14.
[302] ibid, ss 14Z15(2)(b) and (3).
[303] ibid, ss 14Z16(3)(c) and (4).
[304] Department of Health, *Local Authority Health Scrutiny* (2014), para 1.1.1.
[305] Localism Act 2011, Schedule 2, inserting new s 9B into Local Government Act 2000.
[306] Department of Health, n 304, para 3.1.7.
[307] Local Authority (Public Health, Health and Wellbeing Boards and Health Scrutiny) Regulations 2013, SI 2013/218, reg 26(1).
[308] ibid, reg 27(1).
[309] ibid, reg 22(1).
[310] ibid, reg 22(7).
[311] ibid, reg. 23(1).
[312] ibid, reg. 23(2).
[313] NHS England, *Planning and Delivering Service Changes for Patients* (2013), 32.

and the relevant health scrutiny body and it may prove helpful to develop joint protocols or memoranda of understanding in this regard.[314] The authority must be provided with the proposed date of decision and the date by which any comments on the proposal are requested; these dates must also be published.[315] The option of referral (in writing) to the Secretary of State is available where the health scrutiny body has not been consulted,[316] and is not satisfied by the reasons given for lack of consultation; where it has been consulted but content or timing of consultation is inadequate; and where it considers that the proposal would not be in the interests of the health service in its area.[317] Upon receiving such a referral, the minister may, at his discretion, ask for advice from the Independent Reconfiguration Panel, an advisory non-departmental public body sponsored by the Department of Health. Ultimately, the Secretary of State may issue directions requiring consultation or further consultation to take place; the matter to be determined in a particular way; or other steps in relation to the matter to be taken (or not taken).[318]

3. Governance of standards and performance

1.124 To the extent that patients elect to litigate in respect of poor standards of care, the law of negligence may have an influence in improving standards. However, the duty of quality and the concomitant right contained in the NHS Constitution,[319] is not limited to those who bring complaints; indeed, it extends to matters about which there has been no complaint. It requires authorities to introduce systems of clinical governance capable of identifying shortcomings and responding to them appropriately. Three of these will be outlined briefly here: the Care Quality Commission, Monitor, and the Professional Standards Authority for Health and Social Care.[320]

(i) Care Quality Commission (CQC)

1.125 CQC was created in 2009 to perform the functions previously carried out by the Healthcare Commission, the Commission for Social Care Inspection, and the Mental Health Act Commission. Previously, the regulation of NHS providers, private hospitals, nursing and residential homes, and social services was fragmented. As the boundary between NHS and social services care became blurred and private providers were encouraged to provide public services, the need for a common system of regulation became clear.

1.126 The CQC's stated purpose is to 'make sure health and social care services provide people with safe, effective, compassionate, high-quality care and [to] encourage them to improve'.[321] It shall perform its functions in order to encourage '(a) the improvement of health and social care services, (b) the provision of health and social care services in a way that focuses on the needs and experiences of people who use those services, and (c) the efficient and effective use of resources in the provision of health and social care services'.[322] In so doing, the

[314] Department of Health, n 304, para 4.2.2.

[315] Local Authority (Public Health, Health and Wellbeing Boards and Health Scrutiny) Regulations 2013, regs 23(1) (b) and (d).

[316] ibid, pursuant to reg 23(2): see n 312.

[317] ibid, reg 23(9). Note, however, that where the scrutiny body has made a recommendation to the proposer with which the latter disagrees, both parties 'must take such steps as are reasonably practicable to try to reach agreement in relation to the subject of the recommendation': reg 23(5)(b).

[318] ibid, reg 25(3).

[319] See National Health Service Act 2006, ss 1A, 13E, and 14R, imposing a duty as to improvement in quality of services upon the Secretary of State, NHS Commissioning Board, and CCGs respectively. See also NHS Constitution, n 105, sec 3a.

[320] For a more detailed discussion of regulation of health care professionals, see Chapter 2.

[321] <http://www.cqc.org.uk/content/who-we-are>.

[322] Health and Social Care Act 2008, s 3(2).

Commission must have regard to (a) views expressed by or on behalf of members of the public about health and social care services; (b) experiences of people who use health and social care services and their families and friends; (c) views expressed by Local Healthwatch organizations or Local Healthwatch contractors; (d) the need to protect and promote the rights of people who use health and social care services; (e) the need to ensure that action taken is proportionate to the risks against which it would afford safeguards and is targeted only where it is needed; (f) any developments in regulatory action; and (g) best practice among persons performing functions comparable to the Commission; as well as such aspects of Government policy as the Secretary of State may direct.[323]

Standards to which service providers must conform are set out in Regulations,[324] which are underpinned by guidance issued by the Commission under s 23 of the 2008 Act.[325] In response to the recommendations of the inquiry into care at Mid Staffordshire NHS Trust, a new set of 'fundamental standards' has been introduced, below which the provision of regulated activities and the care people receive should never fall. These include standards relating to: person-centred care; dignity and respect; the need for consent; safe care and treatment; safeguarding service users from abuse and improper treatment; meeting nutritional and hydration needs; receiving and acting on complaints; good governance; staffing; and the 'duty of candour'; among others.[326] Breach of certain of these standards (such as those relating to consent, safe care and treatment, safeguarding users from abuse and improper treatment, meeting nutritional and hydration needs, and the duty of candour) may trigger criminal enforcement powers ranging from simple cautions to prosecution; in the case of other standards, CQC may use civil enforcement powers, such as imposing, varying or removing conditions of registration, suspending or cancelling registration and/or placing one or more of a provider's services in special measures.[327] **1.127**

However, consonant with the variety of regulatory approaches adopted in health care as outlined in para 1.86, enforcement is only one component of the operating model which the Commission uses to achieve its purpose and perform its role. A central function of the CQC is the registration of health and social care providers and managers; it is an offence to carry on a 'regulated activity' (defined as involving or connected with, the provision of health or social care in, or in relation to, England),[328] without being registered.[329] In granting an application, the CQC must be satisfied as to the 'fitness' of the person or body seeking registration to carry on a regulated activity,[330] and that there will be compliance with Regulations (including the 'fundamental standards') and any other statutory requirements it considers to be relevant.[331] **1.128**

The CQC also undertakes inspection of providers.[332] Inspections assess whether the requirements set out in Regulations—notably, the 'fundamental standards' are being met, but **1.129**

---

[323] ibid, ss 4(1), (2), as amended by Health and Social Care Act 2012, s 189(6)(a).

[324] Primarily, the Care Quality Commission (Registration) Regulations 2009, SI 2009//3112 and the Health and Social Care Act 2008 (Regulated Activities) Regulations 2014, SI 2014/2396.

[325] CQC, *Guidance for providers on meeting the Regulations* (2015).

[326] Health and Social Care Act 2008 (Regulated Activities) Regulations 2014, Part 3, Section 2.

[327] See CQC, *Enforcement Policy* (2015).

[328] Health and Social Care Act 2008, s 8(2)(a). Regulated activities are specified in Health and Social Care Act 2008 (Regulated Activities) Regulations 2014, Schedule 1.

[329] ibid, s 10(1).

[330] Health and Social Care Act 2008 (Regulated Activities) Regulations 2014, regs 4–7.

[331] Health and Social Care Act 2008, s 12(2).

[332] ibid, s 60. There are supplementary powers of entry onto premises, inspection of documents and items, seizure, and interview: see s 63.

beyond these, the Commission also poses a series of questions about the service to establish its quality: namely, whether it is safe, effective, caring, responsive to people's needs, and well-led.[333] The Commission is obliged to prepare and publish reports on inspections.[334] In most cases, these include ratings (for each of the five key questions and overall) on a four-point scale ranging from 'outstanding' to 'inadequate'. These ratings must be displayed by the provider.[335] The provider is expected to respond to areas of concern that are identified on inspection, to develop an action plan to address them and to make improvements. Improvements may be required through the issuing of a 'requirement notice' which obliges the provider to report upon how they will comply with their legal requirements, or a 'warning notice' in more serious cases;[336] improvements can be forced through the use of civil enforcement powers or placing the provider in special measures, with criminal powers also available.[337]

1.130 The CQC has experienced something of a chequered history. The National Audit Office concluded in 2011 that it did not offer value for money, given failures to meet deadlines in registering providers and to complete planned programmes of reviews and inspections.[338] The Francis Inquiry into standards of care at Mid-Staffordshire NHS Foundation Trust noted evidence of a 'defensive institutional instinct to attack those who criticise it' and identified the importance of 'not ignoring Trusts which have failed to appear on the radar of concern', one means of doing so being to engage in more direct contact with service users and families.[339] Most notably, revelations of criminal abuse of patients by staff at Winterbourne View, near Bristol, and the apparent failure to act upon whistleblowing there,[340] led to the development of a tighter inspection and regulatory regime and more rigorous calling to account of failures to meet legal requirements.[341] The Commission acknowledged the need to 'make major changes to what we do and how we do it',[342] but it continues to be subject to criticism. For example, the British Medical Association's 2015 annual representative meeting passed a motion asserting that it had proven itself 'not fit for purpose' and calling for its abolition, on the basis that its inspection regime was too burdensome and was diverting resources from front line services.[343]

(ii) Monitor

1.131 Monitor was established in 2004 as the 'Independent Regulator of Foundation Trusts',[344] but its role was significantly extended as a consequence of the Health and Social Care Act

---

333 CQC, n 327, 9.

334 Health and Social Care Act 2008, s 46, as inserted by Care Act 2014 s 91(2).

335 Health and Social Care Act 2008 (Regulated Activities)(Amendment) Regulations 2015, SI 2015/64, reg 11.

336 See Health and Social Care Act 2008, s 29.

337 CQC, n 327, 14.

338 National Audit Office, *The Care Quality Commission: Regulating the Quality and Safety of Health and Adult Social Care*, (HC 1665, 2010–12).

339 *Report of the Mid-Staffordshire NHS Foundation Trust Public Inquiry, Executive Summary*, (HC 947, 2013) paras 1.74, 1.79–1.80.

340 See 'Warnings of care home "were ignored for months"' *Daily Telegraph* (1 June 2011).

341 See Department of Health, *Transforming Care: a national response to Winterbourne View Hospital* (2012).

342 CQC, *Raising Standards, Putting People First: our Strategy for 2013 to 2016* (2013), 1. A subsequent report by the National Audit Office concluded that, 'in the face of sustained criticism, the Commission has made substantial progress to change its regulatory model', but that 'further challenges lie ahead to demonstrate value for money', in particular in respect of recruitment of staff, building an organizational culture, and managing public expectations: see National Audit Office, *Capacity and Capability to Regulate the Quality and Safety of Heath and Adult Social Care* (HC 271, 2015–16), paras 20–21.

343 'BMA delegates support call for CQC to be abolished' *Pulse* (22 June 2015).

344 Health and Social Care (Community Health and Standards) Act 2003, s 2.

2012, and it has described itself as the 'sector regulator for health services in England'.[345] Its main duty, as set out in s 62(1) of the 2012 Act, is 'to protect and promote the interests of people who use health care services', which the regulator interprets as meaning 'we must put patient interests first in everything we do'.[346] It is required to carry out this duty by promoting provision of health services which is economic, efficient, and effective and which maintains or improves quality, having regard to likely future demand for services.[347] Hence, its 'job is to help those working on the NHS front-line to improve services continuously so the NHS can provide more and better care for patients within the resources available to it'.[348]

The regulator's functions are detailed further in Chapters 2 to 5 of Part 3 of the 2012 Act. **1.132** Certain of these functions are primarily economic in character. Thus, as noted previously, Monitor is conferred with power concurrently with the Office of Fair Trading (now the Competition and Markets Authority) to protect patients by preventing anti-competitive behaviour by health care providers, but not to promote competition as an end in itself.[349] Additionally, chapter 4 of Part 3 of the Act confers power on Monitor to set the 'national tariff',[350] working alongside the NHS Commissioning Board; the latter specifies which services should be subject to the tariff, while Monitor sets the price.

Other functions enable Monitor to 'make sure public providers of NHS care are well led **1.133** and able to deliver quality care on a sustainable basis'.[351] To this end, chapter 3 of Part 3 of the 2012 Act sets out a licensing regime: the licence has been described as 'Monitor's main tool for regulating providers of NHS services'.[352] Providers of health care services for the purposes of the NHS must hold a licence issued by Monitor,[353] unless exempted under regulations made by the Secretary of State;[354] however, the effect of s 88 of the Act is that NHS Foundation Trusts are automatically licensed without the need to make an application.[355] Monitor may set two types of licence conditions. Standard conditions include matters such as provision of information and documents to the regulator; ensuring that only fit and proper persons become directors or governors; obligation to register with CQC; compliance with the national tariff; ensuring patients are informed where there is a choice of providers, or other similar choices.[356] Special licence conditions can also be set under s 95(1) of the Act: these might be inserted in response to risks specifically identified by the regulator. Such conditions are inserted or modified by agreement with the provider; where this is not

[345] Monitor, *About Monitor* (2014) 2.
[346] ibid.
[347] Health and Social Care Act, ss 61(1), (2).
[348] Monitor, n 345, 5.
[349] See para 1.64.
[350] See Health and Social Care Act 2012, s 116.
[351] Monitor, n 345, 4.
[352] Monitor, *Choice and competition licence conditions: guidance for providers of NHS-funded services* (2014), 6.
[353] Health and Social Care Act 2012, s 81(1).
[354] ibid, s 83. Exempt categories include providers which are not required to register with CQC; providers of solely primary medical and dental services; providers of solely NHS continuing healthcare and NHS-funded nursing care; and providers whose NHS turnover is less than £10 million per year, in each case unless the continuity of the service in question in the event of financial unsustainability is deemed as necessary by CCGs or the NHS Commissioning Board because removal would cause harm to patients and there are no alternative providers. See National Health Service (Licence Exemptions, etc) Regulations 2013, SI 2013/2677 and Department of Health, *Protecting and promoting patients' interests: Licence exemptions: guidance for providers* (2015).
[355] Remaining NHS Trusts are exempt from the licence requirement: see SI 2013/2677, reg 4.
[356] Health and Social Care Act 2012, s 94. See Monitor, *The new NHS provider licence* (2013), Annex A.

forthcoming, the matter may be referred to the Competition and Markets Authority for determination.[357]

1.134 There is oversight of the continuing performance of licensed providers to ensure maintenance of standards. The regulator seeks to 'identify potential problems early on, so as to minimize the risk that a provider eventually fails', monitoring criteria such as financial plans and performance against targets; staff satisfaction, absence, and retention; and major transactions such as mergers and acquisitions.[358] In cases of breaches of licence conditions, Monitor may impose discretionary requirements (which may amount to monetary penalties; to take steps to ensure that a breach does not continue or recur; or to take steps to ensure that the position is restored to what it would have been had the breach not occurred),[359] or accept enforcement undertakings;[360] and additional licence conditions may be imposed upon Foundation Trusts in order to address governance failings.[361]

1.135 Where there are serious failures in quality of care and concerns that existing management cannot make the necessary improvements without support, CQC may recommend that an NHS Trust or Foundation Trust is placed in special measures, 'a series of specific interventions designed to improve the quality of care within a reasonable time'.[362] This process was utilized in 2013 in respect of eleven Trusts which were investigated as outliers on mortality rates in the wake of the inquiry into poor standards of care at Mid-Staffordshire NHS Foundation Trust.[363] The decision to take such measures is made by Monitor (or the NHS Trust Development Authority in the case of the remaining NHS Trusts),[364] and will typically involve the appointment of an improvement director; partner organizations to provide support; review of the capability of leadership (with changes where necessary); and the monthly publication of progress against action plans.[365] Re-inspection by CQC will normally take place within twelve months. At this stage the Trust may be taken out of special measures (with or without some continued support); continue in special measures until the end of an extension period (usually, six months); or remain in special measures while further support is provided or a long-term solution (such as acquisition by another organization, or merger) is found.[366]

1.136 Monitor is also responsible for ensuring that essential services, whether provided by a NHS Foundation Trust or an independent sector provider, continue to be maintained and protected for local patients. The primary responsibility for ensuring continuity of services in local areas lies with commissioners, overseen by the NHS Commissioning Board; in circumstances where providers become financially unstable or unable to provide services of sufficient quality, commissioners should identify services which 'need to be kept running because their withdrawal would adversely impact on health or health inequalities'.[367] The standard licence conditions

---

[357] Health and Social Care Act 2012, s 101.

[358] Monitor, *Monitor's Strategy 2014–17* (2014), 9.

[359] Health and Social Care Act 2012, s 105. See further Monitor, *Enforcement Guidance* (2013).

[360] ibid, s 106.

[361] ibid, s 111.

[362] Monitor/CQC/Trust Development Authority, *A Guide to Special Measures* (2015) 2.

[363] See B Keogh, *Review into the quality of care and treatment provided by 14 hospital trusts in England: Overview Report* (the 'Keogh Review') (2013).

[364] Monitor or the NHS Trust Development Authority (both of which are now part of the NHS Improvement organization) may place a Trust into special measures without a recommendation from the CQC: see Monitor/CQC/Trust Development Authority, n 362, 4. In such cases, advice is taken from CQC.

[365] ibid, 4–5.

[366] ibid, 5–9. In respect of the Trusts placed into special measures following the Keogh Review, see CQC/Monitor/Trust Development Authority, *Special measures: one year on* (2014).

[367] Monitor, *Statutory Guidance for Trust special administrators appointed to NHS Foundation Trusts* (2015).

contain provisions relating to continuity of essential services;[368] Monitor has powers under s 98 of the 2012 Act to impose further conditions relating to continuity, such as requiring cooperation with persons which it may appoint to assist in management of the provider's affairs, business, and property. It is thus able to take a variety of steps to protect the continuity of essential services, such as requiring a provider to appoint a 'turnaround team', or to provide information and access to premises to a continuity team appointed by the regulator. The goal is to return the provider to normal operation as soon as possible and ensure the continuity of essential services.

In exceptional circumstances and as a last resort, a special administration regime may be used, a 'bespoke, time-limited process to provide a solution to intractable problems' in providers which are 'significantly challenged',[369] whether because they are unable to meet their financial obligations or because they are unable to provide services of a sufficient quality. The 2012 Act makes provision for two special administration regimes. Chapter 5 provides for 'health special administration', based upon insolvency law but acting as an alternative to the corporate insolvency procedures set out in the Insolvency Act 1986, for companies providing NHS services which have been licensed by Monitor.[370] 'Trust special administration' applies to Foundation Trusts, and is governed by s 65D of the National Health Service Act 2006.[371] There is a separate process, administered by the Secretary of State, for the remaining NHS Trusts.[372] **1.137**

The stages of the special administration regime for both forms of Trust are similar.[373] Following appointment (by Monitor in the case of Foundation Trusts, by the Secretary of State in the case of NHS Trusts), the special administrator takes over the functions of the chair, directors, and governors of the Trust, these officers being suspended. The administrator runs the organization on a 'business as usual' basis, securing the provision of services for the local population. The administrator prepares recommendations in respect of actions which should be taken to secure the continued provision of high-quality, safe, and sustainable services, publishing a draft report within sixty-five days, which is laid before Parliament. An eight-week consultation period follows, which should involve NHS staff and the wider public. A final report, containing recommendations, must be published no later than fifteen days after the end of the consultation period, and is laid before Parliament. Monitor or the Secretary of State must decide what action to take within twenty days of publication of this report; in the case of Foundation Trusts, the Secretary of State must approve Monitor's recommendations for action. Possible outcomes include restructuring of the Trust, acquisition by or merger with another Trust, or dissolution of the Trust and transfer of its staff and services to another Trust or the Secretary of State. The entire process of special administration is limited to 146 days,[374] unless an extension of time order is made by Monitor or the Secretary of State. **1.138**

---

[368] See Health and Social Care Act 2012, ss 97(1)(i), (j), and (k).

[369] Monitor, n 367, 7.

[370] This regime has not yet been introduced. Following a consultation process, the government decided that, in view of uncertainty in the sector and the fact that instances of independent provider insolvency were rare, it was sufficient to rely upon the existing regime for insolvency at present: see Department of Health, *Protecting patients' interests —ensuring continuity of NHS services: Proposals for a Health Special Administration procedure for companies: Government Response* (2014).

[371] As amended and inserted by Health and Social Care Act 2012, ss 174, 175.

[372] National Health Service Act 2006, s 65B as inserted by Health Act 2009, s 16. This provision is repealed by Health and Social Care Act 2012, s 179(6) and Schedule 14, but the repeal will only take effect once all NHS Trusts have become Foundation Trusts: see para 1.49. Amendments to the process for both of these regimes are made by Care Act 2014, s 120.

[373] See Monitor, n 367 and Department of Health, *Statutory Guidance for Trust Special Administrators appointed to NHS Trusts* (2015).

[374] See Care Act 2014, s 120.

1.139 The special administration regime has been used sparingly. Only two Trusts have been subject to the process to date—South London Healthcare NHS Trust in July 2012 and Mid-Staffordshire NHS Foundation Trust in April 2013. In both instances, the Trust was dissolved and its services transferred to other providers. In the South London case, recommendations made by the special administrator (and accepted by the Secretary of State) that there should be changes in provision in a neighbouring Trust were successfully challenged by way of judicial review on the ground that such recommendations were ultra vires the powers conferred by s 65 of the 2006 Act. This only permitted action in relation to the Trust which had been placed under special administration, the Court of Appeal noting that 'Parliament would have been astute to guard against too broad a power which might be used as a "back door approach to reconfiguration"'.[375] In response to this judgment, s 120(1) of the Care Act 2014 amends s 65O of the 2006 Act to provide that action may be taken in relation to another NHS or Foundation Trust which is 'necessary for and consequential on' action taken in relation to the Trust which is in special administration.

1.140 A review of Monitor undertaken by the National Audit Office in 2014 concluded that it had:

> achieved value for money in regulating NHS Foundation Trusts. Its processes for assessing and monitoring Trusts are robust, its judgments have mostly been sound, and it has refined its approach in the light of experience. The balance of evidence suggests that Monitor has generally been effective in helping Trusts in difficulty to improve.[376]

However, it also considered that it needed to explain more fully how it would exercise its additional responsibilities under the 2012 Act, noting a 'gap in understanding, and therefore concern, about how Monitor will apply its new powers to benefit patients',[377] in particular by making clear 'how it will weigh up the benefits to patients of potential improvements in the quality of care and cost savings that may arise from service reconfiguration and integration against reduced choice and competition'. In April 2016, Monitor became part of the newly-established NHS Improvement organization. While its powers and duties remain the same, there is said to be a 'change of emphasis' as a consequence of creation of the overarching organization, whose 'priority is to offer support to providers and local health systems to help them improve'.[378]

(iii) The Professional Standards Authority

1.141 Previously known as the Council for Healthcare Regulatory Excellence, the Authority came into existence in November 2012 under s 222 of the Health and Social Care Act 2012. It was established with a view to securing strengthened accountability of the performance of other regulatory bodies, to balance promised greater independence and autonomy for those bodies; in addition, it has assumed responsibility for regulation of social workers.[379] Its 'over-arching objective', as specified in s 25(2A) of the National Health Service Reform and Health Care Professions Act 2002,[380] is the protection of the public, pursuit of which involves protection, promotion, and maintenance of the health, safety, and wellbeing of the

---

375 *Trust Special Administrator v London Borough of Lewisham* [2013] EWCA Civ 1409, [20] (Sullivan LJ).

376 National Audit Office, *Monitor: Regulating NHS Foundation Trusts* (HC 2013–14, 1071), para 20. Contrast the CQC, nn 338, 342.

377 ibid, para 22(c).

378 <https://www.gov.uk/government/news/monitor-is-now-part-of-nhs-improvement>.

379 See *Enabling Excellence: Autonomy and Accountability for Healthcare Workers, Social Workers and Social Care Workers*, Cm 8008 (2011); and further, Chapter 2.

380 As substituted by Health and Social Care (Safety and Quality) Act 2015, s 5.

public; promotion and maintenance of public confidence in the professions regulated by the regulatory bodies; and promotion and maintenance of proper professional standards and conduct (as well as specific functions relating to pharmacies and opticians).[381] It pursues these objectives by promoting the interests of users of health care, social care and social work in relation to the performance of functions by regulatory bodies; promoting best practice in the performance of those functions; formulating principles relating to good professional self-regulation and encouraging professional bodies to comply with them; and promoting cooperation between regulatory bodies and between those bodies and others performing corresponding functions.[382]

The Authority is, therefore, a 'meta-regulator': a regulator of other regulators. It has oversight of nine statutory bodies which regulate health and social care professionals in the UK:[383] these include the General Medical Council; the General Dental Council; the Nursing and Midwifery Council; and the General Pharmaceutical Council. The Authority conducts an annual performance review of each of these bodies,[384] assessing performance in relation to guidance and standards, education and training, registration and fitness to practise by reference to its Standards of Good Regulation,[385] with a written report laid before Parliament.[386] It has power to recommend that a regulatory body changes the way in which it performs any of its functions,[387] as well as power to give directions requiring a body to make rules to achieve a specified effect, where it considers that this would be desirable for protection of members of the public.[388] It describes its regulatory approach as 'right touch regulation',[389] summarized as 'the minimum regulatory force required to achieve the desired result'.[390] **1.142**

The Authority's most specific meta-regulatory role relates to fitness to practise procedures operated by the regulatory bodies. It audits cases which the regulatory bodies have closed without reference to a formal fitness to practise process, in order to ensure that such decisions have not exposed patients or service users to unacceptable safety risks and to maintain public confidence in regulation of the profession.[391] The Authority's powers are limited to making general reports or general recommendations as to future cases;[392] it is not empowered to reopen or review individual cases, even where it considers that a formal fitness to practise hearing should have been held.[393] **1.143**

As regards final fitness to practise decisions, the Authority reviews and may refer them to the High Court.[394] This power, which was intended to be used as a last resort,[395] is exercised in **1.144**

[381] National Health Service Reform and Health Care Professions Act 2002, s 25(2)(b), as substituted by Health and Social Care (Safety and Quality Act) 2015, s 5.

[382] ibid, s 25(2), as amended by Health and Social Care Act 2012, s 223(1).

[383] See further the discussion in Chapter 2.

[384] n 381, s 26(2)(a).

[385] Professional Standards Authority, *The Performance Review Standards: Standards of Good Regulation* (2010).

[386] National Health Service Reform and Health Care Professions Act 2002, Sch 7, para 16.

[387] ibid, s 26(2)(c).

[388] ibid, s 27(2). No such directions have as yet been made.

[389] See <https://www.professionalstandards.org.uk/policy-and-research/right-touch-regulation> and Council for Healthcare Regulatory Excellence, *Right-touch Regulation* (2010).

[390] Council for Healthcare Regulatory Excellence, *Performance Review Report* (HC 1084-II, 2011) para 6.2.

[391] Professional Standards Authority, *Audit Process and Guidelines* (2011), para 1.3.

[392] See National Health Service Reform and Health Care Professions Act 2002, s 26(4)(c), as substituted by Health and Social Care Act 2008, s 115.

[393] Professional Standards Authority, n 391, para 1.15.

[394] National Health Service Reform and Health Care Professions Act 2002, s 29.

[395] See J Glynn and D Gomez, *The Regulation of Health Care Professionals: Law, Principle and Process* (Sweet & Maxwell 2012), 472.

cases where the Authority considers that the decision is 'not sufficient (whether as to a finding or a penalty or both) for the protection of the public', taking into consideration the need to protect the health, safety, and wellbeing of the public; maintenance of public confidence in the profession concerned; and maintenance of proper professional standards and conduct for members of that profession.[396] In determining whether the power under s 29 should be used, deference should be shown by the Authority to the expertise of the disciplinary tribunal;[397] the degree of deference is likely to be higher where issues of technical competence or clinical practice arise and lower where the case concerns behavioural issues such as dishonesty or sexual misconduct.[398] Even where a reversal of the original decision is achieved through a successful appeal, the Authority regards its 'longer-term objective [as] forward-looking, with a view to improving the fitness to practise processes and procedures across the regulatory bodies. For this to happen, part of the s 29 process must be the dissemination to regulatory bodies of feedback points from previous cases as well as "near misses"'.[399]

1.145 The Health and Social Care Act 2012 extended the Authority's role to include standard-setting and accreditation of voluntary registers of persons working in health and social care occupations that are not statutorily regulated.[400] By 2015, there were seventeen accredited registers covering 63,000 practitioners.[401] These include organizations for sports rehabilitation, psychoanalysis, psychotherapy, and counselling. The existence of some registers—such as those for hypnotherapy and homeopathy—might be regarded as somewhat controversial given that they are not uniformly accepted as a part of conventional medical practice and that evidence of efficacy is limited.[402]

C. Conclusion

1.146 The Health and Social Care Act 2012 has been described as 'arguably the biggest reorganization the Service has seen in its 63-year history'.[403] It is inevitable that the changes described in this chapter will take some time to 'bed in', and therefore the precise trajectory in the near future is difficult to anticipate. However, some broad observations may be made.

1.147 The centrepiece of the reform, which places GPs at the forefront of commissioning in the NHS, has been criticized on the basis that they may lack the necessary expertise to undertake the task,[404] and that it will lead to greater geographical disparities of care across the

[396] National Health Service Reform and Health Care Professions Act 2002, s 29(4), substituted by General Medical Council (Fitness to Practise and Over-arching Objective) and the Professional Standards Authority for Health and Social Care (References to Court) Order 2015, SI 2015/794, art 18(3).

[397] See *Council for the Regulation of Healthcare Professionals v General Medical Council and Ruscillo* [2004] EWCA Civ 1356, [78] (Lord Phillips MR).

[398] See *Council for the Regulation of Healthcare Professionals v Nursing and Midwifery Council and Grant* [2011] EWHC 927 (Admin), [63] (Cox J).

[399] Professional Standards Authority, *Section 29 Process and Guidelines* (2011), para 2.5.

[400] National Health Service Reform and Health Care Professions Act 2002, s 25G, inserted by Health and Social Care Act 2012, s 229(1).

[401] Professional Standards Authority, *Accredited Registers* (2015), para 1.2.

[402] See, eg, House of Commons Science and Technology Committee, Fourth Report (2009–10), *Evidence Check 2: Homeopathy* (HC 45). For discussion of regulation of complementary and alternative therapies, see J McHale, ch 3 in J McHale and N Gale (eds), *Routledge Handbook of Complementary and Alternative Medicine: Perspectives from Social Science and Law* (Routledge 2015).

[403] N Timmins, *Never Again? The Story of the Health and Social Care Act 2012* (Institute for Government 2012).

[404] See A Davies, 'Beyond New Public Management: Problems of Accountability in the Modern Administrative State', in N Bamforth and P Leyland, *Accountability in the Contemporary Constitution* (Oxford University Press 2013) 342.

Service.[405] Furthermore, the (eventual) transition of all hospital Trusts to Foundation status and the significant role played by the economic regulator, Monitor, would seem to point to enhanced competition between providers within the NHS, even if it is unclear how far the private sector will choose to become involved, especially in a time of financial stringency when profits may be limited.

Thus, while 'liberating the NHS' may indeed serve to empower patients and professionals, as health care is 'run from the bottom up', as was the ambition of the Coalition Government in 2010,[406] concerns over equity in access to, and quality of, services and treatments seem likely to persist. Bodies such as NICE, CQC, Monitor, and the Professional Standards Authority will therefore play a vital role in assuring (relative) consistency of standards and performance across an increasingly fragmented NHS. The longevity and legitimacy of the organizational framework outlined in this chapter may thus, in large part, turn upon the efficacy with which these institutions of NHS governance discharge their tasks. **1.148**

[405] See E Jackson, *Medical Law: Text, Cases and Materials* (3rd edn, Oxford University Press 2013) 66.
[406] Department of Health, n 52, 1.

2

REGULATING HEALTH CARE PROFESSIONS

Paula Case

A. Health Care Professions and Regulation

1. Introduction

There are at least 32 'health care professions' in the UK,[1] to include doctors, nurses, midwives, opticians, dentists, chiropractors, pharmacists, and social workers. Whilst this chapter focuses primarily on the regulation of doctors by the General Medical Council ('GMC') and the legal mechanisms designed to ensure the accountability and transparency of the GMC, many features of the legal framework which governs doctors set out in the Medical Act 1983 (as amended) are replicated in the regulatory structures and procedures set up for other health care professions.[2] **2.01**

All of these professions have seen sweeping changes to their regulatory structures over the last decade or so, with statutory frameworks undergoing constant programmes of revision and a relentless deluge of new regulations regularly crashing at the regulators' door. Many of the changes have been characterized by a welcome move away from the tradition of 'self-regulation',[3] but the ad hoc nature of these reforms prompted the Law Commission's review of health care professions regulation in 2014 to observe that the regulatory framework remained 'fragmented, inconsistent and poorly understood'.[4] Although a harmonized legal framework applicable to all regulators remains a pipe dream, one significant outcome from the Law Commission's review has been that the Health and Social Care (Safety and Quality) Act 2015 has introduced a common objective for all health and social care regulators of 'protection of the public'.[5] Any regulator dealing with fitness to practise issues is required to have regard to this overarching objective. **2.02**

2. The health care 'professions'

Professions are defined by the bargain struck between individual professionals and their regulator, and between the profession collectively and the state.[6] The terms of this bargain often require an extraordinary level of dedication on the part of the practitioner by first completing a long and arduous educational journey to develop the necessary specialist knowledge and skill.[7] The practitioner must first prove him or herself qualified, and otherwise eligible, to be registered as a member of that profession. Thereafter, continuing obligations arise to **2.03**

---

[1] Law Commission, *Regulation of Health Care Professions* (Law Com no 345, 2014) at 1.1.

[2] For an overview of some of these regimes see part 2 of A Foster, G Treverton-Jones, and S Hanif, *Disciplinary and Regulatory Proceedings* (8th edn, Jordan Publishing 2015). For dentists the governing legislation is the Dentists Act 1984, for nurses and midwives see the Nursing and Midwifery Order 2001, for opticians see the Opticians Act 1989, for pharmacists in England, Wales, and Scotland see the Pharmacy Order 2010 and for Northern Ireland see the Pharmacy (Northern Ireland) Order 1976, for osteopaths see the Osteopaths Act 1993, for chiropractors see the Chiropractors Act 1994, and for a number of other health care professionals, eg, speech therapists, podiatrists, radiographers, paramedics, and psychologists, see the Health Professions Order 2001.

[3] See paras 2.05–2.07 and 2.16–2.21.

[4] Law Commission, *Regulation of Health Care Professions* (Law Com no 345, 2014) at 1.2.

[5] S 5 introduces the overarching objective for the Professional Standards Authority (discussed in paras 2.100–2.105) and the schedule introduces the objective for the health care regulators. The 'overarching objective' is further defined as including protection, promotion, and maintenance of the health, safety, and well-being of the public, promoting and maintenance of public confidence in the professions, and promoting and maintenance of proper standards and conduct. The issue of whether the overarching objective should extend to protecting public confidence in the professions and maintaining proper standards provoked the highest number of respondents to the Law Commission's review—see 3.1 onwards of the 2014 report, n 4.

[6] J Flood, 'The Re-Landscaping of the Legal Profession: Large Firms and Professional Re-regulation' (2011) 59 Current Sociology 507 at 509.

[7] See 'Education', para 2.27.

maintain the required level of expertise relative to modern developments,[8] and to stay loyal to the service ethic, placing the needs of the patient or client above his or her own interests. These commitments and more are explicitly set out in codes of conduct drawn up by the profession itself or its regulator, breach of which risk professional sanction and even exclusion from the profession.

2.04 In return for the professional's personal investment in education and training, membership of a profession usually brings a distinctive licence to practise, protected by law,[9] which serves to distinguish the practitioner from less trustworthy or less skilled service providers. This commitment and dedication also trigger other 'rewards' of relatively high levels of remuneration[10] and professional autonomy, although modern self-regulation (if it can still be called that) is of a far paler hue than the self-regulation of twenty years ago.[11]

3. Self-regulation and the medical profession

2.05 Regulation is always a product of competing interests[12] and, in the case of regulating health care professionals, the need to protect patient safety and to preserve and maintain public confidence in the profession must be sensibly balanced against the interests of the practitioner, whose livelihood is at stake. The GMC is the regulatory body responsible for regulating doctors in accordance with the provisions of the Medical Act 1983. The GMC's role was once described as 'guarding the portals of the profession'.[13] This phrase reflects the fact that historically, robust regulation of the profession was allegedly aimed primarily at controlling competition in medical work, with patient protection being of secondary importance.[14] These criticisms were considered to be symptomatic of the fact that the GMC is, or at least was, an example of self-regulation, defined as 'a process whereby an organised group of body regulates the behaviour of its members without interference from the state'.[15]

2.06 Such regimes of self-regulation are inevitably controversial as they appear to depart from the rule of law ideal which requires that doctors be subject to the law in the same manner as any other citizen. The justifications or positive features of self-regulation include suggestions that doctors possess an unusual level of *skill and knowledge,* the fact of which precludes the suitability of non-professionals as regulators,[16] and arguments that the costs of regulation are reduced by self-regulation (expertise being available in-house rather than needing to be commissioned on a task by task basis). Arguments against self-regulation have included that it gives the profession immense power to define what constitutes acceptable medical standards and also what is to be treated as a mishap or misconduct.[17] Those who are opposed

---

[8] eg *Crawford v Charing Cross Hospital, The Times* (8 December 1953).

[9] Medical Act 1983, Part VI (privileges of registered practitioners).

[10] NHS, 'Pay for doctors' at <http://www.nhscareers.nhs.uk/explore-by-career/doctors/pay-for-doctors/>.

[11] See further paras 2.16–2.21 and 2.99–2.105 and also Chapter 4 on breach of duty where, in the context of negligence actions, the courts have asserted greater regulatory oversight of the professions, reserving the right to fix the standard of care rather than deferring to medical opinion—see *Bolitho v City & Hackney Health Authority* [1997] 4 All ER 771 and now *Montgomery v Lanarkshire Health Board* [2015] UKSC 11.

[12] R Baldwin and M Cave, *Understanding Regulation* (Oxford University Press 2012) 30.

[13] M Stacey, *Regulating British Medicine: The General Medical Council* (Wiley & Sons 1992).

[14] ibid, 20. See also J Montgomery, 'Medicine, Accountability and Professionalism' (1989) 16 Journal of Law and Society 319, who in the 1980s pointed to the General Medical Council's preference for the preservation of the profession's reputation above the job of ensuring the profession were accountable: and see the conclusions of Dame Janet Smith in the *Shipman Inquiry: Fifth Report*, in Chapter 16.

[15] Law Commission, *Regulation of Health Care Professions* (Joint Consultation Paper, 2012) at 1.10.

[16] E Freidson, *Profession of Medicine* (University of Chicago Press 1988) 361.

[17] M Davies, *Medical Self-Regulation: Crisis and Change* (Ashgate 2007) 12.

to self-regulation point out that it '... has a poor record of enforcing standards against recalcitrant members'.[18]

As late as 2000 the GMC's 'Council' (the governing body of the GMC) bore the hallmark of self-regulation with 75 per cent of its members being taken from the profession itself, and the remainder being lay people. The changes set out below (at paras 2.16–2.21) make it more difficult to describe the GMC of today as an example of self-regulation. The main statutory objective of the GMC has also been adjusted and now requires the GMC, 'to protect the public'. This move represented a clear attempt to distance the GMC from historical allegations of self-interest.[19] **2.07**

4. Trust in the medical profession

The policy of promoting and maintaining the valuable social capital of public confidence in medicine, and the professions which administer it, has been a prominent driver of recent reforms to medical regulation. The reasons for trust and confidence in the medical profession and its regulation being valued so highly can be found in two assumptions pertinent to the health care professions. First, the patient is incredibly vulnerable in the therapeutic encounter, therefore the potential for abuse or exploitation looms large. It is vital therefore that individual practitioners and the systems that regulate them are trustworthy.[20] Secondly, trust is a matter of public interest because of the detrimental impact on society if citizens do not feel able to trust their doctor. This is because medical treatment relies heavily upon individual cooperation. Trusting patients will 'cooperate' by seeking medical attention in the first instance; confiding their health issues to an appropriately qualified 'stranger'; submitting to physical examination; consenting to the recommended diagnostic/exploratory procedures and, ultimately, treatment, in taking medication unsupervised, and following the doctor's advice. This cooperation benefits not only the *individual* patient but also broader *society* in a number of ways: preventative medicine minimizes the risk that patients pose to others (eg transmission of disease, contagion, or violence); treatment may contribute to maximizing the health of the country's workforce and productivity and reduce dependence on the welfare system[21]; treatment of individuals can also be regarded as providing the raw material for incremental advancements in medical knowledge and development and, indeed, trusting, cooperative patients are far more likely to volunteer to be involved in research which advances the frontiers of medical knowledge.[22] **2.08**

Should trust decline, an array of possibilities have been hypothesized which would impact on the public's health and the public purse, including higher rates of requests for second opinions thereby delaying effective treatment,[23] increased **2.09**

---

[18] A Ogus, 'Re-thinking Self-Regulation' in R Baldwin, C Scott, and C Hood (eds), *A Reader on Regulation* (Oxford University Press 1999) 376.

[19] Medical Act 1983, s 1(1A).

[20] *Makki v GMC* [2009] EWHC 3180 (Admin) is one of the few judgments to address exactly why trust is perceived as so important: 'public trust in doctors is essential to the whole enterprise of medicine. A destruction of that trust would be corrosive to the general attitude to the profession and therefore to the effectiveness overall of treatment. In a questioning and doubting world where trust is at a premium, if public trust in doctors falls generally then people will be likely to suffer as a direct consequence and may not seek help or seek help quickly enough. They may doubt the advice or prescriptions given to them by doctors and fail to follow it, or fail to follow the advice of prescriptions rigorously.' (at [43]).

[21] D Woods, 'UK Workers Took 180 Million Sick Days Last Year Costing The Economy £2.5 Billion' *Human Resources* (7th June 2010).

[22] N Kass et al, 'Trust: The Fragile Foundation of Contemporary Biomedical Research' (1996) 25(5) Hastings Center Report 25.

[23] N Moumjid et al, 'Seeking a Second Opinion: Do Patients Need a Second Opinion When Practice Guidelines Exist?' (2007) 80(1) Health Policy 43.

inclinations to litigate when things go wrong,[24] reluctance to seek medical advice or care,[25] or sourcing non-conventional therapies which are less evidence-based and less well regulated.[26]

2.10 The dominance of 'confidence-enhancing' measures in the reform of professional regulation has been seen as a means of redressing the perceived demise of public confidence prompted by a series of medical scandals.[27] These 'scandals' have included:

2.11 *Harold Shipman*—the infamous serial killer, Harold Shipman, thought to have killed over 200 of his patients whilst working as a general practitioner ('GP') in Hyde, Greater Manchester. The *Smith Inquiry*, which eventually produced no less than six reports,[28] looked, inter alia, at the GMC's role in terms of its 'failure' to stop Shipman earlier—why had the GMC played such a negligible part in bringing Shipman to justice? How had it been possible for a GP, who issued more than double the number of death certificates of any other doctor in the area, to kill so many patients without being detected?

2.12 *Alder Hey organs scandal*[29]—in 1998 the media reported the trauma suffered by parents on learning that their deceased child's organs had been harvested without their knowledge or consent. Thousands of organs had been retrieved from the bodies of children who had died in hospital and these organs had been earmarked to facilitate research, although most of them were stockpiled in archives to gather dust.[30] The Inquiry concluded that it had been general practice to remove organs at post mortem and retain them, that this had been done unlawfully (the profession had not attempted to 'construe' the Human Tissue Act 1961 which in fact required 'reasonable enquiries' to be made to ascertain whether any surviving relative would object[31]) and that the practice of not consulting parents was the manifestation of a paternalistic belief that it would be in the best interests of the parents not to have to answer sensitive questions about their child's body at a time of bereavement.[32]

2.13 *The Bristol Royal Infirmary heart surgery scandal*—a higher than average mortality rate was identified at a specialist unit for paediatric heart surgery. The resulting inquiry, reporting in 2001, suggested that opportunities to report the substandard care were neglected due to a culture of secrecy within the profession and lax monitoring systems. The inquiry concluded that regulatory frameworks had created 'no incentive to admit error, only to cover up'.[33]

---

[24] D Mechanic, 'Some Social Aspects of the Medical Malpractice Dilemma' (1975) Duke Law Journal 1179.

[25] 'those in need of medical assistance may be deterred from revealing such information of a personal and intimate nature as may be necessary in order to receive appropriate treatment and, even, from seeking such assistance, thereby endangering their own health and, in the case of transmissible diseases, that of the community': *Z v Finland* (1997) 25 EHRR 371 at [95]; cited with approval in *Campbell v MGN* [2004] 2 WLR 1232 at [145].

[26] Although see O O'Neill, *Autonomy and Trust in Bioethics* (Cambridge University Press 2002) 121, who argues that opting for this is internally inconsistent, and is sceptical about some of these claims that patients turn away from conventional medicine—saying that withdrawal from the technologies and systems where there is a decline of trust may not even be possible.

[27] See, eg, Department of Health, *Trust, Assurance and Safety: Regulation of Health Professionals in the 21st Century* (Cm 7013, 2007) 2.

[28] *The Shipman Inquiry,* all six reports of which are accessible at <http://webarchive.nationalarchives.gov.uk>.

[29] For further detail of the organs scandal and the legal responses, see Chapter 19 on the legal regulation and use of human material.

[30] *The Royal Liverpool Children's Inquiry Report* (HC 12-II, 2001).

[31] Section 1(2). This Act was repealed in favour of the Human Tissue Act 2004.

[32] *The Royal Liverpool Children's Inquiry Report,* n 30.

[33] Bristol Royal Infirmary Inquiry, *Report of the public inquiry into children's heart surgery at the Bristol Royal Infirmary 1984–1995: learning from Bristol* (Cm 5207, 2001).

Gynaecologists Rodney Ledward and Richard Neale—an independent inquiry in 2000 heard that Rodney Ledward was renowned for boasting about performing seven hysterectomies in just over three hours. He was revealed to have performed hundreds of shoddy operations and to have a particularly callous and domineering attitude towards patients.[34] In 2004 a public inquiry investigated the case of Richard Neale, also a gynaecologist, who had been allowed to practice in the UK by the GMC despite having been 'struck off' in Canada. Again, Neale was accused of performing substandard surgery and using intimidating/threatening behaviour towards his patients.[35] The GMC was criticized for taking no action against either practitioner during much of the period of misconduct.[36] **2.14**

Mid-Staffordshire NHS Foundation Trust—neglect and poor quality care causing the unnecessary suffering of hundreds of patients between 2005 and 2009 was exposed at this trust, the initial investigation being triggered by high standardized hospital mortality statistics.[37] The Inquiry Report published in 2013 attributed this substandard care to a number of factors, including an 'unhealthy and dangerous culture' which included bullying, putting 'cost control' ahead of patient care,[38] low staff morale, lack of candour and denial.[39] Added to these was a toxic mix of failures of communication between the different regulatory agencies, a 'loss of corporate memory' caused by persistent reorganization[40] and a belief that performance management and intervention were someone else's responsibilities. In 2013, Lord Hill speaking in a House of Lords debate questioned why (as yet) none of the staff at this Trust had been struck off by the GMC or Nursing and Midwifery Council.[41] Many of these findings and concerns bear a more than uncanny resemblance to the findings of the Bristol Inquiry (above) published more than ten years earlier. **2.15**

5. Impact of the trust agenda on regulation

The UK government's response to a perceived decline in public trust in the professions has been to increase the regulatory gaze by introducing more monitoring, surveillance, and quality assurance mechanisms at the level of both the regulator and the regulated. The GMC has survived a formidable programme of regulatory reforms, triggered for the most part by the findings of the *Smith Inquiry* into events surrounding the murders attributed to Dr Harold Shipman.[42] These reforms, without exception, aimed at least in part to redress the shortfall of public confidence in regulation of the medical profession and, in particular, to deal with a perceived lack of independence of regulator from regulated. The following offers an indication of the extent and breadth of these changes in the regulatory framework: **2.16**

[34] 'Downfall of Surgeon Who Ruined Lives' *The Guardian* (2 June 2000).

[35] 'Doctor Guilty of Poor Work Spanning a Decade' *The Guardian* (21 July 2000).

[36] See M Davies, *Medical Self-Regulation: Crisis and Change* (Ashgate 2007) at 151 onwards for a detailed discussion of these events.

[37] Healthcare Commission, *Investigation into Mid-Staffordshire NHS Foundation Trust* (2009), acting on the statistics published annually by *Dr Foster's Hospital Guide*—see <http://www.drfoster.com/innovation/hospital-guide/>.

[38] Resulting in an independent inquiry reporting in 2010, followed by a public inquiry (both chaired by Sir Robert Francis QC): *Mid Staffordshire NHS Foundation Trust Public Inquiry* (HC 947, 2013), the final report of which was published in 2013 at <http://www.midstaffspublicinquiry.com/report>.

[39] ibid, vol 3 at 20.14.

[40] ibid, *Executive Summary* (2013) 4.

[41] HL Debates, 6th February 2013 c320.

[42] *The Shipman Inquiry*, accessible at <http://www.the-shipman-inquiry.org.uk/home.asp>. The costs of the Shipman Inquiry alone are understood to be around £21 million: Lady Justice Smith, 'Public Inquiries Seminar—'Shipman: Was it Worth It?' delivered 24th September 2010 at Gresham College.

2.17 *Overarching statutory objective:* in an effort to counter allegations that the GMC acted primarily to protect its members, the reforms introduced an overarching statutory objective, which as recently reconfigured, charges the GMC with the duty to exercise its functions so as to 'protect the public'.[43] The protection of the public entails pursuit of: a) the protection, promotion, and maintenance of the health and safety of the public: b) promotion and maintenance of public confidence in the profession; and c) promotion and maintenance of proper professional standards and conduct for the profession.[44]

2.18 *Composition of Council and appointment of members:* the composition of the GMC's Council was changed so as to include more lay members.[45] The Council is now made up of six registered practitioners and six laity[46] and these members are no longer elected but appointed by the Privy Council.[47]

2.19 *Introducing the umbrella concept of 'impairment':* fitness to practise procedures were streamlined, including an apparent widening of the net by focussing on whether in the light of a doctor's 'conduct' fitness to practise was 'impaired', rather than whether 'serious professional misconduct' or 'seriously deficient performance' had been committed.[48]

2.20 *Divesting the GMC of its adjudicatory role:* in the summer of 2012 the fitness to practise panels were moved out of the GMC into the Medical Practitioners' Tribunal Service (MPTS). This addressed the criticism that the same body should not be responsible for both the bringing of fitness to practise cases and their adjudication. This reform replaced plans to create an *Office of Healthcare Professions Adjudicator* (OHPA).[49] Although the creation of OHPA was a strongly worded recommendation of the Shipman Inquiry, the plan was jettisoned by the Coalition Government, a move thought to be due to cost considerations.[50]

2.21 *Burden of proof:* Section112 of the Health and Social Care Act 2008 now applies the civil standard of proof to all fitness to practise proceedings for the health care professions. This is in order to better promote public confidence in professional regulation (the criminal burden of proof being perceived as extremely difficult to satisfy) but also to address an issue of consistency. The GMC had been one of three regulatory bodies to utilize the criminal standard of proof of proving allegations 'beyond reasonable doubt', whereas the remainder applied the lower civil standard of proving the alleged facts were true 'on the balance of probabilities'.

2.22 Critics have commented that a culture which is resistant to change has meant that attempts to improve the accountability of the professions and the ways they are regulated is having

43 Medical Act 1983, s 1(1A).

44 Medical Act 1983, s 1(1B). For detailed discussion of whether the overarching duty should include promotion of public confidence in doctors, see ch 3 of the Law Commission Report cited at n 1.

45 Based on a model of self-regulation, in 2000 membership of the 'Council' comprised a 75:25 split of professional members and lay members. In 2002 this was amended to a 60:40 split and in 2008 became a 50:50 split (*General Medical Council (Constitution) Order 2008* (2008/2554)).

46 *The General Medical Council (Constitution) (Amendment) Order* 2012/1654. The 50:50 split was achieved in 2008 (*General Medical Council (Constitution) Order 2008* (2008/2554)).

47 Medical Act 1983, Sch 1, Part 1A. Health Act 2006 s 60(1) authorizes the Privy Council to hand over these functions to the Appointments Commission.

48 Reform of the Medical Act 1983—The General Medical Council (Fitness to Practise) Rules, Order of Council 2004 No 2608 and the new s 35(C)(2) of the Medical Act 1983. Misconduct must nevertheless be 'serious' before it will be regarded as sufficient for fitness to practise to be impaired: *Nandi v GMC* [2004] EWHC 2317 (Admin) *per* Collins J.

49 Health and Social Care Act 2008, s 98.

50 *Fitness to Practise Adjudication for Health Professionals: Assessing different mechanisms for delivery* (DoH, August 2010).

limited effect in terms of improving patient safety.[51] Although many of these reforms were triggered by the recommendations of the Smith Inquiry into Harold Shipman's crimes, many have questioned whether reforming medical regulation would stop another Shipman, given the very exceptional and deliberative nature of his offending.[52]

When all is said and done, there is no real consensus on what is meant by the term 'trust', how it can be measured, what events are capable of causing permanent damage to that trust, and what tools are effective in repairing it. In light of these uncertainties it is very difficult to measure the success or otherwise of regulatory efforts to combat the perceived 'crisis'. Surprisingly, MORI poll research into public levels of trust in the professions have consistently documented an enviable trust score for doctors when compared with other professions.[53] Another complicating factor is that increased regulatory surveillance is almost bound to increase rates of complaint, and such rises will be construed in some quarters as further evidence that regulation is not working. As Henaghan states: 'distrust, . . . like any disease, spreads quickly if given too much airtime'.[54] Fitness to practise complaints to the GMC appear to rise year on year with complaints from members of the public increasing by 70 per cent in the five years between 2007 and 2012, albeit that the rise was reported as slowing in 2014.[55] Research by a team based at Plymouth's University Peninsula School of Dentistry and Medicine concluded that likely contributory factors included greater 'name recognition' of the GMC amongst the public, a barrage of negative publicity regarding doctors in the media, and patients taking greater ownership of their health.[56] **2.23**

B. The Fitness to Practise Framework

1. Registration and licensing

Central to the GMC's capacity to regulate individuals is the Register of Medical Practitioners and also the licence to practise.[57] The register operates as a regulatory tool in two ways; first of all, by operating the register the GMC assumes the role of the profession's gatekeeper, allowing entry only to those who have achieved the required standards for a 'registered medical practitioner' ('RMP'). Secondly, complaints about a registrant's conduct may trigger 'fitness to practise' proceedings against RMPs which may, in turn, result in registration being qualified or the practitioner being suspended or erased from the register. **2.24**

Registration with the GMC has, since late 2009, been supplemented by a system of 'licensing'—an additional layer of regulation which facilitates the process of 'revalidating' doctors (on which see below at paras 2.32–2.38). *The General Medical Council (Licence to Practise) Regulations Order of Council 2009* inserted a new s 29 into the Medical Act, making it a legal requirement for virtually anyone practising medicine in the UK to have a valid licence to practise. This means that anyone holding a post as a 'physician', surgeon, or other medical **2.25**

[51] eg C Newdick and C Danbury, 'Culture, Compensation and Clinical Neglect: Probity in The NHS After Mid Staffordshire' (2013) 41 JME 956.

[52] R Fisken, 'Premise is Wrongheaded' (2010) BMJ Letters 341.

[53] Percentage of respondents who trusted doctors to tell the truth were reported as being 90 per cent (2014 survey); 89 per cent (2013 survey); 88 per cent (2011 survey): Source—*Ipsos MORI Research Archive* <http://www.ipsos-mori.com/researchpublications/researcharchive> accessed 11th March 2015 (NB—the 'trust in professions' poll was not conducted in 2012).

[54] M Henaghan, *Health Professionals and Trust* (Routledge 2011) xii.

[55] GMC, *State of Medical Education and Practice in the UK 2014* (2014).

[56] J Archer et al, *Understanding the Rise in Fitness to Practise Complaints from Members of the Public* (CAMERA 2014).

[57] Medical Act 1983, s 2.

officer (except at a hospital supported wholly by voluntary contribution) must be fully registered *and* have a licence to practise.[58] Administering such a system is no mean feat—there were 238,247 licensed doctors in the UK in 2013, with newly qualified doctors and doctors from overseas being admitted to the register each week.[59] The 'privileges' of being registered and having a valid licence include the fact that certificates which require the signature of a 'medical practitioner' are valid only if signed by those who are fully registered with a licence to practise[60] and only those registered and with a licence can bring legal proceedings for non-payment of fees in connection with medical advice or services.[61]

2.26 The 2009 regulations set out the grounds for grant, refusal, or withdrawal of licences. It is an offence to wilfully and falsely 'pretend' to be a medical practitioner/to be registered with the GMC or for someone to expressly or impliedly hold himself or herself out as holding a licence to practise whilst not having such a license.[62] Practitioners can have 'provisional' registration, 'full' registration, 'general practitioner' registration, or 'specialist' registration. Any GP (including locums, but not GPs in training) must be on the General Practitioners Register. To obtain entry the practitioner must provide a Certificate of Completion of Training (CCT) in General Practice. Entry to the Specialist Register is a precondition of being appointed after 1997 as a consultant in the NHS, and access to this Register is via provision of a CCT in the relevant specialism or by demonstration of equivalent qualifications of training in a recognized specialty.[63]

2.27 *Education: getting on the register:* the GMC will only register those who have met its educational criteria for the profession (Part II of the Medical Act 1983). The usual route for qualification would be to take an undergraduate degree of four to five years (the Primary Medical Qualification or 'PMQ') before embarking on Foundation Years 1 and 2. After this time, all being well, full GMC registration and a licence to practise should follow. Each year of the Foundation phase should comprise three periods of four months in different specialties, one of which should usually be in Accident and Emergency. Doctors may then opt to undertake three to seven years of training for a particular specialism. A certain level of specialist training is necessary if the doctor is to work as an 'independent practitioner' (whether as a GP or as a consultant).

2.28 In 2010, the GMC acquired responsibility for supervising all undergraduate and postgraduate medical education and training.[64] It is subject to a legal duty to implement quality assurance monitoring of all programmes leading to a PMQ and organizes 'visits' to the relevant institutions to check that their standards meet those specified in *Tomorrow's Doctors*[65] and *The Trainee Doctor*.[66] Visits are triggered by the proposal for a new medical school, a new programme, or a five-year gap since the last visit. 'Checks' can also be undertaken to respond to specific issues of concern.

---

58 Medical Act 1983, s 47.

59 GMC, *State of Medical Education and Practise 2014* (2014) 27.

60 Medical Act 1983, s 48.

61 Medical Act 1983, s 46.

62 Medical Act 1983, ss 49 and 49A.

63 As provided for in the *Postgraduate Medical Education and Training Order of Council 2010*. For a successful legal challenge of a decision not to register see *General Medical Council v Nakhla* [2014] EWCA Civ 1522.

64 The Postgraduate Medical Education and Training Board becoming merged with the GMC at that time.

65 GMC, (2009).

66 GMC, (2011).

Exclusion from the profession: prior to revalidation, a frequent criticism of the GMC was that its style of regulation was reactive and complaints driven, there being no mechanism for periodic review of a doctor's fitness to practise. A doctor's right to practise would only be forfeited by an order for erasure from the register following an adverse outcome at a fitness to practise hearing. Now, however, a practitioner's licence to practise can also be withdrawn following an unfavourable outcome in revalidation (see paras 2.32–2.38, specifically 2.34). (It is also possible for a doctor to apply for voluntary erasure (see para 2.90)). **2.29**

Registration Appeals Panels ('RAPs') hear doctors' appeals against registration decisions, including refusals to grant a licence to practise, refusal to admit the practitioner to the GP or Specialist registers, and revalidation decisions.[67] The RAPs' procedures are set out in regulations and although the panels are part of the GMC, panellists do not have any other involvement with the registration process and the panel will often include both a medical member and a lay panellist.[68] An appeal against a RAP's decision can be made within twenty-eight days of the decision to the county court.[69] That court has the power to dismiss the appeal, revert the matter to the RAP or order the Registrar to include a practitioner on the register if the court is convinced that this is the only realistic outcome of remitting to a RAP.[70] **2.30**

2. Codes of conduct

All healthcare regulators produce guidance to their members on aspects of their work. The GMC is particularly prolific on this front, frequently updating its overarching guidance, *Good Medical Practice,* but also producing themed guidance on issues such as confidentiality, consent, child protection, and end of life care.[71] The *Good Medical Practice* guidance provides the benchmarks for a doctor's five-yearly revalidation (see below). These documents provide potentially useful regulatory tools in guiding the registered practitioner throughout their career and helping to pre-empt incidents of poor practice. Its effectiveness is, however, heavily reliant upon doctors' voluntary compliance/professionalism in adhering to their provisions. Some research has suggested that many doctors simply do not have time to look at the *Good Medical Practice* guidance, with some respondents saying they had filed their copy until they had the time to read it or that they had read it a year or two ago.[72] Any of the GMC's guidance documents may be referred to by the courts post hoc when determining whether a doctor has been in breach of his or her legal obligations.[73] **2.31**

67 A full list of appealable registration decisions is set out in Schedule 3A of the Medical Act 1983, para 2.

68 The General Medical Council (Registration Appeals Panels Procedures) Rules Order of Council 2010, SI 2010/476.

69 Schedule 3A of the Medical Act 1983, para 5.

70 *Hollingworth v Specialist Training Authority of the Medical Royal Colleges* [2003] EWCA Civ 452 [28].

71 *Good Medical Practice* (2013)*; Confidentiality* (2009); *Consent: Patients and Doctors Making Decisions Together* (2008); *Protecting Children and Young People* (2012); *Treatment and Care Towards the End of Life* (2010); *Guidance for Doctors providing Cosmetic Interventions* (2016).

72 *Setting Standards* (Picker Institute 2006). See also Friedson who treats professional codes of conduct with cynicism viewing their function as one of: ' ... persuading the general public to believe that the members of an occupation are ethical', whilst offering no guarantees that such guidance is translated into performance (E Friedson, *Profession of Medicine* (University of Chicago Press 1988) at 186.

73 eg *W v Edgell* [1989] 1 All ER 1089 at 1103 where Scott J treated GMC guidance on confidentiality as of assistance but not a complete statement of the legal duty of confidentiality. See further Chapter 4 on the relevance of professional guidance to the legal standard of care.

3. Auditing doctors' fitness to practise: revalidation

2.32 Revalidation makes the holding of a licence contingent upon a doctor's regular demonstration that they are up to date and fit to practise,[74] and has been hailed as the single most significant reform to professional regulation in the 150 years since the GMC was created. A new s 29 was inserted into the Medical Act 1983[75] empowering the GMC to set up a system of revalidation and placing the GMC under a duty to make regulations on revalidation. The current system of revalidation involves 'regular' assessment of a doctor's fitness to practise (usually every five years), and successful revalidation of a doctor results in the granting or renewal of the doctor's licence to practise. As such, these measures have the potential to transform the GMC's regulatory role from an incident-led, reactive regulator (taking action against a doctor's registration only when a complaint is made and validated) into a regulator responsible for a continuous, rolling programme of performance review.

2.33 The idea of regular assessment of a doctor's fitness to practise dates back to the *Merrison Committee Report* of 1975.[76] The modern commitment to a scheme of regular revalidation of doctors was prompted by the Bristol Inquiry,[77] but was very slow in becoming a reality.[78] Revalidation commenced in December 2012 and it is expected to take until 2018 for all doctors currently practising in the UK to have been the subject of the revalidation process.[79]

2.34 Two key features of revalidation are the doctor's submission of a portfolio of supporting information and regular workplace appraisals. Doctors are obliged to participate in the revalidation process[80] and must collect a portfolio of 'supporting information' across six identified themes.[81] These themes include colleague and patient feedback, the latter being considered crucial if the public is to have confidence in the new revalidation scheme.[82] For most doctors, revalidation builds upon the annual appraisal process which should already be operated by the doctor's employer. The GMC requires that those appraisals include the four broad domains identified in *The Good Medical Practice Framework for Appraisal and Revalidation*—namely: (1) knowledge, skills, and performance; (2) safety and quality; (3) communication, partnership, and teamwork; and (4) maintaining trust.[83] The doctor's Responsible Officer ('RO') is under a statutory obligation to make a recommendation to the GMC regarding the practitioner's fitness to practise after reviewing the doctor's appraisal records, the doctor's supporting information, and intelligence from other sources (eg patient complaints).[84] The RO can make one of three recommendations to the GMC of either a positive recommendation (that the doctor has demonstrated that they are up to date and fit to practise), recommending a deferral of a recommendation, or reporting on the doctor's

---

[74] GMC, *Ready for Revalidation* (2012), 2.

[75] Originally inserted in 2002 but amended in 2009 by The General Medical Council (Licence to Practise) Regulations Order of Council 2009.

[76] *Report of the Inquiry into the Regulation of the Medical Profession* (Cmnd 6018, 1975).

[77] Department of Health, *Learning from Bristol: The Department of Health's Response to the Public Inquiry into children's heart surgery at the Bristol Royal Infirmary 1984–1995* (2002) at para 25.

[78] It was the longevity of the planning stages on revalidation which prompted Parliament to exercise the nominal power of the Privy Council over the GMC and require the GMC to attend 'annual accountability' hearings before a Select Committee of the House of Commons. See para 2.98 on annual accountability hearings.

[79] GMC, *Starting Revalidation* (2013).

[80] GMC, *Good Medical Practice* (2013), para 6.

[81] GMC, *Supporting information for appraisal and revalidation* (2012).

[82] Ipsos Mori and the King's Fund, *Public and Patient Involvement in Revalidation: Assuring Confidence in Revalidation* (2012).

[83] GMC, *The Good Medical Practice Framework for Appraisal and Revalidation* (updated 2013).

[84] GMC, *The GMC Protocol for Making Revalidation Recommendations* (3rd edn, 2014) at 2.3.

non-engagement with the revalidation process.[85] A recommendation of referral might be appropriate, for example, to give a doctor more time to gather materials or to accommodate maternity leave, or where in the course of revalidation, the RO regards the doctor's fitness to practise as being called into question. This can be on the grounds of any of the matters set out in s 35C(2) of the Medical Act 1983 (i.e. misconduct, deficient professional performance, criminal conviction or caution, not having necessary English language requirements, adverse health, or relevant determination by another regulatory body). Such concerns can then be reported to the GMC and thereafter the usual procedures for dealing with allegations of unfitness to practise come into effect.[86] A decision by the GMC not to revalidate a doctor takes the form of a withdrawal of the practitioner's licence to practise.

Also key therefore to the revalidation scheme are ss 45A and 45B of the Medical Act 1983 (inserted by the Health and Social Care Act 2008) which enable regulations to be made requiring 'designated bodies' (ie employer organizations such as NHS Trusts or Health Boards) to nominate 'Responsible Officers' from amongst their employees (usually senior clinicians). The Responsible Officer ('RO') regulations make it clear that the ROs have a duty to ensure that the 'designated body' (employer) carries out regular appraisals for its registered medical practitioners. Those appraisals must obtain and take into account 'all available information relating to the medical practitioner's fitness to practise in the work carried out by the practitioner for the designated body, *and* for any other body, during the appraisal period'.[87] ROs must additionally fulfil a number of other statutory responsibilities which complement revalidation, including investigating concerns raised in connection with the practitioners they are responsible for, referring those concerns to the GMC (where appropriate), monitoring compliance with any conditions imposed on the doctor's registration and any undertakings the doctor has agreed to. They must also maintain records relevant to those practitioners' fitness to practise evaluations, appraisals, and any other investigations and assessments.[88] **2.35**

For doctors who do not have a connection to a 'designated body' it is the doctor's responsibility to identify a 'suitable person' who might take on the RO's role. 'Suitable persons' must either already be a designated RO or must perform duties similar to those of an RO within their organization, and must be approved by the GMC to act as such.[89] The role of ROs has been touted as the means by which to 'close the gap' in medical regulation, although concerns have been expressed in some quarters that the mechanisms for ensuring the RO's accountability have still to be clarified.[90] The statutory obligations of the RO/suitable person are certainly substantial, even potentially overwhelming, and time will tell how well supported ROs will feel in their revalidation role. **2.36**

The revalidation reforms have done a great deal to address criticisms that the GMC was largely 'reactive' in its approach to regulating doctors, instigating fitness to practise procedures only when a complaint had been brought forward, by which time patients had already been put at risk by poorly performing doctors.[91] Critics of the current scheme suggest that what doctors **2.37**

85 ibid, at 2.2.3.

86 Medical Act 1983, s 29C.

87 Medical Practitioner (Responsible Officer) Regulations 2010, regulation 11(2) and (3) respectively.

88 ibid, regulation 13.

89 The General Medical Council (Licence to Practise and Revalidation) Regulations Order of Council 2012, para 6.

90 House of Commons Health Select Committee, *Tenth Report: Annual Accountability Hearing with the GMC 2013* (2014) at [23] onwards.

91 For a history of revalidation proposals to dip into, see ch 26 of the *Fifth Shipman Report*. Dame Janet Smith concluded on the basis of the revalidation proposals as they stood at that time (2004): 'The public cannot properly have confidence that a doctor who has been revalidated is "up to date and fit to practise". That

are required to 'demonstrate' is an offering which falls short of ensuring fitness to practise. For example, as Dame Janet Smith noted during the Fifth Shipman Report, it is not accurate to describe revalidation as an 'MOT' for doctors, for this would wrongly imply that some kind of test or examination must be passed for the doctor to be revalidated.[92] Concerns have also been expressed that revalidation merely 'piggybacks' on existing employer appraisal mechanisms and therefore perhaps adds little to pre-existing systems for assessing fitness to practise.[93] There are dangers too that doctors may take a cynical view of any scheme based on appraisal, perceiving it to be a 'tick box' exercise which creates an 'impression of accountability,' but does not change or influence practice[94] and merely detracts from the time they could otherwise spend on patients. As to the patient feedback component of revalidation, it has also been noted that there is no robust mechanism for ensuring that negative feedback is not destroyed or omitted from the evidence submitted for revalidation.[95]

2.38 Early evaluations of the revalidation regime have further observed that only a very small number of doctors have been 'referred' to the GMC as a result of the revalidation process.[96] Whilst such low numbers might be a source of disappointment to those expecting revalidation to root out doctors not currently fit to practise, the success of revalidation on this front should not be measured solely by reference to referral rates. Revalidation may well have a deterrent effect and it is noteworthy, for example, that a number of doctors voluntarily relinquished registration when revalidation was announced.[97] Some of those relinquishing registration may well have self-diagnosed themselves as being unable to demonstrate fitness to practise and opted to step off the register.

4. The Medical Practitioner Tribunal Service and fitness to practise adjudication

2.39 In 2012 the GMC set up the Medical Practitioner Tribunal Service ('MPTS') as a committee to deal with the adjudication of fitness to practise cases. The diversion of adjudication to the MPTS was intended to counter allegations that adjudication and investigation of disciplinary cases was not sufficiently distinct to comply with requirements of a 'fair hearing' set out in Article 6 of the European Convention on Human Rights. There is still, however, work to be done on the further separation of the MPTS from the GMC. The MPTS remains funded by the GMC, reports biannually to the Council of the GMC and inherited GMC staff on its Medical Practitioner Tribunals. Recent changes effect further separation by placing the MPTS on a statutory footing (albeit still as part of the GMC) and inserting a new s 40A into the Medical Act giving the GMC power to appeal fitness to practise decisions of the Medical Practitioner Tribunals.[98] The ground for a GMC appeal

position may change in the future, if clinical governance improves, as everyone hopes that it will, and if the culture of one doctor's reluctance to report another's failings can be altered. Those changes may or may not come about. But if the GMC intends that revalidation should give the public a reassurance of real, as opposed to illusory, value it must accept that its present proposals are not adequate and must develop a system of revalidation which, at its first stage, entails a summative evaluation of each individual doctor's fitness to practise.'

[92] *Fifth Report* at 1086.

[93] eg House of Commons Health Select Committee, *Revalidation of Doctors—Fourth Report* (2010–11).

[94] G McGivern and E Ferlie, 'Playing Tick-box Games' (2007) 60(9) Human Relations 1361: researching the consultants' experiences of appraisal.

[95] M Davies, 'The Future of Medical Self-regulation in the United Kingdom: Renegotiating the State–profession Bargain' (2014) 14(4) MLI 236 at 249.

[96] J Archer et al, *Evaluating the Strategic Impact of Medical Revalidation* (CAMERA 2013).

[97] 'Revalidation has forced 63 doctors to quit medicine since January says GMC' (*Pulse,* 19th July 2013) <http://www.pulsetoday.co.uk> accessed 5th March 2015.

[98] The General Medical Council (Fitness to Practise and Over-Arching Objective) and the Professional Standards Authority for Health and Social Care (Referrals to Court) Order 2015.

would arise where the tribunal's decision '*is not sufficient (whether as to a finding or a penalty or both) for the protection of the public*'. The GMC's power of appeal mirrors the Professional Standards Authority's powers to refer a decision to court (see paras 2.99–2.104) and both the GMC and the Professional Standards Authority would be able to register themselves as an 'interested party' in an appeal by the other body, and add its own grounds to the appeal. Although the Health Committee needed some convincing that this additional power was needed,[99] the GMC's thinking seems to have been that it would help the GMC to establish itself as a separate entity from the MPTS.[100] There remain concerns that it will cause unnecessary duplication and confusion of the Professional Standards Authority's role.[101]

C. Fitness to Practise Decision-making

1. Investigating complaints

A doctor's fitness to practise may come under scrutiny from the GMC as a result of a 'complaint' being made to the GMC by a patient, another member of the public, or another healthcare professional. A doctor might also find themselves being the subject of a fitness to practise investigation following a report from their RO in connection with the revalidation process (see paras 2.34–2.36). Complaints are first scrutinized by the Registrar, may then proceed to be assessed by two case examiners, and from there may be resolved or referred to an Investigation Committee or to a full fitness to practise hearing before a panel in the MPTS. **2.40**

Aside from the framework set out in the Medical Act 1983 for administering fitness to practise procedures, the GMC and MPTS must follow the *General Medical Council (Fitness to Practise) Rules 2004*. These rules, which set out in detail the procedures to be followed at the various stages of a fitness to practise investigation, are to be construed in a way that balances 'first and foremost' the statutory duty of the GMC to protect the public against the need to protect doctors from allegations.[102] **2.41**

2. The Registrar stage

Allegations that a doctor's fitness to practise is impaired in some way are considered first by a Registrar.[103] If the complaint is not considered to raise fitness to practise issues it may be concluded, or, alternatively, may be referred on to the doctor's RO. If the GMC decides to investigate, it will inform the doctor of the substance of the complaint and request details of the registrant's employer(s). Until recently, complaints would not be investigated if more than five years had elapsed since the most recent of the events complained of, unless the Registrar considered that it was in the public interest, in the exceptional circumstances of the case, to proceed.[104] In 2015, Parliament agreed that this restriction should be removed, enabling the GMC to pursue cases no matter how long ago the incidents alleged were, *if* it was in the public interest to investigate.[105] **2.42**

[99] Qs 48 to 54.

[100] Law Commission, *Regulation of Health Care Professions* (Joint Consultation Paper, 2012) at 201.

[101] See Law Commission, *Regulation of Health Care Professionals* (2014) para 12.29.

[102] *Zia v General Medical Council* [2011] EWCA Civ 743 (at [35]).

[103] GMC (Fitness to Practise) Rules 2004, rule 4.

[104] GMC (Fitness to Practise) Rules 2004, rule 4(5). See *R (on the application of D) v General Medical Council* [2013] EWHC 2839—quashing waiver of the five-year rule given that the allegation was 21 years old and had been fully investigated by police at the time.

[105] The General Medical Council (Fitness to Practise and Over-Arching Objective) and the Professional Standards Authority for Health and Social Care (Referrals to Court) Order 2015.

3. Case examiners

2.43 Following investigation, two case examiners[106] (one medical and one non-medical) will make a decision as to the appropriate action out of four options. They may decide to: (i) close the case with no further action; (ii) close the case but issue a warning; (iii) agree with the doctor that 'undertakings' should be applied; or (iv) refer the case to a hearing before a Medical Practitioner Tribunal.[107] Undertakings are a form of settlement agreement between the regulator and registrant (sometimes referred to as 'consensual disposal'[108]) and can take the form of requiring the doctor to work under supervision or take a specified programme of retraining. For undertakings to be decided upon, both a medical and non-medical examiner must be satisfied that the undertakings are adequate to protect the public. Failure to agree with or to comply with undertakings will result in the case being referred for formal adjudication by a Medical Practitioner Tribunal. Whilst consensual disposal might be regarded as offering a more efficient resolution of the issue at stake (in avoiding the time and cost for the regulator and practitioner necessitated by a full hearing) it raises concerns about the transparency of fitness to practise decision-making.

4. The Investigation Committee

2.44 If the case examiners cannot agree on the proper outcome for a particular case, it will be referred to the Investigation Committee. That Committee has the same four options as do the case examiners (closing the case, issuing a warning, agreeing undertakings, or referral to a Medical Practitioner Tribunal). The case may also proceed to the Investigation Committee if the case examiners have concluded that a warning should be issued, and the registrant requests it or the registrant disputes the facts which form the basis of the warning. When determining whether a case should proceed to be referred to a Medical Practitioner Tribunal, the case examiners/investigation committee must apply the following test—bearing in mind 'the GMC's duty to protect the public which includes the protection of patients and maintaining public confidence in the profession' is there a realistic prospect of establishing that a doctor's fitness to practise is impaired to a degree justifying action on registration?[109]

5. The Interim Orders Tribunals

2.45 Precautionary suspension is a potent regulatory tool in the administration of the fitness to practise framework. Section 41A of the Medical Act 1983 enables an Interim Orders Tribunal (IOT) (now housed in the MPTS[110]) to impose conditions on registration or suspend a doctor before the case against them has been proved. An IOT is made up of three panellists, a Chair, a medical panellist, and a non-medical panellist. A case can be referred to the IOT at the Registrar stage[111] and all that is needed is for a 'prima facie case' to be

---

[106] Replacing the role of 'screeners'.

[107] Allegations involving a criminal conviction resulting in an immediate or deferred custodial sentence or allegations falling under s 35(2)(e) of the Medical Act 1983 determination by another health care regulator that the registrant's fitness to practise is in effect 'impaired' (or analogous finding) are automatically referred to the Medical Practitioner Tribunals—rule 5, GMC (Fitness to Practise) Rules 2004.

[108] See GMC, *Reform of the fitness to practise procedures of the GMC: changes to the way we deal with cases at the end of an investigation* (2011)—a consultation document which included the proposal to extend the use of consensual disposal.

[109] *GMC Thresholds* (para 11) (GMC) available at <http://www.gmc-uk.org/Guidance_GMC_Thresholds.pdf_48163325.pdf>.

[110] See para 2.39. This power is also available to Medical Practitioner Tribunals.

[111] *GMC (Fitness to Practise) Rules 2004*, rule 6.

made out that fitness to practise is impaired.[112] Such orders can be imposed for up to eighteen months without the involvement of the courts,[113] although s 41A facilitates seemingly indefinite extensions beyond this, provided High Court approval is first obtained.[114] The exercise of these broad ranging powers can have a devastating impact on the doctor's career and the duration of this impact is often fairly substantial (many interim orders can mean years of being unable to practise). It is for these reasons, coupled with the fact that there has been real uncertainty as to the scope of these powers, that the issue of interim sanctions is explored in further detail below.

6. Grounds for imposing interim orders: Section 41A Medical Act 1983

The grounds for imposing an interim order are set out in s 41A of the Medical Act 1983 as being that: **2.46**

i) it is necessary for the protection of members of the public; or
ii) it is otherwise in the public interest; or
iii) it is in the interests of a fully registered person, for the registration of that person to be suspended or to be made subject to conditions.

The third 'public interest' ground was clearly intended to make the power as close to all-encompassing as possible and to vest the IOT with a discretion as broad as the courts would permit. GMC guidance avoids attempting to define any of the grounds set out in s 41A, but does suggest that the 'public interest' ground extends to 'preserving public trust in the profession and maintaining good standards of conduct and performance'.[115]

The possession of such wide-ranging powers available at an interim stage of fitness to practise proceedings enables the GMC to adopt the role of the 'benign big gun', having a wealth of sanctions available and securing the cooperation of doctors through the threat, express or implied, of their use.[116] The existence of formidable powers of interim suspension, and the stigma they attract, may be invaluable in negotiations with doctors who are the subject of complaint, making it clear that sanctions can be imposed at any time if the doctor does not demonstrate the desired level of cooperation. It is perhaps the persuasive value of interim orders that we see at work in the number of cases where an interim order is in place and the doctor applies to relinquish registration. This consensual solution of voluntary erasure saves the cost of lengthy fitness to practise proceedings and avoids the added attention which a formal finding of impairment can bring. Relinquishing registration is always a possible outcome of a complaint against a doctor, but the impact of interim orders provides added incentives to practitioners to step out of the regulator's gaze (for more on voluntary erasure see para 2.90). **2.47**

[112] *R (George) v General Medical Council* [2003] EWHC 1124 (Admin).

[113] It is generally considered to be disproportionate to impose an eighteen-month suspension and a shorter period is preferred in the first instance. Section 41A(2) also states that these orders must be reviewed at least every six months and may also review where new evidence comes to light. The eighteen-month term is significant when compared with earlier versions of the power. Prior to 1997 orders could only be made for two months, although amended to six months by s 3 of the Medical (Professional Performance) Act 1995.

[114] Section 41A(6) and (7). Whilst the court may express dissatisfaction about the time being taken to resolve the fitness to practise allegations, it is unlikely to refuse an application for extension but expresses its dissatisfaction by granting a shorter extension than that requested: *Sheill v GMC* [2006] EWHC 3025 (Admin); *GMC v George* [2009] EWHC 1460 (Admin).

[115] <http://www.gmc-uk.org/concerns/hearings_and_decisions/interim_order_panel_referrals.asp>.

[116] I Ayres and J Braithwaite, *Responsive Regulation: Transcending the Deregulation Debate.* (Oxford University Press 1992), particularly ch 2.

7. When is an interim order in the public interest?

2.48 The three-strand test for interim orders in s 41A of the Medical Act 1983 itself leaves ample room for conflicting interpretations. Whilst the first justification for imposing an interim order (protection of the public) is qualified by a requirement of 'necessity', the second ground (suspension which is 'otherwise in the public interest') is not expressly subject to the same proviso.[117] This raises the question of why the second ground is apparently so much broader? If the second ground is intended to apply where there is no 'necessity', it would surely cover all those cases where it was necessary to protect the public, making the first ground, in effect, redundant.

2.49 A practitioner can appeal against a decision of the IOT, and the appeal court has original jurisdiction, meaning that it is not confined to 'review' of the IOT's decision but can decide for itself whether an interim order is appropriate on the facts.[118] Considering the wording of the three strand test in s 41A, Mr Justice Davis in *R (on the application of Shiekh) v General Dental Council* stated that the bar was set high, that suspension would only be justified as in the public interest 'in a relatively rare case', and that although statute did not explicitly apply a necessity test to the 'public interest' ground, necessity was an appropriate 'yardstick'.[119] Similarly, in an appeal by a social worker against a decision of the General Social Care Council,[120] Justice Robertson regarded the power to suspend on an interim basis as available wherever there was 'the need for speedy and urgent action to protect the public' and commented that it was 'an emergency procedure not an administrative one'.[121] Referring to the power as 'draconian', he went on to decide that he could envisage cases of 'violence, serious breach of trust, mental health issues' where its use would be merited, but that it was not indicated in a case where a social worker was accused of inadequacies in her supervision of an Assessment Team.[122]

8. Endorsement of a narrow construction of 'the public interest'

2.50 In *Yeong v General Medical Council* the High Court distinguished the powers of the Interim Orders Panel (the predecessors of IOTs) from those of the panel which was responsible for hearing the case in full against the doctor and determining whether a sanction is appropriate, stating that:

> It will not typically be appropriate for the Interim Orders Panel at the interim stage . . . to impose sanctions on grounds based simply on the importance in the public interest of maintaining clear standards of behaviour, as distinct from dealing with an immediate risk posed by a practitioner in relation to his treatment of patients.[123]

This judgment portrays the ISO as an emergency provision, not suited to general deployment in the assault on perceived crises of confidence.[124] Where the IOT is considering an

---

[117] See Medical Act 1983, s 41A set out above in the text accompanying notes 27–33. In the case of dentists, the wording of the test is almost identical: Dentists Act 1984 as amended, s 32.

[118] Section 41(10).

[119] [2007] EWHC 2972 (Admin) at [16]. Cf the contrasting approach in *Sandler* discussed below. The General Optical Council's guidance on interim orders seems to assume that 'necessity' is a precondition to the exercise of this power: *FTP Guidance to Panel Members* (General Optical Council) 14 available at <http://www.optical.org>.

[120] As of 31st July, this regulator was abolished and its work taken on by the Health Professions Council.

[121] *Bradshaw v General Social Care Council* [2010] UKFTT 3 (HESC) at [8].

[122] It was also not indicated in a case where an employer had concerns about a social worker's performance but no specific risk to the public had been identified: *Sonia West v GSCC* [2009] 1614. SW-SUS.

[123] *Yeong v GMC* [2009] EWHC 1923 (Admin) at [61].

[124] This sentiment is echoed in a judgment of the First Tier Tribunal in *Roach v General Social Council* which disapproved interim suspension where the only purpose appears to have been protecting the

interim order as being in the public interest, the 'reasonable onlooker' test is to be used. The IOT should therefore consider:

> . . .what a reasonable onlooker would think, in the event of the doctor ultimately being convicted of formal allegations arising from the complaints that had been outlined, about his being allowed to go on practising in the meantime. If this hypothetical onlooker would expect the doctor to be suspended from practice, then it would be legitimate to conclude that it was necessary that he should be suspended in order to maintain confidence in the medical profession.[125]

Until recently, case law was divided on whether the narrow interpretation of this interim jurisdiction should prevail or whether it should be read as a broader, almost all-encompassing power.[126] The momentum now seems to have swung almost definitively in favour of the narrower reading of the IOT's powers. The cases of *Patel v General Medical Council*,[127] *Harry v General Medical Council*,[128] *Houshian v General Medical Council*,[129] *Hussain v General Medical Council*,[130] *Raschid v General Medical Council*,[131] *R (on the application of Shiekh) v General Dental Council*,[132] and *R (on the application of Sosanya) v GMC*[133] each provide an example of successful applications to terminate ISOs, and all demonstrate a reluctance to countenance the use of interim suspension in the absence of a direct risk of harm to patients. Unproven allegations of conspiracy to defraud whilst in the post of school governor in *Patel*, forging Employment Appeal Tribunal documents in *Houshian* and money laundering in *Sosanya* were considered in their respective appeals *not* to merit interim suspension 'in the public interest'. The as yet unproven charges had little to do with the appellants' competence as doctors and the public could not be described as at risk if they were allowed to continue to practice.[134] *R (on the application of Shiekh) v General Dental Council* also concerned a practitioner not regarded as posing a direct risk to the safety of the public.[135] *Shiekh* was convicted of conspiracy to defraud in relation to his handling of his associates' travel expenses claims. The Crown Court judge had concluded: there was sustained dishonesty: there was a conspiracy to defraud but 'I consider it unlikely that you would indulge in making dishonest claims in the future.' Mr Shiekh was subsequently referred to the General Dental Council's Interim Hearings Panel.[136] Balancing Mr Shiekh's interests against the 'damage done to the reputation and public confidence in the profession', the Panel considered it proportionate to impose an eighteen-month suspension order in advance of the fitness to practise hearing. On appeal to the High Court, the fraud allegations were not considered to give rise to a case for suspension in the public interest.[137] **2.51**

---

reputation of the profession of social workers [2010] UKFTT 15 (HESC)—practitioner presented no clear risk to service users as he had removed himself from the profession.

[125] *Bhatnagar v General Medical Council* [2013] EWHC 3412.

[126] P Case, 'Putting Public Confidence First: Doctors, Precautionary Suspension and the General Medical Council.' (2011) 19 Med L Rev 339.

[127] [2012] EWHC 3688.

[128] [2012] EWHC 2762.

[129] [2012] EWHC 3458.

[130] [2012] EWHC 2991.

[131] [2012] EWHC 2682.

[132] [2007] EWHC 2972 (Admin).

[133] [2009] EWHC 2814 (Admin).

[134] [2009] EWHC 2814 (Admin) at [25]. No finding of impairment was made against Dr Sosanya after the quashing of this ISO.

[135] [2007] EWHC 2972 Admin.

[136] Dentists Act 1984, s 32(4) which allows interim orders on similar terms as s 41A of the Medical Act 1983.

[137] Although note that later on the General Dental Council took the decision to erase Mr Shiekh from the register given the scale of his fraudulent activities: *Shiekh v General Dental Council* [2009] EWHC 186.

2.52 There are, however, a number of judgments which countenanced a much broader construction of s 41A as not only for use in cases of emergency, but also as a tool for managing public confidence where there was no clear imminent risk to the public.[138] In *TR v GSCC,* the complainant social worker became the subject of an ISO because of her cohabitation with a man who had served a prison sentence for sexual assault of children in a children's home.[139] Her partner had been consistent in maintaining his innocence and TR believed that he was innocent of all charges. The First Tier Tribunal accepted that an ISO was appropriate and proportionate on the grounds of protecting 'public confidence', making no reference to any potential risk of harm (eg a risk that children might come into contact with TR's partner by virtue of her work). It might be tempting to regard the result in this case as a product of the fact that consensus on the malignance of child abuse means that its mere suggestion can attract hyperbolic responses and a tendency to bypass rational risk assessment. This would not, however, explain the case of *Sandler v GMC.*[140]

2.53 In *Sandler* the allegations against the doctor concerned fraud, although such fraud was distinguishable from the cases of *Shiekh* and *Sosanya* in that the fraud arose in the context of his 'clinical duties' in completing cremation certificates. The interim order had been imposed just as Dr Sandler was about to face prosecution under the Cremation Act 1902, not because of a risk to the public, but because suspension was considered to be 'otherwise in the public interest', having regard to the adverse effect of Sandler's case on the reputation of the profession.[141] The fact that its use was only considered once a decision had been taken to charge Dr Sandler, twelve months after the GMC became aware of the doctor's 'misconduct' further underlines the fact that it was being used here to address concerns related to public confidence and professional reputation.

2.54 *Sandler's* admission of some of the charges and the imminent passage of his case through the criminal courts in the full gaze of the media make the *Sandler* case somewhat exceptional and not necessarily a general endorsement of imposing interim suspension under the rubric of protecting confidence in the medical profession. Connections might have been made between *Sandler* and the Shipman affair in the public's mind. The Shipman Inquiry had criticized the rubber stamping of cremation certificates and had recommended reforms to prevent another 'Shipman' being able to evade detection for so long.[142] As Dr Sandler was allegedly fraudulent in his role of corroborating the cause of death, his case therefore had the potential to reignite media interest in Shipman type scenarios, a factor which may have figured in the panel's decision.[143] Given the weight of recent case law which tends to disapprove interim suspension being used unless there is a clear identified risk to patients, however, cases such as *Sandler* seem less likely to be followed.

2.55 Interim orders are a small cog in a complex regulatory framework, and they would appear to perform a vital function in what has been referred to elsewhere as the 'redemption model of fitness to practise'.[144] The final decision as to whether doctors should be the subject of formal

[138] As does *R (on the application of Steven James Walker) v GMC* [2003] EWHC 2308 Admin. Although mentioned in passing, maintaining public confidence was a factor which the panel was entitled or even bound to take account of (at [30]).

[139] *TR v General Social Care Council* [2010] UKFTT 75 (HESC).

[140] *Sandler v General Medical Council* [2010] EWHC 1029 (Admin).

[141] ibid, at [23].

[142] *The Shipman Inquiry: Third Report: Death Certification and the Investigation of Deaths by Coroners* (Cm 5854, 2003).

[143] For another example of a broad construction of the interim order power, see *Bradshaw v GMC* [2010] EWHC 1296 (Admin).

[144] P Case, 'The Good, the Bad and the Dishonest Doctor: The General Medical Council and the Redemption Model of Fitness to Practise' (2011) 31(4) Legal Studies 591.

sanction is informed by an assessment as to whether their fitness to practise is 'impaired'. The degree of their 'impairment' is assessed at the time of their hearing[145] (if there is one) and the system operates so as to incentivize the development of insight, contrition, and remediation in the time between the incident giving rise to the complaint and the final hearing. The use of interim orders not only serves to protect patients (where necessary), but also gives the doctor the opportunity to reflect and develop these desired values of insight and remorse, and time to prove that since the incident(s) in question they are professionally redeemed and therefore fit to return to practice. The interim order also bridges the gap between the allegations and final determination of the case which often spans a number of years. In this way it helps to counter the allegation that final sanction is devalued because of the passage of time between the incidents triggering the complaint and final sanction. The idea that interim suspension is used as part of a 'sanctions package' so as to complement and facilitate the broader regulatory aim of optimizing the redemption of doctors accused of misconduct is not, however, apparent on the face of the statute.

9. Medical Practitioners Tribunals

Cases involving allegations that the practitioner's fitness to practise is somehow 'impaired,' **2.56** and which have not been considered amenable to resolution by other means, are referred on to a fitness to practise hearing before a Medical Practitioner Tribunal. The panel must include a Chair and at least one medical panellist and one lay panellist.[146] Fitness to practise hearings conducted by the MPTS should normally be held in public, although exceptions may be made, for example, where the issues include the practitioner's physical or mental health.

D. Meaning of 'Impairment'

1. Taking action on registration: When is fitness to practise 'impaired'?

Section 35 of the Medical Act 1983 (as amended)[147] requires all disciplinary charges against **2.57** doctors which reach a fitness to practise hearing to be assessed in terms of whether the practitioner's fitness to practise is 'impaired'. The introduction of the concept of 'impairment' was designed to avoid the earlier compartmentalization of fitness to practise allegations and remove the delay and cumbersome procedural complications that the four predecessor categories of discipline had produced.[148] No definition of 'impairment' is to be found in the statute,[149] merely a declaration in the Medical Act that impairment of fitness to practise may be found *only* by reason of:

a) the doctor's misconduct;
b) criminal conviction or caution;
c) deficient professional performance;
d) adverse physical or mental health;
e) not having the necessary knowledge of English; or
f) a determination by another regulatory body to the effect that fitness to practise is impaired.[150]

---

145 See paras 2.60–2.62.
146 *General Medical Council (Constitution of Panels and Investigation Committee) Rules* 2004, rule 4.
147 Medical Act 1983 (Amendment Order) (SI 3135/2002).
148 They were 'serious professional misconduct', 'seriously deficient performance', 'deficient performance', and health concerns.
149 Nor is there any definition in associated legislation or in the GMC's own guidance.
150 Medical Act 1983, s 35C(2).

2.58 Dame Janet Smith in the Fifth Report of the *Shipman Inquiry* had predicted that the term 'impairment' was likely to cause more problems of definition and identification than the preceding terminology.[151] She also expressed concern that the question of whether fitness to practise was 'impaired' was meaningless in the context of complaints relating to misconduct and criminal convictions unrelated to clinical competence.[152] The Medical Practitioner Tribunals now use Dame Smith's summary of the recurrent features of unfitness to practise as a benchmark. Accordingly, a doctor whose fitness to practise is 'impaired' is either: a risk to patients; has brought the profession into disrepute; has breached one of the fundamental tenets of the profession; or the doctor's integrity cannot be relied upon.[153]

2.59 The assessment of whether a doctor's fitness to practise is 'impaired' involves a sequential four step process. Firstly, the Medical Practitioner Tribunal must ask whether the alleged facts which form the substance of the complaint have been proved on the balance of probabilities[154] (step 1); secondly, do those facts which have been proved to the required standard amount to misconduct or deficient professional performance? (step 2); thirdly, in light of all the facts, is the practitioner's fitness to practise 'impaired'? (step 3) and finally, if impairment is found, what sanction ought to be applied (step 4)? In cases of 'misconduct' the issues of whether misconduct has been established and whether fitness to practise is 'impaired' must be considered separately.[155] A finding of misconduct will not, therefore, automatically result in a finding of impairment, and it is the finding of 'impairment' (rather than the misconduct or deficient performance, etc., itself) which unlocks the sanctions set out in s 35D of the Medical Act.[156]

2. 'Impairment' and the 'redemption model' of fitness to practise

2.60 The concept of 'impairment' requires that the Medical Practitioner Tribunal should focus not solely upon the incident(s) which gave rise to the complaint and whether any sanction should follow. Rather, the Medical Practitioner Tribunal should evaluate the doctor's conduct in the round, including evidence of the doctor's performance prior to and subsequent to the conduct in question.[157] This exercise therefore involves looking forward not back,[158] and taking into account the extent to which the practitioner has gained insight into their shortcomings, the extent to which the issues raised are remediable, any attempts made

[151] *Fifth Shipman Inquiry Report—Safeguarding patients—Lessons from the past: proposals for the future* at 25.43. See eg the Privy Council's laboured attempt to define 'serious professional misconduct' in *Doughty v GDC* [1988] AC 164 at 173.

[152] *Fifth Shipman Inquiry Report*, n 151, at 25.46.

[153] ibid, at 25.50, cited with approval in *Zygmunt v GMC* [2008] EWHC 2643 (Admin) at [29].

[154] Health and Social Care Act 2008, s 112, harmonizing the standard of proof amongst regulators of the health professions and transforming the standard applicable to Medical Practitioner Tribunal hearings from the criminal standard to the civil standard.

[155] *Zygmunt v GMC* [2008] EWHC 2643 (Admin) affirmed in *Cohen v GMC* [2008] EWHC 581 (Admin). It may be that the same facts which give rise to the finding of misconduct are also sufficient to give rise to a finding of impairment and that these two issues do not need to need to be formally separate 'stages' in the decision-making process, although it is advisable that their consideration is clearly separated: *Saha v GMC* [2009] EWHC 1907.

[156] Justice Mitting in *Zygmunt v GMC* stated, however, that perhaps in the great majority of cases, a finding of impairment will (automatically) follow a finding of misconduct: [2008] EWHC 2643 (Admin) at [27].

[157] In *Azzam v GMC* [2008] EWHC 2711 (Admin); (2009) 105 BMLR 142, Mr Justice McCombe stated at [44]: '. . . it must behove a FTP Panel to consider facts material to the practitioner's fitness to practise looking forward and for that purpose to take into account evidence as to his present skills or lack of them and any steps taken, since the conduct criticised, to remedy any defects in skill . . . it is clear . . . that evidence of a doctor's overall ability is relevant to the question of fitness to practise'.

[158] *Yeong v GMC* [2009] EWHC 1923 (Admin) at [21].

by the practitioner to remediate their poor practice or misconduct, and the risk of recurrence.[159] This is a reflection of Dame Janet Smith's reading of s 35D(2) of the Medical Act which gives the Medical Practitioner Tribunal the power to impose a sanction where there is a finding that the doctor's fitness to practise 'is' impaired (ie at the time of the hearing). [160]

A consequence of assessing fitness to practise at the date of the hearing, rather than at the date of the conduct complained of, is that post-incident conduct can be taken into account to determine whether fitness to practise is currently 'impaired'.[161] Judgments on the meaning of 'impairment' indicate that some allegations do not lend themselves to doctors redeeming themselves by demonstrating remorse and attempts at remediation. The 2009 judgment in *Yeong v GMC*, for example, suggested that for misconduct other than clinical errors or incompetence, efforts at remediation would be of muted significance.[162] It is certainly true that conduct characterized by dishonesty or intentional wrongs are considered to be particularly 'egregious'[163] and, consequently, it will be more difficult to persuade the tribunal that the doctor's fitness to practise is not impaired, regardless of any well-meaning gestures in the interim. There is an inherent logic in this position, for where the practitioner has shown themselves to be prone to dishonesty, there is reason to doubt that any expressions of remorse and remediation are genuine. **2.61**

This emphasis on individual redemption entails significant benefits for doctors, patients, and society. It is an example of creative and responsive regulation in using fitness to practise hearings as a means of encouraging compliance for the future and facilitating self-governance within the medical profession. It preserves valued social capital in the form of highly skilled, intensively trained medical professionals and is more consistent with modern expectations of doctors. The redemptive model of fitness to practise also, however, entails certain risks, to include the commodification of sentiments such as remorse and attempts to remediate any harm caused. If not vigilantly supervised, such an approach may result in feigned expressions of insight on the doctor's part into their failure to meet professional standards; a superficial exercise by which regulator and regulated trade offerings of contrition and forgiveness.[164] **2.62**

3. The 'heads' of impairment

As explained above, a doctor's fitness to practise can only be impaired by a) the doctor's misconduct; b) criminal conviction or caution; c) deficient professional performance; d) adverse physical or mental health; e) not having the necessary knowledge of English; or f) a determination by another regulatory body to the effect that fitness to practise is impaired.[165] The following sections provide further exploration of each head of impairment. **2.63**

---

[159] ibid. These matters were not relevant to step 2 of the procedure (ie whether misconduct had been committed, and must be reserved for step 3): *Cohen v GMC* [2008] EWHC 581 (Admin).

[160] *Fifth Shipman Inquiry Report—Safeguarding patients—Lessons from the past: proposals for the future* at 25.48.

[161] *Yeong v GMC* [2009] EWHC 1923 (Admin); *Cohen v GMC* [2008] EWHC 581 (Admin). For analysis of the role of post incident conduct and redemption in tribunal findings, see P Case, 'The Good, the Bad and the Dishonest Doctor: the General Medical Council and the 'Redemption Model' of Fitness to Practise' (2011) 31(4) Legal Studies 591.

[162] [2009] EWHC 1923 (Admin).

[163] *Cheatle v General Medical Council* [2009] EWHC 645 (Admin).

[164] See further on this theme, P Case, 'The Good, the Bad and the Dishonest Doctor: the General Medical Council and the 'Redemption Model' of Fitness to Practise' (2011) 31(4) Legal Studies 591.

[165] Medical Act 1983, s 35C(2).

4. 'Misconduct': Section 35C(2)(a)

2.64 The following sections discuss, in no particular order, some forms of misconduct which might lead to a doctor's fitness to practise being regarded as impaired: sexual relationships with patients; misconduct in private life; dishonesty; and reporting/failing to report patient safety concerns.

5. Misconduct: Sexual relationships with patients

2.65 One type of misconduct which exists at the boundary of professional misconduct concerns relationships with clients/patients. Striking up a personal relationship with a client or patient may take place outside the consulting room but it can still be closely connected to the practitioner's professional practice given that it may conflict with duties towards the patient. Some sources suggest an increase in this form of misconduct, which has been attributed to greater informality in the doctor–patient relationship and a consequent blurring of boundaries.[166] The *Good Medical Practice* guidance prohibits doctors using their position 'to pursue a sexual or improper relationship with a patient'[167] and this is the disciplinary offence which results in the highest rate of erasure.[168] What appears to be a very strict approach to relationships with patients is underlined by the GMC's *Sanctions Guidance* which treats relationships with patients as an aspect of 'sexual misconduct' and fails to clearly distinguish 'consensual' sexual conduct with patients from non-consensual conduct such as sexual assault.[169]

2.66 The judgment in *Yeong v General Medical Council*[170] confirms that sexual relationships with patients are to be regarded as an example of particularly egregious conduct and, unlike clinical failings, doctors' efforts to reduce the risk of reoccurrence and attempts at remediation were of much less weight. This aspect of *Yeong* suggests that the courts do not tolerate this type of misconduct—it is not readily remediable and is more likely to result in a finding of impairment. Having said that, the courts have shown some leniency in cases of doctors having relationships with patients, endorsing erasure as the usual but 'not inevitable'[171] sanction, and repeatedly urging that a less severe penalty should be applied in specific cases of relationships with patients.[172] Suspension would suffice where circumstances suggested some leniency would be appropriate,[173] although the imposition of conditions on a doctor's registration would likely be 'too lenient' in a 'bad' case of pursuing a relationship with a vulnerable patient.[174]

6. Misconduct: Dishonesty

2.67 As Foskett J in *Fish v GMC*[175] recently acknowledged, allegations of dishonesty are particularly serious: 'An allegation of dishonesty against a professional person is one of the

---

[166] See Ost's excellent paper 'Breaching the Sexual Boundaries in the Doctor: Patient Relationship' (2016) 24(2) Med L Rev 206.

[167] Para 53; see also GMC, *Maintaining a Professional Boundary between you and your Patient* (2013).

[168] P Case, 'The Good, the Bad and the Dishonest Doctor: The Redemption Model of Fitness to Practise' (2011) 31(4) Legal Studies 591 at 603.

[169] GMC, *Sanctions Guidance* (2016) paras 136–144.

[170] [2009] EWHC 1923 (Admin).

[171] *Bevan v General Medical Council* [2005] EWHC 174 (Admin) [20].

[172] See, eg, *Giele v General Medical Council* [2005] EWHC 2143 (Admin); *Council for the Regulation of Healthcare Professionals v the General Medical Council and Leeper* [2004] EWHC 1850 (Admin); *CHRE v GMC and Solanke* [2004] EWHC 944 (Admin) finding that a three-month suspension was not 'unduly lenient'; compare the not easily distinguished case of *Wentzel v General Medical Council* [2005] EWHC 87 (Admin)—sanction of erasure endorsed.

[173] *Bevan v General Medical Council* [2005] EWHC 174 (Admin) [20].

[174] *Council for the Regulation of Healthcare Professionals v the General Medical Council and Leeper* [2004] EWHC 1850 (Admin).

[175] *Fish v GMC* [2012] EWHC 1269 (Admin).

allegations that he or she fears most. It is often easily made, sometimes not easily defended and, if it sticks, can be career-threatening or even career-ending.'[176] Whilst dishonesty in professional disciplinary cases was once to be judged according to the standards of the profession,[177] the standard applied today rests on ordinary people's understanding of dishonesty (see the *Ghosh* test below). This again places dishonesty outside the context of professional expertise and firmly within the jurisdiction of the court to take a view on whether dishonesty has been established.[178] In this respect, regulators have less discretion in cases where dishonesty is alleged and their findings of dishonesty are more vulnerable to legal challenge than in the past.

(i) The test to be applied in cases involving allegations of dishonesty

In all cases, where dishonesty is an explicit feature of the allegations, the tribunals apply the test adapted from the criminal law case of *R v Ghosh* and approved for use in disciplinary proceedings in *Bryant v Law Society*[179]—a two-part test requiring: i) the doctor's conduct to be found dishonest according to the ordinary standards of reasonable and honest people (objective); *and* ii) that the doctor must have realized what he or she was doing was dishonest by those standards (subjective). The *Ghosh* test therefore offers a combined test of dishonesty, measuring D's conduct against an objective standard, but requiring some subjective conscious impropriety in the form of the doctor's knowledge that the conduct would be regarded as dishonest according to the objective standard. When alleged dishonesty is not proven, it is very often due to a failure to prove that the subjective second limb has been fulfilled. **2.68**

Recent case law expresses unease with the ritualistic application of the *Ghosh* test in fitness to practise proceedings given that these are civil proceedings and that even in criminal law cases, the *Ghosh* direction is not used in all cases of alleged dishonesty. Justice Singh in *Uddin v General Medical Council*[180] urged caution when applying the test to civil proceedings and his concerns were echoed in *Moseka v Nursing Midwifery Council* where Justice Green noted that the sanction applied in fitness to practise cases may be more severe than many low level criminal punishments.[181] Recent dicta from Lord Justice Longmore also seems to recommend that the *Ghosh* test should be modified so as to apply a distinct standard for doctors: ' . . . it would be right and proper for the first part of the direction to be adapted to read that the panel should decide "whether according to the standard of reasonable and honest doctors [not people] what was done was dishonest"'.[182] It is not, however, clear whether an honest doctor standard is meant to be a raised standard of honesty or a more pragmatic standard. **2.69**

7. Dishonesty and the burden of proof

It is in cases involving allegations of dishonesty that the civil standard of proof appears to converge with the criminal law standard of proving allegations 'beyond reasonable doubt'. In another context, Lord Nicholls, somewhat controversially, determined that the civil standard was to be applied 'flexibly'; 'the court will have in mind as a factor, . . . that *the more* **2.70**

[176] ibid, [68].

[177] *Allinson v General Council of Medical Education and Registration of the United Kingdom* (1894) 1 QB 750, 760–61.

[178] See, eg, *R (on the application of Khan) v GMC* [2008] EWHC 3509 at [78] where the court considered the usual deference to regulatory bodies to be qualified where the issue was whether dishonesty was established.

[179] *R v Ghosh* [1982] EWCA Crim 2; [1982] QB 1053; *Bryant v Law Society* [2007] EWHC 3043 (Admin).

[180] [2012] EWHC 2669 at [30] to [31].

[181] [2014] EWHC 846 at [24].

[182] *Hussain v General Medical Council* [2014] EWCA Civ 2246 at [51].

serious the allegation, the less likely it is that the event occurred and, hence, the stronger should be the evidence before the court concludes that the allegation is established on the balance of probability'.[183] This suggested to some judges that, in the case of serious allegations, a 'heightened' standard of proof operated[184]—and what could be more serious than an allegation of dishonesty? Case law confirms that the principle identified by Lord Nicholls is applicable to allegations of dishonesty in disciplinary proceedings against doctors.[185]

8. Sanctions for proven dishonesty

2.71 The 'dishonesty rule' as expressed in *Bolton v Law Society*[186] states that proven dishonesty should generally be met with the ultimate professional sanction—in the case of doctors this equates to 'erasure' from the register of medical practitioners.[187] Although the *Bolton* judgment concerned dishonesty in the legal profession, case law confirms that no lower standard is to be applied to the medical profession.[188] It is clear, however, that a finding of dishonesty against a registered medical practitioner does *not* invariably result in erasure.[189] Although case law endorses the rule prohibiting dishonesty applying with equal force across professions such as law and medicine,[190] one study suggested that in the sample of cases surveyed, approximately 95 per cent of the cases of proven dishonesty against lawyers resulted in an order excluding the respondent from their profession, whereas only around 40 per cent of cases brought against doctors resulted in an order of erasure.[191]

The reasons behind the reduced likelihood of doctors found guilty of dishonesty being erased from the register are many and varied, and include the wide range of sanctions available to Medical Practitioner Tribunals and the civil standard of proof perhaps generating a more marked reluctance to bring a doctor's career to an end.

2.72 Case law also stipulates that in deciding the appropriate sanction, the public interest in removing a doctor found to have acted dishonestly is to be balanced against the public interest in retaining a skilled doctor. Positive testimonials in support of the doctor facing disciplinary charges can go some way in persuading the panel that the doctor should be allowed to return to practise:

> Thus testimonials which establish that a doctor is, in the view of eminent colleagues and of nursing staff who have worked with him, one who is not only competent but whose loss to the profession and to his potential patients would be serious indeed can, in my opinion, be accorded substantial weight.[192]

183 *Re H (Minors)(Sexual Abuse: Standard of Proof)* [1996] AC 563, 586 (emphasis added).

184 eg Lord Steyn in *R (Mc Cann) v Crown Court at Manchester* [2002] 4 All ER 593—the heightened standard was thought to be potentially applicable to disciplinary decisions against doctors, see, eg, *Sadler v General Medical Council* [2003] UKPC 59.

185 *Sharma v GMC* [2014] EWHC 1471 at [19].

186 [1994] 1 WLR 512 518–19.

187 Medical Act 1983, s 35D(2). Erasure is not necessarily permanent, although applications for restoration to the register cannot be made before five years after the order for erasure.

188 *Gupta v GMC* [2002] 1 WLR 1691, at para 21, *per* Lord Rodger of Earlsferry.

189 For a recent example see *Jasinarachchi v General Medical Council* [2014] EWHC 3570—six-month suspension for a single incident of dishonesty in an otherwise unblemished career (completion of cremation certificate falsely verifying that he had viewed and examined the body of the deceased).

190 See n 183.

191 P Case, 'Doctoring Confidence and Soliciting Trust: Models of Professional Discipline in Law and Medicine' (2013) 29(2) Professional Negligence 87. For further analysis of the distinction in enforcement of the dishonesty rule between professions see D Middleton, 'First Do No Harm or Eat What You Kill? Why Dishonesty Matters Most for Lawyers' (2015) 17(3) Legal Ethics 382.

192 *Council for the Regulation of Healthcare Professionals v GMC & Southall* [2005] EWCA Civ 579 (Admin), *per* Collins J. See also the speech of Lord Hoffmann in *Bijl v General Medical Council* [2002] Lloyds Rep Med 60.

9. Misconduct in the private sphere

The regulator's fitness to practise jurisdiction is broadly defined and encompasses conduct which may have occurred outside the UK and can even relate to events from before the doctor was a registered medical practitioner.[193] In 2002, the heads of charge which could give rise to a fitness to practise enquiry against a doctor were altered so that 'serious professional misconduct' became simply 'misconduct'.[194] Whilst the qualifier of 'seriousness' has in effect been reinserted by court judgments,[195] there has been no re-emergence of the requirement that misconduct should be of a professional nature. In the pre-2002 case of *Roylance v GMC,* Lord Clyde regarded the adjunct of 'professional' misconduct as involving a 'link with the profession of medicine' but that this did not require misconduct in the context of clinical work.[196] In fact the loss of the 'professional' qualifier to misconduct seems simply to underline the fact that the courts have always preserved the GMC's prerogative to take action against any 'disgraceful conduct' which might adversely reflect upon the profession.[197] Modern case law reflects this broad, inclusive construction of misconduct: **2.73**

> Misconduct is of two principal kinds. First, it may involve sufficiently serious misconduct in the exercise of professional practice . . . **Second, it can involve conduct of a morally culpable or otherwise disgraceful kind which may, and often will, occur outwith the course of professional practice** itself, but which brings disgrace upon the doctor and thereby prejudices the reputation of the profession.[198]

This recent exposition of 'misconduct' clarifies the reach of professional discipline into the private sphere, but does not attempt to stratify the types of misconduct—rather, the context of the misconduct (professional or personal) does not appear to provide any indication of how it will be dealt with. A number of reported cases can be referred to in order to demonstrate the extent to which professional regulation regulates the whole person, including in their private lives, for example: the case of the 70-year old general practitioner convicted of concealing the proceeds of crime after opening bank accounts and purchasing property in her own name to assist her daughter,[199] unintentionally providing flawed evidence in a criminal trial,[200] and motoring offences, such as driving whilst disqualified.[201] **2.74**

It seems that for the practice of medicine, the reach of regulatory surveillance is exceedingly broad: it is interested in the whole person and not just the registrant's professional activities, but then this is mitigated by a redemption-based model of discipline whereby doctors can potentially save their career by showing they are reformed characters who have fully internalized the values of the disciplinary regime. Research and academic commentary on the interface between personal conduct and professional discipline is almost nonexistent.[202] Where it exists, it largely explores private misconduct in the context of the legal **2.75**

---

193 Medical Act 1983, s 35C(3).

194 As currently provided in s 35C(2)(a) Medical Act 1983.

195 *Meadow v GMC* [2006] EWCA Civ 1390, [2007] 1 QB 462.

196 [1999] UKPC 16, [38].

197 *A County Council v W (Disclosure)* [1997] 1 FLR 574; *Marten v Royal College of Veterinary Surgeons' Disciplinary Committee* [1966] 1 QB 1.

198 Elias J in *R (on the application of) Remedy UK v GMC* [2010] EWHC 2294 (Admin) [37] *per* Elias LJ (emphasis added).

199 *Fatnani v General Medical Council* [2007] EWCA Civ 46 (cf the earlier case of *Manzur v General Medical Council* [2001] UKPC 55; (2002) 64 BMLR 68).

200 *Meadow v General Medical Council* [2006] EWCA Civ 1390, although the finding of serious professional misconduct was overturned on appeal in this judgment.

201 *Arfan Zia Dad v General Dental Council* (PC) [2000] 1 WLR 1538.

202 See A Woolley, 'Regulatory Legitimacy and Legal Ethics: Regulating Lawyers for Personal Misconduct' in R Mortenson et al (eds), *Alternative Perspectives on Lawyers and Legal Ethics* (Routledge 2011).

profession, yet it is probably the medical profession in the UK that experiences the greatest degree of regulatory surveillance of personal conduct. Woolley, writing about lawyers' discipline in Canada, questions the regulatory legitimacy of using professional disciplinary sanctions against conduct outwith professional practice. Her research uses behavioural psychology to suggest that dishonesty in a personal context provides no evidence that a solicitor is not fit to practise or that such conduct may spill over into the conduct of their professional affairs.[203]

10. Reporting/not reporting concerns about patient safety

2.76 Whilst a finding of impaired fitness to practice can be made where a doctor has failed to raise concerns about colleagues' practice which is putting patients at risk,[204] their fitness to practise can also be questioned if they raise such concerns which were later found to be unjustified.[205] Disparagement of fellow professionals was historically treated as a serious disciplinary offence[206] and even the 1998 version of *Good Medical Practice* had reduced the prohibition on disparagement but still directed that when publishing information about the services of other practitioners, 'doctors must not compare their services with those that their colleagues provide . . .' and 'must not make others doubt a colleague's knowledge or skills by making ***unnecessary or unfair*** comments about them'.[207] A practitioner's professional responsibilities are much clearer now in extending to the reporting of practice by fellow practitioners which is putting patients at risk. Many of the recent changes in this area are responses to the Mid Staffordshire Inquiry (see para 2.08) which recommended 'openness, transparency and candour throughout the system about matters of concern'.[208] Paras 24 and 25 of the GMC's *Good Medical Practice* (2013) state that doctors must 'take prompt action' if they believe that a patient's safety or dignity might be compromised or if they have concerns that a fellow practitioner is not fit to practise. This represents a dramatic change in approach to raising concerns about a colleague's work and has been reinforced by professional and statutory duties of candour (see further paras 2.106–2.117).

2.77 In 2000, the appellant in *Roylance v General Medical Council (No. 2)*[209] was found guilty of 'serious professional misconduct' due to his failure to act upon concerns regarding the heightened mortality rate in paediatric cardiac surgery at the hospital where he was Chief Executive Officer of the NHS Trust (the 'Bristol scandal'). The Privy Council isolated the crucial issue in the appeal as being whether the 'misconduct' in this case was '***professional***' misconduct and upheld the decision to erase the appellant's name from the register. The dual roles of the appellant as both registered medical practitioner and administrator confused the issue of serious professional misconduct, as the concerns which could have been acted upon came to the appellant's attention in his administrative role, and therefore externally to his role as a practitioner. The Privy Council refused to allow this to stand in the way of a finding of serious professional misconduct, and stressed that conduct as an administrator, and therefore outwith his professional practice as a doctor, could nevertheless affect his fitness to

[203] ibid, at 11.2.2.
[204] *Roylance v GMC* [2000] 1 AC 311 (PC): finding of misconduct for failing to report concerns, discussed below.
[205] eg *Dowd v GMC* [2003] EWHC 659—finding of misconduct on grounds of reporting concerns, although quashed by judicial review.
[206] *Allinson v GCMER* [1894] 1 QB 750.
[207] Para 29 (emphasis added).
[208] *Report of the Mid-Staffordshire Foundation Trust Inquiry: Executive Summary* (2013) at 4.
[209] [2000] 1 AC 311 (PC).

practise. Severance of the roles of practitioner and administrator was not permissible 'if the interest of the patient is to remain paramount'.[210]

Roylance provided confirmation of the profession's commitment to self-policing, and of the enforceable duty imposed on members to police each other's activities. It also represented further repudiation of the 'closed ranks', self-interested regulation, that many believed the professions were still prone to. The current version of *Good Medical Practice* referred to above makes it clear that the duty to report practices which might be compromising patient safety or dignity does not only attach to those with an administrative responsibility for the quality of patient care but extends to all registered medical practitioners, regardless of rank. **2.78**

11. Deficient professional performance: Section 35C(2)(b)

The concept of deficient professional performance is distinct from either negligence or misconduct—'it connotes a standard of professional performance which is unacceptably low and which (save in exceptional circumstances) has been demonstrated by reference to a fair sample of the doctor's work'.[211] Where concerns are raised regarding a doctor's competence, the Registrar may direct the doctor to undertake a performance assessment[212] and the results of this assessment, which may include a knowledge test related to that person's area of practice, can provide the evidence from which the tribunal concludes that the doctor's professional performance is deficient in some way. If the evidence of deficient performance is drawn from the doctor's practise, it is worth noting that a single incident or failure in respect of one patient can still equate to misconduct or impairment,[213] although errors in relation to a single patient without further aggravating factors rarely gave rise to a finding of impaired fitness to practise. A finding of deficient professional performance does not need to be tied to observed deficiencies in the doctor's clinical competence—it may equally arise in connection with matters such as record keeping or confidentiality.[214] As with the other heads of impairment, subsequent redeeming conduct can result in a finding that although deficient performance was identified, the doctor is currently fit to practise. **2.79**

12. Criminal cautions and convictions: Section 35C(2)(c)

Conduct which causes the doctor to come into contact with the criminal law, albeit outside of his or her professional life, often results in fitness to practise proceedings. In fact where a doctor has a criminal conviction or caution there is a presumption that he/she will be referred to the MPTS for a fitness to practise hearing[215] and where the conviction results in a sentence of imprisonment (even if sentence is suspended), referral is automatic.[216] In a recent study of fitness to practise sanctions against doctors, it was clear that a significant number of motoring offence cases resulted in suspension and a minority were concluded with the sanction of erasure. In each of these cases where a direction for erasure was ordered, there were significant aggravating factors and the convictions for drink driving appeared to be symptomatic of deeper problems, such as a pattern of risk taking behaviour.[217] Minor **2.80**

---

[210] [2000] 1 AC 311 at 333. Parallels were drawn with the case of *Marten v Disciplinary Committee of the Royal College of Veterinary Surgeons* [1965] 1 All ER 949 where the appellant's conduct as a farmer was considered relevant to his status as a veterinary surgeon.

[211] *Calhaem v GMC* [2008] LS Law Med 96 at [39].

[212] *General Medical Council (Fitness to Practise)Rules 2004*, rule 7(3).

[213] See *Kituma v NMC* [2009] EWHC 373.

[214] eg *Sadler v General Medical Council* [2003] UKPC 59.

[215] *General Medical Council (Fitness to Practise) Rules 2004*, rule 5.

[216] ibid.

[217] P Case, 'The Good, the Bad and the Dishonest Doctor: the General Medical Council and the 'Redemption Model' of Fitness to Practise' (2011) 31(4) Legal Studies 591.

motoring offences not involving alcohol or drugs are not normally considered to raise issues of fitness to practise and will not be investigated further.[218]

13. Sexual abuse/offences

2.81 The recent cases of Dr Myles Bradbury (a haematologist at a children's hospital who in 2014 admitted abusing eighteen young boys in his care)[219] and Dr Salmon (convicted in 2015 of raping and sexually assaulting patients at the Stoke Mandeville Hospital[220]) have focused attention on doctors who commit sexual offences. The GMC's *Sanctions Guidance* states that all doctors involved in child pornography may have some restriction imposed on their registration[221] and where a doctor's conduct is called into question because of sexual offences or offences of child pornography, the usual response will be erasure.[222] Pressure has been exerted on the GMC and other professional regulators to go further and apply a policy of automatic erasure in cases where a doctor is found guilty of sexual offences, but the GMC has so far resisted, stating it does not have that power and automatic erasure could give rise to human rights challenges from the doctor concerned.[223] In cases of fitness to practise impaired by reason of criminal conviction or caution, the tribunal generally ensures that the duration of its professional sanctions exceed any sanction imposed by a criminal court.[224]

14. Adverse health: Section 35C(2)(d)

2.82 Research suggests that the medical profession has a high incidence of mental health problems and that the culture of the profession inhibits those affected from seeking help.[225] This combination of high risk of mental illness and disincentives to disclose, present obvious risks to both doctors and their patients and a supportive framework for dealing with doctors affected by health issues is crucial to minimize these risks. Where a doctor is the subject of a complaint or report which raises health concerns, the GMC can ask a doctor to undergo a health assessment.[226] The assessment is conducted by two health examiners[227] who prepare their reports independently of each other, and in the case of substance dependency or mental health issues, the examiners will normally be consultant psychiatrists. Refusal to undergo a health assessment or to cooperate with the assessment will result in the registrant being referred to a fitness to practise hearing. Registrants cannot be erased from the register where their fitness to practise is found to be impaired because of adverse physical or mental health,[228] but the sanction of indefinite suspension is still available.[229]

---

[218] GMC, *GMC Thresholds* (para 1) available at <http://www.gmc-uk.org/Guidance_GMC_Thresholds.pdf_48163325.pdf>.

[219] 'Children's Doctor Admits Sexual Abuse of Young Cancer Patients' *The Guardian* (15th September 2014).

[220] 'Former Children's Doctor at Stoke Mandeville Found Guilty of Historical Rapes' *The Guardian* (6th February 2015).

[221] GMC, *Sanctions Guidance* (2016) at para 146.

[222] ibid, para 144.

[223] 'Sex Offender Doctors Can't Be Erased in Case It Breaches Human Rights' *The Telegraph* (24th September, 2012) and 'More Than 1,000 Doctors Convicted of Crimes from Child Porn to Sexual Assault Could Still Be Practising Because Banning Them Could Be a Breach of Their Human Rights' *Daily Mail* (21st February, 2015).

[224] Following *CHRP v General Dental Council and Fleischmann* [2005] EWHC 87 (Admin).

[225] S Brooks, C Gerada, and T Chalder, 'Review of Literature on the Mental Health of Doctors: Are Specialist Services Needed?' (2011) Journal of Mental Health 1.

[226] *General Medical Council (Fitness to Practise) Rules 2004*, rule 7(3).

[227] Schedule 2, *General Medical Council (Fitness to Practise) Rules 2004*.

[228] Medical Act 1983, s 35D(2)(a).

[229] Medical Act 1983, s 35D(6).

15. Language competence: Section 35C(2)(da)

The case of Dr Ubani, a German locum doctor who gave his patient ten times the normal dosage of diamorphine, highlighted concerns that the language competence of some doctors practising in the UK was compromising patient safety. The dose had proved fatal and in 2010 Dr Ubani was struck off by the GMC, later admitting that he could not understand what patients were telling him.[230] The 2013 edition of *Good Medical Practice* introduced a duty upon doctors to ensure that they had the necessary language competence, stating at 14.1: 'You must have the necessary knowledge of the English language to provide a good standard of practice and care in the UK.' Practising without the necessary language competence is now treated as a fitness to practise issue and is a potential ground for finding a doctor's fitness to practise to be 'impaired',[231] although a finding that language competence is inadequate cannot of itself result in erasure.[232] In 2014 the GMC was given the power to require a level of English language competence (currently an IELTS score of 7.5) as a condition of granting individuals a 'licence to practice'.[233] This followed amendment of the *Mutual Recognition of Professional Qualifications Directive* 2005/36 (by 2013/55) which enables citizens of the European Union (EU) or European Economic Area (EEA) who are qualified professionals to practise their profession in any other EU/EEA Member State. **2.83**

16. Fitness to practise sanctions: Section 35D

Section 35D of the Medical Act 1983 sets out the sanctions available to the Medical Practitioner Tribunal where impairment is found as: erasure, suspension (for a maximum of twelve months, although renewable),[234] or a direction that conditions be imposed upon the doctor's registration for up to three years. Despite its absence from s 35D, a finding of 'impairment' is treated as a sanction[235] and it is also possible to accept written undertakings from the doctor concerned which will appear on the List of Registered Medical Practitioners (LRMP).[236] Finally, where the hearing concludes without a finding of 'impairment', the tribunal may nevertheless issue a warning. Warnings are in fact only available where the conduct falls below the threshold of 'impairment'. Although not categorized as a 'sanction' by statute (as it does not constitute a 'restriction on registration') the warning serves as a mid-level sanction given that it appears on the publicly accessible sections of the LRMP for five years.[237] **2.84**

The use of erasure represents the pinnacle of the tribunal's enforcement powers, being reserved for cases where the doctor's conduct is regarded as 'fundamentally incompatible' with registration as a medical practitioner. On the assumption that professional sanctions have a communicative or expressive function, the message delivered by a direction for **2.85**

---

230 'Dr Daniel Ubani Unlawfully Killed Overdose Patient' *The Guardian* (4th February 2010).

231 Medical Act 1983, s 35C(2).

232 *Guidance for MPTS fitness to practise panels on dealing with concerns about a doctor's knowledge of English* accessible at <http://www.mpts-uk.org/>.

233 The Medical Act (Amendment) (Knowledge of English) Order 2014/1101.

234 Suspension can be ordered on an indefinite basis in health cases (s 35D(6)), but only at review hearings.

235 Findings of impairment appear on the publicly accessible 'history' section of a doctor's record on the List of Registered Medical Practitioners (LRMP). A finding of misconduct but without a finding that fitness to practise is impaired is not recorded on the publicly available sections of the LRMP.

236 *General Medical Council (Fitness to Practise) Rules 2004*, rule 17(2)(m) and GMC, *Indicative Sanctions Guidance* (updated April 2009) paras 49–55. Undertakings are published on the LRMP.

237 Medical Act 1983 s 35D(3). The warning replaced the reprimand which was not recorded on the register but details of which were available on request. Warnings were introduced as part of the 2002 reforms and first used in 2004. They can be imposed by the tribunal, by Case Examiners or by the Investigation Committee (s 35C(6)).

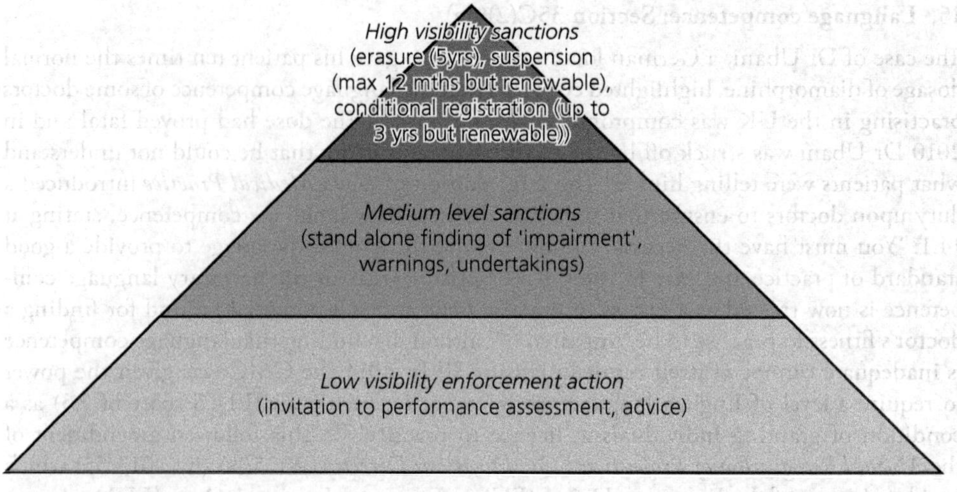

Figure 2.1 The 'Pyramid' of Fitness to Practise Sanctions in Section 35 of the Medical Act 1983

erasure is that this conduct will not be tolerated. In other words, the conduct demonstrated is either not capable of remediation or 'redemption' has not been evidenced on the facts.

2.86 Ayres and Braithwaite in *Responsive Regulation* argue that effective and economically efficient regulators of industry need to be 'Benign Big Guns', able to draw upon a mix of enforcement styles which utilized varying degrees of persuasion and punishment. Crucially, they ought to have a 'pyramid' of regulatory tools with which to secure compliance, ranging from education and persuasion and (low impact) sanctions at the bottom to highly punitive sanctions at the top end, reserved for the recalcitrant few.[238] The GMC and MPTS have at their disposal an impressive pyramid of fitness to practise sanctions (see Figure 2.1 above).

2.87 The jurisprudence surrounding fitness to practise and GMC guidance rigorously rejects punishment as an objective of s 35 sanctions.[239] The stated objectives of sanctioning the defendant doctor are rather to: i) protect patients; ii) maintain public confidence; and iii) declare and uphold standards of professional conduct.[240] Whereas the first of these objectives is a practical one, when a significant objective of the sanction is to uphold standards (deter doctors) or to address public confidence, the sanction takes on a symbolic force and its visibility is key if the sanction is to fulfil its objectives. The high level sanctions of *erasure, suspension,* and *conditions* on registration and also medium level sanctions of a *finding of impairment, warnings,* and *undertakings* are visible on the LRMP which is published on the GMC's website.[241] Whilst until recently fitness to practise sanctions were publishable indefinitely,[242] recent changes will introduce time limits on publication. These will mean that from 2017 a finding of 'impairment' with no sanction will be publishable for five years.

[238] I Ayres and J Braithwaite, *Responsive Regulation: Transcending the Deregulation Debate.* (Oxford University Press 1992), particularly ch 2.

[239] *Raschid and Fatnani v The General Medical Council* [2007] EWCA Civ 46; [2007] 1 WLR 1460 at [18]; *Meadow v GMC* [2006] EWCA Civ 1390; [2007] 1 QB 462 *per* Sir Anthony Clarke MR at [32] (the purpose of the sanction is not to punish but to protect the public).

[240] *Meadow v GMC* [2006] EWCA Civ 1390; [2007] 1 QB 462 at [189].

[241] The GMC is under a statutory duty to publish the register: Medical Act 1983, s 34. *The General Medical Council (Form and Content of the Registers) Regulations No 2 2010* specifies that warnings are to be removed from the register once they have expired, but remain disclosable to enquirers for five years.

[242] The General Medical Council (Form and Content of the Registers) Regulations No 2 2010.

An order imposing conditions or suspensions of less than three months will be published on the GMC/MPTS webpages for ten years and suspensions of more than three months will be published for fifteen years. Orders for erasure will be published for ten years and will be republished should the doctor ever successfully apply to be reinstated on the register.[243]

Whilst the existence of the LRMP in the public's consciousness might be regarded as poor,[244] reporting of sanctions via the LRMP is supplemented by the 'recent decisions' page on the MPTS website, reports of Investigation Committee hearings on the GMC website and regular media reporting of the outcomes of cases against doctors.[245] **2.88**

Warnings issued by either the Investigation Committee or the Medical Practitioner Tribunal stay on the LRMP for five years, after which time they can be disclosed on the request of any employer. **2.89**

17. Appeals: Section 40

A doctor may appeal to the courts from an 'appealable decision', which includes any decision of the GMC or its panels or the MPTS which affect the doctor's registration, including for example a sanction imposing conditions on registration or suspending registration or a decision not to include a doctor on one of the registers.[246] The Privy Council in *McCoan v General Medical Council*[247] asserted that it would require a very strong case to interfere with sanction, because the Committee members of the regulatory body 'are the best possible people for weighing the seriousness of the professional misconduct'. **2.90**

In the course of such appeals, the courts are generally slow to interfere with any findings of the tribunal, in recognition of the expertise and specialism of its members.[248] The High Court can quash the decision appealed from and the test for allowing an appeal is whether the panel's decision was 'wrong'.[249] The appeal court may quash the panel's decision where, for example, the panel's decision is considered 'disproportionate'.[250] A decision of the GMC or MPTS which does not affect registration remains challengeable by way of judicial review.[251] **2.91**

18. Voluntary erasure

The procedure for 'voluntary erasure' is steeped in controversy. A registrant may opt to apply for voluntary erasure at any time during fitness to practise proceedings.[252] The GMC's **2.92**

243 <http://www.gmc-uk.org/List_of_publication_time_limits.pdf_65749892.pdf>.

244 Research into utilization of professional registers suggests that public awareness and therefore use of the registers is very low: *Health Professionals' Regulators' Registers: Maximising their Contribution to Public Protection and Patient Safety.* (CHRE 2010) at 5.1.

245 Although such reporting seems to be skewed by reference to the celebrity status of the story (see, eg, reportage of fitness to practise hearings in *The Guardian* in 2010 which focus disproportionately on the cases of Dr Osborne (brother of George Osborne, current Chancellor of the Exchequer); doctors involved in the case of *Baby P;* Dr Chapman and physiotherapist Steph Brennan, both involved in the Harlequin 'bloodgate' scandal; and Dr Patel (pathologist who examined the body of a patient who died during the G20 protests in 2009, although his fitness to practise case was unrelated to that incident)).

246 Medical Act 1983, ss 31 and 40.

247 [1964] 1 WLR 1107, at 113 agreeing with Lord Goddard in *In re a Solicitor* [1956] 1 WLR 1312.

248 *Raschid v GMC* [2007] EWCA Civ 46.

249 *Cheatle v GMC* [2009] EWHC 645.

250 eg decision that doctor who gave views outside his area of expertise when called as an expert should be suspended from his clinical practice: *Pool v General Medical Council* [2014] EWHC 3791.

251 *R (on the application of Patel) v General Medical Council* [2013] EWCA Civ 327: Court of Appeal compelling the GMC to recognize the applicant's overseas qualification based on a legitimate expectation they had given him.

252 Section 31A of the Medical Act 1983 empowers the GMC to make regulations regarding voluntary erasure: eg the General Medical Council (Voluntary Erasure and Restoration following Voluntary Erasure) Regulations 2004 (SI 2004/2609).

powers to sanction apply only to doctors on the register, therefore voluntary erasure can be viewed as a means of avoiding a finding of culpability and avoiding details of the complaint, allegations, and tribunal's findings becoming a matter of public record.[253] It can also be construed as a means for the regulator to save money at the expense of the need for wrongs to be remedied. Such applications would not normally be considered until at least the investigation phase of the fitness to practise procedure is completed and it is very unlikely that voluntary erasure will be granted where there is suspicion that the doctor may have caused the death of a patient or some other significant harm such as sexual abuse.[254] Reasons for deciding to grant or refuse a voluntary erasure application do not have to be published but a refusal to grant voluntary erasure can be challenged by way of judicial review.[255]

19. The right to a fair hearing and disciplinary proceedings

2.93 Professional regulation must strike a balance between the public interest in protecting patients and the wider public from the risks associated with poorly performing doctors and the practitioners' interests in receiving a fair hearing when allegations are made against them. Increased legalisation and scrutiny has led to some doctors feeling that regulators operate a policy of 'guilty until proven innocent'[256] and recent research has suggested that twenty-four doctors had committed or attempted suicide during a GMC investigation of their medical practice between 2005 and 2013.[257] These findings have prompted a number of initiatives currently exploring how health care professionals might be better supported by their regulatory bodies when complaints have been made against them. The right to a fair hearing is protected by Article 6 of the European Convention on Human Rights (ECHR), and is incorporated into UK law by the Human Rights Act 1998. Article 6 rights apply to the 'determination of civil rights' and they include the guarantee of *'a fair and public hearing within a reasonable time by an independent and impartial tribunal established by law'*.[258]

20. When is Article 6 'engaged'?

2.94 The right to practise a profession is undoubtedly a 'civil right'[259] and disciplinary proceedings are considered sufficiently analogous to criminal proceedings in 'penalising perceived wickedness' that 'something not far from the full rigours of Article 6(2) (presumption of innocence) and (3) (which includes minimum rights such as the right to cross-examine witnesses, to be informed promptly of the case against him, and the right to legal representation) are applied'.[260] Dismissal by an employer would not normally engage Art 6 as it does not prevent the practitioner from practising with other employers,[261] and it does not matter that on the facts the particular employee may find it difficult or nearly impossible

253 See eg 'Insurers Object to Surgeon avoiding GMC Hearing' (2010) BMJ 341.

254 GMC, *Guidance on making decisions on voluntary erasure applications* (2014).

255 eg *R (on the application of Li) v General Medical Council* [2013] EWHC 522: confirming that it was a relevant consideration in this case that the doctor was seeking voluntary erasure to avoid a finding of impairment on the record and hoped to practice overseas in the future.

256 eg G McGivern and M Fischer, 'Medical Regulation, Spectacular Transparency and the Blame Business' (2010) 24(6) Journal of Health Organization and Management 597; and H Williams, C Lees, and M Boyd, *The General Medical Council: Fit to Practise?* (Civitas 2014).

257 S Horsfall, *Doctors Who Commit Suicide Whilst under GMC Fitness to Practise Investigation: Internal Review* (2014).

258 ECHR, Art 6(1).

259 *Le Compte v Belgium* [1982] 4 EHRR.

260 Laws LJ in *International Transport Roth GmbH v Secretary of State for the Home Department* [2002] EWCA Civ 158. See also *Preiss v General Dental Council* [2001] Lloyds Med Rep 491 confirming disciplinary proceedings as determining civil rights.

261 *Matu v The University Hospitals of Coventry and Warwickshire NHS Trust* [2012] EWCA Civ 641 at [52].

to find employment elsewhere.[262] In this context, Article 6 is only engaged by decisions which amount to a legal prohibition on continuing to practise. This means that decisions to suspend or revoke registration or a licence to practise undoubtedly do engage Article 6. The right to practise a profession is also in issue where a trainee is dismissed by a monopoly employer such as the NHS, meaning that s/he is unable to complete his/her training.[263]

Article 6 is therefore engaged by Medical Practitioner Tribunal hearings, but also by any proceedings where the decision has a 'substantial influence or effect on the outcome of subsequent proceedings'.[264] The question then becomes whether those hearings are Article 6 compliant. Article 6 compliance can require the opportunity for legal representation, a right to oral representation, no unreasonable delay and a public hearing and judgment. The view has been expressed that the right to appeal to a court of full jurisdiction under s 40 of the Medical Act means that tribunal proceedings are 'in most cases' Article 6 compliant. The regulatory bodies remain committed to ensuring that even without consideration of the right of appeal, tribunal procedures fulfill the requirements of Article 6.[265] **2.95**

Decisions of the IOT to impose an interim order also engage Article 6, despite the 'temporary' nature of their orders.[266] In any case, the power to impose interim orders in s 41A includes a right of appeal, a right to oral hearing and legal representation. **2.96**

'A *fair* and *public* hearing'—panels are under a duty to give their decision in a form which makes clear to the losing party why they have lost.[267] Depending on the circumstances, a 'fair' hearing can include the opportunity to cross-examine evidence against the registrant.[268] In the case of *R (on the application of) Bonhoeffer v General Medical Council* the fitness to practise panel had acted 'irrationally' in admitting hearsay evidence in a case involving allegations of child abuse. Allowing hearsay evidence in disciplinary proceedings when it would not be permitted in a criminal law hearing would not *necessarily* be a violation of D's right to a fair hearing., However, the 'gravity and complexity' of the charges determine what 'fairness' requires,[269] and the more serious the allegations the greater scrutiny the courts will provide of the fairness of the procedure. It is therefore axiomatic that allegations of serious dishonesty will attract a broader raft of protections for the accused doctor under Article 6. The default position is that Medical Practitioner Tribunal hearings should be held in public unless the circumstances of the case outweigh the public interest in a public determination.[270] This rule should be applied in light of the general commitment to public hearings in Article 6. The GMC must therefore clearly articulate its reasons for departing from a public hearing in terms of the qualifications to Article 6.[271] **2.97**

'Within a reasonable time'[272]—there have been a few disciplinary cases where delays in bringing the fitness to practise proceedings to a conclusion have given rise to a violation of **2.98**

---

[262] ibid.

[263] *Kulkarni v Milton Keynes Hospital NHS Foundation Trust* [2009] EWCA Civ 789.

[264] *R(G) v the Governors of X School* [2012] UKSC 30.

[265] Law Commission, *Regulation of Health Care Professions* (Joint Consultation Paper, 2012) at 9.7.

[266] For authority see *Perry v Nursing v Midwifery Council* [2013] EWCA Civ 145 (Art 6 and Art 8 rights engaged by interim orders). See also *Madan v GMC* [2001] EWHC 577 (Admin); *Micallef v Malta* (2010) 50 EHRR 37; and obiter statements in *R (Wright) v Secretary of State for Health* [2009] 1 AC 739 that interim decisions could engage Art 6 if they had a clear and decisive impact on the exercise of the civil right and the effects were irreversible and incurable, *per* Baroness Hale.

[267] *Phipps v General Medical Council* [2006] EWCA Civ 397.

[268] *R (on the application of Bonhoeffer) v General Medical Council* [2011] EWHC 1585 (Admin).

[269] *R v Securities & Futures Authority Ltd ex parte Fleurose* [2002] IRLR 297.

[270] *GMC (Fitness to Practice) Rules 2004*, rule 41.

[271] *Miller v General Medical Council* [2013] EWHC 1934 (Admin).

[272] *Mahinda v General Medical Council* [2014] EWHC 524 (Admin)—adverse judicial comment on taking eighteen months for proceed to a hearing, during which time practitioner had been suspended on an interim basis.

Article 6. The threshold for delay becoming 'unreasonable delay' is a high one[273] and in assessing whether delay has been reasonable, relevant factors will include the importance of the matter to the registrant, the complexity of the case, and the conduct of the parties. In *Okeke v Nursing and Midwifery Council*[274] a period of four and a half years had elapsed between the allegations being formally notified to the registrant and the fitness to practise hearing where she was struck off the register. The length of time taken was excessive and the remedy was for the sanction to be quashed and remitted to the Professional Conduct Committee for reconsideration in light of the fact that Nurse Okeke's Article 6 rights had been infringed.[275]

2.99 Medical Practitioner Tribunal hearings must normally be adjourned if the practitioner is not fit to attend,[276] but a hearing which continues in the absence of a practitioner is only unlawful if the result is that the practitioner did not receive a fair hearing.[277] Article 6 does not guarantee the opportunity for oral representations, the question is rather whether, in the round, the hearing has been fair.

E. Making Professional Regulation More Accountable

1. Annual accountability hearings

2.100 Over the last five years key regulatory bodies including the GMC, Nursing and Midwifery Council, Care Quality Commission,[278] and Monitor[279] have become subject to a statutory duty to report to Parliament annually on their performance in fitness to practise procedures.[280] These 'annual accountability hearings' take oral and written evidence from the regulators on their efforts to effectively manage the job of regulating the medical profession and health care providers. This measure was first introduced for the GMC following the *House of Commons Report on Revalidation*[281] which expressed deep dissatisfaction with the length of time it was taking to get the revalidation programme off the ground.

2. The Professional Standards Authority and the Section 29 Public Interest Appeal

2.101 Even more significant regulatory accountability mechanisms were introduced by the NHS Reform and Health Care Professions Act 2002. Sections 25–35 of this Act created a new umbrella regulatory body, the 'Council for the Regulation of Healthcare Professions ('CHRP'), more recently known as the 'Council for Health Care Regulatory Excellence' ('CHRE'), but now renamed the Professional Standards Authority for Health and Social Care (or 'PSA').[282] This 'meta-regulator'[283] oversees the work of nine regulatory bodies, the

[273] *Dyer v Watson* [2004] 1 AC 379.

[274] [2013] EWHC 714 (Admin).

[275] For another example of eight-years delay see *Johnson v Nursing and Midwifery Council* [2013] EWHC 2140 (Admin).

[276] *Brabazon-Drenning v United Kingdom Central Council for Nursing Midwifery and Health Visiting* [2001] HRLR 6.

[277] *R v Howson* [1981] 74 Cr App R 172; *R v Jones* [2003] 1 AC 1.

[278] An independent regulator of care services, with responsibility for: monitoring and inspecting the delivery of care at hospitals, care homes, General Practitioner surgeries, and dental surgeries; investigating concerns; and reporting on the quality of these services.

[279] This body oversees the quality of care and financial sustainability of NHS Foundation Trusts.

[280] Medical Act 1983, s 52A.

[281] House of Commons Health Select Committee, *Fourth Report of Session 2010–11: Revalidation of Doctors* (2011).

[282] Health and Social Care Act 2012.

[283] J Black, 'Tensions in the Regulatory State' (2007) Public Law 58.

GMC, General Dental Council, General Chiropractic Council, General Optical Council, General Pharmaceutical Council, General Osteopathic Council, Nursing and Midwifery Council, Health and Care Professions Council, and the Pharmaceutical Society of Northern Ireland. It is an independent body, accountable to Parliament and, at the time of writing, is funded via the Department of Health.[284] The PSA's overarching objective is the 'protection of the public'.[285]

Under s 29(4) of the NHS Reform and Health Care Professions Act 2002 the PSA was vested with the power to appeal the decisions of the nine regulatory bodies it oversees to the High Court, where it considered the regulator's decision to be 'unduly lenient'. That undue lenience could take the form of a 'finding of professional misconduct or fitness to practise on the part of the practitioner concerned (or lack of such a finding) or as to any penalty imposed, or both . . . and . . . it would be desirable for the protection of members of the public for the Council to take action'. The wording of this power has been recently amended so that the challenge can be brought where the decision is thought 'not sufficient (whether as to a finding or a penalty or both) for the protection of the public'.[286] Deciding whether a decision is 'not sufficient' involves consideration of its adequacy in 'protecting the health, safety and wellbeing of the public', in 'maintaining public confidence in the profession concerned' and 'maintaining proper professional standards and conduct for that profession'.[287] This power is exercisable only within the first forty days of the relevant decision becoming final.[288] If the PSA is successful in its appeal, the regulatory body has to consider the matter again, but there is no guarantee it will reach a substantially different decision—it can even make the same decision, but with more detailed reasoning. To avoid duplication of effort, the GMC and PSA must notify each other if they intend to appeal and such notice prevents the other from launching its own appeal.[289] **2.102**

The predecessor test for 'undue leniency' had a high threshold and the court would only interfere with the sanction if it was outside the range of what a reasonable committee would have considered appropriate.[290] This threshold for intervention is therefore similar to judicial review rather than an ordinary appeal, with implications for regulator accountability. The court would, however, employ a lesser degree of deference to the original decision maker where the matters raised concerned 'conduct' (such as dishonesty or sexual misconduct) rather than clinical or technical 'competence'.[291] **2.103**

3. Section 29—a power of last resort?

Initially, the s 29 power was envisaged as being used 'as a last resort to deal with exceptionally grave cases in which there has been a perverse decision or the public interest has not **2.104**

[284] The Coalition Government had planned to introduce changes to funding of the Authority with a fee being levied on the nine regulators which the Authority has oversight of. It is unclear whether these changes will go ahead. See Department of Health, *The Professional Standards Authority for Health and Social Care: Draft Fees Regulations* (2015).

[285] Health and Social Care Act 2015, s 5, amending s 25(2) of the NHS Reform and Health Professions Act 2002.

[286] General Medical Council (Fitness to Practise and Over-arching Objective) and the Professional Standards Authority for Health and Social Care (References to Court) Order 2015, SI 2015/794, para 18.

[287] ibid.

[288] That being forty days after the decision to be appealed being made or forty days from the last day on which the practitioner can appeal from that decision.

[289] ibid.

[290] *CHRE v GMC and Solanke* [2004] EWHC 944 (Admin).

[291] *CHRP v General Dental Council and Fleischmann* [2005] EWHC 87 (Admin).

been fully or properly served'.[292] It was thought that such cases would occur perhaps once or twice a year, notwithstanding that the power spanned the decisions of nine regulators. The Authority's predecessor also took a conservative view as to which decisions could be challenged, stating that it did not regard findings of fact as susceptible to an appeal and possibly not findings regarding whether misconduct is proved, but only decisions on what sanctions should be applied where misconduct was found.[293] Judicial interpretation of the original s 29, however, confirmed that the PSA's power to launch a 'public interest appeal' could be used not only to challenge a sanction as excessively lenient, but could also be used to challenge a finding that the registrant's fitness to practise was not 'impaired'.[294] The power does not currently extend to consensual disposal of cases where case examiners agree with the registrant to resolve the case by undertakings (see para 2.43).[295] This is arguably a significant restriction on the utility of the public interest challenge. However, since 2008 the PSA has been empowered to audit 'early fitness to practise' decisions which involves scrutiny of complaints which do not proceed to a tribunal hearing. Such audits are only undertaken once in every three years and the PSA has no power to require a regulator to reconsider any particular case.[296] If the PSA finds that early resolution of cases is unsatisfactory, the PSA may exercise its power to make recommendations for the future.[297]

2.105 In 2012 it was reported that forty-four referrals had been brought under s 29, resulting in eighteen reasoned court judgments and that the number of referrals being made was reducing over time.[298] There are a number of ways of looking at these statistics. Although the number of court referrals increased from 2013/14 (12) to 2014/15 (21),[299] this number represents less than 1 per cent of the cases reviewed by the PSA. This may be taken as an indicator that the public interest appeal represents a relatively low level form of surveillance. Alternatively, it may be regarded as an indication that, generally, the regulatory structures in place are working well as signified by the fact that there are few cases which the PSA regards as worthy of the court's scrutiny. It is worth noting too that just because a relatively small number of cases are pursued, that does not mean that the impact of the possibility of referral is not felt by the regulators, and that it does not significantly impact on fitness to practise decision-making. The Law Commission's recent review of professional regulation concluded that the PSA's powers had proved useful and offered a 'hard-edged check on whether fitness to practise decisions have been made in a way that promotes the health and wellbeing of the public'.[300]

2.106 Aside from s 29, the PSA has other powers, such as the s 27 power to make directions and the s 28 power to investigate complaints about regulators from the public, although regulations have not been made to set out procedures for the exercise of either of these powers and so they are not

[292] Hansard, House of Commons Standing Committee A, 13 December 2001 (cols 424–27). See also CHRP, *Protecting the Public: Decisions to Refer Regulatory Cases to Court* (2003) at 1.14.

[293] ibid, at 1.7–1.8.

[294] *Council for Healthcare Regulatory Excellence v Nursing and Midwifery Council & Grant* [2011] EWHC 927 (Admin). Unlike many of the other health professions' regulators, the framework for the regulation of nurses at the time did not even allow for the possibility of a warning being issued in the absence of a finding of impairment (*Nursing and Midwifery Council (Fitness to Practise) Rules* 2004 (2004/1761)). This fact in particular meant that a finding of 'no impairment' was, on the facts of *Grant*, unduly lenient.

[295] Although the Law Commission's 2014 report was in favour of extending s 29 to consensual disposals (Law Commission, *Regulation of Health Care Professions* (Law Commission No 345, 2014) at 8.67.

[296] CHRE, *Audit Process and Guidelines: auditing the initial stages of the healthcare regulatory bodies fitness to practise procedures* (2011).

[297] NHS Reform and Health Professions Act 2002, s 26.

[298] Law Commission, *Regulation of Health Care Professions* (Joint Consultation Paper, 2012), 10.42.

[299] PSA, *Annual Report & Accounts 2014/15.*

[300] Law Commission, *Regulation of Health Care Professions* (Law Com No 345, 2014) 12.31.

currently fully utilized.[301] The fact that the PSA's powers are largely non-directive and rely upon oversight, the publication of findings and the making of recommendations means that the PSA in truth cannot probably be referred to as a 'regulator of regulators'. There is consequently a feeling on the part of some stakeholders that the PSA 'lacks teeth' and is sometimes ignored by the regulators it oversees.[302]

F. A Culture of 'Open and Honest Care'

1. Being honest about mistakes

Shortcomings in regulation have frequently been attributed not to deficiencies in the regulatory framework but to a culture of reticence on the part of practitioners to step forward when poor performance or substandard care is observed. The raft of public inquiries into substandard care or the misdemeanours of 'bad apples' in the medical profession demonstrate startling convergence on the theme of an institutional and professional culture in health care which inhibits the disclosure of mistakes and reporting of substandard care and misconduct and which incentivizes concealment. In the history of medical scandals, the Inquiries tell the stories of those members of the public who did not feel they would be believed if they voiced their suspicions to the police or to regulatory authorities and professionals who felt it improper to criticize the conduct of colleagues.[303] In 2013 the Francis Inquiry report concluded that the medical profession had not moved forward in this respect since the findings of the Bristol heart surgery inquiry of 2001.[304] A number of legal measures have been introduced since then to create obligations to be honest when things go wrong and to provide greater protection to those who voice concerns over standards of health care, but for the most part, it is too early to tell whether these changes will be sufficient to neutralize the reported culture of concealment. **2.107**

2. The professional and statutory duties of candour

A key recommendation of the Francis Inquiry report was to introduce a legal duty of candour; an obligation to speak up when failings are observed or mistakes are made.[305] Doctors have been subject to a professional obligation of honesty towards patients for many years, but it has been considered an ethical obligation rather than a legal one.[306] The doctor's duty of care in the tort of negligence would only effectively require the patient to be told the truth about an adverse incident if failure to disclose it had caused some recognized *damage* to the patient.[307] **2.108**

In the aftermath of the Francis Inquiry into events at Mid-Staffordshire, an enforceable statutory duty of candour has been imposed on service providers, to be accompanied by a strengthened professional duty of candour applicable to individual health care professionals. The organizational duty of candour was incorporated into NHS Contracts in 2013.[308] **2.109**

[301] Although the Law Commission's 2014 recommendations were to bring these powers into play: ibid, 12.13.

[302] ibid, 12,13

[303] See *Shipman Inquiry: Fifth Report*, 73.

[304] *Report of the Mid-Staffordshire Foundation Trust Inquiry: Executive Summary* (2013) 107.

[305] ibid, 1.181.

[306] cf *Powell v Boldaz* [1998] Lloyd's Rep Med 116. The House of Commons Health Committee, *Procedures related to Adverse Clinical Incidents and outcomes in Medical Care* (HC 549–I) 6th Report 1998–99 concluded that the *Powell* case meant that there was no duty of care to relatives of a patient to provide them with all the relevant information about what had occurred.

[307] See *Gerber v Pines* (1934) 79 Sol Jo 13 (KB).

[308] *2013/14 NHS Standard Contract: Technical Contract Guidance* with further detail of the candour requirement set out at Annex 4.

This contractual obligation of candour was supplemented by a statutory obligation of candour imposed on health service bodies (NHS Trusts, NHS Foundation Trusts, and Special Health Authorities) backed by criminal sanction. The statutory obligation includes a duty to notify the service user (or anyone acting lawfully on their behalf if the service user is deceased, under 16, or lacks capacity) and to provide 'reasonable support' when a 'notifiable safety incident' has occurred.[309] 'Notifiable safety incidents' are:

> any unintended or unexpected incident that occurred in respect of a service user ... that, in the reasonable opinion of a health care professional, could result in, or appears to have resulted in—(a) the death of the service user, where the death relates directly to the incident rather than to the natural course of the service user's illness or underlying condition, or (b) severe harm, moderate harm or prolonged psychological harm to the service user.

The duty to 'notify' includes a duty to provide an apology.

2.110 As of April 2015, a service provider's failure to comply with the duty of candour is a strict liability criminal offence and may result in a prosecution by the Care Quality Commission. A conviction for breach of the duty of candour can result in a level 4 fine[310] (currently £2,500) and it seems, therefore, that the real sanction will be publication of the fact of prosecution and any damage to the reputation of the service provider which follows.

2.111 The service providers' obligation of candour sits alongside the professional obligation of candour, which in the case of doctors is set out in part, in the GMC's *Good Medical Practice* guidance: doctors 'must take prompt action if [they] think that patient safety, dignity or comfort is or may be seriously compromised.'[311] Moreover, doctors:

> must be open and honest with patients if things go wrong. If a patient under your care has suffered harm or distress, you should a) put matters right (if that is possible); b) offer an apology and c) explain fully and promptly what has happened and the likely short term and long term effects.[312]

One area of potential dispute is the threshold for activating the duty to disclose the incident to the patient (or relevant person). There seems to be a significant difference between the threshold of 'harm or distress' which triggers the professional duty to disclose and apologize to the patient, and the higher threshold of an incident thought to have caused at least 'moderate harm', which applies in both the contractual and statutory duties of candour. Both thresholds require the application of judgment as to what constitutes 'harm' or 'serious harm' and professional guidance will be invaluable as a means of aiding those judgements to be made with a degree of consistency.[313] The duty of candour in its various guises sits within a raft of reforms designed to promote a culture of openness and transparency through organizational learning, training, and education. A joint consultation between the GMC and the Nursing and Midwifery Council has resulted in strengthened professional guidance on the duty of candour, and encouraging a culture where adverse events and near misses are reported.[314]

---

[309] Health and Social Care Act 2008 (Regulated Activities) Regulations 2014, regulation 20.
[310] ibid, regulation 23(6).
[311] GMC, *Good Medical Practice* (2013), para 25.
[312] ibid, at para 55.
[313] On this, reference is made in the statutory/contractual duties to the definitions of harm set out in guidance from 2004 in *Seven Steps to Patient Safety* (National Patient Safety Agency 2004).
[314] *Openness and Honesty When Things Go Wrong: The Professional Duty of Candour* (2014).

3. *'Freedom to Speak Up'*: Protections for whistleblowers

Many of the inquiries which have followed the litany of 'scandals' in modern health care have been accompanied by claims that health care professionals who were aware that patient safety was being compromised by others, feared reprisals if they spoke out, or felt that if they did raise the alarm, they would be ostracized[315] or subject to disciplinary proceedings themselves. In the early 1990s McHale stressed the importance of whistleblowers as a trigger for intervention which might have pre-empted the 'uncaring and demeaning regime' exposed by the enquiry into mental health provision at Ashworth Hospital.[316] McHale referenced the case of Graham Pink as an example of the courage needed to come forward. Pink, a charge nurse at Stepping Hill Hospital, was dismissed after he reported his concerns regarding substandard care caused by understaffing on the geriatric ward to Number 10 Downing Street, a local newspaper, and *The Guardian* . Pink challenged his dismissal at an industrial tribunal and reportedly received a settlement sum equivalent to the maximum the tribunal could have awarded in damages.[317] As McHale notes, successful litigation against the relevant employer is likely to be a 'hollow victory' as very few vindicated whistleblowers find employment again in the NHS.[318] **2.112**

The fear of employment and professional reprisals of the sort experienced by Pink constitutes a substantial obstacle to the profession being truly as self-policing as the *Roylance* judgment (discussed at para 2.75) envisaged. Furthermore, it was, until recently, common practice to rely on 'compromise agreements' or substantial severance payments when terminating the employment of public sector workers and not unknown for such agreements to be purposely used to discourage whistleblowing.[319] Colloquially known as 'gagging clauses', recommendations for a ban on their use were heard in the early 1990s[320] and these arrangements were finally prohibited by the Government as of March 2014. Gagging clauses were associated with the case of Peter Connelly (known in reports of the time as 'Baby P'). Opportunities to intervene to prevent the neglect and cruelty inflicted on Baby P at his home had been missed by several health and social care agencies, including those at Great Ormond Street Hospital. A whistleblowing consultant at the Primary Care Trust responsible for *Baby P's* medical care had been offered £120,000 to leave her employment with a compromise agreement which would have hampered her from speaking up further about her concerns.[321] **2.113**

Added to the prevalence of compromise agreements, the profession's own guidance seemed to lack clarity on where a practitioner's loyalties lay. The 'Ritchie Inquiry' which addressed the issue of why colleagues had failed to report gynaecologist Rodney Ledward's wayward practices sooner, suggested that GMC guidance on fitness to practise and its relationship with reporting concerns had changed repeatedly during Rodney Ledward's misconduct-littered career.[322] As these changes in the guidance were not highlighted, the writers of the **2.114**

[315] eg the experience of Stephen Bolsin who felt the need to move to Australia to escape victimization after reporting his concerns about mortality rates in paediatric heart surgery at Bristol Royal Infirmary.

[316] J McHale, 'Whistleblowing in the NHS Revisited' (1993) 15 JSWFL 52, referring to the *Report of the Committee of Enquiry into Complaints about Ashworth Hospital* (HMSO 1992).

[317] 'NHS Whistleblower Wins 11,000 Damages' *The Independent* (15th June 1993).

[318] J McHale, 'Whistleblowing in the NHS' (1992) 14 JSWFL 363 at 368.

[319] Public Accounts Committee, *Confidentiality Clauses and Special Severance Agreements*, 36th Report (2013–14).

[320] n 309, 368 and Y Cripps, *Legal Implications of Disclosure in the Public Interest* (ESC 1986).

[321] *Public* Accounts Committee, *Confidentiality Clauses and Special Severance Agreements*, 36th Report (2013–14).

[322] Department of Health, *An Inquiry into Quality and Practice within the NHS Arising from the Actions of Rodney Ledward* (2000) at para 19.6.

report surmised that practitioners working with Rodney Ledward were unlikely to have isolated the changes from consecutive editions of guidance, and would perhaps have been unaware of their duty to report Ledward's incompetence.

2.115 The NHS Constitution now includes a pledge to 'encourage and support all staff in raising concerns at the earliest reasonable opportunity about safety, malpractice, or wrongdoing at work'.[323] Whilst this clause may reinforce attempts to change the culture in healthcare, such scaffolding must be accompanied by legal protections for the whistleblower. Such legal protections must strike a balance between the public interest in encouraging workers to come forward with information in the public interest and the interests of employers in protecting their reputation. The right to freedom of expression set out in Art 10 of the European Convention on Human Rights clearly has the potential to protect the communications of concerned health care workers,[324] but Art 10(2) also contains provisos which clearly reduce this right's utility as a mechanism for protecting whistleblowers.[325] Under these provisos qualification of the right is permitted where 'prescribed by law' for the purposes of, inter alia, public safety, protecting confidence, or the protection of health or morals. Legal recognition that duties of confidentiality may be breached 'in the public interest' does little to protect the whistleblower.[326] In any case, the dimensions of the public interest exception are not easily delineated, although it is clear that it would not usually justify informing the public as a whole[327] nor communications to the press.[328]

2.116 The Public Interest Disclosure Act 1998 (PIDA) whilst not intended to directly encourage the reporting of concerns, provides a regime of protection of whistleblowers from victimization by their employer. The Act provides legal protection for public interest disclosures made by workers, including those where the worker has a 'reasonable belief' that 'a person has failed, is failing or is likely to fail to comply with any legal obligation to which he is subject' or 'that the health or safety of any individual has been, is being or is likely to be endangered'.[329] Dismissal for disclosure of protected information is automatically an 'unfair dismissal' and an employer's action short of dismissal, such as deduction in pay or demotion, gives rise to a cause of action.[330]

2.117 The Act, as amended by the Enterprise Regulatory Reform Act 2013, creates a tiered framework of 'protected' disclosures. The recipient of that disclosure is of vital importance, but the further away the recipient is from the employer, the more difficult it will be to demonstrate that the disclosure qualifies for protection. Disclosures to the worker's employer (or 'responsible person' named under the employer's policies) are protected if the worker reasonably believed the disclosure to be in the public interest.[331] If reported externally, a qualifying disclosure must generally be made to a 'prescribed' person or body. The GMC and other healthcare regulators are listed as 'prescribed bodies' under PIDA for the purposes of reporting concerns regarding the fitness to practise of a registrant. In these instances, the

---

[323] NHS Constitution (2013) at s 4, 13.
[324] *Heinisch v Germany* (28274/08)—dismissal of Ms Heinisch for reporting reasonable belief of criminality against employer was infringement of her Art 10 rights.
[325] See J McHale, 'Whistleblowing in the NHS' (1992) 14 JSWFL 363 at 368; and Y Cripps, *Legal Implications of Disclosure in the Public Interest* (ESC 1986).
[326] For further details on obligations of confidentiality and data protection see Chapter 12.
[327] McHale, n 326, at 366.
[328] See, eg, Scott J in *W v Edgell* [1989] 2 WLR 689 at 710D.
[329] Section 1 of PIDA inserting a new s 43B into the Employment Rights Act 1996.
[330] L Vickers, 'Whistling in the Wind: The Public Interest Disclosure Act 1998' (2000) 20 Legal Studies 248.
[331] Employment Rights Act 1996, s 43C.

whistleblower must work harder to show that it is a qualifying disclosure, showing 'reasonable belief' that the disclosure is in the public interest and that it falls within the prescribed person's business and that they believe the substance of the disclosure to be substantially true.[332] Exceptionally, disclosures to other parties (eg the press or police) may be protected. For such disclosures to qualify for protection, the above conditions apply but it must also be 'reasonable' to make the disclosure, and it will only usually be 'reasonable' if the worker has exhausted other avenues first.[333] It must also be the case that either the worker reasonably believes a disclosure to the employer will trigger detriment (eg dismissal) or that where no prescribed person or body is listed for the matter, the worker reasonably believes evidence of the failure will be concealed or destroyed if reported to the employer or that previous disclosure has been made of substantially the same information.[334] A further category of protected disclosures was created to cover 'Exceptionally serious failures' with a less onerous list of qualifying conditions[335] although there is sparse guidance on what might constitute a sufficiently serious failure.[336] It is highly unlikely however, that disclosures to the media would ever be protected.[337]

The limitations of the protection provided by PIDA include that its focus is on providing remedies only *after* the employee has suffered some detriment as the result of a public interest disclosure and that PIDA does not extend protection to a worker who is discriminated against by an employer not recruiting the worker because of previous whistleblowing activities. Writing in 2001, Burrows questioned whether legal change was adequate to counter the culture of protectionism in health care.[338] In almost two decades since PIDA was enacted, it seems that little has changed and that the valuable regulatory tool of information provided by whistleblowing is not being exploited. Research in 2009 suggested that ten years after PIDA came into force, relatively few workers were aware of its existence.[339] **2.118**

In 2014 the House of Commons Public Accounts Committee reported that 'far too often whistleblowers have been shockingly treated, and whistleblowers who have come forward have had to show remarkable bravery'.[340] At the time of writing a review of the GMC's treatment of whistleblowing doctors (the Hooper Review) and an inquiry into whistleblowing in the NHS chaired by Sir Robert Francis QC (*Freedom to Speak Up*) have recently been published. Sir Francis's inquiry was commissioned following the findings of the Mid-Staffordshire Inquiry which suggested that a culture of fear had prevented people from speaking out about the neglect and substandard care exposed at the Mid Staffordshire **2.119**

---

[332] ibid, s 43F. See the government's list at Department of Business, Innovation and Skills, *Blowing the Whistle to a Prescribed Person: List of Prescribed Persons and Bodies* (2015).

[333] Employment Rights Act 1996, s 43G. Indicators of the 'reasonableness' of the disclosure are further included in s 43G(3) which refers to, for example, the seriousness of the allegation and the identity of the person to whom the disclosure is made.

[334] ibid, s 43G(2).

[335] ibid, s 43H.

[336] L Vickers, n 331 at 441, commenting that a revelation of child sex abuse seemed likely to qualify but that no guidance was available on which recipients would qualify the whistleblower for protection.

[337] See, eg, the case of Nurse Haywood involved in BBC Panorama's 2005 documentary *Undercover Nurse* with the motive of exposing substandard care at the NHS Hospital where she worked. (The Nursing and Midwifery Council struck Haywood off the register before later revising the sanction to a caution lasting one year). For further details of the case see <http://news.bbc.co.uk/1/hi/programmes/panorama/4655929.stm> (last accessed 24/5/15).

[338] J Burrows, 'Telling Tales and Saving Lives: Whistleblowing—the Role of Professional Colleagues in Protecting Patients from Dangerous Doctors' (2001) 9 Med L Rev 110.

[339] D Lewis, 'Ten years of Public Interest Disclosure Act 1998 Claims: What Can We Learn from the Statistics and Recent Research?' (2010) ILJ 325.

[340] Public Accounts Committee, *Whistleblowing: 9th Report* (2014).

hospital and those who had spoken out were harassed or their complaints were treated with 'indifference'.[341] The *Freedom to Speak Up* report made a number of recommendations directed specifically at trying to negative any culture of concealment and includes the creation of an Independent National Officer to review how concerns raised by NHS staff are handled and provide leadership in this area.[342]

4. Transparency—published mortality rates

2.120 Both the Bristol heart surgery scandal and the case of substandard care at Mid-Staffordshire NHS Foundation Trust were associated with higher than average mortality which clinicians themselves had not adequately responded to. The publication of standardized mortality rates for hospitals has been a controversial policy, intended to drive the improvement of quality and safety in health care and to inform patient choice when selecting a health care provider.[343] Notwithstanding trenchant criticisms of using mortality statistics as an indicator of care quality in hospitals, the same approach has been applied to individual surgeons. Statistics on mortality rates for UK cardiac surgeons were first published following a Freedom of Information Act 2000 request by *The Guardian* newspaper in 2005,[344] but official league tables for cardiac surgery were introduced shortly afterwards. As of November 2014, mortality rates for surgeons in all thirteen surgery specialities have been published in a browsable format on the *NHS Choices* webpages.[345]

2.121 Mortality rates may be relatively cheap and convenient to compile, but as a regulatory tool they lack precision as there are 'strong signal to noise ratios'[346] (many deaths in hospital are unavoidable and not a product of substandard care) and high mortality statistics tell practitioners nothing about what they might to do improve mortality rates. The Royal College of Surgeons claims that the publication of this data 'will empower patients by providing more public information about the quality of their care', whilst also warning the public that a surgeon who appears as a statistical outlier or even an extreme outlier may not be an indication of poor performance, as further investigation from the employer and professional bodies would be needed to confirm the individual as a 'genuine outlier'.[347] In the absence of information regarding the status of such investigations it is hard to see how a member of the public reading this guidance would avoid the conclusion that the data was useless. There are even suggestions that publishing such data causes risk aversion, with some surgeons avoiding taking on patients where the risks of an adverse outcome are high.[348]

---

[341] eg the experiences reported of the nurse, Ms Donnelly, and Dr Daggett—see 'Whistleblowing' in *Report of the Mid Staffordshire NHS Foundation Trust Public Inquiry*, vol 1, ch 2, 234.

[342] *Freedom to Speak Up: An independent review into creating an open and honest reporting culture in the NHS* (2015).

[343] The right of patients to choose their service provider is part of the broader agenda of further marketization of health services in the UK which is based on the premise that placing providers in a market context will encourage improvements in the quality and efficiency of care. The rights of patients to choose their GP or choose their providing hospital for outpatient appointments is set out in the *Choice Framework 2014* and the NHS Constitution. See further on this M Dent, 'Patient Choice and Medicine in Health Care: Responsibilisation, Governance and Proto-professionalism' (2006) (26) 8 Public Management Review 449.

[344] 'NHS Death Rates: Freedom of Information May Have Saved Lives' *The Guardian* (29th May 2008).

[345] <http://www.nhs.uk/Pages/HomePage.aspx>.

[346] R Lilford and P Pronovost, 'Using Hospital Mortality Rates to Judge Hospital Performance: A Bad Idea that Just Won't Go Away' BMJ (2010) 340.

[347] FAQs on Outcomes Data <https://www.rcseng.ac.uk> last accessed on 23rd March 2015.

[348] 'Surgeons Ask NHS England to Rethink Policy of Publishing Patients' Death Rates' *The Guardian* (30th January 2015).

G. Conclusion

The landscape of professional regulation is constantly shifting and further significant changes will likely have occurred since this chapter went to press. Despite an ongoing programme of review attempting to bring the regulatory structures governing doctors, nurses, and other health care professions closer together, the Law Commission's impressive work culminating in 124 recommendations and a Draft Bill which would consolidate the various regulatory regimes, including the PSA's oversight role, into a single statutory framework, has not made it to Parliament.[349] The Draft Bill would have introduced a harmonized framework for all regulators dealing with such issues as the meaning of 'impairment', fitness to practise procedures, the range of sanctions available to the regulator, the composition of fitness to practise, and interim orders tribunals and availability of appeals. The PSA's role was also key to many of its recommendations—the Law Commission's report had suggested that the PSA should: have oversight over the processes which regulators devised for making or amending their own rules; be involved in supervising the selection processes for appointing members to the regulators, and that the PSA's 'performance reviews' might be tied into the annual accountability hearings (see para 2.98 above) before the House of Commons Health Select Committee. Prior to the May 2015 election, the Coalition Government had expressed its support for the majority of the Law Commission's proposals and stated its commitment to legislation when Parliamentary time allowed,[350] but this leaves the fate of many recommendations uncertain. **2.122**

One limitation of regulation by the GMC (and other regulators cut from the same cloth) is the focus on the conduct of the individual registrant, with some dysfunctional organizational aspects of health care remaining largely out of reach. There are, of course, a number of other statutory bodies which play a role, at least indirectly, in managing the performance of health care professions, but which primarily contribute to the governance of providers in the health care market and are therefore not covered in this chapter (eg National Institute for Health and Care Excellence ('NICE'), NHS England, and the Care Quality Commission[351]). The Health and Social Care Act 2012 contributed to the proliferation of these additional bodies, establishing 'Monitor' (responsible for the regulation of NHS Foundation Trusts and for determining whether NHS Trusts are ready for Foundation status), the 'NHS Trust Development Authority' (responsible for oversight of NHS Trusts), and 'Healthwatch' (a statutory committee of the Care Quality Commission which acts as a 'consumer champion for health and social care').[352] Whatever else this legislation has achieved, it has compounded a legacy of confusing and complex lines of accountability in health care.[353] **2.123**

The 'crisis in trust' which has driven many of the reforms set out in this chapter has been referred to as a 'cliché of our times'.[354] Some commentators have suggested that regulatory **2.124**

---

349 The Bill would have repealed all of the separate statutory regimes and replaced them with a single framework for all health care professions and social workers.

350 *Regulation of Health Care Professionals: Government Response to Law Commission Report 345* (Cm8995, 2015) at 3.

351 See, however, Chapter 1 on the 'Organization of Health Care' for more details of these bodies and their role in clinical governance.

352 Its statutory function is to provide information, advice, or other assistance to CQC or other persons: Health and Social Care Act 2012, s 181.

353 *The NHS Under the Coalition Government* (King's Fund 2015).

354 O O'Neill, *Reith Lectures: A Question of Trust* (2002).

responses to perceived crises of trust endanger patients and compromise trust by triggering reflexive strategies and defensive practices,[355] bolstering unreasonable expectations of medicine, and inciting 'strategic performance' by practitioners designed to meet targets without necessarily improving care; thereby '[deepening] the distrust they seek to remedy'.[356] By the time of the next edition of this text, the duty of candour, the revalidation of doctors, and the GMC's power to appeal MPTS decisions will have had time to bed in, and it might be possible to tell how successful some of these reforms have been in striking the balance between patient care and fairness to practitioners, whilst at the same time facilitating openness and transparency in health care.

[355] M McGivern and M Fischer, 'Reactivity and Reactions to Regulatory Transparency in Medicine, Psychotherapy, and Counselling' (2012) 74 Social Science and Medicine 289.

[356] O O'Neill, *Autonomy and Trust in Bioethics* (Cambridge University Press 2002) ch 6.

PART II

3

DUTIES IN CONTRACT AND TORT

Rachael Mulheron

A. Introduction

Most litigation against doctors concerns actions for medical negligence or, as it is now more commonly known, clinical negligence. It is the principal action by which patients seek compensation for injuries caused within the National Health Service (NHS). The only other action which features to any extent is battery.[1] Actions in battery are however rare, not least because they require the patient to prove the doctor acted without the patient's consent, which is not usually the case. Claims for damages generally arise out of treatment or care to which the patient has consented, but which went wrong or did not produce the desired or expected outcome. The essence of the patient's claim is that the doctor was negligent in that he breached his duty to exercise reasonable care and skill in diagnosing, advising, or treating the patient. **3.01**

The frequency and volume of medical negligence actions has increased considerably in recent years.[2] This development prompted a variety of reactions: recommendations for reform of the medical injuries compensation system;[3] suggestions that a litigation upsurge has given rise to 'defensive medicine', whereby doctors' behaviour towards their patients is modified solely to reduce the risk of legal action;[4] the introduction of 'risk management' systems—defensive practices of a sort—both in clinical and other services provided within the NHS; and the introduction of 'NHS Indemnity' in 1990.[5] The 'Clinical Negligence Scheme for **3.02**

[1] See Chapter 8.

[2] The significant increase in litigation volumes has received recent media attention: '[s]uch are the costs of dealing with legal actions that the NHS has increased the amount of money it retains to deal with claims, up from £8.7 bn in the first year of the coalition government to £15.6 bn in 2013–14 year': 'NHS litigation claims double under coalition' *The Guardian* (13 December 2014).

[3] For discussion of the problems and suggestions for reform see I Kennedy and A Grubb, *Medical Law* (3rd edn, Butterworths 2000), 530–74 and the Chief Medical Officer's Report, *Making Amends* (DoH 2003).

[4] See on 'defensive medicine', M Jones, *Medical Negligence* (4th edn, Sweet & Maxwell 2008), 19–23 and 295–306, and also see para 3.03.

[5] Circular HC (89)34; updated as HSG (96)48. Summary and copy available at: <http://www.nhsla.com/claims/Documents/NHS%20Indemnity.pdf>.

Trusts', administered by the National Health Service Litigation Authority (NHSLA),[6] was introduced on 1 March 1996,[7] as an attempt at more centralized control to effect a rationalization of negligence litigation within the NHS.[8] The NHSLA also produces standards, encompassing organizational, clinical, and non-clinical health and safety risks (most recently for maternity services, which account for a 'significant proportion of the number and costs of claims reported to the NHSLA each year').[9] Recent years have also seen the development of protocols and guidelines by the National Institute for Clinical Excellence (NICE), which have sought to go some way toward standardizing medical responses and informing doctors (and others) on the available options to treat a particular patient[10] (notwithstanding some empirical research which has indicated a number of 'inherent problems' with NICE guidelines, such as low take-up and compliance rates among some doctors, and the variance between guidelines and prevailing clinical practice[11]).

3.03 According to a recent annual review of 2013/14 published by the NHSLA, '[t]he National Health Service Litigation Authority has experienced an unprecedented rise in the number of claims each year, which is placing pressure on internal resources and expenditure'.[12] Indeed, during the course of 2013–14, 11,945 claims of clinical negligence were reported to the NHSLA (which represented a 17.9 per cent increase on the clinical claims received in 2012–13), and for the first time, more than 1,000 claims per month were received, in the first six months of the 2013–14 year.[13] More recently still, the damages paid for clinical negligence claims during 2015–16 (in respect of clinical schemes) totalled £950,400,000 (an increase of £176,000,000, representing a 23 per cent increase, over the damages payments in the previous year).[14] The NHSLA attributed part of this recent 'spike' in claims to the effects of the coming into effect of the Legal Aid, Sentencing and Punishment of Offenders Act 2013 (LASPO) on 1 April 2013, which (amongst other things) prevented claimant solicitors from claiming the success fees and the ATE insurance premiums from the defendant, and banned referral fees. As a result, the NHSLA described the effects on clinical negligence litigation as follows:

> Prior to LASPO, we saw significant marketing campaigns by claimant solicitors to ensure claimants signed up to pre-LASPO no-win, no-fee agreements, which still enable claimant solicitors to charge a success fee on their costs. As a result, the vast majority of claims reported to us throughout the year have been conducted under the pre-LASPO arrangements. The increase in claims received has been challenging for the NHS . . . [15]

[6] National Health Service Litigation Authority (Establishment and Constitution) Order 1995, SI 1995/2800; National Health Service Litigation Authority Regulations 1995, SI 1995/2801. The National Clinical Assessment Service (NCAS), which helps to resolve concerns about the professional practice of doctors, dentists, and pharmacists, became an operating division of the NHSLA on 1 April 2013.

[7] Pursuant to the National Health Service and Community Care Act 1990, s 21. See the National Health Service (Clinical Negligence Scheme) Regulations 1996, SI 1996/251 (as amended).

[8] For the current scope of the Clinical Negligence Scheme for Trusts, in light of the coming into force of the National Health Service (Clinical Negligence Scheme) (Amendment) Regulations 2014, see 'CNST Membership Rules', revised 1 May 2014, available at: <http://www.nhsla.com/Claims/Documents/CNST%20Rules.pdf>.

[9] See *Clinical Negligence Scheme for Trusts Maternity Clinical Risk Management Standards 2013/14* (March 2013), at para 3.3.

[10] See B Hurwitz, *Clinical Guidelines and the Law* (Radcliffe Medical Press 1998).

[11] A Samanta et al, 'The Role of Clinical Guidelines in Medical Negligence Litigation: A Shift from the *Bolam* Standard?' (2006) 14 Med L Rev 321.

[12] See *NHS Litigation Authority Report and Accounts 2013/14* (July 2014), 71.

[13] ibid, 18, and Figure 9.

[14] See *NHS Litigation Authority Annual Report and Accounts 2015/16* (July 2016), Table 1, 11.

[15] *NHS Litigation Authority Report and Accounts 2013/14* (July 2014) 18–19.

On the statutory front, the implementation of two key pieces of legislation in 2006 have, potentially, some interesting ramifications for medical negligence claims. On 8 November 2006, the NHS Redress Act 2006 was enacted, the purpose of which is to establish a scheme of NHS Redress which will offer an alternative means to limited compensation for some patients (a cap of £20,000 has been mooted to apply under any forthcoming scheme). The Act creates framework powers for the Secretary of State to introduce, via statutory instruments, a scheme for 'redress to be provided without recourse to civil proceedings'.[16] The trigger for the application of the scheme to a patient's claim is that there is to be a 'qualifying liability in tort'.[17] This phrase covers liabilities (a) in respect of personal injury or loss arising out of a breach of a duty of care in relation to the diagnosis of illness, or the care or treatment of a patient, and (b) arising as a consequence of any act or omission by a health care professional. 'Redress' under the Act includes an apology.[18] However, since the principal Act's enactment, no redress scheme has been established as yet. In 2011, a House of Commons Select Committee noted the then Governmental view that the NHS Redress Act had 'missed an opportunity . . . [and] should have focused on improving the fact-finding phase prior to pursuit of a claim in order to facilitate faster resolution of claims and leaving it to the parties concerned, or ultimately the courts, to determine cases not resolved by the fact-finding'.[19] If and when any redress scheme is introduced, it is apparently envisaged that only one such scheme for patients will be established in England.[20] In the absence of any formal scheme, however, the NHSLA has produced a guidance to healthcare professionals, to provide a framework on saying 'sorry', and 'how to give an explanation when things go wrong', in order to enhance the transparency and accountability of the NHS.[21] Additionally, new legislation in 2014[22] implemented a duty of candour, whereby organizational providers of regulated healthcare services must act 'as soon as reasonably practicable' after a 'notifiable safety incident' (NSI), and notify the relevant person, provide a truthful account of the NSI and of the investigatory steps and enquiries envisaged, and include an apology. **3.04**

The other statute of note in 2006 was the introduction of the Compensation Act 2006. Section 1 of that statute requires the appropriate standard of care to be determined by having regard, explicitly, to whether a requirement on the defendant's part to meet that standard of care would actually 'prevent a desirable activity from being undertaken at all, to a particular extent or in a particular way'. The provision of health services is surely the paradigm 'desirable activity'. Hence, the effect (if any) of this seemingly defendant-favouring provision upon the substantive law of medical negligence (particularly when the accompanying Explanatory Notes were keen to emphasize that this provision was a mere restatement of existing common law and nothing more) is, as yet, unclear.[23] **3.05**

16 NHS Redress Act 2006, s 1(1).

17 ibid, s 1(2). The phrase itself is defined in s 1(4).

18 ibid, s 3(2).

19 House of Commons Select Committee (Health), *Complaints and Litigation* (2011), ch 7, [182], available at: <http://www.publications.parliament.uk/pa/cm201012/cmselect/cmhealth/786/78610.htm#n187>.

20 Notably, a scheme has been introduced in respect of services provided by, or under arrangements with, the National Health Service in Wales, per the National Health Service (Concerns, Complaints and Redress Arrangements) (Wales) Regulations 2011, SI 704/2011.

21 NHSLA, *Saying Sorry* (2013), available at: <http://www.nhsla.com/claims/Documents/Saying%20Sorry%20-%20Leaflet.pdf>, and see too, *NHS Litigation Authority Report and Accounts 2013/14* (July 2014) 53.

22 Per the Health and Social Care Act 2008 (Regulated Activities) Regulations 2014, SI 2936/2014, reg 20 (in force on 27 November 2014). It is proposed that the duty of candour will be extended to individual doctors and other healthcare professionals too (see, eg, 'New "Duty of Candour" Rules Instruct Medics to Admit Mistakes' *BBC News* (29 Jun 2015)).

23 Compensation Bill, *Explanatory Notes*, cl 13 ('This provision reflects the existing law and approach of the courts as expressed in recent judgments of the higher courts'). To date, the provision has not been examined in the specific context of medical negligence claims.

3.06 More recently, the enactment of the Social Action, Responsibility and Heroism Act 2015, in force on 13 April 2015, may have some (even unintended) consequences on medical negligence litigation. Its sections (of which there are only five) have yet to be judicially considered at the time of writing, but their potential ramifications are referred to later in the chapter.

3.07 Clinical negligence is, in reality, no more than an application of the tort of negligence to professionals such as doctors, nurses, and others involved in the provision of health care services. Hence, the law of negligence is applicable (with some peculiar adaptations) to the medical context and medical negligence is a specific form of negligence liability in the professional context.[24] The general principles of liability in negligence are well known and can be found elsewhere.[25] There are, however, particular factual and legal problems thrown up in the medical context which necessitate a separate account from the general principles of negligence (and professional) liability. A patient may have an action for breach of contract, in the tort of negligence[26] or for misrepresentation.[27]

B. Breach of Contract

1. Treatment under the National Health Service

(i) No contractual relationship

3.08 Historically,[28] the legal obligations of a doctor were derived from his status and 'common calling', that is, to exercise the skill and diligence expected of his calling.[29] Whilst delictual in nature, it was recognized that an action in assumpsit and later contract lay against a doctor who treated a patient for payment.[30] Until the NHS was created in 1948, treatment was either provided privately or on a charitable basis. However, even in the latter instance, when the patient provided no tangible consideration, the courts held that the patient's submission to treatment was sufficient consideration for a contract.[31] Within the NHS today it is generally accepted that there is no contractual relationship between a doctor (whether general practitioner or hospital doctor) and the patient.[32] Equally, there is no contractual relationship between the patient and the hospital, such as the NHS Trust, where the patient

[24] On which, see J Powell and R Stewart, (eds), *Jackson and Powell on Professional Negligence* (6th edn, Sweet & Maxwell 2007, with cumulative supplements); A Dugdale and K Stanton, *Professional Negligence* (3rd edn, Butterworths 1995).

[25] eg S Deakin, A Johnston, and B Markesinis, *Markesinis and Deakin's Tort Law* (7th edn, Oxford University Press 2013); M Lunney and K Oliphant, *Tort Law: Text and Materials* (5th edn, Oxford University Press 2013); J Steele, *Tort Law: Text, Cases and Materials* (3rd edn, Oxford University Press 2014); R Mulheron, *Principles of Tort Law* (Cambridge University Press 2016).

[26] Other actions may include false imprisonment (where the patient is unlawfully restrained) or battery (where the touching is without consent or lawful justification). These torts are discussed in the context of consent and the competent (Chapter 8) and the incompetent patient (Chapter 10).

[27] Under the common law principle in *Hedley Byrne & Co Ltd v Heller & Partners Ltd* [1964] AC 465, or under the Misrepresentation Act 1967, where the patient has been induced to enter into a contract for the provision of the medical services.

[28] See H Teff, *Reasonable Care* (Oxford University Press 1995) 159–60 and 173–80 and references contained therein, and E Picard and G Robertson, *Legal Liability of Doctors and Hospitals in Canada* (4th edn, Carswell 2007), ch 1.

[29] The first reported cases against a doctor is *The Surgeon's Case* (or *Morton's Case*) (1374) 48 Edw 11.

[30] *Everard v Hopkins* (1615) 80 ER 1164 and *Slater v Baker and Stapleton* (1767) 95 ER 860.

[31] *Coggs v Bernard* (1703) 92 ER 107.

[32] Relying on *Pfizer Corporation v Ministry of Health* [1965] AC 512 (HL): medicines supplied under prescription not a 'sale' even if some payment is made. See also *Reynolds v Health First Medical Group* [2000] Lloyd's Rep Med 240 (CC). See also H Teff, *Reasonable Care* (Oxford University Press 1995) 161–62; and Pearson Commission, *Civil Liability and Compensation for Personal Injury* (Cmnd 7054, 1978) para 1313.

is cared for. Any claim for damages based upon a breach of duty lies only in tort and, in particular, in an action for negligence.[33]

(ii) A contrary argument

The basis for the orthodoxy is twofold. First, medical services within the NHS are provided to the patient pursuant to a statutory obligation. Such compulsion to provide a service is considered to be inconsistent with a contractual arrangement.[34] Secondly, the patient fails to provide the consideration in return for the doctor's (or other's) promise to treat which is necessary if a contract is to exist. This position is not, however, beyond challenge. **3.09**

The statutory context, for example, within which a GP functions, is not necessarily inconsistent with a contractual arrangement.[35] In *Dow v Tayside University Hospitals NHS Trust*,[36] the Sheriff Court restated the orthodox propositions that, where medical services were provided under the National Health Service (Scotland) Act 1978, there was no contract between a patient and a Health Board, but the services were provided under a statutory duty created by Parliament and were received by the patient as a right given to them by statute.[37] However, it was possible, in 'unusual circumstances', for an additional contract to be agreed specifically by the patient and doctor themselves, although Sheriff Fletcher questioned why a doctor would enter into such a contract: **3.10**

> I agree that there could possibly be a contractual relationship in addition to the one imposed by statute but I consider that that would be so only where it was clear that the doctor concerned was exceptionally entering into a contract and was not relying on the statutory relationship alone. Having said that it is not easy to envisage a situation in which a doctor providing services under the National Health Service would consider it appropriate to enter into an additional contract in relation to the services. The question arises as to why and in what circumstances the doctor would do so? Perhaps he might find himself being asked by a patient whom he had advised to undergo specific treatment, to guarantee its success before the patient would accept the advice, and in order to persuade the patient to follow the advice he might find himself unwisely guaranteeing it. Clearly that would not be an appropriate response to the patient's misgivings when it might result in its being held that that was a unilateral promise of success. That unlikely scenario in some ways demonstrates the inadvisedness of such a separate contract since the doctors were already under an obligation in terms of the Act to act with proper skill and care so that there would be no need to enter into a contract imposing on themselves additional burdens or duties. The authorities, apart from those dealing with private medical treatment, do no more than leave the door to a contractual relationship slightly ajar.[38]

Subsequently, in *Holdich v Lothian Health Board*,[39] the Scottish Outer House revisited the point in circumstances where the defendant, a statutory provider of health services, stored the claimant's sperm samples in the storage vessels at its sperm bank, but where those samples were damaged because the temperature of the storage vessels rose above the minimum

---

[33] However, a duty may also arise under a contract between a doctor or health institution by virtue of a contractual arrangement if the treatment is provided outside the NHS and the requirements for a legally binding contract are satisfied: namely, (i) there is an intention to create legal relations; (ii) the parties have contractual capacity; (iii) the terms are certain or ascertainable; and (iv) there is consideration. On contractual actions in the medical context, see paras 3.17 *et seq.*

[34] *Pfizer Corporation v Ministry of Health* [1965] AC 512 (HL).

[35] See *Roy v Kensington & Chelsea FPC* [1992] 1 All ER 705 (HL).

[36] 2006 SCLR 865 (Sheriff Ct).

[37] ibid, para 17.

[38] ibid, para 19. In Scottish law (and in contrast to English law), no consideration is required to pass in order to form a contract.

[39] [2013] CSOH 197, 2014 SLT 495.

required level of minus 190 degree centigrade. A threshold question arose as to whether there could be a contract between these parties for the cyro-storage services offered by the defendant where, prima facie, the defendant provided services to users in performance of its statutory functions under the National Health Service (Scotland) Act 1978, and not on a contractual basis. In the opinion of Lord Stewart (which was necessarily couched in non-conclusive terms, given that the question for the court was whether the claimant's pleading disclosed a cause of action), the preferable view was that the parties were not in a contractual relationship, given that the defendant was delivering services which were mandated by the 1978 Act, but there could be 'areas in which contracts might well exist between statutory health providers and service users'.[40]

3.11 Regarding the second point of orthodoxy, it could be argued, for example, that in the case of a GP consideration may indirectly be provided by the patient since his inclusion upon the doctor's medical list will result in remuneration being paid by the relevant Local Authority to the doctor (given that, pursuant to the Health and Social Care Act 2012, local public health services were henceforth commissioned by local authorities[41]).

3.12 In the Canadian decision of *Pittman Estate v Bain*,[42] an Ontario court went even further and held that a contractual relationship existed between the patient and a hospital on the basis that the hospital received funding from the government-funded health insurance scheme. The patient indirectly contributed to this through taxes and health premiums. Further, the hospital obtained a benefit, both financial and in reputation, when patients chose to receive treatment.

3.13 However attractive in principle these arguments may appear, there is, in general, no real reason for an English court to divine a contract between the parties. A contractual claim would not, in most cases, affect the content of the legal rights and obligations of the parties. Even if the courts did determine that a contractual relationship existed, the scope of the duty owed to the patient is unlikely to be any different from that in the tort of negligence.[43]

3.14 In any event, the argument in *Pittman Estate* is most unlikely to be followed by an English court. It stretches the factual boundaries of what amounts to consideration almost to breaking point: the consideration is probably too remote. The English county court case of *Reynolds v The Health First Medical Group*[44] directly addressed these issues in relation to a general practitioner. The claimant sued her GP for failing to advise her that she was pregnant and thereby depriving her of the opportunity to have an abortion. She sued for the costs of raising the child and for general damages arising out of the birth. Seeking to avoid the result in *McFarlane v Tayside Health Board*,[45] she sought to amend her claim to rely upon a contractual basis. The judge held that there was no contract between a GP and his patient.[46] He held that capitation payments to a GP for his NHS patients did not amount to

[40] ibid, paras 53–65, citing (at para 60) paras 3.08–3.14 of the third edition of this book.

[41] A convenient description of the role of local authorities, post-implementation of the Health and Social Care Act 2012, is contained in: Local Government Assn, *Get in on the Act* (June 2012), available at: <http://www.local.gov.uk/c/document_library/get_file?uuid=e0e0321b-49f1-4ec2-9e73-5ba379e0787b&groupId=10180>.

[42] (1994) 112 DLR (4th) 257 (Ont Gen Div); further reasons, (1994) 112 DLR (4th) 482, (1994) 112 DLR (4th) 494, and (1994) 35 CPC (3d) 67.

[43] Subject to the express terms, the law will imply a duty to exercise reasonable care and skill identical to that imposed in the tort of negligence: *Thake v Maurice* [1986] QB 644 (CA); *Eyre v Measday* [1986] 1 All ER 488 (CA); Supply of Goods and Services Act 1982, s 13. See paras 3.23–3.24.

[44] [2000] Lloyd's Rep Med 240 (Judge Simmons).

[45] [2000] Lloyd's Rep Med 1 (HL).

[46] The judge cited and relied upon paras 3.07 and 3.09–3.10 of the first edition of this book.

consideration and that the statutory nature of the relationship negated any intention by the parties to enter into legal relations.[47]

Hence, in England, a contractual basis for the legal obligations of a doctor or hospital is restricted to treatment which is provided privately. It is important to notice that private treatment is not exclusively provided outside NHS facilities. To the extent that it is provided within the NHS in, for example, 'pay beds' then a contractual basis for the parties' legal obligations will apply.[48] **3.15**

2. Private treatment

(i) Express terms

When treatment or other health care is provided privately, a contractual relationship will arise between the doctor and the patient, and usually the clinic or institution and patient. The nature, scope, and terms of these contracts will depend upon the circumstances. Although there are a variety of ways in which contractual relationships may exist for private health care, commonly the patient will make separate arrangements with the doctor (for the treatment and aftercare) and with the clinic for the provision of facilities (such as the operating theatre) and staff (such as nurses). This will be the usual arrangement where the patient consults a doctor privately, who then arranges for the patient to be treated at a clinic with which he (the doctor) has an agreement to admit patients. In other situations the arrangement may be directly with the clinic for the provision of the 'services' sought including the doctors who will carry out the procedure. There may, then, be no separate contractual arrangement with the doctor. Examples of this occur in cases of infertility treatment where the patient seeks treatment at an IVF clinic where particular doctors work.[49] **3.16**

The terms of these contracts will primarily be a matter for agreement between the parties and then subsequently included expressly in the written contract, if one exists. Terms as to payment, the provision of facilities and staff will be common depending upon the circumstances. The consent form, if any, signed by the patient will form part of the contract.[50] The contract may also specify who is to be the treating doctor and, in such circumstances, it will be a breach of contract if another doctor treats the patient.[51] The obligations of the parties will, therefore, be a matter of construing the terms in the contract in each case, subject to the constraints of public policy.[52] **3.17**

One question which has arisen is whether a doctor contractually guarantees the outcome of the treatment. Hence a patient might be able to claim when the treatment does not effect a cure or produce the intended result. An action would certainly be sustainable if the doctor failed to carry out the procedure at all, through oversight or whatever.[53] The possibility of a **3.18**

[47] One reason why Sheriff Fletcher considered, in *Dow v Tayside University Hospitals NHS Trust* 2006 SCLC 865, para 12, that the door had been left 'slightly ajar' to establish a contractual relationship between a patient and a doctor delivering services under the NHS was that, in *Reynolds,* it was said that there was not 'in this instance' a contractual relationship, suggesting that, in other cases, there might be. However, it is doubtful whether much weight should be given to this caveat, in light of the strong views expressed by Judge Simmons as outlined in the accompanying text.

[48] Discussed in relation to 'vicarious liability' and 'primary duty', in Chapter 7.

[49] See, eg, *Thompson v Sheffield Fertility Clinic* (6 March 2001, QBD, Hooper J).

[50] eg *Thake v Maurice* [1986] QB 644 (CA) and *Eyre v Measday* [1986] 1 All ER 488 (CA).

[51] See *Morris v Winsbury-White* [1937] 4 All ER 494.

[52] eg restricting liability: *Tunkl v Regents of the University of California* (1963) 383 P 2d 441 (Cal Sup Ct) and Unfair Contract Terms Act 1977, s 2(1). See also *Thompson v Sheffield Fertility Clinic* (6 March 2001, QBD), discussed in A Grubb, (2001) 9 Med L Rev 170 (Commentary).

[53] See, eg, *Zehr v Haugen* (1994) 871 P 2d 1006 (Ore Sup Ct): action for breach of contract held to be sustainable where doctor had failed to carry out the sterilization operation he had contracted to undertake.

contractual warranty action is important because no such duty arises in negligence: the only obligation of the doctor is to act reasonably. There is no doubt that a doctor may enter into a contractual guarantee.[54] However, in order to do so, he must use explicit and unequivocal words such as 'I guarantee you will be cured', 'I will guarantee to make the hand a 100 per cent perfect hand',[55] or 'I assure you, you will never have children again—you will be infertile'. Absent words of this nature forming part of the contract, the courts will not usually construe contractual terms as amounting to a guarantee of success.

3.19 The US case of *Guilmet v Campbell*[56] illustrates the lengths to which a doctor must go before he warrants an outcome for a patient. The doctor treated the claimant for a bleeding ulcer. Prior to the operation the doctor told the patient:

> Once you have an operation it takes care of all your troubles. You can eat as you want to, you can drink as you want to, you can go as you please . . . there is nothing to it at all—it's a very simple operation. You'll be out of work three to four weeks at most. There is no danger at all in this operation. After the operation you can throw away your pill box.[57]

3.20 Unfortunately, the claimant suffered serious physical after-effects. The Michigan Supreme Court upheld a jury verdict in the claimant's favour that the defendant had contractually guaranteed to cure his peptic ulcer. The court emphasized that it was not saying that a doctor necessarily contracted to produce a cure in these circumstances[58] but rather that there was sufficient evidence for the jury to conclude:

> that the doctor made a specific, clear and express promise to cure or effect a specific result which was in the reasonable contemplation of [the doctors] and the claimant which was relied upon by the claimant.[59]

3.21 The leading English decision concerned with a guarantee of cure or an effect is *Thake v Maurice*.[60] The claimants, a married couple, consulted the defendant, a surgeon, privately in order for the husband to undergo a vasectomy as they did not wish to have any more children. The defendant explained the procedure to the claimants and he pointed out that, although it was possible to restore the husband's fertility, he could not guarantee it, and that the claimants should regard the operation as permanent. The claimants signed a consent form which stated, inter alia, 'I have been told that the object of the operation is to render me sterile and incapable of parenthood. I understand that the effect of the operation is irreversible'. The operation was carried out and appeared successful. However, almost three years later, the wife discovered that she was pregnant. The operation had naturally reversed itself by a process known as late re-canalization and the husband's fertility had been restored. Subsequently, a child was born and the claimants sued the defendant in negligence and for breach of contract.[61] The claimants claimed that they had not been warned of the risk of reversal and that this was negligent. Further, they claimed a breach of contract in that the defendant had guaranteed the success of the operation, namely the

[54] See *Thompson v Sheffield Fertility Clinic* (6 March 2001, QBD), where it was accepted that it was a breach of contract to return three embryos to an IVF patient when she had only agreed to the return of two.

[55] *Hawkins v McGhee* (1929) 146 A 641 (NH).

[56] *Guilment v Campbell* (1971) 188 NW 2d 601 (Mich Sup Ct). See also *Coron v Sandin* (2006) US Dist LEXIS 41276, where the patient alleged that a surgeon told her that back surgery would make her 'one hundred percent' better; summary judgment denied and trial ordered.

[57] *Guilmet v Campbell*, n 56, 606.

[58] ibid, *per* Kavanagh J.

[59] ibid, 607 *per* Kavanagh J.

[60] [1986] QB 644; [1986] 1 All ER 479 (CA). See A Grubb, 'Failed Sterilisation; Is a claim to contract or Negligence a Guarantee of Success?' (1986) 45 CLJ 197.

[61] For a discussion of the 'failed sterilization' cases: see Chapter 10.

husband's infertility. Peter Pain J held the defendant had not, in fact, warned the claimants of the small risk of reversal. He was liable in negligence for this. Also, Peter Pain J held that the defendant was liable in contract as he had given a contractual warranty of success. The Court of Appeal unanimously upheld the judge on the negligence ground but, by a majority,[62] reversed him on the contract claim.

Emphasizing the inexact nature of medical science and unpredictability of medical treatment, Nourse and Neill LJJ held that a doctor would only be held to have guaranteed the success of an operation if he expressly said so in clear and unequivocal terms.[63] Neither the circumstances of the case, nor the use of the word 'irreversible' could lead the court to reach the conclusion that the defendant had guaranteed the husband's sterility.[64] The defendant had only contracted to exercise reasonable care and skill, which he breached by failing to warn the claimants of the risk of reversal as was his normal practice. Nourse LJ said:[65] **3.22**

> a professional man is not usually regarded as warranting that he will achieve the desired result. Indeed, it seems that that would not fit well with the universal warranty of reasonable care and skill, which tends to affirm the inexactness of the science which is professed. I do not intend to go beyond the case of the doctor. Of all sciences medicine is one of the least exact. In my view a doctor cannot be objectively regarded as guaranteeing the success of any operation or treatment unless he says as much in clear and unequivocal terms.

Neill LJ agreed, adding that while both the claimants and the defendant expected that sterility would result, that:[66]

> does not mean, however, that a reasonable person would have understood the defendant to be giving a binding promise that the operation would achieve its purpose or that the defendant was going further than to give an assurance that he expected and believed that it would have the desired result.

In the *Thake* case all the judges accepted that in some circumstances a guarantee of success might be understood from the words used by a doctor.[67] Nourse LJ postulated that a reasonable person might do this where 'the general experience of mankind' was that a particular outcome would, as a matter of fact, result from a procedure. He instanced a surgical procedure to amputate a limb.[68] Nourse LJ contrasted this situation with one 'where an operation is of modern origin, its effects untried over several generations'.[69] There, a reasonable person, even faced with apparently clear and straightforward assurances, would not believe that a guarantee of success was being given. In reality, virtually every medical treatment and procedure will fall into the latter, rather than the former, category. As a result, there is little mileage in couching a claim in contract. It will be a wholly exceptional set of facts where the claimant will be able to persuade a court that the doctor was guaranteeing an outcome. **3.23**

This view is further borne out by the Scottish case of *Dow v Tayside University Hospitals NHS Trust*,[70] in which the pursuer claimed that an operation to terminate a pregnancy with **3.24**

---

62 Nourse and Neill LJJ, Kerr LJ dissenting.

63 *Thake v Maurice* [1986] 1 All ER 479 (CA), 511–12 and 510 respectively, and cited on this point in, eg, *Trebor Bassett Holdings Ltd v ADT Fire and Security plc* [2012] EWCA Civ 1158, para 54.

64 Likewise, therefore, it cannot amount to a misrepresentation so as to found a claim for negligent misrepresentation on the basis of *Hedley Byrne*: see *Gold v Haringay HA* [1988] QB 481; [1987] 2 All ER 888 (CA) at 895–96 *per* Lloyd LJ. See also *Worster v City & Hackney HA*, The Times (22 June 1987).

65 *Thake v Maurice* [1986] 1 All ER 479 (CA), 512.

66 ibid, 510.

67 See also ibid, *per* Kerr LJ at 505.

68 ibid, 511. Kerr LJ, dissenting, considered the instant case as involving 'something in the nature of an amputation', ibid, 505.

69 ibid.

70 *Dow v Tayside University Hospitals NHS Trust* 2006 SCLR 865 (Sheriff Ct).

dizygotic twins was unsuccessful, in that one of the babies remained in the womb and in due course was born by elective Caesarean section. It was claimed, in particular, that the surgeon's discussions that surgical 'termination' was necessary rather than a medical termination by tablet 'clearly implied that the operation would succeed and the success was thus warranted'. However, Sheriff Fletcher rejected this argument, remarking that:

> To equiperate the description of the procedure with a guarantee of success simply because the word 'termination' was used or to suggest that because the word 'termination' was used the pursuer was entitled to take it that success was guaranteed does not bear examination. In my opinion in order to be held to have guaranteed the success of the operation the doctor would have had to have expressly said that he was doing so. He could not be held to have done so impliedly or because he used the word 'termination' per incuriam. I am of the view that he would have to have had the intention to give a warranty of success and it would not matter a great deal what the pursuer subjectively thought the use of the word 'termination' implied.[71]

The court further noted that any warranty of success given by a doctor sufficient to base a contractual claim 'would require to be expressed in clear terms so that the parties would be clear as to exactly what is guaranteed'. A warranty could not arise by mere 'careless use of an expression describing a procedure' or implied from the use of general medical terms used to describe procedures, or from 'the use of simple language understood more readily by patients untutored in medical terms'.[72]

3.25 An exceptional example of a warranty being given in the medical context arose in Canada in respect of cosmetic surgery. In *LaFleur v Cornelis*[73] the defendant, a cosmetic surgeon performed a procedure to reduce the size of the claimant's nose. He failed to inform her that there was a 10 per cent risk of scarring. She was, in fact, scarred. Barry J held the defendant liable in negligence and for breach of contract. He distinguished between 'an ordinary physician' and a cosmetic surgeon.[74] The defendant had told the claimant what she needed done, had drawn a diagram of what he would do and how she would look and had said: 'no problem. You will be very happy.'[75] Barry J concluded that this, in the light of his failure to warn of the risk of scarring, amounted to a warranty of success. Subsequently, Canadian courts have noted that, whilst this line of authority may be argued more frequently in cases of cosmetic surgery, then even so, the clearest possible terms will be required, before the surgeon is taken to have guaranteed a particular outcome.[76] English law would undoubtedly be similarly loath to find that a guarantee or warranty had been given, absent the clearest of evidence. The uncertainties of such surgery are surely no less, usually, than any other. Not every client can be made to look perfect! Absent an undertaking to make the claimant 'stunningly beautiful', 'handsome beyond words', or 'drop-dead gorgeous', even in this context it is suggested that all the surgeon undertakes (as viewed through the eyes of Nourse LJ's perceptive reasonable person) is to exercise reasonable care and skill.

(ii) Implied terms

3.26 More important in practical terms are the terms *implied* in the contract between doctor (or hospital) and patient. The law implies terms in respect of services or goods provided to patients. Many of these obligations are statutory and cannot be excluded: such as those

[71] ibid, para 22.
[72] ibid, para 20.
[73] *LaFleur v Cornelis* (1979) 28 NBR (2d) 569 (QB).
[74] ibid, 577.
[75] ibid.
[76] *Dehekker v Anderson-Penno* [2014] ABQB 95; (2014) 91 Alta LR (5th) 135, para 303.

implied by the Supply of Goods and Services Act 1982 in relation to 'fitness for purpose' and 'satisfactory quality' where goods alone are supplied or together with services, for example, a prosthesis, vaccine, or medicinal product.[77] Further, the law will imply an obligation to respect a patient's confidences which, of course, would otherwise arise by virtue of an equitable obligation alone.[78]

In the context of medical negligence, the important term that the law implies into the contract is, in the case of doctors, to exercise reasonable care and skill when diagnosing, advising, and treating[79] and, in the case of hospitals, for example, in the provision of staff and facilities.[80] These are the very same obligations implied generally in the contracts of other professions and are indistinguishable from the duty of care in the tort of negligence.[81] Hence, in two cases[82] where the patients underwent a sterilization operation, the Court of Appeal held that the contract between the doctor and patient had implied into it a duty to exercise reasonable care and skill in carrying out the operation. In *Eyre v Measday*[83] the Court of Appeal concluded that a warranty of success would not be implied where the doctor had stated that the procedure would be 'irreversible'. No 'intelligent lay bystander' would reasonably infer that the defendant was guaranteeing sterility.[84] **3.27**

3. Contracts with third parties generally

Where a doctor renders medical diagnosis, advice, and treatment to an employee, at the request of an employer, with whom has the doctor entered a contract—employer or employee? This issue arose for examination in *West Bromwich Albion Football Club Ltd v El-Safty*.[85] Michael Appleton, a football player and employee of the West Bromwich Albion Football Club (WBA), suffered a knee injury in practice. He was treated by the defendant, a consultant orthopaedic surgeon specializing in sports injuries and arthroscopic surgery. The defendant diagnosed an injury to Mr Appleton's right posterior cruciate ligament and recommended reconstructive surgery. This was negligent advice, in that the injury should have been treated conservatively, in which case Mr Appleton would have been fit again in about four months. Under the player's contract with WBA, he was required to submit himself to such medical examinations and treatment as might be prescribed by the medical advisers of WBA, and it was WBA's senior in-house physiotherapist who arranged the appointment with the defendant. WBA sued the defendant surgeon for breach of contract and for negligence, claiming millions of pounds in damages for the loss of the value of the player's contract, the cost of replacing him, and lost wages. **3.28**

The Court of Appeal held that, while there was a contract between player and surgeon, there was no contract between WBA and surgeon. There was no express contract, and while there was an intent to create legal relations between WBA and the surgeon,[86] the arrangements **3.29**

[77] See Chapter 18.

[78] eg *W v Egdell* [1990] Ch 359 (CA). For a discussion of 'confidentiality', see Chapter 12.

[79] *Greaves & Co (Contractors) Ltd v Baynham Meikle & Partners* [1975] 3 All ER 99 (CA) 103–04 *per* Lord Denning MR. See also *Platform Funding Ltd v Bank of Scotland plc (formerly Halifax plc)* [2008] EWCA Civ 930, [17]–[18]; *Salkeld Investments Ltd v West One Loans Ltd* [2012] EWHC 2701 (QB) [31].

[80] There appears to be no English case. For a Canadian case in which a hospital was held to have impliedly contracted to exercise reasonable care in providing a safe system of work, see *Osburn v Mohindra* (1980) 29 NBR (2d) 340 (QB). The obligations would be identical to those imposed in the tort of negligence.

[81] Thus little, if anything, turns upon whether the patient pleads the 'negligence' in tort or contract. Indeed, the patient may sue in both tort and contract: see, eg, *Thake v Maurice* [1986] QB 644 (CA).

[82] *Thake v Maurice*, ibid; *Eyre v Measday* [1986] 1 All ER 488 (CA).

[83] *Eyre v Measday*, n 82.

[84] ibid, 495 *per* Slade LJ.

[85] *West Bromwich Albion Football Club Ltd v El-Safty* [2006] EWCA Civ 1299. For comment, see R Griffiths and S Whale, 'Uneasy Bedfellows?' (2006) 156 New Law Journal 1821.

[86] *West Bromwich Albion*, n 85, para 36.

for payment of the defendant's fees (via WBA's health insurer, BUPA) were not determinative, and also, WBA's booking of the appointment could not form the basis of a 'lightly sketched' contract either. In these circumstances, a contract could not be implied, because the test of necessity[87] was not satisfied. Three reasons were given for this conclusion. First, there was no evidence of a past practice under which advice was tendered by the defendant *to WBA*, as distinct from its players (apart from mere courtesy letters). Secondly, there was a danger of conflicts of interest, should a contract exist between WBA and the surgeon as well as between the player and the surgeon, particularly where 'the sportsman may think that his principal interest is tied up in his soonest possible availability to his employer'. This militated against implying a contract with the employer rather than with the patient, or with the employer as well as with the patient. Thirdly, WBA was unable to point to an authoritative example of such a contract between employer and doctor, in spite of the regular practice by which employers paid for medical examinations of their employees.[88]

C. Negligence: Duty of Care

3.30 Actions for breach of contract will be the exception in the medical context. Where a patient is injured allegedly as a result of a doctor's negligence by far the most common basis for a claim will be in the tort of negligence. The claimant (patient) must establish:

(1) that a duty of care was owed to him by the defendant (health professional or hospital[89]);
(2) that the defendant was in breach of that duty by not exercising reasonable care and skill;[90] and
(3) that the breach of duty caused damage, namely the injuries suffered by the patient and that damage was not too remote.[91]

Beyond these—which constitute the legal elements of a claim for medical negligence—there may arise issues concerned with defences to the action,[92] for example, limitation and also calculations of the quantum of damages.[93]

3.31 When will a doctor or other health professional owe a duty of care to another?[94] Usually, this question will not give rise to any difficulty in a medical negligence case. It will be obvious, and accepted, that a duty was owed to the claimant who is the doctor's patient. The real issues in the case will revolve around, for example, breach and causation. There will, however, be problems where the doctor–patient relationship has not been forged fully or at all, for example, where the doctor is employed by another such as an insurance company or a prospective employer to examine the claimant or is a third party who suffers injury as a result of the doctor's negligence (for example, a total stranger injured by the patient or a relative of the patient). Also, legal problems arise where the injury suffered by the patient (or other) is not personal injury arising out of the treatment but rather financial loss or psychiatric harm.

[87] *Baird Textile Holdings Ltd v Marks & Spencer plc* [2001] EWCA Civ 274.
[88] ibid, paras 45–48.
[89] The subject of institutional liability will be discussed in Chapter 7.
[90] Discussed in Chapter 4.
[91] ibid.
[92] Discussed in Chapter 7.
[93] For quantum of damages in general, see H McGregor (ed), *McGregor on Damages* (19th edn, Sweet & Maxwell 2014); and in respect of medical negligence claims, M Jones, *Medical Negligence* (4th edn, Sweet & Maxwell 2008), ch 12.
[94] See also I Kennedy and A Grubb, *Medical Law* (3rd edn, Butterworths 2000), 369–92.

1. To patients

(i) *The general nature of the duty of care*

It may seem blindingly obvious that a doctor owes a duty of care to his patients.[95] It is a duty to exercise reasonable care and skill in diagnosing, advising, and treating the patient.[96] The duty is the same regardless of the experience of the doctor, being instead, as a matter of public policy, tailored to the task that he undertakes and the specialty he professes.[97] Consequently, inexperience is not a defence to a medical negligence action.[98] An action in negligence lies for a breach of this duty which causes injury. The basis for this duty is an 'undertaking' of care of the person as a patient.[99] An undertaking of care may be expressly made by the doctor or implied by the law arising out of the circumstances. As long ago as 1957 Nathan[100] put it as follows: **3.32**

> The medical man's duty of care arises ... quite independently of any contract with his patient. It is based simply upon the fact that the medical man *undertakes the care and treatment of the patient*.

Later Nathan stated that the doctor's duty arises because he has 'assumed responsibility for the care, treatment or examination of the patient'.[101] The language of 'undertaking' and 'assumption of responsibility' reflects the modern approach of the courts when imposing positive duties of care, particularly upon professionals.[102] In general the duty will stem from the doctor's voluntary agreement to 'care for' or 'treat' the person.[103] This will, in turn, lead the law to characterize the doctor's conduct as amounting to 'an assumption of responsibility' to the person. It is important to notice that for a duty to exist, there need be no reciprocation of agreement by the patient. A doctor will equally owe a duty of care to an incompetent adult, for example, an unconscious patient in an Accident and Emergency (A & E) department, or young child brought to his surgery who is too young to consent and whom he examines.[104] **3.33**

The same analysis applies to other health care professionals, such as nurses, who come into contact with a patient: the crucial issue being whether that professional has assumed responsibility by undertaking the 'care' of the person.[105] **3.34**

---

[95] For a discussion of who are a general practitioner's patients, see Chapter 7.

[96] *Sidaway v Bethlem Royal Hospital Governors* [1985] AC 871, [1985] 1 All 643, 657 *per* Lord Diplock, describing it as a 'single comprehensive duty covering all the ways in which a doctor is called on to exercise his skill and judgment in the improvement of the physical or mental condition of the patient'. The duty to advise of risks, as clarified in *Montgomery v Lanarkshire Health Board* [2015] UKSC 11, is discussed in Chapter 4.

[97] *Maynard v West Midlands RHA* [1984] 1 WLR 634 (HL), 638 *per* Lord Scarman.

[98] *Wilsher v Essex AHA* [1987] QB 730 (CA); the point was not raised in the House of Lords. For discussion, see Chapter 6.

[99] *Jones v Manchester Corporation* [1952] QB 852 (CA), 867 *per* Denning LJ (referring to the liability of the hospital). See also *Cassidy v Ministry of Health* [1951] 2 KB 343 (CA), 360 *per* Denning LJ; *R v Bateman* (1925) 94 LJKB 791 (CCA), 794 *per* Lord Hewart CJ.

[100] H Nathan, *Medical Negligence* (Butterworth & Co 1957) 8 (emphasis added).

[101] ibid, 10.

[102] See, eg, *Michael v Chief Constable of South Wales Police* [2015] UKSC 2; [2015] 2 WLR 343; *Selwood v Durham County Council* [2012] EWCA Civ 979; *White v Jones* [1995] 2 AC 207 (HL); *Henderson v Merrett Syndicates Ltd* [1995] 2 AC 145 (HL); *Capital and Counties plc v Hampshire County Council* [1997] 2 All ER 865 (CA); *Kirkham v Chief Constable of Greater Manchester Police* [1990] 2 QB 283 (CA); *Customs and Excise Commissioners v Barclays Bank plc* [2007] 1 AC 181 (HL).

[103] *Capital and Counties plc*, n 102, 883 and 884 *per* Stuart-Smith LJ.

[104] *Re F (Mental Patient: Sterilisation)* [1990] 2 AC 1 (HL), 56 *per* Lord Brandon and at 77 *per* Lord Goff.

[105] See *Barnett v Chelsea and Kensington HMC* [1969] 1 QB 428: nurse in casualty department owed duty to claimant when he presented himself complaining of illness. She was not in breach of her duty because she contacted the duty doctor. See also *Junor v McNicol* The Times, 11 February 1959 (HL) (house surgeon not negligent acting on instructions of consultant); *Wilsher v Essex AHA* [1987] QB 730 (CA) (house officer not negligent as sought opinion of registrar).

(ii) General practitioners

3.35 **(a) To whom is a duty owed?** A general practitioner's patients are determined by the terms of service contained in Schedule 6 to the National Health Service (General Medical Services Contracts) Regulations 2004[106] (the 2004 Regulations). The procedures governing application for inclusion in a list of patients, and the matters such as a patient's preference of practitioner and under what circumstances a doctor may refuse a patient's application to join the list, are set out therein.[107] Under the 2004 Regulations,[108] a GP's patients include, amongst others, 'registered patients', 'temporary residents', those to whom the GP 'is required to provide immediately necessary treatment', and 'any other person' to whom the GP 'has agreed to provide services'. The 2004 Regulations set out a range of duties imposed upon the doctor, including obligations pertinent to 'attendance outside practice premises',[109] 'newly registered patients',[110] 'patients not seen within three years',[111] and patients aged 75 years and over.[112]

3.36 Undoubtedly, the obligations imposed by the 2004 Regulations will guide the courts in determining the scope and content of the doctor's duty at common law, though they will not be determinative or exclusive. They will, for example, be crucial in reaching a view on whether a GP was negligent. However, it does not follow that just because the Regulations impose a duty on a GP, that a duty of care will arise at common law. The 2004 Regulations set out the situations whereby the formal relationship of doctor–patient is created. It would be artificial to state that a GP owes all the patients, for example, on his 'list' a duty of care at all times. Apart from the initial meeting, the GP may never see or hear from the patient subsequently. A GP, in general, only owes his 'formal' patient a duty of care *at common law* when he has knowledge (actual or constructive) of the circumstances which trigger his obligations under the 2004 Regulations. Thus, without a direct or indirect request for 'care' from the patient, the GP does not owe a duty of care.[113]

3.37 Also, the Regulations are not determinative of when a duty of care ceases to a particular patient. The Regulations set out the circumstances in which a doctor may terminate the relationship to his patient, in general[114] or because the patient is violent.[115] Merely complying with this procedure does not necessarily terminate the doctor's duty of care *at common law*. The GP continues to owe his (former) patient a duty at common law until such time as it is reasonable for that treatment to be taken over by another doctor. The common law will

---

106 SI 2004/291, especially Pts 1 and 2. Also: National Health Service (Personal Medical Services Agreements) Regulations 2004, SI 2004/627, Sch 5, Pts 1 and 2. These 2004 Regulations replaced the National Health Service (General Medical Services) Regulations 1992, SI 1992/635.

107 SI 2004/291, Sch 6, Pt 2. The previous regulations pertaining to joining the list of patients, National Health Service (Choice of Medical Practitioner) Regulations 1998, were revoked by the General Medical Services and Personal Medical Services Transitional and Consequential Provisions Order 2004, SI 2004/865.

108 SI 2004/291, Sch 6, Pt 2, and see the definition of 'patient' in Pt 1, 'General', para 2.

109 SI 2004/291, Sch 6, Pt 1, para 3.

110 ibid, para 4.

111 ibid, para 5.

112 ibid, para 6.

113 An alternative analysis would be that the duty always exists and the doctor's knowledge (actual or constructive) is relevant only to the issue of breach of duty. Perhaps it makes no difference in practice which analysis is correct. However, it is suggested that the better one is that postulated in the text. See, eg, analogous situations in relation to a landowner's duty to his neighbours for the state of his premises: *Goldman v Hargrave* [1967] 1 AC 645 (PC) and *Smith v Littlewoods Organisation* [1987] AC 241 (HL), 272–73 *per* Lord Goff.

114 National Health Service (General Medical Services Contracts) Regulations 2004, Sch 6, Pt 2, para 20.

115 ibid, para 21.

not allow a GP to 'abandon' his (former) patient. A duty of care continues until such time as it is reasonable for it to cease although, of course, the content of that duty may be different in the circumstances, for example, where the patient behaves violently towards the doctor.

(b) Emergencies Unlike continental legal systems, English law is chary of imposing positive duties upon individuals.[116] As a consequence, doctors are generally not required to act as 'good Samaritans', going to the aid of others who appear to require medical assistance even in emergency situations.[117] There is no legal duty on a doctor to answer the call 'Is there a doctor in the house?'[118] A doctor 'is not obliged, merely because he is a doctor, to provide . . . medical treatment.'[119] Doctors who come upon an accident may legally 'pass on the other side', though their conduct if it came to the attention of the General Medical Council might lead to disciplinary action.[120] The recent enactment of the Social Action, Responsibility and Heroism Act 2015[121] does not appear to change the law in that respect, limited as it is to circumstances in which a defendant 'was acting for the benefit of society',[122] or was 'carrying out an activity',[123] or when a person was 'acting heroically'.[124] Although the application of this controversial statute is yet to be tested in the courts, its wording seems, on its face, to preclude any application to the 'bad Samaritan' scenario.[125] Instead, English (case) law looks for an 'undertaking' of care or an express or implied assumption of responsibility by the doctor: what has been described as the 'acceptance of the patient as a patient'.[126] Uniquely, in the case of GPs, the terms of service may create a doctor–patient relationship (in the formal sense) between a GP and the victim of an accident.[127] The previous version of these Regulations[128] contemplated *two* situations, the first where an emergency occurred within a GP's practice area and the second where it did not. However, the terms of a GP's obligations were recast somewhat in the 2004 Regulations. **3.38**

A GP is now required to provide 'for the immediately necessary treatment of any person' to whom the GP has been requested to provide treatment, 'owing to an accident or emergency **3.39**

[116] See, eg, *Smith v Littlewoods Organisation Ltd* [1987] AC 241 (HL), 271 *per* Lord Goff. See, generally, B Markesinis, 'Negligence, Nuisance and Affirmative Duties of Action' (1989) 105 LQR 104; R Mulheron, *Medical Negligence: Non-Patient and Third Party Claims* (Ashgate 2010), chs 5, 6.

[117] See *Capital and Counties plc v Hampshire County Council* [1997] 2 All ER 865 (CA), 883 *per* Stuart-Smith LJ.

[118] *Re F (Mental Patient: Sterilisation)* [1990] 2 AC 1, 77–78 *per* Lord Goff.

[119] *R (on the application of Burke) v General Medical Council* [2004] EWHC 1879 (Admin) [84].

[120] As 'serious professional misconduct' under the Medical Act 1983, s 33. See GMC, *Good Medical Practice* (2013), para 26: 'You must offer help if emergencies arise in clinical settings or in the community, taking account of your own safety, your competence, and the availability of other options for care.' Indeed, medical altruism may be alive and well in England, see K Williams, 'Doctors as Good Samaritans: Some Empirical Evidence Concerning Emergency Medical Treatment in Britain' (2003) JLS 258; and see further, by the same author: 'Are Doctors Good Samaritans?' (2004) 71 Medico-Legal Journal 165; 'Litigation against English NHS Ambulance Services and the Rules in *Kent v Griffiths*' (2007) 15 Med L Rev 153.

[121] Social Action, Responsibility and Heroism Act 2015 (in force 13 April 2015).

[122] ibid, s 2.

[123] ibid, s 3.

[124] ibid, s 4.

[125] The *Explanatory Notes* to the Act shed no light at all on the scope of the Act. See generally R Mulheron, 'Legislating Dangerously: Bad Samaritans, Good Society, and the Heroism Act 2015' (2017) 80 Modern Law Review 88.

[126] *Watson v British Boxing Board of Control Ltd* [2001] 1 WLR 1256 (CA), 1269 *per* Lord Phillips MR.

[127] National Health Service (General Medical Services Contracts) Regulations 2004, SI 2004/291, reg 15(6) and (7), and National Health Service (Personal Medical Services Agreements) Regulations 2004, SI 2004/627.

[128] National Health Service (General Medical Services) Regulations 1992, SI 1992/635 (as amended), Sch 2, para 4(1)(h), and discussed in I Kennedy, and A Grubb, *Medical Law* (3rd edn, Butterworths 2000) 81.

at any place in its practice area'.[129] It follows that the definition of 'patient' in the 2004 Regulations includes those persons to whom the GP 'is required to provide immediately necessary treatment'. Failure to provide the treatment will put him in breach of his terms of service and liable to disciplinary action by the PCT. The previous version of the regulations also provided that, where the accident or other emergency, though not in the GP's practice area, was in the locality of his PCT, he had to provide treatment which was 'immediately required' if requested and he agreed to do so. The obligation only arose if the victim did not have a GP to provide the treatment or, if he did, he had been requested to provide it but was 'unable to attend'. Consequently, before the obligation arose, the GP had to be, in effect, the only (or only reasonably) available GP. This particular obligation, however, does not appear in the 2004 Regulations.

3.40 The terms of service are not conclusive of the existence or scope of a duty of care at common law. The common law may take the view that a GP at a site of an accident or emergency within his practice area has *impliedly* assumed a responsibility towards the victim because of his terms of service. By contrast, it is unlikely that a GP owes such a duty if he were elsewhere in the country and happened upon an accident: to impose a duty of care here would be to make the doctor a 'good Samaritan' quite contrary to the general approach of English law.

3.41 An important Australian case raises the possibility that the common law in England might contemplate a duty arising where a doctor is requested in a professional context to provide advice or treatment.[130] In *Lowns v Woods*,[131] the claimant was an 11-year-old boy with a history of epileptic seizures. Whilst on holiday, one morning his mother returned from a walk to find him undergoing a seizure. She sent another of her sons to get an ambulance and her daughter to get a doctor. About five minutes later she arrived at the defendant's surgery. Although it was disputed, the trial judge[132] (Badgery-Parker J) found that the daughter explained the situation and asked the defendant to come but he refused telling her to bring the claimant to him. By the time she returned to her mother, the ambulance had arrived and the claimant was taken to hospital. Unfortunately, the claimant suffered profound brain damage and was quadriplegic as a result of the uncontrolled seizure. It was claimed, inter alia, by the claimant that the defendant was under a duty of care, which included an obligation to attend him, and if he had the defendant would have administered Valium, which would have controlled the seizure and prevented his injuries.

3.42 By a majority,[133] the New South Wales Court of Appeal upheld the trial judge's ruling that the defendant owed the claimant a duty of care. The essence of the court's ruling is stated by Cole JA:[134]

> Dr Lowns accepted that injury ('damage') to a fitting child was foreseeable if he, once requested, did not attend to treat the child. There was obvious physical proximity, for Joanna [the daughter] had come on foot. There also existed an adequate 'circumstantial proximity' in the sense that Dr Lowns was a medical practitioner to whom a direct request for assistance was made in circumstances where, on the evidence presented, there was no reasonable impediment or circumstance diminishing his capacity or indicating significant

[129] SI 2004/291, reg 15(6).

[130] For a discussion of the case and arguments in favour of a duty to treat, see K Williams, 'Medical Samaritans: Is there a Duty to Treat?' (2001) 21 OJLS 393.

[131] [1996] Aust Torts Reports 81-376 (NSW CA). Discussed in L Haberfield, (1998) 6 Tort L Rev 56; and D Mendelson, (1996) 4 Tort L Rev 242.

[132] (1995) 36 NSWLR 344 (NSW Sup Ct).

[133] Kirby P and Cole JA; Mahoney JA dissenting.

[134] [1996] Aust Torts Reports 81-376 (NSW CA).

or material inconvenience or difficulty in him responding to the request, in circumstances where he knew . . . that serious harm could occur to [the claimant] if he did not respond to the request and provide treatment.

Cole JA also relied on the terms of s 27(2) of the Medical Practitioners Act 1938, which imposed a professional obligation (enforceable through disciplinary proceedings) upon a doctor to attend when requested to do so a person in need of urgent medical attention. While the wording of s 27(2) differs from a GP's terms of service, reliance upon it by the court is significant and there is no reason to doubt that an English court would look to the terms of service for guidance. However, the decision is a limited one. The doctor had been requested to provide treatment and had refused. It was accepted (even by him) that in these circumstances he ought to do so and it was not inconvenient or otherwise unreasonable for him to attend. Whether the case can be seen as going much further is not clear.[135] Certainly, Cole JA approved the view of Badgery-Parker J that, in general, a doctor had no duty to rescue another.[136] The trial judge had, nevertheless, been influenced by an argument that a doctor 'in a professional context' should respond to requests for urgent help.[137] The defendant was at his surgery when asked for help. The Court of Appeal did not deal with this point but nothing in the judgment of Cole JA (or of Kirby P) rejected Badgery-Parker J's approach. At least, then, it could be argued that a doctor who is requested to provide help or, even if not, but finds himself 'in a professional context', may have to volunteer help or be liable in negligence. Driving past an accident on the way to the shops with your family is one thing; momentarily stopping at an accident in a car marked 'doctor on call' before driving on, is quite another. English law may well impose a duty of care in the latter situation regardless of the precise requirements of the GP's terms of service. **3.43**

A related, though distinct, point concerns the scope of the GP's duty if he does render help. Properly understood, this must be a matter of what a 'reasonable doctor' would do (or not do) in the circumstances. It is not a question of whether a duty of care exists but rather a question of whether there has been a breach of duty and, therefore, ultimately a matter for determination in each case. In the particular circumstances, a reasonable doctor might only provide temporary relief, such as stemming the flow of blood. In other circumstances, he might have to go further and provide more treatment for the victim. In a number of cases, however, one Court of Appeal judge has in obiter statements suggested that the doctor's 'only duty as a matter of law is not to make the victim's condition worse'.[138] There is no clear basis for stating this as a matter of law and there is no English authority for so limiting the content of the doctor's duty.[139] A doctor who allows a road accident victim to die by failing **3.44**

[135] Subsequently, the Supreme Court of the ACT (Court of Appeal) remarked, in *State of New South Wales v West* [2008] ACTCA 14, para 212, that Cole JA 'did not address his own question as to what was the content of Dr Lowns' duty', while, in a subsequent decision, it was considered that a *Lowns*-type duty would also apply to 'trained rescuers who hold themselves out as skilled, willing and able to assist': *Electro Optic Systems Pty Ltd v State of New South Wales* [2012] ACTSC 184, para 314. In England, such a duty would not, it is suggested, be extended to doctors who happened upon an accident notwithstanding the wording of the GMC's advice, cited above (n 120).

[136] [1996] Aust Torts Reports 81-376 (NSW CA), referring to (1995) 36 NSWLR 344, 354.

[137] (1995) 36 NSWLR 344 (NSW Sup Ct), 357–8, citing English academic authority, inter alia, M Jones, *Medical Negligence* (4th edn, Sweet & Maxwell 2008) para 2.21; and I Kennedy and A Grubb, *Medical Law* (2nd edn, Butterworths 1994) 79.

[138] *Capital and Counties plc v Hampshire County Council* [1997] 2 All ER 865 (CA) *per* Stuart-Smith LJ at 883. See further *Powell v Boladz* (1997) 39 BMLR 35 (CA) *per* Stuart-Smith LJ at 45: 'only a duty not to make the condition of the victim worse' and *Phelps v Hillingdon London Borough Council* (1998) 46 BMLR 100 (CA) *per* Stuart-Smith LJ at 122: 'The extent of the duty is not negligently to create further danger or make the claimant's situation worse.'

[139] Reference was made to the Canadian decision of *Horsley v MacLaren (The Ogopogo)* [1970] 1 Lloyd's Rep 257 (Ont CA); [1971] 2 Lloyd's Rep 410 (Can Sup Ct). This case did not involve a rescue by a

to deal with his injuries does not make the victim's condition 'worse'—assuming he would have died without immediate treatment. Yet, there can be no doubt that medical evidence will in many circumstances suggest that the doctor could reasonably have done something to *improve, or prevent a deterioration in*, the victim's condition. Such a doctor is likely to be in breach of his duty to act reasonably in preventing foreseeable injury to the victim.[140] The effect of the Social Action, Responsibility and Heroism Act 2015 in such cases is also yet to be ascertained. Under that statute, the court 'must have regard to whether the alleged negligence . . . occurred when the person was acting for the benefit of society or any of its members'.[141] Given that doctors will inevitably be acting in that capacity when rendering assistance to others in medical need, the statute will apply, and the court must consider whether that doctor 'demonstrated a predominantly responsible approach towards protecting the safety or other interests of others'.[142] However, the *Explanatory Notes* accompanying the Act state that the statute's provisions 'do not change this overarching framework [of common law negligence]',[143] and hence, were foreshadowed as unlikely to change the scope of a GP's duty to provide assistance.

(iii) Hospital doctors

3.45 Hospital doctors working within an NHS Trust are in a different position to GPs. The 2004 Regulations do not apply to them. Their employment structure is different and there is normally an employment relationship. A patient who is admitted to a hospital under the care of a particular consultant will be owed a duty of care by that consultant. He will have 'undertaken' the care of that patient. As remarked upon in *R (on the Application of Burke) v General Medical Council*: 'it is clear that once a patient has been received or admitted into a National Health Service hospital the duty to provide (and thereafter to go on providing) treatment arises, whether the patient is competent or incompetent, conscious or unconscious.'[144]

3.46 Equally, all those in the consultant's 'team', or 'firm' as it is often known, will owe a duty to the patient as soon as they individually 'undertake' the patient's care. When this happens will depend upon the circumstances but would not necessarily require a 'laying on of hands'. The consultant will, at all times, remain legally responsible for the patient's care. He cannot delegate it to another but given the 'team' nature of hospital care in the modern age, it may well be reasonable for him to leave the patient, at any one time, in the immediate care of a team member whether doctor or other health care professional. He cannot be liable for their acts of negligence as there is no employment relationship giving rise to vicarious liability.[145] Of course, he may be in breach of his own duty if he has entrusted the care to an inappropriate 'team' member who, for instance, lacks experience or competence. Equally, he may

professional but rather, the private owner of a boat whose guest fell overboard. The decision of the Ontario Court of Appeal (the point being left open in the Supreme Court) may be seen as being concerned with the standard of care expected of a rescuer, in effect, not requiring more than not to make the situation worse. Whilst it is obviously correct that less may be expected in an emergency, perhaps even of professionals, it is not at all clear why professional rescuers such as firemen, police, or doctors are given the benefit of the lower duty. For a thorough comparative analysis of 'Samaritan' liability in England and elsewhere, including the liability of medical professionals who fail to intervene or assist, see generally Irish Law Reform Commission, *Civil Liability of Good Samaritans and Volunteers* (LRC 93, May 2009), and its earlier comprehensive consultation paper of the same title (CP 47, November 2007).

140 See *Kent v Griffiths (No 2)* [2000] Lloyd's Rep Med 109 (CA) *per* Lord Woolf MR at [19] (ambulance service is not equivalent to a volunteer).

141 Social Action, Responsibility and Heroism Act 2015, s 2.

142 ibid, s 3.

143 ibid, para 5. See, however, the discussion in R Mulheron, 'Legislating Dangerously: Bad Samaritans, Good Society, and the Heroism Act 2015' (2017) 80 Modern Law Review 88.

144 [2004] EWHC 1879 (Admin), [85].

145 See Chapter 7.

be in breach of his duty if he unreasonably fails to provide any, or adequate, instructions to his 'team' or supervision of its more junior members.[146] These issues are, however, related to breach of his duty rather than to its existence.

More problematic is the question of the point at which a hospital doctor comes under a duty of care, if at all, prior to a patient's admission.[147] Could a patient who collapses in the A & E department of a hospital claim in negligence against the doctor on duty? The answer depends upon whether an express or implied undertaking of care has been given by the doctor. The only relevant English authority is *Barnett v Chelsea and Kensington HMC*.[148] The deceased, along with two workmates, drank some tea and began vomiting. They went to the casualty department of the defendant's hospital. The deceased lay down and looked ill. One of the other men told the nurse on duty what had happened. She telephoned the doctor on duty who, being unwell himself, did not see the deceased but told the nurse to send them home and call their own doctors. Some hours later, the deceased died from arsenic poisoning. Nield J dismissed the action on the basis that even if the doctor had seen them, that would have made no difference because an effective antidote could not have been administered in time. Thus, any negligence had not caused the death. However, on the issue of whether the doctor and nurse owed the deceased a duty of care, Nield J concluded that they did because there was a 'close and direct relationship' between them.[149] Of course, in *Barnett* there is no doubt that both the nurse and doctor assumed a responsibility to the deceased by helping and advising him. The latter, but not the former, was patently negligent in not seeing, examining, and admitting the deceased to hospital. Thus, on its facts, the case is unexceptional. **3.47**

What the *Barnett* case does not determine is whether the doctor will be under a duty of care if he simply refuses to have anything to do with the deceased. There will, in these circumstances, be no express assumption of responsibility of the care of the individual. However, as was suggested earlier a GP 'in a professional context' *impliedly* undertakes the care of emergency patients: a fortiori a doctor in an open A & E department. *Barnett* does not go this far but in principle the duty exists because of the holding out by the doctor that he is there to deal with emergency cases that present themselves.[150] **3.48**

(iv) Liability for financial loss

Generally speaking, an action in negligence against a doctor will be for personal injury or death caused during a medical procedure or it may arise from the illness or disease for which the patient sought advice or treatment. However, a doctor may also cause his patient financial loss. Whether a doctor owes a duty of care in respect of this type of loss will depend upon an application of the complex case law relating to recovery for negligently inflicted **3.49**

[146] eg *Wilsher v Essex AHA* [1987] QB 730 (CA).

[147] For when an ambulance authority comes under a duty of care, see *Kent v Griffiths (No 2)* [2000] Lloyd's Rep Med 109 (CA), and discussed further in, eg, K Williams, 'Litigation against English NHS Ambulance Services and the Rule in *Kent v Griffiths*' (2007) 15 Med L Rev 153. See also *Aitken v Scottish Ambulance Service* [2011] CSOH 49; 2011 Rep LR 42 (a duty of care was arguable on the part of the ambulance).

[148] *Barnett v Chelsea and Kensington HMC* [1969] 1 QB 428, [1968] 1 All ER 1068.

[149] ibid, 1072. The judgment is not entirely clear and he may have been concerned primarily with the hospital's duty to the deceased. Later, he speaks of 'a close and direct relationship between the hospital' and the deceased (ibid).

[150] In the Canadian case of *Egedebo v Windermere District Hospital Association* (1993) 78 BCLR (2d) 63 (BC CA), a doctor who happened to be in a hospital emergency department, but not 'on call', owed a duty of care to a patient whom he knew required attention but whom he left for the 'on call' doctor who was, at that time, busy.

economic loss.[151] If the doctor is consulted by a patient for a particular purpose which the doctor is aware of, then it is likely that, on the basis of *Hedley Byrne*, a duty of care to exercise reasonable care and skill in preparing the report will be owed by the doctor to the patient. More generally, where a doctor advises a patient in circumstances where he knows (or ought to know) that the patient will rely upon it, and the patient thereby suffers economic loss, then under the principle in *Hedley Byrne & Co Ltd v Heller & Partners Ltd*[152] the doctor will owe a duty of care. So, in *Hughes v Lloyds Bank plc*[153] the claimant suffered injury in a road traffic accident. She was treated by her GP whom she later asked to prepare a report detailing her injuries for the purposes of claiming against the other driver. The report understated the claimant's injuries and, as a result, the claim was settled for less than it should have been. The Court of Appeal held that the doctor owed the claimant a duty to take reasonable care in preparing his report.

3.50 However, where the doctor is unaware that the patient intends to rely upon his advice or, more likely, the patient relies upon it for an unrelated and unexpected purpose, then a duty of care will probably not exist.[154] The point is illustrated by *Stevens v Bermondsey and Southwark Group HMC*.[155] The claimant was advised by a casualty officer at a hospital, following an accident, that there was nothing wrong with him. In fact, the claimant had suffered an injury and subsequently developed spondylosis of the spine. However, relying on what he had been told, the claimant had already settled his claim against the local authority which was liable for the accident for a small sum of money. He sued the hospital arguing that the doctor's negligent diagnosis had caused him to suffer economic loss since had he been properly advised he would only have settled his claim for more. Paull J held that the defendant was not liable. The hospital doctor had no duty in respect of the claimant's financial affairs, only his physical condition. The answer would, as the judge acknowledged, have been different if the doctor had been consulted with a view to providing advice about litigation. The case remains good law even in the light of developments since *Hedley Byrne*. The doctor did not know, nor in the circumstances of an A & E department should he have known, that the patient would rely upon his advice in settling his claim. It would have been different if he had known.[156] The doctor had assumed a responsibility to him but only in respect of caring for him *qua* doctor and not as providing the professional services of an expert witness.[157]

3.51 However, a doctor may not only owe a duty of care not to cause his patients financial loss on the basis of a narrow application of the *Hedley Byrne* case. A broader basis of liability was accepted by the House of Lords in *Henderson v Merritt Syndicates Ltd*[158] and *White*

[151] See S Deakin, A Johnston, and B Markesinis, *Markesinis and Deakin's Tort Law* (7th edn, Oxford University Press 2013), 140–77. See also N McBride and A Hughes, '*Hedley Byrne* in the House of Lords: An Interpretation' (1995) 15 LS 376.

[152] [1964] AC 465 (HL).

[153] [1998] PIQR P98 (CA). See further A Grubb, (1998) 6 Med L Rev 368 (Commentary). The report was not covered by the then prevailing rule of witness (including expert witness) immunity either, albeit that the immunity was subsequently overruled by a majority of the Supreme Court in: *Jones v Kaney* [2011] UKSC 13, [2011] 2 AC 398.

[154] See for the general issue, *Caparo Industries plc v Dickman* [1990] 2 AC 605 (HL).

[155] (1963) 107 SJ 478.

[156] On which, see *McGrath v Keily and Powell* [1965] IR 497 (Ir H Ct).

[157] Previously, if a medical expert's report was prepared as a witness in a trial (*Evans v London Hospital Medical College* [1981] 1 WLR 184 (QBD)), or at a pre-trial stage so intimately connected with the conduct of the case that it affected the way a case was to be conducted (*Landall v Dennis Faulkner & Alsop* [1994] 5 Med LR 268 (QBD)), then 'witness immunity' applied (also, *Hughes v Lloyds Bank plc* [1998] PIQR P98 (CA)). However, by majority, the rule of witness (including expert witness) immunity was overruled by the Supreme Court in *Jones v Kaney* [2011] UKSC 13, [2011] 2 AC 398.

[158] [1995] 2 AC 145 (HL).

v Jones,[159] whereby a duty of care may exist where the defendant assumes a responsibility to the claimant.[160] The assumption may be express—arising from an undertaking by the defendant—or implied by the law—arising from the conduct of the defendant and surrounding circumstances. Hence, an employer has been held to owe a duty to an ex-employee when he carelessly produced a reference for the employee's new employer thereby causing the employee to lose the job and suffer financial loss.[161] Likewise, in *Baker v Kaye*, a doctor who was employed by the claimant's potential employer to examine him prior to confirming his job owed a duty of care to the claimant not carelessly to produce a report resulting in the claimant losing the job and suffering financial loss.[162] The claimant in this case was not in a conventional doctor–patient relationship with the doctor and, as will be seen, the issue of what duty is owed in such situations is not clear in England.[163] However, if a doctor assumes a responsibility to an examinee in such a case, a fortiori in the case of a patient when he produces a report at the patient's request or otherwise for a particular purpose. *Baker v Kaye* illustrates that a duty of care may arise for negligent advice given by a doctor to a patient who consults him for the purpose of a 'medical reference' which the doctor knows (or ought to know) will be relied upon by the patient or a third party to whom it is to be supplied.

(v) For psychiatric injury

A patient who suffers emotional distress, grief, or anguish arising out of injuries resulting from medical negligence will, in the usual way, be able to recover general damages to reflect this in addition to the other non-pecuniary and pecuniary damages recoverable for his personal injuries.[164] A patient who does not suffer any personal injury may not, however, recover damages for mere distress or mental anguish.[165] An action could only be brought if psychiatric injury is caused, that is, there is a recognized psychiatric illness.[166] The complex and limiting rules in *McLoughlin*[167] and *Alcock*[168] which are applied to 'secondary victims' who suffer psychiatric injury, do not apply. The doctor owes the patient a duty of care not to cause personal injury which, for this purpose, includes psychiatric injury. The pre-existing duty owed to the patient, as the 'primary victim', will suffice to base an action for psychiatric injuries even where no other injury is suffered.[169] **3.52**

A question arises as to whether a duty would also extend to allow a claim for psychiatric injury caused by the *fear* of being injured by a doctor, for example, on discovering that a doctor who had treated the patient was infected with HIV.[170] In *Creutzfeldt-Jakob Disease* **3.53**

159 [1995] 2 AC 207 (HL).

160 For further endorsement of the 'assumption of responsibility' test, in the context of alleged banking negligence, see: *Customs and Excise Commissioners v Barclays Bank plc* [2007] 1 AC 181 (HL).

161 *Spring v Guardian Assurance plc* [1995] 2 AC 296 (HL).

162 [1997] IRLR 219 (QB, Robert Owen QC) (doctor not liable on facts because he was not careless). Disapproved by the Court of Appeal in *Kapfunde v Abbey National* (1998) 46 BMLR 176 (CA).

163 See paras 3.145–3.154.

164 eg *Kralj v McGrath* [1986] 1 All ER 54 (contract and negligence actions).

165 eg *Reilly v Merseyside RHA* [1995] 6 Med LR 246 (CA). See further R Mulheron, 'Rewriting the Requirement for a "Recognized Psychiatric Injury" in Negligence Claims' (2012) 33 OJLS 1.

166 cf *Grieve v Salford HA* [1991] 2 Med LR 295 (QBD); *Bagley v North Hertfordshire HA* (1986) 136 NLJ 1014. This is usually determined by reference to the *American Diagnostic and Statistical Manual of Mental Disorders* (DSM-V, 2013) or the mental disorders section of the *International Classification of Diseases and Related Health Problems* (ICD-10 1992). The 11th revision is due in 2017.

167 *McLoughlin v O'Brien* [1983] AC 410, [1982] 2 All ER 298 (HL).

168 *Alcock v Chief Constable of South Yorkshire Police* [1992] 1 AC 310; [1991] 4 All ER 907 (HL).

169 ibid, 923–24 *per* Lord Oliver; *Page v Smith* [1996] AC 155 (HL); *White v Chief Constable of the South Yorkshire Police* [1999] 1 All ER 1 (HL).

170 For a discussion of the 'AIDS phobia' cases in an instructive US case, see *Faya and Rossi v Almaraz* (1993) 620 A 2d 327 (My CA), discussed in A Grubb, (1995) 3 Med L Rev 231 (Commentary).

litigation, Group B Plaintiffs v Medical Research Council,[171] several young children who participated in a clinical trial in which they received human growth hormone (HGH) were exposed to the risk of contracting Creutzfeldt-Jakob disease (CJD), a brain-wasting and untreatable condition that (the court said) consigned its sufferers to unimaginable suffering and certain death. As a result of being informed that they were at risk of developing CJD, some of the group sustained psychiatric illnesses. A duty of care to avoid psychiatric injury was found. Morland J declared that the recipients of the HGH were not primary victims of the *Page v Smith* type, because for Mr Page, his awareness of the danger, his participation in the traumatic event of the car accident, his shock, and his resultant psychiatric illness, all happened simultaneously or almost contemporaneously, but not so for the HGH recipients.[172] They learned the terrible news some years after having been injected. This finding clearly had a policy element too, for Morland J observed that if the CJD recipients were indeed *Page v Smith*-type primary victims, then psychiatric injury caused by the apprehension of illness related to exposure to asbestos, radiation, or contaminated food could become actionable on similar principles, even though the claimants had actually suffered no physical injury.[173] However, on classic *Caparo* principles[174] which govern novel duty of care scenarios, the HGH recipients succeeded in proving a duty. There was foreseeability of psychiatric injury, and although the clinicians and the dwarfism sufferers were not in a classic doctor–patient relationship, the relationship was closely analogous, giving rise to relational proximity.[175] Moreover, there was no public policy reason why a claimant should not recover for a psychiatric illness caused by becoming aware of the fact that he was at risk of a lethal disease attributable to a physical event negligently occurring years earlier.[176] Subsequently, the House of Lords confirmed, in *Rothwell v Chemical and Insulating Co Ltd*[177] that these types of fear-of-the-future claimants (who arose there in an employment rather than in a medical context) were properly not to be dealt with as primary victims under the *Page v Smith* framework.

3.54 An illustration of the 'primary victim' approach in the medical context can be found in the case of *Tredget and Tredget v Bexley HA*.[178] The claimants, who were married, suffered psychiatric illness as a result of the defendants' negligence during the birth of their child who subsequently died. Judge White awarded both claimants damages for their psychiatric illnesses. He relied on the participants' category identified by Lord Oliver in *Alcock* which obviously covered the mother but also, he held, the father.[179]

3.55 Another situation in which a doctor might cause psychiatric injury to a patient is where he gives false information or communicates accurate information carelessly to the patient

[171] *Creutzfeldt-Jakob Disease litigation, Group B Plaintiffs v Medical Research Council* [2000] Lloyd's Rep Med 161 (QB).

[172] ibid, 174.

[173] ibid, 163–64.

[174] *Caparo Industries plc v Dickman* [1990] 2 AC 605 (HL) 618.

[175] *Creutzfeldt-Jakob Disease litigation*, n 171, 165.

[176] ibid, 168–69.

[177] [2007] UKHL 39 (also known as *Johnston v NEI Combustion Ltd*).

[178] [1994] 5 Med LR 178. A Grubb, (1995) 3 Med L Rev 213, 215–16 (Commentary). See also *W v Essex County Council* [2000] 2 All ER 237 (HL) (parents of child who was abused by foster child placed in their home who was a known sexual abuser had arguable claim for psychiatric injury as 'primary victims', and as 'secondary victims' under the 'immediate aftermath' doctrine).

[179] *Alcock* [1991] 4 All ER 907 (HL) 923–24 *per* Lord Oliver. Contrast: *Tan v East London and City HA* [1999] Lloyd's Rep Med 389 (Judge Ludlow); *Less v Hussain* [2012] EWHC 3513 (QB); and *Wild v Southend University Hospital NHS Foundation Trust* [2014] EWHC 4053 (QB) [52], discussed at para 3.125.

after treatment.[180] If a doctor did so deliberately, intending to cause harm to the patient, there would be liability under the rule in *Wilkinson v Downton*.[181] This, of course, will be rare. In principle, however, a duty of care exists between a doctor and patient which would encompass negligent postoperative advice whether in its content or in its method of communication.

In *AB v Tameside and Glossop HA*,[182] the parties conceded that the defendant[183] owed a duty of care when negligently communicating accurate information to obstetric patients (present and former) about their possible exposure to a health worker infected with HIV. While noting that no previous case seemed to deal with this point, the Court of Appeal accepted the concession and was content to state that 'we do not have to decide this point, or to consider whether such a duty exists, or the parameters of that duty, where there is no pre-existing relationship of care'.[184] By embarking upon communication with the patient, the doctor assumes a duty of care in respect of what he is undertaking whether it be diagnosis, pre-treatment advice, treatment, or *post-treatment* advice.[185] Providing it is reasonably foreseeable that this negligent advice could cause psychiatric injury, as it may well be depending upon the nature of the advice, then a duty of care will exist. Hence, at least in the case of existing, and even former, patients the concession was surely properly made.[186] **3.56**

Another situation in which the 'primary victim' approach has been applied in the medical negligence context (although not without judicial disagreement) is in the context of where the claimant's sperm was deposited at the defendant's cyro-storage facility, but was negligently damaged due to inadequate temperature controls. As preliminary observations, the English Court of Appeal considered, in *Yearworth v North Bristol NHS Trust*,[187] that the claimant was to be treated as a 'secondary victim', whereas in the factually similar case of *Holdich v Lothian Health Board*,[188] the Scottish Outer House did not consider the claimant to be a 'secondary victim' at all, and indeed, remarked that the primary/secondary victim classification did not operate where there was only one victim of the medical defendant's negligence. **3.57**

2. To third parties

Although a doctor owes a duty of care to his patients, a far more problematical question is whether, and if so to what extent, a doctor will owe a duty of care to third parties who are **3.58**

---

180 See N J Mullany, 'Liability for Careless Communication of Traumatic Information' (1998) 114 LQR 380.

181 [1897] 2 QB 57. See also *Powell v Boladz* (1997) 39 BMLR 35 (CA); and *Wainwright v Home Office* [2003] UKHL 53, [2004] 2 AC 406.

182 [1997] 8 Med LR 91 (CA). See I Kennedy (1997) 5 Med L Rev 338 (Commentary).

183 The case concerned the duty of the hospital but there is no difference, in principle, if the advice is given by a doctor.

184 [1997] 8 Med LR 91 (CA), 93 *per* Brooke LJ.

185 There may be a duty to volunteer information about medical mistakes: *Lee v South Thames RHA* [1985] 2 All ER 385 (CA), 389 *per* Sir John Donaldson MR; *Naylor v Preston AHA* [1987] 2 All ER 353 (CA), 360 *per* Sir John Donaldson MR; *Stamos v Davies* (1986) 21 DLR (4th) 507 (Ont H Ct); *Gerber v Pines* (1934) 79 SJ 13; *Daniels v Heskin* [1954] IR 73 (Ir Sup Ct). For a discussion see G Robertson, 'Fraudulent Concealment and the Duty to Disclose Medical Mistakes' (1987) 25 Alta LR 215.

186 The legal basis of the duty will be negligence if injury is suffered as a result of non-disclosure. If no such injury is caused the duty must rest elsewhere, for example, as an aspect of the parties' fiduciary relationship: *Gerula v Flores* (1995), 126 DLR (4th) 506 (Ont CA). See generally A Grubb, 'The Doctor as Fiduciary' (1994) 47 CLP 311, especially at 335–38.

187 [2010] QB 1 (CA), referring to some similarities in *Attia* v *British Gas plc* [1988] QB 304 (CA), where the claimant's house was badly damaged because of the defendant's negligence during a gas fire installation.

188 [2013] CSOH 197, 2014 SLT 495, paras 87–88.

not his patients.[189] In *Sidaway v Board of Governors of the Bethlem Royal Hospital and the Maudsley Hospital*, Lord Diplock stated that 'a doctor's duty of care, whether he be general practitioner or consulting surgeon or physician is owed to that patient and none other, idiosyncrasies and all'.[190] In *Powell v Boladz* too, speaking on behalf of the Court of Appeal, Stuart-Smith LJ remarked that a doctor only owed a duty of care to his patients and never anyone else, including in that case the parents of the deceased patient.[191] However, in *JD v East Berkshire Community Health NHS Trust*, Lord Bingham questioned the accuracy of Lord Diplock's view, noting that no other member of the court had expressly agreed with it, and that 'in the medical sphere the law is much less clear than Lord Diplock's dictum might suggest'.[192] Furthermore, Stuart-Smith LJ's statement should, perhaps, be understood as merely asserting the limited proposition that a doctor only owes a duty *qua* doctor to *treat* his patients. This is not, of course, the same as saying he does not owe a duty of care, the content of which might include warning or advising others, but not requiring him to act as their doctor.

3.59 In certain circumstances, a doctor may owe a duty of care to someone who is not his patient. It is helpful to consider three situations:

(1) where the doctor is treating a patient whose medical condition is the cause of personal injuries being sustained by third parties ('the dangerous patient' scenario);
(2) where a doctor's medical treatment or examination of a patient causes financial loss to a third party; and
(3) where a doctor's medical treatment or examination of a patient causes psychiatric injury (but not bodily injury) to a third party.

The interesting legal question is whether, and if so why, a doctor owes a duty of care to any of these 'injured' third parties. Dealing with each of the abovementioned categories in turn:

(i) Dangerous patients

3.60 As a result of his treatment and responsibility for the care of a patient, a doctor may know (or reasonably ought to know) that his patient is a danger to others, in the sense that physical harm to third parties is foreseeable. This typically arises in the following scenarios: where the patient suffers from an infectious or contagious disease; where the patient is psychiatrically disturbed; where the patient is physically disabled; where the patient has a genetic predisposition to illness; and where a female sexual partner falls pregnant after a sterilization procedure for her male sexual partner is negligently performed (or where advice about the procedure is negligently given).

3.61 (a) **Infectious diseases** A doctor may know (or ought to have known) that his patient suffered from an infectious disease which he was likely to transmit to others through sexual contact or otherwise. Although relevant cases have arisen in England,[193] Canada,[194] and Australia,[195] it is to the United States that we must look for more developed and longstanding jurisprudence on doctors' liabilities in the context of transmission of infectious

[189] See generally R Mulheron, *Medical Negligence: Non-Patient and Third Party Claims* (Ashgate 2010); D Giesen, *International Medical Malpractice Law* (Kluwer Law International 1988), 157–61.
[190] [1985] AC 871 (HL) 890.
[191] *Powell v Boladz* (1997) 39 BMLR 35 (CA) 45.
[192] [2005] UKHL 23, para 46, citing A Grubb, *Principles of Medical Law* (2nd edn, Oxford University Press 2004), para 5.48.
[193] *Evans v Liverpool Corp* [1906] 1 KB 160.
[194] eg *Pittman Estate v Bain* (1994) 112 DLR (4th) 257 (Ont Gen Div); *Healey v Lakeridge Health Corp* [2006] OJ No 4277 (SCJ); *Bruce Estate v Toderovich* [2011] ABQB 709, (2010) 42 Alta LR (5th) 377.
[195] eg *BT v Oei* [1999] NSWSC 1082.

or contagious diseases by a patient to a third party. In that jurisdiction, courts have held doctors liable for (i) failing to diagnose the disease; (ii) failing to inform the third party (or others) of the danger; (iii) negligently advising the third party that there is no danger; and (iv) failing to prevent the spread of the disease.[196] Usually, however, the courts have restricted the group of potential victims who are owed a duty by the doctor to, for example, close family[197] or sexual partners.[198]

A number of cases have concerned the transmission of diseases by a patient to another.[199] In *DiMarco v Lynch Homes-Chester County*[200] a blood technician accidentally infected herself with hepatitis through a sharps' injury. Her doctors told her that if she remained symptom-free for six weeks, it would mean that she had not been infected. She was not advised to refrain from sexual intercourse, although she did do so for eight weeks. She remained symptom-free and, thereafter, resumed sexual relations with her boyfriend (the claimant), who became infected. The claimant sued the doctors, arguing that they should have advised the patient to refrain from sexual relations for six months, otherwise she could infect her sexual partner. The Pennsylvania Supreme Court (by a majority of 4–3) held that the doctors owed the claimant a duty of care. The court was greatly influenced by public health policy concerns to prevent the spread of communicable diseases and to further that policy by placing responsibility, in these circumstances, on the only person who was aware of the danger—the doctor. One passage in the majority judgment of Larsen J is particularly important:[201] **3.62**

> When a physician treats a patient who has been exposed to or who has contracted a communicable and/or contagious disease, it is imperative that the physician give his or her patient the proper advice about preventing the spread of the disease. Communicable diseases are so named because they are readily spread from person to person. Physicians are the first line of defense against the spread of communicable diseases, because physicians know what measures must be taken to prevent the infection of others. The patient must be advised to take certain sanitary measures, or to remain quarantined for a period of time, or to practice sexual abstinence or what is commonly referred to as 'safe sex'. Such precautions are not taken to protect the health of the patient, whose well-being has already been compromised, rather such precautions are taken to safeguard the health of others. Thus, the duty of a physician in such circumstances extends to those 'within the foreseeable orbit of risk of harm' . . . If a third person is in that class of persons whose health is likely to be threatened by the patient, and if erroneous advice is given to that patient to the ultimate detriment of the third person, the third person has a cause of action against the physician, because the physician should recognize that the services rendered to the patient are necessary for the protection of the third person.

[196] For discussion of doctors' liability toward third parties in the US, see, eg, M Kovalesky, 'To Disclose or Not to Disclose: Determining the Scope and Exercise of a Physician's Duty to Warn Third Parties of Genetically Transmittable Conditions' (2008) 76 U of Cincinnati L Rev 1019; R Mulheron, *Medical Negligence: Non-Patient and Third Party Claims* (Ashgate 2010) ch 4.

[197] eg *Bradshaw v Daniels* (1993) 854 SW 2d 865 (Tenn Sup Ct) ('Rocky Mountain Fever' transmitted by ticks). See Kennedy (1994) 2 Med L Rev 237 (Commentary).

[198] eg *Gammell v US* (1984) 727 F 2d 950 (10th Circ). See A Grubb and D Pearl, *Blood Testing, AIDS and DNA Profiling: Law and Policy* (Jordans 1990), 49–52.

[199] eg *Spina v Jack D Weiler Hospital of the Albert Einstein College of Medicine* (2006) 813 NYS (2d) 406 (App Div) (tuberculosis; no duty); *Candelario v Teperman* (2005) 789 NYS (2d) 133 (App Div) (hepatitis C; no duty); *CW v Cooper Health System* (2006) 906 A 2d 440 (NJ Sup Ct) (HIV; duty to third party sexual partner). For a more unusual case where a laboratory technician became infected with HIV while working for his employer who manufactured two strains of HIV and then infected his spouse, see: *Doe v Pharmacia & Upjohn Co, Inc* (2005) 388 Md 407 (My App Ct) (no duty to spouse).

[200] *DiMarco v Lynch Homes-Chester County* (1990) 525 Pa 558 (Pa Sup Ct).

[201] ibid, 561–62.

The majority emphasized the breadth of their decision. The duty was not owed only to married partners:[202] to so limit it would be 'exalting an unheeded morality over reality'.[203] Also, while it might be thought that in *DiMarco* the claimant was both known and identifiable to the defendants, in fact this played no part in the majority's reasoning.[204] The duty was also not so limited: it was owed to 'anyone who is physically intimate with the patient'.[205]

3.63 Unlike the situation where a patient suffers from a contagious or infectious disease,[206] in an HIV case a duty of care would not be owed to the patient's 'extended family' since they would not be at risk of infection.[207] It may, however, extend to future as well as current sexual partners who are subsequently put at risk of infection. In *Reisner v Regents of the University of California*[208] the California Court of Appeal adopted and applied this reasoning and rejected the argument that to impose a duty on the defendants would not prevent future harm. The patient received a transfusion of blood and blood products infected with HIV antibodies. Her doctor, on discovering this the following day, decided not to tell her or her family. Some years later, she commenced a sexual relationship with the claimant and, unknowingly, infected him with the HIV virus. Shortly before her death, the patient was told she had AIDS and immediately communicated this fact to the claimant, who subsequently learned of his own sero-positive status. In his action in negligence, the California Court of Appeal held that the doctor's duty of care extended to the claimant. Although not readily identifiable, the claimant, as a sexual partner of the patient, was a foreseeable victim even though the injury he complained of occurred some years after the negligent act. The defendant's duty was to warn the patient or her parents, who were likely to have warned the claimant of the risks and thereby have avoided the risk of transmission by abstaining from sexual contact or practising 'safe sex'. Vogel J said:[209]

> Civil liability for a negligent failure to warn under the circumstances of this case may not hasten the day when AIDS can be cured or prevented but it may, in the meantime, protect one or more persons from unnecessary exposure to this deadly virus.

3.64 Subsequently, the Superior Court of New Jersey (Appellate Division) emphasized that, where a duty of care is owed by the doctor to a third party, the duty is not to inform the third party of the risk of contracting the disease per se, but rather, to treat and to advise the immediate patient in a competent manner, the fulfilment of which would have amounted to a reasonable effort to protect the third party against that risk. In *CW v Cooper Health System*[210] the male patient, CW, was admitted into Cooper Hospital complaining of confusion, changes in mental status, and progressive lethargy. He was tested for HIV, and then discharged, without being informed that his HIV test was positive. Subsequently, CW commenced sexual relations with his girlfriend EY, the claimant, and a child was born. After CW and EY separated, EY tested positive for HIV, and the court accepted that she could only have contracted the disease from CW. The child tested negative for the disease. The court held that the duty of care owed by the doctors at Cooper Hospital extended to

---

202 See also *Pittman Estate v Bain* (1994) 112 DLR (4th) 257 (Ont Gen Div); additional reasons, (1994) 112 DLR (4th) 482, (1994) 112 DLR (4th) 494 and (1994) 35 CPC (3d) 767 (duty owed to wife of HIV positive patient).

203 (1990) 525 Pa 558 (Pa Sup Ct) 564 *per* Larson J.

204 ibid, 565 *per* Flaherty J (dissenting).

205 ibid, 563 *per* Larson J.

206 eg *Gammell v US* (1984) 727 F 2d 950 (10th Circ).

207 See *Lemon v Stewart* (1996) 682 A 2d 1177 (Ms Ct Spec App) (claimants were sisters, brothers, nieces, and nephews of HIV-positive patient).

208 *Reisner v Regents of the University of California* (1995) 37 Cal Rptr 2d 518.

209 ibid, 522.

210 (2006) 906 A 2d 440 (NJ Sup Ct). See also *Jarmie v Troncale* (2012) 306 Conn 578.

EY because she was within the class of reasonably foreseeable individuals whose health was likely to have been threatened by the patient's ignorance of his own health status. However, no duty was owed to the child, given that she was born without HIV, and the court rejected the claim that she was at an increased risk for becoming HIV-positive in light of her parents' condition. The Superior Court also refuted the argument (which had succeeded for the hospital at trial) that, even if the doctors had known the identity of the patient's sexual partner (which they did not), they were statutorily precluded by obligations of confidentiality[211] from advising her of CW's HIV status:

> . . . the argument misses the point. The question is not whether defendants have a duty to notify EY directly of CW's HIV test results. The duty of care to a third party such as EY requires the health care provider to take all reasonable measures to notify the patient of the results of his HIV test, and thereafter counsel the infected patient on how to avoid the transmission of the virus. Once this is done, it is up to that individual to act responsibly in his own conduct. Thus, the harm to EY flows from CW's ignorance of his own health status, not from Cooper Hospital's failure to notify EY of CW's medical condition.

(b) Psychiatric Patients Likewise, in cases of dangerous psychiatric patients, some US courts have recognized that a psychiatrist owes a duty of care to potential victims of a dangerous patient.[212] Most famously, the California Supreme Court held such a duty existed in *Tarasoff v Regents of University of California*.[213] The Supreme Court held that a psychotherapist owed a duty of care to his patient's victim (Tatiana Tarasoff, a former girlfriend of the patient) whom he knew was the patient's intended target. Tobriner J stated:[214] **3.65**

> Although . . . under the common law, as a general rule, one person owed no duty to control the conduct of another, nor to warn those endangered by such conduct, the courts have carved out an exception to this rule in cases in which the defendant stands in some special relationship to either the person whose conduct needs to be controlled or in a relationship to the foreseeable victim of that conduct.

The court balanced the public interest in maintaining the confidentiality of the defendant's client against the public interest in protecting others from assaults and concluded that the defendant had a legal duty to take reasonable steps to avert the danger by warning the victim, the police or others who might apprise her of the danger. Tobriner J said:[215] **3.66**

> In this risk-infested society we can hardly tolerate the further exposure to danger that would result from a concealed knowledge of the therapist that his patient was lethal.

In *Tarasoff*, it was important that the victim was known and identified to the defendant by his patient. In other US jurisdictions courts have interpreted *Tarasoff* in different ways. Some have interpreted it widely so as to impose a duty to warn whenever it is foreseeable that a person may be endangered.[216] On the whole, however, courts have taken a more limited view, requiring not only that the victim be foreseeable, but also that the particular victim be identifiable.[217] Some state jurisdictions have rejected the duty altogether,[218] and in some **3.67**

[211] By virtue of the AIDS Assistance Act, NHSA 26:5C-1 to -24.
[212] *Annotation*, 83 ALR 3d 1201.
[213] *Tarasoff v Regents of University of California* (1976) 551 P 2d 334 (Cal Sup Ct).
[214] ibid, 343.
[215] ibid, 347.
[216] eg *Bardoni v Kim* (1986) 390 NW 2d 218 (Mich CA) (foreseeable individual); *Lipari v Sears, Roebuck & Co* (1980) 497 F Supp 185 (DC) (foreseeable class); *Ewing v Northridge Hospital Medical Center* (2004) 120 Cal App (4th) 1289 (Cal App Ct).
[217] See, eg, *Thomson v County of Alameda* (1980) 614 P 2d 728 (Cal Sup Ct).
[218] eg *Cole v Taylor* (1981) 301 NW 2d 766 (Iowa Sup Ct); *Doe v North Central Behavorial Health Systems Inc* (2004) 352 Ill App 3d 284 (Ill App Ct).

instances, the *Tarasoff* duty has been limited or circumscribed by statute.[219] The decision continues to draw fierce academic debate in the United States.[220]

3.68 A duty on the part of a psychiatrist towards a family member of a psychotic patient was recognized in Canadian law too, in the case of *Ahmed v Stefaniu*.[221] Tragically, a brother who was diagnosed with acute psychosis murdered his sister less than two months after his psychiatrist reclassified his psychiatric status from involuntary to voluntary patient, which enabled his release into the community (where he lived with his sister and her family). At the time of the murder, the patient was described by the court as 'in a floridly psychotic, acutely delusional rage in which he believed that his sister was possessed by the devil'. The psychiatrist was liable in negligence towards the sister, although the matter of how the duty of care was to be analysed was not canvassed on appeal.

3.69 In English law too, the liability of a doctor to a third party murdered by a psychiatrically disturbed patient, has been considered, in the decision of *Palmer v Tees HA*[222]—but with the opposite result to that reached in *Tarasoff* and *Ahmed*. The claimant was the mother of a 4-year-old girl who was abducted, sexually abused, and murdered by a psychiatric patient who had been cared for over time by the defendant. The claimant suffered psychiatric injury as a result of discovering her daughter had been abducted, from what she feared had happened and from what she learned had actually happened to her daughter. She sued the defendant alleging it had negligently failed to discover the killer's propensities and to treat him or otherwise prevent him from killing her daughter. She claimed damages on her own behalf for psychiatric injury[223] and on behalf of her daughter's estate. In relation to the latter action, the court considered whether the defendant owed a duty of care to the victim.

3.70 Gage J at first instance,[224] struck out the claimant's action on the basis that no duty of care was owed. First, the judge held that there was no 'proximity' between the victim and defendant. Liability for the actions of a third party only arose if the victim was someone 'who came into a special or exceptional or distinctive category of risk from the activities of the third party'—which she did not. Second, it was not 'fair, just and reasonable' to impose a duty of care on the defendants. He relied upon a number of factors: the danger that doctors might engage in 'defensive medicine', the burden of increased claims upon the health authority and the diversion of resources that defending and dealing with such claims would entail, the limited control the defendant had over the patient, that the defendant might be required to

[219] As discussed in, eg, *Dawe v Bar-Levav* (2008) 279 Mich App 552 (Mich App Ct), with respect to the statutory provision, MCL 330.1946; *Munstermann v Alegent Health-Immanuel Medical Center* (2006) 271 Neb 834 (Neb Sup Ct), referring to Neb Rev Stat §§ 71-1,206.30(1) and 71-1,336; and *Woods v State ex rel Montana State Hospital*, 378 Mont 38, 340 P 3d 1254 (2015), referring to §27-1-1102 Annotated Montana Code.

[220] See, eg, the symposium referenced in A Hubbard, 'The Future of "The Duty to Protect": Scientific and Legal Perspectives on *Tarasoff's* Thirtieth Anniversary: Symposium Introduction' (2006) 75 U of Cincinnati L Rev 429. For English readers, the following article, also arising from the symposium, is of much interest: M Perlin, '"You Got No Secrets to Conceal": Considering the Application of the *Tarasoff* Doctrine Abroad' (2006) 75 U of Cincinnati L Rev 611.

[221] (2006), 275 DLR (4th) 101 (Ont CA); leave to appeal to Supreme Court of Canada dismissed: SCC, 5 Apr 2007.

[222] [1999] Lloyd's Rep Med 351 (CA). See further A Grubb, (1999) 7 Med L Rev 331 (Commentary).

[223] The Court of Appeal held that the claimant's action did not fall within the 'secondary victim' rule in *Alcock v Chief Constable of South Yorkshire* [1992] 1 AC 310—her psychiatric injury was not caused by the sudden appreciation through sight or sound of a horrific event. See paras 3.50 *et seq*.

[224] [1998] Lloyd's Rep Med 447 (QB).

breach the patient's confidence in order to warn others and, finally, the fact that the claimant had a claim for compensation from the Criminal Injuries Compensation Board.

The Court of Appeal dismissed the claimant's appeal. The court held that there was no 'proximity' between the defendant and the victim.[225] Stuart-Smith and Pill LJJ[226] couched their conclusion in terms of the absence of a special relationship or nexus between the defendant and the victim relying on the earlier House of Lords cases of *Home Office v Dorset Yacht* [227] and *Hill v Chief Constable of West Yorkshire*.[228] **3.71**

Stuart-Smith LJ specifically referred to a distinction drawn in *Dorset Yacht* between the assailant who *escapes* from detention and causes harm and the one who is simply *released* or *not caught and detained*—the contrast between the facts of *Dorset Yacht* and *Hill*. What, if anything, is the difference between these situations? One might be that where the patient escapes the defendant's negligence creates a risk of injury (or death) to others. By contrast, where the defendant merely fails to catch or detain an individual in the community, no special risk is created. The former may more readily engage the court's sense of corrective justice that as between the claimant and the defendant, the defendant *ought* to bear responsibility for the harm. However, the same reasoning would seem to be applicable to the patient who is negligently released or allowed out on 'leave'. It is not clear that the judges in *Palmer* would have taken a different view if the psychiatric patient had been detained under the Mental Health Act 1983 and had been negligently released. The earlier decision in *Holgate v Lancashire Mental Hospital Board* [229] was just such a case. Both Stuart-Smith and Pill LJJ considered *Holgate* to be wrongly decided.[230] It may be, however, that the time and geographical gap between release and the harm occurring in that case was significant.[231] Likewise, in *Palmer*, the patient had been released a year before he killed the child and Pill LJ, in particular, noted as important 'the passage of time and distance between [the psychiatric patient's] release and [the child's] murder'.[232] **3.72**

What, then, was the significant factor in *Palmer*? What if the victim had been known to the defendant or could reasonably be identified from the psychiatric patient's threats? Pill LJ, while not wholly persuaded of the point, concluded that *an* important aspect would be whether the victim was known to the defendant. He was not persuaded, however, that there should necessarily be a different legal result where the threat was 'I will kill X' and where it was 'I will kill the first bald-headed man I meet'.[233] Although, he acknowledged that it would be relevant 'to the extent of the duty and the measures necessary to discharge it'.[234] Stuart-Smith LJ also considered that an 'identifiable' victim might satisfy the 'proximity' test.[235] The victim in *Palmer*, of course, was neither identified nor identifiable. She was **3.73**

---

225 The Court of Appeal did not rely on the 'just, fair and reasonable' limb of the *Caparo* test because of the (then) prevailing view that this was prohibited at the striking out stage by the ECtHR's decision in *Osman v UK* (1998) 29 EHRR 245: *Barrett v Enfield LBC* [1999] 3 WLR 79. But see now *Z v UK* (2002) 34 EHRR 3 (ECtHR).

226 Thorpe LJ agreed with Stuart-Smith LJ's judgment.

227 [1970] AC 1004 (HL).

228 [1989] AC 53 (HL).

229 [1937] 4 All ER 19.

230 [1999] Lloyd's Rep Med 351 (CA), 359 and 363 respectively.

231 Contrast *Dorset Yacht* [1970] AC 53 (HL) with *Martin v Smith and Home Office* (1981) 131 NLJ 1028.

232 [1999] Lloyd's Rep Med 351 (CA) 363.

233 ibid.

234 ibid.

235 He left open whether an assumption of responsibility or undertaking towards the victim would also be necessary: [1999] Lloyd's Rep Med 351 (CA), 359.

merely a member of a section of the public, as in *Hill*, which was at risk from the psychiatric patient.

3.74 Subsequent to *Palmer*, the Scottish Outer House considered a somewhat similar tragedy in *Thomson (AP) v Scottish Ministers*.[236] Ann Thomson (AT) was the mother of Catherine Thomson (CT), who was murdered by John Campbell, at AT's house in Moodiesburn, while Mr Campbell was on a short period of 'home leave' from prison. Shortly after his arrest for the murder of CT, Mr Campbell committed suicide. CT had been a friend of the Campbell family—she had known Mr Campbell since childhood, had been his brother's girlfriend for five years, and knew his mother well too. AT argued that CT was within that group of persons that Mr Campbell was likely to 'have dealings with' during his weekend leave, given her close associations with his family, should Mr Campbell become violent during his home release. However, the prisons service did not owe the deceased a duty of care. CT was not at special risk. The Scottish Inner House was at pains to distinguish that other leading prisons case of *Dorset Yacht*, noting that it was from another era, and that 'the law has moved on' since that 1970 decision; that *Dorset Yacht* was a product of the wider 'foreseeability + no public policy reasons' test of *Anns v Merton London BC*;[237] and that it may be that the decision is limited to those persons 'having property in physical proximity to the place where the prisoners were confined'. Importantly, neither of the victims in *Hill* or in *Palmer* knew their attackers; Catherine Thomson did, yet that was not sufficient to fix proximity either, as she was treated as being a member of the general public.

3.75 Hence, it would not be a fair representation of the judgments in *Palmer* to see this issue—'was the victim identified or identifiable?'—as, itself, being a *sufficient* condition for liability. It was, arguably, only seen as a *necessary* condition at least by Stuart-Smith LJ who, in his judgment, set out a number of other important factors militating against a duty of care—the inability to warn the victim or of the authorities to provide protection and the limited powers of control that the defendant had over the patient.[238] It is difficult to see why difficulties over warning an unidentified victim should a priori exclude a duty of care. Warning the victim is only one method by which the duty could be discharged. It may not be the only, or best, one. Why not warn the police? This was, of course, what happened in the US case of *Tarasoff* discussed earlier. Further, the difficulties of involving the compulsory powers of detention may also have been overstated.

3.76 After *Palmer*, there remained a sneaking suspicion that a court would, if the facts were to present themselves, agree with Gage J that liability would arise if 'there existed some distinctive feature or characteristic which demonstrated that [the victim] was at some special risk'.[239] This became manifest in the case of *Selwood v Durham County Council*.[240] Claire Selwood, a senior social worker employed by the Durham CC in their Children in Need team, was the designated social worker for a daughter of Graham Burton, in family proceedings relating to Mr Burton's children. The Tees, Esk and Wear Valley NHS Trust operated a Crisis Resolution Team, staffed by health workers and social workers employed by both. They jointly signed a protocol, 'Working together in the delivery of services to adults and children'. The NHS Trust operated a mental health ward at Cherry Knowle Hospital, to which Mr Burton was admitted as a voluntary patient. During his stay, Mr Burton said that he was 'not pleased' with one of the social workers—the 'nastiest one'—but he did not name

236 [2013] CSIH 63.
237 [1978] AC 728 (HL) 751.
238 [1999] Lloyd's Rep Med 351 (CA), 359.
239 [1998] Lloyd's Rep Med 447 (QB), 461.
240 [2012] EWCA Civ 979.

Ms Selwood specifically. For a case review to be held at the hospital, the managing psychiatrist asked Mr Burton whether Ms Selwood could attend that meeting, but he refused, saying that he would 'kill her on the spot' if he saw her. None of these threats were passed on to Ms Selwood or to her employer, the Durham County Council. Ms Selwood attended the case review, where Mr Burton attacked her, causing very serious injuries (for which he was sentenced to life imprisonment for attempted murder). It was held that the NHS Trust owed Ms Selwood a duty of care. The Court of Appeal was not prepared to hold that Ms Selwood was a member of the general public per se: she 'was not one of the world at large; she was one of a small group of social workers, working in close proximity and cooperation' with both local authority and health authority (plus she was the one who was the subject of Mr Burton's threats, and hence, was in a 'special position'). That also pointed (said the Court of Appeal) to an assumption of responsibility on the NHS Trust's part towards Ms Selwood, because it had, via the joint protocol, assumed responsibility to do what was reasonable to reduce or avoid any foreseeable risk of harm to which an employee of those co-signatories was exposed, in the course of dealing with patients of the Crisis Resolution Team (such as Mr Burton).[241]

Separately from the common law position in negligence, where the claimant (third party's) life is at risk, then in *Osman*,[242] the European Court of Human Rights held that Article 2 of the ECHR will require state authorities to take *positive* action where: **3.77**

> [they] knew or ought to have known at the time of the existence of a real and immediate risk to the life of an identified individual or individuals from the criminal acts of a third party.

The European Court of Human Rights concluded that there had been no violation of Article 2, because there had not been 'any decisive stage in the sequence of the events leading up to the tragic shooting when it could be said that the police knew or ought to have known that the lives of the Osman family were at real and immediate risk'.[243] In *Selwood*, however, the Court of Appeal was prepared to hold that Ms Selwood could conceivably prove, at trial, that she was at real and immediate risk of a serious attack, and hence, the Article 2 claim was permitted to succeed.[244]

Although *Osman* concerned the obligations of the police, *Selwood* illustrates that other state bodies, such as NHS Trusts, also prima facie have the same general obligation.[245] The state's obligation is to do 'all that could be reasonably expected' to avoid the risk. And, of course, the extent of the obligation may depend upon whom the obligation is placed, for example, because the powers and role in society of the police and NHS institutions are different. Nevertheless, arguably the latter could quite reasonably provide warnings or, if necessary, invoke their own powers of detention where the risk presented itself. **3.78**

241 ibid, [54] (Dame Janet Smith).

242 *Osman v United Kingdom* (1998) 29 EHRR [116].

243 See also *Van Colle v Chief Constable of the Hertfordshire Police; Smith v Chief Constable of Sussex Police* [2008] UKHL 50 (no violation of the positive obligation on part of police services under Art 2 to prevent murder of a witness prior to a criminal trial).

244 [2012] EWCA Civ 979, [58].

245 For discussion of different aspects of Art 2 obligations of health authorities and their staff to protect life, see, eg, *Savage v South Essex Partnership NHS Foundation Trust* [2008] UKHL 74 (patient absconded from mental hospital and committed suicide); *Rabone v Pennine Care NHS Trust* [2009] EWHC 1827 QB, aff'd [2010] EWCA Civ 698 (patient released from mental hospital and committed suicide); and *Powell v United Kingdom* (2000) 30 EHRR CD 362 (where a patient dies in a NHS hospital, something more will be required to establish a breach of the Art 2(1) positive obligation to protect life than, simply, a failure on the part of the hospital to meet the standard of care of the patient required by the common law duty of care).

3.79 (c) **Dangerous drivers** A patient may be a danger to others because of his medical condition, for example, if he were to drive a car or other vehicle. To date, no English cases have arisen for consideration. However, in a number of US and Canadian cases, courts have held doctors liable to passengers and other road users who have been injured when a patient lost control of a car or other vehicle when he was physically unfit to drive (by reason of affected vision from wearing an eyepatch[246] or from suffering from a debilitating physical condition[247]). Cases have also concerned driver patients who caused personal injuries to third parties by reason of suffering, for example, an epileptic fit,[248] a diabetic attack,[249] or incapacity to drive brought on by medication prescribed by the doctor.[250] The use of a certain medical procedure or treatment which affects a patient's ability to safely drive immediately after the treatment has also been at issue.[251] Liability has been imposed in three sorts of situations: where the doctor (i) created the 'dangerous' condition, for example, by prescribing drugs;[252] (ii) was aware of the patient's physical condition;[253] and (iii) affirmatively advised the patient that it was safe to drive.[254]

3.80 In those cases in which a duty of care has been imposed toward a third party, the negligence consists, not of failing to warn the third party, but of failing to warn *the patient* of his dangerous condition.[255] Where it has been suggested that the doctor should control the patient by stopping him driving, the courts have been reluctant to impose this onerous (and legally impossible) obligation.[256] The duty is generally held to be owed to all foreseeable road users even though the injured person's precise identity is not known.[257] However, some courts have adopted a more restrictive approach derived, by analogy, from the 'dangerous psychiatric patient' cases such as *Tarasoff*. Consequently, courts have refused to impose a duty of care unless the third party is 'known and identifiable'[258] or where there is a 'special relationship' between the doctor and the patient whereby the doctor has control over the patient.[259] In

246 *Joy v Eastern Main Medical Center* (1987) 529 A 2d 1364 (Me Sup Ct) (failure to warn not to drive wearing an eye-patch); *Bakker v Van Santen* [2003] ABQB 804 (another eyepatch case, in which the possibility of a duty of care was left open).

247 *Toms v Foster* 1994 Ont CA Lexis 346 (driver suffering from cervical spondylosis).

248 eg *Spillane v Wasserman* (1992) 13 CCLT 267 (Ont H Ct).

249 eg *Myers v Quesenberry* (1983) 193 Cal Rptr 733 (Cal CA).

250 *Taylor v Smith* (2004) 892 So 2d 887 (Ala Sup Ct) (outpatient at drug rehabilitation center was administered methadone during programme, when tests during programme indicated that she continued to ingest marijuana and benzodiazepines).

251 *Hardee v Bio-Medical Applications of South Carolina Inc* (2006) 636 SE 2d 629 (SC Sup Ct) (car accident where diabetic patient had undergone almost four hours of dialysis treatment).

252 eg *Gooden v Tips* (1983) 651 SW 2d 364 (Tex CA); *Kaiser v Suburban Transportation System* (1965) 398 P 2d 14 (Wash Sup Ct); *Schuster v Altenberg* (1988) 424 NW 2d 159 (Wis Sup Ct). Cf *Jarmie v Troncale*, 306 Conn 578 (2012).

253 eg *Myers v Quesenberry* (1983) 193 Cal Rptr 733 (Cal CA); *Freese v Lemmon* (1973) 210 NW 2d 576 (Iowa Sup Ct), subsequently, following trial, held no negligence: (1978) 267 NW 2d 680.

254 eg *Freese v Lemmon*, n 253.

255 See *Myers v Quesenberry* (1983) 193 Cal Rptr 733 (Cal CA).

256 eg *Purdy v Estate of Shaw* (1987) 514 NYS 2d 407 (NY App Div) (no duty on health facility to restrain licensed driver).

257 See *Myers v Quesenberry* (1983) 193 Cal Rptr 733 (Cal CA). See also *Duvall v Goldin* (1984) 362 NW 2d 275 (Mich CA); *Freese v Lemmon* (1973) 210 NW 2d 576 (Iowa Sup Ct); *Gooden v Tips* (1983) 651 SW 2d 364 (Tex CA).

258 See *Werner v Varner, Stafford & Seaman* (1995) 659 So 2d 1308 (Fla CA) (duty not owed to public at large); applying *Pate v Threlkel* (1995) 661 So 2d 278 (Fla Sup Ct) (duty to children of patient in respect of the patient's inheritable genetic condition), and see para 3.89.

259 See *Caldwell v Hassan* (1996) 925 P 2d 422 (Kan Sup Ct) (failure to warn patient who suffered from daytime sleep disorder not to drive). The court left open whether liability might exist if the doctor 'created a risk of harm' to the claimant (at 431) but, on the facts, there was no evidence that the medication prescribed by the doctor 'caused or worsened [the patient's] daytime drowsiness problem' (ibid).

context, the latter approach virtually eliminates claims against doctors by injured passengers or other road users. Other courts have also had regard to policy factors in denying a duty of care towards third parties, where 'the benefit of warning an epileptic not to drive is incremental but that the consequences of imposing a duty are great',[260] or that extending physician liability to members of the general public would 'lead to increased litigation and higher health care costs.'[261]

(d) **Genetic conditions** Analogous to the situations of the infectious or dangerous psychiatric patient are those where the patient is not strictly speaking 'dangerous' but, because of information gained during the course of the doctor–patient relationship, the doctor knows that harm may come to another. An illustration of this occurs where the doctor discovers genetic information about his patient which has relevance to the genetic health of members of the patient's family. The increasing potential for determining a patient's genetic 'make-up' will, undoubtedly, increase the incidence of such cases in the future. Although commentators have variously supported the notion that such a duty could be found in English law,[262] recent English authority has held to the contrary. **3.81**

In *ABC v St George's Healthcare NHS Trust*,[263] ABC's father was diagnosed with Huntington's Disease in 2009, which is genetic in origin, and which a child has a 50 per cent chance of inheriting if one of her parents has the disease. At the time of the diagnosis, ABC was in fact pregnant. Additionally, ABC's father was subject to hospital and restriction orders, having killed his wife and been convicted of manslaughter a couple of years prior to this diagnosis. He refused to allow the defendant medical authorities to inform ABC or his other daughter out of concern for their welfare. Although the defendant medical authorities questioned the wisdom of that decision, the wish for confidentiality expressed by their patient was respected. However, in 2010, the information about her father's medical condition was accidentally disclosed to ABC by one of his doctors, and a subsequent test confirmed that ABC also had the disease. ABC claimed that she would have terminated the pregnancy, had she known of her father's diagnosis, and that various economic and psychiatric consequences had followed from the defendant's failure to inform ABC of the genetic condition to which she was at risk. Nicol J struck out the claim as disclosing no reasonable cause of action. There was no duty of care imposed upon the defendants to inform ABC directly of information about her father's genetic condition that would have enabled her to test herself and terminate her pregnancy. To impose a duty towards a non-patient in this way would (said Nicol J) be a 'giant step' from established authority: **3.82**

> this is not a case where the Claimant can show that a novel duty of care would be but an incremental development from some well established duty. It would, on the contrary, be a radical departure to impose liability in circumstances such as these.[264]

Any alternative claim in negligence, that the defendants failed to counsel and advise the father to persuade him that his daughters should be told, was not helpful to ABC's case either, as it was not alleged that, had her father received such counseling, he would have

[260] *Praesel v Johnson* (1998) 967 SW 2d 391, 398.
[261] *Jarmie v Troncale* (2012) 306 Conn 578, 599.
[262] R Gilbar, 'Medical Confidentiality with the Family: The Doctor's Duty Reconsidered' (2004) 18 Intl J of Law, Policy and the Family 195; M Brazier, 'Do No Harm: Do Patients have Responsibilities Too?' (2006) 65 CLJ 397; R Mulheron, *Medical Negligence: Non-Patient and Third Party Claims* (Ashgate Publishing 2010) ch 4.
[263] [2015] EWHC 1394 (QB). The case is under appeal at the time of writing, with the appeal due to be heard in March 2017.
[264] ibid, [27]. This outcome has been followed more recently, in a case involving the genetic transmission of adrenomyeloneuropathy (AMN), in *Smith v University of Leicester NHS Trust* [2016] EWHC 817 (QB).

either told ABC directly, or permitted the defendants to do so. Hence, in the absence of any consent from the patient himself, there was no overriding duty of care imposed on the medical defendants to inform the non-patient of the genetic condition.

3.83 However, in two US decisions, courts have held that a doctor owed a duty of care to the children of a patient whom he discovered had a serious inheritable genetic condition.[265] In *Pate v Threlkel*[266] the defendant treated his patient for thyroid cancer which was genetically inheritable. Three years later, the patient's adult daughter discovered that she suffered from the same condition which was, by this time, incurable. She claimed that if her father had been told, she would have been tested and taken preventative steps which would, more likely than not, have resulted in a cure. The Florida Supreme Court held that a doctor could owe a duty of care to someone who was not his patient. The court concluded that a doctor owed a duty only to 'known' and 'identifiable' individuals who were at risk.[267] Thus, he owed the patient's daughter a duty to warn the patient of the danger of his children inheriting the condition. Further, the court held that the doctor's duty was to warn the patient and not to breach the confidentiality of the patient by directly warning the child. Wells J stated:

> ... the patient ordinarily can be expected to pass on the warning. To require the physician to seek out and warn various members of the patient's family would often be difficult or impractical and would place too heavy a burden upon the physician. Thus, we emphasise that in any circumstances in which the physician has a duty to warn of a genetically transferable disease, that duty will be satisfied by warning the patient.[268]

3.84 The reasoning of the Florida Supreme Court is, however, of limited importance in England. First, the court applied a test for determining a duty of care based, in essence, upon 'foreseeability of risk'.[269] English law would require more to establish a duty of care in this context applying the three-stage test in the *Caparo* case. Secondly, the court relied heavily upon the expert evidence that it was a doctor's professional obligation to warn of the dangers of inheriting the condition.[270] While this may be some evidence supporting the imposition of a legal duty of care, English law would not necessarily adopt the professional standard.[271]

3.85 In the second US case, *Safer v Pack*,[272] a New Jersey appellate court also imposed a duty of care in the context of genetic disease. The defendant treated his patient for a genetically related form of colon cancer from which the patient eventually died. At the time the claimant was aged 10, and 26 years later she was diagnosed as suffering from the same condition. The claimant alleged that the defendant knew of the inheritable nature of the condition and should have warned those at risk so that they might take early preventative measures. The New Jersey court held that the doctor did owe a duty of care to the claimant. Relying on cases concerned with the transmission of infectious disease and physical threats by dangerous patients,[273] the

[265] For discussion of US developments in this area, see, eg, M Kovalesky, 'To Disclose or Not to Disclose: Determining the Scope and Exercise of a Physician's Duty to Warn Third Parties of Genetically Transmittable Conditions' (2008) 76 U of Cincinnati L Rev 1019; S Denbo, 'What Your Genes Know Affects Them: Should Patient Confidentiality Prevent Disclosure of Genetic Test Results to a Patient's Biological Relatives?' (2006) American Business LJ 561.

[266] (1995) 661 So 2d 278 (Fla Sup Ct).

[267] Relying on an 'infectious disease' case: *Hofmann v Blackmon* (1970) 241 So 2d 752 (Fla CA).

[268] *Pate v Threlkel* (1995) 661 So 2d 278 (Fla Sup Ct), 282.

[269] ibid, 280.

[270] ibid, 281 and 282.

[271] But contrast *Baker v Kaye* [1997] IRLR 219 (QB).

[272] (1996) 677 A 2d 1188 (Super Ct App Div).

[273] *McIntosh v Milano* (1979) 403 A 2d 500; *Tarasoff v Regents of University of California* (1976) 551 P 2d 334.

court held that the duty was owed to all 'members of the immediate family of the patient who may be adversely affected'.[274] Kesten J stated[275] that '[t]he individual or group at risk is easily identified, and substantial future harm may be averted or minimized by a timely and effective warning'. The court accepted that the limited duty to warn of an avertible risk those defined by familial connection was 'sufficiently narrow to serve the interests of justice'.[276]

As for the content of the duty, the court concluded that the duty 'require[d] that reasonable steps be taken to assure that the information reaches those likely to be affected or is made available for their benefit'.[277] This, the court contemplated, might be satisfied by warning the patient in a case like *Safer* where the third party was a young child when the genetic condition was discovered. However, unlike the court in *Pate v Threlkel*, the New Jersey court refused to rule out the possibility that the duty might entail an obligation to warn the family member *directly*. Kestin J said:[278] **3.86**

> It may be necessary, at some stage, to resolve a conflict between the physician's broader duty to warn and his fidelity to an expressed preference of the patient that nothing be said to family members about the details of the disease.

For this reason, it has since been said that *Safer* goes much further than did *Pate v Trelkel*, in that *Safer* implemented the notion of the 'genetic family', to whom a doctor owes a duty to warn of genetically transmissible diseases.[279]

(e) **Analytical structure for dangerous patient claims** Where a doctor is charged with negligence causing personal injuries to third parties in the wide variety of scenarios considered in the preceding paragraphs, the analytical structure of English law is clear: it is the 'three-stage' test propounded by the House of Lords in *Caparo Industries plc v Dickman*.[280] For the doctor to owe the third party a duty of care there must be '*foreseeability*' and '*proximity*' of relationship, and the imposition of a duty must be '*fair, just, and reasonable*'.[281] In this context 'foreseeability' of injury is unlikely to be a problem, the real 'battle ground' will be 'proximity' and the policy issues under the third limb. It is probably unduly narrow to see these requirements as wholly distinct and hermetically sealed from each other because particular factors may well influence a court in reaching a view on both requirements. Indeed, in *JD v East Berkshire Community Health NHS Trust*, Lord Bingham opined that questions of proximity and public policy 'cannot be divorced'.[282] Furthermore, English law will develop incrementally by analogy to existing situations of recognized liability. Notwithstanding the successful application by the injured claimant in *Selwood v Durham CC* (a marked contrast **3.87**

[274] *Safer v Pack* (1996) 677 A 2d 1188, 1192 (Super Ct App Div), citing *Schroeder v Perkel* (1981) 87 NJ 53, 65.
[275] ibid, 1192.
[276] ibid, 1192 *per* Kestin J.
[277] ibid, 1192.
[278] ibid, 1192.
[279] J Dolgin, 'The Evolution of the "Patient": Shifts in Attitudes about Consent, Genetic Information, and Commercialization in Health Care' (2005) 34 Hofstra L Rev 137. Notably, in neither case was the family member a 'patient' of the physician's, which can be important when considering the application of state medical malpractice schemes: *Atkinson v Lammico Ins Co*, 63 So 3d 1176 (La App, 2011).
[280] *Caparo Industries plc v Dickman* [1990] 2 AC 605; [1990] 1 All ER 568 (HL), reiterated in, eg, *Customs & Excise Commissioners v Barclays Bank plc* [2006] UKHL 28, [2007] 1 AC 181 (HL), [4] *per* Lord Bingham, and confirmed in *Van Colle v Chief Constable of the Hertfordshire Police; Smith v Chief Constable of Sussex Police* [2008] UKHL 50 as 'currently ... the most favoured test of liability' ([42] *per* Lord Bingham again).
[281] See especially *Caparo*, n 280, *per* Lord Bridge at 574 and *per* Lord Oliver at 585.
[282] [2005] UKHL 23, [20].

from the outcome, and the facts, in *Palmer v Tees HA*), there are, however, a number of formidable difficulties in the way of a claimant establishing such a claim.

3.88 **(f) Omissions and third parties** First, the third party's claim will often be that the doctor *failed* to protect him by, for example, warning him or another of the danger. English law is generally reluctant to impose a duty of care where the defendant is alleged to have failed to act to protect others (ie, for a pure omission).[283] English law does not impose a duty to prevent a person from being harmed by the criminal act of a third party, based simply upon foreseeability of harm to that third party.[284] Moreover, an inability on the doctor's part to convey any effective warning to third parties will militate against a duty of care being owed. As was noted in *Palmer v Tees HA*, the doctors treating the psychotic patient in that case had no ability to warn the mother and murdered child of the dangers posed by the patient: 'the most effective precaution cannot be undertaken as the defendant does not know who to warn.'[285] In *ABC v St George's Healthcare NHS Trust*,[286] Nicol J classified the medical defendants' failure to inform ABC of her father's genetic condition as a pure omission, arising in circumstances where there was no 'special relationship' or any assumption of responsibility towards ABC as family member (daughter).

3.89 Secondly, the claimant may be relying on the doctor's failure to prevent an intermediary voluntarily and intentionally injuring the third party.[287] Generally, this person alone is viewed as responsible for the claimant's injuries.[288] A duty may exist, however, if the defendant could (and should) have controlled that intermediary who was the direct cause of the claimant's harm.[289] This is unlikely unless, for example, the patient is a psychiatric patient who has been detained under the Mental Health Act 1983 and is prematurely released, or should have been but the doctor fails to instigate the procedure for detention under the Act. Another illustration could arise in the area of infectious diseases, but only where the provisions of the Public Health (Control of Diseases) Act 1984 allow for detention.[290] In one case, a hospital[291] was held liable where it released a dangerous patient who assaulted and injured the claimant, having broken into her home.[292] However, the authority of this case is somewhat limited: it was a summing up to a jury and the judge assumed a duty of care arose and was more concerned with the issue of breach. Liability may be restricted to injuries caused to others themselves within the control of the defendant[293] or where, once

[283] See *Smith v Littlewoods Organisation Ltd* [1987] 1 AC 241 (HL); *Mitchell v Glasgow County Council* [2009] UKHL 11.

[284] *Michael v Chief Constable of South Wales Police* [2015] UKSC 2, [2015] 2 WLR 343, para 38; *Van Colle v Chief Constable of Hertfordshire Police; Smith v Chief Constable of Sussex Police* [2008] 3 All ER 977 (HL).

[285] [1999] Lloyd's Rep Med 351 (CA) para 32.

[286] [2015] EWHC 1394 (QB) para 28.

[287] As in the 'dangerous patient' or 'driver' cases or 'infectious disease' cases. Not, however, in the 'genetic' transmission cases.

[288] *Smith v Littlewoods Organisation Ltd* [1987] 1 AC 241 (HL).

[289] *Home Office v Dorset Yacht* [1970] AC 1004, [1970] 2 All ER 294 (HL).

[290] For the set of regulations which complement the 1984 Act, see: the Health Protection (Local Authority Powers) Regulations 2010, SI 657/2010; the Health Protection (Part 2A Orders) Regulations 2010, SI 658/2010; and the Health Protection (Notification) Regulations 2010, SI 659/2010.

[291] The duty is probably that of the institution rather than any particular doctor.

[292] *Holgate v Lancashire Mental Hospitals Board* [1937] 4 All ER 19.

[293] See *Ellis v Home Office* [1953] 2 QB 135 (CA) (injury caused by one prisoner to another). The same reasoning would apply if the injured party was a visitor or, indeed, himself injured: see, eg, *Hay v Grampian Health Board* [1995] 6 Med L Rev 128 (CSOH) and A Grubb, (1995) 3 Med L Rev 299 (Commentary).

escaped, the 'dangerous patient' injures those in close vicinity during his escape.[294] It may, therefore, not be followed in the future.[295]

(g) Increased risk of injury Thirdly, the courts are unwilling to shoulder a doctor with the burden of liability where he has not made the claimant's position worse and they may well insist that he has *increased the risk* of the intermediary harming the claimant.[296] Hence, a doctor who, for example, creates a risk of 'injury' by infecting a patient with HIV[297] could be liable whilst one who merely failed to avert the risk by warning of the danger will not.[298] Ultimately, of course, this is an unsatisfactory distinction. Being the agent of the risk creation is only one indicium of culpability—it increases the moral turpitude of the individual—but there are others. Furthermore, it will inevitably lead to fine distinctions being drawn in cases as to which particular category any given set of facts falls into,[299] but it seems to appeal to the English judiciary as encapsulating a necessary condition for culpability. **3.90**

(h) Identifiable victims Fourthly, liability would not be based upon foreseeability of injury to another alone; certainly if all that is foreseeable is injury to others in general. Even if all the other requirements for liability were in place, English law would seek to limit the range of liability by closely circumscribing the breadth of liability through other control mechanisms.[300] At the very least, foreseeability of harm to a particular person or perhaps a small identifiable group is likely to be essential,[301] although even that may not be sufficient to impose liability.[302] The point was important in *Selwood v Durham County Council*,[303] where the attacked claimant was one of a small group of social workers who was working in close proximity with the council's employees, and was an employee of a co-signatory (and hence, somewhat similar to a 'quasi-employee'), given the joint protocol signed between council and medical defendants. **3.91**

Moreover, by analogy with those cases involving local authorities[304] and police services,[305] not every claimed risk to a third party's life (at the hands of a patient) could require a health authority, under Article 2 of the Convention, to take operational measures to prevent that **3.92**

[294] As in *Home Office v Dorset Yacht* [1970] AC 1004 (HL) itself. Contrast *Marti v Smith and Home Office* (1981) 131 NLJ 1028.

[295] In *Dorset Yacht*, Lord Diplock reserved his opinion on its correctness (at 328) explaining it as a case involving a person not responsible for his actions; Lord Reid appears to have considered it correct as a matter of private law (but doubted the public law issue raised, at 301–02); Lord Morris considered it correct (at 309).

[296] eg *Hill v Chief Constable of West Yorkshire* [1989] AC 53 (HL), explaining Dorset Yacht.

[297] *Reisner v Regents of the University of California* (1995) 37 Cal Rptr 2d 518 (Cal CA).

[298] *Goodwill v BPAS* [1996] 2 All ER 161 (CA).

[299] Hence, a doctor who prescribes a medication to a patient 'creates' a risk to other road users whilst a doctor who only fails to diagnose or inform a patient of an existing condition does not: see its acceptance in *Calwell v Hassan* (1996) 925 P 2d 422 (Kan Sup Ct). The satisfactory nature of this distinction is questionable.

[300] *Dorset Yacht* [1970] AC 1004 (HL); *Hill v Chief Constable of West Yorkshire* [1989] 1 AC 53 (HL); *Caparo Industries plc v Dickman* [1990] 2 AC 605 (HL); *Selwood v Durham County Council* [2012] EWCA Civ 979.

[301] See, eg, *Osman v Ferguson* [1993] 4 All ER 344 (CA), where it was accepted by two judges in the Court of Appeal that there was proximity between the police and a specific individual who was known to them to be at risk: see McCowan LJ at 350; Simon Brown LJ agreed; Beldam LJ at 354 expressing no view.

[302] *Michael v Chief Constable of South Wales Police* [2015] UKSC 2; *Mitchell v Glasgow CC* [2009] UKHL 11.

[303] [2012] EWCA Civ 979.

[304] *Mitchell v Glasgow CC* [2009] UKHL 11.

[305] *Osman v United Kingdom* (1998) 29 EHRR. *Van Colle v Chief Constable of the Hertfordshire Police; Smith v Chief Constable of Sussex Police* [2008] UKHL 500.

risk to the third party from materializing. It would have to be proven that the health authority knew, or ought to have known at the time, of the existence of a real and immediate risk to the life of an identified individual or individuals from the criminal acts of a third party, and that it failed to take measures within the scope of its powers which, judged reasonably, might have been expected to avoid that risk.[306]

3.93 (i) **Conflicts of interest** Fifthly, a doctor's duty to his patient does not permit him to place a third party's interests above those of his patient. Any conflict of duties (actual or potential) will preclude a duty to the third party. In *ABC v St George's Healthcare NHS Trust*,[307] reference was made to the potential for conflicting duties owed by doctors to patients and to non-patient claimants (in that case, if a duty were upheld, then doctors could be sued by their patient if they disclosed information which should have remained confidential, but otherwise could be sued by the aggrieved family member if they failed to disclose information which they should have revealed.) On the other hand, if what is required of the doctor to discharge his duty to the patient would *also* discharge any duty to the third party, then the duties are coincident and aligned, and no conflict arises. That result is more likely if the scope of the doctor's duty is read down, such that, for example, the doctor only has a duty to advise an HIV-positive patient to convey the relevant information and warning about HIV infection to a sexual partner, and not a separate and independent duty to inform the sexual partner of the patient's illness. If the duty to the patient, and the duty to the partner's sexual partner, can be discharged by the diagnosis and provision of proper advice to the patient, then the duties are *aligned*. Notably, the English Court of Appeal was invited to follow a similar line of reasoning in *Palmer v Tees HA*,[308] but declined. Mrs Palmer had argued that the duty imposed on the defendant health authority and hospital was, not to warn her and her child per se, but to provide adequate treatment for the psychotic patient to reduce the risk of his killing a child, and/or to stop him from being released from hospital whilst he posed a risk. It was argued that this duty *coincided* with the duty to mother and child to prevent a mentally ill person in the patient's position from injuring those who lived in close proximity with him. However, the submission failed, and no such duty was owed.

3.94 (j) **Lack of Temporal Proximity** Sixthly, if there has been a considerable time-lag between the alleged wrongdoing of the doctor and the harm caused to a third party by the patient's actions, this may discourage the finding of a sufficient proximity between doctor and third party. The factor figured in *Palmer*, where the murder of the claimant child occurred just over a year from the patient's release. Pill LJ observed that 'the passage of time and distance' between the two events contributed toward the finding of no duty of care. Similarly, in *Goodwill v British Pregnancy Advisory Service*,[309] where the third party (sexual partner) formed a relationship with the patient over three years after the sterilization operation was negligently performed, there was a lack of temporal proximity between the surgeon and the third party. In the words of Thorpe LJ: 'a doctor is entitled to scorn the suggestion that he owes a duty of care to such a band so uncertain in nature and extent and over such an indefinite future span.'[310]

3.95 (k) **Policy and confidentiality** Finally, the courts will investigate the policy arguments that might tell against imposing liability upon the defendant, such as the burdens it would

[306] The Art 2 claim was not struck out in *Selwood*, n 300.
[307] [2015] EWHC 1394 (QB), para 26.
[308] [1999] Lloyd's Rep Med 351 (CA). The submission also failed to gain any support in *ABC v St George's Healthcare NHS Trust*, n 307.
[309] (1996) 31 BMLR 83 (CA).
[310] ibid, 92.

create, the inconveniences that would be generated, and any deleterious effects such a duty might have upon the medical profession. In particular, the courts will be reluctant to impose a duty upon a doctor which requires him to disclose information in breach of confidence. This may not be crucial where the duty only contemplates disclosure to the patient rather than to the third party (or another). Hence, in the *Reisner* case, no breach of confidence was contemplated.[311] In that case, the doctor only has a duty to tell his patient in order for her to act responsibly by desisting from risky behaviour or warning her partners of the risk they might be running. Where a breach of confidence is contemplated (even one which could be justified), however, the preferred position, in negligence law, is to acknowledge that there are exceptional circumstances in which confidentiality may be breached because of danger to others, but not to impose a duty by law.[312] As Nicol J put it in *St George's Healthcare NHS Trust*,[313] the 'starting point' is that medical defendants are obliged to respect a patient's confidential information, albeit that this is 'a qualified duty'. In other words, the law should only provide a justification for a breach of confidence. A permissive approach to disclosure is put forward, for example, by the relevant NHS Code of Practice.[314] Interestingly, however, the ethical guidance issued by the General Medical Council in respect of patients with conditions that could expose a third party to the risk of death or serious harm, in the event that the patient does not disclose or give consent for disclosure to the third party himself, appears to have shifted ground in recent years, from permissive language[315] to more mandatory language (ie, where the safety of others is at risk, then 'you should disclose information promptly to an appropriate person or authority').[316] Similar types of instruction as to what the doctor 'should' do (ie, disclose relevant medical information about the patient to the relevant medical officer), in the event that a patient is medically unfit to drive, and reasonable efforts to persuade him to stop driving have not met with success, are provided by the Driver and Vehicle Licensing Agency.[317]

(ii) For financial loss

A doctor's treatment of, or advice to, a patient may cause financial damage to a third party (where that damage is not consequential upon any physical injury to the third party). For claims of pure economic loss of this type, it may be difficult for the third party to prove that any duty of care to avoid such loss was owed by the doctor, because of a lack of legal proximity between the parties, or because of public policy reasons that preclude a duty of care, or both. A trio of cases show the vastly differing circumstances in which third party claims against doctors for financial losses incurred by those third parties can arise. In all three cases, no duty of care was held to be owed to the relevant third parties. **3.96**

The facts of *West Bromwich Albion Football Club Ltd v El-Safty* have already been considered.[318] The surgeon who negligently advised and treated the football player did not owe a **3.97**

---

[311] See para 3.61. See also *Pate v Threlkel* (1995) 661 So 2d 278 (Fla Sup Ct). This would also be the case in the 'dangerous driver' cases where the duty is to advise the driver/patient himself.

[312] See A Grubb and D Pearl, *Blood Testing, AIDS and DNA Profiling: Law and Policy* (Jordans 1990), 48–55.

[313] [2015] EWHC 1394 (QB), para 17.

[314] Department of Health, *Confidentiality: NHS Code of Practice* (2003), paras 30–34, re-affirmed in NHS, *Confidentiality Policy* (June 2014), para 3.7.1.

[315] GMC, *Serious Communicable Diseases* (GMC, 1998), paras 22–23. This advice was withdrawn on 13 November 2006 *per* Special Notice.

[316] GMC, *Confidentiality* (2009) para 55. See also the guidance on disclosing genetic conditions at para 69.

[317] DVLA, *Assessing Fitness to Drive: A Guide for Medical Professionals* (May 2016) 10, citing the GMC guidelines, n 316.

[318] [2006] EWCA Civ 1299. See text accompanying n 85.

duty in tort to the employer football club to avoid financial losses accrued by the club in the event that the player's career was terminated by reason of the medical negligence. Crucially, there was no assumption of responsibility by the surgeon to advise the football club as to their financial interests. 'The immediate interest here is medical, not financial. WBA is interested, but principally as a good employer not as an investor in player contracts.'[319] The potential conflicts of interest which could arise, should the surgeon owe a duty to both player and club, also precluded a duty of care arising.

3.98 In the case of *Islington London BC v University College London Hospital NHS Trust*,[320] a patient suffered a stroke because of the admitted negligence of a temporary secretary who was working for a cardiac surgeon treating the patient. As a result, the patient was severely disabled, and was provided with residential care by the claimant local authority, which was under a statutory duty to charge for such accommodation unless, as was the case with this patient, the accommodated person was unable to pay. The local authority sought to recover the cost of the patient's care from the defendant NHS Trust. However, by way of preliminary issue, it was held that no duty of care was owed to the claimant by the NHS Trust. Although the provision of care to a patient by a local authority that could not recover the cost of that care from the patient had been reasonably foreseeable by the defendant, there was insufficient legal proximity between these parties to warrant a duty being found.[321] Moreover, where, as here, there was a seemingly inequitable distribution of monetary burdens between two public authorities, then the issue must inevitably involve wider issues of policy which was truly 'a matter for Parliament, or at least for political decision, rather than for a court deciding a particular case.'[322]

3.99 In the Australian case of in *AAA v BBB*,[323] a female patient attended the defendant counsellor for marriage counselling. An affair developed between them, which brought about the breakdown of the patient's marriage. The former husband alleged that he suffered financial damage and emotional distress as a result of the collapse of his marriage. One of the several reasons denying a duty of care here was that any duties which the counsellor may have been found to have owed the former husband were not necessarily coincidental with his duties to his patient.[324]

3.100 A third party financial loss scenario may also arise in cases of negligently managed sterilization or contraception procedures. It appears to remain an open question as to whether a doctor whose medical treatment on his own patient was negligent in this regard, owes any duty of care to the patient's *current* sexual partner for those consequences (the future sexual partner's claim is barred by the decision in *Goodwill v British Pregnancy Advisory Service*[325]). It is one thing if the parental claims are brought jointly for a commonly sustained harm suffered by both of them, but parents may not be able nor willing to do so—for example, because they are separated, or because the financial injury is one parent's only. This leaves open the question of whether a duty of care is owed to the 'other parent', who was not the patient, and upon whom the sterilization operation was not performed. In the wrongful conception case of *McFarlane v Tayside Health Board*,[326] where a failed vasectomy operation occurred, the House of Lords merely noted that the claims for 'financial loss

[319] ibid, [59].
[320] [2005] EWCA Civ 596.
[321] ibid, [44] (Clarke LJ).
[322] ibid, [38].
[323] [2005] WASC 139.
[324] ibid, para 78.
[325] [1996] 2 All ER 161 (CA). See para 3.92.
[326] [2000] 2 AC 59 (HL).

as a consequence of the birth of the said child' were brought by both parents jointly.[327] Since the decision was handed down, it has been said that, just because the surgeon's letter informing that the vasectomy was successful was addressed to Mr McFarlane alone, did not mean that there was no duty to Mrs McFarlane.[328] Subsequently, in the Australian decision in *McDonald v Sydney South West Area Health Service*,[329] the New South Wales Supreme Court remarked that *McFarlane* 'does not assist on the issue of whether the duty of care of the doctor extends to the partner of his patient'[330] (although, in the end, an independent and severable duty of care to husband of the patient, Mr McDonald, was held to be owed).

In a different type of scenario, a doctor who is requested by his patient to provide a medical report to a third party, for example, an insurance company or potential employer, may owe a duty of care to that third party to do so carefully so that the third party does not incur economic loss.[331] Following *Hedley Byrne v Heller*, a doctor, knowing whom the recipient of the report is to be, the purpose for which it will be used, and that the third party will (or is likely to) rely upon it, undertakes (or assumes) a responsibility to the third party sufficient to impose a legal duty to exercise reasonable care and skill in preparing the report.[332] **3.101**

In the unlikely event that the doctor provides a medical report on the patient without knowing what use it will be put to, or if the report is put to an unexpected use or one which could not reasonably be anticipated by the doctor, it may well be that the all important 'assumption of responsibility' is absent. It will not, however, be necessary for the doctor to know the precise identity of the third party providing he knows the nature of the third party's use, for example, that it is an insurance company. **3.102**

The same reasoning would apply if the doctor had no pre-existing relationship with the 'patient' but was specifically engaged directly by the third party to provide the medical report. Here, there would undoubtedly be an undertaking or assumption of responsibility to the third party who requested the report. And, of course, there would almost certainly be a contract between the doctor and third party which would include an implied term which could be the basis for a contractual negligence claim unconstrained by requirements for recovering economic loss in the tort of negligence.[333] **3.103**

(iii) For psychiatric injury

The circumstances in which damages may be recovered for negligently caused nervous shock (psychiatric injury) are confusing and, often, uncertain.[334] A distinction has to be drawn **3.104**

[327] ibid, 98 *per* Lord Clyde, and 107 *per* Lord Millett. The costs of raising daughter Catherine were disallowed. Clearly, the damages for the pain, suffering, and inconvenience of pregnancy and childbirth were the mother's alone, and she was entitled, by majority, to recover those.

[328] *Islington London BC v University College London Hospital NHS Trust* [2004] EWHC 1754 (QB) [37].

[329] [2005] NSWSC 924.

[330] ibid, para 64.

[331] See, eg, *Wharton Transport Corporation v Bridges* (1980) 606 SW 2d 521 (Tenn Sup Ct) (failure by doctor to report to employer the disabilities of an employee resulting in claim by injured person against employer for negligence of employee). See also *North American Co for Life & Health Insurance v Berger* (1981) 648 F 2d 305 (5th Cir) (insurance company had action against doctor for negligent medical assessment of employee entitlement under insurance coverage).

[332] This should follow from the reasoning in *Spring v Guardian Assurance plc* [1995] 2 AC 296; [1994] 3 All ER 129 (HL), but notice the reservation by Lord Goff at 147.

[333] ibid.

[334] For further discussion, see P Handford, *Mullany and Handford's Tort Liability for Psychiatric Damage* (2nd edn, Lawbook Co 2007); S Deakin, A Johnston, and B Markesinis, *Markesinis and Deakin's Tort Law* (7th edn, Oxford University Press 2013), 124–40; EWLC, *Liability for Psychiatric Illness* (No 249, 1998); R Mulheron, *Medical Negligence: Non-Patient and Third Party Claims* (Ashgate Publishing 2010), ch 8, and by the same author, *Principles of Tort Law* (Cambridge University Press 2016), ch 5.

between 'participants' or 'primary victims' and others who are merely 'bystanders' or 'secondary victims' of the defendant's negligence.[335] As regards the latter, the House of Lords in the three cases of *McLoughlin v O'Brien*,[336] *Alcock v Chief Constable of South Yorkshire Police*[337] and *White v Chief Constable of South Yorkshire Police*[338] imposed arbitrary limits upon claims for psychiatric injury not for any logical reason but rather to reflect 'the court's perception of what is the reasonable area for the imposition of liability'.[339] Legislative reform appears to be unlikely, given previous governmental statements that, notwithstanding the difficulties which the area has presented for the courts, it is 'preferable' to allow the area to continue to develop by judicial precedent, rather than by legislative enactment.[340]

3.105 For secondary victims, the courts have explicitly accepted that they are making policy choices about the scope of liability.[341] In particular, the law requires:

(1) a close relationship between the victim and the claimant (either presumed, for example, parent and child, or established in fact, for example, brother and sister) such that psychiatric injury is foreseeable to the claimant;
(2) propinquity in time and space between the victim's 'accident' and the claimant's discovery of the victim's injury (ie at the scene or its 'immediate aftermath');
(3) that the claimant discover that injury by sight and sound; and
(4) that as a result the claimant suffers psychiatric illness through an affront to her senses.

3.106 By contrast, as regards those who are 'participants' or 'primary victims' of the defendant's negligence, *Page v Smith*[342] has made it clear that the *McLoughlin/Alcock* rules do not apply. It suffices that a duty of care arises because it is reasonably foreseeable that the claimant will suffer personal injury whether or not it is also foreseeable that he will suffer psychiatric injury, and the 'proximity' requirements identified in *McLoughlin/Alcock* need not be satisfied.

3.107 These perhaps deceptively simple rules apply in medical negligence cases where the issue is whether a third party, usually a relative of the patient, may recover for the psychiatric injury caused by the doctor's negligence directed towards the patient. As Lord Rodger observed in *JD v East Berkshire Community NHS Trust*, medical mishaps can give rise to a duty on the part of a doctor, not only to the person whom he injures, but also to that person's parents or spouse who suffer psychiatric injury through seeing or hearing the mishap or its immediate aftermath.[343]

3.108 As a prerequisite, any claimant who seeks to recover for negligently caused psychiatric illness must prove that he has, indeed, suffered from a recognizable psychiatric illness.[344] The English legal view is that the suffering of distress, fear, anxiety, irritation, or despondency, is not compensable.[345] However, much will depend upon the psychiatric evidence, and the delineations between compensable and non-compensable injuries can appear, at least to

---

335 See also discussion in paras 3.50–3.55.
336 [1983] AC 410; [1982] 2 All ER 298 (HL).
337 [1992] 1 AC 310; [1991] 4 All ER 907 (HL).
338 [1999] 2 AC 455; [1999] 1 All ER 1 (HL).
339 ibid, *per* Lord Oliver at 926.
340 Department for Constitutional Affairs, *The Law on Damages* (CP 9/07, 4 May 2007), ch 3, para 97.
341 See *White v Chief Constable of South Yorkshire Police* [1999] 2 AC 455, [1999] 1 All ER 1 (HL). In *White*, Lord Hoffmann observed (at 551) that the 'search for principle was called off' earlier in *Alcock*.
342 [1996] AC 155 (HL).
343 [2005] UKHL 23, [107].
344 See para 3.50.
345 *Alcock v Chief Constable of South Yorkshire Police* [1992] 1 AC 310 (HL) 416; *Page v Smith* [1996] AC 155 (HL) 167.

the lay person, to be very fine indeed. In *Ward v Leeds Teaching Hospitals NHS Trust*,[346] Mrs Ward's daughter, Katherine, entered hospital to have her wisdom teeth removed, but failed to regain consciousness after the operation, and died two days later. The NHS Trust admitted negligence, but denied that any duty of care was owed to Mrs Ward in respect of her claim for psychiatric injury (post-traumatic stress disorder). Mrs Ward failed, on the basis, inter alia, that the accepted psychiatric evidence was that she suffered 'a severe and prolonged bereavement reaction', which was described by the court in terms that cast doubt on whether it was a recognized psychiatric illness worthy of compensation.[347] On the other hand, in *Tredget and Tredget v Bexley HA*,[348] the parental claimants were able to recover, for a 'pathological grief reaction'. Mrs Tredget gave birth to a son amid chaos and pandemonium in the delivery theatre. The baby was delivered in a distressed condition (severely asphyxiated) and required immediate resuscitation. Mr Tredget was present in the room, and was requested to encourage his wife in her efforts in delivery. The baby died of his injuries when two days old. Both parents recovered for their psychiatric injuries (£32,500 for Mr Tredget, and £17,500 for Mrs Tredget). The psychiatric evidence was that both parents suffered from 'pathological unresolved mourning'.[349] This claim was entitled to legal compensation, whereas Mrs Ward's grief reaction was not.

We are not, of course, here concerned with the claim by a patient for psychiatric injury arising out of her treatment.[350] Rather, the issue is whether a relative, usually a close relative such as a spouse, partner, or parent, may claim for their psychiatric injury triggered by the negligent care of their relative. The rules stipulated in the preceding paragraphs serve to determine whether (and, if so, why) a duty of care is owed by the doctor to exercise reasonable care to avoid causing psychiatric injury to that particular claimant. The remainder of the negligence action must also be proven, of course, to render the doctor liable. In that regard, in *Toth v Jarman*,[351] the court was not satisfied that the failure of the doctor to give an intravenous glucose injection to a patient, following a hypoglycaemic attack, actually caused the brain damage and death of the 5-year-old patient, and hence, the father's secondary victim psychiatric injury claim against the doctor also fell away. **3.109**

(a) **Participant/primary victim cases** It seems that, in some instances, the courts will regard the relative as so involved in the events of medical negligence that the relative will not be seen as a 'secondary victim' but will be regarded as a 'participant' or 'primary victim'. In *Tredget and Tredget v Bexley HA*,[352] the facts of which are outlined above, Mr Tredget was present throughout the chaotic birth and witnessed what was taking place, and was shaken and stunned by what he saw. After the birth both claimants witnessed the child in intensive care prior to its life-support being switched off. Judge White held that they had each suffered a pathological grief reaction, caused by 'shock' resulting from their involvement in the birth process and subsequent events. Judge White held that it would be unrealistic to isolate the birth from the continuing events leading up to the child's death forty-eight hours later. He applied the 'participant' category identified in *Alcock* which obviously covered the mother but also, he held, the father. As regards the latter, he relied upon 'the degree of involvement in and the immediacy of the parents to the birth of the child'.[353] Hence, in **3.110**

346 [2004] EWHC 2106, [2004] Lloyd's Rep Med 530 (QB).

347 ibid, 535. See also for analogous reasoning and outcome: *Brock v Northampton General Hospital NHS Trust* [2014] EWHC 4244 (QB) para 95.

348 [1994] 5 Med LR 178 (QB).

349 ibid, 181.

350 See paras 3.50–3.55.

351 [2006] EWCA Civ 1028.

352 [1994] 5 Med LR 178 (County Court).

353 ibid, 184.

obstetric cases where a father is present and (as will often be the case) is actively encouraging and supporting his partner, a claim for psychiatric illness caused by negligence in the birth could be brought.

3.111 This will not be the only situation in which a relative will be considered a 'participant', and clearly it will be a matter of fact determined by the closeness and immediacy of involvement of the relative. There are limits, however, upon just who will have the requisite involvement. Merely witnessing the effect of the negligence on the patient will not be sufficient. In *Tredget*, of course, the father was actually involved in his wife's care and it may well be that something of this sort will be necessary for the more restrictive *McLoughlin/Alcock* rules not to apply. Importantly, relatives who merely conduct a vigil at the bedside of the injured patient or are otherwise present at the hospital where the medical negligence occurs will not be considered 'participants'. Rather, their actions for psychiatric injury must fall within the 'secondary victim' rules of *McLoughlin/Alcock* and, as will be seen shortly, are unlikely to succeed.

3.112 A further limitation is that a relative's physical proximity to the actions of an allegedly medically mismanaged patient, witnessing the ramifications of that negligence at close quarters, is also insufficient to render the relative a primary victim. This proposition is particularly illustrated by the cases of three mothers—in *North Glamorgan NHS Trust v Walters*,[354] in *Hall v Gwent Healthcare NHS Trust*,[355] and in *Palmer v Tees HA*[356]—all of whom brought claims for pure psychiatric illness arising out of the death of their children (allegedly as a result of medical negligence), all of whom were closely exposed to and involved with the events surrounding their children's deaths, and all of whom lost their primary victim claims. (Mrs Walters, however, succeeded as a secondary victim, for reasons discussed later in the chapter.) Mrs Hall's scenario is illustrative of the tight ring-fence placed around the term, 'participant', in so far as primary victims in medical negligence scenarios are concerned. Ms Hall's mentally disturbed husband, who was under the care of a local health authority for treatment of his mental illness and for whose family certain care orders were in place, was the target of a cruel hoax played on him by his work colleagues, and it mentally destabilized him. Mr Hall heard 'voices' commanding him to kill his 12-year-old daughter, which he acted upon one night in the family home. Mrs Hall was in the house at the time of the fatal attack, and took the knife from her husband following the fatal stabbing, but she was not herself at risk of physical injury, nor had she unwittingly contributed to her daughter's peril (quite the opposite—she had ensured that no knives were kept in the family home, but her husband purloined one from his sister's house during a brief visit there). This was a strike-out application, and the court was satisfied that Ms Hall could not satisfy the definition of a primary victim.[357]

3.113 **(b) Witnessing a traumatic event** As a secondary victim, damages for psychiatric illness will be recoverable if the claimant witnessed a traumatizing event that comprised the medical negligence: providing always that the other *McLoughlin/Alcock* rules are satisfied, for example, that the claimant has a sufficiently close relationship with the 'primary' victim of the medical negligence. Arguably, in *Tredget* the husband's claim would still have succeeded even if he had only witnessed what the judge described as the 'chaos' and 'pandemonium' at the time of the birth. Thus, seeing a loved one suffer, if sufficiently traumatic, at the hands of

354 [2003] EWCA Civ 1792, [2003] Lloyd's Rep Med 49 (CA).
355 [2004] EWHC 2748 (QB).
356 [1999] Lloyd's Rep Med 351 (CA).
357 [2004] EWHC 2748 (QB) [16]–[17].

a doctor, may do. The decision of the Court of Appeal in *Sion v Hampstead HA*[358] illustrates the application of the 'secondary victim' rules.

The claimant's son was injured in a motorcycle accident and was admitted to hospital. The claimant stayed at his son's bedside for fourteen days watching him deteriorate in health, suffer a heart attack, fall into a coma, and eventually die. The claimant claimed that the hospital had been negligent in that they had failed to diagnose bleeding from his son's left kidney as a result of which he had fallen into a coma. The claimant alleged that he had suffered psychiatric illness as a result of what he had seen whilst at the hospital. The Court of Appeal struck out his action. The claimant's psychiatric illness had not been caused by 'shock' as required under the *McLoughlin/Alcock* rules. There was no evidence that it had arisen from a 'sudden appreciation by sight or sound of a horrifying event'. Instead, the court held that the claimant's condition had arisen from a continuing exposure to the events beginning with his first arriving at the hospital and concluding with the appreciation at the inquest that there had been negligence by the hospital. **3.114**

Sion was an important case even though the claimant was unsuccessful because its judgments (particularly that of Peter Gibson LJ) clarified that a nervous shock claim could arise out of medical negligence[359] (a point reiterated subsequently by the House of Lords in dicta in *JD v East Berkshire Community Health NHS Trust*[360]). Apart from the necessary relationship to the patient, as *Sion* made clear, it is crucial if a claim for psychiatric illness is to have any chance of success that what the claimant sees 'shocks' her. Relatives who suffer recognized psychiatric illness subsequent to the death or illness of their loved one, such as pathological grief disorder (PGD), will be able to recover providing the 'traumatizing' or 'shocking' event was, at least, a contributory cause of their psychiatric illness.[361] Likewise, if the subsequent events aggravate or prolong 'shock'-induced psychiatric illness then damages may be recovered even if this is characterized as PGD.[362] It will be otherwise, however, where the PGD is wholly caused by subsequent events which do not fall within the *McLoughlin/Alcock* rules.[363] Much will therefore turn on the expert evidence of what caused the claimant's psychiatric illness and will require a degree of sophistication. **3.115**

However, the need for a 'shocking' event must not be misunderstood. In *Sion*, it was argued that the defendant's conduct must be 'shocking' in the sense of a sudden and violent incident. The Court of Appeal disagreed. Peter Gibson LJ made this clear, doubting the statement of Auld J in *Taylor v Somerset HA*[364] to the contrary. He said:[365] **3.116**

> I see no reason in logic why a breach of duty causing an incident involving no violence or suddenness, such as where the wrong medicine is negligently given to a hospital patient, could not lead to a claim for damages for nervous shock, for example where the negligence has fatal results and a visiting close relative, *wholly unprepared for what has occurred*, finds the body and thereby sustains a sudden and unexpected shock to the nervous system.

The crucial factor is the unexpected nature of what the claimant *witnesses* through sight or sound rather than the character of the event in itself. Though, of course, merely to be *told* **3.117**

[358] [1994] 5 Med LR 170 (CA). See A Grubb, (1994) 2 Med L Rev 365 (Commentary).
[359] [1994] 5 Med LR 170 (CA), especially at 176.
[360] [2005] UKHL 23, [107].
[361] *Vernon v Bosley (No 1)* [1997] 1 All ER 577 (CA).
[362] ibid.
[363] See *Calascione v Dixon* (1993) 19 BMLR 97 (CA) (claim for PGD not allowed) as explained by the majority of the Court of Appeal in *Vernon v Bosley (No 1)* [1997] 1 All ER 577 (CA), *per* Evans LJ at 600 and *per* Thorpe LJ at 609–10.
[364] (1993) 16 BMLR 63 (QB).
[365] [1994] 5 Med LR 170 (CA) 176 (emphasis added).

the unexpected is quite illogically not enough.[366] In *Sion*, the claimant's psychiatric illness arose from the gradual realization that his son would not survive. Hence, his death was not surprising but expected.[367]

3.118 What is not covered by the 'secondary victim' rules is, as *Sion* itself shows, a situation where the relative's psychiatric illness arises from a vigil at the bedside and the gradual or dawning realization of the victim's fate.[368] A fortiori, a claim would not arise if the claimant's illness arose from the long-term care of the victim of medical negligence at home.[369] In *Taylor v A Novo (UK) Ltd*,[370] which arose from a workplace accident rather than a medical event, the claimant daughter saw her mother (who had been injured when some racking board fell on her at work) die at home. The claimant did not witness the negligent incident at work, but witnessed her mother's collapse and death some three weeks later, from deep vein thrombosis. The claim failed, on the basis that daughter was not sufficiently proximate to the negligent event; witnessing the consequences of the accident is not sufficient, to meet the exacting and restrictive requirements of secondary victim compensation.

3.119 What, precisely, is covered by the requirement of 'shock' was at issue in the Court of Appeal's decision in *North Glamorgan NHS Trust v Walters*.[371] The claimant's 10-month-old son was admitted to hospital suspected of suffering from hepatitis A. In fact, the defendant failed negligently to diagnose he was suffering from acute hepatitis. The claimant stayed with her child in the hospital. She was awoken in the early hours of the morning to discover her son having a major epileptic seizure which, it subsequently transpired, had led to coma and irreparable brain damage. She was told that her son had not suffered brain damage but was to be transferred to a hospital in London for a liver transplant. Following a scan there, she was told that he had severe brain damage, was on a life-support machine, had only a 50/50 chance of survival, and, if he did, would be severely disabled. The next day, following a scan which showed his brain was so severely damaged that he would have no quality of life, the claimant agreed that his life support should be switched off. Thirty-six hours after his fit, he died in the claimant's arms. The claimant suffered a pathological grief reaction.

3.120 The Court of Appeal held that the facts fell within the *McLoughlin/Alcock* rules. First, the thirty-six-hour period amounted to 'an event' as there was an inexorable progression from the moment the fit occurred to the time of the child's death. Second, the claimant's appreciation of the event was 'sudden' and not an accumulation of gradual assaults on her mind. Each event had its impact immediately. This was not a case where the claimant's psychiatric injury arose from a gradual dawning of the realization that her child's life was in danger. The court approved *Tredget* and distinguished *Sion* which had not involved a 'shocking' event but rather a gradual assault on the claimant over a period of time.[372]

---

[366] See *Ravenscroft v Rederiaktiebolaget Transatlantic* [1992] 2 All ER 470 (CA).

[367] See also *Tan v East London and City HA* [1999] Lloyd's Rep Med 389 (Judge Ludlow) (psychiatric injury not 'shock'-induced when arising from planned or expected events). For criticisms of the semantic distinctions between *Sion* and *Walters*, see, eg, R Mulheron, 'Medical Negligence, Secondary Victims and Psychiatric Illness: Family Tragedies and Legal Headaches', in R Probert (ed), *Family Life and the Law* (Ashgate Publishing 2007) ch 5.

[368] See also *Anderson v Smith* (1990) 101 FLR 34 (fifteen-month vigil) and *Beecham v Hughes* (1988) 52 DLR (4th) 625 (BCCA): gradual realization that wife severely injured.

[369] *Alcock* [1992] 1 AC 310 (HL) *per* Lord Ackner at 917; *Andrewartha v Andrewartha* (1987) 44 SASR 1 (South Aus Sup Ct).

[370] [2013] EWCA Civ 194, [2014] QB 150, para 32.

[371] [2003] EWCA Civ 1792; [2003] Lloyd's Rep Med 49 (CA). Discussed in J Laing, (2003) 11 Med L Rev 121 (Commentary).

[372] *North Glamorgan NHS Trust*, *per* Ward LJ at 57–58. He also distinguished the case of *Taylorson v Shieldness Produce Ltd* [1994] PIQR P329 (CA) as involving a gradual dawning of the fate of the relative.

Subsequently, the Court of Appeal held, in *Galli-Atkinson v Seghal*,[373] that *Walters* is illustrative of the proposition that both an event, and its immediate aftermath, can be made up of 'a number of components', all of which can be 'taken together as providing the trigger, if that is the right description, for the shock which produced the psychiatric illness'. However, the *Walters* interpretation of 'shock' has its limits. For example, in *Liverpool Women's Hospital NHS Foundation Trust v Ronayne*,[374] the claimant husband was held not to have suffered a sudden or unexpected assault on his mind, but rather, a gradual realization that his wife's life was in danger as a result of a medical mistake in performing her hysterectomy operation. The timeline, and the circumstances, were very different from *Walters*. Earlier, the District Court of Hong Kong refused to extend it to the scenario in *Wong Fung Sze v Tuen Mun Hospital*,[375] where the claimant wife argued that, although her husband was destined to die of cancer in any event, the quality of his end of life would have been better, and her psychiatric illness would have been prevented, if his doctors had not negligently misdiagnosed his cancer. The claimant argued that she suffered a 'shock' when she learnt in July 2001 that the cancer had spread or, alternatively, that she received a series of shocks between when she thought that her husband was clear of cancer (in May) to the point at which he died (in September). However, the court distinguished *Walters*, and held that this did not constitute the shock necessary to ground a claim for negligently caused psychiatric injury. **3.121**

(c) Witnessing the immediate aftermath In addition to situations where the claimant witnesses the event, the *McLoughlin/Alcock* rules contemplate recovery for psychiatric injury, as secondary victims, as a result of witnessing the 'immediate aftermath'. In *McLoughlin* itself, the House of Lords accepted a claim where the claimant visited the hospital some two hours after the car accident and saw her family in the state they had been brought in. By contrast, in *Alcock* the House of Lords rejected a claim where relatives had visited a mortuary and saw their dead family members eight or nine hours after their death. The distinction between these two factual applications of the 'immediate aftermath' requirement cannot simply be one of time. One important difference is that in *McLoughlin* the victims were in much the same condition as they were immediately following the accident. In *Alcock*, however, the victims had been cleaned up. A further difference is that in *McLoughlin*, the claimant arrived at the hospital not knowing what to expect. In *Alcock*, the claimants knew their relatives were dead and had come to identify them. Applying the 'suddenness' or 'unexpected' requirement of *Sion*,[376] identifying a body will rarely give rise to an *unexpected* shock, unless perhaps in cases where the body is badly mutilated or has not been cleaned up. In *Calascione v Dixon*,[377] the claimant recovered damages for psychiatric injury (post-traumatic stress disorder (PTSD)) as a result of seeing her dead son's body in a hospital following a road accident. His body was described as 'barely recognisable'. **3.122**

Consequently, there will be little scope for applying the 'immediate aftermath' requirement in medical negligence cases. A claimant who arrives at the hospital after the patient has died or been injured will only possibly have a claim if the condition of the claimant creates an unexpected (and immediate) reaction in the claimant. Identifying a dead body is very **3.123**

[373] [2003] EWCA Civ 697, [25].

[374] [2015] EWCA Civ 588, para 40. The *Walters* concept of shock was also distinguished in *Shorter v Surrey And Sussex Healthcare NHS Trust* [2015] EWHC 614 (QB), wherein the claim for secondary victim recovery also failed. More recently, *Walters* was also distinguished in *Owers v Medway NHS Foundation Trust* [2015] EWHC 2363 (QB), again illustrating the difficulties of proving the requisite shock in medical scenarios.

[375] [2004] HKDC 154 (leave to appeal denied, *per* Judge To, on 11 October 2004).

[376] [1994] 5 Med LR 170 (CA).

[377] (1993) 19 BMLR 97 (CA).

unlikely to qualify. In *Taylor v Somerset HA*[378] the claimant's husband suffered a heart attack. He was taken to hospital and died. The claimant was informed that he was ill and had been taken to hospital. She was told after a short time that her husband had died. Not believing what she was told and in shock, she asked to see the body and identified him in the hospital mortuary. The sight of his body caused her shock and distress. She sued the defendant alleging that she had suffered psychiatric injury as a result of the death of her husband which the defendant had negligently caused by failing to diagnose and treat his serious heart condition. Auld J rejected her claim. He held that she could not claim for any psychiatric injury arising from being told that her husband was dead. Further, her visit to the mortuary did not fall within the 'immediate aftermath' requirement. She had gone there to identify her husband and apart from the 'obvious shock to her of the sight of his dead body, it bore no marks or signs to her of the sort that would have conjured up for her the circumstances of his fatal attack'.[379] The absence of the latter was crucial and distinguished the case from *McLoughlin*.

3.124 Likewise, in *Tan v East London and the City HA*,[380] the claimant was the husband of a patient whose baby was stillborn following the alleged negligence of the defendant. The claimant comforted his wife overnight following the news that their baby had died in utero, he held the dead baby after it was delivered the next day and witnessed the disposal of its remains in a metal box. He claimed damages for psychiatric injury. The judge held that he could not recover as a 'secondary victim': (i) the relevant event that he had to witness or be present at the immediate aftermath was the baby's death in utero; (ii) it could not be said the claimant had been present at it or its immediate aftermath; (iii) in any event, he had not suffered psychiatric injury by 'shock' since, apart from being told of his baby's death, the events relied upon were planned and expected.

3.125 The circumstances in *Tan* were extended by analogy, and *Tredget* and *Walters* were distinguished, in the recent case of *Wild v Southend University Hospital NHS Foundation Trust*.[381] Mr and Mrs Wild were expecting their first child. Unfortunately, at forty weeks, it was discovered that the baby had died in utero, and the following morning, Mr and Mrs Wild returned to hospital when Mrs Wild delivered a stillborn child. Mr Wild alleged that, but for the defendant's medical negligence, the child would probably have been born alive, because foetal compromise would have been diagnosed at a sufficiently early date for safe delivery. However, the claim failed. *Walters* was distinguished because in this case, the 'seamless event' ostensibly started with the realization that the child had already died; and *Tredget* was distinguished, because there was no chaos or pandemonium in the delivery room, but only a grim realization that the child would be delivered stillborn (similarly to the tragedy in *Tan*).

3.126 (d) **Delivering 'bad news'**[382] A final situation which should be considered is where a person is negligently told bad news about a relative and, as a consequence, suffers a shock which causes psychiatric injury.[383] The negligence may lie in the way the information is communicated or in its accuracy. It is clear that an action will not lie against the primary defendant where an intermediary acts as a conduit to tell the claimant of injuries that have been inflicted upon the claimant's relative.[384] Unlike that situation, however, we are concerned

---

[378] (1993) 16 BMLR 63 (QB).
[379] ibid.
[380] [1999] Lloyd's Rep Med 389 (County Court).
[381] [2014] EWHC 4053 (QB).
[382] See N Mullany and P Handford, *Tort Liability for Psychiatric Damage* (2nd edn, Lawbook Co 2007); C Witting, *Liability for Negligent Misstatements* (Oxford University Press 2004) ch 6.
[383] See paras 3.53–3.54, for the related issue of liability to the patient.
[384] See para 3.115.

with the liability of the *intermediary* himself. Can a doctor[385] be liable for negligently[386] breaking 'bad news' to the relatives? In principle there is no reason why he should not.[387] The three elements required for a duty of care—'foreseeability', 'proximity', and the 'fair, just, and reasonable' requirement—seem satisfied. It is readily foreseeable that carelessness might produce an adverse psychiatric reaction. There is a 'close and direct' relationship between the doctor and relative sufficient to create a proximate relationship. Finally, it is not obvious what policy reasons mitigate against imposing liability in this particular context. It should not matter whether the negligence lies in the falsity of the communication or in the method or nature of a (true) communication. As regards the latter situation, there is certainly some analogy with the duty of a doctor to exercise reasonable care when informing his patients post-operatively.[388] However, the contrary has been suggested at least where the information is true.[389]

The decision of the Court of Appeal in *Powell v Boladz*[390] appears to limit the scope of a doctor's liability in these circumstances. The claimants, a married couple, brought an action claiming damages for psychiatric injury arising out of the death of their son. He suffered from a rare condition known as 'Addison's disease'. It was accepted that there had been negligence in failing to diagnose and treat his condition and that had he been treated in time he would have survived. Sometime after their son's death, the claimants were told the reason for his death and were shown his medical records. No complaint was made about this. However, they alleged that seven months later they discovered that their son's medical notes had been tampered with by the defendants. They alleged that their GPs had conspired to 'cover-up' the cause of their son's death and that their realization of this caused them each to suffer PTSD. The judge struck out their actions. The Court of Appeal dismissed the appeal on the basis that no duty of care was owed by the defendants in respect of the post-death allegations. The Court of Appeal held that a duty of care would only arise if the defendants had been called upon or undertook to treat the claimants as patients. While the defendants were the claimants' GPs, the court held that at the relevant time they had not been counselling or treating the claimants. Stuart-Smith LJ said: **3.127**

> I do not think that a doctor who has been treating a patient who has died, who tells relatives what has happened, thereby undertakes the doctor–patient relationship towards the relatives. It is a situation that calls for sensitivity, tact and discretion. But the mere fact that the communicator is a doctor, does not, without more, mean that he undertakes the doctor–patient relationship.[391]

Later, he stated that the case law did not establish:

> some kind of free-standing duty of candour, irrespective of whether the doctor– patient relationship exists in a healing or treating context, breach of which sounds in damages, such damages involving personal injury. This would involve a startling expansion of the law of tort.[392]

385 Or other, such as a counsellor.

386 See *Wilkinson v Downton* [1897] 2 QB 57 for malicious communication.

387 *Jinks v Cardwell* (1987) 39 CCLT 168 (Ont H Ct) (doctor held liable for psychiatric injury caused to a wife when he told her, falsely, that her husband had committed suicide).

388 See *AB v Tameside & Glossop Health Authority* [1997] 8 Med LR 91 (CA), and para 3.55.

389 *Mount Isa Mines v Pusey* (1970) 125 CLR 383 (Aust H Ct), *per* Windeyer J at 407. But note *Guay v Sun Publishing Co* [1953] 4 DLR 577 (Can Sup Ct) (no liability for false story published in newspaper).

390 (1997) 39 BMLR 35 (CA).

391 ibid, 45.

392 ibid, 46. Note, however, the statutory duty of candour referenced in para 3.04.

3.128 Three observations on this decision are worth making. First, the claimants only alleged that their discovery of the 'conspiracy' caused them psychiatric injury and not the communication by the GPs to them of false, inaccurate, or insensitively communicated information. Arguably, the claimants' claim would have been stronger if this had been the case. Secondly, the almost mesmeric effect on the Court of Appeal of the label 'doctor–patient relationship' has to be questioned. It is not a necessary condition for a doctor to owe another a duty of care.[393] It is as if the court thought that the claimants were alleging that the defendants had negligently failed to treat them. If they had, the existence of the relationship would have been important, though even then not conclusive, to the action. But this was in fact irrelevant in the case because it was not what they alleged. The real question was whether the defendants owed a duty not to harm the claimants, rather than one not to diagnose or treat them negligently. Thirdly, the Court of Appeal's denial of a duty of care in circumstances such as these was not quite categorical. The court accepted that if the doctor realized that the news he had broken had shocked the recipient such as to call for treatment, he might be liable for not carrying on and treating the individual. Stuart-Smith LJ stated that it would be 'a question of fact and degree in each case whether the doctor–patient relationship came into existence by the doctor undertaking to treat and heal the person as a patient'.[394] It is suggested that the reasoning of the Court of Appeal is so open to question that it is extremely unlikely to survive scrutiny in a future case where a doctor negligently *advises* a relative of a patient's death or injuries and thereby causes psychiatric injury.

3.129 Another way of legally handling the 'bad news' cases is to seek to invoke (albeit, inevitably rather clumsily) the primary and secondary victim classification for the distressed recipients of such news. This occurred, for example, in the unusual case of *Farrell v Avon HA*,[395] where the claimant father attended hospital to see his newborn, and recovered damages for psychiatric injury after he was handed the body of a dead baby that he was wrongly told was his child. One of the most interesting aspects of this case (and there were many) was that the claimant was decreed to be a primary victim, as there was no other primary victim—'the only victim of the incident was the claimant himself' and he had been 'physically involved in the incident'.[396] In *AB v Leeds Teaching Hospital NHS Trust* also,[397] parents who alleged that they suffered psychiatric injury upon learning that their babies who had died at or soon after birth had had organs (brains and hearts) removed and retained for histopathological examinations, without their parents' consent, were classified as primary victims. None of the pathologists or clinicians could have owed the babies a duty of care post-mortem, and hence, if the parents 'are victims at all, they must be primary victims'.[398] Ultimately, two of the three lead claimants failed, because their psychiatric illnesses were not reasonably foreseeable. However, the point is that the victims in these cases hardly resembled the victim in *Page v Smith* at all, yet the courts strained to fit these recipients of bad and unpleasant news into that classification, with consequential detriment to the clarity of the law governing negligently inflicted psychiatric illness.[399]

---

393 See paras 3.56 *et seq.*
394 (1997) 39 BMLR 35 (CA) 45.
395 [2001] Lloyd's Rep Med 458 (QB, HHJ Bursell QC).
396 ibid, 466, and see also 471.
397 [2004] EWHC 644.
398 ibid, [199] *per* Gage J.
399 For further discussion, see, eg, R Mulheron, 'The "Primary Victim" in Psychiatric Illness Claims: Reworking the "Patchwork Quilt"' (2008) King's College LJ 81.

3. Doctors engaged by others

In a number of situations a doctor may be engaged by a third party to examine and provide a report on an individual's health. For example, a doctor may be requested by an insurance company to provide a medical report for a prospective applicant prior to writing a policy, or it may be alleged, for example, that a doctor's assessment of what comprised suitable medical treatment for an insured, following an accident, was negligent.[400] Alternatively, a doctor may be asked by a prospective employer to ensure the individual's fitness for the job,[401] or may be engaged to determine whether an existing employee is still medically suited to the occupation.[402] As a further variation on the occupational theme, medical staff may be given the task of training and developing employees in their workplace at the request of a trade union, and potential claims may arise by those workers who were intended to benefit from the training.[403] Alternatively, a police surgeon may be called upon to examine the person at a police station. Alternatively, a doctor may be requested by a local social services authority to determine whether there is evidence of child abuse,[404] or requested to provide a statutory opinion necessary for the detention of the person under the Mental Health Act 1983.[405] **3.130**

What, if any, duty does the doctor owe the individual examined who is not, in conventional terms, his patient? Where an examination has been performed, is the doctor's duty limited to not harming the individual during the examination or does it go further and require the doctor, for example, to apprise the person of anything relevant to his health discovered during the examination? The answer in England is not clear, for a combination of reasons. For example, there have been conflicting authorities that give rise to an unsatisfactory legal state of affairs; in some cases, a duty of care was assumed rather than argued;[406] and there is a frustrating paucity of English authority in several of the abovementioned situations. By contrast, courts in other jurisdictions, particularly in the United States, have addressed many of these scenarios explicitly. It has, however, been suggested that English law only accepts the limited duty of not harming the person during the examination.[407] **3.131**

(i) Medical examinations re child abuse allegations and for educational needs

It is perhaps unfortunate that the issue of whether a professional can be liable to an individual when he has been engaged by a third party has arisen in a series of House of Lords cases concerned with statutory frameworks in relation to child protection and other local authority functions.[408] Thus, the courts have considered, for example, the liability of psychiatrists and social workers engaged in child abuse investigations and of educational psychologists **3.132**

---

400 *Lowe v Guarantee Co of North America* (2005) 80 OR (3d) 222 (CA).

401 Other examples might include the preparation of a report for the purposes of litigation or for assessing the individual's entitlement under an insurance policy or a statutory benefits scheme.

402 *Ho Ying Wai v Keliston Marine (Far East) Ltd* [2002] HKCFI 543.

403 *Rice v Secretary of State for Trade and Industry* [2006] EWHC 1257 (QB).

404 *X v Bedfordshire County Council* [1995] 2 AC 633, [1995] 3 All ER 353 (HL).

405 *Everett v Griffiths* [1920] 3 KB 163 (CA), [1921] 1 AC 631 (HL).

406 eg in *Harnett v Fisher* [1927] AC 573 (HL), a lunacy certificate committed a farmer to a lunatic asylum for nine years. The certificate was based upon the doctor's observation of the claimant from a window, and a short conversation with him. A jury found negligence, and it was stated (at 593) by the court: 'This action is founded on the assumption that a duty was owed to the applicant.'

407 *X v Bedfordshire County Council* [1995] 2 AC 633; [1995] 3 All ER 353 (HL). See for academic discussion of the issue, eg, A Grubb, 'Doctors Engaged by Third Parties: Duties to Take Care' (1997) 5 Medical L Rev 348; V Harcourt, 'The Doctor, the Third Party and the Examinee: Is There a Duty to Inform?' (2000) 8 Tort LJ 221.

408 *X v Bedfordshire County Council* [1995] 2 AC 633, [1995] 3 All ER 353 (HL); *Phelps v Hillingdon London Borough Council* [2001] 2 AC 619, [2000] 3 WLR 776 (HL); *Barrett v Enfield London Borough Council* [2001] 2 AC 550; *JD v East Berkshire Community Health NHS Trust* [2005] 2 AC 373 (HL).

dealing with children with learning difficulties. There is no doubt that, at least at first, the courts' approach was heavily influenced by the statutory context and their (again initial) reluctance to contemplate damages actions against the employers of these professionals. Since then, however, the courts have reverted to a principled approach of professional liability in these (arguably) controversial statutory contexts. The judicial development of the doctor's duty of care toward an examinee in this scenario can most conveniently be signposted by reference to three key decisions, the reasoning of which manifested both reversals of legal opinion and strong dissents.

3.133 (a) ***X v Bedfordshire County Council*** Whether a doctor engaged by a third party owes a duty to the examinee first arose in the House of Lords' decision in *X v Bedfordshire County Council*.[409] The complex legal and facts issues raised by this case can be found elsewhere.[410] The important issue here, however, is whether a psychiatrist who interviews and examines a child for suspected sexual abuse at the behest of the local social services can be liable to the child for psychiatric injury caused when it is unnecessarily taken into care. The House of Lords held that the psychiatrist did not owe the child a duty of care to avoid psychiatric injury in such circumstances. Beyond the duty not to injure the child during the examination, the psychiatrist's duty was owed solely to the local authority: there was no proximity between the child and doctor.[411] Lord Browne-Wilkinson stated that the psychiatrist did not:

> by accepting the instructions of the local authority, assume any general professional duty of care to the claimant children. The professionals were employed or retained to advise the local authority in relation to the well-being of the claimants but not to advise or treat the claimants.[412]

3.134 Lord Browne-Wilkinson drew an analogy with the situation where a doctor is retained by an insurance company to examine an applicant for life insurance. He said:

> The doctor does not, by examining the applicant, come under any general duty of medical care to the applicant. He is under a duty not to damage the applicant in the course of the examination: but beyond that his duties are owed to the insurance company and not to the applicant. [413]

3.135 No authority was given for this analysis of the relationship in the insurance context; indeed there could not be, since it does not appear that the issue has ever directly arisen in England, either before *Bedfordshire* or since. It was, however, crucial to the view taken by at least four of the judges in the House of Lords.[414] A similar analogy was drawn by a majority of the Court of Appeal.[415] Staughton LJ asserted (and it was no more) that the psychiatrist was in precisely the same position as a doctor who examined a person for insurance purposes or takes a blood sample from a suspected drunk driver at a police station. The doctor owed the person a duty not to cause harm during the examination but 'the general duty to perform the task allocated with reasonable skill and care' was owed to the insurance company or police authority only.[416] By contrast, Sir Thomas Bingham MR dissented on the issue of

[409] [1995] 2 AC 633, [1995] 3 All ER 353 (HL).
[410] See P Cane, 'Suing Public Authorities in Tort' (1996) 112 LQR 13; and K Oliphant, 'Tort' (1996) 49 CLP 29, 31–44.
[411] Lord Nolan dissented on this point [1995] 3 All ER 353 (HL) 400.
[412] ibid, 384.
[413] ibid, 383.
[414] Lord Nolan disagreed that an analogy could be drawn between the relationship of the insurance doctor and an examinee and the psychiatrist in *Bedfordshire* (ibid, 400).
[415] [1994] 2 WLR 554 (CA).
[416] ibid, 582. See also Peter Gibson LJ at 591.

the psychiatrist's duty. He concluded that, while there 'was not on any showing a typical doctor–patient relationship' on the facts, a duty of care was owed to the child because it was for the child alone that the psychiatrist was 'being invited to exercise her professional skill and judgment'.[417]

(b) ***Phelps v Hillingdon London Borough Council*** The law moved on, however, in *Phelps v Hillingdon LBC*[418] and returned to a more principled approach. The case concerned a number of actions by individuals who claimed to have suffered damage as a result of the failure by educational psychologists employed by local authorities to diagnose conditions (such as dyslexia) in the claimants who were schoolchildren. One of the central issues was whether in such circumstances educational psychologists owed the claimants a duty of care such that their employer, local authorities, could be sued in negligence on the basis of vicarious liability. **3.136**

The House of Lords held that a duty of care was owed. The judges specifically referred to the situations of professionals, such as doctors, who are engaged by third parties to individuals. The triangular factual situation was not, in itself, a reason why a duty could not be owed to the examinee. Each case would turn upon its own facts assessing the factors usually relevant to establishing a duty. **3.137**

Like a doctor or other professionals, the educational psychologists were exercising their professional skill and care in dealing with the children. They were specifically called in to advise on the child's condition and there was an assumption of responsibility to the children—all parties knew that the advice was crucial to the children's future. The fact that the psychologists owed a duty to their employer was no impediment to them also owing a duty to the children. The judges considered the potential for a conflict of duties as crucial in their decision. Unlike the *Bedfordshire* case, there was no conflict between the two duties. Lord Nicholls described the case as 'an example par excellence of a situation where the law will regard the professional as owing a duty of care to a third party as well as his own employer' and considered that the two duties 'march[ed] hand-in-hand'.[419] Lord Clyde specifically acknowledged that a doctor examining an individual for insurance purposes would owe them a duty of care.[420] **3.138**

(c) ***JD v East Berkshire Community Health NHS Trust*** Subsequently, in 2003, the Court of Appeal held, in *JD v East Berkshire Community Health NHS Trust*,[421] that the House of Lords' decision in *Bedfordshire*—that is, specifically in the child protection context—could not stand in the wake of the Human Rights Act 1998 and the intellectual pounding it had taken in subsequent House of Lords decisions.[422] This dramatic shift in position was upheld by the House of Lords in the *East Berkshire*[423] decision. The case concerned three appeals, revolving around the liability of health professionals who had mistakenly diagnosed children as being the victims of child abuse. Did the professionals owe the children or their (wrongfully accused) parents/carers a duty of care? The current English legal position is that the former question is to be answered affirmatively, and the latter is to be answered negatively. **3.139**

---

[417] ibid, 660, 570.
[418] [2001] 2 AC 619, [2000] 4 All ER 504 (HL). Discussed in Harris, MC (2001) 117 LQR 25.
[419] *Phelps v Hillingdon London Borough Council*, n 418, 529.
[420] ibid, 537.
[421] [2003] EWCA Civ 1151, [2004] QB 558 (CA).
[422] eg *Barrett v Enfield London Borough Council* [2001] 2 AC 550 (HL) and *Phelps v Hillingdon London Borough Council* [2000] 3 WLR 776 (HL).
[423] [2005] UKHL 23, [2005] 2 AC 373.

3.140 As regards the children, there was no valid public policy reason why a professional should not owe a duty of care to a child who was the subject of investigation. The common law claim raised the same issues which would now arise in a claim under s 6 of the 1998 Act for breach of the child's human rights, in particular under Articles 3 and 8. Interestingly, the Court of Appeal's decision was concerned wholly with issues of policy. 'Proximity' seems to have been assumed. Lord Phillips MR expressed the 'firm conclusion' that:

> it will no longer be legitimate to rule that, as a matter of law, no common law duty of care is owed to a child in relation to the investigation of suspected child abuse and the initiation and pursuit of care proceedings. It is possible that there will be factual situations where it is not fair, just or reasonable to impose a duty of care, but each case will fall to be determined on its individual facts.[424]

3.141 The duty to the child was not the subject of further appeal to the House of Lords (although the parents' claims were). However, during the course of that judgment, and speaking in respect of the duty owed to the examinee child, Lord Rodger observed that the area had moved on 'remarkably swiftly', that local authorities may now owe common law duties to children when exercising child protection duties, and that doctors who examine such children owe them a duty 'to exercise reasonable care and skill in diagnosing and treating any condition from which they may be suffering.'[425]

3.142 Hence, it has followed, from the Court of Appeal's decision in *East Berkshire*, that a social services department may owe a duty to a child who has alleged a breach of a duty of care on the basis of a failure to take reasonable steps to protect him during childhood (by reason, in part, of a 'superficial report' written by a doctor prior to the return of the child from foster care to parental care).[426] Of course, the recognition of a duty of care toward the child does not automatically establish liability, for if no damage to the child can be satisfactorily identified as a result of, say, the separation from the child's parents, then no action in negligence can lie.[427]

3.143 With respect to the parental claimants in *D v East Berkshire Community Health NHS Trust*, both Court of Appeal and House of Lords (by majority, Lord Bingham dissenting) held that no duty of care was owed because the child's interests would conflict with those of the parents and thus public policy required that no duty was owed to them by the doctors in the course of the investigation. The Privy Council had earlier come to the same view, in relation to a father's claim, in *B v Attorney General (New Zealand)*.[428] In *East Berkshire*, the House of Lords posed several other policy reasons militating against a duty of care owed to parents/carers. Among these were: that if a doctor did owe a duty to the parents, then those responsible for the protection of a child against criminal conduct could owe suspected perpetrators a duty of care to prevent foreseeable harm to them;[429] that there was a serious risk that vexatious claims, or even seriously grounded claims with the aim of restoring the parent's reputation, could be brought years after the investigation;[430] that the serious social problem of child abuse was best tackled by relieving doctors from the fear of legal proceedings brought against them by parents/carers;[431] and that doctors already have sufficient burdens (having

---

[424] ibid, [83]–[84].
[425] ibid, [82], [110].
[426] eg *Pierce v Doncaster Metropolitan Borough Council* [2007] EWHC 2968 (QB).
[427] *D v Bury Metropolitan BC* [2006] EWCA Civ 1.
[428] [2003] UKPC 61.
[429] *D v East Berkshire Community Health NHS Trust* [2005] UKHL 23, [78] *per* Lord Nicholls. Point also made in *B v Attorney General (New Zealand)* [2003] UKPC 61, [30].
[430] *East Berkshire*, n 429, [137] *per* Lord Brown.
[431] ibid, [86] *per* Lord Nicholls, [100] *per* Lord Rodger.

to consider both short-term and long-term welfare of the child, making decisions on limited information, deciding what to tell family members) without adding to those burdens by imposing a duty of care toward a wrongfully accused carer.[432]

(d) Developments post-*JD v East Berkshire Community Health NHS Trust* The conjoined appeals in *East Berkshire* arose from facts that predated the coming into force of the Human Rights Act 1998. However, the 'no duty to parents and carers' rule which *East Berkshire* established has withstood a challenge based upon Article 8 of the ECHR, which protects against interference with family life. In *Lawrence v Pembrokeshire County Council*,[433] the Court of Appeal rejected an argument that the rule needed to be revisited, to give proper effect to Article 8, so that the common law should now recognize that doctors, public authorities, and others responsible for the protection of children from abuse by their parents or carers owed a duty of care to parents when investigating and/or taking steps in protection of the children whom they considered to be at risk of parental abuse. Auld LJ observed that, in *East Berkshire*, the common law had been fashioned 'to protect those suspected of it from malice or bad faith, but not from a well-intentioned but negligent mistake', and that to recognize a duty towards parents and carers 'would fundamentally distort the law of negligence in this area, putting at risk the protection for children which it provides in its present form . . . The provision of a discrete convention remedy through the medium of the HRA, does not, on that account, necessitate change of the common law'.[434] **3.144**

Moreover, the House of Lords noted in dicta in *Seal v Chief Constable of South Wales Police*[435] that there could be no suggestion that the protection from liability in negligence which *East Berkshire* afforded to investigating doctors could never be properly characterized as a denial of access to the courts in contravention of Article 6. **3.145**

Quite apart from (unsuccessfully) seeking to challenge the *East Berkshire* rule on the ground that the HRA had consigned it to history, efforts have also been made by parental claimants to distinguish the decision. These attempts, however, have met with little success. For example, in *L v Reading Borough Council*[436] a father was wrongly accused of abusing his daughter. An investigating social worker was accused of negligent operational activities/decisions which (it was argued) did not involve the type of conflicts of duty and finely balanced evaluative judgments discussed in *East Berkshire*. However, the argument failed and no duty was owed by the social worker to the claimant father. A later challenge in the same case to allege that the local authority owed the father a direct duty of care (entailing that the social worker had acted in breach of duty) also failed, as being inconsistent with *East Berkshire*.[437] In *D v Bury Metropolitan Borough Council*[438] the attempts to distinguish *East Berkshire* were judicially described to be the product of 'ingenuity and skill', but the argument that the parents should be owed a duty nevertheless failed. In *Hinds v Liverpool County Court*[439] a negligence suit against a psychologist who had produced a report unfavourable to the father in care proceedings also failed on the basis that no duty of care existed. **3.146**

The upshot of the preceding discussion is that the *Bedfordshire* case no longer presents a bulwark or real obstacle to the courts recognizing that a doctor may owe a duty of care to an **3.147**

432 ibid, [131]–[132] *per* Lord Brown.
433 [2007] EWCA Civ 446, (2007) 96 BMLR 158.
434 *East Berkshire*, n 429, [55].
435 [2007] UKHL 31, [75] *per* Lord Brown.
436 [2006] EWHC 2449 (QB).
437 *B v Reading Borough Council* [2007] EWCA Civ 1313.
438 [2006] EWCA Civ 1, [16].
439 [2008] EWHC 665 (QB).

individual whom, for example, he examines at the behest of another. However, as discussed in the following section, *Bedfordshire* has been influential in denying such a duty in the leading employment-related case in England.

(ii) Examinations for employment and insurance purposes

3.148 Where a person undergoes a medical examination or treatment at the request of a prospective, or existing, insurer or employer, the doctor owes that person a duty of care in negligence not to cause injury in the course of the examination or treatment.[440] Consequently, the doctor who carelessly carries out a medical procedure during the examination, such as taking a blood sample and puncturing an artery, and injures the person, will be liable in negligence. This is not the problematic case. The more difficult question is whether the doctor owes the examinee a broader duty of care than that (eg a duty to inform the examinee of a medical condition that requires treatment or medical intervention, or a duty to prevent foreseeable economic harm flowing from a negligent medical examination). To the extent that a doctor already has a relationship with the person (eg he is that individual's GP), his pre-existing duty of care would extend to all reasonably foreseeable harm.[441]

3.149 In the private, commercial context of insurance and employment the statutory framework which initially inhibited the application of a common law duty of care in *X v Bedfordshire County Council* is absent. It is clear from the decisions in *Phelps*, and subsequently *JD v East Berkshire Community NHS Trust*, that this was the (erroneous in fact) basis of *Bedfordshire*. Equally, there is really no conflict that would arise between the duty owed to the insurance company or employer and the duty which would be owed to the examinee. If there were, then a duty of care should not be imposed.[442] The doctor's duty in relation to both would be to exercise reasonable care in carrying out the examination and in interpreting the results. What is reasonable for the doctor vis-à-vis the insurance company is reasonable vis-à-vis the person examined. The doctor's obligations will be tailored to the tasks he undertakes for the third party and what he could (and should) discover and conclude thereafter. A duty to advise the person on the basis of the examination and assessment of his health is entirely consistent with his legal obligations to the third party.[443]

3.150 However, what case law exists in England is less sanguine in its acceptance of such a duty. Contrast the following two cases.

[440] See, eg, *Leonard v Knott* [1980] 1 WWR 813 (BC CA) (liability for patient who died during annual check-up from an allergic reaction during a procedure); *Dyer v Trachtman* (2004) 470 Mich 45 (medical malpractice claim brought by an examinee who alleged that a physician negligently injured him while performing an independent medical examination, by rotating his shoulder. Claim permitted to proceed); *Appleton v El-Safty* [2007] EWHC 631 (QB) (liability was admitted toward a professional footballer who had to give up football, following a surgeon's negligence both in advising that reconstructive surgery was required for the injury and in performing the surgery). For the employer football club's unsuccessful action against the surgeon, see *West Bromwich Albion FC Ltd v El-Safty* [2005] EWHC 2866 (QB), discussed at paras 3.27–3.28.

[441] The fragmentation of a GP's duty proposed in *Powell v Boladz* (1997) 39 BMLR 35 (CA) 45, (see para 3.127) is unsupportable.

[442] A possible example is where a doctor is requested by an insurance company to consider a person's entitlement under an *existing* policy providing, for example, disability or health coverage. Here, the interests of the company and the individual are, arguably, different. The latter is concerned to minimize exposure (downplaying medical condition) while the individual is concerned to discover the full extent of their condition: see, eg, *Keene v Wiggins* (1977) 138 Cal Rptr 3 (Cal CA), *per* Cologne J at 7. The divergence or conflict of interest does not occur when the policy is only in contemplation.

[443] See Lord Clyde in *Phelps* [2000] 4 All ER 504 (HL), 537.

In *Baker v Kaye*[444] the claimant was a television sales executive. He was offered a job with a company subject to a satisfactory medical report from the company's doctor. On the strength of this offer, the claimant resigned his existing job. The defendant, a GP in private practice, was employed by the company to carry out a medical examination on the claimant. The results of blood tests taken during the examination suggested to the defendant that the claimant had an alcohol problem; consuming excessive amounts of alcohol made him unsuitable for the demanding job with the company. Consequently, the defendant told the company that he could not recommend the claimant for the job. The company, as a result, withdrew their offer of employment to the claimant. The claimant sued alleging that the defendant had negligently interpreted the test results and, as a result, he had suffered economic loss, namely his lost salary. **3.151**

Robert Owen QC (sitting as a deputy High Court judge) held that a duty of care was owed to the claimant by the defendant. There had, obviously, been no reliance by the claimant upon the defendant's advice. It was the company in making its decision to withdraw their offer of employment, who had relied upon the defendant. Nevertheless, applying the three-stage test in *Caparo*,[445] the judge held that a duty of care to the claimant employee existed. First, he held that economic loss to the claimant was foreseeable. Secondly, he concluded that there was a proximate relationship between the parties: (i) the defendant knew the claimant's employment depended upon his medical advice to the company; (ii) the claimant entrusted himself and information to the defendant; and (iii) the defendant regarded himself as under a duty to advise the claimant of anything untoward about his health which he might discover during the examination. Finally, the judge could see no policy reason why it was not 'just, fair and reasonable' to impose a duty of care upon the defendant. In the end, however, he held that the defendant was not liable because he had not been negligent. **3.152**

The decision in *Baker v Kaye* is, however, arguably only of limited importance. It concerned an (allegedly) negligent report produced by a doctor in the knowledge that it would be relied upon and if false was likely to cause loss to the claimant. Thus, liability fell squarely within the case law of the House of Lords beginning with *Hedley Byrne* and, in particular, the employee reference case of *Spring v Guardian Assurance plc*.[446] Nevertheless, in principle, applying the well-known *Caparo* test, there is no difficulty in holding a doctor liable for *all* the immediate consequences of a failure to exercise reasonable care and skill in the course of the examination. Consequently, he could be liable for failing (carelessly) to diagnose a medical condition which could have been treated or its symptoms alleviated if it had been diagnosed earlier. Injury to the person would be foreseeable and there would be a proximate relationship based upon an implied assumption of responsibility by the doctor. The expectation of both examinee and doctor will usually be that the doctor will perform his professional obligations to the person which would include alerting the person to anything untoward. In one US case the court succinctly stated: **3.153**

> In placing oneself in the hands of a person held out to the world as skilled in a medical profession, albeit at the request of one's employer, one justifiably has the reasonable

[444] [1997] IRLR 219 (Robert Owen QC). For factually similar cases in the US, see, eg, *Quisenberry v Compass Vision, Inc* (2007) US Dist LEXIS 97318 (motion to strike dismissed; liability possible); *Olson v Western Airlines Inc* (1983) 191 Cal Rptr 502 (liability); *Armstrong v Morgan* (1976) 545 SW 2d 45 (Tex CA) (liability). Contrast *Rand v Miller* (1991) 408 SE 2d 655 (W Va Sup Ct App) (no liability); *Felton v Schaeffer* (1991) 279 Cal Rptr 713 (Cal CA) (no liability); *Keene v Wiggins* (1977) 138 Cal Rptr 3 (Cal CA) (no liability).

[445] *Caparo Industries plc v Dickman* [1990] 2 AC 605 (HL).

[446] [1995] 2 AC 296 (HL). Notwithstanding the doubts of the judge, the two cases are very close indeed.

expectation that the expert will warn of any incidental dangers of which he is cognizant due to his peculiar knowledge of his specialization.[447]

3.154 Obviously, in this situation the doctor would only be required to exercise *reasonable* care. The doctor's duty would not necessarily, perhaps rarely, be to treat the patient. Rather, it would be sufficient for him to discharge his legal duty if he alerted the patient to the danger and advised him to see his own doctor.

3.155 *Baker v Kaye* was, however, disapproved by the Court of Appeal in *Kapfunde v Abbey National*.[448] In *Kapfunde*, the claimant applied for a job with the first defendant. She completed a confidential medical questionnaire on which she indicated that she had been absent from work for periods of time during the previous two years due to sickle cell anaemia.

3.156 The first defendant passed on the questionnaire to the second defendant, a GP who worked part time for the first defendant. She informed the first defendant that the claimant was likely to have a higher than average absence level. As a result, the first defendant did not give the claimant the job. She sued in tort arguing that the first defendant was vicariously liable for the second defendant's negligence.

3.157 The court held that the second defendant did not owe a duty of care to the claimant to carry out the assessment carefully so as not to negligently inflict economic loss on the latter: first, there was no doctor–patient relationship between the parties; they never met and the claimant did not know of the second defendant; second, the claim was for economic loss; third, the claimant had not entrusted the second defendant with the conduct of her affairs; and finally, in any event, the second defendant was not, on the facts, in breach of duty since her assessment of the claimant was reasonable. Both Kennedy and Millett LJJ considered that the judge in *Baker v Kaye* should not have held that a duty of care was owed.

3.158 The basis of the reasoning in *Kapfunde* is questionable. Both judges who delivered judgments (Kennedy and Millett LJJ)[449] relied on the general position advocated (obiter) by Lord Browne-Wilkinson in *X v Bedfordshire County Council* that a doctor engaged by a third party, whether insurance company, prospective employer, or whatever, owed only the limited duty not to injure the claimant whilst examining the claimant. This, as we have seen, cannot stand with subsequent pronouncements in *Phelps* and should no longer be considered to be sound law—if it ever was!

3.159 The scope of *Kapfunde* is also not clear. There are indications in the judgments of the Court of Appeal that the law may not be so restricted. Both Kennedy and Millett LJJ were anxious to emphasize, and to analyse, the case as being one about economic loss rather than personal injury. Millett LJ also emphasized that it concerned an alleged negligent misstatement for which restrictive rules applied. It is not clear, therefore, what the judges would have held if an examining doctor had failed to discover and/or advise the individual of a deleterious medical condition. Equally, Kennedy LJ (though not Millett LJ) seems to have considered it important that the second defendant had never actually seen, or examined, the claimant. In truth, the Court of Appeal has not in *Kapfunde* examined in depth the situation where a third party engages the doctor, and it is open to a future court to re-examine the decision.

3.160 Other English authority is not entirely helpful on the scope of the doctor's duty to an examinee either, given that relevant decisions have either proceeded upon an admitted duty of

[447] *Webb v TD* (1997) 95 P 2d 1008 (Mont Sup Ct) *per* Trieweiler J (liability for failing to diagnose back condition resulting in injury at work).

[448] (1998) 46 BMLR 176 (CA). Discussed in A Grubb, (1998) 6 Med L Rev 364 (Commentary).

[449] Hutchinson LJ agreed with both judgments.

care or have espoused what the duty *is not*. For example, in *R v Croydon Health Authority*,[450] where a radiologist examined the claimant prior to her employment with the defendant health authority, and failed to report the presence of a significant abnormality, which would have led to a diagnosis of primary pulmonary hypertension, a duty of care by the radiologist toward the examinee to ensure that she was fit for work and would be protected from personal injury whilst employed to look after sometimes violent mentally ill patients was *admitted*. As a result, Kennedy LJ was careful to note that, consequently, 'we are not concerned with the question of what, in reality, was the extent of the duty of care which [the radiologist] owed to [the examinee]'.[451] Subsequently, the High Court confirmed in *Multiple Claimants v Ministry of Defence*[452] that there was no wide duty on the MOD toward former members of the armed forces who alleged combat trauma and psychiatric illnesses and who argued that, had recruitment been adequately conducted by psychologists and other medical screeners, the soldiers' susceptibility to such injury would have been detected, and they would not have been regarded as suitable recruits. In *Cheltenham Borough Council v Laird*,[453] *Kapfunde* was cited for the negative proposition that an employer's medical adviser owes no duty to a prospective employee when reporting to the employer whether or not the applicant was fit for the employment.

In the United States, courts have reached mixed conclusions on the scope of the duty of care owed by a doctor to an examinee.[454] Some courts have dismissed claims brought against doctors engaged by (prospective) employers or insurance companies for failure to diagnose a medical condition or, having done so, to inform or advise the person of it,[455] or to treat the examinee for an identified condition.[456] However, some courts have taken a wider view of liability imposing a duty of care where the doctor undertakes to advise the person of his condition and misrepresents or conceals the results[457] and the advice is relied upon to his detriment.[458] In *Green v Walker*[459] an employee was required to undergo annual health checks. The doctor carried out the tests, found all the results to be normal and classified the employee as 'employable without restriction'. One year later, the employee was diagnosed with lung cancer. He sued the doctor in negligence, alleging that his failure to diagnose the cancer was careless; the failure to disclose these findings and the consequent delay in treatment had reduced his chances of survival. The employee subsequently died. The Fifth Circuit Court of Appeals held that the defendant owed the employee a duty of care notwithstanding the examination occurred ostensibly for the benefit of the employer. The duty required the doctor to carry out the tests and diagnosis carefully and to advise the employee of any findings that 'pose an imminent danger to [his] physical or mental **3.161**

450 (1997) 40 BMLR 40 (CA).

451 ibid, 44.

452 [2003] EWHC 1134 (QB).

453 [2009] EWHC 1253 (QB), para 481.

454 Many of the cases are helpfully collected in the judgment of the Supreme Court of Montana in *Webb v TD* (1997) 95 P 2d 1008. For interesting academic discussion see, eg, P Blake, 'Redefining Physicians' Duties: An Argument for Eliminating the Physician-Patient Relationship Requirement in Actions for Medical Malpractice' (2006) 40 Georgia L Rev 573; N Squillante, 'Expanding the Potential Tort Liability of Physicians: A Legal Portrait of "Nontraditional Patients" and Proposals for Change' (1993) 40 UCLA L Rev 1617.

455 eg *Beaman v Helton* (1990) 573 So 2d 776 (Miss Sup Ct) (no liability for failing to advise examinee that X-ray disclosed cancer); *Ward v Most Health Services Inc* (2008) US Dist LEXIS 61573 (potential liability for failing to diagnose early stages of lung cancer from X-ray).

456 *Joseph v McCann* (2006) UT App 459 (no liability for failing to treat police officer for psychological condition that rendered him unfit to serve as a police officer).

457 *Hoover v Williamson* (1964) 203 A 2d 861 (Md CA).

458 *Heller v Community Hospital* (1993) 603 NYS 2d 548.

459 (1990) F 2d 291 (5th Cir).

well-being'. Subsequent decisions have approved the court's decision.[460] There is a strong argument for finding that a doctor impliedly assumes a responsibility to the individual by examining the patient and refraining from disclosing the results or taking other appropriate action to appraise the individual of the need for further investigation. An individual is as likely to rely upon the silence of the doctor as upon a positive misrepresentation of his good health.[461] One US court persuasively put it as follows:[462]

> When a doctor conducts a physical examination, the examinee generally assumes that 'no news is good news' and relies on the assumption that any serious condition will be revealed.

3.162 A similar recognition that the law will impose upon an examining doctor a duty, somewhat wider than the limited duty not to injure the examinee during the examination, has been reached in Australia,[463] in Hong Kong,[464] and in Canada,[465] in circumstances where the doctor was engaged by a third party.

(iii) Police-related or litigation-related medical examinations

3.163 Although no English case to date has concerned what duty a doctor owes to a patient in a medical examination conducted for police-related or litigation-related purposes, should the examination reveal that the patient has a medical condition that requires treatment, the scenario has been discussed in dicta. In *Re N*,[466] Clarke LJ considered it 'arguable' that the doctor would owe such a patient a duty to inform him or her of the need for treatment if some underlying medical condition was detected, a view which received subsequent approval in the House of Lords.[467]

3.164 The same rationale applies to the police surgeon examining a detained suspect at a police station, with this proviso: the nature of the examination by a police surgeon may be much more limited than for doctors in the other contexts, for example, if the surgeon is merely engaged to take a blood sample. The person's general health condition does not arise. However, if the doctor is engaged to determine the person's fitness to be detained in a police cell overnight, why should not the doctor owe the person a duty to carry out the examination carefully. If a careless mistake is made which leads to the person suffering harm whilst detained, the doctor should, in principle, be liable to the detained person.

3.165 The related question of whether, and if so what scope, of duty of care is owed by doctors towards examinees who undergo medical examinations for the purposes of court-related matters, has arisen in the United States (although not, as yet, in England). For example, in *Greenberg v Perkins*,[468] liability was found against a doctor for an injury caused to the

[460] See, eg, *Woodruff v Gitlow*, 91 A 3d 805 (RI, 2014); *Stanley v McCarver* (2004) 208 Ariz 219 (Ariz Sup Ct); *Daly v US* (1991) 946 F 2d 1467 (9th Cir); *Cleghorn v Hess* (1993) 853 P 2d 1260 (Nev Sup Ct); *Baer v Regents of University of California* (1994) 884 P 2d 841 (NM CA); *Webb v TD* (1997) 951 P 2d 1008 (Mont Sup Ct).

[461] See *Webb v TD*, note 460, *per* Trieweiler J (Leaphart and Gray JJ dubitante).

[462] *Betesh v US* (1974) 400 F Supp 238 (DC Dist Ct), *per* Bryant J at 246 (liability for failing to advise examinee during military pre-induction physical examination of abnormality on X-ray indicating cancer).

[463] *Thomsen v Davison* [1975] Qd R 93.

[464] *Ho Ying Wai v Keliston Marine (Far East) Ltd* [2002] HKCFI 543.

[465] *Parslow v Masters* [1993] 6 WWR 273 (action to obtain medical report). For discussion of the relevant Canadian authorities in this 'evolving' area, see, eg, *Milne v Alberta (Workers' Compensation Board)* [2008] ABQB 710; and *Worthman v Assessmed Inc* (2006), 80 OR (3d) 249 (Gen Div).

[466] [1999] Lloyd's Rep Med 257 (CA).

[467] *JD v East Berkshire Community Health NHS Trust* [2005] UKHL 23, [2005] 2 AC 373 (Lord Bingham).

[468] (1993) 845 P 2d 530 (Colo 1993).

claimant who was undergoing tests during a medical examination for purposes of litigation. Subsequently, in *Harris v Kreutzer*,[469] the Supreme Court of Virginia observed that:

> [a] number of states have addressed the issue whether a physician owes a duty to the person examined in a court-ordered medical examination, which if breached, establishes a cause of action for malpractice. While all the courts addressing this issue have found a cause of action to exist, the denomination of the basis of that cause of action has not been uniform.

In this case, the court held that the clinical psychologist's duty toward the victim of a car accident who was undergoing a court-ordered medical examination to determine the nature and extent of a traumatic brain injury was very limited, viz, 'solely to examine the patient without harming her in the conduct of the examination'. More recently, in *Devitre v Orthopedic Center of St Louis*,[470] it was held that a patient–physician relationship could arise during an independent medical examination for the patient's prospective personal injury action, sufficient to give rise to a negligence action (in that case, an over-rotation of the examinee's arm and shoulder joints was alleged).

(iv) Psychiatric recommendation leading to detention

What is the position of a psychiatrist who negligently recommends that a person be detained under the Mental Health Act 1983? Usually two doctors must recommend detention,[471] at least, one of which will not have a previous relationship with the 'patient'.[472] There is considerable authority to support the view that a doctor owes the (ultimately) detained patient a duty to exercise reasonable care in certifying the patient.[473] The only remaining issues would relate to proof of breach, causation, and damage.[474] In *X v Bedfordshire County Council*, Lord Browne-Wilkinson[475] doubted the authority of one of the earlier 'negligent certification' cases.[476] However, liability falls within the principles already discussed and thus, on balance, a social worker or doctor providing a medical recommendation could be liable in negligence. As Lord Denning put it in his famous dissenting judgment in *Candler v Crane* **3.166**

[469] (2006) 271 Va 188, 198–99.

[470] 349 SW 3d 327 (Mo, 2011).

[471] Under ss 2(3) (assessment), 3(3) (treatment), and 7(3) (guardianship); only one in an emergency (s 4(3)). See discussion in E Jackson, *Medical Law: Text, Cases and Materials* (3rd edn, Oxford University Press 2013) ch 6; B Hoggett, *Mental Health Law* (4th edn, Sweet & Maxwell 1996), 66–71.

[472] Mental Health Act 1983, s 12(2). One doctor must be 'approved': s 12(2).

[473] See *Harnett v Fisher* [1927] AC 573 (HL); *Hall v Semple* (1862) 3 F & F 337 (Crompton J); and *De Freville v Dill* [1927] All ER Rep 205 (McCardie J) and cases cited therein; *Winch v Jones* [1986] QB 296 (CA); *James v Havering LBC* (1992) 15 BMLR 1 (CA). See B Hoggett, *Mental Health Law* (4th edn, Sweet & Maxwell 1996), 248; and L Gostin, *Mental Health Services—Law and Practice* (Shaw & Sons 1986), para 21.04.1. The position of the approved social worker, who initiates the admission process, is no different in all probability and does not raise the kind of policy questions associated with negligence actions arising out of the performance of statutory functions exemplified by *X v Bedfordshire County Council* [1995] 2 AC 633, [1995] 3 All ER 353 (HL), and see *Buxton v Jayne* [1960] 1 WLR 783 (CA) and *James v Havering LBC*, above.

[474] On which see *Everett v Griffiths* [1920] 3 KB 163 (CA) *per* Atkin LJ at 219 (Scrutton LJ disagreed at 196–97); [1921] 1 AC 631 (HL) *per* Viscount Finlay at 666–67 and *De Freville v Dill* [1927] All ER Rep 205, *per* McCardie J at 212–13 (certification is a cause).

[475] [1995] 2 AC 633 (HL), [1995] 3 All ER 353 (HL) 384.

[476] *Everett v Griffiths* [1920] 3 KB 163 (CA) and [1921] 1 AC 631 (HL). The House of Lords held the certifying doctor not liable because he had exercised reasonable care. The Law Lords did not resolve the different views expressed in the Court of Appeal on the duty issue. Bankes LJ had concluded that a duty to exercise reasonable care but not skill existed (at 183–84). Scrutton LJ held that no duty of care was owed (at 195–96) and Atkin LJ held that a duty to exercise reasonable care existed (at 218). In the House of Lords, Viscount Haldane thought it probable a duty to exercise reasonable care existed (at 657). Viscounts Finlay and Cave and Lords Moulton and Atkinson assumed the duty existed (at 669, 680–81, 697, and 681 respectively).

Christmas & Co,[477] the doctor is liable 'because [he] knows that his certificate is required for the very purpose of deciding whether the man should be detained or not'. In modern terminology, there is an assumption of responsibility by the doctors and social worker.

3.167 Nevertheless, it may be that on public policy grounds the courts may not recognize a duty of care owed to detained patients in respect of *the decision to admit* them under the 1983 Act.[478] The statutory (and discretionary) nature of this action, the potential 'chilling' effect of liability in negligence coupled with the spirit of non-liability of hospital managers and others for false imprisonment contained in s 6(3) of the Mental Health Act 1983, could lead a court to decide that no duty is owed. Indeed, the court might accept the argument that the hospital managers are immune because of the quasi-judicial nature of their function.[479]

D. Conclusion

3.168 The principal duty owed to a patient by a doctor (or other healthcare practitioner) is founded in negligence. Actions against a doctor for breach of contract remain exceptional. The duty in tort encompasses a duty to avoid or to minimize personal injury, financial loss, and psychiatric injury, albeit that the latter two categories have been the subject of significant judicially created restrictions. However, doctors may also owe duties of care to those who are not their patients, that is, with parties to whom they have provided no medical treatment, advice, or care whatsoever. The threat of non-patient suits has been judicially held at bay in some instances—for example, where the non-patient is a parent wrongfully accused of physically or sexually abusing his child, and which parent then suffers economic and/or psychiatric damage as a result of that wrongful accusation; and more recently, where the non-patient was a family member who had inherited a genetic condition from the doctor's patient, and about which he was not warned by the doctor (or by the patient). However, a sufficient number of successful cases have been brought (across the categories of personal injury, financial loss, and psychiatric injury) to render the non-patient suit of real concern to medical insurers. More recently, though, key cases in which family members have claimed that the medical treatment of their loved one (the patient) caused them *psychiatric* injury, in circumstances where those non-patients witnessed *the effects* of medical treatment, have failed at appellate level. This suggests that English courts will strive to adopt a strict analysis of those secondary victims who can successfully prove the illogical, but nevertheless deeply embedded, common law requirements (especially the requirement of shock) which govern the imposition of a duty of care in this area of negligently inflicted psychiatric injury.

---

477 [1951] 2 KB 164, [1951] 1 All ER 426 (CA), 435.

478 cf liability for negligence once the patient is detained: M Jones, *Medical Negligence* (4th edn, Sweet & Maxwell 2008), paras 4.129–4.145.

479 See *X v A, B and C and the Mental Health Act Commission* (1991) 9 BMLR 91 (QB, Morland J): Mental Health Act Commission and appointees not liable for negligent certification that treatment fell within s 57. But contrast the liability of 'second opinion doctor' under ss 57 and 58 *per* Morland J at 99.

4

BREACH OF DUTY

Philip Havers QC and Jessica Elliott

A. Reasonableness

1. The reasonable person

The basic test for negligence in domestic law is whether the defendant's conduct was reasonable in all the circumstances of the case. Reasonable conduct is not negligent; unreasonable conduct is culpable. In *Blyth v Birmingham Waterworks Co*[1] Alderson B said that: **4.01**

> Negligence is the omission to do something which a reasonable man, guided upon those considerations which ordinarily regulate the conduct of human affairs, would do, or doing something which a prudent and reasonable man would not do.

This is an objective standard which does not take account of the subjective attributes of the particular defendant.[2] It is sometimes said that the standard required is that of the reasonable person, or the 'man on the Clapham omnibus'.[3] Despite references to the reasonable person, the standard of care is not necessarily determined by the average conduct of people **4.02**

[1] (1856) 11 Exch 781, 784.
[2] *Glasgow Corporation v Muir* [1943] AC 448, 457.
[3] *Hall v Brooklands Auto Racing Club* [1933] 1 KB 205, 217.

in general if that conduct is routinely careless. Nor is there any concept of an 'average' standard of care by which a defendant might argue that he has provided an adequate service on average and should not be held liable for the occasions when his performance fell below the norm. No matter how competent the defendant's conduct was on average, he will be responsible for damage caused by even a single lapse below the standard of reasonable care.[4]

2. The reasonable doctor

4.03 An individual who professes a special skill is judged, not by the standard of the man on the Clapham omnibus, but by the standards of his peers. For the 'reasonable person is substituted the 'reasonable professional', be it doctor, lawyer, accountant, architect, and the like.[5] The classic statement of the test of professional negligence is the direction to the jury of McNair J in *Bolam v Friern Hospital Management Committee*.[6] Now widely known as the '*Bolam* test', this statement of the law has been approved by the House of Lords on many occasions as the touchstone of liability for medical negligence.[7] McNair J said:

> But where you get a situation which involves the use of some special skill or competence, then the test whether there has been negligence or not is not the test of the man on the Clapham omnibus, because he has not got this special skill. The test is the standard of the ordinary skilled man exercising and professing to have that special skill. A man need not possess the highest expert skill at the risk of being found negligent . . . it is sufficient if he exercises the ordinary skill of an ordinary competent man exercising that particular art.[8]

4.04 His Lordship agreed that counsel's statement that 'negligence means failure to act in accordance with the standards of reasonably competent medical men at the time' was an accurate statement of the law, provided that it was remembered that there may be one or more perfectly proper standards:

> A doctor is not guilty of negligence if he has acted in accordance with a practice accepted as proper by a responsible body of medical men skilled in that particular art . . . Putting it the other way round, a doctor is not negligent, if he is acting in accordance with such a practice, merely because there is a body of opinion that takes a contrary view.[9]

---

[4] *Wilsher v Essex AHA* [1986] 3 All ER 801, 810 *per* Mustill LJ. The English courts have not accepted a distinction between 'ordinary' negligence and 'gross' negligence. In *Wilson v Brett* (1843) 11 M & W 113 Rolfe B said that there was no difference: 'it was the same thing with the addition of a vituperative epithet.'

[5] 'The public profession of an art is a representation and undertaking to all the world that the professor possesses the requisite ability and skill. An express promise or express representation in the particular case is not necessary', *per* Willes J in *Harmer v Cornelius* (1858) 5 CB (NS) 236, 246.

[6] [1957] 2 All ER 118. See more generally M Powers, N Harris, and A Barton (eds), *Powers and Harris: Clinical Negligence* (4th edn, Bloomsbury 2008); and M Jones, *Medical Negligence* (4th edn, Sweet & Maxwell 2008).

[7] *Whitehouse v Jordan* [1981] 1 All ER 267; *Maynard v West Midlands RHA* [1984] 1 WLR 634; *Sidaway v Bethlem Royal Hospital Governors* [1985] 1 All ER 643; *Bolitho v City and Hackney HA* [1997] 4 All ER 771; *Chester v Afshar* [2004] UK HL 414, [2005] 1 AC 134. See also *Chin Keow v Government of Malaysia* [1967] 1 WLR 813 (PC); and *The Deep Vein Thrombosis v Air Travel Group Litigation* [2005] UKHL 72, at para 51 (Lord Mance). The Bolam test is not restricted to doctors, but is of general application to any profession or calling which requires special skill, knowledge, or experience: *Gold v Haringey HA* [1987] 2 All ER 888, 894 (CA).

[8] [1957] 2 All ER 118, 121.

[9] ibid, 122. Similar formulations of the standard of care required of the medical profession can be found in other Commonwealth jurisdictions: *Crits v Sylvester* (1956) 1 DLR (2d) 502, 508; aff'd (1956) 5 DLR (2d) 601 (SCC). This standard also allows for differences of view within the medical profession: see *Lapointe v Hôpital Le Gardeur* (1992) 90 DLR (4th) 7, 15 (SCC); *F v R* (1982) 33 SASR 189, 190 *per* King CJ.

There are two important caveats to the *Bolam* test, to be noted at this point and examined in greater detail below. The first is that the test itself is subject to a 'gloss' imposed by the House of Lords in *Bolitho v City and Hackney Health Authority*.[10] The second is that *Bolam* does not apply in the context of determining the adequacy of disclosure of risks associated with medical treatment, an exception confirmed by the Supreme Court in *Montgomery v Lanarkshire Health Board (General Medical Council intervening)*.[11] Those matters aside, *Bolam* provides a test of universal application for determining breach of duty issues in medical cases. **4.05**

In an earlier case, *Hunter v Hanley*,[12] Lord President Clyde had dealt with the question of different professional practices in these terms: **4.06**

> In the realm of diagnosis and treatment there is ample scope for genuine difference of opinion and one man clearly is not negligent merely because his conclusion differs from that of other professional men, nor because he has displayed less skill or knowledge than others would have shown. The true test for establishing negligence in diagnosis or treatment on the part of a doctor is whether he has been proved to be guilty of such failure as no doctor of ordinary skill would be guilty of if acting with ordinary care.

There is a distinction, however, between a test of negligence based on the standards of the *ordinary* skilled professional and one based on the *reasonably* competent professional. The former places emphasis on the standards which are in fact adopted by the profession, whereas the latter makes it clear that negligence is concerned with departures from what *ought* to have been done in the circumstances, which is measured by reference to the hypothetical 'reasonable doctor'.[13] Of course, what the profession does in a given situation will be an important indicator of what ought to have been done, but it should not necessarily be determinative. In the final analysis it is for the court to determine what the reasonable doctor would have done, not the profession, drawing upon the evidence presented. The *Bolam* test fails to make this distinction between the ordinary skilled doctor and the reasonably competent doctor. The distinction is potentially significant when the question arises whether compliance with common professional practice can be negligent. **4.07**

3. Reasonable care

Reasonable care can only be measured by reference to the defendant's conduct in the circumstances. It is meaningless to say that the standard required is reasonable care, without knowing the particular situation with which the defendant was confronted. For example, a defendant faced with an emergency and who has to act on the spur of the moment will not be judged too critically simply because with hindsight a different course of action might have avoided the harm.[14] This clearly applies to medical practitioners.[15] Nonetheless, the test remains reasonable care in all the circumstances. If the error is one which a reasonably competent doctor could have made in the circumstances the defendant is not negligent, but if a **4.08**

---

10 [1997] 4 All ER 771.

11 [2015] UKSC11, [2015] 2 WLR 768.

12 1955 SLT 213.

13 See J L Montrose (1958) 21 MLR 259.

14 *Parkinson v Liverpool Corporation* [1950] 1 All ER 367; *Ng Chun Pui v Lee Chuen Tat* [1988] RTR 298, 302 (both non-medical cases); *Knight v West Kent HA* [1998] Lloyd's Rep Med 18, 23 *per* Kennedy LJ warning against the dangers of hindsight.

15 In *Wilsher v Essex AHA* [1986] 3 All ER 801, 812 Mustill LJ said that an emergency may overburden the available resources, and, if an individual is forced by circumstances to do too many things at once, the fact that he does one of them incorrectly should not lightly be taken as negligence.

reasonably competent doctor would not have made that error, the defendant will be liable, notwithstanding the fact that it occurred in the course of an emergency.[16]

4.09 The obligation is to exercise reasonable care, and therefore doctors do not guarantee a favourable outcome to their efforts.[17] The medical practitioner is not an insurer and cannot be blamed every time something goes wrong. Indeed, it is widely acknowledged that in medicine, in particular, things can go wrong in the treatment of a patient even with the very best available care.[18] The practitioner is not judged by the standards of the most experienced, most skilful, or most highly qualified member of the profession, but by reference to the standards of the ordinarily competent practitioner in that particular field.[19] Nor is the doctor to be judged by the standards of the least qualified or least experienced. It is not a defence that he acted in good faith, or to the best of his ability, if he has failed to reach the objective standard of the ordinarily competent and careful doctor. Nor is it a defence to say that a doctor has committed an 'error of professional judgment' or a 'mere' error of judgment, since this gives no indication as to whether there has been negligence.[20] Some such errors may be consistent with the due exercise of professional skill, but other acts or omissions in the course of exercising 'clinical judgment' may be so glaringly below proper standards as to make a finding of negligence inevitable.[21] If the error of judgment is one that would not have been made by a reasonably competent professional person professing to have the standard and type of skill that the defendant held himself out as having, and acting with ordinary care, then it is negligent. If, on the other hand, it is an error that a person, acting with ordinary care, might have made, then it is not negligent.[22]

4.10 Within the broad term 'reasonable care', it is possible to identify some general principles which the courts have used in the decision-making process about what constitutes negligence. They are, however, no more than guidelines, and competing principles can point to different outcomes. Expert evidence is invariably a vital element in an action for medical negligence, but the importance attached to expert opinion should not obscure the underlying basis for a finding that the defendant has been negligent. This is that, in the light of the expert evidence, the defendant has taken an unjustified risk, for example, or has failed to keep up to date, or has undertaken a task beyond his competence, or conversely that the risk was justified by the potential benefit to the patient, or the harm was unforeseeable, and so on. In other words, expert opinion about the defendant's conduct (whether favourable or unfavourable) should itself be measured against the general principles applied to the question of breach of duty. This point has been emphasized by the House of Lords in *Bolitho v*

---

[16] Where an emergency is foreseeable the hospital authority may be negligent if there is an inadequate system for dealing with the known risks that the emergency is likely to create: *Bull v Devon AHA* (1989), [1993] 4 Med LR 117 (CA); *Meyer v Gordon* (1981) 17 CCLT 1 (BCSC).

[17] In *Dove v Jarvis* [2013] Med LR 284, a case where the Claimant was privately treated, the court rejected the absence of a favourable outcome as an indicator of legal fault even where there had been an express assurance. A statement by a surgeon that a hip operation would be 'well done' was held not to give rise to a higher contractual obligation than the duty of care and skill imposed by tort (at [62]–[64]).

[18] *Hancke v Hooper* (1835) 7 C & P 81, 84 *per* Tindal CJ; *Mahon v Osborne* [1939] 2 KB 14, 31 *per* Scott LJ; *Daniels v Heskin* [1954] IR 73, 84.

[19] *Lanphier v Phipos* (1838) 8 C & P 475, 479 *per* Tindal CJ; *R v Bateman* (1925) 94 LJKB 791, 794 *per* Lord Hewart CJ. See also *Greaves & Co (Contractors) Ltd v Baynham Meikle and Partners* [1975] 3 All ER 99, 103–04 *per* Lord Denning MR.

[20] Even where it is accepted that the exercise of professional judgment is very difficult in the given circumstances, that will not excuse any decision as being a reasonable one. See *Taafe v East of England Ambulance Service NHS Trust* [2012] EWHC 1335 *per* Sir Robert Nelson, at [56].

[21] *Whitehouse v Jordan* [1981] 1 All ER 267, 276 *per* Lord Edmund-Davies.

[22] ibid, 281 *per* Lord Fraser. See also *per* Lord Diplock in *Saif Ali v Sydney Mitchell & Co* [1980] AC 198, 220.

City and Hackney HA,[23] where Lord Browne-Wilkinson made it clear that the court has to weigh expert evidence in a form of risk–benefit analysis:

> the court has to be satisfied that the exponents of the body of opinion relied upon can demonstrate that such opinion has a logical basis. In particular in cases involving, as they so often do, the weighing of risks against benefits, the judge before accepting a body of opinion as being responsible, reasonable or respectable, will need to be satisfied that, in forming their views, the experts have directed their minds to the question of comparative risks and benefits and have reached a defensible conclusion on the matter.

Further, mistakes may occur not because of acts or omissions of individuals but because of failures in the system within which individuals work. Reasonableness remains the yardstick by which a hospital's systems are to be measured.[24] An issue which touches on the adequacy of the system in question is the resources available to fund it. Systems have to be designed to accommodate what can reasonably be foreseen. It is recognized that doctors cannot be in two places at once, and that a system depends on the balanced assessment of likely needs. As Lord Hoffmann put it in *Hall v Simons*:[25]

> the doctor, for example, owes a duty to the individual patient, but he also owes a duty to his other patients which may prevent him from giving one patient the treatment or resources he would ideally prefer.

B. The Standard of Care Required

1. Common professional practice

As a general rule, the fact that a defendant acted in accordance with the common practice of others in a similar situation is strong evidence that he has not been negligent.[26] Following a common practice is only *evidence*, however, it is not conclusive, since the court may find that the practice is itself negligent.[27] There could be many reasons, such as convenience, cost, or habit, why a particular practice is commonly followed, which have nothing to do with exercising reasonable care to avoid harming others.[28] There is no reason in theory why the general approach taken by the courts to compliance with accepted practice should not also apply to actions for medical negligence and it is frequently an issue in such cases. **4.11**

In *Vancouver General Hospital v McDaniel*[29] Lord Alness said that a defendant charged with negligence can 'clear his feet' if he shows that he has acted in accordance with general and approved practice, and there are numerous cases in which actions for medical negligence **4.12**

[23] [1997] 4 All ER 771, 778. For a helpful summary of the appropriate approach following *Bolitho*, see Green J in *C v North Cumbria University Hospitals NHS Trust* [2014] EWHC 61 (QB) at [25]. Of particular note is his observation at [73] that the purpose of assessing the Claimant's evidence is not to ascertain its reasonableness, but to 'determine whether it has the effect of placing the Defendant's expert evidence in such an altogether negative light that I should reject that evidence'.

[24] *Robertson v Nottingham HA* [1997] 8 Med LR 1, para 13.

[25] [2002] 1 AC 690C.

[26] *Morton v William Dixon Ltd* (1909) SC 807, 809; *Morris v West Hartlepool Steam Navigation Co Ltd* [1956] AC 552, 579.

[27] See, eg, *Lloyds Bank Ltd v EB Savory & Co* [1933] AC 201; *Cavanagh v Ulster Weaving Co Ltd* [1960] AC 145; *General Cleaning Contractors v Christmas* [1953] AC 180, 193 per Lord Reid; *Roberge v Bolduc* (1991) 78 DLR (4th) 666, 710 (SCC).

[28] As Lord Tomlin commented in *Bank of Montreal v Dominion Gresham Guarantee and Casualty Co* [1930] AC 659, 666: 'Neglect of duty does not cease by repetition to be neglect of duty'; *Carpenters' Co v British Mutual Banking Co Ltd* [1937] 3 All ER 811, 820 *per* Slesser LJ.

[29] (1934) 152 LT 56, 57–58; *Marshall v Lindsey County Council* [1935] 1 KB 516, 540 *per* Maugham LJ.

have been dismissed on the basis that the doctor conformed to an accepted practice of the profession.[30] Where there is more than one common practice, as the *Bolam* test contemplates, compliance with one of the practices will normally excuse the defendant. In *Maynard v West Midlands RHA*[31] Lord Scarman said that:

> It is not enough to show that there is a body of competent professional opinion which considers that theirs was a wrong decision, if there also exists a body of professional opinion, equally competent, which supports the decision as reasonable in the circumstances . . . Differences of opinion and practice exist, and will always exist, in the medical as in other professions. There is seldom any one answer exclusive of all others to problems of professional judgment. A court may prefer one body of opinion to the other: but that is no basis for a conclusion of negligence.[32]

4.13 It is ostensibly for the court to decide whether, on the evidence before it, the body of opinion which approved of the defendant's conduct could be said to be responsible. However, there are some judicial statements which suggest that the practice of the medical profession is determinative of the issue, and that it is not open to the court to condemn as negligent a commonly adopted practice. In *Maynard* Lord Scarman suggested that the 'seal of approval' of a distinguished body of professional opinion, held in good faith, would acquit the defendant of negligence.[33] His Lordship appeared to equate a *competent* (or 'responsible') body of professional opinion with 'distinguished' or 'respectable' in fact. This tends to conflate accepted practice with the absence of negligence, and, indeed, a 'responsible body of opinion' with the views of distinguished or respectable expert witnesses. This approach is even more apparent in Lord Scarman's speech in *Sidaway v Bethlem Royal Hospital Governors*[34] where he said:

> The *Bolam* principle may be formulated as a rule that a doctor is not negligent if he acts in accordance with a practice accepted at the time as proper by a responsible body of medical opinion even though other doctors adopt a different practice. *In short, the law imposes the duty of care; but the standard of care is a matter of medical judgment.*[35]

As Lord Scarman himself recognized: 'the implications of this view of the law are disturbing. It leaves the determination of a legal duty to the judgment of doctors.'

4.14 Outside the context of medical negligence actions, the courts have had no difficulty with the notion that commonly adopted practices may themselves be negligent. This has been most apparent in cases of employers' liability,[36] but it is also evident in some cases involving

[30] *Vancouver General Hospital v McDaniel* (1934) 152 LT 56; *Whiteford v Hunter* [1950] WN 553; *Bolam v Friern Hospital Management Committee* [1957] 2 All ER 118; *Gold v Haringey HA* [1987] 2 All ER 888.

[31] *Maynard v West Midlands RHA* [1984] 1 WLR 634.

[32] ibid, at 638; *Ratty v Haringey HA* [1994] 5 Med LR 413, 416 (CA); *Dunne v National Maternity Hospital* [1989] IR 91, 109 (Sup Ct Irl); *Kaban v Sett* [1994] 1 WWR 476, 479–80 (Man QB). On the other hand, where there has been no considered clinical judgment, but rather 'a catalogue of errors', the approach in *Maynard* to competing bodies of professional opinion will not be relevant: *Le Page v Kingston and Richmond HA* [1997] 8 Med LR 229, 240.

[33] *Maynard*, n 31, 639.

[34] [1985] 1 All ER 643. Lord Scarman was in the minority in that case. His Opinion has found favour in subsequent cases, however, see in particular *Montgomery v Lanarkshire Health Board* [2015] UKSC 11, [2015] 2 WLR 768, discussed at para 4.70.

[35] [1985] 1 All ER 643, 649 (emphasis added); cf Sir John Donaldson MR in the Court of Appeal, [1984] 1 All ER 1018, 1028: 'The definition of the duty of care is a matter for the law and the courts. They cannot stand idly by if the profession, by an excess of paternalism, denies its patients a real choice. In a word, the law will not permit the medical profession to play God.'

[36] As, eg, in *Cavanagh v Ulster Weaving Co Ltd* [1960] AC 145; *Morris v West Hartlepool Steam Navigation Co Ltd* [1956] AC 552; *Stokes v Guest, Keen & Nettlefold (Bolts & Nuts) Ltd* [1968] 1 WLR 1776, 1783.

professional liability.[37] There is no basis for applying a different rule about the effect of complying with common practice to the medical profession from that which is applied to all other professions, particularly since the Court of Appeal has emphasized that the *Bolam* test applies to all professions equally.[38] In other common law jurisdictions the courts have been careful to ensure that, ultimately, decisions as to what constitutes negligence remain for the court to determine. In *Anderson v Chasney*[39] Coyne JA commented that if general practice was a conclusive defence:

> a group of operators by adopting some practice could legislate themselves out of liability for negligence to the public by adopting or continuing what was an obviously negligent practice, even though a simple precaution, plainly capable of obviating danger which sometimes might result in death, was well known.

Thus, expert evidence from doctors as to a general or approved practice could not be accepted as conclusive on the issue of negligence, especially where the conduct in question did not involve a matter of technical skill and experience.[40] In *F v R*[41] King CJ acknowledged that professions may adopt unreasonable practices. Practices may develop in professions, not because they serve the interests of clients, but because they protect the interests or convenience of members of the profession. The court has an obligation to scrutinize professional practices to ensure that they accord with the standard of reasonableness imposed by the law. The ultimate question was not whether the defendant's conduct was in accord with the practices of the profession or some part of it, but whether it conformed to the standard of reasonable care demanded by the law. That was a question for the court and the duty of deciding it could not be delegated to any profession or group in the community.[42] **4.15**

[37] *Lloyds Bank v Savory & Co* [1933] AC 201, 203; *Edward Wong Finance Co Ltd v Johnson, Stokes and Masters* [1984] AC 296; *Re The Herald of Free Enterprise: Appeal by Captain Lewry, Independent*, 18 December 1987 (Div Ct); *Roberge v Bolduc* (1991) 78 DLR (4th) 666 (SCC).

[38] *Gold v Haringey HA* [1987] 2 All ER 888, 894 *per* Lloyd LJ; *Whitehouse v Jordan* [1981] 1 All ER 267, 276 *per* Lord Edmund-Davies.

[39] [1949] 4 DLR 71, 85 (Man CA); aff'd [1950] 4 DLR 223 (SCC). See also *Hajgato v London Health Association* (1982) 36 OR (2d) 669, 693 *per* Callaghan J.

[40] See also *Crits v Sylvester* (1956) 1 DLR (2d) 502, 514; aff'd (1956) 5 DLR (2d) 601; *Reynard v Carr* (1983) 30 CCLT 42, 68 (BCSC) *per* Bouck J; *Winrob v Street* (1959) 28 WWR 118, 122 (BCSC); *Hajgato v London Health Association* (1982) 36 OR (2d) 669, 693; *Goode v Nash* (1979) 21 SASR 419, 422 (SC of S Aus); *O' Donovan v Cork County Council* [1967] IR 173, 193 *per* Walsh J; *Albrighton v Royal Prince Alfred Hospital* [1980] 2 NSWLR 542, 562–563 *per* Reynolds JA (NSWCA); *Roberge v Bolduc* (1991) 78 DLR (4th) 666, 710 (SCC) *per* L'Heureux-Dubé J.

[41] (1982) 33 SASR 189, 194 (SC of S Aus), approved by Zelling J in *Battersby v Tottman* (1985) 37 SASR 524, 537; and Lockhart, Sheppard, and Pincus JJ in *E v Australian Red Cross Society* (1991) 105 ALR 53, 68, 82–83, 87 (Aus Fed CA).

[42] This view was approved by the High Court of Australia in *Rogers v Whitaker* (1992) 109 ALR 625; [1993] 4 Med LR 79, where it was accepted that, while evidence of acceptable medical practice might be regarded as a useful guide, it was for the court to determine whether the defendant's conduct conformed to the standard of reasonable care demanded by the law; *Trindade* (1993) 109 LQR 352; *McDonald and Swanton* (1993) 67 ALJ 145; *Malcolm* (1994) 2 Tort L Rev 81. In *Naxakis v Western General Hospital* [1999] HCA 22, (1999) 162 ALR 540 the High Court of Australia confirmed that the *Bolam* test had been rejected in *Rogers v Whitaker*. The test for medical negligence was not what other doctors say they would or would not have done in the same or similar circumstances, *per* Gaudron J at [18] and [19]. See also *Dunne v National Maternity Hospital* [1989] IR 91, 109 (Sup Ct Irl), where it was said that reliance on general and approved practice would not exculpate a defendant if the practice has 'inherent defects which ought to be obvious to any person giving the matter due consideration'. In *Collins v Mid-Western Health Board* [2000] 2 IR 154, 156 (Sup Ct Irl) Keane J said that: '. . . a lay tribunal will be reluctant to condemn as unsafe a practice which has been universally approved in a particular profession. The defects in a practice universally followed by specialists in the field are unlikely to be as obvious as the test requires: if they were, it is a reasonable assumption that it would not be so followed. But . . . ultimately, the courts must reserve the power to find as unsafe practices which have been generally followed in a profession.'

4.16 There are, moreover, some English cases in which, on the facts, compliance with common practice has been said to have been negligent. In *Clarke v Adams*[43] the claimant was being treated for a fibrositic condition of the heel and he was warned by the physiotherapist to say if he felt anything more than a 'comfortable warmth'. He suffered a burning injury resulting in the leg being amputated below the knee. Slade J held the defendant liable for giving an inadequate warning to enable the claimant to be safe, although it was the very warning that the defendant had been taught to give. In *Hucks v Cole*, Sachs LJ said that:

> When the evidence shows that a lacuna in professional practice exists by which risks of grave danger are knowingly taken, then, however small the risks, the courts must anxiously examine that lacuna—particularly if the risks can be easily and inexpensively avoided. If the court finds, on an analysis of the reasons given for not taking those precautions that, in the light of current professional knowledge, there is no proper basis for the lacuna, and that it is definitely not reasonable that those risks should have been taken, its function is to state that fact and where necessary to state that it constitutes negligence. In such a case the practice will no doubt thereafter be altered to the benefit of patients.[44]

4.17 His Lordship added that the fact that other practitioners would have done the same thing as the defendant was a weighty factor to be put in the scales on his behalf, but it was not conclusive. The court had to be vigilant to see whether the reasons given for putting a patient at risk were valid in the light of any well-known advance in medical knowledge, or whether they stemmed from a residual adherence to out-of-date ideas.[45]

4.18 This debate was substantially resolved by the House of Lords in *Bolitho v City and Hackney Health Authority*.[46] In that case, a 2-year-old boy had suffered brain damage as a result of cardiac arrest caused by an obstruction of the bronchial air passages. The claimant was in hospital at the time for the treatment of croup. The defendants admitted that there had been negligence, in that a doctor who had been summoned for assistance on more than one occasion had failed to attend. It was also common ground that had the claimant been seen by a doctor and intubated, clearing the obstruction, the brain damage could have been

[43] (1950) 94 SJ 599; see also *Jones v Manchester Corporation* [1952] 2 All ER 125, 129 *per* Singleton LJ citing Oliver J, the trial judge. Some commentators consider *Clarke v Adams* to be of questionable authority on the basis that it predates *Bolam v Friern HMC* [1957] 2 All ER 118: see J Montgomery, 'Medicine, Accountability and Professionalism' (1989) 16 J of Law and Soc 319, 323; A Dugdale and K Stanton, *Professional Negligence* (3rd edn, Butterworths 1998) para 15.26, n 6. The *Bolam* test, however, was not new; it simply encapsulated earlier statements of the law. This, at least, was Lord Diplock's interpretation: *Sidaway v Bethlem Royal Hospital Governors* [1985] 1 All ER 643, 657.

[44] (1968), [1993] 4 Med LR 393, 397.

[45] In *Bolitho v City and Hackney HA* [1993] 4 Med LR 381, 392 Dillon LJ suggested that the court could only adopt the approach of Sachs LJ and reject medical opinion on the ground that the reasons of one group of doctors does not really stand up to analysis if the court, fully conscious of its own lack of medical and clinical experience, was nonetheless clearly satisfied that the views of that group of doctors were *Wednesbury* unreasonable, ie views such as no reasonable body of doctors could have held. In *Joyce v Wandsworth HA* [1996] 7 Med LR 1, 20, however, Hobhouse LJ took a different view: 'In my judgment (*pace* Dillon LJ [1993] 4 Med LR at p. 392), it does not assist to introduce concepts from administrative law such as the *Wednesbury* test; such tests are directed to very different problems and their use, even by analogy, in negligence cases can, in my judgment, only serve to confuse.' In *X (Minors) v Bedfordshire County Council* [1995] 3 WLR 152, 170, in a slightly different context, Lord Browne-Wilkinson commented that: 'I do not believe that it is either helpful or necessary to introduce public law concepts as to the validity of a decision into the question of liability at common law for negligence.'

[46] [1997] 4 All ER 771. For a more detailed discussion of *Bolitho*, see H Teff, 'The Standard of Care in Medical Negligence—Moving on from Bolam?' (1998) 18 OJLS 473; A Grubb, (1998) 6 Med LR 378 (Commentary); M Jones, 'The Bolam test and the Reasonable Expert' (1999) 7 Tort L Rev 226; M Brazier and J Miola, 'Bye-bye Bolam: A Medical Litigation Revolution?' (2000) 8 Med LR 85; A MaClean, 'Beyond Bolam and Bolitho' (2002) 5 Med Law Int 205.

avoided. There were two schools of thought, however, as to whether in the circumstances it would have been appropriate to intubate. The doctor who failed to attend said that *if* she had attended the claimant she would not have intubated, and therefore the cardiac arrest and subsequent brain damage would have occurred in any event. There was evidence from one expert for the defendants, which the trial judge and the Court of Appeal chose to characterize as a responsible body of professional opinion, that he would not have intubated in the circumstances, although five medical experts for the claimant said that the child should have been intubated, and it was agreed that this was the only course of action that would have prevented the damage in this case. In the House of Lords the claimant submitted that the judge had been wrong in law to treat the *Bolam* test as requiring him to accept the views of one truthful body of expert professional advice, even though he was unpersuaded of its logical force, and that ultimately it was for the court, not for medical opinion, to decide what was the standard of care required of a professional in the circumstances of each particular case.

Delivering the judgment of the House, Lord Browne-Wilkinson agreed that the court was not bound to conclude that a doctor can escape liability for negligent treatment or diagnosis just because he leads evidence from a number of medical experts who are genuinely of the opinion that the defendant's treatment or diagnosis accorded with sound medical practice. The court had to be satisfied that the opinion had a logical basis, which would involve the weighing of risks against benefits, in order to reach a defensible conclusion. His Lordship referred to the judgment of Sachs LJ in *Hucks v Cole* and the decision of the Privy Council in *Edward Wong Finance Co Ltd v Johnson Stokes & Master*[47] and commented: **4.19**

> These decisions demonstrate that in cases of diagnosis and treatment there are cases where, despite a body of professional opinion sanctioning the defendant's conduct, the defendant can properly be held liable for negligence (I am not here considering questions of disclosure of risk). In my judgment that is because, in some cases, it cannot be demonstrated to the judge's satisfaction that the body of opinion relied upon is reasonable or responsible. In the vast majority of cases the fact that distinguished experts in the field are of a particular opinion will demonstrate the reasonableness of that opinion. In particular, where there are questions of assessment of the relative risks and benefits of adopting a particular medical practice, a reasonable view necessarily presupposes that the relative risks and benefits have been weighed by the experts in forming their opinions. But if, in a rare case, it can be demonstrated that the professional opinion is not capable of withstanding logical analysis, the judge is entitled to hold that the body of opinion is not reasonable or responsible.[48]

It is rare for the courts to condemn a commonly accepted practice as negligent. Normally, it will only be where the risk was, or should have been, obvious to the defendant so that it would be folly to disregard it that the courts will take this step.[49] The point was stressed by Lord Browne-Wilkinson in *Bolitho v City and Hackney Health Authority*.[50] It would very seldom be right, said his Lordship, for a judge to reach the conclusion that views genuinely held by a competent medical expert were unreasonable. It would be wrong to allow the assessment of medical risks and benefits, which was a matter of clinical judgment, to **4.20**

47 [1984] 1 AC 296.
48 [1997] 4 All ER 771, 779.
49 *Paris v Stepney Borough Council* [1951] AC 367, 382 per Lord Normand ('obvious folly'); *General Cleaning Contractors v Christmas* [1953] AC 180, 193 *per* Lord Reid ('obvious danger'); *Morris v West Hartlepool Steam Navigation Co Ltd* [1956] AC 552, 579 *per* Lord Cohen ('obvious risk'); *Stokes v Guest, Keen & Nettlefold (Bolts & Nuts) Ltd* [1968] 1 WLR 1776, 1783; see also *O'Donovan v Cork County Council* [1967] IR 173, 193 *per* Walsh J; Gent v Wilson (1956) 2 DLR (2d) 160, 165 *per* Schroeder JA (Ont CA).
50 [1997] 4 All ER 771, 779.

deteriorate into seeking to persuade the judge to prefer one of two views both of which are capable of being logically supported: 'It is only where a judge can be satisfied that the body of expert opinion cannot be logically supported at all that such opinion will not provide the bench mark by reference to which the defendant's conduct falls to be assessed.' Thus, *Bolitho* imposes a 'gloss' on the *Bolam* test, by enabling the Court to conclude, in an appropriate case, that the doctor was negligent even though he acted consistently with a number of his peers. This leaves the ultimate question of breach to be determined by the judge as a matter of law, and not to the medical community as a matter of accepted practice.[51]

4.21 In *Marriott v West Midlands HA*[52] the claimant sustained a head injury in a fall and was unconscious for about half an hour. He was admitted to hospital, and, after X-rays and neurological observations he was discharged the next day. At home he was lethargic, and had headaches and no appetite. He did not improve. Eight days after the fall his GP visited the claimant at home, but the neurological tests he carried out showed no abnormality. The GP advised the claimant's wife to telephone him if the claimant deteriorated and suggested analgesics for the headaches. Four days later the claimant's condition suddenly deteriorated and, following emergency surgery on a skull fracture, he was left paralysed and with a speech disorder. The trial judge held that if there was a body of professional opinion which supported the course of leaving a patient at home in these circumstances, then it was not a reasonable body of opinion. The risk might be small, but the consequences if something went wrong would be disastrous for the patient. In the circumstances the only reasonably prudent course where there was a risk of an intracranial lesion, judged from the point of view of the patient, was to readmit the patient to hospital for further testing and observation. The Court of Appeal held that the trial judge was entitled to reject the defendant's expert evidence, applying *Bolitho*. She had considered the small risk of something going wrong, but had weighed that against the seriousness of the consequences for the claimant if the risk did materialize, and the fact that the facilities available in modern hospitals for carrying out scans and other diagnostic procedures were readily available.[53]

4.22 Where the case does not involve difficult or uncertain questions of medical or surgical treatment, or highly technical scientific issues, but is concerned with whether obvious and simple precautions could have been taken, it will be easier for the court to form its own judgment and the practice of experts, though not irrelevant, may be more readily discounted.[54] Where, however, there are difficult, uncertain, highly technical scientific questions requiring information not ordinarily expected of a practitioner, and where the state of medical knowledge

[51] See R Mulheron, 'Trumping Bolam: A Critical Legal Analysis of Bolitho's Gloss' (2010) 69 Cambridge Law Journal 609.

[52] [1999] Lloyd's Rep Med 23; Jones (1999) 15 PN 117.

[53] An expert's views which are based on a mistaken diagnosis are likely to be condemned as illogical: *Drake v Pontefract Health Authority; Wakefield and Pontefract Community NHS Trust* [1998] Lloyd's Rep Med 425, 445 (QBD). See also *Hunt v NHS Litigation Authority* (2000, unreported, QBD), where the defendant's expert's view that the circumstances for the administration of the drug syntocinon to a mother in the course of labour (in order to speed up contractions) had not changed in a forty-seven-minute period during which there were signs of foetal distress on the CTG trace were rejected as 'without logical support', not least because it was inconsistent with other answers that the witness had given in evidence. See further *Reynolds v North Tyneside Health Authority* [2002] Lloyd's Rep Med 459, where the defendants' argument that it was reasonable to ignore a small risk of catastrophic consequences, when the burden of precautions was minimal, was rejected as indefensible. In *Taafe v East of England Ambulance Service NHS Trust* [2012] EWHC 1335 the Defendant's expert evidence that it was reasonable for the paramedics to fail to refer to hospital was rejected as unsustainable in circumstances where the judge had found multiple discreet failings in their assessment and training (at [67]–[68]).

[54] *Anderson v Chasney* [1949] 4 DLR 71, 86–87 *per* Coyne JA (Man CA); aff'd [1950] 4 DLR 223 (SCC); *Chapman v Rix* (1959) 103 SJ 940 *per* Morris LJ (CA).

was highly variable between scientists, public health authorities, and different medical communities, it is not appropriate for the court to find that a practice which conformed to what other similarly situated practitioners were following was negligent.[55] In these circumstances the court should confine itself to the prevailing standards of practice.

Before any question of complying with accepted practice can arise the court must be satisfied on the evidence presented to it that there is a responsible body of professional opinion which supports the practice. It is always open to the court to reject expert evidence applying the ordinary principles of credibility that would be applied in any courtroom.[56] In *Hills v Potter*, Hirst J denied that the *Bolam* test allows the medical profession to set the standard of care: **4.23**

> In every case the court must be satisfied that the standard contended for . . . accords with that upheld by a substantial body[57] of medical opinion, and that this body of medical opinion is both respectable and responsible, and experienced in this particular field of medicine.[58]

Similarly, in *Bolitho v City and Hackney HA* Farquharson LJ pointed out that: **4.24**

> There is of course no inconsistency between the decisions in *Hucks v Cole* and *Maynard's* case. It is not enough for a defendant to call a number of doctors to say what he had done or not done was in accord with accepted clinical practice. It is necessary for the judge to consider that evidence and decide whether that clinical practice puts the patient unnecessarily at risk.[59]

Following accepted practice, or one of several such practices, is strong evidence of the exercise of reasonable care, but ultimately it is for the court to determine what constitutes **4.25**

---

[55] *ter Neuzen v Korn* (1993) 103 DLR (4th) 473, 506 (BCCA); aff'd (1995) 127 DLR (4th) 577 (SCC).

[56] For example, an expert witness should be independent. Evidence which, eg, descends into advocacy may well be treated as less credible. See, eg, *Murphy v Wirral HA* [1996] 7 Med LR 99, 104; *El-Morssy v Bristol and District HA* [1996] 7 Med LR 232, 240; *Wiszniewski v Central Manchester HA* [1996] 7 Med LR 248, 254, 262. In *Gent v Royal Cornwall NHS Trust* (Unreported), 23 April 2012, considerably less weight was accorded to the evidence of the defendant's expert who was 'consistently too ready and willing . . . to suggest an exculpatory explanation' (at [62]). For discussion of the duties of an independent expert see: *National Justice Compania Naviera SA v Prudential Assurance Company Ltd, 'The Ikarian Reefer'* [1993] 2 Lloyd's Rep 68, 81–82; *Sharpe v Southend HA* [1997] 8 Med LR 299, 303. These principles have been expanded upon in the CPR Pt 35, and in particular the Practice Direction that supplements CPR Pt 35, and more recently the *Code of Guidance on Expert Evidence*: see *Civil Procedure* (Sweet & Maxwell 2014), vol 1, 35PD and 35.16. The Code of Guidance is also extracted at (2002) 8 Clinical Risk 60.

[57] In *De Freitas v O'Brien* [1995] 6 Med LR 108 it was argued that this reference to a 'substantial body of medical opinion' meant that the defendant could not rely on a small number of experts in the field as supporting a particular practice. The Court of Appeal rejected this argument. The test is whether there is a 'responsible body' of opinion, which cannot be measured in purely quantitative terms. On the facts, a body of 11 doctors who specialized in spinal surgery, out of a total of well over 1,000 orthopaedic and neurosurgeons in the country, could represent a responsible body of opinion.

[58] [1983] 3 All ER 716, 728. See also *per* Lord Diplock in *Sidaway v Bethlem Royal Hospital Governors* [1985] 1 All ER 643, 659, stating that the court must be satisfied by the expert evidence that a body of opinion qualifies as a 'responsible' body of medical opinion; *Dowdie v Camberwell HA* [1997] 8 Med LR 368, 375 *per* Kay J: 'The mere fact that two distinguished expert witnesses have testified that it was within the range of acceptable practice to proceed in that way does not oblige me to accept their evidence and, on this issue, I accept the evidence of the plaintiff 's experts . . .'

[59] [1993] 4 Med LR 381, 386. In *Chapman v Rix* (1960) [1994] 5 Med LR 239, 247 Lord Goddard said that a doctor cannot avoid a finding of negligence merely by finding two doctors to say that they would have acted as he did, provided there was evidence the other way. In *Gascoine v Ian Sheridan & Co* [1994] 5 Med LR 437, 444 Mitchell J commented that: 'as a matter of common sense . . . simply because a number of doctors gave evidence to the same effect, that does not automatically constitute an established and

negligence. It will be rare for the court to conclude that a common practice was negligent, but when this does happen it will be through a finding that the practice was not 'responsible'. Once the practice followed by the defendant is acknowledged to be a 'responsible' practice it is not open to the court to hold that it was negligent, even where another body of 'responsible' professional opinion is critical of the practice. The inherent danger in the *Bolam* test, however, is that if the courts defer too readily to expert evidence, medical standards may decline, since where there are competing views within the medical profession the *Bolam* test supports the lowest common denominator.

(i) Decisions not involving professional skill or reasoning

4.26 In *JD Williams & Co Ltd v Michael Hyde & Associates Ltd*[60] the Court of Appeal held that the *Bolam* test does not apply where no special skill is required in determining whether there has been negligence (in which case the test would be the usual 'reasonable person' standard of reasonable care in all the circumstances). On the facts of the case (which involved a judgment as to whether further investigation of the risk of discolouration of garments by a particular type of heating system was required or not), it was held that the exercise of judgment required did not involve any architectural skills, and therefore the judge was entitled to conclude that the failure to investigate the risk by the defendant architects was negligent, without reference to the *Bolam* test. The fact that other architects would also have ignored the risk was irrelevant. Sedley LJ commented that the *Bolam* test typically applied where the negligence was said to lie in a conscious choice of available courses made by a trained professional, but it was typically inappropriate where the negligence consisted of an oversight. In many, though not all, cases where there was more than one tenable view of acceptable practice, competence had to be gauged by the lower or lowest of them. But 'to extend the *Bolam* principle to all allegations of professional negligence would be to make the professions, to an extent large enough to accommodate much harm to the public, judges in their own cause'.[61]

4.27 Although Sedley LJ's view is that the *Bolam* test should have a much more restricted ambit, so that it could not be invoked by a professional person where he has not in fact exercised a professional judgment, in *Adams v Rhymney Valley District Council*[62] a majority of the Court of Appeal held that the *Bolam* test applied even where the particular defendant did not have the qualifications of a professional in the relevant field, and even though he did not go through the process of reasoning which a qualified professional would undertake before choosing a particular course of action. Thus, if the defendant had in fact adopted a course of conduct which a responsible body of opinion would have supported, even by accident, he was not to be held negligent. In a dissenting judgment, Sedley LJ said[63] that the purpose of the *Bolam* test was to enable the court to determine whether a person professing and purporting to exercise a particular skill has exercised it with sufficient competence to escape a charge of negligence. A defendant who had failed to set about exercising a professional skill could not expect to be judged by the court as if he had exercised it. The court could not proceed as if an educated choice had been made when it knew that it had not. It was a 'requirement of the *Bolam* test that the defendant should have considered and reflected upon the alternative courses available and made a conscious choice between them'. The question then,

alternative "school of thought" if, for example, the reasons given to substantiate the views expressed do not stand up to sensible analysis: see *Hucks v Cole* [(1968) [1993] 4 Med LR 393] (*per* Sachs LJ).'

[60] [2000] Lloyd's Rep PN 823.

[61] ibid, 835.

[62] [2000] Lloyd's Rep PN 777. See *de Prez* (2001) 17 PN 75.

[63] *Adams*, at [16]–[19].

was whether the defendant's eventual choice of a course of conduct made any difference to the outcome, but that was a question of causation, not professional competence. Thus, if on the balance of probabilities, the professional who should have been consulted would have acted as the defendant did, the negligence did not have any causal effect. But if the professional would probably have done something different which would have affected the outcome, the defendant could not rely on the argument that other responsible professionals might have acted in a way which would not have avoided the damage. The approach of Sedley LJ is out of step with the traditional analysis of negligence. Negligence measures an objective standard of conduct rather than a subjective process of reasoning. If, objectively, the defendant conformed to a standard of care that would have been adopted by a responsible body of professional opinion, the fact that he did so as a result of a flawed process of reasoning, or indeed without any reasoning, is simply irrelevant.[64] An analysis of the reasoning process, the weighing of foreseeable risks and benefits against the burden of precautions, clearly is important when considering whether a particular professional practice constitutes a responsible practice. That, however, is part and parcel of subjecting professional practice to the logical scrutiny required by *Bolitho*.

(ii) Questions of fact

The *Bolam* test does not apply to the resolution of disputes about fact. Thus, where there is a difference of opinion between expert witnesses about a question of fact the court is not precluded from choosing between the expert evidence, even if both views could be characterized as reasonable or responsible. Indeed, the court has a duty to resolve disputes of fact and reach a finding about the facts. In *Penney, Palmer and Cannon v East Kent HA*[65] the claimants alleged that there had been negligence in the screening of cervical smear tests, in that some of the smears were falsely reported as negative, resulting in delay in obtaining treatment for cervical cancer. Screening was carried out by biomedical scientists or by qualified cytology screeners. They did not diagnose, they merely reported what they saw on the slides. If there was an abnormality or if there was doubt as to what was seen, the slide was passed on to a senior screener (a checker). If the checker agreed with the categorization it was passed on to a pathologist. If the pathologist confirmed the abnormality the patient was referred to a gynaecologist for a colposcopy or a biopsy. The expert witnesses (five pathologists) agreed that if a screener was in doubt about what was seen on the slide, it should not be classified as negative. In each case the claimants' smears were reported as normal or negative, but they all developed cervical cancer. The Court of Appeal held that the *Bolam* test applied, subject to the *Bolitho* proviso that expert evidence as to the defendants' conduct had to stand up to logical analysis. The *Bolam* test did not apply, however, to questions of fact, including the question of what could be seen on the individual slides. Thus, the questions that had to be asked were: (i) what could be seen on each slide; (ii) could a reasonably competent cytoscreener have failed to see what was on the slide; (iii) could a reasonably competent cytoscreener, bearing in mind what he or she should have observed, have treated the slide as negative? The answer to the first question required expert evidence, but if there was a dispute amongst the experts as to what was visible on the slides the judge had to make **4.28**

[64] See the comments of Chadwick LJ in *Green v Hancocks (A Firm)* [2001] Lloyd's Rep PN 212 at [60]: 'I do not think it necessary . . . to consider whether it could ever be right to look at the advice given in isolation from the thought process which led to that advice. If the advice is correct, it may well be irrelevant whether the adviser hit upon it as the result of careful and detailed thought, or as the result of experience which overrode the need for a detailed analysis of the reasoning process, or purely by luck. I would not endorse the view that, in every case, a professional adviser will be held negligent because he does not spell out in detail the reasons which lead him to the advice which he gives.'

[65] [2000] Lloyd's Rep Med 41.

his own finding of fact, on the balance of probabilities, a finding which might inevitably involve the rejection of some of the expert evidence. The judge then had to consider the second and third questions in determining whether there had been a breach of duty. Those issues involved an assessment of the expert evidence. All the experts were agreed, however, that an 'absolute confidence' standard should have applied, whereby if there was any doubt in the cytoscreener's mind as to whether the slide was normal it should not have been classified as negative. To the extent that the defendants' experts were saying that it was acceptable to classify a slide as negative when the cytoscreener could not say whether the features of the slide were or were not pre-cancerous, their opinion did not withstand logical analysis. Similarly, if the question is which of two possible explanations for an event having occurred is to be accepted, and there are competing theories from the expert witnesses, the court has to resolve that dispute in determining factual causation.[66]

2. Departures from common practice

4.29 A departure from accepted practice may be evidence of negligence,[67] but it is not conclusive.[68] If deviation from a common professional practice was considered proof of negligence then no doctor could introduce a new technique or method of treatment without facing the risk of a negligence action if something went wrong.[69] The fundamental test remains whether the defendant acted with reasonable care in all the circumstances, and the significance of compliance with or deviation from common professional practice lies in its evidential value. Sometimes, a departure from accepted practice may provide overwhelming evidence of a breach of duty, particularly where the practice is followed as a precaution against a known risk and the defendant has no good reason for not following the normal procedure. If the risk should materialize the defendant will have great difficulty in avoiding a finding of negligence.[70]

4.30 Some instances of departure from accepted practice are quite clearly negligent. In *Chin Keow v Government of Malaysia*[71] a doctor gave a patient an injection of penicillin without making any enquiry about the patient's medical history. Had he done so he would have discovered that she was allergic to penicillin. The patient died due to an allergic reaction to

[66] In *Fallows v Randle* [1997] 8 Med LR 160 an operation to sterilize the claimant failed to achieve sterility. There were competing theories as to how the operation could have failed, one of which involved negligence by the defendant whereas the other did not. The trial judge preferred the claimant's explanation. Stuart-Smith LJ said, at 165, that the *Bolam* principle 'has really no application where what the judge has to decide is, on balance, which of two explanations—for something which has undoubtedly occurred which shows that the operation has been unsuccessful—is to be preferred. That is a question of fact which the judge has to determine on the ordinary basis of a balance of probability. It is not a question of saying whether there was a respectable body of medical opinion here which says that this can happen by chance without any negligence, it is a question for the judge to weigh up the evidence on both sides, and he is, in my judgment, entitled in a situation like this, to prefer the evidence of one expert witness to that of the other.' Naturally there are also disputes of medical facts for which expert witnesses are not required at all: in *Zhang v Homerton Hospitals NHS Trust* [2012] EWHC 1208, where it was common ground that an obstetrician had caused injuries during delivery but in dispute as to how she had done so, the court had regard almost exclusively to oral evidence and subsequent complaints correspondence in determining as a fact that part of the injury had been caused by rotation of the baby's head.

[67] *Robinson v Post Office* [1974] 2 All ER 737, 745.

[68] *Holland v Devitt & Moore Nautical College* The Times, 4 March 1960 (QBD), where a slight departure from the standard textbook treatment was held not negligent, since the doctor had to treat a particular patient, whereas the textbooks deal with a subject generally: *Dunne v National Maternity Hospital* [1989] IR 91, 109.

[69] *Hunter v Hanley* 1955 SC 200, 206 *per* Lord President Clyde.

[70] See *Clark v MacLennan* [1983] 1 All ER 416.

[71] [1967] 1 WLR 813.

the drug. The doctor was aware of the remote possibility of this risk materializing but he carried on with his routine practice of not enquiring because he had not had any mishaps before. He was held to have been negligent. All the medical evidence was to the effect that enquiries, which would have taken no more than five minutes, were necessary. Similarly, in *Landau v Werner*[72] a psychiatrist who engaged in social contact with a female patient who had developed a strong and obsessive emotional attachment to him was held to have been negligent. His conduct was a departure from recognized standards in the practice of psychiatry and led to a serious deterioration in the patient's mental health. Sellers LJ said that:

> ... a doctor might not be negligent if he tried a new technique but if he did he must justify it before the court. If his novel or exceptional treatment had failed disastrously he could not complain if it was held that he went beyond the bounds of due care and skill as recognised generally. Success was the best justification for unusual and unestablished treatment.

One consequence of the *Bolam* test is that where there are two competing responsible bodies of professional opinion and the defendant adheres to one view, but carelessly fails to follow his own normal practice with the result that he complies with the alternative approach, he will not be held negligent because he will have conformed to a practice accepted as proper by a responsible body of professional opinion. Thus, where the doctor fails to give a warning about the risks of treatment which he would usually give, but there is a responsible body of medical opinion which, as a matter of deliberate policy, would not warn the patient of the particular risks, the defendant will not be liable since, though he has departed from his own clinical practice, he has conformed to a practice accepted as proper by a responsible body of professional opinion, albeit by accident.[73] In *Gascoine v Ian Sheridan & Co*[74] a case of alleged negligent overtreatment, Mitchell J commented that: 'If on some hit-and-miss basis [the defendants] treated correctly (or correctly in the opinion of a respected reasonably competent body of thinking in 1978) then liability in negligence could not be established.' **4.31**

Codified standards of professional conduct, though not conclusive, may constitute significant evidence of what constitutes reasonable care.[75] In the context of health care, the introduction of medical audit and NHS clinical governance has led to the development of treatment protocols and best practice guidelines, providing a consensus view of experts in the field as to the proper standards.[76] It might then become increasingly difficult for a doctor to argue that the protocol was rejected in favour of some alternative method, even if there are some doctors prepared to state that they disagree with the protocol produced by the experts.[77] There is already evidence that the courts are prepared to consider, and accept as highly persuasive, guidelines produced by the medical profession on appropriate **4.32**

---

72 (1961) 105 SJ 257 and 1008 (CA).

73 *Moyes v Lothian Health Board* [1990] 1 Med LR 463, 470. See now, for the duty of disclosure, *Montgomery v Lanarkshire Health Board* [2015] UKSC 11, [2015] 2 WLR 768.

74 [1994] 5 Med LR 437, 458. See also *Lachambre v Nair* [1989] 2 WWR 749 (Sask QB).

75 *Lloyd Cheyham & Co Ltd v Littlejohn & Co* (1985) 2 PN 154. See *Gwilliam* (1986) 2 PN 175.

76 One consequence of the introduction of clinical governance has been a proliferation of agencies of the Department of Health issuing guidance, some of which is directly relevant to patient safety. See, eg, the National Patient Safety Agency (<http://www.npsa.nhs>). The General Medical Council ('GMC') publishes extensive Codes of Practice for doctors, ranging from general statements of good practice (eg Good Medical Practice, 2013) to specific advice on how to proceed in particular circumstances. These codes are available from the GMC website (<http://www.gmc-uk.org/guidance/index.asp >).

77 *Harpwood* (1994) 1 Med Law Int 241, 250, 251. Instructive here are the CEPOD Reports into perioperative deaths which have identified certain systematic errors which can occur during surgery: see N Buck, H B Devlin, and J N Lunn, *Report of a Confidential Enquiry into Perioperative Deaths* (Nuffield Provincial Hospitals Trust and the King's Fund 1987); E A Campling, H B Devlin, R W Hoile, and J N Lunn, *Report of the National Confidential Enquiry into Perioperative Deaths* (National Confidential Enquiry into

standards of conduct.[78] Thus where a practitioner can show that he or she acted according to established guidelines (at a national or local level), the only live question is likely to be the reasonableness of those guidelines.[79] In *C v North Cumbria University Hospitals NHS Trust*,[80] Green J gave extensive consideration to the reasonableness of guidelines for administering doses of Prostin, a uterine stimulant. After noting a consensus amongst the experts that the guidelines were incomplete and incoherent in a number of respects, he found that compliance could therefore only amount to *prima facie* evidence of reasonable conduct.

4.33 The fact that a practitioner who departs from the accepted methods of treatment will normally have to provide some justification for doing so could have an inhibiting effect on doctors who seek to employ novel or experimental methods in the interests of their patients where traditional techniques have failed. There is a public interest in allowing the medical profession to develop new, and more effective methods of health care, without the fear that they may be sued for negligence simply for trying something different from established practice.[81] On the other hand, patients should not be recklessly subjected to untried and potentially dangerous experimentation.[82] The law has to reach a balance between these competing considerations. One response has been to say that in such circumstances the courts should be careful not to make a finding of negligence simply because the patient has sustained injury.[83] There is likely to be a time lag between the development of new methods and their acceptance by the profession. Where the new treatment is not yet supported by a responsible body of medical opinion a defendant will have to justify his decision simply by reference to the 'reasonable doctor'. This will depend on the relative risk of the treatment in comparison to the alternative treatments and the nature of the illness for which it was prescribed. Where the patient's condition is very serious and the standard treatment is ineffective, a doctor will be justified in taking greater risks in an attempt to provide some effective treatment. In *Zimmer v Ringrose* Prowse JA said that:

> A physician is entitled to decide that the situation dictates the adoption of an innovative course of treatment. As long as he discharges his duty of disclosure, and is not otherwise in breach of his duties of skill and care, eg has not negligently adopted the procedure given

Perioperative Deaths, 1990). See also H B Devlin, 'Audit in Surgery: The National Confidential Enquiry into Perioperative Deaths' (1995) 1 Clinical Risk 97. On the other hand, rigid adherence to guidelines can be inappropriate. Guidelines and protocols vary in their validity, and attempts to reach professional 'consensus' can result in inadequate and biased guidelines: B Hurwitz, 'Protocols, Guidelines and the Law of Negligence' (1995) 1 Clinical Risk 142; B Hurwitz, 'Legal and Political Considerations of Clinical Practice Guidelines' (1999) 318 BMJ 661.

[78] See *W v Egdell* [1990] 1 All ER 835 in the context of confidentiality; and *Airedale NHS Trust v Bland* [1993] 1 All ER 821 in the context of the treatment for patients in a persistent vegetative state. See also *Pierre v Marshall* [1994] 8 WWR 478 (Alta QB), where the defendant was held to have been negligent for failing to follow the recommendations of the Alberta Medical Association and the Society of Obstetricians and Gynaecologists of Canada that there should be universal screening of pregnant women for gestational diabetes, notwithstanding that there was still controversy about the cost-effectiveness of universal screening.

[79] In *Cowley v Cheshire and Merseyside SHA* [2007] EWHC 48, (2007) 94 BMLR 29, Forbes J found a hospital's policy on the administration of cortico-steroids in labour to be reasonable, a finding which disposed of the claimant's case.

[80] [2014] EWHC 61 (QB).

[81] *Sidaway v Bethlem Royal Hospital Governors* [1985] 1 All ER 643, 657 *per* Lord Diplock.

[82] In *Coughlin v Kuntz* (1987) 42 CCLT 142 (BCSC); aff'd [1990] 2 WWR 737 (BCCA) the defendant was held to have been negligent for adopting a method of performing an operation which was experimental, unsupported by clinical study, and favoured by no other orthopaedic surgeon. The procedure was under investigation by the College of Physicians and Surgeons, which had urged the defendant to undertake a moratorium on the procedure.

[83] *Wilsher v Essex AHA* [1986] 3 All ER 801, 812 *per* Mustill LJ.

the circumstances, the doctor will not be held liable for implementing such a course of treatment.[84]

The defendant's method of sterilization was 'experimental and quite unsupported by clinical study as a method acceptable for human beings'.[85] He was held to have been negligent in failing to inform the claimant that the technique had not been approved by the medical profession.

4.34 It is clear that the patient should not be exposed to excessive risk and there should be some attempt to provide scientific validation for a new technique. In *Hepworth v Kerr* [86] the defendant anaesthetist adopted a new hypotensive anaesthetic technique which he knew had never been attempted routinely before, in order to provide a blood-free field for the operating surgeon. He knew that he was experimenting, but did not embark upon any proper scientific validation of his technique in some 1,500 patients by the time of the claimant's operation. It was not a minor adjustment to well-established techniques, but a step completely outside conventional wisdom which was right at the margins of safety and effectively took patients 'to the very edge of existence'. McKinnon J held the defendant liable for the condition of anterior spinal artery syndrome (spinal stroke) which the claimant was subsequently found to have developed, despite the fact that this amounted to a condemnation of the defendant's 'life-time work'.

4.35 A degree of care is expected which is commensurate with the risk involved, and innovative treatment would be regarded as inherently 'risky' until it has become tried and tested. In *Independent Broadcasting Authority v EMI Electronics Ltd and BICC Construction Ltd*[87] the House of Lords held that a defendant employed to design an experimental television mast had to demonstrate that he had exercised a high degree of care both in assessing the risks of the venture and the possible alternatives. He could not justify his actions simply by saying 'we were taking a step into the unknown and so the risks were unforeseeable'. There was an obligation to think things through and to assess the dimensions of the 'venture into the unknown'.[88] This would apply to claims arising out of a systematic research project, whether therapeutic or non-therapeutic. An allegation of negligence in conducting research would involve proving that the design, the performance, or the follow-up of the experimental procedure was negligent, or that the disclosure of information concerning risks was inadequate. A researcher has a duty to investigate fully the possible consequences of the research using existing published literature and animal experiments where appropriate, prior to conducting research on human subjects.[89] Medical research must seek to minimize the risks to the research subjects, for example by providing for termination of the project if a serious risk of harm became apparent; provision for emergencies; and careful periodic observation of the subjects.[90]

[84] (1981) 124 DLR (3d) 215, 223–24 (Alta CA). See also *Waters v West Sussex HA* [1995] 6 Med LR 362.

[85] *Zimmer v Ringrose* (1978) 89 DLR (3d) 646, 652 *per* MacDonald J. See also *Cryderman v Ringrose* [1977] 3 WWR 109; aff'd [1978] 3 WWR 481 (Alta SC, Appellate Division).

[86] [1995] 6 Med LR 139.

[87] (1980) 14 BLR 1.

[88] ibid, 31 *per* Lord Edmund-Davies.

[89] *Vacwell Engineering Co Ltd v BDH Chemicals* [1971] 1 QB 88, where the defendant was negligent in failing to check all relevant publications dealing with a little-known chemical prior to marketing it.

[90] *Zimmer v Ringrose* (1978) 89 DLR (3d) 646, 656. It is also arguable that a research project which failed to comply with national or international ethical codes on medical experimentation could be found to have been conducted negligently, on the basis that the codes constitute evidence of what is reasonable care, by reference to the accepted practice of the profession: see A M Dugdale and K M Stanton, *Professional Negligence* (3rd edn, Butterworths 1998) para 15.23. Both therapeutic and non-therapeutic medical research are governed by the guidelines of the *Declaration of Helsinki*, extracted in I Kennedy and

4.36 *The Creutzfeldt-Jakob Disease Litigation, Plaintiffs v United Kingdom Medical Research Council*[91] concerned the transmission of the 'slow virus' which causes Creutzfeldt-Jakob Disease (CJD) from human growth hormone (HGH) extracted from the pituitaries of cadavers. Between 1959 and 1985 almost 2,000 children were treated with HGH, and the claimants had all been treated with HGH when they were children. Since 1985, sixteen of the recipients had died of CJD and a further three were expected to do so. Eleven claimants (the group A claimants) had developed CJD as a consequence of receiving HGH contaminated with the CJD virus. There were a further eighty-seven claimants in Group B who had received HGH who had not, as yet, been diagnosed with CJD. The treatment with HGH had originally been a clinical trial under the auspices of the Medical Research Council, but subsequently became a treatment programme for which the Department of Health was responsible. Morland J found that because of the emerging evidence about the transmission of slow viruses the treatment programme should have been partially suspended from 1 July 1977. The defendants had been negligent in permitting the programme to continue, because information about the risk of slow virus infection was conveyed in a cursory manner. In concluding that the department had been negligent on the basis of its lethargy in carrying out enquiries and research into the risk of slow virus transmission, once it had been alerted to that risk, Morland J stated a number of general principles. First, the question of negligence has to be assessed on the basis of the standards and knowledge which could reasonably have been expected at the time of the alleged negligence. Secondly, the risks of the programme had to be weighed against the benefits:

> Many advances in medicine carry with them risk. A risk may be, from a scientific point of view, theoretical and may never become a reality. A risk may be a real risk, but, weighed against the benefit of a drug or treatment, a risk upon careful consideration worth taking, but the risks of a drug or a treatment need constant review in the light of expanding knowledge and experience.[92]

4.37 In assessing that risk the courts had to balance the dangers of too readily condemning novel procedures which went wrong as negligent, against the potential progress that research could produce:

> The courts must be very cautious in condemning a clinical trial or therapeutic programme. Too ready a labelling of an act or omission as negligent by the courts could stultify progress in medical and scientific research and render eminent experts reluctant to serve on committees voluntarily. However, during the clinical trial of a new drug or form of treatment, and especially when the clinical trial is becoming a general therapeutic programme, all reasonably practicable steps should be taken to minimise dangers and side-effects. To discharge this duty, constant alert and inquiring evaluation of the trial or programme is required.[93]

4.38 Thirdly, the standard of care applied to publicly funded or sponsored research should not be lower than that applied to commercial organizations: 'In my judgment, the same duty with the same standard of care is owed to all patients who are the subjects of clinical trials or new therapeutic programmes, whether the responsibility of a pharmaceutical company, government department or other agency.'[94] Finally, in respect of the standard of care that could be expected of an advisory committee Morland J concluded that:

A Grubb, *Medical Law* (3rd edn, Butterworths 2000) 1678. See further the Royal College of Physicians, *Guidelines on the Practice of Ethics Committees in Medical Research Involving Human Participants* (4th edn, RCP 2007). See generally D Giesen, 'Civil Liability of Physicians for New Methods of Treatment and Experimentation: A Comparative Examination' (1995) 3 Med LR 22.

[91] (1996) 54 BMLR 8, [1996] 7 Med LR 309.
[92] (1996) 54 BMLR 8, 14.
[93] ibid, 23.
[94] ibid, 23.

> The standard of care … to be imposed in respect of a committee is that of a reasonably competent and carefully inquiring group of professionals in the relevant disciplines, of sufficient standing to be entrusted with the membership of that committee, bearing in mind it is a committee which is not merely advisory but is carrying out executive and administrative functions.[95]

This applied as much to the scientific and technical staff advising the committee. The medical and scientific staff of both the MRC and the department had a dual role, one administrative, the other in the use of their professional skills. In servicing the committee, they were under a duty to alert the members to current medical and scientific knowledge, and it was the failure to do so which gave rise to negligence. **4.39**

3. Keeping up to date

Professional practice tends to change over time, so that what was once accepted as the correct procedure may no longer be considered to be responsible. Doctors have an obligation to keep up to date with new developments in their particular field, although it can be difficult to determine precisely when a new development will render adherence to the old method negligent; there is a tension between the obligation to keep up to date and the obligation not to subject patients to untried methods of treatment unless the traditional approach has proved ineffective and the anticipated benefits are justified by the risks. Once the risks associated with the old procedure become generally known, so that an ordinary and reasonably competent practitioner can be expected to have altered his practice accordingly, it would be negligent to continue using that procedure. The problem is to identify precisely when it can be said that a risk has become generally known.[96] For example, there may be a difference of knowledge and understanding between research scientists and clinicians, since research scientists are usually better informed about new discoveries in discrete areas of their discipline than practitioners, who have to rely on researchers and professional publications to keep them informed.[97] **4.40**

The obligation is to make a reasonable effort to keep up to date. A doctor cannot realistically be expected to read every article in every learned medical journal,[98] but where a particular risk has been highlighted on a number of occasions the practitioner will ignore it at his peril.[99] The practices adopted or state of knowledge in other countries are not necessarily evidence of the appropriate standard in the UK.[100] **4.41**

---

[95] ibid, 24.

[96] Note that changes in technique or the use of particular instruments may sometimes simply be a matter of fashion, so that the fact that 'new methods become available does not make the continued use of the old negligent unless and until they are shown to be wrong or to carry an unacceptably higher risk to the patient than the new': *Newbury v Bath District HA* (1998) 47 BMLR 138, 162 *per* Ebsworth J.

[97] *ter Neuzen v Korn* (1993) 103 DLR (4th) 473, 497–98 (BCCA); aff'd (1995) 127 DLR (4th) 577 (SCC). Moreover, there may be a lack of effective communication between public health officials and practitioners, again producing a 'time lag' in the knowledge of the profession.

[98] Although it is acknowledged that 'where there is developing knowledge, [the defendant] must keep reasonably abreast of it and not be too slow to apply it': *Stokes v Guest, Keen & Nettlefold (Bolts & Nuts) Ltd* [1968] 1 WLR 1776, 1783 *per* Swanwick J; on the other hand, where the defendant's omission involves an absence of initiative in seeking out knowledge of facts which are not in themselves obvious 'the court must be slow to blame him for not ploughing a lone furrow': *Thompson v Smith Shiprepairers (North Shields) Ltd* [1984] 1 All ER 881, 894 *per* Mustill J.

[99] See, eg, *Roe v Minister of Health* [1954] 2 QB 66; *McLean v Weir* [1977] 5 WWR 609; aff'd [1980] 4 WWR 330; *McCormick v Marcotte* (1971) 20 DLR (3d) 345 (SCC).

[100] *Whiteford v Hunter* [1950] WN 553; *ter Neuzen v Korn* (1993) 103 DLR (4th) 473 (BCCA); aff'd (1995) 127 DLR (4th) 577 (SCC), where it was held that it was not open to a jury to find the common practice of Canadian practitioners to be negligent on the basis of knowledge available in Australia. In *Meiklejohn*

4.42 In *Crawford v Charing Cross Hospital*[101] the claimant developed brachial palsy in an arm following a blood transfusion. At first instance the defendants were held liable on the basis that the anaesthetist had failed to read an article published in *The Lancet* six months earlier, concerning the best position of the arm when using a drip. The Court of Appeal reversed this decision, taking the view that it would be too great a burden to require a doctor to read every article appearing in the current medical press.[102] It was wrong to suggest that a practitioner was negligent simply because he did not immediately put into operation the suggestions made by a contributor to a medical journal, although the time might come when a recommendation was so well proved and so well accepted that it should be adopted. In *Gascoine v Ian Sheridan & Co*[103] Mitchell J commented that a 'shop floor gynaecologist' had a responsibility to keep himself generally informed on mainstream changes in diagnosis, treatment, and practice through the mainstream literature, such as the leading textbooks and the *Journal of Obstetrics and Gynaecology*. However, it was unreasonable to suppose that he had had an opportunity to acquaint himself with the content of more obscure journals.

4. Assessing degrees of risk

4.43 In applying general principles to the assessment of whether a defendant has exercised reasonable care, the courts take into account a number of factors, including the foreseeability of the damage, the magnitude of the risk, the purpose of the defendant's conduct, and the cost or practicability of taking precautions. These issues are just as relevant to an action for medical negligence as any other type of negligence action, despite the heavy reliance which is often placed on expert medical evidence in the former. The decision of the House of Lords in *Bolitho v City and Hackney Health Authority*[104] now makes it clear that medical experts will have to be able to demonstrate that they have addressed the question of assessing the relative risks and benefits of adopting a particular medical practice, and that their opinion stands up to logical analysis.

(i) Foreseeability of risk

4.44 If a particular danger could not reasonably have been anticipated because it was unforeseeable, the defendant did not act negligently, because the reasonable man is not expected to take precautions against unforeseeable consequences. Whether a consequence was foreseeable is not determined by using hindsight but by reference to knowledge at the date of the alleged negligence. Thus, in *Roe v Minister of Health*,[105] heard in 1954, the defendants were found not to have been liable for the injuries inflicted when contaminated anaesthetic was administered to the claimant in 1947, because the anaesthetic had become contaminated in a way which was unforeseeable at the time. The court 'must not look at the 1947 accident

v St George's Healthcare Trust [2014] EWCA Civ 120, Rafferty LJ held that the trial judge had been right to prefer the evidence of the Defendant's UK expert over the Claimant's American expert, where the former had demonstrated relevant differences in standard practice between the UK and the USA (at [97] and [108]).

[101] The Times, 8 December 1953.

[102] See also *Dwan v Farquhar* [1988] 1 Qd R 234, where an article in a journal concerning the risks of contracting the AIDS virus from blood transfusions was published in March 1983, and a patient contracted HIV from a blood transfusion performed in May 1983. It was held that there was no negligence.

[103] [1994] 5 Med LR 437, 447.

[104] [1997] 4 All ER 771, 779.

[105] *Roe v Minister of Health* [1954] 2 QB 66. Sometimes the need for extra precaution on account of the magnitude of the risk is prescribed for in clinical guidelines: eg in *Taafe v East of England Ambulance Service NHS Trust* [2012] EWHC 1335, the relevant guidelines advised a high index of suspicion that any chest pain is cardiac in origin because of the potentially fatal consequences of untreated heart disease.

with 1954 spectacles', even though it would have been negligent to adopt the same practice in 1954 when the risk was more widely known.[106]

(ii) Magnitude of risk

A defendant is not negligent simply because the damage was foreseeable.[107] In some circumstances it may be reasonable to ignore a small risk, because the chance of it materializing is remote and the cost of precautions high. By contrast, where the cost of avoiding a risk is minimal it may be negligent to ignore even a remote risk.[108] **4.45**

A degree of care commensurate with the risk created by the defendant's conduct is required, so that the greater the risk of harm the greater the precautions that must be taken.[109] This principle applies just as much to professional liability as it does to any other category of negligence: **4.46**

> . . . there is a clear relationship between the magnitude of the risk and the duty of care, in particular the standard of care. The greater the risks involved in any proposed course of treatment, the more carefully and anxiously must the medical practitioner weigh and consider the possible alternatives before deciding to resort to the proposed treatment.[110]

Thus, when an anaesthetist was handling a highly inflammable substance and knew of the hazard arising from electrostatic sparks in an operating theatre, the degree of care required was correspondingly high and he was bound to take special precautions to prevent injury to his patient.[111]

The magnitude of the risk involves two elements. First, the likelihood that the harm will occur. The more remote the chance that any damage to the claimant will arise, the more reasonable it will be to take fewer, or even no, precautions against the eventuality. Secondly, the degree of risk also takes into account the severity of the potential consequences. If the harm is likely to be serious, should it occur, then greater precautions must be taken. For example, a risk that a patient may be accidentally infected with HIV from a contaminated blood transfusion will impose a high standard of care upon the supplier of the blood, given the seriousness of the consequences.[112] In *Reynolds v North Tyneside* **4.47**

---

[106] *Roe v Minister of Health* [1954] 2 QB 66, 86; *McLean v Weir* [1977] 5 WWR 609; aff'd [1980] 4 WWR 330 (BCCA). There is some doubt as to whether the contamination of the anaesthetic in *Roe* was in fact caused by the manner in which it was stored: see C D Hutter, 'The Woolley and Roe Case: A Reassessment' (1990) 45 Anaesthesia 859.

[107] *Bolton v Stone* [1951] AC 850, 863 *per* Lord Oaksey.

[108] *Overseas Tankship (UK) Ltd v Miller Steamship Co Pty Ltd, The Wagon Mound (No 2)* [1967] 1 AC 617, 642.

[109] *Read v J Lyons & Co Ltd* [1947] AC 156, 173 *per* Lord Macmillan.

[110] *Battersby v Tottman* (1985) 37 SASR 524, 542 *per* Jacobs J; *Glasgow Corporation v Muir* [1943] AC 448, 456 *per* Lord Macmillan: 'Those who engage in operations inherently dangerous must take precautions which are not required of persons engaged in the ordinary routine of daily life'; *McAllister v Lewisham and North Southwark HA* [1994] 5 Med LR 343, 347 (QBD), where Rougier J commented that: 'The decision whether or not to operate is the product of a tripartite equation: 1. The risks of operating. 2. The benefits of operating. 3. The risks of not operating'; see also *O'Donovan v Cork County Council* [1967] IR 173, 190 *per* Walsh J; *Buchan v Ortho Pharmaceuticals (Canada) Ltd* (1986) 25 DLR (4th) 658, 678–79 *per* Robins JA (Ont CA).

[111] *Crits v Sylvester* (1956) 1 DLR (2d) 502, 511 (Ont CA); aff'd (1956) 5 DLR (2d) 601 (SCC); *Darley v Shale* [1993] 4 Med LR 161, 168 (NSWSC).

[112] *E v Australian Red Cross Society* (1991) 105 ALR 53, 77 (Aus Fed CA) *per* Sheppard J. Despite the high duty, the defendants were found not to have been negligent in this case because of the very limited options for reasonable precautions against infection with HIV at the time (October 1984). A test specifically for HIV did not become available until March 1985. See also *Pittman Estate v Bain* (1994) 112 DLR (4th) 257, 319 *per* Lang J (Ont Ct, Gen Div). Note, however, that the importance of the blood supply in saving lives may justify the taking of greater risk than would otherwise be acceptable.

HA[113] a mother was admitted to hospital for the birth of her child, in circumstances where there was a foreseeable risk, put at between 1 in 250 and 1 in 500, of a cord prolapse. This was considered to be 'low risk', but the potential consequences from foetal hypoxia extended to death or brain damage. The risk materialized and the child suffered from cerebral palsy due to an acute umbilical cord prolapse. The alleged negligence consisted of an omission by the midwife to carry out an immediate vaginal examination given the foreseeable risk. Such an examination was neither difficult nor costly. The defendants argued that the risk of cord prolapse was so slight that it could be ignored. Gross J held that the defendants were not entitled simply to ignore the risk. Although the risk was low, it was not far-fetched or fanciful. It was not a case where a nice clinical balance had to be struck: 'Set against the low risk of cord prolapse were (i) the gravity of the consequences should the risk materialize and (ii) the ease and economy of undertaking an immediate [vaginal examination].'[114] There was a risk of infection from an immediate examination, but a vaginal examination was likely to be conducted at some point during labour and the risks of infection would have been the same whenever it was performed. In any event, said the judge, the risk of infection was heavily outweighed by the risk of cord prolapse. In terms of the gravity of the consequences they were not 'in the same league'.

4.48 Where a doctor has formed an opinion as to the appropriate diagnosis of a patient's condition, he should take into account the possibility that an alternative diagnosis would explain the symptoms, especially where the consequences of the alternative diagnosis, if correct, would be very serious.[115] The defendant must also take account of the known characteristics of the particular claimant where those characteristics make the likelihood of harm occurring greater than would be the case with a normal individual,[116] or where the damage is likely to be more severe.[117] In these circumstances greater precautions will be required than for the average individual.

4.49 The purpose of the defendant's conduct will also be taken into account in assessing what is reasonable. If sufficiently important, it may justify the assumption of abnormal risk.[118] Unsurprisingly, the saving of life and limb is likely to justify taking considerable risk[119] but this does not mean that this purpose can justify taking *any* risk. It is a matter of balancing the risk against the consequences of not taking the risk. If, for example, the patient's condition is such that he will almost certainly die without some form of medical intervention, then treatment with a high degree of risk will be justified, unless, of course, there is an equally effective alternative treatment that carries less risk.

---

[113] [2002] Lloyd's Rep Med 459.

[114] ibid, [43].

[115] *Lankenau v Dutton* (1986) 37 CCLT 213, 232 (BCSC); aff'd (1991) 79 DLR (4th) 707 (BCCA); *Bergen v Sturgeon General Hospital* (1984) 28 CCLT 155 (Alta QB); *Law Estate v Simice* (1994) 21 CCLT (2d) 228, 236 (BCSC).

[116] A 'measure of care appropriate to the inability or disability of those who are immature or feeble in mind or body is due from others, who know of or ought to anticipate the presence of such persons within the scope and hazard of their own operations': *Glasgow Corporation v Taylor* [1922] 1 AC 44, 67 *per* Lord Sumner, approved by Lord Reid in *Haley v London Electricity Board* [1965] AC 778, 793.

[117] Paris v Stepney Borough Council [1951] AC 367.

[118] *Daborn v Bath Tramways Motor Co Ltd* [1946] 2 All ER 333, 336 *per* Asquith LJ.

[119] *Watt v Hertfordshire County Council* [1954] 1 WLR 835. See also the comments of Lang J in *Pittman Estate v Bain* (1994) 112 DLR (4th) 257, 313 (Ont Ct, Gen Div): 'In the case of blood, the societal need for the component produces different considerations. This is not a product that should be removed from the market if inherently dangerous. Blood is an essential source of life to many. Although a biologic, and, therefore, dangerous, the need for the product outweighs the risk.'

(iii) Cost of precautions

A further matter to be considered in assessing whether the taking of a foreseeable risk was justified is the practicability (or cost) of taking precautions. The practicability of taking precautions should be measured on an objective basis: the defendant's impecuniosity is not a defence if objectively a precaution was reasonably required.[120] If the risk can be avoided at small cost or with a trivial expenditure of time and effort, it will be unreasonable to run the risk. Conversely, some risks can only be eliminated or reduced at great expense. A reasonable man would only neglect a risk if he had a valid reason for doing so, for example, if 'it would involve considerable expense to eliminate the risk . . . [h]e would weigh the risk against the difficulty of eliminating it'. However, a reasonable man would not ignore even a small risk 'if action to eliminate it presented no difficulty, involved no disadvantage and required no expense'.[121] In *Hucks v Cole*[122] Sachs LJ said that when risks of great danger are knowingly taken as a matter of professional practice then, however small the risks, the court must carefully examine the practice, particularly where the risks can be easily and inexpensively avoided. In *Coles v Reading and District Management Committee*[123] it was held to be negligent not to have given the patient an anti-tetanus injection, since it was a simple precaution, and the consequences of the infection are serious. **4.50**

Some risks will be unavoidable. In this situation the risks of proceeding have to be weighed against the disadvantages of not proceeding, taking into account the expected benefits to the patient's health. Where the consequences of not treating the patient are potentially very serious, then the doctor will normally be justified in taking greater risks.[124] Conversely, where the treatment is for a minor ailment even small risks should not be disregarded,[125] a fortiori, where a diagnostic test which carries a real risk of an adverse reaction is conducted **4.51**

[120] In *PQ v Australian Red Cross Society* [1992] 1 VR 19, 33 (Vict SC) McGarvie J held that the actual resources of the defendants was not an issue relevant to the practicability of the precautions required to protect the claimant from HIV infection from a transfusion of blood products; cf *Pittman Estate v Bain* (1994) 112 DLR (4th) 257 (Ont Ct, Gen Div), where Lang J held that the conduct of a blood bank should be measured against that of other blood banks, not by reference to commercial organizations, on the basis that it was a 'professional service' not a commercial service. If other 'responsible' blood banks were unable or unwilling through lack of resources to take such precautions, the defendant would probably not be liable for failing to take the same precautions.

[121] *Overseas Tankship (UK) Ltd v Miller Steamship Co Pty Ltd, The Wagon Mound (No 2)* [1967] 1 AC 617, 642; and in the medical context see *Chin Keow v Government of Malaysia* [1967] 1 WLR 813 (PC). In *Hardaker v Newcastle HA and the Chief Constable of Northumbria* [2001] Lloyd's Rep Med 512 at [54] Burnton J held that it was not negligent for the defendant to fail to devote resources, from 'its doubtlessly limited resources', to deal with the claimant's comparatively rare condition (decompression illness). This case is an example of the proposition that the *Bolam* test takes account of what is reasonable in the circumstances, including whether, objectively, precautions against a small risk are reasonably required given the cost of taking those precautions and the degree of risk. It has been argued, however, that the acknowledged under-funding of the NHS should lead the courts generally to adopt a lower standard of care so as to 'ensure that hospitals and their staff are less vulnerable to findings of negligence for systematic failures in care which cannot reasonably be attributed to them': C Witting, 'National Health Service Rationing: Implications for the Standard of Care in Negligence' (2001) 21 OJLS 443, 444. The logic of this argument is that the worse the service provided the less likely it is that a claim for negligence will succeed when a patient is injured by that service. Such an approach would not be considered acceptable in any other sphere of service provision, whether public or private.

[122] (1968) [1993] 4 Med LR 393, 397.

[123] (1963) 107 SJ 115.

[124] *Davidson v Connaught Laboratories* (1980) 14 CCLT 251, 270, where the patient suffered an allergic reaction to a rabies vaccine, having come into contact with a rabid animal. Rabies is almost invariably fatal.

[125] The obvious example would be cosmetic surgery, although there may well be room for disagreement as to the importance to the individual patient of removing certain cosmetic defects. In *La Fleur v Cornelis* (1979) 28 NBR (2d) 569, 573 (NBSC) Barry J commented that cosmetic surgeons do not treat illnesses in

when there are no clinical indications for performing such a test.[126] This balancing exercise must take account of the individual patient. In *Battersby v Tottman*[127] a doctor prescribed a very high dose of a drug to a patient suffering from mental illness. He took the view that the benefits of the drug outweighed the risk of it causing serious and permanent eye damage, since without treatment the patient was 'dangerously suicidal', and other methods of treatment had failed. It was held that in these circumstances the decision to prescribe a dosage that was far in excess of the recommended dosages was not negligent.[128]

5. Specialists and the inexperienced

4.52 A specialist is required to achieve the standard of care of a reasonably competent specialist in his field, exercising 'the ordinary skill of his specialty'.[129] Thus, while a general practitioner must be judged by the standards of general practitioners and not specialists,[130] if a general practitioner were to undertake a specialist task, he would be judged by the standards of that specialty. If he is unable to meet those standards, he will be held negligent for undertaking work beyond his competence. A practitioner of 'alternative medicine' will be judged by reference to the standards of fellow practitioners, not by the standards of conventional medicine, since he does not hold himself out as practising orthodox medicine. Thus, a practitioner of traditional Chinese herbal medicine must conform to the standards of a reasonably competent practitioner of that art. He is not to be held to the standards of orthodox medicine, unless the claimant can prove that the prevailing standard of skill in that art was deficient in the UK having regard to the risks which were not, but should have been taken into account.[131]

4.53 The standard of care within a specialist field is that of the ordinary competent specialist, not the most experienced or most highly qualified within the specialty.[132] Even where the defendant is a leader in his field or otherwise particularly distinguished, it will not be appropriate to impose a top layer on the relevant standard to account for his pre-eminence.[133] However,

---

the ordinary sense, and accordingly a 'doctor who undertakes to operate on the nose of a healthy person for cosmetic purposes has a very high duty indeed'.

[126] *Leonard v Knott* [1978] 5 WWR 511 (BCSC).

[127] (1985) 37 SASR 524; see also Scott LJ in *Mahon v Osborne* [1939] 2 KB 14, 31 on the surgeon's problem of balancing competing risks and objectives when performing an operation.

[128] See also *Vernon v Bloomsbury HA* (1986) [1995] 6 Med LR297.

[129] *Maynard v West Midlands RHA* [1984] 1 WLR 634, 638 *per* Lord Scarman; *Sidaway v Bethlem Royal Hospital Governors* [1985] 1 All ER 643, 660 *per* Lord Bridge; *Whitehouse v Jordan* [1981] 1 All ER 267, 280 *per* Lord Fraser. See also *McCaffrey v Hague* [1949] 4 DLR 291; *Crits v Sylvester* (1956) 1 DLR (2d) 502, 508; aff 'd (1956) 5 DLR (2d) 601 (SCC); *Wilson v Swanson* (1956) 5 DLR (2d) 113, 119 *per* Rand J (SCC).

[130] *Langley v Campbell* (1975) The Times, 5 November 1975; *Sa'd v Robinson* [1989] 1 Med LR 41; *Thornton v Nicol* [1992] 3 Med LR 41; *Gordon v Wilson* [1992] 3 Med LR 401 (CS); *Stockdale v Nicholls* [1993] 4 Med LR 190; *Durrant v Burke* [1993] 4 Med LR 258; *Stacey v Chiddy* [1993] 4 Med LR 216 (NSWSC); aff'd [1993] 4 Med LR 345 (NSWCA).

[131] *Shakoor v Situ (t/a Eternal Health Co)* [2001] 1 WLR 410. The defendant had an obligation to check that there had not been any adverse report on the remedy he used in an orthodox medical journal, but since a general practitioner would not have been negligent in failing to identify the risk, then the defendant had conformed to a reasonable standard of care.

[132] *O'Donovan v Cork County Council* [1967] IR 173, 190 *per* Walsh J (Sup Ct Irl); *Giurelli v Girgis* (1980) 24 SASR 264, 277 *per* White J; *F v R* (1983) 33 SASR 189, 205 *per* Bollen J. In *Dove v Jarvis* [2013] Med LR 284, although the applicable standard was held to be that of an 'orthopaedic surgeon experienced and expert in performing hip arthroplasty' at [28], this observation did not result in the imposition of an enhanced duty over and above that required of an ordinary orthopaedic surgeon.

[133] In *Meiklejohn v St George's Healthcare NHS Trust* [2014] EWCA Civ 120, Rafferty LJ rejected the submission that the relevant comparator for the *Bolam* test was a specialist who was 'a leader in the field of [aplastic anaemia] in the UK and who has an international renown', finding instead that it remained simply 'a tertiary specialist in AA' (at [105] and [107]).

where the defendant has knowledge of some *fact* that makes harm to the claimant more likely than would otherwise be the case, he must take account of that fact as a reasonable man, that is, a greater than average knowledge of the risks entails more than the average or standard precautions.[134] This appears to require that a specialist must take greater precautions than an average doctor when undertaking the same task, if the specialist's actual knowledge and experience gives him a greater knowledge of the risks that ought to be guarded against;[135] a clinician's conduct should not be judged by reference to lesser knowledge than in fact he had. On the other hand, he is not expected to use a higher degree of skill than comparable specialists.[136]

There may come a point where a sub-discipline develops within a specialty such that it can be said that a practitioner undertaking that type of work must achieve the standards of the new 'specialty'.[137] Conversely, where it can be said that a new specialty has developed, the question of whether the defendant has conformed to the practice of a responsible body of professional opinion will be judged by reference to the standards of that specialty rather than the standards of doctors engaged in a more generalized practice. This may make it reasonable, for example, for a specialist surgeon to undertake intricate exploratory surgery, on the basis that this conforms to a practice accepted as proper by a responsible body of surgeons in the specialty, in circumstances where surgeons in other fields might consider the procedure to be too risky.[138] **4.54**

The defendant who is inexperienced or who is just learning a particular task or skill must come up to the standards of the reasonably competent and experienced person. His 'incompetent best' is not good enough.[139] This is a consequence of the rule that the standard of care expected of the reasonable man is objective, not subjective. It takes no account of the particular idiosyncrasies or weaknesses of the defendant.[140] This principle applies with as much force to an inexperienced doctor as it does to, say, an inexperienced motorist. In *Jones v Manchester Corporation*[141] a patient died from an excessive dose of anaesthetic administered by an anaesthetist who had only been qualified for five months. In an action which was concerned with the respective responsibilities of the junior doctor and the hospital authority, the Court of Appeal made it clear that it was no defence to an action by a patient to say that the anaesthetist did not have sufficient experience to undertake the task, or to say that the surgeon in charge was also to blame. **4.55**

134 *Stokes v Guest, Keen & Nettlefold (Nuts & Bolts) Ltd* [1968] 1 WLR 1776, 1783 *per* Swanwick J; *Wilson v Brett* (1843) 11 M & W 113, 115 *per* Rolfe B: 'If a person more skilled knows that to be dangerous which another not so skilled as he does not, surely that makes a difference in the liability.'

135 A point accepted as correct by Webster J in *Wimpey Construction UK Ltd v Poole* [1984] 2 Lloyd's Rep 499, 506–07.

136 In *Duchess of Argyll v Beuselinck* [1972] 2 Lloyd's Rep 172, 183 Megarry J suggested that a solicitor's client might be able to purchase a higher standard of care in contract, the obligation stemming from a contractual term that the solicitor would use the care and skill that he actually possessed rather than the care and skill of the average solicitor specializing in that field of law. Megarry J distinguished contractual duties from the tort of negligence, where 'the unusually careful and highly skilled are not held liable for falling below their own high standards if they nevertheless do all that a reasonable man would have done'; cf *Wimpey Construction UK Ltd v Poole* [1984] 2 Lloyd's Rep 499, 506 *per* Webster J. See also *Matrix-Securities Ltd v Theodore Goddard* [1998] PNLR 290, where Lloyd J held that the obligation of a 'City' firm of solicitors advising tax matters, was to exercise that standard of care which could be expected from a reasonably competent firm of solicitors with a specialist tax department. The fact that the defendants professed very high levels of skill and experience (and presumably charged fees to reflect that) did not lead to an inference that they had undertaken a higher duty.

137 See, eg, *Poole v Morgan* [1987] 3 WWR 217.

138 *De Freitas v O'Brien* [1995] 6 Med LR108.

139 *Nettleship v Weston* [1971] 2 QB 691, 698, 710.

140 *Glasgow Corporation v Muir* [1943] AC 448, 457 *per* Lord Macmillan.

141 [1952] 2 All ER 125.

4.56 The issue arose in *Wilsher v Essex Area HA*,[142] in which a premature baby in a special care baby unit received excess oxygen due to an error in monitoring its supply of oxygen. An inexperienced doctor had inserted a catheter (by which the blood oxygen pressure was to be measured) into a vein rather than an artery. This in itself was not a negligent error. However, on checking the position of the catheter by means of an X-ray, the doctor had failed to spot that the catheter was malpositioned. He did ask a senior registrar in the unit to check the X-ray but the registrar also failed to notice the mistake. The baby was subsequently discovered to be suffering from retrolental fibroplasia, which causes blindness, possibly as a result of the exposure to excess oxygen.[143] There was a marked difference of opinion on the question of the appropriate standard of care to be applied to the junior doctor. Sir Nicolas Browne-Wilkinson V-C, dissenting in the Court of Appeal, said that it was unfair to apply an objective standard to a junior doctor in the first year after qualifying, or to someone who has just started in a specialist field in order to gain the necessary skill in that field. The doctor could not be said to be at fault if he lacked the very skills which he was seeking to acquire. His Lordship would only hold such a doctor liable for acts or omissions which a careful doctor with his qualifications and experience would not have done or omitted.

4.57 However, Mustill LJ said that the notion of a duty tailored to the actor, rather than to the act which he elects to perform, had no place in the law of tort. The effect of applying a subjective test would be that the standard of care that a patient would be entitled to expect would depend upon the level of experience of the particular doctor who happened to treat him. A professional person who assumed to perform a task must bring to it the appropriate care and skill, although his Lordship did add that the standard of care should be related, not to the individual, but to the post which he occupies, distinguishing 'post' from 'rank' or 'status'. It followed that the standard was not just that of the averagely competent and well-informed junior houseman (or whatever the position of the doctor) but of a person who held such a post in a unit offering a highly specialized service, while recognizing that different posts made different demands. The very structure of hospital medicine envisaged that the lower ranks would be occupied by those of whom it would be wrong to expect too much. This approach has generally attracted support in subsequent cases.[144]

4.58 With respect, these comments appear to introduce an inconsistency since, having rejected a subjective test of negligence, his Lordship seems to reintroduce variable standards of care by reference to the 'posts' occupied by different doctors. Glidewell LJ simply applied the *Bolam* test, commenting that this was the standard by which to weigh the conduct of all the doctors in *Wilsher*:

> In my view, the law requires the trainee or learner to be judged by the same standard as his more experienced colleagues. If it did not, inexperience would frequently be urged as a defence to an action for professional negligence.[145]

4.59 It is submitted that this is the correct and long-established approach. A single standard of care for patients can only be achieved by relating the reasonableness of the defendant's

---

142 [1986] 3 All ER 801.

143 The decision of the Court of Appeal on the causation issue was reversed by the House of Lords: [1988] 1 All ER 871. There was no appeal on the issue of the standard of care.

144 In *Djemal v Bexley HA* [1995] 6 Med LR 269 Sir Haydn Tudor Evans held that the standard of care required of a senior houseman in an A&E department was that of a reasonably competent senior houseman acting as a casualty officer, though without any reference to length of experience, applying the view of Mustill LJ.

145 [1986] 3 All ER 801, 831; *Dale v Munthali* (1977) 78 DLR (3d) 588, 594; aff'd (1978) 90 DLR (3d) 763; *Wills v Saunders* [1989] 2 WWR 715 (Alta QB).

conduct to the task that is undertaken, and what is objectively reasonable does not change with the experience of the defendant, or, for that matter, the post he holds.[146] This is at its most obvious if a doctor in a specialist 'post' undertakes some procedure which is completely outside the sphere of that specialty. He would be required to achieve the standard of the reasonably competent doctor in performing the procedure, and if it were a specialized procedure he would have to achieve the standards of the relevant specialty. This has nothing to do with his post. The duty arises by virtue of the fact that he has undertaken to perform the act, and by doing so professes that he has the competence to perform it with skill and care, just as an unqualified person would be held to the standard of a reasonably competent surgeon if he undertook surgery.[147] Thus, undertaking work which is beyond one's competence constitutes negligence. As a matter of practice the inexperienced doctor will normally undertake less complex tasks than his experienced colleagues, but if he does perform tasks beyond the level of his competence, the fault lies not so much in not having the skills, which by definition he does not possess, but in him undertaking the task at all.[148] This principle is not limited to actions against newly qualified doctors. It can apply at any stage where a doctor 'gets in above his head'. The doctor who holds himself out as a specialist will be held to the standards of a reasonably competent specialist, 'even if he is a novice specialist',[149] and even where he is performing the procedure for the first time.[150] A doctor must recognize his limitations and where necessary seek the advice or supervision of more experienced colleagues, or refer the patient to a specialist.[151] The inexperienced doctor will discharge his duty of care by seeking the assistance of his superiors to check his work, even though he may himself have made a mistake.[152] Of course, if the more senior, experienced

[146] See A M Dugdale and K M Stanton, *Professional Negligence* (3rd edn, Butterworths 1998) para 15.11 and para 15.12, making the same point in relation to the standard to be applied to specialists. The objective nature of the standard of care applies to other factors as well as inexperience. If the defendant is unable to measure up to the objectively required standard for any reason, be it stress, overwork, tiredness, or ill health he will nonetheless be found negligent. Thus, old age or infirmity is not a defence for a negligent driver of a motor vehicle: *Roberts v Ramsbottom* [1980] 1 All ER 7, 15; nor is inexperience: *Nettleship v Weston*, n 139. Note however *Mansfield v Weetabix Ltd* [1999] 1 WLR 1263, where the Court of Appeal held that a driver who becomes unable to control a vehicle will not be liable for damage caused by his loss of control if he is unaware of the disabling condition from which he is suffering, whether the disabling event is sudden or gradual. In *Nickolls v Ministry of Health* The Times, 4 February 1955, the surgeon who operated on the claimant was suffering from cancer. The question was whether he was in a fit condition to have undertaken the operation. It was held that, on the facts, he was and therefore he was not negligent. Clearly, if the conclusion had been that he was unfit, and he was aware of that, it would have been negligent to operate. In *Barnett v Chelsea and Kensington HMC* [1968] 1 All ER 1068, 1073 Nield J held that the doctor's failure to see and examine the deceased was negligent, commenting that: 'It is unfortunate that Dr. Banerjee was himself at the time a tired and unwell doctor, but there was no-one else to do that which it was his duty to do.'

[147] *R v Bateman* (1925) 94 LJKB 791, 794 *per* Lord Hewart CJ; *Freeman v Marshall & Co* (1966) 200 EG 777.

[148] In any event, it is possible that a health authority would be in breach of a primary duty of care to the patient for allowing inexperienced staff to practise without adequate supervision: *Jones v Manchester Corporation* [1952] 2 All ER 125; *Wilsher v Essex AHA* [1986] 3 All ER 801, 833 *per* Sir Nicolas Browne-Wilkinson V-C.

[149] *Poole v Morgan* [1987] 3 WWR 217, 254 (Alta QB). The defendant ophthalmologist was held to be inadequately qualified to use laser treatment, a procedure normally performed by a retina vitreous specialist, even though ophthalmologists were permitted to use laser treatment by their governing body.

[150] *McKeachie v Alvarez* (1970) 17 DLR (3d) 87 (BCSC).

[151] *Wilsher v Essex AHA* [1986] 3 All ER 801, 833; *Fraser v Vancouver General Hospital* (1951) 3 WWR 337 (BCCA); aff'd [1952] 3 DLR 785 (SCC); *Payne v St Helier Group HMC* The Times, 12 July 1952; *Dillon v Le Roux* [1994] 6 WWR 280 (BCCA).

[152] It was on this basis that the junior doctor was found not to have been negligent in *Wilsher v Essex AHA*. See also *Junor v McNicol* The Times, 26 March 1959, where the House of Lords held that a house

doctor makes a mistake in checking the junior's work this could be a basis for a finding of negligence.[153]

6. Emergencies

4.60 In an emergency it may well be reasonable for a practitioner inexperienced in a particular treatment to intervene, or indeed for someone lacking medical qualifications to undertake some forms of treatment. For example, a bystander who renders assistance at a road accident does not necessarily hold himself out as qualified to do so. He would be expected to achieve only the standard that could reasonably be expected in the circumstances, which would probably be very low.[154] This approach is clearly born of the emergency since if there was no urgency, the unqualified person who undertook treatment beyond his competence would be held to the standard of a reasonably competent and experienced practitioner. For example, a person who holds himself out as trained in first-aid must conform to the standards of 'the ordinary skilled first-aider exercising and professing to have that special skill of a first-aider'.[155]

7. Defensive medicine

4.61 The increase in medical malpractice litigation over recent years has been accompanied by claims that, in response to the threat of litigation, doctors now practise defensively. This involves undertaking procedures which are not medically justified but are designed to protect the doctor from a claim for negligence. The most commonly cited examples are unnecessary diagnostic tests, such as X-rays, and unnecessary Caesarean section deliveries. However, applying the *Bolam* test, a reasonable doctor would not undertake an *unnecessary* procedure and so a doctor could not avoid a finding of negligence by performing one. In fact, to the extent that the procedure carries some inherent risk, a practitioner acting in this way may increase his chances of being sued.[156] Moreover, there is little clear understanding within the medical profession of what the term 'defensive medicine' means. 'Defensive' may mean simply treating patients conservatively or even 'more carefully', and this begs the question whether that treatment option is medically justified in the patient's interests.

surgeon who had acted on the instructions of a consultant orthopaedic surgeon was not liable; *Tanswell v Nelson* The Times, 11 February 1959, where McNair J said that a dentist was entitled to rely on a doctor's opinion about a patient's response to antibiotics, unless that opinion was clearly inconsistent with the observed facts; *Weir v Graham* [2002] EWHC 2291 (QB), where it was held that a GP was entitled to assume that, where a patient had been referred to hospital for tests, the hospital doctors were aware of the results of the tests and would take them into account in reaching a diagnosis; *Leonard v Knott* [1978] 5 WWR 511 (BCSC), where it was held that a radiologist was entitled to rely on the judgment of the referring physician as to whether a radiological investigation was required, unless there was some obvious problem; cf *Davy-Chiesman v Davy-Chiesman* [1984] 1 All ER 321, 332, 335, stating that solicitors should not rely blindly on the advice of counsel, although in this case the solicitor had failed to detect an 'obvious error'; *Matrix-Securities Ltd v Theodore Goddard* [1998] PNLR 290—a solicitor is entitled to rely on counsel's advice, and would be negligent for failing to do so unless that advice was obviously wrong; *FirstCity Insurance Group Ltd v Orchard* [2002] Lloyd's Rep PN 543 at [82].

153 Which is what happened in *Wilsher v Essex AHA*. See also *Drake v Pontefract HA; Wakefield and Pontefract Community NHS Trust* [1998] Lloyd's Rep Med 425, where a consultant psychiatrist was found to have been negligent in allowing an inexperienced Senior House Officer to interview and treat the claimant without immediate supervision from a more experienced psychiatrist, when the patient had been expressly referred as a suicide risk.

154 See, eg, *Ali v Furness Withy* [1988] 2 Lloyd's Rep 379, where the question was the standard applicable to a ship's master diagnosing insanity in crewman.

155 *Cattley v St John's Ambulance Brigade* (1988, unreported, QBD).

156 If a diagnostic test or procedure is unnecessary by reference to the standards of the medical profession, ie, according to the standards of the reasonably competent doctor exercising and professing to have

Nonetheless, the courts have apparently acknowledged the existence of the phenomenon of defensive medicine, despite the fact that there is virtually no empirical, as opposed to anecdotal, evidence of such practices in this country.[157]

In non-medical cases the courts have occasionally relied on the prospect of unduly defensive practices developing in response to a potential liability in order to deny the existence of a duty of care.[158] This essentially involves a judgment that imposing liability for negligence will tend to 'over-deter' potential defendants, damaging the service in question, rather than contributing to an improvement in standards of conduct, though this is an intuitive judgment rather than being based on empirical evidence.[159] Logically, the same argument would apply to any defendant who is held accountable in the tort of negligence, but no one suggests that imposing a duty of care on, say, motorists makes them drive *too* carefully. The option of denying the existence of a duty of care is not available in most cases of medical negligence, since the doctor undoubtedly owes a duty of care to his patient. In *Barker v Nugent* [160] counsel for the defendant doctor argued that, as a matter of public policy, the courts should be slower to impute negligence to the medical profession than to others, in order to avoid an escalation of defensive medicine. Rougier J rejected the argument, with the comment that: **4.62**

> I can think of only one thing more disastrous than the escalation of defensive medicine and that is the engendering of a belief in the medical profession that certain acts or omissions which would otherwise be classed as negligence can, in a sense, be exonerated.

Similarly, in *Wilsher v Essex AHA* Mustill LJ responded to his own acknowledgement of the risks of defensive practice with the comment that: 'the proper response cannot be to temper the wind to the professional man. If he assumes to perform a task, he must bring to it the appropriate care and skill.' Nonetheless, the judicial perception of the risk of defensive practices developing may be reflected in the standard of proof that claimants have to achieve in practice, although the formal standard of proof remains the same. **4.63**

In *M (a minor) v Newham LBC*[161] the question of defensive practice arose in circumstances where, unusually, it was open to the court to conclude that a duty of care should be held not to exist. A majority of the Court of Appeal held that a psychiatrist and a social worker did not owe a duty of care to a child or its parents when advising a social services authority whether the child had been physically or sexually abused, and as to the identity of the abuser. The child had been needlessly removed from its home into local authority care, and both the child and her mother claimed that they had suffered psychiatric harm as a result. The defendants argued that imposing a duty of care in these circumstances would have **4.64**

that skill, it will be negligence to perform it, and it will be actionable if the patient suffers injury as a consequence. See, eg, *Leonard v Knott* [1978] 5 WWR 511 (BCSC).

[157] *Wilsher v Essex AHA* [1986] 3 All ER 801, 810 *per* Mustill LJ; *Sidaway v Bethlem Royal Hospital Governors* [1985] 1 All ER 643, 653 *per* Lord Scarman. Lord Denning was particularly concerned about the risks of defensive medicine: *Roe v Minister of Health* [1954] 2 QB 66, 86–87; *Lim v Camden and Islington AHA* [1979] 1 QB 196, 217; *Whitehouse v Jordan* [1980] 1 All ER 650, 658; *Hyde v Tameside AHA* (1981) reported at (1986) 2 PN 26; *Hatcher v Black* The Times, 2 July 1954. See also *per* Lawton LJ in *Whitehouse v Jordan* [1980] 1 All ER 650, 659; *Sidaway v Bethlem Royal Hospital Governors* [1984] 1 All ER 1018, 1031, 1035 *per* Dunne and Browne-Wilkinson LJJ.

[158] *Saif Ali v Sydney Mitchell & Co* [1980] AC 198; *Yuen Kun-yeu v Attorney-General of Hong Kong* [1987] 2 All ER 705, 715–16; *Hill v Chief Constable of West Yorkshire* [1988] 2 All ER 238; *Rowling v Takaro Properties Ltd* [1988] 1 All ER 163, 173; *Elguzouli-Daf v Commissioner of Police of the Metropolis* [1995] 1 All ER 833; *Marc Rich & Co v Bishop Rock Marine Co Ltd* [1995] 3 All ER 307.

[159] See *Hartshorne, Smith and Everton* (2000) 63 MLR 502, pointing out that the courts rarely have any empirical evidence to justify assertions about 'defensive' practices.

[160] 1987 (QBD).

[161] *M (a minor) v Newham LBC* [1994] 2 WLR 554.

serious adverse consequences, particularly in terms of: (i) the financial implications for local authorities; and (ii) the reaction of social workers and doctors working the field of child protection to the risk of liability. Peter Gibson and Staughton LJJ accepted that it would not be desirable if actions in such circumstances resulted in a major diversion of resources to defending legal actions. Sir Thomas Bingham MR, dissenting, also accepted that, to a greater or lesser extent, the overstretched resources of local authorities would be diverted from the function of looking after children and wasted on litigation but said:

> . . . this is an argument frequently (and not implausibly) advanced on behalf of doctors: it has not prevailed. Other professions resist liability on the ground that it will in the end increase the cost to the paying customer; that resistance has not on the whole been effective either. Save in clear cases, it is not for the courts to decide how public money is best spent nor to balance the risk that money will be wasted on litigation against the hope that the possibility of suit may contribute towards the maintenance of higher standards.[162]

4.65 The defendants also argued that imposing a duty of care would lead to defensive practices by social workers and doctors engaged in child protection work. Essentially, the question was whether imposing liability in negligence would contribute to a deterioration in standards of conduct or lead to their improvement. It was said that the decisions that have to be taken in the context of child protection are difficult and delicate and involve an exercise of professional judgment. Imposing liability could lead to such decisions being taken in a 'detrimentally defensive frame of mind'. Staughton LJ very much doubted whether the imposition of a duty of care encouraged people not to be negligent, though it might encourage defensive practices. This appears to be inconsistent, for, as Sir Thomas Bingham observed: 'The common belief that the imposition of such a duty may lead to overkill is not easily reconciled with the suggestion that it has no effect.'[163] His Lordship did not accept, as a general proposition, that the imposition of a duty of care makes no contribution to the maintenance of high standards. The task may be difficult, delicate, and judgmental in nature, but this simply means that it is difficult for a claimant to prove negligence. There was no reason, in a case such as *M (a minor) v Newham LBC*, why a doctor's performance of his duty to form the best judgment and give the soundest advice that he could, would be inhibited by the knowledge that he might be held liable to the child:

> He might no doubt be anxious to be as sure as possible before expressing any opinion, and would be careful to express no opinion stronger than the facts in his judgment warranted, but both these results are to be encouraged. I do not think he would be deterred from prompt action where the facts appeared to warrant it, since he would be as vulnerable to criticism for failing to advise urgent action when the facts appeared to call for it as for acting precipitately when the facts did not. The doctor's only certain protection would be sound performance of his professional duty, and that is how it should be.[164]

4.66 In the House of Lords, however, it was accepted that there was a risk of defensive practices developing and that local authorities would adopt a more cautious approach to their duties.[165] In circumstances where a speedy decision to remove a child may be vital there

[162] ibid, 576.

[163] ibid, 572. Staughton LJ's view assumes that, on the one hand, people do not respond to liability rules by acting more carefully, while assuming, on the other, that they do respond to liability rules by being overcareful.

[164] ibid, 571–72. It might be added that the 'frame of mind' with which any professional person approaches the tasks to be carried out is so subjective to the individual as to be almost meaningless. What is 'defensive' for one may well be regarded as good practice by another. What counts is whether *objectively* the professional is exercising reasonable standards of professional conduct; and, moreover, questions of immunity aside, this is the only way in which the professional can be sure of being found not liable.

[165] Sub nom *X (minors) v Bedfordshire County Council* [1995] 3 WLR 152, 184 *per* Lord Browne-Wilkinson.

would be a substantial temptation to postpone making the decision until further enquiries had been made in the hope of getting more concrete facts. This was a factor in the conclusion that a duty of care should not be imposed for reasons of policy. Clearly, it is not in the interests of children that they be negligently left at risk of abuse, but by the same token it is not in their interests that they be wrongly taken into local authority care as a result of negligence. In other words, the exercise of reasonable care by all those engaged in child protection, including doctors, is in the interests of all children, whether they are the victims of abuse or not. As long as it is remembered that the obligation in negligence is only to exercise reasonable care, not to achieve perfection, and that difficult decisions taken in circumstances of some urgency will not lightly be condemned as careless, a duty to exercise reasonable care should hold no terrors for the professional person. The answer to claims about defensive practice lies in the observation of Lord Clyde in *Phelps v Hillingdon LBC*,[166] a case involving allegations of negligence against an educational psychologist in failing to diagnose dyslexia when making an assessment of a pupil's educational needs:

> I am not persuaded that the recognition of a liability upon employees of the education authority for damages for negligence in education would lead to a flood of claims, or even vexatious claims, which would overwhelm the school authorities, nor that it would add burdens and distractions to the already intensive life of teachers. Nor should it inspire some peculiarly defensive attitude in the performance of their professional responsibilities. On the contrary it may have the healthy effect of securing that high standards are sought and secured.

C. Common Types of Error

It is possible for any diagnosis or treatment to be performed in a careless fashion, or for some essential step to be negligently omitted. What follows is a consideration of some of the most common situations in which an action may arise. **4.67**

1. Failure to obtain consent

The Supreme Court has clarified a doctor's obligation to disclose risks associated with medical treatment in *Montgomery v Lanarkshire Health Board (General Medical Council intervening)*.[167] That case concerned a pregnant mother of small stature, with a history of insulin dependent diabetes. The pregnancy was high risk because women suffering from diabetes are likely to have babies that are larger than normal, resulting in a risk of shoulder dystocia where the shoulders of the foetus are too wide to descend through the birth canal. The treating obstetrician did not warn of shoulder dystocia, nor was a caesarian section offered as an alternative mode of delivery. At birth, there was a dystocia, the baby suffered hypoxia and consequent permanent profound brain damage and the mother suffered significant injury in the effort to extract the baby vaginally. The Scots courts (at first instance and on appeal) dismissed the mother's claim accepting that the obstetrician was under no duty to warn of the risk of dystocia or discuss alternative delivery options. The Supreme Court reversed the lower court's decision, and found for the mother, holding that she should have been told of the risk of shoulder dystocia and should have been offered a caesarean section, which she **4.68**

[166] [2001] 2 AC 619, 672. See also *Reynolds v North Tyneside Health Authority* [2002] Lloyd's Rep Med 459 at [43], where Gross J commented that 'in a fault based system, it is indeed necessary both (i) to exclude hindsight and (ii) to recognise the social costs of inadvertently encouraging "defensive" medicine by setting unrealistic standards'. His Lordship concluded, however, that a finding that it was negligent to ignore a small risk of catastrophic consequences (death or brain damage) was neither unfair nor unrealistic.

[167] [2015] UKSC 11, [2015] 2 WLR 768.

would, in the circumstances, have accepted in order to avoid the risk to her and her baby. In a joint Opinion by Lords Kerr and Reid JJSC, with which the other members of the Court concurred, the Court said this:

> 87 . . . An adult person of sound mind is entitled to decide which, if any, of the available forms of treatment to undergo, and her consent must be obtained before treatment interfering with her bodily integrity is undertaken. The doctor is therefore under a duty to take reasonable care to ensure that the patient is aware of any material risks involved in any recommended treatment, and of any reasonable alternative or variant treatments. The test of materiality is whether, in the circumstances of the particular case, a reasonable person in the patient's position would be likely to attach significance to the risk, or the doctor is or should reasonably be aware that the particular patient would be likely to attach significance to it.
>
> 88 The doctor is however entitled to withhold from the patient information as to a risk if he reasonably considers that its disclosure would be seriously detrimental to the patient's health. The doctor is also excused from conferring with the patient in circumstances of necessity, as for example where the patient requires treatment urgently but is unconscious or otherwise unable to make a decision. It is unnecessary for the purposes of this case to consider in detail the scope of those exceptions.

4.69 The Court went on to emphasize that the materiality of the risk reflects a variety of factors beyond its magnitude in percentage terms, so, for example, 'the nature of the risk, the effect which its occurrence would have on the life of the patient, the importance to the patient of the benefits sought to be achieved by the treatment, the alternatives available, and the risks involved in those alternatives'[168] were all factors which might go to materiality. This is an approach which is specific to each doctor and patient, and depends on what is a 'material' risk on the particular facts of the case. The approach does not depend on the application of the *Bolam* test:

> 82 In the law of negligence, this approach entails a duty on the part of doctors to take reasonable care to ensure that a patient is aware of material risks of injury that are inherent in treatment. This can be understood, within the traditional framework of negligence, as a duty of care to avoid exposing a person to a risk of injury which she would otherwise have avoided, but it is also the counterpart of the patient's entitlement to decide whether or not to incur that risk. The existence of that entitlement, and the fact that its exercise does not depend exclusively on medical considerations, are important. They point to a fundamental distinction between, on the one hand, the doctor's role when considering possible investigatory or treatment options and, on the other, her role in discussing with the patient any recommended treatment and possible alternatives, and the risks of injury which may be involved.

4.70 The Supreme Court has thus resolved the uncertainty which had prevailed since *Sidaway v Board of Governors of the Bethlem Royal Hospital and the Maudsley Hospital.*[169] In that case, Lord Diplock (supported by Lords Bridge and Templeman) had concluded that the adequacy of disclosure in medical cases was to be determined by application of the *Bolam* test, by reference to the practice of other similarly qualified medical persons. Lord Scarman had disagreed, and concluded that a doctor must advise his patient of any material risk inherent in the proposed treatment, in order that the individual could make his own decision, recognizing that disclosure was not a *Bolam* question at all. In England and Wales, Lord Scarman's approach had generally found favour in subsequent cases (see, eg, *Pearce v United*

[168] ibid, [89].
[169] [1985] AC 1.

Bristol Healthcare NHS Trust[170]). But *Montgomery* was a Scots case, and the lower courts in Scotland had adhered to the different (majority) view in *Sidaway* in reaching their conclusion. The Supreme Court has now aligned Scots law with the approach in England and Wales, and indeed with the House of Lords' decision in *Chester v Ashfar*[171] in which Lord Bingham had held that even a small risk had to be disclosed (in that case, 1–2 per cent) to enable patients to 'make for themselves decisions intimately affecting their own lives and bodies'.[172]

Thus, it is clear that a surgeon owes a legal duty to a patient to warn of material risks involved in the procedure. The concept of 'medical paternalism' has been rejected and a patient has a right to know of any risk of serious injury which might result, even if that risk is small, so long as it is well established as a risk.[173] Plainly a doctor does not have to warn of every risk. That would be contrary to the interests of patients, overloading them with details of possibly fanciful risks attendant on the procedure. But the doctor does have to warn of any risk which would affect the judgment of a reasonable patient, and which would in consequence be 'material'.[174] In *Khalid v Barnet and Chase Farm Hospital NHS Trust* it was stated that providing *'sufficient information'* does not mean overloading the patient with technical medical information but rather giving a 'simple explanation of what the possibilities were'[175] in the context of advising on whether there would be a need for a caesarean if a 'trial of scar' following an earlier caesarean section was unsuccessful. In some circumstances it may be necessary to explain the comparative risks attendant on an alternative procedure to that which is proposed, so that the patient can assess not only the risks of the proposed procedure but also whether he or she wishes to undergo that procedure at all, or prefers to opt for some other procedure. This was the situation in *Birch v University College Hospital*,[176] where the claimant was consented for catheter angiography, which in the event caused her to suffer a stroke. While there could be no criticism of the hospital undertaking that procedure, even though it exposed the claimant to the risk of stroke, it was held that she should have had explained to her that an alternative means of investigation was by magnetic resource imaging. That explanation should have included the comparative risks of each procedure. Had that been done, this claimant would have opted for MRI and would not have suffered the stroke. The Court of Appeal has confirmed the importance of obtaining consent in medical cases, in *Anita Border v Lewisham and Greenwich NHS Trust*:[177] **4.71**

> The duty to obtain the patient's consent to treatment is a fundamental tenet of medical practice and is inherent in the case-law concerning the duty to take reasonable steps to warn a patient of the risks of treatment so that the patient can make an informed decision about whether to consent to it (see, for example, *Chester v Afshar* [2004] UKHL 41, [2005] 1 AC 134).

2. Failure to attend or treat

A doctor who fails to attend his patient or who is dilatory in attending may be liable in negligence if a reasonable doctor would have appreciated that his attendance was necessary **4.72**

[170] [1999] PIQR p 53 [21], *per* Lord Woolf MR, and see *Birch v University College London Hospital NHS Foundation Trust* (2005) 104 BMLR 168.
[171] *Chester v Ashfar* [2005] 1 AC 134.
[172] ibid, [5]. And see *Montgomery*, n 73, at [86]–[87].
[173] *Chester v Afshar* [2004] 4 All ER 587.
[174] *Pearce v United Bristol Healthcare NHS Trust* (1998) BMLR 118 per Lord Woolf MR at 124, approved in *Chester v Afshar*, n 171, at [15].
[175] [2007] EWHC 644, 97 BMLR 82 (2007), Judge SP Grenfell.
[176] [2008] EWHC 2237, (2008) 104 BMLR 168.
[177] [2015] EWCA Civ 8, [2015] Med LR 48, [24].

in the patient's interests. This will depend upon the precise circumstances of the case: how serious was the patient's condition; what was the doctor told; what commitments to other patients did he have at the time?[178] So it may be negligent to arrange a further appointment to see the patient too long into the future, where the patient's condition is such that an earlier review of the situation is indicated.[179]

4.73 The duty to attend also extends to post-operative treatment. Thus, in *Corder v Banks*[180] a plastic surgeon who allowed the claimant to go home after an operation on the claimant's eyelids, but failed to make any arrangements for the claimant to contact him if bleeding occurred during the first forty-eight hours after the operation, was found to have been negligent. The duty to provide post-operative attendance does not require the doctor to supervise routine procedures carried out by nursing staff.[181] In some circumstances the duty to examine and/or treat the patient may arise independently of any request by or on behalf of the patient. For example, in *Stokes v Guest, Keen and Nettlefold (Bolts and Nuts) Ltd*[182] it was held that a factory medical officer should have instituted six-monthly medical examinations, given his knowledge of the risk to employees of contracting cancer from their working conditions and the fact that early diagnosis gave a significantly better chance of successful treatment. The employers were held vicariously liable for the medical officer's negligence in failing to implement a system of screening employees for the disease.

3. Diagnostic errors

4.74 Diagnostic errors can arise from an inadequate medical history, errors in examining the patient, errors in interpreting the patient's symptoms, a failure to conduct tests or refer the patient for specialist consultation, or a failure to monitor treatment and revise the diagnosis where a treatment is proving ineffective. The duty is not necessarily to get the diagnosis right, but a doctor should be aware of the risk that the initial diagnosis is mistaken and consider the option of referring the patient on for specialist investigation. Diagnosis should be preceded by the taking of a full history from the patient.[183]

---

[178] *Smith v Rae* (1919) 51 DLR 323, 325–26 (Ont SC App Div); see also *Cavan v Wilcox* (1973) 44 DLR (3d) 42, 53 (NBCA), where the information the doctor received over the telephone was not sufficiently serious to alert him to the emergency; *Barnes v Crabtree* The Times, 1 and 2 November 1955, discussed in H Nathan, *Medical Negligence* (Butterworth & Co 1957) 37; on a GP's 'duty to visit' see also: *Kavanagh v Abrahamson* (1964) 108 SJ 320; *Stockdale v Nicholls* [1993] 4 Med LR 190; *Durrant v Burke* [1993] 4 Med LR 258; *Morrison v Forsyth* [1995] 6 Med LR 6 (CS), where the seriousness of the patient's condition was not made clear to the general practitioner.

[179] *Lowe v Havering Hospitals NHS Trust* (2001) 62 BMLR 69, where the patient had a dangerously high and unstable blood pressure, but the doctor arranged a further appointment to see him eight weeks later. The patient suffered a stroke, which could probably have been avoided if the medication had been changed sooner.

[180] The Times, 9 April 1960; *Ocloo v Royal Brompton and Harefield NHS Trust* (2001) 68 BMLR 89 (QBD)—failure to provide clear advice to the patient about a follow-up appointment held to have been negligent; see also *Videto v Kennedy* (1980) 107 DLR (3d) 612, 616–17; rev'd on other grounds (1981) 125 DLR (3d) 127 (Ont CA), where the arrangements made by the defendant doctor for post-operative care in the event of complications were 'just about non-existent'; *Cherewayko v Grafton* [1993] 3 WWR 604, 626 (Man QB) on the failure to provide for 'follow-up'.

[181] *Morris v Winsbury-White* [1937] 4 All ER 494.

[182] [1968] 1 WLR 1776.

[183] In *Collins v Mid-Western Health Board* [2000] 2 IR 154, 164 (Sup Ct Irl) Barron J commented: 'The second defendant [a GP] was not expected to make the correct diagnosis. But he was expected to be in a position to know when his patient should be referred to a specialist . . . if no proper history in the sense of correct questions is taken the chance of an accurate diagnosis or decision to refer is seriously restricted.'

(i) Duty to take medical history

In *Chin Keow v Government of Malaysia*[184] a doctor was held liable in respect of a patient's allergic reaction to penicillin, having administered the injection without first enquiring into the patient's medical history. In *Leonard v Knott*[185] the defendant physician conducted annual 'executive health examinations' for client corporations. He referred the deceased for a radiological examination of the kidneys and urinary tract by means of an intravenous pyelogram. This was part of the 'package' included in the annual check-up, and at that stage the defendant had never even met the deceased, let alone examined him, taken a medical history, done any routine tests, such as urine analysis, or sought any information from the family doctor. The patient died from an allergic reaction to the contrast medium used in the procedure, a risk which was known and foreseeable to the medical profession. The defendant was held liable for exposing the deceased to such a risk without taking a history, examining him, or consulting the family doctor, given that virtually all of the problems could have been thus determined and the deceased had never had any signs or symptoms relating to the kidneys or urinary tract. **4.75**

The patient's medical history may include not only the signs and symptoms of the illness or injury for which the patient is seeking treatment, but also details of any previous treatment either for the same condition or, in appropriate circumstances, a previous injury or disease. In *Coles v Reading and District HMC*[186] a patient was given first aid treatment for a crushing injury to his finger at a cottage hospital but he was not given an anti-tetanus injection. He did not go to another hospital for further treatment, as advised, but saw his own doctor, who did not enquire as to what had happened at the cottage hospital but simply redressed the wound. The patient subsequently died of toxaemia due to tetanus infection. Both the cottage hospital and the GP were held liable for omitting to take the elementary precaution of giving the deceased an anti-tetanus vaccination. The GP was negligent in failing to make enquiries of the hospital or the deceased.[187] **4.76**

The duty to take a full history requires the doctor to *listen* to what the patient is saying. Sometimes, particularly if the patient is considered to be 'difficult', a doctor may disregard or discount what the patient says and this can colour the diagnosis. A failure to listen to a patient who is describing symptoms which would affect diagnosis and treatment will amount to negligence, where harm results.[188] Of course, the patient also bears some responsibility to provide appropriate information when questioned by a doctor. If the information is misleading the doctor will not be held liable for acting upon it, at least where it is reasonable to rely upon the information.[189] But it may not be reasonable to rely on the patient **4.77**

---

[184] [1967] 1 WLR 813.

[185] [1978] 5 WWR 511 (BCSC).

[186] (1963) 107 SJ 115.

[187] In *Meyer v Gordon* (1981) 17 CCLT 1 hospital staff failed to take details of the patient's obstetric history, which would have revealed that her previous labour had been a rapid one and put the staff on notice that the labour must be closely monitored; *Schanczi v Singh* [1988] 2 WWR 465 (Alta QB).

[188] *Giurelli v Girgis* (1980) 24 SASR 264. See also *Cassidy v Ministry of Health* [1951] 2 KB 343, 349 on the question of medical staff ignoring the claimant's complaints of intense and excessive pain; *Reitz v Bruser (No 2)* [1979] 1 WWR 31, where it was held that a doctor should not attribute the claimant's complaints of pain to 'anxiety' until all the possible causes of the symptoms have been explored; *Rhodes v Spokes and Farbridge* [1996] 7 Med LR 135, 145 on the duty to 'keep an open mind' when taking a history. In some cases a judgment that the patient's description of physical symptoms is probably attributable to a psychiatric condition may mislead a doctor into failing to spot a genuine physical problem. See, eg, *Panther v Wharton* (2001, unreported, QBD), where both a GP and a consultant physician fell into this trap.

[189] See, eg, *Venner v North East Essex AHA* The Times, 21 February 1987, where the claimant assured the defendant gynaecologist immediately before a sterilization operation that she could not be pregnant.

where what the patient says is clearly contradicted by the symptoms, or where it is contradicted by information provided by others, such as a spouse or family member.[190] Although a doctor is entitled to rely on what he is told by the patient, that does not absolve him from asking questions to establish that the patient has left nothing out that is material to a proper diagnosis.[191] There is a tendency on the part of patients to 'rationalize' their problem, that is to ascribe the problem to something which they themselves can identify. Thus, it may be dangerous for a doctor to be too ready to put symptoms down to the cause suggested by a patient;[192] and a psychiatrist should not always take at face value what he is told by a patient about how the patient feels.[193]

(ii) Alternative diagnoses

4.78 Whether an error of diagnosis is negligent depends to a large extent upon the difficulty of making the diagnosis given the symptoms presented, the diagnostic techniques available, and the dangers associated with the alternative diagnoses. Where there are two possible diagnoses, one of which is potentially life-threatening but the less likely of the two alternatives, it will not be negligent to undertake diagnostic procedures intended to rule out or confirm that diagnosis before the results of tests for the other possible diagnosis are available.[194] The seriousness of the consequences of the condition proving to be life-threatening would justify the risks associated with the procedure. The difficulty of making a diagnosis will often excuse a defendant.[195] The diagnosis must be judged in the light of the facts at the time and a doctor cannot be expected to possess the vision and wisdom of hindsight.[196] In *Meiklejohn v St George's NHS Trust*,[197] the Claimant was misdiagnosed with aplastic anaemia (AA) in 2003, and alleged a negligent failure on the part of his doctor to raise the index of suspicion to a level which would include a (correct) alternative diagnosis of dyskeratosis congenital (DC). The Claimant was obliged to seek expert evidence from a leading bone marrow doctor in the USA on account of the narrowness of the clinical field. Despite the fact that he presented with none of the triad of symptoms which in 2003 constituted the recognized clinical signs of DC in the UK, his American expert suggested that the presence of other somatic abnormalities should have prevented an alternative diagnosis of DC from being excluded. These abnormalities were first recognized as diagnostic criteria in the UK in 2006, although it was conceded by the treating clinician that new research was starting to identify other routes to diagnosis outside the classic triad. The Court of Appeal upheld the trial judge's conclusion that the Claimant's expert:

The defendant did not perform a dilatation and curettage (D and C) which probably would have terminated any pregnancy. The claimant was in fact pregnant at the time of the sterilization operation, and subsequently gave birth to a healthy child. Tucker J held that the defendant was not negligent in not performing a D and C as a matter of course.

190 *Collins v Mid-Western Health Board* [2000] 2 IR 154, 165 (Sup Ct Irl) *per* Barron J.

191 ibid, 164.

192 *Bova v Spring* [1994] 5 Med LR 120, 127; *Djemal v Bexley HA* [1995] 6 Med LR 269.

193 *Drake v Pontefract HA; Wakefield and Pontefract Community NHS Trust* [1998] Lloyd's Rep Med 425, 443.

194 *Maynard v West Midlands RHA* [1984] 1 WLR 634. See also *Dillon v Le Roux* [1994] 6 WWR 280 (BCCA).

195 *Pudney v Union-Castle Mail SS Ltd* [1953] 1 Lloyd's Rep 73; *Crivon v Barnet Group HMC* The Times, 18 November 1958 (CA); *Walker v Semple* (1993, unreported, CA); *Pilon v Bouaziz* [1994] 1 WWR 700 (BCCA).

196 *Holmes v Board of Hospital Trustees of the City of London* (1977) 81 DLR (3d) 67, 91 (Ont HC); Wilkinson Estate (Rogin) v Shannon (1986) 37 CCLT 181 (Ont HC); *Roe v Minister of Health* [1954] 2 QB 66, 83, per Denning LJ.

197 [2013] EWHC 469, upheld on appeal in [2014] EWCA Civ 120.

had approached this case by reference to standards in the USA rather than in the UK, and, try as she might, she had been unable to consider this case from a prospective basis, but instead has looked at it in retrospect. We all now know that the Claimant has DC.[198]

The judge held that the relevant question was what an AA specialist in the UK would have concluded in March 2003. Adopting a similar prospective approach in other cases of missed diagnosis, the courts have held that the failure to diagnose cancer is not necessarily negligent,[199] nor is to diagnose cancer mistakenly.[200]

Even where a particular condition cannot be diagnosed, the symptoms may indicate that the claimant is suffering from something serious which needs further investigation. The very difficulty of making a diagnosis may in itself suggest that the doctor should take additional precautions such as admitting the patient to hospital for observation, conducting further tests, or referring the patient to a specialist who was capable of making the diagnosis.[201] For example, in *Bova v Spring*[202] a GP diagnosed a muscle strain in the chest of a patient who died two days later from pneumonia. The defendant was held to have been negligent for 'failing to recognise the uncertainties attending his diagnosis'. In *Langley v Campbell*[203] the patient presented with symptoms of fever, headache, and alternate sweating and shivering. His GP diagnosed influenza, but the patient subsequently died from malaria, having recently returned from Uganda. Although GPs did not normally come across malaria, the deteriorating condition of a patient without the recognized complications of influenza should have been the cause of special concern. The defendant might not have been capable of diagnosing malaria, but should have been alerted to the possibility that the patient's illness might not be indigenous. **4.79**

[198] [2014] EWCA Civ 120 [99]–[100].

[199] *Hulse v Wilson* (1953) 2 BMJ 890; *Phillips v Grampian Health Board* [1991] 3 Med LR 16; *Judge v Huntingdon HA* [1995] 6 Med LR 223 (though the defendants were held liable on the facts); cf *Sutton v Population Services Family Planning Programme Ltd* The Times, 7 November 1981, on the diagnosis of cancer; *Stacey v Chiddy* [1993] 4 Med LR 216 (NSWSC); aff'd [1993] 4 Med LR 345 (NSWCA). Where a doctor suspects cancer he should refer the patient to a specialist or arrange for an immediate biopsy: *Wilson v Vancouver Hockey Club* (1983) 5 DLR (4th) 282, 288; aff'd (1985) 22 DLR (4th) 516 (BCCA). In *Taylor v West Kent HA* [1997] 8 Med LR 251 there was a negligent failure to interpret a cytology report correctly. The doctors should have sought clarification of the report, and should have been alerted to the need for further investigations.

[200] *Whiteford v Hunter* [1950] WN 553; *Crivon v Barnet Group HMC* The Times, 18 November 1958 (CA); *Graham v Persyko* (1986) 27 DLR (4th) 699, 703–04, where a doctor who mistakenly diagnosed Crohn's disease was held not to have been negligent. On missed fractures see: *McCormack v Redpath Brown & Co Ltd* The Times, 24 March 1961; *Wood v Thurston* The Times, 5 May 1951; *Newton v Newton's Model Laundry* The Times, 3 November 1959; *Saumarez v Medway and Gravesend HMC* (1953) 2 BMJ 1109; *Fraser v Vancouver General Hospital* (1951) 3 WWR 337 (BCCA); aff'd [1952] 3 DLR 785 (SCC); *Walker v Huntingdon HA* [1994] 5 Med LR 356.

[201] *Barnett v Chelsea and Kensington HMC* [1968] 1 All ER 1068, 1073; *Seyfert v Burnaby Hospital Society* (1986) 27 DLR (4th) 96. In *Dale v Munthali* (1976) 78 DLR (3d) 588; aff'd (1978) 90 DLR (3d) 763 (Ont CA) the defendant diagnosed the patient as suffering from influenza, when in fact he had meningitis. There was no negligence in failing to diagnose meningitis, but the patient was so extremely ill that the defendant should have realized that it was more than gastrointestinal influenza.

[202] [1994] 5 Med LR 120, QBD. See also *Riddett v D'Arcy* (1960) 2 BMJ 1607 where a GP who failed to examine a baby closely enough was held liable for failing to diagnose the early stages of pneumonia. On the failure to diagnose appendicitis see: *Edler v Greenwich & Deptford HMC* The Times, 7 March 1953; *Bergen v Sturgeon General Hospital* (1984) 28 CCLT 155.

[203] The Times, 5 November 1975; see also *Sa'd v Robinson* [1989] 1 Med LR 41; cf *Stockdale v Nicholls* [1993] 4 Med LR 190. On a GP's 'duty to visit' see *Durrant v Burke* [1993] 4 Med LR 258.

(iii) Diagnostic aids

4.80 Where diagnostic aids would assist a doctor in reaching an accurate diagnosis it may well be negligent to fail to use them, if available,[204] although this is not necessarily the case.[205] Where a gynaecologist was aware that his patient could be pregnant, he should have conducted tests before subjecting her uterus to X-rays.[206] Doctors who ordered X-rays to be carried out but then delayed for five days before examining them were held negligent for failing to inform themselves of the factual data which they had themselves identified as pertinent and necessary to the claimant's diagnosis, and which they knew or ought to have known was available.[207] In *Pierre v Marshall*[208] a GP who failed to screen a pregnant woman for gestational diabetes, contrary to the recommendations of the Alberta Medical Association and the Society of Obstetricians and Gynaecologists of Canada, was held to have been negligent. The defendant also had failed to do an ultrasound scan to confirm the expected size of the baby, despite his suspicion that the foetus was slightly larger than it should have been at thirty-six weeks. At a time when screening for gestational diabetes was not routine practice in the UK, a doctor was not necessarily negligent for failing to undertake the standard test for that condition. It is a matter of clinical judgment involving a number of factors.[209] In *X and Y v Pal*[210] it was accepted that an obstetrician who failed to test a patient for syphilis during her pregnancy was negligent.[211]

[204] *Bergen v Sturgeon General Hospital* (1984) 28 CCLT 155; *Lankenau v Dutton* (1986) 37 CCLT 213; (1991) 79 DLR (4th) 707 (BCCA); *Smith v Salford HA* [1994] 5 Med LR 321, QBD, where it was held that the defendant should have undertaken a CT scan prior to performing a spinal fusion operation, because this would have been a far more sophisticated and informative piece of radiology than the X-rays upon which he relied in assessing the need for the operation and the technique that would be required. The simplest diagnostic tool may be a physical examination of the patient. See *Stacey v Chiddy* [1993] 4 Med LR 216, 224–25 (NSWSC); aff'd [1993] 4 Med LR 345 (NSWCA).

[205] *Whiteford v Hunter* [1950] WN 553; *Lakey v Merton, Sutton and Wandsworth HA* (1999) 48 BMLR 18 (CA)—casualty officer not negligent in failing to X-ray a patient who presented with pain in the hip following a fall, when there were no clinical signs of a fracture.

[206] *Zimmer v Ringrose* (1981) 125 DLR (3d) 215, (Alta CA); aff'g (1978) 89 DLR (3d) 646, 656–57; *Gardiner v Mounfield* [1990] 1 Med LR 205, where the defendant dismissed the possibility that the claimant, who was overweight and had a history of amenorrhoea, was pregnant.

[207] *Holmes v Board of Hospital Trustees of the City of London* (1977) 81 DLR (3d) 67 (Ont HC). In *Hutton v East Dyfed HA* [1998] Lloyd's Rep Med 335 a doctor who did not carry out a chest X-ray on a patient with chest pain because she was pregnant and he wrongly thought that it would involve danger to the foetus was held to have been negligent.

[208] [1994] 8 WWR 478 (Alta QB). See also *Tucker v Tees HA* [1995] 6 Med LR 54, where the defendant was held negligent for performing a laparotomy to remove a presumed ovarian cyst without first conducting an ultrasound scan to check whether the claimant was pregnant. On the other hand, a doctor should not be criticized for a refusal to offer a CT scan or any other diagnostic procedure which he considered inappropriate just because the patient was willing to pay and wanted reassurance: *Rhodes v Spokes and Farbridge* [1996] 7 Med LR 135, 146.

[209] *Hallatt v North West Anglia HA* [1998] Lloyd's Rep Med 197, CA.

[210] (1991) 23 NSWLR 26, [1992] 3 Med LR 195 (NSWCA).

[211] There may also be negligence in failing to interpret test results properly: see, eg: *Fraser v Vancouver General Hospital* (1951) 3 WWR 337 (BCCA); [1952] 3 DLR 785 (SCC), and *Roy v Croydon HA* [1998] PIQR Q26 (CA), on the negligent interpretation of X-rays; *Rance v Mid-Downs Health Authority* [1991] 1 All ER 801, an allegedly negligent failure to interpret an ultrasound scan of a foetus; *Penney, Palmer and Cannon v East Kent HA* [2000] Lloyd's Rep Med 41 (CA)—failure to interpret smear tests for cervical cancer accurately. A failure to read a report will be negligent: *Fredette v Wiebe* [1986] 5 WWR 222 (BCSC). On the other hand, a misleading pathology report may result in a finding that a surgeon was not negligent in embarking on radical surgery in a case of suspected cancer: *Abbas v Kenney* [1996] 7 Med LR 47.

(iv) Diagnostic review

The diagnosis should also be kept under review as the treatment progresses. There is a danger in acquiring 'tunnel vision' about the patient's condition.[212] This is even more important where the consequences of the alternative diagnosis, if it turns out to be correct, are likely to be serious.[213] In *Lankenau v Dutton*[214] the medical evidence was that a surgeon confronted with a patient with paralysis after major surgery should not only attempt to diagnose the cause but also 'should make a differential diagnosis, that is to say that he should consider other likely causes of her condition and test them against her symptoms and be ready with an alternative theory to direct her treatment if his first diagnosis and treatment should fail to produce an improvement in her condition'.[215] The defendant had diagnosed an aortic dissection occurring during surgery, which was a reasonable initial diagnosis. As the patient's symptoms progressed, however, he failed to reassess the diagnosis, which resulted in the paralysis becoming permanent. The surgeon was held to have been negligent for clinging to the original diagnosis even though the symptoms should have made him question it, for failing to test his theory by X-ray, and for failing to seek the assistance of neurological experts quickly enough.[216] In *Hutton v East Dyfed HA*[217] a consultant physician was held negligent in failing to revise an initial diagnosis of myopericarditis in a patient with chest pain, having received normal test results for that condition, and in failing to include in his differential diagnosis the risk of pulmonary embolus, despite the real risk of disastrous consequences if a further pulmonary embolus occurred. **4.81**

(v) Obligation to refer

The obligation to refer a patient to a specialist or to seek further advice will arise whenever a doctor is unable to diagnose or treat the patient.[218] Even a consultant in a specialist field may come across a problem that he has never previously encountered and accordingly may have a responsibility to seek advice.[219] In *Poole v Morgan*[220] the defendant ophthalmologist was inadequately trained in the use of a laser, although he had often used it in his practice. The treatment that he gave to the claimant was usually performed by a retina vitreous specialist. Since the **4.82**

[212] *Layden v Cope* (1984) 28 CCLT 140 (Alta QB); *Reitz v Bruser (No 2)* [1979] 1 WWR 31, 47 *per* Hewak J. Tunnel vision was also in evidence in *Panther v Wharton* (2001, QBD), where a GP had formed the view that the patient's symptoms were largely psychiatric in origin, and referred her for a psychiatric assessment, and a consultant physician at the hospital, asked to advise the psychiatric team, failed to approach his physical examination of the patient with an open mind, and so failed to identify a serious vascular problem.

[213] *Bova v Spring* [1994] 5 Med LR 120, 129 (QBD).

[214] *Lankenau v Dutton* (1986) 37 CCLT 213 (BCSC); aff'd (1991) 79 DLR (4th) 707 (BCCA).

[215] ibid, 231 *per* Spencer J.

[216] In *Bergen v Sturgeon General Hospital* (1984) 28 CCLT 155 (Alta QB) a female patient, who was admitted to hospital complaining of pains in her abdomen, died from a ruptured appendix, having been provisionally diagnosed as suffering from acute gastroenteritis, with appendicitis to be checked out. A further diagnosis of pelvic inflammatory disease had been made, but no steps were taken to rule out appendicitis, despite the fact that it explained all the symptoms, the patient's condition was not responding to treatment, and that appendicitis is life-threatening. The defendants were held negligent, not for the initial mistaken diagnosis but for failing to keep the diagnosis under review when the patient's condition did not improve. In *Law Estate v Simice* (1994) 21 CCLT (2d) 228, 236 (BCSC) Spencer J observed that: 'Where a potentially life-threatening condition is included in a differential diagnosis, there is a duty on the physician to take prompt steps to confirm it or rule it out with reasonable dispatch.'

[217] [1998] Lloyd's Rep Med 335.

[218] *MacDonald v York County Hospital* (1973) 41 DLR (3d) 321, 349–50 *per* Dubin JA (Ont CA); aff'd sub nom *Vail v MacDonald* (1976) 66 DLR (3d) 530 (SCC).

[219] *Gascoine v Ian Sheridan & Co* [1994] 5 Med LR 437, 447 *per* Mitchell J.

[220] [1987] 3 WWR 217; *Layden v Cope* (1984) 28 CCLT 140, 148; *Lankenau v Dutton* (1986) 37 CCLT 213; (1991) 79 DLR (4th) 707 (BCCA).

defendant was unable to come up to the standard of that specialty, he had a duty to refer the claimant to such a specialist.

4. Failures of communication

(i) Between doctor and patient

4.83 Failures of communication can arise between doctor and patient or between the various health care professionals involved in a patient's treatment, but in either case the consequences for the patient can be serious. The doctor has an obligation to provide information to a patient about the nature, purpose, and consequences of proposed procedures, but in addition to the duty to warn patients in advance of the risks associated with the treatment, it is possible that in some circumstances the practitioner will be under a duty to inform the patient that something has gone wrong with the treatment.[221] In *Stamos v Davies*[222] the defendant punctured the claimant's spleen while performing a lung biopsy, but did not tell the claimant, who was then discharged from hospital. The claimant was readmitted as an emergency three days later, due to bleeding into his abdominal cavity. The spleen was removed surgically and the claimant recovered uneventfully. Krever J held that the defendant was in breach of a duty to inform the claimant that the spleen had been punctured. The difficulty with any case of this nature, however, is proving that the breach of duty caused the claimant damage. The claimant's ignorance that something untoward has occurred will rarely contribute to any further loss, and since the damage has already occurred, the failure to be candid is not a cause of the harm.[223]

4.84 In some cases the failure to inform may cause further injury as if, for example, the patient takes a risk that he would otherwise have avoided, or if the patient's ignorance leads to delay in diagnosis (resulting in additional harm) or an emergency subsequently arises as a result of the injury of which he is unaware. In *Kiley-Nikkel v Danais*[224] the claimant's breast was removed following a mistaken diagnosis of cancer. She was not informed of the error, with the result that she sought follow-up treatment for cancer in another locality and lived with the belief that she had cancer for a considerable time. Part of the award of damages was for the psychiatric harm resulting from non-disclosure of the error in diagnosis, since the consequences of this would have been much less serious had she known immediately that she was not suffering from cancer. In *Pittman Estate v Bain*[225] a patient received a blood transfusion during the

---

[221] See the comments of Sir John Donaldson MR in *Lee v South West Thames RHA* [1985] 2 All ER 385, and *Naylor v Preston AHA* [1987] 2 All ER 353, 360. In *Gerber v Pines* (1934) 79 SJ 13 Du Parcq J said that as a general rule a patient was entitled to be told at once if the doctor had left some foreign object in his body; cf *Daniels v Heskin* [1954] IR 73, 87 *per* Kingsmill Moore J. But on *Daniels v Heskin* see now *Walsh v Family Planning Services Ltd* [1992] IR 496, 520 (Sup Ct Irl). It has been suggested that there is an obligation to break distressing, though truthful, news to patients in a manner which reduces the risk of patients developing psychiatric illness in response to the news: *AB v Tameside & Glossop HA* [1997] 8 Med LR 91, though the defendants were held not to have been negligent in choosing to inform patients that there was a small risk that they might have contracted HIV from a doctor by letter rather than face-to-face. See S Dziobon and A Tettenborn. 'When the Truth Hurts: The Incompetent Transmission of Distressing News' (1997) 13 PN 70. A fortiori if, as a result of the defendants' negligence, the distressing information was *inaccurate* and the claimant suffered psychiatric harm from this distressing 'news', even where the incorrect information was imparted in a sensitive and appropriate manner: *Allin v City & Hackney HA* [1996] 7 Med LR 167; M Jones, 'Negligently Inflicted Psychiatric Harm: Is the Word Mightier than the Deed?' (1997) 13 PN 111.

[222] (1986) 21 DLR (4th) 507 (Ont HC); G Robertson, 'The Duty to Disclose Medical Mistakes' (1987) 25 Alberta L Rev 215.

[223] *Daniels v Heskin* [1954] IR 73, 81, 88.

[224] (1992) 16 CCLT (2d) 290 (Qué SC).

[225] (1994) 112 DLR (4th) 257 (Ont Ct, Gen Div).

course of heart surgery. It was subsequently discovered that the blood he had received was contaminated with HIV. The defendants were found to have been negligent in failing to inform him that there was a risk, which in fact materialized, that the transfusion had infected him with HIV. Although there was no negligence in the administration of the transfusion, the failure to inform the patient meant that he did not have an opportunity to take measures which could have extended his life expectancy and, moreover, his wife also contracted the infection from unprotected sexual intercourse with her husband. The defendants were held liable for both of these consequences.

A doctor will often need the patient's cooperation, for example, in performing an examination or administering treatment. This may be as simple as requiring the patient to keep still or instructing the patient about taking medication. It may also be necessary to give the patient a warning about any danger signs to look out for, with instructions as to what should be done if they occur, such as stopping the medication or seeking medical assistance immediately.[226] Sometimes this will be absolutely vital. In these circumstances the doctor will be under a duty to take special care in giving the patient instructions, to make sure that the patient understands both the instructions and the importance of strictly adhering to them.[227] In *Joyce v Wandsworth HA*[228] the claimant underwent an operative procedure which resulted in a partially occluded artery, leading three months later to an upper brain stem infarction causing almost total paralysis. The Court of Appeal held that the immediate follow-up care that the claimant had received was negligent because the patient was discharged from hospital without proper instructions and advice. In some instances the risk associated with the treatment may be so great that it will be negligent for a doctor to rely on a patient accurately reporting his symptoms, the obligation being to conduct regular tests.[229] There is also a responsibility to bring home to a patient the importance of obtaining further treatment, if necessary, and the dangers involved in failing to do so.[230] Similarly, where it is unwise for a patient to engage in certain types of activity following treatment, he should be warned of this danger.[231] Indeed, there may be a duty to warn patients to make a lifestyle change. In *Hutchinson v Epson & St Helier NHS Trust*[232] the defendants were held to have been negligent in failing to advise a patient who was a heavy drinker, and at serious risk of developing fatal cirrhosis of the liver, to stop drinking alcohol. Of course, in such a case it would have to be demonstrated that the deceased would probably have heeded the warning. **4.85**

[226] See, eg, *Crossman v Stewart* (1977) 82 DLR (3d) 677, where the defendant doctor was held negligent for failing to identify the indications of side effects.

[227] *Clarke v Adams* (1950) 94 SJ 599; *Stamos v Davies* (1986) 21 DLR (4th) 507. In *Sheridan v Boots Co Ltd* (1980, unreported, QBD), a doctor who prescribed a potent anti-inflammatory drug but failed to give the patient a warning that if he experienced any stomach trouble he should stop taking the drug and consult a doctor immediately, was said to have been negligent, although the action failed on causation.

[228] [1996] 7 Med LR 1.

[229] *Marshall v Rogers* [1943] 4 DLR 68, 77 (BCCA); cf *Battersby v Tottman* (1985) 37 SASR 524 where, in the circumstances, a failure to monitor the known and serious side effects of a drug was held not negligent.

[230] *Coles v Reading and District HMC* (1963) 107 SJ 115.

[231] *Brushett v Cowan* (1987) 40 DLR (4th) 488; aff'd (1990) 69 DLR (4th) 743 (Newfd CA), where the claimant was given crutches to use following a biopsy on her leg, but she was not warned that she should not bear weight on the leg. While engaging in ordinary activity without the crutches the leg broke at the site of the biopsy. The doctor was held negligent.

[232] [2002] EWHC 2363 (QB).

(ii) Between health professionals

4.86 A breakdown in communication between health care professionals with responsibility for a patient can have dangerous consequences for the patient. These errors may be the result of isolated acts of carelessness (such as failing to read the nursing notes[233]) or they may be the product of some organizational failure (for example, relying too heavily on casual exchanges[234]). The system of communication may be so poor that mistakes are almost inevitable, or the methods adopted may fail to take into account the risks of human error by providing some mechanism for checking. Thus, a hospital must have an adequate system for summoning specialist assistance when needed.[235] If a patient is injured by reason of a negligent breakdown in the systems for communicating material information to the clinicians responsible for her care, she is not to be denied redress merely because no identifiable person or persons are to blame for deficiencies in setting up and monitoring the effectiveness of the relevant communication systems.[236] Thus, there must be a system for dealing with a surgeon's patients when the surgeon goes away for a weekend.[237] It is also to be expected that there will be a system for communication between hospitals, or between a hospital and GPs, about the treatment that a patient has received.[238] On the other hand, a GP who is sent the results of a blood test by the hospital is entitled to assume that the hospital doctors are aware of those results and are taking them into account in their investigation of the patient's symptoms, and it is not for the GP to go through hospital notes to check that the hospital has done what it should have done.[239]

4.87 Communication errors can occur from simply mishearing or misreading an instruction. This may be the result of a single lapse of concentration, but the further question will then arise as to whether there was any system for checking for such errors given that it is known that mistakes do sometimes happen. In *Collins v Hertfordshire County Council*[240] a patient died after being injected with cocaine instead of procaine as a local anaesthetic. The surgeon had told a junior, unqualified medical officer over the telephone his requirements for the operation, and the word 'procaine' was misheard for 'cocaine'. The pharmacist dispensing the drug at the hospital pharmacy did not question the order for an 'unheard-of dosage' of a

233 *Holmes v Board of Hospital Trustees of the City of London* (1977) 81 DLR (3d) 67, 94 (Ont HC); *Starcevic v West Hertfordshire HA* [2001] EWCA Civ 192; (2001) 60 BMLR 221—the failure of an occupational therapist and a nurse to pass on information about the condition of the patient's leg to the surgeon, which would have alerted the doctor to the risk of deep vein thrombosis, held to constitute negligence (the patient died from a pulmonary embolism during minor surgery on his leg).

234 *Bergen v Sturgeon General Hospital* (1984) 28 CCLT 155, 175.

235 *Bull v Devon AHA* (1989), [1993] 4 Med LR 117 (CA). Of course, even the best systems may not be foolproof. In *Bolitho v City and Hackney HA* [1997] 4 All ER 771 one doctor failed to attend an emergency call from a nurse because the battery in her bleeper was flat.

236 *Robertson v Nottingham HA* [1997] 8 Med LR 1, 13 *per* Brooke LJ. This may give rise to a 'non-delegable duty' on the part of the hospital to 'set up a safe system of operation in relation to what are essentially management as opposed to clinical matters': ibid.

237 *Cassidy v Ministry of Health* [1951] 2 KB 343, 359 *per* Singleton LJ; *Crichton v Hastings* (1972) 29 DLR (3d) 692, 700 (Ont CA).

238 *Coles v Reading and District HMC* (1963) 107 SJ 115; see also *Schanczi v Singh* [1988] 2 WWR 465 (Alta QB) on a specialist's failure to obtain adequate information about a patient from the referring doctor before proceeding to surgery; cf *Chapman v Rix* (1960), [1994] 5 Med LR 239 (HL).

239 *Weir v Graham* [2002] EWHC 2291 (QB). Similarly, it is not negligent for a GP to fail to advise parents that there was an alternative means of providing immunization of a child against measles, when immunization was not imminent and the GP was aware that the parents would be being advised by another doctor at another practice in twelve to eighteen months about the options for immunization: *Thompson v Blake-James* [1998] PIQR P286 (CA).

240 [1947] 1 KB 598; see also *Strangeways-Lesmere v Clayton* [1936] 2 KB 11, where a nurse who misread her instructions and gave an excess dose was held to be negligent.

dangerous drug, and the surgeon did not check prior to injecting the solution that he was in fact injecting what he had ordered. It was held that both the surgeon and the medical officer were liable, as was the hospital authority for having an unsafe dispensing system.

A pathologist who has been given specimens for testing or analysis owes a duty to the patient not only to conduct the tests in a proper manner but also to take reasonable steps to communicate the results to the referring doctor, and it is irrelevant that the doctor also has a corresponding duty to find out the results.[241] A doctor who prepares a report or medical notes which he is aware may be relied upon by others for the treatment of the patient has a duty to exercise reasonable care in writing the report.[242] This also applies to the writing of a prescription, which should be reasonably legible.[243] A laboratory which is under contract to perform tests should indicate if the sample it receives is in any way inadequate. But a hospital is not necessarily liable for a failure to check that the sample is adequate, if it relied on the laboratory to communicate any such deficiency: *Farraj v King's Healthcare Trust*.[244] In that case, the Jordanian government had procured the NHS Trust to provide genetic foetal testing, which testing the Trust had subcontracted to a private cytogenic laboratory. An inadequate sample was sent for analysis, in the event contaminated by maternal cells. The test results were negative. Had foetal cells been sent for testing, the extent of the child's genetic abnormality would have been revealed and the pregnancy terminated. The Hospital was held (on appeal) not to be liable. The laboratory was solely liable for the error.[245] **4.88**

5. Treatment errors

Errors in treatment can take a multitude of forms. The mere fact that a doctor has departed from the standard treatment will not necessarily indicate negligence, bearing in mind that doctors have to treat the individual patient and not the 'standard' patient found in textbooks; a slight departure from the textbook therefore will not necessarily be a mistake, let alone negligent.[246] On the other hand, a substantial departure from standard practice will place a heavy onus on the defendant to justify this decision.[247] If a doctor has made a considered decision about treatment, it may be more difficult to conclude that there has been negligence[248] than if he has made an unintentional or inadvertent 'error', since in the latter case there has been no balancing of risks and benefits.[249] **4.89**

(i) Operations

The courts have long recognized that the mere fact that something has gone wrong during the course of an operation is not per se indicative of negligence,[250] although knocking **4.90**

---

[241] *Thomsen v Davison* [1975] Qd R 93; see also *McKay v Essex Area HA* [1982] QB 1166 on an alleged omission to communicate test results; *Gregory v Pembrokeshire HA* [1989] 1 Med LR 81 (CA); *Fredette v Wiebe* [1986] 5 WWR 222.

[242] *Everett v Griffiths* [1920] 3 KB 163, 213; *Price v Milawski* (1977) 82 DLR (3d) 130 (Ont CA).

[243] *Prendergast v Sam and Dee Ltd* [1989] 1 Med LR 36 (CA). For similar cases of negligence by a pharmacist failing to spot prescription errors, see *Collins v Hertfordshire County Council* [1947] 1 KB 598 and *Dwyer v Roderick* (1983) 127 SJ 806; A McKevitt, 'Doctors, Pharmacists and Prescriptions: The Standard of Care Owed to the Patient' (1988) 4 PN 185; J Crawford, 'Pharmacists' Liability for Drug-induced Injury' (1995) 2 J Law and Med 293.

[244] *Farraj v King's Healthcare Trust* [2009] EWCH Civ 1203, [2010] PIQR P7.

[245] ibid, [65].

[246] *Holland v The Devitt & Moore Nautical College* The Times, 4 March 1960.

[247] *Clark v MacLennan* [1983] 1 All ER 416.

[248] See, eg, *Darley v Shale* [1993] 4 Med LR 161 (NSWSC).

[249] *Goode v Nash* (1979) 21 SASR 419, 423 (SC of S Aus).

[250] *White v Westminster Hospital Board of Governors* The Times, 26 October 1961; *Ashcroft v Merseyside RHA* [1983] 2 All ER 245; aff'd [1985] 2 All ER 96; see also *Chubey v Ahsan* (1977) 71 DLR (3d) 550 (Man CA); *Kapur v Marshall* (1978) 85 DLR (3d) 567, 573 *per* Robins J (Ont HC).

out four of the patient's teeth during a tonsillectomy was held to be negligent.[251] Where a patient sustains burns in an operating theatre, this is usually the result of negligence.[252] Perforation of the uterus during the course of performing a dilatation and curettage (D and C) is relatively common, and not in itself negligent, but damage to the small bowel during the operation is so rare as to be outside the range of normal practice and does indicate a lack of reasonable care.[253]

4.91 In *Hendy v Milton Keynes HA (No 2)*[254] the evidence showed that it was possible for ureteric damage to occur during an abdominal hysterectomy despite the use of a competent surgical technique, but these rare instances of non-culpable ureteric damage were attributable to anatomical variations outside the normal range. Most cases of ureteric damage where the anatomy was normal were due to poor technique, and therefore the most likely explanation of damage to the claimant's ureter, in the absence of any evidence of abnormal anatomy, was that there had been negligence.

4.92 Obstetric errors are frequently the subject of litigation, partly because the consequences for the child can be extremely serious, and partly because the parents' expectation is to have a normal, healthy child. In *Whitehouse v Jordan*[255] an allegation that the defendant had pulled too long and too hard in the course of a forceps delivery, and thus was negligent in failing to proceed to a Caesarean section delivery, was ultimately rejected on the facts. In *Parry v North West Surrey HA*,[256] on the other hand, the defendant was held liable for attempting to deliver a child by forceps when it was too high in the mother's pelvis, and thus for failing to undertake a Caesarean section delivery. Human error is frequently implicated in obstetric

[251] *Munro v United Oxford Hospitals* (1958) 1 BMJ 167.

[252] *Crits v Sylvester* (1956) 1 DLR (2d) 502; aff'd (1956) 5 DLR (2d) 601 (SCC); *Paton v Parker* (1942) 65 CLR 187; *Crysler v Pearse* [1943] 4 DLR 738; *Clarke v Warboys* The Times, 18 March 1952. Burns to the buttocks following surgery are, apparently, a common type of claim: Medical Defence Union, *Annual Report 1990*, 45; (1993) 9 J of the MDU 95. The Department of Health has issued a specific warning to hospitals about the danger of inflammable liquids igniting during surgery: HC (Hazard) (90) 25.

[253] *Bovenzi v Kettering HA* [1991] 2 Med LR 293 (QBD).

[254] [1992] 3 Med LR 119 (QBD). In *Ratty v Haringey HA* [1994] 5 Med LR 413 the Court of Appeal upheld a finding of negligence where there was damage to the claimant's ureter during the course of colorectal surgery. The negligence consisted, not in the initial damage to the ureter, which could occur even with the exercise of reasonable care, but in failing to discover and correct the damage before the end of the operation. See also *Bouchta v Swindon HA* [1996] 7 Med LR 62; cf *Hooper v Young* [1998] Lloyd's Rep Med 61 (CA).

[255] [1981] 1 All ER 267. See also *Knight v West Kent HA* [1998] Lloyd's Rep Med 18; *Corley v North West Herefordshire HA* [1997] 8 Med LR 45; *Hallatt v North West Anglia HA* [1998] Lloyd's Rep Med 197 (CA); *Hinfey v Salford HA* [1993] 4 Med LR 143, where an allegation that the failure to undertake a Caesarean section delivery constituted negligence was rejected on the evidence; *James v Camberwell HA* [1994] 5 Med LR 253, where a delay in proceeding to a Caesarean section was held not negligent on the facts.

[256] [1994] 5 Med LR 259. See also *Dowdie v Camberwell HA* [1997] 8 Med LR 368, where the defendant was held to have been negligent in failing to proceed to a Caesarean section in a case of shoulder dystocia; *Gaughan v Bedfordshire HA* [1997] 8 Med LR 182—midwife used force for longer than was acceptable in a case of shoulder dystocia; *Sutcliffe v Countess of Chester Hospital NHS Trust* [2002] Lloyd's Rep Med 449—injury to the brachial plexus held to be negligent in a case of undiagnosed shoulder dystocia. See also *Murphy v Wirral HA* [1996] 7 Med LR 99, on the duty of a midwife to monitor the progress of labour by conducting regular vaginal examinations; *Reynolds v North Tyneside HA* [2002] Lloyd's Rep Med 459, a midwife failed to undertake a vaginal examination despite the existence of circumstances in which the risk of cord prolapse was foreseeable; *Simms v Birmingham HA* (2000) 58 BMLR 66, a SHO failed to report the presence of undiluted meconium to the registrar, and left the midwife to interpret the CTG trace in a high-risk situation; *Briody v St Helen's & Knowsley HA* [1999] Lloyd's Rep Med 185; *Wiszniewski v Central Manchester HA* [1998] PIQR P324; *Hill v West Lancashire HA* [1997] 8 Med LR 196; *Bowers v Harrow HA* [1995] 6 Med LR 16. See also *De Martell v Merton and Sutton HA* [1995] 6 Med LR 234 and *Robertson v Nottingham HA* [1997] 8 Med L Rev 1, where the actions failed on causation.

accidents, many of which are avoidable,[257] although establishing the causal link between any negligence and the child's injuries can be extremely difficult.

A doctor may be liable for proceeding to surgery too quickly without first considering conservative treatment.[258] Conversely, a delay in recommending surgery may also be negligent. In *Powell v Guttman*[259] the claimant developed a condition of avascular necrosis following an operation on her leg performed by the defendant orthopaedic surgeon. The defendant failed to advise the claimant to undergo an arthroplasty operation to correct this. A year after the first operation another surgeon performed this operation, and during it the claimant sustained a rotary fracture of the femur. Due to the delay, the condition of the bone had deteriorated as a result of osteoporosis, and this was a 'significant cause' of the fracture that occurred. The defendant was held liable on the basis that the delay in the second operation was attributable to his negligence, and this had caused an increase in the osteoporosis rendering the femur more susceptible to the fracture. **4.93**

(ii) Team negligence

Under modern conditions, most medical treatment is undertaken by a team of health care professionals, and this is invariably true of surgical procedures. In *Wilsher v Essex Area HA*[260] the Court of Appeal rejected the concept of 'team negligence' whereby each of the persons who formed the staff of the unit held themselves out as capable of undertaking the specialized procedures which the unit set out to perform. It would not be right, said Mustill LJ, to attribute to each individual member of the team a duty to live up to the standards demanded of the unit as a whole, because that would expose a student nurse to an action in negligence for a failure to possess the skill and experience of a consultant. Each member of the team will be responsible for his or her own contribution to the joint undertaking. For example, a doctor will not normally be responsible for the negligence of others, such as nurses, in carrying out instructions that have been given with regard to the patient's treatment,[261] and, conversely, nursing staff will not be considered to have acted negligently when faithfully carrying out the instructions of a doctor.[262] Acting under the instructions of a doctor, however, does not excuse a nurse from making any professional judgment. There may be circumstances where a nurse could be negligent when following a doctor's instructions; for example, if a doctor ordered an obviously incorrect and dangerous dosage of a drug and the nurse administered it without obtaining confirmation from the doctor or higher authority.[263] Similarly, a pharmacist has been held to be negligent for failing to **4.94**

257 *Ennis and Vincent* (1990) 300 BMJ 1365. This reflects a number of general problems, including inadequate training and supervision of junior and middle ranking staff in the labour ward: ibid. See further the Department of Health's *Report on Confidential Enquiries into Maternal Deaths in England and Wales* (HMSO 1989).

258 *Schanczi v Singh* [1988] 2 WWR 465, 472 (Alta QB); see also *Coughlin v Kuntz* (1987) 42 CCLT 142 (BCSC); aff'd [1990] 2 WWR 737, 744 (BCCA); *Haughian v Paine* (1987) 37 DLR (4th) 625, 629–35 (Sask CA); *Mann v Judgeo* [1993] 4 WWR 760 (Sask QB), on the performance of aggressive surgery when 'first treatment surgery' was appropriate; *Cherewayko v Grafton* [1993] 3 WWR 604, 619 (Man QB), on an 'unnecessary' operation; *Doughty v North Staffordshire HA* [1992] 3 Med LR 81 (QBD); cf *De Freitas v O'Brien* [1995] 6 Med LR 108, where the defendant's decision to resort to spinal surgery, despite the absence of definite clinical and radiological evidence of nerve compression, was held not to have been negligent.

259 (1978) 89 DLR(3d) 180 (Man CA).

260 [1986] 3 All ER 801, 812–13, reversed on different grounds by the House of Lords [1988] 1 All ER 871.

261 *Perionowsky v Freeman* (1866) 4 F & F 977; *Morris v Winsbury-White* [1937] 4 All ER 494, 498.

262 *Gold v Essex County Council* [1942] 2 KB 293, 299 *per* Lord Greene MR.

263 ibid, at 313 *per Goddard* LJ, although his Lordship added that: 'In the stress of an operation, however, I should suppose that the first thing required of a nurse would be an unhesitating obedience to the

check a request for an 'unheard-of dosage' of cocaine.[264] A doctor may be negligent if he knows or ought reasonably to have known that another person in the team, whether it be the anaesthetist or a nurse, has done something which puts the patient at risk but fails to take any steps to remedy the error.[265] Moreover, it is negligent for a doctor to rely on information provided by a nurse whom he knows or ought to know is overconfident in her own abilities and not qualified to make the clinical judgment in question.[266]

(iii) 'Swab' cases

4.95 The danger of swabs or surgical instruments being left inside a patient at the end of an operation is clearly something which must be guarded against. But even in this type of case a surgeon is not necessarily liable; he only has to exercise reasonable care to see that it does not happen.[267] However, the consequences can be very serious and accordingly the degree of care required in order to satisfy the requirement of reasonableness will be correspondingly high. It is not negligent for a surgeon to delegate the task of counting swabs to a nurse, but a surgeon will not necessarily avoid liability by relying on that count.[268] In *Urry v Bierer*[269] a surgeon conducting a Caesarean section relied almost exclusively on the count by the nurse. He was held to have been negligent in failing to take any additional precautions, such as using swabs with tapes, although it was said that different considerations might apply in an emergency. There was no reason why the surgeon should not have made some mental effort to remember where he had placed the swabs, particularly since he had chosen not to use tapes. In practice, swab cases are usually settled as indefensible, and most of the cases that are litigated end in a finding of negligence.[270] Even if, on the facts, the conclusion is that the surgeon was not negligent in leaving the swab inside the patient, the result will almost invariably be that the nurse conducting the count was negligent.[271]

(iv) Infection

4.96 (a) **In Hospital** Over 6 per cent of hospital patients pick up infections while they are in hospital. Many of these cases are unavoidable, but some are due to medical staff ignoring basic hygiene rules.[272] Cases may arise from cross-infection, where patients acquire a disease

orders of the surgeon.' See also the analogous case of *Davy-Chiesman v Davy-Chiesman* [1984] 1 All ER 321, 332, 335, stating that solicitors should not rely blindly on the advice of counsel.

[264] *Collins v Hertfordshire County Council* [1947] 1 KB 598.

[265] *Perionowsky v Freeman* (1866) 4F & F977, 982; *Wilsher v Essex Area HA* [1986] 3 All ER 801, where the registrar was held to have been negligent in failing to spot the senior house officer's error. *In Jones v Manchester Corporation* [1952] 2 All ER 125 the Court of Appeal took the view that the inexperienced doctor who administered the fatal injection was not as culpable as the experienced doctor who supervised her. See also *Collins v Hertfordshire County Council* [1947] 1 KB 598 on the question of responsibility for injections.

[266] *Wiszniewski v Central Manchester HA* [1996] 7 Med LR 248, 256, a finding that was not challenged on appeal: [1998] PIQRP 324, 328 (CA).

[267] *Mahon v Osborne* [1939] 2 KB 14, 31–32 *per* Scott LJ. Note, however, that Scott LJ dissented on the question of whether *res ipsa loquitur* applied to a swab case.

[268] *Mahon v Osborne* [1939] 2 KB 14, 47 *per* Goddard LJ.

[269] The Times, 15 July 1955 (CA).

[270] See, eg, *James v Dunlop* (1931) 1 BMJ 730, which is considered in *Mahon v Osborne* [1939] 2 KB 14; *Dryden v Surrey County Council* [1936] 2 All ER 535; *Holt v Nesbitt* [1951] 4 DLR 478; *Garner v Morrell* The Times, 31 October 1953; *Urry v Bierer* The Times, 15 July 1955; *Fox v Glasgow South Western Hospitals* 1955 SLT 337; *Cooper v Nevill* The Times, 10 March 1961 (PC); *Anderson v Chasney* 1949] 4 DLR 71 (Man CA); aff'd *sub nom Chasney v Anderson* [1950] 4 DLR 223 (SCC). The position will usually be the same in the case of a surgical instrument inadvertently left inside the patient's body: *Hocking v Bell* [1948] WN 21 (PC); *Gloning v Miller* [1954] 1 DLR 372; cf *McDonald v Pottinger* [1953] NZLR 196.

[271] In *Frandle v MacKenzie* (1990) 5 CCLT (2d) 113 (BCCA) liability for not keeping a proper count of the swabs was ascribed 80 per cent to the surgeon and 20 per cent to the nurses.

[272] *The Times* (4 September 1990). See also Cooke (1989) 5 J of the MDU 62.

from another patient, or they may result from surgical intervention. In the case of post-operative infection, the infection itself cannot be treated as evidence of negligence, because no one can guarantee that post-operative infection will not occur.[273] However, specialists should be quick to recognize the development of infection following surgery.[274] In *Voller v Portsmouth Corporation*[275] the claimant developed meningitis after the administration of a spinal anaesthetic. It was admitted that the illness must have been caused either by contamination of the anaesthetic or by an infection occurring during its administration. It could not be said precisely how the accident occurred but the court concluded that there must have been some failure to follow the appropriate sterilization procedure resulting in contamination from the equipment used.

Unnecessarily exposing a patient to the risk of contracting an infection will be negligent. Thus, bringing a patient into contact with other patients who have an infectious disease can constitute negligence,[276] as can discharging an infectious patient from hospital prematurely, with the result that others who come into contact with him contract the disease.[277] It is not necessarily negligent, however, for a hospital to adopt a system for managing infectious smallpox patients by sterilization rather than isolation, where the defendants conform to a practice accepted as proper by a responsible body of professional opinion.[278] **4.97**

(b) By donor organs or bodily fluid Some cases of infection arise from the transplantation of human organs or the transfusion of bodily fluids from a donor who carried the infection.[279] Before a test for HIV was developed in 1985, there were a number of cases in Commonwealth jurisdictions concerning the liability of blood banks and hospitals for the infection of patients with HIV from blood transfusions.[280] When the risk of infection was unknown or unforeseeable, it could not be negligent to fail to take precautions against the **4.98**

273 *Hajgato v London Health Association* (1982) 36 OR (2d) 669, 681 (Ont HC).

274 ibid, at 682; *Reitze v Bruser* (*No 2*) [1979] 1 WWR 31, 49–50 (Man QB); see also *Hucks v Cole* (1968), [1993] 4 Med LR 393 (CA).

275 (1947) 203 LTJ 264.

276 *Lindsey County Council v Marshall* [1937] AC 97, where the claimant was admitted to the defendants' maternity home notwithstanding an outbreak of puerperal fever in the home a week earlier. See also *Heafield v Crane* The Times, 31 July 1937, where, after the birth of her child, the claimant was moved from the maternity ward to a general ward where a patient was suffering from puerperal fever, and the claimant caught the infection.

277 *Evans v Liverpool Corporation* [1906] 1 KB 160.

278 *Vancouver General Hospital v McDaniel* (1934) 152 LT56.

279 See K McK Norrie, 'Human Tissue Transplants: Legal Liability in Different Jurisdictions' (1985) 34 ICLQ 442 for discussion of both the principles of liability in negligence and the question of consent. See further D Giesen, 'Liability for the Transfusion of HIV-infected Blood in Comparative Perspective' (1994) 10 PN 2. In *Morgan v Gwent HA*, Independent, 14 December 1987 (CA), a young unmarried woman was negligently given a transfusion of Rhesus positive blood instead of Rhesus negative blood, which raised the level of antibodies in her blood and put at risk any future pregnancy. She was awarded £20,000 in damages.

280 The one English case which raised this issue was settled before trial of the substantive matters. See *Re HIV Haemophiliac Litigation* (1990), [1996] PIQR P220, in which haemophiliacs treated with imported HIV-infected blood products commenced proceedings against the Department of Health, the Blood Products Laboratory, and the National Blood Transfusion Service, alleging, inter alia, negligence in screening donors, failing to treat the blood products to minimize the risk of infection, failing to warn donors of the risk, and failing to achieve a self-sufficiency in blood products within the NHS. The action raised novel points on the potential liability of the Department of Health and certain government agencies. Without determining the issues, the Court of Appeal accepted that the claimants had made out at least an arguable case of negligence. For a comparable Canadian case see *Brown v Alberta* [1994] 2 WWR 283 (Alta QB).

risk.[281] Therefore, actions involving allegations that defendants failed to adopt adequate screening of donors from groups known to be at high risk of being infected with HIV or failed to adopt 'surrogate testing'[282] were not particularly successful. Surrogate testing, for example, namely testing blood for Hepatitis B core antibodies (the anti-HBc test) on the basis that there was an association between those who tested positive and those in high-risk groups for AIDS, was highly controversial. It was also not a particularly effective test as there was a risk that introducing surrogate testing could lead to a reduction of the blood supply as a whole, as well as to an increase in the number of undetected donations of HIV-infected blood.[283] In addition, it was alleged that a blood bank or the hospital where a transfusion took place failed to warn doctors and/or patients of the risk of contracting HIV from blood transfusions.[284]

4.99 Between 1982 and 1984 the state of knowledge was in constant flux as scientists and health authorities sought to discover the causes of the newly identified condition of AIDS.[285] However, since the risk of transmission of HIV through blood products has become recognized, the question of negligence turns on whether reasonably practicable steps could have been taken to eliminate or reduce the risk although the standard of care to be expected of a blood bank reflects the fact that it is neither a commercial organization operating for a profit nor a public health organization, with a duty to monitor, investigate, and control the spread of disease.[286] In *Walker Estate v York-Finch General Hospital*[287] the Canadian Red Cross Society was held to have been negligent in the method of screening blood donors for HIV, in that it had asked potential donors about their general health instead of asking about symptom-specific conditions (as the American Red Cross had done in its screening procedures). The Supreme Court of Canada held that the trial judge was entitled to reject expert evidence that the screening procedures were reasonable, because he was not asked to assess complex scientific or highly technical matters. The issue was simply whether the general health question was sufficient to deter an HIV infected donor from donating blood. The issue was not how an expert would have responded to the donor screening questions, but how a lay person would have responded.[288]

---

[281] Thus, in *H v Royal Alexandra Hospital for Children* [1990] 1 Med LR 297 it was not negligent to fail to give a warning of the risk to doctors or patients in 1982, though by 1983 the situation had changed.

[282] *H v Royal Alexandra Hospital for Children* [1990] 1 Med LR 297 (NSWSC); *E v Australian Red Cross Society* (1991)105 ALR 53 (Aus Fed CA); aff'g (1991) 99 ALR 601; [1991] 2 Med LR 303; *PQ v Australian Red Cross Society* [1992] 1 VR 19 (Vict SC); *Pittman Estate v Bain* (1994) 112 DLR (4th) 257 (Ont Ct, Gen Div). On infection with Hepatitis from blood products, see *Kitchen v McMullen* (1989) 62 DLR (4th) 481 (NBCA).

[283] This was because of the possibility of a 'magnet effect' whereby those who were at high risk of having contracted the AIDS virus donated blood for the specific purpose of having the surrogate test performed on them. Given that a positive surrogate test had, at best, a 50 per cent coincidence with HIV infection, the numbers of donations screened out by the surrogate test might be more than offset by the additional donations from high-risk donors.

[284] *H v Royal Alexandra Hospital for Children* [1990] 1 Med LR 297 (NSWSC); *PQ v Australian Red Cross Society* [1992] 1 VR 19 (Vict SC).

[285] See, eg, the comments of Sheppard J in *E v Australian Red Cross Society* (1991) 105 ALR 53, 82 (Aus Fed CA).

[286] *Pittman Estate v Bain* (1994) 112 DLR (4th) 257, 313, 318–19. Lang J commented that the social need for a continued supply of blood created different considerations. It was not a product that could simply be removed from the market if inherently dangerous because it is an essential source of life to many. The need for the product outweighs the risk.

[287] *Walker Estate v York-Finch General Hospital* (2001) 198 DLR (4th) 193 (SCC).

[288] ibid at [82] *per* Major J. Note that the question of whether any NHS body could owe a duty of care in negligence to patients in respect of infected blood has been rendered largely redundant by the ruling of Burton J in *A v National Blood Authority* [2001] 3 All ER 289 that contaminated blood is a defective product to which the strict liability rules of Pt 1 of the Consumer Protection Act 1987 apply. Liability under the Act is strict, in that it does not depend on the proof of fault. The fact that the risk of infection (with

Similar issues have arisen from the possibility of transmitting infection through the donor insemination of semen. In *ter Neuzen v Korn*[289] the claimant contracted HIV from artificial insemination in January 1985. In Australia it was known that HIV could be transmitted through blood transfusion by late 1994, and because the Elisa test for HIV being developed in the US was soon to be available for clinical use, a decision had been taken to impose a moratorium on all bodily fluid and tissue transfers. However, the defendant and North American experts did not learn of the Australian moratorium until after September 1985 and the risk of infection from artificial insemination was not widely known in North America until mid-1985. It was held that this was not a case in which the jury, acting judicially, could find the common practice of competent Canadian doctors to be negligent. The proper test was whether the defendant had conducted himself as a reasonable doctor, and this required the jury to confine itself to prevailing standards of practice in North America. **4.100**

Surgeons who are infected with HIV or Hepatitis B and who knowingly continue to practise surgery, expose their patients to an unacceptable risk of infection, given the seriousness of the consequences, notwithstanding that the risk of passing on the infection is comparatively small. This would almost certainly be deemed to be negligent if a patient were infected in this way, although Public Health England has published guidance on carefully prescribed circumstances in which surgeons infected HIV may continue to perform procedures.[290] **4.101**

(v) Miscalculating drug reactions

Doctors must take account of manufacturers' instructions and known side effects when prescribing drugs, although they should not rely on the manufacturers' information unthinkingly.[291] Where a doctor ignores the manufacturer's instructions and warnings, it is the doctor who is responsible for any adverse reactions, though a decision to exceed the manufacturers' guidelines or dosages indicated in Major Incident Medical Management and Support (MIMMS) in prescribing a drug is not necessarily negligent.[292] The manufacturer will not be liable since a warning addressed to the doctor will normally discharge the manufacturer's duty of care to the patient in the case of prescription drugs.[293] **4.102**

Hepatitis C) was unavoidable, the impracticability and the cost of identifying the potentially harmful virus and taking appropriate precautions, and the fact that blood was supplied by the defendants as a service to society, were all held to be irrelevant to the defendants' liability.

[289] (1993) 103 DLR (4th) 473 (BCCA); aff'd (1995) 127 DLR (4th) 577 (SCC). For discussion of the risks of sexually transmitted disease and HIV infection associated with donor insemination see C L R Barratt and I D Cooke, 'Risks of Donor Insemination' (1989) 299 BMJ 1178 and 1531.

[290] The January 2014 guidance on management of HIV-infected healthcare workers can be found at <https://www.gov.uk/government/uploads/system/uploads/attachment_data/file/333018/Management_of_HIV_infected_Healthcare_Workers_guidance_January_2014.pdf>. Workers who will perform exposure-prone procedures must be tested for the HIV antibody, and are under a duty to seek medical advice if they believe they have been exposed to the virus in the course of their employment. Those health care workers who test positive for HIV may continue to perform exposure-prone procedures if they are either (a) on effective anti-retroviral therapy with a plasma viral load of <200 copies/ml, or (b) an elite controller, and in either case must be subject to viral load monitoring every three months under supervision of two physicians, and must be registered with UKAP Occupational Health Monitoring Register. The guidance reports that there have only been three recorded instances globally of a health care worker infecting a patient with HIV. However, with regard to Hepatitis B, one surgeon who was a carrier had infected nineteen patients and put hundreds of others at risk. He was convicted of the offence of public nuisance and jailed: *The Times* (30 September 1994); see M Mulholland, 'Public Nuisance—A New Use for an Old Tool' (1995) 11 PN 70. See also *R v Thornton* (1993) 13 OR (3d) 744 (SCC).

[291] See, eg, *Buchan v Ortho Pharmaceuticals (Canada) Ltd* (1986) 25 DLR (4th) 658 (Ont CA).

[292] *Vernon v Bloomsbury HA* (1986), [1995] 6 Med LR 297.

[293] *Holmes v Ashford* [1950] 2 All ER 76; *Kubach v Hollands* [1937] 3 All ER 907; *Buchan v Ortho Pharmaceuticals (Canada) Ltd* (1986) 25 DLR (4th) 658, 669 (Ont CA); *Davidson v Connaught Laboratories*

4.103 Ignorance of known side effects is negligent if the defendant ought reasonably to have been aware of them. Some mistakes may be isolated errors,[294] but in other cases the doctor is aware of the risk from side effects, and yet calculates that it is a reasonable risk to run in the circumstances, given the condition for which the drug is prescribed. If the calculation is correct by reference to the standards of the profession he is not negligent, but if the risk was unreasonable in the circumstances he will be liable. For example, in *Battersby v Tottman*[295] a doctor prescribed a very high dose of melleril to a patient who was suffering from a mental illness. He took the view that the benefits of the drug outweighed the risk that the drug would cause serious and permanent eye damage, since without treatment the patient was suicidal, and other methods of treatment had failed. The patient did sustain permanent eye damage. It was held that the decision to prescribe a dosage far in excess of the recommended dosage was not negligent as it was justified by the potential consequences of not using the drug. By way of contrast, in *Graham v Persyko*[296] the defendant gastroenterologist wrongly, but not negligently, diagnosed that the claimant had Crohn's disease, for which there is no cure, and prescribed prednisone, a very potent drug with a multitude of serious adverse effects and a low safety margin. This caused avascular necrosis of the patient's femoral heads, a rare but known complication. The decision to prescribe the drug was held to be negligent, because the risk from the side effects was disproportionate to the anticipated benefit to the patient who was asymptomatic at the time.

4.104 It is also possible for the correct dosage of a drug to be under-calculated. A number of cases have arisen in which patients undergoing surgery have been awake and conscious of pain but unable to communicate with medical staff due to being paralysed by muscle relaxant drugs. This may or may not be due to fault in the administration of the anaesthetic.[297]

(vi) Injections

4.105 Injections may be given in the wrong place, the hypodermic may contain the wrong substance or an excessive dose, or the needle may break.[298] Not all errors, however, will give rise to a claim for negligence. An injection into the patient's surrounding tissues instead of a vein is not necessarily negligent if the vein is difficult to find.[299] On the other hand, a doctor

---

(1980) 14 CCLT 251, 276 (Ont HC); Ferguson (1992)12 OJLS 59; P Peppin, 'Drug/Vaccine Risks: Patient-Decision-Making and Harm Reduction in the Pharmaceutical Company Duty to Warn' (1991) 70 Can Bar Rev 473.

294 See, eg, *Dwyer v Roderick* (1983) 127 SJ 806; *McCaffrey v Hague* [1949] 4 DLR 291.

295 (1985) 37 SASR 524 (SC of S Aus).

296 (1986) 27 DLR (4th) 699 (Ont CA); (1986) 34 DLR (4th) 160 (SCC) leave to appeal refused.

297 See *Ludlow v Swindon HA* [1989] 1 Med LR 104; *Taylor v Worcester and District HA* [1991] 2 Med LR 215; *Ackers v Wigan HA* [1991] 2 Med LR 232; *Phelan v East Cumbria HA* [1991] 2 Med LR 419; *Early v Newham HA* [1994] 5 Med LR 214; *Jacobs v Great Yarmouth and Waveney HA* [1995] 6 Med LR 192. For discussion see A Barton, 'Early v Newham HA' (1995) 1(4) Clinical Risk.

298 A broken needle is not necessarily an indication of negligence, since it may be due to a latent defect in the needle: *Brazier v Ministry of Defence* [1965] 1 Lloyd's Rep 26. See also *Gerber v Pines* (1935) 79 SJ 13; *Galloway v Hanley* (1956) 1 BMJ 580; *Daniels v Heskin* [1954] IR73,79; cf *Cardin v City of Montreal* (1961) 29 DLR (2d) 492 (SCC) where a doctor who administered a vaccine by hypodermic needle to a child who was struggling against his mother's efforts to keep him still was held to have been negligent in not postponing the injection until the child was in a less agitated state. Note that the fact that an instrument, such as a needle, has broken may indicate that the instrument itself was defective in which case there may be an action against the manufacturer either in negligence or under the Consumer Protection Act 1987: see, eg, *G v Fry Surgical International Ltd* (1992) 3(4) AVMA Medical & Legal Journal 12, where the blade of a pair of arthroscopy scissors fractured during the course of an operation and a fragment was lost in the claimant's knee. An action under the Consumer Protection Act 1987 against the importers of the scissors, on the basis that the scissors were defective, was settled.

299 *Williams v North Liverpool HMC* The Times, 17 January 1959; *Prout v Crowley* (1956) 1 BMJ 580; *Gent v Wilson* (1956) 2 DLR (2d) 160.

must take responsibility for what he injects into a patient and administering an excessive dose of a drug having misread the instructions is clearly negligent,[300] as is an excessive dose of anaesthetic given through misjudgment attributable to inexperience.[301] Even when allowing for the fact that the person who provides the hypodermic is skilled in such matters and the solution is made up in the hospital pharmacy, there remains an obligation upon a surgeon carrying out the injection to take reasonable steps to check that he is getting what he ordered.[302] In *Ritchie v Chichester HA*[303] the treatment protocol for the administration of an epidural anaesthetic to a woman in the course of labour required both the midwife and the anaesthetist to check that the correct drug had been selected for injection by reading the name on the ampoule. The defendants were held liable on the basis that the anaesthetist must have injected a neurotoxic substance into the claimant when administering the epidural anaesthetic, despite the fact that there would have to have been a series of errors on the part of the medical staff involved. In *Caldeira v Gray*[304] damage to the sciatic nerve following an injection in the buttocks was found to have been caused by negligence, but in *Wilcox v Cavan*[305] the Supreme Court of Canada held that where gangrene had developed in the claimant's arm following an intra-muscular injection, the nurse who administered the injection was not liable under the principle of *res ipsa loquitur*. Although there was no explanation as to how the injection had found its way into the claimant's circumflex artery, the defendant's version of events was consistent with the absence of negligence.

(vii) Failure to monitor treatment

A doctor has a duty to monitor treatment given to a patient, particularly where the treatment carries a high risk of an adverse reaction.[306] This duty extends to post-operative conditions which the patient may develop.[307] A patient recovering from a general anaesthetic will require careful monitoring. In *Coyne v Wigan HA*[308] the claimant sustained brain damage caused by hypoxia for a period of four to five minutes when she was in the recovery ward following an operation under general anaesthetic. The defendants accepted that the principle of *res ipsa loquitur* applied, seeking to explain the incident on the basis that the hypoxia was the result of silent regurgitation of gastric content. It was held that the evidence did not support the defendants' explanation, which was implausible because there was no recorded instance of silent aspiration leading to brain damage and only one such case was referred to in evidence. Accordingly, the appropriate inference was that there had been negligence in monitoring the patient. **4.106**

[300] *Strangeways-Lesmere v Clayton* [1936] 2 KB 11; *Smith v Brighton and Lewes HMC* The Times, 2 May 1958; *Sellers v Cooke* [1990] 2 Med LR 16, 19.

[301] *Jones v Manchester Corporation* [1952] 2 All ER 125; *Skelton v Lewisham and North Southwark HA* [1998] Lloyd's Rep Med 324, 332 (QBD).

[302] *Collins v Hertfordshire County Council* [1947] 1 KB 598, 607.

[303] [1994] 5 Med LR 187.

[304] [1936] 1 All ER 540.

[305] (1974) 50 DLR (3d) 687 (SCC); *Fischer v Waller* [1994] 1 WWR 83 (Alta QB), where it was held that perforation of the globe of the eye during the course of administering a local anaesthetic prior to cataract surgery was a rare but recognized risk of the procedure which could occur in the absence of negligence.

[306] *Marshall v Rogers* [1943] 4 DLR 68; *Male v Hopmans* (1967) 64 DLR (2d) 105, 113–15 (Ont CA); *Wilsher v Essex AHA* [1986] 3 All ER 801.

[307] *Bayliss v Blagg* (1954) 1 BMJ 709; *Ares v Venner* (1970) 14 DLR (3d) 4 (SCC); and *Harrington v Essex AHA* The Times, 14 November 1984 (QBD), on plaster casts; *Poole v Morgan* [1987] 3 WWR 217; *Cavanagh v Bristol and Weston HA* [1992] 3 Med LR 49 (QBD); *Newbury v Bath District HA* (1998) 47 BMLR 138—defendants negligent in failing to carry out tests for neurological deficit in the immediate post-operative period, in light of the patient's symptoms.

[308] [1991] 2 Med LR 301 (QBD).

D. Psychiatric Patients

4.107 The care and protection of mental patients is nowadays subject to the safeguards of the Human Rights Act 1998, addressed in Section F at the end of this chapter. The *Bolam* test[309] applies to the relationship between a psychiatrist and a psychiatric patient just as it applies to any other doctor–patient relationship. Thus, it was negligent for a psychiatrist to engage in social contact with a female patient who had developed a strong and obsessive emotional attachment to him, leading to a serious deterioration in the patient's mental health, given that this was a departure from recognized standards of practice which no body of professional opinion supported.[310] In some cases the nature of the mental illness makes the patient dangerous, either to himself or to others, and claims can arise out of an alleged failure to exercise control over the patient. A doctor undoubtedly has a duty to take reasonable steps to protect a psychiatric patient from harming himself, and in an institutional setting a hospital authority may be responsible for injuries inflicted on a patient by himself,[311] or by a fellow patient, where the injuries are the result of a failure to provide adequate control and supervision.[312]

1. Self-harm

4.108 This duty can include an obligation to make reasonable efforts to prevent suicide attempts.[313] In *Thorne v Northern Group HMC*[314] the nursing staff on a medical ward of a general hospital were aware that a patient, who was a suspected depressive, had threatened suicide. The patient walked out of the hospital, went home and committed suicide while mentally ill but not legally insane. It was held that there had been no negligence, because, on the facts, constant supervision was not appropriate. In *Selfe v Ilford and District HMC*,[315] on the other hand, it was accepted that reasonable care required continuous observation of a patient who was known to be a serious suicide risk. He was put in a ground floor ward with twenty-seven patients, four of whom were also suicide risks, and there were insufficient nurses available

[309] The claimant in *Bolam v Friern HMC* [1957] 2 All ER 118 itself was a psychiatric patient who sustained serious physical injuries in the course of electro-convulsive therapy administered to treat depression.

[310] *Landau v Werner* (1961) 105 SJ 257 and 1008 (CA).

[311] *Jinks v Cardwell* (1987) 39 CCLT 168 (Ont HC); *Kelly v Board of Governors of St Laurence's Hospital* [1988] IR 402 (Sup Ct Irl).

[312] *Wellesley Hospital v Lawson* (1977) *76* DLR (3d) 688, where the Supreme Court of Canada assumed that such a common law duty existed. In *Ellis v Home Office* [1953] 2 All ER 149 prison authorities were held to owe a duty of care to a prisoner assaulted by another prisoner.

[313] M A Jones, 'Saving the Patient from Himself' (1990) 6 PN 107. Where, on the other hand, the suicide attempt is unforeseeable there will be no liability on the basis that no duty of care is owed: *Orange v Chief Constable of West Yorkshire Police* [2001] EWCA Civ 611, [2002] QB 347 at [41]–[43]; *Lepine v University Hospital Board* (1966) 57 DLR (2d) 701 (SCC). Note that inadequate medical treatment and a lack of effective monitoring of a prisoner who was known to be mentally ill and an identified suicide risk could, in some circumstances, constitute a breach of Article 3 of the ECHR, which provides that 'No one shall be subjected to torture or to inhuman or degrading treatment or punishment': see also *Keenan v UK* (2001) 10 BHRC 319 (ECtHR).

[314] (1964) 108 SJ 484.

[315] (1970) 114 SJ 935. See also *Hay v Grampian Health Board* [1995] 6 Med LR 128 (CS), where the regime for supervising a known suicide risk broke down; *Mahmood v Siggins* [1996] 7 Med LR 76, where a GP was held liable for failing to refer a known manic depressive to a community mental health team for assessment, treatment, and supervision; *Drake v Pontefract HA; Wakefield and Pontefract Community NHS Trust* [1998] Lloyd's Rep Med 425, where an inexperienced psychiatrist was held negligent in failing to diagnose the claimant's condition correctly, failing to assess the risk of suicide, and failing to provide appropriate treatment, though the patient had been referred by the GP as a suicide risk; *Villemure v L'Hôpital Notre Dame* (1972) 31 DLR (3d) 454 (SCC).

to cope with all the circumstances that could be expected to arise. The claimant climbed out of a window and jumped off a roof, sustaining serious injuries. Hinchcliffe J held the defendants liable. The degree of care required was proportionate to the degree of risk, and in this case there had been a breakdown in proper nursing supervision. However, the degree of care must also take into account the level of restraint or supervision appropriate in the light of the patient's mental condition. In some cases imposing restraint on a patient may exacerbate the patient's condition, or at least inhibit effective treatment. If it is against the patient's wishes, it might undermine the trust between doctor and patient. This judgment has to balance competing risks to the patient's health, including the risk of self-harm resulting in death.[316]

If a non-psychiatric patient makes a suicide attempt the question will be whether non-specialist (ie non-psychiatric) staff ought to have realized that there was a genuine risk of a suicide attempt. This will not be judged by reference to whether a psychiatrist could have made this diagnosis but whether in the defendant's position a reasonable doctor or nurse would have identified the risk. In *Hyde v Tameside Area HA*[317] the claimant was admitted to hospital with a painful shoulder. Twelve days later he jumped from a third-floor window, having convinced himself, erroneously, that he had cancer. He suffered catastrophic injuries. It was alleged that the medical staff had negligently failed to identify the claimant's mental distress, and had failed to realize the patient needed psychiatric treatment. The Court of Appeal held that on the particular facts there was no negligence, merely a 'forgivable failure to achieve a standard approaching perfection'. The court will make allowance for the fact that a decision to introduce psychiatric treatment for patients who are not being treated for a psychiatric illness or disorder is one that involves competing considerations. Watkins LJ pointed out that many patients in hospital suffer from anxiety and worry about their medical condition. They may need reassurance and sometimes need drugs to ease pain or stress, but to tell a patient who requires surgery that he also needs psychiatric help may be counterproductive.[318] **4.109**

It has been argued that, quite apart from the question of breach of duty, claims for negligence based on suicide or attempted suicide should not be permitted, on the grounds of causation, *volenti non fit injuria, ex turpi causa non oritur actio*, or simply for policy reasons.[319] The causation argument states that the defendant's negligence merely provided the opportunity for the deceased's act of suicide, which amounted to a *novus actus interveniens*. In *Kirkham v Chief Constable of Greater Manchester Police*[320] Tudor Evans J rejected this contention on the basis that the suicide was the very thing that the defendants had a duty to take precautions against,[321] and concluded that on the evidence the patient's suicide would probably have been prevented.[322] His Lordship commented that although the act of suicide **4.110**

316 *Haines v Bellissimo* (1977) 82 DLR (3d) 215 (Ont HC).

317 *Hyde v Tameside Area HA* (1981), reported at (1986) 2 PN 26.

318 ibid, 30.

319 For consideration of the defences of *volenti non fit injuria* and *ex turpi causa* see Chapter 6, paras 6.73–6.78.

320 [1989] 3 All ER 882; aff'd [1990] 2 WLR 987.

321 Where the intervening conduct is the very thing that the defendant was under a duty to guard against, he cannot avoid liability by arguing that the conduct constituted an intervening act: *Haynes v Harwood* [1935] 1 KB 146, 156; *Perl (Exporters) Ltd v Camden* LBC [1984] QB 342, 353. See also *per* Farquharson LJ in *Kirkham v Chief Constable of Greater Manchester Police* [1990] 2 WLR 987, 997 in relation to the defence of *volenti non fit injuria*.

322 In *Hyde v Tameside AHA* (1986) 2 PN 26 O'Connor LJ said that he did not think that 'the fact that a patient commits suicide or attempts suicide will necessarily break the chain of causation if breach of duty is established against the hospital. It all depends on the circumstances of an individual case.'

was a conscious and deliberate act 'the deceased's mental balance was . . . affected at the time'.[323] This left open the question whether, if the deceased's mind was not 'affected', the suicide could be regarded as a *novus actus interveniens.*

4.111 In *Reeves v Commissioner of Police for the Metropolis*,[324] a case which also involved the suicide of a prisoner who was a known suicide risk, though not found to be mentally ill, the House of Lords held that the suicide did not constitute a *novus actus*. The damage arose from breach of a duty to prevent just such an act and thus did not obliterate the defendants' wrongdoing. It was not a new act, but the very harm that the defendants were under a duty to try to prevent. In cases where the law imposes a duty to guard against loss caused by the free, deliberate and informed act of a human being, 'it would make nonsense of the existence of such a duty if the law were to hold that the occurrence of the very act which ought to have been prevented negatived causal connection between the breach of duty and the loss'.[325] Once it was accepted that a duty to protect a person of full understanding from harming himself was owed, it was self-contradictory to say that the breach could not have been a cause of the harm because the victim caused it to himself.[326] The deceased's mental state was irrelevant to this issue, since the defendant's duty arose out of the fact that the deceased was a known suicide risk, not from any particular mental state. For the same reasons the defence of *volenti non fit injuria* did not apply either.[327] An illustration of breach in the context of a disturbed mental health patient attending an A&E Department, and then being allowed to escape and fall from a ramp sustaining serious personal injury, is given in *Mark Webley v St George's Hospital NHS Trust.*[328] The Trust was held responsible for the Claimant's injuries.

2. Harm to third parties

4.112 It is uncertain whether, in this country, a psychiatrist would be held responsible for foreseeable harm inflicted by a patient on a third party.[329] Even if it were possible to identify reasonably practicable steps that a doctor could have taken (such as seeking compulsory admission for assessment or treatment under the Mental Health Act 1983), it is not clear that a duty of care would be held to exist. Where the patient is compulsorily detained, however, the greater degree of control exercised over the patient may be sufficient to tip the balance in favour of a duty of care being imposed.[330] In *Clunis v Camden and Islington HA*[331] the Court of Appeal rejected a claim in negligence by a patient who had killed an innocent bystander. He alleged that had he received proper psychiatric treatment he would not have committed the offence and therefore he would not have been convicted of a criminal offence

[323] [1989] 3 All ER 882, 889. In *Wright Estate v Davidson* (1992) 88 DLR (4th) 698 (BCCA) the deceased's suicide was held to constitute a *novus actus interveniens* where there was no evidence of disabling mental illness; cf *Costello v Blakeson* [1993] 2 WWR 562 (BCSC).

[324] *Reeves v Commissioner of Police for the Metropolis* [2000] 1 AC 360.

[325] ibid, 367–68 *per* Lord Hoffmann.

[326] ibid, 368.

[327] See Chapter 6, para 6.72. The Court of Appeal in *Reeves* had also rejected the defence of *ex turpi causa* on the same grounds: [1999] QB 169.

[328] [2014] EWHC 299 (QB).

[329] See *Tarasoff v Regents of the University of California* 551 P 2d 334 (1976); *Thompson v County of Alameda* 614 P 2d 728 (1980); *Brady v Hopper* 751 F 2d 329 (1984); cf *Jablonski v US* 712 F 2d 391 (1983).

[330] *Holgate v Lancashire Mental Hospitals Board* [1937] 4 All ER 19. Note, however, that in *Palmer v Tees HA* [1999] Lloyd's Rep Med 351, 358–59 the Court of Appeal dismissed *Holgate* as a case of unsatisfactory authority where little attention was paid to the question of the defendants' duty of care. The case could not be reconciled with *Hill v Chief Constable of West Yorkshire* [1989] 1 AC 53.

[331] [1998] QB 978. This case is not concerned with a claim *by* a third party against the health authority, though it is clear that had the patient's action against the health authority succeeded the deceased's spouse would have had better prospects of obtaining redress from the claimant.

and sent to prison. The claim was struck out as contrary to public policy, because his plea of manslaughter by reason of diminished responsibility still required some degree of personal responsibility, even though it was accepted that his mental responsibility was substantially impaired. The Court of Appeal did, however, contemplate that there could be liability in negligence in such a case if it could be proved that the claimant did not know the nature and quality of his act or that what he had done was wrong.

In *Palmer v Tees HA*[332] a young child was abducted and killed by a mental patient who had previously stated, while a hospital in-patient, that he had sexual feelings towards children and that a child would be murdered after his discharge. The Court of Appeal held that no duty of care was owed by the defendant health authority either to the child herself or the child's mother, in respect of an alleged negligent failure to diagnose that the patient constituted a serious risk to children. The threats made by the patient in *Palmer* were of a general nature. It would at least be arguable that, if a psychiatric patient were to make threats against a specific individual or individuals, where there was a real risk of such threats being carried out, then a duty of care on the part of a psychiatrist or psychologist might arise.[333] In *Buck v Norfolk and Waveney Mental Health NHS Foundation Trust*,[334] the Defendant Trust was the custodian of a psychiatric patient who threw himself under the wheels of the Claimant's bus. The court endorsed a summary of the law in *Palmer* in the following terms: 'a custody authority responsible for the negligent release of a patient did not owe a duty to a victim unless that victim had been identifiable'. In *Selwood v Durham CC & Ors*,[335] the court found that a social worker who had been attacked by a mental patient who had been discharged by the Defendant Trust had a real prospect of success at trial. Smith LJ reiterated that the question remained whether the tripartite test, requiring a claimant to demonstrate foreseeability, proximity, and fairness, as described in *Caparo v Dickman*[336] was satisfied. On the facts of the case, the victim was arguably identifiable as a target of the mental patient, and it was further arguable that the Defendants had assumed responsibility for her safety, so that they were liable for her injuries. **4.113**

Quite apart from a possible right of action in common law, the Human Rights Act 1998 might well provide a basis for arguing state liability in such a case: see later in this chapter. The decision of the House of Lords in *Savage v South Essex Partnership NHS Foundation Trust*[337] concerned a mental patient who absconded from the treating unit and committed suicide. The House of Lords concluded that an action could be brought against the hospital alleging breach of the operational duty owed under Article 2 of the Convention, to protect this patient from the real and immediate risk of suicide. *Savage* concerned a patient compulsorily detained under the Mental Health Act 1983. In *Rabone v Pennine NHS Trust*,[338] the Supreme Court confirmed that the operational duty also applied in cases where the patient was voluntary, but in relation to whom the State had assumed a responsibility. The European Court came to a similar conclusion in *Reynolds v UK*,[339] a case heard shortly after *Rabone* and also involving a mental health patient informally detained.[340] **4.114**

[332] [2000] PIQR P1; [1999] Lloyd's Rep Med 351; See further Jones (2000) 16 PN 3.
[333] As in *Tarasoff v Regents of the University of California* 551 P 2d 334; Sup, 131 Cal Rptr 14 (1976).
[334] HHJ Yelton, Cambridge County Court 27th February 2012, [2012] Med LR 266 at [24], citing with approval a statement taken from M A Jones and A M Dugdale (eds), *Clerk and Lindsell on Torts* (20th edn, Sweet & Maxwell) para 14-43.
[335] [2012] EWCA Civ 979.
[336] [1990] 2 AC 605.
[337] [2009] 2 WLR 11
[338] [2012] UKSC 2; [2012] 2 AC 72
[339] [2012] ECHR 437.
[340] These cases are considered further under Section F, Breach of Convention Rights.

3. Negligent certification

4.115 A doctor who provides a written recommendation supporting the compulsory admission of a patient into hospital under Part II of the Mental Health Act 1983 (as amended by the Mental Health Act 2007) must exercise reasonable care.[341] This necessarily requires that the doctor examine the patient,[342] and make such further enquiries as are necessary.[343] On the one hand, the court must make due allowance for the difficulty in making an accurate diagnosis in some cases of mental illness, and on the other hand, they should require 'very considerable care' to be taken where a person is being deprived of his liberty.[344]

4. Procedural bars

4.116 Section 139(1) of the Mental Health Act 1983 (as amended) provides that no person shall be liable to any civil or criminal proceedings in respect of any act purporting to be done under the mental health legislation unless the act was done in bad faith or without reasonable care.[345] In addition, civil proceedings may not be instituted in respect of such an act without leave of the High Court.[346] Proceedings issued without leave are a nullity,[347] although the requirement for leave applies only to patients who are formally detained under the Act; voluntary patients do not need leave to bring an action.[348] The requirement for leave does not apply to actions against the Secretary of State or a health authority.[349] It had been thought that one consequence of s 139(4) was that, irrespective of the substantive defence provided to an individual doctor by s 139(1), the hospital employing that doctor would be vicariously liable for his actions (for example in the tort of battery) even if the doctor was held not liable because he acted in good faith and with reasonable care.[350] But in *R (on the application of W) v Broadmoor Hospital*[351] Hale LJ suggested that a health authority or NHS Trust could only

---

[341] *Hall v Semple* (1862) 3 F & F 337; *De Frevillev Dill* (1927) 96 LJKB 1056; *Everett v Griffiths* [1921] 1 AC 631; *Harnett v Fisher* [1927] AC 573; *Buxton v Jayne* [1960] 1 WLR 783; [1962] CLY 1167.

[342] Mental Health Act 1983, s 12(1).

[343] *Hall v Semple* (1862) 3 F & F 337, 354 *per* Crompton J.

[344] ibid, 355–56.

[345] J Jaconelli and A Jaconelli, 'Tort Liability Under the Mental Health Act 1983' [1998] 20 JSWFL 151. The section does not apply to an application for judicial review, so that proceedings for judicial review of a decision purportedly taken in the exercise of powers conferred by the Mental Health Act 1983 can be brought even though the applicant does not allege that the decision was made negligently or in bad faith: *Re Waldron* [1986] QB 824. It was conceded in this case that s 139 would not apply to a writ of habeas corpus.

[346] Mental Health Act 1983, s 139(2). It is arguable that a private law action brought under s 7 of the Human Rights Act 1998 would require leave under s 139(2) of the Mental Health Act 1983: *R (on the application of W) v Broadmoor Hospital* [2001] EWCA Civ 1545, [2002] 1 WLR 419 *per* Brooke LJ at [54] and Hale LJ at [61].

[347] *Pountney v Griffiths* [1976] AC 314.

[348] *R v Runighian* (1977) Crim LR 361.

[349] Mental Health Act 1983, s 139(4). Accordingly, it does not apply to the Mental Health Act Commission, which is a special health authority: *X v A, B and C and the Mental Health Act Commission* (1991) 9 BMLR 91, 97 (QBD). See, however, *C v South London and Maudsley Hospital NHS Trust* (2001, unreported, QBD), where McCombe J, having refused to grant leave under s 139(2) to bring proceedings against the individual doctors, held that the proceedings against the defendant NHS Trust would be bound to fail, for the same reasons as given under s 139(2), and therefore it was inevitable that they would either be struck out under the court's case management powers or judgment would be given in favour of the defendants on the basis that the claim had no real prospect of succeeding. This would seem to undermine the effect of s 139(4).

[350] See *R (on the application of W) v Broadmoor Hospital* [2001] EWCA Civ 1545, [2002] 1 WLR 419 at [24] *per* Simon Brown LJ and [58] *per* Hale LJ.

[351] ibid, *per* Hale LJ.

be held vicariously liable for the actions for which the individual doctors would themselves be liable, which would indirectly confer the benefit of s 139(1) on the employers.[352]

In *Winch v Jones*[353] the Court of Appeal held that it was not necessary for the claimant to establish a prima facie case of negligence against the defendant in order to obtain leave, because this would lead to a full dress rehearsal of the action, and at the stage of seeking leave an applicant who has a reasonable suspicion that there has been negligence may be quite unable to put forward a prima facie case before discovery has taken place. The test is whether on the materials immediately available to the court 'the applicant's complaint appears to be such that it deserves the fuller investigation which will be possible if the intended applicant is allowed to proceed'.[354] Parker LJ said that the purpose of the section was to prevent harassment by clearly hopeless actions, not to see that only those actions which would be likely to succeed should go ahead. **4.117**

In *James v LBC*,[355] however, Farquharson LJ suggested that the court did have to decide whether the applicant had a prima facie case. He distinguished *Winch v Jones* and refused the applicant leave under s 139(2) saying that, because it was virtually unarguable that the doctor and the social worker concerned in an emergency compulsory admission for assessment had acted without reasonable care, an action by the applicant would be bound to fail. Farquharson LJ disagreed with the approach of Sir John Donaldson MR, on the ground that the object of s 139 was to protect a defendant from the consequences of a wrong decision made in purported compliance with the Mental Health Act, particularly in circumstances where decisions have to be made quickly for the safety of the patient or others. Section 139 was not only protection against frivolous claims; it was also a protection from error in the circumstances set out in the subsection.[356] It is arguable, however, that requiring a claimant to establish a prima facie case before disclosure, and in circumstances where facts are in dispute, sets the procedural hurdle for claimants too high, a point that had been accepted in *Winch v Jones.* **4.118**

E. Evidence and Proof

1. Proof of negligence

The burden of proving, on the balance of probabilities, that the defendant has been negligent and that the negligence caused damage to the claimant lies with the claimant. If there are two equally possible explanations for an accident, one of which indicates that the **4.119**

[352] Brooke LJ even suggested, provisionally, that a hospital may not be vicariously liable at all for the actions of a responsible medical officer (RMO) in making treatment decisions under ss 57 or 58 of the Mental Health Act, on the basis that the Act vests the duty to carry out the specified functions in the RMO personally. It was not the hospital, through the agency of one of its medical staff, in whom was vested the power to direct treatment without consent, but the RMO himself: ibid, at [42] and [43].

[353] *Winch v Jones* [1985] 3 All ER 97.

[354] ibid, 102 *per* Sir John Donaldson MR.

[355] *James v LBC* (1992) 15 BMLR 1.

[356] ibid, 4. See also *C v South London and Maudsley Hospital NHS Trust* (2001, unreported, QBD), where the claimant argued that the doctors had used the procedure for compulsory admission for assessment (under s 2) in bad faith, in order to avoid the statutory requirements associated with compulsory admission for treatment (under s 3) because it was known that the claimant's mother objected. McCombe J refused leave under s 139(2), on the basis that there was no reason why a doctor could not reasonably and in good faith take the view that the grounds for admission under s 2 were met, even if he thought that in the end a s 3 admission for a longer period would almost inevitably follow.

accident occurred without negligence by the defendant, the claimant's action will fail,[357] although it will only be in an exceptional case that the issue should be decided on the basis of the burden of proof.[358] The claimant does not have to provide direct evidence that the defendant has fallen below the requisite standard of care. He may rely upon any legitimate inferences that can be drawn from the proved facts, and in the absence of evidence to the contrary, the inference may well be that the defendant has been negligent. In the event that a lack of important evidence is the consequence of a defendant's breach of duty, the court will judge the claimant's case benevolently and the defendant's case critically.[359]

2. *Res ipsa loquitur*

4.120 The principle of *res ipsa loquitur* is an evidential principle which enables a claimant who has no knowledge, or insufficient knowledge, of how a medical accident occurred to rely on the accident itself and its surrounding circumstances as evidence of negligence on the part of the defendant. There is no magic in the phrase; it is simply a submission that the facts establish a prima facie case against the defendant which would be sufficient to impose liability in the absence of evidence in rebuttal.[360] Of course, it does not follow that, simply because the claimant is in a position to invoke *res ipsa loquitur*, his action will necessarily succeed. The inference of negligence may be rebutted by evidence adduced by the defendant which explains how the accident occurred without negligence on his part.[361] Indeed, it is not incumbent on the defendant to explain how the accident happened at all, provided there is evidence to show that he exercised reasonable care.[362] As Hobhouse LJ commented in *Ratcliffe v Plymouth and Torbay HA*: 'There is no rule that a defendant must be liable for any accident for which he cannot give a complete explanation.'[363] But the maxim prevents a defendant who does know what happened from avoiding responsibility simply by choosing not to give any evidence.[364]

---

357 *Jones v Great Western Railway Co* (1930) 47 TLR 39, 45 *per* Lord Macmillan; *The Kite* [1933] P 154; *Harrington v Essex AHA* The Times, 14 November 1984 (QBD), where Beldam J felt unable to select either one of two possible explanations for the claimant's necrosis of the skin, and the claimant's action failed on the burden of proof.

358 *Morris v London Iron & Steel Co Ltd* [1987] IRLR 182 (CA); *The Popi M* [1985] 2 Lloyd's Rep 1, 6 (HL).

359 *Raggett v Kings College Hospital NHS Foundation Trust* [2016] EWHC 1604 (QB), [131] *per* Sir Alistair MacDuff.

360 *Roe v Minister of Health* [1954] 2QB 66, 87–88 *per* Morris LJ; *Ballard v North British Railway* Co 1923 SC 43, 56 *per* Lord Shaw: 'If that phrase had not been in Latin, nobody would have called it a principle.'

361 See, eg, *Roe v Minister of Health* [1954] 2 QB 66; *Brazier v Minister of Defence* [1965] 1 Lloyd's Rep 26; *Moore v Worthing District HA* [1992] 3 Med LR 431 (QBD); *Lindsay v Mid-Western Health Board* [1993] 2IR 147 (Sup Ct Irl); *Wilcoxv Cavan* (1974) 50 DLR (3d) 687 (SCC); *Hajgato v London Health Association* (1982) 36 OR (2d) 669; aff'd (1983) 44 OR (2d) 264 (Ont CA).

362 In *Delaney v Southmead HA* [1995] 6 Med LR 355 the claimant suffered a brachial plexus injury in the course of an operation for which, the claimant argued there was no explanation other than that the arm had been hyper-abducted and/or externally rotated. There was no direct evidence as to what the defendant had actually done during the operation, but the Court of Appeal held that a defendant was entitled to rely on evidence as to his normal practice to rebut an inference of negligence, even though there was evidence in the medical literature from 1942 onwards, backed up by expert evidence for the claimant, which suggested that there were effectively only two possible explanations for the claimant's injury, one of which the trial judge found had not in fact occurred, and the other of which was consistent with negligence. The effect of the Court of Appeal's ruling was that there was *no* explanation for the claimant's injury.

363 [1998] PIQR P170 at 187.

364 eg patients under a general anaesthetic are not aware of what is going on about them, and the facts are peculiarly within the knowledge of the anaesthetist and others attending them: *Crits v Sylvester* (1956) 1 DLR (2d) 502, 510 *per* Schroeder JA (Ont CA); see also *Mahon v Osborne* [1939] 2 KB 14, 50 *per* Goddard LJ.

In some cases it has been suggested that the principle has the effect of reversing the burden of proof, requiring the defendant to show that the harm was not the product of his carelessness.[365] The better view would seem to be that this is incorrect. The burden of proof remains with the claimant, but *res ipsa loquitur* requires the defendant to offer some reasonable explanation as to how the accident could have occurred without negligence by him.[366] On this basis, *res ipsa loquitur* 'is no more than the use of a Latin maxim to describe the state of the evidence from which it is proper to draw an inference of negligence'.[367] Where an inference of negligence does arise, a general denial by way of defence will not be sufficient to rebut it.[368] If the defendant adduces no evidence, the claimant will have proved his case. If the defendant does adduce evidence that is consistent with an absence of negligence on his part, then the inference of negligence is rebutted. The claimant then has to produce positive evidence that the defendant has acted without reasonable care[369] although, in practice, it is unlikely that the claimant will be able to do this, since he would not have relied on *res ipsa loquitur* in the first place if he had such evidence. Where the explanation given by the defendant relates to a remote or unusual eventuality,[370] however, this will not necessarily rebut the presumption of negligence. The claimant does not have to disprove every theoretical explanation, however unlikely, that might be devised to explain what happened in a way which absolves the defendant.[371] Just as the claimant is not entitled to rely on conjecture or speculation to establish his case on the balance of probabilities, so the defendant cannot resort to this when he is called upon for an explanation of events, although on occasions the courts are tempted to accept an explanation of events which relies on the occurrence of extremely remote risks.[372] **4.121**

Res ipsa loquitur may apply where the defendant, or someone for whom he is responsible, has 'control' of the thing or circumstances that caused the damage,[373] and the accident is such as 'in the ordinary course of things' is one which does not happen in the absence of negligence.[374] However, if all the facts about the cause of the accident are known, the maxim does not apply. **4.122**

[365] *Henderson v Henry E Jenkins & Sons* [1970] AC 282; *Ward v Tesco Stores Ltd* [1976] 1 WLR 810; Moore v R Fox & Sons [1956] 1 QB 596; *Mahon v Osborne* [1939] 2 KB 14, 50 per Goddard LJ.

[366] *Ng Chun Pui v Lee Chuen Tat* [1988] RTR 298 (PC).

[367] ibid, 300 *per* Lord Griffiths. In *Lloyde v West Midlands Gas Board* [1971] 1 WLR 749, 755, Megaw LJ regarded *res ipsa loquitur* as 'no more than an exotic, although convenient, phrase to describe what is in essence no more than a common sense approach, not limited by technical rules, to the assessment of the effect of the evidence'. See also *Lindsay v Mid-Western Health Board* [1993] 2 IR 147, 183–84 (Sup Ct Irl); *Crits v Sylvester* (1956) 1 DLR (2d) 502, 510 (Ont CA).

[368] *Bergin v David Wickes Television* [1994] PIQR P167, 168 (CA).

[369] *Ballard v North British Railway Co* (1923) SC 43, 54 per Lord Dunedin.

[370] *Holmes v Board of Hospital Trustees of the City of London* (1977) 81 DLR (3d) 67, 82; *Glass v Cambridge Health Authority* [1995] 6 Med LR 91, where the defendant's explanation for the claimant's cardiac arrest under general anaesthetic was rejected as 'at best a highly unlikely possibility'.

[371] *Bull v Devon AHA* (1989), [1993] 4 Med LR117, 138 (CA) *per* Dillon LJ; *Ballard v North British Railway Co* 1923 SC 43, 54 *per* Lord Dunedin; cf *Lindsay v Mid-Western Health Board* [1993] 2 IR 147, 185 (Sup Ct Irl), where it was said that 'it was legitimate ... for the defendant to adduce evidence of possibilities, remote though they might be, as an explanation; in contradistinction to saying that it could not offer *any* explanation of any description whatsoever' (original emphasis).

[372] See, eg, *Howard v Wessex RHA* [1994] 5 Med LR 57 (QBD).

[373] Where the defendant is vicariously liable for all the staff who played some role in the claimant's treatment, this is sufficient control: *Cassidy v Ministry of Health* [1951] 2 KB 343; cf *Morris v Winsbury-White* [1937] 4 All ER 494, 499, where the patient's post-operative treatment was under the control of several people (nurses, and resident medical officers) as well as the defendant surgeon, and it was held that *res ipsa loquitur* did not apply.

[374] *Scott v London & St Katherine Docks Co* (1865) 3 H & C 596, 601; *Cassidy v Ministry of Health* [1951] 2 KB 343, 353–54 per Singleton LJ.

The question in such a case is whether, on the known facts, negligence by the defendant can be inferred.[375]

4.123 Despite the occasional suggestion that, since much of medical practice is outside the common experience of life, *res ipsa loquitur* should not be invoked in the context of a medical negligence action,[376] the principle may be relied upon in an appropriate case, although the court will be cautious about drawing an inference of negligence simply because something has gone wrong with the treatment.[377] The occurrence of injury is not itself necessarily evidence of a lack of reasonable care, since medical treatment carries inherent risks.[378] Nonetheless, even within medicine, there are some circumstances where the maxim *res ipsa loquitur* will apply.[379] For example, leaving swabs or surgical instruments inside a patient after an operation will normally speak of negligence.[380] Where a patient went into hospital for treatment of two stiff fingers but came out of hospital with four stiff fingers, he was entitled to call on the defendants for an explanation of how the injury could have occurred without negligence.[381] Similarly, the heart of a fit child does not arrest under anaesthesia if proper care is taken in the anaesthetic and surgical processes.[382]

---

[375] *Barkway v South Wales Transport Co Ltd* [1950] 1 All ER 392; *Johnston v Wellesley Hospital* (1970) 17 DLR (3d) 139, 146 (Ont HC).

[376] See, eg, Scott LJ in *Mahon v Osborne* [1939] 2 KB 14, 23. In *Delaney v Southmead HA* [1995] 6 Med LR 355, 359 Stuart-Smith LJ doubted whether the maxim was of much assistance 'in a case of medical negligence, at any rate when all the evidence in the case has been adduced'. In *Ritchie v Chichester HA* [1994] 5 Med LR 187, 205 (QBD), Judge Thompson QC did not understand Stuart-Smith LJ to be saying that *res ipsa loquitur* could not apply in cases of medical negligence, or that medical negligence was in a special category which put it outside the ordinary English law of negligence. Rather, the maxim may not be of much help where there has been a lot of medical evidence. See also *Nesbitt v Holt* [1953] 1 DLR 671 (SCC).

[377] *Hucks v Cole* (1968), [1993] 4 Med LR 393, 396 *per* Lord Denning MR.

[378] *Roe v Minister of Health* [1954] 2 QB 66, 80; *O'Malley-Williams v Board of Governors of the National Hospital for Nervous Diseases* (1975) 1 BMJ 635; *Delaney v Southmead HA* [1995] 6 Med LR 355, 360 per Dillon LJ; *Holmes v Board of Hospital Trustees of the City of London* (1977) 81 DLR(3d) 67, 78; *Girard v Royal Columbian Hospital* (1976) 66 DLR (3d) 676, 691 (BCSC).

[379] *Clarke v Warboys* The Times, 18 March 1952 (CA), where a patient sustained a burn from a high frequency electrical current used for 'electric coagulation' of the blood; *Bull v Devon AHA* (1989) [1993] 4 Med LR 117, 131 (CA) *per* Slade LJ, where there was a delay of fifty minutes in obtaining expert obstetric assistance at the birth of twins when the medical evidence was that at the most no more than twenty minutes should elapse between the birth of the first and the second twin; *Coyne v Wigan HA* [1991] 2 Med LR 301 (QBD), where, following an operation under general anaesthetic, a patient in the recovery ward sustained brain damage caused by hypoxia for a period of four to five minutes; *Roe v Minister of Health* [1954] 2 QB 66, where a spinal anaesthetic became contaminated with disinfectant as a result of the manner in which it was stored, causing paralysis to the patient; *Brazier v Ministry of Defence* [1965] 1 Lloyd's Rep 26, 30, when a needle broke in the patient's buttock while he was being given an injection; *Crits v Sylvester* (1956) 1 DLR (2d) 502 (Ont CA); aff'd (1956) 5 DLR (2d) 601 (SCC); *Cavan v Wilcox* (1973) 44 DLR (3d) 42 (NBCA); rev'd on the facts (1974) 50 DLR (3d) 687 (SCC); *Eady v Tenderenda* (1974) 51 DLR (3d) 79 (SCC); *Reitze v Bruser (No 2)* [1979] 1 WWR 31 (Man QB).

[380] *Mahon v Osborne* [1939] 2 KB 14, 50 *per* Goddard LJ; *Cassidy v Ministry of Health* [1951] 2 KB 343, 365–66 *per* Denning LJ; *Garner v Morrell* The Times, 31 October 1953 (CA); *Nesbitt v Holt* [1953] 1 DLR 671 (SCC).

[381] *Cassidy v Ministry of Health* [1951] 2 KB 343; see also *Fraser v Vancouver General Hospital* (1951) 3 WWR 337, 343 *per* O'Halloran JA (BCCA). In *Moore v Worthing District HA* [1992] 3 Med LR 431, 434 (QBD) it was said that where a claimant goes into hospital with no impediment to the use of his upper limbs and no obvious risk to them, but comes out crippled, this creates a prima facie case of negligence; though on the facts the injury was found to be attributable to the claimant's abnormal susceptibility.

[382] *Saunders v Leeds Western HA* (1984) [1993] 4 Med LR 355; *Lindsay v Mid-Western Health Board* [1993] 2 IR 147, 181 (Sup Ct Irl) *per* O'Flaherty J: '. . . it seems to me that if a person goes in for a routine medical procedure, is subject to an anaesthetic without any special features, and there is a failure to return the patient to consciousness, to say that that does not call for an explanation from defendants would be in defiance of reason and justice.' See also *Glass v Cambridge HA* [1995] 6 Med LR 91, where it was held that

In *Ratcliffe v Plymouth and Torbay HA*[383] the Court of Appeal made it clear that *res ipsa loquitur* will rarely be relevant in medical negligence. The issue is rather what weight should be given to the evidence and whether an inference of negligence is appropriate. Brooke LJ summarized[384] the application of the maxim to medical negligence actions: **4.124**

(1) In its purest form the maxim applies where the [claimant] relies on the *res* (the thing itself) to raise the inference of negligence, which is supported by ordinary human experience, with no need for expert evidence.
(2) In principle, the maxim can be applied in that form in simple situations in the medical negligence field (surgeon cuts off right foot instead of left; swab left in operation site; patient wakes up in the course of surgical operation despite general anaesthetic).
(3) In practice, in contested medical negligence cases the evidence of the [claimant], which establishes the *res*, is likely to be buttressed by expert evidence to the effect that the matter complained of does not ordinarily occur in the absence of negligence.
(4) The position may then be reached at the close of the [claimant's] case that the judge would be entitled to infer negligence on the defendant's part unless the defendant adduces evidence which discharges this inference.
(5) This evidence may be to the effect that there is a plausible explanation of what may have happened which does not connote any negligence on the defendant's part. The explanation must be a plausible one and not a theoretically or remotely possible one, but the defendant certainly does not have to prove that his explanation is more likely to be correct than any other. If the [claimant] has no other evidence of negligence to rely on his claim will then fail.
(6) Alternatively, the defendant's evidence may satisfy the judge, on the balance of probabilities, that he did exercise proper care. If the untoward outcome is extremely rare, or is impossible to explain in the light of the current state of medical knowledge, the judge will be bound to exercise great care in evaluating the evidence before making such a finding, but if he does so, the prima facie inference of negligence is rebutted and the [claimant's] claim will fail. The reason why the courts are willing to adopt this approach, particularly in very complex cases, is to be found in the judgments of Stuart-Smith and Dillon LJJ in *Delaney*.[385]
(7) It follows from all this that although in very simple situations the *res* may speak for itself at the end of the lay evidence adduced on behalf of the [claimant], in practice the evidence is then buttressed by expert evidence adduced on his behalf, and if the defendant were to call no evidence, the judge would be deciding the case on inferences he was entitled to draw from the whole of the evidence (including the expert evidence), and not on the application of the maxim in its purest form.

There are cases where, although *res ipsa loquitur* does not strictly apply, the events in question are such as to call for an explanation. One such case was *Lillywhite v University College London Hospitals NHS Trust*,[386] where the claimant's condition of holoprosencephaly, which is accompanied by an absence of certain brain structures, had gone undetected by an experienced brain sonographer on foetal scanning. An explanation was called for (which in the event could not satisfactorily be given and the hospital was found to be in breach).[387] **4.125**

res ipsa loquitur applied to a case where the heart of a healthy man went into cardiac arrest while under general anaesthesia.

383 *Ratcliffe v Plymouth and Torbay HA* [1998] PIQR P170. For comment on *Ratcliffe* see Jones (1998) 14 PN 174.
384 *Ratcliffe*, n 382, 184.
385 *Delaney v Southmead HA* [1995] 6 Med LR 355.
386 [2005] EWCA Civ 1466.
387 See also *Pithers v Leeds NHS Trust* [2004] EWHC 1392 (QB), as to the failure to detect a severely abnormal bladder on fetal ultrasound screening.

(i) Inherent risks of treatment

4.126 As a general rule, *res ipsa loquitur* will not apply where the injury sustained by the claimant is of a kind recognized as an inherent risk of the treatment, since such accidents obviously can occur without negligence.[388] However, if the risk is known but does not normally occur in the absence of negligence, the maxim can apply.[389] As Robins J said in *Kapur v Marshall*,[390] *res ipsa loquitur* only comes into play when common experience or the evidence in the case indicates that the happening of the injury itself may be considered as evidence that reasonable care had not been used; this will not be the case where the complication is a recognized, even if rare, risk inherent in the operation.[391]

3. Standard of proof

4.127 The standard of proof in cases of medical negligence is the same as for any other case of negligence, namely 'on the balance of probabilities', but in practice the cogency of the evidence that the courts require in order to satisfy the test can vary with the issues at stake.[392] It has been suggested that cases of professional negligence create particular problems, and this may result in what is effectively a higher standard of proof than for 'ordinary' cases of negligence.[393] This is particularly true of the medical profession. This may reflect the concern that has been expressed about the effect that findings of negligence can have on the reputation of individual doctors, and the more general consequences of medical malpractice litigation for the practice of medicine. Thus, in *Hucks v Cole* Lord Denning commented that:

> A charge of negligence against a medical man, a solicitor or any other professional man, stands on a very different footing from a charge of negligence against a motorist or employer. The reason is because the consequences for the professional man are far more grave. A finding of negligence affects his standing and reputation. It impairs the confidence which his clients have in him. The burden of proof is correspondingly greater. The principle applies that: 'In proportion as the charge is grave, so ought the proof to be clear': see *Hornal*

[388] *O'Malley-Williams v Board of Governors of the National Hospital for Nervous Diseases* (1975) 1 BMJ 635; *Guertin v Kester* (1981) 20 CCLT 225; *Considine v Camp Hill Hospital* (1982) 133 DLR (3d) 11 (Nova Scotia SC); *Videto v Kennedy* (1980) 107 DLR (3d) 612, 618; rev'd on other grounds (1981) 125 DLR (3d) 127.

[389] *Holmes v Board of Hospital Trustees of the City of London* (1977) 81 DLR (3d) 67 (Ont HC).

[390] (1978) 85 DLR (3d) 566, 574 (Ont HC).

[391] *Fish v Kapur* [1948] 2 All ER 176, dentist broke the claimant's jaw during an extraction; cf *Lock v Scantlebury* The Times, 25 July 1963; *Fletcher v Bench* (1973) 4 BMJ 17 (CA); *Keuper v McMullin* (1987) 30 DLR (4th) 408, part of a dental drill was left embedded in the jaw; *Considine v Camp Hill Hospital* (1982) 133 DLR (3d) 11 (Nova Scotia SC), claimant became incontinent following a prostate operation; *Girard v Royal Columbian Hospital* (1976) 66 DLR (3d) 676, 691 (BCSC), patient suffered permanent partial paralysis of the legs following anaesthesia; *Kapur v Marshall* (1978) 85 DLR (3d) 566 (Ont HC), patient died from haemorrhage during the course of spinal disc surgery when the surgeon pierced an artery with a surgical instrument; *Rocha v Harris* (1987) 36 DLR 410 (BCCA), paralysis occurred following a cervical laminectomy; *Ferguson v Hamilton Civic Hospitals* (1983) 144 DLR (3d) 214, paralysis occurred following arteriography; *Whitehouse v Jordan* [1980] 1 All ER 650, 658, 661; *Goguen v Crowe* (1987) 40 CCLT 212 (Nova Scotia SC), baby suffered cerebral palsy following a forceps delivery; *Grey v Webster* (1984) 14 DLR (4th) 706, sterilization operation failed to render the claimant sterile; *Hobson v Munkley* (1976) 74 DLR (3d) 408, patient's ureter damaged in the course of a tubal ligation operation.

[392] See R Pattenden, 'The. Risk of Non-persuasion in Civil Trials: The Case Against a Floating Standard of Proof' (1988) 7 CJQ 220. It is more difficult, for example, to establish that the defendant has behaved fraudulently than to prove that he was negligent: *Hornal v Neuberger Products Ltd* [1957] 1 QB 247.

[393] In *Dwyer v Roderick* (1983) 127 SJ 806 May LJ said that it was: 'to shut one's eyes to the obvious if one denies that the burden of achieving something more than that mere balance of probabilities is greater when one is investigating the complicated and sophisticated actions of a qualified and experienced lawyer, doctor, accountant, builder or motor engineer than when one is enquiring into the momentary inattention of the driver of a motor car in a simple running-down action.'

> *v Neuberger Products Ltd* [1957] 1 QB 247 . . . A doctor is not to be held negligent simply because something goes wrong . . . He is not liable for mischance, or misadventure. Nor is he liable for an error of judgment . . . He is only liable if he falls below the standard of a reasonably competent practitioner in his field—so much so that his conduct may fairly be held to be—I will not say deserving of censure, but, at any rate, inexcusable.[394]

More rarely, perhaps, the courts also recognize that doctors are only human, and that even a conclusion that a defendant doctor has made a negligent mistake is not to be taken as a statement that the doctor is incompetent to practise medicine. This approach makes it easier for the court to make a finding of negligence without undermining the doctor's professional reputation.[395] **4.128**

F. Breach of Convention Rights

In addition to ordinary common law claims, the Human Rights Act 1998, which incorporated the Convention for the Protection of Human Rights and Fundamental Freedoms ('the Convention') into English law, provides scope for claims to be brought. Articles 2, 3, and 8 are potentially relevant to claims for medical mistreatment. **4.129**

1. Article 2

Article 2 provides: **4.130**

> 1. Everyone's right to life shall be protected by law. No one shall be deprived of his life intentionally save in the execution of a sentence of a court following his conviction of a crime for which this penalty is provided by law.
> 2. Deprivation of life shall not be regarded as inflicted in contravention of this Article when it results from the use of force which is no more than absolutely necessary:
>   (a) in defence of any person from unlawful violence;
>   (b) in order to effect a lawful arrest or to prevent the escape of a person lawfully detained;
>   (c) in action lawfully taken for the purpose of quelling a riot or insurrection.

(i) Protection of hospital patients

Article 2 puts Health Authorities under an overarching obligation to protect the lives of patients in their hospitals. This includes the obligation to employ competent staff trained to a high professional standard, and to ensure that hospitals adopt systems of work which will protect the lives of patients: *Isiltan v Turkey*.[396] However, this positive obligation is to be interpreted in such a way as not to impose an excessive burden upon the state, bearing in mind the unpredictability of human conduct and the operational choices which have to **4.131**

---

394 (1968), [1993] 4 Med LR 393, 396. See also the comments of Lord Denning in *Roe v Minister of Health* [1954] 2 QB 66, 86–87; *Hatcher v Black* The Times, 2 July 1954; *Whitehouse v Jordan* [1980] 1 All ER 650, 658; *Hyde v Tameside AHA* (1981) reported at (1986) 2 PN 26. Similarly, in *Whitehouse v Jordan* [1980] 1 All ER 650, 659 Lawton LJ commented that: 'The more serious the allegation the higher the degree of probability that is required. In my opinion allegations of negligence against medical practitioners should be considered as serious.'

395 In *Whitehouse v Jordan* [1980] 1 All ER 650, 666 Donaldson LJ pointed out that very few professionals can claim never to have been negligent, and that often the only difference between those who are sued and their colleagues is that the error happens to have caused harm to the claimant; see also *Clark v MacLennan* [1983] 1 All ER 416, 433; *Thake v Maurice* [1984] 2 All ER 513, 523.

396 (1995) 81 DR 35. See also *Tarariyeva v Russia* (Application 4353/03) (unreported) given 14 December 2006, para 74, and *Dodov v Bulgaria* (Application 59548/00) (unreported) given 17 January 2008, para 80.

be made in terms of priorities and resources: *Keenan v United Kingdom.*[397] For example, in *Furdik v Slovakia (Admissibility),*[398] the European Court found that it was not incumbent upon the Slovakian state in this instance to impose a time limit within which an air ambulance had to attend at the scene of an emergency mountain rescue. In this context, something more will be required to establish a breach of duty under the Article 2(1) positive obligation to protect life than simply a failure on the part of the hospital to meet the standard of care. In *Powell v United Kingdom*[399] the ECHR stated:

> The court accepts that it cannot be excluded that the acts and omissions of the authorities in the field of health care policy may in certain circumstances engage [the state's] responsibility under the positive limb of article 2. However, where a contracting state has made adequate provision for securing high professional standards among health professionals and the protection of the lives of patients, it cannot accept that matters such as error of judgment on the part of a health professional or negligent co-ordination among health professionals in the treatment of a particular patient are sufficient of themselves to call a contracting state to account from the standpoint of its positive obligations under article 2 of the Convention to protect life.

4.132 Provisions in domestic law for securing high professional standards amongst health professionals must exist in practice as well as in theory. In *Dodov v Bulgaria,*[400] Mr Dodov's mother had disappeared from a nursing home in December 1995 and had never been found. A preliminary investigation was not commenced until December 1997. It was discontinued in April 1998 but was subsequently reinstated twice, following pressure by Mr Dodov, only to be discontinued again on each occasion. The final decision to discontinue the investigation was upheld on the basis that the time limit for prosecuting the alleged perpetrators had expired. The Court found that the legal system as a whole, faced with an arguable case of neglect endangering human life, had failed to provide an adequate and timely response consistent with the state's obligations under Article 2.

(ii) Prisoners

4.133 The state has a duty under Article 2 of the Convention to protect the life of prisoners by providing adequate medical treatment. This extends to the provision of adequate medical records, proper examinations and competent surgery: *Tarariyeva v Russia.*[401]

(iii) The operational duty

4.134 The first sentence of Article 2(1) enjoins the State not only to refrain from the intentional and unlawful taking of life (the 'negative duty'), but also to take appropriate steps to safeguard the lives of those within its jurisdiction (the 'positive duty'): *Osman v United Kingdom.*[402] The much cited 'rule in *Osman's* case' (often referred to as the 'operational' duty) was summarized by the European Court at para 116 of that judgment:

> It must be established to the Court's satisfaction that the authorities knew or ought to have known at the time of the existence of a real and immediate risk to the life of an identified individual or individuals from the criminal acts of a third party and that they failed to take measures within the scope of their powers which, judged reasonably, might have been expected to avoid that risk.[403]

[397] (Application 27229/95) [2001] 33 EHRR 38.
[398] (Application 42994/05) [2009] 48 EHRR SE9.
[399] [2000] 30 EHRR CD 362.
[400] [2008] 47 EHRR 41.
[401] [2009] 48 EHRR 26.
[402] [1998] 29 EHRR 245.
[403] In the recent case of *Daniel v St George's Healthcare NHS Trust* [2016] EWHC 23 Laing J held that an operational duty could arise in the case of patients in detention if certain conditions were met and that

(iv) Protection from self-harm

The rule in *Osman*'s case has been extended to the protection of individuals from harming themselves: *Keenen v United Kingdom.*[404] In *Keenen*'s case, the European Court considered to what extent the *Osman* principle applied in cases where the risk derived from self-harm. The Court concluded that in the context of prisoners, the fact that they are in a vulnerable position by virtue of being in custody made it incumbent on the state to account for any injuries suffered. The obligation was found to be 'particularly stringent' (para 90) when the individual dies. The test, applying *Osman,* was whether the authorities knew or ought to have known that the prisoner posed a real and immediate risk of suicide and, if so, whether they did all that reasonably could have been expected of them to prevent that risk (para 92): see also *Salman v Turkey.*[405] The government, in its 'Response to the Joint Committee on Human Rights' *Third Report of Session 2004–05 on Deaths in Custody,*[406] summarized the position, stating: **4.135**

> [H]uman rights come sharply into focus in the institutional setting where those detained are entirely dependent on their custodians not only to keep them safe but also to provide them with a humane, decent and caring environment . .[407]

The rule has also been applied to military conscripts who commit suicide. As in the case of prisoners, there are two general obligations under Article 2 of the Convention. First, to put in place a legislative and administrative framework which will make for the effective prevention of suicides. Second, to ensure that practical measures are adopted to protect conscripts who could be exposed to the dangers inherent in military life: *Kilinç v Turkey.*[408] In considering whether the military authorities failed in their positive obligation to protect the life of Mr Kilinç, the Court examined first whether there was a real and immediate risk that he would commit suicide, and if so, whether the state had done everything that could reasonably be expected of it to prevent that risk. Particular diligence is also expected when dealing with mentally ill conscripts. In *Araman v Turkey*[409] the Strasbourg Court found that the Turkish authorities had not taken the practical measures that could reasonably have been expected of them, namely preventing the applicant's son from having access to lethal weapons. **4.136**

(v) Psychiatric patients

The European Court has long considered that the position of inferiority and powerlessness which is typical of patients confined in psychiatric hospitals calls for increased vigilance when reviewing whether the Convention has been complied with: *Herczegfalvy v Austria.*[410] However, it is only relatively recently that the British courts have applied the *Osman* principle to psychiatric patients. The case of *Savage v South Essex Partnership NHS Foundation Trust*[411] concerned a mental patient being treated for paranoid schizophrenia under s 3 of the Mental Health Act 1983. She absconded from an open acute psychiatric ward in an NHS hospital and committed suicide. The House of Lords found that there is an **4.137**

---

a failure to provide timely and appropriate medical care to a detainee could be a violation of Article 2 even in cases where the failing was by an individual rather than a systemic failing.

404 [2001] 33 EHRR 913.

405 [2000] 34 EHRR 425, [99].

406 HL Paper 15-I/HC 137-I. See Appendix to the Joint Committee's Eleventh Report of Session 2004–05 (HL Paper 69/HC Paper 416).

407 As referred to by Baroness Hale of Richmond in *Savage v South Essex NHS Trust* [2008] UKHL 74, [97].

408 (Application No 40145/98) 7 June 2005.

409 (Application 46252/99) 27 April 2006.

410 [1992] 15 EHRR 437 at [82].

411 [2009] 2 WLR 11.

operational duty which arises only if a member of staff knew or ought to have known that a particular patient presents a 'real and immediate risk' of suicide: in those circumstances, Article 2 of the Convention requires them to do all that they can reasonably be expected to do to prevent the patient from committing suicide. The Court was keen to stress that the operational duty itself is not particularly stringent, but that the threshold for triggering the duty (real and immediate risk to life) is high: *per* Lord Rodger at paras 40–41. Lord Rodger usefully summed up the relevant obligations of health authorities:

> 68 In terms of article 2, health authorities are under an over-arching obligation to protect the lives of patients in their hospitals. In order to fulfil that obligation, and depending on the circumstances, they may require to fulfil a number of complementary obligations.
>
> 69 In the first place, the duty to protect the lives of patients requires health authorities to ensure that the hospitals for which they are responsible employ competent staff and that they are trained to a high professional standard. In addition, the authorities must ensure that the hospitals adopt systems of work which will protect the lives of patients. Failure to perform these general obligations may result in a violation of article 2. If, for example, a health authority fails to ensure that a hospital puts in place a proper system for supervising mentally ill patients and, as a result, a patient is able to commit suicide, the health authority will have violated the patient's right to life under article 2.
>
> 70 Even though a health authority employed competent staff and ensured that they were trained to a high professional standard, a doctor, for example, might still treat a patient negligently and the patient might die as a result. In that situation, there would be no violation of article 2 since the health authority would have done all that the article required of it to protect the patient's life. Nevertheless, the doctor would be personally liable in damages for the death and the health authority would be vicariously liable for her negligence. This is the situation envisaged by *Powell*'s case 30 EHRR CD 362.
>
> 71 The same approach would apply if a mental hospital had established an appropriate system for supervising patients and all that happened was that, on a particular occasion, a nurse negligently left his post and a patient took the opportunity to commit suicide. There would be no violation of any obligation under article 2, since the health authority would have done all that the article required of it. But, again, the nurse would be personally liable in damages for the death and the health authority would be vicariously liable too. Again, this is just an application of *Powell*'s case.
>
> 72 Finally, article 2 imposes a further 'operational' obligation on health authorities and their hospital staff. This obligation is distinct from, and additional to, the authorities' more general obligations. The operational obligation arises only if members of staff know or ought to know that a particular patient presents a 'real and immediate' risk of suicide. In these circumstances article 2 requires them to do all that can reasonably be expected to prevent the patient from committing suicide. If they fail to do this, not only will they and the health authorities be liable in negligence, but there will also be a violation of the operational obligation under article 2 to protect the patient's life. This is comparable to the position in *Osman*'s case 29 EHRR 245 and *Keenan*'s case 33 EHRR 913. As the present case shows, if no other remedy is available, proceedings for an alleged breach of the obligation can be taken under the Human Rights Act 1998.

4.138 At para 101 of her judgment, Baroness Hale posed some obiter questions about the extent to which the operational duty could apply to different classes of mental patient. She observed that patients could be deprived of their liberty by law, as Mrs Savage was, but that there would also be circumstances where patients were deprived of their liberty by the fact of their condition, or could be deprived of their liberty if they chose to leave. In *Rabone v Pennine Care NHS Trust*,[412] the parents of a mental patient who had committed suicide argued that the Trust owed her an operational duty under Article 2 even though she was not formally

[412] [2012] UKSC 2.

detained. At para 34 of his judgment, Lord Dyson found that a duty was undoubtedly owed on the following bases: (i) that she had been admitted to hospital because she was a real suicide risk; (ii) that by reason of her mental state, she was extremely vulnerable; (iii) that the Trust had assumed responsibility for her; (iv) that she was under its control; (v) that, although she was not detained, it was clear that the authorities could and should have exercised their powers under the Mental Health Act to prevent her from causing harm to herself. He found, in conclusion, that the difference between her position and that of a hypothetical detained mental patient would have been one of form, not substance. On the facts of the case, there was a real and immediate risk that M, the patient, would commit suicide when allowed home, and the Trust was therefore in breach of the operational duty under Article 2. The European Court in Strasbourg came to a similar conclusion, itself referring to the Supreme Court's judgment in *Rabone,* in *Reynolds v United Kingdom,*[413] a case brought by the mother and sister of the deceased who had committed suicide by jumping from a sixth floor window in the intensive support unit where he had been placed by the NHS as a voluntary patient, while suffering from schizophrenia. The Court held that in the circumstances, the State's operational duty to take reasonable steps to protect the deceased from a real and immediate risk of suicide was engaged.

(vi) Right to be informed of a deadly illness

The limits of claims under Article 2 were tested in the case of *Colak and Tsakiridis v Germany.*[414] The Court found unanimously that there had been no breach of Article 2 by Mrs Colak's doctor for failing to inform her that her companion was suffering from AIDS. **4.139**

(vii) Right to die

The ECHR has found that Article 2 cannot, without a distortion of language, be interpreted as conferring the diametrically opposite right, namely the right to die; nor can it create a right to self-determination in the sense of conferring on an individual the entitlement to choose death rather than life: *Pretty v United Kingdom.*[415] However, the Court also stated (at para 31) that it was unclear whether it would be a breach of Article 2 if a state chose to allow assisted suicide: **4.140**

> The extent to which a State permits, or seeks to regulate, the possibility for the infliction of harm on individuals at liberty, by their own or another's hand, may raise conflicting considerations of personal freedom and the public interest that can only be resolved on examination of the concrete circumstances of the case. However, even if circumstances prevailing in a particular country which permitted assisted suicide were found not to infringe Article 2 of the Convention, that would not assist the applicant in this case, where the very different proposition—that the United Kingdom would be in breach of its obligations under Article 2 if it did not allow assisted suicide—has not been established.

The Supreme Court has recently called (by a majority) on Parliament to review our domestic law on assisted suicide, currently contained in the Suicide Act 1961, in *R (Nicklinson) v Ministry of Justice* and combined cases.[416] A Bill to legalize assisted suicide, subject to a number of strict conditions, was introduced in the House of Commons in 2015 but was rejected by substantial majority (330–118). It seems that notwithstanding overwhelming public support for a change in the law, there is no prospect of such a change in the near future and given that Parliament has now debated the issue and rejected such a change it is unlikely that a further challenge in the Courts will succeed. **4.141**

[413] [2012] ECHR 437.
[414] (Application 77144/01; 35493/05), 5 March 2009.
[415] [2002] 35 EHRR 1, [39].
[416] [2014] UKSC 38, and see further later in this section.

2. Article 3

4.142 Article 3 of the Convention provides: 'No one shall be subjected to torture or to inhuman or degrading treatment or punishment.' The prohibition is absolute. There can be no justification for inflicting such treatment on an individual. However, ill-treatment must attain a minimum level of severity if it is to fall within the scope of Article 3. The Commission stated in *East African Asians v United Kingdom*:[417]

> The Commission finally recalls its own statement in the first *Greek Case* (1969) 12 Y.B. Eur. Con v H.R. 1 that treatment of an individual may be said to be 'degrading' in the sense of article 3' if it grossly humiliates him before others or drives him to act against his will or conscience' . . . the word 'grossly' indicates that article 3 is only concerned with 'degrading treatment' which reaches a certain level of severity.

4.143 The assessment of the 'level of severity' is relative: it depends on all the circumstances of the case, such as the duration of the treatment, its physical and/or mental effects, and, in some cases, the sex, age, and state of health of the victim: *Keenan v UK*.[418] Where treatment humiliates or debases an individual, showing a lack of respect for, or diminishing, his or her human dignity or arouses feelings of fear, anguish, or inferiority capable of breaking an individual's moral and physical resistance, it may be considered as degrading and may also fall within the prohibition of Article 3: *Price v United Kingdom*.[419]

(i) Obligations to provide medical care

4.144 Article 3 generates both a negative obligation (to prevent citizens being subjected to inhuman and degrading punishment) and a positive obligation to provide protection against such treatment. A positive obligation has been found to arise in a number of cases: for example, where four child applicants were severely abused and neglected by their parents: *Z and Others v United Kingdom*.[420] The lack of appropriate medical care may amount to inhuman or degrading treatment contrary to Article 3: *R v NW Lancashire HA, ex p A*.[421] Suffering from physical illness in itself may be covered by Article 3, where it is, or risks being, exacerbated by treatment, whether flowing from conditions of detention, expulsion, or other measures, for which the authorities can be held responsible: *Pretty v United Kingdom*.[422]

4.145 The quantum of damages will depend on the level of pain, anxiety, and humiliation suffered. Causation of physical psychiatric harm need not be proven; an assumption of anxiety and suffering may be enough: *Istratii v Moldova*.[423]

(ii) Detained individuals

4.146 As with Article 2, the state is under an additional obligation positively to protect the health of persons deprived of their liberty. The state will be in breach of Article 3 if the medical condition of a person is such that subjecting him to detention would amount to inhuman or degrading treatment: *Farbtuhs v Latvia*.[424] In *Holomiov v Moldova*,[425] the court found

---

[417] [1973] 3 EHRR 76, 81, [195].
[418] [2001] 33 EHRR 913, [90].
[419] [2002] 34 EHRR 53, [24]–[30].
[420] [2001] 34 EHRR 3, [52]
[421] [2000] 1 WLR 977 see also *Daniel v St George's Healthcare NHS Trust* [2016] EWHC 23 where Laing J held that a failure to provide appropriate medical care to detainees may amount to a violation of Article 3.
[422] [2002] 35 EHRR 1.
[423] (Application 8721/05), 27 March 2007, para 105.
[424] (Application 4672/02), 2 December 2004.
[425] (Application 30649/05), 2 February 2007.

that detaining a person suffering serious kidney disease for a long period without appropriate medical care reached the threshold of severity required by Article 3. There were no doctors specialized in the treatment of the applicant's condition either in the prison or in the prison hospital. Having the Applicant seen by doctors without later following up their recommendations was not enough, and the 'resources'-based defence (that the claimant had been offered medical treatment within the '*modest possibilities*' of the prison medical service—para 21) was rejected.

Claims for what effectively amounts to simple medical negligence can sometimes also be brought under Article 3: *Istratti v Moldova.*[426] However, as with claims under Article 2, this has generally been restricted to instances where a claimant is vulnerable and under the control of the state. Where an individual is detained, the court will consider (a) the condition of the inmate, (b) the quality of the care and, (c) the appropriateness of the detention on the basis of the health status of the applicant: *Farbtuhs v Latvia.*[427] In *Istratii*, the ECHR found that the applicant's Article 3 rights had been breached as, during the course of his detention at a remand centre, he had an acute crisis of paraproctitis with rectal haemorrhage. He was then transported to a hospital where he was handcuffed to a wall heater until his surgery the next day. Four hours after the operation he was transferred to a prison hospital despite the fact that he could not move because of pain and the risk of bleeding. The Court found that his treatment amounted to inhuman and degrading treatment within the meaning of Article 3 of the Convention. **4.147**

Handcuffing during medical treatment does not normally give rise to an issue under Article 3 of the Convention. The critical question is whether the risk of a prisoner escaping during a hospital visit was sufficient to justify the use of handcuffs or escort chains, even during medical treatment. That assessment is very much a matter for the prison officials who have to make the assessment: *R (on the application of Faizovas) v Secretary of State for Justice.*[428] **4.148**

As to patients detained in mental hospitals, the general rule is that treatment which can be shown to have been therapeutically necessary cannot be regarded as inhuman or degrading. However, in *Herczegfalvy v Austria*,[429] the Court reserved to the right to satisfy itself that the treatment was in fact medically necessary. It stated (at para 83): **4.149**

> While it is for the medical authorities to decide, on the basis of the rules of medical science, on the therapeutic methods to be used, if necessary by force, to preserve the physical and mental health of patients who are entirely incapable of deciding for themselves and for whom they are therefore responsible, such patients nevertheless remain under the protection of article 3, the requirements of which permit of no derogation.

As to patients detained in care homes, the Court has considered the application of Article 3. In *Stanev v Bulgaria*,[430] the European Court found a breach in circumstances where the applicant had been detained against his will in a care home (despite having capacity) for a period of seven years in the following conditions: **4.150**

> . . . it appears that the food was insufficient and of poor quality. The building was inadequately heated and in winter the applicant had to sleep in his coat. He was able to have a shower once a week in an unhygienic and dilapidated bathroom. The toilets were in an execrable state and access to them was dangerous, according to the findings by the CPT. In addition, the home

426 (Application 8721/05), 27 March 2007.
427 (Application 4672/02), 6 June 2005, para 53.
428 [2008] EWHC 1197 (Admin).
429 15 EHRR 437.
430 Application 36730/06, (2012) 55 EHRR 22.

did not return clothes to the same people after they were washed, which was likely to arouse a feeling of inferiority in the residents.[431]

4.151 In cases involving failed asylum seekers, the threshold for breaches of Article 3 is higher than in other cases: *D v United Kingdom.*[432] In *D,* the Court found that the applicant had to be at a critical stage in a fatal illness before removal to a receiving state without the necessary medical facilities would amount to inhuman treatment in violation of Article 3. The European Court stated in *N v United Kingdom*[433] that aliens who are liable to expulsion cannot claim an entitlement to remain in the territory of a contracting state in order to benefit from medical, social or other forms of assistance and services. The fact that the applicant may have a reduced life expectancy if expelled was not sufficient to give rise to a breach of Article 3. It would require an exceptional case with compelling humanitarian considerations before Article 3 would be engaged. The Court of Appeal has confirmed that the test remains one of exceptional hardship in these cases: *GS (India) v Ors v SSHD,*[434] a case where the Court accepted that the foreign nationals would have drastically reduced life expectancies if returned but held that Article 3 did not prevent their return.

3. Article 8

4.152 Article 8 of the Convention provides:

> Right to respect for private and family life
>
> 1. Everyone has the right to respect for his private and family life, his home and his correspondence.
> 2. There shall be no interference by a public authority with the exercise of this right except such as is in accordance with the law and is necessary in a democratic society in the interests of national security, public safety or the economic well-being of the country, for the prevention of disorder or crime, for the protection of health or morals, or for the protection of the rights and freedoms of others.

4.153 Private life covers the physical and psychological integrity of a person: *Pretty v UK.*[435] The state's obligations under Article 8 might extend to a positive obligation to adopt measures to secure respect for private and family life even as between individuals, having regard to the requirement that a fair balance be struck between their competing interests: *Odievre v France.*[436]

4.154 The causing of psychiatric harm to an individual will not of itself found a claim under Article 8 in circumstances which could not found a claim in negligence. Further, the eggshell skull principle forms no part of the test of breach of duty under the HRA or the Convention. In *Anufrijeva v London Borough of Southwark,*[437] the House of Lords held, at para 143:

> Where a public authority commits acts which it knows are likely to cause psychiatric harm to an individual, those acts are capable of constituting an infringement of article 8. Maladministration will not, however, infringe article 8 simply because it causes stress that leads a particularly susceptible individual to suffer such harm in circumstances where this was not reasonably to be anticipated. No lack of respect for private life is manifested in

431 ibid, [209].
432 (Application 30240/96) [1997] 24 EHRR.
433 [2008] 47 EHRR 39 para 42.
434 [2015] EWCA Civ 40.
435 [2002] 35 EHRR 1, para 61.
436 (Application 42326/98) [2003] 1 FCR 621 (ECHR). Applied by *Evans v United Kingdom,* (Application 6339/05), 10 April 2007.
437 [2003] EWCA Civ 1406.

such circumstances. The eggshell skull principle forms no part of the test of breach of duty under the HRA or the Convention.

As with Articles 2 and 3, the European court has stressed that prisoners enjoy the same rights under the Convention as ordinary citizens. In *Dickson v United Kingdom*,[438] the applicants complained that a refusal of access to artificial insemination was in breach of their Article 8 rights. They had been married while they were serving prisoners. The court upheld the complaint, stating that with regard to both positive and negative obligations under Article 8, regard had to be had to the fair balance to be struck between the competing interests and that prisoners' rights should not be automatically forfeited based purely on what might offend public opinion. **4.155**

In the case of *Juhnke v Turkey*,[439] the applicant had been arrested in Turkey on suspicion of membership of an illegal armed organization, the PKK (Workers' Party of Kurdistan). She claimed, inter alia, that during detention she was subjected to a gynaecological examination against her will. The Court rejected this allegation but found that she had resisted the examination until persuaded to agree to it and that, given the vulnerability of a detainee in such circumstances, she could not have been expected indefinitely to resist agreeing to it. The Court accordingly found that there had been an interference with her private life in that the examination had been imposed on her without her free and informed consent, and that the examination was not 'in accordance with the law'. Therefore, her Article 8 rights had been breached. **4.156**

The right to a 'private life' and the physical and psychological integrity it protects gives rise to an enhanced degree of protection for human dignity: *R (on the Application of (1) A (2) B (By their Litigation Friend the Official Solicitor) (3) X (4) Y) v East Sussex County Council.*[440] In *A, B, X and Y*, Munby J held that in respect of disabled people the 'positive obligation of the State to secure their essential human dignity, calls for human empathy and humane concern as society' (para 93) and that this calls for enhanced protection on behalf of the state. As such, Article 8 has the potential to expand the range of claims that may be brought against healthcare professionals: see, for instance, the *Organ Retention Group Litigation*[441] at para 298, where it was accepted by the Court that Article 8(1) was engaged and possibly breached by the decision to use a retained brain for the purposes of research. However, justifications can be advanced under Article 8(2), and unlike claims brought under Article 3, lack of NHS, Trust, or prison resources may provide such justification. As the Strasbourg Court said in *Pentiacova v Moldova:*[442] **4.157**

> Although the object of Art.8 is essentially that of protecting the individual against arbitrary interference by the public authorities, it does not merely compel the State to abstain from such interference since it may also give rise to positive obligations inherent in effective 'respect' for private and family life. While the boundaries between the State's positive and negative obligations under this provision do not always lend themselves to precise definition, the applicable principles are similar. In both contexts regard must be had to the fair balance that has to be struck between the competing interests of the individual and the community as a whole, and in both contexts the State enjoys a certain margin of appreciation (App. No. 38621/97, *Zehnalová and Zehnal v Czech Republic*, Dec.14.05.2002).

[438] (Application 44362/04), 4 December 2007.
[439] (Application 52515/99), 13 May 2008.
[440] [2003] EWHC 167 (Admin) *per* Munby J at [93].
[441] [2004] EWHC 644.
[442] (Application 14462/03), 30 April 2004.

The Court continued:

> The margin of appreciation referred to above is even wider when, as in the present case, the issues involve an assessment of the priorities in the context of the allocation of limited State resources.

4.158 Article 8 also entails procedural obligations. The scope in the context of a doctor's duty to consult was considered by the Court of Appeal in *R (Tracey) v Cambridge University Hospitals NHS Trust*,[443] where it was the claimant's case that the imposition of a Do Not Attempt Resuscitation (DNACPR) Order without consulting or notifying the patient, without offering a second opinion, and without having or making available a policy which was clear and unambiguous, was in breach of that patient's Article 8 rights. The Court reaffirmed that Article 8 can be engaged in the context of medical treatment,[444] and is certainly engaged where a clinical decision concerns how an individual passes the closing days and moments of his life. With regard to consultation on such decisions there was a presumption in favour of patient involvement, and the question as to whether there was a breach depended on the appropriateness of consultation on the facts of the individual case. In *Tracey*, the Court found that there was no evidence that the treating doctor decided against consultation as a result of concerns about the degree of psychological harm which the patient would sustain, and therefore the failure to consult was a breach of Article 8. Furthermore, with regard to the Trust's policy, it was held in principle that a patient's right to be consulted and notified about DNACPR decisions would be undermined if he were not aware of the criteria which the clinician reached the decision to complete a notice; this required both clear and accessible guidelines. However, the Court rejected the proposition that the guaranteed availability of a second medical opinion was one of the core procedural safeguards of Article 8.

4.159 In *R (on the application of Purdy) v Director of Public Prosecutions*,[445] the House of Lords provided further clarity on the ambit of Article 8 in assisted suicide cases. Ms Purdy suffered from primary progressive multiple sclerosis and intended to travel to a country where assisted suicide was lawful, but did not want her husband to risk prosecution should he travel with her.[446] She sought information from the Director of Public Prosecutions (DPP) as to how he would decide whether it was in the public interest to prosecute those who assisted suicides. Following the ECtHR judgment in *Pretty*,[447] the House of Lords found the Suicide Act 1961 constituted an interference with Mrs Purdy's Article 8(1) right to respect for her private life. The issue was, therefore, whether, in the absence of an offence-specific policy by the DPP, this interference was 'in accordance with the law' under Article 8(2). The House of Lords found that it was not and that the existing guidance was insufficient. The DPP were required to promulgate an offence-specific policy on prosecuting cases of assisted suicide.

---

443 [2014] EWCA Civ 822.

444 Lord Dyson MR clarified that an interpretation of Toulson LJ's judgment in whatever the case is that Article 8 could not be engaged in the context of medical treatment was not sustainable and clearly could not represent the state of the law, at [41].

445 [2009] UKHL 45.

446 The Suicide Act 1961, s 2(1) makes it a criminal offence to 'aid, abet or counsel or procure the suicide of another'. This would cover assisting anyone to travel where assisted suicide was possible. The issues raised by Mrs Purdy, however, related not to s 2(1) of the 1961 Act, but s 2(4), which gives the DPP discretion as to whether or not to pursue a prosecution.

447 *Pretty v United Kingdom* (2002) 35 EHRR 1. Although the ECtHR found that the UK bar on assisted suicide under s 2(1) of the Suicide Act 1961 interfered with Mrs Pretty's Art 8 right to respect for her private life, the House of Lords in *R (on the application of Pretty) v Director of Public Prosecutions (Secretary of State for the Home Department Intervening)* [2002] 1 AC 800 found that, despite such an interference, it was justified under Art 8(2) in order to safeguard life and protect others.

In February 2010, the DPP published a Policy for Prosecutors in respect of Cases of Encouraging or Assisting Suicide. The continuing lack of clarity in these guidelines was the subject of challenge *R(AM) v DPP and ors*,[448] which was joined with a case seeking either a reading of section 2(1) of the Suicide Act 1961 (prohibiting assisted suicide) which made the section compliant with the claimants' Article 8 rights, or a declaration that the section was incompatible with Article 8 (*R (Nicklinson) and anor v Ministry of Justice and ors*.[449] In respect of *Nicklinson*, the Supreme Court held that a prohibition against assisted suicide was within the wide margin of appreciation accorded to states, and that it would be institutionally appropriate at that point for the courts to grant a declaration of incompatibility through assessing whether the interference with the claimants' Article 8 rights was justified in the interests of protecting vulnerable people from being pressured into suicide. Parliament should first be given the opportunity to reconsider section 2 in light of the Supreme Court judgment, which detailed numerous problems with the current state of the law.[450] With regard to *AM*, it was held unanimously that it was not for the Court to dictate what should be in the DPP's policy, albeit that it expected her to clarify any confusion and to review the policy's terms. The public had a right to know what the policy was, and to know whether it was being applied consistently. The policy has since been reviewed and updated.[451] **4.160**

[448] *R (AM) v DPP and ors* [2014] UKSC 38.

[449] ibid.

[450] It was noted that the interference was grave; that the arguments in favour of the current law were not overwhelming; that assisted suicide seemed as a matter of practice to be officially tolerated in certain situations; that these were similar issues to those previously determined under common law; and that the rational connection between the aim and effect of s 2 was fairly weak. Lords Clark, Sumption, Reed, and Hughes dissented on the conclusion that the Court would have power to issue a declaration of incompatibility on this issue in any event owing to the fact that this was a choice involving competing moral values on which there was no consensus.

[451] See Director of Public Prosecutors, Policy for Prosecutors in Respect of Cases of Encouraging or Assisting Suicide (updated in October 2014) available at <http://www.cps.gov.uk/publications/prosecution/assisted_suicide_policy.html>.

5

ACTIONS ARISING FROM BIRTH

Stephen Todd

A. Introduction

5.01 In this chapter we will consider the nature of those events occurring before birth, whether or not preceding conception, which may give a right of action to a child who is eventually born or to a member of his or her family.[1] As will be seen, claims can only be made by or on behalf of children who are born alive or, probably, only by parents and not by other relations.

5.02 Virtually all claims by children in England and Wales will be brought under the Congenital Disabilities (Civil Liability) Act 1976, which replaces the common law in respect of all births after its passing on 22 July 1976.[2] However, it is necessary also to discuss the common law rights of children, partly because of their relevance to other jurisdictions and partly because, under the Limitation Act 1980, some children born before the Act came into effect may have claims which are not and may never become statute barred. Furthermore, all claims by a parent will be brought under the common law.

5.03 The general assumption is that, whether at common law or under statute, children can only claim for disabilities which they have suffered as a result of some prenatal event, and not for the very fact of being born with disabilities or, in other words, for so-called 'wrongful life'. A parent, on the other hand, may have a claim for the so-called 'wrongful conception' or 'wrongful birth' of a child who is born alive but who would not have been born alive but for the defendant's negligence. However, at least in the UK, awards of damages in claims

[1] See generally J K Mason, *The Troubled Pregnancy: Legal Wrongs and Rights in Reproduction* (Cambridge University Press 2007), discussing various medico-legal issues arising out of pregnancy and birth.

[2] Congenital Disabilities (Civil Liability) Act 1976, s 4(5).

of this kind can only be for loss related to the pregnancy and birth, for loss of autonomy in planning whether or when to have children, and, if the child is born with a disability, for expenses related to that disability. What clearly cannot be recovered is the expense of raising the unplanned child. The mother also may have a claim for any personal injuries resulting from the birth and also, in limited circumstances, a claim for psychiatric injury.

It is not always possible to keep these categories of claims completely separate. For example, where one event is responsible both for the conception of, and for a disability in, a child eventually born, the question arises whether that child's claim can succeed as a prenatal injury claim or whether it fails as a 'wrongful life' claim. And further complications can arise, for example in deciding how a claim by a child can dovetail with any claim by a parent arising out of the same event. **5.04**

B. Claims by Living Children for Injuries Caused Before Birth

1. Claims for injuries at common law

(i) The status of the foetus

A foetus[3] has no legal personality. In *Paton v British Pregnancy Advisory Service Trustees*[4] a husband applied to restrain his wife and the British Pregnancy Advisory Service from causing or permitting an abortion, for which she had obtained a certificate under the Abortion Act 1967, from being carried out upon her. The case thus raised directly the question of the rights of the unborn child. Sir George Baker P held that 'in England and Wales the unborn child has no right, no right at all, until birth,'[5] and that the husband could not by injunction stop his wife from having a lawful abortion within the terms of the 1967 Act. **5.05**

In *C v S*[6] a putative father of a foetus once again failed in an application for an injunction to restrain an abortion. Heilbron J considered here whether the unborn child had the locus standi to make the application, and concluded that it did not: **5.06**

> The authorities, it seems to me, show that a child, after it has been born, and only then in certain circumstances, based on his or her having a legal right, may be a party to an action brought with regard to such matters as the right to take on a will or intestacy, or for damages for injuries suffered before birth. In other words, the claim crystallises upon the birth, at which date, but not before, the child attains the status of a legal persona, and thereupon can exercise that legal right.[7]

These views were endorsed by the Court of Appeal in *Re F (in utero)*[8] when deciding the question whether the court had jurisdiction to make a foetus a ward of court. The answer, that it had not, was based on the fact that the unborn child had no existence independent of the mother, and the court could not, therefore, exercise the rights, powers and duties of a

[3] The form 'fetus' is preferred by many purists to 'foetus', though, for consistency, the latter spelling is used throughout this volume. Etymologically the word is connected with the obscure Latin verb 'feo', meaning 'bear' or 'produce', as are the words 'fecundus' (fruitful), 'felix' (fortunate) and 'femina' (woman).

[4] *Paton v British Pregnancy Advisory Service Trustees* [1979] QB 276. The husband later took the case to the European Commission of Human Rights, which rejected his complaint under Arts 2 and 8: *Paton v UK* [1980] EHLR 408.

[5] *Paton*, n 4, 279.

[6] *C v S* [1988] QB 135 (HC and CA).

[7] ibid, 140. The Court of Appeal dismissed the appeal.

[8] [1988] Fam 122 (CA).

parent over the foetus without controlling the mother's actions. Again, the Court of Appeal in *Re MB*[9] and in *St George's NHS Trust v S*[10] held that an unborn child did not have an existence or interest separate from the mother such as would justify a court overriding a competent woman's refusal of a Caesarean section intended to save the child's life.[11]

5.07 The law of Scotland is the same. In *Hamilton v Fife Health Board*[12] Lord McCluskey said that an unborn person, a foetus, was not a person in the eyes of the law—at least in relation to the law of civil remedies—and there could be no liability to pay damages to a foetus for injuries caused by negligent conduct. Decisions elsewhere show a similar refusal to accord legal rights to a foetus.[13]

5.08 So a foetus has no legal personality, and therefore cannot sue or recover damages. However, as we shall see, it does not follow that there is no duty to exercise reasonable care not to injure a foetus. It may lack legal capacity when unborn, but it does not follow that it is unprotected by the common law.

(ii) The civil law

5.09 By contrast, the civil law clearly protects the rights of an unborn child. There is a well-established rule of civil law that an unborn child shall be deemed to be born whenever its interests require it.[14] The application of that maxim is typically in the field of succession. For example, a gift to a class of children living on a particular date is held to benefit a child *en ventre sa mère* at that date but later born alive within that class. The rule appears in certain Latin versions, one of which is ***nasciturus pro iam nato habetur quotiens de eius commodo agitur*** ('one about to be born will be held already to have been born whenever that is to his advantage'). This principle contributed to the decision of the Admiralty Court in *The George and Richard*,[15] where Sir Robert Phillimore held that a child born after the death of its father—in that case a ship's carpenter, drowned in a shipwreck—counted as a 'dependant' for the purposes of bringing an action under the Fatal Accidents Act 1846. As will be seen, the influence of the civil law upon developments in this branch of the common law has been considerable.

(iii) The criminal law

5.10 The criminal law provides sanctions against certain conduct directed against a foetus.[16] The destruction of a foetus by abortion is made unlawful by s 58 of the Offences Against the

---

[9] [1997] 2 FLR 426 (CA); I Kennedy, 'Consent, Adult: Refusal of Consent, Capacity' (1997) 5 Med L Rev 317.

[10] [1999] Fam 26 (CA); R Bailey-Harris, 'Pregnancy, Autonomy and Refusal of Medical Treatment' (1998) 114 LQR 550; J Herring, 'Caesarean Sections and the Right of Autonomy' [1998] 57 CLJ 438; A Grubb, (1998) 6 Med L Rev 361; C Witting, (1999) 7 TLJ 96; and see R Scott, 'The Pregnant Woman and the Good Samaritan' (2000) 20 OJLS 407.

[11] See also *CP v First-tier Tribunal (Criminal Injuries Compensation)* [2015] 2 WLR 463, at [66].

[12] 1993 SC 369.

[13] In Australia see *Attorney-General (Qld) (ex rel Kerr) v T* (1983) 46 ALR 275 (HCA); in Canada see *Trembley v Daigle* [1989] 2 SCR 530 (SCC); in the US, see *Roe v Wade* 410 US 113 (1973) (USSC); *Planned Parenthood of Central Missouri v Danforth* 428 US 52, USSC 1976; in New Zealand see *Wall v Livingstone* [1982] 1 NZLR 734 (CA); *Wilcox v Police* [1994] 1 NZLR 243 (appeal dismissed [1995] 2 NZLR 160 (CA)); *Harrild v Director of Proceedings* [2003] 3 NZLR 289, [117] (CA); *Right to Life NZ Inc v Abortion Supervisory Committee* [2008] 2 NZLR 825, [81]–[87] (on appeal *Right to Life New Zealand Inc v Abortion Supervisory Committee* [2012] 3 NZLR 762 (SC), where the point was not discussed); cf *Re an Unborn Child* [2003] 1 NZLR 115 (injunction to prevent filming of birth of child for a pornographic film).

[14] See *Villar v Gilbey* [1907] AC 139 (HL).

[15] (1871) LR 3 A & E 466; and see *Williams v Ocean Coal Ltd* [1907] 2 KB 422.

[16] See generally J C Smith and B Hogan, *Criminal Law* (13th edn, Oxford University Press 2011) by D Ormerod, 491–93.

Person Act 1861, save in the circumstances set out in the Abortion Act 1967.[17] The Act of 1861 did not criminalize the taking of a child's life while it was being born and before it was fully born, but that loophole was blocked by the Infant Life (Preservation) Act 1929. However, s 5(1) of the 1967 Act provides that no offence is committed under the Act of 1929 if termination is in accordance with the Act of 1967. The grounds for termination under the 1967 Act, as amended, are, broadly, that the pregnancy has not exceeded twenty-four weeks and its continuance poses risk of physical or mental injury to the pregnant woman or children of her family, or that termination is necessary to prevent grave permanent injury to the health of the woman or risk to her life, or that there is a substantial risk of serious handicap to the child. Once the child has 'an existence independent of its mother'[18] its life is protected by the law of homicide. The cord and afterbirth need not have been expelled from the mother nor severed from the child.[19] Generally, the child should have an independent circulation and should have breathed after birth.[20] But the law has eschewed laying down any rigid requirements. In *R v Iby*[21] the New South Wales Court of Appeal recognized that there is no single test for determining what constitutes being born alive. Any indicia of independent life, such as breathing or a heartbeat, satisfies the common law rule. In *Re A*[22] Brooke LJ observed that 'advances in medical treatment of deformed neonates suggest that the criminal law's protection should be as wide as possible'.

5.11 In *R v Tait*[23] the Court of Appeal decided that the threat 'I am going to kill your baby' addressed to a pregnant woman, if meant as a threat to kill the foetus in utero, was not a threat to kill 'a third person' within the meaning of s 16 of the Offences Against the Person Act 1861. The reason was that the foetus in utero was not, in the ordinary sense, 'another person' distinct from its mother.

5.12 If a child is injured in utero but is later born alive and dies of that injury, then assuming the necessary mens rea the person who inflicted it is guilty of manslaughter or murder. In *R v Senior*[24] an incompetent male midwife broke a child's skull with a knife as he became visible during birth and the child died immediately after he was born. It was held that the midwife could properly be convicted of manslaughter. The justification for that result was the 'born alive' rule, namely that the child, having been born alive, then became 'a person' independent of the mother and thus was so at the time of death.

5.13 In *Attorney-General's Reference (No 3 of 1994)*[25] the respondent stabbed his girlfriend, whom he knew was pregnant, in the abdomen, penetrating the foetus. Two weeks later she gave birth at twenty-six weeks' gestation, but the child subsequently died from the complications of prematurity. He was charged with murder, but acquitted on the judge's direction that the facts adduced by the prosecution could not result in a conviction for murder or manslaughter. On a reference to the Court of Appeal the question was whether, assuming proof of a causal link between the wound and the death, the facts could justify such a conviction. It held that a foetus was to be treated as an integral part of the mother, so an injury to the foetus was as unlawful as an injury to any other part of her. So where, having subsequently been born alive, the child died of that injury, the actus reus of homicide would be proved.

[17] As amended by the Human Fertilisation and Embryology Act 1990, s 37. See further Chapter 14.
[18] Infant Life (Preservation) Act 1929, s 1(1).
[19] *R v Reeves* (1839) C & P 25.
[20] For a full discussion see *Rance v Mid-Downs HA* [1991] 1 QB 587, 617–23 *per* Brooke J.
[21] (2005) 63 NSWLR 278, [54]–[62] (NSWCA); and see *R v F* (1996) 40 NSWLR 245 (CCA).
[22] [2001] Fam 147 (CA).
[23] [1990] 1 QB 290 (CA).
[24] [1832] 1 Mood CC 346.
[25] [1996] QB 581 (CA); [1998] AC 245 (HL).

As to mens rea, the court invoked the doctrine of transferred malice[26] (whereby if A intends to kill B but instead kills C, A is as guilty as if he or she had intended to kill C). It was irrelevant that the foetus had no separate existence at the time of the act, and the respondent's intention in relation to the mother could be transferred to the child after its birth.

5.14 This line of reasoning did not commend itself to the House of Lords.[27] In the event it decided that the doctrine of transferred malice simply could not be stretched to what it regarded as a double transfer of intent—from the mother to the foetus and from the foetus to the child as yet unborn.[28] However, as manslaughter was a crime of 'basic intention' an unlawful and dangerous act directed at a woman who later gave birth to living child who died could give rise to a conviction for manslaughter. In so deciding their Lordships roundly rejected the identification of the foetus with the mother, principally on obvious physiological grounds. 'The mother and the foetus were two distinct organisms living symbiotically, not a single organism with two aspects.'[29]

5.15 Comment on *Attorney-General's Reference (No 3 of 1994)* has been critical. It has been pointed out that to hold that it was manslaughter of the child by the unlawful and dangerous act of stabbing the mother looks exactly like transferred malice. Moreover, the act was not merely unlawful and dangerous—it was done with the mens rea of murder, and as it caused the death of the child it is hard to see why it was not in fact murder.[30] The decision also has been criticized as failing to deal convincingly with the relevance of the doctrine of the unforeseen mode (should it matter that the child's death resulted from the premature birth, not from any direct wound?) and of the extended principle of contemporaneity (if the death was part of an unbroken sequence of events following the stabbing, should not D's original intent be connected with the ultimate death?).[31]

5.16 In *CP v First-tier Tribunal (Criminal Injuries Compensation)*[32] the matter in issue was whether a child could claim criminal injuries compensation under the Criminal Injuries Compensation Act 1995 after being born with foetal alcohol spectrum disorder as a direct result of her mother's excessive drinking while pregnant. It was argued on behalf of the child that the mother had committed the offence of maliciously administering poison or other noxious thing to 'any other person' so as to endanger life or inflict grievous bodily harm, contrary to s 23 of the Offences Against the Person Act 1861. The Court of Appeal held, first, that a s 23 offence could not be regarded in the same way as manslaughter, and that Lord Mustill and Lord Hope in *Attorney-General's Reference* were in agreement that a foetus was not to be regarded as 'another person'.[33] Alternatively, it was argued that since *Attorney-General's Reference* had analysed the actus reus of manslaughter as a continuing act running from the attack on the mother to the death of the child after birth, there was no

[26] See, eg, *R v Latimer* [1886] 17 QBD 359; *R v Mitchell* [1983] QB 741.

[27] [1998] AC 245 (HL); S Fovargue and J Miola, 'Policing Pregnancy: Implications of the Attorney-General's Reference (No 3 of 1994)' (1998) 6 Med L Rev 265; S Gough, 'Pre-Natal Injury and Homicide following Attorney-General's Reference (No 3 of 1994)' (1999) 62 MLR 128.

[28] *Attorney-General's Reference*, n 27, 261–62 *per* Lord Mustill.

[29] ibid, 255 *per* Lord Mustill; and see at 267 *per* Lord Hope. In *R v King* (2003) 59 NSWLR 472 the New South Wales Court of Appeal declined to take this approach where the charge was wounding the mother with intent to do bodily harm, in which context it was held that the foetus should be regarded as part of the mother. In so deciding the court approved the decision of the New Zealand Court of Appeal in *Harrild v Director of Proceedings* [2003] 3 NZLR 289, as to which see para 5.162.

[30] Smith and Hogan, n 16, 493.

[31] A Ashworth and J Horder, *Principles of Criminal Law* (7th edn, Oxford University Press 2013), 190.

[32] [2015] 2 WLR 463.

[33] See [1998] AC 245, at 254A, 267F.

good reason why the criminal law should not equally protect a foetus from deliberate conduct causing foreseeable harm which resulted in grievous bodily harm after birth. On this point the Court of Appeal held that an essential element of an offence contrary to s 23 was the infliction of grievous bodily harm on a person. Harm to a foetus would not suffice. On the facts the harm was caused to the child *before* her birth. The distinction between harm or injury caused by an act and the consequences of the harm or injury was critical. If a victim suffered further harm as a result of suffering grievous bodily harm, that did not give rise to a further offence.

Lord Dyson MR recognized, in support of this conclusion, that in English law women did not owe a duty of care in tort to their unborn child,[34] and thought the law would be incoherent if a child were unable to claim compensation from her mother for breach of a duty of care owed during pregnancy, but the mother was criminally liable for causing the harm which gave rise to damage and a right to compensation under the 1995 Act. It was true that tort and crime were conceptually distinct. But the policy reasons underlying the state's view that a child should not be able to claim compensation from her mother for what was done (or not done) during pregnancy should rationally also lead to the conclusion that, save in the exceptional circumstances expressly recognized by Parliament, there should be no criminal liability for what a mother did (or did not do) during pregnancy. The role of the state in these circumstances should be to provide care and support for a child who had suffered harm to the extent that this was necessary. It should not be to pay compensation on the basis that the child was the victim of a crime by her mother. **5.17**

(iv) The common law

(a) Early development Early decisions at common law rejected claims by born-alive children who had suffered injury while still in the womb. Some objections as originally perceived are illustrated by two American decisions. In *Dietrich v Inhabitants of Northampton*[35] a child was born at four or five months' gestation following a fall by the mother, and survived its premature birth only by ten or fifteen minutes. Holmes J declined to follow the criminal and civil law analogies and rejected a claim based on the infant's loss of life, on the grounds that it was not a 'person' recognized by law at the time of its injury. He went on to rule that as the unborn child was a part of the mother at the time of the injury, any damage to it which was not too remote to be recovered for at all was recoverable by her. **5.18**

Similar objections were advanced in *Drobner v Peters*.[36] The plaintiff was an infant allegedly injured when, eleven days before his birth, his mother fell down a coal-hole left uncovered in the sidewalk. The defendant argued that the child's claim should be rejected as lacking in authority, for its practical inconvenience and possible injustice, and because there was no separate person in being apart from the mother at the time of the accident and, therefore, there was no duty of care. It was held that the claim failed, on the ground that the injuries were to the mother and the defendant owed a duty of care to her alone. **5.19**

A turning point came with the decision of the Supreme Court of Canada in *Montreal Tramways v Leveille*[37] concerning prenatal injury under the Civil Code of Quebec. The majority of the court held that the civil law fiction should apply and that a child would be **5.20**

[34] Congenital Disabilities (Civil Liability) Act 1976, ss 1, 2; see para 5.49.
[35] 138 Mass 14 (Mass Sup Jud Ct, 1884).
[36] 25 NY 220 (NYCA, 1921).
[37] *Montreal Tramways v Leveille* [1933] SCR 456 (SCC).

deemed to have been born at the time of the accident of the mother. However, the judgment of Cannon J is of particular interest to the common lawyer. His Honour said:

> [T]he cause of action arose when the damage was suffered and not when the wrongful act was committed. The plaintiff's right to compensation came into existence only when she was born with the bodily disability with which she suffered. It was only after birth that she suffered the injury, and it was then that her rights were encroached upon and she commenced to have rights.[38]

This judgment, as will be seen, contains the genesis of the modern analysis of the problem.

5.21 Eventually, the right of a child when born alive to sue for injuries caused by a prenatal event became recognized not only in Canada[39] but in the US (where every jurisdiction now permits such a claim),[40] Australia,[41] South Africa,[42] Scotland,[43] Ireland (by statute),[44] and England and Wales.[45]

5.22 **(b) The decision in *Watt v Rama*** A close analysis of the law can be found in the influential decision of the Supreme Court of Victoria in *Watt v Rama*.[46] The claim was brought by the infant plaintiff allegedly injured in utero by the negligent driving of the defendant, who took the preliminary point that the allegations disclosed no cause of action. The defendant argued that at the time of the collision he owed no duty of care to the plaintiff, who was then unborn, that he owed the plaintiff no duty not to injure her mother, and that the damages sought to be recovered were in law too remote. The majority (Winneke CJ and Pape J) defined the issue not as whether an action lay in respect of prenatal injuries, but whether a plaintiff born with injuries caused by the prenatal neglect of the defendant had a cause of action in negligence against him in respect of such injuries. The solution was to define the relationship of the defendant to the plaintiff in utero as 'contingent or potential' which would 'crystallize' or 'ripen into a relationship imposing a duty' when the plaintiff's identity as a legal person became defined by birth. At that stage the act of neglect could be treated as a breach of duty, and the prenatal damage as 'merely an evidential fact relevant to the issue of causation and damage': the damage consisted of 'injuries as a living person'.[47] Thus, duty, breach, and damage remained potential until at and after birth, at which point they became actual.

5.23 Gillard J thought that it was immaterial whether at the time of fault the victim was in existence or not, so long as the victim was a member of a class which might reasonably and probably be affected by the act of carelessness. He noted that the pleaded and relevant damage was 'physical disabilities at and after her birth'. From this he inferred that the only

38 ibid, 357.

39 See, further, *Duval v Sequin* (1972) 26 DLR (3d) 418; *Cherry v Borsman* (1992) 94 DLR (4th) 487 (BCCA), *Winnipeg Child and Family Services (Northwest Area) v G (DF)* [1997] 3 SCR 925, 942 (SCC); *Paxton v Ramji* (2009) 299 DLR 4th 614, [38] (Ont CA); *Liebig v Guelph General Hospital* [2010] ONCA 450: and see para 5.34.

40 The change of view seems to have been initiated by *Bonbrest v Kotz* 65 F Supp 138 (1946). The reversal was complete by about 1972: see *Huskey v Smith* 265 So 2d 596 (1972); and see D B Dobbs, *The Law of Torts* (West Group 2000) 781.

41 *Watt v Rama* [1972] VR 353; *X v Pal* (1991) 23 NSWLR 26 (NSWCA); *Lynch v Lynch* (1991) 25 NSWLR 411 (NSWCA).

42 *Pinchin v Santam Insurance Co Ltd* [1963] 2 SA 254.

43 *Hamilton v Fife Health Board* [1993] SC 369; A Grubb, (1993) 1 Med L Rev 392.

44 Civil Liability Act 1961, s 58.

45 *Burton v Islington HA: De Martell v Merton & Sutton HA* [1993] QB 204 (CA); see paras 5.24–5.25.

46 *Watt v Rama* [1972] VR 353.

47 ibid, 360–61, 366.

difference made to a plaintiff by the passage of time was that by birth she acquired capacity to sue. He then went on to provide two linked answers to the contention that prior to birth no duty could be owed to an unborn child because it was not a legal person:

> The first depends on the views I have already expressed. The cause of action for negligence only comes into existence when the damage is suffered. The infant plaintiff at that period . . . is, I repeat, a persona juridica, with capacity to institute proceedings and to whom a duty might be owed. The injury while en ventre sa mère was but an evidentiary incident in the causation of damage suffered at birth by the fault of the defendant . . . As a second answer there is probably at the time of the defendant's fault also damnum contemporaneous with the injuria to a subject which is sufficiently protected by the rules of the common law, so that when it reaches the capacity of a person in being by subsequent birth to institute legal proceedings, it is entitled to bring those proceedings for its own benefit in relation to the damage suffered.[48]

(c) The decisions in *De Martell* and *Burton* The second answer given by Gillard J effectively identifies a complete cause of action at the time of the initial trauma, with the reservation only that it cannot be enforced until after a live birth. This raises without resolving the problem of how a being with no legal identity can possess a chose in action, and is the less preferable analysis. Certainly, it was the first answer of Gillard J which attracted Phillips J at first instance in *De Martell v Merton and Sutton Health Authority*:[49] **5.24**

> To say that the plaintiff suffered his injuries the moment after his birth rather than in the period leading up to his birth involves a legal fiction. But the fiction is that which denies the living creature which became the plaintiff a persona in the period prior to birth. It is that legal fiction which the health authority relies upon in denying liability to the plaintiff. It is not open to the health authority to deny liability on the ground that the organism that they injured was not in law the plaintiff and yet to deny responsibility for the defects with which the plaintiff was born on the ground that they inflicted them before birth. In law and in logic no damage can have been caused to the plaintiff before the plaintiff existed. The damage was suffered by the plaintiff at the moment that, in law, the plaintiff achieved personality and inherited the damaged body for which the health authority (on the assumed facts) was responsible. The events prior to birth were mere links in the chain of causation between the health authority's assumed lack of skill and care and the consequential damage to the plaintiff.

Potts J similarly recognized a born-alive child's cause of action in *Burton v Islington Health Authority*.[50] He respectfully adopted the view of Winneke CJ and Pape J in *Watt v Rama* and held that on the infant plaintiff's birth the defendant's contingent or potential duty crystallized and the wrong to the child was then complete.

Burton and *De Martell* were taken on conjoined appeal to the Court of Appeal,[51] which dismissed both appeals without calling on the respondents. The majority followed *Watt v Rama* without expressing a preference for its different approaches or for either of the two first instance decisions. Dillon LJ recognized that Phillips J was inclined to prefer the approach of Gillard J to that of the Chief Justice and Pape J, but considered that both led to the same conclusion and that the differences were not significant in the context of the instant appeal. **5.25**

(d) Advice to the mother The performance of the duty to avoid injury to the foetus may extend beyond diagnosis and treatment to the provision of advice to the mother. In *Howarth* **5.26**

48 [1972] VR 353, 374–75.
49 [1993] QB 204, 219.
50 [1991] 1 QB 638.
51 [1993] QB 207 (CA); I Kennedy, (1993) 1 Med L Rev 103.

v Adey[52] Winneke J said that once it was accepted that a medical practitioner owed a duty of care both to the mother and to the child, the scope of that duty had to extend to providing advice and information to the mother as to maternal risks affecting the potential well-being of the infant inherent in the proposed management of the delivery. In the circumstances the mother was the only person in the position to make the relevant decision in the interests of the infant. Applying the principle, he permitted an amendment to the case to allow a plaintiff with cerebral palsy secondary to perinatal hypoxia to allege that the mother should have been warned of the risks of continued attempts at vaginal delivery and advised of the alternatives. Again, in *Elayoubi v Zipser*[53] a child deprived of oxygen during the birth process succeeded in a claim against a hospital which had carried out an earlier Caesarean operation, on the ground that it had negligently failed to warn the mother about the ramifications for the management of any future pregnancy.[54]

5.27 The approach taken in *Howarth v Adey* is implicit in the decision of the Supreme Court in *Montgomery v Lanarkshire Health Board*,[55] although not actually discussed in it. A patient who was expecting her first child suffered from diabetes, which condition meant that she was likely to have a baby which was larger than normal, and was placed under the care of an obstetrician and gynaecologist employed by the defendant in order that her pregnancy could be intensively monitored. A prime concern in diabetic pregnancies is a risk of shoulder dystocia, which is the risk that the shoulders of the baby will be too wide to pass through the mother's pelvis without medical intervention. During delivery the baby got stuck, and as a consequence of this he was starved of oxygen and suffered brain damage. The patient brought a claim on behalf of her son, alleging that the obstetrician should have warned her of the risk of shoulder dystocia and informed her of the possibility of delivery by caesarean section.

5.28 A problem facing the patient was the decision of the House of Lords in *Sidaway v Board of Governors of the Bethlem Royal Hospital*,[56] which treated questions about disclosure to patients of the risks of treatment simply as a matter of clinical judgment. On this view a doctor who failed to warn a patient of a risk would not be liable if other reasonable doctors adhering to proper professional practices would have done the same.[57] But Lord Kerr and Lord Reed, delivering the leading judgment, recognized that times had moved on from the 'doctor knows best' approach and determined that *Sidaway* should be abandoned. Matters regarding advice could be distinguished from diagnosis and treatment, as it was the patient's fundamental right to decide whether or not to undergo treatment. It would be a mistake to view patients as uninformed, incapable of understanding medical matters, or wholly dependent upon a flow of information from doctors. To make this the default assumption on which the law should be based was now manifestly untenable. Rather, the doctor was under a duty to take reasonable care to ensure that the patient was aware of any material risks involved in any recommended treatment, and of any reasonable and variant treatments. The test of materiality was whether, in the circumstances of the particular case, a reasonable person in the patient's position would be likely to attach significance to the risk, or the doctor was or should reasonably be aware that the particular patient would be likely

52 [1996] 2 VR 535, 546, Vic CA.

53 (2008) Aust Torts Reports 81–985 (NSWCA).

54 A claim against the doctor who delivered the plaintiff and who had failed to inquire of the first hospital about the mother's medical history also succeeded.

55 [2015] AC 1430.

56 [1985] AC 871.

57 Applying *Bolam v Friern Hospital Management Committee* [1957] 1 WLR 582: see para 5.48.

to attach significance to it. However, the doctor was entitled to withhold information as to a risk if he or she reasonably considered its disclosure would be seriously detrimental to the patient's health. On the instant facts the obstetrician had come under a duty to warn of the material risk of shoulder dystocia, and the evidence established that the patient would have chosen delivery by caesarean section had the risk been properly explained and this alternative option been offered. Their Lordships held, accordingly, that the claim should succeed.

Their Lordships spoke consistently of the duty of disclosure owed to a patient, without drawing any distinction between the patient and her child. However, Lady Hale, giving a brief concurring judgment, said that doctors clearly had to volunteer the pros and cons of vaginal delivery and caesarean section in any case where either the mother or the child was at heightened risk from a vaginal delivery. She added that in this day and age we were not only concerned about risks to the baby. We were equally, if not more, concerned about risks to the mother. And these included the risks associated with giving birth, as well as any after-effects. **5.29**

(e) **Pre-conception occurrences** If we accept that a claim can be made by a living child for the effects of an occurrence which preceded his or her birth, it is but a short step to conclude that a living child can also make a claim for the consequences of an incident which preceded its conception. Our concern at this stage is only with the case where the defendant brings about an injury to a child not yet conceived at the time of the act complained of but who would have been conceived whatever the defendant did. Where a defendant brings about the conception of a child who, having been conceived, is doomed to disability for reasons unconnected with the act of the defendant, or brings about both the conception and the disability, any claim by the child faces the very serious objections to claims for 'wrongful life'.[58] These are discussed later on.[59] **5.30**

In *X v Pal*[60] the New South Wales Court of Appeal considered the claim of an infant plaintiff, born with congenital syphilis, that her disabilities were caused by the negligence of her mother's gynaecologists in failing to screen and treat the mother for syphilis before she became pregnant. The defendants argued that the doctors owed no duty to the infant plaintiff, but the argument was rejected. Clarke JA confirmed that a person may be subjected to a duty of care to a child who was neither born nor conceived at the time of his careless act or omission. Whether or not that duty would arise depended upon whether there was a relevant relationship between the careless person and the class of persons of whom the child was one. So a duty could be owed provided the defendants could reasonably foresee injury to such a child. Of course, if the plaintiff could only ever have been born with injuries caused by syphilis, this would have been an action for wrongful life. But the problem was avoided, and plaintiff was entitled to maintain an action, on the basis that, had the disease been diagnosed, steps could have been taken to prevent the plaintiff from contracting it.[61] **5.31**

Various pre-conception occurrences may give rise to injuries to a child subsequently conceived. For example, a doctor may negligently perform an operation which weakens the patient's uterus so that some years later it ruptures at the end of pregnancy and injures the child. Another possibility may be some trauma to the mother leading to disability in a child **5.32**

[58] However, it sometimes is difficult to draw a clear line between these two kinds of cases: see para 5.93.
[59] See paras 5.81–5.89.
[60] (1991) 23 NSWLR 26 (NSWCA); and see *Kosky v The Trustees of the Sisters of Charity* [1982] VR 961.
[61] However, the evidence did not show that the disease caused the disabilities of which the plaintiff complained.

not yet conceived when it occurs. Or there may be pre-conception exposure to chemicals or radiation which cause gene mutation and consequent disability to children later conceived. However, while claims for such pre-conception injuries are not to be rejected on the basis that the child was not alive or in existence at the time of the damage-producing event, there may nonetheless be difficulty in establishing a sufficiently proximate connection between the defendant and the born-later child as to give rise to a duty of care, or in showing that but for the occurrence complained of the child would have been born and born without the relevant disability.

5.33 In America some decisions refuse to permit such claims to be brought against negligent motorists, on the ground that there is no 'special relationship' between the careless driver and the future child of the woman he injures.[62] But the requisite relationship has been held to exist where the child's disabilities are caused by the conduct of a doctor or pharmaceutical manufacturer.[63] Without the 'special relationship', injury to a future (as yet unconceived) child is treated as unforeseeable, and hence no duty of care is owed to the child.[64] In New York there is a blanket rejection of any duty of this kind.[65]

5.34 In Canada the Ontario Court of Appeal considered that it was reasonably foreseeable that a doctor could cause harm to a future child by prescribing teratogenic medication for acne to a woman who was or might become pregnant, but that there was no relationship of proximity making it fair and just that the doctor should owe a duty to the child.[66] There was the prospect of conflicting duties as between the patient and the child, the relationship between a doctor and a future child was indirect and mediated through the patient, and imposing a duty would interfere with a woman's right to choose to abort a foetus. But a doctor would owe a duty to the mother in prescribing a drug, and would be liable for the damage she suffered in giving birth to a child with disabilities caused by the drug.

5.35 In England the position at common law is unlikely to need to be determined, because any claim will almost certainly be covered by the Congenital Disabilities (Civil Liability) Act 1976. But in principle, in light of the Act making provision for a claim for injuries to a child resulting from an incident which occurred before its conception,[67] it would very arguably be appropriate for the common law to take the same approach. Certainly it is not convincing simply to assert that injury to a child caused by a pre-conception event is unforeseeable. However, any objections of principle seen in the common law cases, like the risk of a conflict of interest between mother and child, would have to be brought into account. As we will see, it may be that this problem can be avoided in relation to a claim under the 1976 Act.[68]

---

[62] *Hegyes v Unjian Enterprises Inc* 286 Cal Rptr 85 (Cal App 2 Dist, 1991) (driver of motor vehicle not liable to child subsequently conceived and suffering disability in utero as a result of mother's injuries sustained in the accident).

[63] See, eg, *Bergstreser v Mitchell* 577 F 2d (8th Cir, 1978) (negligent Caesarean section leading to weakened uterus); *Renslow v Mennonite Hospital* 367 NE 2d 1250 (Ill Sup Ct, 1977) (negligent blood transfusion leading to injury due to its incompatible Rhesus factor); *Hegyes v Unjian Enterprises Inc* 286 Cal Rptr 85 (Cal App 2 Dist, 1991).

[64] *Hegyes v Unjian Enterprises Inc* 286 Cal Rptr 85 (Cal App 2 Dist, 1991), 93, 103 *per* Woods JA (Lillie PJ concurring); cp at 108 *per* Johnson JA, dissenting; and see also *McAuley v Wills* 303 SE 2d 258 (1983) (Ga Sup Ct); *Yeager v Bloomington Obstetrics and Gynaecology Inc* 585 NE 2d 696 (Ct App Indiana, 1992); I Kennedy, (1993) 1 Med L Rev 247.

[65] *Albala v City of New York* 54 NY 2d 269 (1981).

[66] *Paxton v Ramji* (2009) 299 DLR 4th 614 (Ont CA).

[67] See paras 5.45–5.46.

[68] See para 5.55.

(f) Transgenerational claims Something may happen to a person posing a risk not only to his or her child but to succeeding generations. Establishing a causal link between the occurrence and the harm to later generations might be difficult, but in principle a claim by a member of a later generation could be maintainable in the same or a similar way as with pre-conception claims. But there are significant policy objections, as illustrated in the litigation by the American DES daughters. Diethylstilbestrol (DES) was a drug which, between 1947 and its banning in 1971, was given to millions of pregnant women to prevent miscarriages. In utero exposure to DES resulted in genital tract abnormalities to daughters later born, who in turn and as a result suffered obstetric problems including premature births. In *Enright v Eli Lilly & Co*[69] the granddaughter of a woman who had ingested the drug during pregnancy sued the manufacturers, alleging that in consequence her mother had given birth prematurely and as a result she suffered from cerebral palsy. In rejecting the claim the New York Court of Appeals was strongly influenced by policy considerations, and in particular the unquantifiable extent of the potential liability of drug companies to future generations.[70] English courts would very likely reach the same conclusion. **5.36**

(g) Liability of parents Thus far we have considered claims in respect of prenatal injuries where the born-alive child has sued a medical professional or other third party. Suppose now an action is brought on behalf of a child against his or her parent. As a matter of general principle a parent can be liable to a child for failing to take care in looking after the child. The duty arises by reason of the parent having assumed responsibility for the child's welfare. So a parent (or person in loco parentis) must take care to safeguard a child from danger on the road, or from dangerous premises, or from being assaulted or abused.[71] Applying a **5.37**

[69] 570 NE 2d 198 (NYCA, 1991).

[70] But the daughters could have a cause of action. In the decision of the Supreme Court of California in *Sindell v Abbott Laboratories* 607 P (2d) 924 (1980), the plaintiff suffered from vaginal cancerous lesions caused by her mother having taken DES while pregnant. The plaintiff's difficulty lay in proving which of more than 200 manufacturers of DES caused her injury. The court resolved the difficulty by holding that each defendant would be liable in proportion to its share of the market, unless it could demonstrate that it could not have made the product which caused the plaintiff's injury. In effect, the market share equated with the chance that the particular defendant had caused the injury. For discussion of *Sindell*, see J G Fleming, 'Probabilistic Causation in Tort Law' (1989) 68 Can Bar Rev 661; E Handsley, 'Market Share Liability and the Nature of Causation in Tort' (1993) 1 TLJ 24. It has been held in the Dutch Supreme Court that each manufacturer of DES was jointly liable for the whole damage, although market share could be relevant when apportioning damages: J R Spencer and A J O Van Wassenaer, 'Causal Links and Congenital Disabilities' [1993] 52 CLJ 206; J G Teulings, 'D.E.S. and Market Share Liability in the Netherlands' (1994) 110 LQR 228. On the DES litigation generally, see R Goldberg, 'Causation and Drugs: The Legacy of Diethylstilbestrol' (1996) 25 Anglo-Am LR 286.

[71] Parents: *McCallion v Dodd* [1966] NZLR 710 (NZCA); *Tweed SC v Howarth* (2009) Aus Torts Reps 82–010 (NSWCA). Local authority: *Barrett v Enfield London Borough Council* [2001] 2 AC 550 (HL). School: *Barnes v Hants County Council* [1969] 1 WLR 1563 (HL); *Commonwealth v Introvigne* (1982) 150 CLR 258 (HCA); *Myers v Peel County Board of Education* [1981] 2 SCR 21 (SCC). Whether or how far the duty might extend to cover the promotion by parents of a child's general well-being was considered by the New Zealand Court of Appeal in *A v Roman Catholic Archdiocese of Wellington* [2008] 3 NZLR 289. William Young P explained that damages for bad parenting will not be entertained, for reasons associated with parental autonomy and a sense that the issues would not be practicably justiciable. But there could be a duty as to children's physical and psychiatric health and this would encompass emotional abuse. Provided it did not extend to anything approaching a duty to maximize or enhance the emotional well-being of children, it should be reasonably manageable. In *OPO v MLA* [2014] EWCA Civ 1277, at [57], the Court of Appeal rejected a claim alleging a parent owed a duty to a child not to expose him to unacceptable risk of psychological injury. Arden LJ said that it would encompass a whole range of commonplace activities in which a parent was involved in caring for his child. On appeal to the Supreme Court in *Rhodes v OPO* [2015] 2 WLR 1373 the Court of Appeal's finding that there could nonetheless be a claim under the rule in

similar principle, a parent owes his or her child a duty to give or withhold consent to medical treatment in the best interests of the child.[72]

5.38 However, a controversial question is whether a child has a right to sue his or her mother in respect of injuries arising from some antenatal event.[73] The Law Commission was much troubled by the idea.[74] The Commission felt that such a right of action could further stress the already difficult relationship between mother and disabled child, or become a weapon between parents in a matrimonial conflict to its further detriment. It was impressed by the difficulty and unseemliness of possible allegations against mothers, such as those of excessive drinking and smoking, and pointed to the fact that in any event a mother, even if liable, would probably be unsupported by funds. In the end it recommended that a woman should only be liable for causing antenatal injury to her child if she was negligent in driving when she knew or ought reasonably to know herself to be pregnant. But it did not recommend any special exemption for a father.

5.39 Let us consider how the relevant concerns of policy have influenced courts considering a common law claim by a child against a parent for an antenatal injury. In *Dobson v Dobson*[75] a majority in the Supreme Court of Canada[76] held that an expectant mother who was involved in a road accident which caused serious injury to her child before his birth owed no duty of care to the child. It was thought that recognizing a duty would result in extensive and unacceptable intrusions into the bodily integrity, privacy, and autonomy rights of women, and could render the most mundane decision taken in the course of their daily lives subject to judicial scrutiny. And any attempt to carve out an immunity for so-called 'lifestyle' choices of the mother would result in arbitrary line-drawing. By contrast, the minority[77] thought that a distinction could be drawn between the duty to avoid injury which a defendant ordinarily owes to others and duties peculiar to parenthood. In the instant case the mother's freedom of action in respect of her driving was already restricted by her duty of care to users of the highway. She would not have had to take any further precautions to avoid liability to her born-alive child. Any policy concerns about the appropriateness of inter-familial litigation should apply to all members of the family unit, not just born-alive children injured in utero.

5.40 For these latter reasons an absolute immunity arguably is undesirable, and certainly in Australia the minority view has been favoured. In two driving cases similar to *Dobson* the courts have been prepared to impose a duty of care on the mother.[78] In cases such as these the parent's conduct can be assessed by the same tests as those which apply to a non-parent. By contrast, applying a lifestyle immunity, a mother cannot be liable for harm to a foetus caused by smoking or drinking while she is pregnant. For example, in *Winnipeg Child and Family Services (Northwest Area) v G (DF)*[79] a majority in the Supreme Court

Wilkinson v Downton [1897] 2 QB 57 on the facts in this case was reversed: see further S Todd, 'Tortious Intrusions upon Solitude and Seclusion' (2015) 27 S Ac LJ 731, at paras 8–14.

[72] *Re J (Wardship: Medical Treatment)* [1991] Fam 33, 41 (CA).

[73] R Scott, 'Maternal Duties toward the Unborn? Soundings from the Law of Tort' (2000) 8 Med L Rev 1.

[74] Law Commission Report No 60, *Report on Injuries to Unborn Children* (Cmnd 5709, 1974), paras 54–63 (hereinafter 'Report No 60').

[75] [1999] 2 SCR 753 (SCC); D Ginn, 'A Balancing that is Beyond the Scope of the Common Law: A Discussion of the Issues Raised by *Dobson v Dobson*' (2002) 27 Queens LJ 51; M McInnes, (2000) 116 LQR 26; I R Kerr, 'Pregnant Women and the Born Alive Rule in Canada' (2000) 8 Tort L Rev 713; I Malkin, 'A Mother's Duty of Care to Her Foetus while Driving: A Comment' (2001) 9 TLJ 109.

[76] Lamer CJC and L'Heureux-Dubé, Gonthier, Cory, McLachlan, Iacobucci, and Binnie JJ.

[77] Major and Bastarache JJ.

[78] *Lynch v Lynch* (1991) 25 NSWLR 411 (CA); *Bowditch v McEwan* (2002) Aust Torts Reports 81–632.

[79] [1997] 3 SCR 925 (SCC); M Randall, 'Pregnant Embodiment and Women's Autonomy Rights in Law: An Analysis of the Language and Politics of *Winnipeg Child and Family Services v DFG* '(1999) 62

of Canada[80] declined to make an order for the detention of a pregnant woman who was addicted to glue-sniffing for the purpose of preventing harm to the unborn child. There may be more difficult cases, but probably the courts are capable of delimiting an immunity on any particular facts where recognition of a duty would infringe upon a pregnant woman's autonomy. There may also be a problem in some cases in determining the standard of care expected of the mother and the precautions she ought to take to protect her child. But a lifestyle immunity perhaps can take such problems into account. Again, a pregnant woman is entitled to put her own wishes or interests ahead of those of her unborn child in making decisions about medical treatment.[81] By parity of reasoning, it is difficult to envisage a court finding a mother to be negligent in refusing or delaying treatment to herself which might benefit her unborn child.

(h) Defences An unborn child not being a 'person' in law, it is hard to see how any contract term or notice given by a defendant prior to birth can exclude or restrict the defendant's liability for injuries with which the child is born. The mother can hardly be described as an agent, fixing the foetus as a legally non-existent principal with notice or with the terms of a contract to which she was a party. But this conclusion did not attract the Law Commission,[82] which concluded on social grounds that it would be unfair on a defendant if he or she could not limit liability to a child as yet unborn to the same extent as he or she could limit liability to the mother. However, s 2(1) of the Unfair Contract Terms Act 1977 provides that a person cannot by reference to any contract term or to a notice given to persons generally or to particular persons exclude or restrict his liability for death or personal injury resulting from negligence. With the passing of this Act a defendant could not exclude his or her liability to the mother, and the wording is sufficiently broad to include injury arising from a prenatal event as well. The Act originally applied to all contracts, but the Consumer Rights Act 2015 removed all consumer contracts and notices from its coverage and made its own, separate, provision for these contracts and notices. In particular, the 2015 Act bars any exclusion of negligence liability for death or personal injury,[83] as under the Unfair Contract Terms Act. Any dispute is likely to concern a consumer contract or notice, in which case the new Act will apply, but in substance, so far as the present issue is concerned, the law remains the same. **5.41**

The protection afforded to claimants by the Unfair Contract Terms Act 1977 and by the Consumer Rights Act 2015 is expressed to apply only in the case of negligence, including negligence in the performance of a contract.[84] Possibly there could be a stricter statutory or other duty applying in particular circumstances, but even in such a case the defence that liability had been excluded seemingly would still fail on the application of ordinary principle. An unborn child could not be bound by an exclusion clause to which he or she had not consented. **5.42**

Similar principles can apply in the case of a parent's voluntary assumption of a risk to his or her as yet unborn child. The parent's consent would only absolve a defendant of a duty not **5.43**

Sask L Rev 515. The case provoked wide-ranging discussion in a series of comments in (1998) 36 Alberta Law Review 707: see S Rodgers, at 711; F C DeCoste, at 725; L Shanner, at 751; B P Elman and J Mason, at 768; F Baylis, at 785; T Caulfield and E Nelson, at 799. See also *CP v First-tier Tribunal (Criminal Injuries Compensation)* [2015] 2 WLR 463; see paras 5.16–5.17.

[80] Lamer CJC, La Forest, L'Heureux-Dubé, Gonthier, Cory, McLachlan, Iacobucci JJ; Major and Sopinka JJ dissenting.

[81] *St George's Healthcare NHS Trust v S* [1999] Fam 26 (CA); see para 5.06.

[82] Report No 60, n 74, paras 67–71.

[83] Consumer Rights Act 2015, s 65.

[84] Unfair Contract Terms Act 1977, s 1(1); Consumer Rights Act 2015, s 65(4).

to injure an unborn child if he or she was treated as having authority to consent on behalf of the child, and this conclusion would have no basis on ordinary principles of agency. The Law Commission, again, thought it unfair that a defendant should be liable to the child born of a *volens* mother, and proposed that there be legislative provision to counter this perceived injustice.[85] As regards the common law, it is probable that the mother's consent does not in itself prejudice any claim by the child. The doctor's duty to the child alone should be to decline to carry out medical treatment posing a foreseeable and unreasonable risk to the foetus. But it seems unlikely that the question could arise in such a stark form. Rather, the doctor also would owe a duty to treat the mother in accordance with her wishes, and at least normally, as we have seen, the duty will prevail over any possible duty to the child.

2. Claims for injuries under the Congenital Disabilities (Civil Liability) Act 1976

(i) Background

5.44 In 1974 the Law Commission considered in some detail the question of civil liability in respect of prenatal injuries. In its *Report on Injuries to Unborn Children*,[86] the Commission recommended that there should be reforming legislation, for five reasons:[87]

(1) In the absence of English authority there was doubt whether a child had a cause of action at all for injuries caused before birth.
(2) The basis upon which the cause of action existed in other common law jurisdictions varied. American authority was founded on the recognition of the foetus as a legal entity separate from its mother, but in Australia a claim could be brought by a living plaintiff in respect of a disability with which he was born, even though this was caused by the earlier negligent conduct of the defendant.
(3) The cost of law reform should fall upon one individual. There was a strong case for resolving doubts about the existing state of the law.
(4) The first factual situation litigated would almost certainly leave a number of ancillary questions unanswered. It was desirable that as many of these questions as could be foreseen should be answered before they arose.
(5) The proposed reform involved departures on social grounds from the probable results of strict application of legal principles. This point was of particular relevance to the question whether a mother could be liable in negligence in an action by her own child.

It may be that legislation was hardly necessary. As we have seen already, the common law has dealt reasonably satisfactorily with the special problems posed by claims by children in respect of their prenatal injuries. But however that might be, the Commission's recommendations led to the passing of the Congenital Disabilities (Civil Liability) Act 1976, which came into force on 22 July 1976.[88] Where the Act applies it operates to replace the relevant principles of the common law.[89]

(ii) Civil liability to disabled child

5.45 The long title to the 1976 Act states, inter alia, that it is an Act to make provision as to civil liability in case of children born disabled in consequence of some person's fault. This objective is achieved by s 1(1) and (2), which provide:

---

[85] Report No 60, n 74, paras 67–69; for the legislation, see para 5.57.
[86] Report No 60, n 74, paras 67–69.
[87] ibid, para 110.
[88] P Cane, 'Injuries to Unborn Children' (1977) 51 ALJ 704; P J Pace, 'Civil Liability for Pre-Natal Injuries' (1977) 40 MLR 141.
[89] Congenital Disabilities (Civil Liability) Act 1976, s 4(5).

(1) If a child is born disabled as the result of such an occurrence before its birth as is mentioned in subsection (2) below, and a person (other than the child's own mother) is under this section answerable to the child in respect of the occurrence, the child's disabilities are to be regarded as damage resulting from the wrongful act of that person and actionable accordingly at the suit of the child.

(2) An occurrence to which this section applies is one which—

(a) affected either parent of the child in his or her ability to have a normal, healthy child; or

(b) affected the mother during her pregnancy, or affected her or the child in the course of its birth, so that the child is born with disabilities which would not otherwise have been present.[90]

References in the Act to a child being born disabled or with disabilities are to the child being born with 'any deformity, disease or abnormality, including pre-disposition (whether or not susceptible of immediate prognosis) to physical or mental defect in the future'.[91] 'Born' means 'born alive (the moment of a child's birth being when it first has a life separate from its mother)'.[92] So there can be no claim by a stillborn child.

The two parts to s 1(2) were intended to deal with pre-conception occurrences and post-conception occurrences respectively,[93] but they are not mutually exclusive. For example, a badly performed Caesarean section may affect the mother's subsequent ability to have a normal healthy child and also affect her during a later pregnancy. Further, the language of para (b) requires only that the occurrence should 'affect' the mother, not that it should injure her. Gynaecological treatment may injure a foetus without injuring the mother, and this clearly is covered. Indeed, the Act goes on to provide that a child has a right of action even though the mother has not been injured.[94] **5.46**

Disabilities which result from certain infertility treatments are specifically included. By s 1A(1), there may be liability under the Act where a child carried by a woman as the result of the placing in her of an embryo or of sperm and eggs or her artificial insemination is born disabled, and the disability results from an act or omission in the course of selection, or the keeping or use outside the body, of the embryo or of the gametes used to bring about the creation of the embryo.[95] **5.47**

(iii) The standard of care

Section 1(5) of the Act lays down a statutory standard of care. It provides: **5.48**

> The defendant is not answerable to the child, for anything he did or omitted to do when responsible in a professional capacity for treating or advising the parent, if he took reasonable care having due regard to then received professional opinion applicable to the particular class of case; but this does not mean that he is answerable only because he departed from received opinion.

---

[90] For discussion of what may constitute an 'occurrence', see *Multiple Claimants v Sanifo-Synthelabo Ltd* [2007] EWHC 1860, at [55]–[58].

[91] Congenital Disabilities (Civil Liability) Act 1976, s 4(1). The mistaken use of donor sperm coming from a man from a different ethnic background from that of the would-be parents falls outside the Act, because a healthy child born as a result of such sperm cannot be said to suffer from a congenital defect: *A & B v A Health and Social Services Trust* [2011] NICA 28, at [3].

[92] Congenital Disabilities (Civil Liability) Act 1976, s 4(2)(a).

[93] Report No 60, n 74, Appendix 1, note 5 to Clause 1 of the Draft Bill.

[94] Congenital Disabilities (Civil Liability) Act 1976, s 1(3); see para 5.52; and see *The Corby Group Litigation* [2009] EWHC 1944; R Lee, 'Old Iron: Birth Defects Litigation and the Corby Steelworks' Reclamation' (2009) 25 PN 174.

[95] See *A & B v A Health and Social Services Trust* [2011] NICA 28, at [3].

This is an attempted codification of the common law.[96] As explained by the Law Commission, it demands of a professional man that he should exercise such care as accords with the standards of reasonably competent medical men at the time unless he has in fact greater than average knowledge of any risks, in which case his duty will be that much greater.[97] So the subsection is founded both on the standards of the day and on the principle that departure from approved practice is not necessarily a breach of duty.[98] Again, the principle of the common law that compliance with common medical practices is relevant to, but is not determinative of, the question of negligence also can be seen to apply.[99]

(iv) Actions against parents

5.49 With one exception, a child born disabled has no claim against its mother.[100] The exceptional case is where a woman is driving a motor vehicle when she knows (or ought reasonably to know) herself to be pregnant. In this circumstance the mother owes a duty to take care for the safety of her unborn child,[101] who may sue her if later born with disabilities. This right of action extends only to the driving of a motor vehicle and not, for example, to the riding of a bicycle or a horse. The policy behind this provision is to allow claims in respect of prenatal injury which are covered by the mother's compulsory insurance or by the Motor Insurance Bureau.[102] In these circumstances the arguments for disallowing such claims are much diminished.

5.50 A father does not enjoy the same immunity from action as does the mother. This apparent anomaly was justified by the Law Commission's views that, inter alia, there would be fewer ways in which congenital disabilities could be caused by a father than by a mother, a father's responsibility for a child's injuries would be less likely to raise family disputes than a mother's, and a child born disabled as a result of an assault by a man on the mother (even a rape which caused the conception) should have a cause of action against that man.[103]

(v) Damages

5.51 Liability to a child under the preceding provisions is to be regarded as liability for personal injuries sustained by the child immediately after its birth.[104] One purpose of this provision is to exclude a right to compensation for any prenatal suffering, and to provide for damages to be assessed as if the prenatal injury had been inflicted after birth without the disabilities due to the prenatal wrong.[105] The Act also provides that no damages shall be recoverable for loss of expectation of life unless the child lives for at least forty-eight hours.[106] However, the provision is obsolete, for damages in respect of any loss of expectation of life were abolished in 1982.[107]

96 See *Bolam v Friern Hospital Management Committee* [1957] 1 WLR 582; *Bolitho v City and Hackney HA* [1998] AC 232 (HL); *Chinnock v Veale Wasbrough* [2015] EWCA Civ 441, at [52]–[59]. However, questions as to the giving of advice about the risks of treatment are determined not by reference to professional opinion but in accordance with the doctor's duty to disclose material risks: *Montgomery v Lanarkshire Health Board* [2015] AC 1430; see paras 5.27–5.29.

97 Report No 60, n 74, para 94.

98 See I Kennedy and A Grubb, *Medical Law* (Butterworths 2000), 453–55.

99 *Bolitho v City and Hackney HA* [1998] AC 232 (HL). See, eg, *Farraj v King's Healthcare NHS Trust* [2008] EWHC 2468, [84] (a wrongful birth claim).

100 Congenital Disabilities (Civil Liability) Act 1976, s 1(1).

101 ibid, s 2.

102 Report No 60, n 74, paras 59–60.

103 ibid, paras 92–93.

104 Congenital Disabilities (Civil Liability) Act 1976, s 4(3).

105 Report No 60, n 74, para 100.

106 Congenital Disabilities (Civil Liability) Act 1976, s 4(4).

107 Administration of Justice Act 1982, s 1.

(vi) A derivative claim

The basis of liability under the Act is unique. Save in claims against a mother for motoring injuries, a defendant is liable to the child only if the defendant has committed a breach of duty to a parent. This is made clear by s 1(3), which provides: **5.52**

> [A] person . . . is answerable to the child if he was liable in tort to the parent or would, if sued in due time, have been so: and it is no answer that there could not have been such liability because the parent suffered no actionable injury, if there was a breach of legal duty which, accompanied by injury, would have given rise to the liability.[108]

In other words, a child's claim is derivative from a breach of duty to the parent which gives rise to, or would if accompanied by damage give rise to, liability in tort. This liability certainly includes the case where there is a liability in tort which is coextensive with a liability for negligent breach of contract. In addition, the statutory protection in respect of defective products afforded by the Consumer Protection Act 1987 extends to the unborn child. Liability to the child, similarly, is derivative on liability to a parent under the provisions of that Act.[109]

This derivative approach avoids a number of anomalies. For example, an occupier's duty may require a different level of care to be exercised towards lawful visitors from that which is owed to trespassers.[110] Imposing an unrestricted duty of care to unborn children upon an occupier could mean that he or she owed a higher duty to the unborn child than to its trespassing mother. By making the child's action derivative on a breach of duty to a parent, the Act avoids the problem which would arise if a defendant owed two levels of duty in respect of one incident. More importantly, this approach enables the child to sue the maker of a negligent misstatement to the mother. This might not otherwise have been possible, for if the only duty upon which an action could be based was one owed directly to a child as yet unborn, there might be difficulty in imposing liability for negligent advice given to the mother before birth.[111] **5.53**

(vii) Transgenerational claims

The Law Commission thought that there should be no claim for prenatal injury otherwise than at the suit of the first generation,[112] and this was achieved by the meaning given by s 4(5) to the requirement in s 1(3) that the defendant be 'liable in tort' to the parent. Section 4(5) provides: **5.54**

> This Act applies in respect of births after (but not before) its passing, and in respect of any such birth it replaces any law in force before its passing, whereby a person could be liable to a child in respect of disabilities with which it might be born; but in section 1(3) . . . the expression 'liable in tort' does not include any reference to liability by virtue of this Act or to liability by virtue of any such law.

To see how this works, let us take as an example the case where a manufacturer, M, supplies a drug to X at a time when she is pregnant, X gives birth to Y, who suffers an injury caused by the drug, and Y later gives birth to Z who also suffers an injury caused by the drug.

108 See also s 1A(2), which provides similarly in the case of claims in respect of infertility treatments under s 1A(1).

109 Consumer Protection Act 1987, s 6(3).

110 See *Herrington v British Railways Board* [1972] AC 877 (HL); Occupiers' Liability Act 1984, s 1(3).

111 However, *Montgomery v Lanarkshire Health Board* [2015] AC 1430 saw any duty owed by a doctor to disclose the risks of treatment as owed both to the mother and to the child: see para 5.29.

112 Report No 60, n 74, para 80.

Z brings an action against M. Z's parent is Y but the tortious act is committed against X, Z's grandparent. Any liability of M to Y must arise under the 1976 Act (by reason of M's liability in tort to X), and this liability is excluded by s 4(5). So Z cannot sue M. The possibility that, apart from any claim under the Act, Y could also have a claim at common law against M (which would allow a claim under the Act by Z against M) is excluded by the first part of s 4(5), abolishing the common law for births after the Act came into force.[113]

(viii) Defences

5.55 In some circumstances the derivative approach will operate in a way that is disadvantageous to the child. If the parents' actions would have given rise, had they sued, to a defence, then an action by the child also is barred. An example is where a parent has assumed the risk of harm. Suppose a mother refused appropriate treatment such as a Caesarean section in appropriate circumstances, or refused to go into hospital despite a warning that the labour was high risk. Here the child will be without remedy either against the medical professional or against the mother (because she is immune from action save in motoring claims). This conclusion seemingly is a necessary one, for it follows from the principle that a pregnant woman is entitled to put her own interests before those of her unborn child.[114] Undue solicitude for the mother, even at risk to the child, also might not be a breach of any duty to her, in which case the child injured by such excess of care would have no action.[115] Again, a manufacturer of a drug known to create a risk to both mother and foetus may warn the mother of the risk to herself but negligently state that the drug is safe for the foetus. The mother consumes the drug: only the foetus is injured. It has been suggested that because the child's claim is derivative only on an assumed breach of duty to the mother, he or she has no claim against the drug manufacturer.[116] However, prescribing a drug to a mother which injures her unborn child is a breach of duty to the mother,[117] so arguably the child can sue.

5.56 The derivative nature of the child's action is further apparent from a number of particular provisions in the Act which identify the child with the parents for the purpose of determining whether the defendant has a good defence. There are three such provisions.

5.57 **(a) Knowledge of the risk** First, parental knowledge of a risk to the foetus can bar a claim. Section 1(4) of the Act provides:

> [I]n the case of an occurrence preceding the time of conception, the defendant is not answerable to the child if at that time either or both of the parents knew of the risk of their child being born disabled (that is to say, the particular risk created by the occurrence); but should it be the child's father who is the defendant, this subsection does not apply if he knew of the risk and the mother did not.

Seemingly the Law Commission intended this to be a statutory form of ***volenti non fit injuria***,[118] although specific provision would not be necessary for the defence to apply. However, s 1(4) is wider than a *volenti* defence, for mere knowledge of a risk does not make a plaintiff *volens*. In order for a person to be held to have assumed the risk of harm it must be shown that he or

[113] I am indebted to Andrew Grubb for the use of this example.

[114] See para 5.06.

[115] See J Eekelaar and R Dingwall, 'Some Legal Issues in Obstetric Practice' (1984) JSWL 258.

[116] P Cane, 'Injuries to Unborn Children' (1977) 51 ALJ 704, 707–08, note 42.

[117] *Paxton v Ramji* (2009) 299 DLR 4th 614 (Ont CA); see para 5.34.

[118] Report No 60, n 74, paras 71 and 93; and see Appendix 1, note 10 to the Draft Bill, suggesting a defence 'if either or both of the parents knew of the risk of their child being born disabled *and accepted it*'.

she had full knowledge of the risk and, with that knowledge, freely and voluntarily decided to incur it.[119] In the present context, the parent's or parents' knowledge alone will prevent a claim by the child.

Section 1(4) does not apply to a risk attaching to post-conception occurrences, but only to those attaching to occurrences which precede conception. However, in cases where it is the father who is sued, the father cannot claim that his knowledge of the risk amounted to a defence unless that knowledge was shared by the mother. Were the law otherwise, a man who knew he had syphilis, and who in raping a woman infected a child thus conceived with that disease, might be able to plead his own knowledge of it as a defence. This obviously would be absurd. **5.58**

A comparable but not identical provision applies to claims arising out of the infertility treatments referred to in s 1A of the Act.[120] Section 1A(3) provides: **5.59**

> [T]he defendant is not under this section answerable to the child if at the time the embryo, or the sperm and eggs, are placed in the woman or at the time of her insemination (as the case may be) either or both of the parents knew the risk of their child being born disabled (that is to say, the particular risk created by the act or omission).

(b) Exclusion and restriction of liability Second, a defendant may seek to exclude his or her liability. By s 1(6), any contract term having the effect of excluding or restricting liability to the parent also operates to exclude liability to the child. And by s 1A(4), this provision also applies to claims in respect of infertility treatments under s 1A. But the provision is of little impact, because such exclusion of liability operates to the same extent and subject to the same restrictions as liability in the parent's own case: and by virtue of s 2(1) of the Unfair Contract Terms Act 1977 and s 65 of the Consumer Rights Act 2015, as we have seen, a defendant acting in the course of a business cannot by reference to any contract term or notice exclude or restrict his liability for death or personal injury resulting from negligence. In product liability claims under the Consumer Protection Act 1987 the same result is achieved directly, by making s 1(6) inapplicable[121] and by prohibiting exclusions from liability under that Act.[122] **5.60**

(c) Contributory negligence Third, contributory negligence by a parent also is a defence. Section 1(7) provides: **5.61**

> If in the child's action under this section it is shown that the parent affected shared the responsibility for the child being born disabled, the damages are to be reduced to such extent as the court thinks just and equitable having regard to the extent of the parent's responsibility.[123]

This gives a partial or complete defence to a defendant on grounds equivalent to the contributory negligence of a parent. In so providing the Act recognizes an injustice which would otherwise result to a wrongdoer who was made to pay damages in full when his or her fault was slight compared with that of the parent. The result is that (save in motoring claims) a child may have his or her damages severely reduced by reason of the mother's responsibility, and yet because of her exemption from liability have no right to recover the balance of the

---

[119] *Osborne v London and North Western Railway* (1888) 21 QBD 220, 223–34 *per* Wills J; *Smith v Baker* [1891] AC 325, 355 (HL).
[120] See para 5.47.
[121] Consumer Protection Act 1987, s 6(3)(c).
[122] ibid, s 7.
[123] By s 1A(4), this provision also applies to claims in respect of infertility treatments under s 1A.

compensation.[124] It is apparent, then, that just as a mother is entitled to prefer her interests over those of the foetus, so she is not bound to take care for the benefit of the foetus.

(ix) Radiation injuries

5.62 The Nuclear Installations Act 1965 imposes a strict liability on the licensee of a nuclear site to pay compensation to those injured by a nuclear incident, and the Act of 1976 provides for the relevant provisions to apply for the benefit of children subsequently born disabled due to radiation.

5.63 Anything which affects a man in his ability to have a normal, healthy child, or affects a woman in that ability or so affects her when she is pregnant that her child is born with disabilities which would not otherwise have been present, is an injury for the purposes of the 1965 Act.[125] If a child is born disabled as the result of such an injury, and this is caused by a breach of a duty under that Act, then the child's injuries are to be regarded as injuries caused on the same occasion, and by the same breach of duty, as was the injury to the parent.[126] However, and once again, compensation is not payable in cases where the injury to the parent preceded the time of the child's conception and at that time either or both of the parents knew the risk of their child being born disabled.[127] Damages also may be reduced by the contributory fault of the parent within the meaning of the 1965 Act.[128]

C. Claims by Living Children for 'Wrongful Life'

1. 'Wrongful life' claims at common law

(i) Introduction

5.64 In the preceding section we considered a child's claim in respect of prenatal injuries. Quite different is a child's claim for what is usually known as 'wrongful life'. This commonly is a claim by a child who is born with a disability alleging negligence by the medical advisers of his or her mother or father in failing to diagnose or warn about the disability or risk of disability. So the gist of the claim is for the child's loss in being born with an existing disability, not for his or her loss in suffering a prenatal injury which has been caused by the defendant.[129]

(ii) United Kingdom authority

5.65 In *McKay v Essex AHA*[130] the Court of Appeal considered claims arising from the birth of a child born disabled as a result of an infection of rubella suffered by the mother during

[124] See P J Pace, 'Civil Liability for Pre-Natal Injuries' (1977) 40 MLR 141, 157 for arguments that this provision is unfair and inconsistent with the Law Commission's wish to avoid bitterness in the family.

[125] Congenital Disabilities (Civil Liability) Act 1976, s 3(2).

[126] ibid, s 3(3).

[127] ibid, s 3(5).

[128] ibid, s 3(4). 'Fault' in this context means an act which is committed with the intention of causing harm to any person or property or with reckless disregard for the consequences of the act: Nuclear Installations Act 1965, s 13(6).

[129] The expressions 'wrongful life' and, below, 'wrongful conception' and 'wrongful birth' have been criticized as emotive and as implicitly denigrating life; see H Teff, 'The Action for "Wrongful Life" in England and the United States' (1985) 34 ICLQ 423, 427–28. In *Harriton v Stephens* (2006) 226 CLR 52 at [8]–[13] (HCA), Kirby J recommends the expression 'wrongful suffering' rather than 'wrongful life'. The use of these expressions in this text is conventional and is not intended to carry any moral judgment or to point towards any particular conclusion.

[130] *McKay v Essex AHA* [1982] QB 1166 (CA).

pregnancy. One claim brought by the child was that, but for the negligence of the defendants in managing the pregnancy, the mother would have had a lawful abortion and the child would not have suffered entry into a life in which her injuries were highly debilitating, and distress and loss and damage. It was clear that the injuries resulted not from the negligence but from the untreated rubella, and the claim by the child was therefore analysed as one for negligently allowing her to be born alive in an injured condition. The court was satisfied that it should be struck out, for two main reasons.

First, a claim of this kind was thought to be contrary to public policy, as being inconsistent with the concept of the sanctity of human life. As expressed by Stephenson LJ,[131] the claim would mean regarding the life of a handicapped child as not only less valuable than the life of a normal child, but so much less valuable that it was not worth pursuing. Second, a court could not evaluate non-existence for the purpose of awarding damages for life or for the denial of non-existence. Ackner LJ[132] pointed out that the injuries were caused by the rubella and not by the doctor. The child's complaint was that she was allowed to be born at all, given the existence of her prenatal injuries. Thus, compensation had to be based on a comparison between the value of non-existence and the value of her existence in a disabled state. But how could a court begin to evaluate non-existence, 'the undiscovered country from whose bourne no traveller returns?' No comparison was possible and therefore no damage could be established which a court could recognize. This objection went to the root of the whole cause of action. **5.66**

In *Whitehead v Searle*,[133] where a child was born suffering from spina bifida after a health authority had failed to detect his disability, it was common ground, applying *McKay*, that the child had no cause of action against the authority. His mother had a cause of action for disability expenses,[134] but she had committed suicide before her claim had been resolved. Following her death, the child's father took the advice of the defendants, a barrister and a firm of solicitors, and settled a claim by the estate against the health authority. He subsequently brought a claim against the solicitors, both on behalf of the estate and in his personal capacity, alleging, inter alia, negligence in failing to bring the mother's claim to a successful outcome before the date of her death.[135] The father's personal claim will be examined later on.[136] As regards the claim on behalf of the estate, Laws LJ pointed out that the child could not have been substituted as claimant for his mother after her death, and accordingly the court should not proceed in an action on behalf of the estate on the footing that the defendants owed a duty to recover for the mother what would prove, albeit after the event, to exceed the estate's entitlement. The solicitors should not be held liable for failure to secure for the estate what on the full facts amounted to an uncovenanted windfall. The estate could only pursue a wrongful birth action for damages limited to the cost of care and loss of earnings incurred by the mother prior to her death, together with general damages for pain and loss of amenity suffered during her lifetime. Had the action been brought to a successful conclusion before her death, the recoverable damages would have extended to the costs of care into the future. But, Laws LJ said, 'the law should not speculate when it knows'. Here the mother had committed suicide and would not in fact incur the future losses, and they were, therefore, irrecoverable by the estate. **5.67**

[131] ibid, 1180.
[132] ibid, 1189.
[133] [2009] 1 WLR 549 (CA).
[134] See para 5.126.
[135] He also made a secondary claim that owing to the negligence of both defendants the mother's action had been settled at an undervalue.
[136] See paras 5.141–5.144.

(iii) American authority

5.68 A number of American cases were considered in *McKay v Essex AHA*, and some of the thinking is illustrated by three of them. In *Gleitman v Cosgrove*[137] the Supreme Court of New Jersey by a majority rejected a claim by a child born disabled as a result of intra-uterine rubella on the grounds that the action did not give rise to damages cognizable in law, in that a child could not complain that it would have been better off not being born. So *Gleitman* reached the same conclusion as in *McKay*.

5.69 However, a different approach was taken in *Curlender v Bio-Science Laboratories*,[138] where the Californian Court of Appeal considered a case in which it was alleged that, as a result of negligently conducted genetic tests, a child was born suffering from Tay-Sachs disease. The court, accepting that the real crux of the problem was whether the breach of duty was the proximate cause of an injury cognizable at law, was able to identify as such an injury not the physical defect (for which the defendant was not responsible) nor the birth alone, but the composite concept of 'the birth of the plaintiff with such defect'. It therefore ruled that damages could be quantified for the pain and suffering to be endured during the limited lifespan available to the child and any special pecuniary loss resulting from the child's impaired condition.

5.70 This development was curtailed by the Supreme Court of California in *Turpin v Sortini*.[139] In this case the court considered the claim by a child that clinicians had been negligent in failing to advise her parents that the deafness of an elder sister was hereditary. The claim was for 'general damages for being deprived of the fundamental right of a child to be born as a whole, functional human being without total deafness',[140] and special damages were also claimed for expenses necessary to treat the hereditary illness. Unlike the *Curlender* court, that in *Turpin* rejected the claim for general damages. Taking into account the benefits of life itself as well as the detriment of the affliction, it held that because of the incalculable nature of both elements of the harm–benefit equation, a reasoned, non-arbitrary award of general damage was simply not obtainable.[141] But special damages were allowed for the extraordinary expenses of specialized teaching, training, and hearing equipment as there was no benefit or amenity enjoyed by the plaintiff which could fairly be set off against these requirements.

5.71 While the approach taken in the US to claims for wrongful life is not uniform, there is nonetheless a widespread reluctance to countenance the action. In twenty-four states it has been denied,[142] although in two the courts have followed the decision in *Turpin*.[143]

(iv) Australian authority

5.72 In *Harriton v Stephens*,[144] the plaintiff's mother contracted rubella while she was pregnant, and as a consequence of the infection the appellant was born suffering from severe congenital disabilities. She sued her mother's doctor, who had failed to diagnose the rubella,

137 227 A 2d 689 (1967).

138 165 Cal Rptr 477 (Cal CA, 1980).

139 *Turpin v Sortini* 643 P 2d 954 (Sup Ct Cal, 1982).

140 ibid, 956.

141 ibid, 964.

142 For the list, see *Harriton v Stephens* (2006) 226 CLR 52 at n 102 (HCA).

143 *Harbeson v Parke-Davis Inc* (1983) 656 P 2d 483 (Wash Sup Ct); *Procanik v Cillo* (1984) 478 A 2d 755 (NJ Sup Ct).

144 (2006) 226 CLR 52 (HCA); A Grey, '*Harriton v Stephens*: Life, Logic and Legal Fictions' (2006) 28 Syd LR 545; K Warner, (2007) 123 LQR 209; H Teff, (2007) 15 Tort L Rev 7; D Stretton, 'Wrongful Life and the Logic of Non-Existence' (2006) 30 Melb ULR 972; T Faunce and S Jefferys, 'Abandoning the Common Law: Medical Negligence, Genetic Tests and Wrongful Life in the Australian High Court'

alleging that she had suffered damage in living her profoundly disabled life. The claim failed in the High Court of Australia, by a six to one majority. Crennan J was satisfied that the damage claimed was not amenable to being determined by the application of ordinary legal method, for had the respondent not been negligent the appellant would not be living at all. Damages ordinarily were measured on the basis of the compensatory principle, but a comparison between a life with disabilities and non-existence was impossible. Relevant concerns of policy also indicated that the claim should be rejected. First, there would be conflict between the interests of the mother and the interests of the child and, indeed, the prospect of an action by a child against his or her own mother. Second, it was odious and repugnant to devalue the life of a disabled person by suggesting that such a person would have been better off not to have been born into a life with disabilities. Third, there was a lack of certainty about the degree of disability that could potentially give rise to a claim. Fourth, to allow a disabled person to claim his or her own existence as actionable damage would be inconsistent with statutes prohibiting differential treatment of the disabled and with the law's sanction of those who take a life. So the claim could not be reconciled with values expressed generally in the common law and statute. Life with disabilities, like life, was not actionable.

Kirby J delivered a strongly argued dissent. He considered it was arguable that a life of severe and unremitting suffering was worse than non-existence and that, in principle, this was a loss that should be recoverable in an action brought by or for the child. Awarding damages would enable the child to lead a more dignified existence; the action would be unlikely to provoke familial discord; admitting a claim against a health care professional would say nothing about admitting a claim against a mother; the availability of a remedy for the parents was irrelevant; and likely advances in genetic science, making it impossible to know the consequences of accommodating the claim, were not a reason for putting the common law into deep freeze. **5.73**

In *Waller v James*,[145] decided at the same time as *Harriton*, the plaintiff's disability was caused by his father's pre-conception condition. The father had a genetic deficiency known as anti-thrombin 3 deficiency (AT3 deficiency) which was genetically transmittable and could give rise to cerebral thrombosis in his children. He and his wife sought advice from the defendant obstetrician and gynaecologist concerning *in vitro* fertilization, but the defendant did not investigate Mr Waller's AT3 deficiency and did not advise Mr and Mrs Waller about its potential consequences. Mrs Waller became pregnant and gave birth to a son with a genetic AT3 deficiency which, after his birth, caused cerebral thrombosis. Had Mr and Mrs Waller been advised about Mr Waller's AT3 deficiency they would have ensured that an embryo without the AT3 deficiency was implanted in Mrs Waller, or used donor sperm, or obtained a lawful termination of Mrs Waller's pregnancy. And, had another embryo been used, Mrs Waller might have given birth to another child, but that child would not have been the plaintiff. **5.74**

(2007) 14 JLM 469; D Morgan and B White, 'Everyday Life and the Edges of Existence: Wrongs with No Name or the Wrong Name' (2010) 26 PN 39.

[145] (2006) 226 CLR 136 (HCA). The parents in this case also brought a claim, but in *Waller v James* [2015] NSWCA 232 it was held that the risk of the child suffering a stroke was not a risk of the same kind as being born with AT3 deficiency but was encompassed within the normal risks of pregnancy and IVF that the appellants were willing to accept. In those circumstances, the harm suffered by the child as a result of the stroke was not within the scope of the risk created by the respondent's negligence and was not relevantly foreseeable, and it was therefore too remote to be recoverable.

5.75 The High Court of Australia decided, by the same majority, that this claim too should fail. The conclusion reached in *Harriton* that the damage alleged—a life with disabilities—was not legally cognizable in the sense required to found a duty of care applied equally in, and disposed of, the instant case.

(v) New Zealand authority

5.76 *Cumberland v Accident Compensation Corporation*[146] is a decision in New Zealand concerning an accident compensation claim by a mother who gave birth to a child suffering from spina bifida following an ultrasound scan where the radiologist failed to identify the condition. In the first instance judgment Faire J observed, obiter, that any claim by the child would amount to one of 'wrongful life'. His Honour referred to the argument accepted in *McKay*,[147] that to entertain a claim where the mother's position was that she would have aborted the foetus had she not been misadvised would be contrary to public policy as a violation of the sanctity of human life, and expressed his entire agreement with this sentiment.[148]

(vi) Disadvantaged life

5.77 Claims for what has been termed 'disadvantaged life' are particularly controversial. There are a number of examples in the US. In *Zepeda v Zepeda*[149] an illegitimate child sued his father for conferring on him the status of illegitimacy by fraudulently inducing his mother to have sexual relations with a promise of marriage when he was already married. In *Williams v State of New York*[150] a child who was conceived as a result of the rape of the mother when she was a patient in a state mental hospital asserted that the conception resulted from negligence in the hospital, and that in consequence she was deprived of property rights, of a normal childhood and home life, and of proper parental care, support and rearing, and caused to bear the status of illegitimacy. In *Stills v Gratton*[151] a child alleged that, as a result of a negligently performed abortion, he was born out of wedlock and 'various reasons' affected him to his detriment.

5.78 All of these remarkable claims failed. The courts have refused to recognize the social incidents of existence itself as 'injury' for the purposes of the law of negligence. Moreover, and not surprisingly, there has been a strong policy element involved, with the courts drawing attention to the implications of such claims:

> It is not the suits of illegitimates which give us concern, great in numbers as these may be. What does disturb us is the nature of the new action and the related suits which would be encouraged. Encouragement would extend to all others born into the world under conditions which they might regard as adverse. One might seek damages for being born of a certain colour, another because of race; one for being born with a hereditary disease, another for inheriting unfortunate family circumstances; one for being born into a large and destitute family, another because a parent has an unsavoury reputation.[152]

5.79 The objections to allowing claims alleging a disadvantaged life are well illustrated by the decision of the Northern Ireland Court of Appeal in *A & B v A Health and Social Services*

---

146 [2011] NZAR 309 (HC), [2014] 2 NZLR 373 (CA).

147 See para 5.65.

148 [2011] NZAR 309, at [77]. The decision was taken on appeal on the question whether the claimant had suffered a personal injury within the meaning of the scheme, as to which see para 5.115.

149 190 NE 2d 849 (Ill CA, 1963).

150 223 NE 2d 343 (NYCA, 1966).

151 127 Cal Rptr 652 (Cal CA, 1976).

152 *Zepeda v Zepeda* 190 NE 2d 849, 858 (Ill CA, 1963) *per* Dempsey PJ. See also *Cowe v Forum Group Inc* 575 NE 2d 630 (Sup Ct Indiana, 1991), a claim for 'wrongful life' based on the rape of the plaintiff's intellectually disabled mother: see A Grubb, (1993) 1 Med L Rev 261.

Trust.[153] The claimants, who were twins, were children born as a result of IVF treatment provided by the defendant to the plaintiffs' mother. The parents of the claimants were white, and they requested that any children born as a result of IVF treatment should have the same skin colour. The defendants used the wrong sperm, and as a result the claimants were obviously darker in complexion than their parents. They sought damages from the defendant alleging personal injuries, loss, and damage, but the court held that their claim had to fail. Girvan LJ said that it would be perverse and objectionable to suggest that children born with a different skin colour to their parents were in some way damaged, disabled, or injured. The fact that they were subjected to intolerant and offensive remarks did not mean that they were damaged by the factors which led the intolerant to make the comments. Underlying this reasoning, although not articulated, was the point that the children were claiming for their 'wrongful life'. If the mother had been inseminated with the 'correct' sperm, any children born as a consequence would have been a different colour, but they also would have been different persons. They could only exist in this world as a result of what had actually happened.

(vii) Actions against parents

There are special policy implications involved in claims by disabled children against their parents for conceiving them or allowing them to be born. The Californian Court of Appeal in *Curlender v Bio-Science Laboratories*[154] contemplated that there could be an action of this kind, but otherwise there is no judicial support.[155] Certainly, it is very hard to see how, say, a mother's decision not to have an abortion could possibly be treated as an actionable wrong. **5.80**

(viii) Appraisal

Let us consider now the arguments as to whether or not a claim for wrongful life ought to be allowed. We should look first at the question of causation. While the doctor does not cause the existence of the disabilities, he or she does cause the child to be born in a disabled condition, by depriving the parents of the opportunity of preventing the birth. In *Harriton* the claim was put on the basis that the medical practitioner was responsible for a 'life with disabilities', and if this can be regarded as loss or damage the negligence certainly is a cause. So there is no separate issue of causation, and we can move on to the question whether the doctor ought to be held liable for causing 'damage' of that kind. **5.81**

The core, and compelling objection to the claim for wrongful life is that life itself cannot be recognized as amounting to a legal injury. Accepting that there is actionable damage requires us to treat the child being born as harm or, in Crennan J's words in *Harriton*, to recognize 'a right of a foetus to be aborted, or an interest of a foetus in its own termination'. The action required a comparison between life with disabilities and non-existence, and that was impossible. Her Honour pointed out that there was no field of human learning or discourse, including philosophy and theology, which would allow a person experiential access to non-existence. This was a 'practical forensic difficulty' that was independent of arguments about the value or sanctity of human life.[156] **5.82**

The objection is not simply one of difficulty in quantifying the damage, which is a common enough problem. A focus on quantum is misplaced if the damage itself cannot be identified. **5.83**

[153] [2011] NICA 28; Sheldon, S, 'Only Skin Deep? The Harm of Being Born a Different Colour to One's Parents' (2011) 19 Med L Rev 657.

[154] 165 Cal Rptr 477, 488 (Cal CA, 1980).

[155] See, eg, *McKay v Essex AHA* [1982] QB 1166, 1181 (CA); *Harriton v Stephens* (2006) 226 CLR 52, [205], [250] (HCA).

[156] *Harriton v Stephens*, n 155, [245], [254].

This point undermines the decision in California in *Turpin*, and the dissent of Kirby J in *Harriton*, according to which the child can at least recover special damages, on the basis that he or she would not have had any economic needs had the defendant medical adviser exercised reasonable care. But the presence of financial costs is not in itself sufficient to allow the award of damages in the absence of a determination that the defendant has caused legally cognizable harm.[157]

5.84 And what about the measure of damages? Is a comparison between life with disabilities and non-existence necessarily impossible? Kirby J in *Harriton* was prepared to hold that a plaintiff can seek to show that life with disabilities should be treated as being worse than non-existence. But even assuming that we can ask this question, there is no sensible way in which it can be answered. Crennan J pointed out that judges normally can determine that there is physical damage based on their common experience or on the evidence of experts. But in the present case this conclusion can be reached only on the basis of pure hypothesis or imagination. And there can be no comparison between the disabled plaintiff and a hypothetical healthy child,[158] for a plaintiff in a wrongful life action could never have had a different and better life.

5.85 Turning to policy matters, a fundamental concern, expressed in particular in *McKay* in England and *Gleitman* in the US, is that recognition of the claim would offend the deeply held societal belief in the sanctity of human life. This contention must be viewed with considerable caution, for we need to assess it in the light of such societal changes as liberalized abortion laws, developments in the law governing lawful discontinuance of medical treatment, and decriminalization of suicide. Certainly life cannot always be regarded as a blessing, nor the sanctity of life as a moral absolute. Yet an associated and significant concern is the perception that the claim is demeaning to disabled persons. In *Harriton* Crennan J observed that it was 'odious and repugnant' to devalue the life of a disabled person by suggesting that he or she would have been better off not to have been born. Kirby J, by contrast, argued that the claim would provide 'practical empowerment' for the plaintiff, who would gain financial assistance and greater opportunities in life. But disabled persons may well regard the claim as insulting rather than empowering.[159] The negative reaction from groups representing disabled persons to the decision of the Cour de Cassation in the *Perruche* case in France,[160] where a claim was admitted, well illustrates the point.[161]

5.86 Second, if the action is to be allowed, the question whether a claim lies against the child's mother or father must be considered. Numerous commentators support the wrongful life action,[162] but others have noted that there are not similar loud calls to permit disabled children to sue their parents.[163] Indeed, it is not easy to see why parents should not be held liable in just the same way.

[157] N Priaulx, 'Conceptualising Harm in the Case of the Unwanted Child' (2002) 9 European Journal of Health Law 337, 342.

[158] This was the solution favoured by the Israeli Supreme Court in *Zeitzov v Katz* (1986) 40 (2) PD 85; D Heyd, 'Are Wrongful Life Claims Philosophically Valid? A Critical Analysis of a Recent Court Decision' (1986) 21 Israel Law Review 574.

[159] W Hensel, 'The Disabling Impact of Wrongful Birth and Life Actions' (2005) 40 Harvard Civil Rights-Civil Liberties L Rev 174.

[160] *X c Mutuelle d'Assurance du Corps Sanitaire Francais (Perruche)* (2000) JCP 2293; Cour de Cassation Caw No 9913701.

[161] See M Lysaught, 'Wrongful Life? The Strange Case of Nicholas Perruche' (2002) Human Life Review 165; J Ewing, 'The *Perruche* Case' [2002] Journal of Law and Family Studies 317.

[162] See para 5.89.

[163] P Dimopoulos and M Bagaric, 'The Moral Status of Wrongful Life Claims' (2003) 32 CLWR 35, 44; and see *Harriton v Stephens* (2006) 226 CLR 52, [250] (HCA).

This leads us to a third concern, that there is a potential conflict of interest between the mother and the foetus. The defendant's duty, if recognized, requires that advice be given to the mother about risks to the foetus. So the child's interest can only be promoted through the mother, pursuant to her decision to abort. Yet a court cannot infer from a mother's decision to terminate that this course is in the best interest of the foetus.[164] An abortion may well be sought for relatively trivial reasons or purely in the mother's or the father's interests. Further, at the time of the decision the prognosis for the child may be quite uncertain. So it is difficult to see how, in many or most cases, the decision can or will be made in the interests of the foetus. **5.87**

Fourth, we must ask how it can be determined whether a disability is sufficiently serious that non-existence has to be regarded as preferable. The quality of and satisfaction with life of even seriously disabled people is infinitely variable and may be unknowable. A court's decision might be regarded as a 'crude and speculative' value judgment,[165] lacking any adequate evidential foundation. And how can the court decide where the line ought to be drawn? We can reasonably question whether it would be desirable for the courts to make decisions about the 'loss' suffered by claimants in living their lives with their particular capacities and unique genetic profiles. **5.88**

Many commentators consider that the objections to wrongful life claims are overstated and that policy supports the action.[166] They point to the needs of the child, the dictates of justice, the notion that fault should be compensable, the denial of the child's autonomy in having no choice but to lead an impaired life, the analogy that may be drawn with claims for wrongful birth, and the contrast with s 1A of the Congenital Disabilities (Civil Liability) Act 1976.[167] But it is strongly arguable that the objections are intractable and render the claims untenable.[168] The Law Commission was clearly of this view, recommending that wrongful life claims be excluded from its proposed statutory remedy for disabled children,[169] and this recommendation was brought into effect in the ensuing legislation.[170] As **5.89**

164 *Harriton v Stephens*, ibid, [247] (HCA).

165 Dimopoulos and Bagaric, 'The Moral Status of Wrongful Life Claims', n 163, 63.

166 H Teff, 'The Action for "Wrongful Life" in England and the United States' (1985) 34 ICLQ 423; A Jackson, 'Wrongful Life and Wrongful Birth' (1996) 17 J Legal Medicine 349; A Shapira, 'Wrongful Life Lawsuits for Faulty Genetic Counselling: Should the Impaired Newborn Be Entitled to Sue?' [1998] J Medical Ethics 372; M Strasser, 'Wrongful Life, Wrongful Birth, Wrongful Death and the Right to refuse Treatment' (1999) 64 Missouri L Rev 29; A Morris and S Santier, 'To Be or Not to Be: Is That the Question? Wrongful Life and Misconceptions' (2003) 11 Med L Rev 167; G Kapterian, '*Harriton, Waller* and Australian Negligence Law: Is There a Place for Wrongful Life?' (2006) 13 JLM 336; M Fordham, 'A Life Less Ordinary—The Rejection of Actions for Wrongful Life' (2007) 15 TLJ 123; E Ellis and B McGivern, 'The Wrongfulness or Rightfulness of Actions for Wrongful Life' (2007) 15 Tort L Rev 135; A Ruda, 'I Didn't Ask to be Born: Wrongful Life from a Comparative Perspective' (2010) 1 JETL 204; R Scott, 'Reconsidering "Wrongful Life" in England after Thirty Years: Legislative Mistakes and Unjustifiable Anomalies' (2013) 72 CLJ 115.

167 See paras 5.47, 5.101.

168 C Stolker, 'The Limits of Liability and Beyond' (1994) 43 ICLQ 521; Dimopoulos and Bagaric, 'The Moral Status of Wrongful Life Claims', n 163; W Hensel, 'The Disabling Impact of Wrongful Birth and Life Actions' (2005) 40 Harvard Civil Rights-Civil Liberties L Rev 174, 179–80; B Steininger, 'Wrongful Life and Wrongful Birth: Basic Questions' (2010) 1 JETL 125. R Perry, 'It's a Wonderful Life' (2008) 93 Cornell L Rev 329, advocates a contractual solution, basing the child's action on the claim that the defendant promised the parents that the child would be born without a certain defect. The crucial advantage is that this theory depends on a comparison between reality (life with disability) and the promised state (life without disability).

169 Report No 60, n 74, para 90.

170 See paras 5.97–5.98.

for the common law, the overwhelming trend in the decisions is hostile to the action, and *Whitehead v Searle*[171] shows that judicial thinking about the question remains unchanged.

(ix) Events which cause injury and birth

5.90 So far we have considered cases at common law where prenatal occurrences cause injury (in which damages claims by children may lie) and where they cause birth (where *McKay, Harriton* and similar decisions prevent such claims). Situations may, however, arise, particularly in a pre-conception context, in which an occurrence can cause both the injury and the birth. Examples include the negligent supply of damaged sperm for artificial insemination or of a contraceptive pill which proves both ineffective and damaging to a subsequently born child. Or there may be over-prescription of a fertility drug, leading to a multiple pregnancy which, by reason of its multiplicity, results in births so premature that the children suffer the disabilities associated with premature birth. More dramatically, the Law Commission asked whether a child ought to have an action against a man suffering from syphilis who had intercourse with a woman without telling her that he was infected.[172] There is some justice in the Commission's view that in such a case there should be compensation, not for the fact of being born, but for the disability itself. This case, it said, is not properly called a wrongful life action.[173] But this is questionable, for in cases where the defendant has caused both life and injury it may still be true that the child would not otherwise have been born at all, and that he or she sues in respect of a life which could not have been a different and better one.

5.91 The decision of the British Columbia Court of Appeal in *Cherry v Borsman*[174] gives support for a claim of this kind. The defendant attempted an abortion, but negligently failed and in so doing injured the foetus. The child subsequently born sued not for wrongful life but for injuries sustained in the procedure. Before trial the surgeon admitted liability to the mother in failing to conclude that the operation had failed and thus allow her to have a second operation to terminate the pregnancy. As regards the child's claim, it was argued on behalf of the surgeon that he owed no duty to protect the foetus because that was inconsistent with the duty to the mother to terminate. However, the court held that the surgeon owed a duty of care to the mother to perform his task properly but at the same time owed a duty of care to the foetus not to harm it if he should fail in meeting the duty of care he owed to the mother. It is apparent, then, that the court allowed the claim for injuries which resulted from the very procedure which, because it was negligently performed, permitted the pregnancy to continue and the infant plaintiff to be born.

5.92 More recent decisions in Canada recognize that a doctor cannot be held subject to conflicting duties to the mother and to the child. In *Lacroix v Dominique*[175] a doctor failed to warn a patient contemplating pregnancy of the risks to a foetus posed by her medication for epilepsy. The court held that to recognize a duty to the foetus would create a conflict with the doctor's duty to the mother to prescribe a drug she needed. If fully informed, the mother would have avoided pregnancy, so but for the negligence the child would not have been born, and the claim accordingly was held to fail. In *Bovingdon v Hergott*,[176] in another variation, the defendant prescribed a fertility drug to a patient which was the first link in a chain of causation that led to the conception of twins and damage caused by their premature birth. By failing to give full information to the mother to allow her to make an informed decision whether to take the drug, the doctor caused or contributed to the birth, but did not

---

171 [2009] 1 WLR 549 (CA); see para 5.67.
172 Law Commission Report.
173 Report No 60, n 74, para 88.
174 (1992) 99 DLR (4th) 487 (BCCA).
175 (2001) 202 DLR (4th) 121 (Man CA).
176 (2008) 290 DLR (4th) 126 (Ont CA).

cause the damage. It could not be said that the children had a right to a drug-free birth, and the defendant had no duty to the unborn children in prescribing the drug to the mother.

The different ways of analysing claims such as these were considered in *Paxton v Ramji*.[177] In this case, as we have seen, a mother's medication for acne caused severe disabilities in her subsequently conceived child. The court noted that, on the one hand, the duty on the doctor was to ensure the child was not conceived, making her claim one for wrongful life. On the other hand, the doctor's duty was to refuse to prescribe the medication to a woman of child-bearing potential, and if this duty was discharged the child would have been born healthy. So the court preferred not to decide the case by categorizing the claim as one or the other. Rather, it was held that the doctor owed no duty of care to the child, primarily because of the actual or potential conflict of duties which would be owed to the patient and to the child. **5.93**

A comparable problem was considered by the Supreme Court of Massachusetts in *Payton v Abbott Laboratories*.[178] The plaintiffs were women whose mothers had ingested during pregnancy the drug diethylstilbetrol (DES) which was manufactured by the defendants. The drug was designed to prevent the mothers from miscarrying, but it could cause abnormalities in their daughters. Accordingly, the one drug could be responsible both for giving life and for causing injury to the 'DES daughters'. The claims, however, were not for 'wrongful life' but only for injury. The allegation was that the defendants were negligent in marketing the drug without adequate testing or warnings. The plaintiffs contended that, just as rescuers have a duty to exercise reasonable care in their efforts to save or protect the lives of others, so by analogy the defendants as manufacturers of a drug designed to preserve life were under a duty to exercise reasonable care in connection with their drug. It was however pointed out that the analogy was not exact, because whereas in a 'rescue' case the plaintiff might be better off if no attempt had been made to save her than if an attempt had been made negligently, in a DES case she would simply not have been born but for the drug, and just could not say that in those circumstances she would have been better off than if born, albeit injured, as a result of its use by the mother. In those circumstances the claims were rejected as if they had been claims for wrongful life, the court concluding that 'the provider of the probable means of the plaintiff's very existence should not be liable for unavoidable, collateral consequences of the use of that means'.[179] **5.94**

However, it is not in every case that collateral injurious consequences are 'unavoidable'. Perhaps a drug manufacturer could still be liable for negligently failing to eliminate the dangerous side effects from a life-giving drug. More generally, it may be objected that accepting the argument that a disability should be non-compensable because the defendant caused the life which bears the disability, is permitting the defendant to rely on the child's very existence to defeat a claim.[180] Since the courts prevent a plaintiff from relying on his or her existence to raise a 'wrongful life' claim, should they not in fairness prevent a defendant from seeking to rely upon it to defeat a child's claim? But the argument does not meet the objection that legally cognizable damage cannot be identified in cases where, but for the defendant's negligence, the child would not have been conceived or born. **5.95**

---

177 (2009) 299 DLR 4th 614 (Ont CA); see para 5.34.

178 *Payton v Abbott Laboratories* 437 NE 2d 171 (Sup Ct Jud Mass, 1982).

179 ibid, 182.

180 See the remarks of Lord Osborne in *P's Curator Bonis v Criminal Injuries Compensation Board* 1997 SLT 1180, 1200. Considering a child born as a result of incestuous rape with disabilities due to consanguinity he said, obiter: 'I consider that (a jury) would accept that the birth of the child and its disabilities were both directly attributable to the same criminal act.'

5.96 To be distinguished from the above occurrences, each of which may have the double effect of causing both life and injury, are circumstances where one act or event causes injury and another causes life. Let us suppose that a gynaecologist negligently damages a foetus, and then goes on negligently to fail to warn the parents of what has happened with the result that they are deprived of the opportunity, which would have been accepted, of a lawful abortion: in the result the child is born disabled. There is a good argument that in such a case the child could succeed in an action against the gynaecologist by contending that the dominant event was the intra-uterine injury, and that the gynaecologist could not escape liability for the consequences of that act by relying on a further act of negligence, saying that if he had been more careful the plaintiff would never have been born, and that the action was really only one for wrongful life.

2. 'Wrongful life' claims under the Congenital Disabilities (Civil Liability) Act 1976

(i) Intention of the statute

5.97 The Law Commission in its *Report on Injuries to Unborn Children* considered that no claim should lie by statute for wrongful life.[181] The Commission recognized that to justify the action it was necessary to argue that the child would have been better off not to have been born, that it would be difficult to establish a norm with which the disabled plaintiff could be compared, and that any such cause of action could place an almost intolerable burden on medical advisers in their socially and morally exacting role. Furthermore, the danger that doctors would be under subconscious pressures to advise abortions in doubtful cases through fear of an action for damages was thought to be a real one.

5.98 It was therefore the clear intention of the legislature that the Congenital Disabilities (Civil Liability) Act 1976 should allow no such cause of action. It sought to achieve this result by making provision in s 1(1) for civil liability for an 'occurrence' causing a child to be born disabled, and defining the nature of the occurrence in s 1(2).[182] As we have seen already, the occurrence must be one which:

(a) affected either parent of the child in his or her ability to have a normal, healthy child; or
(b) affected the mother during her pregnancy, or affected her or the child in the course of its birth, so that the child is born with disabilities which would not otherwise have been present.

In *McKay v Essex AHA*[183] Stephenson LJ and Ackner LJ, consistently with the views of the Law Commission,[184] interpreted s 1(2)(b) as being worded so as to import the assumption that, but for the occurrence giving rise to a disabled birth, the child would have been born normal and healthy, not that it would not have been born at all. They thus concluded that the Act excluded claims by children for wrongful life.[185] Griffiths LJ took the same view.[186]

(ii) Appraisal

5.99 Commentators have raised three reasons for doubting this conclusion. The first relies on the wording of s 4(5), which states that the Act 'replaces any law in force before its passing, whereby a person could be liable to a child in respect of disabilities with which it might

181 Report No 60, n 74, para 89.
182 See para 5.45.
183 [1982] QB 1166 (CA).
184 Report No 60, n 74, Appendix 1, note 6.
185 *McKay v Essex AHA*, n 183, 1178, 1186–87 (CA).
186 ibid, 1191.

be born'.[187] A 'wrongful life' action is not, so the argument runs, an action 'in respect of disabilities', but rather in respect of life itself: therefore, s 4(5) leaves intact any pre-existing common law right to sue for 'wrongful life'.[188] However, even if the English courts could be persuaded that such actions could be brought at common law, which is extremely doubtful, they would certainly hesitate long before allowing such an interpretation and bypassing the intention of the statute so as to permit a wrongful life claim by a disabled child. In any event the argument fails to convince. We have seen that in *McKay* the claim was formulated on the basis that the medical practitioner was responsible for 'entry into life in which [the plaintiff's] injuries [were] highly debilitating',[189] and in *Harriton* the claim was for the creation of a 'life with disabilities'.[190] The action is in respect of life *and* disabilities. Both come into existence simultaneously at the moment of birth and cannot be separated. Seemingly, then, a 'wrongful life' claim by a child born disabled is 'in respect of disabilities' and is therefore covered by s 4(5) and excluded by s 1(2)(b).

Second, Kennedy and Grubb point out that the *McKay* dicta cited above referred to s 1(2)(b), and not to s 1(2)(a), of the 1976 Act.[191] It is suggested that negligence in a pre-conception context, for example in the course of genetic counselling, could amount to an occurrence which affected the parents' opportunity to have a normal healthy child, and therefore his or her 'ability' so to do within the meaning of s 1(2)(a). By this reasoning, the statute would in fact give the child a remedy in such circumstances, whatever was its intended policy. In this case damages could be computed by reference to the life of the child and not (as in a 'wrongful birth' claim)[192] by reference to the, frequently shorter, life of the caring parent. But there are a number of objections. The 'ability' to have a healthy child in s 1(2)(a) normally refers to a parent's physical capacity to have the healthy child. With this argument it would have to mean the 'opportunity' to have the child. Kennedy and Grubb say that 'ability' could certainly be interpreted in this way, but it seems unlikely that a court would do so.[193] It would clearly be contrary to the intention of the Law Commission and of Parliament, it would lead to an unsatisfactory distinction between pre- and post-conception occurrences, and it would raise intractable difficulties in determining the basis upon which the damages could be computed. It may be added that difficulty in adducing the necessary evidence to establish a right of action of this kind, particularly in relation to proof of cause, would very likely be considerable. **5.100**

Third, Kennedy and Grubb[194] also draw attention to s 1A of the 1976 Act,[195] which allows a child to claim for negligence in the course of infertility treatment, and point to the fact that the section covers negligence in the 'selection' of the embryo that becomes the child. In such a case the child's claim is one for wrongful life, since (but for the negligence) some other embryo would have been selected and the child claimant himself or herself would never have been born. However, it may be that the courts would interpret the whole phrase 'in the course of the selection' so as to restrict claims to those based on acts or omissions during the selection process, rather than on the very act of choice. If they did not, they would have **5.101**

[187] See para 5.54.
[188] J Fortin, 'Is the 'Wrongful Life' Action Really Dead?' (1987) JSWL 306.
[189] See [1982] QB 1166, 1174 (CA).
[190] See (2006) 226 CLR 52, [245] (HCA).
[191] *Medical Law*, n 98, 1551–52.
[192] See para 5.131.
[193] *Medical Law*, n 98.
[194] *Medical Law*, n 98, 1552.
[195] See para 5.47.

no alternative but to quantify the difference between the condition of the disabled claimant as it was in fact on the one hand and his or her non-existence on the other hand, a process from which they will continue to shrink. The alternative, to compare the claimant's disabled state with that of a healthy but hypothetical child who might otherwise have been born had the selection process been different, would be an entirely artificial exercise. The decision at common law of the High Court of Australia in *Waller v James* certainly lends support to the view that such a claim would be rejected.[196]

D. Claims by Parents of Children Born Alive

1. Claims by parents for wrongful conception or birth

(i) Introduction

5.102 Claims against medical professionals by the parents of unwanted children may arise in various factual contexts. Where the patient undergoes an operation designed to prevent conception, there may be negligence in pre-operative counselling (eg a failure to warn of the risk of recanalization of the vas), in the operation itself (eg if the doctor ligates a ligament during an operation for female sterilization rather than a fallopian tube), in post-operative testing (eg a failure to carry out sperm tests properly after vasectomy), or in post-operative counselling (eg if there is a failure to warn of the need to use contraceptives until sperm tests after vasectomy have proved negative).[197] More generally, there may be a failure by an adviser to give appropriate advice about contraception. A claim by the patient in any of these cases may be described as a claim for wrongful conception, because the central allegation is that the defendant ought to be held responsible for not preventing the child from being conceived.

5.103 Claims may also be brought if a child is born after an attempt at an abortion has failed, or if a patient is misinformed that she is not pregnant. Again, there may be negligence in failing to screen for genetic abnormalities, to warn of the risk to a foetus from maternal rubella or chickenpox or to conduct appropriate tests of foetal health during pregnancy. In these cases the mother, or both parents, may allege that negligence by a doctor or radiologist has caused the mother to continue with a pregnancy that is not wanted or no longer wanted and to suffer the expenses of raising the child. These, then, are actions for wrongful birth, as the plaintiff complains about the wrongful continuation of an existing unwanted pregnancy or of an initially wanted pregnancy that the mother would have wished to terminate.

5.104 There is, however, some variation in the terminology. Some commentators have used the term 'wrongful pregnancy' or 'wrongful conception' to denote claims by parents where a child subsequently born is healthy, confining the term 'wrongful birth' to cases where the child is not only unwanted but born with a disability.[198] The distinction between these two categories of claim, however, is not based on any difference in the legal bases for the claims, but only on different factual bases for quantifying damages. Defining 'wrongful conception' claims as those involving an unwanted conception, and 'wrongful birth' claims as

---

[196] See para 5.74.

[197] See A Mullis, 'Wrongful Conception Unravelled' (1993) 1 Med L Rev 320, 321–22.

[198] For example, see *Medical Law*, n 98, 1553, 1586. For the different terminologies see H Teff, 'The Action for "Wrongful Life" in England the United States' (1985) 34 ICLQ 423, 425–26; J K Mason, 'Wrongful Pregnancy, Wrongful Birth and Wrongful Terminology' (2002) 6 Edinburgh L Rev 46.

those where the fault lies in permitting a pregnancy to continue to birth seems preferable as a matter of principle and is supported in the cases.[199]

A further introductory point concerns the question who may be sued in cases of negligently performed sterilizations in the particular circumstances where an action can lie. First, applying ordinary principle, a hospital can be held vicariously liable for the negligence of its employees committed in the course of employment. Second, a hospital may come under a non-delegable duty of care in cases where it has entrusted the care and treatment of its patients to an independent contractor.[200] **5.105**

(ii) The decision in McFarlane

A number of decisions in the 1980s and 1990s allowed parents to recover full damages for the pecuniary and non-pecuniary losses caused by a wrongful conception or birth. For example, in *Emeh v Kensington, Chelsea and Westminster AHA*[201] a mother whose sterilization operation had failed due to the surgeon's negligence, and who subsequently gave birth to a disabled child, recovered damages for her past and future pain and suffering, loss of amenity in looking after the child, loss of earnings, and past and future costs of maintaining the child. In so deciding, the Court of Appeal was satisfied that it was not contrary to public policy to recover damages for the birth of a child. However, in *McFarlane v Tayside Health Board*,[202] where the question was considered for the first time by the House of Lords, the scope for an award of damages was very considerably restricted, and *Emeh* and similar cases were overruled. **5.106**

The facts were straightforward. The pursuers, a married couple with four children, alleged that a surgeon employed by the defendants negligently advised them that a vasectomy had rendered the husband infertile, that they acted on the advice by ceasing to take contraceptive precautions, and that an unplanned child was conceived and born. They then sought to recover damages in respect of various losses associated with the birth of the child. Their Lordships held that the mother could claim general damages for the pain and suffering of pregnancy and childbirth and for certain associated expenses, but that the parents could not recover the costs of bringing up the child. We need to give separate consideration to these two conclusions. **5.107**

(iii) Damages for unwanted pregnancy and birth

(a) The mother's claim The claim in respect of unwanted pregnancy and birth may be called the mother's claim. A majority of their Lordships (Lord Slynn, Lord Steyn, Lord Hope, and Lord Clyde) were agreed that damages could be awarded in respect of the pain, discomfort, distress, and inconvenience of pregnancy and childbirth.[203] There is a degree of support for the recovery as well of some other pregnancy-related expenses: Lord Slynn would allow a claim for associated special damages by way of extra medical expenses, clothes, **5.108**

---

199 *Parkinson v St James and University Hospital NHS Trust* [2002] QB 26 (CA); *Groom v Selby* [2002] Lloyd's Rep Med 1, [18] (CA).

200 *Woodland v Essex County Council* [2014] AC 537; cp *Armes v Nottinghamshire County Council* [2016] QB 739. For an example arising in the present context, see *Byrne v Ryan* [2007] IEHC 207.

201 [1985] QB 1012 (CA); and see *Thake v Maurice* [1986] QB 644 at 670; *Robinson v Salford HA* [1992] 3 Med LR 270; *Allen v Bloomsbury HA* [1993] 1 All ER 651; *Crouchman v Burke* (1997) 40 BMLR 163; *Benaar v Kettering HA* (1988) 138 NLJ Rep 179; cf *Udale v Bloomsbury AHA* [1983] 1 WLR 1098. See generally W V H Rogers, 'Legal Implications of Ineffective Sterilisation' (1985) 5 LS 296.

202 [2000] 2 AC 59 (HL); J Thomson, 'Abandoning the Law of Delict?' 2000 SLT (News) 43; T Weir, 'The Unwanted Child' (2000) CLJ 238; M A Jones, (2001) Tort L Rev 14; A Whitfield, 'The Fallout from *McFarlane*' (2002) 18 PN 234.

203 *McFarlane v Tayside Health Board* [2000] 2 AC 59 (HL), 74, 84, 87, 102; and see generally E Baginska, 'Wrongful Birth and Non-Pecuniary Loss: Theories of Compensation' (2010) 1 JETL 171 at 182.

equipment on birth, and lost earnings;[204] Lord Steyn considered that a claim for the loss suffered by the wife giving up work in the later stages of pregnancy would be sustainable;[205] and Lord Hope would include any financial loss attributable to the pregnancy, including physical or emotional problems or loss of income after birth.[206] On the other hand, Lord Millett would have rejected the claim as formulated, but would have allowed both parents a conventional sum for infringement of their freedom to limit the size of their family.[207] In addition, he would allow the replacement costs of baby equipment if the parents disposed of the items concerned in the belief that they would have no more children.[208] This seemingly would be on ordinary principles relating to liability for negligent advice.

5.109 Damages under this head also have been awarded elsewhere. In the US, broadly speaking, limited damages covering the cost of pregnancy usually are allowed, but the majority of courts draw the line at the costs of rearing the child.[209] In Canada there have been similar developments,[210] and this also is the position in Ireland.[211] In the decision of the High Court of Australia in *Cattanach v Melchior*[212] there was no appeal from an award to the mother of damages for an unwanted pregnancy and birth. And nearly all European systems allow the mother to recover for loss of earnings due to pregnancy.[213]

5.110 **(b) Unwanted pregnancy and birth as personal injury** A separate question is whether unwanted pregnancy and birth can be treated as 'personal injury'. The way in which the harm is classified may affect the outcome in cases not involving a doctor and patient, as where the claimant is the subsequent sexual partner of the patient, or the action is against the manufacturer of a contraceptive. It is clearly relevant to the running of the limitation period.

5.111 Let us consider first some pre-*McFarlane* cases. In *Allen v Bloomsbury HA*[214] Brooke J considered a claim by a mother who was negligently deprived of the opportunity to have a pregnancy terminated to be a claim for damages for personal injuries in relation to the discomfort and pain associated with the continuation of her pregnancy and the delivery of her child, but not in relation to the economic loss in having to pay for the upkeep and care of an unwanted child. The Court of Appeal then considered the matter in *Walkin v South Manchester HA*,[215] where the question in issue was whether a claim for upbringing following a mother's failed sterilization was a claim for 'damages in respect of personal injuries' for limitation purposes.[216] Auld LJ rejected Brooke J's view in *Allen* that an unwanted

[204] *McFarlane*, n 203, 74.
[205] ibid, 84.
[206] ibid, 89.
[207] ibid, 114. See further para 5.135.
[208] ibid, 115.
[209] See, in particular, *Johnson v University Hospitals of Cleveland* 540 NE 2d 1370 (1989), where there is a review of the cases. And see, eg, *Lovelace Medical Center v Mendez* 805 P 2d 603 (1991) (full damages); *Szekeres v Robinson* 745 P 2d 1076 (1986) (no damages); *Public Health Trust v Brown* 388 So 2d 1084 (1980) (limited damages covering the cost of pregnancy but not child rearing costs); *Sherlock v Stillwater Clinic* 260 NW 2d 169 (1977) (child rearing costs allowed but non-financial benefits set off against them). See generally G Sarno, 'Tort Liability for Wrongfully Causing One to be Born' (1978) 83 ALR 3d 15; D Dobbs, *The Law of Torts* (West Group 2000), 794–801.
[210] For a review, see *Kealey v Berezowski* (1996) 136 DLR (4th) 708, 723–41; and see *Bevilacqua v Altenkirk* (2005) 27 CCLT (3d) 75.
[211] *Byrne v Ryan* [2007] IEHC 207.
[212] (2004) 215 CLR 1 (HCA); see para 5.153 below.
[213] C von Bar, *The Common European Law of Torts* (Oxford University Press 1998), vol 1, para 583.
[214] [1993] 1 All ER 651, 658.
[215] [1995] 1 WLR 1543 (CA); A Grubb, (1996) 4 Med L Rev 94.
[216] See para 5.119.

pregnancy created two different causes of action, holding that the unwanted conception, whether caused by negligent advice or negligent surgery, was personal injury in the sense that the resultant physical change in the plaintiff's body was an 'impairment' of her physical condition. Neill LJ agreed, whereas Roch LJ reserved the question as to the nature of the damage in cases of failed male sterilization where the man's loss was purely financial.

Turning now to *McFarlane*, while four of their Lordships accepted that unwanted pregnancy following a failed sterilization amounted to a compensable loss, they did not speak with one voice on the question whether such pregnancy constituted 'personal injury' in an orthodox sense. Lord Slynn said that as the conception and childbirth were unwanted and known to be so by the Health Board it was unnecessary to consider whether there was a personal injury.[217] Lord Steyn rejected a submission that 'the natural processes of conception and childbirth' could not in law amount to personal injury.[218] Lord Hope held that the claim was 'analogous to that which may be made by a pursuer in the case of personal injury'[219] and Lord Clyde thought that the reality of the pain, discomfort, and inconvenience of pregnancy could not be ignored and that this could qualify as a potential head of damages.[220] So there was a variety of approaches, although it is at least clear that the 'pregnancy' claim and the 'upbringing' claim were treated differently, the latter being recognized as a claim for financial loss.[221] **5.112**

In *Parkinson v St James and Seacroft University Hospital NHS Trust*,[222] following *McFarlane*, Hale LJ said that all of their Lordships, in their different ways, recognized that to cause a woman to become pregnant and bear a child against her will was an invasion of her fundamental right to bodily integrity. Some highlighted the interference with bodily autonomy, others the pain, suffering, and loss of amenity. Her Ladyship did not comment on whether this loss can amount to personal injury, but in *Mitchell v Glasgow City Council*[223] (as Baroness Hale) she maintained that an unwanted pregnancy and childbirth were physical harms to the mother. **5.113**

(c) **Personal injury in New Zealand** While the question has not been clearly determined in England, it has however been considered in New Zealand in the context of cover under that country's Accident Compensation Act 2001.[224] There is cover only for 'personal injury', defined as including, inter alia, 'physical injuries to the person',[225] which must be caused, inter alia, by an 'accident' or, in a medical context, be 'medical misadventure' or (since 2005) 'treatment injury'.[226] Where there is cover a common law action is barred,[227] but if there is no cover, any common law action can proceed.[228] Initially, pregnancy was treated simply as a natural physiological condition not amounting to personal injury,[229] but in **5.114**

[217] *McFarlane*, n 203, 74.
[218] ibid, 81.
[219] ibid, 86.
[220] ibid, 102.
[221] See para 5.120. In *Godfrey v Gloucestershire Royal Infirmary NHS Trust* [2003] Lloyd's Rep Med 398, at [35], Leveson J still applied *Walkin* and treated the mother as having a claim for personal injuries.
[222] [2002] QB 206, [58] (CA).
[223] [2009] 2 WLR 481, [75] (HL).
[224] S Todd (gen ed), *The Law of Torts in New Zealand* (7th edn, Thomson Reuters 2016) ch 2.
[225] Accident Compensation Act 2001, s 26(1)(b) (NZ).
[226] ibid, ss 20(2)(b), 32, 33.
[227] ibid, s 317.
[228] *Queenstown Lakes District Council v Palmer* [1999] 1 NZLR 549 (CA).
[229] *L v M* [1979] 2 NZLR 519, 530 *per* Cooke J; *XY v ACC* (1984) 2 NZFLR 376, 380 *per* Jefferies J; *ACC v Auckland Hospital Board* [1980] 2 NZLR 748, 753 *per* Speight J; *SGB v Wellington District Health Board* [2002] NZAR 413; *Accident Compensation Corporation v D* [2008] NZCA 576.

Allenby v H[230] the Supreme Court held, in a unanimous decision, that a patient who suffered mental illness after becoming pregnant following a sterilization procedure carried out by the appellant doctor had suffered 'personal injury', as defined, and was covered for compensation. Elias CJ said that the 2001 Act was concerned with establishing entitlements for impairment, rehabilitation, and treatment; physical impact which was significant enough to support such responses, which clearly included pregnancy, was physical injury within the meaning of the Act. Blanchard J maintained that impregnation was a physical consequence for the victim of a rape, and it followed that impregnation resulting from medical misadventure in the form of a failed sterilization was also a personal injury. It was submitted also that pregnancy was a natural and necessary process and should not be regarded as physical injury to the mother, even if unwanted. But the development of the foetus following impregnation occurred because of medical error, just as in the case of an undetected tumour. It caused significant physical changes to the woman's anatomy which, while natural, still caused discomfort and, ultimately, pain and suffering.[231]

5.115 The principle in *Allenby* was developed in *Cumberland v Accident Compensation Corporation*,[232] where the court held that the continuation of the claimants' pregnancy following the failure by a radiologist to detect spina bifida during an antenatal ultrasound scan was covered for compensation. The misdiagnosis involved significant physical changes to the anatomy of the mother, and bore comparison with an undetected tumour. Assuming that the mother had been deprived of the opportunity lawfully to terminate the pregnancy, and would have taken that opportunity, then, applying *Allenby*, this was personal injury.

5.116 **(d) Appraisal** One commentator has argued that in *McFarlane* the mother's conception was an entirely natural event that her physiological constitution was designed to induce and to accommodate. Furthermore, most women were glad to be able to conceive and to give birth, although this was not true in the instant case. There was an undoubted interference with Mrs McFarlane's autonomy and she suffered pain and anxiety during pregnancy and birth. But her physiological integrity was not compromised and her body returned after delivery to its pre-conception state. So it was difficult to characterize the changes of pregnancy as deleterious or as an impairment of bodily functioning. This was not physical injury in the orthodox sense but was damage of a 'socially constructed' kind.[233] On the other hand, it has been contended that the fact that pregnancy was a 'natural' event was irrelevant, for so were cancer and arthritis. And the objection that some women welcomed pregnancy looked at the question from the wrong perspective: what mattered was whether there was damage to the particular claimant. This admittedly meant that pregnancy might be a personal injury in some cases but not in others, depending on whether the pregnancy was desired, but there was no good reason why this should affect the classification of unwanted pregnancy as actionable damage.[234]

---

[230] [2012] 3 NZLR 425 (SC). The decision says nothing about the costs of bringing up the unplanned child, which very arguably are not covered for compensation: see S Todd, 'Accidental Conception and Accident Compensation' (2012) 28 Jo of Prof Negl 196. *ACC v J* [2016] NZHC 1683 affirms this view.

[231] This conclusion posed a difficulty in potentially opening the door to accident compensation claims in respect of other unwanted pregnancies, such as could result from a bursting condom or from unprotected sexual intercourse, on the argument that the pregnancy would amount to a 'personal injury by an accident'. Blanchard J avoided this conclusion by holding that a woman who chose to engage in sexual intercourse, during which she suffered no physical harm but as a result of which she fell pregnant, could not sensibly be said to have suffered an 'accident' within the statutory definition.

[232] [2014] 2 NZLR 373 (CA).

[233] C Witting, 'Physical Damage in Negligence' [2002] CLJ 189, 192–93.

[234] D Nolan, 'New Forms of Damage in Negligence' (2007) 70 MLR 59, 73–75.

On any view a claim in respect of an unwanted pregnancy is a unique form of 'damage'. Whether it can be characterized as 'physical injury' does not admit of a straightforward answer. The better view perhaps is that while it can be, and has been, treated as an injury, it is not personal injury as ordinarily understood. Taking this view avoids a number of conceptual and practical difficulties arising out of the different ways in which the question can arise. First, personal injury refers naturally to a physical state of affairs that is objectively ascertainable. We can more easily accept that a woman has suffered damage because her pregnancy is unwanted than we can accept that she has been physically injured. Second, how otherwise should we deal with the problem, identified by Roch LJ in *Walkin*, where the only reasons for the pregnancy and subsequent birth being unwanted are financial?[235] In such a circumstance it is not the pregnancy which is unwanted but the financial difficulties. Third, if a claim against a doctor is for failure to diagnose an unwanted pregnancy in time for termination, then the injury (unwanted pregnancy) would pre-date the breach of duty (failure to diagnose), and a condition which was not a physical injury would somehow transmute into a condition which was on the pregnancy continuing. A similar point can be made in relation to a pregnancy that is initially wanted, but there is a failure to diagnose a possible foetal abnormality in time for termination. Fourth, if the criterion for conception amounting to a physical injury is that it is unwanted by the woman, then a woman who wants a child, but has one by a man who does not but becomes a reluctant father only because his vasectomy has, through negligence, failed, would have no personal injury claim herself. Nor would the man, for the failure would have left him as before.[236] His claim, if any, would be for economic loss.[237] **5.117**

If the mother's loss is not personal injury, then arguably this is one good reason why a claim against a doctor by a reluctant mother who is the subsequent sexual partner of the doctor's patient, where the doctor has negligently performed or given advice about the patient's vasectomy operation, will very likely fail.[238] A duty ordinarily is owed with respect to negligently inflicted personal injury, but the recovery of damages is at least much more restricted in the case of damage by way of an invasion of autonomy or which is purely economic. A successful claim against a negligent dispenser of a contraceptive pill or manufacturer of a contraceptive sheath is equally unlikely.[239] **5.118**

The nature of the damage also has limitation consequences. By s 2 of the Limitation Act 1980, the ordinary limitation period for an action founded on tort is six years from the date on which the cause of action accrued.[240] But by s 11(1), in the case of any action for damages for negligence, nuisance or breach of duty where the damages claimed consist of or include 'damages in respect of personal injuries to the plaintiff or any other person', the period is **5.119**

[235] [1995] 1 WLR 1543, 1553 (CA).

[236] *Naylor v Preston AHA* [1987] 1 WLR 938, 971 (CA) *per* Sir John Donaldson MR, cited in *Walkin* [1995] 1 WLR 1543, 1550 *per* Auld LJ.

[237] See Roch LJ in *Walkin* [1995] 1 WLR 1543, 1553 (CA).

[238] See *Goodwill v British Pregnancy Advisory Service* [1996] 1 WLR 1397 (CA), para 5.140. Kennedy and Grubb argue that even if the harm is characterized as physical, liability should still be limited to those within the 'zone of knowledge' of the doctor: *Medical Law*, n 98, 1585.

[239] *Richardson LRC Products* [2000] Lloyd's Rep Med 280 (where a condom was found not to have been defective).

[240] Section 14A provides for an extended time limit in non-personal injury cases where certain facts relevant to the cause of action are not known at the date of accrual. See, for example, *Schumann v Veale Wasbrough* [2013] EWHC 3730 (requirements of s 14A not satisfied in relation to a claim against solicitors and barrister for alleged negligence in giving advice about suing an NHS Trust in respect of the birth of the claimants' disabled child).

three years from the date on which the cause of action accrued or the date of knowledge (if later) of the person injured.[241] In *Pattison v Hobbs*[242] a failed vasectomy case where both parents sued, the Court of Appeal held that the six-year limitation period applied as the claim was not for 'damages in respect of personal injuries' within the meaning of s 11. But as we have seen, in *Walkin v South Manchester HA*,[243] involving a claim for financial loss arising from the birth of a child following a failed laparoscopic tubal diathermy, a majority in the Court of Appeal considered that the claim was 'in respect of personal injuries', that time ran from the moment of conception and that the action was statute-barred. The anomalies and difficulties flowing from this view, as outlined above, are such that it should not be followed. It is arguably inconsistent with the majority view in *McFarlane* in any event.

(iv) Damages for the costs of bringing up an unwanted child

5.120 **(a) The parents' claim** The second head of claim in *McFarlane v Tayside Health Board*[244] was for the costs of bringing up the unplanned child. This, their Lordships were agreed, was a claim for economic loss.[245] It can be called the parents', as opposed to the mother's, claim. We noted at the beginning of this discussion that most of the early decisions at first instance and in the Court of Appeal allowed this kind of claim. But when that of the McFarlanes came before the House of Lords it was unanimously rejected. However, the reasons for this conclusion were varied.

5.121 **(b) Failure to abort or to arrange an adoption** All of their Lordships rejected any suggestion that failure by a pregnant woman to undergo an abortion or arrange an adoption on discovering that she was pregnant could be a new act which broke the chain of causation between the negligence and the birth.[246] Lord Slynn pointed out that there was no legal or moral duty to arrange an abortion or an adoption of an unplanned child.[247] Lord Steyn could not conceive of any circumstances in which the autonomous decision of the parents not to resort to even a lawful abortion could be questioned.[248] And, for similar reasons, the parents' decision not to have the child adopted was plainly natural and commendable. The starting point was the right of parents to make decisions on family planning and, if those plans failed, their right to care for an initially unwanted child. The law respected decisions of parents which were so closely tied to basic freedoms and rights of personal autonomy. Lord Millett said that, save in the most exceptional circumstances (which it was very hard to imagine), it could never be unreasonable for parents or prospective parents to decline to terminate pregnancy or to place the child for adoption.[249]

---

[241] Section 14 defines what is meant by a person's 'date of knowledge'. Further provisions apply if the person injured has died before the expiration of the period.

[242] The Times, 11 November 1985 (CA).

[243] [1995] 1 WLR 1543; see para 5.111.

[244] *McFarlane v Tayside Health Board* [2000] 2 AC 59 (HL); see paras 5.106–5.107.

[245] ibid, 75–76, 79, 89, 99–100, 109; see generally Hogg, M, 'Damages for Pecuniary Loss in Cases of Wrongful Birth' (2010) 1 JETL 156.

[246] In *Emeh v Kensington & Chelsea & Westminster HA* [1985] QB 1012 the Court of Appeal also had taken this view. However, Purchas LJ (at 1027) remarked that if the sole motivation of a plaintiff for continuing a pregnancy was in order to promote an action, that would be at least a factor to be taken into account in deciding whether, on an objective test of unreasonableness, there had been a break in the chain of causation. See also *Goodwill v British Pregnancy Advisory Service* [1996] 2 All ER 161 (CA), where the plaintiff's decision to continue with the pregnancy influenced the court in its view that a claim should be struck out as frivolous, vexatious, and an abuse of process.

[247] *McFarlane,* n 244.

[248] ibid, 81.

[249] ibid, 113.

(c) **Birth of a healthy child as a 'loss'** However, although there was no causal bar, the parents' claim still should fail. Lord Slynn declined to set off the intangible, non-economic benefits of parenthood against the economic costs of caring for the child, regarding this as well-nigh impossible.[250] The choice was between awarding all costs or excluding those for child rearing. He favoured the latter, on the grounds that it was not fair and reasonable to impose liability and the doctor did not assume responsibility for these costs. Lord Steyn focused on the idea of distributive justice.[251] Ordinary citizens would consider that there should be a just distribution of burdens and losses in society and that the law of tort had no business to provide legal remedies consequent upon the birth of a healthy child. This would be founded upon an inarticulate premise as to what was morally acceptable. Lord Hope said that it would not be fair and reasonable to leave the benefits of parenting out of account, yet their value was incalculable.[252] So the costs could not be recovered, because it could not be shown that overall they would exceed the benefits. Lord Clyde thought that relieving the parents of their financial obligations went beyond reasonable restitution for the wrong and that the potential expense was disproportionate to the doctor's culpability.[253] He would allow the mother's claim for solatium, but no other costs. Lastly, Lord Millett accepted the main argument that the birth of a child is a blessing.[254] He said in truth it was a mixed blessing, but society must regard the balance as beneficial. The advantages and disadvantages of parenthood were inextricably bound together, and it would be subversive of the mores of society for parents to enjoy the advantages but transfer the responsibilities to others. His Lordship considered that this reasoning also led to the rejection of the mother's claim for the loss associated with her pregnancy. However, he would allow a conventional sum representing the parents' loss of their personal autonomy and their freedom to limit the size of their family. 5.122

(d) **Loss of earnings** Subsequent cases have tested the limits of the *McFarlane* decision. First, in *Greenfield v Irwin*[255] the principle was held to apply both to a claim for the costs of rearing a child and to a claim for loss of earnings contingent upon the decision of a mother to leave work to care for her child. It was argued for the plaintiff that *McFarlane* had not addressed the issue of earnings loss, and that it was concerned with negligent advice and not, as in the instant case, with an omission in the course of treatment. But the Court of Appeal rejected the suggested distinction, holding that even if the loss could be characterized as one of physical injury caused by omission the policy of *McFarlane* applied in just the same way. 5.123

(e) **Disability expenses** Secondly, the question arose whether a claim might lie where the unplanned child suffers from a disability. In *Parkinson v St James and Seacroft University Hospital NHS Trust*[256] the claimant, a mother of four children living with her husband, 5.124

---

250 ibid, 74–76.

251 ibid, 82.

252 ibid, 97.

253 ibid, 105–06.

254 ibid, 113–14.

255 [2001] 1 WLR 1279 (CA); O Radley-Gardner, 'Wrongful Birth Revisited' (2002) 118 LQR 11; A Grubb, (2001) 9 Med L Rev 54.

256 *Parkinson v St James and Seacroft University Hospital NHS Trust* [2002] QB 206 (CA); O Quick, 'Damages for Wrongful Conception' (2002) 10 Tort L Rev 5; A Grubb, 'Failed Sterilisation: Damages for the Birth of a Disabled Child' (2002) 10 Med L Rev 78. For earlier decisions at first instance, see *Taylor v Shropshire HA* [2000] Lloyd's Rep Med 96 (failed sterilization); *Rand v East Dorset HA* [2000] Lloyd's Rep Med 181 (failure to advise parents of Down's syndrome foetus); *Hardman v Amin* [2000] Lloyd's Rep Med 498 (failure to advise of the risk of foetal deformity due to maternal rubella). For similar decisions in the US, see *Moores v Lucas* 405 So 2d 1022 (1981); *Fassoulas v Ramey* 450 So 2d 822, 824 (1984); *Emerson*

underwent a negligently performed sterilization operation. She later conceived her fifth child, the marriage then broke down, and three months later she gave birth to the child, who suffered from severe disabilities. The Court of Appeal held, in a unanimous decision, that the claimant was entitled to recover damages in respect of the costs of providing for her child's special needs and care relating to his disability, but not for the basic costs of his maintenance. Hale LJ considered that at the heart of *McFarlane* was the feeling that to compensate for the financial costs of bringing up a healthy child was a step too far. A child brought benefits as well as costs, and the only sensible course was to assume that they balanced one another out. Yet there was no reason to take that limitation on recovery any further and to preclude recovery for the extra care and expenditure needed for a disabled child. In so deciding, her Ladyship was concerned not to draw an invidious and unacceptable distinction between the 'worth' of healthy child and of a disabled child. As she observed, 'this analysis treats a disabled child as having exactly the same worth as a non-disabled child. It affords him the same dignity and status. It simply acknowledges that he costs more.'[257]

5.125 If disability expenses were to be allowed, the court needed to give guidance as to how disabled the child needed to be. Brooke LJ said that whether there was a 'significant disability' giving rise to a right to compensation would have to be decided on a case-by-case basis, that the expression would include disabilities of the mind and that it would not include minor defects or inconveniences.[258] Hale LJ referred to the statutory definitions in welfare legislation identifying those whose special needs required special services,[259] and saw no difficulty in using the same definition in the present context.[260] A further question was when the disability needed to arise. Brooke LJ said that his concern was only with the loss that arose when the child's significant disabilities flowed foreseeably from his or her conception.[261] There might well be foreseeable incidents during the time leading up to the birth from which the disabilities had flowed, but these would not in the ordinary way be effective to break the chain of causation. But established principles of causation would need to be applied if there was evidence that the child's disabilities, discernible at birth, were caused by some new intervening cause. Hale LJ concluded, in similar vein, that any disabilities resulting from genetic causes or foreseeable events during pregnancy (such as rubella, spina bifida, or oxygen deprivation during pregnancy or childbirth) up until the child was born alive, and which were not *novus actus interveniens*, would suffice to found a claim.[262]

5.126 In *Whitehead v Searle*,[263] where a mother committed suicide before her claim for disability expenses was resolved, the Court of Appeal assumed that *Parkinson* would have applied to the mother's claim, although it did not decide whether the father would have had an action.[264] However, it is uncertain whether or how far *Parkinson* survives the subsequent

v Magendantz 689 A 2d 409 (1997); see generally M Hogg, 'Damages for Pecuniary Loss in Cases of Wrongful Birth' (2010) 1 JETL 151 at 164.

[257] *Parkinson v St James and Seacroft University Hospital NHS Trust*, n 256, [90].

[258] ibid, [52].

[259] ibid. Hale LJ referred in particular to the Children Act 1989, s 17(1), providing that a child is disabled if he is blind, deaf, or dumb or suffers from mental disorder of any kind or is substantially and permanently handicapped by illness, injury, or congenital deformity or such other disability as may be prescribed.

[260] ibid, [91].

[261] ibid, [53].

[262] ibid, [92]. See also *Less v Hussain* [2012] EWHC 3513, where the court held that had inadequate medical advice caused the claimant to become pregnant, she could have recovered in respect of her suffering a stillbirth, even though there was no direct connection between the negligent advice and the cause of the stillbirth.

[263] [2009] 1 WLR 549 (CA).

[264] See para 5.142.

decision of the House of Lords in *Rees v Darlington Memorial Hospital NHS Trust*.[265] This question will be considered below.[266]

(f) **Intervening medical negligence** In *Groom v Selby*[267] the mother of a premature child who appeared healthy at birth but developed salmonella meningitis at three weeks of age was held entitled to recover in a wrongful birth action, because the child had been exposed to bacteria during delivery and was never born 'healthy'. The chain of causation was accordingly not broken. But if the disability to the unwanted child arises from an injury caused by negligence, then it may be that any claim by the parents for the costs attributable to the disability should fail, on the basis that negligence in relation to the child's conception is not the cause of the loss or that the damage is too remote. **5.127**

Determining whether there is a sufficient causal connection between negligent conduct and ultimate harm where that harm is brought about by the intervening negligence of another necessarily requires a value judgment. A helpful method of approach is to ask whether the claimant's loss is within the scope of the risk created by the defendant's conduct. This approach has gathered support in recent times and is now well accepted.[268] For example, the risk created by a road accident may well encompass further injury stemming from the victim's vulnerable position in the road, even where the intervening event is also negligent.[269] On the other hand, the Court of Appeal has held that a negligently performed eye operation was not a foreseeable consequence of negligence in failing to protect an employee from assault.[270] In the present context, it is unlikely that negligence by a doctor in relation to the conception of a child or to the continuance of a pregnancy will be seen to encompass the risk of a subsequent, negligently inflicted, injury to the child during the pregnancy or birth unless, as in the road accident cases, the child is in some way put in a vulnerable position at special risk of injury.[271] At all events the child will have a claim under the Congenital Disabilities (Civil Liability) Act 1976,[272] and a court will be concerned not to allow full recovery for overlapping loss by different claimants. **5.128**

(g) **Quantification of damages** The mother, or both parents, may seek an award of general damages in respect of the additional anxiety, stress, and burden involved in bringing up a disabled child.[273] There need be no specific knowledge or foresight of the child's disability: it is sufficient that there is a foreseeable risk of congenital abnormality with any pregnancy.[274] **5.129**

Parkinson establishes that special damages are recoverable in respect of the foreseeable loss and expense attributable to the disabilities of an unplanned child. And just as the economic costs attributable to a child's disability, which can include loss of earnings and the cost of professional care, are recoverable by a parent, so the value of care provided by a parent alone **5.130**

---

[265] [2004] 1 AC 309 (HL).
[266] See paras 5.135–5.138.
[267] [2002] Lloyd's Rep Med 1 (CA).
[268] See, in particular, *Environment Agency v Empress Car Co (Abertillary) Ltd* [1999] 2 AC 22, 30–31 (HL); *Kuwait Airways Corporation v Iraqi Airways Co (Nos 4 and 5)* [2002] 2 AC 883, [71] (HL).
[269] *Chapman v Hearse* (1961) 106 CLR 112 (HCA); *Rouse v Squires* [1973] 1 QB 889 (CA).
[270] *Rahman v Arearose Ltd* [2001] QB 351, 365 (CA).
[271] See, eg, *Webb v Barclays Bank Ltd* [2001] Lloyd's Rep Med 500 (no liability for intervening medical negligence which was gross and/or unforeseeable).
[272] See para 5.45.
[273] *Allen v Bloomsbury HA* [1993] 1 All ER 651, 657, 662; *Taylor v Shropshire HA* [2000] Lloyd's Rep Med 96; *Rand v East Dorset HA* [2000] Lloyd's Rep Med 181; *Hardman v Amin* [2000] Lloyd's Rep Med 498.
[274] *Emeh v Kensington AHA* [1985] QB 1012, 1019–20 (CA); *Parkinson v St James and Seacroft University NHS Trust* [2002] 2 QB 206, [50], [92] (CA).

also should be recoverable. In *Hardman v Amin*[275] it was argued that no claim could be brought for the value of care provided by the family of a disabled child, but the argument was rejected.

5.131 Damages are computed by reference to the life of the parent.[276] However, there is no good reason to restrict the claim for disability costs to the period until the child reaches the age of 18, or any other particular age. The test is simply whether the expense is reasonable and foreseeable.[277] The argument that there is no legal obligation on the defendants to compensate for any provision for disability after majority was rejected by Swinton Thomas J at first instance in *Fish v Wilcox*.[278] In this case the child suffered from spina bifida and was likely to survive into adult life. The judge accepted as a matter of general principle that the measure of damages should be a sum of money which would put the party who had been injured in the same position as she would have been in if she had not sustained the wrong, and clearly would have awarded damages for maternal services after the age of 18 had he not found as a fact that the child would not require them. The argument was again rejected in *Rand v East Dorset HA*[279] and in *Nunnerley v Warrington HA*.[280] Certainly parents of children born with disabilities are likely to wish, and indeed feel morally obliged, to make reasonable provision for them throughout the children's lives, and this sense of obligation is supported by the common law.

5.132 In *Rand* the amount of the damages was calculated by reference to the means of the parents. Newman J held that, the claim being for economic loss, it should be limited to the amount which the parents would have been able to pay for in caring for the child in the absence of compensation. However, to categorize the claim as one for economic loss is to do no more than identify the need for control mechanisms on the imposition of liability: it says nothing about the quantification of damages. Such a principle would simply serve to penalize the impecunious parents, and certainly would seem unjust. The better view is that the damages should be based upon the reasonable cost of the services needed, not the ability of the particular parents to pay for them. So *Rand* has not been followed on this point. In *Hardman v Amin*[281] Henriques J concluded that the parents' means were not relevant to the calculation of their claim for costs attributable to their child's disability. The same view was taken by Toulson J in *Lee v Taunton & Somerset NHS Trust*[282] and by Turner J in *Roberts v Bro Taf HA*.[283]

5.133 A final question concerns the application of s 2(4) of the Law Reform (Personal Injuries) Act 1948. This provides:

> In an action for personal injuries (including any such action arising out of a contract) there shall be disregarded, in determining the reasonableness of any expenses, the possibility of avoiding those expenses or part of them by taking advantage of facilities available under the National Health Act 1977 or the National Health Service (Scotland) Act 1978 or of any corresponding facilities in Northern Ireland.

---

275 [2000] Lloyd's Rep Med 498.
276 *Whitehead v Searle* [2009] 1 WLR 549 (CA).
277 Some US authorities allow recovery after the child attains the age of majority only if the parents remain liable under the relevant state law for the support of the child: see *Smith v Cote* 513 A 2d 341 (1986); *Bani-Israeli v Lerman* 505 NE 2d 507 (1987); *Viccaro v Milunsky* 551 NE 2d 8 (1990).
278 9 April 1992.
279 [2000] Lloyd's Rep Med 181.
280 [2000] Lloyd's Rep Med 170. An application for permission to appeal on this point was rejected by the Court of Appeal: *N v Warrington HA* [2003] Lloyd's Rep Med 365.
281 [2000] Lloyd's Rep Med 498.
282 [2001] 1 FLR 419, 433.
283 [2002] Lloyd's Rep Med 163.

The claim for the upbringing costs of a healthy child was recognized in *McFarlane* as being a claim for economic loss, and a claim for disability costs must be of the same kind. In *Lee v Taunton & Somerset NHS Trust*[284] Toulson J expressed the provisional view that the subsection did not apply. He thought that although the action was in part a claim for personal injuries suffered by the mother, the costs of caring for the child were not in truth damages for personal injuries suffered by her. Moreover, as we have seen, it is at least arguable that the mother's claim is not a claim for 'personal injuries' either. But even if this is not right, s 2(4) still cannot apply in a claim for disability costs.

(v) Loss of autonomy

Suppose now that the *mother* suffers from a disability. In *AD v East Kent Community NHS Trust*[285] the claimant was a female psychiatric patient sectioned under s 3 of the Mental Health Act 1983. She had a healthy child, allegedly as the result of negligence on the part of the defendant in failing to protect her from pregnancy. The child was brought up by the maternal grandmother under a residence order, and the claimant claimed all the upbringing costs, arguing that the grandmother incurred them because of her own disability. The court drew no distinction between physical disability and mental disability, but considered that there were no 'extra' costs attributable to the mother's disability. Rather, they were the same costs but borne by the grandmother,[286] and these were not recoverable on the authority of *McFarlane*. **5.134**

In *Rees v Darlington Memorial Hospital NHS Trust*,[287] by contrast, the mother sought to recover additional costs attributable to her disability. She had undergone a sterilization operation because she suffered from a severe visual handicap which she feared would prevent her from properly looking after a child. Having later conceived and given birth to a healthy child, and being a single parent, she sought damages to recover the costs of providing for the child. While ordinary costs were precluded, the question was whether the mother's special difficulties could be taken into account. The Court of Appeal,[288] in a majority decision, held that just as the parent of a child with significant disability was entitled to compensation for providing for the child's special needs associated with his disability, so too was a disabled parent entitled to the extra costs in discharging her responsibility towards a healthy child. However, the House of Lords, in a 4:3 decision, allowed the appeal but also introduced a significant 'gloss' on the holding in *McFarlane*. Lord Bingham accepted and supported a rule of legal policy which precluded recovery of the full cost of bringing up an unplanned child, yet questioned the fairness of a rule which denied the victim of a legal wrong any recompense at all beyond the immediate expenses of pregnancy and birth. The real loss was that the parent, particularly the mother, had been denied by negligence the opportunity to live her life in the way that she wished and planned. His Lordship accordingly supported the suggestion favoured by Lord Millett in *McFarlane*, that there should be a conventional award to mark the plaintiff's injury and lost autonomy. This sum, fixed at £15,000, would not be the product of calculation but would be some measure of recognition for the wrong **5.135**

[284] [2001] 1 FLR 419, 431.

[285] [2003] 3 All ER 1167 (CA); N Priaulx, 'Parental Disability and Wrongful Conception' [2003] Fam Law 117.

[286] For the recoverability of damages where a relative gratuitously provides care for the claimant, see *Hunt v Severs* [1994] 2 AC 350 (HL).

[287] [2004] 1 AC 309 (HL); P Cane, 'Another Failed Sterilisation' (2004) 120 LQR 189; A Morris, (2004) 20 PN 2; A Pedain, 'Unconventional Justice in the House of Lords' (2004) 63 CLJ 19; and see generally E Baginska, 'Wrongful Birth and Non-Pecuniary Loss: Theories of Compensation' (2010) 1 JETL 171 at 186.

[288] [2002] 2 WLR 1483 (CA).

done. It would be in addition to any award for pregnancy and birth and would be applied without differentiation to all cases, including those in which either the child or the parent was disabled. So his Lordship would disallow a separate award for disability expenses.

5.136 Lord Nicholls, Lord Millett, and Lord Scott agreed that there should be a conventional award, but differed on whether disability expenses were recoverable as well. Lord Nicholls agreed with Lord Bingham, Lord Millett did not decide, and Lord Scott said that he might allow them if the purpose of the sterilization was to avoid conception of a disabled child. Lord Steyn, Lord Hope and Lord Hutton, expressing a minority view, rejected a conventional award and would allow the disability costs where either the mother or the child was disabled.

5.137 The view of the dissentients, together with that of Lord Scott, does at least give a majority in favour of allowing disability expenses where the purpose was to avoid conception of a disabled child or, seemingly, in a wrongful birth case where the mother has been negligently misinformed that her foetus is healthy and suffers from no disability. *Whitehead v Searle*[289] is a case in the second category. Here, as we have seen, a health authority failed to detect spina bifida in an unborn child, and the Court of Appeal accepted, without reference to *Rees*, that in principle the mother had a good claim for the expenses of raising the child.[290]

5.138 In summary, as the law now stands, in any case of wrongful birth or conception the mother is entitled to her pecuniary and non-pecuniary losses directly attributable to the pregnancy and birth, and the parents can recover the conventional sum for disruption of their lifestyle.[291] Where the child is disabled the position is uncertain, but at the least *Parkinson* has not been overruled. So it may be that disability expenses in a failed sterilization case are recoverable as well. The idea of an award for loss of autonomy arguably could be developed and applied in analogous kinds of claims, but the courts have shown little sign of wishing to do this.[292]

(vi) Doctor's duty to non-patient

5.139 A doctor does of course owe a duty of care to the patient whom he or she is treating or advising. *McFarlane* decides that that duty is owed to the mother with respect to the physical effects of an unwanted pregnancy or birth, but that no duty is owed to either parent with respect to the unwanted costs of upbringing. However, as we have seen, *Parkinson* allows claims for disability expenses and *Rees* for loss of autonomy. In these cases we have to consider whether a duty also may be owed to the patient's spouse or partner or other person upon whom loss or expense occasioned by the birth of the child may fall.

5.140 (a) **Mothers** The wife or partner of a male patient whose sterilization fails through negligence or who is given negligent advice clearly has a cause of action against the doctor. *McFarlane* itself was a failed vasectomy case where the husband was the patient, and the

---

289 [2009] 1 WLR 549 (CA). See also *Farraj v King's Healthcare NHS Trust* [2006] EWHC 1228, a wrongful birth case (as to which see para 5.147), where the court proceeded on the basis that *Parkinson* represented the law. Counsel for the defendants reserved his argument that it was wrongly decided in the light of *Rees*.

290 But the mother had committed suicide and this intervening event had to be taken into account: see para 5.67.

291 First instance courts in Ireland (*Byrne v Ryan* [2007] IEHC 207) and Canada (*Bevilacqua v Altenkirk* (2005) 27 CCLT 3d 75) have taken the same or at least a similar view.

292 See, for example, *Less v Hussain* [2012] EWHC 3513 (loss of autonomy starts at birth, not conception, so there can be no award where the child is stillborn); *Holdich v Lothian Health Board* [2013] CSOH 197 at [99]–[104] (no authority for 'loss of autonomy' award in 'wrongful sterility' cases).

House of Lords held that the wife had a cause of action in respect of her unwanted pregnancy and birth. But might a doctor owe a duty to a future sexual partner of his or her patient? In *Goodwill v British Pregnancy Advisory Service*[293] the plaintiff had commenced a sexual relationship with a man (M) who, three years earlier, had undergone a vasectomy operation arranged by the defendant and had been advised that the operation had been successful and that he did not need to use contraception in the future. M told the plaintiff about the vasectomy and its purported success and permanency, so she did not use any form of contraception. However, the vasectomy had spontaneously reversed and the plaintiff became pregnant. She brought an action claiming damages for financial loss caused by the birth of the child, alleging negligence in failing to warn M of the possibility of late spontaneous reversal of the vasectomy and its consequences, but the Court of Appeal struck out the claim. It could not be shown that, at the time it was given, the defendant knew that its advice was likely to be acted upon by the plaintiff without independent enquiry, or that it had in fact been acted upon by the plaintiff to her detriment. In so deciding the court considered how far any duty might extend. Peter Gibson LJ said that the doctor who performed a vasectomy on a man was concerned only with the man, his patient, and possibly that man's wife or partner if the doctor intended her to receive and she received advice from the doctor in relation to the vasectomy and the subsequent tests.[294] Whether the avoidance of pregnancy was a benefit or a disadvantage to a sexual partner of the man would depend on her circumstances. If the existence of that partner was known to the doctor and the doctor was aware that she wished not to become pregnant by the man and the vasectomy was carried out to meet her wish as well as the man's wish, it might be said that the doctor was employed to confer that benefit on her. Thorpe LJ considered that the doctor in the circumstances regarded himself as advising the patient and, if a married man, the patient's wife.[295] It could not be said that he knew or ought to have known that he also advised any future sexual partners of his patient who chanced to receive his advice at second-hand. Presented with such a set of facts a doctor was entitled to scorn the suggestion that he owed a duty of care to such a band so uncertain in nature and extent and over such an indefinite future span.[296]

(b) Fathers Applying the *Caparo* test,[297] a doctor may be held to owe a duty to take care where he or she should foresee harm to a sufficiently proximate claimant in circumstances where it is fair, just, and reasonable that a duty of the kind and extent that is alleged should be recognized. Perhaps, then, the husband of a negligently sterilized patient who gives birth to a disabled child has a cause of action together with his wife for the extra expenses in bringing up the disabled child. Certainly there are a number of wrongful birth cases where fathers as well as mothers have obtained judgment.[298] And in *Parkinson* Hale LJ's tentative view was that there was a sufficient relationship of proximity between the tortfeasor and the father who has and meets his parental responsibility to care for the child.[299] **5.141**

[293] *Goodwill v British Pregnancy Advisory Service* [1996] 2 All ER 161 (CA).
[294] ibid, 167.
[295] ibid, 170.
[296] See *Miller v Rivard* 585 NYS 2d 523 (Sup Ct NY, App Div, 1992) on the distinction between known and casual sexual partners.
[297] *Caparo Industries plc v Dickman* [1990] 2 AC 605, 617–18 (HL).
[298] *Salih v Enfield Health Authority* [1991] 3 All ER 400 (CA); *Anderson v Forth Valley Health Board* (1997) 14 BMLR 108; *Rand v East Dorset Health Authority* [2000] Lloyd's Rep Med 181; *Farraj v King's Healthcare NHS Trust* [2008] EWHC 2468; see generally E Baginska, n 287, at 195.
[299] [2002] QB 206, [93] (CA).

5.142 In *Whitehead v Searle*[300] the Court of Appeal discussed the question but did not reach a concluded view. As we have seen,[301] one of the claims was by a father against his wife's former solicitors for negligent delay in pursuing the wife's action against a health authority for the disability expenses in bringing up their child, the period of delay being such that the action had not been settled or resolved at the time when the wife committed suicide. In the view of Laws LJ (with whom Rimer LJ agreed), the defendants owed no duty of care to the father.[302] The defendants had not assumed any responsibility to the father, who had not asked for advice about suing the health authority, would not pay for it, had not retained them, and had other solicitors of his own. His Lordship recognized that the defendants had been concerned to secure support for the child and had considered the possibility of joining the father in a claim by the estate. But he thought that imposing a duty to advise the claimant that he might have a personal claim would be a step too far. The father's claim could be seen as a surrogate for the claim that the child could not bring,[303] and accordingly the duty of the court was specifically not to fill this gap. That conclusion was sufficient to dispose of the claim, but his Lordship went on to consider briefly whether the father would have had a viable claim against the health authority had such a claim been launched on his behalf. He accepted that on the authorities the father's claim was not ruled out. But there were important difficulties. It would be viable if at all only as a secondary claim, and would critically depend upon evidence that had the mother known of the foetus's defect she would have chosen to undergo a termination. Mixed questions of policy and causation would arise, and given the likely depth of the problem the question should be authoritatively concluded in a case calling for its decision, which the present case did not.

5.143 Rix LJ was prepared to go further. He noted that fathers' claims had succeeded in a number of cases, and was satisfied that it could not be said that there was no real chance of the father showing a duty of care. Indeed, he imagined a wrongful birth case where the mother died in childbirth and the father bore all the care costs thereafter. Here the father was living with the mother until several months after the birth, and after the mother's death he had taken up the parental responsibility of looking after the child. There was nothing so unrealistic about his claim against the health authority as to deny its existence. It was appropriate, therefore, to revisit the question of duty of care on the part of the defendant solicitors. The fact that no claim could be made by the child did not lead to the conclusion that it was not fair, just, and reasonable to give proper consideration to whether a father's undertaking of care for the child should not, in part out of concern for the child himself, be made the occasion for a claim. It was not as though the father's and the child's interests were in conflict. But out of respect for the opposing views of Laws LJ, he would not press his concerns to a dissent.

5.144 In weighing up these opinions we should recognize that any parent's disability claim is likely to operate for the benefit of the child, and it should not be dismissed as a surrogate for a non-permissible claim by the child himself or herself. So Rix LJ's judgment, accepting that there can be a claim by a father, gives the preferable view. Of course, any such claim must depend on the father in fact assuming responsibility for the child and for the extra expenses entailed by the child's disability. However, *Whitehead* seems right in holding that on the facts there was no duty owed by the solicitors to the father.

300 [2009] 1 WLR 549 (CA).
301 See para 5.67.
302 See also *Schumann v Veale Wasbrough* [2013] EWHC 3730, at [68]–[73].
303 ibid.

(c) Other persons It is possible that a duty might be owed to other persons. Suppose, adapting Rix LJ's example in *Whitehead*, a single mother dies giving birth to a disabled child, and the child is looked after by a grandparent. In this case there would be a good argument in favour of giving the grandparent, or other person in fact taking care of the child, a right of action.[304] But there can be no doubt that, say, a wrongful conception claim by a sibling, alleging in effect a diversion of resources away from himself or herself, would certainly fail. Following *McFarlane*, the very basis for a claim of this kind would be lacking.[305] **5.145**

(d) Loss of autonomy As for a claim for loss of autonomy, in *Rees* three members of the majority (Lord Bingham, Lord Nicholls, and Lord Millett) spoke of an award to the parent or parents of a conventional sum by way of compensation.[306] Seemingly only one such sum may be awarded, to the mother or to the father or to both, depending on who is claiming and who in fact suffers this loss. A single sum if both parents claim can be seen as fair, as the impact on the autonomy on each parent is likely to be less than the impact on a single parent. And almost certainly a parent who was not the partner of the doctor's patient at the time of the negligent sterilization or advice has no independent claim. **5.146**

(vii) Duty of supplier of services

The supplier of services which lead to the birth of a child with disabilities may owe a duty to a parent. One example perhaps could be an IVF clinic supplying inadequately screened sperm carrying a genetic deficiency of the donor. Another is found in the facts of *Farraj v King's Healthcare NHS Trust*.[307] The claimants, who were Jordanian nationals residing in Jordan, were the parents of a child suffering from Beta Thalassaemia Major (BTM), an inherited blood disorder. The first defendant (KCH), acting pursuant to a contract with the Jordanian Government, undertook genetic testing of a sample of foetal material provided by the mother, and the second defendants (CSL) cultured that sample pursuant to a contract with KCH. The report provided by KCH stated that the foetus would not suffer from BTM. However, the sample was substantially contaminated by maternal cells, so the DNA tested was the mother's. The claimants alleged negligence by both defendants in failing to appreciate that the quality of the sample was so poor that no confidence could be placed in the result. In particular, they alleged negligence by KCH in not asking CSL whether the cultured sample would provide reliable results, and by CSL in not volunteering the relevant information. KCH admitted they owed the claimants a duty to use reasonable care to assess and report on the sample, but denied that they were liable or were under a non-delegable duty with respect to CSL's failures, if any, and also contended that if liability was established against them they would seek an indemnity or contribution from CSL. In their defence CSL denied they owed the claimants any duty of care, and this question was tried as a preliminary issue. **5.147**

It was held by Swift J that there was a sufficient relationship of proximity between the claimants and CSL to satisfy the requirement for the existence of a duty of care. It was also fair, just and reasonable for such a duty to be imposed. If negligence occurred in a hospital laboratory, the hospital trust would be liable to the person who suffered damage as a result, **5.148**

[304] In *Fish v Wilcox* 9 April 1992, n 278, Swinton Thomas J considered obiter the possibility of the father and brothers of a disabled child being joined in a wrongful birth action brought by the mother so that they might recover damages for the services they had provided to the child.

[305] In the US, claims by siblings have been regarded as 'wholly without merit': *Sala v Tomlinson* 422 NYS 2d 506 (Sup Ct App Div, 1979).

[306] [2004] 1 AC 309, [8], [17], [125] (HL).

[307] [2006] EWHC 1228.

and it was difficult to see why a private laboratory which was paid for its services should be in a different position. The duty could include a duty to provide information to KCH for transmission to the parents, and whether it extended that far in the circumstances of the case was a matter for evidence at the trial.[308]

(viii) Claims in contract

5.149 *McFarlane*, *Parkinson*, and *Rees* all concern claims in tort against NHS providers or their employees. The question arises whether or how far the same principles should apply to actions in contract in the case of private medical treatment.[309] There are two issues to consider here.

5.150 First, it may be argued that a doctor performing a sterilization operation has promised that the patient will be rendered sterile. In *Eyre v Measday*[310] the claimant underwent a laporoscopic sterilization after the defendant gynaecologist had emphasized that it was 'irreversible'. The claimant argued that the defendant had contracted to render her absolutely sterile, and that the use of the word 'irreversible' amounted to an express guarantee that the operation would achieve its object of sterilizing her or that there was an implied warranty to that effect. However, the Court of Appeal held that the contract was only to carry out the particular type of operation and not to sterilize. The representation that the operation was 'irreversible' meant only that the operation could not be reversed and not that it would achieve its object. Slade LJ said that in a contract to carry out an operation the court would imply an obligation to exercise reasonable skill and care, but would be slow to imply an unqualified warranty as to the results of an intended operation, because, objectively speaking, it was most unlikely that a responsible doctor would intend to give a warranty of this nature.[311] Again, in *Thake v Maurice*,[312] where both parents sued for breach of warranty and breach of a duty of care in tort following the husband's failed vasectomy, the claim for breach of warranty failed on the basis that no binding promise had been made. Neill LJ said that a reasonable man would have expected the defendant to exercise all the proper skill and care of a surgeon in that speciality: he would not have expected the defendant to give a guarantee of 100 per cent success.[313] Nourse LJ similarly observed that a doctor could not be objectively regarded as guaranteeing the success of any operation or treatment unless he said as much in clear and unequivocal terms.[314]

5.151 These principles do not appear to have been changed by *McFarlane*.[315] Accordingly, an action in contract for breach of a guarantee that a patient will be sterilized is possible in

[308] In *Farraj v King's Healthcare NHS Trust* [2008] EWHC 2468 Burnett J held that both defendants were liable and attributed two-thirds responsibility to CSL and one-third to KCH. However, the Court of Appeal allowed KCH's appeal, holding that CSL was solely liable and that KCH did not owe a non-delegable duty to the claimants: *Farraj v King's Healthcare NHS Trust* (2010) 11 BMLR 131; R Heywood, 'Non-delegable Duties and Hospitals' (2010) 26 PN 49. See also *A (A Child) v Ministry of Defence* [2004] 3 WLR 469 (CA).

[309] In *McFarlane*, n 244 at 99 Lord Clyde recognized that actions in contract may give rise to different issues than those in tort.

[310] *Eyre v Measday* [1986] 1 All ER 488 (CA).

[311] ibid, 495.

[312] *Thake v Maurice* [1986] QB 644 (CA).

[313] ibid, 685.

[314] ibid, 688.

[315] In *McFarlane v Tayside Health Board* [2000] 2 AC 59, 77, Lord Steyn thought that the correctness of the assumption that it is immaterial whether an action is brought in contract or in delict might depend on whether the term amounted to a warranty of an outcome, and did not contemplate that it might depend simply on the cause of action which was asserted.

principle.[316] However, the courts will require clear evidence that any such promise has in fact been made.

The second issue is whether damages for the costs of upbringing are still possible in an action for negligent breach of contract. In *Thake* it was held that the defendant's failure to warn of the risk that the husband might become fertile again amounted to a breach of the duty of care he owed to the parents and was actionable in both contract and tort. But *Thake* was overruled by *McFarlane* at least so far as a claim in tort was concerned, and very arguably an action in contract should fail as well. There may be concurrent liability, subject to any limits or exclusions in the contract, where a cause of action is for negligence,[317] the ambit of an action for negligent breach of contract and an action for negligence normally is co-extensive,[318] compensatory damages may be subject to policy controls in contract as well as in tort,[319] and in contract it is still necessary to ask whether the parents have suffered a 'loss' in law. Furthermore, the courts are unwilling to encourage different rights to compensation as between private and NHS patients.[320] And finally, the same policy as in medical cases clearly ought to apply in the case of an action against the retailer of a contraceptive for breach of an implied warranty of quality. **5.152**

(ix) Australian authority

Contemporary developments in Australia contrast markedly with those in the UK. In *Cattanach v Melchior*,[321] another failed sterilization case, the High Court of Australia, in a 4:3 decision, was not persuaded by the policy considerations against recovery, and upheld a trial judge's decision to award damages against a negligent obstetrician for the cost of raising an unplanned child. The majority view was that the defendant could be held liable on the application of ordinary principles of negligence. McHugh and Gummow JJ thought that the expression 'wrongful birth' was misleading, because what was wrongful was not the birth but the negligence of the doctor.[322] The defendant sought merely the proscription of a particular head of recovery of damages. But no novel head of damages was involved. The plaintiffs' loss was not the coming into existence of the parent–child relationship but simply the expenditure that the plaintiffs had incurred or would incur in the future. If this was causally connected to the negligence and reasonably foreseeable then it ought to be **5.153**

[316] In *Thompson v Sheffield Fertility Clinic* (QB, 6 March 2001, Hooper J), a mother who had three embryos replaced during IVF treatment was able to establish a breach of an agreement that only two should be replaced: A Grubb, (2001) 9 Med L Rev 170.

[317] *Henderson v Merrett Syndicates Ltd* [1995] 2 AC 145 (HL); *Bryan v Maloney* (1995) 182 CLR 609 at 619–22 (HCA); *Riddell v Porteous* [1999] 1 NZLR 1, 9 (NZCA).

[318] See *Frost & Sutcliffe v Tuiara* [2004] 1 NZLR 782 (NZCA).

[319] An example is the continuing debate, going back to *Addis v Gramophone Co Ltd* [1909] AC 488 (HL), about limits upon damages in contract for upset and distress.

[320] See *Hotson v East Berkshire HA* [1987] 1 AC 750, 760, 768.

[321] *Cattanach v Melchior* (2004) 215 CLR 1 (HCA); J Seymour, 'Cattanach v Melchior: Legal Principles and Public Policy' (2003) 11 TLJ 208; K Weston-Scheuber, 'Victory for Reluctant Parents: Cattanach v Melchior' (2003) 26 UNSWLJ 717; P Cane, 'The Doctor, the Stork and the Court: A Modern Morality Play' (2004) 120 LQR 23; B Golder, 'From *McFarlane* to *Melchior* and Beyond: Love, Sex, Money and Commodification in the Anglo-Australian Law of Torts' (2004) 12 TLJ 128; O M Bradfield, 'Healthy law makes for healthy children: Cattanach v. Melchior' (2005) 12 JLM 305; C Witting, 'Tort Law, Policy and the High Court of Australia' (2007) 31 Melb UL Rev 569, 583–90. The opinions in the earlier decision of the New South Wales Court of Appeal in *CES v Superclinics (Aus) Pty Ltd* (1995) 38 NSWLR 47 were split three ways: Kirby ACJ favoured full recovery, Priestley JA would allow damages for the birth but not for subsequent expenses, and Meagher JA thought the claim should fail; J Swanton, (1996) 4 TLJ 1; J A Devereux, 'Actions for Wrongful Birth' (1996) 4 Tort L Rev 107.

[322] *Cattanach v Melchior*, n 321, [67]–[68].

recoverable. Kirby J maintained that in the real world, cases of this kind were about money, not love or the preservation of the family unit.[323] The notion that in every case the birth of a child was a 'blessing' represented a fiction that the law should not accept in the absence of objective evidence bearing it out. In any event the parents' claim was simply for economic loss consequential upon physical injury to the mother. To deny such recovery was to provide a zone of legal immunity to medical practitioners engaged in sterilization procedures that was unprincipled and inconsistent with established legal doctrine. Furthermore, the emotional benefits of parenthood were different in quality from the costs incurred in child-raising and should be ignored in calculating the recoverable damages.[324]

(x) Irish authority

5.154 In Ireland, in *Byrne v Ryan*,[325] the decisions of the House of Lords in *McFarlane* and *Rees* were preferred to the majority view of the High Court of Australia in *Cattanach*. Kelly J was satisfied that this conclusion was in harmony with the majority of decisions in the common law world and with a number of decisions of the civil law courts. His Honour also considered that the value which the Irish Constitution placed upon the family and the dignity and protection it afforded to family life were matters which were better served by a decision to deny rather than to allow damages for the upbringing of children.

(xi) Appraisal

5.155 In Kirby J's view in *Cattanach* the parents had a straightforward claim for financial loss consequential upon physical injury to the mother by way of pregnancy and childbirth.[326] But this assumes, arguably without adequate foundation, that pregnancy is 'physical injury',[327] and it also fails to take proper account of the position of the father, who was also a plaintiff and who certainly suffered no physical consequences. In *McFarlane* the loss was treated as purely financial, and if characterization as one or the other is necessary then this is the better view.[328] The complaint is not about the consequences to the mother of the physical aspects of birth and of any injury and pain that she herself has suffered, but is about the consequences to the parents of the existence of a child and the creation of a relationship pursuant to which there are legal and moral obligations to expend money on and provide support for the child. Perhaps, however, we can recognize in the light of *Rees* that the loss here can be treated as sui generis—that it is the unwanted imposition of responsibility to bring up a child and the accompanying deprivation of autonomy, with the obligation to pay being simply a consequence of that wrong.[329] And even if we treat the mother as having suffered physical damage, her claim involves the unique physiological event of pregnancy and childbirth and can be seen as quite different in nature from an ordinary claim involving physical injury and consequential economic loss.

5.156 Wrongful conception and wrongful birth claims involve contentious issues of law and policy about which opinions may fairly differ.[330] But a choice has to be made. Critics of *McFarlane*

---

[323] ibid, [145], [148], [175].

[324] Political reaction in Australia to *Cattanach* was negative, and legislation in three states reversed it: see Civil Liability Act 2003 (Qld), ss 49A, 49B; Civil Liability Act 2002 (NSW), s 71; Civil Liability Act 1936 (SA), s 67.

[325] [2007] IEHC 207.

[326] (2004) 215 CLR 1, [148]–[150].

[327] See paras 5.110–5.113.

[328] See also *Arndt v Smith* [1997] 2 SCR 539, [75] (SCC).

[329] See also *Parkinson v St James & Seacroft University Hospital NHS Trust* [2002] QB 266, [89] (CA): *Groom v Selby* [2002] Lloyd's Rep Med 1, [31] (CA).

[330] See generally M Hogg, 'Damages for Pecuniary Loss in Cases of Wrongful Birth' (2010) 1 JETL 156; E Baginska, 'Wrongful Birth and Non-Pecuniary Loss; Theories of Compensation' (2010) 1 JETL 171.

and *Rees* argue that the law should favour reproductive autonomy, that legal principle supports the action for costs of upbringing, and that standard rules of tort can be applied to give a remedy.[331] However, a commentator on *Cattanach v Melchior* has remarked that the view that judges do not make law and that 'legal principle' can tell us whether Dr Cattanach should have been held responsible for the cost of rearing Jordan Melchior might be called a fairy tale.[332] And the arguments denying the parent's claim ultimately are persuasive.[333] The key objection is that the existence of a child cannot be treated as legally recognizable loss or damage or that it is impossible to measure any damage: and an associated argument is that treating the existence of a child as a loss to the parents is inconsistent with many other rules affecting the parent–child relationship. As Gleeson CJ remarked in dissent in *Cattanach*, the law imposes many obligations on parents in support and protection of a child which are difficult to reconcile with the idea that creating the parent–child relationship is actionable damage. Again, if a claim is to be allowed, the determination of which expenses are and which are not to be the subject of an award of damages must necessarily be selective and unprincipled. In Gleeson CJ's words once more, the plaintiff cannot select some of the detrimental financial consequences of the relationship and ignore all others, whether financial or non-financial. And, lastly, any damages are potentially indeterminate both as to their nature and their amount. In particular, there would be no reason in principle to restrict claims for upbringing costs to any particular age, nor to exclude any particular form of reasonable discretionary expenditure.

What, then, of the case where the mother or the child is disabled? A special exception if the **5.157** mother is disabled, as argued in *Rees*, would be inappropriate and unworkable. The costs of bringing up a healthy child are infinitely variable, not only according to the needs of the child but according to the circumstances of the parents (including any disability) and of family and friends. Furthermore, costs due to the birth and due to the disability cannot be disentangled; they are a single cost with composite causes.[334] It is different where the child is disabled. Extra costs should at least be recoverable as proposed by Lord Scott in wrongful birth cases, where the defendant's failure to diagnose or to advise that the foetus was suffering from an abnormality means that the mother has lost the opportunity to terminate the pregnancy. Here the risk of disability is the reason for seeking the diagnosis and should be specifically within the contemplation of the defendant.[335] However, disability expenses

[331] K Norrie, 'Failed Sterilisation and Economic Loss: Justice Law and Policy in *McFarlane v Tayside Health Board*' (2000) 16 PN 76; L Hoyano, 'Misconceptions about Wrongful Conception' (2002) 65 MLR 883; P Dimopoulos and M Bagaric, 'Why Wrongful Birth Actions Are Right' (2003) 11 JLM 230; B Golder, 'From *McFarlane* to *Melchior* and Beyond: Love, Sex, Money and Commodification in the Anglo-Australian Law of Torts' (2004) 12 TLJ 128; N Priaulx, 'That's One Heck of an Unruly Horse: Riding Roughshod over Autonomy in Wrongful Conception' (2004) 12 Feminist Legal Studies 317; J K Mason, 'The Reproductive Torts', in *Halsbury's Laws of England Centenary Essays* (Butterworths 2007) 127.

[332] P Cane, n 321, 26. For a review of the basic questions, see B Steininger, 'Wrongful Life and Wrongful Birth: Basic Questions' (2010) 1 JETL 125.

[333] See further T Weir, 'The Unwanted Child' (2000) 59 CLJ 238; Cane, n 321; I Kennedy and A Grubb, *Medical Law*, n 98, 1578. M Vranken, 'Damages for 'Wrongful Birth': Where to after *Cattanach*?' (2003) 24 Adelaide L Rev 243, recognizes that the decision in *Rees* offers a workable compromise.

[334] On these points see *Rees v Darlington Memorial Hospital NHS Trust* [2004] 1 AC 309, [114]–[120] *per* Lord Millett.

[335] On this view it may sometimes be necessary to bring into account the law governing abortion. If at the time of the alleged negligence an abortion would have been illegal the plaintiff's claim must fail, as the lost opportunity could only have been turned to value by a breach of the law: *Rance v Mid-Downs Health Authority* [1991] 2 WLR 159; *CES v Superclinics (Aus) Pty Ltd* (1995) 38 NSWLR 47 (NSWCA); *Farraj v King's Healthcare NHS Trust* [2008] EWHC 2468, [26]–[43]. The circumstances in which an abortion may lawfully be performed are provided for in the Abortion Act 1967: see para 5.10.

arguably can be seen as justifiable in wrongful conception cases as well. Three of their Lordships in *Rees* considered that it was anomalous that the defendant's liability should be related to a disability which the doctor's negligence did not cause, and not to the birth, which it did. But the *McFarlane* rule concerns not cause but the nature of legally cognizable loss: it depends on the inextricable calculus of benefits and burdens associated with the bringing up of a child. Disability expenses can be seen as falling outside that calculus. If this is not accepted the parents must rely on public provision for the consequences of disability.

5.158 Finally, the award of a conventional sum to compensate for the mother's or the parents' loss of autonomy in controlling the size of her or their family certainly is unprecedented, but has something to be said for it. A claim for loss of autonomy is conceptually quite different from a claim for the costs of bringing up a child. The same objections of principle do not apply, and the focus is on the impact of the child on the lives of the parents rather than on the unwanted costs of or expenditure on the child. A conventional award also avoids a key vice of the wrongful conception action, that it can compensate for major discretionary expenditure of well-to-do parents—school fees, presents, holidays, and the like. Indeed, critics of *McFarlane* may well draw the line at such claims notwithstanding that they are both foreseeable and reasonable, yet denying them gives the lie to the argument that ordinary principles of tort liability are being applied. And if damages are limited to 'basic' expenses then awards will tend towards a standard sum, as already achieved (at an admittedly modest figure) by the House of Lords. The *Rees* award recognizes that the parents have suffered a real loss, but evaluates the loss at the same level for all. It introduces a desirable element of certainty and predictability into the quantum of damages.

5.159 There is an unavoidable element of arbitrariness in setting the appropriate sum. In *Rees* no explanation is given for fixing it at £15,000. Of course, the loss is infinitely variable and there can be no 'correct' figure. Even so, the award can be rationalized on the basis that it assists the parents in reordering their lives and adjusting to their new circumstances. In *Rees* the House of Lords was searching for a sum that could be widely recognized as reasonably fair. Fixing general damages in this way had to be impressionistic rather than calculated.

2. Claims by parents for physical and psychiatric injury

(i) Physical injury

5.160 Circumstances which lead to neonatal injury or death may also injure the mother. The damages which may be recovered in a case of this kind were considered in *Kralj v McGrath*.[336] A mother was admitted to hospital for the birth of twins. After attempted internal cephalic version of the second twin without any anaesthetic, a procedure described as horrific and completely unacceptable, he was delivered by Caesarean section, but died eight weeks later. The mother claimed, inter alia, for aggravated damages and damages for grief arising out of the loss of a child. Woolf J held that the concept of aggravated damages should not be introduced into personal injury actions, although to the extent that the mother's experience of her baby's injuries and death made it more difficult for her to overcome the consequences of her own injuries, the award would correspondingly be increased. He further ruled that, while damages could not be awarded for grief in isolation at common law, the mother could be compensated for the shock she had sustained as a result of being told what had happened and of seeing her son, and, to the extent that grief had made her injuries have a more drastic effect on her, that could be taken into account in calculating the personal injury award. The claim also included damages for the consequences, including financial loss, of having

[336] [1986] 1 All ER 54.

another child to replace the one who had died. On the evidence the probability that the mother would become pregnant again was only 66 per cent. However, Woolf J awarded £18,000 under this head to take account of the financial loss which would arise if a pregnancy occurred and the loss of satisfaction of achieving the planned family if it did not.

A doctor's general duty of care requires him or her to tell a patient if a mishap occurs in the course of treatment.[337] And a failure to inform a patient of what has gone wrong can be a factor which increases the amount of an award for the original wrong. In *Greive v Salford HA*[338] a psychiatrically vulnerable unmarried woman had a stillborn child following a negligent obstetric procedure. The stillbirth was held to be particularly damaging because she had been given a variety of inconsistent explanations as to what had been the cause of death, and this aggravating factor was reflected in the quantum of the damages. **5.161**

Even without other injury, it is possible that a mother who gives birth to a child who is stillborn due to the negligence of a medical professional has a cause of action on the basis that the mother herself has suffered personal injury. This at least was the view taken by the New Zealand Court of Appeal in *Harrild v Director of Proceedings*,[339] where the question was whether the mother had suffered personal injury for the purpose of cover under the New Zealand accident compensation scheme. A majority of the court were satisfied that an unborn child could be part of the mother, even though mother and foetus were biologically distinct, and that the mother had suffered personal injury on account of the death of the foetus. Elias CJ was not attracted by the stark choice of treating the unborn child either as the same as the mother or as distinct. She considered that where severance of the physical link between mother and unborn child occurred through the death of the child as a result of medical error, by that loss the mother suffered a personal injury within the meaning of the legislation. Keith and McGrath JJ thought similarly. Blanchard and Glazebrook JJ, by contrast, considered that on the majority view a mother and foetus were treated as a single entity, which ignored biological reality. **5.162**

Harrild was decided in relation to the definition of 'personal injury' in the New Zealand legislation[340] and was not concerned with common law principle, but the majority view possibly could be taken to give a cause of action.[341] However, at least in cases where the mother suffers no separate injury, the view of the minority is the more convincing.[342] **5.163**

(ii) Psychiatric injury

Claims for psychiatric injury are seen as posing their own special problems of policy. A major consideration in determining the ambit of liability is the perceived risk of opening the floodgates of litigation and of imposing a burden of liability that is disproportionate to **5.164**

---

[337] *Lee v South West Thames RHA* [1985] 1 WLR 845, 850–51: *Naylor v Preston AHA* [1987] 1 WLR 958, 967 (CA).

[338] (1991) 2 Med L R 295.

[339] [2003] 3 NZLR 289 (NZCA); and see *Sam v ACC* [2009] 1 NZLR 132.

[340] As to which, see para 5.114.

[341] See also *Winnipeg Child and Family Services (Northwest Area) v G (DF)* [1997] 3 SCR 925, 945 *per* McLachlin J ('The law has always treated the mother and unborn child as one').

[342] It was preferred by Heath J in *Sivasubramanium v Yarrall* [2005] 3 NZLR 268, [68]. In *Cumberland v Accident Compensation Corporation* [2011] NZAR 389 (HC) Faire J refused to extend *Harrild* to cover the case of a born-alive child suffering from spina bifida and rejected the argument that the mother had suffered personal injury in the form of a developing lesion within herself. On appeal ([2014] 2 NZLR 373), the Court of Appeal held that the mother had suffered personal injury by the unwanted continuation of her pregnancy (as to which see para 5.115), and on this view the question whether a developing lesion in the foetus was personal injury to the mother did not need answering.

the tortious conduct involved.[343] Accordingly, the courts view claims for such injury with caution and, certainly, they treat them differently from claims for physical injury. The duty to take care to avoid causing psychiatric harm is hedged by certain limitations beyond the mere requirement that some form of mental harm be foreseeable. And these limitations sometimes will come into operation in medical negligence cases, in particular where a parent sues in respect of psychiatric injury caused by the death or injury of a child.

5.165 (a) **Actionable injury** First, the parent must suffer a recognizable injury. Upset, grief, and distress do not give rise to any cause of action. In any claim for mental harm standing alone, the shock must cause the plaintiff to suffer some medically identifiable psychiatric illness or injury or have some physical consequence, such as a miscarriage.[344]

5.166 In *Bagley v North Herts HA*[345] the negligent failure to carry out a blood analysis in pregnancy deprived the plaintiff of her opportunity of successful delivery by Caesarean section, and the child was stillborn. Simon Brown J considered that the mother was entitled to compensation for 'dashed hopes', that is to say the loss of the satisfaction of bringing her pregnancy, confinement, and labour to a successful conclusion. Furthermore, the parents decided not to attempt another pregnancy, which would have carried a 50 per cent risk of mortality, and he also awarded compensation for loss of the pleasure of bringing up an ordinary healthy child who would now not be born. In *Greive v Salford HA*,[346] in similar circumstances, Rose J came to the same conclusion. However, in *Kerby v Redbridge HA*,[347] a case not of a stillbirth but of a neonatal death resulting from negligence, Ognall J disagreed. He rejected a 'dashed hopes' formulation of the claim partly on the basis that it would duplicate statutory damages for bereavement[348] (which are not available in the event of a stillbirth), but also because it amounted to a claim for damages for 'the normal emotions by way of grief, sorrow, or distress attendant on the loss of a loved one'[349] which were not compensable in law. A claim for damages for 'shattered family plans' was similarly rejected. So there is serious difficulty in treating 'dashed hopes' as the subject matter of a separate head of damages, rather than as a factor in quantifying a personal injury claim.

5.167 (b) **Primary victims** Second, there was formerly a general rule in all mental injury cases that injury by shock must be foreseeable,[350] but in *Page v Smith*[351] the House of Lords held that the requirement did not apply to a victim who was put in danger by the defendant's conduct (who was called a 'primary' victim). Rather, the defendant's duty was the ordinary duty to take care not to cause personal injury, whether physical or psychiatric. And once it was shown that there was a foreseeable risk of one form of personal injury, the rule that defendants take their victims as they find them applied. The plaintiff was not required to be a person of 'ordinary phlegm'. Accordingly, the defendant was liable for the plaintiff's

---

343 See generally *Frost v Chief Constable of the South Yorkshire Police* [1999] 2 AC 455, 493 (HL).

344 *McLoughlin v O'Brian* [1983] 1 AC 410, 418 (HL); *Hicks v Chief Constable of the South Yorkshire Police* [1992] 2 All ER 65 (HL); *Page v Smith* [1996] 1 AC 155, 189 (HL); *Frost v Chief Constable of the South Yorkshire Police* [1999] 2 AC 455, 469 (HL); *Tame v NSW: Annetts v Australian Stations Pty Ltd* (2003) 211 CLR 317, [7], [192]–[194] (HCA); *van Soest v Residual Health Management Unit* [2000] 1 NZLR 179 (NZCA).

345 [1986] NLJ 1014.

346 (1991) 2 Med LR 295.

347 (1993) 4 Med LR 178.

348 See para 5.178.

349 Quoting *McLoughlin v O'Brian* [1983] 1 AC 410, 431 *per* Lord Bridge.

350 *King v Phillips* [1953] 1 QB 429 (CA).

351 [1996] AC 155 (HL); see further *Frost v Chief Constable of South Yorkshire Police* [1999] 2 AC 455 (HL); *W v Essex CC* [2001] 2 AC 592 (HL).

psychiatric injury resulting from a relatively minor road accident caused by the fault of the defendant, even though the plaintiff was especially susceptible to suffering such injury. However, the decision creates difficult problems of classification, and it may yet be reconsidered.[352] There is a substantial body of case law involving plaintiffs who are not secondary victims—those who suffer mental injury because of the death or injury of another person—who have been owed a duty of care in respect of foreseeable psychiatric harm even though they have not been physically endangered.[353] A simple dichotomy between primary and secondary victims cannot cope with the variety of ways in which a person may become the victim of psychiatric harm.

A mother who, through the defendant's negligence, gives birth to a stillborn child is treated as a primary victim.[354] The father of a stillborn child is not a primary victim.[355] **5.168**

(c) **Secondary victims** Third, persons who are not personally in danger who suffer mental injury from perceiving or hearing about the death or injury of another or others (called 'secondary' victims) must show that it was foreseeable by the defendant that, in the circumstances of the case, a person of ordinary susceptibility or fortitude would suffer psychiatric injury.[356] In addition, according to the House of Lords in *Alcock v Chief Constable of South Yorkshire Police*,[357] secondary victims are subject to three particular control mechanisms, which require that the plaintiff should have a close relationship of love and affection with the primary victim, should be physically proximate to the accident or its immediate aftermath,[358] and should suffer a 'sudden' shock. **5.169**

In a series of medical negligence cases the courts have been exercised in determining whether the plaintiff was sufficiently proximate to the accident and whether shock was suffered 'suddenly' or was the result of the cumulative effect of events and a gradual realization of the effect of the defendant's wrong. In *Taylor v Somerset HA*[359] a widow whose husband had died as a consequence of medical negligence was unsuccessful in her claim for damages for psychiatric shock from seeing his body in the hospital mortuary. Auld J held that the plaintiff needed to show that the husband's death had resulted in 'some external, traumatic event in the nature of an accident or violent happening'.[360] In *Sion v Hampstead HA*[361] a claim by a father who stayed by his son's hospital bedside following an accident until his death two weeks later allegedly due to the defendant's misdiagnosis of his injuries, similarly failed. **5.170**

---

352 See *Rothwell v Chemical Insulating Co Ltd* [2008] 1 AC 281, [52], [104] (HL); *Corr v IBC Vehicles Ltd* [2008] 2 WLR 499, [54] (HL).

353 See, eg, *Hunter v British Coal Corporation* [1998] QB 140 (CA); *McLoughlin v Jones* [2002] QB 1312 (CA); *Re Organ Retention Group Litigation* [2005] 2 WLR 358; *Butchart v Home Office* [2006] 1 WLR 1155 (CA).

354 *Wild v Southend University Hospital NHS Foundation Trust* [2014] EWHC 4053, at [22].

355 *Less v Hussain* [2012] EWHC 3513, at [185].

356 *Bourhill v Young* [1943] AC 92 at 110, 117 (HL) and see *Tame v New South Wales; Annetts v Australian Stations Pty Ltd* (2003) 211 CLR 317 (HCA).

357 [1992] 1 AC 310 (HL).

358 In the earlier decision in *McLoughlin v O'Brian* [1983] 1 AC 410 (HL), Lord Wilberforce had said that there needed to be a 'direct perception of some of the events which go to make up the accident as an entire event', and this could include seeing the immediate aftermath of the accident.

359 (1993) 4 Med LR 34, 37.

360 In *Alcock* itself the viewing of bodies of relatives in a mortuary was held to be outside the aftermath. Compare *Galli-Atkinson v Seghal* [2003] Lloyd's Rep Med 285, where the Court of Appeal allowed a claim by a mother who went to the scene of an accident and was told that her daughter had been killed, and who then saw her badly disfigured body in a mortuary. The visit to the mortuary was seen as the last in a sequence of events which went to make up the entirety of the claimant's perception of the accident.

361 *Sion v Hampstead HA* (1994) 5 Med LR 170 (CA); A Grubb, (1994) 2 Med L Rev 365.

Peter Gibson LJ said that it was the sudden awareness, violently agitating the mind, of what was occurring or had occurred that was the crucial ingredient of shock. But he could see no reason in logic why a breach of duty causing an incident involving no violence or suddenness, such as where the wrong medicine was negligently given to a hospital patient, could not lead to a claim for damages for nervous shock, for example where the negligence had fatal results and a visiting close relative, wholly unprepared for what had occurred, found the body and thereby sustained a sudden and unexpected shock to the nervous system.[362] In *Taylorson v Shieldness Produce Ltd*[363] the claim by parents of a 14-year-old boy crushed in an accident who stayed with their son during the two days he was on a life-support machine also failed. The mother had a dawning consciousness that they were going to lose their son, and Kennedy J declined to extend the notion of proximity to 'this elongated process'.

5.171 The same principles have been applied in the case of fathers suing in respect of the birth of their still-born child. For example, there was no sufficient evidence that a father's psychiatric injury following a stillbirth was caused by shock, as opposed to bereavement.[364] Again, a father could not recover for the mental injury he suffered on realizing that his child had died in the mother's womb following the defendant's negligence.[365]

5.172 On the other hand, the requirements of proximity and suddenness were satisfied in *Tredget v Bexley HA*.[366] In this case the defendant's negligence in failing to deliver a child by Caesarean section caused the child to be born severely asphyxiated and to die two days later. The father was present at the birth. The judge found that the actual birth with its 'chaos' or 'pandemonium', the difficulties that the mother had with the delivery, the sense in the room that something was wrong, and the arrival of the child in a distressed condition requiring immediate resuscitation was, for those immediately and directly involved as each of the parents was, frightening and horrifying. He was satisfied that the period from onset of labour until the child's death was effectively one event, that there was no need to invoke the 'aftermath' doctrine, and that the parents were victims of an experience sufficient to establish liability even though a full appreciation of the gravity of that child's condition only developed in the forty-eight hours between birth and death. As that composite event was a powerful factor in contributing to the pathological grief thereafter suffered by the parents, each was entitled to damages for psychiatric injury. Again, in *Walters v North Glamorgan NHS Trust*[367] a claim by a mother who suffered pathological grief reaction after her baby took thirty-six hours to die following negligent treatment succeeded. Ward LJ said that there was an inexorable progression from the moment when the child suffered a fit as a result of the hospital's failure in diagnosis, the fit causing brain damage which shortly afterwards made the termination of the child's life inevitable, and a dreadful climax when the child died in the mother's arms. It was a seamless tale and one drawn-out experience with an obvious beginning and an equally obvious end.

5.173 **(d) Claims in both categories** The *Alcock* rules leave uncompensated the parent whose psychiatric illness develops only as a result of learning of and experiencing the injury to the child a long time after the birth. But if the mother is, as she must be, the patient of the obstetrician, can she qualify as a primary victim? If so, it may be possible for her to claim that her

[362] *Sion v Hampstead HA*, n 361, 176.

[363] [1994] PIQR 329 (CA). See also, eg, *Liverpool Women's Hospital NHS Foundation Trust v Ronayne* [2015] EWCA Civ 588; *Shorter v Surrey and Sussex Healthcare NHS Trust* [2015] EWHC 614.

[364] *Less v Hussain* [2012] EWHC 3513, at [187]–[191].

[365] *Wild v Southend University Hospital NHS Foundation Trust* [2014] EWHC 4053.

[366] (1994) 5 Med LR 178; A Grubb, (1994) 2 Med L Rev 368.

[367] [2003] Lloyd's Rep Med 49.

psychiatric illness was a foreseeable consequence of the long-term stress caused to her by the negligence of her obstetrician. Employees seeking damages for psychiatric injury caused by their employers' breach of duty in not protecting them from work-related stress are treated as primary victims.[368] So it may be that a mother can make a claim on a somewhat similar basis. However, while a mother traumatized by the circumstances of birth can be a primary victim, one injured by developing stress suffers not because of the circumstances of birth but because she later learns of her child's developing disability. It may be hard to establish that such psychiatric illness is a foreseeable consequence of the negligence.

This problem was recognized by Steel J in *Farrell v Merton Sutton and Wandsworth HA*.[369] The claimant gave birth by Caesarean section to a son who developed cerebral palsy. The operation itself was traumatic, and she was not able to see the child for over twenty-four hours, at which time he was in intensive care, when she was told he had irreversible brain damage. A claim by the child was settled, and the mother claimed for psychiatric injury. She succeeded as a primary victim, Steel J being satisfied that there was no break in the chain of causation. She considered that the trauma of the birth encompassed not only the events in the operating theatre but also the position up to and including the mother's first sight of her baby and the realization of his disability. In the alternative she found that, as the delay was attributable to the defendants, in the circumstances the claimant's first sight of the child was in the immediate aftermath of the birth, and she succeeded as a secondary victim. The claimant was held to be entitled in addition to damages for 'loss of a private life far beyond the normal constraints imposed by bringing up a healthy child', but the total award of general damages did not distinguish between the two claims. **5.174**

While a remedy was found in *Farrell*, it may not always be possible to attribute developing psychiatric illness to the event causing the child's injury or its immediate aftermath or to establish that this was a foreseeable consequence of the negligence. The difficulty can be illustrated by the decision of the House of Lords in *Grieves v F T Everard & Sons*,[370] where the claimant had developed a depressive illness on account of his fears from having been exposed to asbestos dust many years earlier. Their Lordships were satisfied that the evidence did not establish that the psychiatric injury was itself foreseeable, and held that the plaintiff could not qualify as a primary victim simply because there was a foreseeable risk of injury by disease. *Page v Smith* could apply only to those within the zone of danger of physical impact, and could not be extended to cover the instant case. Lord Hope said that the category of primary victim should be confined to persons who suffered psychiatric injury caused by fear or distress resulting from involvement in an accident caused by the defendant: and here the causal chain was stretched far beyond what was envisaged in *Page*. **5.175**

(e) **Proposals for reform** It is not difficult to criticize many of the preceding principles. The need to classify all victims of psychiatric injury as primary or secondary, the nature of the dividing line between the two, the restrictions on recovery by those who suffer psychiatric injury on account of physical harm to others, the 'sudden shock' rule, all raise problematic issues. Some solutions were put forward by the Law Commission,[371] which recommended, inter alia: that the courts consider abandoning any practical consequences flowing from the primary/secondary **5.176**

[368] *Walker v Northumberland CC* [1995] 1 All ER 737; *Hatton v Sutherland* [2002] 2 All ER 1 (CA), where the court discusses the principles to be applied in this kind of case (reversed in part sub nom *Barber v Somerset CC* [2004] 1 WLR 1089 (HL)).
[369] (2000) 57 BMLR 158.
[370] [2008] 1 AC 281 (sub nom *Rothwell v Chemical Insulating Co Ltd*).
[371] Law Commission, Report 249 (1998).

distinction;[372] that in secondary victim cases the *Alcock* factors involving proximity to an accident and suddenness of shock be removed and that there be a new statutory duty of care with its elements positively spelt out in the statute;[373] and that other kinds of claims be left to develop by incremental judicial decision.[374]

5.177 There are no plans at present to implement any of these proposals by legislation.[375] And seemingly it is too late to achieve satisfactory development of the law by judicial decision. But a better approach, which is broadly consistent with the Law Commission's recommendations, is the view taken by the High Court of Australia in *Tame v New South Wales: Annetts v Australian Stations Pty Ltd*,[376] that a duty to take care not to cause psychiatric harm turns on whether, in all the circumstances, the defendant should reasonably have foreseen that a person in the position of the plaintiff would sustain a recognizable psychiatric injury. Physical and temporal proximity, suddenness and a close and loving relationship with a physical victim may be relevant to assessing reasonable foreseeability, causation, and remoteness, but are not themselves decisive of liability.

(iii) Bereavement awards

5.178 Where a child has died after 31 December 1982 the parents (if it was legitimate) or the mother (if it was illegitimate) are entitled to a statutory award of damages for bereavement.[377] The award is conventional. In relation to death before 1 April 1991 it is £3,500, in relation to later death before 1 April 2002 it is £7,500, and in relation to subsequent death it is £10,000.[378] Where both parents have an entitlement, the award is to be divided equally between them.[379]

E. Claims on Behalf of the Estate in Cases of Stillbirth and Neonatal Death

1. Stillbirths

5.179 At common law, there can be no actionable breach of duty to those who are stillborn: before they are born they are not 'persons',[380] and after they are born, because they never lived, they have no legal rights. Nor is the position different under statute. First, it is a precondition for recovery under the Congenital Disabilities (Civil Liability) Act 1976 that the child is born alive. Secondly, no right either of bereavement or dependency can arise out of the Fatal Accidents Act 1976, because death is a precondition of such rights. A court will inevitably conclude that one who, in the eyes of the law, has never become a 'person', cannot be said to have obtained life, and therefore cannot be said to have suffered death. Third, for the same reason there will be no claim under the Law Reform (Miscellaneous Provisions) Act 1934 which applies only 'on the death of any person'.[381]

[372] ibid, paras 5.45–5.54.

[373] ibid, paras 6.4–6.53.

[374] ibid, paras 7.1–7.16.

[375] The Government Consultation Paper, *The Law of Damages* CP 09/07, ch 3, para 97 stated that the government considered it preferable to allow the courts to continue to develop the law in this area.

[376] (2003) 211 CLR 317 (HCA); and see *Gifford v Strang Patrick Stevedoring Pty Ltd* (2003) 214 CLR 269 (HCA).

[377] Fatal Accidents Act 1976, s 1A, inserted by Administration of Justice Act 1982, s 3.

[378] Damages for Bereavement (Variation of Sum) (England and Wales) Orders 1990, SI 1990/2775 and 2002, SI 2002/644.

[379] Fatal Accidents Act 1976, s 1A(4).

[380] See paras 5.05–5.08. For the definition of a still-birth, see Births and Registration Act 1926, s 12, as amended by the Still-Birth (Definition) Act 1992.

[381] Law Reform (Miscellaneous Provisions) Act 1934, s 1(1).

2. Neonatal deaths

There may be a claim on behalf of the estate of a child dying as a result of a birth injury for reasonable funeral expenses.[382] A claim for the pain, suffering, and loss of amenity of the child before death will survive for the benefit of the estate but will be modest. In *Kralj v McGrath*[383] the award was £2,500; in *Kerby v Redbridge HA*,[384] where the child survived only for three days, the award was £750. **5.180**

F. Claims for Injuries Preventing the Conception of Children

Claims for injuries which deprive a man or a woman of the chance or ability to have a child are strictly outside the ambit of this chapter, but deserve mention by way of conclusion. Normally claims of this kind are actionable on ordinary principles. Indeed, in *Briody v St Helens and Knowsley Area Health Authority*[385] the Court of Appeal recognized that a woman who, by the negligence of the defendants had been deprived of her womb, had suffered a very serious loss of amenity. The damages should reflect an understanding of the gravity of that detriment. **5.181**

It is clear that injury to a male affecting his reproductive capacity is likewise actionable. However, an unusual variation arose for consideration in *Yearworth v North Bristol NHS Trust*.[386] The six claimants had been diagnosed with cancer and had accepted advice to undergo a course of chemotherapy. Having been advised that the treatment might damage their fertility, they produced samples of semen which the defendant hospital agreed to freeze and store. The defendant negligently allowed the semen to thaw and the sperm contained in it to perish irretrievably. The claimants sought damages, alleging, inter alia, that they had suffered personal injury through destruction of a bodily product which was intended to be kept in a biologically active state in order to fertilize a human egg. But the Court of Appeal rejected the argument, holding that to treat this as personal injury would be a fiction and would generate paradoxes and lead to substantial uncertainty in an area of law which should be simple and clear.[387] And even accepting the principle within the suggested parameters, the law would swim into deep waters in relation to the continued biological activity, and the function, of several other bodily substances or parts. Further, had one of the men died prior to the loss of the sperm the suggested personal injury would have been inflicted upon all of the men save him; and had the loss occurred after the men had recovered their natural fertility, or the sperm had been lawfully destroyed,[388] the suggested personal injury would have been inflicted albeit damage would be absent and the injury would not be actionable. However, the claims nonetheless succeeded on another basis, for the defendants were held liable in their capacity as bailees of the sperm.[389] **5.182**

---

[382] ibid, s 1(2)(c).
[383] [1986] 1 All ER 54.
[384] (1993) 4 Med LR 178.
[385] [2002] 2 WLR 394 (CA).
[386] [2009] 3 WLR 118 (CA). For further discussion, see Chapter 19.
[387] But see the debate in *Holdich v Lothian Health Board* [2013] CSOH 197, at [6]–[8], where Lord Stewart was prepared to contemplate that in Scotland there might be a personal injury claim for damage to gametes.
[388] The Human Fertilisation and Embryology Act 1990, s 14, imposes a maximum statutory storage period of fourteen years.
[389] See generally C Hawes, 'Property Interests in Body Parts: *Yearworth v North Bristol NHS Trust*' (2010) 73 MLR 130. For extensive discussion of the issues arising out of this aspect of *Yearworth*, see *Holdich v Lothian Health Board* [2013] CSOH 197, at [36]–[76].

5.183 A claim for mental injury also may be a possibility. In *Yearworth* the Court of Appeal recognized that on ordinary principles of tort liability the claimants would need to establish that they had suffered such injury as a reasonably foreseeable consequences of the defendant's breach of duty. Furthermore, the question would arise whether, replicating the rule in secondary victim cases, a distinction should be drawn between the person who witnesses damage to his property and in consequence suffers psychiatric injury and the person who receives information about it and suffers similarly. But this did not need to be decided, for the arrangements for the storage of the sperm were closely akin to contracts and should, therefore, fall within the principle allowing recovery for mental distress where the object of the contract was to provide enjoyment, comfort, peace of mind, or other non-pecuniary or family benefits.[390]

[390] Citing, inter alia, *Johnson v Unisys Ltd* [20013] 1 AC 518, at [70]. For discussion of the delictual claim in *Yearworth*, see *Holdich v Lothian Health Board* [2013] CSOH 197, at [77]–[98].

6

CAUSATION AND DEFENCES

Richard Goldberg

A. Causation

1. Introduction

It is trite law that merely to show that a defendant was in breach of a duty owed to the claimant and that the claimant suffered damage does not suffice to ground an action in negligence. The defendant's breach must have caused the claimant's damage and, additionally, the damage must be such that the law regards it proper to hold the defendant responsible for it. These two requirements jointly constitute causation and are often separately referred to as (i) *cause in fact* and (ii) *cause in law* and *remoteness*. **6.01**

The concern here is whether there are considerations specific to medical law which call for a treatment of causation beyond that which can be found in standard works on the law of torts.[1] The answer is that there are.[2] While the principles of causation may ordinarily be relatively straightforward, it is fair to say that causation in the context of medical law is fraught with difficulty.[3] This is due both to the complexity of the factual circumstances themselves and to the (perhaps unnecessarily) complex nature of the law, when the principles come to be applied to the facts. As for the former, the complicated and, to some extent, indeterminate nature of medical science means that the causal nexus between X and Y, while **6.02**

[1] See J Fleming, *The Law of Torts* (9th edn, Law Book Co 1998); K Oliphant (ed), *The Law of Torts* (2nd edn, Butterworths 2007) ch 14 and, particularly on clinical negligence, M Jones, *Medical Negligence* (4th edn, Sweet & Maxwell 2008) ch 5. See also R Goldberg, *Causation and Risk in the Law of Torts: Scientific Evidence and Medicinal Product Liability* (Hart Publishing 1999); L Khoury, *Uncertain Causation in Medical Liability* (Hart Publishing 2006); R Goldberg (ed), *Perspectives on Causation* (Hart Publishing 2011); S Steel, *Proof of Causation in Tort Law* (Cambridge University Press 2015).

[2] For a noteworthy discussion of causation in the medical context, see *Chappel v Hart* (1998) 27 ALJR 1344 (HC Aus), especially the judgment of Kirby J.

[3] It was Lord Bridge in *Hotson v East Berkshire AHA* [1987] 2 All ER 909 who remarked (at 913): 'In some cases, perhaps particularly medical negligence cases, causation may be so shrouded in mystery that the courts can only measure statistical chances.'

suspected, may be hard to demonstrate. Indeed, it could be said that the more medicine is portrayed as a scientific endeavour, rather than as an art or a combination of both art and science, the more difficult it becomes on occasion to demonstrate to the satisfaction of the law a causative link between breach and damage.[4] As for the latter, the law becomes ever more complex as it seeks to serve the twin aims of justice: fairness to the patient and to the doctor.[5] As Leggatt LJ put it in *Tahir v Haringey HA*,[6] 'when a doctor has been at fault no court wishes to send his patient away empty handed'. This, of course, is the crux. A breach of duty is proved, or even admitted, and yet the doctor or hospital is found not liable and the patient recovers nothing. The patient is left bemused. But, equally, if whatever happened to the patient was not the result of the doctor's conduct, it is hard to see why the doctor should be held liable. Only a system which compensated damaged patients on the basis of need rather than proof of someone else's misconduct could square this particular circle.

6.03 There is an 'apparent tension'[7] between the levels of evidential proof of causation for purposes of science and for the law. For the law of negligence, it is enough to show that the balance of probabilities—meaning more than 50 per cent,[8] or on a preponderance of the evidence—indicates a causal connection. It has been sometimes erroneously assumed by lawyers that scientists regard an association as causal if it is 95 per cent certain, but this is a

[4] See, eg, *Bonthrone v Millan* [1985] 2 The Lancet 1137 (Lord Jauncey) (existence of cryptogenic (unknown) causes to eliminate possible causal connection between pertussis vaccine and brain damage); *Loveday v Renton* [1990] 1 Med LR 117 (whooping cough vaccine); *Kay v Ayrshire and Arran Health Board* [1987] 2 All ER 417 (penicillin overdose not capable of causing or aggravating deafness); *Dingley v Chief Constable, Strathclyde Police No 4* 2000 SC (HL) 77, 86, 93 (in the event of there being no proof on a balance of probabilities that trauma could ever trigger the onset of multiple sclerosis, it was inevitable that the pursuer would be unable to establish the specific issue as to whether there had been a causal connection between the pursuer's whiplash injury in a road traffic accident and the subsequent onset of multiple sclerosis). Where a claimant seeks to rely on epidemiological evidence of disease through an expert witness in proving causation, the claimant must impart to the court special knowledge of the subject matter of epidemiology, including published material lying within the witness's field of expertise, so that court can form its own judgment about the alleged causal connection between the disease and the defendant's breach of duty: *McTear v Imperial Tobacco Ltd* 2005 2 SC 1 (OH); followed in *Smith v McNair* [2008] CSOH 154. Discussed in R Goldberg, (2009) 13 Edin LR 282. Even where in principle a connection can be shown between the type of harm suffered by the claimant and a specific hazard, it may be extremely difficult to demonstrate that the individual claimant's condition was caused by exposure to that hazard as opposed to another factor for which the defendant was not responsible: see M Jones, *Medical Negligence* (4th edn, Sweet & Maxwell 2008) 5-020, citing *Plater v Sanotrach* [2004] EWHC 146 (QB), [99] (claimant unable to prove on balance of probability that his HIV infection had been caused by a contaminated needle or syringe after he had been given an intravenous injection at defendant's clinic, since he had been unable to exclude other possible causes of HIV infection). See also *Reay v British Nuclear Fuels; Hope v BNFL* [1994] 5 Med LR 1, 53, where French J held that the plaintiffs had failed to establish that paternal pre-conception irradiation was a material contributory cause of childhood leukaemia of Dorothy Reay or non-Hodgkin's Lymphoma of Vivien Hope. Note also the difficulties in proving both general and specific causation between a product and damage with epidemiological evidence derived from trends in general populations in the decision of the Outer House of the Scottish Court of Session in *McTear v Imperial Tobacco Ltd* 2005 2 SC 1 (OH) The Times, 14 June 2005, in particular, paras 6.180, 6.184–6.185. Discussed in R Goldberg, 'Causation' in G Howells (ed), *The Law of Product Liability* (2nd edn, LexisNexis 2007), para 5.3; and C Miller, 'Causation in Personal Injury: Legal or Epidemiological Common Sense' (2006) 26 LS 544, 566.

[5] See, eg, *Fairchild v Glenhaven Funeral Services Ltd* [2002] 3 All ER 305 (seeking to strike a balance between fairness to the claimant and defendant in an industrial context).

[6] [1998] Lloyd's Rep Med 104, 111. For a Commentary, see A Grubb, (1996) 4 Med LRev 92.

[7] R Goldberg, 'Epidemiological Uncertainty, Causation, and Drug Product Liability' (2014) McGill LJ 777, 784–85.

[8] The expression of the balance of probabilities as more than 50 per cent may 'carry with it a danger of pseudo-mathematics'. While process may include evaluation of scientific evidence it 'is not scientific . . . and to express the probability of some event having happened in percentage terms is illusory': *Milton Keynes Borough Council v Nulty* [2013] EWCA Civ 15, [2013] 1 WLR 1183, [35], per Toulson LJ.

misinterpretation of the so-called p value, which is merely the level of statistical significance required to exclude the possibility that something transpiring in a cohort of cases does so by chance.[9] While neither the claimant nor the defendant has to apply scientific standards of proof when determining causation on a balance of probabilities,[10] courts should be aware of the difficulty that may be encountered by an expert 'in readjusting his focus from the 95 per cent confidence limits approach to the balance of probabilities test'.[11] However, in *Vadera v Shaw,*[12] the Court of Appeal reconciled the legal standard of proof of a balance of probabilities with the scientific standard of statistical significance in showing that a failure to establish a statistically significant connection between the oral contraceptive Logynon and strokes was fatal to the establishment of proof of causation on a balance of probabilities. Henry LJ stated:

> The judge concluded, and in our respectful view was right on the evidence to conclude, that the studies carried out and referred to by Dr Lidegaard [for the plaintiff] did not establish a statistically significant connection between Logynon and strokes. Such evidence cannot be ignored by a judge. It is as common sense a conclusion as one could wish to say that if the connection between 'a' and 'b' cannot be shown with confidence to be other than a coincidence, then it cannot be held on a balance of probabilities that 'a' caused 'b'. This is not to allow scientists or statisticians to usurp the judge's function, but rather to permit him to use their skills to discern a connection, or lack of connection between the two phenomena.[13]

An attempt to reconcile the balance of probabilities standard and the standard for epidemiology has emerged with the theory that causation can be proved on the balance of probabilities by reference to the doubling of risk of injury.[14] In *XYZ v Schering Health Care Ltd*,[15] a trial of seven lead cases involving third generation oral contraceptives, Mackay J applied this so-called doubling of risk theory, and held that a claimant could prove that an exposure to risk caused injury if that exposure had more than doubled the risk of the injury occurring.[16] This method of proving causation has been applied in a case of bladder cancer **6.04**

[9] ibid.

[10] *Carter v Basildon and Thurrock University Hospitals NHS Foundation Trust* [2007] EWHC 1882 (QB), [2007] LS Law Medical 657, [92]. Such a standard must be 'much more than marginal': See *Dingley v The Chief Constable, Strathclyde Police*, 1998 SC 548 at 603, cited in *Sienkiewicz v Grief (UK) Ltd* [2011] UKSC 10, [2011] 2 AC 229, [9] per Lord Phillips.

[11] *Carter v Basildon*, n 10, [97]. A confidence interval or confidence limit is a range within which a study parameter lies 95 per cent of the time: R Goldberg, *Causation and Risk in the Law of Torts: Scientific Evidence and Medicinal Product Liability* (Hart Publishing 1999) 137. See further *Fairhurst v St Helens & Knowsley HA* [1994] 5 Med LR 422, where Judge Clark QC held that the plaintiff's severe mental retardation had been caused by kernicterus (bilirubin encephalopathy) as a consequence of rhesus incompatibility. In coming to this decision, the judge examined the conflicting evidence of the respective experts of the plaintiff and the defendant. In accepting the evidence of the plaintiff's expert, he considered there was some force in counsel for the plaintiff's submission that the approach of the defendant's expert 'was more akin to that of the scientist seeking scientific certainty' (at 426–27).

[12] *Vadera v Shaw* (1998) 45 BMLR 162 (CA).

[13] ibid, 164. However, it is suggested that there was a failure by the trial judge and the Court of Appeal to scrutinize adequately the scientific evidence in respect of causation. The examination of the relevant scientific evidence concerning the increased risk of stroke in a 22-year-old Asian woman with no history of health problems was unsatisfactory. No attempt was made in this case to particularize the evidence to the individual patient: R Goldberg, 'The Contraceptive Pill, Negligence and Causation: Views on *Vadera v Shaw*' (2000) 8 Med L Rev 316, 331–35.

[14] See especially in the context of medicinal products and causation, R Goldberg, 'Epidemiological Uncertainty, Causation, and Drug Product Liability' (2014) McGill LJ 777, 785–93.

[15] *XYZ v Schering Health Care Ltd* [2002] EWHC 1420, (2002) 70 BMLR 88 (QB).

[16] ibid, [21] *per* Mackay J. See further C J Miller and R S Goldberg, RS, *Product Liability* (2nd edn, Oxford University Press 2004) 17.06–17.08.

where the claimant had been tortiously exposed to carcinogens and non-tortiously exposed to cigarette smoke, both of which are potent causes of the condition.[17] In cases of multiple potential causes, Smith LJ opined in the Court of Appeal in *Sienkiewicz v Greif* that, 'saving the expression of a different view by the Supreme Court',[18] a claimant can demonstrate causation by showing that a tortious exposure has at least doubled the risk arising from the non-tortious cause or causes. However, on appeal to the Supreme Court,[19] though there was unanimity in the Justices holding that there was no room for introducing the doubling of risk approach to 'single exposure' mesothelioma cases or multiple defendant mesothelioma cases,[20] the differences in view emerged with the obiter discussion of the general applicability of the doubling of risk theory using epidemiological evidence to determine proof of causation in personal injury cases. While Lord Phillips concluded[21] that there was no scope for the doubling the risk test in cases where two agents operated cumulatively and simultaneously in causing the onset of the disease, since in such cases the material contribution rule in *Bonnington Castings v Wardlaw* [22] would apply, he submitted[23] that there was no reason in principle why the 'doubles the risk test' should not be applied where the initiation of a disease was dose related and there had been consecutive exposures to an agent or agents that cause the disease, for example, *McGhee v National Coal Board*.[24] He also considered[25] that there was no reason in principle why the 'doubles the risk' test should not apply to competing alternative, rather than cumulative potential causes of a disease or injury, such as *Hotson v East Berks Area Health Authority*.[26] However, neither Lord Rodger nor Baroness Hale took

[17] *Novartis Grimsby Ltd v Cookson* [2007] EWCA Civ 1261, [74] *per* Smith LJ. See also *Ministry of Defence v AB* [2010] EWCA Civ 1317, 117 BMLR 101 at 149 [AB]. In the appeal for AB (*AB v Ministry of Defence* [2012] UKSC 9, [2013] 1 AC 78), the Supreme Court found the doubling of risk theory relevant in the context of examining the strength of claimants' cases on causation and in determining whether the trial court's exercise of discretion under s 33 of the Limitation Act 1980 was appropriate: at [100] per Lord Wilson. See further J Stapleton, 'Factual Causation, Mesothelioma and Statistical Validity' (2012) 128 LQR 221, 223–25.

[18] *Sienkiewicz v Greif (UK) Ltd* [2009] EWCA Civ 1159, [2010] 2 WLR 951 (CA), [23] *per* Smith LJ.

[19] *Sienkiewicz v Grief (UK) Ltd* [2011] UKSC 10, [2011] 2 AC 229.

[20] ibid, [106] *per* Lord Phillips, [160] *per* Lord Rodger, [169] *per* Baroness Hale, [188] *per* Lord Mance, [2003] *per* Lord Kerr, [220] *per* Lord Dyson. Cf Stapleton (2012) 128 LQR 221, 224–25, who states that both propositions (using the doubling of the risk approach in mesothelioma cases where there was a single exposure or one with multiple defendants) could have been rejected as invalid on elementary statistical principles. However, in *Heneghan v Manchester Dry Docks Ltd* [2016] EWCA Civ 86, [2016] 1 WLR 2036, [8], Lord Dyson MR, while noting the doubt in *Sienkiewicz* as to the validity of the doubling the risk test for mesothelioma cases, accepted its use in answering the question as to whether the claimant's lung cancer had been caused by asbestos as opposed to smoking.

[21] *Sienkiewicz v Greif* [2011] UKSC 10, [91] *per* Lord Phillips.

[22] *Bonnington Castings v Wardlaw* [1956] AC 613, 620 *per* Lord Reid.

[23] *Sienkiewicz v Greif* [2011] UKSC 10, [92] *per* Lord Phillips.

[24] *McGhee v National Coal Board* [1973] 1 WLR 1. Yet as Professor Stapleton has observed, the basis for the validity of the doubling of the risk approach in this instance would be absent. By way of illustration, she cites the example of a person injured in a road accident who is administered an emergency dose of a medicinal product. The injured person is immediately transferred to a hospital, where the admitting doctor, failing to discover that medications had been administered to the victim, negligently administers a smaller dose of the medication. In that scenario, it is likely that the causal mechanism required a commingling of molecules from the later smaller dose with the innocent molecules, and thus the tortious administration of the medication by the admitting doctor would have made a causal contribution to the death, even though another larger and earlier dose would have been sufficient to cause death: J Stapleton, 'Factual Causation, Mesothelioma and Statistical Validity' (2012) 128 LQR 221, 228–29; see, further, J Stapleton, 'Unnecessary Causes' (2013) 129 LQR 39, 55–56.

[25] *Sienkiewicz v Greif* [2011] UKSC 10, [93] *per* Lord Phillips.

[26] *Hotson v East Berks Area Health Authority* [1987] AC 750.

such a view, and both thought that a doubling of risk approach was not an appropriate test of causation.[27]

In cases where statistics are strongly in favour of causation, while such bare statistics per se may not establish a causal link between negligence and damage, they may form part of the background against which the medical aetiology must be assessed. In *Demery v Cardiff and Vale NHS Trust*,[28] a majority of the Court of Appeal held that the expert evidence should have been considered against a background in which the great majority of cases had a successful outcome. The judge had failed to consider whether on the balance of probabilities the delay which occurred and the consequences of the delay turned what was a routine and normally successful operation into one of these very rare ones in which the outcome was unsuccessful.[29] In group litigation, when causation is being addressed as a generic issue common to a series of claimants, statistical evidence may be determinative. In *Corby Group Litigation v Corby DC*,[30] the claimants alleged that birth defects—consisting of shortened or missing arms, legs, and fingers—had been caused as a result of their pregnant mothers' ingestion or inhalation of harmful substances generated by reclamation works at an extensive industrial site to the east of Corby. The court was required to consider and address specific issues which were generic and common to the claimants and prerequisite to the determination of liability to an individual claimant. In giving judgment for the claimants, it was held that the local authority's failure to exercise reasonable care and skill in and about the execution of the reclamation works had the ability to cause the upper and lower limb defects to the claimants in all but two claimants. This conclusion was supported by evidence of a statistically significant cluster of birth defects to children born to mothers living in Corby in the period 1989 to 1998.[31] **6.05**

However, there is a clear need for caution to be exercised in the use of statistics in establishing causation. When determining liability to an individual claimant, courts must look at that claimant's individual circumstances[32] and not merely focus on general statistics. Accordingly, in *Wardlaw v Farrar*[33] it was alleged that a general practitioner was negligent in his failure to diagnose a pulmonary embolism in a patient and it was claimed that a delay in arranging for the admission of the patient to hospital reduced the patient's chance of survival. The claimant's counsel relied on evidence from the International Co-operative Pulmonary Embolism Registry (ICOPER), which indicated that 85 per cent of patients survived a pulmonary embolism, but that the patient had proved resistant to the usual **6.06**

[27] *Sienkiewicz v Greif* [2011] UKSC 10, [156], [158], [162] *per* Lord Rodger, [170], [172]–[173] *per* Baroness Hale. For further analysis, see R Goldberg, 'Epidemiological Uncertainty, Causation, and Drug Product Liability' (2014) McGill LJ 777, 789–93 (and noting further the cautious attitude by the full Federal Court of Australia towards the use of the doubling of risk rule in the context of specific causation and the anti-inflammatory drug Vioxx in *Merck Sharp & Dohme (Australia) Pty Limited v Peterson* [2011] FCAFC 128, leave to appeal refused, [2012] HCATrans 105.

[28] *Demery v Cardiff and Vale NHS Trust* [2006] EWCA Civ 1131.

[29] ibid, [35]–[36] *per* Pill LJ.

[30] *Corby Group Litigation v Corby DC* [2009] EWHC 1944 (TCC), [2009] NPC 100, [2010] Env LR D2.

[31] ibid, [884]–[885].

[32] For the need to exercise caution in the use of general statistics in establishing causation, and the importance of looking at the claimant's individual circumstances, see the observations of Brooke LJ in *Wardlaw v Farrar* [2003] 4 All ER 1358, [2004] Lloyd's Rep Med 98, [2004] PIQR 19 at [35]–[36]. See further *Amaca v Ellis* [2010] HCA 5, [62], [70]; *Sienkiewicz v Greif* [2011] UK SC 10, [152], [163] *per* Lord Rodger, [170], [172] *per* Baroness Hale, [190]–[192] *per* Lord Mance, [204]–[206] per Lord Kerr; *Benhaim v O'Donovan* 2016 SCC 48, [50], per Wagner J (McLachlin CJ, and Karakatsanis and Gascon JJ concurring).

[33] *Wardlaw v Farrar* [2003] 4 All ER 1358, [2004] Lloyd's Rep Med 98, [2004] PIQR 19.

beneficial effect of anti-coagulation therapy when she received treatment in hospital and subsequently died.[34] The claimant's counsel argued that the fact that the patient was resistant to the anti-coagulation therapy should be ignored, as she submitted that the matter should be determined at the time of the negligent diagnosis, and that it was this diagnosis which allowed the thrombosis to grow.[35] The Court of Appeal rejected this argument. In considering on the balance of probabilities whether the doctor's negligence had caused the patient's death, the judge had to take into account all the relevant evidence. The failure of anti-coagulant therapy to prevent the formation of a massive pulmonary embolism was inevitably a material piece of evidence. This indicated that it was probable that the patient fell into the category of the other 15 per cent of patients who fail to survive despite treatment for unknown reasons.[36]

6.07 Brooke LJ observed:

> While judges are of course entitled to place such weight on statistical evidence as is appropriate, they must not blind themselves to the effect of other evidence which might put a particular patient in a particular category, regardless of the probabilities.[37]

On the basis of these unknown reasons, the Court of Appeal upheld the trial judge's decision that the delay had not materially contributed to the patient's death.[38]

2. Factual causation

(i) The burden of proof

6.08 In any examination of causation, the first question to ask is who bears the burden of proving the causative link between breach of duty and damage. The answer is unequivocally that in this, as in all other aspects of civil litigation, it is the claimant who must prove causation and it must be established on a balance of probabilities.[39] There was a brief period of time in which it was thought that, in certain particular circumstances, medical law provided an exception to this principle by reversing the burden and placing it on the defendant. As will be discussed more fully below, it was Lord Wilberforce's speech in *McGhee v National Coal Board*[40] that gave rise to this strain of reasoning. The claimant had established a breach of duty, the failure to provide showers so as to be able to wash off the brick dust which pervaded the workplace. The presence of the dust in the workplace was not itself a breach of duty. The result was that the brick dust continued to adhere to his skin while he cycled home. He contracted dermatitis. What he could not definitively demonstrate was that the extra time spent cycling home was causative of his dermatitis. Lord Wilberforce's speech was taken to mean that, in such a case, the burden of proof shifted to the defendant to show that his breach of duty did not cause the dermatitis. Certainly Peter Pain J in *Clark v McLennan*[41] interpreted the speech in this way. In *Wilsher v Essex AHA*,[42] however, the House of Lords categorically

[34] ibid, [4], [6]–[7], [33].

[35] ibid, [34].

[36] ibid, [38].

[37] ibid, [35].

[38] ibid, [36]. See also *Anderson v Heatherwood and Wrexham Park Hospitals NHS Trust* [2005] EWHC 1325, [27] *per* Judge Eccles QC.

[39] *Pickford v Imperial Chemical Industries plc* [1998] 3 All ER 362, [1998] 1 WLR 1189 (HL).

[40] [1973] 1 WLR 1, 6. Discussed in E Weinrib, 'A Step Forward in Factual Causation' (1975) 38 MLR 518.

[41] [1983] 1 All ER 416.

[42] [1988] AC 1074, [1986] 3 All ER 801. Discussed in A Grubb, 'Causation and Medical Negligence' [1988] 47 CLJ 350.

reasserted that the burden of proof always remains with the claimant.[43] *McGhee* was distinguished on its facts and Lord Wilberforce's speech was relegated by Lord Bridge to the status of a dissent.[44] That marked the end of that brief period of heresy.

Of course, what *McGhee* and *Wilsher* drew attention to was the well-recognized fact of litigation in medical law, that proof of causation is often an extremely difficult hurdle for the claimant. The law appears to contemplate some kind of linear connection between X and Y, whereas in reality what is involved in medicine is often a series of interdependent and interacting events from which it is at best difficult to pluck one (the defendant's breach) and point to it as 'the cause'. The claimant's increased ill-health may, for example, be as much the consequence of the natural progression of the disease as the defendant's breach. The defendant's breach may be only one of several independent or interacting causal agents, as was the case in *Wilsher*.[45] Or further, the state of medical science may be such that experts may properly disagree as to the exact aetiology of the claimant's condition, as in *Loveday v Renton*.[46] Obvious examples of this in common knowledge are the effects of passive smoking or radiation.[47] **6.09**

(ii) The 'but for' test

The standard approach to causation in the law of torts is represented by the 'but for' test: that the damage suffered by the claimant would not have been suffered *but for* the defendant's breach of duty. The assumption of the law is that it is possible to show (and, therefore, that the law should demand demonstration) that X would not have happened but for Y. The corollary is that if this cannot be demonstrated, causation is not proved and the defendant, regardless of any breach of duty, is not liable. While represented as a principle concerned with fact, it is, of course, self-evident that what is involved is a matter of policy. A limit is placed on the potential liability of the defendant by demanding that a particular form of nexus be shown. And, as has been said, there are numerous circumstances, particularly in medical law, when this policy defeats the claim of the claimant. The clearest example is when the defendant's breach may have been part of the background leading to the claimant's injury. If the defendant can show that the injury would have occurred in any event, regardless of any breach of duty, then the claimant's action will fail. *Barnett v Kensington and Chelsea HMC*[48] was just such a case. The claimant attended an A & E department of **6.10**

---

[43] [1988] AC 1074, 1090–1091.

[44] [1988] AC 1074, 1087.

[45] The House of Lords found that there were at least five possible causes of the retrolental fibroplasia suffered by the claimant. See also *Plater v Sanotrach* [2004] EWHC 146 (QB).

[46] [1990] 1 Med LR 117, where the issue at stake was the relationship (if any) between the pertussis vaccine and brain damage. Discussed in R Goldberg, *Causation and Risk in the Law of Torts: Scientific Evidence and Medicinal Product Liability* (Hart Publishing 1999), 137–43. See also *Kay v Ayrshire and Arran Health Board* [1987] 2 All ER 417.

[47] See, eg, *Reay v British Nuclear Fuels; Hope v BNFL* [1994] 5 Med LR 1, 53, where French J held that the plaintiffs had failed to establish that paternal preconception irradiation was a material contributory cause of childhood leukaemia of Dorothy Reay or non-Hodgkin's Lymphoma of Vivien Hope; also *Davis & Doherty v Balfour Kilpatrick* [2002] EWCA Civ 736, where claimants failed to establish that their alleged radiation sickness was caused by radio frequency emissions. The Court of Appeal confirmed the important point (citing *The Popi M* [1985] 1 WLR 948 (HL)) that the trial court judge was not obliged to make a positive finding as to what *was* the cause of such symptoms. See further *Milton Keynes Borough Council v Nulty* [2013] EWCA Civ 15, [2013] 1 WLR 1183, [34], per Toulson LJ. However, such cases are rare. Cf where there are two competing explanations 'which though they may be uncommon, are not improbable', then once one cause has been eliminated, the judge is entitled to conclude that the other was the probable cause of the damage: *Ide v ATP Sales Ltd* [2008] EWCA Civ 424, [2009] RTR 8, [4], [19]–[20].

[48] [1968] 1 All ER 1068.

a hospital complaining of feeling ill and vomiting after drinking some tea. On the advice of a doctor, a nurse told the claimant to go home and call his own doctor. The claimant was actually suffering from arsenic poisoning and some hours later died. Had the hospital's breach of duty caused the claimant's death? The court found that the claimant would have died in any event, regardless of the defendant doctor's failure to provide proper medical care, because, by the time arsenic poisoning would have been diagnosed, it would have been too late to take any action to save him. Similarly, in *Toth v Jarman*[49] the Court of Appeal held that a general practitioner's failure to administer a glucose injection to a boy suffering glycogen storage disease, while negligent, did not cause the boy's death as by that stage he had suffered irreversible (fatal) brain damage. Further, in *Vernon v Bloomsbury Health Authority*[50] Tucker J held that even if the plaintiff had successfully shown that the defendants had been negligent in failing to monitor his treatment while being administered the drug gentamicin, further assays would probably not have recorded any danger signals of ototoxicity.[51]

6.11 The difficulties associated with the 'but for' test in medical law are at their starkest when there are several concurrent or successive causal factors contributing to the claimant's injury and/or the real cause of the injury is indeterminate. The intrinsic complexity of medical evidence means, therefore, that if the law fails to mitigate the strict application of the 'but for' test, injustice may be done.[52] One obvious mitigating device would be to *reverse the burden of proof*, providing certain conditions were met. As has been seen, tentative steps in this direction were firmly retraced by the House of Lords in *Wilsher*.[53] By contrast, a second mitigating device is an established part of the ordinary tort rules on causation. It may be relevant in medical law. It consists in the claimant being able to succeed if it can be shown that the defendant's breach was a *material* and not *de minimis* contribution to the damage suffered, and thus *a*, if not the only, cause of the damage.[54]

6.12 (a) **Material contribution to the injury** The House of Lords' decision in *Bonnington Castings v Wardlaw*[55] makes it clear that a defendant could be liable if the breach of duty, while not the sole or even a substantial cause, contributed in a material way to the damage suffered by the claimant. This is of some significance to the mitigation of the 'but for' test

---

[49] [2006] Lloyd's Rep Med 397, (2006) 91 BMLR 121.

[50] [1995] 6 Med LR 297.

[51] [1995] 6 Med LR 297, 307. See also *Anderson v Milton Keynes General NHS Trust* [2006] EWHC 2249, [2006] All ER (D) 175 (May) (failure to prescribe antibiotic treatment not cause of injury to claimant's leg since by time antibiotics had been administered, bacteria would have entered the bone and would have been immune from antibiotic attack). The Supreme Court of Canada has reaffirmed the 'but for' test as the primary test for causation in negligence actions: *Hanke v Resurfice Corp* (2007) 278 DLR (4th) 643, [22]. The dangers of taking an over-expansive approach to the 'but for' test should be noted: cf *Crossman v St George's Healthcare NHS Trust* [2016] EWHC 2878 (QB), [45]–[46] *per* Judge Peter Hughes QC (had claimant had operation on different occasion, on a balance of probabilities his operation would have been successful; claim succeeded on conventional 'but for' causation principles).

[52] See D M A Strachan, 'The Scope and Application of the "But For" Causal Test' (1970) 33 MLR 386, 391. This may be true elsewhere also and has led the House of Lords to depart from the 'but for' test in the industrial injury context when the cause of the claimant's injuries was indeterminate but was certainly caused by one or more successive employers who were each at fault: *Fairchild v Glenhaven Funeral Services Ltd* [2002] UKHL 22, [2003] 1 AC 32 (discussed, in J Stapleton, 'Lords A' Leaping Evidentiary Gaps' (2003) 10 Tort LJ 276). See further paras 6.23–6.28. For a possible third judicial development see also paras 6.29 *et seq*.

[53] [1988] AC 1074, 1087.

[54] *Bonnington Castings v Wardlaw* [1956] AC 613.

[55] ibid.

in medical law.[56] In that case, there were two sources of the silica dust which the claimant inhaled, and because of which he contracted pneumoconiosis. The claimant could not point to the source of dust which was dubbed 'guilty', that is, arising from a breach of duty, as being the sole or even the more important source. But the claimant was allowed to succeed in his action by persuading the court to make an inference from the facts that the 'guilty' dust had made a material contribution to his illness. While the material contribution principle applies where negligent and non-negligent components have both contributed to the disease and it is not possible to apportion the harm caused, the claimant can only show the tort made a material contribution to the disease where the disease or harm is 'divisible' so that an increased dose of the harmful agent worsens the disease.[57]

The key factor was the court's preparedness, in the absence of any way of knowing, with any degree of certainty, what actually caused the claimant's illness, to draw an inference of fact favourable to the claimant from all the available evidence. This is clearly, at bottom, a nice issue of judgment for any court. On one level, it can be represented as a matter of extremely technical legal analysis in which certain complex verbal formulae must be applied to the facts and, once applied, the solution to causation will emerge. More realistically, the court **6.13**

[56] Whether the material contribution test is an exception to the but for test, or merely an application of it remains a bone of contention: cf S Bailey, 'Causation in negligence: what is a material contribution?' (2010) 30 LS 167 (an application of the but-for test to cumulative causes) with C Miller, 'Causation in personal injury after (and before) *Sienkiewicz*' (2012) 32 LS 396, 399 (exception to 'but for' test; various combinations of dust concentrations were covered).

[57] *B v Ministry of Defence* [2010] EWCA Civ 1317, (2011) 17 BMLR 101, [134], [150] *per* Smith LJ, giving the judgment of the Court; and, further, *Heneghan v Manchester Dry Docks Ltd* [2016] EWCA Civ 86, [2016] 1 WLR 2036, [46] *per* Lord Dyson MR (the material contribution test is readily demonstrated in the case of divisible injuries like silicosis and pneumoconiosis, 'whose severity is proportionate to the amount of exposure to the causative agent'). Cf the position where the harm is divisible *and* it is possible to apportion the harm caused by the defendant's wrong, with the result that the defendant's negligence can be shown to have caused or contributed to a part only of that injury: *Holtby v Brigham & Cowan (Hill) Ltd* [2000] 3 All ER 421 (CA). Discussed in L Gullifer, (2001) 117 LQR 403. In such cases, the Court of Appeal reaffirmed *McGhee*'s requirement that the claimant must show that the defendant's conduct made a material contribution to the disability but that the defendant is liable only to the extent of that contribution: [2000] 3 All ER 421 (CA), [20] *per* Stuart-Smith LJ. See also *Allen v British Rail Engineering Ltd* [2001] EWCA Civ 242, [2001] ICR 942, [20] *per* Schiemann LJ. It is for the defendant to raise the apportionment issue: *Hatton v Sutherland* [2002] EWCA Civ 76, [2002] 2 All ER 1, [36] and [39] *per* Hale LJ. Note that, other than in the exceptional circumstances prescribed in *Barker v Corus UK Ltd* [2006] UKHL 20, [2006] 2 AC 572 (see para 6.26), proportionate damages are available only in cases classified as ones of 'divisible' injury: L Gullifer, (2001) 117 LQR 403, 407; M Lunney and K Oliphant, *Tort Law: Text and Materials* (5th edn, Oxford University Press 2010) 223. The *Holtby* and *Allen* principles of apportionment 'should be limited to industrial disease or injury cases where there has been successive exposure to harm by a number of agencies, where the effect of harm is divisible, and where it would be unjust for an individual defendant to bear the whole of a loss when in common sense he was not responsible for all of it': *Environmental Agency v Ellis* [2008] EWCA Civ 1117, [2009] PIQR P5, [39] *per* May LJ. In *Wright v Stoddart International plc* [2007] CSOH 138, 2008 Rep LR 2 the Lord Ordinary (Uist) observed that the apportionment point was never argued in *Wardlaw* or *McGhee* 'either because it was never even contemplated or because it was contemplated and considered to be a bad point': [141]. Lord Uist declined to follow the approach of the Court of Appeal in *Holtby* in Scots law: [147]. For criticism, see M Hogg, (2008) Edin LR 99, 103–04. For acceptance of apportionment in the context of psychiatric injury, see *Rahman v Arearose Ltd* [2001] QB 351 and *Hatton v Sutherland* [2002] 2 All ER 1, [36] *per* Hale LJ. But see *per contra, Barker v Somerset County Council* [2004] UKHL 13, [2004] 1 WLR 1089, where Lord Walker expressly declined to endorse Hale LJ's approach to apportionment and quantification of damage, stating that their Lordships had not heard argument on the topic. Further, in *Dickins v O2 plc* [2008] EWCA Civ 1144, [44], the Court of Appeal expressed doubt as to the applicability of the approach taken by Hale LJ in *Hatton* to apportionment in a case of psychiatric harm, where there are multiple causes of a breakdown.

is ultimately in the business of seeking to honour what have been suggested as the two conflicting policy objectives, namely controlling liability while being fair to claimants. Such a view—whether more realistic or cynical—would suggest that the verbal formulae are precisely that and little else. What the claimant and defendant must do is pile up as many factual arguments as they can muster in favour of their view of the case. The more facts, the more a court can find something to infer, or to deny that any inference can be drawn. Of course, once the decision is made, it will be expressed in the appropriate formulaic manner. But, while participating in this process, the parties to the litigation would be unwise to be so mesmerized by the complex taxonomy of causation that they overlook what is really going on.

6.14 **(b) Material increasing the risk of injury** So far, what we have seen is where the material contribution made by the defendant's breach is to the *damage itself* suffered by the claimant. What if the claimant can establish that the defendant's negligence contributed to the *risk of damage*? In *McGhee*, the House of Lords was prepared to infer that the failure to provide showers *materially increased the risk* of contracting dermatitis from the brick dust and that *in itself* established a causal link with the defendant's fault.[58] The reason for doing so was the lack of available evidence, such that the claimant could not meet the 'but for' test and establish that the breach had caused or made a material contribution to the injury.

6.15 In their subsequent 'interpretation' of *McGhee* in *Wilsher*,[59] the House of Lords was anxious, as we saw, to reassert the basic principle that the claimant must show either that the damage would not have occurred 'but for' the defendant's breach, or that the breach made a material contribution to it. For Lord Bridge in *Wilsher*, *McGhee* was merely a 'robust and pragmatic approach'[60] to the undisputed primary facts. Thus, all that the court had done in *McGhee* was to make a common-sense inference of fact that increased exposure to the dust must have materially contributed to the claimant's dermatitis itself.

6.16 Of course, it is all very well to describe *McGhee* as common sense but it places the defendant in a well-nigh impossible situation. If the court is moved to draw an inference of fact because of the inherent uncertainty of the facts, the defendant cannot, *ex hypothesi*, disprove the inference (given the uncertainty!). Furthermore, to claim that a material increase in the risk constitutes a material contribution to the damage is not only to make one step in the dark, but two. This is because it must also be assumed that the risk which was increased in fact materialized, since merely to increase a risk is not logically to cause anything. The underlying triumph of policy over logic is again laid bare.

6.17 The difficult question for the medical lawyer, however, is when will a court draw an inference of fact based on pragmatism or common sense? Unfortunately, there are few pointers in the cases which can serve as reliable guides in the uncertain world which is the reality of medical science. One plausible guide is the distinction which may be drawn between uncertainty created by the existence of a range of contributing factors, any or all of which may be judged cumulatively to have made a material contribution, and uncertainty created by the existence of a number of possible contributing factors each of which is separate and distinct.

6.18 Where the factors are cumulative, the court, following *Bonnington Castings*, has the option to find the defendant liable. If the factors taken together led to the claimant's injury, then the defendant's breach, as a contributing factor, may be held to have made a contribution

58 [1972] 3 All ER 1008, 1011, [1973] 1 WLR 1, 5 *per* Lord Reid and at 1018 and 1012–13 *per* Lord Salmon; see E Weinreb, 'A Step Forward in Factual Causation' (1975) 38 MLR 518, 523.

59 *Wilsher v Essex AHA* [1988] AC 1074, [1986] 3 All ER 801.

60 ibid, 1090.

which can be described as material, if it is not *de minimis*.[61] By contrast, where the injury could have been caused by any one of a number of distinct factors, the material contribution principle will not work in the claimant's favour. This is illustrated by the House of Lords' decision in *Wilsher v Essex AHA*.[62]

In *Wilsher*, the baby's RLF (retrolental fibroplasia) could have arisen from any of at least five separate and distinct factors. The defendant's breach was responsible for only one of these. It was impossible to assert that the breach was the sole cause of the RLF. It was equally untenable to argue that the breach materially contributed to it. It may have had no effect whatsoever. The House of Lords held that to show that the defendant's negligence materially increased the risk of the claimant's injury did nothing to exclude the other causes; therefore, it was impossible for the court to infer that the defendant was the cause of the injuries.[63] **6.19**

It may be that the reasoning in *McGhee*—moving from increased risk of injury to material contribution to the injury—is more likely to work where the risks are cumulative and interact, rather than when they are discrete and separate—*McGhee* versus *Wilsher*. However, *McGhee* itself was a case where it could have been that either/or both causes of the risk actually caused (or contributed to) the dermatitis. **6.20**

Where there is a breach of duty, and uncertainty as to what may have led to what, the court has the choice of favouring the claimant or the defendant. If the court chooses the latter, it can merely decide that the 'but for' test is not satisfied and the case is over. If, on the other hand, it is thought proper to assist the claimant in pursuit of a remedy, once a defendant is judged to have breached his duty, the court in effect has two principal policy options. The most effective option, of course, is to reverse the burden of proof. But this has been rejected in *Wilsher*, where the House of Lords held that *McGhee v National Coal Board* laid down no new principle of law, since the onus remained on the plaintiff to prove the causal link between the defendant's negligence and his injury.[64] The alternative is for the court **6.21**

[61] See the recent successful attempts at utilizing this in the context of multiple causal factors: *Bousted v North West Strategic Health Authority* [2008] EWHC 2375, [2008] LS Law Medical 471, [70]–[71] (since on the evidence there were concurrent cumulative causes of intraventricular haemorrhage, the claimant had satisfied the burden of proving that the defendant's breach of duty in delaying proceeding to a Caesarean section had made a material contribution to his brain damage); *Bailey v Ministry of Defence* [2008] EWCA Civ 83, [2009] 1 WLR 1052 (CA), [46] (cumulative causes (non-negligent pancreatitis and negligent lack of care), where contribution of negligent cause was more than negligible; 'but for' test modified and claimant would succeed), discussed in M Stauch, [2009] CLJ 27 and S Green, (2009) 125 LQR 44; *Canning-Kishver v Sandwell and West Birmingham NHS Trust* [2008] EWHC 2384 (QB), [36]–[37] (contribution of cardiac collapse occasioned by the breach of duty constituted a contribution to the cerebral atrophy that was more than negligible; claim succeeded); *Leigh v London Ambulance Service NHS Trust* [2014] EWHC 286 (QB), [2014] Med LR 134, [28] (cumulative causes: passenger trapped on a bus with dislocated knee for fifty minutes due to negligent failure of ambulance to arrive developed post-traumatic stress disorder (PTSD): contribution of negligent failure of ambulance to arrive was more than negligible and it made a material contribution to the development of the claimant's PTSD). Cf where the issue is whether one substance that *can* cause injury *did* cause injury: in such circumstances, questions of what is a material contribution do not arise: *Amaca Pty Ltd v Ellis* [2010] HCA 5, (2010) 240 CLR 11, [68] (asbestos and lung cancer). The material contribution test has been held not to apply to a claimant's occupational exposure to carcinogens in conjunction with their exposure to carcinogens contained in cigarette smoke and other possible factors, since the causes did not operate cumulatively: *Heneghan v Manchester Dry Docks Ltd* [2016] EWCA Civ 86, [2016] 1 WLR 2036, [39], [41] *per* Lord Dyson MR.

[62] [1988] AC 1074, [1986] 3 All ER 801. Discussed in A Grubb, [1988] CLJ 350 and A Boon, (1988) 51 MLR 508.

[63] *Wilsher v Essex AHA* [1988] AC 1074, 1090–91. See also *Hanke v Resurfice Corp* [2007] 1 SCR 333, [2007] 4 WWR 1, [19] (refusal of Supreme Court of Canada to accept that where there is more than one potential cause of injury, the 'material contribution' test must be used, as this would do away with the 'but for' test altogether).

[64] *Wilsher*, n 63.

to use the principle of material contribution, particularly in its *McGhee* manifestation, to draw appropriate inferences of fact.[65] The drawback for both parties is the lack of certainty such an obviously policy-led approach represents.[66] These difficulties were rehearsed in the judgment of the Canadian Supreme Court in *Snell v Farrell*.[67] In *Snell*, Sopinka J revisited *McGhee* in the light of the House of Lords' decision in *Wilsher*. Beginning from the point that 'proof of causation in medical malpractice cases is often difficult for the patient',[68] Sopinka J took the view that Lord Bridge's endorsement of a 'robust and pragmatic approach to the . . . facts' was a reminder to the courts not to adopt what he described as a 'too rigid application' of the traditional approach to causation.[69] He cited with approval[70] Lord Salmon's view in *Alpha-cell Ltd v Woodward*[71] that causation is 'essentially a practical question of fact which can best be answered by ordinary common sense rather than abstract metaphysical theory'. Relying on the crucial notion of drawing inferences, Sopinka J went on to state that:

> [i]n many medical malpractice cases, the facts lie particularly within the knowledge of the defendant. In these circumstances, very little affirmative evidence on the part of the plaintiff will justify the drawing of an inference of causation in the absence of evidence to the contrary.[72]

6.22 This was not, he emphasized, a matter of shifting the burden of proof or even the burden of adducing evidence:

> The legal or ultimate burden remains with the plaintiff, but in the absence of evidence to the contrary adduced by the defendant, an inference of causation may be drawn, although positive or scientific proof of causation has not been adduced. If some evidence to the contrary is adduced by the defendant, the trial judge is entitled to take account of Lord Mansfield's famous precept [referred to earlier, that] '[i]t is certainly a maxim that all evidence is to be weighed according to the proof which it was in the power of one side to have produced, and in the power of the other to have contradicted it'.[73]

6.23 It could be said that English law could greatly benefit if the courts were more ready to adopt Sopinka J's approach to causation in this most troubling area of litigation.[74] Subsequent to

---

[65] It was Nourse LJ in *Fitzgerald v Lane* [1987] QB 781 who described *Wilsher*'s robust and pragmatic approach as the 'benevolent principle [which] smiles on . . . factual uncertainties and melts them all away'. See further *Lybert v Warrington* [1996] 7 Med LR 71 (CA).

[66] For a summary of propositions relating to causation, see A Grubb, Commentary on *Tahir v Haringey HA* (1996) 4 Med L Rev 92, where it is suggested that in cases of medical negligence, where 'causation is often difficult to establish', 'the plaintiff must establish one of the following: 1. that "but for" the negligence he would not have suffered *any* injury (plaintiff recovers for all his injuries); or 2. that "but for" the negligence he would not have suffered *an identifiable part* (X) or *particular aggravation* (Y) of the injuries (plaintiff recovers for X and Y respectively); or 3. that the negligence *materially contributed* to the whole injury (Z) or an identifiable part (X) or particular aggravation (Y) of the injuries (plaintiff recovers for Z, X and Y respectively)' (emphasis in original).

[67] *Snell v Farrell* (1990) 72 DLR (4th) 289. Discussed in J Fleming, 'Probabilistic Causation in Tort Law: A Postscript' (1991) 70 Can Bar Rev 136, 139.

[68] *Snell v Farrell*, n 67, [19].

[69] ibid, [30].

[70] ibid, [30].

[71] [1972] AC 824, 847, [1972] 2 All ER 475, 490 (HL).

[72] *Snell v. Farrell*, n 67, [31].

[73] ibid, [34], referring to *Blatch v Archer* (1774) 1 Cowp 63, which he had previously cited at [30]. The *Snell v Farrell* inference of causation is one that trial judges are *permitted* to draw, but *not* one that they are *required* to draw: *Benhaim v O'Donovan* 2016 SCC 48, [50].

[74] See the support for inference-drawing as a means of finding (or not finding) cause in fact in R Brown, 'Inferring Cause in Fact and the Search for "Legal Truth"' in R Goldberg (ed), *Perspectives on Causation* (Hart 2011) 93, though stressing that inference drawing necessarily involves both deliberation and explicit justification of a determination of whether cause in fact is demonstrated on the evidence (at 109).

Snell v Farrell, the principles concerning the applicability of the 'material contribution' test were explained by the Supreme Court of Canada in *Hanke v Resurfice Corp*.[75] It held that the Alberta Court of Appeal had erred in suggesting that where there was more than one potential cause of an injury, the material contribution test must be used.[76] The basic test for determining causation remained the 'but-for' test, which applied to multi-cause injuries. The plaintiff bore the burden of showing that 'but for' the negligent act or omission of each defendant, the injury would not have occurred.[77] However, in special circumstances, the law recognized exceptions to the 'but for' test, and applied a 'material contribution' test.[78] There were two requirements to be satisfied. First, it had to be impossible to prove 'but-for' causation, due to factors outside the plaintiff's control, such as the 'current limits of scientific knowledge'. Secondly, the plaintiff's injury had to fall within the ambit of the risk created by the negligent exposure of the plaintiff to an unreasonable risk of injury. Where these two requirements were satisfied, liability could be imposed even though the 'but-for' test is not satisfied, since it would offend basic notions of fairness and justice to deny liability by applying a 'but-for' approach.[79] Subsequent appellate decisions have stated that the 'material contribution' test as adumbrated in *Hanke v Resurfice Corp* can only be relied on where it is impossible to prove on a balance of probabilities that a delay in treatment caused the plaintiff's injuries.[80] However, the material contribution test was applied in special circumstances where, for reasons beyond her control, it was impossible for the plaintiff to prove that a negligent delay in diagnosing and treating breast cancer had caused her injury and the claimant's injury fell within the ambit of the risk created by the negligence in failing to do a biopsy.[81] Subsequent to *Hanke v Resurfice Corp*, the Supreme Court in *Clements v Clements*[82] has restricted the exceptional circumstances where a material contribution to risk approach may be imposed to that of indeterminate defendants.[83] While the 'material contribution' test as adumbrated in *Hanke v Resurfice Corp* was accurate, it was incomplete in providing a 'clear picture of when "but for" causation c[ould] be replaced by material contribution to risk'.[84]In order to obtain such clarity, it was necessary to explore what was meant by 'impossible to prove'.[85] The idea that a material contribution to risk approach was available whenever proof of 'but for' causation was impossible was problematic. Allowing plaintiffs to succeed whenever proof of causation was impossible would undermine the burden of proof being on the plaintiff to show that 'but for' the defendant's negligence she would not have been injured.[86] For it to be impossible to prove 'but for' causation on a balance of probabilities as a precondition to the material contribution to risk approach, each one of a number

[75] *Hanke v Resurfice Corp* [2007] SCC 7, (2007) 278 DLR (4th) 643, [25].

[76] ibid, [19].

[77] ibid, [21].

[78] ibid, [24].

[79] ibid, [25]. For criticism, see V Black and D Cheifetz, 'Through the Looking Glass, Darkly: *Resurfice Corp v Hanke*' (2007) 45 Alta L Rev 241; and L Khoury, 'Causation and Risk in the Highest Courts of Canada, England and France' (2008) 124 LQR 103, 108.

[80] *Barker v Montford Hospital* [2007] ONCA 282, (2007) DLR (4th) 215, [53] (Ontario CA); *Jackson v Kelowna General Hospital* [2007] BCCA 129, (2007) 277 DLR (4th) 385, [23] (British Columbia CA).

[81] *Bohun v Sennewald* 2007 BCSC 269, (2007) 46 CCLT (3d) 138, [94]–[96] (British Columbia SC); see also the High Court of Australia's support for a material contribution test where a wrongful act or omission results in an increased risk of injury to the claimant and that risk eventuates: *Naxakis v Western General Hospital* [1999] HCA 22; (1999) 197 CLR 269, [31], citing *Chappel v Hart* (1998) 195 CLR 232, 244–45 *per* McHugh J.

[82] 2012 SCC 32, (2012) 346 DLR (4th) 577, [2012] 2 SCR 181.

[83] See further S Steel, *Proof of Causation in Tort Law* (Cambridge University Press 2015) 173–74.

[84] *Clements v Clements* 2012 SCC 32, [34].

[85] ibid, citing [2007] SCC 7, (2007) 278 DLR (4th) 643, [25].

[86] ibid, [37].

of tortfeasors, all of whom were negligent in a manner that might have caused the plaintiff's injury, could 'point the finger at the other'.[87]

6.24 (c) **Reinstating *McGhee*** In the landmark decision of *Fairchild v Glenhaven Funeral Services Ltd*,[88] their Lordships refuted the narrow construction of *McGhee* which had been placed upon it by the House of Lords in *Wilsher*.[89] It was, therefore, not to be seen as an application of the traditional 'but for' test, rather as a departure from it in exceptional (and specific) circumstances. The claimants were exposed to asbestos dust over a long period of time whilst working for successive employers. They developed mesothelioma, a cancer of the lung. Claims were brought against some—but not all—of the employers. The evidence was that mesothelioma was caused by exposure to asbestos dust but it was not known whether it was caused by a single fibre or whether multiple fibres were necessary or made development of the cancer more likely. On the evidence, it could not be said which employer's breach of duty in exposing the claimants to asbestos dust had caused, or materially contributed to, their injuries. There was a 'scientific deficit' in the evidence. The House of Lords unanimously held that each of the employers was liable to the claimant for their injuries.[90] The Law Lords held, on policy grounds, that the *McGhee* test of 'material increase in risk' applied to fix each employer with responsibility for the claimants' injuries. Where successive employers had failed to protect an employee from a disease (mesothelioma), but it could not be proved on a balance of probability which employer had caused the injury, the conduct of each employer in exposing the claimant to a material increase in risk to which the claimant should not have been exposed should be treated as if it had made a material contribution to the disease.[91] It was just to depart from the 'but for' test of causation where, as in this case, the injustice of holding an employer responsible for injury that he may not have caused (or contributed to) was outweighed by the injustice of leaving the employees without compensation.[92]

6.25 The narrowness of the exception carved out by the judges to the traditional test was emphasized by the Law Lords. Whilst not incapable of further extension, the circumstances were exceptional (if not uncommon) and the judges advised caution in extending the application of the *McGhee* test. Certainly, the context of employment was important and it was arguably crucial such that the court would not see the merits of extension beyond it.[93] It was suggested that it was unlikely that the *McGhee/Fairchild* principle applied only where all sources of risk to the victim had been 'wrongful',[94] but the question as to whether a single

[87] ibid, [39], [43].

[88] *Fairchild v Glenhaven Funeral Services Ltd* [2002] UKHL 22, [2003] 1 AC 32. Discussed in J Morgan, (2003) 66 MLR 277; T Weir, [2002] CLJ 519; J Stapleton, 'Lords a' Leaping Evidentiary Gaps' (2002) 10 Torts LJ 276; J M Thomson, (2003) 7 Edin LR 80.

[89] With the exception of Lord Hutton who preferred to see *McGhee* as a case where it was proper to make a factual inference of causation: *Fairchild*, n 88, [108] and [109].

[90] ibid. Subject to the issue of contribution proceedings between the defendants *inter se*, which was not before the House.

[91] ibid, [2003] 1 AC 32, [2], [34] *per* Lord Bingham, [42] *per* Lord Nicholls, [47], [65], [67] *per* Lord Hoffmann, [116] *per* Lord Hutton, and [168] *per* Lord Rodger.

[92] ibid, [33]–[34] *per* Lord Bingham, [45] *per* Lord Nicholls, [56], [62] *per* Lord Hoffmann.

[93] ibid. See especially [2] *per* Lord Bingham and [61] *per* Lord Hoffmann. For a suggestion of an even more limited application of the test see J Stapleton, 'Cause-in-Fact and the Scope of Liability for Consequences' (2003) 119 LQR 388, 398. But it is not clear that these limitations would have been accepted by the judges: see especially [72] *per* Lord Hoffmann, and [170] *per* Lord Rodger.

[94] See J Stapleton, 'Lords a' Leaping Evidentiary Gaps' (2002) 10 Torts LJ 276, 292 (comparing Lord Bingham, requiring all risks to be wrongful [2003] 1 AC 32, [2003] 3 All ER 305, [2] with Lord Hoffmann, who does not mention the requirement of risks being wrongful and Lord Rodger, who reserves his position to allow the principle to apply 'where the other possible source of injury is a similar but lawful act or omission of someone else or a natural occurrence' [170]).

type of agent was a requirement remained uncertain. While Lord Rodger distinguished *Wilsher* by stating that the *McGhee/Fairchild* principle was inapplicable 'where the claimant has merely proved that his injury could have been caused by a number of different events, only one of which is the eventuation of the risk created by the defendant's wrongful act or omission',[95] he nevertheless added that usually the claimant in multi-agent cases must prove that his injury was caused 'if not by exactly the same agency as was involved in the defendant's wrongdoing, at least by an agency that operated in substantially the same way'.[96] There was, however, nothing in *Fairchild* to suggest that Lord Hoffmann would contemplate a single type of agent as a requirement.[97] Further uncertainty remained as to whether defendants would be liable *in solidum* to the claimant for the entire indivisible disease or whether they could claim apportionment.[98]

In the light of this uncertainty, the nature and limits of the *Fairchild* principle were further defined by their Lordships in *Barker v Corus UK Ltd*.[99] *Barker* established that the *Fairchild* exception did not require all potential causes of the injury to be tortious, providing one or more employers was at fault or the claimant was at fault himself. It was therefore irrelevant whether the other exposure was tortious or non-tortious, by natural causes or by the claimant himself.[100] More controversially, however, was the determination of the issue of the extent of liability in a *Fairchild*-type case. The majority of their Lordships held that where it could not be shown which defendant's breach of duty caused the damage, but that it could be shown that each defendant exposed the claimant to a significant risk of eventual damage, fairness demanded that the damage should be apportioned between defendants in accordance with their aliquot contribution to the risk or chance of the disease being contracted by the claimant.[101] While joint and several liability applied generally to defendants who were held to have made a material contribution to indivisible injuries such as mesothelioma, Lord Hoffmann characterized the damage as being the *risk* or *chance* of causing the disease, as opposed to the damage being the disease itself.[102] Since the risk or chance of contracting mesothelioma was divisible, damages could be apportioned severally, in accordance with the share of the damage attributable to each defendant.[103] Attributing liability in accordance with the chance of the disease being contracted 'would smooth the **6.26**

[95] *Fairchild*, n 88, [170].
[96] ibid.
[97] ibid, [72]. See J Stapleton, 'Lords a' Leaping Evidentiary Gaps', n 94, 294–99; and M Lunney and K Oliphant, *Tort Law: Text and Materials* (3rd edn, Oxford University Press 2008) 244–45.
[98] See J Stapleton, 'Lords a' Leaping Evidentiary Gaps', n 94, 299–302. Cf the position under the American Federal Employers' Liability Act, which expressly allowed a worker to recover his entire damages from a railroad whose negligence jointly caused his work-related asbestos, thus placing on the railroad the burden of seeking contribution from other tortfeasors: *Norfolk & Western Ry Co v Ayers* 123 S Ct 1210, 1227, 538 US 135 (2003) (US Sup Ct).
[99] *Barker v Corus UK Ltd* [2006] UKHL 20, [2006] 2 AC 572. See J M Thomson, (2006) 10 Edin LR 421; A Kramer, (2006) 122 LQR 553. For support for the *Barker* decision as a general realignment of material increase in risk cases as lost chances, see M Hogg, 'Re-establishing Orthodoxy in the Realm of Causation' (2007) Edin LR 8; cf L Khoury, 'Causation and Risk in the Highest Courts of Canada, England and France' (2008) 124 LQR 103, 117, 119.
[100] *Barker v Corus UK Ltd*, n 99, [17]–[18] *per* Lord Hoffmann, [59] *per* Lord Scott, [101] *per* Lord Rodger, [117] *per* Lord Walker, [128] *per* Baroness Hale.
[101] ibid, [43], [48] *per* Lord Hoffmann, [62] *per* Lord Scott, [103], [113] *per* Lord Walker, [122], [124], [127] *per* Baroness Hale.
[102] ibid, [35] *per* Lord Hoffmann. A disease is indivisible if its severity is not proportionate to the amount of exposure to the causative agent: *Heneghan v Manchester Dry Docks Ltd* [2016] EWCA Civ 86, [2016] 1 WLR 2036, [46] *per* Lord Dyson MR.
[103] ibid, [36] *per* Lord Hoffmann.

roughness of the justice which a rule of joint and several liability creates'.[104] In his dissenting judgment, Lord Rodger stated that by adopting Lord Hoffmann's analysis, their Lordships were 'not so much reinterpreting as rewriting'[105] *McGhee* and *Fairchild*. While he had no quarrel[106] with Lord Hoffmann's view in *Fairchild*[107] that, in the circumstances, a breach of duty which materially increased the risk of disease should be treated as if it had materially contributed to the disease, Lord Rodger rejected[108] Lord Hoffmann's treatment of a material risk as sufficient in the circumstances to satisfy the causal requirements of liability.[109] Lord Rodger concluded that Lord Hoffmann's analysis was open to criticism, since it tended to maximize inconsistencies in the law 'by turning the *Fairchild* exception into an enclave where a number of rules apply which have been rejected for use elsewhere in the law of personal injuries'.[110] Thus, while the gist of the damage was seemingly redefined in *Barker* as the increased risk of contracting the mesothelioma, as opposed to the disease itself, it remains the law that an increased risk or chance of contracting the disease, which is not consequent upon some physical injury, is not damage on which a claim for negligence can be founded.[111] Accordingly, a claimant who suffers an increased risk of mesothelioma cannot establish liability until he actually contracts it.[112] Lord Rodger concluded that there was no compelling connection between the *Fairchild* exception and the introduction of several liability. He would therefore have adhered to the usual rule of liability *in solidum* (joint and several liability), which applies generally to defendants who have made a material contribution to indivisible injuries, such as mesothelioma.[113] In response to pressure from the victims of mesothelioma and their families, s 3 was inserted into the Compensation Act 2006, a statute which was primarily designed to make provision for the regulation of claims management services. The effect of s 3 is the reversal of *Barker*, so far as mesothelioma victims are concerned by substituting several liability with joint and several liability.[114]

[104] ibid, [43] *per* Lord Hoffmann.

[105] ibid, [71].

[106] ibid, [78].

[107] *Fairchild*, n 88, [65].

[108] *Barker v Corus UK Ltd*, n 99, [78], [83].

[109] See *Fairchild*, n 88, [65] *per* Lord Hoffmann.

[110] *Barker v Corus UK Ltd*, n 99, [85].

[111] *Gregg v Scott* [2005] 2 AC 176, [118] *per* Lord Hope; *Rothwell v Chemical and Insulating Co Ltd* [2007] UKHL 39, [2008] 1 AC 281, [2], [12] *per* Lord Hoffmann, [41] *per* Lord Hope, [67] *per* Lord Scott, [88] *per* Lord Rodger, [103] *per* Lord Mance (expressly rejecting increased risk as the gist of negligence). The actual development of mesothelioma is an essential element of the cause of action: see *Durham v BAI (Run Off) Ltd* [2012] UKSC 14, [2012] 1 WLR 867, [65] *per* Lord Mance JSC, discussed below at para 6.30. Accordingly, the development of pleural plaques, whether or not associated with the risk of future disease and anxiety about the future, is not actionable damage in negligence: *Rothwell v Chemical and Insulating Co Ltd* [2007] UKHL 39, [2008] 1 AC 281, [2], [11] *per* Lord Hoffmann, [50] *per* Lord Hope, [68], [74] *per* Lord Scott, [90]–[91] *per* Lord Rodger, [103] *per* Lord Mance; cf where, as a result of the defendant's negligence, there is a risk that the claimant will suffer physical injuries and death in the future and the claimant foreseeably develops a psychiatric injury in consequence of receiving this information, there may be a claim in respect of the psychiatric injury: *CJD Litigation: Group B Plaintiffs v Medical Research Council* [2000] Lloyd's Rep Med 161, (1997) 41 BMLR 157. The Damages (Asbestos-related Conditions) (Scotland) Act 2009 ensures that the decision in *Rothwell* has no effect in Scotland, and that asbestos-related pleural plaques are a non-negligible personal injury for the purposes of the law of delict.

[112] *Barker v Corus UK Ltd* [2006] UKHL 20, [2006] 2 AC 572, [85]. The redefinition of the gist of the damage has therefore given rise to the criticism that such an approach is intellectually incoherent to those who believe that tortious or delictual liability arises when harm is wrongfully caused, since the harm would be the risk of the disease and not its development: see J M Thomson, (2006) 10 Edin LR 421, 426.

[113] *Barker v Corus UK Ltd*, n 112, [85], [91]. In *Wright v Stoddart International plc* [2007] CSOH 138, 2008 Rep LR 2, [149], Lord Uist adopted Lord Rodger's analysis of the law of apportionment in Scots law.

[114] In *Sienkiewicz v Greif* [2011] UK SC 10, [2011] 2 AC 229, a majority of the Justices held that Section 3(1) of the Compensation Act 2006 applied where the responsible person is liable in tort for materially increasing the risk of mesothelioma or for any other person. It did not, however, state that the responsible person will be liable in tort if he has materially increased the risk of a victim of mesothelioma: [70] *per* Lord

The uncertainty as to whether a single type of agent was a limitation to the Fairchild principle was explored further in *Barker*. While there was nothing in *Fairchild* to suggest that Lord Hoffmann would contemplate a single type of agent as a requirement,[115] his view had changed somewhat in *Barker*. He held that it was 'an essential condition' for the *Fairchild* principle to be limited to cases where each potential causative agent must have operated in the same way; that is, the mechanism by which the agents caused the damage must be the same.[116] Accordingly, he considered that the *Fairchild* exception did not apply when the claimant suffered lung cancer that may have been caused not only by exposure to asbestos or other carcinogenic matter, but also may have been caused by smoking, and it could not be proved which was the more likely to have been the causative agent.[117] However, he agreed that the *Fairchild* exception would continue to apply where the agent 'may have been different in some causally irrelevant respect'.[118] The only other judge in *Barker* to address the single type of agent issue was Lord Scott. In his view, *Fairchild* established a narrow exception to causation requirements, applicable only to 'single agent cases'.[119] He was unwilling to extend the exception to cover 'multi-agent cases' as well, particularly since identification of the proportion of risk of the eventual outcome attributable to each particular agent would be 'well nigh impossible and highly artificial'.[120] **6.27**

The extent to which the *Fairchild* principle operates has been subject to judicial discussion in the Court of Appeal. While it has been observed that 'great caution is required before any development of the *Fairchild* exception should be allowed',[121] it is clear that the conditions required to be satisfied for its application were not intended to exclude its application to other conditions and circumstances, and the exception will not be limited to cases of mesothelioma.[122] In *Sanderson v Hull*,[123] Smith LJ attempted to formalize the principles from *Fairchild* by adopting[124] Lord Rodger's conditions[125] for its application. As expressed by Smith LJ, there were five main elements to the *Fairchild* principle operating to relax the need to satisfy the 'but **6.28**

Phillips. So the Act did not determine the proper approach of the common law to questions of causation and liability in mesothelioma cases, but merely altered the apportionment of damages. Whether, and in what circumstances, liability in tort attached to one who has materially increased the risk of a victim contracting mesothelioma remained a question of common law: [70] *per* Lord Phillips, [130]–[132] *per* Lord Rodger, [183] *per* Lord Brown, [223] *per* Lord Dyson.

115 [2003] 1 AC 32, [2002] 3 All ER 305, [72].

116 *Barker v Corus UK Ltd* [2006] UKHL 20, [2006] 2 AC 572, [24].

117 ibid. However, it has been submitted, albeit obiter, that the *Fairchild* principle would operate where different causative agents, viz amines in cigarette smoke and amines in occupational exposure, act on the body in the same way. It was highly arguable that *Fairchild* should apply to bladder cancer and that it would be sufficient for a claimant to prove that the occupational exposure had made a material contribution to the risk of him developing the disease: *Novartis Grimsby Ltd v Cookson* [2007] EWCA Civ 1261, [72] *per* Smith LJ.

118 Lord Hoffmann cites Lord Rodger's example in *Fairchild* ([2003] 1 AC 32, [170]) of a workman's exposure dust being particles of two different substances: *Barker v Corus UK Ltd*, n 116, [24].

119 *Barker v Corus UK Ltd*, n 116, [64].

120 ibid. This would seem to exaggerate somewhat the difficulty of identifying the proportion of risk.

121 *Sanderson v Hull* [2008] EWCA Civ 1211, [2009] PIQR P7, [34] *per* Smith LJ.

122 ibid, [42], [45]. The *Fairchild* principle is 'applicable to any disease which has the unusual features of mesothelioma': *International Energy Group Ltd v Zurich Insurance plc* [2015] UKSC33, [2016] AC 509, [191] *per* Lord Neuberger PSC and Lord Reed JSC. Accordingly, the *Fairchild* exception has been deemed applicable to multiple exposures to asbestos leading to lung cancer, in addition to mesothelioma: *Heneghan v Manchester Dry Docks Ltd* [2014] EWHC 4190 (QB), [71], [72], [2016] EWCA Civ 86, [2016] 1 WLR 2036, [47]–[50] *per* Lord Dyson MR.

123 *Sanderson v Hull* [2008] EWCA Civ 1211, [2009] PIQR P7.

124 ibid, [50], [53].

125 [2002] UKHL 22, [169]–[170], and *Barker v Corus (UK) plc* [2006] UKHL 20, [2006] 2 AC 572, [97].

for' test of causation. First, the claimant must show the current state of scientific knowledge leaves it inherently impossible for the claimant to prove exactly how his injury was caused. Second, the defendant's breach of duty must have materially increased the risk of injury to the claimant.[126] Third, the defendant's conduct must have been capable of causing the claimant's injury. Fourth, the claimant must show that the injury was caused by the eventuation of the kind of risk created by the defendant's wrongdoing. Fifth, the injury must be caused by the same agency as was involved in the defendant's wrongdoing (or an agency which operates in a similar way).[127] It is clear that Lord Rodger's conditions are at a higher level of generality than those of Lord Bingham and Hoffmann,[128] but in their principled approach they arguably provide the clearest guidance to practitioners and litigants as to *Fairchild*'s scope.

6.29 *Barker*'s establishment that it was unnecessary for the *Fairchild* exception to apply to prove that all the exposures to toxic agents were tortious and that it was irrelevant whether the other exposure was tortious or non-tortious, by natural causes or by the claimant himself,[129] was confirmed by the Supreme Court in *Sienkiewicz v Greif*.[130] In two cases, the claimants had been exposed to asbestos dust by, respectively, an employer who manufactured steel drums[131] and a school[132] where there had in addition been a risk of environmental exposure to low-level asbestos dust in the atmosphere. The Supreme Court held that the *Fairchild* exception applied to such 'single exposure cases' (where only one defendant exposed the victim to asbestos, and the only other exposure creating a risk of developing mesothelioma was environmental exposure to low-level asbestos dust in the atmosphere),[133] providing the claimant proved that the defendant's breach of duty materially increased the risk that he would develop mesothelioma.[134] The Court also held that there was no room for the introduction of a doubling of risk approach[135] to single exposure mesothelioma cases or multiple defendant mesothelioma cases.[136]

6.30 The issue of the 'combined effect'[137] of *Fairchild* and *Barker* was addressed in the so-called *Trigger* litigation, *Durham v BAI (Run Off) Ltd*.[138] The question raised was whether insurer's liability in a mesothelioma case was 'triggered' when an employee was exposed to asbestos or at the point when the disease manifested itself, many years after the period of the insurance. To put it another way, the issue was whether employers' liability insurance policies responded to claims by former employees of the insured in respect of negligent exposure to asbestos dust when the employees developed mesothelioma many years later.[139] Some

---

[126] The *Fairchild* threshold of material increase in risk is anything more than *de minimis: Rolls Royce Industrial Power (India) Ltd v Cox* [2007] EWCA Civ 1189 (CA), [21].

[127] [2008] EWCA Civ 1211, [2009] PIQR P7, [53].

[128] See *Fairchild v Glenhaven Funeral Services Ltd* [2002] UKHL 22, [2] *per* Lord Bingham, and [61] *per* Lord Hoffmann.

[129] ibid, [17]–[18] *per* Lord Hoffmann, [59] *per* Lord Scott, [101] *per* Lord Rodger, [117] *per* Lord Walker, [128] *per* Baroness Hale.

[130] *Sienkiewicz v Greif* [2011] UK SC 10, [2011] 2 2 AC 229.

[131] ibid, [115].

[132] ibid, [125].

[133] ibid, [103], [113] *per* Lord Phillips, [160] *per* Lord Rodger, [173] *per* Lady Hale, [184] *per* Lord Brown, [188] *per* Lord Mance, and [203] *per* Lord Kerr.

[134] ibid, [107] *per* Lord Phillips, [160], [165] *per* Lord Rodger, [223] *per* Lord Dyson.

[135] The doubling of risk theory is one that causation can be proved on the balance of probabilities by reference to the doubling of risk of injury. For further analysis, see R Goldberg, 'Epidemiological Uncertainty, Causation, and Drug Product Liability' (2014) McGill LJ 777, 785–793.

[136] *Durham v BAI (Run Off) Ltd* [2012] UKSC 14, [2012] 1 WLR 867.

[137] *Clerk & Lindsell on Torts* (21st edn, Sweet & Maxwell 2014) [2-65].

[138] *Durham v BAI (Run Off) Ltd* [2012] UKSC 14, [2012] 1 WLR 867.

[139] ibid, [3].

of the insurance policies had provided coverage for claims which arose when the injury or disease was 'sustained' during the course of the policy and others for injury or disease 'contracted' during the course of the policy.[140] The answer to whether the insurances responded was partly contingent on construing whether the wording covered the scenario where the exposure to asbestos occurred during the relevant insurance period but the injury to the employees manifested itself many years after the period of insurance, applying principles of contract law. The Supreme Court construed the words 'injury sustained' and 'disease contracted' in the policies as meaning that a disease might be said to have been 'sustained' or 'contracted' by an employee during the period when it was *caused* or initiated, even though it only developed or manifested itself subsequently.[141] This meant that liability would be entailed for harms *caused* by exposure during employment despite the disease only developing or manifesting itself later on.

However, the Supreme Court also had to address the correct approach to causation in the claims in tort against the employees. If the effect of *Barker* was that the essence of the claim was not for damage caused by asbestos, but for liability to the extent that the negligence contributed to the risk of contracting mesothelioma, it was arguable that the insurance policies would not respond to the claims and the claims would fail.[142] On the other hand, if the correct approach of *Fairchild* was that an employer who exposed an employee to asbestos was deemed to have caused that employee's mesothelioma (as opposed to a contribution to the risk of developing mesothelioma) the insurance policies would respond to the claims.[143] Giving the leading speech, Lord Mance JSC (with whom Lord Kerr, Lord Clarke, and Lord Dyson JJSC agreed) reconsidered *Barker* and held that it was inaccurate to speak as of the cause of action recognized in *Fairchild* and *Barker* as being merely for the risk created by exposing someone to asbestos. The cause of action existed because the defendant had exposed the victim to asbestos, because that exposure may have led to mesothelioma and because mesothelioma had been suffered by the victim. The actual development of mesothelioma was an essential element of the cause of action.[144] *Barke*r did not establish a unique principle of legal responsibility. Lord Mance considered that it was 'both possible and appropriate to characterise the position achieved by the common law after *Barker* as one concerned with the issue of the "causal requirements" or "causal link", as between the defendant's conduct and the disease, which the common law requires in order for there to be an action for mesothelioma'.[145] For the purpose of claims for mesothelioma, 'the law accepts a weak or broad causal link which may but cannot be shown on the ordinary balance of probabilities to have played a role in the actual occurrence of the disease'. For the purposes of the policies, the negligent exposure of an employee to asbestos could *'properly be described as having a sufficient causal link or being sufficiently causally connected with subsequently arising mesothelioma for the policies to respond'*.[146] He added: 'The concept of a disease being "caused" during the policy period must be interpreted sufficiently flexibly to embrace the role assigned to exposure by the rule in *Fairchild* and *Barker*'.[147] Lord Mance's judgment seemingly restored the common understanding of the effect of *Fairchild* on the issue of the **6.31**

[140] ibid, [4].
[141] ibid, [47], [49]–[50].
[142] ibid, [53]–[54].
[143] ibid, [53].
[144] ibid, [65], per Lord Mance JSC.
[145] ibid, [64].
[146] ibid, [74].
[147] ibid, [74].

nature of the damage for which the employer is responsible. However, it has been determined unanimously by the Supreme Court that the decision in *Barker* remains good law.[148]

6.32 Since an essential element of the development of *Fairchild* will be the first element, namely the inherent impossibility for the claimant to prove enough to satisfy the 'but for' test,[149] the likelihood is, however, that the *Fairchild* test will have little impact in medical negligence cases. In cases where there is a 'scientific deficit' in the evidence, it is unlikely that the factual context will work in a claimant's favour. Usually, the claimant will be unable to show that the injury suffered was precisely that which flowed from the doctor (or other's) breach of duty but rather that it was the result of one of a number of possible causative events each (or some) of which lacks the same essential characteristics of the risk created by the doctor as in *Wilsher* itself and the Law Lords cast no doubt on the actual outcome in *Wilsher*.[150] Second, and perhaps more significantly, attempting to apply *McGhee* in the medical context may not invoke the same policy response from the judges because of the impact that extending liability would have on the NHS and its budget.[151] The remarks of Lord Hoffmann in *Fairchild* suggest that the *McGhee/Fairchild* approach is unlikely to be imported:[152]

> It is true that actions for clinical negligence notoriously give rise to difficult questions of causation. But it cannot possibly be that the duty to take care in treating patients would be virtually drained of content unless the creation of a material risk of injury were accepted as sufficient to satisfy the causal requirements of liability. And the political and economic

---

148 *International Energy Group Ltd v Zurich Insurance plc* [2015] UKSC33, [2016] AC 509, [27], [29], [31] *per* Lord Mance JSC. As Lord Mance put it: '*Barker*, as analysed in "Trigger", accepted causation in [a] weak or broad sense and none the less held an employer's responsibility to be proportionate to that part for which the employer was responsible of the victim's total exposure to asbestos dust. Trigger cannot therefore be said to affect or undermine the reasoning or decision in *Barker*' [29]. See also Lord Sumption JSC at [135] (the natural reading of the majority speeches in *Barker* is that *Fairchild* is an exception to the ordinary rules of causation alone); [194] *per* Lord Neuberger PSC and Lord Reed JSC (*Barker* a 'pragmatic decision' that each employer was responsible for a proportion of the damages but not for the whole, which 'created a further exception to established legal principles').

149 ibid, [43].

150 ibid: *Wilsher* was approved *per* Lord Bingham, [22]; *per* Lord Hoffmann, [70]; *per* Lord Hutton, [118]; *per* Lord Rodger, [149] and [170]. For an example post-*Fairchild* of a multiple potential cause decision decided in line with *Wilsher*, see *Temple v South Manchester Health Authority* [2002] EWCA Civ 1406, where the claimant alleged that the defendant's negligence had caused his cerebral oedema as a result of diabetic ketoacidosis. Various theories existed as to the possible causes of cerebral oedema. One of the theories was that cerebral oedema might be produced where a patient was infused at less than normal salinity, and it was on this basis that the trial judge had found the defendants negligent. As in *Wilsher*, there were a number of different causes which were in play and which might have operated independently or cumulatively. The state of knowledge was such that it was not known whether the giving of a low saline infusion was ever the cause of cerebral oedema. The Court of Appeal upheld the trial judge's conclusion that no causal link had been established on a balance of probabilities. Note that the *Fairchild* exception has no application to cases where the claimant's injuries arise from a single incident: *Clough v First Choice Holidays and Flights Ltd* [2006] EWCA Civ 15, [2006] PIQR P22, [43].

151 But *quaere* if the claimant was treated in a private hospital or clinic?

152 [2002] UKHL 22, [69]. But contrast *Snell v Farrell* (1990) 72 DLR (4th) 289 (Can Sup Ct). Note the unsuccessful attempt to apply the *Fairchild* exception to a case involving a negligent dispensing of the wrong contraceptive pill. In *Wooton v J Docter Ltd and another* [2008] EWCA Civ 1361, [2009] LS Law Med 63, the claimant contended that because the current state of scientific knowledge precluded her from establishing that 'but for' the erroneous dispensing of the contraceptive Logynon for Microgynon, she would not have become pregnant, she could invoke the alternative and exceptional principles identified in *Fairchild*. Invoking Lord Rodger's principles in *Fairchild* to the facts of the case, (as explained by Smith LJ in *Sanderson v Hull* [2008] EWCA Civ 1211, [53]), counsel for the claimant contended that the current state of scientific knowledge rendered it inherently impossible for the claimant to prove exactly how her injury was caused. The negligent dispensing of Logynon was capable of causing a failure of contraception and materially increased that risk. The claimant's pregnancy was the result of the kind of risk created by the by the pharmacist's wrongdoing, and the pregnancy was caused by the same agency which the reduction

arguments involved in the massive increase in liability of the National Health Service which would have been a consequence of the broad rule favoured by the Court of Appeal in Wilsher's case are far more complicated than the reasons given [in *McGhee*] for imposing liability upon an employer who has failed to take simple precautions.

(iii) Recovering damages for loss of chance

We have already seen a number of attempts—some successful, some not—by the judges to mitigate the rigours of the 'but for' test when the justice of the case demands it. A third would be the issue of whether damages may be recovered for 'loss of a chance'. The argument here is that as a consequence of the defendant's breach of duty, the claimant did not receive any, or any proper, treatment and thereby suffered damage. In ordinary circumstances, there is no reason why the claimant should not be compensated for any such damage, even if it takes the form of not having his condition improved or having it become worse, rather than some discrete, identifiable additional damage. If the claimant can show that this change for the worse in his condition was, on the balance of probabilities, the consequence of the defendant's breach, the 'but for' rule will apply and recovery will follow. **6.33**

The problems arise when the evidence demonstrates that, even if the defendant had complied with his duty of care, it was more likely than not that the claimant's condition would *not* have improved. The claimant's alleged damage, then, is the loss of a *chance* of improvement, but a chance which was less than a 50 per cent chance. Clearly the 'but for' test cannot be satisfied in that the claimant cannot show that, on the balance of probabilities, but for the defendant's breach he would have recovered or his condition would have improved.[153] **6.34**

(a) ***Hotson v East Berkshire AHA*** The question of whether damages could be recovered for 'loss of a chance' of improvement in a patient's health first arose in England in the case of *Hotson v East Berkshire AHA*.[154] It was alleged by the claimant that the delay of five days in diagnosing the fracture of his left femoral epiphysis when he fell from a tree caused him to lose a chance of complete recovery. The chance was put at 25 per cent. The claimant argued that although there was always a 75 per cent chance of permanent injury, the defendant's breach made that a 100 per cent certainty. The defendant's response was straightforward. The claimant's case must be established on a balance of probabilities, that is, that it was at least 51 per cent likely that the defendant's breach caused the damage. The evidence, the defendant argued, failed to meet that criterion. It was the fall from the tree that must have been more likely than not the cause of the claimant's damage. The law treats past facts, established on a balance of probabilities, as certain.[155] Hence, it was certain that the cause of the claimant's damage was not the delay in treatment. Simon Brown J, at first instance, **6.35**

in levonorgestrol permitted to occur. Counsel for the defendant stated that the 'but for' test continued to apply, and that unlike *Fairchild*, '[t]he biology was understood' (at [39]). Statistical analysis failed to establish an increase in risk due to a reduction in the intake of progesterone by 100 mcg or at most 200 mcg. The Court of Appeal held (at [40]) that the claimant had failed to establish that the erroneous intake of two logynon pills materially increased the risk of contraceptive failure. The claimant could not invoke any principle from *Fairchild* or *Barker* to overcome the trial judge's finding that the reduction in intake of progesterone did not increase, let alone materially increase, the risk of contraceptive failure.

153 See J King, 'Causation, Valuation and Chance in Personal Injury Torts Involving Pre-existing Conditions and Future Consequences' (1981) 90 Yale LJ 1353, 1354, 1376, 1381 and 1385 (advocating loss of a less than even chance and suggesting a need for an appropriate method of assigning a value to such a lost chance for it to be a compensable interest).

154 [1987] AC 750.

155 See *Judge v Huntingdon HA* [1995] 6 Med LR 223, citing Lord Diplock in *Mallett v McMonagle* [1970] AC 166: 'Anything that is more probable than not is certain.'

preferred the claimant's argument.[156] He held that the issue before him was not one of causation but of quantification; the proper quantum of damages, given the defendant's breach of duty. Assessing the damages arising from the avascular necrosis caused by the fracture at £46,000, he then awarded the claimant 25 per cent of this amount (£11,500) to compensate for the 25 per cent chance of avoiding permanent injury which had been lost.

6.36 On appeal, the Court of Appeal affirmed the High Court's decision.[157] In the House of Lords, however, their Lordships saw the facts as raising an issue of causation relating to the claimant's *injury*. As Lord Bridge put it: 'on a balance of probabilities the injury caused by the claimant's fall left insufficient blood vessels intact to keep the epiphysis alive. This amounts to a finding of fact that the fall was the sole cause of the vascular necrosis.'[158] Thus, the House of Lords held that the appeal must be allowed 'on the narrow ground that the claimant had failed to establish a cause of action'.[159]

6.37 As a consequence of their view of the evidence, the judges did not take the opportunity to develop the law in a radical way and recognize 'loss of a chance' as being a head of damage recoverable in its own right. It can be argued that, while the claimant is entitled to more than a fair share of sympathy, his position is no different from lots of other situations in which the defendant's breach is egregious but the claimant cannot establish causation and, therefore, loses. *Barnett*[160] is one such well-known example. The answer may be, of course, that the fact that the claimant cannot establish causation is what is under discussion. And, given the policy 'tweaks' which the courts in *Bonnington Castings* and *McGhee* and *Fairchild* were prepared to contemplate, why should they not go a 'tweak' further? The premise again, it will be recalled, is that justice requires that a way be found to compensate a claimant when the defendant is in breach of duty and the claimant has suffered damage—in this case, through the loss of a chance of treatment which could, perhaps, have been beneficial.

6.38 **(b) Developing the law** The judges in *Hotson*, and particularly Lord Mackay, did not rule out the possibility of recovery by the claimant.[161] It remained, therefore, following *Hotson*, a matter for further argument whether a claimant may bring an action based clearly and unequivocally on a claim that a chance of recovery or improvement was lost through the defendant's breach of duty. The claimant would be able to point to the evidence of the lost chance, and to quantify it. The court would be able to respond to this factual evidence and indeed encourage it, rather than see the law continue to favour doubt over some sort of certainty. The damages to be awarded to the claimant would not be the 100 per cent recovery of all that flowed from the damage suffered, but merely 100 per cent of the lost chance, that is the proportion of the total damage attributable to the lost chance.

6.39 The first argument in favour of allowing the claimant to recover is based on analogous cases from the law of contract. The most obvious case is *Kitchen v Royal Air Force Association*,[162] in which the loss of a chance was clearly held to be recoverable. The solicitor's breach of duty in *Kitchen* had prevented the claimant from pursuing a civil action. The claimant recovered damages based on an estimation of his likely chance of success. Lord Bridge in

156 [1985] 3 All ER 167.
157 [1987] 1 All ER 210.
158 *Hotson v East Berkshire AHA* [1987] AC 750, 782.
159 ibid, 782.
160 [1968] 1 All ER 1068.
161 See *Hotson v East Berkshire Area Health Authority* [1987] 1 AC 750, 786, [1987] 2 All ER 909, 916 *per* Lord Mackay; also [1987] 1 AC 750, 782–83, [1987] 2 All ER 909, 914 *per* Lord Bridge.
162 [1958] 1 WLR 563.

Hotson dismissed the analogy somewhat airily, referring to (without specifying) 'formidable difficulties in the way of accepting the analogy'.[163] It would be odd law, however, if a patient treated privately could maintain an action in contract against his doctor and recover damages for the loss of a chance of recovery or improvement, while a patient treated in the public sector and, therefore, restricted to an action in tort could not.

A second argument might be that to contribute materially to the claimant's prospects of permanent injury, denying him the chance of treatment, is just another way of materially increasing the risk of damage. Post-*McGhee* and *Fairchild*, the latter can be the basis for a successful damages claim. The problem is, however, that in those cases the court infers as a matter of law a causal connection between the breach of duty and the claimant's *injury*. Here, the claimant is arguing that there is a causal connection between the breach and the loss of a chance of recovery or improvement. It is as if in those cases the claimant was seeking to recover for *the risk of injury itself*. Perhaps, as a consequence, the analogy breaks down somewhat. What may not be lost, however, is the justice of the claimant's case. In *Hotson*, the claimant had sought to put some estimate on the risk and thereby lost the case by pre-empting the court's ability to draw any factual inference that his injuries had been caused by the defendant's negligence. It could be said that the only difference between *McGhee* and *Hotson* is that in *McGhee* it was impossible to estimate the extent of the increased risk, thereby allowing the court a free hand to draw inferences. But it would be a strange policy if the law preferred the unknown risk (*McGhee*) to the quantifiable (*Hotson*), in circumstances where nothing can be known for sure. **6.40**

There are two matters which may tell against the recognition of 'loss of a chance' claims—one of policy and one of identification. First, Lord Hoffmann's strictures in *Fairchild* against the expansion of liability in the NHS context by utilizing the *McGhee* test will be recalled.[164] They are no less significant here. Indeed, subject to the matter of identification, the threat to NHS budgets is probably greater. This may prove an insuperable policy objection. Second, there is the issue of quantification. In the usual clinical negligence case, the risk will have eventuated and the claimant will have suffered an injury. The factual focus will almost inevitably be upon who, or what, caused that injury. That is the common-sense and sensible approach to evaluating the facts and the law may not be able to refocus elsewhere.[165] To require the claimant to prove this causal connection would not, to borrow Lord Hoffmann's words in *Fairchild*, 'empty [the doctor's] duty of content'.[166] There are many other ways in which the doctor may be held accountable. More importantly, to hold otherwise would erroneously suggest that the doctor's legal duty is to exercise reasonable care and skill so as to increase *the chance* of improvement or benefit to the patient's health. **6.41**

There are, arguably, some situations when these arguments may break down or fall away. For example, the patient's situation may be such that all the doctor is expected to do is to act reasonably in order to improve the patient's chance of survival or deteriorating health. The most obvious is the diagnosis and treatment of cancer. Here, very often, the doctor is at best diagnosing and treating an incurable condition but which, with treatment, may improve the patient's chances of survival. It is no coincidence that it is in these cases that, by and large, **6.42**

[163] [1987] 1 AC 750, 782.
[164] [2002] UKHL 22, [69].
[165] See *Lawson v Laferriere* (1991) 78 DLR (4th) 609 (Can Sup Ct), especially *per* Gonthier J. See also *Naxakis v Western General Hospital* (1999) 197 CLR 269, [36] *per* Gaudron J.
[166] [2002] UKHL 22, [62].

US courts have developed recovery for 'loss of a chance'.[167] These were essentially the facts of the English case of *Gregg v Scott*,[168] which will be discussed shortly.

6.43 (c) **Post-*Hotson* jurisprudence** Subsequently, however, the courts have not interpreted *Hotson* in a benevolent way, preferring instead to see the judges as having excluded the possibility of recovery for loss of a chance.[169] Likewise, the Supreme Court of Canada[170] rejected recovery, and while until 2010 the Australian High Court judges were hopelessly split,[171] they have now come down firmly against loss of a chance of a better outcome being a form of actionable damage.[172] However, an increasing number of US jurisdictions allow recovery.[173]

6.44 (d) ***Gregg v Scott*** Following the decision of the House of Lords in *Fairchild* to take a flexible approach towards the problems of causation on policy grounds, the question of whether a loss of a chance, in the sense of a diminution of life expectancy by reference to worsened statistical chances of survival, should be recognized as damage giving rise to a claim in negligence was addressed by the House of Lords in *Gregg v Scott*.[174] The claimant's GP negligently failed to diagnose that he suffered from non-Hodgkin's lymphoma. The cancer was subsequently diagnosed. The expert evidence was that the negligent delay in diagnosing the condition reduced the claimant's chance of survival for a five-year period from 42 per cent to 25 per cent. Could he recover damages in these circumstances? Following *Hotson*, the trial judge held that the claimant had failed to prove that the delay had made any difference to the outcome for him. As a result, he had failed to prove that the negligence caused or materially contributed to any injury.

6.45 The Court of Appeal (by a majority)[175] rejected the claimant's action for the 'lost chance' of recovery from cancer. By a majority of 3:2, the House of Lords dismissed the claimant's appeal.[176] Two arguments were presented by the claimant. The first, the 'quantification

167 See, eg, *Herskovits v Group Health Cooperative* (1983) 664 P 2d 474 (Wash Sup Ct).

168 [2002] EWCA Civ 1471, [2003] Lloyd's Rep Med 105.

169 See *Tahir v Haringey HA* [1998] Lloyd's Rep Med 104 (CA), 108 *per* Otton LJ. See also *Pearman v North Essex HA* [2000] Lloyd's Rep Med 174. Contrast *Smith v NHS Litigation Authority* [2001] Lloyd's Rep Med 90.

170 *Lawson v Laferriere* (1991) 78 DLR (4th) 609, 658; see also *Cottrelle v Gerrard* (2003) 233 DLR (4th) 45 (Ont CA), [36].

171 *Naxakis v Western General Hospital* (1999) 197 CLR 269: Gaudron J (not recoverable), Callinan and McHugh JJ (recoverable), Glesson and Kirby J (expressing no opinion). Several Australian appellate decisions before 2009 appeared to have accepted the concept of loss of a chance (see, eg, *Gavalas v Singh* [2001] VSCA 23, (2001) 3 VR 404, [15] *per* Callaway JA, [38] *per* Smith AJA and *Rufo v Hosking* [2004] NSWCA 391, [405]–[406] *per* MW Campbell AJA, [9]–[10], [12] *per* Hodgson JA, [53]–[54] *per* Santow JA). However, the approach adopted by *Gavalas* and *Rufo* was rejected by the New South Wales Court of Appeal as involving a departure from conventional principles and to do so was 'plainly wrong': *Gett v Tabet* [2009] NSWCA 76, [389]. The Court of Appeal's decision was upheld by the Australian High Court: *Tabet v Gett* [2010] HCA 12, (2010) 265 ALR 227.

172 *Tabet v Gett* [2010] HCA 12, [58], [63] *per* Gummow ACJ, [67] *per* Hayne and Bell JJ, [101] *per* Crennan J, [151] *per* Kiefel J; cf [98] *per* Heydon J (expressing no opinion).

173 See, eg, *Perez v Las Vegas Medical Center* (1991) 805 P2d 589 (Nev Sup Ct) (where there was a dissent); *Wollen v DePaul Health Center* (1992) 828 SW 2d 681 (Missouri Sup Ct); *Matsuyama v Birnbaum* 890 NE 2d 819, 828, n 23 (Mass 2008), listing majority of states (at least 20, and District of Columbia) that have adopted a version of the loss of chance doctrine and joining that majority to ensure that the fundamental aims and principles of tort law (loss sharing, deterrence, and compensation) remain fully applicable (see Note, (2009) 122 Harv L Rev 1247). But cf the view of Kiefel J in *Tabet v Gett* [2010] HCA 12, [132], who interprets *Matsuyama v Birnbaum* as a case of proportionate damages.

174 *Greg v Scott* [2002] EWCA Civ 1471, [2003] Lloyd's Rep Med 105.

175 ibid. Simon Brown and Mance LJJ; Latham LJ dissenting.

176 *Greg v Scott* [2005] UKHL 2, [2005] 2 AC 176. Discussed in E Peel, (2005) 121 LQR 364; J Stapleton, (2005) 68 MLR 996; Rt Hon Lord Hoffmann, 'Causation' (2005) 121 LQR 592, 600–01.

argument', was that the delay had caused him physical injury in the form of enlargement of the tumour, because the trial judge had found that if he had been treated earlier, the cancer would not have spread as quickly as it did. He was entitled to compensation for this injury, including damages for the reduction in the chance of his survival. The second, the 'loss of a chance argument', was that the reduction in his chance of survival was itself a recoverable head of damage.

A majority of their Lordships rejected the first argument of the claimant, namely, the so-called 'quantification argument'. Lord Hoffmann said that the issue to be addressed was whether the claimant's likely premature death would be attributable to the defendant's delay in treatment.[177] He concluded that the claimant was unable to show on a balance of probabilities that the delay in treatment would have caused his likely premature death, since he would probably have been in the same position of his life being shortened to less than ten years in any event.[178] Lord Hope dissented from this view of the facts. He considered that on a balance of probabilities, the delay in treatment had caused the spread of the tumour with consequent pain and suffering, and that this gave him a cause of action for the pain and suffering caused by that injury and for the effect of the cancer on his life expectancy.[179] **6.46**

A majority of their Lordships also dismissed the claimant's 'loss of a chance argument' that the defendant's negligence in failing to diagnose the cancer tumour had reduced the claimant's chance of survival from 42 per cent to 25 per cent and that this was something of value and recoverable on policy grounds. However, the effect of their ruling on whether loss of a chance of a favourable outcome could ever be a recoverable head of damage in a clinical negligence case remains inconclusive.[180] Lord Hoffmann said that the claimant was attempting to extend the *Fairchild* exception so that damages should be awarded for the possibility that the injury had been caused by the doctor.[181] In his view the outcome of the claimant's disease was determinate in that the cancer would inevitably reduce his life. The outcome was not random, but was governed 'by the laws of causality' and an inability to establish that the delay in diagnosis caused the reduction in expectation of life could not be remedied 'by treating the outcome as having been somewhat indeterminate'.[182] He expressly rejected the adoption of the loss of a chance approach in clinical negligence cases, concluding that adopting such a rule would be a rejection of *Wilsher, Hotson*, and the qualifications and restrictions with which their Lordships hedged the *Fairchild* exception. No new arguments or change of circumstances could justify 'such a radical departure from precedent'[183] which would 'amount to a legislative act'[184] that would have 'enormous consequences for insurance companies and the National Health Service'.[185] Baroness Hale also rejected the loss of a chance approach. In her view, redefining the definition of personal injury from being in outcome terms to one being in loss of opportunity terms 'would cause far more problems in the general run of personal injury claims than the policy benefits are worth'.[186] **6.47**

177 *Greg v Scott* (HL), n 176, [68].
178 ibid, [71]; also [57]–[58] *per* Lord Nicholls, [187], [191] *per* Lord Phillips, [202], [205] *per* Baroness Hale.
179 ibid, [96].
180 See M Jones, *Medical Negligence* (4th edn, Sweet & Maxwell 2008) [5-086]–[5-094]; also *Clerk & Lindsell on Torts* (19th edn, Sweet & Maxwell 2006), [2-62]–[2-65].
181 *Greg v Scott* (HL), n 176, [84].
182 ibid, [80].
183 ibid, [85].
184 ibid, [90].
185 ibid, [90].
186 ibid, [225].

6.48 However, Lord Nicholls and Lord Hope were in favour of a claim succeeding on a loss of a chance basis in a clinical negligence action in a restricted set of circumstances. Lord Nicholls was willing to accept a claim for loss of a chance in cases where the patient's condition 'gave rise to significant medical uncertainty' as to what the outcome would have been in the absence of negligence.[187] He distinguished *Hotson*, where there was no significant uncertainty as to what would have happened to Hotson's leg if treated properly, from *Gregg*, where there was 'considerable medical uncertainty about what the outcome would have been had Mr Gregg received appropriate treatment nine months earlier'.[188] In his view, Mr Gregg's prospects of recovery had he been treated promptly, expressed in percentage terms of likelihood, represented the medical reality of his position. The law, he said, 'should be exceedingly slow to disregard medical reality in the context of a legal duty whose very aim is to protect medical reality'.[189]

6.49 Lord Hope also distinguished *Gregg* from *Hotson*. In *Hotson*, the 'fundamental question of fact to be answered [viz, whether the boy's fall was the cause of his avascular necrosis] related to a point in time before the negligent failure to treat began'.[190] Accordingly, it was to be treated 'as a matter of past fact'.[191] By contrast, the injury which affected the claimant's prospects of a successful recovery, namely the enlargement of the tumour, still lay in the future at the time when the claimant was seen by the doctor.[192] While Lord Phillips upheld the decision of the trial judge on the facts, he left open the possibility of a claim for loss of a chance. On the facts, the case's complications persuaded him that it was 'not a suitable vehicle' to award damages for the reduction of the prospects of a cure, when the long term result of treatment was still uncertain.[193] However, he did not rule out the possibility of a claim for loss of a chance where the medical treatment resulted in an adverse outcome and negligence increased the chance of that outcome, recovery of damages being proportionate to the increase in chance of the adverse outcome.[194]

6.50 It therefore seems arguable[195] that a claim for loss of a chance of a better medical outcome could be made where the patient's condition gives rise to 'significant medical uncertainty' as to what the outcome would have been in the absence of negligence,[196] and 'where medical treatment has resulted in an adverse outcome and negligence increased the chance of that outcome'.[197] In *Barker v Corus UK Ltd*,[198] Lord Hoffmann said that the majority of their Lordships in *Gregg* rejected the claimant's case, not on the ground that there was some conceptual objection to treating diminution in the chances of a favourable outcome as actionable damage, but on the basis that adopting such a rule in *Gregg* 'would in effect have extended the *Fairchild* exception to all cases of medical negligence, if not beyond, and would have been inconsistent with *Wilsher*.'[199] This distinguishing of *Gregg* enabled Lord Hoffmann to characterize the gist of the damage in the *Fairchild*-type case as the creation of the risk or chance of causing the disease, without the possibility of inconsistency between

187 ibid, [38], [44].
188 ibid.
189 ibid, [42].
190 ibid, [108].
191 ibid, [108].
192 ibid, [109].
193 ibid, [190].
194 ibid, [190].
195 See, especially, M Jones, *Medical Negligence* (4th edn, Sweet & Maxwell 2008), [5-095]–[5-100].
196 *Gregg v Scott* (HL), n 176, [38], [44] *per* Lord Nicholls.
197 ibid, [190] *per* Lord Phillips.
198 *Barker v Corus UK Ltd* [2006] UKHL 20, [2006] 2 AC 572, [2006] 2 WLR 1027, [39].
199 ibid.

the decisions.[200] However, it has been argued that Lord Hofmann's formulation in *Barker* 'renders precarious the authority of Hotson'.[201] Accordingly, the position in English law after *Hotson* and *Gregg* remains unresolved.

3. The place of *Bolam* in causation

Bolam[202] has traditionally been seen as the *locus classicus* of the test for the quantum of care required of a doctor by the law, so as to comply with his duty of care.[203] The question arose in the case of *Bolitho v City and Hackney HA*[204] as to whether *Bolam* also had a role to play in determining issues of causation. In *Bolitho*, the responsible doctor failed to attend a child patient, despite two separate requests from the senior nurse. The child suffered total respiratory collapse and a cardiac arrest and subsequently died. It was accepted during the course of the trial that had the child been intubated, the respiratory failure, had it occurred, would not have led to cardiac arrest, and that such intubation would have had to be carried out before the final catastrophic event. The doctor's failure to attend (either in person or through a deputy) was conceded to be a breach of duty. The question then arose whether this breach caused the child's death. **6.51**

It will be noticed that the breach of duty relied on by the claimant was the doctor's failure to attend the child, rather than a failure to intubate. This had significant consequences for the approach to causation adopted by the courts at all levels. The evidence given by the doctor was that, even if she had attended, she would not have intubated the child. Intubation of a 2-year-old child was, she said, a major intervention not free from risks. The symptoms of the child did not warrant it. On a straightforward application of the 'but for' test, the claimant fails at that point, provided, of course, that the defendant's evidence is believed, which it was. There is, however, an obvious reservation to be entered. As a precedent, does not such an approach lend itself to self-serving, *ex post facto* justification? Is it not particularly undesirable to base causation on this approach, when there may be evidence to suggest that the failure to carry out a procedure (on the basis that the defendant states that he would not have carried it out), itself constitutes a further breach of duty? It appears counter-intuitive to allow a defendant to avoid liability by pleading in aid the fact that he would have compounded the original breach of duty with a further breach. **6.52**

Faced with this apparent difficulty, both the Court of Appeal (with Simon Brown LJ dissenting) and the House of Lords (with Lord Browne-Wilkinson speaking for the House), decided that something had to be done. What they decided to do, having asked the first question—would the doctor have attended the child?—and received a negative response, was to ask a second question—*should* the doctor have intubated the child? If the evidence was that she should have, then, their Lordships held, causation would be established. As it happens, the evidence was sufficiently equivocal to absolve the defendant. **6.53**

Lord Browne-Wilkinson referred with approval to the judgment of Hobhouse LJ in *Joyce v Merton, Sutton and Wandsworth HA*.[205] In that case, Hobhouse LJ, commenting on the Court of Appeal's judgment in *Bolitho*, said: '[the situation which arose in *Bolitho*] involves **6.54**

---

200 ibid, [35].

201 See J Stapleton, 'Occam's Razor Reveals an Orthodox Basis for *Chester* v *Afsher*' (2006) 122 LQR 426, 448, n 77.

202 *Bolam v Friern HMC* [1957] 2 All ER 118.

203 But see *Bolitho v City and Hackney HA* [1997] 4 All ER 771.

204 ibid.

205 [1996] 7 Med LR 1.

the factual situation that the original fault did not itself cause the injury but that this was because there would have been some further fault on the part of the defendants.' The response to this line of reasoning must be, first, that the 'original fault', if relied upon as the breach of duty on which the claimant's case is based, is the relevant fault for the law of causation. Secondly, the 'further fault' does not exist save as a hypothesis and is unrelated to the conduct of the particular defendant. While it is understandable that the court would not want to be seen to allow a defendant to 'get away with it', it is at least doubtful whether the law of causation is the appropriate mechanism to achieve this. What the doctor *should* have done may be evidence of what the doctor *would* have done, but it is no more than that. As has been said elsewhere: '[i]t is relevant to know what *should* have been done in deciding what a particular doctor *would* have done, but it cannot be conclusive . . . The fact that some doctors would have intubated the claimant while others would not cannot determine what *this doctor* would have done.'[206]

6.55 The House of Lords' approach, therefore, is at best odd. What the doctor should or should not have done relates to her duty of care to the patient. It has nothing to do with establishing a causative link between breach (non-attendance in this particular case) and the child's injury and death. Causation purports to be a matter of fact, or, in cases of omission such as *Bolitho*, a matter of plausible hypothesis based on evidence of the past practice *of the defendant*. What *others* would have done cannot be conclusive.

6.56 It may seem that this is a somewhat churlish response to *Bolitho*, given that it sought to mitigate the difficulties encountered by the claimant in dealing with an entirely hypothetical situation: did the non-attendance cause the child's injury? The response must be that the route taken by way of mitigation is incoherent even by the standards of the law of causation. It is no answer that it allowed the House of Lords to endorse the move away from *Bolam* as the basis for establishing a breach of duty, which had been signalled by the Court of Appeal. Although this is particularly welcome, it is irrelevant for current purposes. What is relevant is that, in cases in which the breach of duty alleged is an omission to act, the legal enquiry into causation, which is represented as factual, will be converted into a normative investigation as to what the defendant should have done. Admittedly, it is clear from what has gone before, that the supposedly factual enquiry as to causation is not free from an accretion of policy issues. Nonetheless, it has always ultimately resolved itself into a factual issue, even if the courts have sometimes decided to infer one set of facts rather than another. *Bolitho* represents a significant departure from this approach. By introducing a normative element into causation in this way, it has added to the complexity (and, some would say, incoherence) of the law. It only remains to say that the alternative approach for the claimant in *Bolitho* was to have focused on the failure to intubate as the relevant breach of duty—but this was, of course, difficult to establish on the expert evidence. There was little doubt that factual causation could link *this* breach to the child's subsequent injury and death. Had the case been

[206] Commentary (1993) Med LRev 241. For a sustained assault on Hobhouse LJ's judgment in *Joyce*, see, A Grubb, Commentary (1996) Med LRev 86. For further discussion of cases applying the two-limbed *Bolitho* causation test, see *Wiszniewski v Central Manchester HA* [1996] 7 Med LR 248 (doctor would have intervened; sufficient to establish causation under first limb); *Gouldsmith v Mid-Staffordshire General Hospitals NHS Trust* [2007] EWCA 397, [2007] LS Law Med 363, [29] (upon reference to a specialist hospital, appropriate surgery would have been conducted; determinative of causation under first limb) (*sed quaere*?: see M Jones, *Medical Negligence* (4th edn, Sweet & Maxwell 2008) [5-016]). Note that if what the doctor *would* have done would probably have resulted in damage to the claimant, then the question of what *should* have been done would be irrelevant. This is the case, even if the doctor *would* have acted in a way which went beyond the standard of care required to avoid harm. The doctor would have been liable: *Robbins v Bexley LBC* [2013] EWCA Civ 1233, [2014] BLR 11, [47]–[53] *per* Vos LJ, [69] *per* Aikens LJ.

approached in this way, the law of causation may have avoided the strange flirtation with *Bolam*, even at a time when *Bolam*'s death-knell is being rung.

4. Causation and the duty to inform

Where a doctor has breached his duty to obtain a properly informed consent, [207] the patient, if he is to succeed in an action in negligence, must still show that the breach caused the damage complained of. The damage, of course, is the fact that a procedure was carried out without consent. It is immaterial that it may have been carried out with all due skill. The proposition that the breach must cause the damage translates here into the assertion by the claimant that, if he had been properly informed, he would not have gone ahead with the procedure. Obviously, it is open to the claimant, with the benefit of '20:20 vision' to assert that he would not have consented. Provided he is believable, this would clinch the case. Causation would be established on the basis of his say-so. Such a subjective approach to causation, however, may appear to tip the scales too heavily in favour of the claimant. For instance, in the decision of the House of Lords in *Chester v Afshar*[208] it was held that a claimant could recover against a defendant surgeon for failure to warn of the risk of injury through surgery (here, a 1 to 2 per cent risk of cauda equina syndrome), where the injury transpired, despite the fact that the risk was neither created nor increased by the failure to warn, and despite the claimant's inability to show that she would never have undergone surgery carrying the same risk at a later date. While their Lordships held that on conventional causation grounds, failure to warn did not cause the claimant's injury,[209] a majority of their Lordships relied on the policy factors underlying the scope of the defendant's duty to warn his patient of the risk of injury to modify the normal approach to causation.[210] Since the injury was 'intimately involved with'[211] and was within the scope of the very risk that she should have been warned about when her consent to the operation was obtained, the injury could be regarded as having been caused, in the legal sense, by the defendant's breach of duty.[212] The underlying policy of the duty of a medical practitioner to warn the patient of **6.57**

[207] See further Chapter 4, para 4.152.

[208] *Chester v Afshar* [2004] UKHL 41, [2005] 1 AC 134.

[209] ibid, [81] *per* Lord Hope.

[210] ibid [24]–[25] *per* Lord Steyn, [85]–[88] *per* Lord Hope, [93] *per* Lord Walker. Cf the dissenting judgments of Lord Bingham, at [8], and Lord Hoffmann at [29] and [31], concluding that the claimant had failed to establish that 'but for' the failure to warn, she would have not undergone surgery. Lord Hoffmann, at [31], criticized the claimant's argument that it was sufficient that she would not have had the operation at that time or by another surgeon, as being 'about as logical as saying that if one had been told, on entering a casino, that the odds on the number 7 coming up at roulette were only 1 in 37, one would have gone away and come back next week or gone to a different casino'. He added: 'The question is whether one would have taken the opportunity to avoid or reduce the risk, not whether one would have changed the scenario in some irrelevant detail'. For criticism of this reasoning, and for the view that there was sufficient evidence to satisfy the 'but for' test (since Miss Chester would have had the operation, if at all, at a different time, and the a priori estimate of the risk would have been 1 to 2 per cent, so that it would have been more likely than not that, but for the breach, she would not have suffered the syndrome), see J Stapleton, 'Occam's Razor Reveals an Orthodox Basis for *Chester v Afsher*' (2006) 122 LQR 426, 428, 429–30. However, in order to argue successfully that an orthodox approach is an adequate one, Professor Stapleton considers that it is necessary to move from the three-step approach to causation as championed by Hart and Honoré (historical fact, causal connection, and remoteness) to a two-step analysis, viz factual historical involvement and scope of liability for consequences of breach): 426, 436–48.

[211] *Chester v Afshar*, n 208, [87], *per* Lord Hope.

[212] ibid, [87]–[88]. For the application of *Chester v Afshar* in the context of the duty to warn of alternative treatments and causation, see *Birch v University College London Hospital NHS Foundation Trust* [2008] EWHC 2237, (2008) 104 BMLR 168 (QB). The Court of Appeal has emphasized the exceptional and limited application of *Chester* v *Afshar* to cases where there has been a breach of the doctor's duty to advise the patient of the disadvantages and dangers of the proposed treatment so as to enable the patient to give

material risks inherent in a proposed treatment is therefore to protect the patient from the occurrence of physical injury, the risk of which was unacceptable to the patient, as opposed to mere exposure to the risk.[213]

6.58 One option is to insist on an objective test: what would the reasonable person in the claimant's position have done? The difficulty with this alternative is obvious. It rests the test of causation on a fiction, the decision of the reasonable person, rather than on the evidence of the particular patient. A further option is to cleave to the subjective approach, but require that the evidence adduced by the claimant be judged against some test of reasonableness, so as to inject some sort of check on the resort to hindsight. This last, hybrid, position most closely reflects the current position in English law.[214]

5. Legal causation

(i) Intervening acts

6.59 There is little to be said about legal causation for causation and the impact of intervening acts on the defendant's possible liability in medical law.[215] The ordinary rules of tort law apply. The question for the court, where it is alleged that the intervening act of a third party has broken the chain of causation, is clearly a mixed question of law and fact. If the evidence demonstrates that there was some act of a third party which intervened between the defendant's breach of duty and the claimant's injury, the court must decide what degree of responsibility should still reside with the defendant. The word 'responsibility' is used to seek to demonstrate that the court, as ever, has a choice and that, essentially, the choice is a matter of policy. The policy at issue is, of course, that a defendant should only be held liable if his conduct is sufficiently blameworthy. This translates, in any particular case involving allegations of third-party intervention, into whether the defendant's breach of duty is sufficiently blameworthy that he should continue to attract condemnation through an award of damages. As the editors of *Clerk and Lindsell on Torts* have put it in the context of medical negligence: '[O]nly medical treatment so grossly negligent as to be a completely inappropriate response to the injury inflicted by the defendant should operate to break the chain of causation.'[216] Accordingly, in *Webb v Barclays Bank plc and Portsmouth Hospitals*,[217] the Court of Appeal held that there was no general rule that when a claimant is injured by the negligence of a defendant that the defendant's liability is terminated by the intervening negligence of a doctor brought in to treat the original injury, but who in fact made it worse.[218] The claimant, a polio sufferer, had injured her polio-affected left knee as a result of a fall for which the defendants were responsible. The consultant surgeon treating her advised her to

informed consent: *Meikeljohn v St George's Hospital NHS Trust* [2014] EWCA Civ 120, [34]; *Crossman v St George's Healthcare NHS Trust* [2016] EWHC 2878 (QB), [50], [53].

Where there has been failure to warn of two distinct and material inherent risks of surgery, A and B, but the claimant would have chosen to undergo the surgery even if warned of risk A, and risk A eventuated, there will be no liability for failure to warn about risk B since risk B did not eventuate: *Wallace* v *Kam* [2013] HCA 19, (2013) 250 CLR 375 (neuropaxia and paralysis; claimant would have chosen to undergo surgery even if warned of the risk of neuropraxia and neuropraxia eventuated; no liability for failure to warn about paralysis, which did not eventuate).

213 *Wallace* v *Kam* [2013] HCA 19, (2013) 250 CLR 37, [9], [36].

214 See *Smith v Barking, Havering and Brentwood* HA [1994] 5 Med LR 285 and *Smith v Tunbridge Wells HA* [1994] 5 Med LR 334.

215 For a discussion of legal causation and remoteness in the context of medical law see *Chappel v Hart* (1998) 27 ALJR 1344 (HC Aus).

216 *Clerk & Lindsell on Torts* (21st edn, Sweet & Maxwell 2014) 2–92; approved in *Webb v Barclays Bank plc and Portsmouth Hospitals* [2001] EWCA Civ 1141, [2002] PIQR P8.

217 *Webb v Barclays Bank plc and Portsmouth Hospitals* [2001] EWCA Civ 1141, [2002] PIQR P8.

218 ibid, [52]–[53].

have an above-the-knee amputation, which was negligent. The Court of Appeal held that the negligence of the consultant surgeon 'did not eclipse the original wrongdoing'.[219] While the employers were held liable for all the damage due to the fall, their liability for damage attributable to the amputation was assessed at 25 per cent, with the Trust's at 75 per cent.[220] In *Wright v Cambridge Medical Group*,[221] a general practitioner negligently delayed referral of the claimant to hospital, who had developed a bacterial super-infection which attacked her hip. Following negligent treatment by the hospital, the claimant suffered a permanent injury to the hip. The Court of Appeal held that the hospital's failure to treat the claimant properly did not break the chain of causation as '[i]t was not such an egregious event, in terms of the degree or unusualness of negligence, or the period of time for which it lasted, to defeat or destroy the causative link between the defendant's negligence and the claimant's injury'.[222]

Although there is little in the cases in medical law which can add to these general propositions, there are a number of matters which warrant comment. The first is the case of *Knightley v Johns*,[223] in which it was made clear that a subsequent breach of duty by a third party may not break the chain of causation, and thereby absolve the defendant of his breach of duty, if the later breach was reasonably foreseeable.[224] In *Knightley*, Stephenson LJ sought to prescribe some kind of hierarchy of third-party interventions, each of which might have a different effect on the defendant's liability: '[n]egligent conduct is more likely to break the chain of causation than conduct which is not; positive acts will more easily constitute new causes than inaction.'[225] The difficulty with this type of 'analysis by list' is that it omits to identify and analyse the underlying criteria which might give rise to these various conclusions. Given that the criterion is ultimately accepted by Stephenson LJ as being 'common sense rather than logic on the facts and circumstances of each case',[226] it may be wiser to avoid the formulaic approach and concentrate on the complex array of factors which persuade a court to shift responsibility away from a doctor in breach of his duty onto someone else. An illustration of this 'common-sense' approach on the facts of the case is that of *Prendergast v Sam & Dee Ltd*.[227] In that case, the Court of Appeal upheld the trial judge's finding against a doctor and a chemist when a prescription of Amoxil had been wrongly dispensed as Daonil, a drug to control diabetes by reducing the sugar content of the blood. The doctor wrote the word Amoxil, not very legibly, in lower case and the chemist misread the prescription, dispensing Daonil. Having taken six Daonil tablets the plaintiff suffered **6.60**

[219] ibid, [57].

[220] ibid, [59]. See also *Rahman v Arearose Ltd* [2001] QB 351, [29], [34], where the Court of Appeal held that as a matter of law a later negligence did not automatically extinguish the causal link between an earlier act of negligence and subsequent damage and that each tort had played a part in the claimant's suffering; accordingly liability was apportioned between both defendants.

[221] *Wright v Cambridge Medical Group* [2011] EWCA civ 669, [2013] QB 312.

[222] ibid, [37], per Lord Neuberger MR. See also Smith LJ at [131] (the general practitioner's breach of duty 'had an ongoing effect on events which was not completely wiped out by the hospital's failure to act correctly'. Elias LJ concluded, at [111], that the concept of *novus actus interveniens* was inapplicable since it was foreseeable that hospital doctors will be negligent and that it could not be said that the negligence in this case deserved to be characterized as gross or egregious so as to break the chain of causation. However, Elias LJ dissented as to the outcome on the ground that the permanent injury did not fall within the scope of the duty breached by the general practitioner: [111]–[112]. See N McBride and S Steel, 'Suing for the Loss of a Right to Sue: Why *Wright* is Wrong' (2012) 28 PN 27.

[223] *Knightley v Johns* [1982] 1 WLR 349.

[224] ibid, 366.

[225] ibid.

[226] ibid, 367.

[227] [1989] 1 Med LR 36, The Times, 14 March 1989.

hypoglycaemia leading to unconsciousness and irreparable brain damage. The pharmacist had read the error since the doctor's handwriting had been poor enough to invite misreading. The trial judge held that the doctor's writing amounted to negligence since it reasonably permitted the misreading, but also held that the pharmacist was negligent in failing to appreciate the incompatibility of Daonil, in the light of the other items on the prescription. Liability was apportioned 25 per cent to the doctor and 75 per cent to the pharmacist. It was held by the Court of Appeal that although other aspects of the prescription, such as the dosage and number of tablets, should have put the chemist on enquiry as being inconsistent with Daonil, the chain of causation was not broken. It was reasonably foreseeable in the circumstances that Daonil would be prescribed.[228]

6.61 A further matter warranting consideration is what is the status of an intervention by a third party which takes the form of a failure to act—that is, there is no *actus interveniens*. There is some authority in the general law of torts for the proposition that an omission to act by a third party cannot intervene to break the chain of causation. This was the view expressed by Goff LJ in *Muirhead v Industrial Tank Specialities*.[229] In medical law, in the context of a doctor–patient relationship, it is difficult to sustain this approach. Arguably, it gives too much force to a literal interpretation of actus, rather than seeing it as conduct, a more neutral term embracing both commission and omission. Furthermore, given that doctors are liable for omissions once a doctor–patient relationship can be shown to exist, a failure to act, in breach of duty, which causes damage, should be eligible to be regarded as a cause, and in appropriate circumstances, an intervening cause.

6.62 A third issue relates to the claimant's conduct. It will be recalled that what is under discussion here is conduct of another which may break the chain of causation between the defendant's breach of duty and the claimant's damage. So, here, it must be assumed that the doctor is in breach of his duty. It is submitted that, in appropriate circumstances, the unreasonable behaviour of the claimant could be judged to be contributory negligence.[230] Equally, in appropriate circumstances, there seems no reason in principle why it should not be regarded as an intervening cause, absolving the defendant. In such a case, the claimant would become the author of his own misfortune. That said, it is further submitted that, before a claimant would be held in medical law to have brought his own damage on himself, the court would probably demand a high degree of knowledge by the claimant of what he was doing, its implications and that it was not appropriate and would expose him to a risk of harm, and that he acted voluntarily and not under any duress or other factor reducing the capacity to choose. An example can be found in *Sabri-Tabrizi v Lothian Health Board*[231] where an action for damages for a failed sterilization failed because the decision of the claimant to have sexual intercourse knowing that the operation had been unsuccessful was a *novus actus interveniens*. However, a victim's suicide will not break the chain of causation

[228] Cf *Horton v Evans and Lloyds Pharmacy Ltd* [2006] EWHC 2808, [2007] LS Law Medical 212, [53]–[54] (actions of third party physician did not break the chain of causation between pharmacist's negligence in failing to question the correctness of first defendant GP's prescription and the claimant's injuries, caused by an overdose of the corticosteroid, dexamethasone).

[229] [1986] QB 507, 533.

[230] See paras 6.65–6.71.

[231] (1997) 43 BMLR 190 (CS, IH). Cf *Spencer v Wincanton Holdings Ltd* [2009] EWCA Civ 1404, [2010] PIQR P8 (decision of claimant with above-knee amputation to put petrol in his car without using prosthesis or his walking sticks was not unreasonable and thus no *novus actus interveniens*). But note preference of Sedley LJ at [14]–[15] for 'fairness' approach of Lord Bingham *in Corr v IBC Vehicles Ltd* [2008] UKHL 13, [2008] 1 AC 884 at [15] over the 'reasonableness' approach of Lord Reid in *McKew v. Holland and Hannen and Cubitts (Scotland) Ltd* [1969] 3 All ER 1621, 1623. But *quaere* whether fairness any more precise or helpful than reasonableness in determining a *novus actus interveniens*?

where a defendant is under a duty of care to guard against this very act occurring;[232] and where a claimant's capacity to make a reasoned and informed judgment has been impaired, this may indicate that the necessary voluntary element for a *novus actus interveniens* is not present.[233] So, in *Corr v IBC Vehicles*,[234] the House of Lords held that a suicide which was the result of a severe depressive illness that impaired the victim's capacity to make a reasoned and informed judgment did not break the chain of causation, where the defendant's conduct had caused the victim to suffer the accident which resulted in the depression.

A final issue, in the context of intervening cause, is the situation in which the claimant refuses further treatment. Again, the beginning point of analysis is a breach of duty by the defendant doctor. Can the claimant's refusal constitute an intervening cause? Arguing from first principles, it would appear that it should not be so regarded. A patient who is competent is entitled in law to refuse treatment. It is hard to see, therefore, how a refusal to undergo further treatment, so as to rectify a previous breach of duty by the doctor, can be judged adversely. The law may, however, be less simple. The proposition that a competent patient has the right to refuse is, of course, relevant to circumstances in which the patient's personal integrity and inviolability is at stake. Here, it could be argued that the law is concerned with something slightly different. The claimant has had treatment. All that is asked is that the doctor (or another) have the opportunity to take remedial action (for example, intervene surgically to ensure that an operation on the knee which was not done properly does not leave the patient with a permanent limp). Any difference, however, is at best superficial. The integrity of the patient is as much at stake here as in other situations. It would follow that the patient's refusal of further treatment, even if unreasonable or irrational, should not and does not serve as an intervening cause to break the chain of causation. An extreme example in support of this proposition can be found in the case of *Emeh v Chelsea and Kensington AHA*.[235] A doctor was found to be in breach of duty in not performing properly an operation to sterilize the claimant. She became pregnant and brought an action to recover, inter alia, the increased costs associated with the pregnancy and birth of a further child. The trial judge found that her failure subsequently to obtain an abortion was unreasonable and thereby broke the chain of causation. The Court of Appeal in three strongly worded judgments rejected this view. The court went out of its way to make it plain that a woman's choice not to undergo an abortion should not be regarded as a reason for absolving the defendant doctor, whose breach of duty had confronted her with the very dilemma she sought to avoid. **6.63**

(ii) Remoteness

Again, the question here is whether there are any issues of remoteness of damage which are peculiar to medical law. The answer is that the general rules of remoteness in the law of torts and the need to prove that the injury is foreseeable apply. Accordingly, damage to the claimant's interests of the type or kind which occurred must have been foreseeable and it must have materialized in a way which was foreseeable or at least a variant of the foreseeable.[236] **6.64**

---

232 *Reeves v Commissioner of Police of the Metropolis* [2000] 1 AC 306, 367–68, [1999] 3 All ER 897, 902.

233 *Corr v IBC Vehicles Ltd* [2008] UKHL 13, [2008] 1 AC 884. Discussed in G Gordon, (2008) 12 Edin LR 433.

234 *Corr v IBC Vehicles Ltd*, n 233, [16] *per* Lord Bingham, [29] *per* Lord Scott, [42]–[43] *per* Lord Walker, [45]–[46] *per* Lord Mance, [55]–[56] *per* Lord Neuberger.

235 [1984] 3 All ER 1044.

236 See, in general, *Overseas Tankship (UK) Ltd v Morts Dock and Engineering Co Ltd, The Wagon Mound (No 1)* [1961] AC 388, [1961] 1 All ER 404 (PC); *Hughes v Lord Advocate* [1963] AC 837, [1963] 1 All ER 705 (HL). However, determining what constitutes the same type or kind of damage can be problematic: *A-G v Hartwell* [2004] 1 WLR 1273, 1281, [28] *per* Lord Nicholls. The kind of damage should not be too narrowly defined so as to preclude recovery: *Spencer v Wincanton Holdings Ltd* [2009] EWCA Civ 1404,

A number of illustrative examples can be found in the case law: a doctor who negligently fails to discover that his mountaineer patient has a weak knee is not liable for the subsequent injury suffered by the mountaineer as a result of something not related to the knee because the injury is outside the scope of the doctor's duty of care;[237] a patient's injuries suffered when an operating theatre is struck by lightning would not be attributable to any negligence by the doctor or hospital;[238] a doctor would not be liable for an injury resulting from something unrelated to the risk of which the patient is not properly informed, for example, an injury arising from an anaesthetic accident.[239]

6.65 In the context of physical injury to the person, the foreseeability requirement is generally taken to be not that the precise harm, or its extent or the precise concatenation of events which led to it should be foreseeable but that the type or kind of harm should be foreseeable. So, for example, if an injury is not idiosyncratic, and is of a type that ought to be reasonably foreseen, the fact that the claimant suffered an extreme reaction indigenous to him would still result in liability in negligence.[240] This is known as the 'thin skull rule' or the 'eggshell skull rule'. The rule will even apply where the claimant may suffer a major psychiatric condition consequent upon a relatively minor physical injury. Provided there is a causal connection between the physical injury and the psychiatric condition, the defendant is liable in full for all the psychiatric consequences, irrespective of whether they are unforeseeable. Thus in *Shorey v PT Ltd*,[241] the High Court of Australia allowed a plaintiff to recover for the consequences of a conversion disorder, which resulted in paraplegia, although no organic cause was established, where the defendant's negligence had resulted in the plaintiff suffering a fall. It held that while the physical effects of the fall were likely to have resolved within twelve months, the fall was the cause of the conversion disorder since it was the 'main trigger point' or 'sentinel event in the causal chain'. The defendant had to take its victim as it found her.[242]

6.66 Likewise, in *Simmons v British Steel plc*,[243] the pursuer sustained a head injury during the course of his employment by the defenders. After the accident, he experienced an exacerbation of a pre-existing skin condition, and he developed a change in his personality which resulted in a severe depressive illness. The House of Lords held that there was a causal connection between the anger suffered by the pursuer following the accident and his physical and psychiatric injuries.[244] Since the pursuer was a 'primary victim' who had sustained physical injuries in the accident,[245] it was unnecessary to ask whether the psychiatric injury from which he had been suffering was reasonably foreseeable,[246] and the defender had to take his victim as he found him.[247]

[2010] PIQR P8 (personal injury following on from amputation was a kind of consequence that was reasonably foreseeable at the time of the accident: [33] *per* Aikens LJ).

[237] *South Australia Asset Management Corporation v York Montague Ltd* [1996] 3 All ER 365, 371–72 *per* Lord Hoffmann.

[238] *Chester v Ashfar* [2002] 3 All ER 552 (CA), [43] *per* Sir Dennis Henry. See also *Hogan v Bentinick Colleries* [1949] 1 All ER 588, 601 *per* Lord MacDermott—employer not liable where worker injured in employment is burned in hospital fire or in accident whilst in ambulance.

[239] *Chappel v Hart* (1998) 72 ALJR 1344 (HC Aus), [66] *per* Gummow J at and *Chester v Ashfar*, n 238, [43] *per* Sir Dennis Henry.

[240] *Smith v Leech Brain & Co Ltd* [1962] 2 QB 405, [1961] 3 All ER 1159.

[241] *Shorey v PT Ltd.* [2003] HCA 27, (2003) 197 ALR 410.

[242] ibid, [3], [34], [44].

[243] *Simmons v British Steel plc* [2004] UKHL 20, 2004 SC (HL) 94.

[244] ibid, [26]–[27] *per* Lord Hope.

[245] In terms of Lord Lloyd's classification in *Page v Smith* [1996] 1 AC 155, 184, 190.

[246] *R v Croydon HA* [2004] UKHL 20, 2004 SC (HL) 94, [21] *per* Lord Hope.

[247] ibid, [56] *per* Lord Rodger.

6.67 However, the 'thin skull rule' does not require a medical practitioner to be responsible for unforeseeable harm which is not connected to his breach of duty. In *R v Croydon HA*[248] the claimant underwent a pre-employment chest X-ray. The radiographer negligently failed to report a significant abnormality, namely primary pulmonary hypertension (PPH), a potentially fatal condition. The claimant became pregnant and was later admitted to hospital suffering from PPH. The plaintiff gave birth to a healthy child by Caesarean section. She sued in negligence for damages for the birth of the child, the complications arising from the pregnancy and loss of earnings. She argued that had she known about the PPH she would not have become pregnant and incurred the loss and damage. The Court of Appeal held, as regards damages arising out of the birth, the loss was too remote from the radiologist's breach of duty. The latter's duty did not extend to the claimant's private life.

B. Defences

6.68 There are several potential defences available to a defendant in a medical negligence action but in practice, with the exception of limitation, they are rarely relevant, given the nature of the relationship between doctor and patient. The defences that will be considered here are contributory negligence, *volenti non fit injuria, ex turpi causa non oritur actio* and limitation of action.

1. Contributory negligence

6.69 A doctor frequently needs the patient's cooperation, for example, to make an accurate diagnosis or for the purpose of administering treatment. Sometimes this will be absolutely vital. The doctor requires accurate information regarding the patient's symptoms, and medical history. Similarly, the cooperation of the patient may be essential in implementing a treatment regime, for example, with regard to taking medication correctly, or returning for further treatment or tests. If the patient fails to follow proper instructions and this is a cause of his injuries, then it will be possible to argue that the patient has been contributorily negligent, or in an extreme case that his conduct is the sole cause of the damage.[249] Alternatively, where a patient has failed to communicate the nature of the symptoms from which she is suffering, the conclusion may simply be that the doctor was not negligent in failing to make a correct diagnosis on the basis of the available information.[250]

(i) Law Reform (Contributory Negligence) Act 1945

6.70 Section 1 of the Law Reform (Contributory Negligence) Act 1945 provides that where damage is attributable partly to the fault of the defendant and partly to the fault of the claimant, then the award of damages may be reduced by reason of the claimant's contributory negligence.[251] The reduction will be to such extent as the court thinks just and equitable having regard to the

[248] [1998] Lloyd's Rep Med 44 (CA). See also *Brown v Lewisham and North Southwark HA* [1999] Lloyd's Rep Med 110 (CA), 117–18 *per* Beldom LJ; *Thompson v Bradford* [2005] EWCA Civ 1439, [2006] Lloyd's Rep Med 95, [18]–[20], [29]–[31].

[249] *Venner v North East Essex Area HA*, The Times, 21 February 1987; *Murrin v Janes* [1949] 4 DLR 403, 406 (Newfd SC).

[250] *Morrison v Forsyth* [1995] 6 Med LR 6 (CS OH), where a GP was found not liable for failing to visit a patient because the seriousness of the patient's condition was not made clear in the course of a telephone conversation; *Gordon v Wilson* [1992] 3 Med LR 401 (CS, OH); *Friedsam v Ng* [1994] 3 WWR 294 (BCCA).

[251] Section 4 provides that fault means 'negligence, breach of statutory duty or other act or omission which gives rise to a liability in tort or would, apart from this Act, give rise to the defence of contributory negligence'. The Act probably applies to actions in trespass to the person: *Barnes v Nayer*, The Times, 19 December 1986 (CA); *Wasson v Chief Constable of the Royal Ulster Constabulary* [1987] 8 NIJB 34; *Murphy v Culhane* [1977] QB 94; cf *Lane v Holloway* [1968] 1 QB 379.

claimant's share in responsibility for the damage. While there has been controversy about the extent of the Act's applicability to actions in contract,[252] it has been held that it applies to actions in contract where the defendant's negligent breach of contract would have given rise to liability in the tort of negligence independently of the existence of the contract.[253] Accordingly, the defence will be available in virtually all actions arising out of private medical treatment, since the obligations imposed by the contract are normally the same as the duty to exercise reasonable care in the tort of negligence. On the other hand, where:

(a) liability does not depend on negligence but arises from breach of a strict contractual duty; or
(b) liability arises from breach of a contractual obligation which is expressed in terms of exercising reasonable care, but does not correspond to a common law duty of care which would exist independently of the contract,

apportionment under the legislation is not available.[254] Thus, in the rare circumstances where a patient was able to establish that the doctor had given a contractual warranty to achieve a specific result, this would fall into category (a) and the damages could not be apportioned for contributory negligence. It is unlikely that there are circumstances where category (b) could be relevant to the doctor–patient relationship.

6.71 Although, in theory, there is no reason why contributory negligence should not apply in a claim for medical negligence, in practice the defence is rarely invoked successfully, and this is reflected in a comparative dearth of cases. It may be that the plea is considered to be inappropriate, given the inequality between the respective positions of doctor and patient. Patients do not generally question the advice or conduct of their doctors, even when they are aware that their condition is deteriorating or not improving. If the patient has ignored the doctor's advice (eg by discharging himself from hospital or failing to return for further treatment) it may be easier to establish the defence. It would have to be shown that a reasonable person would have been aware of the significance of the advice, which will depend upon the nature of the advice and whether it was clear to the patient. Moreover, in some circumstances there may well be a responsibility upon the doctor to adopt a system for following up patients who do not comply with advice to re-attend for further treatment or tests. The one English reported case in which the claimant's conduct was held to have been negligent is *Pidgeon v Doncaster HA*[255] where a claimant who developed cervical cancer, having been told that the results of a smear test were negative, was held to have been two-thirds contributorily negligent in failing to have a further smear test despite frequent reminders. In fact, by raising a plea of contributory negligence, a defendant may highlight the extent of the doctor's duty to take special care in giving the patient instructions, and making sure that the patient understands both the instructions and the importance of strictly adhering to them. In *Marshall v Rogers*,[256] for example, the defendant alleged that the claimant's injury was caused by his own negligence in failing to follow the instructions that he had been given and to report his symptoms. It was held, however, that where a dangerous remedy was being attempted, the doctor was negligent in delegating his own professional duty to decide the

---

[252] See further A Burrows, *Remedies for Torts and Breach of Contract* (3rd edn, Oxford University Press 2004), 136–43.

[253] *Forsikringsaktieselskapet Vesta v Butcher* [1988] 2 All ER 43 (CA), approving the analysis of Hobhouse J at [1986] 2 All ER 488, 508.

[254] ibid; *Barclays Bank plc v Fairclough Building Ltd* [1994] 3 WLR 1057 (CA).

[255] [2002] Lloyd's Rep Med 130 (Doncaster County Ct).

[256] [1943] 4 DLR 68, 77.

true meaning of the patient's progressive symptoms to the patient himself, especially given that the patient was only able to make a subjective assessment. The defendant should have conducted daily tests.

6.72 Some Canadian courts have made findings of contributory negligence against careless patients. In *Brushett v Cowan*[257] the claimant was contributorily negligent in engaging in ordinary activities without crutches following a bone biopsy on her leg, because she had failed to ask for clear instructions regarding the use of the crutches. A failure to have a post-operative check-up, as suggested by the doctor, has been held to be negligent,[258] as has the failure to pursue physiotherapy when advised to do so.[259] In *Crossman v Stewart*[260] a patient who obtained prescription drugs from an unorthodox source, and continued to use the drugs on a prolonged basis without obtaining prescription renewals or consulting the 'prescribing' physician, was described as 'foolhardy in the extreme'. She was held to be responsible for two-thirds of the damage to her eyesight caused by the side effects of the drug. In *Zhang v Kan*,[261] a doctor failed to arrange an expedited amniocentesis for a 36-year-old woman, who subsequently gave birth to a child with Down's syndrome. While it was held that the failure to take steps to arrange the amniocentesis for his patient was negligent, the patient and her husband were contributorily negligent. The patient was a sophisticated and experienced businesswoman who had researched the topic of amniocentesis because she knew that, at her age, there was a high risk of having a Down's syndrome child. She had already discussed the need for the procedure with another doctor and she doubted the defendant doctor's advice that it was too late in the pregnancy to take the test. Her husband told her to trust the defendant because he was a doctor. She could have sought out another doctor, as she did two months later. The couple knew that there might be a problem if there was no amniocentesis. Accordingly, contributory negligence was assessed at 50 per cent.

6.73 It may be possible for the plea of contributory negligence to apply in cases involving smoking and other forms of addiction. Damages have been reduced under the 1945 Act where the claimant, aware of the dangers of smoking through both health warnings and specific advice, continued to do so, where this had been a substantial cause of his death from lung cancer, which was also caused by the defendant's exposure of him to asbestos.[262] Further, in the Canadian decision of *Dumais v Hamilton*,[263] a patient who was a smoker was given repeated instructions by the defendant surgeon not to smoke for at least one week following a 'tummy tuck' operation, although she was not told why. She ignored this instruction, smoking between two and four cigarettes a day after discharge. The post-operative smoking,

[257] (1987) 40 DLR (4th) 488; affd (1990) 69 DLR (4th) 743 (Newfd CA).

[258] *Fredette v Wiebe* [1986] 5 WWR 222 (BCSC).

[259] *Ibrahim v Hum* [2004] ABQB 420, [2005] 6 WWR 564 (Alta QB), (liability reduced by 25 per cent, notwithstanding the defendant had failed to provide an adequate and effective explanation of why the failure to pursue physiotherapy was critical. Contributory negligence was also found as a result of the patient's failure to volunteer to the defendant that other general practitioners had also treated her post-surgically, which deprived the defendant of the opportunity to obtain useful treatment records from other physicians: [2], [149]–[153], [157]).

[260] (1977) 82 DLR (3d) 677, 686 (BCSC). It is also possible that unreasonable behaviour by a patient after the defendant's negligent conduct could be characterized as a failure to mitigate his loss. In *Brain v Mador* (1985) 32 CCLT 157 (Ont CA) a patient who failed to take steps to seek further medical advice following a vasectomy which had developed complications was held to have acted unreasonably, and his damages were reduced by 50 per cent for failing to mitigate the loss.

[261] [2003] BCSC 5, (2003) 15 CCLT (3d) 1.

[262] *Badger v Ministry of Defence* [2005] EWHC 2941, [2006] 3 All ER 173, [44], [46], [48] (damages reduced by 20 per cent).

[263] *Dumais v Hamilton* (1998) 219 AR 63.

against the surgeon's orders had contributed to skin necrosis attributable to the surgery. While the Alberta Court of Appeal upheld the trial judge's decision that the surgeon had been negligent in not adequately informing the patent of the risks of necrosis before surgery,[264] it allowed an appeal on contributory negligence. The trial judge had erred in suggesting that the patient could only be found to be contributorily negligent by smoking if she reasonably knew the nature and character of the potential injuries that could result. The proper question it should have asked was whether the patient took reasonable care of herself in the circumstances. The fact that the patient persisted in smoking after advice from the surgeon that she should not do so was unreasonable. The patient had been contributorily negligent and damages were reduced by 50 per cent.[265]

6.74 Prior to making a reduction in the damages to a claimant, the court must have regard to whether the claimant's negligence was a potent cause of the harm he has suffered.[266] This important requirement led to a decision not to reduce damages where the fault in the claimant becoming addicted was not such a potent cause in *St George v Home Office*.[267] The claimant, a prisoner, was a drug addict and alcoholic. He told prison staff about his addiction and withdrawal seizures. Nevertheless, he was allocated a top bunk bed in his prison cell. He suffered a withdrawal seizure which caused him to fall from his top bunk and suffer head injuries. The seizure developed into 'status epilepticus' and he sustained severe brain damage. The Court of Appeal held that while the trial judge was entitled to hold that the claimant was at fault in becoming addicted to drugs and alcohol, the fault in becoming addicted was not the potent cause of the brain injury suffered as a result of the defendant's negligent conduct, that of allocating him a top bunk. It was too remote in time, place, and circumstance and was not sufficiently connected or mixed up with, the negligence of the prison staff.[268] In any event, even if the prisoner's addiction had amounted to contributory negligence, it was not just and equitable to reduce his damages having regard to his share in the responsibility for the injury. The staff knew or ought to have known that he might suffer from withdrawal seizures and yet they placed him in a top bunk.[269]

6.75 It would also be possible for a plea of contributory negligence to apply in cases where the claimant attempts suicide and a claim is brought against medical staff on the basis of a negligent failure to prevent the suicide attempt. In *Reeves v Commissioner of Police for the Metropolis*,[270] a similar type of claim brought against the police, the deceased was held 50 per cent contributorily negligent because he was partially responsible for his death, which was the result of the combination of the failure of the police to protect a prisoner who was a known suicide risk from harming himself and his own deliberate decision to end his life. Possibly, where the deceased was of unsound mind his suicide would not give rise to the defence of contributory negligence, by analogy with the position of young children who are not of full understanding.[271] However, the House of Lords were divided as to the applicability of contributory negligence in *Corr v IBC Vehicles Ltd*.[272] In that case, the deceased committed suicide having suffered severe depression after suffering a serious accident caused by the defendant's breach of duty. Lord Bingham and Lord Walker considered that it was

[264] ibid, [9].
[265] ibid, [16]–[17].
[266] *Corr v IBC Vehicles Ltd* [2008] UKHL 13, [2008] 1 AC 884, [44] *per* Lord Walker.
[267] *St George v Home Office* [2008] EWCA Civ 1068, [2009] 1 WLR 1670.
[268] ibid, [56]–[59].
[269] ibid, [60], [63].
[270] *Reeves v Commissioner of Police for the Metropolis* [2000] 1 AC 360.
[271] ibid, 372 *per* Lord Hoffmann.
[272] *Corr v IBC Vehicles Ltd* [2008] UKHL 13, [2008] 1 AC 884.

inappropriate to attach any blame to the deceased when his judgment was impaired by the severe depression brought about by the defendant's negligence.[273] On the other hand, while Lord Scott considered that the deceased's suicidal tendencies had been brought about as a result of his employer's negligence, 'he was not an automaton. He remained an autonomous individual who retained the power of choice'.[274] Accordingly, he would have reduced damages by 20 per cent to reflect the claimant's responsibility for his death.[275] Lord Mance and Lord Neuberger considered that because of the extreme brevity with which the issue had been treated in the case, it was inappropriate to contemplate a deduction.[276] However, Lord Mance and Lord Neuberger left open the possibility that a deduction on the ground of contributory negligence could be appropriate, in some circumstances of deliberate suicide in a state of depression induced by accident.[277]

2. *Volenti non fit injuria*

Volenti non fit injuria consists of a voluntary agreement by the claimant to absolve the defendant from the legal consequences of an unreasonable risk of harm created by the defendant, where the claimant has full knowledge of both the nature and extent of the risk. This should not be confused with *consent* to medical treatment which provides a defence to what would otherwise be the tort of battery. The patient who consents to medical treatment does not thereby consent to run the risk of negligence by the doctor.[278] **6.76**

The one situation where the *volenti* defence could plausibly apply to a medical negligence action is in the case of suicide by a patient in circumstances where the doctor was under a duty to take reasonable precautions to prevent a suicide attempt. The point had been touched upon by the Court of Appeal in *Kirkham v Chief Constable of Greater Manchester Police*,[279] though it was said that the defence would only arise where the person was 'of sound mind'. But in *Reeves v Commissioner of Police for the Metropolis*[280] the House of Lords held that *volenti* does not apply where the claimant's act was the very thing that the defendant was under a duty to take reasonable care to prevent, irrespective of the suicide's mental state. If the defendant owed a duty of care to prevent a suicide attempt, he cannot argue that the act which he was under a duty to prevent gave rise to the defence of *volenti*, because that would undermine the point of imposing a duty of care.[281] **6.77**

[273] ibid, [22] *per* Lord Bingham of Cornhill; [44] *per* Lord Walker of Gestingthorpe.

[274] ibid, [31] *per* Lord Scott. He added: 'The evidence that clinical depression leads often to suicidal tendencies and that between one in ten and one in six persons succumb to those tendencies is evidence that between nine in ten and five in six persons do not.'

[275] ibid, [32]–[33].

[276] ibid, [47] *per* Lord Mance; [57] *per* Lord Neuberger.

[277] ibid, [47], [52] *per* Lord Mance; [64] *per* Lord Neuberger. Lord Mance considered that the conclusion that a person suffering from depressive illness had no responsibility at all for their own suicide, and in effect was acting as an automaton 'may be open to question in law' at least where that person's capacity to make a reasoned and informed judgment was '"impaired" rather than eliminated': [51]. It might be right to consider more closely with the benefit of expert evidence what was involved in 'impairment' and to identify differing degrees of impairment and responsibility. It could be relevant if other factors were also operating on the claimant, independently of the accident: [51]. Lord Neuberger opined that the question to be addressed was the extent to which the deceased's personal autonomy had been overborne by the impairment to his mind attributable to the defendant. When it had not been overborne, the reduction in damages might be 50 per cent. Where it had effectively been overborne, there would be no reduction. In other cases, the answer would be 'somewhere between those two extremes': [69] *per* Lord Neuberger.

[278] See *Freeman v Home Office* [1984] 1 All ER 1036, 1044 *per* Sir John Donaldson MR.

[279] [1990] 2 QB 283.

[280] [2000] 1 AC 360.

[281] In *Corr v IBC Vehicles Ltd* [2008] UKHL 13, [2008] 1 AC 884, [18], Lord Bingham of Cornhill rejected the application of the defence of *volenti* on the facts as an argument which had 'no independent

3. *Ex turpi causa non oritur actio* and other policy factors

(i) *Ex turpi causa*

6.78 The fact that the claimant was involved in committing a criminal offence at the time of sustaining damage may, in some instances, constitute a defence. This is usually expressed in the Latin maxim *ex turpi causa non oritur actio*. It will be extremely rare for a claimant in a medical negligence action to be involved in illegality which is directly linked to the treatment, although in *Kirkham v Chief Constable of Greater Manchester Police* the Court of Appeal accepted that the *ex turpi causa* defence is not confined to criminal conduct, but could apply to illegal or immoral conduct by the claimant if in all the circumstances an award of damages would be an affront to the public conscience.[282] But awarding damages following a suicide would not affront the public conscience, at least where there was medical evidence that the suicide was 'not in full possession of his mind'.[283] Farquharson LJ said that an action could hardly be said to be grounded in immorality where 'grave mental instability' on the part of the victim has been proved, although 'the position may well be different where the victim is wholly sane'.[284] In the context of a claim following a suicide attempt, it would appear that there is considerable overlap between the *ex turpi causa* defence and the *volenti* defence.[285] In *Reeves v Commissioner of Police of the Metropolis*[286] the Court of Appeal held that *ex turpi causa* did not apply in a case where the claimant's conduct was the very act that the defendant was under a duty of care to prevent, whether or not the claimant was of sound mind.[287] However, merely because a defendant is under a duty to protect the claimant from its own criminality does not override the defence of *ex turpi causa* as matter of principle.[288]

6.79 The maxim *ex turpi causa* precludes the recovery for damage which is the consequence of the claimant's own criminal act. In *Clunis v Camden and Islington HA*[289] the claimant was convicted of manslaughter on the basis of diminished responsibility. He sued the health

validity'. The deceased's suicide was 'not something to which [he had] consented voluntarily and with his eyes open but an act performed because of the psychological condition which the employer's breach of duty had induced'. In the context of the principle to be derived from *Clunis v Campden & Islington Health Authority* [1998] QB 978 (see paras 6.75–6.76), volenti has been viewed not as a defence but as a principle of public policy which precludes a claimant from relying upon his illegal act: see *O v Ministry of Defence; West v Ministry of Defence (No 2)* [2006] EWHC 19, [11].

[282] [1990] 2 QB 283, 291 *per* Lloyd LJ. There is controversy about the conceptual basis of the *ex turpi causa* defence, which is sometimes said to rest on the affront to the 'public conscience' if the court is effectively seen to be assisting a criminal, but in other cases depends on whether the claimant has to *rely* on his own criminal act as the basis of the claim. See *Clerk & Lindsell on Torts* (21st edn, Sweet & Maxwell 2014) paras 3–02 to 3–29.

[283] *Kirkham*, n 282, 291 *per* Lloyd LJ; see also *Funk Estate v Clapp* (1986), reported at 68 DLR (4th) 229, and (1988) 54 DLR (4th) 512.

[284] The meaning of the phrases 'grave mental instability' and 'wholly sane' is a matter of some conjecture. *Quaere* whether a person who is not insane, but whose judgment is impaired by an emotional, as opposed to a psychological, disturbance falls into the category of 'not wholly sane'.

[285] In *Hyde v Tameside AHA* (1981), reported at (1986) 2 PN 26, 29–30, Lord Denning MR was opposed to allowing actions based on suicide or attempted suicide, a view that was clearly based on considerations of policy. In *Kirkham*, n 282, 292–93 Lloyd LJ did not share this view.

[286] *Reeves v Commissioner of Police of the Metropolis* [1999] QB 169.

[287] ibid, 185 *per* Buxton LJ; cf para 6.73. There was no appeal on the issue of *ex turpi causa* in the House of Lords, but the reasoning of their Lordships in relation to the argument that the deceased's suicide constituted a *novus actus interveniens* or that the deceased was *volenti* is entirely consistent with the Court of Appeal's approach to *ex turpi causa*.

[288] *Stone and Rolls Ltd (In Liquidation) v Moore Stephens (A Firm)* [2009] UKHL 39, [2009] 1 AC 1391, [177]–[183] *per* Lord Walker, [204] *per* Lord Brown.

[289] *Clunis v Camden and Islington HA* [1998] QB 978. See also *Wilson v Coulson* [2002] PIQR P300.

authority in negligence for failing to treat his mental condition and thereby failing to prevent him from committing the offence, claiming that had he received care he would not have committed the crime and would not therefore have been detained in a special hospital, or at least would not have been detained for as long. The Court of Appeal struck out the claim as contrary to public policy, on the basis that the court would not lend its aid to a litigant who relied on his own criminal or immoral act. A plea of diminished responsibility accepted that the accused's mental responsibility was substantially impaired, but it did not remove liability for his criminal act. There could be no liability in negligence unless it could be shown that he did not know the nature and quality of his act or that what he had done was wrong.[290] On facts similar to *Clunis*, a majority of the New South Wales Court of Appeal in *Hunter Area Health Service v Presland*[291] held that the duty of care that the health authority owed to a psychiatric patient who had been prosecuted for murder but found not guilty by reason of insanity did not extend to the psychiatrist's decision to detain him compulsorily so as to permit recovery for non-physical injury, essentially based on loss of the patient's liberty.[292] While the plaintiff lacked moral culpability by reason of his insanity, his conduct nevertheless constituted an unlawful and wholly unreasonable action. His act was not justifiable homicide but an unlawful homicide for which he was not criminally responsible.[293]

The rule in *Clunis* that *ex turpi causa* precludes the recovery for damage which is the consequence of the claimant's own criminal act is, in its wide form, a view of public policy.[294] **6.80** In its narrower form, the principle of *ex turpi causa* will preclude recovery by the claimant for damage which is the consequence of a sentence imposed on him by way of punishment for a criminal act for which he is personally responsible.[295] In *Gray v Thames Trains Ltd*[296] the claimant suffered injuries including post-traumatic stress disorder as a result of a train crash caused by the defendant's negligence. Whilst suffering from that disorder, the claimant killed a stranger. He pleaded guilty to manslaughter on the grounds of diminished responsibility and was ordered to be detained under the Mental Health Act 1983. While the defendants admitted that they were in principle liable in respect of his losses incurred before the date of the killing, they denied liability in respect of losses incurred after that date, on the basis of *ex turpi causa*. The claimant's case was that all his loss of earnings resulted from post-traumatic stress disorder and that, but for the tort, he would have earned money both before and after the date of the killing and that he was therefore entitled to recover the whole of the loss of earnings from the defendants. The trial judge dismissed the claimant's claim for losses arising after the killing on the grounds of public policy based on *ex turpi causa*. He stated that in order to avoid a finding that the commission of the offence and the incarceration for it broke the chain of causation, the claimant had to rely on the manslaughter and to contend that it was caused by the post-traumatic stress disorder, which in turn was caused by the negligence of the defendants. The claimant was not entitled to loss of earnings after the killing because his claim was closely connected with or inextricably bound up with his own criminal conduct. The Court of Appeal disagreed. It held that the manslaughter was not inextricably linked with the claimant's claim for loss of earnings which was based on his post-traumatic stress disorder both before and after the killing.[297]

290 *Clunis*, n 289, 989–90 *per* Beldam LJ.
291 *Hunter Area Health Service v Presland* [2005] NSWCA 33, (2005) NSWLR 22.
292 ibid, paras 299–300 *per* Sheller JA; paras 324, 377 *per* Santow JA.
293 ibid, para 292 *per* Sheller JA; paras 315, 388 *per* Santow JA.
294 *Gray v Thames Trains Ltd* [2009] UKHL 33, [2009] 1 AC 1339, [32] *per* Lord Hoffmann.
295 ibid.
296 *Gray v Thames Trains Ltd*, n 294.
297 [2008] EWCA Civ 713, [2008] PIQR P20, [22], [24], [28], [35].

The Court of Appeal took the view that, while the case could be distinguished from *Clunis*, there was 'something to be said for the view that the traditional harsh view of public policy expressed in . . . *Clunis* . . . should be revisited in a case in which the crime relied upon by the claimant or the tortfeasor was itself caused by the tort'.[298] The House of Lords reversed the decision of the Court of Appeal. It held that in order to avoid inconsistency in the justice system, the *ex turpi causa* defence precluded a claim for damages for loss of earnings, after imprisonment for an offence, despite the tortious act of the defendant having led the claimant to commit the offence. The criminal court had by its sentence found the claimant to have been personally responsible for the criminal act and it would be inconsistent for a civil court to compensate him for the consequences of such an act, even if he had acted with diminished responsibility.[299]

6.81 Similarly, where a mother had negligently been denied the opportunity to have an abortion, an action for negligence was denied on policy grounds in circumstances where the abortion would not have been lawful under the Abortion Act 1967, since the claimant could not have put the lost opportunity to benefit without breaking the law.[300] For the same reason, a claim for damages in respect of rendering the claimant infertile cannot include the cost of procedures connected with surrogate motherhood if those procedures would be in breach of the Surrogacy Arrangements Act 1985.[301] Accordingly, where potential claims arise out of the negligent performance of procedures which are unlawful, the likelihood is that they will be barred on the grounds of policy, whether or not this is referred to as *ex turpi causa*.[302]

(ii) Other policy factors

6.82 Policy factors may also play a role, though rarely, at other points in a medical negligence action, usually in the form of denying the existence of a duty of care. For example,

[298] [2008] EWCA Civ 713, [2008] PIQR P20, [49]–[50].

[299] [2009] UKHL 33, [2009] 1 AC 1339, [32], [41], [44] *per* Lord Hoffmann, [64], [69] *per* Lord Rodger, [93] *per* Lord Brown. Their Lordships noted that the narrower rule, based on inconsistency, was supported by *British Columbia v Zastowny* 2008 SCC 4 (2008) 290 DLR (4th) 219, [22]–[23] (*ex turpi causa* doctrine barred plaintiff from recovering damages from time spent in prison. Compensation for periods of unemployment due to incarceration for conduct which the criminal law had determined worthy of punishment would create a 'clash' between the criminal and civil law, which would compromise the integrity of the justice system) and *State Rail Authority of New South Wales v Wiegold* (1991) 25 NSWLR 500, 514 (compensation for loss of earnings while in prison and afterwards irrecoverable. 'It would generate the sort of 'clash' between civil and criminal law that is apt to bring the law into disrepute').

[300] *Rance v Mid-Downs HA* [1991] 1 All ER 801, where the period of gestation was such that a termination of the pregnancy would probably have been unlawful. Following amendment of the Abortion Act 1967 by the Human Fertilisation and Embryology Act 1990, s 37, there is no time limit where the termination is necessary to prevent grave permanent injury to the health of the woman, where the pregnancy involves risk to her life, or where there is a substantial risk that the foetus would be seriously handicapped. Where any of these grounds applied the causation issue in *Rance* would be irrelevant. The time limit under s 1(1)(a) of the Abortion Act 1967 is twenty-four weeks.

[301] *Briody v St Helens and Knowsley AHA* [2001] EWCA Civ 1010, [2002] QB 856.

[302] Another possible example would be an unlawful organ transplant operation contrary to the Human Organ Transplants Act 1989. In *Norberg v Wynrib* (1992) 92 DLR (4th) 449 the Supreme Court of Canada held that *ex turpi causa* did not apply to an action where the defendant doctor had supplied drugs to a patient who was addicted to pain-killers and tranquillizers in exchange for sexual contact. The patient had also been obtaining drugs from other doctors, and was convicted of the offence of 'double-doctoring'. The illegality was not causally linked to the harm suffered by the claimant.

'wrongful life' claims on the part of a child whose congenital disabilities the defendant negligently failed to diagnose are not actionable.[303] In *M (a minor) v Newham London Borough Council*[304] a majority of the Court of Appeal held that neither a psychiatrist nor a social worker owed a duty of care in negligence to a child and her mother in respect of the manner in which they conducted an interview with the child for the purpose of identifying whether, and if so by whom, the child had been sexually abused. This was partly on the basis that the child was not the psychiatrist's patient, and therefore the requisite degree of proximity was not established, and partly on the policy grounds first, that such a duty would lead to 'defensive' practices by the professionals involved in child protection, and secondly that actions against local authorities would have an adverse impact on the resources available for the purpose of child protection. This was accepted to be a proper basis for rejecting a duty of care in such circumstances by the House of Lords.[305] However, in *JD v East Berkshire Community Health NHS Trust*[306] Lord Phillips MR, giving judgment for the Court of Appeal, departed from the decision of the House of Lords, and held that the policy reasons justifying the denial of a duty of care did not survive the Human Rights Act 1998.[307] The Court of Appeal held that a local authority owed a common law duty of care to a *child* in relation to the investigation of suspected child abuse and the initiation and pursuit of care proceedings.[308] But the Court of Appeal also held that no duty of care was owed to the child's *parents*, since it would always be in the parents' interests that the child should not be removed and thus the child's interests were 'in potential conflict' with those of the parents. Accordingly, there were 'cogent reasons of public policy for concluding that, where child care decisions are being taken, no common law duty of care should be owed to the parents'.[309] The defendants accepted the existence of a duty of care to the children but appealed the denial of the duty to the parents to the House of Lords. A majority of their Lordships affirmed the decision of the Court of Appeal and held that while local authorities owe common law duties to *children* in exercise of their child protection duties,[310] a local authority did *not* owe a duty of care to *parents* suspected of abusing their

303 *McKay v Essex AHA* [1982] QB 1166; Congenital Disabilities (Civil Liability) Act 1976, s 1(1), (2); also *Harriton v Stephens* [2006] HCA 15, (2006) 226 CLR 52 (where the High Court of Australia held that there was no duty of care owed by the doctor to the child in circumstances similar to *McKay*, where the child's mother contracted rubella during pregnancy: [206] *per* Callinan J, [276]–[277] *per* Crennan J); applied in *Waller v James* [2006] HCA 16, (2006) 226 CLR 136, [86]; M Fordham, 'A Life Less Ordinary—The Rejection of Actions for Wrongful Life' (2007) 15 TLJ 123; and *Lacroix (Litigation Guardian of) v Dominique* 2001 MBCA 122, (2001) 202 DLR (4th) 121, [37] (applying *McKay* and holding action for wrongful life should not be recognized in Canada); cf *Bovington (Litigation Guardian of) v Hergott* (2006) 275 DLR (4th) 168, (2006) 83 OR (3d) 465, [5], [10], [17], [19] (action by children not an action for 'wrongful life', but a case of a negligent failure to disclose material risk of a drug to a patient).

304 [1994] 2 WLR 554.

305 sub nom *X (minors) v Bedfordshire County Council* [1995] 3 WLR 152, 184.

306 *JD v East Berkshire Community Health NHS Trust* [2003] EWCA Civ 1151, [2004] QB 558 (CA).

307 ibid, [83].

308 ibid, [84].

309 ibid, [86].

310 *JD v East Berkshire Community Health NHS Trust* [2005] UKHL 23, [2005] 2 AC 373, [30] *per* Lord Bingham, [82] *per* Lord Nicholls, and [110] *per* Lord Rodger; M A Jones, 'Child Abuse: When the Professionals Get It Wrong' (2006) Med Law Rev 264.

own children and who were being investigated in such cases.[311] Given the seriousness of child abuse as a social problem, health professionals should not be subject to potentially conflicting duties to a child and a parent when deciding whether a child may have been abused or when deciding whether further investigating or protecting steps should be taken. The interests of children should be treated as paramount.[312]

6.83 Another ground of immunity stems from the fact that a witness in legal proceedings has immunity from suit with respect to evidence given in those proceedings,[313] and this immunity applies to a proof or report prepared for trial by a witness.[314] The immunity applies to an expert witness who prepares a joint statement with an expert instructed by the opposing party to the litigation for the purpose of identifying what issues are in dispute between the experts, and this is the case notwithstanding that the expert does not give evidence at the trial.[315] This is based on public policy in protecting the proper administration of justice so that witnesses are able to be frank when giving evidence free from the threat of civil proceedings, and to avoid a multiplicity of actions in which the truth of their evidence would be tried over again.[316] In the case of an expert witness, the immunity extends only to what can fairly be said to be preliminary to giving evidence in court. Thus, the production of a report for disclosure to the other side in litigation is immune, but work done for the principal purpose of advising the client, as to the merits of the claim, for example, is not.[317] In *Landall v Dennis Faulkner & Alsop*[318] the claimant was suing, inter alia, a medical expert who had provided a number of reports on the condition and prognosis of his back for the purpose of a claim being brought by him against a negligent motorist. He alleged that the expert's report and/or advice was negligent in that his opinion relating to the prospects of further successful treatment for the claimant's back condition was unduly optimistic, with the result that the claimant settled his action against the motorist for much less than it was worth. The claimant argued that the reports provided by the expert were not simply for the purposes of the litigation, but also constituted advice to the claimant as to the potential benefits of a spinal fusion operation. This argument was rejected, however. The report constituted:

> pre-trial work . . . so intimately connected with the conduct of the case in court that it could fairly be said to be a preliminary decision affecting the way that the case was to be conducted when it came to a hearing.[319]

[311] *JD*, n 310, [90] *per* Lord Nicholls, [96] *per* Lord Steyn, [115] *per* Lord Rodger, [138] *per* Lord Brown. Their Lordships followed the denial of such a duty of care in the decision of the High Court of Australia in *Sullivan v Moody* (2001) 207 CLR 562, [60], [62]; and in the decision of the Privy Council in *B v Attorney General of New Zealand* [2003] UKPC 61, [2003] 4 All ER 833, [30]. See also *Fairlie v Perth and Kinross Healthcare NHS Trust* 2004 SLT 1200, [31] (OH); and *D(B) v Halton Region Children's Aid Society* (2007) 284 DLR (4th) 682, [41], SCC.

[312] *JD*, n 310, [85]–[86] *per* Lord Nicholls; see further [110] *per* Lord Rodger and [129] *per* Lord Brown.

[313] *Rondel v Worsley* [1969] 1 AC 191, 268; *Saif Ali v Sydney Mitchell & Co* [1980] AC 198.

[314] *Evans v London Hospital Medical College (University of London)* [1981] 1 WLR 184.

[315] *Stanton v Callaghan* [2000] QB 75 (CA).

[316] *Watson v M'Ewan* [1905] AC 480; *Saif Ali v Sydney Mitchell & Co* [1980] AC 198; *Evans v London Hospital Medical College (University of London)* [1981] 1 WLR 184.

[317] *Palmer v Durnford Ford* [1992] 1 QB 483, 488.

[318] *Landall v Dennis Faulkner & Alsop* [1994] 5 Med LR 268 (QBD).

[319] ibid, *per* Holland J, applying *Saif Ali v Sydney Mitchell & Co* [1980] AC 198 and *Palmer v Durnford Ford* [1992] 1 QB 483, 488; cf *Hughes v Lloyds Bank plc* [1998] PIQR P98 (CA), where no proceedings had

Accordingly, the claim was struck out as disclosing no reasonable cause of action.[320]

4. Limitation Act 1980

Where an action is commenced outside the statutory limitation period the defendant can rely on the defence of limitation.[321] An action in tort cannot normally be brought more than six years from the date on which the cause of action accrued,[322] which in the case of an action for negligence is when damage occurs, but in torts actionable per se, such as trespass to the person, the cause of action accrues at the date of the defendant's wrong. In contract the limitation period is also six years from the accrual of the action.[323] These rules are modified, however, in cases of personal injuries and death and claimants under a disability. Medical negligence actions are usually, though not exclusively, concerned with claims for personal injuries or death, which are governed, as a general rule,[324] by the provisions of the Limitation Act 1980, ss 11–14 and 33. The scheme provides for a three-year limitation period running from either (i) the date on which the cause of action accrued, or (ii) if later, the claimant's date of knowledge of certain facts about the cause of action.[325] Additionally, even if this fixed period has expired, the court has a wide discretion to override the time limit and permit the action to proceed.[326] The Law Commission has recommended reform of the law on limitation periods to introduce a single, core limitation regime, applying, as **6.84**

been issued and evidence from the defendant GP had been supplied at the patient's request in the context of negotiations between the patient and a third party's insurers. That advice could not be regarded as preliminary to giving evidence as an expert. The documents supplied by the GP were not for disclosure to the other side in the context of proceedings but purely in the context of negotiation.

[320] In *X (minors) v Bedfordshire County Council* [1995] 3 WLR 152, 188 the House of Lords held that a psychiatrist who, in the course of interviewing a child, was negligent in ascertaining the identity of the person who had sexually abused the child was protected by witness immunity (reversing the decision of the Court of Appeal in *M (a minor) v Newham London Borough Council* [1994] 2 WLR 554). The policy considerations which applied to witnesses in criminal proceedings were equally applicable to a local authority's investigation, in the performance of a public duty, of whether or not there is evidence on which to bring proceedings for the protection of children from child abuse. The psychiatrist knew that if abuse was discovered, proceedings for the protection of the child would ensue and that her findings would be the evidence on which those proceedings would be based. The investigations had an immediate link with possible proceedings in pursuance of a statutory duty, and therefore could not be made the basis of a subsequent action in negligence. Note that subsequently the European Court of Human Rights found that, on these facts, the local authority was in breach of Art 8 of the ECHR, the right to respect for family life, in failing to involve the mother in the decision-making process concerning the care of her daughter: *TP and KM v UK* [2001] 2 FLR 549. See further *JD v East Berkshire Community Health NHS Trust* [2003] EWCA Civ 1151, [2004] QB 558 (CA), [103] and [2005] UKHL 23, [2005] 2 AC 373, [136] *per* Lord Brown on the question of witness immunity.

[321] For a more detailed discussion, see A McGee, *Limitation Periods* (7th edn, Sweet & Maxwell 2014).

[322] Limitation Act 1980, s 2.

[323] ibid, s 5. The action in contract will accrue at the date of the breach of contract.

[324] The Limitation Act 1980 does not apply where a period of limitation is prescribed by other legislation: s 39.

[325] Limitation Act 1980, s 11(3) and (4). New claims which are outside a relevant limitation period cannot be brought by addition to or amendment of existing proceedings since this would have the effect of depriving a defendant of an otherwise valid limitation defence. The Limitation Act 1980, s 35, in combination with CPR 17.4 and 19.5 allows for limited exceptions to this rule.

[326] Limitation Act 1980, s 33. Similar rules apply to claims brought under the Consumer Protection Act 1987 in respect of defective products, except that there is an overall longstop which expires ten years after the product was put into circulation by the defendant. The longstop is an absolute bar, and the court has no discretion to override this limit in personal injuries cases. See Limitation Act 1980, ss 11A(3), 14(1A), 28(7), 32(4A) and 33(1A). The ten-year longstop precludes national law rules (in England and Wales,

far as possible, to all claims for a remedy for a wrong, claims for the enforcement of a right and claims for restitution.[327]

(i) Limitation periods

6.85 Section 11(1) provides that the three-year period applies to 'any action for damages for negligence, nuisance or breach of duty' where the damages claimed by the claimant consist of or include damages in respect of personal injuries. This expressly includes breach of a contractual duty. For several years, the three-year time limit was held to apply to claims in both negligence and in trespass. In *Letang v Cooper*[328] the Court of Appeal held that the wording applied to an action for trespass to the person. However, in *Stubbings v Webb*[329] the House of Lords concluded that s 11(1) was limited to personal injury resulting from accidents caused by negligence, nuisance, or breach of a duty of care.[330] The consequence of this was that cases of 'deliberate assault', such as rape or indecent assault, were not actions for breach of duty within the meaning of s 11(1). However, in *A v Hoare*[331] the House of Lords ushered in a 'new era'[332] in its departure from *Stubbings*. Having reviewed the legislative and judicial history, it considered that the phrase 'breach of duty' had been construed as having a wide meaning, capable of applying to claims for intentional injuries and extending to the case of trespass to the person.[333] Their Lordships concluded that it would be right to depart from the anomalous effect of *Stubbings* and reaffirm the law laid down by the Court of Appeal in *Letang v Cooper*.[334] The decision of their Lordships in *A v Hoare* clearly has consequences for abuse and other intentional assault cases, but will also have relevance to actions for trespass against the person against a doctor; for example, in respect of a failure to obtain a valid consent to treatment. Previously, as a result of the decision in *Stubbings*, such cases were not governed by s 11, but by s 2 of the Limitation Act 1980. This meant that the claimant had to bring the action within six years, without any possibility of the court's discretion under s 33 being available. However, following the decision in *A v Hoare*, such an action would be treated as one of personal injury within s 11(1), and thus subject to a three-year time limit; this would allow the claimant to avail themselves of the date of knowledge provisions in s 14, and, most significantly, the discretionary provisions in s 33.

---

s 35(3) and CPR 19.5) allowing the substitution of one defendant for another during proceedings to permit a producer to be sued, after expiry of the ten-year limitation period, in proceedings brought within that period against another person. However, domestic law can allow an application to substitute a parent company producer of an allegedly defective product as defendant after expiry of the ten-year longstop in place of its wholly owned subsidiary, who was the supplier, but who had been erroneously thought to be the producer, but only where the parent company controlled the supplier and had actually determined when the supplier put the product into circulation: *O'Byrne v Aventis Pasteur MSD Ltd* [2010] UKSC 23, [31], [34], applying Case C-358/08, *Aventis Pasteur SA v OB* [2010] All ER (EC) 522 (ECJ), [44], [49], [52]–[53], [65], and reversing *O'Byrne v Aventis Pasteur MSD Ltd* [2006] EWHC 2562, [2007] 1 WLR 757, [2007] EWCA Civ 966, [2008] 1 WLR 1188. For the previous history of this litigation, see *Horne-Roberts v SmithKline Beecham plc* [2001] EWCA Civ 2006, [2002] 1 WLR 1662; Case C-127/04 *O'Byrne v Sanofi Pasteur MSD Ltd* [2006] 1 WLR 1606, [2006] 2 CMLR 24, [39]; also [2008] UKHL 34, [2008] 4 All ER 881. See further Chapter 18, para 18.72.

[327] *Limitation of Actions* (Law Com 270, July 2001).

[328] [1965] 1 QB 232; *Long v Hepworth* [1968] 1 WLR 1299.

[329] [1993] AC 498.

[330] On the other hand, a daughter's allegation that her mother had been negligent in failing to protect her from sexual abuse by her father during her minority falls within s 11 rather than s 2: *Seymour v Williams* [1995] PIQR P470 (CA).

[331] *A v Hoare* [2008] UKHL 6, [2008] 1 AC 844.

[332] ibid, [84] *per* Lord Brown.

[333] ibid, [9], [19] *per* Lord Hoffmann, [62] *per* Lord Carswell.

[334] ibid, [24]–[25] *per* Lord Hoffmann, [53] *per* Lord Walker, [55] *per* Baroness Hale, [63] *per* Lord Carswell, [80], [84] *per* Lord Brown.

'Personal injuries' includes any disease and any impairment of a person's physical or mental condition.[335] Where the breach of duty does not itself cause the personal injuries, but deprives the claimant of a chance of receiving compensation for the injuries, the three-year period does not apply.[336] So where a patient suffers purely financial loss due to a doctor's negligence (eg as a result of giving up work following a negligent misdiagnosis[337]), the six-year, rather than three-year, period will apply. In *Walkin v South Manchester HA*[338] the Court of Appeal held that a claim for the economic loss attributable to the birth of a child following a failed sterilization operation fell within s 11, as a claim for 'damages in respect of personal injuries'. The unwanted conception was a personal injury because the physical change to the claimant's body was an unwanted condition which she had sought to avoid by being sterilized.[339] This issue was complicated by the ruling of the House of Lords in *McFarlane v Tayside Health Board*[340] that no duty of care is owed to the parents in respect of the financial cost of bringing up a healthy child following negligent advice about, or the negligent performance of, a sterilization operation. Subsequently, in *Parkinson v St James and Seacroft University Hospital NHS Trust*[341] the Court of Appeal held that the parents of a disabled child born following a negligently performed sterilization operation were entitled to the additional costs of raising that child, that is, the additional costs attributable to the disability itself. Thus, such claims are in any event limited to cases involving a disabled child. But in *McFarlane* their Lordships categorized the parents' claim for the cost of raising the child as a claim for pure economic loss, a view adopted by the Court of Appeal in *Greenfield v Irwin*.[342] This led Laws LJ to comment that if the Court of Appeal's reasoning in *Walkin* was at variance with *McFarlane* then it was impliedly disapproved by *McFarlane*.[343] But in *Godfrey v Gloucestershire Royal Infirmary NHS Trust*[344] Leveson J applied *Walkin* to a failed sterilization case where the child had been born disabled. The question was not whether the claim for child-rearing costs was a claim in respect of economic loss, but rather whether it was an action for damages 'consisting of or including damages in respect of personal injuries. That is, or at least could be, different from the question whether the claim for the cost of upbringing of a child is pure or consequential economic loss.'[345] It followed that s 11 of the Act applied, so that the limitation period was three years from the date of the claimant's knowledge, but with the discretionary power to disapply the limitation period. **6.86**

335 Limitation Act 1980, s 38(1).

336 *Ackbar v Green & Co Ltd* [1975] 1 QB 582.

337 See *Hedley Byrne & Co Ltd v Heller & Partners Ltd* [1964] AC 465, 517 *per* Lord Devlin.

338 [1996] 7 Med LR 211.

339 cf *Pattison v Hobbs*, The Times, 11 November 1985, where the Court of Appeal had held that such an action was subject to s 2, as a claim in respect of financial loss. In *Walkin*, Auld LJ said that *Pattison v Hobbs* was a decision of a two-judge Court of Appeal which turned on a point of pleading, whereas the question whether an action was for damages in respect of personal injuries was a matter of substance, not pleading. See also *Bennett v Greenland Houchen & Co (a firm)* [1998] PNLR 458 where the Court of Appeal applied *Walkin* to an action against a firm of solicitors in respect of financial loss alleged to have been caused by the defendants' negligence, where the claimant also alleged that he suffered clinical depression arising out of the defendants' negligent handling of his case against his former employers.

340 [2000] 2 AC 59.

341 [2001] EWCA Civ 530, [2002] QB 266.

342 *Greenfield v Irwin* [2001] EWCA Civ 113, [2001] 1 WLR 1279.

343 ibid, [53].

344 *Godfrey v Gloucestershire Royal Infirmary NHS Trust* [2003] EWHC 549, [2003] Lloyd's Rep Med 398 (QB).

345 ibid, [35].

6.87 Once the limitation period prescribed by s 2 of the Limitation Act 1980 expires, there is no discretion to permit the action to proceed, though the commencement of the limitation period may be postponed in the case of deliberate concealment[346] or latent damage.[347]

(ii) The running of the limitation period

6.88 Time begins to run from either the date on which the cause of action accrued or the date of the claimant's knowledge, if later.[348] Once the period has started to run it cannot be suspended; only the issue of the claim form stops time running. The parties may agree, expressly or impliedly, to extend the time, but the mere fact that negotiations towards a settlement were in progress when the three-year period expired will not constitute such an agreement, unless the defendant's conduct is such that he is estopped from relying on the defence.[349]

---

[346] Where any fact relevant to the claimant's right of action has been deliberately concealed from him by the defendant, the limitation period does not begin to run until the claimant has discovered the concealment or could with reasonable diligence have discovered it: Limitation Act 1980, s 32(1)(b). This includes the deliberate commission of a breach of duty in circumstances in which it is unlikely to be discovered for some time: s 32(2). This covers the commission of a wrong knowingly or recklessly, but mere negligence is not sufficient: *Cave v Robinson Jarvis & Rolf (a firm)* [2002] UKHL 18, [2003] 1 AC 384. Lord Millett observed, at [25], that s 32 'does not deprive a defendant of a limitation defence where he is charged with negligence if, being unaware of his error or that he has failed to take proper care, there has been nothing for him to disclose'; see also *Skerratt v Linfax Ltd* [2003] EWCA Civ 695, [2004] PIQR P10 *per* Waller LJ at [20]: 'it is difficult to conceive of a case of concealment unless that concealment takes place either at the very time that the cause of action is accruing, or unless it takes place after the cause of action was accrued, i.e. unless the defendant is taking some steps to deliberately conceal a fact relevant to the cause of action' (no deliberate concealment within terms of s 32 where defendant required claimant to sign a form of disclaimer before allowing him to ride on a go-karting track); and, further, *Williams v Fanshaw Porter Hazelhurst (A Firm)* [2004] EWCA Civ 157, [2004] 1 WLR 3185, [14], [16] *per* Park J, and at [35]–[39] *per* Mance LJ (conduct of legal executive in deciding not to inform claimant in his clinical negligence claim of the making and agreeing of a consent order whereby a doctor ceased to be a party to proceedings, amounted to a deliberate concealment of facts relevant to the claimant's right of action against the firm of solicitors). In *Sheldon v RHM Outhwaite (Underwriting Agencies) Ltd* [1996] 1 AC 102 the House of Lords held that s 32(1)(b) operated to postpone the running of the limitation period in every case where there is deliberate concealment by the defendant of facts relevant to the claimant's cause of action, regardless of whether the concealment was contemporaneous with or subsequent to the accrual of the cause of action. Thus, subsequent concealment has the effect of bringing s 32 into play, thereby excluding ss 2 and 5, and the claimant has a full six years from the date of discovery of the concealment in which to bring the action, or alternatively, the defendant would be estopped from raising the limitation defence. But if the claimant is aware of the relevant *facts* during the period preceding the concealment, the subsequent acts of the defendant cannot conceal those facts from the claimant: *Sheldon v RHM Outhwaite (Underwriting Agencies) Ltd* [1996] 1 AC 102, 144; *Ezekiel v Lehrer* [2002] EWCA Civ 16, [2002] Lloyd's Rep PN 260.

[347] In cases of latent damage (other than personal injuries) the claimant has three years from the date on which he discovered or ought reasonably to have discovered significant damage, subject to an overall longstop which bars all claims brought more than fifteen years from the date of the defendant's negligence: Limitation Act 1980, ss 14A and 14B. Section 14A is expressed in very similar terms to s 14 (see para 6.85) and the courts' approach to s 14A closely mirrors that taken to s 14: see *Spencer-Ward v Humberts* [1995] 06 EG 148 (CA); *Oakes v Hopcroft* [2000] Lloyd's Rep Med 394 (CA); *Hallam-Eames v Merrett Syndicates Ltd* [2001] Lloyd's Rep PN 178 (CA) (approved in *Haward v Fawcetts (A Firm)* [2006] UKHL 9, [2006] 1 WLR 682). The latent damage provisions do not apply to claims in contract: *Iron Trade Mutual Insurance Co Ltd v JK Buckenham Ltd* [1990] 1 All ER 808; *Société Commerciale de Réassurance v ERAS (International) Ltd (Note)* [1992] 2 All ER 82. Where, however, the defendant owes concurrent duties in contract and tort the claimant is entitled to pursue the action which will give him a practical advantage on the question of limitation: *Henderson v Merrett Syndicates Ltd* [1994] 3 All ER 506, 525 *per* Lord Goff.

[348] For consideration of who has the burden of proof in respect of the limitation defence, see *Fowell v National Coal Board*, The Times, 28 May 1986 (CA); *Nash v Eli Lilly & Co* [1993] 1 WLR 782, 796 (CA); *Driscoll-Varley v Parkside HA* [1991] 2 Med LR 346, 357.

[349] *Deerness v John Keeble & Son Ltd* [1983] 2 Lloyd's Rep 260; *K Lokumal & Sons (London) Ltd v Lotte Shipping Co Pte Ltd* [1985] 2 Lloyd's Rep 28.

In negligence the action accrues when damage occurs, whether or not the damage is discoverable.[350] In the case of minor or trivial harm, it will be a question of fact whether the claimant has sustained 'damage' sufficient for the cause of action to accrue. Damage will only be ignored if it falls within the principle *de minimis non curat lex*.[351] In an action for personal injuries, even if more than three years have elapsed since the action accrued, the primary limitation period will not have expired if the claim form is issued within three years of the claimant's 'knowledge'. By s 14(1), references to a person's date of knowledge are references to the date on which he first had knowledge of the following facts: **6.89**

(a) that the injury in question was significant; and
(b) that the injury was attributable in whole or in part to the act or omission which is alleged to constitute negligence, nuisance or breach of duty; and
(c) the identity of the defendant; and
(d) if it is alleged that the act or omission was that of a person other than the defendant, the identity of that person and the additional facts supporting the bringing of an action against the defendant . . .

The word 'knowledge' does not mean 'know for certain and beyond possibility of contradiction'.[352] Suspicion, particularly if it is vague and unsupported, will not be enough, but reasonable belief will normally suffice.[353] The state of the claimant's belief requires consideration: Such belief must be held with sufficient confidence to justify embarking on the preliminaries to issuing proceedings. This would involve investigating, likely with the assistance of lawyers, whether in law the claimant had a valid claim and it may well involve a search for evidence, including from medical, scientific, or legal experts.[354] The court must assess the intelligence of the claimant, consider his assertions as to how he regarded the information that he had, and determine whether he had knowledge of the facts by reason of his understanding of the information.[355] **6.90**

In *North Essex District HA v Spargo*[356] Brooke LJ set out a number of propositions, taken from previous authorities, about the meaning of the word 'knowledge' for the purpose of s 14: **6.91**

(1) The knowledge required to satisfy s 14(1)(b) is a broad knowledge of the essence of the causally relevant act or omission to which the injury is attributable;

---

350 *Cartledge v Jopling & Sons Ltd* [1963] AC 758.

351 ibid. While previous decisions had held that asymptomatic minor damage was sufficient to give rise to a cause of action (see *Church v Ministry of Defence* (1984) 134 NLJ 623; *Sykes v Ministry of Defence* The Times, 23 March 1984; *Patterson v Ministry of Defence* [1987] CLY 1194), the House of Lords has now held that development of pleural plaques, whether or not associated with the risk of future disease and anxiety about the future, is not actionable damage in negligence: *Rothwell v Chemical & Insulating Co Ltd* [2007] UKHL 39, [2008] 1 AC 281, [2], [11] *per* Lord Hoffmann, [50] *per* Lord Hope, [68], [74] *per* Lord Scott, [90]–[91] *per* Lord Rodger, [103] *per* Lord Mance. Cf Damages (Asbestos-related Conditions) (Scotland) Act 2009, under which asymptomatic asbestos-related conditions constitute material harm for the purposes of the Scots law of delict, ensuring that people with pleural plaques caused by negligent exposure to asbestos can raise an action for damages.

352 *Halford v Brookes* [1991] 3 All ER 559, 573–74 *per* Lord Donaldson MR; *AB and Others v Ministry of Defence* [2012] UKSC 9, [2013] 1 AC 78, [11] *per* Lord Wilson JSC.

353 ibid. For consideration of the degree of 'certainty' required to constitute knowledge, see *Nash v Eli Lilly & Co* [1993] 1 WLR 782, 792 (CA); *Skitt v Khan and Wakefield HA* [1997] 8 Med LR 105; cf *Wilkinson v Ancliff (BLT) Ltd* [1986] 3 All ER 427, 438, and *Stephen v Riverside HA* [1990] 1 Med LR 261, where it was said that reasonable belief is not sufficient to constitute knowledge. But see now *AB and Others v Ministry of Defence* [2012] UKSC 9, [2013] 1 AC 78, [11]–[13] *per* Lord Wilson JSC.

354 *AB and Others v Ministry of Defence* [2012] UKSC 9, [2013] 1 AC 78, [11]–[13] *per* Lord Wilson JSC.

355 *Nash v Eli Lilly & Co* [1993] 1 WLR 782, 792.

356 [1997] PIQR P235, 242. In *AB and Others v Ministry of Defence* [2012] UKSC 9, [2013] 1 AC 78, at [68], Lord Walker observed that summaries such as that of Brooke LJ in *Spargo* 'may be unhelpful if treated as if they were statutory texts'.

(2) 'Attributable' in this context means 'capable of being attributed to' in the sense of being a real possibility;
(3) A plaintiff has requisite knowledge when she knows enough to make it reasonable for her to begin to investigate whether or not she has a case against the defendant. Another way of putting this is to say that she will have such knowledge if she so firmly believes that her condition is capable of being attributed to an act or omission which she can identify (in broad terms) that she goes to a solicitor to seek advice about making a claim for compensation;
(4) On the other hand she will not have the requisite knowledge if she thinks she knows the acts or omissions she should investigate but in fact is barking up the wrong tree; or if her knowledge of what the defendant did or did not do is so vague or general that she cannot fairly be expected to know what she should investigate; or if her state of mind is such that she thinks her condition is capable of being attributed to the act or omission alleged to constitute negligence, but she is not sure about this, and would need to check it with an expert before she could be properly said to know that it was.[357]

6.92 It has been said that these principles were intended not simply as guidelines, but as binding rules.[358] In *O'Driscoll v Dudley HA*[359] the Court of Appeal said that the fourth *Spargo* principle has to be read as 'postulating a situation antithetical to that covered by the third principle; ie the fourth principle postulates a state of mind short of a firm belief which takes a potential claimant to a solicitor'. The reference to 'the need to check with an expert' was a reference to the need for an expert's opinion before even the claimant can be said to know that the attributability of her condition to a particular 'act or omission' was a real possibility. That was not the same investigation as was referred to in the first limb of the third principle, which is an investigation into whether the claimant 'has a case against the defendant', an investigation that has to be carried out whilst the limitation clock is ticking.

6.93 (a) **Significant Injury** An injury is significant if the person whose date of knowledge is in question would reasonably have considered it sufficiently serious to justify his instituting proceedings for damages against a defendant who did not dispute liability and was able to satisfy a judgment.[360] Until recently, this was regarded as a combined subjective/objective test.[361] It was a question of what a reasonable man of the claimant's age, with his background, intelligence, and disabilities would reasonably have known.[362] However, this

[357] In *Ali v Courtaulds Textiles Ltd* [1999] Lloyd's Rep Med 301, the evidence was that the claimant knew he was deaf, knew that exposure to noise could cause deafness, and also knew that the ageing process could cause deafness. The Court of Appeal held that knowledge as to whether his deafness was noise-induced or age-induced was ascertainable only with the help of expert medical advice, and therefore the case fell within the third category of the fourth *Spargo* principle, ie he thought that his condition was capable of being attributed to the act or omission alleged to constitute negligence, but he was not sure, and needed to check it with an expert before he could properly be said to know that it was. See also *Harrild v Ministry of Defence* [2001] Lloyd's Rep Med 117 (QBD).

[358] *Griffin, Lawson and Williams v Clywd HA* [2001] EWCA Civ 818, [2001] PIQR P420; *Corbin v Penfold Metallising Company Ltd* [2000] Lloyd's Rep Med 247, 249 (CA): the court 'intended to lay down, not merely guidelines, but authoritative statements of how s 14 should be interpreted'.

[359] [1998] Lloyd's Rep Med 210, 221–22. See also *Roberts v Winbow* [1999] PIQR P77 (CA) for discussion of the distinction between the *Spargo* principles (3) and (4).

[360] Limitation Act 1980, s 14(2). In *AB and Others v Ministry of Defence* [2009] EWHC 1225 (QB), The Times, 10 June 2009, the defendant argued that when a claim was made in respect of multiple injuries, time started running when the claimant had knowledge that the first injury could be said to be significant. Foskett J was unable to accept the defendant's submission that the first significant injury in time was relevant for the purpose of fixing the date of knowledge: [492].

[361] *McCafferty v Metropolitan Police District Receiver* [1977] 1 WLR 1073, 1081 *per* Geoffrey Lane LJ; *Denman v Essex AHA* (1984) 134 NLJ 264.

[362] *Davis v City and Hackney HA* [1991] 2 Med LR 366.

notion of the test being partly objective and partly subjective was rejected by the Court of Appeal in *McCoubrey v Ministry of Defence*,[363] and then subsequently by the House of Lords in *A v Hoare*.[364] In *McCoubrey*, Neuberger LJ stated that: '[t]he test under section 14(2) is substantially objective, and is not the mixture of subjective and objective in the way in which the analysis of Geoffrey Lane LJ in the *McCafferty* case was interpreted as indicating in a number of cases'.[365] In *A v Hoare*[366] their Lordships held that the test as to what counts as significant injury under s 14(2) was 'an entirely impersonal standard: not whether the claimant himself would have considered the injury sufficiently serious to justify proceedings but whether he would 'reasonably' have done so'.[367] The question is whether a reasonable person would have considered the injury as sufficiently serious, which must be considered objectively without considering the personal circumstances, characteristics, or intelligence of the claimant.[368] Where the claimant's damage consists of psychological harm, there could be some difficulty in determining when a claimant first knew that his injury was significant, particularly where the claimant put the relevant events to the back of his mind, or tried to block or suppress the events. This is a highly fact-sensitive question.[369] In *A v Hoare*[370] it was argued for the claimant that there was considerable difficulty in determining when the claimant first knew that his injury was significant, because 'he had blocked out his memory' or 'put his memories in a box with a tightly sealed lid in the attic', and that this should be taken into consideration. However, Lord Hoffmann indicated that the fact that the claimant may have been 'in denial' about the psychological injuries which he had suffered was not relevant to the application of s 14(2), which 'assumes a practical and relatively unsophisticated approach to the question of knowledge'.[371] Nevertheless, the claimant's subjective reason and beliefs, in particular his psychological state in consequence of the injury, may be relevant to the court's exercise of discretion under s 33.[372]

The third *Spargo* principle[373] appears to treat any claimant who goes to a solicitor as having the requisite degree of knowledge. But it cannot be the case that simply by going to a solicitor **6.94**

[363] *McCoubrey v Ministry of Defence* [2007] EWCA Civ 17, [2007] 1 WLR 1544.

[364] *A v Hoare* [2008] UKHL 6, [2008] 1 AC 844.

[365] *McCoubrey v Ministry of Defence*, n 363, [38]. See, further, [39] and [52].

[366] *A v Hoare*, n 364.

[367] ibid, [34] *per* Lord Hoffmann. He continued: 'You ask what the claimant knew about the injury which he had suffered, you add any knowledge about the injury which may be imputed to him under section 14(3) and then you ask whether a reasonable person with that knowledge would have considered the injury sufficiently serious to justify his instituting proceedings for damages against a defendant who did not dispute liability and was able to satisfy a judgment'; but see, *dubitante*, Baroness Hale, [58]–[61].

[368] ibid, [35] *per* Lord Hoffmann, [68] *per* Lord Carswell.

[369] *KR v Bryn Alyn Community (Holdings) Ltd (in liquidation)* [2003] EWCA Civ 85, [2003] 1 FCR 385.

[370] *A v Hoare*, n 364.

[371] ibid, [43].

[372] ibid, [44], [48] *per* Lord Hoffmann; [68]–[69], [71] *per* Lord Carswell, [87] *per* Lord Brown. See also the further examination of the issue of 'significant injury' in three decisions of the Court of Appeal, viz: *Albonetti v Wirral MBC* [2008] EWCA Civ 783 (the 'injury in question' for purposes of s 14 had to be the injury which the claimant knew about at the time; person who had been seriously sexually abused must know that he had suffered not only a grave wrong but also a significant injury); *AB and others v The Nugent Care Society* [2008] EWCA Civ 795 (correct approach since *A v Hoare* was to determine what the claimant knew about the injury which was imputed to him under s 14(3), and then ask whether a reasonable person with that knowledge would have considered the injury sufficiently serious to justify instituting proceedings: any question as to effect of psychological facts on the claimant's knowledge of injury or his ability to issue proceedings was a matter for consideration under s 33); and *Field v British Coal Corporation* [2008] EWCA Civ 912 (adoption of Lord Hoffmann's approach in *A v Hoare* [2008] UKHL 6, [2008] 1 AC 844 [34] (see n 367)).

[373] See para 6.86.

the claimant necessarily has knowledge of all the relevant *facts*. The claimant may be unsure about the position. In *Sniezek v Bundy (Letchworth) Ltd*[374] the Court of Appeal said that, under the third *Spargo* principle there was a distinction to be drawn between a claimant who has a firm belief that he has a significant injury, attributable to his working conditions (especially a belief that takes him to a solicitor for advice about a claim), a belief that he retains whatever contrary advice he receives, and a claimant who believes that he may have, or even probably has, a significant injury which is attributable to his working conditions, but is not sure and feels it necessary to have expert advice on those questions. The former has knowledge of significant injury and attribution for the purposes of s 14, but the latter does not.[375] In *AB v Ministry of Defence*,[376] the Supreme Court (by a majority of four to three) held that claims by former servicemen for injury or death, allegedly as a result of their exposure to ionizing radiation during nuclear tests carried out in the 1950s, were statute-barred. The majority held that a claimant must be treated as likely to have acquired knowledge of the facts specified in s 14 when he first came reasonably to believe them. Such belief must be held with sufficient confidence to justify embarking on the preliminaries to issuing proceedings. This would involve investigating, likely with the assistance of lawyers, whether in law the claimant had a valid claim and it may well involve a search for evidence, including from experts. The date upon which the claimant first consulted the expert was not, on its own likely to assist the court in determining whether he had by then acquired the requisite knowledge.[377] However, the claimant had to be treated as having knowledge under s 14(1) once he issued proceedings, and not when better evidence of attributability was still to emerge.[378]

6.95 'Significant injury' refers to the gravity of the damage and its monetary value, not to the claimant's evaluation of its cause, nature, or usualness.[379] Section 14(2) makes most injuries significant in monetary terms, since it will not take much to justify instituting proceedings against a solvent defendant who admits liability. Where the injury, though minor, is sufficiently serious to institute proceedings, and the claimant subsequently discovers a far more serious injury caused by the same accident, time will run from the date of the first injury.[380] In *Nash v Eli Lilly & Co*[381] the claimants alleged that they had suffered side effects from the use of the prescription drug Opren. The Court of Appeal accepted that there was a valid distinction between an expected, or accepted, side effect, which would not constitute significant injury, and an injurious or unacceptable consequence. Time would not begin to run until the claimants had knowledge that the side effects were injurious or unacceptable.[382]

---

[374] In *Sniezek v Bundy (Letchworth) Ltd* [2000] PIQR P213, 224.

[375] ibid; also *Secretary of State for Trade and Industry v Mackie* [2007] EWCA Civ 642, [30] (claimant had knowledge of significant injury (noise-induced deafness) when he went for a hearing test despite receiving negative advice from a trade union official about the prospects of his claim); cf *Kew v Bettamix Ltd* [2006] EWCA Civ 1535, [2007] PIQR P16 (claimant did not have knowledge until he was informed by a doctor that he had symptoms which might be attributable to vibration at work).

[376] *AB and Others v Ministry of Defence* [2012] UKSC 9, [2013] 1 AC 78.

[377] ibid, [11]–[13] *per* Lord Wilson JSC.

[378] ibid, [3].

[379] *Dobbie v Medway HA* [1994] 4 All ER 450, 457 *per* Sir Thomas Bingham MR, though his Lordship added that time does not run if the claimant would reasonably have accepted it as a fact of life or not worth bothering about.

[380] *Bristow v Grout*, The Times, 3 November 1986; *Roberts v Winbow* [1999] PIQR P77 (CA). The claimant's appreciation of the seriousness of an injury may depend upon the medical advice which he receives: *Harding v People's Dispensary for Sick Animals* [1994] PIQR P270 (CA).

[381] [1993] 1 WLR 782 (CA).

[382] cf *Briggs v Pitt-Payne & Lias* [1999] Lloyd's Rep Med 1, where the Court of Appeal held that the question of balancing side effects against the overall beneficial effects of a drug was 'simply not relevant' to the question of whether the claimant is aware that he is suffering from 'significant injury'.

(b) Causation The claimant must have knowledge that the injury was attributable in whole or in part to the 'act or omission which is alleged to constitute negligence'. This refers to the claimant's knowledge of factual causation.[383] Ignorance of causation in law is irrelevant. Once the claimant has the broad knowledge that his injuries are attributable to the defendant's acts or omissions, he has sufficient knowledge for the purpose of s 14(1)(b), even if he does not know the specific acts or omissions and is not in a position to draft a fully particularized statement of claim.[384] Moreover, a claimant will be taken to know that his injury was 'attributable' to the defendant's act or omission if he knew that it was 'capable of being so attributed'.[385] **6.96**

Where the claimant has a firm belief that his injuries are due to the acts or omissions of the defendant, but on making enquiries is informed by expert opinion that he is mistaken, the question of whether he had sufficient knowledge to start the limitation period running will be one of degree. If the claimant realized that his belief required further confirmation, then he will not acquire knowledge until he receives that confirmation.[386] On the other hand, if the claimant is convinced in her own mind that there is a causal link, even though objectively that belief is not reasonable in the absence of confirmation from an expert, she nonetheless has the requisite knowledge and it is not open to argue that her knowledge runs from the date of confirmation of that belief by an expert.[387] Moreover, if the claimant has acquired 'knowledge' sufficient to start the limitation period running, he cannot subsequently lose it simply because he receives expert advice which tends to undermine the belief.[388] Everything turns upon the degree of conviction with which the claimant holds his belief, and whether he realized that expert confirmation was required. The Court of Appeal has suggested that where a claimant has sought advice and taken proceedings there would be some difficulty in saying that he did not then have the relevant knowledge.[389] This would mean that where a protective claim form had been issued the claimant would be deemed to have knowledge even where he then received negative expert advice leading him to discontinue the action.[390] In *Nash v Eli Lilly & Co*[391] the Court even went so far as to state that a person who embarks **6.97**

[383] *Dobbie v Medway HA* [1994] 4 All ER 450, 462 *per* Steyn LJ. See, eg, *Marston v British Railways Board* [1976] ICR 124.

[384] *Wilkinson v Ancliff (BLT) Ltd* [1986] 3 All ER 427, 438 (CA); *Hayward v Sharrard* (1998) 56 BMLR 155, 165 (CA).

[385] ibid. 'To "attribute" means "to reckon as a consequence of"': *Halford v Brookes* [1991] 3 All ER 559, 573 *per* Lord Donaldson MR.

[386] See *Davis v Ministry of Defence*, The Times, 7 August 1985; *Sniezek v Bundy (Letchworth) Ltd* [2000] PIQR P213, 224.

[387] *Spargo v North Essex District HA* [1997] PIQR P235, 244 (CA). Brooke LJ said: 'The test is a subjective one: what did the plaintiff herself know? It is not an objective one: what would have been the reasonable layman's state of mind in the absence of expert confirmation?'; *AB and Others v Ministry of Defence* [2009] EWHC 1225 (QB), The Times, 10 June 2009, [521], [523] (knowledge may run from when veteran had earlier formed sufficiently strong belief that radiation had caused his illness, prior to Rowland Report (which was first credible scientific evidence that exposure to radiation above background levels could cause the kind of chromosomal aberrations that evidenced the mechanism for at least some of injuries or conditions claimed by veterans)).

[388] *Nash v Eli Lilly & Co* [1993] 1 WLR 782, 795 (CA).

[389] ibid, 795.

[390] This occurred in *Stephen v Riverside HA* [1990] 1 Med LR 261; and *Davis v Ministry of Defence* The Times, 7 August 1985, but it was held that the claimants did not acquire knowledge until they received further expert advice confirming their original belief that there was a causal connection.

[391] [1993] 1 WLR 782, 792. In *Spargo v North Essex District HA* [1997] PIQR P235, 242, Brooke LJ said that 'attributable in this context means 'capable of being attributed to' in the sense of being a real possibility'. See the quotation at para 6.92.

upon the preliminaries to the making of a claim for compensation by taking legal or other advice may be deemed to satisfy the level of 'certainty' required for acquiring 'knowledge' under s 14. It has now been held that a claimant has knowledge of attributability for the purpose of s 14(1) once he has issued his claim, and not when better evidence of attributability is still to emerge.[392] As Lord Wilson JSC put it: 'it is a legal impossibility for a claimant to lack knowledge of attributability for the purpose of section 14(1) at a time after the date of issue of his claim. By that date he must in law have had knowledge of it'.[393]

6.98 In *Sniezek v Bundy (Letchworth) Ltd*[394] Judge LJ said that *Nash* was not authority for the proposition that time automatically starts to run against a claimant who has taken legal advice. There was nothing in the Limitation Act to suggest that any special consequences must or should be deemed to arise from his doing so. The question remains the individual's state of knowledge of the relevant facts, rather than his adviser's opinion about the prospects of success in legal proceedings. But once time starts to run, it is not postponed even if the claimant sensibly thinks, on the basis of legal and medical advice, that he should not proceed to litigation.[395]

6.99 The issue as to whether the 'knowledge threshold' had been crossed was subjected to the challenge of an unprecedented set of events which were very different from those in a normal personal injuries claim in *AB and Others v Ministry of Defence*.[396] In ten individual lead test cases, the High Court was required to determine as a preliminary issue whether claims against the Ministry of Defence for compensation for injury, disability or death in consequence of the claimants' exposure to ionizing radiation as a result of their presence near nuclear tests carried out by the British Government in the 1950s, were 'statute-barred' under the 1980 Act. Foskett J considered the report of a study carried out by Professor Rowland and his colleagues. The study involved a blind comparison between genetic patterns in chromosomes from blood lymphocytes of a cohort of fifty veterans and fifty men of similar age with either army service or police service background who had not been involved in the tests and who had not been exposed to any significant ionizing radiation. The report relied on the so-called M-FISH (multicolour fluorescent in situ hybridization) assay, which was not available until the late 1990s.[397] It represented the first occasion on which there existed credible scientific evidence that exposure to radiation above background levels caused the kind of chromosomal aberrations that evidenced the mechanism for at least some of the injuries or conditions complained of. Foskett J concluded that the emergence of the Rowland Report represented a 'very significant development in the process of acquiring knowledge generally about the effects of the tests upon humans within range of the tests'.[398] The essential question was whether the Rowland Report had so changed the scientific evidential landscape that it was an inescapable conclusion that the 'knowledge threshold' within the 1980 Act had never (and could never) have been crossed until its promulgation.[399] His Lordship's preferred view was that a claimant would not have knowledge

---

392 *AB and Others v Ministry of Defence* [2012] UKSC 9, [2013] 1 AC 78, [3], per Lord Wilson JSC.

393 ibid.

394 *Sniezek v Bundy (Letchworth) Ltd* [2000] PIQR P213, 229.

395 ibid, 230 *per* Judge LJ.

396 [2012] UKSC 9, [2013] 1 AC 78, [2010] EWCA Civ 1317, (2011) 117 BMLR 101, [2009] EWHC 1225 (QB), The Times, 10 June 2009.

397 *AB and Others v Ministry of Defence* [2009] EWHC 1225, [408]–[410]. The technique involved different chromosomes being 'painted' different colours and visualized using microscopy: [408].

398 ibid, [440].

399 ibid, [172].

unless he appreciated, not only that his injury was capable of being caused by abnormal radiation, but also that 'there [was] some credible evidence that he was exposed to ionizing radiation' at an abnormal level during, or shortly after and in consequence of the nuclear tests.[400] Accordingly, until the Rowland study, there could be no 'knowledge' within s 14, which would mean that none of the cases could be statute-barred. However, following *A v Hoare, Spargo*, and *Sniezek*, Foskett J held that the established authorities precluded that view, and supported the approach that a firm belief, even if unsupported by evidence, in the attributability of an injury or illness could cross the 'knowledge threshold'. [401] Applying the relevant principles of these established authorities, including the objective analysis required by *A v Hoare*, five of the test cases were statute-barred. The Court of Appeal concluded that Foskett J's preferred view had set the knowledge threshold too high, and that the claimant's contention that they did not have knowledge of potential attributability until they received the results of the Rowland study, demonstrated 'a fundamental misunderstanding of the concept of knowledge for limitation purposes'.[402] A majority of the Supreme Court held that a claimant must be treated as likely to have acquired knowledge of the facts specified in s 14 when he first came reasonably to believe them.[403] Each lead claimant had reasonably believed that the injury was attributable to the tests conducted by the defendant and thus they had the requisite knowledge prior to the three year period: the judge had erred in treating the Rowland report as essential rather than evidential.[404]

A particular problem which has arisen in the context of medical negligence actions is the degree of 'specificity' of knowledge required about the causal connection between treatment and the injury. Can it be said that a claimant's knowledge that the injury was attributable to 'medical treatment' is knowledge in 'broad terms' that it was attributable to an act or omission which is alleged to constitute negligence, where the claimant cannot identify the relevant acts or omissions? The difficulty arises because unlike, say, the typical road traffic accident or work accident, the claimant cannot regard the occurrence of injury itself as indicating that there must be a causal connection between the injury and 'act or omission which is alleged to constitute negligence'. Injury following an operation may arise without negligence or without even an error, as an unavoidable complication of the procedure. Alternatively, the operation may simply have been unsuccessful in preventing the claimant's medical condition from deteriorating as a consequence of the original disease or injury which was being treated.[405] Moreover, most people would not regard *successful* medical treatment as constituting an *injury*, so that if a patient is informed that surgery was successful, she would not even consider that she had been injured, let alone address her mind to the question of which acts or omissions had caused the 'injury'. **6.100**

In order to distinguish those injuries which were unavoidable consequences of the procedure and those which are attributable to an 'act or omission which is alleged to constitute negligence', it is strongly arguable that the minimum knowledge a claimant would require is knowledge that 'something has gone wrong' with the treatment. This has been the approach **6.101**

[400] ibid, [514].
[401] ibid, [517]–[521].
[402] [2010] EWCA Civ 1317, (2011) 117 BMLR 101, [85].
[403] [2012] UKSC 9, [2013] 1 AC 78, [11] *per* Lord Wilson JSC, [50] *per* Lord Walker of Gestingthorpe JSC, [69] *per* Lord Brown of Eaton-Under-Heywood JSC, [79] *per* Lord Mance JSC.
[404] [2012] UKSC 9, [2013] 1 AC 78, [62]–[64] *per* Lord Walker of Gestingthorpe.
[405] See, eg, *Harrington v Essex AHA*, The Times, 14 November 1984, where it was held that knowledge by the claimant that he had contracted an infection in the operating theatre, was not knowledge that the infection was attributable to an act or omission constituting negligence, since an infection can be contracted without negligence on the part of anyone.

taken in a number of cases.[406] Conversely, s 14(1) makes it clear that the claimant's ignorance that the defendant's acts or omissions would give rise to a cause of action in law is irrelevant to the running of the limitation period, and it might be argued that requiring knowledge that 'something has gone wrong' would import an element of knowledge about the defendant's negligence.

6.102 In *Broadley v Guy Clapham & Co*[407] the claimant underwent an operation to remove a foreign body from her knee and for at least seven months after the operation she needed two sticks in order to walk. It was held that by this time she had constructive knowledge of a potential cause of action because a reasonable person in her position would have sought further medical assistance or made further enquiries of the doctor. The claimant argued that she did not have knowledge until she knew of:

> some act or omission which could adversely affect the safety of the operation or proper recovery from the operation, such as unreasonable interference with the nerve or failure reasonably to safeguard it from damage, or failure properly to investigate and/or repair the nerve lesion in time.

6.103 Leggatt LJ said that the use of the words 'unreasonable, 'reasonably' and 'properly' could not be justified because s 14(1) provided that 'knowledge that any acts or omissions did or did not, as a matter of law, involve negligence' was irrelevant. The words 'which is alleged to constitute negligence' simply pointed to the relevant act or omission to which the injury was attributable.[408] The situation would be different, said Hoffmann LJ, if the claimant was 'barking up the wrong tree', that is, where the claimant thought that the complications from which she suffered had been caused in one way (eg during the operation) but she later discovered that the real cause was not the operation but the subsequent premature removal of her leg from traction.[409] In these circumstances the issue is the identification of the act which caused the injury and not the appreciation of whether the act was capable of being attributable to negligence or fault. Balcombe LJ said that detailed knowledge (ie sufficient

---

[406] *Bentley v Bristol and Western HA* [1991] 2 Med LR 359, 364 *per* Hirst J: '. . . the performance of a surgical operation . . . is not the act or omission which is itself alleged to constitute negligence. The act or omission which *is* alleged to constitute negligence in operation cases is some conduct or failure which can affect the safety of the operation' (original emphasis); *Nash v Eli Lilly & Co* [1991] 2 Med LR 169, where Hidden J said that there must be a degree of specificity about the act or omission which is alleged to constitute negligence, which in *Nash* consisted of exposing the claimants to a drug which was unsafe in that it was capable of causing persistent photosensitivity and/or in failing to take reasonable steps to protect the claimants from such a condition. The Court of Appeal accepted that this was the appropriate degree of specificity: *Nash v Eli Lilly & Co* [1993] 1 WLR 782, 799 (CA); see also *Driscoll-Varley v Parkside HA* [1991] 2 Med LR 346.

[407] *Broadley v Guy Clapham & Co* [1994] 4 All ER 439 (CA).

[408] ibid, 447. See also *per* Hoffmann LJ at 448. It followed that the decision in *Bentley v Bristol and Western HA* [1991] 2 Med LR 359 was wrong, since it required knowledge on the claimant's part of all matters necessary to establish negligence or breach of duty, and this was too high a test.

[409] See, eg, *Driscoll-Varley v Parkside HA* [1991] 2 Med LR 346, and the comments of Hoffmann LJ on this case in *Broadley v Guy Clapham & Co* [1994] 4 All ER 439, 449; *Khan v Ainslie* [1993] 4 Med LR 319; *Spargo v North Essex District HA* [1997] PIQR P235, 242 *per* Brooke LJ (see the quotation at para 6.92). In *Baig v City and Hackney HA* [1994] 5 Med LR 221, 224, Rougier J commented that: 'It seems to me to be a travesty of language to hold that somebody who approaches his case in a wholly erroneous belief—however strong—as to the cause of his injury could ever have the requisite knowledge. On the contrary, he has the reverse.' In *Rowbottom v Royal Masonic Hospital* [2002] EWCA Civ 87, [2002] Lloyd's Rep Med 173 the claimant believed that complications arising from a wound infection following surgery for a hip replacement, leading eventually to amputation of his leg, were due to the failure of a drain inserted into his leg. He did not acquire knowledge that he had not been given prophylactic antibiotics until he received confirmation of this from a medical expert.

knowledge to enable the claimant's advisers to draft a statement of claim) or qualitative knowledge (ie knowledge that the operation had been performed in such a way as unreasonably to cause injury to a nerve) were not required for the purpose of s 14(1). On the other hand, his Lordship accepted that 'broad knowledge' was required, which consisted of knowledge that the operation had been carried out in such a way that something went wrong.[410]

In *Dobbie v Medway HA*[411] the claimant issued a claim form in 1989 in respect of the removal of her breast during the course of a breast biopsy operation performed in 1973. Although the surgeon believed a lump to be malignant, subsequent pathological examination revealed that it was benign. The claimant was told by medical staff that the breast had been removed to be safe rather than sorry; that the hospital did not have facilities for testing breast lumps while the patient was under anaesthetic; and that she should be grateful that she did not have cancer. She subsequently suffered psychological problems attributable to the loss of her breast. It was argued that since the claimant had been told at the time that she had received the appropriate treatment, she did not know that she should not have had her breast removed until either she received an expert's report to this effect in 1990, or at the earliest in 1988 when she heard about a successful claim in a similar case. The Court of Appeal held that the claimant had sufficient knowledge to start the limitation period running in 1973. Sir Thomas Bingham MR said that knowledge that the breast had been 'unnecessarily' removed, or that something had gone wrong was irrelevant under s 14, because this would conflict with the closing words of s 14(1) that 'knowledge that any acts or omissions did or did not, as a matter of law, involve negligence, nuisance or breach of duty is irrelevant'. Though it was customary in discussing tortious liability to refer to acts and omissions, his Lordship did not believe that the meaning of s 14(1)(b) would be any different had the reference been to 'conduct'.[412] **6.104**

The claimant argued that the word 'injury' should be interpreted in a way which distinguished between the normal or expected consequences of successful medical treatment and the consequences of faulty treatment. The man in the street would not regard himself as 'injured' by a successful operation. He would only regard himself as injured if he suffered consequences other than those normally attributed to the treatment. Beldam LJ rejected this argument because the definition of personal injuries in s 38(1), though not exhaustive, indicated that 'injury' could not be qualified by the addition of words implying its source or aetiology. Nor was there any need to import the perception of the reasonable patient.[413] However, the implication of refusing to draw a distinction between successful and unsuccessful surgery appears to be that any patient who undergoes a surgical operation is, by definition, 'injured' and knows that she has suffered injury immediately. The fact that she does not know that the surgery has gone wrong would be irrelevant to the running of the limitation period. **6.105**

This conclusion is open to question. Consider, for example, a patient who has an appendix removed. She would not consider, and reasonably so, that she had suffered any injury at the hands of the doctor. Appendectomy is a potentially life-saving procedure. The pain and suffering involved in the surgery, and the resultant scar, though clearly 'caused' by the surgeon's **6.106**

[410] [1994] 4 All ER 439, 446–47.

[411] *Dobbie v Medway HA* [1994] 4 All ER 450 (CA). Leave to appeal refused: [1994] 1 WLR 1553.

[412] ibid, 456.

[413] ibid, 461. The Limitation Act 1980, s 38(1) provides that '"personal injuries" includes any disease and any impairment of a person's physical or mental condition, and "injury" and cognate expressions shall be construed accordingly'.

knife would not normally be thought of as an 'injury' when the operation is undertaken on reasonable grounds. If, however, the operation was totally unnecessary on the clinical signs, then a patient would reasonably consider that she had been damaged by having to undergo a needless operation. If the fact that the operation was unnecessary only became apparent much later, the patient only acquired knowledge that she had suffered an *injury* at that time. It is the decision to undertake the operation itself, rather than the performance of the operation (which may have been technically perfect) that is the gist or the 'essence' of her complaint.[414] However, the decision to perform the operation can only be characterized as an 'injury' if the decision was mistaken, and therefore the claimant can only acquire knowledge that she has suffered an injury when she learns that the decision was mistaken. She need not know that it was a careless or negligent mistake, but she has to know that there *was* a mistake, that is, that there was an error or that 'something had gone wrong', before she can have knowledge that she has even suffered an injury.

6.107 While it is correct to say that ignorance of the law does not affect the running of the limitation period, the question of whether the claimant knew that the facts would give her a cause of action in law should not be confused with the question of the claimant being able to identify the relevant act or omission of the defendant as a cause of her injuries. Knowledge that the defendant's acts or omissions have or have not caused the claimant's injuries is knowledge about a fact, not about the law. The question is *which facts* must the claimant have knowledge of, given that s 14(1)(b) clearly does *not* state that it is sufficient to know that the injury was attributable merely to the defendant's *conduct*? The subsection directs attention to the specific conduct of the defendant which it is subsequently alleged by the claimant constitutes negligence, nuisance, or breach of duty. The claimant need not be aware that this conduct would in law give rise to an action for damages, but she must have *some* knowledge of the relevant acts or omissions.[415] In a medical negligence action the claimant needs more than simply knowledge that the 'injury' was attributable to the treatment or operation.

6.108 This point has been made clear by the Court of Appeal in *Hallam-Eames v Merrett*,[416] which was concerned with the interpretation of the analogous provision in s 14A of the Limitation Act 1980 in respect of claims for economic loss. Hoffmann LJ said that:

> If all that was necessary was that a plaintiff should have known that the damage was attributable to an act or omission of the defendant, the statute would have said so. Instead, it speaks of the damage being attributable to 'the act or omission which is alleged to constitute negligence.' In other words, the act or omission of which the plaintiff must have knowledge must be that which is causally relevant for the purposes of an allegation of negligence.

6.109 The words 'which is alleged to constitute negligence' served to identify the facts of which the claimant must have knowledge. It was not sufficient for the claimant to know merely that the relevant damage had been caused by *an* act or omission of the defendant. Commenting on *Dobbie*, Hoffmann LJ said that Mrs Dobbie had to know more than that her breast had

---

[414] See, eg, *Gascoine v Ian Sheridan & Co* [1994] 5 Med LR 437, 442, where Mitchell J considered that the validity of the decision to treat was an 'act' quite independent from the 'act' constituting the conduct of the treatment.

[415] See, eg, *Baig v City and Hackney HA* [1994] 5 Med LR 221, 224, where Rougier J commented that the words of s 14(1)(b) admitted of no interpretation other than that the knowledge required is 'knowledge, at any rate in general outline, of just what it was that the defendant had either done or failed to do which had caused the damage'.

[416] *Hallam-Eames v Merrett*, [1996] 7 Med LR 122, 125.

been removed. She had to know that a healthy breast had been removed. That was the essence of what she was complaining about. Nor did this require knowledge of fault or negligence:

> The plaintiff does not have to know that he has a cause of action or that the defendant's acts can be characterised in law as negligent or as falling short of some standard of professional or other behaviour . . . He must have known the facts which can fairly be described as constituting the negligence of which he complains. It may be that knowledge of such facts will also serve to bring home to him the fact that the defendant has been negligent or at fault. But that in itself is not a reason for saying that he need not have known them.[417]

In *Haward v Fawcetts (A Firm)*[418] the House of Lords approved the approach in *Hallam-Eames v Merett*, holding that for the purposes of s 14A(8), requisite knowledge is knowledge of the facts constituting the essence of the complaint of negligence.[419]

Many of the cases, including several Court of Appeal decisions, refer to a requirement of knowledge of some error relating to safety by the defendant before s 14(1)(b) is satisfied.[420] In *Nash v Eli Lilly & Co*[421] the Court of Appeal accepted that the relevant acts or omissions of the defendants consisted of exposing the claimants to a drug which was *unsafe*. Knowledge that their symptoms were simply attributable to taking a drug could not constitute knowledge by the claimants of any relevant act or omission on the part of the defendant manufacturers. The reference to 'safety' clearly requires that the claimant know more than simply that the defendant's *conduct* caused the injury. It is submitted that she must either know, or have constructive knowledge, that 'something has gone wrong' sufficiently to consider investigating the circumstances.[422] **6.110**

In any event, where the claimant is informed at the time by the medical staff involved that nothing has gone wrong, and that her treatment was consistent with good medical practice, she does not know that she has suffered an injury because there is no basis for challenging either the performance of the treatment itself or the decision to proceed with the treatment. When Mrs Dobbie was informed that she was lucky to be alive, she was not simply being advised that the surgery to remove her breast had been technically competent, she was being advised that the decision to remove her breast was not an error or a mistake. On that information, she did not know that she had suffered an injury.[423] **6.111**

[417] ibid, 126. See also *Ostick v Wandsworth HA* [1995] 6 Med LR 338, where it was held that it was not sufficient that the claimant knew she had received an injury that had not healed. It was necessary to know that there was a causal link between the treatment or lack of treatment and the subsequent physical disability, ie the fact that the injury had not healed.

[418] *Haward v Fawcetts (A Firm)* [2006] UKHL 9, [2006] 1 WLR 682.

[419] ibid, [49] *per* Lord Scott, [120] *per* Lord Mance.

[420] *Davis v Ministry of Defence* The Times, 7 August 1985 (CA); *Wilkinson v Ancliff (BLT) Ltd* [1986] 3 All ER 427, 438 (CA); *Farmer v National Coal Board* The Times, 27 April 1985 (CA).

[421] [1993] 1 WLR 782, 799.

[422] In *Broadley v Guy Clapham & Co* [1994] 4 All ER 439, 446, for example, Balcombe LJ accepted that 'broad knowledge' was required, and that this involved knowledge 'that something went wrong'.

[423] cf *Scuriaga v Powell* (1979) 123 SJ 406; aff'd (1980 (CA)), where, following an unsuccessful abortion on the claimant, the defendant lied to the claimant, telling her that the operation had failed because she had a physical defect. Time did not begin to run until the claimant discovered that the failure was due to the doctor's conduct of the operation. It is apparent that in many of these cases claimants have been given reassurances ranging from statements that nothing further could have been done, implying that the claimant's problem is attributable to the underlying medical condition rather than anything done or omitted by the medical staff, to outright lies. It is unfortunate that claimants should then be caught by the limitation period, having placed reliance on the professional advice of the very defendants that they are now seeking to sue.

6.112 Where the alleged negligence consists of an omission to treat, the claimant must know more than mere fact that he has not been treated. In *Smith v West Lancashire HA*[424] the claimant had been told that the initial treatment had not worked and that there was nothing further that could be done. He presumed that he had received proper treatment, but in fact the operation had been performed too late to achieve full recovery. Russell LJ said that the alleged negligence consisted of the omission to operate promptly, together with the failure properly to diagnose his condition. The reality was that the claimant did not know that there had been an omission to operate at all until he received advice to that effect from his own expert witness:

> True, he knew that he had not had an operation on or about November 12, 1981, but that knowledge cannot, in my judgment, be knowledge of an omission 'which is alleged to constitute negligence'. One cannot know of an omission without knowing what it is that is omitted. In this case, that was an operation to reduce the fracture dislocations, as opposed to conservative treatment. Simply to tell the plaintiff that the first course of treatment had not worked, is not the same as imbuing the plaintiff with the knowledge of an omission to operate.[425]

6.113 Similarly, in *Bates v Leicester HA*[426] it was held that the claimant's knowledge that his disability was caused by the duration of his mother's labour when he was born was not sufficient to give him knowledge of the omission alleged to constitute negligence, that is, the doctors' failure to intervene in a protracted labour. The claimant had to know that the failure to intervene was avoidable, as opposed to knowing that the failure to intervene was negligent, which is irrelevant. Moreover, in determining a claimant's knowledge the court must take into account any advice she has received, because 'until someone or some incident directly challenges the advice, you continue reasonably to assume it was correct'.[427]

6.114 It is also clear that in cases where the claimant mistakenly believed that her injuries were attributable to a particular aspect of her treatment but she subsequently discovered that the injuries were caused by a different aspect of treatment, the claimant does not have knowledge as long as she is 'barking up the wrong tree'.[428] These cases indicate that knowledge that an injury was attributable simply to 'the treatment' or 'the defendant's conduct' is not sufficient.

6.115 (c) **Defendant's identity** Identifying the defendant is not normally a problem in actions for medical negligence, although the claimant may not know which individual in a team caused the injury. However, where the claimant knows that the injuries were caused by one or other of two defendants, but not both, and does not know which defendant is responsible, the claimant would be expected to sue both in the alternative.[429] This will only be

---

424 *Smith v West Lancashire HA* [1995] PIQR P514.

425 ibid, 517. See also *Parry v Clwyd HA* [1997] 8 Med LR 243; *Hind v York HA* [1997] 8 Med LR 377. In *James v East Dorset HA* (1999) 59 BMLR 196 the Court of Appeal held that a patient whose condition had deteriorated following an operation and who inferred that it had not been a success, nonetheless did not acquire knowledge within s 14 when there was nothing to alert him to the fact that he had suffered an injury during the operation. A claimant must know that he has suffered an injury before he can have knowledge that it was a significant injury. Sedley LJ commented, at 201, that: 'I do not believe that in enacting s 14 Parliament intended to reward those alert to assume that every misfortune is someone else's fault and to place at a disadvantage those who do not assume the worst when there is nothing to alert them to it.'

426 *Smith v West Lancashire HA* [1998] Lloyd's Rep Med 93.

427 *Oakes v Hopcroft* [2000] Lloyd's Rep Med 394, [33] *per* Lord Woolf CJ. Clarke LJ commented, at [49]: 'It is not easy to identify what a claimant must know about an omission in order to have knowledge that her loss is capable of being attributed to it.'

428 See the cases cited in n 409 above.

429 *Halford v Brookes* [1991] 3 All ER 559, 574 *per* Lord Donaldson MR.

relevant in cases of private medical treatment or in actions against GPs, since in cases of hospital treatment in the NHS, the claimant will sue the NHS Trust or the health authority which will be vicariously liable for the conduct of all of its staff.

(d) Vicarious liability Section 14(1)(d) refers to the circumstances required to establish an employer's vicarious liability for the torts of employees committed in the course of employment, though the wording is wide enough to cover liability for the conduct of independent contractors where the defendant is under a relevant 'non-delegable' duty. The precise identity of the employee is irrelevant if the claimant is aware that the damage was caused by one or more of the defendant's employees acting in the course of employment.[430] The claimant's ignorance that on the facts the defendant would be held vicariously liable in law is irrelevant. **6.116**

(iii) Constructive knowledge

A person's knowledge includes constructive knowledge, which by virtue of s 14(3) means: **6.117**

> knowledge which he might reasonably have been expected to acquire—
> (a) from facts observable or ascertainable by him; or
> (b) from facts ascertainable by him with the help of medical or other appropriate expert advice which it is reasonable for him to seek;
>
> but a person shall not be fixed under this subsection with knowledge of a fact ascertainable only with the help of expert advice so long as he has taken all reasonable steps to obtain (and, where appropriate, to act on) that advice.

This is a combined subjective/objective test. In *Nash v Eli Lilly & Co*[431] the Court of Appeal said that the claimant is fixed with knowledge which *he* might reasonably have been expected to acquire from facts observable or ascertainable by *him*, but in *Forbes v Wandsworth HA*[432] the Court of Appeal had some difficulty in seeing how the individual character and intelligence of the claimant could be relevant to the question of constructive knowledge (doubting the view expressed by Purchas LJ in *Nash)*. Stuart-Smith LJ said that two alternative courses of conduct may both be perfectly reasonable. Accepting the situation, and saying 'It was just one of those things. The doctors probably did their best' may be reasonable, just as taking a second opinion as to whether there was any lack of care may be reasonable. But a claimant who takes the first option is making a choice. A reasonable man in the claimant's position, who knew that the operation had been unsuccessful, and that he had suffered a major injury which would seriously affect his enjoyment of life in the future (claimant had had his leg amputated following heart bypass surgery) would take advice reasonably promptly (within twelve to eighteen months after he came out of hospital). The fact that a claimant was more trusting, incurious, indolent, resigned or uncomplaining by nature was not a relevant characteristic, since this undermined an objective approach. The problem with this is that it may be very difficult for even a reasonable person to know whether he is being 'too trusting', particularly if there is nothing to put him on notice that he should make enquiry. For example, if a patient is informed after surgery that the injury he sustained in the course of the operation was an inherent risk of the treatment, is he entitled to accept that statement at

[430] Where the defendant is responsible in law for all the staff who played some role in the claimant's treatment, it is unnecessary for the claimant to identify the particular employee who was at fault: *Cassidy v Ministry of Health* [1951] 2 KB 343.

[431] [1993] 1 WLR 782, 799 (CA); *Colegrove v Smyth* [1994] 5 Med LR 111, 114.

[432] [1996] 4 All ER 881. See also *Slevin v Southampton and South West Hampshire HA* [1997] 8 Med LR 175, following *Forbes.*

face value? At what point must the patient question what he is told in order to verify whether his trust is misplaced?[433]

6.118 In *O'Driscoll v Dudley HA*[434] Otton LJ commented that it was not easy to reconcile *Nash* and *Forbes* on the question of the subjective/objective approach, and in *Smith v Leicester HA*[435] the Court of Appeal regarded *Nash* and *Forbes* as conflicting decisions, concluding that the claimant's individual characteristics, which might distinguish her from the reasonable woman, should be disregarded. Constructive knowledge involved an objective test which does not take account of the claimant's individual characteristics (such as her forbearance, or unwillingness to criticize) but does take account of her individual circumstances, such as what she has been told by medical staff. The claimant in *Smith* was told and accepted that the cyst which rendered her tetraplegic was congenital, and that the operation in question had saved her life. She had no reason to suppose that the earlier diagnoses were wrong. In the case of an omission, what the claimant has to know is that there was a lost opportunity to prevent the injury. It was not correct to treat *Forbes* as suggesting that every time a patient has an operation and, following the operation is significantly disabled, the patient has some twelve to eighteen months to decide consciously or unconsciously whether to investigate a possible claim against those who operated. The question was simply whether it was reasonable for the claimant to seek advice, and whether it was reasonable depended on the facts and circumstances of each case, but excluding the character traits of the individual claimant.[436]

6.119 The apparent conflict between *Forbes* and *Nash* on the subjective/objective test for constructive knowledge has now been expressly resolved by the House of Lords in *Adams v Bracknell Forest Borough Council*.[437] Their Lordships established that the objective approach to constructive knowledge in *Forbes* was correct and was to be preferred over the subjective approach in *Nash*. The test under s 14(3) was whether a reasonable person in the situation of the claimant, having suffered the injury, ought reasonably to have acquired knowledge of the relevant facts.[438] While the situation or circumstances of the claimant is relevant, the aspects of character or intelligence which are peculiar to the claimant are not.[439] Personal characteristics, such as shyness or embarrassment, which may have inhibited the claimant from seeking advice but which would not be expected to have inhibited others with a like disability, were irrelevant.[440] Accordingly, Lord Hoffmann concluded: 'section 14(3) requires one to assume that a person who is aware that he has suffered a personal injury, serious enough to be something about which he would go and see a solicitor if he knew he had a claim, will be sufficiently curious about the causes of the injury to seek whatever expert advice is appropriate'.[441] However, if the injury itself would reasonably inhibit him from

433 See the comment of Lord Woolf CJ in *Oakes v Hopcroft* [2000] Lloyd's Rep Med 394, [33]: 'until someone or some incident directly challenges the advice, you continue reasonably to assume it was correct.'
434 [1998] Lloyd's Rep Med 210, 217.
435 *Smith v Leicester HA* [1998] Lloyd's Rep Med 77.
436 ibid, 87.
437 *Adams v Bracknell Forest Borough Council* [2004] UKHL 29, [2005] 1 AC 76.
438 ibid, [71] *per* Lord Scott.
439 ibid, [58] *per* Lord Phillips.
440 ibid, [71] *per* Lord Scott.
441 ibid, [47] *per* Lord Hoffmann; considered and applied in *Miller v Thames Valley Strategic Health Authority* [2005] EWHC 3281 (QB) (claimant alleged failure to diagnose a brain tumour resulting in loss of vision. Butterfield J held that defendant had failed to establish on balance of probabilities that the claimant as a reasonable man of moderate intelligence should have appreciated in all the circumstances that there was a real possibility that the defendant had failed to diagnose the brain tumour in 1963 or 1964

seeking advice, then that was a factor which had to be taken into account.[442] The application of the objective *Adams* test was considered in *Khairule v North West Strategic Health Authority*[443] in determining whether the action of a claimant suffering from athetoid cerebral palsy with preservation of intellect was statute-barred. Cox J held that the person contemplated in s 14(3) was in the same position, in objective terms, as the claimant. Whilst the test was objective, it did not prevent the claimant's objective circumstances being taken into account in asking whether a reasonable person in the circumstances of the claimant, suffering from athetoid cerebral palsy and with the same level of disability and intellect, would have had the curiosity to begin investigating with expert help whether his injury could be considered capable of being attributed to something the hospital did or did not do at the time of his birth. Personal, subjective characteristics were to be disregarded, save to the extent that any such characteristic was a direct result of the injury itself.[444] The claimant's injury could not be regarded as a trigger for fixing his date of knowledge of attributability. Cox J opined that there was a distinction to be drawn between someone who had lived with a disability and its effects from birth and someone who had suffered injury following an adverse incident which occurred in his later years. The claimant's cerebral palsy was part of him and his life and he had lived with it for as long as he could remember.[445] However, the picture had changed over time and by the end of 2002, he had matured and gained independence and experience and secured unrestricted access to the internet.[446] Pursuant to s 14(3), taking into account his circumstances, the claimant had constructive knowledge of attributability by the end of 2002 and his claim was statute-barred unless it could be saved by s 33.[447] The application of the *Adams* test was further considered by the Court of Appeal in *Whiston v London Strategic Health Authority*.[448] It was held that s 14(3) does not provide that actual or constructive knowledge that the injury is significant is determinative of the constructive knowledge issue. It provides that the issue of constructive knowledge should be determined by reference to the knowledge which a person 'might reasonably be expected to acquire'. What was reasonably expected of a claimant must depend on all the circumstances of the case. However, this was not to say that the court should overlook the fact that it must

and that it should have been diagnosed at that time. Nor had the defendant established that this failure had caused or contributed to the claimant's loss of vision.) However, in *Whiston v London Strategic Health Authority* [2010] EWCA Civ 195, [2010] 1 WLR 1582, [55] Dyson LJ held that what Lord Hoffmann said in *Adams* at [47] did not form part of the ratio of *Adams* and that the apparently absolute language used did not appear to lay down a formula to cover every case: see further *Johnson v Ministry of Defence* [2012] EWCA Civ 1505, [2013] PIQR P7, [24] *per* Dame Janet Smith.

442 *Adams*, n 437, [49] *per* Lord Hoffmann. Lord Walker (at [77]) stated that the distinction between circumstances and personal characteristics was intelligible and helpful in many cases but there were bound to be some where the distinction was elided (eg where a claimant who had suffered serious head injuries raised an issue as to whether he had legal capacity to commence or to compromise legal proceedings on his own); and further, *Clerk and Lindsell on Torts* (19th edn, Sweet & Maxwell 2006) [33-51], n 12. Baroness Hale at [91] suggested that there may be a distinction between those personal characteristics which affect the ability to acquire information (to be taken into account) and those which affect a person's reaction to what he does know (to be excluded) and so did not entirely rule out consideration of personal characteristics in determining what knowledge could be imputed to them under s 14(3). Lord Walker at [96] suggested that this distinction would be useful in some cases.

443 *Khairule v North West Strategic Health Authority* [2008] EWHC 1537 (QB).

444 ibid, [59].

445 ibid, [60]; applied in *Whiston v London Strategic Health Authority* [2010] EWCA Civ 195, [2010] Med LR 132, [60] *per* Dyson LJ.

446 *Khairule v North West Strategic Health Authority*, [63].

447 ibid, [68], [70].

448 [2010] EWCA Civ 195, [2010] 1 WLR 1582.

apply an objective test. The decision in *Adams* 'tightened up' the requirements of constructive knowledge in the light of the existence of the s 33 discretion and the 1980 Act policy to avoid injustice to defendants of vexing them with stale claims. *Adams* required the court to expect 'a heightened degree of curiosity' of the reasonable claimant that it would absent s 33.[449]

6.120 A failure to seek legal advice will give rise to constructive knowledge of the facts which would have been discovered after the date at which it would have been reasonable to seek such advice;[450] but where the question is whether it was reasonable for the claimant to seek expert advice, his personal circumstances should be taken into account. Thus, it may well be reasonable for a claimant who is seriously ill or dying not to seek legal advice,[451] though this is a question of degree.[452] Similarly, it may be reasonable for a claimant to delay seeking legal advice where she was still receiving treatment and did not wish to sour relations with the doctors who were treating her.[453] Some account will be taken of the limited resources available to the claimant by way of advice, where, for example, his solicitors could only seek expert advice to the extent that they were authorized to do so by the Legal Aid Board.[454] Constructive knowledge does not include the knowledge of a child's parents during the child's minority.[455] Moreover, an ordinary person of average intelligence and average understanding of medical matters is not expected to infer from the fact that a child is born with cerebral palsy that there was a real possibility that an act or omission of the medical staff was the cause of the injury.[456]

6.121 The proviso to s 14(3) prevents a claimant from being fixed with constructive knowledge where an expert has failed to discover or disclose a relevant fact that ought to have been revealed,[457] but it applies only to facts which are 'ascertainable only with the help of expert advice'. Where the claimant himself could have discovered the information, then he is fixed with any knowledge that the expert acting on his behalf ought to have acquired.[458]

---

449 [2010] EWCA Civ 195, [2010] 1 WLR 1582, [58]–[59] *per* Dyson LJ.

450 *Hills v Potter* [1983] 3 All ER 716, 728.

451 *Newton v Cammell Laird & Co (Shipbuilders and Engineers) Ltd* [1969] 1 All ER 708; *Davis v City and Hackney HA* [1991] 2 Med LR 366; *Driscoll-Varley v Parkside HA* [1991] 2 Med LR 346, 357; *Bates v Leicester HA* [1998] Lloyd's Rep Med 93, where the claimant had significant communication difficulties and relied heavily on his mother who was forcefully dismissive of his chances of a claim and therefore he acted reasonably in not pursuing the matter sooner.

452 In *Forbes v Wandsworth HA* [1996] 4 All ER 881 the Court of Appeal took the view that where the claimant had had his leg amputated following heart bypass surgery he should have sought expert medical advice some twelve to eighteen months after he came out of hospital, by which time he would have had time to overcome his shock at losing his leg and take stock of his disability and its consequences.

453 *Ostick v Wandsworth HA* [1995] 6 Med LR 338.

454 *Khan v Ainslie* [1993] 4 Med LR 319. On the other hand, in *Skitt v Khan and Wakefield HA* [1997] 8 Med LR 105 the Court of Appeal held that though lack of funds to obtain an expert's report could be a factor, that has to be weighed against the seriousness of the injury and its consequences for the claimant in deciding whether objectively it was reasonable to seek expert medical advice. On the facts it was understandable that the claimant did not seek such advice, but it was not reasonable.

455 *Parry v Clwyd HA* [1997] 8 Med LR 243; *Appleby v Walsall HA* [1999] Lloyd's Rep Med 154; cf *O'Driscoll v Dudley HA* [1998] Lloyd's Rep Med 210, 220, where Sir Christopher Slade treated the parents' actual knowledge as imputed to the child, so that her actual knowledge commenced at age 18.

456 ibid.

457 See, eg, *Marston v British Railways Board* [1976] ICR 124; *Stephen v Riverside HA* [1990] 1 Med LR 261; *Davis v Ministry of Defence* The Times, 7 August 1985 (CA).

458 *Leadbitter v Hodge Finance Ltd* [1982] 2 All ER 167, 174–75; *Halford v Brookes* [1991] 3 All ER 559, 565; including any knowledge about the facts that his solicitors ought to have acquired: *Henderson v Temple Pier Co Ltd* [1998] 1 WLR 1540.

Erroneous advice about the law is irrelevant and does not prevent time running.[459] Where the legal advice consists of a failure to discover relevant facts, or a failure to suggest a line of enquiry that would have revealed the facts, then in theory the proviso to s 14(3) applies, although in *Leadbitter v Hodge Finance Ltd*[460] a very narrow view was taken of the facts which are ascertainable only with the help of expert advice. It is also possible that s 14(3)(b) does not apply to *any* form of legal advice, since it has been doubted whether a party's solicitor is an 'expert' within the meaning of the subsection, which is directed to experts in the sense of expert witnesses.[461] This would mean that a claimant is not constructively fixed with the knowledge of his solicitor by virtue of s 14(3), but under the general law of agency it may be that a claimant is fixed with the actual, and even the constructive, knowledge of his solicitor.[462] Of course, it must be reasonable to attribute knowledge to the solicitor. In *Hepworth v Kerr*[463] the claimant suffered paraplegia following an operation under general anaesthetic and, despite a suggestion in the medical notes that his condition might have been attributable to the operation, he was assured on several occasions by the neurosurgeon who subsequently treated him for the paralysis that the operation had not caused his condition. A report by the neurosurgeon to the claimant's solicitors came to the same conclusion. The defendants argued that the claimant had constructive knowledge because a competent solicitor should have realized that the neurosurgeon was the wrong expert and that he had not indicated that he had read the hospital medical notes. This argument was rejected by Latham J. To require the claimant or his solicitor to question whether the expert had obtained sufficient information from the medical notes or to question whether or not he was the appropriate expert was 'asking for a startling degree of scepticism'. Some solicitors might have been sceptical, but that did not mean that it was something that any reasonably competent solicitor would have done.

---

459 Limitation Act 1980, s 14(1); *Farmer v National Coal Board* The Times, 27 April 1985 (CA). See also *Jones v Liverpool HA* [1996] PIQR P251, 266, where Glidewell LJ said that: 'if a person has been advised by one consultant, who considers on the information put before him that the plaintiff probably does not have a cause of action, and years later the plaintiff is advised by another consultant that, upon precisely the same facts, he has a possible cause of action, he cannot thereafter claim that he did not gain knowledge for the purposes of ss 11 and 14 . . . until he received the later opinion.' With respect, this rather assumes that it is the function of medical experts to advise about the law, which, clearly, it is not. If the first expert advised that in his opinion there was no causal connection between the relevant acts or omissions and the claimant's injury, then the advice concerns a fact, notwithstanding that the conclusion would also be that no claim in law would be sustainable because the injury could not be attributed to the defendant's acts or omissions. If this was the only information that the claimant had then he would only acquire the relevant knowledge when informed by the second expert that there was a causal connection.

460 [1982] 2 All ER 167, 174–75.

461 *Fowell v National Coal Board* The Times, 28 May 1986 (CA); *Khan v Ainslie* [1993] 4 Med LR 319, 325.

462 *Simpson v Norwest Holst Southern Ltd* [1980] 2 All ER 471, 476. See *Fowell v National Coal Board* The Times, 28 May 1986, where Parker LJ specifically left this point open. See further the discussion by Hidden J in *Nash v Eli Lilly & Co* [1991] 2 Med LR 169; *Colegrove v Smyth* [1994] 5 Med LR 111; *Khan v Ainslie* [1993] 4 Med LR 319, 325. The Court of Appeal in *Nash v Eli Lilly & Co* [1993] 1 WLR 782, 800 could see no reason to depart from Hidden J's general approach to this issue. Cf the position under s 33, when exercising the discretion there is no rule that anything done by the lawyers must be visited on the client: *Das v Ganju* [1999] PIQR P260, 268 (CA); *Corbin v Penfold Metallising Company Ltd* [2000] Lloyd's Rep Med 247, 251 (CA); *Steeds v Peverel Management Services Ltd* [2001] EWCA Civ 419, The Times, 16 May 2001 (CA).

463 [1995] 6 Med LR 135.

(iv) Section 33 discretion

6.122 Where the primary three-year limitation period has expired, the claimant may seek to persuade the court to exercise its discretion under s 33.[464] It was held by the Court of Appeal that the court's discretion was unfettered,[465] and this was approved by the House of Lords in *Thompson v Brown Construction*.[466] However, the House of Lords then sought to limit the exercise of the discretion where a claimant issued a claim form within the primary limitation period but did not proceed with the action and then issued a second claim form outside the limitation period: in such circumstances, it was held that such a claimant could not rely on this section.[467] In *Walkley v Precision Forgings Ltd*[468] the House of Lords held that s 33(1) directs the court to have regard to the degree to which the operation of the primary limitation period has prejudiced the claimant, but where the claimant has issued a claim form in time and then for some reason the action has not been pursued, he has not been prejudiced by the effect of ss 11 or 12 but by his own dilatoriness. The unfairness of the rule resulted in several innovative attempts to distinguish *Walkley* and limit its application.[469] However, the restrictions on the applicability of the s 33 discretion and the exceptions to such restrictions are no longer applicable since the House of Lords overruled *Walkley* in *Horton v Sadler*.[470] Their Lordships held that s 33 conferred an unfettered discretion to disapply the limitation period where it appeared equitable to allow an action to proceed, which meant 'no more (but also no less) than fair'.[471]

6.123 Under s 33(1) the court may direct that the primary limitation period shall not apply if it would be equitable to allow the action to proceed, having regard to the degree to which (i) ss 11, 11A or, 12 prejudice the claimant and (ii) the decision to allow the action to proceed would prejudice the defendant.[472] The court has to balance the degree of prejudice to the claimant caused by the operation of the primary limitation period against

[464] The burden of proving that it is equitable to allow the action to proceed is the claimant's: *Thompson v Brown Construction (Ebbw Vale) Ltd* [1981] 2 All ER 296, 303; *Sayers v Hunters* [2012] EWCA Civ 1715, [2013] 1 WLR 1695, [55]–[57], per Jackson LJ. It is incorrect to state as a general principle that the burden on the claimant is a particularly heavy one: *AB v Ministry of Defence* [2010] EWCA Civ 1317, (2011) 117 BMLR 101, [96], per Smith LJ; *Sayers v Hunters* [2012] EWCA Civ 1715, [2013] 1 WLR 1695, [55]–[57].

[465] *Firman v Ellis* [1978] QB 886; *Thompson v Brown Construction (Ebbw Vale) Ltd* [1981] 2 All ER 296; *Donovan v Gwentoys Ltd* [1990] 1 All ER 1018, 1023 *per* Lord Griffiths.

[466] *Thompson v Brown Construction (Ebbw Vale) Ltd* [1981] 2 All ER 296; see also *Donovan v Gwentoys Ltd* [1990] 1 All ER 1018, 1023 *per* Lord Griffiths.

[467] *Walkley v Precision Forgings Ltd* [1979] 1 WLR 606.

[468] [1979] 1 WLR 606.

[469] *Thompson v Brown Construction (Ebbw Vale) Ltd* [1981] 2 All ER 296; *Shapland v Palmer* [1999] 1 WLR 2068 (CA); *Piggott v Aulton* [2003] EWCA Civ 24, [2003] PIQR P371; *Adams v Ali* [2006] EWCA Civ 91, [2006] 1 WLR 1330.

[470] *Horton v Sadler* [2006] UKHL 27, [2007] 1 AC 307. Discussed in K Patten, 'Limitation and Discretion in the House of Lords—A Farewell to *Walkley*' [2006] JPIL 295.

[471] *Horton v Sadler*, n 470, [32] *per* Lord Bingham of Cornhill. The reasoning of *Walkley* was 'unsound' and it had 'given rise to distinctions which disfigure the law in this area', the effect of which had 'been to restrict unduly the broad discretion which Parliament conferred': [28] *per* Lord Bingham. The discretion can be exercised where a second claim form is issued outside the limitation period and validly served following the negligent failure to serve the original claim form in time: *Aktas v Adepta* [2010] EWCA Civ 1170, [2011] QB 894; *Davidson v Aegis Defence Services (BVI) Ltd* [2013] EWCA Civ 1586, [2014] 2 All ER 216.

[472] The word 'equitable' is not a term of art, it is simply another way of saying 'fair and just' as between the parties: *Ward v Foss* The Times, 29 November 1993 (CA) *per* Hobhouse LJ. Where the claimant has been untruthful and sought to mislead the court on key issues, it is unlikely that the court will consider it equitable to disapply the limitation period: *Long v Tolchard* [2001] PIQR P18 (CA).

the prejudice to the defendant if the action were to be allowed to proceed. The stronger the claimant's case is on the merits, the greater the prejudice to him, and conversely, the weaker his case, the less he is prejudiced.[473] On the other hand, if the defendant has a good case on the merits, there is probably less prejudice to him in allowing the action to proceed, although in *Thompson v Brown Construction (Ebbw Vale) Ltd*[474] Lord Diplock said that it was still highly prejudicial to a defendant to allow the action to proceed even where he has a good defence on the merits. The loss of the limitation defence *in itself* does not amount to a prejudice to the defendant that has to be taken into account, but rather the effect of the delay on the defendant's ability to defend.[475] The question to ask is: 'To what extent has the defendant been disadvantaged in his investigation of the claim and/or the assembly of evidence, in respect of issues of liability and quantum?'[476] This must be balanced against the prejudice to the claimant of being barred from pursuing the action.[477]

When considering the degree of prejudice to the parties the court is required by s 33(3) to have regard to all the circumstances of the case, and in particular to: **6.124**

(a) the length of and reasons for the delay on the part of the claimant;
(b) the extent to which, having regard to the delay, the evidence . . . is likely to be less cogent . . .;
(c) the conduct of the defendant after the cause of action arose, including the extent (if any) to which he responded to requests reasonably made by the claimant for information or inspection for the purpose of ascertaining facts which were or might be relevant to the claimant's cause of action against the defendant;
(d) the duration of any disability of the claimant arising after the date of the accrual of the cause of action;
(e) the extent to which the claimant acted promptly and reasonably once he knew whether or not the act or omission of the defendant, to which the injury was attributable, might be capable at that time of giving rise to an action for damages;
(f) the steps, if any, taken by the claimant to obtain medical, legal or other expert advice and the nature of any such advice he may have received.

[473] *Dale v British Coal Corporation* [1992] PIQR 373, 380 *per* Stuart-Smith LJ (CA); *Forbes v Wandsworth HA* [1996] 4 All ER 881, 894–95.

[474] [1981] 2 All ER 296, 301.

[475] *Hartley v Birmingham City District Council* [1992] 2 All ER 213, 224 *per* Parker LJ; *Ward v Foss* The Times, 29 November 1993 (CA) *per* Hobhouse LJ. See also *McEvoy v AA Welding and Fabrication Ltd* [1998] PIQR P226, 273 where Pill LJ commented that: 'An important feature of the present case is *the lack of prejudice to the defendants* by reason of the fact that they have, subject to their limitation defence, admitted liability' (emphasis added). In *Shapland v Palmer* [1999] 1 WLR 2068 (CA) the only prejudice to the defendant was being deprived of the limitation defence, and accordingly the court exercised the discretion in the claimant's favour. It cannot always be said that where the ability of a defendant to defend on the merits has not been affected by the delay the defendant suffers no prejudice in having to defend a weak case, since disapplying the primary limitation period will put the defendants to the expense of defending the action. Allowing the action to proceed may simply enable a dilatory claimant to claim from the defendants a sum in settlement which reflects the risk in costs to the defendants rather than the fair value of the claim: *Nash v Eli Lilly & Co* [1993] 1 WLR 782, 804, 808 (CA).

[476] *Cain v Francis* [2008] EWCA Civ 1451, [2009] QB 754, [73], per Smith LJ, cited with approval in *Davidson v Aegis Defence Services (BVI) Ltd* [2013] EWCA Civ 1586, [2014] 2 All ER 216, [10].

[477] *Ward v Foss* The Times, 29 November 1993 (CA) *per* Hobhouse LJ. For an illustration of a trial judge's failure to perform this balancing exercise, see *Whiston v London Strategic Health Authority* [2010] EWCA Civ 195, [2010] 1 WLR 1582 (no explanation by trial judge as to why prejudice to the defendant outweighed prejudice to the claimant).

The court should consider *all* the circumstances of the case, not simply the issues identified by s 33(3).[478] Provided this has been done, the Court of Appeal will be reluctant to interfere with the trial judge's exercise of discretion.[479]

6.125 (a) **Length of and reasons for delay** 'Delay' in s 33(3)(a) and (b) refers to the period between the expiry of the primary limitation period and the issue of the claim form, not the period between the accrual of the action or the claimant's 'knowledge' and the issue of the claim form.[480] However, in weighing the degree of prejudice to the defendant, the court is entitled to take into account the whole period of delay, including that within the primary limitation period, as part of all the circumstances of the case.[481] In these circumstances it is the delay between the commencement of the limitation period and notification to the defendant of the claim, rather than the issue of the claim form, that is significant, the object being to bar 'thoroughly stale claims'. Therefore, there is a distinction between cases where the defendant was notified of the claim fairly promptly, and so had an opportunity to give it full consideration, but the limitation period has expired through an oversight by the claimant's solicitors,[482] and cases where the defendant first heard of the claim some years after the accident.[483]

6.126 A short delay probably causes little prejudice to the defendant:[484] indeed, a very short delay causes no prejudice at all, particularly where the defendant was notified about the claim at an early stage,[485] whereas a delay of five or six years raises a rebuttable presumption of prejudice.[486] The length of the delay is probably of less significance than the reasons for the delay

---

478 *Taylor v Taylor* The Times, 14 April 1984 (CA); *Donovan v Gwentoys Ltd* [1990] 1 All ER 1018 (HL); *KR v Bryn Alyn Community (Holdings) Ltd (In Liquidation)* [2003] EWCA Civ 85, [2003] QB 1441, [74] (v); *Cain v Francis; McKay v Hamlani* [2008] EWCA Civ 1451, [2009] 3 WLR 551 (CA), [2009] RTR 18, [73]; *AB v Ministry of Defence* [2010] EWCA Civ 1317, (2011) 117 BMLR 101, [97]; *Whiston v London Strategic Health Authority* [2010] EWCA Civ 195, [2010] 1 WLR 1582, [80]. The court can take into consideration time elapsed and thus delay before the claimant's date of knowledge as an element of 'all the circumstances of the case', but this should carry less weight than, eg, s 33(3)(b) (loss of cogency of evidence), since the purpose of such a specifically listed factor would be undermined by placing equal weight on an earlier time lapse: *Collins v Secretary of State for Business Innovation and Skills* [2014] EWCA Civ 717, [2014] PIQR P19, [65] *per* Jackson LJ.

479 *Conry v Simpson* [1983] 3 All ER 369; *Bradley v Hanseatic Shipping Co Ltd* [1986] 2 Lloyd's Rep 34, 38; *Burgin v Sheffield City Council* [2005] EWCA Civ 482, [16]. The prejudice to each side may be 'obvious' and may not have to be expressly considered: *Yates v Thakeham Tiles Ltd* [1995] PIQR P135, 139 *per* Nourse LJ (CA); but '[w]here a judge is minded to grant a long 'extension' he should take meticulous care in giving reasons for doing so': *KR v Bryn Alyn Community (Holdings) Ltd (In Liquidation)* [2003] EWCA Civ 85, [2003] QB 1441, [74] (iv).

480 *Thompson v Brown Construction (Ebbw Vale) Ltd* [1981] 2 All ER 296, 301; *Eastman v London Country Bus Services Ltd* The Times, 23 November 1985 (CA); *T v Boys & Girls Welfare Service* [2004] EWCA Civ 1747, [5], [11].

481 *Donovan v Gwentoys Ltd* [1990] 1 All ER 1018, 1024; *McDonnell v Walker* [2009] EWHC Civ 1257, [2010] PIQR P5, [17]; *Davidson v Aegis Defence Services (BVI) Ltd* [2013] EWCA Civ 1586, [2014] 2 All ER 216, [10].

482 *Thompson v Brown Construction (Ebbw Vale) Ltd* [1981] 2 All ER 296; see also *Simpson v Norwest Holst Southern Ltd* [1980] 2 All ER 471, 478; and further *Cain v Francis; McKay v Hamlani* [2008] EWCA Civ 1451, [2009] 3 WLR 551 (CA), [74].

483 *Donovan v Gwentoys Ltd* [1990] 1 All ER 1018, 1024 *per* Lord Griffiths; *Dale v British Coal Corporation* [1992] PIQR P373, 385 (CA); *T v Boys & Girls Welfare Service* [2004] EWCA Civ 1747, [13]–[14].

484 *Firman v Ellis* [1978] QB 886; *Simpson v Norwest Holst Southern Ltd* [1980] 2 All ER 471, 478.

485 *Hartley v Birmingham City District Council* [1992] 2 All ER 213; *Hendy v Milton Keynes HA* [1992] 3 Med LR 114.

486 *Buck v English Electric Co Ltd* [1977] 1 WLR 806; *Pilmore v Northern Trawlers Ltd* [1986] 1 Lloyd's Rep 552. Though note that the Court of Appeal has stated that a *presumption* of prejudice is not justified

and the effect on the evidence. Reasons for the delay will vary considerably, and while the claimant's subjective beliefs are irrelevant to the question of knowledge under s 14, they are taken into account in the court's exercise of discretion under s 33.[487] The claimant may have been unaware of his legal rights,[488] or the injury may not have appeared so serious at first,[489] or he may have felt that he was 'sponging' if he sued and may have wanted to maintain good relations with the defendant,[490] or the claimant may have been in a debilitated physical and mental state throughout the relevant period,[491] or the defendant may have contributed to the delay by withholding information from the claimant.[492] Generally, where the claimant's conduct has not been personally blameworthy, this will carry considerable weight in persuading the court to exercise the discretion in his favour.[493]

(b) Cogency of the evidence The effect of the delay on the cogency of the evidence will be very significant. If documents have been destroyed or witnesses have disappeared, this is a different situation from cases where there is little real dispute about the facts, since the defendant's ability to defend the case has clearly been prejudiced.[494] The essential question under s 33 is whether, given the passage of time, the court could fairly try the claim that the defendant was negligent.[495] Cases which are based on allegations about failures in systems **6.127**

because it would cut down the wide discretion of s 33: *KR v Bryn Alyn Community (Holdings) Ltd (in liquidation)* [2003] EWCA Civ 85, [2003] 1 FCR 385, [79]. But as a general proposition, the longer the delay the more likely it is that the balance of prejudice will swing against disapplying the primary limitation period: ibid, [80].

[487] *Buck v English Electric Co Ltd* [1977] 1 WLR 806; *McCafferty v Metropolitan Police District Receiver* [1977] 1 WLR 1073; *Coad v Cornwall and Isles of Scilly HA* [1997] 8 Med LR 154; *Skerratt v Linfax Ltd* [2003] EWCA Civ 695, [2004] PIQR P10, [26], [31] *per* Waller LJ.

[488] *Brooks v Coates (UK) Ltd* [1984] 1 All ER 702, 713; *Coad v Cornwall and Isles of Scilly HA* [1997] 8 Med LR 154. If one of the reasons for delay were a failure to take legal advice, this should be taken into consideration as a relevant circumstance under s 33(3)(f): *Skerratt v Linfax Ltd* [2003] EWCA Civ 695, [2004] PIQR P10, [31] *per* Waller LJ.

[489] *McCafferty v Metropolitan Police District Receiver* [1977] 1 WLR 1073.

[490] *Buck v English Electric Co Ltd* [1977] 1 WLR 806; *McCafferty v Metropolitan Police District Receiver* [1977] 1 WLR 1073. A patient's natural reluctance to upset the doctor–patient relationship by engaging in litigation is relevant here.

[491] *Mills v Dyer-Fare* (1987, QBD); *Birnie v Oxfordshire HA* (1982) 2 The Lancet 281 (QBD); *Pearse v Barnet HA* [1998] PIQR P39; *Godfrey v Gloucestershire Royal Infirmary NHS Trust* [2003] EWHC 549 (QB), [2003] Lloyd's Rep Med 398, [41] (claimant and family 'were having to cope with a severely disabled baby which will have imposed its own emotional physical and financial constraints on the single-minded pursuit of this litigation').

[492] *Drury v Grimsby HA* [1997] 8 Med LR 38.

[493] *Brooks v Coates (UK) Ltd* [1984] 1 All ER 702; *Bates v Leicester HA* [1998] Lloyd's Rep Med 93, 102; *Ashe Construction v Burke* [2003] EWCA Civ 717, [2004] PIQR P11 (claimant not personally blameworthy, delay being largely attributable to the very unusual circumstances of multiple professional failure of his lawyers. The action was allowed to proceed despite a substantial delay of seven years since the issues at trial would turn on whether there was a 'safe system of work' adopted by the defendants, rather than a dispute as to what happened. The trial judge's exercise of discretion went to the extremity of its margins); *Whiston v London Strategic Health Authority* [2010] EWCA Civ 195, [2010] 1 WLR 1582, [80] (decision of mother of claimant not to sue did not make claimant personally blameworthy; claimant did not make a conscious decision not to start proceedings once he knew he had a claim). Cf *Buckler v Sheffield City Council* [2004] EWCA Civ 920, [2005] PIQR P3 (improper exercise of court's discretion under s 33 where delay of nine years after expiry of limitation period and where claimant had made a conscious decision not to do anything about prosecuting a claim and there was no significant worsening of his medical condition in 2001 from what it had been in 1991).

[494] *Dale v British Coal Corporation* [1992] PIQR P373, 385 (CA); *Hattam v National Coal Board* (1978) 122 SJ 777; cf *Brooks v Coates (UK) Ltd* [1984] 1 All ER 702, 713–14.

[495] *Rowe v Kingston-Upon-Hull City Council* [2003] EWCA Civ 1281, [2004] PIQR P16, [35] *per* Keene LJ.

of work are likely to be better documented than one-off accidents.[496] Cases of medical negligence should, in theory, be reasonably well documented in the medical records,[497] although this is not always the case.[498]

6.128 (c) **Conduct of the defendant** Section 33(3)(c) refers to the extent to which the defendant responded to reasonable requests for information or inspection for the purpose of ascertaining facts which were or might be relevant to the claimant's cause of action. A potential defendant does not have a duty to volunteer information but he should not obstruct the claimant in obtaining information.[499] This includes the conduct of the defendant's solicitors and his insurers. The defendant's conduct is relevant even where he has made an honest mistake in giving misleading information.[500]

6.129 (d) **Duration of the disability** If the claimant is under a disability at the date at which the cause of action accrued, the commencement of the limitation period is postponed until he ceases to be under a disability,[501] but supervening disability does not stop time running. It will be taken into account, however, in the exercise of the discretion. Since

---

[496] *Cotton v General Electric Co Ltd* (1979) 129 NLJ 73; *Pilmore v Northern Trawlers Ltd* [1986] 1 Lloyd's Rep 552; *Buck v English Electric Co Ltd* [1977] 1 WLR 806.

[497] *Bentley v Bristol and Western HA* [1991] 2 Med LR 359; *Farthing v North East Essex HA* [1998] Lloyd's Rep Med 37 (CA); *Smith v Leicester HA* [1998] Lloyd's Rep Med 77 (CA), where the case on liability turned almost entirely on X-rays taken in 1954 and 1955 which did not come to light until 1995. In *Pearse v Barnet HA* [1998] PIQR P39 it was held that there was no prejudice to the defendants from a delay between 1991 and 1994, in dealing with a case based on events in 1970 which would inevitably turn on the medical records (which were virtually complete). But note *KR v Byrn Alyn Community (Holdings) Ltd (In Liquidation)* [2003] EWCA Civ 85, [2003] QB 1441, [74] (vii), where the Court of Appeal stated that the trial judge determining the s 33 issue along with the substantive issues in case should take care not to determine substantive issues, including liability, causation, and quantum before determining the issue of limitation and, in particular, the effect of delay on the cogency of evidence. 'Much of the evidence, by reason of the lapse of time may have been incapable of being adequately tested or contradicted before him. To rely on his findings on those issues to assess the cogency of evidence for the purpose of the limitation exercise would put the cart before the horse': ibid *per* Auld LJ, giving judgment for the Court of Appeal. Where the defendants have had to investigate and prepare to meet another case on liability arising out of the same facts, the cogency of the evidence may not be affected by the delay: *Bowers v Harrow HA* [1995] 6 Med LR 16; *Richardson v Watson* [2006] EWCA Civ 1662, [2007] RTR 21 (the fact that claim of infant children of deceased turned on precisely same issues was an important factor in disapplying s 12 of 1980 Act and allowing action of deceased's spouse to proceed).

[498] In *Forbes v Wandsworth HA* [1996] 4 All ER 881 the Court of Appeal declined to exercise the discretion under s 33 in the claimant's favour having regard to the prejudice to the defendants after a long delay, caused by an inability now to locate medical records and witnesses, fading memories, the difficulty that experts would have in dealing with the appropriate standards of practice of fourteen years earlier, and the fact that the claimant's case was supported by scanty evidence and had only modest prospects of success; cf *Hammond v West Lancashire HA* [1998] Lloyd's Rep Med 146, where the defendants had destroyed the claimant's X-rays because they did not consider them to be part of the patient's medical record, and claimed that they suffered prejudice as a result. The Court of Appeal considered that in these circumstances the prejudice, if anything, was to the claimant and upheld the judge's decision to disapply the limitation period.

[499] *Thompson v Brown Construction (Ebbw Vale) Ltd* [1981] 2 All ER 296, 302. A serious delay in providing the claimant's medical records may be a relevant consideration: *Mills v Dyer-Fare* (1987, unreported, QBD); *Atkinson v Oxfordshire HA* [1993] 4 Med LR 18 (QBD), where a failure to tell the claimant or his mother what had happened during the course of an operation meant that to a large extent the delay was of the defendants' own making.

[500] *Marston v British Railways Board* [1976] ICR 124. The conduct of the defendant prior to the initiation of proceedings may also be relevant: *Kew v Bettamix Ltd* [2006] EWCA Civ 1535, [2007] PIQR P16.

[501] Limitation Act 1980, s 28. The word 'disability' in s 33 has the same meaning as in s 28, ie as defined in s 38 (see para 6.130). It does not include physical disability: *Yates v Thakeham Tiles Ltd* [1995] PIQR P135 (CA); *Thomas v Plaistow* [1997] PIQR P540 (CA).

minority can never supervene, s 33(3)(d) applies to supervening mental incapacity. The claimant's physical disabilities can be considered under s 33(3)(a), as part of the reasons for the delay, or as part of 'all the circumstances of the case'.[502] This was reaffirmed by the House of Lords in *A v Hoare*.[503] The question whether the actual claimant, taking into account his psychological state in consequence of the injury, could reasonably be expected to institute proceedings was not a factor relevant under s 14(2) but was dealt with under s 33.[504] Until Parliament decided to give effect to the Law Commission's recommendation of a more precise definition of psychological incapacity suffered by victims of sexual abuse, it was considered best to leave such considerations to the s 33 discretion.[505] The House of Lords also reaffirmed[506] the unfettered approach to the s 33 discretion laid down in *Horton v Sadler*.[507]

(e) Extent to which claimant acted promptly Until recently, it was thought that if the claimant has acted promptly and reasonably once he became aware of the cause of action, it was not to be counted against him that his lawyers had been dilatory and allowed the primary limitation period to expire.[508] However, this was rejected by Lord Carswell in *Horton v Sadler*,[509] who commented that: 'The claimant must bear responsibility, as against the defendant, for delays which have occurred, whether caused by his own default or that of his solicitors, and in numerous cases that has been accepted.'[510] **6.130**

In *Yates v Thakeham Tiles Ltd*[511] the claimant consulted solicitors after the expiry of the primary limitation period, and the solicitors did not notify the defendants of a potential claim until a year later. The Court of Appeal held that this was proper where the solicitors were obtaining all the relevant information to support the claim, such as advice from counsel, and obtaining legal aid. **6.131**

(f) Steps taken to obtain expert advice This includes legal advice and whether it was favourable or unfavourable.[512] Thus, while erroneous legal advice will not prevent time running under the three-year limitation period, it is relevant under s 33. **6.132**

502 *Yates v Thakeham Tiles Ltd* [1995] PIQR P135 (CA); *Pearse v Barnet HA* [1998] PIQR P39.

503 *A v Hoare* [2008] UKHL 6, [2008] 1 AC 844.

504 ibid, [43]–[44], [48] *per* Lord Hoffmann, [68]–[69], [71] *per* Lord Carswell, [87] *per* Lord Brown; followed in *AB and Others v Nugent Care Society* [2009] EWCA Civ 827, [10], [16].

505 ibid, [48] *per* Lord Hoffmann.

506 ibid, [49] *per* Lord Hoffmann. Lord Brown commented obiter on the sort of considerations which ought clearly to be in mind in exercising the discretion in sexual abuse cases: ibid, [84]–[88]; see further *AB and Others v Nugent Care Society* [2009] EWCA Civ 827, [19].

507 [2006] UKHL 27, [2007] 1 AC 307.

508 *Thompson v Brown Construction (Ebbw Vale) Ltd* [1981] 2 All ER 296, 303; *Das v Ganju* [1999] PIQR P260 (CA); *Corbin v Penfold Metallising Company Ltd* [2000] Lloyd's Rep Med 247, 251 (CA); *Steeds v Peverel Management Services Ltd* [2001] EWCA Civ 419, The Times, 16 May 2001 (CA); s 33(3)(e) is concerned only with the conduct of the claimant, not his advisers: *Davis v Jacobs and Camden and Islington HA and Novartis Pharmaceuticals (UK) Ltd* [1999] Lloyd's Rep Med 72, 86 *per* Brooke LJ.

509 *Horton v Sadler* [2006] UKHL 27, [2007] 1 AC 307, [53].

510 ibid, citing as examples *Firman v Ellis* [1978] QB 886; *Thompson v Brown* [1981] 1 WLR 744 and *Donovan v Gwentoys Ltd* [1990] 1 WLR 472.

511 [1995] PIQR P135 (CA).

512 *Jones v GD Searle & Co Ltd* [1978] 3 All ER 654. The failure of the claimant to consult lawyers to obtain legal advice may count against the exercise of discretion in favour of the claimant. However, if the claimant has been misled by the lawyers as to whether or not there was any cause of action or in relation to any facts which might have given rise to the cause of action, the position will be different: *Skerratt v Linfax Ltd* [2003] EWCA Civ 695, [2004] PIQR P10, [46] *per* Waller LJ.

6.133 **(g) Other factors** The availability of an alternative remedy (for example against the claimant's negligent solicitors) is a 'highly relevant consideration', but it is not conclusive. Even where the claimant would have a cast-iron case against his solicitors, he will suffer some prejudice in having to find and instruct new solicitors, additional delay, and a possible personal liability for costs up to the date of the court's refusal of the application.[513] Where there is any real dispute about the solicitors' liability in negligence, then the chances of the claimant having an alternative remedy should be largely disregarded.[514] It is legitimate to take into account the insurance position of both defendant and claimant, as part of all the circumstances of the case,[515] but the court will not apply different principles to multi-party litigation from the principles applied to ordinary, single claimant actions when exercising the discretion. The merits of each case must be considered individually.[516] The need to give effect to difficulties on proving causation when applying the broad merits test in lead cases was sharply illustrated by the decision of *AB v Ministry of Defence*,[517] which concerned claims for compensation from servicemen in respect of exposure to ionizing radiation as a result of nuclear tests carried out in the 1950s. The trial judge held that in the light of the existence of voluminous contemporaneous documentation relating to the tests, the cogency of the evidence from the defendant's point of view would not be substantially diminished by reason of the deaths of many people who would otherwise have given evidence. There was a need for the issues to be ventilated and the reasonably well-informed and fair-minded layman would consider that the claims should go ahead to trial, and having regard to the overall justice of the situation supported that view. The claim in respect of fall-out radiation, while not a new one, would have been unspecific and largely incapable of proof until the Rowland Report. This report had been a crucial and pivotal event in the potential deployment of a credible fall-out case and that factor had to weigh heavily in the scales when considering the exercise of the discretion. In the circumstances, the s 33 discretion was exercised in five cases that were statute-barred to allow the claimants to proceed to trial.[518] On appeal, the Court of Appeal held that the judge had erred in his exercise of discretion since he had significantly and wrongly underestimated the claimants' difficulties on causation and was thus unlikely to have given appropriate weight to that when applying the broad merits test. In addition, the trial judge had demonstrated an incorrect willingness to give weight to the claimants' contention that there would be a perceived injustice if their cases were not allowed to proceed.[519] The Supreme Court largely agreed with the approach and decision

---

513 *Thompson v Brown Construction (Ebbw Vale) Ltd* [1981] 2 All ER 296, 301–2. The fact that the claimant would have a cast-iron case against his solicitors is not necessarily a reason to use the occasion to teach the solicitors a lesson, particularly where the delay after the expiry of the limitation period was short and had caused the defendants no material prejudice: *Steeds v Peverel Management Services Ltd* [2001] EWCA Civ 419, The Times, 16 May 2001 (CA).

514 *Firman v Ellis* [1978] QB 886, 916 *per* Geoffrey Lane LJ; *Das v Ganju* [1999] PIQR P260, 270 (CA). See further *Conry v Simpson* [1983] 3 All ER 369; *Ramsden v Lee* [1992] 2 All ER 204; *Donovan v Gwentoys Ltd* [1990] 1 All ER 1018.

515 *Firman v Ellis* [1978] QB 886, 916; *Liff v Peasley* [1980] 1 WLR 781, 789; *Hartley v Birmingham City District Council* [1992] 2 All ER 213, 224 (CA); *Horton v Sadler* [2006] UKHL 27, [2007] 1 AC 307, [32] *per* Lord Bingham. In *Kelly v Bastible* [1997] 8 Med LR 15 the Court of Appeal held that the fact that the defendant was insured was one of the factors that could be placed in the scales when weighing prejudice to the parties under s 33, but if, treating the defendant and insurer as a composite unit, the delay had seriously prejudiced their ability to defend the action, and if the court would not have allowed the action to proceed had the defendant not been insured, the weight to be given to the mere fact that the defendant was insured should be nil.

516 *Nash v Eli Lilly & Co* [1991] 2 Med LR 169; aff'd [1993] 1 WLR 782, 810 (CA).

517 *AB v Ministry of Defence* [2009] EWHC 1225 (QB), The Times, 10 June 2009.

518 ibid, [583], [610], [618]–[619], [624]–[625], [867]–[870].

519 [2010] EWCA Civ 1317, (2011) 117 BMLR 101, [157].

of the Court of Appeal, noting that they were unusually well-placed to assess the claimants prospects of establishing causation: the Court of Appeal had been correct in declining to exercise its discretion to extend the limitation period in the light of its conclusion that the claimants faced 'very great difficulties' in establishing causation.[520] The extent to which the public interest in the claims being tried out is material is another factor that may be relevant to the court's exercise of discretion.[521]

The financial consequences to the defendant of the delay itself are a relevant consideration (as opposed to the mere fact that removal of the limitation defence may result in the defendant being required to pay damages), but this has to be balanced against the financial loss that the claimant would suffer if s 11 is not disapplied.[522] The court should also consider the question of proportionality in the exercise of the discretion under s 33, and should be slow to exercise their discretion in favour of a claimant in the absence of cogent medical evidence showing a serious effect on the claimant's health or enjoyment of life or employability, particularly taking into account the amount of damages likely to be awarded.[523] The fact that a medical negligence action is a claim for professional negligence may be a factor in the defendant's favour, because such actions have more serious consequences for defendants and should be prosecuted without delay.[524] This can only be relevant, however, where the defendant has had a claim intimated, but there has been a long delay in issuing the claim form.[525] **6.134**

(v) Death

(a) Fatal Accidents Act 1976 In an action for loss of dependency under the Fatal Accidents Act 1976, if the death occurred before the expiry of the deceased's three-year limitation period, then a new three-year period commences in favour of the dependants. This period runs from the date of death or the date of the dependants' 'knowledge', whichever is later.[526] If the action is not commenced within three years of the death or the date of knowledge of the dependants, the action is barred,[527] although the court may disapply the primary **6.135**

[520] [2012] UKSC 9; [2013] 1 AC 78, [27] *per* Lord Wilson JSC, [65] *per* Lord Walker of Gestingthorpe JSC, [89] *per* Lord Mance JSC.

[521] *AB v Ministry of Defence* [2010] EWCA Civ 1317, (2011) 117 BMLR 101, [110]; *Mutua v Foreign and Commonwealth Office* [2012] EWHC 2678, [15] (QB).

[522] *Smith v Leicester HA* [1998] Lloyd's Rep Med 77 (CA)—where the loss to the claimant would probably have been ten times greater than the additional financial prejudice to the defendants.

[523] *Robinson v St Helens MBC* [2002] EWCA Civ 1099, [2003] PIQR P128, [33]; approved in *Adams v Bracknell Forest Borough Council* [2004] UKHL 29; [2005] 1 AC 76, [54] *per* Lord Hoffmann.

[524] *Jackson & Powell on Professional Negligence* (6th edn, Sweet & Maxwell 2007), para 5.098. In the analogous context of an application to strike out an action for want of prosecution under the old rules of the Supreme Court, prejudice in the form of the worry that professional staff would suffer with the action hanging over them like the 'sword of Damocles', could be taken into account: *Biss v Lambeth HA* [1978] 1 WLR 382 (CA), thought it exceptional to treat the 'mere sword of Damocles' as a sufficient reason in itself to strike out: *Department of Transport v Chris Smaller (Transport) Ltd* [1989] 1 All ER 897, 905 *per* Lord Griffiths. Under the Civil Procedure Rules 'prejudice' is not a requirement on an application to strike out an action for want of prosecution: *Biguzzi v Rank Leisure plc* [1999] 1 WLR 1926, 1934 (CA); *Axa Insurance Co Ltd v Swire Fraser Ltd* [2001] CP Rep 17 (CA), [20]. See further *Slevin v Southampton and South West Hampshire HA* [1997] 8 Med LR 175, 181 on the question of distress to the defendant as a factor in the exercise of the discretion under s 33 in medical negligence cases; and *Sims v Dartford and Gravesham HA* [1996] 7 Med LR 381.

[525] *Dobbie v Medway HA* [1994] 4 All ER 451, 462 *per* Beldam LJ. See *Birnie v Oxfordshire AHA* (1982) 2 *The Lancet* 281 (QBD), Glidewell J.

[526] Limitation Act 1980, s 12. 'Knowledge' is defined in s 14. If dependants have different dates of knowledge, time runs separately against each of them: s 13(1).

[527] ibid, s 12(2).

limitation period under s 33. If the deceased's three-year limitation period had expired before he died, then in theory he could not have maintained an action at the date of his death and the dependants' action is barred by s 12(1). The court can exercise its discretion under s 33, however, having regard to the length of and reasons for the delay on the part of the deceased.[528] The court may disapply s 12 only where the reason why the deceased could no longer maintain an action was because of the time limit in s 11.[529] If he could no longer maintain an action for any other reason, there is no discretion to allow the dependants' action to proceed.

6.136 (b) **Law Reform (Miscellaneous Provisions) Act 1934** The law applicable in the case of an action on behalf of the estate of a deceased person under the Law Reform (Miscellaneous Provisions) Act 1934 is similar to that which applies to Fatal Accident Act claims. If the deceased died before the expiry of his three-year limitation period, a new three-year period commences which runs from either the date of death or the date of the personal representative's knowledge, whichever is later.[530] If this period expires, the personal representative may request the court to exercise its discretion under s 33. Where the deceased died after the expiry of his three-year limitation period, an action by the personal representative is barred by s 11(3), but again the court can exercise its discretion under s 33, having regard to the length of and the reasons for the delay by the deceased.

(vi) Persons under a disability

6.137 A person is under a disability while he is an infant or lacks capacity (within the meaning of the Mental Capacity Act 2005) to conduct legal proceedings[531] An infant is a person under the age of 18.[532] If a person to whom a right of action accrues is under a disability at the date when the action accrued, time does not run until he ceases to be under a disability or dies, whichever occurs first.[533] Thus, an infant has an indefeasible right to bring an action for personal injuries at any time before the age of 21,[534] and where a claimant is under a permanent disability time will not begin to run.[535] The fact that a defendant may suffer prejudice from a long delay is immaterial.[536] If the claimant was not under a disability when the action accrued, supervening lack of capacity will not prevent time running,[537] though the discretion under s 33 is available.

528 ibid, s 33(4).

529 ibid, s 33(2).

530 ibid, s 11(5). If there is more than one personal representative and their dates of knowledge are different, time runs from the earliest date: s 11(7).

531 ibid, s 38(2) (as amended by the Mental Capacity Act 2005).

532 Family Law Reform Act 1969, s 1.

533 Limitation Act 1980, s 28(1) and (6). If the person under a disability dies the primary limitation period starts to run, and there can be no further extension under s 28: s 28(3).

534 *Tolley v Morris* [1979] 2 All ER 561.

535 *Kirby v Leather* [1965] 2 QB 367 (CA). This applies if the lack of capacity arises at any time before the end of the day on which the accident occurred: *Boot v Boot* (1991, unreported, CA); *Turner v WH Malcolm Ltd* (1992) 15 BMLR 40 (CA).

536 *Headford v Bristol and District HA* [1995] 6 Med LR 1, 4 (CA) *per* Rose LJ.

537 *Purnell v Roche* [1927] 2 Ch 142.

7

INSTITUTIONAL LIABILITY

Keith Syrett

A. Introduction

Although medical law has traditionally focused primarily upon the individualized relationship between patient and medical professional, it is readily apparent that health care is, in reality, delivered in an institutional context: either through the component bodies of a health service such as the NHS in England and Wales, or through private health providers (or, increasingly, through a combination of these channels). The consequence is that, while an individual may be held personally liable for negligence, the law may also impose liability upon institutions in private or public law.[1] In private law, NHS bodies and private health facilities may, first of all, be held vicariously liable for tortious conduct (notably, negligence) of employees carried out in the course of their employment, in accordance with the general position at common law. There may also be primary liability for breach of a duty directly owed by the institution to a patient, which may take the form of a non-delegable duty owed by the institution to ensure that reasonable care is taken of patients or relate to organizational deficiencies, such as inadequate equipment or insufficient numbers of staff. **7.01**

The latter connects to a central public policy problem in the modern delivery of health care: the scarcity of resources to meet demand for services and treatment. This issue forms the backdrop to the growing incidence of public law challenges to decisions made at an institutional level, especially those relating to access to treatments and services. Publicly funded health systems worldwide have come under growing pressure as a result of a concatenation of a number of factors, including an ageing population, rising patient expectations, and the cost of new medical technologies,[2] and the NHS is no exception to this general **7.02**

[1] See *Montgomery v Lanarkshire Health Board* [2015] UKSC 11 *per* Lord Kerr and Lord Reed, [75]: 'the treatment which they [health care professionals] can offer is now understood to depend not only upon their clinical judgment, but upon bureaucratic decisions as to such matters as resource allocation, cost-containment and hospital administration: decisions which are taken by non-medical professionals. Such decisions are generally understood within a framework of institutional rather than personal responsibilities, and are in principle susceptible to challenge under public law rather than, or in addition to, the law of delict or tort'.

[2] It has been estimated that, in the absence of any policy action to deal with the rising cost of health care, public spending on health and long-term care will virtually double across OECD countries by 2050. See OECD, *Projecting OECD Health and Long-Term Care Expenditure: what are the main drivers?* (OECD

trend.[3] In response, attempts have been made to utilize resources in a more systematic and rational manner, with priorities for funding being established as a matter of managerial decision—rather than on an individualized level by physicians—and centralized guidance on the cost-effectiveness of medical technologies being issued by the National Institute for Health and Care Excellence (NICE). However, such strategies have also served to bring the 'rationing' of resources for health care to the forefront of public attention, and public law has provided a useful vehicle for the furtherance of the debate on the scope of coverage of the NHS, as well as a means by which individual patients can seek to overturn those decisions which adversely affect them.[4]

B. Liability in Private Law

7.03 In practical terms, it is extremely unlikely that, even where liability is established, an individual medical professional will foot the bill for any award of damages which results, given the existence of NHS Indemnity and the Clinical Negligence Scheme for Trusts (CNST) (described in paras 7.118–7.125). It is true that GPs and doctors working in private practice are not covered by these arrangements, but appropriate indemnity or insurance cover is now a statutory requirement of registration with the relevant regulatory body by all health care professionals.[5] The consequence is that, since costs are borne at an institutional rather than individual level, litigation impacts directly upon the financial resources available to the NHS. For example, in 2014–15, the NHS Litigation Authority (which manages CNST and other schemes which enable NHS bodies to pool the costs of legal liability) received 10,965 claims of clinical negligence and 4,172 claims of non-clinical negligence against NHS bodies, paying out £1,488.5 m and £59.4 m respectively in damages and legal costs.[6]

7.04 Notwithstanding the attempts made by the Authority to avoid formal litigation, with the consequence that fewer than 2 per cent of clinical negligence cases a year reach court,[7] and its view that 'the existing laws of negligence represent a fair balance between claimants and defendants, and therefore require little, if any, amendment',[8] there remains a concern that the assumption of financial responsibility for legal liability by health institutions serves to divert resources away from provision of patient care. This is one of the key arguments underpinning the long-standing debate on reform to the system of clinical negligence, potentially embracing the establishment of a no-fault scheme for the victims of medical misadventure.[9]

EC/WKP (2006/5), 2006), 7. For a discussion of the factors driving increases in health expenditure, see K Syrett, *Law, Legitimacy and the Rationing of Health Care: A Contextual and Comparative Perspective* (Cambridge University Press 2007) 34–43.

[3] See especially the 'Wanless Report': D Wanless, *Securing Our Future Health: Taking a Long-term View* (HM Treasury 2002) para 5.10, estimating that total expenditure on the NHS may need to increase from £68bn in 2002–03 to between £154bn and £184bn in 2022–23, if high-quality clinical standards and rising expectations are to be met. For further analysis, see J Appleby, *Spending on health and social care over the next 50 years: why think long term?* (King's Fund 2013).

[4] For an analysis of the value of public law adjudication in addressing problems of legitimacy to which the rationing of health care may give rise, see Syrett, n 2.

[5] Healthcare and Associated Professions (Indemnity) Order 2014, SI 2014/1887.

[6] NHS Litigation Authority, *Report and Accounts 2015/16* (HC 312, 2016).

[7] <http://www.nhsla.com/Claims/Pages/Handling.aspx>.

[8] House of Commons Constitutional Affairs Committee, Third Report (2005–06), *Compensation Culture* (HC 754-II, Ev. 97) para 5.

[9] See, eg, Department of Health, *Making Amends* (2003); and further, P Cane (ed.), *Atiyah's Accidents, Compensation and the Law* (8th edn, Cambridge University Press 2013), especially chs 7 and 18. Note that the Scottish Government proposes to 'proceed with caution' to explore the scope, shape, and implementation of a no-fault compensation system: see *Consultation on Recommendations for No-Fault Compensation in Scotland for Injuries Resulting from Clinical Treatment* (The Scottish Government 2014). For criticism of this approach, see House of Commons Health Committee, Sixth Report, (2010–12), *Complaints and Litigation* (HC 786-I) paras 153–57.

It was also cited by the government in support of the introduction of the NHS Redress Act 2006.[10] The liability examined in this part of the chapter is accordingly of considerable significance in so far as it serves to exacerbate the already virtually intractable problems of management of the mismatch between the potentially infinite demand for health care and the scarcity of resources for its delivery.

1. Vicarious liability

Institutions providing health care services are in the same position as other employers with respect to vicarious liability of the torts of employees committed in the course of their employment. The three relevant issues in determining the institution's liability are: (i) has the individual committed a tort?; (ii) is the individual an employee of the defendant?; and (iii) did the individual commit the tort in the course of his employment? The first question will not be further examined here.[11] As regards the third, if the negligence occurs on the premises of the institution, it is most unlikely that any question will arise of whether the employee is acting 'in the course of his employment'. He/she will be so acting, for example, where an employee (such as a doctor) injures a patient in the course of diagnosis or treatment, or an employee (such as a porter) drops the patient whilst lifting them onto a trolley. A doctor will be 'acting in the course of his employment' even if he commits a battery (or false imprisonment) when treating a patient, for example, where force[12] or restraint[13] is used upon an incompetent patient in their best interests but it is excessive and unreasonable. Only the most outrageous displays of individualistic behaviour by the employee, such as a porter who punches a patient, could isolate the institution from liability.[14] The second question is the crucial one: is the negligent person an employee of the institution? **7.05**

(i) Hospital staff

Legal systems across the world have been troubled by the question of whether institutional liability should be imposed upon hospitals for the torts of staff, such as surgeons. The difficulty arises from the fact that 'professional' personnel of this type are expected to comply with ethical codes or codes of conduct external to any relationship of employment, such as the Hippocratic Oath or guidance on good practice produced by bodies such as the General Medical Council or the Nursing and Midwifery Council. Relatedly, the exercise of their profession is characterized by personal autonomy and discretion in the treatment of patients. The traditional test for establishing whether a person is an employee (and, therefore, for whom an institution could be vicariously liable), that of 'control over the performance of the individual's duties',[15] bears little relation to the practice of the health care professions. A professional, who is expected to act independently, observe professional ethics, and who may work for a number of institutions, cannot readily be deemed to satisfy the control test. **7.06**

---

[10] See Explanatory Notes to the Act, para 3; and further above n 8, Ev. 105 (Department of Health): 'Money diverted into legal and litigation costs is diverted away from NHS medical care, whilst clinical time diverted into court proceedings is time diverted from the treatment of NHS patients.'

[11] Vicarious liability extends not only to the tort of negligence but also to other torts such as battery committed in the course of employment. See further the discussion in Chapters 3 and 4.

[12] *Re MB (Medical Treatment)* [1997] 2 FLR 426 (CA).

[13] *Re C (Detention: Medical Treatment)* [1997] 2 FLR 180.

[14] eg *Keppel Bus Co v Ahmad* [1974] 1 WLR 1082 (PC); *Mohamud v WM Morrison Supermarkets Plc* [2014] EWCA Civ 116. Contrast situations of authorized force (nn 12 and 13 above) and see generally F Rose, 'Liability for an Employee's Assaults' (1977) 40 MLR 420. For modern and authoritative discussions of the 'scope of employment' requirement, see *Lister v Hesley Hall Ltd* [2002] 1 AC 215 (HL); and *Various Claimants v Catholic Child Welfare Society* [2012] UKSC 56.

[15] The modern 'composite' approach is set out in the Privy Council decision of *Lee Ting Sang v Chung Chi-Keung* [1990] 2 AC 374.

7.07 For this reason, for some time, English law subscribed to the view that hospitals were not vicariously liable for the negligence of 'professional' staff. In the leading case of *Hillyer v Governors of St Bartholomew's Hospital*, the Court of Appeal stated that the only duty undertaken by the governors of a public hospital towards a patient who was treated in the hospital by physicians and surgeons was to use due care and skill in their selection of such staff. Vicarious liability, on this basis, would only exist in relation to 'purely ministerial or administrative duties . . . such as, for example, attendances of nurses in the wards, the summoning of medical aid in cases of emergency, the supply of proper food and the like.'[16] It has been suggested that this stance reflected a desire to relieve charitable hospitals from liabilities which they were unable to afford, such policy rationale being less germane following the establishment of the NHS in 1948.[17] However, prior to this, the decision in *Hillyer* had been rejected in Canada[18] and Australia[19] and reservations had been expressed in the House of Lords.[20]

7.08 In *Gold v Essex County Council*,[21] the Court of Appeal rejected the distinction drawn in *Hillyer*, holding a hospital vicariously liable for the negligence of a qualified radiographer, although the position of doctors was not addressed; while in *Collins v Hertfordshire County Council*,[22] vicarious liability for the negligence of a resident junior house surgeon was established. Then, in the 1950s, *Hillyer* was effectively consigned to the historical dustbin by *Cassidy v Ministry of Health*[23] and *Roe v Minister of Health*.[24]

7.09 In *Cassidy*, it was held that vicarious liability applied to hospitals in the same manner as other employers. Denning LJ stated that:

> whenever [hospital authorities] accept a patient for treatment, they must use reasonable care and skill to cure him of his ailment. The hospital authorities cannot, of course, do it by themselves: they have no ears to listen through the stethoscope, and no hands to hold the surgeon's knife. They must do it by the staff they employ; and if their staff are negligent in giving the treatment, they are just as liable for that negligence as is anyone else who employs others to do his duties for him.[25]

7.10 In *Roe*, Morris LJ considered that liability turned upon the obligations undertaken by the hospital, which was a question of fact to be decided having regard to the particular circumstances of each case. He was of the view that, in this instance, the hospital had undertaken the obligation of anaesthetizing patients for operations on the basis that 'the anaesthetists were members of the 'organisation' of the hospital: they were members of the staff engaged by the hospital to do what the hospital itself was undertaking to do'.[26]

7.11 The correct question, therefore, in determining whether a hospital is vicariously liable for an individual is whether *in the particular case* that member of staff is, or is not, working under

---

16 [1909] 2 KB 820, 829 *per* Kennedy LJ.

17 *Cassidy v Ministry of Health* [1951] 2 KB 343, 361 (CA) *per* Denning LJ. For a critical view, see A Goodhart, 'Hospitals and Trained Nurses' (1938) 54 LQR 533, 575, commenting that: 'This attempt to protect charitable hospitals by judicial legislation has not had a happy result, for it is illogical and has introduced confusion into the law.'

18 *Sisters of St Joseph of the Diocese of London v Fleming* [1938] SCR 172 (SCC).

19 *Henson v Board of Management of Perth Hospital* (1939) 41 WALR 15 (W Aus SC).

20 *Lindsey County Council v Marshall [*1937] AC 97, 124 *per* Lord Wright.

21 [1942] 2 KB 293.

22 [1947] KB 598.

23 [1951] 2 KB 343 (CA).

24 [1954] 2 QB 66 (CA).

25 [1951] 2 KB 343, 360 (CA).

26 [1954] 2 QB 66, 91 (CA).

a contract of service as an employee. The issue is a factual one turning on the nature of the contractual relationship between the parties, having regard to all the circumstances.[27] The court will look for 'indicia' of the employer–employee relationship without regarding any one factor as necessarily conclusive.[28] In practice, however, a hospital will be liable for the negligence of all of its full-time and part-time staff,[29] whether permanently or temporarily engaged, on the basis that they are employees of the hospital.

The one remaining area of doubt relates to the position of visiting or consulting physicians or surgeons. In *Collins*, Hilbery J considered that the position of a consulting surgeon who performs services for a hospital 'as a matter of agreement to which he honourably adheres' rather than on a contractual basis, might be distinguished from the 'situation of qualified persons employed and necessarily employed to fulfil the obligation undertaken by the hospital to give the necessary treatment to a patient'.[30] However, in *Razell v Snowball*, Denning LJ opined that, since the establishment of the NHS, the term 'consultant' did not denote a particular relationship between the doctor and the hospital but was rather a title denoting the former's place in the hierarchy: 'He is a senior member of the staff but nevertheless just as much a member of the staff as the house surgeon.'[31] **7.12**

Although this discrepancy of views has never been judicially resolved, it is of no practical significance. Under the terms of NHS Indemnity, NHS bodies are expected to make arrangements to meet the costs of any liability arising from the negligence of a health care professional who, although not working under a contract of employment, is contracted to an NHS body to provide services to persons to whom that NHS body owes a duty of care.[32] While this does not alter the legal position, NHS institutions did not seek to argue the point as to vicarious liability for consultants even prior to the introduction of the scheme in 1990.[33] **7.13**

(ii) General practitioners

GPs are independent practitioners of health care, not employees. It is unclear whether their relationship with the NHS is contractual in nature,[34] but even if it is, it is not a contract of employment. Accordingly, an NHS institution is not vicariously liable for the negligence of a GP and any claim will lie against the individual although, as noted above, indemnity arrangements are obligatory.[35] GPs will, of course, be liable for the negligence of their employees, such as practice nurses and receptionists, working within the surgery under contracts of service.[36] If a GP works in partnership with other doctors, the partnership will be liable for the negligence of a GP in treating a patient,[37] and each of the partners will be jointly and severally liable for the negligence of the other partners.[38] **7.14**

---

[27] *Ready Mixed Concrete (South East) Ltd v Minister of Pensions and National Insurance* [1968] 2 QB 497 and *Lee Ting Sang v Chung Chi-Keung*, n 15.

[28] See P Atiyah, *Vicarious Liability in Tort* (Butterworths 1967) chs 3–6.

[29] Including occupational physicians: see *Stokes v Guest, Keen and Nettlefold (Bolts and Nuts) Ltd* [1968] 1 WLR 1776 (Birmingham Assizes).

[30] [1947] KB 598, 619. See also *Gold* [1942] 2 KB 293, 302 *per* Lord Greene MR; and *Cassidy* [1951] 2 KB 343, 351 and 358 *per* Somervell and Singleton LJJ.

[31] [1954] 1 WLR 1382, 1386 (CA).

[32] See further paras. 7.118–7.122.

[33] See M Jones, *Medical Negligence* (4th edn, Sweet & Maxwell 2008) para 9-059.

[34] See the differing views expressed by the Court of Appeal and House of Lords in *Roy v Kensington and Chelsea FPC* (1990) 1 Med LR 328 and [1992] 1 AC 624 respectively.

[35] GPs are not covered by NHS Indemnity: see para 7.119.

[36] The legal position of a locum is unclear. In the Canadian case of *Rothwell v Raes* (1988) 54 DLR (4th) 193 (Ont H Ct), Osler J indicated that a locum would be regarded as an independent contractor.

[37] Partnership Act 1890, s 10.

[38] ibid, s 12.

(iii) Private health care

7.15 Two situations call for analysis here: patients who are being treated in an NHS hospital on a private basis, and doctors in private practice.

7.16 A number of NHS Trusts operate 'Private Patient Unit' (PPU) facilities.[39] These may consist of a dedicated ward or wing of an NHS hospital, or a purpose-built facility within the hospital grounds. Alternatively, private beds, perhaps with en-suite facilities, may be provided on NHS wards. Staff, both nurses and doctors, will ordinarily be employees of the hospital in which the patient is being treated. In such a situation, is the NHS institution vicariously liable for their negligence?

7.17 The answer to this question will turn upon whether the staff were acting 'in the course of their employment' with the NHS institution or in a purely private capacity when treating the patient. Factors to be considered might include whether care is provided for the patient outside of the hours allocated for NHS work and whether the services provided differ significantly. A number of PPUs hold themselves out as providing 'the best of both worlds' for patients.[40] It is therefore possible, albeit undecided, that a court might distinguish a patient enjoying such facilities from a patient treated in a wholly private context, and impose vicarious liability upon the hospital.

7.18 A doctor in private practice will frequently be a sole practitioner. He will not be employed by anyone and hence no question of vicarious liability will arise for his negligence. Even in situations where the doctor treats a patient in a private clinic or hospital, it is unlikely that the relationship between the doctor and the clinic or hospital will be one of employment. It is more likely that there will be a contractual arrangement whereby the doctor has 'admission privileges', with the private clinic providing the facilities and, perhaps, nursing staff for the patient's treatment. The doctor's position is likely to be somewhat analogous to the position in other countries where, frequently, doctors are not employees, but operate in private practice, and have 'admissions privileges' at the hospital under an agreement with that hospital.[41] The legal position is illustrated by a case in which an Australian court held that a doctor with 'admission privileges' was not an employee of the hospital.[42] Whilst the doctor was subject to some regulation under the hospital's rules, he was, in essence, in private practice and 'borrowing' hospital space.[43] The clinic will, of course, be liable for the negligence of any of its staff such as the nurses. There may also be a claim for breach of contract, depending upon the existence of a contract between the patient and the clinic and the nature of its terms, for example, if there is fault by the clinic in providing adequate staff

[39] It is estimated that there were 73 dedicated PPUs in operation in 2012, with an estimated capacity of 1,123 beds: A Scott, T Stevenson, and V Chua, 'The Profitability of Private Patients' Health Service Journal (27 September 2012). The Health and Social Care Act 2012, s 165 removed the cap on private income which might be earned by NHS Foundation Trusts, and this has had the effect of increasing private patient revenue in some cases, although with little impact on the NHS overall: see 'Income from Private Patients Soars at NHS Hospital Trusts' *Guardian* (19 August 2014).

[40] See, eg, websites for Orwell Private Cardiothoracic Unit, available at <http://www.orwellppu.co.uk/our_unit.aspx>, Royal Free London PPU, available at <http://www.royalfreeprivatepatients.com/gps-other-referrers/> and Imperial Private Healthcare, *Brochure*, available at< http://imperialprivatehealthcare.co.uk/ >.

[41] Of course, the doctor may be employed by the clinic. Whether or not he is will, in each case, be a question of fact. Even if there is no employment relationship, the clinic may be liable for breach of a direct or primary duty owed to the patient, for which see further paras 7.22–7.63.

[42] *Ellis v Wallsend District Hospital* (1989) 17 NSWLR 553, (1990) 2 Med LR 103 (NSW CA).

[43] See, similarly, *Yepremian v Scarborough General Hospital* (1980) 110 DLR (3d) 513 (Ont CA).

or facilities.[44] Otherwise, liability in tort will depend upon a breach of a primary or direct duty owed to the patient as discussed below.

(iv) Other Situations

(a) Agency staff The total amount spent by the NHS on agency staff amounted to £3.7 bn in 2015–16.[45] Such staff are employed to meet fluctuations in activity levels and to cover short-term absences and may be recruited from 'nursing banks', from the NHS temporary staffing service, or from private agencies. It is therefore increasingly important to establish the nature of any liability for the tortious conduct of such staff. **7.19**

It remains probable that a hospital authority will not be vicariously liable for the negligence of such staff. Any contractual relationship will be with the agency or an independent contractor, unless a contract of service is also entered into with the hospital,[46] and liability of the institution will be for breach of a primary or direct duty owed to the patient. However, some doubt has been cast upon this conclusion by recent authority in other contexts, which has established that relationships which do not amount to contracts of employment or service but are 'akin' to such contracts may still give rise to vicarious liability.[47] The likely extent of this doctrinal development remains, at present, unclear. In any event, such staff are covered by the terms of NHS Indemnity,[48] and the Clinical Negligence Scheme for Trusts will meet the costs of any claim incurred by a member of the scheme in such circumstances on the basis that the individual has been '*engaged*' by the member.[49] **7.20**

(b) 'Borrowed' staff If a doctor is 'loaned' by his employer to work in a hospital operated by another NHS body, previous authority in the law of tort pointed towards liability resting only with one employer.[50] However, in *Viasystems (Tyneside) Ltd v Thermal Transfer (Northern) Ltd*, the Court of Appeal identified that dual liability might exist.[51] This approach was confirmed by the Supreme Court in the *Various Claimants* case.[52] Here, Lord Phillips concurred with the view expressed by Rix LJ in *Viasystems*, that vicarious liability is a doctrine designed for the sake of the claimant, which imposes liability because the employer is treated at law as picking up the burden of an organizational relationship undertaken for his own benefit, and that therefore the test is whether a situation exists in which the employee is so much a part of the work, business, or organization of both employers that it would be just to make both employers answerable for negligence.[53] While the pertinence of this test **7.21**

---

[44] To the extent that 'goods' or 'services' are provided by the clinic under contract, there may be liability under Pt I of the Consumer Rights Act 2015 . There may also be liability in tort for injury caused by a 'defective product', either under common law or Pt I of the Consumer Protection Act 1987.

[45] 'NHS Spending on Agency Staff Increases Despite Control Measures' *Daily Telegraph* (9 May 2016).

[46] In *Brook Street Bureau (UK) Ltd v Dacas* [2004] ICR 1437, the Court of Appeal held that an agency worker did not have a contract of service with the agency. A similar view was taken in the health care context in *Clark v Oxfordshire Health Authority* (1997) 41 BMLR 18 (CA), where a nurse who worked for a Health Authority 'nurse bank' and whose services were supplied to various hospitals within its area was not employed under a contract of service by the Health Authority. It should be noted, however, that both of these cases relate to unfair dismissal. It is possible that, for the purposes of establishing liability for negligence, a court might determine that such an employee held a contract for services or an implied contract of service with the end-user (ie the NHS institution). In practical terms, the situation is covered by NHS Indemnity.

[47] *JGE v Trustees of the Portsmouth Roman Catholic Diocesan Trust* [2012] EWCA Civ 938; *Various Claimants v Catholic Child Welfare Society*, n 14; *Cox v Ministry of Justice* [2014] EWCA Civ 132.

[48] See para 7.119.

[49] National Health Service (Clinical Negligence Scheme) Regulations 1996, SI 1996/251 (as amended). See further paras 7.123–7.125.

[50] See, eg, *Mersey Docks and Harbour Board v Coggins and Griffith (Liverpool) Ltd* [1947] AC 1 (HL).

[51] [2005] EWCA Civ 1151.

[52] *Various Claimants v Catholic Child Welfare Society*, n 14.

[53] ibid, [43].

to the health care context is, as yet, unproven, it is clear that previously restrictive jurisprudence which placed emphasis upon the presence or absence of 'control' has been replaced by a more contextually-sensitive approach, the key question being upon whom it would be fair, just, and reasonable to impose liability.

2. Direct liability

7.22 While vicarious liability for the tortious conduct of an employee represents the most common manner in which institutional liability arises in the health care context, it is also possible for such an institution to be rendered liable for breach of a duty owed *directly* to a patient. Such a duty arises when the institution enters into an 'undertaking' of care for the patient,[54] either expressly or impliedly as a result of the circumstances. For example, the duty of care will arise when the patient is admitted to the hospital,[55] or presents him/herself at the casualty department seeking medical attention.[56] It is doubtful whether a duty will arise prior to this, for example, merely upon receipt of a referral letter by a consultant from a GP or on the making of an appointment at the hospital.[57] There is, in these situations, no assumption of responsibility as yet for the health of the patient.[58] Of course, there may be others who have assumed a duty to the patient at an earlier stage, such as the ambulance service. This duty will clearly exist when the ambulance crew 'assume a responsibility' upon collection of the patient, but it may arise even earlier.

7.23 In *Kent v Griffiths*[59] the Court of Appeal held that a duty of care was owed by the ambulance service when it accepted a call requesting an ambulance but had failed to respond promptly and, as a result of the delay, the claimant had suffered injury. The court distinguished the case law concerned with other public services such as the police and fire service, holding that, unlike these, the ambulance service owed a duty only to the claimant rather than the public at large, and hence no conflict could arise between the claimant's interests and those of the public at large.[60] The court held that the ambulance service was, in effect, in the same position as other parts of the NHS in providing a health service and the duty arose when the ambulance service accepted the call, by which the court seems to have meant 'agreed to send an ambulance'. However, the court left open (but doubted) whether an action could be brought where there were insufficient resources to provide enough vehicles or manpower.[61] Likewise, the court doubted whether a claim would be successful if an ambulance was provided for a serious accident but, due to an error of judgment, a less seriously injured patient

---

[54] *Jones v Manchester Corporation* [1952] 2 QB 852, 867 (CA) *per* Denning LJ; and *Cassidy* [1951] 2 KB 343, 360 *per* Denning LJ.

[55] ibid.

[56] *Barnett v Chelsea and Kensington HMC* [1969] 1 QB 428. Nield J distinguished the situation where the person presents him/herself and the A & E department is closed, when no duty would arise; ibid, 435. It is arguable that a hospital does owe a duty of care in these circumstances as it will have held itself out as being 'willing and able' to receive emergency patients and, thus, must give reasonable notice (or provide reasonable alternative facilities) to the public before closing: see E Picard and G Robertson, *Legal Liability of Doctors and Hospitals in Canada* (3rd edn, Carswell 1996) 10 and 371, citing *Baynham v Robertson* (1993) 18 CCLT (2d) 15 (Ont Gen Div).

[57] *Clunis v Camden and Islington Health Authority* (1997) 40 BMLR 181 (CA) (no duty of care owed to mentally disordered patient referred to hospital and for whom an appointment had been made).

[58] See Chapter 3 for a discussion in the context of a GP's duty.

[59] [2001] QB 36.

[60] See especially *Capital and Counties plc v Hampshire County Council* [1997] QB 1004 (CA) (fire service). Newdick doubts the validity of the distinction drawn in *Kent v Griffiths*, observing that a personal duty of care may equally apply 'to an individual stranded on a canoe at sea, or in a burning block of flats': C Newdick, *Who Should We Treat?* (2nd edn, Oxford University Press 2005) 176.

[61] *Kent v Griffiths* [2001] QB 36, [47].

was transported to hospital first, leaving the more seriously injured to suffer.[62] The basis of this seems to be, not that no duty of care will be owed, but rather that it will be difficult to prove breach, perhaps based upon the need to make a 'snap decision' in an emergency.

There are two broad forms of direct institutional liability existing in private law. First, a *non-delegable duty* may exist in situations where the institution has delegated the performance of a duty to another, but in which responsibility for the manner in which the duty is performed is retained at an institutional level. Here, there is no 'personal' fault on the part of the institution: this is merely a means of allocating liability between parties. There, is, therefore, a degree of overlap between this form of liability and the vicarious form of liability previously discussed. Secondly, there may be *direct liability* for breaches of duty arising from the organization of services. In such situations, the institution itself is at fault and it may, indeed, be impossible to identify a particular individual whose actions have been negligent. In so far as this form of liability relates to failures by the institution, as distinct from an individual, it is more closely akin to the forms of liability in public law to be discussed in the second part of this chapter. In particular, scarcity of resources amounts to a common underpinning theme in both areas of law. **7.24**

(i) Non-delegable duty

Where reasonable care or skill is not taken of a patient by an employee or independent contractor, the institution may be liable for breach of a primary, non-delegable duty owed to the patient. An important policy rationale for development of this form of liability lay in the fact that it enabled responsibility to be established for the actions of independent contractors. This was of particular importance at a time when it was argued that there was no vicarious liability for the breaches of duty arising from those who exercised professional skill and judgment and could not therefore be considered to be employees. **7.25**

The duty was first outlined by Lord Greene MR in *Gold v Essex County Council*. He argued that 'the obligation which [the hospital authorities] undertake is an obligation to treat, and they are liable if the persons employed by them to perform the obligation on their behalf act without due care'.[63] This was so, irrespective of whether the obligation to treat which was in question involved the use of skill. Then, in *Cassidy v Ministry of Health*, Denning LJ stated that: **7.26**

> the hospital authorities accepted the plaintiff as a patient for treatment, and it was their duty to treat him with reasonable care. They selected, employed, and paid all the surgeons and nurses who looked after him. He had no say in their selection at all. If those surgeons and nurses did not treat him with proper care and skill, then the hospital authorities must answer for it, for it means that they themselves did not perform their duty to him.[64]

He declined to determine the case on the basis of whether a surgeon was employed under a contract of service or a contract for services, stating that 'the liability of the hospital authorities should not, and does not, depend on nice considerations of that sort'.[65]

Denning LJ repeated this view in *Roe v Minister of Health*[66] and *Jones v Manchester Corporation*,[67] although the other judges in these cases, as well as those in *Gold*, chose not to rest liability on the basis of a non-delegable duty. However, some forty years later, in **7.27**

62 ibid, [46].
63 [1942] 2 KB 93, 304.
64 *Cassidy v Ministry of Health* [1951] 2 KB 343, 365.
65 ibid.
66 [1954] 2 QB 66, 82 (CA).
67 [1952] 2 QB 852, 869.

X (Minors) v Bedfordshire County Council, Lord Browne-Wilkinson cited with approval the dicta of Lord Greene MR and Denning LJ, stating that:

> It is established that those conducting a hospital are under a direct duty of care to those admitted as patients to the hospital . . . They are liable for the negligent acts of a member of the hospital staff which constitute a breach of that duty, whether or not the member of staff is himself in breach of a separate duty of care owed by him to the plaintiff.[68]

7.28 The approach was further applied in the county court decision of *M v Calderdale and Kirklees Health Authority*, in which a general practitioner employed by the Authority had referred a pregnant woman to a private clinic for a termination, which procedure the latter had negligently failed to carry out. It was held that the NHS institution owed a non-delegable duty to bring about the effective provision of services for the claimant either by itself or by arranging for others to do so. She had never left the care of the Authority and was entitled to:

> remain in the same position as a patient who remains in house relying upon the expectation of an effective provision of services. There will be all the backing of the Authority if things go wrong. There is no need to make enquiries about competence; about standards; about insurance because the umbrella of the authority remains above.[69]

7.29 A different conclusion was reached in *A (A Child) v Ministry of Defence*.[70] The question in this case was whether the Ministry of Defence was liable, by way of a non-delegable duty, for the admitted negligence of a German obstetrician whose actions in the course of delivery of a child of a British soldier had caused irreversible brain damage. From 1996 onwards, the Ministry had ceased to deliver medical care for service personnel and their families itself, instead subcontracting with an NHS Trust that the latter would procure obstetric care in German hospitals. There was no direct contractual relationship between the Ministry and the German hospitals or their staff and no question of vicarious liability arose. It therefore became important for the claimant to establish that the Ministry owed a non-delegable duty, since this would enable a claim to be brought in the English courts. The Court of Appeal held that it did not. Although Lord Phillips MR cited with approval the dictum of Lord Browne-Wilkinson in *X* and opined that 'there are strong arguments of policy for holding that a hospital, which offers treatment to a patient, accepts responsibility for the care with which that treatment is administered, regardless of the status of the person employed or engaged to deliver the treatment',[71] he concluded that any such duty rested with the Ministry only while it continued to undertake the hospital care of personnel and their dependants, not when its 'sole role [was] that of arranging such treatment to be provided by others'.[72] In this regard, his Lordship concluded that the decision in *M* did not represent the current state of English law.[73]

7.30 Similarly, no non-delegable duty arose in *Farraj v King's Healthcare NHS Trust*,[74] Here, the Trust had sent a sample of placental tissue to an independent laboratory for culturing in order to increase the number of available foetal cells such that DNA testing could be carried out by the Trust. Dyson LJ was willing to assume that the state of the law was such that a hospital may generally owe a non-delegable duty to its patients to ensure that they are treated

68 [1995] 2 AC 633, 740 (HL).
69 [1998] Lloyd's Rep Med 157 (HH Judge Garner).
70 *A (A Child) v Ministry of Defence* [2005] QB 183.
71 ibid, [63].
72 ibid, [55].
73 ibid, [52].
74 *Farraj v King's Healthcare NHS Trust* [2009] EWCA Civ 1203.

with skill and care regardless of the employment status of the person who is treating them. However, no such duty existed in this case because the claimants were not receiving medical treatment provided by the Trust, but rather in their home country of Jordan: indeed, there was no evidence that they were even aware that the sample had been sent to the Trust in London. The facts therefore did not fit the 'paradigm of patient and health care provider', but rather 'concern[ed] the provision of analytical and diagnostic laboratory services'.[75]

The preceding authorities must now be read in the light of the decision of the Supreme Court in *Woodland v Essex County Council*,[76] which has served considerably to clarify the law in this area. In this case, a pupil suffered brain damage as a consequence of the negligence of persons independently contracted to provide swimming lessons to schoolchildren. Overturning the decisions at first instance and on appeal, the Court held that a non-delegable duty did arise. Reviewing the English and Australian authorities, Lord Sumption identified two categories of case in which such a duty would attach. First, where the defendant employs an independent contractor to perform some function which is either inherently hazardous or liable to become so during the course of the work. Second, and in point in this case, in situations in which (1) an antecedent relationship exists between defendant and claimant; (2) there is a positive or affirmative duty to protect a particular class of persons against a particular class of risks; and (3) a duty which, by virtue of the relationship, is personal to the defendant: here, delegation makes no legal difference to the defendant's legal responsibility for proper performance of a duty which is, in law, his own.[77] To avoid an anomaly in which liability would exist where there is a contractual relationship between claimant and defendant (such as in a private hospital or school) or vicariously (where the harm is caused by employees of the defendant), but not where the activity has been outsourced by a publicly funded body with whom no contractual relationship exists,[78] the defendant may be taken to assume a liability ***analogous*** to that assumed by a person who contracts to do the work carefully. **7.31**

Lord Sumption endorsed the dicta of Lord Greene MR and Denning LJ in *Gold* and *Cassidy* respectively and indicated that the second form of non-delegable duty was characterized by five defining features:[79] (1) the claimant is a patient or some other person who is 'especially vulnerable or dependent on the protection of the defendant against the risk of injury'; (2) the existence of an antecedent relationship between the claimant and the defendant, independent of the negligent act or omission, which places the claimant in the care of the defendant and from which it is possible to impute the assumption of a positive duty to protect the claimant from harm; such relationships characteristically involve an element of 'control' over the claimant, which varies in intensity from case to case; (3) the claimant has no control over how the defendant chooses to perform those obligations, that is, whether personally or through employees or through third parties; (4) the defendant has delegated some function which is an integral part of the positive duty which he has assumed towards the claimant to a third party, and that party is exercising, for the purpose of the function delegated to him, the defendant's care of the claimant and the element of control that goes with it; and (5) the third party has been negligent in the performance of the very function which the defendant has assumed and delegated to that party, not in some collateral respect. **7.32**

[75] ibid, [103] (Sedley LJ).
[76] *Woodland v Essex County Council* [2013] UKSC 66.
[77] ibid, [7].
[78] See especially ibid, [30]–[32] (Lady Hale).
[79] ibid, [23].

7.33 In applying these tests, his Lordship departed from Lord Phillips MR in *A*, who had opined that a non-delegable duty only arose where injury to the claimant occurred in an environment over which the defendant had control. Rather, he was of the view that 'the essential element . . . [was] not control of the environment in which the claimant is injured, but control over the claimant for the purpose of performing a function for which the defendant has assumed responsibility'.[80] On this basis, *A* was nonetheless correctly decided since the Ministry no longer assumed responsibility for the care and treatment of army personnel and their families (in which instance such care might have been delegated to a third party, giving rise to liability), but rather *arranged* for such care to be undertaken by others. For similar reasons, *Farraj* was also correctly decided.

7.34 The decision in *Woodland* is undoubtedly welcome. It has done much to meet the concerns of Jones, noted in the preceding edition of this text,[81] that liability in negligence should not turn upon the identity of the person who is negligent, given that patients will almost never be aware of the terms upon which providers of health care engage their staff and deliver their functions. However, two minor notes of caution may nonetheless be sounded.

7.35 First, there might be concern that the endorsement of, and new clarity afforded to, the concept of non-delegable duty may exacerbate the problem identified above, of diversion of resources away from patient care, as more claims in negligence are likely to succeed. It is submitted that this is unlikely to be the outcome, for various reasons. First, Lord Sumption indicated that the courts should be sensitive to the imposition of unreasonable financial burdens on those providing critical public services and should, accordingly, impute such a duty only when it was 'fair, just and reasonable' to do so.[82] Second, the liability is not open-ended, but rather restricted to the performance of functions which the provider of health care has assumed a duty to perform (as distinct from being under a duty to arrange the performance of a function, as illustrated by *A* and *Farraj*).[83] Third, the decision in *Woodland* does not significantly widen the scope of liability when viewed in an historical context since, at least until the recent growth of outsourcing to independent contractors, vicarious liability would have arisen in any event in the vast majority of such cases.[84] Fourth, and relatedly, most such instances of negligence have previously been and will continue to be covered by the scope of NHS Indemnity (see paras 7.118–7.122).

7.36 The second concern is, arguably, more worrisome. In emphasizing the importance of 'control' by the defendant over the claimant, Lord Sumption also indicated that the duty would arise only if the ***claimant has no control over how the defendant chooses to perform its obligations***. It is not wholly clear how this requirement sits with the concept of patient choice, which is a fundamental mantra—and, increasingly—a legal requirement—in the contemporary NHS. For example, a 'Choice Framework' indicates that patients can choose GPs, consultant, or specialist for an initial outpatient appointment (and to be referred elsewhere in the event of having to wait longer than maximum waiting times), specialist test facilities, and certain aspects of maternity and community-based care.[85] 'Personal health budgets' are also available for those eligible for NHS continuing health care and for others for whom Clinical Commissioning Groups consider that additional flexibility and control of resources

80 ibid, [24].
81 3rd edn, para 7.35.
82 *Woodland v Essex County Council*, n 76, [25].
83 ibid.
84 ibid.
85 Department of Health, *The NHS Choice Framework: what choices are available to me in the NHS?* (2016).

is appropriate.[86] If a patient exercises choice in any of these situations, does it follow that no liability for breach of a non-delegable duty will arise?[87] Such a patient may be said to exercise a degree of 'control' over the defendant's performance of its obligations by means of exercise of their freedom of choice, but in such cases (save where direct payment under a personal health budget is made to the patient, who then contracts for services), there remains no contractual relationship. Rather, the position appears still to be one in which the individual or facility 'chosen' by the patient assumes a liability which is *analogous* to that assumed by a person who contracts to do the work carefully: that which Lord Sumption considered to constitute the conceptual basis for the imposition of liability in *Woodland.* Put another way, it is unclear that the interposition of patient choice does, or should, make a difference to the question of whether potential liability for breach of a non-delegable duty arises or not. This is particularly so given that, even in light of the accessibility of extensive information via the internet and elsewhere, patients are 'vulnerable' in the manner identified in *Woodland* simply by virtue of their state of ill health, compounded by uncertainty and (perhaps) fear. In consequence, it is highly likely that they will continue to rely upon the expert judgment of treating physicians, especially if they are less articulate.[88] This does not appear to amount to genuine 'control'.

(ii) Organizational errors

In *A*, Lord Phillips MR drew a distinction between the primary duty of the provider of health care to ensure that treatment is administered with reasonable care and skill (the situation considered in section (i) above) and a duty which is 'organizational' in character, namely 'a duty to use reasonable care to ensure that the hospital staff, facilities, and organization provided are those appropriate to provide a safe and satisfactory medical service for the patient'.[89] To put matters somewhat differently, in such cases, negligence is not necessarily traceable to a particular individual, but arises by virtue of the system within which the health professional operates.[90] **7.37**

It is important to bear in mind that the duty is one of *reasonableness* and not an absolute one. The hospital will not be in breach of this duty simply because a doctor or nurse is negligent. A breach of primary duty will only occur if that doctor or nurse is incompetent (in general or in undertaking the particular task) and the hospital has been negligent either in employing him or in allowing him to undertake that task. Hence, an inexperienced doctor who is incapable of performing a particular task will be negligent[91] when he carries it out and the institution will be vicariously liable for his tort.[92] However, the hospital will also be directly liable for its own failure if either it should not have put him in the position of performing a task beyond his abilities,[93] or it has allowed him to carry out the task without adequate supervision by a more experienced practitioner.[94] **7.38**

86 See NHS England, *Guidance on the 'right to have' a Personal Health Budget in Adult NHS Continuing Healthcare and Children and Young People's Continuing Care* (2014); and further, the discussion in Chapter 1, paras 1.31–1.35.

87 For argument to this effect, see A Tettenborn, 'Professional Liability' in M Jones (ed), *Clerk & Lindsell on Torts* (21st edn, Sweet & Maxwell 2014) para 10-95.

88 See M Brazier and J Beswick, 'Who's Caring for Me?' (2006) 7 Medical Law International 183, 195.

89 [2005] QB 183, [32].

90 See Newdick, n 60, 165.

91 Lack of experience is not relevant in setting the standard of care: *Wilsher v Essex Area Health Authority* [1987] QB 730 (CA). For further discussion, see Chapter 4.

92 As would have been the case in *Wilsher,* except for the fact that the inexperienced doctor sought the advice of a more experienced doctor and thereby acted reasonably: see *per* Glidewell LJ, 774.

93 See, eg, *Hinfey v Salford Health Authority* (1993) 4 Med LR 143 (no breach on facts).

94 ibid, and *Wilsher* [1987] QB 730 (CA).

7.39 In *Robertson v Nottingham Health Authority*[95] Brooke LJ emphasized the distinction between the institution's liability based upon vicarious liability and breach of its primary duty. The alleged failure concerned a breakdown in communications between the medical and nursing staff during the confinement of a pregnant woman as a result of which, it was alleged, the plaintiff was born with severe physical and mental disabilities. The judge stated:

> If effective systems had been in place at this hospital for ensuring that so far as reasonably practicable communications breakdowns did not occur in connection with such a significant area of a patient's treatment then the health authority would be vicariously liable for any negligence of those of its servants or agents who did not take proper care to ensure, so far as was reasonably practicable, that the communications systems worked efficiently. If, on the other hand, no effective systems were in place at all . . . then the authority would be directly liable in negligence for this lacuna.[96]

7.40 Such systemic failures may take many forms. Perhaps most self-evidently, an institution may be liable for a failure to supply sufficient numbers of competent and experienced staff to provide safe care for the patient. In *Wilsher v Essex Area Health Authority*, errors were made in the treatment of a premature baby, in part because of inadequate supervision of an inexperienced junior doctor. Although the case was argued as one of vicarious liability, Sir Nicholas Browne-Wilkinson VC could 'see no reason in principle' to refute the claim that 'a health authority which so conducts its hospital that it fails to provide doctors of sufficient skill and experience to give the treatment offered at the hospital may be directly liable in negligence to the patient'.[97]

7.41 However, it is clear that the duty extends further than this, to embrace provision of medical facilities and equipment,[98] procedures to protect patients from cross-infection,[99] systems to minimize errors in the administration of drugs,[100] communications,[101] and managerial and work environments in general.[102]

7.42 The operation of institutional liability in this context is well illustrated by *Bull v Devon Health Authority*.[103] Here, a child, the second of twins, suffered from brain damage which, it was alleged, was caused by asphyxia experienced during a delay in delivery which was attributable to the authority's negligence. The hospital was located over two sites and the responsible obstetrician was on duty at the other site, resulting in a delay in delivery of sixty-eight minutes, despite the existence of a communication system for calling for expert assistance. The Court of Appeal held that the defendant was liable for breach of its primary duty to the plaintiff.

7.43 Slade LJ held that the authority had a duty to provide adequate staff, facilities, and equipment for the provision of maternity services.[104] On the evidence, he held there had been no breach of this duty: at the time, the staffing arrangements were not inadequate, let alone negligently inadequate. It was not necessary, in order for the hospital to comply with its duty, to have a doctor immediately available.[105] However, he determined that the authority

---

[95] *Robertson v Nottingham Health Authority* (1997) 8 Med LR 1 (CA).
[96] ibid, 13.
[97] [1987] QB 730, 778. Glidewell LJ concurred: at 775. The decision was subsequently reversed by the House of Lords on the issue of causation: [1988] AC 1074.
[98] *Vuchar v Trustees of Toronto General Hospital* [1937] 1 DLR 298, 321 (Ont CA).
[99] *Vancouver General Hospital v McDaniel* (1934) 152 LT 56 (PC).
[100] *Collins v Hertfordshire County Council* [1947] KB 598.
[101] *Robertson v Nottingham Health Authority* (1997) 8 Med LR 1 (CA).
[102] *Penny, Palmer and Cannon v East Kent Health Authority* [2000] Lloyd's Rep Med 41.
[103] *Bull v Devon Health Authority* [1993] 4 Med LR 117 (CA).
[104] ibid, 130.
[105] ibid, 131.

also had a duty to provide an adequate system for summoning an appropriate doctor to deal with maternity emergencies. On the facts, he concluded that the system for summoning the doctor must either have broken down, or that a member of staff must have negligently operated it.[106] Consequently, the authority was liable either for breach of its primary duty[107] or on the basis of vicarious liability. Dillon LJ agreed that the authority had a duty to provide adequate staff for its maternity services and the system in place was only acceptable if it worked 'with supreme efficiency',[108] which on the facts, he held it did not: it had been operated negligently.[109] Mustill LJ held that the authority was in breach of its primary duty because the system for summoning a doctor had broken down in its operation.[110] But he went further and concluded that the system itself was inadequate: the duty was to provide immediately a doctor who could have delivered the child. Alternatively, the system was too sensitive to hitches.[111] In either case, the authority was negligent and in breach of its primary duty to the patient.

Somewhat surprisingly,[112] *Bull* was not cited in *Garcia v St. Mary's NHS Trust*,[113] in which a patient suffered brain damage subsequent to extubation following coronary artery bypass surgery. Here, the cardiothoracic registrar on call was not resident in the hospital and arrived by the patient's bedside twenty-seven minutes after being notified. Although the judge considered the argument that inadequacies in the systems operated by the Trust may have resulted in the injury suffered by the patient, he was not prepared to find any breach on the facts. This conclusion was reached on the basis of the rarity of the type of catastrophic post-operative bleeding suffered by the patient in this case. While 'the whole system obviously has to be framed to deal with that which is reasonably foreseeable',[114] it was not negligent to design a system which failed to address a rare occurrence, such as the one in this case. **7.44**

(a) The Relevance of resources One crucial issue which is raised by both *Bull* and *Garcia* is the significance of scarcity of resources to the question of whether the institution is in breach of its primary duty. As noted in the introduction to this chapter, modern health systems of all types—but especially those which are publicly funded—are continually attempting to manage the mismatch between the demand for health care and the finite resources (including staff, equipment, and drugs) available for its delivery. Of course, if, notwithstanding discussions about resources, the manager is nonetheless able to provide and maintain a system which complies with what the law may properly expect of the institution, no further questions arise. But circumstances may be, and usually are, different, and here a question posed by Sir Nicholas Browne-Wilkinson VC in the Court of Appeal decision in *Wilsher* becomes pertinent: 'should the authority be liable if it demonstrates that, due to the financial stringency under which it operates, it cannot afford to fill the posts with those possessing the necessary experience?',[115] or (it might be added) to fill them at all? **7.45**

His Lordship considered that a question of this nature was 'for Parliament, not the courts'.[116] This is indicative of a stance of non-justiciability of allocative questions which, as discussed **7.46**

[106] ibid, 132.
[107] ibid, 132, applying the maxim *res ipsa loquitur*.
[108] ibid, 137.
[109] ibid, 137–38.
[110] ibid, 142. He declined to apply the maxim *res ipsa loquitur*.
[111] ibid, 141–42.
[112] See J Beswick, 'A First Class Service? Setting the Standard of Care for the Contemporary NHS' (2007) 15 Med L Rev 245, 248.
[113] *Garcia v St. Mary's NHS Trust* [2006] EWHC 2314 (QB).
[114] ibid, [96].
[115] *Wilsher v Essex Area Health Authority* [1987] QB 730, 778.
[116] ibid.

later in the context of liability in public law, reflects concerns about the institutional and constitutional competence of the judiciary to adjudicate upon such matters. As will be seen, the courts have now shed much of their traditional deference towards decision-makers on such issues in cases in *public law*, with the consequence that they are more ready to hold institutions liable for defects in the process of decision-making on the allocation of resources. The question to be posed here is: how far will lack of resources be regarded as an answer to a claim in *negligence* which alleges harm caused through failure to provide an adequate or proper service?

7.47 As a starting point it should be noted that, while it is clearly considerably more difficult to make out a claim of negligence when the decision falls within the scope of discretionary policy choices as distinct from situations in which the policy is being practically executed at institutional level, it may not be totally impossible to do so.[117] In any event, it appears that no clear distinction between policy and operations can easily be made, it being preferable to view these areas of decision-making as points on a continuum.[118] This is readily apparent in the health care context, where decisions at the 'macro' level (at which national decisions are taken as to the budgets which are to be allocated to various spending priorities such as health, defence, education etc) clearly impact upon those at the 'meso' level (where commissioners of health care services make decisions as which services and treatments should be given priority: for example should cancer be given precedence over mental health or coronary disease?), which in turn impact upon those at a 'micro' level, 'where those responsible for providing services or making payments decide on who is to get what within the budgetary limits which have been set'.[119]

7.48 This having been said, it is apparent that it is not enough for a claimant merely to allege that injury has been caused as a result of a lack of resources. Some allocative decisions, which might be seen as situated at the extreme end of the continuum outlined above, will simply be non-justiciable in so far as they may be regarded as questions of 'high policy' which are beyond the scope of adjudication.[120] A challenge to a decision to reduce the amount of central government expenditure on the NHS would clearly fall within this category, even if its impact (say) was to reduce the number of intensive care beds available, with the consequence that an individual suffers injury. If there is any legal remedy at all in this situation, it lies in public law as discussed below.

7.49 However, other decisions which involve the exercise of discretion in the allocation of scarce resources may, in principle, be subject to adjudication, with the consequence that a claim of negligence may successfully be made out according to standard principles. This was made clear by Lord Browne-Wilkinson in *X v Bedfordshire CC* when he stated that:

> It is clear both in principle and from the decided cases that the local authority cannot be liable in damages for doing that which Parliament has authorised. Therefore if the decisions complained of fall within the ambit of such statutory discretion they cannot be actionable at common law. However, if the decision complained of is so unreasonable that it falls outside the ambit of the discretionary power conferred upon the local authority, there is no *a priori* reason for excluding all common law liability.[121]

7.50 This indicates that the first requirement in establishing negligence in cases where the allocation of resources is at issue is to establish that the institution is acting outside of the ambit

117 See Newdick, n 60, 178.
118 As noted by Lord Wilberforce in *Anns v Merton LBC* [1978] AC 728, 735 (HL).
119 R Klein, P Day, and S Redmayne, *Managing Scarcity* (Open University Press 1996) 7–10.
120 *X v Bedfordshire CC* [1995] 2 AC 633, 738.
121 ibid, 736.

of its statutory discretion. In some cases this will be impossible, since the decision is too close to the 'policy' end of the continuum and therefore non-justiciable. Elsewhere, it will oblige the court to determine whether the choice made was within or outwith the scope of discretion vested in the institution. Although Lord Browne-Wilkinson expressed reservations as to the introduction of public law concepts relating to the validity of a decision into the question of liability at common law for negligence,[122] it would appear (as the reference to 'reasonableness' in his dictum suggests) that such a determination may turn upon the existence of illegality or (especially) irrationality as defined by Lord Diplock in *Council of Civil Service Unions v Minister for the Civil Service.*[123]

Consequently, an allocative decision which is intra vires and rational will be immune from action in negligence given that it has been established that priority-setting in the NHS is lawful.[124] Conversely, when an institution steps outside the boundaries of its powers, it is not *in itself* an answer to a claim for negligence that the decision involved the allocation of scarce resources. In *Re HIV Haemophiliac Litigation*[125] the Court of Appeal was confronted with a group action by haemophiliacs who had been infected with HIV as a result of using the contaminated blood clotting agent, Factor VIII, imported from the US. The plaintiffs alleged that the defendants (the Secretary of State, health authorities in England and Wales, and the Committee on the Safety of Medicines) had negligently failed to make the UK self-sufficient in blood products and thereby remove the greater risk of infection posed by blood products derived from the US. In reply, it was argued that the claim engaged the allocation of health service resources, which was not justiciable, and that no duty of care was owed. In interlocutory proceedings relating to discovery of documents, it was held that the plaintiffs had made out an arguable case that the policy was unreasonable and amenable to an action in negligence. While recognizing the rarity of a duty of care in this context, the Court of Appeal held that merely because the attack on the government's policy involved questions of resource allocation, this did not, ipso facto, prevent a duty arising. The judges identified the difficulties facing the plaintiffs in making good their case, but they were not prepared to rule out the claim in negligence as unarguable. **7.51**

This case, the significance of which should perhaps not be overstated,[126] suggests that scarcity of resources does not preclude the existence of a duty of care in negligence. However, for negligence to be made out, the claimant must, of course, also demonstrate that there has been breach of that duty. The question in this context is, therefore, whether resources (or, rather, the lack thereof) are relevant in determining the *standard* of care provided by a health institution. **7.52**

Here, resort to first principles would suggest two initial propositions. One is that there must be an irreducible minimum of care which is demanded of any and all institutions. This is reflected in the general law of torts in the well-known case of *Nettleship v Weston.*[127] The case did not involve institutional liability but would appear to apply with equal force here. Indeed, all of the judgments of the Court of Appeal in *Wilsher*[128] seem to suggest, while not **7.53**

[122] ibid. Similar concerns were expressed in subsequent cases: see *Barrett v Enfield LBC* [2000] 2 AC 550, 586 (HL) *per* Lord Hutton; and *Carty v London Borough of Croydon* [2005] 1 WLR 2312, [28] (CA) *per* Dyson LJ.

[123] [1985] AC 374 (HL).

[124] See para 7.68.

[125] [1996] PNLR 290 (CA).

[126] The case was settled before coming to trial. A Grubb and D Pearl, *Blood Testing, AIDS and DNA Profiling* (Family Law 2000) 105, argue that the plaintiffs would have lost the case.

[127] [1971] 2 QB 691 (CA).

[128] *Wilsher v Essex Area Health Authority* [1987] QB 730 (CA).

deciding the point, that an institution may be liable *primarily* if its services do not measure up to that which may properly be expected.[129] Secondly, while every institution must meet a minimum standard of care, if an institution offers more than the minimum, it will be held to whatever is judged to be the proper level of service for what it offers. Thus, an institution which claims to have a specialist unit in, for example, child care will be expected to have available an appropriate range of skilled staff and equipment to meet the needs of such a unit. This proposition is no more than an application of the principle that a defendant will be held to the standard of care which he professes to offer.[130] This is confirmed by Mustill LJ's comment in *Wilsher* that, had the case been argued on the basis of *primary* rather than vicarious liability, the plaintiff would have asserted that 'the defendants owed a duty to ensure that the special baby care unit functioned according to the standard reasonably to be expected of such a unit'.[131]

7.54 However, these observations do not engage directly with the question posed here, of whether negligence standards are resource-dependent. Regrettably, neither *Bull* nor *Garcia* provide clear guidance on this point. In the former case, Mustill LJ expressed 'reservations' as to the contention that the authority 'could be expected to do no more than their best, allocating their limited resources as favourably as possible', arguing that, while hospital medicine was not precisely analogous to other public services, 'in respect of which it is not necessarily an answer to allegations of unsafety that there were insufficient resources to enable the administrators to do everything which they would like to do', there was a danger in 'assuming that it is completely sui generis, and that it is necessarily a complete answer to say that even if the system in any hospital was unsatisfactory, it was no more unsatisfactory than those in force elsewhere'.[132]

7.55 This obiter remark would suggest that resources are irrelevant in determining the standard of care, but Slade LJ appeared to take a different view, opining that the argument that the hospital should have 'ensured' that proper assistance was readily available was an overstatement of the standard of care owed by the institution, given that 'limited manpower' may have made it quite impossible to secure the swift attendance of a specialist because of 'inescapable other commitments'.[133] Spencer J appeared to adopt a similar standpoint in *Garcia*. While no explicit reference to scarcity of resources was made, the judge noted that the Trust 'operated under the provisions of the National Health Service' and, as such its duty to the patient co-existed with a duty owed to other patients.[134] What was therefore required of the systems operated by the Trust was 'a reasonable catering for all to whom the duties are owed'.[135]

7.56 Some support for the latter approach is afforded both by case law and academic argument. In *Knight v Home Office*,[136] personal representatives of a deceased prisoner argued that the facilities provided in prison were inadequate for care of the prisoner's mental health problems by reference to what ought reasonably to have been provided to patients in psychiatric hospitals outside prison. Although Pill J stated that it was 'not a complete defence for a

[129] See further *Brooks v Home Office* (1999) 48 BMLR 109, in which Garland J held that an expectant mother should be entitled to expect the same level of antenatal care while detained in prison as she would have had if at liberty.

[130] *R v Bateman* (1927) 19 Cr App R 8 (CCA).

[131] *Wilsher*, n 128, 747.

[132] *Bull v Devon Health Authority* [1993] 4 Med LR 117, 141.

[133] ibid, 131.

[134] *Garcia v St. Mary's NHS Trust* [2006] EWHC 2314 (QB), [95].

[135] ibid, [96].

[136] *Knight v Home Office* [1990] 3 All ER 237.

government department any more than it would be for a private individual or organization to say that no funds are available for additional safety measures', he was unable to accept the contention that the appropriate standard of care was as high as the standard of care in a psychiatric hospital outside prison. A court must 'bear in mind as one factor that resources available for the public service are limited and that the allocation of resources is a matter for Parliament' and, on this basis, 'there may be circumstances in which the standard of care in a prison falls below that which would be expected in a psychiatric hospital without the prison authority being negligent'.[137]

Witting argues that this is the correct mode of analysis and that the standard of care should be 'adapted to the special position occupied by the NHS': **7.57**

> The particular adaptation that should be made involves simply taking account of the fact of underfunding and its impact upon the health care system in determining whether health authorities and their employees have acted reasonably. The relevant standard of care may be expected to rise or fall depending upon whether a particular hospital or unit is underfunded.[138]

The author justifies this position both by reference to legal principle and policy factors. As regards the former, he contends that hospitals and front-line medical staff are 'causally insignificant parties',[139] who should not be attributed with 'blame' when they have little or no autonomy in the manner in which they discharge their duties, as a result of governmental policies which entail 'the stretching of resources and the pursuit of ever-greater efficiency [which] gives rise to real risks of human failure through under-staffing, fatigue and so on'.[140] As for policy factors, he argues that adoption of a modified or variable standard of care will encourage hospitals to keep facilities open, even if these are not of an ideal standard, rather than to limit access to care by closure of facilities.[141]

The case advanced by Witting, that there should be a variable, resource-dependent standard of care, can be criticized on a number of grounds. First, the argument rests, in part, on an analogy to a deferential approach to resource allocation on the part of courts in public law cases which, he contends, should be extended to private law claims in negligence.[142] This is problematic because matters have moved on: as noted below, courts are now considerably less deferential to institutional choices on resource allocation in judicial review than was once the case—moreover, this development would appear to be characteristic of the field of medical law in general.[143] Second, while it may be accepted that health care institutions and employees work under significant resource constraints, it somewhat overstates the case to argue that autonomy is lacking with the consequence that fault cannot and should not be attributed: 'meso'-level allocative decision-making by those commissioning health care entails that they exercise choice between differing priorities for treatment specifically in order to take account of local particularities; similarly, clinicians and others are expected to exercise discretion in the treatment of individual patients. Third, variability in the standard of care runs the risk of generating a 'postcode lottery' in liability for negligence whereby a **7.58**

[137] ibid, 243. But cf *Brooks v Home Office*, n 129, where Garland J took a contrary view to that of Pill J: especially at 114.

[138] C Witting, 'National Health Service Rationing: Implications for the Standard of Care in Negligence' (2001) 21 OJLS 443.

[139] ibid, 471.

[140] ibid, 466.

[141] ibid, 470.

[142] ibid, 471.

[143] See H Woolf, 'Are the Courts Excessively Deferential to the Medical Profession?' (2001) 9 Med L Rev 1.

patient treated in a better-resourced facility has a greater prospect of success in a claim than one treated under financially straitened circumstances. Given that policy-makers—notably, through the establishment of NICE—have sought to reduce geographical inequity in health care in other respects, such a result seems out of step with the general trend. Fourth, while it might be conceded that attributing 'blame' to institutions or individuals is 'unfair' when there is relatively little that they can do to avoid mistakes in situations of scarce resources,[144] it should be borne in mind that it is virtually certain that they will not, in practice, bear the financial consequence of any such attribution, given that individuals will almost always be covered by NHS or professional indemnity and institutions by the Clinical Negligence Scheme for Trusts. Finally, a resource-dependent standard of care reduces the scope for *accountability* for allocative choices through the legal process.[145] While one might concur with Witting that responsibility for injuries arising from negligence should ideally be placed at the feet of government,[146] the practical difficulty of securing any form of political accountability for funding decisions in view of executive dominance of the legislature and ministerial unwillingness to admit the need for, or existence of, rationing of resources for health care, renders the courtroom a useful alternative forum in which explanations of allocative choices can be demanded and proffered. It would seem invidious to restrict the ability of an individual to obtain such an explanation—even leaving aside the injustice of denying him or her compensation—when alternative avenues of accountability appear relatively ineffective, especially given that the institution or individual is almost invariably protected from the direct financial consequences of liability.

7.59 None of this is to deny that the approach of the courts to the question of whether resources are relevant to the standard of care in negligence is lacking in clarity. Whether one accepts the analysis advanced by Witting or the counter-arguments outlined here, an unambiguous judicial pronouncement on this issue would be highly welcome.

7.60 **(b) Clinical guidelines** A final issue to be considered in this context is the relevance, if any, of clinical guidelines to the standard of care in negligence.[147] It should be noted that these may not only be at issue in cases of direct liability for organizational failure of the type discussed in this section. Failure to introduce a guideline or failure in setting the content of the guideline may give rise to a breach of the hospital's primary duty to the patient. But a failure to follow or implement such a guideline in a particular instance will, if anything, be a question of breach of duty by a member of staff and vicarious liability for that breach of duty. Of course, this is not to say that the hospital might not be liable itself if it negligently allowed, for example, a culture of non-compliance with a guideline by 'turning a blind eye' to its non-implementation.

7.61 Clinical guidelines may be described as 'systematically developed statements to assist practitioner and patient decisions about appropriate health care for specific clinical circumstances'.[148] They have proliferated in recent years as a product of the hegemony of

[144] Witting, n 138, 464–65.

[145] See, eg, J Montgomery, 'Suing Hospitals Directly: What Tort?' (1987) 137 NLJ 703: 'To hold health authorities liable for inadequate systems would provide a mechanism whereby managers can be made accountable for the effects which their activities have on patient care ... Direct liability on the part of health and hospital authorities may present an important tool to unravel the complexities of modern health provision.'

[146] Witting, n 138, 471.

[147] See, generally, J Tingle and C Foster (eds.), *Clinical Guidelines: Law, Policy and Practice* (Cavendish 2002).

[148] M Field and K Lohr (eds), *Clinical Practice Guidelines: from Development to Use* (Institute of Medicine 1992) 2.

'evidence-based medicine'.[149] In the UK, the most influential source of such guidelines is NICE. Its guidance encompasses technology appraisal (evaluations of the clinical and cost-effectiveness of health technologies), medical technologies and diagnostics guidance, interventional procedures guidance, and evidence-based recommendations on a wide range of topics (clinical guidelines). While NHS institutions are mandated to apply funds to implement recommendations contained in technology appraisals,[150] other forms of guidance are not mandatory. Rather, the Institute indicates that 'healthcare professionals should take NICE guidance fully into account when exercising their clinical judgment, but it does not override their responsibility to make decisions appropriate to the circumstances and wishes of the individual patient. The reasons for any differences should be documented'.[151]

Kennedy and Grubb previously argued that: **7.62**

> Increasingly, NICE guidelines will be taken to set the standard and quality of care that a patient is entitled to expect. Thus, while not determinative of the duty of care in negligence, these standards are likely to be seen by courts as the *expected* level of care, such that departure will require some demonstrable justification relating to the individual patient's circumstances.[152]

Similar analysis has been offered by the Institute itself,[153] and by academic commentators **7.63** who argue that guidelines may *inform* the standard of care, while not necessarily being definitive of it, given that:

> clinical guidelines constantly face challenges from dissenting authoritative reinterpretation of existing evidence and from new, relevant evidence that was unavailable at the time the recommendations were developed ... [and that] however-evidence based the process of development may be, a guideline may not easily be applied to a particular patient's care.[154]

It is submitted, however, that the scope for reasonable departure from NICE guidance is narrower in the case of institutional liability than is the case in respect of the individual liability of a clinician. This would appear to follow from the higher level of obligation imposed upon institutions to comply with guidance, as reflected both in the mandatory funding requirement attached to technology appraisal guidance and NICE's ambition to ensure that 'our guidance and advice needs to be put into practice effectively to have any impact on the health of the population and the quality of health care provided', realized through 'a substantial programme of implementation support to motivate and encourage change in practice'.[155] This is distinct from the explicit preservation of individual clinical judgment in the treatment of particular patients.[156] Consequently, it is difficult, albeit perhaps not

[149] For further discussion, see para 7.101.

[150] The National Institute for Health and Care Excellence (Constitution and Functions) Regulations and the Health and Social Care Information Centre (Functions) Regulations 2013, SI 2013/259, regs 7(6) and 8(6).

[151] <http://www.nice.org.uk/about/what-we-do/our-programmes/nice-guidance>. However, see paras 7.101–7.112 for discussion of compliance with clinical guidelines as a duty in public law.

[152] I Kennedy and A Grubb, *Medical Law* (3rd edn, Butterworths 2000) 125 (emphasis in original).

[153] NICE, *The Legal Implications of NICE Guidance* (NICE 2009).

[154] B Hurwitz, 'How Does Evidence-based Guidance Influence Determinations of Medical Negligence?' (2004) 329 BMJ 1024, 1025. See also A Samanta, J Samanta, and M Gunn, 'Legal Considerations of Clinical Guidelines: Will NICE Make a Difference?' (2003) 96 Journal of the Royal Society of Medicine 133; A Samanta, M Mello, C Foster, J Tingle, and J Samanta, 'The Role of Clinical Guidelines in Medical Negligence Litigation: A Shift from the *Bolam* Standard?' (2006) 14 Med L Rev 321; R Fearnley, M Bell, and A Bodenham, 'Status of National Guidelines in Dictating Individual Clinical Practice and Defining Negligence' (2012) 108 British Journal of Anaesthesia 557.

[155] NICE, *NICE Charter* (NICE 2013) para 34.

[156] NICE, n 153, 3.

entirely impossible, to envisage a situation in which non-implementation of guidance by an institution would not amount to an organizational failure which could give rise to direct liability in negligence.

C. Liability in Public Law

7.64 Institutions which provide publicly funded health services may be subject to liability through the mechanisms of public law, in particular by means of the judicial review of administrative action. A successful challenge in judicial review will not normally give rise to an award of damages and the judgment of the court merely obliges the institution to retake its decision in accordance with the law as articulated.[157] Nonetheless, judicial review has, over the past two decades in particular, emerged as a potent tool in the hands of individuals who seek to place pressure on NHS institutions to provide treatments or services to which they have been denied access, generally—albeit not exclusively—on grounds of scarcity of resources. This has prompted institutions to put in place more robust processes for allocative decision-making, especially for the consideration of 'exceptional circumstances' which might justify a departure from a general policy on provision of a particular treatment or service.

7.65 This form of liability raises contentious questions of judicial competence. Judges were formerly deferential toward decision-making on the allocation of resources for health, on grounds that courts lack the institutional expertise to judge questions of clinical and cost-effectiveness, that allocative decisions are necessarily polycentric and thus unsuited to adversarial adjudicatory processes, and that such decisions are the proper constitutional province of elected officials, or those to whom the latter have delegated authority. This stance is reflected in the earlier case law in the field. However, in more recent cases, while continuing to dismiss arguments based upon alleged violation of the Human Rights Act 1998, the courts have evinced a concern for health as an important 'interest' of the individual which warrants protection, primarily through the imposition of certain *procedural* obligations upon the institution, albeit that they remain largely reluctant to disturb the substance of the decision which has been reached.[158]

7.66 Liability in judicial review cases is traditionally classified by way of the grounds adumbrated by Lord Diplock in *Council of Civil Service Unions v Minister for the Civil Service*,[159] consisting of illegality, irrationality, and procedural impropriety. Here, the focus is upon the *categories of institutional actions or decisions* which may give rise to liability and the discussion will be organized accordingly.

1. Failure to provide a service

7.67 Although the legal framework of the NHS is not formulated (at least, primarily)[160] in terms of individual *rights* to treatment, a number of statutory duties arise under the National Health Service Act 2006 (as amended by the Health and Social Care Act 2012),[161] and

[157] See further paras. 7.134–7.138. For a general account of the law relating to judicial review, see H Woolf, J Jowell, A LeSueur, C Donnelly, and I Hare, *De Smith's Judicial Review* (7th edn, Sweet & Maxwell 2013).

[158] For a fuller discussion, see Newdick, n 60, ch 5, and for a conceptual and comparative analysis, see Syrett, n 2.

[159] [1985] AC 374 (HL).

[160] The NHS Constitution (2015) enshrines in one document certain pre-existing statutory and common law rights relating to health care. For further discussion, see paras 1.74–1.84.

[161] See Chapter 1.

institutions operating within this structure must properly comprehend the law which regulates their decision-making powers and give proper effect to it. Failure to do so may give rise to judicial review on grounds of illegality.

The question of whether a failure to provide health services gives rise to a cause of action (here, under the National Health Service Act 1977) first arose in *R v Secretary of State for Social Services, ex p Hincks*,[162] in which it was contended that a decision by the Secretary of State not to provide orthopaedic facilities in the West Midlands area amounted to a failure to comply with the duty to provide a comprehensive health service and hospital accommodation and medical services under ss 1 and 3(1) of the Act respectively. The Court of Appeal held that the statutory duty was not absolute and had to be read subject to an implied qualification relating to the availability of resources. This conclusion was upheld in *R v North and East Devon Health Authority, ex p Coughlan*, in which Lord Woolf MR observed that: **7.68**

> The truth is that, while [the Secretary of State] has the duty to continue to promote a comprehensive free health service and he must never, in making a decision under section 3, disregard that duty, a comprehensive health service may never, for human, financial and other resource reasons, be achievable. Recent history has demonstrated that the pace of developments as to what is possible by way of medical treatment, coupled with the ever increasing expectations of the public, mean that the resources of the NHS are and are likely to continue, at least in the foreseeable future, to be insufficient to meet demand.[163]

This passage makes it clear that it is perfectly lawful to have regard to the scarcity of resources in reaching decisions on the provision of health care services and treatments, even if the consequence is that there is no provision, or limited provision, in certain instances. It follows that it is open to NHS institutions to adopt a policy which gives priority to the funding of certain treatments over others, and in which treatments of lower priority are only funded if sufficient resources remain available, especially in view of their statutory duty not to exceed annual financial allocations.[164] Authority for this proposition comes from *R v North West Lancashire Health Authority, ex p A, D and G*, in which the applicants sought funding for treatment, by means of gender reassignment therapy, for gender identity dysphoria (transsexualism). It was noted that: **7.69**

> it is an unhappy but unavoidable feature of state funded health care that Regional Health Authorities have to establish certain priorities in funding different treatments from their finite resources. It is natural that each Authority, in establishing its own priorities, will give greater priority to life-threatening and other grave illnesses than to others obviously less demanding of medical intervention. The precise allocation and weighting of priorities is clearly a matter of judgment for each Authority, keeping well in mind its statutory obligations to meet the reasonable requirements of all those within its area for which it is responsible. It makes sense to have a policy for the purpose—indeed, it might well be irrational not to have one—and it makes sense too that, in settling on such a policy, an Authority would normally place treatment of transsexualism lower in its scale of priorities than, say, cancer or heart disease or kidney failure.[165]

The apparent implication of this passage is that institutions have virtually unlimited discretion as to the allocation of resources and the establishment of priorities, subject only to a minimal level of judicial scrutiny to ensure that statutory duties are not wholly disregarded and/or that the discretion to allocate resources is not exercised in such a manner that the **7.70**

162 (1980) 1 BMLR 93 (CA).
163 [2001] QB 213, [25] (CA).
164 See National Health Service Act 2006, ss 223B, C, and, H.
165 [2000] 1 WLR 977, 991 (CA) *per* Auld LJ.

decision reached or policy adopted is irrational. This was, indeed, the stance adopted by the courts in early cases in this field, such as *R v Central Birmingham Health Authority, ex p Walker*[166] and *R v Central Birmingham Health Authority, ex p Collier*,[167] two factually similar cases in which minors with clinical needs for heart procedures were denied treatment due to shortages, respectively, of staff and intensive care facilities. Despite expressing sympathy for the children, the Court of Appeal in each instance refused to declare the Health Authority's actions unlawful, implicitly alluding to a lack of constitutional and institutional competence when observing that the 'courts of this country cannot arrange the lists in the hospital',[168] albeit preserving a theoretical capacity to intervene in a situation where the allocation of resources could be considered unreasonable in the extreme, *Wednesbury* sense, viz that the decision is 'so unreasonable that no reasonable authority could ever have come to it'.[169]

7.71 However, in subsequent cases, courts have evinced greater willingness to intervene to control the exercise of institutional discretion in this context. In particular, while remaining largely attentive to the need not to disturb the substance of an allocative decision, judges have sought to impose obligations of explanation upon institutions whose choices serve to deny access to a health care treatment or service. The impetus for this approach was provided by Laws J's judgment in the High Court in the leading case of *R v Cambridge Health Authority, ex p B*, which centred upon the refusal of the authority to provide funding for an admittedly experimental form of treatment for a ten-year-old child's acute lymphoblastic leukaemia. While acknowledging that judges should not make orders which would carry implications for the allocation of health care resources in ignorance of the wider consequences, Laws J drew attention to the fact that the child's right to life was engaged by the refusal to provide the treatment and held that the failure to provide a 'substantial objective justification' for a decision which interfered with that right rendered the decision unlawful: he did not consider that it was sufficient to 'toll the bell of tight resources', holding that the authority 'must explain the priorities which have led them to decline to fund the treatment'.[170]

7.72 Although the decision of the High Court was overturned by the Court of Appeal, which reverted to the passive stance witnessed in *Walker* and *Collier* in holding that '[d]ifficult and agonising judgments have to be made as to how a limited budget is best allocated to the maximum advantage of the maximum number of patients. That is not a judgment which the court can make',[171] the justificatory requirement which characterized the judgment of Laws J has been reiterated—albeit not in identical terms—in a number of subsequent cases. In *R v North Derbyshire Health Authority, ex p Fisher*,[172] a failure to provide treatment by way of beta-interferon for multiple sclerosis was declared unlawful, in part because the authority had failed to provide clear reasons for its departure from government guidance on provision of the drug. In *R v Secretary of State for Health, ex p Pfizer*,[173] the decision to exclude Viagra from availability on the NHS, except in limited circumstances, was held to amount to a failure to comply with the terms of Article 7(3) of Directive 89/105/EEC (the 'Transparency Directive'), which require that any decision to exclude a medicinal product

---

166 (1987) 3 BMLR 32 (CA).

167 *R v Central Birmingham Health Authority, ex p Collier*, 6 January 1988 (CA).

168 ibid *per* Simon Brown LJ.

169 *Associated Provincial Picture Houses v Wednesbury Corporation* [1948] 1 KB 223, 230 (CA) *per* Lord Greene MR.

170 [1995] 1 FLR 1055, 1065.

171 [1995] 1 WLR 898, 906 *per* Sir Thomas Bingham MR.

172 (1997) 8 Med LR 327.

173 [1999] Lloyd's Med Rep 289.

from the coverage of a national health system should 'contain a statement of reasons based on objective and verifiable criteria'. And in the *North West Lancashire Health Authority* case, Buxton LJ stated that, to the extent that treatment by way of gender reassignment procedures continued to occupy a low position in the authority's list of priorities, there was an obligation to 'indicate, at least in broad terms, the reasons for the authority's choice'.[174]

Though couched in the language of 'interests' rather than 'rights'—and notwithstanding that the court had summarily dismissed arguments based upon the Human Rights Act 1998 in this case—Buxton LJ's judgment demonstrates the impact of rights-based reasoning in this field. His Lordship argued that: **7.73**

> the more important the interest of the citizen that the decision affects, the greater will be the degree of consideration that is required of the decision-maker. A decision that, as is the evidence in this case, seriously affects the citizen's health will require substantial consideration, and be subject to careful scrutiny by the court as to its rationality.[175]

In so doing, he was clearly echoing the views of Laws J, both as expressed in *ex p B* and in a 1993 article in which the latter had argued for replacement of the *Wednesbury* standard with proportionality on the basis that this would enable a court to insist that a decision-maker 'accord[s] the first priority to the right in question unless he can show a substantial, objective, public justification for overriding it'.[176] Although the standard of review adopted in these cases is not explicitly labelled as proportionality, the explanatory burden imposed by the courts strongly resembles that which forms a key component of this test. Accordingly, at common law, an institution which seeks to avoid liability for a failure to provide a service or treatment is likely to have to justify its choice (or its policy on priorities) in order to demonstrate to the court that there is an overriding public interest rationale for the interference with an individual's interest (that is, his/her health) which arises from denial of access.

This development is to be welcomed. As commentators have noted,[177] the Court of Appeal decisions in *Walker, Collier* and *ex p B* failed to distinguish adequately between substantive and procedural review, the former being outwith the constitutional competence of the court, but the latter representing a wholly legitimate public law approach. The imposition of an explanatory obligation in cases of this type may be seen as an illustration of the capacity of courts to facilitate decision-making by articulating standards of good administration. By insisting upon a degree of transparency in the allocation of resources, the courts are contributing to the realization of accountability—a value which has commonly been regarded as deficient within the NHS—and furthermore, to the attainment of legitimacy for 'rationing' decisions which are characteristically subject to high levels of moral and political contestation.[178] Simultaneously, they are stopping short of improper involvement in the substance of allocative decisions. **7.74**

The common law position has been reinforced by secondary legislation made by the Secretary of State in connection with the NHS Constitution. The latter, which applies only to the NHS in England, informs a patient that: 'you have the right to expect local decisions on funding of other drugs and treatments to be made rationally following a proper consideration of the evidence. If the local NHS decides not to fund a drug or treatment you **7.75**

[174] *North West Lancashire Health Authority*, [2000] 1 WLR 977, 1000.
[175] ibid, 997.
[176] J Laws, 'Is the High Court the Guardian of Fundamental Constitutional Rights?' [1993] PL 59, 74.
[177] See, eg, R James, and D Longley, 'Judicial Review and Tragic Choices: *ex parte B*' [1995] PL 367; A Parkin, 'Allocating Health Care Resources in an Imperfect World' (1995) 58 MLR 867.
[178] See Syrett, n 2, generally, but especially ch 9.

and your doctor feel would be right for you, they will explain that decision to you.'[179] The Regulations oblige relevant bodies (defined as the NHS Commissioning Board and Clinical Commissioning Groups) to provide, upon request, a written statement of reasons for a general policy on the availability (or otherwise) of a particular health care intervention, except where a statement of reasons for its policy has been published on its website; and to provide an individual whose request for funding for a particular intervention has been refused in accordance with the policy with a written statement of reasons (in such a case, there is no requirement for the individual to issue a request for the statement).[180] The precise nature of the reasons which might be offered is not stipulated, but earlier best practice guidance refers to the need to clearly define and consistently apply standard criteria for decision-making. Such decisions should be based upon the best available evidence (including evidence on clinical, cost-effectiveness, and patient safety), take into account appropriate ethical frameworks, and comply with statutory requirements.[181]

7.76 In a previous edition of this text, it was observed that adherence to Laws J's approach in *ex p B* would have had far-reaching implications since: 'it would, in effect, have meant that Health Authorities do something which they (and central government) have been scrupulous in avoiding. It would have required the Health Authority to make *explicit* the principles by reference to which resource allocation (or rationing) was determined.'[182] Such a statement points to the significance of the politico-economic context in which the law operates in this field: previous judicial reluctance to demand explanation of the principles on which allocative decisions were based might be regarded as appropriate in an environment in which health institutions themselves were unprepared to be transparent about the resource-driven nature of the choices being made. Consequently, any deviation from this approach might have triggered the systemically deleterious outcome of:

> more widely exposing the 'reality' that recommendations purportedly based upon clinical considerations were in fact dictated by limitations upon resources [and] . . . could have had the effect of severely weakening—if not severing altogether—the bonds of trust between physician, patient and public upon which rested the legitimacy of the entire framework of implicit rationing.[183]

7.77 However, the pattern of implicit rationing—in which allocative decisions were concealed behind a 'veil' of clinical judgment—was beginning to break down by the date of the decision in *ex p B* in 1995, primarily as a result of the introduction of the 'internal market' in the NHS which separated the purchasing and provision functions. The establishment of NICE in 1999 added further impetus to the shift to explicit priority-setting in so far as publicly visible criteria and evidence of clinical and cost-effectiveness were applied to decisions on the availability of new treatments on the NHS. In this environment of explicit

[179] NHS Constitution, n 160, s 3(a). This right, which is legally binding, is supported by a non-binding 'pledge' to 'make decisions in a clear and transparent way, so that patients and the public can understand how services are planned and delivered'. There are no directly equivalent instruments to the Constitution elsewhere in the UK, but see, for Scotland, *Making Difficult Decisions in NHS Boards in Scotland: Report of a short-life working group* (2010), especially ch 5; and for Wales, the 'Policy for Interventions Not Normally Undertaken' of each Health Board, eg, Cardiff and Wales University Health Board, Ref. UHB 009 (2014) and NHS Wales, *All Wales Prioritisation Framework* (2011).

[180] The National Health Service Commissioning Board and Clinical Commissioning Groups (Responsibilities and Standing Rules) Regulations 2012, SI 2012/2996, reg. 35.

[181] Department of Health/National Prescribing Centre, *Defining Guiding Principles for Processes Supporting Local Decision Making about Medicines* (2009) 19. See also NICE, *Developing and Updating Local Formularies* (NICE 2012).

[182] 2nd edn, para 8.73.

[183] K Syrett, 'Impotence or Importance? Judicial Review in an Era of Explicit NHS Rationing' (2004) 67 MLR 289, 297.

rationing—which has now, in effect, been enshrined in law by way of the NHS Constitution and its attendant Regulations[184]—it is clearly appropriate that decision-makers should be obliged to be transparent about priority-setting.[185] What is regrettable is that this development has not yet unequivocally had the effect of stimulating 'a development many consider long overdue, a proper, political discussion about rationing'.[186] Commentators and influential stakeholders continue to call for a comprehensive public debate upon the present and future scope of the NHS and upon the principles which should underpin the inevitable choices on the treatments and services which can be provided in the face of scarcity of resources.[187] Yet, although the issue now attracts widespread media and public interest—in part due to court cases such as those discussed here, which have received extensive media coverage—government remains reluctant to instigate a broad debate of this kind, which it judges will prove to be electorally unpopular.[188]

At least to date, the existence of the NHS Constitution has not appeared to make a significant difference to the likelihood of the inception of such a debate, notwithstanding that the 'Guiding Principles' which flesh out the right to expect a rational decision refer to the need for NHS institutions to engage with the public to help to increase understanding of local priority-setting, including the provision of explanations of why prioritization is necessary.[189] **7.78**

Failure to provide a service constitutes, in broad terms, the main basis upon which individuals are likely to bring a public law action against an institution. However, there are a number of variants of this form of challenge which are worthy of specific attention. These will now be examined. **7.79**

2. Blanket bans and exceptionality

As explicit strategies of rationing began to develop in the NHS during the 1990s, a number of Health Authority purchasing plans stated openly that specific (primarily 'marginal') forms of treatment, such as tattoo removal, reversal of sterilization or vasectomy, and breast augmentation, would not be made available to the populations for whom they were responsible.[190] Although this approach was subsequently somewhat modified in so far as managers sought to negotiate guidelines and protocols with clinicians which would specify the conditions which were eligible for treatment by means of a particular intervention,[191] the question nonetheless arose as to whether an institution might lawfully refuse to provide funding for a particular treatment to all categories of patient, irrespective of their clinical need; or, **7.80**

---

[184] See para 7.75.

[185] This is not to argue that all allocative decisions in the NHS are now explicit: 'bedside rationing' by physicians is often implicit (eg denial may be based upon the patient's age, without this fact being explicitly acknowledged) and is widespread. For a discussion of this form of allocation, see M Danis, L Fleck, S Hurst, R Førde, and A-M Slowther (eds), *Fair Resource Allocation and Rationing at the Bedside* (Oxford University Press 2015).

[186] See n 182.

[187] See, eg, British Medical Association, *A Rational Way Forward for the NHS in England* (BMA 2007); B Rumbold, V Akelson, and P Smith, *Rationing Health Care: Is It Time to Set Out More Clearly What Is Funded by the NHS?* (Nuffield Trust 2012); E Bidgood, *Rationing in the NHS in the Current Fiscal Climate* (Civitas 2012); Hansard, HC vol 548 cols. 814–22 (16 July 2012).

[188] One of the best-known attempts to establish an explicit list of services and treatments is the Oregon Health Plan in the USA. For discussion of some of the difficulties to which this has given rise, see J Oberlander, 'Health Reform Interrupted: The Unraveling of the Oregon Health Plan' (2007) 26 Health Affairs w96.

[189] *Defining Guiding Principles for Processes Supporting Local Decision Making about Medicines*, n 181, 24.

[190] See Klein, Day, and Redmayne, n 119, 68–70.

[191] ibid, 71–72.

alternatively, whether all patients exhibiting certain characteristics (such as smokers, alcoholics, or the obese) could be excluded from treatment.[192]

7.81 The issue first arose in the courts in the litigation concerning Viagra,[193] which—for reasons of cost—the government had decided to exclude from availability on the NHS, except in limited clinical circumstances. The unlawfulness here arose, in part, from the fact that the mandatory terminology utilized by the Secretary of State (in guidance which purported merely to be of an advisory nature) acted as an improper constraint upon the professional judgment which GPs were expected to exercise in determining which treatments were necessary and appropriate under their statutory Terms of Service, the court holding that the latter should not be overridden without an explanation of why it was necessary to do so. The court's decision did not, however, preclude the Secretary of State from issuing Regulations under the National Health Service Act 1977 which added Viagra to the schedule of drugs whose availability on the NHS was limited to specified medical conditions or classes of patient ('the grey list'),[194] which action was subsequently undertaken. This decision was also challenged in judicial review,[195] the Court of Appeal stating, obiter,[196] that the decision on non-availability was an essentially 'political' one given its connection to resources, with which the court was not competent to interfere.

7.82 However, use of the 'black' and 'grey' lists does not constitute the primary mechanism by which a generalized policy of non-availability is likely to be effected: indeed, the initial decision on Viagra has been described as 'perhaps the first explicit, national rationing decision in the history of the NHS'.[197] In practice, such a decision is far more likely to occur at local level, as a Trust (or now, a Clinical Commissioning Group) or Health Board sets priorities for funding. Such a scenario arose in the *North West Lancashire Health Authority* case.[198] Here, the authority had placed gender reassignment surgery as a treatment for transsexualism low on its list of priorities for expenditure, alongside 'marginal' interventions such as varicose vein removal, reversal of sterilization and tattoo removal. The policy did not, on its face, wholly eliminate the possibility of treatment by this means, since it provided for exceptional funding in cases of 'overriding clinical need'. However, the Court of Appeal held that there was, in practice, no opportunity for the applicants to demonstrate such need (thereby assigning their cases to the category of exceptionality), since evidence given by the authority indicated that it did not consider transsexualism to amount to an illness, nor gender reassignment surgery an effective form of treatment for it. As Auld LJ noted,

[192] Similar policies have been adopted in more recent times, in the light of the drive for the NHS to make up to £20 billion of efficiency savings by 2015. See, eg, A Robinson, 'The NHS no longer lets GPs like me offer routine operations' *Guardian* (20 January 2012); 'Obese and smokers being denied treatment to "save money"' *Daily Telegraph* (7 March 2012); *Hansard*, HC vol 589 cols. 1089–98 (14 December 2014).

[193] *R v Secretary of State for Health, ex p Pfizer* [1999] Lloyd's Med Rep 289.

[194] For a useful discussion of the 'grey' and 'black' lists, see Newdick, n 60, 113–14 and Chapter 1, paras 1.108–1.109.

[195] *R (on the application of Pfizer Ltd) v Secretary of State for Health* [2003] 1 CMLR 19 (CA). For discussion, see Syrett, n 183.

[196] The primary issue in the case was compliance with the 'Transparency Directive', for which see n 173 and accompanying text. The Court of Appeal held that the statement provided by the UK government to the EC Commission—which referred to the cost of providing Viagra on the NHS but did not seek to prioritize it vis-à-vis other non- life-threatening conditions—was sufficient to comply with the 'fairly modest' degree of transparency required by the Directive: ibid, [27] *per* Buxton LJ.

[197] R Klein, 'Setting Priorities: What is Holding Us Back—Inadequate Information or Inadequate Institutions?' in A Coulter and C Ham (eds), *The Global Challenge of Health Care Rationing* (Open University Press 2000) 25.

[198] *North West Lancashire Health Authority*, [2000] 1 WLR 977.

this stance made a 'nonsense of the policy [of exceptionality] if, as a matter of its medical judgment, there is no effective treatment for it for which there could be an overriding clinical need'.[199] Consequently, it amounted in effect to an over-rigid application of a 'blanket policy' which did not genuinely admit of exceptions based upon consideration of individual circumstances.

The decision in this case has two consequences for institutions which would seek to avoid liability for decisions taken in accordance with a general policy not to provide funding for a particular treatment, or to exclude certain categories of patient from access to treatment. The first is that a simple 'blanket ban' is likely to be unlawful, with the possible exception of situations where the treatment in question is considered by strong medical opinion to be ineffective.[200] Accordingly, any policy on priorities should make provision for the consideration of exceptional cases. This is an application of the general principle of administrative law that mere application of a general policy without proper consideration of whether a particular case should constitute an exception is unlawful as a fetter on discretion.[201] **7.83**

Second—and perhaps more challenging—the institution must give *proper effect* to any policy of exceptionality. It must be genuinely possible for an applicant with exceptional circumstances to persuade the institution to depart from its general policy. In *R (on the application of Rogers) v Swindon NHS Primary Care Trust and Secretary of State for Health*,[202] the PCT, in line with its policy not to fund drugs which had not yet received licensing and regulatory approval by the European Medicines Agency and NICE, refused to fund treatment by means of the breast cancer drug Herceptin. There was provision for departure from the policy in exceptional circumstances, with any application to this effect being considered by the Urgency Panel of the PCT's Clinical Priorities Committee. The applicant's argument of exceptionality having been rejected, she sought judicial review of the PCT's decision to refuse funding. The Court of Appeal found in her favour, holding (on the authority of the *North West Lancashire Health Authority* case) that, while a policy on the prioritization of funding for treatment which provided for exceptions in unidentified circumstances was not per se arbitrary and hence unlawful, a policy of exceptionality would only be rational if 'it is possible to envisage, and the decision-maker does envisage, what such exceptional circumstances might be'.[203] That was not the case in this instance since, absent resource considerations (which the PCT had indicated should be disregarded),[204] the only criterion which could be used to establish exceptionality was clinical need: however, the PCT had not advanced any evidence to suggest that distinctions could in fact be made between patients on clinical grounds. Accordingly, it was impossible to envisage any exceptional circumstances which would justify provision of funding for one patient and denial for another—the policy acted, in effect as a blanket ban on treatment with Herceptin, notwithstanding the purported provision for exceptionality. **7.84**

[199] ibid, 993.

[200] See *R v Sheffield Health Authority, ex p Seale* (1995) 25 BMLR 1, 3, discussed in Newdick, n 60, 106–07. For the relevance of NICE guidance in this regard, see further para 7.109.

[201] See *R v Port of London Authority, ex p Kynoch* [1919] 1 KB 176; *British Oxygen Co. v Board of Trade* [1971] AC 610 (HL).

[202] *R (on the application of Rogers) v Swindon NHS Primary Care Trust and Secretary of State for Health* [2006] 1 WLR 2649. For discussion, see K Syrett, 'Opening Eyes to the Reality of Scarce Resources?' [2006] PL 664.

[203] ibid, [62] *per* Sir Anthony Clarke MR.

[204] This seemingly counter-intuitive stance (given that the total cost of a full course of treatment with the drug was estimated at £26,328.22 including VAT: ibid, [5]) represented a somewhat misguided effort to give effect to guidance issued by the Secretary of State, which had stated that 'PCTs should not refuse to fund Herceptin solely on the grounds of its cost': ibid, [28].

7.85 Similarly, in *R (on the application of Ross) v West Sussex Primary Care Trust*[205] the Trust did not routinely fund treatment of multiple myeloma with the drug lenalidomide, which had not yet been appraised by NICE, but it made provision for exceptionality by means of an Individual Cases Policy. However, the decision to refuse funding for the applicant's treatment on the basis that his case did not fall within the exceptionality policy was held by the High Court to be unlawful, since 'it [was] difficult, if not impossible, to envisage who and in what circumstances might be successful in overcoming this hurdle [viz, of exceptionality] in respect of the drug'.[206] The court reached this conclusion because the Trust's policy provided that an application must be refused when an individual was representative of a group of patients: this meant that a person would automatically be disqualified if he could be likened to another, with the consequence that it would be necessary to show 'uniqueness' to qualify. In addition to the fact that this rendered the decision flawed as a result of a misunderstanding of the meaning of 'exceptional', it was also, in practical terms, impossible for the policy of exceptionality to be fulfilled since it would always be possible for another patient to emerge who was appropriately comparable, depending upon the basis on which comparability was defined.

7.86 The concept of 'exceptionality' is unclear and highly fact-dependent.[207] Case law provides only limited assistance in establishing a definition. In *R (on the application of Gordon) v Bromley NHS Primary Care Trust*,[208] funding for treatment with elotinib for lung cancer was refused by the Trust's Exceptional Cases Group, the claimant not being considered 'radically different' from other patients with the same condition.[209] The court considered that permission to apply for judicial review of this decision should be granted because the basis for the decision was unclear,[210] in line with the principles articulated in the cases considered in paras 7.71–7.72. However, Ouseley J noted that one of the factors which went to this question was the existence of exceptions. He indicated that the need for short-term survival (such as the requirement to make care arrangements for young children) might amount to exceptional circumstances,[211] although the judge also observed that 'the fact that the claimant may have some [clinical] factors suggesting that she could benefit more than many others does not mean that she has to be treated as an exception'.

7.87 Ford is critical of this latter dictum on the basis that 'gaining more benefit from a treatment than might normally be expected is one of the few clinical justifications for treating a patient as an exceptional case'.[212] However, a different stance was taken in *R (on the application of Otley) v Barking and Dagenham Primary Care Trust*,[213] in which the court considered that factors such as the patient's age and relatively fit state of health, absence of side effects, and adverse response to alternative forms of treatment,[214] did point to an increased likelihood of benefitting from the treatment which had been denied and contributed to making her case exceptional.

---

[205] *R (on the application of Ross) v West Sussex Primary Care Trust* (2009) 106 BMLR 1.
[206] ibid, [77] *per* HH Judge Grenfell.
[207] See A Ford, 'The Concept of Exceptionality: a Legal Farce?' (2012) 20 Med L Rev 304. See also now *S v NHS England* [2016] EWHC 1395 (Admin).
[208] *R (on the application of Gordon) v Bromley NHS Primary Care Trust* [2006] EWHC 2462 (Admin).
[209] ibid, [16].
[210] ibid, [43].
[211] ibid, [41].
[212] n 207, 325.
[213] *R (on the application of Otley) v Barking and Dagenham Primary Care Trust* [2007] EWHC 1927 (Admin).
[214] ibid, [20].

One clear principle which emerges from the case law is that it is necessary for decision-makers to consider exceptionality holistically, rather than factor by factor. In *R (on the application of Murphy) v Salford Primary Care Trust*,[215] the patient sought access to a drug for the treatment of kidney cancer which was not routinely funded by the Trust. She had identified seven factors as relevant to her claim of exceptionality, each of which was considered by the Trust but rejected as insufficient on its own. Burnett J observed that 'when any decision-maker is concerned to decide whether a policy exceptionally should be departed from, there will inevitably come a stage in the decision-making process when a general, all-round question must be asked and answered',[216] and while he did not consider that all of the factors advanced by the patient carried weight, it was an error not to look at all of the circumstances in the round. **7.88**

A controversial issue which arose in *Murphy* and several of the other preceding cases is the extent to which social factors may be relevant to a claim of exceptionality. Do circumstances such as caring for a sick husband (*Murphy*),[217] making care arrangements for young children (*Gordon*: obiter),[218] or caring for a disabled child (*Rogers*: obiter)[219] constitute factors which might contribute to establishing the patient's case as exceptional? This question was answered in *R (on the application of Condliff) v North Staffordshire Primary Care Trust*.[220] **7.89**

In this instance, the Trust had adopted a policy which explicitly excluded consideration of social factors from its assessment of exceptionality. The claimant argued that this amounted to a violation of his right to respect for private and family life under Article 8 of the European Convention on Human Rights, as given effect by the Human Rights Act 1998. At first instance,[221] Waksman J held that it was not unlawful for such factors to be excluded, pointing to the practical difficulty of investigating the credibility of claims relating to such factors and the unfairness of taking them into account for the patient when the social factors affecting individuals in the cohort in relation to which exceptionality was being claimed were unknown.[222] He also concurred with the Trust's rationale for exclusion of such factors, viz that they might prove discriminatory (for example, prioritization of treatment which kept individuals in paid work would discriminate against the retired; according preference to carers would tend to favour women over men, etc.).[223] It would therefore appear that it is not unlawful to fail to consider social factors when evaluating exceptionality, save perhaps that it may be obligatory to scrutinize such factors if they have direct clinical implications.[224] **7.90**

The obligation to have regard to individual circumstances in the exercise of discretion on the allocation of funds has now been given statutory force. As part of their arrangements for reaching decisions and adopting policies on whether health care interventions should be made available for their population, Clinical Commissioning Groups and the NHS Commissioning Board are required to 'include arrangements for the determination of requests for the funding of a health care intervention for a person, where there is no relevant NICE recommendation and the relevant body's general policy is not to fund that **7.91**

[215] *R (on the application of Murphy) v Salford Primary Care Trust* [2008] EWHC 1908 (Admin).
[216] ibid, [30].
[217] ibid, [31].
[218] n 211.
[219] n 202, [77].
[220] *R (on the application of Condliff) v North Staffordshire Primary Care Trust* [2011] EWHC 872 (Admin).
[221] The decision was upheld on appeal: [2011] EWCA Civ 910.
[222] *R (on the application of Condliff)*, n 220, [65].
[223] ibid, [10].
[224] ibid, [23]. Ford suggests that relevant factors of this type might include homelessness, domestic abuse or refugee status: n 207, 321.

intervention'.[225] In practice, internal panels have been established to consider 'individual funding requests' of this type, and the handbook on decision-making processes which was issued to accompany the original version of the *NHS Constitution* emphasized that grounds upon which such requests can be made should be clearly defined, that rationales should be provided for decisions, that decisions should be communicated in a timely and sensitive manner and that an appeals process which is independent of the original panel decision should be available.[226]

7.92 NHS institutions appear likely to face an increasing number of high-profile individual funding requests as advances in genetics, stem cell technology, and nanotechnology offer the prospect of tailoring future care more closely to the needs of individual patients (for example, by the use of so-called 'targeted' cancer treatments). Such treatments are unlikely to form part of the normal package of commissioned care for two reasons: first, since they cannot, by definition, be mass-produced, they will inevitably be costly; and secondly, they are likely only to be appropriate to a very small number of patients within a given population. It is therefore important that the commitments to transparent and robust procedures in situations of exceptionality which accompany the right to rational decision-making are honoured as far as is possible, since this should contribute to public understanding and acceptance of the process of priority-setting in this context.[227]

7.93 It should not, however, be readily assumed that the incidence of legal challenges of the type described in this section will necessarily decrease as a consequence of the imposition of these procedural obligations upon decision-makers. Judicial review may continue to offer strategic advantages to patients who seek to establish exceptionality, not least that courts often appear to be more willing than internal panels to favour the individual. This stance is ethically questionable since, as observed by a member of the Individual Cases Review Panel in the *Ross* case, it has the consequence of diverting resources from a larger population of unidentified patients towards a single identified individual.[228] It is therefore to be hoped that courts will be suitably sympathetic to attempts by institutions to fulfil procedural standards and that they will intervene only in circumstances where the decision has been tainted by genuine unfairness to the individual.

3. Withdrawal of service

7.94 'Rationing by denial' normally takes the form of a refusal on the part of a health decision-maker to provide funding for a particular treatment or intervention to which an individual has not previously had access. Withdrawal of treatment once commenced gives rise to particular ethical concerns,[229] and to do so for reasons of resources would appear to be especially problematic. However, issues of liability may be engaged in cases where a decision is taken to close a facility which offers health services to the public.

[225] The National Health Service Commissioning Board and Clinical Commissioning Groups (Responsibilities and Standing Rules) Regulations 2012, n 180, reg 34(2)(b). For Scotland, see *Good Practice Guidance for NHS Boards' Management of Individual Patient Treatment Requests*, SGHD/CMO (2011) 3 (2011); and for Wales, see NHS Wales, *All Wales Policy: Making Decisions on Individual Patient Funding Requests* (2011).

[226] Department of Health/National Prescribing Centre, n 181, 19, 23, 25.

[227] See further, generally, Syrett, n 2.

[228] (2009) 106 BMLR 1, [27]. This may be seen as an illustration of the 'rule of rescue' principle, for discussion of which see, eg, J McKie, and J Richardson, 'The Rule of Rescue' (2003) 56 Social Science and Medicine 2407.

[229] See, eg, General Medical Council, *Treatment and Care Towards the End of Life: good practice in decision-making* (2010), paras 31–36.

Such a situation arose in *Coughlan*.[230] North and East Devon Health Authority operated a residential care facility, Mardon House, which it proposed to close on the grounds that it had become 'a prohibitively expensive white elephant. The unit was not financially viable. Its continued operation was dependent upon the Authority supporting it at an excessively high cost. This did not represent value for money and left fewer resources for other services'.[231] However, the Authority had made representations to the residents that they would be able to remain at the facility for as long as they chose to live there. This promise of a 'home for life' gave rise, in the view of the Court of Appeal, to a legitimate expectation that the facility would not be closed while the residents remained. Such an expectation could have been overridden by a countervailing public interest, and it was argued on behalf of the authority that such an interest did exist in so far as continuation of the facility was uneconomic and diverted resources away from other uses. This argument was rejected by the court, which concluded that frustration of the applicant's expectation in this instance represented 'unfairness amounting to an abuse of power'.[232] Lord Woolf MR also considered that the decision to move the applicant out of the facility would amount to a breach of Article 8 of the European Convention on Human Rights, since it served to deprive her of her only home and could not be justified on the basis that it would reduce public cost, given that any savings made would be limited by the fact that the Authority would continue to be responsible for the costs of her care. This therefore represents a rare example of a court viewing human rights arguments with sympathy in an allocative context, in contrast to the *North West Lancashire Health Authority* and *Condliff* cases, discussed respectively at paras 7.73 and 7.90. **7.95**

Coughlan demonstrates that the courts may be prepared to move beyond scrutiny of decision-making procedures to the enforcement of *substantive allocative obligations* into which health bodies have entered. Clearly, this is controversial, since it entails substitution of a court's view on how limited resources should be allocated for that of the original (and constitutionally competent) decision-maker. Nonetheless, the limitations of the case should be noted. The promise was a very specific one made to a limited group of individuals.[233] It does not follow that promises of a more general kind, such as aspirations to treat all patients with a certain condition within a specified time period, will be regarded as legally enforceable as legitimate expectations, as distinct from targets for which accountability exists, if at all, only in the political arena.[234] However, liability is likely to be incurred if an NHS body promises that it will make treatment available to an individual or group of patients by means of a particular intervention and then resiles upon this on grounds of lack of resources. **7.96**

Suspension or alteration in the provision of health services may also give rise to liability where there has been a failure to consult the public. Section 242 of the National Health Service Act 2006 (as amended) imposes a duty upon Trusts and Foundation Trusts to make arrangements for public involvement in the planning of the provision of services, the development and consideration of proposals for change in the provision of services and decisions affecting the operation of health services; obligations upon NHS England and clinical commissioning groups to secure involvement of those who are or may be provided with services in arrangements for commissioning are similarly imposed by sections 13Q and 14Z2 of the Act. Both These provisions and their precursor, s 11 of the Health and Social Care Act 2001, **7.97**

[230] *Coughlan*, [2001] QB 213 (CA).
[231] ibid, [88] *per* Lord Woolf MR, citing evidence given by the Health Authority.
[232] ibid, [89].
[233] ibid, [71].
[234] Newdick, n 60, 96. For an illustration of the latter approach in another field, see *R v Department of Education and Employment, ex p Begbie* [2000] 1 WLR 1115 (CA), especially *per* Peter Gibson LJ at [56].

have formed the basis of legal challenge in instances where decisions were taken to close or reconfigure health facilities.

7.98 In *Smith v North Eastern Derbyshire Primary Care Trust*[235] the Court of Appeal held that there had been a breach of the statutory duty to consult under s 11, where the Trust had engaged in a tendering process for the provision of GP services but had not properly involved or consulted with the affected population. Recourse to a Patients' Forum,[236] which the judge at first instance had considered to constitute an alternative remedy, non-exhaustion of which was justification for refusal to grant relief, was not considered to be an adequate alternative, since the latter had no power to require the Trust to reverse its decision. Similarly, in *R (on the application of Morris) v Trafford Health Care NHS Trust*,[237] the closure of in-patient facilities without consultation amounted to a breach of s 11, Hodge J rejecting the argument advanced by the Trust that an urgent decision had to be reached on grounds of clinical safety due to a lack of doctors on the wards. However, he refused to issue an order requiring the Trust to reopen the wards pending the outcome of any consultation carried out in response to the judgment. A somewhat different approach was taken in *R (on the application of Royal Brompton and Harefield NHS Foundation Trust) v Joint Committee of Primary Care Trusts*, where the process of consultation was held to be unlawful at first instance on the basis of the frustration of a legitimate expectation that assessment criteria would be used in a particular way in reaching the final decision on configuration of facilities.[238]

7.99 The courts have not always upheld challenges based upon an alleged failure to consult.[239] In the *Brompton and Harefield* case, the Court of Appeal found that no legitimate expectation had, in fact, been created.[240] In *R (on the application of F) v Healthy Futures Joint Committee of Primary Care Trusts*,[241] an application for permission was refused where a process of consultation had taken place, but where certain non-viable options had been discarded and had not therefore been placed before the public. In *R (on the application of Fudge) v South West Strategic Health Authority*,[242] the Court of Appeal observed that the use of two terms, 'involvement' and 'consultation', in s 11 indicated that the statutory obligation was of a variable nature according to the stage which proposals had reached: in some circumstances, provision of information would suffice, while in others full consultation would be necessary.[243]

---

[235] [2006] EWCA Civ 1291.

[236] Patients' Forums were abolished by Local Government and Public Involvement in Health Act 2007, s. 231.

[237] [2006] Lloyd's Rep Med 529.

[238] [2011] EWHC 2986 (Admin).

[239] See also *R (on the application of Unison) v Secretary of State for Health* [2010] EWHC 2655 (Admin) and *R (on the application of London Borough of Ealing) v NHS England* [2013] EWHC 3255 (Admin), in both of which s 242 was used as the basis of challenge, but permission to proceed was not granted. Note also that more limited obligations of consultation exist where a special administration regime is established (for which, see paras 1.137–1.139): see *Trust Special Administrator v London Borough of Lewisham* [2013] EWCA Civ 1409, [16].

[240] [2012] EWCA Civ 472.

[241] [2007] EWHC 1611 (Admin). See further *R (on the application of Enfield BC) v Secretary of State for Health* [2009] EWHC 743 (Admin), [17] *per* Andrews QC: 'It is therefore legitimate for a Primary Care Trust to consider a range of options and to discard some of them on clinical, financial or other grounds without consultation. There is only a duty to consult on a proposal that the NHS body is actively considering it may implement.'

[242] (2007) 98 BMLR 112.

[243] In *Coughlan* and *Fudge*, this was understood to reflect the criteria established in *R v Brent LBC, ex p Gunning* (1985) 84 LGR 168: consultation must be undertaken at a time when proposals are still in a formative stage, sufficient reasons must be provided for particular proposals to permit consultees to give intelligent consideration and response, adequate time must be given and the product of consultation must be conscientiously taken into account when the ultimate decision is taken. See also *R (on the application of Moseley) v London Borough of Haringey* [2014] UKSC 56, [25].

The Local Government and Public Involvement in Health Act 2007 makes clear that the statutory duty is to be viewed as a continuum, in the manner noted by the court in *Fudge*, specifying that the duty to secure involvement of users is discharged 'whether by being consulted or provided with information, or in other ways'.[244]

It might be concluded from the above that NHS institutions which are contemplating reorganization or withdrawal of services—whether on grounds of resources or for some other reason—should remain alert to any specific representations which they have previously made to individuals and to the need to keep the wider population informed of any changes which are proposed to the pattern and menu of local services. However, it is far from certain that any challenge based upon failures in these regards will succeed, and notwithstanding the substantive dimension of review witnessed in *Coughlan*, the primary judicial focus is upon compliance with common law or statutory principles of procedural propriety,[245] as befits the overall character of the judicial review jurisdiction. **7.100**

4. Departure from evidence

'Evidence-based medicine' has come to the forefront of practice in health care over recent decades. Described as 'the conscientious, explicit, and judicious use of current best evidence in making decisions about the care of individual patients',[246] this approach entails the application of clinically relevant research (with the 'gold standard' being the randomized controlled clinical trial) in episodes of patient care. At an institutional level, it takes the form of evidence-based guidelines which offer indications as to best practice in the management of particular conditions, but which also offer a means of addressing the mismatch between the demand for and supply of resources for health care. This is so in so far as guidelines may enable the identification of ineffective treatments and allow resources to be freed from these, as well as serving to reduce inappropriate variations in clinical practice.[247] The resource rationale is most visible in situations where evidence is also gathered of the *cost-effectiveness* of a particular intervention, utilizing the tools of health economics, notably the Quality-Adjusted Life Year (QALY). It is the deployment of such methodologies as a dimension of its work that has led to claims that NICE—which describes itself as providing 'advice on effective, good value health care'[248]—is, in reality, an agent for rationing.[249] **7.101**

In public law, unlawfulness on the ground of irrationality may be established where there is no evidence upon which a decision may be based, or where the evidence is not reasonably capable of supporting the decision. Relatedly, a decision-maker is expected to take account of relevant factors—which might include any evidence which has a bearing upon the choice made—and to disregard any irrelevant considerations. In this context, these fundamental principles of judicial review give rise to the question of whether an institution will be liable if it departs from evidence when reaching a decision on the treatment of an individual, which will necessarily normally be one to deny access to a particular intervention. **7.102**

---

244 s 233(2), substituting sub-s 1B in s 242 of the National Health Service Act 2006.

245 See especially *Unison* and *London Borough of Ealing*, n 239, at [13] and [3] respectively.

246 D Sackett, W Rosenberg, J Muir Gray et al, 'Evidence-based Medicine: What It Is and What it Isn't' (1996) 312 BMJ 71, 71.

247 See, eg, J Grimshaw and A Hutchinson, 'Clinical Practice Guidelines: Do They Enhance Value for Money in Health Care?' (1995) 51 British Medical Bulletin 927; N Freemantle, 'Dealing with Uncertainty: Will Science Solve the Problems of Resource Allocation in the UK NHS?' (1995) 40 Social Science and Medicine 1365.

248 < http://www.nice.org.uk/about/what-we-do>.

249 See especially R Smith, 'The Failings of NICE' (2000) 321 BMJ 1363.

7.103 It might be expected that courts would be reluctant to quash decisions in public law on the basis of a departure from evidence, given that 'uncertainties about the effects of treatments are inevitable',[250] and that even proponents of evidence-based medicine acknowledge that 'excellent external evidence may be inapplicable to or inappropriate for an individual patient'.[251] This is, indeed, the stance that has been adopted in some cases. In the *North West Lancashire Health Authority* case, while acknowledging that it was necessary for a priority-setting body to 'determine the effectiveness of various forms of treatment' for each type of illness, Auld LJ noted that there was 'scope for debate between doctors' as to the issue of the effectiveness of gender reassignment surgery as a treatment for transsexualism:[252] for his Lordship, the unlawfulness lay not in the authority's evaluation of the evidence, but rather in its failure to give effect to its own assessment of the condition as an illness. It is notable, however, that Buxton LJ went somewhat further in obliging the Authority to provide an explanation for its decision to depart from the 'strong and respectable body of medical opinion that considers gender reassignment procedures to be effective in suitable and properly selected cases',[253] although there was no obligation to provide the treatment simply because of the weight of evidence in favour of it.

7.104 A somewhat different issue arose with respect to the evidence of clinical effectiveness in *R (on the application of Longstaff) v Newcastle NHS Primary Care Trust.*[254] The applicant refused treatment for haemophilia with the plasma-based Factor VIII blood product, requesting instead recombinant Factor VIII, given his concerns as to the possible risk of transmission of viruses such as AIDS, hepatitis, and Creuzfeldt-Jacob disease. He sought to argue that it was illogical for the PCT to claim that the plasma-based product was clinically effective given such risks. This argument was rejected, Charles J noting that there were different views on the clinical effectiveness of the treatment and that the view taken by the PCT on the matter—which was in accordance with that of the Department of Health—was within the ambit of its discretion.

7.105 By contrast to the preceding cases, in *R (on the application of Pfizer Limited) v Secretary of State for Health*,[255] the evidence for the clinical effectiveness of Viagra was unequivocal, although it had not been evaluated by NICE for cost-effectiveness. Nonetheless, the Court of Appeal declined to quash the decision of the Secretary of State to limit availability of the treatment on the NHS. Simon Brown LJ held that the decision on the relative priority of Viagra vis-à-vis other treatments was a purely political one, at least while no comprehensive framework of empirical data on clinical and cost-effectiveness existed which would enable the costs and benefits of treatments to be comparatively assessed and NHS priorities ranked.[256] Accordingly, the court could not intervene.

7.106 Simon Brown LJ's dictum might imply that courts would possess competence to review for rationality in an environment where evidence is more routinely available, on the basis that any departure from such evidence must, at minimum, be justified. In fact, an early signal of judicial willingness in this regard is afforded by *Fisher*,[257] in which case the evidence of

[250] I Chalmers, 'Well Informed Uncertainties About the Effects of Treatments' (2004) 328 BMJ 475, 475.

[251] Sackett, Rosenberg, Muir, Gray et al, n 246, 72.

[252] *North West Lancashire Health Authority*, [2000] 1 WLR 977, 992.

[253] ibid, 997.

[254] [2004] Lloyd's Rep Med 400. See also *R v East Lancashire Health Authority, ex p B* (QBD, 27 February 1997), discussed in Newdick, n 60, 105–06.

[255] *R (on the application of Pfizer Limited)*, [2003] 1 CMLR 19.

[256] ibid, [17].

[257] n 172.

clinical and cost-effectiveness of beta interferon was not yet clear-cut; nonetheless, Dyson J considered it unlawful for the health authority to depart from the guidance relating to its introduction to the NHS merely on the grounds that it disagreed with the policy. One might expect judicial intervention of this type to have become still more commonplace as methodologies for gathering and analysing evidence have matured.

There is, indeed, support for such a conclusion from more recent case law. In *R (on the application of Otley) v Barking and Dagenham NHS Primary Care Trust*,[258] a decision to deny the applicant treatment for colorectal cancer by means of the drug Avastin was quashed, in part on the basis that the Trust's Difficult Decisions Panel had reached a decision informed by a critical appraisal of the drug which had accepted NICE guidance that it was not cost-effective to prescribe the drug for front line treatment, but which had omitted that section of the guidance which indicated that prescription of the drug in combination with chemotherapy was capable of giving the patient a slim chance of survival. It should, however, be noted that resource considerations were not to the fore in this instance, since the proposal was only for four or five cycles of treatment. **7.107**

More striking still is the decision in *Ross*,[259] where HH Judge Grenfell intervened on the basis of a 'mistake of fact' committed by the PCT in its assessment of the evidence on clinical and cost-effectiveness. As regards the former, this consisted of a 'failure of any of the Panels to understand the strength of the evidence in favour of treating a patient such as this claimant with lenalidomide in whatever combination of supplementary drugs', probably deriving from a misunderstanding of the results of a randomized clinical trial.[260] This failure made it impossible to assess the cost-effectiveness of the treatment, but the evaluation of the latter was further tainted by a failure to comprehend that the treatment would probably not be continued beyond four cycles if the patient failed to respond, by 'double counting' of those with partial and full responses to the treatment, and by a failure to consider the savings made by discontinuing the previous treatment given to the patient.[261] For these reasons, the judge considered the decision to refuse treatment to be irrational. **7.108**

The drug at issue in *Ross* had not yet been evaluated by NICE. In the case of technology appraisals, there is a mandatory obligation to fund treatments and services recommended by NICE for availability on the NHS.[262] However, no such funding obligation attaches to the other forms of guidance issued by the Institute.[263] How far is it open to an NHS body to depart from such guidance, for example because it differs from NICE on interpretation of the relevant evidence? **7.109**

This question arose in *R (on the application of Rose) v Thanet Clinical Commissioning Group*.[264] Here, the Group had refused a sufferer of Crohn's disease funding for oocyte cryopreservation, notwithstanding that NICE had issued a clinical guideline strongly recommending that patients in this position should be offered the treatment on the basis that it would be clinically effective and beneficial in the majority of cases, as well as cost-effective. It did so because, contrary to NICE, it considered that evidence of effectiveness was 'lacking'. Albeit **7.110**

[258] n 213.
[259] *R (on the application of Ross) v West Sussex Primary Care Trust*, n 205.
[260] ibid, [85].
[261] ibid, [91].
[262] See n 150.
[263] National Institute for Health and Social Care Excellence (Constitution and Functions) and the Health and Social Care Information Centre (Functions) Regulations 2013, SI 2013/259, reg 5.
[264] *R (on the application of Rose) v Thanet Clinical Commissioning Group* [2014] EWHC 1182 (Admin).

obiter,[265] Jay J indicated that, in determining the existence of irrationality, the court would consider not only perversity, but also the 'quality and logicality' of the reasons provided by the decision-maker.[266] On this basis, and following *Fisher*,[267] he did not regard it as open to the Group to depart from the strong recommendation issued by NICE without advancing 'clear, lawful reasons' why it had done so: mere disagreement on the strength of the evidence base was insufficient.[268] The judge did acknowledge that such a conclusion had the consequence that, in reality, the Group could not lawfully disagree with the medical or scientific rationale for NICE's recommendation, although he did not rule out the possibility of lawful reliance upon reasons of a different nature.[269]

7.111 The NHS Constitution obliges NHS bodies in England to make rational funding decisions grounded on a proper appraisal of the evidence base.[270] *Rose* (while not binding on the point) indicates that this obligation should be understood not just in general terms as one to make evidence-based decisions, but as a more stringent obligation in public law not to depart from particular evidence where this is expressed in an authoritative form, such as in NICE clinical guidelines. This is so even though such guidelines are not, in principle, mandatory in character. It should, however, be recalled that the discussion here relates to *institutional* liability. As noted above,[271] it seems probable that courts will continue to permit physicians or other medical professionals to exercise their clinical judgment as to what is necessary in the circumstances of an individual patient's case even where authoritative evidence points to a different mode of treatment, albeit that the legal standard of care will be informed by such evidence and reasons for differing from it will need to be documented.

7.112 The appropriateness of the evolution of this form of review might be queried by some. While connecting to the requirement of transparency examined in paras 7.71–7.78 (in so far as it seeks to ensure that the reasons proffered for allocative choices are logical and robust), judicial intervention on the basis that evidence has been misunderstood (as in *Ross*), or that there has been disagreement with an authoritative source (as in *Rose*) relates much more closely to the *substance* of the decision than the bases of review examined in paras 7.80–7.93 and 7.94–7.100, which clearly speak to the *process* of decision-making. This places such cases at the boundary of what might be regarded as constitutionally and institutionally legitimate within the judicial review jurisdiction, particularly when one considers the uncertainties inherent in all forms of evidence in this context. In this respect, such decisions serve to illustrate just how far English courts have moved away from the stance of passivity which characterized early cases in this field of public policy, such as *Walker* and *Collier*.

5. Waiting lists

7.113 It is, perhaps, at first sight, surprising that the most historically prevalent form of rationing experienced in the NHS, rationing by delay—manifested in the form of the waiting list—has generated little litigation.[272] Three possible explanations might be advanced for this.

[265] The claimant lost the case on the basis that her challenge was not to the general funding policy, but rather to the 'legally unobjectionable' decision not to reopen her individual funding request on grounds of exceptionality, given that she had presented no new clinical information to justify such reopening: ibid, [78]–[80].

[266] ibid, [95].

[267] See n 258.

[268] *Rose*, n 264, [107].

[269] ibid.

[270] n 179. Jay J described this as 'a public law obligation, reflected in the *NHS Constitution*': *Rose*, n 264, [19]. For the position in Scotland and Wales, see n 179.

[271] See para 7.63.

[272] Note, however, that delays in accessing treatments or services were experienced by the claimants in the early cases of *Hincks*, *Walker*, and *Collier*, nn 162, 166, and 167, and accompanying text. However, in

First, the public may find this strategy more tolerable than other forms of rationing merely because they are accustomed to waiting for certain services. This may have been especially true at the inception of the NHS after the Second World War. Secondly, and relatedly, the phenomenon of the waiting list may not be perceived as primarily allocative in character: it is not viewed as a means of management of the mismatch between demand and supply of health resources and is therefore less publicly unacceptable than some of the other institutional strategies analysed above. Thirdly, government initiatives have consistently sought to reduce waiting lists in the NHS. These have met with varying degrees of success, but there is now a statutory obligation, subject to certain exceptions, to commence consultant-led treatment within eighteen weeks of referral in non-urgent cases and to be seen by a cancer specialist within two weeks.[273]

In *R (on the application of Watts) v Bedford Primary Care Trust*,[274] the issue arose as to **7.114** whether the NHS institution was liable to reimburse a patient who had obtained bilateral hip replacement treatment in France, having been informed that there would be a maximum waiting time for the operation on the NHS of twelve months. The European Court of Justice ruled that Article 49 EC (now Article 56 TFEU), the general provision on the free movement of services, applied to the NHS, despite the fact that no direct payments are made by NHS patients for hospital services. The argument advanced by the UK government, that the planning and management of the supply of health services through waiting lists which gave effect to general clinical priorities would be undermined unless authorization for treatment in another member state could be refused, was rejected.[275] Accordingly, the PCT was obliged to reimburse the cost of treatment.

The case therefore establishes that an NHS institution will not avoid liability for reimburse- **7.115** ment simply because treatment is offered within a national waiting time target. It is necessary to establish what an acceptable waiting period may be in light of an objective medical assessment of the patient's medical condition, the history and probable course of the illness, the degree of pain the patient is in, and/or the nature of the disability at the time when the request for authorization is made. This assessment needs to be kept under review while the patient is awaiting treatment.

Directive 2011/24/EU, on the application of patients' rights in cross-border health care, **7.116** now governs this matter.[276] This clarifies the right of patients to receive treatment to which they would be entitled on the NHS in a European Economic Area state and to receive reimbursement for it. As a derogation to the primary objective of the Directive, prior authorization is permissible only in limited circumstances, which are detailed in Article 8(2).[277] Such authorization may be refused where the treatment may be provided on the NHS within a

each of these cases, the basis of the challenge in judicial review was the failure to provide the service. Of course, mere delay is not usually a 'free-standing' ground of review, but may amount to breach of statutory duty, procedural impropriety, or irrationality: see S Lambert and A Strugo, 'Delay as a Ground of Review' (2005) 10 Judicial Review 253.

[273] The National Health Service Commissioning Board and Clinical Commissioning Groups (Responsibilities and Standing Rules) Regulations, n 180, Part 9.

[274] *R (on the application of Watts) v Bedford Primary Care Trust* [2006] QB 667 (ECJ).

[275] ibid, [123].

[276] The Directive is implemented by way of the National Health Service (Cross-Border Healthcare) Regulations 2013, SI 2013/2269. See further the discussion in paras 1.69–1.72. Of course, the withdrawal of the UK from the EU will affect the position in this regard.

[277] These include treatment which requires a stay in hospital accommodation of at least one night and treatment requiring the use of highly specialized and cost-intensive medical infrastructure or equipment.

medically justified period of time,[278] but the discretion to refuse must be exercised proportionately and in a manner which does not undermine the objective of the Directive.

D. Remedy and Redress

7.117 Certain elements of the remedial regimes in private and public law are of particular importance and interest in the institutional context, especially in so far as they impact upon the allocation of resources. The focus here is necessarily selective: readers seeking a full account of the legal framework are directed to specialist texts on remedies in private and public law.[279]

1. Private law

(i) NHS Indemnity

7.118 As was noted on a number of occasions above, the arrangements for NHS Indemnity which have been in place since 1990 mean that NHS institutions assume responsibility for the negligent acts and omissions of their employees and others and that they should have arrangements for meeting any liability which arises.

7.119 Under the scheme, NHS bodies accept full financial liability for negligent acts and omissions occurring in the course of employment of health professionals working under a contract of employment, of professionals not working under a contract of employment but who have been contracted to provide services to persons to whom that NHS body owed a duty of care, and of persons, not employed under a contract of employment and who may or may not be health professionals, who owe a duty of care to the persons injured. The latter category includes 'locums; medical academic staff with honorary contracts; students; those conducting clinical trials; charitable volunteers; persons undergoing further professional education, training and examinations; students and staff working on income generation projects'.[280] Agency staff are also covered.[281] In such cases, the body will not seek to recover its costs either in full or part against the individual concerned or from any indemnity arrangements they may have.

7.120 The terms of NHS Indemnity do not determine the question of whether an institution is, in law, vicariously liable for the negligence of (say) agency staff, but simply specify how the matter is dealt with in practice. If such staff are not in law employees, the scheme cannot deem them to be such. It is, therefore, theoretically possible for an institution to argue the issue in court, though in practice this does not happen (and did not happen prior to 1990).[282]

7.121 NHS Indemnity does not apply to general medical and dental practitioners, except for those who are directly employed by NHS bodies (such as those working as Public Health doctors), nor to other self-employed health professionals such as independent midwives. This is also true of staff employed by general practices.[283] A general practitioner who provides medical

---

[278] Article 8(6)(d).

[279] See, eg, *McGregor on Damages* (19th edn, Sweet & Maxwell 2014); C Lewis, *Judicial Remedies in Public Law* (5th edn, Sweet & Maxwell 2014).

[280] NHS Executive, *NHS Indemnity—Arrangements for Clinical Negligence Claims in the NHS*, HSG 96/48 (1996) paras 5 and 7.

[281] ibid, Annex A, para 24.

[282] See M Jones, *Medical Negligence* (4th edn, Sweet & Maxwell 2008).

[283] *NHS Indemnity—Arrangements for Clinical Negligence Claims in the NHS*, n 280, para 9.

care to patients in hospital under a contractual arrangement (for example, as a clinical assistant) will be covered by NHS Indemnity, but where a hospital merely provides 'hotel facilities' for patients for whom the GP is clinically responsible, the scheme does not apply.[284]

The scheme does not apply to private practice, or to private care delivered in an NHS hospital. Private hospitals have to take commercial insurance cover, and doctors engaging in private practice will normally be members of a defence organization providing indemnity against professional negligence claims. It is accepted that, for the purposes of NHS Indemnity, where junior medical staff are involved in the care of private patients in NHS hospitals, they would normally be doing so as part of their NHS contract. To the extent that NHS employees participate in the treatment, the hospital will be vicariously liable for their negligence.[285] Work which is outside the scope of a junior doctor's employment (such as reports for insurance companies or locum work for a GP) is not covered by the scheme, and the doctor will have to rely on a defence organization for indemnity. **7.122**

(ii) Clinical Negligence Scheme for Trusts

Section 71 of the National Health Service Act 2006 empowers the Secretary of State to establish schemes to enable NHS bodies to make provision to meet liabilities to third parties for loss, damage or injury arising from the exercise of their functions. Such schemes are administered in England by the NHS Litigation Authority, which was established as a Special Health Authority in 1995 to manage negligence claims made against NHS bodies.[286] The Authority operates two principal schemes, the Clinical Negligence Scheme for Trusts (CNST) and the Existing Liability Scheme (ELS), applying respectively to incidents taking place after and before 1 April 1995 (or the date on which a body joined the CNST, if later). Membership of the former is voluntary but currently all Trusts, Foundation Trusts, and Clinical Commissioning Groups in England are members;[287] while independent providers of NHS health care have also been eligible to join the scheme from 1 April 2013. The latter is not a membership scheme, but is funded directly by the Department of Health, and all NHS bodies may apply for support from it, whether or not they are members of CNST. **7.123**

Under the CNST, the NHS body remains the legal defendant, but the Authority assumes full responsibility for handling of the claim and meeting any associated costs. In the case of the ELS, claims may be made against NHS bodies which have ceased to exist because of the restructuring of the NHS. In such cases, the legal defendant will be the legal 'successor' body.[288] However, such claims are again handled centrally by the NHS Litigation Authority. **7.124**

The Litigation Authority's Framework Agreement with the Department of Health obliges it to undertake appropriate and proportionate risk management activities with a view to assisting NHS bodies to minimize their claims and thus improve patient and staff safety.[289] To this end, the Authority seeks to promote settlement out of court with use of mediation or other forms of alternative dispute resolution mechanisms where appropriate. The Authority no longer undertakes assessments of risk management by NHS bodies against standards which reflect issues arising in clinical and non-clinical negligence claims,[290] but it provides **7.125**

[284] ibid, Annex A, para 6.
[285] ibid, Annex A, para 10.
[286] In Wales, similar functions are performed by Welsh Risk Pool Services: see <http://www.wales.nhs.uk/sitesplus/955/page/58513>.
[287] NHS Litigation Authority, *Report and Accounts 2014/15* (HC 293, 2015) 16.
[288] <http://www.nhsla.com/Claims/Pages/Handling.aspx>.
[289] *Framework Agreement between the Department of Health and the NHS Litigation Authority 2013*, para 2.2.
[290] <http://www.nhsla.com/Safety/Pages/Home.aspx>.

a 'Safety and Learning Service' to members and supports the Department of Health's 'Sign Up to Safety' campaign, which seeks to reduce avoidable harm and save 6,000 lives over a three-year period.[291]

(iii) Periodical payments

7.126 Objectives of avoiding large settlements against NHS bodies which might jeopardize patient care in a particular community, and of spreading costs more evenly over time, may be furthered through the use of settlements which provide damages in the form of periodical payments,[292] although the benefits of the latter also accrue to injured patients whose medical prognosis may be uncertain at the date of trial.[293] Prior to 2005, such settlements were voluntary, but s 100 of the Courts Act 2003 substituted a new s 2(1) of the Damages Act 1996, which provides that courts awarding damages for future pecuniary loss in respect of personal injury may order that the damages are wholly or partly to take the form of periodical payments and shall consider whether to make such an order.[294] Any such order may only be made if the court is satisfied that continuity of payment of the order is reasonably secure;[295] this condition is satisfied (inter alia) if the source of the payment is a government or health service body.[296] The NHS Litigation Authority is designated as a body for this purpose.[297]

7.127 (a) **Continuity of Payment** As noted above, membership of the CNST is voluntary. Since CNST is a 'pay as you go' scheme, it possesses no reserves and it is not therefore open to any body which chooses to depart from the scheme to leave liabilities resting with the continuing members. However, once it has departed, the body no longer benefits from the 'reasonable security' provided by the Authority. This problem was previously especially acute in the case of Foundation Trusts which might become insolvent given that transferral of liabilities to the Secretary of State or other body was formerly discretionary in the case of such Trusts.[298]

7.128 In *YM v Gloucestershire Hospitals Foundation NHS Trust; Kanu v King's College Hospital NHS Trust*,[299] Forbes J indicated that he was satisfied that continuity of periodical payments was reasonably secure in the case of orders against Foundation Trusts, on the basis that the NHS Litigation Authority had agreed to be named as the source of the periodical payments and to be made legally responsible for such payments to the claimants. In order

291 <http://www.england.nhs.uk/signuptosafety/>. In particular, a one-off discretionary payment of up to 10 per cent of a body's contribution to CNST in 2015/16 was offered to bodies producing robust safety improvement plans which showed how they would reduce the harm that results in claims.

292 See R Lewis, 'Health Authorities and the Payment of Damages by Means of a Pension' (1993) 56 MLR 844, especially at 847, noting that the fluctuating amounts needed to satisfy lump sum awards can have a significant effect on annual institutional budgets, potentially resulting in the closure of wards or the postponement of major capital expenditure.

293 See, eg, *Wells v Wells* [1999] 1 AC 345, 363–64 (HL) *per* Lord Lloyd; and further Jones, n 282, paras 12-017–12-018.

294 Damages Act 1996, s 2(2) provides that a court awarding other damages in respect of personal injury may make a periodic payments order if the parties consent. For discussion of the statutory regime, see R Lewis, 'The Politics and Economics of Tort Law: Judicially Imposed Periodical Payments of Damages' (2006) 69 MLR 418. The order may provide for variation: see Damages (Variation of Periodical Payments) Order 2005, SI 2005/841.

295 Damages Act 1996, s 2(3).

296 ibid, s 2(4).

297 Damages (Government and Health Service Bodies) Order 2005, SI 2005/474.

298 Health and Social Care (Community Health and Standards) Act 2003, s 25(3). The discretion was removed by the National Health Service Act 2006, s 70.

299 *YM v Gloucestershire Hospitals Foundation NHS Trust; Kanu v King's College Hospital NHS Trust* [2006] PIQR P27.

for the Authority to assume such responsibility, it requires bodies to enter into an agreement to pay a lump sum to cover all continuing future periodical payment liabilities if and when choosing to leave the CNST voluntarily. Where such an agreement is signed, the Secretary of State will put the Authority in funds to meet periodical payments.[300]

Jones notes that the position may differ for medical defence organizations, which may of course be engaged in the case of claims against general practitioners or incidents arising from private medical care. Many such organizations are not covered by the Financial Services Compensation Scheme, which constitutes a scheme under s 213 of the Financial Services and Markets Act 2000 for the purposes of reasonable security of continuity of payments under s 2(4)(b) of the Damages Act 1996, and accordingly additional forms of security will be required.[301] **7.129**

(b) Indexation Once a court has determined that it is appropriate to issue a periodical payment order, an issue as to the appropriate approach to indexation may arise. Section 2(8) of the Damages Act provides that an order shall be treated as providing for the amount of payments to vary by reference to the retail prices index (RPI). This is, however, qualified by s 2(9) which allows for an order to include a provision disapplying or modifying the effect of sub-s (8), giving rise to a question as to the circumstances in which a court may depart from the RPI and apply a different index. **7.130**

The matter was considered in four conjoined cases heard by the Court of Appeal.[302] The claimants had suffered severe injuries at birth as a result of negligence, liability for which had been admitted. It was argued that the RPI was not the appropriate measure of indexation in light of the likelihood that wages of carers would rise at a faster rate than the RPI, thereby increasing care costs. At first instance, each judge had instead indexed care costs by reference to the Office of National Statistics Annual Survey of Hours and Earnings, disaggregated data, standard occupational group classification 6115 care assistants and home carers index (ASHE 6115). This was accepted as the appropriate approach to indexation by the Court of Appeal,[303] following the decision in *Flora v Wakom (Heathrow) Ltd*,[304] in which Brooke LJ had opined that, in enacting s 2 of the Damages Act 1996 (as substituted), Parliament did not intend the courts to depart from the principle that a victim of a tort is entitled to be compensated as nearly as possible in full for all pecuniary losses.[305] **7.131**

Of particular interest from the perspective of the issues discussed in this chapter are the arguments advanced by the NHS institutions as to the resource implications of departing from the RPI as a measure of indexation. At first instance, this issue had been canvassed most extensively in *Corbett v South Yorkshire Strategic Health Authority*.[306] Here, counsel for the Authority had contended that, in deciding whether to exercise its powers of modification under s 2(9), the court should balance the competing needs of persons in the position of the claimant against those of persons requiring a well-resourced and free health service, or 'in blunter terms', that indexation should be adjusted downwards because: **7.132**

300 ibid, [26].

301 Jones, n 282, para 12-025.

302 *Thompstone v Tameside and Glossop Acute Services NHS Trust* [2008] 1 WLR 2207. The other conjoined cases were *South Yorkshire Strategic Health Authority v Corbett; United Bristol Health Care Trust v RH*; and *South West London Strategic Health Authority v De Haas*.

303 In the Scottish case *D's Parent and Guardian v Greater Glasgow Health Board* [2011] CSOH 99, Lord Stewart referred to English precedent for an approach in which indexation was split between care staff costs (linked to ASHE 6115) and nursing staff costs (linked to ASHE 3211).

304 [2007] 1 WLR 482 (CA).

305 Labelled the '100 per cent principle' by Lord Steyn in *Wells v Wells*, n 293, 382–83.

306 *Corbett v South Yorkshire Strategic Health Authority* [2007] LS Law Med 430.

> having regard to the needs of others . . . on the assumption the NHS has finite resources, the more that is to be taken out over the years in payment of compensation, the less will be available to ongoing patient care. Such patients have as much right to look to the NHS to provide appropriate care, as a claimant does to receive a full award of damages.[307]

HH Judge Bullimore rejected this argument on a number of bases, including the absence of authority on distributive justice issues at first instance level, the fact that it would result in a breach of the '100 per cent principle', the injustice and impracticability of the court adopting differing approaches as to indexation according to the identity of the defendant (eg cases involving NHS institutions as distinct from private medicine, or road traffic accidents), the difficulty of establishing evidence as to what the public believed 'justice' required in such an instance, and the social policy character of such questions, which rendered them unsuitable for judicial determination.[308]

7.133 The Court of Appeal (which also received submissions on affordability from interested parties, including the Ministry of Defence and the Medical Protection Society) also rejected the 'distributive justice' argument. Waller LJ indicated that *Flora* should be followed, and cited Brooke LJ's statement in that case that policy arguments based on affordability were a matter for Parliament and not courts, that in any event there was no material upon which the court could establish whether the public perceived it to be fair, reasonable and just to reduce compensation for future pecuniary losses on affordability grounds, and that there was no indication that Parliament had intended such a test to apply when enacting the legislative provision.[309]

2. Public law

(i) Judicial review: Remedies

7.134 Since judicial review is not an appeal process, the court is not empowered to substitute its view for that of the original decision-maker. It follows that it is not normally open to a court to *order* a health institution to provide resources to treat an individual. Rather, the remedies—quashing orders, prohibiting orders, mandatory orders, declarations and injunctions, each of which is awarded at the discretion of the court—seek to remove the unlawful elements of the decision, clearing the way for a new decision to be taken. It is perfectly lawful for the initial decision-maker to arrive at the same conclusion (for example, that a particular form of treatment should not be offered to an individual or group of patients), provided that when it does so, it acts in accordance with the law as articulated by the court.

7.135 However, the practical impact of the award of a remedy to a claimant in judicial review may very well be that the institution reverses its original decision to deny access to treatment. The media coverage attendant upon decisions in this field considerably reduces the scope of manoeuvre of the decision-maker, particularly as the language deployed tends to focus on the notion that the institution has been 'defeated' in court.[310] The institution may well consider that provision of access to treatment is the only realistic response in order to forestall further media and public criticism (which may well be misinformed as to the nature of judicial review) that it has 'not complied' with the court's ruling.

---

307 ibid, [114].

308 ibid, [132]–[143].

309 [2008] 1 WLR 2207, [48], citing *Flora v Wakom (Heathrow) Ltd* n 304, [29].

310 For illuminating discussions of the role of language in this context, see C Burgoyne, 'Distributive Justice and Rationing in the NHS: Framing Effects in Press Coverage of a Controversial Decision' (1997) Journal of Community and Applied Social Psychology 119; V Entwistle, C Watt, R Bradbury, and L Pehl, 'Media Coverage of the Child B Case' (1996) 312 BMJ 1587.

As an illustration of these points, it is instructive to consider the *Rogers* case.[311] The Court of Appeal issued a quashing order in respect of the decision to refuse to treat the patient with Herceptin, but it observed that it 'cannot and should not order the PCT to fund the treatment. As we see it, it is now a matter for the PCT to reconsider its policy and to formulate a lawful policy upon which to base decisions in particular cases, including that of the appellant, in the future.'[312] The response of Swindon PCT, as articulated by its Chief Executive, was that it would 'revisit' its policy taking into account the points made by the court.[313] During this process, it agreed (though not obliged to do so by the court) to provide access to Herceptin to the patient on an interim basis. Revised policy statements on the introduction of new drugs and exceptionality which took account of the court decision were duly issued by the PCT in July and September 2006 respectively,[314] by the date of the latter of which NICE had issued guidance to the NHS recommending use of the drug for most women with early-stage breast cancer.[315] **7.136**

In some instances, and notwithstanding the general proscription on substitution of judgment, there is evidence, albeit limited, of consideration being given to a more interventionist judicial stance on remedies awarded in allocative cases. This might point towards a willingness to utilize mandatory orders to oblige institutions to provide funding for treatment in future cases of this type.[316] In *Otley*,[317] the PCT provided an undertaking to fund five cycles of the drug in question, followed by a review. On this basis, the court accepted that only a quashing order was necessary. In *Ross*, while noting that consideration of relief did not form part of the judgment, the court indicated that 'there should be some mechanism . . . for commencing treatment at the earliest time'.[318] However, it was observed that any such commencement of treatment would necessarily be 'on the strict understanding that, if the PCT properly directing itself in accordance with the reasoning of [the] judgment, nevertheless reached a contrary decision, that the treatment would have to cease, however harsh that may seem'.[319] **7.137**

(ii) Damages

A failure by a public body to comply with the principles of public law does not in itself give rise to an entitlement to damages. The High Court possesses the power to award damages on an application for judicial review if claimed,[320] but in practice a cause of action in tort must be pleaded and proved for such an award to be made. No such award has been made in a case of judicial review of the allocation of resources for health care. Similarly, damages may be awarded in cases where the court holds actions or decisions of a public authority to be unlawful under the Human Rights Act 1998,[321] or where there has been breach of **7.138**

[311] *R (on the application of Rogers) v Swindon NHS Primary Care Trust and Secretary of State for Health* [2006] 1 WLR 2649.

[312] ibid, [84].

[313] See 'Woman Wins Herceptin Court Appeal' *The Independent* (12 April 2006).

[314] Swindon NHS PCT, 'Introduction of New Drugs Policy', PCT06/72; Swindon NHS PCT, Policy Statement No 33, 'Guidance for considering "exceptionality" in individual cases'.

[315] NICE TA107: 'Breast cancer—early: trastuzumab: guidance' (23 August 2006). Interim guidance was issued on 9 June 2006, but was appealed.

[316] See also *S v NHS England* [2016] EWHC 1395 (Admin), [36], where the court issued an interim order for funding for a trial period of three months.

[317] *R (on the application of Otley) v Barking and Dagenham Primary Care Trust* [2007] EWHC 1927 (Admin).

[318] *R (on the application of Ross) v West Sussex Primary Care Trust* (2009) 106 BMLR 1, [95].

[319] ibid.

[320] Senior Courts Act 1981, s 31(4); CPR Pt 54.3.

[321] Human Rights Act 1998, s 8.

European Union law.[322] Again, no such award has been made in the context of the issues discussed in this chapter.[323]

E. Conclusion

7.139 The complexity of modern health care means that the traditional physician-patient focus of medical law appears misplaced, especially beyond primary care. The forms of liability in private and public law which are examined in this chapter are thus likely to prove of increasing importance, requiring courts to consider *systemic* factors as distinct from individual culpability. This, in turn, brings into focus difficult questions of judicial competence in so far as the polycentric nature of such matters, and the managerial expertise which is required to engage with them, would seem to render the courtroom an ill-suited arena for adjudication.[324]

7.140 Yet, while avoiding litigation where feasible may be seen as worthwhile, not least because it minimizes diversion of resources away from the actual provision of health care,[325] patients and families will inevitably continue to pursue health bodies through the courts, simply because of the critical impact which institutional actions and decisions can have upon their lives. Given this, courts should remain closely attentive to the broader consequences of their judgments, balancing the need for redress where there has been fault or unlawfulness against the discretion of clinicians and managers to organize systems and distribute resources to the benefit of the wider population. As this chapter has demonstrated, this is not always an easy task.

[322] See especially Case C-69/80 *Francovich v Italy* [1991] ECR I-5357 (ECJ).

[323] The claim in *Watts*, n 274, was for reimbursement of the costs of treatment, as distinct from compensation for a breach of EU law.

[324] For discussion, see K Syrett, 'Courts, Expertise and Resource Allocation: Is There a Judicial "Legitimacy Problem"?' (2014) 7 Public Health Ethics 112–22.

[325] See, eg, NHS Litigation Authority, n 287, estimating that it saved £1.2 billion for the NHS in 2014/15 in rejecting claims which had no merit: at 9.

PART III

8

CONSENT TO TREATMENT: THE COMPETENT PATIENT

Jean V McHale

A. Consent to Treatment

1. Introduction

The law relating to consent is of central importance in medical law[1]. Under the common law, the legality of a medical treatment or procedure[2] will largely turn upon whether the patient has given a valid consent to it. Treatment without consent may amount to the tort of battery[3] or the crime of assault.[4] Failure to provide information in relation to the risks of a treatment procedure may give rise to liability in negligence. The requirement that a patient with capacity gives consent before being subject to any medical procedure is the legal reflection of the primacy of the principle of respect for autonomy which takes precedence over the duty of care owed by clinicians to their patient.[5] In this particular context, this notion might **8.01**

[1] M Brazier and E Cave, *Medicine, Patients and the Law* (Manchester University Press 2016) ch 5; E Jackson, *Medical Law Text Cases and Materials* (3rd edn, Oxford University Press 2013) ch 4; J Herring, *Medical Law and Ethics* (6th edn, Oxford University Press 2016), ch 4; G Laurie, S E Harmon, and G Porter, *Law and Medical Ethics* (10th edn, Oxford University Press 2016) ch 4; S Pattinson, *Medical Law and Ethics* (4th edn, Sweet & Maxwell 2014) ch 4.

[2] Medical *treatment* involves a procedure carried out by, or on behalf of, a medical or health care practitioner for a therapeutic purpose. By contrast, a medical *procedure* includes interventions where the therapeutic intention may be absent: for example, the taking of blood to test for the benefit of others, organ or tissue donation, and non-therapeutic research. All medical treatment involves a medical procedure.

[3] Battery is the intentional application of physical contact to the person without consent or other lawful justification: see *Faulkner v Talbot* [1981] 3 All ER 468 (DC) *per* Lord Lane CJ at 471 and *Collins v Wilcock* [1984] 3 All ER 374 (DC) *per* Goff LJ at 379. For a discussion of the elements of the tort, see F Trindade, 'Intentional Torts: Some Thoughts on Assault and Battery' (1982) 2 OJLS 211.

[4] The crime of 'common assault' includes an assault *stricto sensu* (ie where the victim merely apprehends a 'touching') and a 'battery' where the 'touching' actually occurs: *DPP v Little* [1992] 1 All ER 299.

[5] For an authoritative ethical statement of the requirement for (and of) consent: see General Medical Council (GMC), 'Good Medical Practice (2013)' (GMC 2013) paras 31–34, 36 at <http://www.gmc-uk.org/guidance/good_medical_practice/contents.asp> and GMC, 'Consent: patients and doctors making decisions together' (GMC June 2008) at <http://www.gmc-uk.org/guidance/ethical_guidance/consent_guidance>.

be better expressed as respect for a person's bodily integrity stemming from a right of self-determination.[6] It is a 'fundamental principle, now long established, that every person's body is inviolate'.[7]

8.02 Article 5 of the European Convention on Human Rights and Biomedicine provides that:

> An intervention in the health field may only be carried out after the person concerned has given free and informed consent to it . . . This person shall beforehand be given appropriate information as to the purpose and the nature of the information as well as its consequences and risks.

Human rights law reinforces the common law's position through the protection of an individual's 'physical integrity' as part of the right to respect for private life protected by Article 8 of the European Convention on Human Rights.[8] In *Pretty v UK*,[9] the European Court of Human Rights stated that:

> In the sphere of medical treatment, the refusal to accept a particular medical treatment might, inevitably, lead to a fatal outcome, yet the imposition of medical treatment, without the consent of a mentally competent adult, would interfere with a person's physical integrity in a manner capable of engaging the rights protected under Article 8.1 of the Convention.

8.03 There is, of course, scope for the state to limit an individual's absolute right to refuse medical treatment within the limited categories set out in Article 8(2). Article 8(1) of the European Convention of Human Rights provides that a Convention right may be subject to interference if justified under Article 8(2) to the extent that such interference is 'necessary in a democratic society'. The 'proportionality' requirement means that a balance has to be struck between the rights of the individual and the legitimate aims specified in Article 8(2). In *R (N and another) v Nottinghamshire Healthcare NHS Trust*[10] the Court of Appeal accepted that action could be justified under Article 8(2) of the Convention to promote an individual's own health as well as to protect the health of others. However, the justification of action by the state to promote a patient's own good health under Article 8(2) has never been suggested to extend to the right to impose medical treatment on a competent patient who refuses consent for a medical procedure. This process requires a balance to be struck on an individual case-by-case basis. There seems little doubt that English judges would take the view that the common law adequately took account of the 'fair balancing' exercise required in Article 8(2), so that balance is always[11] struck in favour of the legally competent individual's right to refuse treatment which is 'paramount' and absolute.[12] The only likely permissible derogations—and then only by Parliament— could be based upon compelling public health considerations, such as the need for public vaccination programmes[13] or in the mental health context, where

[6] *Malette v Shulman* (1990) 67 DLR (4th) 321 (Ont CA) *per* Robins JA at 327–28. See also *Airedale NHS Trust v Bland* [1993] AC 789, [1993] 1 All ER 821 (HL) *per* Lord Goff at 866.

[7] *Re F (Mental Patient: Sterilisation)* [1990] 2 AC 1, [1989] 2 All ER 545 (HL) *per* Lord Goff at 563. See also *Re T (Adult: Refusal of Treatment)* [1993] Fam 95, [1992] 4 All ER 649 (CA).

[8] Other Convention rights may be engaged where treatment is contemplated without a patient's consent, in particular the individual's right to freedom from inhuman or degrading treatment under Art 3. For a general discussion see E Wicks, 'The Right to Refuse Medical Treatment Under the European Convention on Human Rights' (2001) 9 Medical Law Review 17.

[9] Application 2346/02 (2002) 66 BMLR 147 (ECtHR), at para 63. See also *NHS Trust A v M; NHS Trust B v H* [2001] Lloyd's Rep Med 28, [41] *per* Butler-Sloss P.

[10] [2009] HRLR 31, [2009] EWCA Civ 795.

[11] Save in the case of a mentally disordered person subject to compulsory detention.

[12] *Re T (Adult: Refusal of Treatment)* [1993] Fam 95, [1992] 4 All ER 649 (CA) *per* Lord Donaldson MR at 661. See also *Airedale NHS Trust v Bland* [1993] AC 789, [1993] 1 All ER 821 (HL) *per* Lord Keith at 860 and *per* Lord Goff at 866. See also *St George's Healthcare NHS Trust v S* [1998] 3 All ER 673 (CA) *per* Judge LJ at 685–87 (competent adult) and 689–92 (pregnant woman).

[13] See *Acmanne v Belgium* (1984) 40 DR 251 (tuberculosis screening). See also *X v Austria* (1980) 18 DR 154 (compulsory paternity test).

there may be compelling interests justifying the treatment of the patient for his own medical benefit or the protection of others.[14] (See further Chapter 11). However, section 45E of the Public Health (Control of Disease) Act 1984[15] specifically removes the possibility of a person with a transmissible disease being subject to compulsory medical treatment on public health grounds. Such a person could be detained against their will in hospital as long as the public health risk remained[16] but there does not appear to be any power in English law forcibly to medicate a person on public health grounds.

English law may be stated simply as follows: any intentional touching of a person is unlawful and amounts to the tort of battery unless it is justified by consent or other lawful authority. This means that a doctor may only carry out a medical treatment or procedure which involves contact with a patient[17] if there exists a valid consent by the patient (or another person authorized by law to consent on his behalf) or if the touching is permitted notwithstanding the absence of consent.[18] The legal position in England is often stated adopting the famous words of Cardozo J in *Schloendorff v Society of New York Hospital*:[19] **8.04**

> Every human being of adult years and sound mind has a right to determine what shall be done with his own body; and a surgeon who performs an operation without his patient's consent commits an assault, for which he is liable in damages.

English courts have unreservedly accepted that a patient's bodily integrity is inviolable such that any physically invasive medical treatment or procedure, however trivial, is unlawful unless authorized by consent or other lawful authority.[20] In *Re F*, Lord Goff stated that: 'It is well established that, as a general rule, the performance of a medical operation on a person without his or her consent is unlawful . . .'[21] Consequently, the medieval tort of battery—developed to deal with fist and sword fights—is the defining legal framework for determining whether a medical treatment or procedure is lawful. At one time, it was suggested that trespass to the person (here, battery) was irrelevant in the case of medical treatment, because a battery could only be committed if the defendant acted with 'hostility'.[22] If this were so, rarely, if ever, would the medical treatment be caught by battery, even if there was no consent, because the doctor's motives would usually be bona fide, acting, as he would be, in the best interests of the patient. This view has now been conclusively rejected by the House of **8.05**

---

[14] *R (on the application of Wilkinson) v Broadmoor Special Hospital Authority* [2002] 1 WLR 419 (CA). See also *R (on the application of B) v Dr SS and Ors* [2005] EWHC 86 (Admin).

[15] Introduced by s 129 of the Health and Social Care Act 2008.

[16] This power has existed for many years under, eg, s 37 of the Public Health (Control of Disease) Act 1984.

[17] It would have no relevance, therefore, where the medical 'intervention' did not involve a touching even where there has been no consent: for example, causing a patient to take a drug where the patient is unaware that he is part of a research project. Contrast the US case of *Mink v University of Chicago* (1978) 460 F Supp 713 (battery action allowed to continue on these facts) which would not be followed, on this point, in England.

[18] For treatment without consent involving an adult lacking mental capacity or a child see Chapter 10.

[19] (1914) 211 NY 125 at 126. Cited with approval in *Re F* [1989] 2 All ER 545 *per* Lord Goff at 564; and in *Airedale NHS Trust v Bland* [1993] 1 All ER 821 *per* Lord Goff at 866.

[20] For example, *Re F* [1989] 2 All ER 545; *Re T* [1993] Fam 95, [1992] 4 All ER 649; *Re MB* [1997] 8 Med LR 217 (CA). For other recent cases recognizing that a competent patient's right of self-determination entitles him or her to refuse any medical treatment even if life-sustaining see: *St George's Healthcare NHS Trust v S* [1998] 3 All ER 673 (CA); *Re JT (Adult: Refusal of Medical Treatment)* [1998] 1 FLR 48 (Wall J); *Re AK* (2000) 58 BMLR 151 (Hughes J) and *Re B (Adult: Refusal of Treatment)* [2002] EWHC 429 (Fam), (2002) 65 BMLR 149 (Butler-Sloss P).

[21] [1989] 2 All ER 545, 562. See also at 563 and *per* Lord Brandon at 550–51.

[22] *Wilson v Pringle* [1987] QB 237 *per* Croom-Johnson LJ at 253. For a criticism see I Kennedy and A Grubb, *Medical Law* (1st edn, Butterworths 1989), 172–73.

Lords in *Re F.*[23] It is, as we have seen, the issues of consent or other lawful authority (if any) which are determinative of the legality of the treatment or procedure.

8.06 It is important to notice the extent of the relevance of consent. First, a valid consent licenses what would otherwise be unlawful. However, to be a valid consent, the law requires:

(1) that it be given by a competent person (or by someone who can validly give consent on behalf of a person who cannot consent such as a child or by a donee under a Lasting Power of Attorney);
(2) that the person or the substituted decision maker must be adequately informed about the 'nature' of what he is agreeing to; and
(3) that the person or the substituted decision maker should be acting voluntarily and not under the undue influence of another.

Each of these requirements—competence,[24] information,[25] and voluntariness[26]—will be considered separately. In particular, it should be noticed that the first requirement means that adults of sound mind may consent to medical treatment, as may children who are sufficiently mature, but those persons who suffer from mental disorder or disability or are immature such that they are not capable of understanding what is involved in the treatment or procedure, may not give a valid consent in law.[27]

8.07 Secondly, in cases where the patient themselves cannot provide consent, the law will look to another source of justification for the treatment which may, in the case of children, be the consent of a substituted decision maker such as a parent (or person exercising parental authority) or a person acting under a lasting power of attorney. If there is no one who can give or refuse consent for a patient lacking mental capacity, then under the scheme set out by the Mental Capacity Act 2005, which replaced and codified the common law on this subject, medical treatment can, for a patient without legal capacity, lawfully be carried out without the patient's consent by a person who is acting in the patient's best interests (see further Chapter 10). The statutory right to take a decision in a person's best interests where that person does not have capacity has superseded the requirement to rely upon the common law justification based upon 'necessity' to make, what would otherwise be an unauthorized touching, lawful.[28]

8.08 Thirdly, consent is a 'necessary' but it is not a 'sufficient' condition for a patient to be treated. A patient cannot compel a doctor or NHS Trust to provide treatment that is determined by the doctor's clinical judgment not to be in the patient's 'best interests' or which cannot be provided because of limited resources (see further Chapter 1). The courts will not force a doctor or NHS Trust to treat a patient in a manner contrary to their professional judgment.[29] The doctor is entitled to set up his own professional conscience to refuse the treatment. The court has recognized that this is an individual matter for doctors and the outcome can differ between doctors. Hedley J explained this in *Portsmouth Hospitals NHS Trust v Wyatt*[30] as follows:

---

[23] [1989] 2 All ER 545 *per* Lord Goff at 563–64. No other member of the House of Lords commented on this issue.
[24] See paras 8.68–8.89.
[25] See paras 8.70–8.89.
[26] See para 8.8.
[27] See Chapter 9 (competence and adults) and Chapter 10 (children).
[28] See Chapter 4.
[29] *Re J (A Minor) (Wardship: Medical Treatment)* [1993] Fam 15, [1992] 4 All ER 614 (CA); and *Re R (A Minor) (Wardship: Medical Treatment)* [1992] Fam 11, [1991] 4 All ER 177 (CA) *per* Lord Donaldson MR at 187.
[30] [2006] 1 FLR 652, [35].

> Conscience (whether one believes it to be God-given or culturally conditioned), is not a wholly rational sense. It is more in the nature of intuition or a hunch as to whether something is right or wrong. In this context it is brought to bear on the intellectual conclusion by confirming it or undermining it. The professional conscience of a doctor will, of course, have been honed by experience of patients, exposure to the practice of colleagues, and the ethos of his work. But it must be recognised that it has too a truly individual aspect.

In addition it would be impracticable and uncertain for the court to enforce a mandatory order in this context. Finally, the courts are most reluctant to enter into investigations about the proper allocation of resources within the health service. An attempt to introduce a limited 'right to treatment' so as to avoid a breach of Article 3 of the ECHR was proposed by Munby J in *R (Burke) v General Medical Council*.[31] This was not accepted by the Court of Appeal.[32] The Court said:[33] 'Ultimately, however, a patient cannot demand that a doctor administer a treatment which the doctor considers is adverse to the patient's clinical needs.' The Court of Protection should, as a consequence, simply decline to adjudicate in disputes between patients, doctors, and health service institutions arising out of the denial of treatment where, in fact, the issue is one of lack of resources or the allocation of scarce resources to other patients or other forms of treatment.[34] Where the court disagrees with the views of the responsible doctor, the solution lies in finding another doctor who will act on the court's direction, rather than to coerce the patient's existing doctor.[35]

Professional judgment here, however, needs to be distinguished from conscientious objection.[36] There is no general right to opt out of procedures on the basis of conscientious objection that has been recognized in English law in relation to health care procedures; nor has such a right been recognized by the European Court of Human Rights.[37] There are two statutory exceptions—section 4 of the Abortion Act 1967 and section 38 of the Human Fertilisation and Embryology Act 1990—discussed further at paras 14.129–14.133 and 16.133–16.125. Some matters of conscience may fall within protection given to individuals under the Equality Act 2010 as reasonable accommodation of, for example, religious belief.[38] Further guidance on this issue has also been produced by the General Medical Council.[39] **8.09**

[31] See [2004] EWHC 1879 (Admin), [2005] QB 424.

[32] [2005] EWCA Civ 1003, [2006] QB 273.

[33] ibid, [55].

[34] *Re J* [1993] Fam 15, [1992] 4 All ER 614 *per* Lord Donaldson MR at 623, *per* Balcombe LJ at 625, and *per* Leggatt LJ at 626. However, where the decision is either made on resource grounds or there is a refusal to refer the patient to a doctor who made provide the treatment, it may be possible to bring a judicial review action to challenge the legality of the decision. However, this is not a 'best interests' jurisdiction.

[35] Paragraph 9(i) of the GMC Guidance refers to the right of a patient to seek a second opinion which provides a professional basis for the requirement to refer a patient to another doctor who may be prepared to provide the requested treatment. See also here *R (on the application of B) v Cambridge Health Authority* [1995] 1 WLR 898 and discussion in Chapter 1 at paras 1.31, 1.82.

[36] See further S W Smith, 'A Bridge Too Far: Individualised Claims of Conscience' (2015) 23(2) Medical Law Review 283; J R Montgomery, 'Conscientious Objection: Personal and Professional Ethics in the Public Square' (2015) 23(2) Medical Law Review 200; and other articles in "Conscience and Proper Medical Treatment" special edition (2015) 23(2) Medical Law Review.

[37] See further *Dougan v Wood* [2014] UKSC 68; *Pichon and Sajous v France* (App 49853/99) Admissibility decision of 2 October 2001; A Lamackova, 'Conscientious Objection in Reproductive Health Care: Analysis of *Pichon and Sajous v France*' (2008) 15 European Journal of Health Law 7; though see also Council of Europe, The Right to Conscientious Objection in Lawful Medical Care, Parliamentary Assembly Declaration 1763 (2010) <http://assembly.coe.int/main.asp?Link=/documents/adoptedtext/ta10/eres1763.htm>. For commentary on this declaration see M Campbell, 'Conscientious Objection and the Council of Europe' (2011) 19 Medical Law Review 467.

[38] See further J V McHale, 'Faith, Belief, Fundamental Rights and Delivering Health Care in a Modern NHS: An Unrealistic Aspiration?' (2013) 21(3) Health Care Analysis 224.

[39] GMC, 'Personal Beliefs and Medical Practice' (GMC 2013) <http://www.gmc-uk.org/guidance/ethical_guidance/21171.asp>.

Whether matters of conscience should impact on health care decision-making is an issue which goes beyond the scope of this chapter.[40]

2. Burden of proof

8.10 In England, in the only case to consider the point, the High Court concluded that the burden of proving lack of consent is upon the patient. The defendant does not have to prove the patient consented.[41] In other words, intentional touching is not prima facie unlawful unless it is proved to be unjustified.[42] In Canada[43] and Australia the rule is otherwise: the defendant bears the burden of proving consent. In the Australian High Court, McHugh J rationalized this view as follows:

> The contrary view is inconsistent with a person's right of bodily integrity. Other persons do not have the right to interfere with an individual's body unless he or she proves lack of consent to the interference.[44]

Given the importance the law places on the inviolability of the person and the protection of bodily integrity of the individual, it is suggested that the Commonwealth view is the better one and should be adopted in England.[45]

(i) The general principle

8.11 Consent and refusal of consent to treatment are, as expressions of the patient's right to self-determination, opposite sides of the same coin. Where consent to treatment can be provided by a patient, it is a legal necessity. Thus, either a failure to obtain consent or, in particular, a refusal by a competent patient prevents the treatment being lawful.[46] For the doctor to act in the face of such a refusal would be unlawful amounting to a battery and thus liable in criminal and civil law—see discussion below at paras 8.63–8.70.[47] The refusal may be total: 'I don't want any treatment'; or it may be partial: 'I don't want a blood transfusion.' In either case, the refusal is legally effective to prevent the prohibited treatment even if the patient may, or will certainly, die.[48] In *Re T*, Lord Donaldson MR stated:[49]

---

[40] See further in relation to the legal and ethical debate R Dresser, 'Professionals, Conformity and Conscience' (2005) 35(6) Hastings Center Report 9; J Savulescu, 'Conscientious Objection in Medicine' (2006) 332 BMJ 294; M Magellsen, 'When Should Conscientious Objection be Accepted?' (2012) 38 JME 18–21.

[41] *Freeman v Home Office (No 2)* [1984] QB 524 *per* McCowan J at 524. The Court of Appeal did not specifically refer to the point.

[42] However, judges frequently refer to consent being a 'defence': see, eg, *Collins v Wilcock* [1984] 3 All ER 374, 378 *per* Goff LJ.

[43] *Non-Marine, Underwriters, Lloyd's of London v Scalera* [2000] 1 SCR 551 (Can Sup Ct).

[44] *Secretary, Department of Health and Community Services v JWB* (1992) 66 ALJR 300, 337.

[45] Notice the confusing approach in the criminal case of *R v Brown* [1994] 1 AC 212, [1993] 2 All ER 75 (HL) *per* Lord Jauncey at 92, Lord Slynn at 119, and Lord Mustill at 108. It may be, however, that criminal cases are unhelpful in determining upon whom the onus of proof would be in a civil context given the very limited situations where in the former a defendant bears the onus of proof.

[46] *Sidaway v Bethlem Royal Hospital* [1985] AC 871, [1985] 1 All ER 643 *per* Lord Scarman at 649.

[47] eg, *Re T* [1993] Fam 95, [1992] 4 All ER 649 *per* Lord Donaldson MR at 658. See also *Re MB* (n 19) *per* Butler-Sloss LJ at 221.

[48] *Airedale NHS Trust v Bland* [1993] 1 All ER 821 *per* Lord Goff at 866 citing *Nancy B v Hôtel-Dieu de Québec* (1992) 86 DLR (4th) 385 (competent adult patient on ventilator entitled to refuse further intervention). See also *per* Lord Keith at 860 and *per* Lord Mustill at 889. See also *Re B (Adult: Refusal of Treatment)* [2002] EWHC 429 (Fam), (2002) 65 BMLR 149 *per* Butler-Sloss P (tetraplegic patient found competent to refuse life-sustaining treatment—artificial ventilation—court made a declaration that continued treatment was unlawful and made a nominal award of damages for past battery), discussed in A Grubb (2002) 10 Medical Law Review 201 (Commentary) and *Re W (Adult: Refusal of Treatment)* [2002] EWHC 901 (Fam) *per* Butler-Sloss P (prisoner with a psychopathic disorder was competent and entitled to refuse treatment for self-harming injury which might lead to his death).

[49] [1993] 4 All ER 649, 652–53.

> An adult patient who ... suffers from no mental incapacity has an absolute right to choose whether to consent to medical treatment, to refuse it or to choose one rather than another of the treatments being offered ... This right of choice is not limited to decisions which others might regard as sensible. It exists notwithstanding that the reasons for making the choice are rational, irrational, unknown or even non-existent.

Consequently, providing the patient is competent, he or she may refuse any treatment including a life-saving operation such as a blood transfusion,[50] anaesthesia and surgery necessary to prevent harm to her and her foetus,[51] renal dialysis,[52] artificial ventilation,[53] and even artificial feeding.[54] **8.12**

A refusal of medical treatment may be made contemporaneously or in anticipation of becoming incapacitated in the form[55] of an 'advance decision', now recognized by the Mental Capacity Act 2005[56] (see further Chapter 10 at paras 10.97). Such documents were previously known as an advance directive or a 'living will' (although in reality in everyday parlance the words living will and advance directive remain commonly used).[57] A valid advance decision is effective to refuse consent to treatment by a person who, at the time the decision falls to be made, lacks capacity. It must have been made by a patient who was competent at the time the advance decision was made and understood what the treatment-refusal decision entailed. It must have been intended to apply in the circumstances that subsequently arise (ie the patient's current medical condition and the procedure that is required). If the advance decision is 'clearly established',[58] then it is as legally binding upon a doctor as would be a contemporaneous refusal[59] unless it has been effectively revoked.[60] There are special rules about the formalities required to make a valid advance decision in respect of life-sustaining treatment.[61] **8.13**

Section 24 of the Mental Capacity Act sets out what constitutes an 'advance decision'. It applies to those persons over the age of 18.[62] It only applies to treatment refusal. Such a decision has to be made where a person possesses decision-making capacity. Finally, it can be withdrawn at any time while the person possesses decision-making capacity. Section 25 of **8.14**

---

[50] eg *Re T* [1993] Fam 95, [1992] 4 All ER 649 (held to be acting under the undue influence of her mother on facts).

[51] eg *Re MB* [1997] 8 Med LR 217 (held incompetent on facts) and *St George's Healthcare NHS Trust v S* [1998] 3 All ER 673, discussed in A Grubb, (1998) 6 Medical Law Review 356 (Commentary).

[52] eg, *Re JT (Adult: Refusal of Medical Treatment)* [1998] 1 FLR 48.

[53] eg, *Re B (Adult: Refusal of Treatment)* [2002] EWHC 429 (Fam) and *Re AK* (2000) 59 BMLR 151.

[54] *Secretary of State for the Home Department v Robb* [1995] 1 All ER 677 and I Kennedy (1995) 3 Medical Law Review 189 (Commentary).

[55] The Advance Directive may be oral or in writing. One advantage, however, of the latter is that it is more likely to reduce evidential difficulties.

[56] See also the Mental Capacity Act Code of Practice (2007) chapter 9.

[57] Advance Decisions were effective at common law: see *Re AK* (2000) 58 BMLR 151; *HE v A Hospital NHS Trust* [2003] EWHC 1017 (Fam) *per* Munby J. For patients over the age of 18 Advance Decisions are now governed by ss 24–29 of the Mental Capacity Act 2005 and Pt 9 of the Code of Practice. The common law continues to apply in respect of patients between the age of acquiring capacity and reaching the age of 18.

[58] If there is doubt about the patient's capacity or the directive's applicability, then it seems that a doctor may act as if the patient were incompetent in his best interests, particularly if this will preserve his life: see *Re T* [1992] 4 All ER 649 *per* Lord Donaldson MR at 661.

[59] *Re T* [1993] Fam 95, [1992] 4 All ER 649; *Airedale NHS Trust v Bland* [1993] 1 All ER 821 *per* Lord Keith at 860, *per* Lord Goff at 866, *per* Lord Mustill at 892.

[60] On which see *HE v A Hospital NHS Trust* [2003] EWHC 1017 (Fam) *per* Munby J, [36]–[45] and Chapter 4.

[61] See Mental Capacity Act 2005, s 25(5) and the discussion in Chapter 4.

[62] ibid, s 24 (1).

the Act concerns the validity and applicability of advance decisions. They must apply to the specified treatment. They do not apply if the person making the decision has done anything else clearly inconsistent with the decision.[63] The advance decision is not applicable while the person has capacity. [64] While an advance decision may relate to the withdrawal of life-sustaining treatment it will only apply to such treatment if explicitly stated.[65] This is defined in section 4(10) of the Mental Capacity Act as 'treatment which a health care professional who is providing care to the person regards as necessary to sustain life'. The Act also recognizes the gravity of such decisions and requires additional formalities in the case of life-sustaining treatment. The Act provides that they must be in writing/signed by the patient or another in his presence/witnessed and signed by a witness in his presence.[66]Advance decisions may also be operated alongside powers of attorney—as discussed in Chapter 10. The Act provides that the existence of a power of attorney does not prevent an advance directive being binding unless this is expressly stated.[67] One concern in relation to advance directives is that people's views in relation to treatment decisions may change over time. The Mental Capacity Act Code of Practice consequently advises that decisions be updated on a regular basis.[68]

8.15 Section 26 of the Act concerns the effect of advance decisions. The Act provides that an advance decision is as binding as if the person had the capacity at that time to make it. One concern before the Act came into force was that, although advance decisions could be made at common law, clinicians were unwilling to follow them as they were concerned as to whether they were valid and that this might consequently render them liable in criminal or in civil law. The Mental Capacity Act consequently provides that there is no liability for undertaking treatment unless satisfied that an advance directive exists which is valid/applicable.[69] Similarly there is no liability for withholding treatment if s/he reasonably believes that an advance decision exists, which is valid and applicable.[70] If there is uncertainty as to the meaning of the advance decision then the clinicians and NHS Trust can go to court for guidance.[71] The Act also makes express provision stating that it is lawful to continue treatment, that is, life-sustaining treatment, while the NHS trust is in the process of seeking a court order.[72] It is critical that the necessary formalities are complied with although wishes stated in a non-valid advance decision may nonetheless be something which a court subsequently takes into account in determining what is in the patient's best interests.[73]

(ii) The exceptions

8.16 There are a number of exceptions to the competent patient's right to refuse any or all medical treatments.[74]

63 ibid, s 25(2)(c).

64 ibid, s 25(3).

65 ibid, s 25(5).

66 ibid, s 25(6).

67 ibid, s 25(7).

68 Department of Constitutional Affairs, *Mental Capacity Act* 2005: *Code of Practice* (TSO 2007) paras 9.29–9.30.

69 Mental Capacity Act 2005 s 26(2).

70 ibid, s 26(3).

71 ibid, s 26(4).

72 ibid, s 26(5).

73 *An NHS Trust v D* [2012] EWHC 885 COP.

74 In *R v Ashworth Hospital Authority, ex p Brady* [2000] Lloyd's Rep Med 355 (Maurice Kay J) the judge left open whether it would be lawful to force-feed a competent prisoner on hunger strike in the public interest, eg in maintaining institutional discipline. The apparently contrary decision in *Secretary of State for the Home Department v Robb* [1995] 1 All ER 677 (Thorpe J) might be distinguished as only holding that the prison authorities had no *duty* to intervene ([71]–[73]).

8.17 (a) **Children** In the case of child who lacks capacity in respect of the particular decision, a parent (or other person holding parental authority) or the court may override a child's refusal to give consent to treatment if the child lacks capacity and the treatment is in her best interests. At common law either parent can provide valid consent for a child who lacks capacity. However, the parent only gains the right to decide on treatment for the child in order to fill the vacuum where the child is unable to provide consent. It is therefore doubtful that the parent's rights continue once the child has capacity for the specific decision.[75] It can be argued that the parent of a competent child may still have retained the right to provide consent where serious harm or death will ensue if the child's refusal is respected but overall this is unlikely as, once the child has gained capacity, it would probably be a breach of the child's Article 8 rights to override the child's refusal.[76] However if there is any doubt in this context an application should be made in the case of a child to the Family Division or in the case of a child aged 16–18 to the Family Division or to the Court of Protection.

8.18 (b) **Part IV of the Mental Health Act 1983**[77] There are statutory exceptions to the 'right of refusal' of a competent patient, in particular, in Pt IV of the Mental Health Act 1983, where the treatment is for the 'mental disorder' of a detained patient.[78] Section 63 provides that:

> The consent of a patient shall not be required for any medical treatment given to him for the mental disorder from which he is suffering, not being a form of treatment to which section sections 57,[79] 58[80] or 58A[81] above applies, if the treatment is given by or under the direction of the approved clinician in charge of the treatment.

8.19 It is clear, therefore, that section 63 provides in practice a broad exception to the common law rule that medical treatment may only be given to a competent adult patient with consent.[82] Section 63 licenses what would otherwise be trespassory touchings. It is, however, limited to patients 'detained' under the 1983 Act;[83] applies only to treatment 'for the mental disorder'[84] (and not for other physical unconnected ailments or

[75] See Chapter 9 at paras 9.48–9.51.

[76] See *Re W (A Minor) (Medical Treatment: Court's Jurisdiction)* [1993] Fam 64, [1992] 4 All ER 627 (CA); and *Re R (A Minor) (Wardship: Medical Treatment)* [1991] 4 All ER 177 (CA). See also Chapter 4.

[77] For a full discussion of Pt IV see R Jones, *Mental Health Act Manual* (10th edn, Sweet & Maxwell 2009). See also I Kennedy and A Grubb, *Medical Law* (3rd edn, Butterworths 2000) 893–909.

[78] See especially Mental Health Act 1983 ss 63, 58, and 62 (urgent treatment).

[79] ibid, s 57 applies to any surgical operation for destroying brain tissue or for destroying the functioning of brain tissue and the surgical implantation of hormones to reduce male sex drive where both consent *and* a second medical opinion are required for treatment: s 57(1)(a) and the Mental Health (Hospital, Guardianship and Treatment) (England) Regulations 2008, SI 2008/1184, reg 27 and Mental Health (Hospital, Guardianship, Community Treatment and Consent to Treatment) (Wales) Regulations 2008, SI 2008/2439, reg 38.

[80] Mental Health Act 1983 s 58 applies medication given for more than three months where consent *or* a second medical opinion is required: s 58(1)(b).

[81] ibid, s 58A applies to ECT treatment and to medicine delivered as part of ECT therapy. See the Mental Health (Hospital, Guardianship and Treatment) (England) Regulations 2008, SI 2008/1184, reg 27 and Mental Health (Hospital, Guardianship, Community Treatment and Consent to Treatment) (Wales) Regulations 2008, SI 2008/2439, reg 38.

[82] But note the 'throw away' remark in *R (on the application of B) v Ashworth Hospital* [2003] EWCA Civ 547, [2003] 1 WLR 1886 (CA) that the common law of necessity could justify treatment not covered by s 63 where the patient 'cannot or *will not* consent' (emphasis added) *per* Dyson LJ, [44]. Contrast, Simon Brown LJ, [78] and Scott-Baker LJ, [69].

[83] Although it does not apply to all: see s 56(1). Pt IV of the 1983 Act does not apply to a patient 'subject to after-care under supervision' pursuant to ss 25A–25I introduced by the Mental Health (Patients in the Community) Act 1995.

[84] Indeed, it applies only to the mental disorder which justifies the patient's detention: *R (on the application of B) v Ashworth Hospital* [2003] EWCA Civ 547, [2003] 1 WLR 1886 (CA) (s 63 did not justify forcible treatment of patient for a personality disorder when he had been detained on the basis that he was suffering from a mental illness, schizophrenia). It will apply, however, where the non-detained condition

conditions[85]); and the treatment must be given 'by or under the direction' of the responsible clinician in charge of the treatment. Importantly, any treatment must be justified not only as being in the patient's 'best interests' but must also be 'convincingly' shown to be a 'medical necessity'.[86] This is discussed further in Chapter 11.

8.20 (c) **Statutory Authority under the Mental Capacity Act 2005** Interventions (including medical treatment) may be justified by the statutory authority provided by the Mental Capacity Act 2005 (which replaced and codified the common law). Prior to the passing of the Act, the common law justification of 'necessity' came to the aid of the doctor where there was a doubt about a person's capacity. Authority is now provided by the Act, which permits a doctor to make a treatment decision where a lack of capacity is established or the capacity of the patient is unknown. It would not be unlawful, for example, temporarily to restrain a 'suicide jumper' in order to ensure their intentions and competence. Likewise, an apparent suicide victim may be treated to save her life unless it is absolutely clear that the patient was both attempting to kill herself and was competent at the time to make that decision.[87] Even if it subsequently transpired that she was competent and wished to kill herself, the intervention would still be legal.[88] Faced with a patient in a casualty department who has taken a drugs overdose, a doctor would be entitled to entertain these doubts and so act 'out of necessity' to save her life, albeit on a temporary basis. Here is a strong presumption in favour of intervening to save a life, but if a doctor was confident that a person wanted to die, any attempt to revive a person who had attempted to commit suicide may be unlawful. However, a high degree of confidence would be needed before a doctor is likely to stray into the area where s/he could be accused of acting unlawfully or would be subject to professional disciplinary sanctions.

3. Withdrawal of consent

8.21 The law's recognition and protection of the inviolability of the patient's bodily integrity includes the right to withdraw consent after it is given. A withdrawal of consent is indistinguishable, in principle, from an initial refusal of consent. To continue treatment after a patient has validly withdrawn his consent will be unlawful as a battery. There is no relevant English case. However, the issue was considered by the Canadian Supreme Court in *Ciarlariello v Schacter*[89] and it is likely that this approach would be followed in the English courts.[90]

8.22 The claimant was diagnosed with a suspected aneurism. She underwent a diagnostic cerebral angiogram. During the procedure she experienced discomfort and hyperventilation

is treated as part of, or ancillary to, the treatment for the detained condition: ibid, *per* Dyson LJ, [46] and *per* Scott-Baker LJ, [70].

85 eg *Re W (Adult: Refusal of Treatment)* [2002] EWHC 901 (Fam) (renal dialysis).

86 Art 3 of the ECHR and *Herczegfalvy v Austria* (1993) 15 EHRR 437 (ECtHR) applied in *R (on the application of Wilkinson) v Broadmoor Special Hospital Authority* [2002] 1 WLR 419 (CA) and *R (on the application of N) v M* [2003] 1 WLR 562 (CA).

87 For an explanation which would extend further, see P D G Skegg, *Law, Ethics, and Medicine* (Clarendon 1984) 110–16. The more recent recognition of a competent patient's right to refuse all treatment has, probably, superseded Professor Skegg's suggested explanation. But note the reference by Butler-Sloss LJ in *Re T* to 'preventing suicide' ([1992] 4 All ER 649, 665).

88 Of course, if the patient was known to be suffering from a mental disorder which rendered her incompetent, there would be no legal difficulty in treating her under the common law or, if detained, under s 63 of the Mental Health Act 1983 (latter applying even if she is competent): see para 8.13 above and *Re VS (Adult: Mental Disorder)* (1995) 3 Medical Law Review 292.

89 (1993) 100 DLR (4th) 609 (SCC) and I Kennedy (1994) 2 Medical Law Review 117 (Commentary).

90 Kennedy, ibid, 118. Subject to the reservation set out at para 8.28 below.

and she asked the doctor to stop, which he did. When she had calmed down, the claimant told the doctor to continue the procedure. She suffered a rare reaction to the dye which was injected during the course of the procedure. The claimant sued the doctor, inter alia, for battery alleging that she had withdrawn her consent during the procedure and its continuation amounted to a battery. The Supreme Court dismissed her action for battery. The court accepted that a patient had a right to withdraw her consent during a procedure. Cory J stated:[91]

> An individual's right to determine what medical procedures will be accepted must include the right to stop a procedure. It is not beyond the realm of possibility that the patient is better able to gauge the level of pain or discomfort that can be accepted or that the patient's premonitions of tragedy or mortality may have a basis in reality. In any event, the patient's right to bodily integrity provides the basis for the withdrawal of a consent to a medical procedure even while it is underway. Thus, if it is found that the consent is effectively withdrawn during the course of the procedure then it must be terminated.

The court noted that a consent could only validly be withdrawn if the patient was, in law, capable of doing so. A patient's capacity to withdraw consent, just as his capacity to consent, might be affected by the circumstances. Cory J stated that:[92] **8.23**

> If sedatives or other medication were administered to the patient, then it must be determined if the patient was so sedated or so affected by the medication that consent to the procedure could not effectively have been withdrawn. The question whether a patient is capable of withdrawing consent will depend on the circumstances of each case. Expert medical evidence will undoubtedly be relevant, but will not necessarily be determinative of the issue.

Also, the court must decide whether the patient had, in fact, withdrawn his consent. Cory J said: **8.24**

> The words used by a patient may be ambiguous. Even if they are apparently clear, the circumstances under which they were spoken may render them ambiguous. On some occasions, the doctors conducting the process may reasonably take the words spoken by the patient to be an expression of pain rather than a withdrawal of consent.[93]

Cory J referred to two Canadian cases where contrasting views were taken on the evidence before the courts. In *Mitchell v McDonald*[94] the claimant during a cortisone injection into a chest muscle cried out, 'For God's sake stop'. Cory J regarded as 'reasonable' the trial judge's view in that case that the claimant's exclamation was a 'cry of pain' equivalent to 'My God, stop hurting me', rather than an attempt to withdraw consent.[95] By contrast, in *Nightingale v Kaplovitch*[96] the patient was undergoing a sigmoidoscopic examination which had become extremely painful and screamed 'Stop, I can't take this any more'. The doctor continued and was held liable in battery as this amounted to a valid withdrawal of consent by the patient. **8.25**

In the *Ciarlariello* case it was recognized that the patient's right meant that it was incumbent upon a doctor, where there was any question that the patient was attempting to withdraw his consent, to enquire whether this was the case, and not blithely continue.[97] Although the **8.26**

[91] *Ciarlariello v Schacter* (1993) 100 DLR (4th) 609, 619.
[92] ibid 619–20.
[93] ibid, 618.
[94] (1987) 80 AR 16 (Alta QB).
[95] *Ciarlariello v Schacter* (1993) 100 DLR (4th) 609, 618 *per* Cory J.
[96] [1989] OJ No 585 (QL) (HC).
[97] *Ciarlariello v Schacter* (1993) 100 DLR (4th) 609, 618 *per* Cory J.

court did not spell out the implications of not doing so, they are obvious. Continuation in the face of what is subsequently interpreted as a withdrawal of consent will be a battery. It may also expose the doctor to a legitimate complaint to the General Medical Council for breaching the GMC Code of Conduct.[98]

8.27 The Canadian Supreme Court acknowledged that the 'right' to withdraw consent was not absolute where the effect of terminating: 'would be either life threatening or pose immediate and serious problems to the health of the patient'.[99] In this situation, presumably, the court took the view that as a matter of public policy, the 'refusal' is not valid because of the doctor's overriding duty of care to the patient, which would be breached if such serious harm occurred. However, nowhere in the judgment is the basis of this limitation on the 'right' spelt out. In the light of *Re B*[100] the UK courts are likely to take a different view. A valid withdrawal of consent would prevent the continuance of lawful treatment even if the consequence was the death of the patient. Even if the UK courts were to follow the Canadian lead, any permissive continuance of treatment must be limited to allowing continued intervention to secure the patient from the immediate peril, and not necessarily completion of the procedure, when the patient's 'right' will again take precedence.[101] In practical terms, of course, the 'right' to withdraw during a procedure cannot apply to major surgical operations performed under general anaesthetic and is limited to more minor surgery or diagnostic procedures (as in *Ciarlariello* itself) performed, at worst, under a local anaesthetic, and it may be, therefore, that the limitation will not usually apply.

8.28 On the facts, the court held that the claimant had validly withdrawn her consent but this had been complied with by the doctors. The only issue remaining for the court was whether the procedure had been lawfully recommenced. For the court this meant, first, whether there had been a valid consent, and secondly, whether the patient had been sufficiently informed for the purposes of negligence. Cory J concluded both questions in the defendant's favour:[102]

> . . . the patient may still consent to the renewal or continuation of the process. That consent must also be informed. Although it may not be necessary that the doctors review with the patient all the risks involved in the procedure, the patient must be advised of any material change in the risks which has arisen and would be involved in continuing the process. In addition, the patient must be informed of any material change in the circumstances which could alter his or her assessment of the costs or benefits of continuing the procedure. Here, there had been no material change in the circumstances and a valid consent was given to the continuation of the process.

8.29 In England and Wales the law would similarly require that the patient should give a valid consent to continuation and also would impose a duty to provide information relevant to that decision. The content of that duty would be a matter for the law of negligence (discussed below at para 8.71 onwards).[103] While medical evidence of actual (or potential) practices would be highly influential, it would not be determinative.

[98] GMC, 'Good Medical Practice (2013)' (GMC 2013); and see also Chapter 2.
[99] *Ciarlariello v Schacter* (1993) 100 DLR (4th) 609, 619 *per* Cory J.
[100] See [2002] 2 FCR 1.
[101] See DoH, *Reference Guide to Consent for Examination or Treatment* (note 4).
[102] *Ciarlariello v Schacter* (1993) 100 DLR (4th) 609, 624.
[103] See paras 8.70–8.89.

4. Limits to consent

(i) Criminal law

Thus far it has been stated that the presence of a patient's consent[104] determines the legality of a medical treatment or intervention. A medical intervention may amount to the crime of assault or an aggravated form of it under sections 47, 20, and 18 of the Offences Against the Person Act 1861. In England, a person may not consent to anything which is intended to, or which does, cause more than actual bodily harm.[105] Of course, many surgical interventions cause serious injury even though the doctor's intention is to benefit the patient—unlike the usual violent offender charged under the 1861 Act. English law could take the view that 'medical treatment' is wholly outside the violence offences of the 1861 Act because the effects of surgery do not amount to 'injury' or 'harm' when viewed in their totality or in the light of the doctor's intention.[106] The law does not, however, adopt that approach.[107] Instead, it assumes the doctor's actions do prima facie fall within the criminal prohibition but then creates a specific exemption from the law's refusal to accept consent as a defence to anything which amounts to more than actual bodily harm.[108] In *Attorney-General's Reference (No 6 of 1980)*[109] Lord Lane CJ stated that 'reasonable surgical interference' fell outside the criminal law.[110] Subsequently, in *Airedale NHS Trust v Bland*, Lord Mustill stated the 'medical exception' as follows: **8.30**

> ... proper medical treatment stand[s] completely outside the criminal law. The reason why the consent of the patient is so important is not that it furnishes a defence in itself, but because it is usually essential to the propriety of medical treatment. Thus, if consent is absent, and is not dispensed with in special circumstances by operation of law, the acts of the doctor lose their immunity.[111]

In *R v Brown*[112] the House of Lords accepted the existence of the 'medical exception' and Lord Mustill remarked that 'proper medical treatment ... is in a category of its own'.[113] Thus, there is no doubt that the consent of a patient to 'proper medical treatment' is valid notwithstanding that the procedure will cause injury which the patient could not otherwise lawfully consent to. **8.31**

(ii) Therapeutic procedures

The scope of the 'medical exception' remains unclear.[114] In large part this is because a wholly satisfactory account of the basis of the 'medical exception' is elusive, although it must lie in public policy. It is suggested that, in general, the legitimating criterion for an invasion of bodily integrity must be the doctor's 'therapeutic purpose' or his 'intention to benefit' the patient.[115] The criterion is that the procedure is intended to be therapeutic/beneficial to the **8.32**

---

104 Or that of a proxy acting in the patient's 'best interests'.

105 *R v Brown* [1994] 1 AC 212, [1993] 2 All ER 75 (HL).

106 See P D G Skegg, *Law, Ethics, and Medicine* (Clarendon 1984) 30–2.

107 *R v Brown* [1994] 1 AC 212, [1993] 2 All ER 75 (HL).

108 The exception should extend to any qualified *health care practitioner*, for example, a dentist or nurse who is acting within their area of competence (ie providing they have the appropriate qualification, clinical competence, and professional regulation) for example the Medicinal Products: Prescription By Nurses etc Act 1992.

109 [1981] QB 715, [1981] 2 All ER 1057 (CA).

110 ibid, 1059.

111 [1993] 1 All ER 821, 889.

112 [1993] 2 All ER 75.

113 ibid, 110.

114 See P D G Skegg, *Law, Ethics, and Medicine* (Clarendon 1984), chapter 2 and G Williams, *Textbook of Criminal Law* (2nd edn, Stevens 1983), 589–91.

115 See I Kennedy and A Grubb, *Medical Law* (3rd edn, Butterworths 2000), 768–73.

patient, not whether it did actually benefit the patient. The crucial question, in determining whether an intervention falls within the medical exception, must be the doctor's purpose given the patient's decision to consent to the procedure reflecting his judgment about its therapeutic or beneficial character.

8.33 Obviously, within this context, the reference to 'benefit' solely relates to a benefit to the patient's life or physical or mental health.[116] Consequently, a patient could not consent to serious injury, for example the amputation of a leg, in order to enhance her financial interests.[117] A contrasting case which, though superficially similar, falls clearly on the other side of the line, would be where the patient wishes desperately to be rid of his leg, the presence of which he says is causing him severe distress. If the surgeon performs the amputation, honestly intending to benefit the patient's mental health, while many might disagree with that decision, it is not for the criminal law to second guess the patient's own determination of their health interests.

8.34 Providing the therapeutic purpose exists, a patient may consent to serious injury, for example, gender re-assignment surgery.[118] A patient's consent to a procedure will also be valid even if it exposes him to the risk of death providing the procedure, on balance, is considered by his doctors acting in good faith to be in his best medical interests, for example, heart transplant surgery.[119] Of course, if the patient dies as a result of the surgeon's gross negligence, he might be guilty of manslaughter regardless of the validity of the patient's consent.[120]

(iii) Other procedures

8.35 This account does not, however, deal with all procedures which appear to fall within the medical exception. A number of procedures, though not necessarily intended for the medical benefit of the individual, are widely regarded as socially acceptable and ones to which the individual may consent:[121] research,[122] donation of organs and tissue,[123] contraceptive sterilization,[124] abortion,[125] and cosmetic surgery. No doubt the courts would accept—and already do accept—an individual's right to consent to such procedures and that, where such consent is provided, those who carry them out are acting lawfully. There would, of course, be limits: the courts would not allow a person to donate his heart if, as it usually would, this would lead to his death.[126] There is no 'golden thread' or commonality which would

---

[116] See the Female Genital Mutilation Act 2003.

[117] See the guarded comment of Neill LJ in *Re F (Mental Patient: Sterilisation)* [1990] 2 AC 1, 29.

[118] *Corbett v Corbett (Otherwise Ashley)* [1971] P 83; and *Bellinger v Bellinger* [2003] 2 All ER 593 (HL) (legality of gender re-assignment surgery not doubted).

[119] *R v Hyam* [1975] AC 55 (HL) 74 and 77–78 *per* Lord Hailsham.

[120] *R v Adomako* [1995] AC 171, [1994] 3 All ER 79 (HL); and A Grubb, A, (1994) 2 Medical Law Review 362 (Commentary).

[121] See P Lewis, 'Procedures That Are Against the Medical Interests of Incompetent Adults' (2002) 22 OJLS 575 at 575–76 contrasting the position with incompetent adults.

[122] The propriety of non-therapeutic research in prescribed circumstances is recognized in the European Convention on Human Rights and Biomedicine (1996), Arts 16 and 5. There are procedures under the Mental Capacity Act which now govern research which involves performing individually non-therapeutic procedures for adults without capacity. See Chapter 13.

[123] Human Tissue Act 2004.

[124] Originally the National Health Service (Family Planning) Act 1967; now National Health Service Act 2006 s 5(1)(b). Contrast the comments of Denning LJ in *Bravery v Bravery* [1954] 1 WLR 1169 at 1180–81 which no longer can be taken seriously as representing public policy: *Cataford v Moreau* (1978) 114 DLR (3d) 585.

[125] Abortion Act 1967.

[126] Contrast the procedure known as a 'domino transplant' where a person in need of a lung transplant for medical reasons receives both lungs and a new heart, making his heart available for donation. All organ donations of live donors now have to be specifically approved by the Human Tissue Authority as a result of

explain this collection of procedures other than that they are currently socially acceptable and thus, as a matter of public policy, they are, or would be, recognized by the judges as lawful. Without statutory guidance,[127] the courts can do no better than to deal with each procedure, as and when it comes before them, and apply their sense of what are the proper limits of public policy.[128]

B. The Nature of Consent

1. Forms of consent

Consent is a state of mind personal to the patient whereby he agrees to the violation of his bodily integrity.[129] Not every agreement to undergo treatment is, in law, a valid consent because it may be based upon inadequate information to make a meaningful decision whether to undergo the procedure[130] or it may be the product of circumstances, or others' desires, which render the decision involuntary or one which is not really the patient's because of undue influence.[131] **8.36**

A patient's consent need not be given in writing. The common law does not impose such a requirement, although in analogous circumstances statutory provisions may do so.[132] However, 'consent forms' are routinely used in hospitals when a patient undergoes a surgical intervention. They do not, as is sometimes assumed within the medical profession, in themselves constitute a patient's consent. Their function, in law, is purely evidentiary. In stating that the patient has agreed to a particular procedure which has been explained to him and which he has understood, the 'consent' will not be worth the paper it is written on if these recitations are not, in fact, true or the signature has been obtained with inadequate information. Consent expressed 'in form only' is no consent at all.[133] An identical approach is called for in respect of forms which purport to record a patient's refusal of treatment, for example, of a blood transfusion. Speaking of such forms in *Re T,* Lord Donaldson MR stated:[134] **8.37**

> They will be wholly ineffective . . . if the patient is incapable of understanding them, they are not explained to him and there is no good evidence (apart from the patient's signature) that he had that understanding and fully appreciated the significance of signing it.

(i) Express consent

(a) **Actual consent** A patient's consent may be express or implied. Express consent is often treated as synonymous with expressed consent, that is where the patient demonstrates orally or in writing that he agrees to the treatment or procedure. While this will often be **8.38**

the scheme under the Human Tissue Act 2004. Thus lawful authority for an inter vivos organ transplant is now dependent on such specific authority. This requirement does not apply to cadaveric transplants.

[127] Some time ago, the Law Commission provisionally proposed a statutory base, including a statutory list of 'borderline' procedures, for the exception: see *Consent and the Criminal Law* (Consultation Paper No 139, 1995) Pt VIII.

[128] Jurisdictions with Criminal Codes often seek to deal with the 'medical exception' albeit in general terms: see Crimes Act 1961 (NZ) ss 61 and 61A; Criminal Code (Can) ss 45 and 216; Criminal Code (Qld) ss 282 and 288. For a discussion of the latter, see R S O'Regan, 'Surgery and Criminal Responsibility under the Queensland Criminal Code' (1990) 14 Crim LJ 73.

[129] *Sidaway v Bethlem Royal Hospital Governors* [1985] 1 All ER 643, 658 *per* Lord Diplock.

[130] See paras 8.68–8.89.

[131] See para 8.68.

[132] Human Fertilisation and Embryology Act 1990, Sch 8. Discussed in Chapter 10.

[133] *Chatterton v Gerson* [1981] 1 All ER 257, 265 *per* Bristow J.

[134] [1992] 4 All ER 649, 668.

the case, it is sometimes misleading to regard it in these terms. More accurately, the issue is whether the patient has given actual consent to the treatment or procedure whether or not this is demonstrated orally or in writing. Consent is, as was seen earlier, a state of mind of the patient. A valid legal consent is given even where the patient does not demonstrate his agreement providing that the state of his mind was, in fact, that he agreed. In other words, an unexpressed actual consent is, in law, a valid consent. Of course, there may be evidential difficulties in establishing the patient's actual consent if it is not expressed, but this does not detract from the analysis of what consent, in law, really is.

8.39 (b) **Inferred consent** Any other form of consent—sometimes referred to as implied consent—is strictly speaking not a 'consent' given by the patient at all.[135] So, where the patient conducts himself such that it is reasonable to imply that he consented to the treatment or procedure, the law merely prohibits the patient because of his conduct from denying that he consented even though, in fact, he did not.[136] This is not to say that consent cannot be inferred from the patient's conduct and behaviour: it can be, but it should be distinguished from implied consent.[137] The latter is a legal device whereby the legality of a treatment or procedure is recognized even though the patient subjectively does not, in fact, consent. A patient who allows a doctor to carry out a procedure in full knowledge of what is to be done will have given actual consent to the procedure. His consent is not implied but rather inferred. Evidentially, the fact that the patient did not express his consent is not conclusive. Rather, faced with these facts, what other inference is it proper for the court to make other than that the patient was actually consenting?

8.40 The conduct of the patient may lead those providing the treatment to the conclusion that the patient has consented to the treatment or procedure. In these circumstances, it is said that the patient's consent is implied and the doctor has a defence to an action in battery. The classic illustration is found in the US case of *O'Brien v Cunard SS Co.*[138] The claimant was vaccinated against smallpox by a surgeon on board a boat bound for Boston. She joined a line of passengers whom the surgeon was examining and vaccinating if necessary. When the surgeon told her she should be vaccinated she held out her arm and he did so. She sued claiming battery on the basis that she had not consented to the vaccination. The Supreme Judicial Court of Massachusetts dismissed her action. The court held that her consent should be implied from the circumstances and her conduct. Knowlton J said:[139]

> If the claimant's behavior was such as to indicate consent on her part, [the surgeon] was justified in his act, *whatever her unexpressed feelings may have been*. In determining whether she consented, he could be guided only by her overt acts and the manifestations of her feelings.

8.41 Properly understood, O'Brien is almost certainly a case of inferred consent. It might be thought that the claimant's conduct irresistibly led to the inference that she actually had consented to the vaccination. What else was she doing in the line, having spoken to the surgeon, holding her arm out? However, as the words from Knowlton J's judgment show, the court seems not to have inferred that she actually consented. Rather, he conceded that she did not but nevertheless debarred her from relying upon that because of the circumstances and her behaviour: her consent was implied.[140] On the facts, no doubt the court was influenced by the fact that notices had been posted around the ship in various languages that day to indicate the

135 See para 8.48.
136 *Sidaway v Bethlem Royal Hospital Governors* [1985] 1 All ER 643, 658 *per* Lord Diplock.
137 I Kennedy and A Grubb, *Medical Law* (3rd edn, Butterworths 2000), 589–92.
138 (1891) 28 NE 266 (Mass Sup Jud Ct).
139 ibid, 266 (emphasis added).
140 See also *Allan v New Mount Sinai Hospital* (1980) 109 DLR (3d) 634, 641 *per* Linden J.

need for vaccination; the claimant had stood in line and seen what was happening to other passengers and she had not offered any objection to the surgeon when he went to vaccinate her.

Thus, it is suggested that implied consent is not a species of consent at all. To describe the situation in the *O'Brien* case as one of consent would be fictional. Rather, implied consent is more properly understood as a species of estoppel.[141] Where the patient so conducts himself in the circumstances that it is reasonable to conclude that he has consented to a treatment or procedure, the patient will not subsequently be permitted to rely on the fact that she did not in fact have the necessary state of mind to amount to consent, and thus allow her to assert that she did not consent. The doctor will have a defence to what would otherwise be an unlawful touching based upon the patient's appearance of consent. **8.42**

Whether a patient will be taken to have consented to a particular treatment or procedure will be a question of fact in every case. Where a reasonable person looking at the situation would conclude that the patient had agreed to the intervention, even if the patient has not, the doctor will have a defence based upon inferred consent.[142] However it would be dangerous for a doctor to conclude that a patient's silence alone constituted agreement. The issue is one of reasonable deduction based upon all the circumstances, in particular, taking account of the patient's conduct and anything known about the patient. **8.43**

Inferred consent is frequently relied upon by doctors as a justification for carrying out treatments or interventions upon patients. The extent to which consent may be inferred is, often, controversial.[143] Given that inferred consent, even if the patient's state of mind means that he has given no consent at all, nevertheless licenses an interference with the patient's right of self-determination. The circumstances necessary to impute such consent require a clear (perhaps unequivocal) indication that the patient appeared to be giving his consent.[144] Some situations, however, should not be analysed as ones where the patient has impliedly consented: two, in particular, are important. Prior to the passing of the Mental Capacity Act 2005, it was argued that treatment of an unconscious or otherwise incompetent patient may be justified on the basis of implied consent.[145] However it is now clear that where treatment is provided to a person who does not have the capacity to give or withhold consent, legitimacy for the action is provided through the statutory right to act in the best interests of a patient under section 4 of the Act and not on the basis of implied or inferred consent. **8.44**

Inferred consent is also often utilized by doctors to justify treatment or interventions which are considered to be routine by the medical profession. For example, diagnostic tests are regularly performed during maternity care without the explicit consent of the patient. However, the NHS standard consent form asks a patient to consent to 'the procedure or course of treatment described on this form'. Thus any patient who signs the form appears to provide explicit agreement to the treatment as a whole, including diagnostic tests which form of the treatment. There is a part of the form that a patient can say what they do not want. Thus, if the patient disagrees with the routine tests but has remained silent, this is a case of inferred consent. Other examples[146] might include procedures carried out by students as part of their **8.45**

[141] *Sidaway v Bethlem Royal Hospital Governors* [1985] 1 All ER 643, 658, 658 *per* Lord Diplock.

[142] See, eg, *Canadian AIDS Society v Ontario* (1995) 25 OR (3d) 388 ('reasonable blood donor test' used).

[143] eg in the context of HIV testing, see A Grubb and D Pearl, *Blood Testing, AIDS and DNA Profiling—Law and Policy* (Jordans 1991), 11–18.

[144] *Schweiser v Central Hospital* (1974) 53 DLR (3d) 494, 508 *per* Thompson J.

[145] For example, P D G Skegg, 'A Justification for Medical Procedures Performed Without Consent' (1974) 90 LQR 512. Professor Skegg's later views rest more strongly on the doctrine of necessity: see his *Law, Ethics and Medicine* (Clarendon 1984) chapter 5.

[146] An analogous situation is the use of medical records for research, especially epidemiological research.

training. To what extent does the law accept that a medical professional can rely on inferred consent to interventions of this kind when, a fortiori, the patient has not given actual consent? The answer will depend upon the circumstances.

8.46 It will only be proper to infer consent if the reasonable onlooker would conclude, albeit wrongly, that the patient had agreed to the intervention. As a basic minimum, this should require that the patient be given notice of the possibility of the 'extra' intervention and be given an opportunity to 'opt out' which is not taken. Merely being in a teaching hospital would not, on this basis, be sufficient to give rise to an implication that students may engage in touchings for their own benefit. That fact would have to be brought to the patient's attention or reasonable steps be taken to do so.[147]

8.47 Importantly, consent should not be inferred unless the patient has had an opportunity to opt out of the 'extra' intervention. Otherwise, it would not, it is suggested, be reasonable to imply the patient's agreement merely as the result of his silence. Also, it may only be proper to imply the patient's agreement or accord with procedures which involve minor interventions and are not controversial in nature. In other situations, the importance the law places upon the inviolability of the patient's bodily integrity strongly points to the law requiring explicit consent for any substantial invasion of a patient's body. Hence, it would not be proper to infer that a woman in a teaching hospital (even with her knowledge) impliedly consented to intrusive gynaecological investigations by students for the purposes of teaching. Equally, it would be wrong to imply that a patient, by agreeing to the taking of blood, agrees to it being tested for HIV infection or genetic conditions. The implications of the results of such tests for the patient (and others) is such that the law would only countenance explicit consent as justifying the taking from a competent adult.

2. Scope of consent

8.48 The law of consent requires that the patient authorize the procedure which is carried out. A procedure may be unauthorized for a number of reasons and, subject to what is said below, in such circumstances the doctor will commit a battery. As one Canadian judge put it: 'It is the patient, not the doctor, who decides *whether* the surgery will be performed, *where* it will be done, *when* it will be done and *by whom* it will be done.'[148]

8.49 However, it is important to determine what has, or has not, been authorized by the patient. The following situations illustrate the divide between authorized and unauthorized procedures.

(i) Absence of real consent

8.50 A patient may agree to a medical procedure but without understanding the basic 'nature and purpose' of what it involves. It is clear that in this situation a patient's agreement is not a valid consent to the medical touching and a battery action will lie.[149] This issue is explored below.

(ii) In face of a valid refusal

8.51 As was seen above,[150] a valid refusal of treatment by a competent adult patient makes any intervention covered by the refusal unlawful in both the criminal and civil sense. The

[147] Note *Turner v Royal Bank of Scotland plc* [1999] 2 All ER (Comm) 664 (CA) (no implied consent by bank customer to disclosure of confidential information to another bank based upon banking practice of which he was unaware).

[148] *Allan v New Mount Sinai Hospital* (1980) 109 DLR (3d) 634, 642 *per* Linden J (emphasis added).

[149] *Chatterton v Gerson* [1981] QB 432, 443 *per* Bristow J; approved in *Sidaway v Governors of Bethlem Royal Hospital* [1985] AC 871 (HL) and see paras 8.70–8.89.

[150] See paras 8.10–8.12.

refusal may relate to all medical interventions or limit the range of interventions which the doctor may perform by, for example, instructing a doctor not to inject an anaesthetic into a particular arm[151] or not to perform a sterilization.[152] In these circumstances, it will not be a defence that the doctor considered the procedure to be medically desirable.[153] The doctor's duty to act in the best medical interests of the patient is limited by the patient's right to refuse.[154]

(iii) Conditional consent/refusal

Problems can arise in practice where a patient gives only conditional consent to treatment. If the condition is not satisfied and thereafter the treatment is carried out, the procedure will be unauthorized. Hence a battery will have been committed. For example, the patient agrees to a blood transfusion providing the blood is provided by a relative[155] or only if the procedure is performed by a particular doctor.[156] In both cases, when the doctor carried out the surgery he carried out a procedure which, in the circumstances, was unauthorized. Looking at it another way, until the condition upon which consent is dependent is satisfied, the patient, has in fact, refused consent to the procedure. While, in principle, a patient in England could bring a battery action where a different doctor than was anticipated operated,[157] in practice it is unlikely to arise. This is because within an NHS hospital there is no expectation that a particular procedure will be carried out by a particular doctor. This is made plain in the standard consent form used for surgical procedures.[158] Thus, a patient who seeks to set up conditions upon the provision of consent should, unless the clinicians are prepared to accept the conditions and be bound by them, be treated as having refused to provide consent. **8.52**

(iv) 'Further' or 'additional' procedures

What is the legal position when the patient consents to procedure 'X' and the doctor carries out procedure 'Y' (instead of, or in addition to, X)? This could arise, for example, where the doctor discovers condition Y during surgery for condition X. In principle, a patient would have a claim in battery[159] for the performance of the unauthorized procedure.[160] However, it may be that what on the face of it seems an unauthorized[161] procedure was, in fact, authorized or otherwise justified. **8.53**

(a) **Principle of statutory authority**[162] Once the patient has been taken into surgery he will have lost consciousness and thus lack capacity. If the surgeon discovers subsequently **8.54**

[151] *Allan v New Mount Sinai Hospital* (1980) 109 DLR (3d) 634 (Ont HCt).

[152] *Cull v Royal Surrey County Hospital* [1932] 1 BMJ 1195.

[153] *Mulloy v Hop Sang* [1935] 1 WWR 714 (Alta CA) (prohibited amputation which was necessary amounted to a battery).

[154] See *Airedale NHS Trust v Bland* [1993] 1 All ER 821, 866 *per* Lord Goff and (1905) 104 NW 12 (Sup Ct Minn).

[155] *Ashcraft v King* (1991) 278 Cal Rptr 900.

[156] *Perna v Perozzi* (1983) 457 A 2d 431.

[157] *Michael v Molesworth* [1950] 2 BMJ 171.

[158] See *Good Practice in Consent Implementation Guide* (Department of Health 2001).

[159] See also *Williamson v East London and City HA* [1998] Lloyd's Rep Med 6 (Butterfield J) (action in negligence based upon patient's lack of consent when surgeon exceeded P's authority by removing her breast when P had only agreed to less radical surgery).

[160] eg *Mohr v Williams* (1905) 104 NW 12 (Sup Ct Minn) (no consent to operation on left ear during operation on right ear); *Murray v McMurchy* [1949] 2 DLR 442 (BC Sup Ct); *Hamilton v Birmingham RHA* [1969] 2 BMJ 456 (no consent to sterilization during Caesarean section); and *Devi v West Midlands RHA* (1981) (CA Transcript 491) (no consent to sterilization performed during operation to repair ruptured uterus).

[161] See, eg *Abbass v Kenney* (1995) 31 BMLR 157 (Gage J).

[162] More fully discussed in Chapter 9.

that an unauthorized procedure is required, the issue is whether the surgeon can take a decision on behalf of the patient under the Mental Capacity Act 2005. There is a strong presumption under the Act and the Code of Practice that the patient should not have this decision taken for him if it would be possible to bring the patient back to consciousness and then ask for consent. This would avoid the need to take a decision on behalf of a person who lacked consent. However, there may be circumstances where it is manifestly in the patient's best interests to operate immediately and thus a doctor would be justified in taking a best interests decision on behalf of the patient who lacked capacity. The tests under the 2005 Act replace the common law where authority was justified in law if it was necessary in the sense that the patient's medical condition is such that it would have been unreasonable (and not merely inconvenient) to delay the procedure until the patient regains consciousness and can decide for himself.[163] That distinction is highlighted by the Canadian cases of *Marshall v Curry*[164] and *Murray v McMurchy*.[165] The approach under the Mental Capacity Act 2005 is modelled on the common law and is informed by such approaches.

8.55 In *Marshall v Curry*, the doctor discovered a grossly diseased testicle during a hernia operation being performed on the patient. He removed it, as part of the hernia operation, but also because he considered it to be gangrenous and a threat to the patient's life and health. The patient's battery action was dismissed on the basis that a doctor may act without consent 'in order to save the life or preserve the health of the patient'.[166] However, as *Murray v McMurchy* shows, the scope of this apparently broad statement is more limited than providing a justification for exceeding a patient's consent whenever it is considered in his 'best interests' to do so. In the *Murray* case, the patient underwent a Caesarean section, during the course of which she was sterilized because the doctor considered that the condition of her uterus—she had fibroid tumours—would make future pregnancies hazardous for her. The court upheld her battery action. There was no evidence of any immediate danger to her life; it was merely convenient to carry out the sterilization whilst she was unconscious.[167] Thus translated into the language of the Mental Capacity Act, this is an occasion where it would not be justifiable for the doctor to take a decision on behalf of the patient because it was possible for the patient to be brought round from the anaesthetic and then informed about her medical condition and given the choice to give or refuse consent.

8.56 There is no directly relevant English case concerned with the temporarily incapacitated. However, in *Re F* the matter was touched upon both in the House of Lords and the Court of Appeal. Lord Goff, in his speech, stated that the doctor 'should do no more than is reasonably required, in the best interests of the patient, before he recovers consciousness'.[168] While he was prepared to identify the correct legal question he declined to go further and discuss *Marshall* and *Murray*.[169] In the Court of Appeal, having referred to the Canadian cases, Butler-Sloss LJ concluded that where the patient was temporarily incapacitated a procedure which was 'necessary for the preservation of life or for the preservation of health' could be lawfully performed.[170] Neill LJ spoke in terms which mirror the essence of the Canadian cases:

---

163 See *Re F* [1990] 2 AC 1, 37 *per* Butler-Sloss LJ (CA) and at 76–77 *per* Lord Goff (HL). See also P D G Skegg, *Law, Ethics and Medicine* (Clarendon 1984), 102–04.

164 [1933] 3 DLR 260 (Sup Ct NS).

165 [1949] 2 DLR 442 (Sup Ct BC).

166 *Marshall v Curry* (n 164) *per* Chisholm CJ at 265.

167 See also *Parmley v Parmley* [1945] 4 DLR 81 (patient undergoing limited tooth extraction and dentist removed all the patient's teeth because he discovered advanced tooth decay and gum disease—held a battery).

168 *Re F* [1990] 2 AC 1, 77.

169 ibid.

170 ibid, 37.

> The treatment which can be . . . given . . . is, within broad limits, confined to such treatment as is necessary to meet the emergency and as such needs to be carried out at once and before the patient is likely to be in a position to make a decision for himself.[171]

Consequently, the 2005 Act only permits a best interests decision to be taken by a doctor in situations where the patient is temporarily incompetent to permit procedures which it would have been unreasonable to delay because of the imminent danger to the life or health of the patient. **8.57**

(b) Within the 'broad nature' of the consent given It is important to determine precisely what the patient has agreed to prior to the procedure. It may be that, looking at all the circumstances surrounding the patient giving consent, the patient consented to the apparently unauthorized procedure even it is not included on the consent form.[172] Two cases illustrate how the patient's agreement may be interpreted as broad enough to encompass the 'additional' procedure. In *Davis v Barking, Havering and Brentwood HA*[173] the claimant underwent an operation for the removal of a cyst. She signed a consent form in which it was stated that she consented to the 'administration of general, local or other anaesthetics'. She was told that a general anaesthetic would be used. During the procedure, in addition to this, a caudal block was given. After the operation the claimant temporarily lost movement in her legs and control of her bladder, but was left with some minor problems. She sued in battery and negligence alleging, in respect of battery, that the anaesthetist had administered the caudal block without her consent and which had caused her injury. McCullough J dismissed her action in battery. He concluded that it would be wrong to sectionalize what the claimant had consented to. There were not two separate operations which had been performed for which consent to each would have been necessary. The correct question was 'Have the defendants shown that the claimant consented to a procedure the nature and effect of which had in broad terms been explained to her?'[174] The judge held that the claimant had understood in 'broad terms' the nature of what was to be done to her, namely that she would receive an anaesthetic. The judge did not rely upon the broadly drafted terms of the consent form.[175] Instead, his conclusion was that, viewed 'in the round' the caudal block was 'part and parcel' of the anaesthetic she had (with knowledge) agreed to.[176] **8.58**

(c) Consent forms[177] Standard surgical consent forms in England have long contained clauses which indicate, variously expressed, that the patient agrees to 'such further or alternative operative measures or treatment as may be found necessary during the course of the operation or the treatment'.[178] There can be no doubt that these clauses were included on behalf of doctors to license and provide a legal basis for 'further' or 'additional' procedures carried out for the benefit of the patient during an operation. **8.59**

On the face of it, the clause cannot in itself be evidence (let alone amount to) express consent beyond the terms of the express consent. For that, the patient must understand the 'nature and purpose' of the additional or further procedure and have agreed to it.[179] By **8.60**

---

[171] ibid, 30.

[172] See *O'Bonsawin v Paradis* (1993) 15 CCLT (2d) 188.

[173] [1993] 4 Med LR 85; A Grubb, (1993) 1 Medical Law Review 389 (Commentary).

[174] ibid, 91.

[175] See paras 8.61–8.67 and *Pridham v Nash* (1986) 33 DLR (4th) 304.

[176] For a criticism of the case, see A Grubb, (1993) 1 Medical Law Review 389 (Commentary).

[177] For the 'evidentiary' effect of consent forms, see para 8.38.

[178] See, eg the (then) DoH standardized consent form agreed with the medical protection organizations: HSC (IS)197 (October 1975). The form is discussed in W A J Farndale and E C Larman, *Legal Liability for Claims arising from Hospital Treatment* (2nd edn, Ravenswood 1976) 19–29.

[179] eg *Abbass v Kenney* (1995) 31 BMLR 157: on facts held patient consented to operation carried out and no reliance placed upon the clause in consent form stating she consented to 'further or alternative operative measures as may be found to be necessary'.

definition, reliance would only be placed upon this clause when the patient has not understood even in broad terms the nature of the additional procedure. At best, these clauses could only give rise to the argument that the patient had waived his right to the basic information—a claim which is highly problematic legally—or that by signing the consent form containing the clause he is taken thereby to have impliedly consented to the additional or further procedure. The latter arises, as we have seen already, where the patient has conducted himself such that it is reasonable to infer that he agreed and, importantly, understood what would or might happen. A prerequisite of inferred consent is that the patient has actual or constructive notice of the information which he is thereafter estopped from denying. Obviously, this cannot be applied in the context of vaguely drafted clauses in consent forms.[180] Notwithstanding the logic of these arguments, the case law seems to give these clauses some credence. It was referred to as supporting the court's decision in *Brushnet v Cowan*[181] and was the basis for the decision in *Pridham v Nash*.[182]

C. Elements of Consent

8.61 For a consent to treatment, or a refusal of treatment, to be legally valid it must be:

(1) made by a person with capacity;
(2) real, that is, based upon adequate information; and
(3) voluntary and not made under the undue influence of another.

1. Capacity

8.62 See Chapter 9 for a detailed discussion on the law around the capacity of a patient whether adult or child.

2. Information

(i) Battery

8.63 **(a) General principles** An action in battery arises if a patient is touched without consent. The claimant need not demonstrate that any damage has resulted. Simply proving that the touching has taken place is sufficient for an action to be brought. However, the courts are circumspect in relation to extending liability in the tort of battery on public policy grounds, as they have been concerned in relation to the extension of liability in tort and the consequent implications in the area of criminal law. In *Chatterton v Gerson* Mr Justice Bristow held that no liability would arise in battery as long as the patient was informed and understood in broad terms the nature of the procedure that it was proposed to undertake, and she had given consent.[183] Thus in a situation in which such a broad general consent is given, then any further claim that a patient has been given inadequate information should be brought not in battery but in negligence.[184]

180 For the same reasons it would not be conclusive that the form stated that: 'I have been told about additional procedures which may become necessary during my treatment. I have listed below any procedures *which I do not wish to be carried out* without further discussion' (emphasis in original). Unless the patient has been advised about all the possible further procedures he will not have adequate information for his silence in respect of the particular procedure to amount to an 'implied consent'.

181 (1990) 69 DLR (4th) 743, [1991] 2 Med LR 271 (Newfd CA).

182 (1986) 33 DLR (4th) 304.

183 [1981] QB 432.

184 See the comments of Mr Justice Bristow in *Chatterton v Gerson* (n 149), and M Brazier, 'Patient Autonomy and Consent to Treatment: the Role of the Law' (1987) 7 *Legal Studies* 169.

On the face of it, if the patient's consent is not 'real' then the doctor commits battery by touching the patient. However, where the patient does not understand the 'nature' of the procedure, a doctor who mistakenly (and reasonably) believes that the patient is consenting may have a defence in that the patient may be estopped from denying he possessed the information if he has led the doctor 'reasonably to assume the relevant information was known to him'.[185] **8.64**

The only reported English case in which a health care professional has been held liable for battery where, on the face of it, the patient agreed to what was done is *Appleton v Garrett*.[186] The claimants underwent unnecessary dental work at the hands of the defendant. The defendant carried out extensive restorative treatment on teeth which were healthy for financial gain. Dyson J held that the defendant had committed a battery on his patients. In respect of those teeth that were healthy, the judge concluded that the patients' consents were not 'real'. The basis for his decision is not clear but seems, in some part, to be based upon the defendant's fraud and 'bad faith'.[187] However, it is most certainly correct. The patients did not consent even if they were aware of the nature of the 'act' performed by the defendant. They were not aware of its 'intrinsic quality', namely that it was of no benefit to them, in fact rather the contrary was the case. Agreeing to treatment on unhealthy teeth is to agree to a fundamentally different act to that which was carried out.[188] **8.65**

How far the courts will go in atomizing the 'quality' of a touching by a doctor will, ultimately, be a matter of policy and will inevtiably give rise to differences of judicial opinion. In one case,[189] a majority of the Canadian Supreme Court held that a patient had given a valid consent to an intimate examination by a doctor in circumstances where he had done so in the presence of a friend, whom he had told the patient was a medical intern. The judges considered that the patient was aware of the 'nature and quality of the act to be done'. Spence J, however, dissented stating that the patient 'only gave [her] consent to such a serious invasion of her privacy on the basis that [the friend] was a doctor intending to commence practice and who desired practical experience in such matters . . .'[190] At one level the disagreement can be seen as a semantic one but, in truth, it is over the proper scope of battery and the policy of the law. **8.66**

A somewhat similar disagreement could arise in respect of a consent given by a person to the taking of a blood sample which is subsequently used for genetic testing or to determine the individual's HIV status. If the patient is only told about what is descriptively to be done (that is, the taking of blood and the method (the 'act') and that it will be used to 'run some tests'), will the person's consent be valid if they are unaware of the precise purpose that the blood will be put to? Is the person aware of the 'intrinsic quality' of what is being done? On one view, he is because he knows that it will be used for his benefit (the tests). On another view, however, it could be said that the significance of genetic and HIV testing for the person (and indeed others close to him) is such that, without knowledge of that, the quality **8.67**

[185] See *Sidaway v Bethlem Royal Hospital Governors* [1985] 1 All ER 643 *per* Lord Diplock at 658. See discussion in paras 8.71–8.72 (mistake as to capacity). On the related, but distinct point, of whether a patient has to understand information for the purposes of negligence see Kennedy and Grubb, *Medical Law* (n 137), 243–45, and *Ciarlariello v Schacter* (1993) 100 DLR (4th) 609, 622–23 *per* Cory J (positive duty to ensure patient understands).

[186] [1997] 8 Med LR 75 and I Kennedy (1996) 4 Medical Law Review 311 (Commentary).

[187] On these see para 8.89.

[188] On this basis an English court would not follow *R v Mobilio* [1991] 1 VR 339.

[189] *R v Bolduc and Bird* (1967) 63 DLR (2d) 82.

[190] ibid, 87.

of the act is different.[191] Ultimately, however, the issue is a question of policy but given the potential for stigmatization, discrimination, and personal anxiety to the person, it is suggested that the law should require explicit agreement in these situations.

8.68 **(b) Who is carrying out the procedure?** In some situations, who is carrying out the procedure may affect the 'nature' and 'purpose' of what is being done. It is well recognized elsewhere in the law, for example in criminal law, that the identity of the actor may vitiate an individual's consent. Hence, in the law of rape the identity of the man with whom the woman is having sexual intercourse will be relevant.[192] The 'quality' of what is agreed to when a woman consents to sexual intercourse with a man who is impersonating her husband is affected by her misunderstanding. Even though she understands the nature of the 'act' (sexual intercourse), it is of a different 'quality' (adulterous) from that which she believes it to be (marital).[193] Likewise, a patient who consents to be touched by a doctor will not, in law, have given a valid consent when she is touched by that person if he turns out to be impersonating a doctor even if what is actually done is exactly what she expected.[194] The descriptive nature of the 'act' remains the same but its 'intrinsic quality' changes. So, in *R v Tabassum*[195] the defendant, claiming falsely to be a doctor, touched the breasts of a number of women in order to show them how to carry out breast self-examination. The Court of Appeal held that their consents were invalid. The women had consented to the nature of the act but not its quality, since they had (wrongly) been led to believe it was a medical examination.[196]

8.69 However, the identity of the person carrying out the procedure may not always change the 'nature' or 'quality' of what has been agreed to by the patient. It is possible for example, that if a patient who agrees to a therapeutic procedure which, unbeknownst to him, is carried out by a student or trainee, will have given a valid consent since the 'quality' of the act will not change.[197] It would be different if the agreement was to a therapeutic procedure but the student carried out an unnecessary procedure simply in order to learn how to do it or to gain experience.[198] Then, the 'purpose' of the procedure would be radically changed and the patient's consent would not be valid. A change in doctor would not, at least in England,[199] affect the consent given. Even if the patient expected a particular doctor to carry out the procedure, the consent form is likely to indicate that this is a misplaced expectation. In any event, the nature and purpose of what is being done will not change. The only legal relevance of the change in doctor might be that the patient's consent was conditional on that doctor carrying out the procedure: if he did not then there was no consent by the patient at

---

[191] For different views on this, and other analogous situations, of HIV testing, see A Grubb and D Pearl, *Blood Testing, AIDS and DNA Profiling* (Jordans 1990), chapter 1 and J Keown, 'The Ashes of AIDS and the Phoenix of Informed Consent' (1989) 52 MLR 790.

[192] *R v Linekar* [1995] 3 All ER 69 and *R v Elbekkay* [1995] Crim LR 168.

[193] In fact, the criminal law goes further than this and regards any mistake as to identity as vitiating consent: see n 194. *Quaere* whether the 'quality' of the act changes in these cases?

[194] *R v Maurantonio* (1967) 65 DLR (2d) 674. See also *De May v Roberts* (1881) 9 NW 146.

[195] [2000] Lloyd's Rep Med 404 (CA).

[196] But a mere change in status or qualifications will not affect the 'nature' or 'quality of what is being done. For example, in *R v Richardson* (1998) 43 BMLR 21 (CA) the Court of Appeal held that a dentist had not committed an assault when she treated a patient even though, unknown to the patient, she had been suspended from practice by the General Dentist Council. The patient's consent to the treatment was valid. The patient's misunderstanding about 'the qualifications or attributes' of the defendant was irrelevant.

[197] Good practice is, however, that explicit consent be obtained: see *Reference Guide to Consent for Examination or Treatment* (n 4) 5 (para 4.1).

[198] Explicitly informing the patient that the procedure is not part of his care is described as a *legal* requirement: ibid, 5 (para 4.1).

[199] But see *Perna v Pirozzi* (1983) 457 A 2d 431.

all.[200] This may be the case if for example, a patient had agreed to an operation because they wanted a specific medical consultant to undertake that procedure.

(ii) Fraud and misrepresentation

Does fraud or a misrepresentation by the doctor as to information about the procedure to be performed affect the validity of the patient's consent? In Canada, the Supreme Court has held that fraud or misrepresentation (even a negligent one) will unravel what would otherwise be a valid consent.[201] It would seem that in Canada there will not be a valid consent in these circumstances even though it is 'real', in other words, even though the patient understands the 'nature' and 'purpose' of the procedure. Fraud or misrepresentation as to collateral matters will suffice.[202] In England and Wales the position is otherwise. Notwithstanding one or two broader statements at first instance,[203] the only issue in England is whether the patient has understood the 'nature' and 'purpose' of the procedure. A misunderstanding of that may, of course, arise through fraud or misrepresentation, but it may arise simply through mistake by the patient. If fraud or misrepresentation has occurred, that may provide good evidence that the patient's consent was not 'real'. But, it is the non-consent to the procedure rather than the fraud which makes an apparent consent not a real one.[204] Fraud or misrepresentation as to a collateral matter, such as an inherent risk in the procedure or an alternative procedure, will not, however, affect the patient's consent. In *Sidaway*,[205] Sir John Donaldson MR stated that: **8.70**

> [I]t is only if the consent is obtained by fraud or by misrepresentation of the nature of what is to be done that it can be said that an apparent consent is not a true consent.

Of course, the patient may have an action in deceit or negligent misrepresentation in such circumstances but he will not have a claim in battery. In England there is no so-called 'fraud exception' to the 'nature' and 'purpose' rule.[206]

(iii) Liability in negligence

As noted above, as long as what amounts to a consent in broad general terms to the medical procedures being undertaken has been given then there will not be liability in battery. However, consent to treatment in reality goes much further than this. A patient should also be given information regarding the consequent inherent risks that the procedure may go wrong. Without such information being given and in a situation in which a patient suffers harm as a result, an action may be brought in negligence. First, the claimant can assert that there was a duty to provide him/her with information concerning risks of treatment. The claimant would then assert that this duty has been broken due to inadequate provision of information. Finally the claimant would need to demonstrate that s/he had suffered harm as **8.71**

200 ibid.

201 *Reibl v Hughes* (1980) 114 DLR (3d) 1, 11 *per* Laskin CJ.

202 But contrast *Lokay v Kilgour* (1984) 31 CCLT 177 (misrepresentation must go to 'the very nature of the procedure'). See discussion in E Picard and G Robertson, *Legal Liability of Doctors and Hospitals in Canada* (3rd edn, Carswell Thomson 1996), 57–60.

203 *Chatterton v Gerson* [1981] 1 All ER 257, 265 *per* Bristow J; and *Appleton v Garrett* [1997] 8 Med LR 75, 77 *per* Dyson J.

204 See, in the context of rape, *R v Linekar* [1995] 3 All ER 69, 73 *per* Morland J. See also *R v Richardson* (1998) 43 BMLR 21 (CA) *per* Otton LJ at 26.

205 [1984] 1 All ER 1018, 1026. See also Dunn LJ at 1029.

206 Notice, however, the remark of Sir John Donaldson MR in *Freeman v Home Office (No 2)* [1984] 1 All ER 1036, 1044, apparently recognizing a wider 'fraud exception'. *Freeman* was decided two weeks after *Sidaway* in the Court of Appeal and it is most unlikely that the Master of the Rolls intended to recant on his clear statement in *Sidaway*.

had information regarding risks been disclosed then harm subsequently suffered consequent upon those risks arising would have been averted.

(iv) The Supreme Court and informed consent

8.72 Prior to 2015, the law in this area had been the subject of considerable discussion and debate. In the House of Lords decision in *Sidaway v Bethlem Royal Hospital Governors*,[207] the House of Lords took a range of approaches to the basis for the level of disclosure required in relation to informed consent. While the dissenting judge, Lord Scarman, adopted an 'informed consent' approach drawing upon United States of America jurisprudence and having a test rooted in what a information a prudent patient would want to know, a different approach was taken by other members of the House of Lords. The majority rooted the standard of disclosure in the so-called *Bolam* test.[208] This was the test used in standard clinical negligence actions such that a medical practitioner is not guilty of negligence if he has acted in accordance with a practice accepted as proper by a responsible body of medical practitioners (see further discussion of this in chapter 4 of this volume). In the House of Lords, Lord Diplock took the *Bolam* test as the basis, thus essentially leaving a great deal of discretion in the hands of the profession. A broader approach was taken by other members of the House of Lords. So Lord Bridge said that a judge could disagree with the evidence given to him where a disclosure was such that 'no reasonably prudent medical man would fail to make it'. He suggested that such a situation would be an:

> operation involving a substantial risk of grave adverse consequences, as for example, [a] 10 per cent risk of stroke from the operation . . . In such a case, in the absence of some cogent clinical reason why the patient should not be informed, a doctor . . . could hardly fail to appreciate the necessity for an appropriate warning.[209]

8.73 Lord Templeman stated that there could be a distinction between general risks that would normally be known to the patient and special risks that might be required to be disclosed. However, he emphasized that it was for the court itself to determine negligence. In the years which followed *Sidaway*, the courts were generally unwilling to hold that the information disclosed was insufficient such that this constituted negligence.[210] However, in practice, there was a discernible shift towards enhanced disclosure. Some changes were driven by the various reports into health care scandals in the 1990s. For example, the need for consent was something integral to the recommendations made by the Alder Hey Inquiry into the unauthorized retention of human material (see further Chapter 19).[211] Similarly the inadequacy of information provision was highlighted in the Inquiry Report into the events at the cardiac paediatric unit of Bristol Royal Infirmary. The Report emphasized the need for 'respect and honesty' in health care and for the health care professional–patient relationship to be seen as one of partnership.[212] The Report stressed that consent should be seen as something more than a one-off event but rather as a process:[213] It recommended that 'Patients must be given such information as enables them to participate in their care.' Moreover it stressed

---

[207] [1985] 2 WLR 503.

[208] See *Bolam v Friern Hospital Management Committee* [1957] 2 All ER 118.

[209] Note 207 above at para**.

[210] Though see, eg, *Smith v Tunbridge Wells* [1994] 5 Med LR 334.

[211] *Report of the Inquiry into the Royal Liverpool Children's Hospital* (Alder Hey 2001) and *Bristol Inquiry Interim Report Removal and Retention of Human Material* (2000) and the Final Report (2001) available at <http://webarchive.nationalarchives.gov.uk/+/www.dh.gov.uk/en/Publicationsandstatistics/Publications/PublicationsPolicyAndGuidance/DH_4005620 >.

[212] See discussion in A Gallagher and J McHale, 'After Bristol: the importance of Informed Consent' (2001) 97 *Nursing Times* 32.

[213] *Bristol Royal Infirmary Final Report* (2001) 286.

that 'information should be tailored to the needs, circumstances and wishes of the individual'. This Report itself led to a much more individual focused series of informed consent guidance produced by the Department of Health. The Government committed itself to taking this report further and this led to the production of informed consent guidance by the Department of Health.[214] The judiciary themselves however took several years before moving towards an approach which can be seen as 'informed consent' led, with broader developments of enhanced judicial scrutiny in relation to negligence.[215]

In *Pearce v United Bristol NHS Trust*[216] Lord Woolf in the Court of Appeal took a broader approach stating that: **8.74**

> if there is a significant risk which would affect the judgement of a reasonable patient then in the normal course it is the responsibility of a doctor to inform the patient of that significant risk, if the information is needed so that the patient can determine for him or herself as to what course she should adopt.[217]

Subsequently in *Chester v Afshar* in the House of Lords (in a case concerned with causation and the question of informed consent was therefore obiter) Lord Steyn nonetheless framed disclosure here from the perspective of the autonomy of the patient.[218] He stated that **8.75**

> A surgeon owes a legal duty to a patient to warn him or her in general terms of possible serious risks involved in the procedure. The only qualification is that there may be wholly exceptional cases where objectively in the best interests of the patient the surgeon may be excused from giving a warning. This is, however, irrelevant in the present case. In modern law medical paternalism no longer rules and a patient has a prima facie right to be informed by a surgeon of a small, but well established, risk of serious injury as a result of surgery.[219]

In the cases which followed there was a somewhat varied approach to information disclosure. The courts confirmed that while there may be an obligation to inform there was no responsibility on the clinician to ensure that the patient understood the information given.[220] The law in this area has now been recast by the Supreme Court in the recent decision of *Montgomery v Lanarkshire* in 2015.[221] This case builds upon the earlier jurisprudence in the area while reframing the test for consent. **8.76**

Mrs Montgomery brought a claim on behalf of her son, alleging that the obstetrician should have warned her of the risk of shoulder dystocia and informed her of the possibility of delivery by caesarean section. There was disputed medical evidence as to the failure to inform. **8.77**

At first instance and on appeal Mrs Montgomery was unsuccessful. It was held at first instance that the case fell within *Sidaway* and that the obstetrician's approach was in accordance with that of a responsible body of medical practice. Moreover, following *Pearce,* it was held that this would not have been a significant injury to disclose. The Court also rejected evidence that she had questioned the consultant in relation to the risks. A restrictive **8.78**

---

[214] Department of Health, *Learning from Bristol: The Department of Health's Response to the Report of the Public Inquiry into Children's Heart Surgery at Bristol Royal Infirmary 1984–1995* (Cm 5363, 2002) 139–40.

[215] [1997] 3 WLR 1151.

[216] [1999] PIQR P53 (CA); and see further J Jones, 'Informed Consent and Fairy Stories' (1999) 7 Medical Law Review 103.

[217] *Pearce v United Bristol NHS Trust*, ibid.

[218] [2005] 1 AC 234.

[219] ibid.

[220] *Al Hamwi v Johnston and Another* [2005] EWHC 206; and see further J Miola, 'Autonomy Rued OK? Al Hamwi v Johnston and Another' [2006] 14 Medical Law Review 108.

[221] *Montgomery (Appellant) v Lanarkshire Health Board (Respondent) (Scotland)* [2015] UKSC 11; see further A M Farrell and M R Brazier, 'Not so new directions in the law of consent? Examining *Montgomery v Lanarkshire Health Board*' (2015) Journal of Medical Ethics, published online December 18th 2015.

approach was also taken by the Inner and Extra House of Court of Sessions. They rejected evidence that she had repeatedly asked about risks of vaginal delivery and distinguished *Chester v Afshar* on the grounds that it concerned elective surgery.

8.79 Mrs Montgomery was pregnant with her first child. She was a petite woman just over five feet in height. She suffered from diabetes and as a result was likely to give birth to a baby which was larger than normal. An obstetrician and gynaecologist, Dr McLellan, monitored her pregnancy. A major risk in diabetic pregnancies is that of a condition known as 'shoulder dystocia', namely, the risk that the shoulders of the baby will be too wide to pass to enable a standard vaginal delivery without medical assistance with consequent risk of material and fetal abnormality. There was a 9 per cent risk of shoulder dystocia. In addition, there was a further risk to the foetus of a broken shoulder and damage to the nerve roots. While such injury may be limited it can also lead to permanent disability, leaving the child with a useless arm. In cases of shoulder dystocia involving diabetic mothers the risk of such brachial plexus injury, is about 0.2 per cent. There are some instances where the umbilical cord becomes trapped against the woman's pelvis and, in such a situation, there is a small risk of less than 0.1 per cent that where the umbilical cord is occluded prolonged hypoxia may result leading to cerebral palsy or death.

8.80 While Mrs Montgomery was told that she would have a larger than usual baby she was not told the risk of shoulder dystocia. She was not offered a caesarean section as the anticipated birth weight of the baby was lower than her consultant would have normally offered such a procedure. Mrs Montgomery said if she had known of the risk of shoulder dystocia, she would have wanted an explanation and what the risks were and if it was a significant risk, she would have asked for a caesarean section. The baby during the birth became stuck due to shoulder dystocia. In the period of some twelve minutes from the head of the baby emerging and the subsequent delivery, the umbilical cord was completely or partially occluded depriving him of oxygen. The baby was subsequently diagnosed as suffering from cerebral palsy of a form caused by the deprivation of oxygen (this affects all four limbs) and a brachial plexus injury resulting in Erb's palsy (ie paralysis of the arm). Had Mrs Montgomery had an elective caesarean section, her son would have been born uninjured. The court was faced with the question as to what information should have been provided in relation to the risks of harm to the baby.

8.81 In the Supreme Court however the Court allowed the appeal. The judgment of the Court was delivered by Lord Kerr and Lord Reid. There was an additional judgment from Lady Hale. The judgment is fundamentally important in that it confirms that the doctrine of informed consent is indeed today part of English law. Lady Hale in the Supreme Court, quoting from the previous edition of this book, stated that:

> In the third (2010) edition of their leading work on Principles of Medical Law, Andrew Grubb, Judith Laing and Jean McHale confidently announced that a detailed analysis of the different speeches of the House of Lords in *Sidaway v Board of Governors of the Bethlem Royal Hospital and the Maudsley Hospital* [1985] AC 871 was no longer necessary. A combination of the 2008 Guidance provided by the General Medical Council, the decision of the Court of Appeal in *Pearce v United Bristol Healthcare NHS Trust* [1999] PIQR P 53 and the decision of the House of Lords *in Chester v Afshar* [2005] 1 AC 134 meant that it could now be stated 'with a reasonable degree of confidence' that the need for informed consent was firmly part of English law (para 8.70). This case has provided us with the opportunity, not only to confirm that confident statement, but also to make it clear that the same principles apply in Scotland.[222]

[222] ibid, para 107.

What the Supreme Court does in *Montgomery* is to build upon the earlier case law in this area and restructure the test for informed consent. The Court departed from the House of Lords decision in *Sidaway*, which it saw as outdated and not reflective of day-to-day clinical practice today.[223] The Court confirmed that self-determination is a value recognized as underpinning various parts of common law and is also integral to the respect for private life under Article 8 of the European Convention on Human Rights.[224] The shift towards autonomy is highlighted with: **8.82**

> ... an approach to the law which, instead of treating patients as placing themselves in the hands of their doctors (and then being prone to sue their doctors in the event of a disappointing outcome), treats them so far as possible as adults who are capable of understanding that medical treatment is uncertain of success and may involve risks, accepting responsibility for the taking of risks affecting their own lives, and living with the consequences of their choices.[225]

Here the Supreme Court is essentially following the approach taken by Lord Steyn a decade before in *Chester v Afshar*.[226]

One particularly notable aspect of the judgment is that the Supreme Court finally moves away from the *Bolam* test which has underpinned standard clinical negligence actions (see Chapter 4) and makes clear that it does not apply in this context.[227] Instead they build upon the judgments of Lord Scarman in *Sidaway* and Lord Woolf MR in *Pearce*, as well as the decision of the High Court of Australia in *Rogers v Whitaker*.[228] As Lord Kerr and Lord Reid stated: **8.83**

> It follows that the analysis of the law by the majority in *Sidaway* is unsatisfactory, in so far as it treated the doctor's duty to advise her patient of the risks of proposed treatment as falling within the scope of the *Bolam* test, subject to two qualifications of that general principle, neither of which is fundamentally consistent with that test. [229]

Lords Kerr and Reid went onto say that:

> The correct position, in relation to the risks of injury involved in treatment, can now be seen to be substantially that adopted in *Sidaway* by Lord Scarman, and by Lord Woolf MR in *Pearce,* subject to the refinement made by the High Court of Australia in *Rogers v Whitaker*, which we have discussed ... An adult person of sound mind is entitled to decide which, if any, of the available forms of treatment to undergo, and her consent must be obtained before treatment interfering with her bodily integrity is undertaken. [230]

Moreover Lord Kerr and Reid also stated that: **8.84**

> The doctor is therefore under a duty to take reasonable care to ensure that the patient is aware of any material risks involved in any recommended treatment, and of any reasonable alternative or variant treatments. The test of materiality is whether, in the circumstances of the particular case, a reasonable person in the patient's position would be likely to attach significance to the risk, or the doctor is or should reasonably be aware that the particular patient would be likely to attach significance to it.[231]

[223] ibid, para 75.
[224] ibid, para 80.
[225] ibid, para 81.
[226] [2005] 1 AC 234.
[227] *Montgomery* (n 223) para 83.
[228] See generally on the development of the case law in this area J Miola 'On the Materiality of Risks, Paper Tigers and Informed Consent' (2009) 17 Medical Law Review 45.
[229] *Montgomery* (n 223) para 86.
[230] ibid, para 87.
[231] ibid, para 87.

It should be noted that this is a negligence action and the duty is one of reasonable care—not an absolute duty. Not all risks have to be disclosed. Instead here the court is talking about 'material' risks. This will inevitably be context dependant. What is clear from the judgments in *Montgomery* is that information must now be given in relation to treatment alternatives. This is a reasonable patient test but overlaid with that of the information which a particular person would want to know. Here the Supreme Court is itself building upon the approach taken by the General Medical Council in its Good Medical Practice guidance since the late 1990s of what is essentially a very patient-focused approach to disclosure.[232] Clearly we have moved beyond a 10 per cent risk of a stroke—but can percentages at times be actually helpful? Could it be said that some major risks should now be automatically disclosed? While doctors should clearly communicate with their patients, what time scale will this involve? What precise degree of informed consent process will be practicable? In relation to the doctor needing to disclose what factors are relevant to this patient, there are further uncertainties here—to what extent does the doctor have to interrogate the patient as to what factors are relevant? It is clear from the Supreme Court's judgment that the clinician will need to make the information comprehensible. This suggests that this judgment has implicitly overruled the earlier lower court decision in *Al Hamni v Johnston and North West London Hospitals NHS Trust* which stated that doctors did not need to ensure that patients understood the information which was given.[233]

8.85 What will the implications be? Commenting on the judgment Heywood raises concerns in relation to disclosure of 'excessive information which patients may not necessarily need or worse still want'.[234] Spatz commenting on *Montgomery* from a US perspective notes that around a half of all US states have adopted a reasonable patient standard but nonetheless the reality is often far away from patient needs. He argues that in practice informed consent discussions are often 'devoid of details' in relation to risks and so forth and that consent forms tend to be focused on protecting clinicians from litigation and are 'often written at a high reading level and sometimes presented in non-legible print, putting a premium on health literacy and pro-active information seeking behavior'.[235] It remains to be seen whether this will occur in the UK or whether the result of Montgomery may be somewhat different in practice with a more benevolent impact on the doctor-patient relationship. McGrath suggests that there could be:

> a shift in emphasis from practitioner control of information to partnership, that is to say patients choosing for themselves and living with the consequences might draw the motivational sting out of potential litigants . . . [236]

8.86 While *Bolam* has gone in rhetorical terms—the question must be asked whether it has gone in reality—how different will litigation be in practice in the wake of *Montgomery*? One issue will be that this will remain a negligence action and both sides will be adducing evidence to determine whether there has been a breach of a duty of care. In so doing there needs to be a reasonableness test assessment. Evidence will need to be adduced—this evidence will

[232] GMC, 'Good Medical Practice Guidance (2013)' (GMC 2013) 'Communicate Effectively'.

[233] [2005] EWHC 206; and see J Miola, 'Autonomy Rued OK? Al Hamwi v Johnston and Another' (2006) 14 Medical Law Review 108.

[234] R Heywood, 'RIP Sidaway: Patient Oriented Disclosure: A Standard Worth Waiting For' (2015) 23 Medical Law Review 455.

[235] E S Spatz, 'The New Era of Informed Consent: Getting to a Reasonable Patient Standard through Shared Decision-making' (2016) 315(19) Journal of the American Medical Association 2063.

[236] C P McGrath, '"Trust Me I'm a Patient . . . ": Disclosure Standards and the Patients Right to Decide' [2015] 74 Cambridge Law Journal 211, 214.

be brought forward by clinical experts acting for both claimant and defendant as to what information should be disclosed. Clearly the courts will not automatically accept clinical judgment—but that was never the case prior to *Montgomery*. It remains to be seen how this will be interpreted in the future and whether in effect it would become a *Bolam* type professional practice albeit evidence based approach while not being described as such.

(v) Therapeutic privilege

One concept which was introduced by the House of Lords in *Sidaway* but remains post *Montgomery* is that of therapeutic privilege (ie the clinician's discretion to withhold information from the patient where it is in the patient's best interest to do so). Before *Montgomery* it might have been thought that this concept, utilized in US jurisdictions before being discussed in *Sidaway*, might be today regarded as fundamentally outdated, a product of a more paternalistic era. But despite this it was recognized by the Supreme Court in *Montgomery*, holding that: **8.87**

> The doctor is however entitled to withhold from the patient information as to a risk if he reasonably considers that its disclosure would be seriously detrimental to the patient's health. The doctor is also excused from conferring with the patient in circumstances of necessity, as for example where the patient requires treatment urgently but is unconscious or otherwise unable to make a decision. It is unnecessary for the purposes of this case to consider in detail the scope of those exceptions.[237]

Nonetheless, while this is recognized, it is qualified. Lord Kerr commented in the case that: **8.88**

> It is important that the therapeutic exception should not be abused. It is a limited exception to the general principle that the patient should make the decision whether to undergo a proposed course of treatment: it is not intended to subvert that principle by enabling the doctor to prevent the patient from making an informed choice where she is liable to make a choice which the doctor considers to be contrary to her best interests.[238]

The law in this area thus remains uncertain. If information is withheld such that otherwise it would be seriously detrimental to the patient's health—either this is paternalism writ large or it would fall into one of the limited public policy exceptions when consent is not required.[239] Certainly any use of the such a privilege would have to be very carefully justified by a clinician. **8.89**

(vi) Consent and causation

Chester v Afshar brought the law of consent and the law of negligence closer together when it created an exception to the usual rules of causation in a situation where the patient ought to have been warned of a risk and no warning was given. The court decided, following the more flexible approach to causation on a case by case basis developed in *Fairchild v Glenhaven Funeral Services Ltd*[240] that, where a warning of a potential adverse outcome was not given by the doctor, the patient can recover damages, even if the patient is unable to prove that, if the warning had been given, the patient would not have gone ahead with the operation. Lord Hope said:[241] **8.90**

> I start with the proposition that the law which imposed the duty to warn on the doctor has at its heart the right of the patient to make an informed choice as to whether, and if so when and by whom, to be operated on. Patients may have, and are entitled to have, different

237 *Montgomery* (n 223) para 80.
238 ibid, para 91.
239 See ibid, para 80.
240 *Fairchild v Glenhaven Funeral Services Ltd* [2003] 1 AC 32.
241 ibid, [86].

views about these matters. All sorts of factors may be at work here—the patient's hopes and fears and personal circumstances, the nature of the condition that has to be treated and, above all, the patient's own views about whether the risk is worth running for the benefits that may come if the operation is carried out. For some the choice may be easy—simply to agree to or to decline the operation. But for many the choice will be a difficult one, requiring time to think, to take advice and to weigh up the alternatives. The duty is owed as much to the patient who, if warned, would find the decision difficult as to the patient who would find it simple and could give a clear answer to the doctor one way or the other immediately.

8.91 Lord Hope accepted that the decision was one of 'policy' and was intimately connected to the duty on the doctor to provide a warning in the first place. Lord Walker recognized that public attitudes had moved on since 1985. He said:[242]

> The surgeon's duty to advise his patient (and in particular, to warn of unavoidable risks of surgery) is a very important part of his professional duty. In *Sidaway v Board of Governors of the Bethlem Royal Hospital and the Maudsley Hospital* [1985] AC 871, 882, Lord Scarman described the patient's right to make his own decision as a basic human right. Lord Scarman was delivering a dissenting speech, but the whole House recognised this right (see Lord Diplock, at p 895, Lord Bridge of Harwich, at pp 897 and 900, and Lord Templeman, at p 904); and during the 20 years which have elapsed since Sidaway's case the importance of personal autonomy has been more and more widely recognised.

8.92 The surgeon's duty to advise and warn his patient is closely connected with the need for the patient's consent to submit, under anaesthesia, to invasive surgery which would (in the absence of consent) be an assault. The advice is the foundation of the consent. That is why it is so important.

8.93 In *Gregg v Scott*[243] the House of Lords was asked whether the more flexible approach to causation should be extended from the need to provide warnings as part of the consent process to other aspects of clinical negligence. Their Lordships declined to extend the concept and Lady Hale, who was the only judge who referred to *Chester v Afshar*, described it as a 'particular problem which could be remedied without altering the principles applicable to the great majority of personal injury cases'.[244] It should be noted that in only a limited number of cases since *Chester* have informed consent actions succeeded.[245] The issue of causation in many respects has however been subsidiary to the difficulty of establishing breach of duty itself. It remains to be seen whether the issue of causation and consent becomes more problematic in the future.

D. Conclusion

8.94 The law concerning consent to treatment has evolved significantly over the last two decades. The broad parameters remain untouched—the idea that consent itself is protected through criminal and civil law and, moreover, that consent in law has its limits. Public policy can and does circumscribe the boundaries of consent to treatment. What has changed however is both the engagement of patients and health care professionals with consent as a concept, both as a right and as a process. The scandals noted above leading to the reports such as Alder Hey and Bristol Royal Infirmary provided catalysts for the change in approach

[242] ibid, [92].
[243] *Gregg v Scott* [2005] 2 AC 176.
[244] ibid, para 192.
[245] A McLean, 'From *Sidaway* to *Pearce* and Beyond: Is the Legal Regulation of Consent Any Better Following a Quarter of a Century of Judicial Scrutiny?' (2012) 20(1) Medical Law Review 108.

by the General Medical Council Today also consent is clearly underpinned not simply by academic discussion, but also by the courts with respect for fundamental human rights, as exemplified by the provisions of the European Court of Human Rights. Moreover it is the case that patients can no longer be simply regarded as the passive recipients of information. The internet has over the last two decades begun to entirely change the doctor-patient relationship. The NHS itself includes information regarding clinical conditions, diagnosis and treatment on its own website.[246] Information which was traditionally virtually exclusively under clinical control is gradually becoming more accessible. Patients are being encouraged to become partners in their conditions and dialogue around treatments has improved with clinical education facilitating this. However, as we have seen in cases such as *Montgomery* clinicians may still fall short. There is also scepticism among some bioethical commentators as to the nature of informed consent and whether it is a truly meaningful concept.[247] Others have also highlighted the challenges in obtaining consent in a pressurized health service constrained by time and resources.[248] Nonetheless, despite these practical problems and ethical debates, it is clear that English law has today clearly aligned expectations of information disclosure with respect for human rights. The implications of *Montgomery* for informed consent are still to be worked through by academic commentators and subsequently by the courts. The new judicial approach illustrates the changing nature of judicial scrutiny of clinical decision making, though it does follow and very much builds upon Lord Woolf's judgment in *Pearce* and Lord Steyn's approach in *Chester*. Nonetheless its importance cannot be understated—what is clear today is that three decades on from *Sidaway* informed consent is definitely part of English law.

246 <http://www.nhs.uk/Conditions/Pages/hub.aspx>.

247 See, eg N C Manson and O O'Neill, *Rethinking Informed Consent in Bioethics* (Cambridge University Press 2007).

248 R Heywood et al, 'Informed Consent in Hospital Practice: Health Professionals' Perspectives and Legal Reflections' (2010) 18(2) Medical Law Review 152.

9

THE TESTS FOR INCAPACITY

*Neil Allen**

A. Introduction to the Common Law Position

9.01 In this chapter 'mental capacity' is to be distinguished from 'legal capacity'. The former relates to a person's decision-making skills whereas the latter is the ability to hold and exercise rights and duties before the law. Article 12 of the United Nations Convention on the Rights of Persons with Disabilities ('CRPD') requires States to recognize that 'persons with disabilities enjoy legal capacity on an equal basis with others in all aspects of life'. But the UNCRPD Committee has made it clear that *legal* and *mental* capacity are distinct concepts and 'perceived or actual deficits in mental capacity must not be used as justification for denying legal capacity'.[1] The focus in this chapter is therefore upon 'mental capacity' but it will be seen that factors such as age have a bearing upon a child's 'legal capacity'.

9.02 The test for incapacity for those aged 16 and over is now described by the test under Pt 1 of the Mental Capacity Act 2005 ('MCA'). The common law continues to apply to determine

* This is an updated version of the chapter originally written by David Lock QC and Sir James Munby. The author would like to thank the editors for their comments.

[1] See 'General Comment No. 1—Article 12: Equal Recognition before the Law', UN Doc. No. CRPD/C/GC/1, adopted at the 11th Session (April 2014), at para 13.

capacity for children who are under the age of 16.[2] Further, whilst the MCA and its Code of Practice constitute a comprehensive scheme, the concepts described in the Act and the Code are so close to the common law principles that previous cases may still be useful for shedding light on the approach that the Court of Protection should take in interpreting the Act and the Code in any particular situation. This chapter will begin with a consideration of the common law rules of decision-making for the three stages of childhood and adolescence. Following a brief review of the common law position prior to the Mental Capacity Act, it will then go on to consider the present law as it applies to adults.

1. How does the common law start to assess capacity?

Mental capacity or competence to consent to treatment has never been based upon a person's status or age.[3] Consequently, being a child or suffering from a mental disability or disorder did not mean, at common law, that a person was necessarily unable to consent. There was a rebuttable presumption that an adult was competent to consent (or refuse to consent) to treatment.[4] Equally, in relation to those who have attained the age of 16 there is a similar presumption created by s 8 of the Family Reform Act 1969 in relation to 'medical, surgical or dental treatment' including diagnostic and ancillary procedures. However, the presumption is otherwise in respect of children (ie those below 16) where it must be established, following the decision of the House of Lords in *Gillick v Wisbech and Norfolk AHA* ('*Gillick*'),[5] that the particular child has the capacity to consent to the particular treatment contemplated. **9.03**

Mental capacity at common law (and under the Mental Capacity Act) is a question of fact in every case.[6] With children the issue will frequently be a developmental one, namely whether the patient has *acquired* sufficient maturity and intelligence to understand what is involved. The common law did not question the degree of intelligence or education of an adult.[7] In most instances the issue was whether the patient's mental disability or disorder was such that s/he had *lost* the capacity to consent (or refuse) treatment or had never acquired it. A patient may have the capacity to make some but not all treatment decisions both at common law and under the MCA.[8] **9.04**

2. Children and consent

(i) The need for consent

The law normally requires a valid consent before any treatment can lawfully be given to a child. In certain circumstances the law recognizes as valid the child's own consent. In those cases where the child is unable to give a valid consent, the law recognizes as valid a proxy or substitute consent given on behalf of the child either by a parent (or someone having parental responsibility) or by the court. The position regarding those cases where the child **9.05**

[2] Note, however, that the Mental Health Act Code of Practice (2015) states, at para 19.36, that practitioners 'may find it helpful' to consider the equivalent of the functional test of the MCA when considering the capacity of those under 16.

[3] *Gillick v West Norfolk and Wisbech AHA* [1986] AC 112, [1985] 3 All ER 402 (HL); *Johnston v Wellesley Hospital* (1970) 17 DLR (3d) 139, 144–45 *per* Addy J.

[4] *Re T (Adult: Refusal of Medical Treatment)* [1992] 4 All ER 649, 661 *per* Lord Donaldson MR; *Re MB* (1997) 38 BMLR 175, 186 *per* Butler-Sloss LJ; *Re B (Adult; Refusal of Treatment)* (2002) 65 BMLR 149, [28] *per* Butler-Sloss P. However, the burden of proving the continuing validity of an advance refusal (including non-revocation) was upon the patient: *HE v A Hospital NHS Trust* [2003] EWHC 1017 (Fam), [2003] 2 FLR 408 *per* Munby J at [20]. The presumption of capacity is now codified in s 1 of the Mental Capacity Act 2005.

[5] [1985] 3 All ER 402.

[6] *Gillick v West Norfolk and Wisbech AHA* [1986] 3 All ER 402.

[7] *Re T* [1992] 4 All ER 649, 661 *per* Lord Donaldson MR.

[8] *Gillick* [1985] 3 All ER 402 *per* Lord Fraser at 409 and *per* Lord Scarman at 422 and 423–24 (children); *Re T* [1992] 4 All ER 649 *per* Lord Donaldson MR at 661–62 (adults).

is able to give a valid consent but refuses to do so is considered below. In cases of emergency, a doctor can provide treatment notwithstanding the absence of parental or judicial consent.[9]

(ii) The purpose of consent

9.06 The giving of consent to medical treatment has two main functions: one clinical and the other legal:

> The clinical purpose stems from the fact that in many instances the co-operation of the patient and the patient's faith or at least confidence in the efficacy of the treatment is a major factor contributing to the treatment's success. Failure to obtain such consent will not only deprive the patient and the medical staff of this advantage, but will usually make it much more difficult to administer the treatment. I appreciate that this purpose may not be served if consent is given on behalf of, rather than by, the patient. However, in the case of young children knowledge of the fact that the parent has consented may help. The legal purpose is quite different. It is to provide those concerned in the treatment with a defence to a criminal charge of assault or battery or a civil claim for damages for trespass to the person. It does not, however, provide them with any defence to a claim that they negligently advised a particular treatment or negligently carried it out.[10]

9.07 In the case of a child the right of self-determination plays less of a part and the clinical purpose of consent is thus limited. Plainly, except as a legal fiction, a proxy or substitute consent is quite inconsistent with a right of *self*-determination. Moreover, even in those cases where someone under the age of 16 is treated as having the capacity in law to *give* a valid consent to treatment, s/he is not treated as having the capacity effectively to refuse consent to treatment, since such a *refusal* could be overridden by the court.[11]

9.08 As with an adult patient, so with a child, the right to consent is merely a power to consent, not a power to compel. In the case of a child neither the parent nor the child can compel an unwilling doctor or health authority to provide treatment, whether that refusal is based on the doctor's clinical or ethical judgment or on a lack of resources.[12] In such a case, the patient's only remedy is to find another doctor, if s/he can, who is prepared to give the desired treatment.

9.09 Nor is the child any better off by seeking to invoke the assistance of the court. The court, even if it is exercising its inherent *parens patriae* jurisdiction, will never make an order requiring a particular doctor or NHS Trust to treat a child in a manner contrary to their wishes.[13] There are two reasons for this. The first is because, as a matter of policy, the court will never make an order compelling a doctor to treat a patient in a manner contrary to his/her clinical judgment and professional duty.[14] Where the court disagrees with the views of the attending physician the solution is to find another doctor who shares the court's view, not to coerce the existing doctor. Secondly, because, again as a matter of policy, the

---

[9] See Chapter 10, para 10.53.

[10] *Re W (A Minor) (Medical Treatment: Court's Jurisdiction)* [1993] Fam 64, 76 *per* Lord Donaldson of Lymington MR.

[11] See further para 9.18 and Chapter 10, paras 10.78–10.79. It is not advisable to rely on the consent of someone with parental responsibility in such circumstances: see *R (Axon) v Secretary of State for Health* [2006] EWHC 37 (Admin).

[12] *In the matter of X (A Child)* [2014] EWHC 1871 (Fam), [5]–[6].

[13] *Re J (A Minor) (Wardship: Medical Treatment)* [1991] Fam 33, 41, 48; *Re R (A Minor) (Wardship: Consent to Treatment)* [1992] Fam 11, 22, 26; *Re J (A Minor) (Child in Care: Medical Treatment)* [1993] Fam 15, 27, 29, 31.

[14] *Re J (A Minor) (Child in Care: Medical Treatment)* [1993] Fam 15, 26–27, 29–31; affirmed in *Aintree University Hospitals NHS Foundation Trust v James and others* [2014] AC 591, [18]; *Re C (Medical Treatment)* [1998] 1 FLR 384, 390.

court declines to become involved in questions relating to the resource implications of proposed treatment, and refuses to adjudicate in disputes between patients, doctors, and health authorities arising out of the denial of treatment because of a lack of resources or the allocation of scarce resources to other patients or other forms of treatment.[15]

(iii) The effect of consent

In the case of a child it would seem that the effect of a consent will be the same as the effect of a consent given by an adult who is *sui juris* in those cases where the consent is given either by the child him/herself (assuming, that is, that the child in question has the capacity to give a valid consent at all), or by the court on his/her behalf. The effect of a proxy or substitute consent given by a parent (or by someone having parental responsibility) is more limited, for such a consent will not necessarily provide the doctor with an absolute defence. The right of the parent to give a valid proxy or substitute consent is subject to a variety of limitations,[16] and a doctor cannot rely upon a 'consent' which s/he knows, or ought to know, ought not to have been given by the parent: **9.10**

> [B]ecause parents are given authority to act for the benefit of the child, their authority is limited to those acts which advance or protect the welfare of the child. This criterion is a matter which must be determined objectively and not by reference to the good faith opinions of the parent. A parent has no authority, therefore, to consent to medical treatment unless it can be seen objectively that the treatment is for the welfare of the child. If a parent purports to give consent to treatment which is not for the welfare of the child, the consent is of no effect. A person who acts on such 'consent' is guilty of assaulting the child if the treatment involves any physical interference with the child.[17]

---

[15] *R v Secretary of State for Social Services, West Midlands RHA and Birmingham AHA (Teaching), ex p Hinck* (1980) 1 BMLR 93 (patients on waiting list for orthopaedic surgery); *R v Central Birmingham HA, ex p Walker* (1987) 3 BMLR 32 (premature baby requiring heart surgery); *R v Central Birmingham HA, ex p Collier* [1988] CAT 88/1 (4-year-old child in immediate danger to health requiring heart surgery); *Re J (A Minor) (Wardship: Medical Treatment)* [1991] Fam 33, 41; *Re J (A Minor) (Child in Care: Medical Treatment)* [1993] Fam 15, 28, 30–31; *R v Cambridge HA, ex p B* [1995] 1 WLR 898, reversing [1995] 1 FLR 1055 (experimental treatment of 10-year-old child suffering from leukaemia); *R v North Derbyshire HA, ex p Fisher* (1997) 38 BMLR 76 (refusal to fund treatment with beta-interferon of patient suffering from multiple sclerosis). For the more recent general statements of principle see *R v North and East Devon HA, ex p Coughlan* [2001] QB 213 and (addressing the possible impact of Arts 3 and 8 of the ECHR) *R v North West Lancashire HA, ex p A* [2000] 1 WLR 977 (refusal to fund gender reassignment surgery for gender identity dysphoria) and *R (on the application of Watts) v Bedford PCT* [2003] EWHC 2228 (Admin), (2004) 77 BMLR 26 (delays in waiting list for surgery). And, in relation to the Convention, see the important observation of Lord Hoffmann in *Matthews v Ministry of Defence* [2003] UKHL 4, [2003] 1 AC 1163, [26]: 'it is well arguable that human rights include the right to a minimum standard of living, without which many of the other rights would be a mockery. But they certainly do not include the right to a fair distribution of resources or fair treatment in economic terms—in other words, distributive justice. Of course distributive justice is a good thing. But it is not a fundamental human right.' For the distinction in this context between the powers of the Family Division when exercising the inherent *parens patriae* or declaratory jurisdictions and the Administrative Court when exercising its judicial review jurisdiction see *A v A Health Authority, Re J (A Child), R (on the application of S) v Secretary of State for the Home Department* [2002] EWHC 18 (Fam/Admin), [2002] Fam 213, esp at [51]–[53], [89]–[100]. For the impact of Art 49 of the EC Treaty see *R (on the application of Watts) v Bedford PCT* [2003] EWHC 2228 (Admin), (2004) 77 BMLR 26; *R (on the application of Watts) v Secretary of State for Health* [2004] EWCA Civ 166, (2004) 77 BMLR 26; *R (on the application of Watts) v Bedford Primary Care Trust and another* [2006] QB 667 (ECJ). For the same distinction in the context of the Court of Protection, see *In the matter of MN (Adult)* [2015] EWCA Civ 411 (on appeal at the time of writing).

[16] See further Chapter 10, paras 10.49–10.61.

[17] *Secretary, Department of Health and Community Services v JWB and SMB* (1992) 175 CLR 218, 316 *per* McHugh J. To the same effect *Re F (Mental Patient: Sterilisation)* [1990] 2 AC 1, 20 *per* Lord Donaldson of Lymington MR (child would 'undoubtedly have . . . a very substantial claim for damages').

(iv) The role of parental consent

9.11 It will be seen, therefore, that parental consent is only one factor, and except in the case of routine treatment rarely a determining factor, in the treatment of a child. Not even the approval of the court is determinative:

> The doctors owe the child a duty to care for it in accordance with good medical practice recognised as appropriate by a competent body of professional opinion ... This duty is, however, subject to the qualification that, if time permits, they must obtain the consent of the parents before undertaking serious invasive treatment. The parents owe the child a duty to give or to withhold consent in the best interests of the child and without regard to their own interests. The court when exercising the parens patriae jurisdiction takes over the rights and duties of the parents, although this is not to say that the parents will be excluded from the decision-making process. Nevertheless in the end the responsibility for the decision whether to give or to withhold consent is that of the court alone ... No one can dictate the treatment to be given to the child—neither court, parents nor doctors. There are checks and balances. The doctors can recommend treatment A in preference to treatment B. They can also refuse to adopt treatment C on the grounds that it is medically contra-indicated or for some other reason is a treatment which they could not conscientiously administer. The court or parents for their part can refuse consent to treatment A or B or both, but cannot insist upon treatment C. The inevitable and desirable result is that choice of treatment is in some measure a joint decision of the doctors and the court or parents.[18]

No doctor can be required to treat a child which conflicts with the exercise of their own professional judgment. A factor in forming that judgment will be the views and wishes of the child, the importance of which will increase with the increase in the child's intelligence and understanding.[19]

(v) The dwindling right

9.12 Once a child has gained legal capacity and has the right to give or withhold consent for themselves, the right of the parents to take that decision on the child's behalf is no longer required and hence disappears in law. In *Hewer v Bryant*[20] Lord Denning MR said the right of a parent is 'a dwindling right which the courts will hesitate to enforce against the wishes of the child, and the more so the older he is. It starts with a right of control and ends with little more than advice'. In the context of giving consent to medical treatment, Lord Scarman said that 'a parental right yields to the young person's right to make his own decisions when the young person reaches a sufficient understanding and intelligence to be capable of making up his or her own mind in relation to a matter requiring decision'. This led him to the view that:

> ... as a matter of law the parental right to determine whether or not their minor child below the age of 16 will have medical treatment terminates if and when the child achieves a sufficient understanding and intelligence to enable him or her to understand fully what is proposed. It will be a question of fact whether a child seeking advice has sufficient understanding of what is involved to give a consent valid in law.[21]

9.13 However, the reverse view was expressed by Lord Donaldson in *Re R (A Minor) (Wardship: Medical Treatment)*,[22] who said: 'A "Gillick-competent" child or one over the age

[18] *Re J (A Minor) (Wardship: Medical Treatment)* [1991] Fam 33, 41, 48 *per* Lord Donaldson of Lymington MR.

[19] *Re R (A Minor) (Wardship: Consent to Treatment)* [1992] Fam 11, 26 *per* Lord Donaldson of Lymington MR.

[20] [1970] 1 QB 357, 369. This formulation was expressly approved by the majority in the House of Lords in *Gillick*.

[21] *Gillick v West Norfolk and Wisbech* [1986] AC 112, Lord Scarman at 188–89.

[22] [1992] 1 FLR 190.

of 16 will have a power to consent, but this will be concurrent with that of a parent or guardian'.[23] Lord Donaldson's view does not appear to have been accepted by Staughton LJ who said that it was 'not essential to the decision in this case'[24] and the issue was not commented upon by Farquharson LJ. The case is, however, authority for the proposition that, whether or not the parents retain the right to give or withhold consent for a medically competent child, the High Court had power to give authority for the medical treatment of a child who was competent to consent to treatment but who had refused consent.

In the face of considerable academic criticism,[25] Lord Donaldson examined but maintained his view that both a parent and a child had concurrent rights to give consent to medical treatment in *Re W (A Minor) (Consent to Medical Treatment)*[26] but again the issue was not considered by the other two judges. In *Re K, W and H (Minors) (Medical Treatment)*[27] Thorpe J said: 'The decision of the Court of Appeal in Re R (above) made it plain that a child with *Gillick* competence can consent to treatment, but that if he or she declines to do so, consent can be given by someone else who has parental rights or responsibilities.' **9.14**

Despite these authorities, the law appears to be reverting to the decision of Lord Scarman in *Gillick*. The lack of concurrent rights of both child and parent was confirmed by Silber J in *R (on the application of Axon) v Secretary of State for Health and Anor*[28] who referred to the parent's rights terminating when the child gained capacity to make the decision in question. The judge supported his view that the child's rights under Article 8 of the ECHR overrides any similar right that the parent may have[29] and relied on *Yousef v Netherlands*,[30] where the European Court of Human Rights said at para 73 that: **9.15**

> The court reiterates that in judicial decisions where the rights under article 8 of the parents and those of the child are at stake, the child's rights must be the paramount consideration.

Silber J also relied on Article 12 of the United Nations Convention on the Rights of the Child[31] to show that the court is obliged to respect the views of the child on matters concerning consent to treatment in deference to the views of the parents. Despite the doubts expressed by Lord Donaldson, Silber J must be right. A child who has capacity has the right to consent or to refuse consent to medical treatment. It is illogical to permit the parents to retain a concurrent right to give consent and thus nullify the right of the child to refuse **9.16**

[23] ibid, 200.
[24] ibid, 202.
[25] See, eg, A Bainham, 'The Judge and the Competent Minor' (1992) 108 LQR 194, 198–99; R Thornton, 'Multiple Keyholders: Wardship and Consent to Medical Treatment' [1992] CLJ 34; C Dyer, (ed), *Doctors, Patients and the Law* (Blackwell 1992), 58–61, 75–77, 156–57. See also M Brazier and E Cave, *Medicine, Patients and the Law* (6th edn, Manchester University Press 2016) 465–470; S Gilmore and J Herring, '"No" is the Hardest Word: Consent and Children's Autonomy' (2011) 23 Child and Family Law Quarterly 3; and E Cave and J Wallbank, 'Minors' Capacity to Refuse Treatment: A Reply to Gilmore and Herring' (2012) 20(3) Medical Law Review 423.
[26] [1993] 1 FLR 1.
[27] [1993] 1 FLR 854.
[28] [2006] EWHC 37 (Admin). It is unclear from the report whether the cases referred to above concerning concurrent rights were cited to the judge. The decision was endorsed by Keehan J in *PD v SD and others* [2015] EWHC 4103 (Fam). In the context of information disclosure, see also *Local Authority X v HI, IW, I and JAW (Disclosure to Other Parties in Care Proceedings)* [2016] EWHC 1123 (Fam) and A Bainham, 'Keeping Confidences for Children: *Gillick* and Fair Hearings in Care Proceedings' (2016) 46 Family Law 976-83.
[29] See [144], where he referred to *Hendricks v Netherlands* (1992) EHRR 223.
[30] (2003) 36 EHRR 345.
[31] Article 12 of the UNCRC states that: 'States Parties shall assure to the child who is capable of forming his or her own views the right to express those views freely in all matters affecting the child, the views of the child being given due weight in accordance with the age and maturity of the child.'

consent to treatment. However, this raises a difficult issue as to whether the court can still assert a greater right to impose unwanted medical treatment on a competent child than the child's parents. This could be thought to be a policy question as to the level of paternalism the court should adopt to reserve a power to save the young from the consequences of their own decisions. However, the continuing existence of the power to override the views of a competent child, recognized in *Re R (A Minor)(Wardship: Medical Treatment),* is likely to be substantially curtailed following the jurisprudence identified by Silber J in *Axon*.

(vi) The role of the court

9.17 The court is not bound by the wishes or decision of a *Gillick* competent child.[32] Thus the court, if only it chooses to exercise its inherent powers,[33] can always outflank what might appear to be the perfectly clear legislative policy laid down in the Children Act 1989 and can do the very things which the Act has said that it shall not do. It is not easy to reconcile this view of the law with the principle that prerogative power yields to inconsistent statutory provisions.[34]

9.18 Consistently with the principle that the parental right to decide is not absolute, the court is not bound by and can override a parent's decision[35] where this is in the best interests of the child. But, as discussed in Chapter 10, it will tread extremely cautiously in so doing.

B. The Three Stages of Childhood

9.19 Upon attaining the age of 18, a person who is not mentally incapacitated becomes *sui juris* and absolutely entitled to decide whether or not to consent to treatment. Prior to that, the person will have passed through three successive stages of development recognized by the law.

1. The child of tender years

9.20 Manifestly a young child who has not yet reached 'the years of discretion' lacks the capacity to consent to medical treatment, because s/he lacks the intellectual ability to understand what is involved and the maturity to form a balanced judgment. The right to give consent to medical treatment is an aspect of parental responsibility.[36] This is a right which can be

[32] *Re R (A Minor) (Wardship: Consent to Treatment)* [1992] Fam 11, 25, 26, 28, 31, 32; *Re W (A Minor) (Medical Treatment: Court's Jurisdiction)* [1993] Fam 64, 81, 84, 88, 93; *South Glamorgan County Council v W and B* [1993] 1 FLR 574, 584; *Re L (Medical Treatment: Gillick Competency)* [1998] 2 FLR 810, 813. The previous cases bearing on the point were: *B(BR) v B(J)* [1968] P 466; *Re P (A Minor)* [1986] 1 FLR 272; *Re G-U (A Minor) (Wardship)* [1984] FLR 811; *Re E (A Minor) (Wardship: Medical Treatment)* [1993] 1 FLR 386; *Re B (Wardship: Abortion)* [1991] 2 FLR 426.

[33] As in *South Glamorgan County Council v W and B* [1993] 1 FLR 574 (order under inherent jurisdiction for psychiatric examination and assessment of *Gillick* competent child who had validly refused consent under s 38(6)). See also *Re W (A Minor) (Medical Treatment: Court's Jurisdiction)* [1993] Fam 64, 82.

[34] *AG v De Keyser's Royal Hotel Ltd* [1920] AC 508; cf also *Richards v Richards* [1984] AC 174.

[35] *Gillick v West Norfolk and Wisbech AHA* [1986] AC 112, 184, 200; *Re C (A Minor) (Wardship: Medical Treatment) (No 2)* [1990] Fam 39, 46; *Re J (A Minor) (Wardship: Medical Treatment)* [1991] Fam 33, 52; *Re R (A Minor) (Wardship: Consent to Treatment)* [1992] Fam 11, 25; *Re W (A Minor) (Medical Treatment: Court's Jurisdiction)* [1993] Fam 64, 93; *Re Z (A Minor) (Identification: Restrictions on Publication)* [1997] Fam 1, 30–31.

[36] 'It is abundantly plain that the law recognizes that there is a right *and duty* of parents to determine whether or not to seek medical advice in respect of their child, and, having received advice, to give or withhold consent to medical treatment . . .' *per* Lord Scarman in *Gillick v West Norfolk AHA* [1986] 1 AC 112, 184 G.

exercised by either parent where they both hold parental responsibility.[37] In the *Conjoined Twins*[38] case Ward LJ said:

> Since the parents are empowered at law, it seems to me that their decision must be respected and in my judgment the hospital would be no more entitled to disregard their refusal than they are to disregard an adult patient's refusal. To operate in the teeth of the parents' refusal would, therefore, be an unlawful assault upon the child.

Under s 2(7) of the Children Act 1989, where two people have parental responsibility either parent can give a valid consent on behalf of the child. If the parents have a fundamental disagreement between themselves about whether consent should be given or withheld for medical treatment, the matter can be referred to the court for a decision. To the extent that it is reasonable in all the circumstances for the purpose of safeguarding or promoting the child's welfare, consent may also be given by any person who, although s/he does not have parental responsibility, has care of the child.[39] **9.21**

2. The Gillick competent child

The Mental Capacity Act test does not apply to children under the age of 16. So whether a child has the capacity to consent to the particular treatment contemplated continues to be governed by the decision of the majority of the House of Lords in *Gillick.*[40] **9.22**

If and when the child achieves a sufficient understanding and intelligence to enable him or her to understand fully what is proposed, s/he is treated as having the capacity to give a valid consent to medical treatment.[41] The conventional shorthand is to refer to such a child as being '*Gillick* competent'. With children the issue will frequently be a developmental one, namely whether the patient has *acquired* sufficient maturity and intelligence to understand what is involved in the treatment in question. A child will develop capacity with developing maturity. For example, a young child may be sufficiently mature to be able to understand what is involved in a minor form of treatment, such as bandaging a wound, but not a major one, such as a heart by-pass operation. While developmental capacity of a child will be attained once and forever,[42] a competent child or adult's capacity may be lost (or absent) temporarily, for example, through an accident rendering the patient unconscious. It may also be permanently absent, for example, where the patient is born with chronic mental disability. **9.23**

The key to *Gillick* competence is the child's understanding and intelligence.[43] *Gillick* competence in relation to a particular child is a question of fact for the judge (or jury).[44] In determining whether or not a particular child is *Gillick* competent in relation to a particular proposed treatment, what is being looked for is the capacity to reach a mature and balanced judgment; 'the attainment by a child of an age of sufficient discretion to enable him or her **9.24**

---

[37] See s 2(5) of the Children Act 1989.

[38] *Re A (Children)* [2000] EWCA Civ 254, [2001] 2 WLR 480.

[39] Children Act 1989, s 3(5).

[40] [1985] 3 All ER 402, [1986] 1 AC 112 (HL). However, see guidance at para 19.36 of the Mental Health Act Code of Practice (2015).

[41] *Gillick v West Norfolk and Wisbech AHA* [1986] AC 112, 169, 186, 188–89, 195, 201.

[42] See *Re R (A Minor) (Wardship: Medical Treatment)* [1992] Fam 11, [1991] 4 All ER 177 (CA) and *Re W (A Minor) (Medical Treatment)* [1993] Fam 64, [1992] 4 All ER 627 (CA).

[43] *Gillick*, n 41, 171, 186, 189, 201; *Re W (A Minor) (Medical Treatment: Court's Jurisdiction)* [1993] Fam 64, 81.

[44] *Gillick,* n 41, 112, 172, 189. In *An NHS Trust v A and others* [2014] EWHC 1445 (Fam), a 13-year-old child was found to be *Gillick* competent to consent to the continuation or termination of pregnancy. Whereas in *F v F* [2013] EWHC 2683 (Fam) a 15-year-old girl was 'too naïve' to be competent to refuse to consent to the MMR vaccination.

to exercise a wise choice in his or her own interests'.[45] The factors to be taken into account are: the child's understanding and intelligence, his/her chronological, mental and emotional age, intellectual development and maturity, his/her capacity to make up his/her own mind, and his/her ability to understand fully, and to appraise, the medical advice being given, the nature, consequences and implications of the advised treatment, the potential risks to health and the emotional impact of either accepting or rejecting the advised treatment, and any moral and family questions involved:[46]

> I would hold that as a matter of law the parental right to determine whether or not their minor child below the age of 16 will have medical treatment terminates if and when the child achieves a sufficient understanding and intelligence to enable him or her to understand fully what is proposed. It will be a question of fact whether a child seeking advice has sufficient understanding of what is involved to give a consent valid in law . . . When applying these conclusions to contraceptive advice and treatment it has to be borne in mind that there is much that has to be understood by a girl under the age of 16 if she is to have legal capacity to consent to such treatment. It is not enough that she should understand the nature of the advice which is being given: she must also have a sufficient maturity to understand what is involved. There are moral and family questions, especially her relationship with her parents; long term problems associated with the emotional impact of pregnancy and its termination; and there are the risks to health of sexual intercourse at her age, risks which contraception may diminish but cannot eliminate. It follows that a doctor will have to satisfy himself that she is able to appraise these factors before he can safely proceed upon the basis that she has at law capacity to consent to contraceptive treatment.[47]

9.25 Youth and the potential for development may make it difficult, or indeed impossible, to make the relevant findings of fact to the necessary standard of proof. It must also be borne in mind that, even with an adult, there may be considerable barriers, conscious and unconscious, intellectual and emotional, to a full understanding of the implications of accepting or refusing the advised treatment.

9.26 *Gillick* competence reflects the staged development of a child and the progressive transition of the adolescent from childhood to adulthood. The capacity to understand reflects and is conditioned by the gradual acquisition of maturity and the capacity to consent will vary with the gravity of the treatment proposed. A child who has *Gillick* competence to consent to dental treatment, the mending of a broken arm, a tonsillectomy or even an appendectomy, may lack the capacity to consent to more serious treatment:[48]

> [T]he extent of the legal capacity of a young person to make decisions for herself or himself is not susceptible of precise abstract definition. Pending the attainment of full adulthood, legal capacity varies according to the gravity of the particular matter and the maturity and understanding of the particular young person.[49]

(i) Mental disability

9.27 Mental disability is not of itself incompatible with a child having *Gillick* competence, at least for some purposes:

[45] *Gillick*, n 41, 188 *per* Lord Scarman.

[46] ibid, 174, 189, 190, 201; *Re R (A Minor) (Wardship: Consent to Treatment)* [1992] Fam 11, 26.

[47] ibid, 188–89 *per* Lord Scarman.

[48] ibid, 169, 201; *Re R (A Minor) (Wardship: Consent to Treatment)* [1992] Fam 11, 25, 31; *Re W (A Minor) (Medical Treatment: Court's Jurisdiction)* [1993] Fam 64, 81.

[49] *Secretary, Department of Health and Community Services v JWB and SMB* (1992) 175 CLR 218, 293 *per* Deane J.

> The age at which intellectually disabled children can consent will be higher than for children within the normal range of abilities. However, terms such as 'mental disability', 'intellectual handicap' or 'retardation' lack precision. There is no essential cause of disability; those who come within these categories form a heterogeneous group. And since most intellectually disabled people are borderline to mildly disabled, there is no reason to assume that all disabled children are incapable of giving consent to treatment. In the case of children with intellectual disabilities, the situation is further complicated by the need for future, as well as present, assessment . . . It may also be said, in this context, that not only are there widely varying kinds and consequences of intellectual disability but such handicaps, possibly more so than other forms of disability, are often surrounded by misconceptions on the part of others in society, misconceptions often involving an underestimation of a person's ability . . . [I]t is important to stress that it cannot be presumed that an intellectually disabled child is, by virtue of his or her disability, incapable of giving consent to treatment. The capacity of a child to give informed consent to medical treatment depends on the rate of development of each individual.[50]

(ii) Fluctuating capacity

Gillick competence is a developmental concept and will not be lost or acquired on a day-to-day or week-to-week basis. Mental disability must be taken into account particularly where it is fluctuating in its effect[51] or (as with anorexia nervosa) has as one of its features that it is capable of destroying the ability to make an informed choice and creates a wish not to be cured and a compulsion to refuse treatment or accept only ineffective treatment:[52] **9.28**

> But there is no suggestion that the extent of this competence can fluctuate upon a day to day or week to week basis. What is really being looked at is an assessment of mental and emotional age, as contrasted with chronological age, but even this test needs to be modified in the case of fluctuating mental disability to take account of that misfortune. It should be added that in any event what is involved is not merely an ability to understand the nature of the proposed treatment . . . but a full understanding and appreciation of the consequences both of the treatment in terms of intended and possible side effects and, equally important, the anticipated consequences of a failure to treat. On the evidence in the present case . . . even if she was capable on a good day of a sufficient degree of understanding to meet the *Gillick* criteria, her mental disability, to the cure or amelioration of which the proposed treatment was directed, was such that on other days she was not only *Gillick* incompetent, but actually sectionable. No child in that situation can be regarded as *Gillick* competent.[53]

(iii) The standard of proof

The standard of proof must be the more rigorous the more serious the implications for the child of either giving or refusing consent. Where life or serious injury to health is at stake, and the child's decision appears to be unreasonable, the doctor (or the court) may be astute to consider whether there is a lack of capacity to consent: **9.29**

> I find that A is a boy of sufficient intelligence to be able to take decisions about his own well-being, but I also find that there is a range of decisions of which some are outside his ability fully to grasp their implications. Impressed though I was by his obvious intelligence, by his calm discussion of the implications, by his assertion even that he would refuse well knowing that he may die as a result, in my judgment A does not have a full understanding of the whole implication of what the refusal of that treatment involves . . . I am quite

[50] ibid, 238–39 *per* Mason CJ, Dawson, Toohey, and Gaudron JJ.
[51] *Re R (A Minor) (Wardship: Consent to Treatment)* [1992] Fam 11, 26, 31–32.
[52] *Re W (A Minor) (Medical Treatment: Court's Jurisdiction)* [1993] Fam 64, 81, 83.
[53] *Re R (A Minor) (Wardship: Consent to Treatment)* [1992] Fam 11, 25–26 *per* Lord Donaldson of Lymington MR.

satisfied that A does not have any sufficient comprehension of the pain he has yet to suffer, of the fear that he will be undergoing, of the distress not only occasioned by that fear but also—and importantly—the distress he will inevitably suffer as he, a loving son, helplessly watches his parents' and his family's distress. They are a close family, and they are a brave family, but I find that he has no realisation of the full implications which lie before him as to the process of dying. He may have some concept of the fact that he will die, but as to the manner of his death and to the extent of his and his family's suffering I find that he has not the ability to turn his mind to it nor the will to do so. Who can blame him for that? If, therefore, this case depended upon my finding of whether or not A is of sufficient understanding and intelligence and maturity to give full and informed consent, I find that he is not.[54]

9.30 The doctor (or the court) must be astute to the possibility that conscious or subconscious influence is being exerted on a child either by his/her parents or, where religious beliefs are involved, by religious advisers.[55]

3. The 16- and 17-year-old

9.31 Section 8 of the Family Law Reform Act 1969 addresses a developing person's *legal* (as opposed to *mental*) capacity. It provides:

(1) The consent of a minor who has attained the age of sixteen years to any surgical, medical or dental treatment which, in the absence of consent, would constitute a trespass to his person, shall be as effective as it would be if he were of full age; and where a minor has by virtue of this section given an effective consent to any treatment it shall not be necessary to obtain any consent for it from his parent or guardian.

(2) In this section 'surgical, medical or dental treatment' includes any procedure undertaken for the purposes of diagnosis, and this section applies to any procedure (including, in particular, the administration of an anaesthetic) which is ancillary to any treatment as it applies to that treatment.[56]

(3) Nothing in this section shall be construed as making ineffective any consent which would have been effective if this section had not been enacted.

9.32 Thus, all that s 8(1) of the Family Law Reform Act 1969 does is to deem the 16-year-old to have the same *legal* capacity as s/he would have if s/he were 18 ('consent . . . shall be as effective as . . . if he were of full age'). The bare fact of age apart, s 8(1) does not deem the young person to have any *mental* capacity which in fact s/he lacks. Rather, such *mental* capacity is judged by reference to the test set out in the Mental Capacity Act 2005 and principles therein.[57] Accordingly, and significantly, from the age of 16 the MCA assumes that the young person has the *mental* capacity to make the decision unless it can be proven otherwise. In the case of a mentally incapacitated young person, the power to decide will,

---

[54] *Re E (A Minor) (Wardship: Medical Treatment)* [1993] 1 FLR 386, 391 *per* Ward J (15-year-old Jehovah's Witness refusing blood transfusion necessary to save his life). Similarly, *Re S (A Minor) (Consent to Medical Treatment)* [1994] 2 FLR 1065; *Re L (Medical Treatment: Gillick Competency)* [1998] 2 FLR 810.

[55] *Re S (A Minor) (Consent to Medical Treatment)* [1994] 2 FLR 1065 (15½-year-old Jehovah's Witness refusing blood transfusion necessary to save her life).

[56] Section 8 does not extend to the donation of organs, or of blood or other bodily substances, nor even to the taking of a blood sample (for which separate provision is made in s 21(2)), for none of these procedures constitutes either treatment or diagnosis: *Re W (A Minor) (Medical Treatment: Court's Jurisdiction)* [1993] Fam 64, 78, 83, 92, 94; *Re O (A Minor) (Blood Tests: Constraint), Re J (A Minor)* [2000] Fam 139, 147–48.

[57] Where a young person's inability to decide is because of immaturity, rather than an impairment or disturbance in mental functioning, then there is scope for their capacity to be judged according to *Gillick*.

notwithstanding s 8, remain in the parents in collaboration with professionals or the court until the person attains the age of 18.[58]

As in the case of a *Gillick* competent child, and for the same reasons, a parent cannot overrule a 16- or 17-year-old child's consent to treatment but could, in effect, overrule such a child's refusal to consent to treatment.[59] This view of the law has, again, been the subject of severe academic criticism, as involving an inappropriately narrow construction of the language of s 8, which had previously been considered as conferring 'complete autonomy' on the 16- or 17-year-old child. Whether those with parental responsibility can overrule a young person's capacitous refusal in such circumstances must now be seriously open to doubt. In *Re D (A Child) (Deprivation of Liberty)*, for example, it was held that 'the legal authority of a parent to consent to the detention or treatment of a 16- or 17-year-old is severely curtailed, if not removed'.[60] **9.33**

Notwithstanding s 8 of the 1969 Act, the court in the exercise of its inherent *parens patriae* jurisdiction is not bound by the wishes of a 16- or 17-year-old child.[61] For example in *An NHS Foundation Trust Hospital v P*,[62] a 17-year-old with personality disorder and a history of self-harming behaviour took an overdose of paracetamol a week after being discharged from detention under the Mental Health Act 1983. On admission to hospital she refused the antidote. Later that evening she agreed to a first dose of medication but clinicians remained concerned that she might refuse continued treatment which had to be given over a continuous 21-hour period. Serious liver damage would undoubtedly result without it and she would probably die. There was insufficient evidence to disprove her assumed capacity. Her mother consented but, sensibly, the Trust was reluctant to rely upon it to override the young person's refusal. Baker J held: **9.34**

> 15. In this case, balancing the competing factors, I have no hesitation in concluding that the balance comes down firmly in favour of overriding P's wishes. I recognise that this is not to be taken lightly. The wishes of a young person aged seventeen and a half are important. They are, of course, entitled to be taken into account as part of her Article 8 rights under ECHR. On the other hand, those rights are not absolute. Here, they are outweighed by her rights under Article 2—everyone's right to life shall be protected by law. The court is under a positive or operational duty arising from Article 2 to take preventative measures to protect an individual whose life is at risk: *Osman v UK* [1998] 29 EHRR 245: *Rabone v Pennine Care NHS Foundation Trust* [2012] UKSC 2; *A NHS Trust v Dr A* [2013] EWHC 2273 (Fam).
> 16. In those circumstances, this court is under a heavy duty to take what steps it can to protect P's life which is manifestly in danger tonight. Accordingly, I have made an order including a declaration that it is lawful and in P's best interests for the medical practitioners having responsibility for her care and treatment to treat her for the effects of her overdose notwithstanding the fact that she is refusing treatment.
> 17. Furthermore, it is conceivable that in the course of this life-sustaining treatment it may be necessary to sedate or restrain P. I very much hope that this will not be necessary. But if it is, I declare that such steps be lawful, notwithstanding the fact that they amount to a deprivation of liberty.

[58] *Re R (A Minor) (Wardship: Consent to Treatment)* [1992] Fam 11, 24. However, parents cannot consent to the confinement of a young person which, absent a valid consent, would amount to a deprivation of that person's liberty: *Birmingham City Council v D (A Child)* [2016] COPLR 198 at [105].

[59] ibid, 24, 26; *Re W (A Minor) (Medical Treatment: Court's Jurisdiction)* [1993] Fam 64, 74–79, 83–84, 86–87.

[60] [2015] EWHC 922 (Fam) at [39] *per* Keehan J.

[61] *Re R (A Minor) (Wardship: Consent to Treatment)* [1992] Fam 11; *Re W (A Minor) (Medical Treatment: Court's Jurisdiction)* [1993] Fam 64, 81, 83–84, 91–92.

[62] [2014] EWHC 1650 (Fam).

9.35 Thus, by exercising the inherent jurisdiction, the patient's capacitous refusal was overridden by the court. Welfare was the paramount consideration, of which her wishes and feelings were an important component but they were not decisive.

C. The Test for Determining an Adult's Capacity at Common Law

9.36 While it is clear that a patient's capacity to consent to (or refuse) treatment is concerned with his or her *ability to understand* what is involved, how did the common law approach a determination of whether the patient had that ability? The courts developed a three-stage test to assess it. In *Re C (Adult: Refusal of Medical Treatment)*[63] Thorpe J stated that the patient must be able to: (i) *comprehend and retain* the relevant information; (ii) *believe* it; and (iii) *weigh* it in the balance so as to *arrive at a choice*. Subsequent courts applied this so-called '*Re C* three-stage test' and this formed the basis of the test set out in the Mental Capacity Act. The *Re C* test has also been applied in children cases where the issue of the child's capacity is not a developmental one of maturity but is raised by the child's mental disability.[64] In *Re MB* the Court of Appeal authoritatively approved the test.[65] Speaking for the Court of Appeal, Butler-Sloss LJ stated:[66]

> A person lacks capacity if some impairment or disturbance of mental functioning renders the person unable to make a decision whether to consent to or refuse treatment. That inability to make a decision will occur when:
>
> (a) the patient is unable to comprehend and retain the information which is material to the decision, especially as to the likely consequences of having or not having the treatment in question.
>
> (b) the patient is unable to use the information and weigh it in the balance as part of the process of arriving at the decision. If . . . a compulsive disorder or phobia from which the patient suffers stifles belief in the information presented to her, then the decision may not be a true one.

1. Ability to understand versus actual understanding

9.37 Capacity to consent at common law was a question of the person's *ability* to understand that which the law required the patient to understand.[67] The law looked to the person's innate facility or aptitude to understand what was involved in giving consent to (or refusing) the treatment. Of course, it was relevant whether a patient did *actually* understand what was involved. It would be necessary if the patient's consent was to be *real*, and thus, valid. An uncomprehending 'consent' (or 'refusal to consent') was no consent at all but it did not mean necessarily, or otherwise, that the patient was incompetent. The patient may have had the *ability* to understand but did not, perhaps because of the incomplete or inadequate

---

63 [1994] 1 All ER 819, 824; and A Grubb (1992) 2 Med L Rev 92 (Commentary).

64 See *Re C (Detention: Medical Treatment)* [1997] 2 FLR 180; and A Grubb (1997) 5 Med L Rev 227 (Commentary). See also *Re B (A Minor) (Treatment and Secure Accommodation)* [1997] 1 FCR 618; and A Grubb (1997) 5 Med L Rev 233 (Commentary).

65 *Re MB* [1997] 2 FLR 426, 433: 'the test to be applied where the issue arose as to capacity . . .' *per* Butler-Sloss LJ. See also *Re B (Adult; Refusal of Treatment)* (2002) 65 BMLR 149, [33] *per* Butler-Sloss P. For a discussion of 'capacity' after *Re MB*, see I Kennedy, (1997) 5 Med L Rev 317, 320–24 (Commentary).

66 ibid, 437.

67 For a case in which the court looked to the actual understanding of the patient see *Re L (Medical Treatment: Gillick Competency)* [1998] 2 FLR 810 (Stephen Brown P) (14-year-old girl who was a Jehovah's Witness incompetent to refuse treatment—which might include a blood transfusion—for a life-threatening condition). For criticism see A Grubb (1999) 7 Med L Rev 58 (Commentary).

explanation offered by the doctor, *actually* understand the information. The patient was not thereby rendered incompetent and unable to decide for him/herself. Rather, the law imposed an obligation upon the doctor to disclose the information in a reasonably comprehensible way or the consent may be invalid and the touching arising out of the treatment (of the competent patient) may be unlawful. Also, the patient's actual understanding would, of course, assist the doctor and, ultimately, the court in some cases to determine whether the patient was able to understand what was involved. In other words, the patient's actual understanding would be a useful 'yardstick' by which to assess the patient's capacity. But, for the reasons just given, it was no more than that and it was not conclusive.

2. What did the patient need to understand?

If mental capacity required the patient to be able to understand what was involved in the proposed procedure, the question arising at common law was as to precisely what that entailed. Did it require the patient to be able to understand only that information which, if understood, would make the patient's consent real and the doctor's touching not a battery? In other words, the patient must be able to understand the 'broad nature and purpose' of the procedure? This would have a certain legal symmetry about it and would be consistent with decisions of the Court of Appeal that consent in medical law simply had the function of licensing that which would otherwise be a battery. **9.38**

At the other extreme, the law could require the patient to have an ability to understand all information which the law required the patient to have in mind when consenting whether in order to avoid a battery claim or because of the doctor's obligation in negligence to provide information. This would, therefore, encompass much more than the 'broad nature and purpose' of the procedure and include some risks etc. There was a logical basis for this approach since it would be curious if the law required disclosure of information which the patient was simply unable to comprehend. However, as was often the case, the common law took a middle course. The patient must have been able to understand more than the 'broad nature and purpose' of the procedure. S/he must also have been able to understand the likely (or possible) effects or consequences of undergoing (or not) the procedure in question.[68] In one case, the court stated that the patient should have the ability to understand the 'nature, purpose and effects' of the procedure which was the amputation of part of a leg.[69] The Court of Appeal in *Re MB* spoke of the patient having capacity if she was able to understand 'the information which is material to the decision, especially as to the likely consequences of having or not having the treatment in question'.[70] **9.39**

In children cases, there is some suggestion in the case law that the patient must have a much greater ability to understand than has been suggested above.[71] In the *Gillick* case, for example, the child had to understand the 'moral and family questions' associated with her decision to engage in sexual intercourse and to seek contraceptive treatment secretly without involving her parents.[72] To require this of a child is indeed to expect a lot: more, quite frankly, than could, or indeed would, be expected of an adult patient. It is better to understand the remarks in *Gillick*, at best, as restricted to the particular context of contraception **9.40**

[68] See formulation in the Age of Capacity (Scotland) Act 1991, s 2(4).
[69] *Re C (Adult: Refusal of Medical Treatment)* [1994] 1 All ER 819 *per* Thorpe J, 824.
[70] (1997) 38 BMLR 175, 187 *per* Butler-Sloss LJ.
[71] For a discussion of the capacity of children to consent (or refuse) medical treatment, see paras 9.19–9.35.
[72] *Gillick v West Norfolk and Wisbech AHA* [1986] AC 112 at 189.

and the court's desire to move slowly forward in emancipating children or, at worst, as simply wrong, going beyond anything that the law could reasonably expect of anyone.[73]

D. Capacity Under the Mental Capacity Act 2005

1. Introduction to the 2005 Act

9.41 Part 1 of the Mental Capacity Act 2005 codified the common law on mental capacity and provided a statutory test for the first time. When introducing the Bill at Second Reading the junior minister, Mr David Lammy MP, described the common law test on capacity to be 'unsystematic and full of gaps and that it often did not reflect changes in attitudes'.[74] This ill-judged observation, made of course within the parliamentary process, failed to give credit to the sensitivity of judges who developed the common law and singularly failed to acknowledge that the Law Commission had produced a Bill[75] which was a codification of the common principles, rather than any systematic departure from them.

9.42 The Bill was changed and expanded substantially through the parliamentary process from the draft produced by the Law Commission, particularly in the development of the concept of an Independent Mental Capacity Advocate to create a legally useful and robust structure to support the law around medical research involving people who lack capacity. In its final form it represents a fusion of common law principles, systematic input from the Law Commission, and the outcome of a highly active parliamentary process, which allowed the interests of a variety of interest groups to be reflected in the final Act of Parliament.

2. Who comes under the Mental Capacity Act?

9.43 Section 2(5) provides that the powers for those acting on behalf of persons who lack capacity shall not be exercisable 'under this Act' in relation to anyone under the age of 16. Although the test of incapacity in s 2(1) appears to apply to everyone regardless of age, the test is only expressed to be 'for the purposes of this Act'. It follows that the common law tests which have been built up in case law to determine when children gain capacity remain unaffected by the Mental Capacity Act.[76] In relation to those who have attained the age of 16, the presumption created by s 8 of the Family Reform Act 1969—that such children have the capacity to consent in relation to 'medical, surgical or dental treatment' including diagnostic and ancillary procedures—is rebuttable; but the test for determining whether a 16- or 17-year-old has capacity is set out in ss 2–3 of the Mental Capacity Act 2005 and not those at common law.

3. The role of the Code of Practice

9.44 A key mechanism to ensure that the practice of professionals operating in this area is kept up to date is in s 42, which requires the Lord Chancellor to prepare one or more Codes of

[73] See *C v Wren* (1987) 35 DLR (4th) 419 (Alta CA) and *Ney v Attorney-General of Canada* (1993) 102 DLR (4th) 136 (BC Sup Ct).

[74] See *Hansard*, record of Second Reading Debates of 11 October 2004.

[75] For the background, see the Law Commission's reports: '*Mentally Incapacitated Adults and Decision-Making*' (Law Com No 119); '*Mentally Incapacitated Adults and Decision-Making: A New Jurisdiction*' (Law Com No 128); '*Mentally Incapacitated Adults and Decision-Making: Medical Treatment and Research*' (Law Com No 129); '*Mentally Incapacitated and other Vulnerable Adults: Public Law Protection*' (Law Com No 130); and '*Mental Incapacity*' (Law Com No 231).

[76] Note, however, the Mental Health Act Code of Practice (2015) para 19.36 which states that practitioners 'may find it helpful' to consider the equivalent of the functional test of the MCA when considering the capacity of those under 16.

Practice. The statutory purposes include 'for the guidance of persons assessing whether a person has capacity'.[77] Section 42(4) imposes a duty on a range of people to 'have regard to any relevant code' when acting in relation to a person who lacks capacity. The range of persons includes those acting 'for remuneration' and thus will include all health care and caring staff who are paid for their work. This duty is imposed on both the consultant and the ward assistant or untrained care worker in an elderly person's home, and on all staff in between. The Code of Practice was published in 2007[78] and runs to 302 pages. The Lord Chancellor has power to revise the Code. Updating a Code of Practice allows flexibility for the government to respond to emerging issues and to developing practice without having to wait for parliamentary time to amend the main Act or to lay new regulations.

However the duty of those who work with people who lack capacity is to have regard to the current edition of the Code of Practice and to only depart from it if there are cogent reasons for doing so.[79] Thus those who are affected by the Code have a duty to keep themselves up to date with any changes. The text below is based upon the Code of Practice in force at the date of going to press but those using this book would be well advised to cross-check references against any subsequent version before relying on the text set out below. **9.45**

4. Capacity as a decision-specific test

The Act and the Code of Practice stress that the test of incapacity is a test in relation to a specific decision that a person has to take[80] and not their ability to make decisions in general. A person may be able to make some decisions for themselves but lack capacity to take other decisions, depending on the complexity and importance of the particular decision. Thus the test for incapacity is a test which is focused on the individual decision which the person is required to take, judged against the capacity of the person to make that decision, and is not a once and for all decision for a person. The fact that a person lacks capacity to make a decision about serious medical treatment or financial investments does not mean that the person lacks the capacity to make a decision as to where they would prefer to live. Similarly, the fact that a mother could make decisions about surgery and pain relief did not mean she could make decisions about the removal of her child.[81] **9.46**

Affirming the previous position at common law, under the MCA the issue is whether the person lacks the capacity to understand the nature, purpose, and effects of the proposed treatment. As discussed below, the last of these entails understanding the benefits and risks of deciding to have or not to have the treatment, and of not making a decision at all. What is required is 'a broad general, understanding of the kind that is expected from the population at large', for we 'should not ask more of people whose capacity is questioned than of those whose capacity is undoubted'.[82] **9.47**

---

[77] See Mental Capacity Act 2005, s 42(1)(a).

[78] It can be downloaded from <https://www.gov.uk/government/publications/mental-capacity-act-code-of-practice>.

[79] By analogy see *R (on the application of Munjaz) v Mersey Care NHS Trust* [2006] 2 AC 148 at [21]. For a detailed analysis, see Chapter 11.

[80] See para 4.4 of the MCA Code of Practice. The decision that falls to be made will depend upon the options that are or may be available as we 'cannot always have what we want': *Aintree University Hospitals NHS Foundation Trust v James* [2013] UKSC 67, [2014] 1 AC 591, [2013] COPLR 492, at [45]. See also *In the matter of MN (Adult)* [2015] EWCA Civ 411, [2015] COPLR 505 (on appeal at the time of going to press).

[81] *Coventry City Council v C* [2012] EWHC 2190 (Fam), [2013] 1 FCR 54.

[82] *Heart of England NHS Foundation Trust v JB* [2014] EWHC 342 (COP), at [25]–[26].

5. The statutory principles of empowerment

9.48 The Act starts in s 1 with a series of five principles which apply for the purpose of the Act, the first three of which are relevant to the assessment of capacity. They are:

(1) A person must be assumed to have capacity unless it is established that he lacks capacity.
(2) A person is not to be treated as unable to make a decision unless all practicable steps to help him to do so have been taken without success.
(3) A person is not to be treated as unable to make a decision merely because he makes an unwise decision.

(i) Assuming capacity

9.49 Our starting point is to assume, irrespective of any condition the person may have, that those aged 16 and over are able to make the relevant decision at the time it falls to be made. The burden of proof rests on others to disprove that assumption; the person being assessed need prove nothing. Requiring others to assume that a person with, for example, intellectual disability or dementia is capable of deciding for themselves serves to challenge old assumptions when people's capacity was globally written off because of their diagnosis. To rebut the statutory assumption, s 2(4) provides that any decision as to whether a person lacks capacity must be decided on the balance of probabilities. So it must be demonstrated that it is more likely than not that the person is unable to make the decision because of an impairment of, or disturbance in the functioning of, their mind or brain.

(ii) Supported decision-making

9.50 This second principle very much reflects the ethos behind the United Nations Convention on the Rights of Persons with Disabilities. Thus, no finding of incapacity can be made unless and until all practicable steps have first been taken to support the person to make the decision themselves. Chapter 3 of the Code of Practice goes into considerable detail about the steps care staff are expected to take to assist those with questionable capacity who are called upon to take medical treatment decisions to understand the options before a decision is taken that the person lacks capacity. The Code[83] invites staff to consider:

- Does the person have all the relevant information they need to make a particular decision?
- If they have a choice, have they been given information on all the alternatives?

. . .

- Could information be explained or presented in a way that is easier for the person to understand (for example, by using simple language or visual aids)?
- Have different methods of communication been explored if required, including non-verbal communication?
- Could anyone else help with communication (for example, a family member, support worker, interpreter, speech and language therapist or advocate)?

. . .

- Are there particular times of day when the person's understanding is better?
- Are there particular locations where they may feel more at ease?
- Could the decision be put off to see whether the person can make the decision at a later time when circumstances are right for them?

. . .

- Can anyone else help or support the person to make choices or express a view?

[83] The wording is taken from the summary section of the Code, pp.29–30.

What is and is not practicable will depend on the precise circumstances.[84] It is clear from the Code of Practice that professionals are required to plan their work so as to build in enough time and flexibility, where that is clinically appropriate, to deliver on this statutory duty. The argument that, save in a case of medical emergency, staff resources meant that it was not practicable to allow the patient time to make his own decisions is highly unlikely to be accepted. Paragraph 4.16 of the Code explains: **9.51**

> Every effort must be made to provide information in a way that is most appropriate to help the person to understand. Quick or inadequate explanations are not acceptable unless the situation is urgent.

(iii) A lack of wisdom

This third principle in s 1(4) demonstrates the Act's rejection of the outcome approach to determining mental incapacity and provides an important brake on any temptation to conflate capacity with best interests. It ensures that professionals and the court are not unduly influenced by the 'protection imperative'; that is, feeling 'drawn towards an outcome that is more protective of the adult and thus, in certain circumstances, fail to carry out an assessment of capacity that is detached and objective'.[85] To put it another way: **9.52**

> The temptation to base a judgement of a person's capacity upon whether they seem to have made a good or bad decision, and in particular upon whether they have accepted or rejected medical advice, is absolutely to be avoided. That would be to put the cart before the horse or, expressed another way, to allow the tail of welfare to wag the dog of capacity. Any tendency in this direction risks infringing the rights of that group of persons who, though vulnerable, are capable of making their own decisions. Many who suffer from mental illness are well able to make decisions about their medical treatment, and it is important not to make unjustified assumptions to the contrary.[86]

There is an important difference between (a) an unwise decision and (b) a decision based on a lack of understanding of risks or inability to weigh up the information about the decision. Between them is a preserved space within which an individual's autonomy operates.[87] Moreover, to conclude that a person lacks capacity can interfere with their right to respect for private life as guaranteed by Article 8 ECHR.[88] And it is 'of the essence of a free society that people who have capacity can choose lifestyles of which those with health or care responsibilities for them do not approve without on that basis alone being at risk of forfeiting capacity, that is the essence of the Article 8 protection'.[89] As Davis LJ has held:

> It is, of course, of the essence of humanity that adults are entitled to be eccentric, entitled to be unorthodox, entitled to be obstinate, entitled to be irrational. Many are. But the decided authorities show that there can be no power of public intervention simply because an adult

84 Analysing the equivalent provision in the Mental Capacity Act 2010, the Singapore Court of Appeal held in *Re BKR* [2015] SGCA 26 at [103] that 'It directs us to look not at fanciful possibilities but at sensible ones. Hence, if P needs extremes of assistance which he could not realistically expect to receive in order to be able to make decisions, it would not be right to say that he possesses the ability to make decisions.'

85 *CC v KK* [2012] EWHC 2136 at [25] *per* Baker J.

86 *Heart of England NHS Foundation Trust v JB* [2014] EWHC 342 (COP) at [7].

87 *PC and NC v City of York Council* [2013] EWCA Civ 478, [2014] Fam 10 at [54].

88 See *Shtukaturov v Russia* (2012) 54 EHRR 27 at [83].

89 *A Primary Care Trust v P and others* [2009] COPLR Con Vol 956, at [58] *per* Hedley J.

proposes to make a decision, or to tolerate a state if affairs, which most would consider neither wise nor sensible.[90]

9.53 Section 1(4) of the Act states that an inability to decide cannot be found 'merely' because the decision is unwise. A perceived lack of wisdom may therefore not be altogether irrelevant to the assessment process:

> The significance of section 1(4) must not be exaggerated. The fact that a decision is unwise or foolish may not, without more, be treated as conclusive, but it remains in my judgment a relevant consideration for the court to take into account in considering whether the criteria of inability to make a decision for oneself in section 3(1) are satisfied. This will particularly be the case where there is a marked contrast between the unwise nature of the impugned decision and the person's former attitude to the conduct of his affairs at a time when his capacity was not in question.[91]

9.54 Moreover, the principle in s 1(4) is likely to have less weight with regards to the autonomy of young persons aged 16 and 17.[92]

6. The statutory test for determining incapacity

9.55 The test for incapacity in s 2(1) of the Act—the 'core determinative provision'[93]—is as follows:

> For the purposes of this Act, a person lacks capacity in relation to a matter if at the material time he is unable to make a decision for himself in relation to the matter because of an impairment of, or a disturbance in the functioning of, the mind or brain.

9.56 This is a single test whose plain wording looks to the person's inability to decide first. As the Court of Appeal held in *PC and NC v City of York Council:*

> There is, however, a danger in structuring the decision by looking to section 2(1) primarily as requiring a finding of mental impairment and nothing more and in considering section 2(1) first before then going on to look at section 3(1) as requiring a finding of inability to make a decision. The danger is that the strength of the causative nexus between mental impairment and inability to decide is watered down. That sequence—'mental impairment' and then inability to make a decision'—is the reverse of that in section 2(1)—'unable to make a decision . . . *because of* an impairment of, or a disturbance in the functioning of, the mind or brain' (emphasis added). The danger in using section 2(1) simply to collect the mental health element is that the key words 'because of' in section 2(1) may lose their prominence and be replaced by words such as those deployed by Hedley J: 'referable to' or 'significantly relates to'.[94]

9.57 An impairment or disturbance includes, but goes beyond, the concept of 'mental disorder' as defined in s 1 of the Mental Health Act 1983. So, in addition to mental illnesses, learning disabilities, dementias, and delirium, it can include brain damage, physical or medical conditions that cause confusion, drowsiness or loss of consciousness, as well as intoxication, phobias, and the effects of pain, shock, exhaustion, and fear. Indeed, s 2(1) provides that it does not matter whether the impairment or disturbance is permanent or temporary. Although often referred to as the 'diagnostic test', a diagnosis based upon medical

---

[90] *DL v A Local Authority* [2012] EWCA Civ 253, [2013] Fam 1 at [76].

[91] *D v R (the Deputy of S)* [2010] EWHC 2405 (COP) at [40] *per* Henderson J. See also para 4.30 of the Code of Practice.

[92] See *A Local Authority v FG and others* [2011] EWHC 3932 (COP) at [11].

[93] *PC and NC v City of York Council* [2013] EWCA Civ 478, [2014] Fam 10 at [56].

[94] [2014] Fam 10, [58]. It has been suggested that this passage does not seek to reverse the order of the questions but simply stresses the need for a causative nexus: see *Norfolk CC v PB* [2014] EWCOP 14 at [89]–[90].

evidence is not necessarily required, although would be advisable in more borderline or controversial cases.

Section 2(3) provides that a lack of capacity cannot be established merely by reference to: **9.58**

(a) a person's age or appearance, or
(b) a condition of his, or an aspect of his behaviour, which might lead others to make unjustified assumptions about his capacity.

'Appearance' covers all aspects of the way people look, including the way they dress, skin colour, and body piercings, as well as the physical characteristics of certain conditions, such as features linked to Down's syndrome or muscle spasms caused by cerebral palsy.[95] Designed to challenge any unjustified preconceptions an assessor of capacity may have, 'condition' is similarly wide-ranging and includes physical, mental, and temporary conditions. According to the Code of Practice, '[a]spects of behaviour might include extrovert (for example, shouting or gesticulating) and withdrawn behaviour (for example, talking to yourself or avoiding eye contact)'.[96] **9.59**

Section 2(4) provides that any decision as to whether a person lacks capacity must be decided on the balance of probabilities. However, the presumption is that all those aged 16 and over have capacity and thus the onus of proof must lie on another person to prove, on balance, that the person does *not* have capacity. Further, a person, known as 'D' under the Act, has a defence under s 5 to a claim for wrongful interference with the rights of the other person, known as 'P' under the Act, if D had a reasonable belief that P lacked capacity even if that belief turns out to be incorrect when the full facts are known. **9.60**

Section 3(1) provides that a person is unable to make a decision if any one or more of the four functionality criteria are not satisfied.[97] A finding of incapacity is not necessarily 'marginal', simply because the person is unable to do merely one of them.[98] The criteria are that the person is unable: **9.61**

(a) to understand the information relevant to the decision,
(b) to retain that information,
(c) to use or weigh that information as part of the process of making the decision, or
(d) to communicate his decision (whether by talking, using sign language or any other means).

These criteria, now reduced to statutory form, are substantially the same as those set out in the judgments of Thorpe J in *Re C*[99] and of the Court of Appeal in *Re MB*, although 'use or weigh' has replaced the belief requirement.[100] However, as the Act and the Code of Practice now form a comprehensive statutory scheme, there may only be limited benefit in looking back to the cases which preceded the Act concerning the interpretation of these words, although such cases are likely to be useful to resolve ambiguities or to cast light on circumstances which are not comprehensively covered in the Act and the Code of Practice. **9.62**

---

95 See Code of Practice, para 4.8.

96 ibid, para 4.9.

97 Use of the word 'or' in s 3(1)(c) demonstrates that the individual incapacities in s 3(1) are not cumulative: *RT v LT and another* [2010] EWHC 1910 (Fam), [2011] 1 FLR 594 at [40].

98 *Mental Health Trust v DD* [2014] EWCOP 11, [2015] 1 FLR 1430 at [79].

99 *Re C (Refusal of Medical Treatment)* [1994] 1 FLR 31. See also *Re T (An Adult)(Consent to Medical Treatment)* [1993] Fam 95, 102 *per* Lord Donaldson MR.

100 *Re MB (Medical Treatment)* (1997) 38 BMLR 175, where Lady Butler-Sloss P said: 'A person lacks capacity if some impairment or disturbance of mental functioning renders the person unable to make a decision whether to consent to or to refuse treatment.' However, that judgment was influenced by the proposal on Mental Capacity put forward by the Law Commission which eventually led to the 2005 Act.

There is a danger that an over-reliance on pre-Act cases may lead to the Act and the Code of Practice being interpreted in the light of the previous cases rather the previous cases being seen to influence the Law Commission and parliamentary process which led to the Act. However, given the coincidence of language between the leading cases before the Act and the statutory wording, it seems inevitable that, in understanding what Parliament meant by the above expressions, the courts will be influenced by cases which pre-dated the Act.[101] But it is important to bear in mind that:

> The central provisions of the MCA 2005 have been widely welcomed as an example of plain and clear statutory language. I would therefore deprecate any attempt to add any embellishment or gloss to the statutory wording unless to do so is plainly necessary.[102]

7. Understanding the information relevant to a decision

9.63 Section 3(1)(a) of the MCA provides that P does not have capacity if s/he is unable to understand the information relevant to a decision. However, the Act does not define the quantity or quality of the information that is required to be communicated to a patient so that an effective decision can be made as to whether the patient is in a position to give or refuse consent to medical treatment.

9.64 According to s 3(4), relevant information 'includes information about the reasonably foreseeable consequences of— (a) deciding one way or another, or (b) failing to make the decision.' It is not necessary to understand all the details that lie at the periphery of the decision: only the 'salient details' relevant to the decision need to be comprehended and weighed.[103] To assess capacity without having provided those salient details is an inappropriate blank canvass. Instead, the person 'must be presented with detailed options so that their capacity to weigh up those options can be fairly assessed'. Where the choice is between staying in a nursing home or returning home, for example, the choice the person 'should be asked to weigh up is not between the nursing home and a return to the bungalow with no or limited support, but rather between staying in the nursing home and a return home with all practicable support'.[104]

9.65 A failure to provide the relevant information to the person under evaluation may not only lead to an unfair assessment of capacity but also to negligence. This is because, in the context of medical treatment, reasonable care must be taken to ensure that a patient is aware 'of material risks of injury that are inherent in treatment'.[105] Thus:

> 87. [. . .] An adult person of sound mind is entitled to decide which, if any, of the available forms of treatment to undergo, and her consent must be obtained before treatment interfering with her bodily integrity is undertaken. The doctor is therefore under a duty to take reasonable care to ensure that the patient is aware of any material risks involved in any recommended treatment, and of any reasonable alternative or variant treatments. The test of materiality is whether, in the circumstances of the particular case, a reasonable person in the patient's position would be likely to attach significance

[101] *Re MM: Local Authority X v MM* [2007] EWHC 2003, [2009] 1 FLR 443 (Fam); Munby J indicated that there was no relevant distinction between the tests for capacity at common law and those under the Mental Capacity Act.

[102] *PC and NC v City of York Council* [2013] EWCA Civ 478, [2014] Fam 10 at [37] *per* MacFarlane LJ.

[103] *LBL v RYJ and VJ* [2010] EWHC 2665 (COP), [2010] COPLR Con Vol 795, at [58].

[104] *CC v KK* [2012] EWHC 2136 (COP), at [68].

[105] *Montgomery v Lanarkshire Health Board* [2015] UKSC 11, [2015] AC 1430, at [82]. For discussion, see C Hobson, 'No (,) more Bolam please: Montgomery v Lanarkshire Health Board' 79(3) Modern Law Review 488-503. See also, Royal College of Surgeons, 'Consent: Supported Decision-Making: A guide to good practice' (Nov 2016).

> to the risk, or the doctor is or should reasonably be aware that the particular patient would be likely to attach significance to it.
>
> 88. The doctor is however entitled to withhold from the patient information as to a risk if he reasonably considers that its disclosure would be seriously detrimental to the patient's health. The doctor is also excused from conferring with the patient in circumstances of necessity, as for example where the patient requires treatment urgently but is unconscious or otherwise unable to make a decision. It is unnecessary for the purposes of this case to consider in detail the scope of those exceptions.

In determining *how* to relay the material risks to the person, s 3(2) of the MCA provides: **9.66**

> A person is not to be regarded as unable to understand the information relevant to a decision if he is able to understand an explanation of it given to him in a way that is appropriate to his circumstances (using simple language, visual aids or any other means).

This approach reflects the second principle in s 1 that a person is not to be treated as unable to make a decision unless all practicable steps to help him to do so have been taken without success. Care needs therefore to be taken to calibrate the provision of information to the circumstances of the patient. However, there is a tension between (a) ensuring a painted canvass is used to fairly assess capacity, with the detailed options and material risks disclosed, and (b) withholding information that would be seriously detrimental to health. The danger being that the person risks being found to lack capacity because they cannot understand, retain, use, and weigh an undisclosed piece of relevant information. We would suggest, however, that such inability is not because of the person's impairment or disturbance: it is because the capacity assessor has not disclosed a salient detail. Accordingly, the causative nexus (detailed below) could not be established. **9.67**

8. Retaining the information

The requirement that a patient should be able to retain the information was recognized in *Re MB*.[106] Under the MCA, capacity is time specific, s 2(1) providing 'a person lacks capacity in relation to a matter if *at the material time* he is unable to make a decision'. Section 3(3) provides that: 'the fact that a person is able to retain the information relevant to a decision for a short period only does not prevent him from being regarded as able to make the decision.' The Code does little more than repeat the statutory words, stating at para 4.20: **9.68**

> The person must be able to hold the information in their mind long enough to use it to make an effective decision. But s 3(3) states that people who can only retain information for a short while must not automatically be assumed to lack the capacity to decide—it depends on what is necessary for the decision in question. Items such as notebooks, photographs, posters, videos and voice recorders can help people record and retain information.

Thus a person who has fluctuating capacity may be able to make an effective decision to consent or refuse consent to medical treatment in a window of lucidity.[107] That decision will be effective to provide consent for the clinicians both at that time and during the foreseeable period when the patient has lost the capacity to make decisions for themselves. Difficulties may arise where a patient with fluctuating capacity makes a valid consent decision in favour of a course of treatment but, when the treatment comes to be administered, the patient resists or seeks to change their mind. Those administering the treatment will then have to **9.69**

[106] (1997) 38 BMLR 175. Butler-Sloss P said the patient must be able to 'retain the information which is material to the decision'.

[107] Where capacity is fluctuating, it is important to keep the matter under regular review: see *Derbyshire County Council v AC, EC, LC* [2014] EWCOP 38, at [36]; *NHS Trust and another v G* [2015] 1 WLR 1984, 2004. See also paras 4.26–4.27 of the Code of Practice.

decide whether the subsequent refusal is a valid expression of the patient's will or whether the patient has lost capacity. If the former, that is the patient's decision. If the latter, and it is possible to do so, it would be appropriate to wait until the person has regained capacity. But if the patient has lost capacity and it is not practicable to wait, then a best interests decision will need to be made. The reasoning process would be that the earlier decision was taken at a time when the patient appeared to understand the medical issues and give a valid consent, and the later refusal was taken in circumstances which indicated a lack of capacity. Thus, in deciding whether to continue with the treatment, the clinician can take a best interests decision guided by the earlier wishes and feelings expressed with capacity.

9. Using or weighing that information as part of the process of making the decision

9.70 The requirement that a patient must have the ability to use or weigh the information was recognized in *Re MB*, where Butler-Sloss LJ said:

> the patient is unable to use the information and weigh it in the balance as part of the process of arriving at the decision. If, as Thorpe J observed in *Re C*, a compulsive disorder or phobia from which the patient suffers stifles belief in the information presented to her, then the decision may not be a true one.

9.71 The Code of Practice at para 4.22 gives the following instances where this is relevant:

> For example, a person with the eating disorder anorexia nervosa may understand information about the consequences of not eating. But their compulsion not to eat might be too strong for them to ignore. Some people who have serious brain damage might make impulsive decisions regardless of information they have been given or their understanding of it.

9.72 Examples can be taken from the case law much of which comes from abroad or was before the passing of the 2005 Act. Thus, a refusal of treatment by a patient suffering from anorexia nervosa,[108] borderline personality disorder resulting in self-harm,[109] or a 'needle phobia' compelling the patient to panic and refuse the procedure,[110] may not be valid in law because the patient may be incapable of 'weighing' the information relevant to the decision. In contrast, a patient at Kings College Hospital with a tentative suggestion of personality disorder was found to have the capacity to refuse renal dialysis following her suicide attempt. The court disagreed with the clinicians' view that she was unable to use or weigh the information. She was choosing to give no weight to her prognosis, within the context of her own values and outlook, as opposed to failing to believe or weigh her prognosis when making the decision.[111] MacDonald J went on to observe:

> 97. The decision C has reached to refuse dialysis can be characterised as an unwise one. That C considers that the prospect of growing old, the fear of living with fewer material possessions and the fear that she has lost, and will not regain, 'her sparkle' outweighs a prognosis that signals continued life will alarm and possibly horrify many, although I am satisfied that the ongoing discomfort of treatment, the fear of chronic illness and the fear of lifelong treatment and lifelong disability are factors that also weigh heavily in the balance for C. C's decision is certainly one that does not accord with the expectations of many in society. Indeed, others in society may consider C's decision to be unreasonable, illogical or

[108] *Re W (Adult: Refusal of Treatment)* [2002] EWHC 901 (Fam).

[109] *B v Croydon HA* [1995] Fam 133, [1995] 1 All ER 683 (CA). See A Grubb (1995) 3 Med L Rev 191 (Commentary).

[110] *Re MB* (1997) 38 BMLR 175 and *Re L (Patient: Non-Consensual Treatment)* [1997] 2 FLR 837.

[111] *Kings College Hospital NHS Foundation Trust v C* [2016] COPLR 50 at [88].

even immoral within the context of the sanctity accorded to life by society in general. None of this however is evidence of a lack of capacity.

Indeed, even if she had been found to be unable to use or weigh, the evidence was equivocal as to 'whether what was being seen might be the operation of a personality disorder or simply the thought processes of a strong willed, stubborn individual with unpalatable and highly egocentric views'.[112]

Certain mental disorders may result in a patient being deprived of the ability to make a real or true choice. A patient whose mental condition forces or makes the patient feel compelled to reach a particular decision, usually to refuse the treatment, may not in law have capacity to make that decision. The patient may be unable to 'weigh' the information and 'make a choice'. In addition, the patient's mental disorder may cause the patient to 'skew' the information given to her such that she distorts the relevant factors in her own mind. In *A Local Authority v E,* a patient with severe anorexia was able to understand and retain information relevant to the decision to eat and communicate her decision. However: **9.73**

> [T]here is strong evidence that E's obsessive fear of weight gain makes her incapable of weighing the advantages and disadvantages of eating in any meaningful way. For E, the compulsion to prevent calories entering her system has become the card that trumps all others. The need not to gain weight overpowers all other thoughts.[113]

A patient whose mental illness leads her to minimize past events and selectively ignore or distort information given about her condition may be 'unable to weigh treatment information, balancing risks and needs', and hence will be incompetent to make a decision about the treatment for her mental disorder.[114] **9.74**

There is no requirement in the MCA to use or weigh the relevant information to a particular standard. Indeed, having weighed the relevant information a patient may ultimately decide to reject it: to give it no weight, as in *Kings College* above. Whilst there will often be overlap between a finding of incapacity and a lack of insight, this is not necessarily so, particularly in the field of psychiatry where the science is not exact:[115] **9.75**

> Thus a patient could be regarded as having capacity to decide if he wished to have treatment even though . . . he lacked insight or understanding of his problems, which insight might have to be addressed by medication. He could similarly be considered to have capacity not because he was shown to have capacity but because the evidence of, for example, his confused mind, did not go quite far enough to rebut the presumption of capacity.[116]

Other factors, such as religious beliefs, may lead a person to give no weight to information that is considered by others to be relevant to the decision. **9.76**

10. The ability to communicate the decision

The final part of the statutory test considers whether the patient is unable to communicate his or her decision. This factor will only apply on its own if the patient has a total absence of the ability to make any effective communication because s 3(1)(d) allows communication 'by talking, using sign language or any other means'. There are many people who are unable **9.77**

[112] ibid at [93].

[113] [2012] EWHC 1639 (COP), [2012] 2 FCR 523, at [49].

[114] eg, *Re C (Detention: Medical Treatment)* [1997] 2 FLR 180. See also *Re MB* [1997] 2 FCR 541, *per* Butler-Sloss LJ.

[115] *R (on the application of B) v Ashworth Hospital Authority* [2005] 2 AC 278, 292. See also N Allen, 'Is Capacity "In Sight"?' (2009) Journal of Mental Health Law 165.

[116] *R (on the application of B) v Dr. SS, Dr. AC and the Secretary of State for Health* [2005] EWHC 86 (Admin), at [79] *per* Silber J.

to communicate but, in virtually all cases, the impairment or disturbance in the functioning of the mind or brain will also prevent the patient from being able to perform the first three parts of the statutory test. The fourth test is therefore only relevant to those patients who have the ability to understand the information, retain the information and use or weigh it, but nonetheless cannot communicate the outcome of their decision-making process.

9.78 The Code of Practice notes at paragraph 4.23 that:

> This will apply to very few people, but it does include:
>
> a) people who are unconscious or in a coma, or
> b) those with the very rare condition sometimes known as 'locked-in syndrome', who are conscious but cannot speak or move at all.
>
> If a person cannot communicate their decision in any way at all, the Act says they should be treated as if they are unable to make that decision.

9.79 The Code of Practice[117] is stringent in describing the efforts which must be made before a person can be said to lack capacity under this heading alone. It suggests that this might call for the involvement of speech and language therapists, specialists in non-verbal communication or other professionals. The Code says:

> Communication by simple muscle movements can show that somebody can communicate and may have capacity to make a decision. For example, a person might blink an eye or squeeze a hand to say 'yes' or 'no'.

9.80 This aspect of the functional test may not apply to those who, whilst capable of making the decision, are unwilling to communicate it. Only if such unwillingness is because of an impairment of, or disturbance in the functioning of, the mind or brain will the MCA apply. Otherwise the presumption of capacity will not have been displaced.

11. The causative nexus

9.81 If the person is proven to be unable to understand, retain, use or weigh the relevant information, or to communicate their decision, the second element of the incapacity test looks at why. Is it 'because of' an impairment of, or disturbance in the functioning of, their mind or brain? So a finding that the inability to decide is 'referable to' or 'significantly relates to' the impairment or disturbance is insufficient.[118] Similarly, if the inability is solely because of some other reason, such as undue influence or immaturity, the MCA is not generally applicable.

9.82 In *NCC v PB and TB*,[119] one issue was whether the person's inability to use or weigh relevant information was because of an impairment/disturbance or because of the influence exercised over her by her husband. Parker J held that 'the true question is whether the impairment/disturbance of mind is an effective, material or operative cause. Does it cause the incapacity, even if other factors come into play? This is a purposive construction.'[120] However, her Ladyship

---

117 See paras 4.24 and 4.25 of the Code. In *AK (Adult Patient) (Medical Treatment: Consent), Re* [2001] 1 FLR 129, a patient with motor neurone disease was supported to communicate her decision by blinking her eyelids in response to a communication aid.

118 *PC and NC v City of York Council* [2013] EWCA Civ 478, [2014] Fam 10.

119 *NCC v PB and TB* [2014] EWCOP 14.

120 ibid, [86].

went on to decide that the impairment/disturbance was 'the effective cause, the primary cause of her inability to make a decision'.[121] It need not be the *sole* cause of the inability.[122]

E. Specific Areas Concerning Assessments of Capacity

1. Beliefs and value systems

In applying the tests of capacity, the courts are not concerned with the reasonableness of the patient's decision or his reasoning process.[123] Nor is the law concerned with the rationality of the patient's decision or its basis, unless that leads the court to conclude that the patient is unable to understand, retain, use, or weigh the information. The fact that, after conducting that process, the patient comes to a decision which appears to the doctor to be unwise or even irrational is irrelevant.[124] In *Re T (Adult: Refusal of Treatment)* Lord Donaldson MR stated that a competent adult patient had a right to consent to, or refuse, medical treatment based upon reasons which were 'rational, irrational, unknown or even non-existent'.[125] Consequently, religious beliefs which lead patients to refuse some or all medical treatment do not affect a patient's capacity, however irrational the belief may seem.[126] A Jehovah's Witness who refuses a blood transfusion, or a Christian Scientist who refuses all medical intervention is not, by reason of the irrationality or otherwise of their beliefs, unable to make decisions about their medical treatment. Providing they are able to comprehend what is involved, their refusals will be legally binding upon the doctors.[127] There are two explanations of the law's position here. First, the law defers to religiously based decisions made by adults, though not necessarily those made on behalf of children,[128] in discharge of the state's duty to respect the observance of religious views under Article 9 of the European Convention on Human Rights.[129] Such beliefs have to satisfy certain objective minimum thresholds relating to seriousness, coherence, and conformity with accepted standards of human dignity and integrity before the qualified rights under Article 9 are engaged.[130] Article 9 provides an absolute right to hold a religious belief and a qualified right to manifest **9.83**

[121] ibid, [107].

[122] ibid, [101]. Similarly in *Re BKR* [2015] SGCA 26, the Singaporean Court of Appeal held that, where there is interaction between (i) mental impairment on the part of P and (ii) the possibility that P is under the undue influence of other persons, it is only where there is no material question of any mental impairment causing the alleged mental incapacity that a court ought properly to find it has no jurisdiction under the Act.

[123] *Re T (Adult: Refusal of Treatment)* [1993] Fam 95, [1992] 4 All ER 649, 664 (CA) *per* Butler-Sloss LJ: 'a decision . . . does not have to be sensible, rational or well considered.' See also *Smith v Auckland Hospital Board* [1965] NZLR 191 (NZCA), 219 *per* Gresson J.

[124] *Re MB* (para 9.36). See also *St George's Healthcare NHS Trust v S* [1998] 3 All ER 673 (CA); *Re JT (Adult: Refusal of Medical Treatment)* [1998] 1 FLR 48 (Wall J); *Kings College Hospital NHS Foundation Trust v C* [2016] COPLR 50.

[125] *Re T*, n 123 at 102. See also *Re MB, per* Butler-Sloss LJ at [1997] 2 FCR 541 at 549.

[126] *Re W (A Minor) (Consent to Medical Treatment*, [1993] Fam 64, [1992] 4 All ER 627 (CA) 637 *per* Lord Donaldson MR.

[127] *Re T (Adult: Refusal of Treatment)* [1993] Fam 95, [1992] 4 All ER 649 (CA).

[128] See, eg, *Re S (A Minor) (Medical Treatment)* [1993] 1 FLR 376, *Re E (A Minor)* (1990) 9 BMLR 1; *Re R (A Minor)* [1993] 2 FLR 5; *Re L (Medical Treatment: Gillick Competency)* [1998] 2 FLR 810.

[129] Article 9(1) provides: 'Everyone has the right to freedom of thought, conscience and religion; this right includes freedom, either alone or in community with others and in public or private, to manifest his religion or belief, in worship, teaching, practice and observance.' Similarly, in the context of best interests, delusions with a religious component will not automatically reduce the weight to be attached to them, as Article 9 is no less engaged: *Wye Valley NHS Trust v Mr B* [2015] EWCOP 60, [2015] COPLR 843 at [14].

[130] See *R (Williamson) v Secretary of State for Employment and Education* [2005] UKHL 15, [2005] 2 AC 246.

the belief.[131] For an adult with capacity, it is difficult to envisage any medical circumstances where the limited right to override that belief under Article 9(2) could be justified:

> 34. This aspect of the test of capacity must be applied very cautiously and carefully when religious beliefs are in play. In his essay John Stuart Mill speaks of the prohibition in Islam on the eating of pork. He describes how Muslims regard the practice with 'unaffected disgust'; it is 'an instinctive antipathy'. There can be no circumstances where a Muslim could 'weigh' the merit of eating pork. It is simply beyond the pale. So too, it would appear, when it comes to Jehovah's Witnesses and blood transfusions. But it would be an extreme example of the application of the law of unintended consequences were an iron tenet of an accepted religion to give rise to questions of capacity under the MCA.
>
> 35. I therefore place little emphasis on the fact that a tenet of RC's religious faith prevents him from weighing the advantages of a blood transfusion should his medical circumstances indicate that one is necessary.[132]

9.84 Second, and perhaps of more general importance for medical law, such decisions do not stem from any cognitive impairment on the part of the patient and thus cannot be said to be a result of any impairment of or a disturbance in the functioning of the mind or brain. It follows that a person who makes a decision based on religious beliefs is nonetheless making a valid decision within s 2 of the Mental Capacity Act 2005. This is a valid decision which the doctors must respect unless the patient is suffering from a mental impairment having a pathological or psychological aetiology. Where a person's refusal to consent to medical treatment is not driven by a religious belief system which attracts the protection of Article 9 of the ECHR, imposing medical treatment on the person without consent may well be a breach of Article 8 of the ECHR if a person's lack of capacity overrides a cultural set of beliefs. Article 8 of the ECHR emphasizes the right of each person to autonomy over their own bodies. Hence an individual's belief system which leads a person to refuse to give consent to medical treatment, even if not religious in origin, must be respected so as to abide by Article 8 unless it can be said to derive from an impairment of or disturbance in the functioning of the mind or brain (in which case it may be indicative of a lack of capacity). In practice, in a multi-cultural society with a very wide range of belief systems amongst the patient population, it can be fiendishly difficult for doctors, lawyers, and the court to draw the line in a culturally sensitive manner to determine who does and does not have capacity in such circumstances. Relatives, who are often a key source of information about the background and reasoning process of the patient, can have profoundly differing views as to whether a refusal to accept treatment in a patient can be indicative of a lack of capacity. Thus doctors, nurses, and care professionals should, where possible, act cautiously and in accordance with the Code of Practice and their professional obligations in seeking advice before making decisions.

2. Misperception of reality

9.85 In order for a patient to have capacity to decide, s/he must be able to understand the information that is material to making the decision. As part of this, a patient must be able to understand what is wrong with him or her and which requires treatment, and s/he must be able to understand the consequences of undergoing or declining the treatment. However, an irrational belief, whether long-held or of contemporary origin, which affects or influences a patient's judgment about medical treatment will not lead to a finding of incapacity unless it results in an inference that the patient is suffering from a mental impairment. In *Re MB* the Court of Appeal acknowledged that it would not be proper to find a patient incompetent

[131] *R (on the application of Begum) v Denbigh High School* [2006] UKHL 15, [2007] 1 AC 100.

[132] *Nottinghamshire Healthcare NHS Trust v RC* [2014] EWCOP 1317, [2014] COPLR 468 *per* Mostyn J.

merely because his decision was 'irrational', meaning one 'so outrageous in its defiance of logic or of accepted moral standards' that 'no sensible person who had applied his mind to the question to be decided could have arrived at it'.[133] The Court of Appeal accepted, however, that if the patient's irrational decision was based upon a misperception of reality stemming from a mental disorder, then the patient might lack the ability to 'comprehend' or 'believe' the information under the *Re C* test which was in force at the time.[134]

This aspect of the test for capacity was considered by Charles J in *NHS Trust v T*,[135] a case which concerned both the validity of an Advance Directive and the present capacity of the patient to refuse medical treatment. There was a dispute between the experts as to the extent to which the patient was approaching matters on a basis that was eccentric or whether her approach showed she lacked capacity because of her misperception of reality. Charles J concluded that she came down on the lack of capacity side of the line. He said:[136] **9.86**

> . . . it seems to me that Ms T's references to her blood being evil equate to the example given that 'the blood is poisoned because it is red' . . . From that it seems to me that this assertion and belief of Ms T is a misconception of reality which can more readily be accepted to be, and on the present evidence should be accepted to be, a disorder of the mind and afurther or alternatively symptoms or evidence of incompetence.

Another example of this problem was *Doncaster & Bassetlaw Hospitals NHS Trust and Anor v C*,[137] where a patient had a suspected renal carcinoma. However, as a result of the patient's mental health problems, the patient considered she was not ill, refused treatment and wanted to be left in charge of her own body. Her delusions meant that she regarded medical treatment as unnecessary and believed that the proposed medical interventions that were part of a plot against her. Sumner J made an order for the treatment to go ahead despite her trenchant opposition. The court would now be likely to come to the same view saying that the patient lacked capacity because the patient was unable to 'use or weigh' the information under s 3(1)(c) because of her delusions and thus lacked capacity. **9.87**

However, it is essential to a finding of incapacity that the patient's 'disbelief' derives from an impairment of or disturbance in the functioning of the mind or brain. Not every patient who disbelieves their doctor's advice fails the statutory test and lack capacity: indeed, most will retain capacity. An important distinction has to be drawn between outright disbelief due to mental disorder where the patient is 'impervious to reason, divorced from reality, or incapable of adjustment after reflection' and 'the tendency which most people have when undergoing medical treatment to self assess and then puzzle over the divergence between medical and self-assessment'.[138] Merely to take a different view of the world from a doctor may result in a patient 'disbelieving' him but it does not render the patient incapacitated and thus unable to decide, as a matter of law, for themselves.[139] Even a skewed, and indefensible view of the world, does not have this effect *unless* it has its genesis in what was previously termed, mental 'malfunctioning'[140] and now must involve an impairment of or disturbance in the functioning of the mind or brain. **9.88**

[133] See *Re MB* [1997] 2 FCR 541 at 553 *per* Butler-Sloss LJ.
[134] ibid.
[135] *NHS Trust v T* [2004] EWHC 1279 (Fam).
[136] ibid, at [61].
[137] [2004] EWHC 1657 (Fam).
[138] *B v Croydon HA* (1994) 22 BMLR 13, 20 *per* Thorpe J.
[139] *Re C (Adult: Refusal of Medical Treatment)* [1994] 1 All ER 819; *Kings College Hospital NHS Foundation Trust v C* [2016] COPLR 50.
[140] See, eg, *Tameside and Glossop Acute Services Trust v CH* [1996] 1 FLR 762, where the patient had a deluded belief that her doctors were maliciously trying to hurt her and her unborn child. See A Grubb (1996) 4 Med L Rev 193 (Commentary).

9.89 Hence, a patient's irrational fear of surgery[141] or a particular medical procedure are not sufficient in themselves to make the patient incompetent in law to make a decision about their treatment. Only if the 'fear' acts on the patient's mind or brain so as to 'paralyse the will and thus destroy the capacity to make a decision' will a finding of incapacity be justified.[142] In practice, given the statutory focus on the need to show an impairment of or disturbance in the functioning of the mind or brain, a doctor who is faced by a borderline patient would be well advised to seek a psychiatric view to support the decision as to whether the patient has or does not have capacity.

3. Compulsive or driven behaviour

9.90 There are cases which show clearly how fine this line can be. In *R v Ashworth Hospital Authority, ex p Brady*[143] a prisoner refused food by going on a hunger strike. The court decided that he was incompetent to make that decision. The prisoner's paranoid personality disorder had resulted in a 'battle of wills' with the prison authorities such that he was unable to weigh and balance information in relation to food refusal and force-feeding under the third stage of the *Re C* test (since this case preceded the 2005 Act).

9.91 However, caution must be exercised in applying the 'use or weigh' part of the test. It is potentially an open invitation to make a finding of incapacity because the doctor (or court) finds the patient's decision difficult to understand. This is not what the Act intends. The requirement that a patient must have the ability to 'weigh' information does not mean that every incongruous or inexplicable decision is an incapacitated one. The court is not entitled simply to re-weigh the factors relevant to the patient's decision and, because it would come to a different decision, treat the patient as lacking capacity. It is the patient's inability to weigh, rather than the actual weight given to particular factors, which is at the core of the test. A patient may have the ability to weigh the information but, for reasons particular to him, reach a decision that the doctor (or court) would not. That is the patient's choice and the decision may be based upon the patient's own perception of the world or values providing it is not the product of distorted or deluded perceptions stemming from mental malfunctioning, in particular the very mental disorder for which treatment is needed.[144] To do otherwise, would be to introduce a test of unreasonableness or irrationality which the courts have rejected.[145]

4. External factors

9.92 A patient's ability to understand may be temporarily affected by external factors such as confusion, shock, fatigue, pain, or medication.[146] Such factors may render a patient incapable of making a decision because the patient is unable to 'weigh' the information and make

[141] See, eg, *Re Maida Yetter* (1973) 96 D & C 2d 619 (Comm Pleas Pa) and *Lane v Candura* (1978) 376 NE 2d 1232 (Mass App Ct).

[142] *Re MB (Medical Treatment)* [1997] 2 FLR 426, 437 *per* Butler-Sloss LJ. Equally, it must be remembered that: 'common strategies for dealing with unpalatable dilemmas—for example indecision, avoidance or vacillation—are not to be confused with incapacity. We should not ask more of people whose capacity is questioned than of those whose capacity is undoubted': *Heart of England NHS Foundation Trust v JB* [2014] EWHC 342 (COP) at [25] *per* Peter Jackson J.

[143] [2000] Lloyd's Rep Med 355 (Maurice Kay J). Discussed in P Fennell (2000) 8 Med L Rev 251 (Commentary).

[144] See *B v Croydon HA* (1994) 22 BMLR 13, 20 *per* Thorpe J, and see also *Re MB* [1997] 2 FCR 541 at 550 *per* Butler-Sloss LJ.

[145] *St George's Healthcare NHS Trust v S* [1998] 3 All ER 673 (CA), [1999] Fam 26: pregnant woman competent to refuse treatment even though her thinking was bizarre and irrational.

[146] *Re T (Adult: Refusal of Medical Treatment)* [1992] 4 All ER 649, 661 *per* Lord Donaldson MR. See also *St George's Healthcare NHS Trust v S* [1998] 3 All ER 673 (CA), *per* Judge LJ at 693.

a choice.[147] However, if the effect is only temporary and the treatment is not urgent, the doctor must wait until the patient is able to make a decision. Paragraph 4.45 of the Code advises: 'Can the decision be delayed to take time to help the person make the decision, or give the person time to regain the capacity to make the decision for themselves?'

The court will require a demonstrable effect of the patient's ability to reason and decide before such a finding will be permissible. It is not sufficient that the patient's capacity is merely reduced. The patient's capacity must be 'completely erode[d] . . . to such a degree that the ability to decide is absent'.[148] In *Re MB* Butler-Sloss LJ illustrated how the patient's panic and fear could make them incompetent:[149] **9.93**

> Another . . . influence may be panic induced by fear. Again careful scrutiny of the evidence is necessary because fear of an operation may be a rational reason for refusal to undergo it. Fear may also, however, paralyse the will and thus destroy the capacity to make a decision.

The importance of the limited scope of this basis for a finding of incapacity is illustrated by two cases involving obstetric treatment.[150] In one case,[151] a patient in the late stages of labour was held to be incompetent because, in the words of Johnson J, '[s]he was called upon to make the decision at a time of acute emotional stress and physical pain in the ordinary course of labour made even more difficult for her because of her own particular mental history'.[152] The patient denied she was pregnant. Even though the psychiatric evidence was that she was not suffering from a mental disorder within the Mental Health Act 1983, she had a history of psychiatric treatment and it is difficult to believe that her denial of the obvious was based upon a difference of opinion or values rather than having a psychiatric aetiology. Johnson J was not, therefore, relying upon the patient's circumstances in reaching his decision that she was incompetent. However, in another case decided on the same day,[153] the same judge did make such a finding where the patient had no psychiatric history. Despite the consultant obstetrician's view that she was competent to decide, Johnson J held:[154] **9.94**

> The patient was in the throes of labour with all that involved in terms of pain and emotional stress. I concluded that a patient who could, in those circumstances, speak in terms which seemed to accept the inevitability of her own death, was not a patient who was able properly to weigh-up the considerations that arose so as to make any valid decision, about anything of even the most trivial kind, surely less one which involved her life.

In *Re MB*, the Court of Appeal rightly doubted this finding.[155]

(i) Legal obligations when there are doubts about capacity

The GMC Guidance document 'Consent: patients and doctors making decisions together' (2008)[156] sets out the following advice for doctors who have concerns as to whether a patient has capacity: **9.95**

---

[147] An alternative way of determining such cases would be to say that the patient was acting involuntarily or under undue influence: *Beausoleil v Soeur de la Charité de la Providence* (1964) 53 DLR (2d) 65 (patient sedated).

[148] *Re MB* [1997] 2 FCR 541 at 542 *per* Butler-Sloss LJ.

[149] ibid, at 554 *per* Butler-Sloss LJ.

[150] For a thorough and scholarly discussion of the case law, see R Scott, *Rights, Duties and the Body: Law and Ethics of the Maternal-Fetal Conflict* (Hart 2002), especially at 154–63.

[151] *Norfolk and Norwich Healthcare (NHS) Trust v W* [1997] 1 FCR 269.

[152] ibid, 272.

[153] *Rochdale Healthcare (NHS) Trust v C* [1997] 1 FCR 274.

[154] ibid, 275.

[155] See also *St George's Healthcare NHS Trust v S* [1998] 3 All ER 673 (CA).

[156] Available online at < http://www.gmc-uk.org/guidance/ethical_guidance/consent_guidance_index.asp>.

> 73 If your assessment leaves you in doubt about the patient's capacity to make a decision, you should seek advice from:
>
> (a) nursing staff or others involved in the patient's care, or those close to the patient, who may be aware of the patient's usual ability to make decisions and their particular communication needs
> (b) colleagues with relevant specialist experience, such as psychiatrists, neurologists, or speech and language therapists.
>
> 74 If you are still unsure about the patient's capacity to make a decision, you must seek legal advice with a view to asking a court to determine capacity.

9.96 The use of the word 'must' in paragraph 74 is significant. A doctor who is unsure about whether a patient has capacity or not is under a professional duty to seek legal advice. Thus in a borderline case, save in a medical emergency, a doctor who declined to seek legal advice and proceeded to make a best interests decision may be able to rely on a defence to a legal action by reliance on s 5 of the Mental Capacity Act[157] but, whilst acting lawfully, may also be acting in breach of the GMC Code and thus face the possibility of professional sanction.

(ii) A mistake as to capacity

9.97 A doctor who mistakenly believes on reasonable grounds that a patient has capacity to consent to (or refuse) medical treatment does not necessarily act unlawfully if s/he provides treatment without the patient's express consent. Section 5 of the Mental Capacity Act provides that if a person ('D') does an act in connection with the care or treatment of another person ('P'), the act is one to which s 5 applies if:

> (a) before doing the act, D takes reasonable steps to establish whether P lacks capacity in relation to the matter in question, and
> (b) when doing the act, D reasonably believes—
> (i) that P lacks capacity in relation to the matter, and
> (ii) that it will be in P's best interests for the act to be done.

9.98 Whether or not the doctor is judged to have taken reasonable steps may in part depend on whether D has had regard to the Code of Practice in reaching his decision on whether P has capacity or not.[158] Paragraph 6.33 of the Code provides:

> If healthcare and social care staff are involved, their skills and knowledge will affect what is classed as 'reasonable'. For example, a doctor assessing somebody's capacity to consent to treatment must demonstrate more skill than someone without medical training. They should also record in the person's healthcare record the steps they took and the reasons for the finding. Healthcare and social care staff should apply normal clinical and professional standards when deciding what treatments to offer. They must then decide whether the proposed treatment is in the best interests of the person who lacks capacity to consent.

9.99 If a doctor or other health care worker can show that s/he took reasonable steps to establish whether P had capacity, the doctor is treated as if P had had capacity to consent in relation to the matter, and had consented to the treatment. Section 5 provides a defence to an action based on an alleged lack of consent but is no defence to a clinical negligence claim or criminal liability for the act in question.[159]

---

[157] Unless it was unreasonable to have declined to have sought legal advice. See also Royal College of Surgeons, 'Consent: Supported Decision-Making: A guide to good practice' (Nov 2016) para 9, which is drafted in similar terms to para 74.

[158] See Mental Capacity Act, s 42(4).

[159] See Mental Capacity Act, s 5(3).

F. Conclusion

Prior to the Human Rights Act 1998, a parent could lawfully consent to the treatment of a *Gillick* competent child who was refusing to consent.[160] A parent could not overrule a *Gillick* competent child's consent to treatment,[161] but could, in effect, overrule a *Gillick* competent child's refusal to consent to treatment: the parent and the child had concurrent powers to consent and where more than one person had a power of consent, only a failure to, or refusal of, consent by all created a veto.[162] **9.100**

The position today tends to suggest that it is not advisable to rely upon the consent of those with parental responsibility to admit or treat a *Gillick* competent child who refuses. Both Department of Health guidance[163] and the Code of Practice to the Mental Health Act[164] cautions against such reliance. The courts are increasingly recognizing the importance of the rights of children, attaching greater weight to their views, albeit they not determinative.[165] **9.101**

The advent of the MCA, with its principles of empowerment and the causative nexus, has strengthened the ability of those aged 16 and over to make their own decisions. Whether the diagnostic limb of the test for incapacity survives the UN Convention on the Rights of Persons with Disabilities remains to be seen. What is clear, however, is that the effect of the legislation is that far more is required in the way of reasoned clarity before a person's autonomy to decide for themselves can be undermined. Indeed, the future is likely to focus even less on mental incapacity and far more on supported decision making. **9.102**

[160] *Re R (A Minor) (Wardship: Consent to Treatment)* [1992] Fam 11, 23–25, 26; *Re W (A Minor) (Medical Treatment: Court's Jurisdiction)* [1993] Fam 64, 84, 86, 87; *Re K, W and H (Minors) (Medical Treatment)* [1993] 1 FLR 854, 859.

[161] *Re R (A Minor) (Wardship: Consent to Treatment)* [1992] Fam 11, 23, 26; *Re W (A Minor) (Medical Treatment: Court's Jurisdiction)* [1993] Fam 64, 83.

[162] *Re R (A Minor) (Wardship: Consent to Treatment)* [1992] Fam 11, 22, 26. However, now see Department of Health, *Reference Guide to Consent for Examination or Treatment* (2nd edn, 2009) ch 3, para 15: 'The courts have, in the past, also found that parents can consent to their competent child being treated even where the child/young person is refusing treatment. However, there is no post-Human Rights Act 1998 authority for this proposition, and it would therefore be prudent to obtain a court declaration or decision if faced with a competent child or young person who is refusing to consent to treatment, to determine whether it is lawful to treat the child.'

[163] Department of Health, *Reference Guide*, n 162, ch 3, para 15.

[164] Mental Health Act 1983 Code of Practice (2015) para 19.39.

[165] See *In the matter of X (A Child)* [2014] EWHC 1871 (Fam) at [10] *per* Sir James Munby PFD; *An NHS Foundation Trust v A, M, P, A Local Authority* [2014] EWHC 920 at [12] *per* Hayden J; see also *R (Axon) v S/S for Health* [2006] EWHC 37 (Admin).

10

CARE AND TREATMENT OF THOSE LACKING DECISION-MAKING CAPACITY

*Neil Allen**

A. Sources of the Law

10.01 It is a fundamental principle that a doctor who gives medical treatment[1] or performs surgery without the consent of his/her patient is *prima facie* guilty of both a tort and a crime.[2] The adult who is *sui juris* is recognized as having the fundamental human and personal right to control his/her own body, the right to self-determination or right of autonomy, the right to decide for oneself to the exclusion of others.[3] Three classes of patient lack the capacity to give a valid consent and are therefore unable to exercise their right to self-determination.

* This is an updated version of the chapter originally written by Sir James Munby. The author would like to thank the editors and Alex Ruck Keene for their comments.

[1] In this chapter 'treatment' is used as a generic term covering all forms of examination, assessment, diagnosis, treatment, or care, and all procedures, whether surgical, medical, psychiatric, dental, or nursing, which involve any physical touching or penetration of the patient's body, however trivial. 'Doctor' is similarly used as a generic term covering everyone involved in providing 'treatment'.

[2] See Chapter 8.

[3] See, eg, *Border v Lewisham and Greenwich NHS Trust* [2015] EWCA Civ 8 where a doctor in accident and emergency was held to be negligent for inserting a cannula into an objecting patient's arm. For a critical analysis of the way the principle of autonomy is handled in English law, see C Foster, 'Autonomy in the Medico-legal Courtroom: A Principle Fit for Purpose?' (2014) 22(1) Med L Rev 48.

The first is children,[4] who by reason of non-age lack the *legal* capacity to give consent, or whose refusal of consent can be overridden by others. Second are those adults who, because of impaired or disturbed functioning of the mind or brain, lack the *mental* capacity to give a valid consent to treatment. Finally, there are young persons (aged 16 to 17) who, because of immaturity or mental impairment, lack the *legal* and/or the *mental* capacity to give consent.

For these purposes, 'legal capacity' is therefore used to refer to the ability to hold and exercise rights and duties before the law, whereas 'mental capacity' refers to a person's decision-making skills.[5] The unborn child or foetus[6] (in legal terminology the child *en ventre sa mère*) occupies a special position, to be separately considered. **10.02**

1. *Parens patriae*

(i) Children and young people

In relation to those under 18, the Crown retains a prerogative power as *parens patriae* exercisable by the judges of the High Court. This power, often though not necessarily exercised by means of wardship, is of considerable importance in relation to the resolution of difficult or disputed questions about the treatment of this age group.[7] **10.03**

(ii) Adults who lack mental capacity

In relation to adults who lack the mental capacity[8] to make decisions, the Crown's prerogative power as *parens patriae* was abrogated in 1960 upon the coming into force of the Mental Health Act 1959.[9] The resulting 'gap' in the law, which was the subject of many expressions of judicial regret, has been filled by three successive developments: first, by the development of the court's inherent declaratory jurisdiction;[10] second by the judicial 'rediscovery' of the court's *parens patriae* jurisdiction in relation to adults;[11] and, third, by the creation by the Mental Capacity Act 2005[12] of a new Court of Protection (replacing the old Court of Protection[13]) with extended powers, including power to deal with 'personal welfare' issues including the giving or refusing of consent to medical treatment.[14] **10.04**

---

[4] The terminology is capable of confusing, for 'child' has very different meanings in the law of succession, in the law of persons, and in colloquial usage. In this chapter, 'child' is used to refer to those under 16; 'young person' refers to those aged 16 and 17; and 'adult' is aged 18 and over. Note, however, that under the Children Act 1989 s 105(1), a 'child' means a person who is under the age of 18.

[5] Article 12 of the Convention on the Rights of Persons with Disabilities ('CRPD') requires States to recognize that 'persons with disabilities enjoy legal capacity on an equal basis with others in all aspects of life.' The UK ratified the Convention on 8 June 2009. The UNCRPD Committee has made it clear that legal and mental capacity are distinct concepts: 'General Comment No. 1—Article 12: Equal Recognition before the Law', UN Doc. No. CRPD/C/GC/1, adopted at the 11th Session (April 2014), at para 13.

[6] The form 'fetus' is preferred by many purists to 'foetus', though, for consistency, the latter spelling is used throughout this volume.

[7] See further Chapter 9.

[8] For the background, see the Law Commission's reports: *Mentally Incapacitated Adults and Decision-Making* (Law Com No 119); *Mentally Incapacitated Adults and Decision-Making: A New Jurisdiction* (Law Com No 128); *Mentally Incapacitated Adults and Decision-Making: Medical Treatment and Research* (Law Com No 129); *Mentally Incapacitated and other Vulnerable Adults: Public Law Protection* (Law Com No 130); and *Mental Incapacity* (Law Com No 231).

[9] *Re F (Mental Patient: Sterilisation)* [1990] 2 AC 1, 51, 54, 57–58, 70, 71, 83. See also *T v T* [1988] Fam 52, *Re C (Mental Patient: Contact)* [1993] 1 FLR 940, *Airedale NHS Trust v Bland* [1993] AC 789; *A v A Health Authority, Re J (A Child), R (on the application of S) v Secretary of State for the Home Department* [2002] EWHC 18 (Fam/Admin), [2002] Fam 213, [35].

[10] See further paras 10.114–10.116.

[11] See further paras 10.117–10.118.

[12] Since amended by the Mental Health Act 2007. All references hereinafter to the Mental Capacity Act 2005 are to the Act as amended by the Mental Health Act 2007.

[13] As to which see the second edition of this work, Chapter 4, para 4.04.

[14] See further paras 10.110–10.112.

2. Statute

10.05 Certain miscellaneous and socially controversial procedures are specifically governed by statute, for example, tattooing,[15] the taking of blood samples,[16] certain forms of treatment for mental disorder,[17] female genital mutilation,[18] and organ transplants.[19] In addition to the Mental Capacity Act 2005, which is considered below, there are two provisions of general application which are directly relevant to the treatment of young persons or adults who lack mental capacity.

(i) Young persons

10.06 Section 8 of the Family Law Reform Act 1969 deems those aged 16 and over as having the same *legal* capacity as they would have if they were 18 for 'any surgical, medical or dental treatment', including procedures undertaken for the purposes of diagnosis and ancillary treatment. But it does not extend to the donation of organs, or of blood or other bodily substances, nor even to the taking of a blood sample (for which separate provision is made in s 21(2)), for none of these procedures constitutes either treatment or diagnosis.[20]

(ii) Persons suffering from mental disorder

10.07 Section 63 of the Mental Health Act 1983 (which applies in accordance with s 56 of the Act) provides:

> The consent of a patient shall not be required for any medical treatment given to him for the mental disorder[21] from which he is suffering, not being a form of treatment to which section 57, 58 or 58A above applies if the treatment is given by or under the direction of the approved clinician in charge of the treatment.

10.08 Section 145 of the 1983 Act provides that:

> 'medical treatment' includes nursing, psychological intervention and specialist mental health habilitation, rehabilitation and care ... Any reference in this Act to medical treatment, in relation to mental disorder, shall be construed as a reference to medical treatment

[15] Tattooing of Minors Act 1969 s 1 makes it a criminal offence to tattoo a person under 18 'except when the tattoo is performed for medical reasons'.

[16] Family Law Reform Act 1969, s 21(1) (adults with capacity), s 21(2) (minors who have attained the age of 16), s 21(3) (minors under the age of 16), s 21(4) (persons who lack capacity).

[17] See generally Chapter 11. For the treatments in question see the Mental Health Act 1983, s 57(1)(a) (surgical operations for destroying brain tissue or the functioning of brain tissue), s 57(1)(b) and s 58(1)(a) (forms of treatment specified by the Secretary of State), s 58(1)(b) (administration of medicine—as to which see *B v Croydon HA* [1995] Fam 133, 137–38); *R (on the application of N) v M* [2002] EWCA Civ 1789, [2003] 1 WLR 562, s 58A (electro-convulsive therapy). See also the Mental Health Act 1983, ss 56, 59–62, 64.

[18] Female Genital Mutilation Act 2003 makes female genital mutilation in all its forms a criminal offence unless it is either 'necessary for ... physical or mental health' or performed 'for purposes connected with ... labour or birth'. Section 1(5) of the Act draws an interesting distinction between mental health and customary or ritual belief by providing that 'For the purpose of determining whether an operation is necessary for the mental health of a girl it is immaterial whether she or any other person believes that the operation is required as a matter of custom or ritual'.

[19] Human Tissue Act 2004.

[20] The statutory right can be contrasted with the common law right whereby a *Gillick* competent child can consent to the donation of blood or organs: *Re W (A Minor) (Medical Treatment: Court's Jurisdiction)* organ, 78, 83–84, 92, 94; *Re O (A Minor) (Blood Tests: Constraint), Re J (A Minor)* [2000] Fam 139, 147–48. See also Chapter 9 and *Re JM (A Child)* [2015] EWHC 2832 (Fam), [2016] 2 FLR 235 at [13].

[21] As defined in the Mental Health Act 1983, s 1(2). Section 63 permits medical treatment of any mental disorder from which the patient is suffering, irrespective of whether it falls within the form of disorder that justified the compulsory admission in the first place: *R (on the application of B) v Ashworth Hospital Authority* [2005] UKHL 20, [2005] 2 AC 278. For a detailed analysis, see Chapter 11.

the purpose of which is to alleviate, or prevent a worsening of, the disorder or one or more of its symptoms or manifestations.

'Medical treatment' in s 63 thereby includes (a) a range of acts ancillary to the core treatment of the mental disorder; (b) treatment for the symptoms of a mental disorder; and (c) treatment of an unconnected physical disorder only if such treatment is likely to directly affect the mental disorder.[22] It thus includes forcible feeding for the treatment of anorexia nervosa[23] or other psychiatric illnesses[24] and inducing labour and performing a caesarean section where effective treatment of the patient's paranoid schizophrenia required that the patient give birth to a live baby and resume medication necessarily interrupted by her pregnancy, including, if necessary, restraint and the use of reasonable force.[25] **10.09**

3. The Human Rights Act 1998

Section 6 of the Human Rights Act 1998, which gives further effect to the rights and freedoms guaranteed under the European Convention for the Protection of Human Rights and Fundamental Freedoms ('ECHR'), agreed by the Council of Europe at Rome on 4 November 1950, makes it unlawful for a public authority (and the court is for this purpose a public authority) to act, or fail to act, in a way which is incompatible with the rights and fundamental freedoms set out in, inter alia, Articles 2–12 and 14 of the Convention. **10.10**

The provisions of the Convention that are most relevant for the purposes of this chapter are: Article 2 (which provides that, subject to the exceptions in Article 2(2), 'Everyone's right to life shall be protected by law'); Article 3 (which provides in unqualified terms that 'No one shall be subjected to torture or to inhuman or degrading treatment or punishment'); Article 5 (which provides that 'Everyone has the right to liberty and security of person'); Article 8 (which provides that, subject to the exceptions in Article 8(2), 'Everyone has the right to respect for his private and family life, his home and his correspondence'); Article 9 (which provides that, subject to the exceptions in Article 9(2), 'Everyone has the right to freedom of thought, conscience and religion . . . and freedom . . . to manifest his religion or belief, in . . . practice and observance'); and Article 14 (which provides that the enjoyment of Convention rights 'shall be secured without discrimination on any ground'). **10.11**

One example of the potential vulnerability of English law to an ECHR challenge is s 63 of the Mental Health Act 1983. This is because the fact that compulsory admission *automatically* authorizes compulsory treatment for mental disorder gives rise to significant human rights concerns. Provisions similar to s 63 were held to be incompatible with Article 8 ECHR in *X v Finland*[26] as there were no proper safeguards to guarantee against arbitrariness. Indeed, in **10.12**

---

[22] *J v Foundation Trust* [2010] Fam 70, [52].

[23] *Riverside Mental Health NHS Trust v Fox* [1994] 1 FLR 614; *Re KB (Adult) (Mental Patient: Medical Treatment)* (1994) 19 BMLR 144; *B v Croydon HA* [1995] Fam 133, affg [1995] 1 FCR 332.

[24] *Re VS (Adult: Mental Disorder)* 17 August 1995 (Douglas Brown J), [1995] Med L Rev 292; *R v Collins and Ashworth Hospital Authority, ex p Brady* [2000] Lloyd's Rep Med 355 (force-feeding of patient detained in Special Hospital). Contrast *Secretary of State for the Home Department v Robb* [1995] Fam 127 (force-feeding of a prisoner refusing food with mental capacity).

[25] *Tameside and Glossop Acute Services Trust v CH* [1996] 1 FLR 762, 771–74. Contrast *Re C (Adult: Refusal of Treatment)* [1994] 1 WLR 290 (patient with schizophrenia entitled to refuse consent to amputation of gangrenous leg where the gangrene was 'entirely unconnected' with the mental disorder); *B v Croydon HA* [1995] Fam 133, 139; *Re JT (Adult: Refusal of Medical Treatment)* [1998] 1 FLR 48 (adult with learning difficulties and extremely severe behavioural disturbance refusing treatment for renal failure: renal dialysis not treatment for the mental disorder); *St George's Healthcare NHS Trust v S, R v Collins ex p S* [1999] Fam 26, 52 (obstetric treatment of pregnant woman not treatment for mental disorder).

[26] (Application no. 34806/04; 3 July 2012).

Nottinghamshire Healthcare NHS Trust v RC,[27] Mostyn J suggested that it would have been 'an abuse of power' to compel treatment for mental disorder upon a detained, capacitous, refusing patient, and that it was accordingly lawful to withhold it, notwithstanding the existence of s 63 powers.

4. Common law

10.13 Save to the extent to which particular matters are regulated by statute, or by the Crown's prerogative power as *parens patriae*, the treatment of children and adults who lack capacity, and related issues of consent, are regulated, subject to the Human Rights Act 1998, by the general principles of the common law.

B. The Foetus

10.14 As has been said:

> From the earliest times the posthumous child has caused a certain embarrassment to the logic of the law, which is naturally disposed to insist that at any given moment of time a child must either be born or not born, living or not living. This literal realism was felt to bear hardly on the interests of posthumous children and was surmounted in the Civil Law by the invention of the fiction that in all matters affecting its interests the unborn child in utero should be deemed to be already born.[28]

10.15 Perhaps not surprisingly, the law is both unclear and confused.[29] Thus it has been said that the law treats the foetus as being 'an integral part of the mother' until it has a separate existence of its own, so much so that an injury to the foetus is treated as being an injury to a part of the mother in the same way as would be an injury to her arm or leg.[30] That view, however, has since been rejected by the House of Lords in favour of the view that the foetus, although dependent upon the mother for its survival until birth, is, from the moment of conception, an organism separate and distinct from the mother:[31]

> There was, of course, an intimate bond between the foetus and the mother, created by the total dependence of the foetus on the protective physical environment furnished by the mother, and on the supply by the mother through the physical linkage between them of the nutriments, oxygen and other substances essential to foetal life and development. The emotional bond between the mother and her unborn child was also of a very special kind. But the relationship was one of bond, not of identity. The mother and the foetus were two distinct organisms living symbiotically, not a single organism with two aspects. The mother's leg was part of the mother, the foetus was not . . . [T]he foetus does not (for the purposes of the law of homicide and violent crime) have any relevant type of personality but is an organism sui generis lacking at this stage the entire range of characteristics both of the mother to which it is physically linked and of the complete human being which it will later become.[32]

[27] [2014] EWCOP 1317, [2014] COPLR 468 at [42]. For a more detailed analysis of MHA Part 4, see Chapter 11.

[28] *Elliot v Lord Joicey* [1935] AC 209, 238 *per* Lord Macmillan.

[29] For a discussion see *St George's Healthcare NHS Trust v S, R v Collins, ex p S* [1999] Fam 26, 45–46.

[30] *Attorney-General's Reference (No 3 of 1994)* [1996] QB 581, 591, 593, 598 *per* Lord Taylor of Gosforth CJ.

[31] *Attorney-General's Reference (No 3 of 1994)* [1997] 3 WLR 421, 429, 440.

[32] ibid, 428–29 *per* Lord Mustill.

Be that as it may, the criminal law has long protected the foetus and the civil law recognizes that a foetus once born can have an independent and legally enforceable right separate and distinct from any right of its mother.[33] **10.16**

1. The status of the foetus

Both at common law[34] and by statute[35] the criminal law protects the foetus. **10.17**

The position of the foetus in civil law is much less clear.[36] There are in reported cases broad and unqualified statements to the effect that, until it is born, a foetus has no status, that it does not exist as a legal person and has no independent legal personality, that it lacks the status to have any legal right or to be the subject of any legal duty, and that it cannot have a right of action and cannot be a party to an action: **10.18**

> [I]n England and Wales the foetus has no right of action, no right at all until birth . . . [It is] undefined in law and without status.[37]
>
> The human being does not exist as a legal person until after birth. The foetus enjoys no independent legal personality . . . An unborn child lacks the status to be the subject of a legal duty.[38]
>
> It . . . is established beyond doubt for the criminal law, as for the civil law . . . that the child en ventre sa mère does not have a distinct human personality, whose extinguishment gives rise to any penalties or liabilities at common law.[39]

Two judgments, of Sir George Baker P[40] and of Heilbron J[41] at first instance, have been particularly influential: **10.19**

> The foetus cannot, in English law, in my view, have a right of its own at least until it is born and has a separate existence from its mother. That permeates the whole of the civil law of this country (I except the criminal law, which is now irrelevant) . . . For a long time there was great controversy whether after birth a child could have a right of action in respect of pre-natal injury . . . but it was universally accepted . . . that in order to have a right the foetus must be born and be a child . . . [T]here can be no doubt, in my view, that in England and Wales the foetus has no right of action, no right at all, until birth. The succession cases have been mentioned. There is no difference. From conception the child may have succession rights by what has been called a 'fictional construction' but the child must be subsequently born alive: see per Lord Russell of Killowen in *Elliot v Lord Joicey* [1935] AC 209, 233.[42]

---

33 *Schofield v Orrell Colliery Company Ltd* [1909] 1 KB 178, 181; *Watt v Rama* [1972] VR 353, 376. For further details, see Chapter 5.

34 *R v Senior* (1832) 1 Mood 346 (gross negligence by midwife leading to death ex utero); *R v West* (1848) 2 Car & K 784 (murder); *Attorney-General's Reference (No 3 of 1994)* [1997] 3 WLR 421.

35 Offences against the Person Act 1861, ss 58, 59, Infant Life (Preservation) Act 1929, s 1 (as to which see *C v S* [1988] QB 135; *Re F (In Utero)* [1988] Fam 122). The criminal law is, of course, greatly modified by the Abortion Act 1967 (as amended).

36 For a partial survey, see *Burton v Islington HA* [1993] QB 204, 226–27. For the position in Scotland, see *Kelly v Kelly* [1997] 2 FLR 828.

37 *B v Islington HA* [1991] 1 QB 638, 644, 647 *per* Potts J, on appeal [1993] QB 204.

38 *De Martell v Merton and Sutton HA* [1993] QB 204, 213, 218 *per* Phillips J, on appeal [1993] QB 204, 223.

39 *Attorney-General's Reference (No 3 of 1994)* [1997] 3 WLR 421, 434 *per* Lord Mustill. To similar effect see also Lord Mustill at 429 ('foetus does not . . . have any relevant type of personality', 'foetus does not have the attributes which make it a 'person'), 435–36 (foetus 'not a person').

40 *Paton v British Pregnancy Advisory Service Trustees* [1979] QB 276.

41 *C v S* [1988] QB 135.

42 *Paton v British Pregnancy Advisory Service Trustees* [1979] QB 276, 279 *per* Sir George Baker P; followed *C v S* [1988] QB 135, 140 (Heilbron J); approved *Re F (In Utero)* [1988] Fam 122, 138 *per* May LJ; see also at 140–41 *per* Balcombe LJ; applied *B v Islington HA* [1991] 1 QB 638, 644 *per* Potts J.

> The authorities, it seems to me, show that a child, after it has been born, and only then, in certain circumstances, based on he or she having a legal right, may be a party to an action brought with regard to such matters as the right to take, on a will or intestacy, or for damages for injuries suffered before birth. In other words, the claim crystallises upon the birth, at which date, but not before, the child attains the status of a legal persona, and thereupon can then exercise that legal right . . . In my judgment, there is no basis for the claim that the foetus can be a party, whether or not there is any foundation for the contention with regard to the alleged threatened crime.[43]

10.20 There is a line of authority whereby English law appears to adopt, though only for the purpose of enabling the foetus to take a benefit which, if born, it would be entitled to,[44] the fiction of the civil law that:

> Qui in utero est, perinde ac si in rebus humanis esset, custoditur, quoties de commodes ipsius partus quaeritur: quanquam alii, antequam nascatur, nequaquam prosit . . . Qui in utero sunt in toto paene jure civili intelliguntur in rerum natura esse.
>
> [A child in the womb is protected just as if it had been born whenever the question concerns benefits which depend on its existing: but another person cannot be advantaged before the child is actually born . . . Children in the womb are regarded as having been born for almost all the purposes of the civil law.][45]

10.21 The principle was applicable not merely to real and personal property but also to claims by unborn children under Lord Campbell's Act[46] and the Workmen's Compensation Acts[47] and even, it seems, to actions in negligence for prenatal injuries.[48] However, the principle is now governed by the Congenital Disabilities (Civil Liability) Act 1976 which imposes liability for antenatal injuries in certain circumstances. Moreover, the lack of independent foetal rights has been recently reinforced:

> [T]he fact remains that a foetus, in UK law, has no rights of its own until it is born and has a separate existence from its mother. That principle infuses the whole of the criminal and civil law in this country . . . [49]

(i) The foetus as litigant

10.22 In limited circumstances, a child *en ventre sa mère* can be a party to an action,[50] an action for damages or for an injunction can be brought on its behalf, and an injunction can be granted in its favour:[51]

---

43 *C v S* [1988] QB 135, 140–41 *per* Heilbron J; approved *Re F (In Utero)* [1988] Fam 122, 138 (May LJ); see also at 140–41 *per* Balcombe LJ.

44 *Burnet v Mann* (1748) 1 Ves Sen 156; *Doe d Clarke v Clarke* (1795) 2 H Bl 399, 401; *Blasson v Blasson* (1864) 2 De G J & S 665, 670; *Villar v Gilbey* [1907] AC 139, 145–46, 149, 151–52; *Williams v The Ocean Coal Company Ltd* [1907] 2 KB 422, 429; *Schofield v Orrell Colliery Company Ltd* [1909] 1 KB 178, 181–83; *Elliot v Lord Joicey* [1935] AC 209, 215, 222, 226, 231, 233–34, 238–40, 241; *Burton v Islington HA* [1993] QB 204, 226–27, 230.

45 *Blasson v Blasson* (1864) 2 De G J & S 665, 670; *Elliot v Lord Joicey* [1935] AC 209, 238; *Burton v Islington HA* [1993] QB 204, 226.

46 *The George and Richard* (1871) LR 3 A & E 466, 480–82; *Manns v Carlon* [1940] VR 280 (as to which see *Watt v Rama* [1972] VR 353, 358, 375–76). See now the Fatal Accidents Act 1976.

47 *Williams v Ocean Coal Company Ltd* [1907] 2 KB 422, 429, 432; *Schofield v Orrell Colliery Company Ltd* [1909] 1 KB 178 (as to which, see *Watt v Rama* [1972] VR 353, 358, 376).

48 *Montreal Tramways v Leveille* [1933] 4 DLR 337, 346; *Watt v Rama* [1972] VR 353, 376–77; *Burton v Islington HA* [1993] QB 204, 227.

49 *In the matter of DM* [2014] EWHC 3119 (Fam), [15].

50 *Villar v Gilbey* [1907] AC 139, 144 *per* Lord Loreburn LC.

51 *Lutterel's case* temp Lord Bridgman LC cited *Hale v Hale* (1692) Pre Ch 50 (action on behalf of child en ventre sa mère to stay waste: injunction granted); *Musgrave v Parry* (1715) 2 Vern 710, 711; *Wallis v Hodson* (1740) 2 Atk 114, 117; *Thellusson v Woodford* (1799) 4 Ves 227, 322; *The George and Richard* (1871)

The principal reason I go upon in the question is, that the plaintiff was en ventre sa mère at the time of her brother's death, and consequently a person in rerum natura, so that both by the rules of the common and civil law, she was, to all intents and purposes, a child, as much as if born in the father's life-time ... First, as to the common law, there is the trite case of an infant en ventre sa mère being vouched in common recovery; a mother also may justify the detaining of charters on behalf of it; a devise to him is good, by the opinion of Treby and Powell, in Scatterwood and Edge, 1 Salk 229, a bill may be brought in his behalf, and this court will grant an injunction in his favour to stay waste, 2 Vern 710, Musgrave versus Parry et al ... Secondly, as to the civil law, nothing is more clear, than that this law considered a child in the mother's womb absolutely born, to all intents and purposes, for the child's benefit.[52]

The next objection is, that, supposing, he meant a child en ventre sa mère, and had expressly said so, yet the limitation is void. Such a child has been considered as a non-entity. Let us see what this non-entity can do. He may be vouched in a recovery, though it is for the purpose of making him answer over in value. He may be an executor. He may take under the Statute of Distributions. (22 & 23 Ch II c 10.) He may take by devise. He may be entitled under a charge for raising portions. He may have an injunction; and he may have a guardian. Some other cases put this beyond all doubt ... Why should not children en ventre sa mère be considered generally as in existence? They are entitled to all the privileges of other persons.[53]

2. Medical treatment and the foetus

(i) General principles

(a) **Consent** There can be no doubt that, as a general principle, the only consent which is either required or relevant for the medical treatment of either the foetus or its mother is that of the pregnant woman. The giving or refusing of consent by the child's father is legally irrelevant, whether or not he is married to the child's mother. Subject only to the provisions of the criminal law, the consent of a pregnant woman makes any treatment either of her or of the foetus lawful, irrespective of any adverse effects which the foetus may suffer, and whether or not the child's father has consented. Conversely, the refusal of consent by the mother is normally decisive, whatever the adverse implications for the foetus. This reflects the biological fact that, until birth, the foetus lives in a symbiotic relationship with, and is totally dependent for its survival upon, the pregnant woman,[54] the very limited rights of the father, whether or not he is married to the child's mother,[55] and the public policy which recognizes the extreme undesirability of creating conflict between the mother and her unborn child and the insuperable difficulties of attempting to manage the lifestyle or control the actions of an uncooperative mother.[56] **10.23**

LR 3 A & E 466, 468, 473, 474, 480, 481–82 (child en ventre sa mère held entitled to bring claim under Lord Campbell's Act; assessment of damages adjourned until birth of child); *Villar v Gilbey* [1907] AC 139, 144; *Manns v Carlon* [1940] VR 280, 284 (child en ventre sa mère held to have right of action under Victorian equivalent of Lord Campbell's Act; trial of action stayed until birth of child); *Watt v Rama* [1972] VR 353, 358, 375–76.

[52] *Wallis v Hodson* (1740) 2 Atk 114, 117–18 *per* Lord Hardwicke LC (as to which see *Thellusson v Woodford* (1799) 4 Ves 227, 322, (1805) 11 Ves 112, 139; *Villar v Gilbey* [1907] AC 139, 141, 142, 149; *Montreal Tramways v Leveille* [1933] 4 DLR 337, 343; *Watt v Rama* [1972] VR 353, 375; *Burton v Islington HA* [1993] QB 204, 229–30).

[53] *Thellusson v Woodford* (1799) 4 Ves 227, 321–22, 323 *per* Buller J, on appeal (1805) 11 Ves 112 (as to which see *Montreal Tramways v Leveille* [1933] 4 DLR 337, 340).

[54] *Attorney-General's Reference (No 3 of 1994)* [1997] 3 WLR 421, 428–29, 440.

[55] *Paton v British Pregnancy Advisory Service Trustees* [1979] QB 276, 279–81, 282.

[56] *Re F (In Utero)* [1988] Fam 122, 131–32, 138, 143, 144–45.

10.24 In the same way the law, as a general principle, treats the interests of the foetus as being so bound up with the interests of its mother that the mother's best interests are treated as being likewise those of the foetus and vice versa.

10.25 (b) **Wardship and the foetus** Consistently with this principle, it has been held that the court cannot exercise its inherent *parens patriae* jurisdiction in relation to an unborn child or over the mother of an unborn child, nor can it make such a child a ward of court.[57] However, in wholly exceptional circumstances the jurisdiction of the High Court may be invoked to obtain anticipatory declaratory relief as to the legality of a public authority's proposed course of conduct in respect of a foetus.[58]

10.26 (c) **Abortion** There is no doubt that neither the foetus, nor its father, nor the husband of its mother, can obtain an injunction to restrain the performance of a lawful abortion to which the mother has consented.[59]

(ii) Possible exceptions

10.27 Whether, and if so in what circumstances, the law will have regard to the independent medical interests of the foetus, or allow legal intervention by or on its behalf for the purpose of protecting its bodily interests, are questions the answers to which are both uncertain and controversial. There would appear to be no absolute bar as a matter of principle. The law recognizes the foetus as an entity capable of having rights, separate and distinct from the rights of its mother, and capable of suing to vindicate those rights. There is no reason in principle why any distinction should be drawn for this purpose between property interests and bodily welfare:

> I can find no logical reason for rejecting the notion that the common law would protect a child en ventre sa mère against careless acts causing him or her injury. As its property, real or personal, is protected, so should its physical substance be similarly protected.[60]

Moreover, the law does not eschew the application of restraint and the use of reasonable force for the purpose of compelling a pregnant child[61] or a pregnant adult woman[62] who lacks capacity to submit to a Caesarean section.

10.28 Thus it might be thought that a child *en ventre sa mère* could sue for an injunction to restrain violent assaults upon its mother of a kind likely to put it in peril even if the mother, for some reason, was not willing herself to bring proceedings against the assailant. On the other hand, it has been held that the unborn child[63] cannot obtain an injunction to restrain

57 ibid.

58 *Re D (unborn baby) (emergency protection order: future harm)* [2009] 2 FLR 313, considered in *In the matter of DM* [2014] EWHC 3119 (Fam) where it was emphasized at [26] that 'The Courts and Local Authority must be vigilant to ensure that the wholly exceptional nature of this relief is never lost sight of'.

59 *Paton v British Pregnancy Advisory Service Trustees* [1979] QB 276, 280, 281, 282; *Dehler v Ottawa Civic Hospital* (1979) 101 DLR (3d) 686, 694–700, appeal dismissed (1980) 117 DLR (3d) 512; *Medhurst v Medhurst* (1984) 9 DLR (4th) 252, 257–59; *C v S* [1988] QB 135, 140, 141. The position is the same in Scotland: *Kelly v Kelly* [1997] 2 FLR 828. For further details, see Chapter 11, paras 11.108–11.117.

60 *Watt v Rama* [1972] VR 353, 376 *per* Gillard J.

61 *A Metropolitan Borough Council v AB* [1997] 1 FLR 767.

62 *Tameside and Glossop Acute Services Trust v CH* [1996] 1 FLR 762; *Norfolk and Norwich Healthcare (NHS) Trust v W* [1996] 2 FLR 613; *Rochdale Healthcare (NHS) Trust v C* [1997] 1 FCR 274; *Re L (Patient: Non-consensual Treatment)* [1997] 2 FLR 837; *Re MB (Medical Treatment)* [1997] 2 FLR 426; *Great Western Hospitals NHS Foundation Trust v AA, BB, CC, DD* [2014] EWHC 132 (Fam); *The Mental Health Trust and others v DD and BC* [2014] EWCOP 11. Important guidance on invoking the jurisdiction of the Court of Protection was given in *NHS Trust and others v FG* [2014] EWCOP 30, [2015] 2 WLR 1984.

63 Whether the father of an unborn child, or the husband of its mother, can obtain an injunction to restrain the performance of an unlawful (and thus necessarily criminal) abortion is uncertain: *Paton v*

the performance of an unlawful (and thus necessarily criminal) abortion.[64] Other cases are more difficult. Where the woman if with capacity is refusing, or if lacking capacity is unable, to consent to treatment which is in her foetus' interests, to what extent is the foetus' interests to be taken into account, and can proceedings be taken by or on behalf of the foetus for the purpose of authorizing or compelling its mother to undergo treatment—if for example, the foetus requires minor but life-saving treatment in the womb, or if its welfare dictates a Caesarean section, or if the question is whether a pregnant woman who is in an irreversible coma should be kept artificially alive for the sole purpose of enabling her viable foetus to be born?

(a) The foetus and the woman who lacks capacity Such problems are likely to be less acute where the mother lacks capacity or is a child and where there is, accordingly, no question of overriding the decision of a patient with capacity who is sui juris. In such cases the court will be astute to find that a procedure which is medically in the interests of the foetus, even if not of its mother, is nevertheless in the mother's best emotional and psychological interests, so that it can authorize (in the case of a child) or declare lawful (in the case of an adult who lacks capacity) the necessary treatment.[65] But even in this situation the only interests that can properly be taken into account are the interests of the mother, not those of the foetus:[66] **10.29**

> In our judgment the court does not have the jurisdiction to take the interests of the foetus into account in a case such as the present appeal [a case involving an adult mother who lacks capacity] and the judicial exercise of balancing those interests does not arise . . . The foetus up to the moment of birth does not have any separate interests capable of being taken into account when a court has to consider an application for a declaration in respect of a Caesarean section operation.[67]

Thus, this approach will not resolve the problem presented by the mother in an irreversible coma who may, in truth, have no current interests at all.[68]

(b) The foetus and the woman with capacity The difficulties are particularly acute where a mother with capacity is refusing treatment in circumstances gravely prejudicial to the life or welfare of her foetus. The law, however, is clear: the doctor and the court are powerless to act:[69] **10.30**

> A competent woman who has the capacity to decide may, for religious reasons, other reasons, for rational or irrational reasons or for no reason at all, choose not to have medical intervention, even though the consequence may be the death or serious handicap of the

British Pregnancy Advisory Service Trustees [1979] QB 276, 282 (leaving the question undecided); *Medhurst v Medhurst* (1984) 9 DLR (4th) 252, 259–61 (holding that he could); *C v S* [1988] QB 135, 149, 153 (leaving the question undecided).

64 *Dehler v Ottawa Civic Hospital* (1979) 101 DLR (3d) 686, appeal dismissed (1980) 117 DLR (3d) 512; *C v S* [1988] QB 135, 140–01.

65 Consider the analyses in *Tameside and Glossop Acute Services Trust v CH* [1996] 1 FLR 762; *Re Y (Mental Patient: Bone Marrow Donation)* [1997] Fam 110; *Norfolk and Norwich Healthcare (NHS) Trust v W* [1996] 2 FLR 613; *Rochdale Healthcare (NHS) Trust v C* [1997] 1 FCR 274; *A Metropolitan Borough Council v AB* [1997] 1 FLR 767; *Re L (Patient: Non-consensual Treatment)* [1997] 2 FLR 837; *Re MB (Medical Treatment)* [1997] 2 FLR 426.

66 *Norfolk and Norwich Healthcare (NHS) Trust v W* [1996] 2 FLR 613, 616; *Re MB (Medical Treatment)* [1997] 2 FLR 426, 440.

67 *Re MB* [1997] 2 FLR 426, 440, 444.

68 Compare *Airedale NHS Trust v Bland* [1993] AC 789.

69 *Re MB* [1997] 2 FLR 426, 436, 438, 440, 441, 444, overruling the extremely controversial decision in *Re S (Adult: Refusal of Treatment)* [1993] Fam 123; *St George's Healthcare NHS Trust v S, R v Collins, ex p S* [1999] Fam 26, 46–50.

child she bears, or her own death. In that event the courts do not have the jurisdiction to declare medical intervention lawful and the question of her own best interests objectively considered, does not arise . . . If therefore the competent mother refuses to have the medical intervention, the doctors may not lawfully do more than attempt to persuade her. If that persuasion is unsuccessful, there are no further steps towards medical intervention to be taken . . . The only situation in which it is lawful for the doctors to intervene is if it is believed that the adult patient lacks the capacity to decide . . . The law is, in our judgment, clear that a competent woman who has the capacity to decide may, for religious reasons, other reasons, or for no reasons at all, choose not to have medical intervention, even though . . . the consequence may be the death or serious handicap of the child she bears or her own death . . . The court does not have the jurisdiction to declare that such medical intervention is lawful to protect the interests of the unborn child even at the point of birth.[70]

10.31 This clear position has been reaffirmed by the Supreme Court:

A patient is entitled to take into account her own values, her own assessment of the comparative merits of giving birth in the 'natural' and traditional way and of giving birth by caesarean section, whatever medical opinion may say, alongside the medical evaluation of the risks to herself and her baby. She may place great value on giving birth in the natural way and be prepared to take the risks to herself and her baby which this entails. The medical profession must respect her choice, unless she lacks the legal capacity to decide (*St George's Healthcare NHS Trust v S* [1999] Fam 26).[71]

C. Children

1. Who can determine welfare?

(i) Common law

10.32 **(a) Parents and the state** As considered in Chapter 9, the common law imposes responsibility for the care, nurture and protection of children on parents, as their guardians by the law of nature, and on the Crown as *parens patriae*. The powers of the child's parents are limited by law. The prerogative powers of the Crown as *parens patriae* are theoretically without limit, though in practice they are exercised only within recognized limits.[72] The Crown normally chooses not to exercise its *parens patriae* powers in relation to children, being content most of the time to leave responsibility for the care, nurture and protection of a child to its parents.[73]

I would for my part accept without reservation that the decision of a devoted and responsible parent should be treated with respect. It should certainly not be disregarded or lightly set aside. But the role of the court is to exercise an independent and objective judgment. If that judgment is in accord with that of the devoted and responsible parent, well and good.

[70] *Re MB* [1997] 2 FLR 426, 436–38, 444 *per* Butler-Sloss LJ.

[71] *Montgomery v Lanarkshire Health Board* [2015] UKSC 11, [2015] AC 1430, at [115] *per* Lady Hale. See Heywood, R, 'R.I.P. *Sidaway:* Patient-oriented Disclosure—a Standard Worth Waiting For?' (2015) 23(3) Med L Rev 455. See also *CP v Criminal Injuries Compensation Authority* [2015] 2 WLR 463, at [66] *per* Lord Dyson MR: ' . . . in English law women do not owe a duty of care in tort to their unborn child. A competent woman cannot be forced to have a caesarean section or other medical treatment to prevent potential risk to the foetus during childbirth.'

[72] See further para 10.36.

[73] *Re KD (A Minor) (Ward: Termination of Access)* [1988] AC 806, 812 *per* Lord Templeman. Consistently with this approach, the common law gives the child no cause of action against a parent for bad parenting, as opposed to parenting which exposes the child to physical dangers: see the discussion in *Surtees v Kingston-upon-Thames Borough Council* [1991] 2 FLR 559 of *McCallion v Dodd* [1966] NZLR 710, *Hahn v Conley* (1971) 126 CLR 276.

> If it is not, then it is the duty of the court, after giving due weight to the view of the devoted and responsible parent, to give effect to its own judgment. That is what it is there for. Its judgment may of course be wrong. So may that of the parent. But once the jurisdiction of the court is invoked its clear duty is to reach and express the best judgment it can.[74]

In making that decision, the court will always act cautiously, 'acting in opposition to the parent only when judicially satisfied that the welfare of the child requires that the parental rights should be suspended or superseded'.[75] Moreover, 'In most cases, parents are the best people to make decisions about a child and the State—whether it be the court, or any other public authority—has no business interfering with the exercise of parental responsibility unless the child is suffering or is likely to suffer significant harm as a result of the care given to the child not being what it would be reasonable to expect a parent to give'.[76] **10.33**

(b) Parental power At common law responsibility for the care, nurture, and protection of a child (including responsibility for the medical treatment of a child) is an aspect of the parental right of custody, the 'bundle of rights' or 'bundle of powers' which enable a parent to exercise physical control over the person of the child, control over the education, religion, and marriage of the child and control over the administration of the child's property.[77] Custody in all its aspects necessarily comes to an end with the child's majority at the age of 18, but that part of custodial power which enables a parent to exercise physical control over the person of the child (which is that aspect of custody which is most relevant in the context of treatment) ceases when the child reaches 'the years of discretion'.[78] Thus, custody: **10.34**

> is a dwindling right which the courts will hesitate to enforce against the wishes of the child, and the more so the older he is. It starts with a right of control and ends with little more than advice.[79]
>
> It is, in my view, contrary to the ordinary experience of mankind, at least in Western Europe in the present century, to say that a child or a young person remains in fact under the complete control of his parents until he attains the definite age of majority, now 18 in the United Kingdom, and that on attaining that age he suddenly acquires independence. In practice most wise parents relax their control gradually as the child develops and encourage him or her to become increasingly independent. Moreover, the degree of parental control actually exercised over a particular child does in practice vary considerably according to his understanding and intelligence and it would, in my opinion, be unrealistic for the courts not to recognise these facts. Social customs change, and the law ought to, and does in fact, have regard to such changes when they are of major importance.[80]

---

[74] *Re Z (A Minor) (Identification: Restrictions on Publication)* [1997] Fam 1, 32–33 *per* Sir Thomas Bingham MR; adopted in *Re T (A Minor) (Wardship: Medical Treatment)* [1997] 1 WLR 242, 250 *per* Butler-Sloss LJ, 255 *per* Roch LJ.

[75] *Re Z*, n 74, 31 *per* Ward LJ (quoting *Re O'Hara* [1902] 2 IR 232, 240 *per* FitzGibbon LJ; approved in *J v C* [1970] AC 668, 715). The test is, of course, easier to state than to apply: compare the facts and the contrasting decisions in *J v C* [1970] AC 668; and *Re M (Child's Upbringing)* [1996] 2 FLR 441; (further proceedings *Re M (Application for Stay of Order)* [1996] 3 FCR 185; and *Re M (Petition to European Commission of Human Rights)* [1996] 3 FCR 377); and consider the (it might be thought surprising) decision in *Re T (A Minor) (Wardship: Medical Treatment)* [1997] 1 WLR 242.

[76] *Re Aysha King (A Child)* [2014] EWHC 2964 (Fam), [2014] 2 FLR 855 at [31]. See J Bridgeman, 'Misunderstandings, Threats, And Fear, of The Law in Conflicts over Children's Healthcare: *In the matter of Ashya King*' (2015) 23(3) Med L Rev 477.

[77] *Re Z (A Minor) (Identification: Restrictions on Publication)* [1997] Fam 1, 25–26.

[78] *Hewer v Bryant* [1970] 1 QB 357, 372–73 (a classic description and analysis of custody by Sachs LJ approved in *Gillick v West Norfolk and Wisbech AHA* [1986] AC 112, 184).

[79] *Hewer v Bryant* [1970] 1 QB 357, 369 *per* Lord Denning MR; approved in *Gillick v West Norfolk and Wisbech AHA* [1986] AC 112, 172, 186.

[80] *Gillick v West Norfolk and Wisbech AHA* [1986] AC 112, 171 *per* Lord Fraser of Tullybelton.

10.35 Custody of a legitimate child is vested in both its parents; in the case of an illegitimate child custody is vested in the mother alone. Rights of custody vested in both parents can be exercised by either and thus either parent can consent to a child's medical treatment.[81]

10.36 (c) **The Crown as *parens patriae*** The nature and extent of this jurisdiction[82] empowers and obliges the Crown as *parens patriae* 'to protect the person and property of . . . those unable to look after themselves, including infants'.[83] The Sovereign, as *parens patriae*, has a duty to protect those of his/her subjects who are unable to protect themselves, particularly children who are the generations of the future.[84] The powers of the Crown as *parens patriae*, and of the court when exercising the parental power of the Crown as part of its inherent jurisdiction, are theoretically without limit, are more extensive than the custodial powers of a parent, and extend beyond anything that either the child, the child's parents, or even an adult sui juris, could authorize or require, but in practice the court declines to exercise a limitless jurisdiction, even when what is in question is the protection as opposed to the custody of the child.[85]

10.37 The powers of the Crown as *parens patriae* are exercised by the judges of the High Court, prior to 1971 by the judges of the Chancery Division, since then by the judges of the Family Division, as part of their inherent jurisdiction as the successors of the judges of the High Court of Chancery.

10.38 (d) **Wardship** The inherent *parens patriae* jurisdiction is often, though not necessarily, exercised by means of wardship. Wardship is merely machinery by which the court exercises *parens patriae* powers in relation to children: the court can exercise its *parens patriae*

---

[81] *Re L (An Infant)* [1968] P 119, 132, 135, 136, 155, 160, 172. The General Medical Council has ruled that a doctor must obtain the permission of both parents whenever possible, but in all cases obtain valid consent in writing from a person with parental responsibility: 'Guidance for Doctors who are asked to Circumcise Male Children' (Sept 1997). This principle has since been adopted by the courts: *Re J (Specific Issue Orders: Child's Religious Upbringing and Circumcision)* [2000] 1 FLR 571, 576, 577, affg *Re J (Specific Issue Orders: Muslim Upbringing and Circumcision)* [1999] 2 FLR 678, 701–02. See also paras 18 to 23 of the GMC's guidance, 'Personal Beliefs and Medical Practice' (2013). Consistently with this the BMA has advised that both parents must give consent for non-therapeutic circumcision and that where there is parental disagreement doctors should not circumcise the child without the leave of the court: 'The Law and Ethics of Male Circumcision—Guidance for Doctors' (June 2006).

[82] See generally *Re Z (A Minor) (Identification: Restrictions on Publication)* [1997] Fam 1; *A v A Health Authority, Re J (A Child), R (on the application of S) v Secretary of State for the Home Department* [2002] EWHC 18 (Fam/Admin), [2002] Fam 213, esp at [30]–[58]. For illuminating discussions of the Crown as parens patriae, viewed from the perspectives of Canada, Australia, pre-partition Ireland, and Scotland respectively, see *Re Eve* (1986) 31 DLR (4th) 1, 13–22 per La Forest J; *Secretary, Department of Health and Community Services v JWB and SMB* (1992) 175 CLR 218, 258–60 per Mason CJ, Dawson, Toohey and Gaudron JJ, 279–85 per Brennan J, 301–02 per Deane J; *In the matter of a Ward of Court (withholding medical treatment) (No 2)* [1996] 2 IR 79, 102–07 per Hamilton CJ, 139–40 per Blayney J; *Law Hospital NHS Trust v Lord Advocate* [1996] 2 FLR 407, 418–23 per Lord Hope of Craighead LP, 427–31 per Lord Cullen, 434–36 per Lord Clyde.

[83] *Re D (A Minor) (Wardship: Sterilisation)* [1976] Fam 185, 192.

[84] *Re X (A Minor) (Wardship: Jurisdiction)* [1975] Fam 47, 51–52; *Re C (A Minor) (Wardship: Medical Treatment) (No 2)* [1990] Fam 39, 46; *Re J (A Minor) (Wardship: Medical Treatment)* [1991] Fam 33, 50; *Re R (A Minor) (Wardship: Consent to Treatment)* [1992] Fam 11, 25.

[85] *Thomasset v Thomasset* [1894] P 295, 299; *Hewer v Bryant* [1970] 1 QB 357, 372; *Re X (A Minor) (Wardship: Jurisdiction)* [1975] Fam 47, 58, 61; *Re X (A Minor) (Wardship: Injunction)* [1984] 1 WLR 1422; *Re C (A Minor) (Wardship: Medical Treatment) (No 2)* [1990] Fam 39, 46; *Re R (A Minor) (Wardship: Criminal Proceedings)* [1991] Fam 56, 63–64, 66; *Re C (A Minor) (Wardship: Jurisdiction)* [1991] 2 FLR 168, 178–79, 184; *Re R (A Minor) (Wardship: Consent to Treatment)* [1992] Fam 11, 25, 28; *Secretary, Department of Health and Community Services v JWB and SMB* (1992) 175 CLR 218, 259, 302; *Re J (A Minor) (Child in Care: Medical Treatment)* [1993] Fam 15, 29; *Re W (A Minor) (Medical Treatment: Court's Jurisdiction)* [1993] Fam 64, 81, 85, 91; *Re Z (A Minor) (Identification: Restrictions on Publication)* [1997] Fam 1, 14–18, 23.

jurisdiction whether or not the child is a ward of court.[86] The substantive powers of the court are the same whether it is exercising the inherent jurisdiction or the wardship jurisdiction, for the court, when exercising the wardship jurisdiction, is in truth exercising the inherent jurisdiction, albeit in a particular manner. The only practical difference between wardship and an exercise of the inherent jurisdiction not involving wardship is that in the former case, but not in the latter, the child acquires the *status* of a ward of court.[87]

The court cannot exercise its inherent *parens patriae* jurisdiction in relation to an unborn child or over the mother of an unborn child, nor can it make such a child a ward of court.[88] However, such jurisdiction can be invoked in exceptional circumstances to obtain anticipatory declaratory relief in respect of an unborn child.[89] **10.39**

The court cannot exercise its inherent *parens patriae* jurisdiction in relation to a child who has died, nor can it make such a child a ward of court: it can, however, grant declaratory relief in relation to such a child.[90] **10.40**

No 'important' or 'major' step in the life of a ward of court can be taken without the prior consent of the court.[91] What precisely counts as an 'important' or 'major' step has never been defined,[92] but the principle plainly extends to the more significant forms of medical treatment, for example, a sterilization,[93] an abortion,[94] and even a psychiatric examination undertaken for forensic purposes.[95] No doubt it extends to other procedures. Moreover, a child who is a ward of court can neither marry nor leave the jurisdiction without the consent of the court. These matters apart, the status of wardship confers neither disadvantage nor privilege: a child who is a ward of court should be treated medically in exactly the same way as one who is not (though the doctor will be looking to the court rather than to the parent for any necessary consent), and the fact that a child either is or is not a ward of court is totally irrelevant when it comes to choosing how to allocate scarce medical resources.[96] **10.41**

(ii) The Children Act 1989

The effect of the Children Act 1989 was to alter the law in detail but without affecting its substance to any significant extent. **10.42**

(a) Parental responsibility The common law concept of custody was replaced by the statutory concept of parental responsibility, defined in s 3(1) as meaning 'all the rights, duties, **10.43**

[86] *Re N (Infants)* [1967] Ch 512, 530–31; *Re L (An Infant)* [1968] P 119, 156–57; *Re C (A Minor) (Wardship: Medical Treatment) (No 2)* [1990] Fam 39, 46; *Re M and N (Minors) (Wardship: Publication of Information)* [1990] Fam 211, 223; *Re W (A Minor) (Medical Treatment: Court's Jurisdiction)* [1993] Fam 64, 73, 85; *Re Z (A Minor) (Identification: Restrictions on Publication)* [1997] Fam 1, 13–14.

[87] *Re W (A Minor) (Medical Treatment: Court's Jurisdiction)* [1993] Fam 64, 73.

[88] *Re F (In Utero)* [1988] Fam 122.

[89] *Re D (Unborn Baby) (Emergency Protection Order: Future Harm)* [2009] 2 FLR 313, considered in *In the matter of DM* [2014] EWHC 3119 (Fam).

[90] *Re A* [1992] 3 Med L Rev 303 (child brain-stem dead: jurisdiction to make declaration that child dead and accordingly lawful to disconnect ventilator).

[91] *Re S (Infants)* [1967] 1 WLR 396, 407; *Re D (A Minor) (Wardship: Sterilisation)* [1976] Fam 185, 196; *Re G-U (A Minor) (Wardship)* [1984] FLR 811; *Re C (A Minor) (Wardship: Medical Treatment)* [1990] Fam 26, 32, 38; *Re J (A Minor) (Wardship: Medical Treatment)* [1991] Fam 33, 49; *Re R (A Minor) (Wardship: Consent to Treatment)* [1992] Fam 11, 25; *Re W (A Minor) (Medical Treatment: Court's Jurisdiction)* [1993] Fam 64, 73.

[92] cf *Kelly v British Broadcasting Corporation* [2001] Fam 59, 75–76.

[93] *Re D (A Minor) (Wardship: Sterilisation)* [1976] Fam 185, 196.

[94] *Re G-U (A Minor) (Wardship)* [1984] FLR 811.

[95] *Re S (Infants)* [1967] 1 WLR 396, 407.

[96] *Re J (A Minor) (Wardship: Medical Treatment)* [1991] Fam 33, 41, 42; *Re R (A Minor) (Wardship: Criminal Proceedings)* [1991] Fam 56, 65–66.

powers, responsibilities and authority which by law a parent has in relation to the child and his property'. Parental responsibility thus defined plainly includes power to consent to medical treatment.[97] The Act recognizes (s 2(5)) that more than one person may have parental responsibility for the same child at the same time and provides (s 2(7)) that where more than one person has parental responsibility each may act alone and without the other.[98] However, notwithstanding the language of s 2(7), in the absence of agreement by all those with parental responsibility the specific approval of the court must be obtained if the case falls within what has been described as 'a small group of important decisions'.[99]

10.44 The Act provides that the following have parental responsibility: the child's father and mother, where they were married to each other at the time of his/her birth (s 2(1)); the child's mother, but not the father, where they were not so married (s 2(2)), unless the father acquires parental responsibility either by order of the court under s 4(1)(c) or pursuant to a 'parental responsibility agreement' with the mother under s 4(1)(b);[100] a person appointed as the child's guardian (s 5(6)); a person in whose favour the court makes a child arrangements order (s 12(2)); the local authority designated in a care order made with respect to the child (s 33(3)(b));[101] the local authority or other authorized person who has obtained an emergency protection order with respect to the child (s 44(4)(c)).[102]

10.45 (b) **Carers** A person who does not have parental responsibility for a particular child but has care of the child—for example, a relative, a child-minder, a schoolteacher, or even a doctor, if for instance the child is an in-patient in a hospital—may do what is reasonable in all the circumstances of the case for the purpose of safeguarding or promoting the child's welfare (s 3(5)). In an appropriate case such a person can consent to medical treatment on behalf of the child, though it will presumably only be reasonable to act without first obtaining the consent of the child's parents or whoever else has parental responsibility in an emergency or if the treatment is trivial.[103]

10.46 (c) ***Parens patriae*** Section 100(2) of the Act follows the common law in distinguishing between 'the High Court's inherent jurisdiction with respect to children' (that is, the exercise by the High Court of the *parens patriae* jurisdiction) and 'wardship'. Section 100(2)(c), following the common law, recognizes that the High Court can exercise its inherent *parens patriae* jurisdiction without making the child a ward of court.

10.47 In addition to exercising its *parens patriae* powers either under the inherent jurisdiction or in wardship the court can in some cases exercise comparable powers under s 8, by making either a prohibited steps order or a specific issue order.[104]

---

[97] *Re Z (A Minor) (Identification: Restrictions on Publication)* [1997] Fam 1, 25–26.

[98] See n 82.

[99] See further para 10.66.

[100] For children born after 1 December 2003, unmarried fathers may also acquire parental responsibility if they register the child's birth jointly with the mother at the time of birth, re-register the birth, marry the mother, obtain a parental responsibility order, or register with the court for parental responsibility. See also Children Act 1989, ss 4ZA (second female parent) and 4A (step-parents).

[101] For an example of consent by a local authority to the treatment of a child in care (voluntary admission to a mental hospital), see *R v Kirklees Metropolitan Borough Council, ex p C* [1992] 2 FLR 117, [1993] 2 FLR 187.

[102] *Re O (A Minor) (Medical Treatment)* [1993] 2 FLR 149, 151.

[103] *R (on the application of G) v Nottingham City Council* [2008] EWHC 152 (Admin), [2008] 1 FLR 1660, at [23]–[26].

[104] In *Re JM (A Child)* [2015] EWHC 2832 (Fam), [2016] 2 FLR 235 at [20]–[28], Mostyn J held that where an NHS Trust sought final binding declarations concerning the medical treatment of a child to which the parents did not consent, the application should be framed as a combination of an application for a specific issue order under the Children Act 1989 s 8 and an application for declaratory relief under the inherent jurisdiction of the High Court.

(iii) The Mental Capacity Act 2005

One of the consequences of the Mental Capacity Act 2005 is that, from the age of 16, there is a rebuttable statutory assumption that the young person has the mental capacity to make the relevant decision. It is indicative of a tendency to recognize greater autonomy from that earlier age which has a bearing on the exercise of parental responsibility. For example, with reference to s 131 of the Mental Health Act 1983 and s 8 of the Family Law Reform Act 1969, it has been observed that 'the legal authority of a parent to consent to the detention or treatment of a 16 or 17 year old is severely curtailed, if not removed'.[105] **10.48**

2. The ambit of parental consent

Even where the law recognizes the capacity of a parent to give a proxy or substitute consent on behalf of a child or young person, the parental right to decide is not absolute. The parental power to give a valid consent is subject to five limitations. In the first place no parent can consent to any procedure which is unlawful. Secondly, where the child is a ward of court parental power is limited by the principle that it is necessary to obtain the prior consent of the court before any 'important' or 'major' step is taken in the life of the child.[106] Thirdly, any parental giving or refusal of consent must be in the best interests of the child or young person. Fourthly, there are certain procedures, not unlawful in themselves, but which are nonetheless considered to be of such a nature as to require the prior sanction of the court. Fifthly, there are limits to the consent which a parent can give in the case of a child old enough to understand what is involved. **10.49**

(i) Control by the court

As discussed in Chapter 9, consistently with the principle that the parental right to decide is not absolute, the court is not bound by and can override a parent's decision;[107] the court can overrule parental consent to treatment which is not in the best interests of the child[108] and overrule parental refusal to consent to treatment which is in the best interests of the child.[109] However, the court always acts 'extremely **10.50**

[105] *Trust A v X and others* [2015] EWHC 922 (Fam), [2016] 1 FLR 142 at [38].

[106] See para 10.41.

[107] *Gillick v West Norfolk and Wisbech AHA* [1986] AC 112, 184, 200; *Re C (A Minor) (Wardship: Medical Treatment) (No 2)* [1990] Fam 39, 46; *Re J (A Minor) (Wardship: Medical Treatment)* [1991] Fam 33, 52; *Re R (A Minor) (Wardship: Consent to Treatment)* [1992] Fam 11, 25; *Re W (A Minor) (Medical Treatment: Court's Jurisdiction)* [1993] Fam 64, 93; *Re Z (A Minor) (Identification: Restrictions on Publication)* [1997] Fam 1, 30–31.

[108] *Re D (A Minor) (Wardship: Sterilisation)* [1976] Fam 185 (sterilization restrained despite parent's consent: as Heilbron J said, at 194, 'in wardship proceedings parents' rights can be superseded'); *Re C (Medical Treatment)* [1998] 1 FLR 384 (Orthodox Jewish parents wishing 16-month-old daughter suffering from terminal spinal muscular atrophy, type 1, to be ventilated in event of respiratory relapse and not willing to agree to only palliative care as recommended by doctors); *Royal Wolverhampton Hospitals NHS Trust v B* [2000] 1 FLR 953. See also the United Nations Convention on the Rights of the Child 1989, Article 3(1) which requires the best interests of the child to be 'a primary consideration'.

[109] *Re B (A Minor) (Wardship: Medical Treatment)* [1981] 1 WLR 1421 (order directing life-saving operation on 10-day-old Down's syndrome child notwithstanding parents' bona fide decision to let nature take its course); *Re P (A Minor)* [1986] 1 FLR 272 (order directing abortion on 15-year-old girl notwithstanding parents' bona fide objections on religious and other grounds); *Re E (A Minor) (Wardship: Medical Treatment)* [1993] 1 FLR 386 (order directing blood transfusion for 15-year-old leukaemic Jehovah's Witness notwithstanding parents' religious objections); *Re B (Wardship: Abortion)* [1991] 2 FLR 426 (order directing abortion on 12-year-old girl notwithstanding parent's bona fide objections); *Re S (A Minor) (Medical Treatment)* [1993] 1 FLR 376 (order directing blood transfusion for 4-year-old leukaemic child of Jehovah's Witnesses); *Re O (A Minor) (Medical Treatment)* [1993] 2 FLR 149 (order directing blood transfusion for 2-month-old child with respiratory problems of Jehovah's Witnesses); *Re R (A Minor) (Blood Transfusion)* [1993] 2 FLR 757 (order directing blood transfusion for 10-month-old leukaemic child of Jehovah's Witnesses); *Re C (Medical Treatment)* [1998] 1 FLR 384 (Orthodox Jewish parents wishing 16-month-old daughter

cautiously'[110] and will act in opposition to the parent only when judicially satisfied that the parental rights should be suspended or superseded.[111] The question is not whether the parent is acting reasonably but what is in the best interests of the child.[112] But the law recognizes that there is a 'margin of appreciation' within which parental decision-making is unlikely to be superseded by the court:

> The law's insistence that the welfare of a child shall be paramount is easily stated and universally applauded, but the present case illustrates, poignantly and dramatically, the difficulties that are encountered when trying to put it into practice . . . It is not an occasion—even in an age preoccupied with 'rights'—to talk of the rights of a child, or the rights of a parent, or the rights of the court. The cases . . . are uncompromising in their assertion that the sole yard-stick must be the need to give effect to the demands of paramountcy for the welfare of the child. They establish that there are bound to be occasions when such paramountcy will compel the court, acting as a judicial parent, to substitute the judge's own views as to the claims of child welfare over those of natural parents—even in a case where the latter are supported by qualities of devotion, commitment, love and reason . . . All these cases depend on their own facts and render generalisations—tempting though they may be to the legal or social analyst—wholly out of place. It can only be said safely that there is a scale, at one end of which lies the clear case where parental opposition to medical intervention is prompted by scruple or dogma of a kind which is patently irreconcilable with principles of child health and welfare widely accepted by the generality of mankind; and that at the other end lie highly problematic cases where there is genuine scope for a difference of view between parent and judge. In both situations it is the duty of the judge to allow the court's own opinion to prevail in the perceived paramount interests of the child concerned, but in cases at the latter end of the scale, there must be a likelihood (though never of course a certainty) that the greater the scope for genuine debate between one view and another the stronger will be the inclination of the court to be influenced by a reflection that in the last analysis the best interests of every child include an expectation that difficult decisions affecting the length and quality of its life will be taken for it by the parent to whom its care has been entrusted by nature.[113]

10.51 Moreover, even in the case of potentially life-saving treatment, the court may be more willing to overrule parental refusal to consent where the child's life-threatening condition can be cured by a simple 'one-off' operation[114] than where the child requires complicated surgery and the total commitment to the treatment, and many years of special care, by a parent upon whom the child's welfare depends but who has conscientiously come to the conclusion that such treatment, with all that it may entail for the child in terms of risks, discomfort and

suffering from terminal spinal muscular atrophy, type 1, to be ventilated in event of respiratory relapse and not willing to agree to only palliative care as recommended by doctors: order directing palliative care); *Re L (Medical Treatment: Gillick Competency)* [1998] 2 FLR 810 (order directing blood transfusion for 14-year-old Jehovah's Witness suffering from life-threatening burns); *Re C (A Child) (HIV Testing)* [2000] Fam 48 (affd *Re C (HIV Test)* [1999] 2 FLR 1004) (order directing HIV testing of 5-month-old baby daughter of HIV positive mother); *Re MM (Medical Treatment)* [2000] 1 FLR 224 (order for lifetime replacement immunoglobin treatment for primary immuno-deficiency in 7-year-old rather than programme of immunostimulant therapy preferred by parents); *An NHS Trust v SR* [2013] 1 FLR 1297 (order to proceed with radio- and chemotherapy treatment for malignant brain tumour against mother's wishes).

[110] *Re C (A Child) (HIV Testing)* [2000] Fam 48, 58 *per* Wilson J (aff'd *Re C (HIV Test)* [1999] 2 FLR 1004).

[111] *Re Z (A Minor) (Identification: Restrictions on Publication)* [1997] Fam 1, 31. See further para 10.55.

[112] *Re T (A Minor) (Wardship: Medical Treatment)* [1997] 1 WLR 242, 250–51, 253–56.

[113] ibid, at 253–54 *per* Waite LJ.

[114] As in *Re B (A Minor) (Wardship: Medical Treatment)* [1981] 1 WLR 1421. See *Re T (A Minor) (Wardship: Medical Treatment)* [1997] 1 WLR 242, 252 *per* Butler-Sloss LJ.

distress, a lifetime of drugs, and the possibility of further invasive surgery, would not be in the child's best interests.[115]

(ii) Control by the doctor

10.52 In practical terms parental decision-making in relation to the medical treatment of children is subject to control by the doctor. In the final analysis much, if not most, of the ultimate process of decision-making is necessarily borne by the doctor. The doctor is not bound to do what the parent wants, and even if s/he has the parent's consent s/he is not necessarily protected from legal proceedings.

10.53 On the other hand, the doctor who wishes to treat a child is not necessarily fettered by the absence, or even the refusal, of parental consent. Except in an emergency,[116] or where parents have abandoned their parental responsibilities without the child yet having been taken into the care of a local authority or someone else in loco parentis,[117] a doctor should always discuss with the child's parents the treatment s/he proposes and obtain their consent;[118] indeed it is unlawful for a doctor to act in the face of a parental refusal of consent.[119] If a consent which s/he believes is necessary is not forthcoming s/he can invoke the assistance of the court. But in a case of emergency, when there is no time to obtain a decision from the court, a doctor can proceed notwithstanding the absence of parental or judicial consent and, if the parents are acting unreasonably or contrary to the best interests of the child, even despite a parental refusal of consent.[120]

(iii) Unlawful procedures

10.54 Some forms of interference with the body are unlawful, in the sense that even an adult with capacity cannot give a consent which the law recognizes as lawful and effective.[121] The general rule, however, is that 'reasonable surgical interference' is lawful as being in the public interest.[122] Nonetheless, from time to time it has been suggested that certain surgical procedures are unlawful. For example, female genital mutilation is unlawful.[123] On the other hand, there is no doubt that male circumcision, for whatever reason it is performed, is not as such unlawful,[124] nor is a 'sex-change' or 'gender reassignment' operation whether

---

115 As in *Re T (A Minor) (Wardship: Medical Treatment)* [1997] 1 WLR 242 (child suffering from life-threatening liver defect requiring liver transplant). See the critical discussion by Professor Andrew Grubb in [1996] Med L Rev 315. See also *Re A (Children) (Conjoined Twins: Surgical Separation)* [2001] Fam 147, 194–95, 244.

116 *Gillick v West Norfolk and Wisbech AHA* [1986] AC 112, 181–82, 194, 200.

117 ibid, 165, 170, 182, 194.

118 ibid, 169, 173–74, 189; *Re J (A Minor) (Wardship: Medical Treatment)* [1991] Fam 33, 41; *Re R (A Minor) (Blood Transfusion)* [1993] 2 FLR 757, 760.

119 *Re A (Children) (Conjoined Twins: Surgical Separation)* [2001] Fam 147, 178.

120 *Gillick v West Norfolk and Wisbech AHA* [1986] AC 112, 200; *Re J (A Minor) (Wardship: Medical Treatment)* [1991] Fam 33, 41; *Re R (A Minor) (Wardship: Consent to Treatment)* [1992] Fam 11, 26; *R (on the application of G) v Nottingham City Council* [2008] EWHC 152 (Admin), [2008] 1 FLR 1660, [23]–[26].

121 *Attorney-General's Reference (No 6 of 1980)* [1981] QB 715; *R v Brown* [1994] 1 AC 212.

122 *Attorney-General's Reference (No 6 of 1980)* [1981] QB 715, 719.

123 Female Genital Mutilation Act 2003. It is a 'barbarous' practice which is 'beyond the pale' (*Singh v Entry Clearance Officer, New Delhi* [2005] 1 FLR 308, [68]). In *Re B (Children)(Care Proceedings)* [2015] 1 FLR 905 it was held that the infliction of any form of female genital mutilation upon a child amounted to significant harm and could never be reasonable parenting.

124 *R v Brown* [1994] AC 212, 231; *Re J (Specific Issue Orders: Muslim Upbringing and Circumcision)* [1999] 2 FLR 678 (affd *Re J (Specific Issue Orders: Child's Religious Upbringing and Circumcision)* [2000] 1 FLR 571). See also *Hickey v Croydon AHA* The Times, 6 March 1985 (claim for damages for negligence in circumcising adult who sought operation to 'improve his sex life': Michael Davies J justified the legality of the operation by reference to Gen xvii: vv 10–14). It has been argued that the reluctance of Anglo-American law to conceptualize male circumcision as a criminal action has precluded it being regarded in the same light as female genital cutting: see M Fox and M Thomson, 'Older minors and circumcision: questioning the limits of religious actions' (2008) 9 Medical Law International 283.

from male to 'female' (involving castration and removal of the penis)[125] or from female to 'male',[126] nor is a sterilization, for whatever reason it is performed.[127]

(iv) Best interests

10.55 Parental rights exist not for the benefit of the parent or anyone else but for the benefit of the child.[128] The parental power to give a substituted consent to medical treatment for a child must be exercised in the best interests of the child, objectively assessed on a judgment of what is best for the welfare of the particular child.[129]

> Parental rights clearly do exist, and they do not wholly disappear until the age of majority. Parental rights relate to both the persons and the property of the child—custody, care, and control of the person and guardianship of the property of the child. But the common law has never treated such rights as sovereign or beyond review and control. Nor has our law ever treated the child as other than a person with capacities and rights recognised by law. The principle of the law . . . is that parental rights are derived from parental duty and exist only so long as they are needed for the protection of the person and property of the child . . . [P]arental right must be exercised in accordance with the welfare principle and can be challenged, even overridden, if it be not . . . [P]arental right endures only so long as it is needed for the protection of the child.[130]

(v) Community standards and parental views

10.56 In determining what is in the best interests of their children, parents are entitled to follow their own moral and social views within the limits set by the general standards of society.

> [O]ne can identify two broad common law propositions relating to the authority of parents to authorise surgery in the case of . . . a child who is, as a matter of fact, completely unable to make a reasoned decision for herself or himself about the desirability of the particular treatment. The first of those propositions is that parental authority exists to authorise such surgery for the purpose, and only for the purpose, of advancing the welfare of the child. It does not extend to authorising surgery because of a perception that it is in the interests of those responsible for the care of the child or in the interests of society in general (eg for eugenic reasons). That which constitutes the welfare of a child in a particular case falls to be determined by reference to general community standards, but making due allowance for the entitlement of parents, within the limits of what is permissible in accordance with those standards, to entertain divergent views about the moral and secular objectives to be pursued for their children. The second broad proposition is that, at least in relation to a serious matter such as a major medical procedure, parental authority can be validly exercised only after due inquiry about, and adequate consideration of, what truly represents the welfare of the child in all the circumstances of the case.[131]

---

[125] *Corbett v Corbett* [1971] P 83, 99. See also *R v Tan* [1983] QB 1053.

[126] *Re A* (1993) 16 Fam LR 715 (Fam Ct Aus).

[127] Denning LJ's dicta in *Bravery v Bravery* [1954] 1 WLR 1169, 1180–81, if they were ever good law (Evershed MR and Hodson LJ expressed the contrary view, 1175–76), are now universally regarded as no longer representing the law: *Re B (A Minor) (Wardship: Sterilisation)* [1988] AC 199; *Re F (Mental Patient: Sterilisation)* [1990] 2 AC 1; *Secretary, Department of Health and Community Services v JWB and SMB* (1992) 175 CLR 218, 234; *R v Dica* [2004] QB 1257, 1269.

[128] For the suggestion that the parental role is fiduciary, and that a parent with a conflicting interest to that of the child is therefore disqualified from giving consent, see *Secretary, Department of Health and Community Services v JWB and SMB* (1992) 175 CLR 218, 317.

[129] *Gillick v West Norfolk and Wisbech AHA* [1986] AC 112, 170, 173, 183–85, 200; *Secretary, Department of Health and Community Services v JWB and SMB* (1992) 175 CLR 218, 240, 278, 295, 316.

[130] *Gillick v West Norfolk and Wisbech AHA* [1986] AC 112, 183–85 *per* Lord Scarman.

[131] *Secretary, Department of Health and Community Services v JWB and SMB* (1992) 175 CLR 218, 295 *per* Deane J.

This approach is reflected in the cases[132] and is mirrored both by commentators[133] who acknowledge that, in bringing up their children, parents have to address the basic moral issue of what sort of child they wish to raise and have a wide range of discretion to pursue goals which society as a whole may find undesirable, but which it will tolerate, and by those commentators[134] who justify infant male circumcision (in contrast to female genital mutilation) on the basis of immemorial usage and social or religious toleration.[135] **10.57**

(vi) Procedures not contrary to the child's interests

Some commentators have suggested that a parent can lawfully give consent to any procedure to which a 'reasonable parent' would consent and which, even if not positively beneficial to the child, is neither cruel, nor excessive, nor clearly against the child's interests. It is on this basis that some commentators justify routine neonatal male circumcision, in contrast to circumcision for religious or ritual purposes,[136] on the footing that the attendant risks are not so great as to be 'contrary to the child's interest'.[137] Such a principle is said to be supported by the decision of the House of Lords that a child can be blood tested for forensic purposes even if it cannot be shown that a blood test will be in its best interests:[138] **10.58**

> It is a legal wrong to use constraint to an adult beyond what is authorised by statute or ancient common law powers connected with crime and the like. But it is not and could not be a legal wrong for a parent or person authorised by him to use constraint to his young child provided it is not cruel or excessive. There are differences of opinion as to the age beyond which it is unwise to use constraint, but that cannot apply to infants or young children. So it seems to me to be impossible to deny that a parent can lawfully require that his young child should submit to a blood test . . . [S]urely a reasonable parent would have some

[132] See *Re T (A Minor) (Wardship: Medical Treatment)* [1997] 1 WLR 242, esp 254 *per* Waite LJ, quoted at para 10.78.

[133] A McCall Smith, 'Is Anything Left of Parental Rights?' in E Sutherland and A McCall Smith (eds), *Family Rights: Family Law and Medical Advance* (Edinburgh University Press 1990) 4; A Bainham, 'Non-Intervention and Judicial Paternalism' in P Birks (ed), *The Frontiers of Liability, Volume 1* (Oxford University Press 1994) 173.

[134] G Williams, 'Consent and Public Policy' [1962] Crim LR 74, 154, 157; G Williams, *Textbook of Criminal Law* (2nd edn, Stevens 1983), 575, 586; R D Mackay, 'Is Female Circumcision Unlawful?' [1983] Crim LR 717, 719; K Hayter, 'Female Circumcision—Is There a Legal Solution?' [1984] JSWL 323, 326.

[135] For ritual male circumcision see now *Re J (Specific Issue Orders: Muslim Upbringing and Circumcision)* [1999] 2 FLR 678 (affd *Re J (Specific Issue Orders: Child's Religious Upbringing and Circumcision)* [2000] 1 FLR 571); *Re S (Change of Names: Cultural Factors)* [2001] 2 FLR 1005; *Re S (Specific Issue Order: Religion: Circumcision)* [2004] EWHC 1282 (Fam), [2005] 1 FLR 236. See also M Fox and M Thomson, 'The New Politics of Male Circumcision: HIV/AIDS, Health Law and Social Justice' (2012) 32(2) Legal Studies 255; M Fox and M Thomson, 'Older Minors and Circumcision: Questioning the Limits of Religious Actions' (2008) 9 Medical Law International 283.

[136] As to which see now *Re J (Specific Issue Orders: Muslim Upbringing and Circumcision)* [1999] 2 FLR 678 (affd *Re J (Specific Issue Orders: Child's Religious Upbringing and Circumcision)* [2000] 1 FLR 571); *Re S (Change of Names: Cultural Factors)* [2001] 2 FLR 1005; *Re S (Specific Issue Order: Religion: Circumcision)* [2004] EWHC 1282 (Fam), [2005] 1 FLR 236.

[137] P D G Skegg, *Law, Ethics, and Medicine* (2nd edn, Clarendon 1984), 66; S Poulter, *English Law and Ethnic Minority Customs* (Butterworths 1986) para 6.28. This is very questionable given the nature of the attendant risks.

[138] *S v McC, W v W* [1972] AC 24; discussed in *Re Z (A Minor) (Identification: Restrictions on Publication)* [1997] Fam 1, 20, 28–29. See also the Family Law Reform Act 1969, s 21(3); *Re F (A Minor) (Blood Tests: Parental Rights)* [1993] Fam 314; *Re L (A Minor) (Blood Tests)* [1996] 2 FCR 649; *Re H (A Minor) (Blood Tests: Parental Rights)* [1997] Fam 89; *Re T (Paternity: Ordering Blood Tests)* [2001] 2 FLR 1190; *Re H and A (Paternity: Blood Tests)* [2002] EWCA Civ 383, [2002] 1 FLR 1145. For the impact in this context of Art 8 of the ECHR see *Re T (Paternity: Ordering Blood Tests)* [2001] 2 FLR 1190, 1197–99.

regard to the general public interest and would not refuse a blood test unless he thought that would clearly be against the interests of the child.[139]

10.59 This perhaps reflects a suggested wider principle of the child's civic duty:

> Children, whether wards of court or not, are citizens owing duties to society as a whole (including other children), which are appropriate to their years and understanding. Those duties are defined both by the common law and by statute.[140]

10.60 This view of the ambit of parental power, at least if it is to be relied upon as a rule of wide-ranging application, is difficult to reconcile either with basic principle or with more recent cases. It is best treated as confined to procedures which involve no more than 'minimal' or 'negligible' risk and discomfort, for example, the taking of nasal or throat swabs and urine or blood samples (including the taking of a blood sample by venepuncture). Interventions beyond that are likely to raise significant human rights concerns.

(vii) The older child

10.61 There are two further limitations upon the parent's power to consent to treatment in the case of an older child. In the first place, parental consent will not be sufficient in the case of a non-therapeutic procedure if the child is old enough to understand what is involved and is either left uninformed or actually withholds his or her consent. This principle would apply, for example, to a blood test[141] or the ritual circumcision of an older boy.[142] Secondly, and even in the case of therapeutic procedures, the jurisdiction of the court should always be invoked where parents are prepared to consent, but a child capable of understanding what is involved, is refusing to consent to some major form of treatment.[143]

3. The court

(i) When the court is involved

10.62 The court may be involved in matters relating to the medical treatment of a child for a variety of different reasons: if the child is already a ward of court, because the law requires prior judicial consent before any 'important' or 'major' step in the ward's life is taken;[144] if there are disputes between parents and doctor, or between parents and child, or between the parents themselves, so that the court can decide what the best interests of the child require; or in cases falling within the 'special category', so that the court can decide whether or not to give the prior sanction which good practice requires.

10.63 (a) **The need to involve the court** It is necessary to involve the court only if the child is already a ward of court or if the case falls within the 'special category'. In cases not falling within the 'special category' there is no need to involve the court unless the child is already a ward of court.

[139] *S v McC, W v W* [1972] AC 24, 43–44 *per* Lord Reid. See also 48, 51 *per* Lord MacDermott (blood test will not be ordered if it 'would prejudicially affect the health of the infant'), 58–59 *per* Lord Hodson ('protection may be needed for health reasons').

[140] *Re R (A Minor) (Wardship: Criminal Proceedings)* [1991] Fam 56, 65 *per* Lord Donaldson of Lymington MR.

[141] *S v McC, W v W* [1972] AC 24, 45.

[142] The point, at least in this form, seems not to have been considered either in *Re J (Specific Issue Orders: Muslim Upbringing and Circumcision)* [1999] 2 FLR 678 (affd *Re J (Specific Issue Orders: Child's Religious Upbringing and Circumcision)* [2000] 1 FLR 571) or in *Re S (Change of Names: Cultural Factors)* [2001] 2 FLR 1005. Contrast *Re S (Specific Issue Order: Religion: Circumcision)* [2004] EWHC 1282 (Fam), [2005] 1 FLR 236, [83], where the age of the boy (8½) was treated as highly relevant. See also *Re L (Specific Issues: Temporary Leave to Remove from the Jurisdiction; Circumcision)* [2016] EWHC 849 (Fam).

[143] *Re W (A Minor) (Medical Treatment: Court's Jurisdiction)* [1993] Fam 64, 79, 90, 94.

[144] See para 10.41.

10.64 Concern, in particular at the prospect of parents consenting to the non-therapeutic sterilization of children with learning disability,[145] has led the courts in a number of jurisdictions to consider whether there are certain procedures, not unlawful in themselves, but which are nonetheless of such a nature that the prior sanction of the court ought, either as a matter of law or at the very least as a matter of good practice, always to be obtained. Thus at first it was suggested[146] that a court exercising the inherent *parens patriae* jurisdiction is the only authority empowered to authorize such a drastic step as sterilization. And the High Court of Australia has since held that, as a matter of law, a parent lacks the capacity to give a valid consent to the non-therapeutic sterilization of a child.[147] In England, however, it would now seem that, unless the child is already a ward of court, the prior sanction of the court is never required as a matter of law,[148] though 'as a matter of good practice' it should always be obtained[149] in those cases falling within what has been described as a 'special category'.[150] In relation to adults who lack capacity to consent to a non-therapeutic sterilization, the treatment decision is so serious that the Court of Protection has to make it.[151]

10.65 Precisely which cases are to be treated as falling within the special category has deliberately been left undefined, to be considered on a case-by-case basis.[152] Initially, it was suggested that the special category would or might include sterilization, abortion, organ donation, and the disconnection of life-support machines.[153] Subsequent decisions indicate that the special category of cases which require the prior sanction of the court includes a non-therapeutic sterilization,[154] the donation of regenerative tissues (bone marrow),[155] the withdrawal of food from a patient in a (formerly called persistent or permanent) vegetative state[156] or minimally conscious state,[157] cases where the capacity of a pregnant woman to consent to or refuse a Caesarean section is in issue,[158] and any case in which the application of restraint or use of force on a non-compliant patient is envisaged,[159] but that it does not include a brain

[145] There is no doubt that in this country *Re D (A Minor) (Wardship: Sterilisation)* [1976] Fam 185 (in which a highly qualified medical practitioner supported by a caring mother, who were proposing to sterilize a 'mentally handicapped' 11-year-old girl, were held by Heilbron J not to be acting in her best interests, although no one had challenged their skill, bona fides, or quality of care) had a powerful effect in influencing the development of this branch of the law: see *Re F (Mental Patient: Sterilisation)* [1990] 2 AC 1, 20, 41, 69 ('stark warning of the danger'), 79 ('vivid illustration').

[146] *Re B (A Minor) (Wardship: Sterilisation)* [1987] 2 All ER 206, 210, [1988] AC 199, 206.

[147] *Secretary, Department of Health and Community Services v JWB and SMB* (1992) 175 CLR 218.

[148] *R (on the application of Burke) v General Medical Council* [2005] EWCA Civ 1003, [2006] QB 273, [80].

[149] In some cases the court, once it has been able to investigate the matter fully, may be willing to devolve the final decision to the attending doctor subject to suitable safeguards: *Re R (Adult: Medical Treatment)* [1996] 2 FLR 99, 104, 106–10.

[150] *Re F (Mental Patient: Sterilisation)* [1990] 2 AC 1, 19–20, 33, 42, 51, 56–57, 78–80, 83. See also *Airedale NHS Trust v Bland* [1993] AC 789, 805–06, 815–16, 859, 873–74.

[151] *A Local Authority v K and others* [2013] EWHC 242 (COP), [2014] 1 FCR 209.

[152] *Re F (Mental Patient: Sterilisation)* [1990] 2 AC 1, 57.

[153] ibid, 19, 33, 40, 42.

[154] ibid.

[155] *Re Y (Mental Patient: Bone Marrow Donation)* [1997] Fam 110, 116: *quaere* in relation to donations of blood or other regenerative bodily fluids.

[156] This was said to be for 'the protection of patients, the protection of doctors, the reassurance of patients' families and the reassurance of the public': *Airedale NHS Trust v Bland* [1993] AC 789, 815 *per* Sir Thomas Bingham MR, approved, 859 *per* Lord Keith of Kinkel, 874 *per* Lord Goff of Chieveley. See further para 10.192.

[157] *W (by her litigation friend, B) v M (by her litigation friend, the Official Solicitor)* [2011] EWHC 2443 (Fam), [2012] 1 WLR 1653.

[158] *Re MB (Medical Treatment)* [1997] 2 FLR 426.

[159] *Re VS (Adult: Mental Disorder)* (1995) Aug 17 (Douglas Brown J), [1995] Med L Rev 292; *Tameside and Glossop Acute Services Trust v CH* [1996] 1 FLR 762, 774.

scan,[160] psychiatric treatment,[161] an abortion,[162] or a therapeutic sterilization.[163] It is clear that the donation of a non-regenerative organ (eg, a kidney) falls within the special category,[164] so also, it is suggested, would a 'sex-change' or 'gender reassignment' operation.[165] Whether, and if so to what extent and in which circumstances, the withholding of life-saving treatment generally falls within the special category is unclear.[166]

10.66 The special category thus far considered relates to those procedures for which, as a matter of good practice, judicial sanction should be obtained even if *all* the persons who have parental responsibility for the child (for example, both parents) are united in support of what is proposed. More recently the courts have identified a further category of what has been described[167] as 'a small group of important decisions made on behalf of a child which, in the absence of agreement with those with parental responsibility, ought not to be carried out or arranged by a one parent carer', even if that parent has parental responsibility under s 2(7) of the Children Act 1989, and where 'a decision ought not to be made without the specific approval of the court'. Thus far this category has been held to include circumcision, other than in a case of medical necessity,[168] and what have been described as 'hotly contested issues of immunisation'.[169]

10.67 **(b) Involving the court unnecessarily** Where there is no disagreement between the child's parents and the doctor, and the proposed treatment is not one which, either because of its nature or because the child is a ward of court, requires the prior sanction of the court, the court will treat the parents' consent as sufficient authority and protection for the doctor and refuse to grant relief.[170] It has previously been said that the court may decline to act even though there is a dispute between a *Gillick* competent child, who is refusing to consent, and its parents, so long as the parents have given the doctor their consent to the proposed treatment.[171] However, nowadays the court is more likely to be called upon in such circumstances.

---

160 *Re H (Mental Patient: Diagnosis)* [1993] 1 FLR 28 (a case involving an adult who lacked capacity).

161 *Re K, W and H (Minors) (Medical Treatment)* [1993] 1 FLR 854.

162 *Re SG (Adult Mental Patient: Abortion)* [1991] 2 FLR 329 (adult lacking capacity). For a different view see *D v An NHS Trust (Medical Treatment: Consent: Termination)* [2003] EWHC 2793 (Fam), [2004] 1 FLR 1110.

163 *Re E (A Minor) (Medical Treatment)* [1991] 2 FLR 585 (consent of court not necessary for therapeutic hysterectomy to relieve serious menorrhagia of severely disabled 17-year-old girl: parents able to give valid consent, as sterilization would not be the purpose, although the inevitable and incidental result, of the operation). Similarly in the case of a mentally incompetent adult: *Re GF (Medical Treatment)* [1992] 1 FLR 293 (declaration of court not needed regarding legality of hysterectomy to relieve excessively heavy periods which would have the incidental effect of sterilizing a woman of 29 with disability, if two medical practitioners are satisfied that the operation is necessary for therapeutic purposes and in the best interests of the patient, and that there is no practicable less intrusive means of treating the condition).

164 *Re F (Mental Patient: Sterilisation)* [1990] 2 AC 1, 19, 33, 40; *Re W (A Minor) (Medical Treatment: Court's Jurisdiction)* [1993] Fam 64, 79, 94.

165 So held by the Family Court of Australia: *Re A* (1993) 16 Fam LR 715.

166 Compare *Re J (A Minor) (Wardship: Medical Treatment)* [1991] Fam 33, 51; *Re C (A Baby)* [1996] 2 FLR 43, 45; *Re R (Adult: Medical Treatment)* [1996] 2 FLR 99.

167 *Re J (Specific Issue Orders: Child's Religious Upbringing and Circumcision)* [2000] 1 FLR 571, 577 *per* Dame Elizabeth Butler-Sloss P.

168 *Re J (Specific Issue Orders: Child's Religious Upbringing and Circumcision)* [2000] 1 FLR 571, 576, 577, affg *Re J (Specific Issue Orders: Muslim Upbringing and Circumcision)* [1999] 2 FLR 678, 701–02.

169 *Re C* (*Welfare of Child: Immunisation*) [2003] EWCA Civ 1148; [2003] 2 FLR 1095 at [16]–[17] (MMR and other vaccinations and immunizations).

170 *Re SG (Adult Mental Patient: Abortion)* [1991] 2 FLR 329 (abortion—a case involving an adult lacking capacity); *Re E (A Minor) (Medical Treatment)* [1991] 2 FLR 585 (therapeutic sterilization); *Re GF (Medical Treatment)* [1992] 1 FLR 293 (therapeutic sterilization—adult lacking capacity); *Re H (Mental Patient: Diagnosis)* [1993] 1 FLR 28 (brain scan—adult lacking capacity).

171 *Re K, W and H (Minors) (Medical Treatment)* [1993] 1 FLR 854 (psychiatric treatment).

(ii) The jurisdiction of the court

The court may be involved in the exercise of its inherent *parens patriae* jurisdiction, the wardship jurisdiction, or its statutory jurisdiction under the Children Act 1989. In relation to the medical treatment of children, the substantive powers of the court are the same, and are exercised in accordance with precisely the same principles, whichever jurisdiction is being exercised.[172] **10.68**

(a) Invoking the jurisdiction of the court If the child is already a ward of court application is made by summons in the wardship.[173] If the child is not a ward, and there are no other relevant proceedings pending, the court's assistance can be invoked, unless the applicant is a local authority, either under the inherent jurisdiction[174] or by an ad hoc wardship (that is, by making a child a ward of court for the purpose of resolving a question relating to the child's medical treatment)[175] or by an application for either a prohibited steps order or a specific issue order under the Children Act 1989, s 8.[176] Different views have been expressed as to whether, other things being equal, the preferred course is to invoke the inherent jurisdiction or s 8.[177] **10.69**

(b) Applications by local authorities Applications by a local authority are governed by the Children Act 1989, s 100(2)(c) (which prevents a child who is in care from being made a ward of court), s 100(3) (which requires a local authority to obtain the leave of the court before invoking the court's inherent jurisdiction), and s 100(4) (which provides that such leave can be granted only if (inter alia) the result which the local authority wishes to achieve cannot be achieved through the making of (inter alia) a prohibited steps order or a specific issue order under s 8). In the case of a child in care a local authority is precluded by s 9(1)[178] **10.70**

[172] ibid, 859.

[173] As in *Re C (A Minor) (Wardship: Medical Treatment)* [1990] Fam 26; *Re J (A Minor) (Wardship: Medical Treatment)* [1991] Fam 33.

[174] As in *Re J (A Minor) (Child in Care: Medical Treatment)* [1993] Fam 15; *Re W (A Minor) (Medical Treatment: Court's Jurisdiction)* [1993] Fam 64; *South Glamorgan County Council v W and B* [1993] 1 FLR 574; *Re O (A Minor) (Medical Treatment)* [1993] 2 FLR 149; *A Metropolitan Borough Council v AB* [1997] 1 FLR 767; and (arguably incorrectly in the light of *Re R (A Minor) (Blood Transfusion)* [1993] 2 FLR 757) in *Re S (A Minor) (Medical Treatment)* [1993] 1 FLR 376; *Re S (A Minor) (Consent to Medical Treatment)* [1994] 2 FLR 1065; *Re T (A Minor) (Wardship: Medical Treatment)* [1997] 1 WLR 242; *Re C (Detention: Medical Treatment)* [1997] 2 FLR 180; *Re A (Children) (Conjoined Twins: Surgical Separation)* [2001] Fam 147.

[175] As in *Re D (A Minor) (Wardship: Sterilisation)* [1976] Fam 185 (sterilization); *Re B (A Minor) (Wardship: Medical Treatment)* [1981] 1 WLR 1421 (life-saving surgery); *Re P (A Minor)* [1986] 1 FLR 272 (abortion); *Re B (A Minor) (Wardship: Sterilisation)* [1988] AC 199 (sterilization); *Re P (A Minor) (Wardship: Sterilisation)* [1989] 1 FLR 182 (sterilization); *Re E (A Minor) (Wardship: Medical Treatment)* [1993] 1 FLR 386 (blood transfusion); *Re E (A Minor) (Medical Treatment)* [1991] 2 FLR 585 (sterilization); *Re B (Wardship: Abortion)* [1991] 2 FLR 426 (abortion); *Re R (A Minor) (Wardship: Consent to Treatment)* [1992] Fam 11 (psychiatric treatment with anti-psychotic drugs); *A NHS Trust v D* [2000] 2 FLR 677 (resuscitation of dying child).

[176] As in *Re K, W and H (Minors) (Medical Treatment)* [1993] 1 FLR 854; *Re HG (Specific Issue Order: Sterilisation)* [1993] 1 FLR 587; *Re R (A Minor) (Blood Transfusion)* [1993] 2 FLR 757; *Re J (Specific Issue Orders: Muslim Upbringing and Circumcision)* [1999] 2 FLR 678 (affd *Re J (Specific Issue Orders: Child's Religious Upbringing and Circumcision)* [2000] 1 FLR 571).

[177] *Re O (A Minor) (Medical Treatment)* [1993] 2 FLR 149, 155 (inherent jurisdiction preferable); *Re R (A Minor) (Blood Transfusion)* [1993] 2 FLR 757, 760 (s 8 preferable). The Official Solicitor's view was that the procedural and administrative difficulties attaching to applications under s 8 are such that the preferred course is to apply within the inherent jurisdiction: *Practice Note (Official Solicitor: Sterilisation)* [1996] 2 FLR 111, para 2 (now superseded). In *Re JM (A Child)* [2015] EWHC 2832 (Fam), [2016] 2 FLR 235 at [20]–[28] Mostyn J held that where an NHS Trust sought final binding declarations concerning the medical treatment of a child to which the parents did not consent, the application should be framed as a combination of an application for a specific issue order under the Children Act 1989, s 8, and an application for declaratory relief under the inherent jurisdiction of the High Court.

[178] cf also ss 9(2), 9(5), 91(1), 91(2) and 100(2).

from obtaining either a prohibited steps order or a specific issue order. The combined effect of the statutory provisions thus appears to be that an application by a local authority in relation to a child in care must be made under the inherent jurisdiction[179] but an application by a local authority in relation to a child who is not in care must be made by way of an application for a s 8 order.[180]

10.71 (c) **Hearing by High Court Judge** Whichever form of procedure is invoked the proceedings should be commenced in the High Court, not in the Family Proceedings Court or the County Court, and should be heard by a High Court Judge of the Family Division.[181]

(iii) The Official Solicitor

10.72 As part of his wide-ranging duties and responsibilities the Official Solicitor is involved, either *ex officio* or as litigation friend or by instructing an advocate to the court (*amicus curiae*), in many cases relating to the treatment of adults who lack capacity and was (until his functions in this respect were assumed by Cafcass) likewise involved in most cases of any significance relating to the treatment of children. Cases relating to children are now normally handled by Cafcass. Members of the staff of Cafcass are prepared to discuss such cases before proceedings have been issued.

10.73 Generally, it was recognized that the Official Solicitor should be invited to act in all cases of any complexity.[182] No doubt the same principle applies now in relation to Cafcass Legal.

(iv) Exercise of the jurisdiction

10.74 (a) **General principles** The sole and paramount criterion[183] for the exercise by the court of its jurisdiction, whether it be the inherent *parens patriae* jurisdiction, the wardship jurisdiction, or its statutory jurisdiction under the Children Act 1989, is the welfare of the child. This was the rule adopted by the High Court of Chancery and is now given statutory force by the Children Act 1989, s 1(1)(a):[184]

> 'The welfare of this child is the paramount consideration and the court must act in her best interests.'[185] The first and paramount consideration is the well-being, welfare, or interests

[179] *South Glamorgan County Council v W and B* [1993] 1 FLR 574 (explaining, 583–84 that the Children Act, s 100(2)(d), is no bar to exercising the inherent jurisdiction); *Re O (A Minor) (Medical Treatment)* [1993] 2 FLR 149.

[180] *Re R (A Minor) (Blood Transfusion)* [1993] 2 FLR 757; *Re J (Specific Issue Order: Leave to Apply)* [1995] 1 FLR 669, 673; *Re C (A Child) (HIV Testing)* [2000] Fam 48 (affd *Re C (HIV Test)* [1999] 2 FLR 1004). The point seems to have been overlooked in *Re S (A Minor) (Medical Treatment)* [1993] 1 FLR 376; *Re S (A Minor) (Consent to Medical Treatment)* [1994] 2 FLR 1065; *Re T (A Minor) (Wardship: Medical Treatment)* [1997] 1 WLR 242; and *Re C (Detention: Medical Treatment)* [1997] 2 FLR 180 (but see at 190) where local authorities were given leave under s 100(3) to invoke the inherent jurisdiction even though the child was not in care.

[181] *Re HG (Specific Issue Order: Sterilisation)* [1993] 1 FLR 587, 596; *Re O (A Minor) (Medical Treatment)* [1993] 2 FLR 149, 155; *Re R (A Minor) (Blood Transfusion)* [1993] 2 FLR 757, 760. Proceedings in the Administrative Court by way of an application for judicial review are almost always inappropriate in this type of case: *R v Portsmouth Hospitals NHS Trust, ex p Glass* [1999] 2 FLR 905 (affg (1999) 50 BMLR 269); *A v A Health Authority, Re J (A Child), R (on the application of S) v Secretary of State for the Home Department* [2002] EWHC 18 (Fam/Admin), [2002] Fam 213, [71]–[81].

[182] *Re B (Wardship: Abortion)* [1991] 2 FLR 426, 428; *Re HG (Specific Issue Order: Sterilisation)* [1993] 1 FLR 587, 597. For an unsuccessful attempt to have the Official Solicitor removed as a child's guardian *ad litem* see *Re A (Conjoined Twins: Medical Treatment) (No 2)* [2001] 1 FLR 267. For a history of the office of the Official Solicitor, see A Ruck Keene, P Bartlett, and N Allen, 'Litigation Friends or Foes? Representation of "P" before the Court of Protection' (2016) 24(3) Med L Rev 333.

[183] *Re B (A Minor) (Wardship: Sterilisation)* [1988] AC 199, 212.

[184] *Re Z (A Minor) (Identification: Restrictions on Publication)* [1997] Fam 1, 28–29.

[185] *Re D (A Minor) (Wardship: Sterilisation)* [1976] Fam 185, 194 *per* Heilbron J.

(each expression occasionally used, but each, for this purpose synonymous) of the human being concerned, that is the ward himself or herself.[186]

Welfare The courts have traditionally been reluctant to articulate the principles and values to be applied in operating the best interests test,[187] but it is clear that welfare for this purpose must be taken in the widest sense and that it includes the child's ethical, moral, spiritual, and religious welfare:[188] **10.75**

> The dominant matter for the consideration of the Court is the welfare of the child. But the welfare of a child is not to be measured by money only, nor by physical comfort only. The word welfare must be taken in its widest sense. The moral and religious welfare of the child must be considered as well as its physical well-being. Nor can the ties of affection be disregarded.[189]

An Objective Standard[190] In deciding questions of welfare, the court, acting as 'the judicial reasonable parent', acts by reference to the objective standard of the ordinary reasonable and responsible mother and father,[191] but having regard to the subjective needs of the particular child.[192] Thus in deciding whether to authorize or direct medical treatment the court adopts that course which, objectively considered, is in the particular child's best interests.[193] **10.76**

Prevention of Harm 'It has always been the principle of this court, not to risk the incurring of damage to children which it cannot repair, but rather to prevent the damage being done.'[194] Moreover, the court is justified in interfering not only where there is a 'likelihood' of damage to the child but even if there is no more than 'an apprehension or suspicion of it'.[195] **10.77**

(b) The child's wishes In relation to medical treatment generally, the court is bound (whether or not the case strictly falls within the Children Act 1989, s 1(4))[196] to have regard to the ascertainable wishes and feelings of the child, considered in the light of his/her age and understanding.[197] However, the court is not bound by the wishes even of a *Gillick* competent child, or a child who has attained the age of 16, though it will not lightly override the child's decision, particularly if the child's decision is sensible or the treatment is invasive:[198] **10.78**

---

[186] *Re B (A Minor) (Wardship: Sterilisation)* [1988] AC 199, 202 *per* Lord Hailsham of St Marylebone LC.

[187] ibid *Re B* is a well-known and much-criticized example of such reluctance; see also *Re J (A Minor) (Wardship: Medical Treatment)* [1991] Fam 33, 52 and *Re T (A Minor) (Wardship: Medical Treatment)* [1997] 1 WLR 242, 254.

[188] *Re K (Minors) (Children: Care and Control)* [1977] Fam 179, 187, 191.

[189] *Re McGrath* [1893] 1 Ch 143, 148 *per* Lindley LJ.

[190] See further paras 10.121–10.125.

[191] *J v C* [1970] AC 668, 723; *Re D (A Minor) (Wardship: Sterilisation)* [1976] Fam 185, 194; *Re E (A Minor) (Wardship: Medical Treatment)* [1993] 1 FLR 386, 392–93; *Re J (A Minor) (Wardship: Medical Treatment)* [1991] Fam 33, 50; *Re R (A Minor) (Wardship: Consent to Treatment)* [1992] Fam 11, 25; *Re O (A Minor) (Medical Treatment)* [1993] 2 FLR 149, 153.

[192] *Re E (A Minor) (Wardship: Medical Treatment)* [1993] 1 FLR 386, 392.

[193] *Re B (A Minor) (Wardship: Sterilisation)* [1988] AC 199, 210.

[194] *Wellesley v Duke of Beaufort* (1827) 2 Russ 1, 18 *per* Lord Eldon LC (cited in *Re X (A Minor) (Wardship: Jurisdiction)* [1975] Fam 47, 51; *Re D (A Minor) (Wardship: Sterilisation)* [1976] Fam 185, 194).

[195] *Re X (A Minor) (Wardship: Jurisdiction)* [1975] Fam 47, 51 quoting *Chambers on Infants* [ed 1842], 20.

[196] *Re W (A Minor) (Medical Treatment: Court's Jurisdiction)* [1993] Fam 64, 93.

[197] *B(BR) v B(J)* [1968] P 466, 473, 481; *Re P (A Minor)* [1986] 1 FLR 272, 276–279; *Re E (A Minor) (Wardship: Medical Treatment)* [1993] 1 FLR 386, 393; *Re B (Wardship: Abortion)* [1991] 2 FLR 426, 428–429. cf Children Act 1989, s 1(3)(a).

[198] *Re W (A Minor) (Medical Treatment: Court's Jurisdiction)* [1993] Fam 64, 81–82, 84, 88, 93. The court's power to make orders under s 8 of the Children Act 1989 is restricted by s 9(7) to those under 16 unless the circumstances of the case are exceptional.

> This is not, however, to say that the wishes of 16- and 17-year-olds are to be treated as no different from those of 14- and 15-year-olds. Far from it. Adolescence is a period of progressive transition from childhood to adulthood and as experience of life is acquired and intelligence and understanding grow, so will the scope of decision-making which should be left to the minor, for it is only by making decisions and experiencing the consequences that decision-making skills will be acquired. As I put it in the course of the argument, and as I sincerely believe, 'good parenting involves giving minors as much rope as they can handle without an unacceptable risk that they will hang themselves'. As Lord Hailsham of St Marylebone LC put it in *Re B* [1988] AC 199, 202, the 'first and paramount consideration [of the court] is the well being, welfare or interests [of the minor]' and I regard it as self-evident that this involves giving them the maximum degree of decision-making which is prudent. Prudence does not involve avoiding all risk, but it does involve avoiding risks which, if they eventuate, may have irreparable consequences or which are disproportionate to the benefits which could accrue from taking them.[199]

10.79 Thus, in practice, the court is unlikely to overrule the competent child's decision in the ordinary run of relatively routine surgical, medical, or dental treatment, though even then it has the power to do so.[200] Moreover, where the views of a competent child conflict with those of its parents, the court is likely to adopt the views of the child rather than the parents.[201] On the other hand, there will be cases where, having given proper weight to the child's views, it is nonetheless appropriate for the court to overrule either a *Gillick* competent or even a 16- or 17-year-old child's decision, for example where that is necessary in order either to save the child's life or to prevent really serious and irreparable harm to the child, for as a general principle the protection of the child's welfare implies at least the protection of the child's life and it is generally the duty of the court to preserve life and ensure so far as it can that children survive to attain the age of 18.[202] The court has not hesitated, for example, to override the refusal of teenagers to consent to a lifesaving blood transfusion[203] or other essential treatment,[204] and, one imagines, would readily overrule a promiscuous teenager's frivolous decision to be sterilized. Likewise, the court would probably be very slow indeed to allow even a willing and *Gillick* competent teenager to donate an organ.

10.80 *Non-Therapeutic Procedures* Where the procedure in question is non-therapeutic, and the child is old enough to understand, the court should not subject him/her to the operation against his/her will, certainly unless to do so is 'clearly' in the child's interests.[205]

---

[199] ibid, 81–82 *per* Lord Donaldson of Lymington MR.

[200] ibid, 94.

[201] As in *Re P (A Minor)* [1986] 1 FLR 272 (where a pregnant 15-year-old girl of strong personality and mature views, and able to understand the implications, wanted an abortion but was opposed by her Seventh Day Adventist parents on bona fide religious and other grounds: the court treated the child's welfare, but not her views and wishes, as paramount and, although giving weight to her parents' feelings and taking into account their deeply and sincerely held religious objections, directed the abortion) and *Re B (Wardship: Abortion)* [1991] 2 FLR 426 (where a pregnant 12-year-old girl's wish to have an abortion was opposed by her mother: the court directed an abortion). See also *Re W (A Minor) (Medical Treatment: Court's Jurisdiction)* [1993] Fam 64, 90, 94.

[202] *Re B (A Minor) (Wardship: Medical Treatment)* [1981] 1 WLR 1421, 1424–25; *Re W (A Minor) (Medical Treatment: Court's Jurisdiction)* [1993] Fam 64, 88, 94.

[203] *Re E (A Minor) (Wardship: Medical Treatment)* [1993] 1 FLR 386; *Re S (A Minor) (Consent to Medical Treatment)* [1994] 2 FLR 1065; *Re L (Medical Treatment: Gillick Competency)* [1998] 2 FLR 810; *Re P (Medical Treatment: Best Interests)* [2003] EWHC 2327 (Fam), [2004] 2 FLR 1117.

[204] *Re R (A Minor) (Wardship: Consent to Treatment)* [1992] Fam 11; *Re W (A Minor) (Medical Treatment: Court's Jurisdiction)* [1993] Fam 64; *A Metropolitan Borough Council v AB* [1997] 1 FLR 767; *Re C (Detention: Medical Treatment)* [1997] 2 FLR 180 (force-feeding for treatment of anorexia nervosa); *Re M (Medical Treatment: Consent)* [1999] 2 FLR 1097 (heart transplant); *Re P (A Child)* [2014] EWHC 1650 (Fam) (life-sustaining treatment following a paracetamol overdose).

[205] *Re L (An Infant)* [1968] P 119, 140; *B(BR) v B(J)* [1968] P 466, 469, 473–74, 481; *S v McC, W v W* [1972] AC 24, 45. See also *Re D (A Minor) (Wardship: Sterilisation)* [1976] Fam 185.

10.81 **(c) The court's approach to religious issues** Religious belief has been described by the Supreme Court as a belief that there is more to be understood about mankind's nature and relationship to the universe than can be gained from the senses or from science.[206] It is 'based on faith, not reason, and some can strongly influence the believer's attitude to health and medical treatment without in any way suggesting a lack of mental capacity.'[207] The court recognizes no religious distinctions and passes no judgment on religious beliefs so long as they are 'legally and socially acceptable' and not 'immoral or socially obnoxious' or 'pernicious'.[208] Indeed, the court pays every respect and gives great weight to the family's religious principles.[209] The same holds true where the person with religiously-held beliefs lacks capacity to make the decision.[210]

10.82 But, although the parents' views and wishes as to the child's religious upbringing are of great importance, and will be seriously regarded by the court, they will be given effect to by the court only so far as and in such manner as is in accordance with the best interests of the child's welfare. In matters of religion, as in all other aspects of a child's upbringing, the interests of the child are the paramount consideration.[211]

> Parents may be free to become martyrs themselves. But it does not follow that they are free, in identical circumstances, to make martyrs of their children before they have reached the age of full and legal discretion when they can make the choices for themselves.[212]

10.83 Where a child is old enough to be able to express sensible views on the subject of religion, even if not old enough to take a mature decision, the court will pay great regard to (though it cannot be bound by) the child's wishes, and will be slow to dictate the child's religious upbringing.[213] But, just as the court will not allow a parent to make a martyr of his/her child, so the court will be very slow to allow a child to martyr him/herself.[214]

---

[206] *R (Hodkin and another) v Registrar General of Births, Deaths and Marriages* [2014] AC 610 at [57].

[207] *Wye Valley NHS Trust v Mr B* [2015] EWCOP 60 at [15].

[208] *Stourton v Stourton* (1857) 8 DeGM&G 760, 771; *Re T (Minors) (Custody: Religious Upbringing)* (1981) 2 FLR 239, 244–45; *Re B and G (Minors) (Custody)* [1985] FLR 134, 157; *Re R (A Minor) (Residence: Religion)* [1993] 2 FLR 163, 171; *Re G (Children) (Religious Upbringing: Education)* [2012] 1 FLR 677. See also Article 9 of the European Convention on Human Rights.

[209] *Re P (A Minor)* [1986] 1 FLR 272, 281; *Re E (A Minor) (Wardship: Medical Treatment)* [1993] 1 FLR 386, 394; *Re O (A Minor) (Medical Treatment)* [1993] 2 FLR 149, 153. In addition to the various cases involving Jehovah's Witnesses referred to in para 10.78, see also *Re C (Medical Treatment)* [1998] 1 FLR 384 (Orthodox Jewish parents wishing 16-month-old daughter suffering from terminal spinal muscular atrophy, type 1, to be ventilated in event of respiratory relapse and not willing to agree to only palliative care as recommended by doctors); *Re J (Specific Issue Orders: Muslim Upbringing and Circumcision)* [1999] 2 FLR 678 (affd *Re J (Specific Issue Orders: Child's Religious Upbringing and Circumcision)* [2000] 1 FLR 571) (dispute between Muslim father and Christian mother as to circumcision of 5-year-old boy). See also M Fox and M Thomson, 'The New Politics of Male Circumcision: HIV/AIDS, Health Law and Social Justice' (2012) 32(2) Legal Studies 255.

[210] *Wye Valley NHS Trust v Mr B* [2015] EWCOP 60, [2015] COPLR 843 at [15].

[211] *Stourton v Stourton* (1857) 8 DeGMG 760, 771; *Re McGrath* [1893] 1 Ch 143, 148, 149; *Re W, W v M* [1907] 2 Ch 557, 566–67; *Ward v Laverty* [1925] AC 101, 108; *Re Aster* [1955] 1 WLR 465, 468; *Re E (An Infant)* [1964] 1 WLR 51, 57–58; *J v C* [1970] AC 668, 713, 715; *Re P (A Minor)* [1986] 1 FLR 272, 281; *Re E (A Minor) (Wardship: Medical Treatment)* [1993] 1 FLR 386, 391–94; *Re S (A Minor) (Medical Treatment)* [1993] 1 FLR 376, 380; *Re S (A Minor) (Consent to Medical Treatment)* [1994] 2 FLR 1065.

[212] *Prince v Massachusetts* (1944) 321 US 158, 170 *per* Rutledge J (cited in *Re E (A Minor) (Wardship: Medical Treatment)* [1993] 1 FLR 386, 394, where the passage, due to an error by counsel, is wrongly attributed to Holmes J).

[213] *Stourton v Stourton* (1857) 8 DeGMG 760 (where the LJJ themselves interviewed a 9-year-old boy); *Re E (A Minor) (Wardship: Medical Treatment)* [1993] 1 FLR 386, 393, 394 (where the judge interviewed a 15-year-old boy); *Re S (Minors) (Access: Religious Upbringing)* [1992] 2 FLR 313, 321; *Re R (A Minor) (Residence: Religion)* [1993] 2 FLR 163, 173–74, 175, 179–80.

[214] *Re E (A Minor) (Wardship: Medical Treatment)* [1993] 1 FLR 386, 394; *Re W (A Minor) (Medical Treatment: Court's Jurisdiction)* [1993] Fam 64, 88; *Re S (A Minor) (Consent to Medical Treatment)* [1994] 2

10.84 (d) **The court and the doctor** The court will naturally pay great respect to, and will not lightly disregard, the opinion of the doctor treating or proposing to treat the child. However, in the final analysis it is for the court, and not for doctors, however eminent, to reach a decision as to what is in the best interests of the particular child.[215] And where there is a diversity or conflict of medical opinion the court is necessarily obliged to choose which view to adopt.

10.85 The court, depending on the circumstances, can either make an order forbidding something to be done to the child (for example, an order restraining a proposed sterilization)[216] or make an order 'authorizing' or 'authorizing and directing' something to be done to the child (for example, an order authorizing and directing surgery).[217] But the court will never make a compulsive order requiring a particular doctor or health authority to treat a child in a manner contrary to their wishes.[218] It follows that, even when the court 'authorizes and directs' treatment, what it is really doing is to authorize the proposed treatment and to indicate that such authorization is to be effective notwithstanding the absence or refusal of parental consent.[219] To avoid confusion or misunderstanding the court should avoid the 'authorize and direct' form of order and simply make an order 'authorizing' the relevant treatment.[220]

D. Adults Who Lack Mental Capacity

1. General principles

(i) The role of consent

10.86 The patient who lacks mental capacity is, by definition, unable to give a valid consent to treatment. The common law does not recognize anyone else as having the legal capacity to give or refuse consent on his/her behalf. Thus a spouse or relative does not have any power either to consent or to refuse consent to medical treatment on behalf of an adult who lacks mental capacity.[221] Accordingly, the care and treatment of the incapacitated patient is governed by the Mental Capacity Act 2005 ('MCA').

FLR 1065; *Re L (Medical Treatment: Gillick Competency)* [1998] 2 FLR 810; *Re P (Medical Treatment: Best Interests)* [2003] EWHC 2327 (Fam), [2004] 2 FLR 1117.

[215] cf *Re F (Mental Patient: Sterilisation)* [1990] 2 AC 1, 80; *Frenchay Healthcare NHS Trust v S* [1994] 1 WLR 601, 609–10.

[216] *Re D (A Minor) (Wardship: Sterilisation)* [1976] Fam 185.

[217] *Re B (A Minor) (Wardship: Medical Treatment)* [1981] 1 WLR 1421, 1424–25.

[218] See para 10.17.

[219] cf *Secretary, Department of Health and Community Services v JWB and SMB* (1992) 175 CLR 218, 259, 267–68.

[220] *Re J (A Minor) (Wardship: Medical Treatment)* [1991] Fam 33, 48; *Re J (A Minor) (Child in Care: Medical Treatment)* [1993] Fam 15, 29, 31; *Re W (A Minor) (Medical Treatment: Court's Jurisdiction)* [1993] Fam 64, 81.

[221] *Re T (Adult: Refusal of Treatment)* [1993] Fam 95, 103; *A v A Health Authority, Re J (A Child), R (on the application of S) v Secretary of State for the Home Department* [2002] EWHC 18 (Fam/Admin), [2002] Fam 213, [36]; *Re S (Adult Patient) (Inherent Jurisdiction: Family Life)* [2002] EWHC 2278 (Fam), [2003] 1 FLR 292, [14]. See also *T v T* [1988] Fam 52; *Re F (Mental Patient: Sterilisation)* [1990] 2 AC 1; *Re C (Mental Patient: Contact)* [1993] 1 FLR 940; *Hospital Authority v C* [2003] Lloyd's Rep Med 130, [27]–[29]. The advent with the MCA of health and welfare lasting powers of attorney and deputyship now means that family members or friends, for example, could be appointed to make such decisions on the patient's behalf.

(ii) Defence to liability

At common law, in the case of an adult who lacked capacity or was permanently unable to communicate,[222] the principle of necessity[223] rendered lawful, despite the absence of consent, such treatment which in the absence of consent would otherwise be tortious,[224] as a reasonable doctor would in all the circumstances give, acting in the best interests of the patient.[225] But it was not a licence to be irresponsible, would not protect someone who was an officious busybody, and would not apply where there is bad faith or where what is done is unreasonable or not in the best interests of the assisted person.[226] **10.87**

The common law doctrine of necessity has now been given statutory force by the Mental Capacity Act 2005 which offers qualified protection from civil and criminal liability.[227] Where the provisions of the MCA apply, the common law defence of necessity has no application.[228] Instead, if a person ('D') does an act in connection with the care or treatment of another person ('P'), and: (1) before doing the act, D takes reasonable steps to establish whether P lacks capacity in relation to the matter in question; and (2) when doing the act, D reasonably believes that P lacks capacity in relation to the matter, and that it will be in P's best interests for the act to be done, then in those circumstances D does not incur any liability in relation to the act that s/he would not have incurred if P: (a) had capacity to consent in relation to the matter; and (b) had consented to D doing the act. Pervading the defence are the concepts of reasonableness, practicability, and appropriateness: **10.88**

> 40. A striking feature of the statutory defence is the extent to which it is pervaded by the concepts of reasonableness, practicability and appropriateness. Strict liability has no place here. Of particular relevance to the present case is the fact that D is under no liability to P in tort for an act done in connection with the care or treatment of P, if he *reasonably* believes that it will be in P's best interests for the act to be done; and (in the case of restraint) if he *reasonably* believes that it is necessary to do the act in order to prevent harm to P; and he is obliged to take into account the views of, amongst others, anyone caring for P, but only if it is *practicable and appropriate* to consult the carer.[229]

---

[222] The doctrine of necessity also applied if the patient had capacity 'in cases of emergency where the patient is unconscious, and where it is necessary to operate before consent can be obtained': *Schloendorff v Society of New York Hospital* (1914) 105 NE 92, 93 *per* Cardozo J. Necessity applied in such a case if (i) it was impossible to communicate with the patient (eg, because the patient was unconscious or under anaesthetic) and (ii) urgent action was imperative in the best interests of the patient but consent could not be obtained until it was too late and (iii) the doctor or surgeon did no more than was reasonably required in the best interests of the patient in the interim before the patient recovered the ability to communicate: *Re F (Mental Patient: Sterilisation)* [1990] 2 AC 1, 71–77.

[223] For the doctrine of necessity in this context, see generally *Re F (Mental Patient: Sterilisation)* [1990] AC 1 and *R v Bournewood Community and Mental Health NHS Trust, ex p L* [1999] 1 AC 458.

[224] *Re F (Mental Patient: Sterilisation)* [1990] 2 AC 1, 73–76.

[225] ibid, 51, 56, 75.

[226] *In re O (Court of Protection: Jurisdiction)* [2013] EWHC 3932, [2014] Fam. 197, [2014] 3 WLR 453 at [18] and [20] where it was held that there was nothing in the MCA to displace this approach.

[227] MCA s 5. Nothing in s 5 excludes a person's civil liability for loss or damage, or his/her criminal liability, resulting from his/her negligence in doing the act: s 5(3). Furthermore, nothing in s 5 affects the operation of advance decisions to refuse treatment: s 5(4).

[228] *ZH v Metropolitan Police Commissioner* [2012] EWHC 604 (Admin) at [44] which was not disapproved of on appeal: *H v Comr of Police of the Metropolis (Liberty intervening)* [2013] EWCA Civ 69, [2013] 1 WLR 3021. However, note the continued recognition of the doctrine post-MCA in *In re O (Court of Protection: Jurisdiction)* [2013] EWHC 3932, [2014] Fam. 197, [2014] 3 WLR 453 at [18] *per* Sir James Munby P: 'Sections 4 and 5, after all, presuppose that such actions are not unlawful per se; they merely, though very importantly, elaborate what must be done and provide, if certain conditions are satisfied, a statutory defence against liability: see the important analysis of Baker J in *G v E (Deputyship and Litigation Friend)* [2010] COPLR Con Vol 470, especially paras 17–18, 56–57.'

[229] *H v Comr of Police of the Metropolis (Liberty intervening)* [2013] EWCA Civ 69, [2013] 1 WLR 3021 at [40] (emphasis in original).

10.89 The Mental Capacity Act 2005 also provides a similar defence if D does an act that is intended to restrain P if, in addition to (1) and (2) above, two further conditions are satisfied, namely: (i) D reasonably believes that it is necessary to do the act in order to prevent harm to P; and (ii) the act is a proportionate response to the likelihood of P's suffering harm, and the seriousness of that harm. The Act defines 'restraint' in very broad terms. Thus, D restrains P if he: (1) uses, or threatens to use, force to secure the doing of an act which P resists; or (2) restricts P's liberty of movement, whether or not P resists.[230]

10.90 The statutory defence to liability provided by s 5 cannot be used to take steps amounting to a deprivation of liberty.[231] Nor can it circumvent the powers under the Mental Health Act 1983 by removing a person from their home so that a mental health assessment may be conducted in a hospital.[232] Furthermore, the defence cannot be relied on to authorize a person to do an act which conflicts with a decision made by a donee of a lasting power of attorney, or a court-appointed deputy within the scope of his/her authority and in accordance with Part 1 of the Mental Capacity Act 2005. However, this does not stop a person providing life-sustaining treatment, or doing any act which s/he reasonably believes to be necessary to prevent a serious deterioration in P's condition, while a decision as respects any relevant issue is sought from the court, even if such intervention amounts to a deprivation of liberty.[233]

10.91 A doctor is never entitled to give treatment, even in cases of emergency or to a patient who is unconscious or lacks capacity, which is contrary to the known wishes of the patient when s/he had capacity:

> [T]he basic requirements, applicable in these cases of necessity, [are] that, to fall within the principle, not only (1) must there be a necessity to act when it is not practicable to communicate with the assisted person, but also (2) the action taken must be such as a reasonable person would in all the circumstances take, acting in the best interests of the assisted person. On this statement of principle, I wish to observe that officious intervention cannot be justified by the principle of necessity. So intervention cannot be justified when another more appropriate person is available and willing to act; nor can it be justified when it is contrary to the known wishes of the assisted person, to the extent that he is capable of rationally forming such a wish.[234]

This principle also has now been given statutory force by the Mental Capacity Act 2005 which prescribes requirements for the advance refusal of life-sustaining treatment.[235]

(iii) The role of parents of adults lacking capacity

10.92 The scope of parental responsibility extends until a person turns 18. Whereas the MCA generally provides a best interests decision-making process for those lacking capacity from the age of 16. Determining best interests is an informal and collaborative exercise. But where there is disagreement between parents and professionals, who decides within this interface of the Children Act 1989 and the MCA is not clearly prescribed by the legislation. What is clear, however, is that parents are not legally powerless when their child turns 18.

10.93 In *Re S (Adult Patient) (Inherent Jurisdiction: Family Life)*,[236] Munby J observed that, save for a special category of medical procedures, the doctrine of necessity—now reflected in the

[230] MCA, s 6.
[231] MCA, s 4A.
[232] *R (on the application of Sessay) v South London & Maudsley NHS Foundation Trust* [2011] EWHC 2617 (QB), [2012] QB 760, [2012] 2 WLR 1071.
[233] MCA, s 4B.
[234] *Re F (Mental Patient: Sterilisation)* [1990] AC 1, at 75–76 *per* Lord Goff of Chieveley.
[235] MCA, ss 5(4) and 24–26.
[236] [2002] EWHC 2278 (Fam), [2003] 1 FLR 292, [2003] Fam. Law 91 at [20]–[21].

MCA—enables parents 'not merely to assume the responsibility for the day-to-day care of their child, with all the routine decision-making which that entails, but also to decide, no doubt, where appropriate, in conjunction with suitable professional advisers, more important matters . . .'. Examples include residence, contact, services offered by public authorities, and medical treatment. His Lordship went on to state:

> It may be that, in strict legal theory, these rights, duties, powers, responsibilities and authority . . . are vested in such a parent not qua parent but rather because the parent has, in the eyes of the law, reasonably and appropriately intervened in order to care for, or has assumed responsibility for the care of, someone unable to look after himself . . . But that is little more than a technicality.

Similarly in the post-MCA decision of *G v E*, Baker J held:[237] **10.94**

> The Act and Code are, therefore, constructed on the basis that the vast majority of decisions concerning incapacitated adults are taken informally and collaboratively by individuals or groups of people consulting and working together. It is emphatically not part of the scheme underpinning the Act that there should be one individual who as a matter of course is given a special legal status to make decisions about incapacitated persons. Experience has shown that working together is the best policy to ensure that incapacitated adults such as E receive the highest quality of care. This case is an example of what can go wrong when people do not work together.

(iv) Lasting powers of attorney

The Mental Capacity Act 2005 enables an adult patient with capacity to create a lasting power of attorney ('LPA') under which the donee is given authority to make decisions about the donor's personal welfare, including giving or refusing consent to medical treatment, where the donor no longer has capacity.[238] But this is subject to any advance decision to refuse treatment ('advance directive')[239] and does not extend, unless the lasting power of attorney expressly so provides, to the giving or refusing of consent to the carrying out or continuation of life-sustaining treatment.[240] Nor can the power be exercised where the donor's treatment is being regulated by Part 4 of the Mental Health Act 1983.[241] **10.95**

Even though the person must have capacity to understand the purpose and scope of the LPA at the time the power is executed,[242] the LPA is not formally created until it has been registered with the Office of the Public Guardian. So where the person signs an advance directive and a health and welfare LPA on the same day, the subsequent registration of the LPA will render the prior advance directive invalid.[243] **10.96**

---

237 [2010] COPLR Con Vol 470, at [57]. See also *Re DC* [2015] EWCOP 23, at [40].

238 MCA, ss 9, 10, and 11(7)(c). See also ch 7 of the MCA Code of Practice. A person can also appoint an attorney for property and financial affairs which falls outside the scope of this chapter.

239 MCA, s 11(7)(b).

240 MCA, s 11(8).

241 MCA, s 28(1). However, according to para 7.8 of the MHA Code of Practice (2015), it is good practice, where practicable, for those involved in assessing and treating patients detained under the 1983 Act 'to establish effective means of communication to ensure that the attorney or deputy is informed and, where relevant, consulted about the patient's care.' And see MHA s 58A in relation to the role of health and welfare LPAs with regard to electro-convulsive therapy.

242 MCA, s 9(2)(c).

243 MCA, ss 25(2)(b) and 9(2)(b). In *Re E and others* [2014] EWCOP 27 the court retrospectively validated the invalid advance directive in similar circumstances, although the lawful basis for doing so is not apparent from the statutory provisions.

2. Advance directives and the adult who lacks capacity

10.97 An adult patient with capacity has an absolute right (the right of self-determination) to refuse consent to any medical treatment or invasive procedure, whether the reasons are rational, irrational, unknown or non-existent, and even if the result of refusal is the certainty of death.[244] In the absence of clear statutory authority to the contrary, such a right to refuse is as true of a mentally disordered person as of anyone else.[245] Consistently with this, a competent adult patient's anticipatory refusal of consent (a so-called 'advance directive' or 'living will') remains binding and effective notwithstanding that the patient has subsequently become and remains incompetent.[246] This principle, recognized by the common law, was given statutory effect by the Mental Capacity Act 2005.

(i) Advance directives previously at common law

10.98 (a) **Burden and Standard of Proof** The burden of proof was on those who sought to establish the existence and continuing validity and applicability of an advance directive.[247] If there was doubt 'that doubt [fell] to be resolved in favour of the preservation of life'.[248] The evidence must be scrutinized with 'especial care'. Clear and convincing proof was required. Where life was at stake the continuing validity and applicability of the advance directive must be clearly established by convincing and inherently reliable evidence.[249]

10.99 (b) **Formal Validity** There were no formal requirements for a valid advance directive: there was no legal requirement as to form. An advance directive need not have been in, or evidenced by, writing: an advance directive could be oral or in writing and could be proved by

[244] For striking applications of this principle see *Re C (Adult: Refusal of Treatment)* [1994] 1 WLR 290 (patient with schizophrenia held entitled to refuse consent to amputation of gangrenous leg); *Secretary of State for the Home Department v Robb* [1995] Fam 127 (prison authorities not entitled to force-feed an adult who lacks capacity prisoner); *Re JT (Adult: Refusal of Medical Treatment)* [1998] 1 FLR 48 (adult with learning difficulties and extremely severe behavioural disturbance refusing treatment for renal failure); *St George's Healthcare NHS Trust v S, R v Collins, ex p S* [1999] Fam 26 (pregnant woman refusing Caesarean section); *Re AK (Medical Treatment: Consent)* [2001] 1 FLR 129 (adult suffering from motor neuron disease seeking removal of his ventilator); *Re B (Consent to Treatment: Capacity)* [2002] EWHC 429 (Fam), [2002] 1 FLR 1090 (tetraplegic adult seeking removal of her ventilator: the judgment of Dame Elizabeth Butler-Sloss P contains at [14]–[35] a valuable survey of the authorities and at [100] an important restatement of the basic principles with additional guidelines). For the impact in this context of the ECHR see *Re AK (Medical Treatment: Consent)* [2001] 1 FLR 129, 136. See also *Heart of England NHS Foundation Trust v JB* [2014] EWHC 342 (COP) (patient with paranoid schizophrenia entitled to refuse consent to amputation of gangrenous foot).

[245] *R v Hallstrom, ex parte W (No 2)* [1986] QB 1090.

[246] *HE v A Hospital NHS Trust* [2003] EWHC 1017 (Fam), [2003] 2 FLR 408, [20]. For the earlier authorities see *Re T (Adult: Refusal of Treatment)* [1993] Fam 95, 102, 115, 116, 120–21; *Airedale NHS Trust v Bland* [1993] AC 789, 808–09, 816–17, 828, 857, 864, 891–92, 894; *Re C (Adult: Refusal of Treatment)* [1994] 1 WLR 290, 294–95, 295–96; *Re MB (Medical Treatment)* [1997] 2 FLR 426; *St George's Healthcare NHS Trust v S, R v Collins, ex p S* [1999] Fam 26; *Re AK (Medical Treatment: Consent)* [2001] 1 FLR 129; *Re B (Consent to Treatment: Capacity)* [2002] EWHC 429 (Fam), [2002] 1 FLR 1090. The British Medical Association has published guidance on advance directives: 'Advance decisions and proxy decision-making in medical treatment and research' (2007).

[247] *HE v A Hospital NHS Trust* [2003] EWHC 1017 (Fam), [2003] 2 FLR 408, [23], [46]. For background, see A R Maclean, 'Advance directives and the rocky waters of anticipatory decision-making' (2008) 16 Med L Rev 1.

[248] *Re T (Adult: Refusal of Treatment)* [1993] Fam 95, 112 *per* Lord Donaldson of Lymington MR.

[249] *HE v A Hospital NHS Trust* [2003] EWHC 1017 (Fam), [2003] 2 FLR 408, [24], [46], applying *Re T (Adult: Refusal of Treatment)* [1993] Fam 95, 103, 112; *Airedale NHS Trust v Bland* [1993] AC 789, 864; *Re AK (Medical Treatment: Consent)* [2001] 1 FLR 129, 134. English law thus corresponds to the 'specific-subjective-intent rule' applied in the US by the courts of New York and Missouri, which requires 'clear and convincing, inherently reliable evidence': *Re O'Connor* (1988) 531 NE 2d 607, 608, 611–12, 613–14; *Cruzan v Harmon* (1988) 760 SW 2d 408, 414–15, 424–26, appeal dismissed (1990) 497 US 261.

a single witness deposing to a conversation with the patient on a single occasion; there was no requirement of corroboration. However, the court plainly scrutinized with great care the evidence of any witness whose interests conflicted with those of the patient, and it may well have been easier to establish the existence of an oral advance directive if more than one witness was able to depose to more than one conversation with the patient. The question for the court was well summarized as follows:

> [T]he 'clear and convincing' evidence standard requires proof sufficient to persuade the trier of fact that the patient held a firm and settled commitment to the termination of life supports under the circumstances like those presented.[250]

(c) **Revocation** There were no formal requirements for the revocation of an advance directive which could be done either orally or in writing. The burden of proof was on those who sought to establish the existence and continuing validity and applicability of an advance directive, with doubt falling to be resolved in favour of the preservation of life.[251] **10.100**

(d) **Capacity to Make an Advance Directive** The question whether someone could lawfully give his/her consent depended solely upon whether or not s/he had capacity to do so at common law. An adult was presumed to have capacity,[252] and the burden of proof was therefore on those who asserted a lack of capacity.[253] The effect of a valid and applicable advance directive was to prevent treatment being given, without speculation as to the personal or religious convictions or reasons behind its creation.[254] **10.101**

Whatever the context in which the question arose, the test of capacity at common law was essentially one of the person's 'understanding' of the 'nature', 'character' and 'effect' of the act or transaction in question. The test of capacity was in essence the same in relation to medical treatment: the question was whether the patient was 'competent to appreciate the issues involved'[255] so as to be able to exercise a 'right of choice',[256] and whether s/he sufficiently 'understand[s] the nature, purpose and effects of the treatment'.[257] **10.102**

The degree of capacity required varied with the circumstances of the particular treatment; it must be commensurate with the gravity of the decision,[258] for 'the more serious the decision, **10.103**

250 *Re O'Connor* (1988) 531 NE 2d 607, 613 *per* Wachtler CJ.

251 *HE v A Hospital NHS Trust* [2003] EWHC 1017 (Fam), [2003] 2 FLR 408, [35]–[39], [46].

252 *R v Sullivan* [1984] AC 156, 170, 171 (approving M'Naghten's Case (1843) 10 Cl & F 200, 210); *Re T (Adult: Refusal of Treatment)* [1993] Fam 95, 112, 115; *Re C (Adult: Refusal of Treatment)* [1994] 1 WLR 290, 295; *Cambridgeshire County Council v R (An Adult)* [1995] 1 FLR 50, 54; *Re MB (Medical Treatment)* [1997] 2 FLR 426, 436.

253 *HE v A Hospital NHS Trust* [2003] EWHC 1017 (Fam), [2003] 2 FLR 408, [20], [46]. With regard to the common law test of capacity, see *Boughton v Knight* (1873) LR 3 P & D 64, 71–75; *Cambridgeshire County Council v R (An Adult)* [1995] 1 FLR 50, 53; *Re F (Mental Patient: Sterilisation)* [1990] 2 AC 1, 12, 31, 34; *Re C (Adult: Refusal of Treatment)* [1994] 1 WLR 290, 295; *Re MB (Medical Treatment)* [1997] 2 FLR 426, 437; *Re T (Adult: Refusal of Treatment)* [1993] Fam 95, 113, 116.

254 See *Tameside and Glossop Acute Services Trust v CH* [1996] 1 FLR 762, 766, 769; *Norfolk and Norwich Healthcare (NHS) Trust v W* [1996] 2 FLR 613; *Rochdale Healthcare (NHS) Trust v C* [1997] 1 FCR 274; *Re L (Patient: Non-consensual Treatment)* [1997] 2 FLR 837; and, in relation to 16- and 17-year-olds, *A Metropolitan Borough Council v AB* [1997] 1 FLR 767; *Re C (Detention: Medical Treatment)* [1997] 2 FLR 180; and approved by the Court of Appeal in *Re MB (Medical Treatment)* [1997] 2 FLR 426, 433, 437. For a case of temporary incapacity see *Bolton Hospitals NHS Trust v O* [2002] EWHC 2871 (Fam), [2003] 1 FLR 824. For the relevance of ambivalence see *Re B (Consent to Treatment: Capacity)* [2002] EWHC 429 (Fam), [2002] 1 FLR 1090, [34]–[35].

255 *Re F (Mental Patient: Sterilisation)* [1990] 2 AC 1, 12 *per* Lord Donaldson of Lymington MR.

256 ibid, 31, 34 *per* Neill and Butler-Sloss LJJ.

257 *Re C (Adult: Refusal of Treatment)* [1994] 1 WLR 290, 295 per Thorpe J.

258 *Re MB (Medical Treatment)* [1997] 2 FLR 426, 437.

the greater the capacity required'.[259] A high degree of capacity was required to refuse life-saving treatment.[260]

10.104 (e) **Effect of Valid Advance Directive** If an adult with capacity had expressed an unequivocal decision to refuse treatment, it was not for the doctor or the court to speculate as to the strength of the patient's personal or religious convictions or as to his/her reasons for refusing consent. Nor was it for the doctor or the court to speculate as to what the patient's decision might have been if s/he had been alive to the current crisis, or if s/he had been more fully informed, or if s/he had had more forcibly brought home to him all the implications of his/her refusal. If it is not possible to say what the patient's decision would have been if s/he had been given more information, his/her expressed decision, if s/he was competent to make it, is decisive, even if it was not made in contemplation of life-threatening circumstances.[261]

(ii) Advance decisions under the Mental Capacity Act 2005

10.105 The Mental Capacity Act 2005[262] has refined in large measure the above common law principles whilst also regulating the relationship between an advance decision and any lasting power of attorney made by the patient.[263] The test of incapacity is now that set out in the Mental Capacity Act 2005,[264] although the courts may look to the common law test where necessary to interpret the Act's provisions. If a person ('P') has made an advance decision which is valid and applicable to a treatment, the decision has effect as if s/he had made it, and had had capacity to make it, at the time when the question arises whether the treatment should be carried out or continued. It does not affect the liability which a person may incur for carrying out or continuing a treatment in relation to the person unless the decision is at the material time valid and applicable to the treatment.

10.106 An 'advance decision' means a decision made by a person, after s/he has reached 18 and when s/he has capacity to do so, that if: (1) at a later time and in such circumstances as s/he may specify, a specified treatment is proposed to be carried out or continued by a person providing health care for him/her; and (2) at that time s/he lacks capacity to consent to the carrying out or continuation of the treatment, the specified treatment is not to be carried out or continued. Preserving the common law position, P may withdraw or alter an advance decision at any time when s/he has capacity to do so which need not be in writing.[265] In *Nottinghamshire Healthcare NHS Trust v RC*,[266] a 23-year-old prisoner with personality disorder was admitted to a secure psychiatric hospital under the Mental Health Act 1983 after cutting his brachial artery. Whilst in prison he had 'embraced the religion of the Jehovah's Witnesses', though was yet to be baptized, and signed an advance decision in hospital refusing blood products. He was found to have capacity and 'to impose a blood transfusion

[259] *Re T (Adult: Refusal of Treatment)* [1993] Fam 95, 113, 116 *per* Lord Donaldson of Lymington MR.

[260] cf *Re E (A Minor) (Wardship: Medical Treatment)* [1993] 1 FLR 386, 391.

[261] *Malette v Shulman* (1987) 47 DLR (4th) 18, 42–44, 47–48, (1990) 67 DLR (4th) 321, 331–33, 335–38.

[262] Sections 24–26. See A R Maclean, 'Advance Directives and the Rocky Waters of Anticipatory Decision-making' (2008) 16 Med L Rev 1, 22 where it is suggested that the statutory provisions are only effective when 'healthcare professionals and/or the courts are comfortable with the patient's decision'. See also R Heywood, 'Revisiting Advance Decision Making under the Mental Capacity Act 2005: A Tale of Mixed Messages' (2015) 23(1) Med L Rev 81.

[263] MCA, s 25(2)(b) and (7).

[264] MCA, ss 2–3.

[265] MCA, s 24(4), (5).

[266] [2014] EWCOP 1317, [2014] COPLR 468.

would be a denial of a most basic freedom'. Indeed, were clinicians to compel such medical treatment for mental disorder under s 63 of the 1983 Act it would be 'an abuse of power'.[267]

An advance decision may not be valid because the person: (1) has withdrawn the decision at a time when s/he had capacity to do so; (2) has, under a lasting power of attorney created after the advance decision was made, conferred authority on the donee (or, if more than one, any of them) to give or refuse consent to the treatment to which the advance decision relates; or (3) has done anything else clearly inconsistent with the advance decision remaining his/her fixed decision. Nor may it be applicable to the treatment in question if: (1) at the material time P has capacity to give or refuse consent to it; (2) that treatment is not the treatment specified in the advance decision; (3) any circumstances specified in the advance decision are absent; or (4) there are reasonable grounds for believing that circumstances exist which P did not anticipate at the time of the advance decision and which would have affected his/her decision had s/he anticipated them. 10.107

It should be noted (and this is a change in the legal requirements)[268] that an advance decision is not applicable to life-sustaining treatment unless: (1) the decision is verified by a statement by P to the effect that it is to apply to that treatment even if life is at risk; and (2) the decision and statement comply with the following requirements: (a) they are in writing;[269] (b) they are signed by P or by another person in P's presence and by P's direction; (c) the signature is made or acknowledged by P in the presence of a witness; and (d) the witness signs, or acknowledges his/her signature, in P's presence.[270] An additional requirement in the case law is that, for life-sustaining treatment refusals, where there is any doubt regarding capacity, a 'full, reasoned and contemporaneous assessment to make such a momentous decision' should be undertaken and recorded to eliminate the possibility of later doubt.[271] In *X Primary Care Trust v XB*,[272] Theis J endorsed the guidance in paragraph 9.19 of the MCA Code of Practice as to what information should be included in an advance decision. 10.108

The Court of Protection is given express statutory power[273] to make declarations as to whether an advance decision exists, is valid or is applicable to a treatment. Moreover, nothing in an apparent advance decision stops a person (a) providing life-sustaining treatment, or (b) doing any act s/he reasonably believes to be necessary to prevent a serious deterioration in P's condition, while a decision as respects any relevant issue is sought from the court.[274] 10.109

3. The jurisdiction of the Court of Protection

The Court of Protection is a superior court of record which has 'in connection with its jurisdiction the same powers, rights, privileges and authority as the High Court'.[275] In 10.110

[267] To describe it in such a way is interesting because MHA, s 63 expressly enables treatment to be provided in the face of an objecting capacitous patient and calls into question whether s 63 is compatible with article 8 ECHR; see also *X v Finland* (34806/04) (3 July 2012) at [220]–[222].

[268] Previously at common law, there were no formal validity requirements so advance directives refusing life-sustaining treatment did not have to be in writing: see *HE v A Hospital NHS Trust* [2003] EWHC 1017 (Fam), [2003] 2 FLR 408, [33], [46]; cf *Re T (Adult: Refusal of Treatment)* [1993] Fam 95 [102].

[269] For a rare example of the Court of Protection upholding an oral advance decision refusing life-sustaining treatment, see *Newcastle Upon Tyne Hospitals Foundation Trust v LM* [2014] EWHC 454 (COP), [2015] 1 FCR 373.

[270] MCA, s 25(5), (6).

[271] *A Local Authority v E and others* [2012] EWHC 1639 (COP), [2012] 2 FCR 523. For commentary, see J Coggon, 'Anorexia nervosa, best interests, and the patient's human right to a 'wholesale overwhelming of her autonomy' (2014) 22(1) Med L Rev 119.

[272] [2012] EWHC 1390 (Fam) at [34].

[273] MCA, s 26(4).

[274] MCA, s 26(5).

[275] MCA, ss 45(1) and 47(1).

the context of medical treatment, it has statutory power under the Mental Capacity Act 2005: (1) to grant declaratory relief;[276] (2) to make a decision on behalf of an incapacitated patient in relation to the patient's personal welfare, including giving or refusing consent to medical treatment;[277] and (3) to appoint a deputy to make such decisions.[278] It was anticipated that the Court of Protection would exercise its declaratory and personal welfare decision-making powers in accordance with the general principles established by the High Court in relation to its analogous jurisdictions. The Court of Protection's power to appoint a deputy was entirely new, although it can be seen as a development of somewhat similar, if more limited, powers already exercised by the High Court. In practice most applications to the Court of Protection in relation to medical treatment have, as in the High Court, and no doubt for similar reasons, been dealt with by exercising the declaratory jurisdiction.[279]

10.111 The Court of Protection can make declarations as to whether a person has or lacks capacity to make certain decisions, and as to the lawfulness or otherwise of any act done, or yet to be done. The general powers conferred by s 47 probably do not extend to the granting of declarations in a form not provided for by s 15.[280] Nor does s 15 confer any general power to make bare declarations as to best interests: it is confined to declarations as to 'lawfulness'.[281] Moreover, a declaration has no coercive effect and cannot be enforced by committal.[282] With regards to lasting powers of attorney, the court can determine whether one exists, direct one not to be registered, if P lacks the mental capacity to do so, order it to be revoked, and give directions regarding the decisions taken pursuant to it. In so far as advance decisions are concerned, the court can determine whether one exists, is valid, and is applicable to a particular treatment.

10.112 There are certain exclusions. The court is excluded, by s 28, from certain psychiatric treatment matters governed by the Mental Health Act 1983.[283] Nor can the court authorize P's deprivation of liberty if P is ineligible. It cannot give consent under the Human Fertilisation and Embryology Acts of 1990 and 2008. Moreover, those matters referred to in s 27 are too personal so such decisions cannot be taken in P's best interests by anyone, including the court, if P lacks capacity to take them.

4. The jurisdiction of the High Court

10.113 The High Court of Justice has jurisdiction (1) to award damages and/or grant an injunction (including, in appropriate cases, a *quia timet* injunction) in respect of anything tortious;[284] (2) to make a declaration; and (3) to exercise the rediscovered *parens patriae* jurisdiction in relation to adults. Prior to the MCA, most applications to the court in relation to medical treatment were for declaratory relief to determine questions relating to the lawfulness or unlawfulness of the proposed treatment or care, including the proposed medical treatment

[276] MCA, s 15(1)(c). See *Re P (adult patient) (medical treatment)* [2008] EWHC 1403 (Fam), [2009] 1 FCR 567 and *In the matter of MN (Adult)* [2015] EWCA Civ 411 (on appeal at the time of writing).

[277] MCA, ss 16(1)(a), (b), 17(1)(d), (e).

[278] MCA, s 16(2)(b). In relation to the appointment of such a deputy, see further MCA, s 19. For the restrictions on the deputy, see MCA, s 20. In particular, a deputy may not refuse consent to the carrying out or continuation of life-sustaining treatment: MCA, s 20(5).

[279] See *Re P (adult patient) (medical treatment)* [2008] EWHC 1403 (Fam), [2009] 1 FCR 567.

[280] *In the matter of MN (Adult)* [2015] EWCA Civ 411, [89].

[281] ibid, [89].

[282] ibid, [90]. See also *In re M (Incapacitated Adult) (Best Interests Declaration: Potential Contempt)* [2015] Fam 239, [50].

[283] One exception is where the person is an informal patient under the age of 18 who lacks capacity to consent to electro-convulsive therapy: MCA, s 28(1A).

[284] For an example see *Re C (Adult: Refusal of Treatment)* [1994] 1 WLR 290.

or care, of an adult who lacked capacity.[285] Such proceedings had to be commenced and heard in the Family Division.[286]

(i) The declaratory jurisdiction

(a) Scope The declaratory jurisdiction extends to the lawfulness or unlawfulness of all aspects of the 'treatment' and 'care' of an adult who lacks capacity which are not covered by the statutory jurisdiction of the Mental Capacity Act 2005. This is not confined to medical treatment, but includes whatever is 'necessary to preserve . . . life, health or well-being' or 'carried out in order either to save . . . lives, or to ensure improvement or prevent deterioration in . . . physical or mental health'.[287] **10.114**

(b) Effect of a declaration[288] It is axiomatic that a declaration is, as its name indicates, merely declaratory in its effect. A declaration changes nothing; it cannot make lawful that which, absent a declaration, would be unlawful. Conversely, that which is declared lawful by declaration is equally lawful absent a declaration.[289] **10.115**

(c) Precedents The forms of declaration granted in a variety of cases can be found in the reports.[290] Where declaratory relief is being sought against a public authority (for instance, an NHS hospital) care must be taken to ensure that the declaration does not encroach on the authority's public law functions or, if it does, that it can be justified on public law grounds and applying appropriate principles of substantive public law.[291] **10.116**

(ii) The inherent parens patriae jurisdiction

(a) Pre-MCA 2005 Gradual developments in the practical exercise of the declaratory jurisdiction led to the appreciation prior to the 2005 Act that for most practical purposes, the declaratory jurisdiction in relation to adults who lack capacity was the same as that of a court exercising the *parens patriae* jurisdiction.[292] Since then there has been continuing development of what is now overtly recognized as a *parens patriae* jurisdiction in relation **10.117**

---

[285] *Re F (Mental Patient: Sterilisation)* [1990] 2 AC 1; *Airedale NHS Trust v Bland* [1993] AC 789. For detailed surveys of the scope of the declaratory jurisdiction see *A v A Health Authority, Re J (A Child), R (on the application of S) v Secretary of State for the Home Department* [2002] EWHC 18 (Fam/Admin), [2002] Fam 213, esp at [35]–[46]; *Re S (Adult Patient) (Inherent Jurisdiction: Family Life)* [2002] EWHC 2278 (Fam), [2003] 1 FLR 292, [3]–[60]. For a detailed consideration of the declaratory jurisdiction prior to the MCA, see Chapter 10, paras 10.123–10.140 of the second edition of this work.

[286] President's Direction (Declaratory Proceedings Concerning Incapacitated Adults: Medical and Welfare Decisions) [2002] 1 FLR 177; *A v A Health Authority, Re J (A Child), R (on the application of S) v Secretary of State for the Home Department* [2002] EWHC 18 (Fam/Admin), [2002] Fam 213, esp at [71]–[81].

[287] *Re F (Mental Patient: Sterilisation)* [1990] 2 AC 1, 52 *per* Lord Bridge of Harwich, 55 *per* Lord Brandon of Oakbrook.

[288] See generally *St George's Healthcare NHS Trust v S, R v Collins, ex p S* [1999] Fam 26, 58–62.

[289] *Airedale NHS Trust v Bland* [1993] AC 789, esp 888–90 *per* Lord Mustill; *A v A Health Authority, Re J (A Child), R (on the application of S) v Secretary of State for the Home Department* [2002] EWHC 18 (Fam/Admin), [2002] Fam 213, [120].

[290] See, eg, *Re F (Mental Patient: Sterilisation)* [1990] 2 AC 1; *Airedale NHS Trust v Bland* [1993] AC 789; *Tameside and Glossop Acute Services Trust v CH* [1996] 1 FLR 762; *Re R (Adult: Medical Treatment)* [1996] 2 FLR 99; *Re Y (Mental Patient: Bone Marrow Donation)* [1997] Fam 110; *Re G (adult who lacks capacity: withdrawal of treatment)* (2001) 65 BMLR 6.

[291] *A v A Health Authority, Re J (A Child), R (on the application of S) v Secretary of State for the Home Department* [2002] EWHC 18 (Fam/Admin), [2002] Fam 213, [123]–[126].

[292] *Re SA (Vulnerable Adult with Capacity: Marriage)* [2005] EWHC 2942 (Fam), [2006] 1 FLR 867 citing *A v A Health Authority, Re J (A Child), R (on the application of S) v Secretary of State for the Home Department* [2002] EWHC 18 (Fam/Admin), [2002] Fam 213, [45].

to vulnerable adults which is for all practical purposes indistinguishable from the court's *parens patriae* jurisdiction in relation to children.[293]

> It is now clear . . . that the court exercises what is, in substance and reality, a jurisdiction in relation to incompetent adults which is for all practical purposes indistinguishable from its well-established parens patriae or wardship jurisdictions in relation to children. The court exercises a 'protective jurisdiction' in relation to vulnerable adults just as it does in relation to wards of court.[294]
>
> There is little, if any, practical difference between the types of orders that can be made in exercise of the two jurisdictions. The main difference is that the court cannot make an adult a ward of court. So the particular status which wardship automatically confers on a child who is a ward of court—for example, the fact that a ward of court cannot marry or leave the jurisdiction without the consent of the court—has no parallel in the case of the adult jurisdiction. In the absence of express orders, the attributes or incidents of wardship do not attach to an adult. But this apart, the court's powers to make orders under the inherent jurisdiction in relation to adults would seem to be as wide as its powers when exercising its inherent parens patriae jurisdiction in relation to children. Just as there are, in theory, no limits to the court's powers when exercising the wardship jurisdiction I suspect that there are, in theory, few if any limits to the court's powers when exercising the inherent jurisdiction in relation to adults.[295]

The court has power to make a very wide range of declaratory, injunctive, and other orders.[296]

10.118 **(b) Post-MCA 2005** Although there was some initial uncertainty, it now seems clear that the inherent jurisdiction has survived the coming into force of the MCA in relation to (a) vulnerable adults who have mental capacity, and (b) vulnerable adults who lack mental capacity where the Court of Protection lacks the jurisdiction to make an order under

---

293 This development can be traced through the following cases, which are listed in chronological sequence: *Re S (Adult Patient) (Inherent Jurisdiction: Family Life)* [2002] EWHC 2278 (Fam), [2003] 1 FLR 292; *Re S (Adult's Lack of Capacity: Carer and Residence)* [2003] EWHC 1909 (Fam), [2003] 2 FLR 1235; *Re A Local Authority (Inquiry: Restraint on Publication)* [2003] EWHC 2746 (Fam), [2004] Fam 96; *Re G (An Adult) (Mental Capacity: Court's Jurisdiction)* [2004] EWHC 2222 (Fam), [2004] All ER (D) 33 (Oct); *Re Z (Local Authority: Duty)* [2004] EWHC 2817 (Fam), [2005] 1 WLR 959; *Re SK (An Adult) (Forced Marriage: Appropriate Relief)* [2004] EWHC 3202 (Fam), [2006] 1 WLR 81; *E (by her litigation friend the Official Solicitor) v Channel Four, News International Ltd and St Helens Borough Council* [2005] EWHC 1144 (Fam), [2005] 2 FLR 913; *M v B, A and S (by the Official Solicitor)* [2005] EWHC 1681, [2006] 1 FLR 117; *Re SA (Vulnerable Adult with Capacity: Marriage)* [2005] EWHC 2942 (Fam), [2006] 1 FLR 867; *X City Council v MB, NB and MAB (by his litigation friend the Official Solicitor)* [2006] EWHC 168 (Fam), [2006] 2 FLR 968; *Re S (Vulnerable Adult)* [2007] 2 FLR 1095; *B Borough Council v S (by the Official Solicitor)* [2006] EWHC 2584 (Fam), [2007] 1 FLR 1600; *Re ST (Adult Patient)* [2006] EWHC 3458 (Fam), [2008] 1 FLR 111; *St Helens Borough Council v PE* [2006] EWHC 3460 (Fam), [2007] 2 FLR 1115; *Re PS (Incapacitated or Vulnerable Adult)* [2007] EWHC 623 (Fam), [2007] 2 FLR 1083; *Re MM; Local Authority X v MM (by the Official Solicitor) and KM* [2007] EWHC 2003 (Fam), [2009] 1 FLR 443; *Surrey Council v MB and others* [2007] EWHC 3085 (Fam); *A Local Authority v E* [2007] EWHC 2396 (Fam), [2008] 1 FLR 978; *LLBC v TG, JG and KR* [2007] EWHC 2640 (Fam), [2009] 1 FLR 414; *Re MM (An Adult)* [2007] EWHC 2689 (Fam), [2009] 1 FLR 487; *City of Westminster v IC (by his friend the Official Solicitor) and KC and NN* [2008] EWCA Civ 198, [2008] 2 FLR 267; *Re SK; A London Borough Council v KS and LU* [2008] EWHC 636 (Fam), [2008] 2 FLR 720; *Re GJ, NJ and BJ (Incapacitated Adults)* [2008] EWHC 1097 (Fam), [2008] 2 FLR 1295; *A Primary Care Trust and P v AH and a Local Authority* [2008] EWHC 1403 (Fam), [2008] 2 FLR 1196.

294 *Re SA (Vulnerable Adult with Capacity: Marriage)* [2005] EWHC 2942 (Fam), [2006] 1 FLR 867, [37] *per* Munby J.

295 ibid, [84].

296 ibid, [85]–[95]; *St Helens Borough Council v PE* [2006] EWHC 3460 (Fam), [2007] 2 FLR 1115, [16]–[19]; *Re PS (Incapacitated or Vulnerable Adult)* [2007] EWHC 623 (Fam), [2007] 2 FLR 1083, [16], [31].

the MCA.[297] Acting as part of the common law's 'great safety net', it fills the gaps of law where necessary, providing a facilitative, as opposed to dictatorial, approach aimed at re-establishing an individual's autonomy to make decision, thereby enhancing their Article 8 rights.[298]

E. Best Interests

As with assessing capacity, so too with determining best interests; neither should be attempted without first identifying the decision in question. The exact nature of the best interests decision is one which the Supreme Court is considering at the time of writing. But as the law presently stands, the decision will depend upon the options that are currently, and reasonably foreseeably, available.[299] **10.119**

Whether a proposed treatment satisfies the *Bolam* test for negligence[300] is a necessary, but not a sufficient, condition of treatment. The treatment must additionally be in an incapacitated patient's best interests.[301] The best interests principle in MCA, s 1(5) is an essential aspect to all decision-making on behalf of those lacking capacity, not just to the Court of Protection. The statute builds upon the common law and offers further guidance. Owing to the non-exhaustive nature of the checklist of best interests factors in MCA, s 4, general assistance is readily available from the common law. **10.120**

1. Best interests or substituted judgment?

The propriety of an invasive medical procedure proposed to be performed on a child or an adult who lacks capacity is judged by reference to the patient's best interests, not by the application of a substituted judgment. The test of best interests is objective, assessed with respect to the particular patient and from their point of view. **10.121**

Some jurisdictions in the US have applied a substituted judgment test[302] to questions relating to the patient's body.[303] However, English law, in common with a number of other jurisdictions in the US which also apply a best interests test,[304] has rejected the substituted judgment test, so far as this concerns questions relating to the patient's physical and bodily welfare, in favour of a best interests test.[305] **10.122**

The test of best interests is objective.[306] One does not, therefore, attempt to find a speculative answer to the question, 'What would this patient have chosen if s/he had the capacity **10.123**

---

[297] *A Local Authority v DL & Ors* [2012] EWCA Civ 253, [2012] COPLR 504. See also *XCC v AA & Anor* [2012] EWHC 2183 (COP), [2012] COPLR 730.

[298] *A Local Authority v DL &* Ors, n 297, at [67].

[299] *In the matter of MN* [2015] EWCA Civ 411, [80] (on appeal at the time of writing).

[300] *Bolam v Friern Hospital Management Committee* [1957] 1 WLR 582. For a long time, the relationship between *Bolam* and best interests was obscure: See the first edition of this book, Chapter 4, paras 4.133–4.136.

[301] *Re A (Male Sterilisation)* [2000] 1 FLR 549; *Re S (Adult Patient: Sterilisation)* [2001] Fam 15.

[302] Explicitly by adopting the English *property* cases and, in particular, *Ex p Whitbread* (1816) 2 Mer 99.

[303] *Strunk v Strunk* (1969) 445 SW 2d 145, 147–48 (Ky); *Hart v Brown* (1972) 289 A 2d 386, 387 (Conn); *Re Quinlan* (1976) 355 A 2d 647, 663, 664, 666 (NJ); *Superintendent of Belchertown State School v Saikewicz* (1977) 370 NE 2d 417, 431 (Mass); *Re Doe* (1992) 583 NE 2d 1263, 1267, 1273 (Mass).

[304] *Re Richardson* (1973) 284 So 2d 185, 187 (La); *Lausier v Pescinski* (1975) 226 NW 2d 180, 181–82, 184 (Wis); *Little v Little* (1979) 576 SW 2d 493, 497–98 (Tex); *Curran v Bosze* (1990) 566 NE 2d 1319, 1326, 1331 (Ill).

[305] *Airedale NHS Trust v Bland* [1993] AC 789, 871–72, 894–95.

[306] See Explanatory Notes to the Mental Capacity Act 2005, para 28.

to make a choice?'[307] But although the test is objective one is necessarily concerned with the question, 'What is in the best interests of *this* particular patient?' One therefore looks at the case, not from the point of view of a hypothetical person, but from the best-informed point of view of the patient in question.[308] In this sense, the standard is subjective.[309]

10.124 As was made clear in the Law Commission's *Report on Mental Incapacity*,[310] upon which the Mental Capacity Act is based, the test contains 'a strong element of 'substituted judgment'. Although still a 'best interests' rather than a 'substituted judgment' test, it is one 'which accepts that the preferences of the person concerned are an important component in deciding where his best interests lie. To take a simple example, it cannot be in the best interests to give the patient food which he does not like when other equally nutritious food is available'.[311]

10.125 This objective approach from the patient's vantage point can be contrasted with that of the United Nations Convention on the Rights of Persons with Disabilities which, in Article 12, has shifted international thinking towards a 'supported' decision-making model.[312] At least according to the UN CRPD Committee, this "will and preference' paradigm must replace the 'best interests' paradigm to ensure that persons with disabilities enjoy the right to legal capacity on an equal basis with others'.[313]

2. In whose best interests?

10.126 The best interests test governs all aspects of a child's 'upbringing'[314] and all aspects of an adult who lacks capacity's care and treatment. This is not confined to medical treatment. It includes whatever is 'necessary to preserve . . . life, health or well-being' or 'carried out in order either to save . . . lives, or to ensure improvement or prevent deterioration in . . . physical or mental health'.[315] In addition to appropriate medical, dental and surgical treatment, treatment includes, in the case of someone who is permanently or semi-permanently incapable, care, as part of daily life, of a basic, simple or humdrum nature, such as dressing, undressing, feeding, looking after, and putting to bed, and including the actions of the relative, friend, or neighbour who comes in to look after the patient.[316]

10.127 Treatment and care extend to 'action . . . such as a reasonable person would in all the circumstances take, acting in the best interests of the assisted person'[317] and thus to everything

[307] *Re T (Adult: Refusal of Treatment)* [1993] Fam 95, 103.

[308] *Re J (A Minor) (Wardship: Medical Treatment)* [1991] Fam 33, 44, 46–47, 55.

[309] *Re E (A Minor) (Wardship: Medical Treatment)* [1993] 1 FLR 386, 392.

[310] 1995, Law Com No 231 at para 3.25.

[311] *Aintree University Hospitals NHS Foundation Trust v James and others* [2014] AC 591, at [24].

[312] See P Bartlett, 'The United Nations Convention on the Rights of Persons with Disabilities and Mental Health Law' (2012) 75(5) Modern Law Review 752; P Fennell and U Khaliq, 'Conflicting or Complimentary Obligations? The UN Disability Rights Convention, the European Convention on Human Rights and English Law' [2011] EHRLR 662; P Gooding, 'Supported Decision-Making: A Rights-Based Disability Concept and its Implications for Mental Health Law' (2012) Psychiatry, Psychology and Law 1.

[313] UN Committee on the Rights of Persons with Disabilities (2014), 'General Comment No 1, Article 12: Equal Recognition before the Law, CRPD/C/GC/1', at [21]. It should be noted, however, that such General Comments, although of considerable importance, are not legally binding on State Parties.

[314] cf the Children Act 1989, s 1(1)(a); *Re Z (A Minor) (Identification: Restrictions on Publication)* [1997] Fam 1, 28–29.

[315] *Re F (Mental Patient: Sterilisation)* [1990] 2 AC 1, 52 *per* Lord Bridge of Harwich, 55 *per* Lord Brandon of Oakbrook.

[316] ibid, 72, 76 *per* Lord Goff of Chieveley.

[317] ibid, 75 *per* Lord Goff of Chieveley.

that conduces to the welfare and happiness of the patient, including companionship and the patient's domestic and social environment.[318]

An invasive medical procedure can be in a patient's best interests even though: **10.128**

(1) it is not therapeutically required;[319]
(2) it is not, of itself, of any medical benefit at all to the patient;
(3) it is attended with some medical risks or disadvantages;[320] and
(4) the primary purpose of the procedure is to further the interests of a third party.[321]

Factors other than the narrowly therapeutic or medical can therefore properly be taken into account in assessing whether or not an invasive medical procedure is in the patient's best interests.[322] Such a procedure may nonetheless be in the patient's best interests if (i) it is not seriously detrimental to the patient[323] and (ii) it is compensated by sufficient countervailing benefits or advantages to the patient, in other words if, having regard to all relevant factors, the balance of benefit and detriment overall is such that it is in the patient's best interests to subject him to the procedure. **10.129**

Thus a non-therapeutic sterilization may be justified as being for the benefit of an incapacitated child or adult's psychological health and well-being.[324] Likewise the donation of bone marrow to a sibling may be justified as serving the emotional and psychological welfare of an adult who lacks capacity.[325] So also a blood test for purely forensic purposes may be in a child's best interests, if the potential personal or financial benefits to the child of ascertaining his/her paternity outweigh any possible medical disadvantages,[326] and notwithstanding that its primary purpose is to further the interests of another, for example, **10.130**

---

[318] *Re C (Mental Patient: Contact)* [1993] 1 FLR 940; *A v A Health Authority, Re J (A Child), R (on the application of S) v Secretary of State for the Home Department* [2002] EWHC 18 (Fam/Admin), [2002] Fam 213, [39]. For a property and affairs illustration, see *David Ross v A* [2015] EWCOP 46 (P's well-being was influenced by the well-being of the family as a whole, justifying the payment out of P's estate of the brother's school fees).

[319] *Re B (A Minor) (Wardship: Sterilisation)* [1988] AC 199 (non-therapeutic sterilization of minor for contraceptive purposes); *Re F (Mental Patient: Sterilisation)* [1990] 2 AC 1 (non-therapeutic sterilization of adult who lacks capacity for contraceptive purposes).

[320] Thus ritual or other non-therapeutic circumcision of minor male children (eg, the routine non-therapeutic circumcision of neonates for reasons which are social or conventional rather than religious) is permissible even though the preponderance of current medical opinion, at least in the UK, is that circumcision is normally of no medical benefit and devoid of rational justification, and notwithstanding that circumcision is not without risks and that the procedure can lead to complications, serious injury, and even death: see *Gray v LaFleche* [1950] 1 DLR 337; *Iqbal v Irfan* [1994] CLY 1642; *R v Alam* The Independent, 9 July 1994, 15 November 1994; *Re J (Specific Issue Orders: Muslim Upbringing and Circumcision)* [1999] 2 FLR 678 (affd *Re J (Specific Issue Orders: Child's Religious Upbringing and Circumcision)* [2000] 1 FLR 571) where some of the medical literature is discussed.

[321] So the blood testing of a child in order to resolve an issue of adultery in a divorce suit: *B(BR) v B(J)* [1968] P 466. Or the donation of bone marrow in order to save a sibling's life: *Re Y (Mental Patient: Bone Marrow Donation)* [1997] Fam 110.

[322] See *Re T (A Minor) (Wardship: Medical Treatment)* [1997] 1 WLR 242.

[323] cf *S v McC, W v W* [1972] AC 24, 44 *per* Lord Reid (referring to blood testing): 'unless . . . clearly . . . against the interests of the child'.

[324] *Re B (A Minor) (Wardship: Sterilisation)* [1988] AC 199; *Re F (Mental Patient: Sterilisation)* [1990] 2 AC 1.

[325] *Re Y (Mental Patient: Bone Marrow Donation)* [1997] Fam 110.

[326] *Re L (An Infant)* [1968] P 119, 141, 158, 160, 161; *B(BR) v B(J)* [1968] P 466, 473, 477; *S v McC (orse S) and M (DS intervener)* [1970] 1 WLR 672, 675–76, 679, 681–82. These cases were decided before *S v McC, W v W* [1972] AC 24, and thus at a time when it was generally held that a child could be blood tested for forensic purposes only if it was in the child's best interests that it should be. Orders were refused, as not being in the child's best interests, in *M(DK) v M(SV) and G (M intervening)* [1969] 1 WLR 843; *B v B and E* [1969] 1 WLR 1800; *W v W* [1970] 1 WLR 682.

the blood testing of a child in order to resolve an issue of adultery in a divorce suit.[327] Similarly, the ritual circumcision of male children, on the basis that, on balance, the perceived religious advantages outweigh both the absence of medical benefit and the risk of occasionally serious complications.[328] The same can be said of a 'sex-change' or 'gender reassignment' operation.[329]

10.131 There are other applications of the same principle: payment away of trust monies to a third party may be for the 'benefit' of a beneficiary if it enables him thereby to discharge what s/he recognizes to be his/her moral obligation to the third party.[330] Public exploitation in the media of a child's medical problems may be in the best interests of the child if it enables her father, by sale of the story to a newspaper, to raise money needed to pay for the child's further, possibly life-saving, medical treatment.[331]

10.132 Determining best interests involves a welfare appraisal in the widest sense, taking into account, where appropriate, a wide range of ethical, social, moral, emotional, and welfare considerations.[332] Best interests are not limited to best medical interests.[333] They encompass medical, emotional, and all other welfare issues.[334] In deciding what is best for the incapacitated patient the judge must have regard to the patient's welfare as the paramount consideration. That embraces issues far wider than the medical. Indeed, it would be undesirable and probably impossible to set bounds to what is relevant to a welfare determination.[335] As the Supreme Court held in *Aintree*:[336]

> The most that can be said, therefore, is that in considering the best interests of this particular patient at this particular time, decision-makers must look at his welfare in the widest sense, not just medical but social and psychological; they must consider the nature of the medical treatment in question, what it involves and its prospects of success; they must consider what the outcome of that treatment for the patient is likely to be; they must try and put themselves in the place of the individual patient and ask what his attitude to the treatment is or would be likely to be; and they must consult others who are looking after him or interested in his welfare, in particular for their view of what his attitude would be.

---

[327] *B(BR) v B(J)* [1968] P 466.

[328] *R v Brown* [1994] AC 212, 231; *Re J (Specific Issue Orders: Muslim Upbringing and Circumcision)* [1999] 2 FLR 678 (affd *Re J (Specific Issue Orders: Child's Religious Upbringing and Circumcision)* [2000] 1 FLR 571); *Re S (Change of Names: Cultural Factors)* [2001] 2 FLR 1005; *Re S (Specific Issue Order: Religion: Circumcision)* [2004] EWHC 1282 (Fam), [2005] 1 FLR 236. See further *Secretary, Department of Health and Community Services v JWB and SMB* (1992) 175 CLR 218, 297 *per* Deane J (parents 'plainly' able to consent to 'male circumcision for perceived hygienic—or even religious—reasons'). However, it has been argued that the reluctance of Anglo-American law to conceptualize male circumcision as a criminal action has precluded it being regarded in the same light as female genital cutting: see M Fox and M Thomson, 'Older minors and Circumcision: Questioning the Limits of Religious Actions' (2008) 9 Medical Law International 283.

[329] So held by the Family Court of Australia: *Re A* (1993) 16 Fam LR 715.

[330] *Re Clore's Settlement Trusts* [1966] 1 WLR 955.

[331] *R v Cambridge District HA, ex p B (No 2)* [1996] 1 FLR 375. Contrast *Re Z (A Minor) (Identification: Restrictions on Publication)* [1997] Fam 1 (not in best interests of child of prominent public figure to appear in television documentary showing her receiving treatment).

[332] *A v A Health Authority, Re J (A Child), R (on the application of S) v Secretary of State for the Home Department* [2002] EWHC 18 (Fam/Admin), [2002] Fam 213, [43].

[333] *Re MB (Medical Treatment)* [1997] 2 FLR 426, 439 *per* Butler-Sloss LJ.

[334] *Re A (Male Sterilisation)* [2000] 1 FLR 549, 555 *per* Dame Elizabeth Butler-Sloss P.

[335] *Re S (Adult Patient: Sterilisation)* [2001] Fam 15, 30 *per* Thorpe LJ.

[336] *Aintree University Hospitals NHS Foundation Trust v James* [2013] UKSC 67, [2014] 1 AC 591, [2013] COPLR 492 at [39].

3. The statutory checklist

10.133 For those aged 16 and over who lack the capacity to consent, MCA, s 4 provides a non-exhaustive checklist of factors to consider. It does not define 'best interests'; this would be a challenge, given the wide range of acts, decisions, and circumstances covered by the Act. Rather, it sets out a minimum number of relevant considerations to be taken into account *in the process* of formulating the decision. All must be considered, even if some are then found to be irrelevant. And relevant factors not on the checklist must also be included:

S4(1) In determining for the purposes of this Act what is in a person's best interests, the person making the determination must not make it merely on the basis of–
(a) the person's age or appearance, or
(b) a condition of his, or an aspect of his behaviour, which might lead others to make unjustified assumptions about what might be in his best interests.

(2) The person making the determination must consider all the relevant circumstances and, in particular, take the following steps.

(3) He must consider–
(a) whether it is likely that the person will at some time have capacity in relation to the matter in question, and
(b) if it appears likely that he will, when that is likely to be.

(4) He must, so far as reasonably practicable, permit and encourage the person to participate, or to improve his ability to participate, as fully as possible in any act done for him and any decision affecting him.

(5) Where the determination relates to life-sustaining treatment he must not, in considering whether the treatment is in the best interests of the person concerned, be motivated by a desire to bring about his death.

(6) He must consider, so far as is reasonably ascertainable–
(a) the person's past and present wishes and feelings (and, in particular, any relevant written statement made by him when he had capacity),
(b) the beliefs and values that would be likely to influence his decision if he had capacity, and
(c) the other factors that he would be likely to consider if he were able to do so.

(7) He must take into account, if it is practicable and appropriate to consult them, the views of–
(a) anyone named by the person as someone to be consulted on the matter in question or on matters of that kind,
(b) anyone engaged in caring for the person or interested in his welfare,
(c) any donee of a lasting power of attorney granted by the person, and
(d) any deputy appointed for the person by the court, as to what would be in the person's best interests and, in particular, as to the matters mentioned in subsection (6).

(8) The duties imposed by subsections (1) to (7) also apply in relation to the exercise of any powers which–
(a) are exercisable under a lasting power of attorney, or
(b) are exercisable by a person under this Act where he reasonably believes that another person lacks capacity.

(9) In the case of an act done, or a decision made, by a person other than the court, there is sufficient compliance with this section if (having complied with the requirements of subsections (1) to (7)) he reasonably believes that what he does or decides is in the best interests of the person concerned.

(10) 'Life-sustaining treatment' means treatment which in the view of a person providing health care for the person concerned is necessary to sustain life.

(11) 'Relevant circumstances' are those–
(a) of which the person making the determination is aware, and
(b) which it would be reasonable to regard as relevant.

10.134 When deciding what is in the best interests of someone lacking capacity, s 1(6) of the MCA requires that regard must be had to whether there are less restrictive options:

> Before the act is done, or the decision is made, regard must be had to whether the purpose for which it is needed can be as effectively achieved in a way that is less restrictive of the person's rights and freedom of action.

10.135 Thus, the fact that a person lacks capacity to make a decision does not necessarily mean that a decision in their best interests falls to be made. Other options may be available that would be less restrictive than making a decision on their behalf. Or if a decision is required, the fact of incapacity is not an 'off-switch' for the person's rights and freedom of action.[337] Those rights and that freedom to act remain very much alive during the process through which the best interests decision is developed.

4. Factors in the best interests equation

(i) The person's vantage point

10.136 Evaluating best interests will often be assisted by the preparation of a balance sheet listing the weighted advantages and disadvantages for the patient of what is proposed.[338] When making a decision with someone who lacks capacity, it is important to orientate the best interests process from the right perspective: that is, the patient's. According to the Supreme Court:[339]

> The purpose of the best interests test is to consider matters from the patient's point of view. That is not to say that his wishes must prevail, any more than those of a fully capable patient must prevail. We cannot always have what we want. Nor will it always be possible to ascertain what an incapable patient's wishes are. Even if it is possible to determine what his views were in the past, they might well have changed in the light of the stresses and strains of his current predicament . . . But insofar as it is possible to ascertain the patient's wishes and feelings, his beliefs and values or the things which were important to him, it is those which should be taken into account because they are a component in making the choice which is right for him as an individual human being.

10.137 A clear illustration of creating the best interests decision from the perspective of the person is *Wye Valley NHS Trust v Mr B.*[340] Here a 73-year-old man was refusing antibiotics for his putrefying foot. He lacked capacity to decide to refuse the proposed amputation, without which he would succumb to a fatal infection within days. But his views were clear:

> I don't want an operation.
>
> I'm not afraid of dying, I know where I'm going. The angels have told me I am going to heaven. I have no regrets. It would be a better life than this.
>
> I don't want to go into a nursing home, [my partner] died there.

---

[337] *Wye Valley NHS Trust v Mr B* [2015] EWCOP 60, [2015] COPLR 843, [11].

[338] *Re A (Male Sterilisation)* [2000] 1 FLR 549, 560 *per* Thorpe LJ. For an interesting example of such a balance sheet (in the context of a proposed abortion), see *Re SS (Medical Treatment: Late Termination)* [2002] 1 FLR 445, [30]. The balance sheet approach of Thorpe LJ did not include the person's past and present views as a relevant factor. Although the Mental Capacity Act 2005 adopts a similar balance sheet approach (see *Dorset County Council v EH* [2009] EWHC 784 (Fam)), s 4 now *requires* these factors to be taken into account.

[339] *Aintree*, n 336, at [45]. See also *Re M (Best Interests: Deprivation of Liberty)* [2013] EWHC 3456 (COP), [2014] COPLR 35 at [38] *per* Peter Jackson J: 'the court must surely have regard to the person's own assessment of her quality of life'; *Westminster City Council v Sykes* [2014] EWCOP B9; *Newcastle-upon-Tyne Foundation Trust v LM* [2014] EWHC 454 (COP); *Sheffield Teaching Hospitals NHS Foundation Trust v TH and another* [2014] EWCOP 4 at [55].

[340] [2015] EWCOP 60.

> I don't want my leg tampered with. I know the seriousness, I just want them to continue what they're doing.
>
> I don't want it. I'm not afraid of death. I don't want interference. Even if I'm going to die, I don't want the operation.

10.138 Peter Jackson J observed: 'To state the obvious, the wishes and feelings, beliefs, and values of people with a mental disability are as important to them as they are to anyone else, and may even be more important. It would therefore be wrong in principle to apply any automatic discount to their point of view.'

(ii) The person's wishes and feelings, beliefs, and values

10.139 At common law, regard was had to the ascertainable wishes and feelings of the patient, considered in the light of his/her age and understanding.[341] Even if the patient lacked the capacity to decide for him/herself, and had never made an effective advance directive, the personality of the particular patient and the expressed views, wishes and feelings of the patient, whether past or present, were relevant and had to be taken into account as a very material factor in ascertaining his/her best interests.[342]

10.140 The same is true when applying the checklist of MCA, s 4. Indeed, 'it is important to be rigorous and scrupulous' in seeking out the incapacitated person's views.[343] But there is no hierarchy to the statutory checklist. The weighting to be afforded to the individual factors is not prescribed by statute. It has been held that the weight to be attached to the person's wishes, feelings, values, and beliefs will be case and fact specific, dependent upon the degree of incapacity, the strength and consistency of the views expressed, the possible impact on P of not giving effect to them, the extent to which they are rational, sensible, responsible, and pragmatically capable of sensible implementation, and 'crucially' the extent to which they can properly be accommodated within the court's overall best interests assessment.[344] In that regard, 'wishes' and 'best interests' 'should never be conflated, they are entirely separate matters which may ultimately weigh on different sides of the balance sheet'.[345]

10.141 In *Wye Valley* it was held that 'there is no theoretical limit to the weight or lack of weight that should be given to the person's wishes and feelings, beliefs and values'. The 'proper weight' would depend upon the circumstances.[346] Indeed, sometimes one or more factors may be of magnetic importance in influencing or even determining the outcome.[347] Moreover:

> Delusions arising from mental illness may rightly lead to a person's wishes and feelings being given less weight where that is appropriate. However, this cannot be the automatic consequence of the wishes and feelings having a religious component. Mr B's religious sentiments are extremely important to him, even though he does not follow an established

---

341 See further, particularly in relation to children, paras 10.78–10.79.

342 *Re W (A Minor) (Medical Treatment: Court's Jurisdiction)* [1993] Fam 64, 88; *Re T (Adult: Refusal of Treatment)* [1993] Fam 95, 103; *Airedale NHS Trust v Bland* [1993] AC 789, 872; *Hospital Authority v C* [2003] Lloyd's Rep Med 130, [30]–[33].

343 *Sheffield Teaching Hospitals NHS Foundation Trust v TH and another* [2014] EWCOP 4 at [56].

344 *Re M (vulnerable adult) (testamentary capacity)* [2009] EWHC 2525 (Fam), [2011] 1 WLR 344 at [35]; see also *Re P* [2009] 2 All ER 1198. For an illustration of P's views sitting uncomfortably within the court's overall assessment, see *RB v Brighton and Hove City Council* [2014] EWCA Civ 561, [2014] COPLR 629, at [81] where an alcoholic's wish to live independently and resume drinking did not accord with the court's view that his best interests were served by remaining deprived of liberty in a care home.

345 *Sheffield Teaching Hospitals NHS Foundation Trust v TH and another* [2014] EWCOP 4 at [56].

346 For a discussion of the weight of wishes, see A Ruck Keene and C Auckland, 'More Presumptions Please, Wishes, Feelings and Best Interests Decision-Making' (2015) Elder Law Journal 293.

347 See, eg, *Re M (vulnerable adult) (testamentary capacity)* [2009] EWHC 2525 (Fam), [2011] 1 WLR 344 at [32] and [52].

religion. Although the point does not arise for determination in this case, I approach matters on the basis that his Article 9 right to freedom of thought and religion is no less engaged than it would be for any other devout person.[348]

On balance, an enforced amputation was held not to be in Mr B's best interests.

(ii) Personal factors

10.142 An evaluation of best interests involves a welfare appraisal in the widest sense, taking into account, where appropriate, a wide range of ethical, social, moral, emotional, and welfare considerations.[349] In assessing an individual's best interests, relevant factors may, in an appropriate case, include: his/her psychological health, well-being, amenity and quality of life;[350] his/her ethical, moral, spiritual, and religious welfare;[351] his/her relationship with his/her parents or other carers;[352] his/her financial interests;[353] ties of affection;[354] and moral obligations, whether or not they are yet the object of public or social pressure, but only if s/he him/herself recognizes and feels the moral obligation.[355] As Eldergill DJ held in *Re Jones*.[356]

> [I]n the ordinary case the Mental Capacity Act is not a vehicle for imposing on people views, wishes and feelings that clearly are contrary to those they held before losing capacity, do not hold now and would not hold if they regained capacity, however right those views may be, and however unworthy P's views are according to most people's standards. The onset of mental incapacity is not an opportunity for moral correction.

(iii) The views of others

10.143 The best interests in question are those of the adult who lacks capacity, not those of a third party or of society. Benefits accruing to the third party are material only insofar as they further the interests of the patient. But the word 'interests' in the best interests test does not confine the court to considering the self-interest of the patient.[357] Rather, the checklist in MCA, s 4 expressly provides for consultation with carers and others interested in the person's welfare as to what would be in that person's best interests and, in particular, what that person's own views would have been. Such consultation is also part of the procedural safeguards of Article 8 ECHR which require, inter alia, 'involvement of the carers in the decision-making process, seen as a whole, to a degree sufficient to provide them with the requisite protection of the families' interests'.[358]

10.144 But the Act arguably goes further than that. For one consequence of MCA, ss 4(2) and (6)(c) is to enable the decision-maker to take into account the views of others per se. *All* of

---

[348] *Wye Valley*, n 340, at [14].

[349] *A v A Health Authority, Re J (A Child), R (on the application of S) v Secretary of State for the Home Department* [2002] EWHC 18 (Fam/Admin), [2002] Fam 213, [43].

[350] *Re B (A Minor) (Wardship: Sterilisation)* [1988] AC 199, 202–03, 206, 208–10; *Re F (Mental Patient: Sterilisation)* [1990] 2 AC 1, 52, 76 ('life, health or well-being'), 55 (steps taken to 'ensure improvement or prevent deterioration in . . . physical or mental health').

[351] *Re K (Minors) (Children: Care and Control)* [1977] Fam 179, 187, 191.

[352] *Re T (A Minor) (Wardship: Medical Treatment)* [1997] 1 WLR 242.

[353] *R v Cambridge District HA, ex p B (No 2)* [1996] 1 FLR 375.

[354] *Re McGrath* [1893] 1 Ch 143, 148 *per* Lindley LJ quoted in para 10.95.

[355] *Re Clore's Settlement Trusts* [1966] 1 WLR 955, 959–60; *Re CL* [1969] 1 Ch 587, 599–600.

[356] [2014] EWCOP 59 (statutory will).

[357] *Re G(TJ)* [2010] EWHC 3005 (COP), [2010] All ER (D) 218 (Nov). See S Hamilton, 'Best interests in statutory will and gift applications: Practical implications of *Re G (TJ)*' [2011] Elder Law Journal 331.

[358] *G v E and others* [2010] EWHC 621, at [88] *per* Baker J.

the relevant circumstances must be considered, which may include the views of others.[359] And 'the other factors that he would be likely to consider if he were able to do so' might, depending on the person lacking capacity, include the effect the decision will have on those around him or her.

Thus best interests might include 'altruistic sentiments and concern for others'.[360] For example, in *Ahsan v University Hospital Leicester NHS Trust* the family of a patient in a permanent vegetative state wanted her to be cared for at home in a Muslim environment. The judge relied on the beliefs and values of the family 'so far as can be properly attributed to her, those which she herself would have held had she continued to have the capacity to do so'.[361] Where the patient's rights conflict with a third party's rights, the conflict is to be resolved by reference to the patient's best interests; they are determinative.[362] **10.145**

The interests of a third party can legitimately be taken into account in assessing all the relevant facts, choices, and other circumstances which have to be taken into account in determining whether or not what is proposed is in the best interests of the patient.[363] But an invasive medical procedure which is not, of itself, of any medical benefit to the patient cannot be justified as being in his/her best interests merely because it confers a benefit (even a very substantial benefit indeed) on a third party; what has to be shown is some countervailing benefit or advantage *to the patient him/herself*.[364] **10.146**

There is no legal (as opposed to moral, ethical or civic) obligation to provide medical assistance to another[365] or to subject oneself to a medical procedure[366] for the benefit of another.[367] This is merely the application in the medical context of the general principle that, in the absence of special relationship or assumption of responsibility, the law imposes no obligation to go to the assistance of someone in peril, however immediate and mortal the peril to the person in danger and however trivial or even non-existent the possible risk to the rescuer.[368] **10.147**

Thus an invasive medical procedure cannot be justified merely because it will lighten the burden on those who care for the patient.[369] So also the giving or withholding of medical **10.148**

[359] See *London Borough of Redbridge v G and others* [2014] EWCOP 1361, at [27]; B Clough, 'What About Us? A Case for Legal Recognition of Interdependence in Informal Care Relationships' (2014) 36(2) Journal of Social Welfare and Family Law 129.

[360] Law Commission, *Report on Mental Incapacity* (Law Com No 231, 1995) para 3.31; see also *Aintree*, n 336, at [24].

[361] [2006] EWHC 2624 (QB), at [56].

[362] *London Borough of Redbridge v G and others* [2014] EWCOP 1361, at [25].

[363] *Re Z (A Minor) (Identification: Restrictions on Publication)* [1997] Fam 1, 28.

[364] As Dame Elizabeth Butler-Sloss P said in *Re A (Male Sterilisation)* [2000] 1 FLR 549, 555: 'The concept of best interests relates to the mentally incapacitated person.'

[365] *Re F (Mental Patient: Sterilisation)* [1990] 2 AC 1, 77; *Capital & Counties PLC v Hampshire County Council* [1997] QB 1004, 1035. See N Allen, 'The Right to Life in a Suicidal State' (2013) 36 International Journal of Law and Psychiatry 350, which analyses the 'ugly Samaritan' approach of common law systems.

[366] This is so even in the case of a mother with a viable foetus: see further paras 10.29–10.31.

[367] *Re T (Adult: Refusal of Treatment)* [1993] Fam 95, 99, 102 and, in the US, *McFall v Shrimp* (1978) 10 Pa D&C 3d 90 (see I Kennedy and A Grubb, *Medical Law: Text with Materials* (3rd edn, Butterworths 2000), 1776–79; *St George's Healthcare NHS Trust v S, R v Collins, ex p S* [1999] Fam 26, 47); Re AC (1990) 573 A 2d 1235, 1243–44, *Re Baby Boy Doe* (1994) 632 NE 2d 326, 333–34.

[368] *Donoghue v Stevenson* [1932] AC 562, 580; *Home Office v Dorset Yacht Co Ltd* [1970] AC 1004, 1027, 1034, 1042, 1060; *The Ogopogo* [1969] 1 LlR 374, 378, [1970] 1 LlR 257, 261, 265, further appeal [1971] 2 LlR 410.

[369] *Re B (A Minor) (Wardship: Sterilisation)* [1988] AC 199, 204, 212; *Secretary, Department of Health and Community Services v JWB and SMB* (1992) 175 CLR 218, 295–96, 297, 300–01. On the other hand, the easing of that burden may indirectly further the interests of the patient: ibid, 300–301. See further *Re T (A Minor) (Wardship: Medical Treatment)* [1997] 1 WLR 242. The welfare of even an insentient patient may be adversely affected if his/her carers are subjected to pressure or put under emotional or other stress,

treatment is not to be determined by reference to the medical[370] or financial[371] implications of the decision for other members of the patient's family. On the other hand, the court can be astute to find that a procedure which is in the medical interests of a third party, though not necessarily of the patient, is nevertheless in the patient's best interests inasmuch as it furthers the patient's emotional and psychological welfare.[372]

10.149 In relation to the conflicting interests of child siblings, where both the patient and the third party are children (for example, where what is in question is a transplant between minor siblings) it is still the interests of the patient (donor), and not of the third party (donee), which are paramount, for it is the patient (donor) whose interests are directly involved.[373]

(iv) Public interests

10.150 In the same way, the general public interest and the moral and civic obligations of the patient can legitimately be taken into account in determining whether or not what is proposed is in the best interests of the patient.[374] But it is still necessary to show some benefit or advantage *to the patient* from what is proposed.[375]

10.151 The performance of a moral, social, or civic obligation can be of benefit to the patient, and his/her moral, social, or civic obligations are therefore relevant, only if the patient is able to recognize, and in fact him/herself recognizes and wishes to give effect to, the obligation.[376]

10.152 Thus the sterilization of a child or mentally incapacitated adult cannot be justified for eugenic purposes[377] or with a view to population control. So also the public interest in publicizing a unique and specialized form of treatment with a view to bringing strength and encouragement to other patients and encouraging the use of the treatment in the UK did not justify the child of a prominent public figure appearing in a television documentary

eg, as a result of massive media intrusion: *Re C (A Minor) (Wardship: Medical Treatment) (No 2)* [1990] Fam 39, 47–48, 51–52, 54–55.

370 *Re Y (Mental Patient: Bone Marrow Donation)* [1997] Fam 110 (whether adult who lacks capacity should donate bone marrow to be determined by reference to the best interests of the donor and not of the donee, notwithstanding that the donee would die if the operation did not take place).

371 *Airedale NHS Trust v Bland* [1993] AC 789, 879–80 (not proper to alter the time of death of patient in permanent vegetative state in order to manipulate third party property rights). See further para 10.181.

372 See the analyses in *Tameside and Glossop Acute Services Trust v CH* [1996] 1 FLR 762 (Caesarean section); *Re Y (Mental Patient: Bone Marrow Donation)* [1997] Fam 110 (bone marrow donation); *Norfolk and Norwich Healthcare (NHS) Trust v W* [1996] 2 FLR 613; *Rochdale Healthcare (NHS) Trust v C* [1997] 1 FCR 274; *A Metropolitan Borough Council v AB* [1997] 1 FLR 767; *Re L (Patient: Non-Consensual Treatment)* [1997] 2 FLR 837; *Re MB (Medical Treatment)* [1997] 2 FLR 258 (Caesarean section) but note the qualification in para 10.29.

373 *Birmingham City Council v H (A Minor)* [1994] 2 AC 212; *F v Leeds City Council* [1994] 2 FLR 60; *Re F (Contact: Child in Care)* [1995] 1 FLR 510; *Re T and E (Proceedings: Conflicting Interests)* [1995] 1 FLR 581. In the case of conjoined twins, where the interests of both siblings are, in the nature of things, directly involved, their interests have to be balanced: *Re A (Children) (Conjoined Twins: Surgical Separation)* [2001] Fam 147, 190–92, 196–97, 242–43. See also Cherkassky, L, 'The Wrong Harvest: The Law on Savior Siblings' (2015) 29(1) International Journal of Law, Policy and the Family 36.

374 *S v McC, W v W* [1972] AC 24, 44; *Re R (A Minor) (Wardship: Criminal Proceedings)* [1991] Fam 56, 65; *Re Z (A Minor) (Identification: Restrictions on Publication)* [1997] Fam 1, 28. See also MCA, s 4(6).

375 Note the emphatic rejection in English law of the doctrine that the public interests of the state can ever prevail over the patient with capacity's right of self-determination: *Re T (Adult: Refusal of Treatment)* [1993] Fam 95, 102; *Secretary of State for the Home Department v Robb* [1995] Fam 127. Similarly, with regard to the position of those lacking capacity to engage in research, see MCA, s 33(3) which provides: 'The interests of the person must be assumed to outweigh those of science and society.'

376 *Re Clore's Settlement Trusts* [1966] 1 WLR 955; and see para 10.131.

377 *Re B (A Minor) (Wardship: Sterilisation)* [1988] AC 199, 202, 204, 207, 212; *Re M (A Minor) (Wardship: Sterilisation)* [1988] 2 FLR 497; *Secretary, Department of Health and Community Services v JWB and SMB* (1992) 175 CLR 218, 295.

showing her receiving the treatment, bearing in mind the adverse effects upon her of the publicity which the broadcast would generate.[378]

5. Independent Mental Capacity Advocates

The MCA introduced a new scheme that makes available, and in certain circumstances demands, the instruction of an Independent Mental Capacity Advocate ('IMCA').[379] They provide an extra safeguard in those circumstances where an incapacitated person is particularly vulnerable by virtue of the absence of an informal support network around them. There have been wide disparities in the instruction of IMCAs, provoking concerns as to whether the statutory duty to refer has been adequately understood.[380] The House of Lords Select Committee recommended[381] their wider use, and recent years appear to show an upward trend.[382] 10.153

The IMCA is not the best interests decision-maker. Rather, their role is to work with and support the person lacking capacity ('P') and to represent their views to the best interests decision-maker. Thus, ascertaining P's past and present wishes, feelings, values, and beliefs are a central component of the role. To fulfil their functions, IMCAs have the right to obtain and evaluate information by interviewing P in private and examining relevant health and social care records and documents at all reasonable times. They can obtain the views of P's professionals and paid workers; identify alternative courses of action; seek a second medical opinion for serious medical treatment; and can prepare a report which the best interests decision-maker must consider. 10.154

The circumstances in which an IMCA *must* be instructed are governed by MCA ss 37–39. In short, these are where P is unbefriended and (1) the NHS is proposing to provide serious medical treatment, or (2) the NHS or a local authority is proposing to arrange a significant change in P's accommodation. 'Serious medical treatment' means treatment which involves providing, withdrawing, or withholding treatment in circumstances (a) where a single treatment is being proposed, there is a fine balance between its benefits to the patient and the burdens and risks it is likely to entail for him; or (b) where there is a choice of treatments, a decision as to which one to use is finely balanced; or (c) where what is proposed would be likely to involve serious consequences for the patient.[383] 10.155

With regards to accommodation, if the NHS proposes to make arrangements for the provision of accommodation in a hospital for the unbefriended incapacitated patient for a continuous period of twenty-eight days or more, an IMCA must be instructed. Similarly, if the NHS or a local authority propose to provide accommodation in a care home for an unbefriended incapacitated patient for eight weeks or more, an IMCA must be instructed. If an IMCA was not instructed because either (a) the relevant body was satisfied at the time that the accommodation would be for a lesser period, or (b) the arrangements had to be made as 10.156

[378] *Re Z (A Minor) (Identification: Restrictions on Publication)* [1997] Fam 1, 10, 11, 12, 30–31, 32, 33.
[379] MCA, ss 35–41.
[380] Department of Health, *The Fifth Year of the Independent Mental Capacity Advocacy (IMCA) Service—2011–2012* (2013) 6.
[381] House of Lords Select Committee on the Mental Capacity Act, *Report of Session 2013–14: Mental Capacity Act 2005: Post-legislative Scrutiny* (2014, HL 139) para 176.
[382] Department of Health, *The Seventh year of the Independent Mental Capacity Advocacy (IMCA) Service* (2015) 10.
[383] Mental Capacity Act 2005 (Independent Mental Capacity Advocates) (General) Regulations 2006, SI 2006/1832, reg 4; Mental Capacity Act 2005 (Independent Mental Capacity Advocates) (Wales) Regulations 2007, SI 2007/852, reg 4. In 2013–14, there were just 2,132 recorded referrals for serious medical treatment, only 6 per cent of which were made by hospital doctors: Department of Health, *The Seventh year of the Independent Mental Capacity Advocacy (IMCA) Service* (2015) 21.

a matter of urgency, but subsequently has reason to believe that the relevant period *from the date of admission* is likely to be exceeded, it must instruct an IMCA.

10.157 An IMCA *may* be instructed where the NHS body or local authority propose to take, or to arrange to be taken, protective measures in relation to P following receipt of an allegation or evidence that P is being, or has been, abused or neglected by another person if satisfied that it would be of particular benefit to P to be so represented. Similarly, an IMCA *may* be instructed for care reviews.[384] The position with regard to the deprivation of liberty safeguards is considered below.

F. Particular Cases

10.158 Reported cases cover a wide range of different forms of care and treatment. Thus, in addition to cases dealing with the blood testing of children[385] and with the general care of the child or adult with disability (including disputes as to where and with whom an adult who lacks capacity should live and have contact),[386] there are reported cases dealing with: the therapeutic[387] and non-therapeutic sterilization[388] of children and adults who lack capacity; the abortion of children[389] and adults who lack capacity;[390] complications during the labour of children[391] and adult women who lack capacity;[392] the psychiatric assessment and treatment

[384] Mental Capacity Act 2005 (Independent Mental Capacity Advocates) (Expansion of Role) Regulations 2006, SI 2006/2883, regs 4–5.

[385] *S v McC, W v W* [1972] AC 24; *Re F (A Minor) (Blood Tests: Parental Rights)* [1993] Fam 314; *Re L (A Minor) (Blood Tests)* [1996] 2 FCR 649; *Re H (A Minor) (Blood Tests: Parental Rights)* [1997] Fam 89; *Re T (Paternity: Ordering Blood Tests)* [2001] 2 FLR 1190; *Re H and A (Paternity: Blood Tests)* [2002] EWCA Civ 383, [2002] 1 FLR 1145. For the impact in this context of Art 8 of the ECHR see *Re T (Paternity: Ordering Blood Tests)* [2001] 2 FLR 1190, 1197–99.

[386] *Re C (Mental Patient: Contact)* [1993] 1 FLR 940; *Cambridgeshire County Council v R (An Adult)* [1995] 1 FLR 50; *Re S (Hospital Patient: Court's Jurisdiction)* [1995] Fam 26, appeal dismissed [1996] Fam 1, subsequent substantive proceedings *Re S (Hospital Patient: Foreign Curator)* [1996] Fam 23; *Re V (Declaration against Parents)* [1995] 2 FLR 1003; *Re D-R (Adult: Contact)* [1999] 1 FLR 1161; *Re F (Mental Health Act: Guardianship)* [2000] 1 FLR 192; *R v R (Interim Declaration: Adult's Residence)* [2000] 1 FLR 451; *Re F (Adult: Court's Jurisdiction)* [2001] Fam 38; *A v A Health Authority, Re J (A Child), R (on the application of S) v Secretary of State for the Home Department* [2002] EWHC 18 (Fam/Admin), [2002] Fam 213; *Re S (Adult Patient) (Inherent Jurisdiction: Family Life)* [2002] EWHC 2278 (Fam), [2003] 1 FLR 292.

[387] *Re E (A Minor) (Medical Treatment)* [1991] 2 FLR 585; *Re GF (Medical Treatment)* [1992] 1 FLR 293; *Re ZM and OS (Sterilisation: Patient's Best Interests)* [2000] 1 FLR 523.

[388] *Re D (A Minor) (Wardship: Sterilisation)* [1976] Fam 185; *Re B (A Minor) (Wardship: Sterilisation)* [1988] AC 199; *T v T* [1988] Fam 52; *Re M (A Minor) (Wardship: Sterilisation)* [1988] 2 FLR 497; *Re P (A Minor) (Wardship: Sterilisation)* [1989] 1 FLR 182; *Re F (Mental Patient: Sterilisation)* [1990] 2 AC 1; *Re NK* 28 February 1990, (Ewbank J), 4 April 1990, (Scott Baker J); *Re W (Mental patient) (Sterilisation)* [1993] 1 FLR 381; *Re HG (Specific Issue Order: Sterilisation)* [1993] 1 FLR 587; *Re LC (Medical Treatment: Sterilisation)* [1997] 2 FLR 258; *Re S (Medical Treatment: Adult Sterilisation)* [1998] 1 FLR 944; *Re X (Adult Sterilisation)* [1998] 2 FLR 1124; *Re ZM and OS (Sterilisation: Patient's Best Interests)* [2000] 1 FLR 523; *Re A (Male Sterilisation)* [2000] 1 FLR 549 (proposed sterilization of male who lacks capacity); *Re S (Adult Patient: Sterilisation)* [2001] Fam 15 (reversing *Re S (Sterilisation: Patient's Best Interests)* [2000] 1 FLR 465).

[389] *Re P (A Minor)* [1986] 1 FLR 272; *Re B (Wardship: Abortion)* [1991] 2 FLR 426.

[390] *Re SG (Adult Mental Patient: Abortion)* [1991] 2 FLR 329; *Re SS (Medical Treatment: Late Termination)* [2002] 1 FLR 445; *D v An NHS Trust (Medical Treatment: Consent: Termination)* [2003] EWHC 2793 (Fam), [2004] 1 FLR 1110.

[391] *A Metropolitan Borough Council v AB* [1997] 1 FLR 767.

[392] *Re T (Adult: Refusal of Treatment)* [1993] Fam 95; *Tameside and Glossop Acute Services Trust v CH* [1996] 1 FLR 762; *Norfolk and Norwich Healthcare (NHS) Trust v W* [1996] 2 FLR 613; *Rochdale Healthcare (NHS) Trust v C* [1997] 1 FCR 274; *Re L (Patient: Non-Consensual Treatment)* [1997] 2 FLR 837; *Re MB (Medical Treatment)* [1997] 2 FLR 426; *St George's Healthcare NHS Trust v S, R v Collins, ex p S* [1999] Fam 26; *Bolton Hospitals NHS Trust v O* [2002] EWHC 2871 (Fam), [2003] 1 FLR 824; *Hospital Authority v*

of children[393] and adults who lack capacity;[394] the force-feeding of children[395] and adults who lack capacity[396] for the treatment of anorexia nervosa or other psychiatric illnesses; the administration of blood transfusions to child[397] and adult who lacks capacity[398] Jehovah's Witnesses; immunization of children;[399] immunoglobin treatment for primary immunodeficiency;[400] experimental drug treatment for variant Creutzfeldt–Jakob disease;[401] a heart transplant;[402] the separation of conjoined twins;[403] the donation of bone marrow by an incompetent adult;[404] the withholding of life-saving treatment (surgery,[405] a liver transplant,[406] kidney transplant,[407] haemodialysis (kidney dialysis[408]), artificial ventilation,[409] cardio-pulmonary resuscitation,[410] and antibiotics[411]) from a child,[412] those with disability[413]

C [2003] Lloyd's Rep Med 130 (Caesarean section of pregnant woman in coma). For the procedure to be adopted in such cases see *Re MB*, above, 439, 445; *St George's Healthcare NHS Trust v S, R v Collins, ex p S* [1999] Fam 26, 63–65. For the proper approach to the issue of capacity in such cases, now see the Mental Capacity Act 2005.

[393] *Re R (A Minor) (Wardship: Consent to Treatment)* [1992] Fam 11; *Re K, W and H (Minors) (Medical Treatment)* [1993] 1 FLR 854; *South Glamorgan County Council v W and B* [1993] 1 FLR 574; *R v Kirklees Metropolitan Borough Council, ex p C* [1992] 2 FLR 117, [1993] 2 FLR 187; *A Metropolitan Borough Council v AB* [1997] 1 FLR 767.

[394] *Re H (Mental Patient: Diagnosis)* [1993] 1 FLR 28.

[395] *Re W (A Minor) (Medical Treatment: Court's Jurisdiction)* [1993] Fam 64; *Re C (Detention: Medical Treatment)* [1997] 2 FLR 180.

[396] *Riverside Mental Health NHS Trust v Fox* [1994] 1 FLR 614; *Re KB (Adult) (Mental Patient: Medical Treatment)* (1994) 19 BMLR 144; *B v Croydon HA* [1995] Fam 133, affg [1995] 1 FCR 332; *Re VS (Adult: Mental Disorder)* 17 August 1995, (Douglas Brown J), [1995] Med L Rev 292; *R v Collins and Ashworth HA, ex p Brady* [2000] Lloyd's Rep Med 355 (force-feeding of prisoner detained in Special Hospital). For a case involving the force-feeding of an adult with capacity prisoner see *Secretary of State for the Home Department v Robb* [1995] Fam 127; *Re P (Medical Treatment: Best Interests)* [2003] EWHC 2327 (Fam), [2004] 2 FLR 1117.

[397] *Re E (A Minor) (Wardship: Medical Treatment)* [1993] 1 FLR 386; *Re S (A Minor) (Medical Treatment)* [1993] 1 FLR 376; *Re O (A Minor) (Medical Treatment)* [1993] 2 FLR 149; *Re R (A Minor) (Blood Transfusion)* [1993] 2 FLR 757; *Re S (A Minor) (Consent to Medical Treatment)* [1994] 2 FLR 1065; *Re L (Medical Treatment: Gillick Competency)* [1998] 2 FLR 810.

[398] *Re T (Adult: Refusal of Treatment)* [1993] Fam 95. See also *HE v A Hospital NHS Trust* [2003] EWHC 1017 (Fam), [2003] 2 FLR 408 (blood transfusion to adult lacking capacity, former Jehovah's Witness).

[399] *Re C (Welfare of Child: Immunisation)* [2003] EWCA Civ 1148; [2003] 2 FLR 1095 (MMR and other vaccinations and immunizations).

[400] *Re MM (Medical Treatment)* [2000] 1 FLR 224.

[401] *Simms v Simms, A v A (A Child)* [2002] EWHC 2734 (Fam), [2003] Fam 83.

[402] *Re M (Medical Treatment: Consent)* [1999] 2 FLR 1097.

[403] *Re A (Children) (Conjoined Twins: Surgical Separation)* [2001] Fam 147. For the further proceedings, see *Re A (Conjoined Twins: Medical Treatment) (No 2)* [2001] 1 FLR 267.

[404] *Re Y (Mental Patient: Bone Marrow Donation)* [1997] Fam 110.

[405] *Re B (A Minor) (Wardship: Medical Treatment)* [1981] 1 WLR 1421.

[406] *Re T (A Minor) (Wardship: Medical Treatment)* [1997] 1 WLR 242.

[407] *A Hospital NHS Trust v S* [2003] EWHC 365 (Fam), [2003] Lloyd's Rep Med 137.

[408] *Re D (Medical Treatment: Mentally Disabled Patient)* [1998] 2 FLR 22.

[409] *Re J (A Minor) (Wardship: Medical Treatment)* [1991] Fam 33; *Re J (A Minor) (Child in Care: Medical Treatment)* [1993] Fam 15; Re C (A Baby) [1996] 2 FLR 43; *Re C (Medical Treatment)* [1998] 1 FLR 384; *Royal Wolverhampton Hospitals NHS Trust v B* [2000] 1 FLR 953; *A NHS Trust v D* [2000] 2 FLR 677.

[410] *Re R (Adult: Medical Treatment)* [1996] 2 FLR 99. See also the joint guidance of the BMA, Resuscitation Council (UK) and the Royal College of Nursing, 'Decisions relating to Cardiopulmonary Resuscitation' (June 2016).

[411] *Re R (Adult: Medical Treatment)* [1996] 2 FLR 99.

[412] *Re T (A Minor) (Wardship: Medical Treatment)* [1997] 1 WLR 242. The Royal College of Paediatrics and Child Health has published guidance: 'Making Decisions to limit treatment in life-limiting and life-threatening conditions in children: a framework for practice' (2015).

[413] *Re B (A Minor) (Wardship: Medical Treatment)* [1981] 1 WLR 1421, reversing (1982) 3 FLR 117; *R v Arthur* (1981) 12 BMLR 1; *Re J (A Minor) (Wardship: Medical Treatment)* [1991] Fam 33; *Re J (A Minor) (Child in Care: Medical Treatment)* [1993] Fam 15; *Re C (A Baby)* [1996] 2 FLR 43; *Re R (Adult: Medical*

or the dying,[414] and the withdrawal of artificial nutrition and hydration from patients in a (formerly called persistent or permanent) vegetative state[415] or minimally conscious state.[416] There are also reported cases dealing with the circumstances in which detention for the purposes of treatment[417] or the application of restraint or the use of force[418] is permissible in relation to a non-compliant child[419] or incapacitated adult[420] patient either under the

Treatment) [1996] 2 FLR 99; *Re D (Medical Treatment: Mentally Disabled Patient)* [1998] 2 FLR 22; *A Hospital NHS Trust v S* [2003] EWHC 365 (Fam), [2003] Lloyd's Rep Med 137.

414 *R v Bodkin Adams* 8–9 April 1957, (Devlin J), [1957] Crim LR 365; *Re C (A Minor) (Wardship: Medical Treatment)* [1990] Fam 26; *R v Cox* (1992) 12 BMLR 38; *Re C (Medical Treatment)* [1998] 1 FLR 384; *Royal Wolverhampton Hospitals NHS Trust v B* [2000] 1 FLR 953; *A NHS Trust v D* [2000] 2 FLR 677. The BMA has published guidance: 'End of Life Decisions: Views of the BMA' (Sept 2009).

415 *Airedale NHS Trust v Bland* [1993] AC 789; *Frenchay Healthcare NHS Trust v S* [1994] 1 WLR 601; *Re G (Persistent Vegetative State)* [1995] 2 FCR 46; *Swindon and Marlborough NHS Trust v S* The Guardian, 10 December 1994, [1995] Med L Rev 84; *Re C (Adult Patient: Restriction of Publicity after Death)* [1996] 2 FLR 251; *NHS Trust A v M, NHS Trust B v H* [2001] Fam 348; *NHS Trust A v H* [2001] 2 FLR 501; *Re G (adult who lacks capacity: withdrawal of treatment)* (2001) 65 BMLR 6.

416 See further paras 10.202-10.210.

417 *Re R (A Minor) (Wardship: Consent to Treatment)* [1992] Fam 11; *Re W (A Minor) (Medical Treatment: Court's Jurisdiction)* [1993] Fam 64; *South Glamorgan County Council v W and B* [1993] 1 FLR 574; *Re C (Detention: Medical Treatment)* [1997] 2 FLR 180; *Re PS (Incapacitated or Vulnerable Adult)* [2007] EWHC 623 (Fam), [2007] 2 FLR 1083; *Re GJ, NJ and BJ (Incapacitated Adults)* [2008] EWHC 1097 (Fam), [2008] 2 FLR 1295; *Re P (adult patient) (medical treatment)* [2008] EWHC 1403 (Fam), [2009] 1 FCR 567. For the inter-relationship between the court's inherent power to order the detention of a child for the purposes of treatment and its limited power to make a secure accommodation order under the Children Act 1989, s 25, see *Re CB (A Minor) (Wardship: Local Authority)* [1981] 1 WLR 379, 387; *Re SW (A Minor) (Wardship: Jurisdiction)* [1986] 1 FLR 24; *South Glamorgan County Council v W and B* [1993] 1 FLR 574; *A Metropolitan Borough Council v AB* [1997] 1 FLR 767; *Re C (Detention: Medical Treatment)* [1997] 2 FLR 180. For the power of a parent, or a local authority having parental responsibility, to authorize the admission of a child to a secure unit or as a voluntary patient under the Mental Health Act 1983 see *Re K, W and H (Minors) (Medical Treatment)* [1993] 1 FLR 854 (parent—secure unit); *R v Kirklees Metropolitan Borough Council, ex p C* [1992] 2 FLR 117, [1993] 2 FLR 187 (local authority— voluntary patient), and, for the explanation of the underlying principle, *R v Rahman* (1985) 81 Cr App R 349, 353, 354; *R v Deputy Governor of Parkhurst Prison, ex p Hague* [1992] 1 AC 58, 162; *Re M (A Minor) (Secure Accommodation Order)* [1995] Fam 108, 117. For the power to detain a mentally disordered patient without recourse to the powers in the Mental Health Act 1983 see *R v Bournewood Community and Mental Health NHS Trust, ex p L* [1999] 1 AC 458. For the older cases dealing with the common law power to restrain and detain, where appropriate for the purposes of treatment, a lunatic who is a danger either to himself or to others, see *Brookshaw v Hopkins* (1772) Lofft 240; *Anderdon v Burrows* (1830) 4 Car & P 210; *Re Shuttleworth* (1846) 9 QB 651; *Re Greenwood* (1855) 24 LJQB 148; *Fletcher v Fletcher* (1859) 1 El & El 420; *Scott v Wakem* (1862) 3 F & F 328; *Symm v Fraser* (1863) 3 F & F 859; *Townley v Rushforth* (1964) 62 LGR 95; *B v Forsey* [1988] SC(HL) 28, 38–39, 44–45, 52, 56, 59–60, 63, 68.

418 *Riverside Mental Health NHS Trust v Fox* [1994] 1 FLR 614; *Re KB (Adult) (Mental Patient: Medical Treatment)* (1994) 19 BMLR 144; *Re S (A Minor) (Consent to Medical Treatment)* [1994] 2 FLR 1065; *B v Croydon HA* [1995] Fam 133; *Re VS (Adult: Mental Disorder)* 17 August 1995, (Douglas Brown J), [1995] Med L Rev 292; *Tameside and Glossop Acute Services Trust v CH* [1996] 1 FLR 762; *Norfolk and Norwich Healthcare (NHS) Trust v W* [1996] 2 FLR 613; *Rochdale Healthcare (NHS) Trust v C* [1997] 1 FCR 274; *A Metropolitan Borough Council v AB* [1997] 1 FLR 767; *Re L (Patient: Non-Consensual Treatment)* [1997] 2 FLR 837; *Re C (Detention: Medical Treatment)* [1997] 2 FLR 180; *Re MB (Medical Treatment)* [1997] 2 FLR 426, 439; *Re D (Medical Treatment: Mentally Disabled Patient)* [1998] 2 FLR 22; *Re PS (Incapacitated or Vulnerable Adult)* [2007] EWHC 623 (Fam), [2007] 2 FLR 1083; *Re GJ, NJ and BJ (Incapacitated Adults)* [2008] EWHC 1097 (Fam), [2008] 2 FLR 1295; *Re P (adult patient) (medical treatment)* [2008] EWHC 1403 (Fam), [2009] 1 FCR 567.

419 *Re R (A Minor) (Wardship: Consent to Treatment)* [1992] Fam 11; *Re W (A Minor) (Medical Treatment: Court's Jurisdiction)* [1993] Fam 64; *South Glamorgan County Council v W and B* [1993] 1 FLR 574; *Re S (A Minor) (Consent to Medical Treatment)* [1994] 2 FLR 1065; *A Metropolitan Borough Council v AB* [1997] 1 FLR 767; *Re C (Detention: Medical Treatment)* [1997] 2 FLR 180.

420 *Riverside Mental Health NHS Trust v Fox* [1994] 1 FLR 614; *Re KB (Adult) (Mental Patient: Medical Treatment)* (1994) 19 BMLR 144; *B v Croydon HA* [1995] Fam 133; *Re VS (Adult: Mental Disorder)* 17

Mental Health Act 1983, s 63,[421] or at common law,[422] or under the Mental Capacity Act 2005.[423] Other procedures are considered mainly in the academic literature: male circumcision;[424] female genital mutilation;[425] 'sex-change' or 'gender reassignment' operations;[426] ear piercing and cosmetic surgery;[427] ritual incision of the face;[428] and tattooing.[429]

Six topics require more detailed consideration: sterilization; abortion; blood testing; organ and tissue donation; issues of life and death; and deprivation of liberty. **10.159**

August 1995, (Douglas Brown J), [1995] Med L Rev 292; *Tameside and Glossop Acute Services Trust v CH* [1996] 1 FLR 762; *Norfolk and Norwich Healthcare (NHS) Trust v W* [1996] 2 FLR 613; *Rochdale Healthcare (NHS) Trust v C* [1997] 1 FCR 274; *Re L (Patient: Non-Consensual Treatment)* [1997] 2 FLR 837; *Re MB (Medical Treatment)* [1997] 2 FLR 426,439; *Re D (Medical Treatment: Mentally Disabled Patient)* [1998] 2 FLR 22; *Re PS (Incapacitated or Vulnerable Adult)* [2007] EWHC 623 (Fam), [2007] 2 FLR 1083; *Re GJ, NJ and BJ (Incapacitated Adults)* [2008] EWHC 1097 (Fam), [2008] 2 FLR 1295; *Re P (adult patient) (medical treatment)* [2008] EWHC 1403 (Fam), [2009] 1 FCR 567.

421 *Riverside Mental Health NHS Trust v Fox* [1994] 1 FLR 614; *Re KB (Adult) (Mental Patient: Medical Treatment)* (1994) 19 BMLR 144; *B v Croydon HA* [1995] Fam 133; *Re VS (Adult: Mental Disorder)* 17 August 1995, (Douglas Brown J), [1995] Med L Rev 292; *Tameside and Glossop Acute Services Trust v CH* [1996] 1 FLR 762.

422 *Re R (A Minor) (Wardship: Consent to Treatment)* [1992] Fam 11; *Re W (A Minor) (Medical Treatment: Court's Jurisdiction)* [1993] Fam 64; *South Glamorgan County Council v W and B* [1993] 1 FLR 574; *Re S (A Minor) (Consent to Medical Treatment)* [1994] 2 FLR 1065; *Norfolk and Norwich Healthcare (NHS) Trust v W* [1996] 2 FLR 613; *Rochdale Healthcare (NHS) Trust v C* [1997] 1 FCR 274; *A Metropolitan Borough Council v AB* [1997] 1 FLR 767; *Re L (Patient: Non-Consensual Treatment)* [1997] 2 FLR 837; *Re C (Detention: Medical Treatment)* [1997] 2 FLR 180; *Re MB (Medical Treatment)* [1997] 2 FLR 426, 439; *Re PS (Incapacitated or Vulnerable Adult)* [2007] EWHC 623 (Fam), [2007] 2 FLR 1083; *Re GJ, NJ and BJ (Incapacitated Adults)* [2008] EWHC 1097 (Fam), [2008] 2 FLR 1295. For the court's approach in deciding whether or not to adopt coercive measures, and the safeguards to be applied, see *Re C (Detention: Medical Treatment)* [1997] 2 FLR 180, 196–99 (and see the form of the order at 199–201); *Re MB (Medical Treatment)* [1997] 2 FLR 426, 445; *Re PS (Incapacitated or Vulnerable Adult)* [2007] EWHC 623 (Fam), [2007] 2 FLR 1083; *Re GJ, NJ and BJ (Incapacitated Adults)* [2008] EWHC 1097 (Fam), [2008] 2 FLR 1295; *Re P (adult patient) (medical treatment)* [2008] EWHC 1403 (Fam), [2009] 1 FCR 567. For the problem presented by the patient who lacks capacity that is unwilling to submit to treatment see *Re D (Medical Treatment: Mentally Disabled Patient)* [1998] 2 FLR 22 (49-year-old chronic but fluctuating psychotic suffering from chronic renal failure at near-end stage and high blood pressure requiring haemodialysis for four hours three or four times each week to keep him alive but unable because of his mental condition to understand the need for treatment and strongly objecting to procedure: held lawful in the last resort 'not to impose haemodialysis upon him in circumstances in which in the opinion of the medical practitioners responsible for such treatment it is not reasonably practicable so to do', the judge accepting that in the circumstances dialysis, which requires the cooperation of the patient, could only be performed under general anaesthetic which was neither practicable nor desirable in a patient suffering D's disabilities).

423 *Re P (adult patient) (medical treatment)* [2008] EWHC 1403 (Fam), [2009] 1 FCR 567.

424 *Re J (Specific Issue Orders: Muslim Upbringing and Circumcision)* [1999] 2 FLR 678 (affd *Re J (Specific Issue Orders: Child's Religious Upbringing and Circumcision)* [2000] 1 FLR 571); *Re S (Change of Names: Cultural Factors)* [2001] 2 FLR 1005; *Re S (Specific Issue Order: Religion: Circumcision)* [2004] EWHC 1282 (Fam), [2005] 1 FLR 236. The BMA has published guidance: 'The law and Ethics of Male Circumcision—Guidance for Doctors' (Nov 2007). So too has the GMC: 'Personal Beliefs and Medical Practice' (Apr 2013).

425 See para 10.54. The BMA has published guidance: 'Female Genital Mutilation—Caring for Patients and Safeguarding Children' (July 2011).

426 See paras 10.54 and 10.130.

427 *Re a Teenager* (1988) 94 FLR 181, 212 *per* Cook J ('cosmetic surgery to a child with malformed features'); *Re Jane* (1988) 94 FLR 1, 31; but see *Secretary, Department of Health and Community Services v JWB and SMB* (1990) 14 Fam LR 427, 448 *per* Nicholson CJ ('there may well be some limitations upon the power to consent to cosmetic surgery on a child, depending upon its purpose').

428 *R v Adesanya* The Times, 16 July 1974, 17.

429 See para 10.05.

1. Sterilization

(i) *Therapeutic and non-therapeutic sterilization*

10.160 The House of Lords dismissed the suggested distinction between therapeutic and non-therapeutic sterilizations as being 'meaningless', 'irrelevant', 'not helpful', and giving rise to 'arid semantic debate'.[430] The distinction[431] is, nonetheless, of importance for at least two reasons. In the first place, whereas the prior sanction of the court is not required for a therapeutic sterilization[432] (unless, that is, the patient is a child who happens to be a ward of court already[433]), it is required for any non-therapeutic sterilization of a child or incapacitated adults.[434] Secondly, although there may be circumstances[435] in which the court would authorize the therapeutic sterilization of a child who either has, or may in later years have, the capacity to make her own choice (for example if the removal of a cancerous womb was necessary to save the life of a *Gillick* competent girl who was refusing her consent to a hysterectomy), the court will not subject such a child to a non-therapeutic sterilization.[436]

(ii) *Therapeutic sterilizations*

10.161 In cases where it is appropriate to invoke the court's assistance at all, it will readily authorize, in the case of a child,[437] or declare lawful, in the case of an adult who lacks capacity,[438] an operation (for example, a hysterectomy) required for genuine therapeutic reasons, even if such an operation will inevitably result in the sterilization of the patient. In extreme circumstances, the Court of Protection has authorized the forcible entry into and removal from a patient's home and deprivation of her liberty in hospital for the sterilization procedure under general anaethestic.[439]

(iii) *Non-therapeutic sterilizations*

10.162 The court will never sanction a sterilization for eugenic purposes.[440] In the case of a non-therapeutic sterilization for contraceptive purposes the court adopts a rigorous approach. The court will not sanction the non-therapeutic sterilization of a girl[441] who has, or may in later years have, the capacity to make her own choice whether or not to be sterilized.[442]

---

430 *Re B (A Minor) (Wardship: Sterilisation)* [1988] AC 199, 204, 205, 211.

431 For the most comprehensive judicial consideration of the distinction between therapeutic and non-therapeutic sterilization see *Secretary, Department of Health and Community Services v JWB and SMB* (1992) 175 CLR 218, esp, 243, 250, 253, 269, 274, 296–97, 306. See also *Re E (A Minor) (Medical Treatment)* [1991] 2 FLR 585, 587 where Sir Stephen Brown P referred to the 'clear distinction' between therapeutic and non-therapeutic sterilizations.

432 *Re E (A Minor) (Medical Treatment)* [1991] 2 FLR 585; *Re GF (Medical Treatment)* [1992] 1 FLR 293.

433 *Re D (A Minor) (Wardship: Sterilisation)* [1976] Fam 185, 196.

434 *Re F (Mental Patient: Sterilisation)* [1990] 2 AC 1 and *A Local Authority v K and others* [2013] EWHC 242 (COP), [2013] COPLR 194. See also Court of Protection Rules 2007 Practice Direction 9E.

435 By analogy with *Re R (A Minor) (Wardship: Consent to Treatment)* [1992] Fam 11; *Re W (A Minor) (Medical Treatment: Court's Jurisdiction)* [1993] Fam 64.

436 *Re D (A Minor) (Wardship: Sterilisation)* [1976] Fam 185.

437 *Re E (A Minor) (Medical Treatment)* [1991] 2 FLR 585.

438 *Re GF (Medical Treatment)* [1992] 1 FLR 293; *Re ZM and OS (Sterilisation: Patient's Best Interests)* [2000] 1 FLR 523.

439 *Mental Health Trust* et al *v DD and BC* [2015] EWCOP 4.

440 *Re B (A Minor) (Wardship: Sterilisation)* [1988] AC 199, 202, 204, 207, 212; *Re M (A Minor) (Wardship: Sterilisation)* [1988] 2 FLR 497. For a study of the legal acceptance of non-therapeutic sterilizations, see P Lewis, 'Legal Change on Contraceptive Sterilisation' (2011) 32 Journal of Legal History 295.

441 It is a matter for comment, and a revealing insight into societal attitudes to gender, sexuality and contraception, that the vast majority of the known cases of sterilization relate to girls; the question of male sterilization appears first to have arisen in *Re A (Male Sterilisation)* [2000] 1 FLR 549. Another rare example is *An NHS Trust v DE* [2013] EWHC 2562 (Fam), [2013] 3 FCR 343 (CP).

442 *Re D (A Minor) (Wardship: Sterilisation)* [1976] Fam 185 (11-year-old girl suffering from Sotos syndrome, of dull normal intelligence, whose future prospects were unpredictable, but with sufficient capacity to marry and likely to be able to make her own choice in later years).

Where the child is severely mentally disabled, will never have the capacity to decide about sterilization for herself and is likely to be exposed to the risk of a pregnancy which she would not understand and the consequences of which would be harmful to her, and other contraceptive methods are inappropriate, the court may come to the view that a sterilization so as to prevent future pregnancy is necessary in her own best interests.[443] So in the case of an adult lacking capacity.[444] The Court of Protection has, for example, determined that it was in the best interests of a 37-year-old learning disabled man with a long-term partner to have a vasectomy in accordance with his expressed wishes.[445]

2. Abortion

Abortion is not a procedure which of its nature requires the sanction of the court,[446] unless the patient is a child who is already a ward of court.[447] **10.163**

In cases where it is appropriate to invoke the court's assistance at all, it will authorize or declare lawful (as the case may be) an abortion if satisfied that the requirements of the Abortion Act 1967, as amended by the Human Fertilisation and Embryology Act 1990, are met and that an abortion is in the best interests of the pregnant child[448] or adult who lacks capacity.[449] **10.164**

As has already been seen,[450] neither the foetus, nor its father, nor the husband of its mother, can obtain an injunction to restrain the performance of a lawful abortion to which the mother has consented. It makes no difference that the mother is either a child or an adult who lacks capacity; it is quite clear[451] that the only questions which arise in such a case are, first, whether the requirements of the Abortion Act 1967 are met and, secondly, whether an abortion is in the best interests of the mother. This was reiterated in *In the matter of X (A Child)*[452] where it was stated: **10.165**

> Only the most compelling arguments could possibly justify compelling a mother who wished to carry her child to term to submit to an unwanted termination. It would be unwise to be too prescriptive, for every case must be judged on its own unique facts, but I find it hard to conceive of any case where such a drastic form of order—such an immensely invasive procedure—could be appropriate in the case of a mother who does

[443] *Re B (A Minor) (Wardship: Sterilisation)* [1988] AC 199 (17-year-old girl with mental age of 5 or 6); *Re M (A Minor) (Wardship: Sterilisation)* [1988] 2 FLR 497 (17-year-old girl suffering from Fragile X Syndrome with an emotional and psychological age of 5 or 6); *Re P (A Minor) (Wardship: Sterilisation)* [1989] 1 FLR 182 (17-year-old girl with mental age of 6); *Re HG (Specific Issue Order: Sterilisation)* [1993] 1 FLR 587 (17-year-old severely epileptic girl with mental age of an infant).

[444] *T v T* [1988] Fam 52; *Re F (Mental Patient: Sterilisation)* [1990] 2 AC 1; *Re W (Mental patient) (Sterilisation)* [1993] 1 FLR 381; *Re X (Adult Sterilisation)* [1998] 2 FLR 1124; *Re ZM and OS (Sterilisation: Patient's Best Interests)* [2000] 1 FLR 523. In the following cases the court refused to make an order: *Re LC (Medical Treatment: Sterilisation)* [1997] 2 FLR 258; *Re S (Medical Treatment: Adult Sterilisation)* [1998] 1 FLR 944; *Re S (Adult Patient: Sterilisation)* [2001] Fam 15 (reversing *Re S (Sterilisation: Patient's Best Interests)* [2000] 1 FLR 465). In *Re A (Male Sterilisation)* [2000] 1 FLR 549 the court refused to make an order in the case of a male adult who lacks capacity.

[445] *An NHS Trust v DE and others* [2013] EWHC 2563 (Fam).

[446] *Re SG (Adult Mental Patient: Abortion)* [1991] 2 FLR 329. See also *X (A Child)* [2014] EWHC 1871 (Fam).

[447] *Re G-U (A Minor) (Wardship)* [1984] FLR 811.

[448] *Re P (A Minor)* [1986] 1 FLR 272; *Re B (Wardship: Abortion)* [1991] 2 FLR 426.

[449] *Re SG (Adult Mental Patient: Abortion)* [1991] 2 FLR 329; *Re SS (Medical Treatment: Late Termination)* [2002] 1 FLR 445 (order refused).

[450] See para 10.26. For a more detailed analysis, see Chapters 5 and 11.

[451] *Re P (A Minor)* [1986] 1 FLR 272; *Re SG (Adult Mental Patient: Abortion)* [1991] 2 FLR 329; *Re B (Wardship: Abortion)* [1991] 2 FLR 426.

[452] [2014] EWHC 1871 (Fam), [6].

not want a termination, unless there was powerful evidence that allowing the pregnancy to continue would put the mother's life or long-term health at very grave risk. Conversely, it would be a very strong thing indeed, if the mother wants a termination, to require her to continue with an unwanted pregnancy even though the conditions in section 1 of the 1967 Act are satisfied.

A child or incapacitated adult may, in strict law, lack autonomy. But the court must surely attach very considerable weight indeed to the albeit qualified autonomy of a mother who in relation to a matter as personal, intimate and sensitive as pregnancy is expressing clear wishes and feelings, whichever way, as to whether or not she wants a termination.

3. Blood testing

(i) Consent to blood testing

10.166 Consent to the taking of blood and other bodily samples[453] is regulated by statute.[454] In addition the court can authorize the taking of a blood sample from a child,[455] though not from an adult with capacity who refuses.[456]

(ii) Blood testing of children

10.167 The court can authorize the taking of a blood sample from a child even if it cannot be shown that a blood test will be in his/her best interests, unless it is satisfied that it would be against the child's interests.[457] In the case of an older child, however, the court will not order a blood test against the child's will unless it would 'clearly' be in the child's interests.[458] Similar principles would appear to apply to the giving of consent[459] by the parent or other person having the care and control of the child.[460]

---

[453] See the definition in s 25 of the Family Law Reform Act 1969, as amended by the Family Law Reform Act 1987.

[454] Family Law Reform Act 1969, as amended by the Family Law Reform Act 1987 and the Child Support, Pensions and Social Security Act 2000, s 21(1) (adults with capacity), s 21(2) (persons who have attained the age of 16), s 21(3) (persons under the age of 16), s 21(4) (persons who lack capacity within the meaning of the Mental Capacity Act 2005). The Court of Protection can consent to the taking of a bodily sample on behalf of the person lacking capacity notwithstanding the absence of a specific application with the proceedings putting parentage in issue: *LG v DK* [2011] EWHC 2453, [2012] 1 FCR 476. Section 8 of the 1969 Act does not apply to the taking of a blood sample: *Re W (A Minor) (Medical Treatment: Court's Jurisdiction)* [1993] Fam 64, 92; *Re O (A Minor) (Blood Tests: Constraint), Re J (A Minor)* [2000] Fam 139, 147–48.

[455] Family Law Reform Act 1969, s 21(3)(b), reversing the decision in *Re O (A Minor) (Blood Tests: Constraint), Re J (A Minor)* [2000] Fam 139.

[456] *S v McC, W v W* [1972] AC 24, 43.

[457] *S v McC, W v W* [1972] AC 24; *Re F (A Minor) (Blood Tests: Parental Rights)* [1993] Fam 314, 318; *Re L (A Minor) (Blood Tests)* [1996] 2 FCR 649, 653; *Re H (A Minor) (Blood Tests: Parental Rights)* [1997] Fam 89, 103–04. For the approach adopted by the court see *Re H (A Minor) (Blood Tests: Parental Rights)* [1997] Fam 89, 104–08; *Re T (Paternity: Ordering Blood Tests)* [2001] 2 FLR 1190; *Re H and A (Paternity: Blood Tests)* [2002] EWCA Civ 383, [2002] 1 FLR 1145. For the impact in this context of Art 8 of the ECHR see *Re T (Paternity: Ordering Blood Tests)* [2001] 2 FLR 1190, 1197–99. For the approach adopted by the court in relation to testing for HIV see *Re O (Minors) (Medical Examination)* [1993] 1 FLR 860; and, in particular, *Re C (A Child) (HIV Testing)* [2000] Fam 48 (affd Re C (HIV Test) [1999] 2 FLR 1004). The procedure for the hearing of applications for HIV testing as laid down in *Re HIV Tests* [1994] 2 FLR 116 has been revised: see now President's Direction (HIV Testing of Children) [2003] 1 FLR 1299. A DNA test should be ordered only as a last resort: *Re M (A Child) (Paternity: DNA testing)* [2013] EWCA Civ 1131, [2014] 1 FLR 695.

[458] *Re L (An Infant)* [1968] P 119, 140; *B(BR) v B(J)* [1968] P 466, 469, 473–74, 481; *S v McC, W v W* [1972] AC 24, 45; *Brighton and Hove City Council v PM and others* [2011] EWCA Civ 795, [2012] 1 FLR 351.

[459] Under the Family Law Reform Act 1969, s 21(3). Query whether, in the light of ss 21(1), 21(2), and 21(3), a parent can give a valid consent in the case of a child who has attained the age of 16.

[460] *S v McC, W v W* [1972] AC 24, 44, 45.

4. Organ and tissue donation

The donation of organs, tissues, or body fluids[461] is not illegal, in the sense of being, as such, either prohibited by law or criminal. The removal, retention, and use of human body parts and tissue—'relevant material'—is regulated by the Human Tissue Act 2004.[462] Transplants of organs are, for the most part, governed by the broad rules of the Act and, in particular, the authorization of activities provision in s 1.[463] **10.168**

(i) Non-regenerative organs and regenerative tissue or body fluids

There is an important distinction between the donation of a non-regenerative organ (for example, a kidney) and the donation of regenerative tissue or body fluids (eg bone marrow or blood). The donation of regenerative tissue or body fluids by a child or incapacitated adult (eg bone marrow) can, in appropriate circumstances, satisfy the best interests test. Whether the donation of a non-regenerative organ by a child or incapacitated adult can satisfy the best interests test, and would therefore be sanctioned by the court, is an unresolved and very difficult question. After all, the patient's wishes, feelings, values, and beliefs in the best interests equation 'could include altruistic sentiments and concern for others'.[464] Moreover, best interests 'do not cease at the moment of death. We have an interest in how our bodies are disposed of after death, whether by burial, cremation or donation for medical research'.[465] **10.169**

(ii) Donation by children

The extent to which a child or his/her parent can validly consent to the donation of organs, tissues, or body fluids was obscure. Section 8 of the Family Law Reform Act 1969 does not extend to the donation of organs, or of blood or other bodily substances, for none of these procedures constitutes either treatment or diagnosis.[466] The position has however been clarified by the Human Tissue Act 2004. Child organ donations are only permitted in 'extremely rare circumstances' and only with (a) the consent of the child, if *Gillick* competent,[467] or those with parental responsibility, and (b) prior court approval, and (c) after scrutiny by the Human Tissue Authority panel. Whatever may be the position in strict legal theory, it has been said to be 'inconceivable' that any doctor should proceed with an organ transplant in the case of a child donor without the consent of both the child and its parents.[468] **10.170**

---

461 Useful general discussions are to be found in K M Mason and A McCall Smith, *Law and Medical Ethics* (9th edn, Oxford University Press 2013), ch 17; M Brazier and E Cave, *Medicine, Patients and the Law* (6th edn, Manchester University Press 2016), chs 17–18.

462 'Relevant material' is 'material other than gametes, which consists of or includes human cells', excluding embryos outside the human body, hair, and nails: Human Tissue Act 2004, s 53.

463 A person commits a criminal offence if s/he removes organs without the person's '*appropriate* consent' (s 5) or 'gives or receives a reward for the supply of, or for an offer to supply, any controlled material' or is involved in the commercialization of the supply of live organs (s 32). For further details, see Chapter 19: The Legal Regulation of Human Material.

464 *In the matter of G (TJ)* [2010] EWHC 3005 (COP) at [43].

465 *In re M* [2009] EWHC 2525 (Fam), at [38] *per* Munby J. For arguments in support, see J Coggon et al, 'Best Interests and Potential Organ Donors' (2008 BMJ 2008 Jun 14; 336 (7657): 1346–47; J Coggon, 'Elective Ventilation for Organ Donation: Law, Policy and Public Ethics' (2013) 39 Journal of Medical Ethics 130. In contrast, see A J McGee and B P White, 'Is Providing Elective Ventilation in the Best Interests of Potential Donors?' (2013) 39 Journal of Medical Ethics 135. See also the recommendations of the Law Commission in: *Mentally Incapacitated Adults and Decision-Making, Medical Treatment and Research* (Law Com No 129, 1993) para 6.9, and *Mental Incapacity* (Law Com No 231, 1995) para 6.5.

466 *Re W (A Minor) (Medical Treatment: Court's Jurisdiction)* [1993] Fam 64, 78, 83, 92, 94.

467 See Chapter 9 at paras 9.22-9.30.

468 *Re W*, n 466, 78–79 *per* Lord Donaldson of Lymington MR.

(iii) Need to involve the court

10.171 The prior sanction of the court is required for all organ donations by a child or an adult who lacks capacity. If the proposed intervention is declared to be lawful, the Human Tissue Authority panel will then consider the case.[469]

(iv) Best interests

10.172 Consistently with principle, the determining criterion is the best interests of the donor. The interests of the potential recipient, however compelling, are relevant only insofar as they further the interests of the donor:[470]

> The test to be applied in a case such as this is to ask whether the evidence shows that it is in the best interests of the [donor] for such procedures to take place. The fact that such a process would obviously benefit the [potential recipient] is not relevant unless, as a result of the [donor] helping the [recipient] in that way, the best interests of the [donor] are served. The approach is as set out in *In re F (Mental Patient: Sterilisation)* [1990] 2 AC 1 . . . The lawfulness of the action depends upon whether the treatment is in the best interests of the patient . . . This case is different from the case of *In re F (Mental Patient: Sterilisation)* because it involves the concept of donation of bone marrow by a donor who is incapable of giving consent where a significant benefit will flow to another person. There was no other person in *In re F* who would have benefitted directly as a result of the declaration sought, the benefits of sterilisation attaching solely to the mentally incapacitated subject of the application. Nonetheless, I am satisfied that the root question remains the same, namely, whether the procedures here envisaged will benefit the [donor] and accordingly benefits which may flow to the [potential recipient] are relevant only insofar as they have a positive effect upon the best interests of the [donor].[471]

10.173 Decisions in the United States of America[472] are important because of the reliance placed in the only English case which has yet been decided[473] upon the reasoning in a decision of the Supreme Court of Illinois.[474]

---

[469] See Human Tissue Authority 'Code of Practice 2: Donation of solid organs for transplantation', para 69 and Appendix A. With regard to the donation of non-regenerative organs, see also *Re F (Mental Patient: Sterilisation)* [1990] 2 AC 1, 19, 33, 40; *Re W (A Minor) (Medical Treatment: Court's Jurisdiction)* [1993] Fam 64, 79, 94. The storage and use of tissue from adults lacking capacity to consent is permitted in certain circumstances: see the Human Tissue Act 2004 (Persons who Lack Capacity to Consent and Transplants) Regulations 2006/1659. See also 'Code of Practice 6: Donation of allogeneic bone marrow and peripheral blood stem cells for transplantation'.

[470] Thus it would seem that it cannot be lawful to take tissue from a donor who is in an irreversible coma or who is unconscious and dying: compare the problem of the pregnant woman in a coma considered in para 10.29.

[471] *Re Y (Mental Patient: Bone Marrow Donation)* [1997] Fam 110, 113 *per* Connell J. The word 'interest' in the best interests test does not confine the court to considering the self-interest of the patient: see *Re G (TJ)* [2010] EWHC 3005 (Fam).

[472] *Strunk v Strunk* (1969) 445 SW 2d 145 (Court of Appeals of Kentucky, donation of kidney by adult who lacked capacity authorized); *Hart v Brown* (1972) 289 A 2d 386 (Superior Court of Connecticut, donation of kidney by child authorized); *Re Richardson* (1973) 284 So 2d 185 (Court of Appeal of Louisiana, donation of kidney by child refused); *Lausier v Pescinski* (1975) 226 NW 2d 180 (Supreme Court of Wisconsin, donation of kidney by adult who lacked capacity refused); *Little v Little* (1979) 576 SW 2d 493 (Court of Civil Appeals of Texas, donation of kidney by child authorized); *Curran v Bosze* (1990) 566 NE 2d 1319 (Supreme Court of Illinois, donation of bone marrow by children refused).

[473] *Re Y (Mental Patient: Bone Marrow Donation)* [1997] Fam 110, 113–14.

[474] *Curran v Bosze* (1990) 566 NE 2d 1319, containing full discussions, 1322–26 of whether the relevant test was best interests or substituted judgment (holding, 1331 that the test was best interests), 1326–32 of the previous American case law and, 1332–45 of a substantial body of evidence directed to the risks and benefits to the donor of a bone marrow transplant.

The American authorities identify, with varying degrees of enthusiasm or scepticism, five factors potentially relevant to the question of whether or not the donation of an organ or tissue is in the best interests of a child or adult incompetent donor:[475] **10.174**

(1) If the potential recipient dies as a result of the transplant not taking place:
   (a) The adverse emotional or psychological effect on the donor (where the recipient is a sibling with whom the donor has a strong identification, or upon whom the donor is emotionally or psychologically dependent), whether that adverse effect is caused by (i) the mere fact of the sibling's death or (ii) the fact that the relationship no longer continues.
   (b) The loss of a prospective carer for the donor after the donor's parents are dead.
   (c) Feelings of guilt on the part of the donor.

(2) If the transplant does take place:
   (d) The increased happiness and gratification of, and psychological benefit to, the donor from having been able to save another person's life.
   (e) The fact that the donor is better off in a family that is happy (because the recipient is alive) than in a family that is distressed (because the potential recipient has died).

The approach adopted in the American cases accords, broadly speaking, with English law, though, consistently with principle (and, indeed, to an extent recognized in the American cases), factors (a)(i), (c), and (d) cannot be relevant unless the donor has sufficient cognitive and social awareness to be able to understand the abstract concept of death, understands that s/he is in a position to ameliorate the recipient's condition and in fact wishes to do so. **10.175**

The critical task is to evaluate the emotional, psychological, and social effects on the donor of what is proposed.[476] In the typical case,[477] the benefits to the donor which have to be shown if the best interests test is to be satisfied will be found, if at all, in the pre-existing family relationships between the donor, the potential recipient, and other members of their family; the critical factor will be proof that there will be emotional, psychological, or social benefits to the donor in maintaining an existing, close family relationship which will be interrupted or lost if the donation does not take place.[478] **10.176**

(a) The balancing exercise Those benefits then have to be balanced against the possible disadvantages[479] to the donor. The best interests balancing exercise has to be performed by considering (a) if the transplant takes place, (i) the psychological and other benefits to the donor, including any enhancement of his/her relationships with the potential recipient and other members of his/her family, balanced against (ii) the medical risks and other possible disadvantages of the procedure; and (b) if the transplant does not take place, (i) the psychological and other detriments to the donor, including any damage to or loss of his/ **10.177**

---

[475] These may usefully be compared with the factors referred to in para 10.142 identified in English cases.
[476] *Re Y (Mental Patient: Bone Marrow Donation)* [1997] Fam 110, 116.
[477] As in *Re Y* (ibid) where, on the evidence, factor (b) was not material, where the patient's low level of cognitive and social awareness, and lack of ability to understand both her own plight and that of the potential recipient, meant that factors (a)(i), (c), and (d) could not be relevant and where, for the same reason, there could not be any question of the patient benefitting from the performance by her of any perceived moral, social, or civic obligation.
[478] ibid, 114–16, adopting, at 113–14, the approach of Calvo J in *Curran v Bosze* (1990) 566 NE 2d 1319, 1331, 1343–44, 1345.
[479] eg as in *Re Y*, n 476, 115–16.

her relationships with the potential recipient and other members of his/her family, balanced against (ii) the avoidance of the medical risks and other possible disadvantages of the procedure.

> I must look therefore at the situation of the [donor] and ask whether the proposals placed before the court would benefit her and, if yes, whether those benefits outweigh any possible detriment to her.[480]

10.178 **(b) Bone marrow transplants** Applying these principles the court has declared lawful the donation of bone marrow by an adult who lacked capacity.[481]

10.179 **(c) Other procedures** Whether the court would ever be willing to authorize (in the case of a child) or to declare lawful (in the case of an adult who lacks capacity) any procedure more serious than a donation of bone marrow must be open to considerable doubt:[482]

> I should perhaps emphasise that this is a rather unusual case and that the family of the [potential recipient] and the [donor] are a particularly close family. It is doubtful that this case would act as a useful precedent in cases where the surgery involved is more intrusive than in this case, where the evidence shows that the bone marrow harvested is speedily regenerated and that a healthy individual can donate as much as two pints with no long term consequences at all. Thus, the bone marrow donated by the [donor] will cause her no loss and she will suffer no real long term risk.[483]

5. Life and death

(i) General principles

10.180 **(a) The duty to care** A doctor (or layman) who has assumed the responsibility of caring for a helpless patient thereby becomes subject to a duty to care for him/her. The breach of that duty, if it leads to the death of the patient, renders the carer, depending upon his/her mens rea, liable to prosecution for manslaughter or murder.[484] The critical enquiry is, therefore, as to the duration and extent of the duty, because that determines whether or not there has been a breach of duty. The duty to care does not oblige a doctor or other carer to pursue invasive treatment or artificial feeding with a view to prolonging life at all costs and regardless of the circumstances.[485]

10.181 **(b) The crucial question** In determining the duration and extent of the duty where the patient lacks capacity to decide, the question which has to be asked is not, 'Is it in the best interests of the patient that s/he should die?' Instead, the question is this: 'Is it in the best interests of the patient that treatment which has the effect of artificially prolonging his/her life should be continued?' If the answer to that question is that the patient's best interests no

---

480 ibid, 114 *per* Connell J.
481 ibid, 114 *per* Connell J.
482 See para 10.169.
483 *Re Y (Mental Patient: Bone Marrow Donation)* [1997] Fam 110, 116 per Connell J.
484 *R v Gibbins* (1918) 13 Cr App R 134; *R v Stone* [1977] QB 354; *Re F (Mental Patient: Sterilisation)* [1990] 2 AC 1, 55–56, 77; *Airedale NHS Trust v Bland* [1993] AC 789, 858, 866, 881, 893; *Swindon and Marlborough NHS Trust v S* The Guardian, 10 December 1994, [1995] Med L Rev 84.
485 *Re J (A Minor) (Wardship: Medical Treatment)* [1991] Fam 33, 52, 54, 55; *Airedale NHS Trust v Bland* [1993] AC 789, 864, 865, 867. See also the BMA's guidance, 'End of Life Decisions: Views of the BMA' (Sept 2009); the joint guidance of the BMA, Resuscitation Council (UK) and the Royal College of Nursing, 'Decisions relating to Cardiopulmonary Resuscitation' (June 2016); and the GMC guidance, 'Treatment and care towards the end of life: good practice in decision making' (Sept 2014) at <http://www.gmc-uk.org/guidance/ethical_guidance/end_of_life_care.asp>.

longer require that it should be, then the withdrawal of the treatment will be lawful; indeed, the continuation of the treatment will be unlawful:[486]

> The correct formulation of the question is of particular importance in a case such as the present, where the patient is totally unconscious and where there is no hope whatsoever of any amelioration of his condition. In circumstances such as these, it may be difficult to say that it is in his best interests that the treatment should be ended. But if the question is asked, as in my opinion it should be, whether it is in his best interests that treatment which has the effect of artificially prolonging his life should be continued, that question can sensibly be answered to the effect that his best interests no longer require that it should be.[487]

In determining the best interests of an incapacitated patient, those concerned must seek to place themselves in the position of the patient so as to identify the decision that is right for that particular person. As discussed later, this requires careful identification and scrutiny of the patient's ascertainable wishes, feelings, beliefs, and values.[488] **10.182**

(c) **The presumption in favour of life** Although the question is, 'Is it in the best interests of the patient that treatment should be continued?' (and not, 'Is it in the best interests of the patient that treatment be discontinued?'), there is a very strong presumption in favour of taking all steps which will prolong life. In the great majority of cases, save in exceptional circumstances or where the patient is dying, the best interests of an incapacitated patient will require such steps to be taken.[489] The burden of proof is accordingly on those who assert that life-saving treatment or life-sustaining artificial feeding should be discontinued: **10.183**

> There is a very strong presumption in favour of taking all steps which will prolong life, and save in exceptional circumstances, or where the patient is dying, the best interests of the patient will normally require such steps to be taken. In case of doubt that doubt falls to be resolved in favour of the preservation of life. But the obligation is not absolute. Important as the sanctity of life is, it may have to take second place to human dignity.[490]

In human rights terms, therefore, the discontinuance of treatment engages not just the right to life under Article 2 ECHR, but also Articles 3 and 8. **10.184**

[486] *Airedale NHS Trust v Bland* [1993] AC 789, 883–84, 885, 897, 898, cited with approval in *Aintree University Hospitals NHS Foundation Trust v James and others* [2014] AC 591, at [20]–[22]. See also *Re J (A Minor) (Wardship: Medical Treatment)* [1991] Fam 33, 53, 54 *per* Taylor LJ; *Re R (Adult: Medical Treatment)* [1996] 2 FLR 99, 107 *per* Sir Stephen Brown P; A Morris, 'Selective Treatment of Irreversibly Impaired Infants: Decision-Making at the Threshold' (2009) 17(3) Med L Rev 347. It follows that, if the *patient's* best interests no longer require that his/her life be artificially prolonged, s/he cannot lawfully be kept alive with a view to benefiting third parties, eg for the purpose of enabling his/her organs or tissues to be harvested (whether before or after his/her death) or for the purpose of obtaining a financial or fiscal benefit. If the patient is pregnant with a viable foetus: see paras 10.28–10.29.

[487] *Airedale NHS Trust v Bland* [1993] AC 789, 868 per Lord Goff of Chieveley. Endorsed in *Aintree University Hospitals NHS Foundation Trust v James and others* [2014] AC 591, at [20]–[22].

[488] *Aintree University Hospitals NHS Foundation Trust v James and others* [2014] AC 591. For a clear illustration, see *Wye Valley NHS Trust v Mr B* [2015] EWCOP 60, [2015] COPLR 843 (not in patient's best interests to amputate life-threatening infected foot).

[489] *Re J (A Minor) (Wardship: Medical Treatment)* [1991] Fam 33, 46, 51, 53; *Airedale NHS Trust v Bland* [1993] AC 789, 867. See also Mental Capacity Act 2005 s 4 and its Code of Practice at para 5.31 which states: 'All reasonable steps which are in the person's best interests should be taken to prolong their life', there being only 'a limited number of cases where treatment is futile, overly burdensome to the patient or where there is no prospect of recovery.'

[490] *R (on the application of Burke) v General Medical Council* [2004] EWHC 1879 (Admin), [2005] QB 424, [116] *per* Munby J, approved by the Court of Appeal, *R (on the application of Burke) v General Medical Council* [2005] EWCA Civ 1003, [2006] QB 273, [61]. See also *Aintree*, n 488, at [35].

(ii) The dying patient

10.185 (a) **Life-prolonging treatment** In the case of life-prolonging treatment—that is treatment the purpose of which is merely to prolong the life of a terminally ill patient who cannot be expected to recover from a condition which is incurable—the court will authorize or declare lawful (as the case may be) such treatment as is appropriate to the patient's condition. In such a case the goal should be to ease suffering and, where appropriate, to 'ease the passing' rather than to achieve a short prolongation of life:[491]

> If the first purpose of medicine, the restoration of health, can no longer be achieved . . . a doctor . . . is entitled to do all that is proper and necessary to relieve pain and suffering, even if the measures he takes may incidentally shorten life.[492]

10.186 (b) **Withdrawal of treatment** Consistent with this approach, there may be circumstances in which it is appropriate to withdraw life-prolonging treatment from a dying patient,[493] but a doctor is never justified in taking active steps in order to kill his/her patient by the introduction of an external agency (eg the administration of a fatal drug) with the intention of bringing about the patient's death. 'Mercy killing' by active means is murder.[494]

10.187 (c) **Indirect consequences** Also consistent with this approach is the recognition[495] in English law of the theological doctrine of double effect:

> 'Thou shalt not kill' is an absolute commandment in this context. But, to quote the well known phrase of Arthur Hugh Clough in 'The Latest Decalogue,' in this context it is permissible to add 'but need'st not strive officiously to keep alive'. The decision on life and death must and does remain in other hands. What doctors and the court have to decide is whether, in the best interests of the child patient, a particular decision as to medical treatment should be taken which *as a side effect* will render death more or less likely. This is not a matter of semantics. It is fundamental. At the other end of the age spectrum, the use of drugs to reduce pain will often be fully justified, notwithstanding that this will hasten the moment of death. What can never be justified is the use of drugs or surgical procedures with the primary purpose of doing so.[496]

10.188 There is a tension here. In *Woollin*[497] it was held that intention to kill can be inferred from foresight of a virtual certainty of death or really serious harm. Nonetheless, as Lord

---

491 *Re C (A Minor) (Wardship: Medical Treatment)* [1990] Fam 26, 32, 33, 37, 38; *Re C (Medical Treatment)* [1998] 1 FLR 384; *Royal Wolverhampton Hospitals NHS Trust v B* [2000] 1 FLR 953; *A NHS Trust v D* [2000] 2 FLR 677. For the impact in this context of Arts 2 and 3 of the ECHR see *A NHS Trust v D* [2000] 2 FLR 677, 695. The BMA has published guidance: 'End of Life Decisions: Views of the BMA' (Aug 2009).

492 *R v Bodkin Adams* 8–9 April 1957, (Devlin J), [1957] Crim LR 365.

493 cf Airedale *NHS Trust v Bland* [1993] AC 789.

494 *R v Bodkin Adams* 8–9 April 1957, (Devlin J), [1957] Crim LR 365; *R v Cox* (1992) 12 BMLR 38; *Airedale NHS Trust v Bland* [1993] AC 789, 831, 865–66, 892. Accordingly, when determining whether it is in the best interests of a patient lacking capacity to consent to or refuse life-sustaining treatment to continue to provide such treatment, the decision-maker must not be motivated by a desire to bring about the patient's death: Mental Capacity Act 2005 s 4(5) and (10). With regard to children, see V Larcher et al, 'Making Decisions to Limit Treatment in Life-Limiting and Life-threatening Conditions in Children: A Framework for Practice' Arch Dis Child 2015; 100 (Suppl 2): s1–s23.

495 By Devlin *J* in *R v Bodkin Adams* 8–9 April 1957, [1957] Crim LR 365. See the discussion in *Re A (Children) (Conjoined Twins: Surgical Separation)* [2001] Fam 147, 199, 216–18, 251–52.

496 *Re J (A Minor) (Wardship: Medical Treatment)* [1991] Fam 33, 46 *per* Lord Donaldson of Lymington MR. The distinction was central to the issue for the jury in *R v Cox* (1992) 12 BMLR 38. For a case turning on double effect which attracted much publicity, though it never proceeded to judgment, see *Lindsell v Holmes* The Guardian, 29 October 1997. The doctrine of double effect has provoked significant criticism: see, eg, D Price, 'Euthanasia, Pain Relief and Double Effect' (1997) 17 Legal Studies 323.

497 *R v Woollin* [1999] 1 AC 82. See also D Price, 'What Shape to Euthanasia After Bland? Historical, Contemporary and Futuristic Paradigms' (2009) LQR 142.

Neuberger reiterated in *Nicklinson*, 'a doctor commits no offence when treating a patient in a way which hastens death, if the purpose of the treatment is to relieve pain and suffering'.[498]

(iii) The patient whose life is threatened

In the case of life-saving treatment—that is treatment the purpose of which is to enable the patient to recover from a life-threatening condition which is potentially curable—there is usually no difficulty in arriving at the appropriate decision. For reasons which are obvious the court will normally[499] authorize or declare lawful (as the case may be) such treatment in the case of a child or incapacitated adult, for generally the duty of the court is to preserve life. Thus where it is necessary to preserve the patient's life the court, notwithstanding religious or other objections, will authorize or declare lawful (as the case may be) a heart transplant,[500] a bone marrow transplant,[501] the administration of blood transfusions to child[502] and incapacitated adult[503] Jehovah's Witnesses, the force-feeding of children[504] and incapacitated adults[505] for the treatment of anorexia nervosa or other psychiatric illnesses, and the administration, if need be by force, of surgical procedures necessary to preserve the life of a child[506] or an incapacitated woman[507] suffering complications during labour. **10.189**

[498] *R (on the application of Nicklinson) v Ministry of Justice and others* [2015] AC 657, [2014] UKSC 38 at [18]; see A Mullock, 'The Supreme Court Decision in *Nicklinson*: Human Rights, Criminal Wrongs and the Dilemma of Death' (2015) Professional Negligence 18; E Wicks, 'The Supreme Court Judgment in *Nicklinson*: one step forward on assisted dying; two steps back on human rights' (2015) 23(1) Med L Rev 144. Applications to the ECtHR were held to be inadmissible: *Nicklinson v United Kingdom* [2015] ECHR 783 (23 June 2015). Regarding the legality of the blanket prohibition on assisted suicide in Canada, see *Carter v Canada (Attorney-General)* [2015] 1 SCR 331, [2015] SCC 5.

[499] But not always. Thus 'on the most unusual facts' the court in *Re T (A Minor) (Wardship: Medical Treatment)* [1997] 1 WLR 242 refused to overrule the parents' refusal to consent to a liver transplant on a 17-month-old boy suffering from biliary atresia, a life-threatening liver defect, notwithstanding unanimous medical opinion that without a transplant the child would not live beyond the age of 2 to 2 and a half whilst the prospects of a successful operation leading to many years of normal life were good. This decision might be thought surprising: see the critical discussion by Professor Grubb in [1996] Med L Rev 315. See also *Re A (Children) (Conjoined Twins: Surgical Separation)* [2001] Fam 147, 194–95, 244. Different considerations may also apply to adults: see *Wye Valley* at paras 10.137 and 10.141.

[500] *Re M (Medical treatment: Consent)* [1999] 2 FLR 1097.

[501] *NHS Trust v A* [2007] EWHC 1696 (Fam), [2008] 1 FLR 70.

[502] *Re E (A Minor) (Wardship: Medical Treatment)* [1993] 1 FLR 386; *Re S (A Minor) (Medical Treatment)* [1993] 1 FLR 376; *Re O (A Minor) (Medical Treatment)* [1993] 2 FLR 149; *Re R (A Minor) (Blood Transfusion)* [1993] 2 FLR 757; *Re S (A Minor) (Consent to Medical Treatment)* [1994] 2 FLR 1065; *Re P (Medical Treatment: Best Interests)* [2003] EWHC 2327 (Fam), [2004] 2 FLR 1117.

[503] *Re T (Adult: Refusal of Treatment)* [1993] Fam 95.

[504] *Re W (A Minor) (Medical Treatment: Court's Jurisdiction)* [1993] Fam 64; *Re C (Detention: Medical Treatment)* [1997] 2 FLR 180.

[505] *Riverside Mental Health NHS Trust v Fox* [1994] 1 FLR 614; *Re KB (Adult) (Mental Patient: Medical Treatment)* (1994) 19 BMLR 144; *B v Croydon HA* [1995] Fam 133, affg [1995] 1 FCR 332; *Re VS (Adult: Mental Disorder)* 17 August 1995, (Douglas Brown J), [1995] Med L Rev 292; *A Local Authority v E and others* [2012] EWHC 1639 (COP), comment by J Coggon, 'Anorexia Nervosa, Best Interests, and the Patient's Human Right to a 'Wholesale Overwhelming of Her Autonomy' (2014) 22(1) Med L Rev 119. For an example of where it was not in the patient's best interests to compel force-feeding, see *A NHS Foundation Trust v X* [2014] EWCOP 35, (2014) 140 BMLR 41.

[506] *A Metropolitan Borough Council v AB* [1997] 1 FLR 767.

[507] *Re T (Adult: Refusal of Treatment)* [1993] Fam 95; *Tameside and Glossop Acute Services Trust v CH* [1996] 1 FLR 762; *Norfolk and Norwich Healthcare (NHS) Trust v W* [1996] 2 FLR 613; *Rochdale Healthcare (NHS) Trust v C* [1997] 1 FCR 274; *Re L (Patient: Non-Consensual Treatment)* [1997] 2 FLR 837; *Re MB (Medical Treatment)* [1997] 2 FLR 426.

(iv) The disabled patient

10.190 The court does not adopt any different approach merely because a patient has a physical or mental disability.[508] The fact that the patient has a disability cannot of course be ignored, for the question is never what treatment would be appropriate for a non-disabled patient but always, what is the treatment appropriate for this patient given his/her condition?[509] Nonetheless:

> where . . . the child is severely handicapped although not intolerably so and treatment for a discrete condition can enable life to continue for an appreciable period, albeit subject to that severe handicap, the treatment should be given.[510]

10.191 Thus, in the leading case,[511] parents had refused consent to surgery on their 10-day-old Down's Syndrome baby to relieve an intestinal blockage, taking the bona fide view that 'God or nature has given the child a way out'. Without surgery the baby would have died; the surgery, if carried out, would enable the baby to live the same life as any other Down's Syndrome child. The Court of Appeal recognized that the child would have a short life expectancy and would be very severely mentally and physically disabled and thus not able to have anything like a normal existence,[512] but directed surgery, holding that the question was whether it was in the best interests of the child to have the operation and not whether the parents' wishes should be respected:

> If the operation takes place and is successful then the child may live the normal span of a mongoloid child with the handicaps and defects and life of a mongol child, and it is not for this court to say that life of that description ought to be extinguished.[513] The child should be put into the same position as any other mongol child and must be given the chance to live an existence.[514]

The principle has subsequently been explained as being that:

> It [is] not for the court to decide that the child should not have the chance of the normal life span of a mongoloid child with the handicaps, defects and life of such a child.[515]

(v) The gravely ill patient

10.192 On the other hand, there are cases in which the patient's medical condition is so grave that it is not in their best interests to give or to continue (as the case may be) treatment which,

---

[508] For examples of the application of this principle see *NHS Trust v T (adult patient: refusal of medical treatment)* [2004] EWHC 1279 (Fam), [2005] 1 All ER 387 (blood transfusion to treat consequences of self-harming by woman with borderline personality disorder); *W Healthcare NHS Trust v H and others* [2004] EWCA Civ 1324, [2005] 1 WLR 834 (reinsertion of feeding tube in woman suffering from multiple sclerosis and in a 'pitiful state'); *Trust A and Trust B v H (An Adult Patient)* [2006] EWHC 1230 (Fam), [2006] 2 FLR 958 (surgery for removal of large malignant ovarian tumour in delusional schizophrenic woman).

[509] *Re C (A Minor) (Wardship: Medical Treatment)* [1990] Fam 26, 32.

[510] *Re J (A Minor) (Wardship: Medical Treatment)* [1991] Fam 33, 54 per Taylor LJ.

[511] *Re B (A Minor) (Wardship: Medical Treatment)* [1981] 1 WLR 1421, reversing (1982) 3 FLR 117, subsequently considered and explained in *Re C (A Minor) (Wardship: Medical Treatment)* [1990] Fam 26; *Re J (A Minor) (Wardship: Medical Treatment)* [1991] Fam 33.

[512] *Re B (A Minor) (Wardship: Medical Treatment)* [1981] 1 WLR 1421, 1423.

[513] ibid, 1424 *per* Templeman LJ.

[514] ibid, 1424–25 *per* Dunn LJ.

[515] *Re C (A Minor) (Wardship: Medical Treatment)* [1990] Fam 26, 35 *per* Lord Donaldson of Lymington MR. In the light of the decisions in *Re B (A Minor) (Wardship: Medical Treatment)* [1981] 1 WLR 1421; *Re C (A Minor) (Wardship: Medical Treatment)* [1990] Fam 26 and *Re J (A Minor) (Wardship: Medical Treatment)* [1991] Fam 33. It is doubtful whether any useful principles can be extracted from *R v Arthur* (1981) 12 BMLR 1.

if given, will artificially prolong life. In *Airedale NHS Trust v Bland*,[516] the Hillsborough disaster left Tony Bland in a vegetative state for more than two years. Doctors sought declaratory relief to discontinue artificial nutrition and hydration treatment. Lord Goff held that no balancing exercise was needed because the treatment had exhausted its therapeutic benefits, was effectively futile, and so the scales would tip in favour of withdrawal.[517] The judgment is not without its critics, many seeing it as turning on negative judgments about the quality of the patient's life.[518] Controversy also surrounds the distinction drawn between the lawful disconnect of a feeding tube and the unlawful administering of a lethal drug, as illustrated in Lord Browne-Wilkinson's *cri de coeur*:

> . . . the conclusion I have reached will appear to some to be almost irrational. How can it be lawful to allow a patient to die slowly, though painlessly, over a period of weeks from lack of food but unlawful to produce his immediate death by a lethal injection, thereby saving his family from yet another ordeal to add to the tragedy that has already struck them? I find it difficult to find a moral answer to that question. But it is undoubtedly the law . . . [519]

Bland was decided during an era which conflated best interests with *Bolam*. But that jurisprudential tie has since been well and truly decoupled. Developments in the provision of health care services now mean that 'patients are now widely regarded as persons holding rights, rather than as the passive recipients of the care of the medical profession'.[520] In these modern circumstances, the law recognizes three situations where it may not be in the patient's best interests to continue to give treatment. According to para 5.31 of the Code of Practice to the Mental Capacity Act 2005, 'There will be a limited number of cases where treatment is futile, overly burdensome to the patient or where there is no prospect of recovery.' This was confirmed in *Aintree* as an accurate statement of the law and led Supreme Court to conclude: **10.193**

> 39. The most that can be said, therefore, is that in considering the best interests of this particular patient at this particular time, decision-makers must look at his welfare in the widest sense, not just medical but social and psychological; they must consider the nature of the medical treatment in question, what it involves and its prospects of success; they must consider what the outcome of that treatment for the patient is likely to be; they must try and put themselves in the place of the individual patient and ask what his attitude to the treatment is or would be likely to be; and they must consult others who are looking after him or interested in his welfare, in particular for their view of what his attitude would be.

(a) Futility The first situation where treatment may lawfully be withdrawn or withheld is where the disability is such that the treatment would be 'futile', 'useless' or 'pointless'. In such a case it is the futility of the treatment which justifies its withholding or withdrawal. It is on this footing that the withdrawal of artificial nutrition and hydration is justified in the case of patients in a (formerly called persistent or permanent) vegetative state.[521] **10.194**

---

[516] [1993] AC 789, [1993] 1 FLR 1026. For an interesting discussion of the issues going to the heart of the decision, see R Huxtable, 'Autonomy, Best Interests and the Public Interest: Treatment, Non-Treatment and the Values of Medical Law' (2014) 22(4) Med L Rev 459. See also A McGee, 'Does Withdrawing Life-Sustaining Treatment Cause Death or Allow the Patient to Die?' (2014) 22(1) Med L Rev 26.

[517] [1993] AC 789, 869. See R Heywood, 'Moving on from Bland: The Evolution of the Law and Minimally Conscious Patients' (2014) 22(4) Med L Rev 548.

[518] R Huxtable, ***Euthanasia, Ethics and the Law: From Conflict to Compromise*** (Routledge-Cavendish 2007) 134–35.

[519] [1993] AC 789, 885. For a case comment, see J M Finnis, 'Bland: Crossing the Rubicon?' (1993) 109 LQR 329.

[520] *Montgomery v Lanarkshire Health Board* [2015] UKSC 11, [2015] AC 1430, [75] *per* Lords Kerr and Reed (with whom Lords Neuberger, Clarke, Wilson, and Hodge agreed). See R Heywood, 'R.I.P. *Sidaway:* Patient-oriented Disclosure—A Standard Worth Waiting For?' (2015) 23(3) Med L Rev 455.

[521] *Airedale NHS Trust v Bland* [1993] AC 789, 869, 870, 884.

Treatment can properly be categorized as futile if it cannot cure or palliate the disease or illness from which the patient is suffering and thus serves 'no therapeutic purpose of any kind'.[522] Significantly, however, in *Aintree* the Supreme Court held that 'futile' was to be interpreted 'in the sense of being ineffective or being of no benefit to the patient'.[523] Thus, a treatment 'may bring some benefit to the patient even though it has no effect upon the underlying disease or disability'.[524] Every case must therefore be determined upon its own facts. Arguments based upon the 'futility' of treatment seem confined to cases of vegetative states and, even then, best interests should be considered from the patient's point of view.

10.195 Do not attempt cardio-pulmonary resuscitation ('DNACPR') decisions are anticipatorily made by health professionals, usually on the basis of futility. As they potentially deprive the patient of life-saving treatment, there is a strong presumption in favour of patient involvement, with convincing reasons required not to involve them. A likelihood of causing the patient to suffer physical or psychological harm may provide such a reason, although merely causing distress would not. The very decision to complete a notice represents an interference with the patient's private life, protected by Article 8. Where the clinician's decision is based on futility, there is an obligation to tell the patient that this is the decision, as s/he may then seek a second opinion (unless it was the multi-disciplinary team that told the patient).[525] The need for prior consultation applies equally to incapacitated patients. So where it is practicable and appropriate to consult a person identified in MCA s 4(7) before the decision is made or acted on, in the absence of some compelling reason against consultation, a DNACRP notice without consultation will be procedurally flawed and in breach of Article 8.[526]

10.196 **(b) Overly burdensome** The second situation is where the overly burdensome nature of the proposed treatment outweighs its benefits, such as where the incapacitated patient strongly objects to, and is not prepared to submit to, the relevant procedure.[527] At least in the context of incapacitated adults, any decision that a treatment is overly burdensome must be reached against a backdrop of the benefits of a continued existence to that particular patient (rather than by generalized assessments of burdens of treatment). In *Aintree*,[528] for example, with reference to the Judge at first instance, the Supreme Court noted:

> He clearly did consider that the treatments in question were very burdensome. But he considered that those burdens had to be weighed against the benefits of a continued existence. He was also correct to see the assessment of the medical effects of the treatment as

[522] ibid, 869.

[523] *Aintree University Hospitals NHS Foundation Trust v James and others* [2014] AC 591 at [40].

[524] ibid at [43].

[525] *R (on the application of Tracey) v Cambridge University Hospitals NHS Foundation Trust* [2015] QB 543, [2014] EWCA Civ 822. See the joint guidance, 'Decisions relating to cardiopulmonary resuscitation', published by the BMA, Resuscitation Council (UK) and the Royal College of Nursing (June 2016). See also J Samanta, 'Tracey and Respect for Autonomy: Will the Promise Be Delivered?' (2015) 23(3) Med L Rev 467.

[526] *Winspear v City Hospitals Sunderland NHS Foundation Trust* [2015] EWHC 3250 (QB), [2016] QB 691 at [47].

[527] *Re D (Medical Treatment: Mentally Disabled Patient)* [1998] 2 FLR 22 (49-year-old chronic but fluctuating psychotic suffering from chronic renal failure at near-end stage and high blood pressure requiring haemodialysis for four hours three or four times each week to keep him alive but unable because of his mental condition to understand the need for treatment and strongly objecting to procedure: held lawful in the last resort 'not to impose haemodialysis upon him in circumstances in which in the opinion of the medical practitioners responsible for such treatment it is not reasonably practicable so to do', the judge accepting that in the circumstances dialysis, which requires the cooperation of the patient, could only be performed under general anaesthetic which was neither practicable nor desirable in a patient suffering D's disabilities). This decision is likely to now be seen as satisfying the 'overly burdensome' test rather than an 'impracticability' test.

[528] *Aintree*, n 523, at [40].

only part of the equation. Regard had to be had to the patient's welfare in the widest sense, and great weight to be given to Mr James' family life which was 'of the closest and most meaningful kind'.

Considering best interests from the patient's vantage point, also sensitive to the views of her closest friend, led in *A NHS Foundation Trust v X* to the conclusion that it was not in the patient's best interests to compel life-sustaining treatment for anorexia nervosa which she did not want.[529] Similarly, in *Wye Valley* the amputation of a foot so as to prevent the spread of a life-threatening infection was held not to be in the best interests of man with long-standing mental health difficulties who did not have the capacity to make decisions as to his medical treatment but was clear that he did not wish such amputation. As Peter Jackson J held, 'There is a difference between fighting on someone's behalf and just fighting them. Enforcing treatment in this case would surely be the latter'.[530] **10.197**

(c) No prospect of recovery The final situation is where there is no prospect of the patient recovering. In *Aintree*, the Supreme Court held that this means 'no prospect of resuming a quality of life which the patient would regard as worthwhile' and *not*, as the Court of Appeal had held, 'no prospect of recovering such a state of good health as will avert the looming prospect of death if the life-sustaining treatment is given'. Moreover: **10.198**

> where a patient is suffering from an incurable illness, disease or disability, it is not very helpful to talk of recovering a state of 'good health'. The patient's life may still be very well worth living. Resuming a quality of life which the patient would regard as worthwhile is more readily applicable, particularly in the case of a patient with permanent disabilities. As was emphasised in *In Re J* [1991] Fam 33, it is not for others to say that a life which the patient would regard as worthwhile is not worth living.[531]

(vi) The gravely ill but sentient patient

In the leading case of *Re J*, mechanical ventilation was held not to be necessary in the case of a 'gravely damaged' 5-month-old baby who was suffering from an 'appalling catalogue of disabilities'.[532] **10.199**

> [A]ccount has to be taken of the pain and suffering and quality of life which the child will experience if life is prolonged. Account has also to be taken of the pain and suffering involved in the proposed treatment itself... But in the end there will be cases in which the answer must be that it is not in the interests of the child to subject it to treatment which will cause increased suffering and produce no commensurate benefit, giving the fullest possible weight to the child's, and mankind's, desire to survive.[533]
>
> There is only the one test: that the interests of the ward are paramount. Of course the court will approach those interests with a strong predilection in favour of the preservation of life, because of the sanctity of human life. But there neither is, nor should there be, any absolute rule that, save where the ward is already terminally ill, that is dying, neither the court nor any responsible parent can approve the withholding of life-saving treatment on the basis of the quality of the ward's life... [I]t could in certain circumstances be inimical to the interests of the ward that there should be such a requirement: to preserve life at all costs, whatever the quality of the life to be preserved, and however distressing to the ward may be the nature of the treatment necessary to preserve life, may not be in the interests of the ward.[534]

529 [2014] EWCOP 35, (2014) 140 BMLR 41.
530 *Wye Valley NHS Trust v Mr B* [2015] EWCOP 60, [2015] COPLR 843 at [45].
531 *Aintree*, n 523, at [44].
532 *Re J (A Minor) (Wardship: Medical Treatment)* [1991] Fam 33, 49, 56.
533 ibid, 46–47 *per* Lord Donaldson of Lymington MR.
534 ibid, 51–52 *per* Balcombe LJ.

10.200 In the particular circumstances of that case the reasons for arriving at the decision that life-saving treatment should not necessarily be given were that:

> mechanical ventilation is itself an invasive procedure which, together with its essential accompaniments … would cause the child distress. Furthermore the procedures involve taking active measures which carry their own hazards, not only to life but in terms of causing even greater brain damage. This had to be balanced against what could possibly be achieved by the adoption of such active treatment. The chances of preserving the child's life might be improved, although even this was not certain and account had to be taken of the extremely poor quality of life at present enjoyed by the child, the fact that he had already been ventilated for exceptionally long periods, the unfavourable prognosis with or without ventilation and a recognition that if the question of reventilation ever arose, his situation would have deteriorated still further.[535]

10.201 At the end of the day, all these cases are highly fact sensitive, and fall to be decided by reference to the patient's best interests. A very helpful distillation of the ten propositions was provided by Holman J in *An NHS Trust v MB*.[536] Amongst these is the width given to best interests, which 'include every kind of consideration capable of impacting on the decision. These include, non-exhaustively, medical, emotional, sensory (pleasure, pain and suffering) and instinctive (the human instinct to survive) considerations.'

10.202 There are other reported examples of the application of these principles.[537] They provide the basis for the more recent summary of the law by Peter Jackson J in *Re KH (Medical Treatment: Advanced Care Plan)*.[538] With regard to children, the relevant medical guidance is contained in *Making decisions to limit treatment in life-limiting and life-threatening conditions in children: a framework for practice*.[539] It describes three circumstances in which it may be appropriate to limit treatment in a child's best interests: (1) limited quantity of life;

---

[535] ibid, 47–48 *per* Lord Donaldson of Lymington MR.

[536] [2006] EWHC 507 (Fam), [2006] 2 FLR 319, [16]–[17]; followed in *Re B (Medical Treatment)* [2008] EWHC 1996 (Fam), [2009] 1 FLR 1264, [15]; *Re SE (A Child)* [2015] 1 FLR 1316, [23]; *Manchester University Hospitals NHS Foundation Trust v A* [2015] EWHC 2828 (Fam).

[537] In relation to gravely disabled children see *Re J (A Minor) (Child in Care: Medical Treatment)* [1993] Fam 15 (artificial ventilation); *Re C (A Baby)* [1996] 2 FLR 43 (artificial ventilation); *Re L (Medical Treatment: Benefit)* [2004] EWHC 2713 (Fam), [2005] 1 FLR 491 (artificial ventilation and cardiac massage); *An NHS Trust v MB (a child represented by her Cafcass guardian ad litem)* [2006] EWHC 507 (Fam), [2006] 2 FLR 319 (artificial ventilation and tracheostomy); *Re K (Medical Treatment: Declaration)* [2006] EWHC 1007 (Fam), [2006] 2 FLR 883 (total parenteral nutrition); *Re B (Medical Treatment)* [2008] EWHC 1996 (Fam), [2009] 1 FLR 1264 (intensive resuscitation). For the illuminating sequence of judgments in relation to Charlotte Wyatt, reflecting fluctuations in her condition and, after the first two judgments, the impact of the Court of Appeal's decision in *R (on the application of Burke) v General Medical Council* [2005] EWCA Civ 1003, [2006] QB 273, see *Portsmouth NHS Trust v Wyatt and Wyatt, Southampton NHS Trust Intervening* [2004] EWHC 2247 (Fam), [2005] 1 FLR 21; *Wyatt v Portsmouth NHS Trust and Wyatt (by her Guardian) (No 3)* [2005] EWHC 693 (Fam), [2005] 2 FLR 480; *Portsmouth Hospitals NHS Trust v Wyatt and another* [2005] EWCA Civ 1181, [2005] 1 WLR 3995; *Portsmouth NHS Trust v Wyatt* [2005] EWHC 2293 (Fam), [2006] 1 FLR 652; *Re Wyatt* [2006] EWHC 319 (Fam), [2006] 2 FLR 111. For a case where the proceedings were dismissed without the court addressing the merits see *R v Portsmouth Hospitals NHS Trust, ex p Glass* [1999] 2 FLR 905 (affg (1999) 50 BMLR 269); and for the subsequent proceedings in the European Court of Human Rights (holding the UK to have been in breach of Article 8 for its failure to afford a court hearing) see *Glass and another v United Kingdom* [2004] 1 FLR 1019, [2004] 1 FCR 553. For cases involving gravely disabled adults see *Re R (Adult: Medical Treatment)* [1996] 2 FLR 99 (cardio-pulmonary resuscitation and antibiotics); *A Hospital NHS Trust v S* [2003] EWHC 365 (Fam), [2003] Lloyd's Rep Med 137 (kidney dialysis and transplant); *W Healthcare NHS Trust v H and others* [2004] EWCA Civ 1324, [2005] 1 WLR 834.

[538] [2013] 1 FLR 1471.

[539] V Larcher et al, 'Making Decisions to Limit Treatment in Life-Limiting and Life-threatening Conditions in Children: A Framework for Practice' Arch Dis Child 2015; 100 (Suppl 2): s 1–s 23.

(2) limited quality of life, where there is no overall qualitative benefit; and (3) informed, competent, supported refusal of treatment.[540]

(a) Life-saving treatment and the quality of life As can be seen, the Court of Appeal[541] has accepted that the quality of life is something that can be taken into account in deciding whether or not a gravely ill but sentient patient should receive life-saving treatment. But this does not mean that, in the case of a sentient patient, the withholding or withdrawal of life-saving treatment or artificial feeding can ever be justified solely by reference to an assessment of the quality of the patient's life, let alone because of physical or mental disability, however grave. Withdrawal is justified only if the court is satisfied to a high degree of probability that the patient's quality of life (and any prospects of improvement) are demonstrably so very poor as not to be commensurate with the extreme pain, suffering, or distress (physical or mental) being experienced as a result of the patient's condition (including any pain, suffering, and distress resulting from, and any hazards involved in, the treatment itself). In other words, the determining factor is not the patient's quality of life as such but pain, suffering, or distress, whether physical or mental, so extreme that the artificial prolongation of the patient's agony cannot be justified.[542] **10.203**

(b) The patient in a vegetative state The essence of a vegetative state (formerly known as persistent or permanent vegetative state)[543] is that the patient is alive, is not dying (and, if properly treated may live for many years), but is totally insensate, and therefore can feel neither pain nor distress, has no cognitive functions, requires artificial nutrition and hydration to remain alive, and has no hope of either recovery or improvement. **10.204**

Need to involve the court Withdrawal of artificial nutrition and hydration from a patient in a vegetative state requires the prior sanction of the court.[544] This appears to be the case even where all parties agree that withdrawal is in the person's best interests. However, the position is less clear cut where the person has made an advance decision refusing the treatment, or a health and welfare lasting power of attorney has been granted the authority to decide. Indeed, at least insofar as advance decisions are concerned, the terms of MCA s 26 suggest that there is no decision for the Court of Protection to make, and no liability is incurred for withholding or withdrawing treatment if the person so acting reasonably believes that the advance decision is valid and applicable. **10.205**

The Royal College of Physicians has provided 'Prolonged disorders of consciousness: national clinical guidelines'[545] which distinguish three disorders of consciousness with corresponding **10.206**

[540] *Re Jake (A Child)* [2015] EWHC 2442 (Fam), [2016] 2 FCR 118 where the withdrawal of treatment was declared to be lawful with regard to a gravely disabled 10-month old boy.

[541] In *Re J (A Minor) (Wardship: Medical Treatment)* [1991] Fam 33. For comments by the House of Lords on this case see *Airedale NHS Trust v Bland* [1993] AC 789, 858, 868–69, 872, esp Lord Goff of Chieveley's reservation, 869, and see also, 885, 899. For subsequent comments by the Court of Appeal see *Frenchay Healthcare NHS Trust v S* [1994] 1 WLR 601, 607, 610; *Re A (Children) (Conjoined Twins: Surgical Separation)* [2001] Fam 147, 185–88 (an important analysis by Ward LJ).

[542] *Re J (A Minor) (Wardship: Medical Treatment)* [1991] Fam 33, 46, 47–48, 55, 56; *Airedale NHS Trust v Bland* [1993] AC 789, 858, 868.

[543] The state was fully described in *Airedale NHS Trust v Bland* [1993] AC 789, 795–96, 797–98, 806–07, 860–61.

[544] *Airedale NHS Trust v Bland* [1993] AC 789, 805, 815, 824, 833, 859, 873, 875. See now Court of Protection Practice Direction 9E para 5 which provides that cases involving the withdrawal or withholding of artificial nutrition and hydration from someone in vegetative or minimally conscious states 'should' be brought to the court. For arguments against the need to involve the court see D Wade, 'Back to the Bedside? Making Clinical Decisions in Patients with Prolonged Unconsciousness' (2016) J Med Ethics, and J Kitzinger and C Kitzinger, 'Causes and Consequences of Delays in Treatment—Withdrawal from PVS Patients' (2016) J Med Ethics 2016. Not requiring court involvement where there is a valid applicable advance decision refusing treatment was confirmed in *Briggs v Briggs and others* [2016] EWCOP 53, overview para 10 and [22].

[545] RCP Publication, 2013.

criteria: coma (absent wakefulness and absent awareness); vegetative state (wakefulness with absent awareness); and minimally conscious state (wakefulness with minimal awareness). According to a UK survey that informed the guidelines,[546] the Wessex Head Injury Matrix ('WHIM') is the most commonly used tool, followed by the Sensory Modality Assessment and Rehabilitation Technique ('SMART') assessment and then the JFK Coma Recovery Scale—Revised ('CRS-R'). WHIM is designed to monitor changes from coma through to emergence from post-traumatic amnesia; SMART and CRS-R are used to distinguish patients in vegetative states from those in minimally conscious states. However, determining a person's level of consciousness is extremely difficult and modern science appears to suggest there is a spectrum.

10.207 In *W v M*, Baker J observed that standardized testing is always necessary before an application is made to the Court:

> It is of the utmost importance that every step should be taken to diagnose the patient's true condition before any application is made to the Court. In future no application for an order authorising the withdrawal of ANH from a patient in a vegetative state or a minimally conscious state should be made unless a SMART assessment or similarly validated equivalent has been carried out to provide a diagnosis of the patient's disorder of consciousness and in the case of the patient thereby diagnosed as being in the minimally conscious state a series of WHIM assessments have been carried out over time with a view to tracking the patient's progress and recovery if any through the minimally conscious state.[547]

10.208 The need to adhere carefully to such guidance was laid bare in *St George's Healthcare NHS Trust v P and Q* which concerned the proposed withdrawal of life-sustaining renal replacement therapy. The Court agreed with the patient's family following a SMART assessment that the patient was not in a vegetative state, as the Trust had suggested, but a minimally conscious state and decided that treatment should not be withdrawn.[548]

10.209 *Withdrawal of Treatment* Where a patient is diagnosed as being in a vegetative state the court is likely to authorize or declare lawful (as the case may be) the withdrawal of artificial nutrition and hydration.[549] This is essentially on the ground that artificial nutrition and hydration is medical treatment[550] and that in the case of a patient in a vegetative state such treatment is futile: the patient has no further interest in being kept alive, his/her interest in life being in truth null.[551] The primary function of the court is to verify the diagnosis of the patient as being in a vegetative state. The court must then determine whether it is in the patient's best interests to continue artificial nutrition and hydration, although the

---

546 M Delargy, A McCann, F Haughey et al, 'Review of Prolonged Disorder Of Consciousness (PDOC) Rehabilitation Service Provision: A Questionnaire Survey of UK BSRM Members' (Dublin: The PDOC Working Group, National Rehabilitation Hospital, 2013).

547 [2012] 1 WLR 1653. The assessments are not however by themselves determinative of the outcome in a given case: *Re N* [2015] EWCOP 76, [2016] COPLR 88 at [23].

548 [2015] EWCOP 42, [2015] COPLR 561.

549 *Airedale NHS Trust v Bland* [1993] AC 789; *Frenchay Healthcare NHS Trust v S* [1994] 1 WLR 601; *Re G (Persistent Vegetative State)* [1995] 2 FCR 46; *Swindon and Marlborough NHS Trust v S* The Guardian, 10 December 1994, [1995] Med L Rev 84; *Re C (Adult Patient: Restriction of Publicity after Death)* [1996] 2 FLR 251; *NHS Trust A v M, NHS Trust B v H* [2001] Fam 348; *NHS Trust A v H* [2001] 2 FLR 501; *Re G (adult who lacks capacity: withdrawal of treatment)* (2001) 65 BMLR 6; and see also *NHS Trust v D and D* [2005] EWHC 2439 (Fam), [2006] 1 FLR 638 where the court declared lawful the withholding of life preserving treatment from a patient in a permanent vegetative state. For the impact in this context of Arts 2, 3 and 8 of the ECHR see *NHS Trust A v M, NHS Trust B v H* [2001] Fam 348, 355–63. For a case where a short trial of an experimental drug on a patient in a permanent vegetative state was authorized see *An NHS Trust v J* [2006] EWHC 3152 (Fam), (2006) 94 BMLR 15.

550 *Airedale NHS Trust v Bland* [1993] AC 789.

551 ibid, 858, 859, 868, 869, 884, 885, 897, 899.

conventional 'balance sheet' exercise is not normally appropriate because all the factors that are relevant normally fall on one side, with no countervailing factors in support of the continuation of treatment.[552] The views of the patient's relatives or of others close to the patient will be taken into account by the court but cannot act as a veto.[553]

(c) **The patient in a minimally conscious state** Patients in a minimally conscious state are, unlike a vegetative state, aware to some extent of themselves and their environment but do not have full consciousness. They may therefore experience pain. The first case in this country where the court was asked to authorise the withdrawal of ANH from a patient in a minimally conscious state was *W v M*.[554] A 43-year-old woman suffered from viral brain stem encephalitis resulting in extensive and irreparable brain damage. Initially diagnosed as being in a vegetative state, it transpired that she had regained a degree of consciousness and was clinically stable in a minimally conscious state. Her mother sought a declaration that it was lawful to withhold ANH treatment. **10.210**

The court dismissed the application. In all cases other than vegetative states—which favour the withdrawal of treatment—a best interests analysis required a balance sheet approach, comparing the advantages of withdrawing and the advantages of continuing treatment. There was no justification for introducing a requirement of clinical instability before embarking upon the MCA, s 4 test as this would introduce an impermissible gloss. However, what might be seen as components of clinical stability was unquestionably an important factor to be taken into account in the best interests analysis itself.[555] Conducting that analysis required careful scrutiny of important factors: (1) the preservation of life; (2) wishes and feelings; (3) pain; (4) enjoyment of life; (5) prospects of recovery; (6) dignity; (7) wishes and feelings of family members. As regards the second factor, given the importance of the sanctity of life, and the fatal consequences of withdrawing treatment, the absence of an advance decision, it would be wrong to attach significant weight to prior statements made by the patient. The decisive factor in this particular case was the importance of preserving life.[556] **10.211**

6. Deprivation of liberty

(i) Hospitals and care homes: Plugging the Bournewood gap

The Medical Treatment Act 1930 initially paved the way for the informal admission of voluntary and compliant incapacitated, known as 'non-volitional', mental health patients. The recommendations of the Percy Commission,[557] which favoured the absence of legal formality provided the offer of care did not involve deprivation of liberty, led to what is now s 131 of the Mental Health Act 1983. Subject to compliance with Article 5 of the European **10.212**

[552] *Gloucestershire CCG v AB, CD* [2014] EWCOP 49 at 17.

[553] *Bland*, n 550, at 871; *Re G (Persistent Vegetative State)* [1995] 2 FCR 46, 51. In *NHS Trust A v M, NHS Trust B v H* [2001] Fam 348, 361, Dame Elizabeth Butler-Sloss P left open the question of whether the wishes and feelings of the patient's family forms part of the patient's right to respect for family life under Art 8 of the ECHR.

[554] [2011] EWHC 2443, [2012] 1 WLR 1653; for commentary see A Mullock, 'Deciding the Fate of a Minimally Conscious Patient: An Unsatisfactory Balancing Act?' (2012) 20(3) Med L Rev 460.

[555] *W v M*, n 554, at [102]–[103].

[556] ibid at [219], [220], [223], [230], [231], [234], [238], [240], and [242]. See also *St George's Healthcare NHS Trust v P* [2015] EWCOP 42, [2015] COPLR 561 (balance in favour of continuing treatment); *United Lincolnshire Hospitals NHS Trust v N* [2014] EWCOP 16, [2014] COPLR 660 (balance favouring discontinuance of treatment). For a significant decision where the court sanctioned the withdrawal of artificial nutrition and hydration from someone in a minimally conscious state, see *Briggs v Briggs and others* [2016] EWCOP 53.

[557] *Report of the Royal Commission on the Law Relating to Mental Illness and Mental Deficiency* ('The Percy Report') (Cm159,1957); For the background to the 'lunacy legislation', see C R Unsworth, 'Mental Disorder and the Tutelary Relationship: From Pre- to Post-Carceral Legal Order' (1991) 18 Journal of Law and Society 254.

Convention for the Protection of Human Rights and Fundamental Freedoms, a deprivation of liberty for the purpose of treatment may be lawful if authorized by the court under the inherent jurisdiction[558] or if authorized by statute.[559] The Mental Capacity Act 2005 authorizes the detention of an incapacitated person in three situations: when authorized by the Court of Protection; when authorized (either as standard or urgent) under the deprivation of liberty safeguards ('DoLS') set out in s 4A and Schedules A1 and 1A to the 2005 Act; and when detention is necessary for the purpose of giving the person life-sustaining or other emergency treatment pending a decision from the Court of Protection.[560]

10.213 The DoLS were introduced in response to the *Bournewood* litigation.[561] HL was autistic and lacked the capacity to decide whether he should be admitted to a psychiatric hospital for treatment. He was described in the judgments as compliant[562] and was admitted on an informal basis under the common law in his best interests, but his carers challenged his detention. The ECtHR held that HL had been deprived of his liberty in contravention of Article 5(1). His detention had not been 'in accordance with a procedure prescribed by law'. There had also been a contravention of Article 5(4) as there was no formal procedure by which he could seek to review his detention. This so-called '*Bournewood* gap' was remedied, initially by the court exercising its inherent jurisdiction[563] and then by the amendment of the Mental Capacity Act 2005 by the Mental Health Act 2007 to provide a legal framework and safeguards for the deprivation of liberty of incapacitated patients detained in hospitals and care homes.[564] The DoLS have been found to be unfit for purpose[565] and the Law Commission has been tasked with devising their replacement.[566]

10.214 Most of the people covered by the DoLS are adults with significant learning disabilities, or older people who have dementia or some similar disability, but they can also include those who have certain other neurological conditions (for example as a result of a brain injury) or other mental disorder. The DoLS apply only to those detained in a hospital or care home and do not apply to patients under 18 or those who are detained in a hospital under mental health legislation.

10.215 The government published a Code of Practice on the Deprivation of Liberty Safeguards[567] which outlines when and how the safeguards apply. The Code

[558] See paras 10.117–10.118.

[559] MHA 1983 and MCA 2005.

[560] MCA, s 4B. For a detailed discussion of the safeguards see L Gostin et al (eds), *Principles of Mental Health Law and Policy* (Oxford University Press 2010) ch 11.

[561] *R v Bournewood Community and Mental Health NHS Trust, ex p L* [1999] AC 458; *HL v United Kingdom* (Application No 45508/99) (2005) 40 EHRR 32. For comment, see K Keywood, 'Detaining mentally disordered patients lacking capacity: The arbitrariness of informal detention and the common law doctrine of necessity' (2005) 13(1) Med L Rev 108.

[562] The oral evidence from treating clinicians during the Ombudsman's investigation suggests that HL was in fact objecting: see the Health Service Ombudsman's report (Case No. E. 2280/98–99); N Allen, 'The Bournewood Gap (as amended?)' (2010) Med L Rev 78.

[563] *Re PS (Incapacitated or Vulnerable Adult)* [2007] EWHC 623 (Fam), [2007] 2 FLR 1083; *LLBC v TG, JG and KR* [2007] EWHC 2640 (Fam), [2009] 1 FLR 414; *Re GJ, NJ and BJ (Incapacitated Adults)* [2008] EWHC 1097 (Fam), [2008] 2 FLR 1295; *Re BJ (Incapacitated Adult)* [2009] EWHC 3310 (Fam), [2010] 1 FLR 1373.

[564] See *GJ v Foundation Trust, PCT and the Secretary of State for Health* [2009] EWHC 2972 (Fam), [2010] 1 FLR 1251; *G v E, A Local Authority and F* [2010] EWHC 621 (Fam), [2010] 2 FLR 294 (appeal dismissed [2010] EWCA Civ 822).

[565] House of Lords Select Committee on the Mental Capacity Act, *Report of Session 2013–14: Mental Capacity Act 2005: Post-legislative Scrutiny* (HL 139, 2014) para 32.

[566] See Law Commission, *Mental Capacity and Deprivation of Liberty: A Consultation Paper* (Law Com No 222, 2015) and the Commission's 'Interim Statement' (25 May 2016).

[567] Mental Capacity Act 2005: Deprivation of Liberty Safeguards Code of Practice (TSO, 2008).

provides[568] that 'a managing authority' (ie the relevant hospital or care home) must seek authorization from a 'supervisory body' in order to be able lawfully to deprive someone of their liberty. Before giving such an authorization, the supervisory body must be satisfied that the person has a mental disorder and lacks capacity to decide about their residence and treatment. In England, the supervisory body (for both hospitals and care homes) is the local authority where the person is ordinarily resident. In Wales, for hospitals it is the local health board; for care homes it is the local authority. The DoLS make it clear that a person may only be deprived of their liberty in their best interests to protect them from harm, if it is a necessary and proportionate response to the likelihood and seriousness of the harm, having regard to less restrictive alternatives.[569] Any action taken under the DoLS must be in line with the general principles of the 2005 Act.

(ii) The safeguards

Focusing on hospital settings, when it appears that, judged objectively, there is a risk that cannot sensibly be ignored that, within the next twenty-eight days, the relevant circumstances of a patient's care will amount to a deprivation of liberty,[570] the hospital managers must request a standard authorization. If the deprivation is so urgent that it must begin before the request is made or dealt with, the managers can issue an urgent authorization for up to seven days, during which all the standard authorization assessments must be completed.[571] These relate to the person's age, 'no refusals', mental capacity, mental health, eligibility, and best interests.[572] But urgent authorizations 'should normally only be used in response to sudden unforeseen needs' although 'they can be used in care planning (for example, to avoid delays in transfer for rehabilitation, where delay would reduce the likely benefit of the rehabilitation)'.[573] **10.216**

The following principal safeguards are provided by the statutory scheme for patients (referred to as 'detained residents'): **10.217**

1. The authorization to deprive liberty must be sought in advance, thereby avoiding arbitrary detention.
2. The 'cornerstone of the protection' is an independent assessment undertaken of the patient's best interests.[574]
3. Objective medical expertise determines whether the person has a mental disorder.
4. Maximum period of authorization is twelve months at a time.
5. The availability of conditions attached to the standard authorization to reduce the intensity of the deprivation of liberty.
6. The appointment of a representative to maintain contact with the detained resident and represent and support them in matters relating to or connected with DoLS.[575]
7. Non-means tested legal aid to challenge the authorization in the Court of Protection.

568 ibid, para 1.4.
569 ibid, para 1.13.
570 *AM v South London and Maudsley NHS Foundation Trust and Secretary of State for Health* [2013] UKUT 365 (AAC) at [59]; see also MCA, Sch A1 paras 24 and 76; DoLS Code of Practice paras 3.4 and 3.7.
571 The supervisory body can extend the urgent authorization by a further seven days if there are exceptional reasons, but this would not cover staffing shortages; see DoLS Code of Practice para 6.24.
572 DoLS Code of Practice ch 4.
573 DoLS Code of Practice para 6.2; see also *NHS Trust v FG* [2014] EWCOP 30, [2015] 1 WLR 1984 at [101].
574 *London Borough of Hillingdon v Neary and others* [2011] EWCOP 1377 at [174].
575 DoLS Code of Practice ch 7.

8. A clear right of access to the Court of Protection under Article 5(4) ECHR that is not dependent upon the exercise of discretion by a third party.[576]
9. The availability of IMCAs with additional rights and responsibilities compared with an IMCA more generally instructed under the Mental Capacity Act.[577]
10. A requirement on managing authorities to review the continued need for the authorization and to seek a review.

(iii) Restricted movement or 'deprived' of liberty?

10.218 A key issue is determining precisely when a person is deprived of their liberty as opposed to having their liberty merely restricted, the difference being one of 'degree or intensity'.[578] One major criticism identified academically and by the Law Commission is the DoLS' fixation on Article 5 means that the trigger for the safeguards is 'based on case law which continues to be a moving target'.[579] Article 5 is engaged where a trinity of factors are satisfied. First, the objective element is that the person is confined to a particular restricted place for a non-negligible period of time. Second, the subjective element is that the person does not consent to that confinement. And, thirdly, the deprivation is one for which the State is directly or indirectly responsible which will always be the case in hospitals, both NHS and independent.[580] It follows that where a patient consents with capacity to a hospital admission, they are not deprived of their liberty. For those lacking such capacity, whether their hospital care engages Article 5 will depend upon the objective element.

10.219 **(a) The objective element** In *P v Cheshire West and Chester Council* and *P & Q v Surrey County Council*, the Supreme Court confirmed the universal nature of human rights.[581] Thus what it means to be deprived of liberty must be the same for everyone, irrespective of any disability, and because of the extreme vulnerability of those like P, MIG, and MEG, we must err on the side of caution in determining what constitutes a deprivation. The fact that the care arrangements make the person comfortable, and their life as enjoyable as it could possibly be, makes no difference: 'a gilded cage is still a cage'. Whether they comply or object, the relative normality of the placement, and the reason or purpose behind the placement are not relevant. Whether the objective element is satisfied depends upon an 'acid test'. The starting point must be the person's concrete situation, taking into account a range of criteria such as the type, duration, effects and manner of implementation of the restrictive measures in question. But if the person is subject to continuous (or complete) supervision and control and not free to leave, they are confined.[582]

10.220 The judgment has introduced a new era of legalism in health and social care.[583] Overnight, hundreds of thousands of incapacitated people being cared for suddenly met the 'acid test'

[576] *Re AJ (Deprivation of Liberty Safeguards)* [2015] EWCOP 5, [2015] Fam. 291; see also *RD & Ors (Duties and Powers of Relevant Person's Representatives and Section 39D IMCAs)* [2016] EWCOP 49.

[577] DoLS Code of Practice, para 3.22.

[578] DoLS Code of Practice, para 2.3.

[579] Law Commission (Law Com No 222, 2015) para 2.14. See also N Allen, 'Restricting movement or depriving liberty?' (2009) Journal of Mental Health Law 19.

[580] This third element will be satisfied when treatment is provided in an NHS or private hospital, so a detailed analysis is therefore outside the scope of this chapter. In relation to deputies and state imputability, see *Staffordshire CC v SRK* [2016] EWCA Civ 1317.

[581] [2014] UKSC 19, [2014] AC 896 at [45].

[582] Chapter 2 of the MCA DoLS Code of Practice, which includes a helpful non-exhaustive list of factors that can be relevant to identifying a deprivation of liberty, must now be read subject to the Supreme Court's decision. See also 'Deprivation of liberty: a practical guide' (Law Society, 2015), ch 4 (the hospital setting).

[583] For a critical perspective, see N Allen, 'The (not so?) Great Confinement' (2015) Elder Law Journal 45. The scale of the impact of the Supreme Court's decision is reflected in the use of DoLS. According to the figures published by NHS Digital, in England there were 13,715 requests for a standard authorization in 2013–14, compared with 195,840 in 2015–16.

and became 'deprived' of liberty, necessitating safeguards and State authorization. The following are examples of hospital patients lacking the relevant decisional capacity that have been found to be deprived of their liberty:

- Woman transferred by ambulance from a psychiatric unit to the maternity unit of an acute hospital for a caesarean section where the use of restraint was envisaged; obstetric and midwifery staff to be constantly present throughout her labour and delivery; under the continuous control of such staff who, because of her incapacity, take decisions on her behalf in her best interests; and not permitted to leave the delivery suite.[584]
- Being required to remain in a 'section 136' suite of the Maudsley hospital for thirteen hours until being detained under the Mental Health Act 1983. The suite was unlocked but she would have been prevented from leaving had she tried.[585]
- Patient with delusional disorder on hunger strike having to be force fed involving the use of restraint while a nasogastric tube was inserted and to prevent its removal; sedation used on occasions; not allowed to leave the hospital; complete control over his care, treatment, and movements resulting in his loss of a very significant degree of personal autonomy.[586]
- Forcible entry into the patient's home to convey her to a community health service resource and, using physical restraint, to administer a Depo-Provera contraceptive injection.[587]
- Forcible entry into the patient's home, use of restraint to convey her to hospital, and the undertaking of a sterilization procedure by laporoscopic application of Filshie clips across the fallopian tubes to occlude them, whilst the patient was under general anaesthetic.[588]
- Objecting patient required to be transferred to hospital for dental surgery to remove lower teeth and thereafter to remain as an inpatient; five to six days later she would receive cardiac surgery, with the possibility of post-operative physical and sedation to overcome her resistance; most of the monitoring equipment to be removed within forty-eight hours but the recovery period would be ten to fifteen days with intensive care staff.[589]

(b) The subjective element Where a patient does not object to being in hospital, their capacity to decide whether to be there to receive the relevant care or treatment is crucial. If they have capacity and consent, they are not deprived and are free to leave (unless the holding power in s 5 of the Mental Health Act 1983 is invoked to undertake an assessment). If they lack capacity, they will be deprived of liberty if the objective element is met. Broadly speaking, the decision to be admitted to a hospital is likely to include consideration of the relevance of the admission for the relevant purpose, to stay in hospital whilst its purpose is carried out, and to the circumstances relating to a possible deprivation of liberty.[590] These are the salient details of the decision that should be considered when assessing the patient's capacity to make the decision.[591] **10.221**

584 *NHS Trusts v FG* [2014] EWCOP 30, [2015] 1 WLR 1984 at [96]. This was endorsed in *R (Ferreira) v HM Senior Coroner for Inner South London* [2017] EWCA Civ 31, where it was held that there is in general no deprivation of liberty where a person is receiving life-saving treatment in intensive care. This seems to be essentially because it is not covered by Article 5(1), is a commonly occurring restriction on movement, and beyond the State's control. Note, also, that the Police and Crime Act 2017, s 178 exempts authorised deprivations of liberty from 'state detention' for coroner-purposes.

585 *R (Sessay) v South London and Maudsley NHS Foundation Trust and others* [2011] EWHC 2617 (QB), [2012] QB 760.

586 *A NHS Trust v Dr A* [2013] EWHC 2442 (COP), [2014] Fam 161. See also *A Local Authority v E and others* [2012] EWHC 1639 (COP), [2012] 2 FCR 523; for comment, see J Coggon, 'Anorexia nervosa, best interests, and the patient's human right to a 'wholesale overwhelming of her autonomy' (2014) 22(1) Med L Rev 119.

587 *The Mental Health Trust and others v DD* [2014] EWCOP 44.

588 *The Mental Health Trust and others v DD* [2015] EWCOP 5.

589 *A Local Health Board v AB* [2015] EWCOP 31. The validity of the decision with regard to the patient's supposed ineligibility is open the doubt.

590 *AM v South London and Maudsley NHS Foundation Trust and Secretary of State for Health* [2013] UKUT 0365.

591 See also *M v Ukraine* [2012] ECHR 732 at [77]; *A PCT v LDV and others* [2013] EWHC 272 (Fam) at [39]–[40].

10.222 (c) **Other criticisms** In addition to the difficulty in drawing a line between restricting movement and depriving liberty, the Law Commission found that the DoLS' narrow focus on Article 5: (a) assumed that staff could identify and respond to deprivations of liberty; (b) meant DoLS had little to say about Article 8 ECHR; (c) and they ran counter to the policy of prevention. Further criticisms included:

- A disconnect with the MCA, which was in practice being viewed as separate from the DoLS;
- Potential conflicts of interest, particularly where a local authority acted as both the supervisory body and the commissioner of care;
- Being limited in scope to hospitals and care homes, DoLS does not apply to other care settings, such as supported living and shared lives accommodation, where Article 5 could be engaged;
- The scheme imposes a one-size-fits-all approach, so deprivations in intensive care hospital wards are administratively dealt with in the same way as, for example, long-stay care home;
- There is a lack of an effective system of oversight and monitoring, for example with regard to the implementation of conditions, and no system of automatic referral to court;
- The drafting of the legislation is lengthy and complex;
- The language of the law was ill-suited with inadequate terminology;
- DoLS were designed to provide comprehensive safeguards for a relatively small number of cases rather than to the number of those lacking the relevant capacity who, since, may now be deprived of liberty.

(iv) Future reform

10.223 The Law Commission originally proposed a system of 'protective care' consisting of different elements. 'Supportive care' in the community would establish a preventive set of care planning safeguards, aimed at reducing the need for intrusive interventions in the longer term. 'Restrictive care and treatment' would replace the DoLS but be broader in scope with more robust safeguards. And a bespoke system of safeguards was proposed for hospitals and palliative care, which were bolstered if the patient was to remain for more than twenty-eight days. Amendments were also proposed to the Mental Health Act 1983 to enable the admission of compliant incapacitated mental health patients but with greater safeguards than at present.

10.224 A consultation period followed, with 83 nationwide events and 583 written responses from interested persons and organizations. It led to a revised, narrower approach. Where a person is to be deprived of liberty, the commissioning body—usually the local authority or NHS body—will authorize it. The necessary evidence in support will include (a) a capacity assessment; (b) objective medical evidence of the need for a deprivation of liberty on account of the person's mental health; (c) arranging provision of advocacy (or assistance from 'an appropriate person'); (d) consultation with family members and others; (e) an existing care plan. With an increased emphasis on rights and access to advocacy and reviews, the proposed reform would appear to abolish the supervisory body and, controversially, not require an independent best interests assessment as a matter of routine. As such, it risks offending the policy aim of the decision, to provide 'a periodic independent check on whether the arrangements made for them are in their best interests'.[592] However, the Law Commission does envisage this safeguard for a defined group:

[592] *P v Cheshire West and Chester Council* and *P & Q v Surrey County Council* [2014] UKSC 19, [2014] AC 896 at [57].

1.42 In addition we are considering whether a defined group of people should receive additional independent oversight of the deprivation of their liberty, which would be undertaken by an Approved Mental Capacity Professional. Owing to the vast number of people now considered to be deprived of their liberty following *Cheshire West*, it would not be proportionate or affordable to provide such oversight to all those caught by article 5 of the ECHR. Whilst we are still working to develop the precise criteria that would operate to identify this group, we envisage that this group would consist of those who are subject to greater infringement of their rights, including, in particular, their rights to private and family life under article 8 of the ECHR.

The new scheme will therefore apply to incapacitated patients that are deprived of liberty in hospital for *physical* health care in their best interests. But it will not apply to those admitted to hospital for the purpose of assessment and treatment of *mental* disorder. Their admission, including those that are compliant but lack capacity to consent, will in future be governed by the Mental Health Act if the Law Commission's interim proposals are enacted. The purpose of hospital detention will therefore be the key identifier of the relevant scheme of safeguards. **10.225**

(v) Judicial safeguards: Re X

Pending law reform, and in anticipation of a significant number of deprivations of liberty in care settings other than hospitals and care homes requiring judicial authorization, the Court of Protection developed a system of safeguards to protect the Article 5 rights of those deprived of their liberty. In *Re X and others (Deprivation of Liberty)*[593] the President devised a streamlined process for uncontested cases to be dealt with, which provides minimum evidential requirements and a system of review. In *Re NRA*,[594] it was noted that the cost of implementing the Supreme Court's judgment will reduce the numbers and quality of available placements for those lacking capacity. The judgment also addresses[595] the controversial issues of party status, litigation friends, and representatives, and stresses the inquisitorial approach of the court. **10.226**

G. Conclusions

The Mental Capacity Act 2005 has already been influential in modernizing the law. As discussed in Chapter 9, its assumption of capacity from the age of 16 promotes the autonomy of young people and challenges 'condition-stigma' of all ages. The statutory requirement for all practicable steps to promote the exercise of autonomy resonates well with Article 12 CRPD. But with regard to welfare, the Act expressly enables others to make best interests decisions for those lacking mental capacity. At some level, health and social care requires a legal mechanism for co-decision-making; otherwise the most vulnerable risk being subjected to harm, either by act or omission, which would make for a perverse kind of equality. **10.227**

The CRPD provides an international aspiration for our domestic direction of travel. But the Convention must be seen as a whole. The MCA aims to strike a difficult balance between enhancing autonomy and protection from harm. Similarly, Article 12 CRPD requires equal recognition of legal capacity whilst Article 16 CRPD requires the protection of those with **10.228**

593 [2014] EWCOP 25 and [2014] EWCOP 37. See also COPR 2007 Practice Direction 10A: Deprivation of Liberty Applications and *Re X (Court of Protection Practice)* [2015] EWCOP Civ 599. Improvements to be procedure were identified in *Re NRA* [2015] EWCOP 59 at [225]–[229].

594 *Re NRA* [2015] EWCOP 59.

595 ibid at [16]. See also *Re JM* and *Re VE* [2016] 4 WLR 64.

disabilities from all forms of exploitation, violence and abuse. Perhaps the most significant challenge to the MCA (and the MHA) is Article 14 CRPD which provides, 'the existence of a disability shall in no case justify a deprivation of liberty'. Early international signals suggest that they are vulnerable to criticism from the UN Committee which is likely to call for their review.[596]

10.229 There is no doubt that the MCA was visionary for its time, although its origins date back to the 1990s. Of most concern, however, is that it has been 'largely unimplemented'.[597] Cultures of paternalism in health and risk-aversion in social care prevail and its empowering ethos has not been delivered. Whether implementing the thirty-nine recommendations of the House of Lords Select Committee will shield the Act from criticism from the UN seems unlikely. However, the Law Commission's current work may provide an opportunity to at least fine-tune aspects of our domestic law to better comply with our international aspirations. Its revised approach will strengthen Article 8 safeguards. It will give 'greater priority to the person's wishes and feelings when a best interests decision is being made'. Perhaps the most fundamental of the reforms is the proposal to qualify the immunity from legal action in MCA, s 5 'to provide additional procedural safeguards in respect of certain key decisions by public authorities'.[598] For withholding the legal flak jacket of liability may prove to be an effective way of securing the MCA philosophy.

[596] See, eg, UN Committee on Rights of Persons with Disabilities report on Spain (6th session, 19–23 September 2011, Concluding observations, CRPD/C/ESP/CO/1, 19 October 2011); Australia (10th session, 2–13 September 2013, CRPD/C/Aus/CO/1, published 24 October 2013); New Zealand (12th session, 15 September–3 October 2014, CRPD/C/NZL/CO/1, published 31 October 2014).

[597] House of Lords Select Committee on the Mental Capacity Act: Report of Session 2013-14: Mental Capacity Act 2005: Post-legislative Scrutiny (2014), 6.

[598] Law Commission's *Interim Statement* (25 May 2016).

11

MENTAL HEALTH LAW

Judith Laing and Nicola Glover-Thomas

A. Introduction

This chapter will consider the framework for compulsory admission and treatment of patients suffering from mental disorder under the Mental Health Act 1983, as amended by the Mental Health Act 2007. The legislation applies to England and Wales as the Scottish Parliament has passed its own statute, the Mental Health (Care and Treatment) (Scotland) Act 2003 (as amended by the Mental Health (Scotland) Act 2015) which came in to force in 2005. The main purpose of mental health legislation is to ensure that some patients suffering from a mental disorder (as defined) are forced to accept admission to hospital and/or compulsory treatment without their consent. The Mental Health Act 2007 sets out the criteria and procedures to be followed to enable that to take place. The Act permits both 'civil' hospital admissions as well as criminal justice admissions from the courts or prison. The primary focus in the 2007 Act is on the presence of mental disorder and the risk posed by the patient to him/herself or others. The Act tries to strike a balance between individual autonomy and society's right to deprive that individual of their liberty. Most provisions of the 2007 Act came into force in November 2008. It represents the culmination of a protracted and controversial reform process, which began in 1998 and is briefly outlined below. **11.01**

Part II of the 2007 Act has also amended the Mental Capacity Act 2005 (MCA) by introducing new provisions for the deprivation of liberty of adults who lack mental capacity. These changes will not be considered in this chapter as they are discussed elsewhere in this book (see Chapters 9 and 10). However, there is some potential overlap between the two statutes and reference will be made to the 2005 Act where appropriate. In some cases, it may not be entirely clear which statute should be used to deprive an individual of their liberty. As outlined briefly below, the courts have made it clear that the decision should be a matter of professional judgment. The Mental Health Act is clearly the preferred route when the patient does need treatment for a mental disorder and where it is necessary to protect the patient or others. It also applies when the individual is objecting to treatment, irrespective **11.02** of his/her capacity to do so, whereas the 2005 Act would obviously be more appropriate for a patient who lacks capacity to consent to treatment and requires treatment for a physical disorder. However, the dividing line between the two is not always clear. In *GJ v The Foundation Trust*[1] the High Court stated that where there is any doubt which of the two statutes to use, the Mental Health Act has 'primacy' whenever it applies. Charles J declared that it would be unlawful for any professional 'to proceed on the basis that they can pick and choose between the two statutory regimes as they think fit'.[2] Accordingly, the mental health statutory framework would seem to take precedence and potentially has a much broader reach than the mental capacity legislation. However, in *AM v Slam NHA Foundation Trust*[3] the same judge took a rather different approach and cautioned against making general propositions about the interrelationship between the two legislative schemes. Instead, the question of primacy should be case and fact specific, based on a determination of the least restrictive way of best achieving the proposed assessment and treatment:

> In my judgment, the rationale for this more flexible approach, is that in certain circumstances which it has defined in the MHA and the MCA Parliament has provided statutory regimes which may or do provide alternatives and so choices which fall to be considered by the relevant statutory decision makers under the two schemes . . . the theoretical and practical availability of the MCA regime and its DOLS is one of the factors that needs to be considered by the MHA decision maker in carrying out that search, as are their overall impact in best achieving the desired objective when compared with other available choices and so detention under ss. 2 or 3 MHA (at para 75).

11.03 It would appear that the interface between the two Acts is becoming increasingly complex, particularly in light of this judicial recognition that the Mental Capacity Act Deprivation of Liberty regime must be borne in mind by professionals when making decisions about whether detention is warranted under the Mental Health Act. It is clearly difficult to generalize about which is the least restrictive regime and much will depend on the individual facts and proposed care regime in each case. Some additional guidance is provided in the latest Mental Health Act Code of Practice,[4] and makes it clear that a key factor will be whether the individual is *objecting* to the proposed care/treatment, and if so, the Mental Health Act must be used. In all other circumstances, however, the Code simply reinforces that the decision must be made based on the least restrictive alternative available on the facts of each individual case:

> The choice of legal regime should never be based on a general preference for one regime or the other, or because one regime is more familiar to the decision-maker than the other. Such considerations are not legally relevant and lead to arbitrary decision-making. In addition decision-makers should not proceed on the basis that one regime is generally less restrictive than the other. Both regimes are based on the need to impose as few restrictions on the liberty and autonomy of patients as possible. In the particular circumstances of an individual case, it may be apparent that one regime is likely to prove less restrictive. If so, this should be balanced against any potential benefits associated with the other regime.

[1] *GJ v The Foundation Trust* [2009] EWHC 2972 (Fam). See also G Ashton et al, *Mental Capacity: The New Law* (Jordans 2006).

[2] *GJ v The Foundation Trust*, n 1, at para 59. The court also stated that, in deciding which statute is most appropriate, the decision-makers should apply a 'but for' test to determine whether the person was within the scope of the legislation and should focus on the purpose of the treatment in making their decision. For commentary on this case see N Allen, 'The Bournewood Gap (As Amended)' (2010) 18(1) Med L Rev 78–85.

[3] (2013) UKUT 365 (AAC).

[4] Department of Health, *Mental Health Act 1983: Code of Practice* (The Stationery Office 2015) paras 13.49–13.62. See also Welsh Government, *Mental Health Act 1983 Code of Practice for Wales Review* (October 2016) Chapter 14.

In the relatively small number of cases where detention under the Act and a Deprivation of Liberty authorization or Court of Protection order are available, the Code of Practice does not seek to preferentially orientate the decision-maker in any given direction. Such a decision should always be made depending on the unique circumstances of each case.[5]

This chapter will focus on the compulsory detention and treatment provisions in the Mental Health Act 1983 as amended by Pt I of the 2007 Act. It will briefly outline the reform process which culminated in the 2007 Act, followed by a consideration of the primary functions in Pt 1 of the Act including the definition of mental disorder; the grounds, procedures and principles for compulsory detention and treatment of patients both in hospital and the community; the professional roles and safeguards against arbitrary detention such as the presence of advocacy, nearest relatives, and the Mental Health Review Tribunal. The Department of Health has issued a revised Code of Practice in 2015 to guide mental health professionals in implementing the Act correctly, which will also be considered in the discussion below. **11.04**

B. Background

1. Introduction

The Mental Health Act 1983 was based on its predecessor, the Mental Health Act 1959, which had generally been perceived as an enlightened piece of legislation. It endorsed the so-called medical model of mental illness,[6] focusing on prompt treatment of the mentally ill and mandating the role of the medical profession in the admission and treatment process. The role of psychiatrists in making recommendations for compulsory admission and controlling the treatment and discharge process was reaffirmed in the 1983 Act. The 1983 Act also sought to bolster patient rights with detailed criteria and procedures for hospital admission and the presence of Approved Social Workers (ASW) in the admissions process. The ASW was intended to provide a social perspective to counterbalance the medical opinion. Safeguards also included Mental Health Review Tribunals to provide an independent and automatic review of detention (see paras 11.183 et seq). These legislative developments were accompanied by a policy shift away from hospital-based treatment to care in the community. Since the mid-1950s, there has been a massive decline in the number of psychiatric inpatient beds and an increasing reliance on community-based services and support. **11.05**

As the years progressed it became apparent that the 1983 Act was not functioning as effectively as it could have done. A number of highly publicized homicides in the 1990s involving former mental patients who had attacked or killed innocent members of the public, as well as concerns about the high suicide rates among the mentally ill, prompted the government to consider mental health law reform. There were also concerns that community-based services had been very slow to develop and were inadequate to meet the needs of the mentally disordered population. The government published a policy document in January 1998 which stated that 'care in the community has failed' because 'it left far too many walking the streets, often at risk to themselves and a nuisance to others'.[7] The document announced **11.06**

---

[5] ibid. paras 13.58, 13.60.

[6] See further K Jones, *Asylums and After: A Revised History of the Mental Health Services* (Athlone Press 1993); C Unsworth, *The Politics of Mental Health Legislation* (Oxford University Press 1985); P Fennell, 'Mental Health Law: History, Policy and Regulation' in L Gostin et al (eds), *Principles of Mental Health Law and Policy* (Oxford University Press 2010).

[7] *Mental Health Policy: Safe, Sound and Supportive* (DoH 1998).

the government's intention to update the law (i) to ensure that patients who were considered a danger to themselves or others could not refuse to comply with treatment and (ii) to permit the detention of dangerous people with severe and untreatable personality disorder.[8]

2. The reform process

(i) The Richardson Committee Report

11.07 The reform process began in 1998 with the appointment of an expert committee (chaired by Professor Genevra Richardson) to review the 1983 Act.[9] The Richardson Committee suggested that it might be appropriate to change the current structure to reflect modern practice and contemporary patterns of care.[10] Foremost was the Committee's desire to promote the principle of non-discrimination which led to an emphasis on patient rights and autonomy. Specifically, the Committee recommended a broad definition of mental disorder but narrowed the criteria for compulsion. There would be a single pathway to compulsory treatment which could take place either in hospital or in the community. The Mental Health Tribunal would have a central role in authorizing and reviewing compulsion. Following an initial twenty-eight-day assessment, the tribunal would be required to authorize longer-term compulsion in hospital or the community. Accordingly, the Committee recommended that key principles should be included on the face of the legislation as well as in the Code of Practice. The principles included non-discrimination, equality, respect for diversity, informal and consensual care, as well as explicit recognition of the importance of patient autonomy and capacity. The Committee was mindful of the need to provide a framework to protect public safety, but was also keen to provide rights for those subjected to compulsion where appropriate and encourage best practice generally.

(ii) The government response

11.08 Following a lengthy and uncertain period of consultation, Draft Mental Health Bills were published in 2002, 2004, and 2006 which culminated in the Mental Health Act 2007. The government published a White Paper in 2000 which led to a Draft Mental Health Bill in 2002. It was the result of a joint collaboration between the Home Office and Department of Health and rejected many of the Richardson Committee proposals.[11] The then government's initial proposals have been described as 'controlling and cautionary' and signified a 'shift away from patient oriented principles'.[12] Consequently, the focus was placed on risk as a key factor in the compulsion decision, introducing more effective compulsory community powers and ensuring that dangerous and severely personality disordered patients could be subject to detention in the mental health system. As noted by Fennell, '[s]ince the 1990s successive governments have pursued a public safety agenda in relation to mental health services responding to concerns about homicides by mentally disordered people'.[13] Accordingly, the Draft Bill emphasized public protection and risk management at the expense of individual

---

[8] For further discussion of the government's proposals for patients with dangerous and severe personality disorder see J M Laing, 'Detaining the Dangerous: Legal and Ethical Implications of the Government's Proposals to Detain High-risk Individuals' (2002) 66(1) Journal of Criminal Law 64–83.

[9] For further discussion of the reform process, see D Pilgrim, 'New "Mental Health" Legislation for England and Wales: Some Aspects of Consensus and Conflict' (2007) 36(1) Journal of Social Policy 79–95.

[10] Report of the Expert Committee, *Review of the Mental Health Act 1983* (1999).

[11] For a detailed discussion of the main differences between the expert report and the government's response, see J Laing, 'Rights versus Risk? Reform of the Mental Health Act 1983' (2000) 8(2) Medical Law Review 210–50; J Peay, 'Reform of the Mental Health Act 1983: Squandering and Opportunity?' (2000) Journal of Mental Health Law, February, 5–15.

[12] Peay, n 11, 8, 10.

[13] P Fennell, *Mental Health: Law and Practice* (Jordans 2011), para 1.16.

liberty and principles such as non-discrimination.[14] Not surprisingly, the proposals were subject to widespread opposition from a number of sources including professional bodies, mental health charities, carers, and user groups.[15] However, the government pressed ahead with its risk-based agenda and introduced a Draft Bill in 2004 which mirrored the 2002 draft proposals. Following strong criticism from the Parliamentary Joint Committee on Human Rights,[16] the government decided to introduce an amending measure rather than a new piece of legislation. Consequently, a shorter Bill was introduced into the House of Lords in 2006 and the Mental Health Act 2007 was given the Royal Assent in July 2007. Whilst the Act introduced a number of key changes which were intended to bolster patients' rights, such as advocacy services and amendments to the nearest relative provisions, overall many of the new provisions would seem to be focused on public safety, risk management, and ensuring compliance with treatment.

(iii) Key changes introduced by the 2007 Act

The 2007 Act amended the 1983 Act and set out a new framework for determining when and how people will be subject to the use of compulsory powers. It made a number of significant changes, notably broadening and simplifying the definition of mental disorder as well as extending the powers of compulsion in the community—with the introduction of Supervised Community Treatment orders. Supervised Community Treatment (SCT) replaced after-care under supervision and provides a framework for the management of patient care in the community, following a period of detention in hospital. It reflects modern service provision enabling patients with serious mental health problems to be treated outside hospital where it is appropriate. SCT is designed to enable a small number of patients with a mental disorder to live in the community whilst subject to certain conditions under the 1983 Act, to ensure they continue with the medical treatment that they need. Prior to its introduction, some patients left hospital and discontinued their treatment, their health deteriorated and they required detention again—the so-called 'revolving door'. SCT is an attempt to respond to this peripatetic behaviour by providing closer supervision in the community. It is also intended to reduce the risk of social exclusion, which is associated with detention in hospital for long periods of time.[17] This power as well as other means of providing compulsory treatment in the community will be considered further in paras 11.133 et seq. **11.09**

The 2007 Act broadened the group of practitioners who can take on key professional roles in the admission, assessment, and treatment processes under the Act. The Approved Mental Health Professional role includes mental health/learning disability nurses, chartered psychologists, and occupational therapists, as well as social workers. The Act also expanded the **11.10**

[14] Homicides by the mentally ill account for 5–10 per cent of all killings in England and Wales. Whilst they are not increasing (see PJ Taylor and J Gunn, 'Homicides by People with Mental Illness: Myth and Reality' (1999) 174 Br J Psychiatry 9–14) neither are they falling, and research has shown that non-compliance with treatment in the community is an important cause of such tragedies (see L Appleby, J Shaw, J Sherratt et al, *Safety First: Five-Year Report of the Confidential Inquiry Into Suicide and Homicide by People with Mental Illness* (Stationery Office 2001)).

[15] See, eg, the Mental Health Alliance located at <http://www.mentalhealthalliance.org.uk>; R Hargreaves, 'The Mental Health Bill 2006—A Social Work Perspective' (2007) Journal of Mental Health Law 85–96; P Walton, 'Reforming the Mental Health Act 1983: An Approved Social Worker Perspective' (2000) 22(4) The Journal of Social Welfare and Family Law 401–14.

[16] House of Lords, House of Commons Joint Pre-Parliamentary Scrutiny Committee, *Report on the Draft Mental Health Bill* (HL Paper 79(1); HC Paper 95(1) Session 2004–05. See further P Fennell, 'Protection! Protection! Protection! The Government's Response to the Joint Parliamentary Scrutiny Committee on the Mental Health Bill 2004' (2005) Journal of Mental Health Law (Nov) 1–3.

[17] Department of Health, *Mental Health Bill 2006 Summary Guide* (November 2006), 3.

Registered Medical Practitioner role to permit professionals who are not Registered Medical Practitioners (ie doctors) to take on the role, which is now described as the Responsible Clinician (RC). The government envisaged that the roles would be fulfilled by, inter alia, first level nurses, chartered psychologists, and occupational therapists,[18] provided they have undergone relevant training. These changes were designed to reflect modern NHS practices which have moved towards a more 'competency-based' approach to roles and responsibilities. Arguably, the changes may also have been driven by the significant difficulties in recruiting and retaining social workers and psychiatrists, due to the increasing demands of the roles, coupled with high caseloads[19] and increasing degrees of burnout among social workers[20] and consultants.[21]

11.11 The 2007 Act made a number of changes to the role of the nearest relative, who has the power to apply for compulsory admission and challenge the patient's compulsory detention. The nearest relative is determined by virtue of a statutory list which was modified by the 2007 Act to include civil partners as well as same or opposite sex couples living together as man and wife. As a result of a successful challenge to the 1983 Act under the Human Rights Act 1998,[22] the 2007 Act also introduced a new provision to enable the patient to seek displacement of an unsuitable nearest relative. The role of nearest relative is discussed further in paras 11.193–11.201. A key development in the 2007 Act is the introduction of Mental Health Advocates to provide support for all patients subject to the provisions under the Act (with the exception of those held under ss 4, 5, 135, or 136). Section 30(2) places a duty on the Secretary of State (or Welsh Assembly) to provide advocacy services, which includes help in obtaining information about and understanding the provisions of the Act and why they have been applied. Advocacy also includes help in obtaining information about any rights which may be exercised in relation to the patient. Advocacy is perceived to be an important protection for the patient and is discussed further in paras 11.202–11.208. Another important mechanism for safeguarding patients and standards of mental health care was perceived to be the Mental Health Act Commission.[23] It was established in the 1983 Act as a multidisciplinary and independent body to monitor and oversee the use of compulsory powers in the Act. The Commission carried out regular hospital inspection visits, investigated the handling of complaints made by detained patients and produced biennial reports. Significantly, the MHAC was abolished in 2008 and its functions transferred to the Care Quality Commission (CQC), a new integrated health and social care regulator. This step brought together existing health and social care regulators into one body. The role and functions of the CQC are discussed in paras 11.216–11.220.

11.12 The Code of Practice, which accompanies the mental health legislation, has also been amended to reflect all these changes. The Code has been subject to several revisions to date, most recently in 2008, followed by a public consultation[24] and further amendments

[18] NHS Act 2006; MHA 1983, Approved Clinician Directions 2008.

[19] A Dean, *The Consultant Psychiatrist in the New Millennium* (Royal College of Psychiatrists 2001).

[20] See P Huxley et al, 'Stress and Pressures in Mental Health Social Work: The Worker Speaks' (2005) 35 British Journal of Social Work 1063–79.

[21] R Kendell and A Pearce, 'Consultant Psychiatrists who Retired Prematurely 1995 and 1996' (1997) 21 Psychiatric Bulletin 741–45.

[22] See *JT v United Kingdom* (2000) 30 EHRR CD 77 (ECtHR).

[23] See, eg, I Shaw, H Middleton, and J Cohen (eds), *Understanding Treatment Without Consent: An Analysis of the Work of the Mental Health Act Commission* (Ashgate 2007); J McHale, 'Standards, Quality and Accountability – the NHS and mental health: a case for joined-up thinking?' (2003) 25(4) The Journal of Social Welfare and Family Law 313.

[24] Department of Health, *Mental Health Act 1983: Draft Code of Practice for consultation* (TSO 2014) located at <www.gov.uk/government/uploads/system/uploads/attachment_data/file/329778/DoH_Code_of_Practice_accessible.pdf>. See also Department of Health, *Stronger Code: Better Care. Consultation on*

in 2015. The most recent changes were necessary in light of substantial policy, case law, and legislative updates as well as changes to professional practice since 2008. Specifically, the updated Code reflects developments in key areas such as the use of Community Treatment Orders, the use of police powers to detain mentally disordered people and the use of restrictive practices. One of the main changes to the recent editions of the Code is the inclusion of explicit principles to guide decision-making under the Act. The principles are designed to promote respect for mentally disordered individuals and their carers and are discussed more fully in paras 11.14–11.18. Whilst the Code is not legally binding, it is a statutory document, and failure to follow it could lead to legal challenge.[25]

A final important statutory safeguard is the patient's right to appeal against detention to an independent tribunal. Mental Health Review Tribunals were introduced by the Mental Health Act 1959 to provide patients with an opportunity to seek independent review of their continued detention. The tribunal system was left largely untouched by the 2007 Act and the only changes relate to the system of automatic reviews where a patient has not applied for review and the establishment of separate Tribunals for England and Wales. However, the passing of the Tribunals, Courts and Enforcement Act 2007 led to the recent replacement in England of the MHRT by a new First-tier Tribunal (Mental Health). The operation of the tribunal is considered more fully in paras 11.182 et seq. **11.13**

C. The Current Law

1. The guiding principles in the Code of Practice

(i) The principles

Section 118 of the 1983 Act places a duty on the Secretary of State (and the National Assembly in Wales) to prepare, and from time to time, revise a Code of Practice 'for the guidance' of those exercising functions in relation to the admission and treatment of patients under the 1983 Act. The Code in England includes five guiding principles which are set out in Chapter 1. The Welsh Assembly first published a Code of Practice for Wales in 2008. The Code has recently been revised and also lists guiding principles to underpin the legislation, as it applies in the principality.[26] The Welsh Code contains six similarly worded principles, based on the Welsh National Service Framework for Adult Mental Health,[27] with the same emphases as its English counterpart. **11.14**

The principles are intended to inform decisions made under the Act and provide guidance as to how the Act should be implemented. The guiding principles in the Code of Practice in England embrace the following: **11.15**

proposed changes to the Code of Practice: Mental Health Act 1983. (TSO 2014) located at <http://www.gov.uk/government/uploads/system/uploads/attachment_data/file/327653/Doh_Consultation_for_web.pdf>.

[25] *Regina v. Ashworth Hospital Authority (now Mersey Care National Health Service Trust) (Appellants) ex parte Munjaz* (FC) (Respondent) [2005] UKHL 58.

[26] *Mental Health Act 1983 Code of Practice for Wales* (2008); *Mental Health Act 1983 Code of Practice for Wales Review* (October 2016). Similarly, it contains six stated principles to guide the Act's implementation, namely dignity and respect; least restrictive option and maximizing independence; fairness, equality and equity; empowerment and involvement; keeping people safe; and effectiveness and efficiency. Taken together, and in line with the principles in the English Code, they seek to ensure that patients are treated with dignity, fairness, respect, and are central to decision-making under the Act.

[27] Located at <http://www.wales.nhs.uk>.

- Least restrictive option and maximizing independence: where it is possible to treat a patient safely and lawfully without detaining them under the Act, the patient should not be detained. A patient's independence should be encouraged and supported with a focus on promoting recovery wherever possible.
- Empowerment and involvement: patients should be fully involved in decisions about care, support and treatment. The views of families, carers and others, if appropriate, should be fully considered when taking decisions. Where decisions are taken which are contradictory to views expressed, professionals should explain the reasons for this.
- Respect and dignity: patients, their families, and carers should be treated with respect and dignity and listened to by professionals. Purpose principle: decisions under the Act must be made with a view to minimizing the undesirable effects of mental disorder, by maximizing the safety and well-being of patients, promoting recovery, and protecting other people from harm.
- Efficiency and Equity: providers, commissioners, and other relevant organizations should work together to ensure that the quality of commissioning and provision of mental healthcare services are of high quality and are given equal priority to physical health and social care services. All relevant services should work together to facilitate timely, safe and supportive discharge from detention.

11.16 Overall, paragraph 1.23 of the Code states that 'all five sets of principles are of equal importance' and should '*inform* any decision made under the Act' (emphasis supplied), but they are clearly not determinative. Furthermore, in making decisions under the Act, the principles as a whole need to be balanced in different ways according to the particular circumstances of each individual decision.[28] That is not to say that any of the principles should be disregarded but, rather, the weight given to each one will depend upon the particular circumstances of the individual concerned.

11.17 At first glance, the emphasis in the principles would seem to be on inclusivity, respect, encouraging patient participation, and promoting dignity and autonomy wherever possible. The government firmly believes that changes to the Code in 2014 are aimed at increasing patient involvement in decisions about their care and providing more personalized care.[29] The guiding principles have been re-ordered in the most recent edition and the first three principles are now focused on minimizing restrictions, patient empowerment, and involvement in decision making as well as being treated with dignity and respect. Professionals are urged to respect diversity and dignity, communicate effectively, and involve patients as closely as possible in decision-making under the Act. Treatment should be appropriate to patients' needs and it should be provided in safe and supportive environments. Professionals are also reminded of the need to respect patient rights as the Code now, for the first time, includes a specific chapter on equality and human rights. Chapter 3 expressly advises that all decisions must be lawful, which includes compliance with the Equality Act 2010 and the Human Rights Act 1998.[30] Since the 1998 Act came into force, all public authorities are under a legal duty to make decisions which are compatible with the European Convention on Human Rights (hereinafter ECHR), in particular, in this context, Article 5 of the ECHR which includes safeguards against arbitrary deprivation of liberty.

11.18 Despite this rhetorical commitment to patient rights in the Code, interestingly, Fennell has observed that s 118 of the Act contains a list of 'matters' which must be taken into

[28] *Code of Practice*, para 1.23.

[29] Department of Health, *Stronger Code: Better Care—Consultation on proposed changes to the Code of Practice: Mental Health Act 1983* (TSO 2014) para 5.4.

[30] *Code of Practice*, para 1.22.

account by the Secretary of State in preparing the statement of principles in the Code. The list specifically includes the effectiveness of treatment and public safety. As Fennell notes, this certainly includes emphasis on compliance with medication and signals a shift towards ensuring patient compliance with medication and risk management.[31] The purpose principle in the Code also makes explicit reference to the need to make decisions under the Act which *protect other people from harm* (emphasis supplied). Arguably, therefore the Code's commitment to patient rights and autonomy is not as strong as it appears. This is also evinced by the fact that the Richardson Committee had recommended that principles such as these should be included on the face of the Act itself, and the Parliamentary Joint Committee on Human Rights on the Draft Mental Health Bill[32] agreed. However, the government ultimately did not due to 'the technical difficulty of grafting new principles onto existing legislation'.[33] This is regrettable, as the Mental Capacity Act 2005 stands in stark contrast to this. The emphasis in the MCA 2005 is undoubtedly on empowerment and personal autonomy which is spelt out clearly in the five principles on the face of the MCA itself.[34] Section 1 of the Mental Health (Care and Treatment) (Scotland) Act 2003 also enshrines a number of key principles. The approach adopted in the 2007 Act suggests a dilution in the commitment towards the rights and autonomy of mentally disordered patients and is much weaker than an explicit statutory requirement. Instead, the list is relegated to the Code of Practice and, as Fennell notes, 'is a good deal weaker than a statutory requirement to have regard to principles spelt out in statute'. [35] In practice, this could lead to much greater focus on risk than intended by the Code, as Glover-Thomas' qualitative research on perceptions of risk with mental health practitioners in Merseyside has found.[36]

(ii) The status of the Code

Section 118(2D) states that persons exercising functions under the Act should 'have regard' to the Code. The relevance of the Code to decision-making was considered in the case of *R (on the application of Munjaz) v Mersey Care NHS Trust*.[37] The facts related to the use of seclusion to manage disturbed or violent behaviour in Ashworth Hospital and the applicant challenged its use in breach of the previous edition of the MHA Code of Practice. The use of seclusion is not governed by the Act, but is subject to guidance in the Code of Practice.[38] In this case, the majority of the House of Lords found that the Code did not have the binding effect of a statutory provision or instrument. It is guidance and not instruction. Lord Bingham stated that: **11.19**

[31] Fennell, *Mental Health: Law and Practice*, n 13, para 2.46.

[32] Session 2001–02, Joint Committee on Human Rights, *Twenty Fifth Report* para 2.

[33] Session 2006–07 (HL) Debs Vol 690, col 118 *per* Lord Hunt. The government has reinforced this point in the recent consultation on the new Code: Department of Health, *Stronger Code: Better Care. Consultation on proposed changes to the Code of Practice: Mental Health Act 1983* (TSO 2014) para.5.8.

[34] See further Chapter 10.

[35] Fennell, *Mental Health: Law and Practice*, n 13, para 2.46.

[36] N Glover-Thomas, 'The Age of Risk: Risk Perception and Determination following the Mental Health Act 2007 (2011) 19(4) Medical Law Review 581.

[37] *R (on the application of Munjaz) v Mersey Care NHS Trust* [2003] 3 WLR 793.

[38] The latest edition of the Code includes a chapter entitled 'Safe and therapeutic responses to disturbed behaviour' (chapter 26), which covers the range of interventions which may be considered for the safe and therapeutic management of disturbed behaviour. Seclusion is included and is defined as the 'supervised confinement and isolation of a patient, away from other patients, in an area in which the patient is prevented from leaving, where it is of immediate necessity for the purpose of the containment of severe behavioural disturbance which is likely to cause harm to others'. (para 26.103). The Code stipulates that seclusion should be used flexibly, and in the least restrictive manner possible; it should not be used as a punishment, threat or form part of a treatment programme, nor should it be used because of a shortage of staff. It should never be used solely as a means of managing self-harming behaviour (paras 26.107, 26.108, and 26.111).

> ... the Code does not have the binding effect which a statutory provision or a statutory instrument would have [but] ... the guidance should be given great weight. It is not instruction, but it is much more than mere advice which an addressee is free to follow or not as it chooses. It is guidance which any hospital should consider with great care, and from which it should depart only if it has cogent reasons for doing so.[39]

11.20 Consequently, the Code should be observed by all professionals who are using the Act and hospitals cannot depart from it as a matter of policy. Cogent reasons could relate to a hospital departing from the Code in respect of groups rather than individual patients and need not be because of the facts of the individual case. This could be a policy decision arising from the special problems of high security hospitals which contain the most potentially dangerous patients in the country. It could justify differences in the seclusion policy with respect to the special position of such patients whom it was necessary to seclude for longer than a very few days.

11.21 During the parliamentary debates that preceded the 2007 Act, the Minister of State for Health, Lord Hunt made it clear that:

> ... In the light of [Munjaz], no one should be under any illusion that principles expressed in the code can be lightly ignored. They must be properly and carefully considered. We have given effect to this in the duty of practitioners to have regard to the code, a duty that must and will continue to be read in the light of *Munjaz*.[40]

11.22 The amended s 118 should therefore be interpreted in accordance with the dictum in *Munjaz*. Accordingly, departures from the Code will be rare and there must be clear and convincing reasons for justifying such a departure. Similarly, the revised Code of Practice for Wales cautions that any departures from the Code must be well justified and 'appropriately and clearly evidenced'.[41]

2. The definition of mental disorder: 'Any disorder or disability of mind'

(i) A single broad definition

11.23 The definition of 'mental disorder' ensures that only those whose mental health problems 'fit' the criteria can be made subject to the provisions of the Act. Previously, the 1983 Act had contained a detailed definition with various sub-categories. It had a general definition of mental disorder for short term assessment (up to twenty-eight days) and a narrower more elaborate system of sub-categories applied to longer term admission for treatment. This included mental illness and severe mental impairment as well as psychopathic disorder and mental impairment. With the exception of mental illness, the sub-categories required an association with abnormally aggressive or seriously irresponsible conduct. An additional complicating factor was the fact that individuals suffering from mental impairment or psychopathic disorder could only be detained if they were 'treatable'; that is, that medical treatment in hospital was likely to alleviate or prevent deterioration in the patient's condition. The interpretation of treatability was extremely broad and the House of Lords in *Reid v Secretary of State for Scotland*[42] held that it is wide enough to include treatment which alleviates or prevents deterioration in the symptoms of the disorder, not the disorder itself. Accordingly, on the facts of the case itself this included anger management classes in the structured environment of a high security hospital.

---

[39] *R (on the application of Munjaz)*, n 37, [21] *per* Lord Bingham.

[40] Session 2006–07 (HL) Debs, vol 590, col 120.

[41] *Mental Health Act 1983 Code of Practice for Wales Review* (October 2016) p. 4. For further discussion see P Bowen, *Blackstone's Guide to the Mental Health Act 2007* (Oxford University Press 2007), 58–60.

[42] [1999] 1 All ER 481 (HL).

The previous definition had also included a number of specific exclusions relating to drug/alcohol dependence as well as sexual deviancy, promiscuity, and immoral conduct. Most of the exclusions have now been removed and the 2007 Act has adopted a single and simplified broad definition of mental disorder embracing 'any disorder or disability of the mind' (s 1(2)). This applies to all patients subject to the compulsory powers under the Act. The Code of Practice at para 2.4 states that relevant professionals should determine whether a patient has a disorder or disability of the mind in accordance with good clinical practice and accepted standards of what constitutes such a disorder or disability. The Code contains a long list of recognized conditions which could fall within this definition and includes affective disorders such as depression and bipolar disorder, schizophrenia and delusional disorders, neurotic and stress-related disorders such as anxiety, PTSD, and obsessive compulsive disorders; organic mental disorders such as dementia and delirium; personality disorders; eating disorders, learning disabilities, autistic spectrum disorders, and mental and behavioural disorders caused by psychoactive substance use. The Code makes it clear that this definition includes the full range of autistic spectrum disorders, including those existing alongside a learning disability or any other kind of mental disorder. However, it is likely to be very rare for someone on the autistic spectrum to meet the conditions for treatment under the legislation without having any other form of mental disorder, even if it is not associated with abnormally aggressive or seriously irresponsible conduct.[43] 11.24

The list above is not exhaustive but it is certainly comprehensive, which suggests that the definition is extremely broad and over-inclusive. Concerns were expressed during the parliamentary debates that it could potentially lead to an increase in the use of compulsion.[44] Recent statistics would seem to bear this out. Over the past ten years, the number of long term compulsory detentions under the Mental Health Act has increased by 30 per cent and there has been an overall rise in the use of compulsion.[45] The Care Quality Commission has highlighted in successive annual monitoring reports on this disturbing increase in the use of compulsion.[46] Although the Code attempts to guard against this by urging professionals to take care to avoid diagnosing mental disorder based on preconceptions about people or failure to appreciate cultural and social differences.[47] Indeed, the Code emphasizes that difference should not be confused with disorder and no one may be considered to be mentally disordered solely because of his/her political, religious, or cultural beliefs, values, or opinions. The same is true of a person's involvement or likely involvement in illegal, anti-social, or 'immoral' behaviour.[48] 11.25

This broad definition does not delineate precisely who may be detained and leaves considerable discretion in the hands of the professionals. There are few obstacles standing in the way of professionals to apply the Act to a broader group of individuals, particularly those with a personality disorder, than under the previous definition. Of course, this was one of the main driving forces behind the reforms and was reinforced by the government throughout the reform process (discussed below at para. 11.38 et seq). As Fennell has noted: 11.26

43 *Code of Practice*, para 20.19.

44 See, eg, the comments of the Royal College of Psychiatrists, *Briefing on the Mental Health Bill 2006, House of Lords Second Reading 28 November 2006* (RCP, November 2006) para 3.1.

45 HSCIC, *In-patients formally detained in hospitals under the Mental Health Act 1983, and patients subject to supervised community treatment, Annual Report England 2013/14* (October 2014) Figure 4.

46 CQC, *Monitoring the Mental Health Act in 2012/13* (TSO, 2014), 3,4; CQC, *Monitoring the Mental Health Act in 2013/14* (TSO 2015), 9.

47 *Code of Practice*, para 2.7.

48 *Code of Practice*, para 2.8.

> [t]he combined effect of the changes to the definition, the removal of all exclusions save those for addiction, and the replacement of the treatability test with availability of appropriate treatment, is to remove areas of clinical discretion *not to use* compulsory powers. There will be many fewer legitimate reasons for clinicians not to use compulsory powers under the Act with relation to people with personality disorder.[49]

11.27 The definition is nonetheless compatible with the ECHR. Article 5(1) states that no one shall be deprived of his/her liberty unless the deprivation is carried out in accordance with a procedure prescribed by law and is necessary in a democratic society on one of a number of grounds. Article 5(1)(e) provides that one of those grounds is unsoundness of mind. In *Winterwerp v The Netherlands*[50] the European Court of Human Rights (ECtHR) set out the substantive criteria that must be met for the lawful detention under Article 5(1)(e). There are three minimum conditions which must be satisfied:

(1) Except in emergency cases, the individual must be reliably shown to be of unsound mind.
(2) The mental disorder must be of a kind or degree justifying compulsory detention.
(3) The validity of continued confinement depends on the persistence of such mental disorder.

11.28 First, this means that there must be objective medical expertise and evidence of a true mental disorder. Second, the mental disorder must be of sufficient severity to justify the use of compulsion. Finally, the third condition implies that there must be a periodic review of the individual's detention to ensure that the first two conditions are still met.[51] The ECtHR did not provide a definition of 'unsoundness of mind' as it is a flexible concept which changes with advances in psychiatry and societal attitudes.[52] Consequently, the definition has been left to the clinical judgement of psychiatrists, but subject to the minimum conditions outlined in *Winterwerp* above, which are contained in the Act's admission criteria and discussed below.

(ii) Learning disability

11.29 The Act defines a learning disability as a 'state of arrested or incomplete development of mind which includes significant impairment of social functioning' (s 1(4)). This is broadly similar to the ICD-10 and DSM-5 category of intellectual disability/development disorder. The Code of Practice (chapter 20) states that the identification of an individual with a learning disability is a matter for clinical judgement, guided by current professional practice. Those assessing the individual must be satisfied that s/he displays a number of characteristics and it is important to assess him/her holistically. Unlike previous editions of the Code, the current version does not provide any further clarification on the terminology, preferring to leave the interpretation entirely to clinical discretion, although it does suggest that a learning disability has also been described as:

> significantly reduced ability to understand new or complex information, to learn new skills, and reduced ability to cope independently which starts before adulthood with lasting effects on development.

11.30 The Code cautions against the use of the Act for individuals with learning disabilities or autistic spectrum disorders, recognizing that the vast majority of such individuals will never

---

[49] P Fennell, 'The Statutory Definition of Mental Disorder' in L Gostin et al (eds), *Principles of Mental Health Law and Policy* (Oxford University Press 2010) para 2.105.
[50] (1979) 2 EHRR 387 (ECtHR).
[51] See also *X v UK* 1989 4 EHRR 188.
[52] *Winterwerp v The Netherlands* (1979) 2 EHRR 387, para 37.

come into contact with the Act, as the conditions 'share few features with the serious mental illnesses that are the most common reason for using the Act'.[53]

(iii) Seriously irresponsible or abnormally aggressive behaviour

11.31 Individuals diagnosed with a learning disability must still be displaying abnormally aggressive or seriously irresponsible conduct to be detained for longer-term treatment (under s 3), guardianship or Supervised Community Treatment (s 1(2A)). As Fennell notes: 'Although this does not necessarily imply a cause–effect relationship, any such conduct which arises from other sources such as physical disorder or severe toothache is excluded.'[54] Criticism has been levelled at this requirement from both Fennell and Jones, who argue that the preservation of the exclusion does not permit the Act to be used to rescue people with learning disabilities from abusive situations, where the irresponsible conduct of others is putting them at risk.[55]

11.32 **(a) Abnormally aggressive behaviour** This term is not defined in the Act, though the court in *R v Trent Mental Health Review Tribunal ex p Ryan*[56] felt that determining whether conduct amounts to seriously irresponsible or aggressive behaviour goes beyond asking questions 'of a purely clinical nature'. In *R v Hall*[57] the Court of Appeal was required to consider the meaning of the words 'severe impairment of intelligence and social functioning' in the context of the Sexual Offences Act 1956. The court held that these were 'ordinary English words' and that severe impairment should be measured 'against the standard of normal persons' and not by reference to other individuals with learning disability.

11.33 The revised Code provides very little guidance to practitioners, stating that it is 'not possible to define exactly what behaviour would fall into either category'.[58] Inevitably, much will depend on the nature of the behaviour and the circumstances in which it is exhibited, as well as the extent to which it gives rise to a risk to the health and safety of the person, or others, or both.

11.34 However, the Code does list a number of relevant factors in assessing whether a patient's learning disability is abnormally aggressive, including how persistent and severe the aggressive behaviour has been; whether it has resulted in harm or distress to other people or to property; how likely it is to recur; and how common similar behaviour is in the population generally.[59]

11.35 **(b) Seriously irresponsible conduct** Similarly, the Code does not attempt to define seriously irresponsible conduct, but, instead includes a list of relevant factors in assessing how serious and irresponsible the conduct is, including how seriously detrimental to the patient or to other people the consequences of the conduct were, or might have been; how persistent and recent the behaviour has been; is it likely to recur and whether it has resulted in harm to the patient, other people, or damage to property.[60]

[53] *Code of Practice*, para 20.5.
[54] Fennel, *Mental Health: Law and Practice*, n 13, para 3.40.
[55] P Fennell, 'The Statutory Definition of Mental Disorder', in L Gostin et al (eds), *Principles of Mental Health Law and Policy* (Oxford University Press 2010) citing Jones at para 2.71.
[56] [1992] COD 157.
[57] (1987) 86 Cr App R 159 *per* Parker LJ at 162 (CA)
[58] *Code of Practice*, para 20.9.
[59] *Code of Practice*, para 20.10.
[60] *Code of Practice*, para 20.11.

11.36 The meaning of irresponsible conduct has been considered judicially in a number of cases. For example, in *Lewis v Gibson*[61] Thorpe LJ stated that this type of conduct need not be recent or current and consideration must be given to past conduct:

> To make a balanced assessment of the patient's present state some regard must be had to the past history and the future propensity. A conclusion based only on the recent past which might represent a transient phase of quiescence, would be superficial.

11.37 Accordingly, regard may be had to whether this type of conduct has occurred in the past and whether there is a risk that the conduct could manifest itself again in the future, should the patient not comply with medication/treatment.

11.38 Also, in *Re F (Mental Health Act: Guardianship)*[62] the court had to decide whether a 17-year-old girl with learning disability was displaying seriously irresponsible conduct. She wanted to return to a home where she had suffered neglect and abuse. The court concluded that she was not behaving in a seriously irresponsible way, as the urge to return to one's home and family is 'almost universal'. Accordingly, she did not satisfy the detention criteria and could not be made subject to guardianship. However, the court did invoke its inherent jurisdiction to determine where she should reside. This case was applied in *Newham LBC v S (adult: court's jurisdiction)*.[63] Here again the court concluded that 'a lack of road sense and a tendency to rush into the road without looking' was not sufficient to amount to seriously irresponsible conduct under the Act.

(iv) Personality disorder

11.39 Apart from the learning disability qualification, the Act does not distinguish between different forms of mental disorder. Consequently, the term 'psychopathic disorder' (as found in the original 1983 Act) has been removed, and the amended Act's provisions now apply to personality disorder (of all types) in exactly the same way as it applies to mental illness and other mental disorders. Furthermore, there is no longer a requirement that the personality disorder is associated with abnormally aggressive or seriously irresponsible conduct, as was previously the position under the 1983 Act.

11.40 It is clear from the ECtHR decision in *Reid v United Kingdom*[64] that psychopathic/personality disorder amounts to unsoundness of mind within Article 5(1)(e). Psychopathic or personality disorder encompasses a very broad and diverse range of anti-social, dangerous, and disturbed behaviour. The DCM-5 classification of diseases contains a list of different types of personality disorder which includes, borderline, avoidant, anti-social, narcissistic, obsessive compulsive, and schizotypal.[65] The ICD-10 classification groups personality disorders together as:

> . . . a variety of conditions and behaviour patterns which tend to be persistent and appear to be the expression of the individual's characteristic lifestyle and mode of relating to himself or herself and others. Some of these conditions and patterns of behaviour emerge early in the course of individual development, as a result of both constitutional factors and social experience, while others are acquired later in life. Specific personality disorders [] . . ., mixed and other personality disorders [] . . ., and enduring personality changes [] . . . are deeply ingrained and enduring behaviour patterns, manifesting as inflexible responses to a broad range of personal and social situations. They represent extreme or significant

[61] [2005] EWCA Civ 587.
[62] [2000] 1 FLR 192 (CA).
[63] [2003] EWHC 1909 (Fam).
[64] (2003) 37 EHRR 9 (ECtHR).
[65] American Psychiatric Association, *DSM-5 Personality Disorders* located at <http://www.psychiatry.org/psychiatrists/practice/dsm/dsm-5>. Accessed 30 September 2015.

deviations from the way in which the average individual in a given culture perceives, thinks, feels and, particularly, relates to others. Such behaviour patterns tend to be stable and to encompass multiple domains of behaviour and psychological functioning. They are frequently, but not always, associated with various degrees of subjective distress and problems of social performance.[66]

The Code urges professionals not to make assumptions about the suitability of using the Act or providing services in respect of personality disorders or the people who have them.[67] Undoubtedly, this is one of the most controversial aspects of the changes introduced by the 2007 Act. During the early stages of the reform process, the government had made it clear that it wished to introduce proposals to detain dangerous and severely personality disordered individuals and this was one of the main driving forces behind the reform process.[68] The government has for years been concerned about the management of this particular group of individuals, especially paedophiles and sexual predators such as Michael Stone and Robert Oliver. They are thought to pose a particularly significant risk of serious harm due to their severe personality disorder. The problems have stemmed from the fact that personality disorder has not responded as well to traditional forms of psychiatric treatment in hospital and, in some cases, psychiatrists have not been able to state whether treatment might work for particular patients. Consequently, the 'treatability' requirement (ie that medical treatment would be likely to alleviate or prevent deterioration in the patient's condition) in the 1983 Act meant that such patients may have fallen outside the ambit of mental health legislation. Psychiatrists may decide not to detain under Pt II, even though the patient poses a significant risk to him/herself or others, as they have not been convinced that the treatment might work. Consequently, this group of patients may have been denied appropriate treatment/support and members of the public put at unnecessary risk, in particular by sex offenders with personality disorder. The removal of the treatability criterion and sexual deviancy exclusion (see paras 11. 41 et seq) coupled with the broader definition of mental disorder is intended to rectify this position. But it is unlikely to do so unless there is a corresponding increase in the provision of specialist mental health services in prison and hospital for this particular group. Somewhat worryingly, a review of offenders with mental health problems in the criminal justice system in 2009 highlighted that there is no formal provision of services for people with personality disorder in prison nor is there a coherent approach to the management of personality disorder with the criminal justice/health sector.[69] Recent HM Chief Inspector of Prisons annual reports continue to express similar concerns about the overall inadequacy of prison mental health care.[70] The National Institute for Clinical Health and Excellence[71] and the Department of Health/Ministry of Justice[72] have published guidance for commissioning services and to practitioners on working with personality disordered offenders, which outlines various treatment programmes which should **11.41**

[66] Version 2016, Chapter 5 located at <http://apps.who.int>. Date accessed: 30 September 2015.

[67] *Code of Practice*, para. 2.20.

[68] See further J M Laing, 'Legal and Ethical Implications of the Government's Proposals to Detain High-risk Individuals' (2002) 66(1) Journal of Criminal Law 64–83.

[69] See *The Bradley Report: Lord Bradley's review of people with mental health problems or learning disabilities in the criminal justice system, Executive Summary* (DoH 2009) para 51.

[70] See, eg, *HM Chief Inspector of Prisons for England and Wales Annual Report 2012–13* (TSO 2013) HC 682, 39; *HM Chief Inspector of Prisons for England and Wales Annual Report 2013–14* (TSO 2014) HC 680 40.

[71] Located at <http://www.nice.org.uk/guidance/conditions-and-diseases/mental-health-and-behavioural-conditions/personality-disorders>.

[72] Department of Health, *Working with personality disordered offenders: A practitioners guide* (MoJ January 2011) 35.

be available in the custody treatment pathway for personality disordered offenders. Waiting lists for many of these treatment programmes can be very long however.[73]

(v) Dependence on alcohol or drugs exclusion

11.42 The original 1983 Act definition also contained exclusions relating to promiscuity/other immoral conduct, sexual deviancy, or dependence on alcohol or drugs, but most of these have now been removed. Exclusions are intended to clarify what type of behaviour or beliefs should not come under mental health legislation, even though they may fall within the definition of mental disorder. As noted by the Royal College of Psychiatrists:

> Exclusions also guard against people being swept into the Act when their sexual, cultural or social behaviour offends moral norms or is illegal and could be seen by some to reflect a disordered mental state but where there is no therapeutic health intervention for them.[74]

11.43 The government felt that it would be preferable to remove most of these exclusions[75] and the amended Act contains only one exclusion by virtue of 'dependence on alcohol or drugs' (s 1(3)). This means that the Act cannot be used to detain people in hospital simply because they are dependent on alcohol or drugs. However, alcohol or drug dependence is not completely outside the scope of the Act, as it may be accompanied by, or associated with other kinds of mental disorder as defined. Indeed, in some cases the mental disorder in question may result from the person's alcohol or drug dependence and severe intoxication could itself amount to a mental disorder. The Code of Practice recognizes that other mental disorders relating to the use of alcohol or drugs are not excluded, and these include withdrawal state with delirium or associated psychotic disorder, and organic mental disorders associated with prolonged abuse of drugs or alcohol.[76] The latest version of the 'Reference guide to the Mental Health Act 1983' also makes it clear that, although 'drugs' is not defined in the Act, it can be taken to include psychoactive substances like solvents as well as medicines and illicit drugs.[77] Of course, drug/alcohol addicts could still fall within the scope of the legislation as they may be suffering from a recognized mental disorder which is unrelated to their dependence.

11.44 The removal of the sexual deviancy exclusion allows paedophiles and sexual predators to fall within the scope of the Act, as long as all the other criteria are fulfilled. This is evident from the Explanatory Notes which accompanied the Mental Health Bill in 2006:

> . . . there are disorders of sexual preference which are recognised clinically as mental disorders and some of these may be considered 'sexual deviance' in the terms of the current exclusion (for example paraphilias like fetishism or paedophilia) and the Act will now apply to these disorders in the same way as it applies to other mental disorders.[78]

11.45 The removal of promiscuity/immoral conduct was necessary as society's views of what constitutes that behaviour have changed significantly and neither of these by itself is a mental disorder. The government assumes that no professionals would ever use the Act to detain and treat someone purely on these grounds, so the exclusion is obsolete.

11.46 The removal of most of the exclusions does raise questions about precisely where the dividing line between mental disorder and immoral or deviant behaviour lies. But the government is unconcerned about this and is content to leave the line-drawing in the hands of the

[73] ibid.
[74] Royal College of Psychiatrists, *Briefing on the Mental Health Bill 2006*, para 3.1.
[75] Department of Health (London 2006), 5.
[76] *Code of Practice*, para 2.12.
[77] *Reference guide to the Mental Health Act 1983* (DoH 2015) para 1.11.
[78] DoH, Ministry of Justice, Welsh Assembly, *Mental Health Act 2007 Explanatory Notes* (2007) para 24.

professionals. It feels that the simplified definition will make the Act easier to use and will complement the changes it has made to the criteria for the use of compulsion. The changes are also intended to ensure that no one fails to receive the treatment they need because their condition happens not to fall within one of the sub-categories,[79] and particularly if the disorder relates to sexually deviant behaviour which poses a high risk to others. As noted earlier, many cautioned during the reform process that the new broad definition and the removal of some of the exclusions could lead to broadening the scope of compulsory powers. The Joint Parliamentary Committee on Human Rights expressed concerns about the potential consequences and that it would be a 'retrograde step' to permit mental health professionals to become 'guardians of morality' by removing some of the exclusions in this way.[80] The Royal College of Psychiatrists also opined that 'the cumulative effect of all these [changes] is a real likelihood that people may get trapped in a long term system of compulsory care'.[81] The compulsory admission statistics mentioned earlier would suggest that some of these fears were not wholly unfounded, particularly if one considers the recent comments of the House of Commons Health Committee on Post-Legislative Scrutiny of the Mental Health Act 1983. The report noted that there has been a substantial increase in the total population of patients detained under section since the introduction of the 2007 reforms, yet:

> It is of concern to the Committee that the Department of Health does not have a clear picture as to the factors which are driving increased rates of detention.[82]

3. Professional roles

(i) Approved mental health professionals

Approved Mental Health Professionals (AMHPs) replaced Approved Social Workers (ASWs) under the original 1983 Act, and the competence required of an AMHP is broadly similar to that which was required of an ASW. The AMHP role is not, however, restricted to social workers, but extends to other mental health professionals as well, such as mental health and learning disability nurses, occupational therapists, and chartered psychologists, if they meet the required criteria.[83] 'Relevant' professionals therefore include nurses, occupational therapists, psychologists, and social workers (but does not include registered medical practitioners: s 114(2) MHA 1983 (as inserted by s 18 MHA 2007)) to provide a social care perspective and to act independently. The MHAC in its final report noted some take-up of training by professionals other than social workers in the initial training courses for AMHPs in certain areas of the country,[84] and there is some more recent evidence of mental health nurses undertaking the AMHP role.[85] A national AMHP Survey in 2012 reported that 'social workers overwhelmingly continue to take on the AMHP role—government may have committed to training other professionals but it appears that many Trusts have not'.[86] **11.47**

---

[79] Department of Health, *Mental Health Bill 2006 Summary Guide* (2006) 4.

[80] Session 2001–02, *Twenty Fifth Report*, para 10.

[81] Royal College of Psychiatrists, *Briefing on the Mental Health Bill 2006*, para 3.2.

[82] House of Commons Health Committee, *Post-legislative scrutiny of the Mental Health Act 1983: First Report of Session 2013–14*, HC 584 (TSO, 2013) 36.

[83] For more detailed discussion of the roles see N Glover-Thomas and J M Laing, 'Mental Health Professionals' in L Gostin et al (eds), *Principles of Mental Health Law and Policy* (Oxford University Press 2010).

[84] *Coercion and Consent MHAC Thirteenth Biennial Report 2007–2009* (TSO 2009) para 2.21.

[85] D T Bressington et al, 'A concept mapping exploration of social workers' and mental health nurses' understanding of the role of the Approved Mental Health Professional' (2011) 31 Nurse Education Today 564–70; 'New approved mental health professionals discuss the role' in Community Care, 15 June 2009, located at <http://www.communitycare.co.uk/2009/06/15/new-approved-mental-health-professionals-discuss-the-role/>

[86] J Hudson and M Webber, *The National AMHP Survey 2012: Final Report Stress and the statutory role: is there a difference between the professional groups?* (Kings College London 2013) 4.

There is still no reliable national data available to date on take-up and the overall composition of the AMHP workforce, although the Care Quality Commission has reported that, in some Local Authorities, the number of AMHPs is falling.[87]

11.48 This change was intended to 'remove the current demarcation of professional roles, in favour of a new approach which ensures that professionals with the right skills, experience and training can carry out important functions not currently open to them'.[88] This is positive in many respects as it does reflect current mental health practice within the NHS and will, hopefully, ensure more targeted, holistic, and better quality patient-centred care. The recent trend within the mental health service is to move towards a much more skills-based approach and emphasis on multidisciplinary working. The National Institute for Mental Health in England produced a report entitled New Ways of Working,[89] aimed at all mental health staff to help them work more flexibly within teams. It builds on earlier guidance to promote a model where distributed responsibility is shared amongst team members and no longer delegated by a single professional, such as the consultant. The shift has been away from a traditional practice perspective to a modern capability/competence based team. It is believed that this will enable delivery of good modern care through a team approach which requires distribution of responsibility, not delegation. It should mean that more professionals play an equal role in mental health care. As Coffey and Hannigan identified:

> Community mental health nursing has traditionally been subordinate to the powers of psychiatry. New roles in the delivery of mental health care have the potential to challenge this position . . . The advent of the new role of approved mental health professional may be another step towards advancing the independent professional project of community mental health nursing.[90]

But there are some indications that there are tensions in the role and it can be challenging for nurses to incorporate an independent *social* perspective into the decision-making process.[91] Furthermore, the Care Quality Commission has reported that, despite the professional extensions to the role, there are still staff shortages and difficulties in accessing AMHPs in some areas, particularly out of office hours.[92]

11.49 Social services authorities retain responsibility for approving professionals (see reworded s 114 as amended by MHA 2007, s 18). Training courses are subject to statutory regulation and approval by the Health and Care Professions Council (HCPC) for all health and care professionals in the UK and social workers in England or the Care Council (CC), which still regulates social workers in Wales (1983 Act, s 114A). However, the government removed the requirement for ASWs to be employed by Local Authorities (LA). This gives LAs the freedom to approve appropriately trained and qualified people whom they do not employ. The government envisaged that it should also make it easier to recruit AMHPs in areas which are experiencing a shortage of ASWs.[93] Whilst LAs will be responsible for AMHPs, they will continue to be subject to regulation by their own professional body. The HCPC published

87 *Monitoring the Mental Health Act in 2011/12* (2013), 53.

88 *Mental Health Bill 2006 Summary Guide* (DoH 2006), 3.

89 *A Best Practice Implementation Guide* (DoH 2007).

90 M Coffey and B Hannigan, 'New roles for nurse as approved mental health professionals in England and Wales' (2013) 50 International Journal of Nursing Studies 1423–30, 1429.

91 ibid. See also J Rapaport, 'New roles in Mental Health: The Creation of the Approved Mental Health Practitioner' (2006) 14(5) Journal of Integrated Care 37–46.

92 CQC, *Monitoring the Mental Health Act in 2012/13* (TSO 2014), 64.

93 *Mental Health Bill: Amending the Mental Health Act 1983 Briefing Sheet—Professional Roles—A4* (DoH March 2007) 2.

standards and CC Code of Professional Practice for social care lay down the standards of conduct and practice expected of social workers when acting as AMHPs.

Before approving a person as an AMHP, a LA must be satisfied that the person has appropriate competence in dealing with people with a mental disorder and must take into account matters specified by the appropriate authority—eg the qualifications and experience required. The Mental Health (Approved Mental Health Professionals) (Approval) (England) Regulations 2008[94] which came into force on 3 November 2008, stipulate further the precise approval (and re-approval) conditions in England. A LA may only approve a person to act as an AMHP if it is satisfied that the person has appropriate competence in dealing with persons who are suffering from mental disorder (reg 3). This includes ensuring that the person fulfils at least one of the professional requirements and certain matters relating to competence set out in Schedule 2 (see para 11.52). The LA may approve the person to act as an AMHP for a period of five years, which is renewable (reg 4). Similar regulations have been published by the Welsh Assembly which mirror these conditions.[95] **11.50**

(a) **Professional requirements** The 'professional requirements' are set out in Sch 1 and include: (a) a social worker registered with the HCPC; (b) a first level nurse in the Nurses' Part of the register maintained under Art 5 of the Nursing and Midwifery Order 2001, SI 2002/253, whose field of practice is mental health or learning disabilities nursing; (c) an occupational therapist registered in Pt 6 of the Register maintained under Art 5 of the Health Professions Order 2001, SI 2002/254; or (d) a chartered psychologist listed on the British Psychological Society's Register of Chartered Psychologists who holds a relevant practising certificate issued by the Society. **11.51**

Registered Medical Practitioners are specifically excluded from performing the role under s 114(2) MHA 1983, which seeks to ensure a combination of perspectives in the decision to use compulsion. **11.52**

(b) **Determining 'competence'** Schedule 1 to the Regulations lists matters which must be taken into account by LAs to determine competence. These are divided into five key competence areas covering: (1) application of values to the AMHP role; (2) application of legal knowledge; (3) application of knowledge of mental disorder; (4) application of skills and working in partnership; and (5) application of skills in terms of making and communicating informed decisions. Key competence area 1 focuses on redressing discrimination and inequality as well as being sensitive to and respecting individual needs and patient rights. It is encouraging to note that these issues have been specifically included and will therefore be central to daily decision-making about patient care. Key competencies 2 and 3 relate to the AMHP's knowledge and understanding of both the broader legal and policy framework, as well as the range of models of mental disorder. In particular, AMHPs will be required to critically understand and apply the social perspective on mental disorder and mental health needs. The final two competencies relate to the ability of AMHPs to work effectively in partnership with other professions, patients, carers, and relatives as well as making independent and informed decisions, communicating effectively, and sharing appropriate information. Multidisciplinary decision-making is fundamental to the 2007 Act and presents some of the greatest challenges, particularly in light of the tensions which have existed historically between the different professions. **11.53**

---

[94] SI 2008/1206.

[95] The Mental Health (Approval of Persons to be Approved Mental Health Professionals) (Wales) Regulations 2008, SI 2008/2436 (W 209) came into force on 3 November 2008. They include broadly similar approval requirements relating to the relevant professional qualifications and the need to demonstrate key competencies for AMHPs. The Regulations. See further <http://www.newwales.gov.uk>.

11.54 The HCPC in England has duties under the Health and Social Care Act 2012 to approve, monitor and inspect provision for social work education and training. The regulations have been fleshed out by the HCPC in its training requirements for AMHPs.[96] The training requirements state that AMHPs must demonstrate competence across all five key areas. Overall, the criteria focus on the ability of AMHPs to demonstrate sound knowledge and autonomous practice; make informed decisions; respect diversity, equality and promote the rights, dignity and self-determination of service users; communicate and collaborate effectively as well as make appropriate assessments and interventions. [97] The Welsh Assembly issued similar regulations in Wales, which have been accompanied by AMHP training guidance produced by the Care Council in Wales.[98] In essence, the Welsh Regulations mirror the English requirements by focusing on the professional qualifications and five key competence areas.[99] The Care Council course requirements stress the need for candidates to demonstrate a commitment to seeking the least restrictive health and social care; to enable service users to contribute to decisions and to respect individuals' qualities, abilities and diverse backgrounds. In line with the key competencies, the specific learning outcomes will require candidates to demonstrate knowledge, understanding and application in values and ethics; legislation and systems; understanding of mental disorder; professional responsibilities and assessment and intervention.

11.55 The rhetoric contained in the Regulations and training documents produced in England and Wales are broadly comparable and this goes some way towards ensuring consistency in the accreditation and training of AMHPs in both England and Wales.[100] Note however, that the system does not confer automatic reciprocity, as the 'Reference guide to the Mental Health Act 1983'[101] makes it clear that:

> AMHPs approved by an English local authority may only act on behalf of local authorities which are also in England. In order to act on behalf of local authorities in Wales, they would need also to be approved as an AMHP by a local authority in Wales, in accordance with the corresponding regulations made by the Welsh Ministers'.[102]

11.56 (c) **Training, monitoring, and supervision** To be appointed as an AMHP, the person must have completed within the last five years a course approved by the HCPC or Care Council for Wales (reg 3(3)). The HCPC (and CC in Wales) also approve AMHP training on behalf of the Nursing and Midwifery Council and the British Psychological Society. Regulation 5 stipulates that the role is subject to certain conditions, notably that in each year, the AMHP shall complete at least eighteen hours of training agreed with the approving LA as being relevant to their role as an AMHP (reg 5(a)) and the AMHP shall cease to undertake the role and notify the LA if they no longer meet at least one of the professional requirements,

[96] HCPC, *Approval criteria for approved mental health professional (AMHP) programmes* (August 2013) located at <http://www.hcpc-uk.org/assets/documents/1000414DApprovalcriteriaforapprovedmentalhealthprofessional(AMHP)programmes.pdf>.

[97] ibid, s 2.

[98] Care Council for Wales, *Specified Named Course Requirements: Approved Mental Health Professional* at <http://www.ccwales.org.uk> in May 2009.

[99] Mental Health (Approval of Persons to be Approved Mental Health Professionals) (Wales) Regulations 2008, SI 2008/2436 (W 209).

[100] See also Department of Health, *Reference guide to the Mental Health Act 1983* (TSO 2015). Note that the Welsh regulations do stipulate that, in order for an AMHP (who has been approved to act in England) to be eligible to act as such in Wales, s/he must be able to demonstrate that s/he has appropriate competence to act as an AMHP within Wales (SI 2008/2436, reg 3(2)(b)).

[101] (TSO 2015) para 30.29.

[102] In accordance with the Social Services and Well-being (Wales) Act 2014, which came into effect in April 2016. See <http://www.legislation.gov.uk/anaw/2014/4/contents/enacted>.

if their registration is suspended or if they agree to act as an AMHP on behalf of another LA (reg 5(d)). LAs may approve people as AMHPs for five years at a time, after which they must be re-approved.

11.57 (d) **Responsibilities of local authorities** The Regulations impose strict record keeping requirements on LAs for each AMHP, relating to the AMHP's personal details and profession, date of approval, details of any suspension, and completion of training to comply with reg 8.

11.58 The revised MHA Code of Practice provides some limited guidance to LAs in terms of ensuring that there is appropriate AMHP provision, however this is no longer an explicit statutory duty, as the Care Quality Commission has pointed out:

> Before 2008, the Mental Health Act imposed a statutory duty on local authorities to make sure they 'appoint sufficient numbers' of AMHPs. However, the 2007 Act amendments removed this phrase.[103]

Nevertheless, the Code continues to refer to the statutory duty on LAs (in para 4.33) and stresses that LAs should have arrangements in place in their area to provide a 24-hour service that can respond to patients' needs.[104] This is significant, as it does indicate that LAs must ensure that there is some level of 24-hour service provision available, although it is regrettable that the obligation has been diluted and is no longer included on the face of the statute. Section 13 of the 1983 Act places a specific duty on LAs to arrange for an AMHP to consider the case of any patient who is within their area, if they have reason to believe that an application for detention in hospital may need to be made. LAs must also make such arrangements if asked to do so by (or on behalf) of a patient's nearest relative.[105]

11.59 (e) **Functions of Approved Mental Health Professionals** AMHPs have a number of important duties and functions under the legislation. The AMHP's primary responsibility is coordinating the preliminary examination process and providing a non-medical view when considering, with her/his medical colleagues, whether a patient meets the conditions for admission under the 1983 Act. The Code of Practice stipulates that AMHPs must interview the patient in a suitable manner, carry out an assessment, and make a decision whether to make an application for compulsory admission to hospital.[106] It is normally the AMHP who will make the application for compulsory admission and the role of the AMHP in the assessment and admission process is considered more fully in Section 4.

11.60 Under s 11 of the 1983 Act, AMHPs are also required to attempt to identify and notify the patient's nearest relative (as defined in s 26 of the 1983 Act[107]) before or within a reasonable time after an application for admission of a patient for assessment is made. The nearest relative must also be informed that s/he has the power to discharge the patient. Where there

---

[103] *Monitoring the Mental Health Act in 2012/13* (2014), 65: The Mental Health (Amendment) Act 2007 substituted a revision of Mental Health Act 1983 section 114.

[104] *Code of Practice*, para 14.35. The Code makes no reference to any responsibilities of health trusts here which is surprising given that the majority of AMHPs could be employed by the health care sector. Clearly there is no incentive for the health sector to train AMHPs as the responsibility falls solely on the LA's shoulders and this may be one of the reasons for the lower uptake from the health care professions identified in para 11.46 above.

[105] *Code of Practice*, para 14.32.

[106] *Code of Practice*, para 14.49.

[107] 'Relative' is defined as anyone who is the patient's husband/wife or civil partner; son/daughter; father/mother; brother/sister; grandparent; grandchild; uncle/aunt; or nephew/niece. This includes relationships of the whole and half blood and relationships through adoption (though not step-relationships). See further paras 11.193–11.201.

is a failure to consult with the nearest relative, any subsequent detention could be rendered unlawful,[108] and could give rise to a claim for damages under Article 5 of the ECHR.[109] Indeed, in *TW v Enfield London Borough Council*,[110] the Court of Appeal recognized that the AMHP, when considering whether to consult the 'nearest relative' prior to making an application to admit, must strike a balance between the patient's right under Article 5 of the ECHR not to be arbitrarily deprived of his/her liberty and the patient's right to a private and family life under Article 8. The AMHP must consult the person 'appearing to be' the nearest relative; this is judged subjectively, so there is no requirement for reasonable belief.[111] In *GD v The Hospital Managers of the Edgware Community Hospital, London Borough of Barnet*[112] the court made it clear that the duty to consult is a two-way process:

> . . . which exists to enable there to be a dialogue about the action proposed in respect of a mentally ill individual. The person consulted is entitled to have his views taken into account and, importantly, the consultation process should enable the nearest relative to object to the proposed course if he wishes. The consultation must be a real exercise and not a token one.[113]

11.61 This means that AMHPs must endeavour to consult the nearest relative in sufficient time to enable an effective discussion to take place, irrespective of how obstructive the nearest relative is perceived to be.[114] If the nearest relative objects, the AMHP cannot make the application.[115] However, an unreasonable objection by a nearest relative is one of the grounds in s 29 for the county court to transfer the powers to another person (see paras 11.193 et seq).

11.62 With respect to an application under s 3, the requirement to consult the nearest relative does not apply if it appears to the AMHP that such consultation is not 'reasonably practicable' or would involve 'unreasonable delay'. The Code suggests that this could apply where it is not practicable for the AMHP to obtain sufficient information to establish the identity or location of the nearest relative or if doing so would involve an excessive amount of investigation thereby causing unreasonable delay.[116] Furthermore, the Code of Practice stipulates that AMHPs are not required to consult the nearest relative, when consultation is not possible because of the nearest relative's own health or mental incapacity.[117]

11.63 The meaning of 'reasonably practicable' was considered in *R (on the application of E) v Bristol City Council*.[118] In this case, E's nearest relative was her sister, but they did not get on and she

---

[108] *Re S-C (Mental Patient: Habeas Corpus)* [1996] 1 QB 599; *Code of Practice* para 14.59. Consultation with the nearest relative can precede the obtaining of the two medical recommendations which are needed to support the application for admission *Re Whitbread* Times Law Report 14 July 1997; *Reference Guide to the Mental Health 1983* para 8.28.

[109] *TTM (TM) v London Borough of Hackney* [2011] EWCA Civ 4; 'Detained patient wins right to claim damages', *The Independent* (15 January 2011).

[110] [2014] EWCA Civ 362.

[111] *Re D (Mental Patient: Habeas Corpus)* [2000] 2 FLR 848, [15].

[112] *GD v The Hospital Managers of the Edgware Community Hospital, London Borough of Barnet* [2008] EWHC 3572 (Admin).

[113] ibid, at [46].

[114] See further L Davidson, 'Nearest Relative Consultation and the Avoidant Approved Mental Health Professional' (2009) Journal of Mental Health Law, Spring, 70–80.

[115] If the nearest relative objects to the making of the application for admission for treatment, the application cannot be made and if an application is made in the face of such an objection, the detention will be unlawful: *TTM v Hackney BC* [2011] EWCA Civ 4; *CX v A Local Authority* [2011] EWHC 1918 (Admin).

[116] *Code of* Practice, para 14.60.

[117] ibid.

[118] *R (on the application of E) v Bristol City Council* [2005] EWHC 74 (Admin); For analysis of this case, see H Kingston, 'The Balancing Act' (2005) Journal of Mental Health Law, November, 186. See also *TW v Enfield London Borough Council* [2014] EWCA Civ 362.

did not want her to be involved at all with her care. E sought judicial review of Bristol City Council's decision that her sister would have to be informed or consulted on aspects of her care. E argued that it would be unlawful for the council to notify her sister without her consent. Bennet J held that 'practicable' includes taking into account the wishes and well-being of the patient.[119] An earlier edition of the Code had referred to practicability with respect to the availability of the nearest relative and not to the appropriateness of informing or consulting the person concerned. Bennet J felt that this interpretation was 'wrong' and 'far too restrictive'. It could lead to 'positive injustice' in breach of the claimant's rights under Article 8 under the ECHR.[120] Impracticability could include a situation such as this one where the patient was competent and had strongly expressed her wish that her nearest relative was not to be informed or consulted. Accordingly, there may be cases where, though physically possible, it would not be reasonably practicable to inform the nearest relative because there would be a detrimental impact on the patient.[121] The revised Code cites examples of 'detrimental impact' as including cases where patients are likely to suffer emotional distress, deterioration in their mental health, physical harm, or financial or other exploitation as a result of consultation.[122] Therefore, it will also be impracticable to consult with the nearest relative where, in all the circumstances, the benefits to the patient of that consultation do not justify any infringement of the patient's rights under Article 8 of the ECHR to privacy and family life.[123]

In this case, Bennet J reinforced the importance of the nearest relative role and stated that it is 'not lightly to be removed by invoking impracticability'.[124] The revised Code also cautions that consulting and notifying the nearest relative is a 'significant safeguard' for patients,[125] All the more so since cases such as this and *R (M) v. Secretary of State for Health*[126] where this aspect of the previous legislation was declared incompatible with the Human Rights Act 1998. **11.64**

The Code provides that, where the AMHP is the applicant for detention, they have a professional responsibility to ensure that all the necessary arrangements are made for the patient to be conveyed and admitted to hospital. Under s 40 AMHPs have the power to convey patients directly to hospital. They can also return patients who are absent without leave to hospital (under s 18(1)); examine patients who have been removed by the police to a 'place of safety' under s 136 with a view to making arrangements for their care and treatment; and apply for a warrant to search for and remove a patient who is unable to care for him/herself or has/is being neglected or ill-treated under s 135. **11.65**

[119] See para 11.193, and the recent Court of Appeal decision, *TW v Enfield London Borough Council* [2014] EWCA Civ 362; [2014] WLR (D) 145.

[120] *R (on the application of E)*, n 117, at [29].

[121] One example of when it was not practicable to consult is *DP v South Tyneside District Council* (2011) Admin Court 14/7/11 (unreported). Here the patient was perceived to be potentially at risk from the nearest relative (owing to the risk of forced marriage/death) and consultation was not possible without disclosing the patient's location. Moreover, consulting a nearest relative in the face of patient opposition has been considered to be 'unreasonably practicable': *R (on the application of E) v Bristol City Council* [2005] All ER (D) 57 (Jan). Admission to hospital can lawfully occur without consultation if to consult would lead to unreasonable delay.

[122] *Code of Practice*, para. 14.61.

[123] ibid, para 14.61.

[124] ibid, para 14.62. See also *GP v Derby County Council* (2012) EWHC 1451 (Admin) where the court stated that there is a heavy duty on those who carry out these tasks under the Mental Health Act to ensure that the statutory provisions are complied with.

[125] ibid, para 14.62; See also *Code of Practice for Wales Review*, para. 5.1.

[126] [2003] EWHC 1094. See also *JT v UK* [2000] 1 FLR 909 (ECHR).

(ii) Responsible/Approved Clinician

11.66 When a patient is registered under the Act, an Approved Clinician (AC) must be appointed as the patient's clinical supervisor, to be in charge of the assessment of the patient and any treatment provided in accordance with the Act. The clinical supervisor is entrusted with important functions under the Act and has a key role in the exercise of formal powers. ACs are involved in the daily care and treatment of patients, both those who are detained in hospital and those living in the community. The RC has several powers and functions under Pts 2, 3, 4 and 5 of the Mental Health Act 1983, as amended by the Mental Health Act 2007. These include granting leave of absence; recalling a patient from leave and Supervised Community Treatment; renewing detention and Community Treatment Orders; duties regarding the administration of medical treatment and discharging patients. These are discussed more fully in Sections 5, 6, and 7 below.

11.67 The appropriate authority will set qualifying criteria as to who is eligible to become an AC, for example, by profession, qualification, and relevant experience in the diagnosis and treatment of mental disorder. Initially, it was expected that ACs would be psychiatrists and psychologists of consultant status,[127] but ultimately due to staff shortages and resource implications, the role has been extended to other health professionals.[128] However, the Act does leave some decisions, such as those concerning initial detention, in the hands of doctors. Similarly, doctors are required to undertake the 'medical recommendations' for detention, but ACs and Responsible Clinicians (RC) are still left to provide expertise or make decisions that could engage Article 5 issues.[129]

11.68 The MHAC's Twelfth Biennial Report highlighted the shortage of suitably trained consultant psychiatrists to take on the RMO role. The Department of Health's 'New ways of working' initiative[130] de-centres power and responsibility from the consultant psychiatrist and aims to share it among the health care team. As noted by the MHAC: '[t]his aim could be distorted towards saving money or other resources to the detriment of patient care or patient safeguards, but it has the potential to provide a better, more patient orientated and responsive services.'[131] To date, take-up has been predominantly by psychiatrists with some input from psychologists, although there is no firm national data available on the precise numbers.[132] Despite the opportunities offered by these professional changes, overall indications are that the uptake from other professions is still very low, as the Care Quality Commission has observed:

> Four years on from implementation of these changes, there is little evidence of a broadening professional base identified as approved or responsible clinicians and, although CQC still sees some examples of good multidisciplinary team work in supporting patients, more

---

[127] *Mental Health Act 2007 Act, Explanatory Notes*, ch 2, para 48.

[128] Including a first level mental health/learning disability nurse, social worker, and occupational therapist; see *Mental Health Act 1983 Instructions with Respect to the Exercise of an Approval Function in relation to Approved Clinicians 2015* Schedule 1 para 1.4.

[129] See MHAC, *Policy Briefing Issue 17* (July 2007) 3.

[130] Department of Health, *Guidance on new ways of working for psychiatrists in a multi-disciplinary and multi-agency context: National Steering Group interim report, August 2004* (TSO 2004); *New ways of working for psychiatrists: Enhancing effective, person-centred services through new ways of working in multidisciplinary and multi-agency contexts. Final report* (TSO 2005).

[131] MHAC, *Twelfth Biennial Report 2005–2007: Rights, Risk and Recovery*, para 1.45.

[132] See, eg, 'London's first non-medical Approved Clinician', 24th May 2013, located at <http://www.oxleas.nhs.uk/news/2013/5/londons-first-non-medical-appr/>; 'The pilot scheme that could shatter the glass ceiling for mental health social workers', *Community Care*, 27th November 2013, at <http://www.communitycare.co.uk/2013/11/27/mental-health-pilot-scheme-shatter-glass-ceiling-social-workers/>.

progress could be made to ensure that patients' experiences of mental health interventions extend beyond receiving medication.[133]

(a) **Approval and supervision** The introduction of mandatory training to meet 'approval' status is a crucial mechanism for the extension of professional responsibility. Professionals seeking 'approval' must undergo AC training within twelve months preceding approval. However, unlike the training provision available for AMHPs, preparation for training for RCs has been developed from scratch. Training for AMHPs has its foundations upon the well-established training programmes devised over the years for ASWs and continues to be regulated by the HCPC (England) or the Care Council (Wales).[134] This places training provision for RCs at a major disadvantage; however, the need to establish new training curricula for ACs is beneficial as it contributes to the augmentation and enhancement of the role. Yet, reference to the precise training requirements during the reform process was rather vague.[135] For example, the Mental Health Bill 2006: Summary Guide, stated that '[t]he RC will have to be trained and approved to take on their role', yet details of what this training should entail were not specified. The Mental Health Act 1983 (Approved Clinicians) Directions 2008 do not offer any further elucidation on this point; the Directions merely explicate the need for the completion of a course for the initial training of ACs.[136] **11.69**

(b) **Professional requirements** The RC is defined in s 34 of the Mental Health Act 1983. The RC will generally be the AC with overall responsibility for the detained patient's case, the AC who is given authority to act in relation to a patient subject to guardianship, and the AC who acts as the 'nominated medical attendant' for a patient under the guardianship of someone other than a local authority. The RC will have overall charge of the care of the formally detained patient, with powers to grant leave and discharge, an obligation to report to and attend appeal tribunals, and will also have additional responsibilities relating to Community Treatment Orders.[137] All RCs will be ACs but with the elevated status of RC will come the additional, overall responsibility for the patient's case. All ACs, who may not necessarily be medical practitioners, will acquire some of the powers that were previously restricted to doctors alone, such as the ability to hold a voluntary patient who wishes to leave hospital for up to seventy-two hours if the AC believes that an application for formal detention under the Act is warranted,[138] having personally examined the patient.[139] **11.70**

To receive 'approved' status, the applicant must come from one of the relevant professions, as listed in Schedule 1 of the Mental Health (Approved Clinician) Directions 2008. Approval is, therefore, not restricted to medical practitioners and may be extended to nurses, occupational therapists, clinical psychologists, and social workers. Medical training is no longer regarded as central to the provision of appropriate care and treatment,[140] thereby extending professional opportunities within mental health care. **11.71**

---

133 *Monitoring the Mental Health Act in 2011/12* (TSO 2013), 59.

134 See para 11.55.

135 The course materials and methods of delivery are the subject of guidance which has been developed under the auspices of the 'National Advisory Group for Approved Clinicians Guidance', which sets out basic standards for training and the recommended curriculum.

136 The *Code of Practice* also remains silent on this issue.

137 RCs have the power to initiate, with the agreement of the AMHP, a Community Treatment Order: Mental Health Act 1983, s 17A, as inserted by the Mental Health Act 2007, s 32(2).

138 The Mental Health Act 2007, s 9 amends the Mental Health Act 1983, s 5(2) and (3).

139 *Code of Practice*, para 14.71.

140 However, non-medically trained ACs will not be eligible to provide the necessary medical recommendation required for initial detention and guardianship decisions.

11.72 (c) **Determining 'competence'** For 'approved' status, the relevant professional must also demonstrate that s/he possesses the necessary competencies. There must be evidence of clear understanding of what the AC role entails, what legal responsibilities are attached to the role and what the key functions are. The relevant competencies are laid out in Sch 2 of the Mental Health (Approved Clinician) Directions 2008.[141] The professional seeking approval must be able to demonstrate a clear, practical knowledge of the legal framework within which care of the mentally disordered is conducted. There must be an applied knowledge of the Mental Health Act 1983, as amended by the Mental Health Act 2007, the Code of Practice and all related local guidance and policy documentation.[142] There must also be present the ability to apply relevant ancillary legislation on a case-by-case basis: for example, the Children Acts 1989 and 2004 and the Mental Capacity Act 2005. The applicant must be capable of working within this legal framework at ground level in his/her daily professional capacity when conducting mental health assessments and when deciding upon appropriate care and treatment responses. The applicant must also be culturally sensitive to the patient's needs. AC regulations have been approved by the Welsh Assembly and largely reflect the requirements laid down in the English regulations, with the same competencies providing the benchmark for approval.[143]

11.73 The applicant must be able to identify the presence of mental disorder and its severity and be able to determine whether the condition warrants compulsory confinement. Within this diagnostic process, the professional must be able to take account of all medical, social, and cultural influences on the patient and in so doing, may thus be able to offer a greater understanding of the patient's needs. Part of the AC's responsibility is to assess and manage risks associated with patients. Focus is placed increasingly upon risk assessment and its management; the applicant for approved status must be able to demonstrate an ability to assess all levels of clinical risk presented by a patient. Within this process of risk assessment, the applicant must be capable of achieving, as far as possible, an effective balance between the potential risks to the public vis-à-vis the need to protect patients. This process of risk assessment and management reflects the continuing trend towards evidence based care and treatment and as such, the applicant must be able to harness this particular working framework in his/her daily role. The professional must have good responsive skills following a diagnosis and risk assessment, and must be capable of responding to all nature of mental disorders with all appropriate and available treatments. In addition, s/he must be able to assess effectively the capacity of patients with regard to the statutory consent to treatment provisions.[144]

11.74 The professional must demonstrate the ability to consider a patient's needs within the context of a workable care plan, meeting the patient's health and social needs while taking account of practical resource implications. Awareness of and willingness to recognize equality issues is, under the Mental Health (Approved Clinician) Directions 2008, essential. The professional must be able to recognize and identify areas where discrimination and inequality may have arisen and respond appropriately to it. The inclusion of this required competency is welcome and will ensure such issues remain at the heart of daily professional conduct.

---

[141] See also the Mental Health Act 1983, 'Instructions with Respect to the Exercise of Approval Functions 2014' (introduced by Health and Social Care Act 2012, s 38).

[142] Professionals are also expected to have a good working knowledge of current NICE guidelines.

[143] The Mental Health (Approval of Persons to be Approved Mental Health Professionals) (Wales) Regulations 2008 include broadly similar approval requirements relating to the need to demonstrate key competencies for AMHPs. See further <http://www.wales.nhs.uk/sites3/Documents/816/AC%20Directions%202008%20(E).pdf>.

[144] MHA 1983, Pt 4.

However, it is the final competencies that need to be demonstrated: multidisciplinary team working and leadership, and the ability to communicate that often pose the greatest challenge. Multidisciplinary working is, under the 2007 Act, a central tenet to mental health care provision. It is not a new idea, nor should it be regarded as particularly radical. However, the changing roles of mental health care professionals and the extension of professional participation now make it essential in all aspects of daily care. The 2008 Approved Clinician Directions lay down the skills that the professional must demonstrate, such as, 'the ability to assimilate the views and opinions of other professionals', the 'ability to effectively lead' and to understand and recognize the limits of their own skills and when to seek assistance from others. Moreover, the professional must be able to 'communicate effectively with professionals, patients, carers, and others'. However, despite such good intentions, multidisciplinary working presents an historical catalogue of failures. **11.75**

Such working practices should offer 'seamless service' yet, rarely do. Research suggests that multidisciplinary working, in a variety of settings, often suffers from similar difficulties, notably, defensiveness, unclear professional boundaries and responsibilities, and competitive professional tendencies in seeking to achieve professional dominance.[145] The relevant professionals that may seek approval come from a variety of professional backgrounds, with different training and educational histories and will often evaluate patients from different perspectives. Murphy has noted that: **11.76**

> Doctors, nurses, therapists, psychologists and social workers plough their own educational furrows, their courses focused almost exclusively on their own professional contribution to the care of individual patients. They are rarely taught about service development during their basic training years, and multidisciplinary team working is supposed to come naturally after graduation and with experience.[146]

Although examples of multidisciplinary failures abound,[147] such changes to the roles of mental health professionals should not, perhaps, be viewed immediately with suspicion and pessimism. The most frequent impediments to good joint working relations have been the problem of overcoming professional self-interest and reducing defensiveness. It may be that the expansion of professional involvement and authority to play a more homogeneous statutory role will overcome these causes of past multidisciplinary failings. In the short term, it is expected that such competencies will certainly limit the 'approved' status to experienced, senior professionals, given the advanced level of skill that will be required of ACs. However, in the longer term, it must be hoped that the injection of experience from more diverse professional backgrounds will only improve the process of care provision. **11.77**

Where the 'approval' criteria are met for medical practitioners who become ACs, automatic s 12 approved doctor status will also be granted. A s 12 doctor is one who is approved as having special knowledge and experience in the diagnosis and treatment of mental disorder. The formal detention processes under the Mental Health Act 1983 required two medical recommendations for compulsory admission to hospital under ss 2 and 3, of which one recommendation must be made by a s 12 approved doctor. This stringent evidential standard in the formal detention process is still in place under the Mental Health Act 2007. Section **11.78**

[145] N Glover-Thomas, 'Joint Working: Reality or Rhetoric in Housing the Mentally Vulnerable?' (2007) 29 (3&4) Journal of Social Welfare and Family Law 217–31.

[146] E Murphy, 'Mental Illness and Community Care', paper presented at the Conference of the Association of Social Service Directors, Solihull, 1993, as quoted in: A Rogers, and D Pilgrim, *Mental Health Policy in Britain* (2nd edn, Palgrave 2001) 103.

[147] See, eg, S Hayes, 'Scientific Practice Guidelines in a Political, Economic and Professional Context' in K S Dobson and K D Craig (eds), *Empirically Supported Therapies* (Sage 1998).

16 of the Mental Health Act 2007 amends s 12 of the 1983 Act and provides that where a registered medical practitioner has been approved and is an AC, there will also be approval for s 12. Paragraph 62 of the Explanatory Notes explains this automatic conferral of s 12 status on the basis that to become an AC 'special experience in the diagnosis or treatment of mental disorder' must be demonstrated. Such evidence would also meet the same demands of s 12 approval. However, this automatic conferral is limited to ACs who are registered medical practitioners. For ACs who come from the other relevant professions, s 12 status is not available. It is recognized that there are some tasks, particularly those related to initial detention decisions, which lie outside the ambit of non-medical professionals' experience. It is also recognized that given the quite fundamental impact of some decisions on individuals with mental disorders, non-medically trained ACs would lack the necessary qualifications and experience.

11.79 (d) **Training** The training of non-clinical medical professionals should now be aligned with approved doctor training, in an effort to create a universal role specification. Service provider organizations are largely responsible for training, re-training, and refresher training. Training is competence led and incorporates a series of modules covering distinct aspects of the role. CSIP/NIMHE[148] have taken a major lead in the creation of training packages with emphasis being placed upon 'training the trainers'. The training programmes seek to: provide easy access to information about the key legislative changes brought about by the 2007 Act; present information within context; and secure uniform provision across each of the eight Regional Development Centres. The training focuses on the changes brought about by the 2007 Act, closely tied with the Code of Practice using worked case examples, and adopts a values-based training approach, placing the 2007 Act's guiding principles at the heart of decision-making. However, the training has been provided on a regional basis, with limited national oversight, regulation, and governance, which falls dramatically short of the training system for AMHPs.

11.80 Little indication as to the levels and standards of training necessary to meet the requirements of the AC and s 12 role have been made available, nor whether this training will be affected by the individual's professional background. Unlike training for AMHPs, no national body to oversee the training/ regulation of ACs in England has been identified[149] and the approval system is currently reliant on regional centres and professional initiatives.[150] For example, the British Psychological Society has produced specific advice for registered psychologists who wish to apply for AC status,[151] but other professional groups have not, to date, developed such guidelines and are required to submit their portfolio directly to Regional Approval Panels.[152] In England there are four regional approval centres which

[148] Care Services Improvement Partnership/National Institute for Mental Health in England.

[149] The Approved Clinician National Reference Group is designed to provide some guidance on the approval process—however, its precise role is unclear and it would not appear to have an ongoing supervisory function. It is therefore far less proactive and powerful than professional regulators such as the HCPC and CC. There is also some limited information available relating to the National Advisory Group for Approved Clinicians Guidance; however, its precise role is also rather indistinct.

[150] See NHS Wales, *Procedural Arrangements for the Approval and Re-approval of Approved Clinicians in Wales* (June 2013). The Welsh procedures have specific arrangements for governance and ongoing review, although these have not been without difficulty and there is still a need for improved provision of AC training courses in Wales, as well as more rigorous governance arrangements and regular monitoring/ quality assurance assessments (*The Introduction of Approved Clinicians within Wales: A summary review* (Welsh Assembly Government, March 2010) para 56.

[151] B T Taylor and J L Taylor, *Guidance for Registered Psychologists in Making Applications to the British Psychological Society Approved Clinician Peer Review Panel* (BPS January 2010).

[152] National Reference Group on s 12 and Approved Clinician Approval, *Applying for Approved Clinical Approval* (June 2010) 3.

offer courses run by a range of providers, including the Royal College of Psychiatrists, the Education and Training Network, and academic institutions working in collaboration with health care trusts. There is, however, no central approving or coordinating body in England, which does raise questions about the overall quality and consistency of the current AC training provision. This stands in contrast to Wales, where the Betsi Cadwalader University Health Board has been delegated the responsibility to carry out the approval arrangements for s 12(2) doctors and Approved Clinicians for Wales, on behalf of the Welsh Minister.[153] The current approach would seem to be rather opaque and unsystematic, thereby raising concerns about the consistency and uniformity of training programmes and whether a national training standard will ever be achieved and maintained. The approval process waters were muddied even further in 2012, when it became apparent that several Strategic Health Authorities had delegated authority for giving section 12 approval to NHS Trusts in an irregular manner. This fell outside the permitted delegated authority of the Trusts and meant that approximately 12,000 doctors had been making decisions that they were technically not able to make. There has been no suggestion that any of these detentions were clinically inappropriate. But the government responded by passing retrospective legislation in 2013[154] and, since April 2013, the approval functions have been discharged by the Department of Health.[155]

Research has suggested that there are definite areas of training need, however, particularly given the inclusion of risk assessment and management considerations within decision-making under the 2007 Act.[156] **11.81**

It had been anticipated that, with the broadening of the professional base from which RCs can be drawn, the role could potentially be fulfilled by professionals from the same professional discipline, risking their independence.[157] The training of RCs must therefore encompass specific requirements in order to aid independence and objectivity in the decision-making process. It is unfortunate that RC training does not have the same solid foundation as that of the AMHP training provision;[158] and even more concerning that it has not yet been subject to independent scrutiny or kept under regular review. **11.82**

4. Routes to compulsory admission to hospital

This section will outline the powers for admitting patients to hospital for assessment or treatment in Pt II of the 1983 Act, as amended. They include a short-term power of assessment (s 2), longer term treatment (s 3), or urgent admission for treatment (s 4). The vast majority of admissions to hospital are informal and voluntary and the total number of formal admissions to NHS hospitals under Pt II has remained stable since 2000. In 2013–14, there were a total number of 32,781 formal longer-term admissions under Pt II. Of that **11.83**

[153] NHS Wales, *Procedural Arrangements for the Approval and Re-approval of Approved Clinicians in Wales* (June 2013).

[154] Mental Health (Approval Functions) Act 2012.

[155] Department of Health, *Independent review of the arrangements made by SHAs for the approval of registered medical practitioners and approved clinicians under the Mental Health Act 1983* (2013).

[156] J Hurley and P Linsley, 'Proposed Changes to the Mental Health Act of England and Wales: Research Indicating Future Educational and Training Needs for Mental Health Nurses' (2006) 13 Journal of Psychiatric and Mental Health Nursing 48.

[157] See, eg, M Cleary, 'The Challenges of Mental Health Care Reform for Contemporary Mental Health Nursing Practice: Relationships, Power and Control' (2003) 12 International Journal of Mental Health Nursing 139 and M Coffey and E Jenkins, 'Power and Control: Forensic Community Mental Health Nurses' Perceptions of Team-working, Legal Sanction and Compliance' (2002) Journal of Psychiatric and Mental Health Nursing 521–29.

[158] See para 11.55.

total, 77 per cent were under s 2 and 23 per cent under s 3. Uses of Section 4 during 2013–14 decreased by 18 per cent (70) since the previous reporting year, continuing a downward trend in uses over the last five years.[159] The Care Quality Commission has commented on the decline in use of s 3 and increasing use of s 2 in recent years and speculated about the possible reasons for this trend. One factor may be that there is better support in terms of maintaining people in the community which means that patients do not deteriorate to the point of requiring hospital admission, or it could be due to the fact that 'services know less about the patients they are assessing'.[160] The CQC also observed in 2013 that:

> The majority of section 2 detentions result in the patient agreeing to remain in hospital as a voluntary patient—this was the outcome of 69% of section 2 detentions in 2011/12, whereas 23% resulted in further detention under section 3.[161]

11.84 The section below also considers doctors and nurses holding powers (s 5) which can be applied to prevent patients from leaving hospital in certain circumstances. Community treatment and after-care are discussed in Section 6 below.

(i) Admission for assessment—section 2

11.85 Section 2 governs the criteria for short-term admission for assessment. The assessment period lasts up to twenty-eight days and is non-renewable. Although there must be an intention to assess the patient's needs, a patient detained under s 2 may also be treated. Indeed, the Reference Guide to the Mental Health Act 1983 makes it clear that: 'Although there must be an intention to assess the patient's needs if the criteria . . . are to be met, a patient detained for assessment may also be treated. Indeed, treatment may form part of the assessment.'[162] An application for admission for assessment may be made by the patient's nearest relative or an AMHP (discussed in paras 11.46–11.65), supported by two medical recommendations, one of which must be provided by a doctor approved under s 12 as having expertise in the diagnosis and treatment of mental disorder. Approved doctors are usually specialist psychiatrists, but there may also be GPs with relevant expertise in psychiatry on the list. The other recommendation can be provided by any doctor, although it is preferable for one of the recommendations to be provided by someone who 'has previous acquaintance' with the patient.[163] Since 2002–03, there has been an overall steady increase in admissions under s 2. Admissions under s 2 now account for 77 per cent of all longer term Pt II admissions, compared to 54 per cent in 1997–98.[164]

11.86 The grounds for admission under s 2 are that the patient:

(a) Is suffering from mental disorder of a nature or degree[165] which warrants the detention of the patient in a hospital for assessment; and

[159] HSCIC, *Inpatients formally detained in hospitals under the Mental Health Act 1983, and patients subject to Supervised Community Treatment: Annual Report, England, 2013–14*, Table 2 (October 2014) located at <http://www.hscic.gov.uk/>.

[160] *Monitoring the Mental Health Act in 2011/12* (2013) 13.

[161] ibid.

[162] *Reference Guide to the Mental Health Act 1983*, para. 8.5.

[163] Mental Health Act 1983, s 12(2). In *Ann R (By her litigation Friend Joan T v Bronglais Hospital Pembrokeshire and Derwen NHS Trust* [2001] EWHC Admin 792, the court found that this was easily satisfied when the GP had only just accepted and met with the patient at a local social services department. Scott Baker J found that s 12(2) does not require 'personal' acquaintance.

[164] NSIC, *Inpatients formally detained in hospitals under the Mental Health Act 1983 and other legislation, England 1997–98 to 2007–08* (October 2008). See also HSCIC, *Inpatients formally detained in hospitals under the Mental Health Act 1983, and patients subject to Supervised Community Treatment: Uses of the Mental Health Act: Annual Statistics 2014/15*. Figure 2.2 and Table 1 (October 2015).

[165] In *R v Mental Health Review Tribunal for South West Thames Region, ex p Smith* [1999] COD 148 the court stated that this phrase is disjunctive, therefore a disorder of a nature (but not of a degree) that warrants detention does still satisfy this element of the criteria.

(b) He ought to be so detained in the interests of his own health or safety or with a view to the protection of other persons.

As Fennell notes, these grounds are highly paternalistic as there is no need for a threat to the safety of the patient/others, provided the patient is suffering from a mental disorder of appropriate severity, s/he may be detained solely in the interests of their own mental/physical health.[166] There is remarkably little jurisprudence on the precise meaning of the substantive criteria here and there is clearly great flexibility in the interpretation of the terms. Although, in line with case law, the Reference Guide to the Mental Health Act 1983 states that for both sections 2 and 3: **11.87**

> 'nature' refers to the particular mental disorder from which the patient is suffering, its chronicity, its prognosis, and the patient's previous response to receiving treatment for the disorder. 'Degree' refers to the current manifestation of the patient's disorder.[167]

Ultimately, however, the decision is left in the hands of the professionals involved and undoubtedly, in the current climate, risk assessment will feature prominently in the decision to detain. Yet the reliability of the tools currently used to predict risk is questionable and academics have doubted this 'broad discretion' and 'lack of clear definitional parameters' as it 'presents concerns about just how far risk will be perceived and determined'.[168] It has led one such legal commentator to conclude, on the basis of empirical research into risk with mental health practitioners employed by Mersey Care NHS Trust, that: **11.88**

> In light of the Mental Health Act's broad criteria and its wide reliance on professional judgment, it is difficult to resist the conclusion that patient's rights will increasingly become secondary to public safety in the post-2007 Act era.[169]

Part 4 of the 1983 Act (as amended) regulates the treatment for mental disorder of patients detained under s 2, whereas the MCA 2005 regulates the treatment for physical disorder (see further Chapter 10). The patient's nearest relative has no power to veto the admission under s 2 but the patient does have the right to apply to the First-tier Tribunal (Mental Health) for discharge once within the first fourteen days following admission (see further paras 11.183 et seq). **11.89**

(ii) Admission for treatment—section 3

Section 3 governs the criteria for admission for treatment for up to six months. This is renewable for a further six months and thereafter for periods of twelve months at a time under s 20. An application for treatment may be made by the patient's nearest relative/AMHP and supported by two medical recommendations (one of whom is s 12 approved) on the grounds that: **11.90**

(a) He is suffering from mental disorder of a nature or degree which makes it appropriate for him to receive medical treatment in hospital; and
(b) It is necessary for the health or safety of the patient or for the protection of other persons that he should receive such treatment; and
(c) Appropriate medical treatment is available.

166 Fennel, *Mental Health: Law and Practice*, n 13, para 6.108.
167 *Reference Guide*, para. 8.3.
168 See for example N Glover-Thomas, 'The Age of Risk: Risk Perception and Determination following the Mental Health Act 2007 (2011) 19(4) Medical Law Review 581–605, 584.
169 ibid. 605.

11.91 As noted above 'mental disorder' here does not include learning disability unless that learning disability is associated with abnormally aggressive or seriously irresponsible conduct on the part of the patient concerned (see paras 11.28–11.37).

11.92 The criteria make it clear that the intention here is that it is appropriate and necessary for the patient to receive medical treatment in hospital. Consequently, this section cannot be used if the purpose is to admit and detain the patient for a purely nominal period during which no appropriate treatment will be given.[170] Section 3 must only be used for those whose condition is believed to require a period of treatment as an inpatient.

11.93 Patients detained under s 3 for treatment are able to apply to the First-tier Tribunal (Mental Health) for discharge once within the first six months following admission and once in each period in which the detention is renewed. Unlike s 2, the patient's nearest relative does have the power under s 11(4) to block detention under s 3 or guardianship.

11.94 (a) **Nature/degree** The Code stipulates that the criteria require consideration of both the nature and degree of a patient's mental disorder.[171] As noted above, '[n]ature' refers to the particular mental disorder from which the patient is suffering, its chronicity, its progress, and the patient's previous response to receiving treatment for the disorder. 'Degree' refers to the current manifestation of the patient's disorder. However, the terms are disjunctive, as enunciated in *R v Mental Health Review Tribunal for the South Thames Region, ex parte Smith*.[172] In all cases, consideration must be given to: the patient's wishes and views; the patient's age and physical health; any past wishes or feelings expressed by the patient; the patient's cultural background and social/family circumstances; the impact that any future deterioration or lack of improvement would have on the patient's relatives/carers; and the effect on the patient and those close to the patient of a decision to admit or not to admit under the Act.

11.95 The Code makes it clear that when a patient needs to be in hospital, informal admission is usually appropriate when a patient who has the capacity to do so consents to the admission, although 'this should not be regarded as an absolute rule'.[173] Furthermore, consideration must be given to whether there are alternative means of providing the care and treatment which the patient requires, such as guardianship.[174] Foremost, the Code reminds professionals that the threat of detention must not be used to induce a patient to consent to admission to hospital or to treatment, and is likely to invalidate any apparent consent in any event.[175]

11.96 The MHAC had urged the government to update the guidance to clarify that s 3 should only be used to admit a patient who is known to services and has been assessed in the recent past, but this has not been explicitly included in the recent revisions to the Code.[176]

11.97 (b) **The health/safety of the patient** The Code includes a list of factors to consider in deciding whether patients should be detained for their own health/safety, which includes the risk of suicide, self-harm, self-neglect, or jeopardizing their own health/safety accidentally, recklessly or unintentionally. The reliability of the evidence suggesting there is such a risk should be considered as well as the views of the patient, carers, relatives, or close friends,

---

[170] *R v Hallstrom, ex p W; R v Gardner, ex p L* [1986 2 WLR 883.
[171] *Code of Practice,* para 14.6.
[172] [1999] COD 148.
[173] *Code of Practice,* paras 14.14, 14.15.
[174] ibid, para 14.7.
[175] ibid, para 14. 17.
[176] MHAC, para 4.39.

as well as the patient's capacity to consent to or refuse admission and treatment. Ultimately, the Code advises that:

> Professionals must consider available alternatives, having regard to all the relevant circumstances, to identify the least restrictive way of best achieving the proposed assessment or treatment.[177]

(c) **The protection of others** In considering whether detention is necessary for the protection of other people, the relevant factors are the nature of the risk to other people, and likelihood and severity of any potential harm. Harm includes psychological as well as physical harm. Professionals should always bear in mind that it is not always possible to differentiate risk of harm to the patient from the risk of harm to others; the reliability of the available evidence; the willingness and ability of those who live with the patient to cope with and manage the risk and whether other methods of managing the risk are available.[178] Risk prediction, in particular the risk posed to others by the patient will no doubt feature prominently in the decision whether to use compulsory powers. There is remarkably little guidance from the courts on precisely how great a risk the patient must pose and precisely when the mental disorder makes it appropriate for the patient to be detained. The criteria are vague and, yet again, the decision is a matter for clinical discretion. **11.98**

(d) **Availability of appropriate treatment** The 2007 Act replaced the old 'treatability test' with a new test of availability of appropriate treatment. As noted by Fennell,[179] this applies regardless of whether the patient accepts the treatment, so the new test is satisfied even when the patient is refusing to cooperate with the treatment. The main aim of this provision is to seek to ensure that people with a personality disorder are not excluded from compulsory powers due to the lack of appropriate treatment options. **11.99**

Section 3(4) of the MHA as inserted by the 2007 Act states that: **11.100**

> References to appropriate medical treatment, in relation to a person suffering from mental disorder, are references to medical treatment which is appropriate in his case, taking into account the nature and degree of the mental disorder and all the other circumstances of his case.

The Code expressly states that the purpose of this test is to ensure that no one is detained (or remains detained) or is on a Community Treatment Order unless they are actually to be offered appropriate medical treatment for their mental disorder.[180] The test requires a 'balanced and holistic judgement' about whether appropriate medical treatment is available given (1) the nature and degree of the patient's mental disorder, and (2) all the other circumstances of the patient's case.[181] In other words, both the clinical appropriateness of the treatment and its appropriateness more generally (ie social factors) must be considered. According to the Code, 'all the other circumstances' includes factors such as the patient's physical health/ disability, the patient's age, culture, ethnicity, religious beliefs, gender or sexual orientation, as well as the location and implications of the available treatment.[182] The final consideration in the list is the patient's views about what treatment works for them and what doesn't. Whilst the Code seeks to advise professionals on the appropriateness of the treatment, it does not provide any further guidance on the precise meaning of 'availability', **11.101**

---

177 *Code of Practice*, para. 14.13.
178 ibid, para. 14.10.
179 Fennell, *Mental Health: Law and Practice*, n 13, 87.
180 *Code of Practice*, para. 23.8.
181 ibid, para. 23.11.
182 ibid, para. 23.12.

so professionals are given very little help in determining what it entails. Does available simply mean geographically close/available locally or does it mean on offer in the NHS as opposed to the private sector? The Reference Guide to the Mental Health Act 1983 is equally unhelpful on this point suggesting that available means that appropriate treatment is 'actually' available and it is not enough that it 'exists in theory for the patient's condition'.[183] This point is reinforced in the Code, [184] although it does indicate that the treatment must be available 'for the time being'.[185] Again here, much discretion is left in the hands of the clinicians involved to determine precisely what type of treatment is appropriate and available. And no matter what the limited guidance in the Code provides, if the clinician reasonably concludes that there is no medical treatment available which is appropriate for the patient, s/he is unlikely to recommend compulsory admission. Despite the government's contrary intention, this could still leave individuals with a personality disorder falling outside the reach of the mental health legislation. Although the Code seeks to counteract this by reminding professionals that:

> A patient's attitude towards the proposed treatment may be relevant in determining whether the appropriate medical treatment test is met. An indication of unwillingness to co-operate with treatment generally, or with a specific aspect of treatment, does not make such treatment inappropriate.... In particular, psychological therapies and other forms of medical treatments which, to be effective, require the patient's co-operation are not automatically inappropriate simply because a patient does not currently wish to engage with them. Such treatments can potentially remain appropriate and available as long as it continues to be clinically suitable to offer them and they would be provided if the patient agreed to engage.[186]

11.102 The new broader definition of 'medical treatment' now includes 'psychological intervention and specialist mental health habilitation, rehabilitation and care' (s 7 of the 2007 Act). This is not exhaustive so can include a broad range of treatments, including psychotherapy, drug therapy, and electroconvulsive therapy (ECT).[187] It also means that patients with a personality disorder can receive appropriate cognitive behaviour and psychotherapy, even when they may be refusing to cooperate with that treatment. The Code makes it clear that the definition includes treatment of physical health problems only to the extent that such treatment is part of, or ancillary to, treatment for mental disorder.[188] An example would be treating wounds self-inflicted as a result of mental disorder. All other medical treatment for physical health problems falls outside the Act and is regulated by the common law or the Mental Capacity Act 2005.[189]

11.103 The Law Society was concerned during the reform process that 'specialist' intervention should include some level of supervision by a psychiatrist,[190] but this has not been clearly stated in the amended Act or the revised Code of Practice. Consequently, the Law Society cast doubt on whether this provision complies precisely with the ECHR requirement for objective medical expertise[191] when a patient is receiving non-consensual medical treatment for a mental disorder.

---

183 ibid, para. 8.8.

184 ibid, para. 23.14.

185 ibid, para. 23.21.

186 ibid, paras 23.19–23.20.

187 But note that special rules and procedures apply to certain treatments such as ECT, medication beyond an initial three-month period, neurosurgery and surgical hormone implants (ss 57, 58, and 58A). See further Section 5.

188 *Code of Practice*, para. 24.5.

189 See further Chapters 8, 9, and 10.

190 *Parliamentary Brief Mental Health Bill, House of Lords*, 2.

191 See para 11.26.

This amendment received a great deal of criticism from a number of campaign groups. For example, there was concern that using 'availability of appropriate treatment' as a basis for compulsory detention could be misused to exclude patients inappropriately from medical treatment due to the scarcity of mental health resources.[192] The fact that para 23.14 of the Code states that 'it is not sufficient that appropriate treatment could theoretically be provided' and that 'medical treatment must actually be available to the patient . . . for the time being', does seem to reinforce that point. Moreover, there may be long waiting lists for some treatments, but there is no indication of the timescale within which the treatment must actually be made available to the patient. This could result in long delays and patients kept waiting until the 'appropriate' treatment becomes available. There had also been concerns that this test opened up the possibility of detaining people for whom there is no therapeutic benefit (see below).[193] In an attempt to counteract such concerns, the 2007 Act inserted a new sub-s (4) into s 145 which makes it clear that 'medical treatment' must demonstrate some benefit in terms of being for the 'purpose of alleviat[ing], or prevent a worsening of, the disorder or one or more of the symptoms or manifestations'. In addition, para 23.18 of the Code makes it clear that simply detaining someone, even in a hospital, does not constitute medical treatment. Despite this limitation, recent CQC mental health monitoring reports suggest, somewhat worryingly, that the thresholds for admission may well be 'distorted' by external factors, such as the availability of hospital beds, which impact on admission. For example, the 2012/13 report noted that: **11.104**

> We have heard strong anecdotal evidence that in some geographical areas, bed availability or similar systemic pressures are distorting the thresholds for detention. It is accepted the system is running over capacity, and research indicates a relationship between lack of bed capacity and increases in detention . . . The principle of least restriction is a fundamental consideration for professionals making decisions about a course of action under the Act. It would not be lawful to use detention powers solely as a mechanism to secure access to hospital treatment, but in practice the thresholds for detention can be influenced by what alternative provision is available.[194]

The Code of Practice stresses that purpose is not the same as likelihood, which means that there is no need to show in advance that the purpose is likely to be achieved.[195] This differs from the previous treatability test which included a likelihood requirement. Furthermore, and of particular relevance to the discussion about personality disorder at paras 11.38–11.40, the Code reminds professionals that there may well be a range of interventions which are appropriate even if particular mental disorders are likely to persist or get worse despite treatment. Moreover, 'it should never be assumed that any disorders, or any patients, are inherently or inevitably untreatable'.[196] Finally, the Code provides that: '. . . an indication of unwillingness to cooperate with treatment generally, or with a specific aspect of treatment, does not make such treatment inappropriate.'[197] **11.105**

This suggests that the scope of this treatment test is very broad and 'easily met', as the Care Quality Commission has pointed out.[198] The test is unlikely to impede admission in most cases, as long as the clinicians involved conclude that the treatment is appropriate **11.106**

[192] Law Society, *Parliamentary Brief Mental Health Bill Second Reading House of Lords*, 2.
[193] Royal College of Psychiatrists, *Briefing on the Mental Health Bill*, para 3.1.
[194] CQC, *Monitoring the Mental Health Act in 2012/13* (TSO 2014) 14–15.
[195] *Code of Practice*, para 23.4.
[196] ibid, para 23.6.
[197] ibid, para 23.19.
[198] CQC, *Monitoring the Mental Health Act in 2011/12* (TSO 2013) 58.

and available. Given the wide ambit of medical treatment and the low threshold of the new availability of appropriate treatment test, it would appear that, as the Code points out:

> There may be patients whose particular circumstances mean that treatment may be appropriate even though it consists only of nursing and specialist day-to-day care under the clinical supervision of an approved clinician in a safe and secure therapeutic environment with a structured regime.[199]

11.107 Not surprisingly, this aspect of the 2007 reforms has already been the subject of legal challenge. In the case of *MD v Nottinghamshire Healthcare NHS Trust*[200] the Tribunal adopted a broad definition of treatment in this section. Despite the fact that the patient (who had a personality disorder) was unable to engage with psychotherapy, it found that the patient may instead derive benefit from: 'the milieu of the ward both for its short term effects and for the possibility that it would break through the defence mechanisms and allow him later to engage in therapy'.[201] Bartlett and Sandland have noted that this:

> . . . comes perilously close to finding that detention is, itself, appropriate treatment. That in turn goes a long way to undercutting the therapeutic image which the appropriate treatment test was meant to foster.[202]

11.108 In contrast, the Upper Tier Tribunal in *DL-H v Devon Partnership NHS Trust and Secretary of State for Justice*[203] took a narrower and more cautious view, expressing concern that the broad language relating to medical treatment should not create the illusion that appropriate treatment was available, masking decisions based on dangerousness alone. The Upper Tier Tribunal was also concerned that treatment refusals should not be equated with unavailability of treatment. The following advice was offered for Tribunals to make an 'individualised assessment' based on the treatment needs of the particular patient:

> The tribunal must investigate behind assertions, generalisations and standard phrases. By focusing on specific questions, it will ensure that it makes an individualized assessment for the particular patient. What precisely is the treatment that can be provided? What discernible benefit may it have on this patient? Is that benefit related to the patient's mental disorder or to some unrelated problem? Is the patient truly resistant to engagement?[204]

11.109 Whilst the threshold for admission may still be too low, it is regrettable that the new test has failed to remedy the perennial problems of finding an appropriate hospital bed for some patients. That is likely to be a far more crucial factor to securing hospital admission. This pressure on beds has already been highlighted by the House of Commons Health Committee in its post-legislative scrutiny of the 2007 Act.[205] As one former social worker has put it:

> . . . the revisions to the Act have done nothing to pressurise health authorities into ensuring that beds are available for patients where professionals consider admission is necessary.[206]

---

199 *Code of Practice*, para 23.17.

200 *MD v Nottinghamshire Healthcare NHS Trust,* [2010] UKUT 59.

201 ibid, [39].

202 P Bartlett and R Sandland, *Mental Health Law Policy and Practice* (Oxford University Press 2014) 255.

203 *DL-H v Devon Partnership NHS Trust and Secretary of State for Justice* [2010] UKUT 102 (AAC).

204 ibid, [33].

205 *Post-legislative scrutiny of the Mental Health Act 2007* (TSO 2013) HC 584 para 27: 'A disturbing element of the evidence the Committee took was the suggestion that pressure on bed places had made it difficult for patients to be admitted to psychiatric units on a voluntary basis . . . it was possible that a clinician might section a patient who in the past would not have been sectioned in order to access a psychiatric unit'.

206 R Brown, *The Approved Mental Health Professional's Guide to Mental Health Law* (2nd edn, Learning Matters 2009) 13.

Some of the evidence presented by the CQC in the annual mental health monitoring reports mentioned above[207] would suggest that this has become a major problem for practitioners using the Act and external pressures may well be influencing decisions about the use of compulsory admission far more than they should do.

(e) **Section 2 or section 3?** Obviously, the purpose of s 2 is to carry out an assessment whereas s 3 is concerned with treatment. However, the choice between ss 2 and 3 may not always be clear but it can have significant implications for the patient in terms of applications to the review tribunal. As Bartlett has observed, patients admitted for assessment under s 2 and then for treatment under s 3 will have the opportunity for two tribunal review hearings, but a patient admitted under s 3 has only one. Section 2 cases tend to be heard more promptly by the tribunal and a s 3 patient who was initially admitted under s 2 may be in a stronger position at a hearing as the medication has had a greater opportunity to take effect.[208] The Code advises that an application under s 2 should be made if the full extent of the patient's condition is unclear; there is a need to carry out an initial inpatient assessment in order to formulate a treatment plan/reach a judgement about whether the patient will accept treatment on a voluntary basis; or there is a need to carry out a new inpatient assessment in order to reformulate a treatment plan or to reach a judgement about whether the patient will accept treatment on a voluntary basis.[209] The focus here is clearly on the reasons for the admission and the conditions for section 2 admission are not as stringent as for section 3. Section 3 should be the preferred route where the patient is already detained under s 2, or where 'the nature and current degree of the patient's mental disorder, the essential elements of the treatment plan to be followed and the likelihood of the patient accepting treatment as an informal patient are already sufficiently established to make it unnecessary to undertake a new assessment under section 2'.[210] This advice differs from the advice contained in an earlier edition of the Code when it cautioned against using s 2 where an objection to a s 3 by the nearest relative was anticipated as being likely. But this advice has since disappeared.[211] In making a choice between the two sections, professionals should also bear in mind *R v Wilson ex p. Williamson*.[212] The applicant had been admitted to a mental hospital for assessment under s 2. During the maximum twenty-eight-day period of detention, the doctors recommended that the applicant should remain in hospital to receive treatment, but the applicant refused. The patient's nearest relative also objected to a s 3 order being made. The hospital authorities applied for a further s 2 to be made, rather than applying to displace the nearest relative and then making a s 3 order. However, the court made it clear that the practice of using s 2 as a fall back in the face of an objection to s 3 was unlawful. Section 2 cannot therefore be used to extend powers or as a stopgap procedure. This point is reinforced in the Reference Guide to the Mental Health Act 1983: **11.110**

> The powers under section 2 can only be used for the limited purpose for which they were intended. They cannot be used to further detain patients for the purposes of assessment

[207] See, eg, the observations in *Monitoring the Mental Health Act in 2011/12* (TSO 2013) 53–56.

[208] P Bartlett, 'Civil Confinement', in L Gostin et al (eds), *Principles of Mental Health Law and Policy* (Oxford University Press 2010) para 12.229.

[209] *Code of Practice*, para 14.27. This can be contrasted with the Welsh Code of Practice which contains a broader range of factors including the use of s 2 when a judgment is required on whether the patient will accept treatment on a voluntary/informal basis; the condition of a patient who has already been assessed is judged to have changed; the diagnosis and/or prognosis is unclear; and a judgment has to be made on whether a proposed treatment under Pt IV of the Act is likely to be effective (para 5.2).

[210] *Code of Practice*, para 14.28.

[211] R Brown, *The Approved Mental Health Professional's Guide to Mental Health Law* (2nd edn, Learning Matters 2009) 23.

[212] [1996] COD 42; The Independent, 19 April 1995.

beyond the 28 days period. Nor can they be used as a temporary alternative to detention under section 3 merely to allow an application to be made to the county court under section 29 for an order to appoint an acting nearest relative in place of a nearest relative who objects to the use of section 3.[213]

11.111 There has been strong criticism in the past about the widespread use of s 3. Consequently, the MHAC made it clear in its penultimate Biennial Report that s 3 should only be used to admit a patient who is known to services and has been assessed in the recent past.[214] This point has not been precisely translated into recent revisions to the Code of Practice however.

11.112 **(f) Alternatives to detention—patients who lack capacity to consent** The Code of Practice urges doctors and AMHPs who are involved in assessments always to consider the alternative ways of providing the treatment or care that the patient might need.[215] In particular, the fact that patients cannot consent to the admission or to the treatment they need does not automatically mean that the Act must be used. The Mental Capacity Act 2005 may be relied upon instead to provide treatment in the best interests of patients who are over 16 and who lack capacity to consent to treatment. Professionals may consider utilizing the Deprivation of Liberty Safeguards (DoLS) for people (over 18) who need to be deprived of their liberty in their best interests for care and treatment to which they lack the capacity to consent to themselves. Further detailed guidance on the application of these provisions, as well as a flow chart to aid decision-making, is provided in the Code of Practice.[216] The decision as to which statutory regime to use will be left to the doctors and AMHPs involved, and the examination carried out by them (discussed below) could form the basis of an assessment under either statute. The Code of Practice emphasizes that:

> Practitioners should be able to identify the legal framework that governs a patient's assessment and treatment and authorise any appropriate deprivation of a patient's liberty whether the MCA or Metal Health Act (the Act). The legal framework is not static and may change as the patient's circumstances and needs change.[217]

However, this is not as straightforward as it seems, as the discussion above highlighted the difficulties faced by professionals in determining the most appropriate statutory framework, especially in light of the criticisms of and complexities surrounding the DoLS regime.[218] The provisions of the 2005 Act and recent proposals for reform put forward by the Law Commission[219] are considered in detail in Chapter 10.

---

[213] *Code of* Practice, para 8.11.
[214] MHAC, para 4.39.
[215] *Code of Practice*, paras 14.11–14.13.
[216] ibid; and see especially Chapter 13.
[217] *Code of Practice*, para 13.2.
[218] See, eg, the House of Lords Select Committee on the Mental Capacity Act 2005, *Mental Capacity Act 2005 Post-legislative scrutiny*, HL Paper 139 (TSO March 2014) 7: 'The provisions are poorly drafted, overly complex and bear no relationship to the language and ethos of the Mental Capacity Act. The safeguards are not well understood and are poorly implemented.... The only appropriate recommendation in the face of such criticism is to start again. We therefore recommend a comprehensive review of the Deprivation of Liberty Safeguards with a view to replacing them with provisions that are compatible in style and ethos to the rest of the Mental Capacity Act.'
[219] Law Commission, *Mental Capacity and Deprivation of Liberty: A Consultation Paper* (Law Com No 222, 2015).

(iii) The assessment process

An application for detention may be made by an AMHP or the patient's nearest relative. An AMHP is usually a more appropriate applicant given his/her's professional training, experience, and expertise. In particular, AMHPs should have knowledge of local services and appropriate mental health facilities. Applications must be supported by two medical recommendations in accordance with the Act. The objective of the assessment is to determine whether the criteria for detention are met and, if so, whether an application for detention in hospital should be made. Where possible, patients should be seen jointly by the AMHP and at least one of the two doctors involved in the assessment, [220] however, both doctors must examine the patient prior an application for admission to hospital being made.[221] Paragraph 14.49 of the Code of Practice stipulates that AMHPs may only make an application for detention if they: **11.113**

- have interviewed the patient in a suitable manner;
- are satisfied that the statutory criteria for detention are met; and
- are satisfied that, in all the circumstances of the case, detention in hospital is the most appropriate way of providing the care and medical treatment the patient needs.

Interviewing the patient 'in a suitable manner', includes taking into account the patient's age and understanding and any hearing or linguistic difficulties which the patient may have. The AMHP is required to coordinate the process of assessment and the Code of Practice states that, in doing so, the AMHP should be 'sensitive to the patient's age, sex, gender identity, social, cultural, or ethnic background, religion or belief, and/or sexual orientation.[222] S/he should also bear in mind how any disability the patient has may affect the way the assessment needs to be carried out. The Code contains useful guidance on how AMHPs should carry out the interview and stresses the importance of good communication—the AMHP has responsibility to ensure that patients are able to communicate effectively and reliably and prevent potential misunderstandings. This could mean arranging a signer, professional interpreter, or specialist equipment such as a hearing aid in the case of people who are deaf or have linguistic difficulties.[223] There are also additional guidelines for assessing people with dementia, a learning disability or a personality disorder. It is also the responsibility of the AMHP to secure the attendance of other people who the individual wants to be present, for example an advocate or familiar person.[224] **11.114**

In *R (on the application of M) v South West London & St George's Mental Health NHS Trust*[225] the Court of Appeal considered the meaning of assessment under the Act. The patient was detained in hospital under s 2 and had been transferred to another hospital for diagnostic tests. Whilst on the surgical ward of that hospital, she was seen by another social worker and psychiatrist for an assessment for detention under s 3, at the request of her Responsible Clinician. The patient did not feel physically well enough to participate in the assessment and telephoned her solicitor, who asked for the assessment to be deferred. It was not deferred however and the patient subsequently challenged her detention under s 3. She argued that **11.115**

220 See further guidance in paras 14.38–14.56 of the *Code of Practice.*

221 The length and manner of the interview/examination with the patient are flexible and a matter for professional judgment, as the term is not defined in the legislation: *M v Managers, Queen Mary's Hospital* [2008] EWCA Civ 1112.

222 *Code of Practce,* para 14.41. Similar guidance is contained in the *Code of Practice for Wales Review*, ch 14.

223 ibid, para 14.42.

224 ibid, para 14.53.

225 *R (on the application of M)) v South West London & St George's Mental Health NHS Trust* [2008] EWCA Civ 1112.

the social worker and doctor had failed to conduct proper interviews and assessments as required under the Act. The Court of Appeal concluded that a doctor can 'examine' a patient for the purpose of reaching an opinion as to her mental health even if she refuses, for example, to answer questions or submit to a physical examination. Accordingly, where a patient does not respond to an AMHP attempting to communicate with him/her, the AMHP is entitled to infer that the patient does require treatment. The court accepted that this 'strained' construction of the Act was necessary otherwise it would be 'inoperable in many cases where it was most obviously needed'.[226] The court has recognized that it can be difficult for professionals to examine an un-cooperative patient and, for safety and expediency, have set an extremely low threshold for satisfying the examination requirement. This view was reinforced in *GM (patient: consultation)*[227] where the court indicated that in cases where the patient is violent, the AMHP was justified in carrying out an interview that could take only 'seconds' to complete.

11.116 With respect to the assessment itself, the Code urges that doctors and AMHPs undertaking assessments should apply professional judgment and reach decisions independently of each other, but in a framework of cooperation and mutual support.[228] Wherever possible, patients should be seen jointly by the AMHP and at least one of the two doctors involved in the assessment.[229] Once the assessment is complete, a decision must be made as to whether an application should be made under Pt 2 of the Act for assessment/treatment in hospital or guardianship in the community. If the AMHP decides not to make an application, where necessary, alternative proposals should be made for the person's care and/or treatment. If the AMHP decides that it is appropriate to make an application, s/he must implement that decision. However, s 11(5) of the Act states that the AMHP must have 'personally seen' the patient within fourteen days prior to the making of the application. This is usually satisfied by the interview, but it could be a separate personal visit if the interview was conducted prior to that fourteen-day period.

11.117 As identified in 2007 and again in 2009 by the MHAC in its Biennial Reports, one of the main problems with assessment and admission is accessing the required professionals to complete applications for admission under the Act as well as severe difficulties in admitting patients and locating available beds.[230] This could leave ASWs in a difficult and dangerous position of being alone with a person who requires admission under the Act or that person could be left without appropriate support. The Care Quality Commission reports that ASWs continue to experience difficulties in obtaining support from other bodies, particularly the police and ambulance service.[231] The MHAC had recommended that it is imperative that social services and other authorities agree protocols over attendance for Mental Health Act assessments.[232] The updated Code of Practice has responded to this and now explicitly refers to the need for commissioners, providers, local authorities, and the police to have in place joint locally agreed policies on the involvement of the police in the assessment process. This is in line with the Mental Health Crisis Care Concordat[233] and the Code

226 ibid, para 15.

227 [2000] 1 MHLR 41.

228 *Code of Practice*, para 14.44; See also *Code of Practice for Wales Review*, para. 14.102 which emphasises that any professional disagreements must be discussed.

229 *Code of Practice*, para 14.45.

230 MHAC, *Risk, Rights, Recovery Twelfth Biennial Report 2005–2007* (TSO 2008) para 4.1; MHAC, *Coercion and Consent Thirteenth Biennial Report 2007–2009* (TSO 2009), paras 2.22, 2.28–2.29.

231 *Monitoring the Mental Health Act in 2011/12* (TSO 2013) 56–57.

232 MHAC, *Risk, Rights, Recovery Twelfth Biennial Report 2005–2007* (TSO 2008) para 4.5.

233 This is a national agreement between services and agencies involved in the care and support of people in crisis. It sets out how organizations will work together better to make sure that people get the help they need when they are having a mental health crisis. In February 2014, twenty-two national bodies

stipulates that '[t]hese should include a joint risk assessment tool to help determine the level of risk and what (if any) police assistance may be required and how quickly it is needed'.[234] Furthermore, locally agreed policies should include arrangements for transport to hospital 'to ensure that patients can be conveyed without delay'.[235] The Code provides that:

> Where the AMHP is the applicant, they have a professional responsibility to ensure that all the necessary arrangements are made for the patient to be transported to hospital. All relevant agencies should co-operate fully with the AMHP to ensure safe transport to hospital.... Relevant bodies should ensure locally agreed arrangements are in place.[236]

Clear agreements should therefore be in place, in line with the Crisis Care Concordat, to outline the respective roles and obligations of each agency and policies should ensure that AMHPs (in particular) are not left to negotiate arrangements with providers of transport services on an ad hoc basis, in the absence of clear expectations about the responsibilities of all those involved.[237] Unfortunately, the CQC has found that these local arrangements have not always worked well due to difficulties in harmonizing the police and ambulance service response: **11.118**

> In the College of Social Work survey, 66% of AMHPs said their local authority had a formal arrangement with ambulance providers for transport to hospital. However, 42% said the arrangement was not working well enough, and 10% that it was not working at all. This is clearly an area where good practice is hampered by co-ordination problems, as we have noted on some visits.[238]

(iv) The duty to make an application for admission or guardianship

The AMHP does not have to apply for admission just because the statutory criteria are met, as they must only apply if that is the most appropriate way to provide treatment, taking into account all the circumstances of the case. In making that decision, AMHPs are required to consider 'all the circumstances of the case' which might include the patient's past history of mental disorder, the patient's present condition and the social, familial, and personal factors bearing on it, as well as the other options available for supporting the patient's relatives and carers. Accordingly, under s 13 of the 1983 Act (as amended) it is the duty of an AMHP to make an application for admission or guardianship if that professional is (a) satisfied that such an application ought to be made and (b) is of the opinion, having regard to any wishes expressed by relatives of the patient or any other relevant circumstances, that it is necessary and proper for the application to be made by him/her, rather than the nearest relative. This does not affect the rules about consultation with nearest relatives or nearest relative's right to object to an application for admission for treatment, described below in paras 11.193–11.201. **11.119**

(vi) Urgent assessment—section 4

Section 4 governs urgent admission for assessment in cases of emergency. It provides that in any case of urgent necessity, an application for admission for assessment may be made to **11.120**

involved in health, policing, social care, housing, local government, and the third sector came together and signed the Crisis Care Concordat. Since then five more bodies have signed the Concordat, making a total of twenty-seven national signatories. Mental Health Crisis Care Concordat: *Improving outcomes for people experiencing mental health crisis. Department of Health and Concordat signatories* (2014) <https://www.gov.uk/government/uploads/system/uploads/attachment_data/file/281242/36353_Mental_Health_Crisis_accessible.pdf>.

[234] *Code of Practice*, para 14.48.
[235] ibid, para 17.2.
[236] ibid, paras 17.9–17.10.
[237] ibid, para 17.27. See also paras 17.22–17.28.
[238] CQC, *Monitoring the Mental Health Act in 2013/14* (TSO 2014) 66.

detain the patient for up to seventy-two hours on the basis of a single medical recommendation. It is worth noting that the latest statistics reveal that the use of s 4 has declined significantly during the last decade. In 2013–14 the total number of s 4 admissions was slightly above 300,[239] which is down by almost 80 per cent from 1,600 in 1997–98.[240] The Health and Social Care Information Centre attributes the decline to the changes introduced by the 2007 Act, which make it easier for and AMHP and doctors who work in the same hospital to authorize a longer term admission under section 2 or 3: '[t]hese changes make it quicker to field the team required for a section 2 or section 3'.[241]

11.121 Furthermore, the Code advises[242] that this section should only be used in 'very limited circumstances'—that is, 'in a genuine emergency, where the patient's need for urgent assessment outweighs the desirability of waiting for a second doctor'. It should never be used simply for administrative convenience. There is no need for the doctor providing the medical recommendation to be approved under s 12 nor is it necessary that s/he has personal knowledge of the patient, although the Reference Guide to the Mental Health Act does suggest that the doctor should have previous acquaintance with the patient, if practicable.[243] The fact the doctor is not required to have any specialist knowledge/expertise or prior knowledge of the patient raises questions about the appropriateness of using of s 4 as an initial route to hospital admission. The Code recognizes this danger and requires hospital managers and local authorities to monitor the use of section 4 to ensure that it is not 'misused'.[244]

11.122 The Code states[245] that an application for detention under s 4 may be made only when:

- the criteria for detention for assessment under s 2 are met;
- the patient's detention is required as a matter of urgent necessity; and
- obtaining a second medical recommendation would cause undesirable delay.

11.123 The Code cites an emergency as being where the patient's mental state or behaviour presents problems which those involved cannot reasonably be expected to manage while waiting for a second doctor.[246] Essentially, the professionals concerned must be satisfied that there is evidence of an immediate significant risk of mental/physical harm to the patient or others; a danger of serious harm to property; or there is a need for the use of restrictive interventions on a patient.

11.124 There are strict time limits which must be met for an emergency detention. An application under s 4 may be made by an AMHP or nearest relative, but only if the applicant has seen the patient personally within the previous twenty-four hours. The authority to convey the patient to hospital and to commence their s 4 detention there lasts only for twenty-four hours from the last time at which the doctor examined the patient, or, from the time the application was made, whichever is the earlier. The patient may only be detained for a

239 HSCIC, *Inpatients formally detained in hospitals under the Mental Health Act 1983 and patients subject to supervised community treatment: Annual report, England, 2013/14* (October 2014) Figure 12.

240 NSIC, *Inpatients formally detained in hospitals under the Mental Health Act 1983 and other legislation, England 1997–97 to 2007–08* (October 2008) at <http://www.ic.nhs.uk>, para 2.2.

241 HSCIC, *Inpatients formally detained in hospitals under the Mental Health Act 1983 and patients subject to supervised community treatment: Annual report, England, 2013/14* (October 2014), 28.

242 *Code of Practice*, paras 15.2, 15.6.

243 *Reference Guide to the Mental Health Act*, para 8.48. Previous acquaintance need not involve personal acquaintance, provided the doctor in question has some knowledge of the patient and is not 'coming to them cold'. See *AR (by her litigation friend JT) v Bronglais Hospital and Pembrokeshire and Derwen NHS Trust* [2001] EWHC Admin 792.

244 *Code of Practice*, para 15.11.

245 ibid, para 15.2.

246 ibid, para 15.8.

maximum period of seventy-two hours unless a second medical recommendation required for s 2 is provided. The Code urges that patients detained under s 4 should be examined by an appropriate second doctor 'in a timely manner' and as soon as possible, to decide whether they should continue to be detained.[247] If the relevant criteria are met, there is nothing to prevent an application for admission for treatment being made under s 3 while a patient is detained under s 4, but two new medical recommendations would be required.[248]

Even though patients detained on the basis of emergency applications may not be treated without their consent under Pt 4 (unless a second medical recommendation is received) they are deprived of a number of important safeguards under the Act. In particular, they do not have access to the First-tier Tribunal (Mental Health) to review the continued grounds for their detention (discussed in para 11.183 et seq). **11.125**

(vii) Holding powers—section 5

Patients who have initially been admitted consensually and informally but later seek to leave hospital may be restrained from doing so by nurses' and Approved Clinicians' holding powers under s 5. The holding power is intended as a temporary response to an emergency/crisis situation where it is not possible to carry out a full assessment under s 2 or s 3 and is likely to be used for an informal (voluntary) patient on a psychiatric ward. It does not apply to patients who are already detained because of an application under the Mental Health Act or to Supervised Community Treatment patients (ie patients subject to a Community Treatment Order). **11.126**

(a) **Doctor's holding power** Under s 5(2) the doctor or approved clinician in charge of the treatment of an inpatient in any hospital, not necessarily a psychiatric one, may restrain the patient from leaving hospital. The holding power can be used when the doctor or approved clinician in charge of the treatment of a hospital inpatient concludes that an application for detention under the Act should be made. It authorizes the detention of the patient in the hospital for a maximum of seventy-two hours so that the patient can be assessed with a view to such an application being made. The period of detention starts at the moment the doctor/AC's report is furnished to the hospital managers. **11.127**

The scope of the power is broad as it extends beyond inpatients receiving informal treatment for mental disorder. It includes patients who are in hospital by virtue of a deprivation of liberty authorization under the Mental Capacity Act 2005[249] and it does not matter whether or not the patient was originally admitted for treatment primarily for a mental disorder. However, the power cannot be used for an outpatient attending a hospital's A & E department, or any other outpatient. **11.128**

Particular care must be taken in the general hospital setting to ensure that the use of the section is appropriate and lawful. For example, the last report of the MHAC included examples of patients suffering from the secondary symptoms of cancer and alcohol withdrawal, which could not properly be classified as mental disorder within the meaning of the 1983 Act's definition. In such cases, it was clear that the holding power was being used improperly to restrain a patient from leaving hospital so that treatment for physical disorder could be enforced against the wishes of the patient concerned.[250] Bartlett and Sandland have commented on how 'lax' this provision is, particularly as there are no separate substantive **11.129**

[247] ibid, paras 15.9, 15.13.
[248] ibid, para 15.5.
[249] See further Chapter 10.
[250] MHAC, *Risk, Rights Recovery, Twelfth Biennial Report 2005–2007* (TSO 2008) paras 4.9–4.12.

criteria for its use—it is requires only that the doctor thinks that an application under sections 2 or 3 'ought' to be made.[251]

11.130 Section 5(3) allows the doctor or AC in charge of the inpatient's treatment to nominate a deputy to exercise the holding power in their absence. The deputy will then act on their own responsibility. Only one deputy may be authorized at any time for any patient, s/he must be competent to do so and must be on the staff of the same hospital.

11.131 Arrangements for an assessment to consider an application under s 2 or 3 should be put in place as soon as the s 5(2) report is furnished to the hospital managers. Although it lasts for a maximum of seventy-two hours, it should not be used longer than necessary and should come to an end if the doctor/RC decides that no assessment needs to be carried out or a decision is taken not to make an application for the patient's detention.

11.132 The penultimate report of the MHAC noted that there had been a decline in the use of s 5(2), although there has been an increase in detentions under s 3 consequent to s 5(2) over the last 20 years. On the positive side, the MHAC observed that this may signify improved practice, 'it could indicate that the doctor's initial view that an application ought to be made for further detention is well founded and the holding power is not being used simply to keep informal patients in check'.[252] Regrettably, the MHAC also commented on the inappropriate use of this section in general hospitals, where it does seem to be perceived as a 'free standing detention power rather than as a means to facilitate a Mental Health Act assessment'.[253] As noted above, there were a number of examples of unlawful detention in general hospital environments. Consequently, the MHAC recommended that staff in general hospitals should have access to advice, support, and training about the correct use of holding powers from a competent Mental Health Act Administrator.

11.133 **(b) Nurses' holding power** Section 5(4) confers a similar power on a nurse of a 'prescribed class'[254] to hold an inpatient in a psychiatric ward or hospital for not more than six hours. Unlike s 5(2), this power cannot be used on a general hospital ward where the patient is receiving treatment for physical disorder. It can only be used where an informal (ie voluntary) patient is receiving treatment for mental disorder in hospital as an inpatient. Nurses do not have to detain the patient personally but patients may only be detained in the hospital in which they are inpatients. Unlike s 5(2), this power does include substantive criteria before it can be exercised. It may only be used where the patient is still on the hospital premises and the nurse considers that:

- The patient is suffering from mental disorder to such a degree that it is necessary for the patient to be immediately prevented from leaving the hospital either for the patient's health or safety or for the protection of other people; and
- it is not practicable to secure the attendance of a doctor or approved clinician who can submit a report under s 5(2).

11.134 The Code makes it clear that 'the decision to invoke the power is the personal decision of the nurse, who cannot be instructed to exercise the power by anyone else'.[255] There are

[251] P Bartlett and R Sandland, *Mental Health Law Policy and Practice* (Oxford University Press 2014) 270.
[252] MHAC, n 249, para 4.7.
[253] ibid, para 4.9.
[254] The prescribed classes are nurses registered in sub-parts 1 or 2 of the register maintained by the Nursing and Midwifery Council whose entry in the register indicates that their field of practice is either mental health nursing or learning disability nursing.
[255] *Code of Practice*, para 18.27.

strict recording requirements laid down in the Code, which include the nurse recording in writing on a statutory form that the criteria are satisfied and sending the form to the hospital managers as soon as possible. The power can only be used to restrain the patient from leaving the hospital and the nurse may use minimum force to detain the patient and prevent them from leaving.

The Code urges hospital managers to monitor the use of s 5, including: how quickly patients are assessed for detention and discharged from the holding power; the attendance times of doctors and approved clinicians following the use of s 5(4); and, the proportion of cases in which applications for detention are, in fact, made following use of s 5.[256] In the past, the MHAC had stressed the importance of preserving suitably qualified and/or trained nursing staff to exercise this power[257] to prevent misuse and unlawful detention. This is essential, as Bartlett and Sandland have pointed out that '[i]t is certainly not a test which will be met simply because a mentally disordered patient wishes to leave the psychiatric ward at a time when no doctor is at hand. The nurse is placed in a position where he or she must make a decision on the criteria'.[258] The Code does advise hospital managers to ensure that suitably qualified, experienced, and competent nurses are available to all wards where there is a possibility that s 5(4) could be invoked, particularly acute psychiatric admission wards. Furthermore, it is good practice for hospital managers to arrange suitable training in the use of the power in such situations.[259] Despite the comments of the MHAC, official statistics suggest that, over the past five years, the use of both holding powers has increased by a small amount (between 1–4 per cent) each year. In 2013/14, the total number of uses of section 5(2) was just under 9,000 and there were just under 2,000 instances when section 5(4) was used.[260] It is not clear from the HSCIC data what proportion of these resulted in applications for longer term admission under the Act, although the CQC has published data indicating that in 2013/14, there were 14,087 cases of compulsory detention following a hospital stay as an informal patient and/or where a short term or emergency detention order, such as under s 5, had been used.[261] It is troubling to note, however, that the CQC has also expressed concerns about the potentially unlawful and unethical use of section 5, commenting in a recent monitoring report that: **11.135**

> . . . we learned that a factor in the significant local use of holding powers under section 5 was some patients who arrived on the ward on an informal basis, or under the purported authority of the Mental Capacity Act, appeared to be unaware of where or for what purpose they had been brought there. We heard of examples of patients being told they were coming into hospital 'for a nice chat', 'a cup of tea' or 'to see a doctor'. Their subsequent distress on realising their actual situation as an admitted inpatient led to them trying to leave, and holding powers being invoked. Subterfuge or euphemism should never be used to admit a patient into hospital. Such practices breach the guiding principles and specific guidance of the Code of Practice, and must be open to legal challenge in any individual case as unlawful deprivation of liberty.[262]

This would suggest that further training is required for nurses and doctors on the appropriate use of the holding powers to ensure that patients are informed about the basis of their detention and their rights are respected in accordance with the legislation.

256 ibid, para 18.39.

257 MHAC, n 249, para. 4.15.

258 P Bartlett and R Sandland, *Mental Health Law Policy and Practice* (Oxford University Press 2014) 270.

259 *Code of Practice*, para 18.28.

260 HSCIC, ***Inpatients formally detained in hospitals under the Mental Health Act 1983 and patients subject to supervised community treatment: Annual report, England, 2013/14*** (October 2014), Figure 13.

261 Care Quality Commission, *Monitoring the use of the Mental Health Act in 2013/14* (TSO 2014) 35.

262 Care Quality Commission, *Monitoring the use of the Mental Health Act in 2012/13* (TSO 2014) 16.

5. Compulsory treatment in hospital

11.136 As with admission to hospital, most care and treatment for psychiatric problems are provided informally and on a voluntary basis. So, armed with expert support and advice, individuals can choose to receive treatment, while section 131 of the Mental Health Act 1983 enables the provision of such voluntary psychiatric treatment. However, although the number of patients cared for in hospital has dropped steadily over recent years, for those patients who are in hospital, the number of formally detained patients compared with informal patients, has grown.[263] For those patients in hospital, currently around 90 per cent of them are cared for informally, and are hence outside the scope of the Act.[264] For these individuals, their physical and mental health treatment is governed by the common law or the Mental Capacity Act 2005 depending on whether they have or lack capacity.

11.137 Part V of the Mental Health Act 1983 suggests that the provision of psychiatric treatment should be undertaken with compassion and benevolence. As McCullough J observed in *R v Hallstrom, ex parte W*, 'no one is to be detained in hospital or to undergo medical treatment or even to submit himself to a medical examination without his consent. That is as true of a mentally disordered person as of anyone else.'[265] However, despite the significant inroads into the recognition and facilitation of individual autonomy and support in decision-making, seen particularly following the Mental Capacity Act, section 28 of the MCA acknowledges that it does not apply to patients who fall under the parameters of Parts IV and 4A of the Mental Health Act. Notwithstanding the 90 per cent of patients who as informal patients are not subject to the mental health legislation, the remaining 10 per cent of patients detained under the Mental Health Act may be required to submit to treatment for their psychiatric condition without their consent even when they have mental capacity.

11.138 This section will outline the powers within Pts 4 and 4A which are available to authorize the compulsory treatment of patients in hospital.

(i) The application of Part 4

11.139 Section 56 of the Mental Health Act 1983 outlines to whom Pt 4 of the Act applies.[266] Section 57 covers 'special treatments'[267] which tend to be irreversible or have potentially long-term effects, and applies to all patients whether they are formally detained or informally

263 In 2013/14, the Mental Health Act was used 53,176 times to detain patients in hospital for periods longer than seventy-two hours (an increase of 5 per cent from 2012/13 and a 30 per cent increase from 2003/04). 34,806 of cases were detention upon admission to hospital, 14,087 cases were detentions following a hospital stay as an informal patient and/or a short term or emergency detention order had been used; see Health and Social Care Information Centre, *Inpatients Formally Detained in Hospitals Under the Mental Health Act 1983 and Patients subject to Supervised Community Treatment, England—2013–2014*. Available at: <http://www.hscic.gov.uk/searchcatalogue?productid=16329&q=title%3a%22Inpatients+formally+detained+in+hospitals+under+the+Mental+Health+Act%22+&sort=Most+recent&size=10&page=1#top> (accessed on 28 August 2015).

264 Rethink, *Behind Closed Doors—The current state and future vision of acute mental health care in the UK* 11, available at: <http://www.rcn.org.uk/downloads/professional_development/mental_health_virtual_ward/treatments_and_therapies/behind-closed-doors-reportpdf.pdf> (accessed 23/03/2015).

265 [1986] QB 1090 at 1104.

266 Section 56 was introduced through section 34 of the Mental Health Act 2007. Part IV (Sections 56–64) and Part 4A (64A–64K) of the Act are mainly concerned with consent to treatment for long-term detained patients, but certain safeguards in this part of the Act also apply to informal patients. A patient will also be subject to Part IV and 4A if he is a community patient and has been recalled to hospital under section 17E.

267 See P Fennell, *Mental Health: The New Law* (Jordans 2011).

hospitalized.[268] Section 58, applies to medicines for mental disorder. Section 58A,[269] provides special safeguards for the administration of ECT and any other treatment provided for under s 58A(1)(b). Where the patient is 'capable of understanding the nature, purpose and likely effects of the treatment' then ECT must be accompanied by patient consent. Without capacity, a decision to administer ECT would have to be certified as 'appropriate' and should not conflict with an advance decision (which is believed to be valid and applicable) nor must it conflict with a decision made by a donee or deputy or by the Court of Protection.

Several categories of patient are exempt from Part V and 4A. It does not apply: **11.140**

- where a patient has been admitted as an emergency under s 4 and where no second medical opinion has been obtained in order to convert the s 4 into a s 2 detention;
- where the patient is liable to be detained under the AC's or the nurse's holding powers found within s 5;
- where the patient is remanded in hospital for assessment by a criminal court under s 35;
- where the patient has been detained in a place of safety under s 135 or s 136;
- where the patient is detained in a place of safety while pending admission to hospital under a hospital order or a hospital direction (s 37(4) or s 45A(4)); and
- where the patient is a conditionally discharged restricted patient who has agreed to comply with a proposed treatment regime as a condition of the discharge.

Finally, in terms of the scope of Pt 4's applicability, community patients are not subject to the provisions found within this part of the legislation, apart from s 57 (see below, para 11.140) which applies to all. A community patient will only be subject to Pt 4 in the event that he/she is recalled to hospital for treatment under s 17E (see below para 11.175). Furthermore, s 58A (see above para 11.137), which governs the procedures surrounding the administration of ECT, also applies to patients under 18 irrespective of whether they are formally detained or hospitalized informally. **11.141**

When considering whether the consent to treatment provisions within Parts 4 and 4A apply, it is necessary to demonstrate that the proposed treatment would be for a mental disorder. The Mental Capacity Act 2005 and the common law governs all treatment without consent for physical conditions. Section 7 (3) of the Mental Health Act 2007 (see para 4(ii)(d) above), significantly widened the definition of 'medical treatment for mental disorder' (s 145(4)) and now provides scope for a broad interpretation of medical treatment for mental disorder.[270] **11.142**

(ii) Section 57

Section 57 provides two safeguards for the provision of the irreversible treatments of neurosurgery and the surgical implantation of male sexual suppressants, which is likely to have long-term, potentially permanent, consequences for the recipient of the treatment. These treatments are rarely performed. The patient must provide a valid consent to any treatments, **11.143**

---

[268] For an excellent consideration of compulsory treatment under the mental health legislation, see P Bartlett, 'The Necessity Must Be Convincingly Shown to Exist: Standards for Compulsory Treatment for Mental Disorder Under the Mental Health Act 1983' (2011) Medical Law Review 1.

[269] Section 58A was inserted into the Mental Health Act 1983 following s 27 of the Mental Health Act 2007.

[270] Treatments such as psychotherapy are often regarded as the preferred longer term treatment option for many patients. Cognitive Behavioural Therapy (CBT) is used for anxiety disorders, bipolar disorder, eating disorders, and schizophrenia, while Dialectical Behaviour Therapy (DBT) is increasingly used to successfully treat Borderline Personality Disorder (BPT).

which fall under s 57, and it is this consent that provides the necessary authority to treat.[271] In conjunction with this consent, certain safeguards must also be met. A psychiatrist and two Care Quality Commission appointed individuals must certify that the patient is capable of understanding the nature, purpose, and likely effects of the proposed treatment and has indeed consented to it. Furthermore, the medical member of the 'team', the second opinion approved doctor (SOAD), must certify that such treatment is appropriate in the given case. The SOAD must also discuss the proposed treatment with a nurse and another nurse or doctor who has been involved in the patient's past care in order to ascertain whether the treatment does represent the right course of action. It is also notable that unlike any of the other treatment provisions, s 57 applies to formal and informal patients.

11.144 Given the serious nature of these treatments all elements of the s 57 requirements must be met in full. Second opinion support for the treatment must be firmly demonstrated and likewise, should there be any question raised about the patient's capacity to consent to the treatment, the treatment cannot proceed. The Mental Capacity Act 2005 should not be used as a mechanism to fill the gap presented by the patient's incapacity—'a person who lacks capacity to consent to s 57 treatment may not be given it'.[272]

(iii) Section 58

11.145 The SOAD system plays a fundamental role within s 57. However, this is not the case with treatment authorized under s 58. Section 58 authorizes treatment with either patient consent or a second opinion. These mutually exclusive statutory safeguards apply where the patient is given long-term medication (over three months). This three-month period is known as the 'stabilizing period'[273] whereby the RC who is in charge of the patient's case can use this time to achieve the initial stabilization of the condition before a longer term treatment programme can be established, if necessary. Although this period effectively allows treatment to be given without any accompanying professional scrutiny or patient consent, it has always been justified on the basis that immediately successful psychiatric assessment and treatment regimes are rare and often need refinement. Greater flexibility is often required for a successful solution to be found. After the first three months, if the patient refuses to consent to a continuation of treatment, his wishes can be overruled by a SOAD if the treatment is considered to be appropriate. In such instances, the patient is entitled to know the reasons. In *Wooder v Feggerter*[274] it was noted that fairness demands that where the patient's wishes are overridden, written and adequate reasons for certifying that medication should be given against his will, should be disclosed by the SOAD. The disclosure requirement should, however, be excused if the SOAD or the RMO considers that such disclosure would be likely to cause serious harm to the physical or mental health of the patient or any other person.[275] The scope of this discretion should be seen in light of data published in the Care Quality Commission's 2011–12 report, which found that 1 in 10 patients were unlawfully receiving medication beyond that which had been authorized under s 58 of the MHA, of which most second opinions were for medication.[276]

---

[271] See P Fennell, 'Statutory Authority to Treat: Relatives and Treatment Proxies', 1994 2(1) Med Law Rev 30.

[272] Mental Capacity Act 2005 *Code of Practice*, para 13.51.

[273] Also, referred to as the 'three month rule' – see The Royal College of Psychiatrists, *3 Month Rule for Second Opinion Briefing*, Mental Health Alliance at: <http://www.mentalhealthalliance.org.uk/pre2007/documents/Commons_Report_Stage_3MonthRule_Briefing.pdf> (accessed 27 February 2015).

[274] [2002] EWCA Civ 554.

[275] See also Care Quality Commission, *Guidance for SOADs: Giving reasons when certifying appropriate treatment*, as originally issued by the Mental Health Act Commission in October 2008.

[276] Care Quality Commission, *Monitoring the Mental Health Act in 2011/12*, (TSO 2013).

Although the need for a 'stabilizing period' remains a clinical necessity, it should not be assumed by decision-makers that a patient is unable to provide consent. Every effort should be made to ensure the patient is provided with adequate information about the treatment, an opportunity is given for the patient to ask questions and to reflect upon the information provided. It is also essential that following this, sufficient time is provided to enable the patient to give consent. Furthermore, given the continued ambivalence among various mental health stakeholder groups over the stabilizing period, it is important that such efforts to obtain consent are recorded fully in the patient's notes. Under scrutiny, decisions to treat which were made despite refusal by the patient or where the patient withdraws consent, must be able to withstand such inspection.[277] **11.146**

Unlike s 57 where patient consent provides the necessary authority to treat, s 58 allows for treatment to be taken forward even where a patient's consent is not forthcoming. In this situation, the SOAD plays a vital role.[278] The SOAD acts as the doctor who provides a second medical opinion and is not responsible, unlike the AC, for administering or giving the order for treatment to be administered. The SOAD's role is to provide an essential safeguard within the treatment process on behalf of the patient. The SOAD will assess the recommended treatment to ensure it is clinically defensible and that due consideration has been given to the views and rights of the patient.[279] In coming to the decision of whether the proposed treatment is appropriate for the patient concerned, the SOAD must consult with two other professionals who have been involved in the patient's care, either two nurses or a nurse and doctor. There is also an expectation that the SOAD will give written reasons for his/her decision, if s/he is in favour of the treatment going ahead under s 58, which will then be disclosed to the patient concerned unless clear evidence can be provided that such disclosure would be detrimental.[280] **11.147**

(iv) Section 58A

The Mental Health Act 2007 inserted s 58A into the Mental Health Act 1983 which provides a capacity threshold for the administration of ECT (except in emergencies): **11.148**

- If patient has capacity and refuses ECT, it cannot be given;
- If patient lacks capacity, it can be given provided a SOAD approves and it does not conflict with any advance decision, or that of a donee, deputy, or the Court of Protection.

Therefore, when not an emergency, ECT may not be given if the patient is mentally capable and is refusing to consent. The Code of Practice explicitly acknowledges that where a patient is mentally incapable of providing consent, treatment under s 58A cannot be given.[281] However, if a SOAD certifies that the patient lacks capacity to consent and that: **11.149**

- the treatment is appropriate;
- no valid and applicable advance decision has been made by the patient under the Mental Capacity Act 2005 refusing the treatment;
- no suitably authorized attorney or deputy objects to the treatment on the patient's behalf; and

[277] This falls in line with the European Committee for the Prevention of Torture and Inhuman or Degrading Treatment, *The CPT Standards*, Ch VI, para 41.

[278] This system is run by the Care Quality Commission. It is responsible for the appointment of all SOADs and the management of the SOAD service.

[279] *R (on the application of Wilkinson) v Responsible Medical Officer Broadmoor Hospital* [2001] EWCA Civ 1545; [2002] 1 WLR 419.

[280] *R (on the application of Wooder) v Feggetter* [2002] EWCA Civ 554.

[281] *Code of Practice*, para 13.63.

- the treatment would not conflict with a decision of the Court of Protection which prevents the treatment being given,[282] then treatment may be permitted.

11.150 Section 58A applies to patients who are detained under the powers which authorize detention beyond seventy-two hours and who are not conditionally discharged restricted patients or patients subject to remand under s 35. Section 58A applies to patients under the age of 18 though SOAD approval for ECT treatment, whether or not that patient is detained under the Act and whether or not that patient consents to the treatment must first be obtained. Following the 2007 Act the appropriate treatment test applies. Recent data suggests that there has been a declining rate of referrals for ECT. Approximately 30 per cent of SOAD visits to consider treatment with medication (whether or not in combination with ECT) resulted in some change to the proposed treatment plan. Only around 15 per cent of SOAD visits relating to ECT alone resulted in some change. This may be because ECT referrals often present SOADs with more binary decisions to be made. ECT will either be appropriate or not, while medication is often a matter of degree and may take time to fine tune the prescription.[283]

11.151 Most significant about the changes brought about in relation to ECT is the introduction of an additional second medical opinion procedure following the 2007 Act. As noted above, s 57 requires the SOAD to certify the patient is able and willing to consent and that treatment is appropriate; whereas s 58 requires the SOAD to state that the patient is either incapable of consenting to the treatment or is capable and is refusing, but that treatment is necessary. This means that ECT can only be given if an independent, specially approved psychiatrist has looked at the individual's case and has authorized it. This further second medical opinion procedure strengthens the rights of patients significantly.

11.152 However, s 58A relies upon the right of a patient to refuse ECT and this hinges on a finding of capacity. While the patient may be deemed capable because s/he understands the nature, purpose and effects of ECT and thus meets the capacity test in the Mental Health Act 1983, there is the issue of whether the patient's mental disorder is of such severity that it is thought to impede the ability to come to a reasoned decision. If this were found to be the case, would it affect the overall assessment of the patient's capacity?

(v) Section 62

11.153 Section 62 is commonly referred to as the emergency treatment provision which enables treatment to be given to a patient before a second medical opinion is arranged or when the patient does not or cannot provide consent. This provision is largely applied when there is an immediate threat of harm to the patient or others owing to a significant deterioration in the patient's mental state. Section 62(1) provides details of when such treatment can be administered. It applies to treatment which is:

- immediately necessary to save the patient's life; or
- which (not being irreversible) is immediately necessary to prevent a serious deterioration in his condition; or
- which (not being irreversible or hazardous) is immediately necessary to alleviate serious suffering by the patient; or
- which (not being irreversible or hazardous) is immediately necessary and represents the minimum interference necessary to prevent the patient behaving violently or being a danger to himself or others.[284]

---

282 *Code of Practice*, para 24.21.
283 CQC, *Monitoring the Mental Health Act in 2011/12*, (TSO 2013) 74.
284 See *Code of Practice*, para 24.33 for further detail.

Emergency treatment under s 62 may also bypass s 58A. Where treatment is deemed necessary to save the patient's life, is not irreversible but may alleviate serious suffering, then ECT under s 58A may be administered without the patient's consent if the first and second points above are met.[285] The Code of Practice emphasizes the need for decision-makers to view s 62 as a means of last resort and to be used when no other immediately available means exist. Rather, every effort should be made to meet the second medical opinion safeguard, where possible. **11.154**

(vi) Section 63

This provides a general power to treat detained patients without consent. It provides that any medical treatment for mental disorder, which is not covered by ss 57, 58, or 58A, may be given to a patient without their consent.[286] The only limitations on the exercise of this broad discretionary power are: the patient must be detained; the treatment must be 'for the mental disorder' (a vital question of causation); and the approved clinician in charge must sanction the treatment. Where a patient's planned treatment falls outside these limitations, treatment cannot be provided to capacitous patients who refuse it but it can be provided to incapacitated patients if permitted by the Mental Capacity Act 2005. In practice, this statutory power is normally used where patients disagree with psychiatric opinion.[287] Use of s 63 when there is disagreement between the patient and the clinical team contrasts significantly with how s 63 was expected to be used. During its passage through Parliament, it was envisaged that s 63 would be used for 'perfectly routine, sensible treatment'[288] which may explain why explicit safeguards, such as consent and SOAD opinions, were considered unnecessary.[289] **11.155**

Treatment for mental disorder has always been given a broad interpretation. In the early days following the enactment of the Mental Health Act 1983, flexibility was seen as necessary to enable decision-makers to perform their duties effectively, yet concerns have always been linked to the scope of s 63. Significantly the Court of Appeal in *R (B) v Ashworth* held a patient could only be treated under section 63 for the condition under which he had been classified.[290] However, this restrictive interpretation of s 63 was subsequently overturned in 2005 by the House of Lords in *R v Ashworth Hospital Authority and another ex parte B*.[291] Eating disorders, such as anorexia nervosa, are now viewed as a psychiatric condition[292] and, as such, nasogastric tube feeding against the will of the patient is regarded as an ancillary, though closely related, treatment of the psychiatric condition and hence, falls within the scope of s 63.[293] Likewise, the treatment of symptoms as well as the underlying medical **11.156**

[285] Mental Health Act 1983, s 62(1A).

[286] *R (on the application of B) v Ashworth Hospital Authority* [2005] UKHL 20.

[287] G Richardson, 'Autonomy, Guardianship and Mental Disorder: One Problem, Two Solutions' (2002) 65 Modern Law Review 702.

[288] Hansard, HL, Deb, Vol 426, ser 5, cols 1064–65 and col 1071 (1 February 1982).

[289] P Fennell, 'Institutionalising the Community: The Codification of Clinical Authority and the Limits of Rights-Based Approachs', in B McSherry and P Weller (eds), *Rethinking Rights-Based Mental Health Laws* (Bloomsbury Publishing 2010).

[290] (2003) EWCA Civ 547.

[291] *R (on the application of B) v Ashworth Hospital Authority* [2005] UKHL 20.

[292] See R Dresser, 'When Patients Resist Feeding: Medical, Ethical, and Legal Considerations' (1985) 33(11) Journal of the American Geriatrics Society 790; P C Hébert and M A Weingarten, 'The Ethics of Forced Feeding in Anorexia Nervosa' (1991) 144(2) CMAJ 141.

[293] In *Re KB (adult) (mental patient: medical treatment)* (1994) 19 BMLR 144, Ewbank J. accepted that the forced administration of food and fluids by naso-gastric tube 'was related to the mental illness, not to some unconnected physical condition'. In *Re VS (adult: mental disorder)* (1995) 3 Med L Rev 292, the High Court declared that it was lawful for the proposed treatment of a patient by tube feeding and/or nasogastric tube or intravenous rehydration for the purpose of saving life and/or alleviating symptoms and signs of

cause have been found to fall within the remit of s 63. Nevertheless, other treatments, which have gradually edged into the interpretation of s 63, have been less enthusiastically embraced, particularly following the Human Rights Act 1998 and the concern that such treatments may breach the ECHR.[294] In *Tameside and Glossop Acute Services Trust v CH (a patient)*,[295] a pregnant schizophrenic patient risked having a still birth. She was prone to delusions and resisted attempts to monitor her pregnancy in the belief that clinicians were intent on harming the baby. There was also evidence suggesting that the delivery of a healthy child would improve her psychiatric prognosis; whereas a stillbirth would have a deleterious effect on her condition. During pregnancy treatment for the schizophrenia had been interrupted and replaced by a less potent medication. Wall J was satisfied that the performance of a caesarean section was connected to her mental disorder and was hence medical treatment for it. Three evidential grounds were relied upon to establish that the caesarean section fell within s 63:

- an ancillary reason was to prevent deterioration in her mental state;
- it was necessary for her to give birth to a live baby in order for her treatment for schizophrenia to be effective;
- the overall structure of her treatment requires her to receive strong antipsychotic medication which the pregnancy had interrupted.

11.157 The 1996 decision of *Tameside* led to significant levels of concern among many mental health professionals' and users alike.[296] The use of s 63 to authorize a Caesarean section to treat a mental disorder stretched s 63 beyond all expectations. Such broad interpretations may enable effective arguments to be made concerning the connection between the preservation of the patient's physical health and the benefit to or prevention of a deterioration in their mental health. The threat posed to civil liberties resulting from such a broad interpretation of s 63 was realized in *St George's Healthcare NHS Trust v S*.[297] The pregnant patient had a limited psychiatric history with only one earlier diagnosis of moderate depression. She requested a natural birth and retained capacity to refuse treatment at common law. However, the hospital used a s 2 admission to compel her to have a caesarean without any clear evidence of mental illness. The Court of Appeal was far from impressed and took the opportunity to retreat from the expanded interpretation of s 63 as introduced by *Tameside*. The court noted that the mental health legislation cannot be used to achieve a compulsory detention to allow treatment of an individual against her will. Such treatment cannot be authorized by s 63 of the 1983 Act and can only go ahead if the patient lacks capacity to make a decision for him/herself.[298] In such instances, the treatment may be authorized by common

starvation and dehydration. See also M J R Curtice, 'Force-feeding: Implications for the Mental Health Act 1983 and Human Rights Act 1998' (2002) 11 (3) Journal of Mental Health 235.

[294] 'Medical treatment' includes treatment of physical health problems only to the extent that such treatment is part of, or ancillary to, treatment for mental disorder (eg treating wounds self-inflicted as a result of mental disorder). Otherwise, the Act does not regulate medical treatment for physical health problems: *Code of Practice*, para 24.5. See also, M J R Curtice, 'Medical Treatment Under Pt IV of the Mental Health Act 1983 and the Human Rights Act 1998' (2009) 33 Psychiatric Bulletin 111–15.

[295] [1996] 1 FLR 762. See Chapter 10 for further discussion of this and related case law.

[296] For a detailed consideration of this case, see C Widdett and M Thomson, 'Justifying Treatment and Other Stories—*Tameside and Glossop Acute Services NHS Trust v CH (A Patient)*' (1997) 5(1) Feminist Legal Studies 77.

[297] [1999] Fam. 26. See also J J Bailey-Harris, 'Pregnancy, autonomy and medical treatment', (1998) 114 Law Quarterly Review 550.

[298] The authority to treat in such situations would now be authorized and governed by the Mental Capacity Act 2005. This recently hit the headlines when the Mental Capacity Act was used to justify the

law.[299]

6. Compulsory powers and treatment in the community

Community-based care plays a fundamental role in the care of many people suffering mental disorder. Historical accounts of mental health chart community support for people with mental health problems as predating the industrial era.[300] At a statutory level, the Percy Commission, which was established in order to consider the creation of a new regime for mental health law and whose recommendations led to the Mental Health Act 1959, acknowledged the importance of discharging as many patients as possible into the community and using hospital compulsion only in the most severe circumstances.[301] Community-based care has been an explicit ongoing policy objective since the mid-1980s and since this time, further changes and enhancements to the system have taken place. The Care Programme Approach has become an essential aspect to community-based care: it involves all patients being fully assessed in terms of both risk and needs, which is then followed up by a written care plan being established.[302] The assessment was provided under the auspices of the National Health Service and Community Care Act 1990 which provided a legal framework for community support of a range of vulnerable people with various health and welfare needs. Responsibility for this assessment was placed with social care agencies, rather than health authorities, to arrange the planning of care (which included health, housing, and other support needs) for mentally ill patients in the community. When the 1990 Act was initially introduced, local authorities were to have financial responsibilities for securing the client's social care and health authorities would have to provide the financial means for addressing the health needs of patients in the community. This led to considerable disagreements and discussions over whether the provision of a service was 'health' or 'social' care. The 'seamless' services anticipated in the philosophies did not prove to be easily achieved. This division also caused considerable distress for patients. For example, in *R v North & East Devon HA, ex p Coughlan*,[303] the Court of Appeal ruled that the provision of accommodation and ancillary nursing care was not 'health' care to be paid from NHS budgets. Instead it was to be regarded as social care to be provided by local authorities, to which patients may be required to contribute financially.[304] This duty now falls under the remit of the Care Act 2014. Sections 9 to 11 of the Care Act 2014 now govern the duty to undertake assessment 11.158

forced caesarean section operation upon a woman with bipolar disorder: see *AA, Re (Including: Note By Mr Justice Mostyn)* [2013] EWHC 4378 (COP) (23 August 2012). See further Chapter 10.

[299] Since 1998, calls have been made to introduce further guidance and greater regulation by way of SOAD involvement for treatments that have been authorized under s 63. See House of Lords, House of Commons Joint Committee on Human Rights, *Legislative Scrutiny: Mental Health Bill Fourth Report of Session 2006–07* (HL Paper 40, HC Paper 228, 4 February 2007), para 80 and App 3, para 67.

[300] M Foucault, *Madness and Civilization: A History of Insanity in the Age of Reason*, (Random House 1988).

[301] *Royal Commission on the Law Relating to Mental Illness and Mental Deficiency* (Percy Commission) (Cmnd 169, 1957).

[302] See H Killaspy, 'From the asylum to community care: learning from experience' (2006) 79–80 (1) *Br Med Bull* 245.

[303] [2000] 3 All ER 850.

[304] The Care Act 2014 will make some important changes to this area of social care costs. The first changes were implemented in April 2015, with further changes due from April 2016. Importantly, the Care Act 2014 has introduced a new national minimum threshold for access to care and support. It will also give legal rights to carers who provide care and support on an unpaid basis and make care more portable should a patient move to a different area. The legislation will also introduce (from April 2016) a cap on eligible care costs so that once a person has paid £72,000 in eligible costs, the local authority will pay the ongoing costs of care, but not general living costs. Social care is subject to an assessment of need and financial ability to pay, the asset threshold for local authority financial support with residential care will be raised from £23,250 to £118,000.

of needs for care and support. They are augmented by the Care and Support (Assessment) Regulations 2014 and the Care and Support Statutory Guidance of October 2014. Section 9(1) provides that where a local authority believes that an adult may have needs for care and support, the authority must assess: (a) whether the adult does have needs for care and support, and, (b) if the adult does, what those needs are. The duty to assess (defined as a 'needs assessment' by section 9(2) of the Act) replaces the existing duty under section 47 of the NHS and Community Care Act 1990. Despite slight differences in wording the trigger for assessment is very similar to the duty under s 47 and continues to operate as it did under the 1990 Act.

11.159 The Care Programme Approach also works in conjunction with s 117 of the Mental Health Act 1983. It provides free 'aftercare' and is provided to people who have been detained and given treatment under sections 3, 37, 47, or 48 of the Mental Health Act. This includes people who have been granted leave under s 17 and patients discharged onto supervised community treatment (see below, para 11.160). NHS clinical commissioning groups and local social services authorities are jointly responsible for providing and paying for aftercare.[305] Under s 47 of the National Health Service and Community Care Act 1990, the authority must carry out an assessment of the individual's needs for those services; and having regard to the results of that assessment, shall then decide whether his needs require provision of services.[306]

11.160 Under the Mental Health Act 1983, three compulsory community powers are provided:

(1) guardianship;
(2) extended leave; and
(3) after-care under supervision (now repealed and replaced with 'Community Treatment Orders' (see below, para 11.160).[307]

(i) Guardianship

11.161 Guardianship has existed in various guises under mental health law. It has often been likened to an early community treatment order, since it allowed guardians to control the care and treatment of mentally disordered persons living outside of hospital. The expectation was that the guardian would exercise those powers over a mentally disordered person as would be used in relation to a minor under the age of 14. For non-offender patients, guardianship applications are made under s 7 of the Mental Health Act 1983 and can be applied for by the patient's nearest relative or an AMHP (see para 11.46 et seq). This application must also be agreed by two medical professionals. Section 7 requires that the patient be suffering from a mental disorder which warrants reception into a guardianship order and that such an order would aid protection of his/her welfare and/or for the protection of others. Details of the guardian's powers are laid down in s 8. The Code of Practice notes the guardian's powers as being:

---

305 Detention in hospital must be under s 3, detention for treatment; s 37, hospital order (with or without restrictions); s 45A, hospital direction; or ss 47 or 48, after transfer from prison.

306 In *R v Manchester City Council, ex p Stennett* [2002] UKHL 34 the House of Lords made it clear that s 117 after-care services cannot lawfully be charged for. However, other community-based care services may be subject to charging as the LSSA may have the right to use eligibility criteria to assess need (*R v Gloucester County Council, ex parte Barry* [1997] 2 All ER 1 (HL)).

307 In the Mental Health Act 2007, Community Treatment Orders (CTOs) are referred to as Supervised Community Treatment (SCT).

- an exclusive right to decide where a patient should live, taking precedence even over an attorney or deputy appointed under the Mental Capacity Act 2005 (MCA);[308]
- a right to require the patient to attend for treatment, work, training, or education at specific times and places (but they cannot use force to take the patient there);[309]
- a right to demand that a doctor, approved mental health professional (AMHP) or another relevant person has access to the patient at the place where the patient lives.[310]

In the past, guardianship was often regarded as inadequate to meet the needs of patients and practitioners. The guardianship power was reworked in the Mental Health Act 1983 to apply to a narrower range of patients and to contain powers that were geared towards maximizing the patient's welfare. While the power permits the supervision of a person with a mental disorder in community settings and may be conferred on a person who has entered mental health services via the criminal justice system (s 37), it is not used extensively and tends to be invoked for elderly patients with mental health problems.

Although guardianship was seen as offering great hope with the arrival of the Mental Health Act 1959, a hope which continued with the remodelling of its provisions in the Mental Health Act 1983, the perceived lack of sanctions for the guardian has diminished any real expectations that guardianship can offer a means of practical community based control. Yet, despite this, the *Code of Practice* remains firmly of the view that guardianship could '. . . [provide] an authoritative framework for working with a patient, with a minimum of constraint, to achieve an independent a life as possible within the community'.[311] Guardianship seeks to provide a framework within the community setting that enables patients to be supported with a minimum of constraint. It is most likely to be of value to patients who tend to respond positively to authority and who will comply with the treatment needed for their mental disorder. Guardianship is also thought useful when there is a particular need for someone to have the authority to decide where the patient should live[312] or to insist that doctors, AMHPs, or other people be given access to the patient.[313] However, figures suggest that guardianship features rarely in day-to-day community care provision. Between 2001–02 and 2008–09, the number of guardianship cases at the end of the year was 901, which was 8 per cent lower than in 2001–02, but 2 per cent higher than in 2007–08. The overall number of new cases opened during 2008–09 decreased by 11 per cent when compared with 2007–08, and by 33 per cent when compared with 2001–02.[314] The number of new cases increased from 280 cases in 2012–13 to 290 cases in 2013–14 (up 4 per cent). The number of people subject to a guardianship at the end of 2013–14 was 600, a decrease of 4 per cent from 2012–13. There has been a decline in continuing guardianship cases for 9 consecutive years from 950 continuing cases in 2004–05 to 600 cases in 2013–14, a reduction of 37 per cent.[315] Applications are made either by **11.162**

[308] This power includes the right to take and convey a patient to the specified place of residence and also includes the right to return the individual should he/she abscond: Mental Health Act 2007, Sch 3, para 3(5).

[309] It is worth noting that the Mental Health Act 1983 provides no sanctions for the guardian should the patient fail to comply with an agreed treatment programme as the legislation does not allow for treatment to be provided against the will of the patient.

[310] *Code of Practice*, para 30.3. Section 129 also makes it an offence to deny an authorized person access to the patient.

[311] *Code of Practice*, para 30.4.

[312] The Code also clarifies that guardianship cannot be used to deprive a person of their liberty.

[313] See *Code of Practice*, paras 30.3–26.8.

[314] Department of Health, Guardianship under the Mental Health Act 1983, England 2009 (TSO 2009).

[315] See HSCIC, *National Statistics Guardianship under the Mental Health Act 1983, England 2013–14* (National Statistics, 10 September 2014).

the AMHP or the nearest relative under s 7 of the Mental Health Act. While for mentally disordered offenders, the Court has the power to issue a guardianship order under s 37. Certain requirements must be met, namely:

- the patient must be at least 16;
- suffering from mental disorder;
- of a nature or degree which warrants his reception into guardianship; and
- must be in the interests of the welfare of the patient or for the protection of other persons that the patient should be so received.

11.163 A care plan must be formulated that identifies the patient's care and those elements that are provided using the compulsory powers. According to the Code of Practice,[316] the plan should identify the services needed by the patient and who will provide them. It should also indicate which of the powers that guardians have under the Act are necessary to achieve the plan. If none of the powers are required, guardianship should not be used. Key elements of the plan are likely to be:[317]

- suitable accommodation to help meet the patient's needs;
- access to day care, education, and training facilities, as appropriate;
- effective cooperation and communication between all those concerned in implementing the plan;
- (if there is to be a private guardian) support from the LSSA for the guardian.

11.164 Central to the use of guardianship is that it has to be the least restrictive alternative. However, guardianship may not offer the best option for some individuals: where the person lacks capacity to make decisions about their welfare, the provisions of the Mental Capacity Act 2005 might be more appropriate to determine where the patient should live and what support should be provided. Section 5 of the Mental Capacity Act introduces a 'general authority' to act reasonably in doing acts that are in the best interests of a person lacking capacity. These 'acts' can include decisions about where the person lives, with whom they have contact and what they do during the course of the day. The acts can be performed by any person providing support to the individual and so has a much greater degree of flexibility than guardianship. Whereas guardianship powers are normally conferred to one individual. This may offer advantages, particularly when a number of people are involved in the provision of care yet who disagree about the individual's welfare and care needs.[318] Although guardianship allows for a degree of control over the individual in the community, notably through powers to require specified residence and attendance at particular treatment centres, there is no authority to administer medical treatment without the patient's consent. However, if a patient is detained in hospital under the compulsory assessment provisions of the Mental Health Act,[319] the guardianship order does co-exist with these provisions.

11.165 An application for guardianship must have support from the recommendations of two doctors. Given the community-based focus of guardianship, the application is addressed to local social service authorities and must be lodged within fourteen days of relevant medical examinations taking place. The proposed guardian may be any social services authority or a

[316] *Code of Practice*, paras 13.23–13.36.
[317] ibid, para 30.22.
[318] B Hatfield et al, 'Managing severe mental illness in the community using the Mental Health Act 1983: a comparison of Supervised Discharge and Guardianship in England' (2001) 36 Social Psychiatry and Psychiatric Epidemiology 508.
[319] Mental Health Act 1983, s 2 and s 4.

private individual. Furthermore, the nearest relative has the right to veto the application for guardianship, though action can be taken to remove the nearest relative if s/he is making decisions that are contrary to the welfare of the patient. Once guardianship begins, it can last up to six months and can be renewed for a further six months and at twelve-monthly intervals thereafter. Guardianship offers an avenue for accessing community-based care and services to people who may not easily access these services any other way. The statutory framework offers an explicit means of outlining the responsibilities of relevant agencies under guardianship and additionally, offers the prospect of a periodic review of the service user's care and some legal scrutiny of the conditions in which the person is living.[320]

(ii) Extended leave

Leave of absence is governed by s 17 of the Mental Health Act 1983. It enables a patient's responsible clinician (RC) to grant leave of absence for specific occasions or for specific or indefinite periods of time. The RC may also make the leave subject to conditions which must be met as part of the leave package. These conditions tend to be regarded as necessary in the interests of the patient or for the protection of other people. Where these conditions are no longer being met by the patient or the RC has particular concerns about the patient while on leave, the patient may be recalled from leave by the RC as long as the RC gives notice of this recall in writing to the person(s) in charge of the patient while on leave. **11.166**

Leave offers a very flexible tool to a patient's RC. It provides a means by which the patient remains subject to control, while also enabling contacts and routines to be developed in the community, with a view to the patient's eventual discharge there. Leave offers a means by which a patient can gradually be reintegrated into the community. For restricted patients, leave operates differently for the leave must be agreed with the Home Secretary (s 41(3)), who may also impose conditions on the patient's leave. This may result in the operation of conditional discharge being delayed.[321] When weighing up the risks and benefits of leave,[322] consideration will be given to possible conditions, if any, that should be attached to the leave. For example, requiring the patient not to associate with specified persons or to visit particular places may be deemed essential for leave to be a success. The RC concerned should take account of additional factors, when relevant, such as any child protection/welfare issues and other particular risk factors. In addition, successful leave will often be dependent upon appropriate levels of support being provided, a collaborative, joined up approach among relevant agencies[323] being adopted, and adequate consideration being given to the views of the patient and other involved persons in the planning process. **11.167**

Before alternative formal community care provisions were introduced by the Mental Health Act 2007, leave of absence was considered one of the best methods of creating a **11.168**

[320] K Canvin, A Bartlett, and V Pinfold, 'Guardianship Accountability of Compulsory Powers in the Community: The Ethical Considerations of Mental Health Service Users on Supervised Discharge and Guardianship' (2005) 31 Journal of Medical Ethics 457.

[321] See, eg, *OS v Home Office* [2006] EWHC 1903 (Admin). It is worth noting that recommendations by clinical teams that a restricted patient should be given a period of supervised leave have been rejected by the Justice Secretary. Where such disagreements have resulted in legal challenge, the courts have been unwilling to find the justice secretary's decision unlawful: see, eg, *R on the Application of PP v Secretary of State for Justice* [2009] EWHC 2464 (Admin). The Secretary of State was not bound by the professionals' opinion, even where the opinion was unequivocal and unanimous. Nor was the Secretary of State bound to seek a second clinical opinion to substantiate his own judgment on the question of risk. Cf an exception to this approach in *The Queen on the Application of X v Secretary of State for Justice* [2009] EWHC 2465 (Admin).

[322] See *Code of Practice*, para 27.10.

[323] N Glover-Thomas, 'Joint Working; Reality or Rhetoric in Housing the Mentally Vulnerable?' (2007) 29(3–4) Journal of Social Welfare and Family Law 217.

long-term community care order with existing provisions found within the 1983 Act. As noted above, leave can be granted with associated conditions and the condition of compliance with medical treatment was used as a means of extending control over a patient while also harnessing the less restrictive care environment of the community. Failure to meet these conditions by the patient resulted in recall to hospital. Using leave of absence to create a community care provision was ended abruptly with the decision of *R v Hallstrom, ex p W (No 2)*[324] where it was found that recalling to hospital patients who were currently on leave for the sole purpose of renewing the s 3 detention for treatment order (which would then be followed immediately with leave of absence) was unlawful. Admitting patients to hospital for treatment under s 3 of the 1983 Act when the patient would not receive inpatient treatment was found to breach the compulsion criteria set down in s 3, in particular that it should be demonstrated that the individual must require treatment in hospital for their mental disorder. Since Hallstrom, more recent case law indicates that this is no longer the case,[325] suggesting now that treatment[326] does not have to be as an inpatient.[327] It is clear that the courts are increasingly supportive of those care plans that combine community supervision with minimal inpatient assessment to ensure that the patient has a better chance of coping in community settings.[328] However, the Code of Practice reminds decision makers that:

> Leave should normally be of short duration and not normally more than seven days. When considering whether to grant leave of absence for more than seven consecutive days, or extending leave so that the total period is more than seven consecutive days, responsible clinicians should also consider whether the patient should go onto a community treatment order (CTO) instead and, if required, consult any local agencies concerned with public protection.[329]

[324] [1986] 2 All ER 306.

[325] In *B v Barking Havering and Brentwood Community Healthcare NHS Trust* [1999] 1 FLR 106 (CA), it was held by the Court of Appeal that it was lawful to renew the detention of a patient even though her detention amounted to only two nights a week in hospital. Whilst three years later an even wider interpretation of 'hospital treatment' was made in *R (on the application of DR) v Mersey Care NHS Trust* [2002] EWHC 1810 (Admin). In this case, a patient, who was currently living in the community under leave of absence and who was required to see a psychologist weekly and attend a ward round once a month as part of the conditions attached to her leave, still met the requirement of hospital treatment for the purpose of s 3. Pitchford J noted that the MHRT had not erred in its decision to refuse to grant the patient discharge as her condition still necessitated some hospital-based treatment input.

[326] Patients on leave also remain subject to the consent to treatment provisions in Part 4 of the Mental Health Act. As a result, certain treatments for the patient's disorder may be administered without patient consent. There is scope, at least in theory, for compulsory treatment in the community to be possible under the Mental Health Act 1983, although these treatments are administered in hospital and not in the patient's home. The *Code of Practice* (para 27.25) does caution against the use of Part 4 provisions for patients on leave. However, it is suggested that the threat of possible recall would make it more difficult for a patient on leave to 'refuse' treatment. See R J Bonne and J Monahan, 'From coercion to contract: Reframing the debate on mandated community treatment for people with mental disorders' (2005) 29(4) Law and Human Behavior 485; MS Swartz et al, 'Consumers' perceptions of the fairness and effectiveness of mandated community treatment and related pressures' (2004) 55(7) Psychiatric Services 780. It is also worth noting that in *K v UK* [1998] 40 BMLR 20, the Court ruled that patients must not be recalled without the presence of objective medical evidence establishing that the conditions for revoking leave have been fulfilled (ie the *Winterwerp criteria* must be satisfied).

[327] See *KL v Somerset Partnership NHS Foundation Trust* (2011) UKUT 233 (AAC); *R (on the application of DR) v Mersey Care NHS Trust* [2002] EWHC 1810 (Admin).

[328] See *R (on the application of CS) v Mental Health Review Tribunal and another* [2004] EWHC 2958 (Admin.).

[329] See *Code of Practice*, para 27.11.

(iii) Supervised community treatment

Section 17A is principally aimed at preventing the 'revolving door' scenario and the harm which could arise from relapse. It is a more structured system than leave of absence and has more safeguards for patients.[330] Lord Warner observed that the rationale behind CTOs in the Mental Health Act 2007 was that: **11.169**

> We know that some patients stop taking their medication or treatment once they leave hospital, and so relapse and end up being readmitted. This detrimental cycle is often referred to as the revolving door. Patients on supervised community treatment will benefit from a structure designed to promote safe community living. This will reduce the risk of relapse and re-detention. They will be asked to comply with conditions to help prevent relapse, such as living in a certain place, attending an out-patient clinic and agreeing to take medication under the direction of their responsible clinician.[331]

It was estimated that CTOs would plug a very small, yet persistent gap where alternative responses to patient needs were not adequate. Lord Warner predicted that over a five-year period, there would be 3,000 to 4,000 patients on a CTO; yet in the first four months of their implementation, over 2,000 orders had been granted. However, in 2012, 22,267 people were subject to detention or CTO restrictions under the Mental Health Act in NHS and independent sector hospitals. Of this, 4,764 people of which were subject to a CTO with 4,220 CTOs made during 2011–12, an increase of 386 (10 per cent) since 2010–11. During this same period, CTO recalls increased by 30 per cent and it is estimated that around 70 per cent resulted in a revocation.[332] This casts serious doubt on whether CTOs are being used as intended or whether they are fit for purpose. **11.170**

Supervised Community Treatment (SCT) was introduced by the Mental Health Act 2007 to respond to perceived gaps within the 1983 Act, to provide a robust community care provision with an associated treatment compliance mechanism. SCT is provided by means of a Community Treatment Order (CTO) and may be applicable to patients who have been detained under s 3 or who have been the subject of a hospital order, a hospital direction or unrestricted transfer direction.[333] As the Code of Practice notes, supervised community treatment aims to offer a means of patients receiving treatment in the community instead of having to be detained in hospital.[334] The CTO seeks to provide support within the community with the expectation that it will reduce the risk of deterioration in mental state. The CTO provides the RC with the power to recall a patient receiving SCT to hospital for treatment, if necessary. Patients who are on SCT will be subject to conditions whilst living in the community. Most conditions will depend on individual circumstances but must be for the purpose of ensuring the patient receives medical treatment, or to prevent risk of harm to the patient or others. Such conditions will form part of the patient's community treatment order (CTO). Patients on SCT may be recalled to hospital for treatment should this become necessary . . . [where compulsion becomes necessary, the patient should be conveyed to hospital for treatment].[335] **11.171**

330 *Code of Practice*, para 28.5.

331 HL Debs, 28 Nov col 656.

332 HSCIC, *Inpatients formally detained in hospitals under the Mental Health Act 1983, and patients subject to supervised community treatment, Annual figures, England, 2011*/12, (2012) 5.

333 Patients who meet these criteria following a transfer from Scotland, Northern Ireland, the Isle of Man, or the Channel Islands are also eligible for SCT consideration.

334 See *Code of Practice*, para 29.1.

335 Mental Health Act 2007, Explanatory Notes, 20. See also, *Code of Practice*, para 29.45–29.47.

11.172 In order for SCT to apply to a patient, s 17A(1) gives the RC the power to grant a detained patient leave subject to being liable for recall, if:

(a) the patient is suffering from a mental disorder (any disorder or disability of mind) of a nature or degree which makes it appropriate for him to receive medical treatment;
(b) it is necessary for his health or safety or for the protection of other persons that he should receive such treatment;
(c) subject to his being liable to be recalled, such treatment can be provided without his continuing to be detained in a hospital;
(d) it is necessary that the responsible clinician should be able to exercise the power, under s 17E(1) of the Act, to recall the patient to hospital; and
(e) appropriate medical treatment is available for him.[336]

11.173 **(a) Assessment for SCT** It is for the RC to decide whether a patient meets the above criteria. This decision will be made following the agreement of an AMHP that SCT is the appropriate course of action.[337] As the CTO represents a formal 'community care and treatment framework', should it be possible to obtain the desired effects of SCT by using a more informal method, then these avenues should be investigated fully before SCT is sought. It is also important to bring the patient and his/her carers into the initial discussions, when possible, as the success of SCT (as with all forms of community provision) is much more likely to be achieved if the patient cooperates fully and feels engaged with the process.

11.174 Ultimately, the decision to use a CTO as a means of formally engaging with a patient in the community requires the RC to assess the potential risks of a patient being discharged into the community without any formal oversight.[338] One of the greatest concerns for the RC relates to medication compliance and the potential repercussions should the patient not comply. Since community-based provisions are always a matter of weighing up different risks, particularly in terms of how a patient may interact with members of the public and whether he/she would represent a risk to others, this weighing up process is imperative. The RC must take into consideration the patient's medical history and any other relevant factors when making his/her decision. If the patient has a history of non-compliance or has posed a risk to others in the past, this may not necessarily prevent the use of a CTO in the future but rather may inform the planning process and may result in particular conditions being set. Indeed, where a patient is deemed to pose a risk, use of SCT, rather than a more informal agreement, is much more justified[339] and assessment of the value of SCT must be flexibly applied. Other factors that may be relevant might be the mental state of the patient, the level of insight s/he has into the condition and the environment in which it is planned the patient will be placed in the community.

11.175 Good planning is essential for a successful CTO. All involved parties must be included in the consultation process and be made aware that the patient is to be discharged onto SCT. Over recent years, a move towards a more skills-based approach with emphasis on multidisciplinary working has been evident. The National Institute for Mental Health in England's report New Ways of Working[340] aims to help all mental health staff work more flexibly within teams. It promotes a model where distributed responsibility is shared amongst team members

[336] See Mental Health Act 1983, s 17A(5).

[337] Where the AMHP does not agree that SCT is appropriate, then SCT will not be possible, see *Code of Practice*, para 29.25.

[338] *Code of Practice*, para 31.6.

[339] *Code of Practice*, para 25.10.

[340] *A Best Practice Implementation Guide* (DoH 2007). See also S Gillard, C Edwards, S Gibson, J Holley, and K Owen, 'New ways of working in mental health services: a qualitative, comparative case study assessing and informing the emergence of new peer worker roles in mental health services in England' (2014) 2 Health Services and Delivery Research 19.

and no longer delegated by a single professional such as the consultant. Seamless provision and support does rely heavily upon effective joint working between the various care teams and its members; yet, achieving useful and efficient liaison between different providers has always proven problematic in the past. Despite continued statements of support and intent to improve joined-up thinking by various actors within government and the mental health care field,[341] there remains continued concern that implementation problems of the past will hamper how CTOs operate in the future.[342] Patients on CTOs remain entitled to after-care services under s 117 of the 1983 Act and as such, the normal after-care assessment of needs will be carried out and packages of care devised to meet identified need, as far as possible.[343]

As discussed above, SCT may have conditions attached for a variety of reasons, including conditions designed to minimize the potential risk presented by the patient in a community environment. In all cases of supervised community treatment, two conditions are always required: **11.176**

.... Patients are required to make themselves available for medical examination:

- when needed for consideration of extension of the CTO, and
- if necessary, to allow a second opinion approved doctor (SOAD) to provide a part 4A certificate authorising treatment.[344]

Other conditions may be attached if it is required to ensure the patient receives the appropriate medical treatment, as a means of preventing the risk of harm to the patient's health or safety and to protect others. Conditions may include specific places of residence, where the patient is to go to receive treatment and people or places that the patient should avoid. The key with attached conditions is to avoid being too inflexible, to use them to enhance the order's likely overall success and to avoid using too many conditions so as to restrict the patient's liberty in the community unreasonably. Perhaps, most important is to recognize that the setting of conditions, although being a largely clinical decision, should seek to be explained to the patient and his/her carers as fully as possible.[345] Where patients believe they are central to the process and are better engaged and compliant with the conditions, the order is more likely to be successful. However, despite the Code of Practice urging decision-makers to avoid restricting the patient's freedom too much within the community, there is scope for flexibility in terms of the type of conditions that can be attached and this decision is wholly dependent upon the RC's discretion with the agreement of an AMHP. **11.177**

Community patients must be monitored regularly to ensure continued compliance with set conditions.[346] Where there is evidence the patient is not complying with the conditions or **11.178**

[341] eg, in relation to young peoples' mental health care, Department of Health, *Future in mind: Promoting, protecting and improving our children and young people's mental health and wellbeing*, (TSO 2015) and the allied report, Children and Young People's Mental Health and Wellbeing Taskforce, *'Co-ordinated System' Task and Finish Group Report* (2015), where several challenges were identified in relation to effective joint working: complexity and fragmentation within the current system; lack of clarity in relation to roles and responsibilities; a lack of cohesion between the various actors within the system of care; a lack of accountability to meet shared outcomes among and between agencies; unclear funding arrangements with the result that disinvestment in services and non-recurrent funding is a major problem; and lack of information.

[342] See N Glover-Thomas, 'Joint Working: Reality or Rhetoric in Housing the Mentally Vulnerable?' (2007) 29(3) Journal of Social Welfare and Family Law 217. See also J McHale, 'Standards, Quality and Accountability—The NHS and Mental Health: A Case For Joined Up Thinking?' (2003) 24 Journal of Social Welfare and Family Law 369; and M Atkinson et al, *Multi-agency Working: A Detailed Study* (National Foundation for Educational Research 2002).

[343] National Health Service and Community Care Act 1990, s 47. See also *Code of Practice*, para 34.13.

[344] See *Code of Practice*, para 29.27.

[345] *Code of Practice*, para 29.33.

[346] *Code of Practice*, paras 29.37–29.38.

the order is not proving appropriate for the patient's needs, the RC must consider possible responses, including possible recall to hospital. Any such changes would need to be agreed with an AMHP and preferably discussed with and explained to the patient in order to achieve the best possible outcome.

11.179 To a large extent, SCT, as with previous community care provisions, relies heavily upon the input of carers in the community. Included within this is the need for clinicians to listen and take seriously a carer's assessment of the patient's health, whether s/he is complying with the conditions laid down and whether changes to the CTO would be beneficial to the patient. Establishing effective working relations between the clinical care team and the community-based one (both lay and professional) is, therefore, essential for the CTO to work well and for provision to be as seamless as possible. However, applications for CTOs exceeded all expectations and this has consequently affected the ability for timely administration of applications.[347] The Mental Health Act Commission in its posthumously published final biennial report,[348] note that mental health services are struggling to deal with a high demand for community treatment orders which has far exceeded official estimates with more than 1,200 people in England being made subject to compulsory treatment outside hospital five months after the powers were introduced under the Mental Health Act 2007.[349] The Care Quality Commission, which has been responsible for monitoring and reviewing the Mental Health Act since 2009, noted in its 2013/14 report that since 2009 use of the Mental Health Act had grown across all areas, with 23,531 people subject to the Act, either detained in hospital or under a community treatment order at the end of 2013/14 (a 6 per cent increase from 2012/13).[350] This increasing pressure on service provision will continue to have a knock-on effect upon the effectiveness of community based services. There is also evidence that community treatment orders are simply not achieving the desired effects. The government-funded OCTET randomized controlled trial[351] tested whether CTOs reduce admissions compared with use of s 17 leave, and found that at twelve months, despite the significant difference in length of initial compulsory outpatient treatment (median 183 days on CTOs but 8 days on s 17) the number of patients readmitted did not differ between the two groups. It was noted that, 'In well coordinated mental health services the imposition of compulsory supervision does not reduce the rate of readmission of psychotic patients. We found no support in terms of any reduction in overall hospital admission to justify the significant curtailment of patients' personal liberty.'[352]

11.180 **(b) Powers to treat community patients** Ostensibly, CTOs were heralded as a means of achieving less restrictive care for patients while also offering clinicians a means of controlling a patient's condition through legitimate community-based treatment. This image conjured up such significant concerns for many of those working with the mentally disordered in the

[347] See S Lawton-Smith, *A Question of Numbers: The Potential Impact of Community Treatment Orders in England and Wales* (King's Fund 2005); and M Kinton, 'Towards an Understanding of Supervised Community Treatment' (2008) 17 Journal of Mental Health Law 7.

[348] MHAC, *Coercion and Consent—Monitoring the Mental Health Act 2007—09, Thirteenth Biennial Report.*

[349] ibid, para 2.74. See also D Lombard, 'Mental Health Act: Demand for Community Orders Swamps Services: Mental Health Act Commission Says Compulsory Treatment Levels have Exceeded Official Estimates' (2009) Community Care, March.

[350] CQC, *Monitoring the Mental Health Act in 2013/14* (TSO 2015) 9.

[351] T Burns, J Rugkåsa, A Molodynski, J Dawson, K Yeeles, M Vazquez-Montes, M Voysey, J Sinclair, S Priebe, 'Community treatment orders for patients with psychosis (OCTET): a randomised controlled trial' (2013) 381 Lancet 1627.

[352] ibid, 1627. See also M S Swartz, J W Swanson, H R Wagner, B J Burns, V A Hiday, and R Borum, 'Can involuntary outpatient commitment reduce hospital recidivism? Findings from a randomized trial with severely mentally ill individuals' (1999) 156 American Journal of Psychiatry 1968.

community of forcible treatment in the patient's home and teams of carers having to hold down recalcitrant patients that objections flew thick and fast throughout the period of reform which ultimately resulted in the 2007 Act.

The reality of this authority to treat is, however, different. Section 35 of the 2007 Act introduced Pt 4A into the Mental Health Act 1983, which allows for treatment to be given to community patients without their consent. Section 64A–64K authorizes the administration of 'relevant treatment', which amounts to medicines used for mental disorder and ECT. Technically, these treatments may be given in the community without resort back to hospital. However, ECT is not a treatment that can be administered away from a clinical setting and owing to the risks associated with ECT emergency care needs to be close by. Where treatment may be administered in the community settings, strict limits apply to the circumstances in which such treatment is appropriate. Treatment in the community of a community patient is permitted if: **11.181**

- the treatment is immediately necessary and the patient is capable and consents to the treatment;
- the treatment is immediately necessary and there is consent from someone authorized under the Mental Capacity Act 2005 to make decisions on the patient's behalf;
- the patient lacks capacity and force is not necessary to secure compliance; or
- emergency treatment needs to be given, using force if necessary, to a patient who lacks capacity.

Therefore, the provision of treatment is much more limited than the initial fears surrounding CTOs suggested. The focus of such treatment is largely related to 'immediately necessary' treatment as a response to an emergency deterioration of health. In addition, even though such treatment can be administered to a patient with capacity, their consent is required. Mostly, the expectation is that the bulk of this power to administer community treatment will focus on patients who do not have capacity. **11.182**

Furthermore, as discussed above (see para. 11.138 et seq), although Pt 4A introduces a further SOAD certification process as an additional safety mechanism, certificates are not required in a variety of situations including where treatment is 'immediately necessary'. Where a SOAD certificate is required, it is for the clinician who is responsible for the treatment decision to ensure a request is made for a SOAD to visit. A SOAD visit would only normally be required where a certificate is needed because there is a genuine uncertainty about whether the patient has capacity to consent or whether the patient is in fact consenting. Beyond this, a significant degree of discretion is placed with the clinical decision-maker. Inevitably, this raises the question about just how much the additional SOAD certification process has actually increased protection for patient rights. For the most part, where patients have capacity and are living in the community under a CTO who then decide to stop complying with their treatment regime, the only real means of seeking compliance will be for the RC to recall the patient back to hospital. SCT was principally aimed at preventing or at least alleviating the peripatetic behaviour of the 'revolving door' patient, who regularly ricocheted back and forth between hospital and community. However, it seems that CTOs have had little impact on readmission figures, a fact confirmed by the OCTET study.[353] **11.183**

(c) **Power to recall to hospital** The power to recall a patient to hospital when they are subject to a CTO is governed by s 17E. The recall power is primarily seen as a mechanism **11.184**

[353] T Burns et al, 'Community treatment orders for patients with psychosis (OCTET)', n 350.

that offers the RC the ability to act when the patient is showing evidence of a relapse or is exhibiting high-risk behaviour relating to his/her mental disorder.

11.185 The RC can use the recall power if certain criteria are met. These are that in the RC's opinion:

- the patient requires medical treatment in hospital for his mental disorder; and
- there would be a risk of harm to the health or safety of the patient or to others if the patient were not recalled back to hospital.[354]

11.186 The power to recall also includes the situation where a patient fails to comply with a given condition (as discussed above) attached to the CTO. However, the Code of Practice regards recall as a last resort and should not be used as a bargaining tool or as a means of threatened sanction.[355] Where recall is resorted to regularly, it is likely that the patient is not benefiting from SCT and as such, the patient's needs ought to be reviewed.

11.187 When the RC does decide to recall a patient to hospital, it should be communicated to the patient in writing.[356] A patient recalled from a CTO can then be taken and conveyed to hospital by an AMHP, a hospital staff member, a police officer, or anyone authorized in writing by the RC. It is important that appropriate preparations at the hospital be made to receive the patient, the responsibility of which lies with the RC. The RC and clinical team will assess the patient's condition and needs and take steps to provide the necessary treatment. Under recall, the patient may be detained in hospital for up to seventy-two hours and during this time a further, more thorough assessment of the patient is expected to be undertaken. If the RC does not revoke the CTO, then after seventy-two hours the patient may leave hospital and be subject to the same conditions as before, if no variation has been made. However, if the RC decides that SCT has not proved successful, the order can be revoked altogether.

11.188 **(d) Revocation and Discharge of CTO** Following the MHA 2007, revoking a CTO is a separate step from recall of a community patient to hospital. Revocation is governed by s 17F and the RC may revoke a CTO in writing if he/she is of the opinion that the conditions for detention to hospital under s 3 are met. This view must also be shared by an AMHP. Where a revocation takes place under s 17F, the patient will then revert to the status of a detained patient.

11.189 Where it is believed that a patient requires inpatient treatment for longer than seventy-two hours after arrival at hospital, the RC is tasked with the need to assess whether the CTO is offering the necessary support and is appropriate for the patient concerned. Where it is decided that the CTO is not achieving the desired outcome, the RC should consider revoking the CTO. Alternatively, a patient's condition may have improved, their establishment back into the community may be good, or they may simply no longer meet the criteria for SCT. In such cases, consideration must be given to whether the patient should be discharged from SCT. The Code of Practice guides practitioners away from the possibility of simply allowing the order to lapse but rather to be proactive in the ending of the order when it is no longer necessary.[357] A decision to discharge a patient from SCT should be fully

[354] Mental Health Act 1983, s 17E(3) allows for the hospital to which the patient is recalled to be different from the responsible hospital.

[355] In the *Code of Practice*, para 29.37, it is noted that 'recalling the patient to hospital will be an option if the risk justifies it.'

[356] If the patient is difficult to find or simply refuses to receive the recall notice, the notice will still be deemed to have been delivered and received, thereby allowing the RC and clinical team to prepare for the patient's return to hospital.

[357] See *Code of Practice*, para 29.76.

communicated to the patient explaining the reasons for the decision and an opportunity should be made to listen and respond to any concerns that the patient, the patient's carers, or nearest relative might have about the decision. It is also important to note that discharge from a CTO does not remove the responsibility placed on the LSSA to provide appropriate after-care services under s 117.[358]

7. Discharge and tribunal review of the lawfulness of detention

The decision to discharge a patient from psychiatric care can be made by several different actors within the care system, depending on the patient's status and the meeting of the discharge criteria. Section 23 of the Mental Health Act 1983 provides for the absolute discharge of detained patients, patients who are subject to guardianship, and community patients under CTOs. This discharge can be ordered by the patient's RC, the hospital managers (or the LSSA for patients on guardianship), or the patient's nearest relative. The discharge order must be ordered in writing; anything less will be insufficient.[359] **11.190**

(i) Discharge

The decision to discharge should not be one taken lightly or influenced by ancillary issues such as a shortage of hospital facilities or beds.[360] Rather, the RC should consult with all other mental health professionals who are currently working with the patient. A full assessment of the patient's needs, both in terms of medical and social needs, must be carried out and a detailed risk assessment will be necessary to ascertain whether discharge is viable. If all evidence points to the need to discharge the patient from a CTO, then this should follow. A decision to discharge is multi-faceted—both the patient's current status must be assessed in terms of needs and how these are being met combined with an assessment of how these current and future needs will be met and managed in the community following a decision to discharge. As such, in many ways discharge should not be regarded as a single decision but rather should be a series of review decisions. In *South West London and St. George's Mental Health NHS Trust v W*[361] Crane J noted that: **11.191**

> RC[s] should … assess the need for the patient's continued detention by considering whether: (1) the patient is still suffering from mental disorder; (2) the disorder continues to be of a nature or degree which makes assessment or assessment followed by medical treatment or treatment in a hospital appropriate; (3) for s 3 patients, the appropriate treatment test continues to be satisfied; and (4) detention in a hospital is still necessary in the interests of the patient's own health or safety or for the protection of others.[362]

Hospital managers also have discharge powers which may be employed if it is decided that detention is no longer justified under the legislation.[363] In such circumstances, the hospital managers' decision is absolute even where the RC and clinical team disagree.[364] There is no formal process by which a patient seeking discharge from the hospital manager has to follow. A patient merely has to place a request with the managers for a review of the case. **11.192**

---

[358] ibid, para 29.77.

[359] See *Code of Practice*, para 32.17: 'Section 23 of the Act allows responsible clinicians to discharge part 2 patients and unrestricted part 3 patients and all CTO patients by giving an order in writing.'

[360] In *R v Drew* [2003] UKHL 25, it was found that the RC has a duty to discharge a patient from detention if the medical conditions that justified admission are no longer met—it should be these factors which influence the final discharge decision rather than other factors.

[361] *South West London and St. George's Mental Health NHS Trust v W* [2002] EWHC Admin 1770.

[362] ibid, [81].

[363] MHAC, *First Biennial Report*, 1983–85, para 8.13.

[364] See *Code of Practice*, para 35.13: 'Section 23 of the Act gives hospital managers the power to discharge most detained patients and all CTO patients.'

Following such a request, it may be decided that instead of reviewing the case by the managers, the case ought to be referred to the First-tier tribunal, previously known as the Mental Health Review Tribunal (see below, para 11.183). However, when the hospital managers make a decision, it must be justified by the rules of natural justice[365] with reasons given.[366]

11.193 The nearest relative of the patient may also seek discharge. The order of discharge must be preceded by a seventy-two-hour written notice supplied to the hospital managers. Once in receipt of a written notice of intent, the hospital managers will inform the patient's RC who can then nullify the discharge request if s/he provides a written report within the seventy-two-hour window to the managers outlining the RC's concerns and reasons for the views adopted. Section 25(1) provides that if, in the opinion of the RC, 'the patient, if discharged, would be likely to act in a manner dangerous to other persons or himself, any order for the discharge of the patient made by that relative in pursuance of the notice shall be of no effect'.[367] However, where a notice of intent is supplied by the nearest relative to seek a patient's discharge but there is clear evidence that the patient remains unwell and in need of continuing care, the nearest relative may be displaced. Displacement of the nearest relative may be possible on the grounds that:

- the nearest relative is incapable of acting as such because of illness or mental disorder;
- the nearest relative has objected unreasonably to an application for admission for treatment or a guardianship application;
- the nearest relative has exercised the power to discharge a patient without due regard to the welfare of the patient or the interests of the public;[368]
- the nearest relative is otherwise not a suitable person to act as such; or
- the patient has no nearest relative within the meaning of the Act, or it is not reasonably practicable to ascertain whether the patient has a nearest relative or who that nearest relative is.[369]

(ii) Application to the First-tier tribunal for case review

11.194 For patients who are detained beyond seventy-two hours, a right exists to apply to the First-tier tribunal to seek review of the lawfulness of the detention.[370] Hospital managers and LSSAs are under a duty to ensure that patients know that they have this right to apply for case review.[371] Furthermore, under Article 5(4) of the ECHR, anyone deprived of their liberty must have an opportunity to have the lawfulness of the detention reviewed, speedily decided upon, and an effective remedy given should the detention prove to be unlawful. For

[365] The managers must be able to demonstrate that they have acted fairly, in good faith, without bias, and have given the relevant parties adequate opportunity to state their case.

[366] *R (on the application of O) v West London Mental Health NHS Trust* [2005] EWHC 604.

[367] Mental Health Act 1983, s 25(1)(a).

[368] ibid, s 29(3)(d).

[369] See *Code of Practice*, para 5.7.

[370] The First-tier tribunal is the name for what was the Mental Health Review Tribunal (MHRT), following the Tribunals, Courts and Enforcement Act 2007. The MHRT was introduced and set up by the Mental Health Act 1959 in response to the Royal Commission's recommendation that psychiatric patients should be provided with a safeguard against unjustified detention or control under guardianship by means of an independent review conducted by people with both medical and non-medical backgrounds. The Tribunal is an independent judicial body, set up under the Mental Health (Northern Ireland) Order 1986 (the Order), which reviews the cases of patients who are compulsorily detained or are subject to guardianship under the Order. The Tribunal is tasked with providing patients with a safeguard against unjustified detention in hospital or control within the community.

[371] *Code of Practice*, para 32.5.

patients who do not seek review of their case, the case must be automatically referred to the First-tier tribunal.[372]

11.195 The First-tier Tribunal (Mental Health) (as was the MHRT) is an 'independent judicial body . . . to review the cases of detained, conditionally discharged, and SCT patients under the Act and to direct the discharge of any patients where it thinks it appropriate'.[373] The tribunal offers a safeguard for patients by providing a judicial forum to scrutinize whether the detention criteria is still being met. The burden of proof will sit firmly in the hands of the patient's RC. Evidence supporting the argument for continued detention will have to include:

- the information required about the patient;
- the documents required concerning the patient;
- the clinician's report;
- the social circumstances reports;
- if the patient is an inpatient, the nursing report;
- if the patient is subject to SCT, the information must include (inter alia):
    - details of the original authority for the patient's supervised community treatment under the Mental Health Act 1983;
    - the patient's responsible clinician and the length of time the patient has been under their care;
    - the patient's mental state, behaviour and treatment for mental disorder, and relevant medical history;
    - a statement as to whether the patient has ever neglected or harmed himself, or has ever harmed other persons or threatened them with harm, at a time when he was mentally disordered, together with details of any neglect, harm or threats of harm;
    - an assessment of the extent to which the patient or other persons would be likely to be at risk if the patient is discharged by the Tribunal, and how any such risks could best be managed;
    - the reasons why the patient can be treated as a community patient without continued detention in hospital, and why it is necessary that the responsible clinician should be able to exercise the power under s 17E(1) of the Mental Health Act 1983 to recall the patient to hospital.[374]

11.196 The evidence supplied to the tribunal must meet the *Winterwerp v Netherlands*[375] criteria. That is: the lawfulness of continued psychiatric detention under Article 5(1)(e) depends on the continuing persistence of unsoundness of mind of a nature or degree warranting confinement. Where there are questions or concerns raised that the evidence does not resoundingly support a case for continued detention, the tribunal will be required to discharge the patient forthwith.

---

372 The Mental Health Act 2007, s 37(3) amends s 68(5) of the Mental Health Act 1983 to introduce a requirement to refer to the First-tier tribunal the case of any patient who has not applied for a hearing within six months from the 'applicable day', which is the day on which the patient was first detained (this also now includes s 2 detention for assessment).

373 *Code of Practice*, para 12.3.

374 Practice Direction: First-tier Tribunal Health Education and Social Care Chamber: Statements and Reports in Mental Health Cases, October 2013. This Practice Direction applies to a 'mental health case' as defined in Rule 1(3) the Tribunal Procedure (First-tier Tribunal) (Health, Education and Social Care Chamber) Rules 2008 ('the 2008 Rules') (as amended 2014).

375 (1979) 2 EHRR 387 (ECtHR).

11.197 (a) **The Tribunals, Courts and Enforcement Act 2007** The administrative tribunals system (which also includes MHRTs) underwent significant revision and reform following the Leggatt review in 2001 which recommended extensive reorganization to the entire tribunal system.[376] It was suggested that all tribunals should be brought together in a single tribunal system and that this system should be administered by a single tribunal service. The various governmental departments in which the different tribunals were attached in the past would be separated from the tribunals system altogether thereby creating a less complex and more independent administrative framework. The government's response to the Leggatt review was positive. The government's White Paper, Transforming Public Services: Complaints, Redress and Tribunals was published in the summer of 2004.[377] This process of review culminated in the Tribunals, Courts and Enforcement Act 2007.

11.198 The objective of the 2007 Act was to create a 'new, simplified statutory framework for tribunals which provides coherence and will enable future reform'.[378] A streamlined structure would create greater uniformity and efficiency; while enshrined within the Act were three key principles: accessibility, fairness, and efficiency. The Act created two new tribunals—the First-tier Tribunal and the Upper Tribunal. The major changes to the MHRT in England took place from November 2008, specifically:

- The abolition of the MHRT;
- New rules of procedures and practice directions;
- New appeals arrangements.[379]

11.199 The Upper Tribunal is largely, though not exclusively, an appellate tribunal and reviews and decides appeals arising from the First-tier Tribunal. The government expected the Upper Tribunal to reduce the number of mental health Judicial Review (JR) proceedings. These expectations were met with the number of mental health JR proceedings falling significantly in 2008 and numbers have since remained fairly static.

11.200 Mental health cases are considered within the Health, Education and Social Care Chamber with a Chamber President who heads the chamber and a Senior President of Tribunals who heads the tribunal's judiciary. The Act provides a unified appeal structure—a decision of the First-tier Tribunal may be appealed to the Upper Tribunal and this decision may then be appealed to the Court of Appeal.[380] In 2013/14, mental health, within the Health, Education and Social Care Chamber, saw an 8 per cent increase in cases received in 2012/13. The applications included both those made by patients, the nearest relative, and referrals from hospital managers and the Secretary of State.[381] Various changes have been implemented within this jurisdiction to improve efficiency and timeliness within the hearing process. In 2014, the joint Judicial Case Management Board was established, with members

---

376 Sir Andrew Leggatt, *Tribunals for Users—One System, One Service* (August 2001).

377 Department for Constitutional Affairs, *Transforming Public Services: Complaints, Redress and Tribunals* (Cm 6243, July 2004).

378 Mental Health Act 2007 Act, Explanatory Notes, 2.

379 See generally First-tier Tribunal (Health, Education and Social Care Chamber) Rules 2008 (as amended 2014).

380 These appeals, however, must relate to points of law. The difference between JR proceedings and the onward process using the Upper Tribunal is that JR strikes out a decision, whereas, with an onward appeal process, the Upper Tribunal would deal finally with a case without any further delays.

381 A variety of applications were made in 2013–14, including section 2 cases, which rose to nearly 30 per cent of the total case load in 2013–14. This figure, in particular, raises concern as there is a suspicion that patients are being detained under section 2 for assessment, despite many of the patients being already known to mental health services and are hence being detained inappropriately (see *First-tier Tribunals Senior President of Tribunals' Annual Report 2015*, 48).

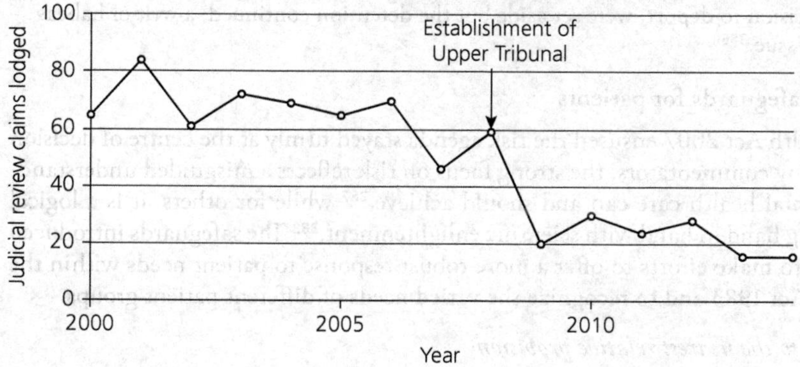

Figure 11.1 The Impact of the Establishment of the Upper Tribunal of Judicial Review Claims.

of the judiciary and administration working together to identify areas that would benefit from direct judicial intervention by a salaried judge or Registrar. The objective of this is to enable better use of valuable judicial time, thus enabling the more complex cases to benefit from significant judicial experience without having to endure significant delays.[382] In line with the above objective, for the mental health jurisdiction, these changes[383] also remove the requirement for a pre-hearing examination by the tribunal doctor in every mental health case, however, the tribunal can retain the examination in particular circumstances or where the patient has requested that such an examination is conducted.

(iii) Habeas corpus and judicial review

With the Upper Tribunal, JR cases have reduced. The number of JR claims lodged has reduced significantly by about two thirds between 2000 and 2014, with a significant dip following the establishment of the Upper Tribunal (see Figure 11.1 above).[384] **11.201**

Habeas corpus claims to the High Court are still available following the establishment of the Upper Tribunal. On the facts of a given case, a mental health patient may be able to apply to the High Court for a writ of habeas corpus or instigate JR proceedings; however, the procedures are separate and very different in nature. In *R v Secretary of State for the Home Department, ex parte Cheblak*,[385] Lord Donaldson MR provides a clear exposition of the differences between the two procedures: **11.202**

> A writ of habeas corpus will issue where someone is detained without any authority or the purported authority is beyond the powers of the person authorizing the detention and so is unlawful. The remedy of judicial review is available where the decisions or action sought to be impugned is within the powers of the person taking it but, due to procedural error, a misappreciation of the law, a failure to take account of relevant matters, a taking account of irrelevant matters or the fundamental unreasonableness of the decision or action, it should never have been taken. In such a case the decision is unlawful, unless and until it is set aside by a court of competent jurisdiction. In the case of detention, if the warrant, or the

[382] *First-tier Tribunals Senior President of Tribunals' Annual Report 2015*, 50.

[383] See generally First-tier Tribunal (Health, Education and Social Care Chamber) Rules 2008 (as amended 2014).

[384] Ministry of Justice, Civil justice statistics quarterly: October to December 2014, available at <https://www.gov.uk/government/statistics/civil-justice-statistics-quarterly-october-to-december-2014>.

[385] [1991] 2 All ER 319, at 322.

underlying decision to deport, were set aside but the detention continued, a writ of habeas corpus would issue.[386]

8. Additional safeguards for patients

11.203 The Mental Health Act 2007 ensured the risk agenda stayed firmly at the centre of decision making. For many commentators, the strong focus on risk reflects a misguided understanding of what mental health care can and should achieve,[387] while for others, it is a logical progression going hand in hand with scientific enlightenment.[388] The safeguards introduced in 2007 sought to make efforts to offer a more robust response to patient needs within the Mental Health Act 1983 and to recognize the varied needs of different patient groups.

(i) *Amendment to the nearest relative provisions*

11.204 The appointment and removal of nearest relatives is governed by ss 26–30 of the Mental Health Act 1983. The nearest relative plays a fundamental role in the operation of the legislation, as noted in paras 11.59–11.64. The nearest relative has a right to apply for an individual to be detained in hospital under ss 2 and 3 and can seek an application of guardianship over the patient. The nearest relative may also veto a decision taken to detain an individual in hospital or admit to guardianship.[389] Also, the nearest relative may also seek the patient's discharge and/or apply to the First-tier Tribunal on behalf of the patient in order to seek a review of the case.[390] Furthermore, there is an expectation that the nearest relative will be consulted during the decision-making process, (as discussed in paras 11.59–11.64). In *TW v LB Enfield*,[391] the applicant argued that her nearest relative ought to have been consulted before her section 3 detention. However, it was thought 'not reasonably practicable' to undertake the consultation process as the patient had repeatedly sent dictated letters instructing Enfield's staff not to involve her family, and had gone so far as to refer to having obtained solicitors' advice about breaches of patient confidentiality.[392] One example of when it was not practicable to consult is *DP v South Tyneside District Council*.[393] Here the patient was perceived to be at risk from the NR (forced marriage/death) and consultation was not

386 It has since been found in *Re S-C (Mental Patient: Habeas Corpus)* [1996] 1 All ER 532 (CA), that where a patient's application is based on the jurisdiction of the decision-maker rather than on the administrative decision itself, an application for habeas corpus is the appropriate remedy rather than JR.

387 P Lepping, 'Ethical Analysis of the New Proposed Mental Health Legislation in England and Wales' (2007) 2 Philosophy, Ethics, and Humanities in Medicine 5.

388 See, eg, A Maden, 'England's new Mental Health Act Represents Law Catching up with Science: A Commentary on Peter Lepping's Ethical Analysis of the New Mental Health Legislation in England and Wales' (2007) 2 Philosophy, Ethics, and Humanities in Medicine 16. See also 'Treating Violence', in A Maden, *A Guide to Risk Management in Mental Health* (Oxford University Press 2007) 1.

389 This occurred most recently in the case of *Kay v Gueli and another* [2009] All ER (D) 128 (Oct). The NR vetoed the patient's admission to hospital under s 3 of the Mental Health Act 1983 partly because she did not accept that the patient had a mental illness and partly because she believed that the patient would cooperate with professionals if treatment were agreed informally. The displacement application was rejected at first instance, but that decision was reversed on appeal.

390 The nearest relative also has the right to be consulted before any application concerning the patient is made by an AMHP (MHA 1983, s 11(3)).

391 (2013) EWHC 1180 (QB), (2013) MHLO 59.

392 In the Court of Appeal decision, *TW v Enfield London Borough Council* [2014] EWCA Civ 362; [2014] WLR (D) 145, it was found that approved social workers should consider whether it is 'reasonably practicable' to consult the 'nearest relative' before making an application to admit a patient, pursuant to sections 3(1) and 13(1) of the Mental Health Act 1983. Section 11(4) of the Act imposed on social workers an obligation to strike a balance between the patient's right under article 5 of the ECHR not to be detained unless it was done by a procedure that was in accordance with the law and the patient's right to a private life under Article 8.

393 (2011) Admin Court 14 July 2011 (unreported).

possible without disclosing the patient's location.[394] In addition, admission can lawfully occur without consultation if consultation would lead to unreasonable delay in the admission of the patient to hospital. The nearest relative therefore plays a central role across the full spectrum of the patient's care yet for the most part, the level of experience and training in psychiatric matters that they have will be extremely limited to the personal relationship shared with the patient.

With the Mental Health Act 2007 came some changes to the nearest relative. Under the 1983 Act, the nearest relative was chosen from a prescribed list of familial relationships beginning with the patient's spouse, through to parents and then children. The list was tightly applied and did not register other 'relationships' which may have resulted in a more informed and appropriately chosen individual to act as nearest relative. The Mental Health Act 2007 sought to respond to this inflexibility by modifying the list to include civil partners as well as same sex partners who live together in the same way as partners in the more 'traditional' sense and opposite sex partners.[395] The role of the nearest relative has not changed with the 2007 Act, but the extension to the list of recognized individuals who may become the patient's nearest relative has offered better opportunities to achieve a good 'fit' with the patient to ensure the patient's welfare is placed at the heart of any decisions. For some patients, contact with spouses, parents, or children may be very limited while stronger relationships with new partners may have developed. It is these newer partners who are likely to have a better sense of the patient's views and wishes; they are also more likely to have a better understanding of the patient's current health and care needs.[396] **11.205**

A criticism commonly levelled at the nearest relative provision was that the nearest relative was automatically appointed under s 26, giving the patient no involvement in the decision. In *JT v United Kingdom*[397] and *R (M) v Secretary of State for Health*,[398] such inflexibility was deemed to be incompatible with Article 8 of the ECHR. The 2007 Act has sought to remedy this partly by expanding the 'list' of relatives (as discussed above), but also, by providing the patient with a means of displacing the nearest relative under s 29.[399] The grounds upon which the nearest relative may now be displaced have been extended to include 'that the nearest relative of the patient is otherwise not a suitable person to act as such'.[400] **11.206**

An application to the county courts under s 29 for displacement of the nearest relative can be made by the patient, any relative of the patient, any other person who lives with the patient or an AMHP acting on behalf of a LSSA.[401] AMHPs need to consider making an application for displacement or appointment if:[402] **11.207**

---

[394] Consulting a NR in the face of clear patient opposition has been considered to be 'unreasonably practicable'; see *R (on the application of E) v Bristol City Council* [2005] All ER (D) 57 (Jan): see paras 11.59–11.64.

[395] *R (on the application of SSG) v Liverpool City Council* (2002) 5 Community Care LR 639; see <http://www.dh.gov.uk/en/Policyandguidance/Healthandsocialcaretopics/Mentalhealth/DH_4077674>.

[396] This relationship must meet the definition of 'partner'—they must have been the partner for at least six months and the relationship will not take precedence where there is a legal spouse or civil partner unless there is evidence of desertion or separation (see Mental Health Act 1983, s 26(1)).

[397] [2000] 1 FLR 909.

[398] [2003] 1 MHLR 88.

[399] This amendment was introduced in the light of the decision of *M v Secretary of State for Health* [2003] EWHC 1094, when the High Court ruled that the Act's provisions concerning the patient's nearest relative breached Article 8 of the European Convention. The fact that a patient has no means of challenging the appointment of a person as nearest relative was in violation of a person's right to respect for their private life. See also *JT v UK* [2000] 1 FLR 909.

[400] Mental Health Act 1983, s 29(3)(e).

[401] The Civil Procedure Rules and the associated Practice Directions govern the procedures which are to be followed in relation to applications to the court in respect of nearest relatives.

[402] See further *Code of Practice*, ch 8; *Code of Practice for Wales*, ch 23.

(a) they believe that a patient should be detained in hospital under s 3 or should become a guardianship patient, but the nearest relative unreasonably objects[403] (s 29(3)(c)); or
(b) they believe that the nearest relative is likely to discharge the patient from detention or guardianship unwisely (s 29(3)(d)).

11.208 AMHPs should also consider doing so if:
(a) the patient has no identifiable nearest relative or it is not reasonably practicable to identify who the nearest relative is (s 29(3)(a)); or
(b) the patient's nearest relative is incapable of acting as such (s 29(3)(b)); or
(c) they have good reasons to think that a patient considers their nearest relative is 'unsuitable' and would like them to be replaced (s 29(3)(e)).

11.209 Applying to displace the nearest relative should be perceived by AMHPs as a last resort[404] as the Code of Practice states that, before making an application for displacement, AMHPs should consider other ways of achieving the same end. This includes whether the nearest relative will agree to delegate the role to someone else, or providing/arranging support for the patient to make an application for themselves, which could include support from an independent mental health advocate.[405]

11.210 The last ground of 'unsuitability' in s 29(3)(e) was introduced by the 2007 Act. Very little guidance is provided in the Code as to precisely what 'unsuitable' means or amounts to for the purposes of the Act. This issue is ultimately one for the courts to determine.[406] However, the Code does helpfully list certain factors that AMHPs should take into account when deciding whether to make an application to displace on the grounds of unsuitability. The list is not exhaustive, but could include whether the patient has suffered/is suspected of suffering abuse at the hands of the nearest relative or is at risk of suffering such abuse;[407] whether there is any evidence that the patient is afraid of/seriously distressed by the nearest relative being involved; and where there is a distant or non-existent relationship between the patient and nearest relative or their relationship has broken down irretrievably.[408] Commentators have argued that 'thorough consideration' is needed as to what is meant by 'damage' to the patient's health and well-being as well as ineffective relationships.[409] Rapaport and Manthorpe also argue that the 'patient's

---

403 The test for unreasonable objection was established in *W v L* [1974] QB 711, where the court held that it is to be determined on an objective basis.

404 This is largely because the process of removing a nearest relative can be very lengthy. In the case of *R (on the Application of M) v Homerton University Hospital* [2008] EWCA Civ. 197, an interim application was granted removing the patient's mother as nearest relative in July 2007. At the time of judgment in this case, the hearing to displace the mother had still not taken place. Patients who lack capacity to instruct a solicitor have no readily available advocate who can petition the hospital managers or a mental health review tribunal for their discharge. The Court of Appeal has suggested that this is in breach of Article 5(4) ECHR: *R (on the application of MH) v Secretary of State for Health and others* [2004] EWCA Civ. 1609. In this case the patient was detained in excess of seven months under s 2 pending determination of the application to displace her nearest relative. On appeal, [2005] UKHL 60, the House of Lords did not endorse this ruling and held that the absence of a nearest relative in such circumstances was not in breach of ECHR law.

405 *Code of Practice*, para 8.15.

406 ibid, para 8.13.

407 See *Kay v Gueli and another* [2009] All ER (D) 128 (Oct).

408 *Code of Practice*, para 8.13.

409 J Rapaport and J Manthorpe, 'Family Matters: Developments Concerning the Role of the Nearest Relative and Social Worker under Mental Health Law in England and Wales' (2008) 38 British Journal of Social Work 1115–31, 1127.

social, economic and care context' is central to the overall assessment of an individual's well-being and an ability to listen to all concerned is essential for the right action to be taken.[410] It is therefore incumbent on LSSAs to provide clear practical guidance to help AMHPs decide whether to make an application and LSSAs should consult the county court and ensure that they have access to the necessary legal advice and support.[411] One would hope that this difficult aspect of the role would feature prominently in the initial AMHP training and refresher courses, particularly over time as expertise and a body of case law under the Act builds up.

The right to apply for displacement of the nearest relative on the grounds of unsuitability extends beyond the patient—the legislation now enables the patient's RC and AMHPs to apply also. Where the nearest relative is displaced, the court can now appoint an acting nearest relative for an indefinite period.[412] **11.211**

What these amendments have brought is the scope for the patient to have greater involvement in the choices made about their own care. The amendments also provide a more robust framework to restrict the involvement of individuals who might act as the patient's nearest relative yet are inappropriate for the role. **11.212**

(ii) Independent mental health advocates (IMHAs)

IMHAs[413] are specialist advocates who are trained to work within the framework of the legislation to assist in meeting the needs of patients. IMHAs offer an important social policy tool. Many charities have established advocacy services for people with mental health problems, in order to support them and represent their wishes and feelings in circumstances where users might find it difficult to do this alone. The 2007 Act introduced a duty on the Secretary of State (or Welsh Assembly) to provide advocacy services for certain groups of detained patients, guardianship patients, and patients subject to supervised community treatment.[414] A duty also exists for service providers to provide qualifying patients with information that advocacy services are available—for patients on guardianship this is likely to be channelled through the AMHP and it will be the responsibility of the hospital managers for patients liable to be detained.[415] Under s 130D of the 1983 Act, AMHPs will have a duty to take whatever steps are practicable to ensure patients understand that help is available to them from IMHAs and how they can obtain that help. This must include giving the relevant information both orally and in writing.[416] IMHAs will have a duty to visit and interview a patient if requested to do so by an AMHP, the patient's nearest relative or responsible clinician.[417] IMHAs will also have the right to interview professionals and look at records, provided it is for the purpose of supporting the patient.[418] The function of IMHAs is overwhelmingly one of facilitation—ensuring the patient is informed about what is going on, their rights and what steps they can take.[419] The duty to provide advocacy services under section 130 applies to detained patients held under longer-term sections (ie those detained in excess of seventy-two hours) as well as for patients subject to guardianship and supervised community treatment orders. Therefore, such services cannot **11.213**

[410] ibid.
[411] *Code of Practice*, para 8.16.
[412] See Mental Health Act 1983, s 30(4B).
[413] These advocacy services were introduced on 1 April 2009.
[414] See further Mental Health Act 1983, ss 130A–130D.
[415] Department of Health, *Reference Guide to the Mental Health Act 1983* (TSO 2008) Table 34.2.
[416] ibid, para 34.20.
[417] Mental Health Act 1983, s 130B(5).
[418] ibid, s 130B(3) and (4).
[419] See ibid, s 130B generally for IMHA functions.

be applied as of right to those to those individuals it is proposed should be admitted to hospital.

11.214 Although non-statutory advocacy services have been available for a while, they have not been monitored and there are national variations in quality and quantity. IMHA services were introduced to complement and work with non-statutory mental health advocacy services, however because of this lack of national coverage and consistency in service provision, the advocacy provision continues to remain patchy with varying levels of guidance, training and capacity available. The Care Quality Commission has commented on this variability and highlighted a number of recurring issues with IMHA provision in recent annual monitoring reports, and the IMHA implementation project has been launched in an attempt to address the gaps in provision.[420]

11.215 A patient will be deemed a 'qualifying patient' and therefore, eligible for support if s/he:

(1) is detained under the MHA (even if they are currently on leave of absence from hospital) apart from those patients detained under ss 4, 5(2), 5(4), 135, or 136;
(2) is a conditionally discharged restricted patient;
(3) is subject to guardianship under the Act; or
(4) is on Supervised Community Treatment (SCT).

11.216 As well as the above, a patient will also be deemed a 'qualifying patient' if s/he is:

(1) being considered for a treatment to which s 57 applies ('a s 57 treatment');
(2) under 18 and being considered for electro-convulsive therapy or any other treatment to which s 58A applies ('a s 58A treatment').[421]

11.217 IMHAs are sought from a variety of sources, but IMHAs will usually have previous qualities and skills that they can bring to the role in order to aid patients. The IMHA regulations state that a person who might be appointed as an IMHA must:[422] have appropriate training or experience or a combination of both; be a person of integrity and good character; be able to act independently of any person who requests an IMHA to visit and interview the patient; be able to act independently of any person who is professionally concerned with a patient's medical treatment; and, in determining if a person is of integrity and of good character, they must have undergone an enhanced Criminal Records Bureau check or, if an enhanced certificate is not required, a Criminal Records Bureau check.[423]

(iii) Children

11.218 The recognition that children should have specially tailored services to meet their particular needs has been present for some time. Indeed, Specialist Child and Adolescent Mental Health Services (CAMHS) are designed to treat and care for children and young people suffering from mental disorder.[424] Yet, ensuring that these needs are fully met has not always

[420] See, eg, ***Monitoring the Mental Health Act in 2013/14*** (TSO 2015) 37, 40–41: typical examples included lack of information on the ward about the IMHA service; lack of awareness of IMHA service; no access to the IMHA service, especially for incapacitated patients and those on a CTO; complaints about the advocate/services; and *Monitoring the Mental Health Act in 2011/12* (2013), 26–27. See also a report on IMHA services by the University of Central Lancashire: K Newbigging et al, *The Right to be Heard: Review of the Quality of Independent Mental Health Advocate Services in England* (June 2012).

[421] See Mental Health Act 1983, s 130C(3).

[422] Mental Health Act 1983 (Independent Mental Health Advocates) (England) Regulations 2008, SI 2008/3166.

[423] ibid, reg 6.

[424] Department of Education and Department of Health, *The Mental Health and Psychological Well-Being of Children and Young People, 2004* (Standard 9 of the National Service Framework for Children and Maternity Services, 2007).

been easy particularly in relation to accommodation where children and young people have needed hospital-based care. In a recent report by NHS England, it was found that the number of NHS-funded child and adolescent mental health services beds increased from 844 in 1999 to 1,128 in 2006, rising further to 1,264 in January 2014. However, shortages were found in the South West and areas such as Yorkshire and Humber, resulting in patients being admitted to services a long way from home.[425]

Several amendments were introduced by the Mental Health Act 2007 to respond to inadequacies within previous provision and to introduce additional safeguards. **11.219**

(a) **Informal admission to hospital** Where a child is 16 or 17 and has mental capacity, they may (as before the 2007 Act) consent to be informally admitted into hospital even where an individual(s) with parental responsibility objects. However, since the 2007 Act, a child with capacity and who does not consent to admission informally to hospital, cannot be so admitted on the basis of consent given by an individual(s) with parental responsibility.[426] Where the child lacks capacity, however, a person with parental responsibility can still consent to the informal admission of the child. **11.220**

(b) **The provision of a suitable environment** The hospital accommodation that children and young people were often provided with in the past was little different from that of adult patients. Indeed, there has been a long-standing debate about the impact of a child's environment on his/her mental health and whether inadequate provision as part of their mental health care may have a negative effect.[427] The Mental Health Act Commission voiced concerns in its biennial reports about the treatment of children and adolescents under the MHA within adult mental health facilities. In its twelfth report, it stated: **11.221**

> ... between October 2004 and November 2006, the Mental Health Act Commission encountered 116 adult wards where one or two children under the age of 18 were detained. In all, 132 children were accommodated in such situations. Eighteen of these wards were psychiatric intensive care units where the most disturbed and dangerous adults are treated.[428]

The concern that children and young people are exposed to abuse in these environments and face intimidation was thought to compromise obligations under Article 3 of the ECHR as such adult wards made it difficult for children to be protected from abuse and the risk of abuse. The Parliamentary Joint Committee on Human Rights recommended an amendment, which would ensure children and young people received age-appropriate assessments and placements. Appropriate accommodation is part of this ideal but the Joint Committee also recognized that given the state of provision and the demands placed on the service, that there would undoubtedly be times when a child or young person's needs could only be met with adult services.

Section 31 of the 2007 Act introduces s 131A, which requires hospital managers to ensure that the patient's environment is suitable having regard to his/her age and subject to his/her **11.222**

---

[425] NHS England, *Child and Adolescent Mental Health Services (CAMHS) Tier 4 Report*, July 2014, available at: <http://www.england.nhs.uk/wp-content/uploads/2014/07/camhs-tier-4-rep.pdf> (accessed 22 February 2015).

[426] Mental Health Act 2007, new s 131(2)–(5).

[427] Office of the Children's Commissioner, *Pushed into the Shadows: Young People's Experience of Adult Mental Health Facilities* (January 2007). See also Department of Health, *Improving the patient experience: Sharing success in mental health and learning disabilities* (The King's Fund's Enhancing the Healing Environment programme) (TSO 2008).

[428] Mental Health Act Commission, *Risk, rights, recovery: the Mental Health Act Commission twelfth biennial report 2005–2007* (TSO January 2008).

needs.[429] The government has made a commitment to commence this provision in England by April 2010.[430] To meet this duty, managers will have to provide appropriate physical facilities; staff with appropriate training; and a hospital routine that will allow their personal, social, and educational development to continue as normally as possible.[431] Depending on the nature of the child's difficulties, different demands may well be placed on the environment. For example, a young patient with anorexia may be facing six months in hospital and will need access to educational facilities. This need should be factored into the needs assessment. Likewise, the accommodation would have to be suitable so that family relations could be more easily maintained with such long periods of separation. However, despite this, there may be occasions where a child's need for a secure and safe environment in which to be cared for and treated becomes more important than ensuring the accommodation is suitable for the child's age. If appropriate accommodation is not available immediately but the child has an immediate need of care and/or treatment, this need will take precedence. The Code of Practice states that in such circumstances:

> . . . the patient's need to be accommodated in a safe environment could, in the short term, take precedence over the suitability of that environment for their age. Furthermore, it is also important to recognise that there is a clear difference between what is a suitable environment for a child or young person in an emergency situation and what is a suitable environment for a child or young person on a longer-term basis. In an emergency, such as when the patient is in crisis, the important thing is that the patient is in a safe environment. Once the initial emergency situation is over, hospital managers, in determining whether the environment continues to be suitable, would need to consider issues such as whether the patient can mix with individuals of their own age, can receive visitors of all ages and has access to education. Hospital managers have a duty to consider whether a patient should be transferred . . . as soon as possible.[432]

11.223 The Mental Health Act Commission in its penultimate Biennial Report[433] suggested that a doctor with specific child and adolescent mental health training should always be involved, even if only in a consultative role, in the care of any detained child or adolescent patient. Although there is no legal requirement for this, but is seen as best practice and one supported by the Royal College of Psychiatrists.[434]

11.224 Within this broader duty to ensure that children and young people are provided with appropriate accommodation, a series of other duties are included and are focused particularly around notification responsibilities. Section 140 of the Mental Health Act 1983 (Section 31 of the MHA 2007) places a duty on NHS bodies to provide sufficient detail to LSSAs of hospitals/facilities in the region that are suitable to enable children and young people to be admitted for emergency care and that offer the necessary environment to meet the needs of this patient group. Where a child or young person is being considered by a criminal court for a hospital order under s 37, remand under ss 35 or 36 or a committal under s 44 of the 1983 Act, the 2007 Act introduces a power of information request from the court about the availability of accommodation or facilities that could meet the needs of the child or

[429] See s 131A(2). This amendment aims at supporting Standard 9 (National Service Framework for Children Young People and Maternity Services: The Mental Health and Psychological Well-being of Children and Young People) of the *National Service Framework for Children and Maternity Services*, 2007.

[430] 'Government invests £31m in children and young peoples' psychiatric wards', Department of Health Press Release (14 November 2007).

[431] Rosie Winterton MP, Minister of State, HC Debs, 18 Jun 2007, col 1144.

[432] *Code of Practice*, para 36.71.

[433] MHAC, *Risk, Rights, Recovery; Twelfth Biennial Report 2005–2007* (2008) para 3.61, rec 21.

[434] Royal College of Psychiatrists, *Safe and Appropriate Care for Young People on Adult Mental Health Wards* (RCP 2009).

young person in question.[435] It is anticipated that by placing duties upon PCTs and LSSAs to notify and/or respond to information requests concerning children's secure facilities, that more resources will be ploughed into this areas of provision so that, combined with the duty to offer appropriate accommodation for children and young people, more facilities will ultimately be available. Special accommodation should become the norm rather than the exception.[436]

(c) Treatment To treat children or young people under the 2007 Act a divide is drawn between hospital-based and community treatment. If a child or young person has been detained in hospital and is subject to Pt 4 of the Act, then treatment may be authorized under s 63 though it will be subject to the safeguards found in ss 57–58A (see paras 11.138–11.148). Children and young people may also be subject to emergency treatment as governed by s 62. The question of capacity/competence is now relevant as with adults. It remains the case that a child who lacks capacity cannot be administered treatments covered by s 57 and for ECT (now governed by s 58A), if the child or young person is capable and refuses that treatment.[437] If the child or young person lacks the necessary competence, then if the RC and SOAD believe that ECT is an appropriate treatment avenue to follow, the treatment may still be given. **11.225**

For children and young people who are community patients and are subject to SCT, treatment may be given to 16- and 17-year-olds if there is the appropriate authority to treat and if the certification requirement is met. Treatment may be given if the patient provides consent. Treatment may also be given when the patient does not consent and if force is not necessary. The patient must lack the necessary capacity, the treatment is 'immediately necessary' and such treatment does not conflict with an advance direction or previous decision of a Court of Protection, health care authority, or deputy. For children under the age of 16 who are community patients, s 64E states that treatment may not be given unless there is authority to give it. Such authority exists if the patient is competent and does consent or if s 64F authorizes it (this covers treatment authorized for patients lacking competence) or the treatment is emergency treatment under s 64G. **11.226**

(iv) Monitoring the MHA and mental health care

The MHAC was established alongside the Mental Health Act 1983[438] to monitor, on behalf of the Secretary of State, the operation of the Act in respect of patients detained in hospital. Its role was focused on safeguarding people who are detained in hospital under the powers of the Mental Health Act 1983. The Commission was introduced as a monitoring body rather than one with regulatory or inspectorate powers. It was primarily concerned with the legality of detention decisions and the protection of individuals' human rights. The Mental Health Act 1983 gave power to the MHAC to visit and interview detained patients **11.227**

[435] Mental Health Act 2007, s 39 (1A) and (1B).

[436] Children Act 1989, ss 85 and 86 provide a duty that where a child or young person is accommodated for three months or more by any Health Authority, NHS Trust, Local Education Authority, independent hospital, or residential care home, the proprietors/body of the facility must notify the appropriate local authority. The local authority is then placed under a duty to ensure the child's welfare is safeguarded; see also *HM Government Statutory Guidance on making Arrangements to Safeguard and Promote the Welfare of Children under section 11 of the Children Act 2004*. Section 11 of the Children Act 2004 requires that all NHS bodies and contracted service providers carry out their functions having regard for the need to safeguard and promote the welfare of the child at all times.

[437] Following the 2007 Act, a distinction has now been drawn between competence and capacity. For children over the age of 16, the test of capacity is used; for under 16s the test is competence. How these two concepts will operate in practice remains to be seen.

[438] See *The Report of the Review of Rampton Hospital* (Cmnd 8073, 1980), which recommended the establishment of such a commission.

in hospital and patients in the community who were subject to a community treatment order. Its work involved the deployment of its independent Commissioners to carry out frequent, short notice, and often unannounced visits to all NHS and independent hospitals and care homes in England and Wales where patients may be detained, to check the legality of detention and to interview patients in private to ascertain whether they are being treated appropriately and within the law. In addition to its visiting programme, it also provided important safeguards to patients who lacked capacity or refused consent to treatment, through the Second Opinion Appointed Doctor Service.[439] Furthermore, the 1983 Act gave the Commission the power to investigate complaints, a duty to administer the Second Opinion Appointed Doctor system that considers the authorization of certain treatments and assist with the production and revision of the Code of Practice.[440] The MHAC was also charged with producing a biennial report which was laid before Parliament; this reported on the MHAC's monitoring programme and its findings. Since the Commission's inception, the reports have provided an authoritative narrative on many matters such as human rights, safe care, and the experience of patients subject to detention (particularly women and children). All the above responsibilities, including the publication of biennial reports, have acted as a means of regular scrutiny and sought to ensure continued and robust checks on the commitment procedures governed by the Mental Health Act. As noted by the Care Quality Commission,[441] the MHAC has 'used its knowledge and expertise to comment on wider issues that have affected the care and treatment experienced by detained patients', such as the balance between hospital and community services, the effective application of the care programme approach in ensuring that patients have individualized care plans, and the question of inequalities around accessing treatment, such as the accessibility of psychological therapies.

11.228 The MHAC ceased to exist in 2009.[442] Its functions are now carried out by the Care Quality Commission (CQC), which act as the health and social care watchdog for England and is a single regulator. Following the changeover, the CQC developed a five-year strategy for the regulation of mental health services, including community care and specialist care. A new vision and direction for the Care Quality was set out in a new strategy for 2013–2016, *Raising standards, putting people first*, to consider new and more radical ways of regulating health and social care services. For mental health monitoring,[443] new priorities have been set for improving how the CQC monitors, inspects, and regulates specialist mental health services. The CQC acknowledge that mental health provision offers particular challenges given that detained mental health patients are the only people who can be treated against their will. The CQC has a critical role to play in using both its regulatory and monitoring

439 From November 2008, the Mental Health Act Commission's remit was extended to include patients subject to the new community treatment orders.

440 'Having access to an expert, independent visiting body is an essential safeguard and source of reassurance to people who are detained or deprived of their liberty': Care Quality Commission briefing, *The Mental Health Act Commission's biennial report 2007–2009—Key lessons and the Care Quality Commission's response* (20 July 2009) 2. Under the *Optional Protocol to the UN Convention against Torture*, the UK Government has made a positive commitment to ensuring that there is unrestricted access to, and independent monitoring of, all those citizens deprived of their liberty, whether in prisons, psychiatric hospitals, care homes, or other settings: see United Nations, *Optional Protocol to the Convention against Torture and other Cruel, Inhuman or Degrading Treatment or Punishmen*t (UN December 2002).

441 Care Quality Commission briefing, *The Mental Health Act Commission's biennial report 2007–2009—Key lessons and the Care Quality Commission's response* (20 July 2009) 3.

442 The cessation of the Commission took place on 31 March 2009.

443 Care Quality Commission, *A fresh start for the regulation and inspection of mental health services: Working together to change how we regulate, inspect, and monitor specialist mental health services* (TSO 2013).

roles to protect patients' rights and interests, although the extent to which it is successfully achieving these aims in relation to mental health care has been questioned.[444]

The functions of the CQC are the same as they were under the Mental Health Act Commission. When the CQC was introduced, it was anticipated that the new, fully integrated reviewing body would enable better joined-up thinking and implementation of provision within health and social care. Since the Mental Health Act 2007, the functions of the Commission have been expanded to include: the extension of the SOADs functions in relation to community patients under SCT; the extension of the SOADs function in relation to informal child patients under s 58A; the requirement of RCs to furnish a report to the Commission under s 61 to be extended to include patients receiving treatment under ss 62A and 58A; the Commission's function in relation to the withdrawal of SOAD certificates issued under Pt 4 is now also expanded to include certificates issued under s 58A and SOAD certificates issued in respect of community patients on SCT; and, the Commission's functions in relation to the visiting of patients and the investigation of complaints have been extended to now include community patients on SCT. **11.229**

D. Conclusion

For the last thirty years many mental health professionals, patients, and lawyers have witnessed at first hand the impact of legal rules that have not always been fit for purpose. Changes in psychiatric practices have meant that the focus of care has radically altered—moving from hospital-based care to community-centred support and the mental health legislation has often struggled to maintain its usefulness in this changing care context. The difficulty of successfully marrying up both law and clinical practice has been recognized for decades and various attempts to reform the law in line with clinical changes have been made, culminating with the Mental Health Act 2007. Yet, the road to reform has been far from easy, with several false starts and the introduction of well intentioned, though toothless provisions, such as supervised discharge under the ill-fated Mental Health (Patients in the Community) Act 1995, included along the way. **11.230**

When the 2007 Act arrived on the statute books, it prompted a mixed response from those variously connected to the mental health system. For some, the nature of the Act as an amending piece of legislation which sought to update and introduce new provisions to meet recognized areas of need, did not offer the root and branch reform that was seen to be so necessary. For others, the 2007 Act represented a shift towards a risk-focused agenda where patient rights (originally of key importance in the 1983 Act) were trumped by a media-fuelled fear that the mentally disordered presented a significant risk to others. **11.231**

The 2007 Act's key changes to the 1983 Act offered both providers and users of mental health services some much-needed benefits. Some changes have been particularly positive in relation to children and young people and through the introduction of Independent Mental Health Advocacy. Also, the commitment procedures have been simplified, largely by changing the definition of mental disorder to allow for a much wider interpretation, thereby accommodating groups that historically were outside the ambit of the 1983 Act. In addition, the inclusion of Supervised Community Treatment was introduced to respond to the needs of patients with frequent rates of admission and discharge who fail to thrive in the community. However, areas for concern continue to exist with a continuing rise in **11.232**

444 See, eg, J M Laing, 'Perspectives on Monitoring Mental Health Legislation in England: A view from the front-line' (2015) 23(3) *Medical Law Review* 400-426.

the number of people under compulsion,[445] with more people being subject to community treatment orders but with fewer people being discharged, and black and ethnic minorities being over represented in patient cohorts. Extreme variations in implementation and resourcing is also problematic across the country.

11.233 The 2007 Act sought to strike a balance between the perceived need to loosen the restrictions and complexities which beset the 1983 Act and those working within it while also recognizing that patients need to have increased involvement in their care and to receive greater levels of information about their position and status. As anticipated in the previous edition of this book, many of the problems anticipated with the Mental Health Act 2007 have revolved around the practical implementation and available resourcing of these new systems. The presence of IMHAs on wards has proven to be beneficial, although the Care Quality Commission is still concerned about the availability and quality of some IMHA provision. The rise in patients drawing up advance statements of their preferences for care and treatment has also risen.[446] However, the Care Quality Commission has also noted that the involvement of patients in their own care planning needs improvement with 27 per cent of care plans showing no evidence of patients being actively involved.[447]

11.234 With the Mental Health Act 2007 operational since 2008, the changes introduced have had some time to bed in and become established into daily practice. Some of the changes which were perceived as impossible to implement have proven highly successful. The introduction of IMHAs was welcomed but there was understandably concern that it would not be possible to train and recruit enough IMHAs to meet the needs of patients. The CQC has noted in recent Mental Health Act monitoring reports that a strong IMHA presence exists within the wards and is making a positive difference to the lives of some detained patients, although there is still much room for improvement. The hopes surrounding other changes, such as CTOs to reduce the number of revolving door patients have been less successful, with detention figures continuing to rise. Indeed, the publication of the OCTET study in 2013 offered a rather bleak evaluation of the effectiveness of CTOs.[448] In addition, the introduction of automatic case reviews by the tribunal was an essential step towards improving the commitment process and consequently, the lives of many detained patients. However, for it to be successful there must be sufficient tribunal judges to sit and review the cases, as the number of reviews increases. Similarly, the opportunities offered by the extensions to professional roles in the 2007 Act have still not been fully harnessed. The Mental Health Act 2007 had its supporters and its opponents, but its longer term success will depend upon how well the changes are supported financially by the government and embraced by those working within the confines of the legislation. The 2007 Act is more easily tolerated by those involved if accompanied by the recognition that legislative changes alone will never be sufficient.

[445] In 2012–13, 27 per cent of recorded outcomes of section 2 detentions showed that the patient continued to be detained, a rise of 3 per cent from the previous year. CTOs since they were introduced in 2008 were used 18,942 times by 31 March 2013 (see CQC, *Monitoring the Mental Health Act in 2012/13* (TSO 2014) 13.

[446] CQC, *Monitoring the Mental Health Act in 2012/13*, (TSO 2014) 3.

[447] ibid, 3.

[448] T Burns and A Molodynski, 'Community treatment orders: background and implications of the OCTET trial' (2014) 38(1) *Psychiatr Bull* 3.

12

CONFIDENTIALITY AND DATA PROTECTION

Mark Taylor

A. Introduction

Any consultation with a patient will result in the doctor (or other health professional) collecting information personal to the patient. It is essential that a patient is able to make a full and frank disclosure to ensure that any medical recommendations take account of all relevant matters. This inevitably means that health professionals will be privy to much that the patient will regard as private and expect to be treated as such. Failure to fulfil those expectations is likely to embarrass, offend, stigmatize, and ultimately deter the patient from disclosing the information or even seeking medical advice in the first place. The private and public interests at stake are too important to leave unaddressed by the law. **12.01**

This chapter considers, first, the manner in which the law regulates the use that the doctor or other health professional may make of the patient's private and confidential information, and the circumstances in which it is lawful to disclose that information to anyone other than the patient. **12.02**

A second issue concerns the extent to which a doctor or other health professional can control information that is collected and recorded in the course of the doctor–patient relationship. A patient's medical record will almost always include information beyond that which the patient has disclosed to the doctor. Much of this information may be sensitive and the health professionals who have contributed to the medical record over the years may be unwilling to disclose their own notes. To what extent do health professionals control access to the patient record by the patient, the patient's advisers, or third parties? **12.03**

This chapter therefore investigates two separate questions: **12.04**

(1) When does the law allow a health professional to disclose information that is personal to the patient?
(2) When does the law require a health professional to disclose information that has been generated through the provision of a patient's medical treatment?

In the process of investigating these questions, this chapter will also consider how the law reconciles the different private and public interests at stake.

B. Confidentiality and Privacy

1. Common law

(i) Basis

12.05 The obligation to protect patients' confidential and private information has a well-recognized ethical basis. The non-absolute duty of confidence has long been regarded as one of the most fundamental ethical principles of medical practice. The Hippocratic Oath states:

> Whatsoever things I see or hear concerning the life of men, in my attendance on the sick or even apart from there from, which ought not to be noised abroad, I will keep silence thereon counting such things to be as sacred as secrets.

This is restated and reaffirmed in the Declaration of Geneva: 'I will respect the secrets which are confided in me, even after the patient has died.' Furthermore, the duty is expressly recognized in the professional codes of conduct and official guidance that are provided to all members of the health professions and NHS staff.[1]

12.06 While ethical duties do not automatically translate into legal duties, the common law has long recognized a *legal obligation* of confidence rooted in equity and protected in the public interest. In *Attorney-General v Guardian Newspapers (No 2)* (the *Spycatcher* case), Lord Griffiths noted that the jurisdiction in confidence rests on the 'the public interest in upholding the right to confidence, which is based on the moral principles of loyalty and fair dealing'.[2] Lord Goff stated that 'the basis of the law's protection of confidence is that there is a public interest that confidences should be preserved and protected by the law'.[3]

12.07 More recently the obligation of confidence has been developed to take account of the European Convention on Human Rights (ECHR), as given domestic effect by the Human Rights Act 1998 (HRA 1998). In *Campbell v Mirror Group Newspapers*,[4] the House of Lords held that the common law action was to be interpreted in line with Article 8 ECHR.[5] The action for 'breach of confidence' was held to protect not only confidential information, but also the informational privacy of individuals. The protection offered by the law has been subsequently transformed and extended to a point where the courts have considered the

[1] See General Medical Council (GMC), *Good Medical Practice* (2013), para 50; GMC, *Confidentiality* (2009); Department of Health, *Confidentiality: NHS Code of Practice* (2003); Nursing & Midwifery Council (NMC), *The Code: Standards of Conduct, Performance and Ethics for Nurses and Midwives* (2015), 6; GDC (General Dental Council), *Standards for the Dental Team* (2013), 35–43; Health and Social Care Information Centre, *A Guide to confidentiality in health and social care,* (2013); *The NHS Constitution for England* (2013), 8; *Care Record Guarantee* (2011).

[2] *Attorney-General v Guardian Newspapers (No 2)* [1990] 1 AC 109, 269.

[3] ibid, 282.

[4] *Campbell v Mirror Group Newspapers* [2004] UKHL 22, [2004] 2 AC 457, 466. See also *A v B Plc and Another* [2002] EWCA Civ 337; [2003] QB 195, 203.

[5] This case is discussed throughout this chapter: see esp paras 12.20 and 12.61.

protection to be better characterized, at least in some circumstances, as a *tort* of misuse of private information. Lord Nicholls advanced the view that the tort itself should be renamed:

> The continuing use of the phrase 'duty of confidence' and the description of the information as 'confidential' is not altogether comfortable. Information about an individual's private life would not, in ordinary usage, be called 'confidential'. The more natural description today is that such information is private. The essence of the tort is better encapsulated now as misuse of private information.[6]

It would appear to remain appropriate, however, to continue to refer to the common law duty of confidence in circumstances where the information would, in ordinary usage, be called 'confidential information' and there would be nothing strained about recognizing a 'duty of confidence': namely, in circumstances where the phrases have traditionally been applied. Indeed, there is a developing view that the action for breach of confidence now encompasses two related causes of action: one protecting confidentiality as traditionally understood and the other protecting privacy.[7] Support for this view is expressed in the speech of Lord Nicholls in *OBJ Ltd v Allan* [2008]: **12.08**

> As the law has developed breach of confidence, or misuse of confidential information, now covers two distinct causes of action, protecting two different interests: privacy, and secret ('confidential') information. It is important to keep these two distinct. In some instances information may qualify for protection both on grounds of privacy and confidentiality. In other instances information may be in the public domain, and not qualify for protection as confidential, and yet qualify for protection on the grounds of privacy . . . Conversely, and obviously, a trade secret may be protected as confidential information even though no question of personal privacy is involved.[8]

There may be a number of advantages to retaining 'a role for 'traditional' breach of confidence alongside a claim for 'extended' breach of confidence or misuse of private information.'[9] One of these is that it may help to clarify the jurisdictional basis of the relevant cause of action. Although the historical roots of an action for breach of confidence lay in equity, in a number of cases 'breach of confidence has been treated as being analogous to a tort'.[10] This has led to query regarding the proper understanding of its jurisdictional basis. *Vidal-Hall and Others* v *Google* [2014] 1 WLR 4155 clarified that although the common law duty of confidence is based in equity and does *not* give rise to an action in tort[11] there *is* an associated tort in the misuse of private information. While, the full consequences of the move to recognize two distinct causes of action are not yet settled, the remainder of this chapter will continue to focus upon the possibilities of a breach of confidence with reference to the tort of misuse of information only where it seems relevant. **12.09**

---

6 *Campbell v Mirror Group*, n 4, [14]. While technically a dissenting judgment (as Lord Nicholls and Lord Hoffman were in the minority) Lady Justice Sharp opined in *Google* v *Vidal-Hall* [2015] EWCA Civ 311 that in this developing area of law the 'speech of Lord Nicholls in *Campbell* has been highly influential' [22] and 'the difference of opinion related to a narrow point arising out of the facts of the case' [22]. See also *McKennitt v Ash* [2006] EWCA Civ 1714, [8] *per* Buxton LJ.

7 T Aplin, 'The Relationship between Breach of Confidence and the "Tort of Misuse of Private Information"' [2007] Kings Law Journal 329–36.

8 [2007] UKHL 21, [2008] 1 AC 1 [255].

9 See Aplin, n 7, 334.

10 *Vestergaard* [2010] FSR 29 [19]. See also, PM North, 'Breach of Confidence: Is There a New Tort' [1972] 12 Journal of Society of Public Teachers of Law 149.

11 See *Kitechnology BV v Unicor GmbH Plastmaschinen* [1995] FSR 765, 777–78.

(ii) Scope

12.10 **(a) General** The action for breach of confidence enables one party who imparts information in confidence to another to obtain relief against the recipient of that information if the latter, without authorization, discloses that information directly or indirectly to a third party. In *Hunter v Mann*, Boreham J considered the question of whether a doctor owed an obligation of confidence to his patients and concluded:

> [I]n common with other professional men . . . the doctor is under a duty not to disclose [voluntarily], without the consent of his patient, information which he, the doctor, has gained in his professional capacity.[12]

12.11 This position was affirmed in subsequent cases and there can now be no question that an obligation of confidence can arise out of the doctor–patient relationship, notwithstanding that the patient may have no contractual or proprietary rights over the information.[13] Where, however, a contractual relationship does exist, the terms of the contract may modify the nature and scope of the obligation of confidence that might otherwise have been owed. A contract that is silent on the matter of confidence will not prevent the recognition of an obligation of confidence.

12.12 English courts have retained great flexibility in interpreting the scope of the doctor's obligation of confidence. First, the obligation is one that is focused upon 'confidential' or 'private' information. Only where the relevant information is confidential or private will the law restrain a doctor from disclosing it. Second, the information must be imparted in particular circumstances. As discussed below, each of these two aspects may increasingly be viewed as part answer to a common question: Would an individual, taking into account all relevant circumstances, have a reasonable expectation of privacy in the information disclosed?

12.13 **(b) Confidential and private information** For some time, English law has imposed an obligation of confidence when the information is 'confidential' *and* has been communicated in particular circumstances.[14] Confidential information includes within its scope all information that has 'the necessary quality of confidence about it, namely, it must not be something which is public property and public knowledge'.[15] Almost any kind of information can therefore be confidential, as long as it is not 'trivial tittle tattle'.[16]

12.14 Once information is in the public domain it will usually cease to be confidential or private. This would only pertain to information communicated in the doctor–patient relationship where any possible disclosure by the doctor would not add anything to that which was already in the public domain. Thus, for example, the fact that the patient had known about her condition for a particular length of time might be confidential notwithstanding that she has disclosed to the public at large that she has the condition. Moreover, it will always be a question of degree whether the information is sufficiently broadly disseminated that it can be said to have lost its confidential character.

12.15 It is also worth noting that in *OBG Ltd v Allan* and *Douglas v Hello!*, Lord Nicholls said, when comparing the circumstances in which the law might now protect 'privacy' as well as 'confidential information', that there may be instances where 'information may be in the

[12] [1974] QB 767, 772. Noted by C Boyle, (1975) 38 MLR 69.

[13] *X v Y* [1988] 2 All ER 648; *W v Egdell* [1990] Ch 359; *Attorney-General v Guardian Newspapers (No 2)* [1990] AC 109, 255 *per* Lord Keith.

[14] *Coco v AN Clark (Engineering)* [1969] RPC 41, 41–48 *per* Megarry J.

[15] *Saltman Engineering Co v Campbell Engineering Co Ltd* (1948) 65 RPC 203, 215. See also *Campbell v MGN* [2004] UKHL 22, esp [92] *per* Lord Hope.

[16] *Coco v AN Clark (Engineers)* [1969] RPC 41, 48 *per* Megarry J.

public domain, and not qualify for protection as confidential, and yet qualify for protection on the grounds of privacy. Privacy can be invaded by further publication of information or photographs already disclosed to the public.'[17] If there is a reasonable expectation of privacy in relation to the information, then the fact that the information has been made public by a third party will not relieve the doctor of any duty of confidence that they owe in relation to it.

In *R (on the application of W, X, Y and Z) v Secretary of State for Health* the High Court offered a relatively restrictive view of what might constitute confidential or private information in the High Court. Mr Justice Silber's view was that the disclosure of specified limited information by NHS Trusts to the Secretary of State for Health, which was then passed to the Home Office for the purposes of imposing an immigration sanction, did not constitute the disclosure of 'confidential or private' information even though that information has been gathered within the context of the doctor patient relationship and was not otherwise in the public domain.[18] The specified limited information contained name and date of birth of the patient and, where available, his or her address, nationality and travel document number with expiry date. The information was disclosed in order to facilitate the administration of an immigration sanction which could be applied in case of certain debts being owed to the NHS. Details about the amount and date of the debt, and the NHS trust to which it was owed, were also included within the specified limited information. **12.16**

Mr Justice Silber was of the opinion that 'the specified limited information transmitted by the NHS bodies falls at the least intrusive end of the spectrum of medical information, because it omits details of the illness or the medical history of the non-resident patient or the treatment administered or the prognosis for that patient'.[19] He concluded that the information was not private or confidential. The Court of Appeal rejected this conclusion. The Court did not: **12.17**

> agree that the fact that the Information was 'at the least intrusive end of the spectrum' indicates that it was not private. The fact that the disclosure may be 'less intrusive' than disclosure of detailed information about an individual's medical condition and treatment does not mean that it is not intrusive at all or that the information is not inherently private. Instead it means that it is likely to be easier to justify disclosure. The conclusion that the Information was not private information at all would be correct only if it were, in privacy terms, entirely trivial which . . . it is not. [20]

The Court of Appeal supported the position taken by professional guidance that all identifiable patient data held by a doctor or a hospital must be treated as confidential. In fact, the Court's position was informed, at least in part, by the fact that this approach *is* taken in *publicly available* professional guidance; which itself can be understood to both reflect and inform the expectations of patients. Indeed, what patients may reasonably expect in the circumstances was of considerable significance to the Court. Despite, supporting an expansive approach to defining private or confidential data in general terms, the Court did *not* consider that in the circumstances of this case that the information disclosed was private vis-à-vis the Secretary of State or the Home Office: **12.18**

> We do not see how overseas visitors who, before they are treated in an NHS hospital, are made aware of the fact that, if they incur charges in excess of £1,000 and do not pay them within 3 months, the Information may be passed to the Secretary of State for onward

[17] [2007] UKHL 21, 255.
[18] *R (on the application of W, X, Y and Z)* [2014] EWHC 1532, (Admin) [46].
[19] ibid, [45].
[20] *R (on the application of W, X, Y and Z)* v *Secretary of State for Health* [2015] EWCA Civ 1034, [34].

transmission to the Home Office for the stated immigration purpose can have any, still less any *reasonable*, expectation that the Information will not be transmitted in precisely that way. They will, however, have a reasonable expectation of privacy in relation to the Information vis-à-vis anyone else.[21]

The Court clearly considered it significant, when determining whether the information was private or confidential, what uses of data an individual could reasonably expect in the circumstances. This suggests a very close relationship between the circumstances of disclosure and characterisation of information as either private or confidential.

12.19 (c) **Requirement for particular 'circumstances'** The requirement that the information be communicated in circumstances of confidence was considered by the House of Lords in the *Spycatcher* case, in which Lord Goff stated:

> a duty of confidence arises when confidential information comes to the knowledge of a person (the confidant) in circumstances where he has notice, or is held to have agreed, that the information is confidential, with the effect that it would be just in all the circumstances that he should be precluded from disclosing the information to others.[22]

This formulation does not require a pre-existing confidential relationship between the parties.[23]

12.20 Although a pre-existing confidential relationship is not required, the courts do appear to consider invasions of privacy to be more serious if they are accompanied by betrayals of trust.[24] In *McKennitt v Ash*, Buxton LJ declared that information about a person's health was clearly private and 'doubly private' when it is imparted in the context of a relationship of confidence.[25] The doctor–patient relationship is one in which it is readily assumed that the information has been communicated in circumstances of confidence (see para 12.10).

12.21 In *Campbell v Mirror Group Newspapers*[26] the House of Lords determined whether an obligation of confidence attached to the information by asking whether the person to whom the information related had 'a reasonable expectation of privacy'.[27] Lord Nicholls, who expressly approved this formulation, also approved that used by Lord Goff in *Spycatcher* and declared:

> Now the law imposes a 'duty of confidence' whenever a person receives information he knows or ought to know is fairly and reasonably to be regarded as confidential.[28]

12.22 His Lordship expressed the view that this alternative formulation was 'awkward', because of its usage of the word 'confidential' to capture 'private information' that would not ordinarily be regarded as confidential. Even with this proviso, these two formulations are potentially incompatible. One turns on the reasonable expectations of the *subject* of the information, whereas the other turns on the actual or inferred knowledge of the *recipient* of the information as to what is fair and reasonable. This incompatibility is, however, more apparent than real. According to Baroness Hale,

21 ibid, [39].

22 *Spycatcher* [1990] 1 AC 109, 281 *per* Lord Goff.

23 ibid.

24 See the discussion in J Loughrey, 'Can You Keep a Secret? Children, Human Rights, and the Law of Medical Confidentiality' (2008) 20 CFLQ 312.

25 [2006] EWCA 1714, [23].

26 *Campbell v Mirror Group Newspapers* [2004] UKHL 22.

27 ibid, [21] *per* Lord Nicholls, [85], [96] *per* Lord Hope, [134] *per* Baroness Hale.

28 ibid, [14].

> The position we have reached is that the exercise of balancing article 8 and article 10 may begin when the person publishing the information knows or ought to know that there is a reasonable expectation that the information in question will be kept confidential.[29]

Thus, a duty of confidence will exist whenever a recipient knows or ought to know that the subject can reasonably expect his or her privacy to be protected. According to Lord Hope, reasonable expectation is determined by reference to 'a person of ordinary sensibilities' in the position of the person to whom the information relates.[30] The circumstances will determine whether a disclosure is consistent with an individual's reasonable expectations: only if a person of ordinary sensibilities could be said to have a reasonable expectation that his or her data will not be disclosed, or not disclosed without authorization, will such disclosure constitute an infringement of privacy. **12.23**

Lord Hope also indicated that the law will readily infer a reasonable expectation where the information is 'obviously private'.[31] Medical information clearly falls into this category. Baroness Hale put it thus: **12.24**

> It has always been accepted that information about a person's health and treatment for ill-health is both private and confidential. This stems not only from the confidentiality of the doctor–patient relationship but from the nature of the information itself.[32]

Her Ladyship specifically referred to the decision of the European Court of Human Rights (ECtHR) in *Z v Finland,*[33] a case concerned with the disclosure of a woman's medical records (revealing her HIV status) during the trial of her husband for the sexual assault and attempted manslaughter of other women. The Strasbourg court specifically addressed the applicability of Article 8 ECHR in the context of medical confidentiality: **12.25**

> Respecting the confidentiality of health data is a vital principle in the legal systems of all the Contracting Parties to the Convention. It is crucial not only to respect the sense of privacy of a patient but also to preserve his or her confidence in the medical profession and in the health services in general. Without such protection, those in need of medical assistance may be deterred from revealing such information of a personal and intimate nature as may be necessary in order to receive appropriate treatment and, even, from seeking such assistance, thereby endangering their own health and, in the case of transmissible diseases, that of the community.[34]

Even before *Campbell*, it was clear that the obligation of confidence will cover information that the doctor receives from the patient in the course of a professional relationship. Both information that is directly communicated by the patient, and information to which the doctor is privy by reason of his or her position, such as diagnostic test results, would be regarded as confidential. Similarly, information that is communicated to the doctor by a third party who is aware of the doctor's professional relationship with the patient might be subject to an obligation of confidence. **12.26**

The position was less clear where the doctor receives information other than in connection with a professional relationship. This situation could arise either where the patient discusses matters with the doctor for purely social purposes, or where a third party discusses the patient with the doctor, but is unaware of the professional relationship between the doctor **12.27**

[29] ibid, [134].
[30] ibid, [99]. See also *Murray v Express Newspapers* [2008] EWCA Civ 446, [35]–[36].
[31] *Campbell v Mirror Group Newspapers* [2004] UKHL 22, [96].
[32] ibid, [145].
[33] *Z v Finland* (1998) 25 EHRR 371.
[34] ibid, [95].

and that patient. The public interest underpinnings of the action for breach of confidence support a strong argument that any information about a patient that the doctor receives should be subject to an obligation of confidence in order to maintain the essential relationship of trust upon which the effective provision of medical treatment depends. This is a view reflected in the Hippocratic Oath, as quoted above, and now reflects the legal position in so far as a person in the patient's position could reasonably consider such information to be private.

12.28 The conventional view is that the obligation of confidence is owed exclusively to the patient and that the right to enforce the confidence is that of the patient rather than the doctor. However, in *Ashworth Hospital Authority v Mirror Group Newspapers*[35] the House of Lords held that an obligation of confidence was owed to a hospital as well as a patient where the patient's medical records contained information and opinions on the patient supplied by other hospital staff.[36] An action for breach of confidence could, therefore, be brought by the hospital against a newspaper that had obtained the records unlawfully from another member of staff.

(iii) Special cases

12.29 (a) **Children** The obligation of confidence owed to children raises a number of complexities. First, very young children are simply not able to form a relationship of confidence or even have an expectation that their information will be kept secret. Second, where the child is not competent to consent to medical treatment, their information will have to be disclosed to their parents for them to be able to consent on their behalf.[37]

12.30 In *Gillick v West Norfolk and Wisbech AHA*[38] the House of Lords recognized that a doctor could, in appropriate circumstances, accede to a competent child's wishes to keep information about her medical treatment from her parents. Lord Fraser declared that the doctor would be 'justified in proceeding without the parents' consent or *even knowledge*', provided that the doctor was satisfied on five matters, including the child being able to understand the advice.[39] The House of Lords was not, however, concerned with confidentiality so much as the question of whether a competent child could consent to contraceptive treatment in the absence of parental consent. Nonetheless, some commentators wish to link the approach taken to consent to medical treatment, resting on the child's competence, with the approach to confidentiality. Kennedy and Grubb have argued that it is 'analytically preferable' to found the duty of confidentiality owed to a child on the child's ability to form a confidential relationship or an expectation that the information will be kept secret.[40] This approach would mean that no obligation of confidence would arise where the child is unable to form such a relationship or expectation. However, even before the HRA 1998, the courts had considered an obligation of confidence to be owed to *all* children.[41] None of these cases explained the precise legal basis for this obligation of confidence,[42] but the action for breach

---

[35] *Ashworth Hospital Authority v Mirror Group Newspapers* [2002] UKHL 29.

[36] ibid, [32] *per* Lord Woolf CJ.

[37] It should be noted, however, that the duty of confidence is owed to the child, as the patient, and not to his or her parents. See *Powell v Boladz* [1998] Lloyds Rep. Med. 116 CA.

[38] *Gillick v West Norfolk and Wisbech AHA* [1986] AC 112.

[39] ibid, 174 (emphasis added).

[40] See I Kennedy and A Grubb, *Medical Law* (3rd edn, Butterworths 2000), 1100–01, 1077–78; M Brazier and E Cave, *Medicine, Patients and the Law* (5th edn, Penguin 2011), 101. See further the discussion in J Loughrey, 'Medical Information, Confidentiality and a Child's Right to Privacy' (2003) 23 LS 510 and J Loughrey, 'Can You Keep a Secret?' n 24.

[41] *Re C* [1990] Fam 39, at 48, 52, and 54; *Venables v NGN* [2001] Fam 430, 469; *Re Z* [1997] Fam 1.

[42] See J Loughrey, 'Medical Information, Confidentiality and a Child's Right to Privacy' (2003) 23 LS 510.

of confidence is now linked to privacy and it is well established that children (even very young children) have a right to respect for private life under Article 8.[43] Any disclosure of a child's medical information must therefore be justified as necessary for the proportionate pursuit of a legitimate aim recognized by Article 8(2).

The case of *R (Axon) v Secretary of State for Health* considered whether the obligation of confidence owed to a competent child permitted the details of her medical consultation on conception or abortion to be kept from her parents.[44] In this case Mrs Axon challenged Department of Health guidance, arguing that the duty of confidence owed to a child was subject to the parents' responsibility for the welfare of their child.[45] Silber J rejected the argument that health professionals were only under an obligation to protect the confidence of a child under 16 on sexual matters where parental knowledge could prejudice a child's physical or mental health.[46] The duty owed to a *Gillick* competent child was said to be a 'high one' that could only be overridden by 'a very powerful reason' beyond 'family factors'.[47] Further, the parents' Article 8 ECHR right to respect for private and family life did not entitle them to be notified when their *Gillick* competent child was given such advice by a health professional. Loughrey has pointed out that questions remain about the extent of the duties owed to children who are not *Gillick* competent against their parents.[48] **12.31**

The General Medical Council (GMC) guidance states that doctors owe 'the same duties of confidence' to children as to adults, and information may only be disclosed without the child's consent where there is an overriding public interest in disclosure, when disclosure is required by law, or when the disclosure is in the best interests of a child or young person who does not have the maturity or understanding to make a decision about disclosure.[49] In contrast, the Department of Health's Code suggests that the appropriate test for determining whether there is a duty of confidence turns on the child's capacity: **12.32**

> Young persons aged 16 or 17 are presumed to be competent for the purposes of consent to treatment and *are therefore entitled* to the same duty of confidentiality as adults. Children under the age of 16 who have the capacity and understanding to take decisions about their own treatment are also entitled to make decisions about the use and disclosure of information they have provided in confidence.[50]

This appears to adopt a much narrower approach than the common law and, in so far as this is the case, it is wrong in law. **12.33**

(b) Incompetent adults Much of the analysis described above with regard to incompetent children applies equally to incompetent adults. Again, the GMC's guidance indicates that there is an ethical obligation of confidence to the incompetent patient that may be breached in the patient's best interests.[51] This view is supported by Hale LJ in *R (on the application of S) v Plymouth City Council*.[52] The case involved an incompetent 27-year-old adult whose **12.34**

---

[43] eg *East Sussex County Council v Stedman and others* [2009] EWHC 935 (Fam); *Murray* v *Big Pictures (UK) Ltd* [2008] 3 FCR 661; *Gaskin v UK* (1990) 12 EHRR 36 and *Glass v UK* [2004] 1 FLR 1019.

[44] *R (Axon) v Secretary of State for Health* [2006] EWHC 37.

[45] Department of Health, *Best Practice Guidance For Doctors and Other Health Professionals on the Provision of Advice and Treatment to Young People Under 16 on Contraception, Sexual and Reproductive Health* (2004).

[46] *R (Axon) v Secretary of State for Health* [2006] EWHC 372, [29].

[47] ibid, [64]. See also *R (on the application of B) v Stafford Combined Court* [2006] EWHC 1645.

[48] J Loughrey, 'Can You Keep a Secret?' n 24.

[49] GMC, *0–18 years: Guidance for All Doctors* (2007), paras 42–52.

[50] Department of Health, *Confidentiality: NHS Code of Practice* (October 2003) 30 (emphasis added).

[51] GMC, *Confidentiality* (2009), paras 57–63, esp 61–62.

[52] [2002] EWCA Civ 388.

mother sought access to his medical records, as his nearest relative under the Mental Health Act 1983. The local authority refused access on the basis that it would be a breach of confidentiality. Hale LJ reviewed the relevant law and concluded that an incompetent person does have a right to confidentiality and to respect for privacy under Article 8 ECHR. These rights had to be balanced against the public and private interests in permitting, indeed requiring, the disclosure of confidential information for certain purposes. On the facts of the case, the interference with the son's right to confidentiality was justified by the mother's right to be involved as a nearest relative in the decision-making process concerning her son's welfare.

12.35 Since the Mental Capacity Act 2005 came into force a person must be assumed to have capacity unless it is established that he or she does not.[53] If an individual lacks the capacity to make a decision (including that relating to the disclosure of confidential patient information), even with appropriate support, then the 2005 Act requires that any decision for or on behalf of that person be made in his or her best interests.[54] In determining what is in a person's best interests, the 2005 Act sets out a number of considerations, detailing both what should, and what should not, be taken into account.[55] These include taking into account, where practicable and appropriate to consult, the views of persons either specifically named or appointed for the purpose or those engaged in caring for the person or interested in his or her welfare.[56]

12.36 **(c) Deceased patients** Ethical guidance from the GMC, the BMA, and the Department of Health is in agreement that confidentiality obligations must continue to apply beyond death.[57] The GMC expressly advises that doctors still have an obligation to keep personal information confidential after a patient dies. The extent to which confidential information may be disclosed after a patient's death will depend on the circumstances, including: the purpose of the disclosure; whether it is already public knowledge or can be anonymized or coded; and whether disclosure may cause distress to, or be of benefit to, the patient's partner or family. Health practitioners who fail to follow the professional guidelines could find themselves facing disciplinary action.

12.37 In *Lewis v Secretary of State for Health* the High Court considered the disclosure of the medical records of deceased patients to an inquiry. Foskett J was satisfied with the prima facie conclusion that 'it is *arguable* that the duty of confidentiality does survive the death of the patient', because both parties were in agreement on the point.[58] This conclusion was reached in the light of the position adopted by the professional guidelines, the general expectations of patients, and the likely consequences of holding otherwise. Foskett J also noted that the Tribunals Service Information Tribunal had reached the same conclusion in an earlier case.[59] While these cases are not conclusive, in practice they have probably settled the question of whether the common law protects the privacy of deceased persons.

12.38 **(d) Anonymized information** The question of whether an obligation of confidence is owed with respect to information in a form that is not capable of identifying the patient was considered in *R v Department of Health, ex p Source Informatics*.[60] The Court of Appeal

---

[53] Mental Capacity Act 2005, s 1(1)

[54] ibid, s 1(5).

[55] ibid, s 4.

[56] Ibid, s 4(7).

[57] GMC, *Confidentiality* (2009), para 67–72; BMA, *Confidentiality and Disclosure of Health Information* (1999); Department of Health, n 50, 29.

[58] [2008] EWHC 2196, [18].

[59] *Bluck v The Information Commissioner* (2007) 98 BMLR 1.

[60] [1999] 4 All ER 185, rev'd [2001] QB 424 (CA).

held that it was not a breach of confidence to disclose anonymized patient information. The applicant was a data collection company, which wished to collect anonymized data from pharmacists about GPs' prescribing habits. The applicant wished to sell these data commercially. It sought a declaration that the Department's policy to advise health authorities and others that it might be a breach of confidence to disclose anonymized patient information was unlawful.

At first instance, Latham J concluded that the policy was lawful. It could be a breach of confidence to disclose anonymized information without a patient's consent. There was a public interest that confidences were respected. It was important that patients were not inhibited from seeking medical assistance, and some patients might feel strongly about the use of information obtained from their prescription forms. The mere unauthorized disclosure was itself a sufficient detriment to found an action for breach of confidence. A patient's consent could not be implied where the information was to be used for commercial gain. It was not necessary to decide, but consent might possibly be 'implied' if the information was to be used for NHS management purposes or for research. **12.39**

On appeal, the decision was reversed. Delivering the judgment of the Court of Appeal, Simon Brown LJ identified the issue for the court as being whether a pharmacist would interfere with the patients' 'personal privacy' in *disclosing* anonymized information to Source Informatics. He concluded that the proposed scheme did not involve a breach of confidence because the patients' identities would be protected: **12.40**

> I would . . . hold simply that the pharmacists' consciences ought not reasonably to be troubled . . . The patient's privacy will have been safeguarded, not invaded. The pharmacist's duty of confidence will not have been breached.[61]

Thus, the Court of Appeal concluded that the obligation of confidence does not apply to fully anonymized information.

The approach of the Court of Appeal has been strongly criticized.[62] It is worth noting that *Source Informatics* was decided before *Campbell* and the implementation of the HRA 1998. As discussed above, the law is now that an obligation of confidence exists where a person in the position of the person to whom the information relates has a reasonable expectation of privacy. In *Pretty v UK* the ECtHR held that 'private life' was concerned with 'the ability to conduct one's life in a manner of one's own choosing'.[63] In *Campbell,* Lord Nicholls noted that the right is wider than protection of private information[64] and Lord Hoffman held that the right is an aspect of 'human autonomy and dignity'.[65] In short, the Article 8 right to respect for one's private life may be engaged by an interference with a person's autonomy in relation to their physical and psychological integrity. In this context, it is interesting to consider whether a patient's reasonable expectations of privacy—and right to informational self-determination—may go beyond concealment of their identity. It is at least arguable that, under the Convention framework, if use of patient data engages the Article 8 right, then anonymization will only be sufficient where the conditions of Article 8(2) are satisfied. That is to say, the use of patient data, without consent, must be shown to be *necessary* and **12.41**

[61] [2001] QB 424, 440.

[62] See D Beyleveld and E Histed, 'Betrayal of Confidence in the Court of Appeal' (2000) 4 Med LI 277. Cf A Grubb, 'Breach of Confidence: Anonymized Information: *R v Department of Health, ex p Source Informatics*' (2000) 8 Med L Rev 115.

[63] (2002) 35 EHRR 1, [62]. See the discussion of the impact of this broad conception of privacy on *Source Informatics* in Pattinson, n 76, 225–26.

[64] *Campbell v Mirror Group Newspapers* [2004] UKHL 22, [15].

[65] ibid, [50], [51].

proportionate for one of the stated interests (see para 12.60). Balanced against this view it should be noted that the European Data Protection Directive, discussed more fully later (para 12.163), itself intended to ensure data processing systems across the European Union respect the fundamental rights and freedoms protected by the European Convention on Human Rights, notably the right to privacy,[66] only recognizes a right to protection in relation to identifiable data.[67]

12.42 Anonymized information is used widely within the NHS and it is recognized good practice to reduce the identifiability of data where possible prior to its use. The Caldicott Committee[68] recommended that patient-identifiable information should not be used unless it is absolutely necessary and this guiding principle has been adopted by the Department of Health. The Department of Health published a detailed Code of Practice for NHS Staff on Confidentiality[69] and more recently the HSCIC (now NHS Digital) published a Code of Practice on Confidential Information.[70] This Code serves as a guide to required practice for health and social care bodies that collect, analyse, publish, or otherwise disseminate confidential patient information in connection with the provision of health or social care in England, and those under contract to them.[71] The Department of Health Code describes the concept of confidentiality, provides a detailed account of the main legal requirements, recommends a generic decision support tool for sharing/disclosing information, and lists examples of particular information sharing scenarios. Central to the Code is the premise that unless there is a robust public interest or legal justification for using information in a form that identifies an individual, it should not be used in that form.[72] The Code also states that once information is *effectively* anonymized, it is no longer confidential and may be used with relatively few constraints.[73] This, of course, reflects the position at common law according to the *Source Informatics* case, discussed above. It is surely reasonable to take the position that any fair and expected use of anonymized data would be unlikely to unjustifiably infringe any right to respect for a private and family life under Article 8 of the ECHR. It may still be preferable, however, to recognize that the law may still have scope to regulate unexpected and unfair use if, in particular circumstances, it was considered inconsistent with a 'reasonable expectation of privacy' (para 12.23).

12.43 The Nuffield Council on Bioethics have noted that, at least in the context of individual level data, the 'irreversible anonymisation of meaningful data is practically unattainable given the availability of data tools and environmental data for contextualization'.[74] While this does not prevent effective anonymization in a particular context, it does encourage reflection upon the risks of re-identification, particularly if data are to be published or contextual controls are otherwise to be reduced, for example, through data sharing. Moreover, from

[66] Data Protection Directive 95/46/EC, Recital 2, Article 1.

[67] ibid, Recital 26, Article 2(a).

[68] Caldicott Committee, *Report on the Review of Patient-Identifiable Information* (December 1997) and subsequent implementation in 'Implementing the Recommendations of the Caldicott Report' (HSC 1998/089) and Caldicott Guardians (HSC 1999/012). See also *For the Record: Managing Records in NHS Trusts and Health Authorities* (HSC 1999/053) and *Preservation, Retention and Destruction of GP General Medical Services Records Relating to Patients* (HSC 1998/217).

[69] Department of Health, *Confidentiality: NHS Code of Practice* (October 2003).

[70] The code is produced in response to s 263 Health and Social Care Act 2012.

[71] HSCIC, *Code of Practice on Confidential Information* (December, 2014) 7.

[72] Department of Health, *Confidentiality*, n 69, 4. The GMC guidance *Confidentiality* (2009) para 9 also advises doctors to anonymize or code data if it is practicable and will serve the purpose.

[73] Department of Health, *Confidentiality*, n 69.

[74] Nuffield Council on Bioethics (2015), The collection, linking and use of data in biomedical research and health care: ethical issues, for which a link is available at <http://nuffieldbioethics.org/wp-content/uploads/Biological_and_health_data_web.pdf>.

an ethical and public interest point of view, even the effective anonymization of a patient's information does not automatically remove the rationale for its protection. Beyleveld and Histed raise the example of a devout Catholic woman who is opposed to the use of chemical contraceptive methods as a matter of religious conviction.[75] If she were to seek medical assistance for her irregular menstrual cycles, her opposition to the use of her data in research on chemical contraceptives would not be placated by anonymization. Similarly, Pattinson asks us to consider the example of a woman who actively campaigns against a company that aggressively markets baby milk in developing countries.[76] If she were to seek medical advice on a lactation problem, anonymization would not remove her opposition to the use of her information in research conducted by the company against which she is campaigning. What is more, effective anonymization (eg through aggregation) does not prevent engagement with the privacy interests of a group or mitigate the risks of 'fresh association' of an individual with characteristics reported at a group level.[77] Failure to attend to a patient's privacy interests in such situations could lead to sections of society losing confidence in the health care system (See para 12.25).

(iv) Lawful disclosure

(a) Disclosure with the patient's consent Disclosure within the parameters of a valid consent will not breach the legal duty of confidence, because the patient's consent operates as a waiver of the duty.[78] The modification of duty of confidence to take into account Article 8 ECHR in no way alters this, as the right to respect for private life is only engaged by *non-consensual* invasions of privacy.[79] **12.44**

When consent can properly be said to have been given requires some unpacking. Consent is a state of mind that could be signalled in a number of ways.[80] The most straightforward situations are those where the patient explicitly signals consent by words of agreement or by equivalent conduct such as the nodding of the head. Disclosure in such circumstances will be with the patient's *explicit* consent. The signal can also be *implied* through an individual's conduct in other situations. **12.45**

Consent is properly described as *implied* where consent is inferred from the person's conduct in a particular context, even though that conduct may not be regarded as sufficiently explicit or indicative of consent in another context. Consent to an injection could, for example, be signalled by a patient holding out an arm in response to the doctor's recommendation of a tetanus injection, even though holding out an arm would not indicate consent to an injection in many other contexts.[81] Consent can also be *implied*, where the activity in question is a necessary means of fulfilling a purpose for which explicit consent has been obtained and the patient is reasonably expected to be aware of this implication. When, for example, a patient consents to a major operation, the patient implies permission for various theatre and ward clinical staff to have access to information about the patient's condition, because this is required for them to appropriately monitor and respond to the patient's medical needs. Understood in this way, implied consent is concerned with the scope and interpretation of **12.46**

[75] See D Beyleveld and E Histed, 'Case Commentary: Anonymisation is Not Exoneration' (1999) 4 Med LI 69 at 73–74.

[76] S D Pattinson, *Medical Law and Ethics* (3rd edn, Sweet & Maxwell 2011) ch 6.

[77] M J Taylor, *Genetic Data and the Law* (Cambridge University Press 2012) esp 149–56.

[78] *C v C* [1946] 1 All ER 562.

[79] See *Z v Finland* (1998) 25 EHRR 371, [112]; *MS v Sweden* (1999) 28 EHRR 313, [34]–[35]; *Peck v UK* (2003) 36 EHRR 719, [81].

[80] The discussion of types of signal heavily draws on Beyleveld and Histed, n 75, and Pattinson, n 76, 213–14. See also D Beyleveld and R Brownsword, *Consent in the Law* (Hart 2007).

[81] Compare *O'Brien v Cunard SS Co* (1891) 28 NE 266 (Mass Sup Jud Ct).

the signal and does not operate in the absence of a relevant signal.[82] In the absence of any signal at all, the patient's consent cannot be anything other than *imputed*. In such circumstances, usage of the language of consent is no more than a fiction.

12.47 The legal requirements for a valid consent to disclosure are surely the same as those for a valid consent in medical law generally: at the time of giving consent the patient must be competent, acting voluntarily, and understand the nature of the disclosure proposed (see further Chapters 8 and 9). The courts have, however, given little attention to what the law regards as a sufficient signal of consent to disclosure.

12.48 There is little doubt that explicit consent is not always required. The General Medical Council (GMC) ethical guidance to doctors emphasizes the importance of obtaining patient consent, but recognizes the acceptability of relying on a patient's implied consent to the sharing of information in the health care team.[83] The guidance advises that doctors:

> should make sure information is readily available to patients explaining that, unless they object, personal information about them will be shared within the healthcare team, including administrative staff and other staff who support the provision of their care.[84]

12.49 The Department of Health adopts a similar approach in its guidance to NHS staff where the purpose of the disclosure is directly concerned with the health care of the patient. Accordingly, the Code on confidentiality provides:

> Where patients have been informed of:
>
> a. the use and sharing of their information associated with their health care; and
> b. the choices that they have and the implications of choosing to limit how information may be used or shared;
>
> then explicit consent is not usually needed for information disclosures needed to provide that health care. Even so, opportunities to check that patients understand what may happen and are content should be taken.[85]

12.50 The Information Governance Review, known as Caldicott2, concluded that 'across the health and social care system, implied consent is only applicable in instances of direct care'.[86] When sharing for the purposes of direct care, it was the view of the panel that 'registered and regulated social workers must also be considered part of the care team covered by implied consent when the social worker has a legitimate relationship to the individual concerned.'[87] Establishing the boundaries of 'implied consent' may prove to be increasingly important given moves to further integrate health and social care.

12.51 The Information Governance Review recommended that the health and social care regulators 'agree upon and publish the conditions under which regulated and registered professionals can rely upon implied consent to share personal confidential data for direct care.'[88]

[82] Note that Beyleveld, Brownsword, and Pattinson would seek to distinguish between use of the term 'implied' and 'implicit' in these different circumstances. See Beyleveld and Histed, n 75, 73–74, Pattinson, n 76, and D Beyleveld and R Brownsword, *Consent in the Law* (Hart 2007).

[83] Note, however, that any definition of consent that is compatible with the absence of a positive signal could not be relied on as explicit consent for the purposes of the Data Protection Act 1998 (see para 12.198).

[84] GMC, *Confidentiality* (2009), para 25.

[85] Department of Health, *Confidentiality*, n 69, para 15.

[86] Caldicott 2, 37. This is consistent with the position described in the NHS Code of Practice on Confidentiality: 'Where the purpose is not directly concerned with the healthcare of a patient however, it would be wrong to assume consent. Additional efforts to gain consent are required or alternative approaches that do not rely on identifiable information will need to be developed.' (2003) 8.

[87] Caldicott 2, Information: To share or not to share, 39.

[88] ibid.

One year on from publication, the Review panel expressed disappointment at the lack of progress in relation to this particular Recommendation.[89] It remains important that the boundaries of implied consent are clarified.

The range of activity associated with a valid implied consent must surely depend upon an understanding of what an individual can reasonably be understood to have intended to imply through their conduct in the circumstances—for example through explicit consent to receive care and treatment. The clearest reason for restricting implied consent to direct care relates to what it is reasonable to understand an individual to have impliedly given consent to through their conduct in the circumstances. Any extension to the activity to which an individual is understood to have given implied consent, beyond direct care, would be dependent upon that being a reasonable expectation in the circumstances: it would need to be fair for a reasonable patient in the circumstances to expect their conduct to be interpreted as such a signal.[90] **12.52**

(b) Providing information to third parties Where doctors are asked to provide information to third parties (such as employers, insurance companies, government departments, or agencies assessing entitlement to benefits), the GMC advises that doctors should obtain, or have seen, the patient's *written* consent beforehand and: **12.53**

> be satisfied that the patient has sufficient information about the scope, purpose and likely consequences of the examination and disclosure, and the fact that relevant information cannot be concealed or withheld.[91]

This paragraph goes on to say that the doctor must offer to show the patient, or provide a copy of, any report written about them for employment or insurance purposes, unless the patient has indicated that they do not want to see it, disclosure would be likely to cause serious harm to the patient or another, or disclosure would be likely to reveal information about another person who does not consent. **12.54**

Although the GMC guidance stresses the importance of written consent to the disclosure in such circumstances, in *Kapadia v Lambeth London Borough Council*[92] the Court of Appeal stated that consent to disclose a medical report may be implied where a person undergoes a medical examination at the request of a third party. The case involved a claim by an employee against an employer for disability discrimination before an Employment Appeal Tribunal. The applicant had called his own expert witnesses and had consented to an examination by an independent medical expert instructed by his employers. The doctor who conducted the examination had refused to disclose the report to the respondent employer without first obtaining the consent of the applicant. The applicant had not been prepared to consent to the disclosure without first seeing the report and the case proceeded with no medical evidence being called on behalf of the respondent. In the opinion of Pill LJ, the report should have been disclosed by the doctor to the employers and no further consent was required from the claimant: **12.55**

> By consenting to being examined on behalf of the employers the claimant was consenting to the disclosure to the employers of a report resulting from that examination. A practice under which a person who has agreed to be examined in circumstances such as these, but

89 <https://www.gov.uk/government/uploads/system/uploads/attachment_data/file/391533/iigop-annual-report.pdf>, 18.

90 For the view that implied consent may extend beyond direct care in such circumstances, see Confidentiality and Security Advisory Group for Scotland *Protecting Patient Confidentiality: Final Report* (CSAG, April 2002) esp 7.6–7.18 <http://www.sehd.scot.nhs.uk/publications/ppcr/ppcr.pdf>.

91 GMC, *Confidentiality* (2009), para 34.

92 *Kapadia v Lambeth London Borough Council* (2000) 57 BMLR 170 (CA).

then claims a veto upon disclosure of the report to those who obtained it is not, in my view, a good practice.[93]

This arguably offers less protection to vulnerable persons than the position taken by the GMC. One must consider how this position by the court relates to withdrawal of consent, and objection to disclosure, more generally.

12.56 **(c) Withdrawal of consent and express prohibition** Where a patient has explicitly objected to particular information being shared with others providing care, the GMC states that doctors involved are advised to respect those wishes.[94] This is echoed by the Department of Health, although the Code of Practice cautions that when patients choose to exercise their right to object, it may mean that the care that can be provided is constrained and that, in extremely rare circumstances, it might not be possible to offer certain treatment options.[95] Formally, it is important to recognize a distinction between the withdrawal of consent and objection. Where consent provides a lawful basis for disclosure, then the withdrawal of consent can deprive a party of an authorization otherwise available to them. This does not mean that there can be no alternative legal basis. If there is an alternative legal basis to consent available to the discloser, then respect for the dissent may be considered usually to be an ethical requirement but not necessarily a legal one.[96]

12.57 Since, in the absence of consent, the lawfulness of disclosure must depend upon whether or not disclosure can be justified on the basis of statutory permission, statutory requirement, or otherwise in the public interest, there may be exceptional circumstances in which even an explicit prohibition on disclosure may be overridden. Clearly, there would be no breach of confidence where disclosure is required by law. It is undoubtedly also lawful to disclose where it is necessary to prevent a real risk of serious harm even in the face of patient objection (see discussion of *Egdell*, para 12.64). However, if the patient objects to the disclosure, then a doctor would not be justified in disclosing the confidential information *for the patient's own benefit*, for example, by informing the patient's GP or other health professionals caring for the patient.[97] Similarly, disclosure contrary to an explicit prohibition for the purposes of teaching or research would probably not be lawful.

12.58 An explicit prohibition may remove what would otherwise be a legal requirement to share under the Health and Social Care (Safety and Quality) Act 2015 (see para 12.100). Whether respect for an explicit prohibition is itself a legal requirement will depend upon whether a failure to respect objection would constitute a breach of s 10 of the Data Protection Act 1998 (see para 12.209) or, if a public body is involved, an unjustified infringement of Article 8 of the ECHR.[98] In this context it is also relevant to note that the NHS Constitution recognizes:

---

93 ibid, 177.

94 GMC, *Confidentiality* (2009), para 27.

95 Department of Health, *Confidentiality*, n 69, para 14.

96 Alternative legal grounds include public interest (from para 12.59) and statutory basis (from para 12.85).

97 On this see also Health and Social Care (Safety and Quality Act) 2015, para 12.100.

98 J Grace and M J Taylor, 'Disclosure of Confidential Patient Information and the Duty to Consult: The Role of the Health and Social Care Information Centre' (2014) 21 Med L Rev 415–47. Also, when establishing the legal basis of processing under the DPA it is relevant to note that the Information Commissioner's Office do not consider it appropriate to rely upon any alternative condition under Sch 3 of the DPA 98 if explicit consent has first been sought from, but not provided by, the data subject. See <http://www.hra.nhs.uk/documents/2013/09/managing-non-response-guidance-v1-2.pdf>.

You have the right to request that your confidential information is not used beyond your own care and treatment and to have your objections considered, and where your wishes cannot be followed, to be told the reasons including the legal basis.[99]

(d) Disclosure in the public interest: General The legal duty of confidence is not absolute. Since the obligation of confidence is largely based upon important public interests favouring confidentiality, it follows that it may be overridden where there are sufficient countervailing public interests favouring disclosure. The courts have tended to articulate the public interest exception in rather broad and inconclusive terms. Exposition of the law is complicated by both the limited nature of judicial dicta on the application of the public interest justification for disclosure in the context of the doctor–patient relationship and by the fact that the public interest justification must now be interpreted in accordance with the ECHR rights given effect by the HRA 1998.[100] **12.59**

Article 8 ECHR similarly regards the right to privacy as non-absolute. While Article 8(1) states that everyone has a right to respect for 'private and family life', Article 8(2) states: **12.60**

> There shall be no interference by a public authority with the exercise of this right except such as is in accordance with the law and is necessary in a democratic society in the interests of national security, public safety or the economic well-being of the country, for the prevention of disorder or crime, for the protection of health or morals, or for the protection of the rights and freedoms of others.

Recognition is therefore given in Article 8(2) to countervailing considerations, including the rights and freedoms of others. In *Campbell,* Lord Hope compared the traditional balancing exercise between the public interest in maintaining confidence and the countervailing public interest favouring disclosure with that involving Articles 8 and 10, and concluded that it is 'essentially the same exercise, although it is plainly now more carefully focussed and more penetrating'.[101] These Articles now form part of the content of the action for breach of confidence and are 'not merely of persuasive or parallel effect'.[102]

The courts balance the public interests favouring confidentiality against those favouring disclosure in the particular circumstances of each case. The balance of the public interest in the context of an action to restrain what was alleged to be a potential breach of medical confidentiality was first considered by English courts in 1987 in the case of *X v Y*.[103] The defendants in that case intended to publish an article identifying two doctors with AIDS who were carrying on general practice in England after having sought and received appropriate medical advice and counselling. The health authority that held the doctors' medical records sought to restrain publication. The question for the court was whether or not the defendants were justified in the public interest in publishing and using the information about the two doctors. **12.61**

Rose J held that it was not necessary to show any detriment to the individual claimants, because the courts were concerned to protect the public interest, rather than purely private interests. It would be unlawful to disclose the information provided the public interest in maintaining confidence, in this case in loyalty and confidentiality both generally and particularly in relation to the hospital records of patients with AIDS, outweighed the public **12.62**

[99] NHS Constitution (March 2013) 8.

[100] See Pattinson, n 76, 215 and, for an example of a rights-based interpretation of the public interest, see D Townend, 'Overriding Data Subjects' Rights in the Public Interest', in D Beyleveld et al (eds), *The Data Protection Directive and Medical Research Across Europe* (Ashgate 2004), 89.

[101] [2004] UKHL 22, [86].

[102] *McKennitt v Ash* [2006] EWCA Civ 1714, [11].

[103] [1988] 2 All ER 648.

interest in disclosure, here having a free press and an informed public debate.[104] (The particular relationship between Article 8 and Article 10 is further considered below from para 12.71).

12.63 Subsequently, the scope of medical confidentiality was considered by the Court of Appeal in *W v Egdell*.[105] The case arose out of the proposed disclosure to the Home Office of a report about the mental condition of a psychiatric patient in a secure hospital. Bingham LJ described the case as establishing:

> (1) that the law recognizes an important public interest in maintaining professional duties of confidence; but
> (2) that the law treats such duties not as absolute but as liable to be overridden where there is held to be a stronger public interest in disclosure.[106]

12.64 W had been convicted of manslaughter on the grounds of diminished responsibility after having shot and killed five people in an indiscriminate display of violence. At the time of the action for breach of confidence, he was compulsorily detained in a secure hospital but was being considered for transfer to a regional secure unit, as a step towards eventual release back into the community. When a recommendation for transfer was refused, W took steps to apply to a mental health review tribunal for conditional discharge. To that end, his solicitors instructed Dr Egdell to report on W's mental state. His report conflicted substantially with that of W's own medical advisers and he recommended further investigation of this conflict in opinion. Further, he recommended that attention should be given to other information, including W's confession that he had a continuing and long-standing interest in explosives, which apparently had not been noted in other reports. W subsequently withdrew his application and his solicitors refused to forward Dr Egdell's report to those responsible for his care and for any future recommendations as to his transfer to a less secure facility or discharge. Dr Egdell nonetheless sent a copy of his report to the hospital and also pressed for a copy to be sent to the Home Office to be considered by those responsible for reviewing W's case.

12.65 W's solicitors commenced an action for breach of confidence against Dr Egdell, claiming damages and injunctive relief. Bingham LJ quoted with approval from the speech of Lord Goff in the *Spycatcher* case:

> although the basis of the law's protection of confidence is that there is a public interest that confidences should be preserved and protected by the law, nevertheless that public interest may be outweighed by some other countervailing public interest which favours disclosure . . . It is this limiting principle which may require a court to carry out a balancing operation, weighing the public interest in maintaining confidence against a countervailing public interest favouring disclosure.[107]

12.66 The court must reach its own decision on the balance. However, in doing so it is legitimate for the court to give 'such weight to the considered judgment of a professional man as seems in all the circumstances to be appropriate'.[108] On the facts, that balance 'clearly lay in the restricted disclosure of vital information to the director of the hospital and to the Secretary of State who had the onerous duty of safeguarding public safety'.[109] In both *W v Egdell* and the earlier case of *X v Y*[110] the courts paid great heed to the advice provided by the GMC

---

104 [1988] 2 All ER 648, 661.
105 [1990] Ch 359.
106 *W v Egdell* [1990] Ch 359, 419.
107 ibid, 389 (quoting from [1990] 1 AC 109, 282).
108 ibid, 422.
109 ibid, 416.
110 [1988] 2 All ER 648.

contained in its ethical guidance to doctors,[111] but the question remains one for the courts and not for professional bodies or the Department of Health.

Although the HRA 1998 had not then been enacted, Bingham LJ expressed the view that the decision was in accordance with Article 8 ECHR.[112] Article 8(2) requires the disclosure of private information to be justified as being in accordance with the law, necessary in a democratic society (proportionate), and for at least one of the specified purposes.[113] Dr Egdell had acted in accordance with the law and, in the judgment of the court, his conduct had been necessary in the interests of public safety and the prevention of crime.[114] **12.67**

The ECtHR has accepted that Article 8 requires competing public interests to be balanced. In *Z v Finland*, a later decision of the ECtHR, it was held that the effect of Article 8 was that only 'an overriding requirement in the public interest' could justify breaching medical confidentiality.[115] This was a case in which the medical records of an HIV-positive patient were disclosed during the trial of her husband for sexual assault and attempted manslaughter. The Court held that there was no breach of Article 8 on the facts as the interference with her right to privacy was justified under Article 8(2) as being 'in accordance with the law and necessary in a democratic society' in the light of the safeguards from abuse, namely, that the proceedings were held in camera and sealed by the court and subject to a requirement that all parties kept the patient's identity confidential. However, a breach of Article 8 had occurred in that the proceedings were only to be sealed for ten years and the patient's identity had been disclosed in the court's judgment. **12.68**

The disclosure in *W v Egdell* was justified by reference to the public interest in ensuring that a properly informed decision was made by those responsible for considering W's detention in order to avert a 'real risk of consequent danger to the public'.[116] This raises the question of what risks of harm might be sufficient to justify disclosure of confidential information in the public interest. It has been suggested that, in order to justify disclosure, the risk of harm must be 'real' and not fanciful, and it must be a risk involving the danger of *physical* harm.[117] In the case of *Lewis v Secretary of State for Health* (see para 12.76), however, Foskett J was prepared to hold that it was in the public interest to disclose confidential information related to deceased patients to an inquiry into human tissue analysis in UK nuclear facilities, holding that he had: **12.69**

> not the slightest doubt that this is an appropriate case in which to hold that the public interest in disclosure of the material sought outweighs the other public interest, namely, that of maintaining the confidentiality of medical records and information, provided, of course, proper safeguards are put in place to ensure that no inappropriate information becomes public.[118]

[111] See GMC, *Confidentiality* (2009) for the latest version of this ethical guidance.

[112] *W v Egdell*, n 112, 424–25.

[113] The interference must be in the interests of national security, public safety, or the economic well-being of the country, for the prevention of disorder or crime, for the protection of health or morals, or for the protection of the rights and freedoms of others.

[114] *W v Egdell*, n 112, 424–25.

[115] *Z v Finland* (1998) 25 EHRR 371, 406.

[116] ibid, 424.

[117] See I Kennedy and A Grubb, *Medical Law* (3rd edn, Butterworths 2000), 1100–01; M Brazier and E Cave, *Medicine, Patients and the Law* (5th edn, Penguin 2011), 101.

[118] [2008] EWHC 2196, [58]. See also the GMC guidelines, *Confidentiality* (2009), which state that there can be a public interest in disclosing information: 'to protect individuals or society from risks of serious harm, such as serious communicable diseases or serious crime; or to enable medical research, education or other secondary uses of information that will benefit society over time' (para 26). See further ibid, paras 37–56.

While Foskett J did not mention the Convention rights, the disclosure of this information to the inquiry was clearly in accordance with the law, proportionate, and for at least one of the specified purposes, which include the interests of public safety and the protection of health. The ECtHR has given a relatively broad scope to the conditions justifying disclosure under Article 8(2) ECHR, though the margin of appreciation to restrict the right will tend to be narrower '[w]here a particularly important facet of an individual's existence or identity is at stake'.[119]

12.70 Even if a doctor considers there to be a real risk of physical harm, it remains unclear whether the doctor is justified in disclosing information on the basis of his or her reasonable belief or must prove objectively that such a risk does in fact exist. This point was not resolved in *W v Egdell*, since it is possible to read the judgments as saying that either might be in the public interest. Brazier and Cave suggest that the test should be based on the reasonableness of the particular doctor's belief:

> When the doctor reasonably foresees that nondisclosure poses a real risk of physical harm to a third party he ought to be free to warn that person, especially if that person too is his patient. The courts should not be over-zealous in proving him wrong.[120]

12.71 **(e) Disclosure in the public interest: Article 10 of the European Convention on Human Rights** The Article 8(1) ECHR right to private and family life is subject to countervailing public interest considerations focused by reference to, inter alia, Article 10. Article 10 provides that everyone has the right to freedom of expression, including the right to receive and impart information. It is also worth pointing out that s 12 of the HRA 1998 makes special provision in relation to applications to restrict freedom of expression. Section 12(4) states that '[t]he court must have particular regard to the importance of the Convention right to freedom of expression'. This right is of particular relevance to the media and their freedom to publish. Further, Article 10(1) is subject, under Article 10(2), to the need to protect the rights and freedoms of others. As Lord Hope points out in *Campbell v MGN*:

> The effect of these provisions is that the right to privacy which lies at the heart of an action for breach of confidence has to be balanced against the right of the media to impart information to the public. And the right of the media to impart information to the public has to be balanced in its turn against the respect that must be given to private life.[121]

12.72 In *Venables v News Group Newspapers,*[122] Dame Elizabeth Butler-Sloss considered the relationship between Articles 8 and 10 with respect to the media's desire to publish the new identities of Jamie Bulger's killers, Jon Venables and Robert Thompson. Butler-Sloss P stated that:

> s 12 of the 1998 Act and art 10(1) of the convention ... together give an enhanced importance to freedom of expression and consequently to the right of the press to publish ... There is no doubt, therefore, that Parliament has placed great emphasis upon the importance of art 10 and the protection of freedom of expression, inter alia for the press and for the media.[123]

However, despite this emphasis, she was prepared to grant an unprecedented lifelong injunction against the whole world, protecting any information leading to the identity, or future

[119] *S v Marper v UK* (2009) 48 EHRR 50, [102]. See also *Z v Finland* (1998) EHRR 313 (discussed in para 12.25) and *MS v Sweden* (1999) 28 EHRR 313 (discussed in para 12.80).

[120] M Brazier and E Cave, *Medicine, Patients and the Law* (5th edn, Penguin 2011), 101. See also *Duncan v Medical Practitioners' Disciplinary Committee* [1986] 1 NZLR 513, 521.

[121] [2004] UKHL 22, [105].

[122] *Venables v News Group Newspapers* [2001] 1 All ER 908.

[123] ibid, 919.

whereabouts, of the claimants. A failure to do so would probably lead to serious physical injury or to the death of the claimants. Consequently, it was necessary to place the right of confidence above the right of the media to publish freely information about the claimants. Butler-Sloss P did, however, stress that her decision was based on the exceptional circumstances of the case.[124]

Brooke LJ in *Douglas v Hello! (No.1)* neatly summed up the approach adopted by the courts in the balancing exercise: 'Although the right to freedom of expression is not in every case the ace of trumps, it is a powerful card to which the courts of this country must always pay appropriate respect.'[125] In other words, there is no presumptive priority given to freedom of expression when it is in conflict with another ECHR right. Courts will deal with applications to restrain the media by balancing the facts on a case-by-case basis and the outcome will be determined principally by considerations of proportionality.[126] However, an order to restrain the media from publication requires a 'strong case'[127] and an injunction will only be granted where it can be 'convincingly demonstrated' that it is 'strictly necessary'.[128] **12.73**

In *Campbell v Mirror Group Newspapers*[129] the House of Lords considered whether the press had breached Naomi Campbell's Article 8 ECHR right, protected by the law of confidentiality, when it had published details about her drug addiction and therapy. Their Lordships were unanimous on the principles to be applied and all concluded that the newspaper in question had been justified (in the light of Ms Campbell's public profile and previous public claims) in publishing the fact that she was a drug addict and receiving treatment. A majority held that the newspaper in question had not been justified in publishing further information relating to the name of the clinic at which she was receiving treatment, the details of that treatment, and a photograph of her leaving a specific meeting with other addicts. The conclusion reached by the majority (Lord Hope, Baroness Hale, and Lord Carswell) on disclosure of this further information differed from that reached by the Court of Appeal. The involvement of more than one ECHR right had made the application of the proportionality test less than straightforward. As Lord Carswell put it: **12.74**

> Weighing and balancing these factors is a process which may well lead different people to different conclusions, as one may readily see from consideration of the judgments of the courts below and the opinions given by the several members of the Appellate Committee of your Lordships' House.[130]

In conclusion, Article 10 considerations will weigh heavily in the balance against Article 8 privacy considerations, but the balance will be struck on a case-by-case basis and freedom of expression is not always the trump card. **12.75**

(f) Disclosure in the public interest: Examples The balancing exercise required by the 'public interest' justification for disclosure, as interpreted in the light of the ECHR rights, is fact specific. It is, nonetheless, possible to put some flesh on the bones of this justification by reference to examples of circumstances when it may outweigh the obligation of confidence. **12.76**

---

[124] However, she subsequently granted the same lifelong injunctions to protect the identity of Mary Bell and her daughter: *X (a woman formerly known as Mary Bell) v SO* [2003] EWHC 1101.

[125] [2001] QB 967, 982.

[126] [2004] UKHL 22, esp at [20] *per* Lord Nicholls, [59] *per* Lord Hoffmann, [113] *per* Lord Hope, and [139] *per* Baroness Hale.

[127] *Venables v News Group Newspapers* [2001] 1 All ER 908, 922 *per* Dame Elizabeth Butler-Sloss.

[128] ibid, 934. For criticism of Butler-Sloss's approach to this issue in *Venables*, see G Phillipson, 'Transforming Breach of Confidence? Towards a Common Law Right of Privacy under the Human Rights Act' (2003) 66 Med L Rev 726, 750–51.

[129] *Campbell v Mirror Group Newspapers* [2004] UKHL 22, rvsg [2002] EWCA Civ 1373.

[130] ibid, [168].

X v Y, W v Egdell, and *Lewis v Secretary of State for Health*, discussed above, are examples of cases where the courts have held the obligation of confidence to be outweighed on the specific facts before them.

12.77 The HSCIC Code of Practice on Confidential Information references a number of sources of guidance on whether a relevant public interest justifies disclosure in particular circumstances.[131] These include guidance originally produced by the Department of Health to supplement the NHS Code of Practice on confidentiality.[132] The Guidance states that decisions about disclosure of confidentially sensitive information in the public interest must be made on the basis of case-by-case considerations, taking into account at least the following in all cases:

- Extent of the information which is to be disclosed—it will be easier to justify disclosure of demographic data or the fact that someone attended a clinic rather than detailed health information.
- The nature and impact of the crime or harm justifying the disclosure—it will be easier to justify disclosure of information relating to a physical attack against a person than it would be for shoplifting.
- Whether the disclosure is for detection or prosecution of crime or harm to others or whether it is preventative—it may be more justifiable to disclose information to support prosecution in relation to a crime that has occurred than to prevent a crime which has not yet occurred.[133]

12.78 The Guidance continues with the advice that a public interest justification for disclosure can be considered where:

- Disclosure would be in the public interest; AND
- The purpose of the disclosure cannot be achieved with anonymised information; AND
- There is no statutory basis for disclosure; AND
- Patient consent has not been given because:
  - It is not practicable to ask the patient(s) for consent eg because, for example, there are no up-to-date contact details for the patient, or the matter is urgent and the patient cannot be contacted; OR
  - It would be inappropriate to ask the patient(s) because, for example, they lack the capacity to give consent, or they are suspect(s) who should not be informed that they are under criminal investigation; OR
  - The patient(s) have been asked for consent and refused.[134]

12.79 While much of this seems sensible advice, the appropriateness of reliance upon the public interest in circumstances where a patient has not given consent because they lack capacity must be considered in the light of the requirements of the Mental Capacity Act 2007 (see 12.35 and further Chapter 10).

12.80 In *MS v Sweden*,[135] the ECtHR applied Article 8 ECHR to personal information, as it had done earlier in the same year in *Z v Finland* (discussed in para 12.25 and 12.81). In this case, a clinic disclosed the patient's records to the Social Insurance Office, which was considering her compensation claim under the appropriate legislation for an injury to her back she claimed had occurred at work. The Court found that: (i) Article 8(1) applied to

[131] HSCIC Code of Practice on Confidential Information (December 2014) 16.
[132] Department of Health, *Confidentiality: NHS Code of Practice—Supplementary Guidance: Public Interest Disclosures* (November 2010).
[133] ibid, 6 (emphasis in original).
[134] ibid, 6.
[135] (1999) 28 EHRR 313.

personal data such as medical information; (ii) the disclosure to the Social Insurance Office was an interference with the right to respect for her private life since it was not connected to her medical treatment; (iii) she had not waived that right by requesting compensation; (iv) nevertheless, the interference was justified under Article 8(2): it was in accordance with the law (having a legal basis) and was 'necessary in a democratic society' in that it was for a legitimate purpose ('economic well-being of the country') and in the light of the safeguards against abuse including the Office's duty of confidentiality, it was not disproportionate to that legitimate purpose.

Z v Finland and *MS v Sweden* represent the minimum required for Convention compliance. **12.81** As noted by Fennell,[136] the approach in *Woolgar v Chief Constable of Sussex Police*[137] goes beyond this minimum. In this case, the Court of Appeal was anxious to ensure that the right to confidentiality is considered by a court when police are seeking access to confidential information. The police were investigating a registered nurse and matron of a nursing home following the death of a patient in her care. The investigation concluded without any charges being brought against Woolgar, but the police referred the matter to the UK Central Council, then the regulatory body for the nursing profession.[138] Woolgar sought an injunction to restrain the police from disclosing details of the investigation. Her application was dismissed and she appealed. The Court of Appeal held that where a regulatory body, operating in the field of public health and safety, asked the police for access to confidential material, the police were entitled to release that material if they were reasonably persuaded that it was of some relevance to the subject matter of an enquiry being conducted by the regulatory body. Whilst emphasizing that the primary decision as to disclosure was for the police, the Court of Appeal stressed that the court should consider the right to confidentiality. If the police refused to disclose, the regulatory body could make an application to the court. Similarly, if the police were minded to disclose, they should normally inform the person affected so as to enable him or her to seek assistance from the court if necessary.[139] Competing interests should therefore be weighed by a court, where this is possible.

Another example of the 'public interest' justification can be found in the context of **12.82** genetic information. The nature of genetic information about one person means that it may be very relevant to other family members because of their common genetic heritage.[140] Consequently, there are competing interests at stake. As noted by Ngwena and Chadwick, a major legal and ethical dilemma is:

> whether to allow a third party access to personal and confidential information that is generated by the doctor from the patient in the course of diagnostic care. The nature of genetic disease, with its vertical transmission down the family tree from one generation to the next, means that at any given point, personal and confidential genetic information generated from a specific individual might be regarded as a legitimate interest by his/her spouse partner, offspring or other relatives such as siblings and grandchildren. Such third parties may claim especially in the context of genetic counselling, to be entitled to access to what would otherwise be confidential information on the ground that knowledge of it is the sine qua non for preventing or ameliorating probable or actual harm from genetic disease.[141]

---

[136] P Fennell, (1999) 7 Med L Rev 346 (which is a case note on *MS v Sweden* (1999) 28 EHRR 313.

[137] [2000] 1 WLR 25.

[138] The UK Central Council was replaced by the Nursing and Midwifery Council in 2002.

[139] On the responsibility to inform see also M J Taylor and J Grace, 'Disclosure of Confidential Patient Information and the Duty to Consult: The Role of the Health and Social Care Information Centre' (2013) Med L Rev (0), 1–33.

[140] Pattinson, n 76, ch 12, esp 413–15, 416–20. See also GMC, *Confidentiality* (2009) paras 67–69.

[141] C Ngwena and R Chadwick, 'Genetic Diagnostic Information and the Duty of Confidentiality: Ethics and Law' (1993) 1 Med LI 73, 74.

12.83 These questions continue to have relevance as genetic testing, including whole genome sequencing, is integrated into mainstream health care.[142] To what extent does the public interest exception justify the disclosure of genetic information about a patient to other members of that patient's family? Both the BMA and the GMC are of the opinion that such disclosure can be justified in exceptional circumstances, where the patient cannot be persuaded to agree and there is a risk of serious harm.[143] The (now abolished) Human Genetics Commission, which was established to develop policy and advise the government on the regulation of genetics, expressed a similar view:

> Disclosure of sensitive personal genetic information without consent may be justified in rare circumstances where a patient refuses to consent to such disclosure but the benefit to other family members or the wider public substantially outweighs the need to respect confidentiality. We would expect this to remain an exceptional situation.[144]

This would be on the basis of the 'harm to others' justification. Ngwena and Chadwick would agree with this view:

> It is apparent from decided cases that the public interest exception can be invoked to protect an open rather than closed category of interests . . . What is crucial is the establishment of tangible anticipated harm to a third party. In principle, therefore, the interest in preventing the deleterious effects of genetic disease in a genetically related third party prima facie falls within the public interest exception.[145]

12.84 It is, therefore, arguable that disclosure of genetic information can be justified where there is a real risk of harm to genetically related third parties.[146] If, as Laurie suggests,[147] the public interest justification applies to avoid harm to others, then one may also conclude that it is only available where it is possible for disclosure to reduce the risk of harm. If the risk of harm cannot be reduced, then it is less clear that there is potential benefit sufficient to justify a breach of confidentiality.

(2) Statutory modifications to the obligation of confidence

12.85 There are three different ways in which a statute may modify a doctor's obligation of confidence. First, it might reinforce the common law obligation of confidence by providing specific penalties for unjustified disclosure, or extend its application to cover circumstances in which the doctor might have been justified in disclosing information at common law. Secondly, it might empower the doctor to disclose information in certain limited circumstances, although not in fact requiring him or her to do so. Thirdly, a statute might positively require disclosure provided specified conditions are satisfied, leaving the doctor no discretion whether or not to disclose.

---

142 An example of the attempts to increasingly integrate genetic testing into mainstream care is the 100 000 Genomes Project, to be delivered through Genomics England Ltd. See <http://www.genomicsengland.co.uk>.

143 BMA, *Human Genetics: Choice and Responsibility* (BMA 1998) 70–2; and GMC, *Confidentiality* (2009), para 69.

144 *Inside Information: Balancing Interests in the Use of Personal Genetic Data* (2002), para 19.

145 Ngwena and Chadwick, n 141, 81.

146 See L Skene, 'Patients' Rights or Family Responsibilities? Two Approaches to Genetic Testing' (1998) 6 Med L Rev 1; 'Genetic Secrets and the Family: A Response to Bell and Bennett' (2001) 9 Med L Rev 162–69. On the question of whether a duty to disclose exists in law see *ABC* v *St George's Healthcare NHS Trust & others* [2015] EWHC 1394 (QB).

147 G T Laurie, 'The Most Personal Information of All: An Appraisal of Genetic Privacy in the Shadow of the Human Genome Project' (1996) 10 International Journal of Law, Policy and the Family 74–101; *Genetic Privacy: A Challenge to Medico-Legal Norms* (Cambridge University Press 2002).

The doctor's duty of confidence may be overridden in circumstances where the doctor is required by law to disclose information that would otherwise be subject to an obligation of confidence. In 1974 in *Hunter v Mann,*[148] Boreham J considered whether or not a statutory obligation to provide information to the police investigating an allegation of dangerous driving could apply to doctors.[149] Having considered both the clear and unambiguous language of the statute and the nature of the doctor's obligation of confidence to his patients, Boreham J concluded that the doctor could be under no obligation of confidence to his patients in relation to information that he was compelled by law to disclose. **12.86**

(i) Section 251 NHS Act 2006 and the Health Service (Control of Patient Information) Regulations 2002

Section 251 of the NHS Act 2006 (which replaces the almost identical s 60 of the Health and Social Care Act 2001) provides a power to ensure that patient identifiable information needed to support essential NHS activity can be used without patient consent. In effect, this measure sets aside the common law obligation of confidentiality. The power can only be used to support medical purposes that are in the interests of patients or the wider public, where consent is not a reasonably practicable alternative and where anonymized information will not suffice. It is designed to support broader medical purposes such as preventative medicine, medical research, and epidemiology and was introduced to cater for situations where patient consent cannot be obtained. For example, important research projects may involve tens of thousands of patients and individual contact would be impracticable. Moreover, excluding those from whom consent could not be obtained might bias data collection to the extent that it loses all value. **12.87**

Section 251 empowers the Secretary of State to make regulations requiring or regulating the processing of patient information for medical purposes as he or she considers necessary or expedient either (a) in the interests of improving patient care; or (b) in the public interest.[150] 'Medical purposes' are defined widely to include, for example, diagnosis, treatment, medical research, preventative medicine, and management of health and social care services.[151] 'Patient information' is defined to include anonymized information.[152] Section 251 provides that: **12.88**

> where prescribed patient information is processed by a person in accordance with the regulations, anything done by him in so processing the information must be taken to be lawfully done despite any obligation of confidence owed by him in respect of it.[153]

This, must, however, be read with the following two subsections:

> (7) Regulations under this section may not make provision for or in connection with the processing of prescribed patient information in a manner inconsistent with any provision made by or under the Data Protection Act 1998 (c 29).
> (8) Subsection (7) does not affect the operation of provisions made under subsection (2)(c).

Thus, where the regulations create conditions that make *a breach of confidence* not unlawful, that breach, *in itself,* will not constitute unlawful processing under the DPA. It is, however, important to note that the requirements of the DPA are otherwise unaffected. Section 251

148 [1974] QB 767.
149 The relevant provision was the Road Traffic Act 1972, s 168(2).
150 NHS Act 2006, s 251(1).
151 ibid, s 251(12).
152 ibid, s 251(10) and (11).
153 ibid, s 251(2)(c).

is restricted to providing an exemption from the common law on confidentiality and does not provide any kind of exemption from the requirements of the DPA.

12.89 Section 251 contemplates, in particular, two types of regulations: (i) those requiring disclosure of specified information to patients or others on their behalf;[154] and (ii) those requiring or authorizing disclosure or other processing of specified information between specified individuals subject to certain conditions.[155] The first is concerned with providing a greater level of information to increase the patient's understanding of their treatment and so forth. The second is more general and is specifically designed (though it is not so restricted) to facilitate transfer of patient information (whether anonymized or not) for medical purposes, including the purposes of medical research, epidemiological purposes, and cancer registries, where this is in the 'public interest'. Where it would be 'reasonably practicable' to anonymize the information, 'having regard to the cost of and the technology available', the regulations must not extend to identifying patient information.[156] Since the abolition of the National Information Governance Board for Health and Social Care all proposed regulations are now to be considered by the Care Quality Commission.[157]

12.90 Regulations were passed in June 2002 under the provision replaced by section 251 (see para 12.87) and they remain in force. The Health Service (Control of Patient Information) Regulations 2002, SI 2002/1438 are of the second type and support processing for medical purposes including the purposes of medical research, the operations of cancer registries, and processing to protect public health with respect to communicable diseases and other similar risks. The regulations set aside the common law duty of confidentiality:

> Anything done by a person that is necessary for the purpose of processing confidential patient information in accordance with these Regulations shall be taken to be lawfully done despite any obligation of confidence owed by that person in respect of it. (reg 4)

Accordingly, processing of identifiable personal information without patient consent is permitted, inter alia, for the establishment of cancer registries[158] and for the recognition, control, and prevention of communicable diseases and other risks to public health.[159]

12.91 Subject to the restrictions contained within Regulation 7, Regulation 5 grants the Secretary of State the power to authorize the processing of 'confidential patient information' for 'medical purposes' in circumstances set out in the Schedule of the Regulations. Decisions in relation to medical research have been delegated to the Health Research Authority (HRA).[160] Confidential patient information cannot be disclosed for the purposes of medical research without a favourable opinion of a research ethics committee. Decisions in relation to all non-research medical purposes remain decisions of the Secretary of State. The HRA is responsible for appointing a committee for the purposes of giving advice to the Secretary of State and the HRA on the application of the Regulations and the disclosure of confidential patient information, for both research and non-research medical purposes, without patient

[154] ibid, s 251(2)(a).

[155] ibid, s 251(2)(b).

[156] ibid, s 251(4).

[157] National Health Service Act 2006, as amended, s 252. See para 12.124.

[158] Health Service (Control of Patient Information) Regulations 2002, reg 2.

[159] There is some question of the scope of reg 3 in this context. See M J Taylor, 'Legal Bases for Disclosing Confidential Patient Information for Public Health: Distinguishing between Health Protection and Health Improvement' Med L Rev (Advance Access, published 20 May, 2015, doi.10.1093/medlaw/fwv018).

[160] Health Service (Control of Patient Information) Regulations 2002, reg 5 as amended by Care Act 2014, s 117(2).

consent.[161] The committee that has been appointed by the HRA for this purpose is known as the Confidentiality Advisory Group (CAG).[162]

Regulation 5 has been subject to judicial consideration. In *Lewis v Secretary of State for Health*,[163] the High Court was asked to consider the disclosure of the medical records of deceased patients to an inquiry. It was argued that the relevant disclosure had been authorized by the Secretary of State under the powers granted by Regulation 5 on the basis that the purpose of the disclosure was the 'audit, monitoring and analysing of the provision made by the health service for patient care and treatment'.[164] Foskett J rejected this claim and queried whether the taking of tissues after death amounted to 'care and treatment', as required by the Regulations.[165] During the course of his judgment, Foskett J also rather tentatively offered the view that the Regulations are restricted to patient information generated within the NHS.[166] As disclosure was authorized on general confidentiality principles, because the disclosure was held to be justified in the public interest, Foskett J did not consider it necessary to consider either argument as closely as he might have done otherwise and expressly recognizes that 'the converse view is at least reasonably arguable'.[167] **12.92**

In 2002 the group responsible for providing independent advice prior to authorization of disclosure of confidential patient information under the Regulations considered an application that concerned disclosure from private hospitals. Members of the group: **12.93**

> were unsure whether the definition of patient information within the Regulations was broad enough to cover private patient information as well as NHS patient information. Members were informed that legal advice had been sought from Department of Health lawyers in relation to this point, as it would set a precedent in terms of applications under the Regulations.[168]

While the minutes of the meeting record that the legal advice had not been received at the time of the meeting, the application was subsequently approved.[169] This would suggest that the advice was that, despite the tentatively offered opinion of Foskett J, the 2002 Regulations can apply to patient information generated outside the NHS context.

(ii) Health and Social Care Act 2012

The Health and Social Care Act 2012[170] establishes a new legal framework for the flow of confidential patient information within England and Wales. Section 252 establishes the 'Health and Social Care Information Centre' (the 'Information Centre'). The Information Centre has been subsequently re-branded NHS Digital. Section 259 provides the Information Centre with the power to *require* confidential patient information (and other information) from health and social care bodies and 'any person (other than a public body) who provides **12.94**

161 Care Act 2014, Sch 7, para. 8.

162 For more information about the committee see the HRA website: <http://www.hra.nhs.uk/about-the-hra/our-committees/section-251/>.

163 *Lewis v Secretary of State for Health* [2008] EWHC 2196.

164 Health Service (Control of Patient Information) Regulations 2002, The Schedule, para 5.

165 *Lewis v Secretary of State for Health*, n 163, [45]–[54].

166 ibid, [46]. See also [48]–[49].

167 ibid, [57].

168 Ethics and Confidentiality Committee (ECC) Meeting (December 2012) 19. Available at <http://www.hra.nhs.uk/about-the-hra/our-committees/section-251/cag-advice-and-approval-decisions/minutes-of-previous-ecc-meetings/>.

169 Approval is recorded in the register of ECC supported approvals. The register is currently held on the HRA website: <http://www.hra.nhs.uk/about-the-hra/our-committees/section-251/cag-advice-and-approval-decisions/>.

170 Pt IX, Ch 2.

health services, or adult social care, in England, pursuant to arrangements made with a public body exercising functions in connection with the provision of such services of care'.[171]

12.95 The Information Centre has this power to *require* information where it is considered 'necessary or expedient'[172] for the purposes of any of its statutory functions *and in the case of confidential patient information*[173] in response to:

(a) a direction from the Secretary of State or the Commissioning Board to establish an 'information system' under s 254, or
(b) a 'mandatory request'[174] from a 'Principal Body'[175] to establish and information system under s 255 and s 256,[176] or
(c) any person, who has requested that the Information Centre collect confidential information,[177] *if* that person has (independent) authority to *require* disclosure of that information (s 256(2)(b)).

12.96 Outside the circumstances in which the Information Centre may *require* the disclosure of confidential patient information[178] it may *request* disclosure of confidential information if the request relates to 'information which may otherwise be lawfully disclosed to the Information Centre or to [the party requesting that the Centre collect the information] by the person holding it'.[179]

12.97 There is a general responsibility upon the Information Centre to publish all information obtained through complying with a direction under s 254 (by the Secretary of State or the Commissioning Board) or a (mandatory) request under s 255 (by any other person) to establish and operate a system for the collection or analysis of information.[180] However, there are exceptions to this general obligation and they include where the information is in a form that would allow an individual to be identified.[181] Therefore, although the Information Centre is empowered to collect, and to require, the disclosure of confidential patient information it will not *publish* that information in identifiable form. Note in this context also the general duty upon the Information Centre to 'respect and promote the privacy of recipients of health services and of adult social care in England'.[182]

12.98 There are further restrictions upon the *dissemination* of identifiable data (other than by way of publication).[183] As a public body, the Information Centre may only disclose information

[171] The Health and Social Care Act 2012, s 259(2).
[172] ibid, s 259(1)(a).
[173] ibid, s 256(1): 'Confidential Information' is defined within the Act as 'information which is in a form which—(a) identifies any individual to whom the information relates who is not an individual who provides health or adult social care, or (b) enables the identity of such an individual to be ascertained.'
[174] ibid, see s 255(4): A request is a mandatory request if it is (a) made by a principal body, and (b) the body considers the information to be necessary or expedient to have in relation to the discharge of a duty in connection with the provision of health or adult social care services in England.
[175] ibid, s 255(9): 'Principal Body' means Monitor, the Care Quality Commission, the National Institute for Health and Care Excellence, and such other persons as may be prescribed in regulations.
[176] ibid. A request of this kind constitutes a 'mandatory request' (s 255(4)) and mandatory requests for confidential information are permitted under s 256(2)).
[177] ibid. Under s 255, *any* person (including a devolved authority) can request that the Information Centre 'establish and operate a system for the collection or analysis of information of a description specified in the request' but s 256 limits requests for confidential information.
[178] ibid, s 259(3).
[179] ibid, s 256(2)(c).
[180] ibid, s 260.
[181] ibid. If the information relates to 'a relevant person' then it must also be considered inappropriate to publish taking into account the interests of the person and the public interest. See s 260(1) and (2).
[182] ibid, s 253(ca)
[183] ibid, s 261(2).

where it has specific power to do so. These circumstances are set out in sections 261 and 262. The Information Centre may only disseminate information if it considers that dissemination to be for the purposes of the provision of health or adult social care or the promotion of health.[184] The Information Centre may also disclose information obtained in the range of circumstances set out in section 262(5)(a)–(f). These include where (a) the information has previously been lawfully disclosed to the public, (b) disclosure is made in accordance with any court order, (c) the disclosure is necessary or expedient for the purposes of protecting the welfare of any individual, (d) the disclosure is made in circumstances where it is necessary or expedient for the person to have the information for the purposes of exercising statutory functions, (e) the disclosure is made in connection with the investigation of a criminal offence, or (f) for the purposes of criminal proceedings. Where information is disclosed under (a), (b), and (f), the common law duty of confidence is expressly set aside.[185] In exercising any function of publishing or otherwise disseminating information, the Information Centre must have regard to any advice given to it by the committee appointed by the Health Research Authority under paragraph 8(1) of Schedule 7 to the Care Act 2014 for the purposes of giving such advice.[186] This committee is known as the Confidentiality Advisory Group (CAG) (and is further discussed in para 12.91).

The Information Centre is under a statutory responsibility to prepare and publish a code of practice on confidential information. The content must relate to the practice to be followed in relation to the collection, analysis, publication and other dissemination of confidential information concerning, or connected with, the provision of health services or adult social care in England.[187] **12.99**

The Health and Social Care (Safety and Quality) Act 2015 ('the 2015 Act'), which introduced various amendments to the Health and Social Care Act 2012, is intended to improve the safety and quality of health services and social care in a number of ways. It includes both a requirement for the use of a consistent service user identifier in individuals' health and social care records in England, and also, a duty to share information in support of people's direct care in England to help ensure more integrated care. **12.100**

Section 2 of the 2015 Act inserts a new section 251A (consistent identifiers) into Part 9 of the Health and Social Care Act 2012. This makes provision for a duty upon relevant persons[188] to include a consistent identifier—likely in practice to be the NHS number[189]—in records whether processed internally or disclosed to other health and social care bodies. The duty extends only so far as the relevant person considers that the inclusion is: **12.101**

(a) likely to facilitate the provision to the individual of health services or adult social care in England, and
(b) in the individual's best interests.[190]

The duty to include a consistent identifier is lifted in certain specified circumstances with the effect that it is only imposed where the relevant person either knows the consistent **12.102**

[184] ibid, s 261(1A).
[185] ibid, s 261(6).
[186] ibid, s 262A.
[187] ibid, s 263.
[188] A 'relevant health or adult social care commissioner or provider' as defined in new s 251C(2) of the Health and Social Care Act 2012.
[189] Health and Social Care Act 2012, s 251A(1) imposes a duty on the Secretary of State to make regulations specifying a description of consistent identifier but an example of a consistent identifier, such as might satisfy the criteria to be specified, is given in the explanatory notes as NHS number.
[190] Health and Social Care Act 2012, s 251(A)(5).

identifier or might learn it through reasonable efforts, the patient does not object to such inclusion, and certain other specific conditions are not satisfied; for instance the patient is not receiving sensitive (eg sexual health) treatments anonymously.[191]

12.103 Section 3 of the 2015 Act inserts new section 251B (duty to share information) into Part 9 of the Health and Social Care Act 2012. The duty is upon any relevant person to disclose information to those working for them or to 'any other relevant health or adult social care commissioner or provider with whom the relevant person communicates about the individual.' As with the previous section, the duty applies only so far as 'the relevant person considers that the disclosure is (a) likely to facilitate the provision to the individual of health services or adult social care in England, and (b) in the individual's best interests.'[192]

12.104 The duty to share information extends only to direct care purposes[193] and is expressly lifted in circumstances where:

(a) the individual objects, or would be likely to object, to the disclosure of the information;
(b) the information concerns, or is connected with, the provision of health services or adult social care by an 'anonymous access provider' (as defined in new section 251C(6));
(c) for any other reason the relevant person is not reasonably able, or should not *be required, to comply with the new duty.*[194]

(iii) Public health

12.105 In addition to the provisions of the Health Service (Control of Patient Information) Regulations 2002 relevant to public health discussed above (para 12.90), there are specific regulations which require the disclosure of confidential information in certain circumstances for public health purposes. Since the nineteenth century there has been a statutory responsibility to notify infectious diseases. The Health Protection (Notification) Regulations 2010[195] extend the responsibility adopting an 'all hazards' approach and there is now a responsibility upon a registered medical practitioner (R) to notify the proper officer of a local authority where they have 'reasonable grounds for suspecting' that a patient (P) has (or has died from):

(a) a notifiable disease;
(b) an infection[196] which, in the view of R, presents or could present significant harm to human health; or has (having) been
(c) contaminated[197] in a manner which, in the view of R, presents or could present significant harm to human health.[198]

12.106 Where a local authority has been so notified, there is a responsibility upon them to disclose the fact and content of that notification to Public Health England, the proper officer in the local authority in which P usually resides, and also the proper officer in the Port Authority or local authority in which P has disembarked (from ship, hovercraft, aircraft or international

---

[191] ibid, s 251(A)(6).
[192] ibid, s 251(B)(3).
[193] ibid, s 251(C)(5).
[194] ibid, s 251(B)(4).
[195] Regulations 2010/659. See also Health Protection (Notification) (Wales) Regulations 2010/1546.
[196] According to s 45A(3) of the Public Health (Control of Disease) Act 1984 ('the 1984 Act') any reference to infection or contamination is 'a reference to infection or contamination which presents or could present significant harm to human health'.
[197] According to the 1984 Act, s 45A(2) contamination includes radiation.
[198] Health Protection (Notification) Regulations 2010, Regulations 2010/659. The duty in relation to the living is contained within reg 2. The duty in relation to the dead within reg 3.

train) if known.[199] Diagnostic laboratories also have a duty to notify Public Health England if they identify any 'causative agent' listed within Schedule 2 of the Regulations or evidence of any infection caused by such an agent.[200]

A local authority has powers to address a public health risk. These powers are conferred by the Public Health (Control of Disease) Act 1984, as amended by the Health and Social Care Act 2008, and the Health Protection (Local Authority Powers) Regulations 2010. The 2008 Act introduced Part 2A into the 1984 Act and this conferred a number of additional powers.[201] Detailed consideration of these powers extends beyond a consideration of data protection and confidentiality but it is worth noting that these powers include, where a justice of the peace is satisfied that an individual represents a significant risk to human health, the power to detain them, to submit them to medical examination, and to ask them questions about their health and circumstances. **12.107**

The NHS (Venereal Diseases) Regulations 1974[202] have been revoked, so far as they apply in England, by the Health and Social Care (Miscellaneous Revocations) Regulations 2015. NHS Trusts and Primary Care Trusts (Sexually Transmitted Diseases) Directions 2000 remain in force but since the reorganization of the NHS the bodies named in the Directions either no longer exist (ie Primary Care Trusts) or are relatively few (and declining) in number (ie NHS Trusts). It is not clear at the time of writing what, if anything, will replace the Regulations and Directions and make specific provision for information relating to sexually transmitted disease. One option appears to be development of the HSCIC Code of Practice to cover the handling of such data.[203] **12.108**

(iv) Injuries at work: The Reporting of Injuries, Diseases and Dangerous Occurrences Regulations 2013/1471

Under these Regulations the 'responsible person'[204] must report an injury, death, or dangerous occurrence[205] involving an employee or other person 'in control of the premises' where the reportable occurrence happened and also diagnosis reportable under Regulation 8, 9, or 10 in relation to certain persons including employees and self-employed persons. Records must be kept of reportable incidents and reportable diagnosis and any injury to a person at work resulting from an accident arising out of or in connection with that work, which incapacitate that person for routine work for more than three consecutive days (excluding the day of the accident).[206] These records must be kept for at least three years.[207] **12.109**

(v) Abortion Regulations 1991

Under the Abortion Regulations 1991,[208] any registered medical practitioner who terminates a pregnancy in England or Wales is required to provide the Chief Medical Officer with **12.110**

199 ibid, reg 6.
200 Ibid, reg 4.
201 The Health Protection (Part 2A) Regulations 2010/658; See also Health Protection (Part 2A) Wales Regulations 2010/1544.
202 SI 1974/29.
203 National AIDS Trust, *HIV Patient Information and NHS Confidentiality in England* (Policy Report, January 2014) 20 <http://www.nat.org.uk/media/Files/Publications/Jan-2014-HIV-Patient-Confidentiality-NHS.pdf>.
204 Reporting of Injuries, Diseases and Dangerous Occurrences Regulations SI 2013/1471, reg 3.
205 ibid. Reportable under regs 4,5, 6, or 7.
206 ibid, reg 12.
207 Ibid, reg 12(2).
208 SI 1991/499. Wilful contravention or wilful failure to comply with these requirements is an offence under s 2(3). See *R v Senior* [1981] 1 QB 283 *per* Lord Russell for a discussion of what amounts to wilful failure in these circumstances.

notice of the termination together with any other information specified in the prescribed form of notification.[209] The regulations also prohibit disclosure of the notice or other information provided to the Chief Medical Officer other than for the purposes set out in the regulations themselves.[210]

(vi) Births

12.111 Any person in attendance on the mother is obliged to give notice of any child born dead or alive after the twenty-fourth week of pregnancy.[211] Notice must be provided to: (a) the NHS Commissioning Board;[212] (b) a local authority whose area includes the whole or part of the registrar's sub-district; and (c) a Clinical Commissioning Group whose area coincides with or includes the whole or part of the registrar's sub-district.[213] This obligation may be discharged by instructing another person to notify the birth.[214]

(vii) Fertility treatment

12.112 There are specific provisions in the Human Fertilisation and Embryology Act 1990 (as modified by the Human Fertilisation and Embryology Act 2008) regulating confidentiality. The Human Fertilisation and Embryology Authority (HFEA)[215] is required by the 1990 Act (as amended) to keep a register of information relating to the provision of licensed treatments.[216] Generally, specific and unambiguous consent is required for the disclosure of identifying information covered by the register of information, but there is a long list of specific exceptions.[217] The HFEA describe the aim of the register is 'to give people conceived through donation an opportunity to learn about their genetic background and to help avoid biological relatives inadvertently marrying or having children'.[218] A person who is 16 years old or over may apply to the HFEA for information about whether they were conceived through donated material and to receive certain information about the donor.[219] The information that may be received is limited to non-identifying information unless the donor has consented to the disclosure of identifying information or the person was conceived on or after 1 April 2005 and they have reached 18 years of age.[220]

(viii) In connection with the investigation and prevention of crime

12.113 Under the Police and Criminal Evidence Act 1984, certain material is excluded from the ordinary provisions enabling courts to make special procedure orders for the production of documents required for criminal investigations.[221] This material is described as 'excluded material' and covers both personal records created or acquired for professional purposes and

---

[209] ibid, reg 4(1). In Wales the 'notice' or 'information' must be provided to the National Assembly for Wales.

[210] ibid, reg 5.

[211] NHS Act 2006, s 269(4).

[212] Since 1 April 2013 the NHS Commissioning Board has used the name NHS England for operational purposes.

[213] National Health Service and Public Health (Functions and Miscellaneous Provisions) Regulations 2013/261, reg 9.

[214] NHS Act 2006, s 269(8).

[215] Human Fertilisation and Embryology Act 1990 (as amended), s 5(1).

[216] ibid, s 31(2).

[217] ibid, ss 31(2), 33A–34. For more information see the HFEA Code of Practice (8th edn, 2015) 30: 'Confidentiality and Privacy'.

[218] Answer to 'Why is there a Register?' on Frequently Asked Question page on HFEA website < http://www.hfea.gov.uk/hfea-questions.html#whyistherearegister>.

[219] Human Fertilisation and Embryology Act 1990, n 215, s 31ZA(2).

[220] ibid, s 31ZA; The Human Fertilisation and Embryology Authority (Disclosure of Donor Information) Regulations 2004.

[221] Police and Criminal Evidence Act 1984, s 9(1).

held in confidence, and human tissue or tissue fluid taken for the purposes of diagnosis or medical treatment and held in confidence.[222] Personal records are in turn defined in s 12 to include records from which an individual can be identified and which relate to his or her physical or mental health.

In *R v Cardiff Crown Court, ex p Kellam*[223] it was held that hospital records detailing which of a psychiatric hospital's patients were absent from the hospital on a particular day fell within the definition of 'personal records', because they enabled patients to be identified by reference to their state of mental health. The fact that the document was created for the purpose of calculating National Insurance payments was not relevant to this enquiry, since the critical question is whether or not the information in the record relates to the physical or mental health of the individual who may be identified therefrom. In the context, the phrase 'relating to physical or mental health' is to be construed broadly. **12.114**

Police may seize excluded material without a court order if they come upon material whilst lawfully on premises for another purpose, provided they have reasonable grounds for believing that it is relevant evidence in relation to an offence and that it is necessary to seize it to prevent it from being destroyed.[224] A court order to produce excluded material will only be given if there are (i) reasonable grounds to believe that there is material which includes excluded or special procedure material on the premises; (ii) a search warrant for that material might otherwise (ie before PACE) have been given; and (iii) the issue of a warrant would, in the circumstances, have been appropriate. The person who is subject to the order must be given notice and cannot then lawfully destroy material.[225] **12.115**

Section 19 of the Terrorism Act 2000 imposes a duty on everyone, including doctors, to inform the police if they believe or suspect certain terrorism offences under the Act to have been committed. The police must be notified 'as soon as is reasonably practicable' and a failure to do so will amount to an offence under the Act. **12.116**

Section 172(2)(b) of the Road Traffic Act 1988 provides that, where the driver of a vehicle, or rider of a bicycle, is alleged to be guilty of a road traffic offence: 'any other person shall if required . . . give such information which it is in his power to give and may lead to identification of the driver.'[226] **12.117**

Hunter v Mann[227] confirmed that this section applied to doctors who received the information in confidence from a patient, and that doctors have the power to disclose such information if so required by statute, even where they might not be entitled otherwise voluntarily to disclose such information without the patient's consent. **12.118**

(ix) Clinical governance and the Care Quality Commission

The Care Quality Commission (CQC) has many oversight duties, including monitoring the detention of mental health patients, assessing the performance of health services, coordinating investigations into whether public funds are being used effectively within health care, and overseeing the NHS complaints procedure. This role of the CQC is addressed in detail in Chapter 1 (para 1.125–1.130). It was established in April 2009 under s 1 of the Health and Social Care Act 2008 and replaces the functions of the Healthcare Commission, the **12.119**

---

222 If, eg, blood was taken to determine an individual's blood-alcohol level it would not be 'excluded material'. Bullets are not excluded material.

223 The Times, 3 May, 1993 (Evans LJ and Morland J). Noted by A Grubb (1994) 2 Med L Rev 370.

224 Police and Criminal Evidence Act 1984, s 19.

225 ibid, Sch 1.

226 Section 172(4) makes it an offence to fail to give information in accordance with such a request.

227 [1974] QB 767.

Commission for Social Care and Inspection, and the Mental Health Act Commission. The Health and Social Care Act 2012 gave CQC new legal responsibilities from 1st April 2013 for monitoring and seeking to improve registered providers information governance (IG) practices. Section 280 of the 2012 Act amended the Health and Social Care Act 2008 to provide the CQC (under S20A of the 2008 Act) with the following functions:

(a) to monitor the practice followed by registered persons in relation to [the processing of patient information or any other information obtained or generated in the course of the provision of the health service or by adult social services, or adult placement schemes made in connection with the provision of personal care, by an English local authority],[228] and
(b) to keep NHS England and Monitor informed about the practice being followed by registered persons in relation to such processing.

12.120 The CQC must 'seek to improve the practice followed by registered persons in relation to the processing of relevant information'.[229] CQC may require persons listed under s 64(2) of the Health and Social Care Act 2008, including an English NHS body, and any person providing health care commissioned by NHS England or a Clinical Commissioning Group, to provide the CQC with 'any information, documents, records (including personal and medical records) or other items which the Commission considers it necessary or expedient to have for the purposes of any of its regulatory functions.'[230] Section 76 of the Act prevents those involved with or assisting the CQC from disclosing confidential information when it relates to and identifies an individual during that individual's lifetime. It is a criminal offence, punishable by fine or up to two years' imprisonment, to knowingly or recklessly contravene the prohibition on disclosure, subject to the defence of reasonable belief that one of the circumstances specified by s 77(2) applies, and the defence that the circumstances specified by s 77(3) apply.

12.121 Disclosure is permitted under s 77(2) where it:

(a) was made in a form in which the individual to whom the information relates is not identified,
(b) was made with the consent of the individual to whom the information relates,
(c) has previously been lawfully disclosed to the public,
(d) was made in accordance with any enactment or court order,
(e) was necessary or expedient for the purposes of protecting the welfare of any individual, or
(f) was made to any person or body in circumstances where such disclosure was necessary or expedient for that body or person to exercise its functions under any enactment.

12.122 Disclosure is permitted under s 77(3), where it was made for the purpose of facilitating the exercise of any functions of the Commission, in connection with the investigation of a criminal offence, or for the purpose of criminal proceedings.

12.123 The prohibition on disclosure seems to be narrower than the common law in one respect: it does not survive the death of the individual to whom it relates. The common law position is otherwise (see para 12.36). The exceptions in s 77(2) largely reflect the common law: consent, disclosure required by law, and disclosure in the public interest.

12.124 The view of the CQC must be sought before Regulations are laid before Parliament under Section 251 of the National Health Service Act 2006.[231]

---

[228] Section 20A(3) defines 'relevant information'.
[229] Section 20A(2).
[230] Health and Social Care Act 2008, s 64(1).
[231] National Health Service Act 2006, s 252.

(x) Monitor and audit of NHS Foundation Trusts

Monitor authorizes, licenses, and regulates NHS foundation trusts. Monitor issues a licence to each NHS foundation trust which set out conditions with which the trust must comply. Audit of NHS foundation trusts must comply with guidance issued by Monitor, and auditors have a responsibility to report certain matters to Monitor.[232] Under Schedule 10, paragraph 2 of the 2006 Act[233] 'An auditor of an NHS foundation trust has a right of access at all reasonable times to every document relating to the trust which appears to him necessary for the purposes of his functions under this Chapter.' The disclosure of information obtained by Auditors during the course of an audit is restricted.[234] The exceptions to the restrictions on the disclosure of information received are: 12.125

(a) with the consent of the person to whom the information relates,
(b) for the purposes of any functions of an auditor of an NHS foundation trust,
(c) for the purposes of the functions of the regulator,
(d) for the purposes of the functions of the Comptroller and Auditor General under this Chapter,
(e) for the purposes of the functions of [the Care Quality Commission],
(f) for the purposes of any criminal proceedings.

Again, the exceptions largely reflect the position at common law: consent, disclosure required by law, and disclosure in the public interest are all permitted. Otherwise disclosure is an offence that carries with it the possibility of imprisonment.[235]

3. Disclosure for the purpose of litigation

(i) Actions against an NHS trust, Foundation trust, or doctor

Before the commencement of litigation a person who is 'likely to be a party to subsequent proceedings' can apply to the High Court to compel a doctor or hospital to make disclosures relevant to an issue arising or likely to arise, provided that the doctor or hospital is also 'likely to be a party to the proceedings'.[236] Such pre-action disclosure is no longer limited to litigation relating to personal injuries or death.[237] 12.126

In the leading case of *Black v Sumitomo Corp,* the Court of Appeal held that it was not necessary to show that proceedings are likely to be issued, but that the person from whom disclosure is sought 'may well' be a party to proceedings *if* those proceedings are issued.[238] It was held that to hold otherwise would be both undesirable and unnecessary: undesirable because the purpose of the application is to enable the litigants to discover whether there is sufficient evidence to bring a claim; and unnecessary, because the court has all the power it needs in the exercise of its discretion to restrain mere fishing expeditions. The Court of Appeal also considered the requirement that the court may order pre-action disclosure 'only where' it is 'desirable' to dispose fairly of anticipated proceedings, assist resolution of the dispute without proceedings, or save costs.[239] This was said to involve a two-stage process.[240] For jurisdictional purposes, the court is only permitted to consider granting pre-action 12.127

232 NHS Act 2006 para 6, Sch 10.
233 ibid, s 62.
234 ibid, para 8, Sch10.
235 Ibid, paras 8(2) and 8(3).
236 Senior Courts Act 1981, s 33, and CPR Pt 31.16. See also County Courts Act 1984, s 52.
237 Civil Procedure (Modification of Enactments) Order 1998, SI 1998/2940 and *Burrells Wharf Freeholds v Galliard Homes* [2000] CP Rep 4.
238 *Black v Sumitomo Corp* [2001] EWCA Civ 1819, [71]–[72] *per* Rix LJ.
239 See CPR Pt 31.16.
240 *Black v Sumitomo Corp*, n 238, [79]–[83] and [88].

disclosure where there is a 'real prospect' of such an order being fair to the parties, or of assisting the avoidance of litigation, or of saving costs. If there is such a real prospect, then the court should go on to consider whether to exercise its discretion in the light of all the facts. According to Rix J:

> the more focused the complaint and the more limited the disclosure sought in that connection, the easier it is for the court to exercise its discretion in favour of pre-action disclosure, even where the complaint might seem somewhat speculative or the request might be argued to constitute a mere fishing exercise.[241]

12.128 Courts considering these applications must balance the public interest in favour of disclosure against the public interest in maintaining the confidentiality of the information, and the relevant legislation empowering the High Court to make such orders prohibits the making of an order for discovery where 'compliance with the order, if made, would be likely to be injurious to the public interest'.[242]

12.129 The burden is on the party seeking to maintain the confidence of the information to establish that the court should refuse to order disclosure, since it is generally the case that the public interest in the administration of justice will be overriding. It is clear that the mere fact of information having been communicated confidentially within the confines of the doctor–patient relationship will not be sufficient to justify the court exercising its discretion. Some further considerations would be required before a court would exercise its discretion to refuse to require medical information to be disclosed in the context of litigation.[243]

(ii) After proceedings have been commenced

12.130 Once litigation has commenced, the High Court has the power (within its inherent jurisdiction) to order disclosure between the parties of any documents that are relevant to an issue arising out of the claim. It also has the power under s 34 of the Senior Courts Act 1981 to order a person who is not a party to the proceedings to disclose certain documents to the claimant, defendant, or their adviser.[244] These powers are, once again, dependent upon a finding that it is not against the public interest to order disclosure,[245] and that disclosure is desirable to dispose of the case fairly, assist resolution of the dispute without proceedings, or to save costs.[246]

12.131 Even as between parties to the litigation, English courts have shown their willingness to exercise their discretion to refuse to order disclosure of information where there is an important public interest in maintaining the confidentiality of the information in the circumstances. Thus, for example, in *D v NSPCC*[247] (an action for breach of duty and negligence against the NSPCC), the House of Lords held that documents disclosing the source of a complaint to the NSPCC should be immune from inspection on discovery, since otherwise the society's capacity to perform its public functions could be put at risk. It may be that, in particular cases, information that would otherwise be confidential—for example, information disclosed for purposes of maintaining public health or containing the spread of infectious diseases—may similarly be immune from disclosure in legal proceedings on the basis that disclosure might jeopardize an important public interest.

---

241 ibid, [95].
242 Senior Courts Act 1981, s 35(1). See also CPR Pt 31.19.
243 For a discussion of the court's discretion in relation to medical information see *Re C (A Minor) (Evidence: Confidential Information)* [1991] 2 FLR 478.
244 See also County Courts Act 1984, s 53.
245 Senior Courts Act 1981, s 35(1).
246 CPR Pt 31.17(3).
247 [1977] 1 All ER 589.

(iii) In the courtroom

It will often be the case that a doctor or other health professional is requested to supply information as evidence orally or in a written statement, either as a witness or in order to defend the claim. In such cases, the doctor is entitled to include confidential information in his or her evidence, provided that it can be shown that it is in the public interest that such information is before the court.[248] As discussed above, the presumption in favour of disclosure rests upon the weight of the public interest in the administration of justice. In order to justify non-disclosure, therefore, a doctor must be able to establish that the public interest in confidentiality in the circumstances outweighs the public interest in disclosure. Doctors who are not able successfully to justify non-disclosure may be liable for contempt of court if they refuse to give evidence in court, regardless of the fact that the information is confidential to the patient.[249] **12.132**

The Canadian Supreme Court in *M(A) v Ryan* held that there is no absolute privilege in communications between a psychiatrist and his or her patient.[250] The court must be satisfied of four requirements for privilege: (i) communication in confidence; (ii) confidence is essential to the full and satisfactory maintenance of the professional relationship; (iii) fostering the relationship is of public importance; and (iv) the interests served by protecting the communications from disclosure outweigh the interest of pursuing the truth and disposing correctly of the litigation. On the facts, in a claim by a patient against her former psychiatrist for abuse, the records of her communications with a subsequent psychiatrist were not privileged since disclosure could be limited to the lawyers and expert witnesses of the defendant and should not be used for any purpose other than defending the claim.[251] **12.133**

4. Confidentiality, warning, and negligence liability

(i) Negligent disclosure

In the New Zealand case of *Furniss v Fitchett*[252] it was held that liability in negligence could arise from disclosure of information in breach of confidence. Barrowclough CJ clearly felt that the obligation to take reasonable care to respect confidences could be owed in any situation in which it was reasonably foreseeable that disclosure might injure the claimant's mental health. **12.134**

> I have not forgotten that the certificate was true and accurate, but I see no reason for limiting the duty to one of care in seeing that it is accurate. The duty must extend also to the exercise of care in deciding whether it should be put in circulation in such a way that it is likely to cause harm to another.

The English courts have considered this issue in the context of negligent disclosure by the police. In *Swinney v Chief Constable of the Northumbria Police*[253] there was an arguable claim for negligent breach of confidence where police allowed an informer's identity held in confidence to be discovered by leaving documents in a car, from which they were subsequently **12.135**

[248] For a consideration of the Crown Court's power to set aside a witness summons which would have required the witness to produce records relating to lawful abortions see *Morrow v DPP* (1993) 14 BMLR 54, noted by I Kennedy, [1994] 2 Med L Rev 99.

[249] See *Duchess of Kingston's Case* (1776) 20 State Trials 355; *Nuttall v Nuttall and Twynan* (1964) 108 Sol J 605. For a discussion of the balancing process, see *D v NSPCC* [1977] 1 All ER 589, 597.

[250] [1997] 1 SCR 157 (Can Sup Ct).

[251] See also the GMC guidance relating to disclosure in connection with judicial or other statutory proceedings in GMC: *Confidentiality* (2009), paras 21–23.

[252] [1958] NZLR 396, 403. Noted by R G Fox, 'Professional Confidences and the Psychologist' (1968) 3(1) University of Tasmania Law Review 12, 34.

[253] [1997] QB 464 (CA).

stolen. Applying the current rules relating to recovery in the tort of negligence to the facts, it was possible that a special relationship existed that rendered the claimants particularly at risk; that the police had in fact assumed a responsibility of confidentiality to the claimants; and that the claimant's claim was not precluded on grounds of public policy. The court confirmed that the police do not have blanket immunity and considerations of public policy, such as the need to preserve the springs of information; to protect informers; and to encourage them to come forward without an undue fear of the risk that their identity will become known to the suspect, carried considerable weight. However, at trial, there was no liability in negligence as there was no breach of duty on the facts.[254]

12.136 No English court has yet considered whether an action in negligence could arise out of a breach of confidence by a doctor. In light of the approach taken by the court in *Swinney*, there is a strong argument that in any case in which it could be shown that a doctor had breached the obligation of confidence owed to a patient, in circumstances where it was foreseeable that this could harm or put a patient a risk, he or she may also have breached the duty of care owed to that patient. Even if other doctors might similarly have disclosed the information, it could hardly be described as 'responsible' medical practice to act unlawfully in breach of a patient's confidence.[255] This is particularly so given that the finding of a breach of confidence itself is predicated upon there being no overriding public interest in disclosure in the circumstances.

12.137 In most cases, however, a claimant will not have suffered damage compensable in the tort of negligence. In order to succeed in a negligence action, a claimant needs to show some personal injury, or possibly economic loss.[256]

(ii) Negligent failure to disclose

12.138 A doctor is sometimes justified in disclosing confidential information in the public interest. Does this mean that a doctor might also have a duty to disclose confidential information in order to avert a risk of harm either from the patient or some other source? The most well-known authority dealing with the doctor's duty to warn of a risk of harm from a patient in this situation is the American case of *Tarasoff v Regents of the University of California*.[257] The California Supreme Court held that a psychotherapist could be held liable in negligence for failing to warn of his patient's intention to kill a named victim. The court accepted that: 'the therapist's obligations to his patient require that he not disclose a confidence unless such disclosure is necessary to avert danger to others'.[258]

12.139 Where, however, there was a real risk of physical harm to a named person:

> If the exercise of reasonable care to protect the threatened victim requires the therapist to warn the endangered party or those who can reasonably be expected to notify him, we see no sufficient societal interest that would protect and justify concealment. The containment of such risks lies in the public interest.[259]

[254] *Swinney v Chief Constable of Northumbria Police (No 2)* (1999) 11 Admin LR 811.

[255] See, eg, the interpretation of *Bolam v Friern HMC* [1957] 2 All ER 118 in *Smith v Tunbridge Wells HA* [1994] 5 Med L Rev 334 (Morland J); and *Pearce v United Bristol NHS Trust* [1999] PIQR 53 (CA).

[256] The recovery of economic loss in actions for medical negligence based upon a breach of confidence would involve a substantial expansion in the law governing the recovery of economic loss which is unlikely given the 'incremental' approach favoured by English courts in this area: see, eg, *Murphy v Brentwood District Council* [1990] 2 All ER 908.

[257] *Tarasoff v Regents of the University of California* (1976) 131 Cal Rptr 14.

[258] ibid, 27.

[259] ibid, 27–28.

Thus, the psychotherapist was held liable in negligence *for failing to warn the patient's victim* (whom the patient later murdered).

The English courts have traditionally been slow to recognize a duty to prevent harm being inflicted by a third party.[260] In *ABC* v *St George's Healthcare NHS Trust & others*[261] a detained mental patient refused permission to disclose his diagnosis of Huntington's Disease to his pregnant daughter. When the daughter subsequently learnt, after giving birth to her own daughter, of her father's diagnosis she claimed the failure to tell her of her father's condition was (a) actionable negligence on the part of the Defendants and (b) a violation of her rights under Article 8 of the European Convention on Human Rights. For the purposes of the application: **12.140**

> the Defendants were prepared to proceed on the basis that the Claimant would be able to establish at trial that injury to her would have been reasonably foreseeable if they failed to inform her that her father had Huntington's Disease. Again, for the purposes of the present application, they were prepared to accept that there was sufficient proximity between the Claimant and the Defendants for a duty of care to arise.[262]

Nonetheless, the Defendants claimed that the action should be struck out as 'there was no reasonable prospect of the Claimant establishing that it would be fair, just or reasonable to impose on the Defendants a duty of care towards the Claimants in this regard.'[263]

Mr Justice Nicol accepted the submission to strike out the claim because it disclosed no reasonable cause of action. He did not consider there to be any relevant assumption of responsibility toward the Claimant by the Defendants but also acknowledged the significance of the description by counsel for the Defendants of a number of potential negative consequences of putting doctors in a position where they were under a duty to disclose confidential information to third parties. While English courts will *allow* disclosure (in the public interest) where there are exceptional circumstances of danger or harm to others, they seem reluctant to *require* it. **12.141**

5. Remedies

(i) Injunction

A patient may apply to the court for an injunction to restrain publication of confidential information, either absolutely or in part. An injunction is available at the discretion of the court and may be granted upon whatever terms the court thinks appropriate. At the interlocutory stage, when most of these issues come to be tried, the availability of an injunction depends upon showing that there is a serious issue to be tried.[264] An interlocutory injunction will be of considerable practical significance for a claimant in a breach of confidence action since, unless publication is restrained, it will usually be pointless for a claimant to continue with the action. **12.142**

[260] See, eg, *Palmer v Trees HA* [2000] PIQR P1; *Home Office v Dorset Yacht* [1970] AC 1004; and *Hill v Chief Constable of West Yorkshire* [1989] AC 53.
[261] *ABC* v *St George's Healthcare NHS Trust & others* [2015] EWHC 1394 (QB).
[262] ibid, [11].
[263] ibid, [11].
[264] Applying the principles laid down in *American Cyanamid Co v Ethicon* [1975] 1 All ER 504. See further para 12.72.

(ii) Declaration

12.143 In some circumstances a claimant may be satisfied with a declaration from the court that a breach of confidence took place, or that a particular disclosure that is reasonably anticipated by the parties would amount to a breach of confidence.

(iii) Damages

12.144 An award of damages for a breach of confidence is, in line with ordinary common law principles, principally intended to be compensatory.[265] If a doctor's breach of confidence caused financial harm to a patient, such as adverse implications for his or her employment or business opportunities, this loss could be compensated in an action for breach of confidence. The appropriateness of awarding damages for mental distress has been the subject of judicial doubt in the past[266] but the courts have now clarified the position.

12.145 In *Cornelius v De Taranto*[267] the High Court awarded the claimant £3,000 as fair and reasonable compensation for the injury to her feelings after a medicolegal expert passed a copy of her psychiatric report to the claimant's GP and a consultant psychiatrist without her agreement, because the expert believed the claimant needed urgent psychiatric treatment. Morland J found that there was a clear contract between both parties and the defendant was in breach of an implied contractual duty of confidence. Having reviewed the relevant case law, Morland J concluded that:

> [i]n the present case in my judgement recovery of damages for mental distress caused by breach of confidence, when no other substantial remedy is available, would not be inimical to considerations of policy but indeed to refuse such recovery would illustrate that something was wrong with the law. Although the object of the contract was the provision of a medicolegal report, that object could not be achieved without the defendant's examination and assessment of confidential material relating to the claimant's private and family life. The duty of confidence was an essential indeed fundamental ingredient of the contractual relationship between the claimant and the defendant which she breached.[268]

12.146 Given that an injunction would be of little use to the claimant because the damage had already been done, Morland J was prepared to award fair and reasonable compensation. He considered this conclusion to be consistent with Article 8 ECHR and opined that any victory would be hollow if confidential information could be disclosed and only nominal damages awarded in respect of distress caused.[269]

12.147 This case was subsequently applied in *Lady Archer v Williams*.[270] In that case the claimant was awarded £2,500 damages for breach of confidence and injury to feelings. The judge accepted that, where a breach of confidence causes injury to feelings, the court has power to award general damages. However, he cautioned that such damages should be kept to a modest level and should be proportionate to the injury suffered, and such awards should be well below the level of general damages for serious physical or psychiatric injury.[271]

---

[265] Although note the comments of Mr Justice Eady in *Mosley v News Group Newspapers* [2008] EWHC 1777 (QB), [2008] ALL ER (D) 322 (Jul) [231].

[266] *W* v *Egdell* [1990] Ch. 359 at 398. Note also that the *Law Commission Report on Breach of Confidence*, at para 4.81, recommended against the recovery of damages for embarrassment or distress caused by a non-contractual breach of confidence. (Law Com No 110, 1981).

[267] *Cornelius v De Taranto* [2001] EMLR 329. Morland J's findings on liability for breach of confidence were upheld on appeal [2001] EWCA Civ 1511.

[268] *Cornelius v De Taranto* [2001] EMLR 329, [69].

[269] ibid, [65].

[270] [2003] EWHC 1670.

[271] See also *Mosley v News Group Newspapers* [2008] EWHC 1777 (QB); [2008] All ER (D) 322 (Jul) [220].

In *Campbell v MGN*[272] Morland J awarded Ms Campbell £2,500 for the distress and injury to her feelings that the newspaper articles had caused, in addition to aggravated damages of £1,000. The House of Lords, in reversing the decision of the Court of Appeal, restored the order of Morland J and thereby affirmed the availability of damages for mental distress. Damages for distress are similarly recoverable in a claim for misuse of private information.[273] Significantly, in *Gulati & Ors* v *MGN Ltd* the Court was willing to award damages for misuse itself (separate from distress) where there was an interference with privacy and infringement of the values protected by the right to respect for a private life.[274] **12.148**

(iv) Restitutionary damages

If a doctor were to profit financially from a breach of patient confidentiality it is possible that he or she might be liable to account for those profits to the patient. The situation could arise, for example, where a doctor sells a patient's story to the press, or makes use of confidential information derived from the patient for personal financial gain from scientific research or development. **12.149**

C. Control of Patient Information

1. The scheme of the Data Protection Act 1998

Alongside the common law on confidentiality we have the Data Protection Act 1998 (DPA), which implements the Data Protection Directive (DPD).[275] The DPD aims to 'protect the fundamental rights and freedoms of natural persons, and in particular their right to privacy with respect to the processing of personal data',[276] in order to provide harmonized minimal protection that will allow a free internal market in personal data within the EU.[277] **12.150**

The following discussion outlines the main provisions of the DPA emphasizing their application to data concerning a person's health.[278] The Act creates a registration (or notification) system with the Information Commissioner (ICO) (and an Information Tribunal).[279] Unregistered processing of personal data is generally a criminal offence,[280] though there are exceptions.[281] The Act lays down eight 'Data Protection Principles',[282] which 'data controllers' must observe. It creates a system of enforcement procedures by the ICO, which are subject to a right of appeal to the Tribunal,[283] and provides personal remedies for 'data subjects', including rectification,[284] the power to prevent the processing of data likely to cause damage **12.151**

[272] [2002] EWHC 499, rvsd [2002] EWCA Civ 1373, rvsd [2004] UKHL 22.
[273] *Vidal-Hall v Google Inc (The Information Commissioner intervening)* [2015] EWCA Civ 311.
[274] [2015] EWHC 1482 (Ch) (21 May 2015), esp [111–45].
[275] Directive 95/46/EC of the European Parliament and of the Council of 24 October 1995 on the protection of individuals with regard to the processing of personal data and on the free movement of such data [1995] OJL 281.
[276] DPD, Article 1(1). The DPA does not mention this.
[277] See DPD, recitals 2–9 and Art 1(2).
[278] The ICO's website provides general and specific guidance: <https://ico.org.uk/for-organisations/guidance-index/data-protection-and-privacy-and-electronic-communications/>.
[279] Prior to the Freedom of Information Act 2000, these were, respectively, known as the 'Data Protection Commissioner' and 'Data Protection Tribunal.'
[280] DPA, ss 17(1) and 21(1).
[281] ibid, s 17(2)–(4).
[282] ibid, Schs 1–4.
[283] ibid, Pt V.
[284] ibid, s 14.

or distress,[285] and compensation for damage caused by non-compliance with the Act.[286] It also creates a right of access to personal data by the data subject.[287]

2. The scope of the Data Protection Act 1998

12.152 The DPA[288] regulates the 'processing' of 'personal data' of 'data subjects' by 'data controllers' and covers not only data held electronically but also some data held in manual/written form.[289] It excludes data processed purely for personal or domestic purposes.[290]

(i) Data controller

12.153 A data controller is 'a person who (either alone or jointly or in common with other persons) determines the purposes for which and the manner in which any personal data are, or are to be, processed.'[291] Within the NHS, Health Service bodies such as NHS Trusts will be 'data controllers.' Individual doctors, especially GPs, may also be such.[292]

(ii) Data

12.154 The DPA covers *all* information that:

(a) is being processed by means of equipment operating automatically in response to instructions given for that purpose,
(b) is recorded with the intention that it should be processed by means of such equipment,
(c) is recorded as part of a relevant filing system or with the intention that it should form part of a relevant filing system, or
(d) does not fall within paragraph (a), (b) or (c) but forms part of an accessible record as defined by section 68, or
(e) is recorded, does not fall within paragraphs (a) to (d), and is held by a public authority.[293]

12.155 A relevant filing system is one in which the information is structured by reference to individuals or criteria relating to individuals such that specific information relating to an individual

---

[285] ibid, s 10.
[286] ibid, s 13.
[287] ibid, s 7.
[288] All UK laws implementing EU Directives must be interpreted in a manner consistent with EU law. See *Marleasing SA v La Comercial Internacional de Alimentacion SA* [1990] ECR I-4135 [8]; *Miret v Fondo de Guarantia Salaria* [1993] ECR I-6911 [20]. If it is not possible to interpret the UK legislation as being in accordance with an 'unconditional and sufficiently precise' provision of an EU Directive, then that requirement may nonetheless be relied on against the State in the domestic courts (vertical direct effect): eg Case C-152/84 *Marshall v Southampton and South West Hampshire AHA* [1986] QB 401, [46]. The State is defined broadly to encompass its organs or emanations, including bodies that have been given responsibility by public authorities and provide public services under their supervision: eg Case C-188/89 *Foster v British Gas* [1990] ECR I-3313 [18]; Case C-279/12 *Fish Legal (and another)* v *The Information Commissioner* [2013] ALL ER (D) 200 (Dec). This clearly captures NHS bodies. No provision in a Directive can, however, be relied upon directly in a case against a private individual or company (horizontal direct effect): eg Case C-91/92 *Faccini Dori v Recreb Srl* [1995] 1 CMLR 665, [20]. In such a case, if harmonious interpretation is not possible, the only recourse for the affected party is to seek damages against the UK: eg Joined Cases C-6/90 and C-9/90 *Francovich and Bonifaci v Italian Republic* [1991] ECR I-5357. See further the discussion in S Weatherill, *Cases and Materials on EU Law* (Oxford University Press 2014) chs 3–6.
[289] DPA, s 1(1).
[290] ibid, s 36 (cf art 3(2) DPD).
[291] ibid, s 1(1). A person processing personal data is not necessarily a data controller. s 1(1) defines a data processor as a person (other than an employee of the data controller) processing data on behalf of the data controller.
[292] See <https://ico.org.uk/for-the-public/health/>.
[293] DPA, s 1(1), as amended. Personal data falling only within para (e) is exempt from many provisions of the DPA. In fact, only those provisions related to accesses and accuracy apply: s 33A.

is readily accessible.[294] An 'accessible record' is defined in s 68(2) to include a 'health record,' namely:

> any record which—
> (a) consists of information relating to the physical or mental health or condition of an individual, and
> (b) has been made by or on behalf of a health professional in connection with the care of that individual.

'Health professional' is defined in s 69 to include doctors, nurses, dentists, opticians, pharmacists, and scientific heads of department of health service bodies. **12.156**

The definition of 'data' covers virtually all health records, whether electronic or written, including such documents as X-rays. However, because some records containing information relating to the physical or mental health or condition of a person might be made other than by or on behalf of a health professional in connection with that person's care, the question of what constitutes a relevant filing system is still pertinent to the application of the DPA. This question was considered by the Court of Appeal in *Durant v FSA*.[295] This concerned a request for access to various manual records in relation to a complaint made by Mr Durant against Barclays Bank, and so has no specific relevance to medical law. In his leading judgement, Auld LJ held that the Act applies 'to manual records only if they are of sufficient sophistication to provide the same or similar ready accessibility as a computerized filing system'.[296] If a file is so structured that a searcher has to leaf through it to find what personal data it contains then the data is not in a relevant filing system.[297] The ICO offer 'the temp test' as a rule of thumb: 'If you employed a temporary administrative assistant (a 'temp'), would they be able to extract specific information about an individual from your manual records without any particular knowledge of your type of work or the documents you hold?'[298] **12.157**

(iii) Personal data

'Personal data' is defined by the DPA as: **12.158**

> data which relate to a living individual who can be identified—
> (a) from those data, or
> (b) from those data and other information which is in the possession of, or is likely to come into the possession of, the data controller,
>
> and includes any expression of opinion about the individual and any indication of the intentions of the data controller or any other person in respect of the individual.[299]

(a) The meaning of 'relating to' In *Durant*[300] the Court of Appeal provided 'guidance' on the meaning of 'relating to'. According to Auld LJ, information only relates to a person if 'it is information that affects his privacy, whether in his personal or family life, business or professional capacity'.[301] It is not enough that a document held by a data controller merely **12.159**

294 ibid, s 1(1).
295 *Durant v FSA* [2003] EWCA Civ 1746.
296 ibid, [48].
297 See ibid.
298 ICO, 'Frequently asked questions and answers about relevant filing systems', Q2 <https://ico.org.uk/media/for-organisations/documents/1592/relevant_filing_systems_faqs.pdf>.
299 DPA, s 1(1).
300 *Durant v FSA*, n 295.
301 ibid, [28].

mentions the data subject.[302] Two notions 'may assist' in deciding whether or not information affects the privacy of an identifiable individual:

> The first is whether the information is biographical in a significant sense, that is, going beyond the recording of the putative data subject's involvement in a matter or an event that has no personal connotations, a life event in respect of which his privacy could not be said to be compromised. The second is one of focus. The information should have the putative data subject as its focus rather than some other person with whom he may have been involved or some transaction or event in which he may have figured or have had an interest, for example, as in this case, an investigation into some other person's or body's conduct that he may have instigated.[303]

12.160 In *Edem* v *The Information Commissioner and The Financial Services Authority*, the Court of Appeal clarified that these notions should only be considered in 'borderline' cases. The Court supported the ICO Data Protection Technical Guidance:

> It is important to remember that it is not always necessary to consider 'biographical significance' to determine whether data is personal data. In many cases data may be personal data simply because its content is such that it is 'obviously about' an individual.[304]

12.161 This may be compared with the approach taken by the Article 29 Working Party. According to the Working Party, for information to relate to an individual is simply for it to be about that individual. It will clearly relate to an individual if it is 'the data of the results of a patient's medical test in his medical records, or the image of a person filmed on a video interview of that person'.[305] The Working Party lists three elements, possession of *any one* of which is sufficient for data to relate to an individual: (i) a 'content' element, present when information is given about a particular person; or (ii) a 'purpose' element, present when the purpose of the data is to evaluate, treat in some way, or influence the status or behaviour of an individual; or (iii) a 'result' element, present when the use of the data is likely to have some (not necessarily major) impact on the person's rights and interests.[306] Consequently, 'the information contained in a company's folder under the name of a certain client clearly relates to him'[307] and 'the same information may relate to different individuals at the same time' and this 'means also that it is not necessary that the data "focuses" on someone in order to consider that it relates to him.'[308]

12.162 (b) **Restriction to the living** The DPA defines personal data only in relation to living individuals and has no provisions about use of personal data on the living once they die. While the DPD makes reference to 'a natural person' (which contrasts with 'a legal person', not 'a deceased person') this does not mean that the Act is incompatible with the DPD in focusing on living individuals.[309]

12.163 (c) **The test of identifiability and anonymization** The DPA specifies that data are personal if the data subject can be identified directly from the data itself or if the data subject can be identified indirectly from that data together with other information possessed by or likely to be possessed by the data controller.[310] This contrasts with the DPD, according to which:

---

[302] ibid, [28].
[303] ibid, [28].
[304] *Edem v The Information Commissioner and The Financial Services Authority* [2014] EWCA Civ 92; 2014 WL 320313 [21].
[305] WP 136, 9, 01248/07/EN WP 136 adopted on 20 June 2007. The Working Party's documents are available at its website <http://ec.europa.eu/justice_home/fsj/privacy/workinggroup/index_en.htm>.
[306] See ibid, 10–11.
[307] ibid at 10.
[308] ibid, 11–12.
[309] ibid, 22.
[310] DPA, s 1(1).

> an identifiable person is one who can be identified, directly or indirectly [taking into account any 'means likely reasonably to be used either by the controller *or by any other person* to identify the said person'[311]], in particular by reference to an identification number or to one or more factors specific to his physical, physiological, mental, economic, cultural or social identity.[312]

The DPA is not explicit about the status of anonymized or anonymous data, but per recital 26 DPD: 'the principles of protection shall not apply to data rendered anonymous in such a way that the data subject is no longer identifiable.' Provided that data is anonymized *in the terms specified by the DPD*, there can be no doubt that the DPA does not apply to data rendered anonymous.[313] But there are complications.[314]

Prima facie, under the DPA, data D is personal for as long as the data controller *(even if only the data controller)* can identify the data subject from D directly or indirectly. Suppose that a data controller X holds personal data D and releases information contained in D to Y in a form (Dm) from which Y cannot identify the data subject directly, while X can do so indirectly. This will often be the case when data is released to medical researchers in coded form by bodies that hold the code while the researchers themselves do not. Is the information released to Y (Dm) personal data? Section 1(2) DPA states: **12.164**

> In this Act, unless the context otherwise requires—
> (a) 'obtaining' or 'recording', in relation to personal data, includes obtaining or recording the information to be contained in the data; and
> (b) 'using' or 'disclosing', in relation to personal data, includes using or disclosing the information contained in the data.

This reinforces the idea that Dm is personal data for as long as X can identify the data subjects from Dm if only with the help of other information X has is or likely to obtain.

The circumstances under which data is personal/rendered anonymous under the DPA was considered by the House of Lords in *Common Services Agency v Scottish Information Commissioner.*[315] A researcher acting on behalf of a member of the Scottish Parliament requested to know the incidence of childhood leukaemia by census ward within the Dumfries and Galloway area from the Common Services Agency (CSA) under s 38 of the Freedom of Information (Scotland) Act 2002 (FOISA).[316] The CSA refused to disclose the information on the grounds that because of the small numbers there was an unacceptable risk that the children could be identified from the statistics, so its disclosure would violate the DPA. The Scottish Information Commissioner (SIC), who is the supervisory authority for the FOISA, ordered disclosure of the data in a 'barnardized' form designed to reduce the risk of identification by recipients. After the Inner House of the Court of Session upheld the SIC's decision, the CSA appealed it to the House of Lords. The House ordered that the application from the researcher be remitted to the SIC, who was to examine whether, in the light of the House of Lords' judgment, the information can be sufficiently **12.165**

311 DPD. See recital 26 (emphasis added).

312 DPD, Article 2(a).

313 See Information Commissioners Office, *Anonymisation: Managing data protection risk* (November 2012). See also *R v Department of Health, ex p Source Informatics* [2001] QB 424, 441 *per* Simon Brown LJ.

314 See D Beyleveld and D Townend, 'When is Personal Data Rendered Anonymous? Interpreting Recital 26 of Directive 96/46/EEC' (2004) Med LI 73, 73–86.

315 *Common Services Agency v Scottish Information Commissioner* [2008] UKHL 47.

316 Section 40 of the Freedom of Information Act 2000 (FOIA), which applies to the rest of the UK, overlaps with s 38 of FOISA, so this case is relevant for the whole of the UK. The ICO is the supervisory authority under the DPA for the whole of the UK, but in relation to the FOIA only for England, Wales, and Northern Ireland, Scotland having its own supervisory authority for the FOISA.

depersonalized so as to be rendered anonymous. If so, it must be disclosed in that form. If not, the SIC is to determine if and under what conditions it can be released lawfully in compliance with the data protection principles.[317]

12.166 Lord Hope, with whom Lord Hoffmann concurred, opined that the effect of para (b) of the s 1(1) definition of 'personal data' is that a data controller (here the CSA):

> cannot exclude personal data from the duty to comply with the data protection principles simply by editing the data so that, if the edited part were to be disclosed to a third party, the third party would not find it possible from that part alone without the assistance of other information to identify a living individual.[318]

It does not matter that *the recipient* of the edited data (here the barnardized data) cannot identify those individuals, because we are 'concerned in this case with its status while it is still in the hands of the data controller [the CSA]'.[319]

12.167 However, according to Lord Hope, on the uncontested premise that the CSA can, from the statistics (D) that have been subjected to barnardization, identify the children, it does not *necessarily* follow that the barnardized information (Dm) is personal data. For Dm to be personal data, the CSA must be able to identify the children from Dm *alone* (per s 1(1)(a)) or from Dm *together with* some other information the CSA holds or is likely to come into possession of (per s 1(1)(b)). But *both* the other information *and* Dm must play a role in the identification.[320]

12.168 In *R (on the application of the Department of Health)* v *Information Commissioner* [2011] EWHC 1430 (Admin), Justice Cranston considers himself bound by Lord Hope's reasoning and follows the view that if data (D) are changed (Dm) so that an individual could not be identified from them, then even if such other information as would allow Dm to be related to a particular individual were held by the data controller, then (so long as Dm do not contribute toward the identification), Dm fall outwith the definition of personal data. Such data could be disclosed by a data controller, as non-personal data. (But note comments on the ICO Code of Practice on Anonymisation at para 12.177).

12.169 What if the data is identifiable by a third party but not the data controller? Suppose that the data controller X discloses data to a recipient Y. X cannot identify the data subject directly or indirectly. Y cannot identify the data subject directly, but can do so indirectly. Under the DPD (via recital 26, because this places no limitation on the person able to identify the data subject either directly or indirectly) this data is still personal data when disclosed by X. But under the DPA, it is anonymous when disclosed by X. This might be an unlikely scenario but it is not impossible. It should be noted, however, that in this case Y will become a data controller, and responsible for meeting the responsibilities imposed by the Data Protection Act 1998, if they are now processing personal data.

12.170 **(d) Genetic data and families** The Article 29 Working Party[321] considers that genetic information is sensitive personal data under Article 2(a) DPD.[322] Furthermore, genetic data might relate to more than one individual, which raises questions about how conflicts

[317] See *Common Services Agency v Scottish Information Commissioner*, n 315, [44] *per* Lord Hope.
[318] ibid, [22].
[319] ibid, [26]. When the courts considered the issue of anonymization in connection with the common law on confidentiality, the presumption was very much that if the recipient cannot identify the confidant then disclosed data is anonymous. (See paras 12.38–12.43).
[320] ibid, [24].
[321] Working Document on Genetic Data WP 91 12178/03/EN, 17 March 2004. (See n 305).
[322] ibid, 5.

between the data protection rights, of say different family members, are to be dealt with. One possibility is to treat other family members as 'data subjects' with all the rights that follow from this. Another is to provide them with rights under different laws.[323] But, in either case, given 'the complexity of the issues, at this stage, consideration should be given to a case-by-case approach in deciding how to address possible conflicts between the interests of the data subjects and those of their biological family'.[324]

(iv) Processing

Section 1(1) DPA defines 'processing' in relation to 'information or data' as: **12.171**

> obtaining, recording or holding the information or data or carrying out any operation or set of operations on the information or data, including—
> (a) organisation, adaptation or alteration of the information or data,
> (b) retrieval, consultation or use of the information or data,
> (c) disclosure of the information or data by transmission, dissemination or otherwise making available, or
> (d) alignment, combination, blocking, erasure or destruction of the information or data.

When read with Article 2(b) DPD, the 'processing' under the DPA covers any operation or set of operations performed on personal information or data, regardless of whether or not the processing is by automatic means. Hence, no operation on personal data can possibly not constitute processing of it.[325]

In *Campbell v MGN*[326] (see para 12.61), the Court of Appeal considered whether or not publication of newspapers and other hard copies previously subjected to data processing is processing under the DPA. According to Lord Phillips MR, who delivered the judgment of the court, given that processing covers any operation or set of operations, at: **12.172**

> one end of the process 'obtaining the information' is included, and at the other end 'using the information'. While neither activity in itself may sensibly amount to processing, if that activity is carried on by, or at the instigation of, a 'data controller', as defined, and is linked to automated processing of the data, we can see no reason why the entire set of operations should not fall within the scope of the legislation. On the contrary, we consider that there are good reasons why it should.[327]

Indeed, considering that publication of personal data is more likely to violate privacy and cause damage or distress than the recording or holding of it: **12.173**

> If publication were not treated as part of a 'processing operation' . . . [Article 23 DPD, which requires Member States to provide penalties for unlawful processing] would be deprived of much of its force.[328]

Johnson v Medical Defence Union[329] raised the question whether manually selecting personal information from documents, some of which are manual and not in a relevant filing system, some of which are already held on computer, and placing the information on various forms for use by the Medical Defence Union (MDU) to make decisions and reflect reasoning about whether or not to allow membership of the MDU to continue, constitutes processing. **12.174**

---

[323] WP 91, Working Document on Genetic Data WP 91 12178/03/EN, 17 March 2004, 8–9. (See n 305).
[324] ibid, 9. See further M J Taylor, n 77.
[325] Anonymization is not explicitly included but see para 12.176.
[326] *Campbell v MGN* [2002] EWCA Civ 1373.
[327] ibid, [104].
[328] ibid, [105].
[329] *Johnson v Medical Defence Union* [2006] EWHC 321.

Mr Johnson, whose membership of the MDU had been terminated, complained that the compilation of three forms (by a Dr Roberts) constituted unfair processing under the DPA. This claim cannot get off the ground unless the activity complained about constitutes processing. In the High Court, Rimer J accepted, on the basis of the statement of the Court of Appeal in *Campbell,* that the effect of s 1(1) as expanded by s 1(2) is that both Dr Roberts' selection of information from the computerized files for inputting into the computer and the selection of material from various manual and microfiche files for inputting into a computer amounted to 'processing'. [330]

12.175 On appeal,[331] Buxton LJ recoiled from what he saw as an implication of Rimer J's view:

> If the judge is correct, any exercise in decision-making by an individual the results of which are then part of the same operation recorded or transmitted in electronic form will be subject to scrutiny under the Data Protection Principles, including the requirements that the processing (such as, on this view, the decision-making is) should be conducted fairly. This leads to many alarming examples: some of these render justiciable decisions that are socially trivial; others render justiciable decisions in respect of which there are good policy reasons why the courts should abstain from interfering . . . [332]

Longmore LJ agreed with Buxton LJ and held that Rimer J was mistaken, but Arden LJ offered a lengthy dissenting judgment. While such disagreement might lead to a referral to the ECJ for a preliminary ruling, the Court was unanimous that if processing had been done it was not unfair (so the outcome of the case did not rest on the processing issue) and it was agreed not to seek a preliminary ruling.[333] So, though there was a majority opinion, this opinion is *obiter.*

12.176 **(a) Anonymization as processing** Anonymization is not explicitly included within an otherwise comprehensive list of things that will constitute 'processing' as defined by the DPA (see para 12.171) and the ICO Code of Practice on Anonymisation notes that:

> As anonymised data has no direct effect on any individual, there can be a tendency not to tell individuals about it, or even to be secretive.[334]

12.177 Despite anonymization not appearing in the definition of processing, the ICO Code of Practice recommends organizations are transparent about the approach taken toward anonymization. The Code lists a number of things that, in the ICO's view, an organization should be clear about. These include recommendations to organizations that they:

> - explain why you anonymise individuals' personal data and describe in general terms the techniques that will be used to do this;
> - make it clear whether individuals have a choice over the anonymisation of their personal data, and if so how to exercise this—including the provision of relevant contact details. (Note though that the DPA does not give individuals a general right to prevent the processing of personal data about them);
> - say what safeguards are in place to minimise the risk that may be associated with the production of anonymised data. In particular, you should explain whether the anonymised data will be made publicly available or only disclosed to a limited number of recipients . . . [335]

330 ibid, [97].
331 *Johnson v Medical Defence Union* [2007] EWCA Civ 262.
332 ibid, [44].
333 ibid, [80] *per* Buxton LJ and [151] *per* Arden LJ.
334 Information Commissioner's Office, *Anonymisation: Managing data protection risk* (November 2012) 40.
335 ibid, p 40–41.

Responsibilities, including 'fair processing', regarding anonymized data were not considered by the House of Lords in *CSA v SIC* (see paras 12.165–12.167). However, the Article 29 Working party have stated that '[a]nonymisation constitutes a further processing of data'[336] and the position described by the ICO in the Code of Practice is consistent with the objective of the DPD to protect fundamental rights and freedoms, in particular the right to respect for private life in the processing of personal data. The ECJ, like the ECtHR, gives a very broad interpretation to private life[337] and family life[338] (see further para 12.41) and control over the uses to which one's data are put, including following anonymization, is consistent with the ideals of informational self-determination. **12.178**

It has been argued by Beyleveld and others that anonymization, like destruction, might interfere with protection.[339] On 'destruction', Advocate General Ruiz-Jarobo Colomer in *College van Burgemeester and Wethouders van Rotterdam v MEE Rijkeboer,* opines that:[340] **12.179**

> As a rule, the destruction of data is a protective act. However, it may lead to different outcomes, since, when files are deleted, all trace of how they have been used disappears with them. Thus, an individual who appears to be protected may also be harmed because he will never know how the holder of his personal data has used them.

It is clear that the ICO consider it to be good practice to provide information, and extend some control to individuals, over any intended anonymization of data whilst it is still in an identifiable form. **12.180**

3. The Data Protection Principles

Eight Data Protection Principles are set out in Sch 1, Pt I to the DPA and elaborated upon in Sch 1, Pt II and Sch 2–4: **12.181**

1. Personal data shall be processed fairly and lawfully and, in particular, shall not be processed unless—
   (a) at least one of the conditions in Schedule 2 is met, and
   (b) in the case of sensitive personal data, at least one of the conditions in Schedule 3 is also met.
2. Personal data shall be obtained only for one or more specified and lawful purposes, and shall not be further processed in any manner incompatible with that purpose or those purposes.
3. Personal data shall be adequate, relevant and not excessive in relation to the purpose or purposes for which they are processed.
4. Personal data shall be accurate and, where necessary, kept up to date.
5. Personal data processed for any purpose or purposes shall not be kept for longer than is necessary for that purpose or those purposes.
6. Personal data shall be processed in accordance with the rights of data subjects under this Act.
7. Appropriate technical and organisational measures shall be taken against unauthorised or unlawful processing of personal data and against accidental loss or destruction of, or damage to, personal data.

---

[336] Opinion 05/2014 on Anonymisation Techniques, 3.

[337] Joined Cases 46/87 and 227/88 *Hoechst v Commission* [1989] ECR 2859, and Case C-94/00 *Roquette Frères* [2002] ECR I-9011.

[338] Case C-60/00 *Carpenter* [2002] ECR I-6279, [38]; and Case C-459/99 *MRAX* [2002] ECR I-6591, [53].

[339] D Beyleveld and D M R Townend, 'When is Personal Data Rendered Anonymous? Interpreting Recital 26 of Directive 95/46/EC', Medical Law International 2004 6: 73; D Beyleveld and E Histed, 'Betrayal of Confidence in the Court of Appeal', Medical Law International 2000 4: 277.

[340] (Case 553/07) 2009, para 2 of the Advocate-General's Opinion 22/12/2008.

8. Personal data shall not be transferred to a country or territory outside the European Economic Area unless that country or territory ensures an adequate level of protection for the rights and freedoms of data subjects in relation to the processing of personal data.

12.182 Our main, but not exclusive, concern is with the 'obtaining', 'storage', 'use', and 'disclosure' of patient information for medical purposes.

(i) First Principle

12.183 Personal data must be processed 'fairly' and 'lawfully'. Here we deal with 'fair' processing. 'Lawful' processing is discussed at paras 12.192–12.207.

12.184 The First Principle requires that for processing to be 'fair', the data controller must 'so far as practicable' provide the data subject with certain information, such as the former's identity and the purposes for which it is intended to process the information.[341] This must be provided when the data is obtained from the data subject or, if obtained from a third party, before it is first processed or disclosed.[342] Therefore, patients must be made aware at the relevant time of the purpose(s) to which data will subsequently be put. Section 33, which provides exemptions for research, provides no exemption from the First Principle, and so use of data for 'research purposes' is covered by this requirement. The DPA, like the DPD, differentiates between cases where data is obtained from the data subject (to which Article 10 DPD applies) and cases where data was not obtained from the data subject (to which Article 11 DPD applies). In the latter case only, the Act (and the DPD) exempts from the duty to inform the data subject of material required for fair processing, when to do so would involve 'disproportionate effort' and certain conditions are satisfied.[343] The Act gives no further guidance on the scope of this exemption, which must, in each case, be a question of fact.[344]

12.185 The need to provide a patient with information about possible uses is reinforced by the requirement under the First Principle that in deciding whether information has been processed 'fairly', regard is to be had to the method by which it has been obtained, including whether the individual has been deceived or misled as to the purposes for which it will be processed.[345] Thus, whilst a use may be compatible with the purposes notified to the ICO (or is covered by s 33 for 'research purposes') and so does not offend the Second Principle, misleading or deceiving the patient about its use may still offend the First Principle.

12.186 The issue of fairness is not confined to the way in which data is *obtained*. The First Principle requires data to be *processed* fairly. But neither the DPA nor the DPD contains anything explicit about the requirements of fairness outside of the context of the provision of information. Given the purposes of the DPD, however, it is reasonable to infer that any processing that violates the fundamental rights and freedoms of the data subject violates the First Principle, whether as being 'unfair' or 'unlawful'. Much of this will be covered by the DPD and DPA under headings other than 'fair processing'.

---

[341] DPA, Sch 1, Pt II, paras 2 and 3.

[342] ibid, Sch 1, Pt II, paras 2(1)(a) and 2(1)(b) and (2) respectively.

[343] ibid, Sch 1, Pt II, para 3 and the Data Protection (Conditions under para 3 of Pt II of Schedule 1) Order 2000, SI 2000/185: '(i) whilst it need not be volunteered, the information must be provided if requested; and (ii) record the reasons why disclosure would involve a 'disproportionate effort.'

[344] General guidance on providing information is contained within the Information Commissioner's Office, *Privacy Notices: Code of Practice* (December 2010).

[345] DPA, Sch 1, Pt II, para 1(1).

(ii) Second Principle

The Second Principle requires information to be 'obtained only for one or more specified and lawful purposes', and not 'further processed' 'in a manner incompatible' with those purposes. These purposes may be specified in the registration with the ICO (under Pt III of the DPA) or in a notice given to the data subject at the time it is obtained.[346] Generally, this will not cause any difficulties within the NHS, provided that the 'registrable particulars' spell out the treatment, management, audit or research purposes, and so forth, to which patient information may be put and, more particularly, by notice given to the patient directly. **12.187**

DPA, s 33 renders further processing of data for 'research', 'statistical or historical purposes' exempt from *that part of* the Second Principle that prohibits further processing in a manner incompatible with the purposes for which it was obtained.[347] 'Compatibility' is nowhere explained. However, one can at least suppose that a hurdle ('compatible processing') is overcome if the conditions for this exemption apply. The exemption applies only where three conditions are met: (i) the data is not processed to 'support measures or decisions with respect to particular individuals'; (ii) the processing is not done in such a way as to cause, or be likely to cause, 'substantial damage or substantial distress' to the data subject; (these two conditions being the so-called 'relevant conditions') and (iii) further processing is solely for research, historical, or statistical purposes. **12.188**

(iii) Fifth Principle

The Fifth Data Protection Principle requires information to be kept for no longer than necessary for the purposes for which it is processed. Section 33(3), however, allows information being processed solely for 'research purposes' (as defined) to be kept indefinitely, provided that the relevant conditions are met. **12.189**

(iv) Eighth Principle

Medical research often involves partners in 'third countries' (those outside the European Economic Area, which comprises the EU States plus Iceland, Liechtenstein, and Norway). Para 8 of Sch1 Pt I[348] prohibits transfers of personal data to any country or territory outside of the EEA unless that country or territory ensures an adequate level of protection for the rights and freedoms of data subjects in relation to the processing of personal data. At the time of writing, only Andorra, Argentina, Canada (commercial organizations), Faroe Islands, Guernsey, Isle of Man, Israel, Jersey, New Zealand, Switzerland, and Uruguay are recognized as third countries providing adequate protection.[349] However, the eighth principle does not apply to a transfer falling within the conditions of Sch 4. These include: the consent of the data subject; transfer in the substantial public interest; and transfer under conditions approved by the Information Commissioner's Office (ICO) (as ensuring adequate safeguards for rights and freedoms). The ICO provides advice on assessing adequacy and, in case of inadequate level of protection, putting in place adequate safeguards to protect the rights of the data subject, possibly using Model Contract Clauses or Binding Corporate Rules.[350] **12.190**

---

346 ibid, Sch 1, Pt II, para 5, referring back to paras 2 and 3.

347 ibid, s 33(1).

348 Compare DPD, Art 25.

349 <http://ec.europa.eu/justice/data-protection/international-transfers/adequacy/index_en.htm>. Arrangements previously taken to assure adequate protection vis-à-vis transfers to organizations signed up to the US Department of Commerce's Safe Harbor Privacy Principles were found inadequate by the Court of Justice of the European Union (CJEU) in *Schrem* v *Data Protection Commissioner* (2015) Case C-362/14.

350 See <https://ico.org.uk/for-organisations/guide-to-data-protection/principle-8-international/>.

(v) Exemptions

12.191 By way of general exemption, disclosures required by law, by statute, or court order or which are made in connection with legal proceedings or seeking legal advice are exempt from the non-disclosure provisions of the Act, *including* the First Principle (except for compliance with the conditions in Schs 2 and 3), and the Second Principle.[351]

4. The conditions for lawful processing

12.192 That processing must be 'lawful' reads into the DPA, inter alia, the common law of confidentiality and the provisions of the HRA 1998. Any disclosure in breach of confidence (unless justified at common law or statute) will involve a breach of the First Principle. In addition, the First Principle requires, as a condition for compliance, that personal data are processed in accordance with Sch 2 and, if they are 'sensitive personal data', also in accordance with Sch 3. Health information is 'sensitive personal data', which includes information about an individual's 'physical or mental health or condition'.[352] Schs 2 and 3 lay down conditions for processing. Any processing of health information must satisfy *one condition in each* of the Schedules. However, satisfaction of some of the conditions of Sch 3 implies satisfaction of a condition of Sch 2. For example, if 'explicit consent' per Sch 3 is satisfied, 'consent' per Sch 2 will also be satisfied. The most relevant conditions are as follows.

(i) Schedule 2

12.193 (a) **Consent of the Data Subject** Condition 1 of Sch 2 is that 'the data subject has given his consent to the processing'. This is not explained in the DPA. However, Article 2(h) DPD defines 'the data subject's' consent as: 'any freely given specific and informed indication of his wishes by which the data subject signifies his agreement to personal data relating to him being processed.' And the corresponding Article 7(1) DPD, actually requires 'unambiguous' consent. Given this, it might still be possible to rely on implied consent to satisfy Sch 2, where implied consent is understood to be given to any actions that are clearly and obviously necessary (or which the data subject has been told, and understands, are necessary) for the performance of an action to which the data subject has directly consented (cf the discussion of consent in relation to confidentiality in paras 12.44–12.52). The important thing here is that there is some behaviour indicating consent to the processing.[353] The Article 29 Working Party have opined that

> It is questionable whether the absence of any behaviour—or perhaps better: passive behaviour—could also be interpreted as an indication [unless?] in very specific circumstances (ie a totally unambiguous context). The notion of 'indication' is wide, but it seems to imply a need for action.[354]

For this reason, the ICO is surely correct that consent cannot be inferred from a non-response to a communication.[355]

12.194 (b) **Compliance with a Legal Obligation** Condition 3 of Sch 2 is that the processing is 'necessary for compliance with any legal obligation to which the data controller is subject, other than an obligation imposed by contract'. An NHS Trust (or GP), required by a binding Direction from the Secretary of State to provide certain patient information, falls within this condition. This also covers disclosures required by statute, court order, or other legal

351 DPA, ss 35 and 27(3) and (4).
352 DPA, s 2(e).
353 Opinion 15/2011 on the definition of consent, WP187 (July 2011), 11.
354 Opinion 15/2011 on the definition of consent, WP187 (July 2011), 12.
355 Information Commissioners Office, *The Guide to Data Protection* (31 March 2015, 2.2.4) 100. See also Opinion 15/2011 on the definition of consent, WP187 (July 2011) 24.

duty, including those established by the Health and Social Care Act 2012 (on which see para 12.94) and disclosure or other processing *required* (not merely *authorized*) under the Health Service (Control of Patient Information) Regulations 2002 (on which see para 12.90).

(c) The vital interests of the data subject Condition 4 of Sch 2 is that the processing is 'necessary in order to protect the vital interests of the data subject'. Disclosure must be 'necessary' and not merely convenient. The relevant purpose must not be reasonably achievable by some other reasonable means.[356] Also, any processing must relate to the patient's 'vital interests'. This should probably not be read so narrowly as to be limited to 'life and death' situations, and should be construed as meaning 'relevant to his life and health'.[357] It would certainly justify a doctor disclosing information in an emergency to protect the life or health of a patient who needed treatment (eg where a GP informs a casualty doctor that the patient is on a particular medication that is relevant to the emergency treatment). But the condition might also be satisfied where disclosure to other health professionals is required for the treatment of the patient. It is generally implausible to apply the condition to research involving a patient's medical records since it will usually not affect *that patient's* 'vital interests' (as against the interests of others when the outcome of the research is known). **12.195**

(d) Legitimate interests of the data controller or others Condition 6 of Sch 2 applies to processing that is 'necessary for the purposes of legitimate interests pursued by the data controller or by the third party . . . to whom the data are disclosed'. This condition would prima facie allow an NHS body to disclose patient information for its, or the recipient's, legitimate interests. This could include disclosure for the purposes of research, financial accounting, management, audit, preventing fraud within the NHS, for maintaining professional standards or pursuing appropriate legal action against another, or defending an action brought against a NHS body. On its wording ('by the data controller or by the third party') disclosure to an individual or other body in order to protect that individual from danger, for example, by the patient, is covered. Importantly, the condition requires that the processing should not be 'unwarranted' by reason of the data subject's rights, freedoms, and legitimate interests. This may well prevent disclosure where the disclosure is not 'tailored' in scope and content to the particular interests to be pursued. Hence, if the purpose could be achieved by using, for example, identity-protecting rather than identifying health data, then this condition is unlikely to be satisfied. This condition can, surely be invoked to justify disclosure for wider NHS purposes (such as audit, management of the Health Services, etc). But the underlying reason, if this provision is invoked, has to be that the legitimate interests of the NHS are not contrary to the legitimate interests of the patient, rather than that the patient has impliedly consented.[358] **12.196**

(ii) Schedule 3

As we have already noted, a condition in Sch 3 must also be satisfied because health information is 'sensitive personal data.' **12.197**

(a) Explicit consent The first condition in Sch 3 is that the data subject has given 'explicit consent' to the processing of the personal data. More than unambiguous 'consent' (as required by Article 7(1) DPD and defined by Article 2(h)) must be contemplated. But neither the DPA nor the DPD explains what this 'more' is. The Article 29 Working Party **12.198**

---

356 Information Commissioners Office *The Guide to Data Protection* (31 March 2015, 2.2.4) 100.

357 But note the ICO's view that it is restricted to matters of 'life and death': ibid, 94.

358 The Article 29 Working Party expressly says that it is misleading to characterize or try to legitimize processing through consent on the grounds that there are interests at stake that would override an objection. See *Working Party Document on the Processing of Personal Data Relating to Health in Electronic Health Records* (EHR) WP 131 para 4(a)(aa), 8, n 305.

rules out 'opt-out' solutions altogether[359] The Working Party does not consider that written consent is required,[360] but suggests that it is necessary that the data subject understand that sensitive personal data has special protection under the law and that by consenting to the processing of such data the data subject is renouncing this protection.[361]

12.199 The ICO considers that the conditions in Sch 3 are not lexically ordered, such that a data controller should look for explicit consent first.[362] The Article 29 Working Party has also recognized the 'need to emphasise that consent is not always the primary or the most desirable means of legitimizing the processing of personal data.'[363] However, account must be taken of the fact that it is the clear and consistent jurisprudence of the ECtHR that any use of a person's health data without their consent is an interference with Article 8(1) ECHR and requires justification in terms of Article 8(2) ECHR to be lawful.[364]

12.200 (b) **Medical and research purposes** DPA, Sch 3 para 8 permits processing for 'medical purposes', when:

(1) The processing is necessary for medical purposes and is undertaken by—
  (a) a health professional, or
  (b) a person who in the circumstances owes a duty of confidentiality which is equivalent to that which would arise if that person were a health professional.
(2) In this paragraph 'medical purposes' includes the purposes of preventative medicine, medical diagnosis, medical research, the provision of care and treatment and the management of health care services.

12.201 DPD, Article 8(1) prohibits the processing of sensitive categories of personal data, and DPD, Articles 8(2), (3), and (4) lift this prohibition in certain circumstances. Sch 3, para 8(2) is controversial because DPD, Article 8(3), from which it derives (unlike Sch 3, para 8(2)) makes no mention of medical research, stating that (under the conditions that Sch 3, para 8(1)) faithfully lists, the prohibition of Article 8(1):

> shall not apply where processing of the data is required for the purposes of preventive medicine, medical diagnosis, the provision of care or treatment or the management of health-care services.

Almost certainly with the DPA in mind, the Article 29 Working Party opines that, because DPD, Article 8(3) lifts a prohibition, the derogation under DPD, Article 8(3) only covers processing of personal data for the specific purposes mentioned therein. 'Not covered is further processing which is not required for the direct provision of such services, such as medical research'.[365]

12.202 According to the Article 29 Working Party,[366] it is via DPD, Article 8(4) which provides:

> Subject to the provision of suitable safeguards, Member States may, for reasons of substantial public interest, lay down exemptions in addition to those laid down in [Article 8 DPD] paragraph 2 either by national law or by decision of the supervisory authority.

---

359 WP 131, n 358, 9. Opinion 15/2011 on the definition of consent, WP187 (July 2011), 25.
360 ibid.
361 ibid.
362 Information Commissioners Office, *The Guide to Data Protection* (31 March 2015, 2.2.4) 101.
363 Opinion 15/2011 on the definition of consent, WP187 (July 2011), 10.
364 See, eg, *Z v Finland* (1998) 25 EHRR 371; *MS v Sweden* (1999) 28 EHRR 313; *Peck v UK* (2003) 36 EHRR 719.
365 00323/07/EN WP 131, n 358, para 6(a), p 10; and see paras 6(d) and (e), p 11.
366 ibid, para 7, p 12.

that the prohibition on processing health data may be lifted for medical research. And, indeed, under Sch 3, para 10, the Data Protection (Processing of Sensitive Personal Data) Order 2000[367] has been passed to just this effect. Article 2, para 9 of the Order covers 'processing' which is 'in the substantial public interest' which is 'necessary for research purposes' (as defined in s 33) providing the processing (i) does not support measures or decisions in respect of a particular individual otherwise than with explicit consent, and (ii) does not cause, nor is likely to cause, substantial damage or distress to the data subject or any other person. The Explanatory Report to the Order suggests archiving as an example of processing in the substantial public interest.

(c) **Vital interests of the data subject or another** DPA, Schedule 3, para 3 applies where processing is in the vital interests of an individual even where the data subject does not consent. It provides for processing that: **12.203**

> is necessary—
> (a) in order to protect the vital interests of the data subject or another person, in a case where—
> (i) consent cannot be given by or on behalf of the data subject, or
> (ii) the data controller cannot reasonably be expected to obtain the consent of the data subject, or
> (b) in order to protect the vital interests of another person, in a case where consent by or on behalf of the data subject had been unreasonably withheld.

To the extent that the disclosure is to protect the vital interests of the patient, this will also usually be covered by the 'medical purposes' condition in para 8. Where, however, it is to protect a third party, this paragraph permits disclosure even where the data subject cannot consent, unreasonably refuses consent, or it is not reasonable to seek consent. In principle, situations concerned with dangerous psychiatric patients, child (or other sexual) abusers or patients carrying an infectious disease would fall within this provision. For the disclosure to be 'necessary', the manner of disclosure must be tailored to the aim to be achieved; hence it must be to the appropriate person or authority. **12.204**

(d) **Legal and other proceedings** DPA, Schedule 3, para 6 allows processing where it is necessary in connection with legal proceedings or to seek legal advice. **12.205**

The Data Protection (Processing of Sensitive Personal Data) Order 2000[368] also adds a further condition to Sch 3 of the DPA, which is of considerable relevance in the health context. This condition allows processing that is in the '*substantial* public interest' where it is 'necessary' for the discharge of functions that are designed for 'protecting members of the public' against 'dishonesty, malpractice, or other seriously improper conduct by, or the unfitness or incompetence of, any person' or 'mismanagement in the administration of, or failures in services provided by, any body'.[369] The scope of these functions encompasses disclosure to, or by, a professional regulatory body such as the GMC as well as, of course, processing by the body once it was received.[370] It covers processing in the context of clinical governance arrangements within the NHS. **12.206**

The only limitations are:[371] processing must be: (i) in the '*substantial* public interest'; (ii) 'necessary' for discharging the stated function; and (iii) carried out without the explicit **12.207**

[367] SI 2000/417.
[368] SI 2000/417.
[369] ibid, Sch, para 2.
[370] The order also adds a further purpose, namely 'the prevention or detection of any unlawful act' (ibid, Sch, para 1).
[371] ibid, Sch, paras 1 and 2.

consent of the individual because this is necessary not to prejudice the discharge of that function. The information that is targeted by these conditions is, principally, that relating to the *health professional* rather than the patient. Information about the latter could probably be processed, for these purposes, with explicit consent.

5. Remedies

12.208 The DPA creates *three* remedies that are of particular interest in the medical context. The first two complement the common law actions for breach of confidence and negligence. The third provides an additional remedy beyond the common law's scope. In addition the DPA creates a number of relevant offences.

12.209 First, s 10 entitles a data subject to serve a notice upon the data controller requiring the data controller to cease, or not to begin, processing personal data relating to him or her. The right does not apply if one of the conditions in paras 1–4 of Sch 2 is satisfied. The basis for such a notice must be that the processing (or its manner) is causing or is likely to cause substantial damage to the data subject or another and that damage or distress is unwarranted.[372] Within twenty-one days, the data controller must give written notice to the data subject that he has complied, or intends to comply, or state why he considers it unjustified.[373] The data subject may apply to the court which may, to the extent it thinks fit, enforce the notice against the data controller if he fails to comply. Certainly, as regards improper disclosure of patient information, the Act may add little to a common law claim for breach of confidence. While it would have the advantage that it may provide a remedy where the 'processing' does not entail a breach of confidence, for example because it is being misused without disclosure, this particular gap may have been narrowed—if not closed entirely—by the development of the common law to provide remedy for misuse of personal information.

12.210 Secondly, an individual may seek compensation for damage suffered as a result of a breach of the DPA by a data controller.[374] The claimant may be the data subject or another who suffers damage, for example, as a result of disclosure in breach of the Act. Compensation is limited to damage and any consequential distress suffered by the data subject.[375] Following *Google v Vidal-Hall*,[376] and despite the express wording of Article 13(2), it is possible to claim compensation for distress even where that is not consequent upon pecuniary loss.[377] It is a defence for the data controller to establish that he took reasonable care in all the circumstances to comply with the Act.[378] Given that the claimant must prove damage and the data controller has a defence of 'no negligence', again the remedy may not add much to the common law.

12.211 Thirdly, the court may order the data controller to 'rectify, block, erase or destroy' inaccurate data including an expression of opinion, which appears to be, based upon inaccurate data'.[379]

12.212 In addition to the remedies described above, the DPA establishes a number of offences. These can only be instituted by the Information Commissioner or with the consent of the

[372] DPA, s 10(1).
[373] ibid, s 10(3).
[374] ibid, s 13.
[375] ibid, s 13(2)(a).
[376] *Google v Vidal-Hall* [2015] EWCA Civ 311.
[377] ibid, [76]–[105].
[378] DPA, s 13(3).
[379] ibid, s 14.

Director of Public Prosecutions. These include offences related to unauthorized disclosure and to the sale of personal information.

According to DPA, s 55: **12.213**

(1) A person must not knowingly or recklessly, without the consent of the data controller—
  (a) obtain or disclose personal data or the information contained in personal data, or
  (b) procure the disclosure to another person of the information contained in personal data.

This does not apply under conditions laid down in s 55(2). There are also relevant exemptions, under s 55(8) in relation to national security (s 28) and manual data held by public authorities (s 33A). However, under s 55(3) it is a criminal offence to contravene s 55(1). Furthermore, s 55(4)–(6) makes it an offence to sell, offer to sell, or advertise an offer to sell personal data in contravention of s 55(1). **12.214**

Section 55(7) states that for the purposes of s 55, s 1(2) (which otherwise defines the meaning of the words 'obtaining' and 'disclosing' in the Act) does not apply but that for the purposes of s 55(4)–(6) (which are concerned with sale of data obtained in contravention of s 55(1)) 'personal data' includes information 'extracted from personal data.' The effect of this is not entirely clear. One possibility is that the disapplication of s 1(2) is intended to narrow the scope of any offence under s 55(1) so that it does not apply to the obtaining or disclosing of information 'contained in' personal data but this restricted reading is not considered appropriate in cases where individuals go on to offer for sale 'information extracted from personal data' where such data have been obtained in contravention of s 55(1). In other words, where personal data are obtained inappropriately, then the effect of s 55(7) may be to extend the scope of data it is an offence to sell to include data 'extracted from personal data.' This raises the interesting possibility that such data need not otherwise fall within the definition of personal data: it may include data no longer in an identifiable form. **12.215**

D. Access to Medical Records

1. General

Here we consider the circumstances in which a patient may be entitled to claim access to medical records *as of right*. We are not concerned with claims for access to medical records made on the basis that: **12.216**

(a) it is allegedly negligent for the doctor or hospital to refuse access to the claimant's medical records, or not to have disclosed certain information therein to the patient,[380] or
(b) litigation has commenced or is in contemplation and access to medical records is sought as part of disclosure under ss 33 or 34 of the Senior Courts Act 1981 and CPR, Pt 31 (on which see para 12.130).

Neither of these involves claims that the patient has a right of access to his or her medical records per se.

380 See *Montgomery v Lanarkshire Health Board* [2015] UKSC 11.

2. Data Protection Act 1998

(i) Background

12.217 In this section, we are concerned with the 'subject information provisions' of the DPA, focusing on their application to health records. But, before looking at the DPA, we must first consider its relationship with the Freedom of Information Act 2000.

(ii) Relationship between the DPA and the Freedom of Information Act 2000

12.218 It is important to appreciate the relationship between the DPA and the Freedom of Information Act (FOIA) 2000. The FOIA 2000 creates a right of access to information held by public authorities[381] subject to certain exemptions,[382] for example, information provided in confidence,[383] where disclosure is prohibited by or under any enactment,[384] or where disclosure is likely to endanger any individual.[385] The FOIA 2000 also amends the DPA 1998 in a number of respects,[386] for example, extending the DPA to cover 'unstructured personal data'.[387] The latter extension does not have an impact on a patient's right of access to his or her medical records since these would fall within the DPA anyway as part of an 'accessible record' under s 68 of that Act.

12.219 The important point is, however, that the FOIA 2000 seeks to create a 'bright line' between access to 'personal information' covered by the DPA and access to other information covered by the FOIA 2000. Hence, an individual who seeks access to 'personal data' relating to himself or herself, which would include medical or health information, has no right of access under the FOIA 2000: it is absolutely exempt from the 2000 Act. The patient's right of access, if any, is under the DPA.[388]

12.220 Where the information is sought by a third party, it is also exempt under the FOIA 2000 if disclosure would contravene the DPA or the person to whom it relates would not have a right of access to it.[389] Taken with the exemption for confidential information in s 41, the effect is that third party access will only be possible if compatible with the DPA.

12.221 The principal importance, therefore, of the FOIA 2000 in the health context must be that it might provide a right of access to non-personal information held by health bodies, for example, policies on access to treatment and so forth.[390]

(iii) Right of access under the DPA

12.222 Section 7 of the DPA confers a right of access upon the 'data subject' to certain information from a 'data controller', that is, the person or persons who control the purposes for which, and the manner in which, the personal data are processed. The data controller is required to supply the information 'promptly' and in any event within forty days.[391] The court may require the data controller to supply the information if he fails to do so.[392] In order to trigger the data controller's obligation to supply: (i) there must be a request in writing to supply

[381] FOIA 2000, Pt I.
[382] ibid, Pt II.
[383] ibid, s 41.
[384] ibid, s 44.
[385] ibid, s 38.
[386] ibid, Pt VII.
[387] ibid, ss 68 and 69 adding a new s 1(1)(e) and inserting s 9A into the DPA.
[388] DPA, s 40(1).
[389] DPA, s 40(2)–(4).
[390] But see *CSA v SIC* [2008] UKHL 47 (discussed at paras 12.165–12.167).
[391] DPA, s 7(8) and (10).
[392] ibid, s 7(9).

information;[393] (ii) the data controller must receive a fee not exceeding the prescribed maximum, which is usually £10;[394] and (iii) the data controller has requested and been supplied with 'further information in order to satisfy himself as to the identity of the person making the request and to locate the information which that person seeks'.[395]

Subject to a number of exemptions and other limitations (see below), the data controller must supply the following information:[396] **12.223**

(i) whether personal data of which the individual is the subject is being processed by or on behalf of the data controller;[397]
(ii) a description of the data, the purposes for which it is being processed, and the recipients (or classes of recipients) to whom it may be disclosed;[398]
(iii) if required by the data subject, where possible and which would not involve disproportionate effort, a copy in a permanent and intelligible form of the information held—including the source of the data—this may include an explanation of any terms used;
(iv) the logic of any process of automated data processing applied to the data.[399]

The court may order a data controller to comply with a request under s 7 if the failure to do so is in contravention of the DPA.[400] **12.224**

(iv) Exemptions and limitations

Part IV of the DPA contains certain exemptions from the subject information access provisions. In relation to medical records the following are relevant. **12.225**

(a) **Harm to the patient or another** Section 30(1) of the Act allows the Secretary of State to exempt (or modify) the subject access provisions where the personal data consist of information about the 'physical or mental health or condition of the data subject'. Pursuant to this, the Secretary of State promulgated the Data Protection (Subject Access Modification) (Health) Order 2000,[401] which does so in a number of ways. The order allows a health professional not to disclose such information[402] where it would be 'likely to cause serious harm to the physical or mental health or condition' of the patient or any other person.[403] Provision is made that where the data controller is not a health professional, he must consult the 'appropriate health professional' and only disclose information or withhold the information in accordance with that professional's opinion.[404] The 'appropriate health professional' is the **12.226**

[393] ibid, s 7(2)(a).
[394] Data Protection (Subject Access) (Fees and Miscellaneous Provisions) Regulations 2000, SI 2000/191, reg 3. Though note the application of reg 6 to some health records which, inter alia, permits a higher fee (£50) where a copy of data is to be supplied from data not held in electronic form.
[395] DPA, s 7(3), as amended.
[396] ibid, ss 7(1) and 8.
[397] In *Johnson v MDU* [2004] EWHC 347, Laddie J ruled that data need only be disclosed at the time of the request if it is still being processed at the time of the request.
[398] In Case 553/07 2009 *College van Burgemeester and Wethouders van Rotterdam v MEE Rijkeboer*, the ECJ provided guidance on the question of how long data should be kept for the purposes of a subject access request. The ECJ ruled that where the period for which data is being held is much longer than the period for which details of the disclosure and use of that data are held, this is unlikely to constitute fair processing, unless it can be shown that longer storage of the latter would place an excessive burden on the data controller. While not making it a rule, this suggests that, without special justification, details about disclosures, etc should not be destroyed for as long as the original data is being kept.
[399] DPA, 7(1)(d). Except in so far as this information constitutes a trade secret (see 8(5)).
[400] ibid, s 7(9).
[401] Data Protection (Subject Access Modification) (Health) Order 2000, SI 2000/413.
[402] ibid, Art 3(1).
[403] ibid, Art 5(1).
[404] ibid, Arts 5(2), 6, and 7.

current or most recent professional responsible for the relevant aspects of the data subject's clinical care.[405]

12.227 The order exempts health information from s 7 where disclosure would be injurious to the patient *or another*. For example, disclosure of information that might lead the patient, on discovering it, to harm another, such as a spouse or child, would fall within the exemption. Indeed, the 'other' might be the doctor. Such an affected individual can also apply to the court to prevent the disclosure of information by the data controller.[406] It is also worth noting that there will be some overlap with the exemption (see para 12.231) covering information about, or provided by, a third party. Not all information that, if disclosed, is likely to injure another need necessarily be information relating to, or identify as the source, that other and thus fall within the more general exemption.

12.228 (b) **Research, statistical, or historical purposes** Personal data that are processed (including held) only for research, statistical, or historical purposes are exempt from the right of access under s 7, provided that three conditions are met: (i) the data is not processed to 'support measures or decisions with respect to particular individuals'; (ii) the processing is not done in such a way as to cause, or be likely to cause, 'substantial damage or substantial distress' to the patient; and (iii) the results of the research are made available in a form that does not identify *any* patient.[407]

12.229 (c) **Infertility treatment** Section 38(1) allows the Secretary of State to exempt by order any personal data whose disclosure is prohibited or restricted by or under any enactment if it is necessary for safeguarding the interests of the data subject or the rights and freedoms of any other individual and the exemption should prevail over the right of access. The Data Protection (Miscellaneous Subject Access Exemptions) Order 2000[408] exempts from the subject access provisions of s 7 information falling within ss 31, 31ZA–31ZE and 33A–33D of the Human Fertilisation and Embryology Act 1990 (as amended).

12.230 (d) **Regulatory bodies** Section 31 exempts certain regulatory activities from the access provisions to the extent that they would be likely to prejudice the proper discharge of their functions. Section 31(2)(a)(iii) covers a statutory body, which protects members of the public against dishonesty, malpractice, or other seriously improper conduct by, or unfitness or incompetence of, persons authorized to carry on any profession of activity.[409] Hence professional regulatory bodies such as the GMC or the Nursing and Midwifery Council will be exempt from the subject information provisions to the extent they would otherwise prejudice the proper discharge of their regulatory function.

12.231 (e) **Third party information** Finally, there are special provisions in respect of so-called 'third party data'. Section 7(4) provides that a data controller need not supply information relating to an identifiable third party, unless that person has consented to it[410] or it is reasonable in all the circumstances to do so without consent. This covers not only information *about* a third party, but also information that identifies the third party as the *source* of the information.[411] Notice that the exemption does not apply to the extent that the information

405 ibid, Art 2.
406 DPA, s 7(9), as amended.
407 ibid, s 33(4).
408 SI 2000/419, made under s 38(1) of the DPA. Relevant sections substituted by SI 2009/1892, art 3, Sch 3, para 1.
409 See also DPA, s 31(4)(b).
410 Such as where the data subject authorizes another to make an application on his behalf.
411 DPA, s 7(5). Identified individual includes someone who could be identified taking account of all the information that is, or is likely to be, in the possession of the data subject: ibid, s 8(7).

can be provided without identifying the individual.[412] Further, s 7(6) states that in deciding whether it is 'reasonable in all the circumstances' to comply with a request without the consent of the third party regard is to be had to: (i) any duty of confidentiality owed to the third party; (ii) any steps taken to obtain the third party's consent; (iii) whether the third party is capable of consenting; and (iv) whether the third party has expressly refused. For health information, the Data Protection (Subject Access Modification) (Health) Order 2000,[413] adds to s 7(4) so that disclosure of data cannot be withheld merely because they relate to, or were provided by, another health professional who has 'compiled or contributed' to the patient's records or has 'been involved in the care' of the individual 'as a health professional'.

(v) Children and incompetent adult patients

(a) The proper interpretation of section 7 Section 7(1) seems to envisage the 'data subject' as the applicant in that it states that 'an individual' is entitled to the statutory information if 'personal data of which *that* individual is the data subject' are being processed.[414] No difficulty arises where the data subject is competent to make such a request, that is to say, is able to understand the nature and likely consequences of seeking his or her medical records. What if the data subject is incompetent? The DPA 1998 itself contains no express provision addressing incompetent adults or children. Does s 7 apply where the request is made by the incompetent patient's legally recognized proxy decision-maker (ie by a person with parental responsibility or a person recognized under the Mental Capacity Act 2005 (MCA 2005) as empowered to make decisions regarding the personal welfare of the incapacitated adult)?[415] **12.232**

The Data Protection (Subject Access Modification) (Health) Order 2000 SI 2000/423 sets out exemptions from disclosure, including those that apply where: 'any person falling within paragraph (4) is enabled by or under any enactment or rule of law to make a request on behalf of a data subject and has made such a request.'[416] A person falls within para (4) where 'the data subject is a child, and that person has parental responsibility for that data subject' or 'the data subject is incapable of managing his own affairs and that person has been appointed by a court to manage those affairs'.[417] The exemption applies to the extent that application of s 7 would disclose information: **12.233**

(a) provided by the data subject in the expectation that it would not be disclosed to the person making the request;
(b) obtained as a result of any examination or investigation to which the data subject consented in the expectation that the information would not be so disclosed; or
(c) which the data subject has expressly indicated should not be so disclosed provided that sub-paragraphs (a) and (b) shall not prevent disclosure where the data subject has expressly indicated that he no longer has the expectation referred to therein.[418]

Paragraph (4) captures all legal proxies that were recognized at the time of the enactment of the order. Under the MCA 2005, proxies can now be appointed to make decisions with regard to the personal welfare of incapacitated adults patients.[419] If an individual grants another person authority (eg through a lasting power of attorney)[420] to act on their behalf, **12.234**

412 ibid, s 7(5).
413 SI 2000/413, Art 8(a).
414 DPA, s 7(1)(a), emphasis added.
415 The Mental Capacity Act 2005 recognizes proxies appointed by individuals before they lose capacity (donees of lasting powers of attorney: ss 9–14) and proxies appointed by the court to act on behalf of incapacitated adults (court-appointed deputies: ss 16–20).
416 SI 2000/413, reg 5(3).
417 ibid, reg 5(4). The wording relating to children differs with regard to Scotland.
418 ibid, reg 5(3).
419 See n 415 above.
420 Mental Capacity Act 2005, s 9.

then the ICO advise that 'it is reasonable to assume that an attorney with authority to manage the property and affairs of an individual will have the appropriate authority [to exercise subject access rights on his or her behalf]'.[421] In such circumstances, they would not fall within para (4) and would also appear, therefore, to escape the exemptions from s 7 contained within the Regulations.[422]

(vi) Remedies

12.235 If a doctor fails to comply with a request under s 7, the data subject (or other person making the request) may make an application to the court for access under s 7(9). The court can order the data controller to comply with the request. The patient may also recover compensation for any 'damage' suffered as a result of the doctor's failure to comply with the request,[423] which may include financial or psychiatric injury. Compensation for 'distress' alone, however, is not recoverable under s 13 in this instance. On application by the data subject, s 14 also gives a court the power to order the data controller to 'rectify, block, erase or destroy' data which is 'inaccurate'.[424]

3. Access to Health Records Act 1990

12.236 The Access to Health Records Act (AHRA) 1990 applied to manual health records created on or after 1 November 1991. Most of the AHRA 1990 was repealed by the DPA. The sole remaining basis for access to manual records by virtue of the AHRA 1990 is under s 3(1)(f) by the personal representatives of a dead patient or by a person who may have a claim arising out of his or her death where the health records are relevant to an action arising out of the patient's death. The subject access provisions of the DPA do not apply *directly* to this situation in the form of a request to access the personal data of the dead patient, since they only cover the personal data of a *living person* (see para 12.162) and it is not entirely clear that anyone other than the data subject may apply for access under s 7 of that act (see paras 12.232–12.233). That said *if* the data in a deceased person's health record *also relates to a living person,* which, according to the Article 29 Working Party they might well do when the living and deceased person are blood relatives (see paras 12.170), then this living person should be able to make a request under DPA, s 7. But, on this rationale, the living person would have to make a request to access his or her own data, not that of the deceased person.

(i) Scope of the right of access

12.237 The AHRA 1990 applies to all records made by or on behalf of a health professional[425] in connection with the care[426] of an individual.[427] The application must be made in writing[428] and contain sufficient information to identify the patient and to establish that the applicant is entitled to make the application.[429] A fee may be charged where access is given to information none of which was recorded during the forty days immediately preceding the application,[430] or where the applicant is supplied with a copy of the

[421] <https://ico.org.uk/for-organisations/guide-to-data-protection/principle-6-rights/subject-access-request/>.

[422] See J Laing and A Grubb, 'Confidentiality and Medical Records' in A Grubb (ed), *Principles of Medical Law* (Oxford University Press 2004) 553, 626 (para 9.214).

[423] DPA, s 13.

[424] DPA, s 14.

[425] Defined in AHRA 1990, s 2 (as amended) to have the same meaning as in DPA, s 69.

[426] Defined in AHRA 1990, s 11 to include 'examination, investigation, diagnosis and treatment'.

[427] AHRA 1990, s 1(1)(b).

[428] ibid, s 11.

[429] ibid, s 3(6).

[430] The fee is £10.

record.[431]

12.238 Depending upon the time frame to which the application relates, the holder of the record has either twenty-one days (if it relates even in part to a record made within 40 days preceding the application) or forty days to respond to the request, either by giving access to the record or part of the record. The applicant must be allowed to inspect the record (or so much of the record as is not excluded) or part of the record to which the application relates, or be supplied with a copy of the record or extract.[432]

(ii) Exemptions and limitations

12.239 There are three exceptions in the Act that are of particular importance here. First, the Act provides that access shall not be given to any part of the record that:

(a) in the opinion of the holder of the record, would disclose—

(i) information likely to cause serious harm to the physical or mental health of any individual.[433]

12.240 Secondly, access should also be excluded in respect of any part of the record that:

(a) in the opinion of the holder of the record, would disclose— . . .

(ii) information relating to or provided by an individual, other than the patient, who could be identified from that information.[434]

An exception to this is made where the individual concerned has consented to the application, or is a health professional who has been involved in the care of the patient.[435]

12.241 Thirdly, access should be excluded where the records contain a note at the deceased's request that the personal representatives should not be granted access.[436]

12.242 Where access under the Act is excluded, the record holder is under no obligation to inform the applicant that information exists and has been excluded. All that is required is that the record holder inform the patient that he does not hold any information that he is required by law to disclose.

4. Access to Medical Reports Act 1988

12.243 The Access to Medical Reports Act (AMRA)1988, which came into force on 1 January 1989, gives patients the right to see certain medical reports prepared about them for employment or insurance purposes.[437] The right of access conferred by the Act is a right to inspect or be supplied with a copy of the report.[438]

(i) Scope of the right of access

12.244 An important limitation on the scope of the Act comes from the fact that 'medical report' is defined to mean: 'a report relating to the physical or mental health of the individual

[431] AHRA 1990, s 3(4)(b). The fee may not exceed the cost of making the copy and, where relevant, the cost of postage.
[432] ibid, s 3(2).
[433] ibid, s (5)(1)(a)(i).
[434] ibid, s (5)(1)(a)(ii).
[435] ibid, s 5(2).
[436] ibid, s 4(3).
[437] AMRA 1988, s 1, defined in s 2(1).
[438] ibid, s 4(4). See also s 5(2), conferring upon the individual the right to request corrections to the report.

prepared by a medical practitioner who is or has been responsible for the clinical care of the individual'.[439]

12.245 'Care' is, in turn, defined in the Act to include 'examination, investigation or diagnosis for the purposes of, or in connection with, any form of medical treatment'.[440] Accordingly, reports prepared by an independent medical practitioner who is not, and has not been, involved in a therapeutic doctor–patient relationship with the individual concerned are not covered by the Act.[441] Difficult questions arise in relation to the position of an occupational health doctor who is employed to advise employers and employees about issues involving health and safety at work. Whether or not reports prepared by such a doctor will fall within the scope of the Access to Medical Reports Act 1988 will most likely depend upon the degree of involvement with the employees and, in particular, whether the physician has, or has had, any direct responsibility in relation to the mental or physical well-being of the individual concerned.

12.246 The Act provides that the employer or insurance company must obtain the individual's consent when it seeks the report, and that the individual may at that time make consent conditional upon being given access to the report prior to the supply to the employer or insurance company.[442] Even if an individual does not so stipulate at the time of consenting, he or she may nonetheless, by notice to the doctor supplying the report, request access prior to the report being given to the employer or insurance company[443] or, again by notice to the doctor, within six months of the report being so supplied.[444]

(ii) Exemptions and limitations

12.247 The individual's right of access to medical reports under the Act is not absolute. There are three situations in which doctors are justified in refusing to provide access. First, where disclosure would: '*in the opinion of the practitioner* be likely to cause serious harm to the physical or mental health of the individual or others . . .'[445] This is similarly worded to the equivalent exception applying to the s 7 right of the DPA, save that this explicitly adopts a subjective test.

12.248 Secondly, where disclosure would 'in the opinion of the practitioner . . . indicate the intentions of the practitioner in respect of the individual'.[446]

12.249 Thirdly, where disclosure would:

> be likely to reveal information about another person, or to reveal the identity of another person who has supplied information to the practitioner about the individual unless—
>
> (a) that person has consented; or
> (b) that person is a health professional who has been involved in the care of the individual and the information relates to or has been provided by the professional in that capacity[447]

439 ibid, s 2(1). Again, 'health professional' is defined in accordance with s 69 of the DPA 1998.
440 AMRA 1988, s 2(1).
441 They may, however, be covered by the DPA 1998.
442 AMRA 1988, s 3(1).
443 ibid, s 4(3).
444 ibid, s 6.
445 ibid, s 7(1) (emphasis added).
446 ibid, s 7(1).
447 ibid, s 7(2).

The doctor is obliged to inform the individual that the request for access has been denied under one of the exceptions.[448] The individual is entitled to apply to the county court for an order that the doctor must provide him or her access under the Act.[449] 12.250

(iii) Relationship with the Data Protection Act 1998

What is the relationship between the DPA and the Access to Medical Reports Act 1988? While a medical 'report' would be a 'record', it might not be a 'health record' within DPA, s 68. The definition of 'health record' excludes medical reports, unless made by a health professional in the course of the patient's care or treatment.[450] It does not follow, however, that the AMRA 1988 confers a greater degree of access and control than the DPA with regard to those medical reports within its ambit (ie medical reports prepared by the patient's doctor for employment or insurance purposes). Any such medical report will also fall under the DPA if it is in a relevant filing system or subject to automatic processing (ie if it falls within paras (a), (b), and (c) of the s 1 definition of 'data'). 12.251

5. The common law

(i) Judicial development of a right of access

The first English decision to deal with the question of a common law right of access to medical records was *R v Mid Glamorgan Family Health Services Authority, ex p Martin*.[451] As we shall see, this case did not consider in any detail the legal basis for asserting a common law right to access.[452] Prior to *Martin*, however, the Supreme Court of Canada in *McInerney v MacDonald*[453] had considered the question and determined that a common law right of action could be found from the general fiduciary nature of the doctor–patient relationship. LaForest J, delivering the judgment of the Canadian Supreme Court, found that the fiduciary qualities of the doctor–patient relationship created a duty upon the physician to grant access to the information the doctor uses in administering treatment,[454] and that this duty extends to requiring the disclosure of information that has been conveyed to the current holder by another doctor.[455] 12.252

The Court of Appeal in the *Martin* case reached a broadly similar conclusion that a patient might have a limited common law right of access to medical records, but this was based on reasoning far removed from that of the Canadian Supreme Court.[456] The claimant sought judicial review of the decision of two health authorities to deny him access to medical records relating to two specific incidents in his past, both of which involved his psychiatric treatment, which he sought in order that he might better come to terms with his own personal development. His repeated requests for access had been refused, on grounds ranging from possible detriment to his overall best interests to a perceived duty to 'protect retired colleagues'. At one stage, access was offered provided that the patient would give an assurance that 'the Authority and/or any of its staff are not implicated in any potential litigation being contemplated by Mr Martin in respect of his South Glamorganshire treatment'. 12.253

[448] ibid, s 7(3).
[449] ibid, s 8.
[450] DPA, s 68(2)(b).
[451] *R v Mid Glamorgan Family Health Services Authority, ex p Martin* [1995] 1 All ER 356; noted by A Grubb (1994) 2 Med L Rev 353 and D Feenan (1996) 59 MLR 101.
[452] See the discussion in Kennedy and Grubb, n 117, 992–1019.
[453] *McInerney v MacDonald* (1992) 93 DLR (4th) 415.
[454] ibid, 424.
[455] ibid, 425.
[456] For argument in favour of the view that the doctor–patient relationship is fiduciary see A Grubb, 'The Doctor as Fiduciary' [1994] CLP 311.

Finally, in 1993, after the patient had instituted proceedings for judicial review of the decision not to give him access to his medical records, the respondents agreed to disclose the patient's medical records to his medical advisers, but not to the patient himself.

12.254 At first instance Popplewell J,[457] in the course of a judgment that denied the existence of a common law right of access to medical records, rejected the fiduciary approach in *McInerney* on the basis that Lord Scarman in the House of Lords (and Browne Wilkinson LJ in the Court of Appeal) in *Sidaway*[458] had rejected this characterization of the doctor–patient relationship.[459] Accordingly, his judgment contains little examination of whether or not English courts should recognize fiduciary qualities in the doctor–patient relationship, and the point was not discussed when the case reached the Court of Appeal.

12.255 The Court of Appeal focused on the question of whether a doctor or a health authority, as the owner of a patient's medical records, is entitled to deny the patient access to his medical records on the ground that their disclosure would be detrimental to him or her.[460] Nourse LJ, with whom Evans LJ and Sir Roger Parker agreed, held that access to medical records could be denied where it was in the best interests of the patient to do so, such as where disclosure would be detrimental to the patient's health. Given that the health authorities had offered to disclose the patient's medical records to his medical advisers, there was clearly no ground for granting the patient the relief sought in his action for judicial review of the health authorities' decisions. Unfortunately, the narrow basis of this question considered by the Court of Appeal precluded any helpful guidance being issued on questions such as who has the onus of proving that disclosure would be harmful to the patient, and upon what other grounds access might lawfully be denied.

12.256 Of greater interest is the Court of Appeal's analysis of the possible bases upon which a patient could claim a common law right of access to his or her medical records. Each of the judges found that a health authority has no absolute right to deal with medical records in any way that it chooses.[461] According to Nourse LJ, this right is limited by a doctor or health authority's general duty to act at all times in the best interests of the patient, a duty which he identifies as resting upon the speech of Lord Templeman in *Sidaway v Bethlem Royal Hospital Governors*.[462] Evans LJ based the duty to disclose upon the need not to frustrate the very purposes for which medical records are created in the first place. In his view those purposes were to enable a patient's doctor and his successors best to treat the patient, and to provide a record of diagnosis and treatment in the case of future enquiry or dispute.[463] Sir Roger Parker preferred not to set out the scope of the doctor's duty of disclosure because 'the circumstances in which a patient or former patient is entitled to demand access to his medical history as set out in the records will be infinitely various'.[464] He gave the example of a patient requiring access in order to facilitate medical treatment if the patient is about

[457] [1993] PIQR P426.

[458] [1985] AC 871, 884: 'There is no comparison to be made between the relationship of doctor and patient with that of solicitor and client, trustee and *cestui qui trust* or the other relationships treated in equity as of a fiduciary character.'

[459] Moreover, Popplewell J criticized the judgment in *McInerney* for failing to distinguish between information in the medical records that had been collected from the patient, and conclusions that a doctor reaches based on that information but which should remain wholly the property of the doctor.

[460] *R v Mid Glamorgan Family Health Services Authority, ex p Martin*, n 451, 359 *per* Nourse LJ, 365 *per* Evans LJ.

[461] ibid, 363 *per* Nourse LJ, 365 *per* Evans LJ, 366 *per* Sir Roger Parker.

[462] [1985] AC 871, 904.

[463] *ex p Martin*, n 451, 365.

[464] ibid, 366.

to emigrate and has a condition that require treatment before a successor doctor can be nominated.

The difficulty with the judgments of the Court of Appeal are that they rest more on assertion of the need to qualify a doctor or health authority's right to deny access to medical records than upon any analysis of the possible basis in the common law for a right of access to medical records. The court, in effect, sought to qualify the scope of the duty without examining the basis of the duty in the first place. **12.257**

The lack of any principled foundation for the right of access to medical records, identified by the Court of Appeal in *Martin*, was recognized by the High Court of Australia in *Breen v Williams*.[465] The case arose after a woman was denied access to her medical records, which had been compiled by her doctor after *private* treatment in connection with complications from a breast augmentation operation that had been performed by another doctor. She sought access to her medical records in order to participate in settlement of breast implant litigation in the US, but access was refused by her doctor unless she agreed to release him from any possible claim which might arise in relation to his treatment of her. In contrast to *McInerney* and *Martin*, there was no suggestion that disclosure of the information in the records could have any adverse effect on the patient's physical or mental health. **12.258**

In *Breen* it was held that, unless a patient had a contractual right of access to her records, or disclosure of the information in the records was in her best interests such that it would be negligent to withhold the information, there was no common law obligation on a doctor or hospital to provide access. Moreover, there was no basis for implying such a term into the contractual relationship between the doctor and the patient. Rejecting the authority of *Martin*, the High Court found that the relationship between a doctor and patient is not such that a patient has a *right* to see her medical records.[466] Also of interest was the High Court's rejection of the argument that the fiduciary qualities of the doctor–patient relationship were such that a doctor would be under a fiduciary obligation to provide a patient with access to her medical records. Whilst accepting that a doctor was a fiduciary in some respects, the High Court held that the fiduciary duty, as understood in Australia, did not provide any foundation for an obligation to provide access to a patient's medical records, or more generally to act in the patient's best interests.[467] **12.259**

(ii) Scope of the common law right of access

In England, the most that can be said with any certainty is that the courts implicitly accept that the owner of medical records does not have an unfettered discretion to deal with them as he or she chooses. The legal basis for qualifying these ownership rights could be based upon a number of possible grounds. First, that patients have a general 'innominate' right of access to medical records subject to certain exceptions. Secondly, that, in certain defined circumstances, doctors are obliged to disclose information in the medical records or hand over the records themselves to patients. These circumstances include where it is necessary to do so to avoid liability in negligence and where so required by the rules governing disclosure for the purposes of litigation. Thirdly, it is still possible that either the Court of Appeal or the House of Lords could adopt the reasoning of the Canadian Supreme Court in *McInerney* and of Kirby P in dissent in *Breen v Williams*, and hold that the fiduciary qualities of the doctor–patient relationship impose an obligation upon doctors to provide **12.260**

[465] (1996) 70 ALJR 772. See P Parkinson (1995) 17 Sydney LR 433 and I Kennedy, (1997) 5 Med L Rev 115.
[466] *Breen v Williams* (1996) 70 ALJR 772, 784, 789–90, 804.
[467] ibid, 776–77, 781–82, 793.

patients with access to their medical records. In any event, given that access to medical records undoubtedly engages Article 8(1) ECHR,[468] the ownership rights of the doctor and NHS in the patient's medical record must be consistent with the patient's right to private and family life.

12.261 By way of conclusion to this discussion, we find it difficult to envisage circumstances where a patient would want to rely on a common law right of access, because the DPA and the other legislation examined above would seem to cover all patient records.

E. Overview

12.262 Dramatic changes in information technology are radically challenging the traditional methods of protecting patient information. 'Ask or anonymize' is rapidly becoming outmoded as a sufficient response to the question of how to appropriately protect the full range of private and public interests engaged by the use of confidential patient information. The law must play its part in constructing conditions under which persons may have confidence, when they disclose confidential information to a health professional, that the information they provide will only be used for purposes that they have reason to expect, to accept as appropriate,[469] and to be respectful of his or her privacy.

12.263 Consideration of the law of confidentiality and data protection shows that a respect for confidentiality and privacy does not mean that data should not be used. It means that data should be used, but used *only* in ways that are consistent with a person's reasonable expectations.

12.264 Both the domestic courts and the ECtHR have identified the right to privacy as protected by Article 8 ECHR as an important underpinning of the duty of confidentiality in relation to the use and disclosure of health data (see paras 12.17–12.18), and the DPD has as its objective the protection of fundamental rights and freedoms, in particular privacy. Yet, the existing regime of data protection may not operate with as broad a conception of the right to privacy as the ECHR. This may limit the ability of the DPA alone to protect reasonable expectations, but also underline the continuing importance of the role of the common law in this context.

12.265 Article 8 ECHR has been interpreted very broadly by the ECtHR (see para 12.27). It covers physical and psychological integrity, therefore embracing multiple aspects of a person's physical and social identity, such as gender identity, name, sexual orientation, and sexual life. A right to personal development, as well as a right to establish and develop relationships with other human beings and the outside world are protected, as is a person's right to his or her image. In short, it provides nothing less than a prima facie right to control virtually all aspects of one's personality (in effect, a right to personal autonomy in relation to all elements related to a person's physical and psychological integrity). This has important implications.

12.266 There is an interference with Article 8 ECHR if health data is used without a patient's consent. In relation to the use of data relating to a person's health, Art 8, in effect, grants a patient a prima facie right to control the use of the data obtained for his or her treatment. This, for example, calls into question the idea that processing of health data can be rendered

[468] *Gaskin v UK* (1990) 12 EHRR 36.

[469] M J Taylor, and N C Taylor, 'Health Research Access to Personal Confidential Data in England and Wales: Assessing Any Gap in Public Attitude between Preferable and Acceptable Models of Consent' (2014) Life Sciences, Society and Policy 10:15. doi.10.1186/s40504-014-0015-6.

legitimate without the patient's consent unless this consent is either impossible, or, if possible, would threaten more important values in unavoidable conflict with it. This has particular relevance to the application of DPA, Sch 3, para 8.

The complete removal of privacy protection on the grounds of anonymization is inappropriate. The law should reflect the position taken by the ICO code of practice and recognize anonymization as relevant processing of personal data (see paras 12.167–12.180). As the common law develops to recognize two separate causes of action, both the traditional duty of confidence and the more recently recognized tort of misuse of personal information, the appropriateness of the narrow construction of privacy (as evident in the reasoning of the Court of Appeal in *Source Informatics*)[470] should also be reconsidered (paras 12.38–12.43). It should be possible for the law to recognize a misuse of information in circumstances that patients would recognize as such and this may not be limited to those cases where information remains in an individually identifiable form. **12.267**

As the limits of perfect anonymization are in any case recognized, it becomes increasingly important that the boundary between appropriate and inappropriate use of data is drawn according to values and principles that are of broad application. The law discussed in this chapter has sought to recognize, accommodate, and reconcile the rights and interests of a broad range of persons to both access and deny access to patient information under different circumstances. Such reconciliation is not best understood as a 'balance' between private interests (eg in an atomistic conception of privacy) and public interests (eg in the public good that might flow from health research). The ideas are instead mutually supportive.[471] After all, under a broad conception of privacy, medical research, by offering the possibility of improved quality of life and improved life options, engages the elements protected by ECHR, Art 8 just as much as does the confidentiality of information given for a patient's treatment. Conversely, in as much as there is a public interest in medical research, there is a public interest in the protection of confidentiality which can be seen to support rather than to conflict with medical research values.[472] **12.268**

The challenge is to identify the appropriate 'norms of exclusivity'[473] that *permit* access to data under conditions that persons have reason to expect, accept, and are respectful of fundamental rights and freedoms: both their own and those of other members of the community. **12.269**

470 [2001] QB 424, 54.

471 M J Taylor, *Genetic Data and the Law* (Cambridge University Press 2012) 13.

472 See, eg, D Beyleveld, 'Conceptualising Privacy in Relation to Medical Research Values' in S A M McLean (ed), *First Do No Harm* (Ashgate 2006) 151–63.

473 M J Taylor, n 471, ch 2.

13

CLINICAL RESEARCH

Jean V McHale

A. Introduction

13.01 The drive for progress in medicine and science has led to a vast increase in the amount of clinical and scientific research undertaken.[1] The importance of clinical research has led

[1] On the legal regulation of clinical research see generally H Biggs, *Healthcare Research Ethics and Law* (Routledge Cavendish 2009); M Brazier and E Cave, *Medicine, Patients and the Law* (Manchester University Press 2016) ch 15; E Jackson, *Medical Law Text Cases and Materials* (3rd edn, Oxford University Press 2013) ch 9; J Herring, *Medical Law and Ethics* (6th edn, Oxford University Press 2016), ch 11; G Laurie, S E Harmon, and G Porter, *Law and Medical Ethics* (10 edn, Oxford University Press 2016) chs 19 and 20; S Pattinson, *Medical Law and Ethics* (4th edn, Sweet & Maxwell 2014) ch 11. For further detailed discussion regarding the interface with the ethical debate, see C Foster, *The Ethics of Medical Research on Humans* (Cambridge University Press 2001); C Foster (ed), *Manual for Research Ethics Committees* (Kings College London 2002); and see also M Brazier, 'Exploitation and Enrichment: The Paradox of Medical Experimentation' (2008) 34 Journal of Medical Ethics 180.

some indeed to argue that individuals have a duty to participate in such research.[2] Such research may lead to incredible discoveries and 'miracle' cures but at the same time this is an area dogged with controversy. The abuses which occurred in Germany during the Second World War have cast a long shadow. Since that time there has been concern at the international level to ensure that, in the future, research practices will be ethical and in accordance with legal principles. This led to the Nuremberg Code in 1949 and the Declaration of Helsinki which was initially produced in 1964.[3] In the European context, statements which have been influential, at least at a rhetorical level include the Council of Europe Convention on Human Rights and Biomedicine—although the UK is still not a signatory to this convention.[4] The Council of Europe has also issued an Additional Protocol to the Convention on Human Rights and Biomedicine.[5] The European Convention on Human Rights is also of undoubted importance and in the UK context is of particular relevance in the light of the Human Rights Act 1998.[6]

Nonetheless, despite the promulgation of such statements internationally scientific research **13.02** has been still dogged with controversy.[7] In the notorious Tuskegee experiment, experiments were undertaken on black US males to determine the progression of syphilis despite the fact that there had been accepted treatment over many years.[8] A further more recent incident was at Johns Hopkins University in 2001.[9] Ellen Roche, a 24-year-old technician, died after acting as a volunteer in a non-therapeutic study of asthma. The review into her death led to major criticisms as to the safety of the trial, the review procedures of the project, inadequate consent procedures as well as inadequate failure to report unexpected adverse events, and the suspension of all federally funded projects until corrective action plans were produced. In a damning statement, the external review committee found that 'many people at Hopkins believe that oversight and regulatory processes are a barrier to research and are to be reduced to the minimum'.[10]

In the UK the main drive towards regulating clinical research practices began in the 1960s. **13.03** In 1968 the then Minister of Health, following a report of the Royal College of Physicians, sent a letter to Health Authorities requesting that they establish research ethics committees (RECs). These bodies sat on a part-time basis and were primarily composed of health professionals. The first major piece of guidance to research ethics committee members was produced in 1984 by the Royal College of Physicians. In 1991 the Department of Health itself finally issued major guidelines to RECs in the form of the so-called 'Red Book'.[11] The DOH guidance was accompanied by a raft of guidance on specific issues produced by health professional bodies. The promulgation of such guidance at times perhaps obscured

[2] See J Harris, 'Scientific Research is a Moral Duty' (2005) 31 Journal of Medical Ethics 242; A Caplan, 'Is There an Obligation to Participate in Biomedical Research?', in S F Spicker, I Alon, A de Vries, and H Tristram Englehardt, (eds), *The Use of Human Beings in Research* (Kluwer 1988).

[3] Adopted by the 18th World Medical Assembly, Helsinki, Finland, 1964.

[4] See further A Plomer, *The Law and Ethics of Medical Research: International Bioethics and Human Rights* (Cavendish Publishing 2005).

[5] Council of Europe Steering Committee on Bioethics, *Additional Protocol to the Convention on Human Rights and Biomedicine on Biomedical Research*, Strasbourg 25 January 2005.

[6] Further recent guidance includes the Council for International Organisations of Medical Sciences, *International Ethical Guidelines for Health-related Research involving Humans* (6 December 2016).

[7] See generally discussion in H Biggs, *Healthcare Research Ethics and Law* (Routledge Cavendish 2009) ch 2.

[8] J Jones, *Bad Blood: The Tuskegee Syphilis Experiment* (Free Press 1981).

[9] 'Death of Research Volunteer at Johns Hopkins' *Bulletin of Medical Ethics* (September 2001) 3.

[10] ibid, 7.

[11] Department of Health, *Local Research Ethics Committees* (DoH 1991); and see discussion in J V McHale, 'Medical Research: Some Ethical and Legal Dilemmas' (1993) 1 Med L Rev 160–86.

the fact that the legal regulation of this area was exceedingly limited. RECs themselves were non-statutory bodies, as was the guidance. Explicit statutory regulation of research activities was rare. One example is that of embryo research regulated under the Human Fertilisation and Embryology Act. Some statutory regulation did exist in relation to those trials which were undertaken on medicinal products under the Medicines Act 1968.[12] But the scope of statutory regulation was limited.

13.04 However, since the publication of the Red Book there has been a movement towards increasingly structuring the work of RECs. Today support is given by a statutory body, the Health Research Authority, discussed at paras 13.09–13.18 and by organizations such as the Association of Research Ethics Committees (AREC). Material on research ethics is increasingly being made available and indeed AREC now has its own refereed academic journal, *Research Ethics*.[13] Nonetheless, the development of legal knowledge in this area, amongst clinicians at least, appears to have been more limited. A study of health care professionals undertaken by Ferguson published in 2003 indicated that while clinical researchers were concerned with ethical issues in clinical trials, their knowledge of the applicable law in this area was limited.[14] One may express some sympathy with the clinicians as much of the applicable law in this area could only be ascertained through extrapolation from related case and statute law, but there was no coherent statutory regulation. While despite the establishment of the Health Research Authority we are still a considerable way from overarching statutory regulation, the conduct of clinical trials was radically impacted through the implementation into English law of the EU Clinical Trials Directive in 2004. The Directive aligns procedures for clinical trials on medicinal products in the EU. The EU Clinical Trials Directive places the establishment of research ethics committees on a statutory basis.[15] It applies to both commercial and non-commercial trials. Clinical Trials are defined as 'an investigation to ascertain the efficacy or safety of a medicine in human subjects'.[16] All clinical trials must be undertaken in accordance with the standards of 'good clinical practice'.[17] The incorporation of the Directive was met with a mixed response, not least because of concerns that it could raise costs in publicly funded trials and reduce the number of such trials in the future.[18] Cave and Holm have argued that the 'industry led' approach of the Directive, which has been followed in the Research Governance Arrangements, places undue emphasis upon the facilitation of research rather than upon safeguarding participants' interests.[19] The Directive is now being replaced by a new EU Regulation which will take forward the approach of the Directive, but in other ways has streamlined the process and will afford less discretion to member states in the future in this area.[20] Whether this will apply to the UK

---

[12] Medicines Exemption from Licence (Special Cases and Miscellaneous Provisions) Order 1972, SI 1972/1200.

[13] There is also much related guidance eg Royal College of Physicians, *Guidelines on the Practice of Ethics Committees in Medical Research Involving Human* Participants (8th edn, RCP 2007); General Medical Council, Good Practice in Research and Consent to Research (GMC 2013).

[14] P Ferguson, 'Legal and Ethical Aspects of Clinical Trials: The Views of Researchers' (2003) 11 Med L Rev 48–69.

[15] As implemented in Pt 2 of the Medicines for Human Use (Clinical Trials) Regulations 2004, SI 2004/1031.

[16] Directive and reg 2, and see explanatory notes, para 4.1.4.

[17] Articles 1(4) and 3–5 of the Directive as incorporated in reg 28 and Sch 1. The statement on GCP is to be found at the Commission website at <http://www.pharmacos/eudra.org>.

[18] See further discussion in T K Hervey and J V McHale, *European Health Law: Themes and Implications* (Cambridge University Press 2015).

[19] E Cave and S Holm, 'New Governance Arrangements for Research Ethics Committees: Is Facilitating Research Achieved at the Cost of Participants' Interest?' (2002) 28 Journal of Medical Ethics 318–21.

[20] Regulation (EU) No 536/2014 of the European Parliament and of the Council of 16 April 2014 on clinical trials on medicinal products for human use, and repealing Directive 2001/20/EC.

in the future of course will depend on the political developments post the EU Referendum in June 2016. This is considered further below at paras 13.111–13.112.

Despite the emphasis in recent years upon the need for practices in clinical research to be seen as 'ethical', the medical and research community in the UK has also been dogged with controversy. The scandals caused by the widespread unauthorized retention of human material led to the consideration of this issue in the Bristol Interim Inquiry Report[21] and also through the establishment of the inquiry into events at the Royal Liverpool Children's Hospital, better known as the Alder Hey inquiry,[22] leading ultimately to the Human Tissue Act 2004 (discussed further in Chapter 19).[23] In the context of clinical research, the process of obtaining consent in a clinical trial came under critical scrutiny in an inquiry into a study involving children, in which it was alleged that adequate parental consent had not been obtained.[24] The risks of clinical trials and the need for careful safety procedures were highlighted in the wake of events at an independent research unit at Northwick Park hospital in London in 2006 where six healthy male volunteers suffered a sudden violent reaction during a trial involving an anti-inflammatory drug, which was being developed for the treatment of arthritis and leukaemia.[25] The six men all suffered multiple organ failure, with two in particular suffering serious complications.[26] **13.05**

Part of the revision of the current research governance guidance derives from these scandals and can also be seen through the current major consideration of reform of the law concerning human material. The area of research has been influenced by the rhetoric of clinical governance; standards and accountability (see further Chapter 1). As in other areas, standards frameworks have been introduced in relation to research governance.[27] The Research Governance Framework (RGF) applies to both health and to social care. It makes reference to 'participants' rather than to 'subjects'. This was a discernible shift in emphasis. The RGF now provides that key elements of such a culture include: **13.06**

- Respect for participants' dignity, rights, safety and well-being;
- Valuing the diversity within society;
- Personal and scientific integrity;
- Leadership;
- Honesty;
- Accountability;
- Openness;
- Clear and supportive management.[28]

The RGF emphasizes the need to safeguard consent,[29] and the protection of personal data.[30] **13.07**
In the light of inquiries at Bristol Royal Infirmary and Alder Hey, it stressed the need for

[21] Bristol Inquiry Interim Report, *Removal and Retention of Human Material* (2000) and the Final Report (2001) available at <http://webarchive.nationalarchives.gov.uk/+/www.dh.gov.uk/en/Publicationsandstatistics/Publications/PublicationsPolicyAndGuidance/DH_4005620>.

[22] *Report of the Inquiry into the Royal Liverpool Children's Hospital* (Alder Hey 2001) (HC-121).

[23] See generally on the Act: D Price, 'The Human Tissue Act 2004' (2005) 68 MLR 798; K Liddell, 'Beyond Bristol and Alder Hey: The Future Regulation of Human Tissue' (2005) 13 Med L Rev 170.

[24] R Griffiths, *NHS Executive West Midlands Regional Office Report of a Research Framework in North Staffordshire Hospital NHS Trust* (NHS 2001).

[25] 'Six Taken Ill After Drug Trial' *BBC News* (6 March 2006) <http://news.bbc.co.uk/1/hi/england/london/4807042.stm>.

[26] See the report of the expert scientific group established by the Secretary of State in the light of the Northwick Park incident, *The Expert Group on Phase One Clinical Trials: Final Report* (2006).

[27] *Research Governance Framework for Health and Social Care* (2nd edn, DoH 2005).

[28] ibid, para 2.7.2.

[29] ibid, para 2.2.3.

[30] ibid, para 2.2.5.

particular care in relation to research involving tissue and organs.[31] The RGF refers to the need for service groups, carers, or their representatives to be involved wherever possible in the design, conduct, analysis, and reporting of research.[32] Alongside the Frameworks there are also the Standard Operating Procedures (SOPs) for Research Ethics Committees which provide further guidance.[33] Each REC is required under GAFREC to adopt SOPs which have been 'approved by or on behalf of its appointing authority'.[34] Moreover, the importance of research itself in the NHS is highlighted in s 1E of the Health and Social Care Act 2012 which provides that:

> In exercising functions in relation to the health service, the Secretary of State must promote—
>
> (a) research on matters relevant to the health service, and
> (b) the use in the health service of evidence obtained from research.

13.08 This chapter sets out the regulatory structure for clinical research in this country—focusing in particular upon the operation of research ethics committees. It considers the clinical trials approval process and problematic issues regarding assessment of risk and consent. The differences in the position at common law regarding consent are contrasted with that of the proposed regulations implementing the Clinical Trials Directive. The provision made today for monitoring clinical trials and the responsibilities of the parties to the clinical trial are outlined. Particular areas which may give rise to difficulty for researchers, namely confidentiality and use of human material, are discussed. Finally, the provision made for compensation in the event of injury to the research subject is considered. The discussion here centres upon clinical trials. But what precisely constitutes research has been the subject of some discussion.[35] Labelling an activity as 'audit' may mean that it becomes immune from research ethics scrutiny. It should be noted that there has over the years been considerable controversy in relation to the pioneering of new experimental therapeutic techniques. These are now the subject of consideration by the National Institute for Health and Clinical Excellence but will not be discussed further in this chapter (see further Chapter 1). The Care Act 2014 now addresses the regulation of research, as we shall see below, and places the regulatory structures on a statutory footing.

B. The Regulation of Clinical Research: Regulatory Structures

1. Regulation and the Health Research Authority

13.09 In the past one of the criticisms of the conduct of research ethics committees was related to the lack of effective coordination of their operation at a national level.[36] Recent initiatives, however, are changing the situation. There is now a Health Research Authority, which was established in 2011 and has now been given a statutory basis by the Care Act 2014. The Act provides that there must be a chair appointed by the Secretary of State.[37] The first chair is

[31] ibid, para 2.2.4.
[32] ibid, para 2.2.6.
[33] Standard Operating Procedures for Research Ethics Committees, Version 6.1 (hereinafter 'SOP V 6.1') January 2015.
[34] SOP V 6.1, January 2015, para 2.
[35] H Biggs, *Healthcare Research Ethics and Law* (Routledge Cavendish 2009), 5–9; National Research Ethics Service, 'Defining Research' (DoH 2007).
[36] M Warnock, 'A National Research Ethics Committee' (1988) 297 BMJ 1626; M Gelder, 'A National Committee for the Ethics of Research' (1990) 16 Journal of Medical Ethics 146.
[37] Care Act 2014, schedule 7, s 1(1)(a).

Professor Jonathan Montgomery of the Faculty of Law at University College London, who is also chair of the Nuffield Council on Bioethics. Three further members are appointed by the Secretary of State and there also two other appointed members.[38] Currently members are appointed from those working in the pharmaceutical and life sciences sector, medicines, NHS research regulation, and the NHS. In addition the Authority must appoint a Chief Executive.[39] The HRA has a number of functions set out in the legislation. Section 110 of the Act provides that:

> The main functions of the HRA are—
>
> (a) functions relating to the co-ordination and standardisation of practice relating to the regulation of health and social care research (see section 111);
> (b) functions relating to research ethics committees (see sections 112 to 115);
> (c) functions as a member of the United Kingdom Ethics Committee Authority (see section 116 and the Medicines for Human Use (Clinical Trials) Regulations 2004 (S.I. 2004/1031)) . . .

The HRA also has functions in concerning disclosure of confidential information concerning patients. Section 110 (2) of the Care Act goes on to set out what are the main objectives of the HRA in undertaking its role:

> (2) The main objective of the HRA in exercising its functions is—
>
> (a) to protect participants and potential participants in health or social care research and the general public by encouraging research that is safe and ethical, and
> (b) to promote the interests of those participants and potential participants and the general public by facilitating the conduct of research that is safe and ethical (including by promoting transparency in research).

The Care Act 2014 also defines what constitutes 'health research' in s 110 (3) as follows:

> (3) Health research is research into matters relating to people's physical or mental health; but a reference to health research does not include a reference to anything authorised under the Animals (Scientific Procedures) Act 1986.

The HRA has a statutory duty to co-operate with a number of named individuals/bodies under s 111 of the Act in relation to 'co-ordinating and standardising practice relating to the regulation of such research'. Such persons/bodies include the Secretary of State, the licensing authority for the purposes of the Medicines Act 1968, the Health and Social Care Information Centre, the Chief Medical Officer of the Department of Health, Human Fertilisation and Embryology Authority, Human Tissue Authority, Care Quality Commission, and the Administration of Radioactive Substances Advisory Committee. In promoting such coordination the HRA must also ensure that such coordination is 'proportionate'.[40] The HRA is obliged to lay an annual report before Parliament.[41] The HRA provides today what is known as 'HRA Approval'. This system, introduced in March 2016, brings together governance and legal requirements assessment by the staff of the Health Research Agency and operates alongside independent REC opinion.[42] The aim is to streamline the research process and reduce costs. Applications must be made through the integrated research application process. **13.10**

[38] Care Act 2014, schedule 7, s 1(1)(b)(c).
[39] Care Act 2014, schedule 7, s 1(1)(c).
[40] Care Act 2014, s 111(3).
[41] Care Act 2014, schedule 7, para 20.
[42] <http://www.hra.nhs.uk/research-community/hra-approval-the-new-process-for-the-nhs-in-england/#sthash.cNng7xDM.dpuf>.

13.11 In 2009 it was announced that the National Research Ethics service (now part of the Health Research Authority) had been asked to establish a new UK body: the National Research Ethics Advisory Panel of nine members. The panel was to be drawn from different disciplines/experiences including previous chair of research ethics committees, clinical research involving patients and healthy volunteers, patient and public involvement, the pharmaceutical industry, public health research ethics, and health care law. Today this body, now called the National Research Ethics Advisors Panel, is established by the HRA under GAFREC. [43] Its aim is 'to help optimize research ethics review and so improve the research environment in the UK'.[44]

13.12 Oversight of the establishment of research ethics committees operating under the Medicines for Human Use (Clinical Trials) Regulations[45] is now undertaken by the Health Research Authority. It has the power to establish or to recognize existing ethics committees as committees which approve trials under the Medicines for Human Use (Clinical Trials) Regulations, where these comply with criteria set out under the regulations.[46] It can revoke recognition of such an ethics committee if it is satisfied that the provisions of Sch 2 have not been complied with, or if the Committee has failed in relation to adequately performing its functions under the regulations or it is 'otherwise necessary or expedient to do so'.[47] The HRA is also charged with monitoring ethics committees' performance in accordance with the regulations.[48]

2. Role of research ethics committees

(i) Remit of research ethics committees

13.13 The Governance Arrangements for NHS REC (GAFREC) provides that:

> REC review as described in this document is required if a specific research project involves:
> (a) potential research participants . . . identified from, or because of, their past or present use of the services listed above (including services provided under contract with the private or voluntary sectors), including participants recruited through these services as healthy controls;
> (b) potential research participants identified because of their status as relatives or carers of past or present users of these services . . . ;
> (c) collection of tissue (i.e. any material consisting of or including human cells) or information from users of these services . . . ; or
> (d) use of previously collected tissue or information from which individual past or present users of these services . . . could be identified, either directly from that tissue or information, or from its combination with other tissue or information in, or likely to come into, the possession of someone to whom the tissue or information is made available, unless any of the exceptions or other exclusions described in paragraph 2.3.9–2.3.14 apply.[49]

Generally, research which concerns staff of health or social care services who have been recruited in relation to their professional role or health care market research are studies

[43] SOP V 6.1, January 2015, para 10. <http://www.hra.nhs.uk/about-the-hra/our-committees/panels-and-advisory-groups/>.
[44] GAFREC, para 3.3.8.
[45] Medicines for Human Use Clinical Trials Regulations 2004 SI 2004/1031, reg 5.
[46] ibid, regs 6 and 7.
[47] ibid, reg 8.
[48] ibid, reg 10.
[49] DoH, Governance Arrangements for Research Ethics Committees: A Harmonised Edition GAFREC (2011) para 2.3.2.

which will fall outside NHS review and will usually be rejected.[50] It should be noted that research governance review applies across the devolved jurisdictions. In the case of Wales, the Welsh Government in addition has agreed with the Health Research Authority to perform certain functions in relation advice and support for research ethics committees in conjunction with [51]

In addition, a REC may, on request, give opinions in relation to other studies. So for example, research which concerns health/social care staff in their professional role would not normally require review, however, such applications may be reviewed where the REC determines that it 'involves serious ethical issues'. [52] In addition, RECs may also consider those applications which have been made in relation to the establishment of research tissue banks and databases in the UK. [53] Finally RECs may review other research involving human participants and 'raises material ethical issues' as 'it is desirable as a matter of public policy that it is ethically reviewed'.[54] In a situation in which a researcher has not got access to ethical review—the example given in the standard operating procedures is a University REC or a professional body's ethics committee—then the SOP provide that 'the REC is encouraged to accept the application and give an ethical opinion on a voluntary basis'.[55] Ultimately however acceptance of such an application is a matter for the REC chair. Where applications are made retrospectively in some instances, for example, in relation to trials concerning medicinal products, this may constitute a criminal offence and in relation to health and social care generally this is an infringement of research governance. As a consequence, the SOP provides that such cases are to be reported to the HRA Improvement and Liaison Manager for consideration.[56] **13.14**

Some REC's are referred to as a 'flagged REC'.[57] Administrative flags operate in relation to research concerning children, research involving prisoners, research on medical devices, research databases, research tissue banks, and qualitative research.[58] Flagging also relates to other types of research. These include trials involving medicinal products. Here, Article 6 of the EU Directive requires that an ethics committee must provide an opinion regarding clinical trials. Regulation 15(5) of the Medicines for Human Use (Clinical Trials) Regulations 2004, which implements the Clinical Trials Directive, is based upon Article 6 of the Directive.[59] It sets out a number of issues which the committee must consider, which includes the following factors: **13.15**

- the relevance and design of the trial;
- any anticipated risks/benefits;
- the trial protocol and investigator's brochure;
- the suitability of investigator and of supporting staff and also the quality of the facilities provided;
- information which is to be given to subjects and 'informed consent' procedures;
- in the case of persons lacking capacity why their inclusion in this trial is justified;
- availability of indemnity and compensation regarding death/personal injury;

---

50 SOP V 6.1, January 2015, para 1.93.
51 <http://www.healthandcareresearch.gov.wales/research-ethics-in-wales/>.
52 SOP V 6.1, January 2015, para 1.93.
53 GAFREC, para 2.3.7, and SOP V 6.1, January 2015, para 1.94.
54 SOP V 6.1, January 2015, para 1.95.
55 ibid, para 1.95.
56 ibid, para 1.99.
57 ibid, para 2.
58 ibid, para 1.10.
59 Medicines for Human Use Clinical Trials Regulations 2004, SI 2004/1031.

- any liability insurance/indemnity cover for investigator/sponsors;
- information regarding rewards/compensation for investigators/trial subjects; and
- the arrangements for the recruitment of subjects.

Research under the Medicines for Human Use (Clinical Trials) Regulations must be approved by an ethics committee which is recognized under the Regulations and is also recognized to review this particular medicinal product. A distinction is also drawn between clinical trials concerning interventional medicinal products and those which are classed as 'non-interventional' and which are not required to be approved by a recognized REC. If there is doubt in relation to the interpretation of a CTIMP then the Chief Investigator or sponsor is required to seek formal advice from the Medicines and Healthcare Products Regulatory Agency helpline.

13.16 Social Care Research Ethics Committees are also established as part of the national Research Ethics Service under GAFREC.[60] Applications in England must be submitted to a Social Care Research Ethics Committee.[61] Social Care RECs review:

(a) adult social care research;
(b) intergenerational studies involving adults and children or families;
(c) use of social care databases; and
(d) other studies conducted with NHS patients using social sciences methodology and not involving any clinical interventions or changes to clinical care.[62]

NHS RECs cannot consider such applications unless they concern NHS patients or their tissue/data. If research concerning NHS patients is submitted to a NHS REC, this may be accepted where it uses social science methodology and does not involve any clinical interventions or changes in clinical practice.[63] Guidance should be sought from the Social Care REC Coordinator on a case-by-case basis. Where such applications are accepted for review, they do not then require separate review by another REC. Ethical review of research concerning UK armed forces or sponsored or funded by the MOD is undertaken by a Research Ethics Committee appointed by the Ministry of Defence.[64]

13.17 RECs are expected to operate independently of the NHS trust Research and Development (R&D structure).[65] The RGF stresses that: 'It is not for research ethics committees or reviewers to give legal advice, nor are they liable for any of their decisions in this respect.'[66] Where there is the prospect that a particular project may give rise to legal issues, it states that the research ethics committee should advise both the Chief Investigator and the 'appropriate authority' and the Chief Investigator and organization are expected to take legal advice.[67] In addition, while the RGF notes that research projects should not proceed without REC approval, that by itself is not the only factor. So, for example, whether research is sanctioned within a particular care organization will be a decision for that organization.[68]

13.18 When considering the appropriateness of the REC remit, one difficult issue remains: the extent to which ethically controversial issues, giving rise to a public policy dimension, should

60 SOP V 6.1, January 2015, Para 1.25.
61 GAFREC, para 1.26.
62 ibid.
63 SOP V 6.1, January 2015, para 1.27.
64 ibid, para 1.30.
65 RGF, para 3.12.4.
66 RGF, para 3.12.7.
67 RGF, para 3.12.7.
68 RGF, para 3.12.6.

be subject to determination by only one committee acting on a localized basis. It is suggested that where there is a proposal to undertake a research project which involves a particularly controversial procedure with public policy dimensions, there should be consideration of such issues at a national level. An illustration of a situation in which the public policy issues raised may suggest that a local consideration of such issues may be insufficient was that of the use made of a video surveillance technique in a Staffordshire hospital to ascertain whether children were victims of Munchausen's syndrome by proxy.[69] This may be an issue which, in the future, is appropriate for consideration by the Health Research Authority.

(ii) Relationship of RECs with other bodies—general

A feature of clinical research over the last two decades has been that of the proliferation of new regulatory bodies.[70] Thus while REC approval is considered essential before a clinical trial is undertaken, authorization may also be required from another appropriate body. There are a number of situations in which an application is required to another body in addition to the REC. Examples of such bodies are the Gene Therapy Advisory Committee, which is concerned with research concerning gene therapy[71] and the Human Fertilisation and Embryology Authority's role regarding embryo research.[72] **13.19**

A further important body in relation to trials of medicinal products is that of the Medicines and Healthcare Products Regulatory Agency (MHRA) (this body was formerly the Medicines Control Agency).[73] Applicants must provide information which relates to the manufacture and control of medicines. Information must also be given to support the specification of the product. **13.20**

In addition to ethics committee approval, trials concerning medicinal products need to receive favourable authorization from the licensing authority.[74] For these purposes the 'Licensing Authority' (LA), defined as the statutory licensing authority established under s 6 of the Medicines Act 1968.[75] To begin a trial without having obtained such authorization is a criminal offence. The sale/supply of medicinal products for use in a clinical trial, unless the sponsor has been authorized to undertake a trial and it has been manufactured/imported by a person with a marketing authorization in UK/EEA, is a criminal offence.[76] Application to the LA must be made in writing and signed by and on behalf of the sponsor.[77] Different rules relate to different classes of product.[78] In relation to general medicinal products[79] a LA is required to inform the sponsor of the decision. This may take the form **13.21**

[69] See further D Evans, 'The Investigation of Life-threatening Child Abuse and Munchausen's Syndrome by Proxy' (1995) 21 Journal of Medical Ethics 9; D Southall and M P Southall, 'Some Ethical Issues Surrounding Covert Video Surveillance—A Response' (1995) 21 Journal of Medical Ethics 104; E Gillon, Editorial: 'Covert Surveillance by Doctors for Life Threatening Munchausen's Syndrome by Proxy' (1995) 21 Journal of Medical Ethics 104; 'Symposium on Covert Video Surveillance' (1996) 22 Journal of Medical Ethics 16.

[70] See further J Montgomery, *Health Care Law* (2nd edn, Oxford University Press 2003) ch 21.

[71] <http://www.dh.gov.uk/ab/GTAC/index.htm>.

[72] <http://www.hfea.gov.uk/>.

[73] <http://www.mhra.gov.uk/index.htm>.

[74] Medicines for Human Use Clinical Trials Regulations 2004, SI 2004/1031, reg 12 and see also European Commission, *Detailed guidance for the request for authorisation of a clinical trial on a medicinal product for human use to the competent authorities, notification of substantial amendments and declaration of the end of the trial European Commission*, Enterprise Directorate-General, Brussels Revision 2 (October 2005).

[75] Medicines Act 1968 s 6, reg 2(1).

[76] n 74, reg 12.

[77] ibid, reg 17.

[78] The Directive and regulations also consider the issue of the manufacture/importation of investigational medicinal products but these are not considered further in this chapter: Art 13 Clinical Trials Directive, reg 35.

[79] Medicines Act 1968 s 6, reg 18.

of acceptance, acceptance subject to condition or rejection.[80] If the sponsor is not informed within thirty days the trial is regarded as authorized.[81] If the request is not accepted the sponsor may submit an amended request to the LA within fourteen days.[82] However, if this is not submitted the request for authorization is deemed rejected and LA will not consider it further. Where an amended request is submitted, the LA must respond within sixty days from the receipt of the original request and must state the grounds for not accepting or conditionally accepting the amended request.[83]

13.22 Where the trial concerns products for gene therapy/somatic cell therapy,[84] while the procedure is similar to general medicinal products, the time periods are longer. In relation to applications these must be dealt within a period of 30 days[85] but where an LA refers this to a relevant committee, the period is then extended up to 120 days.[86] In a situation in which the request has been rejected, the sponsor has 30 days in which to submit an amended request (or such amended period allowed by the LA).[87] Where an amended request has been submitted, the LA must respond within 90 days, or in a situation in which the matter has been referred to the appropriate committee, within 180 days.[88] Again, in such a situation they may alternatively authorize the trial subject to conditions or reject it.[89]

13.23 A separate procedure applies in relation to authorization of those trials involving products with special characteristics other than set out above which do not have a marketing authorization[90] or those medicinal products have active ingredients which are:

(aa) (ii) . . . biological products of human or animal origin, or
(bb) containing biological components of human or animal origin, or
(cc) the manufacturing of which requires such components.

13.24 Alternatively, the licensing authority may have provided written notification that, by virtue of the special characteristics of the material, special authorization is required.[91] The Regulations provide procedures enabling the LA to compulsorily amend the clinical trial conditions:

where necessary to ensure—

(a) the safety or scientific validity of the clinical trial, or
(b) that the conditions and principles of good practice are satisfied or adhered to in relation to the clinical trial.[92]

In such a situation the LA is required to give the sponsor at least fourteen days' notice to enable the sponsor the opportunity to respond in writing.[93] The LA is required to take those responses into account before making its decision.[94]

[80] ibid, reg 18(2).
[81] ibid, reg 18(3).
[82] ibid, reg 18(5).
[83] ibid, reg 18(6).
[84] Including xenogeneic cell therapy and medicinal products containing genetically modified organisms.
[85] Medicines Act 1968 s 6, reg 19(2).
[86] ibid, reg 19(5).
[87] ibid, reg 19(6).
[88] ibid, reg 19(7).
[89] ibid, reg 19(8).
[90] This refers to those products set out in Part A to Annex of Regulation (EEC) No 2309/93.
[91] Medicines Act 1968 s 6, reg 20(1)(b).
[92] ibid, reg 23.
[93] ibid, reg 23(2).
[94] ibid, reg 23(3).

(iii) REC membership

REC members are to be appointed in an open process compatible with Nolan standards[95] after there has been public advertisement of the post.[96] An application form must be completed and the guidance provides that the selection of members is to be subject to standard operating procedures. Appointments are made for fixed periods of five years.[97] Although terms are renewable, the guidance does not envisage that members should serve more than two consecutive terms on the same REC. There is provision for extension of membership however for periods up to a year when new members are appointed.[98] Over the last decade, steps have been taken to ensure, as far as possible, the full and informed participation by REC members. Today members are required as a condition of their appointment to undertake appropriate initial and continuing training.[99] **13.25**

The maximum overall membership of a REC is eighteen. GAFREC provides that RECs are expected to reflect current ethical norms in society as well as their own ethical judgement. REC members may come from groups associated with particular interests but they are not representatives of those groups. REC members are appointed in their own right to participate in the work of a REC as equal individuals of sound judgement, relevant experience and adequate training in research ethics and REC review.[100] **13.26**

GAFREC states that expert members should form part of each REC 'to ensure methodological and ethical expertise about research in care settings and in relevant fields of care, as well as professional expertise as care practitioners'.[101] Moreover, it is stated that the expertise 'should be appropriate to the types of research proposal the REC reviews'.[102] The REC may also establish one or more sub-committees.[103] In addition GAFREC provides for specialist advice to be obtained from specialist referees where a proposal goes beyond the expertise of members.[104] In such situations advice should only be sought in relation to issues of research ethics concerning that particular proposal. **13.27**

GAFREC states that at least a third of the REC membership should be 'lay'. These are defined as being 'people who are independent of care services, either as employees or in a non-executive role. Their primary professional interest is not care-related research'. **13.28**

(iv) REC chair

While GAFREC does provide for the appointment of a chair, a vice-chair, and a deputy vice-chair, it does not state what constituent groups they should be drawn from.[105] In the past there was some debate as to whether such office holders should be 'lay'. The draft of the original Red Book provided that the chair should be a lay member and the Red Book final version stated that chair should be a lay member. One advantage of the appointment of a lay chair is that of perceptible detachment/objectivity. Nonetheless, Marshall and Moodie have commented that there may be some perceived difficulties in a lay chair.[106] These could relate to situations where the proposal submitted was of a very complex technical nature. A lack **13.29**

95 These are the basic ethical standards expected of public office holders.
96 GAFREC, para 4.2.5.
97 GAFREC, para 4.2.15.
98 GAFREC, para 4.3.2.
99 GAFREC, para 4.3.11.
100 GAFREC, para 4.2.2.
101 GAFREC, para 4.2.6.
102 GAFREC, para 4.2.6.
103 SOP V 6.1, January 2015, para 7.8.
104 GAFREC, para 4.2.20
105 GAFREC, para 4.2.13.
106 P Marshall and P Moodie, 'Guidelines for Local Research Ethics Committees' (1992) 304 BMJ 1293.

of specialist knowledge may create difficulties in a situation in which a lay chair was asked to take 'chair's action' between committee meetings, although concerns regarding such lack of expertise may of course be met by thorough consultation by the chair. Individuals who apply for a chair/deputy chair post will be expected to have a year's experience as a REC member.[107] The guidance also states that, where appropriate, supplementary training should be given to chairs before taking up the role.[108] The appointments apply for a period of up to but not exceeding five years.[109]

(v) Research Ethics Committee Procedures

13.30 As noted above there are standard operating procedures regarding RECs for example relating to the constitution, appointment and internal procedures, and the like.[110] One particular issue raised in the EU Clinical Trials Directive was that of time limits. The aim was to ensure the expeditious processing of research applications. In the context of trials on medicinal products, the Regulations now state that ethics committee must normally provide an opinion within sixty days of receipt of the application.[111] Extensions of thirty days may be allowed in relation to those medicinal products which concern gene therapy, somatic cell therapy, or those medicinal products which contain genetically modified organisms.[112] There is also provision for a further ninety-day extension in a situation in which RECs consult an expert group/committee regarding such a trial.[113] Ethics committees may also request supplementary information and where this occurs, the appropriate time limits are suspended. In the case of trials on medicinal products, the Regulations incorporating Article 10(a) of the Directive now provide that the ethics committee will have to provide an opinion on amendments which involve changes to the trial protocol or other related documents used in the application.[114]

13.31 GAFREC stresses the need for independence and impartiality.[115] The Chief Investigator should attend the meeting and other researchers may also do so.[116] REC processes are not however aligned with a judicial decision-making type process. So, for example, GAFREC provides that REC meetings are not public meetings.[117] This approach has however been the subject of some critical comment. It can be argued that there is a legitimate public interest in opening up REC deliberations to public scrutiny. Ashcroft and Pfeiffer have explored the arguments for maintaining secrecy.[118] First, it can be argued that this safeguards clinical confidentiality. But, as they note, this is only likely to be an issue in exceedingly rare cases: for example, if it is a case in which a trial involves a rare or serious condition where it is possible for an individual patient to be identified. Secondly, maintaining confidentiality can be seen in terms of maintaining 'commercial or academic confidentiality'. However, Ashcroft and Pfeffer suggest that, in practice today in drug trials, a vast amount of information does in any case have to be made public. They question the extent to which other researchers could realistically benefit substantially from disclosure of data and methods. In their view,

[107] GAFREC, para 4.2.14.
[108] GAFREC, para 4.2.14.
[109] GAFREC, para 4.2.15.
[110] SOP V 6.1, January 2015.
[111] Medicines for Human Use (Clinical Trials) Regulations 2004, SI 2004/1031, reg 15(10)(b).
[112] ibid, reg 15(10)a(ii).
[113] ibid, reg 15(10)a (i).
[114] ibid, reg 24.
[115] GAFREC, para 3.2.6.
[116] Health Research Authority, *Guidance for Applicants attending a Full REC meeting* HRA (2016).
[117] GAFREC, para 4.2.22.
[118] R Ashcroft and N Pfeffer, 'Ethics Behind Closed Doors: Do Research Ethics Committees Need Secrecy?' (2001) 322 BMJ 1294–296.

there was no risk to the commercial confidentiality of researchers and a strong pressure to ensure that the results of research are made widely known in the NHS. While there may be arguments for safeguarding the privacy of a researcher, nonetheless they suggest that if it is the case that decisions about competence are raised, these could be dealt with under reserved business with a researcher being given a right of reply. Finally, they consider the argument that confidentiality is required to safeguard the privacy interests of REC themselves and promote candour, with for example, analogies being drawn with the operation of the jury system. Ashcroft and Pfeffer persuasively rebut this on the basis that jury secrecy is safeguarded through a raft of policy considerations, such as preserving finality of verdicts and protecting them from the defendant that are not applicable in the research context. They are sceptical of the secrecy as promoting candour argument, pointing to the trend in other public areas to enhanced disclosure. This concern is now met only to a very limited extent by a provision in the standing operating procedures which states that the opinion of the REC on each application for ethical review should be published in the annual report.[119]

(vi) Monitoring REC performance

The RGF provides that those who establish RECs must create systems for the monitoring of RECs' performance. RECs are required to submit annual reports to their reporting authority.[120] This is to include information regarding committee members, meetings, attendance, and information about proposals, including decisions reached and time taken to process such applications. They are to be informed of projects which were completed or terminated during that year, any training which was undertaken by the committee or its members, and the Chair's report of the work they have undertaken that year.[121] The increased transparency of decision-making is to be welcomed. However, this reporting procedure is still very much on a localized basis, with RECs reporting to their appointing authority. It is thus difficult to undertake an effective overview of RECs as a whole. This may militate in the future in favour of a greater structured research ethics overview. It may be (as we shall see later in this chapter) that some recent developments in this area may mean greater centralization in the future (see paras 13.112–13.113). **13.32**

C. Evaluating a Research Protocol: Legal and Ethical Issues

1. Introduction

GAFREC requires RECs, when considering research protocols, to examine a number of factors. The interests of participants are seen as paramount.[122] As is commented,[123] 'The interests of researchers and of research are secondary to the dignity, rights, safety and well-being of people taking part in research.' Nonetheless 'the interests and safety of researchers in addition to the public interest itself' should be taken into consideration.[124] GAFREC also provides that the benefits and risks of participation in research and of research evidence should be fairly distributed across groups.[125] While one can support the sentiment, whether this remains an effective realizable aim remains to be seen. One further issue is the extent to which they should be concerned with the scientific validity of the project. While this is **13.33**

[119] SOP V 6.1, January 2015, para 2.84; GAFREC, para 7.18.
[120] GAFREC, Annex G.
[121] ibid, para 7.20.
[122] GAFREC, para 3.2.1.
[123] GAFREC, para 3.2.2.
[124] GAFREC, para 3.2.2.
[125] GAFREC, para 3.2.3.

review focused on ethical issues, some research suggests that research ethics committees reviewing proposals will consider the scientific merit of the proposals.[126] In this section we consider in particular the issues of risk—which relates to the design of the trial, consent, and confidentiality.

2. Assessing risk

13.34 The Declaration of Helsinki states that:

> Medical research involving human subjects should only be conducted if the importance outweighs the inherent risks and burdens to the subject. This is especially important where the human subjects are healthy volunteers. (General Principles, 18.)

13.35 As noted above, GAFREC emphasizes the need to ensure care and protection of research participants. Prior to consideration by RECs, it is now the practice that protocols will have been subject to prior scientific review by appropriate experts. The risk–benefit calculation is of course problematic.

13.36 English law does not allow the competent adult to consent to the infliction of any harm, however grave.[127] Unlawful infliction of harm may result in prosecution for a range of offences, including battery or one of the statutory offences contained in the Offences Against the Person Act 1961. Difficult issues surround the inclusion of subjects in 'risky' trial procedures. There has, for example, been considerable discussion regarding the legitimacy and legality of the inclusion of subjects in trials for experimental procedures such as xenotransplantation, which involve considerable risks.[128] The precise boundaries of what constitutes a legitimate level of risk are unclear.[129]

13.37 One further factor related to the assessment of risk in clinical trials is that of the inducements which may be offered to participants in the trial, researchers, and research hosts. Whether inducement should be provided is controversial. Concerns have been raised that such inducements could have the effect of increasing willingness to be involved in research, and that involvement in research should not be commodified in this way.[130] Inducements may be other than financial. An illustration is the inclusion of prisoners in clinical research. There have long been concerns that prisoners are potentially vulnerable participants. Their decision as to whether to be included in a clinical trial could be influenced by the fact that such inclusion may facilitate the parole process. At the same time, there are reasons why prisoners may receive considerable benefits from involvement in clinical trials.

13.38 The potential risks to a particular group which is perceived as vulnerable are obviously a matter which should be the concern of RECs. We consider below two further groups which may give rise to particular problematic consideration in this context: children and adults lacking mental capacity.

---

[126] See E L Angell et al, 'An Analysis of Decision Letters by Research Ethics Committees: The Ethics/Scientific Quality Boundary Examined' (2008) 17 Quality and Safety in Health Care 131.

[127] See also *R v Brown* [1993] 2 All ER 75.

[128] See generally discussion in M Fox, 'Clinical Research and Patients' in J Tingle and A Cribb (eds), *Nursing Law and Ethics* (3rd edn, Blackwell Scientific 2007).

[129] See Law Commission, *Consent in the Criminal Law* (Law Com No 139, 1996) paras 8.38–8.52.

[130] See generally P McNeill, 'Paying People to Participate in Research: Why Not?' (1997) 11 Bioethics 391; M Wilkinson and A Moore, 'Inducement in Research' (1997) 11 Bioethics 373; J P Bently and P G Thacker, 'The Influence of Risk and Monetary Payment on the Research Participation Decision Making Process' (2004) 30 Journal of Medical Ethics 293.

3. Consent and the competent adult

(i) Introduction

The latest version of the Declaration of Helsinki provides in paragraph 26 that: **13.39**

> In medical research involving human subjects capable of giving informed consent, each potential subject must be adequately informed of the aims, methods, sources of funding, any possible conflicts of interest, institutional affiliations of the researcher, the anticipated benefits and potential risks of the study and the discomfort it may entail, post-study provisions and any other relevant aspects of the study. The potential subject must be informed of the right to refuse to participate in the study or to withdraw consent to participate at any time without reprisal. Special attention should be given to the specific information needs of individual potential subjects as well as to the methods used to deliver the information.
>
> After ensuring that the potential subject has understood the information, the physician or another appropriately qualified individual must then seek the potential subject's freely-given informed consent, preferably in writing. If the consent cannot be expressed in writing, the non-written consent must be formally documented and witnessed.

This emphasis on informed consent is reflected in a whole series of major ethical guidelines. The EU Clinical Trials Directive, as enacted into English law through the Medicines for Human Use (Clinical Trials) Regulations 2004,[131] contains provision for 'informed consent'.[132] It is defined as being a decision which is 'taken freely after being duly informed of its nature, significance, implications and risks'.

13.40 Of course, what precisely constitutes an informed consent can prove problematic to ascertain. In relation to trials on medicinal products, the EU Directive sets very broad parameters which afford considerable discretion to Member States. Nonetheless, there is the issue as to the extent to which enhanced disclosure equates with enhanced comprehension by research participants. There has been some debate over the extent to which informed consent is an ideal which cannot effectively be realized.[133] Some commentators, such as Thornton, have been sceptical as to the reality of consent and have suggested that the best which may be achieved is partly informed consent.[134] This extent of comprehension by research participants of information which has been given to them by researchers is a relatively undeveloped research area. In a study of patients participating in clinical trials, Ferguson found that a very high proportion of participants were happy with the information given to them by researchers. Ninety-four per cent of the sample were happy with the information which was provided; in terms of patient understanding some 50 per cent stated that they had understood all of the information given and some 49 per cent were of the view that they comprehended most of the information provided.[135] Interestingly, it appeared that patients felt that they were receiving more information because they were involved as participants in a clinical trial. There is, of course, a question as to the extent to which patients' perceptions regarding their comprehension were realistic and as Ferguson notes, this is an issue which requires further research. A further question is the extent to which, in the case of long-term

[131] OJ C 306, 18:10:97.

[132] Article 3, para 2(b).

[133] See generally N C Manson and O O'Neill, *Rethinking Informed Consent in Bioethics* (Cambridge University Press 2007).

[134] See H Thornton, 'Clinical Trials: A Brave New Partnership?' (1994) 20 Journal of Medical Ethics 19; and note the response by M Baum, 'Clinical Trials—A Brave New Partnership; A Response to Mrs Thornton' (1994) 20 Journal of Medical Ethics 23.

[135] P R Ferguson, 'Patients' Perceptions of Information Provided in Clinical Trials' (2002) 28 Journal of Medical Ethics 45.

studies, consent can be seen as a one-off event or as an ongoing dialogue or series of events which raises questions about the nature of the consent form and the validity of the consent process.[136]

13.41 One particular difficulty in the consent process relates to the use of randomization in clinical trials. Randomization can assist the trial process by reducing the prospects of findings illustrating an improvement, whereas this particular improvement may simply be because a new treatment has been given. Provision of information regarding the nature of the trial and that it is a placebo is necessary.[137] The whole notion of randomization is exceedingly problematic in a situation in which a drug which is under trial represents the only known chance of a cure for a life-threatening condition. A notable illustration of this was the controversy of the randomization of drugs under test in the case of HIV. In the USA one trial was rendered ineffective when patients who were desperate for treatment pooled the drugs.[138] The Declaration of Helsinki states that:

> The benefits, risks, burdens and effectiveness of a new method should be tested against those of the best current proven intervention except in the following circumstances:
>
> - The use of placebo or no treatment is acceptable in studies where no current proven intervention exists; or
> - Where for compelling scientific or scientifically sound methodological reasons the use of placebo is necessary to determine the efficacy or safety of an intervention and the patients who receive placebo or no treatment will not be subject to any risk of serious or irreversible harm. Extreme care must be taken to avoid abuse of this option.[139]

(ii) Informed consent: liability in battery

13.42 In relation to consent to treatment, it is accepted at common law that a health professional is only required to provide a patient with a general explanation in broad terms of the nature of a procedure to avoid liability in battery.[140] This concerns a therapeutic procedure. It is possible that the courts may be prepared to take a more rigorous approach in relation to disclosure in non-therapeutic research. A notable Canadian case frequently cited for its support of an approach of broad disclosure to volunteers in clinical trials is *Halushka v University of Saskatchewan*.[141] In this case, Hall J stated that:

> The subject of medical experimentation is entitled to a full and frank disclosure of all the facts, probabilities and opinions which a reasonable man might be expected to consider before giving his consent. It has been suggested that such an approach should be employed in relation to both patients and volunteers.[142]

13.43 It is suggested that this approach should be followed in relation to non-therapeutic procedures. If trials can be seen as being undertaken in the public interest, then surely the position of the volunteer in such a trial should be safeguarded through full and frank disclosure of all applicable risks.

---

136 See, eg, discussion in G Laurie and E Postan, 'Rhetoric or Reality? What Is the Legal Status of the Consent Form in Health Related Research?' (2013) 21(3) Medical Law Review 371.

137 See also T E Chan, 'Regulating the Placebo Effect in Clinical Practice' (2015) 23(1) Medical Law Rev 1.

138 See further discussion in J D Arras, 'Non-compliance in AIDS Research' (1990) Hastings Centre Report 24; and also see A Young and J V McHale, 'The Dilemmas of the HIV Positive Prisoner' (1992) Howard Journal of Criminal Justice 89.

139 Declaration of Helsinki (2008), para 32.

140 *Chatterson v Gerson* [1981] 1 All ER 257.

141 *Halushka v University of Saskatchewan* [1965] 53 DLR (2d) 436, [1965] 55 WWR 608.

142 ibid, 616–17.

The situation regarding therapeutic procedures is more problematic. To allow actions to be brought in battery on the basis of failure to inform in the context of therapeutic procedures would require a different approach to be taken between therapeutic research and therapeutic treatment, as the courts have indicated their unwillingness to extend the boundaries of liability in battery.[143] **13.44**

(iii) Informed consent liability in negligence

Where there is a claim that a research participant was provided with insufficient information regarding the risks of involvement in a clinical trial an action is most likely to be brought in negligence. The leading case on the test for information disclosure is now that of Montgomery *v Lanarkshire*[144] (see Chapter 8). This develops the law from the earlier test rooted in the professional practice standard, though recognizing the need for scrutiny of professional decision making. The new test set out by the Supreme Court today is: **13.45**

> The doctor is therefore under a duty to take reasonable care to ensure that the patient is aware of any material risks involved in any recommended treatment, and of any reasonable alternative or variant treatments. The test of materiality is whether, in the circumstances of the particular case, a reasonable person in the patient's position would be likely to attach significance to the risk, or the doctor is or should reasonably be aware that the particular patient would be likely to attach significance to it.[145]

It is likely that this more critical approach to scrutiny of clinical decision-making may also be reflected in the context of any judicial consideration of disclosure of information provided to participants involved in a therapeutic trial in the future.

Moreover such a movement towards the provision of enhanced information for the research participant has been reflected in professional practice guidance.[146] This suggests a need for a real dialogue with a research participant to ascertain information which would be relevant to him/her in determining what additional information it might be appropriate to provide. It is submitted that researchers today would be at the very least unwise to withhold information from research subjects. Greater disclosure and frankness in spelling out the possibilities is moreover surely the best way to facilitate enhanced participation in research activities in the future. **13.46**

(iv) Non-consensual inclusion

One of the elements of a valid consent is that the consent which is given should be voluntary. Coercion implicitly negates the reality of the consent process. Nonetheless, in the 1990s there were some indications that, in exceptional situations, the judiciary may be prepared in some limited situations to sanction involvement in clinical procedures, despite a competent patient's refusal.[147] However this approach was subjected to judicial criticism in *Re MB*[148] and *St George's NHS Trust v S*,[149] which confirmed the right of the competent adult to refuse treatment, regardless of the consequences. This is now embedded in statute in the Mental Capacity Act 2005 (see Chapter 9). It is thus exceedingly unlikely that the courts would now be prepared to override the refusal of a competent adult to be involved in a research procedure, even where this procedure represented that person's only chance of survival. **13.47**

---

[143] See generally, Tan Keng Feng, 'Failure of Medical Advice: Trespass or Negligence?' (1987) 1 LS 149 and M Brazier, 'Patient Autonomy and Consent to Treatment' (1987) 1 LS 169.
[144] *Montgomery (Appellant) v Lanarkshire Health Board (Respondent) (Scotland)* [2015] UKSC 11.
[145] ibid, at [87].
[146] <insert reference>
[147] *Re S (Adult: Refusal of Medical Treatment)* [1992] 3 WLR 806.
[148] [1997] 2 FLR 426.
[149] [1998] 3 WLR 936.

(v) Pregnancy

13.48 One problematic issue is the extent to which pregnant women should be involved in clinical trials. While research on this subject group may lead to important therapeutic benefits, it is nonetheless a potentially vulnerable group. The inclusion of pregnant women in clinical trials is not an issue directly addressed in the research governance guidelines. In contrast, there is some specific reference to this in the form of the Council of Europe Additional Protocol to the Convention on Human Rights and Biomedicine on Biomedical Research, which provides in Article 18 that:

> 1. Research on a pregnant woman which does not have the potential to produce results of direct benefit to her health or that or the embryo or fœtus or child after birth, may only be undertaken if the following conditions are met;
>   i) the research has the aim of contributing to the ultimate attainment of results capable of conferring benefit to other women in relation to reproduction or to other women in relation to reproduction or to embryos, foetuses or children,
>   ii) research of comparable effectiveness cannot be carried out on women who are not pregnant,
>   iii) the research entails only minimal risk and minimal burden.
> 2. Where research is undertaken on breast feeding women, particular care shall be taken to avoid any adverse impact on the health of the child.[150]

13.49 The involvement of pregnant women in a clinical research project may arise unexpectedly, perhaps following the occurrence of an emergency situation. The Royal College of Physicians' *Guidelines* now provide that:

> 8.39 Pregnant or nursing women should not participate in non-therapeutic research that carries more than minimal risk to the fetus or neonate, unless this is intended to elucidate problems of pregnancy or lactation
>
> 8.40 As a general rule, therapeutic research should only be undertaken in pregnant or nursing women with a view to:
> improving the health of the mother without prejudice to that of the fetus or breast-fed baby, or
> enhancing the viability of the fetus, or
> aiding the baby's healthy development, or
> improving the ability of the mother to nourish it adequately.[151]

They go on to suggest that, 'wherever practical', women should be given information about research during the pregnancy.[152] They do, however, take the approach that, in the case of some 'low risk' studies (they give as examples collection of placental material and amniotic fluid), women should be able to give consent contemporaneously. In addition, they suggest that prior consent may be 'impracticable' where there is a 'rare condition' of woman or neonate.[153]

---

[150] Strasbourg, 2005.

[151] Royal College of Physicians, *Guidelines on the Practice of Ethics Committees in Medical Research with Human Participants* (Royal College of Physicians 2007).

[152] ibid, para 8.42.

[153] ibid.

4. Consent and the child participant: Common law

(i) Introduction

The involvement of children in clinical trials[154] necessitates careful ethical scrutiny.[155] The general principle is that research should not be undertaken on children, unless research can be undertaken on a competent adult. However, it is necessary to undertake certain forms of research using child subjects. This may relate to the fact that the study is to focus on childhood diseases. Alternatively, it may be because a particular drug may have differential effects on children and adults. Inclusion of children may give rise to particularly difficult issues regarding risk assessment. The Royal College of Paediatrics and Child Health guidelines provided that it would not be appropriate to subject a child to a risk which was more than minimal in the case of a non-therapeutic trial.[156] The Clinical Trials Directive, enacted in the Medicines for Human Use (Clinical Trials) Regulations 2004, places explicit limitations on the inclusion of children in clinical trials concerning medicinal products. It provides that research should only be undertaken on children where: 13.50

> some direct benefit for the group of patients is obtained from the clinical trial and only where such research is essential to validate data obtained in clinical trials on persons able to give informed consent or by other research methods: additionally such research should either relate to a clinical condition from which the minor concerned suffers or be of such a nature that it can only be carried out on minors.[157]

While this, as noted earlier, relates to medicinal products, should there be judicial consideration of the common law position it may be speculated that this statement may be influential in relation to the rest of the clinical trials process. 13.51

(ii) Children and consent

Children over the age of 16 have a statutory right to consent to medical and dental treatment under s 8 of the Family Law Reform Act 1969.[158] While children under that age may be competent to consent, this is, however, a decision-relative test under the common law, namely: does the child have sufficient maturity to comprehend the information given and to make a choice.[159] It should be noted that ethical guidance suggests that, in relation to research projects, even where a child may be technically competent to consent, that consent should also be obtained from the child's parents. Non-therapeutic trials are more problematic. It is submitted that it could be problematic for a researcher to justify the conduct of such a trial on a minor without also obtaining parental consent, following the approach taken by the Court of Appeal in *Re W* in 1992.[160] Here the Court of Appeal indicated that s 8(1) referred to 'surgical medical and dental "treatment"'. This suggests that in a case of non-therapeutic research, reference would be required to the position at common law. Thus, in such a situation, parental consent would, in practice, invariably be required. 13.52

A further difficult issue is the extent to which children should ever be compelled to be involved in clinical research. In the vast majority of situations it would be difficult to envisage 13.53

---

[154] See generally on children and clinical research, R Nicholson, *Medical Research and Children* (Oxford University Press 1985); Medical Research Council Ethics Guide, *Medical Research Involving Children* (2004).

[155] See also the Nuffield Council on Bioethics, *Children and Clinical Research* (2015).

[156] Royal College of Paediatrics and Child Health Ethics Advisory Committee, 'Guidelines for the Conduct of Medical Research Concerning Children' (2000) 82 Archives of Disease in Childhood 177.

[157] Clinical Trials Directive, Art 4.

[158] See generally, in relation to consent and children, Chapter 10.

[159] *Gillick v West Norfolk v Wisbech AHA* [1985] 3 All ER 402.

[160] *Re W (A Minor) (Medical Treatment)* [1992] 4 All ER 627.

researchers seeking to continue a project in the face of opposition from a minor. However, there may be exceptional cases, for example involving therapeutic research projects, where this would involve the trial of a potentially life-saving drug/procedure in which compulsion may be sought. In the past in relation to treatment decisions, the Court of Appeal has held that a decision by a competent minor to refuse treatment may be overridden. In *Re W* Lord Donaldson memorably stated that:

> No minor of whatever age has power by refusing to consent to treatment to override a consent to treatment by someone who has parental responsibility for the minor. Nevertheless such a refusal was a very important consideration in making clinical judgments and for parents and the court in deciding whether themselves to give consent.[161]

13.54 Although the judicial willingness to override the refusal of the competent minor has been subject to trenchant academic criticism this principle still holds.[162] Although circumstances in which a protesting adolescent would be compelled to be included in a clinical research project—albeit therapeutic—are likely to be limited. One possible exception is when the procedure itself represents a potentially life-saving therapy and the only chance of survival for a critically ill adolescent.[163]

5. Consent: Adults who lack mental capacity

(i) Introduction

13.55 As with children, the perceived vulnerability of mentally incompetent adults has led to professed concerns regarding their inclusion in clinical research projects.[164] For many years the legality of the inclusion of adults lacking mental capacity in clinical research was uncertain. The situation has been, to some extent, clarified by the enactment of the Mental Capacity Act 2005. This sets out detailed provisions in relation to the regulation of research concerning adults lacking mental capacity. It covers 'intrusive' research involving adults lacking mental capacity over the age of 16 in England and Wales.[165] Research is deemed to be intrusive where it would be unlawful if it was carried out (a) 'on or in relation to a person who had capacity to consent to it, (b) but without his consent'.[166] This research appears to extend to include observational research.[167] In order for such research to be lawful, it must be approved by the 'appropriate body' under the regulations; such a body must be a designated research ethics committee.[168]

13.56 Section 31(2) of the Mental Capacity Act 2005 provides that the research must be connected with:

(a) an impairing condition affecting P; or
(b) its treatment.

---

[161] ibid, 639–40.

[162] See Chapter 10 and see also, eg, A Grubb, 'Treatment Decisions: Keeping it in the Family' in A Grubb (ed), *Choices and Decisions in Healthcare* (John Wiley 1993).

[163] See further Chapter 10.

[164] This is discussed further in J V McHale, 'Research and Mental Capacity: Where Now After the Mental Capacity Act 2005?' (2009) *5* Research Ethics Review 65–70; J V McHale, 'Clinical Research and Mental Illness' in L Gostin, P Bartlett, P Fennell, J V McHale, and R McKay (eds), *Principles of Mental Health Law* (Oxford University Press 2010).

[165] Mental Capacity Act 2005, s 30(1).

[166] ibid, s 30(2).

[167] P Bartlett, *Blackstone's Guide to the Mental Capacity Act 2005* (Oxford University Press 2005) para 2.125.

[168] See further Mental Capacity Act 2005 (Appropriate Body) (England) Regulations 2006, SI 2006/2810 and parallel regulations for Wales.

An impairing condition is defined as a condition which is or may be 'attributable to or which causes or contributes to (or may cause or contribute to) the impairment of or disturbance in the functioning of the mind or brain'.[169] Section 31(4) provides that: '[t]here must be reasonable grounds for believing that research of comparable effectiveness cannot be carried out if the project has to be confined to or relate only to persons who have capacity to consent to take part in it'. Research may be undertaken which is therapeutic. This is defined as being such research which has potential to benefit a person without imposing on them a burden that is disproportionate to the potential benefit.[170] **13.57**

Research can also be undertaken under s 31(5)(b) where it is 'intended to provide knowledge of the causes or treatment of or the care of persons affected by the same or a similar condition'. This can be seen as sanctioning non-therapeutic research. If the research falls with s 31(5)(b) then: **13.58**

> There must be reasonable grounds for believing
> (a) that the risk to P of taking part is negligible and
> (b) that anything done to/in relation to P will not
> (i) interfere with P's freedom of action or privacy in a significant way, or
> (ii) be unduly invasive or restrictive.[171]

(ii) The consultee

The Act provides for someone to be consulted before the person lacking mental capacity is included in the research. Section 32 provides that the researcher must take reasonable steps to identify someone who is engaged in caring for the person without mental capacity or who is interested in their welfare, other than in their professional capacity or for remuneration and who is prepared to be consulted under this legislation. The Act indicates that the consultee can be a family member/carer/friend; an attorney acting under a lasting power of attorney; or a court-appointed deputy as long as they had a relationship with the person/personal knowledge of the person lacking capacity.[172] **13.59**

Section 32(4) provides that the consultee must be provided with information about the project. They must be asked their advice regarding the inclusion of the adult without capacity in the research process, as well as their opinion as to what the adult's views would have been regarding inclusion in the project if s/he had the capacity to make the decision her/himself. **13.60**

(iii) The nominated consultee

If, in a particular situation, the researcher is unable to identify a consultee who has an unpaid/non-professional role in caring for the welfare of the person lacking capacity, then if researchers wish to include that particular person in a research project, they must appoint a 'nominated consultee' under s 32(3) of the Act.[173] Guidance has been issued on this topic by the Department of Health.[174] **13.61**

---

169 Mental Capacity Act 2005, s 31(3).
170 ibid, s 31(5)(a).
171 ibid, s 31(6).
172 ibid, s 32(7).
173 See further DoH, *Guidance on Nominating a Consultee for Research Involving Adults who Lack Capacity to Consent* (DoH 2008) 10; and J V McHale, 'Clinical Research and Mental Illness' in L O Gostin et al, *Principles of Mental Health Law* (Oxford University Press 2010).
174 DoH *Guidance*, n 181, and J V McHale, 'Clinical Research and Mental Illness', n 181.

(iv) Emergency research

13.62 The Act also regulates undertaking research in a situation in which emergency treatment is being provided under s 32(8), (9). In an emergency situation, the Act enables researchers to bypass the role of the consultee. Where treatment is to be provided as a matter of urgency and the researcher is of the opinion that it is necessary to go ahead with the research as a matter of urgency, and it is not reasonably practicable to consult, then the researcher may include the adult without capacity in the research. The section provides that the researcher must obtain the agreement of a registered medical practitioner not involved in the organization or the conduct of the research or, alternatively, may proceed as long as he acts 'in accordance with a procedure approved by an appropriate body at the time when the research was approved under section 31' (s 32(a)). However, the researcher cannot continue to act in accordance with that subsection if the emergency has passed. In such an emergency situation, the only effective check/balance regarding the inclusion of a person in the project will be that of the initial approval given by the research ethics committee or that of the registered medical practitioner.

(v) Loss of capacity during research

13.63 The Mental Capacity Act 2005 (Loss of Capacity During Research Project) Regulations 2007[175] makes provision for cases where a person loses capacity during the course of a research project. For a person to remain in the project, the researcher must submit a protocol to be approved by a Research Ethics Committee detailing the arrangements to be made for the person who has lost capacity to consent. The regulations require that the researcher identifies or nominates a consultee, in order that the participation of the person who lacks capacity can be reviewed. The researcher should provide the consultee with information about the research and the nature of the consent provided at the start of the participant's involvement in the project. They should also seek advice as to whether or not the person lacking capacity should take part in the project. In addition, they should ask the consultee their opinion regarding what the wishes and feelings of the person lacking capacity would be in relation to taking part in the research, if they were able to express a view.

13.64 Where research started before the Act came into force (1 October 2007) and a person originally had capacity to consent and gave consent before 31 March 2008, research involving tissue or data collected from that person before a loss of capacity may continue if the participant later loses capacity before the end of the project.[176] Such research must have procedures for dealing with people who lose capacity during the project who have been approved by the research ethics committee. Approval for the project to continue should be made by submitting a substantial amendment to the relevant REC.

6. Consent and incapacity: Children and adults; the Clinical Trials Directive

(i) Introduction

13.65 A further consequence of the EU Clinical Trials Directive is the introduction of specific provision relating to the inclusion in clinical trials of those persons lacking capacity.[177] The Directive provides that where a person is unable to consent themselves, consent may be obtained from their 'legal representative'. Consent is also required in an emergency

[175] SI 2007/679.

[176] This research is permitted under the Mental Capacity Act 2005 (Loss of Capacity During Research Project Regulations 2007, SI 2007/679.

[177] See further K Liddell et al, 'Medical Research Involving Incapacitated Adults: Implications of the EU Clinical Trials Directive' (2006) 4 Medical Law Review 367.

situation. These provisions were incorporated into English law through the Medicines for Human Use (Clinical Trials) Regulations 2004.[178]

The provisions relating to trials involving medicinal products operate alongside the existing common law and statutory provisions. In the case of the child, the personal legal representative is to be the person who has parental responsibility. Specific provisions relate to adults without mental capacity. These are different provisions for their inclusion in clinical research than the provisions set out under the Mental Capacity Act provisions, which are discussed at paras 13.55–13.64. 13.66

(ii) The legal representative

Individuals may be able to act as a legal representative 'by virtue of their relationship' and they are available to make the decision and are prepared to do so.[179] As noted above, this, in the case of the child, is to be the person with parental responsibility, which has the same meaning in England and Wales as under the Children Act 1989.[180] 13.67

(iii) Professional legal representative

In some instances, while normally the role of the legal representative will be undertaken by a person who is close to the patient, this may not always be the case. In such a situation the patient's doctor will undertake this role, save where the doctor is 'connected with the conduct of the trial'.[181] Persons 'connected with the conduct of the trial' are defined as being: 13.68

(a) The sponsor of the trial;
(b) A person employed or engaged by or acting under arrangements made with, the sponsor and who undertakes activities in connection with the management of the trial;
(c) An investigator for the trial (defined as the authorized health professional responsible for the conduct of the trial at a trial site and if the trial is conducted by a team of authorized health professionals at a trial site, the leader responsible for that team);
(d) A health care professional who is a member of the investigator's team for the purposes of the trial; or
(e) A person who provides health care under the direction or control of a person referred to in paragraphs c or d whether in the course of the trial or otherwise.[182]

Where the health professional responsible for the patient's care is involved in the research, it is provided that they should nominate a person to undertake this role.[183] However, while this may be seen as a practical measure facilitating the operation of the trial, it may prove to be problematic. In such a situation, they may be regarded as not being totally objective in that decision and thus to ask them to nominate a person may not be appropriate. 13.69

(iv) Taking the decision

The basis for such a decision is that of the individual's 'presumed will'.[184] Any explicit decision made by a person prior to becoming incapacitated must be respected. Where the decision is made by a professional legal representative, the doctor may also have knowledge regarding an individual's clinical condition which would suggest that although the application of the test of presumed will may support an individual's inclusion it may in fact be 13.70

178 Medicines for Human Use (Clinical Trials) Regulations 2004, SI 2004/1031.
179 ibid, Sch 1(2)(a)(i) and part 3.
180 ibid, Sch 1(2) and part 4.
181 ibid.
182 ibid, Sch 1(2), para 27.
183 ibid, Sch 1(2), para 3.
184 ibid, Sch 1(5), para 12.

clearly against their own interests. A professional legal representative who is not the clinical carer may consult persons they regard as being appropriate in making a decision in accordance with the 'presumed will' of the potential subject. However, they are not under any obligation to make exhaustive enquiries. Again, if there is a 'valid and applicable advance refusal' this is to be regarded as conclusive of the presumed will of the subject.

(v) Monitoring continued participation

13.71 The legal representative has a right to withdraw the research subject from the trial and this right may be exercised at any time.[185] A maximum period for participation without further review by legal representative is to be established at the start of the trial. Where those with clinical responsibility believe that there should not be continued participation of the subject in the trial, this information should be given to the personal legal representative. Where there is disagreement between clinician and personal legal representative, there should be an attempt to resolve this.[186]

(vi) Emergency situations

13.72 The EU Clinical Trials Directive requires consent from a legal representative in all situations, including an emergency. This prompted some expressions of concern in the research community that this might lead to such trials having, in many instances, to be abandoned.[187] The 2004 Regulations were subsequently amended by the Medicines for Human Use (Clinical Trials) Amendment Regulations No 2 2006.[188] These enable an adult lacking mental capacity to be included, where a person's legal representative has not consented. For the regulations to be satisfied, three criteria need to be complied with. First, urgent action is required; secondly, that it is not reasonably practicable to meet the usual conditions; finally, a research ethics committee must have approved the trial. The regulations provide that this provision will cease to apply where it is no longer necessary to take this action as a matter of urgency.[189]

(vii) Recovery of competence

13.73 If the research subject gains competence, they must be informed regarding their participation in a clinical trial.[190] Their consent must be obtained to any further involvement.

D. Monitoring the Conduct of the Trial: General

13.74 The RGF provides that research ethics committees are to require NHS researchers to provide them with information regarding the progress of studies and, as a consequence, they may review advice which has been given as to the ethical acceptability of the study.[191] If researchers intend to deviate from the protocol, the REC shall be informed. GAFREC provides for exceptions where the reason for the deviation concerns immediate hazards to research participants or where changes are only envisaged to the 'logistical or administrative

[185] ibid, Sch 1(5), para 5.
[186] ibid, Sch 1(5), para 44.
[187] E A Singer, and M Mullner, 'Implications of the EU Directive on Clinical Trials for Emergency Medicine' (2002) 324 BMJ 1169.
[188] SI 2006/2984. See also *Explanatory Memorandum to the Medicines for Human Use (Clinical Trials) Amendment Regulations 2006,* No 2984.
[189] See further discussion of the regulations in M F Bone, 'Ethics of Research in Clinical Emergencies: UK Regulation Inconsistent with European Law' (2007) 3 Research Ethics Review 97.
[190] n 188.
[191] RGF, para 3.12.8.

aspects of the research'.[192] This can be contrasted with the procedures relating to follow-up regarding trials under the Clinical Trials Directive discussed below. Nonetheless, as GAFREC notes, responsibility as to whether a study does follow the protocol and any consequent monitoring on its progress lies with the host NHS institution.[193] Interestingly, in situations in which there are anticipated problems in recruiting subjects, GAFREC states that the REC may also require that there shall be reports regarding the potential subject's perception of the projects 'acceptability'.[194] In addition, in a situation in which a REC member has information that there may have been a possible breach of good practice in research this should be notified to the REC chair and Administrator.[195] The Administrator should also inform the appointing authority of this information. When it approves the application the REC shall state whether it requires progress reports. Within three months of the study having ended it shall require a final report.[196]

E. Monitoring of Trials Concerning Medicinal Products

1. Introduction

In relation to those trials which concern medicinal products, the position is more complex. Under the Directive, the regulatory authority, the Medicines and Health Care Regulatory Agency, has certain obligations. Regular 'good clinical practice' inspections are to be undertaken. Those sites which are involved in clinical trials, which will include those of the investigator/laboratories used for analysis/sponsor's premises, are liable to inspection. It is intended that there will be consequent penalties relating to non-compliance. In addition there will also be an infringement notice procedure. **13.75**

2. Reporting requirements

The implementation of the Clinical Trials Directive can be seen as a development on the existing provisions under the Medicines Act 1968 regarding the reporting of serious adverse reactions to the Licensing Authority.[197] The new provisions relate to serious adverse events and suspected unexpected serious adverse reactions (SUSARs).[198] Investigators must report all serious adverse events to the sponsor, followed with a detailed report.[199] Additional reporting requirements may have been imposed by the trial protocol and, if so, these should also be complied with. SUSARs must be recorded and reported to the LA, to the competent authority, and also to the ethics committee. SUSARs which are 'fatal and life-threatening' must be initially reported within seven days and then additional information within an eight-day period. Trial sponsors are required to inform all investigators who are responsible for conduct of a trial.[200] SUSARs are included in a European database which has been established under Article 11(1) of the Directive.[201] Sponsors are also required to give LA and ethics committee annual reports of all suspected serious adverse reactions at those sites **13.76**

192 GAFREC, para 7.24.
193 ibid, para 7.33.
194 ibid, para 7.31.
195 ibid, para 7.34.
196 ibid, para 7.26.
197 Medicines for Human Use (Clinical Trials) Regulations 2004, SI 2004/1031, regs 32–33.
198 See also European Commission, *Detailed Guidance on the Collection, Verification and Presentation of Adverse Reaction Reports Arising from Clinical Trials on Medicinal Products for Human Use*, Revision 2 (European Commission 2006).
199 Medicines for Human Use (Clinical Trials) Regulations 2004, SI 2004/1031, reg 33.
200 ibid, reg 33(5).
201 See further on this database at <http://www.pharmacos/eudra.org>.

(whether in the UK or elsewhere) for which they are sponsors.[202] Failure to comply with these notification provisions will, in a change to the existing provision, become a criminal offence.[203]

3. Amendments to the trial protocol

13.77 There are various situations in which researchers may seek to amend the trial protocol.[204] First, an amendment may be required for safety reasons. Appropriate urgent measures may be taken by the sponsor or investigator in order to safeguard subjects from immediate hazard to health and safety.[205] Sponsors may also make amendments to the protocol. However, where it is proposed to make a 'substantial amendment' defined in reg 11 as:

> . . . likely to affect to a significant degree:
>
> (a) The safety and personal integrity of the subjects of the trial
> (b) The scientific value of the trial
> (c) The conduct and management of the trial
> (d) The quality or safety of an investigational medical product used in the trial

In such a situation both the Licencing Authority and the Research Ethics Committee need to be informed.[206]

13.78 Where an amendment proposal has been rejected, the sponsor may amend this and give at least fourteen days' notice in writing to LA/relevant ethics committee of their intention to make an amendment.[207] The LA or ethics committee may, within fourteen days of this notice, state why they do not accept the amendment (or in the case of the ethics committee why they are giving an unfavourable opinion in relation to the amendment). Where applications for amendments are refused/accepted, subject to conditions, this can be referred to the Commission on Human Medicines.[208]

4. Infringements of clinical trial protocol requirements

13.79 The licensing authority is to have powers to deal with infringements through the issue of an infringement notice.[209] They can suspend or prohibit a trial. This power arises where authorization conditions have not been complied with or where information raises doubts as to safety/scientific validity/conduct of the trial.[210] Save in a situation in which there is an imminent risk to health and safety, the LA must give written notice to the sponsor or investigator as to its intention to issue a notice.[211]

5. Appeal procedures

13.80 Sponsors may make representations to the appropriate committee in relation to the rejection of request for authorization/failure to obtain amendment/termination of trial.[212] Notice

[202] Medicines for Human Use (Clinical Trials) Regulations 2004, n 207, reg 33(4).
[203] ibid, reg 49.
[204] ibid, reg 22.
[205] ibid, reg 30.
[206] ibid, reg 24.
[207] ibid, reg 25(2).
[208] This body replaced the Medicines Commission and the Committee for the Safety of Medicines in 2005, reg 25, sched 3 para 5.13 <http://www.mhra.gov.uk/Committees/Medicinesadvisorybodies/CommissiononHumanMedicines/index.htm>.
[209] Medicines for Human Use (Clinical Trials) Regulations 2004, n 207, reg 48, implementing Art 12(2).
[210] ibid, reg 31.
[211] ibid, reg 31(5), (6).
[212] ibid, reg 25.

must be given by the sponsor within fourteen days (although there is a discretion for the LA to extend this). After a hearing, the committee will advise the LA. The LA must take the committee's decision into account but is not bound by it. An application may be made to the Medicines Commission, again within a twenty-eight-day period.[213] The LA must consider the report and any advice given by the Commission but is not bound by it. It is also provided that the sponsor may request to appear before the appropriate committee. On request this hearing may be held in public. Again, while the LA is required to take into account the report and consider whether to confirm/alter their decision, they are not bound by it.

6. The end of the trial

Specific provisions relate to trials on medicinal products. Sponsors are required to state in the trial protocol when the trial will end. The sponsor is then required to notify the LA in writing and the ethics committee which had approved the trial, that it has come to an end within ninety days.[214] Where the trial has ended early, this notification must be within fifteen days and reasons should be given for its early termination. Failure to comply with this information is a criminal offence. An obligation is placed upon the sponsor and the Chief Investigator to retain documents contained in the master file of the trial and also the medical files of trial subjects for a period of at least five years after the trial has ended.[215] **13.81**

7. Provision of information

The Clinical Trials Directive contains certain specific provisions regarding the provision of information concerning clinical trials in the EU. Article 11 of the Directive provides that information concerning trials conducted in Member States is to be entered into a central European database, the EUDRACT database, accessible only to competent authorities within Member States and to the Commission.[216] Detailed guidance on the database has been issued by the European Commission,[217] which notes the purposes of the database, including providing an overview of all EU clinical trials, facilitation of communication between Member States, EMEA, and the Commission on clinical trials, the identification of those trials within the EU which are ongoing, completed, and terminated, generation of clinical trial statistics, provision of information concerning GCP, and also of notification to the competent authorities where trials are ended for reasons of safety.[218] Member States are to enter extracts from the request that a trial be authorized,[219] amendments which have been made to the trial protocol,[220] the approval of the ethics committee,[221] inspections which have been undertaken to ensure that the conduct of the trial is in accordance with the principles of good clinical practice,[222] and the declaration that the trial has come to an end.[223] In addition, there is also to be the identification of trials and medicinal products in order **13.82**

[213] ibid, Sch 5, para 2(1).
[214] ibid, reg 27.
[215] Reg 31(A) inserted by the Medicines for Human Use (Clinical Trials) Amendment Regulations 2006, SI 2006/1928.
[216] See further <https://eudract.ema.europa.eu/>.
[217] European Commission, *Detailed Guidance on the European Clinical Trials Database EUDRACT Database* ENTR/6421/01, Brussels, July 2002, see also Eudralex, 'The Rules Governing Medicinal Products in the European Union', Vol 10, ch 5: <http://ec.europa.eu/enterprise/pharmaceuticals/eudralex/vol10_en.htm#>.
[218] European Commission, *Detailed Guidance on the European Clinical Trials Database*, n 225, para 5.
[219] Clinical Trials Directive Art 11(1)(a).
[220] ibid, Art 11(1)(b), (c).
[221] ibid, Art 11(1)(d).
[222] ibid, Art 11(1)(f).
[223] ibid, Art 11(1)(e).

to enable links between with clinical trial information and any reports regarding 'suspected unexpected serious adverse reaction'.[224]

13.83 The European Commission has established a separate database, the Eudravigilance Clinical Trial Module concerning suspected unexpected serious adverse reactions[225] which is provided for under Article 17(3) (a) of the Directive. Its role is comparable with that of the EUDRACT database. It includes provision of an overview of the occurrence of SUSARs, the facilitation of communication between competent authorities in Member States, the Commission, and EMEA, enables a separate review to be undertaken of SUSARs in individual Member States, review of SUSARs, and the generation of statistics and the links between trials and medicinal products to provide links with SUSARs.[226]

8. Specific criminal offences

13.84 Several criminal offences are included in the Regulations implementing the Directive.[227] These include the provision of 'relevant information'[228] which is false or misleading in relation to clinical trial authorizations.[229] It is also an offence for sponsors/investigators/contract research organizations/persons involved in conduct of a trial and so forth to provide information which is false or misleading to the MCA or to an ethics committee.[230] Regulation 51 provides that it is a defence to show that a person undertook all reasonable caution and exercised all due diligence to avoid commission of the offence.

F. Responsibility and Accountability

1. Introduction

13.85 The language of the Research Governance Framework is cast in terms of 'responsibilities'. Interestingly it begins by raising the issue of the responsibility of the research participant. It notes that: 'Anyone using health and social care services should give serious consideration to becoming involved in developing or undertaking research studies.'[231]

13.86 This statement can be seen as very much reflecting principles such as those of social solidarity and the public interest in participation in the research process.[232] One important issue highlighted in the research governance framework is that of the need for clear agreements which set out respective rights and responsibilities and that such agreements are documented.[233] The RGF notes that these particularly need to be in place in relation to studies where there may be:

---

224 European Commission, *Detailed Guidance on the European Clinical Trials Database*, n 225, para 5.

225 <http://www.ema.europa.eu/ema/index.jsp?curl=pages/regulation/general/general_content_000679.jsp&mid=WC0b01ac05800250b5>.

226 ibid, para 5.

227 Medicines for Human Use (Clinical Trials) Regulations 2004, n 207, reg 50.

228 This refers to information relevant regarding the assessment of safety/quality/efficacy of investigational medicinal product/safety/scientific validity of a clinical trial/whether conditions/principles of GCP have been met.

229 Medicines for Human Use (Clinical Trials) Regulations 2004, n 207, reg 37.

230 Offences under these provisions would be liable at the magistrates court for a fine not exceeding £5,000 or term of imprisonment not exceeding three months; in the case of the Crown Court of a fine and/or prison term not exceeding two years, ibid, reg 52.

231 RGF, para 3.4.1.

232 See, eg, O O'Neil, R Chadwick, and K Berg, 'Solidarity and Equity: New Ethical Frameworks for Genetic Databases' (2001) 2 Nature Reviews Genetics 318.

233 RGF, para 3.2.2.

- work on more than one site: and/or
- researchers employed by more than one organisation; and/or
- patients, users and care professionals from more than one care organisation; and/or
- more than one funder.[234]

2. The researchers

Secondly, the RGF focuses upon the responsibility of the researchers themselves:[235] **13.87**

They are responsible:

- for ensuring that any research they undertake follows the agreed protocol,
- for helping care professionals to ensure that participants receive appropriate care while involved in research,
- for protecting the integrity and confidentiality of clinical and other records generated by the research and for reporting any failures in these respects, adverse drug reactions and other events or suspected misconduct through the appropriate systems.[236]

The focus for the conduct of the trial is now placed upon the 'Chief Investigator'.[237] It is this person's responsibility to ensure that: 'The research team gives priority at all times to the dignity, rights safety and well-being of participants.'[238] Thus here, finally, there is a reference to participants' rights, but it is rather anomalous in the light of the fact that such a statement is not included in relation to the responsibilities of the researchers generally. The Chief Investigator is to ensure that the study is in accordance with legal and ethical requirements, that the research is undertaken within the research governance framework, that the trials are registered, and that the person with organizational responsibility such as the Chief Executive is informed. In a situation in which research participants are included while they are under the care of health/social care professionals, those professionals are to be informed as to the research participant's involvement in the study. Service users, carers, and children under the auspices of a local authority are invited to participate. The Chief Investigator is required to ensure that members of the research team are appropriately qualified to undertake their roles and that where the study involves new researchers/students, appropriate training should be given. Other responsibilities outlined include: ensuring that the research should follow the approved protocol but that any proposed changes should be submitted to the ethics committee, research sponsor, and also any appropriate body; that there should be dissemination of findings; and that the researcher accepts a key role in detecting/preventing scientific misconduct by 'acting as guarantor on published outputs'.[239] **13.88**

3. The sponsor

The RGF also refers directly to the role of the research sponsor. This is an issue which derives from the Clinical Trials Directive but, as implemented through the RGF, this is to apply to all clinical trials. From April 2004, any research involving the NHS/social care must involve a research sponsor who has confirmed that it accepts its research responsibilities.[240] The definition of the 'sponsor' flows from the EU Clinical Trials Directive. It is to be 'the individual **13.89**

[234] ibid, para 3.2.3.
[235] ibid, para 3.5.1.
[236] ibid, para 3.5.1.
[237] ibid, para 3.2.14.
[238] ibid, para 3.6.3.
[239] ibid.
[240] ibid, para 3.8.1.

or organization who takes on ultimate responsibility for the initiation and management (or arranging the initiation and management) of, and the financing (or arranging the financing) for that trial'.[241] Their role involves the assessment of the quality of the research, of the research environment and the experience/responsibility of the principal investigator and of other key researchers. Sponsors are charged with ensuring that arrangements are in place in relation to the management and monitoring of the research.[242] The RGF provides that in a situation in which there is no external sponsor, a situation termed 'own account research', health and social organizations must accept the responsibility.[243] The Department of Health has a list of 'recognized sponsors'. The RGF gives as an example that of a student's supervisor who may undertake the function of a sponsor in relation to the student's research.[244] It provides that there must be a clear written agreement which identifies the organization which is responsible for management/coordination of the study.[245] The sponsor must be satisfied about a range of issues. These include that the proposal 'respects the dignity, rights, safety and well-being of participants and the relationship with care providers'.[246] It also provides that agreements should have been reached in relation to the provision of compensation where harm arises. The RGF emphasizes that research sponsors require appropriate systems/ access to such systems for independent review, which may enable them to satisfy themselves regarding the projects standing.[247] The reviews are to be directed at the project's scientific and ethical standing, what 'strategic relevance' it may have, and also 'value for money'.

13.90 A further set of responsibilities is outlined for research funders.[248] This is in line with the division of responsibility under the EU Clinical Trials Directive. The RGF provides that: 'Organisations that fund research have a responsibility for ensuring that the work is a proper use of the funds they control and provides value for money.'[249] It emphasizes that those bodies that want to fund research in collaboration with NHS/social care, must be willing to undertake the responsibilities of research sponsor or to collaborate with another organization which is 'willing and able to do so'.[250] As the Medical Research Council comments, the sponsor role is one which follows the model of the pharmaceutical industry. As it notes, under such a model:

> a single company develops a product, initiates, funds and manages the trials necessary to gain a Marketing authorization and then recoups its costs and profits directly from its sales. It is in the interests of that company to take responsibility for all aspects of trials undertaken for regulatory purposes.[251]

In contrast, the MRC note that, in the context of publicly funded trials, these are by their very nature a collaborative partnership and in, such situations, individuals/organizations have differing levels of sponsorship.

4. Universities/organizations employing researchers

13.91 The RGF emphasizes that those employers, whether private or public sector, of persons undertaking research in health and social care have an obligation to promote and develop a

241 Under the Medicines for Human Use (Clinical Trials) Regulations.
242 RGF para 3.8.3.
243 ibid, para 3.8.5.
244 ibid, para 3.8.6.
245 ibid, para 3.8.6.
246 ibid, para 3.8.7.
247 ibid, para 4.2.
248 ibid, para 3.7.
249 ibid, para 3.7.1.
250 ibid, para 3.7.2.
251 MRC, *Good Regulation of Clinical Trials for Patients* (2003) 12.

quality research culture.[252] It stresses that the employers must support and also, where relevant, hold staff to account in relation to professional conduct of research. This also includes provision regarding training, career planning, and development. It also extends to the use of codes of practice and compliance monitoring systems. Employers are also directed to have provision for dealing with non-compliance and misconduct and in relation to learning from complaints.

The employing organizations are themselves required to ensure that researchers both understand and are able to discharge their responsibilities under the RGF.[253] There is an interface between the responsibilities of the employer and that of the research sponsor. The framework notes that the nature of the employer's responsibilities needs to be agreed with the sponsor and care provider. Moreover, it notes that ultimate responsibility regarding management and monitoring of the study is in the hands of the sponsor. The employers are charged with ensuring that the appropriate agreements are in place between research funders and care organizations regarding intellectual property issues. **13.92**

The university/employers are required to ensure compliance with relevant employment and health and safety legislation and codes of practice regarding other issues.[254] It is the employer who is required to ensure that principal investigators/other staff understand/comply with the RGF. They are required to have systems in place to detect/address fraud and other scientific/professional misconduct. They are also required to ensure that they are in a position to compensate anyone who is harmed through negligent behaviour of their staff. They must permit and sanction investigations where these flow from complaints in respect of employer's actions. **13.93**

5. Responsibilities of organizations providing care

The RGF also sets out the responsibilities of UK health and social care organizations.[255] It requires that such organizations must be aware of the research which is undertaken within their organization or which involves participants/organs/tissues/data through the organization. Appropriate information is to be given to patients, users, and carers where this may impact upon care, experience of care and their work in the organization. Interestingly, the RGF states that 'They should ensure that activities are presented as research only if they are managed formally as research within the provisions of this framework.'[256] **13.94**

It is the organization providing care which is required to ensure that the research undertaken meets Framework standards and that an identifiable research sponsor is in place.[257] The Chief Executive/Agency Director is required to ensure accountability here. Researchers who are not employed by the NHS organization but 'who interact with individuals in a way which has a direct bearing on the quality of their care should hold an NHS honorary contract'.[258] **13.95**

6. Responsibilities of care professionals

The RGF emphasizes that health and social care professionals retain responsibility for the care of patients/users where they are involved in research.[259] Moreover, care professionals **13.96**

[252] RGF, para 3.9.1.
[253] ibid, para 3.9.2.
[254] ibid, para 3.9.4.
[255] ibid, para 3.10.1.
[256] ibid, para 3.10.1.
[257] ibid, para 3.10.2.
[258] ibid, para 3.10.3.
[259] ibid, para 3.11.1.

are also required to ensure that, before patients/clients are involved, the research has been subject to approval by scrutinizing authorities.[260]

G. Confidentiality, Privacy, and Research Participant's Information

1. Introduction

13.97 Health care professionals are required to safeguard the confidentiality of their patient information subject to certain exceptions (see Chapter 12).[261] The obligation of confidentiality is bolstered by other obligations through statute, such as the Data Protection Act 1998 and principles, such as the right to privacy of home and family life in Article 8 of the European Convention on Human Rights.[262] The perceived need to safeguard confidentiality and privacy of research participants' information is reflected in guidance regarding the use of information for clinical research purposes.[263] The GAFREC provides that research protocols should contain information as to who will have access to research participant's data and samples, what measures are to be undertaken to maintain the confidentiality and security of research participant's information, and whether this information will be anonymized. The protocol must address how data/samples will be obtained, kept and used and, if it is intended for this material to be used in other jurisdictions, to which countries the data/samples will be sent. The GAFREC also specifically requires the REC to consider the 'adequacy of the process for obtaining consent for the above'.[264] Use of information for clinical research purposes must comply with existing legal obligations, including the equitable remedy of breach of confidence, the Data Protection Act 1998, and the Human Rights Act 1998. Participant information used in clinical research may be derived from existing clinical information *or* obtained during the study itself.

2. Consent and anonymization

13.98 Generally, the research participant should consent to their information being used to avoid the prospect of an action for breach of confidence. The tenor of guidance issued by professional bodies suggests however, that in a situation in which the patient information is anonymized, it may be legitimately used without further consent being obtained. Such an approach is in line with that taken in the Court of Appeal in *R v Department of Health, ex p Source Informatics*[265] (see Chapter 12). In the context of genetic research the Human Genetics Commission found such an approach to be an attractive one.[266] However, the decision in *Source Informatics* has been subject to criticism.[267] Whether anonymization can be regarded as a satisfactory solution is dependent upon the precise reasons as to why an individual may want to exercise control over their personal information. They may simply be interested in ensuring that they cannot be linked to their own personal information.

---

[260] ibid, para 3.11.2.

[261] See generally *X* v *Y* [1988] 2 All ER 648; *W* v *Egdell* [1990] 1 All ER 835; GMC, *Confidentiality* (GMC 2009).

[262] *Z v Finland* (1998) 25 EHRR 371; *MS v Sweden* (1999) 28 EHRR 313; *Campbell v Mirror Group Newspapers* [2004] 2 All ER 995.

[263] eg Medical Research Council, *Personal Information in Medical Research* (MRC 2000); General Medical Council, *Confidentiality* (GMC 2009). See generally, discussion in H Biggs, *Healthcare Research Ethics and Law* (Routledge Cavendish 2009) ch 6.

[264] GAFREC, para 9.16.

[265] [2000] 1 All ER 786.

[266] Human Genetics Commission, *Inside Information* (HGC 2002).

[267] See further D Beyleveld and E Histed, 'Betrayal of Confidence in the Court of Appeal' (2000) 4 Medical Law International 69.

However, it can be argued that anonymization is not the answer because that does not obviate an individual's wish to exercise control over whether their information should be subsequently used in a particular clinical research project. Some empirical research has indicated that patients have considerable reservations regarding the sanctioning of access to health records for researchers and associated purposes.[268] Particular problems may also arise in a situation in which it is proposed to access and use such material over a much longer period of time. This difficulty can be exacerbated where the research project relates to a longer term use, for example, in relation to genetic databases in relation to major population studies—this issue is returned to below.

What of the situation in which information has not been effectively anonymized? Some research guidelines envisage the possibility of disclosing confidential information for research purposes without the participant's consent having been obtained. GMC guidance on Confidentiality sets out situations in which this may occur.[269] It provides that: **13.99**

42. You may disclose identifiable information without consent if it is required by law, if it is approved under section 251 of the NHS Act 2006, or if it can be justified in the public interest and it is either:
    (a) necessary to use identifiable information, or
    (b) not practicable to anonymize or code the information and, in either case, not practicable to seek consent (or efforts to seek consent have been unsuccessful).

43. In considering whether it is practicable to seek consent you should take account of:
    (a) the age of records and the likely traceability of patients
    (b) the number of records, and
    (c) the possibility of introducing bias because of a low response rate or because particular groups of patients refuse, or do not respond to, requests to use their information.

44. When considering whether the public interest in disclosures for secondary uses outweighs patients' and the public interest in keeping the information confidential, you must consider:
    (a) the nature of the information to be disclosed
    (b) what use will be made of the information
    (c) how many people will have access to the information
    (d) the confidentiality and security arrangements in place to protect the information from further disclosure
    (e) the advice of a Caldicott Guardian or similar expert adviser, who is not directly connected with the use for which disclosure is being considered, and
    (f) the potential for distress or harm to patients.

In the past the courts have taken into account professional guidelines such as those of the GMC in determining what constitutes the public interest,[270] but whether there would today be unquestioning acceptance of such guidelines is more uncertain given that the courts as we have seen in other contexts have demonstrated that they are willing to scrutinize professional practice approaches.[271]

[268] See the discussion in J O'Brien and C Chantler, 'Confidentiality and the Duties of Care' (2003) 29 Journal of Medical Ethics 36.
[269] General Medical Council, *Confidentiality* (GMC 2009).
[270] *W v Edgell* [1990] 1 All ER 835.
[271] See further Chapter 3, paras 3.58–3.129 and Chapter 8, paras 8.63–8.93.

3. Statutory exceptions sanctioning disclosure for research purposes

13.100 As noted in Chapter 12, the disclosure of sensitive personal clinical information without consent may conflict not only with the common law safeguards relating to breach of confidence, but also the Data Protection Act 1998, which concerns personal data held on both computer and manual records. Some regarded this as, effectively, an inhibitor to clinical practice.[272] The impact of the Data Protection Act 1998, particularly in relation to the legality of holding clinical information in, for example, cancer registries and its use for clinical research purposes without further consent being obtained for such use, led to the enactment of s 60 of the Health and Social Care Act 2001, which is now re-enacted as s 251 of the National Health Service Act 2006.[273] This provision enables the Secretary of State to make regulations which allow the processing of 'prescribed patient information for medical purposes as he considers necessary or expedient'. Such regulations may be made in the interests of providing patient care or in the public interest. The regulations provide for disclosure of patient information without consent in relation, for example, to communicable diseases and other public health purposes.[274] Advice is given to the Secretary of State in relation to applications under this section by the Confidentiality Advisory Group of the Health Research Authority; this is discussed further in Chapter 12 at paras 12.91 and 12.98. While s 60 and its successor, s 251, are provisions which have been welcomed by many in the scientific community as facilitating transfer of information for research purposes, in other respects it may be viewed as problematic. It enables the enactment of broad brush exceptions to the equitable remedy of breach of confidence. There remains the prospect that in the future, there may be challenges brought by an individual's objection to automatic use of their information, albeit anonymized with reference to the Human Rights Act 1998 and Article 8.

4. Feedback of clinical information to participants

13.101 One further problematic issue concerns the extent to which an individual about whom information is generated is entitled to any feedback regarding the study which has been undertaken, in a situation in which the study itself may have produced information which may be regarded as relevant to that person's health.[275] The Convention on Human Rights and Biomedicine on Biomedical Research provides in Article 27:

1. Research participants shall be entitled to know any information collected on their health in conformity with the provisions of Article 10 of the Convention.
2. Other personal information collected for a research project will be accessible to them in conformity with the law on the protection of individuals with regard to processing of personal data.

13.102 While such an approach can be regarded as providing respect for autonomy, it can also be viewed as problematic. It may give rise to particular difficulties in a situation in which a study is undertaken over a very long period of time and where the information in question may relate to a person's genetic susceptibility to develop illness/disability. On the one hand, individuals may be interested in such information, particularly if the prediction may enable them to seek treatment. On the other hand, they may as a consequence be entrusted

---

[272] J Strobl, E Cave, T Walley, 'Data Protection Legislation: Interpretation and Barriers to Research' (2000) BMJ 890.

[273] Health Services (Control of Patient Information) Regulations 2002, SI 2002/1438, reg 4; and see also P Case, 'Confidence Matters: The Rise and Fall of Informational Autonomy in Medical Law' (2003) 11 Med L Rev 208–36.

[274] Health Services (Control of Patient Information) Regulations 2002, n 281, reg 3.

[275] See, eg, discussion of this issue in relation to biobanks in C Johnston and J Kaye, 'Does UK Biobank Have a Legal Obligation to Feedback Individual Findings to Participants?' (2004) 12 Med L Rev 239.

with information which they may otherwise not have wanted to receive and indeed may infringe any 'right not to know'. Such information may be regarded as harmful if it is then incorporated into their medical records. The prospect of such feedback then inevitably leads to considerations of exactly how the feedback process should be undertaken. It may be the case that in relation to genetic information, the feedback is in relation to risks rather than certainties and the calibration of such risks may be fundamentally problematic.[276] The MRC are of the view that this is something which must be determined in relation to the individual study.[277] However interestingly they go on to comment that: 'Research results obtained on anonymized unlinked samples cannot have any impact on the interests of an individual donor.'

There is some suggestion that where results have immediate clinical relevance, then a clinician has a duty of care to inform the research participant of this directly or through their doctor. Nonetheless, it has been suggested that, in such a situation, verification of the result should be obtained to obviate the risk of error. The question of the obligation, if any, owed to research participants in such a situation remains at the time of writing under active consideration by UK Biobank. **13.103**

5. Use of information for research purposes after death

While long recognized by the medical profession, it is only recently that judicial authority has suggested that the law concerning patient confidentiality can extend to after the patient's death[278] (see Chapter 12). The Data Protection Act 1998 does not apply in such a situation and access to the records of deceased persons is still governed by the earlier legislation in the form of the Access to Health Records Act 1990. **13.104**

H. Regulating Bad Practice: Fraud in Scientific Research

Scientific research is undertaken in a 'high pressure' competitive environment.[279] Researchers are under pressure to show that the money invested in their project was well spent. Career advancement is dependent upon a prolific publication record. Thus there are risks that particular individuals may be tempted to falsify results. Concerns regarding misconduct in scientific research led to calls over many years for more centralized review.[280] The Committee on Publication Ethics was established in 1997 as a means through which medical and scientific journal editors could manage research fraud.[281] Subsequently, the Academy of Medical Sciences were involved in developing a framework to monitor research misconduct, including a database of information, although there is disagreement as to whether an audit function was appropriate here.[282] While there is the possibility of professional sanctions which will flow from research fraud, for example, through disciplinary action from professional bodies such as the GMC, there is no explicit legal regulation of this issue. **13.105**

---

[276] See further discussion in M P M Richards, 'Issues of Consent and Feedback in a Genetic Epidemiological Study of Women with Breast Cancer' (2003) 29 Journal of Medical Ethics 93–96.

[277] Medical Research Council, *Personal Information in Medical Research* (MRC 2000) para 8.1.

[278] See S Lock and J Loudan, 'A Question of Confidence' (1984) 288 BMJ 123; and now see *Lewis v Secretary of State for Health* [2008] EWHC 2196 (QB).

[279] S Lock (ed), *Fraud and Misconduct in Medical Research* (2nd edn, BMJ 1996).

[280] R Smith, 'Time to Face up to Research Misconduct' (1996) 312 BMJ 789; Editorial, 'Dealing with Deception' (1996) Lancet 843; D Rennie, 'Education and Debate; Dealing with Research Misconduct in the UK' (1998) 316 BMJ 1726–33; and see MRC, *Scientific Misconduct* (1997).

[281] <http://publicationethics.org/>.

[282] S Mayor, 'Proposals for a UK Body to Investigate Research Fraud Lack "Teeth"' (2002) BMJ 325.

13.106 The UK Research Integrity Office (UKRIO) was established by Universities UK in 2006 and is now concerned with furthering good practice in research and also in identifying misconduct.[283] UKRIO is chaired by Professor Bernard Silverman, the Home Office Chief Scientific Advisor. In October 2008 it launched its Procedure for the Investigation of Misconduct in Research, which is currently voluntary.[284] In 2009 it also issued a 'Code of Practice for Research: Promoting good practice and preventing misconduct', this is currently under review.[285] The Code sets out a series of principles to guide organizations and researchers, honesty, integrity, cooperation, accountability, training and skills, and safety.[286] The body is concerned with the promotion of good governance management and conduct of research and the sharing of good practice. UKRIO itself has come under criticism. As has been noted by Biggs, it does not 'investigate allegations of misconduct or to monitor researchers who are suspected of misconduct'.[287]

I. Accountability to the Research Participant

13.107 The decisions of RECs may be subject to review in the courts through what is termed 'judicial review'.[288] Their decisions may be viewed on the basis that they have acted ultra vires, irrationally, or contrary to the rules of natural justice.[289] The decision may, as a result, be struck down or the decision referred back to the ethics committee to redetermine. As Kennedy has noted, REC members are also individually responsible:

> Principal among these duties is the duty of each member to act with due care. The role of each member is to review proposals for research and make recommendations as to the ethical propriety, or otherwise, of them. In carrying out this role, members must take account of the twin aims, referred to above (para 13.70), of fostering research while safeguarding the welfare of research subjects. Members must, therefore, seek to understand, so as to take an ethical view about, complex issues of, inter alia, biomedical science, statistics and moral philosophy. The members' duty, expressed in this way, may seem somewhat daunting. The standard of care demanded by the law, however, is that of reasonableness.[290]

13.108 In a situation in which research participants have been harmed, it is possible that not only could researchers be subject to litigation, but that proceedings may also be brought against research ethics committees and their members in the civil tort of negligence. Brazier has suggested that, in principle, individual REC members owe a duty of care to research subjects.[291] REC members acting in accordance with their duties are covered by NHS indemnity. Nonetheless, while in theory, a REC may be held liable where the committee or its members have acted negligently in scrutinizing the conduct of a clinical trial, in practice establishing liability in the courtroom itself may prove problematic. As Brazier has commented, to establish the action, the research participant would be required to demonstrate that the committee member's negligence in approving the project led to the injury which

---

[283] <http://ukrio.org/>.

[284] (UKRIO 2008).

[285] Code of Practice for Research: Promoting good practice and preventing misconduct (UKRIO 2009) <http://ukrio.org/publications/code-of-practice-for-research/>.

[286] ibid, para 2.0.

[287] H Biggs, *Healthcare Research Ethics and Law* (Routledge Cavendish 2009) 168.

[288] See further J V McHale, 'Guidelines for Medical Research: Some Ethical and Legal Problems' [1993] 1 Med L Rev 160.

[289] *R v St Marys Hospital ex parte Harriot* [1988] 1FLR 512.

[290] I Kennedy and A Grubb, *Principles of Medical Law* (1st edn, Oxford University Press 1998) para 13.70.

[291] M Brazier, 'Liability of Ethics Committees and their Members' (1990) 6 Professional Negligence 186.

this participant suffered.[292] This is likely to be particularly difficult regarding the need to establish causation. Nonetheless, this is an issue which has caused and continues to cause concern within the research ethics community, not least because, while litigation may not necessarily be successful, that does not mean that such litigation may not be brought against research ethics committees and their members.[293]

The Clinical Trials Directive has now led to a reconsideration of the procedures for ensuring that research participants obtain compensation should something go wrong during a clinical trial. The role of the research sponsor is now enshrined in the RGF and, as noted above, RECs, in considering the trial protocol, should examine the availability of indemnity and compensation. In considering the whole area of compensation in the law of tort, the Pearson Commission, while rejecting generally the introduction of a no-fault compensation system in relation to the UK, nonetheless supported the introduction of a specific no-fault compensation system in relation to clinical trials.[294] This proposal was not taken up following the most recent recommendations on reforming the law of clinical negligence in the Chief Medical Officer's report 'Making Amends' in 2003, although these recommendations did pave the way for some resolution of clinical negligence actions outside the courtroom through the NHS Redress Act 2006[295] (see further discussion in Chapter 4). **13.109**

J. Conclusions

In the early 1990s the operation of RECs came under criticism. Neuberger, writing in 1992, commented that 'Some ethical committees are very good indeed but others are not. Overall the system is a mess'.[296] It is undoubtedly the case that, today, the systems in place for review of research protocols are infinitely superior than in 1992. The NHS research ethics system is more comprehensive and there have been greater attempts to standardize the process. The Clinical Trials Directive provided an important catalyst for reform. Provisions such as those of the Mental Capacity Act 2005 have considerably impacted upon this area and have provided some clarification of the position concerning research involving adults lacking mental capacity. Nonetheless, the proliferation of research ethics review has itself led to criticism. Proposals were made by the Ad Hoc Advisory Group on the Operation of NHS Research Ethics Committees in 2005 for reform, but these are yet to be implemented.[297] The Health Research Authority does represent an important statement; health research regulation has now been placed upon a statutory footing. There is a body at national level entrusted with its oversight and review and much potential to evolve and develop policy, and also to have an impact upon the evolution of structures here in the future.[298] **13.110**

---

[292] ibid.

[293] J V McHale, 'Liability in Tort of Research Ethics Committees and their Members' (2005) 1(2) Research Ethics Review 53.

[294] *The Royal Commission on Civil Liability for Personal Injury,* ch 24 'Medical Injury' at para 1341.

[295] Chief Medical Officer, *Making Amends: A Consultation Paper Setting out Proposals for Reforming the Approach to Clinical Negligence in the NHS* (DoH 2003).

[296] J Neuberger, *Ethics and Health Care; the Role of Research Ethics Committees in the UK* (Kings Fund Institute 1992).

[297] *Report of the Ad Hoc Advisory Group on the Operation of NHS Research Ethics Committees* (DoH 2005) and see A J Dawson, 'The Ad Hoc Advisory Group's Proposals for Research Ethics Committees: A Mixture of the Timid, the Revolutionary and the Bizarre' (2005) 31 Journal of Medical Ethics 435; R Ashcroft, 'Reforming Research Ethics Committees' (2005) 331 BMJ 587.

[298] See further J V McHale, 'Reforming the Regulation of Health Research in England and Wales: New Pitfalls and New Challenges' (2013) 1 Journal of Law Medicine and Ethics 23.

13.111 It had been envisaged that further reform of regulation in this area will soon follow the incorporation of the new EU Clinical Trials Regulation into English law.[299] This Regulation replaces the EU Clinical Trials Directive.[300] The aim of the Regulation was to address concerns relating to the operation of the Directive that it had inhibited rather than facilitated trial approval processes and increased costs and so forth in relation to multi-state trials.[301] Unlike its predecessor, it does not make approval by a research ethics committee itself mandatory, although in practice it is very unlikely that the use of research ethics committees will be abandoned, particularly given their mandatory use in other areas, such as human tissue and mental capacity and the fact too that scientific journals today routinely require that studies being considered for publication have been subject to ethics committee approval. The new Regulation is broader in scope than the Directive.[302] There will be new procedures to regulate the conduct of multi-state trials.[303] Perceived administrative inefficiencies will be addressed through a new single computer system for applications for clinical trials, which is to be linked to an EU database—an EU 'portal'. It is hoped that there will be greater clarity in oversight through the introduction of the concept of the 'reporting' Member State.[304] Some aspects will be similar to the position under the Directive. So some issues will require Member State cooperation, while other issues are devolved. Devolved matters will be issues referred to as 'national', such as questions of liability, issues such as compensation and indemnity, and ethical issues, such as informed consent; or, what is termed as 'local', for instance, whether a site for a particular trial is suitable. Separate provisions will, as at present, apply in relation to children and adults lacking mental capacity. One further change is that approval time limits will be much shorter. These will be typically ten days after an initial validation process. It has already been suggested that these will be unrealistic and in turn could lead to criticism of research ethics review if it is impossible to adhere to them.[305] The Regulation will also address the inclusion of individuals in research in emergency situations, something which was not included in the original Directive.[306] The movement from Directive to regulation signals further the intention to move towards centralization of regulation of clinical research across the EU, as opposed to the greater degree of discretion afforded to Member States by the Directive. It was originally envisaged that

[299] Proposal for a Regulation of the European Parliament and of the Council on clinical trials on medicinal products for human use and repealing Directive 2001/20/EU, 2012/0192 (COD). The legal basis for the regulation will be Article 114 TFEU and Article 168(4)(c) para 1.

[300] Regulation (EU) No 536/2014 of the European Parliament and of the Council of 16 April 2014 on clinical trials on medicinal products for human use, and repealing Directive 2001/20/EC.

[301] See 'Assessment of the functioning of the Clinical Trials Directive 2001/20/EC' Brussels 09/10/2009 <http://ec.europa.eu/health/files/clinicaltrials/docs/2009_10_09_public-consultation-paper.pdf>; 'Assessment of the functioning of the Clinical Trials Directive, 2001/20/EC: Summary of Responses to the Public Consultation Paper', Brussels 30/03/2010, <http://ec.europa.eu/health/files/clinicaltrials/2010_03_30_summary_responses.pdf>. And see further J Hearn and R Sullivan, 'The impact of the Clinical Trials Directive on the cost and conduct of non-commercial cancer trials in the UK' (2007) 43 European Journal of Cancer 8–13.

[302] Article 2.

[303] See further discussion in H Nys, 'New European Rules Regarding the Approval of Clinical Trials, the Role of Research Ethics Committees and the Protection of Subjects' (2012) 60 Arch Immunology Ther Exp 405; and T K Hervey and J V McHale, *European Health Law: Themes and Implications* (Cambridge University Press 2015).

[304] Article 5.

[305] See further Statement of the European Group on Ethics in Science and New Technologies on the Proposal for a Regulation of the European Parliament and the Council on Clinical Trials on Medicinal Products for Human Use and repealing Directive 2001/20/EC (COM 2012), 369 final, 2012/0192 (COD).

[306] Article 32.

this would be implemented in the UK in 2018.[307] However, at the time this book goes into production the question of whether this will in fact be implemented in the UK remains highly uncertain post- the UK EU Referendum in June 2016. It can be speculated that post-Brexit some adherence to EU clinical trials regulations may still be undertaken given that companies with bases in the UK who wish to market their pharmaceutical products within the EU would need to comply with the relevant EU regulation in this area. In this area as in relation to other parts of health law where there is an interface between domestic and EU law we await the political developments post-Brexit.

There is now a movement towards addressing concerns in the research community regarding the perceived regulatory burden caused by the establishment of research ethics committees. GAFREC itself now stresses the fact that review is 'proportionate to the scale and complexity of the research proposal'. [308] We saw above how the establishment of the Health Research Authority is forming part of this process. Nonetheless, while much has been done to regulate research, provide information for, and to engage researchers in particular over the last two decades in the UK, this is an area that is still under regulatory evolution and many challenges still remain. Currently, as has been seen in this chapter, regulation in this area remains complex and piecemeal, particularly when set alongside related issues such as the legal regulation of human material (see Chapter 19). Perhaps, in the long term, what is needed is to move towards a new comprehensive single statutory regulatory framework for research across England and Wales to provide greater clarity and protection for research ethics committees, research participants and regulatory agencies alike. **13.112**

[307] See further <http://www.hra.nhs.uk/resources/before-you-apply/types-of-study/clinical-trials-of-investigational-medicinal-products/clinical-trials-investigational-medicinal-products-ctimps-eu-legislation/>.

[308] GAFREC, para 3.2.4.

PART IV

14

MEDICALLY ASSISTED REPRODUCTION

Michael Freeman

A. Introduction

This chapter examines infertility, and the ways in which the law in England and Wales responds to the practices developed by scientists and the medical profession to alleviate the problem. **14.01**

Infertility has been defined as 'the involuntary, significant reduction of reproductive capacity'.[1] The standard medical definition of infertility is the failure to conceive after twelve months of regular, unprotected sexual intercourse, or the occurrence of three or more consecutive miscarriages or stillbirths.[2] But this definition is not, and no definition can be, precise. For example, there is evidence that about half of all couples who qualify as infertile on the twelve-month standard will conceive naturally during the following year.[3] And it has been suggested that the 'twelve month rule is a recent development, partly inspired by **14.02**

[1] *Per* Canadian Law Reform Commission, *Medically Assisted Procreation* (Working Paper 65, 1992). On 'why' people want children, specifically children produced by reproductive technologies, see K Lesnik-Oberstein. *On Making an Own Child* [Karnac 2008]. On whether there is a right to reproduce, see M Quigley, A right to Reproduce? [2014] 24 Bioethics 403–411.

[2] *Black's Medical Dictionary* (38th edn, 1995) 252.

[3] ER Te Velde, R Eijkemans, and HD Habbems, 'Variations in Couple Fecundity and Time to Pregnancy, and Essential Concept in Human Reproduction' (2000) 355 Lancet 1928–29.

"infertility specialists" marketing experimental and expensive new reproductive technologies'.[4] Treatment services may be sought, of course, by those who are not infertile: examples are persons with genetic disease,[5] homosexual couples,[6] individuals with no sexual partner, long-term prisoners,[7] women who fear sexual intercourse, women who wish to postpone pregnancy and want embryos to be created and frozen for later use when they may be past the height of their fertility. It may also be sought by those who in past times would have accepted their infertility, notably post-menopausal women.[8]

14.03 In the UK, previous NICE guidelines define infertility as a failure to conceive after regular unprotected sexual intercourse for two years in the absence of known reproductive pathology.[9]

14.04 Estimates vary as to the incidence of infertility. At the time of the Warnock Inquiry (in the early 1980s), 'a commonly quoted figure [was] that one couple in ten [was] childless'.[10] It, however, conceded that accurate statistics were not available, and noted that the proportion of this figure relating to couples who chose not to have children was not known. Higher estimates have been suggested elsewhere,[11] and it may be that as many as one in seven couples will experience infertility at some stage in, what would be, their normal reproductive lives. Even the 10 per cent estimate would mean 50,000 or so new cases of infertility in Britain each year. Worldwide it is estimated that between 8 and 12 per cent of reproductive aged couples have an unexplained problem of infertility.[12] It is thought that fertility problems affect one in seven couples in the UK.[13]

14.05 Questions might also arise as to whether treatment services should be made available to all forms of fertility compromise. IVF was originally used for inoperably blocked fallopian tubes. In Denmark, Lee and Morgan point out,[14] it was largely confined to such treatment. In the UK 'it is also indicated in endometriosis, ovulation disorders, anti-sperm antibodies and male infertilities, many of which . . . are socially or environmentally caused'.[15] There have been discussions as to whether infertility is an illness.[16] These are now effectively foreclosed as a result of the recommendation of the National Institute for Health and Clinical Excellence (NICE) that at least some infertility treatment should be publicly funded.[17]

14.06 Most infertility treatment fails. Most couples who undergo fertility treatment remain childless. Success rates of clinics relate to a number of variables: not only the skill and expertise

[4] S Faludi, *Backlash: The Undeclared War Against Women* (Chatto and Windus 1992) 47.

[5] See HFEA, *Tenth Annual Report and Accounts* (HFEA 2002) 7.

[6] See <http://www.nhs.uk/Livewell/LGBhealth/Pages/Havingchildren.aspx> and <http://www.telegraph.co.uk/news/health/news/9872984/More-IVF-for-gay-couples-and-over-40s-on-the-NHS.html>.

[7] Though in a case involving a long-term prisoner, *R v Secretary of State for the Home Department, ex p Mellor* (2000) 59 BMLR 1, medically assisted reproduction was not in issue.

[8] About 100 women over 50 are treated at UK clinics each year: *Daily Telegraph* (8 May 2006).

[9] Previous guidelines did not include a specific definition, but recommended that 'A woman of reproductive age who has not conceived after one year of unprotected vaginal sexual intercourse, in the absence of any known cause of infertility, should be offered further clinical assessment and investigation along with her partner, with referral to a specialist if [she] is over 36 years of age.'

[10] See *Report of the Committee of Inquiry into Human Fertilisation and Embryology* (Cmnd 9314, 1953) para 2.1.

[11] Other estimates put it as high as one in six. Some evidence of the causes of male infertility is found in N Jorgensen et al, 'Regional Differences In Semen Quality in Europe' (2001) 16 Human Reproduction 1012.

[12] Ombelet W et al, 'Infertility and the provision of infertility medical services in developing countries' (2008) 14 Human Reprod Update 605–21.

[13] See <http://www.nhs.uk/conditions/Infertility/Pages/Introduction.aspx>.

[14] R G Lee and D Morgan, *Human Fertilisation and Embryology-Regulating: The Reproductive Revolution* (Blackstone 2001) 44.

[15] ibid. On environmental influences see R F A Weber et al, 'Environmental Influences on Male Reproduction' (2002) 89 British Journal of Urology International 143.

[16] On what is, see A Stark, *The Limits of Medicine* (Cambridge University Press 2006).

[17] It has been estimated that full implementation of NICE's proposals would cost £100m a year: *The Guardian* (26 August 2003).

of the clinicians but also 'political' decisions as to whom to treat, the types of infertility to be treated, the risks particular clinics are prepared to take. League tables indicating success rates must thus be viewed cautiously (if not cynically). Robert Winston has expressed the opinion that the very presence of such tables encourages 'a few clinics to be "somewhat economical with the truth"'.[18] According to the data collected by the Human Fertilisation and Embryology Authority[19] the live birth rate per treatment cycle of IVF in 2010 was 32.2 per cent for women aged under 35. It is less successful for older women. For women aged between 35–37 it is 27.7 per cent. For women aged between 38–39 it is 26.8 per cent. For women aged between 40–42 it is 13.6 per cent. For women aged between 43–44 it is 5 per cent. For women aged 45 and over it is 1.9 per cent. More than 250,000 babies have been born in the UK as a result of IVF.[20] For micromanipulation techniques (intracytoplasmic sperm injection is the most commonly used method), the success rate is very similar. For Donor Insemination (DI) (including gamete intra-fallopian transfer (GIFT)) it was only 9.9 per cent. In more than one quarter of cases where a live birth results from IVF or micromanipulation there is a multiple birth.[21] It is estimated that 30 per cent of the causes of infertility can be attributed to men, 60 per cent to women, and 10 per cent to both.

There are a large number of techniques which have been developed—and continue to develop—for treating the infertile. These range from donor insemination (DI or AID as it was once called), which has existed for more than a century[22] to surrogacy, which has claims (dubious it must be said) to biblical roots.[23] It was with the development of *in vitro* fertilization (IVF) in the 1970s[24] that medically assisted reproduction has come to concern policy-makers throughout much of the world.[25] Other technologies which are used, and which will be discussed in this chapter, are cryopreservation, assisted insemination by a husband or partner, oocyte donation, gamete intra-fallopian transfer, and micromanipulation (intracytoplasmic sperm injection and subzonal insemination). Cloning—the use of which in the treatment of infertility has been prohibited—is discussed in the next chapter. **14.07**

1. The Warnock Report

The Warnock Inquiry had its precursors. There were inquiries into DI shortly after the Second World War (the Fisher Report[26] recommended it should be criminalized), and in the late 1950s the Feversham Committee, [27] which reported in 1960, concluded that AID was an undesirable practice to be discouraged. A more positive response was made in the Peel Report in 1973:[28] AID should, it recommended, be available at accredited NHS centres **14.08**

[18] *The IVF Revolution: The Definitive Guide to Assisted Reproductive Techniques* (Vermillion 1999), 163.

[19] Human Fertilisation and Embryology Authority, *Ninth Annual Report and Accounts* (HFEA 2000) 12, table 4.1.

[20] See <https://www.theguardian.com/society/2016/nov/04/more-than-250000-uk-babies-born-ivf> (November 2016).

[21] ibid, 27.3 per cent and 26.9 percent respectively.

[22] There is a claim that the first human donor insemination was in the US in 1884: see R Snowden and G D Mitchell, *The Artificial Family* (Unwin 1983) 13.

[23] See P Singer and D Wells, *New Ways of Making Babies: The Reproduction Revolution* (Oxford University Press 1984) 107–08, citing Genesis 16 (the story of Abram and Sarai).

[24] Louise Brown, the first 'test-tube' baby, was born in 1978. On justice and assisted reproduction see A Donchin [2011] 25 Bioethics 92–101.

[25] See S A M McLean, *Law Reform and Human Reproduction* (Dartmouth 1992); Bonnicksen, AL, *In Vitro Fertilisation: Building Policy from Laboratories to Legislatures* (Columbia University Press 1989).

[26] *Artificial Human Insemination: the Report of a Committee appointed by his Grace the Archbishop of Canterbury* (SPCK 1948).

[27] Home Office and Scottish Department, *Departmental Committee on Human Artificial Insemination* (Cmnd 1105, 1960).

[28] British Medical Association, *Annual Report of the Council*, Appendix V: Report of the Panel on Human Artificial Insemination, *British Medical Journal Supplement*, 7 April 1973, vol II, 3–5. On

for those for whom it was appropriate. But the report led to nothing and no system of accreditation was established. Modern thinking on assisted reproduction begins with the Warnock Report. [29] The Warnock Inquiry was established in 1982 'to consider recent and potential developments in medicine and science related to human fertilization and embryology; to consider what policies and safeguards should be applied, including consideration of the social, ethical and legal implications of these developments; and to make recommendations'.[30] The committee reported in 1984. It took the view that 'actions taken with the intention of overcoming infertility can, as a rule, be regarded as acceptable substitutes for natural fertilization'.[31] Infertility was not to be seen as 'something mysterious, nor a cause of shame, nor necessarily something that has to be endured without attempted cure'.[32] It is, the Inquiry concluded, 'a condition meriting treatment',[33] and, in the light of its analysis, it recommended statutory regulation of medically assisted reproduction. The Warnock Report was predicated upon the assumption that fertility services would be integrated into the NHS (itself a different creature from what it is now). The commercial potential of fertility services was not foreseen. The problems engendered by commercialization were barely addressed in the Warnock Report.[34] Ironically, within months of publication the 'first' commercial surrogacy created a moral panic[35]—and legislation[36]—and alerted the public to issues of commercialization and commodification which barely surfaced in the Warnock Report.[37]

14.09 Although the Warnock Report was debated both in the House of Lords and in the House of Commons in 1984,[38] the Human Fertilisation and Embryology Bill, largely based on it, was not introduced to Parliament until 1989. In the meantime there were two Private Member's Bills,[39] both of which had substantial support (in 1985 and 1986 respectively), which, if passed, would have put an end not just to embryo research, their primary target, but also to most IVF treatment. The relatively liberal 1990 Act might have been derailed had it not been for the Progress Educational Trust (established in November 1985), which successfully worked to increase public understanding of the benefits of embryo research and infertility treatment, and for the fortuitous announcement of successful preimplantation sex diagnosis to prevent the birth of a child suffering from a sex-limited genetic disorder some five days before the House of Commons voted on the Human Fertilisation and Embryology Bill.[40]

---

public funding for assisted reproduction and the appeal to nature implicit in restrictions, see Carter and Braunack-Mayer, 'The Appeal to Nature Implicit in Certain Restrictions on Public Funding for Assisted Reproductive Technology' [2011] 25 Bioethics 463–71.

[29] *Report of the Inquiry into Human Fertilisation and Embryology* (Cmnd 9314, 1984) ('the Warnock Report'), subsequently reprinted with an introduction by the chairwoman as *A Question of Life* (Basil Blackwell 1985). See also M Warnock, *Making Babies* (Oxford University Press 2002).

[30] Warnock Report, n 29, para 1.2.

[31] ibid, para 2.4.

[32] ibid, para 2.4.

[33] ibid, para 2.4.

[34] Outside the context of surrogacy.

[35] See C Dyer, 'Baby Cotton and the Birth of a Moral Panic', *The Guardian* (15 January 1985), and A Hutchinson and D Morgan, 'A Bill Born from Panic', *The Guardian* (12 July 1985).

[36] Surrogacy Arrangements Act 1985.

[37] See M Brazier, 'Regulating the Reproduction Business' (1999) 7 Med L Rev 166, 191. cf N Duxbury, 'Do Markets Degrade?' (1996) 59 MLR 331. See also G Annas, *Some Choice—Law, Medicine and the Market* (Oxford University Press 1998).

[38] See *Hansard*, HL vol 456, cols 524–93; HC vol 68, cols 547–90.

[39] See further M Mulkay, *The Embryo Research Debate: Science and the Politics of Reproduction* (Cambridge University Press 1997), 24–29.

[40] ibid. See also S Franklin, 'Making Representations: The Parliamentary Debate on the Human Fertilisation and Embryology Act and Orphaned Embryos' in J Edwards, S Franklin, E Hirsch, F Price, and M Strathern et al, *Technologies of Procreation: Kinship in the Age of Assisted Conception* (Routledge 1999), 127.

2. History of regulation

One immediate response to the Warnock Report was the establishment by the Medical Research Council and the Royal College of Obstetricians and Gynaecologists of the Voluntary Licensing Authority in 1985. This was subsequently (in 1989) called the Interim Licensing Authority. This body instituted a self-regulatory mechanism for licensing infertility treatment and research on human embryos and gametes. The Voluntary/Interim Licensing Authority operated for six years, approved IVF centres, and licensed research projects. It established voluntary guidelines for such research work, including provisions for donor consent and prior ethical committee approval of the work.[41] It ceased to exist on 1 August 1991 when the Human Fertilisation and Embryology Act 1990 came into force. This established the Human Fertilisation and Embryology Authority. In July 2010 it was announced that the Human Fertilisation and Embryology Authority was to be abolished by 2015.[42] However, following an independent review by Justin McCracken in 2012, the government announced in July 2013 that, 'in order to ensure maintenance of public confidence', the HFEA will be retained as the independent regulator of assisted reproduction and embryo research across the UK.[43] **14.10**

The Human Fertilisation and Embryology Act 1990 (the 1990 Act) regulated infertility treatments that involved the use of donated genetic material, whether sperm, eggs, or embryos, or those that involve the creation of an embryo outside the human body. It does not apply to GIFT[44] (even though this is more likely to result in multiple pregnancy[45] and even though 'stimulation of ovulation *without* IVF is almost certainly the most dangerous of any reproductive treatment').[46] Whether the justification for this omission is clinical freedom, as the then Lord Chancellor, Lord Mackay of Clashfern argued,[47] or the desire to limit expense, as Lee and Morgan suggest,[48] or a combination of these two factors, is immaterial. The end result is that the Act failed to address a major infertility technique. And, concomitantly focused—some might say over-focused[49]—on another, namely IVF. **14.11**

In addition, the 1990 Act regulated the storage of all genetic material, and therefore most obviously cryopreservation. The 1990 Act was not directly concerned with the practice of surrogacy. Only in so far as a surrogate birth is effectuated through the use, in part or whole, of donated genetic material or using IVF techniques was the framework of the 1990 Act applicable. The moral panic fanned by the birth of 'Baby Cotton' in January 1985[50] resulted in an attempt to regulate the practice of surrogacy in legislation passed in 1985 (the Surrogacy Arrangements Act[51]). The 1990 Act effected some amendments to this and **14.12**

---

[41] On its work, see J Gunning and V English, *Human In Vitro Fertilisation* (Dartmouth 1993).

[42] See V Raper, 'New Breed of Fertility Watchdog on Way' *Bionews* (26 July 2010) 568. See also 'HFEA and Health Policy Agency Quangos Face Abolition or Mergers' *The Times* (26 July 2010). Primary legislation will be required: see E Harris, 'The Demise of HFEA—Don't Lament—or Celebrate—Too Soon, It May Never Happen' *Bionews* (2 August 2010) 569.

[43] Department of Health, *Response to the Review of the HFEA and HTA* (July 2013) located at <https://www.gov.uk/government/uploads/system/uploads/attachment_data/file/216946/Government_Response_to_the_report_of_the_independent_review_of_the_HFEAand_HTA_Final.pdf>.

[44] No embryo is created or kept outside a woman's body: see the 1990 Act, s 1(3).

[45] As observed by M Brazier, 'Reproductive Rights: Feminism or Patriarchy?', in J Harris and Holm, S (eds), *The Future of Human Reproduction* (Clarendon Press 1998), 68. Because it is not regulated, more than three eggs can be transferred during a cycle of treatment.

[46] n 14 above, 145.

[47] *Hansard*, HL vol 516, col 1089.

[48] Lee and Morgan, n 14 above, 13.

[49] This is Lord Winston's view: n 14 above.

[50] Reported as *Re C* (1985) FLR 846. A more personal account is Cotton, K and Winn, D, *Baby Cotton: For Love or Money* (Dorling Kindersley, 1985). See Carlos A Ball, *The Right to be Parents* (New York University Press 2002).

[51] On which see M D A Freeman, 'After Warnock: Whither The Law?' (1986) 39 CLP 33, 37–48.

made it clear that surrogacy agreements are unenforceable.[52] But surrogacy is best treated distinctly from other techniques for the relief of infertility, and accordingly is given a separate section later in this chapter.

14.13 There is broad agreement that the 1990 Act worked well. But inevitably there was a need to bring in new legislation to keep abreast of rapid scientific developments and changing public attitudes. Some changes were effected by regulation. For example, within a year of the 1990 Act the maximum storage period for gametes was extended.[53] And in 2007 regulation allowed licences to be made available for non-medical fertility services.[54] There was also legislation: in 2001 the Human Reproductive Cloning Act criminalized any attempt to create a child through any process other than fertilization using sperm and egg.[55]

14.14 However, it had become obvious that new legislation was required, and the Human Fertilisation and Embryology Act 2008 (the 2008 Act) is the result of this thinking. There was a Public Consultation in 2005,[56] and a White Paper followed in December 2006,[57] in which the government set out the aims of the new legislation. These are: (i) to ensure that legitimate applications of human reproductive technologies continue to flourish; (ii) to promote public confidence in the development of human reproductive technologies; and (iii) to secure that regulation accords with better regulation principles and to encourage best regulatory practices.

14.15 A draft Bill (Human Tissue and Embryo (Draft) Bill) was published in May 2007. This was subjected to scrutiny by a Joint Committee of both Houses.[58] It heard evidence from a wide range of organizations. The Joint Committee report was published in August 2007, and responded to by the Government in October 2007.[59] A new Bill, with substantial changes, and now entitled the Human Fertilisation and Embryology Bill, was introduced in November 2007. It received Royal Assent a year later.

14.16 Much of the Bill proved controversial. As the Parliamentary Under-Secretary for the Department of Health, Lord Darzi of Denham, acknowledged when moving the Bill, 'Sincerely held views and opinions differ widely, and sometimes fundamentally, in this area'. And he agreed that: 'We are navigating strong currents of reproductive freedom and responsibility, patient safety, public accountability and professional autonomy, and questions of how best to safeguard the welfare of children.'[60]

14.17 Amongst the principal areas of controversy were human admixed embryos,[61] saviour siblings,[62] and the welfare provision, in particular the proposal to remove from this the need to consider whether the child would have a father.[63] Much of the opposition spoke

---

[52] See para 14.249.

[53] Human Fertilisation and Embryology (Statutory Storage Period) Regulations 1991, SI 1991/1540.

[54] Human Fertilisation and Embryology (Quality and Safety) Regulations 2007, SI 2007/1522.

[55] See Human Reproductive Cloning Act, s I. It created a maximum sentence of ten years' imprisonment.

[56] Department of Health, *Review of the Human Fertilisation and Embryology Act—A Public Consultation* (DoH 2005).

[57] *Review of the Human Fertilisation and Embryology Act: Proposals for Revised Legislation (Including Establishment of the Regulatory Authority for Tissues and Embryos)* (Cm 6989, December 2006).

[58] *First Report from the Joint Committee on the Human Tissue and Embryos (Draft) Bill*, (HC 630, 2006–07).

[59] Cm 7139.

[60] *Hansard*, 19 November 2007, col 663, 664.

[61] eg Geraldine Smith MP, ibid, col 1098.

[62] There was concern that . . . would be created 'just for spare parts', *Hansard*, HC 12 May 2008, eg John Robertson MP, col 1069. See also Andrew Lansley MP at col 1096.

[63] See ibid, eg Andrew Lansley MP at col 1079; Gerald Howarth MP at col 1096.

in exaggerated language about 'Frankenstein Monsters', creating children as 'spare parts', and lesbians availing themselves of fertility treatment.[64] There were also attempts (in 1990 they were successful) to attach abortion reform to the legislation: this was unsuccessful. There was some debate also on the restriction imposed by the government—contrary to the recommendation of NICE—to permit only one cycle of IVF treatment at public expense. NICE had recommended three.[65]

The Act was passed in November 2008. The provisions relating to parenting came into operation in April 2009; the remainder of the Act in October 2009. The Human Fertilisation and Embryology Authority published its accompanying Code of Practice (its 8th such Code) in July 2009, which has been subject to later revisions. **14.18**

B. The Human Fertilisation and Embryology Authority

1. Establishment of the Authority

The 1990 Act established the Human Fertilisation and Embryology Authority (HFEA).[66] This is a body corporate, and consists of a chairman and deputy chairman, and such number of the other members as the Secretary of State appoints. There is no limit on the number of members who may be appointed.[67] In making appointments the Secretary of State is to have regard to the desirability of ensuring that the proceedings of the authority, and the discharge of its functions, are informed by the views of both men and women.[68] S/he must also ensure that there is a majority of members who are neither doctors nor research scientists.[69] Neither the chairman nor deputy chairman may come from either of these professional groups. The first two chairs were both academic lawyers/university heads (Sir Colin Campbell, the Vice-Chancellor of the University of Nottingham and Ruth Deech (now Baroness Deech), the Principal of St Anne's College, Oxford). The third, appointed in 2002, was Suzi Leather (now Dame Suzi Leather). The fourth was Shirley Harrison, the fifth was Professor Lisa Jardine of Queen Mary, University of London, and the current permanent chair is Sally Cheshire. **14.19**

Appointments to HFEA are for renewable periods of three years.[70] A member can resign his or her office at any time by giving notice to the Secretary of State.[71] The Secretary of State may also decide that a member should vacate his or her position.[72] An appointed member may be removed from office if he or she: **14.20**

(a) has been absent from meetings of the Authority for six consecutive months or longer without the permission of the Authority; or
(b) is unable or unfit to discharge the function of a member.[73]

---

64 In 2006 1.4 per cent of the 40,484 IVF treatments were for single women, and 0.5 per cent were for 'registered' lesbians, ie 560 single women and 200 lesbians in one year. See Norman Lamb MP, ibid, col 1089.

65 And see Dari Taylor MP, ibid, at col 1092.

66 1990 Act, s 5. The Authority has been criticized by the House of Commons Science and Technology Committee, *On Developments In Human Genetics and Embryology, Fourth Report of Session 2001–2002*, (HC 791). Now with its imminent demise (see para 14.10), strong defences are being offered: see, eg, R Deech, 'How Not to Save Money: Unscrambling the HFEA' *Bionews* (9 August 2010) 570.

67 1990 Act, s 5(2).

68 ibid, Sch 1, para 4(2).

69 ibid, Sch 1, para 4(4).

70 ibid, Sch 1, para 5(2).

71 ibid,Sch 1, para 5(3).

72 ibid, Sch 1, para 5(5).

73 ibid, Sch 1, para 5(5).

A person is disqualified from being appointed as chair, deputy chair, or as any other member of the Authority if:

(a) he is the subject of a bankruptcy restrictions order or interim order;
(b) a bankruptcy order has been made against him by a court in Northern Ireland or his estate has been sequestrated by a Court in Scotland, or under the laws of either of those countries he has made a composition or arrangement with, or granted a trust deed for, his creditors; or
(c) in the last five years has been convicted in the United Kingdom, the Channel Islands, or the Isle of Man of an offence and has had a qualifying sentence passed on him.[74]

Appointments are to be made on merit[75] and not in order that particular groups should be represented.

14.21 The Authority is not a servant or agent of the Crown, and does not enjoy any status, privilege, or immunity of the Crown.[76] It has the power to do anything which is calculated to facilitate the discharge of its functions, or is incidental or conducive to their discharge, except the power to borrow money.[77]

2. Functions of HFEA

14.22 The principal functions of HFEA are:

(i) to license treatment services, the storage of gametes and embryos, and research on embryos;[78]
(ii) to monitor and inspect premises and activities carried out under statutory licence;[79]
(iii) to submit an annual report to the Secretary of State on its activities;[80]
(iv) to maintain a code of practice as guidance for the proper conduct of activities carried out under a licence (eight editions of this have been published).[81]

In addition, it has the following 'general functions':[82]

(i) to keep under review information about embryos and any subsequent development of embryos and about the provision of treatment services and activities governed by the Act, and advise the Secretary of State, if s/he asks it to do so, about these matters;
(ii) to publicize the services it provides or which are provided in pursuance of licences it grants;
(iii) to provide, to such extent as it considers appropriate, advice and information for persons to whom licences apply or who are receiving treatment services or providing gametes or embryos for use for the purposes of activities governed by the Act, or may wish to do so (it may charge a fee for any advice provided);[83]
(iv) to maintain a statement of general principles which it considers should be followed, in the carrying on of activities governed by the Act, and in the carrying out of its functions in relation to such activities;[84]

[74] ibid, New Sch 1. para 4A.
[75] Following Nolan guidelines.
[76] 1990 Act, Sch 1, para 1.
[77] ibid, Sch 1, para 2.
[78] ibid, s 11.
[79] ibid, s 9.
[80] ibid, s 7.
[81] ibid, s 25.
[82] ibid, s 8(1).
[83] ibid, s 8(2) (inserted by 2008 Act).
[84] ibid, s 8(1)(ca).

(v) to promote, in relation to activities governed by the Act, compliance with the requirements imposed by or under the Act, and the Code of Practice under section 23 of the Act;[85]
(vi) to perform such other functions as may be specified in regulations.

HFEA may be called upon to advise the Secretary of State on any of these functions. Note they are widely drafted. For example, 'any subsequent development of embryos' could place a review of abortion services within HFEA's remit, perhaps even the scope of abortion law. Hitherto, however, the 'general functions' have been interpreted narrowly and such 'review' has been limited to embryos produced as a result of reproductive services. **14.23**

The Authority must carry out its functions 'effectively, efficiently and economically'.[86] It must have regard to the 'principles of best regulatory practice'.[87] **14.24**

It can contract out functions.[88] It may not contract out functions that can only be exercised by members of the Authority[89] or functions excluded by order of the Secretary of State.[90] It cannot contract out decisions relating to the grant, revocation or variation of any licence, or relating to a power or right of entry, search, or seizure of any property.[91] **14.25**

The Authority has a duty to collect data from licensed treatments, and to keep a register of them.[92] The Act provides that the register shall include information relating to: **14.26**

(a) the provision of any identifiable individual or treatment services other than basic partner treatment services;[93]
(b) the procurement or distribution of any sperm, other than sperm which is partner-donated sperm and has not been shared, in the case of providing non-medical fertility services for any identifiable individual;
(c) the keeping of the gametes of any identifiable individual or of an embryo taken from any identifiable woman;[94]
(d) the use of the gametes of any identifiable individual other than their use for the purpose of basic partner treatment services;
(e) the use of an embryo taken from any identifiable woman, or if it shows that any identifiable individual is a relevant individual.[95]

HFEA has a rule as regards the formation of policy. An example is the issue of multiple births. HFEA has formed a multiple birth policy and minimization strategy in 2009 which aims to lower the average national multiple birth rate from its current rate of 24 per cent (of all live birth events following IVF/ ICSI) to 10 per cent over a number of years.[96] As a result, all clinics must have a 'multiple birth policy', which sets out how they intend to reduce their annual multiple birth rates and to ensure that they do not exceed the HFEA-set maximum figure. **14.27**

85 ibid, s 8(1)(cb).
86 ibid, s 8ZA(1).
87 ibid, s 8ZA(2).
88 ibid, s 8C.
89 ibid, s 8C(1)(a).
90 ibid, s 8C(1)(c).
91 ibid, s 8C(2).
92 ibid, s 31(1).
93 ibid, s 31(2)(a) (as amended).
94 ibid, s 31(2)(c) (as amended).
95 ibid, s 31(2)(e) (as amended).
96 Chair's Letter, September 2008, CH(08)03

C. Licensing

1. Types of licence

14.28 The 1990 Act (as amended) provides that HFEA may grant any one of four types of licence authorizing:

(i) activities in the course of providing treatment services;[97]
(ii) activities in the course of providing non-medical fertility services;[98]
(iii) the storage of gametes, embryos, or human admixed embryos;[99]
(iv) activities for the purpose of a project of research.[100]

14.29 In the course of providing treatment services a licence may authorize any of the following:[101]

(i) bringing about the creation of embryos *in vitro*;
(ii) procuring, keeping, testing, processing, or distributing embryos;
(iii) procuring, testing, processing, distributing, or using gametes;
(iv) using embryos for the purpose of training persons in embryo biopsy, embryo storage, or other embryological technologies (HFEA must be satisfied that the proposed use of embryos is necessary for that purpose).
(v) practices designed to secure that embryos are in a suitable condition to be placed in a woman;
(vi) placing any permitted embryo in a woman;
(vii) mixing sperm with the egg of a hamster, or other animal specified in directions, for the purpose of testing the fertility or normality of the sperm, but only where anything which forms is destroyed when the test is complete and, in any event, not later than the two cell stage; and
(viii) such other practices as may be specified in, or determined in accordance with, regulations. This is apart from practices such as mixing human gametes with animal gametes, bringing about the creation of a human admixed embryo or keeping or using a human admixed embryo except in pursuance of a licence (discussed at 14.41–14.42, 14.46).

14.30 A licence may be granted subject to such conditions as may be specified.[102] A licence cannot authorize any activity unless it appears to HFEA to be 'necessary or desirable' for the purpose of providing treatment services.[103] A licence cannot be granted for a period of more that five years.[104] In 1995 HFEA advocated that this period should be reduced where the treatment clinic applying for renewal had not radically changed since the last inspection or committee decision.[105]

14.31 The circumstances in which embryos can be tested in pursuance of a treatment licence are:

(i) to establish whether an embryo has a gene, chromosome, or mitochondrion abnormality that may affect its capacity to result in a live birth;[106]

---

97 1990 Act, s 11(1)(a) and Sch 2, para 2.
98 ibid, s 11(1)(aa).
99 ibid, s 11(1)(b).
100 ibid, s 11(1)(c) and Sch 2, para 3.
101 ibid, Sch 2, para 1(1).
102 See generally ibid, Sch 2, para 1(2).
103 ibid, Sch 2, para 1(3).
104 ibid, Sch 2, para 1(5).
105 See HFEA, *Fourth Annual Report*.
106 1990 Act, Sch 2, para 1ZA(1)(a) (as amended).

(ii) where there is a risk of such genetic abnormality, to establish whether it has that abnormality, or any other gene, chromosome, or mitochondrial abnormality.[107] But only if the Authority is satisfied that in relation to the abnormality for which there is a particular risk and also any other abnormality for which testing is to be authorized that there is a 'significant risk that a person with the abnormality will have or develop a serious physical or mental disability; a serious illness or any other serious medical condition';[108]

(iii) to establish the sex of an embryo, where there is a particular risk that the resulting child will have or develop a gender-related serious or physical or mental disability, serious illness, or other gender-related serious medical condition.[109] A disability, illness, and condition is 'gender-related' if the Authority is satisfied that it affects only one sex or one sex significantly more than the other.[110]

Sex selection is thus permitted for conditions like muscular dystrophy and breast cancer (where a mother does not wish to pass the possibility of this to a daughter, and this genetic condition is prevalent in the family). It is not permitted for social reasons (see para 14.33): **14.32**

(i) to establish whether the embryo would result in a child whose tissue was compatible with that of an existing child.[111] The embryo is often referred to as a 'saviour sibling'.[112] This has provoked controversy. The House of Lords ruled in *Quintavalle (on behalf of Comment on Reproductive Ethics) v HFEA* that a licence could be granted for such treatment,[113] and this is now confirmed by the 2008 legislation[114] (see further Chapter 15, paras 15.42–15.47). The 2008 Act permits this where a person suffers from a 'serious medical condition which could be treated by umbilical cord blood stem cells, bone marrow, or other tissue of any resulting child'. 'Other tissue' does not include a reference to any 'whole organ' of the child, thus ruling out the use of 'spare parts' surgery.

(ii) where uncertainty has arisen as to whether the embryo is one of these whose creation was brought about by using the gametes of particular persons, to establish whether it is.[115]

The policy of the Authority has always been to refuse to allow sex selection techniques to be used, other than for medical reasons. This position is affirmed in the 2008 Act. This states: 'A licence . . . cannot authorize any practice designed to secure that any resulting child will be of one sex rather than the other'.[116] But this provision is subject to the exceptions stated in Sch 2, para 1ZB (inserted by the 2008 Act, s 11(2), Sch 2, para 1ZA).[117] So it is re-emphasized that embryo testing which is permitted under Sch 2 is not prevented by the ban on sex selection testing, where there is a particular risk that a woman will give birth to a child who will have or develop a gender-related serious physical or mental disability, serious illness, or any other gender-related serious medical condition.[118] **14.33**

[107] ibid, Sch 2, para 1ZA(1)(b) (as amended).
[108] ibid, Sch 2, para 1ZA(2) (as amended).
[109] ibid, Sch 2, para 1ZA(1)(c) (as amended).
[110] ibid, Sch 2, para 1ZA(3) (as amended).
[111] ibid, Sch 2, para 1ZA(1)(d) (as amended).
[112] On which see M Freeman, 'Saviour Siblings' in S A M McLean (ed), *First Do No Harm* (Ashgate 2006), 389–406. On saviour siblings dilemmas, K Strong et al [2014] 28 Bioethics 187–93 may be consulted.
[113] [2005] 2 All ER 555.
[114] 1990 Act, Sch 2, para 1ZA(1)(d) and(4) (as amended).
[115] ibid, Sch 2, para 1ZA(1)(e) (as amended).
[116] ibid, Sch 2, para 1ZB(1) (as amended).
[117] ibid, Sch 2, para 1ZB(2) (as amended).
[118] ibid, Sch 2, para 1ZB(3),(4) (as amended).

14.34 There is power to amend para 1ZA by regulation.[119] This includes amendment to the sex selection provisions if this appears to the Secretary of State to be 'necessary or expedient' as a consequence of amendments to para 1ZA.[120] But regulations may not enable the authorization of the testing of embryos for the purpose of establishing their sex or other practices falling within para 1ZB, except on grounds relating to the health of any resulting child.[121] 'Amend' includes 'add to' as well as 'repeal'.[122]

14.35 There is a new provision in the 2008 Act (inserting a sub-para 1A into Sch 2 of the 1990 Act). This deals with licences for non-medical fertility services. It provides that a licence may authorize procuring sperm and distributing sperm in the course of providing non-medical fertility services.[123] But a licence cannot authorize the procurement or distribution of sperm to which there has been applied any process designed to secure that any resulting child will be of one sex rather than the other.[124] This rules out the possibility of using sperm sorting for sex selection purposes.[125]

14.36 The duration of the licence is for such period specified in the licence, but it must not exceed five years.[126]

14.37 There are record-keeping requirements. No information is to be removed from any records maintained in pursuance of the licence before the expiry of such period as may be specified in directions for records of the class in question.[127] Where the 'person' responsible (see paras 14.49, 14.55) does not know if any child was born following treatment, the information must be retained for not less than fifty years from when it was first recorded (under s 24(1) of the 1990 Act). The information to be recorded is set out in s 13(2). This lists:

(a) the persons for whom services are provided in pursuance of the licence;
(b) the services provided for them;
(c) the persons whose gametes are kept or used for the purpose of the services provided in pursuance of the licence or whose gametes have been used in bringing about the creation of embryos so kept or used;
(d) any child appearing to the person responsible to have been born as a result of treatment in pursuance of the licence;
(e) any mixing of egg and sperm and any taking of an embryo from a woman or other acquisition of an embryo;[128]
(f) any consent that is required under Sch 3.[129]

Other matters may be specified by the Authority in directions.

14.38 A licence for the purposes of research may authorize the bringing about of the creation of embryos *in vitro* and the keeping or using of embryos,[130] but it cannot authorize any activity unless it appears to HFEA 'to be necessary or desirable'[131] for the purposes of a project of research specified in the licence.

---

[119] ibid, Sch 2, para 1ZC(1) (as amended).
[120] ibid, Sch 2, para 1ZC(2) (as amended).
[121] ibid, Sch 2, para 1ZC(3) (as amended).
[122] ibid, Sch 2, para 1ZC(4) (as amended).
[123] ibid, Sch 2, para 1A(1) (as amended).
[124] ibid, Sch 2, para 1(1A) (as amended).
[125] And see HFEA, Code of Practice (8th edn), 10.15–10.16.
[126] 1990 Act, Sch 2, para 1(5).
[127] ibid, s 13(4) (as amended).
[128] ibid, s 13(2)(a)–(e) (as amended).
[129] ibid, s 13(3) (as amended).
[130] So long as they have not developed a primitive streak (ibid, s 3(3)(a),(4)).
[131] 1990 Act, Sch 2, para 1(3) (as amended).

14.39 A licence cannot authorize any activity unless the activity appears to the Authority to be necessary or desirable for any of the principal purposes set out in the Act.[132] These are:

(a) to increase knowledge about serious diseases or other serious conditions;
(b) to increase knowledge about the causes of any congenital diseases or congenital medical condition, which does not fall into the category of serious disease or serious medical condition;
(c) to promote advances in the treatment of infertility;
(d) to increase knowledge about the causes of miscarriage;
(e) to develop more effective techniques of contraception;
(f) to develop methods for detecting the presence of gene, chromosome, or mitochondrion abnormalities in embryos before implantation; or
(g) to increase knowledge about the development of embryos.[133]

14.40 A licence may authorize mixing sperm with the egg of a hamster (or another animal specified in directions) in order to develop more effective techniques for detecting the fertility or normality of sperm, but only where anything which forms is destroyed when the research is complete and, in any event, no later than the two-cell stage.[134]

14.41 A licence may authorize bringing about the creation of human admixed embryos *in vitro*, and keeping or using human admixed embryos.[135]

14.42 No licence is to be granted unless the Authority is satisfied that any proposed use of embryos or human admixed embryos is 'necessary' for the purposes of the research.[136]

14.43 Licences may be granted subject to conditions specified in the licence. They may be granted for a period of up to three years.[137]

14.44 A research licence can only authorize activities to be carried on in premises specified in the licence (or in certain cases on relevant third party premises), and under the supervision of an individual designated in the licence.[138] No licence can authorize more than one research project: each proposed research project requires a separate licence.[139] No licence can authorize more than one individual who is to be responsible for the licensed activities,[140] nor apply to premises of the person who holds the licence in different places.[141]

14.45 A licence which authorizes treatment services or a licence which authorizes research can also permit the storage of embryos or gametes. However, a treatment licence cannot authorize research. Nor can a research licence authorize treatment. Each of these activities must be considered in a separate licence application.[142] A storage licence may also be issued in its own right.[143]

14.46 Licences may also be granted for storage. 'Store' in relation to gametes, embryos, or human admixed embryos means 'preserve' by cryopreservation or in any other way;[144] 'storage'

132 ibid, Sch 3A(1)(a) (as amended).
133 ibid, Sch 2, para 3(A)(2) (as amended).
134 ibid, Sch 2, para 3(2) (as amended).
135 ibid, Sch 2, para 3(3) (as amended).
136 ibid, Sch 2, para 3(5) (as amended).
137 ibid, Sch 2, para 3(8) (as amended).
138 ibid, s 12(a).
139 ibid, Sch 2, para 4(2)(b).
140 ibid, Sch 2, para 4(2)(c).
141 ibid, Sch 2, para 4(2)(d).
142 ibid, Sch 2, para 4(2)(a).
143 ibid, Sch 2, para 4(2)(a) (licences for storage come within para 2).
144 ibid, s 2(1) (as amended).

and 'stored' are to be interpreted accordingly.[145] Human admixed embryos may be stored whether the licence holder is permitted by licence to store embryos or gametes.[146] A licence authorizing storage may be granted subject to such conditions as may be specified in the licence, and may authorize storage in such manner as may be so specified.[147] The gametes of a person shall be placed in storage only if:

(i) received from that person;[148]
(ii) acquired in circumstances where the person's consent to storage is not required because of Sch 3, para 9, or 10;[149]
(iii) they are acquired from a person to whom a licence or third party agreement applies;[150]
(iv) stored embryos are not to be supplied to a person otherwise than in the course of providing treatment services unless that person is a person to whom that licence applies;[151]
(v) no gametes, embryos, or human admixed embryos may be kept in storage for longer than the statutory storage period (ten years):[152] at the expiry of this period, they must be allowed to perish;[153]
(vi) the licence for storage is to be granted for such period as specified in the licence but not exceeding five years;[154]
(vii) the Authority may specify in Regulations whose consent is required (under Sch 3 of the Act), the terms of their consent, the circumstances of storage, and other matters (including the keeping of records).[155]

14.47 The circumstances in which human admixed embryos may be stored are:

(i) where created *in vitro* otherwise than in pursuance of a licence only if acquired from a person to whom a licence applies (under Sch 2, para 2, or 3);[156]
(ii) human admixed embryos shall not be supplied to a person unless that person is a person to whom a licence applies;[157]
(iii) no human admixed embryo is allowed to be kept in storage for longer than the statutory storage period, and if stored at the end of this period, to be allowed to perish;[158]
(iv) the statutory storage period for human admixed embryos is such period as may be specified in the licence but this cannot exceed ten years; [159]
(v) the Authority may specify in Regulations whose consent is required under Schedule 3, the terms of their consent and the circumstances of the storage, and other matters including the keeping of records maintained in pursuance of the licence. [160]

14.48 Licences are granted to an individual, described in the 1990 Act as the 'person responsible'.[161] Treatment licences authorize particular classes of treatment to be carried out under

[145] ibid, s 2(1).
[146] ibid, Sch 2, para 2(1A) (as amended).
[147] ibid, Sch 2, para 2(2).
[148] ibid, s 14(1)(a)(i) (as amended).
[149] ibid, s 14(1)(a)(ii) (as amended).
[150] ibid, s 14(1)(a)(iii) (as amended).
[151] ibid, s 14(1)(b).
[152] ibid, s 14(3).
[153] ibid, s 14(1)(c) (as amended).
[154] ibid, Sch 2, para 2, 3.
[155] ibid, s 14(1)(d), (2).
[156] ibid, s 14(1)(ac) (as amended).
[157] ibid, s 14(1)(ba) (as amended).
[158] ibid, s 14(1)(c) (as amended).
[159] ibid, s 14(5).
[160] ibid, s 14(1)(d), (2).
[161] ibid, s 17.

the control of the 'person responsible' at the designated premises. Licences for research are granted for a specific project of research for one or more of the purposes set out in Sch 3, para 2 (and see para 14.47).

2. The licence committee

HFEA is to maintain one or more committees to discharge its functions of granting, varying, suspending, and revoking licences. [162] Other functions may be delegated to a member or to staff of HFEA.[163] HFEA established a licence panel, consisting of members of staff with relevant experience. The panel considers routine applications for treatment, non-medical fertility services, and storage licences, as well as routine applications for research licences. Applications not considered routine will be referred by the panel to a licence committee. The licence committee consists of three or five members of HFEA including the Chair or Deputy Chair: the required quorum is three. It must have a lay majority: lay is defined as persons who are not registered medical practitioners, concerned with keeping or using gametes or embryos outside of the body or directly concerned with research which involves such keeping or use. The committee can run its own procedures in whatever way it sees fit.[164] **14.49**

A member of HFEA who is in any way directly or indirectly interested in a licence granted, or proposed to be granted, must disclose the nature of his/her interest to HFEA,[165] which must record this.[166] The member concerned is not to participate in any deliberation or decision with respect to the licence.[167] If he/she does so, the deliberation or decision will have no effect.[168] There can be no doubt that any breach of these rules would lead to a successful judicial review. **14.50**

3. Licensing procedure

A licence may be granted to any person who meets the following requirements:[169] **14.51**

(a) that the application is for a licence designating an individual (it must be an individual and not a legal person) as the person under whose supervision the activities to be authorized by the licence are to be carried on,
(b) that either the individual is the applicant or—
    (i) the application is made with the consent of that individual, and
    (ii) the Authority is satisfied that the applicant is a suitable person to hold a licence,
(c) that the Authority is satisfied that the character of the individual is such as is required for the supervision of the activities and that the individual will discharge the duty under section 17,
(d) that the Authority is satisfied that the premises in respect of which the licence is to be granted and any relevant third party premises are suitable for the activities, and
(e) that the other requirements of [the] Act in relation to the granting of the licence are satisfied.

The initial fee is decided by HFEA with the approval of the Secretary of State and the Treasury. The Authority may charge a fee for an application for a licence, the grant or renewal of a licence, an application for the revocation or variation of a licence or the exercise by the Authority of any other function conferred on it. In fixing the amount of any fee the **14.52**

[162] ibid, s 9(1).
[163] ibid, s 9A(1).
[164] ibid, Sch 1, para 9(1).
[165] ibid, Sch 1, para 10(1).
[166] ibid, Sch 1, para 10(2).
[167] ibid, Sch 1, para 10(3).
[168] ibid, Sch 1, para 10(3).
[169] ibid, s 16(1).

Authority may have regard in the costs incurred by it.[170] HFEA aims to find 70 per cent of its expenditure through fees. Concerns have been raised that this could compromise HFEA's independence. There is no evidence of this. It has also been said that since patients ultimately foot the bill, this is in effect a 'tax on the infertile'.[171]

14.53 When an application is received, there is a site visit by a team of inspectors, consideration of the application and inspection report by a licence committee, and notification of the outcome to the applicant. If the applicant is not content with the decision, representations may be made to the committee before the decision takes effect. This may be followed by an appeal to the full Authority and, finally on a point of law, an applicant may appeal to the High Court.

14.54 There have been few refusals. Where treatment licences have been refused, the reasons for the refusal have been given to the applicants. According to HFEA: 'Generally these have been cases where the centres failed in significant ways to meet the standards required by the Act and the Code of Practice, and where it appeared to the licence committee that the centre would be unable to meet the required standard within a reasonable period of time.'[172] As HFEA acknowledged in its *Second Annual Report*, 'while much of the licensing procedure is set out in statute [the 1990 Act], the corresponding administrative arrangements are entirely at the discretion of the authority'. It is therefore aware that 'it is important to ensure that the right information is available to centres, to inspectors and to licence committees'. It has accordingly standardized licence conditions 'to maintain consistency',[173] and to show how they relate to particular parts of the Code of Practice.

14.55 The 'person responsible' has a number of duties.[174] S/he must secure:

(i) that the other persons to whom the licence applies are of suitable character and hold suitable qualifications to participate in the activities authorised by the licence. These people are those specified as any person designated in the Act or to whom the licence applies after notice has been given to HFEA. It includes any person acting under the direction of the person responsible,[175]
(ii) that proper equipment is used,
(iii) that proper arrangements are made for the keeping of gametes, embryos, and human admixed embryos and for the disposal of gametes, embryos, and human admixed embryos that have been allowed to perish,[176]
(iv) that the conditions of the licence are complied with.[177]
(v) that conditions of third party agreements relating to the procurement, testing, processing, or distribution of gametes or embryos are complied with,
(vi) that the Authority is notified and provided with a report analysing the cause and existing outcome of any serious adverse event or serious adverse reaction.[178]

170 ibid, s 35B(1), (4), inserted by the 2008 Act.
171 See, in relation to the so-called 'postcode lottery', *The Times* (23 February 1999).
172 HFEA, *Second Annual Report* (HFEA 1993) 7.
173 ibid.
174 1990 Act, s 17.
175 ibid, s 17(1)(a), (2)(c).
176 ibid, s 17(1)(c).
177 ibid, s 17(1)(e).
178 ibid, s 17(1)(g).

4. Licence conditions

Licences may be granted subject to conditions.[179] The 1990 Act lays down both general conditions and conditions for licences for each of treatment,[180] non-medical fertility services,[181] storage,[182] and research.[183] **14.56**

(i) General conditions

The general conditions, which must be imposed, are: **14.57**

(i) licensed activities can only be carried on in the premises to which the licence relates and under the supervision of the 'person responsible'; [184]
(ii) proper records must be maintained in the form specified by HFEA.[185] Copies of extracts from those records or any other specified information is to be provided to HFEA when and how it specifies;[186]
(iii) the requirements as to written consent (see paras 14.138–14.140) must be complied with;[187]
(iv) no money or other benefit is to be given or received in the supply of gametes, embryos, or human admixed embryos other than in accordance with authorization given by HFEA in directions;[188]
(v) any activities to which ss 3(1A)(b) or (1B) or 4(1A) apply must be carried on only on the premises to which the licence relates or on relevant third party premises.[189]

It was suggested[190] that the waiving of charges for private treatment in consideration of the donation of eggs would be waiving a payment for advantage, and not a payment in money or money's worth, and therefore would have fallen outside the province of this provision. 'Money's worth' is not an identical concept to 'other benefit'. The latter is wider so that the example used should accordingly fall within the prohibition in s 12(1)(e). There has been uneasiness surrounding payment but a concern that the entire service might be jeopardized if it were prohibited.[191] Initially, expenses could be reimbursed. So long as expenses were allowed, the question that needed to be answered was how far the concept extended.[192] One view was that compensation for loss of earnings should be acceptable, but more dubious was recompense for inconvenience and discomfort. Morgan and Lee expressed the view that: **14.58**

> there is a good case for allowing financial benefit to be greater where more invasive procedures are used. However, the medical profession has generally disdained payments calibrated according to use. This would seem to militate against large sums of money being offered for the supply of healthy eggs.[193]

---

179 ibid; see generally Sch 2. The general conditions are in the 1990 Act in s 12 (as amended).
180 ibid, s 13.
181 ibid, s 13A, inserted by the 2008 Act.
182 ibid, s 14.
183 ibid, s 15.
184 ibid, ss 16, 17, and Sch 2, para 4(1).
185 ibid, s 12(1)(d).
186 ibid, s 12(1)(g).
187 ibid, s 12(1)(c) and Sch 3.
188 ibid, s 12(1)(e) (as amended).
189 ibid, s 12(1)(aa) (as amended by the 2008 Act).
190 By D Morgan and R Lee, *Blackstone's Guide To The Human Fertilisation and Embryology Act 1990* (Blackstone Press 1991) 99.
191 See R Deech, 'Payment to Gamete and Embryo Donors' (1999) 6(1) Journal of Fertility Counselling 6.
192 It was reported in 1995 that a treatment centre was using an agency to pay women to donate eggs: *The Guardian* (2 November 1995). This led to an amendment of directions in 1996 to cover payments from third parties.
193 N 183 above, 99.

HFEA concluded in 1996 that a donation should be 'a gift, freely and voluntarily given'.[194] It was of the view that donors should not be out of pocket as a result of becoming donors, so that 'reasonable direct expenses', such as for travel and child care should be reimbursed. A Working Party then examined the implementation of this policy in detail. By 1999, however, HFEA concluded that it was not practicable to ban payments and it decided accordingly to allow £15 per donation, plus reasonable expenses, to continue.[195] It should be added that a person to whom a licence applies and who gives or receives any money or any benefit, other than in accordance with HFEA directions, commits an offence.[196] Such persons are liable on summary conviction to imprisonment for six months or to a fine not exceeding level five on the standard scale, or both. The latest Code of Practice rules that donors may be reimbursed all reasonable expenses 'but not excessive expenses if these would be benefits in themselves'.[197] Expenses must be 'directly linked' to the process of donation, for example travel and child care.[198] And donors may be compensated for loss of earnings up to a daily maximum of £61.28, with an overall limit of £250 for each course of cycle of donation.[199] Advertising or publicity aimed at recruiting donors or encouraging donation should not 'refer to the possibility of financial gain or similar advantage'.[200] If an egg donor becomes ill as a direct result of donating, the centre is allowed to reimburse reasonable expenses arising from the illness.[201] Benefits in the form of treatment services may be given to an egg provider.[202] HFEA changed its rules on payment for donation in 2012 following an extensive public consultation 'Donating sperm and eggs; have your say' and review of donation in 2011. The new policy came into effect on 1 April 2012, and allows centres to compensate egg donors £750 per cycle of donation and sperm donors £35 per clinic visit, with the provision to claim an excess to cover higher expenses. The HFEA felt that this was a fair amount to compensate donors whilst not creating an inducement to donate.

14.59 Egg-sharing schemes are permitted and the HFEA's donation review recognized that there is a high value attached to this type of arrangement. A woman who wants IVF treatment may be encouraged to donate eggs retrieved during a cycle in return for free or cheaper treatment for herself. This may be worth many thousands of pounds to her, and therefore amounts to payment, albeit indirect. Of course, one cost to the donor may be having to bear the psychological trauma of knowing that another woman has had a child when her treatment has failed, as will frequently happen. The new policy permits egg-sharing arrangements, but the HFEA reviewed the guidance to make it clear what other benefits might be included (eg free or reduced storage or an opportunity to move up the waiting list). Centres may also offer 'benefits in kind' if a man donates sperm:[203]

(i) where gametes, embryos or human admixed embryos are supplied by one licence holder to another, the supplier is to give to the recipient such information as the Authority may specify in directions;[204]

---

[194] HFEA, *Fifth Annual Report* (HFEA 1996) 23–24.

[195] HFEA, *Eighth Annual Report* (HFEA 1999) 28. The issue of payment 'could not be considered as an issue of principle in isolation from others'.

[196] 1990 Act, s 41(8).

[197] Code of Practice (8th edn, 2009) 13.2.

[198] ibid, 13.3.

[199] ibid, 13.4.

[200] ibid, 13.6.

[201] ibid, 13.9.

[202] ibid, ch 12.

[203] ibid, 12.5.

[204] 1990 Act, s 12(1)(f) (as amended).

(ii) any member or employee of the Authority is to be permitted to enter and inspect premises as well as equipment and records. Such persons may also observe any activity. Inspections are to be carried out at reasonable times. If required to do so, the member or employee must produce identification.[205]

The Authority may also attach further conditions.[206] These can be specific to the centre, and can relate to a range of issues. Many of the conditions imposed have related to security, counselling and confidentiality, as well as to the welfare to the child and information for patients. HFEA has reported that: 'Licence conditions have been used, when appropriate, as a means of applying pressure on centres to conform quickly in areas where there have been observed deficiencies in their practice.'[207] It is HFEA's view that it is 'reasonable for the Authority to recognize that in some centres it may take a little time to develop adequate procedures'.[208] **14.60**

(ii) Treatment licence conditions

The 1990 Act, as amended, prescribes conditions of licences for treatment. These relate to record-keeping. Such information is to be recorded as the Authority may specify in directions which relate to the persons for whom the services are provided in pursuance of the licence; the services provided for them; the persons whose gametes are kept or used for the purposes of services provided in pursuance of the licence or whose gametes have been used in bringing about the creation of embryos so kept or used; any child appearing to the person responsible to have been born as a result of treatment in pursuance of a licence; any mixing of sperm and eggs and any taking of an embryo from a woman or other acquisition of an embryo; and such other matters specified by HFEA in directions.[209] Records are also to record consents required under Sch 3[210] to the 1990 Act.[211] No information may be removed from any records maintained in pursuance of the licence before the expiry of such period as may be specified in directions for records of the class in question.[212] Where a treatment licence holder does not know whether a child has been born following the provision of treatment services, the information held shall be maintained for a period of not less than fifty years from when it was first recorded.[213] **14.61**

Two other conditions of licences for treatment, dealing with counselling and with the prospective welfare of any child born as a result of treatment are considered below (see paras 14.107–14.140 and 14.145). **14.62**

(iii) Research licence conditions

The conditions of research licences are: that the records maintained in pursuance of the licence shall include such information as the Authority may specify;[214] that no information shall be removed from any records maintained in pursuance of the licence before the expiry of such period as may be specified in directions for records of the class in question;[215] that **14.63**

205 ibid, s 12(b). See also the enforcement powers in s 39, which include retaining embryos or gametes (s 39(3)).

206 Those in the 1990 Act, ss 12–15 are those which must be imposed: others may be (and are).

207 HFEA, *Second Annual Report* (HFEA 1993).

208 ibid.

209 1990 Act, s 13(2).

210 As to which see para 14.138.

211 1990 Act, s 13(3).

212 ibid, s 13(4).

213 ibid, s 24(1).

214 ibid, s 15(2).

215 ibid, s 15(3).

no embryo appropriated for the purposes of any project of research shall be kept or used otherwise than for the purposes of such a project.[216] This prohibits another line of research being carried out under the guise of the original research licence.[217]

(iv) Storage licence conditions

14.64 The 1990 Act prescribes conditions of storage licences.[218] Every licence must require that 'gametes of a person shall be placed in storage only if received from that person, or acquired from a person to whom a licence applies', and that 'an embryo the creation of which has been brought about *in vitro* otherwise that in pursuance of that licence shall be placed in storage only if acquired from a person to whom a licence applies'.[219] An embryo may not be placed in storage if it has been created *in vitro* by an unlicensed person. The words 'a person to whom a licence applies' are ambiguous. Literally interpreted, it would include persons not licensed to bring about the creation of embryos (persons, indeed, who may have committed an offence in so doing). The better interpretation must be that it envisages persons licensed to bring about the creation of embryos. In addition, it is a condition of every licence authorizing the storage of gametes or embryos that gametes or embryos which are or have been stored shall not be supplied to a person otherwise than in the course of providing treatment services, unless that person is a person to whom a licence applies.[220]

14.65 The statutory storage (and freezing) period for gametes may not exceed ten years.[221] For embryos the same period is prescribed.[222] If still stored at the end of this period they must be allowed to perish.[223] An embryo created from stored gametes may itself be frozen and stored for five years. Accordingly, an embryo could be used for treatment services, or for the purposes of research, for up to fifteen years after the egg or sperm from which it derives was donated. Regulations may, however, provide for a shorter maximum period of storage,[224] and, in circumstances as may be specified, a longer period.[225]

14.66 Human admixed embryos:

(i) may be stored where created *in vitro* but not in pursuance of a licence, they may be placed in storage only if acquired from a person to which a licence under Sch 2, paras 2 or 3 applied, that is, a storage or research licence;[226]
(ii) may not be supplied to a person unless that person is one to which a licence applies;[227]
(iii) may not be kept in storage for longer than the statutory period (as specified in the licence, subject to a maximum of ten years);[228]
(iv) must be allowed to perish, if in storage at the end of that period;[229]

216 ibid, s 15(4).
217 ibid, Sch 2, para 4(2)(b).
218 ibid, s 14 (as amended).
219 ibid, s 14(1)(a). Unless it was acquired in circumstances in which that person's consent to storage is not required.
220 ibid, s 14(1)(b).
221 ibid, s 14(3).
222 ibid, s 14(4) (as amended). The 1990 Act originally prescribed five years.
223 ibid, s 14(1)(c).
224 ibid, s 14(5)(a).
225 ibid, s 14(5)(b).
226 ibid, s 14(1)(ac) (as amended).
227 ibid, s 14(1)(ba) (as amended).
228 ibid, s 14(4A) (as amended).
229 ibid, s 14(1)(c) (as amended).

Regulations may change the length of period of storage of human admixed embryos, providing a shorter or longer period.[230] The Authority may specify in regulations where consent is required (under Sch 3), the terms of their consent, the circumstances of the storage and other matters, including the keeping of records in pursuance of the licence.[231]

5. Prohibited activities

The 2008 Act (as did the 1990 Act) prohibits a number of activities in connection with: **14.67**

(1) embryos;
(2) gametes;
(3) germ cells;
(4) genetic material which is not of human origin;
(5) mitochondrion donation.

(i) Embryos

Prohibitions relating to embryos are contained in the 1990 Act, s 3. No person may bring about the creation of an embryo, or keep or use an embryo, except in pursuance of a licence.[232] No person may keep without storage, such an embryo, except in pursuance of a third party agreement.[233] Also, it is not permitted to procure or distribute an embryo intended for human application except in pursuance of a licence or third party agreement.[234] 'Human application' means being used in a human recipient.[235] A 'third party agreement' is an agreement in writing between a person who holds a licence and another person which is made in accordance with any licence conditions imposed by the Authority for the purpose of securing compliance with the requirements of Article 24 of the First Directive.[236] A third party agreement enables the other person to perform certain duties on behalf of the licence holder, for example test gametes or embryos. **14.68**

The 2008 Act (s 3(2)(a)) prohibits the placing in a woman of any embryo other than a 'permitted embryo'. 'Woman' includes 'girl'.[237] A 'permitted embryo' is one created by the fertilization of a permitted egg by permitted sperm, whose nuclear or mitochondrial DNA has not been altered, and has not had cells added other than by division of the embryo's own cells.[238] As a result, embryos created by the use of artificial gametes or genetically modified gametes cannot be placed in a woman. Also, it has the effect of banning human reproductive cloning. This was criminalized in 2001.[239] The Human Reproductive Cloning Act 2001 has now been repealed, since as a result of this provision, it is no longer needed.[240] **14.69**

A licence may not authorize the keeping or using of an embryo after the appearance of the primitive streak. The primitive streak is to be taken to have appeared in an embryo not later than the end of the period of fourteen days beginning with the day on which the process of creating the embryo began, not counting any time during which the embryo is stored.[241] **14.70**

[230] ibid, s 14(5).
[231] ibid, s 14(1)(d).
[232] ibid, s 3(1A)(a), (b), (i).
[233] ibid, s 3(1A)(b)(ii).
[234] ibid, s 3(1B).
[235] ibid, s 2(1).
[236] ibid, s 2 A (as amended).
[237] ibid, s 3ZA(6) (as amended).
[238] ibid, s 3ZA(4) (as amended).
[239] By the Human Reproductive Cloning Act 2001.
[240] See further Chapter 15.
[241] 1990 Act, s 3(3)(a), (4) (as amended).

14.71 A licence may not authorize the placing of an embryo in any animal.[242]

14.72 A licence may not authorize the keeping or using of an embryo in any circumstances in which regulations prohibit its keeping or use.[243]

(ii) Gametes

14.73 No person should place any gametes in a woman other than 'permitted eggs' or 'permitted sperm', and this may only be in pursuance of a licence.[244] 'Permitted egg' is an egg produced by or extracted from the ovaries of a woman whose nuclear or mitochondrial DNA has not been altered.[245] 'Woman' includes girl.[246] 'Permitted sperm' are sperm produced or extracted from the testes of a man, whose nuclear or mitochondrial DNA has not been altered.[247] 'Man' includes 'boy' (from birth).[248]

14.74 The effect of this provision is that artificially created gametes and genetically modified gametes cannot be placed in a woman.

14.75 Before gametes may be stored, a licence must be obtained.[249]

(iii) Germ cells

14.76 No person shall, for the purpose of providing fertility services for any woman, use female germ cells taken from or derived from an embryo or a foetus, or use embryos created by using such cells.[250] 'Female germ cells' are cells of the female germ line, of any stage of maturity and include eggs.[251] 'Fertility services' are defined to mean 'medical, surgical or obstetric services provided for the purpose of assisting women to carry children'.[252]

(iv) Genetic material not of human origin

14.77 No person may place in a woman:

(a) a human admixed embryo;
(b) any other embryo which is not a human embryo;
(c) any gametes other than human gametes.[253]

A human admixed embryo may not be placed in an animal.[254] An 'animal' is an 'animal' other than 'man'.[255]

14.78 In order to mix human gametes with animal gametes, or bring about the creation of a human admixed embryo or keep or use a human admixed embryo, it is necessary to have a licence.[256] This cannot authorize keeping or using a human admixed embryo after the appearance of the primitive streak or the end of the period of fourteen days beginning with the day on which the process of creating the human admixed embryo began (not counting any time during

242 ibid, s 3(3)(b).
243 ibid, s 3(3)(c).
244 ibid, s 4(3).
245 ibid, s 3ZA(2) (as amended).
246 ibid, s 3ZA(6)(a) (as amended).
247 ibid, s 3ZA(3) (as amended).
248 ibid, s 3ZA(6)(a) (as amended).
249 ibid, s 4(1)(a).
250 ibid, s 3A(1) (as amended).
251 ibid, s 3A(2) (as amended).
252 ibid, s 3A(2) (as amended).
253 1990 Act, s 4A(1) (as amended).
254 ibid, s 4A(3) (as amended).
255 ibid, s 4A(8) (as amended).
256 ibid, s 4A(2) (as amended).

which it is stored).[257] An embryo is defined as a live embryo, including an egg in the process of fertilization or which is underlying any process capable of resulting in an embryo.[258]

Power is given to the Secretary of State, if it appears to him or her to be necessary or desirable in the light of scientific or medical development, to amend (but not repeal) by regulations the meaning of human admixed embryo. This is set out in the 1990 Act, s 4A(6) (as amended). Also, to include within 'embryo', 'eggs' or 'gametes', things that would not otherwise fall within the definition.[259] **14.79**

(v) Mitochondrion donation

It is now possible to create healthy embryos using a woman's eggs, her partner's sperm, and healthy donated mitochondria.[260] This follows a length period of debate and approval by parliament in February 2015. The UK is the first country to license the new mitochondrial techniques and the new regulations allow clinics to apply to use the techniques of pronuclear transfer (PNT) and maternal spindle transfer (MST). Accordingly, it is provided that regulations[261] may allow an egg to be a permitted egg, an embryo, or permitted embryo, 'even though the egg or embryo has had applied to it a prescribed process designed to prevent the transmission of serious mitochondrial disease'.[262] The regulations provide that any clinic that applies to perform these techniques will have to provide clear evidence that they have both the staff with the experience to perform them and the equipment to do so. Consideration will also be given to the clinic's plans for follow-up of the children born. Each application will be considered by the HFEA on a case-by-case basis, during which the potential patient's specific circumstances will be taken into account. **14.80**

(a) Offences The following are offences. The penalty upon conviction is imprisonment for a term not exceeding ten years, or a fine, or both: **14.81**

(i) to place in a woman an embryo or any gametes except for those permitted embryos, permitted eggs, or permitted sperm;
(ii) to use germ cells or embryos taken from such cells to provide fertility services;
(iii) to place in a woman a human admixed embryo, or any other embryo which is not a human embryo or any gametes which are human gametes;
(iv) to mix human gametes with animal gametes; to create, keep, or use a human admixed embryo without a licence;
(v) to place an embryo in an animal;
(vi) to keep or use an embryo, which is prohibited by regulations.[263]

A prosecution requires the consent of the Director of Public Prosecutions, or his or her decision to bring the prosecution (in Northern Ireland the Director of Public Prosecutions for Northern Ireland).[264] **14.82**

Section 41(11) sets out the following defence: **14.83**

> that at the material time (the person charged) was a person to whom a licence or third party agreement applied or to whom directions had been given, and that he took all

257 ibid, s 4A(3) (as amended).
258 ibid, s 4A(9) (as amended).
259 ibid, s 4A(11) (as amended).
260 Human Fertilisation and Embryology (Mitochondrial Donation) Regulations 2015; *Mitochondrial donation*, Guidance Note 33 available at <http://www.hfea.gov.uk/9931.html>.
261 ibid, s 3ZA(7) (as amended).
262 ibid, s 3ZA(5) (as amended).
263 ibid, s 41 (as amended).
264 ibid, s 42.

such steps as were reasonable and exercised all due diligence to avoid committing the offence.

6. Directions, regulations, and the Code of Practice

14.84 Section 23(1) of the 1990 Act empowers the Authority to give directions for any purpose for which directions may be given under the Act, or directions varying or revoking such directions. A person to whom any requirement contained in directions is applicable must comply with the requirement.[265] Directions may be general or given to a particular person (or clinic). A licence can be revoked if the 'person responsible' fails to comply with directions given in connection with any licence.[266] Directions may be given for a very wide range of regulatory purposes. These are (in order they appear in the 1990 Act):

(i) Maintenance of proper records in the form specified;[267]
(ii) Authorizing payment or other benefit for gametes, embryos, or human admixed embryos,[268] which would otherwise be unlawful (most reported directions are in relation to this);
(iii) Information to be supplied to the licensed recipients of gametes, embryos, or human admixed embryos;[269]
(iv) Information to be recorded in pursuance of a treatment licence;[270]
(v) Length of time for which information must be maintained;[271]
(vi) Records dealing with the storage of gametes or embryos to include the consents required for their storage, the terms of those consents and the circumstances of the storage, and any other matters which the Authority specifies;[272]
(vii) Length of time for which information about the storage of gametes or embryos must be preserved;[273]
(viii) Information to be maintained in research licence records, and the length of time for which such information must be held;[274]
(ix) In respect of treatment licences which involve any of:

(a) bringing about the creation of an embryo *in vitro*,
(b) procuring, keeping, testing, processing, or distributing embryos,
(c) procuring, testing, processing, distributing, or using gametes,
(ca) using embryos for the purpose of training persons in embryo biopsy, embryo storage, or other embryological technique,
(d) any therapeutic practice with an embryo to ensure it is in a suitable condition for transfer to a woman,
(e) placing any permitted embryo in a woman,
(f) using the hamster or other specified test to determine the fertility or normality of sperm, or
(g) any other specified practice.[275]

[265] ibid, s 23(2).
[266] ibid, s 18(2)(c).
[267] ibid, s 12(1)(d).
[268] ibid, s 12(1)(e) (as amended).
[269] ibid, s 12(1)(f) (as amended).
[270] ibid, s 13(2)(a)–(f).
[271] ibid, s 13(4).
[272] ibid, s 14(1)(d).
[273] ibid, s 14(2).
[274] ibid, s 15(2), (3).
[275] ibid, Sch 2, para 1.

Information is to be recorded and given to the Authority in respect of: 14.85

(i) the persons for whom any of these service have been provided;
(ii) the services provided for them;
(iii) the persons whose gametes are kept or used for those purposes or the bringing about the creation of any embryo;
(iv) any child appearing to the person responsible to have been born as a result of the licensed treatment service; and
(v) any mixing of egg and sperm or taking of an embryo from any woman or other acquisition of an embryo from another licensed person, whether inside or outside the United Kingdom;
(vi) any other matters the Authority specifies in directions; [276]
(vii) the receiving or sending of gametes, embryos, or human admixed embryos from the United Kingdom (or to it) to be subject to specified conditions, and the provisions dealing with conditions (in ss 12–14) to be modified accordingly;[277]
(viii) licence committees to direct what is to happen where a licence is to be varied or cease to have effect;[278]
(ix) the draft code of practice, as approved by the Secretary of State, to come into force in accordance with directions.[279]

Where there is a breach of directions or one is alleged, the Authority may make preliminary enquiries and if these establish evidence of a breach, refer its findings to a licence committee (see para 14.49) which will make the decision on further action (if any). Should this lead to a decision to revoke or suspend a licence, there is an appeal to an appeal committee, and to the High Court on a point of law. If enquiries reveal a criminal offence, the matter should be referred to the Director of Public Prosecutions. 14.86

Regulations may be used to inject flexibility into the legislation and to permit changes to reflect scientific knowledge and development. Without such powers there would need to be constant legislative updating. Regulations and the power to make consequential provisions are provided for in the legislation. This includes the power to include transitional, incidental, and supplemental provision. 14.87

The Act makes use of the two forms of parliamentary scrutiny of secondary legislation: 'negative' and 'affirmative' resolutions of Parliament. With the former, regulations will come into force forty days after being lodged in the office of the clerk of each House of Parliament if not made subject to a resolution of annulment passed in either House. The latter requires affirmative approval, and necessitates room being found in the Parliamentary timetable. 14.88

Those questions which require the affirmative resolution procedure are laid down in the 1990 Act, s 45(4A). They are: 14.89

s 1(6)	– redefining 'embryos', 'eggs', 'sperm', 'gametes' for the purposes of s 1. This is subject to the exclusion in s 1(7).
s 3(3)(c)	– stating the circumstances in which a licence cannot authorize the keeping or using of an embryo.
s 3ZA(5) (as amended)	– allowing an egg or embryo to be a permitted egg or embryo even though it has been treated by a process to prevent the transmission of serious mitochondrial disease.

276 ibid, s 13(2)(a)–(e).
277 ibid, s 24(4) (as amended).
278 ibid, s 24(5A) (as amended).
279 ibid, s 26(5).

s 4(2)	– extending the circumstances in which a licence can authorize the storage or use of gametes.
s 4(3)	– extending the circumstances in which a licence is required to place sperm or eggs in a woman.
s 4A(5)(ii) (as amended)	– amending the statutory definitions of 'human admixed embryo', 'embryo', 'eggs' or 'gametes' for the purposes of s 4A.
s 20A(3) (as amended)	– making provision about the membership and proceedings of appeals committees.
s 20B(2) (as amended)	– making provision about the procedure in relation to reconsideration of licensing decisions.
s 24(4B) (as amended)	– requiring or authorizing directions to be given in relation to particular matters specified in regulations relating to activities involving genetic material of animal origin.
s 31ZA(2)(a) (as amended)	– specifying the information that is to be given about a donor when there is a request for information as to genetic parentage.
s 33C (as amended)	– providing for additional exceptions as to where a person may make of disclosure of information from the register under s 33 A(B), and subject to s 33 B(2).
s 33D (as amended)	– making provision for the disclosure of information from the register for the purposes of medical or other research.
s 35A (as amended)	– setting down provisions for other parts of the Act to have effect where there has been mitochondrial donation.
s 43	– providing for the keeping, examining and storage of gametes or embryos in connection with the investigation of offences, wherever committed.
s 42, para (1)(g) (as amended)	– specifying the practices which may be licensed for treatment.
Sch 2, para 1ZC (as amended)	– embryo testing relating to the health of any resulting child.
Sch 2, para 3A(1)(c) (as amended)	– detailing further purposes for which a licence for research may be applied for.

14.90 There are other matters which fall within the negative resolution procedure.[280] These are:

(1) additional functions to be undertaken by HFEA (s 8(1)(d));
(2) composition of HFEA licence committees (s 9(5));
(3) changes in the licensing procedure (s 10(1), (2));
(4) changes in permitted periods for the storage of gametes or embryos (s 14(5));
(5) any changes in the information which HFEA must disclose to an applicant under s 31 (s 31(4)(a)).

14.91 HFEA is obliged to maintain a Code of Practice giving guidance about the proper conduct of activities carried on in pursuance of a licence under this Act, and the proper discharge of the functions of the person responsible and any other persons to whom the licence applies.[281] In particular, the Code is to include guidance 'for those providing treatment services about the account to be taken of the welfare of children who may be born as a result of treatment services (including a child's need for supportive parenting), and of any other children who may be affected by such births'.[282]

[280] ibid, s 45(5).
[281] ibid, s 25(1).
[282] ibid, s 25(2) (as amended).

14.92 The Code is also to give guidance about the giving of a suitable opportunity to receive proper counselling.[283] The Code may also give guidance 'about the use of any technique involving the placing of sperm and eggs in a woman'.[284] HFEA is given the power to revise the whole or part of the Code.[285] It has done this seven times: the Code is now in its eighth edition.[286] The objective of the Code, as stated in the Introduction to the fifth edition:

> . . . is wider than to secure the safety and efficacy of particular clinical or scientific practices which raise fundamental and ethical and social questions. In framing it, we have been guided both by the requirements of the . . . Act and by:
> — the respect which is due to human life at all stages in its development;
> — the right of people who are or may be infertile to the proper consideration of their request for treatment;
> — a concern for the welfare of children, which cannot always be adequately protected by concern for the interests of the adults involved; and
> — a recognition of the benefits, both to individuals and to society, which can flow from the responsible pursuit of medical and scientific knowledge.[287]

The eighth edition of the Code is said to serve as 'a useful reference for patients, donors, donor-conceived people, researchers and those working in the fertility sector'. It is in 32 chapters and is well over 300 pages in length (the pages are not numbered). It consists of regulatory principles for licensed centres, guidance notes, and a useful glossary. There is also a very full index. It offers an interpretation of the law where it is felt 'centres may find it helpful, especially when the law is very complex'. Thirteen regulatory principles are set out. For convenience these are reproduced here.

(i) Regulatory principles for licensed centres

14.93 HFEA expects the person responsible to ensure that their licensed centre demonstrates adherence to the following principles when carrying out activities licensed under the Human Fertilisation and Embryology Act. Licensed centres must:

(1) treat prospective and current patients and donors fairly, and ensure that all licensed activities are conducted in a non-discriminatory way;
(2) have respect for the privacy, confidentiality, dignity, comfort, and well-being of prospective and current patients and donors;
(3) have respect for the special status of the embryo when conducting licensed activities;
(4) take account of the welfare of any child who may be born as a result of the licensed treatment provided by the centre, and of any other child who may be affected by that birth;
(5) give prospective and current patients and donors sufficient, accessible, and up-to-date information to enable them to make informed decisions;
(6) ensure that patients and donors have provided all relevant consents before carrying out any licensed activity;
(7) conduct all licensed activities with skill and care and in an appropriate environment, in line with good clinical practice, to ensure optimum outcomes and minimum risk for patients, donors, and offspring;

[283] ibid, s 25(2A) (as amended).
[284] ibid, s 25(3).
[285] ibid, s 25(4).
[286] This was published in 2009, though it has been subject to further revisions, most recently in October 2015.
[287] HFEA, *Code of Practice* (5th edn) 7. This statement is not found in the 8th edition.

(8) ensure that all premises, equipment, processes, and procedures used in the conduct of licensed activities are safe, secure, and suitable for the purpose;
(9) ensure that all staff engaged in licensed activity are competent and recruited in sufficient numbers to guarantee safe clinical and laboratory practice;
(10) maintain accurate records and information about all licensed activities;
(11) report all adverse incidents (including serious adverse events and serious adverse reactions) and near misses to HFEA, investigate all complaints properly, and share lessons learned appropriately;
(12) ensure that all licensed research by the centre meets ethical standards, and is done only where there is both a clear scientific justification and no viable alternative to the use of embryos, and
(13) conduct all licensed activities with regard for the regulatory framework governing treatment and research involving gametes or embryos within the UK, including:
- maintaining up-to-date awareness and understanding of legal obligations;
- responding promptly to requests for information and documents from HFEA; and
- cooperating fully with inspections and investigations by HFEA or other agencies responsible for law enforcement or regulation of health care.

14.94 Failure to observe the Code will not of itself give rise to civil or criminal liability.[288] However, the Authority may, in considering where it has power to do so whether or not to vary or revoke a licence, take into account any observance of or failure to observe the provisions of the Code. In addition, the Authority shall, in considering whether there has been any failure to comply with any licence conditions, in particular conditions requiring anything to be 'proper' or 'suitable', take account of any relevant provision of the Code.[289]

14.95 Whether the Code of Practice is effective has been questioned. According to research conducted by Savas and Treece,[290] albeit some years ago now, it has not prevented inconsistent decisions. The Code gives scope for different interpretations and leads these researchers to conclude that it is of questionable legal value. But, as Lee and Morgan point out, 'there are local ethics committees and . . . there is a hierarchy of regulatory mechanism, with the Code ranking lowest in terms of its prescription'.[291] The fact that there have been few legal challenges to HFEA must be attributed in part to the success of the Code of Practice.

7. Challenging decisions

14.96 If a condition is imposed which the applicant does not like, s/he may apply for a variation of that condition.[292] Applications may be made by the 'person responsible' or the holder of the licence (if this is a different person).[293] However, the licence can only be varied so far as it relates to the activities authorized by the licence by changing the manner in which the licensed activities are conducted or the conditions of the licence.[294] To the extent that the licence authorizes the conduct of activities of licensed premises, the licence can be varied only so far to extend or restrict the premises to which the licence relates.[295] So an application

[288] ibid, s 25(6)(b) (as amended).
[289] ibid, s 25(6)(a) (as amended).
[290] D Savas and S Treece, S, 'Fertility Clinics: One Code of Practice?' (1998) 3 Medical Law International 243.
[291] R G Lee and D Morgan, *Human Fertilisation and Embryology-Regulating: The Reproductive Revolution* (Blackstone 2001), 112.
[292] 1990 Act, s 18 A.
[293] ibid, s 18 A(2) (as amended).
[294] ibid, s 18A(5)(a) (as amended).
[295] 1990 Act s 18A(1) (as amended).

to vary a licence cannot add new premises which were previously unlicensed, nor can it add new services, nor can it authorize the conduct of an activity, not previously authorized, which will need a separate application for a new licence. However, it may, on an application by the nominal licensee, vary the licence so as to designate another individual in place of the 'person responsible' if the committee is satisfied that the character, qualifications, and experience of the other individual will discharge the duties stipulated in the 1990 Act, s 17.[296]

The other avenue open to an aggrieved applicant is recourse to ordinary public law remedies. Thus, the conditions imposed by HFEA must be '*Wednesbury* reasonable'.[297] As formulated by Lord Greene MR, 'a person entrusted with a discretion must . . . direct himself properly in law. He must call his own attention to the matters which he is bound to consider. He must exclude from consideration matters which are irrelevant to what he has to consider'.[298] In *Secretary of State for Education and Science v Tameside Metropolitan Borough Council* Lord Diplock said that 'the very concept of administrative discretion involves a right to choose between more than one possible course of action upon which there is room for reasonable people to hold differing opinions as to which is to be preferred'.[299] Thus, the conditions that the Authority may lawfully impose are not without limit. They must be properly related to the aims and scheme of the 1990 Act, as amended by the 2008 Act. **14.97**

HFEA must not fetter its discretion.[300] This does not mean that it may not exercise its discretion by means of a policy or rule. But it must 'be prepared to make an exception to that rule or policy in a deserving case'.[301] Thus, if, for example, a decision were taken that a certain category of research within the 1990 Act, Sch 2, para 3(2)(a)–(e) could never be pursued, the courts might be prepared to conclude that this offended against legality by fettering discretion. Interested parties (treatment clinics) must be allowed the opportunity to persuade the licensing authority to amend or deviate from the rule or policy, but the rule against fettering does not extend to the point of requiring any particular form or hearing or any particular technique of making or receiving representations.[302] **14.98**

The case of *R v Human Fertilisation and Embryology Authority, ex p Assisted Reproduction and Gynaecology Centre and H*[303] illustrates this. This was an application for judicial review of HFEA's refusal to deviate from guidance in its Code of Practice that 'no more than three eggs or embryos should be placed in a woman in any one cycle, regardless of the procedure used'. The clinic wished to provide treatment for a 46-year-old woman using five eggs. The authority disagreed that the transfer of more than three was medically necessary or essential and considered that there was a significant risk of multiple births in H's case, because she produced large numbers of good quality embryos. HFEA relied on an American research paper dealing with the transfer of embryos. It was argued by the claimants that the decision and advice was irrational, that it was fettered by a policy drawn so narrowly as to prevent consideration of individual circumstances or that Art 8 (right to a private and family life) and Art 12 (right to marry and found a family) of the European Convention on Human **14.99**

[296] The other individual's consent is also required (see s 18 A(1)(a)).
[297] See *Associated Provincial Picture Houses v Wednesbury Corporation* [1948] 1 KB 223.
[298] ibid, 229.
[299] [1977] AC 1014, 1064.
[300] Lord Woolf, J Jowell, and A Le Sueur, *De Smith's Judicial Review of Administrative Action* (6th edn, Sweet and Maxwell 2007) 479–98.
[301] ibid, 488–89. See also *R v Secretary of State for the Home Department, ex p Venables* [1997] 3 WLR 23, 47.
[302] *R v Secretary of State for the Environment, ex p Brent* LBC [1982] QB 593.
[303] *R v Human Fertilisation and Embryology Authority, ex p Assisted Reproduction and Gynaecology Centre and H* [2002] EWCA Civ 20, [2003] 1 FCR 266.

Rights were applicable. It was the claimants' submission that it would be for HFEA to show that H's human rights had not been breached. Ouseley J held: (i) it was fundamental to the arguability of the claimants' case that there were demonstrated facts that took the case out of the range of available decisions, (ii) the statistics used by the claimants did not arguably contradict the approach adopted by HFEA, namely that the risk of multiple births from pregnancy was greater with a patient who had good eggs if more than three were transplanted; (iii) applying its policy guidance, HFEA had considered H's medical circumstances and age; (iv) the court could not adjudicate between two views of an academic paper or its relationship to the United States Vital Statistics Reports; (v) the claimants' evidence had not answered HFEA's point that any pregnancy would involve overcoming some unknown but adverse factor in the receiving area, which would have been overcome for all the eggs transplanted in one cycle; (vi) the claimants' evidence had not shown that HFEA was irrational but had merely shown that two views were possible (it was not for the court to intervene in a decision on the merits on a level far beyond that necessary for scrutiny of the lawfulness of the decision in which human rights were potentially engaged); (vii) HFEA was entitled to reach the view that two successive cyclical treatments with three eggs as opposed to five eggs in one cycle would achieve better prospects of pregnancy without a greater risk of multiple births; (viii) the decision letter had not shown any fettering of HFEA's views such that the appropriate or proportionate application of the guidelines to H was ignored. The appeal to the Court of Appeal failed.[304] The Court of Appeal noted that this was an area of rapidly developing scientific knowledge and debate in which HFEA, as the licensing body established by Parliament to regulate, made decisions and gave advice. It was not the function of the court to enter the scientific debate, nor was it the function of the court to adjudicate on the merits of HFEA's decisions or any advice it gave. Like any public authority, HFEA was open to challenge by way of judicial review but only if it exceeded or abused the powers and responsibilities given to it by Parliament. It was clear in this case that HFEA had considered the request for advice carefully and thoroughly, and it had produced opinions that were plainly rational. As Wall LJ said in the Court of Appeal, the court had no part to play in the debate, and certainly no power to intervene to strike down any such decision'.[305]

14.100 Decisions may be challenged also for procedural *ultra vires*. This can take two forms: failure to follow the direction of the Act, and failure to observe the principles of natural justice. As regards directions under the Act, there are both mandatory prescriptions (where disobedience will normally render invalid what has been done) and directory ones, in which case disobedience may be treated as an irregularity not affecting the validity of what has been done.[306] It is not always easy to distinguish the two requirements, but it may be said that where statutory words require things to be done as a condition of making a decision, especially when the form of words requires that something *shall* be done, an inference is raised that the requirement is mandatory, so that failure to do the required act renders the decision unlawful.[307] An example would be the failure by the Authority to give notice of a determination of a licence application contrary to the requirements of the 1990 Act, s 19(1). Where the procedures are merely directory, the courts will not normally find committees bound, with the result that failure to meet the procedural requirements will not generally be fatal to the validity of the decision taken. It is important to emphasize that all statutory requirements are prima facie mandatory.[308] In order to decide whether a presumption that a

[304] ibid.
[305] ibid.
[306] See Savas and Treece, n 290, 251 *et seq*. See also *Cullimore v Lyme Regis Corporation* [1962] 1 QB 718.
[307] But the decision is presumed valid until set aside or otherwise held to be invalid by a court of competent jurisdiction: *Smith v East Elloe RDC* [1956] AC 736.
[308] Savas and Treece, n 290, 267.

provision is mandatory is in fact rebutted, the whole scope and purpose of the Act must be considered: one must assess 'the importance of provision that has been disregarded, and the relation of that provision to the general object intended to be secured by the Act'.[309]

A key element of procedural propriety is the duty to observe the principles of natural justice. The Act itself embodies these[310] (there is, for example, a right to be heard in the Act itself), but recourse must also be had to common law principles. It has been said that rules of natural justice 'mean no more than the duty to act fairly'.[311] The courts have offered some guidance as to which interests should be protected by fair procedures. In *McInnes v Onslow Fane*[312] three situations were distinguished: 'forfeiture' or 'deprivation' cases, where there is a decision which takes away some existing right or position (in our context, the operation of an existing licensed treatment clinic); 'application cases', where no interest yet exists, for example to run a treatment clinic; and an intermediate category of 'expectation cases', where there is a reasonable expectation of an existing benefit (the renewal of a licence is an example) which falls short of a right. A fair hearing, the court suggested, should be granted in cases involving 'forfeiture' and, normally, 'expectation', but not in those involving a mere 'application'. A strict application of this reasoning could result in injustice, with one clinic securing a licence and another not, and so the courts have held that deciding bodies are under a duty to give an applicant an opportunity to make representations and to be apprised of all information on which the decision may be founded.[313] It has been argued that 'wherever a public function is being performed there is an inference, in the absence of an express requirement to the contrary that the function is required to be performed fairly'.[314] This inference is all the more compelling where a decision may adversely affect a person's rights or interests, or when a person has a legitimate expectation of being treated fairly, as is clearly the case with applications for licences under the Act. 'The court is the arbiter of what is fair',[315] when fairness is required and what is involved to achieve fairness is a decision for the courts as a matter of law. **14.101**

The question may arise, given the controversial nature of the decision the Authority may be engaged in, as to who has the standing to challenge such decisions. It is not 'a function of the courts to be there for every individual who is interested in having the legality of an administrative action litigated'.[316] The applicant must have 'sufficient interest in the matter to which the application relates'.[317] The courts are increasingly receptive to challenges by public interest groups,[318] even to individual applications. Note Sedley J's remarks that he is 'perfectly entitled as a citizen to be concerned about, and to draw the attention of the court to, what he considers is an illegality'.[319] **14.102**

---

309 *Howard v Bodington* (1877) 2 PD 203, 211. See also *R v Towers Hamlets Health Authority ex p Tower Combined Trades Association* [1994] COD 325.

310 See the 'right to be heard' in the Act and Regulations, and protections against bias (eg the 1990 Act, Sch 1, para 10(1)).

311 *Per* Lord Diplock in *O'Reilly v Mackman* [1983] 2 AC 237, 275.

312 [1978] 1 WLR 1520.

313 See *R v Huntingdon DC, ex p Cowan* [1984]1 WLR 501. The obligation may be qualified by a right to refrain from disclosing the source and precise content of highly confidential information: *R v Gaming Board for Great Britain, ex p Benaim and Khaida* [1970] 2 QB 417, 431.

314 See Savas Treece, n 290, 360.

315 *Per* Woolf and Lloyd LJJ in *R v Panel on Takeovers and Mergers, ex p Guinness* [1990] 1 QB 146. The test is not whether no reasonable body would have thought it proper to dispense with a fair hearing.

316 *R v Secretary of State for the Environment, ex p Rose Theatre Trust Ltd* [1990] 1 All ER 754, 768.

317 RSC Ord 53: see CPR 1998, Sch 1.

318 See, eg, *R v Secretary of State for the Foreign and Commonwealth Office ex p. World Development Movement* [1995] 1 WLR 386, and *R v Inspectorate of Pollution ex p Greenpeace Ltd* [1994] 4 All ER 329.

319 In *R v Somerset CC v ARS Southern Ltd, ex p Dixon* [1997] COD 323, 331.

14.103 With respect to the impact of the Human Rights Act 1998, the HFEA is clearly a public body.[320] It is therefore unlawful for it to 'act in a way which is incompatible with convention rights'.[321] However, 'standing' is more narrowly defined under the Convention and under s 7 of the Human Rights Act. This adopts a 'victim' test.[322] Whether the Society for the Protection of the Unborn Child (SPUC) or LIFE could claim 'victim' status perhaps in an appeal to the 'right to life' provision in Art 2 of the Convention is open to question.[323] But the reality is that such an organization should have little difficulty finding one of its members to stand as a putative victim. The precedent of *Bowman v United Kingdom*[324] is useful to consider here —Mrs Bowman was held to be a victim when the UK government stopped the publication and distribution by an organization of anti-abortion leaflets which provided the opinions of parliamentary candidates—should offer the support to pressure groups wishing to challenge HFEA decisions on embryo research, for example. The courts, which have adopted a liberal position on 'standing', are likely to take a similar stand on 'victim'.[325]

D. Access to Treatment and the Welfare of the Child

1. Introduction

14.104 In a legal text it would not normally be necessary, or some would think appropriate, to spell out the most obvious constraint on access to treatment: namely, that restriction upon NHS funding may confine access to infertility treatment to those with considerable financial resources. But this would be to ignore the European dimension. Those who are denied assisted conception services in the UK may seek treatment abroad: a woman denied treatment on grounds of her age might go to the Czech Republic or Spain. There are at least 24,000–30,000 cross-border fertility treatments carried out each year involving 11,000 to 14,000 patients. Article 59 of the European Treaty only applies to services which are 'normally provided for remuneration'. There is thus no right to publicly funded assisted conception in another Member State, but those who can pay can go abroad and, as Hervey puts it, '"buy their way out" of ethical or moral choices given legislative force in their own Member State'.[326] Thus, those wealthy enough to do so can buy into private infertility treatment in this country, and buy out of our regulatory framework (which is stricter than many countries in the European Union).[327]

---

[320] Within Human Rights Act 1998, s 6.

[321] See Human Rights Act 1998, s 6(1).

[322] See ECHR, Art 34, s 7(1).

[323] cf *F v Switzerland* [1988] 10 EHRR 411.

[324] [1998] 26 EHRR 1.

[325] The *Code of Practice* (8th edn) makes only one reference to the Human Rights Act 1998: see para 29.1 (the HRA 'also relevant when considering broader issues of discrimination').

[326] See T Hervey, 'Buy Baby: The European Union and Regulation of Human Reproduction' [1998] 18 OJLS 207, 229. See D Campbell, 'Destination Spain: The Rise and Rise of Fertility Tourism', *The Guardian* (23 August 2010), 11; R Deonandan, Recent Trends in Reproductive Tourism and International Surrogacy: Ethical Considerations and Challenges for Policy (2015) 8 Risk Management and Healthcare Policy 111–19. Also generally see A Denchin, 'Reproductive Tourism and the Quest for Global Gender Justice' (2010) 24 Bioethics 323–32.

[327] On France, see M Latham, *Regulating Reproduction* (Manchester University Press 2002). See also S Hennette-Vauchez, 'Words Count: How Interest in Stem Cells Has Made the Embryo Available—A Look at the French Law of Bioethics' (2009) 17 Med L Rev 52–75; L Culley et al, What Are You Going to Do, Confiscate Their Passports? Professional Perspectives on Cross-Border Reproductive Travel (2013) 31 (1) Journal of Reproductive and Infant Psychology 46; N Hudson and L Culley, 'Cross-border Reproductive Travel' in N Lundt, J Hanefeld, D Horsfall (eds), *Handbook on Medical Tourism and Patient Mobility* (Edward Elgar Publishing 2015); R G Lee and D Morgan, *Human Fertilisation and Embryology—Regulating The Reproductive Revolution* (Blackstone 2001), ch 11.

The Warnock Committee was 'not prepared to recommend that access to treatment should be based exclusively on the legal status of marriage'.[328] It did, however, express the view that 'as a general rule it is better for children to be born into a two-parent family, with both father and mother'.[329] It concluded that 'eligibility' raised difficult questions, and that 'hard and fast rules' were not applicable to its solution.[330] Instead, the Warnock Committee recommended that where consultants declined to provide treatment 'they should always give the patient a full explanation of the reasons'.[331] During the passage of the 1990 Act through Parliament, an attempt was made to restrict access to infertility treatment to married couples or, at least, to heterosexual couples in a stable relationship, but this failed.[332] Four years later France passed legislation limiting assisted conception services to those whose infertility was 'of a pathological character which has been medically diagnosed' and who were heterosexual married couples or at least able to prove that they have lived together for at least two years.[333] **14.105**

Neither the 1990 Act nor the 2008 Act 'contains any statutory bars upon the treatment of any competent adult, so single, lesbian or post-menopausal women may all lawfully receive assisted conception services'.[334] The 1990 Act only addressed the question of access to treatment in one provision, and then obliquely rather than directly. Section 13(5) of this provided: **14.106**

> A woman shall not be provided with treatment services unless account has been taken of the welfare of any child who may be born as a result of treatment (including the need of that child for a father), and of any other child who may be affected by the birth.

Kennedy and Grubb point to the significance (indeed, uniqueness) of this provision:

> Parliament has required that the clinical judgement of the doctor must be exercised having regard to others and not just the 'best interests' of this patient. In this respect, the 1990 Act departs from what would be the normal understanding of a doctor's duty to his patient.[335]

The provision is incoherent. It refers to the welfare of children as yet unconceived ('who are only a twinkle in the doctor's eye'[336]). It asks us to compare the utilities of not being born to a single mother; surely a nonsense since existence will nearly always (perhaps always) be preferable to non-existence.[337] Jackson finds it difficult, 'perhaps even impossible', to imagine circumstances in which it would be preferable not to be born.[338] And literally interpreted that must be right, but only, I would suggest, because there are circumstances in which the child would be removed from the parents at birth.[339] If the prospective mother had already killed or seriously harmed several of her previous babies, would it not be better **14.107**

[328] *Report of the Committee of Inquiry into Human Fertilisation and Embryology* (Cmnd 9314, 1953) para 2.5.
[329] ibid, para 2.11.
[330] ibid, para 2.13.
[331] ibid, para 2.13.
[332] An amendment moved in the House of Lords to make it an offence to provide treatment services for an unmarried couple was defeated by a single vote (see *Hansard*, HL vol 515, col 787).
[333] See Law 94–654 (29 July 1994).
[334] See G Douglas, *Law, Fertililty and Reproduction* (Sweet & Maxwell 1991), 135.
[335] I Kennedy and A Grubb, *Medical Law—Text with Materials* (Butterworths 2000), 1272.
[336] See Douglas, n 334, 121.
[337] And see D Parfit, *Reasons and Persons* (Oxford University Press 1984); J Harris, *Wonderwoman and Superman* (Oxford University Press 1992).
[338] E Jackson, 'Conception and the Irrelevance of the Welfare Principle' (2002) 65 MLR 176, 181. See also E Jackson, *Regulating Reproduction: Law, Technology and Autonomy* (Hart Publishing 2001) 190 *et seq.*
[339] By means of an emergency protection order (see Children Act 1989, s 44).

to invoke this provision and deny her infertility treatment than allow her this service and then remove the child? But Parliament's concern—and certainly HFEA's—goes beyond ensuring that patients reach a minimal level of parental adequacy. It requires—and here I agree with Jackson—that clinicians take into account 'factors such as the would-be parents' commitment to having and bringing up a child; their ability to provide a stable and supportive environment; their future ability to look after or provide for a child's needs and the possibility of any risk of harm to their child'.[340] This list, drawn from a previous Code of Practice, is modelled on the checklist in the Children Act 1989 (see s 1(3)), but, whilst it is undoubtedly useful there, to resolve a conflict over an existing child, it is difficult to see how apposite it is where there is yet no child.

14.108 Equally incoherent was the emphasis in s 13(5) of the 1990 Act on 'the need of that child for a father'. All children have genetic fathers: what the provision required was a *social* father. Should fertility services therefore be refused if the prospective father cannot fulfil that role? Because he is in prison? Or is a homosexual, not able to offer the 'appropriate' role model? Or is 'just a City workalcoholic?'[341] Or is the reality that what the provision is targeting is lesbians and that 'father' is actually a cloak for a 'man'? And, of course, no fertility clinic can guarantee that a man 'on the scene' at the time of conception will still be about in a year or five years time.

14.109 The 2008 Act has removed the phrase 'need for a father' when considering the welfare of any resulting child, and substituted instead the phrase 'supportive parenting'.[342] This change was controversial and produced alarmist concerns. But, as the Secretary of the State for Health explained, 'this does not signal a desire to diminish fatherhood, nor are we denying children who have been conceived through assisted conception access to information about sperm donors'.[343]

14.110 The Code of Practice defines 'supportive parenting' as 'a commitment to the health, well-being and development of the child. It is presumed that all prospective parents will be supportive parents, in the absence of any reasonable cause for concern that any child who may be born, or any other child, may be at risk of significant harm or neglect. Where centres have concern as to whether this commitment exists, they may wish to take account of wider family and social networks within which the child will be raised'.[344] The provision only requires 'account' to be 'taken of the welfare of any child who may be born as a result of treatment' and 'of any other child who may be affected by their birth'. There is no indication as to the weight, if any, to be attached to the welfare of either set of children. An amendment which would have made the welfare of the child paramount (cf Children Act 1989 s 1(1)) did not pass.[345] But what is mean by account? On whom exactly does the duty fall?[346] What has to be shown to demonstrate that it has been discharged? Who can challenge a decision taken allegedly in breach of the duty? The 1990 and 2008 Acts are both silent on locus standi,[347] either to determine that account has not been taken or to challenge that which has and the resultant conclusion.

[340] E Jackson, ' Conception', n 338, 181.

[341] R G Lee and D Morgan, *Human Fertilisation and Embryology—Regulating The Reproductive Revolution* (Blackstone 2001), 166.

[342] 2008 Act, s 14(2).

[343] *Hansard*, HL vol 517, col 1113.

[344] *Code of Practice* (8th edn).

[345] *Hansard*, HL vol 517, col 1097.

[346] Evidence of the way clinics interpreted the welfare provision in the first years of the Act is found in G Douglas, 'Assisted Reproduction and the Welfare of the Child' (1993) 46 Current Legal Problems 53.

[347] And see paras 14.101–14.102.

The Act does not define 'welfare' (though the Code of Practice, as we shall see in paras 14.114, 14.117) attempts to inject some content into this. Conventionally, 'welfare' is given a broad definition.[348] It includes material welfare, so that the poverty of the prospective parents may be taken into account. But stability, security, warmth, compassion, and commitment of those parents are of greater significance. The directive to take account also of the welfare of the other children who may be affected by the birth means that such extraneous considerations as that an existing child would stand to inherit less as a result of the birth of a new medically assisted sibling may also be considered. **14.111**

The Code of Practice addresses this issue by listing factors to be taken into account during the assessment process. These are factors likely to cause a risk of significant harm or neglect to any prospective child or existing child of the family. These factors include—the list is not therefore exhaustive—such matters as: **14.112**

(a) previous convictions relating to harming children;
(b) child protection measures taken regarding existing children;
(c) violence or serious discord in the family environment;

and circumstances (past or present) likely to lead to an inability to care throughout childhood for any prospective child or that are already seriously impairing the care of any existing child of the family, for example:

(a) mental or physical conditions;
(b) drug or alcohol abuse;
(c) medical history where this indicates that any child who may be born is likely to suffer from a serious medical condition;
(d) circumstances that the centre considers likely to cause serious harm to any child.[349]

But little if any of this was in the minds of those responsible for s 13(5). This was introduced, and passed, expressly to prevent the creation of one-parent families through assisted reproduction, and, in particular, to prevent lesbian women from receiving treatment services. The provision, say Lee and Morgan: 'has all the hallmarks of a profamilist ideology. Assisted conception is to be, for the most part, for the married, mortgaged middle-class'.[350] **14.113**

There is no reference in either Section 13(5) of the 1990 Act nor in the 2008 Act, s 14(2) to the need of the woman for treatment services. What, for example, of the woman who wants a child but who does not wish to have sexual intercourse or genuinely fears sexual relations? Her welfare might dictate the provision of assisted conception to enable her to achieve a 'virgin birth'. The woman's welfare is also an issue where fertility clinics impose age limitations on the provision of services (and see para 14.128). **14.114**

The focus in s 13(5) of the 1990 Act (and in the revamped version in the 2008 Act) is on the welfare of the child. One limitation thus imposed is the best interests of the individual born as a result of assisted conception beyond his/her childhood. This is significant in the context of an individual's quest to construct an identity. 'Welfare' does not seem to address positive self-image or 'genealogical bewilderment'.[351] **14.115**

[348] Lord Mackay of Clashfern, n 337, quoted Hardie Boys J in the New Zealand case of *Walker v Harrison* [1981] New Zealand Recent Law 257.
[349] *Code of Practice* (8th edn) para 8.10.
[350] R G Lee and D Morgan, *Human Fertilisation and Embryology—Regulating The Reproductive Revolution* (Blackstone 2001) 164.
[351] See H Sants, 'Genealogical Bewilderment in Children with Substitute Parents' (1964) 37 British Journal of Medical Psychology 133.

14.116 The width of s 13(5) must also be noted. It extends to any treatment service, including intrauterine insemination. 'Treatment service' is defined in the Act to mean 'medical, surgical or obstetric services provided to the public or a section of the public for the purpose of assisting women to carry children'.[352] In theory, antenatal services could be denied to a lesbian woman on the ground that it would be better for the child if she miscarried. No one, one must assume, would put this construction on s 13(5), but, however extraordinary, it is capable of bearing this meaning.

14.117 Section 13(5) clearly also applies to surrogacy (on which see paras 14.240–14.280). This means that treatment services to a surrogate mother must take account both of the abilities of the commissioning parents (or parent where the surrogate's own egg is being used) to advance the child's welfare and the psychological effect that a woman giving birth and then giving the child away may have on her other children.[353] The surrogate's own welfare is not within the ambit of s 13(5) (and see para 14.114).

14.118 The eighth edition of the HFEA's Code of Practice recognizes that people have the right to be treated fairly.

14.119 So, 'the centre should ensure that all licensed activities are conducted in a non-discriminatory way and with proper respect for the privacy, confidentiality, dignity, comfort and well-being of all prospective and current patients and donors'.[354] It notes that 'attitudes towards the use of gametes and embryos may vary widely among cultures and religions'. It requires all health care professionals to be 'sensitive' to this. 'Each case and decision is individual and personal and must be treated as such.'[355] It requires that 'all prospective and current patients and donors . . . be treated with respect, whatever their life choices or beliefs'.[356] It adds: 'Staff at the centre must not unlawfully discriminate against patients or donors by allowing their personal views to affect adversely the professional relationship with them, or the treatment they arrange or provide.'[357] The Code of Practice also stresses that those seeking treatment are 'entitled to a fair assessment'.[358] As a result, centres are expected to consider 'the wishes of all those involved'.[359] The assessment must be carried out in a 'non-discriminatory way. In particular, patients must not be discriminated against on grounds of gender, race, disability, sexual orientation, religious belief or age.'[360]

14.120 The Code of Practice does not exclude any category of persons as such from access to services for assisted reproduction. But, as can be seen above, it does emphasize 'the child's need for supportive parenting', and stresses that treatment should be refused if the Centre believes that 'it would not be in the interests of any resulting child, or any children already existing'. It leaves decisions to rest with individual centre's assessments of an applicant's suitability.[361] It also emphasizes the importance of giving reasons for decisions. Where these prove inadequate, there may be a challenge by judicial review.

[352] 1990 Act, s 2(1) (as amended).
[353] H Krimmel, 'The Case Against Surrogate Parenting', *Hastings Center Report*, (October 1983) 35, quotes a 9-year-old girl who, when told that the child her mother was carrying would be given away to another family, responded: 'All right . . . But if it's a girl, let's keep it and give Jeffrey away' [her 2-year-old brother].
[354] *Code of Practice* (8th edn), para 29.3.
[355] ibid, para 29.4.
[356] ibid, para 29.6.
[357] ibid, para 29.10.
[358] ibid, para 8.7.
[359] ibid, para 8.7.
[360] ibid, para 8.7.
[361] And see HFEA, *Tenth Annual Report and Accounts* (HFEA 2002).

There are few reported challenges. The first case, which antedates both the 1990 Act, and therefore any Code, is *R v Ethical Committee of St Mary's Hospital (Manchester) ex p Harriott*.[362] The applicant, who had been turned down as a suitable foster or adoptive parent because she had a criminal record involving prostitution offences and a 'poor understanding' of fostering, was removed from the IVF waiting list after the clinic became aware of her background. At this clinic, the criteria for offering treatment was that couples: 'must, in the ordinary course of events, satisfy the general criteria established by adoption societies in assessing suitability for adoption . . .[363] [and there] must be no medical, psychiatric or psychosexual problems which would indicate an increased probability of a couple not being able to provide satisfactory parenting to the offspring or endanger the mother's life or health if she became pregnant.' **14.121**

The applicant sought judicial review of the decision to refuse to treat her. She failed because she had been given an opportunity to make representations against the refusal. There was, accordingly, no procedural unfairness (as to which see paras 14.99–14.100). However, Schiemann J noted that 'it is not, and could not be, suggested that no reasonable consultant could have come to the decision to refuse treatment to the applicant'.[364] The clinic's criteria were therefore not *Wednesbury* unreasonable. He was prepared to accept, obiter, that a blanket policy to refuse treatment to 'anyone who was a Jew or coloured [sic]' might be illegal.[365] Why Schiemann J had any other doubt as to the propriety of a policy which would deny treatment on grounds of race or colour is surprising because such policies were unlawful under the Race Relations Act 1968, and now under the Equality Act 2010. Discrimination on grounds of religion was not then unlawful under any legislation, but is now outlawed by the Equality Act 2010.[366] It may be added that such blanket policies would also fetter discretion and be unlawful for this reason too. **14.122**

Upper age limits for publicly funded treatment are common. This policy was challenged in *R v Sheffield Area Health Authority ex p Seale*.[367] The applicant, who was 37, was outside the age range within which the authority provided treatment (it had an upper age limit of 35). This had been imposed in order to ration treatment, within a limited budget, to women upon whom it was likely to have the greatest benefit. Auld J found the policy to be neither illegal nor irrational 'applying the high test that that word imports under the *Wednesbury* decision'.[368] He also found no fettering of discretion—but his conclusion here is dubious—or procedural impropriety. Although Mrs Seale's challenge failed (she did not even persuade the judge that she had an arguable case that would justify granting leave to bring an application for judicial review), a future challenge to an inflexible age policy may succeed. The policy may be lawful but it should not be applied blindly but rather flexibly, which, it may be argued, did not happen in Mrs Seale's case. **14.123**

It is common to find other criteria employed by NHS clinics. Examples are evidence of the stability of a non-marital relationship (it seems marital relationships are assumed to be stable), and that the woman is close to her ideal body weight.[369] In addition, many NHS clinics will fund no more than one cycle of treatment.[370] As Jackson states, 'although these **14.124**

362 *R v Ethical Committee of St Mary's Hospital (Manchester) ex p Harriott* [1988] 1 FLR 512.
363 See generally M J Campion, *Who's Fit To Be A Parent?* (Routledge 1995). On adoption, see ch 2; on assisted reproduction see ch 4.
364 *ex p Harriott*, n 362, 519.
365 ibid, 518–19.
366 See Equality Act 2010, s 10.
367 *R v Sheffield Area Health Authority ex p Seale* [1994] 25 BMLR 1.
368 ibid.
369 See E Jackson, *Regulating Reproduction* (Hart Publishing 2001) 198.
370 ibid.

eligibility guidelines may seem overly restrictive, it must of course be remembered that funding any infertility treatment is more generous than the norm'.[371] It is unlikely that challenges to any of these criteria will succeed. The latter two (body weight and restriction on the number of courses of treatment) can clearly be medically justified and thus, it would seem, are rational decisions.

14.125 The 1990 Act deals with treatment services only within the UK. However, s 24(4) of the Act does invest HFEA with a discretion to permit a licence-holder to export gametes or embryos. Accordingly, the possibility of using treatment services abroad, most particularly within the European Union, and the legal implications of doing so, has arisen in two cases. In *R v Human Fertilisation and Embryology Authority, ex p Blood*,[372] when Mrs Diane Blood was denied permission to take her dead husband's sperm to Belgium with a view to treatment services being performed in a Brussels clinic, she invoked provisions of the EC.[373] The Court of Appeal held that the prohibition on exporting gametes, imposed by HFEA, was tantamount to a denial of the right of access to medical treatment abroad, and could only be justified if it were absolutely necessary in the public interest. HFEA was entitled to place restrictions on the export of sperm, but such restrictions had to be justified on grounds of public policy. HFEA was accordingly directed to reconsider its position in the light of (what is now) Article 49 of the EC Treaty. Said Lord Woolf MR:

> Parliament has delegated to the Authority the responsibility for making decisions in this difficult and delicate area, and the court should be slow to interfere with its decisions. However, the reasons given by the Authority, while not deeply flawed, confirm that the Authority did not take into account two important considerations. The first being the effect of Article [49] of the Treaty. The second being that there should be, after this judgment has been given, no further cases where sperm is preserved without consent. The Authority is not to be criticised for this because, in relation to the law, it was dependent on the guidance it received. However, the fact remains that having not received the appropriate guidance, the Authority did not take into account two matters which Mrs Blood is entitled to have taken into account.[374]

14.126 Following the decision of the Court of Appeal, HFEA reconsidered its position. It considered that the case would set no precedent since sperm should never again be taken without consent. It also agreed that it had failed to establish a sufficiently compelling public policy exception to Mrs Blood's rights to transfer her dead husband's sperm across borders. Mrs Blood subsequently had treatment in Belgium, and gave birth to a son. She has since done this a second time.[375] The Court of Appeal's decision was criticized for failing to observe that there was surely a presumption that before sperm was exported it have first been obtained and stored in conformity with national law.[376] The government commissioned Professor Sheila McLean to report on the implications of the *Blood* decision. She commented:

> It surely cannot have been intended that the discretion to permit export was intended to cover gametes which were unlawfully obtained and/or unlawfully stored. It would be

[371] ibid.

[372] *R v Human Fertilisation and Embryology Authority, ex p Blood* [1997] 2 All ER 687. See also *L v HFEA* [2008] EWHC 2149 (Fam).

[373] Articles 59 and 60 (now Arts 49 and 50).

[374] *ex p Blood*, n 372, 702.

[375] A second son was born in July 2002. Both boys have a father (see s 13(5) of the 1990 Act, before the 2008 changes), but ironically not a legal father.

[376] See D Morgan and R Lee, 'In The Name of the Father? *Ex parte* Blood: Dealing with Novelty and Anomaly' (1997) 60 MLR 840, 851.

a most unusual piece of legislation which created legislation only to build into itself the power to defeat them by the exercise of discretion.[377]

The government indicated that as a result of the *Blood* case and the McLean Report it would amend the Human Fertilisation and Embryology Act,[378] and it has done so.

This was done in the Human Fertilisation and Embryology (Deceased Fathers) Act 2003. **14.127** This was replaced by s 39 of the 2008 Act which provides that where a woman has a child as a result of the placing in her of an embryo, or sperm and eggs or artificial insemination, and the child was created using the sperm of a man after his death, then the man who provided the sperm is to be treated as the child's father if:

(i) the man consented in writing to the use of his sperm or embryo after his death, and to being treated as the child's father for the purposes of birth registration;[379]
(ii) he did not withdraw his consent;[380]
(iii) the woman must elect in writing that he should be so treated within forty-two days of the child's birth;[381]
(iv) no one else is to be treated as the father by virtue of sections 35, 36, or 38(2) or (3);[382]
(v) no one else is to be treated as a parent of the child by virtue of sections 42 or 43;[383]
(vi) no one else is to be treated as a parent of the child by virtue of adoption.[384]

These provisions apply whether the embryo or gametes were transferred to the woman in the UK or elsewhere.[385] Since Diane Blood did not have her dead husband's written consent, she would encounter similar problems now.

In *Blood* the Court of Appeal predicted that there would be no more such cases. It was **14.128** wrong. In 2008, the court was involved again in a similar case, *L v HFEA* when H died after routine surgery. H and his partner, L already had a child and were keen to have a second. An application was made to Macur J to remove sperm from H. She declared it was lawful to do so. But the decision misunderstood the scope of the Human Tissue Act 2004, which does not apply to gametes. Since there was no written consent, the sperm could not be used in the UK. Before the sperm could be exported to a jurisdiction where it could be used without written consent, it had to be decided whether it could be stored and exported lawfully. It was held by Charles J that (1) the evidence was clear that H would have wanted his sperm to be used posthumously; (2) the law was clear: storage and use of H's sperm in the UK was unlawful but HFEA had a wide discretion to permit export of gametes. HFEA then took account of both European Treaty rights and the Human Rights Act 1998 (ECHR Arts 8 and 12) and permitted export of H's sperm to the USA, where it could be lawfully used.[386]

[377] *Consent and the Law: Review of the Common Law Provisions Relating To The Removal of Gametes and of the Consent, Provisions in the Human Fertilisation and Embryology Act 1990 for the UK Health Ministers* (HMSO 1997) para 7.4.

[378] *Government Response to the McLean Review on Consent to Storage and Use of Human Sperm and Eggs* 2000/0486 (25 August 2000).

[379] 2008 Act, s 39(1)(c). Not for other purposes, such as inheritance.

[380] ibid, s39(1)(c).

[381] ibid, s 39(1)(d).

[382] ibid, s 39(1)(e).

[383] ibid, s 39(1)(e).

[384] ibid, s 39(1)(e).

[385] ibid, s 39(2).

[386] See *L v HFEA* [2008] EWHC 2149 [Fam].

E. Conscientious Objection

14.129 The 1990 Act contains a conscience clause provision designed to permit individuals to opt out of participating in any of the activities covered by the Act. It provides that: 'No person who has a conscientious objection to participating in any activity governed by this Act shall be under a duty, however arising, to do so.'[387] However, 'in any legal proceedings the burden of conscientious objection rests on the person claiming to rely on it'.[388]

14.130 The provision is modelled on s 4 of the Abortion Act 1967, but there is an important difference. The 1990 Act does not contain an exception to the right to object where action is necessary to save a patient's life or prevent grave permanent injury.[389] However, it will be noted that s 38 refers to 'any activity governed by this Act', and abortion is in part governed by the 1990 Act.[390] There is thus a conflict between s 4 of the Abortion Act and s 38 of the 1990 Act. This was created unintentionally but still has to be resolved. The better view must be that the exception does not apply to activities covered by the 1990 Act, except abortion. However, two other points may be noted. First, life-threatening conditions are not likely to arise in the context of infertility treatment. Secondly, were they to do so, there is a common law duty on doctors to intervene to arrest conditions which are life-threatening or are causing grave physical injury.[391] The omission and the conflict are not therefore of overwhelming significance.

14.131 The objection must be 'conscientious'. 'Conscience' is widely interpreted and will include not only religious beliefs but also other principled reasons which impel a person to believe that an activity is inherently wrong.

14.132 The provision states that 'no person' with a conscientious objection is under a duty to participate in any of the Act's activities. This clearly extends to doctors and to nurses,[392] but, in the light of the House of Lords' decision in *Janaway v Salford Area Health Authority*,[393] whether it extends any further will depend on how 'participate' is interpreted. There can be no doubt that a research scientist or laboratory technician may invoke the conscience clause. But, whether a secretary, instructed to type letters or forms in connection with, for example, embryo research to which she takes moral objection, would be similarly protected is generally thought unlikely after *Janaway*.[394] However, the language of the abortion provision, interpreted in *Janaway*, and s 38 are not identical. Section 4 of the Abortion Act refers to participation in *any treatment* authorized by the Act, and s 38 is couched more widely in terms of *any activity* governed by the Act. A secretary does not, so it has been held, participate in treatment, but it is not stretching language too far to hold that she does participate in an activity governed by the 1990 Act. In support of this interpretation it may be noted that Lord Keith in *Janaway* argued that:

---

387 The 1990 Act, s 38(1). And see M Wicclair, 'Conscientious Objection in Medicine' [2000] 14 Bioethics 205. See Special Issue of *Bioethics* [2014] vol 28 [1].

388 1990 Act, s 38(2). Justifications for conscience exemptions are considered by L Kantymir and C McLeod, 'Justification for Conscience Exemptions in Health Care' [2014] 28 *Bioethics* 16–23.

389 As the Abortion Act 1967 does.

390 1990 Act, s 37.

391 See *F v Berkshire Health Authority* [1990] 2 AC 1.

392 See *Royal College of Nursing of the United Kingdom v Department of Health and Social Security* [1981] AC 800.

393 *Janaway v Salford Area Health Authority* [1989] AC 537.

394 Where a doctor's receptionist was held not to be participating in abortion when she typed a letter referring a patient to a second doctor for a second opinion.

> If Parliament had intended the result contended for by the applicant (ie that typing a letter amounted to participating in treatment), it could have procured it very clearly and easily by referring to participation 'in anything authorized by this Act', instead of 'in any treatment [so] authorised'.[395]

In effect this is what Parliament has done in the 1990 Act. It is thus arguable that even activities remote from treatment are covered by the conscience clause in s 38. Whether s 38 in addition reverses the ruling in *Janaway* (note the argument in para 14.132 that abortion is an activity covered by the 1990 Act) must be arguable, although there can be no doubt that Parliament had no such intention.

The conscience clause permits an individual to object to *any* activity governed by the 1990 Act. S/he may thus, for example, object to embryo research on conscientious grounds, without also objecting to assisted reproduction. However, difficult questions arise in relation to this. Most obviously, can an individual who assists assisted reproduction conscientiously object to the use of *in vitro* fertilization in the case of, for example, a single woman or a lesbian woman? Does acceptance of an activity entail acceptance of all instances of that activity? It has been argued that the conscience clause could be successfully invoked by those who do not wish to treat lesbians.[396] This is not very convincing for two reasons. First, such an objection would be rooted in prejudice, rather than based on conscience[397] (though it must be conceded that a definitive understanding of what is meant by 'conscience' awaits clarification by the courts). Secondly, it does not seem that the person invoking conscientious objection is objecting to the activity as such, but rather to the sexual orientation and/or lifestyle of the person who is the potential beneficiary of the activity. It would be straining language to hold that the objection is to the activity of creating unconventional families. This is not the natural meaning of the language used, nor was it Parliament's intention. The Code of Practice makes it clear that the person responsible must ensure that this provision is not being used to perpetrate unlawful discrimination.[398] **14.133**

F. Consent to the Use of Genetic Material

The most firmly entrenched principle of medical law requires that a person consents to treatment. There is probably no more commonly quoted dictum in English medical law than Cardozo J's in *Schloendorff v Society of New York Hospital*: **14.134**

> Every human being of adult years and sound mind has a right to determine what shall be done with his own body; and a surgeon who performs an operation without his patient's consent commits an assault . . . [399]

In the case of medically assisted reproduction, which is regulated by the 1990 Act (as amended), the common law (on which see Chapter 3) is supplemented by the 1990 Act (as amended), and by the Code of Practice. The common law remains important both because it underpins the legislation and therefore may be prayed in aid in its interpretation, and because it needs must govern procedures and techniques which fall outside the legislative framework. It is also important where a question arises (eg whether a withdrawal of consent **14.135**

[395] Janaway, n 393, 570.

[396] See G Douglas, 'Assisted Reproduction and the Welfare of the Child' (1993) 46 *Current Legal Problems* 122.

[397] And see R Dworkin, *Taking Rights Seriously* (Duckworth 1977) ch 10.

[398] *Code of Practice* (8th edn) 29.11.

[399] (1914) 211 NJ 125, 126, cited with approval, inter alia, in *Re F (Mental Patient: Sterilisation)* [1990] 2 AC 1; and in *Airedale NHS Trust v Bland* [1993] AC 789.

was the result of undue influence) which requires recourse to it.[400] The question therefore needs to be raised as to what infertility treatment, which falls outside the remit of the 1990 Act, a person may consent. There is no direct authority on this, but on principle it would seem that one can consent to any 'proper medical treatment'. It may be a matter of some controversy as to what is to be regarded as proper medical treatment. The courts are likely to apply the *Bolam* principle (as to which see Chapter 6) and rely on the views of institutions like the Royal College of Obstetricians and Gynaecologists.[401] The courts have stressed that the *Bolam* principle should not be allowed to inhibit innovative work: this is an especially important ruling in the context of medically assisted reproduction where development of new technologies is an ongoing process.[402]

14.136 The *Blood* litigation in 1996–1997[403] (and see paras 14.129–14.131) re-emphasized the necessity of consent. Sperm was removed from Mr Blood, who was in a coma dying from bacterial meningitis, on the instructions of his wife. According to Lord Woolf MR, in the Court of Appeal, 'humanity dictated that the sperm was taken and preserved first and the legal argument followed'.[404] There was argument that Mr Blood's consent could be implied from conversations that he and his wife had had about starting a family. The Court of Appeal agreed with the Human Fertilisation and Embryology Authority that consent had to be express and written, as stipulated in the 1990 Act,[405] and could not be construed in this way. It also agreed with HFEA that the storage of Mr Blood's sperm was 'technically' a criminal offence: it was contrary to s 41(2)(b) of the Act. Although the Court of Appeal did not address the issue, it is also clear that Mrs Blood had no capacity to consent on behalf of her husband. Such capacity would have to be grounded on the need 'to save life or to ensure improvement or prevent deterioration in physical or mental health',[406] and none of these conditions could possibly have applied. Further, if treating Mr Blood in this way was not in his best interests, it is difficult to see how he would have an interest in treatment which was designed to produce offspring whose lives he would never see.

14.137 The 1990 Act provides in the new s 13(6) that:

> A woman shall not be provided with any treatment services involving—
>
> (a) the use of any gametes of any person, if that person's consent is required under paragraph 5 of Schedule 3 to this Act for the use in question,
> (b) the use of any embryo the creation of which was brought about *in vitro*, or
> (c) the use of any embryo taken from a woman, if the consent of the woman from whom it was taken is required under paragraph 7 of that Schedule for the use in question,
>
> unless the woman being treated and, any man or woman who is to be treated together with her, have been given a suitable opportunity to receive proper counselling about the implications of being provided with treatment services of that kind, and have been provided with such relevant information as is proper.

400 Examples of undue influence in medical law include *Re T* [1993] Fam 95.

401 As courts have done in areas like permanent vegetative state diagnosis. See, eg, *An NHS Trust v M; An NHS Trust v H* [2001] 2 FLR 367; *NHS Trust A v H* [2001] 2 FLR 501. Thus in relation to egg giving, where the 'three embryos' rule does not apply, the question must be raised as to whether consent may be given to more than three embryos being inserted. Dr Ian Craft has admitted to inserting as many as thirteen (*Panorama*, BBC 1, 6 July 2003). It is dubious whether the woman concerned could consent to this if the *Bolam* principle were adhered to, which, it is argued, should be the case.

402 See *JS v An NHS Trust; JA v An NHS Trust* [2003] 1 FLR 879.

403 *R v Human Fertilisation and Embryology Authority, ex p Blood* [1997] 2 WLR 806.

404 ibid, 814.

405 1990 Act, Sch 3, para 8.

406 *Per* Lord Brandon of Oakbrook in *Re F* [1990] 2 AC 1, 55.

The events in connection with which counselling must be offered are: **14.138**

(1) A man gives the person responsible a notice under the agreed fatherhood conditions (on which see para 14.220) in a case where the woman for whom the treatment services are provided has previously given a notice referring to the man.
(2) The woman for whom the treatment services are provided gives the person responsible a notice in a case when the man to whom the notice relates has previously given a notice.[407]
(3) The woman for whom the treatment services are provided gives the person responsible a notice under agreed female parenthood conditions (on which see paras 14.224–14.227) in a case where the woman for whom treatment services are provided has previously given a notice.
(4) A woman for whom treatment services are provided gives the person responsible notice in a case where the other woman to whom the notice relates has previously given a notice.

Consent must be in writing. This is not a requirement of common law, so that procedures outside the 1990 Act do not require consent to be so evidenced. It would be rather foolhardy for a treatment clinic not to insist on written consent to such treatment. Consent can be withdrawn: the withdrawal will be effective, even if there has been pressure, provided this does not amount to undue influence.[408] **14.139**

Section 13(6), as amended, confirms and reinforces the common law, and supplements it by requiring an opportunity for counselling and the provision of relevant information. The need for counselling was recognized in the Warnock Report.[409] It envisaged 'non-directional' counselling aimed at 'helping individuals to understand their situation and to make their own decisions about what steps should be taken next'.[410] The 1990 Act does not state what counselling is to consist of, nor when it is to be made available, nor whether a centre can direct or merely encourage the use of counselling services. However, the Code of Practice is very specific on the content of counselling (see para 3 of the Code). The 1990 Act, as originally formulated, was expressed in the present continuous tense ('being treated'). This raised the question as to whether proper counselling must also be offered each time the patient or patients return for treatment. In the 2008 amendment 'being treated' is replaced by 'who is to be treated', suggesting that counselling needs to be offered each time the patient returns for treatment.[411] But given resource constraints, the better interpretation would be to limit the obligation to before initial treatment is offered. On the question whether counselling may be directed or merely offered, the Code is clear that what is required is the making available of counselling. There must be concern about the adequacy of counselling, and doubt as to whether the Authority has the ability to police this requirement effectively. **14.140**

G. Counselling

1. The Provision of counselling

Counselling should be clearly distinguished from: **14.141**

[407] 1990 Act, Sch 3ZA, Pt 2 (as amended).
[408] *Centre for Reproductive Medicine v U* [2002] 1 FLR 927.
[409] *Report of the Committee of Inquiry in Human Fertilisation and Embryology* (Cmnd 9314 1953) paras 3.3–3.4.
[410] ibid, para 3.4.
[411] 1990 Act s 13(6) (as amended). And see *Code of Practice* (8th edn), 3.5.

(1) the assessment of a person's suitability to receive treatment, or to store or donate their gametes or embryos;
(2) the provision of information before obtaining consent or providing treatment; and
(3) the normal relationship between clinical staff and patients or donors.[412]

14.142 The counselling service should comply with current professional guidance on good practice in fertility counselling. Counselling is to be provided only by qualified counsellors.[413]

14.143 The Code requires counselling to be available from a counsellor attached to the centre, but further states: 'If this is not possible or if the practice prefers to seek counselling elsewhere, the centre should provide lists of counsellors, indicating the services they offer and organizations which can provide relevant information.'[414]

14.144 The Code also stipulates that counselling facilities provide 'quiet and comfortable surroundings for private, confidential and uninterrupted sessions'.[415]

14.145 Information obtained during counselling is confidential. But the Code of Practice acknowledges that it may be disclosed in certain circumstances.[416] The example given[417] is if it gives rise to concerns about the suitability of a person to donate gametes or receive treatment. The duty of confidentiality is not absolute and confidences may be divulged appropriately in the public interest (on which see Chapter 12).

14.146 Prior to the 1990 Act there was, it seems, very little counselling for those who wanted infertility treatment. The 1990 Act provides that counselling arrangements should be set up within the Code of Practice. This accordingly provides in the current edition that:

> 3.1 The centre should normally offer counselling after the individual or couple has received oral and written information about the services to be provided and before they consent to treatment, or to the storage or use of gametes or embryos. The timing and frequency of counselling sessions is up to the counsellor and the person or couple concerned, who should agree to this together.
>
> 3.2 The centre should make patients aware that the offer of counselling is routine. The offer should include written information giving the name(s) of qualified counsellor(s), explaining their role, when they are available and how to access the service. The centre should allow enough time before treatment starts for patients to consider the offer and to take up the opportunity of counselling if they so choose.
>
> 3.3 If the possibility of treatment with donated gametes or embryos arises, the centre should offer counselling about the implications of treatment with donated material separately from counselling about the implications of treatment in general and before treatment with donor gametes start.
>
> 3.4 If the possibility of donating gametes or embryos for the treatment of others, or donating embryos for research or training arises, the centre should continue only if the woman and, if applicable, her partner have been offered counselling about the implications of donation.
>
> 3.5 The centre should take all practicable steps to provide an opportunity for counselling throughout the treatment, donation or storage processes, and afterwards if requested. If a person has previously donated gametes or embryos, or received treatment, requests further counselling at any point, the centre should take all practicable steps to help them obtain it.

---

412 *Code of Practice* (8th edn) 3.7.
413 ibid, 3.8.
414 ibid, 3.9.
415 ibid, 3.11.
416 ibid, 3.12.
417 ibid, 3.12.

> 3.6 The centre should offer people the opportunity to be counselled with a partner, if they have one, individually or both. Group sessions may be offered in addition to individual and couple sessions.
>
> 3.10 The centre should ensure that arrangements are in place to provide, or refer people for, specialist counselling if appropriate, taking account of their duty of confidentiality under the . . . Act. This might include genetic counselling, and counselling for oncology patients or others requiring the longer term storage of gametes or embryos.

It will have been observed that, although there is a great emphasis on counselling, no one is under any obligation to accept it. There is, it seems, a low take-up rate on counselling. There is no duty to make it free of charge. The Code clearly sees counselling as beneficial but there is nothing in it to strengthen participation. There must be a concern—Lee and Morgan also recognize this[418]—that centres do not promote counselling lest it deter potential patients who are, after all, a source of profit. There is concern also that the Authority's enforcement of the counselling code is weak. **14.147**

2. The provision of information

As regards the obligation to give information, the Code of Practice lays down the following: **14.148**

> 4.2 Before treatment is offered, the centre should give the woman seeking treatment and her partner, if applicable, information about:
>
> (a) the centre's policy on selecting patients,
> (b) the centre's statutory duty to take account of the welfare of any resulting or affected child,
> (c) the expected waiting time for treatment,
> (d) fertility treatments available,
> (e) the likely outcomes of the proposed treatment (data provided should include the centre's most recent live birth rate and clinical pregnancy rate per treatment cycle, verified by the HFEA, and the national live birth rate and clinical pregnancy rate per treatment cycle),
> (f) the nature and potential risks of the treatment, including the risk of children conceived having developmental and birth defects,
> (g) the possible side effects and risks to the woman being treated and any resulting child, including ovarian hyperstimulation syndrome (OHSS),
> (h) in the case of fresh egg donation, the screening requirement of the donor and the risk of infection for the recipient,
> (i) the availability of facilities for freezing embryos, and the implications of storing embryos and then using embryos,
> (j) the importance of informing the treatment centre about the eventual outcome of the treatment (including if no live birth results),
> (k) the centre's complaints procedure, and
> (l) the nature and postnatal risks (immediate and/or long term) of IVF/ICSI with *in vitro* matured eggs, including reference to the clinic's experience.

Information is also to be given about the cost of treatment (a 'personalised costed treatment plan'). The centre 'should give patients the opportunity to discuss the plan before the treatment begins' (para 4.3). **14.149**

As will have been observed, the level of detail required by the Code of Practice far exceeds the requirements of common law. The question therefore arises as to the liability of a clinician who fails to comply with the Code of Practice. Section 25(6) of the 1990 Act states **14.150**

[418] R G Lee and D Morgan, *Human Fertilisation and Embryology—Regulating The Reproductive Revolution* (Blackstone 2001).

that: 'A failure on the part of any person to observe any provision of the code shall not of itself render the person liable to any proceedings . . .' On its face this suggests that failure to observe a provision of the Code will not, without more, be sufficient to render a doctor liable to civil or criminal proceedings. However, a case may be made that the Code of Practice establishes what is regarded as good medical practice, and thus what a responsible doctor would do, with the consequence that failure to comply with it could constitute a breach of duty and expose the doctor concerned to a civil action for negligence. [419] The latter is the better view, and, in the absence of a legal ruling to the contrary, should be followed. However, the Act imposes on the Authority the obligation that where it has to consider whether there has been a failure to comply with the conditions of a licence, in particular where the conditions require something to be done that is 'proper' or 'suitable', it is to take into account only relevant provision of the Code of Practice.[420] And, in considering whether or not to vary or revoke a licence, it can take into consideration failure to observe the Code of Practice.[421]

14.151 Where the treatment falls outside the 1990 Act, and thus the Code of Practice, the common law will govern what information must be given. The details of this are found in Chapter 6.

H. Control of Gametes and Embryos

14.152 The 1990 Act (as amended) in Sch 3 sets out an elaborate framework, the purpose of which is to vest control of gametes, embryos, and human admixed embryos in those who provide the genetic material.

14.153 It is a requirement of the 'licence condition' that the consent provisions in Sch 3 are complied with.[422] Failure to observe the provisions will breach the duty upon the 'person responsible' for the licensed activities to ensure that the conditions of the licence are complied with.[423] A breach of such duty, for example, proceeding without an effective consent, is a ground for the revocation of the licence.[424]

14.154 The Schedule requires that a gamete provider must, at the time the gametes are procured, indicate in a written consent to what use or uses the gametes may be put.[425] The gametes, human cells, embryo, or human admixed embryo may only be used in accordance with the consents (this includes those consents as varied).[426]

14.155 A gamete provider must specify the purposes to which the gametes or human cells may be put. They may not be used for treatment services unless there is an 'effective consent'[427] by that person to their being so used, and they are used in accordance with the terms of the consent.[428] Nor may they be kept in storage unless there is an effective consent by that person to their storage, and they are stored in accordance with the consent.[429] Nor may they be used to bring about the creation of an embryo *in vitro* unless there is effective consent by

[419] See *Bolam v Friern Hospital Management Committee* [1957] 1 WLR 582.
[420] 1990 Act, s 26(6)(a).
[421] ibid, s 26(6)(b).
[422] ibid, s 12(c).
[423] ibid, s 17(1)(e).
[424] Under ibid, s 18(2).
[425] ibid, Sch 3, para 2(1).
[426] ibid, Sch 3, para 4 (as amended).
[427] ibid; 'Effective consent' means consent which has not been withdrawn: see Sch 3, para 1.
[428] ibid, Sch 3, para 5.
[429] ibid, Sch 3, para 8(1).

that person to such a creation.[430] In this case, the gamete provider must both consent to the future use and/or storage of the embryo.[431]

14.156 A consent to the use of any embryo may specify conditions subject to which the embryo may be so used.[432] Similarly, a consent to storage of gametes, embryos, or human admixed embryos may specify conditions subject to which they may remain in storage.[433] But may the provider specify any conditions? For example, would a condition which stipulated that the gamete not be used for the treatment of individuals of a particular racial, ethnic, or religious group be valid or invalid? The 1990 Act does not provide an answer to this question. But common law does. There can be little doubt that such a condition would be regarded as invalid.[434] A treatment centre should therefore not accept gametes or embryos subject to such conditions. Whether such a condition would invalidate the 'effective consent' is more contentious. There are two views: one which argues that, if the consent could be valid with the unlawful condition removed, it should be upheld; the second would uphold the consent only if it gave effect to the provider's underlying intention.[435] The better view, it is submitted, is the first one, which would sever the invalid condition. The public interest in making gametes available should prevail over the selfish prejudice of the provider.[436]

14.157 A consent to the storage of any gametes, embryos, or human admixed embryos must specify the maximum period of storage, if less than the statutory storage period[437] (on which see para 14.64), and state what is to be done with the gametes, embryos, or human admixed embryos if the person who gave the consent dies or is unable, because of incapacity, to vary the terms of the consent or to revoke it.[438] The legislation does not state what should happen, only that the provider of gametes and embryos should address the issue.

14.158 Consent can be varied and withdrawn[439] by notice. By implication notice must be in writing[440] (though this is not specifically stated in the legislation). Nor does the Act say what notice must be given: the assumption must be that any notice will suffice. The terms of any consent to the use of any embryo cannot be varied, and the consent cannot be withdrawn, once the embryo has been used in providing treatment services or training persons in embryo biopsy, embryo storage, or other embryological techniques or for the purpose of any project of research.[441]

14.159 An embryo taken from a woman must not be used for any purpose unless there is effective consent by her to the use of her embryo for that purpose, and it is in accordance with the consent,[442] or it is used for the purpose of providing that woman with treatment services.[443] Nor must it be kept in storage unless there is effective consent to this by her.[444]

430 ibid, Sch 3, para 6(1).
431 ibid, Sch 3, para 6(3).
432 ibid, Sch 3, para 2(1) (as amended).
433 ibid, Sch 3, para 2(2) (as amended).
434 See *Re Dominion Students' Hall Trust* [1947] Ch 183; *Re Lysaght* [1966] Ch 191. And see Equality Act 2010.
435 See I Kennedy, and A Grubb, *Medical Law—Text with Materials* (Butterworths 2000), 1294.
436 As happens with charitable trusts. Certainly, this should happen if, once the invalid condition is removed, the public interest in having gametes and embryos preserved could be upheld.
437 1990 Act, Sch 3, para 2(2)(a) (as amended).
438 ibid, Sch 3, para 2(2)(b) (as amended).
439 ibid, Sch 3, para 4(1) (as amended).
440 The definition of 'notice' in the 1990 Act, s 46 does not require notice to be in writing, but the language of s 46(2) ('delivering', 'leaving', 'sending by post') strongly suggests this.
441 1990 Act, Sch 3, para 4(2) (as amended). This provision seeks to overcome the problems which arise where there are disputes over frozen embryos, for example over their 'custody' as happened in *Evans v UK* [2007] 1 FLR 1990, and see paras 14.165–14.167.
442 ibid, Sch 3, para 7(1), (2).
443 ibid, Sch 3, para 7(3) (as amended).
444 ibid, Sch 3, para 8(3).

14.160 A person's gametes must not be kept in storage unless there is effective consent by that person to their storage and they are stored in accordance with the consent.[445] An embryo, the creation of which was brought about *in vitro*, must not be kept in storage, unless there is effective consent to the storage of the embryo by the relevant person in relation to the embryo, and the embryo is stored in accordance with those consents.[446] It follows that, upon the valid withdrawal of consent by at least one gamete provider, any gametes or embryo may no longer be lawfully stored. They must then either be used in accordance with any remaining consents to their use or, if no such consent exists, must presumably be 'allowed to perish'.[447] The legislation is silent as to what should happen in these circumstances, but no other consequence seems possible in terms of general scheme of the Act.

14.161 These issues were litigated in the *Evans* case in the English courts and before the European Court of Human Rights.[448]

14.162 Ms Evans and Mr Johnston underwent *in vitro* fertilization treatment. They were then partners. Embryos created from their gametes were frozen and stored. Ms Evans had her ovaries removed immediately following the harvesting of her eggs, and so the frozen embryos represented her only chance of giving birth to a child which was genetically hers. The relationship came to an end. Ms Evans wished to remove the embryos from storage and have them transferred to her, so that she could become pregnant. Mr Johnston withdrew his consent to the IVF treatment and to the continuing storage of the embryos. He wanted the clinic to allow the embryos to perish. Ms Evans argued that the court had the power both to override the withdrawal of her former partner's consent, and to permit her to use the embryos. Both Wall J. and the Court of Appeal found that Mr Johnston had only ever consented to undergoing 'treatment together' with Ms Evans, and had never consented to her using the jointly created embryos alone. Once the relationship had broken down, and Mr Johnston had indicated that he did not wish the embryos to be preserved or used by Ms Evans, they were no longer being 'treated together'. The Court of Appeal accepted that this was an interference with the private lives of the parties, but they found this to be justified and proportionate. Arden LJ believed that the 'imposition of an invariable and ongoing requirements for consent in the 1990 Act . . . satisfies Article 8(2) of the [European] Convention'.[449] She was of the opinion that fatherhood could no more be forced on Mr Johnston than motherhood on Ms Evans.

14.163 The European Court of Human Rights held that the general interests pursued by the 1990 Act were legitimate and consistent with Art 8. The domestic rules were clear, had been brought to Ms Evans' attention, and struck a fair balance between the competing interests within the margin of appreciation. Respect for human dignity and free will, as well as a desire to ensure a fair balance between the parties to IVF treatment, underlay Parliament's decisions to enact provisions in the 1990 Act which permitted an exception to the rules of consent to ensure that every person donating gametes for the purpose of IVF treatment would know in advance that no use could be made of his or her genetic material without his or her continuing consent. They stressed also that the absolute nature of this rule served

[445] ibid, Sch 3, para 8(1).

[446] ibid, Sch 3, para 8(2) (as amended).

[447] *Code of Practice* (8th edn, 2009) requires the procedure for disposal to be designed with 'appropriate sensitivity', given the 'special status' of the human embryo (see para 15.13).

[448] *Evans v Amicus Healthcare Ltd* [2004] 1 FLR 67 (Wall J); and (2004) 2 FLR 766 (CA); and *Evans v UK* [2007] 1 FLR 1990 (ECtHR).

[449] *Evans v Amicus Healthcare Ltd* (2004) 2 FLR 766 (CA), 795.

to promote legal certainty and to avoid the problems of arbitrariness and inconsistency that would be inherent in weighing, on a case-by-case basis, entirely incommensurable interests.

It is now possible for a woman to freeze her eggs. The HFEA has reported that, by December 2012, 20 babies had been born in the UK as a result of successful egg freezing followed by *in vitro* fertilization.[450] It is estimated that about 2000 babies worldwide have been born as a result of this new technique.[451] This enables women to circumvent the dilemma posed by the recalcitrant former partner. It does also, of course, achieve parity with men, who have long been able to freeze sperm. This arguably prioritizes the man's right to be free from unwanted reproduction (as an American court held also in *Davis v Davis*[452]), rather than the woman's right to bear a child on the grounds that after fertilization, natural or *in vitro*, a man has no rights over the reproductive process (a conclusion arrived at by another American court in *Kass v Kass*[453] and also by the Israel Supreme Court in *Nachmani v Nachmani*[454]). **14.164**

The *Evans* decision has been much criticized.[455] There was a strong dissent in the European Court.[456] Two of the dissenting judges held that the majority had been overly concerned with considerations of public policy and the margin of appreciation open to Member States, and had as a result neglected the individual rights at stake. In their opinion the 'dilemma should instead be resolved through careful analysis of the circumstances of the particular case, to avoid the unjust preservation of one person's right by negating the rights of the other'.[457] Whether there was true consent by Ms Evans has also been questioned. Thus, it has been noted that there was 'lack of space for confidential, private discussions between each party and clinic staff on the one hand, and between the two parties themselves, on the other'.[458] **14.165**

Another consequence of the provisions is that if one partner dies, the other has no right to insist on treatment. **14.166**

A centre which fails to comply with these provisions would be in breach of a condition of its licence. This could be reviewed by HFEA, and revoked. The legislation is silent on whether gamete or embryo providers have any remedy in law. There would appear to be four possibilities.[459] **14.167**

One possible avenue of redress is by way of an application for judicial review, and then to seek a declaration or an order of mandamus. For this to succeed it would be necessary to show that the licence-holder was exercising a public function.[460] Although Kennedy and Grubb characterize it as a private activity[461] and, therefore, not subject to judicial review, **14.168**

[450] See HFEA website available at <http://www.hfea.gov.uk/46.html>.

[451] See <http://factually.gizmodo.com/only-about-2000-babies-have-been-born-using-cryogenic-e-1692707823>; V Kruskop, 'Babies on Ice', *The Guardian* (4 March 2006). Egg freezing is discussed by Harwood, 'Egg freezing: A breakthrough for reproductive autonomy?' [2009] 23 Bioethics 39–46; A case is put by Goold and Savulescu for freezing for non-medical reasons—see I Goold and J Savulescu, Freezing eggs for lifestyle reasons (2008) 8(6) American Journal of Bioethics 32–35.

[452] 842 SW 2d 588 (1992).

[453] 91 NY 2d 554 (1998).

[454] 50(4) PD 661 (Israel Supreme Court).

[455] eg by S Sheldon, 'Evans v Amicus Healthcare—Revealing Cracks in the Pillars?' (2004) 16 Child and Family Law Quarterly 437. The *Evans* case is subjected to a feminist critique by Anne Donchin; see A Donchin, 'In Whose Interest? Policy and Politics in Assisted Reproduction' [2011] 25 Bioethics 92.

[456] By Judges Turmen, Tsatsa-Nikolowska, Spielmann, and Ziemelc.

[457] *Evans v UK* [2007] 1 FLR 1990 (ECtHR), 1997.

[458] By Sheldon, n 455, 440.

[459] And see I Kennedy and A Grubb, *Medical Law—Text with Materials* (Butterworths 2000).

[460] See *R v Panel on Take-Overs and Mergers, ex p Datafin plc* [1987] QB 815.

[461] Kennedy and Grubb, n 459, 1307–08.

there is a strong argument for saying that even a private clinic would be carrying out a public function. It is, after all, licensed by the HFEA, an institution established by the State and is highly regulated.

14.169 A remedy in contract is the second resource. In default of express terms, Kennedy and Grubb argue, it is submitted rightly, that Schedule 3 'could be said to be implied into the contract such that a claim for breach of contract could be brought against the licence-holder'.[462] Remedies would include, injunction, or specific performance as well as damages (which might extend to any distress[463] caused, given the personal nature of the contract). It may be more difficult to argue in contract where treatment or storage is provided under the aegis of the National Health Service: but, even here, whether or not there is payment, it should be possible to proceed in contract.[464]

14.170 Although s 25(6) (and see para 14.154) states that breach of the Code of Practice does not render the person concerned liable to any proceedings, it is arguable that a breach of statutory duty, for example, the duty to allow embryos to perish, could give rise to a private right of action for breach of statutory duty. The 1990 Act imposes a statutory duty upon the licence-holder: 'the conditions of the licence [must be] complied with'.[465] But it is silent on whether civil liability can exist for breach of the Act. Kennedy and Grubb, however, argue that the Act is 'so emphatic'[466] in its commitment to the wishes of the gamete providers that a court might well take the view that a private right of action should arise. The provisions of Sch 3 clearly contemplate gamete providers as the beneficiaries of the obligations imposed upon licence-holders.[467] They add that this argument 'gains force'[468] from the absence of any remedy. However, it is argued that remedies may well exist in judicial review and in contract.

14.171 Whether or not there is a property claim had not been addressed in any English case until *Yearworth v North Bristol NHS Trust* in 2009.[469] A previous edition of this book had raised the question as to how a court would decide a dispute if gametes or embryos were damaged or destroyed or, indeed lost. The possibility of these being regarded as property was raised, and Kennedy and Grubb were quoted to the effect that this was 'a question of metaphysical proportions'.[470] They thought it 'idle to predict the outcome of such a case should these . . . circumstances arise', and this author agreed.[471]

14.172 These circumstances have now arisen, and the Court of Appeal in *Yearworth v North Bristol NHS Trust* has concluded that there is a property interest in gametes, and therefore presumably in embryos (and human admixed embryos). The case centred on six men who were diagnosed with cancer and who were recommended to freeze sperm before they underwent chemotherapy. They provided samples which were duly frozen and stored in the hospital laboratory. But, prior to any attempt to use any of the sperm, the amount of liquid nitrogen in the tanks in which it was stored fell below the requisite level. The semen thawed. The actions against the Trust proceeded on the basis that the sperm then perished irretrievably.

[462] ibid, 1308.
[463] See eg *Hayes and Another v Dodd* [1990] 2 All E R 815, and in particular *Yearworth v North Bristol NHS Trust* [2009] EWCA Civ 372, [2009] 2 All ER 986.
[464] See *Yearworth v North Bristol NHS Trust* [2009] EWCA Civ 372, [2009] 2 All ER 986.
[465] 1990 Act, s 17(1)(e).
[466] Kennedy and Grubb, n 459, 1308.
[467] ibid.
[468] ibid.
[469] *Yearworth v North Bristol NHS Trust*, n 464.
[470] Kennedy and Grubb, n 459, 1315.
[471] *Medical Law* (2nd edn) para 10.143.

The Trust admitted negligence, but denied liability. It did not admit the men had suffered psychiatric injury or that, if they had so suffered, this was consequent on any breach of duty. More importantly, the Trust also averred that, even if its breach of duty had caused the injury or distress, as a matter of law the men were not entitled to recover damages: this was on the basis that loss of the sperm constituted neither 'personal injury' to the men nor damage to their property. It might have sought support in the Warnock Report, which opined that the 'concept of ownership of human embryos' was 'undesirable',[472] but such support was weak because the Warnock Report, rather ambiguously, conceded that a couple who had stored an embryo should have 'rights to the use and disposal of the embryo' (and these are clearly incidents of ownership).[473] **14.173**

It was the Trust's contention that the men's loss did not qualify as the sort of damage which is a necessary constituent of an action in negligence. But the court concluded that the men had ownership of the sperm which they ejaculated. It gave the following reasons: **14.174**

(i) By their bodies, they alone generated and ejaculated the sperm.
(ii) The sole object of their ejaculation . . . was that, in certain events, it might later be used for their benefit . . .
(iii) Ancillary to the object of later possible use of the sperm is the need for its storage in the interim . . .
(iv) . . . while the licence-holder has *duties* which may conflict with the wishes of the men, for example in relation to destruction of the sperm after expiry of the maximum storage period, no person . . . other than each man has any *rights* in relation to the sperm which he has produced.
(v) In reaching our conclusion . . . we are fortified by the precise correlation between the primary, if circumscribed, rights of the men in relation to the sperm, namely in relation to its future use, and the consequence of the Trust's breach of duty, namely preclusion of its future use.[474]

Although strictly unnecessary to do so, the Court of Appeal also investigated the possibility that the men would have a cause of action in bailment, where the measure of damages might be more favourable. Having found: **14.175**

(a) The unit chose to take possession of the sperm . . .
(b) The unit's assumption of responsibility for the careful storage of the sperm was express and unequivocal . . .
(c) The unit acquired exclusive possession of the sperm.
(d) The unit held itself out to the men as able to deploy special skill in preserving the sperm.
(e) . . . the Trust admits that, if the unit was a bailee of the sperm, it was in breach of the duty of care consequent upon the bailment.
(f) The unit . . . broke a particular promise to the men, namely that the sperm 'will be stored . . . at minus 196°C . . .[475]

the court concluded 'without hesitation'[476] that there was a bailment of the sperm by the men to the unit. And the law of bailment provides men in such a situation with a remedy under which they are entitled to compensation for any psychiatric injury (or actionable distress) foreseeably consequent upon the breach.[477]

472 *Report of the Committee of Inquiry in Human Fertilisation and Embryology*, n 409, para 10.11.
473 ibid.
474 *Yearworth v North Bristol NHS Trust*, n 464, 1002.
475 ibid, 1005.
476 ibid, 1005.
477 ibid, 1006.

14.176 The consequences of this decision go far beyond the issues at stake in this case, and are discussed in other chapters of this book.

I. Access to Information

14.177 Section 31 of the 1990 Act, as amended by the 2008 Act, imposes upon the HFEA a statutory obligation to keep a register of information relating to:

(a) The provision of treatment services for any identifiable individual other than basic partner treatment services.
(b) The procurement or distribution of any sperm, other than sperm which is partner-donated sperm and has not been stored, in the course of providing non-medical fertility service for any identifiable individual.
(c) The keeping of the gametes of any identifiable individual. The Act requires licence-holders to collect this information and provide it to the HFEA.[478]
(d) The keeping of an embryo taken from an identifiable woman.
(e) The use of gametes of any identifiable individual other than for their use for basic partner treatment services.
(f) The use of an embryo taken from any identifiable woman.
(g) Identifying an individual who was or may have been born as a result of treatment services, other than basic partner treatment services.
(h) Identifying an individual who was or may have been born as a result of the procurement or distribution of any sperm, other than partner-donor sperm which has not been stored for the use of providing non-medical services.[479]

14.178 Who has access to the statutory information held by the Authority? A person who was conceived as a consequence of gamete donation, and who has reached the age of 16[480] may request by notice to give him/her notice stating whether or not the information contained in the register shows that a person (the donor) other than a parent of the applicant would, or might, but for the relevant statutory provisions, be the parent of the applicant.[481] If it does show that, the Authority must give the applicant so much of the information as relates to the donor as regulations require it to give,[482] or to state whether or not that information shows that there are other persons of whom the donor is not the parent and, if so, the number, sex, and year of birth of those other persons.[483]

14.179 The Authority shall only comply with the request if the information in the register shows the applicant is a 'relevant individual' (that is someone born of treatment services or through the use of sperm which was not partner-donated sperm in the cause of providing non-medical fertility services), and the applicant has been given a suitable opportunity to receive proper counselling about the implications of compliance with the request.[484]

14.180 Applicants who are under 18 (ie who are 16 or 17) cannot receive identifying information.[485]

---

478 1990 Act, s 31(2) (as amended).
479 ibid, s 12(g).
480 ibid, s 31Z A(1) (as amended).
481 ibid, s 31Z A(2) (as amended).
482 ibid, s 31Z A(2)(a) (as amended).
483 ibid, s 31Z A(2)(b) (as amended).
484 ibid, s 31Z A(3) (as amended).
485 ibid, s 31Z A(4) (as amended).

The Authority has a discretion not to comply with a request if it considers that 'special circumstances' exist which increase the likelihood that compliance with the request would enable the applicant to identify the donor or identify any person in a case where under regulations the Authority is not required to give that information.[486] 14.181

In addition, a donor-conceived person may require the Authority to give him/her information as to whether he/she is related to a person whom he/she proposes to marry, or enter into a civil partnership, or is a person with whom he/she is in an intimate physical relationship or with whom he/she proposes to enter into such a relationship.[487] However, such a request may not be made by a person under 16 who is in, or proposes, to be in an intimate physical relationship.[488] If it is made by a person under 16, the Authority must not comply with the request.[489] The age limitation does not apply to marriage and civil partnership, since 16 is the minimum age for such statuses.[490] 14.182

The applicant must specify the person to whom he/she may be related.[491] 14.183

The Authority is to comply with the request if: 14.184

(i) The information in the register shows the applicant is a relevant individual;
(ii) It receives written notice from the specified person consenting to the request being made, and the consent has not been withdrawn;
(iii) The applicant and the specified person have each been given a suitable opportunity to receive proper counselling about the implications of the request.[492]

The 2004 Regulations[493] specify the information the Authority must provide. They distinguish information provided by a donor before 1 April 2005 from that provided on or after this date. If information was provided before 1 April 2005, only certain specified non-identifying information must be provided;[494] where the information was provided on or after 1 April 2005, certain identifying and non-identifying information must be provided.[495] 14.185

The Authority may inform the donor that a donor-conceived person has requested information about him/her, but it may not disclose the identity of the applicant or any information relating to the applicant.[496] 14.186

Donors (including those who donated before the coming into force of this new statutory provision) may request the clinic or the Authority to provide information about the number, sex, and year of birth of children born as a result of their donations.[497] The clinic and the Authority need not comply with the request if special circumstances exist which increase the likelihood that compliance with the request would enable the donor to identify any such person.[498] 14.187

486 ibid, s 31Z A(6) (as amended).
487 ibid, s 31Z B(2) (as amended).
488 ibid, s 31Z B(4) (as amended).
489 ibid, s 31Z B(5) (as amended).
490 Marriage Act 1949.
491 1990 Act, s 31Z B(2) (as amended).
492 ibid, s 31Z B(3) (as amended).
493 Human Fertilisation and Embryology (Disclosures of Information) Regulations 2004 (SI 2004 / 1511).
494 ibid, reg 2(2).
495 ibid, reg 2(3).
496 1990 Act, s 31ZC(1) (as amended).
497 ibid, s 31ZD (as amended).
498 ibid, s 31ZD(5) (as amended). On identity and assisted reproduction with particular reference to Sweden see J Stoll, 'New Challenges Raised by Surrogacy' A Diduck, N Peleg, and H Reece, (eds), *Law in Society: Reflections on Children, Culture, Family and Philosophy* (Brill 2015), 551–70. More generally see M

14.188 There is now (as a result of the 2008 Act) a provision which enables persons conceived as a result of donations to request and obtain identifying information about their genetic half-siblings, that is persons conceived using gametes from the same donor.[499] Two relevant individuals are donor-conceived genetic siblings of each other if the donor who is not the legal parent of either of them would, or might, but for the relevant statutory provisions, be the parent of both of them.[500] In order for information to be disclosed, both of the persons must be 18.[501] The information in the register must show that a donor-conceived individual (A) is the donor-conceived genetic sibling of another donor-conceived individual (B).[502] If A has provided information to the Authority that permits his/her identity to be disclosed to any of his donor-conceived genetic siblings of a specified description which includes B, then the Authority may disclose the information,[503] but only if B has requested disclosure to B of information about any donor-conceived genetic sibling of B, and both A and B have each had a suitable opportunity to receive proper counselling about the implications of disclosure.[504] The Authority is not under an obligation to disclose information if it considers such disclosure will lead to either A or B identifying the donor, unless the donor has consented to his/her identity being disclosed to A or B, or where A or B to make a request under s 31ZA(2)(a), pursuant to which the Authority would be required to give A or B information which would identify the donor.[505]

14.189 The Authority has the power to set up a voluntary contact register.[506] This is a register of persons who have indicated that they wish to receive information about any person to whom they are genetically related as a consequence of the provision to any person of treatment services in the UK before 1 August 1991.[507] The Authority may also arrange with any person or organization which has kept such a register for that person/organization to supply the Authority with that information.[508]

14.190 In relation to the voluntary contact register, the Authority has a number of powers. It may set up and keep a voluntary contact register in such manner as it thinks fit.[509] It may determine the criteria for eligibility for inclusion on the register and the particulars that may be included.[510] It may charge a fee to persons who wish their particulars to be entered on the register.[511] It may arrange for samples of DNA of such persons to be analysed at their request.[512] It may make such arrangements as it thinks fit for the disclosure of information on the register between persons who appear to the Authority to be genetically related.[513] It may impose such conditions as it thinks fit to prevent 'A' from disclosing information to a person to whom A is genetically related (B), where that information would identify any person who is genetically related to both A and B.[514]

Cowden, '"No Harm, no Foul": A Child's Right to Know their Genetic Parents' [2012] 26 International Journal of Law, Policy and the Family 102–26.

499 1990 Act, s 31ZE (as amended).
500 ibid, s 31ZE(1) (as amended).
501 ibid, s 31ZE(3)(a) (as amended).
502 ibid, s 31ZE(2)(a) (as amended).
503 ibid, s 31ZE(3)(b) (as amended).
504 ibid, s 31ZE (as amended).
505 ibid, s 31ZE(4) (as amended).
506 ibid, s 31ZF(2)(a) (as amended).
507 ibid, s 31ZF(1) (as amended).
508 ibid, s 31ZF(3) (as amended).
509 ibid, s 31ZF(2)(a), (b) (as amended).
510 ibid, s 31ZF(2)(c) (as amended).
511 ibid, s 31ZF(2)(d) (as amended).
512 ibid, s 31ZF(2)(e) (as amended).
513 ibid, s 31ZF(2)(f) (as amended).
514 ibid, s 31ZF(2)(g) (as amended).

The Authority is also given the power to give financial assistance to any person who sets up or keeps a voluntary contact register.[515] Financial assistance may take the form of grants, loans, guarantees, and incurring expenditure for the person assisted.[516] A person who receives assistance must comply with the terms and conditions on which it is given.[517] The Authority may enforce compliance.[518] The power to give financial assistance is instead of, not in addition to, the power to keep its own voluntary contact register. **14.191**

The Registrar General [519] may request information from HFEA in fulfilling his statutory functions.[520] The Authority is bound to comply with any request made by the Registrar General by notice[521]—presumably in writing, though the 1990 Act does not so stipulate[522] —to disclose whether any information on the register (which HFEA is obliged by s 31 to keep) tends to show that a particular person may be the parent of the child [523] and, if it does, disclose that information.[524] This provision applies where a claim is made before the Registrar General that a person is or is not the parent of the child and it is 'necessary or desirable' for the purpose of any function of the Registrar General to determine whether the claim is or may be well founded.[525] **14.192**

A court may require the Authority to disclose information, excluding that relating to any donor,[526] where in any proceedings the question of whether a person is or is not the parent of a child by virtue of the status provisions of the 1990 Act (on which see paras 14.208–14.239) falls to be determined. The court cannot do this of its own motion: it requires an application by any party to the proceedings.[527] The court must not comply unless it is satisfied that the interests of justice require it to do so, taking into account any representation by any individual who may be affected by the disclosure and the welfare of the child if a minor and of any other minor who may be affected by the disclosure.[528] If the proceedings are civil proceedings, the court may direct that they (or part of them) be heard in camera,[529] and applications for such a direction must themselves be heard in camera.[530] **14.193**

A court may require the Authority to disclose the identity of a donor when a child wishes to bring a claim for injury caused before birth under s 1 of the Congenital Disabilities (Civil Liability) Act 1976 [531] (see further Chapter 5). The 1976 Act provides for civil liability in the case of children born disabled in consequence of the intentional act, negligence, or breach of statutory duty of some person prior to the birth of the child. The defendant is answerable to the child if he/she was liable to one or both parents in respect of matters which gave rise to the disability at birth. Such matters could arise either before conception, during pregnancy, **14.194**

515 ibid, s 31ZG(1) (as amended).
516 ibid, s 31ZG(2) (as amended).
517 ibid, s 31ZG(4) (as amended).
518 ibid, s 31ZG(4) (as amended).
519 Defined in s 31Z(3) of 1990 Act.
520 1990 Act, s 32(1) (as amended).
521 ibid, s 32(2) (as amended).
522 Though the wording of s 46(2) of the 1990 Act would make it difficult to give or serve a notice, if it were not in writing.
523 By virtue of any of the relevant provisions, discussed below at paras 14.205, 14.210–14.213, 14.216, 14.228.
524 1990 Act, s 32(2) (as amended).
525 ibid, s 32(1) (as amended).
526 ibid, s 34(1) and s 31(2)(b) (as amended).
527 ibid, s 34(1).
528 ibid, s 34(2).
529 ibid, s 34(3).
530 ibid, s 34(4).
531 ibid, s 35(1) (as amended).

or in the process of childbirth. The legislation contemplates the situation where it is necessary to identify a person who is the genetic, but because of the 1990 Act as amended, not the legal parent of the child. The provisions of sub-ss (2)–(4) of s 34 (and see para 14.151) apply to these applications as well. This provision becomes a resource of importance when a child wishes to sue a donor for the donor's negligence.[532]

14.195 The Data Protection Act 1998 (DPA), which regulates the processing of personal data, must be considered here (see also generally Chapter 12). Clinicians are 'data controllers' and 'processing' includes the obtaining, storage, and use of personal data produced in the treatment service environment. The DPA entitles a patient to serve notice on a doctor to stop the processing of personal data, allowing the doctor as data controller to rectify or erase inaccurate data. Individuals have the right to seek compensation for damage. The DPA covers all health records, whether held electronically or in written form. Under an order made under the previous legislation (the 1984 Act),[533] permission was given to withhold data which might otherwise have had to be disclosed. The new legislation is similarly accompanied. The Data Protection (Miscellaneous Subject Access Exemptions) Order 2000,[534] made under s 38(1) of the DPA, exempts from the subject access provisions of s 7 of the DPA information falling within ss 31 and 33 of the 1990 Act, that is 'information about the provision of treatment services, the keeping or use of gametes or embryos and whether identifiable individuals were born in consequence of treatment services'. There are two possible interpretations of this exemption provision. First, it could be said to remove from the regime of the DPA any access questions relating to the relevant personal data. Thus, a child or patient or donor seeking access to this information about him/herself from a licensed clinic or the Authority would only be able to do so in accordance with and, importantly, through the processes provided by the 1990 Act. The right of access—for example the right of someone about to marry to find out whether he is genetically related to his intended wife—would remain under the 1990 Act itself, since it is exempted from s 7 of the DPA by the order. A second interpretation is however possible. The 2000 Order exempts the relevant information covered by ss 31 and 33 of the 1990 Act 'the disclosure of which is prohibited or restricted' (Art 2). It might therefore be said that the exemption from s 7 is more limited: namely, only to the extent that the information covered by the 1990 Act cannot be disclosed under the 1990 Act is it exempt from s 7. Thus, information which can or must be disclosed by a clinic or the Authority under s 31 or 33 remains subject to the right of access by a data subject under s 7 of the DPA. This will be important only when the information is personal data that is health information about the individual seeking access him/herself. If it relates to others, for example, a donor or a child's parents when the applicant is a child, disclosure under the DPA would be modified.

14.196 The 1990 Act as amended imposes a strict secrecy requirement for statutory information held by the Authority and by licence-holders. As regards the Authority, it then provides that information may not be disclosed by:

(a) a member or employee of the Authority;[535]
(b) a person exercising functions of the Authority under contractual or agency arrangements;[536]
(c) any person engaged to provide services to the Authority;[537]

532 ibid, s 33(8), inserting a new s 35A into the Data Protection Act 1984.
533 Data Protection (Subject Access Modification) (Health) Order 2000, SI 2000/413.
534 SI 2000/419.
535 1990 Act, s 33A(1)(a) (as amended).
536 ibid, s 33A(1)(b) (as amended).
537 ibid, s 33A(1)(c) (as amended).

(e) any licence holder;[538]
(f) any person to whom a third party agreement applies;[539]
(g) any person to whom directions have been given.[540]

Disclosure is only permitted if made to one of the persons listed in the new s 33A(2), or in other circumstances specified there. Disclosure may be made to: **14.197**

(a) a person as a member or employee of the Authority or a person exercising functions of the Authority;[541]
(b) a person engaged by the Authority to provide services to the Authority;[542]
(c) a person employed by, or engaged to provide services to a person engaged to provide services to the Authority;[543]
(d) a licence-holder for the purpose of that person's functions as such;[544]
(e) a person to whom a third party agreement applies for the purposes of that person's functions under the agreement.[545]

Disclosure may also be made in pursuance of directions.[546] They may also be made 'so that no individual can be identified from the information[547] (anonymized data most obviously[548]). Disclosure is allowed where it is 'necessary to avert an imminent danger to the health of an individual',[549] and it could be disclosed with the individual's consent.[550] Disclosure is also permitted when it is of information lawfully made available to the public before the disclosure is made.[551] Other circumstances where disclosure is permitted are listed in the legislation.[552] **14.198**

The 1990 Act as amended goes further than the common law in limiting disclosure. In addition, a licence-holder or a person to whom a licence applies who gives or receives any money or other benefit, not authorized by directions, in respect of the supply of gametes, embryos, or human admixed embryos, is guilty of a criminal offence.[553] **14.199**

J. The Status of Children

Until statutory intervention in 1987,[554] parentage was tied by the common law to genetics: a sperm donor was the father, although in practice a combination of a common law presumption (the husband of a mother is presumed to be the father of her child) and pious perjury (the child was often registered as the husband's child) meant that social fatherhood often **14.200**

[538] ibid, s 33A(1)(e) (as amended).
[539] ibid, s 33A(1)(f) (as amended).
[540] ibid, s 33A(1)(g) (as amended).
[541] ibid, s 33A(2)(a) (as amended).
[542] ibid, s 33A(2)(b) (as amended).
[543] ibid, s 33A(2)(c) (as amended).
[544] ibid, s 33A(2)(d) (as amended).
[545] ibid, s 33A(2)(e) (as amended).
[546] ibid, s 33A(2)(f) (as amended). Directions by virtue of s 24.
[547] ibid, s 33A(2)(g) (as amended).
[548] And see *R v Department of Health, ex p Source Informatics Ltd* [2001] QB 424.
[549] 1990 Act, s 33A(2)(i) (as amended). cf the facts of *Tarasoff v Regents of the University of California* 551 P 2d 334 (1976).
[550] 1990 Act, s 33A(2)(i), (ii), (iii) (as amended).
[551] ibid, s 33A(2)(j) (as amended).
[552] See ibid, s 33A(2)(k)–(t) (as amended).
[553] ibid, s 41(8).
[554] Family Law Reform Act 1987, s 27.

prevailed. There was little discussion of egg or embryo donation[555] before the emergence of surrogacy as a recognized problem in the mid-1980s: in theory, the genetic should have prevailed here too, though in practice it is thought the gestational mother was regarded as the legal mother.[556]

14.201 In 1987 the Family Law Reform Act[557] tackled the situation of the married couple who had a child through donor insemination. It reversed the common law rule and made the husband of a woman who was artificially inseminated the father of the child, unless it was proved that he did not consent to the procedure. However, this legislation did not deal with egg or embryo donation or with other techniques such as GIFT. This provision was replaced by a more comprehensive set of provisions in the 1990 Act, and now by complex provisions in the 2008 Act. This has introduced the concepts of 'fatherhood' and 'female parenthood'.[558] There is, it has been said, 'a particular need for certainty in provisions affecting status . . .'[559]

K. Marriage and Civil Partnership

14.202 References to parties to a marriage and to parties to a civil partnership are explained in the 2008 Act, ss 49 and 50 respectively.

14.203 A marriage has to be a subsisting one. It does not subsist if there is a judicial separation (or a legal separation obtained outside the British Islands and recognized in the UK).[560] Marriage includes a void marriage if either or both of the parties reasonably believed at that time that the marriage was valid.[561] And there is a presumption that one of the parties so believed, unless the contrary is shown.[562] An example would be where it was believed reasonably that the wife was 17, but she was in fact 15.[563]

14.204 When legislation was passed in 1990, English law did not know the concept of a civil partnership. This was introduced by the Civil Partnership Act 2004, and the 2008 Act thus needs to accommodate it. It does so in s 50. This provides that references to civil partnership mean a civil partnership that is subsisting, unless there is a separation order in force.[564] It includes parties to a void civil partnership if either or both of the parties reasonably believed at the time that their partnership was valid.[565] It is presumed that one of them did so believe, unless the contrary is shown.[566]

14.205 This applies also where a person is a second parent (see below at 14.226) at the time of artificial insemination or the placing of an embryo or sperm and egg in their partner, but by the time the child is born, the parties have entered a civil partnership, with the result that the child becomes the legitimate child of the second parent.[567]

---

555 See M D A Freeman, 'The Unscrambling of Egg Donation' in S A M McLean (ed), *Law Reform and Human Reproduction* (Dartmouth 1992) 273.
556 As in California: see *Johnson v Calvert* 851 P 2d 776 (1993).
557 Family Law Reform Act, s 27.
558 See paras 14.213–14.230.
559 *Per* Wilson J in *U v W* (*Attorney-General Intervening*) [1997] 2 FLR 282, 303.
560 2008 Act, s 49(1)(a), (2).
561 ibid, s 49(1)(b).
562 ibid. s 49(1)(b).
563 The minimum age for marriage is 16.
564 2008 Act, s 50(1)(a).
565 ibid, s 50(2).
566 ibid, s 50(2).
567 ibid, s 48(6)(b).

1. Statutory motherhood

The 2008 Act provides,[568] as did the 1990 Act,[569] that a woman who is carrying or has carried a child as a result of the placing in her of an embryo or of sperm and eggs, and no other woman, is to be treated as the mother of the child. The gestational woman is thus in law the mother of any child born as a result of IVF procedures or GIFT or ZIFT (zygote intra-fallopian transfer). Where egg donation does not involve IVF, GIFT, or ZIFT, that is, where the egg is directly implanted in the woman for natural fertilization, the Act does not apply and who is the mother is a question that would fall to be determined by the common law, which, as indicated (see para 14.208) can offer no conclusive answer. Where the donation is only sperm (note the wording 'sperm and eggs'), the gestational mother will be the legal mother. **14.206**

Where the mother is a surrogate, the legislation does not achieve the objective of tying legal to social motherhood,[570] and the gestational mother becomes the legal mother even though she is not intended by the parties involved to be the social mother. The social mother, who will rear the child, is denied the status of parent even where her egg, fertilized by the sperm of her husband or partner, is used. She can, if married, seek a parental order under s 30 of the 1990 Act, as amended by s 54 of the 2008 Act (as to which see paras 14.270–14.272). **14.207**

Section 23 of the 2008 Act applies whether the woman was in the UK or not at the time of the placing in her of the embryos or the sperm and eggs or of her artificial insemination.[571] **14.208**

2. Statutory fatherhood

(i) The married mother

The 2008 Act provides[572] that if a married woman becomes pregnant following embryo transfer, GIFT, ZIFT, or DI, her husband is to be treated as the father of any child who results from such treatment. It has been said to be contrary to Parliament's express wish to treat such a man differently from the father of any other child when considering an application for contact.[573] The court held that it would go against the principles of justice to deny rights to a man who had consented to, and participated fully with the mother in, fertility treatment merely because of an absence of a biological link between him and the child. That contact may not always be granted is clear from the case of *Re D*.[574] In this case a man and a woman sought fertility treatment. They acknowledged that he would be the father of any resulting child. The treatment failed, the relationship foundered, and she presented herself the following year without telling the clinic that her new partner was not the man who had signed the consent forms. The treatment using anonymous sperm donation was successful. The first man sought a parental responsibility order and also contact. The man's application for a parental responsibility order was deferred, and it was suggested that an order for contact not be made until the child was at least three years old. It was not in Parliament's mind that mistakes would occur and an embryo would be placed in a woman which used the wrong sperm. That this could happen came to light in 2002 when a white couple who **14.209**

[568] ibid, s 33.
[569] 1990 Act, s 27(1).
[570] Hence the need for the parental order established by s 30 of the 1990 Act, and now in s 54 of the 2008 Act, discussed in 14.267.
[571] 2008 Act, s 35(2).
[572] ibid, s 35.
[573] *Re CH* [1996] 1 FLR 768.
[574] [2001] 1 FLR 972. Indirect contact was ordered in this case. On appeal this case is reported as *Re R* [2003] 1 FLR 1183. The Court of Appeal hoped the parties could reach agreement about what contact, if any, would be best for the child (see at 1193).

had had ICSI treatment gave birth to mixed-race twins.[575] (and see para 14.215). Where a person is to be treated as the father of the child by virtue of s 35, no other person is to be treated as the father of the child.[576]

14.210 If a man can show that he did not consent to the treatment service, he is not be treated as the father under s 35(1)(b) although he will remain the presumed father by virtue of s 38(2), which preserves the common law presumption of paternity. This is a rebuttable presumption,[577] which may be most obviously rebutted by DNA evidence showing the contrary.[578] Although it is not clear, it may be supposed that a husband who consented to the treatment service but changed his mind in the nine months between treatment and birth, will also be the presumed father, if he is not treated as the father under s 38(2). It is not a requirement of treatment that a married woman should get her husband's consent. However, the Code of Practice does advise that this be sought as a matter of good practice.[579] Research indicates that clinics are sensibly reluctant to treat without his consent.[580]

14.211 It is clear that a mistake as to the identity of the embryo being placed in a man's wife vitiates his consent, so that s 35(1)(b) does not apply.[581] In *Leeds Teaching Hospitals NHS Trust v A*, the question arose as to whether the husband could consent retrospectively. The court refused to accept that this was possible.[582] The court accepted that its interpretation of s 28 (now s 35 of the 2008 Act) constituted an interference with the right to respect for private and family life of the mother, her husband and the twins (under Article 8 of the European Convention on Human Rights), and it was the human right of the twins that were 'most obviously and seriously infringed'.[583] But it held that no declaration of incompatibility was needed, since there were domestic remedies available to secure and protect those rights. All concerned agreed that the twins should remain with the family into which they were born and a residence order was granted—giving the husband the parental responsibility he otherwise lacked. The application of the genetic father for a declaration of parentage[584] was adjourned. Dame Elizabeth Butler-Sloss P was of the opinion that:

> truth ... is more important to the rights of the twins and their welfare than a fictional certainty ... To refuse to recognise ... their biological father is to distort the truth about which some day the twins will have to learn through knowledge of their paternal identity.[585]

(ii) The fatherhood conditions

14.212 Where a woman becomes a mother using the sperm of a donor and she is not married, and has no female partner, but does have a male partner who is not her husband, the 2008 Act enables the man to be the father of the child.[586] The following conditions need to be satisfied before he can be treated as the legal father:

---

575 See *Leeds Teaching Hospitals NHS Trust v A* [2003] 1 FLR 1091, 1101 *per* Dame Elizabeth Butler-Sloss P. This case is very far from unique. It is hoped that the introduction of double witnessing will prevent such things recurring again.

576 2008 Act, s 38(1).

577 Rebuttable on a balance of probabilities.

578 As in *Leeds Teaching Hospitals NHS Trust v A*, n 575, 1101.

579 *Code of Practice* (8th edn), para 6.8.

580 See G Douglas, *Access To Assisted Reproduction—Legal and other Criteria for Eligibility* (Cardiff Law School 1992).

581 See *Leeds Teaching Hospitals NHS Trust v A* [2003] 1 FLR 1091, 1101.

582 ibid, 1101–02 *per* Dame Elizabeth Butler-Sloss P.

583 ibid, 1109.

584 Under s 55A of the Family Law Act 1986.

585 *Leeds Teaching Hospitals NHS Trust v A*, n 581, 1109.

586 2008 Act, s 36.

(1) the woman must have had the embryo or sperm and eggs placed in her, or she must have been artificially inseminated in the course of treatment services provided by a licensed clinic in the UK;
(2) the sperm is not that of her unmarried male partner, that is, the man who wishes to become the legal father;
(3) the man who wishes to become the legal father is alive at the time;
(4) the 'fatherhood conditions' in s 37 of the 2008 Act are met.[587]

The 'fatherhood conditions' (set out in s 37(1) of the 2008 Act) are:

(i) at the time the embryo or gametes have been placed in the woman or at the time when she was artificially inseminated, each of them must have given the 'person responsible' notice of consent to his being treated as the father;
(ii) neither must have given notice withdrawing that consent;
(iii) the woman must not, since the giving of the notice, give a further notice stating that she consents to another man being treated as the father or to a woman being treated as the parent of any resulting child;
(iv) the couple must not be within the prohibited degrees of relationship to each other.[588]

These conditions are to ensure that the couple know what they are doing, and there is clear evidence of this. That it must take place in a licensed clinic should also ensure that intentions are properly documented. Notices of consent must be provided to the 'person responsible'[589] and must be in writing and signed.[590] There is a provision that if any of the parties are unable to sign because of illness, injury, or physical disability, the consent will be valid as to the signature if it is signed at the direction of the incapacitated party, in their presence and in the presence of at least one witness who attests the signature.[591] **14.213**

(a) **Posthumous use of sperm** The 1990 Act did not provide for cases where sperm was taken from a man and used posthumously. As a result of the *Blood* case,[592] the Human Fertilisation and Embryology (Deceased Fathers) Act 2003 was passed. This allowed a man to be registered as the father of a child conceived after his death using his sperm or an embryo created with his sperm before his death. **14.214**

The 2003 Act is replaced by s 39 of the 2008 Act. This provides that where a child is carried by a woman as a result of the placing in her of an embryo or sperm and eggs or her artificial insemination, and the creation of the embryo was brought about by using the sperm of a man after his death, or the creation of the embryo was brought about using the sperm of a man before his death but the embryo was placed in the woman after his death, the man is to be treated as the child's father for the purpose of birth registration,[593] if the following conditions are satisfied: **14.215**

(i) the man consented in writing to the use of the sperm or embryo after his death, and to being treated as the child's father for the purpose of birth registration for any resulting child;
(ii) he did not withdraw his consent;

[587] ibid, s 36.
[588] ibid, s 37(1).
[589] ibid, s 37(1).
[590] ibid, s 37(2).
[591] ibid, s 37(5).
[592] *R v Human Fertilisation and Embryology Authority, ex p Blood* [1996] 3 WLR 1176, discussed at paras 14.130–14.131.
[593] Not therefore for other purposes, like inheritance.

(iii) no one else is to be treated as the father of the child by virtue of ss 35, 36, 38(2), that is, marriage, fatherhood provisions, or the common law presumption;
(iv) no one else is to be treated as a parent of the child by virtue of ss 42 or 43 (that is, woman in a civil partnership or agreed female parenthood), or by virtue of adoption.[594]

14.216 These provisions apply whether the embryo or gametes were placed in the woman in the UK or elsewhere.[595]

14.217 (b) **Posthumous use of donated sperm by married couple** There is provision in the 2008 Act for the case where donated sperm has been used to create an embryo and the husband of the woman in whom the embryo was placed dies before the embryo is placed in her. Section 40 ensures that the husband can be treated as the father of the resulting child. The following conditions have to be satisfied:

(i) the woman was married when the embryo was created;
(ii) the husband has died before the placing of the embryo in the woman;
(iii) the husband consented in writing to the placing of the embryo in his wife, and to being treated as the child's father for the purpose of birth registration for any resulting child;
(iv) the woman must elect in writing that he should be treated in this way, and do so not later than forty-two days from the child's birth (it is twenty-one days in Scotland);
(v) no one else is to be treated as the child's father by virtue of ss 35, 36, 38(2), or 38(3) (ie marriage, the parenthood conditions, or the common law presumption);
(vi) no one else is to be treated as a parent of the child by virtue of ss 42 or 43(that is woman in a civil partnership or agreed female parenthood);
(vii) no one else is to be treated as a parent of the child by virtue of adoption.[596]

14.218 (c) **Posthumous use of sperm by unmarried couples** If the woman is not married or a party to a civil partnership at the time when the embryo was created, and donated sperm was used to create the embryo, the conditions in para 14.221 applying to married couples apply to enable the man to be treated as the child's father. In addition, the agreed fatherhood conditions must be met immediately before the man's death, and the embryo must have been created in the course of licensed treatment services provided to the woman in the UK.[597]

14.219 (d) **Persons not to be treated as father** Section 41 of the 2008 Act states (by way of clarification) who is not to be considered is law as the father of a child:

(1) first, a man who donates sperm and has consented to its use for treatment of another person or non-medical fertility services is not to be treated as the father of the child;[598]
(2) secondly, subject to the provision in s 39 on posthumous use of sperm, a man who has not consented to his sperm being used after his death is not to be treated as the father of the child.[599] This applies whether the woman is in the UK or elsewhere at the time of the placing in her of the embryo or the sperm and eggs or of her artificial insemination.[600]

594 2008 Act, s 39(1).
595 ibid, s 39(2).
596 ibid, s 40(1).
597 ibid, s 40(2).
598 ibid, s 41(1).
599 ibid, s 41(2).
600 ibid, s 41(3).

(iii) The female parenthood conditions

Some of the most radical provisions in the 2008 Act, which was not envisaged by Warnock or the drafters of the 1990 Act, concern cases where a woman is to be the other parent. Women have been able to enter into a civil partnership with other women since the Civil Partnership Act 2004 came into operation. The 2008 Act provides for this situation,[601] and also where the relationship between two women is not that of a civil partnership.[602] **14.220**

(a) Civil partnership When a female civil partner gives birth to a child conceived as a result of donor insemination, she is the mother of the child (gestational mothers always are[603]), and her civil partner is to be treated as a 'parent' of the child unless it is shown that she did not consent to the treatment of her partner.[604] This applies whether the mother was in the UK or elsewhere at the time of her placing in her of the embryo or sperm or eggs or her artificial insemination.[605] **14.221**

(b) No civil partnership Where the relationship is not one of civil partnership and (i) no man is treated as the father of the child by virtue of s 35; and (ii) no woman is treated as a parent of the child by virtue of s 42, that is, the mother is not married or in a civil partnership: then, provided conditions are met, a second woman may be the parent of the child.[606] **14.222**

These conditions are: **14.223**

(a) the embryo or sperm and eggs were placed in the woman or she was inseminated in a UK licensed clinic;[607]
(b) at that time the agreed female parenthood conditions were met in relation to the other woman;[608]
(c) the woman who wishes to be the other parent is still alive.[609]

(c) The agreed female parenthood conditions The agreed female parenthood conditions are set out in s 44 of the 2008 Act. The other woman, that is the woman who is not the mother, is referred to in the Act as 'P'. The conditions are: **14.224**

(i) P has given the person responsible a written and signed notice that P consents to P being treated as a parent of any child resulting from treatment provided to the mother under the licence;
(ii) the mother has given the person responsible a notice (also in writing and signed) stating that she agrees to P being so treated;
(iii) neither the mother nor P has, since giving the notice, withdrawn consent;
(iv) the mother has not given notice of consent to another woman being treated as the child's parent;
(v) the mother has not given notice of consent to another man being treated as the child's father;
(vi) the mother and P are not within the prohibited degrees of relationship.[610]

601 ibid, s 42.
602 ibid, s 43.
603 ibid, s 33.
604 ibid, s 42(1).
605 ibid, s 42(2).
606 ibid, s 43.
607 ibid, s 43(a).
608 ibid, s 43(b).
609 ibid, s 43(c).
610 ibid, s 44.

14.225 The law relating to consent is as for those who seek fatherhood.[611] Consent must be in writing, and signed, and given to the 'person responsible'. There is provision (identical to the above—see para 14.217) for those unable to sign because of illness, injury, or physical disability.[612]

14.226 The effect of female parenthood is that where a woman is to be treated by virtue of s 42 or s 43 as a parent of the child, no man is to be treated as the father of the child.[613] But these provisions do not affect who is to be considered the parent of the child by reason of the common law presumption that the child of a married couple is the child of the mother's husband.[614] Nor do these provisions apply to any child to the extent that the child is treated by virtue of adoption as not being the woman's child.[615]

14.227 (d) **Embryo transfer after the death of a civil partner** There is a new provision in the 2008 Act enabling a deceased same-sex partner in a civil partnership to be registered as a child's parent.[616] If a child has been carried by a woman as a result of the placing in her of an embryo, created at a time when she was a party to a civil partnership, and the other party to the civil partnership dies before the placing of the embryo in the woman, and the other party to the civil partnership consented in writing to the placing of the embryo after her death and to being treated for the purpose of birth registration as the parent of any resulting child, the other party to the civil partnership is to be treated as the parent of the child, provided:

(i) consent has not been withdrawn;
(ii) the woman has elected not later than the end of the period of forty-two days (in Scotland twenty-one days) from the day on which the child was born for the other party to the civil partnership to be treated as the parent of the child (for the purpose of birth registration);
(iii) no one else is to be treated as the father of the child by virtue of s 35, s 36, s 45(2) or (3) (that is marriage, fatherhood provisions, or the common law presumption);
(iv) no one else is to be treated as a parent of the child by virtue of s 42 or s 43 (woman in civil partnership or agreed female parenthood) or by virtue of adoption.[617]

This provision applies wherever in the world the woman is when the embryo is placed in her.[618]

14.228 (e) **Embryo transfer after the death of an intended female parent** There is also a new provision in the 2008 Act enabling a deceased same-sex partner not in a civil partnership to be registered as the child's parent.[619] If a child has been carried by a woman as a result of the placing in her of an embryo, created at a time when the woman was not in a marriage or civil partnership, but was created in the course of licensed treatment services in the UK, and another woman consented in writing to the placing of the embryo in the woman after her death, and to being treated for the purpose of birth registration as the parent of any resulting child, and the other woman died before the placing of the embryo in the woman, and immediately before the other woman's death, the agreed female parenthood conditions were

611 ibid, s 44(1), (2), and (3).
612 ibid, s 44(3).
613 ibid, s 45(1).
614 ibid, s 45(2).
615 ibid, s 45(4).
616 ibid, s 46.
617 ibid, s 46(1).
618 ibid, s 46(3).
619 ibid, s 46(2).

met in relation to other woman, then the other woman is to be treated for birth registration purposes as a parent of the child, provided:

(i) consent has not been withdrawn;
(ii) the woman has elected in writing not later than the end of the period of forty-two days (twenty-one days in Scotland) from the day on which the child was born for the other woman to be treated for the purpose of birth registration as the parent of the child;
(iii) no one else is to be treated as the father of the child by virtue of ss 35 or 36 or ss 45(2) or 45(3) (ie marriage, fatherhood provisions, or the common law presumption);
(iv) no one else is to be treated as a parent of the by virtue of ss 42 or 43 (woman in civil partnership or agreed female parenthood), or by virtue of adoption.[620]

This provision applies whether the woman is in the UK or elsewhere when the embryo is placed in her.[621]

(f) Egg donation Section 47 makes it clear that a woman is not to be treated as a parent of a child whom she is not carrying and has not carried merely because she has donated the egg, which is the source of the child. She will only be treated as the parent where she is so treated by virtue of s 42, s 43, s 46, or by virtue of adoption. **14.229**

(g) The effect of the parenthood provisions Section 48 makes it clear that where a person is to be treated as the mother, father, or parent of a child that is 'for all purposes'.[622] Conversely, where a person is not to be treated as a parent of the child, that person is to be treated in law as not being a parent of the child for all purposes.[623] **14.230**

Where the 2008 Act permits a deceased man or woman to be treated in law as the father or parent of a child, this is for the purposes of registration of birth, and not for any other purpose.[624] **14.231**

The new parenthood provisions do not affect the succession to any dignity or title of honour.[625] **14.232**

(h) Transsexual parents Neither the 2008 Act or the updated Code of Practice make any provision for transsexual parents. However, it is possible that an individual may have chosen to freeze and store their gametes or embryos prior to embarking on gender reassignment surgery.[626] In contrast to heterosexual couples, it may not be as clear who has the legal parentage in the case of transsexual parents. **14.233**

L. Surrogacy

Surrogacy, as defined in the Warnock Report, is 'the practice whereby one woman carries a child for another with the intention that the child should be handed over after birth'.[627] It can take a number of forms: the commissioning mother may be the genetic mother, in **14.234**

[620] ibid, s 46(2).
[621] ibid, s 46(3).
[622] ibid, s 48(1).
[623] ibid, s 48(2).
[624] ibid, s 48(3), (4).
[625] ibid, s 48(7).
[626] C Richards and L Seal, Trans People's Reproductive Options and Outcomes (2014) 40 Journal of Family Planning and Reproductive Health Choices 1–3.
[627] *Report of the Committee of Inquiry in Human Fertilisation and Embryology* (the 'Warnock Report') (Cmnd 9314 1953), para 8.1. On whether there is a right to surrogacy, see C Straehle [2006] 33 J Applied Philosophy 146–59. See also D Weinstock and J Wisperlaere, 'State Regulation and Assisted Reproduction: Balancing the Interests of Parents and Children' in C McLeod and F Baylis, eds, Family Making (Oxford University Press 2014), 131–50.

that she provides the egg, or she may make no contribution to the establishment of the pregnancy. The surrogate woman may simply lease her womb. She may also be the genetic mother. The genetic father may be the husband of the commissioning mother (or a partner). He may also be the husband or partner of the gestational mother, or a donor. Surrogacy may involve payment (the Brazier Report found typical payments of between £10,000 and £15,000[628] and higher ones are now found in reported cases) or the reimbursement of expenses. There is also so-called altruistic surrogacy, where, for example, one sister carries the pregnancy for another.

14.235 The practice of surrogacy (or 'contract pregnancy') has proved very controversial.[629] The Warnock Report went so far as to describe 'surrogacy for convenience', of which there is little or no evidence, as 'totally ethically unacceptable'.[630] Even where there are 'compelling medical circumstances', the report castigates the practice of surrogacy using Kantian language: 'That people should treat others as a means to their own ends, however desirable the consequences, must always be liable to moral objection.'[631] Although the committee was more concerned with the commercial exploitation of surrogacy, it recommended the criminalization of surrogacy agencies, both profit and non-profit making organizations.[632] It also recommended that it be provided by statute that all surrogacy agreements are illegal contracts and unenforceable in the courts.[633] Legislation was passed within a year of the Warnock Report,[634] but the speed of response is attributable to the first major surrogacy case in the UK, the 'Baby Cotton' case in January 1985 which caused a 'moral panic'.[635] The Surrogacy Arrangements Act 1985 (the SAA Act), passed in response to this case, did not go as far as Warnock recommended. It distinguished the practice of commercial agencies from those which are non-profit making, and it said nothing about the status of the surrogacy contract. The latter issue was picked up, after the 1987 White Paper had addressed it, in the 1990 Act.[636]

14.236 There is an excellent statement of the law on surrogacy in Hale LJ's judgment in *Briody v St Helen's and Knowsley Area Health Authority*.[637] On the basis of this she concluded that surrogacy 'as such is [not] contrary to public policy'.[638] But the 'issue is a difficult one, upon which opinions are divided, so that it would be wise to tread with caution'.[639] She expressed the view that 'if there is a trend it is towards acceptance and regulation as a last resort rather than towards prohibition'.[640] That surrogacy can cause distress is manifest (the 'Baby M'

628 *Surrogacy: Review for Health Ministers of Current Arrangements for Payments and Regulation* (Cm 4068, 1998) para 5.4.

629 See M Freeman, 'Is Surrogacy Exploitative?' in S A M McLean (ed), *Legal Issues in Human Reproduction* (Gower 1989) 164. See generally M A Field, *Surrogate Motherhood* (Harvard University Press 1988). S Wilkinson, 'Exploitation in International Paid Surrogacy Arrangements' [2006] 33 J Applied Philosophy 125–45.

630 The Warnock Report, n 627, para 8.17. On surrogacy law see A Alghrani, D Griffiths, and M Brazier, 'Surrogacy Law: From Piecemeal Tweaks to Sustained Review and Reform' in A Diduck, N Peleg, and H Reece (eds), *Law in Society* (Brill 2015), 425–52; K Horsey and S Sheldon, 'Still Hazy After All These Years: The Law Regulating Surrogacy' [2012] 20 Medical Law Review 67–89.

631 The Warnock Report, n 627, para 8.17.

632 ibid, para 8.18.

633 ibid, para 8.19.

634 Surrogacy Arrangements Act 1985 (SAA Act).

635 *Re C (A Minor)* [1985] FLR 846.

636 *Human Fertilisation and Embryology: A Framework for Legislation* (Cm 259, 1987) paras 66–75.

637 *Briody v St Helen's and Knowsley Area Health Authority* [2001] 2 FLR 1094, 1098–1100.

638 ibid, 1100. On the changing profile of surrogacy see M Cranshaw, E Blyth, and O van den Akker, 'The Changing Profile of Surrogacy in The UK—Implications for National and International Policy and Practice' (September 2012) 34(3) Journal of Social Welfare and Family Law 267–77.

639 *Briody*, n 637.

640 ibid.

saga in the United States is an egregious example[641]). The mess created in *W and B v H*[642] (discussed in para 14.275) led Hedley J to caution against 'an imbalance between our scientific and ethical capacities'.[643]

1. Surrogacy agreements

The status of surrogacy agreements can be examined from the perspectives of both the criminal law and the civil law. **14.237**

(i) The criminal law

As far as the criminal law is concerned, there are a number of ways in which surrogacy may be thought to be sanctioned. Most obviously, an offence may be committed under s 95 of the Adoption and Children Act 2002 if the commissioning couple intend to adopt the child once born. This provides that: **14.238**

> Any person who—
> (a) makes any payment to which this section applies,
> (b) agrees or offers to make any such payment, or
> (c) receives or agrees to receive or attempts to obtain any such payment is guilty of an offence.

However, in *Re an Adoption Application (Surrogacy)*[644] Latey J put a somewhat liberal construction on this statutory provision's predecessor. He held that whether there is 'any payment or reward' for adoption is 'a question of fact to be decided on the evidence'.[645] He could see 'nothing commercial in what happened',[646] although the couples admitted that sums of £10,000 and £5,000 had changed hands. In his view, it 'was only after the payments had been made and the baby was born that any of them began to turn their minds in any real senses to adoption and the legalities'.[647] 'Legalities' may be a Freudian slip on the judge's part: surely, he meant 'illegalities'. He seems to have been influenced by the absence of a written contract and the fact that lawyers were not consulted until after the baby was born. The arrangement was one of 'trust which was fully honoured on both sides'.[648]

The section applies to any payment, other than an excepted one for, or in consideration of, inter alia, 'the adoption of a child', and 'giving any consent required in connection with the adoption of a child'. The offence is punishable by imprisonment for up to six months or a fine of £10,000, or both. **14.239**

But there is no reason why most commissioning parents should want to go through the adoption process, given the establishment of the parental order.[649] Only those who do not comply with the requirements for obtaining a parental order—fewer since the 2008 Act extended eligibility to those in an 'enduring family relationship' and to civil partners[650]—need to seek adoption of the child, though people may feel more secure with adoption; a **14.240**

[641] On which see L Gostin, *Surrogate Motherhood* (Indiana University Press 1990) 233 and 243 and J Merrick, in D Bartels et al (eds), *Beyond Baby M* (Humana Press 1990) 183.
[642] *W and B v H* [2002] 1 FLR 1008.
[643] ibid, 1009. On licensing see K Trimmings and P Beaumont [2011] 7 J Private International Law 627–47 and A Botterell and C McLeod (2016) 33 J Applied Philosophy 178–96.
[644] *Re an Adoption Application (Surrogacy)* [1987] Fam 81.
[645] ibid, 86.
[646] ibid, 84.
[647] ibid, 86.
[648] ibid, 84.
[649] ibid, 86.
[650] ibid, 84.

concept they may understand, than with a parental order, with which they are likely to be unfamiliar.

14.241 It is not unlawful under the Adoption and Children Act 2002 for a surrogate mother to receive a payment for handing over her child to another, nor is there a crime of 'baby selling'.

14.242 The criminal law might also be invoked if the agreement were thought to constitute a conspiracy to corrupt public morals or outrage public decency.[651] Although a body of opinion would support this,[652] it seems unlikely that such a prosecution would be brought. No English case has addressed this question, and there has been ample opportunity for Directors of Public Prosecutions to have initiated a prosecution should they have wished to do so.

(ii) The civil law

14.243 From the perspective of the civil law it is now clear that a surrogacy arrangement is unenforceable. The 1990 Act inserted a new s 1A into the SAA Act: 'No surrogacy arrangement is enforceable by or against any of the persons making it.' The commissioning parents thus have no right to the child, and the surrogate no right to her emolument (expenses, fee, etc).

(iii) Public policy

14.244 Is the agreement also void on grounds of public policy? In *Re P (Minors) (Wardship: Surrogacy)*, Sir John Arnold P said obiter that there was a view that an element of the surrogacy agreement was 'repellent to proper ideas about the procreation of children, so as to make any such agreement one which should be rejected by law as being contrary to public policy'.[653] *In A v C*, Comyn J held that an agreement made between a prostitute and a man that she would bear his child and hand it over to him was contrary to public policy as 'a purported contract for the sale and purchase of a child'.[654] The Court of Appeal described the arrangement as 'most extraordinary and irresponsible, bizarre and unnatural', 'a sordid commercial bargain',[655] and 'a kind of baby-farming operation of a wholly distasteful and lamentable kind'.[656] An Australian court has been less censorious, arguing that it was 'appropriate [to] take account of the intentions and expectations of the four adults who co-operated to bring about [the] birth'.[657] And Hale LJ in *Briody v St Helen's and Knowsley AHA* interprets the English law as not indicating that surrogacy is contrary to public policy. The law, she says, indicates the issue is a 'difficult' one, upon which opinions are divided, so that it would be 'wise to tread with caution'.[658]

14.245 This question remains of importance despite the insertion of the new provision in the SAA Act (see para 14.247). The new provision applies to 'surrogacy arrangements' as defined in the SAA Act.[659] These do not include agreements reached after the child is conceived and which are intended to result in the child being handed over by the surrogate mother. Such arrangements would remain governed by the common law and on the basis of the

---

651 On which see *Shaw v Director of Public Prosecutions* [1962] AC 220, and *Knuller v Director of Public Prosecutions* [1973] AC 435.

652 Best represented by Lord Devlin, *The Enforcement of Morals* (Clarendon Press 1965).

653 [1987] 2 FLR 421, 425.

654 *A v C* [1985] FLR 445, 449 (decided in 1978).

655 ibid, 455, 457 *per* Ormrod LJ.

656 ibid, 459 *per* Cumming-Bruce LJ.

657 *Re Evelyn* (1998) FLC 92–807, 29 *per* Jordan J. This is discussed by M Otlowski, 'Re Evelyn: Reflections on Australia's First Litigated Surrogacy Case' (1997) 7 Med L Rev 38.

658 *Briody*, n 637, 1100.

659 See s 1(2)(a) of the SAA Act.

case law considered in para 14.247, might be held to be both contrary to public policy and unenforceable.

(iv) Activities connected with surrogacy

English law does not prohibit surrogacy arrangements, but the SAA Act prohibits a number **14.246**
of activities in connection with surrogacy. Where IVF or DI techniques are used to achieve pregnancy (and the latter does not employ DIY), the activities will be licensed under the 1990 Act as amended[660] and, as such, HFEA may regulate the use of the techniques to achieve a surrogate pregnancy.

The British Medical Association's publication, *Changing Conceptions of Motherhood* contains **14.247**
guidelines for practitioners. The attitude to surrogacy is more relaxed than in a previous report published in 1990. No longer are doctors to exercise 'extreme caution' before helping to achieve a surrogate pregnancy: it is still emphasized that they should only do so 'as a last resort'. Surrogacy is described as 'an acceptable option of last resort in cases where it is impossible or highly undesirable for medical reasons for the intended mother to carry a child herself'.[661] The report stresses that the interests of the potential child must be paramount, and the risks to the surrogate mother must be kept to a minimum.

2. Surrogacy agencies

(i) Statutory provisions

The SAA Act, as amended by the 1990 and 2008 Acts,[662] seeks to outlaw commercial sur- **14.248**
rogacy agencies. It provides[663] that:

> No person shall on a commercial basis do any of the following acts in the United Kingdom, that is—
>
> (a) initiate any negotiations with a view to the making of a surrogacy arrangement,
> (aa) take part in any negotiations with the view to the making of a surrogacy arrangement,
> (b) offer or agree to negotiate the making of a surrogacy arrangement, or
> (c) compile any information with a view to its use in making, or negotiating the making of, surrogacy arrangements,
>
> and no person shall in the United Kingdom knowingly cause another to do any of these acts on a commercial basis.

An act is done on a 'commercial basis' if 'any payment is at any time received by himself or another in respect of it' or 'he does it with a view to any payment being received by himself or another in respect of making, or negotiating or facilitating the making of, any surrogacy arrangement'.[664] Contravention of these provisions is a criminal offence.[665] However, a person is not to be treated as doing an act on a commercial basis by reason of having received a payment if it is proved that he did not do the act knowing or having reasonable cause to suspect that any payment had been received in respect of the act or, where payment was received after he did the act, that he did not do the act with a view to payment being received.[666]

---

660 1990 Act, s 2(1).
661 *The Changing Conceptions of Motherhood—The Practice of Surrogacy in Britain* (BMA 1996) 59.
662 SAA Act, s 36(2).
663 ibid, s 3(2) (as amended).
664 ibid, s 2(3).
665 ibid, s 2(2).
666 ibid, s 2(4).

14.249 It is now[667] provided that a non-profit-making body[668] does not contravene the SAA Act merely because it does an act (described in 14.251 above) in respect of which any reasonable payment is received by it or another or does an act with a view to any reasonable payment being received by it or another in respect of facilitating the making of any surrogacy arrangement.[669] Furthermore, it is not an offence knowingly to cause such a body to participate in such an act merely because of reasonable payment being made or contemplated.[670] 'Reasonable payment' is defined as a payment 'not exceeding the body's 'costs reasonably attributable to' the making of any surrogacy arrangement.[671]

(ii) Statutory definition

14.250 For this purpose 'payment' does not include payment 'to or for the benefit of a surrogate mother or prospective surrogate mother'.[672] Both she and the commissioning couple are specifically excluded from the provisions of the legislation under s 2(2).

14.251 It has been seen (para 14.253) that the provision outlawing the negotiation and so forth of surrogacy arrangements is broadly defined. There have been no reported prosecutions, and there was reluctance, it seems, on the part of the Director of Public Prosecutions to get involved in a case many years ago where the payment was (supposedly) for the writing of a pregnancy diary.[673]

14.252 'Surrogate mother' and 'surrogate arrangement' are also broadly defined.[674] 'Surrogate mother' means 'a woman who carries a child in pursuance of an arrangement made before she began to carry the child' with a view to the child being handed over and parental responsibility being met by another person or persons: it therefore does not cover an arrangement reached after conception.

14.253 In determining whether an arrangement is made with a view to the child being handed over, and parental responsibility being met by another person or persons:

> regard may be had to the circumstances as a whole (and, in particular, where there is a promise or understanding that any payment will or may be made to the woman or for her benefit in respect of the carrying of any child in pursuance of the arrangement, to that promise or understanding).[675]

An arrangement may be regarded as made with such a view although there are conditions relating to the handing over of the child.[676] 'Payment' is defined to include 'money's worth'.[677]

(iii) Advertising

14.254 It is a criminal offence to publish an advertisement seeking a surrogate mother or offering to act as a surrogate mother in a newspaper or periodical.[678] The offence is committed by the proprietor, editor, or publisher.[679] The offence is also committed by a person who

667 2008 Act, s 59.
668 ibid, s 59(2), inserting a new s 1(7A) into the SAA Act.
669 ibid, s 59(4).
670 SAA Act, new s 2(2B), inserted by 2008 Act, s 59(4).
671 ibid, new s 2(2C), inserted by 2008 Act, s 59(4).
672 ibid, s 2(3).
673 As reported in *The Daily Telegraph* (15 May 1986).
674 SAA Act, s 1(2) and s 1(3)–(6) respectively.
675 ibid, s 1(4).
676 ibid, s 1(5).
677 ibid, s 1(8).
678 ibid, s 3(4).
679 ibid, s 3(3).

conveys an advertisement through radio or television[680] or through the internet or otherwise (for example, a shopkeeper who places a notice on his or her window would commit an offence).[681] Whether the potential surrogate mother and the commissioning couple also commit offences is far from clear. It could be argued that they 'cause' an advertisement to be 'conveyed' or 'published' or 'distributed' by placing the advertisement with the publisher.[682] This section does not apply to any advertisement placed by, or on behalf of, a non-profit-making body, if the advertisement relates only to the doing of acts that would not contravene s 2(1), even if done as a non-commercial basis.[683]

3. Parentage and parental responsibility for the child

Where a child is born as a result of a surrogacy arrangement who are his/her parents and who has parental responsibility? **14.255**

(i) Maternity

On the question who is the mother, the law in England and Wales is clear and unequivocal. The woman who gives birth is the legal mother. It matters not that she is a surrogate or whose eggs were used.[684] Nor does the law distinguish different types of surrogacy: the same test applies whether the gestational mother is also the genetic mother or not. The woman in the commissioning couple is not the mother even if her eggs are used. As Jackson notes, the consequence of assigning legal status in this way is that 'the presumed interests of the surrogate mother even take priority over the interests of the child'.[685] The surrogate has no interest in bringing up the child, but it is she who has parental responsibility, not the commissioning parents who intend to rear the child. The conservatism of this model is brought strikingly into relief should the commissioning parents reject the child for any reason, perhaps because s/he has special needs or their marriage has broken down.[686] **14.256**

(ii) Paternity

Where artificial insemination has been used and the surrogate is married, her husband is to be treated as the father of the child, unless he can prove that he did not consent to the procedure. The partner of the commissioning couple is not the father even if his sperm is used for DI or IVF.[687] He is treated in such a case in the same way as a sperm donor. By providing for an untruthful conclusion, the law encourages dishonesty. **14.257**

Where the surrogate is unmarried, but has a male partner (and no female partner), there are provisions (as we have seen) to enable him to be the father of the child. But he is unlikely to want to be the father, and anyway will only be the father if the 'fatherhood conditions'[688] are satisfied (see para 14.216). It is unlikely that they will be satisfied. At the point of birth, therefore, such a child will be legally fatherless. **14.258**

(iii) Registration of birth

A child born to a surrogate must be registered as her child and if applicable, that of her partner or the person treated as the father under the 1990 Act. A previous Code of Practice **14.259**

680 ibid, s 3(5).
681 ibid, s 3(4) (and see Kennedy and Grubb, n 459).
682 ibid, see new s 3(1A), inserted by s 59 of the 2008 Act, s 59(7).
683 ibid, s 33. This is discussed at para 14.210.
684 E Jackson, *Regulating Reproduction* (Hart Publishing 2001) 266.
685 See further M Shapiro, 'How (Not) To Think About Surrogacy and Other Reproductive Innovations' (1994) 28 Univ of San Francisco LR 647.
686 2008 Act, s 35(1).
687 ibid, s 38(1).
688 ibid, s 37.

confirmed this: the surrogate must register the baby to which she has given birth in the normal way: 'her husband or partner should normally be registered as the father.'[689] Of course, this is an implicit admission by HFEA that there are situations which fall outside the norm. Most obviously, where the surrogate is a single woman. If the surrogate and the commissioning father were to attend the Registrar of Births and jointly request that his father should be recorded on the birth certificate of the child as his/her father, it is difficult to find a justification for the Registrar to refuse the request. He is the father and DNA tests will confirm this. The latest Code of Practice does not address this question.

4. Acquiring legal parenthood

14.260 In most cases after the birth of the child, he/she will be handed over by the surrogate mother to the commissioning couple. A number of legal avenues are then open to them.[690] They can adopt or acquire a parental order under s 30 of the 1990 Act, as amended. Until they do so, neither the commissioning mother nor the commissioning father will have the status of parent or parental responsibility for the child.

(i) Adoption

14.261 For full details of the law of adoption, standard books on child law should be consulted. In short, much depends on whether the surrogate is married, whether or not assisted procreation was used, and, if she is married, whether or not her husband consented to her becoming a surrogate.

14.262 Adoption is governed by a test which requires the court and the adoption agency to regard the child's welfare throughout his life as the paramount consideration.[691] The critical case will occur where the surrogate changes her mind and refuses to hand over the child to the commissioning parents. The emphasis is on the child's best interests. But there are other interests to be considered: the surrogate's and those of the commissioning parents (and, arguably, their respective families). What is in a child's best interests is not easily determined. Nor is it easy to avoid reference implicit or explicit, to the decision-maker's values. Questions which will arise include (i) are the circumstances of the child's birth relevant? (ii) is there a presumption that it is in a child's best interests to be reared by the woman who gave birth to him/her? (iii) should the residential status quo be disturbed? The length of this is important: (iv) should we be looking to short-term interests, particularly significant if the child has bonded, or the long-term? There are questions of identity to consider here.

14.263 The court and the adoption agency is directed to have regard to a number of considerations.[692] These include the child's wishes and feelings (in the light of the child's age and understanding). Since the child will be a baby, this is unlikely to be of any significance. They also include the child's needs, the likely effect of ceasing to be a member of the surrogate's family and becoming an adopted person, any harm the child has suffered or is at risk of suffering, and the relationship the child has with relatives. In addition, the adoption agency must give due consideration to the child's religious persuasion, racial origin, and cultural and linguistic background.[693]

[689] *Code of Practice* (2001) Annex D, 59.
[690] Assuming they want to cement the relationship. Only adoption will imitate nature and confer total parental status. A s 30 order, however, comes sufficiently close to this to make little difference in practice. With wardship only care and control is conferred.
[691] See Adoption and Children Act 2002, s 1(2).
[692] See ibid, s 1(4).
[693] See ibid, s 1(5).

(ii) The section 30 (now section 54) parental order

The 1990 Act introduced the parental order as an alternative to adoption.[694] Before a court may make this order (which provides for the child to be treated in law as the child of the commissioning parents[695]) a number of conditions, set out now in the 2008 Act, must be satisfied: **14.264**

(i) the child must have been born to a surrogate as a result of assisted procreative techniques;[696]

(The s 30 procedure is not applicable where DIY has been used or the commissioning father has had sexual intercourse with the surrogate.)

(ii) the gametes of at least one of the commissioning couple have been used to bring about the creation of the embryo;[697]

(The child must thus be genetically related to at least one of the commissioning couple.)

(iii) the applicants must be either husband and wife or civil partners or two persons living as partners in an enduring family relationship;[698]

(Under the 1990 Act only married couples could apply. A single person can still not apply and would need to use the adoption route.)

(iv) the applicants must apply within six months of the birth of the child or for births before the 1990 Act came into force within six months of that;[699]

(v) the child must have his or her home with the applicants both at the time of the application and at the time of the order;[700]

(This may prove difficult to establish in a case where the surrogate refuses to hand over the child. It also means that the Act requires persons who have no parental responsibility to look after the child prior to the order.)

(vi) at least one of the applicants must be domiciled in a part of the United Kingdom or in the Channel Islands or the Isle of Man;[701]

(The emphasis on domicile means that even where both applicants are living in the UK or the rest they may not be eligible to apply for a s 30 order: but they may be able to do so when they are not living in the UK.)

(vii) both applicants must be at least 18 years old;[702]

(viii) the court must be satisfied that the child's father, where he is not the husband, and the surrogate mother freely agree to the making of the order. When an unmarried woman, acting as a surrogate for a married couple, carried and gave birth to a child created from the egg of the wife fertilized by sperm donated at a clinic under a licensed arrangement rather than the sperm of the husband, it seems that there is no man who

694 1990 Act, s 30. The law is now in s 54 of the 2008 Act.
695 2008 Act, s 54(1).
696 ibid, s 54(1)(a).
697 ibid, s 54(1)(b).
698 ibid, s 54(2).
699 ibid, s 54(3). This is subject to s 54(11).
700 ibid, s 54(4)(a).
701 ibid, s 54(4)(b). That this can cause problems is illustrated by *Re G* [2008] 1 FLR 1047.
702 ibid, s 54(5).

is to be treated as the father and whose consent is therefore required to the making of the parental order.[703] The agreement must be unconditional and with full understanding of what is involved.[704] No agreement is required of a person who cannot be found or is incapable of giving agreement.[705] The surrogate is not permitted to agree until six weeks have elapsed since the child's birth.[706]

(In contrast to adoption, there is no provision for dispensing with a surrogate's agreement, or her partner's agreement, where the child's welfare requires the consent to be dispensed with. The effect of this is to give the surrogate (which may be understandable) and her partner (which is less easy to defend) a veto over the making of a s 54 order.)

(ix) the court must be satisfied that no money or other benefit (other than for expenses reasonably incurred) has been given or received by the husband or wife for or in consideration of the making of the parental order, any agreement required, the handing over of the child to the applicants or the making of any arrangements with a view to the making of the order.[707] The court can, however, authorize payments. On the clear analogy of the adoption legislation, it may be assumed that courts will do this retrospectively as well as prospectively. And this has happened. Examples of this being done are *Re Q*,[708] where a payment of £8,280 was found to be reasonable and retrospectively authorized, and *Re C*,[709] where £12,000 was held to be not so disproportionately greater than the 'usual' sum.

(It will be observed that reasonable expenses can be paid and that, as in *Re Q* and *Re C*, this is interpreted liberally, but, of course, retrospectively. It has been recommended that a list of 'prescribed' expenses be stipulated. Wall J in *Re C* stressed the need for 'transparency in the definition and true extent of expenses reasonably incurred under s 30(7) of the [1990] Act'.)[710]

14.265 Applications for a s 54 order may be made to the High Court, a County Court or to Family Proceedings Court.[711] There are no regulations as yet to indicate the test which is to be applied. Under the 1990 Act, the court had to 'have regard to all the circumstances, first consideration being given to the need to safeguard and promote the welfare of the child'.[712] It may be assumed that a paramountcy test will replace this. The guardian ad litem[713] must establish whether the s 30 criteria are met and must then determine whether there is any reason why a parental order would not be in the best interests of the child. It is thought that guardians will often confront the dilemma that the criteria are not satisfied (most obviously, because the surrogate has been paid) but the child's best interests mandate an order. Courts, it seems, extricate them from this dilemma by retrospectively authorizing unlawful

[703] *Re Q (Parental Order)* [1996] 1 FLR 369.
[704] 2008 Act, s 54(6).
[705] ibid, s 54(6)(b).
[706] ibid, s 54(7).
[707] ibid, s 54(8).
[708] [1996] 1 FLR 369.
[709] *Re C* [2002] 1 FLR 909.
[710] ibid, 918.
[711] 2008 Act, s 30(9)(a). These are strong grounds for any parental order application involving a foreign element to be transferred to a nominated inter-country adoption county court or the High Court at the first directions hearing: see *Re G* [2008] 1 FLR 1047, 1059.
[712] Parental Orders (Human Fertilisation and Embryology) Regulations 1994, SI 1994/2767, Sch 9(1)(a).
[713] See Local Authority Circular LAC (94) 25.

payments as reasonable expenses.[714] *Re C*[715] is the clearest of examples of this: it was manifestly in the interests of a 'much loved and cherished child' that she be treated in law as the child of the commissioning couple despite £12,000 having passed to a surrogate (who in addition was claiming income support—a fact not known by the couple). But would the court have come to a different conclusion had they known? I suspect not: the welfare of the child would still have dictated the order.

A parental order gives parental responsibility to the applicants.[716]It also extinguishes the parental responsibility which any person has for the child immediately before the making of the order, as well as any order under the Children Act 1989 (eg a residence order or a child arrangements order[717]), and any duty arising by virtue of an agreement or the order of a court to make payments, so far as the payments are in respect of the child's maintenance or upbringing for any period after the making of the order.[718] The child is to be treated for all purposes as if she is the child of the marriage of the applicants for the parental order, and not the child of anyone else.[719] There are a number of exceptions to this. One of these is with regard to prohibited degrees of relationship in relation to marriage and incest as against the genetic relations of the child.[720] Part of the reason for this is to allow for a register of parental orders.[721] **14.266**

The Registrar General is required to maintain a 'Parental Order Register' to record the effects of parental orders made under s 30.[722] The child, upon reaching the age of 18, is entitled to obtain details of his/her birth, including the name of the surrogate mother.[723] Prior to being given this information, the person concerned will be offered counselling.[724] The children of surrogacy arrangements were thus the only children born following medically assisted reproduction to be granted this right until the 2008 Act.[725] Surrogacy is equated for these purposes (and others as we have seen) with adoption. The analogy, however, breaks down where the surrogate leases her womb but does not provide her egg. In such a case the child will at 18 be able to discover his/her gestational mother, but, unless the egg of a third woman has been used, will already know his/her genetic mother. Where the child is born to a surrogate using egg donation from a third party woman, the child will be able to find out the identity of the genetic mother if the commissioning parents who cannot use the s 30 procedure adopted him/her. In addition, a child under 18 who is subject to a 'parental order' may discover whether a person he/she intends to marry is within the prohibited degrees of relationship.[726] For this purpose both the commissioning couple and the surrogate and her partner, if she has one, will be the child's parents. The child is not allowed to marry the surrogate's son or daughter, who are considered siblings even where the surrogate was the gestational mother only.[727] **14.267**

714 The Brazier Report (Cm 4068, 1998) described the reference to expenses reasonably incurred as 'laconic' (para 7.11).
715 *Re C*, n 709, 917.
716 See n 709 above, r. 2.2.
717 See n 712 above.
718 See n 709 above, r. 2.2.
719 ibid.
720 ibid, r.2.3(e).
721 ibid, r.2.4.
722 ibid.
723 ibid, r.2.4(b).
724 ibid.
725 See para 14.183.
726 See r 2.4(b)(11).
727 ibid.

(iii) Children Act 1989

14.268 Proceedings under s 54 are 'family proceedings' within the meaning of the Children Act 1989.[728] This means that the powers available under that Act are also available on an application for a 'parental order', including the power to make s 8 orders.[729] The court could thus grant the applicants a child arrangements order instead of a parental order.[730] It could also make an additional order, for example, a contact order[731] in favour of the surrogate mother, a specific issue order[732] (perhaps relating to the religion in which the child is to be brought up) or a prohibited steps order[733] (for example, relating to the removal of the child from this country).

(iv) Wardship

14.269 If the surrogate mother refuses to hand over the child, the only way the dispute may be resolved is by warding the child.[734] The commissioning parents may invoke the inherent jurisdiction of the High Court as *parens patriae* to decide matters relating to the child's future. In *Re P (Minors) (Wardship: Surrogacy)*, Sir John Arnold P said:

> The court's duty is to decide the case, taking into account as the first and paramount consideration [now the paramount consideration], the welfare of the child or children concerned and if that consideration leads the court to override any agreement that there may be in the matter, then that court is fully entitled to do.[735]

In this case, 'preserving the link with the [surrogate] mother to whom they [there were twins in this case] are bonded and who has exercised over them a satisfactory level of maternal care'[736] tipped the balance in favour of the surrogate and against the commissioning parents. In *Re C(A Minor)* Latey J remarked that 'the moral, ethical and social considerations are for others and not for this court in its wardship jurisdiction'.[737] His only concern was 'what is best for this baby'.[738] He was in no doubt that care and control should be given to the commissioning parents. The surrogate did not disagree: it was the local authority, who had taken a place of safety order, who were obstructing the commissioning parents.

14.270 It is possible for the court to grant commissioning parents contact with the child, whilst leaving him/her in the care of the surrogate mother.[739] In the well-known *Baby M* case[740] in New Jersey, the commissioning parents were awarded custody, but the Supreme Court of New Jersey decided that the surrogate mother should have 'visitation'.[741] The issue has only been considered in one English case (*A v C*), where the Court of Appeal firmly rejected it. To Ormrod LJ, it would lead to 'the whole of this sordid story . . . (be[ing] revived weekly or monthly . . . The mother's position will be handicapped, and the handicapping of her position handicaps the child'.[742] Although the facts were different from almost all surrogacy

---

[728] 2008 Act, s 54(9)(a) and see Children Act 1989 s 8(3), (4).
[729] See M D A Freeman, *Children, Their Families and the Law* (Macmillan 1992) ch 3.
[730] Children Act 1989, s 8(1).
[731] ibid, s 8(1).
[732] ibid, s 8(1).
[733] ibid, s 8(1).
[734] As to which see N Lowe and R A H White, *Wards of Court* (Barry Rose 1986).
[735] *Re P (Minors) (Wardship: Surrogacy)* [1987] 2 FLR 421, 425.
[736] ibid, 427.
[737] *Re C(A Minor)* [1985] FLR 445.
[738] ibid.
[739] Under the Children Act 1989, s 8.
[740] 537 A 2d 1227 (1988).
[741] 'Contact' in English legal terminology.
[742] *A v C*, n 653, 458.

cases (the 'contract' resulted from a casual encounter with a prostitute), courts are unlikely today to make a 'contact order' in favour of commissioning parents if they decide that the child should continue to reside with the surrogate mother. Nor are they likely to follow the precedent of *Baby M* and award contact to a surrogate mother.

(v) Informal transfers

The Brazier Report believed that 'a substantial proportion of commissioning couples are failing to apply to the courts to become the legal parents of the child'.[743] The likeliest reason is that informal transfers have taken place and commissioning parents are ignorant of their lack of status or, less likely, indifferent. The consequences of this are that the surrogate retains parental responsibility.[744] If she has a husband he is likely to have this too. They can, as a result, interfere with decisions the commissioning parents take about the child. The potentiality for acrimonious disputes is obvious. Concomitantly, the commissioning parents will not have parental responsibility. Nor will they be 'parents'. They will have 'care' of the child and may, subject to the provisions of the Children Act, 'do what is reasonable . . . for the purpose of safeguarding or promoting the child's welfare'.[745] With the leave of the court,[746] they may apply for a child arrangements order and acquire parental responsibility in this way.[747] It is also possible for a competent child[748] to seek a child arrangements order in favour of his/her social parents,[749] but then he/she could equally well ask it to be in favour of the surrogate or some other person or persons. **14.271**

(vi) Abductions

If a child is born in England and Wales to a surrogate, the surrogacy agreement and conception having taken place abroad, will an English court return the child to the foreign country? This issue arose in the complex case of *W and B v H*.[750] The surrogacy agreement was entered into in California, by the law of which it was legally binding,[751] between an English surrogate and a Californian couple. The egg was from an anonymous donor. This was fertilized by the commissioning father's sperm. When it was discovered that the surrogate was carrying twins, there was considerable dispute (talk of 'selective reduction' and alternative parents). The surrogate invoked the jurisdiction of the Californian court to divest herself of custody, and, after achieving this, changed her mind, and came to England where she gave birth. The *forum conveniens* for this dispute would appear to be California,[752] but the genetic father sought the protection instead of the Hague Convention on International Child Abduction.[753] He had rights of custody under Californian law but the Convention would not bite unless the children were or ever had been habitually resident in California. They clearly were not nor had ever been. Hedley J held also that they were not habitually **14.272**

[743] *Surrogacy: Review for Health Ministers of Current Arrangements for Payments and Regulations* (Cm 4068, 1998) para 5.7.

[744] Children Act 1989, s 2(1). A defence of the Brazier report is A Alghrani, D Griffiths, and M Brazier, 'Surrogacy Law: From Piecemeal Tweaks to Sustained Review and Reform' in A Diduck, N Peleg, and H Reece, (eds), *Law in Society* (Brill 2015), 425–52.

[745] Children Act 1989, s 3(5).

[746] ibid, s 10(1)(a)(ii).

[747] ibid, s 12(2).

[748] ie a child who has 'sufficient understanding to make the proposed application for the section 8 order' (Children Act 1989, s 10(8)).

[749] See *Re SC* [1994] 1 FLR 96, 100 *per* Booth J.

[750] *W and B v H* [2002] 1 FLR 1008.

[751] ibid,1009.

[752] And so Hedley J held in *W and W v H (Child Abduction: Surrogacy) No 2* [2002] 2 FLR 252.

[753] Brought into English Law by the Child Abduction and Custody Act 1985.

resident in England.[754] This conclusion is less easy to justify. Would he have come to the same conclusion if the surrogate had been the genetic mother? There is reason to doubt this, within his judgment. He concluded that the children were not habitually resident anywhere. (They were presumably domiciled in England[755]—a legal connection that is irrelevant to the problem.) Abduction proceedings failed. In effect an English court refused to uphold a surrogacy agreement valid by its applicable law[756] and at the same time undermined the order of a foreign court giving custody to the commissioning parents. And this, ironically, in an area where comity prevails over paramountcy.[757]

(vii) Surrogacies with a foreign element

14.273 A stumbling block to foolproof regulation is procreative tourism, and this is becoming more common.[758] Surrogacy arrangements are now commonly made between British couples and surrogates abroad. The child herself may face immigration problems. The child may be a foreign national from birth and accordingly not allowed to enter the UK. And it can get even more complicated if under the surrogate's personal law the commissioning couple are regarded as the child's parents. This was the situation in *Re X and Y (Foreign Surrogacy)*.[759] Under Ukrainian law, the commissioning couple were treated as the child 's parents from birth, but under English law they are not so regarded. They cannot become the child's parents until an order (adoption or a parental order) is made by a court. This meant that the child was both stateless and had no parents. Hedley J drew attention to these difficulties. They were exacerbated by the fact that the payment of the surrogate was excessive (€235 a month during pregnancy and €25,000 on the live birth of the twins). Hedley J expressed his discomfort but authorized the payments to enable a parental order to be made. He observed that 'it is almost impossible to imagine a set of circumstances in which by the time the case comes to court, the welfare of any child (particularly a foreign child) would not be gravely compromised (at the very least) by a refusal to make an order.'[760]

14.274 Problems also arise where a foreign domiciled couple make a surrogacy arrangement with a British couple. Since they are not domiciled in the UK they are not eligible for a parental order.[761] There are also restrictions upon foreign nationals adopting British children. In *Re G (Surrogacy: Foreign Domicile)*,[762] McFarlane J found a solution in s 84(2) of the Adoption and Children Act 2002. This permits a court to make an order giving parental responsibility to persons who intend to adopt a child abroad. In addition to granting parental responsibility, s 84 has the effect of terminating the parental responsibility of any other person in the case, notably the surrogate. McFarlane J was critical of COTS, the agency which had arranged the surrogacy. He questioned whether 'the role of facilitating surrogacy arrangements should be left to groups of well meaning amateurs'.[763]

---

[754] A baby was held not to have the habitual residence of his mother (the surrogate). To hold otherwise was to confuse domicile with habitual residence (as had happened, so it was held, in *B v H (Habitual Residence: Wardship)* [2002] 1 FLR 388).

[755] As illegitimate children they would have the domicile of their mother as their domicile of origin.

[756] There was no express choice of applicable law but it seems this contract was more closely connected with California than England, so that even if the surrogate was the characteristic performer (see Rome Convention, Art 4(2)) the presumption would be rebutted by Art 4(5).

[757] See M Freeman, 'Images of Child Welfare in Child Abduction Appeals'. in J Murphy, (ed), *Ethnic Minorities, Their Families and the Law* (Hart Publishing 2000) 3–14.

[758] See the discussion of 'sperm ships' by D Hunter and S Oultram, 'The Challenge of "Sperm Ships": The Need for the Global Regulation of Medical Technology' (2008) 34 Journal of Medical Ethics 552–56. On reproductive tourism and possible policy responses see A Donchin [2010] 24 Bioethics 323–32.

[759] *Re X and Y (Foreign Surrogacy)* [2009] 1 FLR 733.

[760] ibid, 743. See also *Re* S (*Parental Order*) [2010] 1 FLR 1156.

[761] See para 14.270.

[762] *Re G (Surrogacy: Foreign Domicile)* [2008] 1 FLR 1047.

[763] ibid, 1055.

M. The Future?

Whether the law should follow scientific advances or anticipate them is a matter of debate and controversy. But it may be said that the opportunity to provide a framework for some likely developments in assisted reproduction has not been grasped.[764] Three examples are the development of artificial gametes,[765] the possibility of male pregnancy, and the creation of artificial wombs. The implications for the law of each of these possible developments will be briefly considered. **14.275**

Artificial gametes raise ethical concerns as well as legal conundrums. There is a severe shortage of donor gametes so that if artificial ones can be developed this would be enthusiastically embraced by those affected by the current deficit. The development would 'inevitably increase the medicalization of conception and pregnancy'.[766] It would enable people to have children in new ways. For example, male couples could use artificial gametes to create a child genetically related to both of them, but they would still need a woman to gestate the child. Female couples could not use this technology, since sperm cannot be generated in the absence of a Y chromosome. It would, however, enable post-menopausal women to produce eggs and bear children genetically related to them, instead of, as at present, requiring donor eggs. It is also possible that a man could produce a child where he was the only genetic parent. This involves obtaining eggs and sperm from an embryonic clone of the prospective parent. Such a procedure, Newson and Smajdor point out,[767] 'hovers uneasily on the boundary between reproductive and therapeutic cloning'. However, any child born as a result would not be genetically related with the man from whose stem cells the gametes have been obtained. What are the implications of this for childhood? And will the man whose DNA is contained in the egg be the 'biological mother'? Should the line between the concept of 'mother' and 'father' remain distinct? It is at present unlawful to use artificial gametes to achieve a pregnancy.[768] *In vitro*-derived gametes are allowed for the purposes of research, but not for treatment. Criminalization is not the long-term solution to this problem.[769] **14.276**

It may become possible to generate an embryo *in vitro*, in an artificial womb or ectogenic incubator. Ectogenesis has been anticipated for many years, and is a concern in much feminist literature.[770] There are enormous implications, for example for abortion.[771] The use of artificial wombs to gestate a child is unlawful at present. This is because s 3(3) of the 1990 Act prohibits the use of embryos beyond the appearance of the primitive streak, which is deemed by the legislation to be at fourteen days.[772] This provision was retained by the 2008 Act. Artificial wombs raise the possibility of male pregnancy. An artificial womb could be **14.277**

764 See A Alghrani, 'The Human Fertilisation and Embryology Act 2008: A Missed Opportunity?' (2009) 35 Journal of Medical Ethics 218–19.

765 According to M C Tsai et al, 'Alternative Sources of Pregnancy: Reality or Science Fiction?' (2000) 15 Human Reproduction 988–95 (where he says 'it is already a concrete fact').

766 See A I Newson and A R C Smajdor, 'Artificial Gametes: New Paths to Parenthood?' (2005) 31 Journal of Medical Ethics 184.

767 ibid, 185.

768 ibid, 186.

769 See G Hinseff, *The Guardian* (9 March 2008) quoting Evan Harris MP.

770 See, eg, R Rowland, *Living Laboratories—Women and Reproductive Technology* (Lime Tree 1992) and M Stanworth (ed), *Reproductive Technologies—Gender, Motherhood and Medicine* (Polity Press 1987).

771 See, in relation to abortion, A Alghrani, in M Freeman, *Law and Bioethics* (Oxford University Press 2008), 303–28.

772 HFEA 1990, s 3(3) and (4).

implanted into a man. The legislation does not permit such a procedure. This is an activity which the HFEA is not permitted to license by the 1990 Act.[773]

14.278 HFEA has a Horizon Scanning Panel to '. . . identify new developments that may impact on the field of assisted reproduction or embryo research so that the Authority is aware of potential licence applications and prepared, if necessary, with an Authority policy or position'.[774] This was welcomed by the House of Commons Science and Technology Committee in a report in 2004–05.[775] In 2007–08 the Authority identified womb transplants as one such development but rather disappointingly dismissed it without any detailed consideration. However, the first successful womb transplants were carried out in Sweden in 2014[776] which led to the successful birth of a baby boy to one of the recipients in September 2014.[777] The Health Research Authority has now granted ethical approval for ten womb transplants as part of a clinical trial in the UK.[778] In light of this development, the time has surely come for the HFEA to revisit the issues raised by uterus transplantation.

773 1990 Act, Sch 2.

774 See A Caplan et al, 'Moving the Womb' (2007) 37 Hastings Center Report 18–20. See also I Evans, *The Times* (8 September 2006) where it was suggested it may only be a few years away.

775 This was attempted in 2000. See W Fajeeh et al, (2002) 78 International Journal of Gynaecology and Obstetrics 248.

776 *The Guardian* (13 January 2014). See also M Brannstrom et al, 'Livebirth After Uterus Transplantation' (2015) 385 (9968) The Lancet 606–17.

777 *The Guardian* (30 September 2015).

778 'Womb Transplants Approved for Ten UK women' *Bionews* (October 2015) available at <http://www.bionews.org.uk/page_574003.asp>.

15

REPRODUCTIVE GENETICS

Michael Freeman

A. Introduction

Possibilities for human reproduction have been rapidly expanded by reproductive and genetic technologies. This chapter examines the law governing these technologies.[1] Reproductive Genetics (Reprogenetics) has been defined as the 'creation, use, manipulation, or storage of gametes or embryos'.[2] This definition reflects the broad range of technologies which can now be used for reproductive purposes. **15.01**

Reproductive genetics encompasses both technologies which are currently being used for human reproductive purposes, technologies which are currently only permitted for research purposes, and speculative technologies which are on the horizon. As such the boundaries between research and experimental clinical practice in the area of reproductive genetics are not obvious. Technologies are often introduced into clinical practice quickly and in the absence of long term follow-up studies or randomized controlled trials that are usually expected in clinical practice. **15.02**

The Human Fertilisation and Embryology Act 1990 was enacted with an aim to provide a comprehensive and facilitative framework for regulating embryo research and assisted reproduction. Although technology in this area is fast moving, the Human Fertilisation and Embryology Authority (HFEA) has a broad remit with regard to ensuring public trust in reproductive medicine, maintaining standards of care, and rules as regards the formation of policy. For example, the HFEA formed a multiple birth policy and minimization strategy in 2009 which aims to lower the average national multiple birth rate from its current rate of 24 per cent (of all live birth events following IVF/ICSI) to 10 per cent over a number of years.[3] As a result, all clinics must have a 'multiple birth policy', which sets out how they intend to reduce their annual multiple birth rates and to ensure that they do not exceed the **15.03**

[1] See generally L P Knowles and G E Kaebnick, *Reprogenetics—Law, Policy and Ethical Issues* (Johns Hopkins University Press 2007).

[2] E Parens and L P Knowles, 'Reprogenetics and Public Policy Reflections and Recommendations' (2003) 33 The Hastings Center Report S1–S24.

[3] HFEA, Chair's Letter, CH(08)03 (30 September 2008).

HFEA-set maximum figure. The HFEA has also undertaken wide public consultations on the public acceptability of controversial technologies such as sex selection[4] and mitochondria donation.[5]

15.04 As detailed in the previous chapter, notwithstanding several legal challenges the 1990 Act was largely viewed as a success. However, given the rate of scientific advance in the area it became clear that substantial revisions were necessary. In a White Paper published in December 2006 the government set out the aims of new legislation.[6] These are: (i) to ensure that legitimate applications of human reproductive technologies continue to flourish; (ii) to promote public confidence in the development of human reproductive technologies; and (iii) to secure that regulation accords with better regulation principles and to encourage best regulatory practices.

15.05 The Human Fertilisation and Embryology Act 2008 came into force in October 2009. The 2008 Act aims to ensure continued effective regulation in a fast-changing technological landscape.

B. Creating Gametes and Embryos

15.06 Reproductive genetic techniques have given rise to new ways to make both embryos and gametes. This has led to various legal challenges as precise statutory definitions were thrown into legal uncertainty. As a consequence in their review leading to the 2008 Act, the Science and Technology Committee[7] proposed a strict definition of an embryo that could be used for reproduction and a more open-ended definition for research. This recommendation was followed and section 3(2) allows only a 'permitted embryo' to be placed in the body of a woman.[8] Originally a permitted embryo was defined as one created by the fertilization of a permitted egg by permitted sperm, where no nuclear or mitochondrial DNA of any cell of the embryo has been altered, and no cell added to it other than by division of the embryo's own cells.[9] Since 2015 this has been modified to allow for the implantation of embryos following mitochondrial transfer (see 15.57).[10] This illustrates the way current regulations are equipped to accommodate scientific advances in embryology, avoid legal ambiguity, and 'future-proof' the Authority's remit against litigation.[11]

1. *In vitro* derived gametes

15.07 *In vitro* derived gametes (artificial sperm and eggs) are gametes or gamete-like cells derived from pluripotent stem cells in a laboratory. In non-human animal experiments scientists

[4] HFEA, 'Sex Selection: Options for Regulation' (2003) <http://www.hfea.gov.uk/docs/Final_sex_selection_main_report.pdf> (Accessed 30 August 2016).

[5] HFEA, 'Mitochondrial Donation: Public Consultation' (2012) <http://www.hfea.gov.uk/9359.html> (Accessed August 30th 2016).

[6] HFEA, *Review of the Human Fertilisation and Embryology Act: Proposals for Revised Legislation (Including Establishment of the Regulatory Authority for Tissues and Embryos)* (Cm 6989, December 2006).

[7] Science and Technology Committee, *Human Reproductive Technologies and the Law* (HC 2004–05, Fifth Report).

[8] 2008 Act, s 3(2).

[9] ibid, s 3ZA(4) (as amended).

[10] Human Fertilisation and Embryology (Mitochondrial Donation) Regulations 2015; *Mitochondrial donation*, Guidance Note 33 available at <http://www.hfea.gov.uk/9931.html>.

[11] Department of Health, Government Response to the Report from the House of Commons Science and Technology Committee: Human Reproductive Technologies and the Law (2007) para 53. <https://www.gov.uk/government/uploads/system/uploads/attachment_data/file/243182/7209.pdf> accessed 16 March 2015.

have reported success in both deriving these cells and also their use in non-human animal reproduction.[12] This raises the possibility that scientifically, gametes could be also derived from human embryonic stem cells.[13] These gametes have potential uses for both research and treatment. As Testa and Harris point out, this 'could have a very significant impact . . ., enabling infertile individuals to have their own genetic children'.[14]

The 2008 Act permits *in vitro* derived gametes to be created for research purposes,[15] but not to treat patients.[16] This restriction is found in the amended 1990 Act, ss 3 and 3ZA. Section 3(2) allows permitted eggs or sperm to be placed in a woman, and s 3ZA defines a permitted egg as one: 'which has been produced or extracted from the ovaries of a woman and whose nuclear or mitochondrial DNA has not been altered.'[17] Permitted sperm are similarly defined ('from the testes of a man'[18]). **15.08**

Unlike other aspects of the regulations which allow for the possibility that scientific advances can be accommodated there is no power in the legislation to change this by regulation. This means that if it becomes possible to create *in vitro* derived human gametes new legislation will be required. **15.09**

2. Creating embryos without consent

The general rule is that before embryos can be used for research purposes, those who provide them must consent.[19] Such consent must be in writing and can be withdrawn at any time.[20] The person giving consent must have been given a suitable opportunity to receive counselling, and must be given 'such relevant information as is proper'.[21] For guidance on the information to be given see the HFEA Code of Practice,[22] para 22.7. **15.10**

New questions are raised by the possibility of extracting stem cell lines from embryos. These lines may be valuable, for example, to pharmaceutical companies, as well as to clinicians. They are 'potentially immortal'. Thus, it must be made clear to potential donors that 'any stem cell lines created may continue indefinitely' and be used in many research projects. People who donate embryos for stem cell research must be told of the intention to bank stem cell lines derived from their embryos in the UK stem cell bank. **15.11**

There are exceptions to the need to obtain consent to use an embryo in a research project. First, Sch 3, para 15(2)–(5) to the 1990 Act, (as amended by the 2008 Act), provides that, if the 'parental consent conditions' are met, a person with parental responsibility can give consent to the use of their child's cells to create an embryo for research purposes. The child must suffer from, or be likely to develop, a serious disease, a serious mental or physical disability, or any other serious medical condition.[23] The child must not possess decision-making **15.12**

[12] K Hayashi et al, 'Reconstitution of The Mouse Germ Cell Specification Pathway in Culture by Pluripotent Stem Cells' (2011) 146 Cell 519–32.

[13] Hinxton Group, 'Consensus Statement: The Science, Ethics and Policy Challenges of Pluripotent Stem Cell-Derived Gametes' (April 2008).

[14] G Testa and J Harris, 'Ethics and Synthetic Gametes' (2005) 19 Bioethics 155; see also 'Special Section: Stem Cell Derived Gametes' (2014) 40 Journal of Medical Ethics 725–65.

[15] 1990 Act, s 3ZA (as amended).

[16] ibid.

[17] ibid, s 3ZA(2)(b) (as amended).

[18] ibid, s 3ZA(3)(a) (as amended).

[19] ibid, Sch 3 (as amended).

[20] ibid, Sch 3(1) (as amended).

[21] ibid, Sch 3(3) (as amended).

[22] HFEA, *Code of Practice* (8th edn, 2009).

[23] 1990 Act, Sch 3, para 15(2) (as amended).

capacity.[24] Where a child is 16 use may be authorized where such a child must lack the 'capacity to consent to such use of his/her human cells'.[25] Further, the embryo (or human admixed embryo) is to be used in research to increase knowledge about the disease, disability, or medical condition, or the treatment or care of persons affected by the disease, disability, or medical condition, or any similar disease, disability, or medical condition.[26] There must be reasonable grounds for believing that research of 'comparable effectiveness' cannot be carried out if the only human cells that can be used are those of a competent adult or persons under 18 who are competent to deal with the issue of consent to such use of their human cells.[27] This raises questions about the scope of s 8 of the Family Law Reform Act 1969,[28] and about *Gillick* competency,[29] discussed elsewhere in this book, particularly in Chapter 10. Despite s 2(7) of the Children Act 1989, it is thought that the consent of everyone with parental responsibility should be sought.[30]

15.13 There is a similar provision for adults who lack capacity.[31] The person responsible[32] under the licence is required to take reasonable steps to identify a person who is a carer of the incompetent adult or is interested in his/her welfare. If it is the case that such a person cannot be identified, they 'must' nominate an independent person (namely one unconnected with the project) who is prepared to be consulted.[33] The person responsible must ask the carer/person nominated what in their opinion the incompetent adult's wishes and feelings about the use of his/her human cells would be likely to be if he/she had capacity. Since it is unlikely that such a person has ever expressed a view, in reality the decision is being taken by the carer/person nominated.[34] But the person responsible must not have been advised that in the opinion of the carer/nominated person the incompetent adult's wishes and feelings are such that he/she would be likely to decline to consent to the use of his/her human cells for research.[35]

15.14 The third exception—allowing for consent to be dispensed with—is if the person's cells were stored before the 2008 Act came into force (in October 2008), and he/she has since died. The Act requires that there must be no evidence that the person would have objected to the use of their cells and in addition there must also be agreement from someone who is in a qualifying relationship.[36] The list of such persons is in the Human Tissue Act 2004, s 27(4).[37]

3. Reproductive cloning

15.15 The birth of Dolly the sheep in 1996—it was reported in 1997—provoked discussion about human reproductive cloning.[38] The 1990 Act's definition of 'embryo'—'a live human

---

[24] ibid, 15(3)(a) (as amended).
[25] ibid, 15(3)(b) (as amended).
[26] ibid, Sch 3, para 15(4) (as amended).
[27] ibid, Sch 3, para 15(5) (as amended).
[28] Discussed in Chapter 10.
[29] See *Gillick v West Norfolk and Wisbech AHA* [1986] AC 112.
[30] As with non-therapeutic male circumcision: see *Re J* (*Specific Issue Orders: Child's Religious Upbringing and Circumcision*) [2000] 1 FLR 571. See also *Re C* (*Welfare of the Child: Immunisation*) [2003] EWLA Civ 1148, adding immunization as a case when all with parental responsibility are required to consent.
[31] 1990 Act, Sch 3, para 17(2) (as amended).
[32] See ibid, s 17.
[33] ibid, Sch 3, para 18 (as amended).
[34] ibid, para 18(4) (as amended).
[35] ibid, para 18(5) (as amended).
[36] ibid, para 20.
[37] This contains a ranking.
[38] See A J Klotzko, 'The Debate About Dolly' [2007] 21 Bioethics 427–38.

embryo where fertilization is complete'—[39] arguably did not address cloning, since fertilization does not take place when a cell is cloned. However, both the Human Genetics Advisory Commission (HGAC) and HFEA in their 1998 report[40] and the Chief Medical Officer's Report in 2000[41] rejected this argument, and concluded that cloning was either prohibited or subject to licensing, and HGAC and HFEA indicated that no licences for research into reproductive cloning would be issued.[42] HGAC and HFEA concluded in their joint report that while 'the nuclear replacement of eggs (was) not expressly prohibited', it involved 'the use or creation of embryos outside the body', and so fell within the Act and the 'jurisdiction of HFEA'.[43] This interpretation is purposive in that it undoubtedly achieved the result that Parliament intended in 1990.

The claim was made by the Pro-Life Alliance that the definition of 'embryo' in the 1990 Act did not cover embryos created by cell nuclear replacement (CNR); this would mean that creating embryos in this way would fall outside the statutory regime, and would not be subject to regulation. This claim succeeded at first instance.[44] Crane J ruled that an embryo created by CNR was not protected by the 1990 Act, so that no licence was required for the creation or use of embryos created by this process. This ruling so concerned Parliament that within nineteen days it had enacted the Human Reproductive Cloning Act 2001. This made it a criminal offence to place in the womb of a woman a human embryo created other than by fertilization. **15.16**

Shortly afterwards, the Court of Appeal allowed the Secretary of State's appeal against Crane J's judgment.[45] Lord Phillips of Worth Matravers MR said: **15.17**

> The court has to ask, not what would Parliament have enacted if it had foreseen the creation of embryos by CNR, but, do such embryos plainly fall within the genus covered by the legislation and ask the clear purpose of the legislation be defeated if the extension is not made.[46]

He continued:

> The embryo created by cell nuclear replacement and the embryo created by fertilisation are essentially identical as far as structure is concerned . . . It is the capacity to develop into a human being that is the significant factor and that it is one that is shared by both types of embryo.[47]

The House of Lords agreed.[48] In their view, the 1990 Act had to be construed in the light of contemporary scientific knowledge.[49] For Lord Steyn: **15.18**

> there is not a kind of rational explanation why an embryo produced otherwise than by fertilisation should not have the same status as an embryo created by fertilisation. It is a classic case where the new scientific development falls within . . . 'the same genus of facts' and in any event there is clear legislative purpose which can only be fulfilled if an extensive interpretation is adopted.[50]

39 1990 Act, s 1(1)(b) (as amended).
40 HGAC and HFEA, *Cloning Issues in Human Reproduction, Science and Medicine* (1998) para 3.4.
41 Department of Health, *Stem Cell Research: Medical Progress with Responsibility* (Chief Medical Officer's Expert Group, 16 August 2000).
42 HGAC and HFEA, n 40, para 5.4.
43 ibid, para 3.4.
44 *R (on the application of Quintavalle) v Secretary of State for Health* [2001] 4 All ER 1013.
45 [2002] 2 FCR 140.
46 ibid, 150.
47 ibid, 150–51.
48 [2003] 2 All ER 113.
49 eg *per* Lord Steyn, [2003] 2 All ER 113, 124.
50 ibid.

15.19 For the purposes of reproduction an 'embryo' now means 'a live human embryo'.[51] It includes an egg which is in the process of fertilization or undergoing any other process capable of resulting in an embryo.[52] It does not include a human admixed embryo which falls within the definition for the purposes of research. The 2008 Act thus creates the concept of the 'permitted embryo'.[53] This is the only category of embryo that can be transferred to a woman's body. The effect of this is to ban reproductive cloning, and to make the Human Reproductive Cloning Act 2001 redundant. It is accordingly repealed.[54]

4. Hybrid embryos

15.20 The Human Fertilisation and Embryology Act 2008 permits the creation of, what it calls, 'human admixed embryos'[55] which is a term used to describe what are human/animal hybrid embryos.[56] These have been developed using the technique of cell nuclear replacement (CNR) using denucleated animal eggs and human nuclear DNA.[57] These embryos contain only mitochondrial animal DNA. The embryos themselves are 99.9 per cent human. If stem cell lines are extracted from them these will be 100 per cent human.

15.21 HFEA accepted (in September 2007) that it could, within its powers, license the creation of such a hybrid embryo. It invoked the support of Lord Bingham's judgment in *R (on the application of Quintavalle) v Secretary of State for Health*.[58] He had noted that the creation of the human embryos by CNR fell within the 'same genus of facts'[59] as those created by IVF. Lord Steyn, in the same case, had observed that the 'long title of the 1990 Act makes clear, and it is in any event self-evident, that Parliament intended the protective regulatory system in connection with human embryos to be comprehensive'.[60]

15.22 HFEA's research licence committee authorized research projects using animal eggs to create human admixed embryos in 2008. In April 2008 it was reported that the first human/animal hybrid embryo had been created.

15.23 The first licences were challenged by Comment on Reproductive Ethics (CORE). It was argued that HFEA had exceeded its powers. By the time the case got to court, the 2008 Act had been passed—though it was not in operation—so it could not really be maintained that such research was contrary to Parliament's wishes. Permissions for leave to apply for judicial review was refused by Dobbs J in December 2008 in *R (on the application of Quintavalle and CLC) v HFEA*. The judge noted:

> The Act did not seek to define 'human embryo'. What is 'human' will be dependant on the particular facts of any case and informed by scientific knowledge at the time. I do not accept the claimants' submission that the fact that this technique is in a separate category under the new Act means that Parliament did not intend it to fall within the definition of 'human embryo' under section 1 of the 1990 Act . . . The approach advocated by the defendant's lawyers . . . to take a cautious approach by treating the technique as coming within regulation—is . . . in accordance with the spirit and purpose of the 1990 Act.[61]

---

51 2008 Act, s 1(2)(a).
52 ibid, s 1(2)(b).
53 ibid, s 3(5), inserting a new s 3ZA into the 1990 Act. Permitted embryo is now defined in s 3ZA(4) of the 1990 Act (as amended).
54 ibid, Sch 8.
55 1990 Act, s 4A(G) (as amended).
56 Previously called 'late-specifics' embryos, and sometimes referred to as 'hybrid embryos'.
57 Defined in 1990 Act s 2(1) (as amended).
58 [2003] UKHL 13.
59 ibid.
60 ibid.
61 [2008] EWHC 3395 (Admin).

Section 4A of the 2008 Act inserts amends the 1990 Act and defines a human admixed embryo as: 15.24

(a) an embryo created by replacing the nucleus of an animal egg or of an animal cell, or two animal pronuclei, with—
  (i) two human pronuclei,
  (ii) one nucleus of a human gamete or of any other human cell, or
  (iii) one human gamete or other human cell,
(b) any other embryo created by using—
  (i) human gametes and animal gametes, or
  (ii) one human pronucleus and one animal pronucleus,
(c) a human embryo that has been altered by the introduction of any sequence of nuclear or mitochondrial DNA of an animal into one or more cells of the embryo,
(d) a human embryo that has been altered by the introduction of one or more animal cells, or
(e) any embryo not falling within paragraphs (a) to (d) which contains both nuclear or mitochondrial DNA of a human and nuclear or mitochondrial DNA of an animal . . . but in which the animal DNA is not predominant.

'Animal' is defined as 'an animal other than man'.[62] 'Embryo' is defined as 'live embryo, including an egg that is in the process of fertilisation or is undergoing any other process capable of resulting in an embryo'.[63] 15.25

There is power to make regulations to specify new combinations which will be regarded as human admixed embryos, and also to amend, but not repeal, the definitions set out above.[64] 15.26

Human admixed embryos can be created for research purposes and cannot be used for reproduction.[65] HFEA may authorize the bringing about of the creation of human admixed embryos *in vitro*, and the keeping or using of such embryos for the purposes of a project of research specified in the licence.[66] No licence can be granted unless the Authority is satisfied that any proposed use is 'necessary' for the purposes of research.[67] 15.27

C. Embryo Selection Techniques

Reproductive genetic technologies give rise not just to new ways to create embryos and gametes but also enhance techniques for screening embryos for particular traits. The use of such techniques enhances our ability to select traits which future children will or will not have. 15.28

1. Pre-implantation genetic diagnosis

Pre-Implantation Genetic Diagnosis (PGD) is a technique used to test an embryo produced as a result of IVF for particular genetic or chromosomal traits. Most people who use PGD will not be infertile but are rather using the technique because they wish to avoid the birth of a child with a particular genetic disease; indeed PGD reduces chances of a live birth overall. In 2013, the most recent year for which figures are available, 8 clinics provided PGD; 577 cycles of IVF involved PGD; and the live birth rate was 25.7 per cent.[68] 15.29

[62] 1990 Act, s 4A(8) (as amended).
[63] ibid, s 4A(9) (as amended).
[64] ibid, s 4A(11)(a).
[65] ibid, Sch 3(3)(a).
[66] ibid.
[67] ibid, Sch 3A(1).
[68] HFEA, 'Fertility Treatment in 2013: Trends & Figures' (2014) <http://www.hfea.gov.uk/docs/HFEA_Fertility_Trends_and_Figures_2013.pdf> (Accessed 30 August 2016).

15.30 PGD developed after the Warnock Report. The technique was first successfully used in 1990 to produce two sets of twin girls where families were at high risk of passing on a serious X-linked disorder.[69] PGD was not specifically tackled in the 1990 Act. But, since it involves the creation and use of embryos, it had to be licensed by HFEA to be lawful. Since the 1990 Act did not indicate when PGD was permissible, principles were developed by HFEA and set out in the Code of Practice.

15.31 The 2008 Act does now lay down the circumstances in which PGD is permissible. The Act states[70] that a licence cannot authorize the testing of an embryo, except for one or more of the following purposes:

(a) establishing whether the embryo has a gene, chromosome or mitochondrial abnormality that may affect its capacity to result in a live birth.
(b) in a case where there is a particular risk that the embryo may have any gene, chromosome or mitochondrial abnormality, establishing whether it has that abnormality or any other gene, chromosome or mitochondrion abnormality.
(c) in a case where there is a particular risk that any resulting child will have or develop,
   (i) a gender-related serious physical or mental disability,
   (ii) a gender-related serious illness,
   (iii) any other gender-related serious medical condition, establishing the sex of the embryo.

15.32 A physical or mental disability, illness, or other medical condition is gender-related if the Authority is satisfied it affects only one sex, or one sex significantly more than the other.[71]

15.33 A licence cannot authorize the testing of embryos for the purpose in (b) unless the Authority is satisfied in relation to the abnormality of which there is a particular risk, and in relation to any other abnormality for which testing is to be authorized, that there is a significant risk that a person with the abnormality will have or develop a serious physical or mental disability, a serious illness, or any other serious medical condition.[72]

15.34 What is a serious disease? In most cases the answer is obvious. But sometimes it is difficult to draw the line between severe and non-severe conditions. The question arises also in relation to abortion.[73] Inevitably, values will come into play. The Code of Practice accepts this: 'the Centre should consider the circumstances of those seeking treatment, rather than the particular inheritable condition.'[74] And also, the 'perception of the level of risk for those seeking treatment'[75] is seen as an important factor. It advises that the following factors be taken into account:

(a) the views of those seeking treatment, including their previous reproductive experience;
(b) the likely degree of suffering associated with the condition;
(c) the availability of effective therapy, now and in the future;
(d) the speed of degeneration in progressive disorders;
(e) the extent of any intellectual impairment;
(f) the social support available;
(g) the family circumstance of the people seeking treatment.[76]

---

69 See HFEA/ACGT Consultation Document, *Pre-implantation Genetic Diagnosis* (1999), para 10.
70 1990 Act, Sch 2, para 1ZA (as amended).
71 ibid, Sch 2, para 1ZA(3) (as amended).
72 ibid, Sch 2, para 1ZA(2) (as amended).
73 As in *Jepson v The Chief Constable of West Mercia Police Constabulary* [2003] EWHC 3318.
74 *Code of Practice* (8th edn, 2009), para 10.4.
75 ibid, para 10.5. And see R Scott, C Williams, K Ehrich, and B Farsides, 'The Appropriate Extent of Pre-implantation Genetic Diagnosis' [2007] 15 Medical L Rev 320–56.
76 *Code of Practice* (8th edn, 2009), para 10.6.

PGD is permitted for adult-onset genetic conditions such as Huntington's disease. In 2006 HFEA undertook a public consultation in 2006, as a result of which it decided that in principle it is acceptable to use PGD to detect lower penetrance late-onset conditions, such as breast cancer.[77] It has now licensed PGD for several cancer susceptibility genes like BRCA1 and BRCA2. The question remains as to whether PGD is to be permitted for all susceptibility genes. And, if not, where is the line to be drawn? How high must the risk be? In 2014 HFEA agreed 'not to authorise the testing of embryos for Autism Spectrum Disorder'.[78] **15.35**

The Act does not address the problem faced by the carrier embryo. It is possible to detect whether an embryo is the carrier of a recessive disorder. If this embryo were to reproduce with another carrier, their child will have an increased (double) chance of inheriting the disease and also of being a carrier. This case is not covered by the legislation. But if both parents are carriers and PGD is undertaken, it may be possible to avoid using embryos which are affected (if there are any such embryos). **15.36**

We have made the assumption that couples will wish to screen out disabilities, but it is possible they may wish to screen in as well. It is said there are deaf couples who want to have deaf children, and who would wish to use PGD to ensure that only deaf embryos are implanted.[79] Prior to the 2008 Act it had been argued,[80] and there is also judicial support,[81] that s 13(5) of the 1990 Act (now s 14(2) of the 2008 Act)[82] could be invoked to prevent this occurring. If you take account of the welfare of any child who may be born as a result of the treatment, you would not choose deafness (or other disability). **15.37**

The law is now clear. Section 13(9) of the 1990 Act (as amended) states: **15.38**

> Persons or embryos that are known to have a gene, chromosome or mitochondrial abnormality involving a significant risk that a person with the abnormality will have or develop—
> (a) a serious physical or medical disability,
> (b) a serious illness, or
> (c) any other serious medical condition, must not be preferred to those that are not known to have such an abnormality.

This does not ban the transfer of affected embryos, but it does not allow them to be preferred. Thus, if there are two embryos, and only one is deaf, the other should be preferred. If the only embryos which are suitable for transfer are all affected, it is permissible to transfer them to the woman's womb.

Section 13(9) applies to 'persons' as well, most obviously to gamete donors. This means that a deaf woman cannot, for example, prefer a deaf sperm donor. However, it would be difficult to prove that she had preferred him because he was deaf, and not because of his high IQ or his height or athletic prowess. **15.39**

These restrictions have been the subject of much criticism. Some of those who criticise these provisions argue that it is nearly always better to be born than not born.[83] As such there is no **15.40**

---

[77] HFEA, *Choices and Boundaries* (2006).

[78] 'Minutes of the HFEA Statutory Approvals Committee: Item 6' (30 January 2014) <http://guide.hfea.gov.uk/guide/ShowPDF.aspx?ID=5518>.

[79] Several examples have been reported including during the press coverage of the 2008 amendments see *The Observer* (9 March 2008).

[80] M Freeman, 'A Time To Be Born and A Time To Die' (2003) Current Legal Problems 516, 603, 627–28.

[81] Mance, LJ in *R (on the application of Quintavalle) v HFEA* [2003] 3 All ER 257, 286.

[82] On which see Chapter 14, para 14.116.

[83] J Savulescu, 'Deaf Lesbians, "Designer Disability", and the Future of Medicine' (2002) 325 British Medical Journal 771–73. An excellent account is D S Davis, *Genetic Dilemmas* (Routledge 2001)

justification from a child welfare perspective for prohibiting selection for disability. Others argue that destroying embryos because they will produce disabled children sends out a negative message about disability.[84] Similarly it can be argued, as was argued by the deaf couple who wished to have deaf children, that these restrictions place an illegitimate restriction on reproductive choice. However, such restrictions are not surprising when we consider that many of those involved in this field of reproductive medicine do not primarily view themselves as technicians of assisted reproductive technologies but rather as technicians of disease prevention. Peter Braude, an expert in the embryo screening and diagnosis, describes 'PGD is a means of treating genetic disease, not a form of assisted reproduction'.[85]

2. HLA tissue typing

15.41 HLA (Human Leukocyte Antigen) typing (tissue typing) involves taking a cell from an early embryo, and testing it to see if the resulting child would be a good tissue match for a sick sibling. If the selected embryo is a match it is implanted with a view to creating a child often described as a 'saviour sibling' because blood or tissue from the child could be used to treat their sick sibling. [86]

15.42 HFEA initially distinguished between a case (the *Hashmi* case) where the sick child's condition was genetic, and a second case (the *Whitaker* case) where the sick child's condition was not inherited. The parents of both children wanted to use PGD and tissue typing to select an embryo which would be a good tissue match for their child. The Hashmis were allowed to do this: the Whitakers were refused permission. They duly went to the US where treatment proved successful.[87] The decision to allow PGD and tissue typing in the *Hashmi* case was challenged by Josephine Quintavalle on behalf of CORE. It argued that tissue typing was prohibited by the 1990 Act, which defined at that time 'treatment services' as services provided for the 'purposes of assisting women to carry children' including 'practices designed to secure that embryos are in a suitable condition to be placed in a woman or to determine whether embryos are suitable for that purpose'. Maurice Kay J ruled that HFEA was wrong to allow PGD to select an embryo which would be tissue-typed to find the best match for an existing child.[88] His decision would have halted not just tissue typing, but PGD as well. The Court of Appeal[89] and the House of Lords[90] disagreed, and took a purposive approach to the interpretation of the legislation. In the Lords, Lord Hoffmann said:

---

ch 3. Another comment to note is in A Buchanan, D W Brock, N Daniels, and D Wikler, *From Chance to Choice* (Cambridge University Press 2000), 281–84. More generally see K W Anstly, 'Are Attempts to Have Impaired Children Justifiable?' (2003) 28 Journal of Medical Ethics 286–88. See also the challenging thesis of D Benatar, *Better Never To Have Been—The Harm of Coming into Existence* (Oxford University Press 2006).

[84] See E Parens and A Asch (eds), *Prenatal Testing and Disability Rights* (Georgetown University Press 2000); D Wasserman, J Bickenbach, and R Wachbrost (eds), *Quality of Life and Human Difference* (Cambridge University Press 2005).

[85] S Franklin, *Born and Made: An Ethnography of Preimplantation Genetic Diagnosis* (Princeton University Press 2006).

[86] See M Freeman, 'Saviour Siblings' in S A M McLean (ed), *First Do No Harm* (Ashgate 2006), 389–406; C Gavaghan, *Defending The Gamete Supermarket* (Routledge-Cavendish 2007) ch 6; M Smith, *Saviour Siblings and the Regulation of Assisted Reproductive Technology: Harm, Ethics and Law* (Routledge 2015).

[87] The reasoning of HFEA and the alleged distinction between the two cases is severely criticized by S Sheldon and S Wilkinson, 'Hashmi and Whitaker: An Unjustifiable and Misguided Distinction?' (2004) 12 Medical Law Review 137.

[88] [2003] 2 All ER 1, 5.

[89] [2003] 2 All ER 257.

[90] [2003] 2 All ER 555.

The licensing power of the authority is defined in broad terms. Paragraph 1(1) of Sch 2 enables it to authorise a variety of activities . . . provided only that they are done 'in the course of' providing IVF services to the public and appear to the authority 'necessary or desirable' for the purpose of providing these services. Thus, if the concept of suitability in sub-paragraph (d) of s 1(1) is broad enough to include suitability for the purposes of the particular mother, it seems to me clear enough that the authority of determining the genetic characteristics of the embryo by way of PGD or HLA typing would be 'in the course of' providing the mother with IVF services and that the authority would be entitled to take the view that it was necessary or desirable for the purpose of providing such services . . .[91]

The Court of Appeal and House of Lords held that both PGD and HLA typing could lawfully be authorized by the Authority as activities to determine the suitability of the embryo for implantation within the meaning of Sch 2, para 1(1)(d).

Before the House of Lords' decision, HFEA changed its policy. In 2004, guidance did not distinguish the *Hashmi* and *Whitaker* cases (the Fletchers, whose child had the same condition as the Whitaker child, were permitted to use tissue typing, and a tissue-matched child was born). The new guidance also reviewed the requirement that only cord blood could be used. This followed scientific evidence that there might be circumstances in which a bone marrow transplant might also be necessary.[92] Since in any event HFEA cannot control the treatment of a child who is born as a result of licensed treatment, this guidance was superfluous.[93] **15.43**

The 2004 policy is now essentially found in the 2008 Act. Schedule 2, paragraph 1ZA(1) of the 1990 Act, as amended, provides: **15.44**

A licence . . . cannot authorise the testing of an embryo, except for one or more of the following purposes— . . .

(d) in a case where a person ('the sibling') who is the child of the persons whose gametes are used to bring about the creation of the embryo (or either of those persons) suffers from a serious medical condition which could be treated by umbilical cord blood stem cells, bone marrow or other tissue of any resulting child, establishing whether the tissue of any resulting child would be compatible with that of the sibling . . .

The tissue typing process is only permitted in relation to selection of a tissue donor from an older sibling. **15.45**

Schedule 2, para 1ZA(4) makes it clear that the reference to 'other tissue' of the resulting child (in para 1ZA(1)) does not include a reference to 'any whole organ of the child'. 'Spare parts' surgery is thus ruled out. This would not prevent the new child becoming an organ donor for a sibling in the future. On this, see Human Tissue Act 2004, s 2(3) and s 2(7). **15.46**

3. Sex selection

Parents may wish to select the sex of their child for medical reasons, for instance, in relation to a serious genetic disease which is a dominant disorder inherited by the male line. Secondly, parents may wish to select the sex of their child for non-medical including family balancing purposes. There are several ways[94] in which parents may attempt to control the sex of their child. The main methods involve sperm sorting, pre-implantation genetic **15.47**

[91] ibid, 568.
[92] HFEA endorsed with amendment a recommendation of its Ethics and Legal Committee to this effect on 21 July 2004.
[93] Decisions will usually be made by those with parental responsibility, and sometimes by courts.
[94] I ignore 'old wives' tales!

diagnosis, and abortion.[95] It is not known how many abortions are carried out in England for reasons that the child is not the desired sex. The Serious Crime Act 2015 'places a duty on the Secretary of State to assess the evidence of abortions taking place on the grounds of the sex of the foetus'.[96] Sperm sorting could be carried out without a licence in the UK, but since the EU Tissues and Cells Directive requires a licence it should not be possible to obtain a licence: success rates are low, and, since sex selection for social reasons is prohibited, licences should not be granted.

15.48 This leaves pre-implantation sex selection, using pre-implantation genetic diagnosis (PGD). In 2003 HFEA carried out a public consultation.[97] This showed there was 'very widespread hostility to the use of sex selection for non-medical reasons'.[98] There would need to be 'substantial demonstrable benefits'[99] if the State were to challenge the public consensus. The benefits, it concluded, were 'at best debatable'.[100] It therefore advised that sex selection should be 'restricted under licence to cases in which there is a 'clear and overriding medical justification'.[101]

15.49 The 2008 Act now adopts HFEA policy. The Act states:

> (1) A licence . . . cannot authorize any practice . . . to secure that any resulting child will be of one sex rather than the other.[102]

15.50 However, it is expressly provided that this does not prevent the authorization of any embryo testing where this is to establish an abnormality, or where there is a particular risk that any resulting child will have or develop a gender-related disability, serious illness or other gender-related serious medical condition.[103]

15.51 Sex selection is thus permitted for medical reasons, but not for social reasons.

15.52 The Code of Practice (8th edn) offers the following guidance:

> With respect to any PGD programme the following conditions apply . . .
>
> (d) that Centres should not use any information derived from tests on an embryo, or any material removed from it or from the gametes which produced it, to select embryos of a particular sex for social reasons.[104]

15.53 The assumption is made that it is easy to distinguish social and medical reasons for wanting to use PGD to make a choice of the sex of a child. In most cases the line between the two will be clear, particularly since to take advantage of PGD for sex selection purposes the abnormality is required to be 'serious'. But there will be difficult cases. As detailed above, in 2014 the Statutory Approvals Committee considered an application to undertake PGD for autistic spectrum disorder in a situation where a couple with a son affected by autism wished to have a daughter because they believed that she would be less likely to be affected. What about a couple concerned that a boy of theirs is likely to suffer from attention deficit disorder

[95] Sex selection is not, of course, a ground for terminating a pregnancy, but abortions undoubtedly take place where the ostensible reason is couched in terms of the Abortion Act 1967, s 1(1)(a).
[96] Serious Crime Act 2015, s 84.
[97] HFEA, *Sex Selection: Options for Regulation* (2003).
[98] ibid, para 147.
[99] ibid.
[100] ibid.
[101] ibid.
[102] ibid, Sch 2, para 1ZB(1) (as amended).
[103] ibid, Sch 2, para 1ZB(2); 1ZA(1)(a)–(e) (as amended).
[104] HFEA Code of Practice (8th edn 2009) para 13.8.

(ADD) who would prefer to have a girl? Both autism and ADD are more commonly found in boys than girls, but they are not sex-linked disorders.

The policy of the Authority has always been to refuse to allow sex selection techniques to be used, other than for medical reasons. This position is affirmed in the 2008 Act. This states: 'A licence . . . cannot authorize any practice designed to secure that any resulting child will be of one sex rather than the other'.[105] So it is re-emphasized that embryo testing which is permitted under Sch 2 is not prevented by the ban on sex selection testing, where there is a particular risk that a woman will give birth to a child who will have or develop a gender-related serious physical or mental disability, serious illness, or any other gender-related serious medical condition.[106] **15.54**

In summary sex selection is thus permitted for conditions such as muscular dystrophy and breast cancer (where a mother does not wish to pass the possibility of this to a daughter, and this genetic condition is prevalent in the family). It is not permitted for social reasons. **15.55**

There is power to amend para 1ZA by regulation.[107] This includes amendment to the sex selection provisions if this appears to the Secretary of State to be 'necessary or expedient' as a consequence of amendments to para 1ZA.[108] But regulations may not enable the authorization of the testing of embryos for the purpose of establishing their sex or other practices falling within para 1ZB, except on grounds relating to the health of any resulting child.[109] 'Amend' includes 'add to' as well as 'repeal'.[110] **15.56**

D. Mitochondrial Donation

Approximately 1 in 200 children is born with faulty mitochondria. Mitochondrial donation is a technique that enables a woman to avoid the transmission of mitochondrial diseases to her children. There are two key methods: maternal spindle transfer (MST) and pro-nuclear transfer (PNT). These involve the transplantation of nuclear DNA from a patient's egg or embryo to a donor's egg or embryo from which the donor's nuclear DNA has been removed. The reason for this is that the patient's egg or embryo will contain unhealthy mitochondria whereas the donor egg or embryo contains healthy mitochondria. Such techniques are now authorized in the UK.[111] This follows a length period of debate and approval by parliament in 2015. The UK is the first country to license the new mitochondrial techniques and the new regulations allow clinics to apply to carry out MST and PNT. Accordingly, it is provided that regulations[112] may allow an egg to be a permitted egg, an embryo, or permitted embryo, 'even though the egg or embryo has had applied to it a prescribed process designed to prevent the transmission of serious mitochondrial disease'.[113] **15.57**

The regulations provide that any clinic that applies to perform these techniques will have to give clear evidence that they have both the staff with the experience to perform them and the equipment to do so. Consideration will also be given to the clinic's plans for follow-up **15.58**

[105] 2008 Act, Sch 2, para 1ZB(1) (as amended).
[106] ibid, Sch 2, para 1ZB(3), (4) (as amended).
[107] ibid, Sch 2, para 1ZC(1) (as amended).
[108] ibid, Sch 2, para 1ZC(2) (as amended).
[109] ibid, Sch 2, para 1ZC(3) (as amended).
[110] ibid, Sch 2, para 1ZC(4) (as amended).
[111] Human Fertilisation and Embryology (Mitochondrial Donation) Regulations 2015; *Mitochondrial donation*, Guidance Note 33 available at <http://www.hfea.gov.uk/9931.html>.
[112] ibid, s 3ZA(7) (as amended).
[113] ibid, s 3ZA(5) (as amended).

of the children born. Each application will be considered by the HFEA on a case-by-case basis, during which the potential patient's specific circumstances will be taken into account.

15.59 Sections 5 and 8 of the Human Fertilisation and Embryology (Mitochondrial Donation) Regulations 2015 set out the circumstances under which mitochondrial transfer can take place:

> **Permitted egg: circumstances**
>
> 5. The circumstances referred to in regulation 3(b) are that—
>
> (a) the Authority has issued a determination that—
> (i) there is a particular risk that any egg extracted from the ovaries of a woman named in the determination may have mitochondrial abnormalities caused by mitochondrial DNA; and
> (ii) there is a significant risk that a person with those abnormalities will have or develop serious mitochondrial disease; and
>
> (b) egg B was extracted from the ovaries of the woman so named.
>
> **Permitted embryo: circumstances**
>
> 8. The circumstances referred to in regulation 6(b) are that—
>
> (a) the Authority has issued a determination that—
> (i) there is a particular risk that any embryo which is created by the fertilisation of an egg extracted from the ovaries of a woman named in the determination may have mitochondrial abnormalities caused by mitochondrial DNA; and
> (ii) there is a significant risk that a person with those abnormalities will have or develop serious mitochondrial disease; and
>
> (b) embryo B was created by the fertilisation of an egg extracted from the ovaries of the woman so named.

15.60 Clinics must undergo a two-stage process for approval to carry out mitochondrial transfer. First the clinic must apply for a licence variation to carry out mitochondrial transfer. Once the licence has been approved by the HFEA licence committee they may then submit patient applications on a case-by-case basis when they are approached by individuals who wish to be treated using the technique.[114]

E. Conclusion

15.61 Given the advances outlined in this chapter, some people have concerns regarding the spectre of 'designer' babies on the horizon.[115] In the *Quintavalle* case[116] this was one of CORE's concerns. As summarized by Lord Hoffmann:

> It would enable the authority to authorise a single cell biopsy to test the embryo for whatever characteristics the mother might wish to know: whether the child would be male or female, dark or blonde, perhaps even in time to come, intelligent or stupid.[117]

Lord Hoffmann did not think Warnock had totally ruled this out.[118] The White Paper which examined the Warnock Report was adamant that 'designer babies' should not be

114 'Mitochondrial Donation Regulations' <http://www.hfea.gov.uk/9942.html>.

115 On designer babies see R M Green, *Babies By Design* (Yale University Press 2007), R Gosden, *Designing Babies* (WH Freeman 1999). On genetic screening more generally, see RS Cowan, *Heredity and Hope* (Harvard University Press 2008).

116 *R (on the application of Quintavalle) v HFEA* [2005] 2 All ER 555.

117 ibid, [13].

118 ibid, [19].

permitted.[119] However, as Lord Hoffmann acknowledged, there was not a proposal to ban 'the testing of embryos to enable the mother to choose to carry a child with characteristics of her choice'.[120] This is not entirely true, for it was clear that she could not choose 'designer'-type characteristics. In the arguments before the Lords everything hinged on the choice of what characteristics were permissible, on the drawing of a line between saviour siblings and designer babies (and 'more sinister eugenic practices').[121] Lord Hoffmann thought Parliament had intended to leave it for the Authority to decide. Having said it would allow sex selection on social grounds, he added:

> . . . it is impossible to say that selection on the grounds of any other characteristics which the mother might desire was positively excluded from the direction of the Authority, however unlikely it might be that the Authority would actually allow selection on that ground.[122]

Maurice Kay LJ in the Court of Appeal did, however, see a clear distinction between 'screening out alternatives' and screening in preferences'.[123] 'Preferences', he noted, 'suggests personal indulgence or predilection and the luxury of real choice'.[124]

Discussion about the ethics of the designer baby will doubtless continue. It is important to note that to date, at least, such an approach is not reflective of the way in which embryo selection technologies have been used. Legally, limits have been placed such that it is prohibited to use these technologies in order to accommodate what may be considered trivial choices. Instead these technologies have only been used in situations where the aim is to meet particular medical ends. **15.62**

119 *Human Fertilisation and Embryology: A Framework for Legislation* (Cm 259, 1987), para 37.
120 *R (on the application of Quintavalle) v HFEA* [2005] 2 All ER 555, [22].
121 ibid, [25]. A more positive view is M J Mehlman, *Wondergenes* (Indiana University Press 2003).
122 ibid, [29].
123 [2003] 3 All ER 257, 289.
124 ibid.

16

ABORTION

Emily Jackson

A. The Ethics of Abortion

16.01 Abortion is one of the most contentious medical procedures. Some people think that abortion is incompatible with respect for the moral value of the foetus. This view is held with varying degrees of intensity. There are those who believe that a foetus is a person from the moment of conception, and that abortion involves the murder of the 'unborn child'.[1] This is a minority view, however. Very few people believe that a foetus has the same moral status as, say, a ten-year-old child. If the foetus is a person from fertilization onwards, then a woman's reasons for seeking an abortion would be irrelevant, as would its stage of development.[2] If a woman conceives as a result of a violent rape, most people believe that she should be able to terminate the pregnancy. In contrast, the circumstances of a person's conception make no difference to his or her right not to be killed. Most people also believe that there is a difference between terminating a pregnancy in its early stages, and late abortions, carried out when the foetus might be capable of being born alive.[3] Again, this would be inconsistent with the view that a person exists from fertilization onwards, since we do not judge the culpability of murder according to the victim's developmental stage.

16.02 A diametrically opposed stance on the ethics of abortion would instead emphasize the physical invasiveness of pregnancy, and the unprecedented degree of self-sacrifice involved if a woman were to be forced to carry a pregnancy to term and go through childbirth, against

[1] J Finnis, 'The Rights and Wrongs of Abortion: A Reply to Judith Thomson' (1973) 2 Philosophy and Public Affairs 117–45.

[2] R Dworkin, *Life's Dominion* (HarperCollins 1993).

[3] ibid.

her wishes.[4] Because this sort of analysis would always give the pregnant woman's right to self-determination priority over the interests of the foetus, its logical consequence would be that abortion should be available, on demand, throughout pregnancy.

A much more common view than either of these polarized positions is that, while not a person, a foetus is not 'nothing', and its destruction should be treated as a serious matter, requiring justification.[5] Legal personhood is acquired suddenly, as soon as a baby has an existence separate from his mother, but many people instinctively adopt a gradualist approach to moral status,[6] believing that a thirty-six-week-old foetus deserves more protection than a six-week-old embryo. To some extent, this gradualist approach is enshrined in the law relating to abortion. It is possible to terminate a pregnancy until term, but only if the pregnancy poses a grave risk to the pregnant woman's life or health, or if the baby would be born suffering from very serious abnormalities. Earlier in pregnancy, access to abortion is much more straightforward. **16.03**

B. Abortion and the General Law

Abortion is the termination of a pregnancy. As with other medical procedures the general requirements of medical law apply. A competent pregnant woman, whether she is a minor[7] or adult, must give consent to the procedure.[8] *R (on the application of Axon) v Secretary of State for Health*[9] confirms that a Gillick-competent child can give a valid consent to abortion, and that she has a right to confidentiality in relation to the termination, which can take place without her parents' knowledge or consent. **16.04**

In the case of a child who is not Gillick-competent, the consent of the parents[10] or the court[11] must be obtained, acting in the child's best interests.[12] The child's wishes and feelings are nevertheless of central importance. As Sir James Munby P explained in *In the matter of X (A Child)*,[13] a case involving a 13-year-old girl who was fourteen weeks pregnant: **16.05**

> A child or incapacitated adult may, in strict law, lack autonomy. But the court must surely attach very considerable weight indeed to the albeit qualified autonomy of a mother [sic] who in relation to a matter as personal, intimate and sensitive as pregnancy is expressing clear wishes and feelings, whichever way, as to whether or not she wants a termination. . .. 'Consent', of course, is not the appropriate word, for by definition a child of X's age who,

---

[4] E McDonagh, 'My Body, My Consent: Securing the Constitutional Right to Abortion Funding' (1999) 62 Albany Law Review 1057; J Jarvis Thomson, 'A Defence of Abortion' (1971) 1 Philosophy and Public Affairs 47.

[5] R Dworkin, *Life's Dominion* (HarperCollins 1993).

[6] R Gillon, 'Is there a "new ethics of abortion"?' (2001) 26 suppl II Journal of Medical Ethics ii5–ii9, ii8.

[7] Under the Family Law Reform Act 1969, s 8 (aged 16–18) or the common law if *Gillick*-competent (under 16).

[8] While the Court of Appeal's judgment in *Re W (A Minor) (Medical Treatment)* [1992] 4 All ER 627 (CA) implied that the court may, in some circumstances, consent to medical treatment even if a competent child refuses to consent, this is unlikely to happen in practice in relation to termination of pregnancy. Parents almost certainly cannot override the competent child's refusal; ibid, *per* Nolan LJ at 648–9. For discussion, see Chapter 4.

[9] [2006] EWHC 37 (Admin).

[10] A parent or other with 'parental responsibility' under the Children Act 1989. It is impossible to imagine circumstances where the 'carer' provision in the Children Act 1989, s 3(5), could be applied to abortion.

[11] Under its inherent jurisdiction (requiring leave under the Children Act 1989, s 100), under the Children Act 1989, s 8, or, unusually under the wardship jurisdiction if the child is already a ward of court.

[12] See, eg, *Re P (A Minor)* [1986] 1 FLR 272; *Re B (Wardship: Abortion)* [1991] 2 FLR 426.

[13] [2014] EWHC 1871 (Fam).

like X, lacks Gillick capacity, cannot in law give a valid consent. But something of the nature of consent or agreement, using those words in the colloquial sense, is required. The Consultant's word 'accepting' in my judgment captures the nuance very well.

16.06 If the pregnant woman is an adult who lacks capacity, the Mental Capacity Act 2005 applies and an abortion may be performed if, in addition to it satisfying the terms of the Abortion Act 1967, the doctor judges it to be in the woman's best interests. In making this judgment, the doctor should consider the factors set out in s 4, which place particular emphasis upon the patient's values and beliefs and any previously expressed wishes.

16.07 The Mental Capacity Act Code of Practice specifies a number of procedures, such as non-therapeutic sterilization, for which court approval should routinely be sought: termination of pregnancy is not one of them.[14] Where her doctors are clear that the woman lacks capacity and that abortion would be in her best interests, there is no need to seek court approval, but in *An NHS Trust v D*,[15] it was suggested that an application to the court should be made promptly where there is doubt as to either issue, or where there is a realistic prospect of the patient regaining capacity during or shortly after pregnancy; or where there is some other exceptional circumstance, such as the pregnancy being the woman's last chance to bear a child.

16.08 It is worth stressing that a court's decision that termination would be in a patient's best interests does not amount to a court order that a termination should take place.[16] On the contrary, doctors must exercise their professional judgement and, in addition, a termination will be lawful only if all of the criteria set out in the Abortion Act are satisfied.

16.09 *Re SB (A patient; capacity to consent to termination)*[17] is an unusual case in which Holman J, sitting in the Court of Protection, disagreed with the psychiatrists' assessment that a woman who suffered from bipolar disorder and who, at the time of the hearing, was compulsorily detained under the Mental Health Act 1983, lacked capacity in relation to the decision to have a termination. The patient was twenty-three weeks pregnant, adamant that she wanted a termination, and indeed said she was suicidal at the prospect of continuing the pregnancy. Holman J unreservedly accepted that she was mentally unwell, but he found that the wisdom, or otherwise, of her reasoning was irrelevant and that she was, in fact, able to weigh information in order to make a decision:

> even if aspects of the decision making are influenced by paranoid thoughts in relation to her husband and her mother, she is nevertheless able to describe, and genuinely holds, a range of rational reasons for her decision. When I say rational, I do not necessarily say they are good reasons, nor do I indicate whether I agree with her decision, for section 1(4) of the Act expressly provides that someone is not to be treated as unable to make a decision simply because it is an unwise decision.

C. Statutory Regulation of Abortion

1. The Abortion Act 1967

16.10 In addition to the general law, the Abortion Act 1967 regulates the availability and provision of terminations of pregnancy in England, Scotland, and Wales. The Act does not apply in

[14] Mental Capacity Act 2005 Code of Practice, para 8.18 (DH, 2007).
[15] [2003] EWHC 2793.
[16] *Re SB (A patient; capacity to consent to termination)* [2013] EWHC 1417 (COP).
[17] [2013] EWHC 1417 (COP).

Northern Ireland (see below). The Abortion Act 1967 operates by creating a defence to what would otherwise amount to the criminal offence of 'procuring a miscarriage' under ss 58 and 59 of the Offences Against the Person Act 1861[18] or, if the foetus is 'capable of being born alive', to the offence of 'child destruction' contrary to the Infant Life (Preservation) Act 1929.[19]

The Abortion Act 1967 sets out a number of criteria which must be satisfied in order for an abortion to be lawful. First, two doctors must be of the opinion, formed in good faith, that one of four statutory grounds is satisfied.[20] Secondly, the Act lays down the time limits within which an abortion may be carried out.[21] Thirdly, it stipulates who may carry out abortions[22] and where they may be performed, providing for a system of licensing for non-NHS clinics.[23] Finally, it provides for regulatory matters such as reporting requirements and disclosure restrictions.[24] **16.11**

2. Background to the 1967 Act

(i) *Offences Against the Person Act 1861, sections 58 and 59*

The Abortion Act 1967 began life as a Private Member's Bill sponsored by David Steel MP. **16.12** It came into force on 27 October 1967, replacing, in England, Scotland, and Wales, the common law which had been set out in *R v Bourne*[25] (and which still applies in Northern Ireland).[26] At common law, an abortion would not be 'unlawful' under ss 58 or 59 of the Offences Against the Person Act 1861[27] (the '1861 Act') if it was 'done in good faith for the purpose only of preserving the life of the mother'. In his direction to the jury in *Bourne,* Macnaghten J adopted an expansive interpretation of this phrase to include cases where the probable consequence of the continuance of the pregnancy would be to make the woman 'a mental or physical wreck'. Subsequent case law confirmed that a doctor could perform an abortion where this was necessary to preserve the mental or physical health, as well as the life, of the pregnant woman.[28]

---

[18] In Scotland, it is a common law crime.

[19] Abortion ('procuring a miscarriage') has been a statutory offence since 1803. Whether there was a crime of abortion at common law is uncertain, though the better view is that there probably was. For discussions of the common law and the legislation between 1803 and 1861, see J Keown, *Abortion, Doctors and the Law* (Cambridge University Press 1988) and A Grubb, 'Abortion Law in England: The Medicalisation of a Crime' (1990) 18 Law, Medicine and Health Care 146.

[20] Section 1(1).

[21] Sections 1(1)(a) and 5(1).

[22] Section 1(1): only 'registered medical practitioners'.

[23] Section 1(3) and (3A). Notice the emergency exception in s 1(4).

[24] Section 2 and the Abortion Regulations 1991, SI 1991/499 as amended by the Abortion (Amendment) (England) Regulations 2002, SI 2002/887 and the Abortion (Amendment) (Wales) Regulations 2002, SI 2002/2979 (W 275), and the Abortion (Amendment) Regulations 2008/735 and the Abortion (Amendment) (Wales) Regulations 2008/1338

[25] [1939] 1 KB 687. For a judicial account of the law of abortion prior to the 1967 Act see: *R (on the Application of Smeaton on behalf of SPUC) v Secretary of State for Health* [2002] EWHC 610 (Admin); (2002) 66 BMLR 59 *per* Munby J at [78]–[107].

[26] Section 6.

[27] *R v Magira* [2008] EWCA Crim 1939 is an unusual modern example of a conviction under the 1861 Act. In this case, the husband pleaded guilty to administering a poison or noxious drug with intent to procure a miscarriage, having bought 'abortive pills' from a website, and put them in two meals which he gave his wife when she was eleven weeks pregnant. His attempt to 'procure a miscarriage' was unsuccessful, though his wife did suffer from contractions, stomach pain, and bleeding.

[28] *R v Bergmann* [1948] 1 BMJ 1008 (Morris J) and *R v Newton and Stungo* [1958] Crim LR 469 (Ashworth J).

3. Northern Ireland

16.13 The Abortion Act 1967 does not apply in Northern Ireland. There are, therefore, no statutory defences to sections 58 and 59 of the Offences Against the Person Act 1861. However, *R v Bourne* applies and so a defence may exist if the pregnancy is endangering the pregnant woman's life, and for this purpose, it is sufficient if the consequence of carrying the pregnancy to term would be to leave her a 'mental wreck'. Thus individual doctors must decide, on a case-by-case basis, and with the potential threat of criminal prosecution, whether a woman's circumstances are sufficiently grave to fit within the *Bourne* exception.

16.14 Court rulings in Northern Ireland have confirmed that there are circumstances in which abortion will not be a criminal offence, but because there is no specific statutory defence, the parameters within which abortion may lawfully be performed remain unclear.[29]

16.15 The first case to consider the lawfulness of abortion in the abstract was *Re Family Planning Association of Northern Ireland*.[30] This was a case brought by the Family Planning Association of Northern Ireland, which had asked the Department of Health for Northern Ireland for guidance on when abortion could be lawfully performed. Initially, Kerr J rejected their application on the grounds that the medical profession was not unclear about the law, which was governed by the *Bourne* exception—restrictively interpreted—to the Offences Against the Person Act 1861. This was, however, overturned on appeal. The Court of Appeal held that the Department of Health, Social Services and Public Safety could not be compelled to issue guidelines on abortion, but suggested it would be prudent to do so.

16.16 In 2009, guidance was eventually published, but it was immediately challenged by the Society for the Protection of the Unborn Child on the grounds that it misrepresented the law.[31] Girvan LJ found that the guidance was misleading in relation to counselling and conscientious objection and should be withdrawn 'with a view to the Guidance being reconsidered by the Department taking account of the contents of the judgment'.

16.17 Given inevitable uncertainty over whether any risk to the mother's mental health is sufficiently grave to justify abortion in Northern Ireland, and the serious consequences for doctors who break the law, it is not surprising that abortion is largely unavailable in Northern Ireland. It is not uncommon for Northern Irish women who wish to terminate unwanted pregnancies to travel to England, Scotland, or Wales. Officially, 837 women did so in 2014,[32] though because this figure only includes women who gave a Northern Irish address to the abortion clinic, it is undoubtedly an underestimate.

16.18 In addition to being inconvenient, having to travel to the mainland will inevitably delay Northern Irish women's abortions. Women from Northern Ireland are three times more likely than other British women to have abortions after twenty weeks. Northern Irish women are not entitled to NHS abortions, which means that they have to pay for a private abortion, in addition to covering the costs of travel. In *R (on the application of A (A Child)) v Secretary of State for Health*,[33] X and Y, a 15-year-old girl and her mother, applied for judicial review of the English Secretary of State for Health's failure to exercise his power to require free abortion services to be provided to women from Northern Ireland on the same basis as

---

[29] *Northern Health and Social Services Board v F & G* [1993] NILR 268; *Northern Health and Social Services Board v A* [1994] NIJB 1; *Western Health and Social Services Board v CMB* (29 Sept 1995); *Down Lisburn Health and Social Services Board v CH & LAH* (18 Oct 1995).

[30] [2003] NIQB 48.

[31] *Society for the Protection of the Unborn Child (SPUC) v NI* [2009] NIQB 92.

[32] Department of Health, Abortion Statistics 2014 (2015).

[33] [2015] EWCA Civ 771.

they were to women in England. X had had to pay for a private abortion in England. The Court of Appeal held that it was not unlawful or irrational for the Secretary of State to limit access to free NHS services according to residency. As Elias LJ put it: 'It is not irrational to take the view that English taxpayers should not have to bear the cost of providing abortion services to women from Northern Ireland'. The Supreme Court heard an appeal against this decision in 2016.

Not everyone will be able to afford to travel to the mainland for a private termination, and Northern Irish women are also more likely than women living in England, Scotland, or Wales to purchase abortion drugs from offshore internet 'pharmacies'. In 2016, a 21-year-old woman was given a one year suspended prison sentence for procuring a miscarriage with pills purchased online.[34] **16.19**

In 2012, the first private abortion clinic opened in Belfast. Run by Marie Stopes, the clinic announced that it would provide early medical abortions in the first nine weeks of pregnancy within the terms of the law: that is, only to women who fit within the *Bourne* exception. **16.20**

In 2014, the Department of Justice in Northern Ireland sought the public's views on the possibility of decriminalizing abortion in two strictly limited circumstances: where the foetus was suffering from a 'lethal abnormality', and if the woman was pregnant as a result of 'sexual crime'.[35] Most of the responses received were against any change in the law. **16.21**

Nevertheless, in 2015 the Northern Ireland Human Rights Commission applied for judicial review of Northern Ireland's failure to provide for the option of termination in cases of lethal foetal abnormality and sexual crime. In *The Northern Ireland Human Rights Commission's Application*,[36] Horner J held that the prohibition of abortion in Northern Ireland was incompatible with Article 8 in two limited circumstances: fatal foetal abnormality (FFA) at any time, and pregnancies that had resulted from sexual crime, but only until the foetus is viable. The prohibition of abortion in cases of serious malformation of the foetus (SMF) interfered with women's Article 8 rights, but that interference was proportionate. At the time of writing, the Northern Irish Attorney General is planning an appeal. **16.22**

4. The Infant Life (Preservation) Act 1929

Until 1991, the Abortion Act 1967 (hereinafter 'the 1967 Act') had to be read in conjunction with the Infant Life (Preservation) Act 1929 (hereinafter 'the 1929 Act'). The 1929 Act was enacted to close a loophole in the law. If a child was killed in the course of being born, it was neither an offence under the Offences Against the Person Act—it could not be said to be procuring a 'miscarriage'—nor was it murder or manslaughter, because the child would not yet have 'an existence independent of its mother'. In order to fill this gap, the 1929 Act provided that killing the child during childbirth would also be an offence. **16.23**

However, s 1(1) of the 1929 Act is broader in its scope. It provides that 'any person who, with intent to destroy the life of a child capable of being born alive, by any wilful act causes a child to die before it has an existence independent of its mother' shall be guilty of an offence. Aborting a foetus 'capable of being born alive' could therefore amount to the offence under the 1929 Act. **16.24**

[34] H McDonald, 'Northern Irish Woman Given Suspended Sentence over Self-Induced Abortion' *The Guardian* (4 April 2016).

[35] Department of Justice, The Criminal Law on Abortion: Lethal Foetal Abnormality and Sexual Crime (DoJNI 2014).

[36] [2015] NIQB 96.

16.25 As a result, the 1929 Act had the practical effect of setting the upper time limit for an abortion when the foetus was 'capable of being born alive'. What does this mean? The Act itself created a presumption that a 28-week-old foetus is 'capable of being born alive'.[37] That, however, is no more than a presumption and since 1929, a foetus has been deemed capable of being born alive at earlier stages in pregnancy. In 1991, for example, in *Rance v Mid-Downs HA*,[38] Brooke J held that a 26-week-old foetus was 'capable of being born alive' within the terms of the 1929 Act and he rejected an argument that the foetus must have the capacity to survive for a reasonable period of time after birth.

16.26 In *C v S*[39] the Court of Appeal concluded that the 1929 Act required that the foetus should have the capacity to survive and hence did not apply to a foetus of between eighteen and twenty-one weeks gestation, because at that stage, independent survival is impossible.

16.27 Thus, prior to 1991, the time limit for a legal abortion was around twenty-four weeks,[40] unless the abortion was carried out 'in good faith for the purpose only of preserving the life of the mother'.[41]

5. Section 37 of the Human Fertilisation and Embryology Act 1990

16.28 Despite numerous backbench attempts to change its terms, in particular, to lower the upper time limit for abortions and to restrict the grounds upon which an abortion could be carried out, the substance of the 1967 Act remained unaltered until 1991. During the passage of the Human Fertilisation and Embryology Act 1990 the government allocated time in order to allow a full debate on abortion. As a result, s 37 of the Human Fertilisation and Embryology Act 1990, which came into force on 1 April 1991,[42] amended the 1967 Act in four ways:

(i) it substituted (and enlarged) the grounds for abortion contained in s 1(1) of the 1967 Act;[43]
(ii) it disengaged the 1967 Act from the Infant Life (Preservation) Act 1929, so that compliance with the 1967 Act created a defence both to the 1861 and 1929 Acts;[44]
(iii) it set an upper time limit of twenty-four weeks for the most common ground for an abortion under the new s 1(1)(a) of the 1967 Act, and removed any time limit for the other grounds;[45]
(iv) it clarified the legality of selective reduction and foeticide.[46]

6. Abortion and post-coital contraception

16.29 Commonly used contraceptives, such as the oral contraceptive pill and barrier methods like condoms, prevent fertilization from taking place by chemical or physical means. Other methods commonly referred to as contraceptives work differently, and instead prevent a fertilized egg from implanting in the woman's uterus. Examples of these are intra-uterine

[37] The Infant Life (Preservation) Act 1929, s 1(2).
[38] [1991] 1 All ER 801, 817.
[39] [1987] 1 All ER 1230 (Heilbron J and CA).
[40] This will remain important where the legality (or availability) of an abortion prior to 1 April 1991 is still relevant, for example, in a 'wrongful birth' claim arising before that date: see *Rance v Mid-Downs HA* [1991] 1 All ER 801. See discussion in Chapter 12.
[41] 1929 Act, s 1(1).
[42] Human Fertilisation and Embryology Act 1990 (Commencement No 2 and Transitional Provision) Order 1991, SI 1991/480.
[43] See 1967 Act, as amended, s 1(1)(a)–(d).
[44] See ibid, s 5(1).
[45] Combined effect of ibid, ss 1(1)(a) and 5(1).
[46] See ibid, s 5(2).

devices (IUDs) and the so-called 'morning after pill'. It may be more accurate to refer to these methods as contragestive, since they act to prevent gestation rather than fertilization.

In some circumstances, the IUD and the 'morning after pill' may dislodge an implanted embryo from the wall of the uterus. In order to work out whether they might then be acting as abortifacients, and hence be covered by the law relating to abortion, it must be determined whether they could be said to effect a 'miscarriage', and hence fall within the criminal prohibition in the 1861 Act. **16.30**

(i) Miscarriage

It is clear that a purely contraceptive agent does not produce a 'miscarriage'. A failure to fertilize cannot be considered a 'miscarriage'. What about contragestive methods of birth control? Is a failure to implant also a 'miscarriage'? In one sense, the woman has ceased to 'carry' and, hence has 'miscarried'. What was previously within her body will be expelled. This does not tally within the ordinary notion of 'miscarriage', however, which would entail the loss of a pregnancy (that is, one which had become established to the woman's knowledge). This, of course, only occurs once a period is missed, which itself can only follow the implantation of the embryo. **16.31**

Modern medical usage supports the view that a miscarriage can only occur after the embryo has implanted.[47] In addition, there is strong support for this interpretation from the then Attorney-General in a written answer in the House of Commons in 1983: 'it is clear that, used in its ordinary sense, the word "miscarriage" is not apt to describe a failure to implant . . . Likewise, the phrase "procure a miscarriage" cannot be construed to include the prevention of implantation.'[48] In a non-abortion context, there is further statutory support for the conclusion that 'a woman is not to be treated as carrying a child until the embryo has become implanted'.[49] **16.32**

Further, there is no convincing public policy argument for bringing post-coital contraceptive methods within the scope of the law regulating abortions, since the practical result would be to make access to them extremely inconvenient and time consuming, for both the woman herself and for the medical profession. Making post-coital contraception less accessible might be likely to increase the number of unwanted pregnancies, and hence increase the number of abortions. **16.33**

(ii) The morning-after pill case

The point arose for judicial determination in 2002 in *R (on the Application of Smeaton on behalf of SPUC) v Secretary of State for Health*.[50] The claimant, on behalf of the Society for the Protection of Unborn Children (SPUC), sought judicial review of a statutory instrument[51] which allowed pharmacists to dispense the morning-after pill as an emergency contraceptive, without the need for a prescription. The claimant argued that in doing so a pharmacist would commit a criminal offence under ss 58 and 59 of the Offences Against the **16.34**

[47] I Kennedy, *Treat Me Right* (Clarendon Press 1988) ch 3. Contrast V Tunkel,'Late Abortions and the Crime of Child Destruction' [1974] Crim LR 461 and J Keown, '"Morning After" Pills, "Miscarriage" and Muddle' (2005) 25 Legal Studies 296–319.

[48] 42 Parl Deb HC 238, 239.

[49] Human Fertilisation and Embryology Act 1990, s 2(3).

[50] *R (on the Application of Smeaton on behalf of SPUC) v Secretary of State for Health* [2002] EWHC 610 (Admin); (2002) 66 BMLR 59 (Munby J).

[51] The Prescription Only Medicines (Human Use) Amendment (No 3) Order 2000, SI 2000/3231 amending the Prescription Only Medicines (Human Use) Order 1997, SI 1997/1830.

Person Act 1861, as the effect of the pill would be to procure a 'miscarriage' which, he contended, covered any interference with a fertilized egg, whether before or after implantation.

16.35 Munby J, as he then was, analysed the case law[52] and the medical[53] and legal literature[54] at some length. He held that when enacting the nineteenth-century legislation, Parliament had not had in mind the issue of contraception and there was nothing to suggest that Parliament had intended to protect life from conception. Further, the word 'miscarriage'—which was left undefined by Parliament—should be interpreted as it would currently be understood and in the light of the best current scientific knowledge available,[55] according to which 'miscarriage' was the termination of a post-implantation pregnancy. This interpretation, Munby J considered, accorded with normal linguistic usage, since there could be no 'true carriage' before the embryo had attached itself to the woman's uterus, and it was supported by the only English decision on this point.[56]

16.36 Munby J dismissed the application and concluded that a miscarriage could only occur after implantation, which would not be the case when the morning after pill was taken. Because other contraceptives, such as the IUD but also sometimes the oral contraceptive pill inhibit the implantation of a fertilized egg, a finding in favour of SPUC would have had the result that every method of contraception, except the condom, might involve the commission of a criminal offence. According to Munby J, this would mean that 34 per cent of all women between the ages of 16 and 49 (approximately 4.5 million women) could be guilty of criminal offences. It was also relevant that a finding in favour of SPUC would, in practice, delay the use of the morning-after pill, making it less likely to be effective, resulting in an increase in the number of abortions.

(iii) Post-implantation?

16.37 Purely contragestive methods of birth control are not regulated by the 1967 Act. But where the method may work after implantation has taken place, the position may be different. This can occur if an IUD is fitted some time after sexual intercourse took place. The legal issue will then be whether the doctor acts 'with intent' to procure a miscarriage.

16.38 (a) **'Intent to procure a miscarriage'** Certainly, if the doctor fitting the IUD believes that the woman is pregnant, what he is doing falls within the 1861 Act and he must comply with the requirements of the Abortion Act in order to have a defence. In a case in which a doctor fitted an IUD to a woman whom the doctor believed to be about fourteen weeks pregnant, there could be no doubt as to his intention. The Court of Appeal in *R v Price*[57] upheld his conviction under s 58.

16.39 If an IUD is fitted much sooner after sexual intercourse, before the woman has missed a period, the doctor's understanding and knowledge is likely to be less certain. The woman may, of course, not actually be pregnant. For the offence under s 58 to be committed, it is not necessary for the woman to actually be pregnant or, as s 58 quaintly puts it, 'with child'. As is clear from the only case where this issue has arisen, the relevant issue is the doctor's intention. Given that the defendant will be a doctor who can be expected to have some

---

[52] *R (on the Application of Smeaton on behalf of SPUC) v Secretary of State for Health*, n 49, at [226]–[255].

[53] ibid, at [125]–[169] including expert evidence submitted at the hearing.

[54] ibid, at [256]–[277].

[55] Munby J concluded that the 1861 Act was 'always speaking' and in seeking Parliament's intention must, as a matter of construction, be interpreted in the light of advancing knowledge, technology, and social standards: see *Birmingham CC v Oakley* [2001] 1 AC 617, HL, especially *per* Lord Hoffmann at 628 and 631.

[56] *R v Dhingra* (24 January 1991, Birmingham CC, Wright J).

[57] [1969] 1 QB 541 (CA).

knowledge of the physiology of conception and pregnancy, his knowledge of the woman's particular sexual and menstrual history will be evidentially significant.

(b) ***R v Dhingra*** In *R v Dhingra*[58] the defendant doctor inserted an IUD into a woman eleven days after they had had sexual intercourse, which was seventeen days after the start of her last period. He was charged with the offence under s 58 of the Offences Against the Person Act 1861, and the judge held that the issue was: **16.40**

> whether the defendant, at the time he inserted the coil, knew or believed that [the woman] was pregnant, and, accordingly, introduced the instrument with intent to produce a miscarriage; or whether, as is the case for the defence, that he knew or believed that she was not pregnant . . . and that his purpose in inserting the coil was for contraceptive purposes; in other words, to prevent her becoming pregnant thereafter.[59]

Wright J was clear that 'miscarriage' meant dislodging an implanted fertilized egg.[60] On the basis of the expert evidence, the woman could not have been pregnant until at least the twentieth day of her cycle so that, at the time the IUD was fitted, she was almost certainly not pregnant.[61] On the evidence, Wright J concluded that the defendant had been aware that the woman could not have been pregnant when he inserted the IUD, and that he had, in fact, told her as much. Thus, the judge held that the defendant could not possibly have intended to procure a miscarriage when he fitted the IUD,[62] and he withdrew the case from the jury. **16.41**

Factually *R v Price* and *R v Dhingra* lie at opposite ends of a spectrum of knowledge which establish or refute the intention to procure a miscarriage. Cases towards the middle may be more difficult. A doctor may fit an IUD at a time during a woman's cycle when he cannot know—one way or another—whether implantation would have occurred, and hence his intention will be unclear. He may, instead, be unsure and prepared to take the risk of the effect the IUD will have. If the doctor undertakes the procedure prepared, if necessary, to bring about a 'miscarriage', his state of mind is the intent to procure a miscarriage. **16.42**

D. The Abortion Act 1967

Section 1(1) of the 1967 Act[63] (as amended) states that: **16.43**

> Subject to the provisions of this section, a person shall not be guilty of an offence under the law relating to abortion when a pregnancy is terminated by a registered medical practitioner if two registered medical practitioners are of the opinion, formed in good faith—
>
> (a) that the pregnancy has not exceeded twenty-four weeks and that the continuance of the pregnancy would involve risk, greater than if the pregnancy were terminated, of injury to the physical or mental health of the pregnant woman or any existing children of her family; or
> (b) that the termination is necessary to prevent grave permanent injury to the physical or mental health of the pregnant woman; or
> (c) that the continuance of the pregnancy would involve risk to the life of the pregnant woman, greater than if the pregnancy were terminated; or

58 *R v Dhingra* (24 January 1991, Birmingham CC, Wright J).
59 ibid, Transcript, 1.
60 ibid, Transcript, 9.
61 ibid, Transcript, 9.
62 ibid, Transcript, 9–10.
63 Amended by the Human Fertilisation and Embryology Act 1990, s 37, with effect from 1 April 1991.

(d) that there is a substantial risk that if the child were born it would suffer from such physical or mental abnormalities as to be seriously handicapped.

1. The scope of the Act

16.44 The Abortion Act 1967 creates a defence to the offences of 'procuring a miscarriage' under ss 58 and 59 of the Offences Against the Person Act 1861[64] and of 'child destruction' under the Infant Life (Preservation) Act 1929,[65] provided all of the provisions of the 1967 Act are satisfied.

(i) '. . . a pregnancy is terminated . . .': unsuccessful terminations?

16.45 The wording of s 1(1) of the 1967 Act states that the woman's 'pregnancy' must be 'terminated'.[66] Given that the crime to which it provides a defence does not require that a miscarriage must actually occur, this is a curious formulation. Section 58 creates an offence where the person does one of the specified acts[67] 'with intent to procure the miscarriage' of a woman. The crime is committed even if a miscarriage is not procured,[68] provided that was his intention and, in the case of anyone except the woman herself,[69] even if she is not actually pregnant. On the face of it, however, the 1967 Act does not apply where a pregnancy is not, in fact, terminated. Interpreted literally then, a person would have a defence if the abortion was successful but not where it failed or where the woman was wrongly believed to be pregnant. This would be a most bizarre outcome.

16.46 When the issue was raised in the case of *Royal College of Nursing v DHSS*,[70] the Law Lords who discussed it expressed differing views. Lord Diplock considered that the 1967 Act should be interpreted to cover 'the whole treatment undertaken' and not merely, should it occur, the miscarriage.[71] Lord Wilberforce (dissenting) took the opposite view. For him, the 1967 Act did not apply unless a pregnancy was actually terminated: '[t]ermination is one thing; attempted and unsuccessful termination wholly another'.[72] Lord Edmund-Davies (also dissenting) agreed with Lord Diplock on this point: 'Were it otherwise the unavoidable conclusion is that doctors and nurses could in such cases be convicted of what in essence would be the extraordinary crime of attempting to do a lawful act.' It is suggested that the approach of Lords Diplock and Edmund-Davies on this point is the common sense interpretation which would be more likely to be adopted by a court.

[64] Section 6 of the 1967 Act defines 'the law relating to abortion' as meaning the Offences Against the Person Act 1861, ss 58 and 59, and, rather mysteriously, 'any rule of law relating to the procurement of abortion'. It is not clear what this latter phrase relates to.

[65] Abortion Act 1967, s 5(1).

[66] For difficulties in respect of 'selective reduction', see below.

[67] The 'act' means to administer a poison or other noxious thing or use any instrument or other means to procure the miscarriage.

[68] *R v Magira* [2008] EWCA Crim 1939 is an unusual modern example of a conviction under the 1861 Act. In this case, the husband pleaded guilty to administering a poison or noxious drug with intent to procure a miscarriage, having bought 'abortive pills' from a website, and put them in two meals which he gave his wife when she was eleven weeks pregnant. His attempt to 'procure a miscarriage' was unsuccessful, though his wife did suffer from contractions, stomach pain, and bleeding.

[69] If the woman is charged she must be 'with child'. She may, however, commit an attempt if she believed she was pregnant, or be charged an accessory to another's crime or with conspiracy: *R v Sockett* (1908) 24 TLR 893 and *R v Whitchurch* (1890) 24 QBD 420.

[70] *Royal College of Nursing v DHSS* [1981] AC 800; [1981] 1 All ER 545 (HL).

[71] ibid, 828.

[72] ibid, 823.

(ii) '. . . by a registered medical practitioner . . .'

The 1967 Act also requires that the pregnancy is terminated by a registered medical practitioner, that is, a doctor who is registered with the General Medical Council. This requirement is of little significance in relation to surgical abortion, when a surgeon's involvement would simply represent good clinical practice. Medical abortions, where the abortion is terminated using drugs rather than surgery, are a different matter. In early medical abortions, mifepristone is used to dislodge the embryo from the lining of the uterus, with a second drug, misoprostol, taken two days later in order to trigger a miscarriage. Medical abortions are increasingly common: in 2014, 51 per cent of all abortions were carried out in this way.[73] **16.47**

If the woman herself takes the mifepristone, and—as happens in a small minority of cases—miscarries before she returns to hospital for the second drug, has she terminated the pregnancy herself? If she has, she may have committed an offence under the Offences Against the Person Act 1861 to which the Abortion Act could not offer a defence. **16.48**

Medical abortions also take place late in pregnancy, when they involve foeticide followed by the induction of labour using prostaglandins. Because this will resemble a normal delivery, a team of health care professionals, including both doctors and nurses, will be involved. In the *Royal College of Nursing* case, the House of Lords was asked to determine whether nurses' participation in this sort of medical abortion would fall within the defence set out in the 1967 Act. If it did not, it would amount to a criminal offence. By a majority (3–2), the House of Lords held that the Act did apply. The majority (Lords Diplock, Roskill, and Keith) adopted a broad interpretation of s 1(1) so as to take account of modern medical practice and the notion of the health care 'team'. The termination would come within the Act if the treatment was prescribed or determined by a doctor, carried out in accordance with his or her directions and he or she remained in charge throughout. Lord Diplock was clear that which acts were performed by a doctor, and which by others, such as a nurse, did not affect the application of the Act, provided that what was done was 'in accordance with accepted medical practice'.[74] **16.49**

This case effectively establishes that nurses can actively participate in the termination of pregnancy if they are supervised throughout by a medical practitioner. While this case did not address the question of whether the woman who takes an abortion pill is terminating her own pregnancy, the same principle applies, and the defence will exist if the treatment was prescribed or determined by a doctor, carried out in accordance with his or her directions and he or she remained in charge throughout. **16.50**

(iii) '. . . two registered medical practitioners are of the opinion, formed in good faith . . .'

Section 1(1) of the 1967 Act requires that two doctors certify that one or more of the grounds for abortion set out in the Act applies. In an emergency, section 1(4) provides that if one doctor is of the opinion, formed in good faith, that the termination is immediately necessary to save the pregnant woman's life or to prevent grave permanent injury, there is no need for a second doctor's opinion. **16.51**

While the doctor who performs the abortion will commonly be one of the certifying doctors, this is not required by the Act. Section 1(1) only requires that the pregnancy is terminated by a doctor and that two doctors have previously certified that a statutory ground exists. Indeed, there is no legal requirement that the certifying doctors should have seen, **16.52**

[73] Department of Health, *Abortion Statistics 2014* (London, 2015).
[74] [1981] AC 800, 828–9.

let alone examined, the woman, as long as they were nevertheless able to form an opinion of her circumstances in good faith.

16.53 (a) **Pre-signed forms** In 2012, the then Secretary of State for Health, the Rt Hon Andrew Lansley MP, ordered the Care Quality Commission (CQC), at a cost of £1 million, to cancel 600 planned inspections of hospitals and care homes, and instead carry out unannounced inspections at 300 abortion providers. The CQC apparently found evidence that what are known as HSA1 forms had been pre-signed, which Andrew Lansley declared to be unlawful. It is not necessarily self-evident that this is the case. A pre-signed form may raise a suspicion that the doctor does not plan to evaluate the woman's case in order to judge whether her circumstances fit within the statutory grounds, but it does not prove that he will not do so. The Department of Health's previous advice had been that the second doctor does not actually have to see the pregnant woman himself and the 2002 Regulations simply provide that the opinion must specify 'whether or not each practitioner has seen or examined, or seen and examined, the pregnant woman'.[75] A pre-signed form could indicate that the doctor plans to have a telephone consultation with her, before authorizing the use of the pre-signed form.

16.54 In 2014, the Department of Health (DH) produced further guidance on the interpretation of the Abortion Act. This specified that:

> Although there is no legal requirement for at least one of the certifying doctors to have seen the pregnant woman before reaching a decision about a termination, the Department's view is that it is good practice for this to be the case. It is recognised however that, with technological advances, this may well mean that a doctor does not physically see the woman, e.g. there could be a discussion by phone or over a webcam.[76]

The Guidance then specifically addresses the pre-signing of HSA1 forms:

> The pre-signing of HSA1 forms calls into question whether a doctor could turn his or her mind to a specific woman's circumstances and form a good faith opinion which, if any, of the lawful grounds under the Abortion Act might apply . . . DH considers pre-signing of forms (without subsequent consideration of any information relating to the woman) to be incompatible with the requirements of the Abortion Act.[77]

16.55 (b) **Forming an opinion in good faith** The 1967 Act does not require that one of the statutory grounds actually exists. Instead, it merely states that two doctors must each form the opinion 'in good faith' that the woman's circumstances fit within one of the statutory grounds. An abortion will be lawful even if the doctors are mistaken as to the existence of the ground, providing they honestly believe it to exist.[78]

16.56 The Act is silent upon whether the doctors need to agree upon which ground is satisfied, and hence it would appear that an abortion would be lawful if each doctor believes, in good faith, that a different ground is satisfied. Oddly, however, the Abortion (Amendment) (England) Regulations 2002 appear to introduce a fresh requirement that the doctors must agree upon which ground is satisfied. Under para 3(1)(d) the opinion must state 'that each practitioner is of the opinion formed in good faith that at least *one and the same ground* mentioned in paragraph (a) to (d) of section 1(1) of the Act is fulfilled.' (emphasis added). It could be argued that it is illegitimate to alter the meaning of a statute in this way via

[75] Abortion (Amendment) (England) Regulations 2002/887 para 3(1)(c).

[76] Department of Health, *Guidance in Relation to Requirements of the Abortion Act 1967: For all those responsible for commissioning, providing and managing service provision* (DH, 2014) para 6.

[77] ibid, para 17.

[78] *R v Smith* [1974] 1 All ER 376 (CA).

Regulations, especially since what is at stake is the scope of a defence to a criminal offence, which should, in the case of ambiguity, be construed in favour of the defendant, that is the doctor. In practice, cases in which the certifying doctors disagree about which ground is satisfied are likely to be vanishingly rare. Nevertheless, the existence of this anomaly between the wording of the statute and the Regulations is unsatisfactory.

In extreme circumstances, the conduct of the doctor may call into question the bona fides of his opinion. In *R v Smith*,[79] the doctor had carried out a limited examination of the pregnant woman, but he did not obtain a medical history and agreed to carry out the procedure a week later, for cash. No further investigations or enquiries were carried out and a second opinion was not sought before she was seen by the anaesthetist on her admission. The doctor's conviction under s 58 was upheld by the Court of Appeal. On the facts, the Court of Appeal concluded that the jury had been entitled to take the view that the doctor had not, in good faith, attempted to balance the risks of pregnancy and termination. The Court of Appeal appeared to indicate that a doctor will have acted in good faith if he complies with accepted medical practice: 'good faith' thus seems to be synonymous with the *Bolam* test.[80] **16.57**

As a result of the wording of the 1967 Act, it will be very difficult to establish that an abortion does not fall within the Act if two doctors, acting non-negligently, conclude that a ground, usually s 1(1)(a), is satisfied, providing always that the required procedures under the 1967 Act and the Abortion Regulations of 1991, 2002, and 2008 are followed.[81] It is also important to remember that, in a criminal case, the prosecution has the burden of proving beyond reasonable doubt that the 1967 Act was not complied with. In *Paton v BPAS*,[82] a case in which a husband sought an injunction to prevent his wife from having an abortion, Sir George Baker P stated that it would not only: **16.58**

> be a bold and brave judge . . . who would seek to interfere with the discretion of doctors acting under the 1967 Act, but I think he would really be a foolish judge who would try to do such a thing, unless possibly, there is clear bad faith and an obvious attempt to perpetrate a criminal offence.

2. The grounds for abortion

(i) 'Risk of physical or mental injury'—section 1(1)(a)

Section 1(1)(a) is the most commonly relied upon ground for abortions, and is only available where the woman's pregnancy has not exceeded its twenty-fourth week. There are, in fact, two distinct grounds contained within s 1(1)(a) relating first, to a risk to the pregnant woman's health and secondly, to that of the existing children of her family.[83] In 2014, 98 per cent of all abortions were authorized on the grounds that the pregnancy posed a risk to the pregnant woman's own health, and 99.93 per cent of these were authorized solely because of the risk to her mental health. One per cent were authorized because of a risk to her children's health.[84] **16.59**

(a) The comparative exercise This ground for abortion[85] requires the certifying doctors to engage in a comparative exercise and decide whether there is a greater risk to the pregnant **16.60**

[79] ibid. For two unreported prosecutions both ending in acquittals, see *R v Dhingra* (n 57 above) and *R v Dixon*, *The Times*, 22 December 1995 (news report).

[80] See Chapter 4 (breach of duty).

[81] *Paton v BPAS* [1978] 2 All ER 987, 992.

[82] [1978] 2 All ER 987, 992. See also *C v S* [1988] QB 135; [1987] 1 All ER 1230, 1243 *per* Sir John Donaldson MR.

[83] Abortion Regulations 1991, S1 1991/499, Sch 1, distinguishes between these two bases for relying on s 1(1)(a): see Certificate A indication 'C' and 'D' respectively.

[84] *Abortion Statistics 2014* (DH, 2015).

[85] As does s 1(1)(c) relating to risk to the mother's life.

woman's (or existing children's) physical or mental health if the pregnancy continues than if it were terminated.

16.61 **(b) 'Risk to Woman's Mental Health'** As regards the risk to the pregnant woman, the ground is very broad in its scope. It covers any risk of any physical or mental injury, providing the comparative exercise is satisfactorily performed. The doctors must always be satisfied that continuing the pregnancy would have a more negative effect upon her health than termination. Almost by definition, however, a woman with an unwanted pregnancy may suffer distress if she is compelled to carry the pregnancy to term, and hence any unwanted pregnancy may pose a risk to the 'mental health' of a pregnant woman, greater than if her pregnancy is terminated.

16.62 The Act is concerned with the 'risk' to the woman's mental health and not the certainty or even probability of its occurring. For there to be a risk to the pregnant woman's mental health, it is not necessary to show that she would be likely to suffer a recognized psychiatric injury. Rather any interference with her mental wellbeing would be sufficient to establish that the risks of continuing the pregnancy exceeded the risks of termination.

16.63 **(c) The statistical argument** It would even be possible to argue that abortions under s 1(1)(a) are effectively available on request as a result of the so-called 'statistical argument'. This is that the risks of continuing a pregnancy and going through childbirth are generally greater than the risks involved in the termination of pregnancy. In the first months of pregnancy, this is almost always the case. In relation to the pregnant woman's physical health, then, section 1(1)(a) will invariably be satisfied. Ultimately, of course, the two doctors must form an opinion that the ground is satisfied in relation to this individual woman, and not solely on the basis of abstract statistics, though, as we have seen, there is no legal requirement that they examine her. Provided that there is nothing in the individual woman's circumstances to contradict the 'statistical argument', the ground in section 1(1)(a) is therefore very easily satisfied.

16.64 **(d) 'Foreseeable environment'** In applying s 1(1)(a) and assessing the effect on the pregnant woman[86] of continuing the pregnancy, s 1(2) states that 'account may be taken of the pregnant woman's actual or reasonably foreseeable environment'. Consequently, the comparative exercise is not restricted to the risks to her health during the pregnancy itself. As a result, the social, economic, and emotional strain of having another child may be taken into account insofar as this will have an impact upon her physical or mental health after the child is born.

16.65 Thus, the potentially deleterious consequences of having a child in one's teens, or of having too large a family, or of having one's career plans derailed could all be bases for forming a 'good faith' view of injury to the woman's mental health.

16.66 **(e) Sex-selective abortion?** In recent years, there has been considerable controversy over the possibility that an abortion sought on the basis of the foetus's sex might fall within the terms of the Act, if the birth of a child of the 'wrong' sex would adversely affect the woman's mental health. In 2012, undercover reporters from the *Daily Telegraph* filmed abortion providers allegedly agreeing to carry out terminations on the grounds of foetal sex.[87] The reaction of the Secretary of State for Health and the Chief Medical Officer was to declare

[86] Or of 'existing children of her family'.

[87] Claire Newell and Holly Watt, 'Abortion investigation: doctors filmed agreeing illegal abortions "no questions asked"' *Daily Telegraph* (22nd February 2012).

that such abortions are unlawful.[88] The GMC suspended the registration of some of these doctors. Their conduct was reported to the Crown Prosecution Service, which investigated but decided not to prosecute.

Despite the assertions of the Secretary of State and others, the Abortion Act does not specify that abortion on the grounds of foetal sex is unlawful; rather, under section 1(1)(a), a termination's legality depends solely upon two doctors forming the opinion, in good faith, that the woman's health would be at greater risk if she were to continue the pregnancy than it would if her pregnancy was terminated. If a woman's mental health would be at risk if she feared rejection by her family on the grounds of the sex of her newborn child, termination would not necessarily be unlawful. **16.67**

Nevertheless, in its 2014 Guidance, the Department of Health once again asserted that 'Abortion on the grounds of gender alone is illegal. Gender is not itself a lawful ground under the Abortion Act'.[89] With respect, this represents a misunderstanding of the statutory language. A reason for abortion does not need to be expressly stated on the face of the Act for it to fall within the statutory grounds. To take an extreme analogy, the Act does not specify that abortion on the grounds of rape is lawful, but it certainly does not follow that abortion on the grounds of rape is unlawful. Of course, a woman pregnant with a female foetus which she does not want does not automatically satisfy section 1(1)(a). The only relevant question is whether two doctors judge, in good faith, that continuing the pregnancy poses a greater risk to her mental or physical health than termination. **16.68**

In 2015, a backbench Conservative MP, Fiona Bruce, tabled an amendment to the Serious Crime Bill in order to try to put beyond doubt the illegality of abortion on the grounds of foetal sex. In the end, this was defeated, in part as a result of fears that it would have interfered with access to abortion for women with foetuses affected by sex-linked genetic diseases. At the same time, an amendment which would require a review of the incidence of sex selective abortion in England, Wales, and Northern Ireland was passed with a substantial majority. **16.69**

(f) 'Risk to Existing Children of her Family' We have already noted that s 1(1)(a) contemplates an abortion because of the risk the woman's pregnancy poses to the physical or mental health of her existing children. In most circumstances, having a pregnant mother or a new sibling would not pose a risk of physical injury to an existing child. It is more likely that this ground would be satisfied where carrying the pregnancy to term would have a negative impact on the mental health of existing children. During the pregnancy, this would only be plausible if their mother would be seriously incapacitated and unable to care for them, perhaps because she has a history of a debilitating condition such as pre-eclampsia. Abortions in such circumstances would, however, already be lawful on the grounds of the risk to the pregnant woman's health. **16.70**

The risk to existing children's health is more likely to relate to the effect a new sibling would have upon their health after he or she is born. Under this ground, doctors are entitled to take into account the woman's 'actual or reasonably foreseeable environment',[90] so there might **16.71**

[88] Andrew Lansley MP, quoted in Newell and Watt, n 86. Dame Sally Davies letter to GPs, 23rd February 2012, available at <https://www.gov.uk/government/uploads/system/uploads/attachment_data/file/215147/dh_132849.pdf>

[89] Department of Health, *Guidance in Relation to Requirements of the Abortion Act 1967: For all those responsible for commissioning, providing and managing service provision* (DH, 2014) para 25.

[90] Abortion Act 1967, s 1(2).

be a risk to existing children's health where already impoverished family circumstances will be even more stretched by the birth of another baby.

16.72 The risk must be to 'any existing children of her family'. Who does this cover? The Act offers no definition but there is no reason to adopt a restrictive interpretation. Parliament intended to include all those who would be cared for by the pregnant woman and who might therefore be affected by the continuation of her pregnancy and the birth of a child.[91] Hence, it would cover any child for whom the pregnant woman is a primary carer. It is also suggested that the word 'child' should not be narrowly construed, and could also include older 'children' who, perhaps for reasons of serious disability, continue to be dependent upon the pregnant woman.

16.73 (g) **'Pregnancy not exceeded its twenty-fourth week'** As we saw earlier, the 1991 amendment to the 1967 Act resulted in a time limit being introduced into the Act for the first time. Only s 1(1)(a) is subject to a time limit: the pregnancy must not have exceeded its twenty-fourth week. There are no time limits in the other grounds. However, s 1(1)(a) does not specify the point at which the clock starts running in calculating the twenty-four weeks. There are essentially four possibilities:

(A) the first day of the woman's last period;
(B) the date of conception (usually around two weeks later);
(C) the date of implantation (up to ten days after (B)); and
(D) the first day of the woman's first missed period (usually about four weeks after (A)).

16.74 In England the medical profession calculates the length of a foetus's gestation on the basis of (A) because it is the most certain date of any of these alternatives. Options (B) and (C), namely the date of conception and the date the fertilized egg implants itself in the woman's uterus, in contrast, cannot be known for certain. Option (D) could lead to problems if the woman has irregular periods, or if she conceives just before her period, and hence only misses the one after that.

16.75 An interpretation of s 1(1)(a) consistent with the medical profession's approach in (A) would achieve certainty. But there are arguments favouring options (B) or (C). First, option (A) leads to the absurd conclusion that a woman is pregnant in the fourteen days (approximately) between the first day of her last period and the time of conception, when this is patently not the case. Secondly, the medical profession's approach exemplified in option (A) could act to the detriment of a defendant since it results in the shortest possible time for the twenty-four-week period to run. A pregnancy might be calculated on the basis of (A) to be twenty-five weeks, but it is actually likely to be only twenty-three weeks since implantation took place, and the pregnancy began. Ambiguities in criminal statutes should be construed in the defendant's favour, particularly when interpreting what amounts to a defence to a criminal offence.

16.76 On balance, (C) is the most defensible starting point, according, as it does, with the definition of when a 'miscarriage' could first be 'procured'. As a matter of common sense, the Abortion Act should be interpreted so that the defence to the crime in s 58 operates from the point in time when that crime could first be committed, namely after an embryo has implanted.

[91] See A J Hoggett, 'The Abortion Act 1967' [1968] Crim LR 247.

(ii) 'Necessary to prevent grave permanent injury to physical or mental health'—section 1(1)(b)

Section 1(1)(b) introduced a new substantive ground for abortion. Unlike s 1(1)(a), there is no time limit, and so abortions until full term are possible. As with the remaining grounds under the Act, Parliament did not wish to impose a time limit on abortions when the woman's health or life is in grave danger. Although s 1(1)(b) is concerned with the pregnant woman's health, it requires injury of a different order to that contemplated by s 1(1)(a). Parliament clearly intended that it should be available only where there is a serious danger to the pregnant woman's health. In the House of Lords' debates, Lord Mackay LC gave some examples of when 'grave permanent injury' might arise, such as where a woman suffers from severe hypertension and continuation of the pregnancy might result in permanent kidney, brain, or heart damage.[92] **16.77**

For s 1(1)(b) to apply, the certifying doctors must be of the opinion that the termination is 'necessary to prevent grave permanent injury to the physical or mental health' of the woman. Note that it is insufficient that there might be a risk of grave permanent injury, rather the doctors must be satisfied that 'grave permanent injury' would be reasonably certain to occur if the pregnant continued. Equally, a termination will only be 'necessary' if there is no alternative way to avoid the effect on the woman's health. Section 1(1)(b) not only lays down a very stringent requirement of harm—'grave permanent injury'—it also only applies where termination is effectively a last resort. **16.78**

(iii) 'Risk to woman's life'—section 1(1)(c)

Prior to 1991, the ground in s 1(1)(c) was lumped together with what is now s 1(1)(a). Both require the two certifying doctors to engage in the comparative exercise of judging whether the risk to the pregnant woman—here to her 'life'—is greater if the pregnancy is continued than if it is terminated. The risk must be to her; risks to her children are irrelevant under this ground. The ground only requires that the termination reduces the risk to her life. It does not require that the termination eliminates the risk altogether. For example, an abortion will not save a terminally ill woman's life, but it might be justified under this ground if pregnancy and childbirth might be likely to hasten her death. **16.79**

This ground is concerned with the risk to the woman's life, as opposed to her health. Before the passage of the Abortion Act 1967, in *R v Bourne*[93] and subsequent cases,[94] the courts had taken a broad view at common law of what was meant by a risk to a pregnant woman's 'life', so as to include risks to her mental health. This broad interpretation would now be inconsistent with the other grounds in the Act, in particular s 1(1)(a) through which Parliament intended to restrict to twenty-four weeks abortions performed because of a risk to the woman's health. **16.80**

(iv) 'Substantial risk (so as to be) seriously handicapped'—section 1(1)(d)

The final ground for abortion is in s 1(1)(d), according to which a pregnancy may be terminated if two doctors are of the opinion that there is 'a substantial risk' that if the child is born it would be 'seriously handicapped' as a result of 'physical or mental abnormalities'. The interpretation of this ground is not without difficulty. Since 1991, there has been no time limit. In theory at least, an abortion on the basis of foetal abnormality could be carried out up to full-term. In practice very few abortions are performed after twenty-four weeks.[95] **16.81**

[92] *Hansard*, HL vol 522, col 1039.
[93] [1939] 1 KB 687.
[94] *R v Newton and Stungo* [1958] Crim LR 469 and *R v Bergmann* [1948] 1 BMJ 1008.
[95] Such late terminations cannot be performed in independent abortion clinics and are, therefore, only available in NHS hospitals.

Although there are some cases where foetal abnormality is not detected until or after the twenty week anomaly scan, many abnormalities are detected earlier in pregnancy. Some gynaecologists will not be prepared to perform an abortion in the third trimester unless the abnormality is unusually severe as, for example, in the case of anencephaly where most, if not all, of the foetus's higher brain and much of its skull will be missing.

16.82 (a) **Substantial Risk** What degree of risk is contemplated by the need for there to be a 'substantial risk' of 'serious handicap'? Proof of certainty is not essential. Clearly a substantial risk exists if there is more than 50 per cent chance that the child will have the disability, but would a one in four chance of disability suffice? It is not clear from the Act. The interpretative difficulty will be exacerbated in 'double risk' cases where there is a risk that the child will inherit a genetic condition but it is not certain, if it does, how seriously the child would be affected. There may be a 'substantial' risk of inheriting the genetic condition, but if the chances that the child will go on to develop a serious disability are much less, the latter will statistically dilute the former and it is the overall risk (the risk of suffering physical or mental abnormalities so as to be seriously handicapped) which must be 'substantial'.

16.83 When is a risk 'substantial'? Of course the courts would look to medical evidence to determine the risks in a particular situation, but whether they are 'substantial' requires an interpretation of the statute and is a legal question. Two doctors may, in good faith, conclude that a particular risk is substantial but that will not be conclusive that s 1(1)(d) has been complied with. If their mistake is factual, for example, if they thought the risk was 50 per cent when it was only 10 per cent, their honest belief ('good faith') will protect them under the Act., If, however, their mistake is not factual but rather whether 10 per cent is a 'substantial' risk, their 'good faith' will not protect them if a court takes the view that that is a misinterpretation of the Act. In practice, the courts would be likely to give doctors considerable leeway and perhaps consider any risk which a reasonable person would consider material when making an abortion decision to be one which is 'substantial'.

16.84 (b) **Seriously handicapped** A further problem of interpretation arises in relation to the meaning of the phrase 'seriously handicapped'.[96] 'Handicap' is undoubtedly an old-fashioned word; a more modern formulation would be 'serious disability'. Regardless of whether the reference is to handicap or disability, the criterion in the Act is that it must be 'serious'. Again, like the meaning of the phrase 'substantial risk', this would be a question of law for the court, though it is clear that the child does not have to have a life-threatening condition for it to be 'seriously handicapped'.

16.85 At a minimum, it is suggested, a 'serious handicap' would require the child to have a physical or mental disability which would cause significant suffering or impairment of their ability to function in society.

16.86 When must the serious handicap exist? Must it exist at birth or immediately thereafter, or could it be a latent condition which develops later in the child's life. Section 1(1)(d) is concerned with the life of the 'child' 'if born'. Consequently, the condition must exist after birth at some point. However, to require the condition, and its manifestation, to exist at the point of birth or immediately thereafter is too narrow a reading of the Act. The Act is concerned with 'the child'. A reasonable interpretation would allow the doctors to consider whether the child would be likely to suffer 'serious handicap' in the future. Tay-Sach's disease, for example, is a genetic condition that can be detected in utero, but the child who is born will appear to develop normally for the first six months of life. Their health will then rapidly deteriorate,

[96] For a recent evaluation of the logic of this section, see S Mcguinness, 'Law, Reproduction and Disability: Fatally "Handicapped"' (2013) 21 Med Law Rev 213–42.

and they will become blind, deaf, and unable to swallow, before paralysis sets in. Death usually occurs before the age of four. There is no doubt that Tay-Sachs would count as a 'serious handicap' for the purpose of s 1(1)(d), even though the child will be healthy at birth.

Of course, the child must actually be likely to suffer a 'physical or mental abnormality', meaning that s 1(1)(d) could not be used to justify termination where the foetus is a carrier of a recessive defective gene such as cystic fibrosis, which would not manifest itself at all during their lifetime. **16.87**

Unlike Tay-Sachs disease, some genetic conditions do not manifest themselves until much later in life. Huntington's Disease, for example, is a serious neurodegenerative disorder, but it will normally first appear when someone is middle-aged. Does a condition like this fit within s 1(1)(d)? On one view it does not. The Act speaks of the 'child' if born suffering from 'physical or mental abnormalities as to be seriously handicapped'. However, it would be artificial and arbitrary to interpret s 1(1)(d) as only including conditions likely to manifest themselves before a person's 18th birthday, and disallowing terminations for conditions which may develop after the child has reached the age of 18. This would also create practical difficulties where a condition is likely to manifest itself in a person's late teens, when there would inevitably be doubt as to whether the child would be likely to suffer the disabilities before or after they reach the age of majority. **16.88**

The better view is that the limiting factors in s 1(1)(d) are the need for the risk to be substantial and the disabilities to be serious, rather than the age of onset, and that there is no need to confine the use of this section to childhood diseases. Indeed, as is evident from the wording of s 1(1), which specifies that what matters are the two doctors' *opinions* that the ground is satisfied and as we see below from the Jepson case, it is clear that a court will be slow to interfere with doctors' discretion in determining whether the disability is serious and the risk of it occurring substantial. **16.89**

3. Operation of the Abortion Act

The 1967 Act together with the Abortion Regulations 1991[97] provide a statutory regulatory framework for abortion. Any person who wilfully contravenes or wilfully fails to comply with the requirements of the 1991 Regulations commits a summary offence.[98] In particular, Regulations provide for (i) the places where terminations may be performed; (ii) the certification of the grounds for the abortion; (iii) notification to the relevant Chief Medical Officer of information about the abortion performed; and (iv) restrictions on the disclosure of information. **16.90**

(i) Places

Section 1(3) of the Abortion Act 1967 provides that an abortion may only be carried out in an NHS hospital or in a place approved by the Secretary of State. An exception is provided for in cases of emergencies. Section 1(4) states that a termination need not be carried out in such a place where the doctor: **16.91**

> . . . is of the opinion, formed in good faith, that the termination is immediately necessary to save the life or to prevent grave permanent injury to the physical or mental health of the pregnant woman.

[97] SI 1991/499 as amended by the Abortion (Amendment) (England) Regulations 2002, SI 2002/887 and the Abortion (Amendment) (Wales) Regulations 2002, SI 2002/2979 (W 275) (made pursuant to s 2).

[98] Abortion Act 1967, s 2(3). Liable to a fine not exceeding level 5 on the standard scale.

16.92 (a) **The independent sector** In 2014, 98 per cent of abortions were funded by the NHS, 67 per cent of which took place in the independent sector under NHS contract.[99] All clinics and hospitals that provide terminations of pregnancies are regulated by the Care Quality Commission (CQC).

16.93 As part of its inspection function, the CQC requires compliance with Department of Health guidance.[100] These set a number of standards, relating to, inter alia, the provision of oral and written information, confidentiality, the offer of counselling, and ensuring that women have access to timely abortion services. Good practice is to ensure that women are offered the abortion procedure within five working days of the decision to proceed. All providers should have policies on the disposal of foetal tissue, in order to ensure that it is treated with dignity and respect and that a patient's wishes in respect of disposal are taken into account.

16.94 The Regulations place some limits on when a termination may be carried out. Terminations after the twenty-fourth week of gestation may only be carried out in an NHS hospital. Terminations between twenty and twenty-four weeks may only be performed by suitably qualified, skilled and experienced staff and providing that appropriate procedures to deal with a medical emergency are in place.

16.95 (b) **Medical abortions** The Human Fertilisation and Embryology Act 1990[101] introduced a new s 1(3A) into the 1967 Act. It provides that:

> The power under subsection (3) of this section to approve a place includes power, in relation to treatment consisting primarily in the use of such medicines as may be specified in the approval and carried out in such manner as may be specified, to approve a class of places.

16.96 This provision was intended to allow the drug mifepristone, discussed earlier, to be prescribed and taken in places other than NHS Hospitals or approved clinics.

Mifepristone does not require hospitalisation on medical grounds. The drug has been proven to be safe with few side-effects.[102] All that is required is that the woman should ingest the drug, and two days later misoprostol is taken in order to trigger the miscarriage, which usually happens between four and six hours later. While it is essential that the woman should remain under the care of a doctor, there is no clinical reason to require the woman to receive either drug in a hospital or approved clinic.

16.97 Section 1(3) would require the Secretary of State to approve each place (such as a GP surgery or family planning clinic) separately. Section 1(3A) permits the Secretary of State to approve such places as a class, but this has not yet been done. This is noteworthy because it runs counter to the general trend within the NHS of providing more medical treatments in primary care settings, such as GP surgeries, rather than in hospitals.

16.98 Even if the Secretary of State had exercised his power under s 1(3A), a literal interpretation of the Act might still cause difficulties for early medical abortions. It is not clear that 'treatment for the termination of pregnancy' is restricted to the prescription of the drugs. Arguably, the 'treatment' begins with the prescription of the drug and continues until the pregnancy is terminated. In *Royal College of Nursing of UK v DHSS*[103] the House of Lords adopted a broad interpretation of 'treatment' under the Abortion Act to include all the

[99] Abortion Statistics 2014 (DH, 2015).

[100] *Procedures for the Approval Of Independent Sector Places For The Termination Of Pregnancy* (DH, 2014).

[101] Section 37(3).

[102] B Couzinet et al, 'Termination of Early Pregnancy by Antiprogesterone RU486 (Mifepristone)' (1986) 315 New Eng J Med 1565; J Cherfas, J and J Palca, 'The Pill of Choice?' (1989) 245 Science 1319.

[103] [1981] AC 800.

activities, undertaken by the 'hospital team', which were designed to bring about the termination of a pregnancy. 'Treatment for the termination of pregnancy' is, in the case of mifepristone and misoprostol, a process spanning a number of days. In practice, a woman will only be at one of the classes of places which could be approved under s 1(3A) for part of the time that the 'treatment' is taking place.

It would be impossible for the Secretary of State to approve all of the places that a woman might visit between the prescription of mifepristone and the eventual miscarriage. Moreover, it is unlikely that s 1(3A) allows the approval of non-medical locations, such as the woman's home or the bus she catches to go home after taking the first pill. **16.99**

In practice, the Act has not been interpreted literally, and while the drug must be prescribed in a NHS hospital or approved clinic, women's movements are not restricted for the subsequent forty-eight hours, when the drug will be acting to cause, and eventually will cause a miscarriage. **16.100**

A woman could safely take both abortion drugs at home.[104] This would have particular advantages in the case of the second drug, misoprostol, which is taken a few days after the first pill in order to ensure that the pregnancy has been terminated. For an abortion to be lawful, however, it must take place in an NHS hospital or approved clinic, and hence women undergoing early medical abortions must be present in the clinic to take the pills on two separate occasions. This will be especially inconvenient for women with young children or women who live a long way from their nearest clinic. Because in most cases it is the misoprostol which actually triggers the abortion, there is also the concern that women might miscarry on the way home from the clinic. **16.101**

In 2012, one of the largest abortion providers in the UK, the British Pregnancy Advisory Service (BPAS) sought a declaration that it would be lawful to prescribe misoprostol when the woman attended the clinic to take the mifepristone, so that she could take the misoprostol home with her. This, they argued, would be more convenient for women, who could take the second pill at home, safe in the knowledge that they will be at home when the miscarriage actually occurs. According to BPAS, the pregnancy would still be 'terminated by a registered medical practitioner' where the registered medical practitioner had prescribed an abortifacient drug with the intention of terminating a pregnancy. They failed to convince the judge, however.[105] According to Supperstone J, the 'treatment' which had to take place in an approved place was the taking of the drug, not merely its prescription. **16.102**

In 1967, it was eminently sensible to require a surgical procedure to take place in a specialized hospital or clinic. But requiring women to attend a clinic on two separate occasions, sending them home after the second drug is taken, in fact increases the likelihood that they will experience a miscarriage while travelling or in a public place. Indeed it is noteworthy that in its latest evidence-based guideline on the treatment of women requesting abortion, the RCOG suggests that taking misoprostol at home is safe, and that it would be desirable for women to be given the choice about how and where to undergo this sort of abortion.[106] **16.103**

(c) **Purchasing drugs from online pharmacies** Until relatively recently, bypassing the provisions of the Abortion Act by terminating one's own pregnancy would have been difficult. Within the UK, it is a criminal offence to supply a prescription-only medicine without a **16.104**

104 RCOG, *The Care of Women Requesting Induced Abortion: Evidence-based Clinical Guideline number 7* (RCOG, 2011).

105 *British Pregnancy Advisory Service (BPAS) v Secretary of State for Health* [2012] 1 WLR 580.

106 RCOG, *The Care of Women Requesting Induced Abortion: Evidence-based clinical guideline number 7* (RCOG, 2011).

prescription.[107] Online pharmacies, based offshore, now enable consumers to bypass restrictions on the supply of prescription-only medicines, including mifepristone and misoprostol.

16.105 With the exception of certain controlled drugs, the penalties for obtaining prescription-only drugs without a prescription are directed at the supplier rather than the purchaser. It is therefore not an offence to buy misoprostol from an online pharmacy. If, however, misoprostol is judged to be a 'poison or other noxious thing', using it to terminate one's own pregnancy would be a criminal offence under s 58 of the Offences Against the Person Act 1861, to which the Abortion Act 1967 would offer no defence.

16.106 In England, Scotland, and Wales, comparatively few women will be tempted to terminate their own pregnancies with abortion pills purchased over the internet. It would, however, be a mistake to assume that this sort of 'DIY abortion', does not happen in the UK. In Northern Ireland, where abortion continues to be illegal, unless the woman faces a grave risk to her life or health, terminating one's pregnancy with a medicine bought online may be more convenient and affordable than travelling to England, Scotland, or Wales for a private abortion.[108]

16.107 Within England, Scotland, and Wales, there may also be women, such as panic-struck teenagers, who might tempted to buy medicines online in order to terminate their own pregnancies. A woman who is determined to end her pregnancy when to do so would not be lawful under the Abortion Act might also attempt to self-abort. This was the case for Sarah Catt, who bought abortion pills from an internet site in order to terminate her own pregnancy, shortly before she was due to give birth.[109] In doing so, she had 'procured a miscarriage' outside of the statutory defences offered to doctors under the Abortion Act 1967, and thus committed a crime under s 58 of the Offences Against the Person Act 1861. Initially Cooke J sentenced Catt to eight years in prison, but the Court of Appeal held that this sentence was manifestly excessive, and on appeal, her sentence was reduced to three and a half years.

(ii) Certification

16.108 The two doctors' 'good faith' opinions, required under s 1(1) of the 1967 Act, must be given in the prescribed form of the 'certificate of opinion' set out in Sch 1, Pt 1 to the Abortion Regulations 1991. The certificate must be completed 'before the commencement of the treatment for termination of the pregnancy'.[110] Where the termination is to be carried out in an emergency under s 1(4), when a single doctor's opinion will suffice, that opinion must be given in accordance with the certificate set out in Sch 1, Pt II to the 1991 Regulations.[111] In this situation the certificate must be completed before the start of treatment or, if that is not reasonably practicable, not more than twenty-four hours after the termination.

16.109 The certificate must be retained by the practitioner who terminates the pregnancy for not less than three years from the date of the termination[112] and, thereafter, if it is no longer to be preserved it must be destroyed by the person having custody of it.[113] Wilful failure to comply with the Regulations is a criminal offence.[114]

---

107 Human Medicines Regulations 2012, regulation 214.
108 H McDonald, 'Northern Irish women risk jail by admitting use of abortion drugs' *The Observer* (10 March 2013).
109 *R v Sarah Catt* [2013] EWCA Crim 1187.
110 Abortion Regulations, SI 1991/499, reg 3(2).
111 Certificate B and reg 3(1)(b) as substituted.
112 Abortion Regulations, SI 1991/499 reg 3(4).
113 ibid, reg 3(5).
114 Abortion Act 1967, s 2(3), and para 16.61.

(iii) Notification

The Abortion Regulations 1991 provide that a doctor terminating a pregnancy must within fourteen days of the termination provide the relevant Chief Medical Officer[115] with notice of the termination and information relating to it, as required by Sch 2 to the Regulations. **16.110**

(iv) Disclosure of information

(a) **The Restriction** As with other medical treatment, the common law protects the confidentiality of information provided by, or relating to the pregnant woman. However, the 1991 Abortion Regulations give further statutory protection to this information. Regulation 5 imposes a duty not to disclose a 'notice given or any information' supplied to the relevant Chief Medical Officer in pursuance of the Regulations, except as provided in the Regulations. The Regulations are widely drawn. They do not merely prohibit disclosure of the notice under Schedule 2 to the Act but also 'any information' contained in it. The Regulations do not specify upon whom the 'duty' is imposed, however. They merely state that the notice or information 'shall not be disclosed'. There can be little doubt that the duty not to disclose applies to everyone.[116] Of course, the criminal offence created by the 1967 Act if a breach occurs is only committed if the discloser acts 'wilfully'.[117] The Regulations do not specifically create a civil cause of action enforceable by a patient. Given their specificity, however, and the identity of the person they are designed to protect, the courts might be likely to construe the Regulations as creating a civil cause of action so that the pregnant woman[118] could seek an injunction to prevent disclosure in breach of the Regulations, and perhaps damages if disclosure has taken place. **16.111**

(b) **The Exceptions** There are nine circumstances specified in Regulation 5 in which disclosure of the 'notice' or 'information' supplied to the relevant Chief Medical Officer is permitted:[119] **16.112**

(i) to an authorized officer of the Department of Health or the Welsh Assembly Government,[120] or to the National Statistician duly appointed under section 5 of the Statistics and Registration Service Act 2007, or an employee of the Statistics Board (established under section 1 of that Act) authorized by the National Statistician,[121] or, in Wales, to the chairman of the Statistics Board, or a member of the Statistics Board's staff who has been duly authorized by the chairman;[122]

(ii) to the Director of Public Prosecutions (or an authorized member of staff) for the purposes of carrying out his duties in relation to offences under the Abortion Act 1967 or the law relating to abortion;[123]

(iii) to a police officer not below the rank of Superintendent (or a person authorized by him) for the purposes of investigating whether an offence has been committed under the Abortion Act 1967 or the law relating to abortion;[124]

(iv) pursuant to a court order for the purposes of proceedings which have begun;

115 Of England or for Wales: SI 1991/499, reg 4 as amended by SI 2002/887, reg 4 (England) and SI 2002/2979 (W 275), reg 5 (Wales).

116 Including the relevant Chief Medical Officer him- or herself.

117 Abortion Act 1967, s 2(3).

118 Leaving aside the Attorney-General who could do so as the guardian of the public interest.

119 reg 5(a) to (i).

120 Including an authorized person responsible for the relevant CMO's computer system: reg 5(a)(i) added by SI 2002/887, reg 5(b) (England) and SI 2002/2979 (W 275), reg 5(b) (Wales).

121 Abortion (Amendment) Regulations 2008/735.

122 Abortion (Amendment) (Wales) Regulations 2008/1338.

123 Namely, the Offences Against the Person Act 1861, ss 58, 59.

124 ibid.

(v) for the purposes of bona fide scientific research;
(vi) to the medical practitioner who terminated the pregnancy;
(vii) to a medical practitioner, with the consent in writing of the woman whose pregnancy was terminated;
(viii) to the President of the General Medical Council (or an authorized member of staff) when requested by him for the purpose of investigating whether there has been serious professional misconduct by a medical practitioner;
(ix) to the woman whose pregnancy was terminated if she supplies the Chief Medical Office with written proof of her identity including a birth certificate and the place and date of the termination.[125]

(v) Conscientious objection

16.113 The Abortion Act 1967 does not require a doctor to perform an abortion even if the circumstances of the pregnant woman clearly fall within one of the grounds in the Act. Of course, English law never requires a doctor to treat a patient contrary to his or her clinical judgment, so it is unexceptional that the Act does not place doctors under a duty to perform abortions. The Abortion Act is unusual, however, because it specifically allows doctors to refuse to participate in medical treatment on the grounds of conscience.

16.114 Section 4(1) of the Abortion Act 1967 provides that:

> no person shall be under any duty, whether by contract or by any statutory or other legal requirement, to participate in any treatment authorised by this Act to which he has a conscientious objection.

16.115 A conscientious objection cannot be relied upon in an emergency. Section 4(2) provides that:

> [n]othing in subsection (1) . . . shall affect any duty to participate in treatment which is necessary to save the life or to prevent grave permanent injury to the physical or mental health of the pregnant woman.[126]

16.116 Subject to the emergency exception, s 4(1) allows a doctor or nurse not to participate in an abortion when they otherwise would be required to do so by virtue of their employment. The burden of proving the conscientious objection lies upon the individual seeking to rely upon it.[127] There are two essential elements to the 'conscientious objection': first, that the person's objection is conscientious; and secondly, that they would otherwise be asked to participate in an abortion.

16.117 **(a) Matters of Conscience** 'Conscience' refers to a conviction or belief based upon a moral assessment. The *Oxford English Dictionary* refers to:

> [t]he internal acknowledgment or recognition of the moral quality of one's motives and actions; the sense of right and wrong as regards things for which one is responsible; the faculty or principle which pronounces upon the moral quality of one's actions or motives, approving the right and condemning the wrong.

16.118 A matter of 'conscience' is widely understood to cover religious, moral, or other principled beliefs, which lead the individual to conclude that an activity is wrong. Objections based upon prejudice rather than principle would not be covered. A doctor who took a particular view of the sanctity of the early stages of human life would have a conscientious objection, whether that belief was religious or secular.

---

125 reg 5(i) added by SI 2002/887, reg 5(c) (England) and SI 2002/2979 (W 275), reg 5(c) (Wales).
126 ie, falling within s 1(1)(b) and in extreme cases under s 1(1)(c).
127 For proof in Scotland, see s 4(3).

The Act also permits a doctor or a nurse to have a conscientious objection to some but not all abortions. Section 4(1) refers to a person having a conscientious objection to '*any* treatment' covered by the Act. Although it is not free from doubt, this provision would seem to allow a doctor to object to, say, late abortions only, or to terminations on the basis of foetal abnormality, while not objecting to others. Providing the objection is 'conscientiously' based, rather than grounded in prejudice, a person need not participate in such terminations. **16.119**

(b) Who is Covered? Section 4(1) applies to any 'person', and not just the doctor carrying out the termination, providing that they would be 'participat[ing]' in the 'treatment authorised' under the Act. Undoubtedly, nurses and others who take part in the termination, under the direction of the responsible doctor,[128] will be covered by s 4(1). But what of others who are less directly involved? **16.120**

The issue first arose in *Janaway v Salford HA*.[129] The plaintiff was a receptionist/secretary at a health centre. She was asked by one of the doctors to type a referral letter for a pregnant woman seeking an abortion. She refused and was dismissed. She sought judicial review of that decision on the basis that she was entitled to rely on the 'conscientious objection' provision in s 4(1) of the 1967 Act. Nolan J (at first instance) refused her application and her appeal was subsequently dismissed by the Court of Appeal and the House of Lords. The House of Lords held that the word 'participate' had to be given its ordinary and natural meaning. The plaintiff was not entitled to rely on s 4(1) because she was not 'actually taking part in treatment administered in a hospital or other approved place . . . for the purpose of terminating a pregnancy'.[130] **16.121**

In the Scottish case of *Doogan v Greater Glasgow and Clyde Health Board*, two Catholic midwives initially failed to persuade the Court of Session that section 4(1) entitled them to refuse to delegate to, supervise, or support staff who were directly involved with the provision of abortion services.[131] The midwives appealed successfully to an Extra Division of the Inner House,[132] which gave the right to conscientious objection a surprisingly broad interpretation, on the grounds that a 'wide interpretation' was 'in keeping with the reason for the exemption'. That decision was then overturned by the Supreme Court,[133] which instead found that 'the narrow meaning is more likely to have been in the contemplation of Parliament when the Act was passed'. According to the Supreme Court, section 4 is concerned with a conscientious objection to the acts which were made lawful by section 1, that is, to the termination of pregnancy itself, rather than to various administrative, managerial, and ancillary tasks. In giving the judgment of the court, Lady Hale said that '"participate", in my view, means taking part in a "hands on" capacity'. **16.122**

What about a doctor, usually a GP, who refuses to sign a certificate for conscientious reasons. Is he entitled to rely on s 4(1)? In *Janaway*, Lord Keith left the point open, but on the basis of the House of Lords and now the Supreme Court's interpretation of 'participate', such a doctor could not be said to be participating in the treatment authorized under the Act. Indeed, as Lord Keith acknowledged, the certificate must come into existence 'before the commencement of the treatment'.[134] It is logically impossible to construe signing the certificate as 'participation' in treatment which the law insists cannot take place lawfully **16.123**

---

128 See *Royal College of Nursing v DHSS* [1981] AC 800 discussed above.
129 *Janaway v Salford HA* [1989] AC 537 (HL).
130 ibid, 570 *per* Lord Keith.
131 [2012] CSOH 32.
132 [2013] CSIH 36.
133 [2014] UKSC 68.
134 [1989] AC 537, 572. See Abortion Regulations 1991, SI 1991/499, reg 3(2).

unless the form has already been signed. Consequently, such a doctor would not be able to rely upon s 4(1) to relieve him of any duty he would otherwise have to sign the certificate or refer the pregnant woman to another doctor.

16.124 In the Court of Appeal in *Janaway*, Stocker LJ took the view that a doctor had a legal duty to sign the certificate. At the very least, the GP must refer the patient to another doctor. In *Barr v Matthews*,[135] a GP was unsuccessfully sued in negligence for failing to offer or arrange a termination of pregnancy. In the course of his judgment, Alliott J stated that 'once a termination of pregnancy is recognised as an option, the doctor invoking the conscientious objection clause should refer the patient to a colleague at once'.[136]

16.125 Doctors are not legally obliged to publicize their conscientious objections to abortion, so women may not know in advance whether or not their doctor is a conscientious objector. However, the GMC's latest guidance on doctors' personal beliefs suggests that doctors must tell women that they have a right to see another doctor, and that they should take steps proactively to inform all of their patients about their unwillingness to refer for abortion. According to the GMC, if the woman cannot easily make her own arrangements to see another doctor, the doctor is under a duty to assist her.[137]

(vi) Selective reduction

16.126 **(a) The techniques** Sophisticated ultrasound techniques mean that it is now possible to reduce a multiple pregnancy by killing one or more foetuses in utero. The greater the number of foetuses carried by a woman, the greater the risk to her health during pregnancy and at delivery. Multiple pregnancies are also much more risky for babies. Premature birth and low birth weight is common, and there is a considerably increased risk of mortality and morbidity, including cerebral palsy. Particularly for higher order multiple pregnancies, such as triplets and quadruplets, reducing the pregnancy may help to preserve the health and life of both the pregnant woman and the remaining foetuses. This is usually done in the first fourteen weeks of the pregnancy by either injecting potassium chloride into the amniotic sac or into the heart of a foetus or by aspiration. The foetus(es) will die and may be spontaneously expelled or remain in the pregnant woman, wither, and what remains will be expelled when the remaining foetuses are delivered. This procedure is known as 'selective reduction'.

16.127 A similar procedure, selective foeticide, may be used later in pregnancy when one foetus is discovered to be seriously handicapped.

16.128 **(b) Legal position before 1991**

Miscarriage It was not clear under the law prior to 1 April 1991 whether selective reduction and selective foeticide were covered by the law relating to abortion. It could be argued that, in cases where the 'reduced' foetus is not expelled, no 'miscarriage' occurs within the terms of s 58 of the Offences Against the Person Act 1861.[138] The better view, however, is that the term 'miscarriage' does not require immediate expulsion of all the contents of the womb but merely that some or all of the contents cease to be carried alive within it, and will eventually be expelled. This would bring both procedures within s 58 of the 1861 Act.

[135] *Barr v Matthews* (1999) 52 BMLR 217.
[136] ibid, 227.
[137] GMC, *Personal Beliefs and Medical Practice* (GMC 2008).
[138] The argument is put and rejected by J Keown, 'Selective Reduction of Multiple Pregnancy' (1987) 137 NLJ 1165.

Termination of Pregnancy A further complication was that it was not clear whether selective reduction was a 'termination of pregnancy' for the purposes of the Abortion Act 1967 because the woman is still pregnant after the procedure. **16.129**

(c) **Legal Position After 1991** In an attempt to put the matter beyond doubt, s 5(2) of the 1967 Act was amended by the Human Fertilisation and Embryology Act 1990[139] to include the following: **16.130**

> . . . in the case of a woman carrying more than one foetus, anything done with intent to procure her miscarriage of any foetus is authorised by [section 1] if—
>
> (a) the ground for termination of the pregnancy specified in subsection (1)(d) of that section applies in relation to any foetus and the thing is done for the purpose of procuring the miscarriage of that foetus, or
>
> (b) any of the other grounds for termination of pregnancy specified in that section applies.

The effect of this amendment is to bring selective reduction and selective foeticide within the Abortion Act and to require compliance with its terms if a doctor is to act lawfully. Section 5(2) assumes that the procedures do result in a 'miscarriage' for the purposes of the 1861 Act. **16.131**

Selective Foeticide Section 5(2)(a) covers the procedure of selective foeticide where the particular foetus is identified by prenatal screening (using amniocentesis or chorionic villus sampling) as suffering from a physical or mental abnormality which would lead to the child being 'seriously handicapped' within s 1(1)(d) of the Act. As a result of s 5(2)(a), providing the foetus could be aborted on the grounds of foetal abnormality if it had been a singleton, it may be aborted through selective foeticide. **16.132**

Selective Reduction Section 5(2)(b) covers the procedure of selective reduction. If a doctor would be justified in terminating the whole pregnancy under s 1(1) of the Act because of the risk to the pregnant woman's health or life or because of the serious injury she will suffer if the pregnancy continues, he or she may reduce the number of foetuses in the multiple pregnancy in order to remove (or reduce) the risk the pregnancy poses to her. **16.133**

Unlike s 5(2)(a), which requires the doctor to kill only the handicapped foetus, s 5(2)(b) permits the doctor randomly to select which foetus(es) to kill. This difference between the two provisions is inevitable because in the case of selective reduction, no foetus can be singled out as posing the threat to the pregnant woman's health; rather it is the cumulative effect of their presence which creates the risk. **16.134**

One final point to notice. Selective reduction may be desirable because a multiple pregnancy poses a risk of damage to the foetuses themselves. Section 5(2) does not permit selective reduction in this situation because a risk of injury to a foetus is not a ground for abortion under s 1(1).[140] Only a risk to the pregnant woman would satisfy the Act. This criterion is nevertheless easily satisfied because even twin pregnancies significantly increase the risks of pregnancy and childbirth for the pregnant woman. **16.135**

E. The Impact of the Human Rights Act

In practice, the Human Rights Act 1998 has not had very much impact upon the law of abortion in the UK. **16.136**

[139] Section 37(4).

[140] But note the comment by Lord Mackay of Clashfern LC, *Hansard*, HL vol 522, cols 1041–2.

16.137 Two principal Convention issues arise.[141] First, does a foetus have a 'right to life' under Article 2? Secondly, if it does, how should the court give effect to that right if it conflicts with the human rights of the pregnant woman, for example, her own 'right to life' or her 'right to private life' protected by Article 8?

1. Article 2—the 'right to life'

16.138 Article 2(1) of the European Convention on Human Rights states that:

> Everyone's right to life shall be protected by law. No one shall be deprived of his life intentionally ... [emphasis added].

16.139 Does a foetus fall within the terms 'everyone' and 'no one'? The foetus is not a legal person and so it seems likely that it is not protected by Article 2. Before the European Convention on Human Rights was incorporated into English law by the Human Rights Act 1998, in *Paton v UK*[142] the European Commission noted that the term 'everyone' is not defined in the Convention. It appears several times, and in most instances, the word is used so that it could only apply after birth. The Commission declined to decide whether Article 2 could ever offer protection to a foetus, but instead held that Article 2(1) had to be subject to an implied limitation justifying the termination of a pregnancy in order to protect the life and health of the woman.

16.140 *Vo v France*[143] involved a mix-up between two patients with similar names, which led to Mrs Vo's wanted pregnancy being terminated. Mrs Vo instituted criminal proceedings against the doctor responsible, and he was initially convicted of unintentional homicide. On appeal the French Cour de Cassation reversed this judgment, on the grounds that the foetus was not a person and was therefore not entitled to the protection of the criminal law. Mrs Vo then applied to the European Court of Human Rights, arguing that the French authorities had an obligation under Article 2 to pass legislation making the unintentional killing of a foetus a criminal offence. The ECtHR considered that the question of when the right to life begins was a question to be decided at national level by member states. It was not possible to answer in the abstract the question whether the foetus was a person for the purposes of Article 2 of the Convention, in part because there was no European consensus on the scientific and legal definition of the beginning of life. In another non-abortion case, *Evans v UK*,[144] the ECtHR reaffirmed its decision in *Vo v France* and rejected the applicant's claim that frozen embryos had a right to life under Article 2.

16.141 The Council of Europe has suggested that member states' 'margin of appreciation' on the moral status of the foetus should not be sufficiently wide to permit some states to make abortion unlawful.[145] Rather, while member states have the right to restrict access to abortion beyond a 'reasonable gestational limit', they should ensure that all women have access to safe and legal abortion. A number of countries, including Northern Ireland and the Republic of Ireland, do not meet this requirement.[146]

---

[141] Claims by fathers to be involved in termination decisions by virtue of Art 8 and their 'right to private and family life' are considered below.

[142] [1980] 3 EHRR 408.

[143] (2005) 40 EHRR 12.

[144] (App no 6339/05) (2007).

[145] *Access to safe and legal abortion in Europe* Resolution 1607 (2008).

[146] For commentary, see R Fletcher, 'Abortion Needs or Abortion Rights? Claiming State Accountability for Women's Reproductive Welfare' (2005) 13 Feminist Legal Studies 123–34; E Fegan and R Rebouche, 'Northern Ireland's Abortion Law: The Morality of Silence and the Censure of Agency' (2003) 11 Feminist Legal Studies 221–54; B Hewson, 'Therapeutic Abortion: Human Right or Wrong' (2006) 156 New Law Journal 1348–49.

Abortion is illegal in the Republic of Ireland, except where the pregnancy poses a risk to the pregnant woman's life. The Irish Constitution was amended in 1983 by Article 40.3.3, which provides that the 'unborn' and the pregnant woman have an equal right to life. Hence, unless the pregnant woman's life is in danger, the foetus's right to life must take priority. **16.142**

Despite the fact that it has always been lawful to terminate a pregnancy when the woman's life is at risk, in 2012 Savita Halappanavar died after being denied a termination of pregnancy on the grounds that the doctors could still detect a foetal heartbeat. A public opinion survey conducted soon after Mrs Halannanavar's death suggested that 80 per cent of the Irish population would support laws which allow abortion where the mother's life is threatened, including by suicide. **16.143**

Public outcry following Mrs Halappanavar's death resulted in the Protection of Life During Pregnancy Act (PLDPA) 2013, which repealed sections 58 and 58 of the Offences Against the Person Act. Under sections 7, 8, and 9 of the PLDPA, termination will be lawful where there is a real and substantial risk of loss of the woman's life and where the specified number of doctors (which varies according to the nature of the risk) certify that 'in their reasonable opinion (being an opinion formed in good faith which has regard to the need to preserve unborn human life as far as practicable) that risk can only be averted by carrying out a termination'. **16.144**

2. Article 8—'the right to private and family life'

(i) The right

Article 8 protects an individual's right to 'private and family life'. The state is both under a positive duty to 'respect' those rights and also a negative obligation not to 'interfere' with them, except to the extent permitted under Article 8(2). Shifting the human rights debate to Article 8 has the effect that the rights of the pregnant woman become the starting point. Legislative limits upon her right to undergo a termination require justification. Hence all of the restrictions upon access to abortion, such as the grounds for abortion and the time limit, must be defensible. **16.145**

The European Court of Human Rights has recognized that 'private life' is a broad term and includes the 'physical and psychological integrity of a person'.[147] There is no doubt that it includes a pregnant woman's interest in accessing an abortion, and ensuring that, where a state permits therapeutic abortions, this right is a meaningful one. **16.146**

(ii) The justification

Both the notion of 'respect' for an individual's right to private life and the justification for interference by the state with that right, entail the court in a balancing exercise of competing rights and interests which must be weighed to reach a 'proportionate' result. Thus, in determining the compatibility of the Abortion Act with a woman's Article 8 rights, any interference with access to abortion must be (i) in accordance with the law; (ii) for a legitimate aim; and (iii) 'necessary in a democratic society', that is, it must be a proportionate response to achieve a legitimate aim, which must serve a 'pressing social need'. **16.147**

(a) 'In accordance with the law' There is no difficulty with the first of these requirements providing the termination is carried out in accordance with the requirements of the Abortion Act 1967. **16.148**

[147] See, eg, *Pretty v UK* (2002) 12 BHRC 141 at [61].

16.149 (b) **'Legitimate aim'** The legitimate aim of any limitation upon a woman's right to choose may be protection of her own health interests, for example, the restrictions upon the places where terminations may take place.[148] Most limitations, however, such as the grounds for abortion and the time limit of twenty-four weeks, seek to strike a balance between the seriousness of foetal destruction and the pregnant woman's reproductive autonomy. Many people would accept that the state has a legitimate interest in protecting human life, even before birth, and this is not necessarily inconsistent with the law failing to recognize a foetus as a legal person.

16.150 (c) **'Proportionality'** Given the controversial nature of abortion and the moral disagreements that it engenders, it is most unlikely that an English court would try to 'second-guess' Parliament's weighing of the competing interests that finds form in the grounds for abortion in s 1(1) of the Act.

16.151 The UK courts will, therefore, respect the legitimacy of Parliament's choices in setting the grounds for abortion and permitting terminations beyond the point of viability where the pregnant woman's life is at risk[149] or she will suffer grave permanent injury[150] if the pregnancy continues. In these situations, Parliament has decided that protection of the pregnant woman's rights should prevail.

16.152 Interestingly the Article 8 rights of an unidentified group of women were said not to be engaged in a case in which a pro-life pressure group had sought to use the Freedom of Information Act 2000 in order to force the Department of Health to publish statistical data about the conditions that had justified late terminations of pregnancy on the grounds of foetal abnormality. The Department of Health had resisted giving a breakdown of which conditions had justified terminations of pregnancy on the grounds that, if the numbers were very small and the condition extremely rare, it might be possible to identify either the woman or her doctor.

16.153 In *Department of Health v Information Commissioner*,[151] Cranston J held that the chance of identifying individual women was 'remote'—but note, not non-existent—and that, as a result, Article 8 was not engaged. Given the potentially devastating consequences of identifying women who had undergone late abortions, it is interesting that a remote risk of identification was not thought to engage the women's human rights.

3. Article 10—the 'right to free speech'

16.154 The right to freedom of expression of those who are opposed to abortion might receive protection from Article 10. In *R (Prolife Alliance) v British Broadcasting Corporation*,[152] the House of Lords, by a 4–1 majority, held that the BBC's decision to refuse to transmit a party political broadcast which contained graphic footage of an abortion did not amount to a discriminatory, arbitrary, or unreasonable denial of the right to freedom of expression under Article 10(2).

16.155 This question of the freedom to publicize anti-abortion material arose again in *Connolly v Director of Public Prosecutions*,[153] in which the defendant, Mrs Connelly, had sent close-up colour photographs of dead twenty-one-week-old foetuses to pharmacists who stocked the

148 Abortion Act 1967, s 1(3).
149 ibid, s 1(1)(c).
150 ibid, s 1(1)(b).
151 [2011] EWHC 1430 (Admin).
152 [2003] UKHL 23.
153 [2007] EWHC 237 (Admin).

morning-after pill. She was convicted of sending a communication of an indecent or grossly offensive nature with the purpose of causing distress or anxiety, contrary to section 1 of the Malicious Communications Act 1988. Mrs Connelly appealed on the grounds that if communications of a political or educational nature could be 'indecent' or 'grossly offensive', the section breached her rights under Articles 9 and 10 of the Convention. Dyson J held that Article 10 was engaged, but that the interference was justified under 10(2), in order to protect the rights of others, namely the pharmacists' employees' right to be protected from receiving offensive material. He also held that, insofar as the defendant, when sending the images, was exercising her right under Article 9(1) of the Convention to manifest her religious beliefs, any interference with that right was justified under Article 9(2) for the same reasons.

It is, however, worth noting that Dyson J thought the position might have been different if the recipient of the photographs was not a person who requires such protection. He suggested that a doctor who routinely performs abortions might be less likely to find the photographs grossly offensive, and hence might be in a materially different position from an employee in a pharmacy which happens to stock the 'morning-after pill'. **16.156**

F. Injunctions to Prevent Abortions

In what, if any, circumstances, will a court grant an injunction to prevent a woman undergoing an abortion? Courts throughout the world have rejected claims for injunctions by putative 'fathers'.[154] Under the Abortion Act 1967, the decision whether or not to terminate a pregnancy is exclusively one for the patient and two doctors, subject to the various regulatory requirements. Third parties have no legal role to play in that process although, of course, in practice pregnant women often make joint decisions about termination with their sexual partners.[155] **16.157**

There are a number of grounds upon which 'fathers' have sought unsuccessfully to claim an injunction: (i) as a representative of the foetus in order to prevent a wrong being committed against it; (ii) on his own behalf to enforce his right to agree or be consulted as the foetus's 'father'; and (iii) as a public-spirited citizen on the basis that in the particular circumstances the abortion would be a crime. **16.158**

1. As litigation friend of the foetus

In order for a 'father' (or another person) to act on behalf of the foetus, the law would have to regard the foetus as a legal person possessing rights which could be enforced by a 'litigation friend'. In the UK, as elsewhere,[156] the courts have rejected the view that a foetus has legal personality. Hence, for example, a foetus cannot be made a ward of court.[157] It cannot bring an action for prenatal injury until after it is born,[158] and it is not protected by the criminal **16.159**

[154] *Attorney-General of Queensland* (ex rel Kerr) v T (1983) 46 ALR 275 (Aust HCt); *Tremblay v Daiglé* (1989) 62 DLR (4th) 634 (Can Sup Ct); *Kelly v Kelly* 1997 SLT 896 (CS (IH)); *Paton v Trustees of BPAS* [1978] 2 All ER 987 (Baker P) and *C v S* [1987] 1 All ER 1230 (Heilbron J and CA).

[155] R Ingham, E Lee, S Clements, and N Stone, 'Second-Trimester Abortions in England and Wales' (Centre for Sexual Health Research University of Southampton 2007).

[156] See, eg, the Canadian Supreme Court in *Winnipeg Child and Family Services (Northwest Area) v DFG* (1997) 152 DLR (4th) 193. See also *Tremblay v Daiglé* (1989) 62 DLR (4th) 634 (Can Sup Ct).

[157] *Re F (In Utero)* [1988] 2 All ER 193 (CA).

[158] *Burton v Islington HA* [1992] 2 All ER 833 (CA) and Congenital Disabilities (Civil Liability) Act 1976, s 4(2)(a).

law of murder or manslaughter if it is killed in utero.[159] In the context of 'paternal' injunctions, in *Paton v BPAS* [160] (upheld in *Paton v UK*[161]*)* and in *C v S*,[162] the courts have denied injunctions grounded in the foetus's 'rights'. In the latter case, Heilbron J (at first instance) stated that 'there is no basis for the claim that the foetus can be a party, whether or not there is any foundation for the contention with regard to the alleged threatened crime'.[163]

16.160 In the Scottish case of *Kelly v Kelly*[164] a 'father' claimed an interim interdict—the Scottish equivalent of an interlocutory injunction—to prevent his estranged wife from undergoing an abortion. The Inner House of the Court of Session approached his claim by asking whether the foetus had any legal rights at all which could be enforced on its behalf by the 'father'. The court concluded that it did not, since it was not a legal (or juridical) person until birth. The court referred to, and adopted, the English, Commonwealth, and American jurisprudence that denies the foetus legal status, and, as a result, held that the 'father' could have no claim on behalf of the foetus.

2. As the progenitor

16.161 The English courts have also dismissed the idea that the sexual partner of a pregnant woman has any right, common law or otherwise, in the foetus. The Abortion Act 1967 frames abortion as a clinical decision, reached between the two doctors and their patient, and giving a third party any rights in relation to that decision would run counter to basic principles of medical confidentiality.

16.162 Could a 'father' claim that his exclusion from the decision to undergo a termination breached his 'right to private and family life' protected by Article 8 of the Convention? The answer is almost certainly 'no'. In *X v UK*,[165] the European Commission accepted that the pregnant woman's husband's Article 8 rights were engaged in this situation but concluded that their infringement was justified under Article 8(2) as being necessary for the protection of the woman's Article 8 rights, because the termination was carried out to avert a risk to her physical and mental health. Interfering with the man's Article 8 right will be justified readily under Article 8(2) because of the burden to the pregnant woman of being forced—against her wishes—to carry a child to term and go through childbirth. The physical invasiveness of pregnancy and childbirth make it straightforward to justify prioritizing the pregnant woman's right to respect for her private life.

16.163 In *X v UK*, the husband also claimed a right to be consulted about the proposed abortion. Giving a man a right to be consulted would be less intrusive, but the Commission, following an earlier decision,[166] concluded that Article 8 could not be interpreted 'so widely as to embrace such procedural rights'.[167] An equally conclusive argument, it is suggested, lies in the effect such consultation could have on some pregnant women. For victims of domestic violence or women pregnant as a result of rape, there may be good reasons for fearing the

[159] *Attorney-General's Reference (No 3 of 1994)* [1997] 3 All ER 936 (HL). See also *R v Tait* [1989] 3 All ER 682 (CA): foetus not 'a third party' so that a threat to kill the foetus amounts to a crime of threatening to kill 'a third party' under s 16, Offences Against the Person Act 1861, s 16.

[160] [1978] 2 All ER 987 (Baker P).

[161] [1980] 3 EHRR 408.

[162] *C v S* [1987] 1 All ER 1230.

[163] ibid, 1235. The Court of Appeal decided the case on the basis that no crime would be committed under the Infant Life (Preservation) Act 1929. However, the judges did not doubt the approach of Heilbron J or that in *Paton*: see, especially, *per* Sir John Donaldson MR at 1243.

[164] 1997 SLT 896.

[165] *X v UK* [1981] 3 EHRR 408 (also known as *Paton v UK*).

[166] *Bruggemann and Scheuten v Federal Republic of Germany* (1977) DR 10 100, [1977] 3 EHRR 244.

[167] *X v UK*, n 164, at [27].

consequences if 'fathers' had a right to be consulted about a woman's decision to seek an abortion.

3. As guardian of the public interest

The final basis upon which to claim an injunction might be the criminal nature of the proposed abortion. An 'interested' individual might argue that an injunction should be granted to prevent the commission of an offence under s 58 of the Offences Against the Person Act 1861, if the Abortion Act 1967 has not been complied with. Leaving aside the difficulty of substantiating such an allegation where two doctors have, in good faith, concluded that the grounds for abortion in the 1967 Act are satisfied, could such an individual have locus standi? Absent a private wrong, a citizen will only in the most exceptional circumstances, if ever, be allowed by the courts to claim a civil remedy to prevent a criminal offence. In practice, only an application by the Attorney-General will be entertained by the courts, and then rarely. **16.164**

After the abortion has taken place, an interested bystander might want to refer the case to the police to investigate whether the abortion had been lawfully performed. Ultimately it would be for the Crown Prosecution Service to determine whether the evidential criteria for prosecution were satisfied and whether a criminal trial was in the public interest. **16.165**

In 2003, an application for judicial review was brought by the Rev. Joanna Jepson following her discovery that an abortion had been carried out on a foetus with a cleft palate after twenty-four weeks gestation.[168] Her argument was that when Parliament debated the 1990 amendments to the Abortion Act, which enabled abortion until birth for serious abnormalities, its intention had been that third trimester abortions would be justifiable only for extremely serious conditions, and not for fairly minor abnormalities like cleft palate. West Mercia police launched an investigation following her complaint, but no prosecution was instigated. In *Jepson v The Chief Constable of West Mercia Police Constabulary*, [169] Jackson J initially granted her leave to apply for judicial review of the decision not to prosecute, on the grounds that the case raised an issue of public importance, but admitted that she would face considerable obstacles at the full hearing. **16.166**

West Mercia police then conceded that their initial investigation may not have been sufficiently thorough, and the case was reopened under a different team of officers, who referred it to the Crown Prosecution Service (CPS). In 2005, the CPS determined that the doctors who authorized the abortion had acted in good faith.[170] **16.167**

G. Abortion and Homicide

1. Killing in utero

It is neither murder nor manslaughter to kill a foetus in utero. Homicide[171] requires the death of 'a person in being' (or *in rerum naturae*), namely that the child has an existence separate from its mother and is 'breathing and living by reason of its breathing through its own lungs alone, without deriving any of its living or power of living by or through any **16.168**

[168] *Jepson v The Chief Constable of West Mercia Police Constabulary* [2003] EWHC 3318.
[169] ibid.
[170] R Scott, 'Interpreting the Disability Ground of the Abortion Act' (2005) 64(2) CLJ 388.
[171] See P D G Skegg, *Law, Ethics and Medicine* (Clarendon 1994) 19–26.

connection with its mother'.[172] The rule was reaffirmed by the House of Lords in *Attorney-General's Reference (No 3 of 1994)*.[173]

2. Killing ex utero

16.169 What would be the position if the abortion procedure results in the foetus being born alive and dying ex utero? Could this be murder or manslaughter? It is helpful to consider two situations: first, where the doctor terminates the pregnancy intending to kill the foetus in utero, but for whatever reason the child dies after birth; and secondly, where the intention is to produce a live birth and let the child die. Clearly, in both situations it would have to be proved that the doctor's action in terminating the pregnancy caused or substantially contributed to the child's death after birth. This will be a factual matter turning upon expert evidence. More problematic are the questions of whether the doctor has the requisite mens rea for murder or manslaughter and, if he does, whether he has any defence on the basis that what he did was lawful under the Abortion Act 1967.

(i) Death in utero intended

16.170 **(a) Murder and manslaughter** Where a doctor intends to terminate the pregnancy by killing the foetus in utero, he will lack the mens rea of murder, namely an intention to kill or cause serious injury to a legal person since, prior to birth, the foetus is not a legal person. However, could the doctrine of 'transferred intention' apply,[174] that is, could the intention to kill the foetus be transferred to the child once born?[175] In *Attorney-General's Reference (No 3 of 1994)*[176] the House of Lords decided that for murder the doctrine of 'transferred intention' could not be applied where the intention was directed against the pregnant woman, because that would require a 'double transfer': first, from the pregnant woman to the foetus, and secondly, from the foetus to the child who is subsequently born. This was a fiction too far for the House of Lords. However, where the intention is directed against the foetus—as it will be in an abortion—the House of Lords' decision leaves open the possibility of transferring the intention from the foetus to the child who is subsequently born: a single transfer or 'fiction'. The better view is, however, that the doctor's intention cannot be transferred because he does not intend to kill a 'legal person'.

16.171 One possibility of an offence is where the doctor in the course of a termination inadvertently brings about a live birth and the child dies.[177] The doctor could commit the offence of manslaughter by gross negligence if his negligence in bringing about the live birth and subsequent death was sufficiently 'gross', that is, so bad that it should be criminal.[178]

16.172 **(b) A lawful justification** In any event, the law would probably recognize that the doctor would have a defence to a charge of murder or manslaughter if the child died after birth as the result of a lawful abortion. In *Attorney-General's Reference (No 3 of 1994)*,[179] the Court of Appeal stated that a doctor's action in terminating the pregnancy, unlike that of the violent assailant, would not be unlawful if the terms of the 1967 Act were complied with,

[172] *Rance v Mid-Downs HA* [1991] 1 All ER 801, 817 *per* Brooke J. For a discussion of the historical precedents, see S Atkinson,'Life, Birth and Live-Birth' (1904) 20 LQR 134.

[173] [1997] 3 All ER 936, 948 *per* Lord Mustill.

[174] For a discussion of the doctrine in this context see J Tempkin, 'Pre-Natal Injury, Homicide and the Draft Criminal Code' [1986] CLJ 414.

[175] As was held in *R v West* (1848) 2 Cox CC 500 (murder); and *Kwok Chak Ming v R* [1963] HKLR 349 (manslaughter).

[176] [1997] 3 All ER 936 (HL), overruling the Court of Appeal, [1996] 2 All ER 10.

[177] *R v Senior* (1832) 1 Mood CC 346 (gross negligence by midwife leading to death ex utero).

[178] See *R v Adomako* [1994] 3 All ER 79 (HL).

[179] [1996] 2 All ER 10 (CA). The issue was not addressed by the House of Lords.

and hence he would have a defence to a charge of murder or manslaughter. The basis for the defence is not clear, however.[180] The Abortion Act 1967 does not expressly or impliedly create a defence to a charge of murder or homicide. The legislative intention behind the 1967 Act is clear from its provisions, which remove criminal liability for an offence under 'the law relating to abortion' which means under the 1861 Act.[181]

(ii) Death ex utero intended

16.173 In the unlikely event that a doctor carried out an abortion intending the foetus to die after birth, he would commit murder if the child were 'born alive'. It is more likely in practice that a doctor might inadvertently bring about a live birth and the child then dies. If that were to happen, the doctor would commit the offence of gross negligence manslaughter if his negligence in bringing about the live birth and subsequent death was judged to be sufficiently serious.[182] It is arguable that the doctor would not have a defence or lawful justification.

16.174 Once born, the baby would be entitled to the same care from the doctor and protection from the law as any premature baby. Undoubtedly the surest way to avoid a charge of murder or manslaughter is to prevent the situation arising altogether by adopting a method of termination which will kill the foetus in utero. In practice, therefore, if there is any risk that a child might be born alive after a termination, foeticide will take place first.

H. Conclusion

16.175 The Abortion Act 1967 reflects the time at which it was passed. It does not give women the right to a termination, but rather protects doctors' discretion in judging whether a woman's situation justifies the termination of her pregnancy. Now fifty years old, there is also a significant discrepancy between the statute, which appears to allow abortion only where the pregnancy poses a risk to the woman's health, and the reality, which is that abortion is available on request in the first months of pregnancy. In practice, in the first and much of the second trimester, most doctors will accept that simply not wanting to be pregnant is sufficient reason for a woman to have an abortion.

16.176 There is, however, little political enthusiasm for modernizing the Abortion Act 1967.[183] In recent years, most attempts at reform have come from anti-abortion campaigners who have attempted to chip away at access to abortion in various ways: by reducing the time limit, for example, or introducing new counselling requirements. None has thus far been successful, but it could be argued that the recent furore over sex-selective abortions and pre-signed forms points to a new tactic among anti-abortion campaigners, namely to create a climate of suspicion and mistrust of doctors performing abortions. Certain newspapers appear to have embraced this agenda enthusiastically. Abortion in the UK may not be as politically contentious as it has been in the US, but it continues to be a hugely divisive issue.

---

[180] See A Grubb, 'Unborn Child (Pre-Natal Injury): Homicide and Abortion' (1995) 4 Med L Rev 302, 308–10 (Commentary).

[181] Offences Against the Person Act 1861, ss 1(1) and 6(1) and, since 1990, under the Infant Life (Preservation) Act 1929: s 5(1).

[182] *R v Senior*, n 176, and para 16.139.

[183] S Sheldon, 'A Missed Opportunity to Reform an Outdated Law' (2009) 4 Clinical Ethics 3–5.

(D) Death [illegible]

14 Conclusion

[182] Cf Smith, n 179, and para 16.139.

PART V

17

THE REGULATION OF MEDICINAL PRODUCTS AND MEDICAL DEVICES

Christopher Hodges

A. Common Principles of Product Regulation

1. The nature of product regulation

Product regulation is the system of administrative control over the marketing of products. It may potentially cover all the activities of producers and distributors, including design, research, manufacture, labelling, distribution, advertising, post-marketing vigilance, and recall. It does not currently generally impose regulatory duties on users of products (except for some human tissue products), but imposes regulatory duties on producers or others **17.01** responsible for placing products on the market, and sometimes distributors. Breach of such duties is enforceable by regulatory authorities, through sanctions applied by administrative authorities or ultimately by the criminal courts.

2. Overview of this chapter

17.02 There are many detailed legal provisions that regulate the placing on the market and safety of products. The aim of this chapter is to give an overview of the most important features that affect some of the products that are used in the medical context. It does not seek to be an exhaustive discussion but to outline the main points that would be relevant in a medical context. Accordingly, we do not deal with aspects of the legislation that relate to the more commercial aspects of products, such as on the data exclusivity provisions for research-based products, intellectual property, pricing, and approval for state reimbursement.

17.03 Many product types are regulated by specific, vertical regulatory provisions. Thus, medicinal products and medical devices are each subject to specific, and different, regimes. These are outlined respectively in Parts B and E of this chapter, and certain specific provisions for human tissues and cells, and for advanced therapy medicinal products, are respectively in Parts C and D. We do not deal with all product regulatory systems, such as those for personal protective equipment or metrology, nor with the general law on workplace health and safety.

17.04 Consumer products generally are regulated by horizontal provisions contained in the General Product Safety Regulations 2005, which implement Directive (EC) 2001/95. An outline of some aspects of these horizontal provisions is given in Part F of this chapter. The exact overlap between the horizontal general consumer safety (GPS) provisions and the vertical provisions (in Parts B to E) is a complex issue that is not fully clarified. In general, the GPS regime does not apply to medicinal products or to most activities relating to medical devices.

17.05 We begin, however, with an outline of some general features of the legal systems that apply to each of the systems that are discussed subsequently. These aspects need to be understood in order to understand the detail that follows, particularly relating to the overarching provisions of EU law.

3. Basis in EU law

(i) Competing objectives of Common Market trade and safety

17.06 The product regulatory systems that apply in the UK have their legal basis in EU law, as part of the legal rules that harmonize the laws relating to trade within the Community so as to create a common internal market.[1] There is an inherent conflict in the fact that rules which are in social terms intended to ensure the safety of products' users and bystanders are ultimately primarily justified and construed by the courts in legal terms on criteria relating to trading issues, albeit that such laws are required to achieve a high level of health and safety of persons.[2]

(ii) The development of product regulation

17.07 Historically, regulation arose in Europe as a result of safety concerns: regulation of medicinal products began in Europe during the 1960s following concern at phocomelia injuries

[1] Treaty on the Functioning of the European Union (TFEU), Art 114.
[2] ibid: the phrase 'high level of safety' is usually recited in individual product Directives.

caused by thalidomide. The first EU legislation on medicinal products[3] was enacted in 1965 (which did not apply to the UK until it joined the Community in 1972) and the first UK legislation was the Medicines Act 1968, effective from 1971: since then the initial rules have been regularly reformed and extended in scope. There was some confusion between the Community and UK national laws until the mid-1990s, when UK regulations were enacted that essentially applied the Community provisions.[4] The EU codified its legislation in 2001 but subsequent amendments and expansions have been made regularly. In 2008 the UK began a review aimed at modernizing its domestic legislation, which was scattered amongst the 1968 Act and a raft of statutory instruments, and codified the national medicines regulatory legislation in The Human Medicines Regulations 2012.[5]

Regulation of medical devices was introduced during the 1990s, having largely not existed before that time under national laws in Europe, as a result of the desire, which was held jointly by an increasingly multinational manufacturers' sector and the Community trade authorities, to avoid fragmentation of national systems. The legislative model adopted for medical devices was the EU's pre-existing 'new approach' template, which applies to many types of engineered products.[6] Both the 'new approach' and medical devices models were reviewed in the mid-2000s and subsequently extended and reformed as discussed later. **17.08**

Regulation of activities, rather than of products, was introduced for human blood and blood components from 2005[7] and for human tissues and cells from 2006.[8] Regulation of gene therapy medicinal products and somatic cell therapy medicinal products became mandatory from 2012 and of tissue engineered products from 2013.[9] **17.09**

(iii) Relationship between EU legal instruments and national law

The EU legal instruments that form the basis of product regulation are Directives[10] and Council Regulations—the latter being used several times in the pharmaceutical sector but less often in other sectors,[11] although codification of the medical devices legislation is likely in the Regulation in 2017. A Council Regulation has direct effect in the Member States whereas a Directive is binding on each Member State, which is obliged under the EC Treaty to implement the Directive into its national law. A Member State has the discretion to choose the manner in which the Directive may be implemented so long as the effect of the Directive is achieved under its national legal order. Most Member States transpose Directives into their national law by enacting domestic legislation that follows the text of the Directives closely, if not verbatim. However, differences between implementing laws can arise, particularly in relation to enforcement and sanctions for non-compliance, which are aspects almost entirely governed by Directives in broad terms so are mostly matters for the national authorities. It is the national law that is directly binding on people, companies, and operations within a particular state, not the Directive. However, since the Directive **17.10**

[3] Directive (EEC) 65/65. The European model was significantly based on the pre-existing model of the United States of America: see D Carpenter, *Reputational Power: Organizational Image and Pharmaceutical Regulation at the FDA* (Princeton University Press 2010).

[4] Such as the Medicines for Human Use (Marketing Authorisations Etc) Regulations 1994, SI 1994/3144.

[5] The Human Medicines Regulations 2012, SI 2012/1916.

[6] Council Resolution of 7 May 1985 on a new approach to technical harmonization and standards, OJ 1985 No C 136/1, 4.6.85.

[7] Directive (EC) 2002/98 and Commission Directives (EC) 2004/33, (EC) 2005/61, and 2005/62/EC.

[8] Directive (EC) 2004/23 and Commission Directives (EC) 2006/17 and (EC) 2006/86.

[9] Regulation (EC) 1394/2007 and Commission Directive (EC) 2009/120.

[10] Of the Council and the European Parliament: some Commission Directives are sometimes used.

[11] Regulations (EEC) 726/2004, 1394/2007, and 1901/2006.

ultimately governs the national law, people often colloquially refer to the Directive rather than the national law and this approach will be adopted in this chapter. Nevertheless, in any given situation, one must always check the relevant national law and consider, first, what are its provisions, second, to what extent they differ from the Directive and, third, whether any difference constitutes a breach of Community law by the Member State and what consequences might flow, such that the national provision might be unenforceable. As noted above, the primary domestic medicines regulatory provisions are The Human Medicines Regulations 2012. For medical devices, the basic national provisions are The Medical Devices Regulations 2002.

4. Major differences between the systems of regulation of medicinal products and medical devices

17.11 There are significant differences between the regulatory systems for medicinal products and medical devices. First, there is a fundamental difference in the regulatory methodology and architecture of the two systems. For medicinal products, the system requires companies to apply for and hold authorizations granted by competent authorities (ie, governmental licensing authorities) in order to undertake the activities of clinical development, placing a product on the market, manufacture, and wholesale distribution. In contrast, the onus for certifying regulatory compliance for medical devices[12] falls on the manufacturer. In some cases, the manufacturer requires the prior and continuing certification of some activities by a notified body (a private organization with a contractual relationship with the manufacturer but acting in accordance with regulatory powers authorized by a competent authority), and in other, numerically rare, cases the approval of a competent authority is required. The safety rationale for these different approaches to medicines and devices lies in the differences in the nature of the product types, their modes of operation, levels of inherent risk, and availability of safety data.[13] Medicines are fixed biomedical compounds that are ingested, so a level of confidence in their safety can only be assured through a testing regime. Medical devices, in contrast, are engineered products that are usually iterations of previous designs, so previous recorded knowledge can be relied on.

17.12 Secondly, the scope of the medicinal products regulatory system is appreciably wider than that for medical devices. The former regulates almost all commercial activity, encompassing pre-market testing, authorization to market, manufacture, labelling, advertising, distribution, retail supply,[14] post-marketing vigilance, and recall. In contrast, the law relating to medical devices only currently regulates the activities of placing on the market (encompassing certain aspects of pre-market testing, design, production and labelling) and, in part, post-marketing vigilance. The medical device regulatory system currently has no specific rules on advertising[15] or distribution[16] but reform of certain aspects is imminent.

---

[12] As with all Directives that are of the type originally prescribed in Council Resolution of 7 May 1985 on a new approach to technical harmonization and standards [1985] OJ C136/1, and now covered by the New Legislative Framework described below.

[13] A Parvizi and K Woods, 'Regulation of medicines and medical devices: contrasts and similarities' (2014) 14(1) Clinical Medicine 6.

[14] This is not covered directly by Community legislation but in the UK is subject to control partially under the Medicines Act 1968 (eg, licensing of premises) and partially under professional rules of pharmacists (enforced by the General Pharmaceutical Council): see G Appelbe and J Wingfield, *Dale and Appelbe's Pharmacy Law and Ethics* (10th edn, Pharmaceutical Press 2013).

[15] But see Directive (EC) 2005/29 on unfair business-to-consumer commercial practices, implemented by the Consumer Protection from Unfair Trading Regulations 2008, SI 2008/1277.

[16] See discussion below on the New Legislative Framework, 'new approach', medical devices, and general product safety provisions, especially in relation to distributors. Certain Member States have national provisions on distribution of medical devices.

B. Medicinal Products

1. Overview

Both the volume and complexity of the regulatory provisions and control for medicinal products are extensive. The controls extend over the conditions for animal and human research, pre-marketing safety conditions, control of manufacturing quality and distribution, advertising and informational parameters, and post-marketing vigilance requirements. The provisions have grown steadily since their inception in the 1960s[17] and are still being developed. This chapter gives an overview of the scope of the provisions that are of primary importance in relation to medical practice, notably the authorization and safety issues. This discussion covers the primary legal provisions, but there are in addition extensive supplementary guidelines issued by the authorities.[18] **17.13**

Specific measures apply to medicinal products intended for testing or use in paediatric subjects or patients.[19] A simplified registration procedure applies to homeopathic medicinal products that are administered orally, for which no specific therapeutic indication appears on the labelling or in any information relating to the product, and there is a sufficient degree of dilution.[20] A simplified registration procedure applies for herbal medicinal products, notably where evidence is produced of at least thirty years' traditional use.[21] **17.14**

The situation is somewhat confused by the existence of two approval systems for marketing authorizations: a *centralized system*, in which a single marketing authorization valid throughout the EU is granted by the European Commission after advice from the European Medicines Agency (EMA),[22] and a *decentralized* or *mutual recognition system*, in which marketing authorizations valid only for individual Member States are granted by national **17.15**

---

[17] Regulation followed recognition that the tragic effects of phocomelia in children were caused by thalidomide taken as a prophylactic for symptoms of morning sickness by pregnant women in the early 1960s: see H Teff and C R Munro, *Thalidomide: The Legal Aftermath* (Saxon House 1976). As a result, the European Community introduced Directive (EC) 65/65 in 1965 and the UK government introduced a non-statutory Committee on the Safety of Drugs (the 'Dunlop Committee') followed by the Medicines Act 1968. Considerable revision and extension of these provisions has been undertaken on a regular basis.

[18] Guidance documents at Community level comprise a sequence of categories from the less formal Concept Papers and Points to Consider and the more permanent guidelines issued by Working Parties of the European Medicines Agency, to the more formal guidelines authorized by that Agency's Committee for Medicinal Products for Human use in consultation with the competent authorities of the Member States and issued by the European Commission in its series of volumes entitled *The Rules Governing Medicinal Products in the European Union*. Reference should be made to <http://ec.europa.eu/health/documents/eudralex/index_en.htm>

[19] Regulations (EC) 1901/2006 and 1902/2006. See Communication from the Commission: Guideline on the format and content of applications for agreement or modification of a paediatric investigation plan and requests for waivers or deferrals and concerning the operation of the compliance check and on criteria for assessing significant studies: 2008/C 243/01. In the UK see the Human Medicines Regulations 2012, SI 2012/1916, Regs 50(6)(g) and 64(5)(b) and Sch 10.

[20] Directive (EC) 2001/83, Art 14, introduced by Directive (EC) 92/73. The medicinal product may not contain either more than one part per 10,000 of the mother tincture or more than 1/100th of the smallest dose used in allopathy with regard to active substances whose presence in an allopathic medicinal product results in the obligation to submit a doctor's prescription. A Member State may specify its own rules on the toxicological and pharmacological tests and clinical trials for homeopathic medicinal products (Directive (EC) 2001/83, Art 16.2); in the UK see the Medicines for Human Use (National Rules for Homeopathic Products) Regulations 2006, SI 2006/1952.

[21] Directive (EC) 2004/24.

[22] The name was subsequently shortened. Financial penalties for infringement of the centralized system are in Commission Regulation (EC) 658/2007.

competent authorities[23] for which abbreviated procedures of cross-referencing to the first state's assessment and approval are applied to applications for authorization by second and subsequent states. This duality of systems gives rise to two sets of legal instruments, albeit with many virtually identical provisions and considerable overlap. The centralized system is set out in Council Regulation (EC) 726/2004[24] and the mutual recognition system in Directive (EC) 2001/83, which comprises a comprehensive EU code relating to medicinal products for human use,[25] many provisions also applying under the centralized approval system.

17.16 This analysis will focus on medicinal products for human use rather than veterinary use, since this work is concerned primarily with the safety of products for humans. It should, however, be noted that, since the use of veterinary medicines is relevant to the safety of animals in the food chain, particular provisions govern maximum residue limits. The basic structure of the veterinary legislation and much of the detailed provisions are identical to the system governing human products but there are significant differences in matters of detail.

17.17 As discussed in paras 17.01–17.12, almost all of the UK law that governs this area is subject to provisions of EU law. For this reason, the following description and references are primarily based on the applicable EU law provisions, supplemented where necessary by the national provisions. Naturally, if a particular issue arises under UK law, it will be necessary to consider the national law provisions that apply, but it is always relevant to check that the national provisions conform to the governing EU provisions: if there are differences between the two, it is then necessary to consider whether and what legal consequences may flow, but that is an issue of EU law that is outside the scope of the current work.

17.18 The basis of the UK legislation[26] predated this state's entry into the European Economic Community, as it then was, with the result that the original national and Community schemes[27] differed somewhat in conception as well as detail. Although the national scheme has since been aligned as regards the provisions of EU law, there remain differences both in some general aspects and in many details.[28] It is impracticable to give here descriptions or references to many detailed matters, such as the extensive provisions of subsidiary legislation or the criminal enforcement provisions,[29] but the objective is to give a clear outline of the main structure.[30]

---

[23] In the UK the Licensing Authority comprises the Ministers of Health for England and Wales, Scotland, and Northern Ireland, whose functions are assisted by the Medicines Control Agency and who may be advised by expert committees such as the Committee on Safety of Medicines: see Medicines Act 1968, ss 1–4.

[24] Replacing Regulation (EEC) 2309/93.

[25] Since amended by Directives (EC) 2004/24, 2004/27, 2008/29, and 2009/53 and Regulations (EC) 1901/2006, 1394/2007, and 1234/2008. The 2001 Code consolidated and repealed 11 previous Directives. All the current EU legislation is accessible at <http://ec.europa.eu/enterprise/pharmaceuticals/eudralex/vol1_en.htm>.

[26] Medicines Act 1968.

[27] Which began in 1965 with Directive (EEC) 65/65.

[28] The Court of Appeal identified several substantial differences between the national and Community provisions which put the UK in breach of its Treaty obligations: *Organon Laboratories Ltd v Department of Health and Social Security* [1990] 2 CMLR 49. This led to introduction of the Medicines for Human Use (Marketing Authorisations Etc) Regulations 1994, SI 1994/3144, as amended, which confusingly disapplied parts of the Medicines Act 1968 and its various SIs. The position was simplified when a codification was introduced by the Human Medicines Regulations 2012, SI 2012/1916.

[29] See the Human Medicines Regulations 2012, SI 2012/1916; the Medicines Act 1968, ss 45, 67, 84, 91, 123, 124, and 125.

[30] For detailed review of the practical requirements relating to pharmaceutical companies see P Feldschreiber (ed), *The Law and Regulation of Medicines* (Oxford University Press 2008) and J P Griffin,

2. Products covered

(i) Definition of medicinal product

A medicinal product is defined as: **17.19**

(a) Any substance or combination of substances presented as having properties for treating or preventing disease in human beings; or
(b) Any substance or combination of substances which may be used in or administered to human beings either with a view to restoring, correcting or modifying physiological functions by exerting a pharmacological, immunological or metabolic action, or to making a medical diagnosis.[31]

The term 'substance' is defined as any matter, irrespective of origin, which may be human, animal, vegetable, or chemical.[32] There are two distinct tests under this definition of medicinal product: presentation and function, although the Court of Justice has commented that the two limbs cannot be regarded as strictly separate from each other, since a substance which is endowed with properties for treating or preventing disease in human beings or animals falls in principle within the scope of the 'function' limb.[33] Nevertheless, satisfaction of either test is sufficient for a substance to be considered a medicinal product. **17.20**

It is for the relevant competent authorities and the national courts to determine on a case-by-case basis, and consistent with the relevant Directives, the classification of each product having regard to all its characteristics, in particular to its composition, to its pharmacological properties (as they may be ascertained in the current state of scientific knowledge), to the way in which it is used, to the extent to which it is sold, to consumers' familiarity with it, and even to the risks which its use may entail.[34] The Court of Justice has itself recognized that differences in the classification of identical products may occur as between Member States and that this is 'difficult to avoid' under the current system.[35] **17.21**

It is clear that if a product satisfies either of the limbs of the definition of medicinal product it will be subject to the medicinal product legislation, to the exclusion of any other rules, such as those for cosmetics,[36] food,[37] or medical devices.[38] Thus, a product will be subject to the medicinal product regime even if it otherwise satisfies the definition of a cosmetic in Directive (EEC) 76/768 if, for example, it is presented as possessing properties for the treatment or prevention of illness or disease, or if it is intended to be administered with a view to restoring, correcting, or modifying physiological functions.[39] **17.22**

J Posner, and G R Barker (eds), *Textbook of Pharmaceutical Medicine* (7th edn, BMJ Books 2013). For academic analysis of the issue of legal certainty see N Chowdhury, *European Regulation of Medical Devices and Pharmaceuticals: Regulatee Expectations of Legal Certainty* (Ashgate 2014).

[31] Directive (EC) 2001/83, Art 1(2), as amended by Directive (EC) 2004/27.

[32] ibid, Art 1(3); Case C-35/85 *Procureur de la République v Gérard Tissier* [1985] ECR II-1207 (the definition applies not only to substances to be administered as they are but also to substances requiring processing, eg, by mixing, such as carrier constituents of radio-pharmaceuticals).

[33] Case C-290/90 *Re Eye Lotions: EC Commission v Germany* [1995] 2 CMLR 65.

[34] Case C-112/89 *Upjohn Co and Upjohn NV v Farzoo Inc and JAWMJ Kortmann* [1991] ECR I-1703; Case C-212/91 *Angelopharm GmbH v Feie und Hansestadt Hamburg* [1994] ECR I-00171; Case C-60/89 *The Republic v Jean Monteil and Daniel Samanni* [1992] 3 CMLR 425; Case C-290/90, n 33.

[35] Case Case C-290/90 *Re Eye Lotions: EC Commission v Germany* [1995] 2 CMLR 65; Case C-369/88 *Delattre* [1991] ECR I-1487.

[36] Case Case C-60/89 *The Republic v Jean Monteil and Daniel Samanni* [1992] 3 CMLR 425.

[37] Case C-219/91 *Ter Voort* [1995] ECR I-5485.

[38] Directive (EEC) 93/42, Art 1(5)(e).

[39] Case Case C-60/89 *The Republic v Jean Monteil and Daniel Samanni* [1992] 3 CMLR 425.

17.23 The 'presentation' limb of the definition is to be construed broadly.[40] The Court of Justice has held that a product is 'presented for treating or preventing disease' when it is expressly 'indicated' or 'recommended' as such, possibly by means of labels, leaflets, or oral representations: consequently herbal teas which are expressly indicated or recommended as having therapeutic or prophylactic properties are to be regulated as medicines.[41] However, the Court of Justice has also held that it is not necessary that the product be expressly indicated or recommended as suitable for treating or preventing disease, for example by means of labels, leaflets, or oral representation: it is sufficient that any averagely well-informed consumer gains the impression, even impliedly (so long as it is definitive) that the product would, having regard to its presentation, have those properties.[42] However, in one case it was decided that the fact that a product is antiseptic and antibacterial is not conclusive of its medicinal function since many non-medicinal products, including soap, also display such properties.[43]

17.24 The 'function' limb of the definition:

> must be given a sufficiently broad interpretation to cover all substances capable of having an effect on the actual functioning of the body. However, that criterion does not serve to include substances such as certain cosmetics, which while having an effect on the human body, do not significantly affect the metabolism and thus do not, strictly, modify the way in which it functions.[44]

The function limb is 'designed to cover products whose pharmacological properties have been scientifically observed and which are genuinely designed to make a medical diagnosis or to restore, correct or modify physiological functions'.[45] The application of the definition of 'medicinal product' can be far from straightforward and there can, in particular, be room for more than one opinion in relation to the 'function' test, where the result can be very much a question of judgment.[46] Accordingly, the Court of Appeal has said that a competent authority is to be allowed a margin of appreciation in decisions on such questions since, in discharging their initial heavy responsibility of protecting public health, the Agency is an expert body, has accumulated experience in relation to other products and has to develop a consistent policy between similar products.[47]

17.25 A Member State may, at its discretion, enforce national legislation prohibiting or restricting the sale, supply, or use of medicinal products as contraceptives or abortifacients.[48]

(ii) Products not covered

17.26 The regulatory controls in the Community code do not apply to:[49]

---

[40] Case C-227/82 *Van Bennekom* [1983] ECR I-3883; Case C-60/89 *The Republic v Jean Monteil and Daniel Samanni* [1992] 3 CMLR 425.

[41] Case Case C-212/91 *Angelopharm GmbH v Feie und Hansestadt Hamburg* [1994] ECR I-00171.

[42] Case C-227/82 *Van Bennekom* [1983] ECR I-3883 (external form and concentration may be relevant, so as to render a vitamin a medicinal product); Case C-60/89 *The Republic v Jean Monteil and Daniel Samanni* [1992] 3 CMLR 425.

[43] Case C-60/89 *The Republic v Jean Monteil and Daniel Samanni* [1992] 3 CMLR 425.

[44] Case C-112/89 *Upjohn Co and Upjohn NV v Farzoo Inc and JAWMJ Kortmann* [1991] ECR I-1703, 1742; see also C-227/82 *Van Bennekom* [1983] ECR I-3883.

[45] Case C-319/05 *Commission v Germany* ECR [2007] I-09811, holding that a product containing only garlic is not a medicinal product.

[46] *R v Medicines Control Agency, ex p Pharma Nord* (UK) Ltd [1998] 3 CMLR 109 (CA).

[47] ibid. See A Guide To What Is A Medicinal Product: Guidance Note No 8 (MHRA revised 2012).

[48] Directive (EEC) 2001/83, Art 4(4) (introduced by Directive (EEC) 93/39, Art 1(5)).

[49] Directive (EC) 2001/83, Art 3.

(i) any medicinal product prepared in a pharmacy in accordance with a medical prescription for an individual patient (commonly known as the magistral formula);
(ii) a medicinal product which is prepared in a pharmacy in accordance with the prescriptions of a pharmacopoeia and is intended to be supplied directly to the patients served by the pharmacy in question (commonly known as the officinal formula);
(iii) medicinal products intended for research and development trials;
(iv) intermediate products intended for further processing by an authorised manufacturer;
(v) any radionuclides in the form of sealed sources;
(vi) whole blood, plasma or blood cells of human origin, except for plasma which is prepared by a method involving an industrial process.

A Member State may, in accordance with legislation in force and to fulfil special needs, exclude from the provisions of Directive (EC) 2001/83 medicinal products supplied in response to a bona fide unsolicited order, formulated in accordance with the specifications of an authorized health care professional, and for use by his individual patients on his direct personal responsibility.[50] Specific provisions apply to homeopathic medicinal products[51] and to herbal medicinal products.[52] **17.27**

3. Requirement for a marketing authorization: Data requirements

(i) The primary criteria of safety, efficacy and quality

Regulatory decisions in relation to the grant of marketing authorizations are to be based on three criteria,[53] namely safety, efficacy,[54] and quality, which are designed to ensure the protection of public health. This is established as a matter of policy in the recitals to the governing legislation:[55] **17.28**

> In the interest of public health, authorisation decisions . . . should be taken on the basis of the objective criteria of quality, safety and efficacy of the medicinal product concerned, to the exclusion of economic and other considerations. However, Member States should be able exceptionally to prohibit the use on their territory of medicinal products for human use which infringe objectively defined concepts of public policy and public morality . . .

Safety is tested by the authorities in applying a risk–benefit balance for a product. Thus, an application for a marketing authorization shall be refused if, inter alia, the risk–benefit balance is not considered favourable.[56] Recitals to Regulation (EC) 726/2004 stress the **17.29**

---

[50] Directive (EC) 2001/83, Art 5.

[51] ibid, Arts 13–16.

[52] ibid, Arts 16a–16i.

[53] The risks of counterfeit medicines have been an increasing concern, and raise issues of safety, efficacy, and quality: see *Green Paper: Combating Counterfeiting and Piracy in the Single Market*, COM (98) 567, and Communication from the *Commission: Follow-up to the Green Paper on Combating Counterfeiting and Piracy in the Single Market*, COM (2000) 789.

[54] The concept of the protection of public health means that a medicinal product must not only not be harmful but also must be effective, catching products which are not sufficiently effective or which do not have the effect which their presentation might lead to expect: Case C-219/91 *Ter Voort* [1992] ECR I-5485; Order of the President of the Court in Case C-471/00 *Commission of the European Communities and Cambridge Healthcare Supplies Ltd* (11 April 2001); Joined Cases T-74/00, T-76/00, T-83/00 to T-85/00, T-132/00, T-137/00, and T-141/00 *Artegodan GmbH v European Commission* (26 November 2002).

[55] Regulation (EC) 726/2004, recital 13, closely repeated from Regulation (EEC) 2309/93, recital 3; virtually identical wording had been used in Council Directive (EEC) 93/93, third recital, which amended the primary measure, Council Directive (EEC) 65/65. The three criteria are set out in the Medicines Act 1968, s 19, but the Community provisions are applied to nearly all products by virtue of the Medicines for Human Use (Marketing Authorisations Etc) Regulations 1994.

[56] Directive (EC) 2001/83, Art 26 as amended. 'Risk–benefit balance' is defined as an evaluation of the positive therapeutic effects of the medicinal product in relation to the risks. 'Risks related to use of the medicinal product' are defined as (a) any risk relating to the quality, safety or efficacy of the medicinal

importance of making decisions on the basis of criteria of safety, efficacy, and quality, and of making decisions that are of the highest possible quality:

> Provision should be made for the quality, safety and efficacy criteria [in previous Directives] to apply to medicinal products authorized by the Community and it should be possible to assess the risk-benefit balance of all medicinal products when they are placed on the market, at the time of the renewal of the authorization and at any other time the competent authority deems appropriate.
>
> . . .
>
> The chief task of the Agency should be to provide Community institutions and Member States with the best possible scientific opinions so as to enable them to exercise the powers regarding the authorization and supervision of medicinal products conferred upon them by Community legislation in the field of medicinal products. Only after a single scientific evaluation procedure addressing the quality, safety and efficacy of high technology medicinal products has been conducted by the Agency, applying the highest possible standards, should a marketing authorisation be granted by the Community, and this should be done by means of a rapid procedure ensuring close co-operation between the Commission and Member States.

17.30 In considering whether a product can be safely administered, Mustill LJ has commented:

> . . . there is no absolute standard of safety. Very few drugs are entirely free from the risk of inducing adverse side effects in some patients. The question must always be whether the degree of risk is sufficiently low to be acceptable, and this cannot be addressed without an appreciation of the benefits to be gained from taking a risk of that degree.[57]

17.31 The President of the Court of Justice has said that in decisions on grant, variation, suspension, or revocation of a marketing authorization, the requirements of public health unquestionably take precedence over economic considerations, and involve a benefit/risk assessment, in which the degree of harmfulness which the authority may regard as acceptable depends on the benefits which the medicinal product is considered to provide.[58] The means by which the above policy considerations are achieved in practice will now be examined.

(ii) Requirement for a marketing authorization

17.32 No medicinal product may be placed on the market within the Community unless the relevant authority has granted a marketing authorization.[59] For certain medicinal products the relevant authority is the EMA, which commenced operations on 1 January 1995, operating the centralized system.[60] Marketing authorizations granted by the EMA are valid throughout the European Economic Area (EEA). The relevant competent authorities for other medicinal products are those of each Member State,[61] which each has jurisdiction over its national territory.

---

product as regards patients' health or public health, and (b) and risk of undesirable effects on the environment. See Directive (EC) 2001/83, Art 1, points 28 and 28a, inserted by Directive (EC) 2004/27.

[57] *Organon Laboratories Ltd v Department of Health and Social Security* [1990] 2 CMLR 49 (CA), 78.

[58] Order of the President of the Court in Case C-471/00 *Commission of the European Communities and Cambridge Healthcare Supplies Ltd* [2001] ECR I-02865.

[59] Regulation (EEC) 726/2004, Art 3; Directive (EC) 2001/83, Art 6(1); the Medicines for Human Use (Marketing Authorisations Etc) Regulations 1994, reg 3 and Sch 1 (formerly the Medicines Act 1968, s 7) prohibits inter alia the placing on the market of a medicinal product save in accordance with a marketing authorization (product licence), subject to certain exceptions.

[60] Derived from biotechnological processes, specified categories of new products, and certain generic, paediatric use, or orphan medicinal products.

[61] The Licensing Authority for the UK is discussed at para 17.48. The administrative agency is the Medicines and Healthcare products Regulatory Agency (MHRA).

All decisions to grant, refuse, vary, suspend, withdraw, or revoke a marketing authorization shall state in detail the reasons on which they are based and be notified to the party concerned.[62] A marketing authorization shall not be refused, varied, suspended, withdrawn, or revoked except on the grounds set out in the legislation.[63] It may not be dispensed with for imported generic products or granted on grounds of price.[64] Applications for variations of marketing authorizations must be made in accordance with prescribed procedures.[65] **17.33**

(iii) Application for a marketing authorization: Particulars and documents recording the results of tests and clinical trials

In order to obtain a marketing authorization, the person responsible for placing the product on the market must submit an application to the relevant authority accompanied by the particulars and documents referred to in Article 8(3) and Annex I of Directive (EC) 2001/83.[66] Exemption from supplying comprehensive clinical data for a medicinal product may be granted for medicinal products which are subject to, or eligible for, the centralized procedure and which: [67] (a) aim at the treatment, prevention, or medical diagnosis of seriously debilitating diseases or life-threatening diseases; or (b) are to be used in emergency situations in response to public health threats recognized by the World Health Organization of the European Community; or (c) are designated as orphan medicinal products.[68] In such cases, a conditional marketing authorization may be granted for one year where the risk-benefit balance is positive, it is likely that the applicant will be in a position to provide the comprehensive clinical data, unmet medical needs will be fulfilled, and the benefit to public health of the immediate availability of the product outweighs the risk inherent in the fact that data are still required. Conditions may include that the holder complete ongoing studies or conduct new studies. **17.34**

The particulars and documents that must normally accompany an application are: **17.35**

(a) Name or corporate name and permanent address of the applicant, and, where applicable, of the manufacturer;
(b) Name of the medicinal product;
(c) Qualitative and quantitative particulars of all the constituents of the medicinal product in usual terminology, but excluding empirical chemical formulae, with mention of the international non-proprietary name recommended by the World Health Organization where such name exists or a reference to the relevant chemical name;
(d) Environmental risk evaluation and specific arrangements to limit impact;
(d) Brief description of the manufacturing method;

---

[62] Regulation (EEC) 726/2004, Art 81 and Directive (EC) 2001/83, Art 125. A relevant authority or advisory committee must be allowed a broad discretion by the courts in judicial review cases in considering how best to approach scientific evidence (such as evidence of a lack of safety in overdose by the elderly) and what weight to give to it: *In the matter of Organon Laboratories Ltd* (CA Transcript CO/1738/88, 17 February 1989).

[63] Regulation (EEC) 726/2004, Art 81.2 and Directive (EC) 2001/83, Art 126.

[64] Case C-185/10 *European Commission v Republic of Poland*, unreported.

[65] Commission Regulation (EC) 1084/2003 governs products authorized under the centralized procedure, and Commission Regulation (EC) 1085/2003 governs those authorized under the decentralized mutual recognition procedure. The centralized and decentralized procedures for variations are to be subject to harmonized rules under a Commission Regulation by 20 January 2011: Directive 2009/53/EC and Commission Regulation (EC) 1234/2008. See also Commission Guidelines 2013/C 223/01.

[66] See also Regulation 726/2004, Art 6; Medicines Act 1968, s 18; the Human Medicines Regulations 2012, SI 2012/1916, Part 5.

[67] Commission Regulation (EC) 507/2006.

[68] Regulation (EC) 141/2000 sets out the requirements and procedure for designation as an orphan medicinal product.

(e) Therapeutic indications, contra-indications, and adverse reactions;
(f) Posology, pharmaceutical form, method and route of administration, and expected shelf life;
(g) If applicable, reasons for any precautionary and safety measures to be taken for the storage of the medicinal product, its administration to patients and for the disposal of waste products, together with an indication of potential risks presented by the medicinal product for the environment;
(h) Description of the control methods employed by the manufacturer;
(i) Results of:[69]
— pharmaceutical (physico-chemical, biological, or microbiological) tests,
— pre-clinical (toxicological and pharmacological) tests,
— clinical trials;[70]
(ia) A detailed description of the pharmacovigilance and, where appropriate, of the risk-management system which the applicant will introduce;
(ib) A statement to the effect that clinical trials carried out outside the European Union meet the ethical requirements of Directive 2001/20/EC;
(j) A summary, in accordance with Article 11, of the product characteristics, a mock-up of the outer packaging, containing specified details, and of the immediate packaging of the medicinal product, containing specified details, together with a package leaflet in prescribed form;
(k) A document showing that the manufacturer is authorized in his own country to produce medicinal products;
(l) Copies of any authorization obtained in another Member State or in a third country to place the medicinal product on the market together with a list of Member States to whom applications have been submitted, including details of any refusal decisions;
(m) Copy of any orphan designation;
(n) Proof that the applicant has the services of a qualified person responsible for pharmacovigilance and has the necessary means for notification of any adverse reaction suspected of occurring either in the Community or in a third country.

17.36 In summary, a considerable quantity of data must be produced to the competent authority in support of an application for a marketing authorization. The data must record that the required tests and clinical trials on the product have been carried out so as to found an

[69] There are certain exceptions to the provision of pre-clinical tests and clinical trials, notably where an applicant can demonstrate: (i) that the product is a generic (ie the same qualitative and quantitative composition in active substances and the same pharmaceutical form, whose bioequivalence has been demonstrated in bioavailability studies) of a reference medicinal product which has been authorized for not less than eight years in a Member State or the Community, in which case the applicant's medicinal product may not be placed on the market for ten years after the reference product, although the period is extended to eleven years if the original authorization holder has obtained in the first eight years an authorization for one or more new indications that are held to bring a significant clinical benefit in comparison with existing therapies; or (ii) that the active substances have been in well-established medicinal use within the Community for at least ten years, with recognized efficacy and an acceptable level of safety. In the latter case the test and trial results shall be replaced by appropriate scientific literature: Directive (EC) 2001/83, Arts 10 and 10a and Annex I, Pt II, ss 1–3, as amended by Directive (EC) 2004/27. In relation to the second exception, under which the scientific literature in the public domain must be complete, see Case C-440/93 *R v Licensing Authority of the Department of Health and Norgine Ltd, ex p Scotia Pharmaceuticals Ltd* [1995] ECR I-2851: 'the abridged procedure in no way relaxes the requirements of safety and efficacy which must be met.' See also Case C-368/96 *R v The Licensing Authority established by the Medicines Act 1968 (acting by The Medicines Control Agency), ex p Generics (UK) Ltd* [1999] ECR I-7967, which affirmed the same point.

[70] Regulation (EC) 536/2014 will introduce new rules on clinical trials from June 2016, replacing Directive (EC) 2001/20.

opinion that the product affords a sufficient level of safety and efficacy. Production of this data is time-consuming and expensive. The cost of developing a new drug was put in the mid-2000s at over $800 million, and rising at an annual rate of 7.4 per cent above general price inflation.[71]

The requirements for the results of tests and clinical trials in Article 8(3)(i) are considerably amplified in Annex I to Directive (EC) 2001/83[72] and amplified in the Commission's Notice to Applicants.[73] The main headings are set out in Table 17.1. **17.37**

(iv) Expert reports

Signed reports from experts in each of three disciplines for which documents are required (analysis, pharmacology and similar experimental sciences, and clinical trials) are to be submitted with the particulars and documents of the application.[74] These reports fulfil two main functions: first, verification that the experts have carried out the relevant tasks and have described the results objectively; secondly, to describe their observations in accordance with the requirements of Annex I of Directive (EC) 2003/63. **17.38**

Where applicable, the experts must also state the grounds for using published references rather than the results of clinical studies.[75] **17.39**

In effect, therefore, there is expert assessment giving an overview of the scientific aspects. This function effectively constitutes a regulatory verification and assessment prior to that of the competent authority. An expert need not, however, be independent of the applicant. The competent authority may use its power of assessment to ascertain whether or not the applicant, and consequently the expert who prepared the documentation supporting the application, took account of current technical developments and scientific progress and whether or not he or she was satisfied that the scientific publications were up to date.[76] **17.40**

(v) Duration of a marketing authorization

A marketing authorization is valid for five years on and is renewable thereafter for an indefinite period on the basis of a re-evaluation of the risk–benefit balance by the competent authority, unless the competent authority decides, on justified grounds relating to pharmacovigilance, to proceed with one additional five-year renewal.[77] An authorization may be granted in exceptional circumstances subject to conditions, such as the carrying out of further studies or the notification of adverse reactions.[78] **17.41**

---

71 Boston Consulting Group, *A Revolution in R&D: How Genomics and Genetics are Transforming the Biopharmaceutical Industry* (Boston Consulting Group 2001); J DiMasi, R W Hanson, and H G Grabowski, 'The Price of Innovation: New Estimates of Drug Development Costs', (2003) 22 Journal of Health Economics 151–85; D W Light, and R N Warburton, 'Extraordinary Claims Require Extraordinary Evidence' (2005) 24(5) Journal of Health Economics 1030–33.

72 Amended by Directive (EC) 2003/63. First introduced by Directive (EEC) 75/318, then significantly amended by Directive (EEC) 91/507.

73 Available in EudraLex, Vol 2: Pharmaceutical legislation on notice to applicants and regulatory guidelines for medicinal products for human use, at <http://ec.europa.eu/health/documents/eudralex/vol-2/index_en.htm>.

74 Directive (EC) 2001/83, Art 12 (first introduced by Directive (EEC) 75/319, Art 2); Regulation (EC) 726/2004, Art 6.

75 Directive (EC) 2001/83, Art 12(2).

76 Case C-440/93 *R v Licensing Authority of the Department of Health and Norgine Ltd, ex p Scotia Pharmaceuticals Ltd* [1995] ECR I-2851.

77 Regulation (EC) 726/2004, Art 14; Directive (EC) 2001/83, Art 24 as amended; Medicines Act 1968, s 24.

78 Directive (EC) 2001/83, Art 22 and Regulation (EC) 726/2004, Art 14(8).

(vi) Procedures for assessment

17.42 (a) **The centralized procedure and the CHMP** A centralized application is considered by the Committee for Medicinal Products for Human Use (CHMP), which is responsible for formulating the opinions of the EMA[79] on any question concerning the admissibility of the files submitted, the granting, variation, suspension or withdrawal of a marketing authorization and pharmacovigilance.

17.43 The CHMP consists of representatives of the Member States and of the Commission and the EMA and draws up its own rules of procedure.[80] The CHMP prepares its opinion on the application.[81] It is required to verify that the particulars and documents submitted are those required by Article 8 of Directive (EC) 2001/83 and Annex I of Directive (EC) 2003/63 and to examine whether the conditions specified in the Regulation for issuing a marketing authorization for the medicinal product are satisfied. It has power to ask for a test of the medicinal product, its starting materials and, if need be, its intermediate products or other constituent materials to be carried out, in order to ensure that the control methods employed by the manufacturer and described in the application documents are satisfactory. It also has power, where appropriate, to request the applicant to supplement the particulars accompanying the application within a specific time limit.

17.44 Where the opinion of the CHMP is that the application does not satisfy the criteria for authorization, or the summary of product characteristics proposed by the applicant should be amended, or the labelling or package leaflet is not in compliance with Title V of Directive (EC) 2001/83, or the authorization should be granted subject to conditions appropriate for conditional marketing authorization or exceptional circumstances and reviewed annually, the EMA must forthwith inform the applicant, who may appeal to the EMA/CHMP. The EMA forwards the final opinion of the CHMP to the Commission, the Member States, and the applicant, together with a report describing the assessment of the product and stating the reasons for its conclusions.[82] Where the opinion is favourable, the opinion annexes a draft summary of the product characteristics, details of any conditions or restrictions, which are recommended to be imposed, the draft text of the labelling and package leaflet proposed by the applicant, and the assessment report.

17.45 A centralized marketing authorization is issued by the Commission. The Commission issues a draft of the decision and has power to make a decision that is not in accordance with the opinion of the EMA, in which case its draft decision shall annex a detailed explanation of the reasons for the differences.[83] The Commission's draft decision is forwarded to the Member States and the applicant. It is also forwarded to the Standing Committee on Medicinal Products for Human Use, whose function is to 'assist' the Commission. This Committee delivers its opinion on the draft decision, based on weighted majority voting in accordance with Article 148(2) of the Treaty.

17.46 The Commission shall adopt the measures envisaged if they are in accordance with the opinion of the Committee. If the measures envisaged are not in accordance with the opinion of the Committee, or if no opinion is delivered, the Commission shall, without delay, submit a proposal to the Council, which shall act by a qualified majority. If, on the expiry of three months from the date of referral to the Council, the Council has not acted, the

79 Established under Regulation (EC) 726/2004 Art 5.
80 Regulation (EC) 726/2004, Art 61.
81 ibid, Art 6.
82 ibid, Art 9.
83 ibid, Art 10.

Table 17.1 Analytical, Pharmacotoxicological and Clinical Standards and Protocols in Respect of the Testing of Medicinal Products

Table of Contents

(*continued*)

2.	Somatic cell therapy medicinal products (human and xenogeneic)
3.	Specific requirements for gene therapy and somatic cell therapy(human and xenogeneic) medicinal products regarding Modules 4 and 5
3.1.	Module 4
3.2.	Module 5
3.2.1.	Human pharmacology and efficacy studies
3.2.2.	Safety
4.	Specific Statement on Xeno-transplantation Medicinal Products.

Commission shall adopt the proposed measures, save where the Council has decided against the measures by a simple majority.[84] Each Member State may forward written observations to the Commission and where, in the opinion of the Commission, these observations raise important new questions of a scientific or technical nature that have not been addressed in the opinion of the EMA, the matter is referred back to the EMA for further consideration.

(b) The Mutual recognition procedure An application for a marketing authorization may be made to a national competent authority for a marketing authorization that is valid solely in that authority's Member State. The procedure which must be followed, including the particulars and documents which must be submitted, and the criteria which apply to the grant of the application are essentially as set out above. The national authority has similar powers to the EMA in relation to testing the substance and requiring the applicant to supplement the particulars accompanying the application in respect of the items listed in Article 8 of Directive (EC) 2001/83.[85] Similarly, it is authorized to examine the application to verify whether the particulars submitted comply with Article 8 and examine whether the conditions for issuing an authorization are complied with. **17.47**

An application for a marketing authorization for the medicinal substance which applies in a second or further Member State is subject to the decentralized (mutual recognition) procedure. Under this procedure, the applicant for (or holder of) the marketing authorization in the first Member State may request the competent authority of the first Member State, known as the 'reference Member State',[86] to prepare or update an assessment report, and forward it to the other Member States to whom the authorization holder has applied.[87] Any one of the other Member States may oppose the application only if it considers that there are grounds of potential serious risk to public health,[88] giving a detailed explanation of its reasons, after which the matter is referred to a coordination group of Member States, failing which the matter is referred to the CHMP for arbitration. The EMA then reports its opinion to the Commission for a binding decision.[89] **17.48**

[84] ibid, Art 87.

[85] Directive (EC) 2001/83, Art 19.

[86] Directive (EC) 2001/83, Art 28.

[87] ibid, Art 28.

[88] See Guideline on the definition of a potential serious risk to public health in the context of Art 29(1) and (2) of Directive (EC) 2001/83—March 2006.

[89] Directive (EC) 2001/83, Arts 27–34. It is no longer possible for the applicant to prevent this procedure by withdrawing an application in the Member State where an authority raises objections.

(vii) The UK authorities

17.49 The competent authority in the UK responsible for the grant, renewal, variation, suspension, and revocation of authorizations is the licensing authority, which is a body consisting of the Ministers of Health and Agriculture.[90] Any function conferred on the licensing authority under the Medicines Act may be performed by one such Minister acting alone, or by two or more of them acting jointly.[91] The Medicines Commission may give advice to the Ministers on relevant matters.[92] Further committees may be established to advise Ministers on particular issues:[93] one such is the Commission on Human Medicines.[94] The administrative agency is the Medicines and Healthcare products Regulatory Agency (MHRA).

(viii) Grounds for refusal

17.50 The test for refusal of an application for a marketing authorization is different under the centralized and decentralized/mutual recognition procedures. Under the former, the authorization shall be refused if, after verification of the required information and particulars submitted, 'it appears that the applicant has not properly or sufficiently demonstrated the quality, safety or efficacy of the medicinal product'.[95] Authorization shall likewise be refused if the particulars and documents provided by the applicant are incorrect or if the labelling and package leaflets proposed by the applicant are not in accordance with the requirements.[96]

17.51 In contrast, the test under the decentralized/mutual recognition procedure for refusal of an application is if, after verification of the particulars and documents, it is clear that: (a) the risk–benefit balance is not considered to be favourable; or (b) that its therapeutic efficacy is insufficiently substantiated by the applicant; or (c) that its qualitative and quantitative composition is not as declared; or if the particulars and documents do not comply with the requirements.[97]

17.52 It is inexplicable that different tests and concepts are stated, namely 'safety' and 'risk–benefit balance'. It may be argued that there are differences between the two wordings used, in particular that there is a difference between it being *appearing to be demonstrated that a product is safe* and it being *considered that the risk–benefit balance is favourable*. The former test is, perhaps generic with overtones of political reassurance, whereas the latter test is (slightly) more specific and is in fact that used by regulators in practice. In the result, the required level of safety under the centralized procedure test is not defined and is, therefore, legally uncertain, whereas the decentralized/mutual recognition test states a supposedly objective standard, although it still begs many questions.

4. Authorization of research

17.53 It has been said above that an applicant for a marketing authorization must include in the documents submitted the results of physico-chemical, biological or microbiological tests, pharmacological tests, and clinical trials. The carrying out of all these tests and trials is

[90] Medicines Act 1968, ss 6 and 1.
[91] ibid, s 6(2).
[92] ibid, ss 2 and 3.
[93] ibid, s 4.
[94] Established in 2005 under the Medicines Act 1968, s 3 and the Medicines (Advisory Bodies) Regulations 2005, SI 2005/1094, to replace the Committee of Safety of Medicines: see now the Human Medicines Regulations 2012, SI 2012/1916, Part 2.
[95] Regulation (EC) 726/2004, Art 12, see earlier Regulation (EEC) 2309/93, Art 11 and Directive (EEC) 65/65, Art 5.
[96] ibid.
[97] Directive (EEC) 2001/83, Art 26, as amended.

subject to regulatory requirements, which lay down uniform rules for the compilation and presentation of dossiers to competent authorities. A clinical trial should only be conducted if the rights, safety, dignity, and well-being of the subjects involved in them are protected, and the it is designed to generate data that is reliable and robust.[98] The interests of the subjects should always take priority over all other interests.[99] National provisions may provide sanctions on those involved in research for breach of the rules,[100] but the primary issue for the purposes of this discussion is to ensure that reliable data are produced on which sound decisions on the safety and efficacy of products can be based: thus the principal result of non-compliance for product regulatory purposes would be that the data would be wholly or partially invalidated.

(i) Research with animals

First, the individuals, facilities, and performance of animal experiments are regulated.[101] **17.54** Laboratory experiments must be carried out in accordance with the standard of good laboratory practice (GLP),[102] which is linked to the OECD principles of GLP. All test procedures shall correspond to the state of scientific progress at the time and shall be validated procedures, the results of validation studies being provided.[103] GLP[104] also applies to laboratories carrying out tests on chemical products,[105] which are subject to inspection and verification.[106] Provisions also apply regarding the protection of animals used for experimental and other scientific purposes.[107] It is prohibited to sell or supply a medicinal product for the purposes of a medicinal test on animals without an authorization or unless a specified exemption applies.[108]

(ii) Research with humans

Regulation (EU) No 536/2014 sets out the rules on clinical trials on medicinal products for **17.55** human use (the Clinical Trials Directive).[109] A clinical trial may be conducted only where the following conditions are fulfilled:

(a) the anticipated benefits to the subjects or to public health justify the foreseeable risks and inconveniences and compliance with this condition is constantly monitored;
(b) the subjects or, when a subject is not able to give informed consent, his or her legally designated representative, have been informed of the information specified;[110]

---

98 Regulation (EU) No 536/2014, recital 1 and Art 3. See previously Directive (EC) 2001/20, recitals 1 and 2.
99 Regulation (EU) No 536/2014, recital 1.
100 ibid, Art 94. The position in the UK is discussed in Chapter 4.
101 Directive (EEC) 86/609; the Animals (Scientific Procedures) Act 1986.
102 'GLP': Directives (EC) 2004/10 and (EC) 2004/9.
103 Directive (EC) 2001/83; Annex, Pt I, Module 3, as amended.
104 Originating from Annex 2 of the Directive of 12 May 1981 of the Council of the OECD on the mutual acceptance of data for the evaluation of chemical products.
105 Directive (EC) 2004/10, applying Directive (EEC) 67/548.
106 Directive (EC) 2004/9.
107 Directive (EEC) 86/609.
108 Medicines Act 1968, ss 32 and 33.
109 See previously Directive (EC) 2001/20, Art 22 and, in UK, the Medicines for Human Use (Clinical Trials) Regulations 2004, SI 2004/1031 as amended. Practice was established from 1987 (Recommended basis for the conduct of clinical trials of medicinal products in the European Community, III/411/87-EN Rev) and developed in 1990 (Good Clinical Practice for trials on medicinal products in the European Community) and by Directive (EEC) 91/507. For further analysis and history see C J S Hodges, 'Harmonisation of European Controls over Research', in A Goldberg and I Dodds-Smith (eds), *Pharmaceutical Medicine and the Law* (Royal College of Physicians 1991).
110 Regulation (EU) No 536/2014, Arts 2(11) and 4.

(c) the subjects or, when a subject is not able to give informed consent, his or her legally designated representative, have given informed consent, in writing, dated and signed;[111]
(d) the rights of the subjects to physical and mental integrity, to privacy, and to the protection of the data concerning them in accordance with Directive 95/46/EC are safeguarded;
(e) the clinical trial has been designed to involve as little pain, discomfort, fear, and any other foreseeable risk as possible for the subjects and both the risk threshold and the degree of distress are specifically defined in the protocol and constantly monitored;
(f) the medical care provided to the subjects is the responsibility of an appropriately qualified doctor or, where appropriate, a qualified dental practitioner;
(g) the subject or, when a subject is not able to give informed consent, his or her legally designated representative, has been provided with the contact details of an entity where further information can be received in case of need;
(h) no undue influence, including that of a financial nature, is exerted on subjects to participate in the clinical trial.[112]

17.56 The Clinical Trials Directive requires prior approval of a clinical trial through scientific and ethical review and administrative authorization as prescribed,[113] through a single application portal operated by the European Medicines Agency.[114] This arrangement is designed to facilitate single centre or multi-centre studies, and those located in different Member States. The ethical review is undertaken by ethics committees that are independent bodies established in each Member State under its domestic law, empowered to give an opinion that takes into account the views of laypersons.[115] An application dossier submitted to the portal must contain all required documentation and information as required, relating to:

(a) the conduct of the clinical trial, including the scientific context and arrangements taken;
(b) the sponsor investigators, potential subjects, subjects, and clinical trial sites;
(c) the investigational medicinal products and, where necessary, the auxiliary medicinal products, in particular their properties, labelling, manufacturing, and control;
(d) measures to protect subjects;
(e) justification, where this is claimed by the sponsor, as to why the clinical trial is a low-intervention clinical trial.[116]

17.57 The relevant reporting Member State prepares an assessment report on the application and each Member State involved notifies the sponsor through the EU portal whether it authorizes (which may be subject to conditions) or refuses the application.[117] Any substantial modifications to a clinical trial must be authorized.[118]

---

[111] ibid, Art 29(1), (7) and (8).
[112] ibid, Art 28(1).
[113] Regulation (EU) No 536/2014, Arts 4 and 5.
[114] ibid, Art 80.
[115] ibid, Arts 2(11) and 4.
[116] ibid, Art 25 and Annex I. A low-intervention clinical trial involves medicinal products and placebos that are already authorized, used in accordance with the terms of their marketing authorizations, use is evidence-based and supported by published scientific evidence on their safety and efficacy, and the additional diagnostic or monitoring procedures do not pose more than minimal additional risk or burden to the safety of subjects compared to normal clinical practice: ibid, Art 2(3).
[117] ibid, Arts 6–8.
[118] ibid, Art 19(2) to (6). The information is designed to enable a subject to be enabled to give or refuse informed consent. It must include the risks and inconveniences, rights and protections, duration and conditions of the clinical trial, and possible alternative treatments, and it must be kept comprehensive, concise, clear, relevant, and understandable to a layperson.

Provisions require notification of the start of a clinical trial and the end of the recruitment of subjects;[119] notification of the end of a clinical trial, and submission of a summary of its results (in both scientific terms and in a manner understandable to laypersons);[120] recording and reporting by investigators and the sponsor of safety events to the Eudravigilance database, notably suspected unexpected serious adverse reactions;[121] adequately monitoring the conduct of the clinical trial by the sponsor, and ensuring that it is conducted in accordance with the protocol and with the principles of good clinical practice;[122] taking urgent safety measures to protect subjects;[123] keeping a clinical trial master file for at least twenty-five years;[124] labelling[125] and control of manufacture and import of investigational products;[126] and systems for compensation for any damage suffered by a subject resulting from participation in a clinical trial in the form of insurance, a guarantee, or a similar arrangement, and which is appropriate to the nature and the extent of the risk.[127] **17.58**

Member States are required to perform inspections to supervise compliance with the Clinical Trials Directive and to take appropriate corrective measures.[128] **17.59**

(iii) UK arrangements regarding clinical research and research ethics committees

The national provisions relating to research ethics committees are discussed in Chapter 13.[129] **17.60**

5. Manufacturing authorization

The manufacture of medicinal products is subject to the holding of an authorization.[130] The authorization may be granted upon application to a competent authority, although there is some lack of clarity over the criteria. In order to obtain the authorization the applicant 'must meet at least the following requirements' and provide particulars in support of these requirements:[131] **17.61**

(i) specify the medicinal products and pharmaceutical forms to be manufactured or imported and the place where they are to be manufactured or controlled;

---

119 ibid, Art 36.

120 ibid, Art 37 and Annexes IV and V.

121 ibid, Arts 40–46.

122 ibid, Arts 47 and 48. 'Good clinical practice' is defined as a set of detailed ethical and scientific quality requirements for designing, conducting, performing, monitoring, auditing, recording, analysing, and reporting clinical trials ensuring that the rights, safety, and well-being of subjects are protected, and that the data generated in the clinical trial are reliable and robust: ibid, Art 2(30). The basic reference is World Medical Association, Declaration of Helsinki: Recommendations Guiding Physicians in Biomedical Research Involving Human Subjects, 1957 as amended, available at <http://www.wma.net/en/30publications/10policies/b3/>.

123 Regulation (EU) No 536/2014, Art 54.

124 ibid, Arts 57 and 58.

125 ibid, Art 66.

126 ibid, Art 61.

127 ibid, Art 76.

128 ibid, Arts 77 and 76.

129 See in particular *Governance arrangements for research ethics committees: a harmonised edition* (Department of Health 2012).

130 Directive (EC) 2001/83, Art 40, first introduced by Directive (EEC) 75/319, Art 16; Medicines Act 1968, s 8(2). There are exceptions in relation to certain activities of doctors, dentists and pharmacists, notably in relation to a product specially prepared by or to the order of a doctor or dentist for administration to a particular patient of his (Medicines Act 1968, s 9(1)), or in relation to preparing or dispensing a medicinal product in a registered pharmacy or a hospital or health centre in accordance with a prescription given by a practitioner, by or under the supervision of a pharmacist (Medicines Act 1968, s 10). For the national criteria, procedures and conditions, see Medicines Act 1968, ss 19(5) and 20–24, the Human Medicines Regulations 2012, SI 2012/1916.

131 Directive (EC) 2001/83, Art 41.

(ii) have at his disposal for the manufacture or import suitable and sufficient premises, technical equipment and control facilities complying with the legal requirements which the Member State concerned lays down as regards both manufacture and control and the storage of products;[132]

(iii) have permanently and continuously at his disposal the services of at least one qualified person who is responsible for securing[133] that the manufacturer or importer is able to carry out manufacture in accordance with the particulars supplied pursuant to the application for marketing authorisation[134] and/or to carry out controls according to the methods described in the particulars accompanying the application.[135]

17.62 The qualified person must fulfil specified minimum conditions of qualification, including a four-year university course, or its equivalent, in one of the scientific disciplines of pharmacy, medicine, veterinary medicine, chemistry, pharmaceutical chemistry, and technology or biology, plus at least two years' practical experience, in one or more undertakings which are authorized to manufacture medicines, in qualitative and quantitative analysis of and quality testing and checking of medicinal products.[136]

17.63 The scheme of the legislation thus involves a measure of delegation of regulatory responsibility from the competent authority to the qualified person in relation to ensuring the consistent quality, and hence safety, of the products concerned. The qualified person will usually be employed by the holder of the manufacturing authorization but is relied on to exercise personal, professional responsibility independent of the manufacturer.

17.64 Principles and guidelines of good manufacturing practice are to be applied by a manufacturer in the manufacture of medicinal products.[137] Various controls address the circulation of falsified medicinal products and active substances, including requirements for importers, manufacturers, and distributors of active substances to register with national authorities, for the Commission to establish 'white' and 'black' lists of products, and for most products to have safety features verifying authenticity and identifying individual packs (with unique identifiers).[138]

6. Distribution and sale

(i) Wholesale distribution authorization

17.65 The wholesale distribution of medicinal products is subject to the possession of an authorization granted by a competent authority, and subject to checks on the authorization holder and their establishments and inspection of premises.[139] Wholesalers are required in particular to:[140]

(i) have suitable and adequate premises, installations and equipment, so as to ensure proper conservation or distribution of medicinal products;

---

132 Pursuant to Directive (EC) 2001/83, Art 20.

133 ibid, Art 20, which empowers an authority to permit certain variations.

134 ibid, Art 8(3)(d).

135 ibid, Art 8(3)(h).

136 ibid, Art 49.

137 ibid, Art 47: these principles and guidelines are set out in Commission Directive 2003/94.

138 Directive (EU) 2011/62, adding Directive (EC) 2001/83, Art 54(o), implemented by the Human Medicines (Amendment) Regulations 2013, SI 2013/1855.

139 ibid, Art 77, first introduced by Directive (EEC) 92/25, Art 3. In the UK, see Medicines Act 1968, s 8(3) and the Human Medicines Regulations 2012, SI 2012/1916, regs 18 and 42–45. There are exemptions for certain activities of doctors and dentists, notably in relation to products specially prepared for administration to a particular patient of theirs: Medicines Act 1968, s 9(1).

140 Directive (EU) 2011/62, n 138, Arts 79–80.

(ii) have a responsible, designated qualified person and other staff;
(iii) keep records of products received or dispatched, with dates, quantities, and names and addresses of suppliers and consignees;
(iv) have an emergency plan which ensures effective implementation of any recall from the market;
(v) comply with the principles and guidelines of good distribution practice for medicinal products (GDP) published by the Commission.[141]

(ii) Prescription only products

17.66 When a marketing authorization is granted, the competent authority must specify the classification of the medicinal product as one that is, or is not, subject to medical prescription.[142] Medicinal products shall be subject to medical prescription where they:

(i) are likely to present a danger either directly or indirectly, even when used correctly, if utilised without medical supervision; or
(ii) are frequently and to a very wide extent used incorrectly, and as a result are likely to present a direct or indirect danger to human health; or
(iii) contain substances or preparations thereof the activity and/or side effects of which require further investigation; or
(iv) are normally prescribed by a doctor to be administered parenterally.[143]

17.67 Conversely, medicinal products that do not meet the above criteria shall not be subject to prescription.[144] Certain sub-categories may be fixed in relation to availability on renewable or non-renewable prescriptions, or subject to special medical prescription, or restricted prescription reserved for use in certain specialized areas.[145] The authorities have some discretion to waive the classification provisions[146] and products can have different status in different Member States.

17.68 The authorities must draw up a list of products subject to prescription in their territory, update it annually, and must examine and amend the classification on the five-yearly renewal of the marketing authorization or when new facts are brought to their notice.[147]

(iii) Retail sale

17.69 National provisions not harmonized by Community law control pharmacies and the retail sale or supply of medicines to patients. Various matters are covered by English legislation. There are, for example, requirements covering the registration, licensing and inspection of pharmacy premises;[148] a requirement for retail sale and supply of medicines not on the general sale list to be made in registered pharmacy premises by or under the supervision of a pharmacist.[149]

---

141 See European Commission, Guidelines on Good Distribution Practice of Medicinal Products for Human Use 2013/C 343/01.
142 Directive (EC) 2001/83, Art 70, first included in Directive (EEC) 92/26.
143 ibid, Art 71(1).
144 ibid, Art 72.
145 ibid, Art 70(2).
146 ibid, Art 71.4.
147 ibid, Arts 73 and 74; Medicines Act 1968, s 58: it is an offence to sell or supply a medicinal product that is listed within the 'prescription only' category except in accordance with a prescription given by an appropriate practitioner, save subject to specified exceptions. The list is drawn up under the Prescription Only Medicines (Human Use) Order 1997, SI 1997/1830 and the Human Medicines Regulations 2012, SI 2012/1916.
148 Medicines Act 1968, ss 69–83.
149 ibid, s 52. This is subject to certain exemptions for doctors, dentists, hospitals, and health centres: ibid, s 55.

7. Information and promotion

(i) General points

17.70 There are specific and detailed requirements and limitations on both the information provided with medicinal products[150] and on the advertising of medicinal products.[151]

17.71 Information provided with products covers the labelling of product packaging and package leaflets provided to users with products. One or more specimens or mock-ups of the outer packaging and the immediate packaging of a medicinal product, together with the draft package leaflet, must be submitted to the authorities competent for authorizing marketing when the authorization for placing the medicinal product on the market is requested.[152]

17.72 The competent authorities must refuse the authorization for placing the medicinal product on the market if the labelling or the package leaflet do not comply with the code provisions or if they are not in accordance with the particulars listed in the summary of product characteristics (see para 17.76).[153] Where the labelling or leaflet provisions are not complied with, and a notice served on the person concerned has remained without effect, the competent authorities of the Member States may suspend the authorization to place the medicinal product on the market, until the labelling and the package leaflet of the medicinal product in question have been made to comply with the requirements.[154]

17.73 The authorities may exempt labels and package leaflets for specific medicinal products from the obligation that certain particulars appear or that the leaflet must be in an official language, when the product is not intended to be delivered to the patient for self-administration.[155]

17.74 The Commission is required to publish guidelines on various aspects of labelling.[156]

17.75 The outer packaging and the package leaflet may include symbols or pictograms designed to clarify information and information compatible with the summary of the product characteristics which is useful for health education, to the exclusion of any element of a promotional nature.[157]

(ii) Summary of product characteristics

17.76 An application for a marketing authorization must contain a summary of the product characteristics (SmPC),[158] which is approved by the authorities and is made public together with their assessment report.[159] The SmPC and assessment report (which the authorities must update) fulfil the dual function of a public, transparent rationale for the grant of an authorization and an official, uniform, approved statement of those product characteristics which are thought to be important prescribing information for users. The SmPC must contain the information specified,[160] which is summarized in Table 17.2.

---

[150] These were first introduced by Directive (EEC) 92/27 and are now contained in the amended Directive (EC) 2001/83, Title V.

[151] First introduced by Directive (EEC) 92/28 and now contained in the amended Directive (EC) 2001/83, Titles VIII and VIIIa. A national prohibition on advertising which applies solely to foreign medicinal products not authorized in the Member State concerned is contrary to Art 30 of the EC Treaty: Case C-320/93 *Lucien Ortscheit GmbH v Eurim-Pharm Arznemittel GmbH* [1995] 2 CMLR 242. In UK, see the Human Medicines Regulations 2012, SI 2012/1916, Part 14.

[152] Directive (EC) 2001/83, Art 8(3)(j).

[153] ibid, Art 61(2).

[154] ibid, Art 64.

[155] ibid, Art 63(3).

[156] ibid, Art 65.

[157] ibid, Art 62.

[158] ibid, Art 8(2)(j).

[159] ibid, Art 21, as amended by Directive (EC) 2004/27.

[160] Regulation (EC) 469/2009.

Table 17.2 Information to be specified in summary of product characteristics

1	Name of the medicinal product followed by the strength and the pharmaceutical form
2	Qualitative and quantitative composition in terms of the active substances and constituents of the excipient, knowledge of which is essential for proper administration of the medicinal product. The usual common name or chemical description shall be used
3	Pharmaceutical form
4	Clinical particulars
4.1	Therapeutic indications
4.2	Posology and method of administration for adults and, where necessary for children
4.3	Contra-indications
4.4	Special warnings and precautions for use and, in the case of immunological medicinal products, any special precautions to be taken by persons handling such products and administering them to patients, together with any precautions to be taken by the patient
4.5	Interaction with other medicinal products and other forms of interactions
4.6	Use during pregnancy and lactation
4.7	Effects on ability to drive and to use machines
4.8	Undesirable effects
4.9	Overdose (symptoms, emergency procedures, antidotes)
5.	Pharmacological properties
5.1	Pharmacodynamic properties
5.2	Pharmacokinetic properties
5.3	Preclinical safety data
6	Pharmaceutical particulars
6.1	List of excipients
6.2	Major incompatibilities
6.3	Shelf life, when necessary after reconstitution of the medicinal product or when the immediate packaging is opened for the first time
6.4	Special precautions for storage
6.5	Nature and contents of container
6.6	Special precautions for disposal of a used medicinal product or waste materials derived from such medicinal product, if appropriate
7	Marketing authorization holder
8	Marketing authorization number(s)
9	Date of the first authorisation or renewal of the authorization
10	Date of revision of the text
11	For radiopharmaceuticals, full details of internal radiation dosimetry
12	For radiopharmaceuticals, additional detailed instructions for extemporaneous preparation and quality control of such preparation and, where appropriate, maximum storage time during which any intermediate preparation such as an eluate or the ready-to-use pharmaceutical will conform with its specifications

(iii) Labelling

17.77 The following particulars are required to appear on the outer packaging of medicinal products or, where there is no outer packaging, on the immediate packaging:[161]

(i) the name of the medicinal product followed by its strength and pharmaceutical form, and, if appropriate, whether it is intended for babies, children, or adults; where the product contains up to three active substances, the international non-proprietary name (INN) shall be included, or, if one does not exist, the common name. This must also be expressed in Braille format on the packaging:[162]

(ii) a statement of the active substances expressed qualitatively and quantitatively per dosage unit or according to the form of administration for a given volume or weight, using their common names;

(iii) the pharmaceutical form and the contents by weight, by volume or by number of doses of the product;

(iv) a list of those excipients known to have a recognized action or effect and included in the detailed guidance published pursuant to Article 65. However, if the product is injectable, or a topical or eye preparation, all excipients must be stated;

(v) the method of administration and, if necessary, the route of administration. Space shall be provided for the prescribed dose to be indicated;

(vi) a special warning that the medicinal product must be stored out of reach and sight of children;

(vii) a special warning, if this is necessary for the medicinal product concerned;

(viii) the expiry date in clear terms (month/year);

(ix) special storage precautions, if any;

(x) specific precautions relating to the disposal of unused medicinal products or waste derived from such products, where appropriate, as well as reference to any appropriate collection system in place;

(xi) the name and address of the marketing authorization holder and, where applicable, the name of the representative appointed by the holder to represent him;

(xii) the number of the authorization for placing the medicinal product on the market;

(xiii) the manufacturer's batch number;

(xiv) in the case of non-prescription medicinal products, instructions for use.

17.78 The particulars of Article 54 quoted above must appear on immediate packaging other than blister packs or small immediate packaging units. The Article 54 particulars shall appear in the official language or languages of the Member State where the product is placed on the market. This provision shall not prevent these particulars from being indicated in several languages, provided that the same particulars appear in all the languages used.[163]

17.79 The following particulars at least shall appear on immediate packaging that takes the form of blister packs and are placed in an outer packaging that complies with the requirements laid down in Article 54:

(i) the name of the medicinal product as laid down in Article 54(a);

(ii) the name of the holder of the authorization for placing the product on the market;

(iii) the expiry date;

(iv) the batch number.[164]

---

[161] Directive (EC) 2001/83, Art 54; Medicines Act 1968, s 85; the Human Medicines Regulations 2012, SI 2012/1916, Part 13 and Schs 24 and 25.

[162] Directive (EC) 2001/83, Art 56a.

[163] ibid, Art 63.

[164] ibid, Art 55(2).

The following particulars at least shall appear on small immediate packaging units on which the particulars laid down in Article 54 cannot be displayed: **17.80**

(i) the name of the medicinal product and, if necessary, the strength and the route of administration;
(ii) the method of administration;
(iii) the expiry date;
(iv) the batch number;
(v) the contents by weight, by volume or by unit.[165]

All the labelling particulars shall be easily legible, clearly comprehensible, and indelible.[166] **17.81**

(iv) Package leaflets

The inclusion in the packaging of all medicinal products of a package leaflet for the information of users is obligatory unless all the specified information required by Articles 59 and 62 of Directive (EC) 2001/83 is directly conveyed on the outer packaging or on the immediate packaging.[167] **17.82**

The package leaflet must be drawn up in accordance with the summary of the product characteristics,[168] and include, in the following order: **17.83**

(i) for the identification of the medicinal product:
— the name of the medicinal product, followed by its strength and pharmaceutical form, and, if appropriate, whether it is intended for babies, children or adults. The common name shall be included where the product contains only one active substance and if its name is an invented name;
— the pharmaco-therapeutic group or type of activity in terms easily comprehensible for the patient;

(ii) the therapeutic indications;[169]
(iii) a list of information which is necessary before the medicinal product is taken:
— contra-indications,
— appropriate precautions for use,
— forms of interaction with other medicinal products and other forms of interaction (for example, alcohol, tobacco, foodstuffs) which may affect the action of the medicinal product,
— special warnings;

this list must:
— take into account the particular condition of certain categories of users (children, pregnant or breastfeeding women, the elderly, persons with specific pathological conditions),
— mention, if appropriate, potential effects on the ability to drive vehicles or to operate machinery,

---

[165] ibid, Art 55(3).
[166] ibid, Art 56.
[167] ibid, Art 58; Medicines Act 1968, s 86, the Human Medicines Regulations 2012, SI 2012/1916, Part 13 and Schs 24 and 25.
[168] See para 17.76.
[169] According to the Commission packaging information guideline, the competent authorities may decide that certain therapeutic indications shall not be mentioned in the package leaflet, where the dissemination of such information might have serious disadvantages for the patient. However, this appears to be based upon an erroneous reference to Directive (EC) 2001/83, Art 59(2).

— list those excipients, knowledge of which is important for the safe and effective use of the medicinal product and which are included in the guidelines published pursuant to Article 65;

(iv) the necessary and usual instructions for proper use, and in particular:

— the dosage;
— the method and, if necessary, route of administration;
— the frequency of administration, specifying if necessary the appropriate time at which the medicinal product may or must be administered,

and, as appropriate, depending on the nature of the product:

— the duration of treatment, where it should be limited;
— the action to be taken in case of an overdose (such as symptoms, emergency procedures);
— what to do when one or more doses have not been taken;
— indication, if necessary, of the risk of withdrawal effects;
— a specific recommendation to consult the doctor or the pharmacist, as appropriate, for any clarification on the use of the product;

(v) a description of the adverse reactions which may occur under normal use of the medicinal product and, if necessary, the action to be taken in such a case; the patient should be expressly asked to communicate any adverse reaction which is not mentioned in the package leaflet to his doctor or pharmacist;

(vi) a reference to the expiry date indicated on the label, with:

— a warning against using the product after that date;
— where appropriate, special storage precautions;
— if necessary, a warning against concerning certain visible signs of deterioration;
— the full qualitative composition (in active substances and excipients) and the quantitative composition in active substances, using common names, for each presentation of the medicinal product;
— for each presentation of the product, the pharmaceutical form and content in weight, volume or units of dosage;
— the name and address of the marketing authorization holder and, where applicable, the name of his appointed representatives in the Member States;
— the name and address of the marketing authorisation holder and where applicable his representative in the Member States;

(vii) Where the medicinal product is authorized in accordance with the decentralized/mutual recognition procedure under different names in Member States, a list of the names authorized in each Member State;

(viii) the date on which the package leaflet was last revised.

17.84 The package leaflet must be written and designed to be clear and understandable, enabling the users to act appropriately, when necessary with the help of health professionals. The authorization applicant must consult with target patient groups when developing this and submit the results to the competent authority. It must be clearly legible in the official language or languages of the Member State in which the medicinal product is placed on the market. This provision does not prevent the package leaflet being printed in several languages, provided that the same information is given in all the languages used.[170]

[170] Directive (EC) 2001/83, Arts 60, 61, and 63.

(v) Advertising

(a) Definition of advertising Advertising of medicinal products is defined for regulatory purposes[171] as any form of door-to-door information, canvassing activity, or inducement designed to promote the prescription, supply, sale, or consumption of medicinal products; it shall include in particular: **17.85**

(i) the advertising of medicinal products to the general public;
(ii) advertising of medicinal products to persons qualified to prescribe or supply them;[172]
(iii) visits by medical sales representatives to persons qualified to prescribe medicinal products;
(iv) the supply of samples;
(v) the provision of inducements to prescribe or supply medicinal products by the gift, offer or promise of any benefit or bonus, whether in money or in kind, except when their intrinsic value is minimal;[173]
(vi) sponsorship of promotional meetings attended by persons qualified to prescribe or supply medicinal products;
(vii) sponsorship of scientific congresses attended by persons qualified to prescribe or supply medicinal products and in particular payment of their travelling and accommodation expenses in connection therewith.

(b) General provisions Member States are to prohibit any advertising of a medicinal product in respect of which a marketing authorization has not been granted in accordance with EU law.[174] All parts of the advertising of a medicinal product must comply with the particulars listed in the summary of product characteristics.[175] There is a positive obligation that the advertising of a medicinal product: **17.86**

(i) shall encourage the rational use of the medicinal product, by presenting it objectively and without exaggerating its properties;
(ii) shall not be misleading.[176]

Different rules apply to advertising of medicinal products to the general public and to health professionals, as discussed in paras 17.88–17.93. **17.87**

(c) Advertising to the general public[177] Medicinal products which are available on prescription only may not be advertised to the general public. Medicinal products may be advertised to the general public only if, by virtue of their composition and purpose, they are intended and designed for use without the intervention of a medical practitioner for diagnostic purposes or for the prescription or monitoring of treatment, with the advice of the pharmacist, if necessary.[178] Medicinal products may not be distributed direct to the public for promotional purposes.[179] **17.88**

---

[171] ibid, Art 86(1).
[172] See Case C-143/06 *Ludwigs-Apotheke München Internationale Apotheke v Juers Pharma Import-Export GmbH* [2007] ECR I-09623.
[173] See Case C-374/05 *Gintec International Import-Export GmbH v Verband Sozialer Wettbewerb eV* [2007] ECR I-09517.
[174] Directive (EC) 2001/83, Art 87(1); Medicines Act 1968, ss 92–97; the Human Medicines Regulations 2012, SI 2012/1916, reg 279.
[175] Directive (EC) 2001/83, Art 87(2): for the summary of product characteristics, see para 17.76.
[176] ibid, Art 87(3).
[177] See the Human Medicines Regulations 2012, SI 2012/1916, Part 14 and Sch 30.
[178] Directive (EC) 2001/83, Art 88.
[179] ibid, Art 88(6).

17.89 All advertising to the general public of a medicinal product shall:[180]

(i) be set out in such a way that it is clear that the message is an advertisement and that the product is clearly identified as a medicinal product;
(ii) include the following minimum information:
— the name of the medicinal product, as well as the common name if the medicinal product contains only one active substance;
— the information necessary for correct use of the medicinal product;
— an express, legible invitation to read carefully the instructions on the package leaflet or on the outer packaging, as the case may be.

17.90 The advertising of a medicinal product to the general public shall not contain any material which:[181]

(i) gives the impression that a medical consultation or surgical operation is unnecessary, in particular by offering a diagnosis or by suggesting treatment by mail;
(ii) suggests that the effects of taking the medicine are guaranteed, are unaccompanied by side effects or are better than, or equivalent to, those of another treatment or medicinal product;
(iii) suggests that the health of the subject can be enhanced by taking the medicine;
(iv) suggests that the health of the subject could be affected by not taking the medicine; (this prohibition shall not apply to specified vaccination campaigns);
(v) is directed exclusively or principally at children;
(vi) refers to a recommendation by scientists, health professionals, or persons who are neither of the foregoing but who, because of their celebrity, could encourage the consumption of medicinal products;
(vii) suggests that the medicinal product is a foodstuff, cosmetic, or other consumer product;
(viii) suggests that the safety or efficacy of the medicinal product is due to the fact that it is natural;
(ix) could, by a description or detailed representation of a case history, lead to erroneous self-diagnosis;
(x) refers, in improper, alarming, or misleading terms, to claims of recovery;
(xi) uses, in improper, alarming, or misleading terms, pictorial representations of changes in the human body caused by disease or injury, or of the action of a medicinal product on the human body or parts thereof.

17.91 **(d) Advertising to health professionals** Any advertising of a medicinal product to persons qualified to prescribe or supply such products shall include:

(i) essential information compatible with the summary of product characteristics;
(ii) the supply classification of the medicinal product.[182]

17.92 Any documentation which is transmitted as part of the promotion of a product to a person qualified to prescribe or supply it must include the above essential information and supply classification, and must state the date on which it was drawn up or last revised.[183] All this

---

[180] ibid, Art 89(1): Member States may decide that only the name of the product may be included if it is intended solely as a reminder.
[181] ibid, Art 90.
[182] ibid, Art 91(1): Member States may decide that only the name of the product may be included if it is intended solely as a reminder: Art 91(2).
[183] ibid, Art 92(1).

information must be accurate, up to date, verifiable, and sufficiently complete to enable the recipient to form his or her own opinion of the therapeutic value of the product.[184] Quotations, tables, and other illustrative matter taken from medical journals or other scientific works and included in this documentation shall be faithfully reproduced and the precise sources indicated.[185]

Medical sales representatives must have adequate training and scientific knowledge to be able to provide precise and complete information about the medicinal products they promote.[186] They must give the persons visited, or have available to them, summaries of the product characteristics of each medicinal product they present.[187] There are restrictions on promotional activities.[188] 17.93

(e) **Monitoring of advertising** Member States are required to ensure that there are adequate and effective methods to monitor the advertising of medicinal products, optionally including a prior vetting system or by self-regulatory bodies.[189] In the UK, the legal scheme and requirements exist as a backdrop but are very rarely invoked, since two self-regulatory schemes are operated in practice. Manufacturers of prescription products who are members of the Association of the British Pharmaceutical Industry observe its *Code of Practice for the Pharmaceutical Industry*, which is administered by the Prescription Medicines Code of Practice Authority. Manufacturers of over-the-counter products who are members of the Proprietary Association of Great Britain observe its *Code of Standards of Advertising Practice for Over-the-Counter Medicines*. There are also the more generalized *British Code of Advertising, Sales Promotion and Direct Marketing* of the Committee of Advertising Practice, *The TV Advertising Standards Code* and *The Radio Advertising Standards Code* of the Broadcast Committee of Advertising Practice which administers them under contract from the broadcast and telecommunications regulator, Ofcom. 17.94

(f) **Scientific information service** A marketing authorization holder is required to establish within his undertaking a scientific service in charge of information about the medicinal products that he places on the market.[190] 17.95

The person responsible for placing the product on the market shall:[191] 17.96

(i) keep available for, or communicate to, the authorities or bodies responsible for monitoring advertising of medicinal products a sample of all advertisements emanating from his undertaking together with a statement indicating the persons to whom it is addressed, the method of dissemination and the date of first dissemination;
(ii) ensure that advertising of medicinal products by his undertaking conforms to the requirements of Title VIIIa of Directive (EC) 2001/83;
(iii) verify that medical sales representatives employed by his undertaking have been adequately trained and fulfil the obligations imposed upon them referred to above, including the obligation to transmit information about the use of the medicinal products they advertise with particular reference to any adverse reactions reported to them by healthcare professionals whom they visit;[192]

184 ibid, Art 92(2).
185 ibid, Art 92(3).
186 ibid, Art 93(1).
187 ibid, Art 93(2).
188 ibid, Arts 94–96.
189 ibid, Art 97.
190 ibid, (EC) 2001/83, Art 98(1).
191 ibid, (EC) 2001/83, Art 98(2).
192 ibid, Art 93(3).

(iv) supply the authorities or bodies responsible for monitoring advertising of medicinal products with the information and assistance they require to carry out their responsibilities;
(v) ensure that the decisions taken by the authorities or bodies responsible for monitoring advertising of medicinal products are immediately and fully complied with.

8. Post-marketing requirements for safety

(i) Pharmacovigilance

17.97 It is recognized that the safe use of medicinal products is not simply a matter to be assessed at the time of marketing, but that there is a need for the continuous collection and re-evaluation of data relating to a product, throughout the time that its product type is marketed and/or remains on the market.[193] The legislation implicitly recognizes the limitations on the understanding of the level of safety which is possible at the time of authorizing its marketing that use of a product will present in normal, 'practical conditions of use'.[194]

17.98 A sophisticated, integrated pharmacovigilance system is established under the Community legislation and a series of guidelines,[195] which relies on spontaneous reporting by health care professionals and others, and imposes (i) recording and reporting obligations on the commercial enterprises involved, and (ii) surveillance and other regulatory obligations on Member States, the Commission, the EMA, and the CHMP. Different post-marketing obligations for medicinal products apply to the holders of marketing authorizations, the holders of manufacturing authorizations, and the holders of wholesale distribution authorizations. The pharmacovigilance system was reviewed in 2007, reforms were proposed in the first quarter of 2008,[196] and amended in 2010 with effect from 2012.[197]

17.99 The principal provisions are:[198]

> In order to ensure the adoption of appropriate and harmonized regulatory decisions concerning the medicinal products authorised within the Community, having regard to information obtained about adverse reactions to medicinal products under normal conditions of use, the Member States shall operate a pharmacovigilance system. This system shall be used to collect information useful in the surveillance of medicinal products, with particular reference to adverse reactions in human beings, and to evaluate such information scientifically.
> Member States shall ensure that suitable information collected within this system is communicated to the other Member States and the Agency. The information shall be recorded in the [official] database and shall be permanently accessible to all Member States and without delay to the public.

193 See S M Roden, 'An Introduction to Drug Safety Surveillance', in Glaxo Group Research, *Drug Safety: A Shared Responsibility* (Churchill Livingstone 1991).

194 This phrase appeared in Directive (EEC) 93/39, recital 7, which justified the initial introduction into Community legislation of the pharmacovigilance system but was not repeated in recital 54 to Directive (EC) 2001/83. Recital 15 to Regulation (EEC) 2309/93 only referred to the mechanistic 'intensive monitoring of adverse reactions' though it reappears at Art 57(1)(c) of Regulation (EC) 726/2004 in connection with the designation of the EMEA's tasks.

195 See vol 9A of the *Rules Governing Medicinal Products in the European Union: Guidelines on Pharmacovigilance for Medicinal Products for Human Use*, which includes guidelines for competent authorities and the EMEA at Pt II.

196 *Strategy to Better Protect Public Health by Strengthening and Rationalising EU Pharmacovigilance* (European Commission, 2007).

197 Regulation (EU) 1235/2010 and Directive (EU) 2010/84.

198 Directive (EC) 2001/83, Art 102, as amended: adapted from its first introduction in Directive (EEC) 93/39, Art 3(3).

This system shall also take into account any available information on misuse and abuse[199] of medicinal products that may have an impact on the evaluation of their benefits and risks.

17.100 (a) **Primary reporting** Neither the centralized nor decentralized/mutual recognition systems refer specifically to reports emanating from patients, nor place any reporting requirements on patients. Both systems envisage reports emanating essentially from health care professionals.[200] The UK voluntary reporting system is known as the 'Yellow Card' scheme. Under the decentralized/mutual recognition system:

> The Member States shall take all appropriate measures to encourage doctors and other health care professionals to report suspected adverse reactions to the competent authorities.

The Member States may impose specific requirements on doctors and other health care professionals, in respect of the reporting of suspected serious or unexpected adverse reactions.[201]

17.101 In contrast, the legislation on the centralized system curiously includes no provision on reporting by doctors or other health care professionals. Seemingly, therefore, Member States have no power to require any such reporting under the centralized system. The only reference to source data is to all suspected adverse reactions that are reported to the company that holds the marketing authorization.[202]

17.102 (b) **Obligations of marketing companies** A marketing authorization holder is required to have permanently and continuously at his disposal a 'qualified person' responsible for pharmacovigilance, who has the following obligations:

> (a) the establishment and maintenance of a system which ensures that information about all suspected adverse reactions which are reported to the personnel of the company, and to medical representatives, is collected and collated in order to be accessible at least at one point within the Community;
> (b) the preparation for the competent authorities of reports on specified adverse reactions;
> (c) ensuring that any request from the competent authorities for the provision of additional information necessary for the evaluation of the benefits and risks afforded by a medicinal product is answered fully and promptly, including the provision of information about the volume of sales or prescriptions for the medicinal product concerned . . .[203]

17.103 Technical and scientific progress in relation to production and control of a medicinal product must be taken into account by the authorization holder, who must apply for approval of any necessary variations.[204] The holder of the marketing authorization must also forthwith inform the EMA, the Commission, and Member States (in the case of products authorized under the centralized system) and the competent authority of the Member State concerned (for products authorized under the decentralized/mutual recognition procedure), of any new information which might entail the amendment of the particulars and documents that were supplied with the application for marketing approval, or amendment of the summary of product characteristics.[205] He shall, in particular, inform them of any prohibition

---

199 Defined in Directive (EC) 2001/83, Art 1(16) as persistent or sporadic, intentional exercise use of medicinal products which is accompanied by harmful physical or psychological effects.
200 Regulation (EC) 726/2004, Arts 22 and 51; Directive (EC) 2001/83, Art 101.
201 Directive (EC) 2001/83, Art 101.
202 See, eg, Regulation (EC) 726/2004, Art 22.
203 Directive (EC) 2001/83, Art 103; for the centralized procedure see Regulation (EC) 726/2004, Art 23, which is almost identical. These provisions are supplemented by guidance in vol 9A of the Rules Governing Medicinal Products in the European Union.
204 Regulation (EC) 726/2004, Art 16.1; Directive (EC) 2001/83, Art 23.
205 Regulation (EC) 726/2004, Art 16.2; Directive (EC) 2001/83, Art 23.

or restriction imposed by the competent authorities of any country in which the product is marketed and of any other new information that might influence the evaluation of the benefits and risks of the product.[206] Under the centralized system, if the person responsible for placing a medicinal product on the market proposes to make any alteration to the information and particulars submitted to support the grant of the marketing authorization, he must submit an application to the EMA.[207] Under the Code applying to the decentralized/mutual recognition procedure, a marketing authorization holder must apply for the variation of the authorization.[208]

17.104 The following definitions are specified:[209]

(i) 'adverse reaction' means a response to a medicinal product which is noxious and unintended;
(ii) 'serious adverse reaction' means an adverse reaction which results in death, is life-threatening, requires inpatient hospitalization or prolongation of existing hospitalization, results in persistent or significant disability or incapacity, or is a congenital anomaly/birth defect;
(iii) 'unexpected adverse reaction' means an adverse reaction, the nature, severity, or outcome of which is not consistent with the summary of product characteristics.

17.105 All *suspected serious* adverse reactions occurring within the Community to a medicinal product which are brought to the attention of the marketing authorization holder by a health care professional must be recorded and reported immediately to the Member States in whose territory the incident occurred, and in no case later than fifteen days following the receipt of the information.[210] There are further obligations in relation to maintaining detailed records of all *suspected* adverse reactions occurring within or outside the Community that are reported by a health care professional.[211] If a *suspected serious unexpected* adverse reaction to a centrally licensed product occurs in a non-Community country, a report must be made both to all Member States and to the Agency. Commission Guidance covers the collection, verification, and presentation of adverse reaction reports, including technical requirements for electronic exchange of pharmacovigilance information.[212]

17.106 Under the centralized system, arrangements for the reporting of suspected adverse reactions within or outside the Community which are reported by a health care professional to the marketing authorization holder on the following basis:

> Unless other requirements have been laid down as a condition for the granting of the marketing authorisation by the Community, the detailed records of such suspected adverse reactions, which the marketing authorisation holder is required to maintain, must be submitted by the marketing authorisation holder to the Agency and Member States immediately upon request or at least every six months after authorisation until placing on the market. Periodic safety update reports must also be submitted immediately upon request

[206] ibid.

[207] Regulation (EC) 726/2004, Art 16.3.

[208] Directive (EC) 2001/83, Arts 23 and 35.

[209] ibid, Art 1: also adopted in Regulation (EC) 726/2004, Art 21.

[210] Under the centralized procedure, Regulation (EC) 726/2004, Art 24; under the Code, Directive (EC) 2001/83, Art 104; both provisions add that this applies to reactions brought to his attention by a healthcare professional and that separate guidance applies to the reporting and recording of other suspected serious adverse reactions.

[211] Directive (EC) 2001/83, Art 104, and Regulation (EC) 726/2004, Art 24.

[212] Directive (EC) 2001/83, Art 106 and Regulation (EC) 726/2004, Art 26. The suspension or revocation of a marketing authorization may only be decided on the grounds laid down in the Community provisions: Case C-83/92 *Pierrel SpA v Ministerio della Sanita* [1993] ECR I-06419.

or at least every six months during the first two years following the initial placing on the Community market and once a year for the following two years. Thereafter, the reports shall be submitted at three-yearly intervals together with the application of renewal of the authorisation, or immediately upon request. These records shall be accompanied by a scientific evaluation particularly of the risk-benefit balance of the product. The Code sets out broadly equivalent requirements for products authorised nationally or under the decentralised/mutual recognition procedure.[213]

The main reporting requirements under the decentralized/mutual recognition system[214] are shown in Table 17.3. **17.107**

The holder of a manufacturing authorization must, inter alia, have qualifying staff, give prior notice to the competent authority of any changes he may wish to make in his approved particulars on facilities and the product, permit the authority access to his premises at any time, and comply with the principles and guidelines of good manufacturing practice for medicinal products.[215] **17.108**

(c) **Obligations on Member States** Each Member State shall ensure that all *suspected serious* adverse reactions occurring within their territory to a medicinal product authorized under the centralized system which are brought to their attention are recorded and reported promptly to the Agency and the marketing authorization holder, and in no case later than fifteen days following the receipt of the information.[216] This provision is followed, under the centralized system but not the mutual recognition system, by an obligation on the Agency to inform the national pharmacovigilance systems of reports which it receives. Implicitly in this context such reports are received only from Member States—the legislation seemingly does not contemplate that the Agency will receive reports from any source other than Member States or marketing authorization holders, and it does not explicitly require the Agency to inform Member States of any reports which it receives other than those of suspected serious adverse reactions received from Member State authorities. Nevertheless, the legislation specifies a mechanism for the Commission in consultation with the Agency, Member States, and interested parties, to draw up guidance on the collection, verification, and presentation of adverse reaction reports.[217] **17.109**

The Agency, in consultation with the Member States and the Commission, maintains a data-processing network (Eudra-vigilance database) to collate pharmacovigilance information regarding medicinal products, to which authorization holders are required to send their reports.[218] Further, the Agency shall collaborate with the World Health Organization on international pharmacovigilance and shall take the necessary steps to submit promptly to the World Health Organization appropriate and adequate information regarding the measures taken in the Community which may have a bearing on public health protection in third countries and shall send a copy thereof to the Commission and the Member States.[219] **17.110**

The supervisory authority for pharmacovigilance is the competent authority of the Member State in which the pharmacovigilance master file is located, and it is responsible for **17.111**

[213] Regulation (EC) 726/2004, Art 24(3); Directive (EC) 2001/83, Art 104. The suspension or revocation of a marketing authorization may only be decided on the grounds laid down in the Community provisions: Case C-83/92 *Pierrel SpA v Ministerio della Sanita* [1993] ECR I-06419.

[214] Directive (EC) 2001/83, Art 104.

[215] Directive (EC) 2001/83, Title IV.

[216] Regulation (EC) 726/2004, Art 25.

[217] Regulation (EC) 726/2004, Art 26; Directive (EC) 2001/83, Art 106.

[218] Regulation (EC) 726/2004, Art 24; Directive (EC) 2001/83, Art 107. See also detailed provisions in Commission Implementing Regulation (EU) No 520/2012.

[219] Regulation (EC) 726/2004, Art 27.

Table 17.3 Reporting requirements under the Community Code

Type of adverse reaction (AR)	Where occurring	Report to competent authority in	Time limit
All suspected serious ARs brought to his attention by a health care professional		Member State where occurred	Promptly and within 15 days
All other suspected serious ARs which meet the reporting criteria		Member State where occurred	Promptly and within 15 days
All suspected serious and unexpected ARs and any suspected transmission via a medicinal product of any infectious agent	In a third country	The Agency and Member State where product is authorized	Promptly and within 15 days
All adverse reactions		To the competent authorities in a periodic safety update report	Immediately on request, or six monthly for the first two years after authorization, and then once a year for the following two years, and then at three-yearly intervals

inspections of authorization holders.[220] Central coordination of pharmacovigilance in the Community is provided for:

> The Agency, acting in close co-operation with the national pharmacovigilance systems established in accordance with Article 102 of Directive (EC) 2001/83, shall receive all relevant information about suspected adverse reactions to medicinal products which have been authorised by the Community in accordance with the centralised system. Where appropriate the CHMP may, in accordance with Article 5 of Regulation 726/2004, formulate publicly accessible opinions on the measures necessary. These measures shall be adopted in accordance with the procedure laid down in Article 87(3) of the Regulation.

Central responsibility for initial analysis and prioritization of signals of new risks or risks that change the risk–benefit balance rests with the EMA's Pharmacovigilance Risk Assessment Committee, which appoints a rapporteur to assess the periodic safety update reports on individual products.[221] Under the centralized system, that Committee may require a marketing authorization holder to conduct post-authorization studies on safety and efficacy, or to operate a risk management system.[222] The marketing authorization holder and the competent authorities of the Member States shall ensure that all relevant information about suspected adverse reactions to medicinal products authorized in accordance with the Regulation are brought to the attention of the EMEA in accordance with the provisions of the Regulation. Patients shall be encouraged to communicate any adverse reaction to health care professionals.[223]

[220] ibid, Arts 18(c) and 19.
[221] ibid, Art 28*a* and 28.3; Directive (EC) 2001/83, Art 107.
[222] Regulation (EC) 726/2004, Arts 10*a* and 14.8.
[223] ibid, Art 22.

The legislation therefore recognizes that use of medicinal products under normal conditions will always involve adverse reactions. The purpose of the pharmacovigilance system is to monitor and evaluate all adverse reactions systematically so as constantly to review the recorded information on the level of safety of products and to review decisions as to the continuation of marketing authorizations or conditions attaching to them. The advantage of a pharmacovigilance system which covers the whole of the EU Member States lies in the statistical power of a system of this size. **17.112**

(ii) Withdrawal from the Market: Suspension or revocation of a marketing authorization

Under the decentralized/mutual recognition system, Member States: **17.113**

> shall take all appropriate measures to ensure that the supply of the medicinal product is prohibited and the medicinal product withdrawn from the market if the view is taken that:
> (a) the medicinal product is harmful under normal conditions of use; or
> (b) it lacks therapeutic efficacy; or
> (c) its risk-benefit balance is not favourable under the authorized conditions of use; or
> (d) its qualitative and quantitative composition is not as declared; or
> (e) the controls on the medicinal product and/or on the ingredients and the controls at an intermediate stage of the manufacturing process have not been carried out or if some other requirement or obligation relating to the grant of the manufacturing authorisation has not been fulfilled.

The competent authority may limit the prohibition to supply the product, or its withdrawal from the market, to those batches which are the subject of dispute.[224]

Under the centralized system, where any of the above triggering provisions occur, a Member State or the Commission may initiate a procedure involving a CHMP opinion and Commission Decision suspending or revoking the authorization.[225] A Member State may nevertheless suspend the use of a product in its territory where urgent action is essential to protect human or animal health or the environment.[226] **17.114**

It will be seen that the competent authority is required to suspend or revoke the authorization where the criteria are met. The principal test as regards safety is where the product proves to be harmful in the normal conditions of use.[227] As with the criteria for the grant of a marketing authorization, these criteria are problematic. Any medicinal product may prove harmful, either in general use or when used by a particular patient, since it is intended to have pharmacological effect in treating a diseased state. The key issue of what level of harm is or is not acceptable, in the general or particular situation, is not addressed. Decisions on these issues require complex assessments and the relevant Community authority enjoys a wide discretion, which is only subject to limited judicial review, in the course of which the Community judicature may not substitute its assessment of the facts for the assessment made by the authority concerned.[228] **17.115**

---

[224] Directive (EC) 2001/83, Art 117. Member States are also required under Art 116 to suspend or revoke an authorization where one of situations (a)–(d) occurs.

[225] Regulation (EC)/726/2004, Art 22.

[226] ibid, Arts 20(4) and 45(4).

[227] It should be noted that the wording in s 28(3)(g) of the Medicines Act differs from the Community provisions (medicinal products of any description to which the licence relates can no longer be regarded as products which can safely be administered for the purposes indicated in the licence, or can no longer be regarded as efficacious). However, the Community provisions are applied by the Medicines for Human Use (Marketing Authorisations Etc) Regulations 1994, SI 1994/3144, reg 6.

[228] Case C-120/97 *Upjohn Ltd v The Licensing Authority established by the Medicines Act 1968 and Others* [1999] ECR I-223; contrast other situations not involving complex assessments (such as in relation

17.116 The authorization shall also be suspended or revoked where the composition of the product is not as declared or the particulars and documents are incorrect or have not been updated. The justification for these provisions is that authorization is based on a product with a precise specification for which the pharmacological effects and side effects are as anticipated. Any variation in the specification, failure to prepare or control the product by the prevailing scientific standards would not continue to promote safety.

(iii) Suspension or revocation of a manufacturing authorization

17.117 In relation to the manufacturing and quality control aspects of a product, the supervisory authority in the case of a medicine manufactured within the Community is the competent authority of the Member State(s) that has granted the manufacturing authorization for the product.[229] Where a product is imported into the Community, the supervising authority is that of the Member State into which it is imported, where the required quality controls are to be carried out, unless the Community has made appropriate alternative arrangements with the exporting country.[230]

17.118 The competent authority of the relevant Member State *shall* suspend or revoke a manufacturing authorization where any one of the requirements laid down in Article 41 of Directive (EC) 2001/83, for grant of a manufacturing authorization (see above) is no longer met.[231] For products approved under the centralized system, where the supervisory authorities, or the competent authorities of any other Member State, are of the opinion that the manufacturer or importer from third countries is no longer fulfilling the obligations laid down, they shall forthwith inform the CHMP and the Commission, stating their reasons in detail and indicating the course of action proposed.[232] The Commission shall examine the reasons advanced, together with the Agency, and prepare a draft of the decision to be taken.[233] Where urgent action is essential to protect human or animal health or the environment, a Member State may suspend the use of a medicinal product in its territory, and shall then inform the Commission and the other Member States, giving its reasons.[234]

C. Human Tissues and Cells

17.119 The donation, procurement, testing, processing, preservation, storage, and distribution of human tissues and cells are regulated activities (under the SANCO Directive).[235] The central requirement is for the testing, processing, preservation, storage, and distribution activities to be undertaken only by a 'tissue establishment' that has been accredited, designated, authorized, or licensed.[236] Requirements include the designation of a responsible person

to labelling issues) where the above of judicial review is not so limited: Case T-179/00 *A Menarini-Industrie Farmaceutiche Riunite Srl and European Federation of Pharmaceutical Industries and Associations v Commission* [2002] ECR II-2879.

229 Regulation (EC) 726/2004, Art 18.

230 ibid.

231 Directive (EC) 2001/83, Art 118; Medicines Act, s 28.

232 Regulation (EC) 726/2004, Art 20.

233 ibid.

234 ibid, Art 20(4).

235 Directive (EC) 2004/23 on setting standards of quality and safety for the donation, procurement, testing, processing, preservation, storage, and distribution of human tissues and cells became mandatory from 7 April 2007.

236 ibid, Art 6.

who in effect exercises delegated control over the requirements, quality management,[237] traceability, record keeping, labelling, reporting of serious adverse events and reactions, import, and export.[238] In principle, donations should be procured only after all consent or authorization requirements have been met, and be voluntary and unpaid, but compensating expenses and inconveniences is permitted: promotion and publicity is controlled.[239] Some exclusions apply, including autologous grafts within the same surgical procedure, blood, and organs used for the same purpose in the human body.[240] Tissues and cells to be used for industrially manufactured products, including medical devices, are regulated by the SANCO Directive only as far as donation, procurement, and testing are concerned: other measures cover other activities.[241]

D. Advanced Therapy Medicinal Products

A special regime applies to gene therapy medicinal products, somatic cell therapy medicinal products, and tissue engineered products (collectively known as advanced therapy medicinal products (ATMPs)).[242] The rules apply to gene therapy medicinal products and somatic cell therapy medicinal products from January 2009 (mandatory from January 2012), and to tissue engineered products from January 2009 (mandatory from January 2013). A tissue-engineered product is one that contains or consists of engineered cells or tissues, and is presented as having properties for, or is used in or administered to human beings with a view to regenerating, repairing, or replacing a human tissue.[243] Products containing or consisting exclusively of non-viable human or animal cells and/or tissues, which do not contain any viable cells or tissues and which do not act principally by pharmacological, immunological, or metabolic action, are excluded from this definition.[244] Annex I to Directive 2001/83 (the Community Code) is adapted to provide specific dossier requirements for ATMPs.[245] **17.120**

ATMPs are regulated under the Community's centralized procedure, subject to certain extra requirements, including on traceability, labelling, post-authorization follow-up of efficacy and adverse reactions, and risk management.[246] The donation, procurement, and testing of human cells or tissues is regulated by Directive (EC) 2004/23, discussed above. A medical device that forms part of a combined ATMP shall also meet the essential requirements for medical devices.[247] **17.121**

[237] Quality and safety requirements are specified in Commission Directives (EC) 2006/17 and (EC) 2006/86. The Directives were implemented into UK law by the Human Fertilisation and Embryology (Quality and Safety) Regulations, SI 2007/1522 in relation to human reproductive cells (gametes) and the Human Tissue (Quality and Safety for Human Application) Regulations 2007, SI 2007/1523, supplemented by many Human Tissue Act Directions.

[238] Directive (EC) 2004/23, Arts 8, 9, 11, 10, 16, 17, 22.

[239] ibid, Arts 13 and 12.

[240] ibid, Art 2.2.

[241] ibid, Art 2.

[242] Regulation (EC) 1394/2007.

[243] ibid, Art 2.1.

[244] ibid, Art 2.1

[245] Commission Directive (EC) 2009/120.

[246] ibid, Arts 4–15.

[247] ibid, Art 6; see Directive (EEC) 93/42 or for active implantable medical devices, Directive 90/385/EEC (see para 17.127).

E. Medical Devices

1. Overview

17.122 The regulatory system for medical devices is quite different from that for pharmaceuticals. It does not involve the pre-marketing assessment of a product by a medicines agency or the grant of a marketing authorization by a competent authority. Instead, the onus of ensuring and declaring that a product conforms to the legal *essential requirements* is placed on the *manufacturer* himself, but in many instances this is subject to approval by an independent technical organization (known as a *notified body*).

17.123 The manufacturer must apply an appropriate *conformity assessment* procedure to his device in order to ensure that it complies with the essential requirements, after which he must certify this fact by completing a *declaration of conformity*. There is usually a choice of conformity assessment procedures open to a manufacturer, depending on a risk-based *classification* of the class into which his device falls. The two main approaches to conformity assessment are based either on an approved total quality management system audited to ISO 9000 series standard, as customized for medical devices with EN 46000 series standard, or individual product assessment.

17.124 The essential requirements relate to the *safety* in use of the device, including labelling requirements, but are principally expressed in terms of scientific and technical *performance* characteristics. Efficacy, as such, is not a criterion. Confirmation of conformity must include evaluation of clinical data for many devices, generated from either a compilation of scientific literature or the results of *clinical investigations* on the product, for which prior ethical and regulatory approval is required. Conformity of a device with the essential requirements is denoted by affixing *CE marking* to the device. CE marking acts in effect as the passport which authorizes the device to be placed on the market and to circulate freely within the EEA and must be marked on the device.

17.125 The legal obligation is that a product must comply with the relevant essential requirements but where the manufacturer chooses to apply a national standard which adopts a European *harmonized standard* (EN series) to an aspect of his product, conformity will be prima facie presumed in respect of the aspects of the essential requirements covered by that standard. Other national or international standards do not have this regulatory benefit. Compliance with the essential requirements at the time of placing the device on the market, or declaration of this fact, should mean that the device is safe but it may later transpire that this is not the case. Manufacturers therefore have *post-marketing surveillance* and *vigilance* requirements. A Member State has *market surveillance* obligations and, if a marketed device is unsafe, its *competent authority* has power under a *safeguard clause* in each Medical Device Directive to take regulatory action to effect the withdrawal of the product from the market in its jurisdiction: the matter is then referred to the Commission and all Member States who then coordinate their actions.

17.126 Before the Medical Devices Directives came into being, most medical devices were unregulated in most European states. In some states, some were regulated (illogically, but this was the only available mechanism) as if they were medicines. Examples of products formerly regulated as medicines in the UK include contact lens products, intrauterine contraceptives and certain medicated dressings, surgical ligatures and sutures, absorbent or protective materials, and dental filling substances.

2. Law on specific device categories

17.127 The EEA law on the marketing of medical devices is governed by three principal Directives which each adopt the Community's scheme for product regulation known as the New Legislative Framework (NLF), originally called the 'new approach'.[248] The new approach applies to many product sectors, such as machinery, personal protective equipment, low voltage equipment, and electromagnetic compatibility requirements, but not to pharmaceuticals or cosmetics. Generic market surveillance and post-marketing requirements apply to all new approach products, as discussed at para 17.205. The three Medical Device Directives[249] are:

(i) Directive 90/385/EEC on Active Implantable Medical Devices ('AIMDD') came into force on 1 January 1993 and is mandatory from 1 January 1995. This covers all powered implants or partial implants which are left in the human body such as a heart pacemaker.
(ii) Directive 93/42/EEC on medical devices ('MDD') came into force on 1 January 1995 and became mandatory on 14 June 1998. This covers a wide range of devices ranging from first aid bandages, tongue depressors and blood collection bags to hip prostheses and active (powered) devices. The MDD was amended by Directive 2001/104/EC as of 13 June 2002, but subject to further five- and seven-year transition periods, in relation to devices containing stable medicinal substances derived from human blood and plasma.
(iii) Directive 98/79/EEC on *in vitro* diagnostics ('IVDD') came into force on 7 June 2000 and is mandatory from 7 December 2003. This covers products such as pregnancy tests, blood glucose monitoring, and tests for transmissible diseases.

17.128 The IVDD contained amendments to the two earlier Directives. All of these Directives are implemented into UK law as from 13 June 2002 by the Medical Devices Regulations 2002.[250]

---

248 The basis of the NLF package is contained in three measures: Regulation (EC) No 765/2008 of the European Parliament and of the Council of 9 July 2008 setting out the requirements for accreditation and market surveillance relating to the marketing of products and repealing Regulation (EEC) No 339/93; Decision No 768/2008/EC of the European Parliament and of the Council of 9 July 2008 on a common framework for the marketing of products; and repealing Council Decision 93/465/EEC, and Regulation (EC) No 764/2008 of the European Parliament and of the Council of 9 July 2008, laying down procedures relating to the application of certain national technical rules to products lawfully marketed in another Member State, and repealing Decision No 3052/95/EC. These replaced Council Resolution of 7 May 1985 on a new approach to technical harmonization and standards, OJ 1985 No C 136/1, 4.6.85. The NLF applies to a large family of engineered products, all of which are subject to the CE marking regime, albeit with significant differences in complexity between product families. The 2008 package extended the previous 'new approach' matrix in relation to obligations on distributors, on post-marketing surveillance, information and recall of products, strengthening the accreditation system for conformity assessment bodies, and strengthening the Community market surveillance system. Some of these aspects are already covered in the medical devices legislation. For general guidance see *The 'Blue Guide' on the implementation of EU product rules* (European Commission 2014).

249 The European Commission consulted in 2008 on recasting the devices Directives into a single, simplified measure.

250 SI 2002/618 (the Regulations), replacing earlier provisions including the Medical Devices Regulations 1994, SI 1994/3017. The Regulations deal with introductory provisions relating to all medical devices (Pt I), general medical devices (Pt II), active implantable medical devices (Pt III), *in vitro*

17.129 The EU legislation, with the exception of IVDs, is anticipated to be consolidated with certain amendments into an EU Regulation during 2017. The principal differences from the regime discussed below are expected to be a consolidated and centralized reporting and surveillance system, utilizing the advantages of unique device identifiers for every product hence supporting supply-chain security and enhancing vigilance, extended registration requirements on economic operators especially in the supply chain, enhanced supervision of notified bodies, authority for the Commission to issue mandatory guidance (the MEDDEV series), increased pre-market scrutiny of higher risk devices, controls on reprocessing and reprocessed devices, requirements for manufacturers and authorized representatives to have at least one Qualified Person, and clarification of a person who sponsors clinical investigations.[251]

17.130 The basic structure, concepts, and terminology of the three Directives on AIMDs, MDs, and IVDs are identical: such differences as exist between them arise out of the different nature of these products. The following discussion will therefore focus on the MDD, since this is the central Directive and covers most products. Short sections follow on AIMDs and IVDs. Detailed analysis of the relevant provisions would fill a large book: what is intended here is to highlight the important aspects that should be considered.

17.131 The intention behind the legislative scheme is that a product should essentially be regulated under a single product-specific regime as a medicinal product,[252] AIMD, MD, IVD, cosmetic,[253] blood or blood product, or personal protective equipment.[254] However, certain other Directives might apply to particular medical devices, including:

(i) Directive 89/336/EEC on electromagnetic compatibility (the EMC Directive): EMC requirements are included within the essential requirements of the Medical Device Directives so the EMC Directive only applies to medical devices before the relevant Medical Device Directive is applicable.
(ii) Directive 2001/95/EC on general product safety: this applies to all consumer products; some of its obligations apply to medical devices used by consumers (see below).

3. Resolution of uncertainties

17.132 Since this legislation is extensive, complex, frequently written in generalized terms, and seeks to create an entirely new regulatory system for products which were formerly largely unregulated, difficulties of interpretation or application are bound to arise. Since the Directives constitute a legal system, ultimate authority for interpretation rests with the courts, fundamentally with the Court of Justice of the European Communities in Luxembourg, to which questions of interpretation of EU law may be referred by national courts. A mechanism however, exists under the Medical Devices Directives by which measures and interpretations may be formally adopted: in the case of the MDD this is the Article 7 Committee, which is a committee of representatives of Member States chaired by the Commission. Under the Article 7 procedure, the Commission may submit to the Committee a draft of

diagnostic medical devices (Pt IV), notified bodies, conformity assessment bodies and marking of products (Pt V), fees charged by the Secretary of State (Pt VI), and general, enforcement and miscellaneous matters (Pt VII). For reasons of space, the following discussion is largely limited to an overview of and references to the provisions that apply to general medical devices.

[251] See Proposal for a Regulation on medical devices, COM (2012) 542, 26.9.2012.
[252] Directive (EC) 2001/83, replacing Directive (EEC) 65/65 as amended and related Directives.
[253] Directive 76/768/EEC, as amended.
[254] Directive 89/686/EEC, as amended.

measures to be taken, on which the Committee delivers its opinion based on a weighted majority of representatives. The Commission shall adopt the measures envisaged if they are in accordance with the opinion of the Committee. If there is divergence, the Commission shall permit a proposal to the Council of members, which shall act by a qualified majority of votes.

Less formal, non-binding procedures also exist. There are frequent meetings between representatives of the Commission, Member States, and notified bodies. The Commission is also assisted by a Working Group of Experts. A sequence of guidance notes have been issued by the Commission (MEDDEV series), by certain competent authorities (for example, the UK MHRA's Bulletins), arising out of the meeting of notified bodies, by trade associations and others. **17.133**

4. Competent authorities and notified bodies

Each Member State has designated a competent authority, which is the governmental authority responsible for implementing the Directive in that Member State. In the case of the UK, the competent authority is the Medicines and Healthcare Products Regulatory Agency,[255] an executive agency of the Department of Health. The principal function of a competent authority in practice is to ensure the safety and health of patients and users of medical devices. **17.134**

A competent authority is not involved in the assessment or authorization for placing on the market of a medical device. As stated above, the legal responsibility in each case rests with the individual manufacturer. However, in many cases the manufacturer is required to obtain independent certification from a third party testing house, called a notified body. Such testing houses are private, commercial enterprises who may apply for and be approved for the purposes of the legislation by the competent authority in their Member State and are then notified within the Community by their approval being published in the Official Journal. Notified bodies may be approved for all devices or only for specific classes of devices. Criteria which they must satisfy in order to be approved are set out in an Annex to the relevant Directive (Annex XI for the MDD). In effect, therefore, notified bodies, although private entities, perform certain delegated regulatory functions. A manufacturer who is required by law to utilize the services of a notified body may choose any notified body within the Community who has the appropriate certification, irrespective of where either of them is located. The relationship between manufacturer and notified body is based on contract even though certain actions of the notified body have regulatory authority. **17.135**

5. Definition of a medical device

A medical device is defined as: **17.136**

> any instrument, apparatus, appliance, material or other article, whether used alone or in combination, including the software necessary for its proper application intended by the manufacturer to be used for human beings for the purpose of:[256]
>
> — diagnosis, prevention, monitoring, treatment or alleviation of disease,
> — diagnosis, monitoring, treatment, alleviation or compensation for an injury or handicap,
> — investigation, replacement or modification of the anatomy or of a physiological process,
> — control of conception,

[255] This Agency was created in 2003 on the merger of the Medicines Control Agency and the Medical Devices Agency.

[256] The important consideration is not the effect but the intended purpose: *Optident Ltd and Another v Secretary of State for Trade and Industry and Another* [2001] UKHL 32, [35] *per* Lord Slynn of Hadley.

and which does not achieve its principal intended action in or on the human body by pharmacological, immunological or metabolic means, but which may be assisted in its function by such means.[257]

17.137 An accessory is also considered to be a medical device. An accessory is defined as:

an article which whilst not being a device is intended specifically by its manufacturer to be used together with a device to enable it to be used in accordance with the use of the device intended by the manufacturer of the device.[258]

6. The drug and device borderline

17.138 Difficult borderline questions arise in relation to a significant number of products,[259] particularly whether they are to be classified as medicinal products or as medical devices. As a general rule, a relevant product is regulated either under the Medical Devices Directives or by the Medicinal Products Directives (MPDs). Normally, the procedures of both Directives do not apply cumulatively. The Commission has issued Guidelines on this drug–device borderline issue[260] and also on what constitutes medical devices, AIMDs, and accessories. In order to decide which regime applies, the relevant criteria are:

(i) the intended purpose of the product, taking into account the way the product is presented (this is likely to establish if either the MDD or MPD apply, rather than distinguish between the two regimes);
(ii) the method by which the principal intended action is achieved. This is crucial in the definition of a medical device. Typically, the medical device function is fulfilled by physical means (including mechanical action, physical barrier, replacement of or support to organs or body functions). The action of a medicinal product is achieved by pharmacological or immunological means or by metabolism.

17.139 The principal intended action of a product may be deduced from:

(i) the manufacturer's labelling and claims;
(ii) scientific data regarding mechanism of action.

17.140 Although the manufacturer's claims are important, it is not possible to place the product in one or other category in contradiction with current scientific data. Manufacturers may be required to justify scientifically their rationale for classification of borderline products.

17.141 Medical devices may be assisted in their function by pharmacological, immunological, or metabolic means, but as soon as these means are no longer ancillary with respect to the principal purpose of a product, the product becomes a medicinal product. The claims made for a product, in accordance with its method of action may, in this context, represent an important factor for its classification as medical device or medicinal product. Examples of

---

[257] Directive (EEC) 93/42, Art 1.2(a); Directive (EEC) 90/385, Art 1(2)(a); the Regulations, reg 2(1).

[258] Directive (EEC) 93/42, Art 1.2(b); the Regulations, reg 5(1).

[259] The two regimes of regulation of medical device and cosmetics have been described as not only different but intended to be separate and distinct. The decision on whether a product is a cosmetic product or a medical device is to be decided by the competent authorities of a Member State and in the last resort by the courts, irrespective of whether a product bears CE marking. *Optident Ltd and Another v Secretary of State for Trade and Industry and Another* [2001] UKHL 32, [27] and [29] *per* Lord Slynn of Hadley.

[260] Guidelines relating to the Application of: The Council Directive (EEC) 90/385 on Active Implantable Medical Devices [and] The Council Directive (EEC) 93/42 on Medical Devices 'Demarcation between: Directive (EEC) 90/385 on Active Implantable Medical Devices, Directive (EEC) 93/42 on Medical Devices, and Directive (EEC) 65/65 relating to Medicinal Products, and Related Directives', European Commission. MEDDEV. 2.1/3 rev. 3, July 2009.

medical devices incorporating a medicinal substance with ancillary action include catheters coated with heparin or an antibiotic, bone cements containing antibiotic, and blood bags containing anti-coagulant.[261]

7. Products comprising both a drug and a device

For so called drug–device combinations, the MDD specifies the following approach:[262] **17.142**

(i) A device which is intended to administer a medicinal product (such as an unfilled syringe) is a medical device. The medicinal product itself remains regulated as a medicine.

(ii) If the device and the medicinal product form a single integral product which is intended exclusively for use in the given combination and which is not reusable (such as a pre-filled syringe), that single product is regulated as a medicine. An application for a marketing authorization must be made under Directive (EC) 2001/83. However, the safety and performance of the device features of the integral product are assessed in accordance with the essential requirements of Annex I of the MDD.

(iii) Where a device incorporates, as an integral part, a substance which, if used separately, may be considered to be a medicinal product and which is liable to act upon the body with action ancillary to that of the device (such as a heparin-coated catheter), the product is classed as a medical device. However, the medicinal product is to be assessed in accordance with the requirements of Directive (EC) 2001/83. A notified body undertaking conformity assessment on a medical device which incorporates a medicinal substance having ancillary action has a responsibility to consult a national medicines agency about the medicinal substance, to verify its safety, quality and usefulness by analogy with the appropriate methods specified in Directive (EC) 2001/83.

These provisions are explained further in Guidelines issued by the European Commission.[263] **17.143**

8. Classification

The purpose of classification of devices is simply so as to provide options for conformity assessment methods. Under the MDD Directive, medical devices are categorized into four classes, generally according to the degree of risk that they represent. In summary, Class I covers those which do not enter or interact with the body, Classes IIa and IIb are invasive or implantable devices or those which do interact with the body, Class III is for devices which affect the functions of vital organs. Implantables with an energy source are covered by the AIMDD. The detailed classification rules[264] are lengthy and are set out in Annex IX of Directive (EEC) 93/42. A sequence of rules must be worked through: charts and software are available to assist this. **17.144**

The classification system uses three basic criteria, in various combinations: duration of contact with the body, degree of invasiveness, and the anatomy affected by the use of the **17.145**

261 ibid.

262 Directive (EEC) 93/42, Recital 6 and Art 1.3 and 1.4; these provisions are not repeated in this form in the Regulations, which provide in regs 12(4) and 5(1) for the second of the three situations, namely single-use combination products, and in reg 9(8) that the medical device component of a single-use combination product need only comply with those essential requirements that relate to safety and performance, unless the medicinal product which forms part of that product is liable to act on the human body with action ancillary to that of the medical device (ie the third situation), in which case the single-use combination product must comply with all the relevant essential requirements which apply to it.

263 See the Guidelines, n 260.

264 Applied by the Regulations, reg 7.

device. Duration is based on continuous use (ie uninterrupted actual use) and categorized as transient (<60 minutes), short term (±30 days) and long term (>30 days). Invasive devices penetrate wholly or partly inside the body by way of an orifice or via the surface of the body. A body orifice is a natural opening in the body and includes the external surface of the eyeball and any permanent artificial opening, such as a stoma. Surgically invasive devices penetrate via the surface to the inside of the body by surgical intervention. Implantable devices are surgically invasive devices intended to be totally introduced to the body, to replace an epithelial surface or the surface of the eye and intended to remain in place after the procedure and also includes those partially introduced surgically invasive devices remaining in place for at least thirty days. The central circulatory system is defined by the following vessels: ***arteriae pulmonales, aorta ascendens, arteriae coronarieae, arteria carotis communis, arteria carotis externa, arteria carotis interna, arteriae cerebrales, truncus brachicephalicus, venae cordis, venae pulmonales, vena cava superior, vena cava inferior.*** The central nervous system consists of the brain, meninges, and spinal cord. Active medical devices depend on a power source such as electricity for its operation, but not sources of power generated by the human body or gravity.

17.146 Non-invasive devices are covered by rules 1–4 and include the following classes:

Class I, for example, colostomy pouches, wheelchairs, eye glasses, incontinence pads, cups and spoons for administering medicines, wound dressings such as cotton wool and wound strips;

Class IIa, for example, transfusion equipment, storage and transport of donor organs, polymer film dressings, hydrogel dressings;

Class IIb, for example, haemodialysers, dressings for chronic extensive ulcerated wounds.

17.147 Invasive devices are covered by rules 5–8 and include following classes:

Class I, for example, dressings for nose bleeds, hand-held dentistry mirrors, enema devices, reusable surgical instruments;

Class IIa, for example, contact lenses, urinary catheters, tracheal tubes connected to a ventilator, needles used for suturing, infusion cannulae, dental bridges and crowns;

Class IIb, for example, urethral stents, insulin pens, devices supplying ionizing radiation, intraocular lenses, maxillo-facial implants;

Class III for example prosthetic heart valves, rechargeable non-active drug delivery systems, absorbable sutures, spinal stents, neurological catheters, temporary pacemaker leads.[265]

17.148 Active devices, whilst covered under the above rules, are largely covered by rules 9–12 and including the following classes:

Class I, for example, examination lights, surgical microscopes, wheelchairs, thermography devices, recording, processing or viewing of diagnostic images;

Class IIa, for example, suction equipment, feeding pumps, anaesthesia machines, ventilators, hearing aids;

Class IIb, for example, lung ventilators, incubators for babies, surgical lasers, X-ray sources.

[265] Hip, knee, and shoulder joint replacements were reclassified from Class IIb to Class III under Commission Directive (EC) 2005/50, implemented by the Medical Devices (Amendment) Regulations 2007, SI 2007/400.

Special rules 13–18 govern several hazardous characteristics that may be found in certain devices and require a certain level of control and conformity assessment. Rule 13 deals with devices incorporating a medicinal substance whose action is ancillary to that of the device—Class III, for example, antibiotic bone cements, condoms with spermicides, heparin-coated catheters. **17.149**

Rule 14 deals with devices used for contraception or the prevention of transmission of sexually transmitted diseases—Class IIb, for example, condoms, contraceptive diaphragms and if they are implantable or long term invasive—Class III, for example, intra-uterine devices. **17.150**

Rule 15 deals with devices for specific disinfecting, cleaning, and rinsing and includes contact lens disinfecting, cleaning, rinsing, and hydrating—Class IIb, for example, contact lens solutions, comfort solutions, and devices specifically intended for disinfecting medical devices—Class IIa, for example, disinfectants for use with endoscopes. **17.151**

Rule 16 classifies non-active devices specifically intended for recording X-ray diagnostic images as Class IIa, for example, X-ray films. **17.152**

Rule 17 classifies all devices utilizing animal tissues or derivatives rendered non-viable and coming into contact with breached skin as Class III, for example, biological heart valves, porcine xenograft dressings, catgut sutures, collagen implants and dressings. **17.153**

Rule 18 puts blood bags into Class IIb. If several rules apply to a device, the strictest rule resulting in the higher classification applies. **17.154**

It must be reiterated that classification is based on the manufacturer's intended use and thus the listing of devices into classes must be taken as guidance only. No classification system can be perfect and thus the aim is to capture the majority of products whilst recognizing that there will always be products that are borderline either between classes or with other product types such as drugs and cosmetics and also new innovative products that do not fit the criteria laid down. **17.155**

9. Conformity assessment procedures and CE marking

Depending on the class of the device a manufacturer may be able to choose between a number of alternative conformity assessment procedures in the assessment of whether a medical device conforms to the essential requirements. Although the rules should be considered in detail in each case,[266] the basic options can be summarized as follows: **17.156**

(i) For all products in classes IIa, IIb, and III, and AIMDs, a *full quality assurance* system, audited periodically by a notified body (Annex II of the MDD) *which includes* examination and certification by the notified body of the design dossier of each product covered. The manufacturer must keep documentation on the quality system and the design dossier of each product plus other documentation. The quality system obligations include post-marketing and vigilance aspects. Compliance with Annex II may be achieved (this is not mandatory but is invariably adopted voluntarily) by compliance with the EN 29000 and 46000 series standards, which apply the ISO 9000 series.

(ii) For products in classes IIa, IIb, and III, and AIMDs, examination and certification by a notified body of a specimen product (*type examination*: Annex III of the MDD) coupled with a varying degree (partially restricted by product class) of product or production quality assurance (MDD Annexes IV, V and VI) which ensures that the manufacturing

[266] Directive (EEC) 93/42, Art 11; the Regulations, reg 13.

process produces products which conform to the certified type and might involve a quality system for manufacture and final inspection (Annex V) or a quality system for final inspection and testing (Annex VI).

(iii) For products in class I, the manufacturer must have specified technical documentation on the design of the product showing that it conforms to the essential requirements: manufacturing aspects are not covered and a notified body is not involved unless there is a measuring function and/or the product is sterilized. (Annex VII: *EC declaration of conformity*).

17.157 In all cases, the specified documentation must be kept for five years after the last product has been manufactured. The Annex VII procedure is also available for Class IIa devices if coupled with the Annex IV or V or VI procedure.

10. Registration

17.158 The manufacturer of a class I device or of a custom-made device or a person who markets a system or procedure pack must inform his competent authority of his registered place of business and the description of the devices concerned.[267] Such manufacturers who are located outside the EEA must designate persons established with the Community who are responsible for such registration.

11. Harmonized standards

17.159 A manufacturer may voluntarily decide to apply any standard to his product or business. Devices which are in conformity with a national standard adopted pursuant to a harmonized EC standard published in the Official Journal of the European Communities shall be presumed by Member States to comply with those aspects of the essential requirements which are covered by the standard.[268] Harmonized standards are those adopted by the EC standards bodies pursuant to a mandate issued by the Commission,[269] in this case the European Committee for Standardization (CEN) and the European Committee for Electrotechnical Standardization (CENELEC). A large number of standards are contemplated but may take time to be written and adopted. Standards may be horizontal (covering aspects common to all or a number of product types) or vertical (dealing only with a specific aspect or specific product type). Important harmonized standards exist on the following:

EN 13485 medical devices—quality management systems—requirements for regulatory purposes;
EN 1041 information and labelling for medical devices;
EN 980 graphical symbols;
EN 10993 series biological evaluation of medical devices;
EN 14155-1 clinical investigation of medical devices for human subjects—Part 1: general requirements;
EN 14155-2—clinical investigation of medical devices for human subjects—Part 2: clinical investigation plans;
EN 60601 series medical electrical equipment;
EN 14971 medical devices—application of risk management to medical devices.

[267] Directive (EEC) 93/42, Art 14; the Regulations, reg 19.
[268] The Regulations, reg 9 (4).
[269] See the definition of a harmonized standard in the Regulations, reg 2 (1).

12. Custom-made devices

17.160 A new device which is specifically made in accordance with a duly qualified medical practitioner's written prescription and which gives, under his responsibility, specific design characteristics and is intended for the sole use of a particular patient, is permitted to be marketed without CE marking under provisions referring to custom-made devices.[270] The prescription may be made by any person authorized by virtue of his professional qualifications to do so. Mass-produced devices which need to be adapted to meet the specific requirements of the medical practitioner or any other professional user are not considered to be custom-made devices.[271]

17.161 The manufacturer must undertake to keep available for the competent authorities documentation on the design, manufacture, and performance of the product so as to allow assessment of conformity with the essential requirements.[272] He must also draw up a statement containing the following information:[273]

(i) data allowing identification of the device in question;
(ii) a statement that the device is intended for exclusive use by a particular patient, together with the name of the patient;
(iii) the name of the medical practitioner or other authorized person who made out the prescription and, where applicable, the name of the clinic concerned;
(iv) the particular features of the device as specified in the relevant medical prescription;
(v) a statement that the device in question conforms to the essential requirements set out in Annex I of the Directive and, where applicable, indicating which essential requirements have not been fully met, together with the grounds. The manufacturer must inform the competent authorities of his registered place of business and the description of the devices concerned.

13. Systems and procedure packs

17.162 It sometimes occurs that a number of items are assembled and marketed together as a particular system or to be used with a particular medical procedure. The individual items might or might not already bear CE marking.

17.163 Where all the devices bear CE marking and are put together within the intended purposes specified by their manufacturers, a person who puts them together shall draw up a declaration stating that:[274]

(i) he has verified the mutual compatibility of the devices in accordance with the manufacturers' instructions and has carried out his operations in accordance with these instructions; and
(ii) he has packaged the system or procedure pack and supplied relevant information to users incorporating relevant instructions from the manufacturers; and
(iii) the whole activity is subjected to appropriate methods of internal control and inspection.

17.164 The system or procedure pack must not bear additional CE marking and must be accompanied by the original manufacturers' information. The declaration must be kept for five years.

---

270 Directive (EEC) 93/42, Arts 1.2(d), 12.6 and Annex VIII; the Regulations, regs 15 and 5.
271 ibid.
272 ibid, see also Regulations 9(5) and 12(2).
273 ibid.
274 Directive (EEC) 93/42, Art 12; the Regulations, regs 14 and 5.

17.165 Where the above conditions are not met, as in cases where the system or procedure pack incorporates devices which do not bear CE marking or where the chosen combination of devices is not compatible in view of their original intended use, the system or procedure pack shall be treated as a device in its own right and the appropriate conformity assessment procedure must be followed.

14. Essential requirements

17.166 The essential requirements contained in Annex I of each new approach Directive specify the aspects of safety and performance which must be satisfied at the time at which a relevant product is placed on the market.[275] Essential requirements are stated as principles or as generalized aspects and exclude detailed technical requirements. The scheme of the Community's new approach is that detailed technical aspects are not required as legal obligations but, if they are generally accepted, may be applied voluntarily by manufacturers through being included in official standards.[276] The essential requirements are intended to be comprehensive and all must be satisfied save for those requirements which do not apply to a particular product as a matter of common sense.

17.167 The essential requirements in the MDD fall under two headings: general requirements and requirements regarding design and construction.[277] The general requirements include the following provisions:

(i) The devices must be designed and manufactured in such a way that, when used under the conditions and for the purposes intended, they will not compromise the clinical condition or the safety of patients, or the safety and health of users or, where applicable, other persons, provided that any risks which may be associated with their use constitute acceptable risks when weighed against the benefits to the patient and are compatible with a high level of protection of health and safety.

(ii) The solutions adopted by the manufacturer for the design and construction of the devices must conform to safety principles, taking account of the generally acknowledged state of the art. In selecting the most appropriate solutions, the manufacturer must apply the following principles in the following order:
- eliminate or reduce risks as far as possible (inherently safe design and construction),
- where appropriate take adequate protection measures including alarms if necessary, in relation to risks that cannot be eliminated,
- inform users of the residual risks due to any shortcomings of the protection measures adopted.

(iii) The devices must achieve the performances intended by the manufacturer and be designed, manufactured and packaged in such a way that they are suitable for one or more of the functions as specified by the manufacturer.

(iv) The characteristics and performances referred to in sections (i)–(iii) above must not be adversely affected to such a degree that the clinical conditions and safety of the patients and, where applicable, of other persons are compromised during the lifetime of the device as indicated by the manufacturer, when the device is subjected to the stresses which can occur during normal conditions of use.

(v) The devices must be designed, manufactured and packed in such a way that their characteristics and performances during their intended use will not be adversely affected during transport and storage taking account of the instructions and information provided by the manufacturer.

---

[275] The Regulations, reg 8.

[276] Council Resolution of 21 December 1989 on a global approach to conformity assessment, OJ 1989 No C10/1, 16.1.90.

[277] The following paragraphs are taken from Directive (EEC) 93/42, Annex I.

(vi) Any undesirable side-effect must constitute an acceptable risk when weighed against the performances intended.

Section (ii) above implies that a manufacturer must carry out a risk analysis. A harmonized standard is available on this topic, EN 14971, which amplifies the methodology for risk analysis, elimination, or reduction required by section (ii). **17.168**

The essential requirements regarding design and construction are too extensive to be summarized here. They cover the following headings: **17.169**

(i) Clinical, physical and biological properties;
(ii) Infection and microbial contamination;
(iii) Construction and environmental properties;
(iv) Devices with a measuring function;
(v) Protection against radiation;
(vi) Requirements for medical devices connected to or equipped with an energy source;
(vii) Information supplied by the manufacturer (this is discussed further below).

15. Information supplied by the manufacturer

The general principle is that each device must be accompanied by the information needed to use it safely and to identify the manufacturer, taking account of the training and knowledge of the potential users. This information comprises the details on the label and the data in the instructions for use. A series of thirteen particular requirements are specified for inclusion in the label and the same thirteen requirements plus a further fifteen categories of information must be included in the instructions for use. **17.170**

As far as practicable and appropriate, the information needed to use the device safely must be set out on the device itself and/or on the packaging for each unit or, where appropriate, on the sales packaging. If individual packaging of each unit is not practicable, the information must be set out in the leaflet supplied with one or more devices. Instructions for use must be included in the packaging for every device. By way of exception, no such instructions for use are needed for devices in Class I or IIa if they can be used safely without any such instructions. **17.171**

Where appropriate, this information should take the form of symbols. Any symbol or identification colour used must conform to the harmonized standards. In areas for which no standards exist, the symbols and colours must be described in the documentation supplied with the device. **17.172**

It will be noted that in the above three paragraphs, which are quoted verbatim from Annex I, certain flexibility is permitted through use of the words 'where appropriate': this is a feature of many of the other essential requirements. The manufacturer is permitted some discretion over compliance with the essential requirements, based on an application of common sense to the circumstances of his particular product. **17.173**

16. Definition of manufacturer

A manufacturer is defined as the natural or legal person with responsibility for the design, manufacture, packaging, and labelling of a device before it is placed on the EU market under his own name, regardless of whether these operations are carried out by that person himself or on his behalf by a third party.[278] The Directives also apply to those who assemble, package, process, fully refurbish, or label a product and in certain other situations.[279] **17.174**

278 Directive (EEC) 93/42, Art 1.2(f); the Regulations, reg 2 (1).
279 ibid.

17.175 The intention is that the person (more normally, the company) who assumes the legal responsibility of 'manufacturer' need not be the person who assembles the product. One or more of the activities of design, manufacture, packaging, or labelling may be subcontracted by the legal manufacturer. The name or trade name and address of the legal manufacturer must appear on the label and instructions for use.[280] In addition, for devices imported into the Community, the label, or the outer packaging, or instructions for use, must contain the name and address of either the authorized representative of the manufacturer established within the Community, or of the importer established in the Community (this is in effect for devices whose importation is not authorized by the manufacturer), or for the person who has the responsibility to register with the competent authorities in the case of Class I or custom-made devices.[281]

17.176 The Regulations require a manufacturer or, where applicable, his authorized representative to observe the manufacturer's obligations set out in the relevant conformity assessment procedure,[282] and to take account of the results of any assessment or verification operations which have been carried out in accordance with the legislation at an intermediate stage of manufacture.[283]

17.177 A manufacturer located outside the EEA may place a Class I or custom-made medical device or a system or procedure pack on the EU market under his own name provided it has undergone a relevant conformity assessment procedure and bears CE marking and the competent authorities in the relevant Member State have been informed either of (i) his registered place of business in that Member State, if he has one, and the description of the device, or (ii) the registered place of business in that Member State of a person he has designated responsible for marketing the device in the European Union, and the category of the device.[284]

17.178 In relation to devices in Classes II, IIa, and IIb, the manufacturer must certify conformity personally under the Annex II procedure, but his authorized representative established in the European Union may do this in place of the manufacturer under the Annex III and IV procedures.

17.179 The functions of an authorized representative are not precisely defined in the Directives save for the IVD Directive, but he is a person explicitly designated by the manufacturer and acts and may be addressed by authorities and bodies in the Community instead of the manufacturer with regard to the latter's obligations.[285] It would be good practice for the manufacturer and authorized representative to have a written contract recording their relationship.

17. CE marking: Placing on the market and putting into service

17.180 Medical devices may only be placed on the market and put into service if they comply with the requirements laid down in the Directive when duly supplied and properly installed, maintained, and used in accordance with their intended purpose.[286] Devices, other than devices which are custom-made or intended for clinical investigations, which are considered to meet the essential requirements set out in Annex I of the relevant Directive must bear the CE marking of conformity when they are placed on the market.[287]

---

[280] Directive (EEC) 93/42, Annex I, para 13.1.
[281] ibid.
[282] The Regulations, reg 17(1).
[283] ibid, reg 17(2).
[284] Directive (EEC) 93/42, Art 14; the Regulations, reg 19.
[285] Directive (EC) 98/79, Art 1(2)(g).
[286] eg Directive (EEC) 93/42, Art 2; the Regulations, reg 8.
[287] eg Directive (EEC) 93/42, Arts 17 and 3; the Regulations, reg 10.

The CE marking of conformity, as specified in MDD Annex XII, must appear in a visible, legible, and indelible form on the device or its sterile pack, where practicable and appropriate, and on the instructions for use.[288] Where applicable, the CE marking must also appear on the sales packaging.[289] It shall be accompanied by the identification number of the notified body responsible for implementation of the relevant conformity assessment procedure. It is prohibited to affix marks or inscriptions that are likely to mislead third parties with regard to the meaning or the graphics of the CE marking.[290] Any other mark may be affixed to the device, to the packaging or to the instruction leaflet accompanying the device provided that the visibility and legibility of the CE marking is not thereby reduced. **17.181**

The concepts of 'placing on the market' and 'putting into service' are standard in Community 'new approach' Directives. For the purposes of the MDD, they are defined as follows: **17.182**

> 'placing on the market' means the first making available in return for payment or free of charge of a device other than a device intended for clinical investigation, with a view to distribution and/or use on the Community market, regardless of whether it is new or fully refurbished;
>
> 'putting into service' means the stage at which a device has been made available to the final user as being ready for use on the Community market for the first time for its intended purpose.[291]

The European Commission has issued guidance on these concepts in the context of all 'new approach Directives'.[292] In essence, a device is placed on the market when it is first put into the stream of distribution or commerce by its manufacturer. A device which is fully refurbished is treated as if it were a new device and must be subject afresh to the requirements of the Directive. Difficulties arise over the definition of what constitutes refurbishment (simple servicing is clearly not included) and aspects such as upgrading. **17.183**

18. Clinical investigation

Confirmation of conformity with the essential requirements must be based on clinical data in the case of, as a general rule, implantable and long-term invasive devices falling within Classes IIa, IIb, and all Class III devices under the MDD;[293] and all active implantable devices under the AIMDD.[294] **17.184**

The adequacy of such clinical data must be based on either[295] a compilation of the relevant scientific literature and, 'if appropriate', a written report containing a critical evaluation, or the results of all clinical investigations made. **17.185**

---

288 ibid.

289 ibid.

290 The Regulations, reg 10(5).

291 Directive (EEC) 93/42, Art 1.2(h) and (i) as amended by Art 21 of Directive (EC) 98/79; the Regulations, reg 2 (1).

292 European Commission, *Guide to the Implementation of Directives Based on the New Approach and the Global Approach* (2000).

293 Directive (EEC) 93/42, Annex X and Art 15; this somewhat imprecise wording from Annex X is not reproduced in the Regulations. Regulation 9(2) states that 'Where confirmation of conformity with the essential requirements must be based on clinical data, such data must be established in accordance with the requirements set out in Annex X.' There is therefore a legal uncertainty about when and how much clinical investigation is required: the issue remains a matter of scientific and technical judgment.

294 Directive (EEC) 90/385, Art 10 and Annex 7; see also Annex 2, para 4.1 and Annex 3, para 3.

295 Directive (EEC) 93/42, Annex X, para 1.

17.186 Thus, *evaluation* of the clinical safety and performance is required for all devices, whereas a clinical *investigation* of each device may or may not be necessary (the term clinical trial is not used in relation to devices). The Directives give some latitude over the circumstances in which a clinical investigation of a non-CE marked device is required. Guidance issued by the MHRA[296] states that an investigation would be required where:

(i) there is the introduction of a completely new concept of device into clinical practice where components, features and/or methods of action, are previously unknown;
(ii) an existing device is modified in such a way that it contains a novel feature particularly if such a feature has an important physiological effect; or where the modification might significantly affect the clinical performance and/or safety of the device;
(iii) a device incorporates materials previously untested in humans, coming into contact with the human body or where existing materials are applied to a new location in the human body, in which case compatibility and biological safety will need to be considered;
(iv) a device, either CE-marked or non-CE-marked, is proposed for a new purpose or function.

17.187 Clinical investigation will also be required where a CE-marked device is to be used for a new purpose.

17.188 The regime of the Directives is that if clinical evaluation is required, it must be subject to ethical approval in accordance with the principles of the Declaration of Helsinki.[297] The Directives provide[298] that the purpose of clinical investigation is to:

(i) verify that, under normal conditions of use, the performance of the devices conform to [those intended by the manufacturer, namely the device should be designed and manufactured in such a way that it is suitable for the functions specified by the manufacturer],
(ii) determine any undesirable side effects, under normal conditions of use, and assess whether they are acceptable risks having regard to the intended performance of the device.

17.189 The Directives also specify the methodology to be adopted in clinical investigations. Adverse incidents occurring in the investigation must be reported to the competent authority. A general requirement in the MDD is:

> Clinical investigations must be performed on the basis of an appropriate plan of investigation reflecting the latest scientific and technical knowledge and defined in such a way as to confirm or refute the manufacturer's claims for the device; these investigations must include an adequate number of observations to guarantee the scientific validity of the conclusions.[299]

17.190 The primary consideration of a clinical investigation of a device is assessment verification of the manufacturer's claims for the technical performance of the device. Safety considerations are nevertheless relevant in that the clinical investigation should determine and assess any undesirable side effects, but the main thrust of the clinical evaluation, and in particular of the conformity assessment by a notified body or the manufacturer to permit marketing, is on technical performance rather than a complete evaluation of safety. It is an essential

---

[296] MHRA, *Guidance Notes for Manufacturers on Clinical Investigations to be carried out in the UK* (2008).

[297] Directive (EEC) 90/385, Annex 7, para 2.2 and Directive (EEC) 93/42, Annex X, para 2.2.

[298] Directive (EEC) 90/385, Annex 7 and Directive (EEC) 93/42, Annex X.

[299] Directive (EEC) 93/42, Annex X, Requirement 2.3.1.

requirement for marketed devices that '[a]ny undesirable side-effect must constitute an acceptable risk when weighed against the performances intended'.[300]

Both the AIMDD[301] and the MDD[302] specify approval procedures for clinical investigations by the competent authority and relevant ethics committee(s). The manufacturer must submit to the competent authority of the Member State in which the investigation is to be conducted a statement in the specified form (MDD Annex VIII) containing information as detailed as design drawings, manufacturing methods, descriptions and explanations, and the results of calculations and technical tests. For Class II devices and implantable and long-term devices in Classes IIa and IIb the investigation may commence either after sixty days unless the authority has objected, or earlier if the authority so authorizes, provided a favourable ethics committee opinion is available. For devices other than those just specified, the Member State may authorize immediate commencement after receipt of notification, provided a favourable ethics committee opinion has been issued. A device which is intended for clinical investigation must not bear CE marking. **17.191**

Compliance with the requirements relating to clinical investigations (AIMDD Annex VII; MDD Annex X) is assisted by adoption of standards EN 14155-1—Clinical investigation of medical devices for human subjects—Part 1: General requirements and EN 14155-2—Clinical investigation of medical devices for human subjects—Part 2: Clinical investigation plans which are very similar to pharmaceutical GCP. **17.192**

Clinical investigation is not required for IVDs, for which the equivalent procedure is performance evaluation, discussed below. **17.193**

19. *In vitro* diagnostic medical devices

(i) Definition of in vitro diagnostic medical device

An *in vitro* diagnostic medical device is defined as any medical device which is a reagent, reagent product, calibrator, control material, kit, instrument, apparatus, equipment, or system, whether used alone or in combination, intended by the manufacturer to be used *in vitro* for the examination of specimens including blood and tissue donations, derived from the human body, solely or principally for the purpose of providing information concerning a physiological or pathological state, or concerning a congenital abnormality, or to determine the safety and compatibility with potential recipients, or to monitor therapeutic measures.[303] For the purpose of this Directive, a specimen receptacle, whether evacuated or not, specifically intended by its manufacturer to contain a specimen for the purposes of *in vitro* diagnostic examination, is considered to be a device. Products for general laboratory use are not devices unless such products, in view of their characteristics, are specifically intended by their manufacturer to be used for *in vitro* diagnostic examination.[304] **17.194**

(ii) Classification

The IVD Directive follows the same general 'new approach' scheme as the other medical devices Directives with the following major differences. IVDs are divided into two classes: Annex II devices and everything else. Annex II devices are themselves divided into List A (high risk) and List B which include the following (each case also including calibrators and control materials): **17.195**

[300] Directive (EEC) 93/42, Annex I, Requirement 6.
[301] Directive (EEC) 90/385, Art 10; the Regulations, reg 29.
[302] Directive (EEC) 93/42, Art 15; the Regulation, reg 16.
[303] Directive (EC) 98/79, Art 1.2(b); the Regulations, reg 2(1).
[304] ibid.

List A— Reagents and reagent products for determining the following blood groups: ABO system, Rhesus (C, c, D, E, e) anti-Kell.

— Reagents and reagent products for the detection, confirmation and quantification in human specimens of markers of HIV infection (HIV 1 and 2), HTLV I and II, and Hepatitis B, C, and D.

List B— Reagents and reagent products for determining the following blood groups: Anti-Duffy and Anti-Kidd.

— Reagents and reagent products for determining irregular anti-erythrocytic antibodies.

— Reagents and reagent products for the detection and quantification in human samples of the following congenital infections: rubella, toxoplasmosis.

— Reagents and reagent products for diagnosing the following hereditary disease: phenylketonuria.

— Reagents and reagent products for determining the following human infections: cytomegalovirus, chlamydia.

— Reagents and reagent products for determining the following HLA tissue groups: DR, A, B.

— Reagents and reagent products for determining the following turmoral marker: PSA.

— Reagents and reagent products, including software, designed specifically for evaluating the risk of trisomy 21.

— The following device for self-diagnosis: device for the measurement of blood sugar.

(iii) Particular provisions

17.196 One of two conformity assessment procedures may be followed for devices covered by Annex II:

(i) the EC Declaration of Conformity procedure (full quality assurance: Annex IV); or
(ii) the EC type examination procedure (Annex V) coupled with either the EC verification procedure (Annex VI) or the EC Declaration of Conformity (production quality assurance: Annex VII).

17.197 All devices other than those covered by Annex II are subject to the EC Declaration of Conformity procedure (Annex III), which does not involve the intervention of a notified body, but which includes supplementary requirements for devices for self-testing, which does involve a notified body (Annex III).

17.198 Common Technical Specifications (CTS) are to be adopted by the Article 7.2 Committee (a working group of scientific experts appointed by the Member States) which will apply to devices in Annex II List A and, when required, devices in Annex II List B.[305] There is some uncertainty about the circumstances in which the requirement might apply to List B devices. CTS establish appropriate performance evaluation and re-evaluation criteria, batch release criteria, reference methods, and reference materials. If, for duly justified reasons, manufacturers do not comply with the CTS, they must adopt other solutions that are at least equivalent to these specifications. CTS are intended mainly for the evaluation of the safety of the blood supply and organ donations.

[305] Commission Decision of 7 May 2002 on common technical specifications for *in vitro*-diagnostic medical devices, (EC) 2002/364 and Commission Decision of 3 February 2009, amending Decision (EC) 2002/364 on common technical specifications for *in vitro*-diagnostic medical devices, (EC) 2009/108.

Manufacturers shall notify competent authorities: 17.199

(i) for reagents, reagent products, reference and control materials, of information concerning common technological characteristics and/or analytes, as well as any important and subsequent modification, including suspension of marketing authorization;
(ii) for other IVDs, appropriate indications;
(iii) for devices in Annex II and devices for self-testing, all data allowing identification and the analytical parameters and, where applicable, for diagnostic products in Annex I.3, results of evaluation of performance in accordance with Annex VIII and certificates of notified bodies.

(iv) Performance evaluation

Clinical evaluation is not appropriate for IVDs but a procedure is specified for performance evaluation studies in clinical laboratories or in other appropriate environments outside the manufacturer's premises (Annex VIII).[306] A manufacturer who places devices on the market under his own name must notify the competent authorities of the Member State in which he has his registered place of business of the address of that registered place of business, the categories of devices as defined in terms of common characteristics of technology and/or analytes and of any significant change thereto. 17.200

20. Adverse event reporting: Vigilance

All adverse events with medical devices of which the manufacturer becomes aware must be recorded. The detailed legal requirements in relation to recording and reporting are, curiously, more onerous in relation to MDs than AIMDs. However, the Commission's Guidance is that they should be treated the same in practice. In general,[307] a manufacturer of general medical devices should report, and a Member State record and evaluate: 17.201

(i) any malfunction or deterioration in the characteristics and performance of a device, or inadequacy in the labelling, which might lead to, or have led to, the death of a patient or user or to a serious deterioration in his state of health;
(ii) any technical or medical reason in relation to the characteristics or performance of a device for the reasons referred to in (i) above, leading to systematic recall of devices of the same type by the manufacturer.

Guidance is issued by the European Commission on medical device vigilance[308] that includes an explanation of the difficult concept of when a deterioration in state of health should be considered serious: 17.202

(i) life-threatening illness or injury;
(ii) permanent impairment of a body function or permanent damage to a body structure;
(iii) a condition necessitating medical or surgical intervention to prevent permanent impairment of a body function or permanent damage to a body structure.

It is intended that regulatory data will be stored on a European database on medical devices accessible only to competent authorities. This will include data on registration, certificates issued or withdrawn, and vigilance data.[309] 17.203

[306] The Regulations, reg 43.
[307] See, eg, Directive (EEC) 93/42, Annex II, para 3.1, seventh indent; these provisions match obligations imposed on Member States by Art 12.
[308] European Commission, MEDDEV, *Guidelines on a Medical Devices Vigilance System* (2009), 2.12-1 rev 6.
[309] Directive (EEC) 93/42, Art 14a.

21. Recall

17.204 A manufacturer may have a number of post-marketing obligations arising under either the new approach or medical devices legislation and/or the GPS legislation, and under product liability or negligence law. The precise legal provisions constitute a somewhat incomplete matrix, although the MHRA has issued guidance on the corrective action (eg the return, modification, exchange, destruction, or retrofit of a device) which covers in general terms the circumstances in which a recall might be appropriate and how it should best be implemented.[310]

22. Market surveillance

17.205 Generic market surveillance and post-marketing requirements apply to all new approach products, save in so far as there are no specific provisions with the same objective in Community harmonization legislation: this means that the generic rules apply unless specific provisions exist in the relevant medical device legislation.[311] Many of the generic provisions exist within the medical devices legislation, so the latter are the ones that apply, but the result has to be considered on a case-by-case basis and the result is somewhat confusing. The specific general new approach obligations apply to Member States from 1 January 2010, notably to organize and carry out market surveillance, to establish appropriate communication and coordination mechanism, to perform appropriate checks on products, to recall, withdraw, or prohibit the marketing of products that present serious risks.[312] A series of surveillance and post-marketing obligations apply to manufacturers, importers, and distributors that are not all found in the medical devices legislation (and so apply to medical devices).[313]

23. Enforcement and sanctions

17.206 The Medical Device Directives and new approach legislation authorize Member States to take enforcement action against medical devices that prove to be unsafe. The specific powers, offences, sanctions, and penalties are subject to the discretion of Member States. Accordingly, these matters are provided for under national legislation and practice. It must be remembered that relevant national provisions may be found not only within national legislation implementing the relevant Medical Device Directive but also in other provisions such as general consumer protection, trade descriptions or criminal legislation. Where a Member State invokes the 'safeguard clause' under a Medical Device Directive, removing a product from the market on grounds of safety, a mechanism must be followed under which the Commission and other Member States are notified, the position discussed and a unified approach taken by the authorities.

17.207 Enforcement provisions are generally of two types: first, powers to investigate and take action against a product and, secondly, offences which may be committed by individuals for breach of which they may be prosecuted by the authorities and subject to criminal sanctions. In the UK, for example, the first category of provisions arise under the product-specific Regulations and Pt II of the Consumer Protection Act 1987. The offences are as specified in

[310] Medical Devices Agency, Directives Bulletin no 3: *Guidance on the Operation of the EU Vigilance System in the UK* (MDA 2008).

[311] Regulation (EC) 765/2008, Art 15(2) and Decision (EC) 768/2008.

[312] Regulation (EC) 765/2008, Arts 16–26.

[313] Decision (EC) 768/2008. These provisions were largely modeled on the GPS post-marketing provisions for consumer products, but updated: see section F below. It is mooted that future amendments of the medical devices legislation will introduce specific post-marketing and surveillance provisions, and thereby oust the new approach provisions.

the product-specific Regulations. There is a considerable variation between Member States in the number and wording of criminal offences that may be committed and in the penalties that might be imposed.

Different national agencies have different practices on what action they may take when faced with dangerous products. The MHRA, for example, operates a practice of issuing a sequence of three advisory notices to UK health services, for which the criteria for the various safety warning categories are as follows:[314] **17.208**

Hazard Notices are issued: **17.209**

(i) in cases of actual death or serious injury, or where death or serious injury would have occurred but for fortuitous circumstances or the timely intervention of health care personnel (or a carer); and
(ii) where the medical device is clearly implicated; and
(iii) where immediate action is necessary to prevent recurrence.

Device Alerts are issued: **17.210**

(i) in cases where there is the potential for death or serious injury, or there may be implications arising from the long term use of the medical device;
(ii) where the medical device is likely to be implicated; and
(iii) where the recipient is expected to take immediate action on the advice.

Safety Notices are used to recommend or inform: **17.211**

(i) where action by the recipient will improve safety;
(ii) where it is necessary to repeat warnings on long standing problems;
(iii) to support or follow up manufacturers' field modifications.

F. Impact of the General Consumer Product Safety Legislation

1. Complementarity between Community rules

Directive (EC) 2001/95, implemented into UK law by the General Product Safety Regulations 2005,[315] (referred to here as the 'GPS' provisions) imposes general regulatory provisions on producers and distributors of consumer products.[316] These GPS provisions apply to producers and distributors of medicinal products or medical devices which are consumer products to the extent that[317] there are no specific provisions with the same objective in other rules of Community law governing the safety of the products concerned. Proposals to extent the GPS regime were made in 2013 and are uncompleted at the time of writing, but are unlikely to significantly affect the aspects discussed here in relation to medicines and medical devices.[318] **17.212**

[314] MHRA, *Safety Notices*, 2001, as updated.
[315] SI 2005/1803.
[316] For the definition of consumer product, see Directive (EC) 2001/95 Art 2(a). The GPS provisions were introduced into Community law by Directive 92/59/EEC, implemented by the General Product Safety Regulations 1994.
[317] This quotes the wording of Directive (EC) 2001/95, Art 1.2.
[318] See <http://europa.eu/rapid/press-release_IP-13-111_en.htm>.

17.213 The extent to which the GPS provisions apply to medicinal products or medical devices is not entirely clear. European Commission Guidelines partly clarify the position.[319] It is clear that the GPS provisions will not apply to products that are not consumer products, and that certain medical devices may not fall within the definition of consumer products.

17.214 In general, it would seem that medicinal products are totally excluded from the GPS regime, since the sector-specific legislation ousts the GPS provisions. Much, if not all, of the GPS provisions are ousted by the sector-specific legislation on medical devices, with the exception that no device provisions govern distributors. For the sake of completeness, the GPS obligations on producers and distributors will now be summarized. This section omits discussion of the GPS obligations on Member States.

2. GPS obligations on producers

(i) Definition of producer

17.215 Several individuals or entities may qualify to be the producer of a consumer product at the same time. A producer is defined for GPS purposes as:[320]

(i) the manufacturer of the product, when he is established in the Community, and any other person presenting himself as the manufacturer by affixing to the product his name, trade mark, or other distinctive mark, or the person who reconditions the product;
(ii) the manufacturer's representative, when the manufacturer is not established in the Community or, if there is no representative established in the Community, the importer of the product;
(iii) other professionals in the supply chain, insofar as their activities may affect the safety properties of a product.

(ii) Obligations on producers

17.216 Under Directive (EC) 2001/95, producers of consumer products are subject to the following sequence of obligations. First, they must place only safe products on the market.[321] A safe product is defined as[322] any product which, under normal or reasonably foreseeable conditions of use including duration and, where applicable, putting into service, installation, and maintenance requirements, does not present any risk or only the minimum risks compatible with the product's use, considered to be acceptable and consistent with a high level of protection for the safety and health of persons, taking into account the following points in particular:

(i) the characteristics of the product, including its composition, packaging, instructions for assembly and, where applicable, for installation and maintenance;
(ii) the effect on other products, where it is reasonably foreseeable that it will be used with other products;
(iii) the presentation of the product, the labelling, any warnings and instructions for its use and disposal, and any other indication or information regarding the product;

---

[319] Guidance Document on the Relationship Between the General Product Safety Directive (GPSD) and Certain Sector Directives with Provisions on Product Safety, Directorate General Health and Consumer Protection, 2005 at <http://ec.europa.eu/consumers/cons_safe/prod_safe/gpsd/gpsd_2ndchapiter_en.pdf>.

[320] Directive (EC) 2001/95, Art 2(e).

[321] Directive (EC) 2001/95, Art 3.1. There is a hierarchy of rules, standards and guidelines against which the safety of a product is to be presumed assessed: Art 3.

[322] ibid, Art 2(b).

(iv) the categories of consumers at risk when using the product, in particular children and the elderly.

The feasibility of obtaining higher levels of safety or the availability of other products presenting a lesser degree of risk shall not constitute grounds for considering a product to be 'dangerous'.

Secondly, within the limits of their respective activities, producers shall provide consumers with the relevant information to enable them to assess the risks inherent in a product throughout the normal or reasonably foreseeable period of its use, where such risks are not immediately obvious without adequate warnings, and to take precautions against those risks.[323] The presence of warnings does not exempt any person from compliance with the other requirements laid down in this Directive.[324] **17.217**

Thirdly, within the limits of their respective activities, producers shall adopt measures commensurate with the characteristics of the products that they supply, enabling them to:[325] **17.218**

(i) be informed of risks which these products might pose;
(ii) choose to take appropriate action including, if necessary to avoid these risks, withdrawal from the market, adequately and effectively warning consumers, or recall from consumers.

The measures referred to above may include, for example: **17.219**

(i) indication, by means of the product or its packaging, of the identity and details of the producer and the product reference or, where applicable, the batch of products to which it belongs, except where the lack of such an indication is justified; and
(ii) in all cases where appropriate, the carrying out of sample testing of marketed products, investigating and, if necessary, keeping a register of complaints and keeping distributors informed of such monitoring.

Action such as that referred to in (ii) above shall be undertaken on a voluntary basis or at the request of the competent authorities. Recall shall take place as a last resort, where other measures would not suffice to prevent the risks involved, in instances where the producers consider it necessary or where they are obliged to do so further to a measure taken by the competent authority. It may be effected within the framework of codes of good practice on the matter in the Member State concerned, where such codes exist. **17.220**

Fourthly, where producers and distributors know or ought to know, on the basis of the information in their possession and as professionals, that a product that they have placed on the market poses risks to the consumer that are incompatible with the general safety requirement, they must immediately inform the competent authorities of the Member States thereof under the conditions laid down in Annex 1 of the GPS Directive, giving details, in particular, of action taken to prevent risk to the consumer.[326] **17.221**

Finally, producers and distributors shall, within the limits of their respective activities, cooperate with the competent authorities, at the request of the latter, on action taken to avoid the risks posed by products that they supply or have supplied. The procedures for such cooperation, including procedures for dialogue with the producers and distributors concerned on issues related to product safety, shall be established by the competent authorities.[327] **17.222**

---

[323] ibid, Art 5(1), first paragraph.
[324] ibid, Art 5(1), second paragraph.
[325] ibid, Art 5(1), third paragraph.
[326] Directive (EC) 2001/95, Art 5(3).
[327] ibid, Art 5(4).

3. GPS obligations on distributors

(i) Definition of distributor

17.223 A distributor of a consumer product for GPS purposes is defined as: 'any professional in the supply chain whose activity does not affect the safety properties of a product.'

17.224 Comparison of this definition with the definition of a producer, at para 17.215, reveals that a person who distributes a product will be subject to the significantly more onerous obligations of a producer where his activities may affect the safety properties of a product. Examples of activities that would affect the safety properties of a product are transporting, storing, or handling it in a manner that makes it less safe than intended by the manufacturer.

(ii) Obligations on distributors

17.225 The principal obligation on a distributor is:[328]

> Distributors shall be required to act with due care to help to ensure compliance with the applicable safety requirements, in particular by not supplying products which they know or should have presumed, on the basis of the information in their possession and as professionals, do not comply with those requirements. Moreover, within the limits of their respective activities, they shall participate in monitoring the safety of products placed on the market, especially by passing on information on product risks, keeping and providing the documentation necessary for tracing the origin of products, and cooperating in the action taken by producers and competent authorities to avoid the risks. Within the limits of their respective activities they shall take measures enabling them to cooperate efficiently.

17.226 In addition, distributors are subject to the obligations to inform the authorities and to cooperate with the authorities noted at paras 17.217 and 17.222 as for producers.

[328] ibid, Art 5(2).

18

PRODUCTS LIABILITY

Richard Goldberg

A. Introduction

'Products liability[1]' may be broadly defined as the liability of manufacturers and other suppliers of products for injury or loss caused by their defective condition.[2] Liability for medicinal products[3] is thus a particular instance of liability for products which cause injury because of the way in which they have been designed, manufactured, or marketed. In the 1960s an elaborate regulatory structure was established for medicines, in the wake of the thalidomide tragedy.[4] The protracted litigation over thalidomide proved to be a catalyst for **18.01**

[1] See generally R Goldberg, *Medicinal Product Liability and Regulation* (Hart Publishing 2013).

[2] cf the 'civil liability of manufacturers and others where damage or loss is caused by products which fail to meet the standards claimed expressly or impliedly for them or which are dangerous or otherwise defective': C Miller and R Goldberg, *Product Liability* (2nd edn, Oxford University Press 2004) 1. 'The term "products liability" is an American invention. It does not describe a distinct category of law in the United Kingdom': Royal Commission on Civil Liability and Compensation for Personal Injury (the 'Pearson Commission') (Cmnd 7054, 1978), vol 1, para 1216.

[3] The term 'medicinal product' is used in this chapter in conformity with the definition in Article 1(2) of Directive 2001/83/EC Medicinal Products Directive [2001] OJ L311/67 as amended by Dir 2004/27/EC [2004] OJ L136/34. It is defined as a substance or combination of substances (a) presented as having properties for the treatment or prevention of disease in human beings or (b) which may be used in or administered to human beings either with the purpose of restoring, correcting, or modifying physiological functions by exerting a pharmacological, immunological, or metabolic action, or for making a medical diagnosis: Medicines Act 1968, s 130(1), Human Medicines Regulations 2012, SI 2012/1916, reg 2.

[4] Medicines Act 1968.

proposals during the 1970s, both in the UK[5] and in Europe,[6] to introduce strict liability regimes for injuries caused by defective products. The culmination of this activity was the European Community Directive on Products Liability (1985),[7] as implemented in England by Pt I of the Consumer Protection Act 1987 (CPA).[8]

18.02 Products liability may arise by virtue of contract, tort, or statute. In contract, reflecting the development of implied warranties in the nineteenth century, the main focus has been on merchantability—the condition or *quality* of the product in the light of presumed consumer expectations. Tort law, on the other hand, has stressed the defendant's *conduct* and society's interest in product *safety*. The distinction is somewhat superficial, since 'almost all defects in goods can at some level be more accurately described as attributable to human agency'.[9] Most importantly now, in the guise of strict liability, a new statutory framework for the protection of consumers was to emerge in the CPA. The CPA appears to blur the tort/contract divide by defining product *safety* in terms of consumer expectations. Defectiveness under the Act depends on proof that 'the safety of the product is not such as persons generally are entitled to expect . . .'[10] However, it would seem that the CPA's conception of 'defectiveness' is rooted in product safety, rather than merchantability.[11]

18.03 The different sources of civil liability do not blend into a single, coherent body of legal doctrine. Leaving to one side the questionable logic of differentiating between the provision of products and services,[12] the CPA provides only an alternative or additional basis for a cause of action in damages.[13] Actions in tort and contract remain available for situations either not covered or less adequately covered by the 1987 Act. In addition to providing these civil actions, the law endeavours to enhance consumer protection by means of regulatory measures which contain criminal penalties for failure to comply with specified

[5] The Law Commission and the Scottish Law Commission, *Liability for Defective Products* (Cmnd 6831, 1977); Royal Commission on Civil Liability and Compensation for Personal Injury, n 1, ch 22. On 14 January 2010, the UK government finally issued a formal apology and announced a £20 million, three-year pilot scheme to help the needs of thalidomide sufferers: The Minister of State, Department of Health (Mr Mike O'Brien), *Hansard*, HC Deb 14 January 2010, vol 503, col 859. A new ten-year grant in the region of £80 million was announced on 20 December 2012, which came into force in April 2013: The Minister of State, Department of Health (Norman Lamb), *Hansard*, HC Deb 20 December 2012, col 1008. A class action by Australian and New Zealand thalidomide victims against Diageo (which took over the drug's UK distributor, Distillers), was settled for $89 million Australian Dollars and this was approved by the Victorian Supreme Court: S Wilson, 'Australian Thalidomide victims settle class action' *The Telegraph* (2 December 2013); *The Guardian* (7 February 2014). In June 2014, eight claimants filed a negligence claim against Grünenthal, the German manufacturer, and Diageo, the claims being apparently based on new evidence on the causation of injury: C Dyer, 'Eight More People in UK Sue Grünenthal and Diageo over thalidomide' (2014) 348 BMJ 3806.

[6] EEC Draft Directive on products liability [1976] OJ C241 (first draft), [1979] OJ C271 (second draft); Strasbourg Convention on Products Liability in Regard to Personal Injury and Death (1977).

[7] Directive (EEC) 85/374 on the approximation of the laws, regulations and administrative provisions of the Member States concerning liability for defective products [1985] OJ L210/29.

[8] As amended by the Consumer Protection Act 1987 (Product Liability) (Modification) Order 2000, SI 2000/2771. See further n 275. The CPA does not apply to damage caused by defects in products supplied before 1 March 1988: CPA, s 50(7); CPA (Commencement No 1) Order 1987, SI 1987/1680.

[9] J Stapleton, *Product Liability* (Butterworths 1994) 329.

[10] CPA, s 3(1).

[11] Department of Trade and Industry, 'Implementation of the EC Directive on Product Liability: An Explanatory and Consultative Note' (DTI 1985) para 55. Cf EEC Draft Directive (first draft), n 4, Explanatory Memorandum, Art 4.

[12] See generally J Stapleton, 'Three Problems with the New Product Liability', in P Cane and J Stapleton (eds), *Essays for Patrick Atiyah* (Oxford University Press 1991) ch 11.

[13] CPA, s 2(6). See *AB v South West Water Services Ltd* [1993] QB 507 (CA), where, as well as claiming under the CPA, s 2(1), the plaintiffs pleaded breach of statutory duty, *Rylands v Fletcher*, breach of contract, nuisance, and negligence.

standards.[14] In recent years, such provision has become more elaborate following a series of EEC initiatives.[15]

Effective medicines are seldom risk-free. Determining whether or not they have caused harm can present difficulties which, in the case of other products, either do not arise or are typically less pronounced. Problems include the unpredictable long-term or delayed effects of certain drugs,[16] idiosyncratic or allergic reactions, the synergistic effects of some drug interactions with other drugs or foods, and the difficulty of distinguishing the effects of medication from the natural progression of illness.[17] A causal complication of a different kind may arise when vaccines and, increasingly, drugs are generically prescribed, with the result that their source of origin is not readily identifiable.[18] **18.04**

The scope of products liability in the medical sphere may also be affected by the way in which a particular substance is legally defined. For example, though the common law has resisted classifying human bodies as 'goods',[19] there are unresolved doubts over whether human organs can be so regarded, or whether supplying bodily fluids could connote a sale of goods rather than a supply of services. Although it is unclear whether or not transplants and blood transfusions constitute a supply of 'goods' within the Supply of Goods and Services Act 1982,[20] it has been accepted that blood and blood products for transfusion are 'products' within the meaning of the CPA and Directive (EC) 85/374.[21] Similarly, the applicable **18.05**

[14] eg under the Medicines Act 1968. The provisions of this Act may not be construed as conferring a civil right of action in respect of contraventions of the Act or of any regulations or order made under it: s 133(2). By contrast, safety regulations made under the Consumer Protection Act 1961 and the Consumer Safety Act 1978 did entitle a person injured by certain goods, which included cosmetics and asbestos products, to bring an action for breach of statutory duty against any seller in the chain of supply. These two Acts (and the Consumer Safety (Amendment) Act 1986) were repealed by the CPA, which has extended the regulation-making powers and which does permit an individual injured by infringement of a safety regulation to bring an action for breach of statutory duty: CPA, s 41. See, eg, the Active Implantable Medical Devices Regulations 1992, SI 1992/3146 (as amended), and the Medical Devices (Amendment) Regulations 2008, SI 2008/2936. Previously, 'licensed medicinal products' and tobacco were not subject to regulatory control under the CPA: CPA, s 10(7)(e) and s 10(7)(f), respectively. However, the ground previously covered by the general safety requirement of s 10 of the 1987 Act has been superseded by the General Product Safety Regulations 2005, which replace section 10 of the 1987 Act: see Regulation 46(2) of the 2005 Regulations which provides that s 10 of the 1987 Act (general safety requirement) should be omitted. Product-specific legislation for medicinal products and tobacco continues to take precedence in those areas where the provisions have similar objectives to the General Product Safety Regulations: see Product safety for Manufacturers (Department for Business, Innovation and Skills 2015) <https://www.gov.uk/guidance/product-safety-for-manufacturers>. See also C Miller, 'Consumer Protection' in Bridge et al (eds), *Benjamin's Sale of Goods* (9th edn, Sweet & Maxwell 2014) ch 14; and J O'Grady et al, *Medicines, Medical Devices and the Law* (Greenwich Medical Media 1999).

[15] *Benjamin's Sale of Goods*, n 14, para 14–001. See esp the General Product Safety Directive 2001/95/EC [2002] OJ L11/4 as implemented by the General Product Safety Regulations 2005, SI 2005/1803. See generally Chapter 17.

[16] See, eg, *Sindell v Abbott Laboratories* (1980) 26 Cal 3d 588 (DES), and para 18.41.

[17] DHSS, *Product Liability: Special Features of the Medical Sector*, Medicines Division Consultation Paper (DHSS, 1979); C Newdick, 'Defective Medicines: Unavoidable Danger or Unacceptable Risk?' (1990) 1 Intl J of Risk and Safety in Medicine 195.

[18] As in *Loveday v Renton and Wellcome Foundation Ltd* [1990] 1 Med LR 117 (pertussis). On generics, see *Mann and Close v Wellcome Foundation Ltd* (1989, QBD); *Sindell v Abbott Laboratories*, n 16.

[19] See further para 18.20.

[20] A P Bell, 'The Doctor and the Supply of Goods and Services Act 1982' (1984) 4 LS 175, 178. See further para 18.21. In the context of business to consumer contracts, Chapter 2 of Part 1 of the Consumer Rights Act 2015 replaces the provisions of the 1982 Act: See Consumer Rights Act Sch 1, para 39–40. Under s 2(8) of the 2015 Act, goods are defined as 'any tangible moveable items, but that includes water, gas and electricity if and only if they are put up for supply in a limited volume or set quantity'.

[21] The point was conceded in *A v National Blood Authority* [2001] 3 All ER 289, 307 (hepatitis C). See para 18.59.

legal principles will vary according to a product's statutory classification and the manner in which it has been supplied. It may have been sold as a 'medicinal product'[22] on the General Sale List (GSL) or as a pharmacy medicine (P). Alternatively, it may have been a Prescription Only Medicine (POM)[23] made available either under the legal regime for drug prescription under the National Health Service or on private prescription.[24] In some circumstances, it would have been directly administered by way of injection.

18.06 The term 'product(s) liability' is primarily associated with claims against manufacturers or producers. However, in attributing or apportioning responsibility for harm it may be necessary to consider other suppliers in the chain of distribution, including the retailer. In the case of medicinal products, liability may attach to retail or hospital pharmacists, doctors, and independent nurse prescribers. In principle, it would seem that an action could also be brought against a regulatory agency with a licensing function, such as the Licensing Authority and its advisory bodies established under the Medicines Act 1968. Although such an action could not be for breach of statutory duty,[25] it might lie in negligence, a possibility contemplated by the Court of Appeal in respect of haemophiliacs injured by blood products contaminated with HIV.[26]

18.07 Though, in England, numerous claims of drug-induced injury have been settled, none has yet culminated in damages being awarded by the court against a pharmaceutical company. There has been scant judicial analysis of what constitutes an absence of 'reasonable care'

---

[22] Under the Medicines Act 1968, a 'medicinal product' has the meaning given by regulation 2 of the Human Medicines Regulations 2012, SI 2012/1916, viz, 'any substance or combination of substances presented as having properties of preventing or treating disease in human beings' or which 'may be used by or administered to human beings with [the purpose of] (i) restoring, correcting or modifying a physiological function by exerting a pharmacological, immunological or metabolic action, or (ii) making a medical diagnosis', s 130(1). And see Directive 2001/83/EC, Art 1(2). Some biological, surgical, dental, and ophthalmic materials which were medicinal products within the Act or its subordinate legislation are now controlled under the CPA. They include IUDs and contact lens fluids. See Council Directive (EEC) 93/42 and the Medical Devices Regulations 2002, SI 2002/618. *In vitro* diagnostic medical devices are covered by Council Directive (EC) 98/79, given effect to by the Medical Devices Regulations 2002 SI 2002/618, as amended by the Medical Devices (Amendment) Regulations 2007 SI 2007/400. Cosmetics may be defined by the Medicines and Healthcare Products Regulatory Agency as 'medicinal products' by virtue of their remedial or curative functions. See Medicines and Healthcare Products Regulatory Agency, *A Guide to What is a Medicinal Product* (MHRA 2012). The Human Medicines Regulations 2012, SI 2012/1916 implements Regulation (EC) No 1394/2007 on advanced therapy medicinal products, which cover regenerative medicines, viz gene therapy medicinal products, somatic cell therapy medicinal products, and tissue engineered products: see <https://www.gov.uk/guidance/advanced-therapy-medicinal-products-regulation-and-licensing>. On judicial review of classification, see *R v Medicines Control Agency, ex p Pharma Nord (UK) Ltd* [1998] 3 CMLR 109. And see D Longley, 'Who is Calling the Piper? Is there a Tune? The New Regulatory Systems for Medical Devices in the United Kingdom and Canada' (1998) 3 Med L Int 319.

[23] See Medicines Act 1968, s 51 (General Sale list), and s 58 (Prescription Only medicinal products). See also the Medicines (Prescription Only, Pharmacy and General Sale) Amendment Order, SI 1989/1852, and the Medicines Act 1968, s 58A, inserted by the Medicines Act 1968 (Amendment) (No 2) Regulations 1992, SI 1992/3271, reg 2 (implementing Council Directive (EEC) 92/26 [1992] OJ L113/5). See generally Medicines Control Agency, *Towards Safe Medicines* (revd edn, MCA 1997).

[24] For an overview of the regulatory structure, see para 18.43. See further Chapter 17.

[25] See n 14.

[26] *Re HIV Haemophiliac Litigation* (1998) 41 BMLR 171 (decided in 1990), where the Committee on Safety of Medicines, the Licensing Authority, and the Department of Health were joined as defendants. See also *Brown v Alberta* [1994] 2 WWR 283 (Alta QB); cf *H v Royal Alexandra Hospital for Children* [1990] 1 Med LR 297 (SC of NSW). Arguably, however, the only duty (of care) is to the public at large: A Barton, 'The Basis of Liability of the Licensing Authority and its Advisers under the Medicines Act 1968 to an Individual' in A Goldberg and I Dodds-Smith (eds), *Pharmaceutical Medicine and the Law* (RCP 1991). See further para 18.46.

by pharmaceutical manufacturers and still relatively few reported cases of any description involving Pt I of the CPA. However, substantive aspects of medical products liability were examined at length in the notable first instance decision of *A v National Blood Authority*, where, significantly, the European Directive was the almost exclusive focus of analysis.[27] Meanwhile, a number of drug injury claims have highlighted the procedural complexity and funding difficulties commonly associated with multi-party actions.[28]

B. Contractual Liability

Historically, the boundaries of liability for injurious products largely derive from the law on sales warranties. Since, under the doctrine of privity, the seller of a defective product is, at common law, contractually liable only to the buyer, in practice contract has limited relevance to claims for harm caused by medicinal products.[29] Pharmaceutical companies rarely have a contractual relationship with consumers for the supply of goods, unless they are private patients buying medical equipment direct from the manufacturer. Patients injured by the more potent drugs will usually have obtained them through NHS prescription. In such circumstances there is no contract with the prescribing doctor, or with the pharmacist, who is statutorily obliged to dispense drugs on presentation of a prescription and payment of any fixed charge.[30] However, pharmacists could be liable in contract for injury caused by **18.08**

[27] *A v National Blood Authority* [2001] 3 All ER 289. See C Hodges, 'Compensating Patients' (2001) 117 LQR 528; G Howells and M Mildred, 'Infected Blood: Defect and Discoverability—A First Exposition of the EC Product Liability Directive' (2002) 65 MLR 9; R Goldberg, 'Paying for Bad Blood: Strict Product Liability after the Hepatitis C Litigation' (2002) 10 Medical Law Review 165. See further paras 18.52 (n 194), 18.61, and 18.70 below. Since *AB v South West Water Services Ltd* (1993), n 13, few cases on liability under the CPA have reached the Court of Appeal: *Iman Abouzaid v Mothercare (UK) Ltd*, The Times, 20 February 2001 (CA). See also *Tesco Stores Ltd v Pollard* [2006] EWCA Civ 393, *Piper v JRI (Manufacturing) Ltd* [2006] EWCA Civ 1344, *O'Byrne v Aventis Pasteur MSD Ltd sub nom O'Byrne v Aventis Pasteur SA* [2007] EWCA Civ 939, and *Ide v ATB Sales Limited* [2008] EWCA Civ 424. First instance decisions include *Worsley v Tambrands Ltd* [2000] PIQR P95; *Richardson v LRC Products Ltd* [2000] Lloyd's Med Rep 280, and *Foster v Biosil Ltd* (2000) 59 BMLR 178. And see Case C-127/04 *O'Byrne v Sanofi MSD Ltd (formerly Aventis Pasteur MSD Ltd)* [2006] ECR I-1313; [2006] 1 WLR 1606, and *O'Byrne v Aventis Pasteur MSD Ltd* [2008] UKHL 34; [2008] 4 All ER 88, para 18.72. For the ECJ ruling on the UK formulation of the 'development risks' defence in the CPA, s 4(1)(e), see paras 18.68–18.71. See also M Mildred, 'The Impact of the Directive in the United Kingdom' in M Goyens (ed), *Directive 85/374/EEC on product liability: ten years after* (Louvain-la-Neuve 1996) 37–57.

[28] See further para 18.80.

[29] *Dunlop Pneumatic Tyre Co v Selfridge & Co Ltd* [1915] AC 847; *Daniels and Daniels v R White & Sons Ltd and Tarbard* [1938] 4 All ER 258; *Woodar Investment Development Ltd v Wimpey Construction UK Ltd* [1980] 1 WLR 277 (HL). Manufacturers and contract houses might, in principle, be liable in contract to human volunteers for injury arising from drug trials. See M Powers, N Harris, and A Barton, *Clinical Negligence* (4th edn, Bloomsbury Professional 2008) 24.9, 24.166. And see para 18.81. The Contracts (Rights of Third Parties) Act 1999 has little or no application to claims for personal injury resulting from defective medicines, but could, on appropriate facts, apply where damage was caused by medical equipment made to order for a retailer by a manufacturer. Contrast the relaxation of the privity rule in the US Uniform Commercial Code s 2–318, extending the seller's liability for breach of warranty to other members of the purchaser's household (including guests); cf *Henningsen v Bloomfield Motors Inc* 161 A 2d 69 (1960), and most importantly, *Greenman v Yuba Power Products Inc* 377 P 2d 897 (1963), where 'strict' liability in tort heralded the widely adopted rule in s 402A of the Restatement (Second) of Torts (1965), making commercial sellers strictly liable to the ultimate user or consumer for physical harm caused by 'unreasonably dangerous' products. See now Restatement (Third) of Torts: Products Liability (1998), s 2, which restores a negligence standard for design and marketing defects, preserving strict liability only for manufacturing defects. See further D Owen, 'Products Liability Law Restated' (1998) 6 Consumer LJ 161.

[30] *Pfizer Corporation v Ministry of Health* [1965] AC 512, 535–36 *per* Lord Reid; *Appleby v Sleep* [1968] 1 WLR 948, 954–55.

privately prescribed drugs and, together with supermarkets and other outlets, by the increasing range of non-prescription medicines sold over the counter. In recent years, the internet has become a fast-growing source of prescribed and non-prescription drugs and medical devices, raising additional concerns about safety.[31] Equally, a doctor or hospital supplying drugs or other medical materials privately could be contractually liable.

1. General principles of liability

18.09 Sales of medicinal products, being subject to the common law and statutory principles generally applicable to consumer sales, can give rise to liability for innocent misrepresentation[32] or breach of contract. In addition to grounding a claim for the breach of any express or implied terms at common law, such transactions are subject to the statutory terms of the Consumer Rights Act 2015 (CRA 2015), which consolidates the statutory provisions covering business to consumer contracts in the Supply of Goods (Implied Terms) Act 1973, the Sale of Goods Act 1979 (SGA 1979), the Supply of Goods and Services Act 1982 (SGSA) and Sale and Supply of Goods Act 1994.[33] Thus the seller can be held liable if the goods sold do not match their description,[34] are not of 'satisfactory quality'[35] or not fit for their particular purpose.[36] Liability for breach of the terms is 'strict', there being no need to prove fault or negligence on the part of the vendor.[37] There are comparable provisions regarding contracts where a trader provides a service to a consumer in section 49 of the CRA 2015.[38]

18.10 Where a medicinal product is defective because of a manufacturing fault there may be a breach of the term in a contract to supply goods that goods are of satisfactory quality, namely, that the goods 'meet the standard that a reasonable person would regard as satisfactory'.[39] For such liability to arise, there is no need for the buyer to have relied on the seller's skill or judgment. In principle this provision could also ground liability for unforeseen side effects resulting from defective design. However, it might be deemed unreasonable to expect drugs not to present any such dangers, and it would often be difficult to demonstrate that unavoidable risks of a powerful drug are incompatible with 'satisfactory quality'.

---

[31] N Glover-Thomas and J Fanning, 'Medicalisation: The Role of E-Pharmacies in Iatrogenic Harm' (2010) 18 Med L Rev 28. In principle, liability can move back up the chain of supply via third-party proceedings and successive indemnities. See para 18.16. For an analysis of ethical and legal implications of deregulating medicines, see D Prayle and M Brazier, 'Supply of Medicines: Paternalism, Autonomy and Reality' (1998) 24 Journal of Medical Ethics 93.

[32] Misrepresentation Act 1967, s 2(1).

[33] See generally *Benjamin's Sale of Goods* (Special Supplement to 9th edn, 2014, Sweet & Maxwell 2015).

[34] CRA 2015, s 11(1). For contracts made before 1 October 2015, see SGA 1979, 13(1). 'Description' is construed broadly to include the purpose and use to which goods are put; cf *Holmes v Ashford* [1950] 2 All ER 76 (CA); *Kubach v Hollands* [1937] 3 All ER 907.

[35] CRA 2015, s 9. For contracts made before 1 October 2015, see Sale and Supply of Goods Act 1994, s 1. The term 'satisfactory quality' replaced the long-established expression 'merchantable quality' (SGA 1979, s 14(2)), which had been criticized as outmoded and inappropriate for consumer transactions: Law Commission, *Sale and Supply of Goods* (Law Commission 1987), paras 2.9 and 2.10. Section 9 of the 2015 Act does not alter the previous 'satisfactory quality' standard in respect of consumer sales. However, s 9 avoids the previous legal terminology of implied terms, providing that each contract to supply goods is *treated* as including these terms: CRA 2015, s 9(1).

[36] CRA 2015, s 10(1)(3). For contracts made before 1 October 2015, see SGA 1979, s 14(3).

[37] *Frost v Aylesbury Dairy Co Ltd* [1905] 1 KB 608 (CA). See also *Kendall (Henry) and Sons (a firm) v William Lillico and Sons Ltd* [1969] 2 AC 31, 84 *per* Lord Reid; *Vacwell Engineering Co Ltd v BDH Chemicals Ltd* [1971] 1 QB 88.

[38] See paras 18.18 and 18.19.

[39] CRA 2015, s 9(1). For contracts made before 1 October 2015, see, SGA 1979, s 14(2A) and (2B), as amended by the Sale and Supply of Goods Act 1994, s 1.

As regards fitness for purpose, inability of the seller to detect an unforeseen side effect is not in principle a defence.[40] However, under s 10(4) of the CRA 2015,[41] 'where the circumstances show that the buyer does not rely, or that it is unreasonable for him to rely, on the skill or judgment of the trader . . .', a term that the goods are reasonably fit for that purpose is inapplicable. The onus is on the trader to show that there was no such reliance. Thus a dispensing pharmacist might be able to show that the implied condition was negated by a private patient's reliance on the judgment of the prescribing doctor[42] or other prescribing professional.[43] In addition, no liability arises in respect of the buyer's unexpected sensitivity unless it has been expressly or impliedly made known to the seller.[44] A pharmacist would therefore not normally be liable if unaware of a customer's abnormal condition or allergy.[45] **18.11**

Since the terms of satisfactory quality and fitness for purpose are treated as included in 'a contract to supply goods',[46] liability can arise in respect of packaging, containers, and instructions which render goods of unsatisfactory quality and/or unfit for their particular purpose(s).[47] However, the mere fact that a drug is potentially harmful will not ground liability if it is safe when taken according to the instructions. **18.12**

The terms of satisfactory quality, fitness for purpose, and matching the description apply to contracts 'for a trader to supply goods to a consumer'.[48] This expression would appear to cover transactions undertaken by a private hospital. The position with regard to NHS hospitals is less clear. A statutory provision making records relating to a 'business' admissible in criminal proceedings has been held not to apply to the medical records of an NHS hospital,[49] on the ground that its commercial functions were ancillary to its main purpose. However, under legislation concerned to promote consumer protection, which defines a trader as 'a person acting for purposes relating to that person's trade, business, craft or profession'[50] and a 'business' to include and the activities of a 'public authority',[51] there is a strong case for regarding trader to consumer transactions of NHS hospitals (a fortiori as Trusts), as contracts for a trader to supply goods to a consumer.[52] **18.13**

---

[40] *Aswan Engineering Establishment Co v Lupdine Ltd* [1987] 1 WLR 1 (CA); *Hill (Christopher) Ltd v Ashington Piggeries Ltd* [1972] AC 441, 498; *Frost v Aylesbury Dairy Co Ltd* [1905] 1 KB 608 (CA); *Kendall (Henry) and Sons (a firm) v William Lillico and Sons Ltd* [1969] 2 AC 31; cf 'it is well settled that the implied condition as to fitness extends to latent defects': *Young and Marten v McManus Childs Ltd* [1969] 1 AC 454, 479 *per* Lord Wilberforce.

[41] For contracts made before 1 October 2015, see SGA 1979, s 14(3).

[42] Virtually all of the prescribing of drugs in the community is carried out by general practitioners: B Guthrie, C McCowan, P Davey, C R Simpson, T Dreischulte, and K Barnett, 'High risk prescribing in primary care patients particularly vulnerable to adverse drug events: cross sectional population database analysis in Scottish general practice' (2011) 342 BMJ d3514.

[43] Suitably qualified pharmacists and nurses now have extensive independent prescribing rights: see Health and Social Care Act 2001, s 63; National Health Service (Miscellaneous Amendments Relating to Independent Prescribing) Regulations 2006, SI 2006/913 (pharmacists), and Medicines for Human Use (Prescribing) (Miscellaneous Amendments) Order 2006, SI 2006/915 (nurses).

[44] *Griffiths v Conway (Peter) Ltd* [1939] 1 All ER 685 (CA) (sale); cf *Ingham v Emes* [1955] 2 QB 366 (CA) (work and materials).

[45] For constructive knowledge, see P Atiyah, *Sale of Goods* (11th edn, Adams 2005) 203.

[46] CRA 2015 s 3(1), (4), (5).

[47] *Vacwell Engineering Co Ltd v BDH Chemicals Ltd* [1971] 1 QB 88; *Wormell v RHM Agricultural (East)* [1987] 1 WLR 1091 (CA); *Amstrad plc v Seagate Technology Inc* (1997) 86 BLR 34.

[48] CRA 2015 ss 3(1)(4), 9(1), 10(1), 11(1). For contracts made before I October 2015, see SGA 1979, s 14(2), (3) (goods sold 'in the course of a business').

[49] Criminal Evidence Act 1965, s 1(1)(4); *R v Crayden* [1978] 1 WLR 604, 609 (CA).

[50] CRA 2015, s 2(2).

[51] CRA 2015, s 2(7). For contracts made before 1 October 2015, see SGA 1979, s 61(1).

[52] See *Davies v Sumner* [1984] 1 WLR 1301 (HL); *Roberts v Leonard* (1995) 14 Tr LR 536; *Benjamin's Sale of Goods*, n 14, 11–028; cf *E v Australian Red Cross Society* (1991) 105 ALR 53 (FC) (blood contaminated

2. Exclusion of liability

18.14 Any attempt by a trader to contract out of statutory rights and remedies under a goods contract may be caught by section 31 of the CRA 2015.[53] This provides that a term of a contract to supply goods is not binding on the consumer to the extent that it would exclude or restrict the trader's liability in respect of the supply of goods that are not of satisfactory quality, are not fit for their purpose, or do not match their description. The 2015 Act also provides that certain kinds of liability cannot be excluded or restricted either by a term of a consumer contract or a consumer notice. More generally, a trader cannot by a term of a consumer contract or by a consumer notice exclude or restrict liability for death or personal injury resulting from negligence.[54]

3. Privity and collateral contracts

18.15 By virtue of the doctrine of privity,[55] the consumer-purchaser of a medicinal product will not normally have a contractual right of action against the manufacturer unless there is a collateral contract between them. Only rarely have the courts so construed agreements arising from manufacturers' representations about their products.[56] Although in *Carlill v Carbolic Smoke Ball Co*[57] the defendants were held liable on the basis of a very specific collateral warranty in their advertisement, even factual representations contained in promotional material are seldom construed as intended to have contractual effect.[58] A fortiori, English law has not followed those US decisions in which collateral contracts based on implied warranties of quality and fitness have been derived from the mere presence of goods on the market.[59]

18.16 However, the consumer-purchaser may in effect be compensated by the manufacturer via third-party proceedings and successive indemnities. Thus, harm caused by non-prescription products sold by retail pharmacists can result in contractual claims that move back up the chain of supply. Intermediaries may, of course, prove to be insolvent, uninsured, or unidentifiable. Suing them could also prove to be impracticable if they trade exclusively outside the jurisdiction.[60] In sales between non-consumers, the chain of liability may be broken by a 'reasonable' exemption clause.[61]

18.17 Though the seller of a defective product is liable in contract only to the purchaser, very occasionally purchasers have been treated as contracting agents for some other individual who

with HIV): public hospital marginally engaged in business activities a 'trading corporation' within the Commonwealth Trade Practices Act 1974. Cf CPA s 45(1), n 233.

[53] For contracts made before 1 October 2015, see SGA 1979, s 55(1) and the Unfair Contract Terms Act 1977 (UCTA), s 1(3)(a), s 6(2), (3), and s 12.

[54] CRA 2015, s 65; this provision parallels s 2(1) of the Unfair Contract Terms Act 1977, applicable to contracts made before 1 October 2015.

[55] See para 18.08.

[56] eg *Wells (Merstham) Ltd v Buckland Sand and Silica Co Ltd* [1965] 2 QB 170: specific and personal assurance to buyer by manufacturer; *cf Shanklin Pier Ltd v Detel Products Ltd* [1951] 2 KB 854.

[57] [1893] 1 QB 256 (CA).

[58] *Lambert v Lewis* [1980] 2 WLR 299 (CA). Contrast the position in some US and Commonwealth jurisdictions: eg *Baxter v Ford Motor Co* 35 P 2d 1090 (1934); *Henningsen v Bloomfield Motors Inc* 161 A 2d 69 (1960); Rest 2d para 402A (1965); *Murray v Sperry Rand Corporation* (1979) 96 DLR (3d) 113; *Leitz v Saskatoon Drug & Stationery Co Ltd* (1981) 112 DLR (3d) 106. And see in Australia, Schedule 2 to the Competition and Consumer Act 2010 (Cth), s 271 (5). See also Atiyah, *Sale of Goods*, n 45, 268–69.

[59] As in *Henningsen*, n 58; cf C Miller, and R Goldberg, *Product Liability* (2nd edn, Oxford University Press 2004) 79 and Atiyah, *Sale of Goods*, n 45, 268–69. See also CPA, s 3(2)(a), para 18.61 and n 288.

[60] Though there may be 'extended' jurisdiction over foreign manufacturers: *Distillers Co (Biochemicals) Ltd v Thompson* [1971] AC 458 (under RSC Ord 11). See now CPR, r 6.20.

[61] Unfair Contract Terms Act 1977 ss 6(2) and 6(3). See *Lambert v Lewis* [1980], n 58.

has suffered injury.[62] In such situations, they may recover for their own resultant losses[63] or, arguably, as contracting expressly for the benefit of another.[64]

4. Contracts involving the supply of products: Supply or services?

Where a contract for private medical treatment is exclusively for the provision of services, at common law a doctor who has not been negligent will not normally be liable for injury.[65] Similarly, under the CRA 2015, in the context of contracts where a trader provides a service to a consumer, every contract to supply a service is to be treated as including a term that the trader must perform the service with reasonable skill and care.[66] If, for example, an operation on a private patient for sterilization has been unsuccessful, in the absence of negligence there will be no breach of contract unless the doctor has guaranteed a successful outcome.[67] When, however, a doctor supplies or administers drugs or other medical materials to a private patient, as when giving an injection or anaesthetic, or applying an ointment, it may not be clear whether the contract is primarily for the provision of services or for the supply of medicines. The same problem can arise when a private doctor (or hospital) supplies medical equipment, such as a prosthesis or other medical device. Even when such products are supplied, the doctor's professional role in diagnosis, advice, and/or treatment will commonly be regarded as the dominant feature of the transaction, so that it is not viewed as comparable to a contract of sale.[68] **18.18**

However, at common law, a contract which in substance is for the supply of work and materials may contain implied terms analogous to those applicable to sales.[69] In the context of business to consumer contracts, statutory terms apply where a trader agrees to supply goods to a consumer under a contract, which is referred to in s 3(1) of the Consumer Rights Act 2015 as a 'contract to supply goods'.[70] Sections 5 to 8 of the 2015 Act define the types of contract to supply goods to which the particular provisions apply[71] as respectively: a sales contract;[72] a contract for the hire of goods;[73] a hire-purchase agreement;[74] and a contract for the transfer of goods.[75] Accordingly, when goods are supplied (or administered) by a trader to a consumer either by way of transfer, as in the case of drugs, prosthetics, dentures, and **18.19**

---

[62] See, eg, *Lockett v A & M Charles Ltd* [1938] 4 All ER 170.
[63] *Preist v Last* [1903] 2 KB 148 (CA).
[64] *Jackson v Horizon Holidays Ltd* [1975] 1 WLR 1468 (CA). See also *Woodar Investment Ltd v Wimpey UK Ltd* [1980] 1 All ER 571, 576–77 *per* Lord Wilberforce.
[65] Lord Nathan, *Medical Negligence* (Butterworths 1957) 10–11.
[66] CRA, s 49. For contracts made before 1 October 2015, see SGSA, s 13.
[67] *Eyre v Measday* [1986] 1 All ER 488 (CA); *Thake v Maurice* [1986] QB 644 (CA); cf *Grey v Webster* (1985) 14 DLR (4th) 706 (NBCQB).
[68] *Benjamin's Sale of Goods* n 14, para 1–046. And see Nathan, *Medical Negligence*, n 65, 19. Cf Case 353/85 *Commission v UK* [1988] STC 251. But note *Commissioners of Customs and Excise v Wellington Private Hospital Ltd* [1997] STC 445 (CA) (supply of drugs and prostheses to private hospital inpatients constitutes a separate supply of goods for the purposes of VAT).
[69] *Samuels v Davis* [1943] KB 526 (CA); *Dodd v Wilson* [1946] 2 All ER 691. The more like sale the transaction, the stricter the implied obligations: *Young & Marten Ltd v McManus Childs Ltd* [1969] 1 AC 454, 476 *per* Lord Wilberforce. In many American jurisdictions, pharmacists, unlike other retailers, have been characterized as professionals providing a service and not subject to strict liability: eg *Murphy v ER Squibb and Sons Inc* 710 P 2d 247, 251–53 (1985).
[70] Consumer Rights Act 2015, s 3(1), (4). The legal terminology of implied terms is avoided under the new Act but each contract to supply goods is *treated* as including these terms: see s 9(1) (goods to be of satisfactory quality); s 10(1) (goods to be fit for particular purpose); s 11(1) (goods to be as described).
[71] See Consumer Rights Act 2015, s 3(2).
[72] Consumer Rights Act 2015, s 5.
[73] Consumer Rights Act 2015, s 6.
[74] Consumer Rights Act 2015, s 7.
[75] Consumer Rights Act 2015, s 8.

injections, or hire, as in the temporary use of splints or crutches, the contract would now be subject to the statutory rights of the CRA 2015.[76] In practice, most medical contracts for work and materials involve transfer, as the patient becomes the owner of the materials used. In some instances of temporary use, however, the contract will be one of hire.[77]

5. Medical products as 'goods'

18.20 Most of the materials used in medicine are undoubtedly 'goods' which can be the subject of commerce, but the position regarding human body products has not been free from difficulty. Judicial abhorrence at the idea of defining human beings, alive or dead, as 'goods or materials'[78] raised doubts about the legal status of transactions involving human organs and bodily fluids such as blood and semen; although, as noted, blood has been deemed a 'product' within the CPA and the European Directive.[79]

18.21 It is thus possible that organ transplantation and artificial insemination, as well as the transfusion of whole blood and blood products, involve a supply of goods capable of giving rise to strict liability under the CRA 2015. The argument is most cogent where commercial supply of the substance in question is both long-established and socially accepted, as in the case of blood transfusion.[80] In the United States there has been widespread resistance to a strict liability approach, partly in recognition of the need for available and affordable transfusion. Nearly all American jurisdictions have followed *Perlmutter v Beth David Hospital*[81] in defining blood transfusion as a service which does not involve sale.[82] When *Perlmutter* was rejected in *Cunningham v MacNeal Memorial Hospital*,[83] many states enacted 'blood shield statutes' to the effect that supplying blood or blood products constituted a service 'for all purposes', so that neither the manufacturer nor anyone else in the supply chain would be subject to an implied warranty of merchantable quality.[84]

---

[76] CRA ss 9 and 10. For contracts made before 1 October 2015 see SGSA, ss 4 and 9.

[77] See further Bell, 'The Doctor and the Supply of Goods and Services Act 1982', n 20.

[78] *Bourne (Inspector of Taxes) v Norwich Crematorium Ltd* [1967] 1 WLR 691, 695; cf *Williams v Williams* (1882) 20 Ch D 659, 662–63; *Dobson v North Tyneside HA* [1997] 1 WLR 596 (CA). Cf *Doodeward v Spence* (1908) 6 CLR 406 (Aus). It would seem that there can be limited possessory rights in corpses or body parts which have acquired different attributes through the lawful application of work and skill, as in dissection or embalming, for the purposes of teaching or exhibition: *R v Kelly* [1999] QB 621(CA); *AB v Leeds Teaching Hospital NHS Trust* [2004] EWHC 644 (QB). See also *Benjamin's Sale of Goods*, n 14, 1-089; P Skegg, 'Human Corpses, Medical Specimens and the Law of Property' (1976) 4 Anglo-American L Rev 412; K Mason and G Laurie, 'Consent or Property? Dealing with the Body and its Parts in the Shadow of Bristol and Alder Hey' (2001) 64 MLR 710.

[79] See para 18.05 and n 21. See further I Kennedy and A Grubb, *Medical Law* (3rd edn, Butterworths 2000) ch 15; Bell, 'The Doctor and the Supply of Goods and Services Act', n 20, 178; Atiyah, *Sale of Goods*, n 45, 24–26; D Meyers, *The Human Body and the Law* (2nd edn, Edinburgh 1990) ch 7. For a recent analysis of proprietary interests in frozen human sperm samples, see *Yearworth and others v North Bristol NHS Trust* [2009] EWCA Civ 37; and further *Lam v University of British Columbia* 2015 BCCA 2. See also C Hawes, 'Property Interests in Body Parts: Yearworth v North Bristol NHS Trust' (2010) 73 MLR 130; L D Rostill, 'The Ownership that wasn't meant to be: *Yearworth* and property rights in human tissue' (2014) 40 J Med Ethics 14.

[80] Trading in human organs is prohibited by the Human Tissue Act 2004, s 32. See also Chapter 19.

[81] *Perlmutter v Beth David Hospital* 123 NE 2d 792 (1954).

[82] See, eg, *Coffee v Cutter Biological* 809 F 2d 191 (USCA) (1987).

[83] *Cunningham v MacNeal Memorial Hospital* 266 NE 2d 897 (SC of Ill) (1970).

[84] See, eg, *Miles Laboratories v Doe* 556 A 2d 1167 (Md CA) (1989). In *Belle Bonfils Memorial Blood Bank v Hansen* 579 P 2d 1158 (Colo Sup Ct) (1978), supply by a blood bank—as distinct from a hospital—was construed as a sale of goods permitting an action for strict liability and breach of warranty. However, in a subsequent hearing, blood and blood products were held to fall within Comment k of the Restatement (Second) of Torts, s 402A, which excluded the application of strict liability to 'unavoidably unsafe'

Subsequent case law has made it clear that the blood shield statutes apply to blood infected with HIV.[85]

C. Tort: Negligence

1. The duty of care

The expression 'products liability' has most commonly been used to describe the liability in negligence of those who supply products in the course of a business. In practice, the primary target has been the manufacturer who by act or omission has failed to take reasonable care to avoid injury to the ultimate consumer. The classic formulation of the manufacturer's duty is the 'narrow rule' in *Donoghue v Stevenson*: **18.22**

> A manufacturer of products which he sells in such a form as to show that he intends them to reach the ultimate consumer in the form in which they left him, with no reasonable possibility of intermediate examination, and with the knowledge that the absence of reasonable care in the preparation or putting up of the products will result in injury to the consumer's life or property, owes a duty to the consumer to take that reasonable care.[86]

(i) Who owes the duty?

The duty owed by manufacturers has been extended to cover anyone in the chain of distribution and supply.[87] Thus, in respect of drugs it could apply to the product licence holder, a subsequent distributor, the prescribing doctor, or the dispensing pharmacist. Pharmacists, for example, may incur liability if they cause injury by negligently dispensing the wrong drug, or the wrong strength of drug.[88] Likewise, a doctor or other authorized prescriber may be liable in negligence for injury attributable to a carelessly written prescription,[89] or which results from prescribing a drug without having taken reasonable steps to explore the risks of side effects, reactions with other drugs or contra-indications. In principle, it might also be possible to impose liability for negligence on the Licensing Authority and its expert committees.[90] **18.23**

products: *Belle Bonfils Memorial Blood Bank v Hansen* 665 P 2d 118 (Colo Sup Ct) (1983). Restatement (Third) of Torts, n 29, expressly excludes services, human blood and blood tissue: s 19, Comment c.

[85] *Hyland Therapeutics v Superior Court* 175 Cal App 3d 509, 220 Cal Rptr 590 (1985). See further D Giesen, 'Liability for the Transfusion of HIV-infected Blood in Comparative Perspective' (1994) 10 PN 2. See also *E v Australian Red Cross Society* (1991) 105 ALR 53 (FC): blood transfused by hospital not an act 'in trade and commerce' where the defendants had not been paid for the blood as such. Cf *Pittman Estate v Bain* (1994) 112 DLR (4th) 257 (Ont Ct Gen Div); *ter Neuzen v Korn* (1995) 127 DLR (4th) 577 (SCC): no implied warranty of quality by doctor in contract to administer artificial insemination which included the supply of (infected) semen. And see A Grubb and D Pearl, *Blood Testing, AIDS and DNA Profiling* (Jordans 1990) ch 5.

[86] [1932] AC 562, 599 *per* Lord Atkin. For discussion of negligence liability more generally see Part Two of this book.

[87] eg *Watson v Buckley, Osborne, Garrett & Co* [1940] 1 All ER 174; *Fisher v Harrods Ltd* [1966] 1 Lloyd's Rep 500.

[88] eg *Horton v Evans & Lloyds Pharmacy* [2006] EWHC 2808: M A Jones, 'Misprescribing and the Chain of Causation' (2007) 23 PN 257. See also *Wootton v J Docter Ltd* [2008] EWCA Civ 1361, and *Prendergast v Sam & Dee Ltd* [1989] 1 Med LR 36 (CA) (doctor held 25 per cent liable; pharmacist 75 per cent); T McKevitt, 'Doctors, Pharmacists and Prescriptions: The Standard of Care Owed to the Patient' (1988) 4 PN 185. See also Civil Liability (Contribution) Act 1978.

[89] ibid; cf *Dwyer v Roderick* (1983) 127 SJ 806 (CA); C A Langley, 'Pharmacy Legislation: Public Protector or Professional Hindrance' (2013) 22 Med L Rev 87, 102–04 (majority of prescription errors occur as a result of poor prescribing). See also n 43 above.

[90] See paras 18.42–18.47.

(ii) Products sold

18.24 The 'narrow rule' in *Donoghue v Stevenson* represents no more than a particular instance of liability for negligence. There being no separate category of 'products liability' as such at common law, no need arises in cases based on negligence to define 'product'. Though Lord Atkin's dictum refers to 'products', the general principles of negligence liability have been interpreted as covering the whole range of production-related negligent acts.[91] Similarly, there is no reason to confine liability to goods 'sold', as distinct, for example, from free samples distributed by a manufacturer.[92]

2. The standard of care

18.25 In general terms, manufacturers are under an obligation to exercise such care as is reasonable in all aspects of the production process under their control. Liability may arise from inadequate care in matters as diverse as research and design, manufacture, presentation, and instructions for use, including warnings about risks.[93] Determining the requisite standard has sometimes been described as an exercise in cost–benefit analysis,[94] centring on such well-established negligence criteria as magnitude of risk,[95] probability of harm,[96] the burden of taking adequate precautions,[97] and the social utility of the defendant's conduct.[98]

18.26 The attempt to establish where the balance of social interest lies can be unusually difficult in the case of medicinal products, the full risks and benefits of which may not become apparent for many years, if at all. The anticipated utility of any given drug, and the advantages of its early availability, may or may not be outweighed by its potential for harm. The benefits of elaborate safety precautions may or may not outweigh the inhibiting effects on innovation of cost and delay.[99] A marginally more effective new drug may be inherently less safe than available alternatives.[100] Many otherwise valuable drugs present a significant risk to a minority of the public, and it has been suggested that a product which is safe for most people should be considered dangerous 'if it might affect other users who had a higher degree of sensitivity than normal, so long as they were not altogether exceptional'.[101]

---

[91] eg *Herschtal v Stewart and Arden Ltd* [1940] 1 KB 155; *Malfroot v Noxal Ltd* (1935) 51 TLR 551; *Howard v Furness Houlder Argentine Lines Ltd and A and R Brown Ltd* [1936] 2 All ER 781.

[92] *Hawkins v Coulsdon and Purley UDC* [1954] 1 QB 319, 333 *per* Denning LJ; cf *Griffiths v Arch Engineering Co Ltd* [1968] 3 All ER 217, 220. And see C Miller and R Goldberg, *Product Liability* (2nd edn, Oxford University Press 2004), 624–25.

[93] *Cartwright v GKN Sankey Ltd* [1972] 2 Lloyd's Rep 242, 259 (CA); *Devilez v Boots Pure Drug Co Ltd* (1962) 106 SJ 552.

[94] As notably articulated in American case law and literature. See *US v Carroll Towing* 159 F 2d 169, 173 (1947) *per* Judge Learned Hand. See further R Posner, 'A Theory of Negligence' (1972) 1 J of Legal Studies 29, 33. And see Stapleton, *Product Liability*, n 9, chs 5 and 6.

[95] *Paris v Stepney Borough Council* [1951] AC 367; *Wright v Dunlop Rubber Co* (1972) 13 KIR 255.

[96] *Bolton v Stone* [1951] AC 850.

[97] *Latimer v AEC Ltd* [1953] AC 643. And see *PQ v Australian Red Cross Society* [1992] 1 VR 19.

[98] *Buchan v Ortho Pharmaceuticals (Canada) Ltd* (1986) 25 DLR (4th) 658, 668 (Ont CA).

[99] C Newdick, 'The Impact of Licensing Authority Approval on Pharmaceutical Product Liability: A Survey of American and UK Law' (1992) 47 F & D LJ 41; H Teff, 'Regulation under the Medicines Act 1968: A Continuing Prescription for Health' (1984) 47 MLR 303, 309–18, and J Abraham, 'The Pharmaceutical Industry as a Political Player' (2002) 360 The Lancet 1498. For criticism that the highly regulated pharmaceutical sector is suffering an 'innovation deficit' through inconsistent and unpredictable regulatory expectations across international borders, potentially hindering the development of better medicines, see H Naci, A W Carter, E Mossialos, 'Why the drug development pipeline is not delivering better medicines' (2015) 351 BMJ h5542.

[100] See *Nicholson v John Deere Ltd* (1986) 34 DLR (4th) 542, 549 (Ont HC).

[101] *Board v Thomas Hedley* [1951] 2 All ER 431, 432 (CA) *per* Denning LJ. See also *Griffiths v Conway (Peter) Ltd* [1939] 1 All ER 685; C Miller and R Goldberg, *Product Liability* (2nd edn, Oxford University Press 2004), 656–58. For the duty to warn, see paras 18.32 and 18.33.

(i) Common practice

Whether or not the defendant's conduct is deemed negligent is judged by reference to the prevailing state of scientific and technical knowledge.[102] Conformity with industry standards or custom, though prima facie evidence of reasonable prudence on the part of a manufacturer,[103] is not dispositive.[104] A general indication of what constitutes appropriate pre-marketing research for pharmaceutical products is contained in the guidelines produced by the regulatory authorities (the Licensing Authority and its advisory bodies) and the industry (the Code of Practice for the Pharmaceutical Industry). However, compliance with recommended testing procedures, for example, is not ipso facto a defence in any given case. Non-compliance with accepted practice would be strong, though not conclusive, evidence of negligence.[105] Similarly, the views of expert official committees are relevant but not determinative.[106] **18.27**

(ii) Compliance with statutory provisions

Even full compliance with statutory requirements does not conclusively preclude liability for negligence at common law.[107] Hence the issue of a product licence does not automatically constitute a defence to a claim.[108] However, the courts would be loath to impose a standard of care that effectively penalized compliance with specific, statutorily prescribed, standards,[109] and they would be reluctant to hold negligent a manufacturer who had been granted a product licence for a drug after having disclosed to the Licensing Authority all the information deemed relevant to its safety.[110] Nonetheless, as well as reiterating the position that compliance with the regulatory regime does not conclusively preclude liability in negligence, recent Australian case law has emphasized that the regulatory regime for medicines lays down minimum and not optimum standards.[111] **18.28**

(iii) Manufacturing defects

Defects arising from error in the manufacturing process are relatively rare in the pharmaceutical industry. Examples would include a failure to combine ingredients in the correct **18.29**

---

[102] *Vacwell Engineering Co v BDH Chemicals* [1971] 1 QB 88; *Stokes v Guest, Keen and Nettlefold (Bolts & Nuts) Ltd* [1968] 1 WLR 1776, 1783; cf *Fuller v Baxenden Chemical Co Ltd* (1985, QBD): failure to update company literature in line with changed knowledge and practice of others; *Ogden v Airedale HA* [1996] 7 Med LR 153.

[103] cf *R v British Pharmaceutical Industry Association Code of Practice Committee,* The Independent, 1 November 1990.

[104] *Morris v West Hartlepool Navigation Co* [1956] AC 552; *Cavanagh v Ulster Weaving Co Ltd* [1960] AC 145. C Miller and R Goldberg, *Product Liability* (2nd edn, Oxford University Press 2004) 609 et seq.

[105] *Chin Keow v Government of Malaysia* [1967] 1 WLR 813 (PC).

[106] *Thompson v Johnson and Johnson Pty Ltd* [1992] 3 Med LR 148, 171–72 (SC of Victoria, App Div).

[107] *Bux v Slough Metals Ltd* [1973] 1 WLR 1358 (CA); *Dickson v Flack* [1953] 2 QB 464; *Best v Wellcome Foundation Ltd* [1994] 5 Med LR 81 (Irish Sup Ct). As licence holders, manufacturers of medicinal products must comply with the statutory requirements of the Medicines Act 1968 and the Human Medicines Regulations 2012, as well as any other subordinate legislation. See further C Newdick, 'The Impact of Licensing Authority Approval on Pharmaceutical Product Liability: A Survey of American and UK Law' (1992) 47 F & D LJ 41, 52.

[108] cf (EEC) 65/65 OJ 22, 9 Feb 1965, 369.

[109] *Budden v BP Oil and Shell Oil* (1980) 124 SJ 376 (CA); cf the defence under the CPA, s 4(1)(a) (paras 18.62 and 18.63).

[110] cf *R v Licensing Authority Established under Medicines Act 1968, ex p Smith, Kline & French Laboratories Ltd* [1989] 1 All ER 578, 590 *per Lord* Templeman; See further R Goldberg, *Medicinal Product Liability and Regulation* (Hart Publishing 2013) 138–41.

[111] *Merck Sharp & Dohme (Australia) Pty Limited v Peterson* [2011] FCAFC 128, leave to appeal refused, [2012] HCATrans 105, [161]–[163], discussed in R Goldberg, *Medicinal Product Liability and Regulation* (Hart Publishing 2013) 141.

proportions, excessive potency, and toxicity,[112] the presence of some impurity or foreign body,[113] and deterioration of the product from contamination or faulty packaging.[114] Though the full burden of proof is formally on the claimant,[115] once it has been proved that there is a defect in the product[116] which probably did not occur after it had left the manufacturer's control,[117] there is an 'inference of negligence' akin to *res ipsa loquitur*, if not tantamount to automatic liability.[118] In fact, generally speaking, the stronger the evidence that the defendant has a careful quality control system, the more likely is it that a particular defect will be attributed to negligence in the production process.[119] In principle, if manufacturers have an appropriate system for ordering raw materials and components and adequate testing and inspection procedures, they will not incur liability for the negligence of an independent contractor,[120] though occasionally the manufacturer's duty has been treated as non-delegable.[121]

(iv) Design defects

18.30 Manufacturers are liable for harm caused by their failure to take reasonable care to ensure that a product has been safely designed.[122] Though they cannot, by definition, be liable in negligence for not knowing about undiscoverable defects, some cases have suggested that a high standard of care is expected, especially in the research that goes into the design of intrinsically dangerous and novel products.[123] However, though the manufacturer is under a duty to keep abreast of medical and scientific discoveries,[124] proof that design defects are attributable to negligence is often elusive, and seldom more so than in the case of medical products.[125]

18.31 A major obstacle to proof of negligence in medical products litigation is that what counts as 'knowledge' can be both intrinsically problematic and complicated by the fact that scientists

---

[112] *Best v Wellcome Foundation Ltd* [1994] 5 Med L R 81 (Irish Sup Ct) (pertussis component in DTP vaccine).

[113] cf *Donoghue v Stevenson* [1932] AC 562; *Daniels and Daniels v R White & Sons Ltd and Tarbard* [1938] 4 All ER 258.

[114] eg *Fisher v Harrods Ltd* [1966] 1 Lloyd's Rep 500; *Adelaide Chemical & Fertilizer Co Ltd v Carlyle* (1940) 64 CLR 514; *Hill v James Crowe (Cases) Ltd* [1978] 1 All ER 812.

[115] eg *Mason v Williams and Williams Ltd* [1955] 1 All ER 808, relying on *Donoghue v Stevenson* [1932] AC 562, 622 *per* Lord MacMillan.

[116] *Grant v Australian Knitting Mills Ltd* [1936] AC 85; cf *Hill v James Crowe (Cases) Ltd* [1978] 1 All ER 812; *Shandloff v City Dairy Ltd* [1936] 4 DLR 712, 719 (Ont CA).

[117] *Mason v Williams and Williams Ltd* [1955] 1 All ER 808, *Evans v Triplex Glass* [1936] 1 All ER 283.

[118] *Lockhart v Barr* (1943) SC (HL) 1.

[119] *Grant v Australian Knitting Mills Ltd* [1936] AC 85, 101; *Hill v James Crowe (Cases) Ltd* [1978] 1 All ER 812, 816; *Carroll v Fearon* [1999] ECC 73; *Divya v Toyo Tire and Rubber Co Ltd* [2011] EWHC 1993 (QB).

[120] *Taylor v Rover Co* [1966] 1 WLR 1491.

[121] *Winward v TVR Engineering Ltd* [1986] BTLC 366 (CA); *Cynat Products Ltd v Landbuild (Investment and Property) Ltd* [1984] 3 All ER 513.

[122] *Hindustan Steam Shipping Co Ltd v Siemens Bros & Co* [1955] 1 Lloyd's Rep 167.

[123] eg *Vacwell Engineering Co Ltd v BDH Chemicals Ltd* [1971] QB 88, 109: liability imposed for failure 'to provide and maintain a system for carrying out adequate research into scientific literature to ascertain known hazards' and for failure to conduct such research. The defendants had based their research on several modern texts (including the standard work on the industrial hazards of chemicals) which did not mention the explosive hazard documented in earlier literature. Cf *Independent Broadcasting Authority v EMI Electronics Ltd and BICC Construction Ltd* [1981] 14 BLR 1 (HL). And see G Howells, *Comparative Product Liability* (Ashford 1993) 74–75; C Newdick, 'The Future of Negligence in Product Liability' (1987) 103 LQR 288, 293–94.

[124] *Stokes v Guest, Keen & Nettlefold (Bolts & Nuts) Ltd* [1968] 1 WLR 1776, 1783; *Cartwright v GKN Sankey Ltd* [1972] 2 Lloyd's Rep 242, 259.

[125] See para 18.04.

and medical researchers may legitimately hold conflicting views.[126] There will often be a grey area between speculation, hypothesis, or information, on the one hand, and 'hard' knowledge on the other,[127] and the courts are mindful of the need to guard against hindsight.[128] Also, though 'the law requires even pioneers to be prudent',[129] it recognizes the importance attached to innovation. In determining the level of acceptable risk for new drugs, allowance will be made for the fact that they need to be potent to be useful and that there are practical limits on discovering risks at the stage of pre-market testing on relatively small populations in animal studies and clinical trials. By contrast with the approach of the courts towards manufacturing defects, a previous good design safety record is of distinct evidential value to the defendant.

(v) Marketing defects

(a) **Warnings and instructions** An important aspect of due care in the supply of products is the provision of adequate instructions for their use and, where necessary, of warnings about risks of which the defendant has actual or constructive knowledge. 'Failure-to-warn claims are now the most common form of litigated product case in the US.'[130] Since the manufacturer is required to make available such information as will enable products to be used safely,[131] any warnings must be readily intelligible and commensurate with risks,[132] bearing in mind that informing the medical profession normally suffices in respect of prescription medicines. Risks, in turn, must not be minimized by promotional material.[133] The manufacturer would normally be expected to warn of a drug's inherent and irreducible risks, though there is no duty to warn of a danger which is either patent or a matter of common knowledge.[134] There can, however, be liability for injury resulting from reasonably foreseeable misuse which has not been warned against.[135] A warning or instructions may also be needed where the danger is known to the user, but not the means of avoiding the risk. At the same time, the manufacturer may have regard to such factors as the remoteness of any **18.32**

[126] See R Lee, 'Vaccine Damage: Adjudicating Scientific Dispute', in G Howells (ed), *Product Liability Insurance and the Pharmaceutical Industry: An Anglo-American Comparison* (Manchester 1991); C Newdick, 'The Development Risk Defence of the Consumer Protection Act 1987' (1988) 47 CLJ 455, 462. The concept of safety is harder to apply to medicinal products, where safety is a relative concept: I Dodds-Smith, M Spencer, and J Bore, 'Product Liability for Medicinal Products' in M J Powers, N H Harris, and A Barton (eds), *Clinical Negligence* (4th edn, Bloomsbury Professional 2008) para 24.78.

[127] See para 18.71.

[128] *Roe v Minister of Health* [1954] 2 QB 66, 86 (CA) *per* Denning LJ; cf *Thompson v Smiths Shiprepairers (North Shields) Ltd* [1984] 1 All ER 881, 894 *per* Mustill J; *Mann and Close v Wellcome Foundation Ltd* (1989, QBD).

[129] *Independent Broadcasting Authority v EMI Electronics Ltd and BICC Construction Ltd* [1981] 14 BLR 1 (HL) 28 *per* Lord Edmund-Davies.

[130] Stapleton, *Product Liability*, n 9, 252.

[131] *Kubach v Hollands* [1937] 3 All ER 907; *Holmes v Ashford* [1950] 2 All ER 76 (CA); *Devilez v Boots Pure Drug Co* (1962) 106 SJ 552.

[132] *Vacwell Engineering Ltd v BDH Chemicals Ltd* [1971] 1 QB 111 (CA) (varying [1971] 1 QB 88); cf *Ward v Hopkins* [1959] 3 All ER 225, 239 (CA).

[133] *Watson v Buckley, Osborne, Garrett & Co Ltd* [1940] 1 All ER 174; cf *Vacwell Engineering Ltd*, n 132; *Buchan v Ortho Pharmaceuticals (Canada) Ltd* (1986) 25 DLR (4th) 658, 678–79 (Ont CA); *Rothwell v Raes* (1989) 54 DLR (4th) 193, 341–42 (Ont CA); *R v Roussel Laboratories; R v Good* (1989) 88 Cr App R 140. For regulatory requirements on advertising and on information to be provided with medicinal products, see Chapter 17, paras 17.70–17.96.

[134] *McTear v Imperial Tobacco Ltd*, 2005 2 SC 1; *Farr v Butters Bros & Co* [1932] 2 KB 606 (CA); *Devilez v Boots Pure Drug Co* (1962) 106 SJ 552; cf *Deshane v Deere & Co* (1993) 106 DLR (4th) 385 (Ont CA). See also Miller and Goldberg, *Product Liability*, n 2, 585–86. In the US there is some support for the view that manufacturers should provide a warning for any users whom they know or should reasonably expect to be less informed than themselves about the dangers associated with the product. See, eg, *Micallef v Miehle Co* 39 NY 2d 376 (1976). See also Restatement (Third) of Torts (1998) n 29, s 2 Comment i.

[135] *Hill v James Crowe (Cases) Ltd* [1978] 1 All ER 812.

danger and the possibility of causing needless alarm.[136] Where there has been a total failure to warn there is little scope for defences such as contributory negligence[137] or volenti, since the user will normally have been unaware of any danger. In principle, there is some scope for them where an inadequate warning has been given.[138]

18.33 **(b) Allergic reactions** Particular difficulties surround the issue of allergic reactions. If a manufacturer knows or ought to know of the danger, in appropriate circumstances a warning would be required for the benefit of a vulnerable minority.[139] In the United States, courts have often relied on the 'narrow formulaic requirement that a certain percentage of persons must suffer an allergic reaction from the product before the manufacturer will be held liable'.[140] However, in any given case, whether or not failure to warn is reasonable could involve consideration of such factors as the severity of the consequences, the social value of the product, the availability of substitutes, and the claimant's access to information about allergy.

18.34 **(c) Causation** Inadequate warning or failure to warn is normally easier to establish than defective design, and plainly is more easily rectified. It will not, though, result in liability without proof of causation. According to orthodox tort theory, the court must be satisfied that the claimant would not have used the product in question had a proper warning been given.[141] However, it is of interest that in *Chester v Afshar*,[142] the House of Lords held a surgeon liable in negligence for failure to warn of an *unavoidable* minor risk that materialized, even though, had she been warned of it, the patient would probably have had the same operation at some later date. It is at least arguable that this more relaxed approach to causation might be applied to failure to warn in the context of pharmaceutical products.[143]

(vi) Continuing duty of care

18.35 If, after its potential for harm had become apparent, a marketed product caused injury, there could be liability in negligence for not having modified it or made its availability subject to a suitable warning,[144] for not having removed it from the market and, it would seem, for not having warned previous purchasers.[145] As regards prescription drugs, it would

---

[136] *Thompson v Johnson & Johnson Pty Ltd* [1992] 3 Med LR 148 (SC of Victoria, App Div) (tampons and toxic shock syndrome).

[137] But see *Devilez v Boots Pure Drug Co*, n 134.

[138] See Miller and Goldberg, *Product Liability*, n 2, 751–56. See also *Cipollone v Liggett Group Inc* 112 S Ct 2608 (1992) (tobacco).

[139] *Ingham v Emes* [1955] 2 QB 366 (CA); *Parker v Oxolo Ltd and Senior* [1937] 3 All ER 524; *Chin Keow v Government of Malaysia* [1967] 1 WLR 813 (PC). See C Newdick, 'Strict Liability for Defective Drugs in the Pharmaceutical Industry' (1985) 101 LQR 405, 412.

[140] C Rogerson and M Trebilcock, 'Products Liability and the Allergic Consumer: A Study in the Problems of Framing an Efficient Liability Regime' (1986) 36 University of Toronto LJ 52, 57. Typically an 'appreciable number': *Crotty v Shartenberg's New Haven Inc* 162 A 2d 513 (Conn, 1960).

[141] *Buchan v Ortho Pharmaceuticals (Canada) Ltd* (1986) 25 DLR (4th) 658 (Ont CA); *H v Royal Alexandra Hospital for Children* [1990] 1 Med LR 297 (SC of NSW); *Davidson v Connaught Laboratories* (1980) 14 CCLT 251 (Ont HC). In *Buchan*, as in English law, the test of causation was subjective. See also *Hollis v Dow Corning Corporation* (1996) 129 DLR (4th) 609 (SCC). In principle, it would seem that where causation depends on what the prescribing doctor would have done if adequately warned, the test should be subjective to that doctor: M A Jones, *Medical Negligence* (4th edn, Sweet & Maxwell 2008), 10-043–10-050, esp at 10-044.

[142] *Chester v Afshar* [2004] UKHL 41: see Chapter 6, para 6.53; and cf *Wallace* v *Kam* [2013] HCA 19, (2013) 250 CLR 375; and Chapter 8, paras 8.77–8.78. For criticism of *Chester*, and support for the reasoning of the High Court of Australia in *Wallace*, see T Clark, and D Nolan, 'A Critique of *Chester v Afshar*' (2014) 34 OJLS 659.

[143] See further R Goldberg, *Medicinal Product Liability and Regulation* (Hart Publishing 2013) 79–82.

[144] *Wright v Dunlop Rubber Co Ltd* (1972) 13 KIR 255, 272 (CA).

[145] *Walton v British Leyland UK Ltd* (1978 QBD), *Hobbs (E) (Farms) Ltd v Baxenden Chemical Co Ltd* [1992] 1 Lloyds Rep 54, 65; *Carroll v Dunlop Ltd* (1996) Product Liability Intl, Apr 1996, 58–59; *United Central Bakers v Spooner Industries Ltd* [2013] CSOH 150, [88] *per* Lord Hodge. Cf *Rivtow Marine Ltd v*

be negligent not to take reasonable steps to warn prescribing doctors[146] and presumably in certain instances not to issue public warnings.[147] To this end, manufacturers need proper procedures for monitoring adverse reactions and product recall.[148]

(vii) Intermediate examination

Lord Atkin described the manufacturer's liability for a defective product as contingent on there being 'no reasonable possibility of intermediate examination' before it reaches the ultimate consumer.[149] Manufacturers are not liable[150] if it was reasonable for them to have expected that the examination conducted by the intermediary would have been of such a type as to reveal the defect.[151] It is now clear that there must be a reasonable 'probability' of such examination if the manufacturer is to avoid liability.[152] **18.36**

Naturally patients cannot normally be expected to have conducted the kind of inspection of medicinal products that would reveal their potential for harm, but the position of doctors and pharmacists is less clear.[153] The manufacturer will normally be absolved from liability where the pharmacist has failed to observe manifest defects connected with the production or distribution process, such as deterioration or lack of sterility of products that have not been properly packaged or stored. In addition, the manufacturer may be able to invoke the 'learned intermediary' rule against either the doctor or the pharmacist.[154] **18.37**

(viii) The 'learned intermediary' rule

An important aspect of the pharmaceutical manufacturer's duty of care is to see that the ultimate user is adequately warned about risks.[155] However, it is not usually necessary for the relevant information to be communicated directly to the consumer when a product is to be used under expert supervision; adequate warning to a responsible intermediary normally suffices.[156] As regards prescription drugs, in many jurisdictions it has been held sufficient for the manufacturer to warn the doctor as 'learned intermediary'.[157] There is no **18.38**

Washington Iron Works [1973] 40 DLR (3d) 530, 536 (SCC); *Hutton v General Motors of Canada Ltd* [2010] ABQB 606, [2011] 4 WWR 284. See also Restatement (Third) of Torts (1998), n 29, ss 10 and 11.

[146] *Hollis v Dow Corning Corporation* (1996) 129 DLR (4th) 609 (SCC).

[147] *Buchan v Ortho Pharmaceuticals (Canada) Ltd*, n 141, 667, 678.

[148] *McCain Foods Ltd v Grand Falls Industries Ltd* (1991) 80 DLR (4th) 252 (NBCA). For pharmaceuticals, the existence of such procedures is a prerequisite for the grant of a marketing authorization, and part of the marketing authorization holder's obligations post-grant: Human Medicines Regulations 2012, SI 2012/1916, regs 57, 75–77. On the 'yellow card' scheme for reporting adverse reactions to the CSM, see H Teff, 'Regulation under the Medicines Act 1968: A Continuing Prescription for Health' (1984) 47 MLR 303. The scheme was extended in 1999 to include nationwide reporting by community pharmacists: (1999) 319 British Medical Journal 1322, and, since 2005, to include reporting by patients: <https://yellowcard.mhra.gov.uk/the-yellow-card-scheme/>.

[149] *Donoghue v Stevenson* [1932] AC 562, 599. See para 18.22.

[150] Subject to any possibility of apportionment under the Civil Liability (Contribution) Act 1978, or of contributory negligence by the consumer.

[151] *Herschtal v Stewart & Ardern Ltd* [1940] 1 KB 155; *Griffiths v Arch Engineering Co (Newport) Ltd* [1968] 3 All ER 217; *Aswan Engineering Establishment Co v Lupdine Ltd* [1987] 1 All ER 135, 153 (CA) *per* Lloyd LJ.

[152] eg *Paine v Colne Valley Electricity Supply Co Ltd* [1938] 4 All ER 803, 808–09; *Griffiths v Arch Engineering Co Ltd*, n 151.

[153] As is that of certain regulatory bodies in regard to design defects. See paras 18.42–18.47.

[154] See P Ferguson, 'Liability for Pharmaceutical Products: A Critique of the "Learned Intermediary" Rule' (1992) 12 OJLS 59.

[155] See paras 18.32 and 18.33; cf *Thompson v Johnson and Johnson Pty Ltd* [1992] 3 Med LR 148 (SC of Victoria, App Div).

[156] cf *Holmes v Ashford* [1950] 2 All ER 76 (CA).

[157] A term first used in *Sterling Drug, Inc v Cornish* 370 F 2d 82 (8th Cir) (1966). See, eg, *Reyes v Wyeth Laboratories* 498 F 2d 1264, 1276 (5th Cir) (1974); *Buchan v Ortho Pharmaceuticals (Canada) Ltd* (1986) 25 DLR (4th) 658, 680–81 (Ont CA) *per* Robins JA. Cf *H v Royal Alexandra Hospital for Children* [1990] 1

express authority on the rule in England, but its spirit is reflected in the applicable regulatory regime. Any written material accompanying the promotion of a medicinal product to a person qualified to prescribe or supply such a product must contain certain particulars, including a statement of any entries in the summary of product characteristics relating to adverse reactions, precautions, and contra-indications.[158] A drug manufacturer cannot assume that doctors will have read all the relevant scientific literature: 'They rely on the drug companies to supply them with the necessary data.'[159]

18.39 Nevertheless, in any given case, doctors are still required to use their independent judgment in prescribing, based on their knowledge of the individual patient and the drug. Under English law, they have traditionally had considerable leeway as to what information they needed to disclose. By virtue of the '*Bolam* principle' they could normally discharge their duty in this respect by acting in accordance with any standard of practice recognized as proper by a responsible body of medical opinion. It followed that, in England, adherence to the 'learned intermediary' rule could in practice result in patients having less effective legal protection against failure to warn in respect of prescription drugs than in the case of the typically less powerful over-the-counter products.[160] However, more recent case law, and medical practice, point to a more patient-oriented view of disclosure generally.[161] It has been submitted that the principal reason why the doctrine should be retained in the UK is the fact that prescription drugs continue to require the intervention of a medical practitioner.[162] Virtually all of the prescribing of drugs in the community is carried out by general practitioners.[163] In such circumstances, the focus of the law should continue to be on the duty of such practitioners to engage in the informed consent process by discussing the risks and benefits of prescription drugs with their patients when selecting the appropriate

Med LR 297 (SC of NSW); *McKee v Moore* 648 P 2d 21 (Okla) (1982); *Centocar, Inc v Hamilton*, 372 SW 3d 140, 158–59 (Tex 2012). The so-called learned intermediary rule has been adopted by the vast majority of states in the US: see R Goldberg, *Medicinal Product Liability and Regulation* (Hart Publishing 2013) 60–67. See also Restatement (Third) of Torts (1998), n 29, s 6(d) (discussed in R Goldberg, *Medicinal Product Liability and Regulation* (Hart Publishing 2013) 66–67) and Ferguson, 'Liability for Pharmaceutical Products: A Critique of the "Learned Intermediary" Rule', n 154, 61.

[158] Human Medicines Regulations 2012, SI 2012/1916, reg 297 and Schedule 30 (particulars for advertisements to persons qualified to prescribe or supply).

[159] *Davidson v Connaught Laboratories* (1980) 14 CCLT 251, 276 *per* Linden J (Ont HC). Awareness that a report of an official advisory committee has been circulated to medical practitioners does not absolve the manufacturer from a common law duty to inform them: *Buchan v Ortho Pharmaceuticals (Canada) Ltd*, n 157, 680–81 *per* Robins JA. See also *Hollis v Dow Corning Corporation* (1996) 129 DLR (4th) 609 (SCC); (1993) 103 DLR (4th) 520 (BCCA), and Stapleton, *Product Liability*, n 9, 252–55.

[160] *Bolam v Friern Hospital Management Committee* [1957] 1 WLR 582; *Sidaway v Board of Governors of the Bethlem Royal Hospital and the Maudsley Hospital* [1985] AC 871. See Ferguson, n 154, 72.

[161] See now the Supreme Court's departure from *Sidaway* through its rejection of the application of the *Bolam* test to a duty to advise of risks in a medical context, and its imposition of a duty of a doctor to inform a patient of any material risks of injury in *Montgomery v Lanarkshire Health Board* [2015] UKSC 11, [2015] AC 1430, [87]; approving *Pearce v United Bristol Healthcare NHS Trust* (1998) 48 BMLR 118, 124–25 *per* Lord Woolf MR. Cf *Bolitho v City and Hackney HA* [1998] AC 232, discussed in Chapter 8. And see *Chester v Afshar* [2004] UKHL 41, discussed in para 18.34; D Meyers, '*Chester v Afshar*: Sayonara, Sub Silentio, *Sidaway*?', in S McLean, S (ed), *First Do No Harm—Law, Ethics and Healthcare* (Ashgate 2006) ch 16. See further Chapter 8.

[162] R Goldberg, *Medicinal Product Liability and Regulation* (Hart Publishing 2013) 76–77.

[163] B Guthrie, C McCowan, P Davey, CR Simpson, T Dreischulte, and K Barnett, 'High risk prescribing in primary care patients particularly vulnerable to adverse drug events: cross sectional population database analysis in Scottish general practice' (2011) 342 British Medical Journal d3514. Independent prescribing rights have also been extended to suitably qualified pharmacists and nurses: Health and Social Care Act 2001, s 63; National Health Service (Miscellaneous Amendments Relating to Independent Prescribing) Regulations 2006, SI 2006/913 and Medicines for Human Use (Prescribing) (Miscellaneous Amendments) Order 2006, SI 2006/915.

medication.[164] The main benefit of the learned intermediary doctrine is that it encourages this activity.[165]

Considerations of policy may argue against applying the 'learned intermediary' rule to certain medical procedures.[166] For example, in the United States it has not always been applied to mass immunization.[167] Some courts have stressed that voluntary participants in a procedure which benefits society at large should not be deprived of a remedy against the manufacturer; that the injections are not necessarily administered by someone who is indisputably a 'learned intermediary'; and that, even when they are, there may be no 'individualized assessment' of risks and benefits.[168] Nor does the rule invariably hold for the prescription of oral contraceptives, when the case for insisting on communication to the user is underlined by the typically 'heightened participation' of patients in the decision; the danger of doctors giving inadequate information about risks and allowing unmonitored long-term and repeat prescriptions, and the elective, non-therapeutic nature of the treatment.[169] American courts have, however, generally retained the 'learned intermediary' rule for contraceptive devices.[170] A further exception to the learned intermediary rule has emerged concerning the direct marketing of prescription drugs to consumers.[171] Finally, it has been observed[172] that that in the European context, the significance of the learned intermediary rule has to some extent been reduced in the case of medicinal products, since, unless all the required information is on the container or on the packaging, the provision of package leaflets for human medicinal products is obligatory.[173] **18.40**

3. Proving causation

In determining whether or not a medicinal product is responsible for harm, the problems of **18.41** extrapolating from biochemical findings, animal studies, and relatively small-scale tests on humans are frequently compounded by competing scientific views on evidence and the 'mismatch of legal and scientific notions of causation'.[174] As a result, proof that on the balance

164 L Noah, 'This is Your Products Liability Restatement on Drugs' (2009) 74 Brooklyn Law Review 839, 905.

165 J L Peters, (2008) 48 Jurimetrics Journal 285, 302, 308.

166 See further R Goldberg, *Medicinal Product Liability and Regulation* (Hart Publishing 2013) 62–66.

167 *Davis v Wyeth Laboratories Inc* 399 F 2d 121 (9th Cir) (1968); *Reyes v Wyeth Laboratories* 498 F 2d 1264 (5th Cir) (1974).

168 *Givens v Lederle* 566 F 2d 1341 (5th Cir) (1974).

169 eg *Seley v GD Searle & Co* 423 NE 2d 831 (1981); *Lukaszewicz v Ortho Pharmaceutical Corporation* 510 F Supp 961 (Wis) (1981); *Stephens v GD Searle & Co* 602 F Supp 379 (Mich) (1985); *MacDonald v Ortho Pharmaceutical Corporation* 475 NE 2d 65 (Mass) (1985); *Odgers v Ortho Pharmaceutical Corporation* 609 F Supp 867 (DC Mich) (1985). cf *Buchan v Ortho Pharmaceuticals (Canada) Ltd* (1986) 25 DLR (4th) 658, 670, 688–9 (Ont CA).

170 *McKee v Moore* 648 P 2d 21 (Okla) (1982); *contra*, *Hill v Searle Laboratories* 884 F 2d 1064 (8th Cir) (1989).

171 See *Perez v Wyeth Laboratories Inc* 734 A 2d 1245 (NJ 1999); *State, ex rel Johnson & Johnson Corporation v Karl* 647 SE 2d 899, 908, 910–11 (W Va 2007); but cf *Centocar, Inc v Hamilton* 372 SW 3d 140, 164 (Tex 2012); D G Owen, 'Dangers in Prescription Drugs: Filling a Private Law Gap in the Healthcare Debate' (2010) 42 Connecticut Law Review 733, 767.

172 R Goldberg, *Medicinal Product Liability and Regulation* (Hart Publishing 2013) 77.

173 Directive 2001/83/EC on the Community Code Relating to Medicinal Products for Human Use [2001] OJ L311/67, as amended by Dir 2004/27/EC [2004] OJ L136/34, Art 58; Human Medicines Regulations 2012, SI 2012/1916, reg 260; (see generally, Dir 2001/83/EC, Title V, labelling and package leaflets, Arts 54–69).

174 R Lee, 'Vaccine Damage: Adjudicating Scientific Dispute', n 126, and para 18.31; cf *Brock v Merrell Dow Pharmaceuticals Inc* 874 F 2d 307 (5th Cir) (1989). See also R Goldberg, 'Scientific Evidence, Causation and the Law—Lessons of Bendectin (Debendox) Litigation' (1996) 4 Med L Rev 32; R Goldberg, *Causation and Risk in the Law of Torts: Scientific Evidence and Medicinal Product Liability* (Hart Publishing 1999); and R Goldberg, 'Epidemiological Uncertainty, Causation, and Drug Product Liability' (2014) McGill LJ 777.

of probabilities a given product caused or materially contributed to the claimant's injuries[175] is often elusive.[176] The suggestion that, following the decision in *McGhee v National Coal Board*, negligent conduct which *increased the risk* of injury would suffice to ground liability unless the defendant could show that it was not the cause was subsequently rejected in *Wilsher v Essex Area Health Authority*.[177] The burden of proof is on the claimant, who must normally prove that on the balance of probabilities the defendant's negligence caused or materially contributed to the injury. However, where the state of scientific knowledge makes it impossible to prove the causal link, it suffices, in appropriate cases, to establish that the defendant had materially increased the risk of injury. It was on this latter basis that the House of Lords held the defendants liable in *Fairchild v Glenhaven Funeral Services Ltd*, and, more recently, in *Barker v Corus UK Ltd*, where it was also decided that, in such cases of multiple defendants, the damages should be apportioned, each defendant to be liable according to the degree of risk it was deemed to have posed to the claimant.[178] Both of these cases involved workers who had contracted mesothelioma from negligent exposure to asbestos, and who had no means of identifying the culpable employer among the several companies for whom they had worked over many years. Similar evidential problems may arise with certain defective drugs. In *Fairchild* Lord Hoffmann detected a certain resemblance to the facts in the Californian decision of *Sindell v Abbott Laboratories*, and he described its 'imaginative rule that each manufacturer should be liable in proportion to his market share' as worthy of consideration in appropriate cases.[179] In *Sindell*, diethylstilbestrol, a defective

[175] *Bonnington Castings Ltd v Wardlaw* [1956] AC 613.

[176] See, eg, *Kay v Ayrshire and Arran Health Board* [1987] 2 All ER 417 (HL) (penicillin and deafness). On pertussis, see, eg, *Loveday v Renton* [1990] 1 Med LR 117; *Rothwell v Raes* (1988) 54 DLR (4th) 193, aff'd (1990) 76 DLR (4th) 280 (Ont CA). But see also *Best v Wellcome Foundation Ltd* [1994] 5 Med LR 81 (Irish Sup Ct). See generally Jones, *Medical Negligence*, n 141, ch 5. And see C Newdick, 'Strict Liability for Defective Drugs in the Pharmaceutical Industry' (1985) 101 LQR 405, 420–30; *Vadera v Shaw* (1999) 45 BMLR 162 (CA), and R Goldberg, 'The Contraceptive Pill, Negligence and Causation: Views on *Vadera v Shaw*' (2000) 8 Med L Rev 316; *Merck Sharp & Dohme (Australia) Pty Limited v Peterson*: [2011] FCAFC 128, leave to appeal refused, [2012] HCATrans 105, discussed in R Goldberg, 'Epidemiological Uncertainty, Causation, and Drug Product Liability' (2014) McGill LJ 777, 792 et seq.

[177] *McGhee v National Coal Board* [1973] 1 WLR 1 (HL), and *Wilsher v Essex AHA* [1988] AC 1074. For detailed analysis, see Chapter 6.

[178] *Fairchild v Glenhaven Funeral Services Ltd* [2003] 1 AC 32 and *Barker v Corus UK Ltd* [2006] 2 AC 572. In respect of mesothelioma contracted through exposure to asbestos, the attempt in *Barker v Corus* to impose several rather than joint liability was reversed by the Compensation Act 2006, s 3. In *Durham v BAI (Run Off) Ltd* [2012] UKSC 14, [2012] 1 WLR 867, Lord Mance JSC (with whom Lord Kerr, Lord Clarke, and Lord Dyson JJSC agreed) reconsidered Barker and held that it was inaccurate to speak as of the cause of action recognized in *Fairchild* and *Barker* as being merely for the risk created by exposing someone to asbestos. The cause of action existed because the defendant had exposed the victim to asbestos, because that exposure may have led to mesothelioma and because mesothelioma had been suffered by the victim. The actual development of mesothelioma was an essential element of the cause of action: *Durham*, [65] *per* Lord Mance JSC. *Barker* did not establish a unique principle of legal responsibility. Lord Mance considered that it was 'both possible and appropriate to characterise the position achieved by the common law after Barker as one concerned with the issue of the "causal requirements" or "causal link", as between the defendant's conduct and the disease, which the common law requires in order for there to be an action for mesothelioma': *Durham*, [64]. While Lord Mance's judgment seemingly restored the common understanding of the effect of *Fairchild* on the issue of the nature of the damage for which the employer is responsible, it has been determined unanimously by the Supreme Court that the decision in *Barker* remains good law: *International Energy Group Ltd v Zurich Insurance plc* [2015] UKSC33, [2015] 2 WLR 1471, [27], [29], [31], per Lord Mance JSC. As Lord Mance put it: '*Barker*, as analysed in "Trigger", accepted causation in [a] weak or broad sense and none the less held an employer's responsibility to be proportionate to that part for which the employer was responsible of the victim's total exposure to asbestos dust. Trigger cannot therefore be said to affect or undermine the reasoning or decision in *Barker*': *International Energy*, [29].

[179] *Fairchild v Glenhaven Funeral Services Ltd*, n 178, [74] *per* Lord Hoffmann. See *Sindell v Abbott Laboratories* 607 P 2d 924 (1980). Cf *Hymowitz v Eli Lilly & Co* 73 NY 2d 487 (1989); *Doe v Cutter*

generic drug produced by over 200 manufacturers, caused vaginal cancer in the daughters of women who had taken it, but their condition only became apparent after a latency period of some fifteen years or more, and it was not possible for individual claimants to identify which manufacturer had produced the drug taken by their mother. In these circumstances, liability was imposed on the manufacturers in proportion to their share of the national market. The decisions in *Fairchild* and *Barker v Corus* could, in theory, presage the adoption of a 'market share' approach by the English courts in pharmaceutical cases, at least where there is only a single causal agent. However, in *Fairchild*, the House of Lords was clearly of the view that any such approach should be used very sparingly. It poses various problems, not least in calculating proportionate responsibility,[180] and, more fundamentally, there would be judicial reluctance to depart from the orthodox, corrective justice model of tort law.

An emerging issue is the extent to which the apparent tension between the balance of probabilities standard and the standard for epidemiology can be reconciled with the theory that causation can be proved on the balance of probabilities by reference to the doubling of risk of injury. While the so-called doubling of risk theory has been subject to trenchant criticism in the US, its existence appears to be gaining ground in the UK.[181] In *Sienkiewicz v Grief (UK) Ltd*,[182] the Supreme Court unanimously held that there was no room for introducing the doubling of risk approach to 'single exposure' mesothelioma cases or multiple defendant mesothelioma cases,[183] but differences in view emerged with the obiter discussion of the general applicability of the doubling of risk theory using epidemiological evidence to determine proof of causation in personal injury cases. While Lord Phillips concluded[184] that there was no scope for the doubling the risk test in cases where two agents operated cumulatively and simultaneously in causing the onset of the disease, he submitted[185] that there was no reason in principle why the 'doubles the risk test' should not be applied where the initiation of a disease was dose related and there had been consecutive exposures to an agent or agents that cause the disease: for example *McGhee v National Coal Board*.[186] He also considered[187] that there was no reason in principle why the 'doubles the risk' test should **18.42**

Biological Inc 971 F 2d 375 (1992): applied to HIV-infected Factor VIII, despite the fact that the manufactured product is not uniformly dangerous.

180 There would doubtless be an even greater emphasis on the role of statistical evidence in such cases, and the issue would emerge as to whether epidemiological evidence could be used to determine proportionate responsibility.

181 See the discussion of the US position and that of the UK in *XYZ v Schering Health Care Ltd* [2002] EWHC 1420, (2002) 70 BMLR 88 (QB), in R Goldberg, 'Epidemiological Uncertainty, Causation, and Drug Product Liability' (2014) McGill LJ 777, 785–93.

182 *Sienkiewicz v Grief (UK) Ltd* [2011] UKSC 10, [2011] 2 AC 229.

183 ibid, [106] *per* Lord Phillips, [160] *per* Lord Rodger, [169] *per* Baroness Hale, [188] *per* Lord Mance, [2003] *per* Lord Kerr, [220] *per* Lord Dyson. Cf J Stapleton (2012) 128 LQR 221, 224–25, who states that both propositions (using the doubling-of-the-risk approach in mesothelioma cases where there was a single exposure or one with multiple defendants) could have been rejected as invalid on elementary statistical principles.

184 *Sienkiewicz v Greif* [2011] UKSC 10, [91] *per* Lord Phillips.

185 ibid, [92] *per* Lord Phillips.

186 *McGhee v National Coal Board* [1973] 1 WLR 1. Yet as Professor Stapleton has observed, the basis for the validity of the doubling–of-the-risk approach in this instance would be absent. By way of illustration, she cites the example of a person injured in a road accident who is administered an emergency dose of a medicinal product. The injured person is immediately transferred to a hospital, where the admitting doctor, failing to discover that medications had been administered to the victim, negligently administers a smaller dose of the medication. In that scenario, it is likely that the causal mechanism required a commingling of molecules from the later smaller dose with the innocent molecules, and thus the tortious administration of the medication by the admitting doctor would have made a causal contribution to the death, even though another larger and earlier dose would have been sufficient to cause death: J Stapleton, 'Factual Causation, Mesothelioma and Statistical Validity' (2012) 128 LQR 221, 228–29; see further J Stapleton, 'Unnecessary Causes' (2013) 129 LQR 39, 55–56.

187 *Sienkiewicz v Greif* [2011] UKSC 10, [93] *per* Lord Phillips.

not apply to competing alternatives, rather than cumulative potential causes of a disease or injury, such as *Hotson v East Berks Area Health Authority*.[188] However, neither Lord Rodger nor Baroness Hale took such a view, and both thought that a doubling of risk approach was not an appropriate test of causation.[189] A cautious attitude towards the use of the 'doubling of risk' test has been recently been adopted in Australia in the context of specific causation and the anti-inflammatory drug Vioxx,[190] and this has been recently echoed, albeit in a medical negligence context, by the Privy Council.[191]

4. Claims against regulatory authorities

18.43 Legal responsibility for harm caused by products is not necessarily limited to those directly engaged in their production and distribution. It is convenient at this point to outline the statutory framework for the control of safety, quality, and efficacy of medicines, with a view to considering whether any actions might lie against the relevant regulatory bodies.

18.44 Under the Human Medicines Regulations 2012, the manufacture and distribution of medicines is regulated by a Licensing Authority (LA), comprising the Secretary of State and the Minister for Health, Social Services and Public Safety, and the right to grant a product licence or market authorization is vested in the LA.[192] Since 2003, its executive responsibilities for pharmaceuticals have been discharged by the Medicines and Healthcare Products Regulatory Agency (MHRA).[193] The LA used to receive advice from the Medicines Commission and various specialist committees,[194] including the Committee on the Safety of Medicines (CSM), which it consulted on questions of safety, quality, and efficacy of new medicines for human use.[195] If the CSM provisionally advised against granting a licence, the applicant had a right to make representations to it. If still unsuccessful, the applicant had a right to be heard by the CSM and, thereafter, a right of appeal to the Medicines Commission and, finally, to a Person Appointed under the Medicines Act 1968. In 2005, the Medicines Commission and the CSM were merged, as the Commission on Human Medicines (CHM), and a more limited appeals structure was introduced.[196] In addition to the national procedure for validating products to be marketed only in the UK, there have been major developments in European measures designed to achieve a single European

---

[188] *Hotson v East Berks Area Health Authority* [1987] AC 750.

[189] *Sienkiewicz v Greif* [2011] UKSC 10, [156], [158], [162] *per* Lord Rodger, [170], [172]–[173] *per* Baroness Hale.

[190] *Merck Sharp & Dohme (Australia) Pty Limited v Peterson*: [2011] FCAFC 128, leave to appeal refused, [2012] HCATrans 105. For further analysis, see R Goldberg, 'Epidemiological Uncertainty, Causation, and Drug Product Liability' (2014) McGill LJ 777, 789–93.

[191] *Williams v The Bermuda Hospitals Board* [2016] UKPC 4, [48].

[192] Human Medicines Regulations 2012, SI 2012/1916, reg 6(1), (6). Marketing authorizations are initially granted for up to five years: ibid, reg 65(1).

[193] In April 2003, the Medicines Control Agency (MCA) and the Medical Devices Agency (MDA) combined to form the MHRA as a single Executive Agency of the Department of Health.

[194] Medicines Act 1968, s 2 and s 4, respectively. See further Medicines Control Agency, *Towards Safe Medicines*, n 23. See also HC Select Committee on Public Accounts, *Safety, Quality, Efficacy—Regulating Medicines in the UK* (26th Report, Session 2002–03).

[195] Medicines Act 1968, ss 19–20. In respect of the safety, quality, and efficacy of products on the market before the Medicines Act 1968 took effect, the LA was advised by the Committee on the Review of Medicines. The Committee was disbanded in 1992.

[196] Medicines (Advisory Bodies) Regulations 2005, SI 2005/1094, revoked by Human Medicines Regulations 2012/1916, Sch 35 para 1. See now Human Medicines Regulations 2012, SI 2012/1916, regs 9, 10. Now, if, after input from a relevant Expert Advisory Group (Human Medicines Regulations 2012, SI 2012/1916, reg 14(1)), the LA initially rejects an application, there is a right to be heard by a panel of reviewers, who must report to the licensing authority and to the applicant within sixty days of the conclusion of the hearing. The LA must take the report into account in deciding whether to confirm or alter its decision: Human Medicines Regulations 2012, SI 2012/1916, Sch 5, Sch 11, paras 10–11.

market in pharmaceuticals.[197] In 1995, following the establishment of the European Medicines Evaluation Agency (EMEA), a new dual EC licensing system was introduced. There is a centralized procedure, mandatory for most biotechnological medicines and optional for other high-technology medicines and those which contain a new active substance. Applications are submitted to the EMEA and marketing authorization is valid for all Member States. There is also a mutual recognition (decentralized) procedure for all other human medicines, compulsory since 1998, where it is sought to have an existing marketing authorization recognized by one or more other Member States. Recent European initiatives have been highly instrumental in shaping the English regulatory scheme and the European Product Liability Directive has become increasingly influential in matters of substantive liability.[198]

Where injury is attributable to the defective design of medicinal products, it is unclear whether or not an action lies against the LA, which authorizes their sale or supply, and against the other statutory bodies (notably the CHM) which advise on their safety, quality, and efficacy, or where appropriate, against the Department of Health. No such right is conferred under the Medicines Act 1968, but neither does the Act purport to derogate from any pre-existing rights of claimants.[199] Bodies which license or advise on products do not attract liability under the CPA, as they are providers of services, not suppliers of products. Though the licensing authority has occasionally been joined as a defendant in negligence actions, as was the CSM,[200] there has been no definitive ruling. The issue turns primarily on how far regulatory bodies enjoy immunity from suit in discharging their statutory duties. In accordance with the distinction adopted by Lord Wilberforce in *Anns v Merton*, discretionary policy decisions have been deemed non-justiciable and operational ones subject to a common law duty of care,[201] though the dividing line can be elusive. Promoting childhood vaccination has been treated as a non-justiciable exercise of statutory discretion, whereas claims that the DHSS had provided inadequate advice on contra-indications were allowed to proceed, as were comparable claims against the Department of Health in respect of Creutzfeldt-Jakob disease contracted following growth hormone treatment.[202] **18.45**

[197] For a detailed account of the European regulatory system, see Chapter 17.

[198] ibid, and n 27 (and related text) above, respectively. See also Powers et al, *Clinical Negligence*, n 126, paras 24.1–24.2, and R Alder, in P Feldschreiber (ed), *The Law and Regulation of Medicines* (Oxford University Press 2008) paras 3.74–3.86.

[199] Medicines Act 1968, s 133(2).

[200] See *Davies v Eli Lilly & Co* [1987] 3 All ER 94 (CA) (Opren), and *Re HIV Haemophiliac Litigation* (1998) 41 BMLR 171 (decided in 1990) (contaminated blood), where the Court of Appeal considered that the plaintiffs had 'made out at least a good arguable claim in law based upon common law negligence' against, inter alia, the LA, the CSM, and the Department of Health. See also *Attis v Canada* (2008) 300 DLR (4th) 415 (No private law duty of care owed by Health Canada to ensure members of the public were protected from medical devices that might cause them harm) (Ontario CA).

[201] eg *Smith v Secretary of State for Health* [2002] EWHC 200 (QB) (timing of CSM warning about drug discretionary); *XYZ v Schering Health Care Ltd* [2002] EWHC 1420 (QB) para 19. See also *Baric v Tomalk* (2006) 38 CCLT (3d) 300, Ont SCJ. See generally *Anns v Merton London Borough Council* [1978] AC 728, 754 *per* Lord Wilberforce; *Rowling v Takaro Properties* [1988] AC 473 (PC); *Home Office v Dorset Yacht Co Ltd* [1970] AC 1004, 1067–68 *per* Lord Diplock; *Sutherland Shire Council v Heyman* (1985) 157 CLR 424, 469 *per* Mason J. Cf on drug licensing: *R v Licensing Authority Established Under Medicines Act 1968, Ex p Smith, Kline & French* [1990] 1 AC 64, 108; *Gray v US and Eli Lilly & Co* 445 F Supp 337 (DC Tex) (1978); and, further, compliance with a request from the European Medicines Agency (EMA) concerning a marketing authorization holder's breach of an EU pharmacovigilance regulation: *R (on the application of Roche Registration Ltd) v Secretary of State for Health* [2014] EWHC 2256 (Admin), [2015] 1 CMLR 6 [153] (reinspection and supply of reinspection report on Roche's pharmacovigilance system to EMA consistent with MHRA's domestic public law duty to act fairly).

[202] *Department of Health and Social Security v Kinnear* (1984) 134 NLJ 886 (the point was not ultimately pursued to judgment). Cf *Rothwell v Raes* (1989) 54 DLR (4th) 193, 346 (Ont HC). But see *Bonthrone v Secretary of State for Scotland* 1987 SLT 34, where the nature and extent of such warnings was deemed a

18.46 It is uncertain, however, whether, or to what extent, the policy/operational distinction still obtains. Lord Wilberforce's speech in *Anns v Merton* was subjected to considerable criticism and subsequent appellate decisions tended to favour extensive immunity for regulatory bodies in the performance of their statutory functions.[203] Dicta to the effect that, in the context of consumer protection, it was perhaps 'best left to the legislature' to state the extent and limits of any such liability[204] seemed to reflect a general retreat from the expansion of liability for negligence. Regulatory agencies are only indirectly involved in the 'supply' of products, and the courts generally take a relatively strict approach to causation. In the context of prescribed drugs, they may be slow to find negligence against bodies which, in practice, exert only limited control over other potential defendants with more direct causal responsibility; though this argument seems less cogent when applied to those therapeutic categories for which NHS prescription is confined to drugs on the 'selected list' of specific, named conditions.[205]

18.47 Each case must now be considered in its context. There may be more scope for impugning the operational decisions of public bodies in respect of personal injury than for pure economic loss, the primary focus of judicial retrenchment. The courts have often laid much stress on 'statutory purpose' in determining whether or not a private right of action exists.[206] Traditionally, the role of statutory bodies has been to protect the general public interest rather than to confer rights on individuals,[207] though a duty to individuals is now more readily acknowledged where an agency has been established specifically to protect the public from dangerous practices.[208] Granted judicial disinclination to impugn discretionary decisions on the 'distribution of risks',[209] the public interest in early availability of valuable drugs must be set against the risks of allowing dangerous products onto the market, bearing in mind that protection of the public is the primary objective of the statutory bodies

discretionary matter. Cf *Ross v Secretary of State for Scotland* [1990] 1 Med LR 235. Under the Vaccine Damage Payments Act 1979, as amended, anyone suffering at least 60 per cent disablement, who can establish that it was caused by vaccination against certain specified diseases, is entitled to no-fault compensation, up to a maximum of £120,000: Vaccine Damage Payments Act 1979 Statutory Sum Order 2007, SI 2007/1931. Section 6(4) of the Act provides for the deduction of such payment from any award based on negligence. There are very few successful claims under the 1979 Act: see 'Vaccine Damage Payments' (2004) 27 Consumer Law Today 4 (5)(1), R Goldberg, *Medicinal Product Liability and Regulation* (Hart Publishing 2013) 10–11; and further R Goldberg, *Causation and Risk in the Law of Torts: Scientific Evidence and Medicinal Product Liability* (Hart Publishing 1999) 174–75 (analysis of tribunal results 1989–93). For growth hormone treatment, see *N v UK Research Council, sub nom Creutzfeldt-Jakob Disease Litigation* [1996] 7 Med LR 309 and *Group B Plaintiffs v Medical Research Council* (1997) 41 BMLR 157.

[203] For criticism of *Anns v Merton* see, eg, *Yuen Kun-yeu v Attorney-General of Hong Kong* [1988] AC 175; *Murphy v Brentwood District Council* [1991] 1 AC 398. Cf *Hill v Chief Constable of West Yorkshire* [1989] AC 53; *Brooks v Commissioner of Police* [2005] UKHL 24; *Smith v Chief Constable of Sussex* [2008] UKHL 50; *X (Minors) v Bedfordshire County Council* [1995] 2 AC 633; and *Stovin v Wise, Norfolk County Council (Third Party)* [1996] AC 923, 951 *per* Lord Hoffmann. For the impact of the European Convention on Human Rights, see para 18.46, n 213.

[204] eg *Murphy v Brentwood District Council* [1991] 1 AC 398, 472 *per* Lord Keith; cf 491 *per* Lord Oliver, and *D and F Estates Ltd v Church Commissioners for England* [1989] AC 177, 193 and 210 *per* Lord Bridge.

[205] NHS (General Medical Services Contracts) (Prescription of Drugs etc.) Regulations 2004, SI 2004/629, reg 3, Sch 2, as amended. For an example of a peripheral, causally remote defendant, see *Danns v Department of Health* [1998] PIQR P226 (CA). See further A Grubb, (1998) 6 Med L Rev 371 (Commentary). And see *Smith v Secretary of State for Health*, n 201.

[206] See, eg, *Governors of the Peabody Donation Fund v Sir Lindsay Parkinson & Co Ltd* [1985] AC 210.

[207] *Atkinson v Newcastle and Gateshead Waterworks Company* (1877) 2 Ex D 441 (CA).

[208] See *Swanson v The Queen in right of Canada* (1991) 80 DLR (4th) (Fed CA) 741, 750–52 *per* Linden J (commercial airlines).

[209] *Rowling v Takaro Properties Ltd* [1988] AC 473, 501 (PC) *per* Lord Keith. And see P Craig, *Administrative Law* (6th edn, Sweet & Maxwell 2008) 959–78.

entrusted with the safety and licensing of medicinal products.[210] It has been suggested that 'a duty of care, by this test, would appear to be owed to the class of patients as a whole rather than individually'.[211] Equally, there may be 'cogent reasons of social policy'[212] for maintaining that such a 'statutory purpose' supports the case for granting a remedy to individual citizens.[213]

Assuming the existence of such a remedy, on whom would the duty lie and what standard of care would it entail? Though the LA is formally the ultimate decision-making body under the Medicines Act,[214] delegation of its advisory role to the CHM, as statutorily provided for,[215] should normally afford it protection against liability for negligence. It has also been argued that the former CSM was, by the very nature of its composition, a 'responsible body of medical opinion' against which a finding of negligence was effectively precluded under the *Bolam* test.[216] Though the same argument could now be made as regards the CHM, it is not self-evident that the *Bolam* principle, as pertaining to medicine, extends beyond the spheres of professional clinical practice and advice in the context of such practice. It is of interest that there has not, as yet, been a *successful* civil action for damages against either the UK or European regulatory bodies. **18.48**

5. Shortcomings of negligence as a remedy for injurious medicinal products

The complexities of proving causation and negligent conduct, especially in design defect cases, can be powerful disincentives to pursuing a claim. Various factors, such as the limits of clinical trials in predicting adverse effects over time; unavoidable side effects, and the general medical condition of the injured person, can pose acute evidential difficulties. So, too, can uncertainty over the appropriate defendant(s), such that claimants can 'sink in a sea of allegations and counter-allegations between drug company, doctor and pharmacist'.[217] However, to appreciate more fully why negligence claims in this area have so often been protracted, costly, and unsuccessful, some attention needs to be paid to the influence of the **18.49**

[210] eg 'The principal task of the licensing authority is to protect the public . . . its duty [is] to safeguard the health of the nation . . .': *R v Licensing Authority Established Under Medicines Act 1968, Ex p Smith Kline & French Laboratories* [1990] 1 AC 64, 103 *per* Lord Templeman. Cf Council Directive (EEC) 65/65 as amended: '. . . the primary purpose of any rules concerning the production and distribution of proprietary medicinal products must be to safeguard public health . . .'

[211] A Barton, 'The Basis of Liability of the Licensing Authority and its Advisers under the Medicines Act 1968 to an Individual' in A Goldberg and I Dodds-Smith (eds), *Pharmaceutical Medicine and the Law* (RCP 1991) 99.

[212] *Murphy v Brentwood District Council* [1991] AC 398, 482 *per* Lord Bridge. Cf *Re HIV Haemophiliac Litigation*, n 200. And see Jones, *Medical Negligence*, n 141, 824, para 10-018.

[213] To strike out a negligence claim against a public authority on the ground that it did not owe the claimant a duty of care does not, however, infringe the claimant's right of access to a court under Art 6(1) of the ECHR, provided the striking out was not a procedural bar but resulted from the domestic court applying principles of substantive law: *Z v UK* (2002) 34 EHRR 3 and *TP and KH v UK* (2002) 34 EHRR 2, departing from *Osman v UK* (1998) 29 EHRR 245. See now *JD v East Berkshire Community Health NHS Trust* [2005] 2 AC 373. Though the English courts have been very reluctant to strike out such claims since *Osman*—see *Phelps v Hillingdon London Borough Council* [2000] 3 WLR 776 (HL) and *Barrett v Enfield London Borough Council* [2002] AC 550—they can grant a defendant summary judgment when it is clear from the documentary evidence before them that the claimant has no real prospect of success: *S v Gloucestershire County Council* [2001] 2 WLR 90 (CA).

[214] Medicines Act 1968, s 6.

[215] See para 18.43 and n 168.

[216] *Bolam v Friern HMC* [1957] 1 WLR 582. See Barton, n 26, 101. See also *AB v Tameside and Glossop HA* [1997] 8 Med L R 91, 98–99 *per* Brooke LJ; and M Mildred, 'Responsibilities and Liabilities of Regulatory Agencies' in J O'Grady et al (eds), *Medicines, Medical Devices and the Law* (Greenwich Medical Media 1999) 166–67.

[217] M Brazier and E Cave, *Medicine, Patients and the Law* (6th edn, Manchester University Press 2016) 294.

pharmaceutical industry in health care provision. Clearly, the public benefits from pharmaceutical innovation and, within limits, from the early availability of new drugs. That said, commercial priorities, and the extent of company control over research, production, and marketing, prompt further reservations about negligence as a remedial mechanism in the pharmaceutical sphere, as well as raising broader issues of an ethical nature.

18.50 A number of these issues were examined a few years ago by a House of Commons Health Select Committee. It cited concerns about the design and conduct of some clinical trials, the commercial incentive to reduce target samples and end trials prematurely, inadequate or delayed reporting to the MHRA of unpublished data, and instances of suppressed negative findings.[218] The Committee also criticized the use of various promotional techniques, including ghost-written' reports, conferences with lavish hospitality, where 'key opinion leaders' are paid to speak about products,[219] and 'disease awareness campaigns' that urge people to visit their GPs, synchronized with the promotion to doctors of newly-launched brand-name 'prescription-only' drugs, undermining the ban on direct advertising to the public.[220] Much company-sponsored information appears in key medical journals, for which drug advertisements and reprints of favourable company-funded trials are a significant source of revenue.[221] The potential for unduly optimistic claims of safety and efficacy can, in turn, affect the regulatory process. Despite the recent growth in regulation, the Health Select Committee expressed concern about the level of rigour in the drug approval process and post-marketing surveillance. It questioned whether a system heavily reliant on company-generated information and entirely funded by user fees was appropriate for difficult decisions about the safety of new and licensed drugs.[222]

18.51 These various linkages in the marketing of medicinal products have implications for the effectiveness of negligence-based actions. Whatever the incidence of the activities described, and however responsibility should be allocated in particular cases, when exaggerated assertions of safety culminate in litigation, claimants often find it very difficult and costly to acquire the information needed to prove negligence. The sheer volume of material (including e-data), often spanning many years, can itself entail much wrangling over what are 'necessary' documents for the purpose of discovery, and whether a defendant company has a right or duty to withhold inspection.[223] Consequently, access to unpublished reports of adverse reactions have historically been denied or long delayed. Similarly, although the MHRA, as a public body, is subject to the provisions of the Freedom of Information Act 2000, it

[218] HC Health Select Committee, *The Influence of the Pharmaceutical Industry*, Fourth report of session 2004–05 (Stationery Office 2005); cf J Lexchin et al, 'Pharmaceutical Industry Sponsorship and Research Outcome and Quality: Systematic Review' (2003) 326 British Medical Journal 167, and 'Bias in sponsored research seemed to be endemic': Royal College of Physicians, *Innovating for Health: Patients, Physicians, the Pharmaceutical Industry and the NHS* (Working Party Report) (Royal College of Physicians, 2009) para 1.9. See also L McGoey and E Jackson, 'Seroxat and the Suppression of Clinical Trial Data: Regulatory Failure and the Uses of Legal Ambiguity' (2009) 35 Journal of Medical Ethics 107.

[219] cf '[the] picture of relentless pressure on doctors, exerted by pharmaceutical marketing masquerading as education': Royal College of Physicians, n 218, 3.31. See also R Moynihan, 'Doctors' education: the invisible influence of drug company sponsorship' (2008) 336 British Medical Journal 416.

[220] HC Health Select Committee, n 218, para 211.

[221] R Smith, 'Medical Journals are an extension of the marketing arm of pharmaceutical companies' (2005) 2(5) PLoS Medicine 138. Cf 'Editors of medical journals report examples of manipulation, distortion, bias, secrecy, overt promotion, and ghost writing in publishing medical research': Royal College of Physicians, n 218, para 5.20.

[222] HC Health Select Committee, n 218, paras 276–84, 296–302; Royal College of Physicians, n 218, paras 1.10–1.12, and McGoey and Jackson, n 218, at 110–11. *Contra* A Breckenridge and K Woods, 'Medicines Regulation and the Pharmaceutical Industry' (2005) 331 British Medical Journal 834–36.

[223] Civil Procedure Rules, rr 31 and 31.3(1)(b), respectively.

has resisted production of information on unpublished clinical trial data and clinical trials authorization data, unless it deems their release to be in the public interest. It also has a qualified right not to disclose information where trade secrets or commercial sensitivity are in issue.[224] However, there have been several recent measures in the EU to improve transparency in the regulation of medicinal products by introducing a more democratic approach[225] by supporting public participation, albeit within the constraints of a technocratic model of decision making. Prompted by the increased burden of adverse drug reactions in the EU,[226] changes to pharmacovigilance legislation[227] have come into effect across the EU in 2012, as a consequence of changes set out in an EU Regulation[228] and a Directive.[229] The aim of this legislation is to improve the health of EU citizens by strengthening and rationalizing pharmacovigilance, thereby reducing the burden of ADRs and optimizing the use of medicinal products.[230] While the scope of changes is considerable, and includes the new extension of Risk Management Plans (RMPs) to all new medicinal product applications,[231] the centralization of the recording and reporting of suspected ADRs in the EudraVigilance database,[232] and the creation of a new scientific committee, the Pharmacovigilance Risk Assessment Committee (PRAC),[233] such reforms have been subject to criticism.[234] Moreover, the recent

[224] Freedom of Information Act 2000, Part II. See L-A Mulcahy and P Feldschreiber, in P Feldschreiber (ed), *The Law and Regulation of Medicines* (Oxford University Press 2008) at paras 8.142 and 12.96, respectively. The degree of secrecy surrounding the regulation of medicinal products in the EU (as well as the US) has been criticized as detrimental to both science and democratic accountability: See C Davies and J Abraham, *Unhealthy Pharmaceutical Regulation: Innovation, Politics and Promissory Science* (Palgrave Macmillan 2013) 283.

[225] This may foster what has been described as a 'technological citizenship' by Frankenfield (see P J Frankenfeld, 'Technological Citizenship: A Normative Framework for Risk Studies' (1992) 17 Science, Technology & Human Values 459) where the public feels obligated to be informed about the risks of medicinal products): see further J Abraham and J Sheppard, 'Democracy, Technocracy, and the Secret State of Medicines Control: Expert and Nonexpert Perspectives' (1997) 22 Science, Technology, & Human Values 139, 143.

[226] The public health burden of adverse drug reactions (ADRs) amounts to the death in hospital of 100,800–197,000 annually in the EU. A reasonable estimate of the total societal cost of ADRs in the EU is €79 billion: Commission Staff Working Document, Accompanying document to the Proposal for a Regulation of the European Parliament and of the Council amending, as regards pharmacovigilance of medicinal products for human use, Regulation (EC) No 726/2004 laying down Community procedures for the authorisation and supervision of medicinal products for human and veterinary use and establishing a European Medicines Agency, and the Proposal for a Directive of the European Parliament and of the Council amending, as regards pharmacovigilance, Directive 2001/83/EC on the Community code relating to medicinal products for human use, IMPACT ASSESSMENT, Brussels, 10 December 2008SEC (2008) 2670, vol I, 12.

[227] See generally: <www.mhra.gov.uk/Howweregulate/Medicines/Pharmacovigilancelegislation/index.htm>. The legislation has been transposed into UK law in the Human Medicines Regulations 2012, SI 2012/1916, Part II.

[228] Regulation (EU) No 1235/2010 of the European Parliament and of the Council of 15 December 2010 amending, as regards pharmacovigilance of medicinal products for human use, Regulation (EC) No 726/2004 laying down Community procedures for the authorisation and supervision of medicinal products for human and veterinary use and establishing a European Medicines Agency, and Regulation (EC) No 1394/2007 on advanced therapy medicinal products [2010] OJ L348/1.

[229] Directive 2010/184/EU of the European Parliament and of the Council of 15 December 2010 amending, as regards pharmacovigilance, Directive 2001/83/EC on the Community code relating to medicinal products for human use [2010] OJ L348/74.

[230] IMPACT ASSESSMENT, Brussels, 10 December 2008 SEC(2008) 2670, vol I, 20.

[231] Directive 2001/83, Art 104(3)(d), 104a(2).

[232] Ibid, Art 107. It will be a legal obligation for all reports of suspected adverse reactions to come centrally to the EudraVigilance database only: ibid.

[233] Regulation (EC) No 726/2004, Art 56(1)(aa).

[234] B Goldacre, *Bad Pharma* (Fourth Estate 2012) 161 (describing the legislation as 'a very mixed bag'); S Garattini and V Bertele, 'Anything new in EU pharmacovigilance?' (2011) 67 European Journal of Clinical Pharmacology 1199–1200; A Herxheimer, 'Looking at EU Pharmacovigilance' (2011) 67

Avandia scandal suggests that pharmaceutical companies continue to be undeterred from unlawful behaviour.[235] The most significant measure to introduce transparency has been an adoption of a new clinical trials regulation, which introduces strict transparency requirements for data access and reporting of clinical trials by ensuring that all trials are registered, and information on clinical trials is publically available on an EU database, though this is again qualified by the need to protect commercially confidential information.[236]

D. Liability under the Consumer Protection Act 1987

1. The European Directive on Product Liability

18.52 The lengthy process of reassessing products liability law which began in the 1970s culminated in the European Directive on Product Liability of 1985,[237] on which Pt I of the Consumer Protection Act 1987 is substantially based.[238] The preamble to the Directive expressed concern that divergences between the laws of Member States could distort competition and result in differential protection of consumers. It also asserted that the imposition of liability without fault on producers was the fairest method of apportioning risk.[239] Accordingly, with a view to harmonizing national laws, the Directive required all members of the European Community to introduce a strict liability regime for defective products.

18.53 Though Pt I of the CPA implements the EC Directive, there are some significant differences of wording, most notably on the 'development risk defence.[240] English law subscribes to

European Journal of Clinical Pharmacology 1201–02; S Frau, M Font Pous, and M R Luppino, 'Risk Management Plans: are they a tool for improving drug safety?'(2010) 66 European Journal of Clinical Pharmacology 785–90; and, further, R Goldberg, *Medicinal Product Liability and Regulation* (Hart Publishing 2013) 164–65.

[235] K Thomas and M S Schmidt, 'Glaxo Agrees to Pay $3 Billion in Fraud Settlement', *The New York Times* (2 July 2012) (detailing GlaxoSmithKline's agreement to plead guilty to criminal charges and pay US$3 billion in fines for promoting two anti-depressant drugs (Paxil and Wellbutrin) for unapproved uses, and failing to report safety data about Avandia).

[236] Regulation (EU) No 536/2014 of the European Parliament and of the Council of 16 April 2014 on clinical trials on medicinal products for human use, and repealing Directive 2001/20/EC, [2014] OJ L 158/1, especially Art 81 (2)(EU database to enable cooperation between competent authorities and to search for clinical trials and to enable citizens of the EU to have access to clinical information about medicinal products) and Art 81 (4) (EU database to be publicly accessible unless confidentiality justified on the grounds of, inter alia, 'protecting commercially confidential information, in particular through taking into account the status of the marketing authorisation for the medicinal product, unless there is an overriding public interest in disclosure'. The EMA's Management Board plan to have the database available for independent audit by August 2017 (see ibid, Arts 82, 89), and if the systems pass the audit, the Regulation will come into force by October 2018: See 'Delivery time frame for the EU portal and EU database' (endorsed by EMA's Management Board), (European Medicines Agency, 17 December 2015) EMA/760345/2015. For further discussion of justification for data transparency, its evolution in the EU and Canada's hitherto reluctance to move toward full transparency of data, see T Lemmens and S Gibson, 'Decreasing the Data Deficit: Improving Post-Market Surveillance in Pharmaceutical Regulation' (2014) 59 McGill LJ 943, 973–85.

[237] (EEC) 85/374. See generally Goyens (ed), *Directive 85/374/EEC on product liability: ten years after* (n 27).

[238] See Stapleton, *Product Liability*, n 9, ch 3; C Miller and R Goldberg, *Product Liability* (2nd edn, Oxford University Press 2004) ch 7. The Act's provisions extend to the whole of the UK. See Consumer Protection (Northern Ireland) Order 1987, SI 1987/2409. No liability arises under the Act in respect of goods put into circulation by the producer prior to 1 March 1988: CPA, s 50(7); SI 1987/1680.

[239] '... liability without fault on the part of the producer is the sole means of adequately solving the problem peculiar to our age of increasing technicality, of a fair apportionment of the risks inherent in modern technological production ...'

[240] See paras 18.68–18.71. The term 'development risk' is normally used to refer to undiscoverable defects which come to light only after a product has been in use. It may be distinguished from 'state of

the doctrine of 'indirect effect', whereby any ambiguity in the domestic legislation which implements directives is, as far as possible, construed so as to conform with Community law obligations.[241] In fact, the CPA itself states that Pt I of the Act 'shall have effect for the purpose of making such provision as is necessary in order to comply with the product liability Directive and shall be construed accordingly'.[242] This novel form of stipulation seemingly invites English courts to apply the Directive whenever the terms of the CPA appear to be incompatible with it. At the same time, assistance in construing ambiguous or obscure statutory wording may now be derived from clear Parliamentary statements of a Minister or other promoter of a Bill.[243] On the 'development risk' defence, in particular, several such statements suggest that the UK Government intended the Act to have a different meaning from that generally attributed to the Directive. The European Commission brought an action against the UK, under Article 169 of the EC Treaty, seeking a declaration of non-compliance. However, the European Court of Justice ruled that the UK formulation of the defence did not clearly conflict with the Directive.[244]

The European Court of Justice has held that non-discretionary provisions in a Directive which are unconditional and sufficiently precise may be relied on directly by an individual against the state, if the state has failed to implement the directive correctly.[245] In addition, in certain circumstances, the state might be liable in damages.[246] In practice, the potential application of the doctrine of direct effect to products liability is severely limited. It could not apply to the 'development risk' defence, as the Directive permits derogation from it.[247] **18.54**

the art', an expression which commonly signifies the most up-to-date technology and standards in a given industry. In both the Directive and the CPA, the defence actually refers to discoverability of the defect, not of a risk: Art 7(e) and s 4(1)(e), respectively.

241 Case 14/83 *Von Colson and Kamann v Land Nordrhein-Westfalen* [1984] ECR 1891, para 26; *Garland v British Railway Engineering Ltd* [1983] 2 AC 751, 771 *per* Lord Diplock; *Pickstone v Freeman plc* [1989] AC 66; *Litster v Forth Dry Dock & Engineering Co Ltd* [1990] 1 AC 456. And see J Steiner, 'Coming to Terms with EEC Directives' (1990) 106 LQR 144. See also Case C-106/89 *Marleasing SA v La Comercial Internacional de Alimentation SA* [1990] ECR 1-4135, para 8. In several decisions the ECJ has held that Member States may not have rules more protective of consumers than is permitted by the Directive: see Case C-52/00 *Commission v France* [2002] ECR 1-3827, paras 17–20; Case C-154/00 *Commission v Greece* [2002] ECR 1-3879, paras 13–16; Case C-183/00 *Gonzalez Sanchez v Medicina Asturiana SA* [2002] ECR 1-3901, paras 26–29; Case C-402/03 *Skov AEG v Bilka Lavprisvarehus A/S* [2006] ECR 1-199, paras 42 and 44; Case C-495/10, *Centre hospitalier universitaire de Besançon v Dutreux* [2012] 2 CMLR 1, [20]; and Case C-310/13, *Novo Nordisk Pharma GmbH v S* ECLI:EU:C:2014: 2385, [23] (CJEU). However, the wording of the CPA prevails if it is irreconcilable with that of the Directive: see A Arnull et al, *Wyatt and Dashwood's European Union Law* (5th edn, Sweet & Maxwell 2006), para 5-029. It should be noted that while the Directive is a maximal harmonization measure, it does not seek to harmonize the sphere of liability for defective products beyond the matters regulated by it. Accordingly this does not preclude the existence of parallel liability regimes in respect of damage which is not covered by the Directive: Case C-285/08, *Moteurs Leroy Somer v Dalkia France and Ace Europe* [2009] ECR I-4733, [24]–[25] [30]–[32]; Case C-495/10, *Centre hospitalier universitaire de Besançon v Dutreux* [2012] 2 CMLR 1, [21], [32], [39]. Case C-310/13; *Novo Nordisk Pharma GmbH v S* ECLI:EU:C:2014: 2385, [24], [29] (CJEU) (amended German national legislation of liability for pharmaceutical products Arzneimittelgesetz (AMG) under which the consumer had the right to require the manufacturer to provide information on the adverse effects of a medicinal product fell outside the scope of the Directive).

242 CPA, s 1(1). See also Case C-300/95 *Commission v United Kingdom* [1997] ECR I-2649. And see *A v National Blood Authority* [2001] 3 All ER 289, [2]. cf '[t]he judge in effect by-passed the wording of the Act and addressed himself to the Directive itself': G Howells and M Mildred, 'Infected Blood: Defect and Discoverability—A First Exposition of the EC Product Liability Directive' (2002) 65 MLR 95, 96.

243 *Pepper (Inspector of Taxes) v Hart* [1993] AC 593.

244 Case C-300/95 *European Commission v UK* [1997] All ER (EC) 481. See further paras 18.68–18.71.

245 Case 103/88 *Fratelli Costanzo SpA v Comune di Milano* [1989] ECR 1839, [29]; Case 8/81 *Becker v Finanzamt Munster-Innenstadt* [1982] ECR 53. And see European Communities Act 1972, ss 2(1), (4).

246 Cases C-6, C-9/90 *Francovich v Italy* [1991] ECR I-5357, [1993] 2 CMLR 66.

247 European Directive on Product Liability, Art 15(1)(b). And see para 18.68.

More generally, directives have direct effect only in so far as a state body is the defendant.[248] However, the doctrine could in principle apply to a health authority,[249] in the capacity, for example, of producer or supplier of pharmaceuticals, aids, appliances, and blood products, or where equipment or products have been substantially modified by health authority employees.

2. The Act

(i) The 'strict liability' regime under the CPA

18.55 A general principle of strict civil liability is contained in s 2(1) of the Act: 'Where any damage is caused wholly or partly by a defect in a product, every person to whom [s 2(2)] applies shall be liable for the damage.' This wording points to the Act's stated focus on the condition of the product rather than on the conduct or state of mind of its producer. Once the claimant has proved that there is a 'defect' in the product and that the relevant damage was wholly or partly caused by it, the onus shifts to the defendant(s), for whom several specific defences are available under the Act.[250] Liability under Pt I of the Act may not be limited or excluded by any contract term, notice, or other provision.[251]

(ii) Causation

18.56 Many of the more intractable problems associated with proving causation in drug-related claims based on negligence[252] remain under the Act. Moreover, its silence on causation and remoteness leaves a number of issues unresolved. For example, though, unlike negligence, the Act does not confine recovery to damage of a foreseeable kind,[253] the courts might still be disposed to treat 'cause' as importing foreseeability of consequences.[254] Medicinal products which cause injury through unforeseeable misuse would presumably not be deemed 'defective'. It should be noted that whereas, in negligence, intermediate examination is seen as breaking the chain of causation as regards defects existing when the manufacturer put a product into circulation, under the Act the manufacturer would be jointly and severally liable with any culpable intermediary.[255] Where damage is caused partly by a defect in the product and partly through the claimant's fault, contributory negligence may be invoked as a partial defence.[256] Any consequent reduction in the claimant's damages might be less than in negligence, given that, under the Act, the defendant's liability is not contingent on negligence.

---

[248] Case 152/84 *Marshall v Southampton and South-West Hampshire AHA* [1986] ECR 723.

[249] ibid.

[250] CPA, s 4. See paras 18.62–18.71.

[251] CPA, s 7.

[252] See paras 18.04 and 18.41, and further, R Goldberg, *Causation and Risk in the Law of Torts: Scientific Evidence and Medicinal Product Liability* (Hart Publishing 1999); R Goldberg, 'Epidemiological Uncertainty, Causation, and Drug Product Liability' (2014) McGill LJ 777; R Goldberg, *Medicinal Product Liability and Regulation* (Hart Publishing 2013) ch 5, 6. See *Richardson v LRC Products Ltd* [2000] Lloyd's Med Rep 280 (no recovery against a manufacturer under the CPA for the consequences of pregnancy following the failure of a condom, in part because the claimant could reasonably have obtained the 'morning after pill' and thereby avoided the pregnancy). See also *XYZ v Schering Health Care Ltd* [2002] EWHC 1420 (QB).

[253] *Overseas Tankship (UK) Ltd v Morts Dock & Engineering Co Ltd, The Wagon Mound (No 1)* [1961] AC 388.

[254] See S Whittaker, 'The EEC Directive on Product Liability' (1985) 5 Yearbook of European Law 233, 253–54.

[255] CPA s 2(5); and see n 266 below.

[256] Law Reform (Contributory Negligence) Act 1945, s 6(4).

(iii) Who may sue?

The Act confers a right of action on any person[257] who suffers damage from a defective product. 'Damage' is defined so as to cover death, personal injury, and loss of or damage to property.[258] The description of 'personal injury', as including 'any disease and any other impairment of a person's physical or mental condition',[259] is broad enough to cover claims for psychiatric damage.[260] No remedy is provided for loss of or damage to the product itself,[261] or for pure economic loss. **18.57**

(iv) Who may be strictly liable?

Primary liability is imposed on the 'producer',[262] 'own brander',[263] and any person who has imported a product into the EC in order to supply it to another in the course of a business.[264] In addition, any persons in the chain of supply can be held strictly liable if they have failed, on request, to identify within a reasonable time either the 'producer' or their own supplier, where identification is not reasonably practicable for the person who has suffered the damage.[265] Typically, it is the manufacturer of the finished product who would incur liability, as 'producer'; but the manufacturer of a defective component part (or the producer of some raw materials) responsible for the damage caused by the finished product is also liable as a 'producer',[266] as is a person who has 'abstracted' a 'substance which has not been manufactured'.[267] So, too, is the processor where the 'essential characteristics' of a product are attributable to an industrial or other process.[268] Depending on the circumstances, assembling products might fall within the definition, though not basic packaging. **18.58**

257 Including persons who have suffered ante-natal injury: CPA, s 6(3).

258 CPA, s 5(1). Actionable damage to property is limited to property of a kind ordinarily intended for private use, occupation, or consumption and mainly so intended by the plaintiff, where the amount to be awarded exceeds £275: s 5(3)(4). For a discussion of 'damage' under Art 9 of Council Directive (EEC) 85/374, see Case C-203/99 *Henning Veedfald v Arhus Amtskommune* [2001] ECR I-3569 (kidney intended for transplantation into claimant damaged and rendered unusable by defective flushing agent produced by hospital within Danish health service); and Cases C-503/13 and C-504/13, *Boston Scientific Medizintechnik GmbH v AOK Sachsen-Anhalt-Die Gesundheitskasse and Others* ECLI:EU: C: 2015:148, [55] (CJEU), (5 March 2015) (cost of an operation to remove and replace a defective medical device, such as a pacemaker or an implantable cardioverter defibrillator, constitutes damage caused by death or personal injuries, providing such an operation is necessary to overcome the defect in the product in question).

259 CPA, s 45(1).

260 *Alcock v Chief Constable of the South Yorkshire Police* [1992] 1 AC 310; *Page v Smith* [1996] AC 155; *White v Chief Constable of South Yorkshire Police* [1999] 2 AC 455. It is arguable that the special 'proximity' restrictions on recovery in negligence for psychiatric harm do not apply under the CPA, and that 'any other impairment of a person's . . . mental condition' could extend the scope for liability beyond the prevailing threshold of a 'recognisable psychiatric illness'.

261 See CPA, 5(2). But see *Hems v Poly Implants Prosthesis* [2007] CLY 1063, Nottingham Co Ct (cost recoverable of both the operation to replace defective silicone breast implants and of the replacements) and Cases C-503/13 and C-504/13, *Boston Scientific Medizintechnik GmbH v AOK Sachsen-Anhalt-Die Gesundheitskasse and Others* ECLI:EU: C: 2015:148, [55] (CJEU), (5 March 2015).

262 CPA, s 1(2).

263 ibid, s 2(2)(b).

264 ibid, s 2(2)(c).

265 ibid, s 2(3); see further Case C-358/08, *Aventis Pasteur SA v OB* [2010] All ER (EC) 522 (ECJ), [58] (supplier to be treated as a producer if it did not inform the injured person 'on its own initiative and promptly of the identity of the producer or its own supplier').

266 CPA, s 1(2). Where two or more persons are liable for the same damage their liability is joint and several: s 2(5), subject to any rights of contribution or indemnity. See s 2(6) and the Civil Liability (Contribution) Act 1978.

267 CPA, s 1(2)(b).

268 ibid, s 1(2)(c).

18.59 It is apparent that the application of the Act to the production and supply of medicinal products is, in principle, far-ranging. In addition to pharmaceutical companies, hospital pharmacies and individual pharmacists manufacturing their own finished products, it would seem that doctors and dentists who mix drugs for a prescription or an injection, or who modify a piece of equipment, could be deemed producers. The European Court of Justice has indicated that there can be more than one 'producer' where a number of entities have been engaged in 'different production activities'.[269] This conclusion sits awkwardly with Article 3(1) of the Directive, where 'producer' is centrally defined as the 'manufacturer of a finished product'. Read literally, this provision would make the last entity involved, even if engaged in a relatively minor process, the sole producer, unless the separate requirements for being a 'producer' qua 'own-brander' or importer were present.[270] In the case of pharmacists, it might not always be clear whether 'packaging' (including inserts of product information) was a routine part of the distribution process or the last stage in producing the finished dosage.[271] The nature of packaging is also relevant to whether pharmacists might be deemed 'own-branders', since the containers of all medicines prepared or dispensed must be labelled with the name and address of the supplying chemist.[272] Despite a Department of Health assurance that dispensing from bulk with such labelling would not be equated with holding out as a producer, the position is not entirely clear. Pharmacists, doctors, or dentists dispensing drugs, and other health care personnel supplying medical equipment, could alternatively be held liable under the Act as suppliers if unable to identify the 'producer' or their own supplier.[273] All suppliers are now well advised to keep adequate records of their source of supply, and producers are similarly advised to label otherwise 'anonymous' products. Identification of source can pose acute problems in the distribution of pharmaceuticals, especially as, increasingly, generic drugs and blood products supplied in bulk originate from a variety of companies, and over 60 per cent of prescription items are dispensed generically.[274]

(v) The meaning of 'product'

18.60 'Product' is broadly defined under the Act, as 'any goods or electricity', including 'a product which is comprised in another product'.[275] Moreover 'goods' include 'substances', defined as

[269] Case C-127/04 *O'Byrne v Sanofi Pasteur MSD Ltd (formerly Aventis Pasteur MSD Ltd)* [2006] ECR I-1313, 1 WLR 1606, paras 29–30.

[270] C Hodges, (2006) 122 LQR 393, 395–96.

[271] See M Powers, N Harris, and A Barton, *Clinical Negligence* (n 126) ch 24, para 24.49. In *O'Byrne*, n 269, the ECJ held that a product has been 'put into circulation . . . when it leaves the production process operated by the producer and enters a marketing process *in the form in which it is offered to the public* in order to be used or consumed': para 27 (emphasis added). In a further reference to the ECJ, it was held that a parent company 'producer' could be substituted for its mistakenly sued wholly-owned subsidiary only if the putting into circulation of the product was 'determined' by the producer. Whether it was so determined would be for the national court to assess: Case C-358/08, *Aventis Pasteur SA v OB* [2010] All ER (EC) 522 (ECJ), [52]–[53], [65].

[272] In particular, where there is no clear indication that a product was manufactured by others, it might be more difficult for any supermarkets and retail chemist chains whose 'get-up' is designed to promote brand identity to rebut the inference of holding out. See Powers et al, n 271, para 24.53. For labelling requirements generally, see Medicines (Labelling) Regulations 1976 SI 1976/1726, as amended; and Human Medicines Regulations 2012, SI 2012/1916, regs 257–71. And see Chapter 17, paras 17.77–17.81.

[273] 'Supplying goods' is, inter alia, defined as providing them 'in or in connection with the performance of any statutory function': CPA, s 46(1)(e). In the case of NHS employees, the effective 'producer' or 'supplier' will be the health authority. Pt I of the CPA binds the Crown: s 9. The activities of a 'public authority' are included within the definition of 'business' for the purpose of producer or supplier liability: CPA, s 45(1).

[274] 76.5 per cent in 2014: Health and Social Care Information Centre, *Prescriptions Dispensed in the Community Statistics for 2004–2014: England* (Health and Social Care Information Centre 2015) paras 252, 259.

[275] CPA, s 1(2). Primary agricultural produce, originally excluded under the Act (s 2(4)), was subsequently made subject to the strict liability regime: Dir 1999/34/EC (OJ L141/20); Consumer Protection Act 1987 (Product Liability) (Modification) Order 2000, SI 2000/2771.

'any natural or artificial substance',[276] which, together with the still broader definition in the Directive—'electricity' and 'all movables'[277]—might be invoked in respect of problematic substances.[278] Now that it has been conceded that blood and blood products are covered by both the Act and the Directive,[279] it seems probable that the same would hold for human tissue and organs.[280] The inclusion of the term 'substances' strengthens the case for regarding them as 'products' within the Act, more especially when they have been abstracted,[281] for example by a surgeon. Equally, the processor of such products might be deemed a producer.[282] But, depending on the facts, any of these transactions might be more appropriately characterized as a provision of services. Initially, the (former) Department of Trade and Industry (DTI) maintained that 'medicinal materials used in trials before marketing' would 'generally be exempt', not having been put into circulation in the normal course of business.[283] In fact, use for research purposes would seem to fall within the statutory definition of 'supply',[284] though, in any event, a product which is still being researched would rarely be deemed 'defective'.[285]

(vi) The meaning of 'defect'

Proof by the claimant that a product has a 'defect'[286] is essential to liability under the Act. **18.61**
Under s 3(1), a product is deemed defective if 'its safety is not such as persons generally are entitled to expect . . .', a purportedly objective, if elusive, test, which has been construed as the 'expectations of the public at large, as determined by the Court'.[287] In determining the issue, 'all the circumstances shall be taken into account . . .'[288] These include 'the manner

[276] CPA, s 45(1).

[277] European Directive on Product Liability, Art 2. 'Movables' have elsewhere been defined by the ECJ as anything capable of money valuation and of being an object of commercial transactions: Case 7/68 *European Commission v Italy* [1968] ECR 423.

[278] ie under CPA, s 1(1). See para 18.52.

[279] *A v National Blood Authority*, n 242.

[280] See paras 18.20 and 18.21. See further Grubb and Pearl, n 85, ch 5; A Grubb, (1993) 1 Med L Rev 259; and K Stern, 'Strict Liability and the Supply of Donated Gametes' (1994) 2 Med L Rev 261. See also *Henning Veedfald v Arhus Amtskommune*, n 258; and the decision under New York product liability holding that sperm is a product: *Donovan v Idant Laboratories* 625 F.Supp.2d 256, 273 (E.D.Pa 2009).

[281] CPA, s 1(2)(b). See also Pearson Commission, n 2, (Cmnd 7054, 1978), vol 1, para 1276.

[282] CPA, s 1(2)(c).

[283] Department of Trade and Industry, *Implementation of EC Directive on Product Liability—An Explanatory and Consultative Note* (DTI 1985) 14, para 56(a). This statement does not appear in a subsequent DTI Guide: *Guide to the Consumer Protection Act 1987* (2001) (<http://webarchive.nationalarchives.gov.uk/20090609003228/>).

[284] CPA, s 46(1). See J McHale and M Fox, *Health Care Law* (2nd edn, Sweet & Maxwell 2007) 719. And see para 18.64.

[285] See CPA, ss 3(1), (2), and para 18.61 below. See also CPA, s 4(1)(e) ('development risk' defence), paras 18.68–18.71, and para 18.81 (research subjects).

[286] See generally R Goldberg, *Medicinal Product Liability and Regulation* (Hart Publishing 2013) ch 2.

[287] *Iman Abouzaid v Mothercare (UK) Ltd* The Times, 20 February 2001 (CA) [25] *per* Pill LJ. See also the European Directive, Art 6 and Recital 6, and *A v National Blood Authority*, n 242, [31]. And see *Scholten v Foundation Sanquin of Blood Supply* H/98.0896 (3 Feb 1999, County Court of Amsterdam). Contrast *Tesco Stores Ltd v Pollard* [2006] EWCA Civ 393, where the Court of Appeal arguably adopted too narrow a view of what persons generally were entitled to expect. See M Mildred, 'Pitfalls in Product Liability' (2007) JPIL 141, 146. But see, now, Wilkes v DePuy International Limited [2016] EWHC 3096 (QB), below, where Higginbottom J emphasised that the reference to what persons were entitled to expect was 'to an entitlement as a matter of law, not actual individual or even general expectation': ibid, [69].

[288] CPA, s 3(2). cf Directive, Art 6(1).

in which, and purposes for which, the product has been marketed, its get-up . . .' and any instructions or warnings concerning its use;[289] 'what might reasonably be expected to be done with or in relation to the product',[290] and 'the time when the product was supplied by its producer to another . . .'[291] The choice of the date of supply as a factor in the evaluation of defectiveness means that, under the Act, no less than in negligence, the claimant has the burden of establishing what safety standards were acceptable at some time in the past, perhaps many years previously in the case of drugs. The Act does not 'require' an inference of defectiveness to be drawn from the fact 'alone' that a product marketed at a later date is more safe,[292] though, where appropriate, liability could be imposed on the producer of the original product for its continued supply.

(vii) The 'legitimate expectation' test

18.62 As the 'learned intermediary' principle implies, with many medicinal products there is a certain artificiality in trying to determine what 'persons generally are entitled to expect'.[293] Section 3(2)'s formulation—that 'all the circumstances shall be taken into account', including how and why a product has been marketed and the nature of any instructions or warnings—had a familiar ring. It seemed to indicate that determinations on defectiveness of design and adequacy of warning would continue to revolve around issues of relative safety, reasonable care and foreseeability, thereby perpetuating the kind of balancing act characteristic of negligence and of American 'strict' products liability regimes alike.[294] However, the judgment of Burton J in *A v National Blood Authority* seemed to mark a distinct shift towards the enhanced consumer protection to which the Directive aspires.[295] Virtually confining himself to the wording of the Directive, he held that blood and blood products infected with Hepatitis C were defective within Article 6 because the public at large was entitled to expect that transfusions would be free of such infection.[296] The test, being the public's 'legitimate', not 'actual', expectation, public awareness of the remote but inevitable risk of a 'non-standard' or 'rogue' product did not preclude liability.[297] Nor did it matter that doctors giving transfusions were aware at the time of a 1 per cent to 3 per cent risk of Hepatitis C in the UK, since this risk had not been communicated to the public. In effect, the 'learned intermediary' rule was deemed inapplicable under the statutory regime.[298] Furthermore, 'taking all circumstances into account' meant all 'relevant' circumstances. These did not

[289] CPA, s 3(2)(a). See, eg, *Worsley v Tambrands Ltd* [2000] PIQR P95; *Wilkes v DePuy International Limited* [2016] EWHC 3096 (QB), [103]. For a detailed analysis of warning and instruction defects and medicinal products, see R Goldberg, *Medicinal Product Liability and Regulation* (Hart Publishing 2013) ch 4.

[290] CPA, s 3(2)(b). This subsection would permit liability for foreseeable misuse.

[291] ibid, s 3(2)(c).

[292] ibid, s 3(2).

[293] See generally R Goldberg, *Medicinal Product Liability and Regulation* (Hart Publishing 2013) ch 2.

[294] cf '. . . even where strict liability is ostensibly the chosen regime, doctrine is likely to reflect the long and enduring reach of negligence principles': Rogerson and Trebilcock, 'Products Liability and the Allergic Consumer: A Study in the Problems of Framing an Efficient Liability Regime', n 140, 52. Cf Whittaker, 'The EEC Directive on Product Liability', n 254, 233; J Stapleton, 'Products Liability Reform—Real or Illusory?' (1986) 6 OJLS 392; Newdick, 'The Future of Negligence in Product Liability', n 123; A Stoppa, 'The Concept of Defectiveness in the Consumer Protection Act 1987: a Critical Analysis' (1992) 12 LS 210; Atiyah, *The Sale of Goods*, n 45, 278–80. See also the special liability rules for prescription drugs and medical devices now established in *Restatement, Third, Torts: Products Liability* § 6.

[295] See n 21. But see further paras 18.77–18.78.

[296] See *A v National Blood Authority*, n 242, [31]. And see n 242 above. See also *Richardson v LRC Products Ltd*, n 252, where the analysis of 'defect' seems to reflect a negligence rather than strict liability approach.

[297] *A v National Blood Authority*, n 242, [31 vi]. Burton J considered the terms 'standard' and 'non-standard' products more appropriate for construing the Directive than the categories of design and manufacturing defects as developed in US case law: ibid, [36] and [39]. See also nn 294 and 29 above.

[298] See the criticism by C Hodges, 'Compensating Patients' (2001) 117 LQR 528; and cf. now *Wilkes v DePuy International Limited* [2016] EWHC 3096, [106] (QB), per Higginbottom J (learned intermediary rule applicable under CPA).

include unavoidability, for example the unavailability of a test to detect the presence of the virus; or impracticability, in terms of the cost or difficulty of preventing the defect, or the social benefits of the product.[299] The shift towards enhanced consumer protection through the legitimate expectations test in A v National Blood Authority was emphatically rejected by the recent decision of Higginbottom J in Wilkes v DePuy International Limited [2016] EWHC 3096 (QB). In Wilkes, which concerned a metal component of an artificial hip, a steel femoral shaft called a 'C-Stem', the claimant contended that the steel shaft was defective. In rejecting the claim, Higginbottom radically departed from the approach of Burton J in A, holding that a test of what persons were 'entitled to expect' required no gloss on the Act and did not benefit from being redescribed as a 'legitimate expectation' test.[300] The test for safety required an objective approach, taking into account the information and circumstances before it, whether or not an actual or notional patient or indeed other members of the public would have considered each of those factors and all of that information.[301] The approach of Burton J to a claimant's task in proving damage, defect, and the causal relationship between the defect and the damage in terms of Article 4 of the Directive by identifying the 'harmful characteristic which caused the injury' and the determination of whether the product was 'standard' or 'non-standard' was deemed incorrect, as it concentrated on causation before investigating defectiveness.[302] In respect of the circumstances to be taken into account in determining whether the safety of a product was at an appropriate level, and the weight to be given to each, Higginbottom J held that a 'holistic' and 'flexible' approach should be adopted, involving the balancing of all relevant considerations.[303] While over time cases could indicate which characteristics may be relevant in particular circumstances, such as whether the product is a prescription-only medicine, any attempt at formal rigid categorization of such products was contrary to the 'inherent flexibility' of the Directive and was likely to be both difficult and unwise.[304] However, in what appears to be a major development in the determination of defectiveness, the Wilkes decision establishes that risk-benefit may lie at the heart of the question of what is the appropriate level of safety for a medicinal product for the purposes of the CPA.[305] This risk-benefit balance together with 'the ease and extent to which a risk can be eliminated or mitigated' (avoidability) were potential circumstances in the assessment of a product's safety.[306] However, asking whether the product was 'standard'or 'non-standard' in accordance with the dichotomy adumbrated by Burton J in A v National Blood Authority was rejected as 'unnecessary and undesirable'.[307] Higginbottom also radically departed from A in concluding that the presence of a learned intermediary was a relevant circumstance for the purposes of determining defectiveness.[308]

---

[299] See *A v National Blood Authority*, n 242, [57], [58], [63], and [68]. For a critique which advocates combining consumer expectation with risk-utility analysis, see R Goldberg, 'Paying for Bad Blood: Strict Product Liability after the Hepatitis C Litigation' (2002) 10 Med L Rev 165. In the context of design defects, the German Supreme Court held in 2009 that a cost–benefit analysis may be appropriate to determine whether a product is defective in design. It stated that the court should have regard inter alia to 'the costs of production, the marketability of the alternative design as well as a cost–benefit balance' and in this respect expressly referred to 'the risk utility test under US law': BGH, 16 June 2009, VI ZR 107/08, 18. While the design defect in question was not in the context of medicinal products. the case indicates that the notion of risk–benefit is relevant to liability for design defects. See, further, R Goldberg, Medicinal Product Liability and Regulation (Hart Publishing 2013) ch 2, 3.

[300] ibid, [71].

[301] ibid, [72].

[302] ibid, [59], following C Miller and R Goldberg(n238) at 10.92.

[303] ibid, [78].

[304] ibid, [79].

[305] ibid, [65].

[306] ibid, [82], [89].

[307] ibid, [94].

[308] ibid, [108]

18.63 That product liability in respect of medicinal products and medical devices may be becoming technologically specific in the context of determining defects is suggested by the first ever guidance as to the circumstances in which a product may be deemed defective in two joined cases before the CJEU:[309] *Boston Scientific Medizintechnik GmbH v AOK Sachsen-Anhalt-Die Gesundheitskasse and Others*. The issue that was addressed by the Court was whether a product was defective if it belonged to or formed part of a product group which had a significant increased risk of failure, but where the defect had not been detected in the specific product in question. The two related cases concerned two types of implanted medical devices—a pacemaker and an implantable cardioverter defibrillator (ICD)—which were both manufactured by Boston Scientific. In each case, the manufacturer identified a risk of failure[310] and treating physicians were written to in the form of a safety notification. Consequent upon these notifications, the devices were explanted and replaced. The patients' health insurers sought damages for the costs relating to the replacement of the devices.[311] In both cases, it had not been determined whether the devices themselves had malfunctioned.[312] In construing Art 6 of the Directive, the Court of Justice of the European Union held that in determining whether a product was defective in accordance with the consumer expectations test, regard had to be made to the reasonable expectations of the public at large.[313] This would appear, at first blush, to be consistent with the legitimate expectations test laid down by Burton J in *A v National Blood Authority*.[314] However, the Court then notably shifted its emphasis from the expectations of the public at large to taking into consideration, inter alia, 'the specific requirements of the group of users for whom the product was intended'; that is, patients.[315] In addition, account was to be taken of 'the intended purpose, the objective characteristics and properties of the product in question'.[316] The Court found that in the light of their function, and of the particularly vulnerable situation of patients using such medical devices, patients were entitled to expect particularly high safety requirements.[317] The Court held that where it is found that products belonging to the same group or same production series have a potential defect, it is possible to classify as defective all products in that group or series, without there being any requirement to show that the product is defective in each individual case.[318] While emphasis was placed on the specific risks associated with the medical devices in issue, in reaching its conclusion the Court couched its reasoning in broader language which would appear to apply more generally, and at the very least to health care products, including medicinal products. Adopting the analysis of Advocate General Bot,[319] the Court stated that the potential lack of safety which could give rise to liability under the Directive stemmed, 'for products

[309] Cases C-503/13 and C-504/13, *Boston Scientific Medizintechnik GmbH v AOK Sachsen-Anhalt-Die Gesundheitskasse and Others* ECLI:EU:C:2015:148 (CJEU), (5 March 2015).

[310] The pacemakers implanted belonged to a product group which had a risk of failure 17 to 20 times greater than was normal for this kind of device: Cases C-503/13 and C-504/13, *Boston Scientific Medizintechnik GmbH v AOK Sachsen-Anhalt-Die Gesundheitskasse and Others* ECLI:EU:C:2014:2306, [24], (Opinion of AG Bot).

[311] Cases C-503/13 and C-504/13, *Boston Scientific Medizintechnik GmbH v AOK Sachsen-Anhalt-Die Gesundheitskasse and Others* ECLI:EU:C:2015:148, [14], [17], [19].

[312] ibid, [25].

[313] ibid, [37].

[314] *A v National Blood Authority* [2001] 3 All ER 289, [31]. See R Goldberg, *Medicinal Product Liability and Regulation* (Hart Publishing 2013) 21–23.

[315] Cases C-503/13 and C-504/13, *Boston Scientific Medizintechnik GmbH v AOK Sachsen-Anhalt-Die Gesundheitskasse and Others* ECLI:EU:C:2015:148, [14], [17], [19], [38].

[316] ibid, [14], [17], [19], [38].

[317] Ibid, [39].

[318] Ibid, [41], [43].

[319] Cases C-503/13 and C-504/13, *Boston Scientific Medizintechnik GmbH v AOK Sachsen-Anhalt-Die Gesundheitskasse and Others* ECLI:EU:C:2014:2306, [30], (Opinion of AG Bot).

such as those at issue in the main proceedings, from the abnormal potential for damage' which they might cause to the person concerned.[320] The final sentence of Advocate General Bot's analysis is instructive as it would appear to support the argument that it is the *risk* of damage which affects legitimate expectations. He explains abnormal potential for damage as being 'a risk of damage of such a degree that it affects the public's legitimate expectations in so far as concerns safety'.[321] Thus a risk of damage affects legitimate expectations, and is arguably consistent with the view that legitimate public expectations may be shaped by a risk–utility assessment.[322] Accordingly, the Court is stating that in certain circumstances, a product may be regarded as defective if it presents an abnormal potential for damage, and that there will be no requirement to show that an individual product contains a defect. It is difficult to predict how national courts will interpret this decision. Nonetheless, there are some observations that can be made with its approach. First, while there may be an abnormal potential for damage in a group of products, such general statistics of failure do not point to there being a defect in the individual product and arguably the claimant should have been required to establish that this was so.[323] Secondly, if the interpretation here is only relevant to particular *types* of product, that is, health care products, then this would lend support to the view that technologically specific approaches to defects are needed in this area in the context of medicinal products and devices. This would appear to be confirmed by AG Bot's submission that 'the function of health care products for human use lends such products an indisputable specific character, which must be taken into account in assessing the concept of defect.'[324]

Thirdly, the notion that a medicinal product with an abnormal potential for damage if it belongs to a group of products with significant risk of failure is defective would seem to be potentially devastating to whole groups of medicinal products of a particular therapeutic class, each one of may operate in a different way on different patients. Fourthly, that notion of 'abnormality' poses the question as to from whose perspective it would need to be determined and presumably quantified. In the instance of technological products, especially medicinal products and devices, it is arguable that one would need to look at this from not only the patient's perspective but also from that of informed users, such as physicians. Whilst it has been argued by Professor Borghetti, that the notion of abnormal potential to cause damage is to be determined by reference to the risks inherent in comparable products,[325] this is highly problematic in the context of medicinal products and devices.[326] It is submitted that the only way in which this notion could operate in a way consistent with a fair apportionment of the risks inherent in modern technological production[327] would be **18.64**

[320] Cases C-503/13 and C-504/13, *Boston Scientific Medizintechnik GmbH v AOK Sachsen-Anhalt-Die Gesundheitskasse and Others* ECLI:EU:C:2015:148, [40].

[321] ibid.

[322] See R Goldberg, 'Paying for Bad Blood: Strict Product Liability after the Hepatitis C Litigation' (2002) 10 Medical Law Review 165.

[323] See Miller and Goldberg, *Product Liability* (2nd ed, Oxford University Press 2004), 10.79.

[324] Cases C-503/13 and C-504/13, *Boston Scientific Medizintechnik GmbH v AOK Sachsen-Anhalt-Die Gesundheitskasse and Others* ECLI:EU:C:2014:2306, [42], (Opinion of AG Bot).

[325] See J-S Borghetti, 'Some views on CJUE, 5 March 2015 Cases C-503/13 and C-504/13, *Boston Scientific Medizintechnik GmbH*', Product Liability Forum, British Institute of International and Comparative Law, 1 July 2015,

[326] See M D Green, 'Statutory Compliance and Tort Liability: Examining the Strongest Case' (1997) 30 University of Michigan Journal of Law Reform 461, 471; M D Green, 'Prescription Drugs, Alternative Designs and the Restatement (Third): Preliminary Reflections' (1999) 30 Seton Hall Law Review 207, 208–11; D G Owen, 'Dangers in Prescription Drugs: Filling a Private Law Gap in the Healthcare Debate' (2010) 42 Connecticut Law Review 733, 739, and further R Goldberg, *Medicinal Product Liability and Regulation* (Hart Publishing 2013) 36–37.

[327] See Recital 2 to the Directive.

if the determination of legitimate public expectations in conjunction with the notion of abnormal potential for damage is shaped by a risk–benefit assessment. To this end, avoidability and foreseeability must seemingly play a role in the process.[328]

(viii) Defences

18.65 Under s 7 of the Act, liability cannot be 'limited or excluded by any contract term, by any notice or by any other provision'. If the claimant can prove that damage has been caused by a 'defective product' (as defined above) for which the defendant is responsible under the Act, the burden shifts to the defence to establish any of six specific defences listed in s 4.

18.66 (a) **Section 4(1)(a)** That the defect 'is attributable to compliance with any requirement imposed by or under any enactment or with any Community obligation'.[329] Compliance with such a requirement is not in itself a defence. The defendant must show that the defect was caused by the compliance. Thus mere compliance with the Human Medicines Regulations 2012 is not a defence, though it will often be strong evidence that the 'consumer expectation' test of safety has been met, and some indication that the producer has demonstrated the degree of scientific and technical knowledge needed to satisfy the 'development risks' defence.[330] The requirement relied upon must be mandatory.[331]

18.67 (b) **Section 4(1)(b) and section 46** That the defendant 'did not at any time supply the product to another'.[332] This defence derives from Article 7(a) of the Directive, under which a producer can avoid liability by proving that 'he did not put the product into circulation'. It could be relied on where, for example, damage has arisen from the theft of drugs or from the use of defective products, provided that they were not yet in the distribution chain.[333] However, the view that the defence would generally be available when medicinal materials are provided to participants in pre-marketing clinical trials[334] is open to question.[335]

---

[328] The opinion of AG Bott would seem to suggest that avoidability and foreseeability will play a role, in that the concept of safety which a person is entitled to expect refers to 'a product that poses risks jeopardising the safety of its user and having an abnormal, unreasonable character exceeding the normal risk inherent in its use': Cases C-503/13 and C-504/13, *Boston Scientific Medizintechnik GmbH v AOK Sachsen-Anhalt-Die Gesundheitskasse and Others* ECLI:EU:C:2014:2306, [30], (Opinion of AG Bot).

[329] CPA, s 4(1)(a).

[330] See Wilkes v DePuy International Limited [2016] EWHC 3096, [100]–[101] (QB)(regulatory approval 'may be evidence (and in an appropriate case, powerful evidence) that the level of safety of the product was that which persons generally were entitled to expect'). See further paras 18.68–18.71.

[331] cf 'mandatory regulations issued by the public authorities': Directive (n 237 above), Art 7(d). More generally, in its third review of the application of the Directive, the European Commission stated that 'stakeholders, and in particular representatives of the pharmaceutical industry, have argued strongly for the introduction of a defence of regulatory compliance . . .': European Commission, *Third Report on the application of Council Directive 85/374 on the approximation of laws, regulations and administrative provisions of the Member States concerning liability for defective products*, COM (2006) 496 final, 11.

[332] CPA, ss 4(1)(b) and 46(1). Under the CPA, promotional samples, being 'gifts', would appear to be 'supplied' within the meaning of s 46(1)(f). It is not so clear that they are 'put into circulation', as required under the Directive, art 7(a). See C Hodges (ed), *Product Liability: European Laws and Practice* (Sweet & Maxwell 1993) 72.

[333] In *Henning Veedfald v Arhus Amtskommune*, n 258, the defective fluid, having been used in the provision of a specific medical service, was held to have been 'put into circulation' for the purposes of Art 7(a) of the Directive, even though it had never left the 'sphere of control' of the hospital.

[334] See para 18.59.

[335] As Miller and Goldberg point out, such provision might be interpreted as a transfer of goods in exchange for consideration, or in connection with performance of a statutory function, or as making a gift: CPA, ss 46(1)(d), (e), and (f), respectively. See Miller and Goldberg, *Product Liability*, n 2, para 13.09. It has been suggested that medicinal materials supplied to testing institutions will not have been 'put into circulation' within the meaning of Art 7a of the Directive, since 'quality control will not have been completed' and the product 'is not ready to be exposed to potential customers': Case C-127/04 *O'Byrne v*

(c) **Section 4(1)(c)** That the defendant did not supply the product 'in the course of a business' and, in the case of the producer, 'own-brander' or importer (ie a s 2(2) defendant), with a view to profit. 'Business' in this context includes NHS provision.[336] **18.68**

(d) **Section 4(1)(d) and section 4(2)** That the defect 'did not exist in the product at the relevant time'.[337] It is a defence for s 2(2) defendants to prove[338] that the defect was not present when they supplied the product to another. In *Piper v JRI (Manufacturing) Ltd*,[339] the claimant's hip replacement prosthesis fractured eighteen months after an apparently successful implantation. The Court of Appeal found the manufacturer not liable, in the light of evidence of the comprehensive nature of its quality control systems and, crucially, of a possible alternative cause for the defect. It accepted that the quality control would probably have revealed, and rectified, any defect prior to the prosthesis being supplied to the hospital that might otherwise have been responsible for the fracture. It was not necessary for the manufacturer to establish how or when the defect arose. A supplier[340] can succeed under the defence by showing that the defect did not exist when the product was last supplied by the producer, 'own-brander' or importer. The supplier is thus apparently not liable, under the Act, for introducing the defect into the product. The defence would be available to a pharmaceutical manufacturer where, for example, a product had deteriorated because of inadequate storage or poor handling by a wholesaler or pharmacist, or where injury was shown to have resulted from a pharmacist having removed a patient leaflet. It could also cover situations where a supplier had altered the original specifications of a product, as well as instances of criminal tampering with tamper-resistant products. **18.69**

(e) **Section 4(1)(f)** That the defect in a component is wholly attributable to the design of the finished product in which it was comprised or to compliance with the instructions of that product's producer.[341] Components manufacturers (and producers of raw materials) are not liable, under the Act, if their product is defective only as a consequence of the design of the finished product or of compliance with instructions given by its producer. In the European Directive, unlike the CPA, the defence that the defect was attributable to instructions is not confined to instructions given to the component manufacturer, and could cover instructions for use.[342] **18.70**

(f) **Section 4(1)(e)** The 'Development Risks' defence:[343] That: '… the state of scientific and technical knowledge at the relevant time was not such that a producer of products of the **18.71**

Sanofi Pasteur MSD Ltd (formerly Aventis Pasteur MSD Ltd [2006] ECR I-1313; 1 WLR 1606, Opinion of A-G Geelhoed, para 36 (and see n 271 above, and n 270 and related text). However, this now seems very unlikely: see Miller and Goldberg n 2, at paras 8.57–8.59, 13.07, and 13.09 (at n 22).

336 See para 18.58, n 273. The defence would not be available for promotional free samples. The equivalent defence under Art 7(c) of the Directive makes no reference to the product not being supplied 'with a view to profit' but applies where it was not made for an 'economic purpose' or in the course of a business. Art 7(c) has been held not to apply where the product had been manufactured and used in the course of a specific medical service financed entirely from public funds and for which the claimant did not pay directly: *Henning Veedfald v Arhus Amtskommune*, n 258, para 22. See also *A v National Blood Authority*, n 314.

337 CPA, s 4(1)(d), (2).

338 The evidential burden of proving that there was no defect at the time of supply lies on the defendant: *Love v Halfords Ltd* [2014] EWHC 1057 (QB), [2014] RTR 32, [29].

339 [2006] EWCA Civ 1344; (2006) 92 BMLR 141.

340 CPA, s 2(3).

341 CPA, s 4(1)(f).

342 Art 7(f).

343 CPA, s 4(1)(e). See R Goldberg, 'The Development Risk Defence and Medicinal Products', in R Goldberg, *Medicinal Product Liability and Regulation* (Hart Publishing 2013) 168–204; C Newdick, 'The Development Risk Defence of the Consumer Protection Act 1987', n 126, 455; C Newdick, 'Risk,

same description as the product in question might be expected to have discovered the defect if it had existed in his products while they were under his control . . .'

This provision has been the most contentious feature of the legislation. The pharmaceutical industry was very prominent in the intensive lobbying to have a 'development risks' defence, emphasizing concern about innovation and insurability. The availability of such a defence in the European Directive[344] was a key factor in obtaining the agreement of all Member States, especially the UK, to the introduction of a strict liability regime.[345] At the same time, there has been much criticism that it signified a reversion to negligence, was conceptually incompatible with strict liability and threatened to undermine the social and economic objectives of products liability reform.[346] These concerns were reflected in the Directive's requirement that, after ten years,[347] the European Commission would have to report on how 'consumer protection and the functioning of the common market' had been affected by court rulings of Member States based on the defence, to determine whether or not Article 7(e) should be repealed.[348]

18.72 **(g) Section 4(1)(e) and Article 7(e)** The controversy was exacerbated by the difference in terminology between s 4(1)(e) and Article 7(e).[349] Under the Act, manufacturers need only show that the state of knowledge when they supplied the product was not such that 'a producer of products of the same description . . . might be expected' to have discovered the defect.[350] The Directive requires the defendant to prove that the state of knowledge 'was not such as to *enable* the existence of the defect to be discovered'.[351] The Directive is concerned with what is objectively discoverable; the CPA only with what might be expected of producers of a particular category of products.

Uncertainty and "Knowledge" in the Development Risk Defence' (1991) Anglo-American L Rev 127; Stapleton, 'Products Liability Reform—Real or Illusory?', n 294, 392; Stapleton, *Product Liability*, n 9, 236–42; Whittaker, 'The EEC Directive on Product Liability', n 254, 233; Stoppa (1992), 'The Concept of Defectiveness in the Consumer Protection Act 1987: A Critical Analysis', n 294, 218–21, M Mildred, 'The Development Risks Defence' in D Fairgrieve (ed), *Product Liability In Comparative Perspective* (Cambridge 2005) 169.

344 Art 7(e).

345 Under Art 15(1)(b), Member States were given the option of adopting or derogating from the defence.

346 See references at n 294 above.

347 ie in 1995.

348 Art 15(3). In its first report on the application of the Directive, the Commission did not propose any amendments to it: *First Report on the application of Council Directive on the approximation of laws, regulations and administrative provisions of the Member States concerning liability for defective products* (85/374/EEC): COM (95) 617 final, 13 December 1995, 2. See also M Mildred, 'The Impact of the Directive in the United Kingdom' in M Goyens (ed), *Directive 85/374/EEC on product liability: ten years after* (Louvain-la-Neuve 1996) 37–57. In its Second and Third Reports, the Commission concluded that the defence was one among several issues that required further monitoring: COM (2000) 893 final, and COM (2006) 496, final, at 28–29 and 10–11, respectively. See also Lovells, *Product Liability in the European Union: A Report for the European Commission*, MARKT/2001/11/D (2003); Fondazione Rosselli, *Analysis of the Economic Impact of the Development Risks Clause as provided by Directive 85/374/EEC on Liability for Defective Products* (2004): and D Fairgrieve and G Howells, 'Rethinking Product Liability: A Missing Element in the European Commission's Third Review of the European Product Liability Directive' (2007) 70 MLR 962.

349 See references at n 334.

350 It is not entirely clear what is meant by 'a producer of products of the same description as the product in question'. In the pharmaceutical context, it could refer to drug manufacturers in general or might be limited to producers of drugs of the same therapeutic class, always assuming that they exist.

351 Emphasis added. Art 7(e) reads in full, 'that the state of scientific and technical knowledge at the time when he put the product into circulation was not such as to enable the existence of the defect to be discovered'.

Clearly, this is a distinction which could have had major implications for the pharmaceutical industry in cases of defective design.[352] The imprecise wording of the CPA defence appeared to permit exactly the kind of balancing act which is familiar in negligence analysis. It seemed to leave the court free to consider what are appropriate standards within the industry, having regard to such factors as the resources of the producer and the feasibility of discovering a particular defect at the pre-marketing stage, in the light of the various financial and scientific constraints on investigative procedures. It has often been asserted that, by virtue of s 4(1)(e), the thalidomide victims might not have recovered damages under an Act which was in part prompted by their struggle. Certainly it is possible that Distillers could have shown that pharmaceutical manufacturers of comparable products might not have been expected to conduct the kind of tests that would have revealed the defect.[353] On the other hand, the reverse onus of proof and the expectations engendered by a strict liability regime would have made their task harder. In 1996, two experienced practitioners in the field observed: **18.73**

> There is widespread expectation that any court would feel obliged to construe the defence in accordance with the Directive and thus in effect to override the literal words of the Act. Indeed, insurance is widely believed to be on this basis.[354]

The following year, in response to infringement proceedings brought by the European Commission, the European Court of Justice ruled that the test of scientific and technical knowledge under Article 7(e) is an objective one. It includes the most advanced level of such knowledge at the time when the product was put into circulation, provided that knowledge was accessible at that time. The Court found that s 4(1)(e) did not impose any restriction on the state of scientific and technical knowledge to be taken into account and, more particularly, did not suggest that the availability of the defence depended on the subjective knowledge of a producer taking reasonable care in the light of standard precautions in the industrial sector in question. The Court further noted that s 1(1) of the Act expressly provided that relevant provisions be construed in conformity with the Directive. It therefore concluded that s 4(1)(e) did not clearly conflict with Article 7(e).[355] In *A v National Blood Authority*, Burton J invoked s 1(1) and the Court of Justice ruling to resolve the development risks issue in the case by reference to Article 7(e). Mindful that the Directive sought to prevent injury and facilitate compensation for injury, he observed that 'Article 7(e) provides a very restricted escape route'.[356] Crucially, he held that when a product is known to be

[352] CPA, s 4(1)(e) would seem to have no application to the risk of manufacturing defects, which already effectively attract strict liability at common law. See *A v National Blood Authority*, n 314, where the existence of the generic defect was known. See Newdick, 'The Development Risk Defence of the Consumer Protection Act 1987', n 126, 472–73. The comparable German provision under the ***Produkthaftungsgesetz*** (Product Liability Act 1990) has been held not to apply to unavoidable manufacturing defects: Bundesgerichtshof (VI ZR 158/94, 9 May 1995) NJW 1995, 2162. See further *A v National Blood Authority*, n 314, [53(iii)]. Contrast *Graham Barclay Oysters Pty v Ryan* [2000] FCA 1099 (9 August 2000) (Aust Fed Ct), interpreting the Australian Trade Practices Act 1974, s 75AK(1)(c). See also J Stapleton, 'Restatement (Third) of Torts: Products Liability, an Anglo-Australian Perspective' (2000) 39 Washburn LJ 363, 379–85. Stapleton considers that there is no role for the defence in failure to warn cases. In her view, since a failure to warn claim is assessed according to the reasonableness of including a warning at the time of supply, there will therefore be no role for the Art 7(e) defence, and Art 7(e) only has a role in the context of design defect claims: J Stapleton, 'Liability for Drugs in the US and EU: Rhetoric and Reality' (2007) 26 Review of Litigation 991, 1018. The view is a controversial one: see R Goldberg, Medicinal Product Liability and Regulation (Hart Publishing 2013) 71–73.

[353] See generally H Teff and C Munro, *Thalidomide: The Legal Aftermath* (Saxon House 1976).

[354] M Mildred and R Pannone, 'Liability in Tort: Class Actions' in C J Miller, ***Product Liability and Safety Encyclopaedia*** (Butterworths 1996) Division IIIA, para 94.

[355] Case C-300/95 ***European Commission v UK*** [1997] ECR I-2649.

[356] *A v National Blood Authority*, n 314, [64]. This restrictive view of the Art 7(e) defence has been criticized by Goldberg, 'Paying for Bad Blood: Strict Product Liability after the Hepatitis C Litigation', n 322.

generically susceptible to a defect, the defendant cannot rely on Article 7(e) merely because of inability to detect the defect in an *individual* product. Put another way, once the risk of a defect occurring is known, it cannot be a development risk.

18.74 This is not to say that the wording of the Directive is free from ambiguity; there are practical difficulties in trying to apply it in a literal fashion. What does it mean to say that the state of scientific and technical knowledge enables the existence of a defect to be discovered? How reliable and beyond challenge must findings be, what level of recognition must they have achieved within the scientific community, before they can be said to constitute 'knowledge' at all, let alone 'the most advanced level of such knowledge'?[357] It has been forcefully argued that 'scientific and technical knowledge' cannot be said to exist merely because of what someone, somewhere knows, or may have published in an obscure journal. A court assessing the relevant state of scientific and technical knowledge would hardly 'require the defendant to prove . . . a worldwide absence of knowledge of the defect'.[358] The ruling by the European Court of Justice that the knowledge in question must have been 'accessible' indicates that, even under the Directive, only reasonably discoverable knowledge is in issue.[359]

(ix) Limitation of actions

18.75 The normal principles of limitation of actions apply under the Act, except in two respects.[360] First, the limitation period for damage to property is the same as for personal injury, namely three years from the date that the claimant became aware or should reasonably have become aware of the material facts relating to the damage.[361] Secondly, an action may not be brought

---

For narrow interpretations of s 4(1)(e), see *Richardson v LRC Products Ltd* [2000] Lloyd's Rep Med 280, at 285, and *Iman Abouzaid v Mothercare (UK) Ltd* The Times, 20 February 2001 (CA) [29] *per* Pill LJ.

357 Newdick, 'Risk, Uncertainty and "Knowledge" in the Development Risk Defence', n 343. Cf para 18.31.

358 Newdick, 'The Development Risk Defence of the Consumer Protection Act 1987', n 126, 459, and see 461–67; C Pugh and M Pilgerstorfer, 'The Development Risks Defence—Knowledge, Discoverability and Creative Leaps' [2004] JPIL 258. Cf Atiyah, *Sale of Goods*, n 45, 280–83; Stapleton, *Product Liability*, n 9, 236–42. While there has been a more liberal interpretation of the notion of the state of scientific and general knowledge by the Paris Court of Appeal, focusing on the need for an 'international consensus' being required to alert practitioners of a risk of an adverse effect (see CA Paris 23 September 2004, *Société Ferring v Mauduit* N° 02/16713, *Dalloz* 2005 1012), the Cour de Cassation was not required to determine whether the Paris Court of Appeal had correctly understood and applied the development risk defence on the facts (Cass Civ 1, 15 May 2007, *Société Ferring v Mauduit* N° 05-10234). See R Goldberg, *Medicinal Product Liability and Regulation* (Hart Publishing 2013) 184–85.

359 *European Commission v UK*, n 355, Opinion of AG Tesauro, paras 23–24. In *A v National Blood Authority*, n 414, Burton J, obiter, may have sought to restrict inaccessible knowledge to that contained in 'an unpublished document or unpublished research not available to the general public, retained within the laboratory or research department of a particular company' (at [49(i)]). A decision of the Italian Courts has reaffirmed the importance of accessibility to the objective state of scientific and technical knowledge as laid down by the European Court of Justice in the context of medicinal products and the defence: see Court of Sassari, Judgment of 12 July 2012, noted in J Bartolomeo, 'Pharmaceutical company's liability for injuries caused by a defective drug: the new trend in Italy' (2012) 49 International Product Liability Review 13.

In the US a number of jurisdictions permit a development risks defence along the lines of the European Directive. Since the mid-1980s, the American courts have largely retreated from strict liability in cases based on defective design and failure to warn. Contrast *Beshada v Johns-Manville Products Corporation* 447 A 2d 539, 546 (1982) (Sup Ct of New Jersey) with the same court's holding in *Feldman v Lederle Laboratories* 479 A 2d 374, 387 (1984). In *Brown v Superior Court (Abbott Laboratories)* 751 P 2d 470, 480–2 (1988), the California Supreme Court held that the exemption from strict liability for 'unavoidably unsafe' products in Comment k to s 402A of the Restatement (Second) of Torts covered all prescription drugs in respect of failure to warn. Contrast *Shanks v Upjohn Co* 835 P 2d 1189 (Alaska 1992). See also J Stapleton, *Product Liability*, n 9, ch 2. See now Restatement (Third) of Torts (1998), ss 2 and 6. And see n 29 above.

360 See s 6(6) and Sch 1, amending the Limitation Act 1980.

361 Limitation Act 1980, ss 11A(4) and 14(1A).

under the Act after ten years from when the defendant supplied the actual defective product which caused the damage; the right of action is 'extinguished'. [362] This cut-off point is of particular significance in respect of drugs, since the latency period for adverse effects can be considerable.[363] Where proceedings have been instituted but there has been a mistake as to the name of the producer, it had been held that the court has discretion to permit substitution of a new party after the expiry of the ten-year limit, in accordance with domestic procedural rules.[364] In *O'Byrne v Sanofi Pasteur MSD Ltd*,[365] the claimant was seriously injured by a defective vaccine produced by a French manufacturer. Within the ten-year limitation period, O'Byrne sued the English distributor (a wholly owned subsidiary of the manufacturer), in the mistaken belief that it was the producer. He subsequently sought to have the manufacturer substituted as the defendant, outside the ten-year period. The matter was referred to the ECJ for a preliminary ruling on when the product had been 'put into circulation' and whether the substitution was permissible. Under Article 11 of the Directive, the right to institute proceedings expires ten years from when the 'producer put into circulation the actual product which caused the damage.' The claimant argued that the relevant date was when the *subsidiary* had supplied the vaccine to the receiving hospital, such that the claim was not out of time; not, as the manufacturer maintained, the date on which it was transferred to the subsidiary company prior to distribution. The ECJ held that a product is 'put into circulation' at the point when it 'leaves the production process operated by the producer and enters a marketing process in the form in which it is offered to the public in order to be used or consumed'.[366] In essence, the ECJ found that it was for the national court to decide, as a question of fact, whether the subsidiary was involved in a production activity or was merely acting as a distributor. Though the Court viewed the issue of substitution as generally a matter of national procedural law, it also reasserted the quest for 'complete harmonization' and 'due regard for the personal scope of the Directive'.[367] It has been argued that the ten-year limitation period could contravene the right to a fair trial under Article 6 of the European Convention on Human Rights, which includes access to the courts to

[362] ibid, ss 11A(3) and 33(1A)(a). Cf Directive, Art 11.

[363] See, eg, *Sindell v Abbott Laboratories* 607 P 2d 924 (Cal 1980).

[364] Limitation Act 1980, s 35(5)(b) and (6)(a) and CPR 19.5(3)(a): *Horne-Roberts v SmithKline Beecham plc* [2002] 1 WLR 1662 (CA). But see now *OB v Aventis Pasteur SA* [2010] UKSC 23; discussed in n 358 and related text.

[365] Case C-127/04 *O'Byrne v Sanofi Pasteur MSD Ltd (formerly Aventis Pasteur MSD Ltd)* [2006] ECR I-1313, [2006] 1 WLR 1606. See G Howells, [2009] JBL 97 (commentary); C Hodges, 'Product Liability: Suppliers, Limitation and Mistake' (2006) 122 LQR 393; and H Preston, 'Product Liability' [2006] 150 SJ 878, 7 July.

[366] *O'Byrne v Sanofi*, n 365, [27] and [32].

[367] ibid, [34], [35], and [38], respectively. The Court of Appeal subsequently upheld the substitution of the manufacturer (*O'Byrne v Aventis Pasteur MSD Ltd* (2007) EWCA Civ 966: see Limitation Act 1980, s 35(5)(b) and (6)(a), and CPR 19.5(3)(a)), and there followed another reference to the ECJ, by the House of Lords, seeking further clarification (*O'Byrne v Aventis Pasteur MSD Ltd* [2008] UKHL 34, [2008] 4 All ER 88). The ECJ reiterated its earlier finding (see text at n 357) precluding substitution under the Limitation Act of a producer who had not been proceeded against within the ten-year period. However, the ECJ also indicated that when a distributor was closely controlled by the manufacturer, or integral to the manufacturing process, the manufacturer could be a 'producer' within Art 3(1) of the Directive, if the national court, in accordance with domestic rules of proof, concluded that it had effectively determined when the distributor (supplier) put the product into circulation: Case C-358/08 *Aventis Pasteur SA v OB* [2010] All ER (EC) 522, [2010] 2 CMLR 16. The Supreme Court subsequently set aside the substitution of the producer as defendant. It readily accepted that Art 11 precluded such substitution under the Limitation Act, s 35, and did not find the distributor to have been 'integrated into the manufacturing process and so tightly controlled' that proceedings against it could be deemed to be proceedings against the producer, under Art 3(1): *OB v Aventis Pasteur SA* [2010] UKSC 23, [11] and [14] and [32]–[34], respectively.

determine civil rights.[368] Clearly, in the pharmaceutical context, more than ten years will sometimes elapse before damage occurs or before the injured party can be expected to be aware of it.[369] However, a ten-year long-stop could still be regarded as proportionate, having regard to the underlying aim in the Directive of balancing producer and consumer interests 'across the broad range of products';[370] and since the statutory cause of action is *extinguished* beyond the ten-year period, it might be argued that no substantive right remains in issue.[371] The ten-year limit under the Act does not, of course, exclude the possibility of an action in negligence.

(x) Jurisdiction

18.76 For the purposes of determining jurisdiction, liability under Pt I of the Act is treated as liability in tort,[372] and the normal rules as to conflict of laws apply.[373] In England, there being no special provisions for product liability in the Directive or elsewhere, the applicable sets of jurisdictional rules are largely to be found in the harmonized European regime for civil and commercial matters[374] and, to a limited extent, in the common law. Generally speaking, and despite the scope for derogation under the Directive, there has not been such a degree of divergence in its implementation by Member States as to encourage widespread forum shopping. However, potential procedural advantages, notably in multiparty actions involving mass exposure to drugs, and the prospect of higher awards, particularly in the US, may provide an incentive to sue abroad when there is a sufficiently close and substantial connection between the litigation and the forum in question.[375] Apart from any extrinsic considerations as to choice of forum, several points merit attention. First, because the Directive applies only to products put into circulation once the domestic implementing law has come into force, liability for products supplied prior to that date is based on the applicable national law at the relevant time. Secondly, though nearly all Member States have implemented a 'development risk' defence, the UK's version is the one most open to a broad interpretation. However, specifically in respect of pharmaceutical products, Germany has a statutory scheme under which manufacturers are subject to strict liability.[376]

[368] cf Human Rights Act 1998 Art 6(1). And see C Ovey and R C A White, *Jacobs and White's The European Convention on Human Rights* (4th edn, Oxford University Press 2006) 170–71.

[369] See G Howells (ed), *The Law of Product Liability* (2nd edn, Butterworths 2007) ch 4, para 4.320, noting that the Polish Constitutional Court has indicated that a general tort limitation rule could be deemed unconstitutional if a party lost the right to act even before damage had occurred: E Rutkowska and L Nowak, 'Statute of Limitation for Tort Claims Declared Unconstitutional' (2006) European Product Liability Review 25/34.

[370] cf *Royal Commission on Civil Liability and Compensation for Personal Injury (Pearson Report)* (London, 1978) Cmnd 7054, vol 1, para 1269.

[371] Howells (ed), *The Law of Product Liability*, n 369.

[372] CPA, s 6(7).

[373] See J Fawcett, 'Jurisdiction' in G Howells (ed), *The Law of Product Liability*, n 369, ch 6; and J Harris, 'Product Liability and the Conflict of Laws' in Miller and Goldberg, *Product Liability*, n 2, ch 18.

[374] Regulation 1215/2012 on jurisdiction and the recognition and enforcement of judgments in civil and commercial matters [2012] OJ L 351/1 ('Brussels Ia Regulation'), replacing the Regulation on Jurisdiction and the Recognition and Enforcement of Judgments in Civil and Commercial Matters Reg (EC) 44/2001 ('Brussels I Regulation'); Lugano Convention on Jurisdiction and the recognition and enforcement of judgments in civil and commercial matters [2007] OJ L339/3 ('Lugano Convention').

[375] An attempt to bring a product liability claim concerning the cardiovascular problems linked to Vioxx in New Jersey on behalf of ninety-eight plaintiffs residing in England and Wales was rejected by the Supreme Court of New Jersey on *forum non conveniens* grounds. The UK was held to provide an adequate alternative forum for products liability litigation in terms of both substantive and procedural law: *In re Vioxx Litigation* 928 A 2d 935, 937, 944 (NJ Sup AD 2007).

[376] Drug Administration Act (*Arzneimittelgesetz*) 1976 BGBI, 1S 2445, amended 20 July 1988 BGBI, IS 1050. The issue of jurisdiction in the context of product liability claims under the Brussels I Regulation

3. To what extent has the CPA enhanced patient protection?

The Preamble to the Directive asserted that 'liability without fault' was to be the 'sole means' for 'fair apportionment of the risks', and Article 1 states that '[t]he producer shall be liable for damage caused by a defect in his product'. These pronouncements appeared to signal a major advance in consumer protection. The title of the 1987 Act also conveyed the impression that shortcomings of the negligence action would be overcome by a shift to a strict, or at least substantially stricter, liability regime. However, and despite the thalidomide disaster as a catalyst for reform, the political and economic interests at stake were such that a compromise solution was always highly likely. Elements of the Preamble; the negotiations preceding the Directive's adoption, and the formulation of key concepts in the CPA, pointed to a liability regime still wedded to a balance of interests, based on perceived costs and benefits.[377] **18.77**

A balancing approach was implicit in determining 'defectiveness' by reference to the level of safety that 'persons generally are entitled to expect', taking 'all the circumstances . . . into account'.[378] It had been made explicit in Recital 7 of the Directive: '. . . a fair apportionment of the risk between the injured person and the producer implies that the producer should be able to free himself from liability if he furnishes proof as to the existence of certain exonerating circumstances'. The emergence and wording of the CPA's development risk defence in s 4(1)(e) illustrate the forces at work. Vigorously lobbied for by the pharmaceutical industry, the UK's seeming reversion to a negligence criterion was not incompatible with the EU vision of innovation as an inclusive concept, producing social benefits for citizens such that they could be expected to share some of the risks.[379] From this perspective, it becomes easier to understand the ECJ's subsequent finding that s 4(1)(e) did not necessarily contravene the Directive.[380] **18.78**

Initially, the sparse English case law showed scant evidence of a significant shift towards strict liability. For manufacturing defects, liability had already long been more or less strict under the negligence framework. As regards design defects and failure to warn, lingering judicial attachment to a negligence mindset would have been fortified by the Act's nebulous 'definition' of defectiveness and its broad version of the development risk defence.[381] That said, there have been some conscious efforts to give substance to the rhetoric of enhanced consumer protection. In *Abouzaid v Mothercare (UK) Ltd* Chadwick LJ was at pains to criticize the use of fault-based reasoning under the Act,[382] and the Court's view that the risk of the particular injury was too small to have reasonably been foreseen did not preclude liability under the Act. Nor did the unavoidability of infection in a very small minority of patients in *A v National Blood Authority*. Burton J was determined that the Directive should not be 'toothless' or 'pointless',[383] and, at the time, his purposive interpretation of it appeared to herald a turning point. **18.79**

---

was addressed by the CJEU in Case C-45/13, *Kainz v Pantherwerke AG* EU:C:2014:7 [2015] QB 34, [26], which held that with regard to product liability claims, the place of the event giving rise to the damage was the place where the product in question had been manufactured; followed in *Allen v Deputy International Ltd* [2014] EWHC 753 (QB), [2015] 2 WLR 442, [13].

[377] J Stapleton, 'Products Liability in the United Kingdom: The Myths of Reform' (1999) 34 Texas International Law Journal 45, esp at 56–58.

[378] CPA, s 3(2).

[379] *Green Paper on Innovation*, COM (95) 688 final, 20 December 1995. And see C Hodges, 'Development Risks: Unanswered Questions' (1998) MLR 560, 561–62.

[380] Case C-300/95 *European Commission v UK* [1997] ECR I-2649.

[381] cf 'the more reasonable interpretation of the ambiguous words of the Directive means that [the producer] will in practice virtually always escape liability if he has used all reasonable care': Stapleton, 'Products Liability in the United Kingdom: The Myths of Reform' (1999) 34 Texas International Law Journal 45, 53, n 74 (and related text).

[382] [2000] All ER (D) 2436 *per* Chadwick LJ, paras 43–44.

[383] *A v National Blood Authority*, n 314, [69].

18.80 How influential the judgment will prove in the long term, either generally or in assisting claimants harmed by medicinal products, remains unclear. Largely because consumer protection is not, on its face, the Directive's sole aim, Burton J's near equation of *actual* and *legitimate* expectations, his treatment of avoidability of the harm as irrelevant to defectiveness, and his refusal to make any concessions to a risk/utility analysis has been subjected to criticism.[384] On the facts of *A v National Blood Authority*, the rejection of the development risks defence for known or foreseeable but unavoidable risks was also open to question. It was not beyond doubt from the wording of Article 7(e) that the 'existence of the defect' related to the 'generic' defect, as Burton J had held, rather than to the unidentifiable harmful batches.[385] It would appear that the criticism of Burton J's reasoning has been emphatically taken on board with the decision of Wilkes v DePuy International Limited, which abandons the legitimate expectation test in favour of an objective approach, including risk-utlity.

18.81 Some of the unease about the refusal to countenance a risk/utility approach in *A v National Blood Authority* stemmed from the policy issues raised by its specific context. As well as the plight of the claimants, the case highlights the predicament of a public body, under a legal duty to provide a vital commodity, but unable to spread its losses.[386] Its significance for claims arising from prescribed is now likely to eclipsed by the decision of Wilkes v DePuy International Limited, in so far as courts are reluctant to deem it a 'legitimate expectation' that they are 'risk-free'. As has been previously noted,[387] it is difficult to predict how national courts will interpret the *Boston Scientific* decision of the CJEU, and whether it will be only applicable to devices, or more widely to medicinal products and other health care products. Generally speaking, claimants could potentially benefit under the Act from its broad definition of 'producer', the strict liability of suppliers and reversal of the burden of proof, especially in the development risk defence. However, persons injured by defective medicinal products are among those most likely to be disadvantaged by the absence of any equivalent to the continuing duty of care in negligence, and by the ten-year long-stop rule.

18.82 More importantly, even in the now unlikely event that if Burton J's radical stance was to prevail, over that of Higginbottom J common features of claims for drug-induced injury can make them as daunting to pursue under the CPA as in negligence. The intrinsic difficulties of proving causation and apportionment of responsibility may be compounded by the complexity of voluminous documentation, as well as by the inaccessibility of negative trial data. Consequently, funding can be prohibitive,[388] and group actions may also encounter formidable organizational problems.[389] The prolonged controversy over the

[384] See, eg, J Stapleton, 'Bugs in Anglo-American Products Liability' (2002) *South Carolina Law Review* 1225, at 1249–52; Goldberg, 'Paying for Bad Blood: Strict Product Liability after the Hepatitis C Litigation', n 319, 199–200; Hodges, 'Compensating Patients', n 298; R Goldberg, *Medicinal Product Liability and Regulation* (Hart Publishing 2013) 28–37, 49–53, 75–76, 195–204.

[385] See Miller and Goldberg, *Product Liability*, n 2, paras 13.96–13.97.

[386] It will be recalled that, in response to public policy concerns over the availability of blood products, 'blood shield' statutes have been introduced in some jurisdictions: para 18.21. For a comparative analysis of products liability doctrine on pathogenically infected products, see Stapleton, 'Bugs in Anglo-American Products Liability', n 384.

[387] See para 18.63.

[388] Note that since 1 April 2013, personal injury claims against pharmaceutical companies will no longer be eligible for legal aid funding in England and Wales: Legal Aid, Sentencing and Punishment of Offenders Act 2012, Sc 1(2), para 1. This does not extend to Scotland: s 152(1). Conditional Fee Arrangements (CFAs), of which 'no win, no fee' agreements are the most common, will be available, but it in the light of the costs involved in such litigation, and the fact that no claim has resulted in damages being awarded by a court against a pharmaceutical company, it seems few lawyers would wish to enter into such arrangements: See E Jackson, *Law and the Regulation of Medicines* (Hart Publishing 2012) 119; R Goldberg, *Medicinal Product Liability and Regulation* (Hart Publishing 2013) 9.

[389] See further para 18.83.

anti-depressant, paroxetine, is but one among many examples. Numerous people have alleged that they suffered harm due to difficulty in withdrawing from the drug. They include many women of child-bearing age, to whom it was prescribed from the early 1990s, who claim that their dependence in early pregnancy resulted in birth defects. Animal studies from the late 1980s, subsequent human studies, and adverse reports from clinical use all raised concerns that the drug was teratogenic. In 2005, the *Lancet* published a data analysis of cases which indicated an association between selective serotonin reuptake inhibitors (SSRIs) taken during pregnancy and neonatal convulsions or withdrawal syndrome. The most marked effects were associated with paroxetine, manufactured as Seroxat by GlaxoSmithKline (GSK), and used in sixty-four of the ninety-three suspected cases.[390] After a protracted process of obtaining public funding, having it withdrawn and then restored for the generic issues, a group action against GSK under the CPA was due to be heard in the autumn of 2010,[391] but Legal Aid for the claims was later withdrawn in England.[392] Since the collapse of the MMR Litigation,[393] in the few other product liability cases which the Legal Services Commission was prepared to fund (Vigabratrin, and the Fetal Anti-Convulsant Litigation[394]), the funding has become considerably more limited in scope.[395] Six years in preparation and three weeks before the Fetal Anti-Convulsant Litigation case was due to come to trial in November 2010, the Legal Services Commission withdrew legal aid.[396] In respect of claims against Merck concerning the cardiovascular problems linked to Vioxx, while claims were brought in Australia[397] and the US, legal aid was refused in England and Wales (though not Scotland,[398] where public funding was granted to a pursuer who alleged that Vioxx caused him to suffer a stroke).

---

390 E J Sanz et al, 'Selective serotonin reuptake inhibitors in pregnant women and neonatal withdrawal syndrome: a database analysis' (2005) 365 Lancet 482. This study was based on cases reported to the WHO's drug monitoring centre.

391 Seroxat Group Litigation Order No 68 29.10.08. Over 500 claimants joined the Group Litigation Order (GLO) against GlaxoSmithKline UK, alleging to have suffered withdrawal symptoms when reducing, discontinuing or attempting to discontinue use of the antidepressant Seroxat. In principle, claims would also be possible against prescribing doctors for failure to warn of risks and, under the Congenital Disabilities Act 1976, on behalf of children injured by the drugs taken by their mothers. On the issue of GSK's five-year delay in disclosing to the MHRA evidence that, if used to treat childhood depression, Seroxat lacked efficacy and increased the risk of suicidal ideation and behaviour, see McGoey and Jackson, 'Seroxat and the Suppression of Clinical Trial Data: Regulatory Failure and the Uses of Legal Ambiguity', n 218.

392 D Body, 'Product Liability Claims Under the Consumer Protection Act 1987: Some Practical Problems' [2012] Journal of Personal Injury Law 79, 81, n 8.

393 See R Goldberg, Medicinal Product Liability and Regulation (Hart Publishing 2013) ch 6.

394 *Multiple Claimants v Sanofi Synthelabo Ltd* [2007] EWHC 1860 (QB); (2007) 98 BMLR 192; *Claimants Registered to the GLO v Sanofi Synthelabo Ltd* [2009] EWHC 95 (QB) (application by claimants to adduce expert evidence of a forensic accountant concerning the worldwide value of sales of Epilim and its profitability, together with evidence of the pricing structures in place which governed sales to the NHS, rejected).

395 D Body, 'Product Liability Claims Under the Consumer Protection Act 1987: Some Practical Problems' n 383, 81.

396 See J Meikle, 'Legal Aid Withdrawal Means Epilim Case Likely to be Dropped' *The Guardian* (8 November 2010); J Robins, 'The Epilim Compensation Case Joins a Dismal Roll Call' *The Guardian* (1 February 2011): <www.guardian.co.uk/law/2011/feb/01/epilim-compensation-case-roll-call>, accessed 15 April 2013.

397 See R Goldberg, Medicinal Product Liability and Regulation (Hart Publishing 2013) chapters 2, 4, 5, 7, and 8.

398 See *Cooper v Merck Sharp & Dohme Ltd* [2012] CSOH 48 and *Hamilton and Others v Merck Sharp & Dohme Ltd* [2012] CSOH 144, [5], discussed in R Goldberg, *Medicinal Product Liability and Regulation* (Hart Publishing 2013), 8–9.

E. Multi-Party Actions

18.83 Our substantive law, the rules of the Supreme Court, and the legal aid system were all essentially designed to deal with individual claims. Because defective medical products and devices can cause injury on a large scale, they are liable to generate multi-party actions which may raise comparable, but often not identical, issues of liability:

> In the case of pharmaceutical products . . . patients of differing susceptibilities will have taken different quantities of the drug over differing periods of time and during different stages of the advancement of scientific knowledge, so that the issue of negligence or 'defective product' will vary. Equally, patients taking the same drug may complain of different ill-effects, and so the issue of causation may vary.[399]

Such cases can pose intractable problems of procedure and case management.[400] Recourse to a representative action—where 'numerous persons have the same interest in any proceedings'[401]— is problematic, especially where individual claims are made for damages.[402] In a legal system which does not provide for 'class actions',[403] early attempts at formalizing group litigation relied on 'coordinated arrangements' organized by the presiding judge. The first such case, in the mid-1980s, concerned the diverse injuries allegedly caused by the non-steroidal anti-inflammatory drug Opren.[404] Such ad hoc arrangements tended to involve protracted and costly hearings,[405] and the imbalance in financial resources and expertise between multinational corporations and claimants continues to pose formidable problems in funding large-scale group litigation. The civil procedure reforms, at the turn of the century, introduced the more elaborate mechanism of Group Litigation Orders (GLOs), which require that claimants need only have 'common or related' issues.[406] The introduction of GLOs would seem to offer a preferable, more flexible approach. However, claimants may find it difficult to persuade the court that the cost–benefit ratio justifies the exercise of its discretion to grant a GLO.[407] In 2008, the Civil Justice Council (CJC) in their report

---

[399] Supreme Court Procedure Committee, *Guide for Use in Group Actions* (1991) 6.

[400] See generally C Hodges, *Multi-Party Actions* (Oxford University Press 2000), and M Mildred, 'Group Actions' in Howells (ed), *The Law of Product Liability*, n 369, ch 8. On cost-sharing, see Civil Procedure Rules, Pt 48.6A; *Andrews v Secretary of State for Health* (1998) 54 BMLR 111 (CJD); *Sayers v Merck SmithKline Beecham plc* [2002] 1 WLR 2274 (CA) (MMR vaccine); and M Mildred, 'Cost-sharing in Group Litigation: Preserving Access to Justice' (2002) 65 MLR 597. See also *Nash v Eli Lilly & Co* [1991] 2 Med LR 169 (Opren); *AB v John Wyeth & Brother Ltd* [1994] 5 Med LR 149, CA (benzodiazepine). And see K Oliphant, 'Innovation in Procedure and Practice in Multi-Party Medical Cases' in A Grubb (ed), *Choices and Decisions in Health Care* (Wiley 1993); Legal Aid Board, *Issues arising for the Legal Aid Board and the Lord Chancellor's Department from Multi-Party Actions* (LAB 1994).

[401] Civil Procedure Rules, r 19.6.

[402] Contrast *Markt & Co Ltd v Knight Steamship Co Ltd* [1910] 2 KB 1021, 1040 (CA): 'absolutely inapplicable' *per* Fletcher Moulton LJ, with *Prudential Assurance Co Ltd v Newman Industries Ltd* [1979] 3 All ER 507 and *Irish Shipping Ltd v Commercial Union Assurance Co plc* [1991] 2 QB 206 (CA).

[403] See, eg, *Davies v Eli Lilly & Co* [1987] 1 WLR 1136, 1139 (CA) *per* Lord Donaldson MR. Contrast the position in the US and certain Commonwealth jurisdictions which provide for numerous claimants with related claims against the same defendant to have them disposed of in a single action. See further Mildred and Pannone, 'Liability in Tort: Class Actions', n 354.

[404] *Davies v Eli Lilly & Co* [1987] 1 WLR 1136 (CA). In the thalidomide claims, individual proceedings had been issued in every case.

[405] See generally Mildred, 'Group Actions', in Howells (ed), *The Law of Product Liability*, n 369, ch 8.

[406] As distinct from the 'same interest' required in a representative action.

[407] A Prynne, A, 'The Rise and Fall of Group Actions: A front-line view' (2008) 152 SJ 9, 22 July. And see R Mulheron, 'Reform of Collective Redress in England and Wales: A Perspective of Need' (Civil Justice Council, 2008) <https://www.judiciary.gov.uk/related-offices-and-bodies/advisory-bodies/cjc/collective-action-reform >.

Improving Access to Justice through Collective Actions supported to the introduction of a generic collective action, and that collective claims could be brought on an opt-in or opt-out basis, subject to certification of the process by the court. It conceded that with mass tort claims, which are factually complex and raise differing issues of causation, it might be better to proceed either a number of discrete opt-in actions or to proceed as an opt-out action on common issues, with decertification to follow.[408] However, the Ministry of Justice rejected the introduction of a generic right of action, preferring a sector based approach to the introduction of collective rights, and concluded that the distinction between opt-in and opt-out was not as clear cut as was suggested by the CJC.[409] The European Commission its Green Paper on Consumer Collective Redress highlighted the weaknesses of the existing redress and enforcement framework in the EU, concluding that 'a significant proportion of consumers who have suffered damage do not obtain redress'.[410] In the absence of collective compensatory relief instruments at EU level, and in order to increase policy coherence,[411] the Commission introduced a Recommendation for Collective Redress, which sets out common principles be applied by Member States in their respective national collective redress systems.[412] Member States have been asked to implement the principles by 26 July 2017,[413] but the Recommendation is not binding and it remains to be determined as to whether changes to existing national laws will indeed take place.

F. Compensation for Injured Research Subjects

Ex gratia compensation for research subjects injured in clinical trials has been examined elsewhere.[414] Here we note the potential entitlement to damages, whether for breach of contract, negligence, or under the CPA. Liability in contract could, in principle, arise under terms agreed between voluntary participants in a trial and the manufacturer and/or contract house responsible for conducting it. Equally, there could be liability in negligence for injury due to lack of reasonable care in conducting a trial, or failure to choose a suitably equipped company to conduct it. However, there is a dearth of relevant English authority on the matter, partly due to ex gratia provision and out-of-court settlements, but also because such research requires prior approval by the MHRA and an ethics committee. Without clear evidence of non-compliance with standard codes of practice, it would be difficult to establish negligence. That said, in the light of modern appellate decisions stressing **18.84**

---

[408] M Black, I G Gubbay, A Kinley, R Musgrove, and J Sorabji, *Improving Access to Justice through Collective Actions: Developing a More Efficient and Effective Procedure for Collective Actions* (Civil Justice Council 2008) 21 (Recommendation, 1, 3) and 145–50.

[409] Ministry of Justice, *The Government's Response to the Civil Justice Council's Report; 'Improving Access to Justice through Collective Actions'* (Ministry of Justice 2009), Responses to Recommendations, paras 9–12, 27–35. Note that the Consumer Rights Act 2015, Sch 7, introduces opt-out collective actions for cases of anti-competitive behaviour brought before the Competition Appeals Tribunal (CAT).

[410] See Commission Green Paper on Collective Redress COM (2008) 794 final, 27.11.2008, para 15.

[411] European Commission, *Communication: Towards a European Horizontal Framework for Collective Redress* COM (2013) 401, 1.3.

[412] European Commission, *Recommendation on Common Principles for Injunctive and Compensatory Collective Redress Mechanisms in the Member States Concerning Violations of Rights Granted under Union Law* 2013/396/EU, (OJ L201/60), 26.7.2013; European Commission, *Communication: Towards a European Horizontal Framework for Collective Redress* COM (2013) 401.

[413] European Commission, *Recommendation on Common Principles for Injunctive and Compensatory Collective Redress Mechanisms in the Member States Concerning Violations of Rights Granted under Union Law* 2013/396/EU, (OJ L201/60), 26.7.2013, Recital 24.

[414] See Chapter 13. See, eg, Brazier and Cave, *Medicine, Patients and the Law*, n 217, ch 16.

the importance of patient autonomy and patient-centred treatment,[415] courts should now be more receptive to claims by healthy volunteers that there has been inadequate disclosure of the risks of an experimental drug.[416] As for the applicability of the CPA, the DTI, as indicated above,[417] appeared to withdraw from its initial view that injury caused by 'medicinal materials used in pre-trial marketing' would not generally ground a claim. However, it would, in any event, usually be difficult to show that a product still under research was 'defective', within the meaning of the Act, given the correspondingly reduced expectations as to its level of safety.[418] Even if defectiveness were established, the manufacturer might well be able to rely on the development risk defence.[419] There remains a cogent moral case for healthy volunteers, in particular, and participating patients, having an enforceable legal right to no-fault compensation.[420]

G. Concluding Remarks

18.85 In the pharmaceutical sphere, there have been few advances in consumer protection under the Directive, and the European Commission's somewhat anodyne reviews on its application[421] have held out little prospect of significant development. In its most recent report, in 2011,[422] apart from stating that it would continue monitoring *'any development likely to affect the balance'* between consumer protection and producers' interests,[423] the Commission broadly endorsed the status quo. The Report noted an increase in both the absolute number of cases brought on grounds of product liability and an increase in the relative use of the Directive against cases brought on the traditional grounds of civil or contractual liability.[424] The Commission considered a series of classic issues, including the issue of the burden of proof and noting consumers emphasis on the difficulty in establishing a causal link between the defect and damage when damage is complex in nature.[425] The report commented on implied reiteration of support for a regulatory compliance defence from representatives of the pharmaceutical industry in Europe, who opined that the Directive 'does not sufficiently take into consideration that the medical products sector is very strictly regulated'.[426] As well

---

[415] *Montgomery v Lanarkshire Health Board* [2015] UKSC 11, [2015] AC 1430, [87]; *Chester v Afshar* [2005] 1 AC 134, 143–44 *per* Lord Steyn.

[416] cf *Halushka v University of Saskatchewan* [1965] 53 DLR (2d) 436, 443 *per* Hall JA, where the defendant was held liable in battery. See also Jones, *Medical Negligence*, n 141, para 3-060.

[417] See para 18.57 and n 275.

[418] CPA ss 3(1) and 3(2).

[419] For a recent case study that considers how negligence or strict liability might apply in the clinical research context, see P Ferguson, 'Clinical Trials and Healthy Volunteers' (2008) 16 Medical Law Review 23 (TGN1412, Phase 1 clinical trial).

[420] See, eg, Brazier and Cave, n 217, 431–33, para 16.15; cf Royal Commission on Civil Liability and Compensation for Personal Injury ('Pearson Commission') (1978) Cmnd 7054, paras 1340–41.

[421] Described as 'flimsy and lacking in conviction' by D Fairgrieve and G Howells, in 'Rethinking Product Liability: A Missing Element in the European Commission's Third Review of the European Product Liability Directive' (2007) 70 MLR 962, 978.

[422] European Commission, *Fourth Report on the application of Council Directive 85/374/EEC on the approximation of laws, regulations and administrative provisions of the Member States concerning liability for defective products* (COM (2011) 547).

[423] ibid, 11.

[424] ibid, 4.

[425] ibid, 7–8. See further D Fairgrieve, G Howells, and M Pilgerstorfer, 'The Product Liability Directive: Time to Get Soft' (2013) Journal of European Tort Law 1.

[426] European Commission, *Fourth Report on the application of Council Directive 85/374/EEC*, n 422, 8. The Fourth Report betrays a misunderstanding of Article 7(d) of the Directive, which provides a defence on proving 'that the defect is due to compliance of the product with mandatory regulations issued by the

as highlighting a divergence in how national courts apply the defence to different types of defect,[427] the Commission reiterated the doubt expressed in its Third Report as to the way the development risk defence should be interpreted.[428] It noted criticism from representatives of pharmaceutical companies of the French case law, holding that the defence should not be invoked for identical products put into circulation between 1988 and 1998 (the date of the transposition legislation), the representatives reasoning that the ground for invocation of the defence cannot be contingent on the date of the putting into circulation of products that are identical.[429]

Whether the Directive 'offers a real possibility of filing a claim for appropriate remedy and compensation for damage caused by a defective product'[430] is contestable, and its ability to do so may vary according to the nature of the product under consideration. It bears repeating that, in England, none of the many claims for drug-induced injury has culminated in a damages award against a pharmaceutical company. Article 13 of the Directive permits the retention by Member States of applicable pre-existing laws,[431] including special liability systems for specific types of products. In this connection, it is of interest that Germany's pre-existing statutory no-fault regime for pharmaceuticals has survived the introduction of the Directive, with the consequence that the regime can be further developed.[432] Sweden and Finland have voluntary insurance schemes for them; Norway has a statutory scheme, and Spain opted to exclude medical products from the development risks defence.[433] It is evident that the kind of issues raised in the Seroxat litigation are far from unique. Today, as in the past, such cases commonly entail prolonged controversy over pre-licensing studies and adverse reactions after clinical use, as well as allegations of concealed data and over-promotion. Aside from the occasional settlement, they ultimately founder, often over proof of defect or causation or simply for lack of adequate funding, compounded in multi-party actions by procedural and organizational problems.[434] Now 18.86

public authorities' (see para 18.66, n 331), by classifying Art 7(d) in a heading as a 'defence of regulatory compliance': ibid. The Fourth Report also noted the pharmaceutical industry's view that the fact that use of a medicinal product is generally subject to external examination by health professionals (including doctors, nurses, or pharmacists) and that the producer does not have any control over the way in which medicines are prescribed or administered, 'should be taken into account when analysing the defect of the product and the producer's liability': ibid. While these comments may relate to the question of whether the learned intermediary rule is applicable under the Directive, they seem to bear little relation to the question of a regulatory compliance defence: R Goldberg, Medicinal Product Liability and Regulation (Hart Publishing 2013) 159.

[427] Noting in particular how the German Bundesgerichtshof has ruled that the defence can never apply in cases of manufacturing defect: German Bottle case BGHZ 129.

[428] European Commission, *Fourth Report on the application of Council Directive 85/374/EEC*, n 422, 8–9. This uncertainty had been previously noted in the Third Report: *Third Commission Report of 31 January 2001 on the Application of Directive 85/374 on liability for defective products* (COM (2006) 496 final) 10–12.

[429] *Fourth Commission Report of 8 September 2011 on the Application of Directive 85/374*, n 428, 8–9. However, this appears inconsistent with European law which suggests that in the context of optional features of a Directive (in this case Art 15(1)(b) of Directive 85/374), the Community law principle of harmonious interpretation is inapplicable: Case 14/83 *Von Colson and Kamann v Land Nordrhein-Westfalen* [1984] ECR 1891, para 26 and Case C-106/89 *Marleasing SA v La Comercial Internacional de Alimentacion SA* [1990] ECR I-4135, para 8. See further Miller and Goldberg, n 59, paras 7.33–7.36.

[430] *Fourth Commission Report of 8 September 2011 on the Application of Directive 85/374*, n 428, 11.

[431] cf CPA, s 2(6).

[432] *Novo Nordisk Pharma GmbH v S* ECLI:EU:C:2014:2385, [24], [29] (CJEU) (amended German national legislation of liability for pharmaceutical products Arzneimittelgesetz (AMG) under which the consumer had the right to require the manufacturer to provide information on the adverse effects of a medicinal product fell outside the scope of the Directive).

[433] Howells (ed), *The Law of Product Liability*, n 369, 4.282.

[434] See para 18.80.

that personal injury claims against pharmaceutical companies will no longer be eligible for legal aid in England and Wales, and in the light of the costs involved in such litigation, and the fact that not one claim has resulted in damages being awarded by a court against a pharmaceutical company, it seems unlikely that solicitors will be keen to enter into 'no win, no fee' arrangements in the near future, unless the probability of success in the particular case is high.[435] Nonetheless, a case against GlaxoSmithKline is being brought on a 'no win, no fee' basis in respect of claims for compensation for death or harm in the form of heart failure and heart attacks allegedly caused by the diabetes drug Avandia.[436] It is arguable that, in the light of such difficulties, medicinal products should be viewed as a special case in the UK.[437] However, apart from the scope for divergence in the Directive itself, Member States may not introduce new laws to increase the level of consumer protection,[438] if, as the ECJ case law indicates, the Directive's objective is economic and requires maximal harmonization.[439]

H. ConclusionConclusion

18.87 In the sphere of medical products liability, especially for drug-induced injury, contract has only a limited role, and the acknowledged shortcomings of negligence as a remedial mechanism prompted calls for reform. The additional regime under the Directive has produced few visible signs of major change. This should occasion little surprise, since neither the Directive nor the CPA depart radically from the position at common law on harm caused by producers. There is still a dearth of fully litigated claims, and no hard data is available on the incidence of settlements. Procedural reform would still, in principle, be possible, and there has been a recent upsurge of interest in collective redress, with the Commission's Recommendation setting out common principles be applied by Member States in their respective national collective redress systems.[440] However, given the prevailing economic climate, and the relative lack of institutional pressure for change, substantially enhanced consumer protection through stricter liability seems improbable in the near future.

[435] R Goldberg, *Medicinal Product Liability and Regulation* (Hart Publishing 2013) 9; E Jackson, *Law and the Regulation of Medicines* (Hart Publishing 2012) 119; see further R Goldberg, 'Medical Malpractice and Compensation in the UK' (2012) 87 Chicago-Kent Law Review 101, 130–31. The President of the Law Society of England and Wales has claimed that withdrawal of legal aid funding in England and Wales will 'leave pharmaceutical companies beyond the reach of the law': 'Legal aid cuts "deprive drug claimants of day in court"' *BBC News* (18 January 2011) <http://www.bbc.co.uk/news/health-12212234>.

[436] S Boseley, 'Families Battle with GSK Over Danger Drug' *The Guardian* (30 January 2013) 1.

[437] See generally R Goldberg, *Medicinal Product Liability and Regulation* (Hart Publishing 2013).

[438] Except in respect of their own domestic producers.

[439] Case C-402/03 *Skov AEG v Billa Lavprisvarehus* [2006] ECR 1-199; Case C-154/00 *Commission v Greece* [2002] ECR 1-3879, para 20; Case C-183/00 *Gonzales Sanchez v Medicinia Asturiana SA* [2002] ECR 1-3901, para 24. See further Miller and Goldberg, *Product Liability*, n 2, paras 7.25–7.32; Stapleton, *Product Liability*, n 9, 60–65, and S Whittaker, 'The EEC Directive on Product Liability' (1985) 5 Yearbook of European Law 233, 238. However, this does not preclude the existence of parallel liability regimes in respect of damage which is not covered by the Directive: Case C-285/08, *Moteurs Leroy Somer v Dalkia France and Ace Europe* [2009] ECR I-4733, [30]–[32] (parallel system of liability which compensates damage to an item of property intended for professional use and employed for that purpose); Case C-495/10, *Centre hospitalier universitaire de Besançon v Dutreux* [2012] 2 CMLR 1, [32], [39] (parallel system of strict liability of service provider (hospital) using defective product (heated mattress with defective temperature control system), of which it is not a producer).

[440] See above, n 412; and further, eg, D Fairgrieve and G Howells, 'Collective Redress Procedures—European Debates' (2009) ICLQ 379, esp 394–99, and Mulheron, 'Reform of Collective Redress in England and Wales: A Perspective of Need', n 407.

PART VI

19

THE LEGAL REGULATION OF HUMAN MATERIAL

Jean V McHale

A. Introduction

English law concerning the regulation of the use of human material has developed over time in what has been largely an ad hoc fashion, driven by a perceptible desire to regulate due to concerns regarding new scientific developments or driven by specific scandals.[1] The involvement of English law in the use of human bodies for scientific purposes has a long history.[2] In 1540 the College of Barbers and Surgeons was granted bodies of four convicted felons a year. The availability of corpses, however, did not equate with the demand. The shortage of corpses resulted in attempts to obtain bodies by whatever means, leading to body snatchers or 'resurrectionists' grave robbing and, in some instances, committing murder. There was, moreover, considerable outrage at the time at the mutilation of the bodies of criminals. Rioting at the gallows resulted as relatives attempted to stop the bodies of their loved ones being used in this manner. A number of incidents led finally to legislation. In March 1828 an anatomist was prosecuted at the Lancaster Assizes for the unlawful possession of a dead body. Meanwhile, Burke and Hare in Edinburgh were prosecuted for murder. It was, however, as Richardson notes, not until a further prosecution in London in which it was claimed **19.01**

[1] For background see: M Brazier and E Cave, *Medicine, Patients and the Law* (Manchester University Press 2016) chs 17 and 18; E Jackson, *Medical Law Text Cases and Materials* (4th edn, Oxford University Press 2016) ch 11; J Herring, *Medical Law and Ethics* (6th edn, Oxford University Press 2016) ch 8; G Laurie, S E Harmon, and G Porter, *Law and Medical Ethics* (10th edn, Oxford University Press 2016) chs 14 and 17; S Pattinson, *Medical Law and Ethics* (4th edn, Sweet & Maxwell 2014) chs 12 and 13.

[2] See R Richardson, 'Fearful Symmetry: Corpses for Anatomy, Organs for Transplantation?' in S J Youngner, R C Fox, and L J O'Connell (eds), *Organ Transplantation: Meanings and Realities* (University of Wisconsin Press 1996); R Richardson, *Death, Dissection and the Destitute* (2nd edn, University of Chicago Press 2001).

that some sixty people had been murdered that legislation was passed in the form of the Anatomy Act 1832 which sanctioned use of bodies of those persons who had died without relatives or with insufficient money to pay for their own funeral.[3] The next significant recent step in terms of formal legal regulation of the use of human material came in the form of the Human Tissue Act 1961, itself following from the scientific developments leading to the first organ transplantation. This legislation governed the use of organs removed from cadavers. It enabled people to choose to donate material before their death through a declaration in writing or orally in the presence of two witnesses[4] or enabled the person 'lawfully in possession' of the body to authorize removal after their death where such enquiries had been made as were reasonably practicable of spouse and surviving relatives.[5] Over time the 1961 Act became the subject of criticism. Difficulties identified with the legislation included the nature and extent of inquiries to be made, what constituted such enquiries as were 'reasonably practicable'. Secondly, the Act was outdated in that while enquiries were to be made of the spouse and surviving relatives it did not cover persons who were in long-term non-marital relationships.[6]

19.02 In more recent times it was another scandal, the Crocket case—albeit less dramatic than that of Burke and Hare—which led to the partial regulation of live organ transplantation.[7] Poor Turkish organ donors were brought over to the UK and were paid to donate organs for transplantation. The doctors who were involved in this practice including Crocket were subject to GMC disciplinary proceedings. The controversy over the case led to the government passing the Human Organs Transplant Act 1989. The 1989 Act introduced a blanket ban on commercial dealing in organs. It criminalized commercial dealing and the advertising of commercial dealing.

19.03 In contrast to the legal regulation of the use of reproductive material which, following the Warnock Report,[8] was placed on a statutory basis, the applicable law in relation to the use of other human material, whether from live donors or cadavers had developed over time with, until very recently, no attempt having been made to undertake a single coherent overview of the regulation in this area. As we shall see in this chapter, the law was instead a disparate series of principles derived from common law and statute. It was also characterized by its low visibility and also considerable uncertainty regarding its application.

19.04 The current law which regulates this area, the Human Tissue Act 2004, was also framed through a scandal. This time the controversy centred on the unauthorized retention of human material. The reform culminating in the Human Tissue Act 2004 followed revelations that there were vast stores of human material at Alder Hey hospital, Bristol Royal Infirmary, and a large number of hospitals around the UK which had been retained without the knowledge of the persons from whom they had been taken or their relatives. The revelations were triggered by the discovery of the unconsented retention of human organs at one hospital in Bristol but this then snowballed as revelation followed revelation in a series

[3] See Richardson in Youngner et al, n 2. The Royal College of Surgeons museum apparently contains specimens from the time of John Hunter in the eighteenth century and has been commented 'without these the teaching of pathology would have been considerably hampered'. See J L Brennan, *Medico-Legal Problems in Hospital Practice* (Ravenswood Publications 1980) 52.

[4] Human Tissue Act 1961, s 1(1).

[5] ibid, s 1(2).

[6] See further PDK Skegg, 'Human Tissue Act 1961' (1976) 16 Medicine, Science and Law 197; G Dworkin, 'The Law Relating to Organ Transplantation in England' (1970) 30 Modern Law Review 353.

[7] See D Brahams, 'Kidneys for Sale by Living Donors' (1989) Lancet 285, and 'Kidneys for Sale' (1989) New LJ 159.

[8] Report of the Committee of Inquiry into Human Fertilisation and Embryology (Cmnd 9314, 1984).

of major inquiries. The controversy led to investigations by Professor Ian Kennedy in his Interim Bristol Inquiry Report and by Michael Redfern QC in the Alder Hey Inquiry.[9] A census undertaken by the Chief Medical Officer, Professor Liam Donaldson, revealed the full extent of the retention of human material.[10] It found that there were over 105,000 body parts, stillbirths, and foetuses stored in English hospitals and medical schools. The census revealed that around 88 per cent of the collections were in 25 NHS Trusts and medical schools. Nearly half were brains and one-sixth were eyes. In Alder Hey itself some 2,128 hearts were stored at the Institute of Child Health, and 1,564 still births or foetuses were stored which had been collected pre-1973. There were also a further 445 at the foetal collection in Myrtle Street. Other body parts included 147 brains, and in the words of Michael Redfern QC 'perhaps the most disturbing specimen is the head of an 11-year-old boy'.[11] Considerable criticism was levelled at the way in which material had been retained and, in particular, over the lack of information given to parents regarding the extent of the retention and use of human material. The Bristol and Alder Hey Inquiries led to the establishment of the Retained Organs Commission which placed a moratorium upon the handing back of organs until the full scale of the retention had been realized.[12] The retention of human material also led to inquiries in Scotland[13] and Northern Ireland.[14] But the controversy over retention did not end there. Further inquiries followed into organ retention by Manchester hospitals[15] and in 2003 Her Majesty's Inspector of Anatomy published a report revealing the extensive non-consensual retention of brains.[16] The government in summer 2002 issued a consultation document 'Human Bodies: Human Choices' reviewing the legal regulation of human organs and tissue.[17] This was followed by the publication of the Human Tissue Bill 2003. This Bill was subject to considerable criticism during its passage through Parliament from some in the scientific community. It was argued that the provisions were unduly restrictive and could harm research.[18] A number of notable amendments were made to the Bill as a consequence, which will be discussed below. The Human Tissue Act 2004 now represents the most comprehensive regulatory framework of human material to date. However, the legislation does not cover all the law in the area. Alongside the statutory principles set out in the 2004 Act there remains a complex series of common

[9] *Report of the Inquiry into the Royal Liverpool Children's Hospital* (Alder Hey) (30 January 2001) <https://www.gov.uk/government/publications/the-royal-liverpool-childrens-inquiry-report>. Bristol Inquiry Interim Report *Removal and Retention of Human Material* (2000) and the Final Report at <http://webarchive.nationalarchives.gov.uk/+/www.dh.gov.uk/en/Publicationsandstatistics/Publications/PublicationsPolicyAndGuidance/DH_4005620 >.

[10] *The Investigation into Retained Organs, Chief Medical Officer's Report on Organ Retention* (Department of Health, Social Services and Public Safety 2001).

[11] ibid, para 20.5.

[12] The Retained Organs Commission, *Remembering the Past, Looking to the Future: The Final Report of the Retained Organs Commission Including the Summary Accountability Report for 2003/4*, March 2004. See also J V McHale, 'Exploring the legacy of the Retained Organs Commission a decade on: Lessons learned and the dangers of lessons lost' in C Stanton et al (eds), *Pioneering Healthcare Law: Essays in Honour of Margaret Brazier* (Routledge 2015).

[13] Scottish Executive, *Final Report of the Independent Review on the Retention of Organs at Post Mortem* (Scottish Executive 2002).

[14] *Report of the Human Organ Inquiry* (2002). Organ retention has also provoked controversy in other jurisdictions: see, eg, G D Jones, *Speaking for the Dead* (Ashgate 2000) regarding the New Zealand position.

[15] Retained Organs Commission, *Organ Retention at Central Manchester and Manchester Children's University Hospitals Trust* (July 2002).

[16] *The Investigation of the Events that followed the Death of Cyril Mark Issacs* (TSO 2003).

[17] See generally the discussion in D Price, 'From Cosmos and Damien to Van Velzen: The Human Tissue Saga Continues' (2003) 11 Med L Rev 1.

[18] S Pinnock, 'Human Tissue Bill Could Jeopardise Research, Scientists Warn' (2004) 328 BMJ 1034; and see K Liddell and A Hall, 'Beyond Bristol and Alder Hey: The Future Regulation of Human Tissue' (2005) 13 Med L Rev 170, 172–73.

law principles concerning property in the human body. The current regulatory position can also be seen as problematic, in that there is no interrelationship between the legal principles concerning confidentiality and privacy and those concerning the use of human material, which can have practical problems in the research context, not least in relation to the operation of human genetic databases.[19] It should be noted that separate legislation operates in Scotland in the form of the Human Tissue (Scotland) Act 2006 and also in Wales through the introduction of a new 'opt-out scheme' in the Human Transplatation (Wales) Act 2013 (see discussion at para 19.57)

19.05 This chapter considers how the Human Tissue Act regulates the use of human material in general. Secondly, it examines the specific legal issues relating to organ and tissue transplantation. Thirdly, it also considers the operation of the common law provisions concerning property in human material which lie outside the legislation.

B. Regulating the Use of Human Material

1. The Human Tissue Authority

19.06 The Human Tissue Act 2004 provided for the establishment of a new regulatory body for human material, the Human Tissue Authority.[20] The new Human Tissue Authority came into operation in 2006. Originally the government had intended that the Human Tissue Authority should be a relatively short-lived body as it intended to combine this body with the Human Fertilisation and Embryology Authority, to establish a new overarching regulatory authority—the Regulatory Authority for Tissue and Embryology (RATE).[21] This option, while initially abandoned, was revisited by the Conservative-Liberal Democrat Coalition in 2010 as part of their review of arm's length bodies.[22] However, after considerable opposition being expressed to the changes and a further review undertaken it was decided ultimately not to take this forward.[23]

19.07 The regulatory functions of the Human Tissue Authority exclude blood, which in this part of the Act was excluded from the category of 'relevant material'. The Human Tissue Authority must inform the public and the Secretary of State in relation to matters which fall within its remit.[24] Section 15(a) provides it must produce a statement of general principles regarding activities within its remit. It is to provide guidance and oversight. It also has the task of overseeing requirements imposed under the legislation and the Codes of Practice, providing to the public, and to persons carrying on activities within its remit, such information and advice as it considers appropriate about the nature and purpose of such activities. The similarities with the regulatory body for reproductive technology and embryology—the Human Fertilisation and Embryology Authority (HFEA) here are obvious. As with the

[19] See, eg, the discussion in J V McHale, 'Regulating Genetic Databases: Some Legal and Ethical Issues' (2004) 12(1) Med L Rev 70.

[20] Human Tissue Act 2004, s 13 and Sch 2.

[21] Department of Health, *Reconfiguring the Department of Health's Arm's-length Bodies* (DoH 2004).

[22] Department of Health, *Report of the Arm's-length Bodies Review Gateway reference 14482* (DoH 2010). See also 'Tissue Watchdog Crisis: Leading Academics Voice Concern over Future of HTA' *Sunday Times* (20th February 2011) <http://www.hta.gov.uk/newsandevents/htanews.cfm/970-Sunday-Times-letter.html>.

[23] The Cracken Review, *Review of the Human Fertilisation and Embryology Authority and Human Tissue Authority* (DoH 2013) <https://www.gov.uk/government/publications/review-of-human-fertilisation-embryology-authority-and-human-tissue-authority>.

[24] Human Tissue Act 2004, s 15.

HFEA, the Act includes a licensing structure.[25] This is also mandated today through the enactment into national law of the EU Tissue and Cells Directive.[26] The Human Tissue Authority (HTA) is also the 'competent authority' for the UK in relation to implementation of the EU Directive 2010/53/EU on the standards of quality and safety of human organs intended for transplantation. The Directive has been implemented into UK law under the Quality and Safety of Organs Intended for Transplantation Regulations 2012.[27] The HTA has broad licensing powers concerning anatomical examinations,[28] post-mortems,[29] other removal of material from deceased persons during anatomical examinations and post-mortems other than for transplantation,[30] storage of anatomical specimens,[31] storage of bodies or material from bodies for scheduled purposes,[32] and the use of bodies or material from bodies for public display.[33] Its licensing powers extend to cover such holdings as cord blood and stem cells.[34] Individuals must be licensed to undertake this work.[35] They have responsibility to ensure that persons who are working under the licence are suitable to undertake the work and that the conditions of the licence are complied with.[36] In some limited situations, the HTA may allow activities to be undertaken without a licence under the Human Tissue (Quality and Safety for Human Application) Regulations 2007.[37] This relates to procurement, testing, processing, import, and export. It applies where these will be undertaken for less than forty-eight hours, where the body is acting on behalf of a licensed establishment, and where it has a third party agreement under the Human Tissue Authority Directions 002/2007 with the established licensee.[38] Initially licences were given on a three-year basis, but the HTA subsequently moved towards awarding licences on a continuous basis with fixed-term licences intended for exceptional situations.[39] Examples given are temporary mortuaries or exhibitions. The HTA has issued position statements on specific areas such as cord blood and stem cells.[40]

The statute provides that various activities including anatomical examinations, definition **19.08**
of death, and post-mortems are to be the subject of Codes of Practice drawn up by the Authority.[41] The existing Codes were published in 2014; however, when this book was going

---

[25] ibid, ss 16–25.

[26] Directive (EC) 2004/23 and see also the Human Tissue (Quality and Safety for Human Application) Regulations 2007, SI 2007/1523.

[27] SI 2012 1501.

[28] Human Tissue Act 2004, s16(2)(a).

[29] ibid, s 16(2)(b).

[30] ibid, s 16(2)(c).

[31] ibid, s 16(2)(d).

[32] ibid, s 16(2)(e).

[33] ibid, s 16(f).

[34] See further <http://www.hta.gov.uk/licensingandinspections/sectorspecificinformation/stemcellsandcordblood.cfm?>.

[35] Human Tissue Act 2004, s 17.

[36] ibid, s 18.

[37] SI 2007/1523.

[38] *Directions given under the Human Tissue Act 2004 implementing the Human Tissue Quality and Safety for Human Application) Regulations 2007* Ref 002/2007.

[39] See further <http://www.hta.gov.uk/licensingandinspections/continuouslicensingsystem.cfm>.

[40] *Human Tissue Authority Position Statement on Regulating Human Embryonic Stem Cell Lines*, originally issued 3 May 2007, updated May 2008, <http://www.hta.gov.uk/licensingandinspections/sectorspecificinformation/humanapplication/positionstatementonregulatinghumanembryonicstemcelllinesforhumanapplication.cfm>; *Human Tissue Authority Position Statement on Cord Blood Collection, March 2010*, <http://www.hta.gov.uk/legislationpoliciesandcodesofpractice/positionstatementoncordbloodcollection.cfm>.

[41] Human Tissue Act 2004, s 26. Human Tissue Authority, *Code of Practice 3 Post Mortems* (Human Tissue Authority, July 2014: Human Tissue Authority *Code of Practice 4: Anatomical Examinations*, (Human Tissue Authority) July 2014.

to press the Human Tissue Authority announced it was undertaking a consultation in relation to the production of revised streamlined codes. It is envisaged that new Codes of Practice will be produced and come into force during 2017. The Act specifically requires that the Authority produces a Code concerning the procedures in relation to consent, where this relates to consent by persons in a 'qualifying relationship'—discussed at para 19.26.[42] It should be noted, that Codes are guidance documents. There is no direct penalty attached to failure to follow the Codes,[43] however, should they be departed from this is something which may impact, for example, on subsequent licensing decisions made by the Authority.

2. Scope of the Human Tissue Act

(i) Relevant material

19.09 The legislation applies to 'relevant material'. This is defined in s 53 of the Act as being 'material other than gametes which consists of or includes human cells'. It excludes hair and nails from living persons, gametes, and embryos—which are separately regulated by the Human Fertilisation and Embryology Act 1990, as amended.[44] Pattinson has questioned the exclusion of hair and nails while other material such as saliva and urine which are 'routinely discarded' do come within the legislation.[45] It has been noted that hair may be valuable and, for example, contain cells which produce keratin.[46] The Act explicitly excludes material created outside the human body. This includes cell lines.[47] The Act includes blood (though it excludes acellular serum and plasma, sputum, lung washouts, and urine). Tissue blocks and slides are also included.[48]

(ii) Appropriate consent

19.10 The legislation provides that use of human material must be subject to 'appropriate consent'.[49] It should be noted that the word 'consent' is used rather than words such as 'gift' or 'donation'. Schedule 1 sets out those purposes for which consent is required. They are listed as being:

PURPOSES REQUIRING CONSENT: GENERAL

1. Anatomical examination.
2. Determining the cause of death.
3. Establishing after a person's death the efficacy of any drug or other treatment administered to him.
4. Obtaining scientific or medical information about a living or deceased person which may be relevant to any other person (including a future person).
5. Public display.
6. Research in connection with disorders, or the functioning, of the human body.
7. Transplantation.

PURPOSES REQUIRING CONSENT: DECEASED PERSONS

8. Clinical audit.

---

[42] Human Tissue Act 2004, s 27.
[43] ibid, s 28.
[44] ibid, s 53(2).
[45] S Pattinson, *Medical Law and Ethics* (4th edn, Sweet & Maxwell 2014) 421.
[46] See D Price, 'The Human Tissue Act 2004' (2005) 68 Modern Law Review 798, 800.
[47] Human Tissue Act 2004, s 54(7).
[48] These have been excluded from regulation under the Human Tissue (Scotland) Act 2006, following the recommendations made in the *Final Report of the Independent Review Group on Retention of Organs at Postmortem* 2000 in Scotland. See discussion in D Price, *Human Tissue in Transplantation and Research* (Cambridge University Press 2009), 38–40.
[49] Human Tissue Act 2004, Sch 1(1).

9. Education or training relating to human health.
10. Performance assessment.
11. Public health monitoring.
12. Quality assurance.

While the Act sets out a series of situations in which consent will itself be required it does not define what constitutes 'appropriate consent'. The specifics of the consent process are something which is left to the Codes of Practice produced by the Human Tissue Authority and to clinicians and researchers. **19.11**

(iii) General and specific consent: Particular problems for regulation of research

One major practical issue facing those persons collecting and storing material for research use is how general or how specific the consent obtained from the research participant should be and indeed can be.[50] Where it is intended that consent is for a single use in one project, then the consent process may be relatively straightforward. However, there are some situations in which researchers may seek to retain and use material over what is a much longer time frame. Notable examples are the storage of material in genetic databases.[51] In such a situation is one-off consent sufficient or should researchers return to the individual to ask permission for subsequent use of the material? Opinions on this are divided.[52] It may be that individuals do not wish to be approached for subsequent consent. However, others could argue that general consent could undermine individual autonomy. Concerns relate to the diversity of possible uses of material where material is held over an extended period, for example, a twenty-year period in genetic databases. **19.12**

The Human Tissue Act 2004 does not state whether consent should be specific or generic consent, although it should be noted that in the debates on the legislation in the House of Lords, Lord Warner commented, on behalf of the government: **19.13**

> Let me state clearly that the Bill does not require consent to be specific to each research project for which tissue might be used. Consent can be broad. Consent to research can be generic and enduring.[53]

The Human Tissue Authority Code of Practice, *Code 1, Consent* states that: 'Consent may differ in its scope as it may be generic or specific.'[54] It then provides:

> 40. Generic consent typically only applies to research. If conducting research on samples of tissue, it is good practice to request generic consent because this avoids the need to obtain further consent in the future. It is still important however that the consent is valid (see the Code of Practice on Research for further guidance).[55]

The Human Tissue Authority Code of Practice on Research goes on to further provide that

> To facilitate the use of valuable human tissue in research, the HTA advises, in line with the MRC and HRA that consent should be generic because this avoids the need to obtain

[50] See further discussion in D Price, *Human Tissue in Transplantation and Research* (Cambridge University Press, 2009) 181–87; and see also N C Manson and O O'Neill, *Rethinking Informed Consent in Bioethics* (Cambridge University Press 2007) 10–12.

[51] See further discussion in J V McHale, 'Regulating Genetic Databases: Some Legal and Ethical Issues' (2004) 11 Med L Rev 70, and J Kaye, 'Abandoning Informed Consent: The Case of Genetic Research in Population Collections' in R Tutton and O Corrigan, *Genetic Databases: Socio-Ethical Issues in the Collection and Use of DNA* (Routledge 2004).

[52] See, eg, discussion in Human Genetics Commission, *Inside Information* (HGC 2002).

[53] HL Deb vol 664 col 370, 22 July 2004. See also Dr Ladyman, HC Standing Committee G col 51, 27 Jan 2004.

[54] *Human Tissue Authority Code 1 Consent* (Human Tissue Authority, July 2014) para 39.

[55] ibid, para 40.

> further consents. It is still important however that consent is valid. If the intention is to store the tissue for an as yet unknown research purpose or as part of a tissue bank for research then this should be explained, setting out the types of research that may be involved, any wider implications and the circumstances under which the tissue will be disposed of.[56]

This represents an important shift of emphasis from the previous Code of Practice on Consent of the Authority and is not uncontroversial.

19.14 It is uncertain to what extent a blanket generic consent policy could prove subject to subsequent Human Rights Act 1998 challenges. For example, litigants may attempt to use Article 8 of the European Convention on Human Rights to challenge this provision in the future. Article 8 safeguards the right to privacy of home and family life. It includes both respect for informational privacy and also for decision-making autonomy.[57] There is the possibility that an individual may claim that they have been given insufficient information to determine how their human material should be used when they consented and that this has consequently undermined their privacy rights.

19.15 It is particularly important if any potential uses of the human material are likely to be particularly sensitive or possibly controversial in some way, that the research participant is informed of such intended uses. One illustration is provided in the Human Tissue Act Code of Practice 1 'Consent' in relation to subsequent use of human material for commercial purposes, where it is stated that:

> Donors should be told if their samples will or could be used for research involving the commercial sector. They should be given appropriate information on the range of activities and researchers which may be involved, and whether these include commercial establishments. [58]

The HTA also advises that is good practice that donors are provided with adequate information upon giving consent, should their samples be exported for use abroad.[59]

19.16 A person may also have a particular religious or cultural dimension to the use of human material and thus to the consent process itself.[60] Respect for principles of faith and belief is inherent in Article 9 of the European Convention on Human Rights as safeguarded under the Human Rights Act 1998. In recognition of the sensitivities of such issues the Code of Practice states that:

> Attitudes towards the use of tissue, and especially towards post mortems, can vary widely among cultures and religions. All healthcare professionals must be sensitive to this. However, each case and decision is an individual and personal one, and must be treated as such. Trusts and other establishments should ensure that their employees are given the necessary training and support to help them identify and meet the widest possible range of needs and wishes.[61]

19.17 There is obviously a practical issue here and, of course, obtaining consent involves time for those involved in the research process. However, in drawing up research protocols and

---

56 Human Tissue Authority, *Code of Practice 9: Research* (Human Tissue Authority, July 2014) para 58.
57 See, eg, the discussion in *Pretty v UK* [2002] FLR 45.
58 Human Tissue Authority *Code of Practice 1, Consent* (Human Tissue Authority, July 2014) para 161.
59 ibid, para 161.
60 See further discussion in Medical Research Council, *Public Perception of the Use of Human Biological Samples* (MRC 2001).
61 *Human Tissue Authority Code of Practice 1, Consent* (Human Tissue Authority, July 2014) para 66.

information sheets, researchers and research ethics committees need to ensure that they are aware and responsive to possible religious and cultural objections.

(iv) Withdrawal of consent

Just as the requirement of consent can be seen as a means of maximizing autonomy, so also can the need of the individual to revoke their consent and withdraw their material from the research process. While this may appear obvious, the practical problems which may result from the withdrawal process may prove problematic for researchers in general and those operating genetic databases in particular. What precisely constitutes the withdrawal of consent? Some guidance on this issue is contained in the Human Tissue Act Code of Practice 1 on Consent. This states that: **19.18**

> Consent may be withdrawn at any time whether it is generic or specific. Withdrawal should be discussed at the outset when consent is being sought. The practicalities of withdrawing consent and the implications of doing so should be made clear, for example, for potential recipients if the donated tissue is for clinical use. Withdrawal of consent cannot be effective where tissue has already been used.[62]

If someone gives consent for their tissue to be stored or used for more than one scheduled purpose and then withdraws consent for a particular scheduled purpose (eg research) this does not necessarily mean that the sample or samples have to be removed or destroyed. However, the samples may no longer be stored or used for the particular purpose for which consent has been withdrawn. In addition, if someone withdraws consent for samples to be used in any future projects this does not mean that information and research data should be withdrawn from any existing projects.[63]

It is important for researchers to ensure that potential research participants are clear both in relation to the initial consent to the use of their material and also as to the prospects and extent of any subsequent withdrawal from the project at the start of the project, *before* the individual decides to become a research participant. Unless there is such clarity from the outset, there is a risk that controversy over withdrawal and the nature of the withdrawal process could inhibit research practices in the future. Furthermore, it can be argued that, regardless of this, applying Article 8 of the ECHR and drawing analogies with the ECHR approach to unauthorized retention of DNA samples in the context of criminal law investigations, an applicant could legitimately demand that the samples be destroyed.[64] **19.19**

(v) Storage and use of material without consent

Where human material from a live person is stored for purposes set out in Part II of Schedule 1 to the Human Tissue Act 2004, then 'appropriate consent' is not required. These purposes are where material is stored or is used for the purpose of clinical audit, education or training relating to human health, performance assessment, public health monitoring, or quality assurance. However, it should be noted that this does apply only to material from living persons. **19.20**

(vi) 'Deemed consent'

In a situation in which it is not reasonably possible to trace the person from whom the material is derived, the Human Tissue Authority may 'deem' consent.[65] This applies where: (i) the Authority is satisfied that the material is from the body of a living person;[66] (ii) it is in the **19.21**

62 ibid, para 43.
63 ibid, para 40.
64 *S & Marper v UK* [2008] ECHR1581.
65 Human Tissue Act 2004, s 7.
66 ibid, s 7(1)(a), (b).

interests of another person (this includes the interests of a future person) to obtain scientific or medical information about the individual;[67] (iii) there is no reason to believe either that the person has died,[68] that they have made a decision not to consent to the use of the material,[69] or that they lack capacity to consent to its use.[70] In addition consent may be deemed in a situation in which the material comes from a living person and that, as before, it is in the interests of the person to obtain scientific or medical information, there is no reason to believe that they have died, have refused consent, or lack capacity, and reasonable attempts have been made to get the person to decide what they wish to happen to their material, but they have not made a decision.[71]

(vii) Use of material under a High Court order

19.22 Section 7(4) of the Human Tissue Act 2004 provides that appropriate consent can be deemed by the High Court for 'research purposes in connection with disorders or the functioning of the human body' where the Secretary of State has enacted regulations to this effect. Such orders may apply in the context of both dead and living persons and also extend to removal and use of relevant material. It appears that it is intended that this provision should be used in what are exceptional circumstances.[72]

(viii) Use of anonymized material for research purposes

19.23 One area of considerable legal uncertainty prior to the Human Tissue Act 2004 was the extent to which 'spare' material left after surgical procedures etc could subsequently be used for research purposes.[73] During the passage of the Human Tissue Bill concerns were expressed that, should it be necessary to obtain consent for use of every spare piece of tissue, this could inhibit research practices. As a consequence, the Bill was amended at Committee stage. Sections 1(7), (8), and (9) of the Human Tissue Act 2004 now allow storage and use of relevant material which has come from a living body *without* consent where: it is ethically approved in accordance with regulations made by the Secretary of State and where research is to be carried out where 'the person carrying it out is not in possession and not likely to come into possession of information from which the person from whose body the material had come can be identified'.[74] The effect of the legislation is to enable use of non-identifiable material for research purposes without consent subject to relevant ethical safeguards. Regulations provide that such material may be used where approved by a research ethics committee.[75] It was thought that by anonymization the use of the material would be Human Rights Act compliant and not infringe the privacy rights of the individual, following the approach taken by the Court of Appeal in *Source Informatics* which held that the use of anonymized patient prescribing data without consent did not constitute an invasion of privacy.[76] However, some question marks surround the legitimacy of the decision in *Source Informatics*, and the validity of extrapolating from this judgment on the use of anonymized

67 ibid, s 7(1)(c).
68 ibid, s 7(1)(d)(i).
69 ibid, s 7(1)(d)(ii).
70 ibid, s 7(1)(d)(iii).
71 ibid, s 7(1)(2).
72 See D Price, 'The Human Tissue Act 2004' (2005) 68(5) MLR 798, 801.
73 See further, eg, Nuffield Council on Bioethics, *Human Tissue; Ethical and Legal Issues* (1995) and J McHale, 'Waste, Ownership and Bodily Products' (2000) 8 Health Care Analysis 123.
74 Human Tissue Act 2004, s 1(9).
75 Human Tissue (Ethical Approval, Exceptions from Licensing and Supply of Information about Transplants) Regulations 2006, SI 2006/1260.
76 *R v Department of Health, ex p Source Informatics* [2001] QB 424.

GP prescribing data to the use of human material (see Chapter 12).[77] One argument is that it is not in line with human rights principles if respect for privacy is considered to include not simply identity but also respect for autonomy and control of personal information. In addition, it is not envisaged that this material would be totally anonymous, simply that the prospect of identification would be reduced. Total anonymization would render the material of less use, as some basic information as to the individual from whom that material has been derived is frequently of great importance to researchers. In the Parliamentary debates on the Human Tissue Bill it was indicated that it was not intended that the material be totally unlinked.[78] The Human Tissue Authority does not envisage total anonymity. For example, Human Tissue Authority Code of Practice 9 on Research provides that:

> There may be occasions when a clinician involved in research may also have access to a secure database that would permit identification of a sample used in research and the identity of the patient whose material is being used. Providing the research material is not identifiable to the researcher (e.g. coded by a laboratory accession number) and the researcher does not seek to link the sample to the patient, it will still be regarded as non-identifiable and the research will be permissible without consent if approved by a recognised research ethics committee.[79]

A further issue is that research participants may be concerned not simply as to identity but also regarding control of the material itself.[80] A person may potentially object even to the use of material which is anonymized because they may argue that they are particularly opposed on ethical grounds—perhaps religious or cultural—to a particular form of research/type of use of human material itself, because the use violates their autonomy in the sense of their personal control rights regarding the use of the material.

(ix) Existing holdings

Concerns arose during the passage of the Human Tissue Bill regarding the legality of existing holdings of human material and their usage. It was suggested that the consent imperative could result in large databases containing valuable material for researchers collected over many years having to be destroyed. The government therefore included a provision to legitimate the use of such holdings. Section 9 of the Human Tissue Act 2004 provides that holdings of human material in existence prior to the Act coming into force on 1 September 2006 do not have to be subject to 'appropriate consent'.[81] **19.24**

(x) Who can consent to use of relevant material under the Human Tissue Act?

(a) Adults Appropriate consent must be given by an adult under s 3 of the Human Tissue Act 2004. In the case of a deceased adult consent in writing must be given for anatomical examination (save for excepted material) or storage for public display.[82] In order for consent in writing to be valid it must be signed in the presence of at least one witness, signed on their direction and in the presence of at least one witness, or contained in a valid will. Otherwise, although consent is necessary, this does not have to be given in writing. If a person has died without consent having been given, then a person who is in a qualifying relationship can be approached to give consent.[83] **19.25**

---

77 See D Beyleveld and E Histed, 'Betrayal of Confidence in the Court of Appeal' (2000) 4 Medical Law International 277.

78 *Hansard*.

79 Human Tissue Authority, *Code 9, Research* (Human Tissue Authority, July 2014) para 52.

80 See McHale, n 72.

81 See further discussion in D Price, *Human Tissue in Transplantation and Research* (Cambridge University Press 2009) 190–91.

82 Human Tissue Act 2004, s 3(4).

83 ibid, s 3(6)(c).

19.26 **(b) The person in a qualifying relationship** Who is included in this category is set out in s 27(4) of the legislation. Those included are listed in order of priority. Section 27(4) lists these as being:

(a) spouse or civil partner;
(b) parent or child;
(c) brother or sister;
(d) grandparent or grandchild;
(e) child of a person falling within paragraph (c);
(f) stepfather or stepmother;
(g) half-brother or half-sister;
(h) friend of long-standing.

19.27 Those seeking consent must first approach those who are higher up in the list.[84] Relatives are not, however, compelled to make a decision. Section 27(8) provides that:

> (8) In applying the principles set out above, a person's relationship shall be left out of account if—
>
> (a) he does not wish to deal with the issue of consent,
> (b) he is not able to deal with that issue.

In addition, the Act provides that the relationship can also be disregarded in a situation in which it is not reasonably practicable to communicate with them within the time available if consent in relation to the activity is to be acted on.[85]

(xi) Children

19.28 In contrast to the Human Tissue Act 1961, the Human Tissue Act 2004 includes specific consent provisions in relation to children in s 2. The provisions in many respects mirror those in relation to adults. As with adults, the legislation regulates both use of material from the living and the deceased. In the case of living children, then the child may consent him or herself.[86] However where the child has not decided whether to consent or to refuse and they are not competent to decide or, if competent to decide, they have not dealt with the issue, then the decision may be made by the person with parental responsibility.[87] The critical issue here will be that of capacity. The Act does not set a specific age at which children can be deemed to give consent themselves. The explanatory notes to the legislation provide that this is something which will be determined by reference to the common law principles set out in the House of Lords decision of *Gillick v West Norfolk and Wisbech AHA*—discussed further in Chapter 9.[88] In the case of deceased children, they can give consent during their lifetime if they have capacity,[89] or alternatively, consent may be given by the person with parental responsibility immediately before the child's death, or by the person in a qualifying relationship.[90] Specific provisions relate to consent in the context of storage or use for public display or in relation to an anatomical examination (where this is not excepted material). Here consent must be given in writing by the child before death[91] and that signature must

[84] ibid, s 27(6).
[85] ibid, s 27(8)(c).
[86] ibid, s 2(2).
[87] ibid, s 2(3).
[88] Explanatory Notes to the Human Tissue Act 2004, para 16.
[89] Human Tissue Act 2004, s 2(7)(a).
[90] ibid, s 2(7)(b).
[91] ibid, s 2(4)(5).

be witnessed; alternatively it can be signed at the direction of the child before death and that signature must also be witnessed.[92]

(xii) The nominated representative

Section 4 enables an adult to appoint a person to act as a decision-maker after their death. Only adults are able to be appointed as nominated representatives.[93] The appointment can be general or the deceased may impose limitations.[94] The nominated representative can be appointed orally or in writing.[95] In order for an oral appointment to be valid this must have been made in the presence of two witnesses who are both present at the same time.[96] In relation to a written appointment, one of three criteria must have been complied with. First, it is valid if signed by the person who made it with at least one witness present to attest the signature.[97] Secondly, it is valid if 'signed at the direction of the person making it, in his presence and in the presence of at least one witness who attests the signature'.[98] Thirdly, it can be included in a valid will.[99] More than one person can be appointed to act as a nominated representative.[100] In such a situation those persons who have been appointed can act jointly or separately, unless it is stated that they must act jointly. An appointment of a nominated representative can be revoked at any time.[101] The nominated representative can at any time decide that they do not want to fulfil this role and can resign.[102] In addition, where there is a nominated representative they do not have to be consulted if, in the particular situation, it 'is not reasonably practicable to contact them'.[103] **19.29**

(xiii) Adults lacking mental capacity

Originally, the Human Tissue Bill did not make specific provision for adults lacking mental capacity but provisions were introduced as the legislation was passing through Parliament. It should be noted that contemporaneous with the Human Tissue Bill passing through Parliament, the Mental Capacity Bill was also under consideration. Section 6 of the Human Tissue Act 2004 now deals with the issue. In a situation in which an adult lacks mental capacity and s/he has not executed any consent statement prior to lacking capacity then this is subject to regulations.[104] In some instances, consent to storage and use of relevant material can be 'deemed': (i) for the purposes of obtaining scientific or medical information concerning a living or deceased person which could be relevant for another person, and it is reasonably believed that it is in the best interests of the person lacking capacity; (ii) for the purposes of a clinical trial under the Medicines for Human Use Clinical Trials Regulations (discussed further in Chapter 13); (iii) for research where this is provided for under ss 30–34 of the Mental Capacity Act 2005 (this is discussed further in Chapter 13, paras 13.55–13.63). **19.30**

[92] ibid, s 2(6).
[93] ibid, s 4(10).
[94] ibid, s 4(2).
[95] ibid, s 4(3).
[96] ibid, s 4(4).
[97] ibid, s 4(5)(a).
[98] ibid, s 4(5)(b).
[99] ibid, s 4(5)(c).
[100] ibid, s 4(6).
[101] ibid, s 4(7).
[102] ibid, s 4(9).
[103] ibid, s 3(8).
[104] Human Tissue Act 2004 (Persons who Lack Capacity to Consent and Transplants) Regulations 2006, SI 2006/1659.

3. Organ transplantation

(i) Introduction

19.31 Organ transplantation is in many respects one of the great medical miracles of the last sixty years.[105] The first successful kidney transplant was in 1954 and the first lung transplant in 1963. Vast publicity followed the first heart transplant in 1967 by Christian Barnard in South Africa. The development of the technology was considerably facilitated by the development of immuno-suppressant drugs which reduced the prospect of the recipient's body rejecting the implanted tissue from another. The first successful partial face transplant took place in 2005, giving a new face to a woman whose face had been savaged by a dog.[106] This was followed in 2010 by the first full face transplant which was undertaken in Spain on a man whose face had been seriously damaged in a shooting incident.[107] The latest developments include uterine transplants.[108] Transplant technology has still not been matched, however, with a proportionate increase in the availability of human material for transplantation. The law itself has been blamed by some commentators as a reason for this shortage and that there needs to be more radical legal reform.[109] The law in this area was first regulated by two pieces of legislation: the Human Tissue Act 1961, which dealt with cadaver donation, and by the Human Organ Transplants Act 1989, which had been triggered by a major controversy regarding commercial dealing in organs and which specifically regulated organ transplants between genetically unrelated donors. Today it is now regulated through the Human Tissue Act 2004. This Act covers all organ transplants and bone marrow transplants.[110] This section of the chapter examines, first, specific issues relating to consent and deceased donors, secondly, transplantation and live donors, thirdly, commercial dealing in material for the purposes of transplantation, and finally, issues concerning proposals for reform of the law in this area.

(ii) Transplantation from deceased donors

19.32 (a) **Adults *The Basic Principles*** Organs can be removed from deceased adults in one or two circumstances. First, organs may be removed for transplantation where an individual has consented before his death.[111] Typically this will be in a situation in which an organ donor card has been executed. This provision mirrors the provision contained in the Human Tissue Act 1961. Secondly, organs may be removed from an individual in a situation in which they have not made a decision during their life-time where consent is obtained from the person who is in a 'qualifying relationship' (discussed at para 19.26).[112] Here the crucial difference is that under the 1961 Act, in a situation in which it was not reasonably practical to communicate with the spouse or surviving relative, the person lawfully in possession of the body, who could include the hospital authorities, could make the decision regarding

[105] See, generally, D Price, *Organ Transplants and Ethics* (Cambridge University Press 2000).

[106] B Devauchelle, L Badet, and B Lengele, 'First Human Face Allograft; Early Report' (2006) 368 The Lancet 203.

[107] 'Full face transplant a success' *BBC News* (23 April 2010) <http://news.bbc.co.uk/1/hi/health/8639437.stm>.

[108] 'First Womb Transplant Baby Born' *BBC News* (4th October 2014) <http://www.bbc.co.uk/news/health-29485996>.

[109] See, eg, V English and A Somerville, 'Presumed Consent for Transplantation: A Dead issue after Alder Hey?' (2003) 29 Journal of Medical Ethics 147: I Kennedy, R Sells, A Daar, et al 'The Case for Presumed Consent in Organ Donation' (1998) Lancet 1650.

[110] See further the Human Tissue Authority, *Code 2: Donation of Solid Organs for Transplantation* (July 2014) and Human Tissue Authority, *Code 6: Donations of Allergenic Bone Marrow and Peripheral Blood Stem Cells for Transplantation* (July 2014).

[111] Human Tissue Act 2004, s 3.

[112] ibid, s 3(6).

donation. In contrast, here the clinical team will need to approach the next person on the list. Under the Human Tissue Act 2004 consent cannot be given unless it is by someone in the qualifying relationship category.

This is a very sensitive issue. On the one hand, where organs are sought for transplantation it is often the case that the potential donor has died due to an unexpected traumatic event. This is obviously a particularly stressful time for loved ones. On the other hand, if approaches are not made, then many potential donor organs could be lost. One problem which may arise is if relatives disagree. The views of higher-ranking relatives under the ranking list contained in s 27(4) according to the Act take precedence. But what if two relatives on the same level disagree? The Code states that: **19.33**

> Where there is a conflict between those accorded equal ranking, then this needs to be discussed sensitively with all parties, whilst explaining clearly that so far as the HT Act is concerned, the consent of one of those ranked equally in the hierarchy is sufficient for the procedure to go ahead.[113]

A further consideration here when consulting family members is the possibility that some family members may also have very strong religious and cultural objections to the procedure. **19.34**

Conditional Organ Donation The Human Tissue Act 2004 is silent on conditional donation. This was an issue which arose under the previous law—the Human Tissue Act 1961. In one incident a family stated that they would only agree to organs being used for the purposes of transplantation if the organs were made available to a white donor. This led to an investigation by the DoH.[114] The issue of conditional donation under the Human Tissue Act 2004 arose in 2008. Press reports noted that a woman, Rachel Leake, who had kidney failure was denied use of her daughter's kidneys. Her daughter Laura had died at 21 after suffering brain damage consequent upon an asthma attack. Laura was on the organ donor register and she had spoken of wanting to help her mother although she had not formally recorded her wish that her mother should benefit. The Human Tissue Act issued a policy statement following this incident. This provided that: **19.35**

> The central principle of matching and allocating organs from the deceased is that they are allocated to the person on the UKT waiting list who is most in need and who is the best match with the donor. This is regardless of gender, race, religion or any other factor.[115]

The statement went on to provide that:

> In line with this central principle a person cannot choose to whom their organ can be given when they die; nor can their family. However the HTA recognises that there may be exceptional situations when this rule might be reconsidered, but the importance of maintaining the central principle means that such exceptional situations would need to be considered with the greatest care before any part of the current rules were to be changed.[116]

The Nominated Representative The Human Tissue Act 2004 enables the deceased to enact a provision to bypass the qualifying relationship category by allowing them to appoint a specific person to decide as to whether the organs should be removed for transplantation.[117] This is discussed further at para 19.26. This may be of particular help if an individual wants **19.36**

[113] Human Tissue Authority, *Code of Practice 2: Donation of Solid Organs for Transplantation* (Human Tissue Authority July 2014) para 115.
[114] *An Investigation into Conditional Organ Donation: The Report of the Panel* (HMSO 2000). See further D Price, *Human Tissue in Transplantation and Research* (Cambridge University Press 2009) at 276–81.
[115] 'HTA Statement on Directed Donation of Organs after Death' (Human Tissue Authority, 2008).
[116] ibid.
[117] Human Tissue Act 2004, s 4(1).

to appoint someone such as a close friend who would be the last on the priority list for the qualifying relationship as the decision-maker.

19.37 (b) **Children** The provisions concerning transplantation from the deceased child donor in many respects are similar to those concerning adults. First, organs may be removed for transplantation in a situation in which the child has consented before death, for example by executing an organ donor card.[118] Secondly, if consent has not been given by the child then the person with parental responsibility may consent.[119] Thirdly, in a situation in which there is not a person who has parental responsibility immediately before the death, then the person who is in a qualifying relationship may consent.

19.38 (c) **Adults lacking mental capacity** Use of adults lacking mental capacity as organ donors has long been a controversial issue and there is considerable divergence in approaches to this issue across Europe.[120] Prior to the Human Tissue Act in 1996, the English courts were asked to rule as to whether an adult lacking mental capacity could act as a bone marrow donor in the case of *Re Y (Mental Patient: Bone Marrow Donation)*.[121] This case concerned a 25-year-old woman with impaired mental capacity. It was proposed that she should act as a bone marrow donor for her 36-year-old sister. It was likely that without the transplant the sister would develop acute myeloid leukaemia within three months. Connell J authorized the performance of tests on Y to ascertain her suitability as a donor and, if necessary, a bone marrow harvesting operation. His decision was on the basis of whether the procedure in question could be seen to be in Y's best interests. Here he looked at the fact that this was a very closely knit family. He noted the impact that the death of Y's sister would have on Y's mother. It was suggested that if Y's sister died then this would reduce Y's mother's ability to assist Y because she would also have to care for Y's sister's child—her granddaughter. Also fundamental to the decision was the fact that this case concerned bone marrow, not solid organ transplantation, the former of course being regenerative while the latter is not. The English courts have not to date had to rule on the issue of donation of a solid organ by an adult lacking mental capacity.[122] Now the question of donation is regulated under the Human Tissue Act 2004 and related regulations. The regulations provide that where it is proposed that an adult lacking mental capacity can act as an organ donor then first the matter must be referred to the court under the Mental Capacity Act 2005 to determine whether the donation can be seen as being in the best interests of the individual.[123] Much will thus depend upon the approach taken by the court of what precisely constitutes best interests in this context and it remains uncertain as to whether the approach in *Y* would be followed. Secondly, where such approval has been given there is then a second stage in that the transplant will require approval by a special panel of three members of the Human Tissue Authority.

19.39 (d) **Role of the coroner** The role of the coroner is discussed further in Chapter 22 below. Here it is mentioned in respect of transplantation procedures. The Human Tissue Act 2004 provides that the transplantation provisions are subject to the authority of the coroner. Section 11 of the Act provides that:

---

118 ibid, s 2(7).

119 ibid, s 2(7)(b)(i).

120 K V Assche, G Genicot, and S Sterckx, 'Using Mentally Incompetent Adults and Organ Donors: Widely Diverging Regulations in Europe' (2012) (19)(5) European Journal of Health Law 441–66.

121 [1996] FLR 791.

122 Contrast the US case of *Strunk v Strunk* (1969) 445 SW2d 145.

123 Human Tissue Act 2004 (Persons who Lack Capacity to Consent and Transplants) Regulations 2006, SI 2006/1659.

(1) Nothing in this Part applies to anything done for purposes of functions of a coroner or under the authority of a coroner.

(2) Where a person knows, or has reason to believe, that—
  (a) the body of a deceased person, or
  (b) relevant material which has come from the body of a deceased person, is, or may be, required for purposes of functions of a coroner, he shall not act on authority under section 1 in relation to the body, or material, except with the consent of the coroner.

Liddell and Hall have suggested that coroners acting without authority may commit an offence under s 5(4) of the Act (see Part 4 of the present chapter). They also suggest that coroners may need to have regard to codes which the Human Tissue Authority prepare.[124] The Human Tissue Authority Code of Practice states that: **19.40**

> In order to ensure that conflicts do not arise between the provisions of section 43 of the HT Act for the preservation of organs and the lawful powers or authority of the coroner when a body is lying in the coroners' jurisdiction, a generic memorandum of understanding should be pre-emptively agreed with the local coroner where possible. Specific notification of the coroner should also occur on a case-by-case basis where appropriate.[125]

This is clearly good practice, but it is uncertain as to what extent this has been adopted in practice nationally to date.

(iii) Transplantation from live donors

In the case of living adults they must give consent.[126] Indeed, failure to obtain consent would, in addition, be actionable both in civil and criminal law. (See further Chapter 5.) The issue as to whether adults can in fact lawfully consent to donation has been the subject of some discussion.[127] English law does not allow an individual to consent to the infliction of harm, however grave.[128] Nonetheless, it appears today that Parliament at least envisages the legality of live organ donation through the enactment of the Human Tissue Act 2004 itself. It has been suggested that it is unlikely that a decision to undertake a transplant operation involving a living donor where the provisions of the legislation were complied with would result in any subsequent criminal prosecution.[129] Nonetheless, Price suggests that to sustain this position much may depend upon the transplantation procedure in question. Clearly, an individual cannot consent to be killed in order to act as a donor. As a less extreme example and one given by Price, 'while the removal of regenerative material such as part of a liver may be legitimate this must surely depend upon the percentage of liver taken and the donor's remaining reserves'.[130] Prior to the Human Tissue Act 2004 live organ transplants were separately regulated by the Human Organ Transplants Act 1989. This provided that while transplants between persons who were genetically related could be undertaken without specific safeguards, in the case of those between non-genetically related donors these had to be the subject of the regulatory body established by the 1989 Act: the Unrelated Live Transplants Regulatory Authority (ULTRA). One of the reasons for this were concerns regarding commercial dealing in organs which the '1989 Act had been introduced **19.41**

[124] See further K Liddell and A Hall, 'Beyond Alder Hey: The Future Regulation of Human Tissue' [2005] 13 Med L Rev 170, 209.

[125] Human Tissue Authority, *Code of Practice 2, Donation of Solid Organs For Transplantation* (Human Tissue Authority July 2014) para 135.

[126] Human Tissue Act 2004, s 3(1).

[127] D Price, *Human Tissue in Transplantation and Research* (Cambridge University Press 2009), 209–11.

[128] *R v Brown* [1994] 2 All ER 79.

[129] See further Law Commission, *Consent in the Criminal Law* (Law Com No 139, 1995) para 8.32.

[130] See D Price, n 127, 210.

to prohibit'. There was the suggestion that persons who were not genetically related may be less driven by altruism in the decision as to whether to donate. However, equally the legislation did not address the issue that genetically related donors may feel under considerable emotional pressure to donate to a sick relative in a situation in fact in which they may not themselves be happy to go ahead and donate.[131]

19.42 ULTRA was abolished by the Human Tissue Act 2004. Today live organ transplantation is regulated by the Human Tissue Authority under s 33. It is a criminal offence under that section to remove or use transplantable material from a living person unless the Human Tissue Authority itself is satisfied that no reward has been or is to be given in contravention of s 32 or that such other criteria as set out in regulations has been complied with.[132] There is a defence under s 33(5) where a person reasonably believes that the exception to the prohibition applies. Under para 10 of Human Tissue Act 2004 (Persons who lack Capacity to Consent and Transplant) Regulations 2006,[133] transplantable material is defined as:

(a) an organ or part of an organ if it is to be used for the same purpose as the entire organ in the human body,
(b) bone marrow, and
(c) peripheral blood stem cells.

Paragraph 2(2) defines an organ as being 'a differentiated part of the human body, formed by different tissues, that maintains its structure, vascularization and capacity to develop physiological functions with a significant level of autonomy'. This definition is considerably more limited than that of 'relevant material'. As Pattinson notes 'it excludes materials such as blood plasma, heart valves removed from a patient receiving a donated heart, and bone removed for bone grafting into another.'[134] In addition, para 10(2) of the Regulations provides that where the primary purpose of the removal is for the medical treatment of a person from whose body the organ was removed it does not fall within s 33. Thus where the transplant is a 'domino' transplant this does not have to be approved under the provisions under s. 33.[135] Also, the regulations only extend to bone marrow and peripheral stem cells in the context of transplants from children or adults lacking mental capacity[136] and such donations from competent adults are not covered under s 33.

19.43 All the provisions concerning live organ transplantation are subject to the consent provisions set out earlier in the legislation and also the common law concerning consent to treatment. The appropriate consents must be obtained before transplantation can go ahead. The regulations set out the procedure which must be complied with.[137] The doctor who has clinical responsibility for the donor must refer this to the Human Tissue Authority.[138] Secondly, the Authority must be satisfied that there has been no reward given in contravention of s 32 and the decision to donate was not subject to duress. Finally, the Authority must give notice of its decision. In addition, in those situations where the transplant has

[131] See, eg, discussion in M Evans, 'Organ Donation Should Not Be Restricted to Relatives' (1989) 15 Journal of Medical Ethics 17.

[132] Human Tissue Act 2004, s 33(3).

[133] SI 2006/1659.

[134] S Pattinson, *Medical Law and Ethics* (4th edn, Sweet & Maxwell 2014) at para 12-030.

[135] This typically arises in a case such as cystic fibrosis where clinically it is more straightforward to transplant both heart and lungs. The recipient's removed heart which may be healthy can then itself be transplanted into a recipient in need of a heart transplant.

[136] Human Tissue Act 2004 (Persons Who Lack Capacity to Consent and Transplants) Regulations 2006, SI 2006/1659, reg 10(3).

[137] ibid.

[138] ibid, reg 11(2).

not been authorized by the court, it is to take into account interviews with the donor and recipient.[139] Where it is proposed to undertake a live organ transplant operation, then the donor and recipient of the organs must be separately interviewed by an independent assessor who has been appointed by the Human Tissue Authority.[140] The independent assessor must be assured that the doctor has explained the nature and risks of the procedure to the donor. The donor must have capacity to consent. The assessor must also be satisfied that there has been no evidence of reward or of coercion.[141] The independent assessor must then submit a report to the HTA who will then make its decision. In very rare instances it is the case that organs cannot be transplanted into an intended recipient. In such a case guidance from the HTA then provides that living organ donors should be asked in advance of surgery as to their wishes in relation to the organ: namely, as to whether it should be transplanted into another recipient on the waiting list, reimplanted in the donor where clinically possible, used for research, or disposed of.[142]

Specific procedures apply in relation to certain forms of donation where the HTA's approval will be required before the donation can go ahead.[143] First, 'paired donation': paired donation matches donor and recipient with a similar donor–recipient in a situation in which a close relative is prepared to donate their organ to their relative but their organ is not compatible.[144] Secondly, 'pooled donation' arises in similar situations to paired donation but where there is more than one pair.[145] Again in such a situation HTA approval is required. Thirdly, specific approval is also required in relation to a situation in which a person donates an organ for altruistic reasons and there is not at the time of donation a designated recipient. **19.44**

In relation to children, the Code of Practice states that they are only to be considered as live organ donors 'in extremely rare circumstances' and court approval should be sought.[146] Such transplants must be subject to specific approval by a panel of three members of the Human Tissue Authority.[147] Prior judicial approval must be sought in addition to approval by a special panel of the Human Tissue Authority in relation to donation from an adult lacking mental capacity.[148] This position can be contrasted with the Council of Europe Biomedicine Convention which provides that organ and tissue removal should only be undertaken from persons lacking mental capacity if it is regenerative material and legislative prohibitions are in existence in relation to such donations in relation to certain other European jurisdictions.[149] **19.45**

---

[139] ibid, reg 11(4)–(10).

[140] Human Tissue Act 2004 (Persons Who Lack Capacity to Consent and Transplants) Regulations 2006, SI 2006/1659, reg 11(6).

[141] ibid, reg 11(8).

[142] Human Tissue Authority, 'Organ or Part of Organ that Cannot be Transplanted into the Intended Recipient '(2011) 4 <http://www.hta.gov.uk/policies/organpartoforgan-cannot-be-transplanted-intended-recipient>.

[143] Human Tissue Act 2004 (Persons Who Lack Capacity to Consent and Transplants) Regulations 2006, SI 2006/1659, reg 12(4), (5).

[144] ibid, reg 12(4), (5).

[145] ibid, reg 12(4), (5).

[146] Human Tissue Authority, *Code of Practice 2: Donation of Solid Organs for Transplantation* (Human Tissue Authority July 2014) para 49.

[147] ibid, para 52. Human Tissue Act 2004 (Persons Who Lack Capacity to Consent and Transplants) Regulations 2006, n 139, reg 12(2), (3).

[148] ibid.

[149] Council of Europe, Convention for the Protection of Human Rights and Dignity of the Human Being with regard to the Application of Biology and Medicine (1997 Oviedo) Art 20 and see also discussion in D Price, *Human Tissue in Transplantation and Research* (Cambridge University Press 2009) 30.

(iv) Trafficking in human material for the purposes of transplantation

19.46 The legitimacy of commercial dealing in human material has long been the subject of academic debate and controversy[150] and it as also been considered by policy makers.[151] Some commentators have strongly argued in favour of a market in organs for transplantation.[152] It has been suggested that by allowing a free market this may increase the available supply of human material for transplantation. Secondly, any infringement on commercial dealing can be seen as an unjustifiable limitation upon personal autonomy, something which is of course safeguarded under Article 8 of the ECHR, the right to privacy. Titmuss argued in the context of blood donation that a market in blood had adverse consequences.[153] Poor individuals and groups were exploited through commercialization. In contrast, others have argued that rather than regarding commercial dealing in human material as being exploitative it can be seen as a means by which the poor can alleviate their situation.[154] Veatch has powerfully argued:

> if we are a society that deliberately and systematically turns its back on the poor; we must confess our indifference to the poor, and lift the prohibition on the one means they have to address their problems themselves.[155]

19.47 Initially this argument may be regarded as attractive. But on closer examination it proves to be more rhetorical than real in its effect. In practice, it appears that such alleviation from poverty is likely to be only temporary, as research regarding organ trading from India illustrates.[156] One possible response to some of the express concerns of exploitation is that of the introduction of a 'regulated market'. This approach has been advocated by Harris and Erin in the context of organ transplantation.[157] They propose that such a market could operate within a defined area such as an individual state. Only resident citizens would be able to sell and sales would be to a single defined purchaser such as the NHS. The organs would be made available to the citizens in the defined area. This has the advantage that health and safety concerns regarding paid donors may be addressed through appropriate transplantation procedures being utilized. However, it can be argued that this argument does not sufficiently address the issue, that effective regulation is impossible in a global community.

19.48 In contrast, others following Titmuss have argued that transplantation should be seen as a 'gift' relationship, an act of fundamental altruism.[158] Some regard commercial dealing

---

[150] See, eg, D Lamb, *Organ Transplants and Ethics* (Routledge 1990) 133–40; J Stacey Taylor, *Stakes and Kidneys: Why Markets in Human Body Parts are Morally Imperative* (Ashgate 2005); D Price, *Organ Transplants and Ethics* (Cambridge University Press 2000); S Wilkinson, *Bodies for Sale: Ethics and Exploitation in the Human Body Trade* (Routledge 2003).

[151] See, eg, Nuffield Council of Bioethics *Human Bodies: Donation for Medicine and Research* (2011) <http://www.nuffieldbioethics.org/donationat> para 6.40. See further D Price, 'Exploitation, Akrasia and Goldilocks: How Many Pounds of Flesh for Medical Uses?' [2013] 21(4) Medical Law Review 519.

[152] See, eg, J Radcliffe-Richards, A Daar, R Guttman et al, 'The Case for Allowing Kidney Sales' (1998) 351 The Lancet 1950.

[153] See further R Titmuss, *The Gift Relationship from Human Blood to Social Policy* (Allen and Unwin 1970).

[154] See, eg, J Radcliffe Richards, et al, n 152.

[155] R Veatch, 'Why Liberals Should Accept Financial Incentives for Organ Procurement' (2003) 13 Kennedy Institute of Ethics Journal 19.

[156] See discussion in D Dickenson, *Body Shopping Converting Body Parts to Profit One World* (Oxford University Press 2008) 154.

[157] C Errin and J Harris, 'A Monopsonistic Market; Or How to Buy and Sell Human Organs, Tissues and Cells Ethically' in I Robinson (ed), *Life and Death Under High Technology Medicine* (Manchester University Press 1994).

[158] See further R Titmuss, *The Gift Relationship from Human Blood to Social Policy* (Allen and Unwin 1970).

as wholly abhorrent trading in human flesh. Concerns have been expressed regarding the commodification of the body which can be seen as an infringement of human dignity.[159] Furthermore, a market-based approach may be seen as 'degrading'.[160] This has been reflected in the approach generally taken internationally to the commercial dealing in human material. A large number of countries have prohibitions upon commercial dealing in organs and only one, Iran, has an operational market in organs.[161] This is also reflected in international statements regarding the use of human material. For example the Council of Europe Convention on Human Rights and Biomedicine provides (Article 21) that: 'The human body and its parts shall not, as such, give rise to financial gain.'

The EU Charter on Fundamental Rights similarly provides in Article 3, which concerns the integrity of the person, that: **19.49**

> 2. In the fields of medicine/biology the following must be respected: . . .
>
> The prohibition on making the human body and its parts as such a source of financial gain . . .

The EU Tissue and Cells Directive also emphasizes the need for voluntary and unpaid donation,[162] anonymity of both donor and recipient, altruism of the donor and solidarity between donor and recipient.[163] Member States are urged to take steps to encourage a strong public and non-profit sector involvement in the provision of tissue and cell application services and related research development.[164] Similarly the EU Organ Transplantation Directive provides in its Preamble that: Altruism is an important factor in organ donations. To ensure the quality and safety of organs, organ transplantation programmes should be founded on the principles of voluntary and unpaid donation. This is essential because the violation of these principles might be associated with unacceptable risks. Where donation is not voluntary and/or is undertaken with a view to financial gain, the quality of the process of donation could be jeopardized because improving the quality of life or saving the life of a person is not the main and/or the unique objective. Even if the process is developed in accordance with appropriate quality standards, a clinical history obtained from either a potential living donor or the relatives of a potential deceased donor who are seeking financial gain or are subjected to any kind of coercion might not be sufficiently accurate in terms of conditions and/or diseases potentially transmissible from donor to recipient. This could give rise to a safety problem for potential recipients since the medical team would have a limited capability for performing an appropriate risk assessment.[165] Building upon these principles the Directive provides that donation should be voluntary and unpaid.[166] **19.50**

Commercial dealing in human organs for transplantation came under the spotlight at a national level in the UK following GMC disciplinary proceedings in the *Crocket* case in the late 1980s. Poor Turkish organ donors were brought over to the UK and were paid to **19.51**

[159] See, eg, J P Khan and F L Delmonico, 'The Consequences of Public Policy to Buy and Sell Organs for Transplantation' (2004) 4(2) American Journal of Transplantation 178.

[160] See further discussion of this issue and ultimate rejection of this argument in N Duxbury, 'Do Markets Degrade?' (1996) 59 MLR 33.

[161] See further E J Gordon and J S Gill, 'Where There is Smoke There is Fire' (2013) 13(2) American Journal of Transplantation 3867.

[162] EU Tissue and Cells Directive, Article 12.

[163] ibid, Recital 13.

[164] ibid, Recital 13.

[165] Directive 2010/53/EU of the European Parliament and of the Council of 7 July 2010 on standards of quality and safety of human organs intended for transplantation [2010] OJ L207/14, Recital 19.

[166] ibid, Article 13, although note that there are different approaches in different Member States as to the practical interpretation of this provision. See further Chapter 14.

donate organs for transplantation.[167] The doctors who were involved in this practice including Crocket were subject to GMC disciplinary proceedings. The controversy over the case led to the government introducing the Human Organs Transplant Act 1989. The 1989 Act introduced a blanket ban on commercial dealing in organs. It criminalized commercial dealing and the advertising of commercial dealing. The original Human Tissue Bill 2003 had contained a broad provision banning trafficking in human materials. This could be seen as in line with international statements such as Article 21 of the Council of Europe Convention on Human Rights and Biomedicine. It also went much further than the previous ban on commercial dealing in human material which had been contained in the Human Organ Transplants Act 1989. However, this provision was the subject of considerable lobbying and debate when the legislation was passing through Parliament not least by the biotechnological community. During the debates the government minister Rosie Winterton stated that it was:

> never our intention to interfere with commercial activities that had been lawfully and ethically carried on for many years. We therefore propose to amend the Bill to confine the offences connected with advertising and supply of human tissue for reward to transplantable tissue only.[168]

19.52 The final provision contained in the legislation is consequently much more restrictive and relates to trafficking in material for the purposes of transplantation. Section 32 of the Human Tissue Act 2004 creates various offences. It applies to 'controlled material' which refers to human material which is intended to be used for transplantation, subject to limited exceptions.[169] It is an offence to give and receive reward for supply or offer to supply any controlled material.[170] The first prosecution under the section occurred in 2007. A salesman who was in debt, Daniel Tuck, was successfully prosecuted for offering to sell a kidney for transplantation on an internet chatroom website and was given a twelve-month suspended jail sentence.[171] It is an offence to seek to find a person who is willing to supply controlled material for reward.[172] It is also an offence to initiate or negotiate any arrangement which involves the supply or offer to supply of any controlled material. It is an offence to take part in the management or control of any organization concerned in the negotiation of such an arrangement. Specific offences also relate to advertising for the sale of such material. Section 32(2) provides that it is an offence to publish or to cause to be published advertisements inviting persons to supply or offer to supply controlled material for reward. Interestingly, in contrast to the law regulating commercial surrogacy arrangements (the Surrogacy Arrangements Act 1985 which excludes the main parties to the agreement—surrogate and commissioning couple—from criminality), the Human Tissue Act, consistent with the approach taken under the 1989 Act, does apply to the donor and donee. The 1985 Act may be distinguished from the Human Tissue Act in that, in relation to the former piece of legislation, the surrogate and commissioning couple were excluded on policy grounds following the recommendations of the Warnock Report, because it was felt that otherwise a child could be born subject to the taint of criminality.[173]

[167] See D Brahams, 'Kidneys for Sale by Living Donors' (1989) Lancet 285, and 'Kidneys for Sale' (1989) New LJ 159.

[168] House of Commons Hansard Debates 28 June 2004, col 115.

[169] Human Tissue Act 2004, s 32(8), (9).

[170] ibid, s 32(1)(a).

[171] *R v Tuck* (2007) and see 'Body Parts Sale Man Avoids Jail' *BBC News* (11 May 2007) <http:///news.bbc.co.uk/1/hi/england/west_midlands/6646467.stm>.

[172] Human Tissue Act 2004, s 32(1)(b).

[173] *Report of the Committee of Inquiry into Human Fertilisation and Embryology* (Cmnd 9314, 1983) para 8.19.

It is not clear as to whether these provisions were intended also to apply when individuals left the jurisdiction and paid for receiving an organ for transplant outside the UK.[174] The question of extra-territorial enforcement of organ trafficking offences is now an issue which is the concern of the international community and has been the subject of a recent non-binding declaration by the Council of Europe in 2014.[175] 19.53

The Act excludes from the definition of 'payment' expenses in connection with transporting, removing, preserving, preparing, or storing the material.[176] The section also explicitly excludes from the definition of 'controlled material' gametes, embryos, and material which has been the subject of the application of human skill.[177] An exclusion applies under s 32(3) where the Human Tissue Authority grants a body permission to traffic in such material. So, for example, as Pattinson notes, this means that the National Blood Service is thus able to buy blood from abroad.[178] Licence holders can also be given permission by the Human Tissue Authority to receive payment other than expenses 'where it relates to transporting, removing, preparing, preserving or storing controlled material', and its receipt is not prohibited by the licence holder.[179] 19.54

(vi) Preserving organs for transplantation and non-heart beating donation

Section 43 of the Human Tissue Act 2004 addresses what was previously an issue of legal uncertainty namely, retaining and preserving bodies prior to transplantation in order, for example, that relatives can be contacted. This may arise, for example, in the case of non-heart beating donation.[180] The section provides that it is lawful to take minimal steps to preserve the cadaver for transplantation purposes until either consent has been given or that it has not or will not be given. The Human Tissue Act Code of Practice 2 on the Donation of Solid Organs for Transplantation provides that, in the situation of non-heart beating donation, the coroner's powers will arise automatically (see further Chapter 22 for discussion of the powers of the Coroner).[181] The Code states that 'what constitutes minimal steps should be considered in terms of both what is least invasive to the donor and also in terms of what may be seen as appropriate by the family'.[182] 19.55

(vii) Reforming the law

Despite considerable efforts by the transplantation community the number of organs available falls well short of that required. One issue is whether the law itself is inhibiting transplantation and whether radical legal changes would facilitate an enhanced supply. Some have questioned this. It is certain that the law in this area is only part of what is a much broader picture. The Kings Fund Report in 1994 identified a number of factors as being 19.56

[174] J V McHale and S McGuinness, 'Transnational Crimes Related to Health: How Should the Law Respond to the Illicit Organ Tourism?' (2014) 34(4) Legal Studies 682; J V McHale, 'Organ Transplantation, the Criminal Law and the Health Tourist: A Case for Extra-Territorial Jurisdiction?' (2013) 22(1) Cambridge Quarterly of Healthcare Ethics 64–76.

[175] Council of Europe Convention on Trafficking in Human Organs, adopted by the Council of Ministers, 9th July 2014.

[176] Human Tissue Act 2004, s 32(7).

[177] ibid, s 32(9).

[178] S Pattinson, *Medical Law and Ethics* (4th edn, Sweet & Maxwell 2014) 456.

[179] Human Tissue Act 2004, s 32(6).

[180] In relation to discussion of the ethical issues around non-heart beating donation see D Price and J Samanta, 'Supporting Controlled Non-Heart Beating Donation' (2013) 22 Cambridge Quarterly of Healthcare Ethics 22.

[181] Human Tissue Authority, *Code of Practice 2: Donation of Solid Organs for Transplantation* (Human Tissue Authority July 2014) at para 125.

[182] ibid, para 131.

influential in determining the availability of organs for transplantation.[183] First, the death rates from relevant causes. One effective source of organs is road traffic fatalities. However, English roads have become notably safer in recent years and in contrast to other European countries the road traffic death rates are much lower. Secondly, demographic considerations such as age of population can be a factor. People are living longer but older persons are not necessarily suitable organ donors if they themselves have suffered illness and disease. Thirdly, critical to transplant levels is the funding available. Transplantation is an expensive technology and requires not simply the relevant equipment but teams of highly trained dedicated personnel led by the transplant surgeon. Some in the transplant community have become concerned in recent years that transplant surgery is a less 'in demand' profession amongst young doctors. Fourthly, effective procurement arrangements are also critically important in ensuring that organs are speedily transferred between donor and recipient. Currently the NHS Blood and Transplant Authority, which was established in 2005 as a special health authority, is concerned with the day-to-day regulation of the transplant process.[184] Its arm 'UK Transplant' manages transplant waiting lists, allocates organs, and collects and analyses transplant data. However, while it provides leadership to transplant co-ordinators it does not employ or manage them. In 2008 a DOH task force recommended the creation of a UK-wide Organ Donation organization.[185] While oversight is also provided by NHS Blood and Transplant, which is a special health authority in many respects, there is still fragmentation in the system with some functions performed by NHS Blood and Transplant and others by the Human Tissue Authority. It is suggested that, in the future, the alignment of the boundaries between these organizations warrant some reconsideration.

19.57 A number of alternative approaches for the increase in the supply of donor organs have been proposed. First is the introduction of an 'opt-out' or 'presumed consent' system[186] which enables cadaver organs to be used for transplantation unless there is some 'opt-out' from the scheme. Such opt-out schemes operate in a number of other countries. They fall into three broad categories. First, systems of strict presumed consent as in Austria. Organs may be removed for transplantation as long as someone has not opted out during their lifetime. Secondly, those schemes which enable opt-out by the relatives of the deceased after their death if they have not opted out during their lifetime. A notable example of such a scheme is operational in Belgium.[187] Whether presumed consent will ultimately be introduced in England remains a live issue. Its introduction was considered but rejected by the UK Government-established task force in 2008.[188] However, more recently a different approach has been taken in Wales. The Human Transplant (Wales) Act 2013 came into effect in December 2015.[189] This represents a considerable change in Wales. It applies to Welsh Residents. Transplantation is lawful with express consent or with 'deemed' consent,[190]

[183] B New, M Solomon, R Dingwall, and J McHale, *Kings Fund Research Report No 18: A Question of Give and Take* (Kings Fund Institute 1994).

[184] <http://www.nhsbt.nhs.uk>.

[185] Department of Health, *Organs for Transplant Organ Donation Task Force* (2008) <http://www.dh.gov.uk/en/Publicationsandstatistics/Publications/PublicationsPolicyAndGuidance/DH_082122>.

[186] V English and A Somerville, 'Presumed Consent for Transplantation: A Dead Issue After Alder Hey?' (2003) 29 Journal of Medical Ethics 147: J Harris, 'Organ Procurement; Dead Interests; Living Needs' (2003) 29 Journal of Medical Ethics 125; I Kennedy, R Sells, A Daar, et al, 'The Case for Presumed Consent in Organ Donation' (1998) Lancet 1650.

[187] See, eg, discussion in P Michelsen, 'Presumed Consent to Organ Donation: Ten Years Experience in Belgium' (1996) 89(2) Journal of the Royal Society of Medicine 662.

[188] The Organ Donation Task Force, *The Potential Impact of an Opt-Out System for Organ Donation in the UK: An Independent Report from the Organ Donation Task Force* (2008).

[189] See also Human Tissue Authority, Code of Practice on the Human Transplantation (Wales) Act 2013 (HTA 2014).

[190] Human Transplantation (Wales) Act 2013, s 3.

unless a person has opted out prior to their death. To avoid concerns that individuals may be unaware of the legislation it places a duty placed upon the Welsh Minister to promote transplantation as a means of improving the health of the public in Wales and also to inform them in relation to deemed consent—including a campaign every twelve months.[191] Under section 4, consent in the case of adults is 'deemed' consent unless it falls under one of the exceptions. These are, in relation to a living person, that they have consented. In relation to a deceased person, consent or refusal of consent has been given during their lifetime. Consent is also not deemed consent if someone has appointed someone else to consent on their behalf. In addition section 4 also provides that consent will also not be deemed if:

> S4 (4)(a) a relative or friend of long standing of the deceased objects on the basis of views held by the deceased and
>
> (b) A reasonable person would conclude that the relative or friend knows that the most recent view of the deceased before death on consent for transplantation activities was that the deceased was opposed to consent being given.

Express consent is also required under section 5 in relation to an 'excepted adult' which is:

(a) an adult who has died and is not ordinarily resident in Wales for a period of 12 months immediately before dying.

(b) an adult who has died and who for a significant period before dying lacked capacity to understand the notion that consent to transplantation activities can be deemed to be given.

What constitutes a 'significant period' is explored further in the HTA guidance developed in relation to the statute. This states that:

> 68. The exact duration that a person lacked capacity is not specified in the Human Transplantation (Wales) Act, but the period must be significant and this means a sufficiently long period as to lead a reasonable person to conclude that it would be inappropriate for consent to be deemed to be given. The significant period test is, therefore, an objective test in the sense that it must be based on the circumstances of each case and the facts presented. The significant period only negates deemed consent; if the person had made a decision to consent, or not to consent, then that express consent remains in force regardless of a subsequent loss of capacity.
>
> 69. In practice, a significant period should mean that the person did not have capacity to understand the notion of deemed consent for a period of at least twelve months before their death. The person's family, friends or carers should consider the significant period to be a period which is long enough that the person's decision not to register a decision in regard to organ donation could not be said to be a conscious decision.[192]

In relation to children under s 6 of the Act, express consent is also required. Here the general consent provisions are analogous to the Human Tissue Act 2004. Section 8 sets out provisions concerning 'appointed representatives' which are analogous to the provisions concerning 'nominated representatives' under s 4 of the Human Tissue Act 2004. Section 9 provides that any transplantation from persons lacking mental capacity will be subject to regulations. Any extension of deemed consent in relation to this group is also likely to be exceedingly controversial. Section 14 provides that, as with the Human Tissue Act 2004, all the powers under the Welsh Act are subject to the powers of the coroner. Thus, while the legislation contains no provision for relative veto as such, families will be involved in the process and consent will not be 'deemed' without this taking place. Relatives can state

[191] Human Transplantation (Wales) Act 2013, s 2.

[192] Human Tissue Authority, *Code of Practice on the Human Transplantation (Wales) Act 2013* (HTA 2014).

that the person did not want to be a donor, but this will not be objection by the relatives as such; rather, they will be indicating what the deceased would have wanted. There are limitations; for example, it will not apply to 'novel' procedures such as hand/face transplants. Interestingly and controversially there is no automatic exclusion for adults lacking mental capacity. Rather, provision is made for adults lacking mental capacity to be excluded after consultation with family. The introduction of an opt-out scheme forces us to confront conceptions as to the status of the body after death and whether individuals or indeed their relatives can be seen as having continuing interests in controlling the use of the body.[193] It is possible that the Welsh legislation ultimately becomes a model for the rest of the UK. One particular concern which has been expressed regarding the introduction of an opt-out scheme is that it may be difficult to reconcile a presumed consent scheme in such a diverse multicultural society as in England and Wales, where different perspectives exist concerning the use of the body after death. While objections from certain religious and cultural groups were made during the passage of the Welsh legislation, these questions were not ultimately determinative in formulating policy. A further approach is that of 'mandated choice'.[194] This has been adopted in the past in certain US states. Here, as the name suggests, the individual is required to make the decision as to whether or not to donate. This in itself is not ethically uncontroversial in that it is compelling an individual to make a choice.

19.58 Alternative options canvassed include the use of genetically modified organs from animals by the development of xenotransplantation. While this has been the subject of serious consideration in the UK, leading to the establishment of a regulatory body, the UK Xenotransplantation Interim Regulatory Authority (UKXIRA), the concerns regarding the risk that such technology could pose through the cross-species transmission of viruses has meant that such trials have not gone ahead.[195] UK XIRA initially placed a moratorium on trials. This body was abolished in 2006 and there have not been recent attempts to take this technology forward in the UK. A further option is that of elective ventilation, the practice of transferring terminally ill patients to intensive care units and ventilating them until death was diagnosed and thus preserving their organs for transplantation. Such a practice was utilized in some UK hospitals in the 1990s but was stopped because this was deemed to be a non-therapeutic procedure which was not in the best interests of the patient (rather than of the organ recipient) and thus such a procedure constituted a battery.[196] Despite some support for this approach there has not been a recent attempt to legalize the practice.[197] Other

---

[193] For discussion of such issues see, eg: S McGuinness and M Brazier, 'Respecting the Living Means Respecting the Dead Too' (2008) 28 Oxford Journal of Legal Studies 297; J Harris, 'Organ Procurement: Dead Interests: Living Needs' (2003) 29 Journal of Medical Ethics 125.

[194] See discussion in D Price, *Human Tissue in Transplantation and Research* (Cambridge University Press 2009) 82; and also P Chouhan and H Draper, 'Modified Mandated Choice for Organ Procurement' (2003) 29 Journal of Medical Ethics 150.

[195] See generally Nuffield Council on Bioethics, *Animal to Human Transplants: The Ethics of Xenotransplantation* (1996); *Animal Tissue into Humans*, A Report by the Advisory Group on the Ethics of Xenotransplantation (1996); M Fox and J McHale, 'Xenotransplantation: The Ethical and Legal Ramifications' (1998) Med L Rev 43; S McLean and L Williamson, *Xenotransplantation Law and Ethics* (Ashgate 2005), S McLean and L Williamson, 'The Demise of UKXIRA and the Regulation of Solid Organ Transplantation in the UK' (2008) 34 Journal of Medical Ethics 373; M Fox, 'Legal Regulation of New Technologies: Re-thinking Xenotechnologes in the Twenty First Century' in G Laurie and P R Ferguson (eds), *Inspiring a Medico-Legal Revolution: Essays in Honour of Shelia McLean* (Ashgate 2015).

[196] See J V McHale, 'Elective Ventilation—Pragmatic Solution or Ethical Minefield' (1995) Professional Negligence 28; and J K Mason, 'Contemporary Issues in Organ Transplantation' in S McLean (ed), *Contemporary Issues in Law, Medicine and Ethics* (Dartmouth 1996).

[197] See discussion in British Medical Association, *Building on Progress: Where Next for Organ Donation Policy in the UK?* (BMA 2012).

more radical suggestions such as lethally injecting patients who are in a persistent vegetative state are very unlikely to be taken forward.[198] Other responses to the shortage include the use of artificial organs although this has not been a great success to date. Ultimately it has been suggested that the organ shortage may be ameliorated through the advances in stem-cell technology enabling compatible tissue and organs to be grown for the recipient (see Chapter 15) or the use of bioprinting devices to enable organs to be machine–printed to order.[199]

4. Criminal offences

The Human Tissue Act 1961 incorporated no specific criminal sanctions for contravention of the statute. For some years it was thought that breach of a statutory provision could lead to a prosecution for the common law offence of disobedience to a statute, although this appeared not to be the case in the light of more recent case authority.[200] The absence of effective criminal penalties for breach of the legislation was highlighted in the Alder Hey inquiry report.[201] The Human Tissue Act 2004 now incorporates criminal penalties. Section 5 provides that it is an offence to undertake an activity which is regulated by the legislation unless the individual reasonably believes that she or he has undertaken the activity with appropriate consent,[202] or that she or he reasonably believes that what is being done is not an activity to which the section applies.[203] It is also an offence for a person to falsely represent that there has been appropriate consent or that the activity does not require consent in a situation in which they know that this representation is false or they believe it not to be true.[204] Contravention of this provision includes penalties of a fine or term of imprisonment for a period up to three years. The Human Tissue Act 2004 also includes a specific offence of using relevant material other than for purposes under Sch 1, medical diagnosis or treatment, decent disposal, or for purposes included in regulations made by the Secretary of State.[205] Under s 8(2) of the Human Tissue Act 2004 it is not, however, an offence where the person reasonably believes that this is not donated material. There are also offences relating to commercial dealing in material for the purposes of transplantation (see para 19.05). **19.59**

There is in addition a specific criminal offence in relation to the use of material for DNA analysis contained in s 45. It is an offence to have human material intending that DNA be analysed without qualifying consent and the results are to be used for other than a qualifying purpose.[206] There is no offence if the material is 'excepted' under s 45(2) and the person reasonably believes that the material is excepted. Section 45(2) provides that: **19.60**

(2) Bodily material is excepted if—

(a) it is material which has come from the body of a person who died before the day on which this section comes into force and at least one hundred years have elapsed since the date of the person's death,

[198] See R Hoffenburg et al, 'Should Organs from Patients in Permanent Vegetative State be Used For Transplantation?' (1997) 350 Lancet 1320.

[199] H Ledford, 'The Printed Organs Coming to a Body Near You' *Nature* (15 April 2015) <http://www.nature.com/news/the-printed-organs-coming-to-a-body-near-you-1.17320>.

[200] *R v Lennox Wright* [1973] Crim LR 529; *R v Horseferry Justices ex p IBA* [1987] QB 54; and see discussion in I Kennedy, 'Liability and the Human Tissue Act 1961', in I Kennedy, *Treat Me Right* (Oxford University Press 1989).

[201] See earlier at para 19.04.

[202] Human Tissue Act 2004, s 5(1)(a).

[203] ibid, s 5(1)(b).

[204] ibid, s 5(2).

[205] ibid, s 8.

[206] ibid, s 45(1).

(b) it is an existing holding and the person who has it is not in possession, and not likely to come into possession, of information from which the individual from whose body the material has come can be identified, or

(c) it is an embryo outside the human body.

19.61 Section 45(2) follows the recommendations made by the Human Genetics Commission in their report 'Inside Information' in 2002 in relation to the unauthorized use of genetic material for purposes including paternity testing.[207] Section 45(5) relates to 'any material which consists of or includes human cells'. As Price notes: 'Thus although extracted DNA is not "relevant material", the non-consensual keeping or handling of any bodily material for the purpose of extracting or analyzing DNA may be.'[208] Price questions why extracted DNA is excluded from the general definition.[209] He suggests a number of possible reasons. It may be to try to limit the scope of the legislation. Alternatively, he suggests it may be because the material is regarded as information itself rather than the material from which information has been obtained. To undertake activities which require a licence from the HTA without possessing such licence is also a criminal offence.[210]

C. Property and Human Material

1. Property and the corpse

19.62 Whether the human body should be the subject of property is the subject of considerable ethical debate and is an issue which goes beyond the scope of this chapter.[211] The law concerning property in the human body and its parts is complex and at present under a state of evolution. While the law regulated the use of corpses for scientific purposes, statutory provision established mechanisms for authorization of use. But while some control rights were given regarding the use of human material what English law did not do was confer proprietary rights upon the families of the deceased. At common law, from *Dr Handyside's* case through a notable series of cases—the *Haynes* case, *Re Sharpe*,[212] *Williams v Williams*[213]—English law has made clear that there is no property in a corpse. In *Dr Handyside's* case[214] two female infants were born conjoined in the stomach. The doctor who delivered them took them away. This case was actually settled but the doctor returned the twins to the father. In the report of the case it is stated that: 'in the case of Dr Handyside, where trover was brought against him for two children that grew together: Lord CJ Willes held that the action would not lie as no person had any property in corpses.'[215]

19.63 Although this decision has been much cited in later cases, the extent to which this case is authority for the proposition cited has been questioned.[216] Nonetheless, despite the powerful

207 (HGC 2002). see further K Liddell, 'Beyond Bristol and Alder Hey: The Future Regulation of Human Tissue' (2005) 13 Med L Rev 170, 184–89.

208 D Price, *Human Tissue in Transplantation and Research* (Cambridge University Press 2009), 37.

209 ibid.

210 Human Tissue Act 2004, s 16.

211 See generally D Beyleveld and R Brownsword, *Human Dignity in Bioethics and Biolaw* (Oxford University Press 2001) ch 8; R Gold, *Body Parts: Property Rights and the Ownership of Human Biological Materials* (Georgetown University Press 1996).

212 (1856–7) Dears and B 160.

213 (1882) 20 Ch D 659.

214 2 East PC 652.

215 ibid.

216 See P Matthews, 'Whose Body; People as Property' (1983) 36 Current Legal Problems 195; and see also P D K Skegg, 'Human Corpses, Medical Specimens and the Law of Property' (1976) Anglo-Am LR 412.

arguments advanced by academic commentators, notably Matthews,[217] as Grubb has commented: 'It is now almost certainly far too late for English law to re-examine Coke's antecedents or rationale for his statement.'[218] They have been affirmed in more recent cases.[219]

2. Property rights in excised human material

In contrast to the legal position concerning the corpse the issue of property rights in samples is considerably more complex. Certain bodily products/parts have been held to be capable of theft for example, hair,[220] blood,[221] and urine.[222] In *R v Welsh*,[223] D provided police with a urine sample. He then tipped it down the sink. He was convicted of theft of urine from the police. In 1984 a doctor amongst others was convicted of conspiracy to steal blood from the NHS.[224] Persons with a hair fetish have been convicted of 'stealing' hair by cutting it off the heads of young women standing at bus stops.[225] In 1997 an artist, Anthony-Noel Kelly, was prosecuted for theft of body parts.[226] Along with a junior laboratory technician he had smuggled anatomical specimens from the Royal College of Surgeons in black bin bags. As press reports noted these amounted to 'an "alphabet" of body parts: a head and torso, two more heads, part of a brain, as well as a collection of arms, hands, legs and feet.'[227] The removal was not discovered by the college authorities. The artist made casts from the body parts and exhibited them at the London Contemporary Art fair in Islington. The theft was only brought to the attention of the authorities when Her Majesty's Inspector of Anatomy, who had spotted it in an article in a Sunday paper, had appreciated that one particular cast, that of a silver-coated head and upper torso of an old man, was such that it could have only have been cast from, as the press report noted, 'an expertly dissected body part'. The artists and the technician were prosecuted. **19.64**

At the prosecution of Kelly and Lindsay the defence also submitted that the specimens were not in the lawful possession of the college at the time they were taken because they had been retained beyond the period of two years for burial which was stipulated by the Anatomy Act 1832.[228] However, it was held by Rose LJ that the judge at trial had been correct in holding that the college had sufficient possession under s 5(1) of the Act. They did not regard the issue of time as determinative and stated rather that the college here were in factual possession of the body parts. It was also unnecessary for the judge in the case to have directed the jury as to what did or what did not constitute lawful possession. **19.65**

The *Kelly* case is of considerable importance in the determination of what constitutes 'property' in human material today. But while human material may be considered to be property, whose property? Is it the property of the person from whom the human material has been removed or is it the property of the clinician or scientist who has retained, used it or developed it? **19.66**

[217] See Matthews, n 216; A Grubb, (1997) Med L Rev 111, though, as he notes, the position in Scotland appears to be different see *HM Advocate v Dewar* 1945 5 (HCt Just).
[218] Contrast P D K Skegg, 'Medical Uses of Corpses and the No-Property Rule' (1992) 312 Medicine, Science and Law 311.
[219] See, eg, *Dobson v North Tyneside Health Authority* [1996] 4 All ER 474 and *R v Kelly* [1998] 3 All 741.
[220] *R v Herbert* (1961) 25 JCL 163.
[221] *R v Rothery* [1976] RTR 550.
[222] *R v Welsh* [1974] RTR 478.
[223] [1974] RTR 478 See G Dworkin and I Kennedy, 'Human Tissue: Rights in the Body and its Parts' (1993) 1 Med L Rev 291.
[224] Matthews, P The Times, 7 July 1984.
[225] *R v Luff* The Times, 13 December 1960; *R v Herbert* The Times, 22 December 1960.
[226] [1999] QB 621.
[227] *Guardian* (Saturday 4 April 1988).
[228] This Act applied as the specimens predated the existing Anatomy Acts.

3. Acquiring property rights from work done on human material

19.67 Property interests may be acquired in human material[229] through work being undertaken on that material. In such situations the proprietary rights are acquired by the person who has undertaken the work. The exact extent of the 'work' which is required to be undertaken on a sample/specimen in such a situation is the subject of some discussion. In *Doodeward v Spence* in 1908 the plaintiff asked for the return of the corpse of stillborn conjoined twins which he had bought from a doctor who had preserved the corpse and placed it in a jar. The plaintiff placed the corpse on public display. This was then confiscated by a police inspector—the defendant in this case. The plaintiff claimed that he had property in that exhibit and it should be returned to him.[230] On appeal to the High Court of Australia Griffiths CJ held that:

> when a person has by the lawful exercise of work or skill so dealt with a human body or part of a human body in his lawful possession that it has acquired some attributes differentiating it from a mere corpse awaiting burial, he acquires a right to retain possession of it, at least as against any person not entitled to have it delivered for the purpose of burial, but subject of course to any positive law which forbids its retention under particular circumstances.[231]

19.68 Barton J agreed with Griffiths while his reasoning was more restrictive. Griffiths LJ suggested that mere preservation would be sufficient; however, another judge in the case, Higgins J, thought that it would not and placed reliance on earlier English case law which rejected property in the body. Alternative legal principles have been used to explain the acquisition of property rights once work is undertaken upon human material. Here we consider 'specificatio' and 'accession'. First, the doctrine of specification. Hardcastle comments that the origin of specificatio is rooted in Roman law 'specification'. He comments that:

> Specificatio is a medieval neologism from the Latin phrase speciem facere (to produce a new species). Roman texts refer to speciem facere and the principle is located in the title of Justinian's Institutes 'On the Acquisition of Ownership'.[232]

Matthews comments that:

> Where the change wrought in A's goods is purely a physical one, so that the shape or form of them is altered, but the substance is not, such authorities as there are agreed that A's property in them should continue. In a very early case the case of leather it was stated that:
>
> 'In every case where the thing itself be known, there the party may take it, notwithstanding that some other thing be joined or mingled with it. So if one take a piece of cloth and make himself a coat the owner may rightfully retake it, for the reason that it is the same things and not different.'[233]

19.69 But where the goods are 'changed into a different species' then the situation is different. This gives rise to the doctrine of specification.[234] As Blackstone stated while the product belongs to the operator 'there must be compensation paid to A for the loss of his goods'. Tests here include: Is it chemically different? Is it different in substance? Can the new goods be reversed into the state of the old? Where such a change has taken place then it is the person who has undertaken the change, not the person whose materials are used, who owns the final

---

229 There is further discussion of property in human material in Chapter 20 in this volume 'Patenting and the Human Body'.

230 *Doodeward v Spence* (1908) 6 CLR 406. See discussion in R Hardcastle, *Law and the Human Body: Property Rights, Ownership and Control* (Hart 2007), at 28–30.

231 *Doodeward v Spence*, n 224.

232 See Hardcastle, n 224, at 131.

233 See P Matthews, 'Specificatio in the Common Law' (1981) 10 Anglo-American Law Review 121.

234 See Hardcastle, n 224 at 131–43.

product. In determining whether specification has occurred courts look to the uses, values, and common names of the starting material and finished product. Hardcastle suggests that:

> There are three options: (1) the owner of the original material that no longer exists; (2) the maker of the new item and (3) no one.[235]

Matthews has argued that the Roman doctrine of 'specificatio' has no place in the common law. He suggests that the

> true principle should be one of identification. If the plaintiff can identify his goods in the defendant's hands, even if their nature can be chemically different from previously then his right to possession of those goods prima facie continues unabated.[236]

Hardcastle suggests that the current work and skill exception may be seen as a 'misguided application of the specification doctrine'.[237] Secondly, there is the doctrine of accession. This is a civil law doctrine and refers to a principle under which the owner of property is entitled to all which it produces and to anything which is linked to or added, whether naturally or by labour or skill, even if this leads to a change in the nature of the material. Hardcastle has defined it as follows: 'Accession involves the bringing together of entities that belong to different people with the result that one contribution merges into the other and loses its legal identity.'[238] Case law to date has not utilized these principles expressly in relation to property in human material. However, Price has suggested that:

> While there may be a paucity of precedent to determine whether natural materials may be subject to the doctrine, in principle there is no reason why not, provided that the original material is subsumed into another item. The doctrine of accession could apply, for instance, to amplified DNA and cell lines.[239]

The scope of the work and skill exception in *Doodeward* was considered in subsequent English cases. In *Dobson v North Tyneside* the Court of Appeal suggested that the work done on the brain in that case, preserving it in paraffin, was not enough—it was not comparable with stuffing/embalming and the like and thus did not fall under *Doodeward*.[240] However, as Grubb has commented: 'what is the difference? There must, it would seem, be an intention to create a novel item with a use of its own.'[241] Admittedly, however, interpreting *Doodeward* broadly would itself have given rise to what were considerable problems. If undertaking any work would give rise to property rights this could have led to difficulties as some work is undertaken on most bodies prior to burial, and this would have given rise to an issue as to whether the person undertaking the embalming would have obtained property rights in the corpse. But this has to be contrasted with *R v Kelly*, where it was suggested that using techniques of preservation or undertaking dissection is sufficient.[242] In the *Kelly* case the court also took another step. It was proposed that body parts which have a use/significance beyond their mere existence may constitute property. In *Kelly* Rose J gave the examples of those body parts which were intended for use in an organ transplant operation, samples for DNA extraction, or as an exhibit to be used at trial.[243] This broader interpretation has itself come under some criticism. Grubb has suggested that: 'This would however, **19.70**

[235] See ibid, at 137.
[236] See P Matthews, n 227, at 121, 127.
[237] See Hardcastle, n 224, at 143.
[238] See Hardcastle, n 224, at 131; and also *Rendell v Associated Finance Pty Ltd* [1967] VR 604 (Vic SC).
[239] See Price, n 184, at 260.
[240] *Dobson v North Tyneside HA* [1997] 1 WLR 596 (CA), per Peter Gibson LJ.
[241] A Grubb, 'Theft of Body Parts; Property and Dead Bodies' (1998) 6 Med L Rev 247.
[242] *R v Kelly* [1999] QB 621.
[243] ibid at 631.

in effect, to re-write the "no-property" rule itself.'[244] In *Re Organ Retention Litigation* actions were brought in relation to retention of human material from deceased children after statutory or hospital post-mortems.[245] Here Gage J agreed that where there had been preservation and dissection of the material into tissue blocks, this vested property rights in relation to the material in the defendants.[246] In *Yearworth v N Bristol NHS Trust.*[247] Clarke LCJ held that the storage of sperm by a fertility unit in liquid nitrogen did constitute 'an application to the sperm of work and skill which conferred on it a substantially different attribute'.[248] However, interestingly here the Court of Appeal took a different approach and did not see the application of work and skill as the critical issue in determining ownership. Here rather they were fundamentally concerned with the question of the control exercised by the individuals who had provided the sperm.

19.71 Thus, to summarize, it is clear that there is in English common law no property in the corpse, but at the same time excised material from both cadaver and live persons may constitute 'property'. It is clear that they may become property if some work/improvement has been undertaken upon them. The application of doctrines such as specification and accession remains to be explored by the English courts in relation to property in human material. But *R v Kelly* raises the issue as to what extent material may constitute property because of its own innate quality even in a situation in which further work has not be undertaken on that material. Moreover even if it may be property, 'whose' property? English law does recognize that undertaking work gives rise to proprietary rights supporting/recognizing the relativity of proprietary rights in relation to human material. *Yearworth* appears to root concern here in the concept of individual control. It also suggests a move away from the *Doodeward v Spence* approach (this case is discussed further at para 19.77). We move below to exploring some of the consequences which may arise if there are property rights in human material.

4. Consequences of recognizing proprietary rights in human material

19.72 If human material may be the property of the person from which it is removed then various legal consequences may follow, not least the prospect of a legal action if there has been unauthorized commercial exploitation of that property. Here we explore the prospect of actions which may result in the tort of conversion and in the action of bailment where material is removed and/or subsequently used without an individual's consent. Before we consider the prospect for such actions in more detail in the context of English law it is instructive to consider a classic case in the USA—that of *Moore v University of California.*[249] Moore had hairy cell leukaemia. Blood, bone marrow, and other samples were taken as part of the process of confirming the diagnosis. He subsequently consented to the removal of his spleen in 1976 but he was not informed nor did he give consent in relation to research being undertaken on his spleen. This was then removed. He also returned to the medical centre at the university over a subsequent period of seven years in which he provided further samples of blood, serum, skin, and bone marrow. Research was undertaken without his knowledge on T-lymphocyte cells. The cells from Mr Moore's spleen were used to develop a cell line which proved to be extremely commercially lucrative. The Regents of the University of California were granted a patent consequent upon this cell line in 1984. Only in 1984 was Moore asked to sign a consent form in relation to the use of his material for research purposes.

---

244 A Grubb, 'Theft of Body Parts; Property and Dead Bodies' (1998) 6 Med L Rev 247.
245 [2005] QB 506, see also discussion in Hardcastle, n 224, at 34–35.
246 This approach was also followed in *Yearworth v North Bristol NHS Trust* [2009] EWCA Civ 37.
247 ibid; and M Quigley, 'Property: The Future of Human Tissue' (2009) 17 Med L Rev 457.
248 *Yearworth v North Bristol NHS Trust*, n 240, at 45.
249 *Moore v University of California* (1990) 793 P 2d 479.

He refused to do so. In the subsequent litigation he claimed that these cells were removed without consent. He alleged that he was told that the procedures undertaken were for therapeutic purposes. He also claimed that there was a breach of the fiduciary duty which was owed to him. He also brought an action in the tort of conversion. The case was heard in the Supreme Court of California. Moore succeeded on the grounds that the cells were removed without his consent. When they removed the tissue the doctors were aware that it could provide 'competitive, commercial and scientific advantages'. He failed, however, to establish a proprietary interest in the cells.

The Supreme Court rejected the proprietary interest. Panelli J (with whom Lucas CJ, Eagelson, Kennard, and Arabian JJ agreed) stated that had Moore: **19.73**

> been permitted to have decision making authority and a financial interest in the cell-line he would then have the unlimited power to inhibit medical research that could potentially benefit humanity. He could conceivably go from institution to institution seeking the highest bid and, if dissatisfied, claim the right simply to prohibit the research entirely.[250]

They noted that Moore did not expect to keep possession when he donated the cells to his physicians.[251] Panelli J made reference to the provision of the Health and Safety Code which provided that:

> Notwithstanding any other provision of law, recognisable anatomical parts, human tissues, anatomical human remains or infectious waste following conclusions of scientific use shall be disposed of by internment, incineration or any other method determined by the state department [of health services] to protect public health and safety.[252]

Although it was the case that this statute was primarily directed at handling of biological waste, Panelli J held that:

> By restricting how excised cells may be used and requiring their eventual destruction, the statute eliminates many of the rights ordinarily attached to property that one cannot simply assume that what is left amounts to 'property' or 'ownership' for purposes of conversion law.[253]

Panelli J distinguished the patented cell line from the cells: cells themselves are not patentable. The difference, as Dickens notes, is that cells by themselves were without value and required development before they could be the subject of commercial exploitation.[254] However, as was noted in the dissent of Broussard J in that case:

> the majority's analysis cannot rest on the broad proposition that a removed part is not property but on the proposition that a patient retains no ownership interest in a body part once the body part has been removed.[255]

He suggested that transplanted organs can be regarded as property for example, if an organ was designated for a specific donor. Broussard took the approach that the patient's control rights over their human material should be protected by the tort of conversion.[256] It should

250 ibid.

251 Cal Health and Safety Code S 7054.4, West Supp 1992.

252 (1990) 793 P 2d 479; see generally B Dickens, 'Living Tissue and Organ Donors and Property Law: More on Moore' (1992) Journal of Contemporary Health Law and Policy 73–93; R S Magnusson, 'Proprietary Rights in Human Tissue' in N Palmer and E McKendrik (eds), *Interests in Goods* (2nd edn, LLP 1998).

253 *Moore v University of California*, n 243.

254 ibid, 186.

255 ibid.

256 See also the dissent of Mosk J, ibid.

be noted however that the court in *Moore* drew back from holding that excised cells could never be property. The court talked in terms of the fact that regulation was necessary for individual parts rather than it being the case that these issues should be left to be dealt with as general property law principles.

19.74 *Moore* is of interest in the UK situation for a number of reasons. The first is the rejection of the proprietary interest approach by the Californian Supreme Court. While the conversion action failed in that case, there is the possibility that such an action could be brought in the UK. Dworkin and Kennedy have discussed the prospects for a claimant in an analogous situation to Moore of bringing an action in the UK.[257] They suggest that prior to removal the patient could have expressly abandoned tissue or impliedly done so. They suggest that in most situations the fact that the physician has not disclosed the possibility of the economic potential of the tissue is unlikely to affect the norm of implied abandonment. However, they argue that there may be two situations in which the position is somewhat different. First, if a patient had explicitly addressed the question of what will or should happen to tissue after its removal. Alternatively, in some rare situations use of tissue may amount to blatant deception, a category into which they suggest the *Moore* case falls:

> In such unusual circumstances it is likely that the failure to disclose known information about commercial potential could be regarded as so important to the patient's decision to undergo the medical procedures as to affect the validity of Moore's consent and so justify an action against the physician for trespass.[258]

In two subsequent US cases, *Greenberg v Miami Children's Hospital*[259] and *Washington University v Catalona*[260] the courts have suggested that property rights may arise once material has become detached, although in neither case was an action in conversion successful.[261]

19.75 Where an action is brought by a claimant who alleges their material has been exploited for commercial purposes it has been suggested that equitable principles of fraud, duress, and undue influence could be used in the claimant's favour or that the plaintiff could avoid the transaction and bring proceedings in conversion.[262] Conversion was defined by Lord Porter in *Caxton Publishing Co v Sutherland Ltd*[263] as 'an act intentionally done inconsistent with the owner's right, though the doer may not know of or intend to challenge the property or possession of the true owner'.

19.76 There may, however, as Dworkin and Kennedy note, be considerable practical difficulties in bringing such an action.[264] Assessment of damages relates very much to the circumstances of the case. Generally, the value of goods at the time of the conversion is the measure of damages along with any consequential and non-remote damage incurred. The problem is that the value of cells at the time of conversion will be negligible; assessment at a later date would be necessary. A further issue is how far the extent to which the defendants have undertaken any work in improving the cell line can be taken into account in reducing the amount of compensation paid.[265] Section 6 of the Torts (Interference with Goods) Act

[257] G Dworkin and I Kennedy, 'Human Tissue: Rights in the Body and its Parts' (1993) 1 Med L Rev 291, 311.

[258] ibid.

[259] 264 F Supp 2d 1064 (US DC Florida 2003).

[260] 437 F Supp 2d 985(USDC Ed Mo 2006).

[261] See further discussion in Hardcastle at n 224 above 71–78.

[262] See Dworkin and Kennedy, n 251.

[263] [1939] AC 178, 202, as quoted by D Brahams in 'Bailment and Donation of Parts of the Human Body' (1989) NLJ 803.

[264] See Dworkin and Kennedy, n 251.

[265] Work undertaken has reduced compensation. *Reid v Fairbanks* (1853) 13 CB 692.

1977 provides that allowance may be made to a defendant for any increase which has been incurred in the value of the goods, due to expenditure or work on them by a person who was acting in what was a mistaken, but honest belief that he had good title to the goods. There is the possibility also of other actions including equitable remedies such as delivery up, account of profits, constructive trust/unjust enrichment, and the like. In some cases persons who obtain patents where unlawful acts have been performed may be ordered to hold that patent on trust for a wronged person.[266] Another possibility is that it could constitute theft.[267] If the approach taken in *Kelly* is followed, then it is suggested that unless there is clear release of any property interest there may in the future be the prospect of an action in conversion in this country along similar lines to that in *Moore*.

A further possibility is that an action can be rooted in bailment. This has been discussed by Brahams. Brahams was of the view that organs/tissues are not abandoned at the point of removal from the body. She suggests that here it may be that there is a gratuitous bailment. This has been as 'created whereby there is a delivery of goods or chattels to somebody who is to carry them or to do something about them gratis, without any reward for such his work or carriage'.[268] As she notes, if the terms of the bailment are breached then the right to immediate possession will revert to the bailor, who in this case would be the patient. The issue, were a *Moore*-type case to be litigated in this country, would be whether it was general practice as to their use. Brahams suggests that if patients were asked they would probably say that they would expect the tissue to be decently treated/disposed of. As she goes on to say: **19.77**

> Any transfer (whether by bailment or gift) would be unlikely to authorise the doctor to e.g. feed the diseased organ to his dog or laboratory animals. It is also doubtful whether any implied agreement would entitle the doctor to display the organ for gain though if the display is in the hospitals medical school this would probably be acceptable provided confidentiality was maintained.[269]

She goes on to argue that:

> While it may be acceptable that the doctor tots for biological gems on an altruistic basis aimed at serving the public good, it is arguable that the same research done without consent and with a view to the doctor's personal financial enrichment may not be either lawful or ethical. If the researcher is passed the material by the doctor who did not know of his financial aspirations the legal tangle could be more complex. Arguably though at one or two more removes the bailment would still lapse once any terms are breached.[270]

The prospect of actions in tort and bailment has been considered most recently in *Yearworth v N Bristol NHS Trust*.[271] In 2008 a group of men successfully sued an NHS trust following the destruction of frozen sperm stored in an NHS trust freezer. The men had been treated for cancer and had undergone chemotherapy. They were advised that the treatment would be likely to render them infertile and that prior to treatment they should store some sperm. This they did. In June 2003, however, the liquid nitrogen levels in the tank storing the sperm fell and no attempt had been made to manually top up the levels. As a consequence the sperm was rendered useless. The men brought an action in tort against North Bristol NHS Trust. The Court of Appeal was asked to consider the ability of the men (and in one **19.78**

[266] *Seager v Copydex* [1967] RPC 349.
[267] See Brahams, n 257.
[268] ibid, Brahams cites Holt's sixth category in (1703) 2 Ld Raynr 909.
[269] ibid.
[270] ibid, 803.
[271] (2009) EWCA Civ 37; and M Quigley, 'Property: The Future of Human Tissue' (2009) 17 Med L Rev 457.

case their executor) to sue in tort and bailment regarding the sperm. The Court of Appeal confirmed that such actions could be brought and referred the matter to the lower court to determine the case. Notably they held that the men had ownership of the sperm and this was the case even though, under the Human Fertilisation and Embryology Act 1990, they could not direct total control over its use for all purposes. As noted above, they were fundamentally concerned with the issue of control. Here, as the men had rights in tort, thus the court held that they were able to have 'Such lesser rights in relation to it as would render them capable of having been bailors of it'.[272] The Court of Appeal held that there was a gratuitous bailment by the fertility unit and thus here the hospital had 'held itself out to the men as able to deploy special skill in preserving the sperm'.[273] Quigley has suggested that the prospect of an action in bailment has considerable advantages for the litigant as the Court of Appeal in the case took the approach that any assessment of damages could also include damages for psychiatric injury and mental distress, something which is exceedingly difficult to establish in the law of tort.[274]

5. Waste property

19.79 If human material may be regarded as 'property', in legal terms at least, then we perhaps need to consider carefully the implications of the fact that people can get rid of their property. Can we regard and indeed should we regard bodily parts/products as 'waste' and what are the legal implications of so doing? The language of 'waste' is certainly used to describe bodily parts and bodily products through the term 'clinical waste'.[275] As the Nuffield Report notes:

> Inevitably prudence dictates some over-collection, and there may be tissue left over after sampling or surgery once sufficient has been assured for diagnosis and therapy. This surplus is normally discarded as clinical waste.[276]

19.80 Again something such as urine may be seen generally as a 'waste' product but not if specifically collected and sent for scientific analysis. Blood is in some instances a precious commodity, is the odd drop of blood from a cut on the fingers, waste? What about genetic information derived from body parts; can this be differentiated? Can waste be defined from the point of view of the person discarding it rather than the recipient? But can this be the case totally—if you knew that the material would be wanted by another for example, would this change your perception of that material? One factor is of course the manner in which the waste may be used subsequently. Moreover, the use of discarded material may have religious and cultural dimensions.[277]

19.81 Recognition of bodily parts/products as property has legal consequences. What is the consequence of conceptualization of bodily parts/products as 'waste'? Is it the case that if something is classified as being 'waste' then this by itself would not mean that an individual would lose an interest, in particular a legal interest in the material which has been removed? This, again, is dependent upon the circumstances and thus we need in particular to examine what are the consequences of definition as 'waste'.

---

272 ibid para 47.
273 ibid para 49.
274 Quigley, n 265, at 464.
275 This was considered in the Nuffield Report on Human Tissue in 1995 as including: (1) Blood/bone marrow used for diagnostic purposes; (2) Amniotic fluid/chorion villus pieces for, eg, diagnostic tests during pregnancy; (3) Small pieces of tissue taken by biopsy for pathological exam/diagnosis.
276 Nuffield Council on Bioethics, *Human Tissue* (1995), para 4.2.
277 Wellcome/MRC, *Public Perceptions of the Collection of Human Biological Samples* (MRC 2001).

The first approach which could be taken is that of arguing that bodily parts/products are *res nullius*. This idea was mooted in the Nuffield Report in 1995. If the tissue is *res nullius* then it is the case that the tissue belongs to no one when it is removed,[278] which is to say that it then belongs to the first person into whose hands it falls. As Dickens stated: **19.82**

> A philosophical approach to the origination from a living body of independently tangible material or of fluids capable of isolation may be to consider them res nullius, that is corporeal items in the legal ownership of nobody.[279]

Bracton lists certain things which are treated to be *res nullius*—wild birds, fish, beasts, and the like. He then states that: 'Things taken as derelict are otherwise said to be res nullius.' He also states that things can become *res nullius* after a period of time has gone by, for example, treasure trove. It appears that there was some questioning of this in later cases motivated by concern at persons seizing the contents of wrecks and so forth, but, interestingly, it was many years before this was actually made a felony (this was in conflict with the later doctrine that all property without an owner went to the king).[280] **19.83**

The application of the concept of *res nullius* has been the subject of trenchant criticism by Matthews.[281] He has stated that 'there is no English authority for treating human tissue as *res nullius*, as if it were some sort of wild animal or plant'. He has argued that it has only been used in certain specific areas of law (theft, wreck, salvage, treasure trove) and that it is doubtful whether it could be said that it was of general application. Also he comments that it presumes that when the doctor removes the tissue etc he does so independently of P. This criticism is echoed by Dickens who suggests that: **19.84**

> The characterisation of separated body materials as *res nullius* may serve the interests of neither the human source or others. To suggest that material immediately passes into the absolute ownership of the hospital or physician undertaking or supervising its removal or intending to appropriate it might defeat the source's justifiable interest in its use or disposition and the purpose of its specific donation, for instance of diagnosis, transplantation or a particular research project . .?[282]

Also what if a limb is severed and then reattached to the body itself? 'His claim to it should not be impaired by the chance of the item falling upon another's land or being retrieved and retained by a stranger not implicated in causing the loss.'[283]

An alternative approach is that a bodily part/product can be regarded as having been abandoned. Interestingly, Blackstone later stated that in circumstances in which moveables are found on the surface of land/on the sea and are unclaimed by an owner then these are: **19.85**

> supposed to be abandoned by the last proprietor and as such, are returned into the common stock and mass of things: and therefore, they belong as in a state of nature to the first occupant or fortunate finder, unless they fall within the description of waifs or strays or wreck or hidden treasure: for these . . . are vested by law in the sovereign.[284]

---

278 Nuffield Council on Bioethics, *Human Tissue* (1995), para 9.8.
279 B M Dickens, 'The Control of Living Bodily Materials' (1977) 27 University of Toronto Law Journal 142, 180.
280 A Hudson, 'Abandonment', in N Palmer and E McKendrick, *Interests in Goods* (2nd edn, Lloyd's of London Press 1998) 429.
281 ibid, 263.
282 ibid, 181.
283 ibid, 183.
284 Comm Bk II ch 26.2.402.

19.86 Abandonment and a category of ownerless property is recognized in criminal law. There is a category of material which may not be stolen.[285] As Smith has stated it arises where the owner 'has evidenced an intention to relinquish his entire interest in the property, without conferring an interest on anyone else'.[286] For example, in *R v Reede* a woman was charged with the larceny of a £5 note found in the street by her daughter. Coleridge J held that 'If the circumstances under which property is found be such that the ownership has been abandoned, the thing is bonum vacans and anyone may take it.'[287] It appears to be the case that the courts will be concerned to ensure that there has been clear evidence to show abandonment.[288] So in *Ellerman Wilson Line v Webster* a lighterman was charged with the theft of scrap copper.[289] Lord Goddard CJ delivered the judgment of the Divisional Court and said that the stipendiary magistrate could find that the copper had been abandoned. He also said that: 'if the property has been abandoned you cannot be charged with stealing abandoned property, but it ought, of course to be abandoned in the sense or under circumstances which would show that the owner had definitely abandoned it and did not intend to retrieve it.'

19.87 There are a number of specific situations in which abandonment may affect possessory/proprietary rights. First, that of treasure trove. If there is simple loss—owner does not divest title; then the claim of the occupier of land on which it is found prevails. If this is not the case or if it is found on the highway then the claim of the finder prevails.[290] Secondly, estrays/strays—tame/reclaimable animals found wandering where the owner is unknown. These belong to the Crown or to the Lord of the Manor in which they were found if the lord is entitled to strays by grant or prescription. As Hudson notes:[291]

> This may compensate the Crown or the Lord of the manor for any damage the animals may have done and for the expense of keeping them. The claim of the Crown or the lord only becomes absolute if the animals have been proclaimed in the church and two nearby market towns and no-one has claimed them within a year and a day. The Crown or lord is bound to keep the animals and may milk or shear them but not use them for work. On claiming the animals the owner must pay the reasonable costs of their upkeep and of proclaiming them.

19.88 The Nuffield Council on Bioethics in their 1995 *Report on Human Tissue* suggested that:

(1) Tissue removed during treatment to which the patient consents is abandoned.
(2) Tissue removed otherwise than during treatment is a gift if voluntarily donated.
(3) Tissue removed and intended to be used for the benefit of the donor will, as a result belong to the donor.
(4) Claims to tissue removed without explicit knowledge and consent (i.e. not within (1)–(3) above must depend upon how far P can be said to have impliedly consented to removal and its subsequent use.
(5) Where a person cannot lawfully consent and no one can consent on his behalf, the Report would prefer to see legislation, but since that is unlikely, suggests that the courts rely on the notion of 'public interest'. Thus it would be legally justified to remove and use tissue from an incompetent adult if the use was a 'justifiable use'.

---

[285] See A Hudson, 'Abandonment', in N Palmer and E McKendrick, *Interests in Goods* (2nd edn, Lloyd's of London Press 1998), 433.
[286] J C Smith, *Law of Theft* (7th edn, Oxford University Press 1993) 33, para 2-52.
[287] (1842) Car & M 307.
[288] See Hudson, n 274, 603.
[289] [1952] Lloyd's Report 179.
[290] See also Treasure Act 1996.
[291] Hudson, n 274, 445.

The Nuffield Report made reference to a US case, *Venners v Maryland*, in which Powers J stated that: **19.89**

> By the force of social custom . . . when a person does nothing and says nothing to indicate an intention to assert his right of ownership possession or control over (bodily) materials, the only rational inference is that he intends to abandon the material.[292]

In another earlier US case, *Paul v Gulf Red Cedar Co*, it was stated that: 'It may be said that abandonment is made up of two elements, act and intent and the intent must be gathered from the fact and circumstances of the case.'[293]

Dworkin and Kennedy suggest that the consequence of the recognition of abandonment would be that property interest would pass to the medical authorities.[294] They state that: **19.90**

> It is submitted that, at common law, in most cases where a patient has consented to medical procedures without more, the presumption of abandonment of all property or other rights in removed tissue could apply, leaving the patient with no further legal rights in the material, whatever may subsequently be done to it. Whilst the recipients of the tissue may be bound by ethical and professional constraints as to its acquisition and use they are not subject to any continuing legal control by the patient.[295]

However, as they note, the notion of abandonment may be modified by the fact that the individual has reserved certain rights.[296]

Others, however, have taken a different approach. Matthews has argued that: **19.91**

> what P intends or does not intend in consenting to an operation must depend upon the precise circumstances. This will include the nature of the operation, the material to be used, the usefulness of such material in the current state of medical science and so on. It cannot be laid down as a general proposition that (for example) consent to the removal of tissue necessarily entails an intent to abandon it.[297]

Matthews also questions the reliance placed in the Nuffield Report on the doctrine of abandonment. He suggests that the status of the doctrine in English law is doubtful and that the cases are 'equivocal'. Moreover, he states that there has never been said to be a general doctrine of abandonment rather, recognition in individual cases for specific circumstances such as earlier cases concerning, for example, theft or wreck. In addition, in most of these cases he states that: 'English law has changed its mind at least once as to whether abandonment should or should not be possible.'

There are considerable divisions over the legitimacy of certain research practices and it is thus quite conceivable that a person may be perfectly happy to 'abandon' the use of their human material for one research project while they view another as being ethically unacceptable.[298] Individuals may be hesitant to 'abandon' their bodily parts if there is the **19.92**

---

292 (1976) 354 A 2d 483 (Md CA).

293 Quoted by J A Rothman in the Intermediate Appeal Court in *Moore* (n 243).

294 G Dworkin and I Kennedy, 'Human Tissue: Rights in the Body and its Parts' (1993) 1 Med L Rev 291.

295 ibid.

296 See also the discussion in B M Dickens, 'The Control of Living Bodily Materials' (1977) 27 University of Toronto Law Journal 142.

297 P Matthews, 'The Man of Property' (1995) 3 Med L Rev 251, 294–95.

298 On 9 February 2001 it was revealed that skin removed from patients during plastic surgery in hospitals in the south of England had been sold to a research centre at Portland Down Defence Evaluation and Research Agency. The skin, which had been removed during breast and abdominal surgery, was used in chemical absorption studies as well as investigation of drug delivery and barrier cream formulation. 'Skin Sold for Chemical Research' *BBC News* (9 February 2001) <http://news.bbc.co.uk/1/hi/health/1162587.stm>.

prospect that money will be made out of that human material.[299] As we have seen earlier in this chapter, the Human Tissue Act 2004 has framed the use of human material in terms of consent. Any assumption of abandonment may prove problematic and the extent to which researchers will in the future be able to assume that such a principle applies may thus be questionable.

19.93 Section 44 of the Human Tissue Act 2004 now provides that where material has been removed in the course of treatment or of diagnostic tests or research it then can be dealt with as waste. Here consent does not need to be obtained before it is disposed of. However, it is unclear as to the extent to which this relates to the common law in this area. Hardcastle suggests that rather than assuming abandonment:

> A better reading suggests that under section 44 surplus materials must be disposed of where the consent provided by the individual has not specified what is to happen to such materials.[300]

Specific provisions are made in relation to disposal of remains from still births and abortions in guidance issued by the Human Tissue Authority.[301] While these are covered by section 44 the guidance recognizes that this may be particularly problematic. The Guidance states that:

> Although under the HT Act, consent is not required for the disposal of pregnancy remains, the particularly sensitive nature of this tissue means that the wishes of the woman and her understanding of the disposal options open to her, are of paramount importance and should be respected and acted upon.[302]

It provides that 'pregnancy' remains mean

> all pregnancy losses, for example as a result of ectopic pregnancy, miscarriage or early intra-uterine fetal death; it also applies to terminations of pregnancy that have not exceeded the 24th week of pregnancy.[303]

Excluded are still births (babies born dead after the 24th week of pregnancy) and neonatal deaths and disposa of IFV created embryos which are regulated by the Human Fertilisation and Embryology Authority (HFEA). The Guidance states that women should be given information in relation to the options for disposal which should be provided in an appropriately sensitive manner. It goes onto state that

> The information provided should include an explanation of how the pregnancy remains will be disposed of if the woman does not wish to make a decision and would prefer the hospital to handle the matter. It should also explain who to contact to request a particular disposal option and the timescale for this. Personal, religious or cultural needs relating to the disposal of the pregnancy remains should be met wherever possible.[304]

---

[299] Instances of this were reported in 2001 that Alder Hey hospital and Birmingham Children's Hospital admitted that they had routinely removed thymus glands during heart surgery and had passed them to representatives of Aventis Pasteur, a French drug company. The company had paid £5 per tissue/organ and the material was used to produce drugs for the treatment of children's immune disorders. The practice had ended when the pharmaceutical company identified a superior material for the production of the drugs. 'Milburn Condemns Body Parts Trade' *BBC News* (26 January 2001) <http://news.bbc.co.uk/1/hi/health/1137764.stm>.

[300] See Hardcastle, n 224, at 111.

[301] Human Tissue Authority *Guidance on the disposal of pregnancy remains following pregnancy loss or termination Issued* (March 2015).

[302] ibid at para 4.

[303] ibid at para 2.

[304] ibid, para 9.

While the Guidance provides that information should be provided it is also recognized that equally some women may not want to be make such a decision and that such a choice itself should be respected.[305] In addition it is also stated that policies and procedures should recognize that this is an emotional time for the woman and that she may not want to make the decision at that time. The guidance provides that in a situation in which the woman has not made a disposal decision

> within a locally specified period of time since the pregnancy loss or termination (which should not exceed 12 weeks), the hospital responsible for the woman's care should make arrangements for disposal in line with this guidance.[306]

It is provided that the woman should be informed of the time period when information about disposal options is initially given. Hospitals are to develop disposal policies.[307] Staff are to be provided with appropriate training so that they can support the woman in the most appropriately sensitive manner.[308]

6. Actions consequent upon the unauthorized interference with a dead body/ unauthorized use of human material from a dead body

It has been suggested that any unauthorized interference with the right to possession of a dead body, for example, an unauthorized post-mortem will constitute a trespass to the person. Such an action could be brought without having to show actual damage.[309] An action may be brought for the tort of intentional infliction of nervous shock.[310] However, it appears that in practice establishing such a claim would be exceedingly difficult. This is because one element of this tort—the necessary intention to inflict harm—would be almost impossible to prove. While there has been some judicial suggestion that there is scope in English law to develop a tort in relation to the intentional infliction of emotional distress this is yet to be developed by the courts.[311] A spouse or other close relative may bring an action in negligence claiming damages for psychiatric injury caused due to the mutilation of the body by transplantation. In principle such an action may succeed if it can be shown that some recognizable psychiatric illness has been caused.[312] 19.94

A number of actions were brought consequent upon the retention of human materials following the Alder Hey Inquiry. It was announced in February 2003 that most claims had been settled with a settlement of £5m, an apology, the announcement that a commemorative plaque would be erected at Alder Hey hospital, and a donation to charity.[313] But families of children whose organs had been retained in other hospitals were offered lower sums. These families continued to pursue litigation. In *Re Organ Retention Litigation* actions were brought in relation to retention of human material from deceased children.[314] It was alleged that the unauthorized retention constituted an infringement of the tort of wrongful interference with the body drawing upon Scottish, Canadian, and US case law. It was argued that there was a duty upon a parent to bury a child, and that the defendants interfered with 19.95

[305] ibid, para 10.
[306] ibid, para 19.
[307] ibid, para 14.
[308] ibid, para 17.
[309] See P D K Skegg, 'Liability for the Unauthorised Regard of Cadaveric Transplant Material' (1974) Medicine, Science and Law 53.
[310] *Wilkinson v Downton* [1897] 2 QB 57; *Janvier v Sweeney* [1919] 2 KB 316.
[311] See further *Hunter v Canary Wharf* [1997] AC 655 per Lord Hoffmann.
[312] *Alcock v Chief Constable of South Yorkshire Police* [1991] 4 All ER 907.
[313] 'Alder Hey Parents Accept out of Court Settlement' *The Guardian* (Thursday, 27 February 2003).
[314] *Re Organ Retention Litigation* [2005] QB 506.

that duty by retaining or disposing of the body parts without authority. Gage J rejected this on the grounds that no such cause of action was currently part of English law. However, Gage J held that alongside the statutory requirements under the 1961 Act there was a duty of care in the law of negligence to inform the parents of the nature of retention. The duty of care involved some explanation of the nature of the procedures of the post-mortem of which the removal and retention is a relevant part. He commented that the 'practice of not warning parents and in particular the mother that a post-mortem right involved removal and subsequent retention of an organ cannot be justified'.[315] He found that consequent upon such a breach of duty an action could be brought by the claimants as primary victims. One of the lead claimants successfully established that psychiatric harm had resulted from the breach of duty, however the other claimants failed on that point which, as Hardcastle rightly comments, illustrates the fundamental difficulties in bringing that type of action.[316] It should however be noted that in the Scottish courts an analogous action, that of affront to feelings, has succeeded in *Stevens v Yorkhill Hospital NHS Trust*.[317] Gage J also stated that the decision to use the child's human material did engage Article 8. While this was not further considered Gage J stated that, in his view, claimants were in his view 'more likely than defendants to succeed in such cases'. This raises an important issue—alluded to earlier in relation to the discussion of the use of material for research purposes—which is whether the ECHR could be utilized as the basis for a claim in the future. Certainly some research organizations operating within the NHS, as Hardcastle notes, are likely to fall under the definition of a 'public body' under the Human Rights Act 1998.[318] Furthermore, Gage J also indicated that there was the prospect of a future action in the law of conversion. This litigation is groundbreaking and also indicates the potential scope for further actions in this area in the future.

D. Conclusions

19.96 The law concerning the regulation of human materials has radically evolved over the last decade and a half. There is a clear statutory structure in relation to consent processes with associated guidance from the regulatory authority, the Human Tissue Authority. In many respects this model has worked very well. Moreover, the use of criminal law provisions as a regulatory tool, though as noted earlier a matter of considerable concern when the legislation was initially enacted, has not in practice proved an inhibitor to scientific research. What remains uncertain however is the raft of legal principles concerning property in human material. The Human Tissue Act itself did not comprehensively regulate the question of property in the body and its parts and as we have seen this remains a complex issue. The whole question too of the interface between human rights and the Human Tissue Act remains something which may be the subject of further future consideration. The Human Tissue Act 2004 introduced what of course is a consent-based law. Whether this will totally remain the case in the future has perhaps been called somewhat into question by the Wales Organ Transplant Act 2013. Should opt-out legislation prove successful in relation to organ transplantation in Wales then it is likely that there will be increasing pressure to change the law in the rest of the United Kingdom. Any such change at a time when transplant technology extends far beyond harvesting kidneys, hearts, and lungs would require a major

[315] ibid.
[316] See Hardcastle, n 224, at 189.
[317] (2006) SLT 889. See also N Whitty, 'Rights of Personality, Property Rights and the Human Body in Scots Law' (2005) 9 Edin LR 194.
[318] See Hardcastle, n 224, at 185 and see generally discussion at 184–85.

public debate. Recently, suggestions that the body may be subject to cryopreservation after death give rise to potential new challenges in the future as to the question. Storage and subsequent potential revival of a 'dead' body would mean that society would not only need to revisit questions of the boundaries of 'life' and 'death' but also the very question of control and ownership of the body itself. In a case decided as this book was going to press a teenage girl dying of cancer was given permission for her body to be exported, subjected to cryopreservation, and stored after her death.[319] The matter was referred to the family courts and is something not covered by the Human Tissue Act 2014. The full legal implications of cryopreservation remain for consideration in a future edition of this book, as they arise. What is clear is that the debates which have dominated this area over many years, namely, the demands for use of human material for clinical and scientific purposes, the question of patient rights and respect for autonomous decision-making, and the need for consequently, effective, clear, consistent, and robust legal regulation in this area will remain.

[319] *JS v M and F (Cryonic Case)* [2016] EWHC 2859 (Fam). This is not a practice currently regulated by the Human Tissue Act 2004. See also Human Tissue Authority Statement on a Family Court Case Regarding Cryo-Preservation of a Child, 17 November 2016 <https://www.hta.gov.uk/news/hta-statement-family-court-case-regarding-cryo-preservation-child>.

20

MEDICAL INNOVATION, PATENTING AND THE HUMAN BODY

*Amanda Warren-Jones**

A. Introduction

20.01 If the last century was globally defined by war and the internet, then this century will be similarly defined by how well health care and health innovation are managed. Access to medical treatments and medicinal products, the availability of new diagnostic tools, and the future direction of biomedical research are all profoundly influenced by the existence and exercise of intellectual property rights (IPRs). This understanding of health care management is already apparent in the trilateral co-operation of the World Health, World Intellectual Property, and the World Trade Organisations (WHO, WIPO, and WTO respectively) on Public Health, IP, and Trade, which resulted in the 2013 report, *Promoting Access to Medical Technologies and Innovation*;[1] as well as being evident within EU wide policies such as the Innovation Union introduced in 2013 under the EU's *Europe 2020 Initiative*;[2] and nationally in the UK forming the basis of reports such as the UK's 2011 Department of Health Report on *Innovation, Health and Wealth: accelerating adoption and diffusion in the NHS*,[3] and legal instruments such as the UK's Health and Social Care Act 2012, which treats health care as a commercial market. This chapter focuses on some of the most pressing issues which arise from that nexus between commerce, health and social responsibility, but specifically directed to the strongest market-based rights granted.[4]

---

* This chapter has been amended and added to (up to January 2016), albeit extensively, to reflect the fast pace of change in this area of innovation and a slightly different focus from the earlier chapter written by Prof Graeme Laurie, to whom I give my thanks.

[1] WHO, WIPO, WTO, *Promoting Access to Medical Technologies and Innovation* (2013).

[2] European Commission, *Innovation Union Competitiveness Report* (2013); European Commission, *Elements for the setting-up of headline indicators for innovation in support of the Europe 2020 strategy* (2013).

[3] UK Department of Health, *Innovation, Health and Wealth: accelerating adoption and diffusion in the NHS* (2011).

[4] This excludes consideration of additional post-market exclusivity mechanisms such as those provided by the European Medicines Agency for data and market exclusivity, which can add up to an additional eleven years of exclusivity: see Regulation 726/2004/EC laying down Community procedures for the authorization and supervision of medicinal products (2004) OJ L136/1, and Directive 2004/27/EC

20.02 The philosophy of the intellectual property regime is disarmingly simple: the promise of a private property right to control the exploitation of a new creation—be it a drug, the maker's brand on its packaging, or the information leaflet within[5]—encourages others to create and make their creations available to the community, all in the name of the public good. The reward to the innovator is a monopoly right, limited in time, to exclude competitors from the marketplace. The strength of the monopoly varies depending on the particular IPR in question. For example, copyright only prevents direct copying of the work that is protected, whereas patent protection confers an absolute monopoly which makes it possible to exclude even innocent infringers who have independently and unknowingly invented the same product. Compensation for this uneven breadth of protection between these IPRs is reflected in the duration of the respective rights. Strong patent protection lasts a maximum of twenty years,[6] while weaker copyright in original works subsists for the life of the author and seventy years after the author's death. It is clear from this that intellectual property law is about seeking a balance between potentially competing interests. On the one hand, there is the need to regulate competing private interests between property right holders and other entrepreneurs who may, as a result, be excluded from the market. This, in turn, has consequences for the public interest lest excessive monopolistic control reduces consumer choice and services. Relatedly, there is the perennial problem of striking an acceptable balance between the offer of attractive and effective IPRs and the restriction on the grant and exercise of those rights when protection of them no longer serves the public good. Nowhere is the tension felt more acutely than in the realm of patent law, and it is this area of intellectual property law that impacts most directly on the provision of health care and the carrying out of medical research.

20.03 Enduring debate has focused on the patentability of biotechnological inventions, most notably genes and gene fragments, and on the impact of aggressive patenting policies on research.

amending Directive 2001/83/EC on the Community code relating to medicinal products for human use (2004) OJ L136/34.

5 As well as different IPRs arising in different contexts of medicine: ie copyright subsists in all notes, records, photographs, X-rays, prescriptions, and charts because these are protected as literary or artistic works under the Copyright, Designs and Patents Act 1988, ss 3–4. Similarly, the design of many instruments or other pieces of equipment might be the subject of design rights under the Registered Designs Act 1949 or the Copyright, Designs and Patents Act 1998, Pt III, while the Trade Marks Act 1994 is the legal basis for the grant of UK trade mark rights, the existence of which is responsible for the maintenance of high prices on drugs to which a successful brand is attached. Indeed, it is a global policy of pharmaceutical companies to ensure that drugs are marketed under a distinctive brand so that, once other protective rights expire, their market share is defended by brand loyalty against competitors producing generics (unbranded equivalents). Further trade mark and patenting disputes affect the pricing and availability of drugs through regulation of the practice of parallel importing, which refers to a re-seller of patented goods who sells in competition with the right holder. Furthering the freedom of movement of goods within the EU, parallel traders have been protected from infringement; see, eg, Case C-143/00 *Boehringer Ingleheim KG v Swingward Ltd (joined actions); Glaxo Group Ltd v Dowelhurst Ltd* [2002] 3 WLR 1697, 65 BMLR 177; but not where such trade has resulted in shortages of medicines in favour of gluts in more profitable markets: see (Joining Cases C-2/01 and C-3/01) *Bayer Adalat case* [2004] ECR I-23; and Case C-53/03 *Syfait v GlaxoSmithKline* [2005] ECR I-4609.

6 Supplementary Protection Certificates (SPCs) are available for pharmaceuticals and agrochemicals to enable any trials period which exceeds five years to be reclaimed, up to a maximum of five years. The rationale is that rigorous safety standards should not compromise the value of the patent in securing exclusivity once the product is marketed. In Europe, see Regulations: 469/2009/EC (2009) OJ L152/1 for pharmaceuticals; 1610/96/EC (1996) OJ L198/30 for agrochemicals; and 1901/2006/EC (2006) OJ L378/1 and 1902/2006/EC (2006) OJ L378/20 allowing an additional 6 months for medicinal products for paediatric use. For a recent ruling on the limits of an SPC by the Court of Justice of the EU (CJEU), see Case C-577/13 *Actavis v Boehringer Ingelheim* [2015] handed down on 12 March 2015 and confirming Case C-443/12 *Actavis v Sanofi* [2014] C 52 OJ EU 30.

This is exacerbated by many blockbuster medicines coming to the end of their patent terms, prompting a need to 'evergreen' patent rights[7] in order to bridge the gap until the new generation of personalized and niche-buster medicines come onto the health care market. How are regulators to resist this evergreening, whilst still ensuring technology proliferation? Protection of *combination inventions* (ie newly claiming known devices/medicines in tandem with unrelated known medicines/cells/tissue/elements), *selection inventions* (allowing new claims to existing chemicals, starting materials and elements with ranged properties),[8] and the statutory implementation of second/subsequent medical uses for known medicines form the most notable landscape for this debate and the subject of potential disparities between European and UK patent law practice. Objections to patenting in the medical sphere have been directed to both (i) *absolute* grounds of objection, that is, arguing that certain inventions should not be patentable at all, and (ii) *relative* grounds of objection, that is, arguing that medical patents should not be exploited in a particular manner—the objection to the latter being that the exercise of the monopoly is unacceptable relative to other social values, such as access to medicines and health care. The structure of this chapter reflects these broad themes. Consideration is also given to the role and rights of research subjects or patients when their participation in research or treatment has led to a patentable invention. While there has been ideological opposition to the prospect of patents in the medical sphere for quite some time, there is now a more pressing need to consider if patents are the right practical tool for managing medical innovation appropriately.

B. Obtaining and Exploiting a Patent

20.04 Patents are intended to facilitate innovation and this is inherently linked to requirements to mediate competing rights and encouraging technological proliferation. This is a consequence of innovation being a competitive process caused by many researchers aiming to meet the same health needs, and patent rights being restrictive to different extents.

1. Patentability criteria

20.05 Patents protect inventions and improvements. *Invention* is not defined in the law;[9] rather, a patent will be granted if a prospective product or process can overcome three significant hurdles. First, it must meet a stringent set of positive criteria for patentability, namely, that the invention must be *new* (in the sense of never before having been made available to the public[10] or being a mere discovery),[11] it must involve an *inventive step* (ie that the invention

[7] This refers to reclaiming innovations which are already known (ie 'me too' medicines) as if they are valuable new products, enabling patents to be granted for an additional twenty years over existing technology.

[8] Selection must either be from 'two-lists' of elements (meaning at least two) or relate to a specific selection from a generic range which provides appropriate advantages: see European Patent Office (EPO) Guidelines for Examination (November 2014) (EPO Guidelines), Part G-IV: 8, also comprised within the UK Intellectual Property Office (UK-IPO) *Examination Guidelines for Patent Applications relating to Medical Inventions in the Intellectual Property Office* (May 2013) (UK-IPO Guidelines).

[9] Patents Act 1977 (as amended) (PA 1977), (consolidated version 2014).

[10] ibid, s 1(1)(a), s 2.

[11] ibid, s 1(2)(a). EPO Guidelines, Part G-IV:3.1: '. . . if a substance found in nature can be shown to produce a technical effect, it may be patentable. An example of such a case is that of a substance occurring in nature which is found to have an antibiotic effect. In addition, if a microorganism is discovered to exist in nature and to produce an antibiotic, the microorganism itself may also be patentable as one aspect of the invention. Similarly, a gene which is discovered to exist in nature may be patentable if a technical effect is revealed, e.g. its use in making a certain polypeptide or in gene therapy.' This division between the natural world which is identified by technical means or may be recreated by technical means is at the heart of the division between biological material which is unpatentable as a discovery (Article 5(1)) and material which

does not merely represent an obvious technical development to an expert in the relevant field),[12] it should be capable of *industrial application* (ie it can be made or used in any kind of industry),[13] it must be sufficiently *disclosed* (ie a single embodiment/version of the invention must be described well enough to be recreated by someone of average aptitude in that area of expertise and other versions must be reasonably capable of being extrapolated),[14] and biotechnological inventions must additionally have *plausibility* (ie the link between the product and its use must be believable).[15] Second, an invention must not be excluded from protection according to a specified list of non-patentable entities; most particularly the invention must not be a method of treatment.[16] Finally, a patent shall not be granted 'for an invention the commercial exploitation of which would be contrary to public policy or morality',[17] and this general prohibition also extends to a non-exhaustive list of specific immoral innovations (ie human cloning or using human embryos commercially).[18] Whilst the second and third hurdles are subject to absolute objections and are explored later in paras 20.40–20.79, medical innovations place particular strains upon the concept of *novelty* as distinguished from *discovery* and this requires further exploration here.

2. Concepts of invention and value

It is essential to understand the wider context of patenting in the health sphere in order to **20.06**
appreciate how and why there are divisions made between what is patentable and what is unpatentable. All medical products (such as medicines, advanced therapy medicinal products like stem cells, and devices) as well as some processes (ie methods of manufacturing medical products) are capable of being patented. It is only where the 'method of treatment of the human . . . body'[19] must be claimed—either because that is the nature of the process that has been invented, or because that is the only means of distinguishing the invention from what is already known—that patentability is restricted. While the extent of the exclusion will be considered below, the issue for consideration in this section is why would a distinction need to be made between products and processes on the basis of how closely they

is the result of technical effort and is patentable (Article 5(2)) within Directive 98/44/EC on the legal protection of biotechnologjcal inventions (1998) OJ L213/13.

[12] PA 1977, s 1(1)(b), s 3.

[13] ibid, s 1(1)(c), s 4.

[14] *Conor Medsystems v Angiotech Pharma* [2008] RPC 28. In *Eli Lilly v Human Genome Sciences* [2012] 1 All ER 1154, the UK Supreme Court followed the EPO jurisprudence (T18/09 Neutrokine/HGS [2009] (unpublished)) to clarify that plausibility of function is an aspect of exploitation (biochemical, cellular, or biological) and is relative to what is known and valued in the specific context. For example, the relationship of a newly identified protein to its family/superfamily determines the level of proof required: where there is a shared function (known and well characterized) between the claimed protein and the superfamily, or where the value to the pharmaceutical industry is in the sequencing of the protein, its function does not need to be proven; but where there is no shared function across the group, or the protein's membership of the superfamily is unproven, the function claimed must be proven. In addition, discharging this proof could rely on evidence which arose after the priority date and this is highly contentious, because validity is generally required to be assessed at the priority date (the earliest filing date). In the EPO, European Patent Convention (EPC) Art 123(2) and the EPO Guidelines, Part H-V:2.2 make it clear that evidence after the earliest filing date can be used, but the UK-IPO initially adopted a more stringent approach (UK-IPO Guidelines, para 119) and it was only in 2015 that later evidence could be considered (following *Generics v Yeda Research and Development* [2013] EWCA Civ 925).

[15] Biotech Directive, (98/44/EC, (1998) OJ L213/13), Art 9; and see Case C-428/08 *Monsanto Technology v Cefetra* [2011] All ER (EC) 209.

[16] PA 1977 (as amended), s 4A(1) and (2).

[17] ibid, s 1(3).

[18] ibid, Schedule A2, s 3(b)-(d).

[19] ibid, s 4A(1).

are tied to a method of treatment? The intent of the exclusion to methods of treatment was summed up by the Court of Appeal in the *Taxol* case[20]

> [It] has the limited purpose of ensuring that the actual use, by practitioners, of methods of medical treatment when treating patients should not be the subject of restraint or restriction by patent monopolies. The difficulty is to decide whether the restraint concerns a method of treatment as opposed to that which is available for treatment.

The law reflects an understanding that patents are necessary to incentivize innovation and technological development, so the availability of these rights for new medical innovations is crucial. On the other hand, patents cannot be so closely tied to contexts of medical practice (ie treatments by surgery, therapy, or diagnosis) that they inhibit a medical professional from making treatment decisions based on the best interests of the patient.

20.07 Section 4A(2) of the Patents Act 1977 (as amended) ensures that 'what is available for treatment' can also be protected, so the prohibition on methods of treatment '. . . does not apply to an invention consisting of a substance or composition for use in any such method'. Pharmaceuticals are the most obvious and important example of such patentable products. The inclusion of this provision is entirely due to the lobbying power of the pharmaceutical industry and its insistence on the need for strong patent protection to maintain the incentive to develop an ever-burgeoning range of drugs. The threat that innovation will dry up if patent protection is not available is a powerful argument which is used across a range of industries that avail themselves of the benefits of the patent system, but nowhere is that threat more effective than in the realm of pharmaceuticals. Although there is precious little empirical evidence that the denial of a patent has a disproportionately negative effect on innovation,[21] the cost is thought to be too great to challenge the fixity of the pharmaceutical sector.[22]

20.08 Some European countries such as Spain and Italy traditionally denied patent protection to pharmaceuticals for reasons similar to those that underpin the exclusion of methods of treatment. Innovative medicines producers tend to avoid such markets if their products are easy to copy, creating pressures to monitor the movement of their goods between countries. As such, it runs counter to international and European Union commitments to trade and the free movement of goods which results in such countries being pressurized into bringing their laws in line with other western states. While a number of developing and least developed countries continue to exclude patent protection in this field, their membership of the WTO and attendant obligations under the international Agreement on Trade-Related Aspects of Intellectual Property Rights 1994 (*TRIPS Agreement*) mean that this is also changing. In particular, TRIPS requires that: 'patents shall be available for any inventions, whether products or processes, in all fields of technology'.[23] Least Developed Countries currently have until 2033 to provide patent protection for pharmaceutical inventions and test data. Meanwhile in Developed Countries, the current drive is towards greater accessibility of global markets and stronger patent protection in more contexts of application. So

[20] *Bristol-Myers Squibb v Baker Norton Pharmaceuticals* [2001] RPC 1, 17.

[21] See generally HM Treasury, *Gowers Review of Intellectual Property* (2006).

[22] See generally European Commission, *Study on evaluating the knowledge economy: what are patents actually worth? The value of patents for today's economy and society* (2006) <http://ec.europa.eu/internal_market>.

[23] TRIPs Agreement, Art 27(1). Note that Art 27.3 allows signatory states to exclude from patentability 'diagnostic, therapeutic and surgical methods for the treatment of humans and animals', while Art 27.2 permits exclusions from patentability of inventions '. . . the commercial exploitation of which is necessary to protect *ordre public* or morality, including to protect human, animal or plant life or health . . .'.

regulators are prompted to steer a line between facilitating more innovation, and ensuring that medical practice is not inhibited by creating requirements to obtain licenses or having limited availability of higher priced products. Novelty is a fundamental patent law mechanism for steering this line, because it changes the pace and proliferation of innovation by determining what threshold inventions need to achieve to attract legal protection and by identifying what technology can be reclaimed as if it is new.

(i) New products and processes

Novelty requires that protection should only be given to inventions which are 'new'. In technical terms, the invention should not form part of the 'state of the art',[24] and this is generally taken to be the sum total of human knowledge available anywhere and by any means before the application for a patent.[25] New medicines, whether they are traditional chemical-based drugs or new DNA-based biologics, are protectable under the Patents Act 1977 (as amended), s 4A(2) as *substances* or *compositions.* This is true even though they are used in an excluded method of treatment or diagnosis.[26] For medical devices (such as MRI or CAT scanners) or combination inventions (ie DNA-based diagnostic test kits) that rely upon new products/elements the novelty requirement is easy to comply with,[27] and this is similarly true of new processes for the production of medical products or devices. Ideally innovators want both product and process patents to be granted to the same technology, giving the strongest form of protection. For products, 'product *per se*' protection offers the strongest right, because it protects the product no matter how it is made or what it is used for. This is only narrowed where it is necessary to exclude known innovations or existing technology (ie by disclaimers). Understanding how an existing product patent can run in tandem with the creation of subsequent rights rests on understanding innovation as comprising: products (distinguished from starting materials), *technical effects* (its technical properties) and uses. **20.09**

Before exploring these concepts, it is important to distinguish that granting rights which follow existing product *per se* patents does not erode the right already given, but it does reduce the potential for further developments being reserved to the original patent holder. This is about technology proliferation. Giving product *per se* protection to a single innovator may inhibit the full social value of the invention being realized and this could be due to a whole raft of reasons. For example, there may be a resource or skills deficit in taking the existing product invention into a new or expanded field of expertise. The patent right enables the patent holder to license others to exploit these possibilities, but this is limited to the inventive knowledge identified in the patent which adds to existing knowledge (the *technical teaching*).[28] This can be more easily understood in a hypothetical situation: 'Product X' is invented as a new substance and the patent application identifies that it has a *technical effect of combustion* making it suitable for *use as a fuel,* and the version explained in the patent relates to refined fuels. As a product per se patent, product X is owned no matter what use it is put to or how it is made. The patent holder may factually exploit product X **20.10**

[24] PA 1977, s 2(2).

[25] The relevant date is the *priority date.* Normally, this is the date when the application is filed with the intellectual property office, but it can be up to twelve months earlier if a patent has been filed in another WTO country and the later application is 'supported by matter' contained in the earlier application; for the UK position see PA 1977, s 5(1) and (2).

[26] See now the PA 1977, s 4A(2) and EPC, Art 53(c).

[27] Legally the same criteria applies in individual European countries and for European patents, although there may be disparities in applying the law factually: see *AGA Medical Corp v Occlutech (UK) Ltd* [2014] EWHC 2506 where the UK court revoked a patent to a device for blocking holes in the heart on the basis that its use in clinical trials had disclosed it, but which was regarded as undisclosed by the EPO Opposition Division.

[28] *Case Law of the Boards of Appeal* (7th edn, EPO 2013), I.A.1.1.

as a refined fuel for farming equipment, but although product X as a non-refined fuel may be beyond the expertise of the patent holder, if it is within the technical teaching of the patent it is suitable for licensing by him. Simply identifying a new use which the product *per se* patent holder is not exploiting but is identified[29] by the patent application is not novel, because this is part of the patent right that was originally granted and it represents no useful additional technical teaching. So the creation and proliferation of innovation hinges on what is considered to be new.

20.11 Understanding innovation in this way leads to questions about what is capable of resulting in novelty, particularly where the product is not clearly different. Existing patent law in Europe and the UK recognizes novelty in three marginal instances: (1) a difference in the product even if it results from incremental changes; (2) identification of a new technical effect which exceeds a mere discovery; or (3) a known product with an undisclosed change in the use. While the first and third instances are shared by UK Intellectual Property Office (UK-IPO) and European Patent Office (EPO) practice, accepting technical effects can give rise to novelty has proven controversial.[30]

20.12 **(a) Changing the Product** Once a medical product has been patented, developing it further[31] relies upon affecting sufficient changes for it to be considered a new product—attracting its own protection—and this occurs either when the patent holder is improving the invention or a competitor has 'invented around' it. Inventions which are incremental particularly test the division between known/new and this is most closely defined in *combination inventions* and *selection inventions*.

20.13 *Combination inventions* arise in the context of medicines where a known product has been combined with: at least one other existing product (ie using two known Active Pharmaceutical Ingredients (APIs)); and/or with at least one known element (starting materials such as chemical elements or a compound). A recent example is the case of *Teva v Leo*,[32] the novelty for which was in combining two known substances for treating psoriasis with an existing solvent which stabilized the different pH's of the components to permit joint use of the substances. Although simply combining existing products/ingredients may not appear to be a valuable contribution to medical knowledge, there are clear instances in which the creation of such combinations have proven invaluable even where the resulting medicine is not more effective in treating. For example, combining AIDS medication facilitated a simplified use regimen, making it more suitable for global up-take; in other instances such combinations may reduce the potential for adverse reactions. In the *Teva v Leo* case, like many such cases, novelty was evident in the difference between the claimed combined invention and what was known, and that difference offered an important medical value. So combination inventions can be considered as new products, but they may still fail to obtain a patent if that difference is obvious.[33] This is because the application of the inventive step

---

[29] In the UK this includes inherently disclosing: *Merrell Dow v Norton* [1996] RPC 76, but inherent disclosure is not considered to destroy novelty at the EPO: T509/04 *ALLERGAN* (unreported), cited in UK-IPO Guidelines, para 145.

[30] Discussed in para 20.21.

[31] For non-patent holders, presuming there is either a license or the activity is within research exemptions: see the Bolar exemptions for EPO applications (ie Directive 2001/83/EC (as amended) on the community code relating to medicinal products for human use, (Consolidated: (2012) ec.europa.eu/health/documents/eudralex/vol-1/index_en.htm), Art 10); and newly expanded in the UK by the UK Legislative Reform (Patents) Order 2014.

[32] *Teva UK Ltd & Teva Pharmaceuticals Ltd v Leo Pharma & Leo Labs* [2014] EWHC 3096; [2015] EWCA Civ 779.

[33] eg *Glenmark Generics (Europe) Ltd v Wellcome and Glaxo* [2013] EWHC 148: and this was a consistent ground for challenge of the patent in other Member States, eg, Germany, Italy, the Netherlands, Sweden:

criteria requires that the innovation cannot be something that an ordinarily skilled person in the relevant field of expertise would have considered doing,[34] and simply combining what is already known is likely to fall foul of this.

Selection inventions are commonly found in claiming pharmaceuticals (ie identifying new chemical elements). Generalized families of chemical compounds are narrowed into fewer and fewer suitable target compounds as trials progress, until a lead drug emerges (creating an original product *per se* patent). Subsequent research commonly goes back through the compounds that were also being considered during the innovation process, looking for other potential medicines (creating selection inventions). Selection inventions also extend to any form of starting materials and any elements which have ranged properties (ie enzymes) and includes different forms of selecting. The result is that new rights may be created as these developments evolve and they tend to go to the original patent *per se* holder who made good use of his lead in the field, although they can be awarded to a competitor overtaking that lead. **20.14**

Selection inventions can be distinguished from combination inventions: the latter identify a new assemblage of products into a single item; the former identify a product or known material with new detail. Selection inventions are often about pulling an obscure family member from generic known lists of chemicals and supplying new information that makes the specific chemical valuable. This new value could be about identifying new drugs which avoid contra-indications (ie arising from taking a cocktail of other medicines for the same/related condition); or side effects (ie arising from existing allergies, genetic predispositions, or mild toxicity). In common with combination inventions, selection inventions can be considered new and still fail for being obvious additions (inventive step) if the selection was 'purely arbitrary'.[35] This appears to introduce a requirement for intentional innovation, but is more about needing to have an identifiable addition to knowledge or value which correlates to the choice of element(s) made.[36] Although the selection can rely upon evidence obtained after the patent application is filed to prove its value,[37] there is no possibility for adding 'unexpected bonus effects' from subsequent research to expand the selection invention applied for.[38] **20.15**

One danger with both combination and selection inventions is that they can easily become a basis for abusing the availability of patent rights, which are commercially valuable to 'evergreen' inventions. This means that innovation already patented can be reclaimed without adding any value and the only effect is to supplement the twenty-year protection granted to the original product with additional periods of protection. The best way of understanding this is to compare two cases: one of a legitimate selection invention and one attempting to reclaim an existing innovation. In *Dr Reddy's Labs v Eli Lilly*[39] the documentary evidence used to attack Eli Lilly's patent came from their own published research and earlier patent documents. So this was a classic case of an innovator patenting one drug in a class and then exploring in more detail some of the other chemicals within the same research looking for an alternative drug for the same treatment. The UK Court of Appeal rejected claims that the chemical—olanzapine, which promised to overcome some of the problems experienced **20.16**

EPO, 'European Patents Subject to Litigation in Multiple Jurisdictions' (2015) 2 OJEPO Supplementary Publication 149–54.

[34] UK-IPO Guidelines, paras 87 and 176–79; *Schlumberger Holdings Ltd v Electromagnetic Geoservices AS* [2010] RPC 33, upheld in *Medimmune v Novartis* [2013] RPC 27.

[35] UK-IPO, *Manual of Patent Practice* 2015, PART I, para 3.89(iv).

[36] See, eg, T939/92 *Triazoles/AGREVO* [1996] OJEPO 309.

[37] UK-IPO, *Manual of Patent Practice* 2015, PART I, para 3.89(vi).

[38] ibid, para 3.91.

[39] *Dr Reddy's Laboratories (UK) Ltd v Eli Lilly & Co Ltd* [2010] RPC 9.

with existing drugs treating schizophrenia—lacked novelty because it was already disclosed within a general class of 86,000 compounds. The court also decided that olanzapine was not obvious because, before the chemical was selected, insufficient information was known about the benefits of using it in treating psychoses. Comparatively, in the *Hospira v Genentech* case,[40] the court of first instance revoked a selection patent to a purified form of a monoclonal antibody therapy (branded 'Herceptin'), which had already been patented by Genentech for breast cancer use. The issue in this case was not that purification is an incredibly minor change, because purification of active ingredients/substances can lead to more effective treatments or opportunities to treat different conditions. The issue was that the stated level of purification was already within the tolerances identified in the original patent, which meant there was no additional value in the subsequent selection patent. So how was it granted in the first place? Getting patent protection right is often a matter of interpreting the potential implications of scientific values in fields which are continuing to be explored. So information arising after the patent or a variable appreciation of potential impacts can easily lead to patents being granted when they perhaps should not. Often it is down to competitors to monitor such infractions.

20.17 Consequences arising from allowing 'me too' medicines, created from reclaiming existing innovation under the guise of combination or selection inventions, can also be demonstrated by the *Hospira v Genentech* case. The existence of the selection invention (together with one to a new dosage regime) obtained during the life of the original Genentech patent to Herceptin had the effect of preventing Hospira, a generic drug producer, from commercializing the generic copy when the original patent expired in 2014. So, while there are clearly gains in promoting the development of these types of variations which fall outside of the original scope of the patent, many are used strategically by the original medicine innovator to keep competitors out of the market.

20.18 Although a combination or selection invention which results in a new use can easily be justified as providing important social value, the somewhat thornier issue is whether a known product—or a combination or selection invention—can be justifiably granted a patent where there is only a new technical effect and the use is already known.

20.19 **(b) Changing the technical effect** Having a new technical effect is at the heart of any innovation, because it is this which provides the basis of the technical teaching that warrants the patent and takes it outside of the realms of theoretical knowledge. The issue is how much else is required by the law in addition to a new technical effect. Patenting a known compound or an existing substance (ie an API or a sequence of DNA)[41] alone when all that is added is an unknown technical effect which results in a non-medical use[42] would not be permitted. This approach is designed to bring medical compositions and substances[43] into line with established rules on non-medical chemical compounds, which do not permit subsequent claims merely on the basis of a new technical effect on the grounds that this is a mere discovery.[44]

[40] *Hospira UK Ltd v Genentech Inc* [2014] EWHC 1094; the main claims confirmed as obvious on appeal: [2016] EWCA Civ 780. The dosage patent was also dismissed on appeal and remains unpatentable for being obvious: [2015] EWCA Civ 57.

[41] EPO Guidelines, Part G-VI: 7; UK-IPO Guidelines, para 172.

[42] ibid.

[43] Albeit that this categorization includes products which are technically not discoveries as such: ie APIs are regarded as equivalent to a single compound (which is usually considered a discovery) even though they are combinations of chemical compounds), see *ICH Harmonised Tripartite Guideline: Good Manufacturing Guide for Active Pharmaceutical Ingredients Q7*, (10 November 2000).

[44] *Case Law of the Boards of Appeal* (7th edn, EPO 2013) 1.C.6.3.1(f). T360/07 *Magnesium Omeprazole/SHERMAN* [2010] (unpublished) is an example of the medical application of this principle, because

As such, it is a consequence of a compound or substance relating to naturally occurring elements, which require technical effort before they can be considered patentable products. This approach can also be distinguished from combination and selection inventions, which are considered to be new products that are tangibly/intangibly different to what is known.

Outside of medical contexts, where a known product already has a specific use the EPO consider that a new technical effect which was not disclosed—even without a new use—can be the basis of a new patent right.[45] These innovations result in a narrower right than a product *per se* patent, and contemplates the creation of a 'purpose-bound' claim because the legal right is bound by the 'use for the purpose claimed.' For example, in the *MOBIL/Friction Reducing Additive* case[46] a publication identified a known product as having rust inhibiting properties (its technical effect) when applied to metals. The subsequent identification that the same product reduced friction (a new technical effect) when used in the same way was considered by the EPO's Enlarged Board of Appeal (EBA)[47] to be sufficient to warrant protection. Where the known product can be usefully employed for social benefit beyond what is already understood about it, there is a good reason to protect that valuable addition. The EPO have adopted the same approach in dealing with medical uses[48] and perhaps one of the most extreme examples was granting a patent on a known toxin with a new technical effect of promoting muscle growth in a known use context (the treatment of cerebral palsy patients), the only difference being in the change of technical effect—its known effect was as a muscle relaxant.[49] The determining factor for the EPO was that the new technical effect was not previously known or disclosed. Difficulties arise in considering how the creation of a purpose-limited right relates to infringement proceedings and in identifying instances where a new technical effect offers new value which is sufficient to justify granting a patent. **20.20**

The UK has been reticent to accept that a new technical effect on its own can be the basis of novelty. The danger became apparent in the *Merrell Dow v Norton* case,[50] where Lord Hoffmann considered the Enlarged Board's judgment in the *Mobil* case (above) and wondered '[h]ow does one tell whether the person putting the additive into his engine is legitimately using it to inhibit rust or infringing by using it to reduce friction?'.[51] Infringing patent rights are strictly liable in the UK, so the intention of the user cannot become a distinguishing feature of the law. In the *Merrell Dow v Norton* case this resulted in the court deciding that novelty is destroyed even if the earlier disclosure was only *inherent,* and not just if it was specifically stated. As will become apparent in section (b) below, the EPO does not share this approach to inherent disclosures. More recent cases have identified that even 'the EPO itself ha[s] come to appreciate the distinction between "true new uses" and cases of "mere more information about old uses"'.[52] So a known product with a new technical effect which only relates to precisely the same use would be unpatentable in the UK, but could be patentable if its new technical effect related to additional uses even if they overlap with the existing use.[53] **20.21**

identifying a different purity utilizing existing purification techniques discovers a difference but adds no technical teaching.

[45] G2/88 *MOBIL/Friction Reducing Additive* [1990] EPOR 73; G6/88 *BAYER/Plant Growth Regulating Agent* [1990] OJEPO 114.

[46] G2/88 *MOBIL/Friction Reducing Additive* [1990] EPOR 73.

[47] The EBA is the highest appeal board.

[48] T290/86 *ICI/Cleaning plaque* [1992] OJEPO 414.

[49] T509/04 *ALLERGAN* (unreported), cited in UK-IPO Guidelines, para 145.

[50] *Merrell Dow v Norton* [1996] RPC 76.

[51] ibid, 92.

[52] *Actavis v Janssen* [2008] EWHC 1422, at para 93.

[53] T231/85 *Triazole Derivatives/BASF* [1989] OJEPO 74.

20.22 In the context of medical applications, paras 20.12–20.17 identified that combination and selection inventions must be new and an inherent part of this is to provide some value from a new technical effect. For example, a new product could comprise a known API within a new mix of compounds if there is a new technical effect which results in a new shape that works more effectively because of its release profile,[54] and this would be given a product *per se* patent. If 'substances or compositions' are entirely known products—irrespective of whether it is within a medical or non-medical use previously—merely identifying new benefits (ie a shorter infusion time for chemotherapy drugs resulting in fewer side effects)[55] which are obvious advantages are unpatentable; but providing new technical knowledge that translates into new value which are not obvious (ie debunking existing knowledge and leading to new applications or uses)[56] is patentable. So even where a known medicine undergoes no physical changes, novelty can still lie in new technical effects which lead to new uses/value and this will be explored in paras 20.25–20.35.

20.23 (c) **Changing the Use** A known product[57] (as distinct from an element) can be regarded as new if there is a new technical effect leading to a new non-medical use.[58] This gives rise to a 'use claim',[59] because the subsequent patent holder only owns rights to the new use/properties of the product[60] and these can be justified on the basis that the use falls outside of the technical teaching of existing patent rights or is not part of mankind's existing knowledge. What is anomalous on this point of the law is why a known product which is not a 'substance or composition' used in an excluded[61] medical context (ie surgery, therapy, or diagnosis)—such as a known medical device—is seemingly excluded from a use claim and can only be protected where the product is new.[62] The answer hinges on why patents on 'substances or compositions' in medical contexts are patentable and relates to requirements for manufacturing: a medicine is expended in its use, creating a need to manufacture more; but a device is not expended and can be reused.[63] This distinction suggests that known devices which are expended during use could be reclaimed for a new use, but the central difficulty would be in how to word the claim so that it did not become excluded as a 'method of treatment'.[64]

---

[54] UK-IPO Guidelines, paras 167–69.

[55] *Bristol–Myers Squibb v Baker Norton Pharmaceuticals* [2001] RPC 1 and this includes the identification of new mechanisms which do not result in new products/applications/uses: UK-IPO Guidelines, para 141.

[56] See UK-IPO Guidelines, para 147; and *Case Law of the Boards of Appeal* (7th edn, EPO 2013), I.A.1.1.

[57] Although Justice Jacob speculated in *Union Carbide Corp v BP Chemicals Ltd* [1999] 11 RPC 409 that this could extend to process patents, it has not been extended to date.

[58] Depending upon what has already been claimed and may be owned by another party, which could result in liability for infringement.

[59] This would not apply to new products such as combination and selection inventions discussed above. These selection inventions—which relate to chemicals/starting materials/ranged properties previously claimed as part of a generic group/sub-group, bringing them closest to being known—are granted product *per se* protection when they are specifically claimed (well characterized with new value either as new products with new technical effects, or additionally in new uses), because the earlier generic disclosure does not destroy their novelty: *Dr Reddy's Laboratories v Eli Lilly* [2010] RPC 9; see also the EPO Guidelines, Part G-VI: 5 and 8.

[60] In contrast to normal use claims, medical use claims require specific legislative provisions ensuring their patentability. This is because normal use claims are treated as process patents, which—unlike normal process patents—do not extend to protecting the products to which they relate, only the methods of use. It is because a use claim relates to a process that—in medical contexts—they must be treated differently in order to circumvent the prohibition on patenting 'methods of treatment'. See EPO Guidelines, Part F-IV: 3.1 and 4.16.

[61] On the potential to replace exclusions with exceptions to rights see L Bently, 'Exclusions from Patentability and Exceptions to Patentees' Rights: Taking Exceptions Seriously' [2011] Current Legal Problems doi: 1010.93/clp/cur011.

[62] UK-IPO Guidelines, paras 71–73.

[63] T227/91 *CODMAN/Second surgical use* [1994] OJEPO 491.

[64] UK-IPO Guidelines, para 73.

Encouraging innovation which allows the full value of products to be realized can be essential to treating/curing different conditions and, as elucidated above, new and marginally new products (combination and selection inventions) which have excluded uses are patentable.[65] In addition, protection of known products with new/known excluded medical uses can be reclaimed provided they are 'substances or compositions': the Patents Act 1977 (as amended) under s 4A(3), protects a first medical use; and s 4A(4), protects second or subsequent medical uses.[66] Although these types of use rights are only for 'substances or compositions' which fall within the excluded methods of treatment, having an excluded and non-excluded medical use would be given protection[67] provided it was worded to the excluded medical use.[68] So what is the nature of these additional exceptions? **20.24**

(b) New uses of known substances and compositions

First medical use is when a known substance—not previously known or used for medical treatment—is newly claimed for medical use. Thus, a patent application would not be granted if there was evidence of *any* prior use of the substance in treatment. The corollary is that a claim to *first* medical use, in the correct form, can claim *any* use so long as at least one effective medical use can be shown.[69] The correct form of claim is: 'Substance X for use. . . .' followed by either 'as a medicament' or 'in therapy/surgery/diagnosis'. As such, they are relatively straightforward in their application and equate to a non-medical use claim. **20.25**

Second or subsequent medical uses of a known substance which has already had a medical application can be claimed for a novel and *specific* use of the substance. A typical type of claim would be: 'Substance X for use in the treatment of medical condition Y.' Note how this is narrower than a first medical use claim. This provision is the result of changes introduced by the European Patent Convention (EPC),[70] and the removal of Swiss-type claims from January 2011,[71] which obviate the need to adopt the fiction that novelty vested in the manufacture of the medicine in order to distinguish it from being an excluded method of treatment. Comparatively with first medical use, a second medical use is also a purpose-bound claim. **20.26**

How novel and specific must a second or subsequent medical use be to qualify for protection? Does any prior claim to use in 'cancer treatment', for example, automatically disqualify a substance for a new claim to a specific use for a specific type of cancer? The EPO ruled that: '[t]he disclosure that a particular treatment is effective against one or more cancer types would not normally indicate a 'reasonable expectation of success' in the treatment of an unrelated form of cancer.'[72] This means that novelty and obviousness hinge on the pathology of diseases: the way in which they work. So prior knowledge that a treatment works for one type of cancer (ie squamous cell carcinoma) provides a 'reasonable likelihood of success' in pathologically related forms of cancer (ie basal cell carcinoma), but using the same treatment for cancers with different pathologies (ie myeloma) could be considered a new use if they are pathologically unrelated. **20.27**

---

65 UK-IPO Guidelines, para 87 (even if the combination is not applied simultaneously: T9/81 *ASTA/Cytostatic combination* [1983] OJEPO 372) and 151; EPO Guidelines, Part G-VI: 7.1.2.

66 *Pfizer Ltd's Patent* [2001] FSR 16.

67 T144/83 *DU PONT/Appetite Suppressant* [1987] EPOR 6.

68 G1/07 *MEDI-PHYSICS/Treatment by Surgery* [2011] OJEPO 134; G02/10 *Scripps/Disclaimer* [2012] OJEPO 376.

69 *Hoffman-La Roche/Pyrrolidine-derivatives* [1984] OJEPO 164. On proof of efficacy, see the UK-IPO Hearing Officer in *Hoffmann-La Roche's Application* BL O/192/04.

70 These were incorporated into UK domestic law by the Patents Act 2004, amending the 1977 Act.

71 EPO Notice dated 20 September 2010, (2010) 10 OJEPO 514.

72 T385/07 *PHARMA MAR* (unreported), cited in the UK-IPO Guidelines, para 113.

20.28 Similarly, what if a new target patient group can be identified for a known substance? This can be sufficient to allow patenting as a second or subsequent medical use, but there is some disagreement between the EPO and UK-IPO as to when this would be allowed. The EPO ruled that the use of a compound to prevent bleeding could be patented specifically for use on non-haemophiliac patients, even though it was already known in all respects for haemophiliac patients.[73] In common with their approach to technical effect relative to use, the EPO allow that claims to specific patient groups must be distinct in terms of their physiological or pathological relevance to the new therapeutic effect of the known substance, and this means that different patient groups can overlap on certain characteristics. For example, the EPO allowed claims to a particular concentration of viral infection in a sub-strain of virus[74] irrespective of it including patients that would have been in the patient population for the known product for the main-strain of the same virus. The UK-IPO is more cautious both with respect to the issue of overlap and on the need to define clearly the target groups and the sub-group stating that: 'the discovery that the treatment works particularly well for that group of patients does not render such a claim novel.'[75]

20.29 The need to consider the relationship between a new technical effect and sub-uses may appear to be a minor legal difference, but there are a raft of *personalized/stratified medicines* being developed for which it is crucial that these distinctions are properly balanced to give a fair level of protection. Patentable personalized medicines arise in two contexts: (i) medicines which are more effective because they are designed for patients' specific genotype/phenotype;[76] or (ii) medicines which are more effective because they are administered by a method which directly relates to patients' physiology.[77]

20.30 **(a) Personalized medicine in geno- or phenotype** In the first category, claims will likely be hinged on the identification of patient groups in terms of specific gene-coding regions (ie product x (new/known) for the treatment of breast cancer in individuals with BRCA1 genes) or other biomarkers that are used to identify patients with the relevant genetic mutations. The EPO are already clearly mindful of such claims in flexing the boundaries between patient populations, but if personalized medicines are to result in the creation of niche-busters to replace the dwindling number of blockbuster medicines which are coming off patent, the concept of novelty cannot require even partially overlapping patient groups. Instead, novelty will need to relate to these additional distinctions in genotype/biomarkers. This is an unprecedented fragmentation of rights, which will undoubtedly form the basis of much controversial debate in coming years.

20.31 **(b) Personalized medicine in method of administration** A method of administering medicines relates to different forms, the timing, intervals, and amounts (general and unit dosage)[78] in which medicines can be taken.[79] The EPO position on method of administration was identified in the *GENENTECH/Method of administration of IGF-1* case,[80] which allowed a patent where the only novelty was in the intermittent administration of a known

---

[73] T893/90 *QUEEN'S UNIVERSITY KINGSTON/Controlling bleeding* [1993] (unreported).

[74] T1399/04 *Schering/Combination therapy HCV* [2006] (unreported).

[75] UK-IPO Guidelines, paras 138–40, at 140.

[76] Given a 'thin' interpretation to distinguish it from physiology: phenotype meaning the way genes interact with environmental factors.

[77] Distinguished from phenotype: physiology meaning the normal mechanisms of the human body, ie metabolism and endocrinology.

[78] Unit dosage relates to a confined amount of a drug (ie as a tablet, within an ampoule or a sealed injection or pump device) and are specifically recognized as protectable: UK-IPO Guidelines, paras 173–75.

[79] Confirmed in the EPO Guidelines, Part G-VI: 7.1.2.

[80] T1020/03 *GENENTECH/Method of administration of IGF-1* [2007] OJEPO 204.

medicine for a known therapeutic treatment. The value of the invention was that the technical effect in the frequency of giving the medicine was beneficial for the patient and was not obvious. This judgment was confirmed by the EBA in *ABBOTT RESPIRATORY/Dosage Regime,*[81] in deciding that a dosage regime or a change in administration method should not be treated differently.

The UK Court of Appeal in the *Taxol* case[82] considered a claim to a novel dosage regime related to giving medical practitioners instructions, rather than in relating to manufacturing, making it unpatentable. However, a subsequent decision by the same court in *Actavis v Merck* pointedly refused to follow *Taxol* and adopted the approach of the EPO: novelty in just the dosage regime could be patented; the court also decided the claim was factually directed to manufacture because it specified the dosage amount; and the innovation was not obvious, because the 'treatment for the condition with the substance had ceased to be worth investigating with *any* dosage regime'.[83] The exploration of dosage regimes are a normal part of clinical trials, so innovation on the basis of novelty in the dosage alone will struggle to not appear obvious, unless it is paired with a specific phenotype/genotype which was not considered relevant to explore within the patient population trialled. **20.32**

Similarly, not being obvious over the inventor's own patent rights elsewhere in the world, or even just submitted earlier in the UK or Europe, will provide a significant hurdle for dosage claims. This was the situation in *Novartis v Focus Pharmaceuticals,*[84] concerning a skin patch for administering a staged dosage of rivastigmine for treating Alzheimers, which was novel over its own PCT patent[85] only in its unit size (stipulating specific starting doses). The first instance decision concluded that this missing information would have been obvious with some experimentation, so the patent fails in the UK and it is left to other proceedings to determine which countries or regions the patent may be protected in. This highlights the limited scope of a patent right, which is territorial in nature—including in Europe until the unitary patent right is fully implemented[86]—and this territoriality inevitably necessitates enforcement through multiple litigation proceedings. The net effect is that the improvement (in this case of a staged dosage which simplifies administration and reduces potential side effects) falls within the original patent right, but even if that patent right is still active, it may not be enforceable in the jurisdictions in which it is used. **20.33**

These second medical use cases ably demonstrate that it is not always possible to find clarity or consistency in the decisions of patent bodies. Indeed, challenges in multiple jurisdictions throughout Europe only accentuate the disparities between Member States' courts and the decisions of the EPO Boards in applying the same general legal provisions.[87] A case in point **20.34**

[81] G2/08 *ABBOTT RESPIRATORY/Dosage Regime* [2010] OJEPO 456.

[82] *Bristol-Myers Squibb v Baker Norton Pharmaceuticals* [2001] RPC 1, 17; followed in *El-Tawii's Application* [2012] EWHC 185, relating to the alleviation of symptoms by a known treatment.

[83] *Actavis v Merck* [2008] EWCA Civ 444, at [32].

[84] *Novartis v Focus Pharmaceuticals* [2015] EWHC 1068, particularly [134].

[85] Centrally submitted for dissemination to the countries or regions identified on the application, permitting at their widest global patent rights, although they must be enforced through national or regional courts where the right is unitary.

[86] Regulation 1257/2012/EU implementing enhanced cooperation in the area of the creation of unitary patent protection (2012) OJL361/1; Unified Patent Court Agreement (2013) OJEPO C175/1 (the Unitary Patent taking effect when the UPC Agreement is ratified by thirteen Member States including the UK, Germany, and France).

[87] In *Conor Medsystems v Angiotech Pharma* [2008] RPC 28 the UK House of Lords acknowledged that it is inevitable that national courts would reach different decisions to the EPO on questions of applying the fact of particular cases to the principles of patent law, but national courts should attempt to adhere to the same interpretations as the EPO on points of law. In *Eli Lilly v Human Genome Sciences* [2010] RPC 14 the Court of Appeal clarified that this did not mean that the EPO Appeal Boards decisions had precedent

was the sustained release formulation to Quetiapine (a treatment for psychosis) which was decided differently in Germany, the Netherlands, as well as the UK, and led the Belgian District Court judge to comment on the lack of agreement in outcomes and disparate reasons even where outcomes aligned.[88]

20.35 Even before the additional fragmentation of rights which will occur with the introduction of personalized medicines, there are already consequences of having these *follow on* medical use rights. This is evident in the *Warner-Lambert v Actavis*[89] litigation, which in its fourth outing included an order for the NHS to issue guidance to GPs, hospitals, and pharmacies on prescription behaviour. Warner-Lambert owned patents to pregabalin—branded as Lyrica—which had been protected for three different medical uses. As the patent rights expired for two of the medical uses, Actavis—a generic producer—sought the right to market a copy of pregabalin. This creates what is known as a 'skinny label', because the generic drug can only be marketed for a reduced list of medical applications in comparison with the original patents. The Court Order requires that the NHS ensures that any prescription for use of pregabalin for neuropathic pain is written to the branded Lyrica only—to respect the remaining patent right. This is a means of making the NHS enforce medical use claims and purpose-bound rights, which comes at an obvious cost where it must additionally be embedded within relevant databases. Notably the infringement of IPRs within public procurement is the subject of an EU Commission consultation which closed in July 2015[90] and which is likely to give rise to specific guidance on avoiding infringement of commercial rights.

20.36 *Summarizing* and noting the relevance of novelty in granting patents: even in the context of known products, novelty rests on finding a new technical effect (a new property) which leads either to a significant change in the product or a change in use and this is accepted in both the UK and Europe. The EPO have additionally allowed that a technical effect alone may suffice, but it must still be coupled with some social value (ie greater efficacy, the avoidance of contra-indications, or a new dosage). Even then, the contribution must not be obvious to someone skilled in that particular field of expertise. New technologies test the boundaries of accepted divisions in applying patent law and it is in the nature of the pharmaceutical industry to push for increasingly preferential rights. The EPO's accommodation of a more generous understanding of novelty, both in not being destroyed by an inherent disclosure and in permitting barely perceptible changes in patient populations for second/subsequent medical uses, appears to accommodate this push and yet still falls short of clearly delineating the boundaries that will be necessary to usher in personalized medicines. How broad the right granted is (ie product *per se*, purpose-bound use claim, or with disclaimers) is relative to how new the product is: this is assessed from what is already known and what the innovation technically teaches. To accommodate new definitions of novelty, the patent systems in the UK and Europe are increasingly fragmenting the rights granted and this risks pushing the pharmaceutical industry back into greater reliance on trade secrecy.

value even on points of legal principle and the Supreme Court in the same decision ([2012] 1 All ER 1154) pointed out that consistent decisions at the EPO should be followed, but individual decisions should not be blindly followed as precedent.

[88] *Case Law of the Boards of Appeal* (7th edn, EPO 2013), 135–42, at 135.

[89] *Warner-Lambert v Actavis* [2015] EWHC 485.

[90] EU Commission, *Consultation on the respect of intellectual property in public procurement procedures* (2015) <http://ec.europa.eu/growth/tools-databases/newsroom/cf/itemdetail.cfm?item_id=8231&lang=en&title=Consultation-on-the-respect-of-intellectual-property-in-public-procurement-procedures>.

This section explored some of the most relevant positive requirements for patents, the next section focuses on some of the strongest grounds for what should not be patented within medical and biotechnological contexts. 20.37

C. Medical and Biotechnological Inventions

Both medical and biotechnological inventions raise public policy concerns. Medical innovations have traditionally required divisions in protection based on not interfering in patient treatment. [91] Yet, in being directed to phenotype or genotype, modern and personalized medicines bridge the distinction between medical and biotechnological innovation in health care contexts. The consequence is that existing policies of non-interference are increasingly challenged by new opportunities for commercial innovation and pressures to proliferate technology earlier. Purely biotechnological inventions continue to be the subject of controversy, because they relate to biological material meaning 'any material containing genetic information and capable of reproducing itself or being reproduced in a biological system'.[92] Put another way, these inventions embody (or are derived from) material taken from living organisms from the plant or animal (including human) kingdoms. A number of objections have been raised to the application of patent law in this realm.[93] These have often been confused and conflated under the emotive term 'patenting life',[94] the use of which is unhelpful and, for the most part, has served only to muddy the waters. 20.38

The interrelationship of medicine and biotechnology in practice negates distinctions being drawn between these categories. Instead broader legal—and social—objections are assessed according to their aims, of which there are two. First, *absolute* grounds of objection have been raised to exclude these inventions from patent protection because it is argued either: (i) they are prohibited as 'methods of treatment'; (ii) they are immoral within either general or specific prohibitions; and/or (iii) they do not meet the criteria for patentability (exemplified here through consideration of consent). Second, *relative* grounds of objection have been raised challenging the effects of patenting medical innovations either because of: (i) the breadth of the monopoly that has been granted; (ii) the ways in which the invention is exploited; and/or (iii) the knock-on effects of patents on continued research. Each of these will be considered in turn. 20.39

1. Absolute grounds for objection

(i) Methods of medical treatment or diagnosis

Patents should only be granted to inventions that are not already available, which add value to the sum total of human knowledge, and which do not offend public sensibilities. The letter of the law pays particular attention to policy concerns surrounding equitable access to health care. For example, s 4A(1) of the Patents Act 1977 (as amended)[95] provides that: 20.40

[91] See D Thums, 'Patent Protection for Medical Treatment: A Distinction between Patent and Medical Law' (1996) 27 International Review of Intellectual Property and Competition Law 423; and A Sims, 'The Case Against Patenting Methods of Medical Treatment' [2007] European Intellectual Property Review 43.

[92] Biotech Directive, (98/44/EC, (1998) OJ L213/13), Art 2(1)(a).

[93] eg C Brabin, 'Intellectual property law in the realm of biology—striking the right balance' (2014) 36(11) European Intellectual Property Review 687–92; J Hitchcock and C S de Sousa e Brito, 'Should Patents Determine When Life Begins?' (2014) 36(6) European Intellectual Property Review 390.

[94] Made popular by Non-Governmental Organizations such as Greenpeace International: see 'Patents on Life' (2004) <http://www.greenpeace.org/international/en/campaigns/agriculture/problem/genetic-engineering/ge-agriculture-and-genetic-pol/patents-on-life/>.

[95] Previously, methods of treatment were excluded from protection because they were considered not capable of industrial application, see PA 1977, s 4(2). This was amended by the Patents Act 2004, s 1, in turn

A patent shall not be granted for the invention of—

(a) a method of treatment of the human or animal body by surgery or therapy, or
(b) a method of diagnosis practised on the human or animal body.

Various practices have been denied patent protection on these grounds, including a method for operating and monitoring heart pacemakers,[96] improved dosage regimes of established treatments,[97] and a method for vaccination against disease.[98] How, then, should the exclusion be read? The answer is, closely and carefully, keeping in mind that the broader the exception, the less likely it is patentable. The EBA's ruling in *MEDI-PHYSICS/Treatment by Surgery*[99] confirms that there is no principle in European patent law that *requires* narrow interpretation of exclusions from patentability. This is not the same thing as saying that courts and legislatures will not continue to narrow exclusions as a matter of practice, but it does mean that there is no duty to consider a narrow interpretation that would increase what is patentable. Fundamentally, each provision must be interpreted in good faith according to its ordinary meaning.

20.41 Paras. 20.04–20.37 discussed how medical products and their processes of manufacture can be patented. This exclusion only extends to *methods* of treatment *of* the human or animal body, a process of use, so it is already a fairly narrow exclusion in light of all possible medical innovations. In addition, the treatments refer to living bodies and not to anything relating to cadavers.[100] Furthermore, anything done to (or created from) samples *derived from* the body is patentable, so long as the substances are not to be returned to the same body.[101] The difference is displayed in this example from the EPO: 'the treatment of blood for storage in a blood bank or diagnostic testing of blood samples is not excluded, whereas a treatment of blood by dialysis with the blood being returned to the same body would be excluded.'[102]

20.42 It must be remembered that if a method is to be patentable it must be *neither* treatment *nor* surgical, therapeutic, *nor* a diagnostic method. These are cumulative provisions; even if something does not fall within the definition of a 'treatment by surgery' or a 'diagnostic method' it might still fall foul of the 'therapy' provision. Equally, surviving these exclusions does not prevent exclusion under other patent law provisions.

20.43 (a) **Surgery** Surgery is generally regarded as having an ordinary English definition (key elements of which are identified in para 20.46), which focuses upon the nature of the intervention and not the reason for it. This means that there is no distinction made between a medical or cosmetic treatment and the law hinges instead upon whether the treatment is surgical. The lead case is the EBA decision in *MEDI-PHYSICS*,[103] which overruled earlier

introduced as a result of the reforms of European Patent Convention, Art 53(c). This was to better reflect the underlying reasons for such an exclusion, namely, to ensure that patents do not unduly interfere with matters of public health; on this rationale see G 05/83 *EISAI/Second medical use* [1985] OJEPO 64.

[96] *Tectronics/Pacemaker* [1996] OJEPO 274.

[97] *Bristol-Myers Squibb v Baker Norton Pharmaceuticals* [2001] RPC 1, 17; (The Court of Appeal in *Actavis v Merck* [2008] EWCA Civ 444 did not overrule this case on a general basis) and [2003] EWCA Civ 1545.

[98] *Unilever's (Davis') Application* [1983] RPC 219.

[99] G1/07 *MEDI-PHYSICS/Treatment by Surgery* [2011] OJEPO 134.

[100] T 182/90 *SEE-SHELL/Blood flow* [1994] OJEPO 641.

[101] EPO Guidelines, Part G-II: 4.2.1.

[102] ibid, 4.8.1. For the UK position, see *Schultz's Application* BL O 174/84, discussed in the UK-IPO Guidelines, para 4116.

[103] G1/07 *MEDI-PHYSICS/Treatment by Surgery* [2011] OJEPO 134.

broad interpretations of surgery directed to securing 'life and health'[104] and changed the practice of both the EPO and the UK-IPO, which had permitted that:

> methods involving irreversible damage to or destruction of living cells or tissues of the living body are regarded as non-insignificant interventions and thus as surgical treatments, irrespective of the underlying mechanism (ie, mechanical, electrical, thermal, chemical).[105]

Ultimately it was this approach of the EPO—amassed from a range of judgments—which resulted in the creation of a distinction between 'life and health' interventions (unpatentable) and enhancements (patentable). This distinction meant that the reason for the intervention became the distinguishing feature—as opposed to being oriented to the nature of the procedure—and this can clearly be seen in the pre-*MEDI-PHYSICS* decision in *General Hospital/Hair Removal Method*.[106] The invention concerned a method of hair removal from the skin by optical radiation, and the EPO's Technical Board of Appeal (TBA) sought out the original intention of the drafters of the EPC through its *travaux préparatoires*.[107] The Appeal Board held that: 'the intention of the legislator was that only those treatments ... maintaining or restoring the health, the physical integrity, and the physical well-being of a human'[108] should be excluded. This meant the hair removal method was patentable, because it was cosmetic rather than securing well-being. **20.44**

The EBA in *MEDI-PHYSICS*[109] challenged this interpretation of legislative intention, declaring instead that the rationale for the exclusion is 'to free [medical] practitioners from being potentially hampered by patents in the application of the best possible treatment on their patients'. The invention concerned a method of imaging the heart for diagnostic purposes and, ahead of this diagnostic procedure, the invention included the injection of a contrast agent into the heart (a surgical procedure). So it involved a multi-step process (diagnosis) with an attendant procedure (surgery). Among the questions asked was whether the surgical procedure made it unpatentable when that step, in itself, did not have the aim of maintaining life and health. The EBA decision resolved around two fundamental issues: (1) what counts as 'surgical'; and (2) does it make a difference if the surgery is only one part of the treatment? **20.45**

In addressing the first point, the EBA stopped short of providing a general definition of surgery, but it did point to key elements that should be weighed in the balance: **20.46**

(1) *The nature of the intervention*—which should be decided on a case-by-case basis. EPO practice guidelines hinge on the exclusion of procedures that are critical, performed on a critical part of the body, or would normally be carried out in a medical context;[110] and the UK-IPO provides that surgery means 'incision or manipulation', so the skin does not have to be pierced;[111]

---

[104] Notably: G1/04 *CYGNUS/Diagnostic methods* [2006] 5 OJEPO334, broadly construing surgery as 'any physical interventions on the human ... body in which maintaining the life and health of the subject is of paramount importance' (para 6.2.1); which accepted the wording from the earlier decision of the TBA in T35/99 *GEORGETOWN UNIVERSITY/Pericardial access* [2000] OJEPO 447, (para 4.3) and T 182/90 *SEE SHELL/Blood flow* [1994] EPOR 320, which listed 'endoscopy, puncture, injections, excision and catheterisation' (para 2.3).

[105] G1/07 *MEDI-PHYSICS/Treatment by Surgery* [2011] OJEPO 134, at para 3.4.2.1.

[106] T383/03 *General Hospital/Hair Removal Method* [2005] OJEPO 159.

[107] Meaning the preparatory documents which precede legislative instruments giving an insight into legislative intent.

[108] T383/03 *General Hospital/Hair Removal Method* [2005] OJEPO 159, 4 of judgment.

[109] G1/07 *MEDI-PHYSICS/Treatment by Surgery* [2011] OJEPO 134, at para 3.3.7.

[110] EPO Guidelines, Part G-II: 4.2.1.1.

[111] UK-IPO Guidelines, para 45.

(2) *The complexity of the procedure*—complexity relates to the procedure raising an expectation of professional medical skill for execution, rather than to what type of medical professional (ie doctor, nurse, or dentist) performed it or who could perform it. This amalgamates previous case law: In *Occidental Petroleum's Application*[112] the court decided that the involvement of a surgeon necessarily meant that the procedure was surgical in nature; and in *Allen's Application*[113] the court decided that performance of a surgical procedure by a non-surgeon could be unpatentable; and

(3) *The degree of risk involved*—the EPO and UK-IPO arguably converge in requiring a procedure with a significant risk,[114] which relates to the risk(s) arising from the type of procedure, rather than any risk resulting from who is performing it.[115]

20.47 The EBA in the *MEDI-PHYSICS* case considered the relationship of the procedure to the invention and confirmed that—unlike diagnosis—surgery is not a stepped procedure. The relevance of which is that any invention that is surgical will automatically be unpatentable. In addition, the EBA identified that a surgical procedure which is merely collateral to a diagnostic invention (which is inherently a multi-step procedure) would not make the invention surgical, just as using a device during surgery does not make the product unpatentable: to be considered as unpatentable, the surgical procedure would have to be an 'essential feature' of the innovation.[116] The significance of this is that an essential surgical procedure becomes 'toxic' to any type of treatment invention into which it is put and makes the whole thing unpatentable. Determining if it is indeed 'essential' will likely rely on whether it inhibits medical professionals from freely selecting the best method of treatment;

20.48 (b) **Therapy** If the method does not involve *treatment* of the human or animal body—in the sense of having a curative or prophylactic effect (ie vaccinations or the removal of plaque)[117] on a disease or malfunctioning of the body—then it is patentable. Thus, 'therapy' revolves around the purpose of the treatment. As such, being focused to its purpose only replicates the requirement for an inherent relationship between the procedure and its negative impact on medical practice, before it is excluded.[118]

20.49 Everything else rests on the meaning of 'therapy' and this is far from straightforward. An example of something patentable would be administering a chemical product for purely cosmetic reasons, such as colouring or care of the skin, hair, or nails.[119] The distinction can be a fine one and, in *Roussel-UCLAF/Thenoyl Peroxide,*[120] it was possible to distinguish a method of cleansing the skin of comedones (blackheads) as personal hygiene (patentable) from a use of the method as a treatment for acne (unpatentable). Methods of removing parasites or plaque from the body are unpatentable.[121]

---

112 *Occidental Petroleum's Application* BL O 35/84; see UK–IPO Guidelines, para 45.

113 *Allen's Application* BL O 59/92; UK-IPO Guidelines, para 47 (method of inserting markers in body for NMR and CT scans).

114 The use of needles for the extraction of blood or administration of medicines is considered 'insignificant' for these purposes: see T182/90*SEE-SHELL/Blood Flow* [1994] OJEPO 641; but a lumbar puncture to the spine in giving an epidural would be unpatentable: UK-IPO Guidelines, para 46; EPO Guidelines, Part G-II: 4.2.1.1.

115 EPO Guidelines, Part G-II: 4.2.1.1.

116 G1/07 *MEDI-PHYSICS/Treatment by Surgery* [2011] OJEPO 134; UK-IPO Guidelines, para 47.

117 T290/86 *ICI/Cleaning plaque* [1992] 8 OJEPO 414.

118 T245/87 *SIEMENS/Flow measurement* [1989] 5 OJEPO 171.

119 T144/83 *DU PONT/Appetite Suppressant* [1987] EPOR 6.

120 T36/83 *Roussel-UCLAF/Thenoyl Peroxide* [1986] OJEPO 295. Similarly, see T144/83 *DU PONT/Appetite Suppressant* [1987] EPOR 6.

121 This is contrary to old authority in the UK decided under the Patents Act 1949, see *Stafford-Miller's Application* [1984] FSR 258.

Methods of contraception are patentable because pregnancy is not a disease and hence it is not 'therapy' to prevent its occurrence.[122] Conversely, methods to terminate pregnancy or to induce labour are unpatentable, as are infertility treatments such as *in vitro* fertilisation; the difference is that these procedures would be expected to be performed under medical supervision,[123] making them recognized forms of therapy. **20.50**

(c) **Diagnosis** Fundamentally the exclusion to methods of treatment by 'diagnosis' only relates to a determination about health in a pathological sense (ie identifying disease or an absence of disease), as opposed to health in a physiological sense (ie assessing general or healthy functioning). *CYGNUS/Diagnostic methods*[124] represents the primary authority and the crucial question was whether 'diagnostic methods practised on the human ... body' excluded only those claims to methods containing all of the procedural steps necessary to a medical diagnosis—(i) the examination and the data collection phase; (ii) the comparison phase; (iii) the identification of deviation from a norm; and (iv) the deductive clinical decision phase—or whether the exclusion applied if any one of these steps could be used for diagnostic purposes or related to diagnosis. The EBA decided that: **20.51**

> The method steps to be carried out prior to making a diagnosis ... are related to examination, data gathering and comparison ... If only one of the preceding steps which are constitutive for making such a diagnosis is lacking, there is no diagnostic method, but at best a method of data acquisition or data processing that can be used in a diagnostic method.[125]

Expressed more simply, only claims which encompass all of the steps required to provide a definitive diagnosis are excluded from protection.[126] The EBA made clear that step (iv) is already excluded as a mental process,[127] so falling within the exclusion relies on *all* of the technical steps between (i) to (iii) being performed on the patient.[128]

Neither is it possible to simply exclude one of the steps, because essential and inherent steps are considered before granting a patent.[129] Similarly, methods which represent mere interim steps will be patentable in themselves, so long as they do not lead directly to a diagnosis. Examples include the taking of a sample, methods of internal imaging (eg X-rays or MRI scanning), and methods for measuring temperature. So too, pharmacological trials either in the lab or in the clinic are not considered diagnostic.[130] This is a far narrower interpretation of diagnostic methods than had previously been applied. **20.52**

In consequence of diagnoses being considered a multi-step process, one unpatentable step does not mean that the whole diagnostic invention fails. Yet, as already identified in paras. 20.43–20.50, if a method of treatment by diagnosis additionally involves steps which are excluded as surgical or therapeutic, then the whole method will be unpatentable.[131] This apparent disparity between 'diagnostic methods' and methods of treatment involving **20.53**

---

[122] *Schering's Application* [1971] RPC 337. Confirmed in the EPO, T820/92 *GENERAL HOSPITAL/Contraceptive Method* [1995] OJEPO 113 and T74/93 *BRITISH TECHNOLOGY/Contraceptive Method* [1995] OJEPO 712. Note, however, such methods are excluded if they involve an element of therapy as well as mere prevention.

[123] *UpJohn (Kirton's) Application* [1976] RPC 324.

[124] G1/04 *CYGNUS/Diagnostic methods* [2006] EPOR 15.

[125] ibid, para 6.2.2.

[126] Although there is no need to identify the actual disease to fall within the exclusion: T125/02 *AEROCRINE* (unreported).

[127] PA 1977, s 1(2)(c).

[128] Confirmed in EPO Guidelines, Part G-II:4.2.1.3.

[129] *Aerotel Ltd v Telco Holdings, Macrossan's Application* [2007] RPC 7.

[130] UK-IPO Guidelines, para 66.

[131] ibid, para 68.

'surgery' or 'therapy' had already been acknowledged by the EBA in *CYGNUS/Diagnostic Methods* ahead of being confirmed in *MED-PHYSICS*. As such, it means that both surgery and therapy are 'toxic' to any innovations that rely upon them, but the same is not true of diagnostic phases.

20.54 *Summarizing* and noting the significance of the absolute objections to methods of treatment: it is clear that the types of innovations which are excluded are very narrow, but not fully rationalized. For example, as discussed in paras. 20.04–20.37, known devices which are expended during use in a new surgical/therapeutic/diagnostic process are not justified as falling within the exemption, but would inevitably be caught by it. In addition, industry is incredibly resourceful in inventing around exclusions. For example, the exclusion for treatment by therapy catches gene therapy performed on a patient, but products are being developed which remove a patient's cells—resulting in autologous cells which are processed in a closed device before being returned to the same patient for a different biological purpose (heterologously) or for the same biological purpose (homologously). This circumvents the exclusion by shifting the innovation away from being a procedure and into being considered a product, which does not fall within the exclusion.

20.55 Technology constantly challenges the legal boundaries between medical interventions which should not be the basis for profit, and procedures which are subject to tradable commercial rights. Policing that boundary during patenting is difficult, because it requires balancing the needs of medical practitioners with the need to incentivize innovation. In doing so, it inevitably creates a conundrum for regulators involved in other stages of progressing medical innovation to market:[132] how can standards similarly aimed at mediating between medical practice and innovation proliferation be comparable between different forms of regulation if different regulators unilaterally rebalance those competing priorities? Understanding that regulating health innovation is spread across many bodies is crucial to ensuring that regulation is effective in protecting the common good.

20.56 For example, the extent of protection given for advanced therapies that can circumvent market authorization under the ***hospital exemption*** (introduced in Article 28(2)[133] of Regulation 1394/2007 on Advanced Therapy Medicinal Products)[134] is analogous to the 'method of treatment' exclusion in patent law. A normal expectation would be that it adopts a similar approach to that of patent law in mediating between the public interest in innovative treatment and opportunities for commercial rights. A public consultation in 2013[135] highlighted that the industry position is that the hospital exemption deters innovation and should only apply when there is no authorized product:[136] the consequences of which would be to reserve the development of these advanced therapies to industry, reduce the scope of the exemption and the amount of innovation being carried out within public hospitals. The exemption was intended to permit hospitals to treat small disease groups and innovate new

[132] Such as funding, market authorization, health technology assessment, and remuneration bodies.

[133] Importing a new Article 3(7) into Directive 2001/83 on the Community Code relating to medicinal products for human use: Consolidated (2012) ec.europa.eu/health/documents/eudralex/vol-1/index_en.htm.

[134] These loosely concern what are referred to as: 'gene therapy', 'somatic cell therapy', and 'tissue engineering', but which do not accord with scientific meanings and the boundaries of which are still being identified both by the European Commission and the Committee on Advanced Therapies.

[135] European Commission Health and Consumers Directorate-General, *Regulation 1394/2007 on Advanced Therapy Medicinal Products: summary of responses to the public consultation* (2013) SANCO/D5/RSR/iv (2013)ddg1.d5.

[136] Although it is ambiguous whether this means that an autologous treatment (involving the patient's own materials) would be prevented where there is an allogeneic treatment (using someone else's biological materials).

medical treatments without the intensive regulatory requirements which exceed considerations of safety. So it is of some concern that the 2014 European Commission report simply redefined the exemption as permitting 'patients to receive an . . . [advanced therapy] under controlled conditions in cases where no authorised medicinal product is available'.[137] While the method of treatment exclusion is being gradually eroded to benefit industry interests, the hospital exemption is a wholesale prioritization of industry interests at the expense of those of the public. The consequence of such failures to coordinate regulatory practices discharging equivalent policy objectives arising in the contexts of different regulatory bodies (exemplified here through the EPO and the EU Commission) is to make regulation more difficult for industry to navigate. Such mixed messages have the long-term effect of inhibiting innovation, because industry will not invest in areas of technological development if regulation is likely to change.

(ii) Morality of commercial innovation

In contrast to the approach adopted in the US and in many other jurisdictions,[138] European patent law has long contemplated a role for moral considerations in the decision-making process on the grant of patents.[139] These provisions lay more or less dormant in the EPC until the advent of biotechnological patents whereupon objectors seized the opportunity to challenge the patentability of these inventions. The response within Europe was the creation and eventual adoption of the Directive 98/44/EC on the protection of biotechnological inventions (*Biotech Directive*), which was subsequently adopted by the Administrative Council of the European Patent Organization in order to align European Patent Law as far as possible with EU law. Consequently, the general morality provision within the EPC is aligned with Article 6(1) and specific moral exclusions within Article 6(2) (prohibiting processes for cloning humans; for effecting germ-line gene therapy; for using human embryos commercially; or for causing unjustified harm when genetically altering animals) are imported into the Rules of the EPC. **20.57**

To future-proof the regulation of such a complex and rapidly evolving area of technology, the Directive required the Commission to monitor and report on developments in Biotechnology under Article 16c,[140] and a Group of Experts was established to monitor and advise on patenting biotechnology in Europe and to assist the Commission in preparing its reports.[141] So integral was this technology considered to future innovation that the Biotech **20.58**

[137] European Commission, *Report from the Commission to the European Parliament and The Council in accordance with Article 25 of Regulation (EC) No 1394/2007 of the European Parliament and of the Council on advanced therapy medicinal products and amending Directive 2001/83/EC and Regulation (EC) No 726/2004*, (28.3.2014) COM (2014) 188 final, at para 4.2.

[138] Art 27.2 of the TRIPS Agreement (1994) permits signatory countries to voluntarily include morality exceptions in their patent law in similar terms to those found in the European Patent Convention. In China, the Patent Law of the People's Republic of China (2009), Chapter I, Article 5 states that 'any invention-creation that is contrary to the laws or social morality or that is detrimental to public interest' is unpatentable and genetic resources are specifically cited as an example. In the UK, s 1(3) of the PA 1977 provides that a 'patent shall not be granted for an invention the commercial exploitation of which would be contrary to public policy or morality.'

[139] Article 53(a), European Patent Convention (as well as its 1973 predecessor and the Strasbourg Convention 1963 on which it was based).

[140] For the first Report from the Commission to the European Parliament and the Council, *Development and Implications of Patent Law in the Field of Biotechnology and Genetic Engineering*, COM (2002) 545 final, 7 October 2002.

[141] This Group reported for the first time in October 2002. In essence, the Group reiterated the need, as it saw it, to maintain competitiveness through full and proper implementation of the Directive, lest Europe lose out on the enormous potential of the biotechnology market: see <http://ec.europa.eu/internal_market/indprop/invent/index_en.htm#reports>.

Directive provoked the establishment of a Union-wide Biotechnology Strategy.[142] Over time initially broad ambitions resolved into more specific policy objectives, such as the current policy aimed at: securing unifying standards (ie the unitary patent right and standard licensing practices which facilitate the dissemination of research innovation); enforcement of IPRs; security against counterfeits; and support for Small and Medium-Sized Enterprises (SMEs) in both incubating and funding innovation.[143] Any intention to secure a European or EU-wide policy on biotechnology has already been demonstrated to be difficult to implement in the context of applying the same legal patent criteria to medical innovations consistently. This disparity between European nations is further exacerbated in the context of assessing a shared understanding of morality and this requires further consideration in paras. 20.59–20.63 below.

20.59 (a) **General moral objections** The Biotech Directive, Article 6(1) excludes from patentability inventions:

> where their commercial exploitation would be contrary to *ordre public* or morality; however, exploitation shall not be deemed to be so contrary merely because it is prohibited by law or regulation.

The first problem was to persuade patent examiners in the EPO that considerations of morality were within their sphere of responsibility and competence. The issue most publicly arose in *HARVARD/Oncomouse*[144] in which the EPO upheld a patent on a transgenic mouse bred to develop cancer as a research tool. The EPO relied on the strictly utilitarian analysis that the potential benefit to mankind outweighed the suffering of the animal, and accordingly there was no bar to patent protection. Proceedings were immediately instituted against the ruling which remained unresolved for over a decade, during which time the patent remained in force. A solution was eventually found in 2001 when the scope of the patent was restricted to 'transgenic rodents containing an additional cancer gene' rather than 'any non-human transgenic mammal'[145] and this was further restricted in 2004 simply to 'transgenic mice'.[146] This case exemplifies that, long after the initial objections to the morality of the invention are resolved, it is only the unfairness of claiming a commercial right that is unwarranted by the technical teaching which gains any weight in ongoing litigation.

20.60 The *HARVARD/Oncomouse* case is most significant because it established the approach for many future challenges on the grounds of morality. It confirmed, for example, that the notion of '*ordre public*' extends to the protection of public security, the physical integrity of individuals in society, and protection of the environment; its crude *felicific calculus* has been adopted and refined in other cases, and almost always in the vein of interpreting

[142] See, eg, Communication from the Commission to the Council, the European Parliament, the European Economic and Social Committee and the Committee of the Regions on the mid term review of the Strategy on Life Sciences and Biotechnology, COM (2007) 175 final, 10 April 2007.

[143] See, eg, 'Communication from the Commission to the European Parliament, the Council, the European Economic and Social Committee and the Committee of the Regions, *A Single Market for Intellectual Property Rights Boosting creativity and innovation to provide economic growth, high quality jobs and first class products and services in Europe*, COM (2011) 0287 final and the Commission's growth agenda detailed at: <http://ec.europa.eu/growth/industry/intellectual-property/index_en.htm>.

[144] T19/90 *HARVARD/Oncomouse* [1991] EPOR 525.

[145] By way of contrast the Supreme Court of Canada revoked the Harvard patent over Oncomouse itself (but not the process to manufacture it) in December 2002, claiming that, '[a] higher life form is not patentable because it is not a "manufacture" or "composition of matter"': see *Harvard College v Canada (Commissioner of Patents)* [2002] SCJ No 77. This ruling cannot now be changed except by express legislation.

[146] T315/03 *HARVARD/Transgenic animal* (*Oncomouse II)* [2005] EPOR 31.

the morality exclusion narrowly.[147] Indeed, in *PLANT GENETIC SYSTEMS/Glutamine Synthetase Inhibitors*,[148] the EPO stated that it was only prepared to entertain challenges on grounds of morality if actual evidence of harm to society could be demonstrated. Yet, survey evidence and opinion polls indicating distaste for patents over genetically modified organisms were considered insufficient evidence by which to judge the overall European moral tone.

In *MICHIGAN STATE UNIVERSITY/Euthanasia compositions*[149] a patent for a composition for administering humane euthanasia in lower animals was challenged. Various ethical objections were lodged, ranging from the concern that 'lower animal' could encompass 'human', that the product might be used more broadly in society, and that it was an affront to the human right to life under Article 2 of the European Convention on Human Rights. All arguments were rejected and the position stated that exceptions should be interpreted narrowly. The hearing body reiterated that its remit was narrow in that the letter of the law at the time concerned only the morality of ***publication or exploitation*** of an invention (interpreting EPC 1973, Article 53(a)). It was not for consideration if the development of the composition itself was immoral or if the act of granting a patent to it was immoral. The narrowness of interpreting the exclusion and excluding consideration of the development of the innovation have since been reversed in decisions considering specific moral prohibitions (discussed at para 20.62 below). In the *Michigan State* case the claims in the patent were considered to be unambiguous in their application to lower mammal life forms and not humans, so in light of the practice of humane euthanasia in animals being widely accepted—indicating that it is in conformity with societal notions of morality—the patent was granted. **20.61**

The current EPO Guidelines provide the following on the morality clause: **20.62**

> This provision is likely to be invoked only in rare and extreme cases. A fair test to apply is to consider whether it is probable that the public in general would regard the invention as so abhorrent that the grant of patent rights would be inconceivable.[150]

This stems in large part from the ruling in *HOWARD FLOREY/Relaxin*.[151] Here the TBA declared that the morality measure should be applied to prevent the grant of patents only in the case of inventions which would universally be regarded as outrageous. Accordingly, it upheld the grant of a patent over a genetically engineered human protein, H2 relaxin, which is produced by women during childbirth to relax the pelvis. The patent had been objected to on a number of grounds. First, that the granting of the patent was tantamount to slavery of women because it involved the 'dismemberment of women and the sale of their parts'; second, that it was offensive to human dignity to use pregnant women for profit; and finally that, because DNA was life itself, patenting of human DNA was intrinsically immoral.[152]

[147] See *R v LELAND STANFORD/Modified Animal* [2002] EPOR 2 in which the patent was upheld for an immuno-compromised chimera mouse. The EPO took the position that the controversial nature of the technology was not a bar to patenting in and of itself.

[148] T356/93 *PLANT GENETIC SYSTEMS/Glutamine Synthetase Inhibitors* [1995] EPOR 357.

[149] T866/01 [2005] (unpublished).

[150] EPO Guidelines, Part G-II: 4.1. The UK-IPO Patents Manual could scarcely be more direct on the interpretation of the PA 1977, s 1(3), which embodies the morality clause: 'what is to be regarded as contrary to public policy or morality will vary according to changes in social attitudes and on no account ought examiners to allow their own personal and individual beliefs to colour their judgment on this matter . . . Only in the clearest cases should examiners invoke this subsection and then only following consultation with their Deputy Director. Any genuine doubt should be exercised in favour of the applicant with an appropriate minute being created.' See UK-IPO, *Manual of Patent Practice* 2015, para 1.41.

[151] T272/95 *Howard Florey/Relaxin* [1995] EPOR 541.

[152] ibid.

The TBA rejected each of these claims on a narrow construction of the morality exclusion. It decided that DNA is not life, nor was the taking and modification of samples anything approximating to slavery. Importantly, the Appeal Board placed considerable store in the fact that consent had been obtained from the women to take the samples from which the patentable subject matter was derived. This, in itself, was thought to be enough to accord respect to human dignity. Interestingly, however, it is not clear what the women consented to, and in particular whether they were ever told of the prospect of patents being granted over material derived from them and the consequent economic potential.[153] We return to the matter of consent in paras 20.80–20.91.

20.63 In developing its jurisprudence, the European Boards created two distinct tests for the general morality provision;[154]

(1) the 'public abhorrence' test;[155] and
(2) the 'unacceptability' test.[156]

These are clearly different standards, involving diverse approaches to applying the standards (rebuttable presumption or a balancing exercise) and to different types of decision-makers (a trusted proxy relying on an intuitive/shared understanding, or one justifying a decision by close reference to evidence). It was only in the referral by the EBA to the (former) President of the EPO in the *Wisconsin Alumni Research Foundation (WARF)/stem cell* case[157] that these matters were addressed. The President rejected both standards in favour of an understanding of *ordre public* as being the 'fundamental principles of the legal order' (ie inherent within instruments such as the European Convention on Human Rights) and morality as being 'an ethically established norm of vital significance, the binding force of which is generally accepted and recognised.'[158] The President specifically rejected a 'balancing test' or an intuitive understanding of shared values: instead he identified a commitment to specific moral principles protecting human life, dignity, and rights which may/may not be evidenced by

[153] See further *Moore v Regents of the University of California* (1990) 51 Cal 3d 120.

[154] Notably, the decisions regarding stem cells have been determined almost wholly on the basis that they comply with Article 6(2)(c) of the Biotech Directive, (98/44/EC, (1998) OJ L213/13), uses of human embryos, and therefore do not require additional consideration under Article 6(1)'s core morality provision (see T1079/03 *Edinburgh University* [2003] (unreported); T1374/04 *WARF* [2007] OJEPO 313, G2/06 [2009] EPOR 15; T522/04 *California Institute of Technology* (*CIT*) [2003] (unreported); and T2221/10 *TECHNION Culturing Stem Cells* [2014] EPOR 23); but in as much as the Opposition Division in the *Edinburgh patent* case referred to the Technical Board of Appeal's decision in the *PGS* case (T356/93 *Greenpeace v Plant Genetic Systems NV* (*PGS*) [1993] 24 International Review of Intellectual Property and Competition Law 618) as authority for the interpretation of the morality provision, they can perhaps be regarded as falling within the 'unacceptability' category.

[155] Adopted in Case T320/87 *Lubrizol Genetics Inc* (*Lubrizol II*) ([1992] EP-B1-122 791 (Opposition Division) (unreported); by the Opposition Division in T356/93 *Greenpeace v Plant Genetic Systems NV* (*PGS*) [1993] 24 International Review of Intellectual Property and Competition Law 618; by the Opposition Division in T272/95 *Howard Florey/Relaxin* [1995] 6 OJEPO 388; [2002] TB EP 83307553.4; it is certainly arguable that the requirement in the *Human Stem Cell/BIOCYTE* case (Opposition Division Decision 15 July 1999 (unreported): revoking European Patent No: 0343217; OD EP 89900042.6: at 32 that the invention be 'in clear conflict with basic legal and ethical values' in all of its envisaged uses before it fails equates to an 'abhorrence' standard; and it is undoubted that the Opposition Division adopted 'abhorrence' in the *R v LELAND STANFORD/Modified Animal* [2002] EPOR 2, at point 51.

[156] To balance the respective advantages and disadvantages to society of the patent which was adopted in the T19/90 *HARVARD/Oncomouse* [1991] EPOR 525, reaffirmed by the T BA in T315/03 *HARVARD/Transgenic animal* (*Oncomouse II*) [2005] EPOR, at 34: and the more specific 'unacceptability' to the 'moral norms that are deeply rooted in European culture' test adopted by the TBA in the *PGS* case (T356/93 *PLANT GENETIC SYSTEMS/Glutamine Synthetase Inhibitors* [1995] 8 OJEPO 545, at 557 and 561 respectively).

[157] T1374/04 *WARF* [2007] OJEPO 313, G2/06 [2009] EPOR 15.

[158] G2/06 *WARF* [2009] EPOR 15, 49–57 and Question 3, point 2 of summary.

norms within law. As such this is akin to Recital 36 of the Biotech Directive, which states that morality is designed to 'protect human . . . life or health or to avoid serious prejudice to the environment'. The opinion of the President is anomalous on these points for two key reasons: (1) the judgment departs from the decision-making methods adopted by the Appeal Boards and Patent Divisions to provide some form of 'just is' approach which is unsubstantiated by any formal decision-making;[159] and (2) the meaning of 'human life' and 'human dignity' are very open to interpretation.[160] Many of the issues raised in the context of the general morality provision are similarly raised in the context of the specific moral prohibitions, and it is for this reason that these aspects form the focus for consideration here.

(b) Specific moral prohibitions Article 6(2) of the Biotech Directive identifies specific exclusions to patenting: 'processes for cloning human beings'; modifying the human germ-line; to 'uses of human embryos for industrial or commercial purposes', as well as to any 'processes for modifying the genetic identity of animals which are likely to cause them suffering without any substantial medical benefit to man or animal'. The list is non-exhaustive and represents the few, most contentious issues that all concerned could agree upon at the time of the adoption of the Directive. The enumeration of specific immoralities was intended to placate moral objectors, while at the same time bringing certainty for the biotechnology industry by legislatively prioritizing patenting innovation in all but a few narrowly defined circumstances. These provisions now also form part of the EPC as rule 28, but all of the provisions remain ambiguous in certain respects. **20.64**

Preventing patenting of 'processes for cloning human beings' is not clearly limited to reproductive cloning only, but EPO Guidelines clarify that it extends to 'embryo splitting'[161] which indicates that reproduction is how it is generally understood. Therapeutic cloning (ie whether for research, for the manufacture of cellular materials, or for treatment) is more notably an issue which is caught by the prohibition on stem cells and so is expanded upon below. Neither does the human cloning prohibition make clear whether 'human beings' would include cloning human admixed embryos (ie the use of an animal ova in combination with a human nucleus). Again EPO Guidelines are focused on preventing full-term human replication and this is supported by Recital 38 of the Directive, which prohibits processes resulting in chimeras (human-animal hybrids). In the UK admixed embryos are only permitted within research,[162] so this would arguably fall outside the prohibition. **20.65**

While somatic cell gene therapy (ie genetically altering heart cells) is permitted, germ-line procedures (ie altering ova) are prohibited on the basis that they risk permanently impacting the 'gene pool' of mankind. This is a precautionary provision which exhibits a focus on not dabbling in human genomes before properly knowing long-term impacts. The often cited example is sickle cell anaemia, which is a debilitating disease presenting in childhood and considerably shortens lifespan: carrier status, however, conveys immunity to malaria. In some respects this is a reflection of ethical principles such as non-maleficence (ie do no harm) **20.66**

[159] eg judicial decision-making relies upon either a right-minded man (correlating to a proxy relying on intuition/shared values), or a reasonable man (correlating to a decision rationally based on identifiable evidence) and ethical decision-making, such as principlism, relies upon both a weighing and a reflective equilibrium to resolve conflicts (see T L Beauchamp and J F Childress, *Principles of Biomedical Ethics* (7th edn, Oxford University Press 2013).

[160] eg the UK Human Fertilisation and Embryology Act 2008 inserts a new s 1(6) into the 1990 Act which allows that the meaning of 'embryo' may be changed by the Secretary of State as scientific knowledge and research progress; and in terms of human dignity see for example on the ambiguity of this concept D Beyleveld and R Brownsword, *Human Dignity in Bioethics and Biolaw* (Oxford University Press 2001).

[161] EPO Guidelines, Part G-II:5.3.

[162] UK Human Fertilisation and Embryology Act 1990 (as amended), notably s 4A(1)(a) and (2), s 11(1)(b).

in the Anglo-American tradition of principlism, but it can be distinguished from eugenics in not being focused on improving human physiological norms. On a practical level, these arguments face serious problems in light of the rise of Cell Banks, which mean that specific DNA could be deposited to guard against the risk of its removal from all mankind (ie presuming that every symptomatic person and carrier receives germ-line therapy). Instead, the high-resource option of treating the individual is permitted, but the ability to prevent their future children from inheriting the same dreadful disease is forbidden. Arguably, this is a subversion of the notion of utilitarianism and striving for the greater good.

20.67 The prohibition on 'modifying the genetic identity of animals which are likely to cause them suffering without any substantial medical benefit to man or animal' affects medical research and is treated as involving a ratio of any-pain to substantial-benefit (rather than a cost-benefit analysis which incrementally balances pain-to-benefits).[163] The *LELAND STANFORD/Non-invasive localization* case,[164] arising after the Opinion of the EPO President in the *WARF* case, notably did not depart from the earlier cases on the general morality provision. The case involved testing cancer treatments on mice (which may/may not have been genetically modified) using light emitting markers and photon detectors to identify and monitor the effectiveness of therapeutic compounds. For those claims which related to genetically modified animals, the Board had to consider the case analogously under the specific prohibition; and to additionally consider for all claims whether the innovation fell within the balancing test of the general morality provision. In assessing the prohibition, the Board noted the presence of harm in the intentional introduction of cancer cells into the mice—which was analogous to the facts in the *Oncomouse* cases—and they were satisfied that there were significant benefits in the potential to identify treatments for cancer.[165] In satisfying the balancing test of the general morality provision, the Board considered the same evidence identifying the scientific and therapeutic benefits of the innovation as for the previous assessment, but additionally included consideration of the need to use fewer test animals.[166] What is perhaps most interesting is that this case confirms that the President's Opinion in WARF has been confined to stem cells only.

20.68 On stem cell patents, Rule 28(c) and Recital 42 of the Biotech Directive make clear that the prohibition does not extend to treatments or diagnostic products/processes which are beneficial to the embryo. The European Group on Ethics in Science and New Technologies (EGE), which is charged with advising the European Commission on all ethical aspects of new biotechnologies,[167] produced Opinions Nos 12 and 22 identifying that funding stem cell research from either banked or supernumerary sources could be ethically acceptable, where it is permitted nationally and providing it respects the donor's rights.[168] In its Opinion No 15, the EGE noted that it is important to respect European pluralism,[169] which is impossible to amalgamate where countries such as the UK and Italy represent polar opposites on issues such as embryonic research.[170] In Opinion No 16, the EGE recommended that patenting on stem cells should not be banned, as this would have an adverse consequence on valuable medical research.[171]

---

[163] T19/90 *HARVARD/Oncomouse* [1991] EPOR 525 and T315/03 *HARVARD/Transgenic animal (Oncomouse II)* [2005] EPOR 31; T606/03 *ARTEMIS/Gene trap,* [2005] (unreported).

[164] T1262/04 *LELAND STANFORD/Non-invasive localization* [2012] (unreported).

[165] ibid, paras 19–21.

[166] ibid, para 22.

[167] Biotech Directive (98/44/EC, (1998) OJ L213/13) Recital 44.

[168] EGE, *Ethical Aspects of Research involving the Use of Human Embryos in FP5,* Opinion No 12 (1998); EGE, *Ethics Review of Human Embryonic Stem Cells in FP7 Research Projects,* Opinion No 22 (2007).

[169] EGE, *Ethical Aspects of Human Stem Cell Research and Use,* Opinion No 15 (2000).

[170] In the UK: the Human Fertilisation and Embryology Act 1990 (as amended); in Italy: Italian Civil Code, Law 40/2004 (Regulation of Medically Assisted Reproduction (2004)), Arts 1 and 13.

[171] EGE, *Ethical Aspects of Patenting Inventions Involving Human Stem Cells,* Opinion No 16 (2002).

The Commission identified the obvious immorality to which there was general agreement—including within the scientific community[172]—with respect to totipotent stem cells, ie those from which a complete human can be derived.[173] Similarly, there was general agreement that multipotent stem cells (which are not embryonic, but have only a limited range of cellular roles) could ethically be patented in the same way that any other type of somatic (adult) cell can be. All ambiguity focused on the issue of pluripotent stem cells (which can develop into almost any type of cell except a whole human, but the harvesting of which could involve embryonic destruction), on which the Commission stipulated that it is for individual Member States to decide and funding should be determined on a case-by-case basis.[174] **20.69**

The progression of the early case law through the EPO demonstrates various attempts to learn from past experience in patent drafting and in utilizing science to circumvent the existing law. The first notable case was the *Edinburgh Patent*,[175] which made the mistake of including the destruction of embryos in its claims relating to the creation and modification of human stem cell lines, which formed the basis for the Opposition Division's refusal to patent. The subsequent *California Institute of Technology* application[176] removed these references by claiming stem cells only after isolation and, although they were excluded from the claims in the *WARF*[177] application, the description included IVF surplus and overseas banked cells (forming the basis for its refusal before the Examining Division and confirmed by the EBA). In addition, the *WARF* claims were about primate stem cells, which include ethically acceptable multipotent stem cells, but again this was identified in the application as applying to human embryonic stem cells.[178] **20.70**

In consequence, *WARF* became the test case for all stem cell applications which—even by 2002—the EGE identified as extending to over 500 embryonic stem cell patent applications lodged globally, a quarter of which had been granted.[179] The Opinions of the EGE suggest that these cases could have been decided differently had they been submitted to individual Member States' with permissive approaches to embryonic research. For example, the UK-IPO would likely have taken its lead from research being permitted nationally with banked cell lines and embryos which are superfluous to IVF treatment.[180] In pushing for a European-wide view on morality, such cases prompted the (former) President of the EPO to **20.71**

[172] Human embryonic research—even at its most liberal—sources embryonic stem cells from blastocysts, which have already passed the totipotent phase of development. Notably the current patent application submitted to WIPO by the SALK Institute for Biological Studies claiming Totipotent Stem Cells (WO2013181641 A1: available through Espacenet) is for those artificially regressed from somatic cells and other patents on embryonic stem cells have been aimed at commercial ownership of pluripotent stem cells rather than totipotent stem cells.

[173] Report from the Commission to the Council and the European Parliament, *Development and implications of patent law in the field of biotechnology and genetic engineering* (2005) (SEC(2005)943) COM/2005/0312 final) (Second Article 16c Report); Biotech Directive, (98/44/EC, (1998) OJ L213/13), Recital 38.

[174] Report from the Commission to the Council and the European Parliament, *Development and implications of patent law in the field of biotechnology and genetic engineering,* COM (2005) 312 final, 14 July 2005 (*Second Article 16c Report*) para 2.2.

[175] T1079/03 *Edinburgh University* [2003] (unreported).

[176] T522/04 *California Institute of Technology* (*CIT*) [2003] (unreported); and T2221/10 *TECHNION Culturing Stem Cells* [2014] EPOR 23.

[177] G2/06 *WARF* [2009] EPOR 15.

[178] Notably in the US the WARF patents have withstood the most recent challenge: *Consumer Watchdog v WARF* (23 February 2015) US Supreme Court Order List 574, 14–516 Order for Certiorari denied; D Jensen, 'California's Consumer Watchdog Loses U.S. Supreme Court Challenge to WARF Stem Cell Patents' (24 February 2015) <http://californiastemcellreport.blogspot.co.uk/2015/02/californias-consumer-watchdog-loses-us.html>.

[179] EGE, *Ethical Aspects of Patenting Inventions Involving Human Stem Cells,* Opinion No 16 (2002), para 1.16.

[180] In 2002, the UK Human Fertilisation and Embryology Authority granted Edinburgh University a license to develop human embryonic stem cell lines for deposit in the Medical Research Council's Stem

advise the EBA in the *WARF* case that the Opinions of the EGE are not legally binding[181] and that exclusionary provisions should not be presumptively narrow in relating to morality,[182] signalling the need for more caution.

20.72 In contrast to the general morality provision, part of the contention which was accepted by the Boards in the trilogy of stem cell cases was about the morality of the *development* of the innovation. The EBA in the *WARF* case[183] decided it makes no difference if the destruction of embryos is not claimed (or not repeated post-development), if—at the date of filing—the only means of recreating the invention relies on embryonic destruction, then the invention is immoral.[184] The fact that science had moved on and created pluripotent stem cells by biologically regressing multipotent stem cells (ie induced pluripotent stem cells (iPS) and protein induced pluripotent stem cells (piPS)), was immaterial to the EBA, because the science arose after the relevant date.[185] The EBA pointed out that the term 'embryo' was undefined, leaving it to be determined in individual decisions.[186]

20.73 This discretion was soon removed by the Court of Justice of the European Union (CJEU) on a referral from the German Patent Court in the *Brüstle* case,[187] which stated that the absence of a definition in the Directive did not derogate determining its scope to Member States, but required uniform application.[188] The CJEU defined a 'human embryo' as derived from fertilization, without fertilization (ie Cell Nucleus Replacement), or obtained through parthenogenesis (stimulating cellular division of an unfertilized ova).[189] In addition, the court identified that research is a 'use' within the meaning of the Directive; following the EBA decision in the *WARF* case, the CJEU stated that the destruction of an embryo precludes patenting even if it is not claimed; and the CJEU went further than the EBA to identify that embryonic destruction—no matter how remote from the innovation being claimed—taints the chain of innovation, making it unpatentable.[190] However, the court left it to individual Member States to decide—in the light of scientific developments—whether the derivative cells could give rise to humans, bringing them within the prohibition.[191]

20.74 Although only Member States are required to follow the decision, it was also voluntarily accepted by the (current) President of the EPO and new Guidelines were issued to incorporate the CJEU ruling,[192] on the back of which the *Brüstle* patent was revoked by the EPO.[193]

Cell Bank: Commission Staff Working Paper, *Report on Human Embryonic Stem Cell Research*, SEC (2003) 441, 3 April 2003, at 31.

[181] G2/06 *WARF* [2009] EPOR 15, at Question 3, point 7 (conclusion).

[182] ibid, at Question 2, point 1 (conclusion).

[183] For commentary on the decision, see P Treichel, 'G2/06 and the Verdict of Immorality' (2009) 40(4) International Review of Intellectual Property and Competition Law 450; and R Rowlandson, 'WARF/Stem cells (G2/06): The *Ordre Public* and Morality Exception and its Impact on the Patentability of Human Embryonic Stem Cells' (2010) 32(2) European Intellectual Property Review 67.

[184] T1374/04 *WARF* [2007] OJEPO 313, para 22.

[185] ibid, para 33.

[186] ibid, para 20.

[187] *Brüstle v Greenpeace* C-34/10 [2011]; [2012] All ER 809.

[188] *Brüstle v Greenpeace* C-34/10 [2011], paras 25–29.

[189] ibid, paras 35–36.

[190] ibid, para 52.

[191] ibid, para 38.

[192] EPO Guidelines (2012), G-II:15.

[193] EPO, 'EPO revokes patent in the "*Brüstle*" case', 11 April 2013, <http://www.epo.org/news-issues/news/2013/20130411a.html>, even though the German Bundesgerichtshof allowed it in part: J Dombrowski, 'Bundesgerichtshof Rules that Patents on Embryonic Stem Cells Are Partially Valid' 29 November 2012, <http://www.eplawpatentblog.com/eplaw/2012/11/de-bundesgerichtshof-rules-that-patents-on-embryonic-stem-cells-are-partially-valid-.html#more>.

Under the Biotech Directive this is presented as an issue of human dignity and the CJEU decision in the *Brüstle* case was specific about the definition of a human embryo being a legal rather than a moral issue.[194] This presumes that adopting a wide biological definition of an embryo as 'any cell that could give rise to a human being' is morally neutral and this is simply not the case.[195]

In 2014 the TBA had the opportunity to apply this new approach to stem cells in the *TECHNION/Culturing Stem Cells* case.[196] The claim was about a method of keeping stem cells unspecialized and the specification outlined three methods of obtaining pluripotent stem cells: (1) isolating them from human blastocysts—which was rejected by the TBA as being factually the same as those rejected in the *WARF* case; (2) obtaining them from existing stem cell lines—which was rejected on the basis that the destruction of the original embryo giving rise to the cell line tainted the chain; and (3) obtaining them from embryonic germ cells (embryonic cells which produce sperm/ova)— which was rejected on the grounds that it did not match the wording of the claim to 'embryonic stem cells'. **20.75**

This has not prevented cases from continuing to test the boundaries of the meaning of an 'embryo'. A referral to the CJEU in the *International Stem Cell Corp v Comptroller of Patents* case[197] distinguished that 'embryo' does not include the derivative cells (parthenotes) which result from stimulating an ova into replication during parthenogenesis. This is because the ova used is unfertilized, which means that the nucleus only has a single complement of chromosomes (haploidy) rather than the usual double complement (diploidy), the significance of which is that it cannot develop into a human. However, the CJEU recognized that subsequent recombination could have the effect of enabling the parthenotes to develop fully (evidenced in the case by early trials with mice), in which case, parthenotes would also be regarded as immoral. In consequence, the CJEU indicated that it would be for Member States to determine each case based on the current state of development in this area of science. Following the decision, the UK-IPO Guidance was rewritten to implement the discretion concerning parthenogenesis.[198] **20.76**

The law has influenced scientific progress and the science has developed the law. This is evident in the changing industry profile during the same period as the case law evolved. In 2012, the UK National Stem Cell Network reported that the UK is leading European countries in this area of technology, which is moving from a profile of patents relating to multipotent and pluripotent stem cells to one which now includes induced pluripotent cells.[199] In the process, the law has delayed developments in harnessing stem cells, for example in keeping viable cell populations and in identifying how these stem cells can be encouraged to develop into specific cells. The cost is that we are one step further away from realizing the promises of personalized medicine and 'off the shelf' organs and tissues. Pro-life campaigners argue that this is a delay that is warranted by the need for ethical development, which cannot justifiably include commodifying embryos.[200] Others will counter that this is prioritizing an unshared **20.77**

---

[194] *Brüstle v Greenpeace* C-34/10 [2011], [2012] All ER 809, para 30.

[195] B Van Roermun, 'The Embryo and its Rights: Technology and Teleology' (2013) 14 German Law Journal 1939; S H E Harmon, G Laurie, and A Courtney, 'Dignity, Plurality and Patentability: The Unfinished Story of Brustle v Greenpeace' (2013) 38(1) European Law Review 92.

[196] T2221/10 *TECHNION/Culturing Stem Cells* [2014] EPOR 23.

[197] C-364/13 *International Stem Cell Corp v Comptroller of Patents* [2014]; [2013] EWHC 807.

[198] UK-IPO Statutory Guidance, 'Inventions involving human embryonic stem cells: 25 March 2015 <https://www.gov.uk/government/publications/inventions-involving-human-embryonic-stem-cells-25-march-2015/inventions-involving-human-embryonic-stem-cells-25-march-2015>.

[199] UKNSCN, *Stem Cells: UKNSCN patent watch landscape* (2012) <https://www.gov.uk/government/publications/stem-cells>.

[200] eg, Campaign Life Coalition asserts that embryonic stem cell research is motivated by profit and is scientifically flawed: <http://www.campaignlifecoalition.com/index.php?p=Stem_Cells>.

spiritual morality over the shared secular morality of alleviating death and suffering of those with an actual—rather than a potential—life.[201] Either way, the issue should be moot now that scientific resourcefulness has enabled compliance with the law and potential immorality is reduced to being on par with use of any genetic material. In the meantime, ethics has once again given way to concern regarding the impact of exclusivity on the proliferation of innovative research, demonstrated by lead iPS cell rights already being challenged.[202]

20.78 So where does this leave the morality provision in European patent law? The EBA has stated that:

> it is important to point out that it is not the fact of the patenting itself that is considered to be against *ordre public* or morality, but it is the performing of the invention, which includes a step (the use involving its destruction of a human embryo) that has to be considered to contravene those concepts.[203]

This limits whether patent law can regulate the morality of innovation. It must be borne in mind that the purpose of the patent system is to grant private rights to facilitate the public exploitation of inventions through control of the market. That is, a patent only gives the right to exclude others from the marketplace. The only effect of a successful challenge to a patent is the denial of this market advantage. Anyone is then at liberty to produce and exploit the invention. Those who object to patenting because they object to the invention itself therefore cannot prevent the creative or exploitative process by challenging the patent.

20.79 The only hope is that the previous refusal to grant patent protection might act as a disincentive to invent, but there are many examples of industrial developments that never qualify for patent protection and yet are not hindered by this fact. In the context of stem cells, it was only in identifying that embryonic destruction will taint the chain of innovation that the courts created any incentive to ensure that multipotent or non-destructive pluripotent stem cells can result in the innovation claimed. Yet, even here the question is who enforces this? The patent system cannot do so, because applicants only need describe *a way* of developing the invention, not *the way they factually did it*. So patent morality is hardly anything to do with ensuring moral behaviour within research communities and is arguably far more about ensuring that products appear reassuringly morally acceptable to the most markets. The problem stems from a misguided desire to use the patent system as a tool for the regulation of science, industry, and medicine.[204] To say that the system is ill-equipped for the task is an understatement of considerable proportion.

(iii) Consent to patenting

20.80 **(a) The European dimension** The *HOWARD FLOREY/Relaxin* case[205] was decided largely on the ethical importance and value of consent. The issue of consent also arose in the negotiations on the draft of the Biotech Directive. Initial proposals required that specific consent to patenting be obtained from individuals who provided samples that might lead to the manufacture of patentable products, but, after much lobbying from industry and the research community, no such measure appears in the body of the Directive. However, recitals in the preamble to any Directive serve as aids to interpretation of the Articles contained therein and Recital 26 of the Biotech Directive provides:

---

[201] eg, G Dolin, 'A Defense of Embryonic Stem Cell Research' (2009) 84 Indiana Law Journal 1203.

[202] *BioGatekeeper v Kyoto University* (2015) 37 C.F.R. § 42.108, Trials@uspto.gov.

[203] G2/06 *WARF* [2009] EPOR 15, para 41.

[204] European Group of Advisors on the Ethical Implications of Biotechnology, Opinion on Ethical Questions Arising from the Commission Proposal for a Council Directive on Legal Protection for Biotechnological Inventions, Opinion No 3, 30 September 1993.

[205] T272/95 *Howard Florey/Relaxin* [1995] EPOR 541.

> Whereas if an invention is based on biological material of human origin or if it uses such material, where a patent application is filed, the person from whose body the material is taken must have had an opportunity of expressing free and informed consent thereto, in accordance with national law.

While the legal status of recitals is unclear,[206] the UK implementing regulations are silent on this requirement for consent.[207] Moreover, the recital itself is opaque as to what consent should relate to: is it the taking of the material or the filing of the patent application? The former is merely a reflection of sound ethical research practice, while the latter is a potentially more onerous requirement, not only for the researcher who must obtain such consent, but also for the patentee (who will not necessarily be the same person). Indeed, the intellectual property office itself could feel the weight of such a provision: upon whom should the onus lie to ensure the provision is complied with, and what sanction, if any, would apply if it is not? The Biotech Directive is silent on these matters, but the burden of examination for intellectual property offices could be considerable if this became a ground on which to challenge the validity of a patent. **20.81**

Nonetheless, it is the Opinion of the European Group of Advisors on the Ethical Implications of Biotechnology that, when someone contributes a biological element that might later be included in an invention, then information disclosure must be 'complete and specific' for the consent to be valid. In particular, there must be information 'on the potential patent application on the invention which could be made from the use of this element'.[208] The Group further opined that a patent should be refused if there is evidence of disrespect for individual rights or human dignity.[209] **20.82**

Concern about the consent provisions in the Recital to the EC Directive was a central feature of the Dutch challenge before the CJEU in 2001.[210] The Netherlands, joined by Italy and Norway, argued that the fundamental right to self-determination was breached by the 'absence of a provision requiring verification of the consent of the donor or recipient'. This addressed only the question of the legal status of consent provisions in the Directive and not their meaning. Even so, Advocate General Jacobs endorsed the Dutch view when he stated that: **20.83**

> [t]he fact that there is nothing in the body of the Directive ensuring that human material is managed carefully . . . [through consent] . . . must be considered contrary to fundamental right . . . [of human integrity and self-determination].[211]

The CJEU disagreed. It saw the patent regime as a system apart from other systems of regulation and control—concerned only with the grant of a patent. The reach of this system did **20.84**

[206] Case C-162/97 *Criminal proceedings against Nilsson, Hagelgren and Arrborn* [1998] ECR I-7477. For a compelling argument for this particular recital being given force of law see: D Beyleveld, 'Why Recital 26 of the EC Directive on the Legal Protection of Biotechnological Inventions should be implemented in National Law' [2000] 1 Intellectual Property Quarterly 1–26.

[207] Patents Regulations 2000, SI 2000/2037.

[208] European Group of Advisors on the Ethical Implications of Biotechnology to the European Commission, *Ethical Aspects of Patenting Inventions Involving Elements of Human Origin*, Opinion No 8 (1996), para 2.4. This body was succeeded by the EGE which reiterated this position in its Opinion No 16: EGE, *Ethical Aspects of Patenting Inventions Involving Human Stem Cells*, Opinion No 16 (2002), para 2.6.

[209] EGE, *Ethical Aspects of Patenting Inventions Involving Human Stem Cells*, Opinion No 16 (2002), para 2.1.

[210] C-377/98 *Kingdom of the Netherlands v Council of the European Union and the European Parliament* [2002] All ER (EC) 97.

[211] See the Opinion of Advocate General Jacobs in C-377/98 *Kingdom of the Netherlands v Council of the European Union and the European Parliament* [2001] ECR I-7079, para 192.

'not . . . extend to activities before and after that grant, whether they involve research or the use of the patented products'. In support, the Court claimed that:

> [t]he grant of a patent does not preclude legal limitations or prohibitions applying to research . . . [t]he purpose of the Directive is not to replace the restrictive provisions which guarantee, outside the scope of the Directive, compliance with certain ethical rules which include the right to self-determination by informed consent.[212]

Accordingly, the Directive was not deemed to be insufficient for lack of direct commitment to the principle of requiring informed consent (broadly defined).[213] More recently, the TBA decided that the absence of consent to patenting from the individuals who provide human material which is used to create a patentable invention is irrelevant in European patent law.[214]

20.85 It does not follow that the power of consent, or refusal, cannot or will not have an impact on patenting practice. As the ethical imperative to obtain fully informed consent grows all the stronger within research communities worldwide, attention has become focused on the utility of this device to give research participants: (1) some degree of continuing control over the materials they contribute to medical science; and (2) some mechanism to curb some of the excess of profiteering often associated with research in the sector. Considering consent as a mechanism of control is evident in a growing body of commentary highlighting the inequality of seminal contributions going unrewarded. For example, Henrietta Lack's cancer cells formed the HeLa cell line without her consent, but this line was instrumental in curing polio and has become a foundational medical research tool.[215] Similarly, in an international context obtaining 'prior informed consent' is one of the fundamental principles underpinning access to genetic resources between countries and cultures,[216] as are requirements for 'mutually agreed terms' which create an origin requirement. Seeing consent as a key to ensuring that benefits from genetic innovation are shared are exemplified in a domestic context by calls for clinical trial participants to sign consent forms only where there are assurances that the trial results will be widely available.[217] It is the same attitude which underpins the removal of confidentiality on trial data, facilitating the creation of a new database in the Clinical Trials Regulation, implemented in 2016.[218]

20.86 There is growing sociological evidence about what research participants think about commercialization practices. In some quarters, for example, there is a belief that any materials

[212] Case C-377/98 *Kingdom of the Netherlands v Council of the European Union and the European Parliament* [2001] ECR I-7079, para 80.

[213] For general comment, see G Laurie, 'Patents, Patients and Consent: Exploring the Interface Between Regulation and Innovation Regimes', in H Somsen, (ed), *The Regulatory Challenge of Biotechnology: Human Genetics, Food and Patents* (Edward Elgar 2007), 214–37.

[214] See T1213/05 *UNIVERSITY OF UTAH/Linked breast and ovarian cancer susceptibility gene* [2007], (unreported). For comment see A Odell-West, 'The Absence of Informed Consent to Commercial Exploitation for Inventions Developed from Human Biological Material: A Bar to Patentability?' [2009] 3 Intellectual Property Quarterly 273.

[215] R Skloot, *The Immortal Life of Henrietta Lacks* (Crown Publishing 2010).

[216] Nagoya Protocol on Access to Genetic Resources and the Fair and Equitable Sharing of Benefits Arising from their Utilization to the Convention on Biological Diversity 2010. eg, Article 5 makes consent part of the ABS; Article 7 embeds it within Traditional Knowledge; Article 6 makes it a condition of accessing genetic resources; Article 10 requires it for transboundary sharing; and Article 14.2(c) makes it a requirement within the Clearing House system.

[217] See, eg, P Andanda, 'Managing Intellectual Property Rights over Clinical Trials Data to Promote Access and Benefit Sharing in Public Health' [2013] 44(2) International Review of Intellectual Property and Competition Law 140, particularly at 154–55.

[218] Regulation 536/2014/EU on clinical trials on medicinal products for human use (2014) OJ L 158/1, Art 81, Recitals 67 and 68.

contributed are free of all claims.[219] Equally, there are studies that suggest that the prospect of profit from research is not well received.[220] Dixon-Woods *et al*[221] and Haddow *et al*[222] found, for example, that there can be marked differences in attitudes between groups suffering from disease and their healthy counterparts, both with respect to attitudes towards property claims and towards the prospect of others profiting from their contributions. Groups which have experienced ill-health are usually very supportive of research and can be more tolerant of its commercial aspects than healthy groups (although see the US cases discussed below). Where intolerance does arise, research groups have found it difficult to find a suitable legal mechanism to address their grievances. The role of consent in such disputes is central but, as the following cases demonstrate, it is unlikely to be sufficiently robust to deliver the control or influence that is sought.

(b) The US Dimension Consent and patenting were classically considered together in the Supreme Court of California ruling in *Moore v Regents of the University of California*.[223] Although this case is now over-debated, it nonetheless serves an important purpose in setting up the issues in the current debate. Briefly, the plaintiff failed in his attempt to claim property rights in his excised spleen cells from which his doctor and other researchers had profited after developing and patenting a cell line using those cells. The Court pointed to the hindrance to research that recognition of property rights in such material could create, and preferred instead to grant Moore remedies for lack of informed consent and breach of fiduciary duty. The court concluded that: **20.87**

> (1) a physician must disclose personal interests unrelated to the patient's health, whether research or economic, that may affect the physician's professional judgment; and (2) a physician's failure to disclose such interests may give rise to a cause of action for performing medical procedures without informed consent or breach of fiduciary duty.[224]

While this is not tantamount to requiring a disclosure of an intention to patent per se, the reference to economic interests indicates that it would be sound practice to alert patients at least to the prospect. This is particularly so when: '[t]he scope of the physician's communication to the patient … must be measured by the patient's need, and that need is whatever information is material to the decision.'[225] It is important to note, too, that there was no question of the court in *Moore* revoking the patent over the cell-line. It was held to be both 'legally and factually distinct'[226] from the cells taken from the plaintiff's body and the resultant financial gain was a valid reward for the inventive effort of the researchers. Thus, not only was Moore denied the recognition of property rights in his own cells, but he was also deprived of the opportunity to ensure that other forms of property right did not pass to other parties.

Similar arguments arose in *Greenberg v Miami Children's Hospital Research Institute Inc*.[227] This was a class action by families of sufferers of Canavan's disease, a rare genetic disorder, **20.88**

[219] M Dixon-Woods et al, 'Tissue Samples as "Gifts" for Research: A Qualitative Study of Families and Professionals' (2008) 9(2) Medical Law International 131.

[220] G Haddow et al, 'Tackling Community Concerns about Commercialisation and Genetic Research: A Modest Interdisciplinary Proposal' (2007) 64 Social Sciences & Medicine Journal 272.

[221] M Dixon-Woods et al, n 219.

[222] G Haddow et al, n 220.

[223] *Moore v Regents of the University of California* (1990) 51 Cal 3d 120.

[224] ibid, 129.

[225] *Cobbs v Grant* (1972) 8 Cal 3d 229, 245.

[226] *Moore v Regents of the University of California* n 223, 141.

[227] *Greenberg et al v Miami Children's Hospital Research Institute Inc et al* 264 F Supp 2d 1064 (SD Fla, 2003).

brought against the researchers and the hospital who patented the Canavan disease gene after carrying out extensive research on samples and information provided by the families. Arguments were advanced in the tort of conversion,[228] on the basis of lack of informed consent and breach of fiduciary duty.[229] A motion at the behest of the defendants to strike out the action was refused, but the grounds for complaint were reduced to the unjust enrichment of the defendants at the expense of the plaintiffs, and the case subsequently settled out of court.[230] Nonetheless, the overarching aim throughout the proceedings had been to obtain an injunction to prevent the defendants relying on the patent. It is to be regretted that a full judicial hearing did not materialize, because there were always at least two reasons to suspect that the case would not blindly follow the precedent in *Moore*. First, the suit was being heard in Florida, and *Moore* is only binding authority in California. The tendency to assume that *Moore* encapsulates a universal precedent is, of course, erroneous. Second, the policy arguments are not as clear-cut as the Supreme Court of California suggested a decade previously. Its concern was to avoid erecting barriers to research and to ensure the development of medicines. The *Greenberg* case was representative of a groundswell of opinion against the use of patents in the medical sphere when these are used to block research by others or to limit access to health care. The owners of the Canavan patent, for example, charged a fixed royalty of $12.50 per test and placed a limit on the number of tests that could be carried out annually by any licensee. Research uses were also tightly controlled through licensing. The plaintiffs in *Greenberg* were challenging the patent precisely because of these practices and not for personal profit. They did so to ensure that further research is carried out and, in this sense, the policy arguments in *Moore* are turned on their head.

20.89 *Washington University v Catalona et al* was not concerned with intellectual property rights as such, but it does raise interesting points about consent as control.[231] This dispute concerned the ownership of physical samples provided by research participants in cancer studies. The US District Court[232] and the Court of Appeals for the Eighth Circuit[233] found that ownership vested in the university under whose auspices the research was originally conducted and that the samples could not be taken by Dr Catalona when he moved institution, even with the express consent of the participants. The courts were satisfied that the university had sufficiently exerted its ownership to the samples—notably through the informed consent materials and in its intellectual property policy—and that the participants had freely given consent to donate samples for research at the university. The District Court cited both *Moore* and *Greenberg* as authority that research participants retain no ownership of biological materials they contribute for research. While *Catalona* might be viewed as another defeat for research participants to claim control, it does move the debate forward in that it presumes prima facie property-type claims. The university won because it brought convincing evidence of possession and control of the samples and because the participants could not show that they had any expectations other than outright gift. The unanswered question is

[228] This is a common law tort which allows someone with a legal interest in property to sue for the return of the property and/or damages.

[229] Meaning a relationship recognized in equity as being one of trust and confidence, giving rise to rights. Examples include doctors and patients.

[230] *Greenberg et al v Miami Children's Hospital*, n 227, settled action; for comment see M R Anderlik and M A Rothstein, 'Canavan Decision Favors Researchers Over Families' (2003) 313 Journal of Law, Medicine and Ethics 450.

[231] For commentary, see L Andrews, 'Rights of Donors: Who Owns your Body? A Patient's Perspective on *Washington University v Catalona*' (2006) 34 Journal of Law, Medicine and Ethics 398.

[232] *Washington University v Catalona* 437 F Supp 2d 985 (2006, US Dist).

[233] *Washington University v Catalona* 490 F.3d 667 (2007); US Supreme Court, certiorari was denied, *Catalona v Washington University* 128 SCt 1122, 169 L Ed 2d 949 (2008).

whether there is room for some form of conditional gift[234] or some other pseudo-property claim which might complement, rather than replace, the role of consent.

(c) **The UK dimension** No such disputes have arisen in the UK, but this may just be a matter of time in light of companies such as 23andMe/23andWe, who provide genetic services and entice individuals to participate in research, but then sell the information to the pharmaceutical industry and patent gene sequences themselves.[235] A related ruling by the Court of Appeal suggests that property-type claims by individuals may be on the horizon thereby offering another control device with respect to parts of the human body, their exploitation and possible commercialization. In *Yearworth v North Bristol NHS Trust*[236] the court accepted a property claim for men who had deposited sperm prior to cancer treatment and who sought legal recourse when it accidentally perished. The specifics of the ruling are dealt with elsewhere in this volume (see Chapter 19), but the interest in the case for present purposes concerns the activism of the court. While recognizing that the common law has been 'noticeably silent' about property in parts or products of the living human body, it suggested that this has been because medical science has not endowed them with any great significance or value. As the cases discussed above demonstrate, this is no longer true. Moreover, the inadequacies of existing mechanisms, and more particularly consent, were recognized and led the court to opine: **20.90**

> In this jurisdiction developments in medical science now require a re-analysis of the common law's treatment of an approach to the issue of ownership of parts or products of a living human body, whether for present purposes (viz. an action in negligence) or otherwise.[237]

The implications of this for individuals or for intellectual property are uncertain. This case was particular on its facts—being concerned with sperm where there was a clear expectation of return of the material—and also complicated by the provisions of the UK Human Fertilisation and Embryology Act 1990 (as amended); notwithstanding, as a matter of principle and logic, it is difficult to see how the call for re-analysis of the law would not be extended further. Notably, the court saw property and consent claims as complementary, not mutually exclusive. The door is therefore open for individuals to claim some degree of continuing control over their body parts as physical property[238] and this may lead to some difficult negotiations down the line for intangible intellectual property arising from the use of such parts.

What is often not appreciated within this debate is that, even where the innovation may result from little more than simple synthesis of biological source materials, this belies the effort required to get the innovation onto the market. Product development requires substantial investment, ingenuity, time, and manpower to be expended in getting the innovation through complex regulations; through often prolonged animal and clinical trials; and through marketing authorization and marketing strategies which become ever more **20.91**

[234] N Kanellopoulou, 'Advocacy Groups as Research Organisations: Novel Approaches in Research Governance' in C Lyall, T Papaioannou, and J Smith (eds), *The Limits of Governance: The Challenges of Policy-making for the New Life Sciences* (Ashgate 2009), ch 9.

[235] For more on this see H C Howard, S Sterckx, and J Cockbain, 'The Convergence of Direct-to-Consumer Genetic Testing Companies and Biobanking Activities' in M Wienroth and E Rodriguez (eds), *Knowing New Biotechnologies: Social Aspects of Technological Convergence* (Routledge 2015).

[236] *Yearworth v North Bristol NHS Trust* [2009] 3 WLR 118, 107 BMLR 47.

[237] *Yearworth v North Bristol NHS Trust* [2009] 3 WLR 118, 107 BMLR 47, at para 45.

[238] M Quigley, 'Propertisation & Commercialisation: On Controlling the Uses of Biomaterials' (2014) 77(5) Modern Law Review 677; For the legal interplay between property, liability, and inalienability see L I Palmer, 'Should Liability Play a Role in Social Control of Biobanks?' (2005) 33 The Journal of Law, Medicine & Ethics 70.

difficult where there are burgeoning numbers of competitor products already in the market and regulators keep introducing additional gatekeepers between the industry and commissioners.[239] In light of all this, claims to determinative value being given by the simple donation of DNA pale in comparison. The inequity of value/benefits received not being commensurate with the value added/burdens adopted is likely to be an enduring issue, which reaches far beyond the interface between researchers and participants. For example, there is an increasing amount of genetic data being gathered through public/charitable organizations,[240] which is being restricted for the benefit of public research and yet it is inescapable that this research will form the basis of rights which are going to have to become commercialized in order to achieve marketability. Without determinatively changing existing regulatory mechanisms, the greatest financial benefits will follow the commercial rights rather than the value of the contributions.

2. Relative grounds of objection

20.92 Assessing the breadth of the monopoly in the market has very many aspects to it, only some of which can be dealt with in this chapter. Paras. 20.09–20.37 already considered how the type of patent claimed relates to its technological proliferation. However, there are other aspects of dissemination which are cause for concern and are collateral to the patent system or cannot form the basis of a legal challenge, making them relative grounds. First, there is the moral issue of having a monopoly right which can exclude access to medical products/processes/devices or adversely affect the flow of research. Secondly, the limitations of legal mechanisms for dealing with patents which are underworked (meaning that they are not proliferated as effectively as possible) must be explored. Finally, paras. 20.107–20.114 consider key mechanisms for ensuring that research is not unduly inhibited by exclusivity rights.

(i) *Morality of monopoly*

20.93 The basis of this objection is that the abusive exercise of the private property right given by a patent undermines certain valued public interests. Access to medicines and diagnostic tools and the pursuit of medical research are undeniably public goods, while the control of drug and therapeutics markets and the impact on research are equally obvious concerns that are raised by the grant of pharmaceutical and biotechnological patents. The scene is set, then, for a classic conflict scenario. No example illustrates the problem better than the case of Myriad Genetics, which concerned worldwide patents over the breast cancer genes BRCA1 and BRCA2. The Nuffield Council on Bioethics characterized the challenges thus:

> The opposition is aimed at curtailing any possible deleterious consequences which might stem from sanctioning the monopoly conferred on Myriad Genetics, including the possible threat to the development of research and the identification of new tests and diagnostic methods. It has also been argued that the patent will have a serious impact on equitable access to testing. It is suggested that the monopoly is antithetical to an approach to public health that is based on a commitment to the comprehensive care of patients at high-risk.[241]

---

[239] eg in the UK accessing Clinical Commissioning Groups within the NHS for innovative drugs must now be approached through fifteen new Academic Health Science Networks and proliferation of technology throughout the NHS relies upon being listed on a scorecard.

[240] This can be exemplified in the UK: the UK Biobank; Cell Banks in which patented biological materials are required to be deposited; in the recent launch of the 100,000 Genomes Project; and the Care. Data initiative being run through the Health and Social Care Information Centre.

[241] Nuffield Council on Bioethics, *The Ethics of Patenting DNA* (2002) para 4.6.

As the Council point out, and as is also raised in *Association for Molecular Pathology et al v US Patent & Trademark Office, Myriad Genetics et al*,[242] because of the way Myriad Genetics initially used its patent monopolies worldwide, there were 'no other methods of diagnosing the presence of the breast cancer susceptibility gene BRCA1 that [could] be used without infringing the patents'.[243]

A European Parliament resolution from October 2001 called upon the EPO to reconsider the grant of patents and for amendment to the EPC, which would allow the Office to revoke patents on its own initiative.[244] The Office replied by pointing to the role of opposition proceedings, which in Europe can be invoked by any party with a valid concern about a patent. It also stressed that its policy is not to make a special case of biotechnological inventions.[245] Certainly, the concern over monopolistic control is not restricted to these kinds of invention, and pharmaceutical patents are open to precisely the same grounds of objection. The dilemma for any intellectual property office and the state in whose name patents are granted is to strike a balance between encouraging sufficient investment and research through the availability of patent protection while not being seen to prejudice, and so dissuade, patentees by making the qualifying criteria too onerous. An additional problem is that wholesale challenges that go to the heart of the patent only offer an all or nothing option: either the patent stands or it does not. Other strategies are, however, available which leave more scope for balance, as discussed in paras. 20.105–20.114. **20.94**

Myriad Genetics's patents on BRCA1 and BRCA2 genes caused considerable outcry globally, but particularly within Europe and the US for two main reasons: (1) the breadth of the patent claims; and (2) Myriad's trading strategies. **20.95**

(a) Breadth of claims Myriad filed its US patents and subsequently filed three European patent applications: a **use claim** over the BRCA1 gene for any method of diagnostic testing for the risk of breast or ovarian cancers (EP 699754); claims to the BRCA1 gene (**product *per se***) with a wide range of possible uses (EP 705902); and a claim to a long list of BRCA1 mutations (EP 705903, **a selection invention**). The use claim (EP 699754) was revoked in 2004, but successfully appealed to the TBA. It was allowed on a reduced claim to *a method* of diagnosing breast and ovarian cancer; and further limited to 'frameshift mutations', which are the most severe forms of mutation, because they are responsible for cells producing abnormal proteins.[246] This was the patent most of interest to Myriad, because diagnostic testing is their primary area of business. Of the three patents, the strongest is EP 705902 because it is to the product *per se*, so it represents the greatest threat to the freedom of other researchers and geneticists. This patent was similarly allowed, but the TBA imposed the same limitation to the frameshift mutation.[247] The raft of BRCA1 mutations (thirty-four at one point) in the selection invention was similarly eventually accepted, but in a very much amended form, as claims to diagnostic methods, probes and specific mutations most prevalent in Ashkenazi Jews.[248] There is no further avenue of appeal through the EPO. **20.96**

[242] *Association for Molecular Pathology v Myriad Genetics, Inc*, 133 S Ct 2107 (US 2013) ('*Myriad V*'), US Supreme Court, 13 June 2013.
[243] Nuffield Council on Bioethics, *The Ethics of Patenting DNA* (2002) para 5.4.
[244] European Parliament resolution on the patenting of BRCA1 and BRCA2 (breast cancer) genes, 4 October 2001, B5-0633, 0641, 0651 and 0663/2001.
[245] EPO Declaration of 17 October 2001, AC/145/01.
[246] T80/05 *UNIVERSITY OF UTAH/Method of Diagnosis* [2008] (unreported).
[247] T1213/05 *UNIVERSITY OF UTAH/Breast and ovarian cancer* [2007] (unreported).
[248] T666/05 *UNIVERSITY OF UTAH/Mutation* [2008] (unreported).

20.97 In 2010, Myriad successfully opposed Cancer Research Technology's patent to the BRCA2 gene and it was revoked on appeal. The problem was that the sequence had not been cited in the documents on which it was claiming priority: this meant that disclosure at the actual filing date failed for lack of novelty, because the sequence had already been disclosed.[249] The significance of this decision is that Myriad are left owning the only BRCA2 patent.

20.98 Both the European and US litigation has been protracted, but the US cases had the unfortunate effect along the way of moving the point at which 'products of nature' (discoveries) become patentable. On the legal point, the US has finally returned to its original position, arguably bringing it back in line with European practice: claims to DNA sequences as they exist in nature are unpatentable; conversely synthesized DNA (cDNA) does not occur in nature because it transposes a base,[250] and excludes introns (non-coding regions); and purified DNA which is not naturally occurring (ie where the introns have been removed) is also patentable,[251] subject to the normal qualification requirements. Arguably Europe does not make such fine distinctions in requiring purification to additionally be tangibly different to the naturally occurring DNA,[252] but the significance of the difference is negligible in the context of achieving patentability in medical innovations. In 2014, additional litigation involving Myriad clarified that DNA primers are unpatentable, because these small sections of single-strand DNA have identical bases to those which are naturally occurring. Primers can be distinguished from probes, because the latter usually contain markers which mean they are not naturally occurring. In addition, on the facts of the case, Myriad's method claims were either already known or abstract ideas.[253]

20.99 The consequence of the litigation on both sides of the Atlantic is that the market for diagnostic test kits is once again open to competitors, but innovators like Myriad will maintain a strong licensing position for other follow on innovations. This is already evident in competitor products emerging which adopt alternative diagnostic strategies or utilize different gene sequences.[254] However, the Myriad litigation demonstrates the negative impact on technological proliferation which ensues from patent claims which are too wide or which *reach through* to too much follow on development.[255] In claiming so many mutations and such strong patent rights, Myriad was patenting itself into an unwarranted position of market control, which could take years to get to the point at which it would come to the attention of competition/antitrust authorities. Considering the patent system as being impassive in affecting any form of market control is naive in the extreme. In the past the EPO has consistently reiterated its position that it is not its role to consider the economic effects of

[249] T902/07 *BRCA2/Breast cancer technology* [2010] (unreported).

[250] Meaning A, C, G, or T.

[251] *Association for Molecular Pathology v Myriad Genetics, Inc*, 133 S Ct 2107 (US 2013) ('*Myriad V*'), US Supreme Court, 13 June 2013.

[252] T272/95 *Howard Florey/Relaxin* [1995] EPOR 541

[253] *Myriad v Ambry* [2014] Federal Court, <http://www.cafc.uscourts.gov/images/stories/opinions-orders/14-1361.Opinion.12-15-2014.1.PDF>.

[254] See, eg, those discussed in J Conley, D Vorhaus, and R Cook-Deegan, 'How Will Myriad Respond to the Next Generation of BRCA Testing?' (2011) Genomics Law Report, <http://www.genomicslawreport. com/>.

[255] *Reach through* occurs during patenting where a product per se patent claim is drafted so widely that it provides the foundation for subsequent generations of technological development. This *reach through* effect can also be achieved in licensing non-foundational technology through agreement clauses such as: (i) royalties on the sales of future products; (ii) options to take out exclusive or non-exclusive licences on future patents; and (iii) full ownership of future inventions as a condition of the initial access: (Organization for Economic Cooperation and Development OECD, *Genetic Inventions, Intellectual Property Rights and Licensing Practices: Evidence and Policies* (OECD Publishing, 2002), 92.

a patent in deciding on its validity,[256] but the appointment in 2013 of their fourth Chief Economist indicates that the EPO are very well attuned to the link between the administration of the patent system and the impact of patents in the market. It is because of the nexus between the rights granted and their potential market impact that the trilateral co-operation between the WHO, WIPO, and WTO (identified at the very beginning of this chapter) is so necessary.

(b) Trading strategy It was the high cost of licensing the technology, $3,120 per test (including full genome sequencing, re-testing, and personal consultation),[257] which prompted much of the Myriad litigation. It was also the fact that the patents were applied for globally, but until 2011 Myriad was a predominantly US company (only 2 per cent of its revenue coming from outside of the United States),[258] which indicates that the patent rights are not being effectively exploited. Patent holders who sit on their rights without exploiting them are referred to as *trolls* and the mechanisms for dealing with them will be looked at in para 20.105–20.106. Before doing so, it is important to glimpse into the broader approach to regulating agreements concerning patents and know-how.[259] Licensing is an under-regulated area given the reality of commerce, which actually gives such agreements a greater significance than the patents on which they are founded. The 2014 Report of the Organization for Economic Cooperation and Development (OECD) identified major concerns over some OECD countries being unable to translate innovation into commercial goods, on the evidence of patent and licensing practices.[260] So this indicates just how important licenses are as indicators of technological proliferation and economic potential. **20.100**

On an EU level, patents and know-how (which is generally protected through trade secrecy) come within the remit of technology transfer regulations. The 2014 EU Commission Regulation on Technology Transfer (*TTBER*)[261] continues the presumption that licensing encourages competition. This is evident throughout, but Recitals 10 and 11 exemplify this presumption by stating that—irrespective of whether licenses are between competitors or not—they 'lead to an improvement in production or distribution and allow consumers a fair share of the resulting benefits'. In accepting the new version of the TTBER, the Commission was keen to highlight the virtues of licenses in promoting trade and proliferating technology.[262] **20.101**

On the back of this justification, the Regulation lays down a block exemption from liability for unfair competitive practices arising from trade between EU Member States involving two parties. For the pharmaceutical industry, which trades globally and throughout Europe, this is an essential legal shield, which is similarly found in other jurisdictions. The main provisions of the TTBER impose market share limitations (Article 3); hardcore **20.102**

[256] *NOVARTIS II/ Transgenic Plant* [2000] EPOR 303, para 3.9, as well as in the *R v LELAND STANFORD/Modified Animal* [2002] EPOR 2, at para 49.

[257] R Cook-Deegan et al, 'Impact of gene patents and licensing practices on access to genetic test of inherited susceptibility to cancer: comparing breast and ovarian cancers to colon cancers' (2010) 12(4, Suppl) Genetic Medicine 15–38.

[258] J Conley, D Vorhaus, and R Cook-Deegan, 'How Will Myriad Respond to the Next Generation of BRCA Testing? (2011) Genomics Law Report <http://www.genomicslawreport.com/>.

[259] Know-how refers to technical information or skills which are unprotectable through formal property rights such as patents, but which have commercial value and are usually protected through confidentiality or restraint of trade clauses.

[260] OECD, *OECD Science, Technology and Industry Outlook* (OECD Publishing 2014) 211.

[261] Regulation 316/2014/EU on the application of Article 101(3) of the Treaty on the Functioning of the European Union to categories of technology transfer agreements (2014) OJ L93/17.

[262] European Commission, 'Antitrust: Commission adopts revised competition regime for technology transfer agreements', 21 March 2014 <http://europa.eu/rapid/press-release_IP-14-299_en.htm>.

restrictions (Article 4) which prevent practices such as price fixing or supply restrictions; and the 2014 version also includes a prohibition on *grant backs* (Article 5(1)(a)) which prevent licenses requiring that follow on development must be licensed back to the licensor. The obvious consequence of *grant back* provisions is that they easily create an impenetrable web, which makes later developments prohibitively expensive: important medical innovations may never reach the patient.

20.103 As an additional security, Article 4(d) stipulates that the exemption is not available where the license restricts research and development, with the caveat that such clauses are permitted if they protect the confidentiality of know-how. In consequence, for medical developments which have complex specifications governing their operation—for example, neural implants which operate bio-engineered prosthetics or increasingly complex scanning equipment—know-how becomes more important than patent rights even, because know-how is legally protected without being time-limited. Although, in the event that the confidentiality is lost, the know-how falls outside of the block exemption.

20.104 The trilateral report of the WHO, WIPO, and WTO in 2013 paints a very positive picture of the progress that has been made in licensing medical innovation, summarizing as follows:

> [p]ublic–private partnerships have resulted in creative licensing agreements that forgo profit maximization in favour of providing essential technologies to poorer countries at affordable prices. Voluntary licenses also form part of corporate social responsibility programmes, especially for HIV/AIDS treatments. The Medicines Patent Pool has reinforced the trend towards voluntary licensing programmes that increase access to medicines by enabling new formulations and enhancing provision of cheaper generic medicines for developing countries.[263]

The difficulty is that these are exceptions rather than the norm. Critiquing these presumptions and the limitations of the TTBER, or even of more fundamental regulation of trading practices[264] is best summed up by the inherent flaw within all such measures: health care is not a normal competitive market. Even in the context of the current neo-liberalism governing health care regulation, which gives primacy to patient choice, there are clear limitations on choice and there is also a disconnect between users and providers. Primary health care providers within the NHS adopt catchment-style restrictions, which means that patient choice is limited to NHS or private practitioners, rather than being a choice between GPs. Health care is not a choice purchase in most instances, but the purchasing power of the patient (consumer) is non-existent when the purchase is essential. This raises questions about how the push to regulate health care, as if it is the equivalent of buying a pair of shoes, may affect the ability to mediate between the need for cost-effective health care provision now and the development of health innovation for the future. Understanding how pressing this is requires an appreciation of key legal measures which regulate getting innovation to the market now and in the future.

(ii) Underworking innovation

20.105 While the link between the innovation and the market cannot be guaranteed, patents that are not exploited are regulated. For example, *patent trolls* sit on their rights in the hope of selling them at an exorbitant market value, or developing themselves even though they have woefully inadequate resources. Regulating is not as simple as enabling access by letting

[263] WHO, WIPO, and WTO, *Promoting Access to Medical Technologies and Innovation* (2013), Executive Summary and Chapter IV, section C.2.

[264] eg, Articles 101 (unfair competitive practices) and Article 102 (dominant market position) of the Treaty on the Functioning of the European Union.

third parties use/exploit the invention where the innovator fails to do so. This is because inherently, a compulsory license removes the benefit (the exclusivity) granted in the patent, so it must only be done where it is truly necessary. Although there are provisions facilitating compulsory licenses within the TRIPs Agreement, the US and elsewhere,[265] within Europe enforcement is devolved to individual Member States.[266] For example, legal provisions in the UK are divided between WTO innovators[267] (who are required to work innovatively and not detrimentally affect progress)[268] and non-WTO proprietors (additionally constrained to ensure UK innovation is manufactured/processed in the UK and marketed widely).[269] In both contexts, a patent holder is permitted to sit on their rights for three years before a compulsory license can be triggered[270] and this represents a limitation on potential competitors. In the context of most modern commercial enterprises in a digital business world, financing, manufacturing, and marketing take considerably less than three years to reach a point which demonstrates innovation is being worked. Conversely, for medicines there are additional requirements for market authorization, which rely upon clinical trials that can take ten years or more to produce and this means that there can be a very significant gap between innovation creation and anyone realizing that it is not being worked properly. Compulsory licensing does not realistically enforce access in any circumstance: against trolls; or against innovators who are unable to fund progress. In the context of medical devices, it provides too long a delay; whereas in the context of medicines, the delay would be considerably longer than the statutory three years. This is clearly not in the interests of either the public or the pharmaceutical industry.

Ensuring that patent rights are worked relies upon competitors or the public alerting the Comptroller of Patents to a problem. The effect is that the regulator grants and enforces only patents that have marketability, because this is where the economic benefits exist. This demonstrates that patents are granted and licensed by regulators to maximize the potential for marketing, with no account being taken of how important the innovation is or what its time-line to market is. Product life-cycle management within pharmaceutical companies is already part of normal commercial practice: for spin-outs/start-ups and SMEs this may be more rudimentary to meet the needs of investors, but such strategies are progressively more developed the larger the company is. There is no reason why such operating policies cannot become part of the evidence which would enable regulatory oversight which preempts failures to work medical innovation. Instead there is considerable opposition towards compulsory licensing by both patentees and intellectual property offices alike. In 2002, the OECD[271] noted that the role of compulsory licenses, although not popular, should be **20.106**

[265] eg TRIPs Agreement 1994, Article 31 and the Doha Declaration (discussed in Part D below); in the US there are 'march-in' rights: 35 USC §200-212.

[266] Regulation 1257/2012/EU (2012) OJL361/1, Recital 10 states that it is decided by provisions in Member States' law.

[267] PA 1977, ss 48–54; on this point ss 48 and 48A.

[268] Production is not meeting demand: (PA 1977, s 48(1)(a)); refusal to license results either in adversely affecting the economic exploitation of a dependent patented technology (PA 1977, s 48(1)(b)(i); see also *Monsanto CCP Patent* [1990] FSR 93); or inhibiting industrial/commercial growth (PA 1977, s 48(1)(b)(ii)); or that licensing conditions adversely affect the proliferation of unpatented technology or industrial/economic growth (PA 1977, s 48(1)(c)).

[269] PA 1977, s 48B(1). In addition, it is open to the patent holder to willingly grant licenses to third parties by placing an entry on the Patent Register (PA 1977, s 46), or to the Comptroller of Patents in the UK to impose a Register entry (PA 1977, s 48) and use by the Government is secured in emergencies (ss 55–59; *Pfizer v Ministry of Health* [1965] RPC 261).

[270] PA 1977, s 48(1), albeit that this can be altered by Parliament: PA 1977, s 48(6); UK-IPO, *Manual of Patent Practice* 2015, point 48.23.

[271] Development OECD, *Genetic Inventions, Intellectual Property Rights and Licensing Practices: Evidence and Policies* (OECD Publishing 2002). This was then followed by recommendations specific to licensing

revisited, partly because the power of the threat of the compulsory license could be enough to force a patentee's hand, prompting them to negotiate with potential licensees.[272] This places an inordinate amount of faith in one legal mechanism, which is clearly too generalized to be of much value in the context of medical innovations.

(iii) Inhibiting research

20.107 It is also worth noting the role of research exemptions in patent law worldwide, as a result of which things done on, or to, an invention for purely experimental purposes are not considered to be an infringement of the patent. There is, for example, a long history of antipathy in the US towards any attempt to limit the private rights of the patent holder.[273] Getting the balance right between patent holders (who must be able to exclude others from competing in the market) and researchers (who must be able to use patented inventions to expand knowledge and explore the potential for future innovation), as well as generic producers (who must be able to enter the market competitively on expiry of the patent) is essential for maximizing the public good in medical innovation. Consequently, so-called Bolar exemptions and research exemptions are crucial mechanisms for achieving this balance. The Bolar exemption provides protection for 'uses reasonably related to the development and submission of information under a Federal law which regulates the manufacture, use, or sale of drugs or veterinary biological products',[274] but this only extends to measures aimed at obtaining regulatory approval for the rapid release of generics onto the market at the expiry of any existing patent. Furthermore, the scope of the common law research exemption—which as its name suggests allows research to be carried out on a patented invention without fear of an infringement suit—has tended to be interpreted progressively more restrictively over the years.

20.108 The research exemption received its strictest interpretation to date in the Federal Circuit decision on *Madey v Duke University*[275] where the court limited the scope of the exemption 'strictly to philosophical enquiry only'. In particular, the exemption does not apply where the use 'furthers the researcher's legitimate business'; a concept that the court interpreted widely to exclude any use if it has the 'slightest commercial implication'.[276] In this particular instance, the court held that the status of the defendant as a non-profit educational institution was not determinative—the research work was lucrative for the university in terms of increasing prestige and attracting further research monies and future students. Doubtless in response to such measures, the Supreme Court ruled in *Merck KGaA v Integra LifeSciences Ltd*[277] that there is an immunity from infringement proceedings in respect of preclinical research and experimentation which is 'reasonably related' to obtaining necessary information for regulatory approval before the US Food and Drug Administration (FDA). This has

genetic technology: OECD, *Recommendation on the Licensing of Genetic Inventions* (OECD Publishing 2006), (2005)149/Rev1.

[272] Development OECD, *Genetic Inventions, Intellectual Property Rights and Licensing Practices: Evidence and Policies* (OECD Publishing 2002), 81.

[273] R S Eisenberg, 'Patents and the Progress of Science: Exclusive Rights and Experimental Use' (1989) 56(3) The University of Chicago Law Review 1017; T A Hemphill, 'The Biotechnology Sector and US Gene Patents: Legal challenges to intellectual property rights and the impact on basic research and development' (2012) S39(6) Science and Public Policy 815.

[274] cf *Roche Products, Inc v Bolar Pharmaceutical Co* (1984) 733 F.2d 858 (CA Fed) and the Act which overturned the ruling to create the 'Bolar exemption': the Drug Price Competition and Patent Term Restoration Act 1984 (Waxman-Hatch Act) 21 USC, § 301 et seq.

[275] *Madey v Duke University*, 307 F.3d 1351 (Fed Cir 2002).

[276] Citing *Embrex Inc v Service Engineering Corp*, 216 F.3d 1343 (Fed Cir 2000), 1353.

[277] *Merck KGaA v Integra LifeSciences Ltd* 545 US 193 (2005), interpreting 35 USC §271(e)(1)—The Drug Price Competition and Patent Term Restoration Act 1984 (also known as the Hatch-Waxman Act).

since been expanded on by the Federal Circuit in *Momenta Pharm v Amphastar Pharm,*[278] where the exemption was held to include post-marketing tests which are required by the FDA, even if they are never in fact submitted.

So, while generics are provided for in conducting tests ahead of establishing therapeutic- or bio-equivalence, it is less clear whether this extends to combination inventions and whether it exempts from infringement the use of proprietary research tools needed to develop therapeutic agents. While Bolar clearly exempts testing, does this extend to other activities, such as manufacture, supply, and importation? The pharmaceutical industry has become increasingly specialized as more and more of its traditional development activities are out-sourced, begging questions about whether Bolar will extend to third parties to the market approval process, such as clinical research organizations (CROs). Similarly, could the research exemption be stretched far enough to cover not only requirements attendant to obtaining market authorization, but including uses attendant to health technology assessments (HTAs)? **20.109**

The position in Europe remained patchy[279] even after the introduction of the EU Bolar exemption[280] because of the lack of detail and the scope to provide more protection. Member States' Bolar/research exemptions categorize into broad or narrow.[281] Germany exemplifies a broad interpretation, exempting from liability for infringement any experimental activities with a patented medicine, irrespective of whether it is commercial, and including clinical trials to obtain market authorization for first or subsequent medical uses, or a generic.[282] **20.110**

Traditionally, the UK exemplified the narrow interpretation. The research exemption which predated the implementation of the EU Bolar exemption distinguished between testing and discovery (within the exemption) and merely confirming or seeking market authorization (as falling outside).[283] This latter aspect was amended in the context of truly novel medicines (*originators)* to accommodate the EU Bolar exemption, which was construed narrowly to exclude activities relating to market authorization of new medical uses, but allowed any activities necessary to obtaining market authorization of generics (including manufacture, import, and supply of samples).[284] Arguably research tools (defined as the use of protected products 'on another invention') were excluded from the exemption.[285] This interpretation is supported by the need to construe the exemption so that it did not impinge upon marketability. For research tools the interim research market is their end market, so an exemption which includes such tools would have the effect of stopping them from being developed or traded because they would not need to be licensed for use. Suggestions that the Bolar exemption should include research tools (because it is intended to expedite generic entry and tools can delay this) [286] are undermined by the range of tools generally available, the **20.111**

[278] *Momenta Pharm v Amphastar Pharm* (2012) 686 F.3d 1348.

[279] See generally G van Overwalle (ed), *Gene Patents and Public Health* (Bruylant 2007).

[280] Directive 2004/27 amending Directive 2001/83 (2004) OJ L136/34, importing a new Article 10(6) into Directive 2001/83/EC (2004) OJ L136/34.

[281] For more detail, see L Cohen and L Peirson, 'The UK Research and "Bolar" Exemptions: Broadening the Scope for Innovation?' (2013) 8(11) Journal of Intellectual Property Law & Practice 837.

[282] *Clinical Trials I* [1997] RPC 623; *Clinical Trials II* [1998] RPC 423 (respectively)

[283] See Unified Patent Court Agreement (2013) OJEPO C175/1, Art 27(d); PA 1977, s 60(5)(b); *Monsanto v Stauffer Chemical Co* [1985] RPC 515, para 3.

[284] UKIPO Guidance on the Bolar exemption, <www.ipo.gov.uk/p-policy-pharmaceutical.htm>; Medicines and Health care products Regulatory Agency (MHRA) Guidance, <www.mhra.gov.uk/home/groups/comms-ic/documents/website resources/con007679.pdf>.

[285] *Smith, Kline and French v Evans Medical* [1989] FSR 513; MHRA Guidance, <www.mhra.gov.uk/home/ groups/>; UK-IPO, *The Patent Research Exemption: A consultation* (HMSO, 2008) 5; UK-IPO Guidance on the Bolar exemption, <www.ipo.gov.uk/p-policy-pharmaceutical.htm>.

[286] L Cohen and L Peirson, 'The UK Research and 'Bolar' Exemptions: Broadening the Scope for Innovation?' (2013) 8(11) Journal of Intellectual Property Law & Practice 837, 842.

licensing fees being considerably cheaper than those for originator medicines and the reality that tools without rights will cease to be developed.

20.112 The UK Legislative Reform (Patents) Order 2014[287] introduced supplementary provisions which broaden the pre-existing exemption considerably. The intention is to remove barriers to conducting clinical trials in the UK and lessen the burden of litigation on the industry.[288] The main provision, in addition to the existing general research exemption, stipulates that 'anything done in or for the purposes of a medicinal product assessment . . . is to be regarded as done for experimental purposes'.[289] This is an extremely broad approach to activities and, in tandem with the following provision, extends the exemption to trials for new medical uses of known substances.[290] The context of testing is extended from the market authorization already permitted by the Bolar exemption to include HTAs and regulatory requirements necessary for market entry that may additionally apply, and this is irrespective of whether it occurs in the UK or abroad. [291] The changes adopt a broad interpretation of medicinal products, including originator medicines, combination medicines, advanced therapies, and combination advanced therapies.[292] The absence of stipulations on whose activities are exempt suggests that it extends to CROs, but this is open to debate. Whether third party supply of active ingredients are covered by the Bolar exemption is a question that was referred to the CJEU by the German Court of Appeal[293] but has since been withdrawn and so misses a prime opportunity for clarification.

20.113 These provisions will undoubtedly benefit access to the market of competitors (eg facilitating inclusion in trials as comparators) and new medical use medicines (first, second/subsequent). These changes mean that generics/biosimilars (irrespective of whether they additionally require trials to demonstrate equivalence) and copies of advanced therapies will be able to put authorization in place, ready for market entry as soon as market exclusivity rights expire. Mediating between researchers (wanting access to products/processes) and patent holders (preserving the value of patent rights where researchers are the end-market) is incredibly difficult. Clearly the balance has changed in widening the research exemption to accommodate changing economic priorities.[294] It is unfortunate that the new provisions do not clarify that research tools fall outside the exemption. The reality at present is that many pharmaceutical companies waste money obtaining legal advice to ensure they are within the research exemption, and those at the smaller end of the field simply ignore the potential for liability and hope not to get caught infringing. The new provisions in the UK will at least allay some of these fears.

20.114 The absolute and relative grounds for objections to medical innovation demonstrate that regulation is a mix between moral and economic considerations. The need to encourage economically beneficial medical developments is resulting in regulation which flexes legal

[287] UK Legislative Reform (Patents) Order 2014 implemented on 1 October 2014, <www.legislation.gov.uk/ukdsi/2014/9780111114537>.

[288] Impact Assessment No 142 (2014), <www.legislation.gov.uk/ukdsi/ 2014/9780111114537/impacts>.

[289] UK Legislative Reform (Patents) Order 2014 implemented on 1 October 2014, <www.legislation.gov.uk/ukdsi/2014/9780111114537>, including a new sub-section 6D into PA 1977, s 60.

[290] ibid, sub-section 6E.

[291] ibid.

[292] ibid, sub-section 6F.

[293] *Polypharma Pharmaceutical Works v Astellas Pharma* [2014], <https://docs. google.com/>.

[294] The European Federation of Pharmaceutical Industries and Association, *The Pharmaceutical Industry in Figures* report (2013), <www.efpia.eu/uploads/Figures_Key_Data_2013.pdf>.

parameters to accommodate innovation with the best or most easily exploitable markets. This is clearly prioritized over the need to ensure that new technologies are achieved morally or in the interests of everyone. The changing nature of that innovation—transitioning from traditional to modern medicine—puts pressure on the relationships between industry, regulators, and the public. As such, patents are only one of the commercial tools utilized in the evolving dynamic of control and value, and this chapter has explored some of the strengths and weaknesses of that right in shepherding new technology to market. Clearly the need to incentivize innovation is intrinsically linked with the need to maximize access to that innovation and, in exploring that, a final consideration must be how access can be accommodated in an international context.

D. Access to Medicines: The International Dimension

The trilateral report of the WHO, WIPO, and WTO identified that: **20.115**

> [l]arge declines in mortality from principal communicable, maternal, perinatal and nutritional causes are projected for 2030 ... [an] ageing of populations in low- and middle-income countries (LMICs) will result in more deaths due to non-communicable diseases leading to a double burden of disease.... The focus on access to medicines—which in the past has been on communicable diseases such as HIV/AIDS and malaria—has broadened.[295]

Providing innovative health care for that double disease burden is the focus of a very dense tranche of policy and regulatory documents by international, regional, and national bodies, and so this section is confined to the role of compulsory licensing. It has already been suggested in paras. 20.105–20.106 that the impact of compulsory licensing schemes domestically in countries such as the UK has been marginal in the health sector. Nonetheless, internationally there is growing support for their use as a fair and reasonable restriction on the effects of patent monopoly control.

The Doha Declaration is designed to address some of the issues arising from the existence and exercise of IPRs as these relate to public health. The Declaration stresses the importance of interpreting and implementing the TRIPS Agreement in ways that both promote access to existing medicines and encourage the creation of new medicines.[296] The primary effects of the Declaration, and a separate Declaration on public health,[297] make it incumbent on the TRIPS Council to address the use of compulsory licenses by developing countries in the pharmaceutical realm, and to extend the deadline for least-developed countries to provide pharmaceutical patent protection under the TRIPS Agreement until 1 January 2033.[298] Doha reiterates the underlying principle of Article 8 of TRIPS that 'members may ... adopt **20.116**

[295] WHO, WIPO, and WTO, *Promoting Access to Medical Technologies and Innovation* (2013), Executive Summary.

[296] For an account of the history of Doha and its future direction, see WTO, *The Road to DOHA and Beyond* (2002).

[297] Declaration on the TRIPS Agreement and Public Health, November 2001.

[298] This, of course, does not deal with the problem of individual (western) countries finding other means to ensure that developing countries provide the sort of protection they would wish, for example, by forcing the issue of bilateral treaties, linked perhaps to aid or other trade incentives, in return for 'adequate' patent protection.

measures *necessary* to protect public health and nutrition'.[299] Thus, para 4 of the Declaration on the TRIPS Agreement and Public Health provides that:

> We agree that the TRIPS Agreement does not and should not prevent members from taking measures to protect public health. Accordingly, while reiterating our commitment to the TRIPS Agreement, we affirm that the Agreement can and should be interpreted and implemented in a manner supportive of WTO members' right to protect public health and, in particular, to promote access to medicines for all.

Such measures include restricting patentability or imposing conditions on the use of a patent, for example, by permitting compulsory licenses to be granted. However, attempts to rely on these provisions[300] have met with vigorous opposition from pharmaceutical companies in some states, and most notably in the US. This in turn led to a further round of negotiations between members of the WTO as to the precise meaning of Article 8 of TRIPS and para 4 of Doha. When, for example, are measures *necessary* to protect public health? Who should decide this? And, how far can a state go to *promote* access to medicines for all?

20.117 The problem is particularly acute for developing and least developed countries, as is recognized by para 6 of the Declaration on Public Health:

> We recognize that WTO members with insufficient or no manufacturing capacities in the pharmaceutical sector could face difficulties in making effective use of compulsory licensing under the TRIPS Agreement.

The stumbling block in this regard has been Article 31(f) of the TRIPS Agreement which provides that production under compulsory license must be predominantly for the domestic market. How, then, can drugs be produced in developing countries—even with the exemption of compulsory license protection—if those countries do not possess the infrastructure to manufacture such drugs? Moreover, how can other states assist if their own generics production should be limited to their own market?

20.118 The TRIPS Council was given the difficult task of finding an equitable solution to this problem before the end of 2002. This did not happen. Negotiations reached stalemate when the US emerged as the sole country to reject an EU proposal to amend TRIPS so as to allow members to grant compulsory licenses for the export of medicines to countries that do not have any substantial manufacturing capacity of their own.[301] The US objected to the fact that developing countries could declare for themselves when measures were necessary, and sought to limit the regime only to medicines for the treatment of HIV/AIDS, malaria, and tuberculosis. A further suggestion from the European Union that an extended list of twenty-two diseases should be introduced, subject to review and extension on the advice of the WHO, was also rejected. The debacle demonstrated only too well the power of disparate political agendas which influence and shape intellectual property law and policy at all levels. It highlighted too

[299] Author's emphasis added.

[300] eg, the South African Medicines and Related Substances Control Amendment Act 1997 sought to improve access to medicines, and in particular treatments for HIV/AIDS, by authorizing parallel imports of drugs from other countries where they are available more cheaply and by restricting the rights exercisable under a patent in respect of designated medicines. In Brazil Art 68 of the Industrial Property Law, Law No 9.279 of 14 May 1996 introduced an obligation on drug patentees to produce the patented drug in the country or face a compulsory licensing scheme, except where production was economically 'unfeasible'. This was challenged by the US as an abuse of TRIPS, the resolution being agreed negotiations between the countries should Brazil seek to invoke the licensing scheme against a US company.

[301] Currently, the TRIPS Agreement 1994, Art 31(f) restricts the legitimate use of compulsory licences to the supply of a domestic market.

the serious incongruities that arise in the search for a fair balance of the interests at stake: economic and moral agendas are notoriously difficult to accommodate together.

This having been said, a compromise was eventually reached on 30 August 2003. This took the form of enabling countries to waive their obligations under Article 31(f) of TRIPS and to allow countries producing generics under compulsory license to export to eligible importing countries. This is subject to the caveat that it is done in good faith and in the name of public health and public research use. Notably, there is no longer a need to show an emergency nor is there a list of qualifying diseases, although para 6 is exemplified in very restricted instances of being triggered. In accordance with sub-section 5 of Paragraph 6, twenty-three countries immediately declared that they would not allow importation under the waiver. In doing so, these countries limit the potential for medicines manufactured under the waiver to be sold through 'black markets' attracted by the potential for profiteering and collaterally preventing those medicines from meeting the medical need they are created to address.[302] The measure has been hailed as an equitable solution to the global problem of access to medicines, but this is a narrow exception in an increasingly widening gap between the West and the rest. While Western companies continue to tighten their grip over their domestic markets, new markets are simultaneously opening up to them, but with only limited means to influence or control the prices of their products. **20.119**

An Oxfam report claims that little changed in the first five years after the adoption of the Doha Declaration.[303] This is partly because the provisions and protections of TRIPS can be circumvented in bilateral or regional agreements between countries between whom there is an imbalance of bargaining power and weaker states agree to so-called TRIPS-plus obligations—tying them further into intellectual property protection—in return for economic or trade benefits. This kind of evidence suggests that, in the absence of measures to ensure that generic production takes place, developing countries will have precious little option but to trade on terms driven by the intellectual property owners and thereby accentuating the power imbalance endemic in this area of law. **20.120**

Some of the urgency to accommodate the needs of developing and least developed countries may have been overshadowed by the recognition that a double disease burden may deter the implementation of the TRIPS Agreement still further, or result in a floodgate of low- and middle-income countries taking advantage of the Doha loophole. Although it is perhaps more likely that the *Nagoya Protocol on Access to Genetic Resources and the Fair and Equitable Sharing of Benefits Arising from their Utilization (ABS) to the Convention on Biological Diversity* 2010 (*Nagoya Protocol*), implemented in 2014, is perceived as being a more valuable tool. In mediating the exchange of genetic resources in fair exchanges (ie for money, commercial advantages over competitor countries, or domestic capacity building through technology transfer) the Nagoya Protocol is destined to secure the interests of countries who fear TRIPS compliance. Such countries are perhaps rightly concerned, given that TRIPs compliance spells the end of access to cheap generics which are still in patent elsewhere in the world and the risk of domestic markets being flooded with overly expensive branded and patented products. Perhaps more pressingly, compliance risks suppressing the development of their own medical industries, while imposing a financial burden from **20.121**

[302] These include the US, Canada, Australia, Japan, and Europe (for the latter see: Regulation 816/2006/EC on compulsory licensing of patents relating to the manufacture of pharmaceutical products for export to countries with public health problems (2006) OJ L157/1).

[303] Oxfam International, *Patents v Patients: Five Years After the Doha Declaration* (2006): <http://www.oxfam.org.uk/resources/policy/health/downloads/bp95_patents.pdf>.

having to enforce patent rights domestically. For developed countries, the Nagoya Protocol offers an end to the stalemate over TRIPs compliance, but brings with it the requirement to teach other countries—often with more resources and cheaper manpower—how to cater to health markets. Only time will tell if the dissemination of capacity, which creates more competitors globally, will result in a fairer world in which to cultivate medical innovation.

E. Conclusion

20.122 Managing health innovation effectively requires an appreciation of a complex mix of factors, only some of which have been briefly touched upon in this chapter focusing upon patent rights. Fundamentally, administering patent rights so that they incentivize the most socially valuable innovations in health care is a goal not easily achieved. Patents must be balanced against equally pressing needs of researchers, health care providers, participants, patients, and generic producers; as well as ensuring the maintenance of a healthy, competitive market. What mechanisms can be utilized in achieving this balance change radically relative to whether a domestic, European or global perspective is adopted.

20.123 Within Europe, patent protection is being expanded to include combinations of known products, selection inventions, and new uses of known medicinal products in an effort to get the most social value from existing technological innovation. This potential benefit comes with inherent risks both in protecting innovation that is merely keeping competitors out of markets for an unwarranted extension of exclusivity, and in fragmenting the right granted to the point at which it is of no commercial value to the pharmaceutical industry. The new generation of personalized medicines only promises to exacerbate this latter risk, by prompting regulators to hinge novelty on increasingly marginal differences. Conversely, no real effort is being made to ensure that the existing patent legislation reflects the increasingly diverse nature of technology, to extend protection to devices on a par with those available for substances in instances where the device is expended during use for example.

20.124 Patent regulation similarly struggles to mediate the commercial interest in exclusivity with the need to respect competing interests. In particular, exclusionary provisions are increasingly being eroded and redevised to prioritize commerciality over the need to protect the public interest by: not encroaching upon the ability of health care professionals to choose the best treatment options for the patient; neglecting to take account of the resourcefulness of industry in circumventing exclusions; undermining the relevance of morality provisions within patent legislation; and failing to recognize the contributions of others in the innovation process. The next generation of medical innovation is necessarily the result of a collaborative effort, but regulation recognizes only the commercial investment and not the social value of contributions.

20.125 It is a symptom of this focus on financial investment that prompts patent challenges to coalesce around the need to ensure that the patent does not become the source of impeding future development. This includes an impetus to litigate where strong monopoly rights are granted, particularly where the trading strategies of right holders are unduly restrictive. Domestically, compulsory licensing and research exemptions have proven inadequate in supporting those struggling to innovate around existing rights, although the expansion of the research exemption in the UK is a step in the right direction. Patent regulation is only one part of the regulatory framework that shepherds innovation to market, yet there is a real absence of coordination between regulators, discussed in this chapter in terms of linking patents with potential market impact.

From an international perspective there is a risk that political posturing will derail the opportunity to bring real change to countries suffering severe public health problems from communicable and, increasingly, also from non-communicable diseases. The opportunity to open up global markets to medicines must be negotiated in increments, in the context of benefits being shared and domestic capacity being nurtured. For Europe this may mean that market opportunities are increasingly being eroded by a greater number of emerging competitor countries, but this only enhances the need to innovate effectively in order to continually create new technology and retain market lead. **20.126**

PART VII

21

ENDING LIFE

Jonathan Herring

A. Introduction

The debates over end of life issues are among the fiercest that rage in medical law. The arguments often collapse into two diametrically opposed camps: those who believe in the principle of the sanctity of life and argue that it is never permissible to kill an innocent person, even if they strongly desire to die; and those who emphasize the principle of autonomy and believe that people should be allowed to choose for themselves when and how they will die.[1] The issues are, in fact, far more complicated than that summary may suggest and the amount of material written on the law and ethics on end of life decisions is indeed voluminous.[2] This reflects not only the complexity, but also the importance of the issues at stake. **21.01**

[1] M Charlesworth, *Bioethics in a Liberal Society* (Cambridge University Press 1993) ch 1.

[2] For just a small selection of the more recent literature see: K Yuill, *Assisted Suicide: The Liberal Humanist Case against Legalisation* (Palgrave 2014); E Wicks, *The Right to Life and Conflicting Interests* (Oxford University Press 2010); E Jackson and J Keown, *Debating Euthanasia* (Hart 2012); S Smith, *End-of-Life Decisions in Medical Care* (Cambridge University Press 2012); C Peterson, *Assisted Suicide and Euthanasia* (Ashgate 2008); D Jeffrey, *Against Physician Assisted Suicide: A Palliative Care Perspective* (Radcliffe Publishing 2008); M Warnock and E MacDonald, *Easeful Death: Is There a Case for Assisted Dying?* (Oxford University Press 2008); R Young, *Medically Assisted Death* (Cambridge University Press 2007); P Lewis, *Assisted Dying and Legal Change* (Oxford University Press 2007); S Woods, *Death's Dominion—Ethics at the End of Life* (Open University Press, 2007); R Huxtable, *Euthanasia, Ethics and the Law: From Conflict to Compromise* (Routledge-Cavendish 2007); S McLean, *Assisted Dying: Reflections on the Need for Law Reform* (Routledge-Cavendish 2007); G Williams, *Intention and Causation in Medical Non-Killing: The Impact of Criminal Law Concepts on Euthanasia and Assisted Suicide* (Routledge-Cavendish 2006); N Gorsuch, (2006) *The Future of Assisted Suicide and Euthanasia* (Princeton University Press 2006); N Biggar, *Aiming to Kill: The Ethics of Suicide and Euthanasia* (Pilgrim Press 2004); S Ost, *An Analytical Study of the Legal, Moral, and Ethical Aspects of the Living Phenomenon of Euthanasia* (Oxford University Press 2004); J Keown, *Euthanasia, Ethics and Public Policy* (Cambridge University Press 2002); M Sommerville, *Death Talk* (McGill Queen's University Press 2001); H Biggs, *Euthanasia* (Hart 2001); R Cohen-Almagor, *The Right To Die With Dignity* (Rutgers University Press 2001); L van Zyl, *Death and Compassion* (Ashgate 2001); M Otlowski, *Voluntary Euthanasia and the Common Law* (Oxford University Press 1997); R Dworkin, *Life's Dominion* (Harper Collins 1993).

21.02 Most deaths occur within a medical setting. Every day medical professionals make death-related decisions: whether that be to withdraw life-sustaining treatment; not to intervene with life-saving treatment; or even to provide medication that it is known will speed a person's death. Indeed in one survey of GPs it was found that 63 per cent of deaths in England involved an 'end of life decision' by a medical practitioner. Of these, 32.8 per cent involved a medical professional intervening to alleviate pain or undesirable symptoms, with potentially life-shortening effect and 30.3 per cent were cases where potentially life-saving treatment was not given;[3] 0.16 per cent involved euthanasia with the request of the patient and 0.33 per cent euthanasia without the patient's consent. It has been suggested that about 18,000 patients in Britain are medically assisted to die.[4] While care must be taken when using such statistics[5] what they reveal is the extent of 'end of life' decisions-making engaged in by health professionals. This makes the legal regulation of the area all the more important.

21.03 This chapter will focus on end of life decision-making in relation to patients who have capacity. Issues surrounding the end of life decisions concerning those who lack capacity are considered in Chapter 10 and those concerning refusal of life-saving treatment are considered in Chapter 8. This chapter will start with a summary of the legal regulation of the end of life for those who have capacity. It will then turn to the ethical and legal disputes concerning the current law. Many lawyers and ethicists are unhappy with the current state of the law, which is uncertain in many places and commonly seen to lack a sound ethical foundation.[6] A popular view is that the law is in a state of flux and we may be experiencing the start of a liberalization of the law in this area.

B. Terminology

21.04 Before setting out the law on ending life, it will be useful to highlight two fundamental distinctions that are drawn by the law.[7] These will be explored in more detail later in the chapter. First, a basic distinction is drawn between suicide, assisted suicide, and euthanasia. [8] Suicide is the killing of a person by themselves. Assisted suicide involves a person helping another to commit suicide. Euthanasia involves a person killing another person. There is therefore a fundamental distinction between a case where a doctor gives a patient a lethal dose of medication that the patient administers to themselves, which would be assisted suicide; and a case where the doctors administers a lethal dose of medication, which would be regarded as euthanasia. Both euthanasia and assisted suicide are illegal in most circumstances. The distinction was supported by Lord Neuberger in ethical terms in *R (on the application of Nicklinson) v Ministry of Justice*[9] where he stated:

> To my mind, the difference between administering the fatal drug to a person and setting up a machine so that the person can administer the drug to himself is not merely a legal

[3] C Seale, 'National Survey of End-of-life Decisions Made by UK Medical Practitioners' (2006) 20 Palliative Medicine 3.

[4] D Price, 'What Shape to Euthanasia after Bland?' (2009) 125 Law Quarterly Review 125, 145.

[5] It may be, for example, that the percentages of euthanasia were under-reported for fear of criminal investigation.

[6] Notably while strongly disagreeing on many issues in their book summarising competing sides of the debate over euthanasia (E Jackson, and J Keown, *Debating Euthanasia* (Hart 2012)) neither Jackson nor Keown find agreement in accepting that the current law unsupportable.

[7] A useful overview of the ethical and legal issues can be found in D Price, 'What shape to euthanasia after Bland?' (2009) 125 Law Quarterly Review 125.

[8] Euthanasia comes from Greek 'eu' (good) and thanatos (death).

[9] [2014] UKSC 38 at [94].

distinction. Founded as it is on personal autonomy, I consider that the distinction also sounds in morality. . .

A second basic distinction is between cases where the euthanasia or assisted suicide is voluntary, non-voluntary or involuntary. A case of voluntary death would be where the patient has specifically requested it, with full capacity to do so; a non-voluntary death would be where the patient has not expressed a view and lacks capacity to do so; an involuntary death would be where the patient has specifically stated that they do not want to die. There are very few, if any, lawyers or ethicists who would think that involuntary euthanasia or assisted suicide would ever be acceptable. However, as discussed in Chapter 10, the law has recognized that it can be legitimate to withdraw or withhold treatment from a patient lacking capacity, leading to their death. **21.05**

C. Legal Regulation of Ending Life

The starting point of a consideration of the legal regulation of the end of life is the criminal law.[10] A health care professional who deliberately kills a patient can be convicted of murder.[11] But the extent to which the normal criminal law principles apply to medical professionals is far from clear.[12] Glenys Williams has made a powerful argument that criminal law concepts are sufficiently vague to enable the courts to reach what the judge regards as 'the right decision'.[13] In other words, what determines whether a medical professional is guilty of murder is not, so much, the substantive criminal law itself, as the interpretation that is given to the open-ended legal concepts by the judge and jury. She argues that the normal criminal law principles are not appropriate to deal with the issues medical professionals face when making end of life decisions. Indeed, several commentators have noted the reluctance of the courts to convict medical professionals for murder, except in the most extreme cases.[14] It is not surprising that one doctor working in the field has complained that the law is 'confusing and conflicting'.[15] **21.06**

1. Murder

A defendant is guilty of murder if he or she causes the death of a victim with an intention to cause death or grievous bodily harm.[16] Where the defendant kills a patient, but has no intention to kill or cause grievous bodily harm, he or she may nevertheless be guilty of manslaughter. Criminal law recognizes no defence of 'euthanasia' or 'mercy killing'. Lord Goff in *Airedale NHNS Trust v Bland*[17] made that clear: **21.07**

> it is not lawful for a doctor to administer a drug to his patient to bring about his death, even if that course is prompted by the humanitarian desire to end his suffering, however great that suffering may be.

---

[10] See also General Medical Council, Treatment and Care Towards the End of Life (GMC 2010).

[11] Crown Prosecution Service, *Nurse found Guilty of Killing his Patients* (CPS 2008).

[12] M Otlowski, *Euthanasia and the Common Law* (Oxford University Press 1997) 182.

[13] G Williams, *Intention and Causation in Medical Non-Killing: The Impact of Criminal Law Concepts on Euthanasia and Assisted Suicide* (Routledge-Cavendish 2006) 2.

[14] ibid.

[15] M Wilks, 'Medical Treatment at the End of Life—A British Doctor's Perspective' in C Erin and S Ost, *The Criminal Justice System and Health Care* (Oxford University Press 2007) 166.

[16] For a detailed discussion of the law of murder see J Herring, *Criminal Law* (6th edn, Oxford University Press 2015) ch 5.

[17] [1993] AC 789, 865 (HL).

The elements of the offence as they might apply in a euthanasia type context will be discussed further.

(i) Causation: Acts

21.08 To be guilty of murder, it must be shown that the defendant caused the death of the victim. This requires proof that the defendant's actions were an operating and substantial cause of death.[18] In some cases in the medical context this will be unproblematic. There would be no difficulty in showing that a doctor who administered an inappropriate amount of a lethal drug killing a healthy patient caused the death. Less straightforward are cases where the patient is already seriously ill and it is shown that the medical treatment may somewhat have hastened the death of the patient.[19] In such cases it need only be shown that the defendant's act was *a* cause of death; it does not need to be the only cause.[20] The fact, therefore, that the maladministration of the medicine led to death was in part because the victim was very ill would not provide a defence, if it could be shown that the defendant's act was a more than a minimal contribution to the death. However, there would come a point where the contribution to the death was so minimal that the defendant's actions are not regarded as a cause. Some commentators have suggested that the law is more willing to accept this in the case of medical treatment than in other cases.[21] However, in *R v Adams*[22] Devlin J, in a trial of a doctor charged with murder, stated: 'If the acts done are intended to kill and do, in fact kill, it does not matter if a life is cut short by weeks or months, it is just as much murder as if it were cut short by years.' That said, it is generally thought that if the medical treatment has only led to a shortening of life of a seriously ill patient of a matter of minutes, then causation will not be established.[23]

(ii) Causation: Omissions

21.09 Generally in the criminal law a person is not liable for an omission. If they come across a sick person, they are entitled to pass on by and not incur criminal liability. This is, however, subject to an important exception, where the there is a duty of care between the defendant and victim.[24] There would be a duty of care owed between a health care professional and a patient they were treating. Health care professionals are, therefore, unusually open to prosecutions for failing to treat patients. However, this potential liability is limited. It will only arise where the failure to treat was a breach of their duty.

21.10 A health care professional could not, therefore, be liable for failing to offer treatment to a competent patient who was refusing to accept any treatment. It would simply be unlawful for them to do so and so the failure to treat would not breach their duty.[25] A slight question mark might hang over this absolute prohibition. In *An NHS Foundation Trust Hospital v P*[26] a seventeen and a half year old took an overdose of paracetamol but refused all treatment to counter its effects, saying she wanted to die. Baker J accepted that the patient had a right under Article 8 to make decisions for herself, but:

---

[18] *R v Cheshire* [1991] 3 All ER 670 (CA).

[19] *R v Cox* (1992) 12 BMLR 38.

[20] *R v Mellor* [1996] 2 Cr App R 245 (CA).

[21] G Williams, *Intention and Causation in Medical Non-Killing: The Impact of Criminal Law Concepts on Euthanasia and Assisted Suicide* (Routledge-Cavendish 2006).

[22] Unreported, but discussed in H Palmer, 'Dr Adams' Trial for Murder' (1957) *Criminal Law Review* 365.

[23] H Palmer, n 23.

[24] For a detailed discussion of the law see J Herring, *Criminal Law* (Oxford University Press 2014) ch 2.

[25] *Ms B v An NHS Trust* [2002] EWHC 429.

[26] [2014] EWHC 1650 (Fam).

> they are outweighed by her rights under Article 2—everyone's right to life shall be protected by law. The court is under a positive or operational duty arising from Article 2 to take preventative measures to protect an individual whose life is at risk.

It was presumably crucial to the reasoning in the case that patient was under the age of 18, although, in the rapidly prepared judgment, that was not made clear. It may be that in other cases of borderline capacity a patient's refusal can be overridden, relying on Article 2.[27]

Similarly, a doctor is not required to give treatment which will not benefit a patient. In the end of life context it might even be determined that receiving life-prolonging or sustaining treatment will not benefit the patient. As Lord Browne-Wilkinson held in *Airedale NHS Trust v Bland*: **21.11**

> [I]f there comes a stage where the responsible doctor comes to the reasonable conclusion (which accords with the views of a responsible body of medical opinion) that further continuance of an intrusive life support system is not in the best interests of the patient, he can no longer lawfully continue that life support system: to do so would constitute the crime of battery and the tort of trespass to the person.[28]

Although those *dicta* were considering the specific case of those receiving life support while suffering from persistent vegetative state, presumably they can be applied in a broader context. There will be other cases at the end of life where a responsible body of medical opinion would determine that it would not be in the interests of a patient to receive the treatment.[29] In such a case the failure to provide treatment would not amount to a breach of duty and so criminal liability would not ensure. That would be so even if the patient were requesting the life-saving treatment.[30]

Even where it is established that the doctor breached the duty of care through not offering treatment the prosecution may face a difficulty in establishing that the breach caused the death. It would be necessary to show that had the correct treatment been given the patient would have lived. In many critical cases it may be hard to prove what would have happened had treatment been provided. **21.12**

As we have just seen, the law draws a fundamental distinction between acts and omissions.[31] One survey of UK medical practitioners suggests that 75 per cent accept a moral distinction between active and passive euthanasia as of important moral significance.[32] This distinction is one which has attracted considerable ethical debate. As we have seen in law it is rarely lawful to do an act which causes the death of the victim. However, not providing treatment for a patient is lawful, indeed required, when the patient with clear capacity has refused to consent to the treatment or the treatment is not beneficial. The distinction can be supported in terms of causation. An omission, it is said, cannot cause death, because death is caused by the underlying medical condition. By contrast an actor can take over authorship and full responsibility for what happens.[33] **21.13**

---

[27] G Richardson, 'Mental capacity in the shadow of suicide' (2013) 9 International Journal of Law in Context 87.

[28] [1993] 1 All ER 821, 882 (HL).

[29] See further Chapter 10.

[30] *R (on the application of Burke) v General Medical Council* [2005] EWCA Civ 1003.

[31] E Garrard and S Wilkinson, 'Passive Euthanasia' (2005) 29 Journal of Medical Ethics 297; J Coggon, 'On Acts, Omissions and Responsibility' (2008) 34 Journal of Medical Ethics 576.

[32] J Coulson, 'Till Death Us Do Part' (1996) BMA News Review 23.

[33] M Stauch, 'Causal Authorship and the Equality Principle: A Defence of the Acts/Omissions Distinction in Euthanasia' (2000) 26 Journal of Medical Ethics 237.

21.14 Despite the popularity of the distinction it has proved difficult to justify and explain at a theoretical level. It is far less popular among philosophers, than among lawyers.[34] Two leading medical ethicists, Beauchamp and Childress, state: 'the distinction between killing and letting die suffers from vagueness and moral confusion. The language of killing is so thoroughly confusing—causally, legally, and morally—that it can provide little if any help in discussion of assistance in dying.'[35] Lord Mustill likewise was not convinced by the distinction and feared that because of the weight attached to it the law is 'morally and intellectually misshapen'.[36] Lord Goff in *Bland* admitted that the distinction between acts and omissions can produce some apparently arbitrary results:

> it can be asked why, if the doctor, by discontinuing treatment, is entitled in consequence to let his patient die, it should not be lawful to put him out of his misery straight away, in a more human manner, by a lethal injection, rather than let him linger on in pain until he dies. But the law does not feel able to authorise euthanasia, even in circumstances such as these, for, once euthanasia is recognised as lawful in these circumstances, it is difficult to see any logical basis for excluding it in others.[37]

Most recently, Lord Neuberger in *R (on the application of Nicklinson) v Ministry of Justice*[38] seemed similarly troubled by the distinction and referred to 'a certain and understandable discomfort with the notion that switching a machine off actually is an omission.'

21.15 Even some opponents of euthanasia are critical of the distinction between acts and omissions. To John Keown[39] the focus on acts and omissions avoids the key question: did the doctor intend to produce death? He argues that if a doctor intends to kill this is wrong. Whether the doctor intended to produce death by an act or an omission is just a detail about the method of killing which should not carry moral weight.

21.16 A further difficulty with the distinction is that it can be difficult to know where to draw it. Is switching off a life support machine an act or an omission? Glanville Williams makes the point in this way:[40]

> The question then arises whether stopping a respirator is an act of killing or a decision to let nature take its course? Common sense suggests it is the latter. Suppose that the respirator worked only as long as the doctor turned a handle. If he stopped turning, he would be regarded as merely commencing to omit to save the patient's life. Suppose, alternatively, that the respirator worked electrically but was made to shut itself off it would be an omission. It can make no moral difference that the respirator is constructed to run continuously and has to be stopped. Stopping the respirator is not a positive act of killing the patient, but a decision not to strive any longer to save him.

21.17 Some commentators argue that the difficulties in making the distinction between an act and omission reveals that the moral principles governing a doctor's decision on how to treat or not treat a patient should not focus on the distinction between withholding or withdrawing treatment, but rather what duties a physician owes her or his patient. Emily Jackson argues:

---

[34] For arguments supporting the distinction between killing and letting die see M Stauch, 'Causal Authorship and the Equality Principle: A Defence of the Acts/Omissions Distinction in Euthanasia' (2000) 26 Journal of Medical Ethics 237; A Mcgee, 'Does Withdrawing Life-Sustaining Treatment Cause Death or Allow the Patient to Die?' (2014) Medical Law Review 26.

[35] T Beauchamp and J Childress, *Principles of Biomedical Ethics* (Oxford University Press 2003) 146.

[36] *Airedale NHS Trust v Bland* [1993] AC 789, 885 (HL).

[37] ibid, 905.

[38] [2014] UKSC 38 at [22].

[39] J Keown, *Euthanasia, Ethics and Public Policy* (Cambridge University Press 2002) 14.

[40] G Williams, *The Sanctity of Life and the Criminal Law* (Faber and Faber 1957) 237.

> Imagine a doctor has two competent adult patients connected to the same artificial ventilator. Patient A wants to continue living, and patient B wants to die. The doctor switches off the machine and both patients die. In relation to Patient A, because the doctor is under a duty to treat her, switching off the machine is characterized as an action, and the doctor might be guilty of murder. But in relation to patient B, switching off the machine is an omission . . .. the morally relevant fact is not whether what the doctor does is an omission or an action, but rather whether the background against which the decision has been taken justifies the doctor's conclusion that life, in these circumstances, should not be artificially prolonged.[41]

She goes on to argue that once we accept that sometimes it is better for a person to be allowed to die than for them to be offered treatment we are accepting that in some cases it would be better for a person to die. If we are willing to make that assessment in relation to those patients where the issue is withdrawal of life-sustaining treatment, the same principle should apply to cases where a patient needs a positive act to achieve death.[42] That argument takes us to the debate over the validity of the sanctity of life principle, which will be discussed shortly.

(iii) Mens rea: Intention

To be guilty of murder it must be shown that the defendant intended to cause death or grievous bodily harm. There will be no difficulty in cases where it was the purpose of the defendant's actions to cause the death of the victim. Harder are cases of so-called 'oblique intention' where the defendant foresees that death will result from his or her action, but acts for some other purpose.[43] In the medical context it is rare that a medical professional will be giving treatment wanting to kill the patient. More common will be the scenario where the professional's primary purpose was to give treatment to lessen pain, but they were aware that a side consequence of doing so was that the medication would hasten death. **21.18**

Generally the law on oblique intention in criminal law is governed by the decision of the House of Lords in *R v Woollin*.[44] This states that a jury are only entitled to find a defendant intended death or grievous bodily harm if that was a virtually certain consequence of the defendant's actions and the defendant realized this.[45] It is important to appreciate that this leaves the jury with a discretion to determine whether or not to find the necessary intention. It is perfectly open to the jury to conclude that although death or grievous bodily harm was the virtually certain consequence of the defendant's actions they will not find intention.[46] To the consternation of some academics the courts have refused to offer guidance to juries on how to decide whether or not to find intent.[47] **21.19**

It is unclear whether the *Woollin* direction is to be used in cases of medical professionals providing lethal doses of pain-relieving medication. If it does it would mean that a doctor who provided a pain-relieving drug, foreseeing that it would be bound to shorten life, but **21.20**

[41] E Jackson, 'Whose Death is it Anyway? Euthanasia and the Medical Profession' (2005) 57 Current Legal Problems 415.

[42] E Jackson, 'Secularism, Sanctity and the Wrongness of Killing' (2008) 3 Biosocieties 125, 126.

[43] Notably in the Mental Capacity Act 2005, s 4(5) a person, in deciding whether to provide life-sustaining treatment to someone who lacks capacity, 'must not, in considering whether the treatment is in the best interests of the person concerned, be motivated by a desire to bring about his death'.

[44] [1991] 1 AC 82 (HL).

[45] Where it is the defendant's purpose to cause death there is no reason to give the 'virtual certainty direction' because purpose will amount to intention automatically.

[46] *R v Matthews and Allayne* [2003] Cr App R 30 (CA).

[47] The judge should not seek to tell the jury how to exercise their discretion: *R v Wright* [2000] *Crim LR* 928 (CA).

that not being their purpose, would be at the mercy of the jury, who would, under the *Woollin* direction, need to conclude whether or not this was a case where they would choose to find intention. However, it seems from the reported cases of doctors charged with murder or attempted murder following the administration of pain relieving drugs, that judges avoid giving the direction on oblique intention that is normally given in criminal law. Instead juries are told that if the doctor did not act for the purpose of causing death, then he or she cannot be guilty of murder.[48] The trials of Doctors Carr;[49] Adams,[50] and Moor,[51] all of whom had provided patients with lethal amounts of drugs, resulted in acquittals. It, is, however difficult to determine whether these are because of a difference in the way trial judges presented the law to juries, or the attitudes of juries themselves, or perhaps both.

21.21 Indeed it seems that the cases where doctors or other medical professionals have been convicted of murder fall into two primary categories. First, those where an individual appears to have been acting for the purpose of killing. A good example is *R v Cox*[52] where a doctor injected a patient with a lethal amount of potassium chloride. He was convicted of attempted murder. The expert evidence was that the amount of the drug given was sufficient to kill the patient and that it had no analgesic value. Further, the victim was found not to be terminally ill. However much one may have been willing to be flexible with the notion of intention it was difficult to get away from the conclusion that Dr Cox intended to kill. There was no other reason for acting in the way he did. Notably in this case he was given a suspended sentence. To be convicted of attempted murder, but not to be given a sentence of immediate custody is unusual, and reflects the facts that these cases are not seen by the judiciary in the same light as 'normal' murders.

21.22 It may be that the judges in these cases are simply failing to give the correct direction that the criminal law requires. However, some commentators have suggested that the general law on intention does not apply to cases involving health care professionals and that where a health care professional is following an accepted body of medical practice it cannot be said that they have committed a crime.[53] Lord Goff's statements in *Airedale NHS Trust v Bland*[54] might suggest this:

> [It is] the established rule that a doctor may, when caring for a patient who is, for example, dying of cancer, lawfully administer painkilling drugs despite the fact that he knows that an incidental effect of that application will be to abbreviate the patient's life. Such a decision may properly be made as part of the care of the living patient, in his best interests; and, on this basis, the treatment will be lawful.

To similar effect, Lord Neuberger in *R (on the application of Nicklinson) v Ministry of Justice*[55] stated 'a doctor commits no offence when treating a patient in a way which hastens death, if the purpose of the treatment is to relieve pain and suffering (the so-called "double effect")'.

21.23 Similar issues arise when the courts are dealing with cases where a relative has administered a lethal medication to a terminally ill patient. There have been cases where, in fact, the motivation of the relative has been to obtain an inheritance. In such a case the juries will

[48] See the discussion in R Huxtable, *Euthanasia, Ethics and the Law: From Conflict to Compromise* (Routledge Cavendish 2007) ch 2.

[49] Unreported, Sunday Times, 30 November 1986.

[50] The case is recorded in H Palmer, 'Dr Adams' Trial for Murder' (1957) Criminal Law Review 365.

[51] Discussed in C Dyer, 'British GP Cleared of Murder Charge' (1999) 318 British Medical Journal 1306.

[52] (1992) 12 BMLR 38.

[53] This was the view of the Attorney-General in evidence to House of Commons Select Committee, *On the Assisted Dying for the Terminally Ill Bill* (*Hansard*, 2005), para 13.

[54] [1993] 1 All ER 821 (HL).

[55] [2014] UKSC 38 at [18].

not hesitate to convict of murder.[56] Where, however, there is a case of 'mercy killing', the court may be more reluctant to find an intention to kill, or to use a defence to a charge of murder.[57] These will be discussed later.

The distinction the law draws between intention and foresight is controversial. Some commentators believe that if a person does an act aware it will cause death they must be held to account for it, whether it happened to be their purpose for acting or not.[58] Most commentators who make this point are in fact supporters of euthanasia. Their point is that given that nearly everyone agrees that giving pain-relieving medication is permissible, even if it shortens life, we should also accept that intentional shortening of life is permissible. The precise nature of the medical professional's state of mind should not matter. **21.24**

Many supporters of the current law support the doctrine of double effect.[59] There is no one approved definition of the doctrine, although all versions accept that in some circumstances a person who is doing an act with the purpose of producing result A, but foreseeing that result B will also result from their actions, will be held to intend result A, but not result B. John Keown's version is representative of many formulations. He refers to four principles that render it permissible to do an act which produces a bad consequence: **21.25**

(1) The act one is engaged in is not itself bad.
(2) The bad consequence is not a means to the good consequence.
(3) The bad consequence is foreseen but not intended.
(4) There is sufficiently serious reason for allowing the bad consequence to occur.[60]

It will be noted that this test is not simply one of assessing 'intention'. The fourth factor demonstrates that there is an element of moral assessment that takes place to determine whether the act is permitted. There is, therefore, a degree of ambiguity over whether the doctrine should be understood as a definition of intention, or rather, as seems more likely, a definition of the circumstances in which it is permissible to do an act which is very likely to lead to a bad consequence. Its application in the case of pain-relieving medication involves an assessment that the pain-relieving qualities of the medication are a good enough reason to permit the use of the medication, despite its likelihood to cause death.[61]

Those who support the distinction between foresight and intention argue that our moral assessment of an act will often hinge on it. Compare, for example, the friend who makes an unpleasant remark about your appearance intending to hurt you, from the friend who made the same remark, not intending to hurt you but wanting to tell the truth, but realizing you might be distressed. The first person is unlikely to remain a friend, while the second may well be forgiven for their insensitivity. **21.26**

Supporters of the distinction between intention and foresight argue that with intention the result is the reason for which a person acts and hence it shows that it was a key element in their moral evaluation. Whereas a foreseen result is not one which has motivated the actor and therefore they have less to account for. This argument is often supported by examples of **21.27**

---

[56] *R v Cumming* [2006] EWCA 3223.

[57] H Biggs, 'Criminalising Carers: Death Desires and Assisted Dying Outlaws' in B Brooks-Gordon, F Ebtehaj, J Herring, M Johnson, and M Richards, M (eds), *Death Rites and Rights* (Hart 2007).

[58] C Foster, J Herring, K Melham, and T Hope, 'The Double Effect Effect' (2011) 20 Cambridge Quarterly Healthcare Ethics 56.

[59] For a useful discussion see D Price, 'Euthanasia, Pain Relief and Double Effect' (1997) 17 Legal Studies 323.

[60] J Keown, *Euthanasia, Ethics and Public Policy* (Cambridge University Press 2002) 20.

[61] C Foster, J Herring, K Melham, and T Hope, 'The Double Effect Effect' (2011) 20 Cambridge Quarterly of Healthcare Ethics 56.

cases where we would say the actor foresaw the result but did not intend it: the binge drinker may foresee a hangover but does not intend to produce it; the law lecturer may foresee her students will be bored, but not intend that; the police officer breaking bad news to relatives of a traffic victim accident may foresee their distress, but does not intend it. Indeed, supporters of double effect, argue, to suggest that in these cases there is intention to produce these undesirable results is absurd.[62] These examples, they argue, show how important the difference between intention and foresight is to our moral intuitions.

21.28 There are, however, plenty of commentators who reject the distinction between intention and foresight. Baroness Warnock has described it as 'absurdly pedantic'.[63] John Harris[64] argues that it places too much weight on how one expresses the problem. If a doctor was to say 'My intention was to end the pain of the patient, by killing him. I realized that the medication would kill him, but that was not my motivation' is death intended or foreseen? While most supporters of the distinction would argue that there is a fundamental difference between a case where a doctor intended to end pain, by killing, and where a doctor intends to end pain but realizes death will result at the same time, to opponents the distinction involves playing with words.

21.29 Even if one accepts the distinction is of fundamental moral importance there is another question and that is whether it is one the law can rely on.[65] It is important to appreciate that the law cannot necessarily match precisely all the sophistication that a perfect ethical analysis may wish to rely on. The law must utilize tests that are capable of proof and are comprehensible to people who will be guided by them. Such concerns are less of an issue for those dealing with high ethics. So one could conclude that whatever the theoretical merit of the double effect doctrine it fails to provide sufficient guidance to those who must seek to comply with the law; and fails to provide sufficient clarity to courts who must decided whether there has been a breach the law. If a doctor, for example, administers a pain-relieving drug intending to kill a patient, how are we to know whether it was his or her intention to kill or not? Indeed, can a doctor be able to separate out their own intentions and foresight? As one doctor has written:

> Physicians are driven by a fundamental imperative to reduce pain and suffering. When faced with a patient who is suffering both physically and mentally, the primary effort will be to give whatever treatment is appropriate to achieve this aim, providing net benefit in terms of best interest. It is unrealistic to think that the doctor at all times keeps from his mind the thought that part of that benefit includes death. Obviously, whether the doctor acts on this thought will define whether he or she remains within accepted ethical and legal practice, but that these thoughts will arise must be simply a natural part of a doctor's professionalism. They are particularly difficult to deal with when the patient also articulates a wish to discuss assisted dying.[66]

While these are important points, one should recall that everyone agrees that a line must be drawn somewhere between which killings are permitted and which are not. Although there are difficulties with the place where the line is currently drawn, there may be ambiguity and difficulties of proof wherever it is drawn.

[62] J Finnis, 'Intention and Side-effects' in R Frey and C Morris (eds), ***Liability and Responsibility*** (Oxford University Press 1991).

[63] M Warnock, ***An Intelligent Person's Guide to Ethics*** (Duckbacks 2001) 39.

[64] J Harris, *The Value of Law* (Oxford University Press 1984) 44.

[65] C Foster, J Herring, K Melham, and T Hope, 'The Double Effect Effect' (2011) 20 Cambridge Quarterly of Healthcare Ethics 56.

[66] M Wilks, 'Medical Treatment at the End of Life—A British Doctor's Perspective' in C Erin and S Ost, *The Criminal Justice System and Health Care* (Oxford University Press 2007) 170.

(iv) Defences to murder

Criminal law provides a number of defences to a charge of murder. Most are not relevant in the context of medical law. Before going into the detail of defences which might apply, it is important to recognize there is no general defence of mercy killing.[67] Lord Neuberger in *R (on the application of Nicklinson) v Ministry of Justice*[68] explained: 21.30

> Mercy killing is a term which means killing another person for motives which appear, at least to the perpetrator, to be well-intentioned, namely for the benefit of that person, very often at that person's request. Nonetheless, mercy killing involves the perpetrator intentionally killing another person, and therefore, even where that person wished to die, or the killing was purely out of compassion and love, the current state of the law is that the killing will amount to murder or (if one or more of the mitigating circumstances are present) manslaughter.

In fact, it is rare for cases of 'mercy killing' to result in a murder conviction;[69] normally defences are available which reduce the charge to manslaughter, especially in the case of carers who kill their seriously ill relative or friend.

Before considering these defences, it is useful to have in mind the distinction, important to criminal lawyers, between a justification and an excuse.[70] In short, a justification involves an argument that the killing was morally right, or at least that it was morally permissible. On the other hand, an excuse finds that the killing was not morally permissible but that the actor does not deserve blame. This distinction is, perhaps most relevant in a case where a spouse, civil partner, or other family member kills a loved one after a long period of care. In such a case there are two kinds of defences the family member may seek to raise in response to such a charge. The first is that he or she was lawfully permitted to do the action. The second is that she was driven to despair by the circumstances and was not wholly responsible for her actions. This may lead to a defence based on, for example, diminished responsibility.[71] 21.31

(a) Diminished responsibility The defence of diminished responsibility is set out in s 2(1) Homicide Act 1957, as amended by the Coroners and Criminal Justice Act 2009: 21.32

> (1) A person ('D') who kills or is a party to the killing of another is not to be convicted of murder if D was suffering from an abnormality of mental functioning which—
> (a) arose from a recognised medical condition,
> (b) substantially impaired D's ability to do one or more of the things mentioned in subsection (1A), and
> (c) provides an explanation for D's acts and omissions in doing or being a party to the killing.
> (1A) Those things are—
> (a) to understand the nature of D's conduct;
> (b) to form a rational judgment;
> (c) to exercise self-control.
> (1B) For the purposes of subsection (1)(c), an abnormality of mental functioning provides an explanation for D's conduct if it causes, or is a significant contributory factor in causing, D to carry out that conduct.'

[67] J Horder, 'Mercy Killings—Some Reflections on Beecham's Case' (1988) Journal of Criminal Law 309.
[68] [2014] UKSC 38 at [17].
[69] Although see *R v Inglis* [2011] WLR 1110 and *R v Cocker* (1989) *Criminal Law Review* 740 (CA).
[70] J Herring, *Criminal Law* (6th edn, Oxford University Press 2014) ch 12.
[71] H Biggs, 'Criminalising Carers: Death Desires and Assisted Dying Outlaws' in B Brooks-Gordon, F Ebtehaj, J Herring, M Johnson, and M Richards, (eds), *Death Rites and Rights* (Hart 2007).

There have been cases where a person has been caring for a terminally ill relative and has suffered depression or other abnormality of the mind, as a result of the exhaustion and stress that twenty-four-hours-a-day care can produce.[72] The defence is only a partial defence and so even if it is successfully raised a defendant will be convicted of manslaughter, but then usually face only a minimal sentence.[73] In one notorious case[74] a 100-year-old man killed his dependent wife after she kept being moved between care homes. The Crown Court Judge, Mr Justice Leveson described the killing as an act of love and he was given a community rehabilitation order.

21.33 (b) Necessity In exceptional circumstances the defence of necessity may be available to a criminal charge. Generally speaking there is no defence in the criminal law that a defendant produced a greater good by killing the victim. For example, it would not be lawful for a doctor to kill one patient so that her organs could be transplanted into several other patients and thereby save their lives. However, it seems that in highly exceptional cases the defence of necessity, that the defendant acted in way which was the lesser of two evils, will succeed.

21.34 In *Re A (Conjoined Twins)*[75] the Court of Appeal were required to determine the fate of Jodie and Mary, who were conjoined twins. Jodie was the stronger of the two. Mary's heart and lungs did not function adequately and it was only because she shared a common artery with Jodie that she was alive. Their condition meant that, in effect, Jodie's heart was pumping blood for Mary as well as herself. The medical evidence indicated that Jodie's heart was under strain and that without a separation operation the twins would die within a few months. If an operation were performed the consequence would be that Mary would die, but Jodie could be expected to have a relatively normal life. In short the alternatives were to do the operation which would kill Mary; or not to intervene which would lead, in a few months time, to both Mary and Jodie dying. The medical team caring for the girls wanted to perform the operation, but the parents objected, primarily on religious grounds. The case was ultimately heard before the Court of Appeal, who declared that the operation would be lawful.

21.35 The Court of Appeal held that no criminal offence would be committed by performing the operation. It was accepted that the operation would cause the death of Mary. Even though her death was not part of the doctors' aim or purpose, Lord Justices Ward and Brooke held that because they realized that it was a virtually certain consequence of the procedure they could be taken to have intended it.[76] In reaching this conclusion they failed to analyse in detail the *Woollin* test (which they purported to apply). In particular they failed to emphasize that the *Woollin* test gives the jury the option not to find intention, even where the result is appreciated as a virtually certain consequence of their act. It may be that they thought that this was a case where it would be appropriate to find intention, but if so no explanation is provided for why they thought that.

---

[72] *R v Taylor* [1979] CLY 570, where a man who killed his autistic child was put on probation. For a further helpful discussion see H Biggs, 'Criminalising Carers: Death Desires and Assisted Dying Outlaws', in B Brooks-Gordon, F Ebtehaj, J Herring, M Johnson, and M Richards (eds), *Death Rites and Rights* (Hart 2007).

[73] *R v Jones*, The Guardian, 4 December 1979; a conviction for manslaughter in a case of mercy killing was punished with a conditional discharge.

[74] S Ost, 'Euthanasia and the Defence of Necessity', in C Erin and S Ost, *The Criminal Justice System and Health Care* (Oxford University Press 2007).

[75] [2001] Fam 147 (CA).

[76] Lord Justice Robert Walker held that there was no intention, relying on the doctrine of double effect (discussed at para 21.25).

All of the members of the Court of Appeal agreed that if the doctors did the operation they would have a defence to any potential murder charge. Lord Justice Robert Walker argued that the defence of private defence could apply. He regarded Mary to be, in effect, attacking or at least threatening Jodie in an unjustified way. The doctors could therefore perform the operation to protect Jodie from the threat. The majority of the Court of Appeal thought that as Mary and Jodie had been born the way they were it could not be said that Mary was posing an unjust threat or attacking Jodie. However, Lord Justices Ward and Brooke thought this was a case where the doctors could rely on the defence of necessity. There was some reluctance to state precisely when such a defence may be available. Indeed, probably the best interpretation of the case is that there will be rare circumstances where the defence of necessity will be available, but these will be determined on a case-by-case basis and require highly unusual facts. **21.36**

The decision in *Re A* has generated substantial academic debate.[77] The issues raised are complex. To some commentators the case is an unwelcome departure from the principle that necessity is not a defence to murder and that a person can never be killed simply in order to benefit others.[78] On such a view the courts should be criticized for placing greater value on Jodie's life than they did on Mary's.[79] Other commentators have criticized the decision for failing to place sufficient weight on the views of the parents, given the fact that strong moral arguments could be made both in favour of performing the operation and opposing it.[80] The decision has been seen to raise broader issues by other academics. Vanessa Munro suggests that the decision demonstrates in dramatic form how individualistic conceptions of rights can fail to capture sufficiently the interconnection between individuals.[81] While to Barbra Hewson the case shows how the cultural norm of individuality and restoring 'physical normality' dominated the decision.[82] **21.37**

It has been suggested by some commentators that the defence of necessity could be used in the euthanasia context.[83] Tony Hope uses a striking example to make the point: **21.38**

> A driver is trapped in a blazing lorry. There is no way in which he can be saved. He will soon burn to death. A friend of the driver is standing by the lorry. This friend has a gun and is a good shot. The driver asks the friend to shoot him dead. It will be less painful for him to be shot than to burn to death.[84]

---

[77] See, eg, J McEwan, 'Murder by Design: The "Feel-Good Factor" and the Criminal Law' (2001) 9 Medical Law Review 246; B Hewson, 'Killing off Mary: Was the Court of Appeal Right?' (2001) 9 Medical Law Review 281; J Harris, 'Human Beings, Persons and Conjoined Twins: An Ethical Analysis of the Judgment in Re A' (2001) 9 Medical Law Review 221; R Huxtable, 'Separation of Conjoined Twins: Where next for English Law?' [2002] Criminal Law Review 459; V Munro, 'Square Pegs and Round Holes: The Dilemma of Conjoined Twins and Individual Rights' (2001) 10 Social and Legal Studies 4; S Michalowski, 'Sanctity of Life—Are Some Lives More Sacred Than Others?' (2002) 22 Legal Studies 377; K Mason, 'Conjoined Twins: A Diagnostic Conundrum' (2001) 5 Edinburgh Law Review 226.

[78] J McEwan, 'Murder by Design: The "Feel-Good Factor" and the Criminal Law' (2001) 9 Medical Law Review 246.

[79] S Michalowski, 'Sanctity of Life—Are Some Lives More Sacred than Others?' (2002) 22 Legal Studies 377.

[80] R Gillon, 'Imposed Separation of Conjoined Twins—Moral Hubris by the English Courts' (2001) 27 Journal of Medical Ethics 3.

[81] V Munro, 'Square Pegs and Round Holes: The Dilemma of Conjoined Twins and Individual Rights' (2001) 10 Social and Legal Studies 4.

[82] B Hewson, 'Killing off Mary: Was the Court of Appeal Right?' (2001) 9 Medical Law Review 281.

[83] S Ost, 'Euthanasia and the Defence of Necessity' in C Erin and S Ost, *The Criminal Justice System and Health Care* (Oxford University Press 2007).

[84] T Hope, *A Very Short Introduction to Medical Ethics* (Oxford University Press 2004), 15.

On the assumption that the reader believes it would be appropriate to shoot the driver, Hope suggests that the same response should be made to a doctor who gives a terminally ill patient in great pain a lethal injection. In both cases the actor is simply choosing the lesser of two evils. However, given the great reluctance of the courts to use necessity as a defence in criminal law[85] it seems very unlikely that the courts will take this route. Indeed in *R (Nicklinson) v Ministry of Justice*[86] at first instance the argument that necessity could apply in an end of life case was firmly rejected.[87]

21.39 (c) Prosecutorial discretion In other cases of 'mercy killing' a prosecution may not even be brought. The Crown Prosecution Service will only bring proceedings if it is in the public interest. In the case of Rachel Heath the judge asked the CPS to reconsider whether it was in the public interest to try for attempted murder an elderly cancer patient who was in pain and was killed by a professional carer. The CPS decided to withdraw the prosecution.[88] Statistics for the years 1982 and 1991 show that only twenty-four cases of 'mercy killings' were brought to court. Of these, only one led to a murder conviction and sixteen to a manslaughter conviction. Of the latter category only three defendants were sent to prison. As shall be discussed shortly in *R (on the application of Purdy) v DPP*[89] the House of Lords decided that the DPP needed to issue clearer guidance on what factors would be taken into account when deciding whether to prosecute someone for assisting suicide. As a result the DPP has produced new guidelines, which will be summarized later.[90]

2. Suicide

21.40 The law's response to suicide is somewhat uneasy. It used to be a crime to commit suicide. Suicide was regarded as murder of the self.[91] Indeed, bizarrely, attempted suicide at one time carried the death sentence.[92] The current law, found in the Suicide Act 1961, states that is not a crime to commit suicide nor attempt to commit suicide.

The reasoning behind the decriminalization of suicide was explained by Lord Sumption in *R (on the application of Nicklinson) v Ministry of Justice*[93]:

> The reason for decriminalising suicide was not that suicide had become morally acceptable. It was that imposing criminal sanctions was inhumane and ineffective. It was inhumane because the old law could be enforced only against those who had tried to kill themselves but failed. The idea of taking these desperate and unhappy individuals from their hospital beds and punishing them for the attempt was as morally repugnant as the act of suicide itself. It was ineffective because assuming that they truly intended to die, criminal sanctions were incapable by definition of deterring them.

So it is wrong to suggest the decriminalization of suicide recognized a right to kill oneself.[94] Rather, the change in the law recognized that the stress of the prosecution is likely to work

[85] S Gardner, 'Direct Action and the Defence of Necessity' (2005) *Criminal Law Review* 371.
[86] [2012] EWHC 2381 (Admin)
[87] For an argument that necessity should be available see J Herring, 'Escaping the Shackles at the End of Life' (2013) 21 Medical Law Review 48
[88] Unreported, but discussed in H Biggs, *Euthanasia* (Hart 2001) 46.
[89] [2009] UKHL 45, discussed in K Greasley, 'R(Purdy) v DPP and the Case for Willful Blindness' (2010) Oxford Journal of Legal Studies 301.
[90] Director of Public Prosecutions, *Policy for Prosecutors in Respect of Cases of Encouraging or Assisting Suicide* (Crown Prosecution Service 2014).
[91] J Stephen, *A History of the Criminal Law of England* (Routledge 1996, 1883) 16.
[92] G Williams, *The Sanctity of Life and the Criminal Law* (Faber and Faber 1957) 274.
[93] [2014] UKSC 38 at [212]
[94] For a discussion of the ethical issues see J Vong, 'On Whether Suicide is Immoral: In Defence of Kant's Moral Prohibition on Suicide Solely to Avoid Suffering' (2008) 34 Journal of Medical Ethics 655.

against the benefits of the treatments being offered by the medical profession. It is therefore rather concerning to read of the use of Anti-Social Behaviour Orders against those who attempt to commit suicide.[95] Lord Sumption's explanation also solves a dilemma that the law does not outlaw suicide but it does prohibit the encouragement or assistance of suicide, as we shall discuss later.

The definition of suicide is complex.[96] It is generally understood to occur when a person intentionally kills themselves. This would indicate that it would be not be suicide for a person to undertake a highly risky activity, aware that it carried the danger of death, at least unless it was their purpose to die as a result. In *Secretary of State for the Home Department v Robb*,[97] Thorpe LJ did not regard the death of a prisoner from a hunger strike as suicide. He provided no reasons for this conclusion, but presumably it is a recognition that the individual's purpose was not to die, but to achieve their mark of protest. This would seem to indicate that a person who wished to undertake a risky form of treatment which carried a risk of death, hoping it would not kill them, would not be committing suicide. A doctor providing that treatment would, likewise, not be assisting a suicide, if the patient were to die.[98] **21.41**

It is not clear whether suicide can be committed by omission. In particular whether a person who refuses life saving treatment because they want to die, is committing suicide. This is a potentially very significant question because if it is suicide, then a person who encourages or helps a patient to make such a decision could be convicted of assisting suicide. There are two primary issues. The first relates to intention. Where the patient was refusing treatment in order to avoid the pain or indignity of the treatment, rather than to die, is that suicide?[99] Second, there is still debate over whether 'letting nature take its course' and not having treatment can be regarded as amounting to suicide. As we saw earlier, normally in criminal law an omission is not regarded as causally significant unless there is a duty to act. So suicide by omission could only exist when or if there is a duty to receive treatment to keep alive. Although the courts have not directly considered the issue in this context, it is generally well established in medical law that a person is entitled to refuse treatment and, therefore, the law does not appear to recognize a duty to accept treatment.[100] It seems, therefore, unlikely that the courts would find a patient who refused treatment to be committing suicide and therefore unlikely that a medical professional who assisted or encouraged someone to refuse treatment would be guilty of assisting suicide.[101] **21.42**

3. The duty to prevent suicide

It is generally assumed that a person is entitled to prevent another person from committing suicide. In some cases the law goes further and imposes an obligation to prevent a person from committing suicide. Uncontroversially this applies where a person lacking capacity is attempting to commit suicide. Doing so would fall under the general obligation to promote the best interests of those lacking capacity. However, the obligation extends to cases where a person has capacity. The duty arises where a person is in the care of a state authority, and **21.43**

[95] S MacDonald, 'A Suicidal Woman, Roaming Pigs and a Noisy Trampolinist: Refining the ASBO's Definition of Anti-Social Behaviour' (2006) 69 Modern Law Review 183.

[96] J Donnelly, *Suicide: Right or Wrong* (Prometheus Books 1998).

[97] [1995] Fam 127 (FD).

[98] There would be a possibility of gross negligence manslaughter if there was no body of professional opinion which regarded the risky form of treatment as appropriate.

[99] See *R v Blaue* [1975] 1 WLR 1411 (CA), where a patient who died after refusing a blood transfusion on account of religious beliefs was said not to have committed suicide.

[100] *Ms B v An NHS Trust* [2002] EWHC 429.

[101] For a contrary view see J Keown, 'A Futile Defence of Bland: A Reply to Andrew McGee' (2005) 13 Medical Law Review 393.

then there is a duty to take reasonable steps to ensure they do not commit suicide. For example, in *Reeves v Commissioner of the Police of the Metropolis*[102] the House of Lords held that the prison services were under a duty to prevent a sane prisoner committing suicide. Similar reasons would apply in relation to a hospital in relation to patients detained under the Mental Health Act 1983. In *Rabone v Pennine NHS Foundation Trust*[103] it was held that Article 2 of the European Convention on Human Rights imposed such an obligation. The case was brought by parents of young a woman who suffered from depression and had been informally admitted to hospital following a suicide attempt. She was assessed at high risk of suicide but the hospital allowed her home for two days leave, during which she committed suicide. The Supreme Court confirmed that there was a duty to protect people from a real and immediate risk of suicide when they were under the control of the state. It did not matter that she was not formally detained under the 1983 Act.

21.44 Less straightforward are cases where the would-be suicide is not under the care of a state authority. It seems in such cases that the state authorities are not obliged to intervene, but in some cases they may. In *Re Z (An Adult: Capacity)*[104] Mrs Z, aged 65, suffered from cerebella ataxia. This was an incurable and terminal condition which caused her to become increasingly disabled. She had become determined that she wanted to commit suicide. She was no longer physically capable of killing herself and so wanted to travel to Switzerland where assisted suicide was permitted. Her husband, Mr Z, made the travel arrangements and planned to travel with her. When the local authority learned of their plans the local authority became concerned. Mrs Z's social worker believed Mrs Z to be competent but also was concerned that Mr Z would be committing the criminal offence of aiding and abetting suicide by making the arrangements. The local authority therefore applied to court, seeking to invoke its inherent jurisdiction to prevent Mr Z from removing Mrs Z from the jurisdiction. An interim injunction was ordered until a full hearing could take place.

21.45 By the time of the hearing there was evidence which established that Mrs Z had legal capacity to make her own decisions. Justice Hedley lifted the interim injunction. He held that in cases of this kind the duties of the local authority were:

(i) to investigate the position of a vulnerable adult to consider what was her true position and intention;
(ii) to consider whether she was legally competent to make and carry out her decision and intention;
(iii) to consider whether any other (and if so, what) influence may be operating on her position and intention and to ensure that she has all relevant information and knows all available options;
(iv) to consider whether she was legally competent to make and carry out her decision and intention;
(v) to consider whether to invoke the inherent jurisdiction of the High Court so that the question of competence could be judicially investigated and determined;
(vi) in the event of the adult not being competent, to provide all such assistance as may be reasonably required both to determine and give effect to her best interests;
(vii) in the event of the adult being competent to allow her in any lawful way to give effect to her decision although that should not preclude the giving of advice or assistance in accordance with what are perceived to be her best interests;

[102] [2000] AC 360. An obligation on the prison authorities to prevent suicide will also arise under the Human Rights Act 1998: *Savage v South Essex NHS Trust* [2008] UKHL 74.
[103] [2012] UKSC 2.
[104] [2004] EWHC 2817.

(viii) where there are reasonable grounds to suspect that the commission of a criminal offence may be involved, to draw that to the attention of the police;
(ix) in very exceptional circumstances, to invoke the jurisdiction of the court under the Local Government Act 1972, section 222 (which enables a local authority to bring proceedings to a court in relation to inhabitant in their area).[105]

Considerable media attention was paid to a case in December 2008 where Daniel James[106] died in a Dignitas Swiss Clinic.[107] He was a 22-year-old student who had suffered a serious spinal injury during a rugby training session, causing paralysis from the chest down and a range of other mobility problems. Before his visit to Dignitas he had tried unsuccessfully to commit suicide. His parents and a friend had helped with the arrangements for him to travel there. The Director of Public Prosecution decided against a prosecution of his parents and the friend for assisting his suicide.[108] His case highlighted the uncertainty over when the CPS would prosecute in a case of assisted suicide. This uncertainty has been to some extent removed by subsequent clarifications to the DPP guidance, discussed below (at para 21.61).

4. Assisting suicide

As already mentioned it is an offence under s 2 of the Suicide Act 1961 to assist or encourage suicide. However s 2 (as amended by the Coroners and Criminal Justice Act 2009) states: **21.46**

(1) A person ('D') commits an offence if—
  (a) D does an act capable of encouraging or assisting the suicide or attempted suicide of another person, and
  (b) D's act was intended to encourage or assist suicide or an attempt at suicide.
(1A) The person referred to in subsection (1)(a) need not be a specific person (or class of persons) known to, or identified by, D.
(1B) D may commit an offence under this section whether or not a suicide, or an attempt at suicide, occurs.
(1C) An offence under this section is triable on indictment and a person convicted of such an offence is liable to imprisonment for a term not exceeding 14 years.

The offence includes providing equipment or advice to another to commit suicide. Where a defendant forced a person to commit suicide, that could be charged as manslaughter or even murder.[109] Aiding suicide would be charged where a defendant gave a person assistance and, as a result, the victim chose in a free, voluntary, and informed way to commit suicide. A straightforward case, one might think, would be where a health care professional gives a lethal dosage of drugs to an individual, aware that they intend to use them to commit suicide. Although even that example is not beyond doubt. In *R v Chard*[110] a doctor gave tablets to a patient at her request. The patient committed suicide by taking the tablets. The doctor was acquitted of assisting suicide because he had just given the patient the option **21.47**

[105] At [19].
[106] The Daniel James case is discussed in A Mullock, 'Overlooking the criminally compassionate: what are the implications of prosecutorial policy on encouraging or assisting suicide?' (2010) 18 Medical Law Review 442 and S Ost, 'The de-medicalisation of assisted dying: is a less medicalised model the way forward?' (2010) 18 Medical Law Review 497.
[107] Dignitas is an organization that has facilities to assist those who wish to commit suicide (<http://www.dignitas.ch/>).
[108] Director of Public Prosecutions, *Decision On Prosecution—The Death By Suicide Of Daniel James* (Director of Public Prosecutions 2009). For a discussion of the discretion of the DPP in relation to assisted suicide see R Tur, 'Legislative Technique and Human Rights' [2003] Criminal Law Review 3 and Calvert-Smith and O'Doherty, 'Legislative Technique and Human Rights: A Response' [2003] Criminal Law Review 384.
[109] *R v Kennedy* [2007] UKHL 38.
[110] The Times, 23 September 1993.

of committing suicide. Such an argument would, however, mean that it would be very rare that a person could be convicted of assisting suicide. It may be that the explanation of the result in *R v Chard*[111] is that the doctor did not intend to help the victim to commit suicide. To be guilty as an accomplice to suicide it must be shown that suicide was foreseen and that the defendant intended to assist that suicide.[112] In *Gillick v West Norfolk and Wisbech AHA*[113] it was stated that a doctor who gave contraception to an under-16-year-old girl would not be regarded as assisting unlawful sexual intercourse because he would not want her to engage in sex. Similarly, if a doctor gave pain relief pills to a patient, not wanting to use them to commit suicide, but foreseeing that the patient might, he or she might, in the same way, escape criminal liability.

21.48 Significantly, s 2(4) of the Suicide Act requires the consent of the DPP to commence any prosecution for assisting suicide.[114] That implies an acceptance by Parliament that there will be cases where prosecution for assisting suicide would not be appropriate. It is this discretion which in recent years has become the focal point for legal proceedings in this area.

21.49 In *R (on the application of Purdy) v DPP*[115] Debbie Purdy was aged 45 and suffering from progressive multiple sclerosis. She stated that she was becoming weaker and suffering great pain. She foresaw that she might at some time in the not too distant future decide to end her life and travel overseas to a country that permitted assisted suicide. One possibility was to go to Switzerland to use the services of Dignitas (an organization that makes arrangements for people who wish to commit suicide). If she were to pursue that plan, she would need the assistance of her husband, but was concerned that if he was involved he might face a prosecution for assisting suicide. She sought from the DPP a reassurance that if her husband were to assist her in travelling overseas he would not be prosecuted. The DPP was unwilling to do more than refer to the Code of Prosecutors which set out the general guidance on when prosecutions of crimes will be brought. The couple challenged that decision in court. The case went to the House of Lords, which found in Ms Purdy's favour.

21.50 At the heart of their reasoning was the conclusion that Debbie Purdy's decision to seek assisted suicide fell within Article 8(1). Any interference in that right could be justified under Article 8(2) but that interference had to be justified by law. To amount to 'law' the legal obligation had to be sufficiently clear. The guidance offered by the DPP failed to be sufficiently clear. This was especially unsatisfactory because the issues surrounding assisted suicide were sensitive and controversial and so officials needed clear guidance. In particular there was insufficient guidance as to what factors would indicate whether a prosecution was in the public interest. The court therefore ordered the DPP to produce clear guidance on how he would exercise his discretion on whether to prosecute for assisting suicide.

21.51 Perhaps the most significant aspect of the decision in Purdy is that a decision to end one's life falls within Article 8(1) and is, therefore, protected as a right. In reaching this decision their Lordships overturned their conclusion in *R (on the application of Pretty) v DPP*[116] that Article 8 did not cover a decision to commit suicide. They justified their change in position by reference to the decision in the ECtHR in *Pretty v UK*.[117] It must be admitted that that

---

111 ibid.
112 *R v Bryce* [2004] EWCA Crim 1231; *R v S* [2005] EWCA Crim 819.
113 [1985] 3 All ER 402.
114 For a good example of when the offence will be prosecuted see *R v Howe* [2014] EWCA Crim 114.
115 *R (on the application of Purdy) v DPP* [2009] UKHL 45.
116 [2001] UKHL 61.
117 *Pretty v UK* [2002] 2 FCR 97.

judgment was not as clear as it could have been on the question of the extent to which Article 8 covered end of life decisions.[118] The European Court there stated:

> The very essence of the Convention is respect for human dignity and freedom. Without in any way negating the principle of sanctity of life protected under the Convention, the Court considers that it is under article 8 that notions of the quality of life take on significance. In an era of growing medical sophistication combined with longer life expectancies, many people are concerned that they should not be forced to linger on in old age or in states of advanced physical or mental decrepitude which conflict with strongly held ideas of self and personal identity.[119]

Whatever debates might be had about the dicta in the case, their Lordships in *Purdy* regarded it as sufficient to justify a reinterpretation of Article 8.

It is important not to exaggerate the significance of *Purdy*. Their Lordships were not saying there was a right to die.[120] The decision does not cast doubt on the interpretation of Article 2 given by the ECtHR in *Pretty v UK*.[121] The ECtHR saw Article 2 as imposing an obligation to protect life and so it could be taken to include a right to die. At the same time the courts have confirmed that Article 2 does not generate an absolute right to all treatment that could sustain life. If, in a doctor's medical opinion, such treatment would be futile or inappropriate it need not be given.[122] **21.52**

Nor were their Lordships saying that it should not be an offence to assist a person in committing suicide. The finding was that the decision to commit suicide fell within Article 8. This is significant because Article 8(2) permits an interference with Article 8 rights. Indeed their Lordships in *Purdy* were in no doubt that there could be circumstances in which it was necessary to interfere in a person's decision to commit suicide. Baroness Hale stated: **21.53**

> Clearly, the prime object must be to protect people who are vulnerable to all sorts of pressures, both subtle and not so subtle, to consider their own lives a worthless burden to others. . . .. But at the same time, the object must be to protect the right to exercise a genuinely autonomous choice. The factors which tell for and against such a genuine exercise of autonomy free from pressure will be the most important.[123]

Their Lordships were simply stating that the law on assisting suicide needed to be sufficiently clear to enable a person to know whether they would be guilty of an offence if they were to assist suicide.

The significance of the ruling in *Purdy* is that any outlawing of assisting suicide must be justified. Lord Brown emphasized that it should not be assumed that all acts of assistance are wrong: **21.54**

---

118 *R (on the application of Purdy)*, n 115. At [67] it stated: 'The applicant in this case is prevented by law from exercising her choice to avoid what she considers will be an undignified and distressing end to her life. The Court is not prepared to exclude that this constitutes an interference with her right to respect for private life as guaranteed under Article 8 § 1 of the Convention.' But confusingly later at [87]: 'The Court has found above that the applicant's rights under Article 8 of the Convention were engaged' (at [61–67]).

119 *Pretty v UK*, n 117, at [65].

120 For discussions on 'a right to die' see: A du Bois-Pedain, 'Is There a Right to Die?' in B Brooks-Gordon, F Ebtehaj, J Herring, M Johnson, and M Richards (eds), *Death Rites and Rights* (Hart 2007); J Coggon, 'Ignoring the Moral and Intellectual Shape of the Law after Bland: The Unintended Side-effect of a Sorry Compromise' (2007) 27 Legal Studies 100.

121 [2002] 2 FCR 97.

122 *R (on the application of Burke) v General Medical Council* [2005] EWCA Civ 1003; *Re OT* [2009] EWHC 633 (Fam).

123 *Purdy*, n 115, at [65].

> suppose, say, a loved one, in desperate and deteriorating circumstances, who regards the future with dread and has made a fully informed, voluntary and fixed decision to die, needing another's compassionate help and support to accomplish that end (or at any rate to achieve it in the least distressing way), is assistance in *those* circumstances necessarily to be deprecated? Are there not cases in which (although no actual defence of necessity could ever arise) many might regard such conduct as if anything to be commended rather than condemned? In short, as it seems to me, there will on occasion be situations where, contrary to the assumptions underlying the Code, it would be possible to regard the conduct of the aider and abettor as altruistic rather than criminal, conduct rather to be understood out of respect for an intending suicide's rights under article 8 than discouraged so as to safeguard the right to life of others under article 2. (para 83)

21.55 One final significance of the *Purdy* decision is that it might give strength to claims in future which rely on Article 14 of the ECHR. In *Pretty v UK*[124] Ms Pretty, relying on Article 14, claimed that the English law had not placed a criminal bar on those physically capable of doing so from committing suicide, but that those who lacked the physical capacity for doing so were unable to commit suicide. This it was claimed was discrimination on the grounds of disability. The argument was rejected by the ECtHR who found that even if there was discrimination it was objectively reasonably justifiable in order to protect vulnerable people:

> . . . there is, in the court's view, objective and reasonable justification for not distinguishing in law between those who are and those who are not physically capable of committing suicide. Under art 8 of the Convention, the court has found that there are sound reasons for not introducing into the law exceptions to cater for those who are deemed not to be vulnerable. Similar cogent reasons exist under art 14 for not seeking to distinguish between those who are able and those who are unable to commit suicide unaided. The borderline between the two categories will often be a very fine one and to seek to build into the law an exemption for those judged to be incapable of committing suicide would seriously undermine the protection of life which the 1961 Act was intended to safeguard and greatly increase the risk of abuse.[125]

21.56 It should be emphasized that generally, a stronger justification is required for discriminatory treatment than for other interferences in a person's rights. Indeed it is notable that Lord Bingham in his judgment in the House of Lords stated:

> If article 2 does confer a right of self-determination in relation to life and death, and if a person were so gravely disabled as to be unable to perform any act whatsoever to cause his or her own death, it would necessarily follow in logic that such a person would have a right to be killed at the hands of a third party.[126]

This may be taken as an acceptance that Article 14 arguments in relation to assisted suicide would carry weight, if only the right to commit suicide can be found to exist within the Convention. As *Purdy* has now found that suicide decisions fall within Article 8, that argument might well be brought before the courts again.

21.57 It is important to emphasize that *Purdy* was not suggesting that all decisions to commit suicide are covered by Article 8. The wish of a person lacking capacity to commit suicide would not fall within Article 8. Also their Lordships in their discussion had in mind a case where a person who was terminally ill wished to commit suicide. Whether they would conclude that a person, with capacity, who wished to commit suicide for what others would regard as a frivolous reason fell within Article 8 may be open to debate. Baroness Hale stated somewhat

---

124 *Pretty v UK* [2002] 2 FCR 97.
125 ibid, at [89].
126 [2002] 1 All ER 1, 6–7.

elliptically in *Purdy*: 'It is not for society to tell people what to value about their own lives. But it may be justifiable for society to insist that we value their lives even if they do not.'[127]

Since *Purdy,* the European Court has offered further clarification on the human rights dimension. In *Koch v Germany*[128] it was clear that a person with a close relationship to the person who wishes to die (eg a partner) will be able to invoke a right under Article 8 in connection with the person's wish to die. Similarly, it has been confirmed that if a person wishes to commit suicide, the state is not under a duty to provide them with their chosen means to do so.[129] However, if the state does provide assistance in some cases, there must be clear guidance setting out when assistance is or is not to be made available.[130] **21.58**

The ECtHR has, therefore, established a reasonably clear approach to end of life issues. Article 8 does protect a right to determine how to end one's life, but a state is permitted to outlaw assisted suicide, providing there is sufficient justification under paragraph 2. However, the precise balancing between the rights falls within a state's 'margin of appreciation'. **21.59**

The Supreme Court in *R (on the application of Nicklinson) v Ministry of Justice*[131] is currently the leading case on the issue of human rights and assisted suicide. However, it is a broad ranging judgment involving some complex issues of human rights and constitutional law, as well as the discussion of medical matters. The case was brought by two appellants. The best known was Tony Nicklinson, who died following the hearing of the case at the High Court, but in whose name the litigation continued. He suffered from 'locked-in syndrome' and was paralysed below the neck and could not speak. He communicated by blinking to indicate a letter on a board held up by his wife or an eye blink computer. He told the court:

> My life can be summed up as dull, miserable, demeaning, undignified and intolerable. . . . it is misery created by the accumulation of lots of things which are minor in themselves but, taken together, ruin what's left of my life. Things like . . . constant dribbling; having to be hoisted everywhere; loss of independence, . . . particularly toileting and washing, in fact all bodily functions (by far the hardest thing to get used to); having to forgo favourite foods; . . . having to wait until 10.30 to go to the toilet . . . in extreme circumstances I have gone in the chair, and have sat there until the carers arrived at the normal time.[132]

The other appellant, known as Martin, also suffered from locked-in syndrome. They both appealed against the findings of the lower courts that the current law on assisted suicide did not infringe their human rights. The Director of Public Prosecutions appealed against an order in the Court of Appeal that the prosecution guidance on assisted suicide needed further clarification as it applied to professionals.

The majority of their lordships (seven of the nine; Lady Hale and Lord Kerr dissenting) rejected an argument that the ban on assisted suicide imposed a 'blanket ban' and so was impermissible under the European Convention on Human Rights. The majority took the view that the European Court of Human Rights had made it clear that the precise regulation of assisted suicide was within the margin of appreciation, meaning that each country could determine for it the balance of rights on the regulation of assisted suicide under Article 8. The majority held that ideally parliament would address the issue and determine what balance was appropriate for England. Only if it refused to would it fall to the courts **21.60**

---

[127] *Purdy*, n 115, at [68].
[128] (2013) 56 EHRR 6.
[129] *Haas v Switzerland* (2011) 53 EHRR 33.
[130] *Gross v Switzerland* (2014) 58 E.H.R.R. 7.
[131] [2014] UKSC 38.
[132] *R (on the application of Nicklinson and another) (Appellants) v Ministry of Justice* [2012] EWHC 2381 (Admin) at [13].

to make the determination. The majority held that the court could, in theory, determine that the ban on assisted suicide infringed convention rights, but that parliament should be given the opportunity to consider amending the law first. Lord Neuberger summarized the conclusion for why as follows:

> First, the question whether the provisions of section 2 should be modified raises a difficult, controversial and sensitive issue, with moral and religious dimensions, which undoubtedly justifies a relatively cautious approach from the courts. Secondly, this is not a case like *Re G* where the incompatibility is simple to identify and simple to cure: whether, and if so how, to amend section 2 would require much anxious consideration from the legislature; this also suggests that the courts should, as it were, take matters relatively slowly. Thirdly, section 2 has, as mentioned above, been considered on a number of occasions in Parliament, and it is currently due to be debated in the House of Lords in the near future; so this is a case where the legislature is and has been actively considering the issue. Fourthly, less than thirteen years ago, the House of Lords in *Pretty v DPP* gave Parliament to understand that a declaration of incompatibility in relation to section 2 would be inappropriate, a view reinforced by the conclusions reached by the Divisional Court and the Court of Appeal in this case: a declaration of incompatibility on this appeal would represent an unheralded *volte-face.*[133]

The holding of the Supreme Court was very limited. The majority (Lady Hale and Lord Mance dissenting) thought it was not appropriate at this point in time to issue a declaration of incompatibility. [134] However, a majority indicated that in the future it could hold that the bar on assisted suicide was contrary to the European Convention on Human Rights, as interpreted by the English courts. There was clearly a degree of disagreement on this issue. Lady Hale and Lord Mance appeared willing to issue a declaration of incompatibility immediately. However, the rest of the Justice were not willing to do so. Lords Neuberger, Mance, and Wilson, while indicating that a declaration of incompatibility could not currently be made, leave strong hints that unless compelling new arguments are made they would be minded to make a declaration of incompatibility. Lords Sumption, Hughes, Reed, and Clarke appear currently less inclined to make to issue of incompatibility, believing the issue to be one for the legislature.

21.61 The Supreme Court did however recommend that the DPP review her guidance in so far as it applied to professionals assisting suicide. Following the decision in *Nicklinson* the Director of Public Prosecutions updated its guidance that it had produced following the Purdy decision. The guidance lists factors which will be taken into account when deciding when to prosecute in a case of assisted suicide.[135]

A prosecution is more likely to be required if:

1. the victim was under 18 years of age;
2. the victim did not have the capacity (as defined by the Mental Capacity Act 2005) to reach an informed decision to commit suicide;
3. the victim had not reached a voluntary, clear, settled, and informed decision to commit suicide;

---

133 ibid, at [116].

134 By contrast in Carter v A-G [2015] SCC 5 the Canadian Supreme Court held the prohibition on assisted dying void as contrary to the Canadian Charter of Rights 'insofar as it deprives a competent adult of such assistance where (1) the person affected clearly consents to the termination of life; and (2) the person has a grievous and irremediable medical condition (including an illness, disease or disability) that causes enduring suffering that is intolerable to the individual in the circumstances of his or her condition': [4].

135 Director of Public Prosecutions, *Policy for Prosecutors in Respect of Cases of Encouraging or Assisting Suicide* (2014).

4. the victim had not clearly and unequivocally communicated his or her decision to commit suicide to the suspect;
5. the victim did not seek the encouragement or assistance of the suspect personally or on his or her own initiative;
6. the suspect was not wholly motivated by compassion; for example, the suspect was motivated by the prospect that he or she or a person closely connected to him or her stood to gain in some way from the death of the victim;
7. the suspect pressured the victim to commit suicide;
8. the suspect did not take reasonable steps to ensure that any other person had not pressured the victim to commit suicide;
9. the suspect had a history of violence or abuse against the victim;
10. the victim was physically able to undertake the act that constituted the assistance him or herself;
11. the suspect was unknown to the victim and encouraged or assisted the victim to commit or attempt to commit suicide by providing specific information via, for example, a website or publication;
12. the suspect gave encouragement or assistance to more than one victim who were not known to each other;
13. the suspect was paid by the victim or those close to the victim for his or her encouragement or assistance;
14. the suspect was acting in his or her capacity as a medical doctor, nurse, other healthcare professional, a professional carer [whether for payment or not], or as a person in authority, such as a prison officer, and the victim was in his or her care;
15. the suspect was aware that the victim intended to commit suicide in a public place where it was reasonable to think that members of the public may be present;
16. the suspect was acting in his or her capacity as a person involved in the management or as an employee (whether for payment or not) of an organization or group, a purpose of which is to provide a physical environment (whether for payment or not) in which to allow another to commit suicide.

A prosecution is less likely to be required if: **21.62**

1. the victim had reached a voluntary, clear, settled, and informed decision to commit suicide;
2. the suspect was wholly motivated by compassion;
3. the actions of the suspect, although sufficient to come within the definition of the offence, were of only minor encouragement or assistance;
4. the suspect had sought to dissuade the victim from taking the course of action which resulted in his or her suicide;
5. the actions of the suspect may be characterized as reluctant encouragement or assistance in the face of a determined wish on the part of the victim to commit suicide;
6. the suspect reported the victim's suicide to the police and fully assisted them in their enquiries into the circumstances of the suicide or the attempt and his or her part in providing encouragement or assistance.

The guidance goes on to explain how these factors should be used.

The DPP made it clear that in issuing these guidelines he was not changing the law. The Suicide Act 1961 had made it clear that it was not necessarily correct to prosecute in every case of assisted suicide. The DPP emphasized that the list of factors provided had to be used with care: **21.63**

> Assessing the public interest is not simply a matter of adding up the number of factors on each side and seeing which side has the greater number. Each case must be considered on its own facts and on its own merits. Prosecutors must decide the importance of each public interest factor in the circumstances of each case and go on to make an overall assessment. It is quite possible that one factor alone may outweigh a number of other factors which tend in the opposite direction. Although there may be public interest factors tending against prosecution in a particular case, prosecutors should consider whether, nonetheless, a prosecution should go ahead and for those factors to be put to the court for consideration when sentence is passed.[136]

D. Slippery Slopes

21.64 One important issue in the current debate surrounds slippery slopes. A slippery slope argument states that even if it is morally acceptable to permit A, it should not be permitted because it would lead to B, which is morally unacceptable.[137] The application of such an argument to euthanasia is then made that even though we might be able to conceive of individual cases or categories of cases where it would be appropriate to allow euthanasia, legalizing the practice would inevitably result in it being used in circumstances which would be unacceptable.

21.65 John Keown[138] has argued that are two kinds of slippery slope arguments that can be made in this context. First, that as a matter of logic, once voluntary euthanasia is permitted there are no arguments which would justify opposing involuntary euthanasia and so one will necessarily lead to another. Second, as a matter of practice, it is not possible to put in place procedures to ensure that there is no involuntary euthanasia. Indeed, in considering the position in countries where voluntary euthanasia has been allowed critics claim that there is evidence that involuntary euthanasia has occurred.[139]

21.66 The first of Keown's arguments is that supporters of euthanasia are on the horns of a dilemma. Either they accept that autonomy is the key principle and then anyone who wishes to die should be allowed to do so. Or we restrict euthanasia to only those who are in great pain or facing a terminal illness. He suspects that most euthanasia supporters, would favour the latter option. But by so restricting autonomy, he claims, we are impliedly saying that in those cases the decision that is being made is a good one. The slippery slope comes in because once we allow this we must accept that it will be sensible for incompetent people in a similar situation to be killed. So, we start off by allowing a small group of people to exercise their autonomy to kill themselves or be killed, but we end up authorizing the killing of those lacking capacity who are terminally ill. Keown might find support for his view in evidence that in Holland where euthanasia has been made lawful under certain circumstances (see para 21.69) there is now much debate over when it is appropriate to kill disabled neonates.[140] Not everyone is convinced by Keown's argument. One response is to suggest that it is perfectly coherent for the law to only allow euthanasia when we have both an exercise of autonomy *and* a belief that the decision is a reasonable one.[141] Whether this attempt to combine autonomy and beneficence is sustainable is one of the central themes in the debate.

---

136 ibid, at [39].

137 D Lamb, *Down the Slippery Slope* (Croom Helm 1988).

138 J Keown, *Euthanasia, Ethics and Public Policy* (Cambridge University Press 2002).

139 See the discussion at para 21.66 *et seq*.

140 E Verhagen and P Sauer, 'The Groningen Protocol—Euthanasia in Severely Ill Newborns' (2005) 352 New England Journal of Medicine 959.

141 H Lillehammer, 'Voluntary Euthanasia and the Logical Slippery Slope Argument' [2002] Cambridge Law Journal 545.

The second slippery slope argument is about the impact of any change in the law on practice. If the law permits euthanasia or assisted suicide in certain fixed situations, is it inevitable that the safeguards will be bypassed and there will be an ever-increasing number of people dying under the scheme? For example, people may be pressurized into agreeing to being killed when that is not their wish; doctors may be willing to allow patients to be killed, even though the patient's condition does not fall exactly within the parameters of the rules; and the need to save resources may increase the pressures on doctors and patients to engage in euthanasia. **21.67**

Both supporters and opponents of euthanasia have referred to what has happened in Netherlands and Oregon, US. In the former, euthanasia has been permitted in certain circumstances and in the latter, assisted suicide. Perhaps not surprisingly to opponents these countries show that safeguards put in place to prevent the slippery slopes just mentioned have been ineffective,[142] while to supporters these examples show how it is possible to have a well regulated regime which protects vulnerable people. **21.68**

1. The Netherlands

Holland has permitted euthanasia in certain circumstances.[143] Essentially, the Dutch law permits a doctor to kill a patient who has produced a request which is voluntary and well-considered; who is suffering in a way which is lasting and unbearable; and where there is no prospect of improvement in his or her condition. Both doctor and patient must believe that there is no reasonable solution to his or her plight apart from assisted suicide or euthanasia. An independent physician must be consulted and confirm that the conditions are met. **21.69**

While there has been considerable attention paid to the Dutch scheme, perhaps predictably there has been no consensus over the lessons to be learned from it. It certainly seems that some doctors are performing euthanasia or assisted suicide without completing the appropriate paperwork and registering it with the authorities. Whether this is a sign of doctors simply avoiding bureaucracy or of a slippery slope with killings taking place outside the scope of the scheme is a matter of fierce debate.[144] John Finnis has argued that in Holland there is a considerable level of non-voluntary euthanasia: **21.70**

> when you look at those figures, the bottom line is this: we find that not just 1,300 or 2,300 or another 1,000 but 25,306 cases of death were accelerated by medical intervention intended wholly or partly to terminate life . . . And of these Dutch deaths, well over half, or fifty eight percent—14,691—were without any explicit request.[145]

[142] J Keown, 'Euthanasia in the Netherlands' in J Keown (ed), *Euthanasia Examined: Ethical, Clinical and Legal Perspectives* (Cambridge University Press 1995).

[143] The Termination of Life on Request and Assisted Suicide (Review Procedures) Act 2001, amending Art 293 of the Penal Code of the Netherlands.

[144] For a detailed discussion of the Dutch law, see J Griffiths, H Weyers, and M Adams, *Euthanasia and the Law in Europe* (Hart 2008); B Onwuteaka-Philipsen, A van der Heide, M Muller, M Rurup, C Rietjens, J Georges, A Vrakking, J Cuperus-Bosma, G van der Wal, and P van der Maas, 'Dutch Experience of Monitoring Euthanasia' (2005) 331 British Medical Journal 24; A Van der Heide, B Onwuteaka-Philipsen, M Rurup, H Buiting, J van Delden, J Hanssen-de Wolf, A Janssen, R Pasman, J Rietjens, C Prins, I Deerenberg, J Gevers, P van der Maas, and G van der Wal, 'End-of-life Practices in the Netherlands under the Euthanasia Act' (2007) 356 New England Journal of Medicine 1957; S Smith, 'Evidence for the Practical Slippery Slope in the Debate on Physician-assisted Suicide and Euthanasia' (2005) 13 Medical Law Review 17; S Smith, 'Fallacies of the Logical Slippery Slope in the Debate on Physician-assisted Suicide and Euthanasia' (2005) 13 Medical Law Review 224.

[145] J Finnis, 'Euthanasia, Morality and the Law' (1998) 31 Loy L A L Rev 1123.

Indeed, concern about the Dutch scheme has been expressed by the United Nations Human Rights Committee[146] and the Committee on Legal Affairs and Human Rights of the European Parliament.[147] The latter body stated that the studies:

> have demonstrated a disturbingly high incidence of euthanasia being carried out without the patient's explicit request and an equally disturbing failure by medical professionals to report euthanasia cases to the proper regulatory authority.[148]

21.71 Many commentators have not been persuaded that the evidence from Holland is concerning, particularly in the light of more recent studies which have found greatly improved rates of reporting. The reporting rate of euthanasia and physician-assisted suicide increased from 41 per cent in 1995, to 54 per cent in 2001 and to 80 per cent in 2005.[149] In 2005, 1.7 per cent of all deaths in Netherlands were reported to be euthanasia and 0.1 per cent assisted suicide. These were lower than 2001, which if accurate, would suggest some of the slippery slope arguments are not supported by the evidence from Holland. However, the figures also show that of all deaths 0.4 per cent were end of life decisions with no explicit request from the patient.[150] Also, 7.1 per cent of all deaths involved the use of palliative sedation and these were significantly up on the figures for 2001, which might indicate an increase in the use of physician involvement in death.

21.72 A study in 2007 of relatives of those who had died under the Dutch euthanasia laws found 92 per cent saying they believed that lawful euthanasia or assisted suicide had contributed favourably to the patient's end of life.[151] Another study claimed that there was no evidence from Holland that vulnerable people were being pressurized into euthanasia without their consent.[152] It is, therefore, difficult at this point to be entirely sure what the picture is of death practices in a state which permits euthanasia. Penney Lewis, after a thorough review of the evidence writes:

> There is no evidence from the Netherlands that the legalization of voluntary euthanasia caused an increase in the rate of non-voluntary euthanasia . . . Evidence in relation to other jurisdictions is mixed; while rates of non-voluntary euthanasia in some prohibitive jurisdictions are higher than the Dutch rate, in other prohibitive jurisdictions the rates are lower. Lacking solid baseline evidence, the current evidence does not support the drawing of inferences either that legalization causes an increase in the rate of non-voluntary euthanasia or that such rates are higher under a prohibitive approach. Furthermore, it seems likely that cultural factors may significantly influence baseline rates, thus further decreasing the possibility of drawing inferences from evidence in one jurisdiction as to what will happen in another.[153]

---

146 The United Nations Human Rights Committee, *Concluding Observations of the Human Rights Committee: Netherlands* (United Nations 2001).

147 European Parliamentary Assembly, Social, Family Affairs and Health Committee (2003) *Euthanasia* (European Parliament 2003).

148 ibid, para 1.

149 Van der Heide et al, 'End-of-Life Practices in the Netherlands' n 144.

150 ibid.

151 J-J Georges, B Onwuteaka-Philipsen, M Muller, G van der Wal, A van der Heide, and P van der Maas, 'Relatives' Perspective on the Terminally Ill Patients who Died after Euthanasia or Physician-assisted Suicide: A Retrospective Cross-sectional Interview Study in the Netherlands' (2007) 31 Death Studies 1.

152 Van der Heide et al, 'End-of-life practices in the Netherlands, n 144.

153 P Lewis, 'The Empirical Slippery Slope from Voluntary to Non-voluntary Euthanasia' (2007) Journal of Law, Medicine and Ethics 197.

2. Oregon

In 1994 Oregon, a State in the US, passed the Death with Dignity Act 1994.[154] This permitted doctors to provide a patient with a lethal quantity of drugs for the purpose of assisting a patient's suicide. However, this was only permitted in certain carefully proscribed circumstances and it did not allow the doctor to administer the drug her- or himself. In other words the legislation permitted physician-assisted suicide, not euthanasia. The patient must be found to be acting voluntarily and be competent. **21.73**

A total of 1173 people have died since the law was passed. In 1998, 16 Oregonians used physician-assisted suicide. This increased to 27 in 1999, 37 in 2004 and to 71 in 2013. This means that 2.19 in a thousand Oregonians die through physician-assisted suicide. [155] **21.74**

Some interesting information has emerged from Oregon about the individuals who typically seek physician-assisted suicide: **21.75**

- The most common medical conditions among those using to Act to commit suicide were those suffering from cancer and motor neurone disease.[156]
- The most common reason given for wanting to die was loss of autonomy and not being able to do the things which made life enjoyable and a loss of dignity. Forty-four per cent of those using the Act mentioned fears about being a burden to their family or friends as a major factor leading them to seek suicide:[157] In 2013 around 70 per cent of those who died were aged 65 or over. Younger people with terminal illnesses were more likely to seek PAS than older people with terminal illnesses.
- There was a significant difference between rates of men and women seeking PAS.in 2013. 62 per cent were men and 38 per cent were female.
- Asian Oregonians were three times more likely than white Oregenians to seek PAS. Divorced and never married people were two times more likely than married people to do so.
- There was a strong association between having attended higher education and seeking PAS.[158]

So far it does not appear from the evidence that there is widespread abuse of the system,[159] but Bonnie Steinbock believes it as yet unproven whether the benefits of the Oregon system outweigh the disadvantages of potential abuse.[160] In 2013, no cases were referred to the Board of Medical examiners, with complaints that the paperwork for prescriptions under the Act was inadequately completed.[161]

---

154 R Cohen-Almagor and M Hartman, 'The Oregon Death With Dignity Act: Review and Proposals for Improvement' (2001) 27 *Journal of Legislation* 269.

155 Oregon Public Health Division, *Death with Dignity Act* (Oregon, PHD 2014).

156 This condition is also known as ALS (amyotrophic lateral sclerosis) or Lou Gehrig's disease.

157 Department of Human Services, *Fifth Annual Report on Oregon's Death with Dignity Act* (DHS 2003) 20.

158 Department of Human Services, *Annual Report* (Salem: Oregon, DHS 2013).

159 E Dahl and N Levy, 'The Case for Physician Assisted Suicide: How Can It Possibly be Proven?' (2006) 32 Journal of Medical Ethics 335.

160 M Battin, A van der Heide, L Ganzini, G van der Wal, and B Onwuteaka-Philipsen, 'Legal Physician-assisted Dying in Oregon and the Netherlands: Evidence Concerning the Impact on Patients in "Vulnerable" Groups' (2007) 33 Journal of Medical Ethics 591.

161 Ibid.

3. Conclusions

21.76 Looking at the international evidence it is hard to form definitive conclusions. Lord Neuberger provided a thoughtful conclusion in *R (on the application of Nicklinson) v Ministry of Justice:*[162]

> It is true that the Falconer Report, supported by the reports of the two Canadian panels, states that in the Netherlands, Oregon and Switzerland there is no evidence of abuse of the law, which permits assisting a suicide in prescribed circumstances and subject to conditions. However, negative evidence is often hard to obtain, there is only a limited scope for information given the few jurisdictions where assisted suicide is lawful and the short time for which it has been lawful there, and different countries may have different potential problems. In other words, the evidence on that point plainly falls some way short of establishing that there is no risk. The most that can be said is that the Falconer commission and the Canadian panels could find no evidence of abuse.

21.77 Before we leave the slippery slope argument we should note that it should not be assumed that countries which outlaw euthanasia are immune from slippery slopes. As the Shipman case shows, even in England an enormous number of patients can be killed without the authorities being alerted.[163] It has been suggested that the rates of euthanasia and assisted suicide in England and Holland are little different: the real difference being that in Holland it is done openly and in a regulated way, while in England it is done in secret.[164]

E. Vulnerable People

21.78 There is general agreement that if euthanasia or assisted suicide is to be made legal in England there would need to be a scheme in place to ensure that vulnerable people were not pressurized into agreeing to be killed against their genuine wishes. Beauchamp and Childress[165] suggest that it should be accepted that assisted suicide should not be simply permitted in every case where a patient wishes to die. However, they suggest that assisted suicide is justified if the following nine conditions are satisfied:

(1) A voluntary request by a competent patient;
(2) An ongoing patient–physician relationship;
(3) Mutual and informed decision-making by patient and physician;
(4) A supportive yet critical and probing environment of decision-making;
(5) A considered rejection of alternatives;
(6) Structured consultation with other parties in medicine;
(7) A patient's expression of a durable preference for death;
(8) Unacceptable suffering by the patient;
(9) Use of a means that is as painless and comfortable as possible.

21.79 The difficulty in seeking to protect the vulnerable is that the expression of a desire to be killed can result from a range of complex social and psychological phenomena.[166] As already mentioned those who desire death may be suffering depression, pain, and isolation and

[162] [2014] UKSC 38 at [88].
[163] J Thunder, 'Quiet Killings in Medical Facilities' [2003] Issues in Law and Medicine 211.
[164] E Jackson, *Medical Law* (Oxford University Press 2012) 958. Although see R Magnusson, *Angels of Death: Exploring the Euthanasia Underground* (Yale University Press 2002) for evidence of "underground euthanasia" in Australia.
[165] T Beauchamp and J Childress, *Principles of Biomedical Ethics* (Oxford University Press 2003) 151.
[166] A Street and D Kissane, 'Dispensing Death, Desiring Death' (2000) 41 Omega 231.

their decisions may not reflect a full exercise in autonomy.[167] There have been concerns that those choosing to die may be greatly influenced by concerns over the cost of the patient's treatment, especially if it means a great reduction in the inheritance that can be left to their children. Those who make arguments like these often emphasize the number of people who change their minds over end of life issues.[168] Further, it is not unknown for relatives desperate for an inheritance to encourage or enable suicide.[169]

Katrina George has argued that women especially are liable to make choices about euthanasia which are not voluntary.[170] She refers to 'structural inequalities and disparities in power—most evident in women's experience of violence—and social and economic disadvantage and oppressive cultural stereotypes that idealize feminine self-sacrifice and reinforce stereotyped gender roles of passivity and compliance'.[171] These concerns may be supported by a study of assisted suicide in Dignitas and Exit Deutsche (assisted suicide organizations in Switzerland) which found that 65 per cent of those using their services were women.[172] By contrast there is no evidence of gender affecting those who seek assisted suicide in Oregon or the Netherlands.[173] **21.80**

Perhaps the most valid concern is that there will be a change in social attitudes and expectations that will impact on vulnerable people. Such pressure will be hard to detect. This fear was well captured by Lord Sumption in *R (on the application of Nicklinson) v Ministry of Justice*:[174] **21.81**

> The vulnerability to pressure of the old or terminally ill is a more formidable problem. The problem is not that people may decide to kill themselves who are not fully competent mentally. I am prepared to accept that mental competence is capable of objective assessment by health professionals. The real difficulty is that even the mentally competent may have reasons for deciding to kill themselves which reflect either overt pressure upon them by others or their own assumptions about what others may think or expect. The difficulty is particularly acute in the case of what the Commission on Assisted Dying called 'indirect social pressure'. This refers to the problems arising from the low self-esteem of many old or severely ill and dependent people, combined with the spontaneous and negative perceptions of patients about the views of those around them. The great majority of people contemplating suicide for health-related reasons, are likely to be acutely conscious that their disabilities make them dependent on others. These disabilities may arise from illness or injury, or indeed (a much larger category) from the advancing infirmity of old age. People in this position are vulnerable. They are often afraid that their lives have become a burden to those around them. The fear may be the result of overt pressure, but may equally arise from a spontaneous tendency to place a low value on their own lives and assume that others do so too. Their feelings of uselessness are likely to be accentuated in those who were once highly active and engaged with those around them, for whom the contrast between

---

[167] J Menikoff, 'The Vulnerability of the Very Sick' (2009) Journal of Law, Medicine and Ethics 51.

[168] J Pacheco, P Hershberger, R Markert, and G Kumar, 'A Longitudinal Study of Attitudes Toward Physician-assisted Suicide and Euthanasia Among Patients with Noncurable Malignancy' (2003) American Journal of Hospice and Palliative Care 99.

[169] *R v McShane* (1977) 66 Cr App R 97 (CA).

[170] K George, 'A Woman's Choice? The Gendered Risks of Voluntary Euthanasia and Physician-assisted Suicide' (2007) 15 Medical Law Review 1.

[171] ibid, 2–3; H Biggs and K Diesfled, 'Assisted Suicide for People with Depressions: An Advocate's Perspective' (1995) Medical Law International 2.

[172] S Fisher, C Huber, L Imhof, R Mahrer Imhof, M Furter, S Ziegler, and G Bosshard, 'Suicide Assisted by Two Swiss Right-to-die Organisations' (2008) 23 Journal of Medical Ethics 810.

[173] M Battin, A van der Heide, L Ganzini, G van der Wal, and B Onwuteaka-Philipsen, 'Legal Physician-assisted Dying in Oregon and the Netherlands: Evidence Concerning the Impact on Patients in "Vulnerable" Groups' (2007) 33 Journal of Medical Ethics 591.

[174] [2014] UKSC 38 at [228].

now and then must be particularly painful. These assumptions may be mistaken but are none the less powerful for that. The legalisation of assisted suicide would be followed by its progressive normalisation, at any rate among the very old or very ill. In a world where suicide was regarded as just another optional end-of-life choice, the pressures which I have described are likely to become more powerful. It is one thing to assess some one's mental ability to form a judgment, but another to discover their true reasons for the decision which they have made and to assess the quality of those reasons. I very much doubt whether it is possible in the generality of cases to distinguish between those who have spontaneously formed the desire to kill themselves and those who have done so in response to real or imagined pressure arising from the impact of their disabilities on other people. There is a good deal of evidence that this problem exists, that it is significant, and that it is aggravated by negative modern attitudes to old age and sickness-related disability. Those who are vulnerable in this sense are not always easy to identify (there seems to be a consensus that the factors that make them vulnerable are variable and personal, and not susceptible to simple categorisation).

F. Refusal of Treatment and Death

21.82 As discussed in Chapter 8, once it is determined that a person has capacity to refuse treatment their wishes must be respected.[175] Giving them treatment without their consent is unlawful. This is so even where doing so will result in their death. As the Court of Appeal in *R (on the application of Burke) v General Medical Council*[176] explained:

> a patient who is in desperate clinical need of a blood transfusion and who has no wish to die may, for religious reasons, not wish to receive one although the consequence is almost certain death. Where a competent patient makes it clear that he does not wish to receive treatment which is, objectively, in his medical best interests, it is unlawful for doctors to administer that treatment. Personal autonomy or the right of self determination prevails.[177]

However, this does not mean that a doctor must provide treatment to a patient which is needed to keep them alive. As explained in Chapter 10 in the case of a person lacking capacity the treatment will be determined on what is in a person's best interests. If the person has capacity and has requested treatment, they do not automatically have a right to it. It may be determined that it is not appropriate for them to be given it. Even if a competent person requests treatment the doctor may determine not to give it to them because the fundamental duty of the doctor is to comply with their duty of care towards the patient. The Court of Appeal in *Burke* explained, discussing the provision of artificial nutrition and hydration (ANH):

> So far as ANH is concerned, there is no need to look far for the duty to provide this. Once a patient is accepted into a hospital, the medical staff come under a positive duty at common law to care for the patient. The authorities cited by Munby J . . . establish this proposition, if authority is needed. A fundamental aspect of this positive duty of care is a duty to take such steps as are reasonable to keep the patient alive. Where ANH is necessary to keep the patient alive, the duty of care will normally require the doctors to supply ANH. This duty

[175] *R (on the application of Burke) v General Medical Council* [2005] EWCA Civ 1003. See further A McGee, 'Finding a Way Through the Ethical and Legal Maze: Withdrawal of Medical Treatment and Euthanasia' (2005) 13 Medical Law Review 357; P de Cruz, 'The Burke Case: The Terminally Ill Patient and The Right To Life' (2007) 70 Modern Law Review 306; H Biggs, '"Taking Account of the Views of the Patient", But Only if the Clinician (and the Court) Agrees - R (Burke) v General Medical Council' [2007] Child and Family Law Quarterly 225.

[176] *R (on the application of Burke)* n 175.

[177] ibid, at [30].

> will not, however, override the competent patient's wish not to receive ANH. Where the competent patient makes it plain that he or she wishes to be kept alive by ANH, this will not be the source of the duty to provide it. The patient's wish will merely underscore that duty.[178]

As a result, the Court of Appeal refused to make a declaration that given Mr Burke's desire to be given ANH this would never be withdrawn unless he expressly so requested. He took his case to the ECtHR (*Burke v UK*[179]) but was not successful. The ECtHR found that he had not demonstrated that there was a real or imminent risk that his concern that artificial nutrition and hydration would be withdrawn. The court noted the presumption in favour of prolonging life in UK law and the fact that doctors would take into account his previous wishes when determining what treatment to provide, meant that it would be very unlikely that ANH would be withdrawn from him.

G. Reform of the Law

1. Autonomy

(i) Autonomy-based arguments

To those who take a more liberal approach to end of life decisions, it is the principle of autonomy which is central to the ethical debates over euthanasia. In short, people should be allowed to lead their own lives as they wish and have control over their bodies. If a person wishes to die it is not for anyone else to reject their decision on the basis that it is seen as foolish or contrary to some kind of quasi-religious view on the sanctity of life. We respect people's choices about how they wish to live their lives not because they are necessarily good choices, but because it is their choice.[180] John Harris writes that prohibition of euthanasia is: **21.83**

> simply a form of tyranny; an attempt to control the life of a person who has her own autonomous view about how that life should go. The evil of tyranny does not require explication in terms of the nature of sanctity of life, but rather in terms of respect for persons and of their autonomy. Euthanasia should be permitted, not because everyone should accept that it is right, nor because to rail to do so violates a defensive conception of the sanctity of life, but because to deny a person control of what, on any analysis, must be one of the most important decisions of life, is a form of tyranny, which like all acts of tyranny is an ultimate denial of respect for persons.[181]

Autonomy-based views accept that we all have different views of what a good death is. For some that will be ending their life before they feel they start to lose control of their bodies and become undignified, for others it might be striving to keep alive until the very end. But, we should allow each person to decide for themselves how they wish to die and the law should not intervene to restrict that choice, especially over a matter of such intimate and personal importance as the style of death.[182] Opponents of euthanasia, it is claimed, are seeking to impose their own ethical or religious beliefs on others.[183] **21.84**

[178] ibid, at [32].

[179] Application 19807/06, July 7 2006.

[180] A Pedain, 'The Human Rights Dimension of the Diane Pretty Case' (2003) Cambridge Law Journal 181.

[181] J Harris, 'Euthanasia and the value of life', in J Keown (ed), *Euthanasia Examined* (Cambridge University Press 1995) 202.

[182] J Raz, 'Death in Our Life' (2013) 30 Journal of Applied Philosophy 1.

[183] M Williams, 'Death Rites: Assisted Suicide and Existential Rights' (2005) 1 International Journal of Law in Context 183.

21.85 Ronald Dworkin[184] has sought to explain further why decisions over death are those which are particularly deserving of respect. He distinguishes between critical interests and experiential interests. Experiential interests are those a person has in pursuing things that a person enjoys doing in and of themselves: for example, eating ice cream; watching a favourite TV show. Critical interests are those things which we believe make us what we are and are central to our understanding of ourselves and our identity. Critical interests, he argues, are especially important to a person, and there need to be particularly good reasons if the state is to interfere in decisions relating to them. Hence it is that especial protection is given to religious belief or sexual practices because these tend to be central to a person's identity of who they are. By contrast, restrictions on a person's experiential interests are easier to justify. He argues that a person's views over how they will die are critical interests and, therefore, deserve especial respect. As he and some other philosophers have put it:

> Certain decisions are momentous in their impact on the character of a person's life—decisions about religious faith, political and moral allegiance, marriage, procreation, and death, for example. Such deeply personal decisions pose controversial questions about how and why human life has value. In a free society, individuals must be allowed to make those decisions for themselves, out of their own faith, conscience, and convictions . . . Most of us see death—whatever we think will follow it—as the final act of life's drama, and we want that last act to reflect our own convictions, those we have tried to live by, not the convictions of others forced on us in our most vulnerable moment . . .[185]

(ii) Responses to the autonomy argument

21.86 Some of the most common responses to the autonomy argument will now be considered. First, there are those who argue that the autonomous wishes of an individual who wishes to be killed need to be weighed against the wider interests of society. Our society does not allow people to do anything they want, we restrict autonomy when its exercise will cause a serious harm to others or the wider society. What, however, is the harm that allowing euthanasia will produce?

21.87 The House of Lords Select Committee on Medical Ethics has stated:

> We acknowledge that there are individual cases in which euthanasia may be seen by some to be appropriate. But individual cases cannot reasonably establish the foundation of a policy which would have such serious and widespread repercussions. Moreover dying is not only a personal or individual affair. The death of a person affects the lives of others, often in ways and to an extent which cannot be foreseen. We believe that the issue of euthanasia is one in which the interests of the individual cannot be separated from the interests of society as a whole.[186]

That, however, fails to make clear what the harm to society is. There is an implied reference to the distress that relatives and friends of the deceased may feel at their death, but it is not clear that that will be any more or less if euthanasia is permitted or not. Alternatively it may be argued that there is a basic moral value of principle which underpins society's moral order and must be protected by the law.[187] However, the argument that the criminal law should be used to uphold moral standards and principles is one that has largely fallen from favour in other areas of the law.[188]

184 R Dworkin, *Life's Dominion* (Harper Collins 1993) 231.

185 R Dworkin, T Nagel, R Nozick, J Rawls, T Scanlon, and J Jarvis Thomson, 'The Philosophers' Brief' in M Battin, R Rhodes, and A Silvers (eds), *Physician Assisted Suicide* (Routledge 1998).

186 House of Lords Select Committee on Medical Ethics, *Paper No 21* (Hansard 1994), discussed in J Keown, *Euthanasia, Ethics and Public Policy* (Cambridge University Press 2002) ch 16.

187 J Keown, *Euthanasia, Ethics and Public Policy* (Cambridge University Press 2002) ch 5.

188 J Herring, *Great Debates: Criminal Law* (Palgrave 2014) ch 1.

Perhaps the strongest case for a state interest in prohibiting euthanasia is that allowing euthanasia will mean that some patients will feel pressurized into saying they want to die. The argument can be put this way: if we allow euthanasia although this will mean that some people will be able to exercise their autonomy and die as they wish, there would be others who would be pressurized into agreeing to be killed. It would be preferable, the argument goes, to have a system which interfered in the autonomy of those who wished to die, than have a system which allowed people to be killed, even though that may not have actually been what they wanted. Being killed against your true wishes is a greater interference in your autonomy than not be allowed to be killed when you would wish to be. **21.88**

This last point raises a broader question which is the extent to which a person can, or at least people do, make informed decisions about their death. It has, for example, been argued that many close to death are so confused by pain, anguish, and a rush of varied emotions that they lack the capacity to make an autonomous choice.[189] Another argument is that many people say they want to die because they fear suffering pain,[190] but are unaware of the possibility of effective pain relief[191] and hospice care which can make the reality of the last few weeks far less unpleasant than people predict.[192] Finally, and perhaps most significantly, there is evidence that those seeking death suffer depression and that once the depression is treated the desire for death falls. Indeed in one study it was found that a remarkable 99 per cent of those who were suffering depression and stating they wished to die changed their mind following treatment for depression.[193] It is notable that a major concern among medical professionals is whether safeguards can be put in place to ensure that decisions reached are genuinely autonomous.[194] **21.89**

Even if one accepted these points[195] they do not provide a 'knock out' blow for the anti-euthanasia camp. It may be argued that these points only demonstrate that if euthanasia is to be permitted we need to have in place a very careful set of procedures to ensure that only those whose decision to die is made in a fully informed way, after due deliberation and with treatment for any depression. But that assumes we can put in place mechanisms which ensure that only fully autonomous choices are respected. The European Parliamentary Assembly, Committee on Legal Affairs and Human Rights had this to say:[196] **21.90**

> Medical professionals working within the palliative care sector have expressed the fragility of patients' desire for death and the rapid changes that, in their experience, may occur in response to good symptom control of psychological interventions. The dangers of acceding to rare requests for voluntary active euthanasia and physical assisted suicide should not be underestimated.

---

189 B Gordijn, B Crul, and Z Zylicz, 'Euthanasia and Physician-assisted Suicide', in H ten Have and D Clarke (eds), *The Ethics of Palliative Care* (Open University Press 2002).

190 E Jackson, *Medical Law* (Oxford University Press 2012) at 948 states that in Oregon the most common reason people seek assisted suicide is not pain, but the loss of autonomy.

191 F Hicks and E Rees, 'A "Pain-free" Death' (2008) 88 British Medical Bulletin 23.

192 F Randall and R Downie, *The Philosophy of Palliative Care* (Oxford University Press 2006); H ten Have and D Clarke (eds), *The Ethics of Palliative Care* (Open University Press 2002).

193 Royal College of Psychiatrists, Statement from the Royal College of Psychiatrists on Physician Assisted Suicide (RCP 2006).

194 C Seale, 'Legalisation of Euthanasia or Physician-assisted Suicide: Survey of Doctors' Attitudes' (2007) 33 Journal of Medical Ethics 742.

195 House of Lords Select Committee, *On The Assisted Dying For The Terminally Ill Bill* (TSO 2005) found however that care could not remove all pain in every case.

196 European Parliamentary Assembly, Social, Family Affairs and Health Committee, *Euthanasia* (European Parliament 2003), para 1.

Certainly it must be accepted that the reasons a person may want to die are complex and may be subject to significant change.[197] Still, supporters of euthanasia may respond that it is not impossible to imagine a case where a person has made a consistent and fully informed choice to die and it is no response to say that others will be less informed or less consistent.

21.91 There is a more theoretical issue here. There is something rather uncomfortable about autonomy being relied upon as the basis of a claim to justify euthanasia. This is because autonomy is all about enabling people to make the most of their lives and to flourish and develop as people.[198] Dying is the very antithesis of autonomy.[199] By dying a person is removing all their future autonomy and it cannot be seen as promoting giving people a range of choices over their life. Sometimes an analogy is drawn with slavery. We do not allow people to exercise their autonomy in order to become slaves. In part that is because in so doing their will robs themselves of their autonomy. There is the same issue in relation to euthanasia. Although Peter Singer has denied the analogy and argued that what makes enforced slavery objectionable is the enforcement of it.[200] Another response is that the way one dies is an important part of how a person organizes their live. Indeed a good death may be regarded by some people as a central part of their life story. Death will end autonomy in any event; in allowing euthanasia one would be allowing a person to determine when and how their closure would be.

21.92 There is a further potential difficulty in relying on autonomy as the basis for euthanasia and that is this: if autonomy is the key moral principle, would we allow anyone who wishes to be killed to die, even the love-sick teenager, who appears so frequently in the literature? Most supporters of euthanasia would not go that far and would restrict access to euthanasia to those who are suffering from a terminal illness or are in grave pain.[201] The problem is that if we are saying that euthanasia should be regarded as a matter of individual choice, then that should be so whatever the personal characteristics of the individual. Indeed, once access to euthanasia or assisted suicide is limited to those who are in a certain state of health or of a certain age the question is raised whether or not autonomy is the sole principle at play.[202]

2. Sanctity of life

21.93 To some ethicists, the sanctity of life is the key principle in the euthanasia debate.[203] However, interestingly, there is little consensus over its correct meaning among commentators or judges. John Keown has suggested that it is useful to separate the following views:[204]

(1) Vitalism. This view holds that human life has an absolute moral value. It can never, therefore, be justifiable to kill a person[205] and indeed all reasonable steps should be taken to keep a person alive. Such a view would firmly reject the idea that there comes

---

[197] H Chochinov, D Tataryn, J Clinch, and D Dudgeon, 'Will to Live in the Terminal Dying' (1999) 354 The Lancet 816.

[198] L Gormally, 'Walton, Davies, Boyd and the Legalization of Euthanasia' in J Keown (ed), *Euthanasia Examined* (Cambridge University Press 1995).

[199] C Foster, *Choosing Life, Choosing Death* (Hart 2009) 149.

[200] P Singer, 'Is the Sanctity of Life Ethic Terminally Ill?' (1995) 9 Bioethics 307.

[201] S Frileux, C Lelievre, M Sastre, E Mullet, and P Sorum, 'When is Physician-assisted Suicide or Euthanasia Acceptable?' (2003) 29 Journal of Medical Ethics 330.

[202] J Ackernman, 'Assisted Suicide, Terminal Illness, Severe Disability, and the Double Standard', in M Battin, R Rhodes, and A Silvers (eds), *Physician Assisted Suicide* (Routledge 1988).

[203] C Foster, 'What is Man, that the Judges are Mindful of Him? Lessons from the PVS Cases' (2005) Journal of Philosophy, Science and Law 1.

[204] J Keown, *Euthanasia, Ethics and Public Policy* (Cambridge University Press 2002) ch 4.

[205] Some vitalists would provide an exception where a person kills in self-defence to save their own life. For a general discussion see J McMahan, *The Ethics of Killing* (Oxford University Press 2003).

a point when a person's life is not worth living. Vitalists would therefore argue that it is never permissible to take steps to shorten a person's life nor to withhold treatment which could keep a person alive.

(2) Sanctity of life. This view holds that human life is a fundamental basic good. It shares many aspects of vitalism in that is also rejects suggestions that a person's life may become not worth living. It holds that a person should never be killed intentionally, be that through an act or an omission. It can, however, be distinguished from vitalism in two ways. First, it would permit an act which shortens life if the act was justified under the principle of double effect (see para 21.25). Under that doctrine a doctor would be permitted to give a lethal amount of medication if his or her purpose was to reduce pain, rather than kill the patient. Second, it might accept the withdrawal of treatment if the treatment was not worth providing. It would therefore, under this view, be acceptable to withdraw treatment if the benefit of the treatment was negligible. However, it would not be acceptable to withdraw treatment on the basis that the person's life was not worth living.[206]

(3) Quality of life. Under this approach it is not life per se that is of value but only the things that one can do, experience and enjoy with life. If, therefore, a person is in such pain that they are unable to appreciate or experience any pleasure then their life will lose its value. In such a case it is permissible to end life.

The principle of sanctity of life has received some judicial support. In *Airedale NHS Trust v Bland*[207] Lord Hoffmann held: **21.94**

> I start with the concept of the sanctity of life . . . [W]e have a strong feeling that there is an intrinsic value in human life, irrespective of whether it is valuable to the person concerned or indeed to anyone else. Those who adhere to religious faiths which believe in the sanctity of all God's creation and in particular that human life was created in the image of God himself will have no difficulty with the concept of the intrinsic value of human life. But even those without any religious belief think in the same way. In a case like this we should not try to analyse the rationality of such feelings. What matters is that, in one form or another, they form part of almost everyone's intuitive values. No law which ignores them can possibly hope to be acceptable.
>
> Our belief in the sanctity of life explains why we think it is almost always wrong to cause the death of another human being, even one who is terminally ill or so disabled that we think that if we were in his position we would rather be dead. Still less do we tolerate laws such as existed in Nazi Germany, by which handicapped people or inferior races could be put to death because someone else thought that their lives were useless.
>
> But the sanctity of life is only one of a cluster of ethical principles which we apply to decisions about how we should live. Another is respect for the individual human being and in particular for his right to choose how he should live his own life. We call this individual autonomy or the right of self determination. And another principle, closely connected, is respect for the dignity of the individual human being: our belief that quite irrespective of what the person concerned may think about it, it is wrong for someone to be humiliated or treated without respect for his value as a person. The fact that the dignity of an individual is an intrinsic value is shown by the fact that we feel embarrassed and think it wrong when someone behaves in a way which we think demeaning to himself, which does not show sufficient respect for himself as a person.

[206] Although some are not convinced that the distinction between an act and omission is sufficiently robust to play such a key role in this area of the law: see eg J Keown, *Euthanasia, Ethics and Public Policy* (Cambridge University Press 2002) ch 4.

[207] [1993] AC 789, 826 (HL).

> ... the fundamental principle is the principle of the sanctity of human life—a principle long recognised not only in our own society but also in most, if not all, civilised societies throughout the modern world, as indeed evidenced by its recognition both in article 2 of the European Convention for the Protection of Human Rights and Fundamental Freedoms (Cmd 8969) and in article 6 of the International Covenant of Civil and Political Rights 1966.
>
> But this principle, fundamental as it is, is not absolute ... We are concerned with circumstances in which it may be lawful to withhold from a patient medical treatment or care by means of which his life may be prolonged. But here too there is no absolute rule that the patient's life must be prolonged by such treatment or care, if available, regardless of the circumstances.[208]

Lord Wilson in *R (on the application of Nicklinson) v Ministry of Justice*[209] claimed that the principle 'is hard-wired into the minds of every living person. It lies at the heart of the common law and of international human rights and it is also an ethical principle of the first magnitude.'

21.95 John Keown has complained that such judicial comments, holding that the principle of sanctity of life is not an absolute one in English law, are based on a misunderstanding of what the doctrine teaches.[210] He argues that these statements have wrongly equated sanctity of life with vitalism. He argues that if the notion of sanctity of life was properly understood it would be regarded as an absolute principle in English law.

21.96 Supporters of the doctrine of sanctity of life argue that we must recognize that every life has value in itself. Many of those supporting this view write from a religious perspective, arguing that everyone's life is equally precious in God's eyes. However, the principle has been supported from a non-religious viewpoint. Somerville writes of the 'deeply intuitive sense of relatedness or connectedness to other people and to the world and the universe in which we live'. She sees the prohibition on euthanasia and assisted suicide reflecting an acceptance of the mysteries of life and death.[211] By contrast, Emily Jackson has argued that the sanctity of life doctrine has 'no coherent secular basis' and that 'the sanctity principle, with its commitment to the intrinsic value of lives which have ceased to contain anything of value, does not make sense, other than as an article of religious faith'. She rejects the view that 'human life is always intrinsically valuable, and that its deliberate destruction is always necessarily a bad thing'.[212] She, and other supporters of euthanasia, tend to argue that although life is precious and valuable, that does not mean that all life must be valued for its own sake.[213] To keep a person alive when they long for death and are wracked with pain is not to treasure life, but to demean it.[214]

21.97 Critics of the sanctity of life principle argue that although supporters of it are entitled to their views, they should not impose them on others who reject the view that life has inherent value.[215] They insist that respect should also be shown to those who hold the view that for them life only has value in the experiences of the person whose life it is. Ronald Dworkin has written of a person suffering Alzheimer's:

[208] [1993] AC 789 (HL).

[209] [2014] UKSC 38 at [199].

[210] J Keown, 'Restoring the Moral and Intellectual Shape to the Law after Bland' (1997) 113 Law Quarterly Review 418.

[211] M Sommerville, *Death Talk* (McGill Queen's University Press 2001) 134.

[212] E Jackson, 'Secularism, Sanctity and the Wrongness of Killing' (2008) 3 Biosocieties 125, 126.

[213] J Harris, *The Value of Life* (Oxford University Press 1984).

[214] J Rachels, *The End of Life* (Oxford University Press 1986).

[215] E Jackson, n 212, 125.

> [He] is no longer capable of the acts or attachment that can give [life] value. Value cannot be poured into a life from the outside; it must be generated by the person whose life it is, and this is no longer possible for him.[216]

Contrast that view with the following comment of John Finnis who supports the sanctity of life view:

> Human Life is indeed the concrete reality of the human person. In sustaining human bodily life, in however impaired a condition, one is sustaining the person whose life it is. In refusing to choose to violate it, one respects the person in the most fundamental and indispensable way. [217]

The contrast between the two views is notable. To Finnis, sustaining life is important and valuable in itself, but for Dworkin, the value is only found if the life is so valued by the person themselves.

3. Dignity

This is a concept which is used by those on both sides of the debate. For supporters of euthanasia it is crucial that we support euthanasia in order to protect the dignity of the dying. As a person dies they gradually lose control of physical and mental functions. This can increase the degree of helplessness and dependence. This can lead to a person's inability to care for themselves or others. Richard Tur cites the following description of a prolonged painful death: **21.98**

> . . . death is dreadful to watch. The skin and mucosa dry out: the blood thickens; the kidneys no longer produce urine and gradually die. The eyes become damaged for the lack of tears; the mouth is infested by fungal infections because the natural cleaning by saliva is lost. The body is gradually poisoned by the breakdown of products which can no longer be excreted. In the airways crusts of dried mucus develop which makes breathing steadily more difficult and so the unconscious patient fades away under the eyes of doctors, nurses and family. It can well take ten days or more before death arrives and in dying the patient becomes a monument to medical and judicial cowardice and hypocrisy.[218]

The argument is then made that it is more dignified to allow a person to die at a time and in a manner of their choosing than to go through such an undignified death.

The importance of the notion of dignity has even received judicial support. Munby J in *R (on the application of A, B, X and Y) v East Sussex CC and the Disability Rights Commission (No 2)*[219] stated: **21.99**

> The recognition and protection of human dignity is one of the core values—in truth the core value—of our society and, indeed, of all the societies which are part of the European family of nations and which have embraced the principles of the Convention. It is a core value of the common law, long pre-dating the Convention . . . The invocation of the dignity of the patient in the form of declaration habitually used when the court is exercising its inherent declaratory jurisdiction in relation to the gravely ill or dying is not some meaningless incantation designed to comfort the living or to assuage the consciences of those involved in making life and death decisions: it is a solemn affirmation of the law's and of society's recognition of our humanity and of human dignity as something fundamental.

---

[216] R Dworkin, *Life's Dominion* (Harper Collins 1993), 230.

[217] J Finnis, 'Bland: Crossing the Rubicon?' (1993) 109 Law Quarterly Review 329.

[218] Dr B Smalhout, quoted in R Tur, 'Special Defence Based on the Ethics of Doctors: "The Doctor's Defence and Professional Ethics"' (2002) 13 King's College Law Journal 75, 95. No doubt some experts in palliative care would deny that such a death could occur with good care.

[219] [2003] EWHC 167 (Admin) at [86].

21.100 It is not clear what dignity adds to autonomy-based arguments.[220] Presumably, the claim is not that a person who is dependent on others lacks dignity. That would mean a person who was perfectly happy in their state of dependency was automatically undignified which would be problematic. It might mean that many disabled people were automatically undignified. In the light of that, if what is meant is that dignity is in its nature undignified, then only a very extreme state of illness where a person's body was so invaded by medical procedures that their humanity has been stripped away. That would apply to few cases. It may, therefore, be better to see dignity as an argument to bolster an autonomy-based argument, rather than being an argument in its own right. Where a person feels they lack dignity then there is a particularly strong case for allowing them to exercise their autonomy to avoid it.

21.101 The argument against euthanasia also seeks to rely on the notion of dignity. Amarasekara and Bagaric argue:

> It could be suggested that allowing a patient to die in pain against his or her wish is undignified. But killing a person hardly seems to be according him or her much concern or respect or placing much valued on the person's life—it would seem to be the antithesis of respecting one's dignity.[221]

Indeed, opponents of euthanasia argue that good palliative care and effective pain relief can mean that death does not need to be undignified.[222] But, again, that may depend on who is deciding what dignity means.

21.102 For a long time deaths have taken place in the medical context in a largely unregulated way. It is perhaps understandable that people had rather looked the other way than addressed what happened. As John Robertson has noted:

> As long as we can dress the choice to take life in other clothes, such as refusing treatment or relieving pain, then we can acknowledge it. But naked decisions to take life as such are, to paraphrase T.S. Eliot, too much 'reality' to bear openly. We must hide the reality of how we made end of life decisions for fear of what we will find. Yet in doing so, society risks even greater harm. Many persons who need assisted suicide to relieve their suffering will not receive it. Some persons may still receive such assistance covertly, but without the advantages of openly following medical protocols that can assure efficacy and prevent arbitrary and abusive practices . . . If we practice and tolerate assisted suicide and euthanasia, we certainly need to do it openly to reassure the public and prevent abuse. At the same time, as T.S. Eliot reminds us, 'humankind cannot bear very much reality.' We also cannot tolerate the notion that doctors will openly take life, even with proper reporting and bureaucratic oversight. We are caught in the dilemma that we can permit assisted suicide only by not admitting it . . .[223]

We have probably reached the stage in our history where turning the other way is no longer an option in relation to legal regulation of ending life in the medical context. Hence we have seen an increase in calls to reform the law. In a recent study, 80 per cent of members of the public questioned would support doctors assisting patients to die if requested.[224] Lady Hale in *R (on the application of Nicklinson) v Ministry of Justice)*:[225]

> It would not be beyond the wit of a legal system to devise a process for identifying those people, those few people, who should be allowed help to end their own lives. There would

---

220 C Foster, *Human Dignity in Bioethics and the Law* (Hart 2013).
221 K Amarakekara and M Bagaric, *Euthanasia, Morality and the Law* (Peter Lang 2002).
222 S Woods, *Death's Dominion—Ethics at the End of Life* (Open University Press 2007) ch 1.
223 J Robertson, 'Respect of Life in Bioethical Dilemmas' (1997) Santa Clara Law Review 329, 342–43.
224 D Price, 'What Shape to Euthanasia after Bland?' (2009) 125 Law Quarterly Review 125, 145.
225 [2014] UKSC 38, at [314].

be four essential requirements. They would firstly have to have the capacity to make the decision for themselves. They would secondly have to have reached the decision freely without undue influence from any quarter. They would thirdly have had to reach it with full knowledge of their situation, the options available to them, and the consequences of their decision: that is not the same, as Dame Elizabeth pointed out in *Re B (Treatment)*, as having first-hand experience of those options. And they would fourthly have to be unable, because of physical incapacity or frailty, to put that decision into effect without some help from others. I do not pretend that such cases would always be easy to decide, but the nature of the judgments involved would be no more difficult than those regularly required in the Court of Protection or the Family Division . . .

There has been a trickle of private members bills which have been introduced to amend the law in this area, none of which have been passed. The latest is the Assisted Dying Bill 2014, the first clause of which states: **21.103**

(1) A person who is terminally ill may request and lawfully be provided with assistance to end his or her own life.
(2) Subsection (1) only applies where the person—
(a) has a clear and settled intention to end his or her own life;
(b) has made a declaration to that effect in accordance with section 3; and
(c) on the day the declaration is made—
(i) is aged 18 or over; and
(ii) has been ordinarily resident in England and Wales for not less than one year.

There was not time to pass the bill before the 2015 general election. It is clearly drafted with a significant number of safeguards which are designed to mitigate fears about the impact on vulnerable people. However, these restrictions mean that someone facing years of a painful illness would not fall under its remit because it only applies to a person who has six months or less to live.

By contrast the Medical Treatment (Prevention of Euthanasia) Bill proposed in 1999 stated in clause 1: **21.104**

It shall be unlawful for any person responsible for the care of a patient to withdraw or withhold from the patient medical treatment or sustenance if his purpose or one of his purposes in doing so is to hasten or otherwise cause the death of the patient.

This Bill attempted to tighten the law in that it prevents a doctor withholding treatment from a patient if the purpose is to hasten death. It would have outlawed the present treatment of patients suffering from PVS, unless doctors could claim that the treatment is withheld not to produce death, but because the treatment is not producing any benefit to the patient. The use of the word 'purpose' rather than 'intend' was designed to make it clear that a doctor who foresaw death being the result of her or his treatment or non-treatment would not be breaking the law if death was not her or his purpose. However, some commentators felt the Bill (if enacted) would have placed doctors in a difficult position.[226]

Of course, a strong case can be made for leaving the law as it is. McCall Smith accepts the present law as a satisfactory, if a little untidy, compromise between the different arguments.[227] He even finds the uncertainty in the present law a benefit: **21.105**

[226] A Morris, 'Easing the Passing: End of Life Decisions and the Medical Treatment (Prevention of Euthanasia) Bill' (2000) 8 Medical Law Review 300.

[227] A McCall Smith, 'Euthanasia: The Strength of the Middle Ground' (1999) 7 Medical Law Review 194.

> Doctors know full well what they are doing when they increase a dose of diamorphine, but they need not describe their act, to themselves or to others as an act of killing. This approach has been described as hypocritical, but it accords with a moral distinction which is meaningful for doctors, then why should they be denied the comfort it affords them? The moral life is possibly more subtly nuanced than some of the proponents of euthanasia would have us believe. We live by more metaphor, and the metaphor of helping rather than killing, may be a valuable one to those whose duty it is to look after the terminally ill.[228]

Hazel Biggs,[229] however, finds the uncertainty and complexity of the law problematic: 'Sophistry and creative legalism may be effective in the court room, but medical practice cannot always be tailored to take advantage of them.'[230] She is particularly critical of the failure of the law to provide clear guidance to those working day-to-day in the area. But to some commentators this uncertainty is a benefit. Martha Minow writes:

> I think the most honest statement of the issues presented in the physician-assisted suicide cases is this: the Court faced a choice of two lies to countenance. By lie I mean knowing misrepresentation; by countenance to extend approval or toleration. The first lie is that physicians do not already, and regularly, participate in assisting dying patients to end their lives. Every physician I have encountered acknowledges as much; many have written about it . . . The second lie is that permitting such assistance would not systematically and routinely be used to push dying people into death. The problem is not merely risks of abuse; the problem arises from the inauguration of a regime in which people would have to justify continuing to live . . . It is better to live with the lie that prohibition works so that, at the margin, those who engage in it do so with trembling.[231]

Minow's quotation issues a challenge to those on both sides of the debate. To those who support the current law she asks whether we can be sure the current system of unregulated unacknowledged killing adequately protects patients, while to those who support liberalizing legislation she asks whether we can be entirely confident that any reform will not inevitably involve the killing of at least a few people who are not genuinely consenting to die. Whether and when reform comes may depend on which side of the debate is more effective in answering these challenges.

H. Conclusion

21.106 This chapter has sought to outline the current law on issues relating to euthanasia and assisted suicide. A helpful summary was provided by Lord Sumption *R (on the application of Nicklinson) v Ministry of Justice)*:[232]

> (1) In law, the state is not entitled to intervene to prevent a person of full capacity who has arrived at a settled decision to take his own life from doing so. However, such a person does not have a right to call on a third party to help him to end his life.
> (2) A person who is legally and mentally competent is entitled to refuse food and water, and to reject any invasive manipulation of his body or other form of treatment, including artificial feeding, even though without it he will die. If he refuses, medical practitioners must comply with his wishes. . .. A patient (or prospective patient) may express his wishes on these points by an advance decision (or 'living will').

---

228 ibid, 206–07.
229 H Biggs, *Euthanasia* (Hart 2001).
230 ibid, 5.
231 M Minow, 'Which Question? Which Lie? Reflections on the Physician Assisted Suicide Cases' (1997) 1 Supreme Court Review 1, 20–22, 30.
232 [2014] UKSC 38 at [225].

(3) A doctor may not advise a patient how to kill himself. But a doctor may give objective advice about the clinical options (such as sedation and other palliative care) which would be available if a patient were to reach a settled decision to kill himself. The doctor is in no danger of incurring criminal liability merely because he agrees in advance to palliate the pain and discomfort involved should the need for it arise. This kind of advice is no more or less than his duty. The law does not countenance assisted suicide, but it does not require medical practitioners to keep a patient in ignorance of the truth lest the truth should encourage him to kill himself. The right to give and receive information is guaranteed by article 10 of the Convention. If the law were not as I have summarised it, I have difficulty in seeing how it could comply.

(4) Medical treatment intended to palliate pain and discomfort is not unlawful only because it has the incidental consequence, however foreseeable, of shortening the patient's life . . .

(5) Whatever may be said about the clarity or lack of it in the Director's published policy, the fact is that prosecutions for encouraging or assisting suicide are rare. . . .

However, even that summary is not uncontroversial. The very first point appears to overlook the fact that there can be a duty on the state to stop people committing suicide (see para 21.44).

The law is being subject to powerful human rights challenges and it is likely that it will continue to face such challenges in the future. *R (on the application of Nicklinson) v Ministry of Justice)*[233] has clearly put the ball in Parliament's court. Some kind of reform seems almost inevitable in the not too distant future. **21.107**

[233] [2014] UKSC 38.

22

DEATH

Murray Earle

A. Introduction

1. A social perspective

22.01 In an interesting review of attitudes to the diagnosis and the demonstration of death, Powner and his colleagues[1] suggested that neither the controversy nor the process had changed substantially over the past 250 years. Change, it was posited, lies not in the solution of the essentially technical fundamental of when does death occur and how can we be sure that it *has* occurred but, rather, in the philosophical, theological, technological, and political environment in which decisions are made and, by extension, the legal context in which decisions are required to be made. And yet from the eighteenth century, legal demands for greater precision on time of death, to a more nuanced understanding of death itself, definitions have evolved in favour of greater emphasis on brain function. The last twenty-five years have seen changes in definitions of death that have occurred alongside a greater emphasis on patient autonomy as the dominant principle of health care. At the same time, the growth of moral

[1] D J Powner, B M Ackerman, and A Grenvik, 'Medical Diagnosis of Death in Adults: Historical Contributions to Current Controversies' (1996) 348 Lancet 1219.

pluralism, together with the waning influence of theism, has contrived to expand the range of choices on both sides of the doctor/patient relationship that are *acceptable* to society.

The principles of moral pluralism and individual autonomy are, of course, demonstrated most often and significantly in life. They do, however strongly influence our modern approach to death not only in terms of our moral and physical outlook but also, in particular, as to how far we should manage and control the time and the mode of dying. Our powers to accelerate and to delay the time of death are steadily increasing and, as a corollary, the ability of and the opportunities for the healthcare professionals to modify the way in which we die, are widening. Paradoxically, at the same time they are being restricted, as the patient's wishes,[2] and those of close relatives, assume greater significance in decision making. Along with this, society's attitudes to the dignity due to the dead body and to the disposal of dead human tissue are also changing, albeit not always without an element of ambivalence.[3] **22.02**

The need for professional and legal overview of these developments is self-evident and provides the setting for this chapter. Even so, it must be appreciated that its scope is limited to death itself. Decisions that affect the mode of death are made in life; they are subjects in themselves and they are analysed in detail in other chapters in this book—most notably, perhaps, in Chapters 19 and 21, but also significantly in Chapter 10. Accordingly, this chapter confines itself to considerations of death per se. The chapter is, effectively, in two parts. The first concerns the diagnosis of death and, concurrently, the more philosophical concept of what *constitutes*—and what does *not* constitute—death; the second addresses the more mundane administrative law concerned with the lawful disposal of the dead. Continuity between the two themes is provided by consideration of how we do and how we ought to care for the dying and the dead body itself. **22.03**

B. The Medical Definition of Death

1. Contexts of definition

Death is defined in the *Oxford English Dictionary* as 'the action or fact of dying or being killed; the end of the life of a person or organism'. An immediate conceptual difficulty emerges when we consider the additions in *Steadman's Medical Dictionary*, to the effect that, 'in multicellular organisms, death is a gradual process at the cellular level with tissues varying in their ability to withstand deprivation of oxygen'. How one defines death depends to a large extent on the purpose of the definition and the context in which it is applied. The former, lay version is no more than a useful social construct; the latter addition, however, raises medical and scientific issues which barely concern—and may, indeed, confuse—the layman or the lawyer who merely want to know: 'Is that *person* now dead?' At the other end of the scale, however, the pure scientist—and, most proximately, the transplant surgeon—will be concerned with so-called *cellular death*, that is, the irrecoverable loss of function of the individual cells of the body. The bedside doctor stands somewhere between these extremes. Certainly, the immediate problem lies in the diagnosis of *somatic* death—or death of the *person*; put another way, when can he or she say to the relatives: 'the patient is dead'? The doctor is, however, also well aware that death is a process; the specific dilemma lies in **22.04**

[2] A valid advance directive as to terminal treatment is now statutorily binding on the care provider: Mental Capacity Act 2005, s 26.

[3] For an intriguing survey of the ethics of the mortuary and the anatomy room, see D G Jones and M I Whitaker, *Speaking for the Dead: the Human Body in Biology and Medicine* (2nd edn, Ashgate 2009).

the search for a definable and acceptable endpoint to that process, that will allow the two forms to coalesce.

2. Cellular death

22.05 Cell function ultimately depends upon an efficient supply of oxygen. Without oxygen, the active elements within the cell become devitalized and its structure disintegrates. The diagnostic criteria for both somatic and cellular death are, accordingly, satisfied by the *ultimate* conclusion that death is 'a permanent state of tissue anoxia'.[4] Clearly, however, this definition is unhelpful in a practical situation and, even at the theoretical level, it derives from a misleading simplification of a process that is further complicated in two main ways. First, the response of different cell types to a similar anoxic—or, more commonly, hypoxic[5]—insult varies. Since oxygen is the body's source of energy, this variability depends, to a very large extent, on the amount of work cells do in life. Thus, we are presented with a more basic philosophical problem. In speaking of 'tissue anoxia', are we referring to *all the tissues* or to a select few? Or, alternatively, can we say that the body is dead when *some* of its tissues are alive? Second, and collateral to this, cells that have been rendered dysfunctional due to a similar degree of oxygen starvation may be able to recover to different degrees when the oxygen supply is restored. Thus, the definition begs the question of what is permanent and, logically, that question is one that can only be answered in retrospect—any other approach is by way of surmise. Moreover, the degree of certainty within that surmise is time-dependent—the longer the delay, the more sure one can be that successful, or useful, re-oxygenation is impossible.

22.06 The present writer is grateful to Professor Kenyon Mason who observed in the previous edition of this book that these distinctions are demonstrated very well in the kidney, which consists, in essence, of glomerular and tubular components. The former have the relatively passive task of filtering the macromolecules of protein in the blood so that they are not lost in the urine; the latter, by contrast, are constantly active in controlling the reabsorption or rejection of the blood electrolytes that have passed through the glomerular filter. If, therefore, the kidney is starved of oxygen, as so often occurs during crushing injury, the glomeruli may be spared but the tubules will necrose. Equally, however, the tubular cells have remarkable powers of recovery. The life of a person suffering from renal tubular necrosis may, then, be saved by temporary dialysis; persons whose glomeruli have been destroyed, on the other hand, will require either lifetime dialysis or renal transplantation therapy.

22.07 Considerations of cellular death are, of course, vital to the practice of transplantation therapy (a topic which receives comprehensive critique in Chapter 19). For present purposes, their importance stems from the fact that they lie at the heart of the concept of brain or brain-stem death, to which we return below. What has been said so far is enough to show that the definition of death in terms of *cellular* death does little to help the grieving relative at the bedside; in addition, there may be times when, for both medical and social reasons, we *need* to know the earliest point at which we can say that life is extinct. Cellular death is a process which, if it is to be applied to the *whole* body, can be long and drawn-out. As a result, the majority of the modern discussion of death is concerned with whether or not, and to what extent, we can pre-empt the ultimate truism and declare the *person* to be dead.

[4] S A M McLean and J K Mason, *Legal and Ethical Aspects of Healthcare* (Cambridge University Press 2003) 192.

[5] Situations in which the living body is exposed to *total* deprivation of oxygen (anoxia) are relatively rare. In practice, cellular damage results far more commonly from diminished oxygen supply (hypoxia).

3. Death of the person

In practical and social terms, the declaration of death requires not only certainty, but also immediacy. Near kin need to know if their *relative* is dead and the law requires to know *when*—and how—he or she died. We have moved away from academic considerations of the nature of death and are looking at the *fact* of death of the human *being*. To do this, we must refer to what Powner and his colleagues[6] identified as the 'centralist theorem' whereby the 'vital principle' of life is held to reside in a single organ or organ system, as opposed to a decentralist theorem that supports the idea of the soul, or makes reference to personhood. Death occurs, then, when that single organ permanently ceases to function. Looked at in these terms, the identification of somatic death depends on which organ is regarded as the keeper of the vital principle, and this dilemma is best appreciated through what may be conveniently called the triadic approach to death. **22.08**

4. The triadic approach to the diagnosis of death

Given an adequate oxygen supply, the heart will continue to beat independently of higher control—it did, for instance, often beat for some twenty minutes following the broken neck of judicial hanging; the cause of acute, natural cardiac failure, therefore, lies within the heart itself. Respiration, on the other hand, depends upon and is controlled by the respiratory centre—a nervous 'battery' situated in the brain stem—and, in practice, acute respiratory failure of the type which is important in the present context is almost invariably the result of central damage—that is, damage to the brain stem.[7] Oxygenation of the tissues, or cellular life, is, thus, based on a servo-type mechanism: the heart depends for its own tissue oxygen on the lungs which, in turn, are useless without the distributive function of the heart. Together they supply oxygen to the brain which, therefore, cannot function in the absence of competent heart and lungs—yet the lungs, themselves, depend upon a functioning brain stem. The only segment of this triad which cannot be substituted is the brain. For this reason, it has been suggested that all death is, and always has been, brain-stem death and that circulatory arrest just happens to be the most common way by which such death is brought about.[8] **22.09**

It is, however, simpler to visualize the brain, the heart, and the lungs as forming a 'cycle of life' which can be broken at any point. Looked at in this way, it is fundamentally wrong to speak of two *types* of death, that is, cardiorespiratory or brain death; it is simply that different criteria, and different tests, can be used for identifying that the cycle has been broken.[9] And it cannot be overemphasized that this is a *basic* premise having no necessary association with the justification of beating-heart organ donation. Be that as it may, it is, nonetheless, also clear that we *must* separate the constituents of the triad as circumstances demand. Thus, while we would normally use the heart and lungs as the medium through which to make the diagnosis, we are forced to turn to the brain when the natural functional condition of either is obscured by the intervention of a machine, not least because the brain is the 'body's **22.10**

---

6 See n 1 above. And see another relatively early British contribution to the debate: K Boyd, 'Attitudes to Death: Some Historical Notes' (1977) 3 J Med Ethics 124.

7 Primary *respiratory* failure is now a relatively rare cause of death and, when it occurs, it is the result of muscular paralysis due to generalized motor neurological disease. Moreover, respiratory failure per se can be readily replaced by the respirator or ventilator. By contrast, it is an inevitable consequence of cardiac failure and, for the purposes of this chapter, cardiovascular and cardiorespiratory death or failure can be regarded as synonymous.

8 C Pallis, 'Return to Elsinore' (1990) 16 J Med Ethics 10.

9 This was much the view taken by the original US President's Commission for the Study of Ethical Problems in Medicine, *Defining Death: Medical, Legal and Ethical Issues in the Definition of Death* (1981).

central controller'.[10] It is, therefore, still necessary to discuss the diagnosis as if it comprised distinct entities.

5. Cardiorespiratory death

22.11 Despite the amount of attention that is spent on discussion of alternatives, this is the definition of somatic death that is relied upon in almost all cases—indeed, any alternative policy would be unsustainable in practice. At the same time, it is in many ways surprising that a diagnosis of such importance is commonly made using the simplest of tools—the finger tips and the stethoscope.

22.12 So much of what has been said depends, however, on the circumstances of death. Currently, most occur in hospital or at home where the dying person has been the object of constant attention. Death is anticipated and it is the common experience of both health care professionals and relatives that one knows instinctively when a person has died; he or she stops breathing and the struggle to survive ceases abruptly, the life-force apparently 'switching off'. Yet even within this apparently uncomplicated scenario, instinct fails to accommodate an essential element of cardiorespiratory death: its irrevocability. In natural circumstances, the build-up of carbon dioxide following respiratory failure may, of itself, be sufficient to reignite a flagging respiratory centre and a heart block may correct itself spontaneously, even if only for a short time. Beyond this, active intervention can, as is well known, restore cardiac function and result in cardioversion, along with cerebral perfusion. The problems associated with the 'do not resuscitate order' are discussed elsewhere in this book; here, it need only be remarked that the mere existence of such orders acknowledges the possibility of reversal. The definitive report on the subject from the Academy of Royal Medical Colleges[11] indicates that a period of five minutes following cardiorespiratory arrest and the absence of pupillary reflexes will be sufficient to determine permanent failure.

22.13 A ventilator is always available unless its use would be futile and this introduces the further complication in the scenario of cardiorespiratory death that is illustrated by the patient who 'dies' during the process of resuscitation following cardiac collapse. Normally, such a patient will be undergoing intensive care and the indicator of a terminal condition will be a 'flat' electrocardiogram. The ECG, however, cannot foretell the future. In particular, it cannot indicate whether or not further attempted resuscitation will be successful. What degree of resuscitative measures must, then, be employed in order to satisfy the criterion of irreversibility? Effectively, this can be answered only in terms of clinical experience.[12]

(i) Apparent death

22.14 These remarks, however, cover only what might be seen as the ideal situation—the death in hospital that is anticipated. Establishing the *fact of death* in other circumstances may not always be so easy. This is because certain conditions minimize the body's need for cellular energy and, in the extreme of such circumstances, *functional* physiological *arrest* may lead to *apparent* death. Typical examples of such conditions include the presence of metabolic disease per se, hypothermia, malnutrition, and drug overdose—and the presence of these,

---

[10] The 'Central Controller Thesis' adopted by the 1981 study cited above, and reiterated in subsequent US President's Commission studies that also reject the 'concept of higher brain death'. See A G Thomas, 'Continuing the Definition of Death Debate: the Report of the President's Council on Bioethics on Controversies in the Determination of Death' (2012) 26(2) Bioethics 101–07.

[11] *A Code of Practice for the Diagnosis and Confirmation of Death* (2008). We return to the subject in a different context at para 22.22.

[12] For which, see the Guidance from the British Medical Association, the Resuscitation Council (UK), and the Royal College of Nursing, *Decisions Relating to Cardiopulmonary Resuscitation* (October, 2014).

either alone or in combination, is not uncommon given the standards to which many are reduced even in a modern society. 'Suspended animation' of some degree, is a rare, but real, possibility.[13]

It is arguable that death should not be certified until there is some unequivocal objective evidence that it has occurred. Such a sign would be the appearance of post-mortem lividity due to hypostasis—that is, discoloration of the skin due to pooling of the blood in dependent parts of the body following cessation of its circulation. Post-mortem lividity, however, takes up to an hour to develop to a recognizable extent; moreover, as a sign of death, it depends on defining death in terms of cardiovascular collapse. The modern stethoscope is a major advance on its predecessors that gave rise to the likes of the London Society for the Prevention of Premature Burial, established in 1896, and the establishment in the eighteenth century of hospitals for the dead in Germany and Austria, to house corpses until decomposition had started,[14] and it would be close to absurd to insist on further corroboration of clinical observation—what matters is that medical practitioners should be *aware* of the possibility of 'apparent death', and should act accordingly.[15] That does not mean, however, that 'real' death may not be preceded by apparent death. Indeed, such a transition may well be seen as within the natural order of dying—which is a subject that merits consideration of itself. **22.15**

(ii) The agonal period

It will be apparent that, given a cardiorespiratory definition of death, the tissues will, in normal circumstances, have been at least partially oxygenated up to the moment when the distribution of oxygen ceases. Thus, there will be a time following somatic death and prior to cellular death when the tissues are still functioning—and it is appropriate to regard, and to define, this as the agonal period, coming as it does from the Greek 'to struggle' and pertaining in medicine to death, dying, or extreme suffering. **22.16**

In general, while this is of obviously profound significance in the field of transplantation therapy, it has, with one major exception, no clinical or ethical importance. The exception lies in the near-metaphysical relationship between 'life'—or the 'vital principle'—and brain function. The brain consists of cellular tissue. As such, its constituents will die when deprived of oxygenated blood; but the speed at which they do so will depend, on the one hand, on the oxygen needs of the individual cells and, on the other hand, on how well supplied with oxygen those cells were immediately before the supply was cut off. In short, what were their reserves of oxygen? There is no simple answer to this question. In this respect, the brain is to be distinguished from any other organ by way of its cognitive function. It is virtually undeniable that at least some cognitive function is maintained between irreversible cardiorespiratory failure and functional brain failure and, if one believes (as many do and **22.17**

[13] See, eg, J Pejares and F Merayo, 'Unique Clinical Case Both of Hypoxia and Hypothermia Studied in an 18-year-old Aerial Stowaway' (1970) 41 Aerospace Med 1416. Although this is an extreme example, it is a not infrequent one, with regular press reports of survival of so-called 'wheel-well passengers', where the cold protects the brain without stopping the heart. Note that a fall in body temperature would not be an objective test of death were environmental hypothermia—which has this protective quality—to be a possible cause.

[14] See, eg, M Alexander, '"The Rigid Embrace of the Narrow House": Premature Burial and the Signs of Death' (1980) 10 Hastings Center Rep 25. The first *vitae dubiae asylum* (Hospital for Doubtful Life), opened in Weimar in 1792; see M P Park and R H R Park, 'Fear and Humour in the Art of Cholera' (2010) 103(12) J R Soc Med 481–83.

[15] Note that the problem of apparent death extends further into the realm of brain-stem death; this is discussed in greater detail at paras 22.26–22.32.

which will be discussed later) that 'life' depends on cognitive brain function,[16] one must accept that 'death' depends on failure of the latter rather than of the former.

22.18 It is to be emphasized that this discussion is not, as yet, concerned with the *diagnosis* of death by way of the measurement of brain function. Rather it refers to how the diagnosis by way of cardiorespiratory function should be regarded as confirmed.[17] Looked at in this way, it is a *clinical* problem—or a matter of managing the dying process. This period of potential 'consciousness-in-dying' may represent the ultimate, and a significant, period of a person's 'life'; as such it is, in many ways, surprising how little *legal* attention it has attracted. At what point in time after cardiorespiratory failure does respect for the dignity of the human being pass to the lesser, albeit still important, degree of respect that is attributable to the human corpse?

22.19 The subject has received far greater attention in the US following the introduction of the Uniform Determination of Death Act 1980 which, in essence, states that an individual who has sustained either:

(1) irreversible cessation of circulatory and respiratory functions, or;
(2) irreversible cessation of all functions of the entire brain, including the brain stem, is dead.

The Act serves to combine the common law definition with the *alternative* medically sustainable definition of the loss of *all* brain functions. This definition may be used when the use of life-sustaining medical technology precludes recourse to the common law definition.

22.20 Undoubtedly, the Act was intended to identify two *diagnostic methods* by which to define death and which could be used according to the circumstances. The fallacy inherent in confusing the admission of 'brain death' as a diagnostic criterion of death, with the needs of transplant therapy has, however, become so ingrained that the Act has often been interpreted as defining two *types of death* which could be called in aid of organ procurement as and when needed. Redefinitions for the purposes of organ transplantation, it is and has been argued, are legal fictions that may be untenable in the long term.[18]

22.21 Although the result has been confusion, not only in the public but also the professional mind,[19] it should also be recognized that there has in recent years been evidence of greater consensus among medical professionals in a 'unifying concept of human death'. While different sets of criteria might be employed, where there is consensus is in the requirement of an irreversible loss of two capacities in combination: the capacity to breathe and the capacity for consciousness.[20] Confusion and contention are still to be found within the debate surrounding the use of non-heart-beating organ donors (NHBD)—latterly known as Donation after Cardiac Death (DCD)—in which, essentially, the dying patient is treated

---

[16] This would be linked logically to the credible belief, for example, that a guillotined head has some understanding of its condition.

[17] See, in particular, C Pallis, n 8.

[18] See, eg, D J Hill and D W Evans, Letter in response to D Gardiner, S Schmie, A Madara, and H Opdam, 'International Perspective on the Diagnosis of Death' (2012) 108 (S1) Br J Anaesthesia i14–i28.

[19] A M Capron, 'Brain Death—Well Settled Yet Still Unresolved' (2001) 344 New Engl J Med 1244, quotes, as an illustration of judicial vagary, 'when the life-supporting measures were suspended, death ensued [although the person] was legally dead even before heroic life-support procedures were discontinued' *Commonwealth v Kostra* 502 A 2d 1287 (Pa, Super Ct, 1985) at 1291.

[20] D Gardiner, S Schmie, A Madara, and H Opdam, 'International Perspective on the Diagnosis of Death' (2012) 108 (S1) Br J Anaesthesia i14–i28. The dual irreversibility of the capacity to breath and the capacity for consciousness in UK and US standards is further considered in J Oram and P Murphy, 'Diagnosis of Death' (2011) 11 (5) Contin Educ Anaesth Crit Care Pain 193.

and prepared for organ donation once his or her heart has stopped beating. The confusion and controversy may stem from the medico-legal need to provide the 'best service' as a defence against litigation in negligence; it may also be due to a conflict with the requirement of irreversibility, which if not yet met implies the possibility of effective Cardiopulmonary Resuscitation (CPR). Prior to the evolution of beating-heart donation, NHBD *was* the optimum treatment; subsequently, however, the efficacy of the latter has to be measured against that of the former, where the transplant surgeon will be anxious to reduce the warm-anoxic interval to as close to zero as is practicable. All of which may appear relevant to transplantation therapy and irrelevant to the philosophy surrounding the diagnosis of death—yet it is trite to remark that the two are intertwined, as is illustrated in this quotation:

> [D]eclarations of death using circulatory-respiratory criteria typically wait for fifteen minutes or more of cardiac arrest and apnoea before retroactively assigning a time of death. . . . The situation *necessarily* changes in cases of non-heart-beating donors, because the need to avoid ischemic damage to organs requires that a significantly shorter waiting period be used. (emphasis added)[21]

Clearly there is both a practical and an ideological conflict as to which should take precedence, but this should not affect the ultimate *diagnosis* of death. The present writer takes the view that this should involve loss of cognitive ability followed by irreversible circulatory arrest, but that both should be present for a definitive diagnosis.

Again, it will rightly be said that, in the circumstance envisaged, absence of higher brain function following cardiorespiratory collapse cannot be proven save in unusual conditions—it would, for example, be bizarre to suggest that every death in hospital should be confirmed by electroencephalography. Yet it will be thought that some standardization is important, if not essential, and it is surprising how little guidance is available. The great majority of guidelines are based not so much on residual brain function as on, first, the remaining possibility of auto-resuscitation[22] of the circulatory system and, second, on the consequential availability of the corpse as a source of fresh organs. Thus, while, as indicated above, the general clinical belief is that cerebral function will have completely ceased after some fifteen minutes of anoxia,[23] the widely accepted report of the prestigious US Institute of Medicine recommends an anoxic period of only five minutes, along with ECG and arterial pressure monitoring, for the purposes of providing non-heart-beating organ donors;[24] the influential 'Pittsburgh Protocol'[25] reduces this to two minutes' pulselessness and the standard in Australia is between two and five minutes, in which death is to be determined based on immobility, apnoea, absent skin perfusion, and the absence of circulation. The UK standard remains that under the AMRC Code[26] there is 'a minimum observation period of 5 **22.22**

[21] J M DuBois, 'Non-heart-beating Organ Donation; A Defense of the Required Determination of Death' (1999) 27 J Law Med Ethics 126, 133.

[22] Which, itself, it to be distinguished from cardioversion using modern technologies.

[23] See also President's Commission for the Study of Ethical Problems in Medicine, *A Report on the Medical, Legal and Ethical Issues in the Determination of Death* (US Government Printing Office 1981) and The President's Council on Bioethics, *Controversies in the Determination of Death* (US Government Printing Office 2008).

[24] Institute of Medicine Non-Heart-Beating Organ Transplantation: Medical and Ethical Issues in Procurement (National Academy Press: Washington, DC 1997).

[25] For description, see, among others, N Zamperetti, R Bellomo, and C Ronco, 'Defining death in non-heart beating organ donors' (2003) 29(3) J Med Ethics 182–85. It should be noted that this protocol is concerned with patients who are being ventilated.

[26] *Code of Practice for the Diagnosis and Confirmation of Death*, Academy of Medical Royal Colleges (2008). See also *An ethical framework for controlled donation after circulatory death*. Academy of Medical Royal Colleges (2011), which is concerned with donation that follows planned withdrawal of treatment.

minutes between diagnosis and confirmation of death'. And yet the Institute of Medicine[27] has disclosed that some centres required no waiting time at all before procurement of organs was initiated. It is, indeed, surprising how little attention has, in practice, been paid to the metaphysical significance of the agonal period.[28] The importance of obtaining good quality cadaver donations cannot be denied; the alternative view is that the dignity of those with, albeit terminal, brain function merits respect equivalent to that accorded to the living. This chapter is about death, not about transplantation. The two subjects are intertwined[29] but, as has been repeatedly emphasized, care must be taken to stifle the misconception that there are two types of death, and that the type accepted depends upon the use to which the diagnosis of death is to be put.[30] As the eminent bioethicist, Paul Ramsey, said early in the development of the transplantation programme:

> [T]he canons of highest loyalty to the [doctor's] primary patient can best be secured if neither the procedures for stating death nor a decision that death has occurred are distorted by reference to someone else's need for organs.[31]

6. Brain death and brain-stem death

(i) Development of the concept

22.23 The difficulties surrounding sole use of a cardiopulmonary standard, leads us to defining brain function as the alternative 'vital principle' by which to judge whether the *person* is alive or dead. The concept of 'brain death' has been increasingly widely accepted by both the medical and the legal professions and one wonders if there is any real purpose in reviewing it once again. Nonetheless, there are still sizeable academic and clinical minorities which find 'brain death' hard to accommodate on both moral and physiological grounds. Moreover, there is still some confusion both as to the use and the meaning of the principle. Thus we cannot yet dismiss it as a *fait accompli*.

22.24 As to its use, it cannot be over-emphasized that, in referring to brain death, we are referring to a diagnostic tool using neurological criteria, and not to an unusual medical condition—or indeed the philosophical speculation that it amounts to a *form* of death *different* to biological death. As we have already discussed, no one should consider a person to be dead *unless* it were assumed that his or her brain was dead. The diagnosis of death *by way of* tests of brain function is no more than an uncommon method that is applied only when the alternative is, for whatever reason, unavailable—and, for practical purposes, this will be when the cardiorespiratory system is being overridden by mechanical means.

22.25 The Harvard group,[32] which was the first to identify the need for accepting a brain-based definition of death, was also the first to spread confusion when they introduced it under

[27] See n 24 above.

[28] For trenchant criticism of this disregard, see J Menikoff, 'Doubts About Death: The Silence of the Institute of Medicine' (1998) 26 J Law Med Ethics 157.

[29] On the relationship between the definition of death and organ transplantation, see S D Shemie, 'Clarifying the paradigm for the ethics of donation and transplantation: was 'dead' really so clear before organ donation?' (2007) 2 Philos Ethics Hummanit Med 18.

[30] A useful analysis of the philosophical argument is to be found in W Chiong, 'Brain Death without Definitions' (2005) 35 Hastings Center Rep 30. Ultimately, the author concludes that 'death eludes definition'.

[31] P Ramsey, *The Patient as Person* (Yale University Press 1970) 112. Quoted by A Jotkowitz, 'Theological Reflections on Donation after Circulatory Death: The Wisdom of Paul Ramsey and Moshe Feinstein' (2008) 34 J Med Ethics 706.

[32] H K Beecher (chairman), 'A Definition of Irreversible Coma', Report of the ad hoc Committee of the Harvard Medical School to examine the definition of brain death (1968) 205 J Amer Med Ass 337.

the rubric of 'irreversible coma',[33] which is equated with conditions such as permanent (or persistent) vegetative state.[34] But, as will be seen when we come to a discussion of 'cognitive death', it is essential that coma, no matter what its depth, is not equated with death;[35] and it soon became clear that the committee was, in fact, describing what other Americans—and later the British Royal Colleges—dubbed 'brain death'.[36] Even this term can be misinterpreted. In particular, it can be taken as including 'partial brain death' and, if death is to be adjudged by way of cerebral non-function, we must be certain, not only that there is *permanent* physical destructive damage, but also that it involves the *whole* brain.

The practical difficulty here is that it is virtually impossible to certify death of the *whole* brain in the circumstances envisaged.[37] The alternative, then, is to speak only in terms of 'brain-stem death',[38] a term which derives from the assumption that somatic life is impossible in the absence of a functioning brain stem and is a conceptual imperative if we are to maintain the triadic model of death described above. Thus, it is fair to say that a major residual concern as to the ethics and legality of the concept of brain death rests on what practical differences there may be between 'brain-stem death' and 'whole-brain death'. **22.26**

Authoritative UK opinion is that any distinction is a matter of semantics only, and it is perhaps for this reason that the UK code for the diagnosis of brain-stem death has come to be referred to as 'diagnosis of death by neurological criteria'.[39] The only unnatural ways in which death or destruction of the brain stem can reasonably be expected in the presence of a normal higher brain are accidents involving the cervical spine and the underlying cord.[40] Natural disease in the form of haemorrhage, thrombosis, or embolism that is localized to the brain stem is rare and is either partial in type or, more commonly, rapidly fatal; in the event of survival, the resulting 'locked in' syndrome, characterized by quadriplegia and inability to speak but with preservation of consciousness and some eye movements, is a terrifying condition but its existence is well appreciated by neurologists and will be eliminated if the *primary* protocol for the diagnosis of brain-stem death is meticulously followed.[41] Again **22.27**

33 Prior to the influential Harvard Report, there were studies that published criteria for 'death of the nervous system' that used the term *coma dépassé* to refer to irreversible coma and apnoea. See P Mollaret and M Goulon, 'Le coma dépassé depassed coma (mémoire préliminaire)' 1959 (101) Rev Neurol (Paris) 3–15, cited by Gardiner, n 20.

34 The condition, generally arising from whole-body hypoxia, in which the cortex of the brain is destroyed but sub-thalamic and brain stem function is preserved; none of the criteria for the diagnosis of death are present. The medico-legal aspects have been fully described in para 10.221 *et seq*. For terminological confusion, see R Cohen-Almagor, 'Language and Reality at the End of Life' (2000) 28 J Law Med Ethics 267. See also, para 22.40, and chapters 10 and 1 of this book.

35 And there is a further distinction to be made between coma, the minimally conscious state, and the permanent vegetative state, although the management of death will be similar in these circumstances. See *Report of a Working Party of the Royal College of Physicians:* Prolonged Disorders of Consciousness (2013). Coma classically presents as eyes-closed unconsciousness and sleep-wake cycles are absent.

36 Conference of Medical Royal Colleges and their Faculties in the UK, 'Diagnosis of Brain Death' (1976) 2 BMJ 1187.

37 Particularly if this includes, as many US commentators would insist, the elimination of pockets of living cells.

38 Originally introduced by A Mohandas and SN Chou (1971) 35 J Neurosurg 211.

39 Academy of the Medical Royal Colleges, *A Code of Practice for the Diagnosis and Confirmation of Death* (2008).

40 It probably occurred as part of the process of dying following judicial hanging. For further discussion see J A Robertson, 'The Dead Donor Rule' (1999) 29 Hastings Center Rep 6. For critique of the rule itself see F G Miller, R D Truog, and D W Brock, 'The Dead Donor Rule: Can It Withstand Critical Scrutiny?' (2010) 35 J Med Philos 299–312. and A S Iltis and M J Cherry, 'Death Revisited: Rethinking Death and the Dead Donor Rule' (2010) 35 J Med Philos 223–41.

41 E Smith and M Delargy, 'Locked-in Syndrome' (2005) 330 BMJ 406. *Vadera v Shaw* (1999) 45 BMLR 162 (CA) provides a tragic example, as does the more recent case of Nicklinson, n 42.

it must be stressed that cases such as that of *Nicklinson* fall among cases involving minimally conscious patients; they involve end-of-life care and decision-making on the withdrawal of treatment, rather than death per se, and are more properly discussed in Chapter 21 of this book.[42]

22.28 Fatal generalized damage to the brain occurs in two main ways. First, external injury to the head may result in either intra-cranial haemorrhage[43] or primary brain swelling—so-called diffuse axonal injury. The consequence is that the expanding brain is trapped within a rigid skull; its vascular supply may then be compressed and the brain tissue will sustain *secondary* hypoxic damage. The important practical point is that, although damage to the brain tissue following direct violence *may* be all-embracing, it may, equally, be selective according to the blood vessels involved. Thus, establishing permanent whole-brain damage may be more difficult, and the diagnostic criteria correspondingly more strict, when it is associated with direct violence, than with the second main reason for destruction of cerebral tissue—that is, *primary* diffuse cerebral hypoxia.

22.29 This is generally associated with whole-body oxygen starvation which may, in turn, result from a number of conditions ranging from the multiple forms of obstruction of the airways (asphyxia) to metabolic hypoxia—of which, drug overdose is a potent cause.[44] 'Brain death' then becomes a conceptual reality because, as we have already seen, the brain is the essential organ that is the most sensitive to oxygen lack. Moreover, the brain stem is that part of the brain that is most *resistant* to hypoxia. Equation of the relatively easily diagnosable brain-stem death with whole-brain death thus relies upon the physiological infeasibility of a generalized, fundamentally hypoxic condition that will destroy the brain stem but which will, at the same time, spare the highly specialized tissue of the cerebral cortex. Thus, authoritative medical and judicial[45] UK opinion is that the terms 'brain-stem death' and 'whole-brain death', can be regarded as synonymous in both practice and theory—in effect, the former is a convenient marker of the latter. But, since, as we have already noted, the tests devised for the diagnosis of brain death—including those in use in countries where the law speaks in terms of 'death of the whole brain[46]—are, essentially, tests of brain-stem function, the former term is to be preferred and has always been used in the UK. Indeed, the Academy of Royal Medical Colleges stated quite baldly: '[C]essation of the integrative function of the

[42] *R (on the application of Nicklinson) v Ministry of Justice, R (on the application of AM) v DPP and others* [2012] 3 FCR 233; (2012) 127 BMLR 107, para 21.59. The same point of exclusion can be made in respect of *W v M and others* [2011] EWHC 2443 (Fam) and *M (Adult Patient) (Minimally Conscious State: Withdrawal of Treatment)* [2012] 1WLR 165. For an in-depth analysis, see W Chiong, n 30 above, and responses at (2006) 36 Hastings Center Rep 4.

[43] Intra-cranial haemorrhage may, of course, arise naturally and one form—spontaneous subarachnoid haemorrhage—occurs in young, otherwise fit persons. *An NHS Trust v J* (2007) 94 BMLR 15 is a good example of a case which came to court. Such cases, therefore, are important non-accidental deaths which fulfil all the criteria for organ donation.

[44] The reader must refer to one of the standard works on forensic medicine for a full list. Since it is written with him or her in mind, the lawyer may find H L Whitwell, K Thorne, and A Kolar, *Mason's Forensic Medicine for Lawyers* (6th edn, Bloomsbury Professional 2015) ch 9, helpful.

[45] *Re A* (1992) 3 Med LR 303, discussed at para 22.37; for Northern Ireland, see *Re T C (a minor)* (1993) 2 Med L Rev 376. There seem to be no comparable decisions in Scotland although, should the question be raised, there is no doubt that *Re A* would be followed.

[46] See para 22.34. This is not to deny that the term does nothing to satisfy those who cannot accept that a person whose cardiorespiratory system is maintained by mechanical means is dead—and it would be wrong to dismiss these sincerely held views without acknowledgement: M Potts and D W Evans, 'Does it Matter that Organ Donors are not Dead? Ethical and Policy Implications' (2005) 31 J Med Ethics 406. See also n 40 on critique of the dead donor rule.

brain-stem equates with the death of the individual and allows the medical practitioner to diagnose death.'[47]

(ii) Diagnostic criteria for brain-stem death

The diagnostic criteria are, however, strict and their scope is often misunderstood—particularly the fact that their application involves three equally important phases.[48] First, as already mentioned, there is the exclusion of coma being due to reversible causes including drug overdose, hypothermia, and metabolic disorders. Secondly—and this is of fundamental importance—the physician responsible must make a *positive* diagnosis of the disorder which has caused the brain damage and must ensure not only that it was *capable* of causing brain stem death but also that it is irremediable. Thirdly, a number of tests specifically designed to demonstrate destruction of the several components of the brain stem must be carried out—thus, all importantly, confirming death of the respiratory centre, as well as the absence of brainstem reflex activity.[49] To this end, a carefully controlled protocol is included whereby a patient's inability to breathe spontaneously is proven—including tests specifically designed to demonstrate the effects of carbon dioxide tension in the blood stream. These tests of brain stem function *must* be repeated, although the recommendations as to the time interval are, of necessity, somewhat open. **22.30**

These criteria have been criticized on the ground that the patient is 'being asked to prove he is alive' rather than that the physician is proving death. Positive tests, such as an electroencephalogram (EEG) or an angiogram—by which cessation of the blood flow in the brain can be visualized[50]—are therefore often sought, and indeed one or other is mandatory in some countries of the European Union.[51] Indeed, use of neurological criteria in the determination of death increasingly requires whole brain death, including brain-stem death. Yet it is hard to believe that an EEG, which measures the surface electrical activity of the cerebral cortex, would be positive in the presence of properly performed confirmatory tests for brain-stem death, but there is no reason why such a test should not be added if it would serve to allay any fears among the next of kin as to the certainty of death.[52] Such public misgiving as persists in the UK may well relate to the link between brain-stem activity and the capacity for consciousness and respiratory control, and which might be further allayed if the purposes of defining brain-stem death were more clearly understood.[53] It is perhaps **22.31**

[47] See n 10 above at 2.1. Interestingly, W F Haupt and J Rudolf, n 51, find the UK to be unique in this respect in Europe.

[48] See the guidance from the AMRC, building on its codes of practice, and a useful summary by Oram and Murphy, n 20.

[49] D Gardiner, S Schmie, A Madara, and H Opdam, 'International Perspective on the Diagnosis of Death' (2012) 108 (S1) Br J Anaesthesia i14, i19–i20.

[50] It may be useful when coma from other causes is a possibility: A I Qureshi et al, 'Computed Tomographic Angiography for Diagnosis of Brain Death' (2004) 62 Neurology 652.

[51] W F Haupt and J Rudolf, 'European Brain Death Codes: A Comparison of National Guidelines' (1999) 246 J Neurol 432, state that an angiogram is mandatory in France and Luxembourg; an EEG is required in France, Luxembourg, Italy, and the Netherlands. The authors admit that their list may be incomplete. A later investigation comparing procedures for the determination of brain death among thirty-three European countries, led to the conclusion that international consensus is called for, due to the current variation in practice. See G Citerio, I A Crippa, A Bronco, A Vargiolu, and M Smith, 'Variability in brain death determination in Europe: looking for a solution' (2014) 21(3) Neurocritical Care 376–82.

[52] EEG activity can, however, be present where brain death criteria are met: D A Shewmon, 'Recovery from "brain death": a neurologist's apologia' (1997) 64 Linacre Q 30–96.

[53] For a historical analysis, see C Machado, J Korein, Y Ferrer, L Portela, M de la C Garcia, and J M Manero, 'The Concept of Brain Death did Not Evolve to Benefit Organ Transplants' (2007) 33 J Med Ethics 197. A lack of understanding among patents' families of the concept of brain death is noted in A Vincent and L Logan, 'Consent for Organ Donation' (2012) 108 Br J Anaesth 125–28.

to that end that the NICE guidelines on organ donation for transplantation recommend discussion of 'withdrawal of life-sustaining treatment or neurological death before, and at a different time from, discussing organ donation unless those close to the patient initiate these discussions in the same conversation.'[54] The original purpose of the diagnostic procedure was to establish a consensus by which patients who can no longer benefit from ventilator support can be removed from intensive care. This option is essential if the patient is to die with dignity, if the relatives are to be spared wholly unnecessary suffering, if resources, both mechanical and human, are to be properly apportioned and, finally, if the physician is to be absolved from the threat of the criminal courts. It follows that there is a need for the concept of brain-stem death irrespective of any transplant programme, and this would persist even in the currently unlikely event that the requirement for human organs was dissipated by the widespread use of animal tissues.[55] Meanwhile, it is essential that the diagnosis of death does not become confused with the application of an 'organ procurement model'. Accepting brain-stem death is not a way of 'hurrying death along'; rather, the ventilator allows the pace of investigation, assessment, and prognosis to be slackened; when it comes to the point, the diagnosis of brain stem death is, in the great majority of cases, only confirming what is clear from clinical observation—that the patient is dead.

22.32 Nonetheless, there are those who believe that the word 'death' should be reserved for those whose heart has stopped beating and it has been mooted that, while those who are diagnosed as brain dead are not 'dead' in the accepted meaning of the term, they are, nevertheless, in the 'near death' situation and should be legally available as organ donors.[56] To follow such a course my give rise to the suspicion that different concepts of death are being used by the profession and by the public and that special criteria apply in association with transplantation.[57] Understanding, or its lack, lies at the root of the problem. Yet, in simply calling for better 'education' of the public, it is easy to minimize the importance of religious and cultural traditions.[58] For example, transplant operations involving brain dead donors have been legalized only since 1997 in Japan and a major reason for this must lie in the unique attitudes to death and to the unity of the family that are widely held in that country.[59] A similar rationale may explain the Indian requirement for a diagnosis of brain-stem death prior to discontinuing artificial ventilation and seeking relatives' consent to organ donation.[60] Islamic jurisprudence requires *either* irreversible medically certified cessation of the heart and respiration, *or* irreversible cessation of all functions of the brain.[61] There is

---

[54] National Institute for Health and Clinical Excellence, Organ Donation for Transplantation: Improving Donor Identification and Consent Rates for Deceased Organ Donation (2011) at para 1.124. <http://www.nice.org.uk/guidance/CG135>.

[55] Others would hold, however, that this is the answer to the brain death paradox: R D Truog, 'Brain Death—Too Flawed to Endure, Too Ingrained to Abandon' (2007) 35 J Law Med Ethics 273, 280.

[56] R D Truog, and W M Robinson, 'Role of Brain Death and the Dead-donor Rule in the Ethics of Organ Transplantation' (2003) 31 Crit Care Med 2391. See n 40 on critique of the dead donor rule and Chapter 19 on transplantation.

[57] Potts and Evans, n 46.

[58] See a debate led by D Inwald, I Jakobovits, and A Petros, 'Brain Stem Death: Managing Care When Accepted Medical Guidelines and Religious Beliefs are in Conflict' (2000) 320 BMJ 1266.

[59] Current Japanese law is that the individual can choose the definition of death that is to be applied in his or her particular case—though even that is dependent on family agreement: A Bagheri, 'Individual Choice in the Definition of Death' (2007) 33 J Med Ethics 146. That author suggests that the Japanese model could be adopted globally.

[60] A D Dhanwate, 'Brainstem death: A comprehensive review in Indian perspective' (2014) 18(9) Indian Journal of Critical Care Medicine 596–606.

[61] Third Session of the Council of the Islamic Fiqh Academy, Amman, Jordan (1986). It has been argued that advances in transplant medicine led to the move away from a previous resistance the equivalency of brain stem and death of the person: V Brainhoo, J L Bernat, and R Beresford (eds), 'Ethical and Legal Issues in Neurology' in *Handbook of Clinical Neurology Series* (Elsevier 2013). For a contrary view, see

no consensus among Halachic (Jewish) scholars, some of whom make exclusive use of cardiac death (Orthodox), while the Chief Rabbinate has approved organ donation in circumstances of brain death.[62] The western critic should be wary before suggesting that centuries of cultural tradition should be swept aside in the name of modern medical technology. Perhaps the major practical result of this discussion—which, in the end, is centred on public trust in the system—is to be found in the current advice that the diagnosis of brain—stem death should be made by two doctors with specialist expertise, one of whom, at least, should be a consultant; neither may be associated with a relevant transplant team. Interestingly, the 'two doctor' protocol is satisfied if one observes the other and the positions are reversed for a mandatory second, confirmatory examination.[63] Even so, while the vast majority of practitioners would abide by authoritative guidelines, there is no definitive UK law on the point.[64]

C. The Legal Diagnosis of Death

1. Development of the law

Given that there is such ambivalence as to the clinical diagnosis of death, it is unsurprising that the law is, at least, not anxious to expose its hand and that, when it does so, it does little to resolve the clinical dilemma. And yet Laurie *et al* have observed that there exists a widely canvassed case for a statutory definition of death, but one which grapples with a form of definition that can include all modes of death.[65] Such definitions, they argue, comprise no more than a statement of good medical practice; that is specifically so in the case of the American Act. **22.33**

The US Uniform Determination of Death Act 1980 has been quoted above.[66] Nearer to our own jurisdiction, we have, as an example of Commonwealth legislation, the Human Tissue Act 1983 of New South Wales, s 33 of which states: **22.34**

> For the purposes of the law of New South Wales, a person has died when there has occurred:
> (a) irreversible cessation of all function of the person's brain, or
> (b) irreversible cessation of circulation of blood in the person's body.[67]

It is interesting, and it has already been noted, that both examples define brain death in terms of *whole-brain* death yet, in practice, the diagnosis will always be made on the basis of tests for *brain-stem* death. Indeed, the US Act perpetuates the confusion by including a tautological reference to the latter; as a result, it is unclear whether a diagnosis of brain-stem death is sufficient or merely a necessary part of the evidence of whole-brain death. It has been argued that in effect defers to the medical profession; the physician is empowered to

A Badir and S Alsoy, 'Brain death revisited: It is not "complete death" according to Islamic sources' (2011) 37 J Med Ethics 290.

[62] G Baeke, J-P Wils, and B Broeckaert, 'American Jewish approaches to contemporary ethical issues in medicine: the case of organ retrieval from brain-dead donors' (2011) 16(4) Mortality 365.

[63] See n 10 above at 6.3, Repetition of Testing. The majority of European countries demand that the diagnosis be made either by two doctors or by a specialist practitioner.

[64] It is arguable, however, that use is made in transplant medicine of a legal fiction (see n 18), that treat the patient as if dead. S K Shah, R D Truog, and F G Miller, 'Death and legal fictions' (2011) 37 J Med Ethics 719–22; S K Shah and F Miller, 'Can we handle the truth? Legal fictions in the determination of brain death' (2010) 36 Amer J Law Med 540.

[65] G T Laurie, S H E Harmon, and G Porter, *Mason & McCall Smith's Law and Medical* Ethics (10th edn, Oxford University Press 2016) paras 16.32–34.

[66] See para 22.19. See also 12 Uniform Laws Annotated (ULA) 589 (West 1993 and West Supp 1997).

[67] See also, Human Tissue Act 1982 (Victoria), s 41.

use his or her own expertise and to vary this according to the circumstances of the individual case. Significantly, there is no attempt to distinguish either the brain or the heart as providing the *ultimate* model on which to hang the diagnosis of death.

22.35 In such circumstances, one can reasonably wonder whether statute law achieves any useful purpose and whether this explains why the UK jurisdiction has no comparable enactment. The answer is apparent from what has been implied already—the law *cannot* make what is a clinical decision, and to attempt to make it do so isolates the diagnosis of death from other such decisions; the result may be to perpetuate uncertainty and distrust.[68] Nonetheless, a significant proportion of the public—and this includes the professional public—still feels the need for some form of legal recognition of the fact that a warm, pink body whose heart is beating and whose metabolic processes are clearly active is, in fact, dead in the accepted sense of the word. In short, an answer is still sought to the question, 'Would you bury such a body and, by implication, would doing so amount to a criminal offence?'

22.36 The matter was first addressed, and partially solved in the complementary cases of *Finlayson* in Scotland and those of *Malcherek* and *Steel* in England.[69] Both concerned the removal from ventilator support of persons who were the victims of criminal activity and whose continued treatment was considered medically futile. All three men were convicted and appealed on the grounds that removal from the ventilator broke the chain of causation; all the appeals failed. At that time, however, the concept of 'brain death' was still being developed and discontinuance of treatment was, at least in the case of *Finlayson*, based on severe brain damage. It was decided in all three cases that this was, in the circumstances, good medical practice. Nevertheless, the cases were, essentially, seen as deciding causation and the question of the *diagnosis of death* was, at best, peripheral to the arguments. A need for some form of reassurance on the topic remained and it is widely held that this lies in the UK in the surprisingly poorly reported case of *Re A*.[70]

2. The case of *Re A*

22.37 *Re A* was an unusual case. A was a 19-month-old child who was admitted to hospital, not for the first time, with symptoms and signs suggestive of non-accidental injury. The admitting hospital could detect no heartbeat but he was, nevertheless, provided with intensive medical care. He was subjected to double hospital transfer but, although there was no evidence of recovery, he was found not to be brain-stem dead when finally admitted to Guy's Hospital twenty-four hours later. In the meantime, an application had been made under the Children Act 1989 for an emergency protection order, the effect of which, under s 44(4)(c), was to confer parental responsibility for A on the local authority. Unfortunately, however, this neither determined, nor indeed diminished, the extent of the residual responsibility of the parents who then applied for a prohibited steps order, which was granted in the following terms:

> No person with parental responsibility, namely the parents and the local authority, shall give consent to the switching off a life-support machine in respect of A without consent of those others with parental responsibility and after consultation with the *guardian ad litem*.[71]

[68] It is notable that the opportunity to legislate on the matter was not taken in either the Human Tissue Act 2004 or the Human Tissue (Scotland) Act 2006.

[69] *Finlayson v HM Advocate* 1979 JC 33; *R v Malcherek; R v Steel* [1981] 1 All ER 422 (CA).

[70] [1992] 3 Med LR 303. The limited reporting can probably be attributed to the fact that, although the underlying reasoning was fully explained, the judgment was *extempore*.

[71] At Med LR 304.

This order was granted on the same day that the hospital finally declared A to be brain-stem dead using accepted medical criteria. In view of the obvious differences of opinion and interests of the hospital and the parents—including the former's doubts as to their legal position when faced with there being apparent dual parental responsibility for the child[72]—the case came before Johnson J in the Family Division five days after the diagnosis of death had been made. The hospital staff were, by then, becoming increasingly distressed through having to ventilate and to feed a child that was believed to be dead—indeed, the consultant in charge stated that she had never previously known parents to refuse removal of a child in A's condition from intensive care support. The parents, on the other hand, were concerned that removal of A from the ventilator would compromise the quality of any evidence later adduced as to the cause of his death and they were, in effect, seeking time in which to arrange for an independent examination of the child.

Johnson J was, however, unhesitatingly of the view that A had been dead for over a week, that the results of all the tests done were available, that there could be no sensible issue between doctors as to whether A was or was not brain-stem dead and, in passing, that the cause of his death would be ascertained better by post-mortem pathological examination than by further clinical examination. To hold otherwise would not be in the interests of the child and would be unfair to the nursing and medical staff of the hospital. Accordingly, the judge made a declaration that A was dead for all legal and medical purposes and that the staff would not be acting contrary to law should they consider it appropriate to disconnect him from the ventilator. **22.38**

Significantly, in *Re A*, Johnson J did not hold that the legal definition of death in England and Wales was to be couched in brain-stem death terms.[73] Rather, he confirmed that, in certain circumstances—in particular, when physiological functions were maintained artificially—a person could be declared dead purely on the ground that the brain stem was dead, thereby incorporating brain-stem death into the common law. Even so, in *Smeaton v Secretary of State for Health*, Munby J found that, 'Once upon a time the law, following medical science, treated death as marked by the cessation of breathing or of heartbeat. At present the law treats death as meaning brain stem death.'[74] The decision in *Re A* differs from those statutory definitions cited above, insofar as it disposes of the brain-stem/whole-brain argument as far as the UK is concerned. The diagnostic tests employed by the clinicians and approved by the judge were tests of brain-stem function; quite properly and logically, therefore, Johnson J referred throughout to brain-stem death; the problem of whole-brain death did not arise. Although the use of brain-stem criteria to define the clinical status of the ventilated patient had been in practical use for many years, as has been described above in respect of *Malcherek*,[75] *Re A* was the first firmly relevant judicial pronouncement as to their legal acceptance in the UK. **22.39**

3. Cognitive death

It is apparent from what has been argued above that *all* death is, ultimately, 'brain death'. It is also clear that, given a scenario such as a hypoxic insult to the brain followed by **22.40**

[72] The legal framework involved is important and logical. Once the child was declared dead, the options of exercising the inherent jurisdiction of the court or of originating a summons in wardship were no longer available. It remained open to the court to make the declarations sought, set out in para 22.38.

[73] As is often suggested. See for example, I H Kerridge, et al, 'Death, dying and donation: organ transplantation and the diagnosis of death' (2002) 28 J Med Ethics 89–94.

[74] *Smeaton v Secretary of State for Health* [2002] EWHC 610 (Admin), para 57, citing both *Re A* [1992] 3 Med LR 303 and *Airedale NHS Trust v Bland* [1993] AC 789.

[75] [1981] 1 All ER 422 (CA). See para 22.36 above.

re-oxygenation followed by survival, we may well be confronted with a situation pictured as 'partial brain death' in the presence of a functioning cardiorespiratory system. Given, again, that the cells of the brain will succumb differentially to the effects of oxygen starvation roughly in proportion to their activity, the higher brain, or neocortex, which controls our cognitive ability, may well be dead while the more primitive brain-stem survives—the result being what is now known as the permanent vegetative state. Our concern at this point, however, is not with that condition per se but, rather, with its relationship to the legal definition of death.

22.41 The repeated, mainly trans-Atlantic, attempts to convert the concept of death of the neocortex to that of neocortical—or, derivatively, cognitive—*death of the person*, serve to extend the definition of brain death far beyond the boundaries which its originators were anxious to preserve.[76] Indeed, in practical terms, cognitive death is almost impossible to define with any certainty or consistency, as indicated by some of the difficulties of precedent in the case law.[77] Such a concept also dictates the co-existence of a legally dead person in a biologically living body and such a contradiction is unacceptable.[78] High profile cases such as *Conroy*[79] in the US and *Bland*[80] in the UK, in which court approval has been given for the withdrawal of life-preserving treatment from patients in a permanent vegetative state, do not represent judicial approval of 'cognitive death'. They do, however, acknowledge that it can be lawful to withhold or withdraw treatment from *living* patients that is agreed to be medically futile—and this on a case to case basis.[81] No matter how it is diagnosed, death must remain an absolute; a 'living death' is semantic imagery that cannot become a legal precept.

22.42 A very similar analysis must, in logic, apply to the anencephalic infant although, in practice, the management of such a child will be modified by the principles governing withdrawal of futile treatment from severely disabled neonates,[82] which, again, gives rise to the inference that the patient is in fact still alive. Anencephalics seldom survive more than a few days, and very few would now advocate the use of heroic efforts to prolong that period. Many attempts[83] have been made to justify the use of such infants as organ donors[84] and

---

76 There is a mass of literature, mainly from the US, on the progression of the definition of death from cardiovascular death to brain death to cognitive death. A complete and informative example is D R Smith, 'Legal Recognition of Neocortical Death' (1986) 71 Cornell L Rev 850. That this progression is generally recognized is seen in L R Samuel, *Death, American Style: a Cultural History of Dying in America* (Rowman and Littlefield 2013) p 120 *et seq.*

77 Consider, for example, the erosion of the stringent criteria for diagnosing the permanent vegetative state established after *Airedale NHS Trust v Bland* [1993] AC 789, the later case of *Frenchay Healthcare NHS Trust v S* [1994] 1 WLR 601 (CA), and the Irish case *Re a Ward* [1996] 2 IR 79. That disputes over the precision of diagnosis can affect judicial proceedings is noted in C Dyer, 'Court case adjourned after diagnosis of persistent vegetative state changes' (2012) BMJ e5803.

78 See, eg, J Fisher, 'Re-examining Death: Against a Higher Brain Criterion' (1999) 25 J Med Ethics 473.

79 *Re Conroy* 486 A 2d 1209 (NJ, 1985).

80 *Airedale NHS Trust v Bland* [1993] AC 789.

81 This topic is discussed more fully elsewhere in this book, in particular in Chapter 10, at paras 10.221 and 10.214.

82 Royal College of Paediatricians and Child Health, *Withholding or Withdrawing Life Saving Treatment in Children: A Framework for Practice* (RCPCH 2015). For an analysis of guidelines and decided cases, see G T Laurie, S H E Harmon and G Porter, *Mason and McCall Smith's Law and Medical Ethics* (10th edn, Oxford University Press 2016), para 15.42 *et seq.* It is also considered in Chapter 10 at paras 10.203 *et seq* and 21.06 *et seq.*

83 The high-profile US case *Re T A C P* 609 So 2d 588 (Fla, 1992) is a good example in which permission was refused.

84 For discussion, see D N Medearis and L B Holmes, 'On the Use of Anencephalic Infants as Organ Donors' (1989) 321 New Engl J Med 391. See also Chapter 19 at para 19.37.

despite argument to the effect that anencephalic donation does not occur in the UK,[85] it has recently been successfully carried out in Cardiff, with the donated kidneys given to an adult recipient in Leeds.[86]

4. The time of death

The greater part of this discussion has led to the inevitable conclusion that, in philosophical terms, death must be regarded as a process; the 'time of death' is, therefore, both difficult to establish in practice and theoretically difficult to define. Fortunately, there are relatively few occasions where a precise statement is required by law—it need not, for example, be stated on the English certificate as to the cause of death.[87] A retrospective estimate may be needed in the practice of criminal investigations, and it is worth noting that, absent circumstantial evidence, this can seldom be done with an accuracy of less than one hour's variation. **22.43**

(i) Simultaneous death

The least uncommon requirement in civil practice, however, lies not in determining the actual but, rather, in assessing the *relative* time of death as between two or more persons in respect of succession rights—the problem of 'simultaneous death' or *commorientes*. In general, this question arises most frequently in the context of accidental death; it has, however, a special significance in the present discussion—that is, as to the time of death when two ventilated patents are declared brain-stem dead. **22.44**

In the words of Lord Grieve, 'Prior to the coming into effect of section 31 of the Succession (Scotland) Act 1964 there was no presumption in the law of Scotland as to the survivorship amongst persons whose death occurred in a common calamity.'[88] The legal solution to simultaneous death in England and Wales lies in the Law of Property Act 1925, s 184 of which states in general that, in the event of two (or more) persons dying in circumstances that make the sequence of death uncertain, the younger will be presumed to have survived the older.[89] This follows the Roman law principle of presumed survivorship following the natural course of life events; it contrasts with the more widely held rule in the majority of countries in the European Union that, in similar circumstances, neither will be deemed to have survived the other.[90] The distinction is important because the English rule clearly introduces the possibility that a finding of uncertainty as to which spouse or civil partner survived the other may result in their estates being distributed in a way contrary to that which was anticipated.[91] This is because the test in deciding if the rule applies is not whether **22.45**

---

[85] See J Brierley, 'Current status of potential organ donation in cases of lethal fetal anomaly' (2013) 15 The Obstetrician & Gynaecologist 184–88.

[86] 'Newborn baby is UK's youngest ever organ donor' (2015) 350 BMJ 2210.

[87] See Appendix A for specimen medical certificate as well as Sch 1 to The Registration of Births and Deaths (Amendment) Regulations 2006, SI 2006/2827. It must, however, be stated or estimated on the Scottish equivalent. See the Schedule to The Registration of Births, Still-births, Deaths and Marriages (Prescription of Forms) (Scotland) Amendment Regulations 2014, SSI 2014/141.

[88] *Lamb v Lord Advocate and others* 1976 SC 110. See n 92 and n 93.

[89] If, however, one or other spouse is intestate, it will be assumed that neither survived the other: Administration of Estates Act 1925, s 46 as amended by the Estates Act 1952, s 1(4). This rule was applied following the double murder of both parents by their only son, in *Re DWS (deceased); Re EHS (deceased); TWGS v JMG and others* [2000] 2 All ER 83; the case was more concerned with the passing of the estate to the grandson of the victims, who was an infant at the time, in the event that the son could not inherit as a result of his conviction.

[90] eg, in France, *Code Civil*, arts 720–22.

[91] Scots law has recognized this imperfection and has excluded spouse or civil partner commorientes from the general rule (Succession (Scotland) Act 1964, s 31). Under s 31 (b), in any other case, the presumption is that the younger person survived the elder unless the contrary us provided for in a testamentary disposition. It has been recommended that Scots law should be altered so as to follow the general European

there was a *simultaneous* death but, rather, whether there was *uncertainty* as to which of two or more persons survived the others—the courts appear to take the view that simultaneous death cannot be proved pathologically and will, in fact, be an extreme rarity.[92] A 'survivorship clause' is, therefore, a near essential in an English will.[93] From the evidential angle, however, it is not the legal precepts that matter so much as the fact that, whatever rule is adopted, all have it in common that the legal presumption is rebuttable by the evidence, and that evidence of survival will be taken into consideration by the courts; such evidence must be mainly medical[94] and the difficulties are compounded by the fact that no limit of time is set—survival for seconds is as significant in law as is survival for days—and it is to be noted that the evidence will not be evidence as to the time of death but, rather, as to that of survival.[95]

22.46 This introduces dilemmas and anomalies both as to discovery of the evidence and of its interpretation, and it is for the court to determine whether there is uncertainty—that is to say that survivorship is not proven—so as to render s 184 applicable. Consider, for instance, the precise cause of death, which can give rise to a further understanding of time of death and likely sequence of death. In the Irish High Court case of *Kennedy*,[96] both spouses were killed in a car accident that ended with the car being discovered under water. Each had by will appointed the other as sole executor. They left neither issue nor parent. The applicant was Mrs Kennedy' sister, and the respondents the seven siblings and ten nephews and nieces surviving Mr Kennedy. Autopsy reports concluded that Mr Kennedy's death was due to acute cardio–respiratory failure associated with coronary atheroma, and Mrs Kennedy's was due to drowning. Whereas in Mr Kennedy's case the time interval between onset and death was said to be 'seconds', in Mrs Kennedy's case it was said to be 'minutes'. It was for that reason that the application was lodged, on the presumption that Mrs Kennedy had survived her spouse. The Probate Officer sought further clarification, which came from the consultant pathologist who compiled the initial pathology reports. On the evidence of the policeman finding the car that Mr Kennedy's head and shoulder were outside the driver's door window, the pathologist found that his heart attack may have been due to his struggle to open the car door, rather than the sudden immersion in cold water; he could therefore not be certain which death had come first. Kearns J found that the evidence had established 'more than an element of uncertainty'. As such, he found that the presumption in section

rule that neither survived the other in all cases: Scottish Law Commission *Report on Succession* (Scot Law Com No 215, April 2009, Recommendation 57).

[92] *Re Lindop; Lee-Barber v Reynolds* [1942] Ch 377. Note that, in this case, 'death' was equated with cessation of breathing. The seminal case is *Hickman v Peacey* [1945] AC 304, [1945] 2 All ER 215, which involved several deaths from a bomb that fell on a house on 14 September 1940, exploding in the basement and killing five people sheltering there, three of whom were testators; it demonstrates the difficulties the courts have experienced in applying the 1925 Act. See also *Re Pringle; Baker v Matheson* [1946] Ch 124 at 129–31 *per* Cohen J where the common-sense interpretation of simultaneous death was adopted.

[93] See *Inland Revenue Commissioners v Trustees of Sir John Aird's Settlement* [1984] Ch. 382. It seems that, whenever possible, opportunity will be taken to adopt the 'neither survived' rule—as, eg, when one of the commorientes dies intestate, n 90.

[94] There may, however, be admissible non-medical evidence. For example, in *Re Bate (deceased), Chillingworth v Bate* [1947] 2 All ER 418, evidence was led as to the habit of the wife in preceding her husband to the kitchen, where they both died of carbon monoxide poisoning. The admissibility of that evidence was inconsequential, however, as there was 'no certainty that the gas jet was turned on before the husband entered the kitchen'.

[95] For an early case showing that medical evidence is required to rebut the presumption in s 184 of the 1925 Act See *Re Bate (deceased), Chillingworth v Bate* n 94.

[96] *Re Kennedy* [2000] IEHC 12, [2000] 2 IR 571.

5 of the Succession Act 1965 did apply, insofar as it was deemed that the Kennedys died simultaneously.[97]

Pathological observations designed to distinguish in time between apparently simultaneous accidental deaths thus require very careful analysis. But they cannot be interpreted unless they are sought; this may imply the need for post-mortem dissection and for time-consuming and technically difficult follow-up investigations—a daunting prospect in circumstances such as airline accidents that may involve hundreds of families possibly being involved in a single disastrous incident. Opposing results as to the likelihood of relative survival may be obtained depending on the diligence and motivation of individual medical investigators—and of the senior coroners of the future.[98] It is unsatisfactory to have to conclude that the disposal of a family estate may, as things stand, depend to a large extent on such uncertainties. 22.47

The complex relationship between brain-stem death and simultaneous death is of an entirely different nature and arises from the fact that, establishing brain-stem death being a *retrospective* exercise, it is impossible to state the precise moment of death—if there ever was such a thing. The best that can be done pragmatically is to identify that time as the time the heart ceased to beat after removal of ventilator support. Even this may be modified if the dead body is to be used as an organ donor and, in so far as the time at or the order in which ventilators may be closed down is an arbitrary choice, it is an unacceptable parameter on which to apply the *commorientes* rule of whatever type that is operative. We are left with the very state of affairs that, so far as is known, the issue has never been decided in court and that, when it is, the authority will be breaking new ground. 22.48

D. Administrative Aspects of Death

1. Death certification and registration

Many comments have been made as to the relatively casual administrative approach to the disposal of the dead that has been adopted in the UK. A major and comprehensive analysis of the procedure was undertaken in 1971 under the chairmanship of Mr Justice Brodrick,[99] the main concern of which was, rather strangely, to simplify the procedural aspects of cremation. The Brodrick Report had a somewhat turbulent history and, in the end, it had remarkably little effect—there was, in fact, no structured follow-up for more than thirty-five years until the Luce Committee was established by the Health Minister in 2001 and reported in 2003.[100] By this time, of course, the case of Dr Shipman—who was convicted of the murder of fifteen of his patients and was probably responsible for the deaths of many times that number—had burst upon the scene. The Luce Report was overshadowed not only by the 22.49

[97] Section 5 provides: 'Where . . . two or more persons have died in circumstances rendering it uncertain which of them survived the other or others, then, for the purposes of the distribution of the estate of any of them they shall all be deemed to have died simultaneously'.

[98] Although regulations may still be needed to accord with the restrictive elements of the Human Tissue Act 2004 in respect of retention of tissues and post-mortem investigations, The Coroners (Investigations) Regulations 2013, SI 2013/1629 have been made under the Coroners and Justice Act 2009. These are discussed at paras 22.83 and 22.99. Regulations have also been passed under The Human Tissue (Scotland) Act 2006: see The Human Tissue (Removal of Body Parts by an Authorised Person) (Scotland) Regulations 2006.

[99] N J L Brodrick (Chairman), *Report of the Committee on Death Certification and Coroners* (HMSO 1971) Cmnd 4810.

[100] T Luce (Chair), *Death Certification in England, Wales and Northern Ireland. Report of a Fundamental Review* (Cm 5831, 2003).

publicity surrounding the case itself but also by the massive report by Dame Janet Smith which was commissioned specifically to examine the relationship between Dr Shipman's remarkable evasion of the law and the current regulation of disposal of the dead.[101]

22.50 There is no doubt, however, that the Luce Report strongly influenced the government in drawing up its proposals for new and consolidating legislation in this area and many of its recommendations were reproduced virtually verbatim in the Coroners and Justice Bill 2008–09.[102] The Bill became the Coroners and Justice Act 2009 and was followed by several Regulations subordinate to that Act, dealing for the most part with the alteration and designation of Coroner areas,[103] and regulations setting out dates for the commencement of certain provisions, such as consequential legislative amendments. A novel development under the Act provides for the appointment of a Chief Coroner, under Part 1 of the Act, which also introduces the concept of a 'coroner's investigation' into a death. The practice and procedure governing such investigations is set out in Regulations, made by the Lord Chancellor and with the agreement of the Lord Chief Justice, the first of which came into force in 2013.[104]

2. The formalities of death

22.51 No matter what be the mode of death—be that natural, accidental, homicidal, or suicidal—a medical certificate[105] as to the cause, or as to the fact that the cause is unknown, must always be provided by the registered—and, now, licensed[106]—medical practitioner who attended the deceased during his or her last illness.[107] Strictly speaking, the doctor in England and Wales should deliver the certificate to the registrar while, at the same time, providing the qualified informant with a notice that he or she has done so; it is then the duty of the informant to deliver the notice to the registrar within five days of the death (eight days in Scotland).[108] In practice, it is usual for the doctor to provide the informant with both the notice and the certificate as to the cause of death; that way the process has the

---

[101] Dame Janet Smith, *The Shipman Inquiry, third report: Death Certification and the Investigation of Deaths by Coroners* (Cm 5854, 2003).

[102] The Luce Report and the Smith Report, although commissioned entirely independently, are complementary. However, Lady Smith subsequently, and unofficially, criticized the resulting Bill as being weaker than she would have wished: see n 126.

[103] See, eg, The Coroners and Justice Act 2009 (Alteration of Coroner Areas) Order 2015, SI 2015/658, combining certain English Coroners' districts. See also SI 2014/3157, SI 2013/1626, and SI 2013/1625, which have a similar effect.

[104] The Coroners (Investigations) Regulations 2013, SI 2013/1629, made under s 43 of the 2009 Act, and which should be read alongside the Coroners (Inquests) Rules 2013, SI 2013/1616 and the Coroners Allowances, Fees and Expenses Regulations 2013, SI 2013/1615. This is discussed more fully in para 22.82.

[105] The certificate must be of prescribed form (Registration of Births and Deaths) Regulations 1987, SI 1987/2088, r 40(1)(a)(i). In England and Wales, a different certificate is required in the case of a child dying within the first twenty-eight days of life: r 40(1)(a)(ii) (Appendix A).

[106] Medical Act 1983, Pt IIIA, inserted by Medical Act 1983 (Amendment) Order 2002/3135. The regulations governing the license to practise have been amended by different Regulations. See The General Medical Council (Licence to Practise and Revalidation) Regulations Order of Council 2012, SI 2012/2685 and The General Medical Council (Licence to Practise and Revalidation) (Amendment) Regulations Order of Council 2014, SI 2014/1273, and information on the General Medical Council web site at <http://www.gmc-uk.org/about/legislation/registration_legislation.asp>.

[107] Births and Deaths Registration Act 1953, s 22, as amended by the Coroners Acts of 1980 and 1988. A modified certificate of the cause of death is used in Scotland where, under the Births, Deaths and Marriages (Scotland) Act 1965, s 24(2), as amended, any medical practitioner who is able to do so may provide a certificate in the absence of the practitioner who attended the deceased during his or her last illness. As a result, deaths in England and Wales which must be referred to the coroner simply because of the non-availability of the deceased's doctor, often do not need to be referred to the procurator fiscal.

[108] The list of qualified informants is given in the 1953 Act, s 16 (death in a house) and s 17 (death elsewhere), as amended most recently by the Coroners and Justice Act 2009, Sch 21, paras 8 and 9 respectively. The *duty* to inform falls, in order of availability, on any person who is a relative or the partner of the

benefit of synchrony. Similarly, the certificate of the cause of death has space for indicating to the registrar that the death has been reported to the coroner (or the procurator fiscal in Scotland); in practice, much time and confusion can be avoided by the medical practitioner reporting directly to the medico-legal authority, thus avoiding the need to issue a certificate which the registrar is bound to reject.

A précis of the cases which should be reported is provided on the reverse of the English certificate.[109] These are when the death was: **22.52**

- of unknown cause;
- violent, unnatural or suspicious;
- possibly due to an accident;
- possibly due to self-neglect or neglect by others;
- possibly due to industrial disease or to the deceased's employment;
- possibly due to an abortion—presumably whether lawful or unlawful;
- during an operation or while recovering from the effects of an anaesthetic;
- possibly due to suicide;
- one which occurred during or shortly after detention in police or prison custody.

In addition, the English list includes when the deceased was not seen by the certifying doctor *either* after death *or* within the fourteen days before death. This would not be a specific reason for reporting the death to the Scottish procurator fiscal but it is notable that in neither jurisdiction is it as yet obligatory for the certifying practitioner to have seen the body after death.[110]

Before considering the implications of the Coroners and Justice Act, it will be helpful to analyse the practical objections to the procedure as it was. In the first place, the wording of the death certificate depends on one person who, having been, by need of statute, the deceased's medical attendant, may have a personal involvement in the mode and cause of death; second, and as a corollary to this, it is that person's choice as to whether or not the death should be reported to the medico-legal authority; and third, even where a second certificate is required—as, for instance, when, as will be discussed below, the body is to be cremated—the primary certifier is unlikely to invite anyone other than a friend to confirm his or her findings. In short, there is very little in the way of independent assessment underlying the certificate of cause of death in England and Wales.[111] This position changed in Scotland under the Certification of Death (Scotland) Act 2011. That Act provides for a system of medical review of certificates of cause of death not subject to investigation by the Procurator Fiscal, both randomly as a duty of the Registrar General, or following a referral by a district registrar or an application by an interested person. A reviewer will determine that a certificate is in order, if satisfied on the available evidence that the stated cause(s) of death represent(s) a reasonable conclusion and other information on the certificate is correct.[112] If the certificate is not in order, the Reviewer is required to inform the **22.53**

deceased present at the death or resident in the same registration district, any person present at the death or the occupier of the house, any inmate of the house or the person causing the disposal of the body. The list in the event of death taking place outside a house includes the person finding or taking charge of the body.

[109] And see also Whitwell, Thorne, and Kolar, n 44, Appendix C.

[110] Neither would the 'fourteen-day rule' necessarily apply in Scotland where it would be quite legitimate for the pathologist to provide the certificate following a 'hospital autopsy' and s/he *would* do so following a medico-legal autopsy.

[111] It is emphasized that this chapter does no more than record the *common* bases for criticism of the regulations.

[112] Certification of Death (Scotland) Act 2011, s 8.

medical practitioner who signed the certificate and invite him or her to attest a replacement certificate.[113]

(i) Flirting with the law

22.54 It is not contended here that every intentional error in a certificate as to the cause of death will be inserted for the benefit or protection of the certifying doctor. The certificate of registration of a death,[114] which contains details as to the cause of death, is a public document and there is no doubt that a number of certificates will be falsified in an attempt to spare the next of kin distress or to preserve the reputation of the deceased. This is no doubt inexcusable but it is, at the same time, understandable. The more difficult case is that in which the doctor has, in fact, flirted with the law by recourse to the doctrine of double effect whereby, in brief, current medical practice may,[115] in carefully delineated circumstances, condone treatment which has a bad effect so long as it is justified by a concomitant—and superior—good effect.[116] This is, however, part of the debate surrounding assisted dying and is fully addressed in Chapter 21. For present purposes, it need only be remarked that, provided the intention has been to allay the symptoms associated with the underlying disease, it may be morally—and legally[117]—acceptable to record the latter as the cause of death.

22.55 The categories of necessity, euthanasia, and mercy-killing are however not clearly delineated, as the seminal case of *R v Adams* demonstrated.[118] Indeed, a major reason for harbouring doubts as to the efficiency of the current system of death certification derives not so much from fear of the doctor's psychopathy as from his or her anxiety to save a patient from prolonged suffering—but to do so in such a way as to circumvent the law relating to mercy-killing. This aspect was well exemplified in the case of Dr Cox.[119] Dr Cox's elderly patient was suffering from rheumatoid arthritis and was in severe and incessant pain. She had repeatedly expressed a wish to die and he, eventually, injected her with a large dose of potassium chloride—a potent cardiotoxin which has no place in the treatment of pain. He was reported by a third party and was tried, and convicted, on a charge of attempted murder—'attempted' because the body had been cremated before the case came to public notice and no evidence as to murder was available. This is not the place to discuss the medico-legal ethics of Dr Cox's actions—for which, see Chapter 21; suffice it to say that his punishment was minimal in both the Crown Court and the General Medical Council. Here, we will do no more than outline those disturbing aspects of administrative medical law which were highlighted by the case.

---

113 ibid, s 10.

114 See para 22.61.

115 One might be more positive in the light of the very firm statement by Lord Goff in *Airedale NHS Trust v Bland* [1993] AC 789 at 867 were it not for the doubt raised in the more recent *R v Woolin* [1999] 1 AC 82, in which it was found that if the bad effect was inevitable, it cannot be regarded as unintentional. These cases are discussed in Chapter 10.

116 In the common scenario, the 'bad effect' is accelerated death and the 'good' is the relief of intractable pain. It is to be noted that the very authoritative Glanville Williams was of the view that the moral doctrine of double effect was better replaced by the legal concept of necessity: G Williams, *Textbook of Criminal Law* (2nd edn, Stevens 1983) 581.

117 A classic example being the case of Dr Moor—for which, see A Arlidge, 'The Trial of Dr David Moor' [2000] Crim LR 31.

118 H Palmer, 'Dr Adams' Trial for Murder' [1957] Crim LR 365. Dr Adams' index patient died from an overdose of opiate drugs. He was acquitted of her murder following a direction to the jury that incorporated the classic definition of 'double effect'. Given that the patient was not terminally ill, it is doubtful that he would have been treated similarly today. See C Foster, J Herring, K Melham, and T Hope, 'The Double Effect Effect' (2011) 20 Camb Q Health Care Ethics 56.

119 *R v Cox* (1992) 12 BMLR 38.

First, Dr Cox did not give the correct cause of death and the fact that he had failed to do so went unrecorded for several days. Second, he did not report the case to the medico-legal authority, which was mandatory on several grounds. And, third—and this is vital to the analysis—the doctor who signed the confirmatory cremation certificate was the pathologist from the same hospital and professional environment, who had already performed an inadequate autopsy and who had clearly undertaken no critical assessment of the manner of dying. In short, and without prejudice to Dr Cox's motives, his case illustrates graphically how the system depends on the integrity of the medical profession and how it is trusted. Many people now see that trust as having been undermined. **22.56**

(ii) Current practice and action for reform

The administration's riposte now lies in chapter 2 of the Coroners and Justice Act 2009. The Act, however, makes surprisingly few direct alterations to current practice and, in general, operates by way of empowering the Lord Chancellor and appropriate Ministers to make regulations, some of which have already been discussed, in respect of coroners area changes,[120] and will be discussed in respect of coroners investigations.[121] There have, at time of writing, not been any regulations passed under Chapter 2 of the 2009 Act. The requirement for the medical practitioner who attended the deceased before his or her death (the attending practitioner) to prepare an 'attending practitioner's certificate' stating the cause of death to the best of his or her knowledge and belief or to refer the case to a (future) senior coroner is retained[122] but there is, following the coming into force of the 2009 Act, a further duty to provide a copy of the certificate to a medical examiner.[123] **22.57**

Medical examiners will be appointed—in sufficient numbers, and with adequate resources—by local authorities in England and Local Health Boards in Wales.[124] The only requirements for appointment yet promulgated are that they must be *active* practitioners of at least five years standing (s 19(3)—from which it follows that the incumbent will also have to hold a licence to practise).[125] Their major functions will include confirming the cause of death as recorded by the attending practitioner and notifying the registrar to that effect or, in appropriate cases, inviting the attending practitioner to issue a fresh certificate. When he or she cannot confirm the cause of death, the medical examiner may refer the case to a senior coroner; alternatively, he or she will be empowered to issue a 'medical examiner's certificate' in cases referred to him or her by a senior coroner. Most innovatively, the Secretary of State may, by regulations, require the medical examiner to discuss the cause of death with the informant or another appropriate person, and to give them the opportunity to mention any fact that might cause the death to be investigated under s 1—that is, where there is reason to suspect that the person died a violent or unnatural death, where the cause of death is unknown, or where the death occurred in custody or state detention.[126] **22.58**

---

[120] See n 103.

[121] At para 22.82 *et seq.*

[122] Coroners and Justice Act, 2009, s 20(1)(a) (not yet in force at time of writing), currently Births and Deaths Registration Act 1953, s 22, as amended by the Coroners Acts of 1980 and 1988—see n 107.

[123] Coroners and Justice Act, 2009, s 20(1)(b) (not yet in force at time of writing). This post must not be confused with the American medical examiner who is appointed in several states and who has powers similar to but considerably extended beyond those of the English coroner.

[124] Coroners and Justice Act 2009, s 19 (not yet in force at time of writing), as amended by the Health and Social Care Act 2012, s 54, which changes 'Primary Care Trust' to 'local authority'. The Secretary of State may also appoint a National Medical Examiner (2009 Act, s 21) whose function may be paraphrased as ensuring the provision of an efficient and uniform service throughout England and Wales.

[125] Medical Act 1983, Pt IIIA inserted by Medical Act (Amendment) Order 2002, SI 2002/3135, art 10.

[126] 2009 Act, s 20(1)(k). As sections 18–21 are not yet in force at time of writing and, by extension, no such regulations will have been published. Even so, their passage may lead to well-founded concerns of increased workload among practitioners. Nevertheless, Dame Janet Smith, who was largely responsible for

(iii) Certifying the cause of death

22.59 The current certificate as to the cause of death (Appendix A) is designed to define the cause of death in consequential form. Thus, the immediate cause of death—for example, internal haemorrhage—may be a relatively useless piece of information from the point of view of the National Statistics Office;[127] it is, therefore, further certified as 'due to'—say, rupture of the aorta. The cause of the haemorrhage in this example could, however, have been 'stab wound'; clearly, then, it will be this precipitating cause given in the last line of the certificate which is of major interest to the registrar and the medical examiner of the future; medico-legal practice has, however, evolved so as to raise some doubts as to the scope of the 'bottom line'. A major reason for this is that, as will be apparent from several other chapters in this book, good modern medical practice has evolved so that terminal decisions are being made which are lawful, but which are only lawful as a result of extensive legal analysis.

22.60 There are now numerous examples of such cases: classic instances include the discontinuance of ventilator support in cases of respiratory paralysis[128] and the removal of nutrition and hydration from persons in the permanent vegetative state.[129] The tendency in all such cases, on an international level, has been to attribute death to the cause of the condition for which treatment was being abandoned—for example, in the case of Mr Bland, to crush asphyxia—whereas, in fact, the subject could have lived for at least some further time given continued support. There is a need to know how often and in what circumstances such essentially iatrogenic deaths occur. For this reason, and in the interests not only of transparency but also of statistical accuracy, it seems that such deaths should be recorded as what they are—for example, 'due to lawful removal of nutrition and hydration'. This is the sort of problem that the new office of Chief Coroner will, no doubt, be prepared to consider.[130]

(iv) Registration of the death

22.61 In any event, certification of the cause of death is but a prelude to its registration, which is a near essential before a body can be finally disposed of[131]—the only exception being when a body is returned to England or Wales from abroad and no further investigation is contemplated, when a certificate to that effect must be provided.[132] Otherwise, and always subject to the possibility of later medico-legal intervention, and in the case of Scotland a review of the medical certificate of the cause of death,[133] the registrar must provide the informant with a disposal certificate to the effect that the death has been registered, where there has

---

the changes (see n 101) still has expressed doubts as to the efficacy of the anticipated measures: C Dyer, 'Reform of Death Certificate System Doesn't go Far Enough, says Judge' (2009) 338 BMJ 435.

[127] The particulars required of the relevant Registrar by the Secretary of State, do not extend to the cause of death, but concern among other particulars the deceased's name, address, and date of death. See The Social Security (Notification of Deaths) Regulations 2012, SI 2012/1604.

[128] An educational example being the seminal New Zealand case *Auckland Area Health Board v Attorney-General* [1993] 1 NZLR 235, [1993] 4 Med LR 239. See Chapter 10, para 10.224 and Chapter 21, para 21.60.

[129] Despite the number of cases that have followed it, *Airedale NHS Trust v Bland*, n 77, remains the most closely argued and authoritative instance.

[130] Those parts of the 2009 Act relevant to the new role of Chief Coroner, were implemented on 25 July 2013, under the Coroners (Investigations) Regulations 2013, SI 2013/1629 and the Coroners (Inquests) Rules 2013, SI 2013/1616. See also The Coroners and Justice Act 2009 (Commencement No. 14) Order 2013, SI 2013/1628.

[131] Births and Deaths Registration Act 1953, s 15. For Scotland, see Registration of Births, Deaths and Marriages (Scotland) Act 1965, s 25.

[132] 1953 Act, s 24(2).

[133] Under the Certification of Death (Scotland) Act 2011. See para 22.53.

been no report to the coroner.[134] The disposal certificate is in two parts, one of which is, essentially, an authority for the person responsible to dispose of the body;[135] the other must be returned to the registrar certifying that disposal has, in fact, been effected. In the event that the latter has not been returned within fourteen days, the registrar is required to institute inquiries into the matter.[136] Given any very unusual circumstances which may emerge as part of the increasing pluralism of modern British society, final disposal of the body will be by way of burial or cremation.[137] Indeed, no burial or cremation may take place without the certificates mentioned above.[138]

E. Disposal of the Dead

1. Responsibility for disposal

For reasons that become clearer below, no general statutory requirement is imposed on any particular individual to dispose of a body[139] and there is nothing that says that a body must be buried or cremated. There is a common law right to be buried in one's parish churchyard but there is nothing that dictates that a person be buried in a recognized burial ground.[140] There is, however, an obligation at common law 'in the nature of a public duty' that rests on persons in possession of a dead body to dispose of it in a manner suitable to the estate.[141] Such ambiguity is clearly a matter for concern. It is widely assumed that the responsibility rests on the executors,[142] but this is based on what is, by any standards, elderly case law; moreover, there is no certainty that the deceased would have *had* an executor. This was one matter raised by the government in its consultation paper *Burial Law and Policy in the 21st Century: The Need for a Sensitive and Sustainable Approach.*[143] In general, the government's response to the consultation was remarkably laissez-faire but it *was* agreed that whether there should be a statutorily defined responsibility for disposing of a dead body was an issue that would benefit from clarification. Nonetheless, the only conclusion was that further work should be done before action was taken.[144] In the event, at time of writing it seems that nothing has been determined and, in view of the difficulty the Ministry of Justice is clearly **22.62**

---

[134] Registration of Births and Deaths Regulations 1987, SI 1987/2088, as amended by The Registration of Births and Deaths (Amendment) (England and Wales) Regulations 2009, SI 2009/2165, r 42.

[135] ibid, r 49.

[136] ibid, r 51.

[137] In acknowledging the multiculturalism of today's society, the Scottish Government set up a Burials and Cremation and Review Group, with a view to bringing legislation after 2015. That, in turn, led to the passage of the Burial and Cremation (Scotland) Act 2016, asp 20. The Act aims to incorporate the recommendations of Lord Bonomy's Infant Cremation Commission (2014), and streamline record-keeping in Scotland. The provisions of the Act came into force on 28 December 2016, SSI 2016/417.

[138] Cremation (England and Wales) Regulations 2008, SI 2008/2841.

[139] There is an exception in that a parent who can afford to do so is bound to provide for the burial of his or her deceased child: *R v Gwynedd County Council, ex p B* [1992] 3 All ER 317 (CA).

[140] The reader who would enjoy some light relief is referred to B Hilliard, 'Last Rights' (1997) 147 NLJ 1566, which also contains some little known facts as to burial at sea.

[141] *Rees v Hughes* [1946] 1 KB 517. Preventing the burial of a body is also an offence at common law: M Hirst, 'Preventing the Lawful Burial of a Body' (1996) Crim LR 96.

[142] *Williams v Williams* (1882) 20 Ch D 659; *Conway v Dalziel* (1901) 3 F 918.

[143] Home Office, January 2004, Q10. The paper followed investigations which had been ongoing since 2001.

[144] Ministry of Justice, Burial Law and Policy in the 21st Century—The Way Forward (5 June 2007). On the question of the role of executor (Q10), the government response was to the effect that, '. . . there would be benefits in making clearer the responsibilities of the family and/or the executor of the estate of the deceased, although further work would be required to determine what those responsibilities should be and how they might be enforced'.

having with the issue, it appears to have been left at that.[145] Most people have a recognizable 'nearest relative' and, if all else fails, we are fortunate in knowing that the local authority stands at the end of the line.[146]

22.63 On the other side of the coin, a person cannot will how his or her body is to be disposed of; no testamentary directions are binding on those with whom the responsibility rests.[147] Here again, however, we can see how the common law established more than a century ago is now open, at least, to amendment. It is, for example, obvious that such a generalization conflicts with the Human Tissue Act 2004[148]—although it could be argued that it still provides a potential legal basis for familial objection to organ donation (see Chapter 19).

2. Burial

22.64 The lack of substantive law as to the burial of human remains in England and Wales is very surprising—at least to this author. Much of it dates from the nineteenth century and such as there is deals with the administration of cemeteries rather than with the respect that is, or is not, due to the human body.[149] The legislation of that era now persists in fragmentary form only. Most significantly, the Burial Act 1857 and associated statutes established the principle that disposal of the dead was a matter of local policy; as a result, there never has been a national system for its regulation. In addition, the Registration of Burials Act 1864, s 1, dictated that all burials in burial grounds in England were to be registered—and this remains in force. Section 7 of the same Act defined a burial ground as including a vault or other place in which a body was buried—which clearly indicates that a body may be buried outside a recognized burial ground.[150]

145 Although the Government did say in 2012 that it was 'committed to keeping the situation under review', albeit specifically in respect of re-use of graves, which was not considered to be a critical issue at the time. See C Fairbairn, 'Reuse of Graves', House of Commons Standard Note SN/HA/4060, 15 May 2014.

146 A duty lies on the local authority to arrange for the burial or cremation of any body for which alternative arrangements cannot be made: Public Health (Control of Diseases) Act 1984, s 46. That this 'bears no resemblance to what was once known as a 'pauper's burial', and that the nature of the provision differs among local authorities, were among the findings in as found in *Stewart v Secretary of State for Work and Pensions* [2011] EWCA Civ 907. The current funeral payment scheme is part of the Social Fund, which provides part payment of funeral costs on a means-tested basis. More than 35,000 such payments (£43m) were made in 2012–13. See S Kennedy, 'Social Fund Funeral Payments', House of Commons Standard Note SN01419, 1 November 2013. The onus lies on the Health Authority if the death occurs in hospital.

147 *Williams v Williams*, n 142.

148 Under which, of course, a person can give 'appropriate consent' to his or her body being used, inter alia, as a transplant donor (s 3). Note that the comparable Scottish legislation (Human Tissue (Scotland) Act 2006) speaks in terms of 'authorisation' rather than 'consent'.

149 In fact, the government had been reconsidering the matter since the report of the House of Commons Select Committee on Environment, Transport and Regional Affairs, Eighth Report, 2 April 2001. See also the follow-up consultation paper of 2004, *Burial law in the 21st century*: <http://www.dca.gov.uk/consult/buriallaw/buriallaw_cp.pdf>. In February 2015 the Scottish Government published a consultation on its legislative proposals for a new Bill relating to burial and cremation, which led to the Burial and Cremation (Scotland) Act 2016, asp 20 (n 137 above). Note, however, that under Part 3 of that Act, account may be taken of the wishes expressed by the deceased while alive, in respect of their burial. The Act also establishes a hierarchy of relatives who may make arrangements for the burial or cremation of the deceased adult or child. Scottish Ministers may under s 6 make Regulations for the management, regulation and control of burial grounds by a burial authority (as defined under s 2).

150 The Select Committee made the interesting distinction between a burial ground—which is, essentially, an area of ground closely associated with a church and managed by the religious denomination concerned—and a cemetery which is established as, and governed as, a commercial undertaking. For legal purposes, however, the former is accommodated within the latter (Local Government Act 1972, s 214(8)). The prospective Burial and Cremation (Scotland) Act 2016, asp 20 (n 137 above), s 1 defines 'burial ground' as land that is or has been used or intended to be used primarily for the burial of human remains.

22.65 Beyond this, however, the statutory control of burial now in England and Wales lies in the Local Government Act 1972, s 214 which transferred the provision and control of burial grounds to the local authority functioning as a burial authority. Even so, the Act does no more than empower the local authority, and the same is true under the 2016 Scottish legislation. As a consequence, practical regulations as to the burial of bodies will be made on a local basis by means of by-laws[151] and it is impossible to generalize as to policy; there is, however, nothing to prevent the Secretary of State making orders as to the general management of cemeteries in the control of burial authorities.[152] In the event, the government has decided, largely on the grounds of convenience and contrary to the replies to their consultation document, against introducing a free standing 'Burial Bill';[153] opportunity to use existing legislation will, however, be taken whenever possible. In this connection, regulations are promised empowering local authorities to re-use graves by way of exhumation licences in defined circumstances.[154] For the present, it is only necessary to remind the reader, as above, that life's chapter is closed by the issue of a disposal certificate—and this applies whether disposal is by way of burial or cremation.

(i) Burial other than in a burial ground or cemetery

22.66 Subject to registration and compliance with any orders or by-laws, there is nothing to prevent the use of land as private burial grounds or cemeteries run on commercial lines. Occasionally, however, the question arises as to whether a body can be buried other than in such a designated area. In Scotland it is an offence to bury human remains other than in a burial ground or in a private burial ground, subject to statutory provisions.[155] In so far as it is possible to generalize, this is permissible although the law in England and Wales, such as obtains, is piecemeal and is, effectively, a conflation of public health and environmental law, largely as expressed in the Environmental Agency's various prevention of pollution guidelines.[156] It is generally assumed that burial in the absence of compliance with these guidelines could result in compulsory exhumation. It would be essential to raise a 'burial register' in order to comply with the Act of 1864 and also to ensure that sufficient details are available when the land is resold.[157] In addition a number of derivative complications need to be considered—for example, whether planning permission would be required in the event that a change of 'principal use' of the garden was contemplated, and whether the burial was compliant with the existing deeds of the property—but this is no place in which to go into such detail. Interestingly, however, other than in respect of any monument erected, close neighbours would have no legal right to object to the burial, provided the environmental requirements were satisfied.

[151] Local Government Act 1972, s 235. For Scotland, see n 150 ibid, and Part 1 of the Burial and Cremation (Scotland) Act 2016.

[152] ibid, s 214(3).

[153] n 144.

[154] n 144, Ministerial Statement attached. Powers are available under Deregulation and Contracting Out Act 1994.

[155] That is, burials carried out subject to the prospective Burial and Cremation (Scotland) Act 2016, asp 20 (n 137 above), s 8 for burial grounds and s 22 for private burial grounds.

[156] There is no PPG specific to burial at home. But see Environment Agency *Funeral Practices, Spreading Ashes and caring for the Environment* archived at <http://www.nhs-chaplaincy-spiritualcare.org.uk/Recent_Guidance/Environment_Agency_Funeral_practices_spreading_ashes.pdf>.

[157] The Ministry of Justice has published guidance on, for example, natural burial which notes that, 'The Registration of Burials Act 1864 requires all cemeteries not otherwise subject to a legal requirement to do so to keep a register of burials': *Natural burial grounds: Guidance for Operators* (2009) 5.

(ii) Burial at sea

22.67 Burial at sea cannot be common, although a case can be made for seeing it as a 'greener' option in view of the decreasing availability of ground for burial. However, in contrast to the more usual form of burial, the process is strictly controlled as an aspect of potential environmental pollution, the authority for such control being derived from the Food and Environment Protection Act 1985, Pt II. There are five areas in British coastal waters for applications for burial at sea: off The Needles, Isle of Wight; between Hastings and Newhaven; off Tynemouth, North Tyneside; 210 miles due West of Oban; and 15 miles West of John O'Groats[158] (although it is also possible to propose a new site when applying to bury someone at sea off the English coast).[159] In respect of England and Wales, a licence must be obtained from the Department for Food and Rural Affairs before a body may be deposited therein.[160] The application will need support from a certificate of freedom from infection, and an embalmed body may not be so disposed of in this way. In respect of burials off the Scottish coastline, licences are issued by the Marine Scotland Licensing Operations team in Aberdeen.[161] There are also a number of specifications as to the coffin and its contents, the general concern being that only biodegradable materials are used and that the coffin should sink to the seabed rapidly and intact.[162] Burial at sea is certainly not a simple process and there is much to be said, from many aspects, for the alternative of cremation with later scattering of the ashes on the sea—for which no licence is required.

3. Cremation

22.68 As a reflection of its finality, cremation as a method of disposal of the dead has always been carefully regulated.[163] It is, admittedly, the ultimate method of concealing an unnatural cause of death; on the other hand, it has many advantages over burial as a legal method of disposal of the dead, and is now the preference of the majority of those responsible. Regulation of cremation must, therefore, be so designed as to permit without undue hindrance a process that is in the public interest yet must, at the same time, safeguard that interest in respect of criminality.[164] The Cremation Acts 1902 and 1952 still represent the

158 See Scottish Government, Burial and Cremation Review Group Report (2007) 38 <http://www.gov.scot/Resource/0039/00398254.pdf>.

159 Though regulations apply if the body is deposited anywhere in the sea from a British vessel or aircraft (s 5). (Note that, inter alia, the Coroner will have to be informed if the body is to be removed from England or Wales (Removal of Bodies Regulations 1954, SI 1954/448 as amended by SI 1971/1354).) Interestingly, a licence may also be required for incineration of substances in British waters or in a British vessel anywhere at sea; incineration in this context must involve the *purpose* of thermal destruction (s 6).

160 <https://www.gov.uk/burial-at-sea>.

161 See the Marine and Coastal Access Act 2009, c 23 and the Marine (Scotland) Act 2010, asp 5.

162 See Marine Management Organisation, *Burial at Sea: Coffin Requirements*, Statutory Guidance (11 June 2014).

163 In contrast to the surprisingly lax attitude to burial, the burning of the remains of a deceased human are prohibited in any place other than a crematorium the opening of which has been notified to the Secretary of State (Cremation (England and Wales) Regulations 2008, SI 2008/2841, r 13).

164 Times change in a multicultural society, however, and, recently, a Mr Ghai protested his right to a Hindu funeral pyre by way of judicial review: *Times Online* (24 March, 2009). Predictably, the case was lost on the grounds that the Cremation Regulations render the burning of a body outside a crematorium a criminal offence; moreover, the fact that a significant proportion of the public would find the procedure a matter of offence was sufficient to justify the application of the Human Rights Act 1998, Sch 1, Art 9.2. One is less impressed by the somewhat sophistic argument that Art 9.1 was not engaged because open-air cremation is a matter of Sikh custom rather than religious belief: *R (on the application of Ghai) v Newcastle upon Tyne City Council* [2009] EWHC 978 (Admin), [2009] NLJR 713. The High Court decision was, however, reversed, largely on the ground that a 'building' need not be fully enclosed in order to comply with the Cremation (England and Wales) Regulations 2008: *R (on the application of Ghai) v Newcastle City Council* [2010] 3 All ER 380. For comment on this case see R Arlow and W Adam (eds), case note in (2009) 11(3) Ecc LJ 367.

law in both England and Wales and in Scotland, but the operation of the Acts for the purposes of England and Wales is now consolidated in the Regulations of 2008.[165] It is re-emphasized that any exceptional discretionary powers under which a body can be buried without certification as to the cause of death and prior to registration of the death do not apply to cremation—the process of cremation cannot be set in motion until the registration of the death is complete. Subject to that proviso, the regulation of cremation can be described conveniently by way of the forms that must be completed before it can proceed.[166]

(i) The cremation process

Cremation 1[167] constitutes an application for cremation which sets out, inter alia, the relationship of the applicant to the deceased, the wishes of the next of kin, the details of the death, an affirmation to the effect that there is no reason to suspect foul play or the need for further examination of the body, and a statement by those who have been in medical charge of the deceased. The application must be countersigned by a householder who knows the applicant. **22.69**

Cremation 4 is the certificate of the medical attendant during the deceased's last illness who has eighteen questions to answer relating to the mode and cause of death, the scope of his attendance on the deceased, and operative treatment and nursing care in the recent past. The doctor must certify that he or she has no reason to suppose that further inquiry is needed and must also affirm that there is no relationship to, nor any pecuniary interest in, the death of the deceased. Despite its comprehensiveness, Cremation 4 does not replace the medical certificate as to cause of death; the latter is essential for the registration of the death whereas Cremation 4 is related only to the process of cremation. **22.70**

Cremation 5 is a confirmatory medical certificate which must be completed by a fully registered practitioner of at least five years' standing[168] who has no family or professional relationship with the practitioner signing Cremation 4. He or she must state whether the body has been seen and whether a careful external examination has been carried out. There is no statutory requirement for this to have been done but the Regulations clearly indicate the need; a negative answer would certainly result in the rejection of the certificate. There is provision for stating whether or not the certifier has performed a post-mortem dissection. There are five questions relating to having questioned various categories of person as to the circumstances of the death; there must be a positive reply to at least one of these. Finally, the certifying doctor must affirm his or her satisfaction as to the cause of death. The unsatisfactory situation whereby the choice of the confirming medical practitioner lies with the certifier of death has been noted above. Cremation 5 can be dispensed with if the patient died in hospital where he was an in-patient and a post-mortem examination was made by a pathologist who would have otherwise been qualified to complete a Cremation 5; the practitioner completing Cremation 4 must, in these circumstances, know the result of the post-mortem examination before giving his certificate.[169] **22.71**

[165] Schedule 1 to the Cremation (England and Wales) Regulations 2008, SI 2008/2841. All previous regulations and amending regulations are revoked. The Cremation (Scotland) Regulations 1935 and 1952, SR & O 1935/247, SI 1952/1639, as amended, are currently extant.

[166] Cremation (E & W) Regulations 2008, Sch 1.

[167] Cremation 2 is used when cremating body parts and Cremation 3 for the disposal of stillborn babies by cremation.

[168] Within the meaning of the Medical Act 1983, s 55, as amended by the European Qualifications (Health and Social Care Professions) Regulations 2007/3101 and the Health Care and Associated Professions (Miscellaneous Amendments) Order 2008/1774. In future, he or she will also be required to have held a licence to practice for at least five years or since the relevant order (Medical Act 1983 (Amendment) Order 2002, Sch 1, para 10) has come into force.

[169] 2008 Regulations, r 17(3).

22.72 In the event that the case has been reported to the coroner or procurator fiscal, the certificate of those officials, Cremation 6, replaces Cremation 4 and 5 and clears the case for consideration by the Medical Referee (see para 22.73). Cremation 6 may be issued before the conclusion of the medico-legal inquiries but, in England and Wales, it does not state the cause of death; it does not replace either the coroner's death certificate or Certificate after Inquest.[170]

22.73 A medical referee is appointed by the Secretary of State[171] for each crematorium authority and is, in effect, the last line of defence against improper destruction of the cadaver. He or she must be a medical practitioner of at least five years' standing and, again, this will include the holding of a current licence to practise; the not uncommon use of retired practitioners for the purpose is, therefore, likely to stop. It is notable, however, that the 2008 Regulations await the guidance of the Secretary of State as to the character and further qualifications the medical referee will be expected to have. This is an important consideration as the regulations give very wide powers to referees. In an emergency, they can either complete the confirmatory certificate or withhold authority for cremation.[172] In normal circumstances, however, any further inquiries considered fitting may be made; the case can be reported to the coroner or procurator fiscal; and the medical referee can invite a pathologist to perform a post-mortem examination or can make such an examination him- or herself.[173] In the last circumstances, the person performing the autopsy completes Cremation 11, which will then replace Cremation 5 and will also override Cremation 4. The remains can be cremated once the referee is satisfied that the regulations have been complied with, that the cause of death has been established and that no further examination is required. This is achieved by way of Cremation 10, the completion of which by the medical referee or deputy medical referee clears the road for final disposal of the body. In this respect, each crematorium authority must appoint a registrar who will keep a permanent register of cremations performed and will send a notification of cremation to the registrar for births and deaths. The register must also include information as to the disposal of the ashes.

22.74 It is noted, finally, that a body that has been buried for not less than a year may be disinterred and cremated without further documentation or authorization; the situation is subject only to the requirements for exhumation.[174] Beyond that time, it is an offence to remove the interred remains from a place of burial, without the grant of a licence from the Secretary of State.[175] In view of the number of 'cold' police cases that are reopened, it might be thought that there is a case for involving the medical referee in such cases—at least for a slightly longer period. The circumstances in which the imposition of such a further administrative burden would be 'effort-effective' must, however, be extremely rare.

---

170 The version of Cremation 6 provided by the procurator fiscal does indicate the cause of death but, notwithstanding, a normal certificate of cause of death must also be provided by his or her medical adviser.

171 Or the Scottish Ministers in Scotland.

172 But, in such circumstances, a written explanation must be given to the applicant: 2008 Regulations, r 28. It seems slightly paradoxical that, whereas the applicant can make representations to the medical referee about any matter contained in the medical certificate or confirmatory medical certificate, r 22 of the 2008 Regulations is silent as to a refusal of authority to cremate.

173 Subject to him or her having a licence to do so and to obtaining the appropriate consent under the terms of the Human Tissue Act 2004.

174 2008 Regulations, r 21. Under the prospective Burial and Cremation (Scotland) Act 2016, asp 20 (n 137 above), s 27, the Scottish Ministers may under regulations provide for the exhumation of human remains, including those persons or descriptions of persons who may apply.

175 Burial Act 1857 s 25, as amended by the Care of Cathedrals Measure 2011 (No. 1) and substituted by the Church of England (Miscellaneous Provisions) Measure 2014 No. 1, SI 2014/2077, s 2. These provisions were considered in the application to exhume and reinter elsewhere the remains of a venerated Polish priest, following the sale of the property on which he had been buried, in *R (on the application of Rudewicz) v Ministry of Justice* [2012] EWCA Civ 499; [2013] QB 410; [2012] 3 WLR 901.

(ii) Cremation of body parts

Regulation of the cremation or incineration of body parts depends on whether the parts come from a deceased or a living person. In the former instance,[176] no cremation is allowed in the absence of certificates as to the cause of death, that there is no need for any further investigation, and of authorization by the medical referee.[177] As to the latter, a crematorium cannot cremate any human tissue or organs from a living person and incineration of such tissues[178] is subject to the Environmental Permitting (England and Wales) Regulations 2007.[179] No other permit is, however, required. **22.75**

(iii) Disposal of the ashes

The cremation authority must offer the ashes to the applicant or to his or her nominee. In the event that neither wishes to receive them, the ashes must be decently interred at the crematorium in a space reserved for the purpose or scattered thereon. This does not, however, prevent controversies arising from the 'incorrect' ashes being handed over in the case of cremated infants.[180] Otherwise, as has already been noted, there is no environmental regulation of the practice, although the Environment Agency issues authoritative guidelines as to the scattering of ashes on water; these are concerned, in the main, with protecting the feelings of others and with the disposal of associated non-degradable memorabilia such as plastic or metal components of wreaths—otherwise, environmental pollution is not a major issue.[181] **22.76**

F. The Coroner

1. Development of the office

The office of coroner in England and Wales developed from the twelfth century, at which time the coroner was largely responsible for supervising the material interests of the Crown in criminal cases. As these could well be affected by the status of the dead person and by the precise conditions surrounding the death, the coroner's office became intimately concerned with the investigation of suspicious deaths. The financial connotations of sudden death gradually relaxed, or were diverted to other offices, and the status of the coroner declined until the office was revived in the Middle Ages. At that time, the coroner's attention was specifically directed to the establishment or exclusion of criminality in relation to death, a principle that persisted until the nineteenth century.[182] The present-day coroner can be **22.77**

176 Cremation (England and Wales) Regulations 2008, r 19.

177 ibid, r 25.

178 ibid, r 29.

179 SI 2007/ 3538, now for the most part revoked by the Environmental Permitting (England and Wales) Regulations 2010/675, except for the purposes of definitions. See also List of Waste (England) Regulations 2005, SI 2005/895, Annex, List of wastes pursuant to Article 1(a) of Directive 75/442/EEC on waste and Article 1(4) of Directive 91/689/EEC on hazardous waste. Under the Burial and Cremation (Scotland) Act 2016, asp 20 (n 137 above), s 56, the Scottish Ministers may make regulations for the retention, return and disposal of ashes by a cremation authority or funeral director.

180 At time of writing there is an ongoing investigation into such issues across crematoria in Scotland, leading to a national investigation under Dame Eilish Angiolini around the provisions of ashes to parents who had lost babies following miscarriage, stillbirth, or neonatal death. See 'New national specialist team to probe baby ashes scandal', *The Herald* (Glasgow, 18 June 2014) and <http://www.gov.scot/About/Review/national-cremation-investigation>. It follows Dame Eilish's Mortonhall Investigation Report (Scottish Government, 2014) into events at that crematorium in Edinburgh. A consultation on a proposed Bill relating to burial and cremation and other related matters in Scotland, led to the Burial and Cremation (Scotland) Act 2016, asp 20 (n 137 above).

181 See para 22.66.

182 And one that still motivates the comparable office of the procurator fiscal in Scotland.

either medically or legally qualified but, in future, a medical qualification will be insufficient evidence of eligibility (see para 22.80).

22.78 The system as it stands was established in the Coroners Act 1887 which stated (s 3(1)):

> Where a coroner is informed that the dead body of a person is lying within his jurisdiction, and there is reasonable cause to suspect that such person has died either a violent or an unnatural death, or has died a sudden death of which the cause is unknown, or has died in prison, or in such place or under such circumstances as require an inquest in pursuance of any Act, the coroner, whether the cause of death arose in his jurisdiction or not, shall, as soon as practicable, issue his warrant for summoning [a jury].

The 1887 Act was significantly amended by the Coroners (Amendment) Act 1926 which, in particular, empowered a coroner to order a post-mortem examination if he had reason to suppose that a death occurring within his jurisdiction was a sudden death of which the cause was unknown and that the examination might prove an inquest to be unnecessary. The 1926 Act also restricted the coroner's mandate when dealing with deaths due to homicide and his power to charge a named person with murder, manslaughter or infanticide was removed by the Criminal Law Act 1977, s 56.

(i) The Coroners and Justice Act 2009

22.79 These requirements, and others derived from several other statutes, were consolidated into the Coroners Act 1988 while the major regulations were to be found in the Coroners Rules 1984.[183] Those provisions remained in effect until the coming into force—in July 2013—of the Coroners and Justice Act 2009 and the Coroners (Inquests) Rules 2013.[184] What follows, then, is based on the 2009 Act as it relates to the coroner's office.[185]

22.80 The most important and far-reaching changes are to be found in the administrative rather than the practical arena and, to this end, arrangements were made for the Lord Chief Justice to appoint a Chief Coroner (and deputies) who must be a High Court or a Circuit Judge (a deputy may also be an existing Senior Coroner).[186] Those office holders must be under the age of 70. The hierarchy of office holders is preserved from the 1988 Act, with changed titles, such that the 1988 hierarchy comprised (in descending order), coroners, deputy coroners, and assistant deputy coroners, while under the 2009 Act the hierarchy comprises senior coroners, area coroners, and assistant coroners. The new hierarchy is based on coroner areas and, to this end, the local authority appoints a senior coroner for each area beneath whom there are appointed a number of area coroners and assistant coroners.[187] In either case, the appointee must be aged under 70 and have possessed a relevant legal qualification for five years.[188]

---

[183] SI 1984/552.

[184] SI 2013/1616. At time of writing not all of the 2009 Act is in force; most notably those provisions in Part 1, Chapter 2 dealing with the powers of the Lord Chancellor or Secretary of State to make regulations regarding the notification, certification, and registration of deaths.

[185] The existing law is outlined in H L Whitwell, K Thorne, and A Kolar, *Mason's Forensic Medicine for Lawyers* (6th edn, Bloomsbury Professional 2015). See also P Mathews, *Jervis on Coroners* (13th edn, Sweet & Maxwell 2014) and C Dorries, *Coroners Courts* (3rd edn, Oxford University Press 2014).

[186] 2009 Act, Sch 8. The term of office of the Chief Coroner is decided by the Lord Chief Justice, in consultation with the Lord Chancellor, but must expire before 70th birthday of the Chief Coroner.

[187] 2009 Act, s 23. All may perform any of the duties of the senior coroner when he or she is absent or at the request of the senior coroner. Thus, for the purposes of statutory interpretation, the use of the word senior coroner is to include area and assistant coroners: ibid, Sch 3, s 8.

[188] ibid, Sch 3; that is, satisfying the judicial-appointment eligibility condition. See Tribunals, Courts and Enforcement Act 2007, s 50. Note that a person may not now be appointed as a coroner simply on the basis of a medical qualification. At the same time, the Lord Chancellor will be able to appoint a person to

22.81 The common law duty that currently rests on 'any person about the deceased' to inform the coroner of circumstances that indicate the need for an inquiry is likely to be significantly affected in the future as the 2009 Act only empowers the Lord Chancellor to make regulations requiring *a medical practitioner*, in prescribed cases or circumstances, to notify a senior coroner of a death of which he or she is aware.[189] Neither the cases nor the circumstances have, as yet, been prescribed but it is fairly safe to assume that they will follow existing advice and will include:

- death resulting from self-harm and neglect (excluding deaths from alcohol or nicotine abuse where the death would not be investigated but for those reasons);
- death resulting from neglect or abuse where there is an established duty of care by a public authority, other organizations, and individuals;
- death occurring during or shortly after a period of detention;
- death caused or contributed to by the conduct of the police or any other state authority or public organization;
- death relating to past or present employment;
- death resulting from lack of care or appropriate treatment, defective treatment, and adverse reaction to prescribed medicine;
- death of a child where it is unexpected;
- death where a violent crime is suspected;
- sudden and accidental death, and deaths resulting from traffic incidents;
- where a death has not been certified as the doctor is unable to identify with any confidence the cause of death;
- death where there is reason to believe it may have been caused or contributed to by a disease or condition that has been specified as being reportable to the coroner because of regional social history, for example lung disease caused through working in the coal industry; and
- death associated with pregnancy and childbirth.[190]

This will fill the gap which, surprisingly, now exists in that there is no legal obligation on a doctor to report a death directly to the coroner although, in practice, it is commonly done when he or she judges it to be expedient.[191] The main statutory duty to do so is currently vested in the Registrar.[192] The only other statutory duty to report directly to today's coroner—that which is imposed on governors of prisons, borstals, detention centres, and other similar institutions—will also be removed, although the governmental response to consultation states clearly that there is nothing to prevent them so doing should they feel it to be in the public interest.

be Medical Adviser to the Chief Coroner and as many Deputy Medical Advisers as is thought necessary (2009 Act, s 38, Sch 9, not yet in force at time of writing).

189 2009 Act, s 18, not yet in force.

190 Ministry of Justice Statutory Duty for Doctors and other Service Personnel to Report Deaths to the Coroner: Response to consultation (21 May, 2008) para 6.

191 Many coroners distribute a list of cases suitable for direct reporting but none has more than advisory standing. See Whitwell, Thorne, and Kolar, n 184, Appendix C.

192 Registration of Births and Deaths Regulations 1987, r 41, SI 1987/2088, which details the circumstances in which he must do so.

2. The coroner's investigation

22.82 A senior coroner who is made aware that the body of a person is within his or her area[193] must conduct an investigation into the death if there is reason to suspect that:

the deceased died a violent or unnatural death,
the cause of death is unknown, or
the deceased died in custody or otherwise in state detention.[194]

It is, however, to be noted that the scope of the investigation is limited to ascertaining:

(a) who the deceased was;
(b) how, when and where the deceased came by his or her death;[195]
(c) the particulars (if any) required by the 1953 Act to be registered concerning the death.[196]

In particular, a determination may not be framed in such a way as to appear to determine any criminal liability on the part of a named person or civil liability in general.[197] According to the Explanatory Notes to the 2009 Act,[198] the continuity in the statutory treatment of the two verdicts or conclusions can be traced from the 1887 Act to the 2013 Rules,[199] 'which suggests that in all the statutory references to justifiable and then lawful killing, Parliament has intended such a conclusion to amount to a positive finding that the death did not result from homicide.'

22.83 The Lord Chancellor was given the power in the 2009 Act to make Coroners' Regulations dealing with investigations, examinations, and exhumations. Those regulations were applicable from 25 July 2013,[200] but do not invalidate any post-mortem examinations held before that date.[201] The senior coroner is required to keep a register of all deaths reported in their area, which contains the particulars identifying the deceased, and is required to attempt to identify and notify the deceased's next of kin that an investigation is to begin.[202] While the investigation is under way, or has been discontinued, the coroner may issue an interim death

[193] Note that it is the locality of the body that is definitive. The duty exists irrespective of where the death occurred; hence, it applies when, for example, a body is returned from abroad: *R v West Yorkshire Coroner, ex p Smith* [1983] QB 335.

[194] 2009 Act, s 1(2). In respect of deaths in custody in Scotland, see the Inquiries into Fatal Accidents and Sudden Deaths etc. (Scotland) Act 2016, asp 2.

[195] In *R v HM Coroner for North Humberside and Scunthorpe, ex p Jamieson* [1995] QB 1, it was said that 'how' was restricted to 'by what means' and not 'in what broad circumstances'. The 2009 Act, however, states at s 5(2) that this purpose is to be read as including the purpose of ascertaining in what circumstances the deceased came by his or her death—this being a consequence of the Human Rights Act 1998. In *Chief Constable of Devon and Cornwall v HM Coroner for Plymouth, Torbay and South Devon* [2013] EWHC 3729 (Admin), Stuart-Smith J endorsed the view of Etherton LJ in *R v Mid and North Shropshire Coroner, ex p. Lewis* [2010] 1 WLR 1836, that this change had been brought when para 7(1) of Sch 5 to the 2009 Act had superseded rule 43 of the Coroners Rules 1984, and which was 'doubtless' with Article 2 obligations in mind. To that end, see Part 7 of the Coroners (Investigations) Regulations 2013, SI 2013/1629, in relation to action to prevent other deaths.

[196] 2009 Act, s 5(1). The coroner and the jury may, however, *explore* facts bearing on civil and criminal liability; the prohibition applies only to the *determination*, hence the current, somewhat bizarre, situation where a coroner in England can criticize military commanders in cases of dead combatants whose bodies are repatriated from battle zones several thousand miles away.

[197] 2009 Act, s 10(2).

[198] 2013 Rules at para 69.

[199] Coroners (Inquests) Rules 2013, SI 2013/1616.

[200] Coroners' Rules which are concerned with the practice and procedures in inquests have been set out in The Coroners (Inquests) Rules 2013, SI 2013/1616, discussed below, and the Coroners (Investigations) Regulations 2013, SI 2013/1629 (2009 Act, s 43). By virtue of s 45 of the 2009 Act coroners Rules can also be made by virtue of the Constitutional Reform Act 2005, Sch 1.

[201] SI 2013/1629, r 3.

[202] SI 2013/1629, Part 2.

certificate, of the fact of death, and must notify the next of kin and other interested persons of the resumption of the investigation.[203] Where a coroner considers that a post-mortem examination should be carried out under s14,[204] she or he must request the examination by suitable practitioner, and must do so in consultation with the chief officer of police where a homicide is suspected. In such circumstances, certain persons are required to be notified of the date, time, and place of the post-mortem examination.[205] Further provisions have been made in respect of the preservation or retention of material from a post-mortem examination. These include written notification of the fact that the material has been retained as relating to the cause of death and a view as to how long the material should be preserved or retained.[206] The provisions applicable to notification require the coroner to also notify the next of kin or personal representative of the deceased that the material is being retained and for how long it requires to be retained. Options available for dealing with the material include disposal (burial or cremation), return to the personal represented or next of kin, and further retention with the consent of those persons. Further provisions apply to the provision of information and documentation,[207] and in relation to bodies, which are required to be released for burial or cremation as soon as is reasonably practicable.[208] Forms available to the coroner have been set out in regulations, covering *inter alia* the certification of the fact of death, and an order for the burial of the deceased.[209]

As a consequence of an investigation he or she has made, the senior coroner has certain options open. She or he can decide that no further action is called for; in this case, she or he notifies the Registrar to accept the certificate of death granted by the medical practitioner. She or he can order a post-mortem dissection[210] and, if it is decided as a result of this that no further investigation is required, the senior coroner must discontinue the investigation and will certify the cause of death as indicated by the autopsy;[211] this coroner's certificate invalidates any previous medical certificate as to the cause of death.[212] Note, however, that these exemptions do not apply if there is reason to suppose that the death was violent or otherwise unnatural or that it occurred in custody.[213] In any other circumstances, the senior coroner must hold an inquest without a jury[214] or with a jury if it is considered appropriate. But there *must* be a jury if: **22.84**

- the death occurred in custody or otherwise in state detention and that either the death was unnatural or the cause was unknown;

203 SI 2013/1629, r 9, 10.
204 See para 22.84.
205 SI 2013/1629, r 13. Those persons include the next of kin or the personal representative of the deceased, the deceased's regular medical practitioner, the hospital in which the deceased died (if applicable), and the appropriate authority where the death may have been caused by an accident or disease which must be reported.
206 SI 2013/1629, r 14.
207 SI 2013/1629, Part 6.
208 SI 2013/1629, Part 5.
209 SI 2013/1629, Schedule.
210 2009 Act, s 14. Note that the person nominated to perform the post-mortem examination must not only be approved by the coroner but must also be licensed to do so: Human Tissue Act 2004, s 16(2)(b). The Lord Chancellor is empowered under s 43 to make regulations in respect of the practice and procedure around post-mortem examinations.
211 2009 Act, s 4(1)(a).
212 It is to be noted, particularly, that the authority to order a post-mortem examination prior to deciding whether or not to hold an inquest extends to the situation in which it is uncertain whether the death was violent or natural and that the examination may be directed to solving the problem.
213 2009 Act, s 4(2), s 7.
214 ibid, s 6. An inquest will form part of an investigation. Where s 6 applies, there is a duty to open an inquest as soon as is reasonably practicable, to be completed within six months of the coroner having been made aware of the death, or as soon as reasonably practicable thereafter: SI 2013/1616, r 5(1), r 8. The coroner conducting the inquest may make use of an assessor who should not, however, combine his role

- the death resulted from an act or omission of a police officer or an armed forces equivalent in the purported execution of their duty;
- the death was caused by a notifiable accident, poisoning, or disease.[215]

22.85 The senior coroner will have discretion as to additional reasons for calling a jury if there is sufficient reason for so doing[216]—one governing principle is that the case should be put before a jury if a recurrence could be prevented or safeguarded against as a result of action taken by some authority.[217] On the other hand, the senior coroner will still be restricted in cases of murder, manslaughter, infanticide, fatal road traffic offences, suicide in which there may have been abetment, or causing the death of a child or vulnerable adult. In the event of a person being charged or being likely to be charged with such offences in relation to the death of the deceased, the coroner must accede to a request from the relevant prosecuting authority to adjourn the inquest;[218] the coroner need not resume the inquest after the relevant criminal proceedings but, if she or he does so, the finding of the inquest must not be inconsistent with the outcome of those proceedings.[219]

22.86 Rules for the conduct of inquests were made by the Lord Chief Justice, in agreement with the Lord Chancellor. Like the regulations applicable to coroners investigations, discussed above,[220] the rules are applicable from 25 July 2013.[221] The rules apply where a coroner is under a duty to hold an inquest by virtue of the 2009 Act,[222] which is a duty that exists as part of the duty to hold an investigation. As such, similar notification and disclosure provisions apply as apply to coroners inquests,[223] but more specific provisions have been made for the taking of evidence at the inquest. These provisions apply, for example, to evidence by video link, written evidence, and evidence given from behind a screen, as directed by the coroner.[224] The sequence of examination of witnesses is also set out in the regulations. Unless otherwise determined by the coroner, witnesses must be examined first by the coroner, then by any interested person, and finally by the witness's representative, if applicable.[225] Regulations also set out relevant forms, such as those applicable to the coroners records,[226] and for the summons to be sent to jurors and to witnesses.[227]

22.87 Following the inquest, the coroner provides the registrar with a certificate after inquest which includes the circumstantial as well as the medical causes of death. Statements signed

with that of an expert witness: *R v HM Coroner for Surrey, ex p Wright* [1997] QB 786 (QBD); (1997) 35 BMLR 57 (CA). The procedure may, therefore, be very similar to that adopted in the Scottish Fatal Accident Inquiry.

[215] 2009 Act, s 7(2). The current requirements in relation to the safety of the public are now provided as a general part of an investigation (ibid, Sch 5, para 7 and Part 7 of the investigation regulations, SI 2013/1629).

[216] ibid, s 7(3).

[217] *R v HM Coroner for Hammersmith, ex p B Peach (No 1)* [1980] QB 211 (CA).

[218] 2009 Act, Sch 1, part 1. Somewhat similar restrictions apply in the case of a death being subject to an inquiry under the Inquiries Act 2005 and the Lord Chancellor so requests.

[219] 2009 Act, Sch 1, para 8(5). A list of recommended conclusions open to the coroner's inquest is to be found in The Coroners (Inquests) Rules 2013, SI 2013/1616. Determinations and findings are required under s 10 of the 2009 Act using Form 2 of the 2013 Rules, the latter being reproduced in Appendix B.

[220] At para 22.83.

[221] SI 2013/1616, r 3.

[222] 2009 Act s 6.

[223] SI 2013/1616, Part 2 and 3. See para 22.83.

[224] SI 2013/1616, rr 17–19.

[225] SI 2013/1616, r 21.

[226] SI 2013/1616, Part 6.

[227] SI 2013/1616, Schedule.

by both the witness and the coroner are known as depositions and can be used in subsequent legal proceedings, provided that they were taken in the presence of the person who is accused at any later criminal trial.

3. Exhumation

The role of the coroner is not yet done, as the office has much to do with the lawful disturbance of a body that is supposedly resting in peace. The law on exhumation is a strange mixture of administrative, criminal, ecclesiastical, and common law jurisdictions. Generally speaking, it is an offence at common law to remove a body from a burial ground in the absence of authority to do so.[228] As to that authority, much depends on the distinction between the power to order and the power to authorize recovery of a dead body. **22.88**

The main power to order is now to be found in the 2009 Act[229] which states, somewhat baldly, that a senior coroner may order the exhumation of a person's body if he or she thinks it necessary in respect of any coronial investigation of a death or, particularly, for the purposes of any criminal proceedings that have been instituted in respect of that person's death, or of another person whose death was connected with the death of that person. **22.89**

Unless an exhumation is regulated by another piece of legislation or it is a matter only of moving the body from one consecrated piece of ground to another,[230] the process of authorizing the procedure is governed by the Burial Act 1857, s 25, under which it is not lawful to remove any body from any place of burial without licence from, now, the Ministry of Justice. The exceptions that apply under s 25 are removal in accordance with a faculty granted by the court and, more recently, a body or remains removed following a proposal under the Care of Cathedrals Measure.[231] When granting a licence under s 25, the Secretary of State is under a duty to act both rationally and in accordance with the general principles of public law on the exercise of a statutory discretion.[232] There is now some doubt as to the interpretation of the words 'any place of burial' as the Ministry itself appears to limit this to 'places' of burial that are recognizable as such.[233] The problem is, however, peripheral to the present discussion; it appears mainly to be concerned with archaeological excavation and will no doubt be addressed in the anticipated reconsideration of burial laws.[234] **22.90**

---

[228] D A Smale, Davies' *Law of Burial, Cremation and Exhumation* (6th edn, Shaw & Sons 1997) 191, quoting, inter alia, *R v Jacobsen* (1880) Cox CC 522. Note, however, that the 7th edition was published in 2007 and an 8th edition is due in 2018. But see also Burial Act 1857, s 25, discussed in para 22.90, and sections 27-31 of the Burial and Cremation (Scotland) Act 2016, asp 20 (n 137 above), empowering the Scottish Ministers to make regulations for or in connection with the exhumation of human remains.

[229] Sch, 5, para 6.

[230] In which case all that is required is a faculty granted by way of the ecclesiastical Consistory Court for the diocese. Case law over the decades suggests that a fairly liberal attitude is adopted in family matters. Elsewhere—eg for scientific research—a compelling case must be made in order to displace a presumption against exhumation: compare *Re Holy Trinity, Bosham* [2004] Fam 125 (DNA testing for archaeological purposes—faculty refused) with *Re St Mary's, Sledmere* [2007] 1 WLR 1538 (viral epidemiological study—faculty granted). For guidance, see *Re Atkins* [1989] 1 All ER 14.

[231] Care of Cathedrals Measure 2011 (No 1). S 25 substituted by the Church of England (Miscellaneous Provisions) Measure 2014, SI 2014/1, s2.

[232] *R (on the application of Plantagenet Alliance Ltd) v Secretary of State for Justice* [2014] EWHC 1662 (QB), which dealt with the exhumation of the remains of King Richard III. See also n 173 and the decision in *R (on the application of Rudewicz) v Ministry of Justice* [2012] EWCA Civ 499; [2013] QB 410, on the role of religion in respect of exhumation and reburial.

[233] See S Gallagher and F Cosgrove-Wilson, 'Exhuming Justice' (2008) 158 NLJ 90.

[234] See n 144. It is noteworthy that the bodies of combatant servicemen which are unburied are protected by the Protection of Military Remains Act 1986.

22.91 Otherwise, the disposal of remains in church-owned burial grounds that are to be built over is controlled by the Disused Burial Grounds (Amendment) Act 1981. Basically, the surviving relatives, if any, of those who have been buried for more than twenty-five years must be given the opportunity to reinter the remains. Alternatively, the church itself may reinter the remains or the grave may be rendered inaccessible. Similar conditions apply to the use of non-religious burial grounds under the terms of the Town and Country Planning Act 1990, ss 238–40.

G. Post-mortem Examination and the Disposal of Body Parts

1. Post-mortem examinations

22.92 For all practical purposes, post-mortem examinations can be regarded as being of two types—those that are ordered by the coroner and those that are loosely known as 'hospital post-mortems'.[235]

(i) The coroner's autopsy

22.93 The former have been discussed already under the heading of 'The Coroner' but, in addition, it is to be noted that the provisions of the Human Tissue Act 2004 do not apply if the case is under investigation by the coroner, and a person may not take any action in respect of the use of human remains without the coroner's authority if he or she has reason to believe that the case may be one which comes within the coroner's remit.[236] However, the majority of examinations which were the subject of complaint at Alder Hey and elsewhere derived from coroners' cases and, as a result, distinct and stringent regulations have been introduced as to the disposal of tissues following a medico-legal autopsy. These are discussed in para 22.98.

(ii) The hospital autopsy

22.94 A hospital autopsy is the ultimate audit of a patient's disease process and its treatment. It also has a strong public interest dimension as it will provide information that can be applied in future similar cases and, as such, is a near essential component of medical education. For these reasons it is, at best, incomplete unless it is combined with the retention of tissues of which the very small fragments used for the preparation of microscopy slides form an integral part.[237] On the other hand, a procedure that clearly involves mutilation of the body may well be offensive to the next of kin. The balance between the public need and private antipathy is, therefore, particularly delicate and post-mortem examinations as a whole are now subject to the governance of the Human Tissue Authority established under the Human Tissue Act 2004, Pt 2 which, inter alia, must also provide a Code of Practice.[238] The current Code pays particular attention to ensuring the relatives' understanding of what the procedure involves[239] and to the often forgotten profound cultural distinctions that exist in this sensitive area—in general, for example, post-mortem examinations are not willingly acceptable within Islam while orthodox Jewish law views an autopsy as a desecration of the body which should be avoided so far as is possible.[240]

---

[235] In so far as 'post-mortem' is adjectival in this context, it would be more correct to speak of coroner's or hospital autopsies. But the term is in popular use and can be regarded as synonymous with 'autopsy' in this context. As regards coroners investigations and inquests, see paras 22.83 and 22.86, above, respectively.

[236] Human Tissue Act 2004, s 11.

[237] In Scotland, such slides are regarded as part of the patient's clinical notes and are retained as such. As to the preservation or retention of material from a post-mortem examination, see The Coroners (Investigations) Regulations 2013, SI 2013/1629, r 14, discussed at para 22.83.

[238] Human Tissue Authority *Code of Practice—Post mortem examination*, Code 3 (July, 2006).

[239] See also *AB v Leeds Teaching Hospital NHS Trust* [2005] QB 506.

[240] S Hollins, *Religions, Culture and Healthcare* (Radcliffe 2006).

Statutory regulation of the hospital autopsy lies in the 2004 Act where determining the cause of death is but one of the twelve scheduled purposes for which appropriate consent, with its extended requirements as described in para 22.99 below, is an essential prerequisite to legality. The pathologist performing the autopsy must have a licence to do so, and one who fails to reach the high standards set by the Code of Practice may well forfeit his or her licence.[241] All these changes are to be welcomed as bringing pathology into line with the modern standards of ethical medical practice. At the same time, it cannot be denied that arranging for a hospital autopsy is now a more complicated process than was once the case and there is no doubt that their number has dropped since the new regulations came into force; this may be, however, coincidental and no more than part of a worldwide trend.[242] **22.95**

(iii) The disposal of body parts

Until recently, the common law understanding that there is no property in a dead body or its parts has dominated the law in respect of their disposal.[243] Effectively, there was no certainty as to who owned or possessed the cadaver and its parts, the extent of any possessory rights being determined by the specific conditions. Thus, for example, the executors were generally, but not universally, agreed to be in possession of the body for the purpose of its disposal.[244] Clearly, however, the body and its parts will, from time to time, be in the possession of someone else for other purposes—perhaps the most obvious example being the coroner and his or her pathologist for the purposes of a coroner's investigation. In the present context, we are most concerned with the body which has been held for post-mortem examination of whichever type and, then, particularly in respect of ownership, with those body parts that have been removed and retained for further study. The special significance of body parts derives from the now well-established rule that *ownership* of them can pass to a person who, while in legitimate possession of the body as a whole, did such work on that part as to endow it with characteristics that differentiate it from mere dead tissue—a rule which greatly concerns the pathologist and which lay at the heart of the Alder Hey and other controversies.[245] **22.96**

Conditions have, however, combined to cast considerable doubt on the viability of the 'no property' aphorism which, because of its negative nature, was never very helpful. In the first place, the escalation of medical and scientific skills, particularly in the fields of biomedicine and organ transplantation has shown that, given the concept of property as being something that has value and that can be bartered, the statement is simply no longer true.[246] Secondly, the outcry at the retention of body parts after death—and especially those of children[247]—was such as to demonstrate that, irrespective of financial considerations, body parts have **22.97**

[241] Human Tissue Act 2004, s 16(2). At the time of writing it is unclear whether he or she will require a licence under the 2004 Act in addition to a licence to practise under the Medical Act 1983 (see para 22.51) or whether they can be combined.

[242] J L Burton and J C Underwood, 'Necropsy Practice after the "Organ Retention Scandal": Requests, Performance and Tissue Retention' (2003) 56 J Clin Pathol 537; G O'Grady, 'Death of the Teaching Autopsy' (2003) 327 BMJ 802.

[243] See M Quigley, 'Property in Human Biomaterials—Separating Persons and Things?' (2012) 32 OJLS 659–83, which offers a philosophical challenge to the traditional distinction between persons and things; and I Goold, L Skene, J Herring, and K Greasley, 'The Human Body as Property? Possession, Control and Commodification' (2014) 40(1) J Med Ethics 1–2. For an overall treatment of the field, see N Hoppe, *Bioequity: Property and The Human Body* (Ashgate 2009).

[244] The proposition appears to rest on *Williams v Williams* [1881–85] All ER Rep 840.

[245] The origin of this lies in the otherwise very unsatisfactory Australian case *Doodeward v Spence* (1908) 6 CLR 406. It has been confirmed more recently in two UK cases: *Dobson v North Tyneside Health Authority* [1997] 1 WLR 596 (CA) and *R v Kelly* [1998] 3 All ER 741; (2000) 51 BMLR 142.

[246] In recent times, it was, apparently, not uncommon practice to sell pituitary glands removed at autopsy: P Ellis, 'Organ Retention Scandals' (2001) 3 J Pers Inj L 261.

[247] eg House of Commons Report of the Royal Liverpool Children's (Alder Hey) Inquiry (January 2001).

an *emotional* value that is recognizable as such. They can no longer be dismissed as mere *res nullius*.[248]

22.98 The time may have come, therefore, for regarding human remains as property[249]—at least in respect of possession and disposal by the variously interested parties—and, thus, introducing some coherence and uniformity into the currently inconsistent law.[250] The alternative is to formulate a system of control of body parts based on a rigidly applied consent model[251] and this is the route that has been adopted in the Human Tissue Act 2004.[252] The Human Tissue Authority has also Published guidance on the Disposal of Human Tissue.[253]

22.99 Section 1 of the 2004 Act governs those activities which shall be lawful if done for 'scheduled purposes' with appropriate consent; there are twelve such activities pertaining to the deceased.[254] Although these vary considerably as to significance in the present context, they are listed here *in toto* for sake of completeness:

(1) Anatomical examination;[255]
(2) Determining the cause of death;
(3) Establishing after a person's death the efficacy of any drug or other treatment administered to him;
(4) Obtaining scientific or medical information about a living or deceased person which may be relevant to any other person (including a future person);
(5) Public display;
(6) Research in connection with disorders, or the functioning, of the human body;

[248] Both these points are exemplified in *AB v Leeds Teaching Hospital NHS Trust* [2005] QB 506, where damages could be awarded in such circumstances on the grounds of psychiatric injury, although it was stated that there was no case in England and Wales involving the tort of interference with a dead body. A similar claim based on *actio inuriarum* has probably always been available in Scotland: *Stevens v Yorkhill NHS Trust* (2007) 95 BMLR 1. On that topic, see N Whitty, 'Rights of Personality, Property Rights and the Human Body in Scots Law' (2005) 9 Edin LR 194.

[249] There is some evidence that judicial views are, in fact, changing—at least in respect of the living: *Yearworth v North Bristol NHS Trust* (2009) 107 BMLR 47 (CC and CA)—a case subsequently used by the Supreme Court of British Colombia in respect of the ownership of donor sperm, in *JCM v ANA* 2012 BCSC 584. If and how *Yearworth* can be extrapolated to the dead remains to be seen, in particular in respect of the interaction of the law of bailment and the law of probate, and the fact that the stored gametes were the property of the men that had them stored. For analysis, see S H E Harmon and G T Laurie, '*Yearworth v North Bristol NHS Trust*: Property, Principles, Precedents and Paradigms' (2010) 69 The Cambridge Law Journal 476–93.

[250] For a recent full discussion from this aspect, see R J Hardcastle, *Law and the Human Body: Property Rights, Ownership and Control* (Hart 2007), and for a more recent consideration that post-dates *Yearworth*, see I Goold, K Greasley, J Herring, and L Skene (eds), *Persons, Parts and Property* (Hart 2014). See also Chapter 14, paras 14.173–14.176 and Chapter 19, paras 19.69–19.70.

[251] Mason and Laurie argued the merits of the two models before the Act was passed and concluded in favour of a modified property model: J K Mason and G T Laurie. 'Consent or Property? Dealing with the Body and its Parts in the Shadow of Bristol and Alder Hey' (2001) 64 MLR 711. For further analysis of alternatives, see C H Harrison, 'Neither *Moore* Nor the Market: Alternative Models for Compensating Contributors of Human Tissue' (2002) 28 Am J L and Med 77.

[252] See also the Human Tissue (Scotland) Act 2006. There are some differences in that the English Act deals almost exclusively with the retention of rather than the therapeutic use of body parts; it is, as a result, rather more appropriate to the present discussion and the 2006 Act is not considered further.

[253] Human Tissue Authority *Code of Practice 5—Disposal of Human Tissue* (July 2014, reviewed July 2016, revised codes in effect from April 2017). See also The Royal College of Pathologists and the Institute of Biomedical Science guidance: *The retention and storage of pathological records and specimens* (4th edn, 2009).

[254] Human Tissue Act 2004, Sch 1. For a discussion of the application of s 1, see *CM v EJ's Executor* [2013] Med LR 321, (2013) 133 BMLR 203.

[255] Note that the Anatomy Act is repealed by the 2004 Act and its provisions are incorporated therein. The Anatomy Act remains in force in Scotland. The regulation of anatomy schools is not considered further in this chapter.

(7) Transplantation;
(8) Clinical audit;[256]
(9) Education or training relating to human health;
(10) Performance assessment;
(11) Public health monitoring;
(12) Quality assurance.

Thus, the 2004 Act is dominated by consent to the storage and use of body parts (see Chapter 19) but what is 'appropriate consent' differs as to whether the body is that of a child (s 2) or an adult (s 3). In either case, any extant consent which was provided in writing by the dead person in life, prevails.[257] If, however, there is no such evidence, power to consent in the case of a child passes to those having parental responsibility[258] or, failing this, to a person in a qualifying relationship.[259] In the case of an adult who has made no decision in life, consent is vested in his or her representative nominated for this purpose under s 4 of the Act or, if there is no such appointment in force, to a person in a qualifying relationship. Special regulations apply in the case of an adult who lacks the capacity to consent[260]—in general, such a person will be deemed to have consented if it is adjudged in good faith to be in his or her best interests. Finally, it will be lawful for any material retained under Sch 1 to the 2004 Act to be dealt with as waste when it ceases to be used, or stored for use, for its original purpose[261] and, in this connection, disposal as waste constitutes decent disposal.[262]

We have, however, already noted that no consent is required for the coroner's investigations and, as a corollary, that the conditions of the Human Tissue Act have no relevance in such procedures. Nonetheless, the sensitivities of surviving relatives must be respected and this is reflected in the new coroners' rules[263] which now insist on certain safeguards which were, previously, conspicuous by their absence. These include: **22.100**

(1) The responsible pathologist must make provision, so far as possible, for the preservation of material which in his opinion bears upon the cause of death or the identification of the deceased and he must notify the coroner when this has been done;
(2) He or she must identify the material being preserved, explain the reasons for so doing and specify the period for which it is believed the material should be preserved;
(3) The coroner must notify the pathologist of the period for which he requires the material to be preserved, this being such period as in the coroner's opinion the material needs to be preserved for the purpose of fulfilling his functions under, now, the Coroners and Justice Act 2009,[264] and he may specify different periods for different materials;

[256] This and subsequent activities relate to deceased persons only.
[257] In the case of an adult, a provision in a will qualifies as 'consent': s 3(5)(c).
[258] But the consent in writing is essential if storage or use is intended for public display or anatomical dissection: s 2(5) in the case of a child, s 3(4) in that of an adult. As to wills and the provisos of the 2004 Act, see *CM v EJ's Executor* [2013] Med LR 321, (2013) 133 BMLR 203.
[259] A qualifying relationship is defined in s 54(9) and runs in hierarchal fashion from a spouse or civil partner, through other familial relations to a friend of long-standing.
[260] Human Tissue Act 2004 (Persons who Lack Capacity to Consent and Transplants) Regulations 2006, SI 2006/1659, as amended by the Quality and Safety of Organs Intended for Transplantation Regulations 2012/1501.
[261] 2004 Act, s 44(3)(b).
[262] ibid, s 54(4).
[263] Coroners Rules 1984, r 9, SI 1984/552, as amended by the Coroners (Amendment) Rules 2005, r 3, SI 2005/420.
[264] See para 22.83, above, on retention and disposal of material following a coroners investigation and inquiry.

(4) The coroner must also notify a close relative[265] or representative of the deceased that the material is being preserved, the period for which it is required to be preserved and the options for dealing with the material on expiry of that period. These include lawful disposal of the material by the pathologist, return of the material to a person who requests that the material be returned to him or her, or retention of the material with the consent of the responsible surviving relative for medical research or other purposes. Confirmation that one of these has been done is now obligatory.

22.101 Further regulations refer to retention of tissues in relation to criminal activity, for the purposes of public inquiries, and for variation in the periods for retention of the tissues.[266] Acknowledging that there is an ethical basis for the retention of tissues for research following coroners' autopsies[267] is particularly welcome. An immense amount of research material is available in the tissues of persons dying from violence. This is particularly so, for example, as to the study of pathology as it occurs in the 'normal' population or, as a corollary, the morbid anatomy of pre-symptomatic disease; it can surely be comforting to surviving relatives to know that violent and unexpected deaths have not been wholly purposeless when the tissues have been put to such use. It was the uncertainty of the need for consent to such activity that caused the problems of the recent past and it is good that that lacuna has been filled.

H. Conclusion

1. Death and the medico-legal curriculum

22.102 What has become evident in the composition of this chapter, is the incremental increase in emphasis placed on death, not only in the medico-legal curriculum, but also by the legislatures of the United Kingdom. By that it should be understood that reference is to the consequences of death itself, rather than those events that precede death—which are more properly considered to be end-of-life issues. It is therefore important first to understand what is meant by death, in terms of its definition, prior to being able to consider the consequences of the event at the end of the process that culminates in the death of the human organism. Such a consideration will, in turn, inform the philosophical and practical relationship between cardiorespiratory and brain death outwith the ambience of transplantation therapy.

22.103 The formalities following a death will depend on the circumstances—or likely circumstances—surrounding that death, and which will, in turn, hinge on a range of legislative instruments. It may be self-evident that both the medico-legal and the medical curricula will require to keep pace with these changes, yet it is difficult to see how the subject can be properly accommodated, when the more ethically and legally contentious—and in the views of some, more interesting—subjects are, technically speaking, end-of-life issues, rather than issues directly applicable to death itself. This applies to the Permanent Vegetative State just as it does to organ donation, each of which was dealt with in previous chapters of this book. The end result is the fact that the medico-legal administrative aspects of death are likely to be neglected. All hope is not lost, however, not least following the recent and ongoing unmasking and control of criminality, particularly, and unexpectedly,

[265] SI 1984/552, r 20(2)(a).
[266] SI 1984/552, r 9A.
[267] ibid, r 12(7)(c).

within the health-caring professions themselves. Another 'unmasking' involving the medical profession in recent years has been the retention of human tissue. Both of these issues have impelled both legislative and professional regulation, albeit that the former has at times driven the latter.

While the Coroners and Justice Act may have been an over-reactive measure, and Dr Shipman may have been unique as a murderer, it is beyond question that there was at the time no mechanism—other than by way of a suspicious relative—by which his activities would be exposed.[268] But the fact that he had *so many* victims can also be attributed to failure on the part of the large number who signed the necessary secondary certificates for those who *were* cremated.[269] Such persons were not criminals. They were either lax in, or they were ill-informed as to, their duties—and the latter is important because it is a remediable fault. **22.104**

The Coroners and Justice Act may turn out to be a much needed and enlightened item of medical law; on the other hand, it could, by reason of its complex structure, become another administrative albatross around the neck of a hard-pressed profession. In either case, it is social attitudes which are of fundamental importance in moulding the way in which we manage the process of dying—and this could well provide a fitting coda to the chapter. **22.105**

2. The ways we die

According to the Office for National Statistics, there were more than 500,000 deaths reported in England and Wales[270] in 2015—and, significantly from the point of view of planning for their care and ultimate disposal, that number is likely to rise to 530,000 by 2030.[271] While most people say they would prefer to die at home, it is to be remembered that such a preference is expressed when the individual is fit and in a happy family relationship. We do not know what will be the circumstances nor how we are likely to feel when death is imminent. In England and Wales in 2012, 22 per cent of deaths took place at home, 20 per cent in care homes, and 6 per cent in hospices.[272] Perhaps the saddest feature is that an almost equal number of deaths take place at home as occur in care homes, receiving neither expert medical care nor familial love—but this is probably inevitable given the conditions of modern urban life. It is also somewhat disheartening to read that only 6 per cent of deaths occur in dedicated hospices, which is surely a reflection of the fact that the great majority of hospices are run as charities and that, as a result, their number in no way meets their need. There is, however, some evidence of a change that may have a positive effect, insofar as there is a drive towards more integrated health and social care. **22.106**

[268] It is, currently, no part of the Registrar's *duties* to question a certificate of a *natural* cause of death—and it would have been a particularly astute Registrar who would have noted, as appeared later in the Report, that the 'natural' death rate among Dr Shipman's female patients aged 65–74 was some ten times that in comparable practices. In point of fact, his ultimate exposure can be attributed to a suspicious relative who happened to be legally qualified.

[269] 208 of the 260 cases of Dr Shipman that were considered in the Smith Report were, in fact, cremated.

[270] <http://www.ons.gov.uk/peoplepopulationandcommunity/birthsdeathsandmarriages/deaths/bulletins/deathsregistrationsummarytables/2015>.

[271] B Gomes and I J Higginson, 'Where People Die (1974–2030): Past Trends, Future Projections and Implications for Care' (2008) 22 Palliative Medicine 33–41. Note, too, the change in the declining trend in the statistics in n 270, above.

[272] Mortality Statistics: Deaths Registered in England and Wales (Series DR), 2012. Office for National Statistics, quoted in *The end of life care strategy: New ambitions* (The National Council for Palliative Care, 2013).

22.107 The UK Government announced increased funding in the 2013 spending round to ensure greater integration of health and social care.[273] In the end, however, there is no real substitute for devoted family care of the dying. The immovable difficulty is, as a leading article in *The Times* once put it, that: 'You cannot legislate for love'.[274]

[273] The £5.3bn Better Care Fund aims to place the cared for person at the centre of service delivery, which at policy level is not dissimilar to the Scottish Government's legislative integration of health and social care, under the Public Bodies (Joint Working) (Scotland) Act, 2014 asp 9, that received royal assent on 1 April 2014. The Care Act 2014, c 23 is also notable in this regard in respect of England and Wales.

[274] Leading Article 'Who Cares?' *The Times* (14 January 2009) 2.

APPENDIX A

MED A 22 482371

BIRTHS AND DEATHS REGISTRATION ACT 1953

(Form prescribed by the Registration of Births and Deaths Regulations 1987)

Registrar to enter No. of Death Entry

MEDICAL CERTIFICATE OF CAUSE OF DEATH

For use only by a Registered Medical Practitioner WHO HAS BEEN IN ATTENDANCE during the deceased's last illness, and to be delivered by him forthwith to the Registrar of Births and Deaths.

Name of deceased ....

Date of death as stated to me .... day of .... Age as stated to me ....

Place of death ....

Last seen alive by me .... day of ....

1 The certified cause of death takes account of information obtained from post-mortem.
2 Information from post-mortem may be available later.
3 Post-mortem not being held.
4 I have reported this death to the Coroner for further action.
[See overleaf]

Please ring appropriate digit(s) and letter

a Seen after death by me.
b Seen after death by another medical practitioner but not by me.
c Not seen after death by a medical practitioner.

CAUSE OF DEATH

The condition thought to be the 'Underlying Cause of Death' should appear in the lowest completed line of Part I.

These particulars not to be entered in death register

Approximate interval between onset and death

I (a) Disease or condition directly leading to death† ....

(b) Other disease or condition, if any, leading to I(a) ....

(c) Other disease or condition, if any, leading to I(b) ....

II Other significant conditions CONTRIBUTING TO THE DEATH but not related to the disease or condition causing it. ....

SPECIMEN

The death might have been due to or contributed to by the employment followed at some time by the deceased. ☐ Please tick where applicable

†This does not mean the mode of dying, such as heart failure, asphyxia, asthenia, etc: it means the disease, injury, or complication which caused death.

I hereby certify that I was in medical attendance during the above named deceased's last illness, and that the particulars and cause of death above written are true to the best of my knowledge and belief.

Signature .... Qualifications as registered by General Medical Council ....

Residence .... Date ....

For deaths in hospital: Please give the name of the consultant responsible for the above-named as a patient ....

Complete where applicable

A	B
I have reported this death to the Coroner for further action. Initials of certifying medical practitioner.	I may be in a position later to give, on application by the Registrar General, additional information as to the cause of death for the purpose of more precise statistical classification. Initials of certifying medical practitioner. ....

The death should be referred to the coroner if:

- the cause of death is unknown
- the deceased was not seen by the certifying doctor *either* after death *or* within the 14 days before death
- the death was violent or unnatural or was suspicious
- the death may be due to an accident (whenever it occurred)
- the death may be due to self-neglect or neglect by others
- the death may be due to an industrial disease or related to the deceased's employment
- the death may be due to an abortion
- the death occurred during an operation or before recovery from the effects of an anaesthetic
- the death may be a suicide
- the death occurred during or shortly after detention in police or prison custody

LIST OF SOME OF THE CATEGORIES OF DEATH WHICH MAY BE OF INDUSTRIAL ORIGIN

MALIGNANT DISEASES	Causes include
(a) Skin	– radiation and sunlight – pitch or tar – mineral oils
(b) Nasal	– wood or leather work – nickel
(c) Lung	– asbestos – chromates – nickel – radiation
(d) Pleura and peritoneum	– asbestos
(e) Urinary tract	– benzidine – dyestuff manufacture – rubber manufacture
(f) Liver	– PVC manufacture
(g) Bone	– radiation
(h) Lymphatics and haematopoietic	– radiation – benzene
POISONING	
(a) Metals	e.g. arsenic, cadmium, lead
(b) Chemicals	e.g. chlorine, benzene
(c) Solvents	e.g. trichlorethylene

INFECTIOUS DISEASES	Causes include
(a) Anthrax	– imported bone, bonemeal hide or fur
(b) Brucellosis	– farming or veterinary
(c) Tuberculosis	– contact at work
(d) Leptospirosis	– farming, sewer or under-ground workers
(e) Tetanus	– farming or gardening
(f) Rabies	– animal handling
(g) Viral hepatitis	– contact at work
CHRONIC LUNG DISEASES	
(a) Occupational asthma	– sensitising agent at work
(b) Allergic alveolitis	– farming
(c) Pneumoconiosis	– mining and quarrying – potteries – asbestos
(d) Chronic bronchitis and emphysema	– underground coal mining

NOTE:—The Practitioner, on signing the certificate, should complete, sign and date the Notice to the Informant, which should be detached and handed to the informant. Where the informant intends giving information for the registration outside of the area where the death occurred, the notice may be handed to the informant's agent. The Practitioner should then, without delay, deliver the certificate itself to the Registrar of Births and Deaths for the sub-district in which the death occurred. Envelopes for enclosing the certificates are supplied by the Registrar.

MED 1 B 354777

Registrar to enter No. of Death Entry

BIRTHS AND DEATHS REGISTRATION ACT 1953

(Form prescribed by the Registration of Births and Deaths Regulations 1987)

MEDICAL CERTIFICATE OF CAUSE OF DEATH OF LIVE-BORN CHILD DYING WITHIN THE FIRST TWENTY-EIGHT DAYS OF LIFE

For use only by a Registered Medical Practitioner WHO HAS BEEN IN ATTENDANCE during the deceased's last illness, and to be delivered by him forthwith to the Registrar of Births and Deaths.

Name of child ....

Date of death .... day of .... Sex ....

Age at death .... days (completed period of 24 hours) .... hours

Place of death ....

Place of birth ....

Last seen alive by me .... day of ....

1 The certified cause of death has been confirmed by post-mortem
2 Information from post-mortem may be available later.
3 Post-mortem not being held.
4 I have reported this death to the Coroner for further action. *[See overleaf]*

Please ring appropriate digit and letter.

a Seen after death by me.
b Seen after death by another medical practitioner but not by me.
c Not seen after death by a medical practitioner.

CAUSE OF DEATH

SPECIMEN

a. Main diseases or conditions in infant ....

b. Other diseases or conditions in infant ....

c. Main maternal diseases or conditions affecting infant ....

d. Other maternal diseases or conditions affecting infant ....

e. Other relevant causes ....

I hereby certify that I was in medical attendance during the above named deceased's last illness, and that the particulars and cause of death above written are true to the best of my knowledge and belief.

Signature .... Qualifications as registered by General Medical Council ....

Address .... Date ....

For deaths in hospital: Please give the name of the consultant responsible for the above-named as a patient ....

APPENDIX B[275]

Conclusions of the coroner/jury as to the death[276]

[275] Reproduced from The Coroners (Inquests) Rules 2013, SI 2013/1616, Schedule, Form 2.

[276] ibid. As regards unlawful killing, see, eg, the jury verdict in *Inquest on Conrad Code, Oxford, May 1992, The Times* (19 May 1992) 1. Note, too, that the distinction between accident and misadventure has in the past been deprecated: *R v Coroner for City of Portsmouth, ex p Anderson* [1987] 1 WLR 1640.

Form 2
Record of an inquest

The following is the record of the inquest (including the statutory determination and, where required, findings)—

1. Name of the deceased (if known):

2. Medical cause of death:

3. How, when and where, and for investigations where section 5(2) of the Coroners and Justice Act 2009 applies, in what circumstances the deceased came by his or her death: (see note (ii)):

4. Conclusion of the coroner/ jury as to the death: (see notes (i) and (ii):

5. Further particulars required by the Births and Deaths Registration Act 1953 to be registered concerning the death:

1.	2.	3.	4.	5.	6.
Date and place of death	Name and surname of deceased	Sex	Maiden surname of woman who has married	Date and place of birth	Occupation and usual address

Signature of coroner (and jurors):

NOTES:

(i) One of the following short-form conclusions may be adopted:—

I. accident or misadventure

II. alcohol / drug related

III. industrial disease

IV. lawful/ unlawful killing

V. natural causes

VI. open

VII. road traffic collision

VIII. stillbirth

IX. suicide

(ii) As an alternative, or in addition to one of the short-form conclusions listed under NOTE (i), the coroner or where applicable the jury, may make a brief narrative conclusion.

(iii) The standard of proof required for the short form conclusions of "unlawful killing" and "suicide" is the criminal standard of proof. For all other short-form conclusions and a narrative statement the standard of proof is the civil standard of proof.

INDEX